RCL

RESOURCES *for* COLLEGE LIBRARIES

2007

This Edition of *Resources for College Libraries* was prepared by:

ACRL & Choice:
Project Editor: Marcus Elmore
Editorial Director, Choice: Francine Graf
Editor & Publisher, Choice: Irving Rockwood

Special Thanks to Our Proofreaders:
Monika Maslowski, Jinna Anderson, Chris Sullivan, Jennifer Donahue, Judith Douville,
Rebecca Bartlett, and Carolyn Wilcox

Record Entry Completed By:
Monika Maslowski, Laurie Trulock, and Sheila Laverty

R. R. Bowker LLC:
John Krafty: Product Manager, RCL
Ashley Ludwig: Managing Editor, RCL
Frank Morris: IT Director
Minh Huynh: Senior Programmer Analyst
Robert Zeisler: Senior Programmer Analyst

Editorial Staff:
Ian Singer: Vice President, Data Services
Roy Crego: Senior Managing Director, Editorial
Eleanor Schubauer: Managing Editor
Michael Olenick: Managing Editor
Beverly Palacio: Associate Editor

Production Department:
Doreen Gravesande: Senior Director, Production
Ralph Coviello, Manager, Manufacturing Services
Myriam Nunez: Project Manager, Product Development & Content Integrity
Kennard McGill: Production Consultant

Research Completed By:
Pat Diaz, Bobbie Ferraro, Kathy Griner, Becky Housel, and Diane Johnson.

Record Entry Completed By:
Jenny Marie DeJesus, Dorothy Perry-Gilchrist, Anthony Giuffra, and Steven Zaffuto

RESOURCES *for* COLLEGE LIBRARIES

2007

Volume 6:
Interdisciplinary and Area Studies

Mary Ellen Davis, Executive Director, ACRL

Published by
R. R. Bowker LLC
630 Central Avenue, New Providence
New Jersey 07974

Annie Callanan, President and CEO

Portions of this publication may be photocopied for the noncommercial purpose of scientific or educational advancement granted by Sections 107 & 108 of the Copyright Act of 1976 as amended.

URL: http://www.rclweb.net
E-mail address: rclfeedback@bowker.com

Readers may send any corrections and/or updates to the information in this work to:
rclfeedback@bowker.com

The best efforts have been made in collecting and preparing material for inclusion in **Resources for College Libraries**, but the American Library Association and R.R. Bowker LLC do not warrant that the information herein is complete or accurate, and do not assume, and hereby disclaim, any liability to any persons for any loss or damage caused by errors or omissions in **Resources for College Libraries**, whether such omissions result from negligence, accident, or any other cause.

International Standard Book Number:

7 Volume Set:	ISBN: 0-8352-4855-0
	ISBN13: 978-0-8352-4855-6
Vol. 1: Humanities:	ISBN: 0-8352-4856-9
	ISBN13: 978-0-8352-4856-3
Vol. 2: Language & Literature:	ISBN: 0-8352-4857-7
	ISBN13: 978-0-8352-4857-0
Vol. 3: History:	ISBN: 0-8352-4858-5
	ISBN13: 978-0-8352-4858-7
Vol. 4: Social Sciences:	ISBN: 0-8352-4859-3
	ISBN13: 978-0-8352-4859-4
Vol. 5: Science and Technology:	ISBN: 0-8352-4860-7
	ISBN13: 978-0-8352-4860-0
Vol. 6: Interdisciplinary & Area Studies:	ISBN: 0-8352-4861-5
	ISBN13: 978-0-8352-4861-7
Vol. 7: Indexes:	ISBN: 0-8352-4862-3
	ISBN13: 978-0-8352-4862-4

Printed and bound in the United States of America

Table of Contents

Resources for College Libraries: General Introduction

Like its predecessors, the three editions of *Books for College Libraries* (BCL) that appeared in 1988, 1975, and 1964, *Resources for College Libraries* (RCL) is a bibliography of carefully selected works spanning the college curriculum and comprising a recommended core collection for all academic libraries. In the tradition of its predecessors, which drew on the such sources as the published catalog of Harvard's Lamont Library (1954), the shelflist of the undergraduate library of the University of Michigan, and, crucially, Charles Shaw's *List of Books for College Libraries* (1931), RCL attempts to balance multiple, often contradictory demands. It seeks to provide a balanced set of recommendations that take note of the weight of the various academic disciplines within the undergraduate curriculum, the degree to which those various disciplines depend on book materials for their essential teaching and research resources, and the extensive pattern of changes that have reshaped the academic curriculum since 1988, the year in which BCL3, the most recent edition of *Books for College Libraries,* appeared.

Of necessity, RCL also embodies a paradox identified by the late Virginia Clark, editor of BCL3: it "can fully succeed only by failing. It would be disastrous should the collection it suggests serve perfectly to ratify the finished work of book selection in any library."[1] Not only will individual institutions create collections significantly larger than the roughly 65,000 titles recommended by RCL, but they will tailor those collections to reflect the size and strength of their own individual departments, majors, and programs. RCL attempts to make general recommendations, within individual subject areas, of those titles most necessary for teaching the subject to undergraduates. In many cases, this means a foundation to which the smallest institutions should aspire but which larger collections will far surpass.

We describe RCL as a successor to, rather than a new edition of, BCL for two reasons. The first is formal, and lies behind the change in nomenclature: RCL includes in its recommendations a variety of electronic resources, including Web sites, subscription databases, e-books, and other electronic materials. The second, procedural reason follows from this: unlike its predecessors, RCL will appear as both a multivolume print edition and a searchable, continuously updated electronic database. In addition, there is a third, tacit distinction which may be made

between RCL and the various editions of BCL: although bibliographers compiling subject lists for RCL often took the titles listed in BCL3 as a starting point, our bibliographic work emphasized building a comprehensive, retrospective list of titles by reference to the current undergraduate curriculum, and thus much of the work on RCL was from scratch. In contrast, the relationship between the various editions of BCL was demonstrably that of revision; from one edition to the next, there was an expectation that a title would be retained unless it was actively removed (if, for instance, it had been superseded by a more recent work). Because so much more time had passed between the appearance of BCL3 and the development of RCL than between any successive editions of BCL, bibliographers faced the simultaneously daunting and liberating prospect of creating a subject list *de novo.* That this same period (1988-2006) has seen momentous sea changes in many of the academic disciplines in the humanities and the sciences, as well as the growth of interdisciplinary study across all the academic disciplines, made this an opportunity to take measure of the way subjects are taught to undergraduates, as well as the sorts of subjects which are taught, when developing our core list.

One result of this reassessment was the decision to recognize and include as separate subject divisions in RCL a number of interdisciplinary fields, e.g., Environmental Studies and Gender Studies. The decision about which fields to include was based primarily on the degree to which those subjects function as areas of formal study at undergraduate institutions in the U.S., whether as major programs, academic minors, or areas of concentration housed within another department (film studies, for instance, is often offered as a program or concentration within the departments of English, Comparative Literature, or Theater). We recognized that the lists of titles recommended for teaching interdisciplinary subjects, e.g., Asian American Studies, might overlap significantly with the corresponding title lists for related traditional fields, e.g., American Literature. At the same time, we were confident that many of the recommended interdisciplinary titles would be unique, and so it has proved. The degree of overlap between the various sections of RCL is, throughout, fortuitous and reflects actual overlap between various undergraduate curricula. Effort was made to regularize the editions selected, but the work of compiling the various subject lists proceeded on an independent basis.

1. Virginia Clark, "Introduction," *Books for College Libraries: A Core Collection of 50,000 Titles,* (3rd ed., Chicago: American Library Association, 1988), vii.

The other dramatic difference between RCL and BCL is the decision to move away from Library of Congress classification as the primary framework for the selection and classification of titles. Though this is bound to be regarded by many librarians as a controversial decision, we are confident that it will prove in retrospect to be a sound one. The rationale for doing so is the desire to have titles classified in a fashion which closely follows the contours of the undergraduate curriculum. While LC accomplishes this for some subjects (for instance, British or American Literature, which are taught by chronological periods, and within periods by major authors and by forms such as poetry or drama), other curricula fail to mesh well with LC classification: Business Administration, for example, is responsible for the largest portion of baccalaureate degrees conferred by U.S. colleges and universities,[2] yet the classification of materials in the business curriculum in LC class HB-HJ, while sufficient for cataloging purposes, offers no insight on the relationship between materials so classified and the curriculum in which they are used. It is, furthermore, an arrangement which makes perfect sense to, but only to, librarians. Not all copies of BCL resided in technical services departments, but it seems unlikely that they were much consulted by students or faculty. Our hope is that the new classification scheme will work to the advantage of all the academic library's constituencies: librarians, especially those lacking strong background in a given subject, will be able to see not only the recommended titles but also, in the subject taxonomy, a map of the undergraduate curriculum; faculty will find recommendations of essential works in a form more accessible than LC, and bearing a closer correspondence to the way their courses and departments are organized; students, searching for a place to begin research on a particular topic, will also be able to recognize in the classification scheme something corresponding to their own encounter with the subject matter in the classroom and laboratory. Finally, since each entry in RCL retains its LC classification, those who prefer to search for materials in this fashion will still be able to.

RCL is the result of the collaborative efforts of 332 contributors, almost exclusively teaching faculty or librarians at U.S. colleges and universities. There were three kinds of contributors: subject editors, bibliographers, and referees. Subject editors were selected on the basis of their subject expertise and teaching or collection development experience: eighteen hold doctorates, four are members of the teaching faculty at research universities, two are independent scholars, and the remainder are academic librarians. Many have previously contributed to or authored major bibliographies in their subject areas. They were responsible for developing the subject classification taxonomy for their respective subject areas, for recruiting bibliographers and coordinating their efforts, and for reviewing the results. The subject editors represented a change from the various editions of BCL, where the bibliographers (mainly Choice reviewers) dealt directly with the project editor. By inserting a layer of subject experts we sought to ensure that the titles selected and the taxonomies in which they were classified reflected as much as possible the realities of the contemporary undergraduate curriculum. The second class of RCL contributors, bibliographers, was responsible for the bulk of the actual selection of titles. Like the subject editors, they were faculty and librarians selected for their subject knowledge, often with particular expertise in one specific aspect of a field. Finally, a pool of sixty-four referees, senior faculty or subject-specialist librarians, provided independent assessment of the initial lists developed by the bibliographers; the subject editors used this feedback to further refine their lists prior to publication.

The development of RCL had presumed from the beginning that bibliographers would be manipulating electronic bibliographic records in some sort of online environment, but the decision of the Association of College and Research Libraries (ACRL) Board of Directors to partner with publisher R. R. Bowker to produce RCL allowed us access to Bowker's massive database of bibliographic records, as well as the extensive technical support and expertise Bowker deployed on behalf of the project. Bibliographers selected titles in Bowker's *booksinprint.com* database, in a particular edition, and then imported them to the online RCL Authoring System, where they assigned subject headings and recommended audience levels. In those instances where no bibliographic record existed for a desired title, one was created from a reliable source (preferably with book in hand, though this was not always possible). At the same time, bibliographers submitted corrections to Bowker records when they identified errors or inconsistencies. While this system allowed us to avoid much of the brute effort which was expended on the creation of bibliographic records for the various editions of BCL, it also meant that bibliographers spent thousands of person-hours in the *booksinprint.com* database, identifying the most recent and reliable edition of particular works; in some cases, editors elected to include multiple editions, especially where the differences between them are significant for undergraduate teaching (see, for instance, the decision to include multiple, equally worthwhile translations of Dante's *Divine Comedy* in the Italian literature section).

The use of an online system for the manipulation of electronic bibliographic records was in part a matter of efficiency, but more importantly, it finally addresses one longstanding issue faced by BCL, that of obsolescence.

---

2. http://nces.ed.gov/fastfacts/display.asp?id=37: U.S. Department of Education, National Center for Education Statistics. (2006). *Digest of Education Statistics, 2005* (NCES 2006-030), chapter 3.

When *Choice* magazine was founded in 1964, it was envisioned as, among other things, an ongoing supplement to BCL1. This approach did not prove practical, and the second and third editions of BCL were required. In contrast, RCL will be updated on an ongoing basis beginning almost immediately after its initial publication; bibliographic records will reflect changes in print status, and new titles will be introduced at regular intervals, to supplement or replace extant titles.

In addition to the tireless efforts of the contributors, on whom I cannot lavish sufficient praise, special thanks to the ACRL Board of Directors and Mary Ellen Davis, ACRL Executive Director, without whose approval and generous support this project would not have been possible. Oversight and advice were provided throughout the project by the RCL Editorial Board: Carolyn Sheehy, North Central College, Chair; and other members Joan Ellen Broome, Georgia Southern University; Barbara Burd, College Misericordia; Brian E. Coutts, Western Kentucky University; Bradford Lee Eden, University of California, Santa Barbara; Stacey Marien, American University; and Richard Shaw, Technical College of the Lowcountry.

Thanks are also due the editorial staff of *Choice*, all of whom contributed effort and advice to the production of this work in varying degrees (and all of whom exhibited tremendous kindness in their efforts, especially in the final days): Becky Bartlett, Judith Douville, Fran Graf, Lisa Mitten, and Carolyn Wilcox. Fran Graf and Irv Rockwood, the Publisher of *Choice*, deserve another helping of praise for their advice, encouragement, and oversight of the project, as well as for handling negotiations of our partnership with R. R. Bowker. Judith Douville made superhuman contributions to a number of subject areas in addition to her own responsibilities in Chemistry. Although almost every member of the *Choice* office staff contributed to this work, Sheila Laverty deserves special praise for her work on the Dance section. Finally, the work would not have been completed if it had not been for the tireless effort of a small cadre of freelance staff, namely Jennifer Donahue, Monika Maslowski, Teri Staab, and Laurie Trulock, who proofread and edited subject headings and section notes, entered titles, cataloged records, and helped maintain communication with subject editors, with extraordinary care, intelligence, and persistence.

With our partners at R. R. Bowker, we enjoyed the highest degree of collegiality and cooperation. Special thanks are due to Angela D'Agostino, Vice-President of Marketing; John Krafty, Product Manager of *Books In Print*; Ashley Ludwig, Managing Editor; Todd Rudloff, Project Manager of *Books In Print*; Frank Morris, Senior Programmer; Minh Huynh, Senior Programmer Analyst, all of whom made significant contributions to bringing this work to the light of day.

Finally, my deep thanks to my family, Colleen and Graham, for their patience and support throughout this project.

Marcus Elmore,

Editor

A Note on the RCL Subject Taxonomy

One of the distinctive features of *Resources for College Libraries* is the subject taxonomy used to organize the titles included in RCL. Developed specifically for RCL by the RCL editorial team, and in particular by the subject editors, the RCL taxonomy reflects the contours of today's undergraduate curriculum. The RCL taxonomy's major headings, therefore, generally correspond to academic majors, departments, or courses of study, e.g., anthropology, business administration, or physics. (In some cases an academic discipline has been further subdivided in order to create sections of manageable size, e.g., the subdivision of History by geographical region.) The goal is a classification scheme, which organizes materials as they would be taught by faculty and encountered in the classroom and the laboratory by undergraduate students.

In some subject areas, e.g. British and American literature, the RCL subject taxonomy closely resembles the Library of Congress classification scheme used in *Books for College Libraries,* 3rd edition. In most cases, however, the differences between LC and today's undergraduate curriculum, have been so substantial as to require the development of a new taxonomy from scratch. This has been especially true for the interdisciplinary subjects such as African American Studies, Criminal Justice, and Native American Studies, which draw upon materials from a dizzying range of LC classes. Gender Studies, for example, draws from a large array of academic disciplines, including (but not limited to) psychology, sociology, literature, philosophy, political science, medicine, and history.

The coverage of interdisciplinary subjects in RCL is another of its distinguishing features, and one deemed essential from the very inception of the project. Although there is some overlap between the interdisciplinary title lists and those of related traditional subjects, e.g., American literature and Chicano/a literature (a subsection of Latino Studies), the interdisciplinary sections inevitably include many unique titles. In addition, the inclusion of the interdisciplinary subjects makes it possible to distinguish those titles which have been selected as essential resources for a traditional subject such as American literature (e.g., Carson McCullers' *Collected Novels*), from those selected for an interdisciplinary area (e.g., Pat Mora's *Communion,* selected for Latino Studies > Humanities > Literature > Chicano/a Literature), and also from those selected for both (e.g., Mora's *Borders*).

By making the ways in which titles are actually used in the classroom the focus for our classification of titles in RCL, we hope to both dramatically increase its usefulness to students and faculty members and also to underscore the extent to which titles were selected on the basis of their importance to undergraduate study and teaching.

RCL Contributors

John Abbott, Graduate Student, GSLIS, University of Illinois, Urbana-Champaign.
Subject Editor: European History.

Randy Abbott, Head Reference Librarian, University of Evansville.
Referee.

Anthony Adam, Assistant Director, John B. Coleman Library, Prairie View A&M University.
Bibliographer: GLBT Studies.

Jan Adamczyk, Slavic Reference Service, University of Illinois.
Bibliographer: Russian Languages and Literatures.

Michael Adams, Librarian, CUNY Graduate Center.
Bibliographer: American Literature.

Paulita Aguilar, Curator, Indigenous Nations Library Program, University of New Mexico.
Bibliographer: Native American Studies.

Flavia Alaya, Professor of English, Ramapo College of New Jersey.
Referee.

Jean Alexander, Head of Reference, Hunt Library, Carnegie Mellon University.
Referee.

Duncan Alford, Head of Reference, Law Library, Georgetown University.
Bibliographer: Law.

Karen Antell, Head, Reference Department, University of Oklahoma.
Bibliographer: Technology and Engineering.

Ralph Arcari, Director Emeritus, Health Center Library, University of Connecticut.
Subject Editor: Medicine.

Susan Ariew, University Librarian, University of South Florida.
Bibliographer: Education.

Jan Armstrong, Professor of Education, University of New Mexico.
Referee.

Teresa Arrington, Associate Professor of Modern Languages, Blue Mountain College.
Bibliographer: Spanish Language and Literature.

Susan Awe, Director of Parish Memorial Library, University of New Mexico.
Referee.

David Azzolina, Reference librarian, University of Pennsylvania.
Bibliographer: General Language and Literature.

Pete Banholzer, Technical Information Specialist, NASA.
Bibliographer: Geology.

Ron Banks, Human Subjects Coordinator, Institutional Review Board, University of Illinois.
Bibliographer: Education.

David Bantz, Chief Information Architect, University of Alaska.
Referee.

Adele Barsh, Business and Economics Librarian, Carnegie Mellon University.
Bibliographer: Business Administration.

Jennifer Bartlett, Head of Research & Instructional Services, Murray State University.
Bibliographer: American Literature.

Edwin Battistella, Dean of Arts and Letters and Professor of English, University of Southern Oregon.
Bibliographer: General Language and Literature.

Frederic Baumgartner, Professor of History, Virginia Tech University.
Bibliographer: European History.

Robert Beauregard, Professor, Urban Policy Analysis and Management, New School University.
Referee.

Linda Behrend, Cataloging Librarian, University of Tennessee, Knoxville.
Bibliographer: American Literature.

Penny Beile, Head, Curriculum Materials Center, University of Central Florida.
Bibliographer: Education.

Dean Bell, Dean and Chief Academic Officer, Spertus Institute of Jewish Studies.
Bibliographer: European History.

Dennis Benamati, Director, Ryan-Matura Library, Sacred Heart University.
Referee.

Riva Berleant-Schiller, Professor emerita of Anthropology, University of Connecticut, emerita.
Subject Editor: Anthropology.

Jay Bernstein, Reader Services Librarian, Kingsborough Community College.
Referee.

John Berry, Native American Studies Librarian, University of California, Berkeley.
Subject Editor: Native American Studies.

Sharon Black, Librarian, Annenberg School for Communication, University of Pennsylvania.
Bibliographer: Journalism and Communication.

Steve Blackburn, Library Director, Hartford Seminary.
Referee.

Robert Bland, Associate University Librarian
Automation and Technical Services, University of North
Carolina, Asheville.
Bibliographer: Philosophy.

Richard Bleiler, Humanities Bibliographer, University of
Connecticut.
Bibliographer: General Language and Literature.

Laurel Blewett, Manager of Library Services,
Edward Hospital.
Referee.

Christopher Bloss, Instructional Services Librarian,
University of South Dakota.
Bibliographer: American Literature.

Ellen Bosman, Head of Technical Services, New Mexico
State University.
Subject Editor: GLBT Studies.

Jesús Bottaro, Instructor, CUNY / Medgar Evers
College.
Bibliographer: Spanish Language and Literature.

Steven Botterill, Professor of Italian, University of
California, Berkeley.
Referee.

Sally Bowdoin, Head of Serials, Brooklyn College.
Subject Editor: British Literature.

Linda Bowles-Adarkwa, Subject Specialist, Black
Studies and Women Studies, San Francisco State
University.
Bibliographer: African American Studies.

James Boxall, Director, GIS Centre, Dalhousie University.
Subject Editor: Geography.

James Bracken, Assistant Director for Main Library
Research and Reference Services, Ohio State University.
Subject Editor: Other Literatures in English.

Laura Braunstein, Research and Reference Services,
Dartmouth University.
Bibliographer: General Language and Literature.

Tony Bremholm, Life Sciences Librarian, Texas
A&M University.
Referee.

Karl Bridges, Coordinator of Electronic Instruction
Resources, University of Vermont.
Bibliographer: U.S. and Canadian History.

JoEllen Broome, Reference Specialist, Georgia Southern
University.
Subject Editor: Environmental Studies.

Mitchell Brown, Research Librarian for Chemistry and
Earth System Sciences, University of California,
Irvine.
Referee.

Mary Jane Brustman, Bibliographer for Social Welfare
and Criminal Justice, SUNY Albany.
Subject Editor: Criminal Justice.

Mark Bullock, Graduate Student, History Department,
University of Illinois at Chicago.
Bibliographer: European History.

Merry Burlingham, Chief Bibliographer and Collections
Officer, University of Texas.
**Bibliographer: Asian History, Languages, and
Literatures.**

Angela Cannon, Reference Librarian, Library of
Congress.
**Bibliographer: Russian Languages and
Literatures.**

Karen Cary, Head, Collection Management, Virginia
Commonwealth University.
Bibliographer: Sociology.

Melissa Cast, Reference Librarian and Subject Specialist
for Education, University of Nebraska Omaha.
Bibliographer: Education.

Rafaela Castro, Bibliographer, University of California,
Davis.
Subject Editor: Latino Studies.

Tina Ching, Reference Librarian, Arizona State
University.
Referee.

Diana Chlebek, English and Modern Languages and
Literature Bibliographer, University of Akron.
Bibliographer: French Language and Literature.

Michael Chromey, Humanities Librarian, Atlanta
University Center.
Bibliographer: African American Studies.

Hui Hua Chua, US Documents Librarian, Michigan
State University.
Bibliographer: Journalism and Communication.

Alan Church, Professor of English, University of
Texas at Brownsville.
Referee.

Janet Clarke, Asian American Studies Selector, Stony
Brook University.
Bibliographer: Asian American Studies.

Kim Clarke, Assistant Librarian, Selector for Women's
Studies, University of Minnesota, Twin Cities.
Subject Editor: Gender Studies.

Rudolph Clay, Subject Librarian, African and
African-American Studies, Washington University.
Bibliographer: African American Studies.

Ana Maria Cobos, Library Department Chair, Saddleback
College.
Subject Editor: Latino Studies.

Francesca Colecchia, Professor of Spanish, Duquesne
University.
Referee.

Gerardo Colmenar, Associate Librarian, Asian American Studies, University of California, Santa Barbara.
Subject Editor: Asian American Studies.

Mark Connell, Director, Center for Advancement of Technology in Education, SUNY College at Cortland.
Referee.

Paul Connors, Research Analyst, Michigan Legislative Service Bureau.
Bibliographer: U.S. and Canadian History.

Miriam Conteh-Morgan, Collection Manager for African Studies, Ohio State University.
Bibliographer: African American Studies.

Kate Corby, Education and Psychology Bibliographer, Michigan State University.
Subject Editor: Education.

Ronald Cormier, Professor of French, Longwood College.
Referee.

Alice Crosetto, Acquisitions Librarian, University of Toledo.
Bibliographer: British Literature.

Cynthia Crosser, Social Sciences and Humanities Librarian, University of Maine.
Bibliographer: Education.

Gwyneth Crowley, Coordinator of Collection Development, Social Science Libraries, Yale University.
Subject Editor: Economics.

Alice Daugherty, Reference Librarian, Louisiana State University.
Bibliographer: American Literature.

Stephanie Davis, Librarian, Spring Arbor University.
Bibliographer: Education.

Judith de Luce, Professor of Classics, Miami University of Ohio.
Referee.

Kathy Dean, Humanities Bibliographer, Ohio State University.
Bibliographer: Other Literatures in English.

Louise Deis, Science & Technology Reference Librarian, Princeton University.
Subject Editor: Environmental Sciences; General Science.

JoAnn DeVries, Associate Librarian, Reference/Bibliographer, University of Minnesota.
Bibliographer: Agriculture.

Jan Dixon, Reference Librarian, University of Arkansas.
Bibliographer: Geology.

Deborah Dolan, Social Science Librarian, Hofstra University.
Bibliographer: Psychology.

Travis Dolence, Instruction Librarian, Minnesota State University Moorhead.
Referee.

Michael Doorley, Associate Lecturer in Humanities, American College, Dublin.
Bibliographer: European History.

Judith Douville, Visual Arts, Science and Technology Editor, CHOICE.
Subject Editor: Chemistry.

Bill Drew, Associate Librarian, Systems and Reference, SUNY – Morrisville.
Referee.

Heather Dubnick, Field Bibliographer, Modern Language Assoc.
Subject Editor: Spanish Language and Literature.

Dana Dunn, Professor of Psychology, Moravian College.
Referee.

Lisa Dunn, Head of Reference, Colorado School of Mines.
Bibliographer: Geology.

Karin Durán, Teacher Curriculum Center Librarian, California State University Northridge.
Bibliographer: Latino Studies.

David Eastman, Doctoral Candidate, Department of Religious Studies, Yale University.
Bibliographer: Religion.

Mary Edsall, Professor of Library and Information Science, Catholic University of America.
Subject Editor: Dance.

Marcus Elmore, CHOICE.
Subject Editor: General Language and Literature.

Robert Elsie, Independent scholar.
Bibliographer: European History.

Kimberly Embelton, Literature and Languages Librarian, California State University Northridge.
Bibliographer: British Literature.

Michael Emery, Professor of English, Cottey College.
Bibliographer: GLBT Studies.

Mark Emmons, Head, Instruction Services, University of New Mexico.
Subject Editor: Film.

Carlene Engstrom, Director, D'Arcy McNickle Library, Salish Kootenai College.
Bibliographer: Native American Studies.

Pam Enrici, Associate Librarian, University of Maryland.
Bibliographer: Technology and Engineering.

Robert Entenmann, Professor of History, St. Olaf College.
Referee.

Isabel Espinal, Librarian for Afro American Studies, Anthropology, Native American Indian Studies, University of Massachussetts.
Bibliographer: African American Studies.

James Allan Evans, Professor Emeritus of Classical Near Eastern and Religious Studies, University of British Columbia.
Bibliographer: European History.

Angel Falcon, Harvard University, formerly.
Bibliographer: African American Studies.

David Feldman, Professor of Mathematics, University of New Hampshire.
Referee.

Robert Fernekes, Information Services Librarian, Business Specialist, Georgia Southern University.
Bibliographer: Business Administration.

Anne Fields, OSU Libraries Coordinator for Research and Reference, Ohio State University.
Bibliographer: Education.

Jenifer Flaxbart, Head Librarian, Reference and Information Services, University of Texas, Austin.
Bibliographer: Journalism and Communication.

Adonna Fleming, GIS / Maps Librarian, University of Nebraska – Lincoln.
Bibliographer: Geology.

Nicole Fluhr, Professor of English, Southern Connecticut State University.
Referee.

Michael Fosmire, Science Librarian, Purdue University.
Subject Editor: Physics.

Stephen Foster, University Librarian, Wright State University.
Referee.

Gerri Foudy, Government and Politics, Public Affairs, and Law Librarian, University of Maryland.
Bibliographer: Political Science.

Kathleen Fountain, Political Science and Social Work Librarian, California State University, Chico.
Bibliographer: Political Science.

Kristine Fowler, Mathematics Librarian, University of Minnesota, Twin Cities.
Subject Editor: Mathematics.

Stephen Fowlkes, Bibliographer for Sociology, Social Work and Reference, Tulane University.
Bibliographer: Sociology.

Ann Fox, Professor of English, Davidson College.
Referee.

Joe Fugate, Professor of German, Kalamazoo College.
Referee.

Steve Fullwood, Manuscripts Librarian, Schomburg Center for Research in Black Culture, New York Public Library.
Bibliographer: African American Studies.

Ronald Ganze, Professor of English, Valparaiso University.
Bibliographer: Medieval Studies.

Bill Gargan, Reference Librarian and Bibliographer, Brooklyn College.
Bibliographer: British Literature.

Meryle Gaston, Islamic and Middle Eastern Studies Librarian, University of California, Santa Barbara.
Subject Editor: Middle Eastern History, Languages, and Literatures.

Cameron Gearen, Lecturer in English, Yale University.
Bibliographer: General Language and Literature.

Caroline Geck, Librarian, Kean University.
Referee.

Jennifer Geddes, Research Associate Professor of Religious Studies, University of Virginia.
Bibliographer: General Language and Literature.

Mary Gilles, Business Reference Librarian, Washington State University.
Subject Editor: Law.

David Giovacchini, Arabic Librarian, Middle East Collection, Stanford University.
Referee.

Ed Goedeken, Humanities Bibliographer, Iowa State University.
Subject Editor: U.S. and Canadian History.

Melissa Goldsmith, Lecturer, Louisiana State University.
Referee.

Millie Gonzalez, Reference Librarian, Framingham State College.
Bibliographer: Business Administration.

Olympia Gonzalez, Professor of Spanish, Loyola University of Chicago.
Referee.

David Goodman, Professor of Library and Information Science, Long Island University.
Subject Editor: Biology.

Candice Goucher, Professor of History, Washington State University, Vancouver.
Referee.

Malaika Grant, Reference/Instruction Librarian, University of Minnesota, Twin Cities.
Bibliographer: Gender Studies.

Laura Graves, Professor of History, South Plains College.
Bibliographer: Native American Studies.

Chip Green, Professor of Geology, University of South Carolina Upstate.
Referee.

Susan Green, Professor of History, California State University, Chico.
Referee.

Cheryl Grossman, Electronic Services Supervisor, LearningWork Connection, Ohio State University.
Bibliographer: Education.

Anna Marie Guengerich, Librarian, College of Education, University of Iowa.
Bibliographer: Psychology.

Richard Hacken, European Studies Bibliographer, Brigham Young University.
Referee.

Michael Handis, Associate Librarian for Collection Management, CUNY Graduate Center.
Bibliographer: European History.

Shaun Hardy, Librarian, Carnegie Institution of Washington.
Bibliographer: Geology.

Sara Harrington, Art Librarian, Rutgers University.
Referee.

Jon Harrison, Social Sciences Collections Coordinator, Missouri State University.
Bibliographer: Criminal Justice.

Elizabeth Hartung, Professor of Sociology, California Sate University Channel Islands.
Bibliographer: Sociology.

Laurence Hauptman, Professor of History, SUNY New Paltz.
Bibliographer: Native American Studies.

Peter Hayes, Professor of History, Northwestern University.
Bibliographer: European History.

Charles Hayford, Research Fellow, Department of History, Northwestern University.
Subject Editor: Asian History, Languages, and Literatures.

Jeremy Hein, Professor of Sociology, University of Wisconsin – Eau Claire.
Referee.

Eileen Herring, Agriculture Librarian, University of Hawaii.
Bibliographer: Agriculture.

Martin Hewitt, Head of History Department, Trinity and All Saints College, University of Leeds.
Referee.

Terry Hill, Customer Representative for North America, OTTO HARRASSOWITZ GmbH & Co. KG.
Bibliographer: Political Science.

Baraba Hillson, Public and International Affairs and Psychology Liaison Librarian, George Mason University.
Referee.

Lee Hilyer, Mathematics Subject Librarian, University of Houston.
Bibliographer: Education.

Keith Hitchins, Professor of History, University of Illinois.
Bibliographer: European History.

Adrian Ho, Assistant Librarian, University of Houston.
Bibliographer: Journalism and Communication.

David Hogg, Astronomer, National Radio Astronomy Observatory.
Referee.

Jane Holmquist, Astrophysics Librarian, Princeton University.
Subject Editor: Astronomy.

Emily Horning, Librarian for Philosophy, Religious Studies and Anthropology, Yale University.
Subject Editor: Religion.

John Hunter, Science/Engineering Librarian, Rice University.
Bibliographer: Geology.

Carol Hutchins, Head Librarian, Courant Institute of Mathematical Sciences, New York University.
Subject Editor: Computing.

Robin Imhof, Reference Librarian, University of the Pacific.
Bibliographer: GLBT Studies.

Richard Irving, Associate Librarian, SUNY Albany.
Bibliographer: Criminal Justice.

Kristin Jacobi, Head, Catologing Department, Eastern Connecticut State University.
Bibliographer: Native American Studies.

James Jaffe, Professor of History, University of Wisconsin – Whitewater.
Bibliographer: European History.

Arif Jamal, Social Sciences Bibliographer, University of Pittsburgh.
Bibliographer: African American Studies.

Sylvia James, Sylvia James Consultancy.
Bibliographer: Business Administration.

Fred Jenkins, Head of Collection Management, University of Dayton.
Subject Editor: Ancient History; Classics.

Donald Clay Johnson, Curator, Ames Library of South Asia, University of Minnesota.
Bibliographer: Asian History, Languages, and Literatures.

Melissa Johnson, Reference and Instruction Librarian, Lynn University.
Bibliographer: European History.

Sarah Johnson, Librarian, Eastern Illinois University.
Bibliographer: General Language and Literature.

Lisa Johnston, Head of Public Services, Sweet Briar College.
Bibliographer: British Literature.

Scott Johnston, Librarian, CUNY Graduate Center.
Subject Editor: Urban Studies.

David P. Jordan, Professor of History, University of Illinois at Chicago.
Bibliographer: European History.

Jonathan Judaken, Professor of History, University of Memphis.
Bibliographer: European History.

Jeannie Kamerman, Director, Curriculum Materials Library, University of West Florida.
Bibliographer: Education.

James Kelly, Humanities Bibliographer, University of Massachussetts.
Subject Editor: American Literature.

Marcia Keyser, Instruction and Reference Librarian, Drake University.
Bibliographer: Education.

Shayee Khanaka, Librarian, Middle Eastern Collection, University of California Berkeley.
Bibliographer: Middle Eastern History, Languages, and Literatures.

Sherise Kimura, Reference Librarian, University of San Francisco.
Bibliographer: Asian American Studies.

Douglas King, Librarian, University of South Carolina.
Bibliographer: American Literature.

Laura Kinner, Coordinator, Cataloging Services, University of Toledo.
Bibliographer: British Literature.

Harold Kirkwood, Librarian, Purdue University.
Bibliographer: Business Administration.

Patricia Kirkwood, Science Librarian, University of Arkansas.
Bibliographer: Technology and Engineering.

Sheila Kirven, Education Services Librarian, New Jersey City University.
Bibliographer: Education.

Linda Klein, Reference Librarian, Eastern Kentucky University.
Bibliographer: British Literature.

Michael Knee, Science Bibliographer and Reference Librarian, University of Albany.
Bibliographer: Computing.

Norma Kobzina, Head of Information Services, Marian Koshland Bioscience and Natural Resources Library, University of California, Berkeley.
Subject Editor: Agriculture.

David Koenigstein, Librarian, Brooklyn College.
Bibliographer: British Literature.

Gayla Koerting, Special Collections Librarian, University of South Dakota.
Bibliographer: U.S. and Canadian History.

Laura Koltutsky, Information Services Librarian, University of Houston.
Bibliographer: Education.

Kwasi Konadu, Professor of History, Winston Salem State University.
Bibliographer: African History, Languages, and Literatures.

Svetlana Korolev, Science Librarian, University of Wisconsin, Madison.
Referee.

Wade Kotter, Social Sciences Librarian, Weber State University.
Bibliographer: Criminal Justice.

Joe Kraus, Science Librarian, University of Denver.
Referee.

Eiko Kuwana, Professor of IIistory, University of the Sacred Heart, Tokyo.
Bibliographer: European History.

Sharon Ladenson, Gender Studies and Communications Bibliographer, Michigan State University.
Bibliographer: Journalism and Communication.

Carolyn Laffoon, Earth and Atmospheric Sciences Librarian, Purdue University.
Bibliographer: Geology.

Blake Landor, Bibliographer for Philosophy, Classics, and Religion, University of Florida.
Subject Editor: Philosophy.

Jeffry Larson, Librarian for Romance Languages and Literatures, Linguistics, and Classics, Yale University.
Subject Editor: French Language and Literature; Italian Language and Literature.

Jason E. Lavery, Professor of History, Oklahoma State University.
Bibliographer: European History.

Bernadette Lear, Behavioral Sciences and Education Librarian, Pennsylvania State University.
Bibliographer: Psychology.

Patrick Leary, Research Fellow, Department of History, Northwestern University.
Subject Editor: Victorian Studies.

Richard S. Levy, Professor of History, University of Illinois at Chicago.
Bibliographer: European History.

Kevin Lindstrom, Behavioral Sciences and Education Librarian, University of British Columbia.
Bibliographer: Geology.

Ken Liss, Communication Librarian, Boston College.
Bibliographer: Journalism and Communication.

Carol Loranger, Professor of English, Wright
State University.
Referee.

Jack Lynch, Professor of English, Rutgers University.
Bibliographer: British Literature.

Karen MacDonald, Business Subject Specialist
Librarian, Texas A&M University.
Bibliographer: Business Administration.

Peter Magierski, Librarian for the Middle East Studies,
New York University.
**Bibliographer: Middle Eastern History, Languages,
and Literatures.**

Diane Maher, University Archivist, University of San
Diego.
**Bibliographer: American Literature; British
Literature.**

Janice Mathews, Librarian for Urban Studies and Social
Work, University of Connecticut.
Referee.

Rhonda McGinnis, Business and Economics Librarian,
Wayne State University.
Bibliographer: Business Administration.

Glenn McGuigan, Business Reference Librarian, Penn
State University.
Subject Editor: Business Administration.

Peter McKay, Business Librarian, University of Florida.
Bibliographer: Business Administration.

Paula McMillen, Social Sciences Librarian, Oregon State
University.
Bibliographer: Education.

Lori Mestre, Digital Learning Librarian, University of
Illinois.
Bibliographer: Education.

Sue Metcalf, Social Sciences Librarian, New Mexico
State University.
Referee.

Marion Miller, Professor of History, University of Illinois
at Chicago, emerita.
Bibliographer: European History.

Lisa Mitten, CHOICE.
Subject Editor: Native American Studies.

Sandy Mooney, Design Librarian, Louisiana State
University.
Referee.

Fred Muratori, Bibliographer for Anglo-American and
Comparative Literature and Film, Cornell
University.
Bibliographer: Drama and Theater.

Paula Murphy, Library Consultant.
Referee.

Linda Musser, Head, Fletcher L. Byrom Earth and
Mineral Sciences Library, Pennsylvania State University.
Bibliographer: Geology.

Theodore Natsoulas, Professor of History, University of
Toledo.
Bibliographer: European History.

Sharon Naylor, Education, Psychology and TMC
Division Head, Illinois State University.
Bibliographer: Education.

Antoinette Nelson, Branch Manager, Science and
Engineering Library, University of Texas Arlington.
Subject Editor: Technology and Engineering.

Jan Newberry, Professor of Anthropology, University of
Lethbridge.
Referee.

Shawn Nicholson, Bibliographer for Sociology, Social
Work, Urban Planning, Michigan State University.
Referee.

Jim Niessen, World History Librarian, Rutgers
University.
Bibliographer: European History.

Byron Nordstrom, Professor of History, Gustavus
Adolphus University.
Bibliographer: European History.

Akilah Nosakhere, Manager, Reference and Research
Division, Auburn Avenue Research Library of
African American Culture and History.
Subject Editor: African American Studies.

Nancy O'Brien, Head, Education and Social Science
Library, University of Illinois.
Subject Editor: Education.

Darby Orcutt, Collection Manager for the Humanities
and Data Analysis, North Carolina State
University.
Bibliographer: Journalism and Communication.

Harriet Ottenheimer, Professor of Anthropology,
Kansas State University.
Bibliographer: Anthropology.

Mark Padnos, Coordinator of Public Services, Bronx
Community College.
**Subject Editor: Germanic Languages and
Literatures.**

John Page, Associate Dean, Learning Resources
Division, University of the District of Columbia.
Bibliographer: African American Studies.

Tim Parrish, Professor of English, Southern Connecticut
State University.
Bibliographer: General Language and Literature.

Lucy Patrick, Head of Special Collections, Florida
State University.
Referee.

Christopher Peebles, Associate Vice President for
Information Technology and Professor of Anthropology,
Indiana University.
Bibliographer: Anthropology.

Ed Peters, Professor of History, University of
Pennsylvania.
Bibliographer: European History.

Carmelita Pickett, African American Studies Librarian,
Emory University.
Bibliographer: African American Studies.

Lisa Pillow, Collection Development Librarian, University
of Wisconsin – River Falls.
Bibliographer: African American Studies.

Chestalene Pintozzi, Science-Engineering Librarian,
University of Arizona.
Bibliographer: Geology.

Don Polzella, Professor of Psychology and Associate
Dean for Faculty Development and Graduate Programs,
University of Dayton.
Subject Editor: Psychology.

Diethelm Prowe, Professor of History, Carleton College.
Bibliographer: European History.

Eleanor Randall, Reference Librarian, Edinboro
University of Pennsylvania.
Bibliographer: Biology.

Brenda Reed, Public Services Librarian, Education
Library, Queen's University.
Bibliographer: Education.

Ira Revels, Instruction Librarian, Cornell University.
Bibliographer: African American Studies.

Leslie Reynolds, Director of Policy Sciences and
Economics Library, Texas A&M University.
Bibliographer: Business Administration.

Amy Robb, Field Librarian for Women's Studies and
Communication, University of Michigan.
Bibliographer: Journalism and Communication.

Gloria Roberson, Reference Librarian, Adelphi
University.
Bibliographer: African American Studies.

Beth Roberts, Earth and Mineral Sciences Librarian,
Pennsylvania State University.
Bibliographer: Geology.

Elizabeth Robertson, Professor of English, University of
Colorado.
Bibliographer: British Literature.

Martin Roden, Professor emeritus of Engineering,
UCLA.
Bibliographer: Technology and Engineering.

Raquel Rodriguez, Librarian for the African American
Collection, University of Pittsburgh.
Bibliographer: African American Studies.

Lisa Romero, Communications Librarian, University of
Illinois.
Subject Editor: Journalism and Communication.

Lana Kay Rosenberg, Director, Dance Theatre,
Miami University of Ohio.
Referee.

Tony Rosso, Professor of English, Southern Connecticut
State University.
Bibliographer: British Literature.

Dana Roth, Chemistry Librarian, Caltech.
Bibliographer: Chemistry.

Linda Salem, Education Librarian, San Diego State
University.
Bibliographer: British Literature.

Mark Sanders, Student Outreach Reference Librarian,
East Carolina University.
Bibliographer: Environmental Studies.

Rachel Sandoval, Historical Records Project Archivist,
University of California, Irvine.
Bibliographer: Latino Studies.

Victoria Santana, Electronic Services Librarian,
Oklahoma City University.
Bibliographer: Native American Studies.

Román Santillán, Reference/Instruction Librarian,
CUNY / College of Staten Island.
Bibliographer: Spanish Language and Literature.

Vernon Schlotzhauer, Social Science Librarian,
Pennsylvania State University.
Bibliographer: Psychology.

Geoff Schmidt, Professor of English, Illinois State
University – Edwardsville.
Bibliographer: General Language and Literature.

Alan Schroeder, Business Librarian, California
State University Northridge.
Bibliographer: Business Administration.

Kate Schroeder, Doctoral Candidate, History Department,
Indiana University.
**Subject Editor: African History, Languages, and
Literatures.**

Friedrich Schuler, Professor of History, Portland State
University.
Subject Editor: Latin American History.

Katrin Schultheiss, Professor of History, University of
Illinois at Chicago.
Bibliographer: European History.

Jason Schultz, Communications Librarian, Georgia
State University.
Bibliographer: African American Studies.

Catherine Shreve, Librarian for Public Policy and Political
Science, Duke University.
Subject Editor: Political Science.

Jack Shreve, Professor of English, Allegany College.
Bibliographer: GLBT Studies.

Adam Siegel, Reference Librarian, University of California, Davis.
Bibliographer: Native American Studies.

Dorothy Siles, Librarian, Taylorville Public Library.
Bibliographer: Native American Studies.

Jane Sloan, Media Librarian, Rutgers University.
Subject Editor: Film.

Becky Smith, Head, Business and Economics Library, University of Illinois.
Bibliographer: Business Administration.

Helen Smith, Life Sciences Librarian, Penn State University.
Bibliographer: Agriculture.

Michael Smith, Business Librarian, Texas A&M University.
Bibliographer: Business Administration.

Jacqueline Snider, Librarian, ACT.
Bibliographer: Education.

Doug Southard, DRA International.
Bibliographer: Business Administration.

Roland Spickermann, Professor of History, University of Texas, Permian Basin.
Bibliographer: European History.

Jill Spreitzer, Assistant Librarian, Public Services, University of Detroit Mercy.
Bibliographer: Technology and Engineering.

Jennifer Stevens, Humanities Liaison Librarian, George Mason University.
Bibliographer: Other Literatures in English.

David Stoloff, Professor of Education, Eastern Connecticut State University.
Referee.

Fred Stoss, Biological Science Librarian, SUNY Buffalo.
Subject Editor: Biology.

Stephen Stratton, Head of Collection Development, California State University, Channel Islands.
Subject Editor: Sociology.

Cindy Stretch, Professor of English, Southern Connecticut State University.
Referee.

Leanne Strum, Library Liaison to the School of Business, Regent University.
Bibliographer: Business Administration.

Mila Su, Coordinator of Reference Services, Pennsylvania State University.
Subject Editor: Sport and Recreation.

Helen Sullivan, Head, Slavic Reference Service, University of Illinois.
Subject Editor: Russian Languages and Literatures.

Sarah Sussman, Curator, French and Italian Collections, Stanford University.
Bibliographer: European History.

Marek Suszko, Professor of History, Purdue University North Central.
Bibliographer: European History.

Laura Taddeo, Reference Librarian, SUNY Buffalo.
Bibliographer: British Literature.

Kornelia Tancheva, Director of Instructional Services, Cornell University.
Subject Editor: Drama and Theater.

Wendy Tann, Librarian, Federal Reserve Bank.
Bibliographer: Business Administration.

Cornelia Akins Taylor, Special Collections Librarian, Florida A & M University.
Bibliographer: African American Studies.

Betty Taylor-Thompson, Professor of English, Texas Southern University.
Referee.

Edward Teague, Head, Architecture & Allied Arts Library, University of Oregon.
Subject Editor: Visual Arts.

Samantha Teplitzky, Earth Sciences Librarian and Bibliographer, Stanford University.
Bibliographer: Geology.

Stephen Thompson, Co-Leader, Technical Services Department, Brown University.
Bibliographer: American Literature.

Erik Thomson, Collegiate Assistant Professor, Social Sciences, University of Chicago.
Bibliographer: European History.

Charles Thurston, Reference Librarian and Bibliographer, University of Texas at San Antonio.
Bibliographer: Education.

Judie Triplehorn, Librarian, Geophysical Institute, University of Alaska.
Bibliographer: Geology.

Markel Tumlin, English and American Literature Librarian, San Diego State University.
Bibliographer: American Literature.

Andrea Twiss-Brooks, Bibliographer for Chemical and Geophysical Sciences, University of Chicago.
Subject Editor: Geology.

Kent Underwood, Music Librarian, New York University.
Subject Editor: Music.

Alan Unsworth, Reference Librarian, University of Rochester.
Referee.

David Vaccari, Professor of Engineering, Stevens Institute of Technology.
Bibliographer: Technology and Engineering.

Susan Vega Garcia, Reference & Instruction Librarian, Bibliographer, Iowa State University.
Bibliographer: Latino Studies.

Tom Volkening, Engineering Librarian, Michigan State University.
Bibliographer: Technology and Engineering.

Heather Ward, University of Oregon, formerly.
Subject Editor: Medieval Studies.

Diane Warner, Monographs and Special Formats Cataloger, Texas Tech University.
Bibliographer: American Literature.

Gary Wasdin, Library Director, New School University.
Referee.

Matthew Wayman, Instruction Coordinator, Penn State University.
Bibliographer: U.S. and Canadian History.

Jeneen Willemssen, Librarian, Conserve School.
Bibliographer: Education.

Wendy Williamson, Economics Librarian, University of Minnesota.
Referee.

Suzanne Wise, Collection Development Librarian, Appalachia State University.
Referee.

Ada Woods, Reference Librarian, Towson University.
Bibliographer.

Peng Xu, Reference Librarian, Michigan State University.
Bibliographer: Business Administration.

Lisa Yuro, Reference Librarian/Humanities and Social Sciences Coordinator, University of Alabama.
Bibliographer: Journalism and Communication.

Ann Zawistoski, Reference and Instruction Librarian, Carleton College.
Bibliographer: Geology.

Linda Zellmer, Head, Geology Library, Indiana University.
Subject Editor: Geology.

HOW TO USE
RESOURCES FOR COLLEGE LIBRARIES

Resources for College Libraries (RCL) was designed to be easily searchable by author, title, and the RCL subject taxonomy. The set consists of seven volumes, Volumes 1-6 arranged by RCL Subject, and sorted alphabetically by author. Volume 7 is a comprehensive author, title and subject index. The volumes are arranged by *Resources for College Library* Subject Headings, a full listing of which is present in the Subject Headings Index in volume 7.

Each title in *Resources for College Libraries* has been classified with a specific RCL Subject and/or subjects. Titles can and often do appear within more than one RCL Subject area. Titles have been given a specific readership level through audience code: g=general, l=lower-division undergraduate, u=upper-division undergraduate graduate, and/or f=faculty level resources. Titles previously mentioned in *Books for College Libraries, 3rd Edition*, have been noted with a specific BCL3 icon ℬ. Non-book entries can be easily identified with the icons for Web ▢, Ebook 🄴, or CD/DVD-ROM 🗋.

Classification Number, Dewey Decimal Number, Library of Congress Control Number, Audience Code, and whether it has been reviewed in Choice Magazine.

Entries in the Author Index can include the following bibliographic information when available: author, co-author, editor, co-editor, translator, co-translator, along with page number(s) and volume number(s) of the selected works within the 6-volume set. Entries are not cross-referenced by other than primary author and/or first contributor. Entries in the Title Index include the title, page number(s) and volume number(s) of the selected works within the 6-volume set.

Titles in *Resources for College Libraries* have been alphabetized using the following rules:

- Initial articles of titles in English, French, German, Italian, and Spanish are not included for sorting purposes.

- Titles beginning with acronyms appear before those

SAMPLE RCL ENTRY

❶ DRAMA AND THEATER ❯ Western Drama ❯ United States

❷ Wilmeth, Don B. & Bigsby, Christopher (Editors)   PN2221

❸ The Cambridge History of American Theater: ❹ 1870-1945. ❺ Ed. 2
❻ Don B. Wilmeth & Christopher Bigsby (Contribution by). ❼ Trade Paper.
❽ Cambridge University Press. ❾ New York, NY. ❿ 2006. ⓫ 608p.
⓬ Cambridge History of American Theater Ser. ⓭ ISBN: 0-521-67984-2,
ISBN13: 978-0-521-67984-8. ⓮ Dewey:792/.0973.
⓯ LCCN: 00-000000

⓰ Audience: l,u,f. ⓱ *Choice, 2005* ℬ

1. RCL Subject Heading
2. Author/First Contributor
3. Title
4. Subtitle
5. Ed. Info
6. Additional Contributors
7. Binding Type
8. Publisher
9. Publisher Location
10. Publication Date
11. Number of Pages
12. Series Title
13. ISBN, ISBN-13
14. Dewey
15. LCCN
16. Audience Code
17. Choice Review and Date

Title entries can include the following bibliographic information, when available: author, co-author, editor, co-editor, translator, co-translator, title, number of volumes, edition, series information, binding type, publisher, publisher location, date of publication, number of pages, ISBN, ISBN-13, Library of Congress

beginning with words. For example, B E A M A Directory would precede Baal, Babylon.

- As a general rule, U.S. and UN are filed in strict alphabetical order.

- Numeric Titles may be found near the end of the Title Index

Authors in *Resources for College Libraries* have been alphabetized using the following rules:

- Proper names beginning with "Mc" and "Mac" are filed in strict alphabetical order. For example, entries for contributors' names such as MacAdam, MacAvory, and MacCarthy are located prior to the pages with entries for names such as McAdam, McCoy, and McDermott.

- When author names are represented with initials, they are alphabetized before author first names. For example, Smith, H. C. appears before Smith, Harold A.

Any errors in bibliographic data should be E-mailed directly to: rclwebfeedback@bowker.com

ABBREVIATIONS AND CODE LIST:

BCL3	*Books for College Libraries, 3rd Edition*
Bk.(s.)	Book(s)
Ed.	Edition
F	Faculty
G	General
Inc.	Incorporated
Jr.	Junior
ISBN	International Standard Book Number
L	Lower-Division Undergraduate
LCCN	Library of Congress Control Number
p.	Pages
RCL	Resources for College Libraries
Ser.	Series
Sr.	Senior
U	Upper-Division Undergraduate

Geographical Abbreviations

AL	Alabama	NJ	New Jersey
AK	Alaska	NM	New Mexico
AB	Alberta	NSW	New South Wales
AE	American Europe	NY	New York
AS	American Samoa	NF	Newfoundland
AZ	Arizona	NC	North Carolina
AR	Arkansas	ND	North Dakota
ACT	Australian Capital Territory	NP	Northern Marianas
BC	British Columbia	N.T.	Northern Territory (Australia)
CA	California	NT	Northwest Territory
CM	Central Marianas	NS	Nova Scotia
CO	Colorado	NU	Nunavut
CT	Connecticut	OH	Ohio
DE	Delaware	OK	Oklahoma
DC	District Of Columbia	ON	Ontario
FM	Federated States Of Micronesia	OR	Oregon
FL	Florida	TT	Pacific Territories
GA	Georgia	PW	Pacific West
GU	Guam	PA	Pennsylvania
HI	Hawaii	PE	Prince Edward Island
ID	Idaho	PR	Puerto Rico
IL	Illinois	PQ	Quebec
IN	Indiana	QLD	Queensland
IA	Iowa	RI	Rhode Island
KS	Kansas	SK	Saskatchewan
KY	Kentucky	SA	South Australia
LA	Louisiana	SC	South Carolina
ME	Maine	SD	South Dakota
MB	Manitoba	TAS	Tasmania
MH	Marshall Islands	TN	Tennessee
MD	Maryland	TX	Texas
MA	Massachusetts	UT	Utah
MI	Michigan	VT	Vermont
MP	Middle Pacific	VIC	Victoria
MN	Minnesota	VI	Virgin Islands
MS	Mississippi	VA	Virginia
MO	Missouri	WA	Washington
MT	Montana	WV	West Virginia
NE	Nebraska	W.A.	Western Australia
NV	Nevada	WI	Wisconsin
NB	New Brunswick	WY	Wyoming
NH	New Hampshire	YT	Yukon Territory

AFRICAN AMERICAN STUDIES

The resources included in this section reflect the phenomenal growth and breadth of African American Studies as a discipline. The explosion of mass-marketed resources in a variety of formats requires close examination by librarians and Africana scholars in general to ensure the use of sound research methodology in development of materials for library collections.

Since the publication of BCL3 in 1988, the demand for Black materials in U.S. institutions of higher education has grown significantly. The discipline, now called African American Studies, has a more narrow focus and has gained some acceptance by American colleges and universities as a legitimate field of study with a body of scholarship to be taught, collected, and managed. Therefore, today mainstream publishers seek to produce series of quality monographs and develop resources in digital formats to capture this market while providing materials of lasting value.

While librarians may find the new RCL African American Studies list valuable in collection development, some Africana scholars have expressed mixed feelings about such lists. A few have stated that African American studies should not be limited by the confines of the traditional subject groupings and such lists neglect the growing international aspect of the discipline and limit the growth of the discipline in other areas. Perhaps they are right. Unless African American Studies programs are providing an education for the development of economic, social, and political policy and policymakers for Africa and her diasporic descendants, what is the point?

Resources selected for this edition were examined in light of the current curricular needs of key African American Studies programs and faculty members nationwide. When possible, the credentials and research specialties of authors were researched before recommending inclusion on the RCL list. Both monographs and databases were examined to ascertain their appropriateness for this seminal reference resource. Librarians from major university and public research libraries contributed to the development of this list and it would not have been possible without their assistance. Many thanks to all.

— Akilah Nosakhere

History

Ani, Marimba CB203.A56 1994
Yurugu: An Afrocentric Critique of European Cultural Thought and Behavior. Trade Cloth. Africa World Press. Trenton, NJ. 1994. 636p. ISBN:0-86543-249-X, ISBN13: 978-0-86543-249-9. Dewey:940/.01. LCCN:91-071027.

Audience: **u,f.**

Arnesen, Peter J. & E185.6.A76 2003
Arnesen, Eric
Black Protest and the Great Migration: A Brief History with Documents. Trade Paper. Bedford/Saint Martin's. New York, NY. 2002. 226p. The Bedford Series in History and Culture ISBN:0-312-39129-3, ISBN13: 978-0-312-39129-4. Dewey:305.896/073. LCCN:2002-104745.

Audience: **l,u.**

Asante, Molefi Kete & E185
Mattson, Mark T.
Historical and Cultural Atlas of African Americans. Compact Disc. Macmillan Publishing Company, Inc. Old Tappan, NJ. 1992. 208p. ISBN:0-02-897029-2, ISBN13: 978-0-02-897029-5. Dewey:973/.0496073.

Audience: **g,l,u,f.** *Choice, 1991.*

Bailey, Anne C. HT1331
African Voices of the Atlantic Slave Trade: Beyond the Silence and the Shame. Beacon Press. 2005. ISBN:0-8070-5513-1, ISBN13: 978-0-8070-5513-7.

Audience: **l,u,f.**

Baraka, Amiri & Jones, ML3556.B16 1999
LeRoi
Blues People: Negro Music in White America. Trade Paper. HarperCollins Publishers. New York, NY. 1999. 256p. ISBN:0-688-18474-X, ISBN13: 978-0-688-18474-2. Dewey:780/.89/96073. LCCN:98-049663.

Audience: **g,l,u,f.** *B*

Bennett, Lerone Jr. E185.B4 2000
Before the Mayflower: A History of Black America. Ed. 7. Trade Cloth. Johnson Publishing Company, Inc. Chicago, IL. 2001. 796p. ISBN:0-87485-091-6, ISBN13: 978-0-87485-091-8. Dewey:973/.0496073. LCCN:00-036530.

Audience: **g,l,u.** *B*

Berlin, Ira F446
Many Thousands Gone: The First Two Centuries of Slavery in North America. Trade Paper. Harvard University Press. Cambridge, MA. 2000. 512p. Belknap Press Ser. ISBN:0-674-00211-3, ISBN13: 978-0-674-00211-1. Dewey:306.3/62/097309032.

Audience: **g,l,u.**

Berlinerblau, Jacques DF78.B3983B47 1999
Heresy in the University: The Black Athena Controversy and the Responsibilities of American Intellectuals. Paper Text. Rutgers University Press. Piscataway, NJ. 1999. 304p. ISBN:0-8135-2588-8, ISBN13: 978-0-8135-2588-4. Dewey:949.5. LCCN:98-008499.

Audience: **u,f.** *Choice, 1999.*

Berry, Mary Frances E185.97.H825B47 2005
My Face Is Black Is True: Callie House and the Struggle for Ex-Slave Reparations. Trade Cloth. Alfred A. Knopf Inc. New York, NY. 2005. 336p. ISBN:1-4000-4003-5, ISBN13: 978-1-4000-4003-2. Dewey:323/.092 B. LCCN:2004-051330.

Audience: **g,l,u,f.** *Choice, 2006.*

Berry, Mary F. & E185
Blassingame, John W.
Long Memory: The Black Experience in America. Paper Text. Oxford University Press, Inc. New York, NY. 1982. 508p. ISBN:0-19-502910-0, ISBN13: 978-0-19-502910-9. Dewey:973/.0496073. LCCN:80-024748.

Audience: **g,l,u.** *B*

Bin Wahad, Dhoruba, et E185.615.B516 1993
al.
Still Black, Still Strong: Survivors of the War Against Black Revolutionaries. Mumia Abu-Jamal & Assata Shakur (Authors). Trade Paper. Semiotexte/Smart Art. Los Angeles, CA. 1993. 272p. Semiotext(e)/Active Agents Ser. ISBN:0-936756-74-8, ISBN13: 978-0-936756-74-5. Dewey:322.4/2/092396073. LCCN:2002-510804.

Audience: **g,l,u.**

Blassingame, John W. E443
The Slave Community: Plantation Life in the Antebellum South. Ed. 2. Paper Text. Oxford University Press, Inc. New York, NY. 1979. 432p. ISBN:0-19-502563-6, ISBN13: 978-0-19-502563-7. Dewey:975/.00496073. LCCN:78-026890.

Audience: **g,l,u.** *B*

Bogle, Donald PN1995.9.N4
Toms, Coons, Mulattoes, Mammies, and Bucks: An Interpretive History of Blacks in American Films. Trade Cloth. Continuum International Publishing Group, Ltd. London, 2003. 480p. ISBN:0-8264-1518-0, ISBN13: 978-0-8264-1518-9. Dewey:791.43652.

Audience: **g,l,u.**

Boyd, Herb E185.A97 2000
Autobiography of a People: Three Centuries of African American History Told by Those Who Lived It. Doubleday. 2000. ISBN:0-385-49278-2, ISBN13: 978-0-385-49278-2.

Audience: **g,l,u.**

Bracey, John H. & E184.6.A333 2004
Sinha, Manisha
African American Mosaic: A Documentary History from the Slave Trade to the Twenty-First Century. Paper Text. Pearson Education. Boston, MA. 2003. 416p. ISBN:0-13-092287-0, ISBN13: 978-0-13-092287-8. Dewey:973/.0496073. LCCN:2003-022536.

Audience: **g,l,u.**

Bracey, John H. & E184.6.A333 2004
Sinha, Manisha
African Americans Mosaic: A Documentary History from the Slave Trade to the Twenty-First Century. Trade Paper. Pearson Education. Boston, MA. 2003. 544p. ISBN:0-13-092288-9, ISBN13: 978-0-13-092288-5. Dewey:973/.0496073. LCCN:2003-022536.

Audience: **g,l,u.**

Brophy, Alfred L. F704.T92B76 2003
Reconstructing the Dreamland: The Tulsa Riot of 1921: Race, Reparations, and Reconciliation. Randall Kennedy (Foreword by). Trade Paper. Oxford University Press, Inc. New York, NY. 2003. 208p. ISBN:0-19-516103-3, ISBN13: 978-0-19-516103-8. Dewey:976.6/86.

Audience: **f.**

Broussard, Jinx PN4872.B76 2003
Coleman
Giving a Voice to the Voiceless: Four Pioneering Black Women Journalists. Paper over Boards. Routledge. New York, NY. 2003.

228p. Studies in African American History and Culture Ser. ISBN:0-415-94717-0, ISBN13: 978-0-415-94717-6. Dewey:070.92/273 B. LCCN:2003-010320.

Audience: **g,l,u.**

Brown, William Wells　　　　**E185.96**
📧 The Black Man, His Antecedents, His Genius, and His Achievements. CD-ROM, E-Book. AFCHRON. Minneapolis, MN. 2006. ISBN:1-892824-79-5, ISBN13: 978-1-892824-79-0. Dewey:970.009.

Audience: **g,l,u.**

Brown, William Wells　　　　**E540.N3B8 2003**
The Negro in the American Rebellion: His Heroism and His Fidelity. John David Smith (Editor). Trade Paper. Ohio University Press. Athens, OH. 2003. 336p. ISBN:0-8214-1528-X, ISBN13: 978-0-8214-1528-3. Dewey:973.7/415. LCCN:2003-058008.

Audience: **g,l,u.** *Choice, 2004.*

Christian, Charles M.　　　　**E185.C519 1999**
Black Saga: The African American Experience: A Chronology. Trade Paper. Basic Books. New York, NY. 1998. 624p. ISBN:1-58243-000-4, ISBN13: 978-1-58243-000-3. Dewey:973/.0496073/0202. LCCN:98-045495.

Audience: **g,l,u.**

Cole, Johnnetta B. &　　　　**E185.86.C58154 2003**
Guy-Sheftall, Beverly
Gender Talk: The Struggle for Women's Equality in African American Communities. Trade Cloth. Ballantine Books. New York, NY. 2003. 336p. ISBN:0-345-45412-X, ISBN13: 978-0-345-45412-6. Dewey:305.48/896073. LCCN:2002-040875.

Audience: **g,l,u.** *Choice, 2003.*

Conyer, James L. Jr. &　　　　**E175.5.C59P36 2004**
Thompson, Julius Eric
Pan African Nationalism in the Americas: The Life and Times of John Henrik Clarke. Trade Cloth. Africa World Press. Trenton, NJ. 2004. 256p. ISBN:1-59221-225-5, ISBN13: 978-1-59221-225-5. Dewey:973/.0496073/0092 B. LCCN:2004-001776.

Audience: **g,l,u,f.**

Crowder, Ralph L.　　　　**E185.97.B895C76 2004**
John Edward Bruce: The Legacy of a Politician, Journalist, and Self-Trained Historian of the African Diaspora. Trade Cloth. New York University Press. New York, NY. 2004. 256p. ISBN:0-8147-1518-4, ISBN13: 978-0-8147-1518-5. Dewey:973/.0496073/0092 B. LCCN:2003-020499.

Audience: **g,l,u.** *Choice, 2004.*

Dandridge, Rita B.　　　　**PS374.N4D36 2004**
Black Women's Activism: Reading African American Women's Historical Romances. Trade Cloth. Peter Lang Publishing, Inc. New York, NY. 2004. 136p. African-American Literature and Culture Ser., Vol. 5 ISBN:0-8204-6734-0, ISBN13: 978-0-8204-6734-4. Dewey:813.009/9287. LCCN:2002-156547.

Audience: **g,u,f.**

Dawson, Michael C.　　　　**E185.61**
Behind the Mule: Race and Class in African-American Politics. Trade Paper. Princeton University Press. Princeton, NJ. 1995. 246p. ISBN:0-691-02543-6, ISBN13: 978-0-691-02543-8. Dewey:323.1/196073. LCCN:93-044088.

Audience: **g,l,u,f.** *Choice, 1995.*

Douglass, Frederick　　　　**E449.D738 2003**
The Frederick Douglass Papers: Autobiographical Writings. John W. Blassingame, John R. McKivigan & Peter P. Hinks (Editors). Cloth over Boards. Yale University Press. Cumberland, RI. 2003. 528p. The Frederick Douglas Papers, Vol. 2 ISBN:0-300-09173-7, ISBN13: 978-0-300-09173-1. Dewey:973.7092. LCCN:2003-005833.

Audience: **g,l,u,f.**

Du Bois, W. E. B.　　　　**E185**
📧 The Souls of Black Folk. E-Book. Bantam Books. New York, NY. 2005. ISBN:0-553-90176-1, ISBN13: 978-0-553-90176-4. Dewey:973/.0496073.

Audience: **g,l,u.** 𝕭

Du Bois, W. E. B.　　　　**E668**
Black Reconstruction in America 1860-1880: An Essay Toward a History of the Part Which Black Folk Played in the Attempt to Reconstruct Democracy in America. Cedric Robinson (Introduction by). Library Binding. University of Notre Dame Press. Notre Dame, IN. 2001. 776p. The African American Intellectual Heritage Ser. ISBN:0-268-02165-1, ISBN13: 978-0-268-02165-8. Dewey:973.8.

Audience: **g,l,u,f.**

Duberman, Martin　　　　**PS3554.U25D83 2005**
Paul Robeson: A Biography. Trade Paper, Perfect. New Press, The. New York, NY. 2005. 804p. Lives of the Left Ser. ISBN:1-56584-941-8, ISBN13: 978-1-56584-941-9. Dewey:791/.092.

Audience: **g,l,u.**

Early, Gerald L.　　　　**E185.615.E16 2003**
This Is Where I Came In: Black America in the 1960s. Trade Cloth. University of Nebraska Press. Lincoln, NE. 2003. 160p. Abraham Lincoln Lecture Ser. ISBN:0-8032-1823-0, ISBN13: 978-0-8032-1823-9. Dewey:323.1/196073/009046. LCCN:2003-047302.

Audience: **g,l,u.**

Finkenbine, Roy E.　　　　**E184.6.F56 2003**
Sources of the African American Past: Primary Sources in American History. Ed. 2. Trade Paper. Longman Publishing. Boston, MA. 2003. 240p. ISBN:0-321-16216-1, ISBN13: 978-0-321-16216-8. Dewey:973/.0496073. LCCN:2003-047680.

Audience: **g,l,u.**

Franklin, John H. &　　　　**E185**
Moss, Alfred A.
From Slavery to Freedom: A History of Negro Americans. Ed. 8. Mixed Media, Trade Paper, CD-ROM. McGraw-Hill Higher Education. Burr Ridge, IL. 2000. 768p. ISBN:0-07-243046-X, ISBN13: 978-0-07-243046-2. Dewey:973/.0496073.

Audience: **g,l,u.** 𝕭

Galle, Jillian E. &　　　　**E185.E555 2004**
Young, Amy L. (Editors)
Engendering African American Archaeology: A Southern Perspective. Trade Cloth. University of Tennessee Press. Knoxville, TN. 2005. 336p. ISBN:1-57233-277-8, ISBN13: 978-1-57233-277-5. Dewey:975/.00496073. LCCN:2003-026431.

Audience: **g,l,u,f.**

Gates, Henry Louis　　　　**E185.96**
African-American Century: How Black Americans Shaped Our Country. West, Cornel. Free Press. 2000. ISBN:0-684-86414-2, ISBN13: 978-0-684-86414-3.

Audience: **g,l,u.**

George, Nelson E185.615.G465 2004
Post-Soul Nation: The Explosive, Contradictory, Triumphant, and Tragic 1980s As Experienced by African Americans (Previously Known As Blacks and Before That Negroes). Trade Cloth. Penguin Group (USA) Inc. New York, NY. 2004. 288p. ISBN:0-670-03275-1, ISBN13: 978-0-670-03275-4. Dewey:973/.049607309/046. LCCN:2003-061606.
Audience: **g,l,u.**

Gibson, Aliona L. E185.96
Nappy: Growing up Black and Female in America. Trade Paper. Writers & Readers Publishing, Inc. New York, NY. 1998. 176p. ISBN:0-86316-329-7, ISBN13: 978-0-86316-329-6. Dewey:973/.0496073/092.
Audience: **g,l,u,f.**

Gray, Fred D. R853.H8
The Tuskegee Syphilis Study: The Real Story and Beyond. Trade Cloth. NewSouth, Inc. Montgomery, AL. 2002. 176p. ISBN:1-58838-089-0, ISBN13: 978-1-58838-089-0. Dewey:364.142.
Audience: **g,l,u,f.**

Green, Robert P.
  (Editor) KR4756
Equal Protection and the African-American Constitutional Experience: A Documentary History. Cloth Text. Greenwood Publishing Group, Inc. Portsmouth, NH. 2000. 368p. Primary Documents in American History and Contemporary Issues Ser. ISBN:0-313-30350-9, ISBN13: 978-0-313-30350-0. Dewey:342.73/0873. LCCN:99-051319.
Audience: **g,l,u,f.**

Griggs, William E. D769.335
The World War II Black Regiment That Built the Alaska Military Highway: A Photographic History. Philip J. Merrill (Editor), Douglas Brinkley (Introduction by). Trade Cloth. University Press of Mississippi. Jackson, MS. 2006. 128p. ISBN:1-57806-504-6, ISBN13: 978-1-57806-504-2. Dewey:940.54/03. LCCN:2002-009425.
Audience: **g,l,u.**

Haley, Alex CS71
Roots: The Saga of an American Family. Library Binding. Buccaneer Books, Inc. Cutchogue, NY. 1994. ISBN:1-56849-471-8, ISBN13: 978-1-56849-471-5. Dewey:929/.2/0973.
Audience: **g,l,u.**

Hall, Perry A. E184.7
In the Vineyard: Working in African American Studies. Trade Paper. University of Tennessee Press. Knoxville, TN. 2005. 264p. ISBN:1-57233-368-5, ISBN13: 978-1-57233-368-0. Dewey:305.896073/071.
Audience: **g,l,u,f.** *Choice, 2000.*

Hanson, Joyce Ann E185.97.B34H36 2003
Mary McLeod Bethune and Black Women's Political Activism. Trade Cloth. University of Missouri Press. Columbia, MO. 2003. 256p. ISBN:0-8262-1451-7, ISBN13: 978-0-8262-1451-5. Dewey:370/.92 B. LCCN:2002-153613.
Audience: **g,l,u.** *Choice, 2003.*

Harding, Vincent E185
There Is a River: The Black Struggle for Freedom in America. Harcourt Brace Jovanovich. 1992. ISBN:0-15-689089-5, ISBN13: 978-0-15-689089-2.
Audience: **g,l.**

Harley, Sharon E185
The Timetables of African-American History: A Chronology of the Most Important People and Events in African-American History. Trade Paper. Simon & Schuster. New York, NY. 1996. 400p. ISBN:0-684-81578-8, ISBN13: 978-0-684-81578-7. Dewey:973/.0496073. LCCN:94-022571.
Audience: **g,l,u.**

Harley, Sharon & E185.86
  Terborg-Penn, Rosalyn (Editors)
The Afro-American Woman: Struggles and Images. Trade Paper. Black Classic Press. Baltimore, MD. 1997. 160p. ISBN:1-57478-026-3, ISBN13: 978-1-57478-026-0. Dewey:305.4889607. LCCN:96-086019.
Audience: **l,u.**

Harris, Stephen L. D570.33
Harlem's Hell Fighters: The African-American 369th Infantry in World War I. Trade Paper, Perfect. Potomac Books, Inc. Dulles, VA. 2005. 301p. ISBN:1-57488-635-5, ISBN13: 978-1-57488-635-1. Dewey:940.4/1273. LCCN:2002-156003.
Audience: **g,l,u.**

Henson, Matthew A. G635.H4A3 2001
A Negro Explorer at the North Pole: The Autobiography of Matthew Henson. Booker T. Washington (Preface by), Robert E. Peary (Foreword by), Robert A. Bryce (Introduction by). Trade Paper. Cooper Square Publishers, Inc. New York, NY. 2001. 272p. ISBN:0-8154-1125-1, ISBN13: 978-0-8154-1125-3. Dewey:910/.92. LCCN:2001-028916.
Audience: **g,l,u.**

Hill, Patricia Liggins, et al. PS508.N3
Call and Response: The Riverside Anthology of the African American Literary Tradition. Bernard W. Bell, Trudier Harris, William J. Harris, R. Baxter Miller, Sondra J. O'Neale & Horace Porter (Authors). Mixed Media, CD-ROM, Cloth Text, Compact Disc. Houghton Mifflin College Division. Boston, MA. 2003. 1024p. ISBN:0-618-45171-4, ISBN13: 978-0-618-45171-5. Dewey:810.8/0896073.
Audience: **g,l,u.**

Hine, Darlene Clark E185.86.B542 1993
  (Editor), et al.
Black Women in America: An Historical Encyclopedia. Elsa B. Brown & Rosalyn Terborg-Penn (Editors). Trade Cloth. Carlson Publishing, Inc. Brooklyn, NY. 1993. 1600p. ISBN:0-926019-61-9, ISBN13: 978-0-926019-61-4. Dewey:920.72/08996073. LCCN:92-039947.
Audience: **g,l,u,f.** *Choice, 1993.*

Hine, Darlene Clark, et al. E185
The African-American Odyssey, Vol. I (Chapters 1-13). Ed. 3. William C. Hine & Stanley Harrold (Authors). Trade Paper. Prentice Hall PTR. Upper Saddle River, NJ. 2005. 416p. ISBN:0-13-192215-7, ISBN13: 978-0-13-192215-0. Dewey:973.04/96073.
Audience: **g,l,u.**

Hine, Darlene Clark E185.86.W435 1995
  (Editor), et al.
We Specialize in the Wholly Impossible: A Reader in Black Women's History. Wilma King & Linda Reed (Editors). Trade Paper. Carlson Publishing, Inc. Brooklyn, NY. 1995. 624p. Black Women in United States History Ser., Vol. 17 ISBN:0-926019-81-3, ISBN13: 978-0-926019-81-2. Dewey:305.48/896073/09. LCCN:94-041968.
Audience: **g,l,u.**

Hine, Darlene Clark &   **E185.86**
Thompsom, Kathleen
A Shining Thread of Hope: The History of Black Women in
America. Trade Paper. Broadway Books. New York, NY. 1999.
368p. ISBN:0-7679-0111-8, ISBN13: 978-0-7679-0111-6.
Dewey:305.48/896/073.
       Audience: **g,l,u.** *Choice, 1999.*

Hine, Darlene Clark   **E185.H535 1996**
Speak Truth to Power: Black Professional Class in United States
History. Joe W. Trotter (Preface by). Trade Cloth. Carlson
Publishing, Inc. Brooklyn, NY. 1996. 222p.
ISBN:0-926019-91-0, ISBN13: 978-0-926019-91-1.
Dewey:305.896/073073. LCCN:95-047307.
       Audience: **g,l,u,f.**

Holloway, Joseph E.   **E185.A26 2005**
(Editor)
Africanisms in American Culture. Ed. 2. Trade Paper, Perfect.
Indiana University Press. Bloomington, IN. 2005. 312p. Blacks
in the Diaspora Ser. ISBN:0-253-21749-0, ISBN13:
978-0-253-21749-3. Dewey:973/.0496073. LCCN:2004-020284.
       Audience: **g,l,u,f.** *Choice, 1990.*

Homan, Lynn M. &   **UG834.A37H64 2001**
Reilly, Thomas
Black Knights: The Story of the Tuskegee Airmen. Louis R.
Purnell (Foreword by). Trade Cloth. Pelican Publishing
Company, Inc. Gretna, LA. 2001. 336p. ISBN:1-56554-828-0,
ISBN13: 978-1-56554-828-2. Dewey:940.54/4973.
LCCN:00-047850.
       Audience: **g,l,u.** *Choice, 2001.*

Hopkins, Dwight N.   **BT82.7**
Heart and Head: Black Theology—Past, Present, and Future.
Michael Eric Dyson (Foreword by). Trade Paper. Palgrave
Macmillan. New York, NY. 2003. 240p. Black
Religion/Womanist Thought/Social Justice Ser.
ISBN:1-4039-6292-8, ISBN13: 978-1-4039-6292-8.
Dewey:230/.089/96073.
       Audience: **g,l,u.**

Hornsby, Alton (Editor)   **E185.C66 2005**
Companion to African American History. Trade Cloth. Blackwell
Publishing, Inc. Malden, MA. 2005. 584p. Blackwell
Companions to American History Ser. ISBN:0-631-23066-1,
ISBN13: 978-0-631-23066-3. Dewey:973/.0496073.
LCCN:2004-011680.
       Audience: **g,l,u.** *Choice, 2005.*

Hornsby, Alton Jr.   **E185.92.H67 2004**
Southerners, Too?: Essays on the Black South, 1733-1990. Trade
Cloth. University Press of America, Inc. Lanham, MD. 2004.
342p. ISBN:0-7618-2871-0, ISBN13: 978-0-7618-2871-6.
Dewey:305.896/073075. LCCN:2004-102176.
       Audience: **g,u,f.**

Hughes, Louis   **E185.97.T8**
🄴 Thirty Years a Slave: From Bondage to Freedom. E-Book.
Digital Antiquaria, Inc. Morristown, NJ. 2004. 94p.
ISBN:1-58057-305-3, ISBN13: 978-1-58057-305-4.
Dewey:305.5/67/092 B.
       Audience: **g,l,u.**

Humez, Jean McMahon   **E444.T82H86 2003**
Harriet Tubman: The Life and the Life Stories. Trade Paper.
University of Wisconsin Press. Chicago, IL. 2005. 488p.
Wisconsin Studies in Autobiography ISBN:0-299-19124-9,

ISBN13: 978-0-299-19124-5. Dewey:973.7/115/092 B.
LCCN:2003-005676.
       Audience: **g,l,u.** *Choice, 2004.*

Hunter, Tera W.   **HD6057.5.U52G45 1997**
To Joy My Freedom: Southern Black Women's Lives and
Labors after the Civil War. Trade Cloth. Harvard University
Press. Cambridge, MA. 1997. 322p. ISBN:0-674-89309-3,
ISBN13: 978-0-674-89309-2. Dewey:331.4/089/9607307582.
LCCN:96-051473.
       Audience: **g,l,u.** *Choice, 1997.*

Hurston, Zora Neale   **PS3515.U789Z465 2006**
Dust Tracks on a Road: An Autobiography. Trade Paper.
HarperCollins Publishers. New York, NY. 2006. 336p. P. S. Ser.
ISBN:0-06-085408-1, ISBN13: 978-0-06-085408-9.
Dewey:813/.52 B. LCCN:2005-052616.
       Audience: **g,l,u.** *𝓑 Choice, 1985.*

Hurt, R. Douglas   **E185.6.A257 2003**
(Editor, Introduction by)
African American Life in the Rural South, 1900-1950. Trade
Cloth. University of Missouri Press. Columbia, MO. 2003. 264p.
ISBN:0-8262-1471-1, ISBN13: 978-0-8262-1471-3.
Dewey:975/.0049607301734. LCCN:2003-002150.
       Audience: **g,u,f.** *Choice, 2004.*

Jackson, Jonathan Jr.   **HV9468.J3A4 1994**
(Foreword by)
Soledad Brother: The Prison Letters of George Jackson. Trade
Paper. Chicago Review Press, Inc. Chicago, IL. 1995. 368p.
ISBN:1-55652-230-4, ISBN13: 978-1-55652-230-7.
Dewey:365/.6/092 B. LCCN:94-028264.
       Audience: **g,l,u.**

Jackson, Ronald L. II   **P94.5.A37A367 2003**
(Editor)
African American Communication and Identities: Essential
Readings. Cloth Text. SAGE Publications, Inc. Thousand Oaks,
CA. 2003. 368p. ISBN:0-7619-2845-6, ISBN13:
978-0-7619-2845-4. Dewey:302.2/089/96073.
LCCN:2003-013998.
       Audience: **g,l,u,f.**

James, C. L. R.   **F1923.T85**
The Black Jacobins: Toussaint L'Ouverture and the San
Domingo Revolution. Ed. 2. Trade Paper. Knopf Publishing
Group. New York, NY. 1989. 448p. ISBN:0-679-72467-2,
ISBN13: 978-0-679-72467-4. Dewey:972.9403.
       Audience: **g,l,u.**

James, Stanlie M. &   **HQ1190.T47 1993**
Busia, Abena P. (Editors)
Theorizing Black Feminisms: The Visionary Pragmatism of
Black Women. Johnnetta B. Cole (Foreword by). Paper over
Boards. Routledge. New York, NY. 1993. 312p.
ISBN:0-415-07336-7, ISBN13: 978-0-415-07336-3.
Dewey:305.4208996. LCCN:92-047346.
       Audience: **g,l,u.**

Johnson, James Weldon   **PS3519.O2625Z463**
Along This Way: The Autobiography of James Weldon Johnson.
Sondra K. Wilson (Introduction by). Trade Paper. Da Capo
Press, Inc. Cambridge, MA. 1999. 440p. ISBN:0-306-80929-X,
ISBN13: 978-0-306-80929-3. Dewey:818/.5209 B.
LCCN:99-058436.
       Audience: **g,l,u.**

Jones, Jacqueline   HD6057.5.U5J66 1986
Labor of Love, Labor of Sorrow: Black Women, Work and the
Family from Slavery to the Present. Trade Paper. Knopf
Publishing Group. New York, NY. 1986. 464p.
ISBN:0-394-74536-1, ISBN13: 978-0-394-74536-7.
Dewey:305.4/8896073. LCCN:85-040860.
                          Audience: **g,l,u.** ℬ Choice, 1985.

Jordan, Winthrop D.   E185.J69
White over Black: American Attitudes Toward the Negro,
1550-1812. Trade Paper. University of North Carolina Press.
Chapel Hill, NC. 1995. 671p. Published for the Institute of
Early American History and Culture Ser. ISBN:0-8078-4550-7,
ISBN13: 978-0-8078-4550-9. Dewey:305.8/96073.
LCCN:68-013295.
                          Audience: **g,l,u.** ℬ

Katz, William Loren   E185.925.K37 2004
The Black West: A Documentary and Pictoral History of the
African American Role in the Westward Expansion of the
United States. Trade Paper, Perfect, Dust Jacket. Broadway
Books. New York, NY. 2005. 318p. ISBN:0-7679-1231-4,
ISBN13: 978-0-7679-1231-0. Dewey:978/.00496073/00922.
LCCN:2003-061218.
                          Audience: **g,l,u.**

Katz, William Loren   E185.6
Breaking the Chains: African-American Slave Resistance.
Library Binding. Sagebrush Education Resources. Caledonia,
MN. 1998. ISBN:0-613-04637-4, ISBN13: 978-0-613-04637-4.
Dewey:975/.00496073.
                          Audience: **g,l,u.**

Lanning, Michael L.   UB418.A47L36 2004
The African-American Soldier. Trade Paper. Kensington
Publishing Corporation. New York, NY. 2004. 320p.
ISBN:0-8065-2629-7, ISBN13: 978-0-8065-2629-4.
Dewey:355/.008996/073. LCCN:2004-558374.
                          Audience: **g,l,u.**

Larson, Kate Clifford   E444.T82
Bound for the Promised Land: Harriet Tubman, Portrait of an
American Hero. Trade Paper. Ballantine Books. New York, NY.
2004. 432p. ISBN:0-345-45628-9, ISBN13: 978-0-345-45628-1.
Dewey:973.7/115/092 B. LCCN:2004-111071.
                          Audience: **g,l,u.** Choice, 2004.

Lincoln, C. Eric   BP221
The Black Muslims in America. Ed. 3. Trade Cloth. Africa
World Press. Trenton, NJ. 1996. 307p. ISBN:0-86543-399-2,
ISBN13: 978-0-86543-399-1. Dewey:297/.87.
                          Audience: **g,l,u.** ℬ

Lincoln, C. Eric &   BR563.N4L55 1990
  Mamiya, Lawrence
The Black Church in the African American Experience. Trade
Paper. Duke University Press. Durham, NC. 1990. 536p.
ISBN:0-8223-1073-2, ISBN13: 978-0-8223-1073-0.
Dewey:277.3/08/08996073. LCCN:90-034050.
                          Audience: **g,l,u.** Choice, 1991.

Locke, Alain L.   PS153.N5
The New Negro. Trade Paper. Simon & Schuster. New York,
NY. 1999. 452p. ISBN:0-684-83831-1, ISBN13:
978-0-684-83831-1. Dewey:810.9/896073. LCCN:91-033377.
                          Audience: **g,l,u.**

Logan, Rayford W.   E185.61.L64 1997
The Betrayal of the Negro: From Rutherford B. Hayes to
Woodrow Wilson, Vol. 1. Trade Paper. Da Capo Press, Inc.
Cambridge, MA. 1997. 480p. ISBN:0-306-80758-0, ISBN13:
978-0-306-80758-9. Dewey:973/.0496073. LCCN:96-044577.
                          Audience: **g,l,u.**

Lowry, Beverly   HD9970.5.C672W3558
Her Dream of Dreams: The Rise and Triumph of Madam C. J.
Walker. Trade Cloth. Alfred A. Knopf Inc. New York, NY. 2003.
496p. ISBN:0-679-44642-7, ISBN13: 978-0-679-44642-2.
Dewey:338.7/66855/092 B. LCCN:2002-027494.
                          Audience: **g,l,u.**

Lynch, Katherine A.   H1.S612
  (Editor)
African American Fraternal Associations and the History of
Civil Society in the United States. Bayliss J. Camp, Marshall
Ganz, Orit Kent, Ariane Liazos, Jennifer Lynn Oser, Theda
Skocpol & Joe W. Trotter (Contribution by). Trade Paper. Duke
University Press. Durham, NC. 2004. 200p.
ISBN:0-8223-6611-8, ISBN13: 978-0-8223-6611-9.
Dewey:366.0089607.
                          Audience: **g,l,u,f.**

Marable, Manning   E184.7.D57 2000
Dispatches from the Ebony Tower: Intellectuals Confront the
African American Experience. Trade Paper. Columbia University
Press. New York, NY. 2001. 352p. ISBN:0-231-11477-X,
ISBN13: 978-0-231-11477-6. Dewey:305.896/073/0711.
LCCN:99-055525.
                          Audience: **g,l,u,f.** Choice, 2000.

Marable, Manning, et al.   E184.6.F74 2003
Freedom on My Mind: The Columbia Documentary History of
the African American Experience. John McMillian & Nishani
Frazier (Authors). Trade Cloth. Columbia University Press. New
York, NY. 2003. 900p. ISBN:0-231-10890-7, ISBN13:
978-0-231-10890-4. Dewey:973/.0496073. LCCN:2003-051605.
                          Audience: **g,l,u.** Choice, 2003.

Mazrui, Ali Al'Amin   DT38
The African Predicament and the American Experience: A Tale
of Two Edens. Trade Cloth. Greenwood Publishing Group, Inc.
Portsmouth, NH. 2004. 136p. ISBN:0-275-97828-1, ISBN13:
978-0-275-97828-0. Dewey:303.48/26073. LCCN:2003-044220.
                          Audience: **g,l,u,f.**

Middleton, Stephen   E185
  (Editor)
Black Congressmen During Reconstruction: A Documentary
Sourcebook. John David Smith (Foreword by). Cloth Text.
Greenwood Publishing Group, Inc. Portsmouth, NH. 2002. 464p.
ISBN:0-313-32281-3, ISBN13: 978-0-313-32281-5.
Dewey:328.73/092/396073. LCCN:2002-067753.
                          Audience: **g,l,u,f.**

Miller, Ericka M.   PS169.L95M55 1999
The Other Reconstruction: Where Violence and Womanhood
Meet in the Writings of Ida B. Wells-Barnett, Angelina Weld
Grimke, and Nella Larsen. Cloth Text. Garland Publishing, Inc.
New York, NY. 1999. 176p. Studies in African American
History and Culture ISBN:0-8153-3495-8, ISBN13:
978-0-8153-3495-8. Dewey:810.9/355. LCCN:99-029874.
                          Audience: **g,l,u.**

Mjagkij, Nina (Editor)   E185.96.P67 2003
Portraits of African American Life since 1865. Book, Other.
Rowman & Littlefield Publishers, Inc. Lanham, MD. 2003.

252p. The Human Tradition in America Ser., No. 16
ISBN:0-8420-2966-4, ISBN13: 978-0-8420-2966-7.
Dewey:920/.009296073 B. LCCN:2002-152539.

Audience: **g,l,u.**

Moore, Christopher   **D810.N4M65 2005**
Fighting for America: Black Soldiers—The Unsung Heroes of
World War II. Trade Cloth. Ballantine Books. New York, NY.
2004. 400p. ISBN:0-345-45960-1, ISBN13: 978-0-345-45960-2.
Dewey:940.54/03.

Audience: **g,l,u.** *Choice, 2006.*

Murdy, Anne-Elizabeth   **PS374.N4M87 2003**
Teach the Nation: Public School, Racial Uplift, and Women's
Writing in the 1890's. Paper over Boards. Routledge. New York,
NY. 2002. 196p. Studies in African American History and
Culture ISBN:0-415-93534-2, ISBN13: 978-0-415-93534-0.
Dewey:813/.4099287. LCCN:2002-068254.

Audience: **g,l,u.**

Nalty, Bernard C.   **VB324.A47N35**
Long Passage to Korea: Black Sailors and the Integration of the
U. S. Navy. William S. Dudley (Foreword by). Trade Paper.
DIANE Publishing Company. Collingdale, PA. 2004. 51p.
ISBN:0-7567-4404-0, ISBN13: 978-0-7567-4404-5.
Dewey:359/.008996/073.

Audience: **g,l,u.**

Neal, Mark Anthony   **E185.615.N35 2001**
Soul Babies: Black Culture and the Post-Soul Aesthetic. Trade
Paper. Routledge. New York, NY. 2001. 256p.
ISBN:0-415-92658-0, ISBN13: 978-0-415-92658-4.
Dewey:305.896/073. LCCN:2001-020490.

Audience: **g,l,u.** *Choice, 2002.*

Painter, Nell Irvin   **E185.P15 2005**
Creating Black Americans: African American History and Its
Meanings, 1619 to the Present. Oxford University Press. 2005.
ISBN:0-19-513755-8, ISBN13: 978-0-19-513755-2.

Audience: **l,u.**

Palmer, Colin A.   **E185P16 1998**
Passageways: An Interpretive History of Black America. Paper
Text. Thomson Wadsworth. Belmont, CA. 1998. 336p.
Passageways Ser., Vol. 2 ISBN:0-15-502483-3, ISBN13:
978-0-15-502483-0. Dewey:973/.0496073. LCCN:97-074864.

Audience: **g,l,u.**

Peterson, Carla L.   **PS153.N5P443 1998**
Doers of the Word: African-American Women Speakers and
Writers in the North (1830-1880). Paper Text. Rutgers
University Press. Piscataway, NJ. 1998. 284p.
ISBN:0-8135-2514-4, ISBN13: 978-0-8135-2514-3.
Dewey:810.9/9287/08996073. LCCN:97-041838.

Audience: **g,l,u.**

Reverby, Susan M.   **R853.H8T87 2000**
  (Editor)
Tuskegee's Truths: Rethinking the Tuskegee Syphilis Study.
James H. Jones (Foreword by). Trade Paper. University of North
Carolina Press. Chapel Hill, NC. 2000. 656p. Studies in Social
Medicine ISBN:0-8078-4852-2, ISBN13: 978-0-8078-4852-4.
Dewey:174/.28/0976149. LCCN:99-056379.

Audience: **g,l,u.** *Choice, 2000.*

Rose, Willie L.   **F279.P6R67 1998**
Rehearsal for Reconstruction: The Port Royal Experiment. Trade
Paper. University of Georgia Press. Athens, GA. 1999. 464p.

Brown Thrasher Bks. ISBN:0-8203-2061-7, ISBN13:
978-0-8203-2061-8. Dewey:975.7/99. LCCN:98-003851.

Audience: **g,l,u.**

Schechter, Patricia A.   **E185.97.W55S34 2001**
Ida B. Wells-Barnett and American Reform, 1880-1930. Trade
Paper. University of North Carolina Press. Chapel Hill, NC.
2001. 408p. Gender and American Culture Ser.
ISBN:0-8078-4965-0, ISBN13: 978-0-8078-4965-1.
Dewey:323/.092 B. LCCN:00-068313.

Audience: **g,l,u.**

Stewart, Jacqueline   **PN1995.9.N4S74 2005**
  (Author, Illustrator)
Migrating to the Movies: Cinema and Black Urban Modernity.
Trade Cloth. University of California Press. Berkeley, CA. 2005.
360p. ISBN:0-520-23350-6, ISBN13: 978-0-520-23350-8.
Dewey:791.43/652996073. LCCN:2004-016541.

Audience: **g,l,u.** *Choice, 2005.*

Tate, Gayle T.   **E185.9.T38 2003**
Unknown Tongues: Black Women's Political Activism in the
Antebellum Era, 1830-1860. Trade Cloth. Michigan State
University Press. East Lansing, MI. 2003. 416p. Black American
and Diasporic Studies ISBN:0-87013-652-6, ISBN13:
978-0-87013-652-8. Dewey:974/.00496073/0082.
LCCN:2002-155167.

Audience: **g,l,u.** *Choice, 2003.*

Till-Mobley, Mamie &   **HV6465.M7T55 2003**
  Benson, Christopher
Death of Innocence: The Story of the Hate Crime That Changed
America. Jesse Jackson (Foreword by). Trade Cloth. Random
House Adult Trade Publishing Group. New York, NY. 2003.
320p. ISBN:1-4000-6117-2, ISBN13: 978-1-4000-6117-4.
Dewey:364.1/34. LCCN:2003-046928.

Audience: **g,l,u.**

Timberlake, Andrea   **Z7964.U49**
  (Editor), et al.
Women of Color and Southern Women: A Bibliography of
Social Science Research 1975-1988. Annual Supplement, 1989.
Lynn W. Cannon, Rebecca F. Guy & Elizabeth Higginbotham
(Editors). Trade Paper. University of Memphis, The, Center for
Research on Women. Memphis, TN. 1990. 175p.
ISBN:0-9621327-1-3, ISBN13: 978-0-9621327-1-1.
Dewey:16.3054. LCCN:89-063010.

Audience: **g,l,u.**

Trotter, Joe (Editor), et al.   **HT123.A66168 2004**
The African American Urban Experience: Perspectives from the
Colonial Period to the Present. Tera W. Hunter & Earl Lewis
(Editors). Cloth over Boards. Palgrave Macmillan. New York,
NY. 2004. 352p. ISBN:0-312-29464-6, ISBN13:
978-0-312-29464-9. Dewey:307.76/089/96073.
LCCN:2003-051739.

Audience: **l,u,f.** *Choice, 2004.*

Valelly, Richard M.   **E185.2.V35 2004**
The Two Reconstructions: The Struggle for Black
Enfranchisement. Trade Cloth. University of Chicago Press.
Chicago, IL. 2004. 348p. American Politics and Political
Economy Ser. ISBN:0-226-84528-1, ISBN13:
978-0-226-84528-9. Dewey:323.1196/073/009.
LCCN:2004-010380.

Audience: **g,l,u.** *Choice, 2005.*

Van Sertima, Ivan   **Q127.A4**
Blacks in Science: Ancient and Modern. Trade Paper.
Transaction Publishers. Somerset, NJ. 1983. 333p.
ISBN:0-87855-941-8, ISBN13: 978-0-87855-941-1.
Dewey:509/.6. LCCN:83-071004.

Audience: **g,l,u.**

Van Sertima, Ivan   **E109.A35V35 1998**
Early America Revisited. Trade Paper. Transaction Publishers.
Somerset, NJ. 1998. 235p. African-American Studies
ISBN:0-7658-0463-8, ISBN13: 978-0-7658-0463-1.
Dewey:970.01/9. LCCN:98-013110.

Audience: **g,l,u.**

Van Sertima, Ivan   **DT14.J68**
(Editor)
Great Black Leaders: Ancient and Modern. Trade Paper.
Transaction Publishers. Somerset, NJ. 1988. 433p.
ISBN:0-88738-739-X, ISBN13: 978-0-88738-739-5.
Dewey:305.8. LCCN:91-127942.

Audience: **g,l,u.**

Van Sertima, Ivan   **E109.A35V36 2003**
They Came Before Columbus: The African Presence in Ancient
America. Trade Paper. Random House Adult Trade Publishing
Group. New York, NY. 2003. 336p. ISBN:0-8129-6817-4,
ISBN13: 978-0-8129-6817-0. Dewey:970.01/9.
LCCN:2003-278224.

Audience: **g,l,u.**

Walker, David   **E446**
David Walker's Appeal: To the Coloured Citizens of the World
but in Particular, and Very Expressly, to Those of the United
States of America. James Turner (Introduction by). Trade Paper.
Black Classic Press. Baltimore, MD. 1993. 104p.
ISBN:0-933121-38-5, ISBN13: 978-0-933121-38-6. Dewey:360.
LCCN:92-081885.

Audience: **g,l,u.**

Walters, Ronald W.   **JK1924.W343 2005**
Freedom Is Not Enough: Black Voters, Black Candidates, and
American Presidential Politics. Trade Cloth. Rowman &
Littlefield Publishers, Inc. Lanham, MD. 2005. 256p. American
Political Challenges Ser. ISBN:0-7425-3837-0, ISBN13:
978-0-7425-3837-5. Dewey:324.6/2/08996073.
LCCN:2005-008343.

Audience: **g,l,u,f.** *Choice, 2006.*

Walters, Ronald W.   **DT16.5.W35 1993**
Pan Africanism in the African Diaspora: An Analysis of Modern
Afrocentric Political Movements. Trade Cloth. Wayne State
University Press. Detroit, MI. 1993. 452p. African American
Life Ser. ISBN:0-8143-2184-4, ISBN13: 978-0-8143-2184-3.
Dewey:320.5/49/096. LCCN:92-030256.

Audience: **g,l,u.** *Choice, 1994.*

Washington, Booker T.   **E185.6.W316**
& Du Bois, W. E. B.
The Negro in the South: His Economic Progress in Relation to
His Moral and Religious Development. Herbert Aptheker
(Introduction by). Trade Paper. Carol Publishing Group.
Secaucus, NJ. 1970. ISBN:0-8065-0219-3, ISBN13:
978-0-8065-0219-9. Dewey:330.975.

Audience: **g,l,u.**

Wells-Barnett, Ida B.   **HV6457.W393 2002**
On Lynchings. Patricia Hill Collins (Introduction by). Trade
Paper. Prometheus Books, Publishers. Amherst, NY. 2004. 202p.

Classics in Black Studies ISBN:1-59102-008-5, ISBN13:
978-1-59102-008-0. Dewey:364.1/34. LCCN:2002-020554.

Audience: **g,l,u.**

White, E. Francis   **HQ1426.W465 2001**
Dark Continent of Our Bodies: Black Feminism and the Politics
of Respectability. Library Binding. Temple University Press.
Philadelphia, PA. 2001. ix, 194p. Mapping Racisms Ser.
ISBN:1-56639-879-7, ISBN13: 978-1-56639-879-4.
Dewey:305.42/0973. LCCN:00-053212.

Audience: **g,l,u.**

White, Shane & White,   **E443.W59 2005**
Graham J.
The Sounds of Slavery: Discovering African American History
Through Songs, Sermons, and Speech. Beacon Press. 2005.
ISBN:0-8070-5026-1, ISBN13: 978-0-8070-5026-2.

Audience: **g,l,u,f.**

Willis, Deborah   **TR23.W55 2000**
Reflections in Black: A History of Black Photographers, 1840 to
the Present. Robin D. G. Kelley (Introduction by). Trade Cloth.
W. W. Norton & Company, Inc. New York, NY. 2000. 368p.
ISBN:0-393-04880-2, ISBN13: 978-0-393-04880-3.
Dewey:770/.8996/073. LCCN:99-055185.

Audience: **g,l,u,f.** *Choice, 2001.*

Wilson, Amos N.   **E185.615.W54 1998**
Blueprint for Black Power: A Moral, Political and Economic
Imperative for the Twenty-First Century. Trade Cloth. Afrikan
World InfoSystems. Brooklyn, NY. 1998. ISBN:1-879164-07-8,
ISBN13: 978-1-879164-07-9. Dewey:305.896/073.
LCCN:98-022964.

Audience: **g,l,u,f.**

Woodward, C. Vann   **E185.61**
The Strange Career of Jim Crow. Library Binding. Sagebrush
Education Resources. Caledonia, MN. 2002.
ISBN:0-613-58674-3, ISBN13: 978-0-613-58674-0.
Dewey:305.896/073/09034.

Audience: **g,l,u,f.** *B*

Wright, Richard   **E185.6.W9 2002**
Twelve Million Black Voices: A Folk History of the Negro in
the U. S. Douglas Brinkley, Noel Ignatiev & Michael Eric
Dyson (Preface by). Trade Paper. Avalon Publishing Group.
New York, NY. 2002. 184p. ISBN:1-56025-446-7, ISBN13:
978-1-56025-446-1. Dewey:973/.0496073. LCCN:2003-269647.

Audience: **g,l,u.** *Choice, 1989.*

Zips, Werner   **F1921.H13 1999**
Black Rebels: African-Caribbean Freedom Fighters in Jamaica.
Shelley Frisch (Translator), Franklin Knight (Introduction by).
Trade Cloth. Markus Wiener Publishers, Inc. Princeton, NJ.
1999. 352p. ISBN:1-55876-212-4, ISBN13: 978-1-55876-212-1.
Dewey:972.9/2/00496. LCCN:00-270150.

Audience: **g,l,u.** *Choice, 2000.*

History > Africa

Ben-Jochannan, Yosef   **GN645.B45 1989**
Black Man of the Nile and His Family. Trade Paper. Black
Classic Press. Baltimore, MD. 1989. 381p. ISBN:0-933121-26-1,
ISBN13: 978-0-933121-26-3. Dewey:909/.0496.
LCCN:89-061274.

Audience: **g,l,u,f.**

Bernal, Martin   PR6029.C33F4
Black Athena: The Afroasiatic Roots of Classical Civilization:
The Linguistic Evidence. Trade Cloth. Rutgers University Press.
Piscataway, NJ. 2006. 704p. ISBN:0-8135-3655-3, ISBN13:
978-0-8135-3655-2. Dewey:822.912.

Audience: **g,u,f.**

Clarke, John Henrik   DT25.C58 1993
African People in World History: A Lecture and Illustrated
History. Trade Paper. Black Classic Press. Baltimore, MD. 1993.
100p. ISBN:0-933121-77-6, ISBN13: 978-0-933121-77-5.
Dewey:909/.0496. LCCN:90-082687.

Audience: **g,l,u,f.**

Clarke, John Henrik   E441
Critical Lessons in Slavery and the Slavetrade: Essential Studies
and Commentaries on Slavery, in General and the African
Slavetrade, in Particular. Ed. 2. Trade Cloth. Native Sun
Publishers, Inc. Richmond, VA. 1997. 208p. Truth and Sanity
Reprint Ser. ISBN:1-879289-06-7, ISBN13: 978-1-879289-06-2.
Dewey:306.362/. LCCN:96-068505.

Audience: **g,l,u,f.**

Diop, Cheikh Anta   GN479.5
The Cultural Unity of Black Africa. Ed. 2. John Henrik Clarke
(Introduction by). Trade Paper. Third World Press. Chicago, IL.
1987. ISBN:0-88378-049-6, ISBN13: 978-0-88378-049-7.
Dewey:960. LCCN:77-012276.

Audience: **g,l,u.**

Diop, Cheikh Anta   DT61
The African Origin of Civilization: Myth or Reality. Mercer
Cook (Editor, Translator). Trade Paper. Chicago Review Press,
Inc. Chicago, IL. 1989. 317p. ISBN:1-55652-072-7, ISBN13:
978-1-55652-072-3. Dewey:932.01. LCCN:73-081746.

Audience: **g,l,u,f.**

Diop, Cheikh Anta   DT14.D5613 1990
Civilization or Barbarism: An Authentic Anthropology. Harold J.
Salemson & Marjolijn de Jager (Editors), Yaa-Lengi Meema
Ngemi (Translator), John Henrik Clarke (Introduction by). Trade
Cloth. Chicago Review Press, Inc. Chicago, IL. 1991. 440p.
ISBN:1-55652-049-2, ISBN13: 978-1-55652-049-5. Dewey:960.
LCCN:90-004141.

Audience: **g,l,u.** *Choice, 1991.*

Fanon, Frantz   DT33.F313 2004
The Wretched of the Earth. Trade Paper. Grove/Atlantic, Inc.
New York, NY. 2004. 256p. ISBN:0-8021-4132-3, ISBN13:
978-0-8021-4132-3. Dewey:960/.0971244. LCCN:2004-042476.

Audience: **g,l,u,f.** *B*

Herskovits, Melville   E185.H52 1990
  Jean
The Myth of the Negro Past. Sidney W. Mintz (Introduction by).
Trade Paper. Beacon Press. Boston, MA. 1990. 416p.
ISBN:0-8070-0905-9, ISBN13: 978-0-8070-0905-5.
Dewey:973/.0496073. LCCN:89-043083.

Audience: **g,l,u,f.**

Jackson, John G.   DT21
Introduction to African Civilizations. Runoko Rashidi (Foreword
by), John Henrik Clarke (Introduction by). Trade Paper.
Kensington Publishing Corporation. New York, NY. 2001. 400p.
ISBN:0-8065-2189-9, ISBN13: 978-0-8065-2189-3. Dewey:960.

Audience: **g,l,u.**

James, George   B178.5
Stolen Legacy. Trade Paper. African American Images. Chicago,
IL. 2002. 192p. ISBN:0-913543-78-0, ISBN13:
978-0-913543-78-8. Dewey:180.

Audience: **g,l,u.**

Jenkins, Everett Jr.   E185.2.J46 1998
Pan-African Chronology 1865-1915: A Comprehensive
Reference to the Black Quest for Freedom in Africa, the
Americas, Europe and Asia, 1865-1915. Cloth Text. McFarland
& Company, Incorporated Publishers. Jefferson, NC. 1998.
582p. Pan-African Chronology Ser. ISBN:0-7864-0385-3,
ISBN13: 978-0-7864-0385-1. Dewey:909/.049608/0202.
LCCN:95-8294.

Audience: **g,l,u,f.** *Choice, 1998.*

Jenkins, Everett Jr.   E185.18
Pan-African Chronology 1914-1929: Reference to the Black
Quest for Freedom in Africa, the Americas, Europe, Asia, and
Australia, 1914-1929. Cloth Text. McFarland & Company,
Incorporated Publishers. Jefferson, NC. 2001. 640p. Pan-African
Chronology Ser. ISBN:0-7864-0835-9, ISBN13:
978-0-7864-0835-1. Dewey:909/.04/96. LCCN:95-8294.

Audience: **g,l,u,f.** *Choice, 2001.*

Jenkins, Everett Jr.   E185.18.J46 1996
Pan-African Chronology, 1400-1865: A Comprehensive
Reference to the Black Quest for Freedom in Africa, the
Americas, Europe and Asia, 1400-1865. Cloth Text. McFarland
& Company, Incorporated Publishers. Jefferson, NC. 1996.
448p. Pan-African Chronology Ser. ISBN:0-7864-0139-7,
ISBN13: 978-0-7864-0139-0. Dewey:909/.0496/00202.
LCCN:95-8294.

Audience: **g,l,u,f.**

Langley, J. Ayodele   DT353.L33
  (Editor)
Ideologies of Liberation in Black Africa, 1856-1970. Trade
Paper. Africa Book Centre. Brighton, 2004. 858p.
ISBN:0-86036-039-3, ISBN13: 978-0-86036-039-1.
Dewey:320.5/096. LCCN:80-458475.

Audience: **g,l,u.**

Lefkowitz, Mary   DT14.L44 1997
Not Out of Africa: How Afrocentrism Became an Excuse to
Teach Myth As History. Trade Paper. Basic Books. New York,
NY. 1997. 320p. ISBN:0-465-09838-X, ISBN13:
978-0-465-09838-5. Dewey:949.5. LCCN:97-183099.

Audience: **g,l,u.**

Mazrui, Ali Al'Amin   DT38
The African Predicament and the American Experience: A Tale
of Two Edens. Trade Cloth. Greenwood Publishing Group, Inc.
Portsmouth, NH. 2004. 136p. ISBN:0-275-97828-1, ISBN13:
978-0-275-97828-0. Dewey:303.48/26073. LCCN:2003-044220.

Audience: **g,l,u,f.**

Poe, Richard   D62.P63
Black Spark, White Fire: Did African Explorers Civilize Ancient
Europe? Trade Paper. Crown Publishing Group. New York, NY.
1999. 576p. ISBN:0-7615-2163-1, ISBN13: 978-0-7615-2163-1.
Dewey:936.

Audience: **l,u,f.**

Sims, James L., et al.   DT634.A37 2003
African-American Exploration in West Africa: Four
Nineteenth-Century Diaries. George L. Seymour & Benjamin J.
K. Anderson (Authors), James Fairhead (Editor). Trade Cloth.
Indiana University Press. Bloomington, IN. 2003. 440p.

ISBN:0-253-34194-9, ISBN13: 978-0-253-34194-5.
Dewey:916.66204/2. LCCN:2002-152631.

Audience: **l,u,f.** *Choice, 2004.*

Wesseling, H. L. **DT28**
Divide and Rule: The Partition of Africa, 1880-1914. Arnold J.
Pomerans (Translator). Trade Cloth. Greenwood Publishing
Group, Inc. Portsmouth, NH. 1996. 464p. ISBN:0-275-95137-5,
ISBN13: 978-0-275-95137-5. Dewey:960.3/12.
LCCN:95-038253.

Audience: **g,l,u,f.** *Choice, 1996.*

Williams, Chancellor **DT14.W53 1987**
The Destruction of Black Civilization. Ed. 3. Trade Cloth. Third
World Press. Chicago, IL. 1987. 384p. ISBN:0-88378-030-5,
ISBN13: 978-0-88378-030-5. Dewey:916/.0696.
LCCN:96-208553.

Audience: **g,l,u.**

History > Diaspora

Anderson, S. E. **HT861**
The Black Holocaust for Beginners. Vanessa Holley (Illustrator).
Trade Paper. Writers & Readers Publishing, Inc. New York, NY.
1995. 192p. ISBN:0-86316-178-2, ISBN13: 978-0-86316-178-0.
Dewey:306.3/62.

Audience: **g,l,u,f.**

Conniff, Michael L. & **E29.N3C68 1994**
Davis, Thomas J.
Africans in the Americas: A History of the Black Diaspora.
Trade Cloth. Palgrave Macmillan. New York, NY. 1994. 400p.
ISBN:0-312-10275-5, ISBN13: 978-0-312-10275-3.
Dewey:973/.0496. LCCN:92-062717.

Audience: **g,l,u,f.** *Choice, 1994.*

Dubois, Laurent & **F1923**
Garrigus, John
Slave Revolution in the Caribbean, 1789-1804: A Brief History
with Documents. Cloth over Boards. Palgrave Macmillan. New
York, NY. 2006. 208p. The Bedford Series in History and
Culture Ser. ISBN:1-4039-7157-9, ISBN13: 978-1-4039-7157-9.
Dewey:972.9403.

Audience: **l,u.**

Gomez, Michael A. **DT16.5.G66 2004**
Reversing Sail: A History of the African Diaspora. Martin Klein
(Contribution by). Cloth Text. Cambridge University Press. New
York, NY. 2004. 248p. New Approaches to African History Ser.,
Vol. 3 ISBN:0-521-80662-3, ISBN13: 978-0-521-80662-6.
Dewey:909/.0496. LCCN:2004-051992.

Audience: **g,l,u,f.** *Choice, 2005.*

Holloway, Joseph E. **E185.A26 2005**
(Editor)
Africanisms in American Culture. Ed. 2. Trade Paper, Perfect.
Indiana University Press. Bloomington, IN. 2005. 312p. Blacks
in the Diaspora Ser. ISBN:0-253-21749-0, ISBN13:
978-0-253-21749-3. Dewey:973/.0496073. LCCN:2004-020284.

Audience: **g,l,u,f.** *Choice, 1990.*

Jenkins, Everett Jr. **E185.2.J46 1998**
Pan-African Chronology 1865-1915: A Comprehensive
Reference to the Black Quest for Freedom in Africa, the
Americas, Europe and Asia, 1865-1915. Cloth Text. McFarland
& Company, Incorporated Publishers. Jefferson, NC. 1998.
582p. Pan-African Chronology Ser. ISBN:0-7864-0385-3,

ISBN13: 978-0-7864-0385-1. Dewey:909/.049608/0202.
LCCN:95-8294.

Audience: **g,l,u,f.** *Choice, 1998.*

Jenkins, Everett Jr. **E185.18**
Pan-African Chronology 1914-1929: Reference to the Black
Quest for Freedom in Africa, the Americas, Europe, Asia, and
Australia, 1914-1929. Cloth Text. McFarland & Company,
Incorporated Publishers. Jefferson, NC. 2001. 640p. Pan-African
Chronology Ser. ISBN:0-7864-0835-9, ISBN13:
978-0-7864-0835-1. Dewey:909/.04/96. LCCN:95-8294.

Audience: **g,l,u,f.** *Choice, 2001.*

Jenkins, Everett Jr. **E185.18.J46 1996**
Pan-African Chronology, 1400-1865: A Comprehensive
Reference to the Black Quest for Freedom in Africa, the
Americas, Europe and Asia, 1400-1865. Cloth Text. McFarland
& Company, Incorporated Publishers. Jefferson, NC. 1996.
448p. Pan-African Chronology Ser. ISBN:0-7864-0139-7,
ISBN13: 978-0-7864-0139-0. Dewey:909/.0496/00202.
LCCN:95-8294.

Audience: **g,l,u,f.**

Lovejoy, Paul E. **E29.N3T73 2002**
Trans-Atlantic Dimensions of Ethnicity in the African Diaspora.
Trotman, David Vincent. Continuum. 2003.
ISBN:0-8264-4907-7, ISBN13: 978-0-8264-4907-8.

Audience: **g,l,u,f.**

Mullen, Bill **E185.615.M75 2004**
Afro-Orientalism. Trade Cloth. University of Minnesota Press.
Minneapolis, MN. 2004. 256p. ISBN:0-8166-3748-2, ISBN13:
978-0-8166-3748-5. Dewey:305.896/073. LCCN:2004-014985.

Audience: **l,u,f.** *Choice, 2005.*

Pybus, Cassandra **E450.P99 2006**
Epic Journeys of Freedom. Beacon Press. 2006.
ISBN:0-8070-5514-X, ISBN13: 978-0-8070-5514-4.

Audience: **g,l,u,f.**

Scruggs, Afi-Odelia E. **E185.97**
Claiming Kin: Confronting the History of an African American
Family. Trade Paper. St. Martin's Press. Gordonville, VA. 2003.
208p. ISBN:0-312-30252-5, ISBN13: 978-0-312-30252-8.
Dewey:976.8/5600496073/009.

Audience: **g,l,u.**

Terborg-Penn, Rosalyn **HQ1787.W65 1996**
& Rushing, Andrea B. (Editors)
Women in Africa and the African Diaspora: A Reader. Ed. 2.
Trade Paper. Howard University Press. Washington, DC. 1996.
ISBN:0-88258-194-5, ISBN13: 978-0-88258-194-1.
Dewey:305.42/096. LCCN:96-046285.

Audience: **g,l,u.**

Thompson, Kathleen & **E185.86.F33 1999**
Mac Austin, Hilary (Editors)
The Face of Our Past: Images of Black Women from Colonial
America to the Present. Darlene Clark Hine (Introduction by).
Trade Cloth. Indiana University Press. Bloomington, IN. 2000.
xiv, 258p. ISBN:0-253-33635-X, ISBN13: 978-0-253-33635-4.
Dewey:920.72/08996073. LCCN:99-024662.

Audience: **g,l,u.**

Van Sertima, Ivan **DT14.J68**
(Editor)
African Presence in Early Europe. Trade Paper. Transaction
Publishers. Somerset, NJ. 1986. 345p. ISBN:0-88738-664-4,

ISBN13: 978-0-88738-664-0. Dewey:940/.0496.
LCCN:85-028870.

Audience: **g,l,u.**

History > Civil Rights Movement

Branch, Taylor   **E185.61.B7914 1989**
Parting the Waters: America in the King Years, 1954-1963.
Trade Paper. Simon & Schuster. New York, NY. 1989. 1088p.
ISBN:0-671-68742-5, ISBN13: 978-0-671-68742-7.
Dewey:973/.0496073. LCCN:97-130525.

Audience: **g,l,u.** *Choice, 1989.*

Carson, Clayborne   **E185.92**
In Struggle: SNCC and the Black Awakening of the Nineteen
Sixties. Trade Paper. Harvard University Press. Cambridge, MA.
1982. 373p. ISBN:0-674-44726-3, ISBN13: 978-0-674-44726-4.
Dewey:322.420973. LCCN:80-016540.

Audience: **g,l,u.** *B*

Carson, Clayborne   **E185**
  (Editor)
The Student Voice, 1960-1965: Periodical of the Student
Nonviolent Coordinating Committee. Cloth Text. Greenwood
Publishing Group, Inc. Portsmouth, NH. 1990. 264p.
ISBN:0-313-28050-9, ISBN13: 978-0-313-28050-4.
Dewey:378.1981. LCCN:89-049690.

Audience: **g,l,u.**

Clar, D.   **E185.615.E95 1991**
The Eyes on the Prize Civil Rights Reader: Documents,
Speeches, and Firsthand Accounts from the Black Freedom
Movement, 1954-1990. Clayborne Carson, David J. Garrow,
Gerald Gill, Vincent Harding & Darlene Clark Hine (Editors).
Trade Paper. Penguin Group (USA) Inc. New York, NY. 1991.
784p. Eyes on the Prize Ser. ISBN:0-14-015403-5, ISBN13:
978-0-14-015403-0. Dewey:323.1196073. LCCN:91-009507.

Audience: **g,l,u.**

Collier-Thomas, Betty   **E185.61.S615 2001**
  & Franklin, V. P. (Editors)
Sisters in the Struggle: African-American Women in the Civil
Rights and Black Power Movements. Trade Cloth. New York
University Press. New York, NY. 2001. 376p.
ISBN:0-8147-1602-4, ISBN13: 978-0-8147-1602-1.
Dewey:323.1/196073/0922. LCCN:2001-001550.

Audience: **g,l,u.** *Choice, 2002.*

Davidson, Bruce   **TR647.D375A4 2002**
Bruce Davidson: Time of Change: Civil Rights Photographs,
1961-1965. John Lewis (Foreword by), Deborah Willis
(Introduction by). Trade Cloth. Saint Ann's Press. Los Angeles,
CA. 2003. 172p. ISBN:0-9713681-1-2, ISBN13:
978-0-9713681-1-8. Dewey:323.09730222.

Audience: **g,l,u.**

McNeil, Genna Rae   **KF373.H644**
Groundwork: Charles Hamilton Houston and the Struggle for
Civil Rights. University of Pennsylvania Press. 1983.
ISBN:0-8122-7878-X, ISBN13: 978-0-8122-7878-1.

Audience: **g,l,u.**

Ogletree, Charles Jr.   **KF4757**
All Deliberate Speed: Reflections on the First Half Century of
Brown v. Board of Education. W.W. Norton and Co.. 2004.
ISBN:0-393-05897-2, ISBN13: 978-0-393-05897-0.

Audience: **g,u,f.**

Olson, Lynne   **E185.O43 2002**
Freedom's Daughters: The Unsung Heroines of the Civil Rights
Movement from 1830 to 1970. Trade Paper. Simon & Schuster.
New York, NY. 2002. 464p. ISBN:0-684-85013-3, ISBN13:
978-0-684-85013-9. Dewey:323/.092/275.

Audience: **g,l,u.**

White, Deborah Gray   **E185.86.W43875**
Too Heavy a Load: Black Women in Defense of Themselves,
1894-1994. Trade Paper. W. W. Norton & Company, Inc. New
York, NY. 1999. 320p. ISBN:0-393-31992-X, ISBN13:
978-0-393-31992-7. Dewey:305.4/8896073. LCCN:98-006518.

Audience: **g,l,u.**

Williams, Juan   **JC599.U5**
Eyes on the Prize: America's Civil Rights Years, 1954-1965.
Library Binding. Sagebrush Education Resources. Caledonia,
MN. 1988. ISBN:0-8335-1431-8, ISBN13: 978-0-8335-1431-8.
Dewey:323.4/0973.

Audience: **g,l,u.** *Choice, 1988.*

Williams, Juan   **E184.A1**
My Soul Looks Back in Wonder: Voices of the Civil Rights
Experience. David Halberstam (Foreword by), Marian Wright
Edelman (Afterword by). Trade Paper, Perfect. Sterling
Publishing Co., Inc. New York, NY. 2005. 248p.
ISBN:1-4027-2233-8, ISBN13: 978-1-4027-2233-2.
Dewey:323.173/09/045.

Audience: **g,l,u.**

History > Black Nationalism

Alkalimat, Abdul
☐ Malcolm X: A Research Site.
http://www.brothermalcolm.net/
University of Toledo and Twenty-first Century Books.

Audience: **g,l,u.**

Flowers, Sandra H.   **PS153.N5F56 1996**
African American Nationalist Literature of the 1960s: Pens of
Fire. Cloth Text. Garland Publishing, Inc. New York, NY. 1996.
216p. Studies in American Popular History and Culture
ISBN:0-8153-2474-X, ISBN13: 978-0-8153-2474-4.
Dewey:810.9/896073. LCCN:96-005278.

Audience: **g,l,u.**

Garvey, Marcus   **E185.97.G3A25 2004**
Selected Writings and Speeches of Marcus Garvey. Bob
Blaisdell (Editor). Trade Paper. Dover Publications, Inc.
Mineola, NY. 2005. 224p. Dover Thrift Editions Ser.
ISBN:0-486-43787-6, ISBN13: 978-0-486-43787-3.
Dewey:320.54/6. LCCN:2004-056231.

Audience: **g,l,u.**

Garvey, Marcus   **E185.97.G3A25 1986**
The Philosophy and Opinions of Marcus Garvey: Or, Africa for
the Africans. Amy J. Garvey (Compiled by), Tony Martin
(Preface by). Trade Cloth. Majority Press, Incorporated, The.
Dover, MA. 1986. 600p. New Marcus Garvey Library, No. 9
ISBN:0-912469-24-2, ISBN13: 978-0-912469-24-9.
Dewey:973/.0496073. LCCN:86-018031.

Audience: **g,l,u.**

Jones, Charles E.   **E185.615.B5464**
  (Editor)
Black Panther Party Reconsidered. Trade Paper. Black Classic

Press. Baltimore, MD. 2005. 519p. ISBN:0-933121-97-0, ISBN13: 978-0-933121-97-3. Dewey:322.420973.

Audience: **g,l,u,f.**

Mezu, S. Okechukwu &   **QC171.G29**
  Mezu, Rose Ure (Editor, Contribution by)
Black Nationalists: Reconsidering Du Bois, Garvey, Booker T. and Nkrumah. Amiri Baraka, Jamal-Harrison Bryant, Bernard W. Bell, Etta Hill, Abraham M. Smith, Chinwe Okoro-Effiong & Yuichiro Onishi (Contribution by). Paper Text. Black Academy Press, Inc. Baltimore, MD. 1999. 232p. ISBN:0-87831-093-2, ISBN13: 978-0-87831-093-7. Dewey:539.

Audience: **l,u.**

Moses, Wilson J.   **E184.6.C62 1996**
  (Editor)
Classical Black Nationalism: From the American Revolution to Marcus Garvey. Trade Cloth. New York University Press. New York, NY. 1996. 267p. ISBN:0-8147-5524-0, ISBN13: 978-0-8147-5524-2. Dewey:973/.0496073. LCCN:95-044335.

Audience: **l,u,f.**

Moses, Wilson J.   **E185.89.N**
The Golden Age of Black Nationalism, 1850-1925. Paper Text. Oxford University Press, Inc. New York, NY. 1988. 348p. ISBN:0-19-520639-8, ISBN13: 978-0-19-520639-5. Dewey:323.1/196073.

Audience: **g,l,u.**

Newton, Huey P.   **E185.615.N4 1995**
To Die for the People: The Writings of Huey P. Newton. Morrison, Toni (Editor). Readers and Writers Publishers. 1995. ISBN:0-86316-327-0, ISBN13: 978-0-86316-327-2.

Audience: **g,l,u.**

Seale, Bobby   **E185.615.S37**
Seize the Time: The Story of the Black Panther Party and Huey P. Newton. Random House. 1970.

Audience: **l,u.**

Smethurst, James   **PS153.N5S56 2005**
  Edward
The Black Arts Movement: Literary Nationalism in the 1960s and 1970s. Trade Paper. University of North Carolina Press. Chapel Hill, NC. 2005. 480p. The John Hope Franklin Series in African American History and Culture Ser. ISBN:0-8078-5598-7, ISBN13: 978-0-8078-5598-0. Dewey:810.9/896073. LCCN:2004-027170.

Audience: **g,l,u.** *Choice, 2005.*

Tyson, Timothy B.   **F264.M75T97 1999**
Radio Free Dixie: Robert F. Williams and the Roots of Black Power. University of North Carolina Press. 1999. ISBN:0-8078-2502-6, ISBN13: 978-0-8078-2502-0.

Audience: **g,l,u.**

History > Pan-Africanism

Martin, Guy   **DT30.5.M275 2000**
Africa in World Politics: A Pan-African Perspective. Trade Paper. Africa World Press. Trenton, NJ. 2003. 328p. ISBN:0-86543-858-7, ISBN13: 978-0-86543-858-3. Dewey:327/.096. LCCN:00-030616.

Audience: **g,l,u,f.**

Poe, Daryl Zizwe   **DT512.3.N57P64 2003**
Kwame Nkrumah's Contribution to Pan-African Agency: An Afrocentric Analysis. Paper over Boards. Routledge. New York,

NY. 2003. 204p. African Studies, :History, Politics, Economics and Culture ISBN:0-415-94643-3, ISBN13: 978-0-415-94643-8. Dewey:341.24/9. LCCN:2003-004068.

Audience: **g,l,u.**

Sherwood, Marika &   **DT30.S515 2003**
  Adi, Hakim
Pan-African History: Political Figures from Africa and the Diaspora since 1787. Trade Paper. Routledge. New York, NY. 2003. 224p. ISBN:0-415-17353-1, ISBN13: 978-0-415-17353-7. Dewey:320.54/9/092396. LCCN:2002-011566.

Audience: **g,l,u,f.** *Choice, 2003.*

Temple, Christel N.   **PN849.A35T46 2003**
Literary Pan-Africanism: History, Context and Criticism. Trade Paper. Carolina Academic Press. Durham, NC. 2004. 208p. ISBN:0-89089-848-0, ISBN13: 978-0-89089-848-2. Dewey:809/.8896/009045. LCCN:2003-065296.

Audience: **g,l,u.**

Africana Studies

Alkalimat, Abdul   **E184.6**
The African American Experience in Cyberspace: A Resource Guide to the Best Web Sites on Black Culture and History. Trade Cloth. Pluto Press. London, 2003. 304p. ISBN:0-7453-2223-9, ISBN13: 978-0-7453-2223-0. Dewey:025.06/305896073. LCCN:2004-298825.

Audience: **g,l,u,f.** *Choice, 2004.*

Alkalimat, Abdul   **E184.7**
  (Editor)
Paradigms in Black Studies: Intellectual History, Cultural Meaning and Political Ideology. Cloth Text. Twenty-First Century Books & Publications. Chicago, IL. 1987. 190p. Annual Theoretical Review in Afro-American Studies ISBN:0-940103-02-8, ISBN13: 978-0-940103-02-3. Dewey:305.89607.

Audience: **u,f.**

Asante, Molefi K. &   **E185.E554 2004**
  Mazama, Ama
Encyclopedia of Black Studies. SAGE Publications. 2005. ISBN:0-7619-2762-X, ISBN13: 978-0-7619-2762-4.

Audience: **g,l,u.**

Asante, Molefi Kete   **P94.5.A37A78 1998**
The Afrocentric Idea. Ed. 2. Paper Text. Temple University Press. Philadelphia, PA. 1998. 256p. ISBN:1-56639-595-X, ISBN13: 978-1-56639-595-3. Dewey:909/.0496. LCCN:97-040735.

Audience: **u,f.**

Bobo, Jacqueline   **E185.625**
  (Editor), et al.
The Black Studies Reader. Cynthia Hudley & Claudine Michel (Editors). Paper over Boards. Routledge. New York, NY. 2004. 504p. ISBN:0-415-94553-4, ISBN13: 978-0-415-94553-0. Dewey:305.896/073. LCCN:2003-027162.

Audience: **g,l,u.**

Brown, Lorene Byron   **Z695.1.B57B76 1995**
Subject Headings for African American Materials. Libraries Unlimited, Inc. 1995. ISBN:1-56308-252-7, ISBN13: 978-1-56308-252-8.

Audience: **u,f.**

Conyers, James L.   E184.7.A35 2003
   (Editor)
Afrocentricity and the Academy: Essays on Theory and Practice.
Paper Text. McFarland & Company, Incorporated Publishers.
Jefferson, NC. 2003. 320p. ISBN:0-7864-1542-8, ISBN13:
978-0-7864-1542-7. Dewey:973/.0496073. LCCN:2002-156433.
                 Audience: **u,f.** *Choice, 2004.*

Fossett, Judith J. &   E185.R23 1997
   Tucker, Jeffrey A. (Editors)
Race Consciousness: African-American Studies for the New
Century. Robin D. Kelley (Foreword by), Arnold Rampersad &
Nell I. Painter (Preface by). Trade Cloth. New York University
Press. New York, NY. 1997. 224p. ISBN:0-8147-4227-0,
ISBN13: 978-0-8147-4227-3. Dewey:305.896/073.
LCCN:96-042999.
                 Audience: **u,f.**

Gates, Henry Louis Jr.   E185.96
   & Burton, Jennifer (Editors)
African American Studies Reader. Paper Text. W. W. Norton &
Company, Inc. New York, NY. 2006. ISBN:0-393-97578-9,
ISBN13: 978-0-393-97578-9. Dewey:920/.009296073/00904.
                 Audience: **g,l,u,f.**

Hall, Perry A.   E184.7
In the Vineyard: Working in African American Studies. Trade
Paper. University of Tennessee Press. Knoxville, TN. 2005.
264p. ISBN:1-57233-368-5, ISBN13: 978-1-57233-368-0.
Dewey:305.896073/071.
            Audience: **g,l,u,f.** *Choice, 2000.*

Henderson, Errol A.   D13
Afrocentrism and World Politics: Towards a New Paradigm.
Trade Cloth. Greenwood Publishing Group, Inc. Portsmouth,
NH. 1995. 240p. ISBN:0-275-95127-8, ISBN13:
978-0-275-95127-6. Dewey:907/.2. LCCN:94-046170.
                 Audience: **g,u,f.**

Hornsby, Alton (Editor)   E185.C66 2005
Companion to African American History. Trade Cloth. Blackwell
Publishing, Inc. Malden, MA. 2005. 584p. Blackwell
Companions to American History Ser. ISBN:0-631-23066-1,
ISBN13: 978-0-631-23066-3. Dewey:973/.0496073.
LCCN:2004-011680.
            Audience: **g,l,u.** *Choice, 2005.*

Karenga, Maulana   E185
Introduction to Black Studies. Ed. 3. Perfect. University of
Sankore Press, The. Los Angeles, CA. 2002. 578p.
ISBN:0-943412-23-4, ISBN13: 978-0-943412-23-8.
Dewey:973.0496.
                 Audience: **g,l,u,f.**

Keto, C. Tsehloane   DT21.K49 2000
Vision and Time: Historical Perspective of an Africa-Centered
Paradigm. University Press of America. 2001.
ISBN:0-7618-1893-6, ISBN13: 978-0-7618-1893-9.
                 Audience: **u,f.**

Logan, Rayford W. &   E185.96.D53 1982
   Winston, Michael R. (Editors)
Dictionary of American Negro Biography. Trade Cloth. W. W.
Norton & Company, Inc. New York, NY. 1983. 680p.
ISBN:0-393-01513-0, ISBN13: 978-0-393-01513-3.
Dewey:920/.009296073 B. LCCN:81-009629.
            Audience: **g,l,u,f.** *B*

Marable, Manning   E184.7.N48 2005
The New Black Renaissance: The Souls Anthology of Critical
African-American Studies. Ed. 6. Trade Paper. Paradigm
Publishers. Boulder, CO. 2005. 400p. ISBN:1-59451-142-X,
ISBN13: 978-1-59451-142-4. Dewey:305.8/0973.
LCCN:2005-021804.
                 Audience: **g,l,u,f.**

Mazama, Ama (Editor)   DT15.A365 2002
The Afrocentric Paradigm. Trade Cloth. Africa World Press.
Trenton, NJ. 2002. 300p. ISBN:1-59221-017-1, ISBN13:
978-1-59221-017-6. Dewey:960/.01. LCCN:2002-010372.
                 Audience: **g,l,u,f.**

New York Public   E185.N57 1999
   Library
The New York Public Library African American Desk
Reference. J. Wiley & Sons. 1999. ISBN:0-471-23924-0,
ISBN13: 978-0-471-23924-6.
                 Audience: **g,l,u,f.**

New York Public   E185
   Library, ProQuest Information and Learning
☐ Black Studies Center: Schomburg Studies on the Black
Experience.
http://www.proquest.com/products_pq/descriptions/
schomburg.shtml
Dodson, Howard; Plamer, Colin. ProQuest Information and
Learning.
                 Audience: **g,l,u,f.**

Nosakhere, Akilah   Z1361.N39
   Shukura (Compiled by), et al.
African-American Studies Core List of Resources. M. Elaine
Hughes & Anne Page Mosby (Compiled by). Perfect. Blackburn
Press, The. Caldwell, NJ. 2004. 95p. ISBN:1-932846-01-8,
ISBN13: 978-1-932846-01-0. Dewey:016.305896/0703.
LCCN:2004-109342.
            Audience: **g,l,u,f.** *Choice, 2005.*

ProQuest Company   Z6944.N39
☐ International Index to Black Periodicals Full Text (IIBP).
http://www.proquest.com
                 Audience: **g,l,u,f.**

Rooks, Noliwe   E184.7
White Money/Black Power: The Surprising History of African
American Studies and the Crisis of Race in Higher Education.
Beacon Press. 2006. ISBN:0-8070-3270-0, ISBN13:
978-0-8070-3270-1.
                 Audience: **l,u,f.**

Africana Studies > Diaspora

Alexander Street Press   E185
☐ Black Thought and Culture.
http://www.alexanderstreetpress.com/products/bltc.htm
Alexander Street Press.
                 Audience: **g,l,u,f.**

Africana Studies > Africa

Karenga, Maulana &   DT61.A84 1984
   Carruthers, Jacob
Kemet and the African Worldview: Research, Rescue and
Restoration. Trade Paper. University of Sankore Press, The. Los

Angeles, CA. 1986. 197p. ISBN:0-943412-07-2, ISBN13: 978-0-943412-07-8. Dewey:932. LCCN:91-135971.

Audience: **g,l,u,f.**

Art

Bearden, Romare &   **N6538.N5B38 1993**
  Harry Henderson
A History of African-American Artists: From 1792 to the Present. Pantheon Books. 1993. ISBN:0-394-57016-2, ISBN13: 978-0-394-57016-7.

Audience: **g,l,u,f.**

Driskell, David C.   **N6538.N5**
Harlem Renaissance: Art of Black America. Abradale Press. 1994. ISBN:0-8109-8128-9, ISBN13: 978-0-8109-8128-7.

Audience: **l,u.**

Art > Performing Arts/Cinema/Television

Anderson, Lisa M.   **PS338.W6A53 1997**
Mammies No More: The Changing Image of Black Women on Stage and Screen. Trade Cloth. Rowman & Littlefield Publishers, Inc. Lanham, MD. 1997. 160p. ISBN:0-8476-8419-9, ISBN13: 978-0-8476-8419-9. Dewey:791.4/3652/0396073. LCCN:97-009782.

Audience: **g,l,u,f.** *Choice, 1998.*

Bean, Annemarie   **PN2270.A35S68 1999**
Sourcebook of African-American Performance. Routledge. 1999. Worlds of Performances ISBN:0-415-18234-4, ISBN13: 978-0-415-18234-8.

Audience: **u,f.**

Bogle, Donald   **PN1995.9.N4**
Toms, Coons, Mulattoes, Mammies, and Bucks: An Interpretive History of Blacks in American Films. Trade Cloth. Continuum International Publishing Group, Ltd. London, 2003. 480p. ISBN:0-8264-1518-0, ISBN13: 978-0-8264-1518-9. Dewey:791.43652.

Audience: **g,l,u.**

Brown-Guillory,   **PS628**
  Elizabeth (Editor)
Wines in the Wilderness: Plays by African American Women from the Harlem Renaissance to the Present. Book, Other. Greenwood Publishing Group, Inc. Portsmouth, NH. 1990. 272p. Contributions in Afro-American and African Studies Ser., No. 135 ISBN:0-313-26509-7, ISBN13: 978-0-313-26509-9. Dewey:812/.5080352042. LCCN:89-025857.

Audience: **g,l,u.** *Choice, 1991.*

Early, Gerald L.   **E185.615.E16 2003**
This Is Where I Came In: Black America in the 1960s. Trade Cloth. University of Nebraska Press. Lincoln, NE. 2003. 160p. Abraham Lincoln Lecture Ser. ISBN:0-8032-1823-0, ISBN13: 978-0-8032-1823-9. Dewey:323.1/196073/009046. LCCN:2003-047302.

Audience: **g,l,u.**

Gavin, Christy   **PS153.N5G29 1999**
African American Women Playwrights: A Research Guide. C. James Trotman (Editor). Cloth Text. Garland Publishing, Inc. New York, NY. 1999. 264p. Critical Studies in Black Life and

Culture, Vol. 31 ISBN:0-8153-2384-0, ISBN13: 978-0-8153-2384-6. Dewey:812/.54099287. LCCN:98-040865.

Audience: **g,l,u.** *Choice, 2000.*

Grant, William R.   **PN1995.9.N4G69 2003**
Post-Soul Black Cinema: Discontinuities, Innovations and Breakpoints, 1970-1995. Paper over Boards. Routledge. New York, NY. 2004. 112p. Studies in African American History and Culture Ser. ISBN:0-415-94768-5, ISBN13: 978-0-415-94768-8. Dewey:791.43/652996073. LCCN:2003-017036.

Audience: **g,l,u.**

Gugler, Josef   **PN1993**
Afican Film: Reimaging a Continent. Indiana University Press. 2003. ISBN:0-85255-562-8, ISBN13: 978-0-85255-562-0.

Audience: **g,l,u.**

Hill, Errol G. & Hatch,   **PN2270.A35H55 2003**
  James V.
A History of African American Theatre. Cambridge University Press. 2003. ISBN:0-521-62443-6, ISBN13: 978-0-521-62443-5.

Audience: **l,u.**

Manatu, Norma   **PN1995.9.N4M28 2002**
African American Women and Sexuality in the Cinema. Paper Text. McFarland & Company, Incorporated Publishers. Jefferson, NC. 2002. 245p. ISBN:0-7864-1431-6, ISBN13: 978-0-7864-1431-4. Dewey:791.43/652042. LCCN:2002-015421.

Audience: **g,l,u.** *Choice, 2003.*

Marsh-Lockett, Carol P.   **PS338.N4B57 1999**
  (Editor)
Black Women Playwrights: Visions on the American Stage. Cloth Text. Garland Publishing, Inc. New York, NY. 1998. 240p. Studies in Modern Drama, Vol. 11 ISBN:0-8153-2746-3, ISBN13: 978-0-8153-2746-2. Dewey:812.0099287. LCCN:98-042553.

Audience: **g,l,u.**

Perkins, Kathy A.   **PS628.N4**
  (Editor)
[e] Black Female Playwrights: An Anthology of Plays Before 1950. E-Book. Indiana University Press. Bloomington, IN. 1990. 298p. Blacks in the Diaspora Ser. ISBN:0-253-20623-5, ISBN13: 978-0-253-20623-7. Dewey:812/.008/09287. LCCN:88-046040.

Audience: **g,l,u,f.** *Choice, 1990.*

Smith-Shomade, Beretta   **PN1992.8.A34S48 2002**
  E.
Shaded Lives: African American Women and Television. Trade Cloth. Rutgers University Press. Piscataway, NJ. 2002. 256p. ISBN:0-8135-3104-7, ISBN13: 978-0-8135-3104-5. Dewey:791.45/652042. LCCN:2001-048840.

Audience: **g,l,u.**

Stewart, Jacqueline   **PN1995.9.N4S74 2005**
  (Author, Illustrator)
Migrating to the Movies: Cinema and Black Urban Modernity. Trade Cloth. University of California Press. Berkeley, CA. 2005. 360p. ISBN:0-520-23350-6, ISBN13: 978-0-520-23350-8. Dewey:791.43/652996073. LCCN:2004-016541.

Audience: **g,l,u.** *Choice, 2005.*

Williams, Dana A.   **Z1229**
Contemporary African American Female Playwrights: An Annotated Bibliography. Cloth Text. Greenwood Publishing Group, Inc. Portsmouth, NH. 1998. 152p. Bibliographies and Indexes in Afro-American and African Studies, Vol. 37

ISBN:0-313-30132-8, ISBN13: 978-0-313-30132-2.
Dewey:016.812/540809287/08. LCCN:98-017542.

Audience: **g,l,u.** *Choice, 1998.*

Art > Visual arts

Bearden, Romare &   **N6538.N5B38 1993**
Harry Henderson
A History of African-American Artists: From 1792 to the
Present. Pantheon Books. 1993. ISBN:0-394-57016-2, ISBN13:
978-0-394-57016-7.

Audience: **g,l,u,f.**

Davidson, Bruce   **TR647.D375A4 2002**
Bruce Davidson: Time of Change: Civil Rights Photographs,
1961-1965. John Lewis (Foreword by), Deborah Willis
(Introduction by). Trade Cloth. Saint Ann's Press. Los Angeles,
CA. 2003. 172p. ISBN:0-9713681-1-2, ISBN13:
978-0-9713681-1-8. Dewey:323.09730222.

Audience: **g,l,u.**

Farrington, Lisa E.   **N6538.N5F27 2004**
Creating Their Own Image: The History of African-American
Women Artists. Trade Cloth. Oxford University Press, Inc. New
York, NY. 2004. 368p. ISBN:0-19-516721-X, ISBN13:
978-0-19-516721-4. Dewey:704/.042/08996073.
LCCN:2003-066171.

Audience: **g,l,u,f.** *Choice, 2005.*

Feelings, Tom   **ND237.F32A4 1995**
The Middle Passage: White Ships/Black Cargo. John Henrik
Clarke (Introduction by). Trade Cloth. Penguin Group (USA)
Inc. New York, NY. 1995. 80p. ISBN:0-8037-1804-7, ISBN13:
978-0-8037-1804-3. Dewey:759.13. LCCN:95-013866.

Audience: **g,l,u,f.**

Griggs, William E.   **D769.335**
The World War II Black Regiment That Built the Alaska
Military Highway: A Photographic History. Philip J. Merrill
(Editor), Douglas Brinkley (Introduction by). Trade Cloth.
University Press of Mississippi. Jackson, MS. 2006. 128p.
ISBN:1-57806-504-6, ISBN13: 978-1-57806-504-2.
Dewey:940.54/03. LCCN:2002-009425.

Audience: **g,l,u.**

Logan, Fern   **TR681.A7L635 2001**
Images of Contemporary African American Artists. Margaret
Rose Vendryes (Foreword by), Deborah Willis (Introduction by).
Trade Cloth. Southern Illinois University Press. Carbondale, IL.
2001. 144p. The Artist Portrait Ser. ISBN:0-8093-2379-6,
ISBN13: 978-0-8093-2379-1. Dewey:779/.2. LCCN:00-056323.
Audience: **g,l,u.** *Choice, 2001.*

Willis, Deborah   **TR23.W55 2000**
Reflections in Black: A History of Black Photographers, 1840 to
the Present. Robin D. G. Kelley (Introduction by). Trade Cloth.
W. W. Norton & Company, Inc. New York, NY. 2000. 368p.
ISBN:0-393-04880-2, ISBN13: 978-0-393-04880-3.
Dewey:770/.8996/073. LCCN:99-055185.

Audience: **g,l,u,f.** *Choice, 2001.*

Anthropology and Archeology

Bontemps, Arna   **GR111.A47B66**
Book of Negro Folklore. Hughes, Langston. Dodd, Mead. 1958.

Audience: **l,u.**

Galle, Jillian E. &   **E185.E555 2004**
Young, Amy L. (Editors)
Engendering African American Archaeology: A Southern
Perspective. Trade Cloth. University of Tennessee Press.
Knoxville, TN. 2005. 336p. ISBN:1-57233-277-8, ISBN13:
978-1-57233-277-5. Dewey:975/.00496073. LCCN:2003-026431.

Audience: **g,l,u,f.**

Hurston, Zora Neale   **GR111.A47H86 1990**
Mules and Men. Miguel Covarrubias (Illustrator), Arnold
Rampersad (Foreword by), Franz Boas (Preface by). Trade
Paper. HarperCollins Publishers. New York, NY. 1990. 336p.
ISBN:0-06-091648-6, ISBN13: 978-0-06-091648-0.
Dewey:398.2/09759. LCCN:89-045672.

Audience: **g,l,u,f.** *B*

Hurston, Zora Neale   **GR55.H86A3 1995**
Folklore, Memoirs, and Other Writings. Cheryl A. Wall (Editor).
Trade Cloth. Library of America, The. New York, NY. 1995.
1024p. Library of America, Vol. 75 ISBN:0-940450-84-4,
ISBN13: 978-0-940450-84-4. Dewey:398/.092 B.
LCCN:94-021384.

Audience: **g,l,u.**

Kaplan, Carla (Editor)   **PS3515.U789Z48 2001**
Zora Neale Hurston: A Life in Letters. Trade Paper. Knopf
Publishing Group. New York, NY. 2003. 912p.
ISBN:0-385-49036-4, ISBN13: 978-0-385-49036-8.
Dewey:813/.52. LCCN:00-065671.

Audience: **g,l,u.**

Biography

Alkalimat, Abdul
☐ Malcolm X: A Research Site.
http://www.brothermalcolm.net/
University of Toledo and Twenty-first Century Books.

Audience: **g,l,u.**

Bassey, Magnus O.   **BP223.Z8L5718 2005**
Malcolm X and African American Self-Consciousness. Trade
Cloth. Edwin Mellen Press, The. Lewiston, NY. 2004. 226p.
Black Studies, 26 ISBN:0-7734-6281-3, ISBN13:
978-0-7734-6281-6. Dewey:320.54/6/092. LCCN:2004-060955.

Audience: **g,l,u.**

Bontemps, Arna   **PS3503.O474.Z486**
Wendell
Arna Bontemps-Langston Hughes Letters, 1925-1967. Trade
Cloth. Dodd, Mead & Company, U. S.. London, 1980. 529p.
ISBN:0-396-07687-4, ISBN13: 978-0-396-07687-2.
Dewey:818/.5209. LCCN:79-017341.

Audience: **l,u.** *B*

Boyd, Valerie   **PS3515.U789Z63 2002**
Wrapped in Rainbows: The Life of Zora Neale Hurston. Trade
Cloth. Simon & Schuster. New York, NY. 2002. 528p.
ISBN:0-684-84230-0, ISBN13: 978-0-684-84230-1.
Dewey:813/.52 B. LCCN:2002-017011.

Audience: **g,l,u.**

Bundles, A'Lelia   **HD9970.5.C672**
On Her Own Ground: The Life and Times of Madam C. J.
Walker. Trade Paper. Simon & Schuster. New York, NY. 2002.
416p. ISBN:0-7434-3172-3, ISBN13: 978-0-7434-3172-9.
Dewey:338.7/66855/092 B.

Audience: **g,l,u.**

Carson, Ben &   RD592.9.C37A3 1990
  Murphey, Cecil B.
Gifted Hands: The Ben Carson Story. Zondervan. 1996.
ISBN:0-310-54650-8, ISBN13: 978-0-310-54650-4.
                                          Audience: **g,l.**

Carter, Robert L.   KF373.C378
A Matter of Law: A Memoir of Struggle in the Cause of Equal
Rights. New Press. 2005. ISBN:1-56584-830-6, ISBN13:
978-1-56584-830-6.
                                          Audience: **g,l.**

Conyer, James L. Jr. &   E175.5.C59P36 2004
  Thompson, Julius Eric
Pan African Nationalism in the Americas: The Life and Times
of John Henrik Clarke. Trade Cloth. Africa World Press.
Trenton, NJ. 2004. 256p. ISBN:1-59221-225-5, ISBN13:
978-1-59221-225-5. Dewey:973/.0496073/0092 B.
LCCN:2004-001776.
                                          Audience: **g,l,u,f.**

Crowder, Ralph L.   E185.97.B895C76 2004
John Edward Bruce: The Legacy of a Politician, Journalist, and
Self-Trained Historian of the African Diaspora. Trade Cloth.
New York University Press. New York, NY. 2004. 256p.
ISBN:0-8147-1518-4, ISBN13: 978-0-8147-1518-5.
Dewey:973/.0496073/0092 B. LCCN:2003-020499.
                                 Audience: **g,l,u.**   *Choice, 2004.*

DeCosta-Willis, Miriam   E185.97.W55A3 1995
  (Editor)
The Memphis Diary of Ida B. Wells. Mary Helen Washington
(Foreword by), Dorothy Sterling (Afterword by). Trade Cloth.
Beacon Press. Boston, MA. 1996. 240p. Black Women Writers
Ser. ISBN:0-8070-7064-5, ISBN13: 978-0-8070-7064-2.
Dewey:323/.092 B. LCCN:94-009087.
                                 Audience: **g,l,u.**   *Choice, 1995.*

Douglass, Frederick   E449.D738 2003
The Frederick Douglass Papers: Autobiographical Writings. John
W. Blassingame, John R. McKivigan & Peter P. Hinks (Editors).
Cloth over Boards. Yale University Press. Cumberland, RI.
2003. 528p. The Frederick Douglas Papers, Vol. 2
ISBN:0-300-09173-7, ISBN13: 978-0-300-09173-1.
Dewey:973.7092. LCCN:2003-005833.
                                          Audience: **g,l,u,f.**

Duberman, Martin   PS3554.U25D83 2005
Paul Robeson: A Biography. Trade Paper, Perfect. New Press,
The. New York, NY. 2005. 804p. Lives of the Left Ser.
ISBN:1-56584-941-8, ISBN13: 978-1-56584-941-9.
Dewey:791/.092.
                                          Audience: **g,l,u.**

Gibson, Aliona L.   E185.96
Nappy: Growing up Black and Female in America. Trade Paper.
Writers & Readers Publishing, Inc. New York, NY. 1998. 176p.
ISBN:0-86316-329-7, ISBN13: 978-0-86316-329-6.
Dewey:973/.0496073/092.
                                          Audience: **g,l,u,f.**

Handy, W. C.   ML410.H18A3 1991
Father of the Blues: An Autobiography. Arna Bontemps (Editor),
Abbe Niles (Introduction by). Trade Paper. Da Capo Press, Inc.
Cambridge, MA. 1991. 340p. Quality Paperbacks Ser.
ISBN:0-306-80421-2, ISBN13: 978-0-306-80421-2.
Dewey:784.5/3/00924 B. LCCN:90-026262.
                                          Audience: **g,l,u,f.**

Hanson, Joyce Ann   E185.97.B34H36 2003
Mary McLeod Bethune and Black Women's Political Activism.
Trade Cloth. University of Missouri Press. Columbia, MO.
2003. 256p. ISBN:0-8262-1451-7, ISBN13: 978-0-8262-1451-5.
Dewey:370/.92 B. LCCN:2002-153613.
                                 Audience: **g,l,u.**   *Choice, 2003.*

Harley, Sharon   E185
The Timetables of African-American History: A Chronology of
the Most Important People and Events in African-American
History. Trade Paper. Simon & Schuster. New York, NY. 1996.
400p. ISBN:0-684-81578-8, ISBN13: 978-0-684-81578-7.
Dewey:973/.0496073. LCCN:94-022571.
                                          Audience: **g,l,u.**

Hemenway, Robert E.   PS3515.U789Z
Zora Neale Hurston: A Literary Biography. Alice Walker
(Foreword by). Trade Paper. University of Illinois Press.
Champaign, IL. 1980. 408p. ISBN:0-252-00807-3, ISBN13:
978-0-252-00807-8. Dewey:813/.52. LCCN:77-009605.
                                 Audience: **g,l,u,f.** *B*

Henson, Matthew A.   G635.H4A3 2001
A Negro Explorer at the North Pole: The Autobiography of
Matthew Henson. Booker T. Washington (Preface by), Robert E.
Peary (Foreword by), Robert A. Bryce (Introduction by). Trade
Paper. Cooper Square Publishers, Inc. New York, NY. 2001.
272p. ISBN:0-8154-1125-1, ISBN13: 978-0-8154-1125-3.
Dewey:910/.92. LCCN:2001-028916.
                                          Audience: **g,l,u.**

Homan, Lynn M. &   UG834.A37H64 2001
  Reilly, Thomas
Black Knights: The Story of the Tuskegee Airmen. Louis R.
Purnell (Foreword by). Trade Cloth. Pelican Publishing
Company, Inc. Gretna, LA. 2001. 336p. ISBN:1-56554-828-0,
ISBN13: 978-1-56554-828-2. Dewey:940.54/4973.
LCCN:00-047850.
                                 Audience: **g,l,u.**   *Choice, 2001.*

Hughes, Louis   E185.97.T8
e Thirty Years a Slave: From Bondage to Freedom. E-Book.
Digital Antiquaria, Inc. Morristown, NJ. 2004. 94p.
ISBN:1-58057-305-3, ISBN13: 978-1-58057-305-4.
Dewey:305.5/67/092 B.
                                          Audience: **g,l,u.**

Humez, Jean McMahon   E444.T82H86 2003
Harriet Tubman: The Life and the Life Stories. Trade Paper.
University of Wisconsin Press. Chicago, IL. 2005. 488p.
Wisconsin Studies in Autobiography ISBN:0-299-19124-9,
ISBN13: 978-0-299-19124-5. Dewey:973.7/115/092 B.
LCCN:2003-005676.
                                 Audience: **g,l,u.**   *Choice, 2004.*

Hurston, Zora Neale   PS3515.U789Z465 2006
Dust Tracks on a Road: An Autobiography. Trade Paper.
HarperCollins Publishers. New York, NY. 2006. 336p. P. S. Ser.
ISBN:0-06-085408-1, ISBN13: 978-0-06-085408-9.
Dewey:813/.52 B. LCCN:2005-052616.
                          Audience: **g,l,u.**   *B* *Choice, 1985.*

Hurston, Zora Neale   GR55.H86A3 1995
Folklore, Memoirs, and Other Writings. Cheryl A. Wall (Editor).
Trade Cloth. Library of America, The. New York, NY. 1995.
1024p. Library of America, Vol. 75 ISBN:0-940450-84-4,
ISBN13: 978-0-940450-84-4. Dewey:398/.092 B.
LCCN:94-021384.
                                          Audience: **g,l,u.**

James, C. L. R.   **F1923.T85**
The Black Jacobins: Toussaint L'Ouverture and the San
Domingo Revolution. Ed. 2. Trade Paper. Knopf Publishing
Group. New York, NY. 1989. 448p. ISBN:0-679-72467-2,
ISBN13: 978-0-679-72467-4. Dewey:972.9403.
Audience: **g,l,u.**

Johnson, James Weldon   **PS3519.O2625Z463**
Along This Way: The Autobiography of James Weldon Johnson.
Sondra K. Wilson (Introduction by). Trade Paper. Da Capo
Press, Inc. Cambridge, MA. 1999. 440p. ISBN:0-306-80929-X,
ISBN13: 978-0-306-80929-3. Dewey:818/.5209 B.
LCCN:99-058436.
Audience: **g,l,u.**

Jones, Kirkland C.   **PS3503**
Renaissance Man from Louisiana: A Biography of Arna Wendell
Bontemps, 151. Trade Cloth. Greenwood Publishing Group, Inc.
Portsmouth, NH. 1992. 232p. Contributions in Afro-American
and African Studies Ser., No. 151 ISBN:0-313-28013-4,
ISBN13: 978-0-313-28013-9. Dewey:818.5209.
LCCN:91-047062.
Audience: **g,l,u,f.** *Choice, 1993.*

Kaplan, Carla (Editor)   **PS3515.U789Z48 2001**
Zora Neale Hurston: A Life in Letters. Trade Paper. Knopf
Publishing Group. New York, NY. 2003. 912p.
ISBN:0-385-49036-4, ISBN13: 978-0-385-49036-8.
Dewey:813/.52. LCCN:00-065671.
Audience: **g,l,u.**

Larson, Kate Clifford   **E444.T82**
Bound for the Promised Land: Harriet Tubman, Portrait of an
American Hero. Trade Paper. Ballantine Books. New York, NY.
2004. 432p. ISBN:0-345-45628-9, ISBN13: 978-0-345-45628-1.
Dewey:973.7/115/092 B. LCCN:2004-111071.
Audience: **g,l,u.** *Choice, 2004.*

Lowry, Beverly   **HD9970.5.C672W3558**
Her Dream of Dreams: The Rise and Triumph of Madam C. J.
Walker. Trade Cloth. Alfred A. Knopf Inc. New York, NY. 2003.
496p. ISBN:0-679-44642-7, ISBN13: 978-0-679-44642-2.
Dewey:338.7/66855/092 B. LCCN:2002-027494.
Audience: **g,l,u.**

Lumumba, Patrice   **DT657.L813**
Congo, My Country. Paper Text. Textbook Publishers. Temecula,
CA. 2003. 195p. ISBN:0-7581-6191-3, ISBN13:
978-0-7581-6191-8. Dewey:967.5.
Audience: **g,l,u,f.**

Manning, Kenneth R.   **QH31.C33**
Black Apollo of Science: The Life of Ernest Everett Just. Trade
Paper. Oxford University Press, Inc. New York, NY. 1985. 416p.
ISBN:0-19-503498-8, ISBN13: 978-0-19-503498-1.
Dewey:574/.092/4.
Audience: **g,l,u.**

Miller, Ericka M.   **PS169.L95M55 1999**
The Other Reconstruction: Where Violence and Womanhood
Meet in the Writings of Ida B. Wells-Barnett, Angelina Weld
Grimke, and Nella Larsen. Cloth Text. Garland Publishing, Inc.
New York, NY. 1999. 176p. Studies in African American
History and Culture ISBN:0-8153-3495-8, ISBN13:
978-0-8153-3495-8. Dewey:810.9/355. LCCN:99-029874.
Audience: **g,l,u.**

Nelson, Emmanuel S.   **PS153**
(Editor)
African American Authors, 1745-1945: A Bio-Bibliographical
Critical Sourcebook. Cloth Text. Greenwood Publishing Group,
Inc. Portsmouth, NH. 2000. 544p. ISBN:0-313-30910-8,
ISBN13: 978-0-313-30910-6. Dewey:810.9/896073 B.
LCCN:99-032527.
Audience: **g,l,u,f.** *Choice, 2000.*

Nelson, Emmanuel S.   **PS374**
(Editor)
Contemporary African American Novelists: A
Bio-Bibliographical Critical Sourcebook. Cloth Text. Greenwood
Publishing Group, Inc. Portsmouth, NH. 1999. 552p.
ISBN:0-313-30501-3, ISBN13: 978-0-313-30501-6.
Dewey:813/.5409896073. LCCN:98-026438.
Audience: **g,l,u,f.** *Choice, 1999.*

Otieno, Wambui   **DT433.582.O75A3 1998**
Waiyaki
Mau Mau's Daughter: A Life Story. Presley, Cora Lynn (Editor,
Introduction by). Lynn Rienner Publishers. 1998.
ISBN:1-55587-722-2, ISBN13: 978-1-55587-722-4.
Audience: **l,u.**

Parks, Gordon   **TR140.P35**
Voices in the Mirror: An Autobiography. Anchor Books. 1992.
ISBN:0-385-26699-5, ISBN13: 978-0-385-26699-4.
Audience: **g,l.**

Perkins, Kathy A.   **PS628.N4**
(Editor)
🄴 Black Female Playwrights: An Anthology of Plays Before
1950. E-Book. Indiana University Press. Bloomington, IN. 1990.
298p. Blacks in the Diaspora Ser. ISBN:0-253-20623-5,
ISBN13: 978-0-253-20623-7. Dewey:812/.008/09287.
LCCN:88-046040.
Audience: **g,l,u,f.** *Choice, 1990.*

Peterson, Bernard L. Jr.   **PS153**
Early Black American Playwrights and Dramatic Writers: A
Biographical Directory and Catalog of Plays, Films and
Broadcasting Scripts. Cloth Text. Greenwood Publishing Group,
Inc. Portsmouth, NH. 1990. 328p. ISBN:0-313-26621-2,
ISBN13: 978-0-313-26621-8. Dewey:812.009/896073.
LCCN:90-002961.
Audience: **g,l,u,f.** *Choice, 1991.*

Pilsner, Brenda   **PS153.N5A3444 2000**
African-American Writers: A Dictionary. Shari Dorantes Hatch
& Michael R. Strickland (Editors). Library Binding. ABC-CLIO,
Inc. Santa Barbara, CA. 2000. 0484p. Literary Companions Ser.
ISBN:0-87436-959-2, ISBN13: 978-0-87436-959-5.
Dewey:810.9/896073/03 B. LCCN:00-024422.
Audience: **g,l,u,f.** *Choice, 2000.*

Poe, Daryl Zizwe   **DT512.3.N57P64 2003**
Kwame Nkrumah's Contribution to Pan-African Agency: An
Afrocentric Analysis. Paper over Boards. Routledge. New York,
NY. 2003. 204p. African Studies, :History, Politics, Economics
and Culture ISBN:0-415-94643-3, ISBN13: 978-0-415-94643-8.
Dewey:341.24/9. LCCN:2003-004068.
Audience: **g,l,u.**

ProQuest Company   **E185.96**
▢ African American Biographical Database (AADB).
http://www.proquest.com
Proquest Company.
Audience: **g,l,u,f.**

Rampersand, Arnold   **PS3537.T323**
The Life of Langston Hughes, Set. Ed. 2. Trade Cloth. Oxford
University Press, Inc. New York, NY. 2002.
ISBN:0-19-521936-8, ISBN13: 978-0-19-521936-4.
Dewey:818/.5209 B.
Audience: **u,f.**

Ridlon, Florence   **R695.M35R53 2005**
Black Physicians Struggle for Civil Rights: Edward C. Mazique,
M. D. Trade Cloth. University of New Mexico Press.
Albuquerque, NM. 2005. 392p. ISBN:0-8263-3339-7, ISBN13:
978-0-8263-3339-1. Dewey:610/.89/96073 B.
LCCN:2004-023086.
Audience: **g,l,u.** *Choice, 2005.*

Robeson, Paul   **E185.97**
Here I Stand. Beacon Press. 1971. ISBN:0-8070-6406-8,
ISBN13: 978-0-8070-6406-1.
Audience: **g,l.**

Roses, Lorraine E.   **PS147**
Harlem Renaissance and Beyond: Literary Biographies of One
Hundred Black Women Writers, 1900-1945. Trade Paper.
Harvard University Press. Cambridge, MA. 1997. 432p.
ISBN:0-674-37255-7, ISBN13: 978-0-674-37255-9.
Dewey:810.9/9287/03. LCCN:89-038731.
Audience: **g,l,u.** *Choice, 1990.*

Salem, Dorothy C.   **E185.96.A45 1993**
(Editor)
African American Women: A Biographical Dictionary. Paper
over Boards. Garland Publishing, Inc. New York, NY. 1993.
664p. Biographical Directories of Minority Women Ser., Vol. 2
ISBN:0-8240-9782-3, ISBN13: 978-0-8240-9782-0.
Dewey:920.7208996073. LCCN:92-045727.
Audience: **g,l,u,f.** *Choice, 1994.*

Schechter, Patricia A.   **E185.97.W55S34 2001**
Ida B. Wells-Barnett and American Reform, 1880-1930. Trade
Paper. University of North Carolina Press. Chapel Hill, NC.
2001. 408p. Gender and American Culture Ser.
ISBN:0-8078-4965-0, ISBN13: 978-0-8078-4965-1.
Dewey:323/.092 B. LCCN:00-068313.
Audience: **g,l,u.**

Shakur, Assata   **E185.97.S53A3 2001**
Assata: An Autobiography. Angela Davis & Angela Lennox S.
Hinds (Foreword by). Trade Paper. C C H, Inc. Riverwoods, IL.
1999. 320p. ISBN:1-55552-074-3, ISBN13: 978-1-55552-074-7.
Dewey:305.8/96073. LCCN:2002-278291.
Audience: **g,l,u,f.** *Choice, 1988.*

Smith, Jessie C.   **E185.96.E65 1993**
Epic Lives: One Hundred Black Women Who Made a
Difference. Trade Cloth. Visible Ink Press. Canton, MI. 1992.
661p. ISBN:0-8103-9426-X, ISBN13: 978-0-8103-9426-1.
Dewey:920.72/089/96073 B. LCCN:93-106495.
Audience: **g,l,u.**

Smith, Jessie Carney   **E185.96.N68 1992**
(Editor)
Notable Black American Women. Ed. 3. Trade Cloth. Thomson
Gale. Farmington Hills, MI. 2002. 775p. ISBN:0-7876-6494-4,
ISBN13: 978-0-7876-6494-7. Dewey:920.72/08996073.
LCCN:91-035074.
Audience: **g,l,u.**

Smith, Jessie Carney   **E185.86.N68 1998**
Notable Black Men. Gale Research. 1998. ISBN:0-7876-0763-0,
ISBN13: 978-0-7876-0763-0.
Audience: **g,l,u.**

Soyinka, Wole   **PR9387.9.S6**
Isara, a Voyage Around. Random House. 1989.
ISBN:0-394-54077-8, ISBN13: 978-0-394-54077-1.
Audience: **g,l.**

Van Sertima, Ivan   **DT14.J68**
(Editor)
Great Black Leaders: Ancient and Modern. Trade Paper.
Transaction Publishers. Somerset, NJ. 1988. 433p.
ISBN:0-88738-739-X, ISBN13: 978-0-88738-739-5.
Dewey:305.8. LCCN:91-127942.
Audience: **g,l,u.**

Washington, Booker T   **E185.97.W4**
Up from Slavery. Trade Paper. Kessinger Publishing, LLC.
Whitefish, MT. 2004. ISBN:1-4191-9216-7, ISBN13:
978-1-4191-9216-6. Dewey:370/.92 B.
Audience: **g,l,u.**

Wells-Barnett, Ida B., et   **E185.97.W55A3 1995**
al.
[e] The Memphis Diary of Ida B. Wells. Miriam Decosta-Willis
& Mary Helen Washington (Authors). E-Book. Beacon Press.
Boston, MA. 1995. ISBN:0-8070-7018-1, ISBN13:
978-0-8070-7018-5. Dewey:323/.092.
Audience: **g,l,u.**

Wideman, John Edgar   **PS3573**
Brothers and Keepers: A Memoir. Trade Paper. Houghton Mifflin
Company Trade & Reference Division. Boston, MA. 2005.
272p. ISBN:0-618-50963-1, ISBN13: 978-0-618-50963-8.
Dewey:813/.54 B. LCCN:2005-272204.
Audience: **g,l,u.**

Yellin, Jean Fagan   **E185.97.T8**
Harriet Jacobs: A Life. Trade Paper. Basic Books. New York,
NY. 2005. 432p. ISBN:0-465-09289-6, ISBN13:
978-0-465-09289-5. Dewey:306.3/62/092 B.
Audience: **g,l,u.** *Choice, 2004.*

Civilization

Ani, Marimba   **CB203.A56 1994**
Yurugu: An Afrocentric Critique of European Cultural Thought
and Behavior. Trade Cloth. Africa World Press. Trenton, NJ.
1994. 636p. ISBN:0-86543-249-X, ISBN13: 978-0-86543-249-9.
Dewey:940/.01. LCCN:91-071027.
Audience: **u,f.**

Bernal, Martin   **PR6029.C33F4**
Black Athena: The Afroasiatic Roots of Classical Civilization:
The Linguistic Evidence. Trade Cloth. Rutgers University Press.
Piscataway, NJ. 2006. 704p. ISBN:0-8135-3655-3, ISBN13:
978-0-8135-3655-2. Dewey:822.912.
Audience: **g,u,f.**

Gates, Henry Louis   **E185.96**
African-American Century: How Black Americans Shaped Our
Country. West, Cornel. Free Press. 2000. ISBN:0-684-86414-2,
ISBN13: 978-0-684-86414-3.
Audience: **g,l,u.**

Lefkowitz, Mary   **DT14.L44 1997**
Not Out of Africa: How Afrocentrism Became an Excuse to Teach Myth As History. Trade Paper. Basic Books. New York, NY. 1997. 320p. ISBN:0-465-09838-X, ISBN13: 978-0-465-09838-5. Dewey:949.5. LCCN:97-183099.
Audience: **g,l,u.**

Poe, Richard   **D62.P63**
Black Spark, White Fire: Did African Explorers Civilize Ancient Europe? Trade Paper. Crown Publishing Group. New York, NY. 1999. 576p. ISBN:0-7615-2163-1, ISBN13: 978-0-7615-2163-1. Dewey:936.
Audience: **l,u,f.**

West, Cornel   **E185.86.W4384 1999**
The Cornel West Reader. Basic Civitas Books. 1999. ISBN:0-465-09109-1, ISBN13: 978-0-465-09109-6.
Audience: **l,u.**

Communication

Jackson, Ronald L. &   **PE3102.N42U53 2003**
  Richardson, Elaine B. (Editors)
Understanding African-American Rhetoric: Classical Origins to Contemporary Innovations. UK-B Format Paperback. Routledge. New York, NY. 2003. 304p. ISBN:0-415-94387-6, ISBN13: 978-0-415-94387-1. Dewey:427/.973/08996073. LCCN:2002-015432.
Audience: **g,l,u,f.** *Choice, 2004.*

Economics

                   E185.86
The Debtors: Whites Respond to the Call for Black Reparations. Perfect. Caucasians United for Reparations & Emancipation Cure. Red Oak, GA. 2005. 256p. ISBN:0-9765909-1-3, ISBN13: 978-0-9765909-1-0. Dewey:305.896073.
Audience: **g,l,u.**

Brophy, Alfred L.   **F704.T92**
Reconstructing the Dreamland: The Tulsa Riot of 1921: Race, Reparations, and Reconcilation. Oxford University Press. 2002. ISBN:0-19-514685-9, ISBN13: 978-0-19-514685-1.
Audience: **l,u.**

Butler, John Sibley   **E185.8**
Entrepreneurship and Self-Help among Black Americans: A Reconsideration of Race and Economics. State University of New York. 2005. ISBN:0-7914-5893-8, ISBN13: 978-0-7914-5893-8.
Audience: **l,u.**

Casserly, Catherine M.   **E185.86**
African-American Women and Poverty: Can Education Alone Change the Status Quo? Garland. 1998. ISBN:0-8153-3055-3, ISBN13: 978-0-8153-3055-4.
Audience: **u,f.**

Corlett, J. Angelo   **HT1523**
Race, Racism, and Reparations. Cornell University Press. 2003. ISBN:0-8014-4160-9, ISBN13: 978-0-8014-4160-8.
Audience: **g,l,u.**

Darity, William A. Jr. &   **HD4903.5.U58D37 1998**
  Myers, Samuel L. Jr.
Persistent Disparity: Race and Economic Inequality in the U. S. since 1945. Trade Cloth. Edward Elgar Publishing, Inc. Northampton, MA. 1998. 208p. ISBN:1-85898-658-3, ISBN13: 978-1-85898-658-6. Dewey:331.13/3/097309045. LCCN:97-030626.
Audience: **g,l,u,f.** *Choice, 1999.*

Gilbert, Charlene   **E185.8**
Homecoming: The Story of African-American Farmers. Quinn Eli. Beacon Press. 2000. ISBN:0-8070-0962-8, ISBN13: 978-0-8070-0962-8.
Audience: **l,u.**

Mazrui, Alamin M. &   **E185.89.R45M39**
  Mazuri, Ail A.
Reparations in the Time of Globalization. Trade Cloth. Africa World Press. Trenton, NJ. 2004. 464p. ISBN:1-59221-269-7, ISBN13: 978-1-59221-269-9. Dewey:305.896/073.
Audience: **g,l,u.**

Mullins, Paul R.   **F189.A6**
Race and Affluence: An Archaeology of African America and Consumer Culture. Kluwer Academic/Plenum Publishers. 1999. ISBN:0-306-46089-0, ISBN13: 978-0-306-46089-0.
Audience: **l,u.**

Rexroat, Cynthia   **E185.86.R48 1994**
The Declining Economic Status of Black Children. Joint Center for Political and Economic Studies. 1994. ISBN:0-941410-96-X, ISBN13: 978-0-941410-96-0.
Audience: **g,l,u.**

Shapiro, Thomas M.   **E185.8**
The Hidden Cost of Being African American. Trade Paper. Oxford University Press, Inc. New York, NY. 2005. 253p. ISBN:0-19-518138-7, ISBN13: 978-0-19-518138-8. Dewey:330.973/0089/96073.
Audience: **g,l.**

Williams, Eric   **HC254.5.W5 1994**
Capitalism and Slavery. Colin Λ. Palmer (Introduction by). Trade Paper. University of North Carolina Press. Chapel Hill, NC. 1994. 307p. ISBN:0-8078-4488-8, ISBN13: 978-0-8078-4488-5. Dewey:338.0941. LCCN:94-008722.
Audience: **g,l,u.**

Wilson, Amos N.   **E185.615.W54 1998**
Blueprint for Black Power: A Moral, Political and Economic Imperative for the Twenty-First Century. Trade Cloth. Afrikan World InfoSystems. Brooklyn, NY. 1998. ISBN:1-879164-07-8, ISBN13: 978-1-879164-07-9. Dewey:305.896/073. LCCN:98-022964.
Audience: **g,l,u,f.**

Winbush, Raymond   **E185.89.R45**
  (Editor)
Should America Pay? Slavery and Raging Rebate over Reparations. Amistad. 2003. ISBN:0-06-008311-5, ISBN13: 978-0-06-008311-3.
Audience: **g,l,u.**

Zalokar, Nadja   **HD6057.5.U5**
The Economic Status of Black Women: An Exploratory Investigation. U.S. Commission on Civil Rights. 1990.
Audience: **g,l,u.**

Education

Benjamin, Lois (Editor)   LB2332.3.B53 1997
Black Women in the Academy: Promises and Perils. Trade
Cloth. University Press of Florida. Gainesville, FL. 1997. 424p.
ISBN:0-8130-1500-6, ISBN13: 978-0-8130-1500-2.
Dewey:378.1/2/082. LCCN:96-047388.
                                 Audience: **u,f.** *Choice, 1998.*

Berlinerblau, Jacques   DF78.B3983B47 1999
Heresy in the University: The Black Athena Controversy and the
Responsibilities of American Intellectuals. Paper Text. Rutgers
University Press. Piscataway, NJ. 1999. 304p.
ISBN:0-8135-2588-8, ISBN13: 978-0-8135-2588-4.
Dewey:949.5. LCCN:98-008499.
                                 Audience: **u,f.** *Choice, 1999.*

Conyers, James L.   E184.7.A35 2003
 (Editor)
Afrocentricity and the Academy: Essays on Theory and Practice.
Paper Text. McFarland & Company, Incorporated Publishers.
Jefferson, NC. 2003. 320p. ISBN:0-7864-1542-8, ISBN13:
978-0-7864-1542-7. Dewey:973/.0496073. LCCN:2002-156433.
                                 Audience: **u,f.** *Choice, 2004.*

Fashola, Olatokunbo S.   LC2731.E34 2005
 (Editor)
Educating African American Males: Voices from the Field.
Trade Cloth. Corwin Press. Thousand Oaks, CA. 2005. 320p.
ISBN:1-4129-1433-7, ISBN13: 978-1-4129-1433-8.
Dewey:371.829/96073. LCCN:2004-024084.
                                 Audience: **g,l,u,f.** *Choice, 2005.*

Franklin, V. P. (Editor)   LC2707.C85 2004
Cultural Capital and Black Education: African American
Communities and the Funding of Black Schooling, 1860 to the
Present. Trade Cloth. Information Age Publishing, Inc.
Greenwich, CT. 2004. 20p. Research on African American
Education Ser. ISBN:1-59311-041-3, ISBN13:
978-1-59311-041-3. Dewey:371.829/96073. LCCN:2004-020281.
                                 Audience: **g,l,u,f.**

Lawson, Ellen N.   LC2801.T57 1984
The Three Sarahs: Documents of Antebellum Black College
Women. Library Binding. Edwin Mellen Press, The. Lewiston,
NY. 1984. 350p. Studies in Women and Religion, Vol. 13
ISBN:0-88946-536-3, ISBN13: 978-0-88946-536-7.
Dewey:371.1/009/22 B. LCCN:84-018914.
                                 Audience: **g,l,u.**

Marable, Manning   E184.7.D57 2000
Dispatches from the Ebony Tower: Intellectuals Confront the
African American Experience. Trade Paper. Columbia University
Press. New York, NY. 2001. 352p. ISBN:0-231-11477-X,
ISBN13: 978-0-231-11477-6. Dewey:305.896/073/0711.
LCCN:99-055525.
                                 Audience: **g,l,u,f.** *Choice, 2000.*

McNeil, Genna Rae   KF373.H644
Groundwork: Charles Hamilton Houston and the Struggle for
Civil Rights. University of Pennsylvania Press. 1983.
ISBN:0-8122-7878-X, ISBN13: 978-0-8122-7878-1.
                                 Audience: **g,l,u.**

Murdy, Anne-Elizabeth   PS374.N4M87 2003
Teach the Nation: Public School, Racial Uplift, and Women's
Writing in the 1890's. Paper over Boards. Routledge. New York,
NY. 2002. 196p. Studies in African American History and

Culture ISBN:0-415-93534-2, ISBN13: 978-0-415-93534-0.
Dewey:813/.4099287. LCCN:2002-068254.
                                 Audience: **g,l,u.**

Obiakor, Festus E. &   LB2376.3.A33
 Gordon, Jacob U. (Editors)
African Perspectives in American Higher Education: Invisible
Voices. Trade Paper. Nova Science Publishers, Inc. Hauppauge,
NY. 2003. 138p. ISBN:1-59033-683-6, ISBN13:
978-1-59033-683-0. Dewey:378.108996. LCCN:2003-271746.
                                 Audience: **g,l,u,f.**

Ogletree, Charles Jr.   KF4757
All Deliberate Speed: Reflections on the First Half Century of
Brown v. Board of Education. W.W. Norton and Co.. 2004.
ISBN:0-393-05897-2, ISBN13: 978-0-393-05897-0.
                                 Audience: **g,u,f.**

Ramirez, J. David   LC2778.L34E26 2005
Ⓔ Ebonics: The Urban Education Debate. Ed. 2. E-Book.
Multilingual Matters Ltd. Clevedon, 2005. xii, 207p. New
Perspectives on Language and Education Ser.
ISBN:1-85359-798-8, ISBN13: 978-1-85359-798-5.
Dewey:427/.973/08996073. LCCN:2004-017325.
                                 Audience: **g,l,u,f.**

Williams, Clarence G.   T171.M49.W55
Technology and the Dream: Reflections on the Black Experience
at MIT, 1941-1999. Library Binding. Sagebrush Education
Resources. Caledonia, MN. 2003. ISBN:0-613-91124-5,
ISBN13: 978-0-613-91124-5. Dewey:378.744/4.
                                 Audience: **g,l,u.** *Choice, 2001.*

Williams, Heather   LC2802.S9W55 2004
 Andrea
Self-Taught: African American Education in Slavery and
Freedom. Trade Cloth. University of North Carolina Press.
Chapel Hill, NC. 2005. 320p. The John Hope Franklin Series in
African American History and Culture Ser.
ISBN:0-8078-2920-X, ISBN13: 978-0-8078-2920-2.
Dewey:370/.89/96073075. LCCN:2004-022755.
                                 Audience: **g,l,u.** *Choice, 2005.*

Woodson, Carter   HS310.Z6
 Godwin
The Mis-education of the Negro. Daryl Michael Scott (Editor);
V. P. Franklin (Foreword by). ASALH Press. 2005.
ISBN:0-9768111-0-3, ISBN13: 978-0-9768111-0-7.
                                 Audience: **g,l,u,f.**

Health

Harley, Debra A. &   RC451.5.N4C66 2005
 Dillard, John M.
Contemporary Mental Health Issues among African Americans.
Trade Cloth. American Counseling Association. Alexandria, VA.
2004. xx, 336p. ISBN:1-55620-236-9, ISBN13:
978-1-55620-236-0. Dewey:616.89/0089/96073.
LCCN:2004-015611.
                                 Audience: **g,u,f.**

Jenkins, Sharron   RA448.5.N4
African American Health Disparities. Paper Text. McGraw-Hill
Primis Custom Publishing. Hightstown, NJ. 2003.
ISBN:0-07-291823-3, ISBN13: 978-0-07-291823-6.
Dewey:362.108996073.
                                 Audience: **g,l,u.**

Livingston, Ivor L.   **RA448**
(Editor)
Handbook of Black American Health: The Mosaic of
Conditions, Issues, Policies, and Prospects. Cloth Text.
Greenwood Publishing Group, Inc. Portsmouth, NH. 1994. 496p.
ISBN:0-313-28640-X, ISBN13: 978-0-313-28640-7.
Dewey:362.108996073. LCCN:93-004852.
Audience: **g,l,u.** *Choice, 1994.*

Logan, Sadye Louise &   **RA448.5.N4H385 2000**
Freeman, Edith M. (Editors)
Health Care in the Black Community: Empowerment,
Knowledge, Skills and Collectivism. Trade Cloth. Haworth
Press, Incorporated, The. Binghamton, NY. 2000. 300p.
ISBN:0-7890-0456-9, ISBN13: 978-0-7890-0456-7.
Dewey:362.1/089/96073. LCCN:00-038882.
Audience: **g,l,u,f.** *Choice, 2001.*

Mickel, Elijah   **RC489.R37M53 2003**
Africa-Centered Reality Therapy and Choice Theory. Trade
Cloth. Africa World Press. Trenton, NJ. 2003. 248p.
ISBN:1-59221-127-5, ISBN13: 978-1-59221-127-2.
Dewey:616.89/14/08996073. LCCN:2003-012522.
Audience: **l,u,f.**

Rosenblatt, Paul C. &   **RC451.5.N4R67 2005**
Wallace, Beverly R.
African-American Grief. UK-B Format Paperback. Routledge.
New York, NY. 2005. 224p. The Series in Death, Dying, and
Bereavement ISBN:0-415-95152-6, ISBN13:
978-0-415-95152-4. Dewey:155.9/37/08996073.
LCCN:2004-022552.
Audience: **g,l,u,f.**

Sammons, Vivian O.   **Q141.B58 1990**
Blacks in Science and Medicine. Hemisphere Publishing Corp..
1990. ISBN:0-89116-665-3, ISBN13: 978-0-89116-665-8.
Audience: **g,l,u,f.**

Smith, Susan L.   **RA448.5.N4S65 1995**
Sick and Tired of Being Sick and Tired: Black Women's Health
Activism in America, 1890-1950. Trade Cloth. University of
Pennsylvania Press. Philadelphia, PA. 1995. 288p. Studies in
Health, Illness, and Caregiving ISBN:0-8122-3237-2, ISBN13:
978-0-8122-3237-0. Dewey:362.1. LCCN:95-011310.
Audience: **g,l,u.** *Choice, 1996.*

Law

Brooks, Roy L.   **E185.89.R45B76 2004**
Atonement and Forgiveness: A New Model for Black
Reparations. Trade Cloth. University of California Press.
Berkeley, CA. 2004. 336p. ISBN:0-520-23941-5, ISBN13:
978-0-520-23941-8. Dewey:973/.049673. LCCN:2004-041239.
Audience: **g,l,u.** *Choice, 2005.*

Carter, Robert L.   **KF373.C378**
A Matter of Law: A Memoir of Struggle in the Cause of Equal
Rights. New Press. 2005. ISBN:1-56584-830-6, ISBN13:
978-1-56584-830-6.
Audience: **g,l.**

McNeil, Genna Rae   **KF373.H644**
Groundwork: Charles Hamilton Houston and the Struggle for
Civil Rights. University of Pennsylvania Press. 1983.
ISBN:0-8122-7878-X, ISBN13: 978-0-8122-7878-1.
Audience: **g,l,u.**

Ogletree, Charles Jr.   **KF4757**
All Deliberate Speed: Reflections on the First Half Century of
Brown v. Board of Education. W.W. Norton and Co.. 2004.
ISBN:0-393-05897-2, ISBN13: 978-0-393-05897-0.
Audience: **g,u,f.**

Literature

Aberjhani, et al.   **PS153.N5A24 2003**
Encyclopedia of the Harlem Renaissance. Sandra West &
Clement Alexander Price (Authors). Trade Cloth. Facts On File,
Inc. New York, NY. 2003. 448p. ISBN:0-8160-4539-9, ISBN13:
978-0-8160-4539-6. Dewey:810.9/896073. LCCN:2002-152067.
Audience: **g,l,u,f.** *Choice, 2004.*

Adell, Sandra   **PS153.N5A29 1994**
Double Consciousness - Double Bind: Theoretical Issues in
Twentieth-Century Black Literature. Trade Cloth. University of
Illinois Press. Champaign, IL. 1994. 184p. ISBN:0-252-02109-6,
ISBN13: 978-0-252-02109-1. Dewey:810.9/896073/0904.
LCCN:93-049578.
Audience: **l,u,f.**

Alexander Street Press   **PN6120.92.B45**
☐ Black Short Fiction.
http://www.alexanderstreetpress.com/products/blfi.htm
Alexander Street Press.
Audience: **g,l,u,f.**

Andrews, William L.   **PS153.N5C59 2000**
(Editor), et al.
The Concise Oxford Companion to African American Literature.
Frances Smith Foster & Trudier Harris-Lopez (Editors). Trade
Paper. Oxford University Press, Inc. New York, NY. 2001. 512p.
ISBN:0-19-513883-X, ISBN13: 978-0-19-513883-2.
Dewey:810.9/896073/003. LCCN:00-065201.
Audience: **g,l,u,f.** *Choice, 2001.*

Baldwin, James   **PS3552.A45A16 1998**
James Baldwin: Collected Essays. Toni Morrison (Contribution
by). Trade Cloth. Library of America, The. New York, NY.
1998. 869p. Library of America, Vol. 98 ISBN:1-883011-52-3,
ISBN13: 978-1-883011-52-9. Dewey:814/.54. LCCN:97-023496.
Audience: **g,l,u,f.**

Bambara, Toni Cade   **PS3552.A473**
The Salt Eaters. Random House. 1980. ISBN:0-394-50712-6,
ISBN13: 978-0-394-50712-5.
Audience: **g,l.**

Bloom, Harold   **PS153.N5B5335 1995**
(Introduction by)
Black American Poets and Dramatists of the Harlem
Renaissance. Trade Cloth. Chelsea House Publishers. Langhorne,
PA. 1995. 180p. Writers of English Ser. ISBN:0-7910-2207-2,
ISBN13: 978-0-7910-2207-8. Dewey:810.9/896073/09041 B.
LCCN:94-005881.
Audience: **g,l,u.**

Bloom, Harold (Editor,   **PS153.N5H225 2003**
Translator, Introduction by)
The Harlem Renaissance. Trade Cloth. Facts On File, Inc. New
York, NY. 2003. 350p. Bloom's Period Studies Ser.
ISBN:0-7910-7679-2, ISBN13: 978-0-7910-7679-8.
Dewey:810.9/896073. LCCN:2003-016873.
Audience: **l,u.**

Blunk, Tim &   **PS508.P7H38 1990**
Levasseur, Raymond L.
Hauling up the Morning: Writings and Art by Political Prisoners
and Prisoners of War in the U. S. Jacobin Books Staff (Editor),
Assata Shakur (Introduction by), William M. Kunstler (Preface
by). Trade Cloth. Red Sea Press. Trenton, NJ. 1990. 350p.
ISBN:0-932415-59-8, ISBN13: 978-0-932415-59-2.
Dewey:810.8/0920692. LCCN:90-061145.

Audience: **g,l,u.**

Bolton, Ruthie   **F279.C49N414 1994**
Gal: A True Life. Harcourt Brace. 1994. ISBN:0-15-100104-9,
ISBN13: 978-0-15-100104-0.

Audience: **g,l,u.**

Bontemps, Arna   **PS591.N4 B58**
(Editor)
American Negro Poetry. Library Binding. Sagebrush Education
Resources. Caledonia, MN. 1996. ISBN:0-8085-7747-6,
ISBN13: 978-0-8085-7747-8. Dewey:811/.5/08.

Audience: **l,u,f.**

Bontemps, Arna   **PS3503.O474.Z486**
Wendell
Arna Bontemps-Langston Hughes Letters, 1925-1967. Trade
Cloth. Dodd, Mead & Company, U. S.. London, 1980. 529p.
ISBN:0-396-07687-4, ISBN13: 978-0-396-07687-2.
Dewey:818/.5209. LCCN:79-017341.

Audience: **l,u.** *B*

Bontemps, Arna   **PN6109.7.H8 1970**
Wendell
Poetry of the Negro, 1746-1970. Doubleday. 1970.
ISBN:0-385-05554-4, ISBN13: 978-0-385-05554-3.

Audience: **l,u.**

Bontemps, Arna   **E185.6.B75**
Wendell
Anyplace but Here. Conroy, Jack. Hill and Wang. 1966.

Audience: **l,u.**

Bontemps, Arna   **GR111.A47B66**
Book of Negro Folklore. Hughes, Langston. Dodd, Mead. 1958.

Audience: **l,u.**

Bontemps, Arna   **PS3503.O474B5 1992**
(Editor)
Black Thunder: Gabriel's Revolt: Virginia 1800. Arnold
Rampersad (Introduction by). Trade Paper. Beacon Press.
Boston, MA. 1992. 256p. ISBN:0-8070-6337-1, ISBN13:
978-0-8070-6337-8. Dewey:813/.54. LCCN:91-034123.

Audience: **g,l,u,f.**

Boyd, Valerie   **PS3515.U789Z63 2002**
Wrapped in Rainbows: The Life of Zora Neale Hurston. Trade
Cloth. Simon & Schuster. New York, NY. 2002. 528p.
ISBN:0-684-84230-0, ISBN13: 978-0-684-84230-1.
Dewey:813/.52 B. LCCN:2002-017011.

Audience: **g,l,u.**

Brooks, Gwendolyn &   **PS508.N3C5 2001**
Malcolm X
Black Voices: An Anthology of African-American Literature.
Abraham Chapman (Editor). Mass Market. Penguin Group
(USA) Inc. New York, NY. 2001. 720p. Signet Classics Ser.
ISBN:0-451-52782-8, ISBN13: 978-0-451-52782-0.
Dewey:810.809.

Audience: **l,u,f.**

Brooks, Joanna   **PS153.N5B668 2003**
American Lazarus: Religion and the Rise of African-American
and Native American Literatures. Trade Cloth. Oxford
University Press, Inc. New York, NY. 2003. 264p.
ISBN:0-19-516078-9, ISBN13: 978-0-19-516078-9.
Dewey:810.9/96073. LCCN:2002-013708.

Audience: **g,l,u,f.** *Choice, 2004.*

Brooks, Joanna &   **PS647.A35F47 2002**
Saillant, John (Editor, Introduction by)
Face Zion Forward: First Writers of the Black Atlantic,
1785-1798. Trade Cloth. Northeastern University Press. Boston,
MA. 2005. x, 242p. Library of Black Literature
ISBN:1-55553-539-9, ISBN13: 978-1-55553-539-1.
Dewey:818/.20809896073. LCCN:2002-007482.

Audience: **g,l,u.** *Choice, 2003.*

Brown, Lois   **PS153.N5B675 2005**
Encyclopedia of the Harlem Literary Renaissance: The Essential
Guide to the Lives and Works of the Harlem Renaissance
Writers. Saddle Stitched, Cloth over Boards. Facts On File, Inc.
New York, NY. 2005. 612p. Literary Movements Ser.
ISBN:0-8160-4967-X, ISBN13: 978-0-8160-4967-7.
Dewey:810.9/896/07307471. LCCN:2004-022097.

Audience: **g,l,u.** *Choice, 2006.*

Brown, William Wells   **PS1139.B9.C53 2004**
Clotel, or, the President's Daughter. Trade Paper. Dover
Publications, Inc. Mineola, NY. 2004. 160p.
ISBN:0-486-43859-7, ISBN13: 978-0-486-43859-7.
Dewey:813/.4. LCCN:2004-052791.

Audience: **g,l,u.**

Brown-Guillory,   **PS628**
Elizabeth (Editor)
Wines in the Wilderness: Plays by African American Women
from the Harlem Renaissance to the Present. Book, Other.
Greenwood Publishing Group, Inc. Portsmouth, NH. 1990. 272p.
Contributions in Afro-American and African Studies Ser., No.
135 ISBN:0-313-26509-7, ISBN13: 978-0-313-26509-9.
Dewey:812/.5080352042. LCCN:89-025857.

Audience: **g,l,u.** *Choice, 1991.*

Butler, Octavia   **PS3552.U827**
Fledgling: A Novel. Seven Stories Press. 2005.
ISBN:1-58322-690-7, ISBN13: 978-1-58322-690-2.

Audience: **g,l.**

Chase-Riboud, Barbara   **PS3553.H336**
Sally Hemings. Avon. 1980. ISBN:0-380-48686-5, ISBN13:
978-0-380-48686-1.

Audience: **g,l.**

Chesnutt, Charles   **PS1292.C6**
Waddell
The Conjure Woman, and Other Conjure Tales. Brodhead,
Richard H. (Editor). Duke Universiry Press. 1993.
ISBN:0-8223-1378-2, ISBN13: 978-0-8223-1378-6.

Audience: **g,l.**

Clark, Keith   **PS153.N5C49 2002**
Black Manhood in James Baldwin, Ernest J. Gaines, and August
Wilson. Trade Cloth. University of Illinois Press. Champaign,
IL. 2002. 176p. ISBN:0-252-02727-2, ISBN13:
978-0-252-02727-7. Dewey:810.9/896073. LCCN:2001-004431.

Audience: **g,l,u.** *Choice, 2002.*

Clark, Keith (Editor)   PS153.N5C645 2001
Contemporary Black Men's Fiction and Drama. Trade Cloth.
University of Illinois Press. Champaign, IL. 2001. 256p.
ISBN:0-252-02676-4, ISBN13: 978-0-252-02676-8.
Dewey:810.9/9286/08996073. LCCN:2001-000518.
               Audience: **g,l,u.** *Choice, 2002.*

Clarke, Cheryl   PS310.N4C48 2004
"After Mecca": Women Poets and the Black Arts Movement.
Trade Cloth. Rutgers University Press. Piscataway, NJ. 2005.
208p. ISBN:0-8135-3405-4, ISBN13: 978-0-8135-3405-3.
Dewey:811/.509896073. LCCN:2004-007530.
               Audience: **g,l,u,f.** *Choice, 2005.*

Clarke, John Henrik   PS647.A35B56 1993
   (Editor)
Black American Short Stories. Trade Paper. Farrar, Straus &
Giroux. New York, NY. 1993. 448p. American Century Ser.
ISBN:0-374-52354-1, ISBN13: 978-0-374-52354-1.
Dewey:813/.01/08896073. LCCN:92-016249.
               Audience: **g,l,u.**

Clarke, John Henrik   PS647.A35H37 1993
Harlem Voices from the Soul of Black America. Ed. 2. Paper
Text. A & B Distributors & Publishers Group. Brooklyn, NY.
1993. 222p. ISBN:1-881316-23-8, ISBN13: 978-1-881316-23-7.
Dewey:813/.0108896073. LCCN:2001-278780.
               Audience: **g,l,u.**

Croft, Robert W.   PS3515.U789Z6 2004
A Zora Neale Hurston Companion. Trade Cloth. University
Press of Florida. Gainesville, FL. 2004. 272p.
ISBN:0-8130-2793-4, ISBN13: 978-0-8130-2793-7.
Dewey:813/.52. LCCN:2004-049335.
               Audience: **g,l,u.** *Choice, 2003.*

Cruse, Harold   E185.6.C96 2005
The Crisis of the Negro Intellectual: A Historical Analysis of the
Failure of Black Leadership. Stanley Crouch (Introduction by).
Trade Paper, Perfect. New York Review of Books, Incorporated,
The. New York, NY. 2005. 616p. New York Review Books
Classics ISBN:1-59017-135-7, ISBN13: 978-1-59017-135-6.
Dewey:305.896/073. LCCN:2004-029508.
               Audience: **g,l,u,f.**

Cullen, Countee   PS3505.U287
My Soul's High Song: The Collected Writings of Countee
Cullen, Voice of the Harlem Renaissance. Early, Gerald.
Doubleday. 1991. ISBN:0-385-41295-9, ISBN13:
978-0-385-41295-7.
               Audience: **g,l,u,f.**

Dash, Julie   PN1997.D325
Daughters of the Dust: The Making of an African Woman's
Film. New Press. 1992. ISBN:1-56584-030-5, ISBN13:
978-1-56584-030-0.
               Audience: **l,u.**

Dawson, Alma & Van   PS153.N5A3364 2004
   Fleet, Connie (Editors)
African American Literature: A Guide to Reading Interests.
Trade Cloth. Libraries Unlimited, Inc. Westport, CT. 2004. 496p.
Genreflecting Advisory Ser. ISBN:1-56308-931-9, ISBN13:
978-1-56308-931-2. Dewey:810.9/896073. LCCN:2004-048928.
               Audience: **g,l,u.**

DeVeaux, Alexis   PS3562.O75Z66 2004
Warrior Poet: A Biography of Audre Lorde. Trade Cloth. W. W.
Norton & Company, Inc. New York, NY. 2004. 512p.

ISBN:0-393-01954-3, ISBN13: 978-0-393-01954-4.
Dewey:811/.54 B. LCCN:2003-023349.
               Audience: **g,l,u.** *Choice, 2004.*

Dickson-Carr, Darryl   PS374.N4D533 2005
ⓔ The Columbia Guide to Contemporary African American
Fiction. E-Book. Columbia University Press. New York, NY.
2005. 400p. The Columbia Guides to Literature since 1945 Ser.
ISBN:0-231-51069-1, ISBN13: 978-0-231-51069-1.
Dewey:813/.540986073.
               Audience: **g,l,u.** *Choice, 2006.*

Douglass, Frederick   E449.D738 2003
The Frederick Douglass Papers: Autobiographical Writings. John
W. Blassingame, John R. McKivigan & Peter P. Hinks (Editors).
Cloth over Boards. Yale University Press. Cumberland, RI.
2003. 528p. The Frederick Douglas Papers, Vol. 2
ISBN:0-300-09173-7, ISBN13: 978-0-300-09173-1.
Dewey:973.7092. LCCN:2003-005833.
               Audience: **g,l,u,f.**

Douglass, Frederick   E449.D749 1994
Autobiographies: Narrative of the Life, My Bondage and My
Freedom, Life and Times. Henry Louis Gates Jr. (Editor). Trade
Cloth. Library of America, The. New York, NY. 1994. 1100p.
Library of America, Vol. 68 ISBN:0-940450-79-8, ISBN13:
978-0-940450-79-0. Dewey:973.8/092 B. LCCN:93-024168.
               Audience: **g,l,u,f.**

Draper, James P.   PS153.N5B556
Black Literature Criticism, Set. Ed. 2. Trade Cloth. Thomson
Gale. Farmington Hills, MI. 1998. xvi, 489p. Black Literature
Criticism Ser. ISBN:0-8103-8574-0, ISBN13:
978-0-8103-8574-0. Dewey:809/.89896. LCCN:98-027492.
               Audience: **g,l,u.**

Egar, Emmanuel Edame   PS310.N4E37 2003
Black Women Poets of Harlem Renaissance. Trade Paper.
University Press of America, Inc. Lanham, MD. 2003. 124p.
ISBN:0-7618-2617-3, ISBN13: 978-0-7618-2617-0.
Dewey:811/.52099287. LCCN:2003-055237.
               Audience: **g,l,u.**

Ellison, Ralph   PS3555.L625I5 2002
Invisible Man. Trade Cloth. Random House, Inc. New York,
NY. 2002. 448p. ISBN:0-375-50791-4, ISBN13:
978-0-375-50791-5. Dewey:813/.54. LCCN:2001-048541.
               Audience: **g,l,u,f.**

Ervin, Hazel Arnett   PS153.N5A33 1999
   (Editor)
African American Literary Criticism: 1773-2000. Trade Cloth.
Thomson Gale. Farmington Hills, MI. 1999. xxix, 475p.
ISBN:0-8057-1683-1, ISBN13: 978-0-8057-1683-2.
Dewey:810.9/896073. LCCN:99-029491.
               Audience: **g,l,u,f.** *Choice, 2000.*

Ervin, Hazel Arnett   PS153.N5E78 2004
The Handbook of African American Literature. Trade Cloth.
University Press of Florida. Gainesville, FL. 2004. 256p.
ISBN:0-8130-2750-0, ISBN13: 978-0-8130-2750-0.
Dewey:810.9/896073. LCCN:2004-049332.
               Audience: **g,l,u,f.**

Evans, Mari   PS147
Black Women Writers, 1950-1980: A Critical Evaluation. Trade
Paper. Doubleday Publishing. New York, NY. 1999.

ISBN:0-385-50005-X, ISBN13: 978-0-385-50005-0.
Dewey:810/.9/9287.

Audience: **g,l,u,f.** *B*

Flowers, Sandra H.   **PS153.N5F56 1996**
African American Nationalist Literature of the 1960s: Pens of
Fire. Cloth Text. Garland Publishing, Inc. New York, NY. 1996.
216p. Studies in American Popular History and Culture
ISBN:0-8153-2474-X, ISBN13: 978-0-8153-2474-4.
Dewey:810.9/896073. LCCN:96-005278.

Audience: **g,l,u.**

Gaines, Ernest J.   **PS3557.A355**
A Lesson Before Dying. A.A. Knopf. 1993.
ISBN:0-679-41477-0, ISBN13: 978-0-679-41477-3.

Audience: **g,l.**

Gates, Henry Louis   **PS866.W5Z595 2003**
The Trials of Phillis Wheatley: America's First Black Poet and
Her Encounters with the Founding Fathers. Trade Cloth. Basic
Books. New York, NY. 2003. 144p. ISBN:0-465-02729-6,
ISBN13: 978-0-465-02729-3. Dewey:811/.1 B.
LCCN:2003-002717.

Audience: **g,l,u,f.** *Choice, 2003.*

Gates, Henry Louis Jr.   **PS508.N3**
Afro-American Women Writers. Trade Cloth. Thomson Gale.
Farmington Hills, MI. 1998. ISBN:0-8161-1848-5, ISBN13:
978-0-8161-1848-9. Dewey:810.8089607.

Audience: **g,l,u,f.**

Gates, Henry Louis Jr.   **PS3568.O243**
  & Appiah, Anthony (Editors)
Ann Petry: Critical Perspectives Past and Present. Trade Cloth.
HarperCollins Publishers. New York, NY. 1994. Literary Ser.
ISBN:1-56743-054-6, ISBN13: 978-1-56743-054-7.
Dewey:813/.54.

Audience: **l,u,f.**

Gates, Henry Louis Jr.   **PS3515.U274Z672 1993**
  & Appiah, Anthony
Langston Hughes: Critical Perspectives Past and Present. Trade
Cloth. HarperCollins Publishers. New York, NY. 1993. 255p.
Literary Ser. ISBN:1-56743-016-3, ISBN13: 978-1-56743-016-5.
Dewey:818/.5209. LCCN:92-045756.

Audience: **l,u.** *Choice, 1994.*

Gavin, Christy   **PS153.N5G29 1999**
African American Women Playwrights: A Research Guide. C.
James Trotman (Editor). Cloth Text. Garland Publishing, Inc.
New York, NY. 1999. 264p. Critical Studies in Black Life and
Culture, Vol. 31 ISBN:0-8153-2384-0, ISBN13:
978-0-8153-2384-6. Dewey:812/.54099287. LCCN:98-040865.

Audience: **g,l,u.** *Choice, 2000.*

Giddings, Paula J.   **E185.86.G49 1996**
When and Where I Enter: The Impact of Black Women on Race
and Sex in America. Ed. 2. Trade Paper. HarperCollins
Publishers. New York, NY. 1996. 416p. ISBN:0-688-14650-3,
ISBN13: 978-0-688-14650-4. Dewey:305.4/8896073.
LCCN:96-019349.

Audience: **g,l,u.**

Gilyard, Keith &   **PS508.N3A58 2004**
  Wardi, Anissa Janine
African American Literature. Trade Paper. Longman Publishing.
Boston, MA. 2004. 1376p. ISBN:0-321-11341-1, ISBN13:
978-0-321-11341-2. Dewey:810.8/0896073. LCCN:2003-020621.

Audience: **g,l,u.**

Giovanni, Nikki   **PS3557.I55.A6 2003**
The Collected Poetry of Nikki Giovanni: 1968-1998. Trade
Cloth. HarperCollins Publishers. New York, NY. 2003. 496p.
ISBN:0-06-054133-4, ISBN13: 978-0-06-054133-0.
Dewey:811/.54. LCCN:2004-302269.

Audience: **g,l,u,f.**

Giovanni, Nikki   **PS3557.I55**
Racism 101. Fowler, Virginia (Editor). W. Morrow. 1994.
ISBN:0-688-04332-1, ISBN13: 978-0-688-04332-2.

Audience: **g,l.**

Graham, Maryemma   **PS374.N4C36 2004**
Cambridge Companion to the African American Novel.
Cambridge University. 2004. ISBN:0-521-81574-6, ISBN13:
978-0-521-81574-1.

Audience: **g,l,u.**

Graham, Maryemma   **PS3545.A517Z67 2001**
Fields Watered with Blood: Critical Essays on Margaret Walker.
University of Georgia Press. 2001. ISBN:0-8203-2254-7,
ISBN13: 978-0-8203-2254-4.

Audience: **l,u.**

Graham, Maryemma   **PS3555.L625Z464 1995**
Conversations with Ralph Ellison. Singh, Amritjit. University
Press of Mississippi. 1995. ISBN:0-87805-780-3, ISBN13:
978-0-87805-780-1.

Audience: **l,u.**

Greenlee, Sam   **PS3568.O243**
The Spook Who Sat by the Door. Trade Cloth. Kayode
Publications, Ltd. New York, NY. 1991. 248p.
ISBN:1-879831-01-5, ISBN13: 978-1-879831-01-8.
Dewey:813/.5/4.

Audience: **g,l,u.**

Griffin, Farah J.   **PS374.N4G75 1995**
Who Set You Flowin'?: The African-American Migration
Narrative. Trade Paper. Oxford University Press, Inc. New York,
NY. 1996. 248p. Race and American Culture Ser.
ISBN:0-19-508897-2, ISBN13: 978-0-19-508897-7.
Dewey:810.9/355/08996/073. LCCN:94-022860.

Audience: **g,l,u.**

Gruesser, John   **PS153.N5G78 2005**
Confluences. Trade Cloth. University of Georgia Press. Athens,
GA. 2005. 216p. ISBN:0-8203-2603-8, ISBN13:
978-0-8203-2603-0. Dewey:810.9/896073. LCCN:2004-028321.

Audience: **g,l,u.** *Choice, 2006.*

Gruesser, John Cullen   **PS159.A35G78 2000**
Black on Black: Twentieth-Century African American Writing
about Africa. Trade Cloth. University Press of Kentucky.
Lexington, KY. 2000. 205p. ISBN:0-8131-2163-9, ISBN13:
978-0-8131-2163-5. Dewey:810.9/326/08996073.
LCCN:99-047796.

Audience: **g,l,u.** *Choice, 2000.*

Handy, W. C.   **ML410.H18A3 1991**
Father of the Blues: An Autobiography. Arna Bontemps (Editor),
Abbe Niles (Introduction by). Trade Paper. Da Capo Press, Inc.
Cambridge, MA. 1991. 340p. Quality Paperbacks Ser.
ISBN:0-306-80421-2, ISBN13: 978-0-306-80421-2.
Dewey:784.5/3/00924 B. LCCN:90-026262.

Audience: **g,l,u,f.**

Harris, Trudier   **PS153.N5H29 2001**
Saints, Sinners, Saviors: Strong Black Women in
African-American Literature. Trade Paper. Palgrave Macmillan.
New York, NY. 2001. 224p. ISBN:0-312-29303-8, ISBN13:
978-0-312-29303-1. Dewey:810.9/352042. LCCN:2001-036009.
Audience: **g,l,u.**

Harris, Trudier   **E185.97.H365**
Summer Snow: Reflections from a Black Daughter of the South.
Beacon Press. 2003. ISBN:0-8070-7254-0, ISBN13:
978-0-8070-7254-7.
Audience: **u.**

Hill, Patricia Liggins, et   **PS508.N3**
al.
Call and Response: The Riverside Anthology of the African
American Literary Tradition. Bernard W. Bell, Trudier Harris,
William J. Harris, R. Baxter Miller, Sondra J. O'Neale &
Horace Porter (Authors). Mixed Media, CD-ROM, Cloth Text,
Compact Disc. Houghton Mifflin College Division. Boston, MA.
2003. 1024p. ISBN:0-618-45171-4, ISBN13:
978-0-618-45171-5. Dewey:810.8/0896073.
Audience: **g,l,u.**

Himes, Chester   **PS3515.I713**
If He Hollers Let Him Go: A Novel. Thunder's Mouth. 1986.
ISBN:0-938410-32-6, ISBN13: 978-0-938410-32-4.
Audience: **g,l.**

Hogue, W. Lawrence   **PS153.N5H59 2003**
The African American Male, Writing, and Difference: A
Polycentric Approach to African American Literature, Criticism,
and History. Cloth Text. State University of New York Press.
Albany, NY. 2003. xiii, 291p. ISBN:0-7914-5693-5, ISBN13:
978-0-7914-5693-4. Dewey:810.9/9286/08996073.
LCCN:2002-075873.
Audience: **g,l,u.**   *Choice, 2003.*

hooks, bell   **E185.86.H735 1991**
Breaking Bread: Insurgent Black Intellectual Life. West, Cornel.
South End Press. 1991. ISBN:0-89608-415-9, ISBN13:
978-0-89608-415-5.
Audience: **l,u,f.**

Hudson-Weems,   **HQ1190.H83 1994**
Clenora
Africana Womanism: Reclaiming Ourselves. Ed. 2. Bedford
Publishers. 1994. ISBN:0-911557-11-3, ISBN13:
978-0-911557-11-4.
Audience: **l,u.**

Hurston, Zora Neale   **GR111.A47H86 1990**
Mules and Men. Miguel Covarrubias (Illustrator), Arnold
Rampersad (Foreword by), Franz Boas (Preface by). Trade
Paper. HarperCollins Publishers. New York, NY. 1990. 336p.
ISBN:0-06-091648-6, ISBN13: 978-0-06-091648-0.
Dewey:398.2/09759. LCCN:89-045672.
Audience: **g,l,u,f.** *B*

Hurston, Zora Neale   **GR55.H86A3 1995**
Folklore, Memoirs, and Other Writings. Cheryl A. Wall (Editor).
Trade Cloth. Library of America, The. New York, NY. 1995.
1024p. Library of America, Vol. 75 ISBN:0-940450-84-4,
ISBN13: 978-0-940450-84-4. Dewey:398/.092 B.
LCCN:94-021384.
Audience: **g,l,u.**

Hurston, Zora Neale   **PS3515.U789A6 1995**
Novels and Stories: Jonah's Gourd Vine; Their Eyes Were
Watching God; Moses, Man of the Mountain; Seraph on the
Suwanee. Cheryl A. Wall (Editor). Trade Cloth. Library of
America, The. New York, NY. 1995. 1054p. Novels and Stories
Ser., Vol. 74 ISBN:0-940450-83-6, ISBN13: 978-0-940450-83-7.
Dewey:813/.52. LCCN:94-025757.
Audience: **g,l,u,f.**

Jackson, Jonathan Jr.   **HV9468.J3A4 1994**
(Foreword by)
Soledad Brother: The Prison Letters of George Jackson. Trade
Paper. Chicago Review Press, Inc. Chicago, IL. 1995. 368p.
ISBN:1-55652-230-4, ISBN13: 978-1-55652-230-7.
Dewey:365/.6/092 B. LCCN:94-028264.
Audience: **g,l,u.**

James, Joy (Author,   **PS153.N5B5536 2000**
Editor)
The Black Feminist Reader. Tracey Denean Sharply-Whiting
(Editor). Trade Paper. Blackwell Publishing, Inc. Malden, MA.
2000. 320p. ISBN:0-631-21007-5, ISBN13: 978-0-631-21007-8.
Dewey:305.48/896073. LCCN:99-051385.
Audience: **g,l,u.**

Kuyk, Betty M.   **E185.K89 2003**
African Voices in the African American Heritage. Trade Paper.
Indiana University Press. Bloomington, IN. 2003. 280p.
ISBN:0-253-21576-5, ISBN13: 978-0-253-21576-5.
Dewey:973/.0496073. LCCN:2002-012902.
Audience: **g,l,u.**   *Choice, 2004.*

Leeming, David   **PS3552.A45.Z77**
James Baldwin: A Biography. Alfred A. Knopf. 1994. A Borzoi
Book ISBN:0-394-57708-6, ISBN13: 978-0-394-57708-1.
Audience: **l,u.**

Levin, Amy K.   **PS374.N4L48 2003**
Africanism and Authenticity in African-American Women's
Novels. Trade Cloth. University Press of Florida. Gainesville,
FL. 2003. 208p. ISBN:0-8130-2631-8, ISBN13:
978-0-8130-2631-2. Dewey:813/.5099287. LCCN:2003-040190.
Audience: **g,l,u.**

Lewis, David Levering   **E185.97.D73**
W. E. B. Du Bois: Biography of a Race, 1868-1919. Trade
Paper. Henry Holt & Company. New York, NY. 1994. 752p.
ISBN:0-8050-3568-0, ISBN13: 978-0-8050-3568-1.
Dewey:973/.0496/073/092. LCCN:93-016617.
Audience: **l,u.**   *Choice, 1994.*

Liddell, Janice   **PS153.N5A87 1999**
Arms Akimbo: African Women in Contemporary Literature.
Trade Cloth. University Press of Florida. Gainesville, FL. 1999.
240p. ISBN:0-8130-1728-9, ISBN13: 978-0-8130-1728-0.
Dewey:810.9/352042. LCCN:99-038712.
Audience: **g,l,u.**

Magill, Frank Northen   **PS153.N5M264 1992**
Masterpieces of African American Literature. HarperCollins.
1992. ISBN:0-06-270066-9, ISBN13: 978-0-06-270066-7.
Audience: **l,u.**

McBride, Dwight A.   **PS3552.A45Z74 1999**
(Editor)
James Baldwin Now. Trade Paper. New York University Press.
New York, NY. 1999. 356p. ISBN:0-8147-5618-2, ISBN13:
978-0-8147-5618-8. Dewey:818/.5409 B. LCCN:99-006546.
Audience: **u,f.**

McDowell, Deborah E.   PS374.N4M37 1995
The Changing Same: Black Women's Literature, Criticism, and
Theory. Trade Cloth. Indiana University Press. Bloomington, IN.
1995. 224p. ISBN:0-253-33629-5, ISBN13: 978-0-253-33629-3.
Dewey:813.009/896073. LCCN:94-010663.
Audience: **g,l,u.** *Choice, 1995.*

McHenry, Elizabeth   PS153.N5M36 2002
Forgotten Readers: Recovering the Lost History of
African-American Literary Societies. Trade Cloth. Duke
University Press. Durham, NC. 2002. 352p. New Americanists
Ser. ISBN:0-8223-2980-8, ISBN13: 978-0-8223-2980-0.
Dewey:028/.9/08996073. LCCN:2002-004448.
Audience: **g,l,u.** *Choice, 2003.*

Morrison, Toni   PS3563.O8749Z464 1994
Conversations with Toni Morrison. Taylor-Guthrie, Danille
(Editor). University of Mississippi. 1994.
Audience: **g,l,u.**

Napier, Winston   PS153.N5A335 2000
African American Literary Theory: A Reader. Trade Paper. New
York University Press. New York, NY. 2000. 576p.
ISBN:0-8147-5810-X, ISBN13: 978-0-8147-5810-6.
Dewey:810.9/896073. LCCN:00-025201.
Audience: **g,l,u.**

Nemiroff, Robert   PS3564.E48
To Be Young, Gifted and Black: A Portrait of Lorraine
Hansberry in Her Own Words. S. French. 1971.
Audience: **g,l.**

Newton, Huey P.   E185.615.N4 1995
To Die for the People: The Writings of Huey P. Newton.
Morrison, Toni (Editor). Readers and Writers Publishers. 1995.
ISBN:0-86316-327-0, ISBN13: 978-0-86316-327-2.
Audience: **g,l,u.**

Nugent, Richard Bruce   PS3527.U34.G39
Gay Rebel of the Harlem Renaissance: Selections from the
Work of Richard Bruce Nugent. Wirth, Thomas H. (Editor);
Gates, Henry Louis, Jr. (Foreword by). Duke University Press.
2002. ISBN:0-8223-2886-0, ISBN13: 978-0-8223-2886-5.
Audience: **l,u.**

Ostrom, Hans A. &   PS153.N5G73 2005
  Macey, J. David
The Greenwood Encyclopedia of African American Literature.
Trade Cloth. Greenwood Publishing Group, Inc. Portsmouth,
NH. 2005. lxii, 2010p. ISBN:0-313-32976-1, ISBN13:
978-0-313-32976-0. Dewey:810.9/896073. LCCN:2005-013679.
Audience: **g,l,u,f.**

Parks, Gordon   TR140.P35
Voices in the Mirror: An Autobiography. Anchor Books. 1992.
ISBN:0-385-26699-5, ISBN13: 978-0-385-26699-4.
Audience: **g,l.**

Pereira, Kim   PS3573.I45677Z83
August Wilson and the African-American Odyssey. Trade Cloth.
University of Illinois Press. Champaign, IL. 1995. 136p.
ISBN:0-252-02137-1, ISBN13: 978-0-252-02137-4.
Dewey:812/.54. LCCN:94-025855.
Audience: **g,l,u.** *Choice, 1996.*

Rampersad, Arnold   PS591.N4O97 2005
Oxford Anthology of African-American Poetry. Hilary Herbold.
Oxford University Press, Inc. 2005. ISBN:0-19-512563-0,
ISBN13: 978-0-19-512563-4.
Audience: **g,l.**

Rampersand, Arnold   PS3537.T323
The Life of Langston Hughes, Set. Ed. 2. Trade Cloth. Oxford
University Press, Inc. New York, NY. 2002.
ISBN:0-19-521936-8, ISBN13: 978-0-19-521936-4.
Dewey:818/.5209 B.
Audience: **u,f.**

Reed, Ishmael   PS3568.E365
Mumbo Jumbo. Trade Paper. Simon & Schuster. New York, NY.
1996. 224p. ISBN:0-684-82477-9, ISBN13: 978-0-684-82477-2.
Dewey:813.54.
Audience: **g,l,u,f.** *B*

Reed, Ishmael   PS3568.E365
New and Collected Poems, 1966-2006. Cloth over Boards.
Avalon Publishing Group. New York, NY. 2006. 384p.
ISBN:0-7867-1788-2, ISBN13: 978-0-7867-1788-0.
Dewey:811.54.
Audience: **g,l,u,f.**

Reed, Ishmael   PS3568.O243
Reed Reader. Trade Paper. Basic Books. New York, NY. 2001.
524p. ISBN:0-465-06894-4, ISBN13: 978-0-465-06894-4.
Dewey:813/.54.
Audience: **g,l,u,f.**

Reed, Ishmael   PS3568.E365
Writin' Is Fightin': Thirty-Seven Years of Boxing on Paper.
Atheneum. 1988. ISBN:0-689-11975-5, ISBN13:
978-0-689-11975-0.
Audience: **g,l.**

Reid-Pharr, Robert F.   HQ76.2.U5R45 2001
Black Gay Man. Trade Cloth. New York University Press. New
York, NY. 2001. 214p. Sexual Cultures Ser.
ISBN:0-8147-7502-0, ISBN13: 978-0-8147-7502-8.
Dewey:305.38/96642. LCCN:2001-000080.
Audience: **g,l,u.** *Choice, 2002.*

Roses, Lorraine E.   PS147
Harlem Renaissance and Beyond: Literary Biographies of One
Hundred Black Women Writers, 1900-1945. Trade Paper.
Harvard University Press. Cambridge, MA. 1997. 432p.
ISBN:0-674-37255-7, ISBN13: 978-0-674-37255-9.
Dewey:810.9/9287/03. LCCN:89-038731.
Audience: **g,l,u.** *Choice, 1990.*

Rowell, Charles Henry   PS508.N3
Making Callaloo: 25 years of Black Literature. St. Martin's
Press. 2002. ISBN:0-312-28898-0, ISBN13: 978-0-312-28898-3.
Audience: **l,u,f.**

Shannon, Sandra &   PS3573.I45677Z57
  Williams, Dana
August Wilson and Black Aesthetics. Cloth over Boards.
Palgrave Macmillan. New York, NY. 2004. 240p.
ISBN:1-4039-6406-8, ISBN13: 978-1-4039-6406-9.
Dewey:812/.54. LCCN:2003-068822.
Audience: **g,l,u.** *Choice, 2005.*

Smethurst, James   **PS153.N5S56 2005**
  Edward
The Black Arts Movement: Literary Nationalism in the 1960s
and 1970s. Trade Paper. University of North Carolina Press.
Chapel Hill, NC. 2005. 480p. The John Hope Franklin Series in
African American History and Culture Ser.
ISBN:0-8078-5598-7, ISBN13: 978-0-8078-5598-0.
Dewey:810.9/896073. LCCN:2004-027170.
Audience: **g,l,u.** *Choice, 2005.*

Smith, Katharine   **PS153.N5S62 2004**
  Capshaw
🄴 Children's Literature of the Harlem Renaissance. E-Book.
Indiana University Press. Bloomington, IN. 2004. xxvi, 338p.
Blacks in the Diaspora Ser. ISBN:0-253-34443-3, ISBN13:
978-0-253-34443-4. Dewey:810.9/9282. LCCN:2003-025351.
Audience: **g,l,u.** *Choice, 2005.*

Spillers, Hortense J.   **PS153.N5S67 2003**
Black, White, and in Color: Essays on American Literature and
Culture. Trade Paper. University of Chicago Press. Chicago, IL.
2003. 570p. ISBN:0-226-76980-1, ISBN13: 978-0-226-76980-6.
Dewey:810.9/896073/00904. LCCN:2002-014268.
Audience: **g,u,f.**

Standley, Fred L.   **PS3552.A45Z464 1989**
Conversations with James Baldwin. Pratt, Louis H.. University
of Mississippi. 1989.
Audience: **l,u.**

Temple, Christel N.   **PN849.A35T46 2003**
Literary Pan-Africanism: History, Context and Criticism. Trade
Paper. Carolina Academic Press. Durham, NC. 2004. 208p.
ISBN:0-89089-848-0, ISBN13: 978-0-89089-848-2.
Dewey:809/.8896/009045. LCCN:2003-065296.
Audience: **g,l,u.**

Thomas, Lorenzo   **PS310.N4T48 2000**
Extraordinary Measures: Afrocentric Modernism and
Twentieth-Century American Poetry. University of Alabama.
2000. ISBN:0-8173-1014-2, ISBN13: 978-0-8173-1014-1.
Audience: **u,f.**

Tilden, Paul Q.   **PS153.N5T55 2003**
African-American Literature: Overview and Bibliography. Trade
Paper. Nova Science Publishers, Inc. Hauppauge, NY. 2003.
192p. ISBN:1-59033-566-X, ISBN13: 978-1-59033-566-6.
Dewey:810.9/896073. LCCN:2003-042069.
Audience: **g,l,u.**

Walker, Alice   **PS3568.O243**
The Color Purple. Ed. 10. Cloth over Boards. Harcourt Trade
Publishers. New York, NY. 1992. 304p. ISBN:0-15-119154-9,
ISBN13: 978-0-15-119154-3. Dewey:813/.54. LCCN:91-047202.
Audience: **g,l,u,f.** 𝓑

Walker, Alice   **PS3573.A425**
The Same River Twice: Honoring the Difficult: A Meditation on
Life, Spirit, Art, and the Making of the Film The Color Purple,
Ten Years Later. Scribner. 1996. ISBN:0-684-81419-6, ISBN13:
978-0-684-81419-3.
Audience: **g.**

Wall, Cheryl A.   **PS153.N5W33 1995**
Women of the Harlem Renaissance. Cloth Text. Indiana
University Press. Bloomington, IN. 1995. 256p. Women of
Letters Ser. ISBN:0-253-32908-6, ISBN13: 978-0-253-32908-0.
Dewey:810/.9/896073. LCCN:95-003132.
Audience: **g,l,u.** *Choice, 1996.*

Wideman, John Edgar   **PS3573**
Brothers and Keepers: A Memoir. Trade Paper. Houghton Mifflin
Company Trade & Reference Division. Boston, MA. 2005.
272p. ISBN:0-618-50963-1, ISBN13: 978-0-618-50963-8.
Dewey:813/.54 B. LCCN:2005-272204.
Audience: **g,l,u.**

Wilson, Harriet E. &   **PS3334**
  Gates, Henry Louis Jr.
Our Nig: Or, Sketches from the Life of a Free Black. Ed. 3.
Trade Paper. Random House, Inc. New York, NY. 2002. 304p.
ISBN:1-4000-3120-6, ISBN13: 978-1-4000-3120-7.
Dewey:813.3.
Audience: **g,l,u,f.**

Wintz, Cary D. &   **NX512.3.A35E53 2004**
  Finkelman, Paul (Editors)
Encyclopedia of the Harlem Renaissance. Ed. 2. Library
Binding. Fitzroy Dearborn Publishers, Inc. Chicago, IL. 2004.
1392p. ISBN:1-57958-389-X, ISBN13: 978-1-57958-389-7.
Dewey:700/.89/9607307471. LCCN:2004-016353.
Audience: **g,l,u,f.** *Choice, 2005.*

Young, Kevin (Editor)   **PS508.N3G53 2000**
Giant Steps: The New Generation of African American Writers.
Trade Paper. HarperCollins Publishers. New York, NY. 2000.
384p. ISBN:0-688-16876-0, ISBN13: 978-0-688-16876-6.
Dewey:810.8.
Audience: **g,l,u.**

Literature > Africa

Alexander Street Press   **PN6119.7**
⬜ Black Drama.
http://www.alexanderstreetpress.com/products/bldr.htm
Alexander Street Press.
Audience: **g,l,u,f.**

Alexander Street Press   **PN6120.92.B45**
⬜ Black Short Fiction.
http://www.alexanderstreetpress.com/products/blfi.htm
Alexander Street Press.
Audience: **g,l,u,f.**

Gates, Henry Louis Jr.   **ND237.R725A93 1983**
  (Editor)
In the House of Osubgo: Critical Essays on Wole Soyinka.
Trade Cloth. Oxford University Press, Inc. New York, NY. 2000.
288p. ISBN:0-19-503349-3, ISBN13: 978-0-19-503349-6.
Dewey:759.13. LCCN:83-002268.
Audience: **u,f.**

Johnson-Odim, Cheryl   **HQ1815.5.Z75**
For Women and the Nation: Funmilayo Ransome-Kuti of
Nigeria. Mba, Nina Emma. University of Illinois. 1997.
ISBN:0-252-02313-7, ISBN13: 978-0-252-02313-2.
Audience: **l,u,f.**

Laye, Camara   **PQ3989.C27**
The Dark Child. Kirkup, James; Jones, Ernest (Translators).
Noonday Press. 1994. ISBN:0-8090-1548-X, ISBN13:
978-0-8090-1548-1.
Audience: **g,l,u,f.**

Lumumba, Patrice   DT657.L813
Congo, My Country. Paper Text. Textbook Publishers. Temecula, CA. 2003. 195p. ISBN:0-7581-6191-3, ISBN13: 978-0-7581-6191-8. Dewey:967.5.

Audience: **g,l,u,f.**

Mandela, Winnie   DT1949.M36A3 1985
Part of My Soul Went with Him. Benjamin, Anne (Editor); Benson, Mary (Adapted by). Norton. 1985. ISBN:0-393-02215-3, ISBN13: 978-0-393-02215-5.

Audience: **g.**

Otieno, Wambui   DT433.582.O75A3 1998
  Waiyaki
Mau Mau's Daughter: A Life Story. Presley, Cora Lynn (Editor, Introduction by). Lynn Rienner Publishers. 1998. ISBN:1-55587-722-2, ISBN13: 978-1-55587-722-4.

Audience: **l,u.**

Soyinka, Wole   PR9387.9.S6
Isara, a Voyage Around. Random House. 1989. ISBN:0-394-54077-8, ISBN13: 978-0-394-54077-1.

Audience: **g,l.**

Soyinka, Wole   DT49 .W516
The Essential Soyinka: A Reader. Henry Louis Gates Jr. (Author, Introduction by). Trade Cloth. Knopf Publishing Group. New York, NY. 1997. 416p. ISBN:0-679-43990-0, ISBN13: 978-0-679-43990-5. Dewey:330.9662605.

Audience: **g,l,u,f.**

Wilentz, Gay   PS153.N5W48 1992
Binding Cultures: Black Women Writers in Africa and the Diaspora. Paper Text. Indiana University Press. Bloomington, IN. 1992. 176p. Blacks in the Diaspora Ser. ISBN:0-253-20714-2, ISBN13: 978-0-253-20714-2. Dewey:810.9/9287/08996. LCCN:91-027069.

Audience: **g,l,u.** *Choice, 1992.*

Literature > Diaspora

Alexander Street Press   PN6119.7
☐ Black Drama.
http://www.alexanderstreetpress.com/products/bldr.htm
Alexander Street Press.

Audience: **g,l,u,f.**

Alexander Street Press   PN6120.92.B45
☐ Black Short Fiction.
http://www.alexanderstreetpress.com/products/blfi.htm
Alexander Street Press.

Audience: **g,l,u,f.**

Coles, Robert   PS153.N5C56 1999
Black Writers Abroad: A Study of Black American Writers in Europe and Africa. Cloth Text. Garland Publishing, Inc. New York, NY. 1999. 176p. Studies in African American History and Culture ISBN:0-8153-2751-X, ISBN13: 978-0-8153-2751-6. Dewey:810.9/896073. LCCN:98-055445.

Audience: **g,l,u.**

De Jesus, Carolina M.   HN290.S33
Child of the Dark: The Diary of Carolina Maria de Jesus. David St. Clair (Translator), Robert S. Levine (Afterword by). Mass Market. Penguin Group (USA) Inc. New York, NY. 2003. 208p. ISBN:0-451-52910-3, ISBN13: 978-0-451-52910-7. Dewey:306/.0981/61.

Audience: **g,l.**

Massaquoi, Hans J.   DD78.B55
Destined to Witness: Growing up Black in Nazi Germany. Morrow. 1999. ISBN:0-688-17155-9, ISBN13: 978-0-688-17155-1.

Audience: **g,l.**

Rowell, Charles Henry   PS508.N3
Making Callaloo: 25 years of Black Literature. St. Martin's Press. 2002. ISBN:0-312-28898-0, ISBN13: 978-0-312-28898-3.

Audience: **l,u,f.**

Music

Alexander Street Press   M1670
☐ African American Music Reference.
http://www.alexanderstreetpress.com/products/aamr.htm

Audience: **g,l,u,f.**

Alexander Street Press   M1670
☐ African American Song.
http://www.alexanderstreetpress.com/products/black.htm
Alexander Street Press.

Audience: **g,l,u,f.**

Baraka, Amiri & Jones,   ML3556.B16 1999
  LeRoi
Blues People: Negro Music in White America. Trade Paper. HarperCollins Publishers. New York, NY. 1999. 256p. ISBN:0-688-18474-X, ISBN13: 978-0-688-18474-2. Dewey:780/.89/96073. LCCN:98-049663.

Audience: **g,l,u,f.** *B*

Cone, James H.   ML3556
The Spirituals and the Blues. Trade Paper. HarperCollins Publishers. New York, NY. 1984. ISBN:0-8164-2073-4, ISBN13: 978-0-8164-2073-5. Dewey:781.62/96073.

Audience: **g,l,u.**

Davis, Angela Y.   ML3521
Blues Legacies and Black Feminism: Gertrude "Ma" Rainey, Bessie Smith, and Billie Holiday. UK-Trade Paper. Alfred A. Knopf Inc. New York, NY. 1999. 464p. ISBN:0-679-77126-3, ISBN13: 978-0-679-77126-5. Dewey:782.4/2/1643/082.

Audience: **g,l,u.**

Dyson, Michael Eric   ML420.S529D97 2001
Holler If You Hear Me: Searching for Tupac Shakur. Trade Cloth. Basic Books. New York, NY. 2001. 304p. ISBN:0-465-01755-X, ISBN13: 978-0-465-01755-3. Dewey:782.4/2/1649/092. LCCN:2001-036564.

Audience: **g,l,u.**

Glenn, Darryl   ML400.N49 2003
African American Concert Singers Before 1950. Paper Text. McFarland & Company, Incorporated Publishers. Jefferson, NC. 2003. 199p. ISBN:0-7864-1467-7, ISBN13: 978-0-7864-1467-3. Dewey:782/.0092/396073 B. LCCN:2003-001307.

Audience: **g,l,u,f.**

Handy, W. C.   ML410.H18A3 1991
Father of the Blues: An Autobiography. Arna Bontemps (Editor), Abbe Niles (Introduction by). Trade Paper. Da Capo Press, Inc. Cambridge, MA. 1991. 340p. Quality Paperbacks Ser. ISBN:0-306-80421-2, ISBN13: 978-0-306-80421-2. Dewey:784.5/3/00924 B. LCCN:90-026262.

Audience: **g,l,u,f.**

Kirchner, Bill   ML3507.O94 2000
Oxford Companion to Jazz. Oxford University Press. 2000.
ISBN:0-19-512510-X, ISBN13: 978-0-19-512510-8.
Audience: **g,l,u.**

Larkin, Colin   ML102.J3
Virgin Encyclopedia of Jazz. Virgin Books. 2004.
ISBN:1-85227-183-3, ISBN13: 978-1-85227-183-1.
Audience: **g,l,u.**

Maultsby, Portia &   ML3508.1.A37 2005
  Burnim, Mellonee V.
African American Music; An Introduction. Routledge. 2005.
ISBN:0-415-94137-7, ISBN13: 978-0-415-94137-2.
Audience: **l.**

Reagon, Bernice   ML3187.R43 2001
  Johnson
If You Don't Go, Don't Hinder Me: The African American
Sacred Song Tradition. Trade Paper. University of Nebraska
Press. Lincoln, NE. 2001. 155p. Abraham Lincoln Lecture Ser.
ISBN:0-8032-8983-9, ISBN13: 978-0-8032-8983-3.
Dewey:782.25/4. LCCN:00-055231.
Audience: **g,l,u.** *Choice, 2002.*

Reagon, Bernice   ML390.W274 1992
  Johnson (Editor)
We'll Understand It Better by and By: Pioneering African
American Gospel Composers. Trade Paper. Smithsonian
Institution Press. Washington, DC. 1992. 396p.
ISBN:1-56098-167-9, ISBN13: 978-1-56098-167-1.
Dewey:782.25092273. LCCN:91-037954.
Audience: **g,l,u.** *Choice, 1993.*

Simmons, Margaret R.   M1629
  (Editor, Music by)
A New Anthology of Art Songs by African American Composer.
Jeanine Wagner (Editor). Compact Disc, Trade Cloth. Southern
Illinois University Press. Carbondale, IL. 2004. 224p.
ISBN:0-8093-2523-3, ISBN13: 978-0-8093-2523-8.
Dewey:782.4/2/0973.
Audience: **g.**

Southern, Eileen   ML3556.S74 1997
Music of Black America: A History. Ed. 3. Trade Cloth. W. W.
Norton & Company, Inc. New York, NY. 1997. 702p.
ISBN:0-393-03843-2, ISBN13: 978-0-393-03843-9.
Dewey:780/.89/96073. LCCN:96-028811.
Audience: **g,l,u.**

Southern, Eileen &   ML3556.S738 2000
  Wright, Josephine
Images: Iconography of Music and Musicians in
African-American Culture 1770s-1920s. Cloth Text. Garland
Publishing, Inc. New York, NY. 2000. 288p. Music in African
American Culture Ser., Vol. 1 ISBN:0-8153-2875-3, ISBN13:
978-0-8153-2875-9. Dewey:780/.89/96073. LCCN:00-029362.
Audience: **g,l,u,f.** *Choice, 2001.*

Walker-Hill, Helen   ML390.W16 2002
From Spirituals to Symphonies: African-American Women
Composers and Their Music. Cloth Text. Greenwood Publishing
Group, Inc. Portsmouth, NH. 2002. 432p. Jazz Companions Ser.
ISBN:0-313-29947-1, ISBN13: 978-0-313-29947-6.
Dewey:780.89/96073. LCCN:2001-040600.
Audience: **g,l,u,f.** *Choice, 2003.*

Walker-Hill, Helen   ML128.W7W35 1995
Music by Black Women Composers: A Bibliography of
Available Scores. Trade Cloth. Columbia College Chicago.
Chicago, IL. 1995. 118p. CBMR Monographs, No. 5
ISBN:0-929911-04-0, ISBN13: 978-0-929911-04-5.
Dewey:016.78/082. LCCN:95-005613.
Audience: **g,l,u.**

Performing Arts

Alexander Street Press   PN6119.7
☐ Black Drama.
http://www.alexanderstreetpress.com/products/bldr.htm
Alexander Street Press.
Audience: **g,l,u,f.**

Bean, Annemarie   PN2270.A35S68 1999
Sourcebook of African-American Performance. Routledge. 1999.
Worlds of Performances ISBN:0-415-18234-4, ISBN13:
978-0-415-18234-8.
Audience: **u,f.**

Davis, Natalie Zemon   PN1995.9.S557D38
Slaves on Screen: Film and Historical Vision. Harvard
University Press. 2000. ISBN:0-674-00444-2, ISBN13:
978-0-674-00444-3.
Audience: **u,f.**

Gugler, Josef   PN1993
Afican Film: Reimaging a Continent. Indiana University Press.
2003. ISBN:0-85255-562-8, ISBN13: 978-0-85255-562-0.
Audience: **g,l,u.**

Hill, Errol G. & Hatch,   PN2270.A35H55 2003
  James V.
A History of African American Theatre. Cambridge University
Press. 2003. ISBN:0-521-62443-6, ISBN13: 978-0-521-62443-5.
Audience: **l,u.**

Politics

    E185.86
The Debtors: Whites Respond to the Call for Black Reparations.
Perfect. Caucasians United for Reparations & Emancipation
Cure. Red Oak, GA. 2005. 256p. ISBN:0-9765909-1-3, ISBN13:
978-0-9765909-1-0. Dewey:305.896073.
Audience: **g,l,u.**

A History of N'cobra and the Reparations Movement: The
Demand for Black Reparations. Trade Paper. Conquering Books.
Drewyville, VA. 2004. ISBN:1-56411-244-6, ISBN13:
978-1-56411-244-6.
Audience: **g,l,u.**

Baldwin, Kate A.   E185.61.B224 2002
Beyond the Color Line and the Iron Curtain: Reading
Encounters Between Black and Red, 1922-1963. Trade Cloth.
Duke University Press. Durham, NC. 2002. 352p. New
Americanists Ser. ISBN:0-8223-2976-X, ISBN13:
978-0-8223-2976-3. Dewey:810.9/3247/08996073.
LCCN:2002-003974.
Audience: **l,u,f.**

Barker, Lucius   **E185.615.B33 1998**
  Jefferson, et al.
African Americans and the American Political System. Ed. 4.
Mack Jones & Katherine Tate (Authors). Trade Paper. Prentice
Hall PTR. Upper Saddle River, NJ. 1998. 372p.
ISBN:0-13-779562-9, ISBN13: 978-0-13-779562-8.
Dewey:323.1/196073. LCCN:98-025287.

                          Audience: **g,l,u.**

Bin Wahad, Dhoruba, et   **E185.615.B516 1993**
  al.
Still Black, Still Strong: Survivors of the War Against Black
Revolutionaries. Mumia Abu-Jamal & Assata Shakur (Authors).
Trade Paper. Semiotexte/Smart Art. Los Angeles, CA. 1993.
272p. Semiotext(e)/Active Agents Ser. ISBN:0-936756-74-8,
ISBN13: 978-0-936756-74-5. Dewey:322.4/2/092396073.
LCCN:2002-510804.

                          Audience: **g,l,u.**

Collins, Patricia Hill   **HQ1426.C633 2000**
Black Feminist Thought: Knowledge, Consciousness and
Politics of Empowerment. Ed. 2. Paper over Boards. Routledge.
New York, NY. 1999. 352p. ISBN:0-415-92483-9, ISBN13:
978-0-415-92483-2. Dewey:305.42/01. LCCN:99-029144.

                          Audience: **l,u,f.**

Collins, Patricia Hill   **HQ801**
Black Sexual Politics: African Americans, Gender, and the New
Racism. Trade Paper. Routledge. New York, NY. 2005. 384p.
ISBN:0-415-95150-X, ISBN13: 978-0-415-95150-0.
Dewey:306.7/089/96073.

          Audience: **g,l,u,f.** *Choice, 2005.*

Cone, James H.   **BT734.2.C6 1997**
Black Theology and Black Power. Trade Paper. Orbis Books.
Maryknoll, NY. 1997. 200p. ISBN:1-57075-157-9, ISBN13:
978-1-57075-157-8. Dewey:230/.08996073. LCCN:97-220426.

                   Audience: **g,l,u.** *B*

Cone, James H.   **BT83.57.C67 1997**
God of the Oppressed. Trade Paper. Orbis Books. Maryknoll,
NY. 1997. 280p. ISBN:1-57075-158-7, ISBN13:
978-1-57075-158-5. Dewey:261.8/34896073. LCCN:97-030468.

                         Audience: **g,l,u**

Cone, James H. &   **BT82.7.B56 1993**
  Wilmore, Gayraud S.
Black Theology: A Documentary History, 1980-1992. Ed. 2.
Trade Paper. Orbis Books. Maryknoll, NY. 1993. 400p.
ISBN:0-88344-773-8, ISBN13: 978-0-88344-773-4.
Dewey:230/.089/96. LCCN:92-044927.

                      Audience: **g,l,u,f.**

Cone, James H. &   **BT82.7**
  Wilmore, Gayraud S.
Black Theology: A Documentary History, 1966-1979. Ed. 2.
Trade Paper. Orbis Books. Maryknoll, NY. 1993. 400p. Black
Theology Ser., Vol. 1 ISBN:0-88344-853-X, ISBN13:
978-0-88344-853-3. Dewey:230/.089/96. LCCN:92-044927.

                    Audience: **g,l,u,f.**

Dawson, Michael C.   **E185.61**
Behind the Mule: Race and Class in African-American Politics.
Trade Paper. Princeton University Press. Princeton, NJ. 1995.
246p. ISBN:0-691-02543-6, ISBN13: 978-0-691-02543-8.
Dewey:323.1/196073. LCCN:93-044088.
          Audience: **g,l,u,f.** *Choice, 1995.*

Du Bois, W. E. B., et al.   **E185.61.A239 1996**
African American Political Thought, 1890-1930: Washington,
Du Bois, Garvey, and Randolph. Booker T. Washington, Marcus
Garvey & A. Philip Randolph (Authors), Cary D. Wintz
(Editor). Trade Cloth. M. E. Sharpe Inc. Armonk, NY. 1996.
360p. ISBN:1-56324-178-1, ISBN13: 978-1-56324-178-9.
Dewey:973/.0496073. LCCN:95-033287.

          Audience: **g,l,u.** *Choice, 1996.*

Gill, LaVerne M.   **E840.6.G55 1997**
African American Women in Congress. Cloth Text. Rutgers
University Press. Piscataway, NJ. 1997. 256p.
ISBN:0-8135-2352-4, ISBN13: 978-0-8135-2352-1.
Dewey:328.73/092/2 B. LCCN:96-029294.

                      Audience: **g,l,u.**

Henderson, Errol A.   **D13**
Afrocentrism and World Politics: Towards a New Paradigm.
Trade Cloth. Greenwood Publishing Group, Inc. Portsmouth,
NH. 1995. 240p. ISBN:0-275-95127-8, ISBN13:
978-0-275-95127-6. Dewey:907/.2. LCCN:94-046170.
                      Audience: **g,u,f.**

Langley, J. Ayodele   **DT353.L33**
  (Editor)
Ideologies of Liberation in Black Africa, 1856-1970. Trade
Paper. Africa Book Centre. Brighton, 2004. 858p.
ISBN:0-86036-039-3, ISBN13: 978-0-86036-039-1.
Dewey:320.5/096. LCCN:80-458475.

                      Audience: **g,l,u.**

Martin, Guy   **DT30.5.M275 2000**
Africa in World Politics: A Pan-African Perspective. Trade
Paper. Africa World Press. Trenton, NJ. 2003. 328p.
ISBN:0-86543-858-7, ISBN13: 978-0-86543-858-3.
Dewey:327/.096. LCCN:00-030616.

                  Audience: **g,l,u,f.**

Middleton, Stephen   **E185**
  (Editor)
Black Congressmen During Reconstruction: A Documentary
Sourcebook. John David Smith (Foreword by). Cloth Text.
Greenwood Publishing Group, Inc. Portsmouth, NH. 2002. 464p.
ISBN:0-313-32281-3, ISBN13: 978-0-313-32281-5.
Dewey:328.73/092/396073. LCCN:2002-067753.
                  Audience: **g,l,u,f.**

Moses, Wilson J.   **E185.M87 2004**
Creative Conflict in African American Thought: Frederick
Douglass, Alexander Crummell, Booker T. Washington, W. E. B.
Du Bois, and Marcus Garvey. Trade Paper. Cambridge
University Press. New York, NY. 2004. 326p.
ISBN:0-521-53537-9, ISBN13: 978-0-521-53537-3.
Dewey:305.896/073/00922. LCCN:2003-058434.

                    Audience: **g,l,u.**

Pohlmann, Marcus D.   **E185.A2536 2002**
  (Editor, Introduction by)
African American Political Thought. Paper over Boards.
Routledge. New York, NY. 2003. 2112p. ISBN:0-415-94284-5,
ISBN13: 978-0-415-94284-3. Dewey:320.5/089/96073.
LCCN:2002-031810.

                    Audience: **g,l,u.**

Springer, Kimberly   **E185.86.S766 1999**
  (Editor)
Still Lifting, Still Climbing: African American Women's
Contemporary Activism. Beverly Guy-Sheftall (Preface by),
Loretta Ross (Afterword by). Trade Cloth. New York University

---

Press. New York, NY. 1999. 360p. ISBN:0-8147-8124-1,
ISBN13: 978-0-8147-8124-1. Dewey:305.48/896073.
LCCN:99-006173.

Audience: **g,l,u.**

Tate, Gayle T.   **E185.9.T38 2003**
Unknown Tongues: Black Women's Political Activism in the
Antebellum Era, 1830-1860. Trade Cloth. Michigan State
University Press. East Lansing, MI. 2003. 416p. Black American
and Diasporic Studies ISBN:0-87013-652-6, ISBN13:
978-0-87013-652-8. Dewey:974/.00496073/0082.
LCCN:2002-155167.

Audience: **g,l,u.** *Choice, 2003.*

Terborg-Penn, Rosalyn   **JK1896.T47 1998**
African American Women in the Struggle for the Vote,
1850-1920. Trade Paper. Indiana University Press. Bloomington,
IN. 1998. 224p. Blacks in the Diaspora Ser.
ISBN:0-253-21176-X, ISBN13: 978-0-253-21176-7.
Dewey:324.6/23/08996073. LCCN:97-041896.

Audience: **g,l,u,f.** *Choice, 1998.*

Valelly, Richard M.   **E185.2.V35 2004**
The Two Reconstructions: The Struggle for Black
Enfranchisement. Trade Cloth. University of Chicago Press.
Chicago, IL. 2004. 348p. American Politics and Political
Economy Ser. ISBN:0-226-84528-1, ISBN13:
978-0-226-84528-9. Dewey:323.1196/073/009.
LCCN:2004-010380.

Audience: **g,l,u.** *Choice, 2005.*

Walters, Ronald W.   **JK1924.W343 2005**
Freedom Is Not Enough: Black Voters, Black Candidates, and
American Presidential Politics. Trade Cloth. Rowman &
Littlefield Publishers, Inc. Lanham, MD. 2005. 256p. American
Political Challenges Ser. ISBN:0-7425-3837-0, ISBN13:
978-0-7425-3837-5. Dewey:324.6/2/08996073.
LCCN:2005-008343.

Audience: **g,l,u,f.** *Choice, 2006.*

Walters, Ronald W.   **DT16.5.W35 1993**
Pan Africanism in the African Diaspora: An Analysis of Modern
Afrocentric Political Movements. Trade Cloth. Wayne State
University Press. Detroit, MI. 1993. 452p. African American
Life Ser. ISBN:0-8143-2184-4, ISBN13: 978-0-8143-2184-3.
Dewey:320.5/49/096. LCCN:92-030256.

Audience: **g,l,u.** *Choice, 1994.*

Walters, Ronald W. &   **Z1361**
  Johnson, Cedric
Bibliography of African American Leadership: An Annotated
Guide. Cloth Text. Greenwood Publishing Group, Inc.
Portsmouth, NH. 2000. 304p. Bibliographies and Indexes in
Afro-American and African Studies, Vol. 41
ISBN:0-313-31314-8, ISBN13: 978-0-313-31314-1.
Dewey:016.3033/4/08996073. LCCN:00-021554.

Audience: **g,l,u.** *Choice, 2000.*

Walton, Hanes Jr &   **E185.615.W317 2005**
  Smith, Robert C.
American Politics and the African American Quest for Universal
Freedom. Ed. 3. Trade Paper. Longman Publishing. Boston, MA.
2005. 336p. ISBN:0-321-29237-5, ISBN13: 978-0-321-29237-7.
Dewey:320.973/089/96073. LCCN:2004-024776.

Audience: **g,l,u.**

Washington, Booker T   **E185.97.W4**
Up from Slavery. Trade Paper. Kessinger Publishing, LLC.
Whitefish, MT. 2004. ISBN:1-4191-9216-7, ISBN13:
978-1-4191-9216-6. Dewey:370/.92 B.

Audience: **g,l,u.**

West, Cornel   **JC423.W384 2004**
Democracy Matters: Winning the Fight Against Imperialism.
Penquin Press. 2004. ISBN:1-59420-029-7, ISBN13:
978-1-59420-029-8.

Audience: **g,l,u.**

Wilson, Amos N.   **E185.615.W54 1998**
Blueprint for Black Power: A Moral, Political and Economic
Imperative for the Twenty-First Century. Trade Cloth. Afrikan
World InfoSystems. Brooklyn, NY. 1998. ISBN:1-879164-07-8,
ISBN13: 978-1-879164-07-9. Dewey:305.896/073.
LCCN:98-022964.

Audience: **g,l,u,f.**

Psychology

Bassey, Magnus O.   **BP223.Z8L5718 2005**
Malcolm X and African American Self-Consciousness. Trade
Cloth. Edwin Mellen Press, The. Lewiston, NY. 2004. 226p.
Black Studies, 26 ISBN:0-7734-6281-3, ISBN13:
978-0-7734-6281-6. Dewey:320.54/6/092. LCCN:2004-060955.

Audience: **g,l,u.**

Belgrave, Faye Z. &   **E185.625.B425 2005**
  Allison, Kevin W.
African American Psychology: From Africa to America. Paper
Text. SAGE Publications, Inc. Thousand Oaks, CA. 2005. 464p.
ISBN:0-7619-2471-X, ISBN13: 978-0-7619-2471-5.
Dewey:155.8/496073. LCCN:2005-007118.

Audience: **l,u,f.**

Fanon, Frantz   **DT33.F313 2004**
The Wretched of the Earth. Trade Paper. Grove/Atlantic, Inc.
New York, NY. 2004. 256p. ISBN:0-8021-4132-3, ISBN13:
978-0-8021-4132-3. Dewey:960/.0971244. LCCN:2004-042476.

Audience: **g,l,u,f.** *B*

Fashola, Olatokunbo S.   **LC2731.E34 2005**
  (Editor)
Educating African American Males: Voices from the Field.
Trade Cloth. Corwin Press. Thousand Oaks, CA. 2005. 320p.
ISBN:1-4129-1433-7, ISBN13: 978-1-4129-1433-8.
Dewey:371.829/96073. LCCN:2004-024084.

Audience: **g,l,u,f.** *Choice, 2005.*

Ferguson, Carroy U.   **E185.625**
Transitions in Consciousness from an African American
Perspective. Trade Paper. University Press of America, Inc.
Lanham, MD. 2004. 256p. ISBN:0-7618-2700-5, ISBN13:
978-0-7618-2700-9. Dewey:305.896073. LCCN:2003-114128.

Audience: **g,l,u,f.**

Jackson, Ronald L. II   **P94.5.A37A367 2003**
  (Editor)
African American Communication and Identities: Essential
Readings. Cloth Text. SAGE Publications, Inc. Thousand Oaks,
CA. 2003. 368p. ISBN:0-7619-2845-6, ISBN13:
978-0-7619-2845-4. Dewey:302.2/089/96073.
LCCN:2003-013998.

Audience: **g,l,u,f.**

Jones, Reginald L.   E185.625.A36 1999
  (Editor)
Advances in African American Psychology. Library Binding.
Cobb & Henry Publishers. Oakland, CA. 1997. xvii, 380p.
ISBN:0-943539-09-9, ISBN13: 978-0-943539-09-6.
Dewey:155.8/496073. LCCN:98-020669.
                                        Audience: **u,f.**

Mickel, Elijah   RC489.R37M53 2003
Africa-Centered Reality Therapy and Choice Theory. Trade
Cloth. Africa World Press. Trenton, NJ. 2003. 248p.
ISBN:1-59221-127-5, ISBN13: 978-1-59221-127-2.
Dewey:616.89/14/08996073. LCCN:2003-012522.
                                        Audience: **l,u,f.**

Rosenblatt, Paul C. &   RC451.5.N4R67 2005
  Wallace, Beverly R.
African-American Grief. UK-B Format Paperback. Routledge.
New York, NY. 2005. 224p. The Series in Death, Dying, and
Bereavement ISBN:0-415-95152-6, ISBN13:
978-0-415-95152-4. Dewey:155.9/37/08996073.
LCCN:2004-022552.
                                        Audience: **g,l,u,f.**

Siddle Walker, Vanessa   E185.86.R244 2004
  & Snarey, John R.
Race-Ing Moral Formation: African American Perspectives on
Care and Justice. Trade Paper. Teachers College Press, Teachers
College, Columbia University. New York, NY. 2004. 208p.
ISBN:0-8077-4449-2, ISBN13: 978-0-8077-4449-9.
Dewey:170/.89/96073. LCCN:2003-070315.
                                Audience: **l,u,f.** *Choice, 2004.*

Reference

Accessible Archives, Inc.   E184.6
☐ African American Newsapers: the 19th century.
http://www.accessible.com/about/aboutAA.htm
Accessible Archives, Inc.
                                        Audience: **g,l,u,f.**

Alkalimat, Abdul   E184.6
The African American Experience in Cyberspace: A Resource
Guide to the Best Web Sites on Black Culture and History.
Trade Cloth. Pluto Press. London, 2003. 304p.
ISBN:0-7453-2223-9, ISBN13: 978-0-7453-2223-0.
Dewey:025.06/305896073. LCCN:2004-298825.
                                Audience: **g,l,u,f.** *Choice, 2004.*

Appiah, Kwame   DT14
  Anthony; Gates, Henry Louis
💾 Microsoft Encarta Africana 2000. 1999.
                                        Audience: **g,l.**

Magill, Frank Northen   PS153.N5M264 1992
Masterpieces of African American Literature. HarperCollins.
1992. ISBN:0-06-270066-9, ISBN13: 978-0-06-270066-7.
                                        Audience: **l,u.**

Wilson, Dreck Spurlock   NA736.A47 2003
African American Architects: A Biographical Dictionary,
1865-1945. Routledge. 2004. ISBN:0-415-92959-8, ISBN13:
978-0-415-92959-2.
                                        Audience: **g,l,u.**

Reference > General

Aberjhani, et al.   PS153.N5A24 2003
Encyclopedia of the Harlem Renaissance. Sandra West &
Clement Alexander Price (Authors). Trade Cloth. Facts On File,
Inc. New York, NY. 2003. 448p. ISBN:0-8160-4539-9, ISBN13:
978-0-8160-4539-6. Dewey:810.9/896073. LCCN:2002-152067.
                                Audience: **g,l,u,f.** *Choice, 2004.*

Andrews, William L.   PS153.N5C59 2000
  (Editor), et al.
The Concise Oxford Companion to African American Literature.
Frances Smith Foster & Trudier Harris-Lopez (Editors). Trade
Paper. Oxford University Press, Inc. New York, NY. 2001. 512p.
ISBN:0-19-513883-X, ISBN13: 978-0-19-513883-2.
Dewey:810.9/896073/003. LCCN:00-065201.
                                Audience: **g,l,u,f.** *Choice, 2001.*

Asante, Molefi Kete &   E185
  Mattson, Mark T.
Historical and Cultural Atlas of African Americans. Compact
Disc. Macmillan Publishing Company, Inc. Old Tappan, NJ.
1992. 208p. ISBN:0-02-897029-2, ISBN13: 978-0-02-897029-5.
Dewey:973/.0496073.
                                Audience: **g,l,u,f.** *Choice, 1991.*

Brown, Lorene Byron   Z695.1.B57B76 1995
Subject Headings for African American Materials. Libraries
Unlimited, Inc. 1995. ISBN:1-56308-252-7, ISBN13:
978-1-56308-252-8.
                                        Audience: **u,f.**

Draper, James P.   PS153.N5B556
Black Literature Criticism, Set. Ed. 2. Trade Cloth. Thomson
Gale. Farmington Hills, MI. 1998. xvi, 489p. Black Literature
Criticism Ser. ISBN:0-8103-8574-0, ISBN13:
978-0-8103-8574-0. Dewey:809/.89896. LCCN:98-027492.
                                        Audience: **g,l,u.**

Greenwood Electronic   E443
  Media
☐ American Slavery: A Composite Autobiography.
http://www.gem.greenwood.com
Rawick, George P.. Greenwood Publishing Group, Inc.
                                        Audience: **g,l,u,f.**

Logan, Rayford W. &   E185.96.D53 1982
  Winston, Michael R. (Editors)
Dictionary of American Negro Biography. Trade Cloth. W. W.
Norton & Company, Inc. New York, NY. 1983. 680p.
ISBN:0-393-01513-0, ISBN13: 978-0-393-01513-3.
Dewey:920/.009296073 B. LCCN:81-009629.
                                        Audience: **g,l,u,f.** *B*

Marable, Manning, et   E184.6.F74 2003
  al.
Freedom on My Mind: The Columbia Documentary History of
the African American Experience. John McMillian & Nishani
Frazier (Authors). Trade Cloth. Columbia University Press. New
York, NY. 2003. 900p. ISBN:0-231-10890-7, ISBN13:
978-0-231-10890-4. Dewey:973/.0496073. LCCN:2003-051605.
                                Audience: **g,l,u.** *Choice, 2003.*

Nelson, Emmanuel S.   PS153
  (Editor)
African American Authors, 1745-1945: A Bio-Bibliographical
Critical Sourcebook. Cloth Text. Greenwood Publishing Group,
Inc. Portsmouth, NH. 2000. 544p. ISBN:0-313-30910-8,

ISBN13: 978-0-313-30910-6. Dewey:810.9/896073 B.
LCCN:99-032527.

         Audience: **g,l,u,f.** *Choice, 2000.*

Nelson, Emmanuel S.   **PS374**
   (Editor)
Contemporary African American Novelists: A
Bio-Bibliographical Critical Sourcebook. Cloth Text. Greenwood
Publishing Group, Inc. Portsmouth, NH. 1999. 552p.
ISBN:0-313-30501-3, ISBN13: 978-0-313-30501-6.
Dewey:813/.5409896073. LCCN:98-026438.

         Audience: **g,l,u,f.** *Choice, 1999.*

New York Public   **E185.N57 1999**
   Library
The New York Public Library African American Desk
Reference. J. Wiley & Sons. 1999. ISBN:0-471-23924-0,
ISBN13: 978-0-471-23924-6.

         Audience: **g,l,u,f.**

New York Public   **E185**
   Library, ProQuest Information and Learning
☐ Black Studies Center: Schomburg Studies on the Black
Experience.
http://www.proquest.com/products_pq/descriptions/
schomburg.shtml
Dodson, Howard; Plamer, Colin. ProQuest Information and
Learning.

         Audience: **g,l,u,f.**

Nosakhere, Akilah   **Z1361.N39**
   Shukura (Compiled by), et al.
African-American Studies Core List of Resources. M. Elaine
Hughes & Anne Page Mosby (Compiled by). Perfect. Blackburn
Press, The. Caldwell, NJ. 2004. 95p. ISBN:1-932846-01-8,
ISBN13: 978-1-932846-01-0. Dewey:016.305896/0703.
LCCN:2004-109342.

         Audience: **g,l,u,f.** *Choice, 2005.*

Ostrom, Hans A. &   **PS153.N5G73 2005**
   Macey, J. David
The Greenwood Encyclopedia of African American Literature.
Trade Cloth. Greenwood Publishing Group, Inc. Portsmouth,
NH. 2005. lxii, 2010p. ISBN:0-313-32976-1, ISBN13:
978-0-313-32976-0. Dewey:810.9/896073. LCCN:2005-013679.
         Audience: **g,l,u,f.**

Oxford University Press   **E184.6**
☐ Oxford African American Studies Center.
http://www.oup.com/online/
Oxford University Press.

         Audience: **g,l,u,f.**

Perkins, Kathy A.   **PS628.N4**
   (Editor)
ⓔ Black Female Playwrights: An Anthology of Plays Before
1950. E-Book. Indiana University Press. Bloomington, IN. 1990.
298p. Blacks in the Diaspora Ser. ISBN:0-253-20623-5,
ISBN13: 978-0-253-20623-7. Dewey:812/.008/09287.
LCCN:88-046040.

         Audience: **g,l,u,f.** *Choice, 1990.*

Peterson, Bernard L. Jr.   **PS153**
Early Black American Playwrights and Dramatic Writers: A
Biographical Directory and Catalog of Plays, Films and
Broadcasting Scripts. Cloth Text. Greenwood Publishing Group,
Inc. Portsmouth, NH. 1990. 328p. ISBN:0-313-26621-2,

ISBN13: 978-0-313-26621-8. Dewey:812.009/896073.
LCCN:90-002961.

         Audience: **g,l,u,f.** *Choice, 1991.*

Pilsner, Brenda   **PS153.N5A3444 2000**
African-American Writers: A Dictionary. Shari Dorantes Hatch
& Michael R. Strickland (Editors). Library Binding. ABC-CLIO,
Inc. Santa Barbara, CA. 2000. 0484p. Literary Companions Ser.
ISBN:0-87436-959-2, ISBN13: 978-0-87436-959-5.
Dewey:810.9/896073/03 B. LCCN:00-024422.

         Audience: **g,l,u,f.** *Choice, 2000.*

ProQuest Company   **E185.96**
☐ African American Biographical Database (AADB).
http://www.proquest.com
Proquest Company.

         Audience: **g,l,u,f.**

ProQuest Company   **Z6944.N39**
☐ International Index to Black Periodicals Full Text (IIBP).
http://www.proquest.com
         Audience: **g,l,u,f.**

Roses, Lorraine E.   **PS147**
Harlem Renaissance and Beyond: Literary Biographies of One
Hundred Black Women Writers, 1900-1945. Trade Paper.
Harvard University Press. Cambridge, MA. 1997. 432p.
ISBN:0-674-37255-7, ISBN13: 978-0-674-37255-9.
Dewey:810.9/9287/03. LCCN:89-038731.

         Audience: **g,l,u.** *Choice, 1990.*

Salem, Dorothy C.   **E185.96.A45 1993**
   (Editor)
African American Women: A Biographical Dictionary. Paper
over Boards. Garland Publishing, Inc. New York, NY. 1993.
664p. Biographical Directories of Minority Women Ser., Vol. 2
ISBN:0-8240-9782-3, ISBN13: 978-0-8240-9782-0.
Dewey:920.7208996073. LCCN:92-045727.

         Audience: **g,l,u,f.** *Choice, 1994.*

Sammons, Vivian O.   **Q141.B58 1990**
Blacks in Science and Medicine. Hemisphere Publishing Corp..
1990. ISBN:0-89116-665-3, ISBN13: 978-0-89116-665-8.

         Audience: **g,l,u,f.**

Smith, Jessie C.   **E185.96.E65 1993**
Epic Lives: One Hundred Black Women Who Made a
Difference. Trade Cloth. Visible Ink Press. Canton, MI. 1992.
661p. ISBN:0-8103-9426-X, ISBN13: 978-0-8103-9426-1.
Dewey:920.72/089/96073 B. LCCN:93-106495.

         Audience: **g,l,u.**

Smith, Jessie Carney   **E185.96.N68 1992**
   (Editor)
Notable Black American Women. Ed. 3. Trade Cloth. Thomson
Gale. Farmington Hills, MI. 2002. 775p. ISBN:0-7876-6494-4,
ISBN13: 978-0-7876-6494-7. Dewey:920.72/08996073.
LCCN:91-035074.

         Audience: **g,l,u.**

Smith, Jessie Carney   **E185.86.N68 1998**
Notable Black Men. Gale Research. 1998. ISBN:0-7876-0763-0,
ISBN13: 978-0-7876-0763-0.

         Audience: **g,l,u.**

Southern, Eileen   **ML3556.S74 1997**
Music of Black America: A History. Ed. 3. Trade Cloth. W. W.
Norton & Company, Inc. New York, NY. 1997. 702p.

ISBN:0-393-03843-2, ISBN13: 978-0-393-03843-9.
Dewey:780/.89/96073. LCCN:96-028811.

Audience: **g,l,u.**

Walker-Hill, Helen   **ML128.W7W35 1995**
Music by Black Women Composers: A Bibliography of
Available Scores. Trade Cloth. Columbia College Chicago.
Chicago, IL. 1995. 118p. CBMR Monographs, No. 5
ISBN:0-929911-04-0, ISBN13: 978-0-929911-04-5.
Dewey:016.78/082. LCCN:95-005613.

Audience: **g,l,u.**

Walters, Ronald W. &   **Z1361**
  Johnson, Cedric
Bibliography of African American Leadership: An Annotated
Guide. Cloth Text. Greenwood Publishing Group, Inc.
Portsmouth, NH. 2000. 304p. Bibliographies and Indexes in
Afro-American and African Studies, Vol. 41
ISBN:0-313-31314-8, ISBN13: 978-0-313-31314-1.
Dewey:016.3033/4/08996073. LCCN:00-021554.

Audience: **g,l,u.** *Choice, 2000.*

Williams, Dana A.   **Z1229**
Contemporary African American Female Playwrights: An
Annotated Bibliography. Cloth Text. Greenwood Publishing
Group, Inc. Portsmouth, NH. 1998. 152p. Bibliographies and
Indexes in Afro-American and African Studies, Vol. 37
ISBN:0-313-30132-8, ISBN13: 978-0-313-30132-2.
Dewey:016.812/540809287/08. LCCN:98-017542.

Audience: **g,l,u.** *Choice, 1998.*

Wintz, Cary D. &   **NX512.3.A35E53 2004**
  Finkelman, Paul (Editors)
Encyclopedia of the Harlem Renaissance. Ed. 2. Library
Binding. Fitzroy Dearborn Publishers, Inc. Chicago, IL. 2004.
1392p. ISBN:1-57958-389-X, ISBN13: 978-1-57958-389-7.
Dewey:700/.89/9607307471. LCCN:2004-016353.

Audience: **g,l,u,f.** *Choice, 2005.*

Reference > Bibliography

Ervin, Hazel Arnett   **PS153.N5A33 1999**
  (Editor)
African American Literary Criticism: 1773-2000. Trade Cloth.
Thomson Gale. Farmington Hills, MI. 1999. xxix, 475p.
ISBN:0-8057-1683-1, ISBN13: 978-0-8057-1683-2.
Dewey:810.9/896073. LCCN:99-029491.

Audience: **g,l,u,f.** *Choice, 2000.*

Ervin, Hazel Arnett   **PS153.N5E78 2004**
The Handbook of African American Literature. Trade Cloth.
University Press of Florida. Gainesville, FL. 2004. 256p.
ISBN:0-8130-2750-0, ISBN13: 978-0-8130-2750-0.
Dewey:810.9/896073. LCCN:2004-049332.

Audience: **g,l,u,f.**

Thomas, Veronica G.   **Z1361**
  (Compiled by), et al.
African American Women: An Annotated Bibliography. Kisha
Braithwaite & Paula Mitchell (Compiled by). Cloth Text.
Greenwood Publishing Group, Inc. Portsmouth, NH. 2000. 232p.
Bibliographies and Indexes in Afro-American and African
Studies, Vol. 42 ISBN:0-313-31263-X, ISBN13:
978-0-313-31263-2. Dewey:016.30548/896073.
LCCN:00-030884.

Audience: **g,l,u,f.** *Choice, 2001.*

Religion and Philosophy

Blyden, Edward Wilmot   **DT4**
Christianity, Islam and the Negro Race. Trade Paper. Black
Classic Press. Baltimore, MD. 1993. 441p. ISBN:0-933121-41-5,
ISBN13: 978-0-933121-41-6. Dewey:291.17. LCCN:93-074112.

Audience: **g,l,u,f.**

Brooks, Joanna   **PS153.N5B668 2003**
American Lazarus: Religion and the Rise of African-American
and Native American Literatures. Trade Cloth. Oxford
University Press, Inc. New York, NY. 2003. 264p.
ISBN:0-19-516078-9, ISBN13: 978-0-19-516078-9.
Dewey:810.9/96073. LCCN:2002-013708.

Audience: **g,l,u,f.** *Choice, 2004.*

Collier-Thomas, Bettye   **BR563.N4C64 1997**
Daughters of Thunder: Black Women Preachers and Their
Sermons, 1850-1979. Trade Cloth. John Wiley & Sons, Inc.
Hoboken, NJ. 1997. 368p. Religion in Practice Ser.
ISBN:0-7879-0918-1, ISBN13: 978-0-7879-0918-5.
Dewey:251/.0082. LCCN:97-004850.

Audience: **g,l,u.**

Cone, James H.   **BT734.2.C6 1997**
Black Theology and Black Power. Trade Paper. Orbis Books.
Maryknoll, NY. 1997. 200p. ISBN:1-57075-157-9, ISBN13:
978-1-57075-157-8. Dewey:230/.08996073. LCCN:97-220426.

Audience: **g,l,u.** *B*

Cone, James H.   **BT83.57.C67 1997**
God of the Oppressed. Trade Paper. Orbis Books. Maryknoll,
NY. 1997. 280p. ISBN:1-57075-158-7, ISBN13:
978-1-57075-158-5. Dewey:261.8/34896073. LCCN:97-030468.

Audience: **g,l,u.**

Cone, James H.   **ML3556**
The Spirituals and the Blues. Trade Paper. HarperCollins
Publishers. New York, NY. 1984. ISBN:0-8164-2073-4, ISBN13:
978-0-8164-2073-5. Dewey:781.62/96073.

Audience: **g,l,u.**

Cone, James H. &   **BT82.7.B56 1993**
  Wilmore, Gayraud S.
Black Theology: A Documentary History, 1980-1992. Ed. 2.
Trade Paper. Orbis Books. Maryknoll, NY. 1993. 400p.
ISBN:0-88344-773-8, ISBN13: 978-0-88344-773-4.
Dewey:230/.089/96. LCCN:92-044927.

Audience: **g,l,u,f.**

Cone, James H. &   **BT82.7**
  Wilmore, Gayraud S.
Black Theology: A Documentary History, 1966-1979. Ed. 2.
Trade Paper. Orbis Books. Maryknoll, NY. 1993. 400p. Black
Theology Ser., Vol. 1 ISBN:0-88344-853-X, ISBN13:
978-0-88344-853-3. Dewey:230/.089/96. LCCN:92-044927.

Audience: **g,l,u,f.**

Frazier, E. Franklin &   **BR563.N4**
  Lincoln, C. Eric
The Negro Church in America/the Black Church since Frazier.
Trade Paper. Knopf Publishing Group. New York, NY. 1974.
224p. Sourcebooks in the Negro History Ser.
ISBN:0-8052-0387-7, ISBN13: 978-0-8052-0387-5.
LCCN:72-096201.

Audience: **g,l,u,f.**

Gyekye, Kwame   **B5619.G4G84 1995**
An Essay on African Philosophical Thought: The Akan
Conceptual Scheme. Ed. 2. Library Binding. Temple University
Press. Philadelphia, PA. 1995. 288p. ISBN:1-56639-383-3,
ISBN13: 978-1-56639-383-6. Dewey:199/.6. LCCN:95-034827.
       Audience: **l,u,f.** *Choice, 1996.*

Hopkins, Dwight N.   **BT82.7**
Heart and Head: Black Theology—Past, Present, and Future.
Michael Eric Dyson (Foreword by). Trade Paper. Palgrave
Macmillan. New York, NY. 2003. 240p. Black
Religion/Womanist Thought/Social Justice Ser.
ISBN:1-4039-6292-8, ISBN13: 978-1-4039-6292-8.
Dewey:230/.089/96073.
       Audience: **g,l,u.**

Langley, J. Ayodele   **DT353.L33**
  (Editor)
Ideologies of Liberation in Black Africa, 1856-1970. Trade
Paper. Africa Book Centre. Brighton, 2004. 858p.
ISBN:0-86036-039-3, ISBN13: 978-0-86036-039-1.
Dewey:320.5/096. LCCN:80-458475.
       Audience: **g,l,u.**

Lincoln, C. Eric   **BP221**
The Black Muslims in America. Ed. 3. Trade Cloth. Africa
World Press. Trenton, NJ. 1996. 307p. ISBN:0-86543-399-2,
ISBN13: 978-0-86543-399-1. Dewey:297/.87.
       Audience: **g,l,u.** *B*

Lincoln, C. Eric &   **BR563.N4L55 1990**
  Mamiya, Lawrence
The Black Church in the African American Experience. Trade
Paper. Duke University Press. Durham, NC. 1990. 536p.
ISBN:0-8223-1073-2, ISBN13: 978-0-8223-1073-0.
Dewey:277.3/08/08996073. LCCN:90-034050.
       Audience: **g,l,u.** *Choice, 1991.*

Mbiti, John S.   **BL2462.5.M36 1990**
African Religions and Philosophy. Ed. 2. Trade Paper.
Heinemann. Portsmouth, NH. 1992. 288p. ISBN:0-435-89591-5,
ISBN13: 978-0-435-89591-4. Dewey:299.6. LCCN:89-48596.
       Audience: **g,l,u.**

Mbiti, John S.   **BL2400.M383 1991**
Introduction to African Religion. Ed. 2. Trade Paper.
Heinemann. Portsmouth, NH. 1991. 216p. ISBN:0-435-94002-3,
ISBN13: 978-0-435-94002-7. Dewey:299/.6. LCCN:91-028675.
       Audience: **g,l,u.**

Pierce, Yolanda Nicole   **BR563.N4P47 2005**
Hell Without Fires: Slavery, Christianity, and the Antebellum
Spiritual Narrative. Trade Cloth. University Press of Florida.
Gainesville, FL. 2005. 192p. History of African-American
Religions Ser. ISBN:0-8130-2806-X, ISBN13:
978-0-8130-2806-4. Dewey:277.3/081/08996073.
LCCN:2004-066133.
       Audience: **g,l,u.** *Choice, 2005.*

Pinn, Anthony B.   **BL2490.P46 1998**
Varieties of African-American Religious Experience. Trade
Paper. Augsburg Fortress, Publishers. Minneapolis, MN. 2003.
256p. ISBN:0-8006-2994-9, ISBN13: 978-0-8006-2994-6.
Dewey:200/.89/96073. LCCN:98-044408.
       Audience: **g,l,u.**

Roberts, Diane   **PR408.R34R6 1994**
The Myth of Aunt Jemima: Representations of Race and
Religion. Paper over Boards. Routledge. New York, NY. 1994.

240p. ISBN:0-415-04918-0, ISBN13: 978-0-415-04918-4.
Dewey:820.9/9287. LCCN:93-050574.
       Audience: **g,l,u.** *Choice, 1995.*

Turner, Richard Brent   **BP67.U6T87 2003**
Islam in the African-American Experience. Ed. 2. Trade Cloth.
Indiana University Press. Bloomington, IN. 2003. 336p.
ISBN:0-253-34323-2, ISBN13: 978-0-253-34323-9.
Dewey:297/.089/96073. LCCN:2003-009791.
       Audience: **g,l,u.**

West, Cornel & Glaude,   **BR563.N4A364 2004**
  Eddie S. (Editors)
African American Religious Thought: An Anthology. Trade
Paper. Westminster John Knox Press. Louisville, KY. 2004.
1080p. ISBN:0-664-22459-8, ISBN13: 978-0-664-22459-2.
Dewey:230/.089/96073. LCCN:2003-053468.
       Audience: **g,l,u.**

Whelchel, L. H.   **BR563.N4W485 2002**
Hell Without Fire: Conversion in Slave Religion. Abingdon
Press. 2002. ISBN:0-687-05283-1, ISBN13: 978-0-687-05283-7.
       Audience: **g,l,u.**

Williams, Juan & Dixie,   **BR563.N4**
  Quinton
This Far by Faith: Stories from the African American Religious
Experience. Trade Cloth. DIANE Publishing Company.
Collingdale, PA. 2005. 326p. ISBN:0-7567-9326-2, ISBN13:
978-0-7567-9326-5. Dewey:200/.89/96073.
       Audience: **g,l,u.** *Choice, 2003.*

Reparations

Brooks, Roy L.   **E185.89.R45B76 2004**
Atonement and Forgiveness: A New Model for Black
Reparations. Trade Cloth. University of California Press.
Berkeley, CA. 2004. 336p. ISBN:0-520-23941-5, ISBN13:
978-0-520-23941-8. Dewey:973/.049673. LCCN:2004-041239.
       Audience: **g,l,u.** *Choice, 2005.*

Brophy, Alfred L.   **F704.T92**
Reconstructing the Dreamland: The Tulsa Riot of 1921: Race,
Reparations, and Reconcilation. Oxford University Press. 2002.
ISBN:0-19-514685-9, ISBN13: 978-0-19-514685-1.
       Audience: **l,u.**

Corlett, J. Angelo   **HT1523**
Race, Racism, and Reparations. Cornell University Press. 2003.
ISBN:0-8014-4160-9, ISBN13: 978-0-8014-4160-8.
       Audience: **g,l,u.**

Hakim, Ida, et al.   **E185.8.R47 1994**
Reparations: The Cure for America's Race Problem. Dorothy B.
Fardan, Jamil Hakeem & Len Moritz (Authors). Trade Paper.
Conquering Books. Drewyville, VA. 1994. 283p.
ISBN:1-56411-088-5, ISBN13: 978-1-56411-088-6.
Dewey:305.896/073. LCCN:95-140905.
       Audience: **g,l,u.**

Mazrui, Alamin M. &   **E185.89.R45M39**
  Mazuri, Ail A.
Reparations in the Time of Globalization. Trade Cloth. Africa
World Press. Trenton, NJ. 2004. 464p. ISBN:1-59221-269-7,
ISBN13: 978-1-59221-269-9. Dewey:305.896/073.
       Audience: **g,l,u.**

Winbush, Raymond   E185.89.R45
  (Editor)
Should America Pay? Slavery and Raging Rebate over
Reparations. Amistad. 2003. ISBN:0-06-008311-5, ISBN13:
978-0-06-008311-3.

Audience: **g,l,u.**

Slavery and Slave Trade

Bailey, Anne C.   HT1331
African Voices of the Atlantic Slave Trade: Beyond the Silence
and the Shame. Beacon Press. 2005. ISBN:0-8070-5513-1,
ISBN13: 978-0-8070-5513-7.

Audience: **l,u,f.**

Berlin, Ira   E446
Many Thousands Gone: The First Two Centuries of Slavery in
North America. Trade Paper. Harvard University Press.
Cambridge, MA. 2000. 512p. Belknap Press Ser.
ISBN:0-674-00211-3, ISBN13: 978-0-674-00211-1.
Dewey:306.3/62/097309032.

Audience: **g,l,u.**

Blassingame, John W.   E443
The Slave Community: Plantation Life in the Antebellum South.
Ed. 2. Paper Text. Oxford University Press, Inc. New York, NY.
1979. 432p. ISBN:0-19-502563-6, ISBN13: 978-0-19-502563-7.
Dewey:975/.00496073. LCCN:78-026890.

Audience: **g,l,u.** *B*

Clarke, John Henrik   E441
Critical Lessons in Slavery and the Slavetrade: Essential Studies
and Commentaries on Slavery, in General and the African
Slavetrade, in Particular. Ed. 2. Trade Cloth. Native Sun
Publishers, Inc. Richmond, VA. 1997. 208p. Truth and Sanity
Reprint Ser. ISBN:1-879289-06-7, ISBN13: 978-1-879289-06-2.
Dewey:306.362/. LCCN:96-068505.

Audience: **g,l,u,f.**

Davis, Natalie Zemon   PN1995.9.S557D38
Slaves on Screen: Film and Historical Vision. Harvard
University Press. 2000. ISBN:0-674-00444-2, ISBN13:
978-0-674-00444-3.

Audience: **u,f.**

Dunaway, Wilma A.   E443.D86 2003
The African-American Family in Slavery and Emancipation.
Cloth Text. Cambridge University Press. New York, NY. 2003.
380p. Studies in Modern Capitalism ISBN:0-521-81276-3,
ISBN13: 978-0-521-81276-4. Dewey:306.3/62/0973.
LCCN:2002-071484.

Audience: **g,l,u.**

Feelings, Tom   ND237.F32A4 1995
The Middle Passage: White Ships/Black Cargo. John Henrik
Clarke (Introduction by). Trade Cloth. Penguin Group (USA)
Inc. New York, NY. 1995. 80p. ISBN:0-8037-1804-7, ISBN13:
978-0-8037-1804-3. Dewey:759.13. LCCN:95-013866.

Audience: **g,l,u,f.**

Greenwood Electronic   E443
  Media
□ American Slavery: A Composite Autobiography.
http://www.gem.greenwood.com
Rawick, George P.. Greenwood Publishing Group, Inc.

Audience: **g,l,u,f.**

Mitchell, Angelyn   PS374.S58M58 2002
The Freedom to Remember: Narrative, Slavery and Gender in
Contemporary Black Women's Fiction. Cloth Text. Rutgers
University Press. Piscataway, NJ. 2002. 192p.
ISBN:0-8135-3068-7, ISBN13: 978-0-8135-3068-0.
Dewey:813/.54099287. LCCN:2001-048609.

Audience: **g,l,u.** *Choice, 2003, 2002.*

Pybus, Cassandra   E450.P99 2006
Epic Journeys of Freedom. Beacon Press. 2006.
ISBN:0-8070-5514-X, ISBN13: 978-0-8070-5514-4.

Audience: **g,l,u,f.**

Stampp, Kenneth M.   E441.S8
The Peculiar Institution: Slavery in the Ante. Paper Text.
Textbook Publishers. Temecula, CA. 2003. xi, 435p.
ISBN:0-7581-0830-3, ISBN13: 978-0-7581-0830-2.
Dewey:326.975.

Audience: **g,l,u.** *B*

Walker, David   E446
David Walker's Appeal: To the Coloured Citizens of the World
but in Particular, and Very Expressly, to Those of the United
States of America. James Turner (Introduction by). Trade Paper.
Black Classic Press. Baltimore, MD. 1993. 104p.
ISBN:0-933121-38-5, ISBN13: 978-0-933121-38-6. Dewey:360.
LCCN:92-081885.

Audience: **g,l,u.**

Whelchel, L. H.   BR563.N4W485 2002
Hell Without Fire: Conversion in Slave Religion. Abingdon
Press. 2002. ISBN:0-687-05283-1, ISBN13: 978-0-687-05283-7.

Audience: **g,l,u.**

White, Shane & White,   E443.W59 2005
  Graham J.
The Sounds of Slavery: Discovering African American History
Through Songs, Sermons, and Speech. Beacon Press. 2005.
ISBN:0-8070-5026-1, ISBN13: 978-0-8070-5026-2.

Audience: **g,l,u,f.**

William Still   E450
  Underground Railroad Foundation
□ William Still Underground Railroad Foundation Website.
http://www.undergroundrr.com/foundation/main.htm
William Still Underground Railroad Foundation.

Audience: **g,l,u,f.**

Williams, Eric   HC254.5.W5 1994
Capitalism and Slavery. Colin A. Palmer (Introduction by).
Trade Paper. University of North Carolina Press. Chapel Hill,
NC. 1994. 307p. ISBN:0-8078-4488-8, ISBN13:
978-0-8078-4488-5. Dewey:338.0941. LCCN:94-008722.

Audience: **g,l,u.**

Williams, Heather   LC2802.S9W55 2004
  Andrea
Self-Taught: African American Education in Slavery and
Freedom. Trade Cloth. University of North Carolina Press.
Chapel Hill, NC. 2005. 320p. The John Hope Franklin Series in
African American History and Culture Ser.
ISBN:0-8078-2920-X, ISBN13: 978-0-8078-2920-2.
Dewey:370/.89/96073075. LCCN:2004-022755.

Audience: **g,l,u.** *Choice, 2005.*

Yee, Shirley J.   E449.Y44 1992
Black Women Abolitionists: A Study in Activism, 1828-1860.
Library Binding. University of Tennessee Press. Knoxville, TN.

1992. 216p. ISBN:0-87049-735-9, ISBN13: 978-0-87049-735-3. Dewey:305.48/896073. LCCN:91-024795.

Audience: **g,l,u**. *Choice, 1992.*

Yellin, Jean Fagan   **E185.97.T8**
Harriet Jacobs: A Life. Trade Paper. Basic Books. New York, NY. 2005. 432p. ISBN:0-465-09289-6, ISBN13: 978-0-465-09289-5. Dewey:306.3/62/092 B.

Audience: **g,l,u**. *Choice, 2004.*

Sociology

Asante, Molefi Kete &   **HM51**
  Vandi, Abdulai S.
Contemporary Black Thought: Alternative Analyses in Social and Behavioral Science. Trade Cloth. SAGE Publications, Inc. Thousand Oaks, CA. 1980. 294p. Focus Editions Ser., Vol. 26 ISBN:0-8039-1500-4, ISBN13: 978-0-8039-1500-8. Dewey:301. LCCN:80-015186.

Audience: **g,l,u,f**.

Bent-Goodley, Tricia B.   **HV3181.A374 2003**
  (Editor)
African-American Social Workers and Social Policy. Trade Cloth. Haworth Press, Incorporated, The. Binghamton, NY. 2003. 211p. ISBN:0-7890-1621-4, ISBN13: 978-0-7890-1621-8. Dewey:362.84/96/073. LCCN:2002-027333.

Audience: **u,f**. *Choice, 2004.*

Byrd, Ayana D. &   **E185.86.B96**
  Tharps, Lori
Hair Story: Untangling the Roots of Black Hair in America. Trade Paper. Holtzbrinck Publishers. Gordonsville, VA. 2002. 208p. ISBN:0-312-28322-9, ISBN13: 978-0-312-28322-3. Dewey:306.4.

Audience: **g,l,u**.

Collins, Catherine   **HV9471**
  Fisher
Imprisonment of African American Women: Causes, Conditions and Future Implications. Paper Text. McFarland & Company, Incorporated Publishers. Jefferson, NC. 2005. 166p. ISBN:0-7864-2159-2, ISBN13: 978-0-7864-2159-6. Dewey:365.973.

Audience: **g,l,u,f**.

Delroy,   **HQ76.3U5**
  Constantine-Simms
The Greatest Taboo: Homosexuality in Black Communities. Alyson Books. 2001. ISBN:1-55583-564-3, ISBN13: 978-1-55583-564-4.

Audience: **l,u,f**.

Du Bois, W. E. B.   **E185**
🅮 The Souls of Black Folk. E-Book. Bantam Books. New York, NY. 2005. ISBN:0-553-90176-1, ISBN13: 978-0-553-90176-4. Dewey:973/.0496073.

Audience: **g,l,u**. 𝓑

Dunaway, Wilma A.   **E443.D86 2003**
The African-American Family in Slavery and Emancipation. Cloth Text. Cambridge University Press. New York, NY. 2003. 380p. Studies in Modern Capitalism ISBN:0-521-81276-3, ISBN13: 978-0-521-81276-4. Dewey:306.3/62/0973. LCCN:2002-071484.

Audience: **g,l,u**.

Dyson, Michael Eric   **ML420.S529D97 2001**
Holler If You Hear Me: Searching for Tupac Shakur. Trade Cloth. Basic Books. New York, NY. 2001. 304p. ISBN:0-465-01755-X, ISBN13: 978-0-465-01755-3. Dewey:782.4/2/1649/092. LCCN:2001-036564.

Audience: **g,l,u**.

Feagin, Joe R. &   **E185.86**
  McKinney, Karyn D.
The Many Costs of Racism. Trade Paper, Perfect. Rowman & Littlefield Publishers, Inc. Lanham, MD. 2005. 250p. ISBN:0-7425-1118-9, ISBN13: 978-0-7425-1118-7. Dewey:305.896/073/0019.

Audience: **g,l,u,f**. *Choice, 2003.*

Ferguson, Carroy U.   **E185.625**
Transitions in Consciousness from an African American Perspective. Trade Paper. University Press of America, Inc. Lanham, MD. 2004. 256p. ISBN:0-7618-2700-5, ISBN13: 978-0-7618-2700-9. Dewey:305.896073. LCCN:2003-114128.

Audience: **g,l,u,f**.

Franklin, V. P. (Editor)   **LC2707.C85 2004**
Cultural Capital and Black Education: African American Communities and the Funding of Black Schooling, 1860 to the Present. Trade Cloth. Information Age Publishing, Inc. Greenwich, CT. 2004. 20p. Research on African American Education Ser. ISBN:1-59311-041-3, ISBN13: 978-1-59311-041-3. Dewey:371.829/96073. LCCN:2004-020281.

Audience: **g,l,u,f**.

Freeman, Edith M. &   **HV3181.R43 2004**
  Logan, Sadye Louise
Reconceptualizing the Strengths and Common Heritage of Black Families: Practice, Research, and Policy Issues. Trade Cloth. Charles C. Thomas Publisher, Ltd. Springfield, IL. 2004. 352p. ISBN:0-398-07488-7, ISBN13: 978-0-398-07488-3. Dewey:362.84/96073. LCCN:2003-071199.

Audience: **g,l,u**.

George, Nelson   **E185.615.G465 2004**
Post-Soul Nation: The Explosive, Contradictory, Triumphant, and Tragic 1980s As Experienced by African Americans (Previously Known As Blacks and Before That Negroes). Trade Cloth. Penguin Group (USA) Inc. New York, NY. 2004. 288p. ISBN:0-670-03275-1, ISBN13: 978-0-670-03275-4. Dewey:973/.049607309/046. LCCN:2003-061606.

Audience: **g,l,u**.

Giddings, Paula J.   **E185.86.G49 1996**
When and Where I Enter: The Impact of Black Women on Race and Sex in America. Ed. 2. Trade Paper. HarperCollins Publishers. New York, NY. 1996. 416p. ISBN:0-688-14650-3, ISBN13: 978-0-688-14650-4. Dewey:305.4/8896073. LCCN:96-019349.

Audience: **g,l,u**.

Grant, William R.   **PN1995.9.N4G69 2003**
Post-Soul Black Cinema: Discontinuities, Innovations and Breakpoints, 1970-1995. Paper over Boards. Routledge. New York, NY. 2004. 112p. Studies in African American History and Culture Ser. ISBN:0-415-94768-5, ISBN13: 978-0-415-94768-8. Dewey:791.43/652996073. LCCN:2003-017036.

Audience: **g,l,u**.

Hakim, Ida, et al.   **E185.8.R47 1994**
Reparations: The Cure for America's Race Problem. Dorothy B. Fardan, Jamil Hakeem & Len Moritz (Authors). Trade Paper. Conquering Books. Drewyville, VA. 1994. 283p.

ISBN:1-56411-088-5, ISBN13: 978-1-56411-088-6.
Dewey:305.896/073. LCCN:95-140905.
Audience: **g,l,u.**

Harley, Sharon (Editor) HD6057.5.U5S576 2002
Sister Circle: Black Women and Work. Black Women and Work
Collective Staff (Contribution by), Nellie Y. McKay (Foreword
by). Cloth Text. Rutgers University Press. Piscataway, NJ. 2002.
320p. ISBN:0-8135-3060-1, ISBN13: 978-0-8135-3060-4.
Dewey:331.4/089/96073. LCCN:2001-048613.
Audience: **g,l,u.** *Choice, 2003.*

Hine, Darlene Clark E185.H535 1996
Speak Truth to Power: Black Professional Class in United States
History. Joe W. Trotter (Preface by). Trade Cloth. Carlson
Publishing, Inc. Brooklyn, NY. 1996. 222p.
ISBN:0-926019-91-0, ISBN13: 978-0-926019-91-1.
Dewey:305.896/073073. LCCN:95-047307.
Audience: **g,l,u,f.**

Hogue, W. Lawrence PS153.N5H59 2003
The African American Male, Writing, and Difference: A
Polycentric Approach to African American Literature, Criticism,
and History. Cloth Text. State University of New York Press.
Albany, NY. 2003. xiii, 291p. ISBN:0-7914-5693-5, ISBN13:
978-0-7914-5693-4. Dewey:810.9/9286/08996073.
LCCN:2002-075873.
Audience: **g,l,u.** *Choice, 2003.*

Holloway, Joseph E. E185.A26 2005
(Editor)
Africanisms in American Culture. Ed. 2. Trade Paper, Perfect.
Indiana University Press. Bloomington, IN. 2005. 312p. Blacks
in the Diaspora Ser. ISBN:0-253-21749-0, ISBN13:
978-0-253-21749-3. Dewey:973/.0496073. LCCN:2004-020284.
Audience: **g,l,u,f.** *Choice, 1990.*

Hurston, Zora Neale GR55.H86A3 1995
Folklore, Memoirs, and Other Writings. Cheryl A. Wall (Editor).
Trade Cloth. Library of America, The. New York, NY. 1995.
1024p. Library of America, Vol. 75 ISBN:0-940450-84-4,
ISBN13: 978-0-940450-84-4. Dewey:398/.092 B.
LCCN:94-021384.
Audience: **g,l,u.**

Hurt, R. Douglas E185.6.A257 2003
(Editor, Introduction by)
African American Life in the Rural South, 1900-1950. Trade
Cloth. University of Missouri Press. Columbia, MO. 2003. 264p.
ISBN:0-8262-1471-1, ISBN13: 978-0-8262-1471-3.
Dewey:975/.0049607301734. LCCN:2003-002150.
Audience: **g,u,f.** *Choice, 2004.*

Jackson, Ronald L. II P94.5.A37A367 2003
(Editor)
African American Communication and Identities: Essential
Readings. Cloth Text. SAGE Publications, Inc. Thousand Oaks,
CA. 2003. 368p. ISBN:0-7619-2845-6, ISBN13:
978-0-7619-2845-4. Dewey:302.2/089/96073.
LCCN:2003-013998.
Audience: **g,l,u,f.**

Jenkins, Sharron RA448.5.N4
African American Health Disparities. Paper Text. McGraw-Hill
Primis Custom Publishing. Hightstown, NJ. 2003.
ISBN:0-07-291823-3, ISBN13: 978-0-07-291823-6.
Dewey:362.108996073.
Audience: **g,l,u.**

Jewell, K. Sue E185.86.J48 1992
From Mammy to Miss America and Beyond: Cultural Images
and the Shaping of U. S. Social Policy. Trade Paper. Routledge.
New York, NY. 1992. 256p. ISBN:0-415-04253-4, ISBN13:
978-0-415-04253-6. Dewey:305.48896073. LCCN:92-011917.
Audience: **g,l,u.** *Choice, 1993.*

Jewell, K. Sue E185
Survival of the African American Family: The Institutional
Impact of U. S. Social Policy. Trade Cloth. Greenwood
Publishing Group, Inc. Portsmouth, NH. 2003. 320p.
ISBN:0-275-95769-1, ISBN13: 978-0-275-95769-8.
Dewey:306.85/089/96073. LCCN:2003-052895.
Audience: **g,l,u,f.** *Choice, 2004.*

Ladner, Joyce A. E185.86.L331 1998
(Editor)
The Death of White Sociology. Trade Paper. Black Classic
Press. Baltimore, MD. 1998. 500p. ISBN:1-57478-007-7,
ISBN13: 978-1-57478-007-9. Dewey:309.173092.
LCCN:97-073660.
Audience: **l,u,f.**

Livingston, Ivor L. RA448
(Editor)
Handbook of Black American Health: The Mosaic of
Conditions, Issues, Policies, and Prospects. Cloth Text.
Greenwood Publishing Group, Inc. Portsmouth, NH. 1994. 496p.
ISBN:0-313-28640-X, ISBN13: 978-0-313-28640-7.
Dewey:362.108996073. LCCN:93-004852.
Audience: **g,l,u.** *Choice, 1994.*

Locke, Alain L. PS153.N5
The New Negro. Trade Paper. Simon & Schuster. New York,
NY. 1999. 452p. ISBN:0-684-83831-1, ISBN13:
978-0-684-83831-1. Dewey:810.9/896073. LCCN:91-033377.
Audience: **g,l,u.**

Lovejoy, Paul E. E29.N3T73 2002
Trans-Atlantic Dimensions of Ethnicity in the African Diaspora.
Trotman, David Vincent. Continuum. 2003.
ISBN:0-8264-4907-7, ISBN13: 978-0-8264-4907-8.
Audience: **g,l,u,f.**

Lynch, Katherine A. H1.S612
(Editor)
African American Fraternal Associations and the History of
Civil Society in the United States. Bayliss J. Camp, Marshall
Ganz, Orit Kent, Ariane Liazos, Jennifer Lynn Oser, Theda
Skocpol & Joe W. Trotter (Contribution by). Trade Paper. Duke
University Press. Durham, NC. 2004. 200p.
ISBN:0-8223-6611-8, ISBN13: 978-0-8223-6611-9.
Dewey:366.0089607.
Audience: **g,l,u,f.**

Manatu, Norma PN1995.9.N4M28 2002
African American Women and Sexuality in the Cinema. Paper
Text. McFarland & Company, Incorporated Publishers. Jefferson,
NC. 2002. 245p. ISBN:0-7864-1431-6, ISBN13:
978-0-7864-1431-4. Dewey:791.43/652042. LCCN:2002-015421.
Audience: **g,l,u.** *Choice, 2003.*

Manring, M. M. HF5813.U6 M25
Slave in a Box: The Strange Career of Aunt Jemima. Trade
Paper. University Press of Virginia. Charlottesville, VA. 1998.
221p. American South Ser. ISBN:0-8139-1811-1, ISBN13:
978-0-8139-1811-2. Dewey:659.1/664753. LCCN:97-033355.
Audience: **g,l,u.** *Choice, 1998.*

McDaniel, Anita K. &   E185.86
  McDaniel, Clyde O.
21st Century African American Social Issues: A Reader. Ed. 2.
Paper Text. Thomson Learning. Independence, KY. 2003.
ISBN:0-7593-3695-4, ISBN13: 978-0-7593-3695-7.
Dewey:305.896073.
                                                Audience: **g,l,u.**

Mitchell, Angelyn   PS374.S58M58 2002
The Freedom to Remember: Narrative, Slavery and Gender in
Contemporary Black Women's Fiction. Cloth Text. Rutgers
University Press. Piscataway, NJ. 2002. 192p.
ISBN:0-8135-3068-7, ISBN13: 978-0-8135-3068-0.
Dewey:813/.54099287. LCCN:2001-048609.
                          Audience: **g,l,u.** *Choice, 2003, 2002.*

Moore, Lois   E185.86.M595 2004
  Merriweather
Voices of Successful African American Men. Trade Cloth.
Edwin Mellen Press, The. Lewiston, NY. 2004. 129p. Black
Studies, Vol. 25 ISBN:0-7734-6349-6, ISBN13:
978-0-7734-6349-3. Dewey:305.38/896073. LCCN:2004-048047.
                                                Audience: **g,l,u.**

Mullings, Leith   E185.86.M945 1996
On Our Own Terms: Race, Class and Gender in the Lives of
African-American Women. Paper over Boards. Routledge. New
York, NY. 1996. 224p. ISBN:0-415-91285-7, ISBN13:
978-0-415-91285-3. Dewey:305.48/896073. LCCN:96-028853.
                                                Audience: **g,l,u.**

Neal, Mark Anthony   E185.615.N35 2001
Soul Babies: Black Culture and the Post-Soul Aesthetic. Trade
Paper. Routledge. New York, NY. 2001. 256p.
ISBN:0-415-92658-0, ISBN13: 978-0-415-92658-4.
Dewey:305.896/073. LCCN:2001-020490.
                          Audience: **g,l,u.** *Choice, 2002.*

Outlaw, Lucius T. Jr.   HM585.O97 2005
In Search of Critical Social Theory in the Interests of Black
Folk. Trade Cloth. Rowman & Littlefield Publishers, Inc.
Lanham, MD. 2005. 208p. New Critical Theory Ser.
ISBN:0-7425-1343-2, ISBN13: 978-0-7425-1343-3.
Dewey:305.896/073. LCCN:2005-005634.
                                              Audience: **g,l,u,f.**

Reid-Pharr, Robert F.   HQ76.2.U5R45 2001
Black Gay Man. Trade Cloth. New York University Press. New
York, NY. 2001. 214p. Sexual Cultures Ser.
ISBN:0-8147-7502-0, ISBN13: 978-0-8147-7502-8.
Dewey:305.38/96642. LCCN:2001-000080.
                          Audience: **g,l,u.** *Choice, 2002.*

Rexroat, Cynthia   E185.86.R48 1994
The Declining Economic Status of Black Children. Joint Center
for Political and Economic Studies. 1994. ISBN:0-941410-96-X,
ISBN13: 978-0-941410-96-0.
                                                Audience: **g,l,u.**

Roberts, Diane   PR408.R34R6 1994
The Myth of Aunt Jemima: Representations of Race and
Religion. Paper over Boards. Routledge. New York, NY. 1994.
240p. ISBN:0-415-04918-0, ISBN13: 978-0-415-04918-4.
Dewey:820.9/9287. LCCN:93-050574.
                          Audience: **g,l,u.** *Choice, 1995.*

Roberts, Dorothy   HQ766.5.U5
Killing the Black Body: Race, Reproduction, and the Meaning
of Liberty. Trade Paper. Knopf Publishing Group. New York,

NY. 1998. 384p. ISBN:0-679-75869-0, ISBN13:
978-0-679-75869-3. Dewey:363.9/6/0973.
                                                Audience: **g,l,u.**

Rooks, Noliwe M.   TT972.R66 1996
Hair Raising: Beauty, Culture, and African American Women.
Trade Paper. Rutgers University Press. Piscataway, NJ. 2003.
156p. ISBN:0-8135-2312-5, ISBN13: 978-0-8135-2312-5.
Dewey:391/.5/08996073. LCCN:95-051395.
                          Audience: **g,l,u.** *Choice, 1997.*

Rooks, Noliwe M.   PN4882.5.R66 2004
Ladies' Pages: African American Women's Magazines and the
Culture That Made Them. Trade Cloth. Rutgers University
Press. Piscataway, NJ. 2004. 208p. ISBN:0-8135-3425-9,
ISBN13: 978-0-8135-3425-1. Dewey:051/.082.
LCCN:2003-018868.
                          Audience: **g,l,u.** *Choice, 2005.*

Ruiz, Vicki L.   HQ1410.U54 2000
Unequal Sisters: A Multicultural Reader in U. S. Women's
History. Ed. 3. Ellen Carol DuBois (Editor). Paper over Boards.
Routledge. New York, NY. 1999. 696p. ISBN:0-415-92516-9,
ISBN13: 978-0-415-92516-7. LCCN:99-016825.
                                                Audience: **g,l,u.**

Salem, Dorothy   E185.86.B543
To Better Our World: Black Women in Organized Reform,
1890-1920. Trade Cloth. Carlson Publishing, Inc. Brooklyn, NY.
1990. 416p. Black Women in United States History Ser., Vol. 14
ISBN:0-926019-20-1, ISBN13: 978-0-926019-20-1.
Dewey:973/.0496073 s. LCCN:90-001397.
                          Audience: **g,l,u.** *Choice, 1990.*

Scruggs, Afi-Odelia E.   E185.97
Claiming Kin: Confronting the History of an African American
Family. Trade Paper. St. Martin's Press. Gordonville, VA. 2003.
208p. ISBN:0-312-30252-5, ISBN13: 978-0-312-30252-8.
Dewey:976.8/5600496073/009.
                                                Audience: **g,l,u.**

Shapiro, Thomas M.   E185.8
The Hidden Cost of Being African American. Trade Paper.
Oxford University Press, Inc. New York, NY. 2005. 253p.
ISBN:0-19-518138-7, ISBN13: 978-0-19-518138-8.
Dewey:330.973/0089/96073.
                                                Audience: **g,l.**

Smitherman, Geneva   E185.86.A3344 1995
  (Editor)
African American Women Speak Out on Anita Hill - Clarence
Thomas. Trade Paper. Wayne State University Press. Detroit,
MI. 1995. 278p. African American Life Ser.
ISBN:0-8143-2530-0, ISBN13: 978-0-8143-2530-8.
Dewey:305.48/89073. LCCN:94-048645.
                                              Audience: **g,l,u,f.**

Till-Mobley, Mamie &   HV6465.M7T55 2003
  Benson, Christopher
Death of Innocence: The Story of the Hate Crime That Changed
America. Jesse Jackson (Foreword by). Trade Cloth. Random
House Adult Trade Publishing Group. New York, NY. 2003.
320p. ISBN:1-4000-6117-2, ISBN13: 978-1-4000-6117-4.
Dewey:364.1/34. LCCN:2003-046928.
                                                Audience: **g,l,u.**

Van Deburg, William L.   HV6791.V36 2004
Hoodlums: Black Villains and Social Bandits in American Life.
Trade Cloth. University of Chicago Press. Chicago, IL. 2004.

304p. ISBN:0-226-84719-5, ISBN13: 978-0-226-84719-1.
Dewey:305.896/073. LCCN:2004-003549.

Audience: **g,l,u,f.** *Choice, 2005.*

Wallace, Maurice O.   **E185.625.W355 2002**
Constructing the Black Masculine: Identity and Ideality in
African American Men's Literature and Culture, 1775-1995.
Trade Cloth. Duke University Press. Durham, NC. 2002. 240p.
A John Hope Franklin Center Book Ser. ISBN:0-8223-2854-2,
ISBN13: 978-0-8223-2854-4. Dewey:305.38/896073.
LCCN:2001-006934.

Audience: **g,l,u.** *Choice, 2003.*

Wallace, Michelle   **E185.86.W34 1990**
Black Macho and the Myth of the Superwoman. Trade Paper.
Analytical Psychology Club of San Francisco, Inc. San
Francisco, CA. 1990. 300p. ISBN:0-86091-518-2, ISBN13:
978-0-86091-518-8. Dewey:305.3/08996073. LCCN:90-042080.

Audience: **g,l,u.**

Walters, Ronald W. &   **E185.615.W314 1999**
  Smith, Robert C.
African American Leadership. Cloth Text. State University of
New York Press. Albany, NY. 1999. 352p. SUNY Series in
Afro-American Studies ISBN:0-7914-4145-8, ISBN13:
978-0-7914-4145-9. Dewey:303.3/4/08996073.
LCCN:98-026840.

Audience: **g,l,u.** *Choice, 2000.*

West, Cornel   **E185.86.W4384 1999**
The Cornel West Reader. Basic Civitas Books. 1999.
ISBN:0-465-09109-1, ISBN13: 978-0-465-09109-6.

Audience: **l,u.**

West, Cornel (Editor)   **E185.615.W43 2001**
Race Matters. Trade Cloth. Beacon Press. Boston, MA. 2001.
144p. ISBN:0-8070-0972-5, ISBN13: 978-0-8070-0972-7.
Dewey:305.8/00973. LCCN:2001-025310.

Audience: **g,l,u.**

Woodward, C. Vann   **E185.61**
The Strange Career of Jim Crow. Library Binding. Sagebrush
Education Resources. Caledonia, MN. 2002.
ISBN:0-613-58674-3, ISBN13: 978-0-613-58674-0.
Dewey:305.896/073/09034.

Audience: **g,l,u,f.** ℬ

Wright, Richard   **E185.6.W9 2002**
Twelve Million Black Voices: A Folk History of the Negro in
the U. S. Douglas Brinkley, Noel Ignatiev & Michael Eric
Dyson (Preface by). Trade Paper. Avalon Publishing Group.
New York, NY. 2002. 184p. ISBN:1-56025-446-7, ISBN13:
978-1-56025-446-1. Dewey:973/.0496073. LCCN:2003-269647.

Audience: **g,l,u.** *Choice, 1989.*

Sports

Davis, Michael D.   **GV697.A1.D38 1992**
Black American Women in Olympic Track and Field: A
Complete Illustrated Reference. Trade Cloth. McFarland &
Company, Incorporated Publishers. Jefferson, NC. 1992. 188p.
ISBN:0-89950-692-5, ISBN13: 978-0-89950-692-0.
Dewey:796.4208996073. LCCN:91-50946.

Audience: **g,l,u.** *Choice, 1992.*

Heaphy, Leslie A.   **GV875.N55H43 2003**
The Negro Leagues 1869-1960. McFarland and Company. 2003.
ISBN:0-7864-1380-8, ISBN13: 978-0-7864-1380-5.

Audience: **g,l,u.**

Holway, John   **GV875.N35H65 2001**
The Complete Book of Baseball's Negro Leagues: The Other
Half of Baseball History. Hastings House Publishers. 2001.
ISBN:0-8038-2007-0, ISBN13: 978-0-8038-2007-4.

Audience: **g,l,u.**

Kennedy, John H.   **GV964.A1K46 2000**
A Course of Their Own: A History of African American Golfers.
Andrews McMeel Publishing. 2000. ISBN:0-7407-0857-0,
ISBN13: 978-0-7407-0857-2.

Audience: **g,l,u.**

Plowden, Martha Ward   **GV697.A1P56 1996**
Olympic Black Women. Ronald Jones (Illustrator). Trade Cloth.
Pelican Publishing Company, Inc. Gretna, LA. 1995. 160p.
ISBN:1-56554-080-8, ISBN13: 978-1-56554-080-4.
Dewey:796/.092/2 B. LCCN:95-032067.

Audience: **g,l,u.**

Shropshire, Kenneth L.   **GV706.32**
In Black and White: Race and Sports in America. New York
University Press. 1996. ISBN:0-8147-8016-4, ISBN13:
978-0-8147-8016-9.

Audience: **g,l,u.**

Ward, Geoffrey C.   **GV1196.J64W37 2004**
Unforgivable Blackness: The Rise and Fall of Jack Johnson.
A.A. Knopf. 2004. ISBN:0-375-41532-7, ISBN13:
978-0-375-41532-6.

Audience: **g,l,u.**

Wiggins, David K.   **GV583.A567 2003**
African Americans in Sports. M.E. Sharpe Inc. 2004.
ISBN:0-7656-8055-6, ISBN13: 978-0-7656-8055-6.

Audience: **g,l,u.**

Women

Anderson, Lisa M.   **PS338.W6A53 1997**
Mammies No More: The Changing Image of Black Women on
Stage and Screen. Trade Cloth. Rowman & Littlefield
Publishers, Inc. Lanham, MD. 1997. 160p. ISBN:0-8476-8419-9,
ISBN13: 978-0-8476-8419-9. Dewey:791.4/3652/0396073.
LCCN:97-009782.

Audience: **g,l,u,f.** *Choice, 1998.*

Andrews, William L.   **PS647.A35C56 2002**
  (Editor)
Classic African American Women's Narratives. Trade Paper.
Oxford University Press, Inc. New York, NY. 2003. 432p.
ISBN:0-19-514135-0, ISBN13: 978-0-19-514135-1.
Dewey:818/.308099287. LCCN:2002-003767.

Audience: **g,l,u,f.**

Bambara, Toni Cade   **PS3552.A473**
The Salt Eaters. Random House. 1980. ISBN:0-394-50712-6,
ISBN13: 978-0-394-50712-5.

Audience: **g,l.**

Benjamin, Lois (Editor)   **LB2332.3.B53 1997**
Black Women in the Academy: Promises and Perils. Trade
Cloth. University Press of Florida. Gainesville, FL. 1997. 424p.

ISBN:0-8130-1500-6, ISBN13: 978-0-8130-1500-2.
Dewey:378.1/2/082. LCCN:96-047388.

Audience: **u,f.** *Choice, 1998.*

Bolton, Ruthie   **F279.C49N414 1994**
Gal: A True Life. Harcourt Brace. 1994. ISBN:0-15-100104-9,
ISBN13: 978-0-15-100104-0.

Audience: **g,l,u.**

Broussard, Jinx   **PN4872.B76 2003**
  Coleman
Giving a Voice to the Voiceless: Four Pioneering Black Women
Journalists. Paper over Boards. Routledge. New York, NY. 2003.
228p. Studies in African American History and Culture Ser.
ISBN:0-415-94717-0, ISBN13: 978-0-415-94717-6.
Dewey:070.92/273 B. LCCN:2003-010320.

Audience: **g,l,u.**

Brown, Eurnestine &   **E185.86.A3343 2000**
  Burgess, Norma J. (Editors)
The African-American Woman: An Ecological Perspective.
Cloth Text. Garland Publishing, Inc. New York, NY. 1999. 212p.
MSU Series on Children, Youth and Families, No. 6
ISBN:0-8153-1591-0, ISBN13: 978-0-8153-1591-9.
Dewey:305.48/896073. LCCN:99-030094.

Audience: **g,l,u.**

Bundles, A'Lelia   **HD9970.5.C672**
On Her Own Ground: The Life and Times of Madam C. J.
Walker. Trade Paper. Simon & Schuster. New York, NY. 2002.
416p. ISBN:0-7434-3172-3, ISBN13: 978-0-7434-3172-9.
Dewey:338.7/66855/092 B.

Audience: **g,l,u.**

Butler, Octavia   **PS3552.U827**
Fledgling: A Novel. Seven Stories Press. 2005.
ISBN:1-58322-690-7, ISBN13: 978-1-58322-690-2.

Audience: **g,l.**

Byrd, Ayana D. &   **E185.86.B96**
  Tharps, Lori
Hair Story: Untangling the Roots of Black Hair in America.
Trade Paper. Holtzbrinck Publishers. Gordonsville, VA. 2002.
208p. ISBN:0-312-28322-9, ISBN13: 978-0-312-28322-3.
Dewey:306.4.

Audience: **g,l,u.**

Casserly, Catherine M.   **E185.86**
African-American Women and Poverty: Can Education Alone
Change the Status Quo? Garland. 1998. ISBN:0-8153-3055-3,
ISBN13: 978-0-8153-3055-4.

Audience: **u,f.**

Chase-Riboud, Barbara   **PS3553.H336**
Sally Hemings. Avon. 1980. ISBN:0-380-48686-5, ISBN13:
978-0-380-48686-1.

Audience: **g,l.**

Clarke, Cheryl   **PS310.N4C48 2004**
"After Mecca": Women Poets and the Black Arts Movement.
Trade Cloth. Rutgers University Press. Piscataway, NJ. 2005.
208p. ISBN:0-8135-3405-4, ISBN13: 978-0-8135-3405-3.
Dewey:811/.509896073. LCCN:2004-007530.

Audience: **g,l,u,f.** *Choice, 2005.*

Cole, Johnnetta B. &   **E185.86.C58154 2003**
  Guy-Sheftall, Beverly
Gender Talk: The Struggle for Women's Equality in African
American Communities. Trade Cloth. Ballantine Books. New

York, NY. 2003. 336p. ISBN:0-345-45412-X, ISBN13:
978-0-345-45412-6. Dewey:305.48/896073. LCCN:2002-040875.

Audience: **g,l,u.** *Choice, 2003.*

Collier-Thomas, Bettye   **BR563.N4C64 1997**
Daughters of Thunder: Black Women Preachers and Their
Sermons, 1850-1979. Trade Cloth. John Wiley & Sons, Inc.
Hoboken, NJ. 1997. 368p. Religion in Practice Ser.
ISBN:0-7879-0918-1, ISBN13: 978-0-7879-0918-5.
Dewey:251/.0082. LCCN:97-004850.

Audience: **g,l,u.**

Collier-Thomas, Betty   **E185.61.S615 2001**
  & Franklin, V. P. (Editors)
Sisters in the Struggle: African-American Women in the Civil
Rights and Black Power Movements. Trade Cloth. New York
University Press. New York, NY. 2001. 376p.
ISBN:0-8147-1602-4, ISBN13: 978-0-8147-1602-1.
Dewey:323.1/196073/0922. LCCN:2001-001550.

Audience: **g,l,u.** *Choice, 2002.*

Collins, Catherine   **HV9471**
  Fisher
Imprisonment of African American Women: Causes, Conditions
and Future Implications. Paper Text. McFarland & Company,
Incorporated Publishers. Jefferson, NC. 2005. 166p.
ISBN:0-7864-2159-2, ISBN13: 978-0-7864-2159-6.
Dewey:365.973.

Audience: **g,l,u,f.**

Collins, Patricia Hill   **HQ1426.C633 2000**
Black Feminist Thought: Knowledge, Consciousness and
Politics of Empowerment. Ed. 2. Paper over Boards. Routledge.
New York, NY. 1999. 352p. ISBN:0-415-92483-9, ISBN13:
978-0-415-92483-2. Dewey:305.42/01. LCCN:99-029144.

Audience: **l,u,f.**

Collins, Patricia Hill   **HQ801**
Black Sexual Politics: African Americans, Gender, and the New
Racism. Trade Paper. Routledge. New York, NY. 2005. 384p.
ISBN:0-415-95150-X, ISBN13: 978-0-415-95150-0.
Dewey:306.7/089/96073.

Audience: **g,l,u,f.** *Choice, 2005.*

Dandridge, Rita B.   **PS374.N4D36 2004**
Black Women's Activism: Reading African American Women's
Historical Romances. Trade Cloth. Peter Lang Publishing, Inc.
New York, NY. 2004. 136p. African-American Literature and
Culture Ser., Vol. 5 ISBN:0-8204-6734-0, ISBN13:
978-0-8204-6734-4. Dewey:813.009/9287. LCCN:2002-156547.

Audience: **g,u,f.**

Dash, Julie   **PN1997.D325**
Daughters of the Dust: The Making of an African Woman's
Film. New Press. 1992. ISBN:1-56584-030-5, ISBN13:
978-1-56584-030-0.

Audience: **l,u.**

Davis, Angela Y.   **ML3521**
Blues Legacies and Black Feminism: Gertrude "Ma" Rainey,
Bessie Smith, and Billie Holiday. UK-Trade Paper. Alfred A.
Knopf Inc. New York, NY. 1999. 464p. ISBN:0-679-77126-3,
ISBN13: 978-0-679-77126-5. Dewey:782.4/2/1643/082.

Audience: **g,l,u.**

Davis, Michael D.   **GV697.A1.D38 1992**
Black American Women in Olympic Track and Field: A
Complete Illustrated Reference. Trade Cloth. McFarland &
Company, Incorporated Publishers. Jefferson, NC. 1992. 188p.

ISBN:0-89950-692-5, ISBN13: 978-0-89950-692-0.
Dewey:796.4208996073. LCCN:91-50946.
Audience: **g,l,u.** *Choice, 1992.*

DeCosta-Willis, Miriam   E185.97.W55A3 1995
   (Editor)
The Memphis Diary of Ida B. Wells. Mary Helen Washington
(Foreword by), Dorothy Sterling (Afterword by). Trade Cloth.
Beacon Press. Boston, MA. 1996. 240p. Black Women Writers
Ser. ISBN:0-8070-7064-5, ISBN13: 978-0-8070-7064-2.
Dewey:323/.092 B. LCCN:94-009087.
Audience: **g,l,u.** *Choice, 1995.*

DeVeaux, Alexis   PS3562.O75Z66 2004
Warrior Poet: A Biography of Audre Lorde. Trade Cloth. W. W.
Norton & Company, Inc. New York, NY. 2004. 512p.
ISBN:0-393-01954-3, ISBN13: 978-0-393-01954-4.
Dewey:811/.54 B. LCCN:2003-023349.
Audience: **g,l,u.** *Choice, 2004.*

Egar, Emmanuel Edame   PS310.N4E37 2003
Black Women Poets of Harlem Renaissance. Trade Paper.
University Press of America, Inc. Lanham, MD. 2003. 124p.
ISBN:0-7618-2617-3, ISBN13: 978-0-7618-2617-0.
Dewey:811/.52099287. LCCN:2003-055237.
Audience: **g,l,u.**

Evans, Mari   PS147
Black Women Writers, 1950-1980: A Critical Evaluation. Trade
Paper. Doubleday Publishing. New York, NY. 1999.
ISBN:0-385-50005-X, ISBN13: 978-0-385-50005-0.
Dewey:810/.9/9287.
Audience: **g,l,u,f.** *B*

Farrington, Lisa E.   N6538.N5F27 2004
Creating Their Own Image: The History of African-American
Women Artists. Trade Cloth. Oxford University Press, Inc. New
York, NY. 2004. 368p. ISBN:0-19-516721-X, ISBN13:
978-0-19-516721-4. Dewey:704/.042/08996073.
LCCN:2003-066171.
Audience: **g,l,u,f.** *Choice, 2005.*

Gates, Henry Louis   PS866.W5Z595 2003
The Trials of Phillis Wheatley: America's First Black Poet and
Her Encounters with the Founding Fathers. Trade Cloth. Basic
Books. New York, NY. 2003. 144p. ISBN:0-465-02729-6,
ISBN13: 978-0-465-02729-3. Dewey:811/.1 B.
LCCN:2003-002717.
Audience: **g,l,u,f.** *Choice, 2003.*

Gates, Henry Louis Jr.   PS508.N3
Afro-American Women Writers. Trade Cloth. Thomson Gale.
Farmington Hills, MI. 1998. ISBN:0-8161-1848-5, ISBN13:
978-0-8161-1848-9. Dewey:810.8089607.
Audience: **g,l,u,f.**

Gates, Henry Louis Jr.   PS3568.O243
   & Appiah, Anthony (Editors)
Ann Petry: Critical Perspectives Past and Present. Trade Cloth.
HarperCollins Publishers. New York, NY. 1994. Literary Ser.
ISBN:1-56743-054-6, ISBN13: 978-1-56743-054-7.
Dewey:813/.54.
Audience: **l,u,f.**

Gavin, Christy   PS153.N5G29 1999
African American Women Playwrights: A Research Guide. C.
James Trotman (Editor). Cloth Text. Garland Publishing, Inc.
New York, NY. 1999. 264p. Critical Studies in Black Life and

Culture, Vol. 31 ISBN:0-8153-2384-0, ISBN13:
978-0-8153-2384-6. Dewey:812/.54099287. LCCN:98-040865.
Audience: **g,l,u.** *Choice, 2000.*

Gibson, Aliona L.   E185.96
Nappy: Growing up Black and Female in America. Trade Paper.
Writers & Readers Publishing, Inc. New York, NY. 1998. 176p.
ISBN:0-86316-329-7, ISBN13: 978-0-86316-329-6.
Dewey:973/.0496073/092.
Audience: **g,l,u,f.**

Giddings, Paula J.   E185.86.G49 1996
When and Where I Enter: The Impact of Black Women on Race
and Sex in America. Ed. 2. Trade Paper. HarperCollins
Publishers. New York, NY. 1996. 416p. ISBN:0-688-14650-3,
ISBN13: 978-0-688-14650-4. Dewey:305.4/8896073.
LCCN:96-019349.
Audience: **g,l,u.**

Gill, LaVerne M.   E840.6.G55 1997
African American Women in Congress. Cloth Text. Rutgers
University Press. Piscataway, NJ. 1997. 256p.
ISBN:0-8135-2352-4, ISBN13: 978-0-8135-2352-1.
Dewey:328.73/092/2 B. LCCN:96-029294.
Audience: **g,l,u.**

Giovanni, Nikki   PS3557.I55.A6 2003
The Collected Poetry of Nikki Giovanni: 1968-1998. Trade
Cloth. HarperCollins Publishers. New York, NY. 2003. 496p.
ISBN:0-06-054133-4, ISBN13: 978-0-06-054133-0.
Dewey:811/.54. LCCN:2004-302269.
Audience: **g,l,u,f.**

Giovanni, Nikki   PS3557.I55
Racism 101. Fowler, Virginia (Editor). W. Morrow. 1994.
ISBN:0-688-04332-1, ISBN13: 978-0-688-04332-2.
Audience: **g,l.**

Graham, Maryemma   PS3545.A517Z67 2001
Fields Watered with Blood: Critical Essays on Margaret Walker.
University of Georgia Press. 2001. ISBN:0-8203-2254-7,
ISBN13: 978-0-8203-2254-4.
Audience: **l,u.**

Hanson, Joyce Ann   E185.97.B34H36 2003
Mary McLeod Bethune and Black Women's Political Activism.
Trade Cloth. University of Missouri Press. Columbia, MO.
2003. 256p. ISBN:0-8262-1451-7, ISBN13: 978-0-8262-1451-5.
Dewey:370/.92 B. LCCN:2002-153613.
Audience: **g,l,u.** *Choice, 2003.*

Harley, Sharon (Editor)   HD6057.5.U5S576 2002
Sister Circle: Black Women and Work. Black Women and Work
Collective Staff (Contribution by), Nellie Y. McKay (Foreword
by). Cloth Text. Rutgers University Press. Piscataway, NJ. 2002.
320p. ISBN:0-8135-3060-1, ISBN13: 978-0-8135-3060-4.
Dewey:331.4/089/96073. LCCN:2001-048613.
Audience: **g,l,u.** *Choice, 2003.*

Harley, Sharon &   E185.86
   Terborg-Penn, Rosalyn (Editors)
The Afro-American Woman: Struggles and Images. Trade Paper.
Black Classic Press. Baltimore, MD. 1997. 160p.
ISBN:1-57478-026-3, ISBN13: 978-1-57478-026-0.
Dewey:305.4889607. LCCN:96-086019.
Audience: **l,u.**

Harris, Trudier   **PS153.N5H29 2001**
Saints, Sinners, Saviors: Strong Black Women in
African-American Literature. Trade Paper. Palgrave Macmillan.
New York, NY. 2001. 224p. ISBN:0-312-29303-8, ISBN13:
978-0-312-29303-1. Dewey:810.9/352042. LCCN:2001-036009.
                                    Audience: **g,l,u.**

Harris, Trudier   **E185.97.H365**
Summer Snow: Reflections from a Black Daughter of the South.
Beacon Press. 2003. ISBN:0-8070-7254-0, ISBN13:
978-0-8070-7254-7.
                                    Audience: **u.**

Hine, Darlene Clark   **E185.86.B542 1993**
  (Editor), et al.
Black Women in America: An Historical Encyclopedia. Elsa B.
Brown & Rosalyn Terborg-Penn (Editors). Trade Cloth. Carlson
Publishing, Inc. Brooklyn, NY. 1993. 1600p.
ISBN:0-926019-61-9, ISBN13: 978-0-926019-61-4.
Dewey:920.72/08996073. LCCN:92-039947.
                          Audience: **g,l,u,f.** *Choice, 1993.*

Hine, Darlene Clark   **E185.86.W435 1995**
  (Editor), et al.
We Specialize in the Wholly Impossible: A Reader in Black
Women's History. Wilma King & Linda Reed (Editors). Trade
Paper. Carlson Publishing, Inc. Brooklyn, NY. 1995. 624p.
Black Women in United States History Ser., Vol. 17
ISBN:0-926019-81-3, ISBN13: 978-0-926019-81-2.
Dewey:305.48/896073/09. LCCN:94-041968.
                                    Audience: **g,l,u.**

Hine, Darlene Clark &   **E185.86**
  Thompsom, Kathleen
A Shining Thread of Hope: The History of Black Women in
America. Trade Paper. Broadway Books. New York, NY. 1999.
368p. ISBN:0-7679-0111-8, ISBN13: 978-0-7679-0111-6.
Dewey:305.48/896/073.
                          Audience: **g,l,u.** *Choice, 1999.*

hooks, bell   **E185.86**
Ain't I a Woman: Black Women and Feminism. Trade Cloth.
South End Press. Cambridge, MA. 1981. 205p.
ISBN:0-89608-130-3, ISBN13: 978-0-89608-130-7.
Dewey:305.4/8/896073. LCCN:81-051392.
                                    Audience: **g,l,u.**

hooks, bell   **PN1995.9.S6H66 1996**
Reel to Real: Race, Sex and Class at the Movies. UK-B Format
Paperback. Routledge. New York, NY. 1996. 256p.
ISBN:0-415-91824-3, ISBN13: 978-0-415-91824-4.
Dewey:302.23/43. LCCN:96-026474.
                                    Audience: **l,u.**

hooks, bell   **E185.86**
Talking Back: Thinking Feminist, Thinking Black. Trade Cloth.
South End Press. Cambridge, MA. 1989. 186p.
ISBN:0-89608-353-5, ISBN13: 978-0-89608-353-0.
Dewey:305.4/8896/073. LCCN:88-042874.
                                    Audience: **l,u.**

Hudson-Weems,   **HQ1190.H83 1994**
  Clenora
Africana Womanism: Reclaiming Ourselves. Ed. 2. Bedford
Publishers. 1994. ISBN:0-911557-11-3, ISBN13:
978-0-911557-11-4.
                                    Audience: **l,u.**

Hunter, Tera W.   **HD6057.5.U52G45 1997**
To Joy My Freedom: Southern Black Women's Lives and
Labors after the Civil War. Trade Cloth. Harvard University
Press. Cambridge, MA. 1997. 322p. ISBN:0-674-89309-3,
ISBN13: 978-0-674-89309-2. Dewey:331.4/089/9607307582.
LCCN:96-051473.
                          Audience: **g,l,u.** *Choice, 1997.*

Hurston, Zora Neale   **PS3515.U789A6 1995**
Novels and Stories: Jonah's Gourd Vine; Their Eyes Were
Watching God; Moses, Man of the Mountain; Seraph on the
Suwanee. Cheryl A. Wall (Editor). Trade Cloth. Library of
America, The. New York, NY. 1995. 1054p. Novels and Stories
Ser., Vol. 74 ISBN:0-940450-83-6, ISBN13: 978-0-940450-83-7.
Dewey:813/.52. LCCN:94-025757.
                                    Audience: **g,l,u,f.**

James, Joy (Author,   **PS153.N5B5536 2000**
  Editor)
The Black Feminist Reader. Tracey Denean Sharply-Whiting
(Editor). Trade Paper. Blackwell Publishing, Inc. Malden, MA.
2000. 320p. ISBN:0-631-21007-5, ISBN13: 978-0-631-21007-8.
Dewey:305.48/896073. LCCN:99-051385.
                                    Audience: **g,l,u.**

James, Stanlie M. &   **HQ1190.T47 1993**
  Busia, Abena P. (Editors)
Theorizing Black Feminisms: The Visionary Pragmatism of
Black Women. Johnnetta B. Cole (Foreword by). Paper over
Boards. Routledge. New York, NY. 1993. 312p.
ISBN:0-415-07336-7, ISBN13: 978-0-415-07336-3.
Dewey:305.4208996. LCCN:92-047346.
                                    Audience: **g,l,u.**

Jewell, K. Sue   **E185.86.J48 1992**
From Mammy to Miss America and Beyond: Cultural Images
and the Shaping of U. S. Social Policy. Trade Paper. Routledge.
New York, NY. 1992. 256p. ISBN:0-415-04253-4, ISBN13:
978-0-415-04253-6. Dewey:305.48896073. LCCN:92-011917.
                          Audience: **g,l,u.** *Choice, 1993.*

Johnson-Odim, Cheryl   **HQ1815.5.Z75**
For Women and the Nation: Funmilayo Ransome-Kuti of
Nigeria. Mba, Nina Emma. University of Illinois. 1997.
ISBN:0-252-02313-7, ISBN13: 978-0-252-02313-2.
                                    Audience: **l,u,f.**

Jones, Jacqueline   **HD6057.5.U5J66 1986**
Labor of Love, Labor of Sorrow: Black Women, Work and the
Family from Slavery to the Present. Trade Paper. Knopf
Publishing Group. New York, NY. 1986. 464p.
ISBN:0-394-74536-1, ISBN13: 978-0-394-74536-7.
Dewey:305.4/8896073. LCCN:85-040860.
                          Audience: **g,l,u.** **B** *Choice, 1985.*

Kaplan, Carla (Editor)   **PS3515.U789Z48 2001**
Zora Neale Hurston: A Life in Letters. Trade Paper. Knopf
Publishing Group. New York, NY. 2003. 912p.
ISBN:0-385-49036-4, ISBN13: 978-0-385-49036-8.
Dewey:813/.52. LCCN:00-065671.
                                    Audience: **g,l,u.**

Larson, Kate Clifford   **E444.T82**
Bound for the Promised Land: Harriet Tubman, Portrait of an
American Hero. Trade Paper. Ballantine Books. New York, NY.
2004. 432p. ISBN:0-345-45628-9, ISBN13: 978-0-345-45628-1.
Dewey:973.7/115/092 B. LCCN:2004-111071.
                          Audience: **g,l,u.** *Choice, 2004.*

Lawson, Ellen N.   LC2801.T57 1984
The Three Sarahs: Documents of Antebellum Black College
Women. Library Binding. Edwin Mellen Press, The. Lewiston,
NY. 1984. 350p. Studies in Women and Religion, Vol. 13
ISBN:0-88946-536-3, ISBN13: 978-0-88946-536-7.
Dewey:371.1/009/22 B. LCCN:84-018914.
                                        Audience: **g,l,u.**

Levin, Amy K.   PS374.N4L48 2003
Africanism and Authenticity in African-American Women's
Novels. Trade Cloth. University Press of Florida. Gainesville,
FL. 2003. 208p. ISBN:0-8130-2631-8, ISBN13:
978-0-8130-2631-2. Dewey:813/.5099287. LCCN:2003-040190.
                                        Audience: **g,l,u.**

Liddell, Janice   PS153.N5A87 1999
Arms Akimbo: African Women in Contemporary Literature.
Trade Cloth. University Press of Florida. Gainesville, FL. 1999.
240p. ISBN:0-8130-1728-9, ISBN13: 978-0-8130-1728-0.
Dewey:810.9/352042. LCCN:99-038712.
                                        Audience: **g,l,u.**

Lowry, Beverly   HD9970.5.C672W3558
Her Dream of Dreams: The Rise and Triumph of Madam C. J.
Walker. Trade Cloth. Alfred A. Knopf Inc. New York, NY. 2003.
496p. ISBN:0-679-44642-7, ISBN13: 978-0-679-44642-2.
Dewey:338.7/66855/092 B. LCCN:2002-027494.
                                        Audience: **g,l,u.**

Manatu, Norma   PN1995.9.N4M28 2002
African American Women and Sexuality in the Cinema. Paper
Text. McFarland & Company, Incorporated Publishers. Jefferson,
NC. 2002. 245p. ISBN:0-7864-1431-6, ISBN13:
978-0-7864-1431-4. Dewey:791.43/652042. LCCN:2002-015421.
                          Audience: **g,l,u.** *Choice, 2003.*

Mandela, Winnie   DT1949.M36A3 1985
Part of My Soul Went with Him. Benjamin, Anne (Editor);
Benson, Mary (Adapted by). Norton. 1985.
ISBN:0-393-02215-3, ISBN13: 978-0-393-02215-5.
                                        Audience: **g.**

Marsh-Lockett, Carol P.   PS338.N4B57 1999
  (Editor)
Black Women Playwrights: Visions on the American Stage.
Cloth Text. Garland Publishing, Inc. New York, NY. 1998. 240p.
Studies in Modern Drama, Vol. 11 ISBN:0-8153-2746-3,
ISBN13: 978-0-8153-2746-2. Dewey:812.0099287.
LCCN:98-042553.
                                        Audience: **g,l,u.**

McDowell, Deborah E.   PS374.N4M37 1995
The Changing Same: Black Women's Literature, Criticism, and
Theory. Trade Cloth. Indiana University Press. Bloomington, IN.
1995. 224p. ISBN:0-253-33629-5, ISBN13: 978-0-253-33629-3.
Dewey:813.009/896073. LCCN:94-010663.
                          Audience: **g,l,u.** *Choice, 1995.*

Mitchell, Angelyn   PS374.S58M58 2002
The Freedom to Remember: Narrative, Slavery and Gender in
Contemporary Black Women's Fiction. Cloth Text. Rutgers
University Press. Piscataway, NJ. 2002. 192p.
ISBN:0-8135-3068-7, ISBN13: 978-0-8135-3068-0.
Dewey:813/.54099287. LCCN:2001-048609.
                       Audience: **g,l,u.** *Choice, 2003, 2002.*

Morrison, Toni   PS3563.O8749Z464 1994
Conversations with Toni Morrison. Taylor-Guthrie, Danille
(Editor). University of Mississippi. 1994.
                                        Audience: **g,l,u.**

Mullings, Leith   E185.86.M945 1996
On Our Own Terms: Race, Class and Gender in the Lives of
African-American Women. Paper over Boards. Routledge. New
York, NY. 1996. 224p. ISBN:0-415-91285-7, ISBN13:
978-0-415-91285-3. Dewey:305.48/896073. LCCN:96-028853.
                                        Audience: **g,l,u.**

Murdy, Anne-Elizabeth   PS374.N4M87 2003
Teach the Nation: Public School, Racial Uplift, and Women's
Writing in the 1890's. Paper over Boards. Routledge. New York,
NY. 2002. 196p. Studies in African American History and
Culture ISBN:0-415-93534-2, ISBN13: 978-0-415-93534-0.
Dewey:813/.4099287. LCCN:2002-068254.
                                        Audience: **g,l,u.**

Nemiroff, Robert   PS3564.E48
To Be Young, Gifted and Black: A Portrait of Lorraine
Hansberry in Her Own Words. S. French. 1971.
                                        Audience: **g,l.**

Olson, Lynne   E185.O43 2002
Freedom's Daughters: The Unsung Heroines of the Civil Rights
Movement from 1830 to 1970. Trade Paper. Simon & Schuster.
New York, NY. 2002. 464p. ISBN:0-684-85013-3, ISBN13:
978-0-684-85013-9. Dewey:323/.092/275.
                                        Audience: **g,l,u.**

Otieno, Wambui   DT433.582.O75A3 1998
  Waiyaki
Mau Mau's Daughter: A Life Story. Presley, Cora Lynn (Editor,
Introduction by). Lynn Rienner Publishers. 1998.
ISBN:1-55587-722-2, ISBN13: 978-1-55587-722-4.
                                        Audience: **l,u.**

Peterson, Carla L.   PS153.N5P443 1998
Doers of the Word: African-American Women Speakers and
Writers in the North (1830-1880). Paper Text. Rutgers
University Press. Piscataway, NJ. 1998. 284p.
ISBN:0-8135-2514-4, ISBN13: 978-0-8135-2514-3.
Dewey:810.9/9287/08996073. LCCN:97-041838.
                                        Audience: **g,l,u.**

Plowden, Martha Ward   GV697.A1P56 1996
Olympic Black Women. Ronald Jones (Illustrator). Trade Cloth.
Pelican Publishing Company, Inc. Gretna, LA. 1995. 160p.
ISBN:1-56554-080-8, ISBN13: 978-1-56554-080-4.
Dewey:796/.092/2 B. LCCN:95-032067.
                                        Audience: **g,l,u.**

Quashie, Kevin Everod   PS153.N5.Q37 2004
Black Women, Identity, and Cultural Theory: (Un)becoming the
Subject. Library Binding. Rutgers University Press. Piscataway,
NJ. 2004. 240p. ISBN:0-8135-3366-X, ISBN13:
978-0-8135-3366-7. Dewey:810.9/9287/08996073.
LCCN:2003-007035.
                          Audience: **g,l,u.** *Choice, 2004.*

Roberts, Diane   PR408.R34R6 1994
The Myth of Aunt Jemima: Representations of Race and
Religion. Paper over Boards. Routledge. New York, NY. 1994.
240p. ISBN:0-415-04918-0, ISBN13: 978-0-415-04918-4.
Dewey:820.9/9287. LCCN:93-050574.
                          Audience: **g,l,u.** *Choice, 1995.*

Roberts, Dorothy   HQ766.5.U5
Killing the Black Body: Race, Reproduction, and the Meaning
of Liberty. Trade Paper. Knopf Publishing Group. New York,
NY. 1998. 384p. ISBN:0-679-75869-0, ISBN13:
978-0-679-75869-3. Dewey:363.9/6/0973.

> Audience: **g,l,u.**

Rooks, Noliwe M.   TT972.R66 1996
Hair Raising: Beauty, Culture, and African American Women.
Trade Paper. Rutgers University Press. Piscataway, NJ. 2003.
156p. ISBN:0-8135-2312-5, ISBN13: 978-0-8135-2312-5.
Dewey:391/.5/08996073. LCCN:95-051395.

> Audience: **g,l,u.** *Choice, 1997.*

Rooks, Noliwe M.   PN4882.5.R66 2004
Ladies' Pages: African American Women's Magazines and the
Culture That Made Them. Trade Cloth. Rutgers University
Press. Piscataway, NJ. 2004. 208p. ISBN:0-8135-3425-9,
ISBN13: 978-0-8135-3425-1. Dewey:051/.082.
LCCN:2003-018868.

> Audience: **g,l,u.** *Choice, 2005.*

Ruiz, Vicki L.   HQ1410.U54 2000
Unequal Sisters: A Multicultural Reader in U. S. Women's
History. Ed. 3. Ellen Carol DuBois (Editor). Paper over Boards.
Routledge. New York, NY. 1999. 696p. ISBN:0-415-92516-9,
ISBN13: 978-0-415-92516-7. LCCN:99-016825.

> Audience: **g,l,u.**

Salem, Dorothy   E185.86.B543
To Better Our World: Black Women in Organized Reform,
1890-1920. Trade Cloth. Carlson Publishing, Inc. Brooklyn, NY.
1990. 416p. Black Women in United States History Ser., Vol. 14
ISBN:0-926019-20-1, ISBN13: 978-0-926019-20-1.
Dewey:973/.0496073 s. LCCN:90-001397.

> Audience: **g,l,u.** *Choice, 1990.*

Salem, Dorothy C.   E185.96.A45 1993
  (Editor)
African American Women: A Biographical Dictionary. Paper
over Boards. Garland Publishing, Inc. New York, NY. 1993.
664p. Biographical Directories of Minority Women Ser., Vol. 2
ISBN:0-8240-9782-3, ISBN13: 978-0-8240-9782-0.
Dewey:920.7208996073. LCCN:92-045727.

> Audience: **g,l,u,f.** *Choice, 1994.*

Schechter, Patricia A.   E185.97.W55S34 2001
Ida B. Wells-Barnett and American Reform, 1880-1930. Trade
Paper. University of North Carolina Press. Chapel Hill, NC.
2001. 408p. Gender and American Culture Ser.
ISBN:0-8078-4965-0, ISBN13: 978-0-8078-4965-1.
Dewey:323/.092 B. LCCN:00-068313.

> Audience: **g,l,u.**

Shakur, Assata   E185.97.S53A3 2001
Assata: An Autobiography. Angela Davis & Angela Lennox S.
Hinds (Foreword by). Trade Paper. C C H, Inc. Riverwoods, IL.
1999. 320p. ISBN:1-55652-074-3, ISBN13: 978-1-55652-074-7.
Dewey:305.8/96073. LCCN:2002-278291.

> Audience: **g,l,u,f.** *Choice, 1988.*

Smith, Jessie C.   E185.96.E65 1993
Epic Lives: One Hundred Black Women Who Made a
Difference. Trade Cloth. Visible Ink Press. Canton, MI. 1992.
661p. ISBN:0-8103-9426-X, ISBN13: 978-0-8103-9426-1.
Dewey:920.72/089/96073 B. LCCN:93-106495.

> Audience: **g,l,u.**

Smith, Jessie Carney   E185.96.N68 1992
  (Editor)
Notable Black American Women. Ed. 3. Trade Cloth. Thomson
Gale. Farmington Hills, MI. 2002. 775p. ISBN:0-7876-6494-4,
ISBN13: 978-0-7876-6494-7. Dewey:920.72/08996073.
LCCN:91-035074.

> Audience: **g,l,u.**

Smith, Susan L.   RA448.5.N4S65 1995
Sick and Tired of Being Sick and Tired: Black Women's Health
Activism in America, 1890-1950. Trade Cloth. University of
Pennsylvania Press. Philadelphia, PA. 1995. 288p. Studies in
Health, Illness, and Caregiving ISBN:0-8122-3237-2, ISBN13:
978-0-8122-3237-0. Dewey:362.1. LCCN:95-011310.

> Audience: **g,l,u.** *Choice, 1996.*

Smith-Shomade,   PN1992.8.A34S48 2002
  Beretta E.
Shaded Lives: African American Women and Television. Trade
Cloth. Rutgers University Press. Piscataway, NJ. 2002. 256p.
ISBN:0-8135-3104-7, ISBN13: 978-0-8135-3104-5.
Dewey:791.45/652042. LCCN:2001-048840.

> Audience: **g,l,u.**

Smitherman, Geneva   E185.86.A3344 1995
  (Editor)
African American Women Speak Out on Anita Hill - Clarence
Thomas. Trade Paper. Wayne State University Press. Detroit,
MI. 1995. 278p. African American Life Ser.
ISBN:0-8143-2530-0, ISBN13: 978-0-8143-2530-8.
Dewey:305.48/89073. LCCN:94-048645.

> Audience: **g,l,u,f.**

Springer, Kimberly   E185.86.S766 1999
  (Editor)
Still Lifting, Still Climbing: African American Women's
Contemporary Activism. Beverly Guy-Sheftall (Preface by),
Loretta Ross (Afterword by). Trade Cloth. New York University
Press. New York, NY. 1999. 360p. ISBN:0-8147-8124-1,
ISBN13: 978-0-8147-8124-1. Dewey:305.48/896073.
LCCN:99-006173.

> Audience: **g,l,u.**

Tate, Gayle T.   E185.9.T38 2003
Unknown Tongues: Black Women's Political Activism in the
Antebellum Era, 1830-1860. Trade Cloth. Michigan State
University Press. East Lansing, MI. 2003. 416p. Black American
and Diasporic Studies ISBN:0-87013-652-6, ISBN13:
978-0-87013-652-8. Dewey:974/.00496073/0082.
LCCN:2002-155167.

> Audience: **g,l,u.** *Choice, 2003.*

Terborg-Penn, Rosalyn   JK1896.T47 1998
African American Women in the Struggle for the Vote,
1850-1920. Trade Paper. Indiana University Press. Bloomington,
IN. 1998. 224p. Blacks in the Diaspora Ser.
ISBN:0-253-21176-X, ISBN13: 978-0-253-21176-7.
Dewey:324.6/23/08996073. LCCN:97-041896.

> Audience: **g,l,u,f.** *Choice, 1998.*

Terborg-Penn, Rosalyn   HQ1787.W65 1996
  & Rushing, Andrea B. (Editors)
Women in Africa and the African Diaspora: A Reader. Ed. 2.
Trade Paper. Howard University Press. Washington, DC. 1996.
ISBN:0-88258-194-5, ISBN13: 978-0-88258-194-1.
Dewey:305.42/096. LCCN:96-046285.

> Audience: **g,l,u.**

Thomas, Veronica G.   **Z1361**
(Compiled by), et al.
African American Women: An Annotated Bibliography. Kisha
Braithwaite & Paula Mitchell (Compiled by). Cloth Text.
Greenwood Publishing Group, Inc. Portsmouth, NH. 2000. 232p.
Bibliographies and Indexes in Afro-American and African
Studies, Vol. 42 ISBN:0-313-31263-X, ISBN13:
978-0-313-31263-2. Dewey:016.30548/896073.
LCCN:00-030884.

Audience: **g,l,u,f.** *Choice, 2001.*

Thompson, Kathleen &   **E185.86.F33 1999**
Mac Austin, Hilary (Editors)
The Face of Our Past: Images of Black Women from Colonial
America to the Present. Darlene Clark Hine (Introduction by).
Trade Cloth. Indiana University Press. Bloomington, IN. 2000.
xiv, 258p. ISBN:0-253-33635-X, ISBN13: 978-0-253-33635-4.
Dewey:920.72/08996073. LCCN:99-024662.

Audience: **g,l,u.**

Timberlake, Andrea   **Z7964.U49**
(Editor), et al.
Women of Color and Southern Women: A Bibliography of
Social Science Research 1975-1988. Annual Supplement, 1989.
Lynn W. Cannon, Rebecca F. Guy & Elizabeth Higginbotham
(Editors). Trade Paper. University of Memphis, The, Center for
Research on Women. Memphis, TN. 1990. 175p.
ISBN:0-9621327-1-3, ISBN13: 978-0-9621327-1-1.
Dewcy:16.3054. LCCN:89-063010.

Audience: **g,l,u.**

Walker, Alice   **PS3573.A425**
The Same River Twice: Honoring the Difficult: A Meditation on
Life, Spirit, Art, and the Making of the Film The Color Purple,
Ten Years Later. Scribner. 1996. ISBN:0-684-81419-6, ISBN13:
978-0-684-81419-3.

Audience: **g.**

Walker, Margaret   **PS3545.A517Z468 2002**
Conversations with Margaret Walker. Maryemma Graham
(Editor). Trade Cloth. University Press of Mississippi. Jackson,
MS. 2002. 224p. Literary Conversations Ser.
ISBN:1-57806-512-7, ISBN13: 978-1-57806-512-7.
Dewey:818/.5209. LCCN:2002-016898.

Audience: **l,u.**

Walker, Margaret   **E185.92.W35 1997**
On Being Female, Black and Free: Essays by Margaret Walker,
1932-1992. Maryemma Graham (Editor). Trade Paper.
University of Tennessee Press. Knoxville, TN. 1997. 272p.
ISBN:0-87049-981-5, ISBN13: 978-0-87049-981-4.
Dewey:975/.00496073. LCCN:96-051235.

Audience: **l,u.**

Walker-Hill, Helen   **ML390.W16 2002**
From Spirituals to Symphonies: African-American Women
Composers and Their Music. Cloth Text. Greenwood Publishing
Group, Inc. Portsmouth, NH. 2002. 432p. Jazz Companions Ser.
ISBN:0-313-29947-1, ISBN13: 978-0-313-29947-6.
Dewey:780.89/96073. LCCN:2001-040600.

Audience: **g,l,u,f.** *Choice, 2003.*

Walker-Hill, Helen   **ML128.W7W35 1995**
Music by Black Women Composers: A Bibliography of
Available Scores. Trade Cloth. Columbia College Chicago.
Chicago, IL. 1995. 118p. CBMR Monographs, No. 5
ISBN:0-929911-04-0, ISBN13: 978-0-929911-04-5.
Dewey:016.78/082. LCCN:95-005613.

Audience: **g,l,u.**

Wall, Cheryl A.   **PS153.N5W33 1995**
Women of the Harlem Renaissance. Cloth Text. Indiana
University Press. Bloomington, IN. 1995. 256p. Women of
Letters Ser. ISBN:0-253-32908-6, ISBN13: 978-0-253-32908-0.
Dewey:810/.9/896073. LCCN:95-003132.

Audience: **g,l,u.** *Choice, 1996.*

Wallace, Michelle   **E185.86.W34 1990**
Black Macho and the Myth of the Superwoman. Trade Paper.
Analytical Psychology Club of San Francisco, Inc. San
Francisco, CA. 1990. 300p. ISBN:0-86091-518-2, ISBN13:
978-0-86091-518-8. Dewey:305.3/08996073. LCCN:90-042080.

Audience: **g,l,u.**

White, Deborah Gray   **E185.86.W43875**
Too Heavy a Load: Black Women in Defense of Themselves,
1894-1994. Trade Paper. W. W. Norton & Company, Inc. New
York, NY. 1999. 320p. ISBN:0-393-31992-X, ISBN13:
978-0-393-31992-7. Dewey:305.4/8896073. LCCN:98-006518.

Audience: **g,l,u.**

White, E. Francis   **HQ1426.W465 2001**
Dark Continent of Our Bodies: Black Feminism and the Politics
of Respectability. Library Binding. Temple University Press.
Philadelphia, PA. 2001. ix, 194p. Mapping Racisms Ser.
ISBN:1-56639-879-7, ISBN13: 978-1-56639-879-4.
Dewey:305.42/0973. LCCN:00-053212.

Audience: **g,l,u.**

Williams, Dana A.   **Z1229**
Contemporary African American Female Playwrights: An
Annotated Bibliography. Cloth Text. Greenwood Publishing
Group, Inc. Portsmouth, NH. 1998. 152p. Bibliographies and
Indexes in Afro-American and African Studies, Vol. 37
ISBN:0-313-30132-8, ISBN13: 978-0-313-30132-2.
Dewey:016.812/540809287/08. LCCN:98-017542.

Audience: **g,l,u.** *Choice, 1998.*

Wilson, Harriet E. &   **PS3334**
Gates, Henry Louis Jr.
Our Nig: Or, Sketches from the Life of a Free Black. Ed. 3.
Trade Paper. Random House, Inc. New York, NY. 2002. 304p.
ISBN:1-4000-3120-6, ISBN13: 978-1-4000-3120-7.
Dewey:813.3.

Audience: **g,l,u,f.**

Yee, Shirley J.   **E449.Y44 1992**
Black Women Abolitionists: A Study in Activism, 1828-1860.
Library Binding. University of Tennessee Press. Knoxville, TN.
1992. 216p. ISBN:0-87049-735-9, ISBN13: 978-0-87049-735-3.
Dewey:305.48/896073. LCCN:91-024795.

Audience: **g,l,u.** *Choice, 1992.*

Yellin, Jean Fagan   **E185.97.T8**
Harriet Jacobs: A Life. Trade Paper. Basic Books. New York,
NY. 2005. 432p. ISBN:0-465-09289-6, ISBN13:
978-0-465-09289-5. Dewey:306.3/62/092 B.

Audience: **g,l,u.** *Choice, 2004.*

Zalokar, Nadja   **HD6057.5.U5**
The Economic Status of Black Women: An Exploratory
Investigation. U.S. Commission on Civil Rights. 1990.

Audience: **g,l,u.**

Science

Carson, Ben & Murphey, Cecil B. RD592.9.C37A3 1990
Gifted Hands: The Ben Carson Story. Zondervan. 1996.
ISBN:0-310-54650-8, ISBN13: 978-0-310-54650-4.

Audience: **g,l.**

Manning, Kenneth R. QH31.C33
Black Apollo of Science: The Life of Ernest Everett Just. Trade
Paper. Oxford University Press, Inc. New York, NY. 1985. 416p.
ISBN:0-19-503498-8, ISBN13: 978-0-19-503498-1.
Dewey:574/.092/4.

Audience: **g,l,u.**

Ridlon, Florence R695.M35R53 2005
Black Physicians Struggle for Civil Rights: Edward C. Mazique,
M. D. Trade Cloth. University of New Mexico Press.

Albuquerque, NM. 2005. 392p. ISBN:0-8263-3339-7, ISBN13:
978-0-8263-3339-1. Dewey:610/.89/96073 B.
LCCN:2004-023086.

Audience: **g,l,u.** *Choice, 2005.*

Sammons, Vivian O. Q141.B58 1990
Blacks in Science and Medicine. Hemisphere Publishing Corp..
1990. ISBN:0-89116-665-3, ISBN13: 978-0-89116-665-8.

Audience: **g,l,u,f.**

Van Sertima, Ivan Q127.A4
Blacks in Science: Ancient and Modern. Trade Paper.
Transaction Publishers. Somerset, NJ. 1983. 333p.
ISBN:0-87855-941-8, ISBN13: 978-0-87855-941-1.
Dewey:509/.6. LCCN:83-071004.

Audience: **g,l,u.**

AFRICAN HISTORY, LANGUAGES, AND LITERATURES

The Africa section contains general and specific texts suitable for undergraduate scholarship. The emphasis is on African history, but the cross-disciplinary nature of the field has been taken into account during the selection process. While periodization and regional definitions are often fluid in the field of scholarship, the taxonomy has used the more broadly accepted categories for organizational purposes. The bibliography includes works meant to aid in teaching and beginning study of African history, but is limited by the available published scholarship. Titles include general works which cover large parts of the continent, not individual countries, and are divided by time period; general works which provide basic knowledge for all students and a strong base for the more specific collection; specific works which are divided by region and then by country; in some cases, more advanced texts are included for advanced undergraduates and teaching faculty. Secondary works are the main focus of the bibliography, but due to the importance of primary sources in historical study, they have been included whenever possible. The most relevant works for undergraduates have been chosen, regardless of publication date and country of origin. All materials are in English, whether original or in translation.

— Kate Schroeder

History of Africa > General Works

DT18
African Biographical Dictionary. Trade Cloth. Grey House Publishing. Millerton, NY. 2006. ISBN:1-59237-112-4, ISBN13: 978-1-59237-112-9. Dewey:920.06 B.

Audience: **g,l,u,f.**

Clark, Leon E.   **DT1**
Through African Eyes: Culture and Society: Continuity and Change. Library Binding. Center for International Training & Education. New York, NY. 2000. 346p. ISBN:0-938960-45-8, ISBN13: 978-0-938960-45-4. Dewey:960.

Audience: **g,l,u,f.**

Cornwall, Andrea   **HQ1240.5.A35**
(Editor)
Readings in Gender in Africa. Trade Cloth. Indiana University Press. Bloomington, IN. 2005. 264p. Readings In... Ser. ISBN:0-253-34517-0, ISBN13: 978-0-253-34517-2. Dewey:305.3096.

Audience: **l,u,f.**

Falola, Toyin   **DT20**
Key Events in African History: A Reference Guide. Cloth Text. Greenwood Publishing Group, Inc. Portsmouth, NH. 2002. 376p. ISBN:0-313-31323-7, ISBN13: 978-0-313-31323-3. Dewey:960. LCCN:2001-058644.

Audience: **g,l,u,f.** *Choice, 2003.*

Fung, Karen   **DT3**
☐ Africa South of the Sahara.
http://www-sul.stanford.edu/depts/ssrg/africa/guide.html
Audience: **g,l,u,f.**

Fung, Karen   **DT3**
☐ Africa South of the Sahara.
http://www-sul.stanford.edu/depts/ssrg/africa/guide.html
Audience: **g,l,u,f.**

Johnson, Donald J., et al.   **DS407**
Through African Eyes: Culture and Society: Continuity and Change. Jean E. Johnson & Leon E. Clark (Authors). Trade Paper. Center for International Training & Education. New York, NY. 2000. 346p. ISBN:0-938960-02-4, ISBN13: 978-0-938960-02-7. Dewey:954.

Audience: **g,l,u,f.**

Martin, Phyllis M. &   **DT3.A23 1995**
O'Meara, Patrick (Editors)
Africa. Ed. 3. Trade Paper. Indiana University Press. Bloomington, IN. 1995. 472p. ISBN:0-253-20984-6, ISBN13: 978-0-253-20984-9. Dewey:960. LCCN:95-005772.

Audience: **g,l,u,f.** *B*

Oliver, Roland Anthony   **DT20**
& Crowder, Michael (Editors)
The Cambridge Encyclopedia of Africa. Trade Cloth. Cambridge University Press. New York, NY. 1981. 500p. Cambridge Regional Encyclopedias Ser. ISBN:0-521-23096-9, ISBN13: 978-0-521-23096-4. Dewey:960. LCCN:79-042627.

Audience: **g,l,u,f.** *B*

Philips, John Edward   **DT19.W75 2005**
(Editor)
Writing African History. Trade Cloth. University of Rochester Press. Rochester, NY. 2005. 552p. Rochester Studies in African History and the Diaspora, Vol. 20 ISBN:1-58046-164-6,

ISBN13: 978-1-58046-164-1. Dewey:960/.072. LCCN:2005-000377.

Audience: **g,l,u,f.** *Choice, 2006.*

Stewart, John   **DT31.S7859 1999**
African States and Rulers. Ed. 2. Cloth Text. McFarland & Company, Incorporated Publishers. Jefferson, NC. 1999. 415p. ISBN:0-7864-0613-5, ISBN13: 978-0-7864-0613-5. Dewey:960.03. LCCN:99-31678.

Audience: **g,l,u,f.**

History of Africa > Description and Travel

G2445 .W6
Africa Today: An Atlas of Reproducible Papers. Ringbound. World Eagle. Littleton, MA. 1996. 252p. World Eagles Today Ser. ISBN:0-930141-60-1, ISBN13: 978-0-930141-60-8. Dewey:912.6.

Audience: **g,l,u,f.**

Ajayi, Jacob Festus Ade   **G2446.S1H5 1985**
& Crowder, Michael (Editors)
Historical Atlas of Africa. Trade Cloth. Cambridge University Press. New York, NY. 1985. 168p. ISBN:0-521-25353-5, ISBN13: 978-0-521-25353-6. Dewey:911/.6. LCCN:83-675975.

Audience: **g,l,u,f.** *B Choice, 1986.*

Binns, Tony (Editor)   **GF701.P46 1995**
People and Environment in Africa. Ed. 1. Trade Paper. John Wiley & Sons, Inc. Hoboken, NJ. 1995. 286p. ISBN:0-471-95100-5, ISBN13: 978-0-471-95100-1. Dewey:304.2/096. LCCN:94-038627.

Audience: **g,l,u,f.**

Grove, A. T.   **DT12.25.G755**
The Changing Geography of Africa. Ed. 2. Paper Text. Oxford University Press, Inc. New York, NY. 1993. 252p. ISBN:0-19-913386-7, ISBN13: 978-0-19-913386-4. Dewey:916.

Audience: **g,l,u,f.**

Hall, Richard Seymour   **DT351.S9 H27 1975**
Stanley: An Adventurer Explored. Houghton Mifflin. 1975. ISBN:0-395-19426-1, ISBN13: 978-0-395-19426-3.

Audience: **g,l,u,f.**

Moorehead, Alan   **DT156.3**
The Blue Nile. Trade Paper. HarperCollins Publishers. New York, NY. 2000. 368p. ISBN:0-06-095640-2, ISBN13: 978-0-06-095640-0. Dewey:962.6/4/02.

Audience: **g,l,u,f.** *B*

Moorehead, Alan   **DT117.M6**
The White Nile. Trade Paper. HarperCollins Publishers. New York, NY. 2000. 448p. ISBN:0-06-095639-9, ISBN13: 978-0-06-095639-4. Dewey:962.93.

Audience: **g,l,u,f.** *B*

Murray, Jocelyn   **G2446**
Cultural Atlas of Africa. Ed. 2. Trade Cloth. Facts On File, Inc. New York, NY. 1998. 240p. Cultural Atlas Ser. ISBN:0-8160-3813-9, ISBN13: 978-0-8160-3813-8. Dewey:960. LCCN:98-035463.

Audience: **g,l,u,f.** *B Choice, 1999.*

Newman, James   **DT363.2.S755N47 2006**
Imperial Footprints. Trade Paper. Potomac Books, Inc. Dulles, VA. 2006. 416p. ISBN:1-57488-723-8, ISBN13:

978-1-57488-723-5. Dewey:916.704/23/092 B.
LCCN:2004-051838.

Audience: **g,l,u,f.** *Choice, 2005.*

Stanley, Henry M.　　　　　　　**DT351.S73**
The Exploration Diaries of H M Stanley, Now First Published
from the Original Manuscripts. Paper Text. Textbook Publishers.
Temecula, CA. 2003. 208p. ISBN:0-7581-1000-6, ISBN13:
978-0-7581-1000-8. Dewey:916.7.

Audience: **g,l,u,f.** *B*

Stichter, Sharon B. &　　　　　**HQ1788.A57 1995**
　Hay, Jean
African Women South of the Sahara. Ed. 2. Paper Text.
Longman Publishing Group. White Plains, NY. 1995. 328p.
ISBN:0-582-21241-3, ISBN13: 978-0-582-21241-1.
Dewey:305.4/8896. LCCN:95-016886.

Audience: **g,l,u,f.**

History of Africa > History

Berger, Iris, et al.　　　　　　**HQ1787.B47 1999**
Women in Sub-Saharan Africa. E. Frances White & Cathy
Skidmore-Hess (Authors). Cloth Text. Indiana University Press.
Bloomington, IN. 1999. 168p. Restoring Women to History Ser.
ISBN:0-253-33476-4, ISBN13: 978-0-253-33476-3.
Dewey:305.4/0967. LCCN:98-053906.

Audience: **g,u,f.**

Clark, J. Desmond　　　　　　**DT20 .C28**
　(Editor)
The Cambridge History of Africa, Set. J. D. Fage & Roland
Oliver (Editor, Contribution by), Richard Gray, John E. Flint &
G. N. Sanderson (Editors). Quantity Pack, Cloth Text.
Cambridge University Press. New York, NY. 1986. The
Cambridge History of Africa Ser. ISBN:0-521-33460-8, ISBN13:
978-0-521-33460-0. Dewey:960. LCCN:76-002261.

Audience: **g,l,u,f.**

Collins, Robert 0.　　　　　　**DT20**
　(Editor, Contribution by)
Problems in African History: The Precolonial Centuries. Ed. 2.
Paper Text. Markus Wiener Publishers, Inc. Princeton, NJ. 2005.
ISBN:1-55876-360-0, ISBN13: 978-1-55876-360-9. Dewey:960.

Audience: **g,l,u,f.**

Collins, Robert O.　　　　　　**DT30.C567 1996**
　(Editor, Introduction by)
Problems in the History of Modern Africa. James M. Burns &
Erik C. Chung (Editors). Paper Text. Markus Wiener Publishers,
Inc. Princeton, NJ. 1997. 320p. Problems in African History
Ser., Vol. III ISBN:1-55876-124-1, ISBN13: 978-1-55876-124-7.
Dewey:960.3/2. LCCN:96-028368.

Audience: **g,l,u,f.**

Collins, Robert O.　　　　　　**DT29.H57 1994**
　(Editor, Introduction by)
Historical Problems of Imperial Africa. Paper Text. Markus
Wiener Publishers, Inc. Princeton, NJ. 1994. 320p.
ISBN:1-55876-060-1, ISBN13: 978-1-55876-060-8.
Dewey:960.3. LCCN:93-027132.

Audience: **g,l,u,f.**

Connah, Graham　　　　　　**DT352.3.C66 2001**
African Civilizations: An Archaeological Perspective. Ed. 2.
Douglas Hobbs (Illustrator). Cloth Text. Cambridge University

Press. New York, NY. 2001. 356p. ISBN:0-521-59309-3,
ISBN13: 978-0-521-59309-0. Dewey:967/.01. LCCN:00-033704.

Audience: **g,u,f.**

Coquery-Vidrovitch,　　　　　**HT148.A357**
　Catherine
History of African Cities South of the Sahara: From Origins to
Colonization. Mary Baker (Translator). Trade Cloth. Markus
Wiener Publishers, Inc. Princeton, NJ. 2005. 440p.
ISBN:1-55876-302-3, ISBN13: 978-1-55876-302-9.
Dewey:307.76/0967. LCCN:2004-022622.

Audience: **g,l,u,f.** *Choice, 2005.*

Coquery-Vidrovitch,　　　　　**HQ1787.C6613 1997**
　Catherine
African Women: A Modern History. Beth G. Raps (Translator).
Trade Paper. Westview Press. Boulder, CO. 1997. 336p. Social
Change in Global Perspective Ser. ISBN:0-8133-2360-6,
ISBN13: 978-0-8133-2360-2. Dewey:305.4/0967.
LCCN:96-047847.

Audience: **g,l,u,f.** *Choice, 1997.*

Davidson, Basil
　(Performed by)
Africa, Pt. 2. Video, VHS Format. Facets Multimedia, Inc.
Chicago, IL.

Audience: **g,l,u,f.**

Davidson, Basil
　(Performed by)
Africa, Pt. 1. Video, VHS Format. Facets Multimedia, Inc.
Chicago, IL.

Audience: **g,l,u,f.**

Davidson, Basil　　　　　　**DT20.D28**
　Risbridger
Africa in History. Trade Paper. Simon & Schuster. New York,
NY. 1995. 480p. ISBN:0-684-82667-4, ISBN13:
978-0-684-82667-7. Dewey:960.

Audience: **g,l,u,f.**

Davidson, Basil　　　　　　**HT1321**
　Risbridger
African Slave Trade. Trade Paper. Little Brown & Company.
New York, NY. 1988. 304p. ISBN:0-316-17438-6, ISBN13:
978-0-316-17438-1. Dewey:306.3/62/096.

Audience: **g,l,u,f.**

Davidson, Basil　　　　　　**DT352.4**
　Risbridger
Lost Cities of Africa. Trade Paper. Little Brown & Company.
New York, NY. 1988. 366p. ISBN:0-316-17431-9, ISBN13:
978-0-316-17431-2. Dewey:960.

Audience: **g,l,u,f.**

Diop, Cheikh Anta　　　　　　**DT61**
The African Origin of Civilization: Myth or Reality. Mercer
Cook (Editor, Translator). Trade Paper. Chicago Review Press,
Inc. Chicago, IL. 1989. 317p. ISBN:1-55652-072-7, ISBN13:
978-1-55652-072-3. Dewey:932.01. LCCN:73-081746.

Audience: **g,l,u,f.**

Ehret, Christopher　　　　　　**DT14.E36 2002**
The Civilizations of Africa: A History to 1800. Trade Cloth.
University Press of Virginia. Charlottesville, VA. 2002. 480p.
ISBN:0-8139-2084-1, ISBN13: 978-0-8139-2084-9.
Dewey:960.1. LCCN:2001-005038.

Audience: **g,u,f.**

Fage, J. D. & Tordoff, William   DT20.F33 2001
A History of Africa. Ed. 4. Paper over Boards. Routledge. New York, NY. 2001. 640p. ISBN:0-415-25247-4, ISBN13: 978-0-415-25247-8. Dewey:960. LCCN:2001-031915.
Audience: **g,l,u,f.** *B*

Falola, Toyin (Editor)   DT20.A61785 2000
Africa, Vol. 4. Trade Paper. Carolina Academic Press. Durham, NC. 2002. 564p. ISBN:0-89089-202-4, ISBN13: 978-0-89089-202-2. Dewey:960. LCCN:00-035789.
Audience: **g,l,u,f.**

Falola, Toyin (Editor)   DT20.A61785 2000
Africa: African Cultures and Societies Before 1885. Trade Paper. Carolina Academic Press. Durham, NC. 2000. 356p. ISBN:0-89089-769-7, ISBN13: 978-0-89089-769-0. Dewey:960. LCCN:00-035789.
Audience: **g,l,u,f.**

Falola, Toyin (Editor)   DT20 .A61785 2000
Africa: Contemporary Africa, Vol. 5. Trade Cloth. Carolina Academic Press. Durham, NC. 2002. ISBN:0-89089-203-2, ISBN13: 978-0-89089-203-9. Dewey:960. LCCN:00-035789.
Audience: **g,l,u,f.**

Falola, Toyin (Editor)   DT20.A61785 2000
Africa: African History Before 1885. Trade Paper. Carolina Academic Press. Durham, NC. 2000. 468p. ISBN:0-89089-768-9, ISBN13: 978-0-89089-768-3. Dewey:960. LCCN:00-035789.
Audience: **g,l,u,f.**

Falola, Toyin (Editor)   DT20
Africa: Colonial Africa 1885-1939, Vol. 3. Trade Paper. Carolina Academic Press. Durham, NC. 2002. 480p. ISBN:0-89089-770-0, ISBN13: 978-0-89089-770-6. Dewey:960. LCCN:00-035789.
Audience: **g,l,u,f.**

Falola, Toyin & Jennings, Christian (Editors)   DT15
Sources and Methods in African History: Spoken, Written, Unearthed. Trade Paper. University of Rochester Press. Rochester, NY. 2004. 300p. Rochester Studies in African History and the Diaspora Ser. ISBN:1-58046-140-9, ISBN13: 978-1-58046-140-5. Dewey:960/.01.
Audience: **g,l,u,f.** *Choice, 2003.*

Fyle, C. Magbaily   DT20.F95 1999
Introduction to the History of African Civilization: Precolonial Africa. Trade Paper. University Press of America, Inc. Lanham, MD. 1999. 192p. ISBN:0-7618-1456-6, ISBN13: 978-0-7618-1456-6. Dewey:960. LCCN:99-034960.
Audience: **g,l,u,f.**

Fyle, C. Magbaily   DT20
Introduction to the History of African Civilization: Colonial and Post-Colonial Africa. Trade Paper. University Press of America, Inc. Lanham, MD. 2001. 202p. ISBN:0-7618-2107-4, ISBN13: 978-0-7618-2107-6. Dewey:960.
Audience: **g,l,u,f.**

Geiger, Susan (Editor), et al.   HQ1787.W655 2002
Women in African Colonial Histories: An Introduction. Nakanyike Musisi & Jean Marie Allman (Editors). Trade Paper. Indiana University Press. Bloomington, IN. 2002. 352p.

ISBN:0-253-21507-2, ISBN13: 978-0-253-21507-9. Dewey:305.4/096. LCCN:2001-003447.
Audience: **g,l,u,f.** *Choice, 2002.*

Hargreaves, John D.   DT29.H37 1996
Decolonization in Africa. Ed. 2. Trade Paper. Pearson Education. Boston, MA. 2002. 320p. The Postwar World Ser. ISBN:0-582-24917-1, ISBN13: 978-0-582-24917-2. Dewey:960.3/2. LCCN:95-041858.
Audience: **g,l,u,f.** *Choice, 1989.*

Henige, David P.   DT19 .H46
The Chronology of Oral Tradition: Quest for a Chimera. Trade Cloth. Oxford University Press, Inc. New York, NY. 1974. xiii, 265p. Oxford Studies in African Affairs ISBN:0-19-821694-7, ISBN13: 978-0-19-821694-0. Dewey:960/.072. LCCN:74-171156.
Audience: **g,l,u,f.** *B*

Isaacman, Allen & Roberts, Richard (Editors)   DT352.7.C68 1995
Cotton, Colonialism, and Social History in Sub-Saharan Africa. Trade Cloth. Heinemann. Portsmouth, NH. 1995. 314p. Social History of Africa Ser. ISBN:0-435-08966-8, ISBN13: 978-0-435-08966-5. Dewey:330.967/03. LCCN:94-45083.
Audience: **u,f.**

Levtzion, Nehemia   BP64.A1H62 2000
The History of Islam in Africa. Randall L. Pouwels (Contribution by). Trade Paper. Ohio University Press. Athens, OH. 2000. 601p. ISBN:0-8214-1297-3, ISBN13: 978-0-8214-1297-8. Dewey:297/.096/09. LCCN:99-027729.
Audience: **u,f.** *Choice, 2000.*

Lovejoy, Paul E.   HT1321 .L68 2000
Transformations in Slavery: A History of Slavery in Africa. Ed. 2. David Anderson, Carolyn Brown, Christopher Clapham, Michael Gomez, Patrick Manning, David Robinson & Leonardo A. Villalon (Contribution by). Cloth Text. Cambridge University Press. New York, NY. 2000. 352p. African Studies Ser., Vol. 36 ISBN:0-521-78012-8, ISBN13: 978-0-521-78012-4. Dewey:306.3/62/096. LCCN:99-059862.
Audience: **u,f.** *B*

Mazrui, Ali (Hosted by)
The Africans Series. Video, VHS Format. Filmic Archives. Botsford, CT.
Audience: **g,l,u,f.**

Miers, Suzanne & Roberts, Richard L. (Editors)   HT1323.E53 1988
The End of Slavery in Africa. Cloth Text. University of Wisconsin Press. Chicago, IL. 1989. 448p. ISBN:0-299-11550-X, ISBN13: 978-0-299-11550-0. Dewey:306/.362/096. LCCN:88-040192.
Audience: **u,f.**

Neale, Caroline   DT19
Writing: African Historiography, 1960-1980. Trade Cloth. Greenwood Publishing Group, Inc. Portsmouth, NH. 1985. 208p. Contributions in Afro-American and African Studies Ser., No. 85 ISBN:0-313-24652-1, ISBN13: 978-0-313-24652-4. Dewey:960/.072. LCCN:84-015756.
Audience: **g,l,u,f.** *B* *Choice, 1985.*

Oliver, Roland   DT20.O386 2000
African Experience: From Olduvai Gorge to the 21st Century. Ed. 2. Trade Paper. Westview Press. Boulder, CO. 2000. 368p.

ISBN:0-8133-9042-7, ISBN13: 978-0-8133-9042-0. Dewey:960.
LCCN:00-044775.

Audience: **g,l,u,f.**

Oliver, Roland &   **DT28.O4 2004**
  Atmore, Anthony
Africa Since 1800. Ed. 5. Trade Paper. Cambridge University
Press. New York, NY. 2005. 414p. ISBN:0-521-54474-2,
ISBN13: 978-0-521-54474-0. Dewey:960/.23.
LCCN:2003-063544.

Audience: **g,l,u,f.**

Phillipson, David W.   **GN861.P47 2004**
African Archaeology. Ed. 3. Cloth Text. Cambridge University
Press. New York, NY. 2005. 404p. ISBN:0-521-83236-5,
ISBN13: 978-0-521-83236-6. Dewey:960/.1.
LCCN:2004-049657.

Audience: **g,l,u,f.** *B Choice, 1985.*

Robinson, David   **BP64.A1R63 2004**
Muslim Societies in African History. Martin Klein (Contribution
by). Trade Paper. Cambridge University Press. New York, NY.
2004. 240p. New Approaches to African History Ser.
ISBN:0-521-53366-X, ISBN13: 978-0-521-53366-9.
Dewey:297/.096. LCCN:2003-055137.

Audience: **g,l,u,f.**

Shillington, Kevin   **DT20**
  (Editor)
Encyclopedia of African History, Set. Library Binding. Fitzroy
Dearborn Publishers, Inc. Chicago, IL. 2004. 1912p.
ISBN:1-57958-245-1, ISBN13: 978-1-57958-245-6.
Dewey:960/.03. LCCN:2004-016779.

Audience: **g,l,u,f.** *Choice, 2005.*

Shillington, Kevin   **DT20 .S47 2005**
History of Africa. Ed. 3. Trade Paper. Palgrave Macmillan. New
York, NY. 2005. 450p. ISBN:0-333-59957-8, ISBN13:
978-0-333-59957-0. Dewey:960. LCCN:2005-284260.

Audience: **g,l,u,f.**

Stahl, Ann (Editor)   **DT13**
African Archaeology: A Critical Introduction. Trade Paper.
Blackwell Publishing, Inc. Malden, MA. 2004. 512p. Blackwell
Studies in Global Archaeology ISBN:1-4051-0156-3, ISBN13:
978-1-4051-0156-1. Dewey:960/.1/072. LCCN:2004-003052.

Audience: **g,l,u,f.** *Choice, 2005.*

Temu, A. J. & Swai, B.   **DT19**
Historians and Africanist History: A Critique. Trade Cloth. Zed
Books, Ltd. London, 1981. 206p. ISBN:0-905762-78-9, ISBN13:
978-0-905762-78-4. Dewey:960/.07206.

Audience: **g,l,u,f.**

History of Africa > History > Since 1945

Carter, Gwendolen M.   **DT30.5.A356 1985**
  & O'Meara, Patrick (Editors)
African Independence: The First Twenty-Five Years. Paper Text.
Indiana University Press. Bloomington, IN. 1986. 380p.
ISBN:0-253-20348-1, ISBN13: 978-0-253-20348-9.
Dewey:960/.32. LCCN:84-048457.

Audience: **g,l,u,f.** *B Choice, 1985.*

Cooper, Frederick   **DT30.C595 2002**
Africa since 1940: The Past of the Present. Martin Klein
(Contribution by). Trade Paper. Cambridge University Press.
New York, NY. 2002. 230p. New Approaches to African History

Ser. ISBN:0-521-77600-7, ISBN13: 978-0-521-77600-4.
Dewey:960.3/2. LCCN:2001-043657.

Audience: **g,l,u,f.** *Choice, 2003.*

Davidson, Basil   **BL1245.S5S58**
  Risbridger
The Black Man's Burden: Africa and the Curse of the
Nation-State. Trade Paper. Crown Publishing Group. New York,
NY. 1993. 368p. ISBN:0-8129-2210-7, ISBN13:
978-0-8129-2210-3. Dewey:181/.4. LCCN:92-038427.

Audience: **u,f.**

Gifford, Prosser &   **DT30.5.D42 1988**
  Louis, William Roger
Decolonization and African Independence: The Transfers of
Power 1960-1980. Trade Cloth. Yale University Press.
Cumberland, RI. 1988. 736p. ISBN:0-300-04070-9, ISBN13:
978-0-300-04070-8. Dewey:960/.32. LCCN:87-014756.

Audience: **g,l,u,f.** *Choice, 1989.*

Gifford, Prosser &   **DT30**
  Louis, William Roger
The Transfer in Power of Africa: Decolonization, 1940-1960.
Trade Paper. Yale University Press. Cumberland, RI. 1988.
656p. ISBN:0-300-04348-1, ISBN13: 978-0-300-04348-8.
Dewey:960/.324. LCCN:81-001931.

Audience: **g,l,u,f.**

Jackson, Robert H. Jr.   **JQ1879.A15**
  & Rosberg, Carl G.
Personal Rule in Black Africa: Prince, Autocrat, Prophet, Tyrant.
Trade Paper. University of California Press. Berkeley, CA. 1982.
350p. ISBN:0-520-04209-3, ISBN13: 978-0-520-04209-4.
Dewey:321.6. LCCN:80-025439.

Audience: **u,f.** *B*

July, Robert   **JA71**
The Origins of Modern African Thought. Trade Cloth. Africa
World Press. Trenton, NJ. 2004. 524p. ISBN:1-59221-199-2,
ISBN13: 978-1-59221-199-9. Dewey:320/.01.

Audience: **u,f.**

July, Robert W.   **DT14.J85 1987**
An African Voice: The Role of the Humanities in African
Independence. Paper Text. Duke University Press. Durham, NC.
1987. xii, 270p. ISBN:0-8223-0769-3, ISBN13:
978-0-8223-0769-3. Dewey:960/.3. LCCN:87-005358.

Audience: **u,f.** *Choice, 1987.*

Le Vine, Victor T.   **JQ3360.L425 2004**
Politics in Francophone Africa. Library Binding. Lynne Rienner
Publishers, Inc. Boulder, CO. 2004. 425p. ISBN:1-58826-249-9,
ISBN13: 978-1-58826-249-3. Dewey:320.966/0917/541.
LCCN:2004-001833.

Audience: **g,l,u,f.** *Choice, 2005.*

Mazrui, Ali A. & Tidy,   **DT30**
  Michael
Nationalism and New States in Africa: From about 1935 to the
Present. Trade Paper. Heinemann. Portsmouth, NH. 1984. xxix,
402p. ISBN:0-435-94146-1, ISBN13: 978-0-435-94146-8.
Dewey:960/.32. LCCN:84-107948.

Audience: **u,f.** *B*

Nkrumah, Kwame   **DT30.N45 1970**
Africa Must Unite. Trade Cloth. International Publishers
Company, Inc. New York, NY. 1970. 248p.

ISBN:0-7178-0295-7, ISBN13: 978-0-7178-0295-1. Dewey:960. LCCN:70-140209.

Audience: **u,f.** *B*

Nugent, Paul　　　　　　　　　　　**DT30.5.N84 2004**
Africa since Independence: A Comparative History. Cloth over Boards. Palgrave Macmillan. New York, NY. 2004. 624p. ISBN:0-333-68272-6, ISBN13: 978-0-333-68272-2. Dewey:960.3/2. LCCN:2004-044503.

Audience: **g,l,u,f.** *Choice, 2005.*

Setel, Philip (Editor), et al.　　　　　　　　　　　**RA644**
Histories of Sexually Transmitted Diseases and HIV/AIDS in Sub-Saharan Africa. Milton Lewis & Maryinez Lyons (Editors). Trade Cloth. Greenwood Publishing Group, Inc. Portsmouth, NH. 1999. 280p. Contributions in Medical Studies, Vol. 44 ISBN:0-313-29715-0, ISBN13: 978-0-313-29715-1. Dewey:616.95/1/00967. LCCN:98-038207.

Audience: **u,f.**

History of Africa > History > Diplomatic and Political History

Boahen, A. Adu　　　　　　　　　　**JV246.B63 1989**
African Perspectives on Colonialism. Trade Paper. Johns Hopkins University Press. Baltimore, MD. 1995. 144p. The Johns Hopkins Symposia in Comparative History Ser. ISBN:0-8018-3931-9, ISBN13: 978-0-8018-3931-3. Dewey:325.6. LCCN:87-002769.

Audience: **u,f.** *Choice, 1988.*

Coleman, James S.　　　　　　　　**JQ1879.A15C64 1994**
Nationalism and Development in Africa: Selected Essays. Richard L. Sklar (Editor). Trade Cloth. University of California Press. Berkeley, CA. 1994. 380p. ISBN:0-520-08374-1, ISBN13: 978-0-520-08374-5. Dewey:320.96. LCCN:93-025774.

Audience: **u,f.** *Choice, 1995.*

Decalo, Samuel　　　　　　　　　**DT30.5.D39 1990**
Coups and Army Rule in Africa: Motivations and Constraints. Ed. 2. Trade Paper. Yale University Press. Cumberland, RI. 1990. 368p. ISBN:0-300-04045-8, ISBN13: 978-0-300-04045-6. Dewey:322/.5/096. LCCN:89-049077.

Audience: **u,f.**

Falola, Toyin　　　　　　　　　　　**DT14**
Nationalism and African Intellectuals. Trade Paper. University of Rochester Press. Rochester, NY. 2004. 256p. Rochester Studies in African History and the Diaspora Ser. ISBN:1-58046-149-2, ISBN13: 978-1-58046-149-8. Dewey:305.5/52/096.

Audience: **u,f.** *Choice, 2001.*

Geiss, Imanuel　　　　　　　　　**DT31.G5513**
The Pan-African Movement: A History of Pan-Africanism in America, Europe and Africa. Trade Cloth. Holmes & Meier Publishers, Inc. Teaneck, NJ. 1974. 546p. ISBN:0-8419-0161-9, ISBN13: 978-0-8419-0161-2. Dewey:320.5/4/096. LCCN:74-078310.

Audience: **g,l,u,f.** *B*

Howard, Rhoda E.　　　　　　　**JC599.A36H68 1986**
Human Rights in Commonwealth Africa. Trade Cloth. Rowman & Littlefield Publishers, Inc. Lanham, MD. 1986. 264p. ISBN:0-8476-7433-9, ISBN13: 978-0-8476-7433-6. Dewey:323.4/096. LCCN:86-003860.

Audience: **g,l,u,f.** *Choice, 1987.*

Leonard, David K. & Straus, Scott　　　　　　**HC800.L465 2003**
Africa's Stalled Development: International Causes and Cures. Paper Text. Lynne Rienner Publishers, Inc. Boulder, CO. 2003. 150p. ISBN:1-58826-116-6, ISBN13: 978-1-58826-116-8. Dewey:338.967. LCCN:2002-031839.

Audience: **u,f.** *Choice, 2003.*

Mamdani, Mahmood　　　　　　　**JV246.M35 1996**
Citizen and Subject: Contemporary Africa and the Legacy of Late Colonialism. Trade Paper. Princeton University Press. Princeton, NJ. 1996. 368p. Princeton Studies in Culture/Power/History Ser. ISBN:0-691-02793-5, ISBN13: 978-0-691-02793-7. Dewey:960. LCCN:95-025318.

Audience: **u,f.** *Choice, 1996.*

Markovitz, Irving L. (Editor)　　　　　　**JQ1872.S78 1987**
Studies in Power and Class in Africa. Paper Text. Oxford University Press, Inc. New York, NY. 1987. 415p. ISBN:0-19-504130-5, ISBN13: 978 0 19 504130-9. Dewey:306/.2/096. LCCN:86-008573.

Audience: **u,f.** *Choice, 1987.*

Martin, Guy　　　　　　　　　　**DT30.5.M275 2000**
Africa in World Politics: A Pan-African Perspective. Trade Paper. Africa World Press. Trenton, NJ. 2003. 328p. ISBN:0-86543-858-7, ISBN13: 978-0-86543-858-3. Dewey:327/.096. LCCN:00-030616.

Audience: **g,l,u,f.**

McCarthy-Arnolds, Eileen (Editor), et al.　　　　　　　**JC599**
Africa, Human Rights, and the Global System: The Political Economy of Human Rights in a Changing World, 15. David R. Penna & Debra Joy Cruz Sobrepena (Editors). Trade Cloth. Greenwood Publishing Group, Inc. Portsmouth, NH. 1993. 288p. Studies in Human Rights Ser. ISBN:0-313-29007-5, ISBN13: 978-0-313-29007-7. Dewey:323/.096. LCCN:93-001643.

Audience: **u,f.** *Choice, 1994.*

Rodney, Walter　　　　　　　　　**HC800.R62 1981**
How Europe Underdeveloped Africa. Vincent Harding, Robert Hill & William Strickland (Introduction by). Trade Paper. Howard University Press. Washington, DC. 1982. 312p. ISBN:0-88258-096-5, ISBN13: 978-0-88258-096-8. Dewey:330.96. LCCN:81-006240.

Audience: **g,l,u,f.**

Sherwood, Marika & Adi, Hakim　　　　　　**DT30.S515 2003**
Pan-African History: Political Figures from Africa and the Diaspora since 1787. Trade Paper. Routledge. New York, NY. 2003. 224p. ISBN:0-415-17353-1, ISBN13: 978-0-415-17353-7. Dewey:320.54/9/092396. LCCN:2002-011566.

Audience: **g,l,u,f.** *Choice, 2003.*

Sithole, Ndabaningi   DT31
African Nationalism. Ed. 2. Trade Cloth. Oxford University
Press, Inc. New York, NY. 1969. ISBN:0-19-501053-1, ISBN13:
978-0-19-501053-4. Dewey:320.1/58/096. LCCN:68-133467.
Audience: **g,l,u,f.** *B*

History of Africa > History > Relations with Particular Countries

Birmingham, David   DT36.B56 2004
Portugal and Africa. Trade Paper. Ohio University Press. Athens,
OH. 2004. 216p. Papers in International Studies: Africa Ser.
ISBN:0-89680-237-X, ISBN13: 978-0-89680-237-7.
Dewey:960/.09712469. LCCN:2004-004405.
Audience: **g,l,u,f.**

Clough, Michael   DT38.7 .C57 1992
Free at Last?: U. S. Policy Toward Africa and the End of the
Cold War. Trade Paper. Council on Foreign Relations. New
York, NY. 1992. 160p. ISBN:0-87609-104-4, ISBN13:
978-0-87609-104-3. Dewey:327.73067. LCCN:91-043338.
Audience: **u,f.**

Cohen, William B.   DT33.3
The French Encounter with Africans: White Response to Blacks,
1530-1880. James D. Le Sueur (Foreword by). Trade Cloth.
Indiana University Press. Bloomington, IN. 2003. 384p.
ISBN:0-253-21650-8, ISBN13: 978-0-253-21650-2.
Dewey:325/.344/096. LCCN:2003-278283.
Audience: **g,l,u,f.** *B*

Digre, Brian   D651.A4D54 1990
Imperialism's New Clothes: The Repartition of Tropical Africa,
1914-1919. Cloth Text. Peter Lang Publishing, Inc. New York,
NY. 1990. XIV, 225p. American University Studies, Ser. IX,
Vol. 79:History ISBN:0-8204-1120-5, ISBN13:
978-0-8204-1120-0. Dewey:940.3/1424. LCCN:89-028908.
Audience: **u,f.** *Choice, 1990.*

Fanon, Frantz   DT33.F313 2004
The Wretched of the Earth. Trade Paper. Grove/Atlantic, Inc.
New York, NY. 2004. 256p. ISBN:0-8021-4132-3, ISBN13:
978-0-8021-4132-3. Dewey:960/.0971244. LCCN:2004-042476.
Audience: **g,l,u,f.** *B*

Gifford, Prosser   DT32
(Editor)
France and Britain in Africa: Imperial Rivalry and Colonial
Rule. Trade Cloth. Yale University Press. Cumberland, RI. 1972.
xix, 989p. ISBN:0-300-01289-6, ISBN13: 978-0-300-01289-7.
Dewey:960. LCCN:70-151574.
Audience: **u,f.** *B*

Gifford, Prosser &   DT0032.B73
Louis, Roger W. (Editors)
Britain and Germany in Africa: Imperial Rivalry and Colonial
Rule. Trade Paper. Books on Demand. Ann Arbor, MI. 847p.
ISBN:0-8357-7405-8, ISBN13: 978-0-8357-7405-5.
Dewey:325.6. LCCN:67-024500.
Audience: **u,f.**

Lugard, Frederick J.   DT32.5
Dual Mandate in British Tropical Africa. Cloth Text. Taylor &
Francis Group. Abingdon, 1965. 643p. ISBN:0-7146-1690-7,
ISBN13: 978-0-7146-1690-2. Dewey:325.341096.
Audience: **u,f.**

MacQueen, Norrie   DT36.5.M33 1997
The Decolonization of Portuguese Africa: Metropolitan
Revolution and the Dissolution of Empire. Paper Text. Longman
Publishing Group. White Plains, NY. 1997. 266p.
ISBN:0-582-25993-2, ISBN13: 978-0-582-25993-5.
Dewey:960/.097569. LCCN:96-034685.
Audience: **u,f.** *Choice, 1997.*

Manning, Patrick   DT532.5 .M365 1998
Francophone Sub-Saharan Africa, 1880-1995. Ed. 2. Cloth Text.
Cambridge University Press. New York, NY. 1999. 258p.
ISBN:0-521-64255-8, ISBN13: 978-0-521-64255-2.
Dewey:966/.0097541. LCCN:98-038091.
Audience: **g,l,u,f.**

McKinley, Edward H.   DT38.M33
The Lure of Africa: American Interests in Tropical Africa,
1919-1939. Trade Cloth. Macmillan Publishing Company, Inc.
Old Tappan, NJ. 1974. x, 293p. ISBN:0-672-51736-1, ISBN13:
978-0-672-51736-5. Dewey:301.29/73/067. LCCN:73-001789.
Audience: **g,l,u,f.** *B*

Newitt, M. D. D.   DT36.5
Portugal in Africa: The Last Hundred Years. Longman. 1981.
ISBN:0-582-64379-1, ISBN13: 978-0-582-64379-6.
Audience: **g,l,u,f.**

Ohaegbulam, Festus   DT38.7.O39 2005
Ugboaja
Dimensions of U.S. Role in Conflict Resolution: Four Case
Studies in Post-Colonial Africa. Trade Cloth. Peter Lang
Publishing, Inc. New York, NY. 2004. 296p.
ISBN:0-8204-7091-0, ISBN13: 978-0-8204-7091-7.
Dewey:327.7306/09/045. LCCN:2003-025258.
Audience: **u,f.** *Choice, 2005.*

Robinson, Ronald   DT32.R55
Edward
Africa and the Victorians: The Climax of Imperialism in the
Dark Continent,. Paper Text. Textbook Publishers. Temecula,
CA. 2003. xii, 491p. ISBN:0-7581-3581-5, ISBN13:
978-0-7581-3581-0. Dewey:325.342096.
Audience: **g,l,u,f.**

Snow, Philip   DT38.9.C5S56 1989
The Star Raft: China's Encounters with Africa. Trade Paper.
Cornell University Press. Ithaca, NY. 1989. 288p.
ISBN:0-8014-9583-0, ISBN13: 978-0-8014-9583-0.
Dewey:303.4/8251/06. LCCN:88-043399.
Audience: **g,l,u,f.** *Choice, 1989.*

Stoecker, H. (Editor)   DT34.5.D713 1986
German Imperialism in Africa: From the Beginnings until the
Second World War. Cloth Text. Brill Academic Publishers, Inc.
Boston, MA. 1987. 448p. ISBN:0-391-03383-2, ISBN13:
978-0-391-03383-2. Dewey:325/.343/09609034.
LCCN:86-000280.
Audience: **g,l,u,f.**

Worger, William H., et   DT353.5.E9A34 2001
al.
Africa and the West: A Documentary History from the Slave
Trade to Independence. Nancy L. Clark & Edward A. Alpers
(Authors), Barbara A. Burg, Richard Newman & Elizabeth E.
Sandager (Editors). Book, Other. Greenwood Publishing Group,
Inc. Portsmouth, NH. 2001. 400p. The Great Cultural Eras of
the World Ser. ISBN:1-57356-247-5, ISBN13:
978-1-57356-247-8. Dewey:967/.02. LCCN:00-010718.
Audience: **g,l,u,f.** *Choice, 2001.*

History of Africa > Egypt

Abu-Lughod, Janet L.   DT143.A26
Cairo: One Thousand-One Years of the City Victorious. Cloth Text. Princeton University Press. Princeton, NJ. 1971. 304p. Near East Studies ISBN:0-691-03085-5, ISBN13: 978-0-691-03085-2. Dewey:962/.16. LCCN:73-112992.
Audience: **g,l,u,f.** *B*

Baines, John & Malek,   DT60.B34 2000
Jaromir
Cultural Atlas of Ancient Egypt. Trade Cloth. Facts On File, Inc. New York, NY. 2000. 240p. Cultural Atlas Ser. ISBN:0-8160-4036-2, ISBN13: 978-0-8160-4036-0. Dewey:932. LCCN:99-057588.
Audience: **g,l,u,f.**

Breasted, James Henry   DT57.B76
Ancient Records of Egypt: Historical Documents from the Earliest Times to the Persian Conquest. Paper Text. Textbook Publishers. Temecula, CA. 2003. ISBN:0-7581-4349-4, ISBN13: 978-0-7581-4349-5. Dewey:932.
Audience: **g,l,u,f.** *B*

Dunand, Francoise &   BL2441.3.D8613 2004
Zivie-Coche, Christiane
Gods and Men in Egypt: 3000 B. C. E. to 395 C. E. David Lorton (Translator). Book, Other. Cornell University Press. Ithaca, NY. 2005. 400p. ISBN:0-8014-4165-X, ISBN13: 978-0-8014-4165-3. Dewey:299/.31. LCCN:2004-001927.
Audience: **u,f.** *Choice, 2005.*

Erman, Adolf   DT61
Life in Ancient Egypt. Trade Paper. Kessinger Publishing, LLC. Whitefish, MT. 2003. ISBN:0-7661-7660-6, ISBN13: 978-0-7661-7660-7. Dewey:913.32/03/1.
Audience: **g,l,u,f.**

Fraser, P M   DT73.A4
Ptolemaic Alexandria. Oxford University Press, Inc. 1985. ISBN:0-19-814278-1, ISBN13: 978-0-19-814278-2.
Audience: **u,f.** *B*

Harris, James E. &   DT62.M7H37
Weeks, Kent R.
X-Raying the Pharaohs. Trade Cloth. Simon & Schuster. New York, NY. 1980. 265p. Encore Editions Ser. ISBN:0-684-16899-5, ISBN13: 978-0-684-16899-9. Dewey:913.32. LCCN:72-001180.
Audience: **g,l,u,f.** *B*

Ikram, Salima   DT62.T6
Death and Burial in Ancient Egypt. Cloth Text. Longman Publishing Group. White Plains, NY. 2003. 256p. ISBN:0-582-77216-8, ISBN13: 978-0-582-77216-8. Dewey:393/.0932.
Audience: **g,l,u,f.** *Choice, 2003.*

James, T. G. H.   DT61
Pharaoh's People: Scenes from Life in Imperial Egypt. Trade Paper. I. B. Tauris & Company, Ltd. London, 2003. 282p. ISBN:1-86064-832-0, ISBN13: 978-1-86064-832-8. Dewey:932.
Audience: **g,l,u,f.**

Mertz, Barbara   DT61.M54 1990
Red Land, Black Land: Daily Life in Ancient Egypt. Trade Paper. School Specialty Publishing. Columbus, OH. 1990. 386p.

ISBN:0-87226-222-7, ISBN13: 978-0-87226-222-5. Dewey:932. LCCN:89-017875.
Audience: **g,l,u,f.** *B*

Meskell, Lynn   DT61
Private Life in New Kingdom Egypt. Trade Paper. Princeton University Press. Princeton, NJ. 2004. 256p. ISBN:0-691-12058-7, ISBN13: 978-0-691-12058-4. Dewey:932/.014. LCCN:2001-096893.
Audience: **g,l,u,f.** *Choice, 2003, 2002.*

Raymond, Andre   DT143
Cairo. Trade Cloth. Universe Publishing. New York, NY. 2003. 496p. ISBN:0-7893-1022-8, ISBN13: 978-0-7893-1022-4. Dewey:962/.16.
Audience: **u,f.** *Choice, 2001.*

Redford, Donald B.   DT83.R4 2004
From Slave to Pharaoh: The Black Experience of Ancient Egypt. Trade Cloth. Johns Hopkins University Press. Baltimore, MD. 2004. 232p. ISBN:0-8018-7814-4, ISBN13: 978-0-8018-7814-5. Dewey:932/.015. LCCN:2003-010639.
Audience: **u,f.** *Choice, 2005.*

Smith, Craig B. &   DT63.S6 2006
Hawass, Zahi
How the Great Pyramid Was Built. Trade Paper. HarperCollins Publishers. New York, NY. 2006. 288p. ISBN:0-06-089158-0, ISBN13: 978-0-06-089158-9. Dewey:932. LCCN:2005-057970.
Audience: **g,l,u,f.**

Tyldesley, Joyce A.   HQ1137.E3
Daughters of Isis: Women of Ancient Egypt. Trade Paper. Penguin Group (USA) Inc. New York, NY. 1995. 336p. ISBN:0-14-017596-2, ISBN13: 978-0-14-017596-7. Dewey:932/.01/082. LCCN:95-047067.
Audience: **u,f.**

Verner, Miroslav   DT63
The Pyramids: The Mystery, Culture, and Science of Egypt's Greatest Monuments. Steve Rendall (Translator). Trade Paper. Grove/Atlantic, Inc. New York, NY. 2002. 512p. ISBN:0-8021-3935-3, ISBN13: 978-0-8021-3935-1. Dewey:932.
Audience: **g,l,u,f.**

Wilson, John A.   DT60 .W65
Signs and Wonders Upon Pharaoh. Trade Cloth. University of Chicago Press. Chicago, IL. 1964. ISBN:0-226-90149-1, ISBN13: 978-0-226-90149-7. Dewey:913.32. LCCN:64-023535.
Audience: **g,l,u,f.**

Wilson, John Albert   DT61.W56
The Burden of Egypt: An Interpretation of Ancient Egyptian Culture. Paper Text. Textbook Publishers. Temecula, CA. 2003. xix, 332p. ISBN:0-7581-2479-1, ISBN13: 978-0-7581-2479-1. Dewey:913.32.
Audience: **g,l,u,f.** *B*

History of Africa > Egypt > History

Vatikiotis, Panayiotis J.   DT107
The History of Egypt. Ed. 2. Baltimore: Johns Hopkins University Press. 1980. Asia Africa Series of Modern Histories ISBN:0-8018-2339-0, ISBN13: 978-0-8018-2339-8.
Audience: **g,l,u,f.**

Audience: g=general, l=lower division undergraduate, u=upper division undergraduate, f=faculty.

57

Al-Sayyid-Marsot,   JQ3811
  Afaf L.
Egypt's Liberal Experiment, 1922-1936. Trade Cloth. University
of California Press. Berkeley, CA. 1977. xii, 276p.
ISBN:0-520-03109-1, ISBN13: 978-0-520-03109-8.
Dewey:320.9/62/05. LCCN:75-022659.

                          Audience: **u,f.** *B*

Aldred, Cyril   DT87.5
Akhenaten: King of Egypt. Trade Paper. Thames & Hudson.
New York, NY. 1991. 320p. ISBN:0-500-27621-8, ISBN13:
978-0-500-27621-1. Dewey:932/.014. LCCN:87-051153.

                   Audience: **u,f.** *Choice, 1989.*

Bagnall, Roger S.   DT93
Egypt in Late Antiquity. Trade Paper. Princeton University
Press. Princeton, NJ. 1995. 382p. ISBN:0-691-01096-X,
ISBN13: 978-0-691-01096-0. Dewey:932/.022.

                   Audience: **u,f.** *Choice, 1994.*

Breasted, James Henr   DT83.B782
History of Egypt from the Earliest Time. Trade Paper. Kessinger
Publishing, LLC. Whitefish, MT. 2003. ISBN:0-7661-7720-3,
ISBN13: 978-0-7661-7720-8. Dewey:932.

                   Audience: **g,l,u,f.**

Chauveau, Michel   DT61.C4613 2000
Egypt in the Age of Cleopatra: History and Society under the
Ptolemies. David Lorton (Translator). Book, Other. Cornell
University Press. Ithaca, NY. 2000. 240p. ISBN:0-8014-8576-2,
ISBN13: 978-0-8014-8576-3. Dewey:932/.021.
LCCN:99-049898.

               Audience: **g,l,u,f.** *Choice, 2000.*

Crabbs, Jack A. Jr.   DT100.C73 1984
The Writing of History in Nineteenth Century Egypt: A Study in
National Transformation. Trade Paper. Wayne State University
Press. Detroit, MI. 1984. 230p. ISBN:0-8143-1761-8, ISBN13:
978-0-8143-1761-7. Dewey:962/.03. LCCN:84-002176.

                   Audience: **u,f.** *B*

Daly, Okasha El   DT74-107.87
Egyptology: The Missing Millennium - Ancient Egypt in
Medieval Arabic Writings. Paper over Boards. Taylor & Francis
Group. Abingdon, 2005. 256p. ISBN:1-84472-063-2, ISBN13:
978-1-84472-063-7. Dewey:932. LCCN:2006-361686.

               Audience: **u,f.** *Choice, 2005.*

Fahim, Hussein M.   DT133.N79 F33 1983
Egyptian Nubians: Resettlement and Years of Coping. Trade
Cloth. University of Utah Press. Salt Lake City, UT. 1983. xiv,
197p. ISBN:0-87480-215-6, ISBN13: 978-0-87480-215-3.
Dewey:305.8/931. LCCN:82-024723.

                   Audience: **u,f.** *B*

Fernea, Robert A. &   DT135.N8
  Gerster, Georg
Nubians in Egypt: Peaceful People. Trade Cloth. University of
Texas Press. Austin, TX. 1973. 160p. ISBN:0-292-75504-X,
ISBN13: 978-0-292-75504-8. Dewey:962/.3. LCCN:73-003078.

               Audience: **g,l,u,f.** *B*

Haykal, Muhammad   DT107.83
  Hasanayan
The Road to Ramadan. Collins. 1975. ISBN:0-00-211653-7,
ISBN13: 978-0-00-211653-4.

                   Audience: **u,f.**

Hholbl, Ghunther   DT92.H6513 2000
History of the Ptolemaic Empire. Tina Saavedra (Translator).
Paper over Boards. Routledge. New York, NY. 2000. 416p.
ISBN:0-415-20145-4, ISBN13: 978-0-415-20145-2.
Dewey:932/.021. LCCN:00-020437.

               Audience: **g,l,u,f.** *Choice, 2001.*

Hopwood, Derek   DT107.825 .H66 1991
Egypt: Politics and Society, 1945-1990. Ed. 3. Audio Cassette.
G T Publishing Corporation. New York, NY. 1992. 219p.
ISBN:0-00-302028-2, ISBN13: 978-0-00-302028-1.
Dewey:962.05. LCCN:92-125105.

                   Audience: **g,l,u,f.**

Jankowski, James   DT107.827.J36 2001
Nasser's Egypt, Arab Nationalism and the United Arab
Republic. Library Binding. Lynne Rienner Publishers, Inc.
Boulder, CO. 2001. 230p. ISBN:1-58826-034-8, ISBN13:
978-1-58826-034-5. Dewey:962.05/3. LCCN:2001-031628.

               Audience: **u,f.** *Choice, 2002.*

Lewis, Naphtali   DT61
Life in Egypt under Roman Rule. Trade Paper. Oxford
University Press, Inc. New York, NY. 1986. 256p.
ISBN:0-19-814872-0, ISBN13: 978-0-19-814872-2.
Dewey:932/.02. LCCN:82-019034.

                   Audience: **g,l,u,f.**

Marsot, Afaf Lutfi   DT104 .S38 1984
  al-Sayyid
Egypt in the Reign of Muhammad Ali. Edmund Burke, Michael
C. Hudson, Walid Kazziha, Rashid Khalidi, Serif Mardin, Roger
Owen, Basim Musallam, Avi Shlaim & Malcolm Yapp
(Contribution by). Trade Paper. Cambridge University Press.
New York, NY. 1984. 320p. Cambridge Middle East Library,
No. 4 ISBN:0-521-28968-8, ISBN13: 978-0-521-28968-9.
Dewey:962/.03. LCCN:83-005241.

                   Audience: **g,l,u,f.**

Perry, Glenn E.   DT100
The History of Egypt. Cloth Text. Greenwood Publishing Group,
Inc. Portsmouth, NH. 2004. 216p. The Greenwood Histories of
the Modern Nations Ser. ISBN:0-313-32264-3, ISBN13:
978-0-313-32264-8. Dewey:962. LCCN:2004-004719.

                   Audience: **g,l,u,f.**

Russell, Mona L.   HQ1793.R87 2004
Creating the New Egyptian Woman: Consumerism, Education,
and National Identity, 1863-1922. Cloth over Boards. Palgrave
Macmillan. New York, NY. 2004. 256p. ISBN:1-4039-6262-6,
ISBN13: 978-1-4039-6262-1. Dewey:305.42/0962.
LCCN:2004-041687.

               Audience: **u,f.** *Choice, 2005.*

Shaw, Ian (Author,   DT83.O9 2003
  Editor)
The Oxford History of Ancient Egypt. Trade Paper. Oxford
University Press, Inc. New York, NY. 2004. 544p.
ISBN:0-19-280458-8, ISBN13: 978-0-19-280458-7. Dewey:932.
LCCN:2004-270015.

               Audience: **g,l,u,f.** *Choice, 2001.*

Tyldesley, Joyce A.   DT87.45.T95 1999
Nefertiti: Egypt's Sun Queen. Trade Cloth. Penguin Group
(USA) Inc. New York, NY. 1999. 300p. ISBN:0-670-86998-8,
ISBN13: 978-0-670-86998-5. LCCN:98-035469.

               Audience: **g,l,u,f.** *Choice, 1999.*

Wilkinson, Toby A. H.   **DT85**
Early Dynastic Egypt: Strategies, Society and Security. Trade
Paper. Routledge. New York, NY. 2001. 440p.
ISBN:0-415-26011-6, ISBN13: 978-0-415-26011-4.
Dewey:932/.012.
                              Audience: **u,f.**

Winter, Michael   **HN786.A8W56 1992**
Egyptian Society under Ottoman Rule, 1517-1798. Paper over
Boards. Routledge. New York, NY. 1992. 336p.
ISBN:0-415-02403-X, ISBN13: 978-0-415-02403-7.
Dewey:301.0962. LCCN:91-036457.
                        Audience: **g,l,u,f.** *Choice, 1993.*

History of Africa > Sudan

Beswick, Stephanie   **DT159.6.S73B47 2006**
Sudan's Blood Memory: The Legacy of War, Ethnicity, and
Slavery in South Sudan. Trade Paper. University of Rochester
Press. Rochester, NY. 2006. 224p. Rochester Studies in African
History and the Diaspora Ser. ISBN:1-58046-231-6, ISBN13:
978-1-58046-231-0. Dewey:962.9/023.
                        Audience: **u,f.** *Choice, 2004.*

Bianchi, Robert S.   **DT159**
Daily Life of the Nubians. Cloth Text. Greenwood Publishing
Group, Inc. Portsmouth, NH. 2004. 312p. The Greenwood Press
Daily Life Through History Ser. ISBN:0-313-32501-4, ISBN13:
978-0-313-32501-4. Dewey:939/.78. LCCN:2004-013208.
                        Audience: **g,l,u,f.** *Choice, 2005.*

Collins, Robert O.   **DT108.7.C64 2006**
The Southern Sudan in Historical Perspective. Trade Paper.
Transaction Publishers. Somerset, NJ. 2006. 101p.
ISBN:1-4128-0585-6, ISBN13: 978-1-4128-0585-8.
Dewey:962.9. LCCN:2005-044772.
                              Audience: **g,l,u,f.**

Edwards, David N.   **DT154.8.E35 2004**
The Nubian Past: An Archaeology of the Sudan. Paper over
Boards. Routledge. New York, NY. 2004. 360p.
ISBN:0-415-36987-8, ISBN13: 978-0-415-36987-9.
Dewey:939/.78. LCCN:2003-025443.
                              Audience: **u,f.**

Evans-Pritchard,   **DT132 .E78**
Edward E.
The Azande: History and Political Institutions. Trade Cloth.
Oxford University Press, Inc. New York, NY. 1971. xviii, 444p.
ISBN:0-19-823170-9, ISBN13: 978-0-19-823170-7.
Dewey:916.7. LCCN:70-889223.
                              Audience: **u,f.** ℬ

Evans-Pritchard,   **DT132**
Edward E.
The Nuer: A Description of the Modes of Livelihood and
Political Institutions of a Nilotic People. Cloth Text. Oxford
University Press, Inc. New York, NY. 1969. 284p.
ISBN:0-19-500322-5, ISBN13: 978-0-19-500322-2.
Dewey:306/.09629/3.
                              Audience: **u,f.**

Johnson, Douglas   **DT157.67.J64 2003**
Hamilton
The Root Causes of Sudan's Civil Wars. Trade Paper. Indiana
University Press. Bloomington, IN. 2002. xx, 234p. African

Issues Ser. ISBN:0-253-21584-6, ISBN13: 978-0-253-21584-0.
Dewey:962.404. LCCN:2002-027316.
                        Audience: **u,f.** *Choice, 2003.*

Prunier, Gerard   **DT159.6.D27P78 2005**
Darfur: The Ambiguous Genocide. Saddle Stitched, Cloth over
Boards, Dust Jacket. Cornell University Press. Ithaca, NY. 2005.
312p. Crises in World Politics Ser. ISBN:0-8014-4450-0,
ISBN13: 978-0-8014-4450-0. Dewey:962.7.
LCCN:2005-048490.
                        Audience: **g,l,u,f.** *Choice, 2006.*

Welsby, Derek A.   **DT159.9.N83W45 1998**
The Kingdom of Kush: The Napatan and Meroitic Empires.
Trade Cloth. Markus Wiener Publishers, Inc. Princeton, NJ.
1998. 240p. ISBN:1-55876-181-0, ISBN13: 978-1-55876-181-0.
Dewey:932/.015. LCCN:97-050451.
                        Audience: **g,l,u,f.** *Choice, 1998.*

Welsby, Derek A.   **DT159.6.N83W45 2002**
The Medieval Kingdoms of Nubia: Pagans, Christians and
Muslims on the Middle Nile. Trade Cloth. British Museum
Press. London, 2002. 304p. ISBN:0-7141-1947-4, ISBN13:
978-0-7141-1947-2. Dewey:962.5/022. LCCN:2002-405581.
                              Audience: **g,l,u,f.**

Woodward, Peter   **DT156.7.W67 1990**
Sudan, 1898-1989: The Unstable State. Library Binding. Lynne
Rienner Publishers, Inc. Boulder, CO. 1990. 273p.
ISBN:1-55587-193-3, ISBN13: 978-1-55587-193-2.
Dewey:962.4. LCCN:89-010953.
                        Audience: **u,f.** *Choice, 1990.*

History of Africa > Sudan > Anglo-Egyptian Sudan

Adams, William   **DT159.6.N83 A32**
Yewdale
Nubia: Corridor to Africa. Princeton University Press. 1977.
ISBN:0-691-09370-9, ISBN13: 978-0-691-09370-3.
                              Audience: **g,l,u,f.**

Evans-Pritchard,   **DT155.2.A93E92 1976**
Edward E.
Witchcraft, Oracles and Magic among the Azande. Paper Text.
Oxford University Press, Inc. New York, NY. 1976. 260p.
ISBN:0-19-874029-8, ISBN13: 978-0-19-874029-2.
Dewey:133.4/0967. LCCN:76-375196.
                              Audience: **u,f.** ℬ

Ruay, Deng D. Akol   **DT108.7.R83 1994**
The Politics of Two Sudans: The South and the North,
1821-1969. Nordiska Afrikainstitutet. 1994.
ISBN:91-7106-344-7, ISBN13: 978-91-7106-344-1.
                              Audience: **u,f.**

History of Africa > North Africa > General History

                                    DT269.C32C37 1987
Carthage Mosaic of Ancient Tunisia. Trade Cloth. W. W. Norton
& Company, Inc. New York, NY. 1988. ISBN:0-393-02549-7,
ISBN13: 978-0-393-02549-1. Dewey:939/.73. LCCN:87-071760.
                        Audience: **g,l,u,f.** *Choice, 1988.*

Abun-Nasr, Jamil M.　　　DT194 .A23 1987
(Editor)
A History of the Maghrib in the Islamic Period. Ed. 3. Trade
Paper. Cambridge University Press. New York, NY. 1987. 471p.
ISBN:0-521-33767-4, ISBN13: 978-0-521-33767-0. Dewey:961.
LCCN:86-024407.
Audience: **g,l,u,f.** *Choice, 1988.*

Burgat, Francois &　　　BP64.A4
Dowell, William
The Islamic Movement in North Africa. Trade Paper. University
of Texas Press. Austin, TX. 1993. 300p. Middle East
Monograph Ser., No. 10 ISBN:0-292-70793-2, ISBN13:
978-0-292-70793-1. Dewey:320.5/5.
Audience: **g,l,u,f.** *Choice, 1994.*

Fasi, Allal　　　DT204
The Independence Movements in Arab North Africa. Paper Text.
Textbook Publishers. Temecula, CA. 2003. xi, 414p.
ISBN:0-7581-7424-1, ISBN13: 978-0-7581-7424-6.
Dewey:320.1/59/61.
Audience: **g,l,u,f.** *B*

Fisher, Godfrey　　　DT201 .F5 1974
Barbary Legend. Trade Cloth. Greenwood Publishing Group,
Inc. Portsmouth, NH. 1982. 349p. ISBN:0-8371-7617-4,
ISBN13: 978-0-8371-7617-8. Dewey:961/.02. LCCN:74-009166.
Audience: **g,l,u,f.**

Hess, Andrew C.　　　DP86.A/
The Forgotten Frontier: A History of the Sixteenth Century
Ibero-African Frontier. Trade Cloth. University of Chicago
Press. Chicago, IL. 1978. xiv, 278p. Publications of the Center
for Middle Eastern Studies, No. 10 ISBN:0-226-33028-1,
ISBN13: 978-0-226-33028-0. Dewey:301.29/46/061.
LCCN:77-025517.
Audience: **u,f.** *B*

Merrills, A. H.　　　DT198.V36 2004
Vandals, Romans and Berbers: New Perspectives on Late
Antique North Africa. Trade Cloth. Ashgate Publishing, Ltd.
Aldershot, 2004. 364p. ISBN:0-7546-4145-7, ISBN13:
978-0-7546-4145-2. Dewey:939/.703. LCCN:2004-003418.
Audience: **u,f.** *Choice, 2005.*

Milton, Giles　　　HT1346.M55 2005
White Gold: The Extraordinary Story of Thomas Pellow and
Islam's One Million White Slaves. Saddle Stitched, Cloth over
Boards, Dust Jacket. Farrar, Straus & Giroux. New York, NY.
2005. 336p. ISBN:0-374-28935-2, ISBN13: 978-0-374-28935-5.
Dewey:306.3/62/0964. LCCN:2004-026427.
Audience: **g,l,u,f.**

Mostyn, Trevor &　　　DS44.C37 1988
Hourani, Albert H. (Editors)
The Cambridge Encyclopedia of the Middle East and North
Africa. Trade Cloth. Cambridge University Press. New York,
NY. 1988. 504p. Cambridge World Encyclopedias Ser.
ISBN:0-521-32190-5, ISBN13: 978-0-521-32190-7. Dewey:956.
LCCN:88-010866.
Audience: **g,l,u,f.** *Choice, 1989.*

Picard, Gilbert C. &　　　DT168 .C4823
Picard, Colette
Life and Death of Carthage: A Survey of Punic History and
Culture from Its Birth to the Final Tragedy. Trade Cloth.

Taplinger Publishing Company, Inc. Marlboro, NJ. 1969.
ISBN:0-8008-4750-4, ISBN13: 978-0-8008-4750-0.
Dewey:939/.73. LCCN:69-012303.
Audience: **u,f.**

Zartman, I. William　　　DT176 .P6
Political Elites in Arab North Africa. Cloth Text. Longman
Publishing Group. White Plains, NY. 1981.
ISBN:0-582-28251-9, ISBN13: 978-0-582-28251-3.
Dewey:306/.2/096. LCCN:81-000145.
Audience: **g,l,u,f.** *B*

History of Africa > North Africa > Libya

Ahmida, Ali Abdullatif　　　DT233 .A38 1994
The Making of Modern Libya: State Formation, Colonization,
and Resistance, 1830-1932. Paper Text. State University of New
York Press. Albany, NY. 1994. 222p. SUNY Series in the Social
and Economic History of the Middle East ISBN:0-7914-1762-X,
ISBN13: 978-0-7914-1762-1. Dewey:961.2/02.
LCCN:93-018526.
Audience: **u,f.** *Choice, 1994.*

Wright, John & Wright,　　　DT236 .W74 1982
Richardson
Libya: A Modern History. Trade Cloth. Johns Hopkins
University Press. Baltimore, MD. 1992. 304p.
ISBN:0-8018-2767-1, ISBN13: 978-0-8018-2767-9.
Dewey:961/.2. LCCN:81-048183.
Audience: **g,l,u,f.** *B*

History of Africa > North Africa > Tunisia (Tunis)

Perkins, Kenneth J.　　　DT245.P47 1986
Tunisia: Crossroads of the Islamic and European Worlds. Cloth
Text. Westview Press. Boulder, CO. 1986. 192p. Profiles -
Nations of Contemporary Middle East Ser. ISBN:0-86531-591-4,
ISBN13: 978-0-86531-591-4. Dewey:961/.1. LCCN:86-005590.
Audience: **u,f.** *Choice, 1987.*

History of Africa > North Africa > Algeria

Connelly, Mathew　　　DT295.C6115 2002
A Diplomatic Revolution: Algeria's Fight for Independence and
the Origins of the Post-Cold War Era. Trade Cloth. Oxford
University Press, Inc. New York, NY. 2002. 418p.
ISBN:0-19-514513-5, ISBN13: 978-0-19-514513-7.
Dewey:965/.0462. LCCN:2002-001234.
Audience: **g,l,u,f.** *Choice, 2002.*

Feraoun, Mouloud　　　DT295.F3813 2000
Journal, 1955-1962: Reflections on the French-Algerian War.
James D. Le Sueur (Editor, Introduction by), Mary Ellen Wolf
& Claude Fouillade (Translators). Cloth Text. University of
Nebraska Press. Lincoln, NE. 2000. 340p. ISBN:0-8032-2002-2,
ISBN13: 978-0-8032-2002-7. Dewey:965/.046/092 B.
LCCN:99-053747.
Audience: **g,l,u,f.**

Keenan, Jeremy   **DT283.6.T83**
The Tuareg: People of Ahaggar. Cloth Text. Palgrave
Macmillan. New York, NY. 1978. ISBN:0-312-82200-6,
ISBN13: 978-0-312-82200-2. Dewey:965/.004933.
LCCN:77-077139.

Audience: **u,f.** ℬ

Roberts, Hugh   **DT295.5.R628 2003**
The Battlefield: Algeria 1988-2002: Studies in a Broken Polity.
Trade Cloth. Verso Books. London, 2002. 320p.
ISBN:1-85984-684-X, ISBN13: 978-1-85984-684-1.
Dewey:965.05. LCCN:2003-374190.

Audience: **g,l,u,f.** *Choice, 2004.*

Stora, Benjamin   **DT295**
Algeria, 1830-2000: A Short History. Jane M. Todd (Translator),
William B. Quandt (Foreword by). Trade Paper. Cornell
University Press. Ithaca, NY. 2004. 283p. ISBN:0-8014-8916-4,
ISBN13: 978-0-8014-8916-7. Dewey:965/.046.

Audience: **g,l,u,f.** *Choice, 2002.*

Wolf, John Baptist   **DT291**
The Barbary Coast: Algiers under the Turks, 1500 to 1830. New
York: Norton. 1979. ISBN:0-393-01205-0, ISBN13:
978-0-393-01205-7.

Audience: **g,l,u,f.**

History of Africa > North Africa > Morocco

Baker, Alison   **HQ1791.B35 1998**
Voices of Resistance: Oral Histories of Moroccan Women. Paper
Text. State University of New York Press. Albany, NY. 1998.
352p. SUNY Series in Oral and Public History
ISBN:0-7914-3622-5, ISBN13: 978-0-7914-3622-6.
Dewey:305.4/0964. LCCN:97-002649.

Audience: **g,l,u,f.** *Choice, 1998.*

Gellner, Ernest &   **DT313.2 .A7 1973**
  Micaud, Charles Antoine
Arabs and Berbers: From Tribe to Nation in North Africa. Trade
Cloth. Gerald Duckworth & Company, Ltd. London, 1973.
448p. ISBN:0-7156-0639-5, ISBN13: 978-0-7156-0639-1.
Dewey:301.29/64. LCCN:73-165872.

Audience: **u,f.**

Ling, Dwight L.   **DT315.L47**
Morocco and Tunisia: A Comparative History. Trade Cloth.
University Press of America, Inc. Lanham, MD. 1979. iii, 204p.
ISBN:0-8191-0873-1, ISBN13: 978-0-8191-0873-9. Dewey:961.
LCCN:79-005364.

Audience: **g,l,u,f.** ℬ

Maxwell, Gavin   **DT324.M38**
Lords of the Atlas: The Rise and Fall of the House of Glaoua,
1893-1956. Geoffrey Moorhouse (Introduction by). Library
Binding. Hippocrene Books, Inc. New York, NY. 1985. 312p.
Travel Classics Ser. ISBN:0-317-19640-5, ISBN13:
978-0-317-19640-5. Dewey:964.04.

Audience: **u,f.**

Munson, Henry Jr.   **BP64.M6M86 1993**
Religion and Power in Morocco. Cloth over Boards. Yale
University Press. Cumberland, RI. 1993. 256p.
ISBN:0-300-05376-2, ISBN13: 978-0-300-05376-0.
Dewey:322.10964. LCCN:92-040202.

Audience: **u,f.** *Choice, 1994.*

Pennell, C. R.   **DT324**
Morocco Since 1830: A History. Trade Paper. New York
University Press. New York, NY. 2001. 400p.
ISBN:0-8147-6677-3, ISBN13: 978-0-8147-6677-4.
Dewey:964/.03.

Audience: **g,l,u,f.**

Porch, Douglas   **DT324.P6 2005**
The Conquest of Morocco. Trade Paper. Farrar, Straus &
Giroux. New York, NY. 2005. 368p. ISBN:0-374-12880-4,
ISBN13: 978-0-374-12880-7. Dewey:964/.04.
LCCN:2005-040055.

Audience: **u,f.**

History of Africa > North Africa > Sahara

Clarke, Thurston   **DT346.T7.C55 1978**
The Last Caravan. Other. Penguin Group (USA) Inc. New York,
NY. 1978. 286p. ISBN:0-399-11900-0, ISBN13:
978-0-399-11900-2. Dewey:966/.004/933. LCCN:77-009533.

Audience: **g,l,u,f.** ℬ

De Villiers, Marq &   **DT333**
  Hirtle, Sheila
Sahara: A Natural History. Trade Paper. McClelland & Stewart.
Toronto, ON. 2004. 336p. ISBN:0-7710-2638-2, ISBN13:
978-0-7710-2638-6. Dewey:916.604/329.

Audience: **g,l,u,f.** *Choice, 2003.*

Hodges, Tony   **DT346.S7**
Western Sahara: Roots of a Desert War. Trade Cloth. Chicago
Review Press, Inc. Chicago, IL. 1984. 400p.
ISBN:0-88208-151-9, ISBN13: 978-0-88208-151-9.
Dewey:964.8. LCCN:83-008565.

Audience: **u,f.**

History of Africa > Central Africa > General History

Birmingham, David &   **DT352.8.H57 1998**
  Martin, Phyllis
History of Central Africa: The Contemporary Years. Trade
Paper. Addison-Wesley Longman, Inc. Boston, MA. 1998. 328p.
ISBN:0-582-27607-1, ISBN13: 978-0-582-27607-9.
Dewey:967/.032. LCCN:97-025419.

Audience: **g,l,u,f.**

Birmingham, David &   **DT352.5**
  Martin, Phyllis M. (Editors)
History Central Africa, Vol. 2. Ed. 1. Paper Text. Longman
Publishing Group. White Plains, NY. 1983. 432p.
ISBN:0-582-64675-8, ISBN13: 978-0-582-64675-9. Dewey:967.
LCCN:83-000745.

Audience: **g,l,u,f.**

Birmingham, David &   **DT352.5.H58 1983**
  Martin, Phyllis M. (Editors)
History of Central Africa, Vol. 1. Trade Cloth. Longman
Publishing Group. White Plains, NY. 1983. 332p.
ISBN:0-582-64673-1, ISBN13: 978-0-582-64673-5. Dewey:967.
LCCN:83-000745.

Audience: **g,l,u,f.** ℬ

Audience: g=general, l=lower division undergraduate, u=upper division undergraduate, f=faculty.

61

Vansina, Jan DT352.65.V355 2004
How Societies Are Born: Governance in West Central Africa Before 1600. Trade Cloth. University Press of Virginia. Charlottesville, VA. 2004. 320p. ISBN:0-8139-2279-8, ISBN13: 978-0-8139-2279-9. Dewey:967/.01. LCCN:2004-001001.
Audience: **u,f.**

Vansina, Jan DT352.65.V36 1990
Paths in the Rainforests: Toward a History of Political Tradition in Equatorial Africa. Paper Text. University of Wisconsin Press. Chicago, IL. 1990. 400p. ISBN:0-299-12574-2, ISBN13: 978-0-299-12574-5. Dewey:967. LCCN:90-050100.
Audience: **u,f.**

Wright, Marcia HT1326.W75 1993
Strategies of Slaves and Women. Paper Text. Lilian Barber Press. New York, NY. 1993. 238p. ISBN:0-936508-28-0, ISBN13: 978-0-936508-28-3. Dewey:305.5/67/09676. LCCN:91-032722.
Audience: **u,f.** *Choice, 1993.*

History of Africa > Central Africa > Cameroon

Bjomson, Richard PQ3988.5.C27
ⓔ The African Quest for Freedom and Identity: Cameroonian Writing and the National Experience. E-Book. Indiana University Press. Bloomington, IN. 1994. 528p. ISBN:0-253-20908-0, ISBN13: 978-0-253-20908-5. Dewey:840.9/96711. LCCN:90-039423.
Audience: **u,f.** *Choice, 1991.*

Joseph, Richard A. JQ3529.A8
Radical Nationalism in Cameroon: Social Origins of the U. P. C. Rebellion. Clarendon Press. Oxford:. 1977. Oxford Studies in African Affairs ISBN:0-19-822706-X, ISBN13: 978-0-19-822706-9.
Audience: **u,f.**

Levine, Victor T. DT574 .L4 1977
The Cameroons from Mandate to Independence. Library Binding. Greenwood Publishing Group, Inc. Portsmouth, NH. 1977. ISBN:0-8371-8764-8, ISBN13: 978-0-8371-8764-8. Dewey:320.9/67/1103. LCCN:76-030362.
Audience: **g,l,u,f.**

Rudin, Harry R. DT574 .R8
Germans in the Cameroons, Eighteen Eighty-Four to Nineteen Fourteen: A Case Study in Modern Imperialism. Library Binding. Greenwood Publishing Group, Inc. Portsmouth, NH. 1969. ISBN:0-8371-0640-0, ISBN13: 978-0-8371-0640-3. Dewey:325.3/43/096711. LCCN:39-005914.
Audience: **g,l,u,f.** 𝓑

History of Africa > Central Africa > Central African Republic

O'Toole, Thomas DT546.322.O86 1986
Central African Republic: The Continent's Hidden Heart. Cloth Text. Westview Press. Boulder, CO. 1986. 130p. Profiles - Nations of Contemporary Africa Ser. ISBN:0-86531-564-7, ISBN13: 978-0-86531-564-8. Dewey:967. LCCN:86-004099.
Audience: **g,l,u,f.**

History of Africa > Central Africa > Chad

Nolutshungu, Sam C. DT546.48.N65 1996
Limits of Anarchy: Intervention and State Formation in Chad. Cloth Text. University Press of Virginia. Charlottesville, VA. 1996. 392p. Carter G. Woodson Institute Series in Black Studies ISBN:0-8139-1628-3, ISBN13: 978-0-8139-1628-6. Dewey:967.4304. LCCN:95-016954.
Audience: **u,f.** *Choice, 1996.*

History of Africa > Central Africa > Congo

Gauze, Rene DT546.275
The Politics of Congo-Brazzaville. Virginia Thompson & Richard Adloff (Translators). Trade Cloth. Hoover Institution Press. Stanford, CA. 1973. 283p. Publication Ser., No. 129 ISBN:0-8179-6291-3, ISBN13: 978-0-8179-6291-3. Dewey:320.9/67/2405. LCCN:73-075886.
Audience: **g,l,u,f.** 𝓑

Martin, Phyllis GV143.C66 M37 1995
Leisure and Society in Colonial Brazzaville. David Anderson, Carolyn Brown, Christopher Clapham, Michael Gomez, Patrick Manning, David Robinson & Leonardo A. Villalon (Contribution by). Trade Paper. Cambridge University Press. New York, NY. 2002. 295p. African Studies ISBN:0-521-52446-6, ISBN13: 978-0-521-52446-9. Dewey:790/.01/35/096724.
Audience: **u,f.**

History of Africa > Central Africa > Democratic Republic of Congo

Edgerton, Robert DT652.E34 2002
The Troubled Heart of Africa: A History of the Congo. Cloth over Boards. St. Martin's Press. Gordonville, VA. 2002. 320p. ISBN:0-312-30486-2, ISBN13: 978-0-312-30486-7. Dewey:967.24. LCCN:2002-069933.
Audience: **g,l,u,f.**

Gondola, Ch. Didier DT652
The History of Congo. Cloth Text. Greenwood Publishing Group, Inc. Portsmouth, NH. 2002. 248p. The Greenwood Histories of the Modern Nations Ser. ISBN:0-313-31696-1, ISBN13: 978-0-313-31696-8. LCCN:2002-075316.
Audience: **g,l,u,f.**

Library of Congress, DT644.Z3425 1994
Federal Research Division Staff (Editor), et al.
Zaire Country Studies: Area Handbook. Ed. 4. Sandra W. Meditz & Tim L. Merrill (Editors). Trade Cloth. Library of Congress. Washington, DC. 1994. 452p. Area Handbook DA Pam Ser., 550-67 ISBN:0-8444-0795-X, ISBN13: 978-0-8444-0795-1. Dewey:967.51. LCCN:94-025092.
Audience: **g,l,u,f.**

Lumumba, Patrice DT657.L813
Congo, My Country. Paper Text. Textbook Publishers. Temecula, CA. 2003. 195p. ISBN:0-7581-6191-3, ISBN13: 978-0-7581-6191-8. Dewey:967.5.
Audience: **g,l,u,f.**

Lumumba, Patrice   DT663.L8 A2513
Lumumba Speaks: Speeches and Writings, 1958-1961. Trade
Cloth. University Place Book Shop. New York, NY. 1972.
ISBN:0-685-77060-5, ISBN13: 978-0-685-77060-3.
Dewey:967.5/1/03.

Audience: **g,l,u,f.**

O'Ballance, Edgar   DT658.O28 1999
The Congo-Zaire Experience, 1960-98. Cloth over Boards.
Palgrave Macmillan. New York, NY. 2000. 234p.
ISBN:0-312-22795-7, ISBN13: 978-0-312-22795-1.
Dewey:967.5/103. LCCN:99-033523.

Audience: **u,f.**

Packard, Randall M.   DT650.B366.P3
Chiefship and Cosmology: An Historical Study of Political
Competition. Trade Cloth. Indiana University Press.
Bloomington, IN. 1981. 256p. African Systems of Thought Ser.
ISBN:0-253-30831-3, ISBN13: 978-0-253-30831-3.
Dewey:967.5/17. LCCN:81-047013.

Audience: **u,f.** ℬ

Slade, Ruth M.   DT655
King Leopold's Congo: Aspects of the Development of Race
Relations in the Congo Independent State. Paper Text. Textbook
Publishers. Temecula, CA. 2003. xi, 230p. ISBN:0-7581-6964-7,
ISBN13: 978-0-7581-6964-8. Dewey:967.5.

Audience: **u,f.** ℬ

Turnbull, Colin M.   DT650.B36
The Forest People. Paper Text. Textbook Publishers. Temecula,
CA. 2003. 288p. ISBN:0-7581-3790-7, ISBN13:
978-0-7581-3790-6. Dewey:305.8/967515.

Audience: **g,l,u,f.**

History of Africa > Central Africa > Gabon

Barnes, James F.   DT546.18.B37 1992
Gabon: Beyond the Colonial Legacy. Trade Paper. Westview
Press. Boulder, CO. 1992. 163p. Profiles - Nations of
Contemporary Africa Ser. ISBN:0-8133-0430-X, ISBN13:
978-0-8133-0430-4. Dewey:967.2104. LCCN:91-046627.

Audience: **g,l,u,f.**

Gray, Christopher J.   DT546.175.G73 2002
Colonial Rule and Crisis in Equatorial Africa: Southern Gabon,
C. 1850-1940. Trade Cloth. University of Rochester Press.
Rochester, NY. 2002. 304p. Rochester Studies in the History of
the African Diaspora, Vol. 13 ISBN:1-58046-048-8, ISBN13:
978-1-58046-048-4. Dewey:967.21/02. LCCN:2002-022554.

Audience: **u,f.** *Choice, 2003.*

History of Africa > East Africa > General History

Chrétien, Jean-Pierre   DT365.5.C4613 2003
The Great Lakes of Africa: Two Thousand Years of History.
Scott Straus (Translator). Trade Cloth. Zone Books. Brooklyn,
NY. 2003. 503p. ISBN:1-890951-34-X, ISBN13:
978-1-890951-34-4. Dewey:967.6. LCCN:2002-191001.

Audience: **u,f.** *Choice, 2004.*

Freeman-Grenville, G.   DT365.A3 F73
S. (Editor)
The East African Coast. Ed. 2. Trade Cloth. Rowman &
Littlefield Publishers, Inc. Lanham, MD. 1976. 314p.
ISBN:0-8476-1233-3, ISBN13: 978-0-8476-1233-8. Dewey:967.

Audience: **g,l,u,f.**

Glassman, Jonathon   DT365.65.G57 1995
Feasts and Riot: Revelry, Rebellion, and Popular Consciousness
on the Swahili Coast. Trade Cloth. Heinemann. Portsmouth, NH.
1995. 293p. Social History of Africa Ser. ISBN:0-435-08956-0,
ISBN13: 978-0-435-08956-6. Dewey:967.6. LCCN:94-34509.

Audience: **u,f.** *Choice, 1995.*

Horton, Mark &   DT429.5.S94H67 2000
Middleton, John
The Swahili. Trade Cloth. Blackwell Publishing, Inc. Malden,
MA. 2001. 288p. The Peoples of Africa Ser.
ISBN:0-631-18919-X, ISBN13: 978-0-631-18919-0.
Dewey:967.6004/96392. LCCN:00-009633.

Audience: **u,f.** *Choice, 2001.*

Ibn Batuta, et al.   DT365.2.I262513 2004
Ibn Battuta in Black Africa: Expanded Edition for the 700th
Anniversary of Ibn Batutta's Birth. Ed. 500. Said Hamdun &
Noel Quinton King (Authors). Trade Paper. Markus Wiener
Publishers, Inc. Princeton, NJ. 2005. 200p.
ISBN:1-55876-336-8, ISBN13: 978-1-55876-336-4.
Dewey:916.704/21. LCCN:2004-054224.

Audience: **g,l,u,f.**

Newitt, M. D. D.   DT365.65.E35 2002
(Editor)
East Africa: Portuguese Encounters with the World in the Age of
Discoveries. Trade Cloth. Ashgate Publishing, Ltd. Aldershot,
2002. 224p. Portuguese Encounters with the World in the Age of
the Discoveries Ser. ISBN:0-7546-0181-1, ISBN13:
978-0-7546-0181-4. Dewey:967.6/01. LCCN:2001-053589.

Audience: **g,l,u,f.**

Spear, Thomas   BR1440.E27 1999
East African Expressions of Christianity. Isaria N. Kimambo
(Contribution by). Trade Cloth. Ohio University Press. Athens,
OH. 1999. 351p. Eastern African Studies ISBN:0-8214-1273-6,
ISBN13: 978-0-8214-1273-2. Dewey:276.7/6/08.
LCCN:98-032021.

Audience: **u,f.** *Choice, 1999.*

Thornton, John   **IN PROCESS**
Africa and Africans in the Making of the Atlantic World,
1400-1800. Ed. 2. Michael Adas, Edmund Burke III & Philip D.
Curtin (Contribution by). Trade Paper. Cambridge University
Press. New York, NY. 1998. 378p. Studies in Comparative
World History ISBN:0-521-62724-9, ISBN13:
978-0-521-62724-5. Dewey:303.482604. LCCN:97-039728.

Audience: **u,f.**

Trimingham, J. Spencer   BP64.A4.E27 1980
Islam in East Africa. Library Binding. Ayer Company
Publishers, Inc. Manchester, NH. 1980. xii, 198p. Islam Ser.
ISBN:0-8369-9270-9, ISBN13: 978-0-8369-9270-0.
Dewey:297/.0967. LCCN:79-052567.

Audience: **u,f.** ℬ

History of Africa > East Africa > Burundi

Lemarchand, Reni   **DT450.64 .L46 1994**
Burundi: Ethnic Conflict and Genocide. Lee H. Hamilton
(Contribution by). Trade Cloth. Cambridge University Press.
New York, NY. 1994. 232p. Woodrow Wilson Center Press Ser.
ISBN:0-521-45176-0, ISBN13: 978-0-521-45176-5.
Dewey:323.1/67572. LCCN:93-037592.
Audience: **u,f.** *Choice, 1994.*

Louis, William Roger   **DT449.R8.L6 1979**
Ruanda-Urundi, 1884-1919. Trade Cloth. Greenwood Publishing
Group, Inc. Portsmouth, NH. 1979. xvii, 290p.
ISBN:0-313-20905-7, ISBN13: 978-0-313-20905-5.
Dewey:967/.57. LCCN:78-027637.
Audience: **u,f.** *ℬ*

History of Africa > East Africa > Ethiopia

Gabre-Sellassie, Zewde   **DT386.7.Z48 1997**
Yohannes IV of Ethiopia: A Political Biography. Trade Cloth.
Red Sea Press. Trenton, NJ. 1997. 352p. ISBN:1-56902-043-4,
ISBN13: 978-1-56902-043-2. Dewey:963/.04/0924.
LCCN:97-011227.
Audience: **g,l,u,f.** *ℬ*

Ghebre-Ab, Habtu   **DT394 .E84**
(Compiled by, Introduction by)
Ethiopia and Eritrea: A Documentary Study. Trade Cloth. Red
Sea Press. Trenton, NJ. 1993. 270p. ISBN:0-932415-87-3,
ISBN13: 978-0-932415-87-5. Dewey:963/.5. LCCN:92-036168.
Audience: **g,l,u,f.**

Henze, Paul B.   **DT381.H465**
Layers of Time: A History of Ethiopia. Trade Paper. Palgrave
Macmillan. New York, NY. 2004. 399p. ISBN:1-4039-6743-1,
ISBN13: 978-1-4039-6743-5. Dewey:963.
Audience: **g,l,u,f.** *Choice, 2001.*

Jones, A. H. M. &   **DT381**
Monroe, Elizabeth
A History of Ethiopia. Trade Cloth. Oxford University Press,
Inc. New York, NY. 1979. viii, 196p. ISBN:0-19-822716-7,
ISBN13: 978-0-19-822716-8. Dewey:963.
Audience: **g,l,u,f.** *ℬ*

Marcus, Harold G.   **DT387.9**
Ethiopia, Great Britain and the United States, 1941-1974: The
Politics of Empire. Trade Cloth. University of California Press.
Berkeley, CA. 1983. 256p. ISBN:0-520-04613-7, ISBN13:
978-0-520-04613-9. Dewey:327.63/06. LCCN:82-008522.
Audience: **u,f.** *ℬ*

Marcus, Harold G.   **DT387.M37 1995**
The Life and Times of Menelik II: Ethiopia 1844-1913. Trade
Cloth. Red Sea Press. Trenton, NJ. 1995. 306p.
ISBN:1-56902-009-4, ISBN13: 978-1-56902-009-8.
Dewey:963/.043/092 B. LCCN:94-048485.
Audience: **u,f.** *ℬ*

Pausewang, Siegfried   **JQ3766.E84 2003**
(Editor), et al.
Ethiopia since the DERG: A Decade of Democratic Pretension
and Performance. Kjetil Tronvoll & Lovise Aalen (Editors).

Trade Paper. Zed Books, Ltd. London, 2003. 272p.
ISBN:1-84277-177-9, ISBN13: 978-1-84277-177-8.
Dewey:320.963. LCCN:2002-031133.
Audience: **u,f.** *Choice, 2003.*

Prouty, Chris   **DT387.R585 1986**
Empress Taytu and Menilek II: Ethiopia, 1883-1910. Trade
Cloth. Red Sea Press. Trenton, NJ. 1987. 430p.
ISBN:0-932415-11-3, ISBN13: 978-0-932415-11-0.
Dewey:963/.04/0922 B. LCCN:87-119384.
Audience: **u,f.** *Choice, 1988.*

Sellassie, Haile   **DT387.7**
My Life and Ethiopia's Progress: The Autobiography of Haile
Sellaissie, Vol. 2. Perfect. Research Associates School Times
Publications. Chicago, IL. 1996. ISBN:0-948390-32-8, ISBN13:
978-0-948390-32-6. Dewey:963/.05/0924 B.
Audience: **g,l,u,f.**

Sellassie, Haile   **DT387.7**
My Life and Ethiopia's Progress 1892-1937: The Autobiography
of Haile Sellassie. Trade Cloth. Research Associates School
Times Publications. Chicago, IL. 1998. ISBN:0-948390-40-9,
ISBN13: 978-0-948390-40-1. Dewey:963/.055.
Audience: **g,l,u,f.**

Spencer, John H.   **DT387.7**
Ethiopia at Bay: A Personal Account of the Haile Sellassie
Years. Anne Fredericks (Editor). Trade Paper. Reference
Publications, Inc. Algonac, MI. 1987. 400p.
ISBN:0-917256-36-0, ISBN13: 978-0-917256-36-3.
Dewey:963/.055. LCCN:87-020488.
Audience: **g,l,u,f.** *ℬ*

Tiruneh, Andargachew   **DT387.95 .T57 1993**
The Ethiopian Revolution 1974-1987: A Transformation from an
Aristocratic to a Totalitarian Autocracy. Christopher Greenwood,
Michael Leifer, Margot Light, Ian Nish, David Stephenson,
Andrew Walter, Dominic Lieven, James Mayall & Donal Watt
(Contribution by). Trade Cloth. Cambridge University Press.
New York, NY. 1993. 452p. London School of Economics
Monographs in International Studies ISBN:0-521-43082-8,
ISBN13: 978-0-521-43082-1. Dewey:963.07. LCCN:92-006554.
Audience: **u,f.** *Choice, 1994.*

Zewde, Bahru   **DT386.B27 2001**
A History of Modern Ethiopia, 1855-1991. Ed. 2. Trade Paper.
Ohio University Press. Athens, OH. 2002. 254p. Eastern African
Studies ISBN:0-8214-1440-2, ISBN13: 978-0-8214-1440-8.
Dewey:963/.04. LCCN:2001-054878.
Audience: **g,l,u,f.** *Choice, 2003.*

Zewde, Bahru   **HN789.Z9.E43 2002**
Pioneers of Change in Ethiopia: The Reformist Intellectuals of
the Early Twentieth Century. Trade Cloth. Ohio University
Press. Athens, OH. 2002. 288p. ISBN:0-8214-1445-3, ISBN13:
978-0-8214-1445-3. Dewey:305.5/52/09630904.
LCCN:2002-074938.
Audience: **u,f.** *Choice, 2003.*

History of Africa > East Africa > Kenya

Anderson, David   **DT433.522**
Histories of the Hanged: The Dirty War in Kenya and the End
of Empire. Trade Paper, Perfect. W. W. Norton & Company, Inc.
New York, NY. 2005. 448p. ISBN:0-393-32754-X, ISBN13:
978-0-393-32754-0. Dewey:967.62.
Audience: **u,f.**

Bravman, Bill   **DT433**
Making Ethnic Ways: Communities and Their Transformations in Taita, Kenya, 1800-1950. Trade Cloth. Greenwood Publishing Group, Inc. Portsmouth, NH. 1998. 284p. Social History of Africa Ser. ISBN:0-325-00105-7, ISBN13: 978-0-325-00105-0. Dewey:967.6/2/00496395. LCCN:98-012377.
Audience: **u,f.** *Choice, 1999.*

Goldsworthy, David   **DT433.582.M35**
Tom MBoya: The Man Who Kenya Wanted to Forget. Trade Cloth. Holmes & Meier Publishers, Inc. Teaneck, NJ. 1982. 308p. ISBN:0-8419-0787-0, ISBN13: 978-0-8419-0787-4. Dewey:967.6/204/0924. LCCN:81-022870.
Audience: **g,l,u,f.**

Kenyatta, Jomo   **DT434.E2K45**
Facing Mount Kenya. Trade Paper. Knopf Publishing Group. New York, NY. 1962. 352p. ISBN:0-394-70210-7, ISBN13: 978-0-394-70210-0. Dewey:572.96765.
Audience: **g,l,u,f.**

Kyle, Keith   **DT433.575.K95 1999**
The Politics of the Independence of Kenya. Cloth over Boards. Palgrave Macmillan. New York, NY. 1999. 278p. Contemporary History in Context Ser. ISBN:0-312-22201-7, ISBN13: 978-0-312-22201-7. Dewey:967.6/2/03. LCCN:98-050837.
Audience: **g,l,u,f.** *Choice, 1999.*

Mboya, Tom   **DT434.E27**
Freedom and After. Little, Brown. 1963.
Audience: **g,l,u,f.**

Munro, J. Forbes   **DT433.542.M83 1975**
Colonial Rule and the Kamba: Social Change in the Kenya Highlands, 1889-1939. Trade Cloth. Oxford University Press, Inc. New York, NY. 1975. vi, 276p. ISBN:0-19-821699-8, ISBN13: 978-0-19-821699-5. Dewey:301.24/1/0967626. LCCN:76-352691.
Audience: **u,f.** *B*

Muriuki, Godfrey   **DT433.542**
A History of the Kikuyu, 1500-1900. Trade Cloth. Oxford University Press, Inc. New York, NY. 1974. viii, 190p. ISBN:0-19-572314-7, ISBN13: 978-0-19-572314-4. Dewey:301.29/676/26. LCCN:74-186971.
Audience: **g,l,u,f.** *B*

Murray-Brown, Jeremy   **DT433.576.K46**
Kenyatta. Ed. 2. Trade Cloth. Routledge. New York, NY. 1979. 381p. ISBN:0-04-920059-3, ISBN13: 978-0-04-920059-3. Dewey:967.6/204/0924. LCCN:79-316123.
Audience: **g,l,u,f.** *B*

Nottingham, John   **DT434.E27**
Myth of the Mau Mau: Nationalism in Kenya. Trade Paper. Penguin Group (USA) Inc. New York, NY. 1974. ISBN:0-452-00297-4, ISBN13: 978-0-452-00297-5. Dewey:967.6203.
Audience: **u,f.**

Oded, Arye   **BP64.K42O34 2000**
Islam and Politics in Kenya. Library Binding. Lynne Rienner Publishers, Inc. Boulder, CO. 2000. ix, 236p. ISBN:1-55587-929-2, ISBN13: 978-1-55587-929-7. Dewey:322/.1/096762. LCCN:00-031094.
Audience: **u,f.**

Percox, David   **DT433.563.G7**
Britain, Kenya and the Cold War: Imperial Defence, Colonial Security and Decolonisation. Cloth over Boards. I. B. Tauris & Company, Ltd. London, 2004. 200p. Tauris Academic Studies ISBN:1-85043-460-3, ISBN13: 978-1-85043-460-3. Dewey:327.4106762. LCCN:2005-295207.
Audience: **u,f.** *Choice, 2005.*

Robertson, Claire C.   **DT433.545.K55R63**
e Trouble Showed the Way: Women, Men, and Trade in the Nairobi Area, 1890-1990. E-Book. Indiana University Press. Bloomington, IN. 1997. 384p. ISBN:0-253-21151-4, ISBN13: 978-0-253-21151-4. Dewey:338.9/0089/963954067. LCCN:97-040099.
Audience: **u,f.** *Choice, 1998.*

Spear, Thomas G.   **DT433.565 .S68 1981**
Kenya's Past. Ed. 1. Cloth Text. Longman Publishing Group. White Plains, NY. 1981. 240p. African History Studies ISBN:0-582-64696-0, ISBN13: 978-0-582-64696-4. Dewey:967.6/201. LCCN:81-201509.
Audience: **g,l,u,f.** *B*

Willis, Justin   **DT434.M7W55 1993**
Mombasa, the Swahili, and the Making of the Mijikenda. Cloth Text. Oxford University Press, Inc. New York, NY. 1993. 256p. Oxford Studies in African Affairs ISBN:0-19-820320-9, ISBN13: 978-0-19-820320-9. Dewey:967.62/3. LCCN:92-023255.
Audience: **u,f.** *Choice, 1993.*

History of Africa > East Africa > Rwanda

Gourevitch, Philip   **DT450.435.G68 1999**
We Wish to Inform You That Tomorrow We Will Be Killed with Our Families: Stories from Rwanda. Trade Paper. Picador. New York, NY. 1999. 368p. ISBN:0-312-24335-9, ISBN13: 978-0-312-24335-7. Dewey:364.15/1/0967571. LCCN:2004-559125.
Audience: **g,l,u,f.** *Choice, 1999.*

Hatzfeld, Jean   **DT450.435**
Machete Season: The Killers in Rwanda Speak. Linda Coverdale (Translator), Susan Sontag (Preface by). Trade Paper. Picador. New York, NY. 2006. 272p. ISBN:0-312-42503-1, ISBN13: 978-0-312-42503-6. Dewey:967.57104/31.
Audience: **g,l,u,f.** *Choice, 2006.*

Vansina, Jan   **DT450.34.V3813 2004**
Antecedents to Modern Rwanda: The Nyiginya Kingdom. Trade Cloth. University of Wisconsin Press. Chicago, IL. 2004. 320p. Africa and the Diaspora Ser. ISBN:0-299-20120-1, ISBN13: 978-0-299-20120-3. Dewey:967.571/01. LCCN:2004-007798.
Audience: **u,f.** *Choice, 2005.*

History of Africa > East Africa > Somalia

Cassanelli, Lee V.   **DT402.3.C37 1982**
The Shaping of Somali Society: Reconstructing the History of a Pastoral People, 1600 to 1900. Trade Cloth. University of Pennsylvania Press. Philadelphia, PA. 1982. 328p.

ISBN:0-8122-7832-1, ISBN13: 978-0-8122-7832-3.
Dewey:967/.7301. LCCN:81-043520.

Audience: **u,f.** ℬ

Lewis, Ioan M.   **DT0403.L395**
A Modern History of Somalia: Nation and State in the Horn of
Africa. Trade Paper. Books on Demand. Ann Arbor, MI. 289p.
ISBN:0-608-13143-1, ISBN13: 978-0-608-13143-6.
Dewey:967/.73. LCCN:79-040569.

Audience: **g,l,u,f.**

Lowe Besteman,   **DT409.Q27B47 1999**
  Catherine
Unraveling Somalia: Race, Violence and the Legacy of Slavery.
Book, Other. University of Pennsylvania Press. Philadelphia, PA.
1999. 296p. Ethnography of Political Violence Ser.
ISBN:0-8122-1688-1, ISBN13: 978-0-8122-1688-2.
Dewey:967.73. LCCN:98-033372.

Audience: **u,f.** *Choice, 1999.*

History of Africa > East Africa > Tanzania

Amin, Mohamed;   **DT448.25.N9**
  Smyth, Annie & Seftel, Adam
Tanzania: The Story of Julius Nyerere through the Pages of
Drum. Mkuki na Nyota Publishers. 1998. ISBN:9976-973-52-7,
ISBN13: 978-9976-973-52-5.

Audience: **g,l,u,f.**

Bennett, Norman R.   **DT435.5**
A History of the Arab State of Zanzibar. Trade Cloth.
Routledge. New York, NY. 1978. viii, 304p. Studies in African
History ISBN:0-416-55080-0, ISBN13: 978-0-416-55080-1.
Dewey:967.8/1. LCCN:78-326151.

Audience: **g,l,u,f.** ℬ

Clayton, Anthony   **DT435.75.C58 1981**
The Zanzibar Revolution and Its Aftermath. Trade Cloth. Shoe
String Press, Inc. North Haven, CT. 1981. xvi, 166p.
ISBN:0-208-01925-1, ISBN13: 978-0-208-01925-7.
Dewey:967.8/104. LCCN:81-003486.

Audience: **u,f.** ℬ

Fair, Laura   **DT499.Z28F35 2001**
Pastimes and Politics: Culture, Community and Identity in
Post-Abolition Urban Zanzibar, 1890-1945. Trade Paper. Ohio
University Press. Athens, OH. 2001. 386p. Eastern African
Studies ISBN:0-8214-1384-8, ISBN13: 978-0-8214-1384-5.
Dewey:967.8/103. LCCN:00-067756.

Audience: **u,f.** *Choice, 2002.*

Feierman, Steven   **DT450.49.L87F85 1990**
Peasant Intellectuals: Anthropology and History in Northern
Tanzania. Trade Paper. University of Wisconsin Press. Chicago,
IL. 1997. 320p. Badger Reprint Edition Ser.
ISBN:0-299-12524-6, ISBN13: 978-0-299-12524-0.
Dewey:967.8/22. LCCN:90-050086.

Audience: **u,f.**

Geiger, Susan   **HQ1236.5.T34G45 1998**
Tanu Women: Gender and Culture in the Making of
Tanganyikan Nationalism, 1955-1965. Trade Cloth. Heinemann.
Portsmouth, NH. 1997. 217p. Social History of Africa Ser.

ISBN:0-435-07254-4, ISBN13: 978-0-435-07254-4.
Dewey:967.8/2/03/082. LCCN:97-27010.

Audience: **g,l,u,f.** *Choice, 1998.*

Gray, John Milner   **DT435 .G7**
History of Zanzibar, from the Middle Ages to 1856. Paper Text.
Textbook Publishers. Temecula, CA. 2003. 314p.
ISBN:0-7581-6939-6, ISBN13: 978-0-7581-6939-6.

Audience: **g,l,u,f.** ℬ

Middleton, John &   **DT435**
  Campbell, Jane
Zanzibar: Its Society and Its Politics. Oxford University Press.
1965.

Audience: **g,l,u,f.**

Nyerere, Julius K.   **DT448.2**
Freedom and Development, Uhuru Na Maendeleo: A Selection
from Writings and Speeches, 1968-73. Trade Cloth. Oxford
University Press, Inc. New York, NY. 1974. xvii, 400p.
ISBN:0-19-572323-6, ISBN13: 978-0-19-572323-6.
Dewey:967.8/04/08.

Audience: **u,f.**

Sheriff, Abdul   **DT449.Z27Z36 1991**
Zanzibar under Colonial Rule: Eastern African Studies. Ed
Ferguson (Contribution by). Trade Paper. Ohio University Press.
Athens, OH. 1991. 317p. Eastern African Studies
ISBN:0-8214-0996-4, ISBN13: 978-0-8214-0996-1.
Dewey:325.341096781. LCCN:90-025407.

Audience: **u,f.**

Shetler, Jan Bender   **DT449.M365S53 2003**
Telling Our Own Stories: Local Histories from South Mara,
Tanzania. Trade Paper. Brill Academic Publishers. Leiden, 2003.
xiv, 336p. African Sources for African History Ser., 4
ISBN:90-04-12625-2, ISBN13: 978-90-04-12625-1.
Dewey:967.8/27. LCCN:2003-271265.

Audience: **g,l,u,f.** *Choice, 2003.*

Sunseri, Thaddeus   **HD5856**
Vilimani: Labor Migration and Rural Change in Early Colonial
Tanzania. Trade Paper. Greenwood Publishing Group, Inc.
Portsmouth, NH. 2001. 264p. Social History of Africa Ser.
ISBN:0-325-00182-0, ISBN13: 978-0-325-00182-1.
Dewey:331.5/44/09678. LCCN:2001-024563.

Audience: **u,f.** *Choice, 2002.*

Willis, Roy   **DT443 .W49**
A State in the Making: Myth, History, and Social
Transformation in Pre-Colonial Ufipa. Trade Cloth. Indiana
University Press. Bloomington, IN. 1981. 352p. African Systems
of Thought Ser. ISBN:0-253-19537-3, ISBN13:
978-0-253-19537-1. Dewey:967.8/28. LCCN:80-008155.

Audience: **u,f.** ℬ

Yeager, Rodger   **DT448.2**
Tanzania: An African Experiment. Paper Text. Westview Press.
Boulder, CO. 1983. 136p. Nations of Contemporary Africa Ser.
ISBN:0-86531-694-5, ISBN13: 978-0-86531-694-2.
Dewey:967.8/04.

Audience: **u,f.** ℬ

History of Africa > East Africa > Uganda

Hanson, Holly Elisabeth   **DT433**
Landed Obligation: The Practice of Power in Buganda. Trade
Cloth. Heinemann. Portsmouth, NH. 2003. 288p. Social History

of Africa Ser. ISBN:0-325-07037-7, ISBN13:
978-0-325-07037-7. Dewey:967.61/01. LCCN:2003-056676.
Audience: **u,f.** *Choice, 2004.*

Melady, Thomas &   **DT433.282.A55.M44**
Melady, Margaret
Idi Amin Dada: Hitler in Africa. Trade Cloth. Andrews McMeel
Publishing. Kansas City, MO. 1977. vii, 184p.
ISBN:0-8362-0783-1, ISBN13: 978-0-8362-0783-5.
Dewey:967.6/104/0924. LCCN:77-011706.
Audience: **u,f.** *B*

Mutibwa, Phares   **DT433.275 .M88 1992**
Uganda since Independence. Trade Cloth. Africa World Press.
Trenton, NJ. 1992. 150p. ISBN:0-86543-356-9, ISBN13:
978-0-86543-356-4. Dewey:967.61. LCCN:92-053941.
Audience: **g,l,u,f.**

Ray, Benjamin C.   **DT433.245.G35R39**
Myth, Ritual, and Kingship in Buganda. Trade Cloth. Oxford
University Press, Inc. New York, NY. 1991. 264p.
ISBN:0-19-506436-4, ISBN13: 978-0-19-506436-0.
Dewey:306.6/99689639570676. LCCN:90-007127.
Audience: **u,f.** *Choice, 1991.*

Reid, Richard J.   **JQ2951.A99B847 2002**
Political Power in Pre-Colonial Buganda: Economy, Society and
Welfare in the Nineteenth Century. Trade Paper. Ohio University
Press. Athens, OH. 2003. 288p. Eastern African Studies
ISBN:0-8214-1478-X, ISBN13: 978-0-8214-1478-1.
Dewey:967.61. LCCN:2002-074343.
Audience: **u,f.** *Choice, 2003.*

Tosh, John   **DT433.29.L36.T67**
Clan Leaders and Colonial Chiefs in Lango: The Political
History of an East African Stateless Society C. 1800-1939.
Cloth Text. Oxford University Press, Inc. New York, NY. 1979.
310p. Oxford Studies in African Affairs ISBN:0-19-822711-6,
ISBN13: 978-0-19-822711-3. Dewey:301.5/92/096761.
LCCN:78-040243.
Audience: **u,f.** *B*

Twaddle, Michael   **DT433.27.T87 1993**
Kakungulu and the Creation of Uganda, 1868-1928. Trade
Cloth. Ohio University Press. Athens, OH. 1993. 320p. Eastern
African Studies ISBN:0-8214-1058-X, ISBN13:
978-0-8214-1058-5. Dewey:967.61. LCCN:92-047361.
Audience: **u,f.** *Choice, 1994.*

History of Africa > East Africa > Other East African Countries

Allen, Philip M.   **DT469.M285A45 1995**
Madagascar: Conflicts of Authority in the Great Island. Trade
Paper. Westview Press. Boulder, CO. 1994. 254p.
ISBN:0-8133-0258-7, ISBN13: 978-0-8133-0258-4.
Dewey:969.1. LCCN:94-038426.
Audience: **g,l,u,f.** *Choice, 1995.*

Brown, Mervyn   **DT469.M285B76 2001**
A History of Madagascar. Trade Cloth. Markus Wiener
Publishers, Inc. Princeton, NJ. 2001. ISBN:1-55876-292-2,
ISBN13: 978-1-55876-292-3. Dewey:969.1.
LCCN:2001-026978.
Audience: **g,l,u,f.**

Campbell, Gwyn   **HC895.C36 2004**
An Economic History of Imperial Madagascar, 1750-1895: The
Rise and Fall of an Island Empire. J. M. Lonsdale, John David
Yeadon Peel, John Sender, David Anderson, Carolyn Brown,
Christopher Clapham, Michael Gomez, Patrick Manning, David
Robinson & Leonardo A. Villalon (Contribution by). Cloth Text.
Cambridge University Press. New York, NY. 2005. 432p.
African Studies, Vol. 106 ISBN:0-521-83935-1, ISBN13:
978-0-521-83935-8. Dewey:330.9691/01. LCCN:2003-069667.
Audience: **u,f.** *Choice, 2005.*

Covell, Maureen   **DT469.M343**
Madagascar: Politics, Economics, and Society. New York: F.
Pinter. 1987. Marxist Regimes Series ISBN:0-86187-429-3,
ISBN13: 978-0-86187-429-3.
Audience: **g,l,u,f.**

Erlich, Haggai   **DT397.E75 1983**
The Struggle over Eritrea, 1962-1978: War and Revolution in
the Horn of Africa. Trade Paper. Hoover Institution Press.
Stanford, CA. 1982. 176p. Publication Ser., No. 260
ISBN:0-8179-7602-7, ISBN13: 978-0-8179-7602-6.
Dewey:963/.06. LCCN:81-081169.
Audience: **g,l,u,f.** *B*

Larson, Pier Martin   **DT469.M277M475 2000**
History and Memory in the Age of Enslavement: Becoming
Merina in Highland Madagascar, 1770-1822. Trade Paper.
Greenwood Publishing Group, Inc. Portsmouth, NH. 2000. 440p.
Social History of Africa Ser. ISBN:0-325-00216-9, ISBN13:
978-0-325-00216-3. Dewey:969.1004/993. LCCN:99-049241.
Audience: **u,f.** *Choice, 2001.*

Metz, Helen C. (Editor)   **DS349.8.I5 1995**
Indian Ocean: Five Island Countries. Ed. 3. Trade Cloth. Library
of Congress. Washington, DC. 1995. 440p. Area Handbooks
Ser.: DA Pam Ser., Vol. 550-154 ISBN:0-8444-0857-3, ISBN13:
978-0-8444-0857-6. Dewey:909/.09824. LCCN:95-016570.
Audience: **g,l,u,f.**

Mutibwa, Phares M.   **DT469.M32 M89**
The Malagasy and the Europeans. Cloth Text. Brill Academic
Publishers, Inc. Boston, MA. 1974. 395p. Ibadan History Ser.
ISBN:0-391-00348-8, ISBN13: 978-0-391-00348-4.
Dewey:327.69/1.
Audience: **g,l,u,f.** *B*

Pateman, Roy   **DT397**
Eritrea: Even the Stones Are Burning. Trade Cloth. Red Sea
Press. Trenton, NJ. 1998. 252p. ISBN:1-56902-026-4, ISBN13:
978-1-56902-026-5. Dewey:963.5/07.
Audience: **g,l,u,f.**

Pool, David   **DT397.P66 2001**
From Guerrillas to Government: The Eritrean People's
Liberation Front. Trade Paper. Ohio University Press. Athens,
OH. 2001. 222p. Eastern African Studies ISBN:0-8214-1387-2,
ISBN13: 978-0-8214-1387-6. Dewey:963.507.
LCCN:00-053028.
Audience: **u,f.** *Choice, 2002.*

Wrong, Michela   **DT397.W76**
I Didn't Do It for You: How the World Betrayed a Small
African Nation. Trade Paper. HarperCollins Publishers. New
York, NY. 2006. 480p. P. S. Ser. ISBN:0-06-078093-2, ISBN13:
978-0-06-078093-7. Dewey:963.507.
Audience: **u,f.**

History of Africa > West Africa > General History

Ajayi, Jacob Festus Ade   **DT475 .H57 1985**
& Crowder, M.
History of West Africa, Vol. 1. Ed. 3. Cloth Text. Longman Publishing Group. White Plains, NY. 1985. 752p. ISBN:0-582-64683-9, ISBN13: 978-0-582-64683-4. Dewey:966. LCCN:88-193404.

Audience: **g,l,u,f.** ℬ

Ajayi, Jacob Festus Ade   **DT475.A76 1976**
& Crowder, M.
History of West Africa, Vol. 2. Ed. 2. Cloth Text. Longman Publishing Group. White Plains, NY. 1987. 780p. ISBN:0-582-01604-5, ISBN13: 978-0-582-01604-0. Dewey:966. LCCN:77-350304.

Audience: **g,l,u,f.** ℬ

Blake, W. John   **DT476.B55 1977**
West Africa: Quest for God and Gold, 1454-1578. Ed. 2. Trade Cloth. Rowman & Littlefield Publishers, Inc. Lanham, MD. 1977. 246p. ISBN:0-87471-965-8, ISBN13: 978-0-87471-965-9. Dewey:966. LCCN:77-373248.

Audience: **g,l,u,f.** ℬ

Brooks, George E.   **DT476.B75 1993**
Landlords and Strangers: Ecological Adjustment. Trade Paper. Westview Press. Boulder, CO. 1994. 360p. ISBN:0-8133-1263-9, ISBN13: 978-0-8133-1263-7. Dewey:966.02. LCCN:92-047445.

Audience: **u,f.**

California University at   **HB2331 .C33 1977**
Los Angeles African Studio Staff & Kuper, Hilda (Editors)
Urbanization and Migration in West Africa. Trade Cloth. Greenwood Publishing Group, Inc. Portsmouth, NH. 1977. ISBN:0-8371-8762-1, ISBN13: 978-0-8371-8762-4. Dewey:304.8/2/0966. LCCN:76-051201.

Audience: **u,f.**

Chafer, Tony   **DT352.5.C48 2002**
The End of Empire in French West Africa: France's Successful Decolonization? Cloth over Boards. Berg Publishers. Oxford, 2002. 256p. ISBN:1-85973-552-5, ISBN13: 978-1-85973-552-7. Dewey:960/.917541. LCCN:2002-001531.

Audience: **u,f.** *Choice, 2003.*

Cruise O'Brien, Donal   **DT476.5 .C66 1990**
(Editor, Editor)
Contemporary West African States. John Dunn & Richard Rathbone (Editors), David Anderson, Carolyn Brown, Christopher Clapham, Michael Gomez, Patrick Manning, David Robinson & Leonardo A. Villalon (Contribution by). Trade Paper. Cambridge University Press. New York, NY. 1990. 235p. African Studies ISBN:0-521-36893-6, ISBN13: 978-0-521-36893-3. Dewey:966.03/27. LCCN:89-009695.

Audience: **g,l,u,f.** *Choice, 1991.*

Curtin, Philip D.   **DT474**
(Editor)
Africa and the West: Intellectual Responses to European Culture. Trade Paper. University of Wisconsin Press. Chicago, IL. 1974. 272p. ISBN:0-299-06124-8, ISBN13: 978-0-299-06124-1. Dewey:916/.03/308. LCCN:77-176409.

Audience: **g,l,u,f.** ℬ

Fage, J. D.   **DT475**
A History of West Africa: An Introductory Survey. Ed. 4. Trade Cloth. Ashgate Publishing, Ltd. Aldershot, 1993. 260p. Modern Revivals in African Studies ISBN:0-7512-0102-2, ISBN13: 978-0-7512-0102-4. Dewey:966.

Audience: **g,l,u,f.**

Forde, Daryll &   **DT476**
Kaberry, P. M. (Editors)
West African Kingdoms in the Nineteenth-Century. Trade Cloth. Oxford University Press, Inc. New York, NY. 1971. ISBN:0-19-724187-5, ISBN13: 978-0-19-724187-5. Dewey:966.

Audience: **g,l,u,f.**

Hargreaves, John D.   **DT476.2.H37 1974**
West Africa Partitioned: The Loaded Pause, 1885-1889, Vol. 1. Trade Cloth. University of Wisconsin Press. Chicago, IL. 1974. 288p. ISBN:0-299-06720-3, ISBN13: 978-0-299-06720-5. Dewey:325/.366/094. LCCN:74-010451.

Audience: **g,l,u,f.** ℬ

Hargreaves, John D.   **DT0476.2.H37**
West Africa Partitioned: The Elephants and the Grass, Vol. 2. Trade Paper. Books on Demand. Ann Arbor, MI. 1985. 293p. ISBN:0-608-07013-0, ISBN13: 978-0-608-07013-1. Dewey:325/.34/0966. LCCN:74-010451.

Audience: **g,l,u,f.** *Choice, 1986.*

Hiskett, Mervyn   **BP64.A4W4**
Development of Islam in West Africa. Ed. 1. Paper Text. Longman Publishing Group. White Plains, NY. 1984. 353p. ISBN:0-582-64694-4, ISBN13: 978-0-582-64694-0. Dewey:297/.0966. LCCN:82-006545.

Audience: **g,l,u,f.** ℬ

Hopkins, A. G.   **HC517.W5 H66**
An Economic History of West Africa. Trade Paper. Columbia University Press. New York, NY. 1973. 450p. Economic History of the Modern World Ser. ISBN:0-231-08345-9, ISBN13: 978-0-231-08345-4. Dewey:330.9/66.

Audience: **g,l,u,f.** ℬ

Klein, Martin A.   **HT1396 .K54 1998**
Slavery and Colonial Rule in French West Africa. Trade Cloth. Cambridge University Press. New York, NY. 1998. 378p. African Studies, Vol. 94 ISBN:0-521-59324-7, ISBN13: 978-0-521-59324-3. Dewey:306.3/62/09660917541. LCCN:98-144038.

Audience: **u,f.** *Choice, 1999.*

Langley, Jabez Ayodele   **DT30**
Pan-Africanism and Nationalism in West Africa, 1900-1945: A Study in Ideology and Social Classes. Trade Cloth. Oxford University Press, Inc. New York, NY. 1973. x, 421p. ISBN:0-19-821689-0, ISBN13: 978-0-19-821689-6. Dewey:320.5/4/0966. LCCN:74-155448.

Audience: **u,f.** ℬ

Law, Robin   **GN652.5 .L38**
The Horse in West African History: The Role of the Horse in the Societies of Pre-Colonial West Africa. Trade Cloth. Oxford University Press, Inc. New York, NY. 1981. IARC Scientific Publications ISBN:0-19-724206-5, ISBN13: 978-0-19-724206-3. Dewey:306/.3. LCCN:81-129421.

Audience: **u,f.**

Levtzion, Nehemiah   **DT476.C67 2000**
Corpus of Early Arab Sources for West African History. J. F. P. Hopkins (Editor). Paper Text. Markus Wiener Publishers, Inc.

Princeton, NJ. 2000. 516p. ISBN:1-55876-241-8, ISBN13: 978-1-55876-241-1. Dewey:966. LCCN:00-040895.

Audience: **g,l,u,f.**

Lovejoy, Paul E.   **HD9213.A56**
Salt of the Desert Sun: A History of Salt Production and Trade in the Central Sudan. David Anderson, Carolyn Brown, Christopher Clapham, Michael Gomez, Patrick Manning, David Robinson & Leonardo A. Villalon (Contribution by). Trade Paper. Cambridge University Press. New York, NY. 2003. 367p. African Studies ISBN:0-521-52433-4, ISBN13: 978-0-521-52433-9. Dewey:338.2/763/0966.

Audience: **g,l,u,f.** *Choice, 1987.*

McIntosh, Roderick J.   **GN652.M25M35 1998**
The Peoples of the Middle Niger: The Island of Gold. Trade Cloth. Blackwell Publishing, Inc. Malden, MA. 1998. 384p. The Peoples of Africa Ser. ISBN:0-631-17361-7, ISBN13: 978-0-631-17361-8. Dewey:305.8/009662. LCCN:98-010817.

Audience: **u,f.** *Choice, 1999.*

Niane, D. T.   **DT532.2**
Sundiata: An Epic of Old Mali. Ed. 2. Trade Paper. Longman Publishing Group. White Plains, NY. 1995. 101p. Longman African Writers Series ISBN:0-582-26475-8, ISBN13: 978-0-582-26475-5. Dewey:398.2096.

Audience: **g,l,u,f.**

Rodney, Walter   **DT477 .R6 1982**
A History of the Upper Guinea Coast, 1545-1800. Trade Paper. Monthly Review Press. New York, NY. 1980. ISBN:0-85345-546-5, ISBN13: 978-0-85345-546-2. Dewey:966/.5. LCCN:79-048070.

Audience: **l,u,f.**

Sanneh, Lamin   **BR1460 .S36**
West African Christianity: The Religious Impact. Trade Paper. Orbis Books. Maryknoll, NY. 1983. 304p. ISBN:0-88344-703-7, ISBN13: 978-0-88344-703-1. Dewey:276.6.

Audience: **u,f.**

Smith, Robert S.   **DT476.S6 1989**
Warfare and Diplomacy in Pre-Colonial West Africa. Ed. 2. Trade Paper. University of Wisconsin Press. Chicago, IL. 1989. 186p. ISBN:0-299-12334-0, ISBN13: 978-0-299-12334-5. Dewey:327/.0966/0903. LCCN:89-016510.

Audience: **u,f.**

Webb, James L. Jr.   **HC1002.W43 1995**
Desert Frontier: Ecological and Economic Change along the Western Sahel, 1600-1850. Trade Cloth. University of Wisconsin Press. Chicago, IL. 1994. 254p. ISBN:0-299-14330-9, ISBN13: 978-0-299-14330-5. Dewey:330.966. LCCN:94-010506.

Audience: **u,f.**

History of Africa > West Africa > Cote d'Ivoire

Foster, Philip J.;   **JQ3023 1971**
  Zolberg, Aristide R.
Ghana and the Ivory Coast; Perspectives on Modernization. Chicago: University of Chicago Press. 1971. ISBN:0-226-25752-5, ISBN13: 978-0-226-25752-5.

Audience: **u,f.**

Bassett, Thomas J.   **HD9087.C852 B37 2000**
The Peasant Cotton Revolution in West Africa: Cotte D'Ivoire, 1880-1995. David Anderson, Carolyn Brown & Christopher Clapham (Contribution by). Trade Cloth. Cambridge University Press. New York, NY. 2001. 266p. African Studies Ser., No. 101 ISBN:0-521-78313-5, ISBN13: 978-0-521-78313-2. Dewey:338.1/7351/096668. LCCN:00-031276.

Audience: **u,f.** *Choice, 2002.*

Launay, Robert   **DT545.45.D85L37**
Beyond the Stream: Islam and Society in a West African Town. Paper Text. Waveland Press, Inc. Prospect Heights, IL. 2004. 258p. ISBN:1-57766-343-8, ISBN13: 978-1-57766-343-0. Dewey:306.6970899634.

Audience: **u,f.** *Choice, 1993.*

Shank, David A.   **BV3785.H348S43 1994**
Prophet Harris, the "Black Elijah" of West Africa. Jocelyn Murray (Editor). Trade Cloth. Brill Academic Publishers, Inc. Boston, MA. 1994. xv, 309p. Studies of Religion in Africa, 10 ISBN:90-04-09980-8, ISBN13: 978-90-04-09980-7. Dewey:269/.2/092 B. LCCN:94-026022.

Audience: **u,f.**

Weiskel, Timothy C.   **DT545.7**
French Colonial Rule and the Baule Peoples: Resistance and Collaboration, 1889-1911. Trade Cloth. Oxford University Press, Inc. New York, NY. 1981. 344p. Oxford Studies in African Affairs ISBN:0-19-822715-9, ISBN13: 978-0-19-822715-1. Dewey:966.6/8. LCCN:79-040886.

Audience: **u,f.**

History of Africa > West Africa > Gambia

Elmer, Laurel   **DT509.4.E43 1983**
The Gambia, a Cultural Profile. Banjul, The Gambia: American Embassy. 1983.

Audience: **g,l,u,f.**

Gamble, David P.;   **DT509.45.W64**
  Salmon, Linda K. & Njie, Alhaji Hassan
Peoples of the Gambia:. I, The Wolof. San Francisco State University, Dept. of Anthropology. 1985. Gambian Studies, No. 17

Audience: **g,l,u,f.**

Wright, Donald R.   **DT532.23.W75 2004**
The World and a Very Small Place in Africa: A History of Globalization in Niumi, the Gambia. Ed. 2. Trade Cloth. M. E. Sharpe Inc. Armonk, NY. 2004. 368p. Sources and Studies in World History Ser. ISBN:0-7656-1007-8, ISBN13: 978-0-7656-1007-2. Dewey:966.51. LCCN:2003-061604.

Audience: **g,u,f.**

History of Africa > West Africa > Ghana

Adjaye, Joseph K.   **DT507.A34 1996**
Diplomacy and Diplomats in Nineteenth Century Asante. Trade Cloth. Africa World Press. Trenton, NJ. 1996. 310p. ISBN:0-86543-504-9, ISBN13: 978-0-86543-504-9. Dewey:327.2/09667/09034. LCCN:96-018448.

Audience: **u,f.**

Berry, Sara   DT507.B47 2000
Chiefs Know Their Boundaries: Essays on Property, Power, and
the Past in Asante, 1896-1996. Trade Cloth. Heinemann.
Portsmouth, NH. 2000. xxxix, 226p. Social History of Africa
Ser. ISBN:0-85255-694-2, ISBN13: 978-0-85255-694-8.
Dewey:966.7. LCCN:00-035036.

Audience: **u,f.**

Boateng, Charles Adom   DT512.3.N57B63 2003
The Political Legacy of Kwame Nkrumah of Ghana. Trade
Cloth. Edwin Mellen Press, The. Lewiston, NY. 2003. 208p.
African Studies, Vol. 66 ISBN:0-7734-6812-9, ISBN13:
978-0-7734-6812-2. Dewey:966.705. LCCN:2002-191241.

Audience: **g,l,u,f.**

Busia, K. A.   JS7649.G62 B8
The Position of the Chief in the Modern Political System of
Ashanti: A Study of the Influence of Contemporary Social
Changes on Ashanti Political Institutions. Paper Text. Textbook
Publishers. Temecula, CA. 2003. xii, 233p.
ISBN:0-7581-5387-2, ISBN13: 978-0-7581-5387-6.
Dewey:354.6674.

Audience: **u,f.**

Daaku, Kwame Yeboah   HF3899.G64
Trade and Politics on the Gold Coast, 1600-1720: a Study of the
African Reaction to European Trade. Clarendon London,. 1970.
ISBN:0-19-821653-X, ISBN13: 978-0-19-821653-7.

Audience: **g,l,u,f.**

McCaskie, T. C.   DT507 .M34 1995
State and Society in Pre-Colonial Asante. David Anderson,
Carolyn Brown, Christopher Clapham, Michael Gomez, Patrick
Manning, David Robinson & Leonardo A. Villalon (Contribution
by). Trade Paper. Cambridge University Press. New York, NY.
2003. 512p. African Studies ISBN:0-521-89432-8, ISBN13:
978-0-521-89432-6. Dewey:966.7/018.

Audience: **u,f.** *Choice, 1995.*

Rathbone, Richard   DT511.R28 2000
Nkrumah and the Chiefs: The Politics of Chieftaincy in Ghana,
1951-1960. Trade Cloth. Ohio University Press. Athens, OH.
2000. 188p. West African Ser. ISBN:0-8214-1305-8, ISBN13:
978-0-8214-1305-0. Dewey:320.9667/09/045. LCCN:99-046031.
Audience: **g,l,u,f.** *Choice, 2001.*

Wilks, Ivor   DT507.W48 1989
Asante in the Nineteenth Century. Trade Paper. Cambridge
University Press. New York, NY. 1989. 680p. African Studies,
No. 13 ISBN:0-521-37994-6, ISBN13: 978-0-521-37994-6.
Dewey:966.7/01. LCCN:74-077834.

Audience: **u,f.** 𝓑

Wilks, Ivor   DT507 .W49
Forests of Gold: Essays on the Akan and the Kingdom of
Asante. Trade Paper. Ohio University Press. Athens, OH. 1995.
405p. ISBN:0-8214-1135-7, ISBN13: 978-0-8214-1135-3.
Dewey:966.7. LCCN:93-000473.

Audience: **u,f.**

History of Africa > West Africa > Liberia

Blyden, Edward Wilmot   DT4
Christianity, Islam and the Negro Race. Trade Paper. Black
Classic Press. Baltimore, MD. 1993. 441p. ISBN:0-933121-41-5,
ISBN13: 978-0-933121-41-6. Dewey:291.17. LCCN:93-074112.
Audience: **g,l,u,f.**

Campbell, Mavis C.   DT516.72.R67 A3 1993
Back to Africa: George Ross and the Maroons: From Nova
Scotia to Sierra Leone. Trade Cloth. Africa World Press.
Trenton, NJ. 1993. 150p. ISBN:0-86543-384-4, ISBN13:
978-0-86543-384-7. Dewey:966.4. LCCN:93-012742.

Audience: **g,l,u,f.** *Choice, 1994.*

Gifford, Paul   BR1463.L7 G54 1993
Christianity and Politics in Doe's Liberia. Duncan Forrester &
Alistair Kee (Contribution by). Trade Paper. Cambridge
University Press. New York, NY. 2002. 367p. Cambridge
Studies in Ideology and Religion Ser. ISBN:0-521-52010-X,
ISBN13: 978-0-521-52010-2. Dewey:261.7/096662/09048.

Audience: **u,f.**

Hlophe, Stephen S.   HN835.Z9.S65
Class Ethnicity and Politics in Liberia: A Class Analysis of
Power Struggles in the Tubman and Tolbert Administrations
from 1944-1975. Trade Paper. University Press of America, Inc.
Lanham, MD. 1979. 336p. ISBN:0-8191-0721-2, ISBN13:
978-0-8191-0721-3. Dewey:306/.2/096662. LCCN:79-063261.
Audience: **u,f.** 𝓑

Liebenow, J. Gus   DT631.L53 1987
Liberia: The Quest for Democracy. Trade Cloth. Indiana
University Press. Bloomington, IN. 1987. 350p.
ISBN:0-253-33436-5, ISBN13: 978-0-253-33436-7.
Dewey:966.6/2. LCCN:86-045956.
Audience: **g,l,u,f.** *Choice, 1987.*

Lynch, Hollis R.   CT2750.B4L9
Edward Wilmot Blyden: Pan-Negro Patriot, 1832-1912. Trade
Paper. Oxford University Press, Inc. New York, NY. 1970. 288p.
West African History Ser. ISBN:0-19-501268-2, ISBN13:
978-0-19-501268-2. Dewey:966/.602/0924 B.

Audience: **g,l,u,f.**

Riley, Stephen P.   DT476.5
Liberia and Sierra Leone: Anarchy or Peace in West Africa?
Research Institute for the Study of Conflict and Terrorism. 1996.
Conflict Studies, No. 287

Audience: **g,l,u,f.**

History of Africa > West Africa > Mauritania

Stewart, Charles   BP64.M3
  Cameron & Stewart, E. K.
Islam and Social Order in Mauritania: A Case Study from the
Nineteenth Century. Oxford: Clarendon Press. 1973. Oxford
Studies in African Affairs ISBN:0-19-821688-2, ISBN13:
978-0-19-821688-9.

Audience: **u,f.**

Cleaveland, Timothy   HN773
Becoming Walata: A History of Saharan Social Formation and
Transformation. Trade Cloth. Greenwood Publishing Group, Inc.
Portsmouth, NH. 2001. 256p. ISBN:0-325-07027-X, ISBN13:
978-0-325-07027-8. Dewey:306/.0966. LCCN:00-061331.
Audience: **u,f.**

History of Africa > West Africa > Niger

Baier, Stephen   HC547.N5
An Economic History of Central Niger. Trade Cloth. Oxford
University Press, Inc. New York, NY. 1980. 340p. OSAA Ser.

ISBN:0-19-822717-5, ISBN13: 978-0-19-822717-5.
Dewey:330.966/26. LCCN:79-041134.

Audience: **g,l,u,f.**

Cooper, Barbara M.   **DT547.45.H38C66 1997**
Marriage in Maradi: Gender and Culture in a Hausa Society in
Niger, 1900-1989. Trade Paper. Heinemann. Portsmouth, NH.
1997. 278p. Social History of Africa Ser. ISBN:0-435-07413-X,
ISBN13: 978-0-435-07413-5. Dewey:306.8/089937.
LCCN:97-1610.

Audience: **u,f.** *Choice, 1997.*

Fuglestad, Finn   **DT547.5**
A History of Niger, Eighteen Fifty to Nineteen Sixty. David
Anderson, Carolyn Brown & Christopher Clapham (Contribution
by). Trade Cloth. Cambridge University Press. New York, NY.
1983. 280p. African Studies, No. 41 ISBN:0-521-25268-7,
ISBN13: 978-0-521-25268-3. Dewey:966/.2603.
LCCN:83-001809.

Audience: **g,l,u,f.** *B*

Van Beusekom,   **HD1516**
 Monica M.
Negotiating Development: African Farmers and Colonial Experts
at the Office du Niger, 1920-1960. Trade Cloth. Greenwood
Publishing Group, Inc. Portsmouth, NH. 2001. 256p. Social
History of Africa Ser. ISBN:0-325-07046-6, ISBN13:
978-0-325-07046-9. Dewey:338.1/096623. LCCN:2001-026388.

Audience: **u,f.**

History of Africa > West Africa > Nigeria

Anthony, Douglas A.   **DT5156**
Poison and Medicine: Ethnicity, Power, and Violence in a
Nigerian City, 1966 To 1986. Trade Paper. Heinemann.
Portsmouth, NH. 2002. 288p. Social History of Africa Ser.
ISBN:0-325-07051-2, ISBN13: 978-0-325-07051-3.
Dewey:966.9/78. LCCN:2001-057765.

Audience: **u,f.** *Choice, 2003.*

Awolowo, Obafemi   **DT515.83.A96.A2 1987**
Awo: The Nigerian Colossus. Trade Cloth. A. Onibonoje.
Ibadan, 1987. 80p. ISBN:978-2366-41-2, ISBN13:
978-978-2366-41-2. Dewey:966.905/092. LCCN:87-210161.

Audience: **g,l,u,f.**

Azikiwe, Nnamdi   **DT515.6.A9**
My Odyssey: An Autobiography. Praeger. 1970.

Audience: **g,l,u,f.**

Berry, Sara   **DT515.45.Y67**
Fathers Work for Their Sons: Accumulation, Mobility, and Class
Formation in an Extended Yorùbá Community. University of
California Press Berkeley:. 1985. ISBN:0-520-05164-5, ISBN13:
978-0-520-05164-5.

Audience: **u,f.**

Brown, Carolyn A.   **HD8039**
We Were All Slaves: African Miners, Culture and Resistance at
the Enugu Government Colliery, Nigeria. Trade Paper.
Greenwood Publishing Group, Inc. Portsmouth, NH. 2003. 376p.
Social History of Africa Ser. ISBN:0-325-07006-7, ISBN13:
978-0-325-07006-3. Dewey:331.7/622334/0966949.
LCCN:2001-051630.

Audience: **u,f.** *Choice, 2003.*

Coles, Catherine &   **DT515.45.H38H38 1991**
 Mack, Beverly (Editors)
Hausa Women in the Twentieth Century. Trade Cloth. University
of Wisconsin Press. Chicago, IL. 1991. 310p. Wisconsin
Publications in the History of Science and Medicine, No. 6
ISBN:0-299-13020-7, ISBN13: 978-0-299-13020-6.
Dewey:305.48/8937. LCCN:91-014182.

Audience: **g,l,u,f.** *Choice, 1992.*

Connah, Graham   **DT515.9.B4**
The Archaeology of Benin: Excavations and Other Researches
in and Around Benin City, Nigeria. Oxford: Clarendon Press.
1975. ISBN:0-19-920063-7, ISBN13: 978-0-19-920063-4.

Audience: **g,l,u,f.**

Dike, K. Onwuka   **HC517.N48**
Trade and Politics in the Niger Delta, 1830-1885: An
Introduction to the Economic and Political History of Nigeria.
Oxford: Clarendon Press. 1956. Oxford Studies in African
Affairs

Audience: **g,l,u,f.**

Falola, Toyin (Editor)   **DT515.65 .W37 1992**
Warfare and Diplomacy in Pre-Colonial Nigeria: Essays in
Honor of Robert Smith. Trade Paper. University of
Wisconsin-Madison, African Studies Program. Madison, WI.
1992. ISBN:0-942615-14-X, ISBN13: 978-0-942615-14-2.
Dewey:966.9/01. LCCN:92-013651.

Audience: **u,f.**

Gbadamosi, T. G. O.   **DT513**
The Growth of Islam among the Yoruba, 1841-1908. Humanities
Press. 1978. Ibadan History Series ISBN:0-391-00834-X,
ISBN13: 978-0-391-00834-2.

Audience: **u,f.**

Hackett, Rosalind I.   **BL2470.N5N49 1987**
 (Editor)
New Religious Movements in Nigeria. Trade Cloth. Edwin
Mellen Press, The. Lewiston, NY. 1987. 245p. African Studies,
Vol. 5 ISBN:0-88946-180-5, ISBN13: 978-0-88946-180-2.
Dewey:291.9/09669. LCCN:86-031080.

Audience: **u,f.**

Johnson, Samuel   **DT513**
The History of the Yorubas. Cloth Text. CSS Bookshops,
Limited, Agency & Publishing Division. Lagos, 1997. 684p.
ISBN:978-32292-9-X, ISBN13: 978-978-32292-9-7.
Dewey:966.9/2.

Audience: **g,l,u,f.**

Laitin, David D.   **DT515.45.Y67L35 1986**
Hegemony and Culture: Politics and Change among the Yoruba.
Trade Paper. University of Chicago Press. Chicago, IL. 1986.
266p. ISBN:0-226-46790-2, ISBN13: 978-0-226-46790-0.
Dewey:966.9/2004963. LCCN:85-028871.

Audience: **u,f.**

Lovejoy, Paul E. &   **HT1334.N6 L68 1993**
 Hogendorn, Jan S.
Slow Death for Slavery: The Course of Abolition in Northern
Nigeria, 1897-1936. David Anderson, Carolyn Brown,
Christopher Clapham, Michael Gomez, Patrick Manning, David
Robinson & Leonardo A. Villalon (Contribution by). Trade
Paper. Cambridge University Press. New York, NY. 1993. 411p.
African Studies, No. 76 ISBN:0-521-44702-X, ISBN13:
978-0-521-44702-7. Dewey:326.096. LCCN:92-018406.

Audience: **u,f.** *Choice, 1994.*

Matory, J. Lorand   **DT515.45.Y67**
Sex and the Empire That Is No More: Gender and the Politics
of Metaphor in Oyo Yoruba Religion. Ed. 2. Trade Cloth.
Berghahn Books, Inc. New York, NY. 2004. 320p. Studies in
Applied Anthropology Ser. ISBN:1-57181-307-1, ISBN13:
978-1-57181-307-7. Dewey:306.6/9968333. LCCN:2004-046221.
                         Audience: **u,f.** *Choice, 1994.*

Mba, Nina E.   **HQ1815.5 .M32 1982**
Nigerian Women Mobilized: Women's Political Activity in
Southern Nigeria, 1900-1965. Paper Text. University of
California, International & Area Studies. Berkeley, CA. 1982.
xii, 348p. Research Ser., No. 48 ISBN:0-87725-148-7, ISBN13:
978-0-87725-148-4. Dewey:305.4/2/09669. LCCN:82-015477.
                         Audience: **u,f.**

Okorocha, Cyril C.   **BL2480.I2**
The Meaning of Religious Conversion in Africa: The Case of
the Igbo of Nigeria. Avebury. Brookfield, USA :. 1987.
ISBN:0-566-05030-7, ISBN13: 978-0-566-05030-5.
                         Audience: **u,f.**

Peel, John David   **BV3625.N5P44 2000**
  Yeadon
Religious Encounter and the Making of the Yoruba. Trade Cloth.
Indiana University Press. Bloomington, IN. 2005. 496p. African
Systems of Thought Ser. ISBN:0-253-33794-1, ISBN13:
978-0-253-33794-8. Dewey:266/.009669/09034.
LCCN:00-037031.
                         Audience: **u,f.** *Choice, 2001.*

Tasie, G. O.   **BV3625.N5 T27 1978**
Christian Missionary Enterprise in the Niger Delta, 1864-1918.
Cloth Text. Brill Academic Publishers, Inc. Boston, MA. 1978.
Studies on Religion in Africa, No. 3 ISBN:90-04-05243-7,
ISBN13: 978-90-04-05243-7. Dewey:266/.009669/3.
LCCN:79-302634.
                         Audience: **u,f.**

Watson, Ruth   **DT515.9.I2W38 2002**
'Civil Disorder Is the Disease of Ibadan': Chieftaincy and Civic
Culture in a Colonial City. Trade Paper. Ohio University Press.
Athens, OH. 2003. 256p. Western African Studies
ISBN:0-8214-1451-8, ISBN13: 978-0-8214-1451-4.
Dewey:303.6/2/0966925. LCCN:2002-074827.
                         Audience: **u,f.**

Zartman, I. William   **HC1055**
  (Editor)
The Political Economy of Nigeria. Trade Cloth. Greenwood
Publishing Group, Inc. Portsmouth, NH. 1983. 298p.
ISBN:0-275-91595-6, ISBN13: 978-0-275-91595-7.
Dewey:330.9669/05.
                         Audience: **u,f.**

History of Africa > West Africa > Senegal

Boone, Catherine   **HC1045 .B65 1992**
Merchant Capital and the Roots of State Power in Senegal,
1930-1985. Trade Cloth. Cambridge University Press. New
York, NY. 1992. 317p. Studies in Comparative Politics
ISBN:0-521-41078-9, ISBN13: 978-0-521-41078-6.
Dewey:338.9663. LCCN:91-046536.
                         Audience: **u,f.** *Choice, 1993.*

Colvin, Lucie G.   **HB2125**
The Uprooted of the Western Sahel: Migrants' Quest for Cash in
the Senegambia. Trade Cloth. Greenwood Publishing Group,
Inc. Portsmouth, NH. 1981. 385p. ISBN:0-275-90597-7,
ISBN13: 978-0-275-90597-2. Dewey:304.8/2/09663.
LCCN:81-005005.
                         Audience: **u,f.**

Echenberg, Myron   **RC179**
Black Death, White Medicine: Bubonic Plague and the Politics
of Public Health in Colonial Senegal, 1914-1945. Trade Paper.
Greenwood Publishing Group, Inc. Portsmouth, NH. 2001. 328p.
Social History of Africa Ser. ISBN:0-325-07016-4, ISBN13:
978-0-325-07016-2. Dewey:614.5/732/009663.
LCCN:2001-024564.
                         Audience: **u,f.** *Choice, 2002.*

Klein, Martin A.   **DT549.7**
Islam and Imperialism in Senegal: Sine-Saloum, 1847-1914.
Stanford University Press. 1968.
                         Audience: **u,f.**

Markovitz, Irving   **DT549.6.S4**
  Leonard
Léopold Sédar Senghor and the Politics of Negritude.
Atheneum. 1969.
                         Audience: **g,l,u,f.**

Robinson, David   **DT541.65.R63 2000**
Paths of Accommodation: Muslim Societies and French Colonial
Authorities in Senegal and Mauritania, 1880-1920. Trade Cloth.
Ohio University Press. Athens, OH. 2000. 377p. Western
African Studies ISBN:0-8214-1353-8, ISBN13:
978-0-8214-1353-1. Dewey:966.1/01. LCCN:00-044614.
                         Audience: **u,f.** *Choice, 2001.*

Searing, James F.   **DT549**
God Alone Is King: Islam and Emancipation in Senegal: The
Wolf Kingdoms of Kajour and Bawol, 1859-1914. Trade Paper.
Greenwood Publishing Group, Inc. Portsmouth, NH. 2001. 336p.
Social History of Africa Ser. ISBN:0-325-07073-3, ISBN13:
978-0-325-07073-5. Dewey:966/.3. LCCN:2001-026389.
                         Audience: **u,f.** *Choice, 2002.*

Senghor, Léopold Sédar   **JQ3396.A91**
On African Socialism. Praeger. 1964.
                         Audience: **g,l,u,f.**

Villalon, Leonardo A.   **BP64.S42 F388 1995**
  (Contribution by), et al.
Islamic Society and State Power in Senegal: Disciples and
Citizens in Fatick, Senegal. David Anderson, Carolyn Brown,
Christopher Clapham, Michael Gomez, Patrick Manning &
David Robinson (Contribution by). Trade Cloth. Cambridge
University Press. New York, NY. 1995. 359p. African Studies,
No. 80 ISBN:0-521-46007-7, ISBN13: 978-0-521-46007-1.
Dewey:320.5/5/09663. LCCN:94-013358.
                         Audience: **u,f.** *Choice, 1995.*

History of Africa > West Africa > Sierra Leone

Abraham, Arthur   **JQ3121**
Mende Government and Politics under Colonial Rule: A
Historical Study of Political Change in Sierra Leone, 1890-1937.
Freetown, Sierra Leone: Sierra Leone University Press. 1978.
ISBN:0-19-711638-8, ISBN13: 978-0-19-711638-8.
                         Audience: **u,f.**

Ayandele, Emmanuel   DT504.J64
Ayankanmi
Holy Johnson: Pioneer of African Nationalism, 1836-1917.
Humanities Press. 1970. Africana Modern Library, No. 13
ISBN:0-391-00041-1, ISBN13: 978-0-391-00041-4.

Audience: **u,f.**

Fyfe, Christopher   DT516.5 .F85
A History of Sierra Leone. Paper Text. Textbook Publishers.
Temecula, CA. 2003. vii, 773p. ISBN:0-7581-7245-1, ISBN13:
978-0-7581-7245-7. Dewey:966.4.

Audience: **g,l,u,f.** β

Kilson, Marion   DT510.42
African Urban Kinsmen: The Ga of Central Accra. St. Martin's
Press. 1974.

Audience: **u,f.**

Reno, William   JQ3121.A56C6 1995
Corruption and State Politics in Sierra Leone. Cloth Text.
Cambridge University Press. New York, NY. 1995. 242p.
African Studies, 83 ISBN:0-521-47179-6, ISBN13:
978-0-521-47179-4. Dewey:320.9664/09/04. LCCN:94-012865.

Audience: **u,f.** *Choice, 1996.*

Spitzer, Leo   DS135.A9S65 1989
Lives in Between: Assimilation and Marginality in Austria,
Brazil, and West Africa, 1780-1945. Trade Paper. Cambridge
University Press. New York, NY. 1990. 262p. Cambridge
Studies in Comparative World History ISBN:0-521-37827-3,
ISBN13: 978-0-521-37827-7. Dewey:303.48/2.
LCCN:89-024004.

Audience: **u,f.** *Choice, 1990.*

Wyse, Akintola J.   DT516.18
The Krio of Sierra Leone: An Interpretive History. Trade Paper.
Howard University Press. Washington, DC. 1991. 157p.
ISBN:0-88258-162-7, ISBN13: 978-0-88258-162-0.
Dewey:966.4. LCCN:91-034770.

Audience: **u,f.**

History of Africa > West Africa > Other West African Countries

Adamolekun, 'Ladipo   HN810.G8
Sekou Toure's Guinea: An Experiment in National Building.
Trade Paper. Routledge. New York, NY. 1976. 200p. Studies in
African History, No. 12 ISBN:0-416-77850-X, ISBN13:
978-0-416-77850-2. Dewey:309.1/66/5205. LCCN:76-017220.

Audience: **u,f.**

Akinjogbin   DT541.65 .A6
Dahomey and Neighbours. Trade Cloth. Cambridge University
Press. New York, NY. 1967. ISBN:0-521-04016-7, ISBN13:
978-0-521-04016-7. Dewey:916.6/8.

Audience: **u,f.**

Allen, Christopher;   DT54.22
Radu, Michael; Baxter, Joan & Somerville, Keith
Benin. New York : Pinter Publishers. 1989.
ISBN:0-86187-481-1, ISBN13: 978-0-86187-481-1.

Audience: **g,l,u,f.**

Brenner, Louis   BP64.M29B73 2001
Controlling Knowledge: Religion, Power and Schooling in a
West African Muslim Society. Trade Cloth. Indiana University

Press. Bloomington, IN. 2001. xv, 343p. ISBN:0-253-33917-0,
ISBN13: 978-0-253-33917-1. Dewey:297/.096623.
LCCN:00-063464.

Audience: **u,f.**

Cabral, Amilcar   DT613.62 .C32
Revolution in Guinea. Trade Cloth. Africa Fund. New York, NY.
1974. 110p. ISBN:0-317-36674-2, ISBN13: 978-0-317-36674-7.
Dewey:320.1/58/096657.

Audience: **g,l,u,f.**

Cabral, Amilcar   DT613.75 .C32
Return to the Source: Selected Speeches. Africa Information
Service Staff (Editor). Trade Paper. Monthly Review Press. New
York, NY. 1974. 128p. ISBN:0-85345-347-0, ISBN13:
978-0-85345-347-5. Dewey:320.9/66/5702.

Audience: **g,l,u,f.**

Cabral, Amilcar   DT0613.75.C3
Unity and Struggle: Speeches and Writings. Michael Wolfers
(Translator), PAIGC Staff (Selected by). Trade Paper. Books on
Demand. Ann Arbor, MI. 1979. 334p. ISBN:0-7837-9602-1,
ISBN13: 978-0-7837-9602-4. Dewey:320.9/66/5702.
LCCN:79-002337.

Audience: **g,l,u,f.**

Cordell, Dennis D. &   HB2126.4.A3
Gregory, Joel W.
Hoe and Wage: A Social History of a Circular Migration System
in West Africa. Paper Text. Westview Press. Boulder, CO. 1998.
400p. African Moderniztion and Development Ser.
ISBN:0-8133-3608-2, ISBN13: 978-0-8133-3608-4.
Dewey:304.8/2/0966.

Audience: **u,f.** *Choice, 1997.*

Derman, William   DT543.42 .D47
Serfs, Peasants, and Socialists: A Former Serf Village in the
Republic of Guinea. Trade Cloth. University of California Press.
Berkeley, CA. 1973. 292p. ISBN:0-520-01728-5, ISBN13:
978-0-520-01728-3. Dewey:301.45/19/6306652.
LCCN:78-117148.

Audience: **u,f.**

Dhada, Mustafah   DT613.78.D47 1993
Warriors at Work: How Guinea Was Really Set Free. Trade
Cloth. University Press of Colorado. Boulder, CO. 1993. 352p.
ISBN:0-87081-287-4, ISBN13: 978-0-87081-287-3.
Dewey:966.57/02. LCCN:94-139187.

Audience: **u,f.** *Choice, 1994.*

Galli, Rosemary &   HC1080
Jones, Jocelyn
Guinea-Bissau: Politics, Economics, and Society. Boulder: L.
Rienner. 1987. Marxist Regimes Series ISBN:1-55587-025-2,
ISBN13: 978-1-55587-025-6.

Audience: **g,l,u,f.**

Irwin, Paul B.   DT0553.U79L5
Liptako Speaks: History from Oral Tradition in Africa. Trade
Paper. Books on Demand. Ann Arbor, MI. 234p.
ISBN:0-8357-3695-4, ISBN13: 978-0-8357-3695-4.
Dewey:966/.2501. LCCN:80-007531.

Audience: **g,l,u,f.**

Knoll, Arthur J.   DT582.7
Togo under Imperial Germany, 1884-1914: A Case Study in
Colonial Rule. Hoover Institution Press. 1978. Hoover Colonial

Studies; Hoover Institution Publication, No. 190
ISBN:0-8179-6901-2, ISBN13: 978-0-8179-6901-1.

Audience: **g,l,u,f.**

Law, Robin　　　　　　　　　　**HT1332.L38 1991**
The Slave Coast of West Africa, 1550-1750: The Impact of the
Atlantic Slave Trade on an African Society. Trade Cloth. Oxford
University Press, Inc. New York, NY. 1991. 388p. Oxford
Studies in African Affairs ISBN:0-19-820228-8, ISBN13:
978-0-19-820228-8. Dewey:306/.0966. LCCN:91-012676.

Audience: **u,f.** *Choice, 1992.*

Manchuelle, Francois　　　　　**DT549.45.S66M35 1997**
Willing Migrants: Soninke Labor Diasporas, 1848-1960. Trade
Cloth. Ohio University Press. Athens, OH. 1997. 388p. Western
African Studies ISBN:0-8214-1201-9, ISBN13:
978-0-8214-1201-5. Dewey:331.6/2367/044. LCCN:97-027492.

Audience: **u,f.** *Choice, 1998.*

Manning, Patrick　　　　　　　**HC1010.M36 2004**
Slavery, Colonialism and Economic Growth in Dahomey,
1640-1960. David Anderson, Carolyn Brown, Christopher
Clapham, Michael Gomez, David Robinson & Leonardo A.
Villalon (Contribution by). Trade Paper. Cambridge University
Press. New York, NY. 2004. 464p. African Studies, Vol. 30
ISBN:0-521-52307-9, ISBN13: 978-0-521-52307-3.
Dewey:330.96683/01. LCCN:2005-277523.

Audience: **u,f.**

McCulloch, Jock　　　　　　　**DT613.76.C3**
In the Twilight of Revolution: The Political Theory of Amilcar
Cabral. Boston : Routledge & Kegan Paul. 1983.
ISBN:0-7100-9411-6, ISBN13: 978-0-7100-9411-7.

Audience: **u,f.**

Nugent, Paul　　　　　　　　　**DT582.45.E93N84 2002**
Smugglers, Secessionists and Loyal Citizens on the Ghana-Toga
Frontier: The Life of the Borderlands since 1914. Trade Cloth.
Ohio University Press. Athens, OH. 2003. 302p. Western
African Studies ISBN:0-8214-1481-X, ISBN13:
978-0-8214-1481-1. Dewey:966.7/03. LCCN:2002-029079.

Audience: **u,f.** *Choice, 2003.*

Piot, Charles　　　　　　　　　**DT582.45.K33P56 1999**
Remotely Global: Village Modernity in West Africa. Trade
Paper. University of Chicago Press. Chicago, IL. 1999. 238p.
ISBN:0-226-66969-6, ISBN13: 978-0-226-66969-4.
Dewey:966.81. LCCN:99-011071.

Audience: **u,f.**

Ronen, Dov　　　　　　　　　　**DT541.5**
Dahomey: Between Tradition and Modernity. Book, Other.
Cornell University Press. Ithaca, NY. 1975. 320p. Africa in the
Modern World Ser. ISBN:0-8014-0927-6, ISBN13:
978-0-8014-0927-1. Dewey:966/.83. LCCN:74-025375.

Audience: **u,f.**

Saul, Mahir　　　　　　　　　　**DT532.5.S38 2001**
West African Challenge to Empire: Culture and History in the
Volta-Bani Anti-Colonial War. Patrick Yves Royer (Contribution
by). Trade Cloth. Ohio University Press. Athens, OH. 2002.
417p. Western African Studies ISBN:0-8214-1413-5, ISBN13:
978-0-8214-1413-2. Dewey:966/.0314. LCCN:2001-037449.

Audience: **g,l,u,f.** *Choice, 2002.*

Silla, Eric　　　　　　　　　　**RC154.8.M42S56 1998**
People Are Not the Same: Leprosy and Identity in
Twentieth-Century Mali. Trade Cloth. Greenwood Publishing
Group, Inc. Portsmouth, NH. 1998. 272p. Social History of

Africa Ser. ISBN:0-325-00005-0, ISBN13: 978-0-325-00005-3.
Dewey:362.1/96998/0096623. LCCN:97-039954.

Audience: **g,l,u,f.** *Choice, 1998.*

Urdang, Stephanie　　　　　　**HQ1818.U69**
Fighting Two Colonialisms: Women in Guinea-Bissau. Trade
Cloth. Monthly Review Press. New York, NY. 1979. 320p.
ISBN:0-85345-511-2, ISBN13: 978-0-85345-511-0.
Dewey:301.41/2/096657. LCCN:79-002329.

Audience: **u,f.** *B*

History of Africa > Southern Africa > General History

Barnard, Alan　　　　　　　　**DT1058.S36B37 1992**
Hunters and Herders of Southern Africa: A Comparative
Ethnography of the Khoisan Peoples. Meyer Fortes, Jack Goody,
Edmund Leach & Stanley Tambiah (Contribution by). Trade
Cloth. Cambridge University Press. New York, NY. 1992. 379p.
Cambridge Studies in Social and Cultural Anthropology, No. 85
ISBN:0-521-41188-2, ISBN13: 978-0-521-41188-2.
Dewey:305.896/1068. LCCN:91-017705.

Audience: **u,f.**

Bauer, Gretchen &　　　　　　**JQ2720.A58B38 2005**
Taylor, Scott D.
Politics in Southern Africa: State and Society in Transition.
Trade Cloth. Lynne Rienner Publishers, Inc. Boulder, CO. 2005.
400p. ISBN:1-58826-332-0, ISBN13: 978-1-58826-332-2.
Dewey:320.968. LCCN:2004-024451.

Audience: **g,l,u,f.** *Choice, 2005.*

Birmingham, David　　　　　　**DT1402.B57 1992**
Frontline Nationalism in Angola and Mozambique. Trade Cloth.
Africa World Press. Trenton, NJ. 1992. 122p.
ISBN:0-86543-367-4, ISBN13: 978-0-86543-367-0.
Dewey:320.5409673. LCCN:92-032977.

Audience: **u,f.**

Hall, Martin　　　　　　　　　**DT1107.H35 1990**
Farmers, Kings, and Traders: The People of Southern Africa,
200-1860. Martin West (Foreword by). Trade Paper. University
of Chicago Press. Chicago, IL. 1990. 176p.
ISBN:0-226-31326-3, ISBN13: 978-0-226-31326-9. Dewey:968.
LCCN:90-039017.

Audience: **g,l,u,f.**

Hanlon, Joseph　　　　　　　　**HF1613.4.Z4A4355**
Beggar Your Neighbours: Apartheid Power in Southern Africa.
Trade Cloth. Indiana University Press. Bloomington, IN. 1986.
364p. ISBN:0-253-33131-5, ISBN13: 978-0-253-33131-1.
Dewey:327/.0968. LCCN:86-045581.

Audience: **g,l,u,f.** *Choice, 1987.*

Kitchen, Helen A.　　　　　　　**E183.8.A5**
Angola, Mozambique, and the West. New York: Praeger. 1987.
The Washington Papers,; 130 ISBN:0-275-92879-9, ISBN13:
978-0-275-92879-7.

Audience: **g,l,u,f.**

Omer-Cooper, John D.　　　　　**DT1787.O44 1987**
History of Southern Africa. Paper Text. Heinemann. Portsmouth,
NH. 1987. 298p. ISBN:0-435-08010-5, ISBN13:
978-0-435-08010-5. Dewey:968. LCCN:86-32007.

Audience: **g,l,u,f.**

Ransford, Oliver   **DT351**
David Livingstone: The Dark Interior. Cloth Text. Palgrave
Macmillan. New York, NY. 1978. ISBN:0-312-18379-8,
ISBN13: 978-0-312-18379-0. Dewey:916.7/04.
LCCN:78-050673.

Audience: **g,l,u,f.**

Saul, John S.   **HX450.A6S38 1990**
Socialist Ideology and the Struggle for Southern Africa. Trade
Cloth. Africa World Press. Trenton, NJ. 1990. 200p.
ISBN:0-86543-099-3, ISBN13: 978-0-86543-099-0.
Dewey:320.5/31/096. LCCN:88-071175.

Audience: **u,f.** *Choice, 1991.*

Schreuder, Deryck M.   **DT746**
The Scramble for Southern Africa: Eighteen Seventy-Seven to
Eighteen Ninety-Five. Cloth Text. Cambridge University Press.
New York, NY. 1980. 400p. Cambridge Commonwealth Ser.
ISBN:0-521-20279-5, ISBN13: 978-0-521-20279-4.
Dewey:968.04. LCCN:78-058800.

Audience: **g,l,u,f.** ℬ

Vail, Leroy (Editor)   **GN656.C74 1989**
The Creation of Tribalism in Southern Africa. Trade Cloth.
University of California Press. Berkeley, CA. 1989. 436p.
Perspectives on Southern Africa Ser. ISBN:0-520-06284-1,
ISBN13: 978-0-520-06284-9. Dewey:320.5. LCCN:88-004753.

Audience: **u,f.** *Choice, 1989.*

History of Africa > Southern Africa > Angola

Bender, Gerald J.   **DT611.42.B46**
Angola under the Portuguese: The Myth and the Reality. Trade
Cloth. Africa World Press. Trenton, NJ. 2004. 326p.
ISBN:1-59221-257-3, ISBN13: 978-1-59221-257-6.
Dewey:325/.3469/09673.

Audience: **u,f.** ℬ

Birmingham, David   **DT604**
Trade and Conflict in Angola: The Mbundu and Their Neighbors
under the Influence of the Portuguese, 1483-1790. Oxford:
Clarendon Press. 1966. Oxford Studies in African Affairs

Audience: **u,f.**

Brittain, Victoria   **DT1428 .B75 1998**
Death of Dignity: Angola's Civil War. Trade Cloth. Africa
World Press. Trenton, NJ. 1998. 200p. ISBN:0-86543-636-3,
ISBN13: 978-0-86543-636-7. Dewey:967.304.
LCCN:97-030309.

Audience: **u,f.**

Heywood, Linda M.   **DT1373.H49 2000**
Contested Power in Angola, 1840s to the Present. Trade Cloth.
University of Rochester Press. Rochester, NY. 2000. 330p.
Rochester Studies in African History and the Diaspora, No.
1092-5228 ISBN:1-58046-063-1, ISBN13: 978-1-58046-063-7.
Dewey:323.1/19639320673/09. LCCN:00-027765.

Audience: **g,l,u,f.** *Choice, 2001.*

James, W. Martin   **DT1428.J36 1991**
A Political History of the Civil War in Angola, 1974-1990.
Trade Cloth. Transaction Publishers. Somerset, NJ. 1991. 314p.
ISBN:0-88738-418-8, ISBN13: 978-0-88738-418-9.
Dewey:967.304. LCCN:90-023709.

Audience: **g,l,u,f.** *Choice, 1992.*

Maier, Karl   **CT1428**
Angola: Promises and Lies. Trade Paper. Serif. London, 2002.
224p. ISBN:1-897959-22-2, ISBN13: 978-1-897959-22-0.
Dewey:967.304092.

Audience: **u,f.**

Miller, Joseph C.   **HT1221.M55 1988**
Way of Death: Merchant Capitalism and the Angolan Slave
Trade, 1730-1830. Cloth Text. University of Wisconsin Press.
Chicago, IL. 1988. 796p. ISBN:0-299-11560-7, ISBN13:
978-0-299-11560-9. Dewey:382.4/4/09469. LCCN:87-040368.

Audience: **u,f.** *Choice, 1989.*

Wheeler, Douglas L. &   **DT611**
  Pelissier, Rene
Angola. Trade Cloth. Greenwood Publishing Group, Inc.
Portsmouth, NH. 1978. 296p. Praeger Library of African Affairs
ISBN:0-313-20011-4, ISBN13: 978-0-313-20011-3.
Dewey:967/.3/03. LCCN:77-020095.

Audience: **g,l,u,f.** ℬ

History of Africa > Southern Africa > Botswana

Morton, Fred &   **DT2490**
  Ramsay, Jeff
The Birth of Botswana: A History of the Bechuanaland
Protectorate from 1910 to 1966. Longman Botswana. 1987.
ISBN:0-582-00584-1, ISBN13: 978-0-582-00584-6.

Audience: **g,l,u,f.**

Parsons, Neil   **DA125.N4P37 1998**
King Khama, Emperor Joe, and the Great White Queen:
Victorian Britain Through African Eyes. Trade Cloth. University
of Chicago Press. Chicago, IL. 1998. 340p.
ISBN:0-226-64744-7, ISBN13: 978-0-226-64744-9.
Dewey:327.4106883. LCCN:97-037111.

Audience: **u,f.** *Choice, 1998.*

Pennington, Renee &   **DT2458.H47**
  Harpending, Henry
The Structure of an African Pastoralist Community:
Demography, History, and Ecology of the Ngamiland Herero.
Cloth Text. Oxford University Press, Inc. New York, NY. 1993.
288p. Research Monographs in Human Population Biology, No.
11 ISBN:0-19-852286-X, ISBN13: 978-0-19-852286-7.
Dewey:304.608996399. LCCN:93-015644.

Audience: **u,f.**

Sillery, A.   **DT791**
Botswana: a Short Political History. Methuen London:. 1974.
ISBN:0-416-75480-5, ISBN13: 978-0-416-75480-3.

Audience: **g,l,u,f.**

Tlou, Thomas &   **DT791**
  Campbell, Alec C.
History of Botswana. Macmillan Botswana. 1984.
ISBN:0-333-36531-3, ISBN13: 978-0-333-36531-1.

Audience: **g,l,u,f.**

History of Africa > Southern Africa > Lesotho

Eldridge, Elizabeth A.   **DT2630 .E44 1993**
A South African Kingdom: The Pursuit of Security in
Nineteenth-Century Lesotho. Trade Cloth. Cambridge University
Press. New York, NY. 1993. 268p. African Studies, No. 78
ISBN:0-521-44067-X, ISBN13: 978-0-521-44067-7.
Dewey:968.8501. LCCN:92-031675.
                    Audience: **u,f.** *Choice, 1994.*

Machobane, L. B.   **DT2638.M33 1990**
Government and Change in Lesotho, 1800-1966. Cloth Text.
Palgrave Macmillan. New York, NY. 1990. 260p.
ISBN:0-312-03680-9, ISBN13: 978-0-312-03680-5.
Dewey:968.85/02. LCCN:89-029461.
                    Audience: **g,l,u,f.**

History of Africa > Southern Africa > Malawi

McMaster, Carolyn   **DT862.2 .M33**
Malawi: Foreign Policy and Development. Cloth Text. Palgrave
Macmillan. New York, NY. 1974. 288p. ISBN:0-312-50925-1,
ISBN13: 978-0-312-50925-5. Dewey:327.689/7.
LCCN:74-080653.
                    Audience: **g,l,u,f.** *ℬ*

Pachai, Bridglal   **DT0859.P3**
Malawi: The History of the Nation. Trade Paper. Books on
Demand. Ann Arbor, MI. 336p. ISBN:0-8357-6200-9, ISBN13:
978-0-8357-6200-7. Dewey:916.89/7. LCCN:73-173415.
                    Audience: **g,l,u,f.** *ℬ*

Page, Melvin E.   **D549.5.M36**
Chiwaya War: Malawians in the First World War. Trade Paper.
Westview Press. Boulder, CO. 1999. 296p. History and Warfare
Ser. ISBN:0-8133-0735-X, ISBN13: 978-0-8133-0735-0.
Dewey:940.4.
                    Audience: **u,f.** *Choice, 2000.*

Schoffeleers, J. Matthew   **BL2470.M34.S364 1992**
River of Blood: The Genesis of a Martyr Cult in Southern
Malawi, C. A. D. 1600. Library Binding. University of
Wisconsin Press. Chicago, IL. 1992. 340p. ISBN:0-299-13320-6,
ISBN13: 978-0-299-13320-7. Dewey:299.67096897.
LCCN:92-050258.
                    Audience: **u,f.** *Choice, 1993.*

White, Landeg   **DT865.M35W44 1987**
Magomero: Portrait of an Africa Village. Cloth Text. Cambridge
University Press. New York, NY. 1987. 288p.
ISBN:0-521-32182-4, ISBN13: 978-0-521-32182-2.
Dewey:968.97. LCCN:86-024427.
                    Audience: **u,f.** *Choice, 1987.*

Williams, T. David   **DT862.2.W54**
Malawi: The Politics of Despair. Book, Other. Cornell
University Press. Ithaca, NY. 1978. 416p. Africa in the Modern
World Ser. ISBN:0-8014-1149-1, ISBN13: 978-0-8014-1149-6.
Dewey:320.9/689/7. LCCN:77-090915.
                    Audience: **g,l,u,f.** *ℬ*

Ó Máille, Pádraig   **DT3232**
Living Dangerously: A Memoir of Political Change in Malawi.
Dudu Nsomba Publications. 1999. ISBN:0-9532396-1-6,
ISBN13: 978-0-9532396-1-0.
                    Audience: **g,l,u,f.**

History of Africa > Southern Africa > Mozambique

Hanlon, Joseph   **HC890.H36 1991**
Mozambique: Who Calls the Shots? Trade Cloth. Indiana
University Press. Bloomington, IN. 1991. 316p.
ISBN:0-253-32696-6, ISBN13: 978-0-253-32696-6.
Dewey:338.9679. LCCN:91-017006.
                    Audience: **u,f.**

Isaacman, Allen F. &   **DT3328**
  Isaacman, Barbara
Slavery and Beyond: The Making of Men and Chikunda Ethnic
Identities in the Unstable World of South-Central Africa,
1750-1920. Trade Cloth. Heinemann. Portsmouth, NH. 2004.
384p. Social History of Africa Ser. ISBN:0-325-00261-4,
ISBN13: 978-0-325-00261-3. Dewey:967.9/02.
LCCN:2003-057122.
                    Audience: **u,f.** *Choice, 2004.*

Newitt, Malyn   **DT3341.N48 1995**
A History of Mozambique. Cloth Text. Indiana University Press.
Bloomington, IN. 1995. 400p. ISBN:0-253-34006-3, ISBN13:
978-0-253-34006-1. Dewey:967.9. LCCN:96-007477.
                    Audience: **g,l,u,f.** *Choice, 1995.*

Sheldon, Kathleen E.   **HQ1799.S44 2002**
Pounders of Grain: A History of Women, Work, and Politics in
Mozambique. Trade Paper. Heinemann. Portsmouth, NH. 2002.
344p. ISBN:0-325-07101-2, ISBN13: 978-0-325-07101-5.
Dewey:305.4/09679. LCCN:2001-059388.
                    Audience: **u,f.** *Choice, 2003.*

History of Africa > Southern Africa > Namibia

Gewald, Jan-Bart   **DT1558.H47G47 1999**
Herero Heroes: A Socio-Political History of the Herero of
Namibia, 1890-1923. Trade Paper. Ohio University Press.
Athens, OH. 1999. 320p. ISBN:0-8214-1257-4, ISBN13:
978-0-8214-1257-2. Dewey:968.8/1. LCCN:98-048351.
                    Audience: **u,f.**

Gordon, Robert J. &   **DT1558.S38G67 2000**
  Sholto-Douglas, Stuart
Bushman Myth: The Making of a Namibian Underclass. Ed. 2.
Trade Paper. Westview Press. Boulder, CO. 1999. 368p. Conflict
and Social Change Ser. ISBN:0-8133-3581-7, ISBN13:
978-0-8133-3581-0. Dewey:306.4/089961. LCCN:99-049180.
                    Audience: **u,f.**

Pendleton, Wade C.   **DT1680.P46 1996**
Katutura: A Place Where We Stay: Life in a Post-Apartheid
Towns. Paper Text. Ohio University Press. Athens, OH. 1995.
238p. Monographs in International Studies, No. 65

ISBN:0-89680-188-8, ISBN13: 978-0-89680-188-2.
Dewey:968.81. LCCN:95-051498.

Audience: **u,f.** *Choice, 1996.*

Silvester, Jeremy &　　　　　　**DT1603.S68 2003**
　Gewald, Jan-Bart
Words Cannot Be Found: German Colonial Rule in Namibia: An
Annotated Reprint of the 1918 Blue Book. South-West Africa,
Administrator's Office Staff (Contribution by). Trade Cloth. Brill
Academic Publishers. Leiden, 2003. xxxvii, 370p. Sources for
African History Ser., Vol. 1 ISBN:90-04-12981-2, ISBN13:
978-90-04-12981-8. Dewey:323.1/6881/09034.
LCCN:2003-044435.

Audience: **g,l,u,f.** *Choice, 2003.*

Smith, Andrew　　　　　　**DT1058.S36B87 2000**
The Bushmen of Southern Africa: A Foraging Society in
Transition. Candy Malherbe, Matt Guenther & Penny Berens
(Contribution by). Trade Paper. Ohio University Press. Athens,
OH. 2000. 120p. ISBN:0-8214-1341-4, ISBN13:
978-0-8214-1341-8. Dewey:968/.004961. LCCN:00-055081.

Audience: **u,f.**

Suzman, James　　　　　　**DT1558.S38**
Things from the Bush: A Contemporary History of the Omaheke
Bushmen. Basel: Schlettwein. 1999. Basel Namibia Studies
Series ISBN:3-908193-06-0, ISBN13: 978-3-908193-06-7.

Audience: **u,f.**

History of Africa > Southern Africa > Zambia

Mwanakatwe, J. M.　　　　　　**DT3119**
End of Kaunda Era. Lusaka, Zambia: Multimedia Zambia. 1994.
ISBN:9982-30-065-2, ISBN13: 978-9982-30-065-0.

Audience: **g,l,u,f.**

Burdette, Marcia M.　　　　　　**DT963**
Zambia: Between Two Worlds. Westview Press. Boulder, Colo..
1988. Profiles.; Nations of Contemporary Africa
ISBN:0-86531-617-1, ISBN13: 978-0-86531-617-1.

Audience: **g,l,u,f.**

Mainga, Mutumba　　　　　　**DT963.42.M3**
Bulozi under the Luyana Kings; Political Evolution and State
Formation in Pre-Colonial Zambia. Trade Cloth. Longman
Publishing Group. White Plains, NY. 1973. xvii, 278p.
ISBN:0-582-64073-3, ISBN13: 978-0-582-64073-3.
Dewey:968.9/4/01. LCCN:73-174757.

Audience: **u,f.** *ℬ*

Prins, Gwyn　　　　　　**DT963.42**
The Hidden Hippopotamus: Reappraisal in African History, the
Early Colonial Experience. Trade Cloth. Cambridge University
Press. New York, NY. 1980. 323p. African Studies, No. 28
ISBN:0-521-22915-4, ISBN13: 978-0-521-22915-9.
Dewey:303.4/826894. LCCN:79-041658.

Audience: **u,f.** *ℬ*

Pritchett, James A.　　　　　　**DT3058.N44P75 2001**
The Lunda-Ndembu: Style, Change and Social Transformation
in South Central Africa. Trade Cloth. University of Wisconsin
Press. Chicago, IL. 2001. 424p. ISBN:0-299-17150-7, ISBN13:
978-0-299-17150-6. Dewey:305.896/3977. LCCN:00-012230.

Audience: **u,f.** *Choice, 2002.*

Roberts, Andrew　　　　　　**DT963.5.R62 1976**
A History of Zambia. Trade Cloth. Holmes & Meier Publishers,
Inc. Teaneck, NJ. 1976. 288p. ISBN:0-8419-0291-7, ISBN13:
978-0-8419-0291-6. Dewey:968.9/4. LCCN:76-040923.

Audience: **g,l,u,f.** *ℬ*

Roberts, Andrew D.　　　　　　**DT963.42.R62 1973**
A History of the Bemba: Political Growth and Change in
North-Eastern Zambia Before 1900. Trade Cloth. University of
Wisconsin Press. Chicago, IL. 1974. 454p. ISBN:0-299-06450-6,
ISBN13: 978-0-299-06450-1. Dewey:916.89/4/06963.
LCCN:73-005813.

Audience: **u,f.** *ℬ*

Turner, Victor W.　　　　　　**DT963.42**
The Forest of Symbols: Aspects of Ndembu Ritual. Trade Paper.
Cornell University Press. Ithaca, NY. 1970. 417p.
ISBN:0-8014-9101-0, ISBN13: 978-0-8014-9101-6.
Dewey:392/.09689/4. LCCN:67-012308.

Audience: **u,f.** *ℬ*

Van Onselen, Charles　　　　　　**HD8039.M61R488**
Chibaro: African Mine Labour in Southern Rhodesia 1900-1933.
Paper Text. Ravan Press. Johannesburg, 1986. 326p.
ISBN:0-902818-96-1, ISBN13: 978-0-902818-96-5.
Dewey:331.6/9/96891.

Audience: **u,f.**

History of Africa > Southern Africa > Zimbabwe

Beach, David　　　　　　**DT2913.S55 B43 1994**
The Shona and Their Neighbors. Trade Cloth. Blackwell
Publishing, Inc. Malden, MA. 1994. xviii, 246p. The Peoples of
Africa Ser. ISBN:0-631-17678-0, ISBN13: 978-0-631-17678-7.
Dewey:968.91004963975. LCCN:92-036819.

Audience: **g,l,u,f.**

Chan, Stephen　　　　　　**DT3000.M28C47 2003**
Robert Mugabe: A Life of Power and Violence. Trade Cloth.
University of Michigan Press. Chicago, IL. 2003. 242p.
ISBN:0-472-11336-4, ISBN13: 978-0-472-11336-1.
Dewey:968.9105/1/092 B. LCCN:2002-073242.

Audience: **g,l,u,f.** *Choice, 2003.*

Ellert, H.　　　　　　**HD9536.Z552**
Rivers of Gold. Mambo Press. 1993. Zambeziana

Audience: **u,f.**

Iliffe, John　　　　　　**HC910.Z9**
Famine in Zimbabwe, 1890-1960. Mambo Press. 1990.
Zambeziana Series, Vol. 20 ISBN:0-86922-459-X, ISBN13:
978-0-86922-459-5.

Audience: **u,f.**

Maxwell, David　　　　　　**BR1367.H94M39 1999**
Christians and Chiefs in Zimbabwe: A Social History of the
Hwesa People. Trade Cloth. Greenwood Publishing Group, Inc.
Portsmouth, NH. 1999. 304p. ISBN:0-275-96626-7, ISBN13:
978-0-275-96626-3. Dewey:276.891. LCCN:98-054355.

Audience: **u,f.** *Choice, 1999.*

Owomoyela, Oyekan　　　　　　**DT2908**
Culture and Customs of Zimbabwe. Cloth Text. Greenwood
Publishing, Inc. Portsmouth, NH. 2002. 192p. Culture
and Customs of Africa Ser. ISBN:0-313-31583-3, ISBN13:
978-0-313-31583-1. Dewey:968.91. LCCN:2001-055647.

Audience: **g,l,u,f.**

Pikirayi, Innocent   DT2942.P55 2001
The Zimbabwe Culture: Origins, Growth, and Decline of
Precolonial States in Southern Zambezia. Joseph O. Vogel
(Foreword by). Trade Cloth. AltaMira Press. Walnut Creek, CA.
2001. 336p. ISBN:0-7591-0090-X, ISBN13: 978-0-7591-0090-9.
Dewey:967/.9. LCCN:00-049340.

Audience: **u,f.** *Choice, 2001.*

Ranger, Terence   DT3020.M39R36 1999
Voices from the Rocks: Nature, Culture and History in the
Matopos Hills of Zimbabwe. Trade Cloth. Indiana University
Press. Bloomington, IN. 1999. 320p. ISBN:0-253-33527-2,
ISBN13: 978-0-253-33527-2. Dewey:968.91. LCCN:98-040424.

Audience: **u,f.**

Schmidt, Elizabeth   DT2913.S55S36 1992
Peasants, Traders, and Wives: Shona Women in the History of
Zimbabwe, 1870-1939. Trade Paper. Heinemann. Portsmouth,
NH. 1992. 304p. Social History of Africa Ser.
ISBN:0-435-08066-0, ISBN13: 978-0-435-08066-2.
Dewey:305.488963975. LCCN:91-41251.

Audience: **u,f.** *Choice, 1993.*

Staunton, Irene   DT2990.M69 1990
  (Compiled by)
Mothers of the Revolution: The War Experiences of Thirty
Zimbabwean Women. Trade Cloth. Indiana University Press.
Bloomington, IN. 1991. 320p. ISBN:0-253-35450-1, ISBN13:
978-0-253-35450-1. Dewey:968.91/04. LCCN:91-009980.

Audience: **g,l,u,f.** *Choice, 1992.*

History of Africa > Southern Africa > Swaziland

Bonner, Philip   DT971.7
Kings, Commoners and Concessionaires: The Evolution and
Dissolution of the Nineteenth-Century Swazi State. David
Anderson, Carolyn Brown, Christopher Clapham, Michael
Gomez, Patrick Manning, David Robinson & Leonardo A.
Villalon (Contribution by). Trade Paper. Cambridge University
Press. New York, NY. 2002. 326p. African Studies
ISBN:0-521-52300-1, ISBN13: 978-0-521-52300-4.
Dewey:968.8/7/02.

Audience: **u,f.**

Crush, Jonathan   HC925 .C78 1987
The Struggle for Swazi Labour, 1890-1920. Trade Cloth.
McGill-Queen's University Press. Montreal, PQ. 1987. 320p.
ISBN:0-7735-0569-5, ISBN13: 978-0-7735-0569-8.
Dewey:331.88/09681/3. LCCN:88-165515.

Audience: **u,f.**

History of Africa > Southern Africa > South Africa

Bhana, Surendra &   DT764.E3D63 1984
  Pachai, Bridglal
A Documentary History of Indian South Africans. Trade Paper.
Hoover Institution Press. Stanford, CA. 1985. xiii, 306p.
Publication Ser., No. 310 ISBN:0-8179-8102-0, ISBN13:
978-0-8179-8102-0. Dewey:968/.00491411. LCCN:84-009154.
Audience: **g,l,u,f.** *Choice, 1985.*

Biko, Steve   DT1949.B55A25 2002
I Write What I Like: Selected Writings. C.R., Aelred Stubbs
(Editor). Trade Paper. University of Chicago Press. Chicago, IL.
2002. 240p. ISBN:0-226-04897-7, ISBN13: 978-0-226-04897-0.
Dewey:305.8/00968. LCCN:2002-023951.

Audience: **g,l,u,f.**

Byrnes, Rita M.   KF27 .B5364 2000C
South Africa: A Country Study. Trade Cloth, Box or Slipcased.
United States Government Printing Office. Washington, DC.
1997. 586p. ISBN:0-16-061206-3, ISBN13: 978-0-16-061206-0.
Dewey:968.

Audience: **g,l,u,f.**

Frueh, Jamie   HN801.A8F78 2002
Political Identity and Social Change: The Remaking of the
South African Social Order. Nicholas Onuf (Foreword by).
Paper Text. State University of New York Press. Albany, NY.
2002. 6p. SUNY Series in Global Politics ISBN:0-7914-5548-3,
ISBN13: 978-0-7914-5548-7. Dewey:303.4/0968.
LCCN:2002-017730.

Audience: **u,f.** *Choice, 2003.*

Lester, Alan   DT1727
From Colonization to Democracy: A New Historical Geography
of South Africa. Trade Paper. I. B. Tauris & Company, Ltd.
London, 1998. 288p. ISBN:1-86064-176-8, ISBN13:
978-1-86064-176-3. Dewey:968.

Audience: **u,f.**

Mandela, Nelson   DT1949.M35A3
Long Walk to Freedom: The Autobiography of Nelson Mandela.
Trade Paper. Little Brown & Company. New York, NY. 1995.
656p. ISBN:0-316-54818-9, ISBN13: 978-0-316-54818-2.
Dewey:968.06092. LCCN:94-079980.

Audience: **g,l,u,f.** *Choice, 1995.*

Meredith, Martin   DT1974
Coming to Terms: South Africa's Search for Truth. Trade Paper.
PublicAffairs. New York, NY. 2001. 400p. ISBN:1-903985-09-9,
ISBN13: 978-1-903985-09-0. Dewey:968.06/5.

Audience: **u,f.**

Sampson, Anthony   E185.97.T8
Mandela: The Authorized Biography. Trade Paper. Knopf
Publishing Group. New York, NY. 2000. 736p.
ISBN:0-679-78178-1, ISBN13: 978-0-679-78178-3.
Dewey:968.06/5/092 B.

Audience: **g,l,u,f.** *Choice, 2000.*

Wilson, Richard A.   DT1974.2 .W55 2001
The Politics of Truth and Reconciliation in South Africa:
Legitimizing the Post-Apartheid State. Chris Arup, Martin
Chanock, Sally Engle Merry, Pat O'Malley & Susan Silbey
(Contribution by). Trade Paper. Cambridge University Press.
New York, NY. 2001. 294p. Cambridge Studies in Law and
Society ISBN:0-521-00194-3, ISBN13: 978-0-521-00194-6.
Dewey:305.8/00968. LCCN:2001-018100.

Audience: **u,f.** *Choice, 2002.*

History of Africa > Southern Africa > South Africa > History

Bozzoli, Belinda &   DT1058.B34B69 1991
  Nkotsoe, Mmantho
Women of Phokeng: Consciousness, Life Strategy, and
Migrancy in South Africa, 1900-1983. Cloth Text. Heinemann.

Portsmouth, NH. 1991. 304p. Social History of Africa Ser.
ISBN:0-435-08054-7, ISBN13: 978-0-435-08054-9.
Dewey:305.4/0968.2/94. LCCN:91-009326.
Audience: **u,f.** *Choice, 1992.*

Carter, Gwendolen   **DT 779.7 .C3**
 Margaret
The Politics of Inequality: South Africa Since 1948. Paper Text.
Textbook Publishers. Temecula, CA. 2003. 541p.
ISBN:0-7581-3207-7, ISBN13: 978-0-7581-3207-9. Dewey:968.
Audience: **g,l,u,f.** *B*

Cope, Richard   **DT1875.C67 1999**
The Ploughshare of War: The Origins of the Anglo-Zulu War of
1879. Trade Paper. University of Natal Press. Scottsville, 1999.
282p. ISBN:0-86980-944-X, ISBN13: 978-0-86980-944-0.
Dewey:968.4/045. LCCN:99-456901.
Audience: **u,f.** *Choice, 2000.*

Crais, Clifton C.   **DT1787 .C73 1992**
White Supremacy and Black Resistance in Pre-Industrial South
Africa: The Making of the Colonial Order in the Eastern Cape,
1770-1865. Carolyn Brown, Christopher Clapham, Michael
Gomez, Patrick Manning, David Robinson, Leonardo A. Villalon
& David Anderson (Contribution by). Cloth Text. Cambridge
University Press. New York, NY. 1992. 302p. African Studies,
No. 72 ISBN:0-521-40479-7, ISBN13: 978-0-521-40479-2.
Dewey:968. LCCN:90-025694.
Audience: **u,f.** *Choice, 1992.*

Davenport, T. H. R. &   **DT1787.D38 2000**
 Saunders, Christopher
South Africa: A Modern History. Ed. 5. Trade Paper. Palgrave
Macmillan. New York, NY. 2000. 680p. ISBN:0-312-23376-0,
ISBN13: 978-0-312-23376-1. Dewey:968. LCCN:00-024339.
Audience: **g,l,u,f.** *Choice, 2001.*

Etherington, Norman   **DT1837.E84 2001**
The Great Treks: The Transformation of Southern Africa,
1815-1854. Trade Paper. Longman Publishing Group. White
Plains, NY. 2001. 400p. ISBN:0-582-31567-0, ISBN13:
978-0-582-31567-9. Dewey:968.04/2. LCCN:2001-038831.
Audience: **g,l,u,f.**

Juckes, Tim J.   **DT1938**
Opposition in South Africa: The Leadership of Z. K. Matthews,
Nelson Mandela and Stephen Biko. Trade Cloth. Greenwood
Publishing Group, Inc. Portsmouth, NH. 1995. 240p.
ISBN:0-275-94811-0, ISBN13: 978-0-275-94811-5.
Dewey:320.968. LCCN:94-032918.
Audience: **u,f.** *Choice, 1995.*

Judd, Denis & Surridge,   **DT1896.J83 2003**
 Keith
The Boer War. Cloth over Boards. Palgrave Macmillan. New
York, NY. 2003. 384p. ISBN:1-4039-6150-6, ISBN13:
978-1-4039-6150-1. Dewey:968.04/8. LCCN:2003-276027.
Audience: **u,f.** *Choice, 2004.*

Keegan, Timothy J.   **DT1756.K44 1997**
Colonial South Africa and the Origins of the Racial Order.
Paper Text. University Press of Virginia. Charlottesville, VA.
1997. 357p. Reconsiderations in Southern African History Ser.
ISBN:0-8139-1736-0, ISBN13: 978-0-8139-1736-8.
Dewey:305.8/00968. LCCN:96-035827.
Audience: **u,f.** *Choice, 1997.*

Laband, John   **DT2400.Z85L32 1997**
Rise and Fall of the Zulu Nation. Trade Cloth. Arms & Armour
Press. London, 1997. 532p. ISBN:1-85409-421-1, ISBN13:
978-1-85409-421-6. Dewey:968.4/04. LCCN:97-190382.
Audience: **u,f.**

Lowry, Donal (Editor)   **DT1896.T43 1999**
The South African War Reappraised. Trade Paper. Manchester
University Press. Manchester, 2000. 256p. Studies in
Imperialism ISBN:0-7190-5825-2, ISBN13: 978-0-7190-5825-7.
Dewey:968.04/8. LCCN:2001-427242.
Audience: **u,f.**

Luthuli, Albert   **GV1580**
Let My People Go. C. Hooper (Introduction by). Trade Paper.
Penguin Group (USA) Inc. New York, NY.
ISBN:0-452-00404-7, ISBN13: 978-0-452-00404-7.
Dewey:322.4/4/0924.
Audience: **g,l,u,f.**

Meli, Francis   **JQ1998.A4M45 1989**
South Africa Belongs to Us: A History of the ANC. Trade Paper.
Indiana University Press. Bloomington, IN. 1989. 290p.
ISBN:0-253-28591-7, ISBN13: 978-0-253-28591-1.
Dewey:322.4/2/0968. LCCN:88-039946.
Audience: **g,l,u,f.** *Choice, 1990.*

Moodie, T. Dunbar   **DT1768.A57**
The Rise of Afrikanerdom: Power, Apartheid, and the Afrikaner
Civil Religion. Trade Paper. University of California Press.
Berkeley, CA. 1974. Perspectives on Southern Africa Ser., No.
11 ISBN:0-520-03943-2, ISBN13: 978-0-520-03943-8.
Dewey:323.1/13/936068. LCCN:72-085512.
Audience: **u,f.**

Morris, Donald R.   **DT2400.Z85M67 1998**
The Washing of the Spears: The Rise and Fall of the Zulu
Nation. Mangosuthu Buthelezi (Introduction by). Trade Paper.
Da Capo Press, Inc. Cambridge, MA. 1998. 650p.
ISBN:0-306-80866-8, ISBN13: 978-0-306-80866-1.
Dewey:968.4/91. LCCN:98-020022.
Audience: **u,f.**

Shell, Robert C.   **HT1394.S6S48 1994**
Children of Bondage: A Social History of the Slave Society at
the Cape of Good Hope, 1652-1838. Library Binding. Wesleyan
University Press. Middletown, CT. 1994. 560p.
ISBN:0-8195-5273-9, ISBN13: 978-0-8195-5273-0.
Dewey:305.5/67/09687. LCCN:94-002194.
Audience: **u,f.** *Choice, 1995.*

Smith, David M.   **DT763**
Apartheid in South Africa. Ed. 3. Trade Paper. Cambridge
University Press. New York, NY. 1990. 95p. Update Ser.
ISBN:0-521-39720-0, ISBN13: 978-0-521-39720-9.
Dewey:305.8/00968. LCCN:90-036147.
Audience: **u,f.**

Swan, Maureen   **DS481.G3S89 1985**
Gandhi: The South African Experience. Paper Text. Ravan
Press. Johannesburg, 1985. 320p. ISBN:0-86975-232-4, ISBN13:
978-0-86975-232-6. Dewey:968.04. LCCN:85-219389.
Audience: **u,f.**

Switzer, Les (Editor)   **PN5477.U53 S68 1997**
South Africa's Alternative Press: Voices of Protest and
Resistance, 1880-1960. David Culbert, Garth Jowett & Kenneth
Short (Contribution by). Trade Cloth. Cambridge University
Press. New York, NY. 1997. 416p. Cambridge Studies in the

History of Mass Communications ISBN:0-521-55351-2, ISBN13: 978-0-521-55351-3. Dewey:302.2/322/0968. LCCN:95-044814.

Audience: **u,f.** *Choice, 1997.*

Szalay, Miklós　　　　　　　　**DT1768.S36**
The San and the Colonization of the Cape 1770-1879: Conflict, Incorporation, Acculturation. Köln R. Köppe. 1995. Research in Khoisan Studies ISBN:3-927620-58-0, ISBN13: 978-3-927620-58-2.

Audience: **u,f.**

Thompson, Leonard　　　　　　　**DT1787.T48 2001**
　Monteath
A History of South Africa. Ed. 3. Trade Cloth. Yale University Press. Cumberland, RI. 2001. xxiv, 358p. Yale Nota Bene Ser. ISBN:0-300-08775-6, ISBN13: 978-0-300-08775-8. Dewey:968. LCCN:00-032101.

Audience: **g,l,u,f.**

Van Onselen, Charles　　　　　　**HT807**
The Seed Is Mine: The Life of Kas Maine, a South African Sharecropper, 1894-1985. Trade Paper. Farrar, Straus & Giroux. New York, NY. 1997. 672p. ISBN:0-8090-1594-3, ISBN13: 978-0-8090-1594-8. Dewey:306.3/65/092.

Audience: **u,f.**

Waldmeir, Patti　　　　　　　　**DT1967.W35 1999**
Anatomy of a Miracle: The End of Apartheid and the Birth of the New South Africa. Paper Text. Rutgers University Press. Piscataway, NJ. 2003. 304p. ISBN:0-8135-2582-9, ISBN13: 978-0-8135-2582-2. Dewey:968/.064. LCCN:98-015607.

Audience: **u,f.** *Choice, 1997.*

Woods, Donald　　　　　　　　**DT779.8.B48W67 1991**
Biko. Ed. 3. Trade Paper. Henry Holt & Company. New York, NY. 1991. 432p. ISBN:0-8050-1899-9, ISBN13: 978-0-8050-1899-8. Dewey:322.4/4/0924. LCCN:91-026551.

Audience: **g,l,u,f.** *B*

Worden, Nigel　　　　　　　　**DT1787.W67 1995**
The Making of Modern South Africa: Conquest, Segregation and Apartheid. Ed. 2. Trade Paper. Blackwell Publishing, Inc. Malden, MA. 1995. 192p. Historical Association Studies ISBN:0-631-19882-2, ISBN13: 978-0-631-19882-6. Dewey:968. LCCN:95-192998.

Audience: **u,f.** *Choice, 1994.*

African Languages and Literatures

Abrahams, Roger D.　　　　　　**GR350**
　(Editor)
African Folktales: Traditional Stories of the Black World. Trade Cloth. Knopf Publishing Group. New York, NY. 1983. 384p. Fairy Tale and Folklore Library ISBN:0-394-50236-1, ISBN13: 978-0-394-50236-6. Dewey:398.2/096. LCCN:83-002474.

Audience: **g,l,u,f.**

Batibo, Herman　　　　　　　**P40.45.A35B38 2005**
Language Decline and Death in Africa: Causes, Consequences and Challenges. Trade Cloth. Multilingual Matters Ltd. Clevedon, 2005. 176p. ISBN:1-85359-809-7, ISBN13: 978-1-85359-809-8. Dewey:306.44/096. LCCN:2004-022674.

Audience: **u,f.** *Choice, 2005.*

Brenzinger, Matthias　　　　　**PL8002.E63 1998**
Endangered Languages in Africa. R. Köppe. 1998. ISBN:3-89645-305-X, ISBN13: 978-3-89645-305-1.

Audience: **u,f.**

Childs, G. Tucker　　　　　　**PL8005.C45 2003**
An Introduction to African Languages. Trade Cloth, CD-ROM. John Benjamins Publishing Company. Philadelphia, PA. 2003. xx, 265p. ISBN:1-58811-421-X, ISBN13: 978-1-58811-421-1. Dewey:496. LCCN:2003-060704.

Audience: **l,u,f.**

Dathorne, O. R.　　　　　　　**PL8010**
The Black Mind: A History of African Literature. Trade Cloth. University of Minnesota Press. Minneapolis, MN. 1974. xi, 527p. ISBN:0-8166-0719-2, ISBN13: 978-0-8166-0719-8. Dewey:809/.8967. LCCN:74-076744.

Audience: **g,l,u,f.** *B*

Gikandi, Simon (Editor)　　　　**PL8010.E63 2002**
Encyclopedia of African Literature. Paper over Boards. Routledge. New York, NY. 2002. 648p. ISBN:0-415-23019-5, ISBN13: 978-0-415-23019-3. Dewey:809/.896/03. LCCN:2002-072757.

Audience: **g,l,u,f.**

Greenberg, Joseph H.　　　　　**PL8005**
Languages of Africa. Ed. 3. Paper Text. Research Institute for Inner Asian Studies, Indiana University. Bloomington, IN. 1970. General Publications, Vol. 25 ISBN:0-87750-115-7, ISBN13: 978-0-87750-115-2. Dewey:496. LCCN:62-063505.

Audience: **g,l,u,f.**

Hay, Margaret Jean　　　　　　**PL8010.6.A34 2000**
　(Editor)
African Novels in the Classroom. Library Binding. Lynne Rienner Publishers, Inc. Boulder, CO. 2000. vi, 314p. ISBN:1-55587-853-9, ISBN13: 978-1-55587-853-5. Dewey:809.3/0096. LCCN:00-022780.

Audience: **f.** *Choice, 2001.*

Heine, Bernd & Nurse,　　　　　**PL8005 .A24 2000**
　Derek (Editors)
African Languages: An Introduction. Trade Paper. Cambridge University Press. New York, NY. 2000. 406p. ISBN:0-521-66629-5, ISBN13: 978-0-521-66629-9. Dewey:496. LCCN:99-056881.

Audience: **u,f.** *Choice, 2001.*

Heywood, Christopher　　　　　**PL8014.S6H49 2004**
A History of South African Literature. Trade Cloth. Cambridge University Press. New York, NY. 2004. 310p. ISBN:0-521-55485-3, ISBN13: 978-0-521-55485-5. Dewey:809/.8968. LCCN:2004-045669.

Audience: **g,l,u,f.** *Choice, 2005.*

Irele, Abiola　　　　　　　　**PQ3980.I74 1990**
African Experience in Literature and Ideology. Trade Cloth. Indiana University Press. Bloomington, IN. 1990. 234p. ISBN:0-253-33124-2, ISBN13: 978-0-253-33124-3. Dewey:840.9/896. LCCN:89-024586.

Audience: **u,f.**

Jemi, Onwuchekwa &　　　　　**PL8010**
　Madubuike, Ihechukwu
Toward the Decolonization of African Literature: African Fiction and Poetry and Their Critics. Trade Cloth. Kegan Paul

International, Ltd. London, 1998. 320p. ISBN:0-7103-0123-5, ISBN13: 978-0-7103-0123-9. Dewey:896.

Audience: **g,l,u,f.**

Larson, Charles R.   **PR9340.L37 2001**
The Ordeal of the African Writer. Trade Paper. Zed Books, Ltd. London, 2001. 192p. ISBN:1-85649-931-6, ISBN13: 978-1-85649-931-6. Dewey:820.9/896. LCCN:00-043476.

Audience: **u,f.** *Choice, 2002.*

Larson, Charles R.   **PL8011**
(Editor, Introduction by)
Under African Skies: Modern African Stories. Trade Paper. Farrar, Straus & Giroux. New York, NY. 1998. 336p. ISBN:0-374-52550-1, ISBN13: 978-0-374-52550-7. Dewey:808.8/31/0896.

Audience: **g,l,u,f.** *Choice, 1998.*

Moore, Gerald   **PL8010.M63 1980**
Twelve African Writers. Trade Cloth. Indiana University Press. Bloomington, IN. 1980. 328p. ISBN:0-253-19619-1, ISBN13: 978-0-253-19619-4. Dewey:809/.896. LCCN:80-007988.

Audience: **u,f.** *ℬ*

Ojaide, Tanure &   **PL8013.E5N478**
Sallah, Tijan M. (Editors)
The New African Poetry: An Anthology. Trade Paper. Lynne Rienner Publishers, Inc. Boulder, CO. 2000. 233p. ISBN:0-89410-891-3, ISBN13: 978-0-89410-891-4. Dewey:896.

Audience: **g,l,u,f.**

Owomoyela, Oyekan   **PL8010.H57 1993**
(Editor)
A History of Twentieth-Century African Literatures. Trade Paper. University of Nebraska Press. Lincoln, NE. 1993. 411p. ISBN:0-8032-8604-X, ISBN13: 978-0-8032-8604-7. Dewey:809.8896. LCCN:92-037874.

Audience: **g,l,u,f.** *Choice, 1994.*

Soyinka, Wole (Editor)   **PL8011.P6 1975**
Poems of Black Africa. Trade Paper. Farrar, Straus & Giroux. New York, NY. 1975. 384p. ISBN:0-8090-1376-2, ISBN13: 978-0-8090-1376-0. Dewey:821.

Audience: **g,l,u,f.** *ℬ*

Webb, Vic &   **P381.A3A33 2000**
Kembo-Sure (Editors)
African Voices: An Introduction to the Languages and Linguistics of Africa. Paper Text. Oxford University Press, Inc. New York, NY. 2001. 400p. ISBN:0-19-571681-7, ISBN13: 978-0-19-571681-8. Dewey:496. LCCN:00-420215.

Audience: **u,f.**

Wehrs, Donald R.   **PR9344.W44 2001**
African Feminist Fiction and Indigenous Values. Trade Cloth. University Press of Florida. Gainesville, FL. 2001. xiii, 259p. ISBN:0-8130-1884-6, ISBN13: 978-0-8130-1884-3. Dewey:823/.91099287/096. LCCN:00-053664.

Audience: **u,f.** *Choice, 2001.*

ASIAN AMERICAN STUDIES

This section contains scholarly and creative works germane to the undergraduate Asian American Studies curriculum. While most of the works are in the disciplinary domains of the Humanities and Social Sciences, topics related to health and physical sciences are also included.

As an interdisciplinary field, Asian American Studies lends itself to multiple points of inquiry. While some works fit well into the conventional taxonomy such as Hall and Okazaki's Asian American Psychology, many critique traditional frameworks and categories, such as Kingston's Woman Warrior. As such, the current taxonomy is a reflection of the heterogeneity of the works represented here. For example, "Race" and "Ethnic Groups" are primary categories along with "History" and "Psychology" under the Social Sciences.

Where possible, works are recommended in their newest, most reliable edition. Since the publication of BCL3, there has been an exciting and intense proliferation of scholarly and literary publications in Asian American Studies. Therefore the emphasis here is on contemporary works, published in the late 1980s to the present. Some older, yet classical texts are included, though they may be out of print. A few works are only available as reprints.

— Gerardo Colmenar

General Works

PS628.A85

☐ Asian American Drama.
http://www.alexanderstreetpress.com/
Alexander Street Press.

Audience: **g,l,u,f.**

Chan, Sucheng   **E184.O6C47 1991**
The Asian Americans: An Interpretive History. Trade Cloth.
Thomson Gale. Farmington Hills, MI. 1991. 240p. Twayne's
Immigrant Heritage of America Ser. ISBN:0-8057-8426-8,
ISBN13: 978-0-8057-8426-8. Dewey:973/.0495.
LCCN:90-044174.

Audience: **l.**   *Choice, 1991.*

Chan, Sucheng (Editor)   **E184.O6R46 2003**
Remapping Asian American History. Trade Cloth. AltaMira
Press. Walnut Creek, CA. 2003. 304p. Critical Perspectives on
Asian Pacific Americans Ser. ISBN:0-7591-0479-4, ISBN13:
978-0-7591-0479-2. Dewey:973/.0495/0072.
LCCN:2003-012018.

Audience: **l.**   *Choice, 2004.*

Chin, Soo-Young   **E184.O6R48 1995**
(Editor), et al.
Reviewing Asian America: Locating Diversity. Wendy L. Ng,
James S. Moy & Gary Y. Okihiro (Editors). Trade Paper.
Washington State University Press. Pullman, WA. 1995. 214p.
Association for Asian American Studies Ser., No. 6
ISBN:0-87422-118-8, ISBN13: 978-0-87422-118-3.
Dewey:305.895/073. LCCN:95-015751.

Audience: **l,u.**

Danico, Mary Yu & Ng,   **E184**
Franklin
Asian American Issues. Cloth Text. Greenwood Publishing
Group, Inc. Portsmouth, NH. 2004. 216p. Contemporary
American Ethnic Issues Ser. ISBN:0-313-31965-0, ISBN13:
978-0-313-31965-5. Dewey:305.895/073. LCCN:2004-016133.

Audience: **g,l.**

Espiritu, Yen Le   **E184.O6**
Asian American Panethnicity: Bridging Institutions and
Identities. Trade Paper. Temple University Press. Philadelphia,
PA. 1993. 222p. Asian American History and Culture Ser.
ISBN:1-56639-096-6, ISBN13: 978-1-56639-096-5.
Dewey:305.895/073.

Audience: **l,u,f.**   *Choice, 1993.*

Fong, Timothy P.   **E184.O6F66 2002**
The Contemporary Asian American Experience: Beyond the
Model Minority. Ed. 2. Trade Paper. Prentice Hall PTR. Upper
Saddle River, NJ. 2001. 358p. ISBN:0-13-091834-2, ISBN13:
978-0-13-091834-5. Dewey:973/.0495. LCCN:2001-036239.

Audience: **l.**

Gee, Emma (Editor)   **E184.O6C68**
Counterpoint: Perspectives on Asian America. Trade Cloth.
University of California, Los Angeles, Asian American Studies
Center. Los Angeles, CA. 1976. ISBN:0-934052-03-4, ISBN13:
978-0-934052-03-0. Dewey:301.45/19/5073. LCCN:76-041528.

Audience: **g,l,u,f.** *B*

Hu-DeHart, Evelyn   **E184.O6A28 1999**
(Editor)
Across the Pacific: Asian Americans and Globalization. Cloth
Text. Temple University Press. Philadelphia, PA. 2000. 232p.

Asian American History and Culture Ser. ISBN:1-56639-710-3,
ISBN13: 978-1-56639-710-0. Dewey:305.895073.
LCCN:98-053900.

Audience: **g,l,u.**   *Choice, 2001.*

Hune, Shirley (Editor),   **E184.O6A843 1991**
et al.
Asian Americans: Comparative and Global Perspectives.
Hyung-chan Kim, Stephen S. Fugita & Amy Ling (Editors).
Trade Paper. Washington State University Press. Pullman, WA.
1991. 290p. Association for Asian American Studies
ISBN:0-87422-071-8, ISBN13: 978-0-87422-071-1.
Dewey:973/.0495. LCCN:91-000056.

Audience: **l,u,f.**

Lee, Jennifer & Zhou,   **E184.A75A84264 2004**
Min (Editors)
Asian American Youth: Culture, Identity and Ethnicity. Paper
over Boards. Routledge. New York, NY. 2004. 376p.
ISBN:0-415-94668-9, ISBN13: 978-0-415-94668-1.
Dewey:305.235/089/95073. LCCN:2004-007207.

Audience: **g,l.**

Min, Pyrong Gap   **E184.A75A84325 2005**
Asian Americans: Contemporary Trends and Issues. Ed. 2. Paper
Text. Pine Forge Press. Newbury Park, CA. 2005. 368p.
ISBN:1-4129-0556-7, ISBN13: 978-1-4129-0556-5.
Dewey:973/.0495. LCCN:2005-006492.

Audience: **l.**

Ng, Franklin (Editor),   **E184.O6N39 1994**
et al.
New Visions in Asian American Studies: Diversity, Community,
Power. Judy Yung, Elaine H. Kim & Stephen S. Fugita
(Editors). Trade Paper. Washington State University Press.
Pullman, WA. 1994. 296p. Association for Asian American
Studies ISBN:0-87422-102-1, ISBN13: 978-0-87422-102-2.
Dewey:973/.0495. LCCN:93-036427.

Audience: **l.**

Okihiro, Gary Y.   **E184.O6O38 1994**
Margins and Mainstreams: Asians in American History and
Culture. Trade Cloth. University of Washington Press. Seattle,
WA. 1994. 222p. ISBN:0-295-97338-2, ISBN13:
978-0-295-97338-8. Dewey:973/.0495. LCCN:93-044382.

Audience: **g,l,u,f.**   *Choice, 1995.*

Ong, Paul M. (Editor)   **E184.O6**
The State of Asian Pacific America: Transforming Race
Relations. Trade Paper. University of California, Los Angeles,
Asian American Studies Center. Los Angeles, CA. 2000. 507p.
ISBN:0-934052-33-6, ISBN13: 978-0-934052-33-7.
Dewey:973.0495.

Audience: **g,l.**

Takaki, Ronald T.   **E184.O6T35 1998**
Strangers from a Different Shore: A History of Asian Americans.
Trade Paper. Little Brown & Company. New York, NY. 1998.
640p. ISBN:0-316-83130-1, ISBN13: 978-0-316-83130-7.
Dewey:973/.0495. LCCN:98-218270.

Audience: **l.**

General Works > Databases

PS628.A85

☐ Asian American Drama.

http://www.alexanderstreetpress.com/
Alexander Street Press.

Audience: **g,l,u,f.**

E184.A1

☐ Ethnic Newswatch.
http://www.proquest.com/products_pq/descriptions/
ethnic_newswatch.shtml
Proquest.

Audience: **g,l,u,f.**

General Works > Reference Works

Cheung, King-Kok &   **Z1229.A75C47 1988**
   Yogi, Stan (Editors)
Asian American Literature: An Annotated Bibliography. Trade
Cloth. Modern Language Association of America. New York,
NY. 1988. x,276p. ISBN:0-87352-960-X, ISBN13:
978-0-87352-960-0. Dewey:016.81/08/0895073.
LCCN:88-005355.

Audience: **g,l,u,f.** *Choice, 1989.*

Fenton, John Y.   **BL1055**
South Asian Religions in the Americas: An Annotated
Bibliography of Immigrant Religious Traditions. Cloth Text.
Greenwood Publishing Group, Inc. Portsmouth, NH. 1995. 256p.
Bibliographies and Indexes in Religious Studies, Vol. 34
ISBN:0-313-27835-0, ISBN13: 978-0-313-27835-8.
Dewey:016.294/097. LCCN:94-039769.

Audience: **l,u,f.** *Choice, 1995.*

Garoogian, David   **E184.A75 2005**
Asian Databook. Trade Cloth, CD-ROM. Grey House
Publishing. Millerton, NY. 2004. 1p. ISBN:1-59237-044-6,
ISBN13: 978-1-59237-044-3. Dewey:305.895/073/021.
LCCN:2004-559197.

Audience: **l,u.** *Choice, 2005.*

Huang, Guiyou (Editor)   **PS153**
Asian American Short Story Writers: An A-to-Z Guide. Cloth
Text. Greenwood Publishing Group, Inc. Portsmouth, NH. 2003.
392p. ISBN:0-313-32229-5, ISBN13: 978-0-313-32229-7.
Dewey:813/.0109895/03 B. LCCN:2002-192772.

Audience: **g,l,u,f.** *Choice, 2003.*

Huang, Guiyou   **PS153.A84C65 2006**
The Columbia Guide to Asian American Literature since 1945.
Trade Cloth. Columbia University Press. New York, NY. 2006.
264p. Columbia Guides to Literature since 1945 Ser.
ISBN:0-231-12620-4, ISBN13: 978-0-231-12620-5.
Dewey:813.5409895073. LCCN:2005-051996.

Audience: **l,u,f.**

Huang, Guiyou (Editor)   **PS366**
Asian American Autobiographers: A Bio-Bibliographical Critical
Sourcebook. Shirley Geok-Lin Lim (Foreword by). Cloth Text.
Greenwood Publishing Group, Inc. Portsmouth, NH. 2001. 464p.
ISBN:0-313-31408-X, ISBN13: 978-0-313-31408-7.
Dewey:818/.540809895. LCCN:00-064056.

Audience: **l,u,f.** *Choice, 2001.*

Kim, Hyung-chan   **Z1361**
   (Editor)
Asian American Studies: An Annotated Bibliography and
Research Guide. Cloth Text. Greenwood Publishing Group, Inc.
Portsmouth, NH. 1989. 514p. Bibliographies and Indexes in

American History Ser., No. 11 ISBN:0-313-26026-5, ISBN13:
978-0-313-26026-1. Dewey:016.973/0495. LCCN:89-001925.

Audience: **g,l,u,f.** *Choice, 1990.*

Kim, Hyung-chan   **E184**
   (Editor)
Distinguished Asian Americans: A Biographical Dictionary.
Dorothy C. L. Cordova, Stephen S. Fugita, Franklin Ng & Jane
Singh (Other Adaptation by). Cloth Text. Greenwood Publishing
Group, Inc. Portsmouth, NH. 1999. 448p. Ethnographic
Reference Bks. ISBN:0-313-28902-6, ISBN13:
978-0-313-28902-6. Dewey:920.009295073. LCCN:98-041423.

Audience: **g,l.** *Choice, 2000.*

Lai, Eric Yo Ping   **E184.O6L35 2003**
   (Editor)
The New Face of Asian Pacific America: Numbers, Diversity,
and Change in the 21st Century. Trade Cloth. AsianWeek Books.
San Fransisco, CA. 2003. viii, 283p. ISBN:0-9665020-4-3,
ISBN13: 978-0-9665020-4-6. Dewey:305.895/073/090511.
LCCN:2002-156209.

Audience: **l,u.**

Lai, Him Mark   **E184.O6A84265**
A History Reclaimed: An Annotated Bibliography of Chinese
Language Materials on the Chinese of America. Russell Leong
& Jean P. Yip (Editors). Cloth Text. University of California,
Los Angeles, Asian American Studies Center. Los Angeles, CA.
1986. 160p. ISBN:0-934052-32-8, ISBN13: 978-0-934052-32-0.
Dewey:973.0495.

Audience: **l,u,f.**

Leonard, George J.   **PS153.A84A87 1999**
   (Editor)
The Asian Pacific American Heritage: A Companion to
Literature and Arts. Trade Cloth. Garland Publishing, Inc. New
York, NY. 1998. 690p. Reference Library of the Humanities,
Vol. 2109 ISBN:0-8153-2980-6, ISBN13: 978-0-8153-2980-0.
Dewey:996. LCCN:98-033468.

Audience: **l,u,f.** *Choice, 1999.*

Liu, Miles Xian (Editor)   **PS338**
Asian American Playwrights: A Bio-Bibliographical Critical
Sourcebook. Cloth Text. Greenwood Publishing Group, Inc.
Portsmouth, NH. 2002. 424p. ISBN:0-313-31455-1, ISBN13:
978-0-313-31455-1. Dewey:812/.509895/03 B.
LCCN:2001-037680.

Audience: **g,l,u,f.** *Choice, 2003.*

Min, Pyong Gap   **E184**
   (Editor)
Encyclopedia of Racism in the United States. Cloth Text.
Greenwood Publishing Group, Inc. Portsmouth, NH. 2005.
1024p. ISBN:0-313-32688-6, ISBN13: 978-0-313-32688-2.
Dewey:305.8/00973/03. LCCN:2005-008523.

Audience: **g,l,u,f.** *Choice, 2006.*

Nakanishi, Don T. &   **E184**
   Wu, Ellen D.
Distinguished Asian American Political and Governmental
Leaders. Cloth Text. Greenwood Publishing Group, Inc.
Portsmouth, NH. 2002. 240p. Distinguished Asian Americans
Ser. ISBN:1-57356-325-0, ISBN13: 978-1-57356-325-3.
Dewey:920/.009295073. LCCN:2002-016957.

Audience: **g,l,u,f.** *Choice, 2003.*

Ng, Franklin (Editor)   **E184.O6A827 1995**
The Asian American Encyclopedia, Set. Trade Cloth. Marshall
Cavendish Corporation. Tarrytown, NY. 1994. 1,900p.

ISBN:1-85435-677-1, ISBN13: 978-1-85435-677-2.
Dewey:973/.0495/003. LCCN:94-033003.

Audience: **l,u.** *Choice, 1995.*

Odo, Franklin   **E184.O6C63 2002**
The Columbia Documentary History of the Asian American
Experience. Trade Cloth. Columbia University Press. New York,
NY. 2002. 688p. ISBN:0-231-11030-8, ISBN13:
978-0-231-11030-3. Dewey:973/.0495. LCCN:2002-019208.

Audience: **g,l,u,f.** *Choice, 2003.*

Okihiro, Gary Y.   **E184.O6C64 2001**
The Columbia Guide to Asian American History. Trade Cloth.
Columbia University Press. New York, NY. 2001. 352p. Guides
to American Indian History and Culture ISBN:0-231-11510-5,
ISBN13: 978-0-231-11510-0. Dewey:973/.0495.
LCCN:2001-028952.

Audience: **g,l,u,f.** *Choice, 2002.*

Sakata, Yasuo   **Z1361.J2**
Fading Footsteps of the Issei: An Annotated Checklist of the
Manuscript Holdings of the Japanese. Trade Paper. University of
California, Los Angeles, Asian American Studies Center. Los
Angeles, CA. 1992. 358p. ISBN:0-934052-20-4, ISBN13:
978-0-934052-20-7. Dewey:16.9173.

Audience: **l,u,f.**

Schultz, Jeffrey D.   **E184.A1E574 2000**
(Editor), et al.
Encyclopedia of Minorities in American Politics: African
Americans and Asian Americans. Andrew L. Aoki & Kerry L.
Haynie (Editors). Cloth Text. Greenwood Publishing Group, Inc.
Portsmouth, NH. 2000. 376p. The American Political Landscape
Ser. ISBN:1-57356-148-7, ISBN13: 978-1-57356-148-8.
Dewey:305.8/00973/03. LCCN:99-043451.

Audience: **l,u,f.**

Singh, Jane (Editor,   **E49.2.S68**
Preface by)
South Asians in North America: An Annotated and Selected
Bibliography. Emily Hodges (Editor), Kenneth R. Logan (Editor,
Introduction by), Bruce La Brack, Mark Juergensmeyer & N.
Gerald Barrier (Editors). Trade Paper. University of California,
Berkeley, Centers for South & Southeast Asia Studies. Berkeley,
CA. 1988. 200p. Occasional Papers, No. 14
ISBN:0-944613-03-9, ISBN13: 978-0-944613-03-0.
Dewey:016.97/0004914. LCCN:87-073457.

Audience: **g,l.**

Smith, Henrietta M. &   **HC102**
Hirahara, Naomi
Distinguished Asian American Business Leaders. Cloth Text.
Greenwood Publishing Group, Inc. Portsmouth, NH. 2003. 256p.
Distinguished Asian Americans Ser. ISBN:1-57356-344-7,
ISBN13: 978-1-57356-344-4. Dewey:338.0973/092/395.
LCCN:2002-067835.

Audience: **g,l.** *Choice, 2003.*

Tong, Benson (Editor)   **E184**
Asian American Children: A Historical Handbook and Guide.
Cloth Text. Greenwood Publishing Group, Inc. Portsmouth, NH.
2004. 288p. Children and Youth Ser., :History and Culture
ISBN:0-313-33042-5, ISBN13: 978-0-313-33042-1.
Dewey:305.23/089/950730904. LCCN:2004-043643.

Audience: **g,l.**

Trudeau, Lawrence J.   **PS153.A84A82 1999**
(Editor)
Asian American Literature: Reviews and Criticism of Works by
American Writers of Asian Descent. Trade Cloth. Thomson
Gale. Farmington Hills, MI. 1998. xii,536p. Asian American
Literature Ser., Vol. 1 ISBN:0-7876-0296-5, ISBN13:
978-0-7876-0296-3. Dewey:810.9/895. LCCN:98-042124.

Audience: **g,l,f.** *Choice, 1999.*

Wong, Sau-Ling   **PS153.A84R47 2001**
Cynthia & Sumida, Stephen H. (Editors)
Resource Guide to Asian American Literature. Trade Cloth.
Modern Language Association of America. New York, NY.
2001. vi, 345p. ISBN:0-87352-271-0, ISBN13:
978-0-87352-271-7. Dewey:810.9/895. LCCN:00-040223.

Audience: **l,u,f.**

Zane, Nolan W.   **E184.O6H36 1998**
Handbook of Asian American Psychology. Lee C. Lee (Editor).
Trade Cloth. SAGE Publications, Inc. Thousand Oaks, CA.
1998. 600p. ISBN:0-8039-4963-4, ISBN13: 978-0-8039-4963-8.
Dewey:155.8/4951073. LCCN:98-008967.

Audience: **u,f.** *Choice, 1998.*

Arts and Humanities > Arts and Culture

Foster, Jenny Ryun   **PN771**
(Editor), et al.
Century of the Tiger: One Hundred Years of Korean Culture in
America. Heinz Insu Fenkl & Frank Stewart (Editors). Trade
Cloth. University of Hawaii Press. Honolulu, HI. 2003. 256p.
Manoa Ser., 14:2:A Pacific Journal of International Writing
ISBN:0-8248-2644-2, ISBN13: 978-0-8248-2644-4.
Dewey:973.04957.

Audience: **g,l.**

Kawakami, Barbara F.   **GT617.H3**
Japanese Immigrant Clothing in Hawaii, 1885-1941. Trade
Paper. University of Hawaii Press. Honolulu, HI. 1993. 272p.
ISBN:0-8248-1730-3, ISBN13: 978-0-8248-1730-5.
Dewey:391/.0089/9560969. LCCN:92-042593.

Audience: **g,l.** *Choice, 1994.*

Yang, Alice, et al.   **N7260.Y36 1998**
Why Asia?: Contemporary Asian and Asian American Art.
Jonathan S. Hay & Mimi Young (Authors). Trade Cloth. New
York University Press. New York, NY. 1998. 256p.
ISBN:0-8147-3579-7, ISBN13: 978-0-8147-3579-4.
Dewey:709/.5/0904. LCCN:97-033892.

Audience: **l,u,f.** *Choice, 1998.*

Arts and Humanities > Arts and Culture > Art

Creef, Elena Tajima   **NX652.J37C74 2004**
Imaging Japanese America: The Visual Construction of
Citizenship, Nation, and the Body. Trade Cloth. New York
University Press. New York, NY. 2004. 256p.
ISBN:0-8147-1621-0, ISBN13: 978-0-8147-1621-2.
Dewey:700/.4529956073. LCCN:2003-016328.

Audience: **l,u,f.**

Duus, Masayo   **NB237.N6D8813 2004**
The Life of Isamu Noguchi: Journey Without Borders. Peter
Duus (Translator). Trade Cloth. Princeton University Press.

Princeton, NJ. 2004. 432p. ISBN:0-691-12096-X, ISBN13: 978-0-691-12096-6. Dewey:709/.2. LCCN:2004-044532.

Audience: **g,l,u,f.** *Choice, 2005.*

Gesensway, Deborah &   **D769.8.A6**
Roseman, Mindy
Beyond Words: Images from America's Concentration Camps. Book, Other. Cornell University Press. Ithaca, NY. 1988. 192p. ISBN:0-8014-9522-9, ISBN13: 978-0-8014-9522-9. Dewey:940.54/72/73. LCCN:86-029088.

Audience: **g,l,u,f.** *Choice, 1987.*

Kim, Elaine H., et al.   **N6538.A83 K56**
Fresh Talk/Daring Gazes: Conversations on Asian American Art. Margo Machida & Sharon Mizota (Authors), Lisa Lowe (Prologue by). Trade Paper. University of California Press. Berkeley, CA. 2005. 234p. ISBN:0-520-24485-0, ISBN13: 978-0-520-24485-6. Dewey:704.03950730904. LCCN:2003-001854.

Audience: **l,u,f.**

Lee, Anthony W.   **N8214.5.U6L43 2001**
Picturing Chinatown: Art and Orientalism in San Francisco. Trade Cloth. University of California Press. Berkeley, CA. 2001. 362p. ISBN:0-520-22592-9, ISBN13: 978-0-520-22592-3. Dewey:704.9/4997461. LCCN:2001-027087.

Audience: **g,l,u,f.** *Choice, 2002.*

Ling, Amy (Editor)   **NX512.3.A83C74 1999**
Yellow Light: The Flowering of Asian American Arts. Trade Cloth. Temple University Press. Philadelphia, PA. 2000. 384p. Asian American History and Culture Ser. ISBN:1-56639-670-0, ISBN13: 978-1-56639-670-7. Dewey:700/.92/3951073 B. LCCN:98-029511.

Audience: **l,u,f.** *Choice, 1999.*

Obata, Chiura   **N6537.O22A2 2000**
Topaz Moon: Chiura Obata's Art of the Internment. Kimi Kodani Hill (Editor), Rutha Asawa (Foreword by), Timothy Anglin Burgard (Introduction by). Trade Paper. Heyday Books. Berkeley, CA. 2000. 168p. ISBN:1-890771-26-0, ISBN13: 978-1-890771-26-3. Dewey:760/.092 B. LCCN:99-089212.

Audience: **g,l,u.**

Poon, Irene   **N6538.A83P66 2001**
Leading the Way: Asian American Artists of the Older Generation. Trade Paper. Gordon College. Wenham, MA. 2001. 108p. ISBN:0-9707487-0-1, ISBN13: 978-0-9707487-0-6. Dewey:704.03/95073. LCCN:2001-368910.

Audience: **g,l,u,f.** *Choice, 2002.*

Wechsler, Jeffrey   **N6538.A83A84 1997**
Asian Traditions Modern Expressions: Asian American Artists and Abstraction, 1945-1970. Trade Cloth. Harry N. Abrams, Inc. New York, NY. 1997. 224p. ISBN:0-8109-1976-1, ISBN13: 978-0-8109-1976-1. Dewey:704/.0395/073. LCCN:96-027195.

Audience: **g,l,u,f.** *Choice, 1997.*

Arts and Humanities > Arts and Culture > Media

Hwang, David Henry   **PN1997.A1P26 2005**
(Foreword by)
Robot Stories: And More Screenplays. Greg Pak (Screenplay by). Trade Paper. Immedium. San Francisco, CA. 2005. 232p.

ISBN:1-59702-000-1, ISBN13: 978-1-59702-000-8. Dewey:791.43/75. LCCN:2004-112738.

Audience: **g,l,u,f.**

Lee, Robert G.   **E184.O6L48 1998**
Orientals: Asian Americans in Popular Culture. Cloth Text. Temple University Press. Philadelphia, PA. 2000. 288p. Asian American History and Culture Ser. ISBN:1-56639-658-1, ISBN13: 978-1-56639-658-5. Dewey:305.895/073. LCCN:98-025853.

Audience: **l,u,f.** *Choice, 1999.*

Leong, Russell   **PN1995.9.M56M68 1991**
(Introduction by)
Moving the Image: Independent Asian Pacific American Media Arts 1970-1990. Linda Mabalot (Preface by). Trade Paper. University of California, Los Angeles, Asian American Studies Center. Los Angeles, CA. 1992. 312p. ISBN:0-934052-13-1, ISBN13: 978-0-934052-13-9. Dewey:791.43/089/95073. LCCN:90-071789.

Audience: **g,l,u,f.** *Choice, 1992.*

Minh-ha, Trinh T.   **PN1995.T66 1991**
When the Moon Waxes Red: Representation, Gender and Cultural Politics. Paper over Boards. Routledge. New York, NY. 1991. 240p. ISBN:0-415-90430-7, ISBN13: 978-0-415-90430-8. Dewey:791.43/01. LCCN:91-014059.

Audience: **u,f.**

Arts and Humanities > Arts and Culture > Media > Film, Cinema

Creef, Elena Tajima   **NX652.J37C74 2004**
Imaging Japanese America: The Visual Construction of Citizenship, Nation, and the Body. Trade Cloth. New York University Press. New York, NY. 2004. 256p. ISBN:0-8147-1621-0, ISBN13: 978-0-8147-1621-2. Dewey:700/.4529956073. LCCN:2003-016328.

Audience: **l,u,f.**

Feng, Peter X.   **PN1995.9.A77F46 2002**
Identities in Motion: Asian American Film and Video. Trade Cloth. Duke University Press. Durham, NC. 2002. 304p. ISBN:0-8223-2983-2, ISBN13: 978-0-8223-2983-1. Dewey:791.43/6520395. LCCN:2002-003056.

Audience: **u,f.** *Choice, 2003.*

Feng, Peter X. (Editor),   **PN1995.9.A77S79 2002**
et al.
Screening Asian Americans. Charles Affron, Mirella Jona Affron & Robert Lyons (Editors). Trade Cloth. Rutgers University Press. Piscataway, NJ. 2002. 304p. Depth of Field Ser. ISBN:0-8135-3024-5, ISBN13: 978-0-8135-3024-6. Dewey:791.43/6520395073. LCCN:2001-031785.

Audience: **l,u,f.** *Choice, 2002.*

Hwang, David Henry   **PN1997.A1P26 2005**
(Foreword by)
Robot Stories: And More Screenplays. Greg Pak (Screenplay by). Trade Paper. Immedium. San Francisco, CA. 2005. 232p. ISBN:1-59702-000-1, ISBN13: 978-1-59702-000-8. Dewey:791.43/75. LCCN:2004-112738.

Audience: **g,l,u,f.**

Leong, Karen J.   **E183.8.C5**
The China Mystique: Pearl S. Buck, Anna May Wong, Mayling Soong, and the Transformation of American Orientalism. Trade

Cloth. University of California Press. Berkeley, CA. 2005. 304p. ISBN:0-520-24422-2, ISBN13: 978-0-520-24422-1. Dewey:305.48/8951073/0922. LCCN:2004-024699.

Audience: **g,l,u,f.** *Choice, 2006, 2005.*

Liu, Sandra &   **PN1995.9.A78C68 2000**
Hamamoto, Darrell Y. (Editors)
Countervisions: Asian American Film Criticism. Trade Cloth. Temple University Press. Philadelphia, PA. 2000. xiv, 317p. Asian American History and Culture Ser. ISBN:1-56639-775-8, ISBN13: 978-1-56639-775-9. Dewey:791.43/6520395. LCCN:00-020630.

Audience: **g,l,u,f.** *Choice, 2001.*

Marchetti, Gina   **PN1995.9.A78M37 1993**
Romance and the "Yellow Peril": Race, Sex, and Discursive Strategies in Hollywood Fiction. Trade Paper. University of California Press. Berkeley, CA. 1994. 270p. ISBN:0-520-08495-0, ISBN13: 978-0-520-08495-7. Dewey:791.436520395. LCCN:92-010878.

Audience: **l,u,f.** *Choice, 1994.*

Minh-ha, Trinh T.   **PN471.T75 1989**
Woman, Native, Other: Writing Postcoloniality and Feminism. Trade Cloth. Indiana University Press. Bloomington, IN. 1989. 184p. ISBN:0-253-36603-8, ISBN13: 978-0-253-36603-0. Dewey:809/.89287. LCCN:88-045455.

Audience: **l,u,f.**

Xing, Jun   **PN1995.9.A77H75 1998**
Asian America Through the Lens: History, Representations and Identity. Trade Cloth. AltaMira Press. Walnut Creek, CA. 1998. 248p. Critical Perspectives on Asian Pacific Americans Ser., Vol. 3 ISBN:0-7619-9175-1, ISBN13: 978-0-7619-9175-5. Dewey:384/.8/089935073. LCCN:98-019694.

Audience: **g,l,u.**

Arts and Humanities > Arts and Culture > Media > Internet

Ignacio, Emily   **E184.F4I37 2005**
Building Diaspora: Filipino Community Formation on the Internet. Trade Cloth. Rutgers University Press. Piscataway, NJ. 2005. 184p. ISBN:0-8135-3513-1, ISBN13: 978-0-8135-3513-5. Dewey:305.89/921073/090511. LCCN:2004-011749.

Audience: **l,u,f.** *Choice, 2005.*

Lee, Rachel C. & Wong,   **T173.8.A815 2003**
Sau-Ling Cynthia (Editors)
Asian America.Net: Ethnicity, Nationalism and Cyberspace. Paper over Boards. Routledge. New York, NY. 2003. 336p. ISBN:0-415-96559-4, ISBN13: 978-0-415-96559-0. Dewey:303.483. LCCN:2002-153218.

Audience: **l,u,f.**

Arts and Humanities > Arts and Culture > Media > Television

Hamamoto, Darrell Y.   **PN1992.8.A78H36 1994**
Monitored Peril: Asian Americans and the Politics of TV Representation. Book, Other. University of Minnesota Press. Minneapolis, MN. 1994. 320p. ISBN:0-8166-2368-6, ISBN13:

978-0-8166-2368-6. Dewey:791.45/6520395073. LCCN:93-038700.

Audience: **l,u,f.** *Choice, 1995.*

Arts and Humanities > Arts and Culture > Music

Reyes, Adelaida   **ML3560.V5R49 1999**
Songs of the Caged, Songs of the Free: Music and the Vietnamese Refugee Experience. Trade Cloth. Temple University Press. Philadelphia, PA. 1999. 248p. ISBN:1-56639-685-9, ISBN13: 978-1-56639-685-1. Dewey:780/.89/9592073. LCCN:98-054778.

Audience: **l,u.** *Choice, 1999.*

Arts and Humanities > Arts and Culture > Popular Culture

Bonus, Rick   **E184.F4B66 2000**
Locating Filipino Americans: Ethnicity and Cultural Politics of Space. Trade Cloth. Temple University Press. Philadelphia, PA. 2000. xiii, 217p. Asian American History and Culture Ser. ISBN:1-56639-778-2, ISBN13: 978-1-56639-778-0. Dewey:305.89/921073. LCCN:99-462220.

Audience: **l,u.**

Creef, Elena Tajima   **NX652.J37C74 2004**
Imaging Japanese America: The Visual Construction of Citizenship, Nation, and the Body. Trade Cloth. New York University Press. New York, NY. 2004. 256p. ISBN:0-8147-1621-0, ISBN13: 978-0-8147-1621-2. Dewey:700/.4529956073. LCCN:2003-016328.

Audience: **l,u,f.**

Feng, Peter X.   **PN1995.9.A77F46 2002**
Identities in Motion: Asian American Film and Video. Trade Cloth. Duke University Press. Durham, NC. 2002. 304p. ISBN:0-8223-2983-2, ISBN13: 978-0-8223-2983-1. Dewey:791.43/6520395. LCCN:2002-003056.

Audience: **u,f.** *Choice, 2003.*

Feng, Peter X. (Editor),   **PN1995.9.A77S79 2002**
et al.
Screening Asian Americans. Charles Affron, Mirella Jona Affron & Robert Lyons (Editors). Trade Cloth. Rutgers University Press. Piscataway, NJ. 2002. 304p. Depth of Field Ser. ISBN:0-8135-3024-5, ISBN13: 978-0-8135-3024-6. Dewey:791.43/6520395073. LCCN:2001-031785.

Audience: **l,u,f.** *Choice, 2002.*

Galang, M. Evelina   **PS508.A8S37 2003**
(Editor)
Screaming Monkeys: Critiques of Asian American Images. Trade Paper. Coffee House Press. Minneapolis, MN. 2003. 500p. ISBN:1-56689-141-8, ISBN13: 978-1-56689-141-7. Dewey:810.9/895. LCCN:2003-061251.

Audience: **l.**

Hamamoto, Darrell Y.   **PN1992.8.A78H36 1994**
Monitored Peril: Asian Americans and the Politics of TV Representation. Book, Other. University of Minnesota Press. Minneapolis, MN. 1994. 320p. ISBN:0-8166-2368-6, ISBN13:

978-0-8166-2368-6. Dewey:791.45/6520395073. LCCN:93-038700.

Audience: **l,u,f.** *Choice, 1995.*

Kondo, Dorinne K.				**E184.O6K65 1997**
About Face: Performing Race in Fashion and Theater. Paper over Boards. Routledge. New York, NY. 1997. 288p. ISBN:0-415-91140-0, ISBN13: 978-0-415-91140-5. Dewey:391/.00952. LCCN:96-043837.

Audience: **u,f.**

Lee, Anthony W.				**N8214.5.U6L43 2001**
Picturing Chinatown: Art and Orientalism in San Francisco. Trade Cloth. University of California Press. Berkeley, CA. 2001. 362p. ISBN:0-520-22592-9, ISBN13: 978-0-520-22592-3. Dewey:704.9/4997461. LCCN:2001-027087.

Audience: **g,l,u,f.** *Choice, 2002.*

Lee, Rachel C. & Wong,			**T173.8.A815 2003**
  Sau-Ling Cynthia (Editors)
Asian America.Net: Ethnicity, Nationalism and Cyberspace. Paper over Boards. Routledge. New York, NY. 2003. 336p. ISBN:0-415-96559-4, ISBN13: 978-0-415-96559-0. Dewey:303.483. LCCN:2002-153218.

Audience: **l,u,f.**

Lee, Robert G.				**E184.O6L48 1998**
Orientals: Asian Americans in Popular Culture. Cloth Text. Temple University Press. Philadelphia, PA. 2000. 288p. Asian American History and Culture Ser. ISBN:1-56639-658-1, ISBN13: 978-1-56639-658-5. Dewey:305.895/073. LCCN:98-025853.

Audience: **l,u,f.** *Choice, 1999.*

Leong, Karen J.				**E183.8.C5**
The China Mystique: Pearl S. Buck, Anna May Wong, Mayling Soong, and the Transformation of American Orientalism. Trade Cloth. University of California Press. Berkeley, CA. 2005. 304p. ISBN:0-520-24422-2, ISBN13: 978-0-520-24422-1. Dewey:305.48/8951073/0922. LCCN:2004-024699.

Audience: **g,l,u,f.** *Choice, 2006, 2005.*

Shimakawa, Karen				**E184.O6.S55 2002**
National Abjection: The Asian American Body on Stage. Trade Cloth. Duke University Press. Durham, NC. 2002. 224p. ISBN:0-8223-2937-9, ISBN13: 978-0-8223-2937-4. Dewey:305.895/073. LCCN:2002-006795.

Audience: **u,f.** *Choice, 2003.*

Xing, Jun				**PN1995.9.A77H75 1998**
Asian America Through the Lens: History, Representations and Identity. Trade Cloth. AltaMira Press. Walnut Creek, CA. 1998. 248p. Critical Perspectives on Asian Pacific Americans Ser., Vol. 3 ISBN:0-7619-9175-1, ISBN13: 978-0-7619-9175-5. Dewey:384/.8/089935073. LCCN:98-019694.

Audience: **g,l,u.**

Arts and Humanities > Arts and Culture > Theater, Performance

								PS628.A85
☐ Asian American Drama.
http://www.alexanderstreetpress.com/ Alexander Street Press.

Audience: **g,l,u,f.**

Cho, Margaret				**PN2287.R74**
I'm the One That I Want. Trade Cloth. DIANE Publishing Company. Collingdale, PA. 2005. 213p. ISBN:0-7567-8750-5, ISBN13: 978-0-7567-8750-9. Dewey:792.7/028/092 B.

Audience: **g,l.**

Escobar, Dario (Editor)			**NX512.U94**
Denise Uyehara: Maps of City and Body. Trade Paper. Kaya Production. New York, NY. 2005. 184p. ISBN:1-885030-38-X, ISBN13: 978-1-885030-38-2. Dewey:709.04074.

Audience: **g,l,u.**

Kondo, Dorinne K.				**E184.O6K65 1997**
About Face: Performing Race in Fashion and Theater. Paper over Boards. Routledge. New York, NY. 1997. 288p. ISBN:0-415-91140-0, ISBN13: 978-0-415-91140-5. Dewey:391/.00952. LCCN:96-043837.

Audience: **u,f.**

Lee, Josephine D.				**PS338.A74L44 1997**
Performing Asian America: Race and Ethnicity on the Contemporary Stage. Trade Cloth. Temple University Press. Philadelphia, PA. 1997. 256p. Asian American History and Culture Ser. ISBN:1-56639-502-X, ISBN13: 978-1-56639-502-1. Dewey:812/.5409035073. LCCN:96-031621.

Audience: **g,l,u.** *Choice, 1997.*

Minh-ha, Trinh T.				**PN1995.T66 1991**
When the Moon Waxes Red: Representation, Gender and Cultural Politics. Paper over Boards. Routledge. New York, NY. 1991. 240p. ISBN:0-415-90430-7, ISBN13: 978-0-415-90430-8. Dewey:791.43/01. LCCN:91-014059.

Audience: **u,f.**

Shimakawa, Karen				**E184.O6.S55 2002**
National Abjection: The Asian American Body on Stage. Trade Cloth. Duke University Press. Durham, NC. 2002. 224p. ISBN:0-8223-2937-9, ISBN13: 978-0-8223-2937-4. Dewey:305.895/073. LCCN:2002-006795.

Audience: **u,f.** *Choice, 2003.*

Arts and Humanities > Literature

Cheung, King-Kok &			**Z1229.A75C47 1988**
  Yogi, Stan (Editors)
Asian American Literature: An Annotated Bibliography. Trade Cloth. Modern Language Association of America. New York, NY. 1988. x,276p. ISBN:0-87352-960-X, ISBN13: 978-0-87352-960-0. Dewey:016.81/08/0895073. LCCN:88-005355.

Audience: **g,l,u,f.** *Choice, 1989.*

Huang, Guiyou				**PS153.A84C65 2006**
The Columbia Guide to Asian American Literature since 1945. Trade Cloth. Columbia University Press. New York, NY. 2006. 264p. Columbia Guides to Literature since 1945 Ser. ISBN:0-231-12620-4, ISBN13: 978-0-231-12620-5. Dewey:813.5409895073. LCCN:2005-051996.

Audience: **l,u,f.**

Nomura, Gail M.				**E184.O6F76 1989**
  (Editor)
Frontiers of Asian American Studies: Writing, Research, and Commentary. Trade Cloth. Washington State University Press. Pullman, WA. 1989. 341p. Association for Asian American

Studies ISBN:0-87422-064-5, ISBN13: 978-0-87422-064-3.
Dewey:973/.0495. LCCN:93-219858.

Audience: **l,u,f.**

Wong, Sau-Ling   **PS153.A84R47 2001**
  Cynthia & Sumida, Stephen H. (Editors)
Resource Guide to Asian American Literature. Trade Cloth.
Modern Language Association of America. New York, NY.
2001. vi, 345p. ISBN:0-87352-271-0, ISBN13:
978-0-87352-271-7. Dewey:810.9/895. LCCN:00-040223.

Audience: **l,u,f.**

Arts and Humanities > Literature > Anthologies

Asian Women United of   **E184.O6M24 1989**
  California Staff (Editor)
Making Waves: An Anthology of Writings by and about Asian
American Women. Trade Cloth. Beacon Press. Boston, MA.
1989. 480p. ISBN:0-8070-5904-8, ISBN13: 978-0-8070-5904-3.
Dewey:305.4/8895073. LCCN:88-047661.

Audience: **g,l,u,f.** *Choice, 1990.*

Bao, Quang &   **PS508.A8.T35**
  Yanagihara, Hanya (Editors)
Take Out: Queer Writing from Asian Pacific America. With
Timothy Liu. Asian American Writers' Workshop; Temple
University Press. 2001. ISBN:1-889876-12-7, ISBN13:
978-1-889876-12-2.

Audience: **g,l,u,f.**

Carbo, Nick & Tabios,   **PR9550.5.B33 2000**
  Eileen (Editors)
Babaylan: An Anthology of Filipina and Filipina American
Writers. Trade Paper. Aunt Lute Books. San Francisco, CA.
2000. 240p. ISBN:1-879960-59-1, ISBN13: 978-1-879960-59-6.
Dewey:820.8/09287/09599. LCCN:00-035525.

Audience: **g,l,u,f.** *Choice, 2001.*

Chan, Jeffery P
The Big Aiiieeeee!. Jeffery P. Chan (Editor). A A C P, Inc. 1992.
ISBN:0-685-61040-3, ISBN13: 978-0-685-61040-4.

Audience: **g,l.**

Chan, Jeffrey P., et al.   **PS508.A8A4 1997**
Aiiieeeee: An Anthology of Asian-American Writers. Frank Chin
& Lawson Fusao Inada (Authors). Trade Paper. Penguin Group
(USA) Inc. New York, NY. 1997. 336p. ISBN:0-452-01176-0,
ISBN13: 978-0-452-01176-2. Dewey:810.8/095073.
LCCN:96-029875.

Audience: **g,l,u,f.**

Fenkl, Heinz Insu &   **PS647.K67**
  Lew, Walter K. (Editors)
Kori: The Beacon Anthology of Korean American Fiction. Trade
Paper. Beacon Press. Boston, MA. 2002. 288p.
ISBN:0-8070-5917-X, ISBN13: 978-0-8070-5917-3.
Dewey:813/.540808957073.

Audience: **g,l,u,f.**

Francia, Luis H. &   **PS508.F53F58 1996**
  Gamalinda, Eric (Editors)
Flippin': Filipinos on America. Trade Paper. Asian American
Writers' Workshop. New York, NY. 1996. 377p.
ISBN:1-889876 01 1, ISBN13: 978 1 889876 01 6.
Dewey:810.8089921. LCCN:96-078962.

Audience: **g,l,u,f.** *Choice, 1997.*

Geok-lin Lim, Shirley &   **PS508.A8T55 2000**
  Chua, Cheng Lok (Editors)
Tilting the Continent: Southeast Asian American Literature.
Trade Paper. New Rivers Press. Moorhead, MN. 2000. 220p.
ISBN:0-89823-206-6, ISBN13: 978-0-89823-206-6.
Dewey:810.8/095. LCCN:99-068471.

Audience: **l,u,f.**

Geok-lin Lim, Shirley &   **PS153.A84F66 1988**
  Tsutakawa, Mayumi (Editors)
The Forbidden Stitch: An Asian-American Women's Anthology.
Trade Cloth. Calyx Books. Corvallis, OR. 1989. 290p.
ISBN:0-934971-10-2, ISBN13: 978-0-934971-10-2.
Dewey:810/.8/09287. LCCN:88-008117.

Audience: **g,l,u,f.**

Hagedorn, Jessica   **PS647.A75C484 2004**
  (Editor)
Charlie Chan Is Dead: At Home in the World an Anthology of
Contemporary Asian American Fiction. Elaine Kim (Preface by).
Trade Paper. Penguin Group (USA) Inc. New York, NY. 2004.
592p. ISBN:0-14-200390-5, ISBN13: 978-0-14-200390-9.
Dewey:813/.54080895. LCCN:2003-058225.

Audience: **g,l,u,f.**

Hong, Maria   **PS508.A8**
Growing up Asian American: Stories of Childhood, Adolescence
and Coming of Age. Prebound. Turtleback Books. Madison, WI.
1993. ISBN:0-606-06429-X, ISBN13: 978-0-606-06429-3.
Dewey:810.8/0895. LCCN:93-014033.

Audience: **g,l,u,f.**

Hongo, Garrett K.   **PS591.A76**
The Open Boat: Poems from Asian America. Trade Paper.
Doubleday Publishing. New York, NY. 1993. 352p.
ISBN:0-385-42338-1, ISBN13: 978-0-385-42338-0.
Dewey:811/.54080895. LCCN:92-011089.

Audience: **g,l,u,f.**

Houston, Velina H.   **PS628.A85S75 1997**
  (Editor)
But Still, Like Air, I'll Rise: New Asian American Plays. Trade
Cloth. Temple University Press. Philadelphia, PA. 1997. 512p.
Asian American History and Culture Ser. ISBN:1-56639-537-2,
ISBN13: 978-1-56639-537-3. Dewey:812/.54080895073.
LCCN:96-048729.

Audience: **l,u,f.** *Choice, 1997.*

Keller, Nora (Editor)   **PS508.K67**
Yobo: Korean American Writing in Hawai'i. Trade Paper.
Bamboo Ridge Press. Honolulu, HI. 2003. 382p.
ISBN:0-910043-65-5, ISBN13: 978-0-910043-65-6. Dewey:813.

Audience: **l,u,f.**

Kim, Elaine H. & Kang,   **PS508.K67**
  Laura Hyun Yi (Editors)
Echoes upon Echoes: New Korean American Writings. Trade
Cloth. Asian American Writers' Workshop. New York, NY.
2003. 288p. ISBN:1-889876-13-5, ISBN13: 978-1-889876-13-9.
Dewey:810.8/08957073. LCCN:2002-113033.

Audience: **l,u,f.** *Choice, 2004.*

Kim, Elaine H. (Editor),   **PS508.A8M35 1997**
et al.
Making More Waves: New Writing by Asian American Women.
Lilia Villanueva & Asian Women United of California Staff
(Editors), Jessica Hagedorn (Foreword by). Trade Paper. Beacon
Press. Boston, MA. 1997. 328p. ISBN:0-8070-5913-7, ISBN13:

978-0-8070-5913-5. Dewey:810.8/09287/08995073.
LCCN:96-052670.

Audience: **g,l,u,f.**

Kono, Juliet S. & Song,   **PS571.H3B4 1991**
Cathy (Editors)
Sister Stew, Fiction and Poetry by Women. Trade Paper.
Bamboo Ridge Press. Honolulu, HI. 1991. 330p. Bamboo Ridge
Ser., Nos. 50-51 ISBN:0-910043-22-1, ISBN13:
978-0-910043-22-9. Dewey:810.9/9287. LCCN:91-011471.

Audience: **g,l,u,f.**

Leong, Russell (Editor)   **HQ76.2.U5A75 1996**
Asian American Sexualities: Dimensions of the Gay and Lesbian
Experience. Paper over Boards. Routledge. New York, NY.
1995. 256p. ISBN:0-415-91436-1, ISBN13: 978-0-415-91436-9.
Dewey:306.8/08995/073. LCCN:95-000538.

Audience: **l,u,f.**

Lew, Walter K. (Editor)   **PS591.A76P74 1995**
Premonitions: The Kaya Anthology of New Asian American
Poetry. Trade Cloth. Kaya Production. New York, NY. 1995.
616p. ISBN:1-885030-13-4, ISBN13: 978-1-885030-13-9.
Dewey:811/.54080895. LCCN:94-075916.

Audience: **g,l,u,f.**

Lim, Shirley   **PS508.A8A83 2000**
Asian-American Literature: An Anthology. Trade Paper.
McGraw-Hill Higher Education. Burr Ridge, IL. 2000. xxii,
563p. ISBN:0-8442-1729-8, ISBN13: 978-0-8442-1729-1.
Dewey:810.8/0895. LCCN:99-016872.

Audience: **g,l,u,f.**

Lim-Hing, Sharon   **PS509.L47V47 1994**
(Editor)
The Very Inside: An Anthology of Writings by Asian and Pacific
Islander Lesbians. Trade Paper. Sister Vision Press. Toronto,
ON. 1994. 760p. ISBN:0-920813-97-6, ISBN13:
978-0-920813-97-3. Dewey:810.8/09206643. LCCN:95-163883.

Audience: **g,l,u,f.**

Maira, Sunaina &   **E184.S69C66 1996**
Srikanth, Rajini (Editors)
Contours of the Heart: South Asians Map North America. Trade
Paper. Asian American Writers' Workshop. New York, NY.
1996. 480p. ISBN:1-889876-00-3, ISBN13: 978-1-889876-00-9.
Dewey:305.891/4073. LCCN:96-078960.

Audience: **l,u,f.** *Choice, 1997.*

Moua, Mai Neng   **PS508.H63B36 2002**
(Editor)
Bamboo among the Oaks: Contemporary Writing by Hmong
Americans. Trade Cloth. Minnesota Historical Society Press.
Saint Paul, MN. 2002. 215p. ISBN:0-87351-436-X, ISBN13:
978-0-87351-436-1. Dewey:810.9/895942. LCCN:2002-004320.

Audience: **g,l,u,f.**

Nelson, Brian (Editor)   **PS628.A85A88 1997**
Asian American Drama: 9 Plays from the Multiethnic
Landscape. David Henry Hwang (Foreword by). Trade Paper.
Applause Theatre Book Publishers. New York, NY. 2000. 432p.
ISBN:1-55783-314-1, ISBN13: 978-1-55783-314-3.
Dewey:812/.54080895. LCCN:97-027054.

Audience: **l,u,f.**

Realuyo, Bino A.   **PS509.N5N54 1999**
(Editor), et al.
The Nuyorasian Anthology: Asian American Writings on New
York City. Kendal Henry & Rahna Reiko Rizzuto (Editors).

Trade Paper. Asian American Writers' Workshop. New York,
NY. 1999. 472p. ISBN:1-889876-07-0, ISBN13:
978-1-889876-07-8. Dewey:810.8/0327471/08995.
LCCN:98-072300.

Audience: **g,l.**

Srikanth, Rajini &   **PS508.A8B65 2001**
Iwanaga, Esther Y. (Editors)
Bold Words: A Century of Asian American Writing. Cloth Text.
Rutgers University Press. Piscataway, NJ. 2001. 480p.
ISBN:0-8135-2965-4, ISBN13: 978-0-8135-2965-3.
Dewey:810.8/0895/0904. LCCN:00-068346.

Audience: **l,u,f.** *Choice, 2002.*

Tran, Barbara (Editor),   **PS508.V54**
et al.
Watermark: Vietnamese American Poetry and Prose. Monique
Truong & Luu T. Khoi (Editors). Cloth Text. Asian American
Writers' Workshop. New York, NY. 1998. 225p.
ISBN:1-889876-05-8, ISBN13: 978-1-889876-05-4.
Dewey:810.8/089592. LCCN:97-078154.

Audience: **g,l,u,f.** *Choice, 1998.*

Watanabe, Sylvia &   **PS647.A75H58 1990**
Bruchac, Carol (Editors)
Home to Stay: Asian American Fiction by Women. Trade Paper.
Greenfield Review Literary Center, Inc. Greenfield Center, NY.
1990. 300p. ISBN:0-912678-76-3, ISBN13: 978-0-912678-76-4.
Dewey:813/.540809287. LCCN:89-084368.

Audience: **g,l,u.**

Women of South Asian   **PS153.A84O97 1993**
Descent Collective Staff (Editor)
Our Feet Walk the Sky: Women of the South Asian Diaspora.
Trade Paper. Aunt Lute Books. San Francisco, CA. 1998. 380p.
ISBN:1-879960-32-X, ISBN13: 978-1-879960-32-9.
Dewey:810.8/09287/08995. LCCN:93-036354.

Audience: **g,l,u,f.**

Wong, Shawn   **PS508.A8A8 1996**
Asian American Literature: A Brief Introduction and Anthology.
Ishmael Reed (Foreword by). Trade Paper. Longman Publishing
Group. White Plains, NY. 1997. 400p. Literary Mosaic Ser.
ISBN:0-673-46977-8, ISBN13: 978-0-673-46977-9.
Dewey:810.8/0895. LCCN:95-009632.

Audience: **g,l,u,f.**

Arts and Humanities > Literature > Biography, Personal Narrative, Memoir

Alexander, Meena   **PR9499.3.A46Z466**
Fault Lines: A Memoir. Ed. 2. Ngugi wa Thiong'o (Preface by).
Trade Paper. Feminist Press at The City University of New
York. New York, NY. 2003. 336p. The Cross-Cultural Memoir
Ser. ISBN:1-55861-454-0, ISBN13: 978-1-55861-454-3.
Dewey:811/.54 B. LCCN:2003-049504.

Audience: **l,u,f.**

Birchall, Diana   **PR9199.3.W3689Z58**
Onoto Watanna: The Story of Winnifred Eaton. Trade Cloth.
University of Illinois Press. Champaign, IL. 2001. 296p. The
Asian American Experience Ser. ISBN:0-252-02607-1, ISBN13:
978-0-252-02607-2. Dewey:813/.52 B. LCCN:00-012167.

Audience: **l,u,f.** *Choice, 2002.*

Bulosan, Carlos   PR9550.9.B8.A8 1973
America Is in the Heart. Trade Cloth. University of Washington
Press. Seattle, WA. 2003. 352p. Washington Papers, Vol. 68
ISBN:0-295-95289-X, ISBN13: 978-0-295-95289-5.
Dewey:818/.5/209. LCCN:73-013007.

Audience: **g,l.**

Bulosan, Carlos   PS3503.U5627
The Laughter of My Father. Trade Paper. Books on Demand.
Ann Arbor, MI. 201p. ISBN:0-598-44144-1, ISBN13:
978-0-598-44144-7. Dewey:617.52. LCCN:44-040087.

Audience: **g,l,u,f.**

Chan, Sucheng (Editor)   E184.V53V55 2006
The Vietnamese American 1.5 Generation: Stories of War,
Revolution, Flight and New Beginnings. Trade Cloth. Temple
University Press. Philadelphia, PA. 2006. 344p. Asian American
History and Culture Ser. ISBN:1-59213-500-5, ISBN13:
978-1-59213-500-4. Dewey:973/.04959200922 B.
LCCN:2005-055985.

Audience: **l,u.**

Chin, Tung Pok &   E184.C5P27 2000
  Chin, Winifred C.
Paper Son: One Man's Story. K. Scott Wong (Introduction by).
Trade Cloth. Temple University Press. Philadelphia, PA. 2000.
xx, 147p. Asian American History and Culture Ser.
ISBN:1-56639-800 2, ISBN13: 978-1-56639-800-8.
Dewey:973.04/951. LCCN:00-034347.

Audience: **l,u,f.** *Choice, 2001.*

Cho, Margaret   PN6165.C56 2005
I Have Chosen to Stay and Fight. Trade Cloth. Penguin Group
(USA) Inc. New York, NY. 2005. 256p. ISBN:1-57322-319-0,
ISBN13: 978-1-57322-319-5. Dewey:792.702/8/092.
LCCN:2005-051042.

Audience: **g,l.**

Cho, Margaret   PN2287.R74
I'm the One That I Want. Trade Cloth. DIANE Publishing
Company. Collingdale, PA. 2005. 213p. ISBN:0-7567-8750-5,
ISBN13: 978-0-7567-8750-9. Dewey:792.7/028/092 B.

Audience: **g,l.**

DasGupta, Shamita D.   E184.S69P38 1998
  (Editor)
A Patchwork Shawl: Chronicles of South Asian Women in
America. Cloth Text. Rutgers University Press. Piscataway, NJ.
1998. 256p. ISBN:0-8135-2517-9, ISBN13: 978-0-8135-2517-4.
Dewey:305.48/8914073. LCCN:97-049650.

Audience: **g,l,u,f.** *Choice, 1999.*

DeBonis, Steven   DS556.45.A43D43 1995
Children of the Enemy: Oral Histories of Vietnamese
Amerasians and Their Mothers. Trade Cloth. McFarland &
Company, Incorporated Publishers. Jefferson, NC. 1994. 309p.
ISBN:0-89950-975-4, ISBN13: 978-0-89950-975-4.
Dewey:959.7/00413. LCCN:94-28735.

Audience: **l,u.** *Choice, 1995.*

Duus, Masayo   NB237.N6D8813 2004
The Life of Isamu Noguchi: Journey Without Borders. Peter
Duus (Translator). Trade Cloth. Princeton University Press.
Princeton, NJ. 2004. 432p. ISBN:0-691-12096-X, ISBN13:
978-0-691-12096-6. Dewey:709/.2. LCCN:2004-044532.

Audience: **g,l,u,f.** *Choice, 2005.*

Espiritu, Yen Le   F869.S22E9 1995
Filipino American Lives. Library Binding. Temple University
Press. Philadelphia, PA. 1995. 256p. Asian American History
and Culture Ser. ISBN:1-56639-316-7, ISBN13:
978-1-56639-316-4. Dewey:305.89/921073/0922 B.
LCCN:94-048081.

Audience: **l.** *Choice, 1995.*

Faderman, Lillian &   E184.H55
  Xiong, Ghia
I Begin My Life All Over: The Hmong and the American
Immigrant Experience. Trade Paper. Beacon Press. Boston, MA.
1999. 288p. ISBN:0-8070-7235-4, ISBN13: 978-0-8070-7235-6.
Dewey:305.895/942073.

Audience: **g,l,u,f.**

Fujino, Diane Carol   E184.J3F8335 2005
Heartbeat of Struggle: The Revolutionary Life of Yuri
Kochiyama. Trade Cloth. University of Minnesota Press.
Minneapolis, MN. 2005. 432p. Critical American Studies
ISBN:0-8166-4592-2, ISBN13: 978-0-8166-4592-3.
Dewey:979.4/004956/0092 B. LCCN:2004-026943.

Audience: **g,l,u,f.**

Han, Arar & Hsu, John   E184.A75A8426 2004
  Y. (Editors)
Asian American X: An Intersection of Twenty-First Century
Asian American Voices. Trade Cloth. University of Michigan
Press. Chicago, IL. 2004. 264p. ISBN:0-472-09874-8, ISBN13:
978-0-472-09874-3. Dewey:305.895/073. LCCN:2004-003463.

Audience: **g,l.**

Han, Hyun Sook &   CT275.H35854A3 2004
  Ruth, Kari
Many Lives Intertwined: A Memoir. Trade Cloth. Yeong &
Yeong Book Company. Saint Paul, MN. 2004.
ISBN:0-9638472-9-5, ISBN13: 978-0-9638472-9-4.
Dewey:973/.04957/0092 B. LCCN:2004-022094.

Audience: **g,l.**

Hayslip, Le Ly   E184.V53
Child of War, Woman of Peace. Trade Paper. Doubleday
Publishing. New York, NY. 1999. ISBN:0-385-50006-8,
ISBN13: 978-0-385-50006-7. Dewey:959.704/38.

Audience: **g,l,u.**

Hayslip, Le Ly &   DS556.93.H39A3 2003
  Wurts, Jay
When Heaven and Earth Changed Places: A Vietnamese
Woman's Journey from War to Peace. Trade Paper. Penguin
Group (USA) Inc. New York, NY. 1993. 400p.
ISBN:0-452-27168-1, ISBN13: 978-0-452-27168-5.
Dewey:959.704/38 B. LCCN:89-013711.

Audience: **g.**

Houston, Jeanne   D769.A6H68 2002
  Wakatsuki & Houston, James D.
Farewell to Manzanar. Trade Cloth. Houghton Mifflin Company
Trade & Reference Division. Boston, MA. 2002. 208p.
ISBN:0-618-21620-0, ISBN13: 978-0-618-21620-8.
Dewey:940.54/72/7309794. LCCN:2002-727748.

Audience: **g,l,u,f.**

Huang, Guiyou (Editor)   PS366
Asian American Autobiographers: A Bio-Bibliographical Critical
Sourcebook. Shirley Geok-Lin Lim (Foreword by). Cloth Text.
Greenwood Publishing Group, Inc. Portsmouth, NH. 2001. 464p.

ISBN:0-313-31408-X, ISBN13: 978-0-313-31408-7.
Dewey:818/.540809895. LCCN:00-064056.
Audience: **l,u,f.** *Choice, 2001.*

Kang, Younghill PS3521.A444E27 1997
East Goes West: The Making of an Oriental Yankee. Paper Text.
Kaya Production. New York, NY. 1998. 425p.
ISBN:1-885030-11-8, ISBN13: 978-1-885030-11-5.
Dewey:813/.54. LCCN:94-075597.
Audience: **g,l,u,f.**

Kim, Elaine M. & Yu, E184.K6E27
Eui-Young
East to America: Korean American Life Stories. Anna Deveare
Smith (Foreword by). Trade Paper. DIANE Publishing
Company. Collingdale, PA. 2004. 386p. ISBN:0-7567-9113-8,
ISBN13: 978-0-7567-9113-1. Dewey:973/.04957.
Audience: **g,l,u,f.**

Kingston, Maxine Hong E184.C5K5 2005
The Woman Warrior and China Men. Mary Gordon
(Introduction by). Trade Cloth. Knopf Publishing Group. New
York, NY. 2005. 560p. ISBN:1-4000-4384-0, ISBN13:
978-1-4000-4384-2. Dewey:973/.04951/0092.
LCCN:2004-061143.
Audience: **g,l,u,f.**

Kiyooka, Roy PS536.3
Pacific Rim Letters. Smaro Kamboureli (Editor). Trade Paper,
Perfect. NeWest Publishers, Ltd. Edmonton, AB. 2005. 359p.
ISBN:1-896300-70-7, ISBN13: 978-1-896300-70-2. Dewey:810.
Audience: **g,l.**

Kumashiro, Kevin K. HQ75.7R47 2003
(Editor)
Restoried Selves: Autobiographies of Queer
Asian-Pacific-American Activists. Trade Paper. Haworth Press,
Incorporated, The. Binghamton, NY. 2005. 138p. Haworth Gay
& Lesbian Studies ISBN:1-56023-463-6, ISBN13:
978-1-56023-463-0. Dewey:305.895073. LCCN:2002-151325.
Audience: **g,l,u,f.**

Lam, Andrew E184.V53L36 2005
Perfume Dreams: Reflections on the Vietnamese Diaspora.
Richard Rodriguez (Foreword by). Trade Paper, Perfect. Heyday
Books. Berkeley, CA. 2005. 143p. ISBN:1-59714-020-1,
ISBN13: 978-1-59714-020-1. Dewey:305.895/92073/092 B.
LCCN:2005-012942.
Audience: **l,u.**

Lee, Mary P. E184.K6L445 1990
Quiet Odyssey: A Pioneer Korean Woman in America. Sucheng
Chan (Introduction by). Trade Cloth. University of Washington
Press. Seattle, WA. 1990. 264p. Samuel and Althea Stroum Bks.
ISBN:0-295-96946-6, ISBN13: 978-0-295-96946-6.
Dewey:973.00495702 B. LCCN:89-028077.
Audience: **g,l,u,f.**

Lee, Wen Ho & Zia, QC774.L44 A3
Helen
My Country Versus Me: The First Hand Account by the Los
Alamos Scientist Who Was. Trade Paper. Hyperion Press. New
York, NY. 2003. 352p. ISBN:0-7868-8687-0, ISBN13:
978-0-7868-8687-6. Dewey:327.1251073/092.
Audience: **g,l,u,f.**

Leong, Karen J. E183.8.C5
The China Mystique: Pearl S. Buck, Anna May Wong, Mayling
Soong, and the Transformation of American Orientalism. Trade

Cloth. University of California Press. Berkeley, CA. 2005. 304p.
ISBN:0-520-24422-2, ISBN13: 978-0-520-24422-1.
Dewey:305.48/8951073/0922. LCCN:2004-024699.
Audience: **g,l,u,f.** *Choice, 2006, 2005.*

Lin, Yutang & Chua, PR9470.9.L5C5 2006
Cheng Lok
Chinatown Family. Trade Cloth. Rutgers University Press.
Piscataway, NJ. 2007. Multi-Ethnic Literatures of the Americas
Ser. ISBN:0-8135-3913-7, ISBN13: 978-0-8135-3913-3.
Dewey:823/.912. LCCN:2006-005587.
Audience: **g,l,u,f.**

Liu, Eric E184.C5
The Accidental Asian: Notes of a Native Speaker. Trade Paper.
Alfred A. Knopf Inc. New York, NY. 1999. 224p. Vintage Bks.
ISBN:0-375-70486-8, ISBN13: 978-0-375-70486-4.
Dewey:305.8951/073.
Audience: **g,l.**

McCunn, Ruthanne PS3568.O243
Lum
Thousand Pieces of Gold: A Biographical Novel. Library
Binding. Sagebrush Education Resources. Caledonia, MN. 1988.
ISBN:0-613-03325-6, ISBN13: 978-0-613-03325-1.
Dewey:813/.54.
Audience: **g,l,u,f.**

Mura, David DS811
Turning Japanese: Memoirs of a Sansei. Trade Paper.
Grove/Atlantic, Inc. New York, NY. 2006. 384p.
ISBN:0-8021-4239-7, ISBN13: 978-0-8021-4239-9.
Dewey:915.204/48.
Audience: **g,l,u,f.**

Nakanishi, Don T. & E184
Wu, Ellen D.
Distinguished Asian American Political and Governmental
Leaders. Cloth Text. Greenwood Publishing Group, Inc.
Portsmouth, NH. 2002. 240p. Distinguished Asian Americans
Ser. ISBN:1-57356-325-0, ISBN13: 978-1-57356-325-3.
Dewey:920/.009295073. LCCN:2002-016957.
Audience: **g,l,u,f.** *Choice, 2003.*

Nam, Vickie E184.O6.Y45 2001
Yell-Oh Girls!: Emerging Voices Explore Culture, Identity, and
Growing up Asian American. Phoebe Eng (Foreword by). Trade
Paper. HarperCollins Publishers. New York, NY. 2001. 336p.
ISBN:0-06-095944-4, ISBN13: 978-0-06-095944-9.
Dewey:305.235. LCCN:2001-018164.
Audience: **g,l,u,f.**

Nguyen, Kien E184.V53N36 2001
The Unwanted: A Memoir. Trade Cloth. Little Brown &
Company. New York, NY. 2001. 352p. ISBN:0-316-28664-8,
ISBN13: 978-0-316-28664-0. Dewey:973/.049592.
LCCN:00-057997.
Audience: **g,l,u.**

Pham, Andrew X. DS556.39
Catfish and Mandala: A Two-Wheeled Voyage Through the
Landscape and Memory of Vietnam. Trade Paper. Picador. New
York, NY. 2000. 352p. ISBN:0-312-26717-7, ISBN13:
978-0-312-26717-9. Dewey:915.9704/44. LCCN:99-022711.
Audience: **g,l,u,f.**

Robinson, Katy E184.K6R63 2002
A Single Square Picture: A Korean Adoptee's Search for Her Roots. Trade Paper. Penguin Group (USA) Inc. New York, NY. 2002. 304p. ISBN:0-425-18496-X, ISBN13: 978-0-425-18496-7. Dewey:973/.04957/0092. LCCN:2001-052922.
Audience: **g,l.**

Scharlin, Craig & HD6515.A292U547 2000
Villanueva, Lilia V.
Philip Vera Cruz: A Personal History of Filipino Immigrants and the Farmworkers Movement. Ed. 3. Trade Paper. University of Washington Press. Seattle, WA. 2000. xxviii, 167p. ISBN:0-295-97984-4, ISBN13: 978-0-295-97984-7. Dewey:331.88/13/092 B. LCCN:00-029902.
Audience: **g,l,u.**

Sone, Monica Itoi F899.S49.J376 1979
Nisei Daughter. Trade Cloth. University of Washington Press. Seattle, WA. 1979. 238p. ISBN:0-295-95688-7, ISBN13: 978-0-295-95688-6. Dewey:979.7/77. LCCN:79-004921.
Audience: **g,l,u,f.**

Tenhula, John E184.I43T46 1990
Voices from Southeast Asia: The Refugee Experience in the United States. Liv Ullmann (Foreword by). Trade Cloth. Holmes & Meier Publishers, Inc. Teaneck, NJ. 1991. 270p. Ellis Island Ser. ISBN:0-8419-1110-X, ISBN13: 978-0-8419-1110-9. Dewey:305.895/9073. LCCN:90-040696.
Audience: **g,l,u,f.**

Tomita, Mary Kimoto E184.J3T65 1995
Dear Miye: Letters Home from Japan, 1939-1946. Robert G. Lee (Editor). Trade Cloth. Stanford University Press. Palo Alto, CA. 1995. 464p. Asian America Ser. ISBN:0-8047-2419-9, ISBN13: 978-0-8047-2419-7. Dewey:940.5/3151/092. LCCN:94-024110.
Audience: **l,u,f.** *Choice, 1996.*

Trenka, Jane Jeong E184.K6T74 2003
The Language of Blood: A Memoir. Trade Paper. Minnesota Historical Society Press. Saint Paul, MN. 2003. 226p. ISBN:0-87351-466-1, ISBN13: 978-0-87351-466-8. Dewey:977.6/004957/0092 B. LCCN:2003-005135.
Audience: **g,l.**

Uchida, Yoshiko D769.8.A6
Desert Exile: The Uprooting of a Japanese-American Family. Trade Cloth. University of Washington Press. Seattle, WA. 2003. 160p. ISBN:0-295-96190-2, ISBN13: 978-0-295-96190-3. Dewey:940.5472. LCCN:81-016187.
Audience: **g,l,u,f.**

Ung, Loung DS554.83.P65
First They Killed My Father: A Daughter of Cambodia Remembers. Trade Cloth. Mainstream Publishing. Snohomish, WA. 2001. 224p. ISBN:1-84018-415-9, ISBN13: 978-1-84018-415-0. Dewey:959.6/042/092.
Audience: **g,l.**

Ung, Loung E184.K45U54 2005
Lucky Child: A Daughter of Cambodia Reunites with the Sister She Left Behind. Trade Cloth. HarperCollins Publishers. New York, NY. 2005. 388p. ISBN:0-06-073394-2, ISBN13: 978-0-06-073394-0. Dewey:973/.049593/0092. LCCN:2004-054346.
Audience: **g,l.**

White-Parks, Annette PR9199.2.S93Z97 1995
Sui Sin Far - Edith Maude Eaton: A Literary Biography. Roger Daniels (Foreword by). Trade Cloth. University of Illinois Press. Champaign, IL. 1995. 288p. The Asian American Experience Ser. ISBN:0-252-02113-4, ISBN13: 978-0-252-02113-8. Dewey:813/.4 B. LCCN:94-006448.
Audience: **l,u,f.** *Choice, 1996.*

Wong, Jade NK4210.W55A2 1989
Fifth Chinese Daughter. Trade Cloth. University of Washington Press. Seattle, WA. 2003. 256p. ISBN:0-295-96826-5, ISBN13: 978-0-295-96826-1. Dewey:738/.092/4 B. LCCN:50-009740.
Audience: **g,l,u,f.**

Yamauchi, Wakako HD1531.M6G83
Songs My Mother Taught Me: Stories, Plays and Memoir. Garrett Hongo (Editor, Introduction by), Valerie Miner (Editor, Afterword by). Trade Cloth. Feminist Press at The City University of New York. New York, NY. 1994. 272p. ISBN:1-55861-085-5, ISBN13: 978-1-55861-085-9. Dewey:322.4/4/097273. LCCN:93-045383.
Audience: **g,l,u,f.**

Arts and Humanities > Literature > Criticism and Theory

Bow, Leslie PS153.A84B69 2001
Betrayal and Other Acts of Subversion: Feminism, Sexual Politics, Asian American Women's Literature. Trade Paper. Princeton University Press. Princeton, NJ. 2001. 224p. ISBN:0-691-07093-8, ISBN13: 978-0-691-07093-3. Dewey:810.9/9287/08995. LCCN:00-058488.
Audience: **l,u,f.**

Cha, Theresa Hak PS3566.L27
Kyung
Dictee. Trade Cloth. Tanam Press. New York, NY. 1982. 176p. ISBN:0-934378-10-X, ISBN13: 978-0-934378-10-9. Dewey:811/.54.
Audience: **l,u,f.**

Chen, Tina PS153.A84C47 2005
Double Agency: Acts of Impersonation in Asian American Literature and Culture. Trade Cloth. Stanford University Press. Palo Alto, CA. 2005. 280p. ISBN:0-8047-5185-4, ISBN13: 978-0-8047-5185-8. Dewey:810.9/353. LCCN:2005-000563.
Audience: **l,u,f.** *Choice, 2006.*

Cheung, King-Kok PS153.A84 I58 1997
(Editor)
An Interethnic Companion to Asian American Literature. Trade Paper. Cambridge University Press. New York, NY. 1996. 430p. ISBN:0-521-44790-9, ISBN13: 978-0-521-44790-4. Dewey:810.9/895. LCCN:95-043092.
Audience: **l,u,f.** *Choice, 1998.*

Cheung, King-Kok PS153.A84W67 2000
(Editor)
Words Matter: Conversations with Asian American Writers. Trade Cloth. University of Hawaii Press. Honolulu, HI. 2000. 408p. Intersections Ser. ISBN:0-8248-2134-3, ISBN13: 978-0-8248-2134-0. Dewey:810.9/895/0904. LCCN:99-036654.
Audience: **g,l,u,f.**

Cheung, King-Kok PS153.A84C48 1993
Articulate Silences: Hisaye Yamamoto, Maxine Hong Kingston, Joy Kogawa. Maxine Hong Kingston (Contribution by). Book,

Other. Cornell University Press. Ithaca, NY. 1993. 216p.
Reading Women Writing Ser. ISBN:0-8014-8147-3, ISBN13:
978-0-8014-8147-5. Dewey:810.99287. LCCN:92-046452.
Audience: **l,u,f.** *Choice, 1994.*

Chiu, Monica   **PS153.A84C483 2004**
Filthy Fictions: Asian American Literature by Women. Ed. 11.
Book, Other. AltaMira Press. Walnut Creek, CA. 2004. 210p.
Critical Perspectives on Asian Pacific Americans Ser.
ISBN:0-7591-0455-7, ISBN13: 978-0-7591-0455-6.
Dewey:810.9/9287/08995. LCCN:2003-016791.
Audience: **g,l,u,f.** *Choice, 2004.*

Christopher, Renny   **PS228.V5C47 1995**
The Vietnam War - the American War: Images and
Representations in Euro-American and Vietnamese Exile
Narratives. Cloth Text. University of Massachusetts Press.
Amherst, MA. 1996. 360p. ISBN:1-55849-008-6, ISBN13:
978-1-55849-008-6. Dewey:813/.5409358. LCCN:95-019687.
Audience: **l,u,f.** *Choice, 1996.*

Chu, Patricia P.   **PS153.A84C485 2000**
Assimilating Asians: Gendered Strategies of Authorship in Asian
America. Trade Cloth. Duke University Press. Durham, NC.
2000. 280p. New Americanists Ser. ISBN:0-8223-2430-X,
ISBN13: 978-0-8223-2430-0. Dewey:810.9/895073.
LCCN:99-033229.
Audience: **l,u,f.** *Choice, 2000.*

Duncan, Patti   **PS153.A84D86 2004**
Tell This Silence: Asian American Women Writers and the
Politics of Speech. Trade Cloth. University of Iowa Press. Iowa
City, IA. 2004. 276p. ISBN:0-87745-856-1, ISBN13:
978-0-87745-856-2. Dewey:810.9/895. LCCN:2003-050739.
Audience: **l,u,f.** *Choice, 2004.*

Eng, David L.   **E184.O6E53 2001**
Racial Castration: Managing Masculinity in Asian America.
Trade Cloth. Duke University Press. Durham, NC. 2001. 368p.
Perverse Modernities Ser. ISBN:0-8223-2631-0, ISBN13:
978-0-8223-2631-1. Dewey:305.38/895073. LCCN:00-057807.
Audience: **u,f.** *Choice, 2001.*

Galang, M. Evelina   **PS508.A8S37 2003**
(Editor)
Screaming Monkeys: Critiques of Asian American Images.
Trade Paper. Coffee House Press. Minneapolis, MN. 2003. 500p.
ISBN:1-56689-141-8, ISBN13: 978-1-56689-141-7.
Dewey:810.9/895. LCCN:2003-061251.
Audience: **l.**

Gee, Emma (Editor)   **E184.O6C68**
Counterpoint: Perspectives on Asian America. Trade Cloth.
University of California, Los Angeles, Asian American Studies
Center. Los Angeles, CA. 1976. ISBN:0-934052-03-4, ISBN13:
978-0-934052-03-0. Dewey:301.45/19/5073. LCCN:76-041528.
Audience: **g,l,u,f.** *B*

Geok-Lin Lim, Shirley   **PS153.A84**
& Ling, Amy (Editors)
Reading the Literatures of Asian America. Trade Cloth. Temple
University Press. Philadelphia, PA. 1992. 384p. Asian American
History and Culture Ser. ISBN:0-87722-935-X, ISBN13:
978-0-87722-935-3. Dewey:810.9/895. LCCN:92-016844.
Audience: **g,l,u,f.**

Kang, L. H. & Kim,   **PS3553.H13D538 1994**
Elaine H.
Writing Self, Writing Nation. Norma Alarcón (Editor), Yong S.

Min (Illustrator). Trade Paper. Third Woman Press. Oakland,
CA. 1994. 176p. ISBN:0-943219-11-6, ISBN13:
978-0-943219-11-0. Dewey:811/.54. LCCN:94-004916.
Audience: **u,f.**

Kang, Laura Hyun Yi   **E184.O6K36 2002**
Compositional Subjects: Enfiguring Asian/American Women.
Trade Cloth. Duke University Press. Durham, NC. 2002. 344p.
ISBN:0-8223-2883-6, ISBN13: 978-0-8223-2883-4.
Dewey:305.895073. LCCN:2001-007612.
Audience: **u,f.** *Choice, 2002.*

Kim, Elaine   **PS153.A84K55**
Asian-American Literature: An Introduction to the Writings and
Their Social Context. Trade Paper. Temple University Press.
Philadelphia, PA. 1984. 241p. ISBN:0-87722-352-1, ISBN13:
978-0-87722-352-8. Dewey:810/.9/895.
Audience: **g,l,u,f.**

Koshy, Susan   **PS374.M53K67 2004**
Sexual Naturalization: Asian Americans and Miscegenation.
Trade Cloth. Stanford University Press. Palo Alto, CA. 2005.
224p. Asian America Ser. ISBN:0-8047-4728-8, ISBN13:
978-0-8047-4728-8. Dewey:813.009/3552. LCCN:2004-018764.
Audience: **l,u,f.** *Choice, 2005.*

Lawrence, Keith &   **PS153.A84R44 2005**
Cheung, Floyd (Editors)
Recovered Legacies: Authority and Identity in Early Asian
American Literature. Trade Cloth. Temple University Press.
Philadelphia, PA. 2005. 304p. Asian American History and
Culture Ser. ISBN:1-59213-118-2, ISBN13: 978-1-59213-118-1.
Dewey:810.9/895. LCCN:2004-062557.
Audience: **u,f.** *Choice, 2006.*

Lee, Josephine D.   **PS338.A74L44 1997**
Performing Asian America: Race and Ethnicity on the
Contemporary Stage. Trade Cloth. Temple University Press.
Philadelphia, PA. 1997. 256p. Asian American History and
Culture Ser. ISBN:1-56639-502-X, ISBN13: 978-1-56639-502-1.
Dewey:812/.5409035073. LCCN:96-031621.
Audience: **g,l,u.** *Choice, 1997.*

Lee, Rachel C.   **PS153.A84L44 1999**
The Americas of Asian American Literature: Gendered Fictions
of Nation and Transnation. Cloth Text. Princeton University
Press. Princeton, NJ. 1999. 208p. ISBN:0-691-05960-8, ISBN13:
978-0-691-05960-0. Dewey:810.9/895. LCCN:99-014575.
Audience: **l,u,f.** *Choice, 2000.*

Leonard, George J.   **PS153.A84A87 1999**
(Editor)
The Asian Pacific American Heritage: A Companion to
Literature and Arts. Trade Cloth. Garland Publishing, Inc. New
York, NY. 1998. 690p. Reference Library of the Humanities,
Vol. 2109 ISBN:0-8153-2980-6, ISBN13: 978-0-8153-2980-0.
Dewey:996. LCCN:98-033468.
Audience: **l,u,f.** *Choice, 1999.*

Leong, Karen J.   **E183.8.C5**
The China Mystique: Pearl S. Buck, Anna May Wong, Mayling
Soong, and the Transformation of American Orientalism. Trade
Cloth. University of California Press. Berkeley, CA. 2005. 304p.
ISBN:0-520-24422-2, ISBN13: 978-0-520-24422-1.
Dewey:305.48/8951073/0922. LCCN:2004-024699.
Audience: **g,l,u,f.** *Choice, 2006, 2005.*

Li, David Leiwei   PS153.A84L5 1999
Imagining the Nation: Asian American Literature and Cultural
Consent. Trade Cloth. Stanford University Press. Palo Alto, CA.
1998. 364p. Asian America Ser. ISBN:0-8047-3400-3, ISBN13:
978-0-8047-3400-4. Dewey:810.9895. LCCN:98-024578.
Audience: **l,u,f.** *Choice, 1999.*

Lim, Shirley (Editor), et al.   PS153.A84T73 2005
Transnational Asian American Literature: Sites and Transits.
Gina Valentino, John Gamber & Stephen Sohn (Editors). Trade
Cloth. Temple University Press. Philadelphia, PA. 2006. 336p.
ISBN:1-59213-450-5, ISBN13: 978-1-59213-450-2.
Dewey:810.9/895. LCCN:2005-049680.
Audience: **l,u,f.**

Ling, Amy   PS153.C45L56 1990
Between Worlds: Women Writers of Chinese Ancestry. Cloth
Text. PPI-UK. Oxford, 1990. 292p. Athene Ser.
ISBN:0-08-037464-6, ISBN13: 978-0-08-037464-2.
Dewey:810.9/9287. LCCN:89-070968.
Audience: **g,l,u,f.** *Choice, 1991.*

Ling, Jinqi   PS153.A84L56 1998
Narrating Nationalisms: Ideology and Form in Asian American
Literature. Cloth Text. Oxford University Press, Inc. New York,
NY. 1998. 224p. ISBN:0-19-511116-8, ISBN13:
978-0-19-511116-3. Dewey:810.9/895. LCCN:97-034558.
Audience: **l,u,f.** *Choice, 1999.*

Liu, Sandra &   PN1995.9.A78C68 2000
  Hamamoto, Darrell Y. (Editors)
Countervisions: Asian American Film Criticism. Trade Cloth.
Temple University Press. Philadelphia, PA. 2000. xiv, 317p.
Asian American History and Culture Ser. ISBN:1-56639-775-8,
ISBN13: 978-1-56639-775-9. Dewey:791.43/6520395.
LCCN:00-020630.
Audience: **g,l,u,f.** *Choice, 2001.*

Lowe, Lisa   PS153.A84L69 1996
Immigrant Acts: On Asian American Cultural Politics. Cloth
Text. Duke University Press. Durham, NC. 1996. 264p.
ISBN:0-8223-1858-X, ISBN13: 978-0-8223-1858-3.
Dewey:810.9/895. LCCN:96-020952.
Audience: **l,u,f.**

Ma, Sheng-mei   E184.O6M22 2000
The Deathly Embrace: Orientalism and Asian American Identity.
Trade Paper. University of Minnesota Press. Minneapolis, MN.
2000. 208p. ISBN:0-8166-3711-3, ISBN13: 978-0-8166-3711-9.
Dewey:305.895073. LCCN:00-008866.
Audience: **l,u,f.** *Choice, 2001.*

Minh-ha, Trinh T.   PN471.T75 1989
Woman, Native, Other: Writing Postcoloniality and Feminism.
Trade Cloth. Indiana University Press. Bloomington, IN. 1989.
184p. ISBN:0-253-36603-8, ISBN13: 978-0-253-36603-0.
Dewey:809/.89287. LCCN:88-045455.
Audience: **l,u,f.**

Moraga, Cherríe &   PS509.F44T5 2001
  Anzaldúa, Gloria (Editors)
This Bridge Called My Back: Writings by Radical Women of
Color. Ed. 3. Trade Paper. Third Woman Press. Oakland, CA.
2002. 370p. ISBN:0-943219-22-1, ISBN13: 978-0-943219-22-6.
Dewey:810.8/09287. LCCN:2001-053486.
Audience: **g,l,u,f.** *B*

Nguyen, Viet Thanh   PS153.A84N48 2002
Race and Resistance: Literature and Politics in Asian America.
Trade Cloth. Oxford University Press, Inc. New York, NY. 2002.
240p. ISBN:0-19-514699-9, ISBN13: 978-0-19-514699-8.
Dewey:810.9/895. LCCN:2001-035851.
Audience: **l,u,f.** *Choice, 2002.*

Sabine, Maureen   PS3561.I52Z87 2004
Maxine Hong Kingston's Broken Book of Life: An Intertextual
Study of the Woman Warrior and China Men. Trade Cloth.
University of Hawaii Press. Honolulu, HI. 2004. 264p.
ISBN:0-8248-2784-8, ISBN13: 978-0-8248-2784-7.
Dewey:813/.54. LCCN:2003-018420.
Audience: **l,u,f.** *Choice, 2004.*

Said, Edward W.   DS5
Orientalism. Ed. 25. Trade Paper. Knopf Publishing Group. New
York, NY. 1979. 432p. ISBN:0-394-74067-X, ISBN13:
978-0-394-74067-6. Dewey:950. LCCN:79-010497.
Audience: **g,l,u,f.**

San Juan, E.   E184.A1
Racial Formations/Critical Transformations: Articulations of
Power in Ethnic and Racial Studies in the United States. Trade
Cloth. Prometheus Books, Publishers. Amherst, NY. 1994. 172p.
ISBN:1-57392-486-5, ISBN13: 978-1-57392-486-3.
Dewey:305.8.
Audience: **l,u,f.**

San Juan, E. Jr.   PL5531.S25 1996
The Philippine Temptation: Dialectics of Philippines - U. S.
Literary Relations. Library Binding. Temple University Press.
Philadelphia, PA. 1996. 256p. Asian American History and
Culture Ser. ISBN:1-56639-417-1, ISBN13: 978-1-56639-417-8.
Dewey:809/.89599. LCCN:95-047191.
Audience: **u,f.** *Choice, 1996.*

San Juan, E., Jr.   PL5531.S25 1996
The Philippine Temptation: Dialectics of Philippines - U. S.
Literary Relations. Temple University Press. 1996.
ISBN:1-56639-417-1, ISBN13: 978-1-56639-417-8.
Audience: **l,u.**

Skandera-Trombley,   PS3568.O243
  Laura E.
Critical Essays on Maxine Hong Kingston. Trade Cloth.
Thomson Gale. Farmington Hills, MI. 1998.
ISBN:0-8057-7828-4, ISBN13: 978-0-8057-7828-1.
Dewey:813/.54.
Audience: **l,u,f.** *Choice, 1999.*

Song, Min   F869.L89A27 2005
Strange Future: Pessimism and the 1992 Los Angeles Riots.
Trade Cloth. Duke University Press. Durham, NC. 2005. 280p.
ISBN:0-8223-3579-4, ISBN13: 978-0-8223-3579-5.
Dewey:305.8/009794/94. LCCN:2005-006511.
Audience: **l,u.**

Spivak, Gayatri   HM101
  Chakravorty
In Other Worlds: Essays in Cultural Politics. Trade Paper.
Methuen & Company, Ltd. London, 1987. xiix, 309p.
ISBN:0-416-01661-8, ISBN13: 978-0-416-01661-1. Dewey:306.
LCCN:86-028625.
Audience: **u,f.**

Srikanth, Rajini   PS153.S68S73 2004
The World Next Door: South Asian American Literature and the
Idea of America. Trade Cloth. Temple University Press.

Philadelphia, PA. 2005. 304p. Asian American History and Culture Ser. ISBN:1-59213-080-1, ISBN13: 978-1-59213-080-1. Dewey:810.98914. LCCN:2003-070260.

Audience: **l,u,f.** *Choice, 2005.*

Sumida, Stephen H.   **PS283.H3S86 1991**
And the View from the Shore: Literary Traditions of Hawaii. Cloth Text. University of Washington Press. Seattle, WA. 1991. 330p. Samuel and Althea Stroum Bks. ISBN:0-295-97078-2, ISBN13: 978-0-295-97078-3. Dewey:810.9/9969. LCCN:90-046127.

Audience: **g,l.**

Trudeau, Lawrence J.   **PS153.A84A82 1999**
   (Editor)
Asian American Literature: Reviews and Criticism of Works by American Writers of Asian Descent. Trade Cloth. Thomson Gale. Farmington Hills, MI. 1998. xii,536p. Asian American Literature Ser., Vol. 1 ISBN:0-7876-0296-5, ISBN13: 978-0-7876-0296-3. Dewey:810.9/895. LCCN:98-042124.

Audience: **g,l,f.** *Choice, 1999.*

Ty, Eleanor Rose &   **PS153.A84A86 2004**
   Goellnicht, Donald C. (Editors)
🄴 Asian North American Identities: Beyond the Hyphen. E-Book. Indiana University Press. Bloomington, IN. 2004. 212p. ISBN:0-253-34380-1, ISBN13: 978-0-253-34380-2. Dewey:810.9/895. LCCN:2003-017925.

Audience: **g,l.** *Choice, 2004.*

Wong, Sau-Ling   **PS153.A84**
   Cynthia
Reading Asian American Literature: From Necessity to Extravagance. Trade Paper. Princeton University Press. Princeton, NJ. 1993. 268p. ISBN:0-691-01541-4, ISBN13: 978-0-691-01541-5. Dewey:810.9895. LCCN:92-042251.

Audience: **l,u,f.** *Choice, 1994.*

Wu, William F.   **PS374.C46 W8**
The Yellow Peril: Chinese Americans in American Fiction, 1850-1940. Trade Cloth. Elliot's Books. Northford, CT. 1982. 241p. ISBN:0-208-01915-4, ISBN13: 978-0-208-01915-8. Dewey:813/.009/35203951. LCCN:81-012701.

Audience: **g,l,u,f.**

Yamamoto, Traise   **PS153.J34Y36 1999**
Masking Selves, Making Subjects: Japanese American Women, Identity, and the Body. Trade Paper. University of California Press. Berkeley, CA. 1999. 320p. ISBN:0-520-21034-4, ISBN13: 978-0-520-21034-9. Dewey:810.9/9287/089956. LCCN:98-014154.

Audience: **u,f.** *Choice, 1999.*

Yin, Xiao-Huang   **PS153.C45Y56 2000**
Chinese American Literature since the 1850s. Trade Cloth. University of Illinois Press. Champaign, IL. 2000. 336p. The Asian American Experience Ser. ISBN:0-252-02524-5, ISBN13: 978-0-252-02524-2. Dewey:810.9/8951. LCCN:99-006512.

Audience: **l,u,f.** *Choice, 2000.*

Yoshihara, Mari   **E184.A1Y78 2002**
Embracing the East: White Women and American Orientalism. Trade Cloth. Oxford University Press, Inc. New York, NY. 2002. 256p. ISBN:0-19-514533-X, ISBN13: 978-0-19-514533-5. Dewey:305.4/0973. LCCN:2002-017060.

Audience: **l,u,f.** *Choice, 2003.*

Zhou, Xiaojing &   **PS153.A84F67 2005**
   Najmi, Samina
Form and Transformation in Asian American Literature. Trade Paper. University of Washington Press. Seattle, WA. 2005. 320p. The Scott and Laurie Oki Series in Asian American Studies ISBN:0-295-98504-6, ISBN13: 978-0-295-98504-6. Dewey:810.9/895. LCCN:2004-027906.

Audience: **g,l,u.** *Choice, 2006.*

Arts and Humanities > Literature > Drama

PS628.A85
🖵 Asian American Drama.
http://www.alexanderstreetpress.com/
Alexander Street Press.

Audience: **g,l,u,f.**

Chin, Frank   **PS3545.I5365**
Chickencoop Chinaman and Year of the Dragon: Two Plays. Trade Paper. University of Washington Press. Seattle, WA. 1981. 172p. ISBN:0-295-95833-2, ISBN13: 978-0-295-95833-0. Dewey:812/.54. LCCN:81-000985.

Audience: **g,l,u,f.**

Chong, Ping, et al.   **PS628.A85B4 1990**
Between Worlds: Contemporary Asian-American Plays. Philip G. Kan, Jessica Hagedorn, David Hwang, Wakako Yamauchi & Laurence Yep (Authors), Misha Berson (Introduction by). Trade Paper. Theatre Communications Group, Inc. New York, NY. 1989. 272p. ISBN:1-55936-004-6, ISBN13: 978-1-55936-004-3. Dewey:812/.5409895. LCCN:90-010821.

Audience: **g,l,u,f.**

Gotanda, Philip Kan   **PS3557.O7934F57 1995**
Fish Head Soup and Other Plays. Trade Cloth. University of Washington Press. Seattle, WA. 1995. 272p. ISBN:0-295-97417-6, ISBN13: 978-0-295-97417-0. Dewey:812/.54. LCCN:95-018878.

Audience: **l.**

Houston, Velina H.   **PS628.A85S75 1997**
   (Editor)
But Still, Like Air, I'll Rise: New Asian American Plays. Trade Cloth. Temple University Press. Philadelphia, PA. 1997. 512p. Asian American History and Culture Ser. ISBN:1-56639-537-2, ISBN13: 978-1-56639-537-3. Dewey:812/.54080895073. LCCN:96-048729.

Audience: **l,u,f.** *Choice, 1997.*

Houston, Velina H.   **PS628.A85**
   (Editor, Introduction by)
The Politics of Life: Four Plays by Asian American Women. Trade Cloth. Temple University Press. Philadelphia, PA. 1993. 288p. Asian American History and Culture Ser. ISBN:1-56639-000-1, ISBN13: 978-1-56639-000-2. Dewey:812/.540809287. LCCN:92-013090.

Audience: **l,u,f.**

Hwang, David Henry   **PS3558.W83**
M. Butterfly: With an Afterword by the Playwright. Trade Paper. Penguin Group (USA) Inc. New York, NY. 1993. 112p. ISBN:0-452-27259-9, ISBN13: 978-0-452-27259-0. Dewey:812.54.

Audience: **g,l,u,f.**

Hwang, David Henry   PS3558.W83F6 1990
F. O. B. and Other Plays. Maxine Hong Kingston (Foreword
by). Trade Paper. Penguin Group (USA) Inc. New York, NY.
1990. 32p. ISBN:0-452-26323-9, ISBN13: 978-0-452-26323-9.
Dewey:812/.54. LCCN:89-013319.

Audience: **g,l,u,f.**

Kondo, Dorinne K.   E184.O6K65 1997
About Face: Performing Race in Fashion and Theater. Paper
over Boards. Routledge. New York, NY. 1997. 288p.
ISBN:0-415-91140-0, ISBN13: 978-0-415-91140-5.
Dewey:391/.00952. LCCN:96-043837.

Audience: **u,f.**

Lee, Josephine D.   PS338.A74L44 1997
Performing Asian America: Race and Ethnicity on the
Contemporary Stage. Trade Cloth. Temple University Press.
Philadelphia, PA. 1997. 256p. Asian American History and
Culture Ser. ISBN:1-56639-502-X, ISBN13: 978-1-56639-502-1.
Dewey:812/.5409035073. LCCN:96-031621.

Audience: **g,l,u.**   *Choice, 1997.*

Liu, Miles Xian (Editor)   **PS338**
Asian American Playwrights: A Bio-Bibliographical Critical
Sourcebook. Cloth Text. Greenwood Publishing Group, Inc.
Portsmouth, NH. 2002. 424p. ISBN:0-313-31455-1, ISBN13:
978-0-313-31455-1. Dewey:812/.509895/03 B.
LCCN:2001-037680.

Audience: **g,l,u,f.**   *Choice, 2003.*

Nelson, Brian (Editor)   PS628.A85A88 1997
Asian American Drama: 9 Plays from the Multiethnic
Landscape. David Henry Hwang (Foreword by). Trade Paper.
Applause Theatre Book Publishers. New York, NY. 2000. 432p.
ISBN:1-55783-314-1, ISBN13: 978-1-55783-314-3.
Dewey:812/.54080895. LCCN:97-027054.

Audience: **l,u,f.**

Shimakawa, Karen   E184.O6.S55 2002
National Abjection: The Asian American Body on Stage. Trade
Cloth. Duke University Press. Durham, NC. 2002. 224p.
ISBN:0-8223-2937-9, ISBN13: 978-0-8223-2937-4.
Dewey:305.895/073. LCCN:2002-006795.

Audience: **u,f.**   *Choice, 2003.*

Uno, Roberta   PS628.A85U53 1993
e Unbroken Thread: An Anthology of Plays by Asian American
Women. E-Book. NetLibrary, Inc. Boulder, CO. 1993.
ISBN:0-585-21735-1, ISBN13: 978-0-585-21735-2.
Dewey:812/.540809287.

Audience: **l.**   *Choice, 1994.*

Yamauchi, Wakako   HD1531.M6G83
Songs My Mother Taught Me: Stories, Plays and Memoir.
Garrett Hongo (Editor, Introduction by), Valerie Miner (Editor,
Afterword by). Trade Cloth. Feminist Press at The City
University of New York. New York, NY. 1994. 272p.
ISBN:1-55861-085-5, ISBN13: 978-1-55861-085-9.
Dewey:322.4/4/097273. LCCN:93-045383.

Audience: **g,l,u,f.**

Arts and Humanities > Literature > Fiction

Bacho, Peter   PS3552.A2573C4 1991
Cebu. Cloth Text. University of Washington Press. Seattle, WA.
1991. 212p. ISBN:0-295-97113-4, ISBN13: 978-0-295-97113-1.
Dewey:813/.54. LCCN:91-000323.

Audience: **g,l,u,f.**

Bacho, Peter   PS3552.A2573D3 1997
Dark Blue Suit: And Other Stories. Trade Cloth. University of
Washington Press. Seattle, WA. 1997. 192p.
ISBN:0-295-97664-0, ISBN13: 978-0-295-97664-8.
Dewey:813/.54. LCCN:97-024806.

Audience: **g,l,u,f.**

Bulosan, Carlos   PR9550.9.B8C79 1995
The Cry and the Dedication. E. San Juan Jr. (Editor,
Introduction by). Library Binding. Temple University Press.
Philadelphia, PA. 1995. 304p. Asian American History and
Culture Ser. ISBN:1-56639-295-0, ISBN13: 978-1-56639-295-2.
Dewey:813/.52. LCCN:94-029767.

Audience: **l,u,f.**

Chang, Diana   PS3553.H2719F76 1994
The Frontiers of Love. Trade Paper. University of Washington
Press. Seattle, WA. 1993. 246p. ISBN:0-295-97326-9, ISBN13:
978-0-295-97326-5. Dewey:813/.54. LCCN:93-035512.

Audience: **g,l.**

Chang, Lan Samantha   PS3553.H2724H86 1998
Hunger. Trade Cloth. W. W. Norton & Company, Inc. New
York, NY. 1998. 160p. ISBN:0-393-04664-8, ISBN13:
978-0-393-04664-9. Dewey:813.5/4. LCCN:98-013547.

Audience: **g,l,u,f.**   *Choice, 1999.*

Chin, Frank   PS3553.H4897C49 1988
Chinaman Pacific and Frisco R. R. Co. Trade Paper. Coffee
House Press. Minneapolis, MN. 1988. 224p.
ISBN:0-918273-44-7, ISBN13: 978-0-918273-44-4.
Dewey:813/.54. LCCN:88-030326.

Audience: **g,l,u,f.**

Chin, Frank   PS3553.H4897G86 1994
Gunga Din Highway. Trade Cloth. Coffee House Press.
Minneapolis, MN. 1995. 400p. ISBN:1-56689-024-1, ISBN13:
978-1-56689-024-3. Dewey:813/.54. LCCN:94-012597.

Audience: **g,l,u,f.**

Chu, Louis   PS3568.O243
Eat a Bowl of Tea. Trade Paper. Kensington Publishing
Corporation. New York, NY. 2002. 256p. ISBN:0-8184-0395-0,
ISBN13: 978-0-8184-0395-8. Dewey:813.5/4.

Audience: **g,l,u,f.**

Divakaruni, Chitra   PS3568.O243
  Banerjee
The Mistress of Spices. Trade Paper. Random House Children's
Books. New York, NY. 1998. 352p. ISBN:0-385-48238-8,
ISBN13: 978-0-385-48238-7. Dewey:813.5/4. LCCN:96-023767.

Audience: **g,l,u,f.**

Fenkl, Heinz Insu &   **PS647.K67**
Lew, Walter K. (Editors)
Kori: The Beacon Anthology of Korean American Fiction. Trade Paper. Beacon Press. Boston, MA. 2002. 288p. ISBN:0-8070-5917-X, ISBN13: 978-0-8070-5917-3. Dewey:813/.540808957073.

Audience: **g,l,u,f.**

Galang, M. Evelina   **PS3557.A375H47 1996**
Her Wild American Self. Trade Paper. Coffee House Press. Minneapolis, MN. 1996. 192p. ISBN:1-56689-040-3, ISBN13: 978-1-56689-040-3. Dewey:813/.54. LCCN:96-033694.

Audience: **g,l.** *Choice, 1996.*

Hagedorn, Jessica   **PS3568.O243**
Dogeaters. Trade Paper. Penguin Group (USA) Inc. New York, NY. 1991. 272p. Contemporay American Fiction Ser. ISBN:0-14-014904-X, ISBN13: 978-0-14-014904-3. Dewey:813/.54. LCCN:89-016195.

Audience: **g,l,u,f.**

Hagedorn, Jessica   **PS3568.O243**
Dream Jungle. Trade Paper. Penguin Group (USA) Inc. New York, NY. 2004. 336p. ISBN:0-14-200109-0, ISBN13: 978-0-14-200109-7. Dewey:813/.54.

Audience: **g,l,u,f.**

Hahn, Kimiko   **PS3558.A32357.E27**
Earshot. Trade Cloth. Hanging Loose Press. Brooklyn, NY. 1992. ISBN:0-914610-84-8, ISBN13: 978-0-914610-84-7. Dewey:811/.54.

Audience: **g,l.**

Huang, Guiyou (Editor)   **PS153**
Asian American Short Story Writers: An A-to-Z Guide. Cloth Text. Greenwood Publishing Group, Inc. Portsmouth, NH. 2003. 392p. ISBN:0-313-32229-5, ISBN13: 978-0-313-32229-7. Dewey:813/.0109895/03 B. LCCN:2002-192772.

Audience: **g,l,u,f.** *Choice, 2003.*

Jen, Gish   **PS3560.E474L685 2004**
The Love Wife. Trade Cloth. Alfred A. Knopf Inc. New York, NY. 2004. 400p. ISBN:1-4000-4213-5, ISBN13: 978-1-4000-4213-5. Dewey:FIC. LCCN:2004-040917.

Audience: **g,l.**

Jen, Gish   **PS3568.O243**
Mona in the Promised Land: A Novel. Trade Paper. Knopf Publishing Group. New York, NY. 1997. 320p. ISBN:0-679-77650-8, ISBN13: 978-0-679-77650-5. Dewey:813.5/4. LCCN:95-044447.

Audience: **g,l.**

Jen, Gish   **PS3568.O243**
Typical American. Trade Paper. Penguin Group (USA) Inc. New York, NY. 1992. 1p. Plume Contemporary Fiction Ser. ISBN:0-452-26774-9, ISBN13: 978-0-452-26774-9. Dewey:813.5/4. LCCN:91-033814.

Audience: **g,l.**

Kadohata, Cynthia   **PS3561.A3615F5**
The Floating World. Cloth Text. DIANE Publishing Company. Collingdale, PA. 1997. 196p. ISBN:0-7881-5046-4, ISBN13: 978-0-7881-5046-3. Dewey:813.54.

Audience: **g,l,u,f.**

Keller, Nora O.   **PS3561.E38574.C66**
Comfort Woman. Trade Paper. Penguin Group (USA) Inc. New York, NY. 1998. 240p. ISBN:0-14-026335-7, ISBN13: 978-0-14-026335-0. Dewey:813/.54. LCCN:96-035458.

Audience: **g,l,u,f.**

Kim, Ronyoung   **PS3568.O243**
Clay Walls. Library Binding. Sagebrush Education Resources. Caledonia, MN. 1996. ISBN:0-613-50288-4, ISBN13: 978-0-613-50288-7. Dewey:813/.54.

Audience: **g,l,u,f.**

Kingston, Maxine Hong   **PS3561.I52T7 1990**
Tripmaster Monkey: His Fake Book. Trade Paper. Knopf Publishing Group. New York, NY. 1990. 352p. Vintage International Ser. ISBN:0-679-72789-2, ISBN13: 978-0-679-72789-7. Dewey:813/.54. LCCN:89-040550.

Audience: **g,l,u,f.**

Kingston, Maxine Hong   **E184.C5K5 2005**
The Woman Warrior and China Men. Mary Gordon (Introduction by). Trade Cloth. Knopf Publishing Group. New York, NY. 2005. 560p. ISBN:1-4000-4384-0, ISBN13: 978-1-4000-4384-2. Dewey:973/.04951/0092. LCCN:2004-061143.

Audience: **g,l,u,f.**

Kogawa, Joy   **PR9199.3.K63I87 1994**
Itsuka. Trade Paper. Alfred A. Knopf Inc. New York, NY. 1993. 352p. ISBN:0-385-46885-7, ISBN13: 978-0-385-46885-5. Dewey:813/.54. LCCN:93-026076.

Audience: **g,l,u,f.**

Kogawa, Joy   **PS3568.O243**
Obasan. UK-Trade Paper. Knopf Publishing Group. New York, NY. 1993. 320p. ISBN:0-385-46886-5, ISBN13: 978-0-385-46886-2. Dewey:813/.54. LCCN:93-026081.

Audience: **g,l,u,f.**

Kudaka, Geraldine &   **PS648.E7O5 1995**
Leong, Russell
On a Bed of Rice: An Asian American Erotic Feast. Book, Other. Knopf Publishing Group. New York, NY. 1995. 528p. ISBN:0-385-47640-X, ISBN13: 978-0-385-47640-9. Dewey:813/.01083538. LCCN:95-015723.

Audience: **g,l,u,f.**

Lahiri, Jhumpa   **PS3562.A316I58 1999**
Interpreter of Maladies. Trade Cloth. Houghton Mifflin Company Trade & Reference Division. Boston, MA. 2000. 160p. ISBN:0-618-10136-5, ISBN13: 978-0-618-10136-8. Dewey:813.54. LCCN:98-050895.

Audience: **g,l,u,f.**

Lahiri, Jhumpa   **PS3562.A316N36 2003**
The Namesake: A Novel. Trade Cloth. Houghton Mifflin Company Trade & Reference Division. Boston, MA. 2003. 304p. ISBN:0-395-92721-8, ISBN13: 978-0-395-92721-2. Dewey:813/.54. LCCN:2003-041718.

Audience: **g,l,u,f.**

Lee, Chang-Rae   **PS3562.E3347A79 2004**
Aloft. Trade Cloth. Penguin Group (USA) Inc. New York, NY. 2004. 352p. ISBN:1-57322-263-1, ISBN13: 978-1-57322-263-1. Dewey:813/.54. LCCN:2003-058630.

Audience: **g,l,u,f.**

Lee, Chang-Rae   **PS3562.E3347G4 1999**
A Gesture Life. Trade Cloth. Penguin Group (USA) Inc. New York, NY. 1999. 356p. ISBN:1-57322-146-5, ISBN13: 978-1-57322-146-7. Dewey:813.5/4. LCCN:99-028382.
                                        Audience: **g,l,u,f.**

Lee, Chang-Rae   **PS3562.E3347N38 1995**
Native Speaker. Trade Paper. Penguin Group (USA) Inc. New York, NY. 1996. 368p. ISBN:1-57322-531-2, ISBN13: 978-1-57322-531-1. Dewey:813.5/4. LCCN:94-032241.
                                        Audience: **g,l,u,f.**

Lee, Don   **PS3562.E339Y45 2001**
Yellow: Stories. Trade Cloth. W. W. Norton & Company, Inc. New York, NY. 2001. 192p. ISBN:0-393-02562-4, ISBN13: 978-0-393-02562-0. Dewey:813/.6. LCCN:00-050047.
                                        Audience: **g,l.**

Lee, Y. C.   **PS3523.E3158F5 2002**
The Flower Drum Song. David Henry Hwang (Introduction by). Trade Paper. Penguin Group (USA) Inc. New York, NY. 2002. 272p. ISBN:0-14-200218-6, ISBN13: 978-0-14-200218-6. Dewey:813/.54. LCCN:2002-028994.
                                        Audience: **g,l,u,f.**

Leong, Russell Charles   **PS3562.E5745P49 2000**
Phoenix Eyes and Other Stories. Trade Cloth. University of Washington Press. Seattle, WA. 2000. 172p. The Scott and Laurie Oki Series in Asian American Studies ISBN:0-295-97944-5, ISBN13: 978-0-295-97944-1. Dewey:813/.6. LCCN:00-037711.
                                        Audience: **g,l.**

Ling, Amy &   **PR9199.2.S93M77 1995**
  White-Parks, Annette (Editors)
Mrs. Spring Fragrance and Other Writings. Trade Cloth. University of Illinois Press. Champaign, IL. 1995. 312p. The Asian American Experience Ser. ISBN:0-252-02133-9, ISBN13: 978-0-252-02133-6. Dewey:813/.52. LCCN:94-014202.
                            Audience: **g,l,u,f.** *Choice, 1996.*

Linmark, R. Zamora   **PS3576.A475R65 1995**
Rolling the R's. Trade Cloth. Kaya Production. New York, NY. 1996. 168p. ISBN:1-885030-02-9, ISBN13: 978-1-885030-02-3. Dewey:813/.54. LCCN:94-075595.
                                        Audience: **g,l.**

Louie, David W.   **PS3562.O818P36 1991**
Pangs of Love: And Other Stories. Trade Cloth. Alfred A. Knopf Inc. New York, NY. 1991. ISBN:0-394-58957-2, ISBN13: 978-0-394-58957-2. Dewey:813/.54. LCCN:90-053544.
                                        Audience: **g,l,u,f.**

Louie, David Wong   **PS3562.O818B37 2000**
The Barbarians are Coming. Trade Cloth. Penguin Group (USA) Inc. New York, NY. 2000. 336p. ISBN:0-399-14603-2, ISBN13: 978-0-399-14603-9. Dewey:813/.54. LCCN:99-036902.
                                        Audience: **g,l.**

Lum, Darrell H. Y.   **PS3562.U468**
Pass on, No Pass Back!. Trade Paper. Bamboo Ridge Press. Honolulu, HI. 1990. 128p. Bamboo Ridge Ser., Nos. 48-49 ISBN:0-910043-19-1, ISBN13: 978-0-910043-19-9. Dewey:811.54. LCCN:90-085158.
                                        Audience: **g,l.**

Mori, Toshio & Inada,   **PS3568.O243**
  Lawson Fusao
Yokohama, California. Trade Paper. University of Washington Press. Seattle, WA. 1985. 176p. ISBN:0-295-96167-8, ISBN13: 978-0-295-96167-5. Dewey:813/.54. LCCN:84-021987.
                                        Audience: **g,l,u,f.**

Mukherjee, Bharati   **PR9499.3.M77D47 2002**
Desirable Daughters. Trade Cloth. Hyperion Press. New York, NY. 2002. 310p. ISBN:0-7868-6598-9, ISBN13: 978-0-7868-6598-7. Dewey:813.54. LCCN:2001-053061.
                                        Audience: **g,l,u,f.**

Mukherjee, Bharati   **PS3568.O243**
Jasmine. Trade Paper. Grove/Atlantic, Inc. New York, NY. 1999. 256p. ISBN:0-8021-3630-3, ISBN13: 978-0-8021-3630-5. Dewey:813.5/4.
                                        Audience: **g,l,u,f.**

Murayama, Milton   **PS3563.U723A79 1988**
All I'm Asking for Is My Body. Franklin Odo (Introduction by). Trade Paper. University of Hawaii Press. Honolulu, HI. 1988. 120p. Kolowalu Bks. ISBN:0-8248-1172-0, ISBN13: 978-0-8248-1172-3. Dewey:813/.54. LCCN:88-006967.
                                        Audience: **g,l,u,f.**

Ng, Fae M.   **PS3568.O243**
Bone: A Novel. Trade Cloth. Hyperion Press. New York, NY. 1993. 208p. ISBN:1-56282-944-0, ISBN13: 978-1-56282-944-5. Dewey:813/.54.
                                        Audience: **g,l.**

Nieh, Hualing   **PL2856.N4S213 1998**
Mulberry and Peach: Two Women of China. Jane P. Young & Linda Lappin (Translators), Sau-ling Wong (Afterword by). Trade Paper. Feminist Press at The City University of New York. New York, NY. 1997. 224p. ISBN:1-55861-182-7, ISBN13: 978-1-55861-182-5. Dewey:895.1/352. LCCN:98-012259.
                                        Audience: **g,l,u,f.**

Nunez, Sigrid   **PS3568.O243**
A Feather on the Breath of God: A Novel. Trade Paper. Picador. New York, NY. 2005. 192p. ISBN:0-312-42273-3, ISBN13: 978-0-312-42273-8. Dewey:813.5/4.
                                        Audience: **g,l.**

Okada, John   **PS3565.K33 N6 1981**
No-No Boy. Trade Cloth. University of Washington Press. Seattle, WA. 2003. 176p. ISBN:0-295-95525-2, ISBN13: 978-0-295-95525-4. Dewey:813/.54. LCCN:79-055834.
                                        Audience: **g,l,u,f.**

Otsuka, Julie   **PS3615.T88W48 2002**
When the Emperor Was Divine: A Novel. Trade Cloth. Alfred A. Knopf Inc. New York, NY. 2002. 160p. ISBN:0-375-41429-0, ISBN13: 978-0-375-41429-9. Dewey:813/.6. LCCN:2002-020814.
                                        Audience: **g,l.**

Ozeki, Ruth L.   **PS3565.Z45**
All over Creation. Trade Paper. Penguin Group (USA) Inc. New York, NY. 2004. 432p. ISBN:0-14-200389-1, ISBN13: 978-0-14-200389-3. Dewey:813.54.
                                        Audience: **g,l,u,f.**

Ozeki, Ruth L.   **PS3565.Z45M99 1998**
My Year of Meats. Trade Paper. Penguin Group (USA) Inc. New York, NY. 1999. 400p. ISBN:0-14-028046-4, ISBN13: 978-0-14-028046-3. Dewey:813/.54. LCCN:97-052319.
                                        Audience: **g,l.**

Pak, Gary   PS3566.A39R53 1998
A Ricepaper Airplane. Trade Paper. University of Hawaii Press. Honolulu, HI. 1998. 180p. Intersections Ser. ISBN:0-8248-1301-4, ISBN13: 978-0-8248-1301-7. Dewey:813/.54. LCCN:97-050407.
Audience: **g,l.** *Choice, 1999.*

Pak, Gary   PS3566.A39W37 1992
The Watcher of Waipuna and Other Stories. Trade Paper. Bamboo Ridge Press. Honolulu, HI. 1992. 180p. Bamboo Ridge Ser., Nos. 55-56 ISBN:0-910043-28-0, ISBN13: 978-0-910043-28-1. Dewey:813/.54. LCCN:92-000426.
Audience: **g,l.**

Phan, Aimee   PS3616.H36W4 2004
We Should Never Meet: Stories. Cloth over Boards. St. Martin's Press. Gordonville, VA. 2004. 256p. ISBN:0-312-32266-6, ISBN13: 978-0-312-32266-3. Dewey:813/.6. LCCN:2004-051295.
Audience: **g,l.**

Roley, Brian Ascalon   PS3568.O5333A84 2001
The American Son: A Novel. Trade Paper. W. W. Norton & Company, Inc. New York, NY. 2001. 256p. ISBN:0-393-32154-1, ISBN13: 978-0-393-32154-8. Dewey:813/.6. LCCN:00-053307.
Audience: **g,l.**

Santos, Bienvenido N.   PR6019.O9
Scent of Apples: A Collection of Stories. Leonard Casper (Illustrator). Trade Paper. University of Washington Press. Seattle, WA. 1979. 250p. ISBN:0-295-95695-X, ISBN13: 978-0-295-95695-4. Dewey:823/.9/1. LCCN:79-004857.
Audience: **g,l,u,f.**

Sasaki, R. A.   PS3569.A745L66 1991
The Loom and Other Stories. Trade Paper. Graywolf Press. St. Paul, MN. 1991. 118p. Graywolf Short Fiction Ser. ISBN:1-55597-157-1, ISBN13: 978-1-55597-157-1. Dewey:813/.54. LCCN:91-015574.
Audience: **g,l,f.** *Choice, 1992.*

Sze, Arthur   PS3569.Z38
Dazzled. Trade Paper. Floating Island Publications. Cedarville, CA. 1982. 60p. ISBN:0-912449-07-1, ISBN13: 978-0-912449-07-4. Dewey:811.54.
Audience: **g.**

Tan, Amy   PS3570.A48J6 1989
The Joy Luck Club. Trade Cloth. Penguin Group (USA) Inc. New York, NY. 1989. 288p. ISBN:0-399-13420-4, ISBN13: 978-0-399-13420-3. Dewey:813.5/4. LCCN:88-026492.
Audience: **g,l,u,f.**

Truong, Monique   PS3620.R86B66 2003
The Book of Salt: A Novel. Dust Jacket. Houghton Mifflin Company Trade & Reference Division. Boston, MA. 2003. 272p. ISBN:0-618-30400-2, ISBN13: 978-0-618-30400-4. Dewey:813/.6. LCCN:2002-192152.
Audience: **g,l.**

Watanabe, Sylvia &   PS647.A75H58 1990
Bruchac, Carol (Editors)
Home to Stay: Asian American Fiction by Women. Trade Paper. Greenfield Review Literary Center, Inc. Greenfield Center, NY. 1990. 300p. ISBN:0-912678-76-3, ISBN13: 978-0-912678-76-4. Dewey:813/.540809287. LCCN:89-084368.
Audience: **g,l,u.**

Watanna, Onoto   PR9199.3.W3689A6
A Half Caste and Other Writings. Linda Trinh Moser & Elizabeth Rooney (Editors). Trade Cloth. University of Illinois Press. Champaign, IL. 2002. 208p. The Asian American Experience Ser. ISBN:0-252-02782-5, ISBN13: 978-0-252-02782-6. Dewey:813/.52. LCCN:2002-006416.
Audience: **l,u,f.** *Choice, 2003.*

Wong, Shawn   PS3573.O583A8 2005
American Knees. Trade Cloth. University of Washington Press. Seattle, WA. 2005. 240p. ISBN:0-295-98496-1, ISBN13: 978-0-295-98496-4. Dewey:813/.54. LCCN:2004-029424.
Audience: **g,l,u.**

Wong, Shawn   PS3573.O583H66 1979
Homebase. Trade Paper. Penguin Group (USA) Inc. New York, NY. 1991. 112p. Plume Contemporary Fiction Ser. ISBN:0-452-26529-0, ISBN13: 978-0-452-26529-5. Dewey:813/.54. LCCN:90-006526.
Audience: **g,l,u.**

Yamamoto, Hisaye   PS3568.O243
Seventeen Syllables and Other Stories. King-Kok Cheung (Introduction by). Trade Cloth. Kitchen Table: Women of Color Press. Brooklyn, NY. 1988. 170p. ISBN:0-913175-15-3, ISBN13: 978-0-913175-15-6. Dewey:813/.54.
Audience: **g,l,u,f.**

Yamanaka, Lois-Ann   PS3568.O243
Blu's Hanging. Trade Paper. HarperCollins Publishers. New York, NY. 1998. 272p. ISBN:0-380-73139-8, ISBN13: 978-0-380-73139-8. Dewey:813/.54.
Audience: **g,l,u,f.**

Yamanaka, Lois-Ann   PS3568.O243
Heads by Harry. Trade Paper. HarperCollins Publishers. New York, NY. 2000. 320p. ISBN:0-380-73316-1, ISBN13: 978-0-380-73316-3. Dewey:813/.54.
Audience: **g,l.**

Yamashita, Karen T.   PS3575.A44T4 1990
Through the Arc of the Rain Forest. Trade Paper. Coffee House Press. Minneapolis, MN. 1990. 192p. ISBN:0-918273-82-X, ISBN13: 978-0-918273-82-6. Dewey:813/.54. LCCN:90-040471.
Audience: **g,l,u,f.** *Choice, 1991.*

Arts and Humanities > Literature > Poetry

Alexander, Meena   PR9499.3.A46
Raw Silk. Trade Cloth. Northwestern University Press. Evanston, IL. 2004. 112p. ISBN:0-8101-5156-1, ISBN13: 978-0-8101-5156-7. Dewey:811/.54. LCCN:2004-052056.
Audience: **g,l,u,f.**

Cha, Theresa Hak   PS3566.L27
Kyung
Dictee. Trade Cloth. Tanam Press. New York, NY. 1982. 176p. ISBN:0-934378-10-X, ISBN13: 978-0-934378-10-9. Dewey:811/.54.
Audience: **l,u,f.**

Chang, Juliana (Editor)   PS591.A76Q54 1996
Quiet Fire: Asian American Poetry, 1892-1970. Trade Paper. Asian American Writers' Workshop. New York, NY. 1996. 164p. ISBN:1-889876-02-X, ISBN13: 978-1-889876-02-3. Dewey:811.008/0895. LCCN:96-078961.
Audience: **g,l,u,f.** *Choice, 1997.*

Chang, Victoria M.   PS591.A76A83 2004
(Editor)
Asian American Poetry: The Next Generation. Marilyn Chin
(Foreword by). Trade Paper. University of Illinois Press.
Champaign, IL. 2004. 232p. ISBN:0-252-07174-3, ISBN13:
978-0-252-07174-4. Dewey:811/.6080895. LCCN:2003-019685.

Audience: **g,l,u,f.** *Choice, 2005.*

Chin, Marilyn   PS3553.H48975R48
Rhapsody in Plain Yellow. Trade Cloth. W. W. Norton &
Company, Inc. New York, NY. 2002. 128p.
ISBN:0-393-04167-0, ISBN13: 978-0-393-04167-5.
Dewey:811/.54. LCCN:2001-044211.

Audience: **g,l,u,f.**

Chin, Marilyn   PS3553.H48975P48
The Phoenix Gone, the Terrace Empty: Poems. R. W. Scholes
(Illustrator). Trade Paper. Milkweed Editions. Minneapolis, MN.
1994. 104p. ISBN:0-915943-87-5, ISBN13: 978-0-915943-87-6.
Dewey:811/.54. LCCN:93-033206.

Audience: **g,l,u,f.**

Chin, Marilyn   MLCS 87/7903 (P)
Dwarf Bamboo. Philip Toy (Photographer). Trade Paper.
Greenfield Review Literary Center, Inc. Greenfield Center, NY.
1987. 84p. ISBN:0-912678-71-2, ISBN13: 978-0-912678-71-9.
Dewey:811.54. LCCN:87-080181.

Audience: **g,l,u,f.**

Dinh, Linh   PS3554.I494A79 2003
All Around What Empties Out. Trade Paper. 'A 'A Arts.
Brooklyn, NY. 2003. 92p. ISBN:1-930068-19-0, ISBN13:
978-1-930068-19-3. Dewey:811/.6. LCCN:2004-274444.

Audience: **g,l.**

Divakaruni, Chitra   PS3554.I86L43 1997
Banerjee
Leaving Yuba City: Poems. Trade Paper. Random House
Children's Books. New York, NY. 1997. 128p.
ISBN:0-385-48854-8, ISBN13: 978-0-385-48854-9.
Dewey:813.54. LCCN:97-006308.

Audience: **g,l,u,f.**

Hagedorn, Jessica   PS3558
Danger and Beauty: Dangerous Music, Pet Food and Tropical
Apparitions and New Writings. Trade Paper. City Lights Books.
San Francisco, CA. 2002. 240p. ISBN:0-87286-387-5, ISBN13:
978-0-87286-387-3. Dewey:813/.54. LCCN:2001-042125.

Audience: **g,l,u,f.**

Hahn, Kimiko   PS3566.L27
Mosquito and Ant Poems. Trade Paper. W. W. Norton &
Company, Inc. New York, NY. 2000. 104p.
ISBN:0-393-32062-6, ISBN13: 978-0-393-32062-6.
Dewey:811/.54. LCCN:98-041003.

Audience: **g,l,u,f.**

Hongo, Garrett   TD426.G721
The River of Heaven. Trade Cloth. Carnegie Mellon University
Press. Pittsburgh, PA. 2001. 67p. Classic Contemporaries Ser.
ISBN:0-88748-358-5, ISBN13: 978-0-88748-358-5.
Dewey:363.7394. LCCN:00-111579.

Audience: **g,l,u,f.**

Hongo, Garrett K.   PS591.A76
The Open Boat: Poems from Asian America. Trade Paper.
Doubleday Publishing. New York, NY. 1993. 352p.

ISBN:0-385-42338-1, ISBN13: 978-0-385-42338-0.
Dewey:811/.54080895. LCCN:92-011089.

Audience: **g,l,u,f.**

Hongo, Garrett K.   PS3558.O48 Y4
Yellow Light: Poems. Trade Paper. Wesleyan University Press.
Middletown, CT. 1982. 78p. Wesleyan Poetry Ser.
ISBN:0-8195-1104-8, ISBN13: 978-0-8195-1104-1.
Dewey:811/.54. LCCN:81-016050.

Audience: **g,l,u,f.**

Inada, Lawson Fusao   PS3559.N3D73 1997
Drawing the Line. Trade Paper. Coffee House Press.
Minneapolis, MN. 1997. 128p. ISBN:1-56689-060-8, ISBN13:
978-1-56689-060-1. Dewey:811/.54. LCCN:96-053370.

Audience: **g,l,u,f.**

Inada, Lawson Fusao   PS3559.N3.L43 1993
Legends from Camp. Trade Paper. Coffee House Press.
Minneapolis, MN. 1993. 112p. ISBN:1-56689-004-7, ISBN13:
978-1-56689-004-5. Dewey:811/.54. LCCN:92-038871.

Audience: **g,l,u,f.** *Choice, 1993.*

Jin, Ha   PS3560.I6F3 1996
Facing Shadows. Trade Cloth. Hanging Loose Press. Brooklyn,
NY. 1996. ISBN:1-882413-25-3, ISBN13: 978-1-882413-25-6.
Dewey:811/.54. LCCN:95-049710.

Audience: **g,l,u,f.** *Choice, 1996.*

Kim, Myung Mi   PS3561.I414U53 1991
Under Flag. Patricia Dienstfrey & Rena Rosenwasser (Editors),
Norine Nishimura (Illustrator). Trade Paper. Kelsey Street Press.
Berkeley, CA. 1991. 56p. ISBN:0-932716-27-X, ISBN13:
978-0-932716-27-9. Dewey:811/.54. LCCN:91-023726.

Audience: **g,l,u,f.**

Lai, Him M., et al.   PL3164.5.E5L35 1991
Island: Poetry and History of Chinese Immigrants on Angel
Island, 1910 to 1949. Genny Lim & Judy Yung (Authors). Trade
Cloth. University of Washington Press. Seattle, WA. 2003. 174p.
ISBN:0-295-97109-6, ISBN13: 978-0-295-97109-4.
Dewey:895.1/15108. LCCN:91-008372.

Audience: **g,l,u,f.**

Lee, Li-Young   PS3562.E35438B66
Book of My Nights. Trade Cloth. BOA Editions, Ltd. Rochester,
NY. 2001. 64p. American Poets Continuum Ser.
ISBN:1-929918-07-0, ISBN13: 978-1-929918-07-2.
Dewey:811/.54. LCCN:2001-037760.

Audience: **g,l,u,f.**

Lee, Li-Young   PS3562.E35438C58
The City in Which I Love You. Trade Cloth. BOA Editions, Ltd.
Rochester, NY. 1990. 89p. American Poets Continuum Ser., No.
20 ISBN:0-918526-82-5, ISBN13: 978-0-918526-82-3.
Dewey:811/.54. LCCN:90-061416.

Audience: **g,l,u,f.** *Choice, 1991.*

Lee, Li-Young   PS3562.E35438
Rose. Gerald Stern (Foreword by). Trade Paper. BOA Editions,
Ltd. Rochester, NY. 1986. 71p. New Poets of America Ser., No.
9 ISBN:0-918526-53-1, ISBN13: 978-0-918526-53-3.
Dewey:811/.54.

Audience: **g,l,u,f.** *Choice, 1987.*

Lee, Priscilla **PS3562.E359W57 2000**
Wishbone. Trade Paper. Heyday Books. Berkeley, CA. 2000.
88p. California Poetry Ser., Vol. 5 ISBN:0-9666691-4-2,
ISBN13: 978-0-9666691-4-5. Dewey:811/.6. LCCN:00-008264.
Audience: g,l.

Lew, Walter K. (Editor) **PS591.A76P74 1995**
Premonitions: The Kaya Anthology of New Asian American
Poetry. Trade Cloth. Kaya Production. New York, NY. 1995.
616p. ISBN:1-885030-13-4, ISBN13: 978-1-885030-13-9.
Dewey:811/.54080895. LCCN:94-075916.
Audience: g,l,u,f.

Lew, Walter K. **PS3612**
Treadwinds: Poems and Intermedia Works. Library Binding.
University Press of New England. Lebanon, NH. 2002. 136p.
Wesleyan Poetry Ser. ISBN:0-8195-6509-1, ISBN13:
978-0-8195-6509-9. Dewey:811/.6. LCCN:2002-016760.
Audience: g,l,u,f.

Lim-Wilson, Fatima **PS3562.I4595C76 1995**
Crossing the Snow Bridge. Trade Paper. Ohio State University
Press. Columbus, OH. 1995. 105p. ISBN:0-8142-0681-6,
ISBN13: 978-0-8142-0681-2. Dewey:811/.54. LCCN:95-017599.
Audience: g,l,u,f. Choice, 1996.

Lum, Wing T. **PS3562.U4685E9 1987**
Expounding the Doubtful Points. Trade Paper. Bamboo Ridge
Press. Honolulu, HI. 1987. 108p. Bamboo Ridge Ser., Nos.
34-35 ISBN:0-910043-14-0, ISBN13: 978-0-910043-14-4.
Dewey:811/.54. LCCN:87-072145.
Audience: g,l.

Mirikitani, Janice **PS3563.I696L68 2002**
Love Works, Vol. 2. Trade Paper. City Lights Foundation. San
Francisco, CA. 2004. 112p. Poet Laureate Ser.
ISBN:1-931404-02-X, ISBN13: 978-1-931404-02-0.
Dewey:811/.54. LCCN:2001-058165.
Audience: g,l,u,f.

Mirikitani, Janice **PS3566.L27**
Shedding Silence. Trade Cloth. Celestial Arts Publishing
Company. Berkeley, CA. 1987. 176p. ISBN:0-89087-496-4,
ISBN13: 978-0-89087-496-7. Dewey:811/.54.
Audience: g,l,u,f.

Mirikitani, Janice **PS3563.I696W43 1995**
We the Dangerous: New and Selected Poems. Trade Cloth.
Little, Brown Book Group Ltd. London, 1995. 164p.
ISBN:1-85381-771-6, ISBN13: 978-1-85381-771-7.
Dewey:811.54. LCCN:95-194957.
Audience: g,l,u,f.

Song, Cathy **PS3569.O6539L36 2001**
The Land of Bliss. Trade Paper. University of Pittsburgh Press.
Pittsburgh, PA. 2001. 136p. Pitt Poetry Ser.
ISBN:0-8229-5770-1, ISBN13: 978-0-8229-5770-6.
Dewey:811/.54. LCCN:2002-277117.
Audience: g,l,u,f.

Song, Cathy **PS3566.L27**
Picture Bride. Richard Hugo (Foreword by). Trade Paper. Yale
University Press. Cumberland, RI. 1983. 89p. Younger Poets
Ser., No. 78 ISBN:0-300-02969-1, ISBN13: 978-0-300-02969-7.
Dewey:811/.54. LCCN:82-048910.
Audience: g,l,u,f.

Tagami, Jeff **PS3570.A28O28 1990**
October Light. Trade Paper. Kearny Street Workshop. San
Francisco, CA. 1990. ISBN:0-9609630-3-0, ISBN13:
978-0-9609630-3-4. Dewey:811/.54. LCCN:87-073338.
Audience: g,l.

Villa, Jose G. **PR9550.9.V48A6 1999**
The Anchored Angel: Selected Writings by Jose Garcia Villa.
Eileen Tabios (Editor). Paper Text. Kaya Production. New York,
NY. 1999. xv, 255p. ISBN:1-885030-28-2, ISBN13:
978-1-885030-28-3. Dewey:821/.912. LCCN:99-066355.
Audience: g,l,u.

Yamada, Mitsuye **PS3575.A4**
Camp Notes and Other Poems. Trade Cloth. Kitchen Table:
Women of Color Press. Brooklyn, NY. 1992.
ISBN:0-913175-24-2, ISBN13: 978-0-913175-24-8.
Dewey:811.5.
Audience: g,l,u,f.

Yamada, Mitsuye **PS3575.A4 D5 1988**
Desert Run: Poems and Stories. Trade Cloth. Kitchen Table:
Women of Color Press. Brooklyn, NY. 1988. 112p.
ISBN:0-913175-13-7, ISBN13: 978-0-913175-13-2.
Dewey:811/.54.
Audience: g,l,u,f.

Yamanaka, Lois-Ann **PS3575.A434**
Saturday Night at the Pahala Theatre. Trade Paper. Bamboo
Ridge Press. Honolulu, HI. 1993. 140p. Bamboo Ridge Ser.,
Nos. 58-59 ISBN:0-910043-31-0, ISBN13: 978-0-910043-31-1.
Dewey:811/.54. LCCN:93-009139.
Audience: g,l.

Yau, John **PS3575.A9H39 1995**
Hawaiian Cowboys. Trade Cloth. David R. Godine Publisher.
Boston, MA. 1995. 169p. ISBN:0-87685-957-0, ISBN13:
978-0-87685-957-5. Dewey:813/.54. LCCN:94-039213.
Audience: g,l,u,f.

Arts and Humanities > Literature > Prose

Alexander, Meena **E184.E2A44 1996**
The Shock of Arrival: Reflections on Postcolonial Experience.
Trade Cloth. South End Press. Cambridge, MA. 1996. 224p.
Literature Ser. ISBN:0-89608-546-5, ISBN13:
978-0-89608-546-6. Dewey:973.04914. LCCN:96-015058.
Audience: l,u,f.

Cha, Theresa Hak Kyung **PS3566.L27**
Dictee. Trade Cloth. Tanam Press. New York, NY. 1982. 176p.
ISBN:0-934378-10-X, ISBN13: 978-0-934378-10-9.
Dewey:811/.54.
Audience: l,u,f.

Chin, Frank **E184.C5C473 1998**
Bulletproof Buddhists and Other Essays. Trade Cloth. University
of Hawaii Press. Honolulu, HI. 1998. 438p. Intersections Ser.
ISBN:0-8248-1999-3, ISBN13: 978-0-8248-1999-6.
Dewey:305.895/1. LCCN:97-039399.
Audience: g,l,u.

Juan, E. San Jr. **PR9550.9.B8A6 1995**
On Becoming Filipino: Selected Writings of Carlos Bulosan.
Cloth Text. Temple University Press. Philadelphia, PA. 1995.

240p. Asian American History and Culture Ser. ISBN:1-56639-309-4, ISBN13: 978-1-56639-309-6. Dewey:818/.5209. LCCN:94-048937.

Audience: **l,u,f.**

Song, Min　　　　　　　　　　**F869.L89A27 2005**
Strange Future: Pessimism and the 1992 Los Angeles Riots. Trade Cloth. Duke University Press. Durham, NC. 2005. 280p. ISBN:0-8223-3579-4, ISBN13: 978-0-8223-3579-5. Dewey:305.8/009794/94. LCCN:2005-006511.

Audience: **l,u.**

Wong, Nellie, et al.　　　　　　　　　　**HQ1426**
Three Asian American Writers Speak Out on Feminism. Merle Woo & Mitsuye Yamada (Authors). Stapled. Radical Women Publications. Seattle, WA. 2003. ISBN:0-9725403-5-0, ISBN13: 978-0-9725403-5-3. Dewey:305.420973.

Audience: **g,l,u,f.**

Yamauchi, Wakako　　　　　　　　　　**HD1531.M6G83**
Songs My Mother Taught Me: Stories, Plays and Memoir. Garrett Hongo (Editor, Introduction by), Valerie Miner (Editor, Afterword by). Trade Cloth. Feminist Press at The City University of New York. New York, NY. 1994. 272p. ISBN:1-55861-085-5, ISBN13: 978-1-55861-085-9. Dewey:322.4/4/097273. LCCN:93-045383.

Audience: **g,l,u,f.**

Zia, Helen　　　　　　　　　　**E184.O6**
Asian American Dreams: The Emergence of an American People. Trade Paper. Farrar, Straus & Giroux. New York, NY. 2001. 368p. ISBN:0-374-52736-9, ISBN13: 978-0-374-52736-5. Dewey:305.895073.

Audience: **g,l,u,f.**

Arts and Humanities > Philosophy

Manalansan, Martin F.　　　　　　　**E184.O6C85 2000**
IV (Editor)
Cultural Compass: Ethnographic Explorations of Asian America. Trade Cloth. Temple University Press. Philadelphia, PA. 2000. 241p. Asian American History and Culture Ser. ISBN:1-56639-772-3, ISBN13: 978-1-56639-772-8. Dewey:305.895073. LCCN:99-087506.

Audience: **u,f.**

Okihiro, Gary Y.　　　　　　　　**E175.9.O38 2001**
Common Ground: Reimagining American History. Trade Cloth. Princeton University Press. Princeton, NJ. 2001. xvi, 158p. ISBN:0-691-07006-7, ISBN13: 978-0-691-07006-3. Dewey:973. LCCN:00-049112.

Audience: **l,u,f.**　*Choice, 2002, 2001.*

Arts and Humanities > Religion

Cadge, Wendy　　　　　　　　　**BQ734.C33 2004**
Heartwood: The First Generation of Theravada Buddhism in America. Trade Cloth. University of Chicago Press. Chicago, IL. 2004. 278p. Morality and Society Ser. ISBN:0-226-08899-5, ISBN13: 978-0-226-08899-0. Dewey:294.3/91/0973. LCCN:2004-000207.

Audience: **l,u,f.**　*Choice, 2005.*

Carnes, Tony & Yang,　　　　　　**BL2525.A84 2004**
Fenggang (Editors)
Asian American Religions: The Making and Remaking of Borders and Boundaries. Trade Cloth. New York University Press. New York, NY. 2004. 432p. ISBN:0-8147-1629-6, ISBN13: 978-0-8147-1629-8. Dewey:200/.89/95073. LCCN:2003-023815.

Audience: **l.**

Coward, Harold　　　　　　　　**BL1055.S68 2000**
(Editor), et al.
The South Asian Religious Diaspora in Britain, Canada, and the United States. John R. Hinnells & Raymond Brady Williams (Editors). Cloth Text. State University of New York Press. Albany, NY. 2000. viii, 301p. SUNY Series in Religious Studies ISBN:0-7914-4509-7, ISBN13: 978-0-7914-4509-9. Dewey:200/.89/914. LCCN:99-039476.

Audience: **l,u,f.**　*Choice, 2000.*

Fenton, John Y.　　　　　　　　　**BL1055**
South Asian Religions in the Americas: An Annotated Bibliography of Immigrant Religious Traditions. Cloth Text. Greenwood Publishing Group, Inc. Portsmouth, NH. 1995. 256p. Bibliographies and Indexes in Religious Studies, Vol. 34 ISBN:0-313-27835-0, ISBN13: 978-0-313-27835-8. Dewey:016.294/097. LCCN:94-039769.

Audience: **l,u,f.**　*Choice, 1995.*

Guest, Kenneth J.　　　　　　　**BL2527.N7G84 2003**
God in Chinatown: Religion and Survival in New York's Evolving Immigrant Community. Trade Cloth. New York University Press. New York, NY. 2003. 237p. Religion, Race, and Ethnicity Ser. ISBN:0-8147-3153-8, ISBN13: 978-0-8147-3153-6. Dewey:200/.89/95107471. LCCN:2003-000761.

Audience: **l,u,f.**　*Choice, 2004.*

Iwamura, Jane &　　　　　　　**BL2525.R475 2003**
Spickard, Paul (Editors)
Revealing the Sacred in Asian and Pacific America. Paper over Boards. Routledge. New York, NY. 2003. 368p. ISBN:0-415-93807-4, ISBN13: 978-0-415-93807-5. Dewey:200/.89/95073. LCCN:2003-549453.

Audience: **l,u,f.**

Jeung, Russell　　　　　　　　　**BL2525.J48 2005**
Faithful Generations: Race and New Asian American Churches. Trade Cloth. Rutgers University Press. Piscataway, NJ. 2004. 240p. ISBN:0-8135-3502-6, ISBN13: 978-0-8135-3502-9. Dewey:277.3/083/08995. LCCN:2004-003827.

Audience: **l,u,f.**　*Choice, 2005.*

Jung Ha Kim　　　　　　　　　**BR563.K67K52 1997**
Bridge-Makers and Cross-Bearers: Korean-American Women and the Church. Trade Cloth. Oxford University Press, Inc. New York, NY. 1996. 168p. AAR Academy Ser., No. 92 ISBN:0-7885-0165-8, ISBN13: 978-0-7885-0165-4. Dewey:306.6/73. LCCN:95-038598.

Audience: **l,u,f.**

Kim, Kwang Chung &　　　　　　**BL2525.K67 2001**
Warner, R. Stephen
Korean Americans and Their Religions: Pilgrims and Missionaries from a Different Shore. Ho Youn Kwon (Editor). Trade Cloth. Pennsylvania State University Press. University Park, PA. 2001. 307p. ISBN:0-271-02072-5, ISBN13: 978-0-271-02072-3. Dewey:200/.89/957073. LCCN:00-037452.

Audience: **l,u,f.**　*Choice, 2001.*

Lawrence, Bruce B.   **BL2525.L39 2002**
New Faiths, Old Fears: Muslims and Other Asian Immigrants in American Religious Life. Trade Cloth. Edinburgh University Press. Edinburgh, 2002. 192p. American Lectures on the History of Religions Ser. ISBN:0-231-11520-2, ISBN13: 978-0-231-11520-9. Dewey:200/.89/95073. LCCN:2002-073450.
Audience: **l,u,f.** *Choice, 2003.*

Mann, Gurinder Singh,   **BL2525.M356 2001**
et al.
Buddhists, Hindus, and Sikhs in America. Raymond B. Williams & Paul David Numrich (Authors). Book, Other. Oxford University Press, Inc. New York, NY. 2002. 160p. Religion in American Life Ser. ISBN:0-19-512442-1, ISBN13: 978-0-19-512442-2. Dewey:294/.0973. LCCN:2001-045151.
Audience: **l,u,f.** *Choice, 2002.*

Min, Pyong G. & Kim,   **BL2525.M56 2001**
Jung H. (Editors)
Religions in Asian America: Building Faith Communities. Trade Cloth. AltaMira Press. Walnut Creek, CA. 2001. 224p. Critical Perspectives on Asian Pacific Americans Ser. ISBN:0-7591-0082-9, ISBN13: 978-0-7591-0082-4. Dewey:200/.89/95073. LCCN:2001-022788.
Audience: **l,u,f.**

Muse, Erika A.   **BR563.C45M87 2005**
The Evangelical Church in Boston's Chinatown: A Discourse of Language, Gender, and Identity. Paper over Boards. Routledge. New York, NY. 2005. 226p. Asian Americans Ser., :Reconceptualizing Culture, History, Politics ISBN:0-415-97406-2, ISBN13: 978-0-415-97406-6. Dewey:289.9/5/089951074461. LCCN:2004-030687.
Audience: **l,u,f.**

Suh, Sharon A.   **BQ6377.L672S84 2004**
Being Buddhist in a Christian World: Gender and Community in a Korean American Temple. Trade Cloth. University of Washington Press. Seattle, WA. 2004. 256p. American Ethnic and Cultural Studies ISBN:0-295-98378-7, ISBN13: 978-0-295-98378-3. Dewey:294.3/089/95709494. LCCN:2003-065751.
Audience: **l,u,f.** *Choice, 2005.*

Tweed, Thomas A. &   **BL2525.T83 1998**
Prothero, Stephen (Editors)
Asian Religions in America: A Documentary History. Paper Text. Oxford University Press, Inc. New York, NY. 1998. 432p. ISBN:0-19-511339-X, ISBN13: 978-0-19-511339-6. Dewey:200/.973. LCCN:98-017674.
Audience: **l,u,f.**

Williams, Raymond B.   **BR563.E27W55 1996**
Christian Pluralism in the United States: The Indian Immigrant Experience. Trade Cloth. Cambridge University Press. New York, NY. 1996. 315p. Cambridge Studies in Religious Traditions, No. 9 ISBN:0-521-57016-6, ISBN13: 978-0-521-57016-9. Dewey:277.3/082. LCCN:95-051450.
Audience: **l,u,f.** *Choice, 1997.*

Yang, Fenggang   **BR563.C45Y36 1999**
Chinese Christians in America: Conversion, Assimilation and Adhesive Identities. Trade Cloth. Pennsylvania State University Press. University Park, PA. 1999. 272p. ISBN:0-271-01916-6, ISBN13: 978-0-271-01916-1. Dewey:280/.4/0899510753. LCCN:98-037365.
Audience: **l,u,f.** *Choice, 2000.*

Social Sciences > Business

Chin, Margaret   **HD6073.C62U5365 2005**
ⓔ Sewing Women: Immigrants and the New York City Garment Industry. Gary Okihiro (Editor). E-Book. Columbia University Press. New York, NY. 2005. 208p. Columbia Comparative Studies on Ethnicity and Race Ser. ISBN:0-231-50803-4, ISBN13: 978-0-231-50803-2. Dewey:331.4/887/097.471.
Audience: **l,u,f.**

Kwong, Peter   **HD8081.C5K85 1998**
Forbidden Workers: Illegal Chinese Immigrants and American Labor. Trade Cloth. New Press, The. New York, NY. 1998. 288p. ISBN:1-56584-355-X, ISBN13: 978-1-56584-355-4. Dewey:331.6/251073. LCCN:97-026301.
Audience: **l,u,f.** *Choice, 1998.*

Lee, Jennifer   **F128.9.A1L44 2002**
Civility in the City: Blacks, Jews, and Koreans in Urban America. Trade Cloth. Harvard University Press. Cambridge, MA. 2002. 288p. ISBN:0-674-00897-9, ISBN13: 978-0-674-00897-7. Dewey:305.8/0097471. LCCN:2002-024259.
Audience: **l,u,f.** *Choice, 2003.*

Light, Ivan H. &   **HD2346.U52L64**
Bonacich, Edna
Immigrant Entrepreneurs: Koreans in Los Angeles, 1965-1982. Trade Cloth. University of California Press. Berkeley, CA. 1991. 506p. ISBN:0-520-07656-7, ISBN13: 978-0-520-07656-3. Dewey:338/.04/089957079493. LCCN:87-025541.
Audience: **l,u.** *Choice, 1989.*

Min, Pyong Gap   **F128.9.K6M56 1996**
Caught in the Middle: Korean Merchants in America's Multiethnic Cities. Trade Paper. University of California Press. Berkeley, CA. 1996. 274p. ISBN:0-520-20489-1, ISBN13: 978-0-520-20489-8. LCCN:95-047020.
Audience: **l,u,f.** *Choice, 1997.*

Min, Pyong G. & Kim,   **E184.O6S76 1999**
Rose
Struggle for Ethnic Identity: Narratives by Asian American Professionals. Trade Cloth. AltaMira Press. Walnut Creek, CA. 1999. 240p. Critical Perspectives on Asian Pacific Americans Ser., Vol. 4 ISBN:0-7619-9066-6, ISBN13: 978-0-7619-9066-6. Dewey:305.8/95/073. LCCN:98-040171.
Audience: **l,u,f.**

Ong, Paul & Hee,   **F869.L89K68 1993**
Suzanne
Losses in the Los Angeles Civil Unrest, April 29-May 1, 1992: Lists of the Damaged Properties and Korean Merchants and the L. A. Riot - Rebellion. Trade Paper. University of California, Los Angeles, Asia Institute. Los Angeles, CA. 1993. 138p. ISBN:1-883191-00-9, ISBN13: 978-1-883191-00-9. Dewey:929/.3/089957079494. LCCN:93-070183.
Audience: **l,u,f.**

Park, Kyeyoung   **HD2346.U52N547 1997**
The Korean American Dream: Immigrants and Small Business in New York City. Book, Other. Cornell University Press. Ithaca, NY. 1997. 224p. Anthropology of Contemporary Issues Ser. ISBN:0-8014-3343-6, ISBN13: 978-0-8014-3343-6. Dewey:338.6/422/0899570747. LCCN:97-003083.
Audience: **l,u,f.** *Choice, 1998.*

Park, Lisa Sun-Hee   **E184.K6P365 2005**
Consuming Citizenship: Children of Asian Immigrant
Entrepreneurs. Trade Cloth. Stanford University Press. Palo
Alto, CA. 2005. 184p. Asian America Ser. ISBN:0-8047-5247-8,
ISBN13: 978-0-8047-5247-3. Dewey:305.895/7073.
LCCN:2005-013560.
                                        Audience: **l,u.**

Smith, Henrietta M. &   **HC102**
Hirahara, Naomi
Distinguished Asian American Business Leaders. Cloth Text.
Greenwood Publishing Group, Inc. Portsmouth, NH. 2003. 256p.
Distinguished Asian Americans Ser. ISBN:1-57356-344-7,
ISBN13: 978-1-57356-344-4. Dewey:338.0973/092/395.
LCCN:2002-067835.
                              Audience: **g,l.** *Choice, 2003.*

Talwar, Jennifer Parker   **HD6300**
Fast Food, Fast Track: Immigrants, Big Business, and the
American Dream. Trade Paper. Westview Press. Boulder, CO.
2003. 240p. ISBN:0-8133-4155-8, ISBN13: 978-0-8133-4155-2.
Dewey:331.6/2/0973.
                              Audience: **g,l.** *Choice, 2002.*

Woo, Deborah   **HD8081.A8W66 2000**
Glass Ceilings and Asian Americans: The New Face of
Workplace Barriers. Trade Paper. AltaMira Press. Walnut Creek,
CA. 2000. 256p. ISBN:0-7425-0335-6, ISBN13:
978-0-7425-0335-9. Dewey:331.6/395/073.
                              Audience: **u,f.** *Choice, 2001.*

Yoon, In-Jin   **HD2346.U5Y66 1997**
On My Own: Korean Businesses and Race Relations in
America. Trade Cloth. University of Chicago Press. Chicago, IL.
1997. 276p. ISBN:0-226-95927-9, ISBN13: 978-0-226-95927-6.
Dewey:338.6/422/089957073. LCCN:96-039395.
                              Audience: **l,u,f.** *Choice, 1998.*

Yu, Renqiu   **HD9999.L383U639 1992**
To Save China, to Save Ourselves: The Chinese Hand Laundry
Alliance of New York. Trade Cloth. Temple University Press.
Philadelphia, PA. 1992. 253p. Asian American History and
Culture Ser. ISBN:0-87722-996-1, ISBN13: 978-0-87722-996-4.
Dewey:338.4/76481/097471. LCCN:92-009205.
                              Audience: **l,u,f.** *Choice, 1993.*

Social Sciences > Civil Rights, Activism

                                        LC2633.6
Department of Education: Efforts by the Office for Civil Rights
to Resolve Asian-American Complaints. Paper Text. DIANE
Publishing Company. Collingdale, PA. 1996. 56p.
ISBN:0-7881-3215-6, ISBN13: 978-0-7881-3215-5.
Dewey:378.1208995.
                                        Audience: **g,l,f.**

Aguilar-San Juan,   **E184.O6S7 1994**
Karin (Editor)
The State of Asian America: Activism and Resistance in the
1990s. David Henry Hwang (Foreword by), M. Annette Jaimes
(Afterword by). Trade Cloth. South End Press. Cambridge, MA.
1994. 504p. Race and Resistance Ser. ISBN:0-89608-477-9,
ISBN13: 978-0-89608-477-3. Dewey:305.8/95.
                              Audience: **g,l.** *Choice, 1994.*

Ancheta, Angelo N.   **KF4757.A75A53 1998**
Race, Rights and the Asian American Experience. Trade Cloth.
Rutgers University Press. Piscataway, NJ. 1998. xv, 209p.

ISBN:0-8135-2463-6, ISBN13: 978-0-8135-2463-4.
Dewey:342.73/0873. LCCN:97-024855.
                              Audience: **l,u,f.** *Choice, 1998.*

Boggs, Grace L.   **F574.D49C53 1998**
Living for Change: An Autobiography. Book, Other. University
of Minnesota Press. Minneapolis, MN. 1998. 344p.
ISBN:0-8166-2954-4, ISBN13: 978-0-8166-2954-1. Dewey:[B].
LCCN:97-027296.
                                        Audience: **l,u.**

Chang, Robert S.   **KF4757.5.A75C48 1999**
Disoriented: Asian Americans, Law and the Nation State. Trade
Cloth. New York University Press. New York, NY. 1999. 248p.
Critical America Ser. ISBN:0-8147-1521-4, ISBN13:
978-0-8147-1521-5. Dewey:342.73/0873. LCCN:98-058131.
                              Audience: **l,u,f.** *Choice, 2000.*

Fujino, Diane Carol   **E184.J3F8335 2005**
Heartbeat of Struggle: The Revolutionary Life of Yuri
Kochiyama. Trade Cloth. University of Minnesota Press.
Minneapolis, MN. 2005. 432p. Critical American Studies
ISBN:0-8166-4592-2, ISBN13: 978-0-8166-4592-3.
Dewey:979.4/004956/0092 B. LCCN:2004-026943.
                                        Audience: **g,l,u,f.**

Ho, Fred W. (Editor)   **HN90.R3**
Legacy to Liberation: Politics and Culture of Revolutionary
Asian/Pacific. Trade Paper. AK Press. Edinburgh, 2000. 415p.
ISBN:1-902593-24-3, ISBN13: 978-1-902593-24-1.
Dewey:320.5/3/0973.
                                        Audience: **g,l,u,f.**

Kumashiro, Kevin K.   **HQ75.7R47 2003**
(Editor)
Restoried Selves: Autobiographies of Queer
Asian-Pacific-American Activists. Trade Paper. Haworth Press,
Incorporated, The. Binghamton, NY. 2005. 138p. Haworth Gay
& Lesbian Studies ISBN:1-56023-463-6, ISBN13:
978-1-56023-463-0. Dewey:305.895073. LCCN:2002-151325.
                                        Audience: **g,l,u,f.**

Louie, Steven G. &   **E184.A75**
Omatsu, Glenn K. (Editors)
Asian Americans: The Movement and the Moment. Trade Paper.
University of California, Los Angeles, Asian American Studics
Center. Los Angeles, CA. 2001. 322p. ISBN:0-934052-34-4,
ISBN13: 978-0-934052-34-4. Dewey:973.0495.
                                        Audience: **g,l,u.**

Muller, Eric L.   **D810.C82M85 2001**
Free to Die for Their Country: The Story of the Japanese
American Draft Resisters in World War II. Trade Cloth.
University of Chicago Press. Chicago, IL. 2001. 250p. The
Chicago Series in Law and Society ISBN:0-226-54822-8,
ISBN13: 978-0-226-54822-7. Dewey:940.53/162.
LCCN:2001-027405.
                              Audience: **l,u,f.** *Choice, 2002.*

Ong, Aihwa   **DS732.O54 1999**
Flexible Citizenship: The Cultural Logics of Transnationality.
Library Binding. Duke University Press. Durham, NC. 1998.
272p. ISBN:0-8223-2250-1, ISBN13: 978-0-8223-2250-4.
Dewey:303.48/2. LCCN:98-033678.
                                        Audience: **u,f.**

Park, John   **JV6450.P35 2004**
Elusive Citizenship: Immigration, Asian Americans, and the
Paradox of Civil Rights. Trade Cloth. New York University

Press. New York, NY. 2004. 240p. Critical America Ser.
ISBN:0-8147-6714-1, ISBN13: 978-0-8147-6714-6.
Dewey:325.73/095. LCCN:2003-026400.

Audience: **l,u,f.**

Pulido, Laura   **HN79.C23R336 2006**
Black, Brown, Yellow, and Left: Radical Activism in Los
Angeles. Trade Cloth. University of California Press. Berkeley,
CA. 2006. 352p. American Crossroads Ser., Vol. 19
ISBN:0-520-24519-9, ISBN13: 978-0-520-24519-8.
Dewey:305.8/009794/909047. LCCN:2005-002624.

Audience: **l,u,f.** *Choice, 2006.*

Shah, Sonia (Editor)   **HQ1426.D845 1997**
Dragon Ladies: Asian American Feminists Breathe Fire. Yuri
Kochiyama (Preface by), Karin Aguilar-San Juan (Foreword by).
Trade Cloth. South End Press. Cambridge, MA. 1997. 241p.
Asian-American Studies ISBN:0-89608-576-7, ISBN13:
978-0-89608-576-3. Dewey:305.48/895073. LCCN:97-022918.

Audience: **l,u,f.**

Võ, Linda Trinh   **F869.S22V6 2004**
Mobilizing an Asian American Community. Trade Cloth. Temple
University Press. Philadelphia, PA. 2004. 288p. Asian American
History and Culture Ser. ISBN:1-59213-261-8, ISBN13:
978-1-59213-261-4. Dewey:305.895/0794985.
LCCN:2003-068669.

Audience: **g,l.** *Choice, 2005.*

Wei, William   **E184.O6**
The Asian American Movement: A Social History. Paper Text.
Temple University Press. Philadelphia, PA. 1993. 376p. Asian
American History and Literature Ser. ISBN:1-56639-183-0,
ISBN13: 978-1-56639-183-2. Dewey:305.895/073.
LCCN:92-029438.

Audience: **g,l,u.** *Choice, 1994.*

Wu, Frank   **E184.O6W84 2003**
Yellow: Race in America Beyond Black and White. Trade Paper.
Basic Books. New York, NY. 2003. 416p. ISBN:0-465-00640-X,
ISBN13: 978-0-465-00640-3. Dewey:305.8/95073.

Audience: **l,u,f.**

Yun, Grace   **E184.O6 L66 1989**
(Introduction by)
A Look Beyond the Model Minority Image: Critical Issues in
Asian America. Paper Text. Minority Rights Group (New York),
Incorporated, Asian & Pacific American Project. New York, NY.
1989. 155p. ISBN:0-318-65927-1, ISBN13: 978-0-318-65927-5.
Dewey:305.8/95073.

Audience: **g,l,u.**

Social Sciences > Education

LC2633.6
Department of Education: Efforts by the Office for Civil Rights
to Resolve Asian-American Complaints. Paper Text. DIANE
Publishing Company. Collingdale, PA. 1996. 56p.
ISBN:0-7881-3215-6, ISBN13: 978-0-7881-3215-5.
Dewey:378.1208995.

Audience: **g,l,f.**

Adler, Susan M.   **E184.J3A35 1998**
Mothering, Education, and Ethnicity: The Transformation of
Japanese American Culture. Cloth Text. Garland Publishing, Inc.
New York, NY. 1998. 203p. Asian Americans Ser.,
:Reconceptualizing Culture, History and Politics

ISBN:0-8153-3159-2, ISBN13: 978-0-8153-3159-9.
Dewey:305.48/8956073. LCCN:98-008583.

Audience: **l,u,f.**

Aguilar-San Juan,   **E184.O6S7 1994**
Karin (Editor)
The State of Asian America: Activism and Resistance in the
1990s. David Henry Hwang (Foreword by), M. Annette Jaimes
(Afterword by). Trade Cloth. South End Press. Cambridge, MA.
1994. 504p. Race and Resistance Ser. ISBN:0-89608-477-9,
ISBN13: 978-0-89608-477-3. Dewey:305.8/95.

Audience: **g,l.** *Choice, 1994.*

Butler, Johnnella E.   **E184.A1C54 2001**
Color-Line to Borderlands: The Matrix of American Ethnic
Studies. Trade Cloth. University of Washington Press. Seattle,
WA. 2001. 288p. American Ethnic and Cultural Studies
ISBN:0-295-98090-7, ISBN13: 978-0-295-98090-4.
Dewey:305.8/0071/173. LCCN:00-068320.

Audience: **l,u,f.** *Choice, 2003, 2002.*

Cheng, Lilly, et al.   **LC2637.C2 1993**
Myth or Reality: Adaptive Strategies of Asian Americans in
California. Henry T. Trueba & Kenji Ima (Authors). Paper Text.
Taylor & Francis Group. Philadelphia, PA. 1992. 212p.
ISBN:0-7507-0073-4, ISBN13: 978-0-7507-0073-3.
Dewey:371.97/95/073. LCCN:92-038080.

Audience: **l,u,f.** *Choice, 1993.*

Chin, Soo-Young   **E184.O6R48 1995**
(Editor), et al.
Reviewing Asian America: Locating Diversity. Wendy L. Ng,
James S. Moy & Gary Y. Okihiro (Editors). Trade Paper.
Washington State University Press. Pullman, WA. 1995. 214p.
Association for Asian American Studies Ser., No. 6
ISBN:0-87422-118-8, ISBN13: 978-0-87422-118-3.
Dewey:305.895/073. LCCN:95-015751.

Audience: **l,u.**

Hirabayashi, Lane R.   **E184.O6T43 1998**
(Editor)
Teaching Asian America: Diversity and the Problem of
Community. Gary Y. Okihiro, Ben Kobashigawa, David L. Eng,
Patricia A. Sakurai, Keith Osajima, Diane C. Fujino, Jachinson
W. Chan & Madhulika S. Khandelwal (Contribution by). Book,
Other. Rowman & Littlefield Publishers, Inc. Lanham, MD.
1998. 256p. Pacific Formations Ser. ISBN:0-8476-8734-1,
ISBN13: 978-0-8476-8734-3. Dewey:305.895/073.
LCCN:97-035604.

Audience: **l,u,f.**

James, Thomas   **D769.8.A6J345 1987**
Exile Within: The Schooling of Japanese Americans. Trade
Cloth. Harvard University Press. Cambridge, MA. 1987. 224p.
ISBN:0-674-27526-8, ISBN13: 978-0-674-27526-3.
Dewey:370/.89956/073. LCCN:86-025792.

Audience: **l,u,f.** *Choice, 1988.*

Kim, Elaine H. & Lowe,   **DS501;E184.A75**
Lisa (Editors)
New Formations, New Questions - Asian American Studies:
Positions Special Issue, Vol. 5. Paper Text. Duke University
Press. Durham, NC. 1997. 200p. ISBN:0-8223-6450-6, ISBN13:
978-0-8223-6450-4. Dewey:973.0495.

Audience: **l,u,f.**

Lee, Stacey J.   **LC2633.4.L44 1996**
Unraveling the "Model Minority" Stereotype: Listening to Asian
American Youth. Cloth Text. Teachers College Press, Teachers

College, Columbia University. New York, NY. 1996. 160p. ISBN:0-8077-3510-8, ISBN13: 978-0-8077-3510-7. Dewey:371.97/95/073. LCCN:96-002129.

Audience: **g,l.**

Lew, Jamie   **LC3501.K6L49 2006**
Asian Americans in Class: Charting the Achievement Gap among Korean American Youth. Trade Cloth. Teachers College Press, Teachers College, Columbia University. New York, NY. 2003. 144p. ISBN:0-8077-4694-0, ISBN13: 978-0-8077-4694-3. Dewey:371.82995/7073. LCCN:2005-046747.

Audience: **l,f.**

Louie, Vivian S.   **E184.C5L685 2004**
Compelled to Excel: Immigration, Education, and Opportunity among Chinese Americans. Trade Cloth. Stanford University Press. Palo Alto, CA. 2004. 272p. ISBN:0-8047-4984-1, ISBN13: 978-0-8047-4984-8. Dewey:305.895/1073. LCCN:2004-011167.

Audience: **l,u,f.**

Nakanishi, Donald T. &   **LC2632.A85 1995**
 Nishida, Tina Y. (Editors)
The Asian American Educational Experience: A Sourcebook for Teachers and Students. Trade Paper. Routledge. New York, NY. 1994. 424p. ISBN:0-415-90872-8, ISBN13: 978-0-415-90872-6. Dewey:371.97/073. LCCN:94-016361.

Audience: **g.**

Ng, Franklin (Editor),   **E184.O6N39 1994**
 et al.
New Visions in Asian American Studies: Diversity, Community, Power. Judy Yung, Elaine H. Kim & Stephen S. Fugita (Editors). Trade Paper. Washington State University Press. Pullman, WA. 1994. 296p. Association for Asian American Studies ISBN:0-87422-102-1, ISBN13: 978-0-87422-102-2. Dewey:973/.0495. LCCN:93-036427.

Audience: **l.**

Nomura, Gail M.   **E184.O6F76 1989**
 (Editor)
Frontiers of Asian American Studies: Writing, Research, and Commentary. Trade Cloth. Washington State University Press. Pullman, WA. 1989. 341p. Association for Asian American Studies ISBN:0-87422-064-5, ISBN13: 978-0-87422-064-3. Dewey:973/.0495. LCCN:93-219858.

Audience: **l,u,f.**

Okihiro, Gary Y.   **E184.O6P75 1995**
 (Editor)
Privileging Positions: The Sites of Asian American Studies. Trade Paper. Washington State University Press. Pullman, WA. 1995. 416p. ISBN:0-87422-124-2, ISBN13: 978-0-87422-124-4. Dewey:973/.0495. LCCN:95-031475.

Audience: **g,l,u.**

Okihiro, Gary Y.   **E184.O6**
Teaching Asian American History. Nell I. Painter & Antonio Rios-Bustamante (Editors). Trade Paper. American Historical Association. Washington, DC. 1997. 57p. Teaching Diversity Ser., :People of Color ISBN:0-87229-077-8, ISBN13: 978-0-87229-077-8. Dewey:907/.095073. LCCN:97-073462.

Audience: **l,u,f.**

Ong, Paul M. (Editor)   **E184.O6**
The State of Asian Pacific America: Transforming Race Relations. Trade Paper. University of California, Los Angeles,

Asian American Studies Center. Los Angeles, CA. 2000. 507p. ISBN:0-934052-33-6, ISBN13: 978-0-934052-33-7. Dewey:973.0495.

Audience: **g,l.**

Pang, Valerie Ooka &   **LC2632.S87 1998**
 Cheng, Li-Rong Lilly (Editors)
Struggling to Be Heard: The Unmet Needs of Asian Pacific American Children. Cloth Text. State University of New York Press. Albany, NY. 1998. 334p. SUNY Series in the Social Context of Education ISBN:0-7914-3839-2, ISBN13: 978-0-7914-3839-8. Dewey:371.829/95. LCCN:97-047482.

Audience: **u,f.**

Rong, Xue Lan &   **LC3731.X84 1998**
 Preissle, Judith
Educating Immigrant Children: What We Need to Know to Meet the Challenges. Trade Paper. Corwin Press. Thousand Oaks, CA. 1997. 200p. Immigrants Students Ser. ISBN:0-8039-6306-8, ISBN13: 978-0-8039-6306-1. Dewey:371.826/91. LCCN:97-021202.

Audience: **l,u,f.** *Choice, 1999.*

Shin, Sarah J.   **P115.2.S5 2004**
Developing in Two Languages: Korean Children in America. Trade Cloth. Multilingual Matters Ltd. Clevedon, 2004. 180p. Child Language and Child Development Ser., Vol. 5 ISBN:1-85359-747-3, ISBN13: 978-1-85359-747-3. Dewey:404/.2/08309073. LCCN:2004-002920.

Audience: **l,u,f.** *Choice, 2005.*

Takagi, Dana Y.   **LB2351.52.U6**
The Retreat from Race: Asian Admissions and Racial Politics. Cloth Text. Rutgers University Press. Piscataway, NJ. 1993. 260p. ISBN:0-8135-1913-6, ISBN13: 978-0-8135-1913-5. Dewey:378.1/616. LCCN:92-013377.

Audience: **l,f.**

Walker-Moffat, Wendy   **LC3501.H56W35 1995**
The Other Side of the Asian American Success Story. Trade Cloth. John Wiley & Sons, Inc. Hoboken, NJ. 1995. 240p. Education Ser. ISBN:0-7879-0122-9, ISBN13: 978-0-7879-0122-6. Dewey:371.9795. LCCN:95-021568.

Audience: **u.** *Choice, 1996.*

Wallace, Kendra R.   **LC3731**
Relative/Outsider: The Art and Politics of Identity among Mixed Heritage Students. Trade Cloth. Greenwood Publishing Group, Inc. Portsmouth, NH. 2001. 200p. Contemporary Studies in Social and Policy Issues in Education ISBN:1-56750-550-3, ISBN13: 978-1-56750-550-4. Dewey:371.829/00973. LCCN:00-049343.

Audience: **l,f.** *Choice, 2002.*

Weinberg, Meyer   **LC2632.W45 1997**
Asian-American Education: Historical Background and Current Realities. Cloth over Boards. Lawrence Erlbaum Associates, Inc. Mahwah, NJ. 1997. 352p. ISBN:0-8058-2775-7, ISBN13: 978-0-8058-2775-0. Dewey:371.82995/073. LCCN:97-008974.

Audience: **l,u.**

Zhou, Min & Bankston,   **E184.V53Z48 1998**
 Carl L. III
Growing up American: How Vietnamese Children Must Adapt to Life in the United States. Trade Cloth. Russell Sage Foundation. New York, NY. 1998. 296p. ISBN:0-87154-994-8, ISBN13: 978-0-87154-994-5. Dewey:305.23/0973. LCCN:97-036932.

Audience: **u,f.** *Choice, 1998.*

Social Sciences > Family

Adler, Susan M.   **E184.J3A35 1998**
Mothering, Education, and Ethnicity: The Transformation of
Japanese American Culture. Cloth Text. Garland Publishing, Inc.
New York, NY. 1998. 203p. Asian Americans Ser.,
:Reconceptualizing Culture, History and Politics
ISBN:0-8153-3159-2, ISBN13: 978-0-8153-3159-9.
Dewey:305.48/8956073. LCCN:98-008583.

                        Audience: **l,u,f.**

Bacon, Jean   **F548.9.E2B33 1996**
Life Lines: Community, Family, and Assimilation among Asian
Indian Immigrants. Cloth Text. Oxford University Press, Inc.
New York, NY. 1997. 320p. ISBN:0-19-509972-9, ISBN13:
978-0-19-509972-0. Dewey:305.8/94/073. LCCN:95-049367.

         Audience: **l,u,f.** *Choice, 1997.*

Dorow, Sara K.   **HV875.58.C6D67 2006**
Transnational Adoption: A Cultural Economy of Race, Gender,
and Kinship. Trade Cloth. New York University Press. New
York, NY. 2006. 344p. Nation of Newcomers Ser.
ISBN:0-8147-1971-6, ISBN13: 978-0-8147-1971-8.
Dewey:362.7340951. LCCN:2005-034182.

                     Audience: **l,u.**

Han, Hyun Sook &   **CT275.H35854A3 2004**
  Ruth, Kari
Many Lives Intertwined: A Memoir. Trade Cloth. Yeong &
Yeong Book Company. Saint Paul, MN. 2004.
ISBN:0-9638472-9-5, ISBN13: 978-0-9638472-9-4.
Dewey:973/.04957/0092 B. LCCN:2004-022094.

                     Audience: **g,l.**

Kibria, Nazli   **E184.C5K45 2003**
Becoming Asian American: Second-Generation Chinese and
Korean American Identities. Trade Paper. Johns Hopkins
University Press. Baltimore, MD. 2003. 232p.
ISBN:0-8018-7744-X, ISBN13: 978-0-8018-7744-5.
Dewey:305.8951073. LCCN:2001-002795.

        Audience: **l,u,f.** *Choice, 2003.*

Koh, Frances M.   **HV881**
Oriental Children in American Homes: How Do They Adjust?
Trade Paper. EastWest Press. Minneapolis, MN. 1984. 132p.
ISBN:0-9606090-0-8, ISBN13: 978-0-9606090-0-0.
Dewey:362.7/34/08995073. LCCN:81-066194.

                     Audience: **g,l.**

Lee, Jennifer & Zhou,   **E184.A75A84264 2004**
  Min (Editors)
Asian American Youth: Culture, Identity and Ethnicity. Paper
over Boards. Routledge. New York, NY. 2004. 376p.
ISBN:0-415-94668-9, ISBN13: 978-0-415-94668-1.
Dewey:305.235/089/95073. LCCN:2004-007207.

                     Audience: **g,l.**

Leonard, Karen I.   **F870.P36L46 1992**
Making Ethnic Choices: California's Punjabi Mexican
Americans. Trade Cloth. Temple University Press. Philadelphia,
PA. 1992. 368p. Asian American History and Culture Ser.
ISBN:0-87722-890-6, ISBN13: 978-0-87722-890-5.
Dewey:305.891/420794. LCCN:91-024482.

        Audience: **g,l,u.** *Choice, 1993.*

Maira, Sunaina   **F128.9.E2M35 2002**
Desis in the House: Indian American Youth Culture in New
York City. Trade Cloth. Temple University Press. Philadelphia,
PA. 2002. 256p. Asian American History and Culture Ser.

ISBN:1-56639-927-0, ISBN13: 978-1-56639-927-2.
Dewey:305.89140747. LCCN:2001-034071.

        Audience: **l,u.** *Choice, 2003, 2002.*

Min, Pyong Gap &   **F128.9.K6**
  Foner, Nancy
Changes and Conflicts: Korean Immigrant Families in New
York. Trade Paper. Allyn & Bacon, Inc. Boston, MA. 1997.
133p. ISBN:0-205-27455-2, ISBN13: 978-0-205-27455-0.
Dewey:305.895/707471.

                   Audience: **g,l,u,f.**

Park, Lisa Sun-Hee   **E184.K6P365 2005**
Consuming Citizenship: Children of Asian Immigrant
Entrepreneurs. Trade Cloth. Stanford University Press. Palo
Alto, CA. 2005. 184p. Asian America Ser. ISBN:0-8047-5247-8,
ISBN13: 978-0-8047-5247-3. Dewey:305.895/7073.
LCCN:2005-013560.

                     Audience: **l,u.**

Parrenas, Rhacel   **HQ792.P5P37 2005**
  Salazar
Children of Global Migration: Transnational Families and
Gendered Woes. Trade Cloth. Stanford University Press. Palo
Alto, CA. 2005. 232p. ISBN:0-8047-4944-2, ISBN13:
978-0-8047-4944-2. Dewey:306.85/09599. LCCN:2004-016220.

        Audience: **l,u.** *Choice, 2006.*

Robinson, Katy   **E184.K6R63 2002**
A Single Square Picture: A Korean Adoptee's Search for Her
Roots. Trade Paper. Penguin Group (USA) Inc. New York, NY.
2002. 304p. ISBN:0-425-18496-X, ISBN13: 978-0-425-18496-7.
Dewey:973/.04957/0092. LCCN:2001-052922.

                     Audience: **g,l.**

Rojewski, Jay W. &   **HV875**
  Rojewski, Jacy L.
Intercountry Adoption from China: Examining Cultural-Heritage
and Other Postadoption Issues. Paper Text. Greenwood
Publishing Group, Inc. Portsmouth, NH. 2001. 232p.
ISBN:0-89789-812-5, ISBN13: 978-0-89789-812-6.
Dewey:362.73/4/0951. LCCN:2001-025176.

        Audience: **g,l.** *Choice, 2002.*

Tong, Benson (Editor)   **E184**
Asian American Children: A Historical Handbook and Guide.
Cloth Text. Greenwood Publishing Group, Inc. Portsmouth, NH.
2004. 288p. Children and Youth Ser., :History and Culture
ISBN:0-313-33042-5, ISBN13: 978-0-313-33042-1.
Dewey:305.23/089/950730904. LCCN:2004-043643.

                     Audience: **g,l.**

Tung, May Paomay   **E184.C5T85 2000**
Chinese Americans and Their Immigrant Parents: Conflict,
Identity and Values. Trade Cloth. Haworth Press, Incorporated,
The. Binghamton, NY. 2000. 112p. ISBN:0-7890-1055-0,
ISBN13: 978-0-7890-1055-1. Dewey:305.8951073.
LCCN:99-056008.

        Audience: **l,u,f.** *Choice, 2001.*

Volkman, Toby Alice   **HV875.5.C86 2005**
  (Editor)
Cultures of Transnational Adoption. Trade Cloth. Duke
University Press. Durham, NC. 2005. 232p.
ISBN:0-8223-3576-X, ISBN13: 978-0-8223-3576-4.
Dewey:362.734. LCCN:2004-026187.

                     Audience: **l,u.**

Social Sciences > Gender and Sexuality

Abraham, Margaret   **HV6626.2.A27 2000**
Speaking the Unspeakable: Marital Violence among South Asian
Immigrants in the United States. Trade Cloth. Rutgers
University Press. Piscataway, NJ. 2004. 256p.
ISBN:0-8135-2793-7, ISBN13: 978-0-8135-2793-2.
Dewey:362.84/914073. LCCN:99-045632.
                              Audience: **u,f.** *Choice, 2000.*

Adler, Susan M.   **E184.J3A35 1998**
Mothering, Education, and Ethnicity: The Transformation of
Japanese American Culture. Cloth Text. Garland Publishing, Inc.
New York, NY. 1998. 203p. Asian Americans Ser.,
:Reconceptualizing Culture, History and Politics
ISBN:0-8153-3159-2, ISBN13: 978-0-8153-3159-9.
Dewey:305.48/8956073. LCCN:98-008583.
                                          Audience: **l,u,f.**

Alexander, Meena   **E184.E2A44 1996**
The Shock of Arrival: Reflections on Postcolonial Experience.
Trade Cloth. South End Press. Cambridge, MA. 1996. 224p.
Literature Ser. ISBN:0-89608-546-5, ISBN13:
978-0-89608-546-6. Dewey:973.04914. LCCN:96-015058.
                                          Audience: **l,u,f.**

Bao, Quang &   **PS508.A8.T35**
  Yanagihara, Hanya (Editors)
Take Out: Queer Writing from Asian Pacific America. With
Timothy Liu. Asian American Writers' Workshop; Temple
University Press. 2001. ISBN:1-889876-12-7, ISBN13:
978-1-889876-12-2.
                                          Audience: **g,l,u,f.**

Bao, Xiaolan   **HD6073.C6U533 2001**
Holding up More Than Half the Sky: Chinese Women Garment
Workers in New York City, 1948-92. Trade Cloth. University of
Illinois Press. Champaign, IL. 2001. 360p. The Asian American
Experience Ser. ISBN:0-252-02631-4, ISBN13:
978-0-252-02631-7. Dewey:331.48870899510747.
LCCN:00-010607.
                              Audience: **l,u,f.** *Choice, 2002.*

Bow, Leslie   **PS153.A84B69 2001**
Betrayal and Other Acts of Subversion: Feminism, Sexual
Politics, Asian American Women's Literature. Trade Paper.
Princeton University Press. Princeton, NJ. 2001. 224p.
ISBN:0-691-07093-8, ISBN13: 978-0-691-07093-3.
Dewey:810.9/9287/08995. LCCN:00-058488.
                                          Audience: **l,u,f.**

Bui, Hoan N.   **HV6626**
In the Adopted Land: Abused Immigrant Women and the
Criminal Justice System. Trade Cloth. Greenwood Publishing
Group, Inc. Portsmouth, NH. 2004. 176p. Criminal Justice,
Delinquency, and Corrections Ser. ISBN:0-275-97708-0,
ISBN13: 978-0-275-97708-5. Dewey:362.82/92/0899592073.
LCCN:2003-062430.
                              Audience: **g,l,u.** *Choice, 2005.*

Chin, Margaret   **HD6073.C62U5365 2005**
Ⓔ Sewing Women: Immigrants and the New York City Garment
Industry. Gary Okihiro (Editor). E-Book. Columbia University
Press. New York, NY. 2005. 208p. Columbia Comparative
Studies on Ethnicity and Race Ser. ISBN:0-231-50803-4,
ISBN13: 978-0-231-50803-2. Dewey:331.4/887/097.471.
                                          Audience: **l,u,f.**

Choy, Catherine Ceniza   **RT17.P6C48 2003**
Empire of Care: Nursing and Migration in Filipino American
History. Trade Cloth. Duke University Press. Durham, NC.
2003. 280p. American Encounters/Global Interactions Ser.
ISBN:0-8223-3052-0, ISBN13: 978-0-8223-3052-3.
Dewey:610.73/09599. LCCN:2002-012388.
                              Audience: **l,u,f.** *Choice, 2003.*

Comas-Diaz, Lillian &   **RC451.4.M58W66 1994**
  Greene, Beverly (Editors)
Women of Color: Integrating Ethnic and Gender Identities in
Psychotherapy. Cloth over Boards. Guilford Publications, Inc.
New York, NY. 1994. 518p. ISBN:0-89862-371-5, ISBN13:
978-0-89862-371-0. Dewey:616.89/14/08693. LCCN:94-010840.
                              Audience: **l,u,f.** *Choice, 1995.*

De Jesus, Melinda L.   **E184.F4P547 2004**
Pinay Power: Peminist Critical Theory. Paper over Boards.
Routledge. New York, NY. 2005. 416p. ISBN:0-415-94982-3,
ISBN13: 978-0-415-94982-8. Dewey:305.48/89921073.
LCCN:2004-021270.
                                          Audience: **l,u,f.**

Donnelly, Nancy D   **E184.H55**
Changing Lives of Refugee Hmong Women. University of
Washington Press. 1997. ISBN:0-295-97621-7, ISBN13:
978-0-295-97621-1.
                                          Audience: **l,u,f.**

Duncan, Patti   **PS153.A84D86 2004**
Tell This Silence: Asian American Women Writers and the
Politics of Speech. Trade Cloth. University of Iowa Press. Iowa
City, IA. 2004. 276p. ISBN:0-87745-856-1, ISBN13:
978-0-87745-856-2. Dewey:810.9/895. LCCN:2003-050739.
                              Audience: **l,u,f.** *Choice, 2004.*

Eng, David L.   **E184.O6E53 2001**
Racial Castration: Managing Masculinity in Asian America.
Trade Cloth. Duke University Press. Durham, NC. 2001. 368p.
Perverse Modernities Ser. ISBN:0-8223-2631-0, ISBN13:
978-0-8223-2631-1. Dewey:305.38/895073. LCCN:00-057807.
                              Audience: **u,f.** *Choice, 2001.*

Eng, David L. & Hom,   **HQ76.3.U5Q4 1998**
  Alice Y. (Editors)
Q and A: Queer in Asian America. Cloth Text. Temple
University Press. Philadelphia, PA. 1998. 432p. Asian American
History and Culture Ser. ISBN:1-56639-639-5, ISBN13:
978-1-56639-639-4. Dewey:306.76/6/08995073.
LCCN:98-014990.
                                          Audience: **l,u,f.**

Espiritu, Yen Le   **E184.O6 E875**
Asian American Women and Men. Trade Paper. SAGE
Publications, Inc. Thousand Oaks, CA. 1996.
ISBN:0-8080-3972-5, ISBN13: 978-0-8080-3972-3.
Dewey:305.895073.
                                          Audience: **l,u,f.**

Espiritu, Yen Le   **E184.O6E875 1996**
Asian American Women and Men: Labor, Laws and Love. Sage
Publications, Ltd. 1996. Gender Lens Ser. ISBN:0-8039-7254-7,
ISBN13: 978-0-8039-7254-4.
                                          Audience: **l,u,f.**

Geok-lin Lim, Shirley &   **PS153.A84F66 1988**
  Tsutakawa, Mayumi (Editors)
The Forbidden Stitch: An Asian-American Women's Anthology.
Trade Cloth. Calyx Books. Corvallis, OR. 1989. 290p.

ISBN:0-934971-10-2, ISBN13: 978-0-934971-10-2.
Dewey:810/.8/09287. LCCN:88-008117.

Audience: **g,l,u,f.**

Glenn, Evelyn N.   **HD6072.2.U52 C24**
Issei, Nisei, War Bride: Three Generations of Japanese American
Women in Domestic Service. Trade Paper. Temple University
Press. Philadelphia, PA. 1988. 312p. ISBN:0-87722-564-8,
ISBN13: 978-0-87722-564-5. Dewey:331.4/8164046/089956.
LCCN:85-025107.

Audience: **l,u,f.**

Hune, Shirley &   **E184.O6A855 2003**
Nomura, Gail M. (Editors)
Asian/Pacific Islander American Women: A Historical
Anthology. Trade Cloth. New York University Press. New York,
NY. 2003. 448p. ISBN:0-8147-3632-7, ISBN13:
978-0-8147-3632-6. Dewey:973/.0495/082. LCCN:2003-002436.

Audience: **l,u,f.**

Jung Ha Kim   **BR563.K67K52 1997**
Bridge-Makers and Cross-Bearers: Korean-American Women
and the Church. Trade Cloth. Oxford University Press, Inc. New
York, NY. 1996. 168p. AAR Academy Ser., No. 92
ISBN:0-7885-0165-8, ISBN13: 978-0-7885-0165-4.
Dewey:306.6/73. LCCN:95-038598.

Audience: **l,u,f.**

Kang, L. H. & Kim,   **PS3553.H13D538 1994**
Elaine H.
Writing Self, Writing Nation. Norma Alarcón (Editor), Yong S.
Min (Illustrator). Trade Paper. Third Woman Press. Oakland,
CA. 1994. 176p. ISBN:0-943219-11-6, ISBN13:
978-0-943219-11-0. Dewey:811/.54. LCCN:94-004916.

Audience: **u,f.**

Kang, Laura Hyun Yi   **E184.O6K36 2002**
Compositional Subjects: Enfiguring Asian/American Women.
Trade Cloth. Duke University Press. Durham, NC. 2002. 344p.
ISBN:0-8223-2883-6, ISBN13: 978-0-8223-2883-4.
Dewey:305.895073. LCCN:2001-007612.

Audience: **u,f.** *Choice, 2002.*

Kim, Elaine H. & Choi,   **HQ1765.5.D36 1998**
Chungmoo (Editors)
Dangerous Women: Gender and Korean Nationalism. Paper over
Boards. Routledge. New York, NY. 1997. 250p.
ISBN:0-415-91505-8, ISBN13: 978-0-415-91505-2.
Dewey:305.420951. LCCN:96-049259.

Audience: **l,u,f.**

Kumashiro, Kevin K.   **HQ75.7R47 2003**
(Editor)
Restoried Selves: Autobiographies of Queer
Asian-Pacific-American Activists. Trade Paper. Haworth Press,
Incorporated, The. Binghamton, NY. 2005. 138p. Haworth Gay
& Lesbian Studies ISBN:1-56023-463-6, ISBN13:
978-1-56023-463-0. Dewey:305.895073. LCCN:2002-151325.

Audience: **g,l,u,f.**

Lee, Rachel C.   **PS153.A84L44 1999**
The Americas of Asian American Literature: Gendered Fictions
of Nation and Transnation. Cloth Text. Princeton University
Press. Princeton, NJ. 1999. 208p. ISBN:0-691-05960-8, ISBN13:
978-0-691-05960-0. Dewey:810.9/895. LCCN:99-014575.

Audience: **l,u,f.** *Choice, 2000.*

Leong, Karen J.   **E183.8.C5**
The China Mystique: Pearl S. Buck, Anna May Wong, Mayling
Soong, and the Transformation of American Orientalism. Trade
Cloth. University of California Press. Berkeley, CA. 2005. 304p.
ISBN:0-520-24422-2, ISBN13: 978-0-520-24422-1.
Dewey:305.48/8951073/0922. LCCN:2004-024699.

Audience: **g,l,u,f.** *Choice, 2006, 2005.*

Leong, Russell (Editor)   **HQ76.2.U5A75 1996**
Asian American Sexualities: Dimensions of the Gay and Lesbian
Experience. Paper over Boards. Routledge. New York, NY.
1995. 256p. ISBN:0-415-91436-1, ISBN13: 978-0-415-91436-9.
Dewey:306.8/08995/073. LCCN:95-000538.

Audience: **l,u,f.**

Lim-Hing, Sharon   **PS509.L47V47 1994**
(Editor)
The Very Inside: An Anthology of Writings by Asian and Pacific
Islander Lesbians. Trade Paper. Sister Vision Press. Toronto,
ON. 1994. 760p. ISBN:0-920813-97-6, ISBN13:
978-0-920813-97-3. Dewey:810.8/09206643. LCCN:95-163883.

Audience: **g,l,u,f.**

Linmark, R. Zamora   **PS3576.A475R65 1995**
Rolling the R's. Trade Cloth. Kaya Production. New York, NY.
1996. 168p. ISBN:1-885030-02-9, ISBN13: 978-1-885030-02-3.
Dewey:813/.54. LCCN:94-075595.

Audience: **g,l.**

Manalansan, Martin F.   **HQ76.2.P6M36 2003**
Global Divas: Filipino Gay Men in the Diaspora. Trade Cloth.
Duke University Press. Durham, NC. 2003. 224p. Perverse
Modernities Ser. ISBN:0-8223-3204-3, ISBN13:
978-0-8223-3204-6. Dewey:305.38/9664/09599.
LCCN:2003-009459.

Audience: **l,u,f.**

Marchetti, Gina   **PN1995.9.A78M37 1993**
Romance and the "Yellow Peril": Race, Sex, and Discursive
Strategies in Hollywood Fiction. Trade Paper. University of
California Press. Berkeley, CA. 1994. 270p.
ISBN:0-520-08495-0, ISBN13: 978-0-520-08495-7.
Dewey:791.436520395. LCCN:92-010878.

Audience: **l,u,f.** *Choice, 1994.*

Minh-ha, Trinh T.   **PN1995.T66 1991**
When the Moon Waxes Red: Representation, Gender and
Cultural Politics. Paper over Boards. Routledge. New York, NY.
1991. 240p. ISBN:0-415-90430-7, ISBN13: 978-0-415-90430-8.
Dewey:791.43/01. LCCN:91-014059.

Audience: **u,f.**

Minh-ha, Trinh T.   **PN471.T75 1989**
Woman, Native, Other: Writing Postcoloniality and Feminism.
Trade Cloth. Indiana University Press. Bloomington, IN. 1989.
184p. ISBN:0-253-36603-8, ISBN13: 978-0-253-36603-0.
Dewey:809/.89287. LCCN:88-045455.

Audience: **l,u,f.**

Moon, Ailee & Song,   **E184**
Young I. (Editors)
Korean American Women: From Tradition to Modern Feminism.
Trade Cloth. Greenwood Publishing Group, Inc. Portsmouth,
NH. 1998. 312p. ISBN:0-275-95977-5, ISBN13:
978-0-275-95977-7. Dewey:305.42. LCCN:97-026184.

Audience: **l,u,f.**

Moraga, Cherríe &   **PS509.F44T5 2001**
Anzaldúa, Gloria (Editors)
This Bridge Called My Back: Writings by Radical Women of
Color. Ed. 3. Trade Paper. Third Woman Press. Oakland, CA.
2002. 370p. ISBN:0-943219-22-1, ISBN13: 978-0-943219-22-6.
Dewey:810.8/09287. LCCN:2001-053486.

Audience: **g,l,u,f.** *B*

Mura, David   **E184.J3**
Where the Body Meets the Memory: An Odyssey of Race,
Sexuality and Identity. Trade Paper. Doubleday Publishing. New
York, NY. 1997. 288p. ISBN:0-385-47184-X, ISBN13:
978-0-385-47184-8. Dewey:305.895/6073.

Audience: **g,l,u,f.**

Nam, Vickie   **E184.O6**
A Yell-Oh Girls! Emerging Voices Explore Culture, Identity and
Growing up Asian. Library Binding. Sagebrush Education
Resources. Caledonia, MN. 2001. ISBN:0-613-49389-3,
ISBN13: 978-0-613-49389-5. Dewey:305.235.

Audience: **g,l.**

Parrenas, Rhacel   **HQ792.P5P37 2005**
Salazar
Children of Global Migration: Transnational Families and
Gendered Woes. Trade Cloth. Stanford University Press. Palo
Alto, CA. 2005. 232p. ISBN:0-8047-4944-2, ISBN13:
978-0-8047-4944-2. Dewey:306.85/09599. LCCN:2004-016220.

Audience: **l,u.** *Choice, 2006.*

Shah, Sonia (Editor)   **HQ1426.D845 1997**
Dragon Ladies: Asian American Feminists Breathe Fire. Yuri
Kochiyama (Preface by), Karin Aguilar-San Juan (Foreword by).
Trade Cloth. South End Press. Cambridge, MA. 1997. 241p.
Asian-American Studies ISBN:0-89608-576-7, ISBN13:
978-0-89608-576-3. Dewey:305.48/895073. LCCN:97-022918.

Audience: **l,u,f.**

Tong, Benson   **HQ146.S4T66 1994**
Unsubmissive Women: Chinese Prostitutes in
Nineteenth-Century San Francisco. Trade Cloth. University of
Oklahoma Press. Norman, OK. 1994. 320p.
ISBN:0-8061-2653-1, ISBN13: 978-0-8061-2653-1.
Dewey:306.74/2/0979461. LCCN:94-016168.

Audience: **l,u,f.** *Choice, 1995.*

Wat, Eric C.   **HQ76.2.U52C38 2002**
Making of a Gay Asian Community: An Oral History of
Pre-AIDS Los Angeles. Book, Other. Rowman & Littlefield
Publishers, Inc. Lanham, MD. 2002. 224p. Pacific Formations
Ser., :Global Relations in Asian and Pacific Perspectives
ISBN:0-7425-1109-X, ISBN13: 978-0-7425-1109-5.
Dewey:305.8950794/94. LCCN:2001-041928.

Audience: **g,l,u,f.**

Wong, Nellie, et al.   **HQ1426**
Three Asian American Writers Speak Out on Feminism. Merle
Woo & Mitsuye Yamada (Authors). Stapled. Radical Women
Publications. Seattle, WA. 2003. ISBN:0-9725403-5-0, ISBN13:
978-0-9725403-5-3. Dewey:305.420973.

Audience: **g,l,u,f.**

Yamamoto, Traise   **PS153.J34Y36 1999**
Masking Selves, Making Subjects: Japanese American Women,
Identity, and the Body. Trade Paper. University of California
Press. Berkeley, CA. 1999. 320p. ISBN:0-520-21034-4, ISBN13:
978-0-520-21034-9. Dewey:810.9/9287/089956.
LCCN:98-014154.

Audience: **u,f.** *Choice, 1999.*

Yung, Judy   **F869.S39C597 1999**
Unbound Voices: A Documentary History of Chinese Women in
San Francisco. Trade Paper. University of California Press.
Berkeley, CA. 1999. 560p. ISBN:0-520-21860-4, ISBN13:
978-0-520-21860-4. Dewey:979.4/61004951/00922.
LCCN:99-031772.

Audience: **l,u,f.** *Choice, 2000.*

Social Sciences > History

Ablemann, Nancy &   **F869.L89**
Lie, John
Blue Dreams: Korean Americans and the Los Angeles Riots.
Trade Paper. Harvard University Press. Cambridge, MA. 1997.
288p. ISBN:0-674-07705-9, ISBN13: 978-0-674-07705-8.
Dewey:979.4/94004957. LCCN:94-023034.

Audience: **l,u,f.** *Choice, 1995.*

Chan, Sucheng   **E184.O6C47 1991**
The Asian Americans: An Interpretive History. Trade Cloth.
Thomson Gale. Farmington Hills, MI. 1991. 240p. Twayne's
Immigrant Heritage of America Ser. ISBN:0-8057-8426-8,
ISBN13: 978-0-8057-8426-8. Dewey:973/.0495.
LCCN:90-044174.

Audience: **l.** *Choice, 1991.*

Chan, Sucheng (Editor)   **E184.O6R46 2003**
Remapping Asian American History. Trade Cloth. AltaMira
Press. Walnut Creek, CA. 2003. 304p. Critical Perspectives on
Asian Pacific Americans Ser. ISBN:0-7591-0479-4, ISBN13:
978-0-7591-0479-2. Dewey:973/.0495/0072.
LCCN:2003-012018.

Audience: **l.** *Choice, 2004.*

Chin, Margaret   **HD6073.C62U5365 2005**
[e] Sewing Women: Immigrants and the New York City Garment
Industry. Gary Okihiro (Editor). E-Book. Columbia University
Press. New York, NY. 2005. 208p. Columbia Comparative
Studies on Ethnicity and Race Ser. ISBN:0-231-50803-4,
ISBN13: 978-0-231-50803-2. Dewey:331.4/887/097.471.

Audience: **l,u,f.**

Chun, Gloria H.   **E184.C5C56 2000**
Of Orphans and Warriors: Inventing Chinese-American Culture
and Identity. Cloth Text. Rutgers University Press. Piscataway,
NJ. 2000. ix, 198p. ISBN:0-8135-2708-2, ISBN13:
978-0-8135-2708-6. Dewey:305.895/1073/0904.
LCCN:99-033563.

Audience: **l,u,f.** *Choice, 2000.*

Dirlik, Arif & Yeung,   **E184.C5C496 2001**
Malcolm (Editors)
Chinese on the American Frontier. Book, Other. Rowman &
Littlefield Publishers, Inc. Lanham, MD. 2001. 544p. Pacific
Formation Ser., :Global Relations in Asian and Pacific
Perspective ISBN:0-8476-8532-2, ISBN13: 978-0-8476-8532-5.
Dewey:973.04/951. LCCN:00-034199.

Audience: **l,u,f.** *Choice, 2001.*

Eymann, Marcia &   **F866.2.W48 2004**
Wollenberg, Charles
What's Going On?: California and the Vietnam Era. Oakland
Museum of California Staff (Contribution by). Trade Cloth.
University of California Press. Berkeley, CA. 2004. 240p.
ISBN:0-520-24243-2, ISBN13: 978-0-520-24243-2.
Dewey:959.704. LCCN:2004-006308.

Audience: **g,l,u,f.** *Choice, 2005.*

Hune, Shirley &   E184.O6A855 2003
   Nomura, Gail M. (Editors)
Asian/Pacific Islander American Women: A Historical
Anthology. Trade Cloth. New York University Press. New York,
NY. 2003. 448p. ISBN:0-8147-3632-7, ISBN13:
978-0-8147-3632-6. Dewey:973/.0495/082. LCCN:2003-002436.
                         Audience: **l,u,f.**

Joyce, Patrick D.   E185.615.J695 2003
No Fire Next Time: Black-Korean Conflicts and the Future of
America's Cities. Book, Other. Cornell University Press. Ithaca,
NY. 2003. 240p. ISBN:0-8014-3941-8, ISBN13:
978-0-8014-3941-4. Dewey:305.895/7073/091732.
LCCN:2003-002345.
               Audience: **l,u,f.** *Choice, 2004.*

Kwong, Peter   HD8081.C5K85 1998
Forbidden Workers: Illegal Chinese Immigrants and American
Labor. Trade Cloth. New Press, The. New York, NY. 1998.
288p. ISBN:1-56584-355-X, ISBN13: 978-1-56584-355-4.
Dewey:331.6/251073. LCCN:97-026301.
               Audience: **l,u,f.** *Choice, 1998.*

Lee, Josephine (Editor),   E184.O6R43 2002
   et al.
Re/Collecting Early Asian America: Essays in Cultural History.
Imogene Lim & Yuko Matsukawa (Editors). Cloth Text. Temple
University Press. Philadelphia, PA. 2002. 400p. Asian Americal
History and Culture Ser. ISBN:1-56639-963-7, ISBN13:
978-1-56639-963-0. Dewey:973/.0495/001. LCCN:2001-050821.
                         Audience: **l.**

Lee, Mary P.   E184.K6L445 1990
Quiet Odyssey: A Pioneer Korean Woman in America. Sucheng
Chan (Introduction by). Trade Cloth. University of Washington
Press. Seattle, WA. 1990. 264p. Samuel and Althea Stroum Bks.
ISBN:0-295-96946-6, ISBN13: 978-0-295-96946-6.
Dewey:973.00495702 B. LCCN:89-028077.
                     Audience: **g,l,u,f.**

Min, Pyong Gap   F128.9.K6M56 1996
Caught in the Middle: Korean Merchants in America's
Multiethnic Cities. Trade Paper. University of California Press.
Berkeley, CA. 1996. 274p. ISBN:0-520-20489-1, ISBN13:
978-0-520-20489-8. LCCN:95-047020.
               Audience: **l,u,f.** *Choice, 1997.*

Okihiro, Gary Y.   E184.O6C64 2001
The Columbia Guide to Asian American History. Trade Cloth.
Columbia University Press. New York, NY. 2001. 352p. Guides
to American Indian History and Culture ISBN:0-231-11510-5,
ISBN13: 978-0-231-11510-0. Dewey:973/.0495.
LCCN:2001-028952.
             Audience: **g,l,u,f.** *Choice, 2002.*

Okihiro, Gary Y.   E175.9.O38 2001
Common Ground: Reimagining American History. Trade Cloth.
Princeton University Press. Princeton, NJ. 2001. xvi, 158p.
ISBN:0-691-07006-7, ISBN13: 978-0-691-07006-3. Dewey:973.
LCCN:00-049112.
           Audience: **l,u,f.** *Choice, 2002, 2001.*

Okihiro, Gary Y.   E184.O6O38 1994
Margins and Mainstreams: Asians in American History and
Culture. Trade Cloth. University of Washington Press. Seattle,
WA. 1994. 222p. ISBN:0-295-97338-2, ISBN13:
978-0-295-97338-8. Dewey:973/.0495. LCCN:93-044382.
            Audience: **g,l,u,f.** *Choice, 1995.*

Okihiro, Gary Y; Ito,   D753.8.O38 1999
   Leslie A
Storied Lives: Japanese American Students and World War II.
Leslie A. Ito (Contribution by). University of Washington Press.
1999. The Scott and Laurie Oki Series in Asian American
Studies ISBN:0-295-97796-5, ISBN13: 978-0-295-97796-6.
                     Audience: **g,l,u,f.**

Palumbo-Liu, David   E184.O6P26 1999
Asian/American: Historical Crossings of a Racial Frontier. Trade
Cloth. Stanford University Press. Palo Alto, CA. 1999. 534p.
ISBN:0-8047-3444-5, ISBN13: 978-0-8047-3444-8.
Dewey:973/.0495073. LCCN:98-048250.
               Audience: **u,f.** *Choice, 1999.*

Patterson, Wayne   DU624.7.K67P36 2000
The Ilse: First-Generation Korean Immigrants in Hawaii,
1903-1973. Trade Cloth. University of Hawaii Press. Honolulu,
HI. 2000. 288p. Hawai'i Studies on Korea ISBN:0-8248-2093-2,
ISBN13: 978-0-8248-2093-0. Dewey:996.9/00495.
LCCN:99-037153.
               Audience: **l,u,f.** *Choice, 2000.*

Said, Edward W.   DS5
Orientalism. Ed. 25. Trade Paper. Knopf Publishing Group. New
York, NY. 1979. 432p. ISBN:0-394-74067-X, ISBN13:
978-0-394-74067-6. Dewey:950. LCCN:79-010497.
                     Audience: **g,l,u,f.**

San Juan, Epifanio, Jr.   E184.F4S258 2000
After Postcolonialism: Remapping Philippines - U. S.
Confrontations. Rowman & Littlefield Publishers, Inc. 2000.
ISBN:0-8476-9860-2, ISBN13: 978-0-8476-9860-8.
                         Audience: **l,u,f.**

Takaki, Ronald T.   DU624.7.A85
Raising Cane: The World of Plantation Hawaii. Library Binding.
Chelsea House Publishers. Langhorne, PA. 1993. 120p. The
Asian American Experience Ser. ISBN:0-7910-2178-5, ISBN13:
978-0-7910-2178-1. Dewey:996.9/00495. LCCN:93-005307.
                   Audience: **g,l,u,f.**

Takaki, Ronald T.   E184.O6T35 1998
Strangers from a Different Shore: A History of Asian Americans.
Trade Paper. Little Brown & Company. New York, NY. 1998.
640p. ISBN:0-316-83130-1, ISBN13: 978-0-316-83130-7.
Dewey:973/.0495. LCCN:98-218270.
                         Audience: **l.**

Tamura, Linda   F882.H9
The Hood River Issei: An Oral History of Japanese Settlers in
Oregon's Hood River Valley. Roger Daniels (Foreword by).
Trade Paper. University of Illinois Press. Champaign, IL. 1993.
384p. The Asian American Experience Ser.
ISBN:0-252-06359-7, ISBN13: 978-0-252-06359-6.
Dewey:979.5/61004956. LCCN:92-034546.
               Audience: **l,u,f.** *Choice, 1994.*

Tchen, John Kuo Wei   PR4148.P6
New York Before Chinatown: Orientalism and the Shaping of
American Culture, 1776-1882. Trade Cloth. DIANE Publishing
Company. Collingdale, PA. 2004. 385p. ISBN:0-7567-7146-3,
ISBN13: 978-0-7567-7146-1. Dewey:821/.7.
                   Audience: **g,l,u,f.**

Tomita, Mary Kimoto   E184.J3T65 1995
Dear Miye: Letters Home from Japan, 1939-1946. Robert G.
Lee (Editor). Trade Cloth. Stanford University Press. Palo Alto,
CA. 1995. 464p. Asian America Ser. ISBN:0-8047-2419-9,

ISBN13: 978-0-8047-2419-7. Dewey:940.5/3151/092.
LCCN:94-024110.
Audience: **l,u,f.** *Choice, 1996.*

Tsuda, Takeyuki   **DS832.7.B73T78 2003**
Strangers in the Ethnic Homeland: Japanese Brazilian Return
Migration in Transnational Perspective. Trade Cloth. Columbia
University Press. New York, NY. 2003. 432p.
ISBN:0-231-12838-X, ISBN13: 978-0-231-12838-4.
Dewey:305.8956081. LCCN:2002-067460.
Audience: **l,u,f.** *Choice, 2003.*

Uchida, Yoshiko   **D769.8.A6**
Desert Exile: The Uprooting of a Japanese-American Family.
Trade Cloth. University of Washington Press. Seattle, WA. 2003.
160p. ISBN:0-295-96190-2, ISBN13: 978-0-295-96190-3.
Dewey:940.5472. LCCN:81-016187.
Audience: **g,l,u,f.**

Wat, Eric C.   **HQ76.2.U52C38 2002**
Making of a Gay Asian Community: An Oral History of
Pre-AIDS Los Angeles. Book, Other. Rowman & Littlefield
Publishers, Inc. Lanham, MD. 2002. 224p. Pacific Formations
Ser., :Global Relations in Asian and Pacific Perspectives
ISBN:0-7425-1109-X, ISBN13: 978-0-7425-1109-5.
Dewey:305.8950794/94. LCCN:2001-041928.
Audience: **g,l,u,f.**

Wei, William   **E184.O6**
The Asian American Movement: A Social History. Paper Text.
Temple University Press. Philadelphia, PA. 1993. 376p. Asian
American History and Literature Ser. ISBN:1-56639-183-0,
ISBN13: 978-1-56639-183-2. Dewey:305.895/073.
LCCN:92-029438.
Audience: **g,l,u.** *Choice, 1994.*

Wilson, Rob   **DU18.W55 2000**
Reimagining the American Pacific: From South Pacific to
Bamboo Ridge. Trade Cloth. Duke University Press. Durham,
NC. 2000. xix, 295p. New Americanists Ser.
ISBN:0-8223-2500-4, ISBN13: 978-0-8223-2500-0.
Dewey:909/.09823. LCCN:99-056924.
Audience: **u,f.** *Choice, 2001.*

Wong, K. Scott &   **E184.C5C57 1998**
   Chan, Sucheng (Editors)
Claiming America: Constructing Chinese American Identities
During the Exclusion Era. Cloth Text. Temple University Press.
Philadelphia, PA. 1998. 256p. Asian American History and
Culture Ser. ISBN:1-56639-575-5, ISBN13: 978-1-56639-575-5.
Dewey:973/.04951. LCCN:97-002539.
Audience: **l,u.** *Choice, 1998.*

Yoo, David K.   **F870.J3Y66 2000**
Growing up Nisei: Race, Generation and Culture among
Japanese Americans of California, 1924-49. Trade Paper.
University of Illinois Press. Champaign, IL. 1999. 264p. The
Asian American Experience Ser. ISBN:0-252-06822-X, ISBN13:
978-0-252-06822-5. Dewey:305.895/6073/0904.
LCCN:99-006263.
Audience: **l,u,f.** *Choice, 2000.*

Yoshihara, Mari   **E184.A1Y78 2002**
Embracing the East: White Women and American Orientalism.
Trade Cloth. Oxford University Press, Inc. New York, NY. 2002.
256p. ISBN:0-19-514533-X, ISBN13: 978-0-19-514533-5.
Dewey:305.4/0973. LCCN:2002-017060.
Audience: **l,u,f.** *Choice, 2003.*

Yu, Eui-Young (Editor)   **F869.L89N319 1994**
Black-Korean Encounter: Toward Understanding and Alliance.
Trade Paper. Regina Books. Claremont, CA. 1994. viii, 160p.
ISBN:0-941690-60-1, ISBN13: 978-0-941690-60-7.
Dewey:979.4/9400496073. LCCN:94-019786.
Audience: **g,l,u,f.**

Yu, Henry   **E184.O6**
Thinking Orientals: Migration, Contact, and Exoticism in
Modern America. Trade Paper. Oxford University Press, Inc.
New York, NY. 2002. 288p. ISBN:0-19-515127-5, ISBN13:
978-0-19-515127-5. Dewey:305.8/95/073.
Audience: **u,f.** *Choice, 2001.*

Yung, Judy, et al.   **E184.C5C479 2006**
Chinese American Voices: From the Gold Rush to the Present.
Gordon H. Chang & H. Mark Lai (Authors). Trade Cloth.
University of California Press. Berkeley, CA. 2006. 474p.
ISBN:0-520-24309-9, ISBN13: 978-0-520-24309-5.
Dewey:973/.04951. LCCN:2005-021227.
Audience: **l,u,f.** *Choice, 2006.*

Zhu, Liping   **E184.C5Z48 1997**
A Chinaman's Chance: The Chinese on the Rocky Mountain
Mining Frontier. Trade Cloth. University Press of Colorado.
Boulder, CO. 1997. 200p. ISBN:0-87081-467-2, ISBN13:
978-0-87081-467-9. Dewey:305.8/951078. LCCN:97-019879.
Audience: **l,u,f.** *Choice, 1998.*

Social Sciences > History > War

Chan, Sucheng (Editor)   **E184.V53V55 2006**
The Vietnamese American 1.5 Generation: Stories of War,
Revolution, Flight and New Beginnings. Trade Cloth. Temple
University Press. Philadelphia, PA. 2006. 344p. Asian American
History and Culture Ser. ISBN:1-59213-500-5, ISBN13:
978-1-59213-500-4. Dewey:973/.04959200922 B.
LCCN:2005-055985.
Audience: **l,u.**

Christopher, Renny   **PS228.V5C47 1995**
The Vietnam War - the American War: Images and
Representations in Euro-American and Vietnamese Exile
Narratives. Cloth Text. University of Massachusetts Press.
Amherst, MA. 1996. 360p. ISBN:1-55849-008-6, ISBN13:
978-1-55849-008-6. Dewey:813/.5409358. LCCN:95-019687.
Audience: **l,u,f.** *Choice, 1996.*

Irons, Peter H.   **KF7224.5**
Justice at War: The Story of the Japanese-American Internment
Cases. Trade Paper. University of California Press. Berkeley,
CA. 1993. 432p. ISBN:0-520-08312-1, ISBN13:
978-0-520-08312-7. LCCN:92-037238.
Audience: **l,u,f.**

Kashima, Tetsuden   **D769.8.A6**
Judgment without Trial: Japanese American Imprisonment
during World War II. Trade Cloth. University of Washington
Press. Seattle, WA. 2004. 328p. The Scott and Laurie Oki Series
in Asian American Studies ISBN:0-295-98451-1, ISBN13:
978-0-295-98451-3. Dewey:940.53/17/089956073.
Audience: **g,l,u,f.**

Ng, Wendy L.   **D769**
Japanese American Internment During World War II: A History
and Reference Guide. Cloth Text. Greenwood Publishing Group,
Inc. Portsmouth, NH. 2001. 232p. ISBN:0-313-31375-X,

ISBN13: 978-0-313-31375-2. Dewey:940.53/17/0973. LCCN:00-069128.
Audience: **l,u.** *Choice, 2002.*

Odo, Franklin S.   **D753.8**
No Sword to Bury: Japanese Americans in Hawaii During World War II. Trade Paper. Temple University Press. Philadelphia, PA. 2004. 344p. Asian American History and Culture Ser. ISBN:1-59213-270-7, ISBN13: 978-1-59213-270-6. Dewey:305.895/60969/09041.
Audience: **g,l,u,f.**

Okihiro, Gary Y.   **D769.8.A6O36 1996**
Whispered Silences: Japanese Americans and World War II. Trade Paper. University of Washington Press. Seattle, WA. 1996. 256p. Samuel and Althea Stroum Bks. ISBN:0-295-97498-2, ISBN13: 978-0-295-97498-9. Dewey:940.53/1503956073. LCCN:95-021895.
Audience: **g,l,u,f.** *Choice, 1996.*

Wong, K. Scott   **E184.C5W65 2005**
Americans First: Chinese Americans and the Second World War. Trade Cloth. Harvard University Press. Cambridge, MA. 2005. 272p. ISBN:0-674-01671-8, ISBN13: 978-0-674-01671-2. Dewey:940.54/089/951073. LCCN:2004-059790.
Audience: **l,u,f.** *Choice, 2006.*

Yuh, Ji-Yeon   **E184.K6Y85 2002**
Beyond the Shadow of Camptown: Korean Military Brides in America. Trade Cloth. New York University Press. New York, NY. 2002. 302p. Nation of Newcomers Ser., :Immigrant History as American History ISBN:0-8147-9698-2, ISBN13: 978-0-8147-9698-6. Dewey:305.48/8957073. LCCN:2002-002674.
Audience: **l,u,f.** *Choice, 2003.*

Social Sciences > Labor

Bao, Xiaolan   **HD6073.C6U533 2001**
Holding up More Than Half the Sky: Chinese Women Garment Workers in New York City, 1948-92. Trade Cloth. University of Illinois Press. Champaign, IL. 2001. 360p. The Asian American Experience Ser. ISBN:0-252-02631-4, ISBN13: 978-0-252-02631-7. Dewey:331.48870899510747. LCCN:00-010607.
Audience: **l,u,f.** *Choice, 2002.*

Bonacich, Edna   **JV6926.L67N49 1994**
(Editor), et al.
The New Asian Immigration in Los Angeles and Global Restructuring. Lucie Cheng & Paul P. Ong (Editors). Cloth Text. Temple University Press. Philadelphia, PA. 1994. 336p. Asian American History and Culture Ser. ISBN:1-56639-217-9, ISBN13: 978-1-56639-217-4. Dewey:305.895/079494. LCCN:93-049863.
Audience: **l,u.**

Chan, Sucheng   **HD8039.F32**
This Bittersweet Soil: The Chinese in California Agriculture, 1860-1910. Trade Cloth. University of California Press. Berkeley, CA. 1987. ISBN:0-520-05376-1, ISBN13: 978-0-520-05376-2. Dewey:338.1/089951/0764.
Audience: **g,l.**

Choy, Catherine Ceniza   **RT17.P6C48 2003**
Empire of Care: Nursing and Migration in Filipino American History. Trade Cloth. Duke University Press. Durham, NC. 2003. 280p. American Encounters/Global Interactions Ser.

ISBN:0-8223-3052-0, ISBN13: 978-0-8223-3052-3. Dewey:610.73/09599. LCCN:2002-012388.
Audience: **l,u,f.** *Choice, 2003.*

Friday, Chris   **HD6515.C27F75 1994**
Organizing Asian American Labor: The Pacific Coast Canned-Salmon Industry, 1870-1942. Trade Cloth. Temple University Press. Philadelphia, PA. 1994. 296p. Asian American History and Culture Ser. ISBN:1-56639-139-3, ISBN13: 978-1-56639-139-9. Dewey:331.6/25079. LCCN:93-029471.
Audience: **g,l.** *Choice, 1994.*

Fujita-Rony, Dorothy B.   **F899.S49F85 2003**
American Workers, Colonial Power: Philippine Seattle and the Transpacific West, 1919-1941. Trade Cloth. University of California Press. Berkeley, CA. 2003. 320p. ISBN:0-520-23094-9, ISBN13: 978-0-520-23094-1. Dewey:979.7/7720049921. LCCN:2001-052279.
Audience: **l,u.** *Choice, 2003.*

Kwong, Peter   **HD8079**
Chinatown, N. Y.: Labor and Politics, 1930-1950. Trade Paper. New Press, The. New York, NY. 2001. 208p. ISBN:1-56584-640-0, ISBN13: 978-1-56584-640-1. Dewey:331.6/251/07471. LCCN:79-002327.
Audience: **l,u,f.**

Kwong, Peter   **HD8081.C5K85 1998**
Forbidden Workers: Illegal Chinese Immigrants and American Labor. Trade Cloth. New Press, The. New York, NY. 1998. 288p. ISBN:1-56584-355-X, ISBN13: 978-1-56584-355-4. Dewey:331.6/251073. LCCN:97-026301.
Audience: **l,u,f.** *Choice, 1998.*

Min, Pyong Gap   **F128.9.K6M56 1996**
Caught in the Middle: Korean Merchants in America's Multiethnic Cities. Trade Paper. University of California Press. Berkeley, CA. 1996. 274p. ISBN:0-520-20489-1, ISBN13: 978-0-520-20489-8. LCCN:95-047020.
Audience: **l,u,f.** *Choice, 1997.*

Min, Pyong G. & Kim,   **E184.O6S76 1999**
Rose
Struggle for Ethnic Identity: Narratives by Asian American Professionals. Trade Cloth. AltaMira Press. Walnut Creek, CA. 1999. 240p. Critical Perspectives on Asian Pacific Americans Ser., Vol. 4 ISBN:0-7619-9066-6, ISBN13: 978-0-7619-9066-6. Dewey:305.8/95/073. LCCN:98-040171.
Audience: **l,u,f.**

Parrenas, Rhacel   **HQ792.P5P37 2005**
Salazar
Children of Global Migration: Transnational Families and Gender Woes. Stanford University Press. 2005. ISBN:0-8047-4944-2, ISBN13: 978-0-8047-4944-2.
Audience: **l,u,f.**

Parrenas, Rhacel   **HD6072.P27 2001**
Salazar
Servants of Globalization: Women, Migration, and Domestic Work. Stanford University Press. 2001. ISBN:0-8047-3921-8, ISBN13: 978-0-8047-3921-4.
Audience: **l,u.**

Pulido, Laura   **HN79.C23R336 2006**
Black, Brown, Yellow, and Left: Radical Activism in Los Angeles. Trade Cloth. University of California Press. Berkeley, CA. 2006. 352p. American Crossroads Ser., Vol. 19

ISBN:0-520-24519-9, ISBN13: 978-0-520-24519-8.
Dewey:305.8/009794/909047. LCCN:2005-002624.
Audience: **l,u,f.** *Choice, 2006.*

Saxton, Alexander　　　　　　**HD8081.C5S3 1995**
The Indispensable Enemy: Labor and the Anti-Chinese
Movement in California. Trade Paper. University of California
Press. Berkeley, CA. 1975. 304p. ISBN:0-520-02905-4, ISBN13:
978-0-520-02905-7. Dewey:331.6/21510794. LCCN:72-115494.
Audience: **l,u.**

Scharlin, Craig &　　　　　　**HD6515.A292U547 2000**
Villanueva, Lilia V.
Philip Vera Cruz: A Personal History of Filipino Immigrants and
the Farmworkers Movement. Ed. 3. Trade Paper. University of
Washington Press. Seattle, WA. 2000. xxviii, 167p.
ISBN:0-295-97984-4, ISBN13: 978-0-295-97984-7.
Dewey:331.88/13/092 B. LCCN:00-029902.
Audience: **g,l,u.**

Takaki, Ronald T.　　　　　　**DU624.7.A85**
Raising Cane: The World of Plantation Hawaii. Library Binding.
Chelsea House Publishers. Langhorne, PA. 1993. 120p. The
Asian American Experience Ser. ISBN:0-7910-2178-5, ISBN13:
978-0-7910-2178-1. Dewey:996.9/00495. LCCN:93-005307.
Audience: **g,l,u,f.**

Talwar, Jennifer Parker　　　　　　**HD6300**
Fast Food, Fast Track: Immigrants, Big Business, and the
American Dream. Trade Paper. Westview Press. Boulder, CO.
2003. 240p. ISBN:0-8133-4155-8, ISBN13: 978-0-8133-4155-2.
Dewey:331.6/2/0973.
Audience: **g,l.** *Choice, 2002.*

Tyner, James A.　　　　　　**HD6305.F55T94 2004**
Made in the Philippines: Gendered Discourses and the Making
of Migrants. Cloth Text. Routledge. New York, NY. 2004. 176p.
RoutledgeCurzon Pacific Rim Geographies Ser., Vol. 5
ISBN:0-415-70015-9, ISBN13: 978-0-415-70015-3.
Dewey:331.6/2599. LCCN:2003-010299.
Audience: **l,u.**

Wu, Diana T.　　　　　　**HD8081.P33W8 1997**
Asian Pacific Americans in the Workplace. Trade Cloth.
AltaMira Press. Walnut Creek, CA. 1997. 276p. Critical
Perspectives on Asian Pacific Americans Ser.
ISBN:0-7619-9121-2, ISBN13: 978-0-7619-9121-2.
Dewey:331.6/3994073. LCCN:97-033727.
Audience: **g,l.**

Social Sciences > Law

Ancheta, Angelo N.　　　　　　**KF4757.A75A53 1998**
Race, Rights and the Asian American Experience. Trade Cloth.
Rutgers University Press. Piscataway, NJ. 1998. xv, 209p.
ISBN:0-8135-2463-6, ISBN13: 978-0-8135-2463-4.
Dewey:342.73/0873. LCCN:97-024855.
Audience: **l,u,f.** *Choice, 1998.*

Bui, Hoan N.　　　　　　**HV6626**
In the Adopted Land: Abused Immigrant Women and the
Criminal Justice System. Trade Cloth. Greenwood Publishing
Group, Inc. Portsmouth, NH. 2004. 176p. Criminal Justice,
Delinquency, and Corrections Ser. ISBN:0-275-97708-0,
ISBN13: 978-0-275-97708-5. Dewey:362.82/92/0899592073.
LCCN:2003-062430.
Audience: **g,l,u.** *Choice, 2005.*

Chang, Robert S.　　　　　　**KF4757.5.A75C48 1999**
Disoriented: Asian Americans, Law and the Nation State. Trade
Cloth. New York University Press. New York, NY. 1999. 248p.
Critical America Ser. ISBN:0-8147-1521-4, ISBN13:
978-0-8147-1521-5. Dewey:342.73/0873. LCCN:98-058131.
Audience: **l,u,f.** *Choice, 2000.*

Lee, Wen Ho & Zia,　　　　　　**QC774.L44 A3**
Helen
My Country Versus Me: The First Hand Account by the Los
Alamos Scientist Who Was. Trade Paper. Hyperion Press. New
York, NY. 2003. 352p. ISBN:0-7868-8687-0, ISBN13:
978-0-7868-8687-6. Dewey:327.1251073/092.
Audience: **g,l,u,f.**

Nakanishi, Don T. &　　　　　　**E184.O6A84145 2002**
Lai, James S.
Asian American Politics: Law, Participation, and Policy. Book,
Other. Rowman & Littlefield Publishers, Inc. Lanham, MD.
2002. 496p. Spectrum Ser., Vol. 3:Race and Ethnicity in
National and Global Politics ISBN:0-7425-1849-3, ISBN13:
978-0-7425-1849-0. Dewey:323.1/195073/09.
LCCN:2002-009334.
Audience: **g,l,u,f.** *Choice, 2003.*

Park, Edward J. W. &　　　　　　**JV6483.P37 2004**
Park, John S. W.
Probationary Americans: Contemporary Immigration Policies
and the Shaping of Asian American Communities. Paper over
Boards. Routledge. New York, NY. 2004. 152p.
ISBN:0-415-94750-2, ISBN13: 978-0-415-94750-3.
Dewey:305.895/073/090511. LCCN:2004-010472.
Audience: **l,u,f.**

Park, John　　　　　　**JV6450.P35 2004**
Elusive Citizenship: Immigration, Asian Americans, and the
Paradox of Civil Rights. Trade Cloth. New York University
Press. New York, NY. 2004. 240p. Critical America Ser.
ISBN:0-8147-6714-1, ISBN13: 978-0-8147-6714-6.
Dewey:325.73/095. LCCN:2003-026400.
Audience: **l,u,f.**

Yamamoto, Eric K.　　　　　　**E184.A1Y36 1999**
Interracial Justice: Conflict and Reconciliation in Post-Civil
Rights America. Trade Cloth. New York University Press. New
York, NY. 1999. 352p. Critical America Ser.
ISBN:0-8147-9674-5, ISBN13: 978-0-8147-9674-0.
Dewey:305.8/00973. LCCN:98-039108.
Audience: **l,u,f.** *Choice, 1999.*

Social Sciences > Migration

Alba, Richard D. &　　　　　　**JV6475.A433 2003**
Nee, Victor
Remaking the American Mainstream: Assimilation and
Contemporary Immigration. Trade Cloth. Harvard University
Press. Cambridge, MA. 2003. 384p. ISBN:0-674-01040-X,
ISBN13: 978-0-674-01040-6. Dewey:303.48/273.
LCCN:2002-191300.
Audience: **l,u,f.** *Choice, 2004.*

Alexander, Meena　　　　　　**E184.E2A44 1996**
The Shock of Arrival: Reflections on Postcolonial Experience.
Trade Cloth. South End Press. Cambridge, MA. 1996. 224p.
Literature Ser. ISBN:0-89608-546-5, ISBN13:
978-0-89608-546-6. Dewey:973.04914. LCCN:96-015058.
Audience: **l,u,f.**

Bates, Crispin   **DS339.4.S66 2001**
💻 Community, Empire and Migration: South Asians in Diaspora. E-Book. Palgrave Macmillan. New York, NY. ISBN:0-333-97729-7, ISBN13: 978-0-333-97729-3. Dewey:305.8914.

Audience: **l,u.**

Bayor, Ronald H.   **E184.A1R244 2003**
Race and Ethnicity in America: A Concise History. Trade Cloth. Eastern European Monographs. Bradenton, FL. 2003. 288p. ISBN:0-231-12940-8, ISBN13: 978-0-231-12940-4. Dewey:305.8/00973. LCCN:2003-046164.

Audience: **l,u,f.**   *Choice, 2004.*

Bonacich, Edna   **JV6926.L67N49 1994**
(Editor), et al.
The New Asian Immigration in Los Angeles and Global Restructuring. Lucie Cheng & Paul P. Ong (Editors). Cloth Text. Temple University Press. Philadelphia, PA. 1994. 336p. Asian American History and Culture Ser. ISBN:1-56639-217-9, ISBN13: 978-1-56639-217-4. Dewey:305.895/079494. LCCN:93-049863.

Audience: **l,u.**

Chan, Sucheng   **E184.C5C478 2005**
Chinese American Transnationalism: The Flow of People, Resources, and Ideas Between China and America During the Exclusion Era. Trade Cloth. Temple University Press. Philadelphia, PA. 2005. 312p. Asian American History and Cultu Ser. ISBN:1-59213-434-3, ISBN13: 978-1-59213-434-2. Dewey:973/.04951. LCCN:2005-041834.

Audience: **l,u.**   *Choice, 2006.*

Chin, Ko-lin   **E184.C5C474 1999**
Smuggled Chinese: Clandestine Immigration to the United States. Douglas S. Massey (Foreword by). Trade Cloth. Temple University Press. Philadelphia, PA. 1999. 296p. Asian American History and Culture Ser. ISBN:1-56639-732-4, ISBN13: 978-1-56639-732-2. Dewey:304.873051. LCCN:99-036086.

Audience: **g,l,u,f.**

Choy, Catherine Ceniza   **RT17.P6C48 2003**
Empire of Care: Nursing and Migration in Filipino American History. Trade Cloth. Duke University Press. Durham, NC. 2003. 280p. American Encounters/Global Interactions Ser. ISBN:0-8223-3052-0, ISBN13: 978-0-8223-3052-3. Dewey:610.73/09599. LCCN:2002-012388.

Audience: **l,u,f.**   *Choice, 2003.*

Daniels, Roger   **JV6483.D36 2003**
Guarding the Golden Door: American Immigration Policy and Immigrants since 1882. Cloth over Boards. Farrar, Straus & Giroux. New York, NY. 2004. 344p. ISBN:0-8090-5343-8, ISBN13: 978-0-8090-5343-8. Dewey:325.73. LCCN:2003-007714.

Audience: **g,l,u,f.**   *Choice, 2004.*

Gyory, Andrew   **E184.C5G9 1998**
Closing the Gate: Race, Politics and the Chinese Exclusion Act. Trade Cloth. University of North Carolina Press. Chapel Hill, NC. 1998. 368p. ISBN:0-8078-2432-1, ISBN13: 978-0-8078-2432-0. Dewey:325.73089951. LCCN:97-047746.

Audience: **l,u,f.**   *Choice, 1999.*

Hein, Jeremy   **HV640.5.I5H44 1995**
From Migrants to Ethnic Minorities: The Settlement of Refugees from Vietnam, Laos, and Cambodia in the United States. Trade Cloth. Thomson Gale. Farmington Hills, MI. 1995. 193p. Twayne's Immigrant Heritage of America Ser.

ISBN:0-8057-8432-2, ISBN13: 978-0-8057-8432-9. Dewey:362.87/089/959. LCCN:94-041960.

Audience: **g,l,u,f.**   *Choice, 1995.*

Hing, Bill Ong   **JV6493.H55 1993**
Making and Remaking Asian America Through Immigration Policy, 1850-1990. Trade Cloth. Stanford University Press. Palo Alto, CA. 1993. 354p. Asian America Ser. ISBN:0-8047-2118-1, ISBN13: 978-0-8047-2118-9. Dewey:325/.25/0973. LCCN:92-025507.

Audience: **l,u,f.**   *Choice, 1993.*

Hing, Bill Ong & Lee,   **E184.O6**
Ronald (Editors)
The State of Asian America: Reframing the Immigration Debate. Cloth Text. University of California, Los Angeles, Asian American Studies Center. Los Angeles, CA. 1996. 322p. ISBN:0-934052-26-3, ISBN13: 978-0-934052-26-9. Dewey:973.0495.

Audience: **g,l,u,f.**

Hirabayashi, Lane Ryo   **E29.J3N49 2002**
(Editor), et al.
New Worlds, New Lives: Globalization and People of Japanese Descent in the Americas and from Latin America in Japan. Akemi Kikumura-Yano & James A. Hirabayashi (Editors). Trade Cloth. Stanford University Press. Palo Alto, CA. 2003. 384p. Asian America Ser. ISBN:0-8047-4461-0, ISBN13: 978-0-8047-4461-4. Dewey:305.895/607. LCCN:2001-008166.

Audience: **l,u,f.**

Hopkins, MaryCarol   **E184**
Braving a New World: Cambodian (Khmer) Refugees in an American City. Trade Cloth. Greenwood Publishing Group, Inc. Portsmouth, NH. 1996. 192p. Contemporary Urban Studies ISBN:0-89789-392-1, ISBN13: 978-0-89789-392-3. Dewey:305.895/93073. LCCN:96-015353.

Audience: **g,l,f.**   *Choice, 1997.*

Hsu, Madeline Y.   **E184.O6H78 2000**
Dreaming of Gold, Dreaming of Home: Transnationalism and Migration Between the United States and South China, 1882-1943. Trade Cloth. Stanford University Press. Palo Alto, CA. 2000. xx, 271p. Asian America Ser. ISBN:0-8047-3814-9, ISBN13: 978-0-8047-3814-9. Dewey:973/.04951. LCCN:00-056355.

Audience: **l,u.**   *Choice, 2001.*

Hu-DeHart, Evelyn   **E184.O6A28 1999**
(Editor)
Across the Pacific: Asian Americans and Globalization. Cloth Text. Temple University Press. Philadelphia, PA. 2000. 232p. Asian American History and Culture Ser. ISBN:1-56639-710-3, ISBN13: 978-1-56639-710-0. Dewey:305.895073. LCCN:98-053900.

Audience: **g,l,u.**   *Choice, 2001.*

Kumar, Amitava   **E184.E2**
Passport Photos. Trade Paper. University of California Press. Berkeley, CA. 2000. 290p. ISBN:0-520-21817-5, ISBN13: 978-0-520-21817-8. Dewey:305.8914073. LCCN:99-031257.

Audience: **l,u,f.**   *Choice, 2000.*

Lai, Him M., et al.   **PL3164.5.E5L35 1991**
Island: Poetry and History of Chinese Immigrants on Angel Island, 1910 to 1949. Genny Lim & Judy Yung (Authors). Trade Cloth. University of Washington Press. Seattle, WA. 2003. 174p.

ISBN:0-295-97109-6, ISBN13: 978-0-295-97109-4.
Dewey:895.1/15108. LCCN:91-008372.

Audience: **g,l,u,f.**

Lasker, Bruno   **JV6891.F54**
Filipino Immigration to the Continental United States and to
Hawaii. J. Ishotwell (Foreword by). Trade Cloth. Ayer Company
Publishers, Inc. Manchester, NH. 1976. American Immigration
Collection, :Series 1 ISBN:0-405-00531-8, ISBN13:
978-0-405-00531-2. Dewey:325.2914. LCCN:69-018783.

Audience: **g,l.**

Lee, Erika   **E184.C5L523 2003**
At America's Gates: Chinese Immigration During the Exclusion
Era, 1882-1943. Trade Paper. University of North Carolina
Press. Chapel Hill, NC. 2003. 352p. ISBN:0-8078-5448-4,
ISBN13: 978-0-8078-5448-8. Dewey:325/.251073.
LCCN:2002-013375.

Audience: **l,u,f.** *Choice, 2004.*

Lim, Shirley (Editor), et al.   **PS153.A84T73 2005**
Transnational Asian American Literature: Sites and Transits.
Gina Valentino, John Gamber & Stephen Sohn (Editors). Trade
Cloth. Temple University Press. Philadelphia, PA. 2006. 336p.
ISBN:1-59213-450-5, ISBN13: 978-1-59213-450-2.
Dewey:810.9/895. LCCN:2005-049680.

Audience: **l,u,f.**

Ma, Laurence J. C. &   **DS732.C5563 2002**
  Cartier, Carolyn L.
The Chinese Diaspora: Space, Place, Mobility and Identity.
Book, Other. Rowman & Littlefield Publishers, Inc. Lanham,
MD. 2003. 400p. Why of Where Ser. ISBN:0-7425-1755-1,
ISBN13: 978-0-7425-1755-4. Dewey:909/.04951.
LCCN:2002-151795.

Audience: **l,u,f.** *Choice, 2003.*

McIllwain, Jeffrey Scott   **HV6452.N7**
Organizing Crime In Chinatown: Race and Racketeering in New
York City, 1890-1910. Paper Text. McFarland & Company,
Incorporated Publishers. Jefferson, NC. 2004. 260p.
ISBN:0-7864-1626-2, ISBN13: 978-0-7864-1626-4.
Dewey:364.1/06/08995107471. LCCN:2003-021121.

Audience: **l,u,f.** *Choice, 2004.*

Min, Pyong Gap &   **F128.9.K6**
  Foner, Nancy
Changes and Conflicts: Korean Immigrant Families in New
York. Trade Paper. Allyn & Bacon, Inc. Boston, MA. 1997.
133p. ISBN:0-205-27455-2, ISBN13: 978-0-205-27455-0.
Dewey:305.895/707471.

Audience: **g,l,u,f.**

Ngai, Mae M.   **KF4800.N485 2005**
Impossible Subjects: Illegal Aliens and the Making of Modern
America. Trade Paper. Princeton University Press. Princeton, NJ.
2005. 400p. Politics and Society in Twentieth Century America
Ser. ISBN:0-691-12429-9, ISBN13: 978-0-691-12429-2.
Dewey:342.73/083.

Audience: **l,u,f.** *Choice, 2004.*

Odo, Franklin   **E184.O6C63 2002**
The Columbia Documentary History of the Asian American
Experience. Trade Cloth. Columbia University Press. New York,
NY. 2002. 688p. ISBN:0-231-11030-8, ISBN13:
978-0-231-11030-3. Dewey:973/.0495. LCCN:2002-019208.

Audience: **g,l,u,f.** *Choice, 2003.*

Okamura, Jonathan Y.   **E184.F4O36 1998**
Imagining the Filipino American Diaspora: Transnational
Relations, Identities, and Communities. Cloth Text. Garland
Publishing, Inc. New York, NY. 1998. 168p. Asian Americans
Ser., :Reconceptualizing Culture, History and Politics
ISBN:0-8153-3183-5, ISBN13: 978-0-8153-3183-4.
Dewey:305.89921073. LCCN:98-028383.

Audience: **g,l,u.**

Ong, Aihwa   **DS732.O54 1999**
Flexible Citizenship: The Cultural Logics of Transnationality.
Library Binding. Duke University Press. Durham, NC. 1998.
272p. ISBN:0-8223-2250-1, ISBN13: 978-0-8223-2250-4.
Dewey:303.48/2. LCCN:98-033678.

Audience: **u,f.**

Parrenas, Rhacel   **HQ792.P5P37 2005**
  Salazar
Children of Global Migration: Transnational Families and
Gender Woes. Stanford University Press. 2005.
ISBN:0-8047-4944-2, ISBN13: 978-0-8047-4944-2.

Audience: **l,u,f.**

Parrenas, Rhacel   **HD6072.P27 2001**
  Salazar
Servants of Globalization: Women, Migration, and Domestic
Work. Stanford University Press. 2001. ISBN:0-8047-3921-8,
ISBN13: 978-0-8047-3921-4.

Audience: **l,u.**

Roth, Joshua Hotaka   **DS832.7.B73R68 2002**
Brokered Homeland: Japanese Brazilian Migrants in Japan.
Book, Other. Cornell University Press. Ithaca, NY. 2002. 192p.
The Anthropology of Contemporary Issues Ser.
ISBN:0-8014-4010-6, ISBN13: 978-0-8014-4010-6.
Dewey:952/.004698. LCCN:2002-001539.

Audience: **l,u.**

San Juan, E.   **E184.F4S26 1998**
From Exile to Diaspora: Versions of the Filipino Experience in
the United States. Harper Collins Publishers Canada, Ltd. 1998.
ISBN:0-8133-3169-2, ISBN13: 978-0-8133-3169-0.

Audience: **l,u.**

San Juan, Epifanio, Jr.   **E184.F4S258 2000**
After Postcolonialism: Remapping Philippines - U. S.
Confrontations. Rowman & Littlefield Publishers, Inc. 2000.
ISBN:0-8476-9860-2, ISBN13: 978-0-8476-9860-8.

Audience: **l,u,f.**

Scharlin, Craig &   **HD6515.A292U547 2000**
  Villanueva, Lilia V.
Philip Vera Cruz: A Personal History of Filipino Immigrants and
the Farmworkers Movement. Ed. 3. Trade Paper. University of
Washington Press. Seattle, WA. 2000. xxviii, 167p.
ISBN:0-295-97984-4, ISBN13: 978-0-295-97984-7.
Dewey:331.88/13/092 B. LCCN:00-029902.

Audience: **g,l,u.**

Takaki, Ronald T.   **E184.K6T33 1994**
From the Land of Morning Calm: The Koreans in America.
Library Binding. Chelsea House Publishers. Langhorne, PA.
1994. 120p. The Asian American Experience Ser.
ISBN:0-7910-2181-5, ISBN13: 978-0-7910-2181-1.
Dewey:973/.04957. LCCN:93-043713.

Audience: **g,l.**

Tenhula, John   E184.I43T46 1990
Voices from Southeast Asia: The Refugee Experience in the
United States. Liv Ullmann (Foreword by). Trade Cloth. Holmes
& Meier Publishers, Inc. Teaneck, NJ. 1991. 270p. Ellis Island
Ser. ISBN:0-8419-1110-X, ISBN13: 978-0-8419-1110-9.
Dewey:305.895/9073. LCCN:90-040696.
                               Audience: **g,l,u,f.**

Tyner, James A.   HD6305.F55T94 2004
Made in the Philippines: Gendered Discourses and the Making
of Migrants. Cloth Text. Routledge. New York, NY. 2004. 176p.
RoutledgeCurzon Pacific Rim Geographies Ser., Vol. 5
ISBN:0-415-70015-9, ISBN13: 978-0-415-70015-3.
Dewey:331.6/2599. LCCN:2003-010299.
                               Audience: **l,u.**

Van Sant, John E.   E184.J3V3 2000
Pacific Pioneers: Japanese Journeys to Hawaii and America,
1850-80. Trade Cloth. University of Illinois Press. Champaign,
IL. 2000. 208p. The Asian American Experience Ser.
ISBN:0-252-02560-1, ISBN13: 978-0-252-02560-0.
Dewey:304.8/73052/09034. LCCN:99-006829.
                     Audience: **l,u,f.** *Choice, 2000.*

Vo, Linda Trinh &   E184.O6C666 2002
  Bonus, Rick (Editors)
Contemporary Asian American Communities: Intersections and
Divergences. Paper Text. Temple University Press. Philadelphia,
PA. 2002. 280p. Asian American History and Culture Ser.
ISBN:1-56639-938-6, ISBN13: 978-1-56639-938-8.
Dewey:305.895073. LCCN:2001-052506.
                     Audience: **l,u,f.** *Choice, 2003.*

Yu, Henry   E184.O6
Thinking Orientals: Migration, Contact, and Exoticism in
Modern America. Trade Paper. Oxford University Press, Inc.
New York, NY. 2002. 288p. ISBN:0-19-515127-5, ISBN13:
978-0-19-515127-5. Dewey:305.8/95/073.
                     Audience: **u,f.** *Choice, 2001.*

Zhao, Xiaojian   E184.C5Z43 2002
Remaking Chinese America: Immigration, Family and
Community, 1940-1965. Cloth Text. Rutgers University Press.
Piscataway, NJ. 2002. 256p. ISBN:0-8135-3010-5, ISBN13:
978-0-8135-3010-9. Dewey:305.895/1073/0904.
LCCN:2001-019844.
                     Audience: **l,u,f.** *Choice, 2002.*

Social Sciences > Politics

Ancheta, Angelo N.   KF4757.A75A53 1998
Race, Rights and the Asian American Experience. Trade Cloth.
Rutgers University Press. Piscataway, NJ. 1998. xv, 209p.
ISBN:0-8135-2463-6, ISBN13: 978-0-8135-2463-4.
Dewey:342.73/0873. LCCN:97-024855.
                     Audience: **l,u,f.** *Choice, 1998.*

Chang, Gordon H.   E184.O6A8427 2001
  (Editor)
Asian Americans and Politics: Perspectives, Experiences,
Prospects. Trade Cloth. Woodrow Wilson Center Press.
Washington, DC. 2000. xiv, 425p. ISBN:0-8047-4051-8,
ISBN13: 978-0-8047-4051-7. Dewey:323.1/195073.
LCCN:00-012465.
                     Audience: **l,u,f.** *Choice, 2001.*

Daniels, Roger   JV6483.D36 2003
Guarding the Golden Door: American Immigration Policy and
Immigrants since 1882. Cloth over Boards. Farrar, Straus &
Giroux. New York, NY. 2004. 344p. ISBN:0-8090-5343-8,
ISBN13: 978-0-8090-5343-8. Dewey:325.73.
LCCN:2003-007714.
                     Audience: **g,l,u,f.** *Choice, 2004.*

Espiritu, Yen Le   E184.O6
Asian American Panethnicity: Bridging Institutions and
Identities. Trade Paper. Temple University Press. Philadelphia,
PA. 1993. 222p. Asian American History and Culture Ser.
ISBN:1-56639-096-6, ISBN13: 978-1-56639-096-5.
Dewey:305.895/073.
                     Audience: **l,u,f.** *Choice, 1993.*

Ho, Fred W. (Editor)   HN90.R3
Legacy to Liberation: Politics and Culture of Revolutionary
Asian/Pacific. Trade Paper. AK Press. Edinburgh, 2000. 415p.
ISBN:1-902593-24-3, ISBN13: 978-1-902593-24-1.
Dewey:320.5/3/0973.
                               Audience: **g,l,u,f.**

Kwong, Peter   HD8079
Chinatown, N. Y.: Labor and Politics, 1930-1950. Trade Paper.
New Press, The. New York, NY. 2001. 208p.
ISBN:1-56584-640-0, ISBN13: 978-1-56584-640-1.
Dewey:331.6/251/07471. LCCN:79-002327.
                               Audience: **l,u,f.**

Lai, James &   E184.O6
  Nakanishi, Don T. (Editors)
National Asian Pacific American Political Almanac 2005-2006.
Ed. 12. Trade Paper. University of California, Los Angeles,
Asian American Studies Center. Los Angeles, CA. 2005. 228p.
ISBN:0-934052-40-9, ISBN13: 978-0-934052-40-5.
Dewey:973.0495.
                               Audience: **g,l,u.**

Lien, Pei-Te   E184.O6L53 2001
The Making of Asian America Through Political Participation.
Library Binding. Temple University Press. Philadelphia, PA.
2001. 304p. ISBN:1-56639-894-0, ISBN13: 978-1-56639-894-7.
Dewey:305.895073. LCCN:00-066679.
                     Audience: **l,u,f.** *Choice, 2002.*

Lien, Pei-Te, et al.   E184.A75L54 2004
The Politics of Asian Americans: Diversity and Community. M.
Margaret Conway & Janelle Wong (Authors). Paper over
Boards. Routledge. New York, NY. 2004. 320p.
ISBN:0-415-93464-8, ISBN13: 978-0-415-93464-0.
Dewey:324/.089/95073. LCCN:2003-013136.
                               Audience: **l,u,f.**

Loule, Steven G. &   E184.A75
  Omatsu, Glenn K. (Editors)
Asian Americans: The Movement and the Moment. Trade Paper.
University of California, Los Angeles, Asian American Studies
Center. Los Angeles, CA. 2001. 322p. ISBN:0-934052-34-4,
ISBN13: 978-0-934052-34-4. Dewey:973.0495.
                               Audience: **g,l,u.**

Nakanishi, Don T. &   E184
  Wu, Ellen D.
Distinguished Asian American Political and Governmental
Leaders. Cloth Text. Greenwood Publishing Group, Inc.
Portsmouth, NH. 2002. 240p. Distinguished Asian Americans

Ser. ISBN:1-57356-325-0, ISBN13: 978-1-57356-325-3.
Dewey:920/.009295073. LCCN:2002-016957.

Audience: **g,l,u,f.** *Choice, 2003.*

Patterson, Wayne   **DU624.7.K67P36 2000**
The Ilse: First-Generation Korean Immigrants in Hawaii,
1903-1973. Trade Cloth. University of Hawaii Press. Honolulu,
HI. 2000. 288p. Hawai'i Studies on Korea ISBN:0-8248-2093-2,
ISBN13: 978-0-8248-2093-0. Dewey:996.9/00495.
LCCN:99-037153.

Audience: **l,u,f.** *Choice, 2000.*

San Juan, Epifanio, Jr.   **E184.F4S258 2000**
After Postcolonialism: Remapping Philippines - U. S.
Confrontations. Rowman & Littlefield Publishers, Inc. 2000.
ISBN:0-8476-9860-2, ISBN13: 978-0-8476-9860-8.

Audience: **l,u,f.**

Saxton, Alexander   **HD8081.C5S3 1995**
The Indispensable Enemy: Labor and the Anti-Chinese
Movement in California. Trade Paper. University of California
Press. Berkeley, CA. 1975. 304p. ISBN:0-520-02905-4, ISBN13:
978-0-520-02905-7. Dewey:331.6/21510794. LCCN:72-115494.

Audience: **l,u.**

Schultz, Jeffrey D.   **E184.A1E574 2000**
(Editor), et al.
Encyclopedia of Minorities in American Politics: African
Americans and Asian Americans. Andrew L. Aoki & Kerry L.
Haynie (Editors). Cloth Text. Greenwood Publishing Group, Inc.
Portsmouth, NH. 2000. 376p. The American Political Landscape
Ser. ISBN:1-57356-148-7, ISBN13: 978-1-57356-148-8.
Dewey:305.8/00973/03. LCCN:99-043451.

Audience: **l,u,f.**

Takagi, Dana Y.   **LB2351.52.U6**
The Retreat from Race: Asian Admissions and Racial Politics.
Cloth Text. Rutgers University Press. Piscataway, NJ. 1993.
260p. ISBN:0-8135-1913-6, ISBN13: 978-0-8135-1913-5.
Dewey:378.1/616. LCCN:92-013377.

Audience: **l,f.**

Võ, Linda Trinh   **F869.S22V6 2004**
Mobilizing an Asian American Community. Trade Cloth. Temple
University Press. Philadelphia, PA. 2004. 288p. Asian American
History and Culture Ser. ISBN:1-59213-261-8, ISBN13:
978-1-59213-261-4. Dewey:305.895/0794985.
LCCN:2003-068669.

Audience: **g,l.** *Choice, 2005.*

Social Sciences > Politics > Public Policy

Hing, Bill Ong   **JV6493.H55 1993**
Making and Remaking Asian America Through Immigration
Policy, 1850-1990. Trade Cloth. Stanford University Press. Palo
Alto, CA. 1993. 354p. Asian America Ser. ISBN:0-8047-2118-1,
ISBN13: 978-0-8047-2118-9. Dewey:325/.25/0973.
LCCN:92-025507.

Audience: **l,u,f.** *Choice, 1993.*

Nakanishi, Don T. &   **E184.O6A84145 2002**
Lai, James S.
Asian American Politics: Law, Participation, and Policy. Book,
Other. Rowman & Littlefield Publishers, Inc. Lanham, MD.
2002. 496p. Spectrum Ser., Vol. 3:Race and Ethnicity in
National and Global Politics ISBN:0-7425-1849-3, ISBN13:

978-0-7425-1849-0. Dewey:323.1/195073/09.
LCCN:2002-009334.

Audience: **g,l,u,f.** *Choice, 2003.*

Park, Edward J. W. &   **JV6483.P37 2004**
Park, John S. W.
Probationary Americans: Contemporary Immigration Policies
and the Shaping of Asian American Communities. Paper over
Boards. Routledge. New York, NY. 2004. 152p.
ISBN:0-415-94750-2, ISBN13: 978-0-415-94750-3.
Dewey:305.895/073/090511. LCCN:2004-010472.

Audience: **l,u,f.**

Zhan, Lin   **E184.O6A8446 2002**
Asian Americans: Vulnerable Populations, Model Interventions,
Clarifying Agendas. Paper Text. Jones & Bartlett Publishers,
Inc. Sudbury, MA. 2002. 330p. Other Nursing Titles of Interest
Ser. ISBN:0-7637-2241-3, ISBN13: 978-0-7637-2241-8.
Dewey:305.895/073. LCCN:2002-028642.

Audience: **l,u.**

Zhan, Lin & National   **RA448.5.A83A86 1997**
League for Nursing Staff
Asian Voices: Asian and Asian American Health Educators
Speak Out. Trade Cloth. National League for Nursing Press (N
L N Press). New York, NY. 1998. 227p. ISBN:0-88737-741-6,
ISBN13: 978-0-88737-741-9. Dewey:362.1/089/95073.
LCCN:97-034603.

Audience: **l,u.**

Social Sciences > Psychology

Balls-Organista, Pamela   **RC451.5.A2R42 1998**
& Chun, Kevin M. (Editors)
Readings in Ethnic Psychology. Paper over Boards. Routledge.
New York, NY. 1998. 432p. ISBN:0-415-91962-2, ISBN13:
978-0-415-91962-3. Dewey:155.8/2. LCCN:97-044675.

Audience: **l,u,f.**

Bernal, Guillermo   **GN502.H3635 2003**
(Editor), et al.
Handbook of Racial and Ethnic Minority Psychology, Vol. 4.
Joseph E. Trimble, Ann Kathleen Burlew & Frederick T. L.
Leong (Editors). Trade Cloth. SAGE Publications, Inc.
Thousand Oaks, CA. 2002. 720p. Racial and Ethnic Minority
Psychology Ser., Vol. 4 ISBN:0-7619-1965-1, ISBN13:
978-0-7619-1965-0. Dewey:155.8/2. LCCN:2002-006456.

Audience: **l,u,f.** *Choice, 2003.*

Chin, Jean L., et al.   **RC451**
Transference and Empathy in Asian American Psychotherapy:
Cultural Values and Treatment Needs. George K. Hong, Joan
Huser Liem & Mary Anna Domokos-Cheng Ham (Authors).
Trade Cloth. Greenwood Publishing Group, Inc. Portsmouth,
NH. 1993. 168p. ISBN:0-275-94493-X, ISBN13:
978-0-275-94493-3. Dewey:616.891408995. LCCN:92-048757.

Audience: **u,f.**

Choi, Namkee G.   **E184.O6P79 2001**
(Editor)
Psychosocial Aspects of the Asian-American Experience:
Diversity Within Diversity. Paper Text. Haworth Press,
Incorporated, The. Binghamton, NY. 2000. 340p. Journal of
Human Behavior in the Social Environment Monograph, Vol. 3,
Nos. 3-4 ISBN:0-7890-1150-6, ISBN13: 978-0-7890-1150-3.
Dewey:305.895073. LCCN:00-047217.

Audience: **l,u,f.**

Comas-Diaz, Lillian &   **RC451.4.M58W66 1994**
  Greene, Beverly (Editors)
Women of Color: Integrating Ethnic and Gender Identities in
Psychotherapy. Cloth over Boards. Guilford Publications, Inc.
New York, NY. 1994. 518p. ISBN:0-89862-371-5, ISBN13:
978-0-89862-371-0. Dewey:616.89/14/08693. LCCN:94-010840.
Audience: l,u,f. Choice, 1995.

Hall, Gordon C.   **E184.O6A8416 2002**
  Nagayama & Okazaki, Sumie (Editors)
Asian American Psychology: The Science of Lives in Context.
Trade Cloth. American Psychological Association. Washington,
DC. 2003. 223p. ISBN:1-55798-902-8, ISBN13:
978-1-55798-902-4. Dewey:155.8/495073. LCCN:2002-001965.
Audience: u,f. Choice, 2003.

Han, Arar & Hsu, John   **E184.A75A8426 2004**
  Y. (Editors)
Asian American X: An Intersection of Twenty-First Century
Asian American Voices. Trade Cloth. University of Michigan
Press. Chicago, IL. 2004. 264p. ISBN:0-472-09874-8, ISBN13:
978-0-472-09874-3. Dewey:305.895/073. LCCN:2004-003463.
Audience: g,l.

Kurasaki, Karen S.   **RC451.5.A75A83 2002**
  (Editor), et al.
Asian-American Mental Health: Assessment Theories and
Methods. Sumie Okazaki & Stanley Sue (Editors). Trade Cloth.
Springer. New York, NY. 2002. 360p. International and Cultural
Psychology Ser., :Topics, Issues, and Directions Ser.
ISBN:0-306-47268-6, ISBN13: 978-0-306-47268-8.
Dewey:362.2/089/95073. LCCN:2002-025685.
Audience: u,f.

Lee, Stacey J.   **LC2633.4.L44 1996**
Unraveling the "Model Minority" Stereotype: Listening to Asian
American Youth. Cloth Text. Teachers College Press, Teachers
College, Columbia University. New York, NY. 1996. 160p.
ISBN:0-8077-3510-8, ISBN13: 978-0-8077-3510-7.
Dewey:371.97/95/073. LCCN:96-002129.
Audience: g,l.

Min, Pyong Gap   **E184.O6M57 2001**
The Second Generation: Ethnic Identity among Asian
Americans. Trade Cloth. AltaMira Press. Walnut Creek, CA.
2002. 280p. Critical Perspectives on Asian Pacific Americans
Ser. ISBN:0-7591-0175-2, ISBN13: 978-0-7591-0175-3.
Dewey:305.895073. LCCN:2001-022783.
Audience: l,u,f.

Nam, Vickie   **E184.O6**
A Yell-Oh Girls! Emerging Voices Explore Culture, Identity and
Growing up Asian. Library Binding. Sagebrush Education
Resources. Caledonia, MN. 2001. ISBN:0-613-49389-3,
ISBN13: 978-0-613-49389-5. Dewey:305.235.
Audience: g,l.

Sandhu, Daya Singh   **RC451.5.A75 A8351999**
  (Editor)
Asian and Pacific Islander Americans: Issues and Concerns for
Counseling and Psychotherapy. Trade Cloth. Nova Science
Publishers, Inc. Hauppauge, NY. 1999. 335p.
ISBN:1-56072-663-6, ISBN13: 978-1-56072-663-0.
Dewey:616.89/14. LCCN:2003-271509.
Audience: u,f.

Tompar-Tiu, Aurora &   **RC451.5.F54T56 1995**
  Sustento-Severicher, Juliana
Depression and Other Mental Health Issues: The Filipino
American Experience. Trade Cloth. John Wiley & Sons, Inc.
Hoboken, NJ. 1994. 180p. Social and Behavioral Science Ser.
ISBN:0-7879-0041-9, ISBN13: 978-0-7879-0041-0.
Dewey:616.89/0089/9921073. LCCN:94-027879.
Audience: l.

Uba, Laura   **RC451.5.A75U23 1994**
Asian Americans: Personality Patterns, Identity, and Mental
Health. Cloth over Boards. Guilford Publications, Inc. New
York, NY. 1993. 302p. ISBN:0-89862-372-3, ISBN13:
978-0-89862-372-7. Dewey:362.2/08995073. LCCN:93-041723.
Audience: l,u,f.

Uba, Laura   **E184.O6U23 2002**
A Postmodern Psychology of Asian Americans: Creating
Knowledge of a Racial Minority. Cloth Text. State University of
New York Press. Albany, NY. 2002. 192p. SUNY Series,
Alternatives in Psychology ISBN:0-7914-5295-6, ISBN13:
978-0-7914-5295-0. Dewey:155.8/495073. LCCN:2001-032202.
Audience: u,f. Choice, 2002.

Vargas, Luis A. &   **RJ507.M54 W67 1992**
  Koss-Chioino, Joan D. (Editors)
Working with Culture: Psychotherapeutic Interventions with
Ethnic Minority Children and Adolescents. Trade Cloth. John
Wiley & Sons, Inc. Hoboken, NJ. 1992. 416p. Social and
Behavioral Science Ser. ISBN:1-55542-469-4, ISBN13:
978-1-55542-469-5. Dewey:618.92/89/008693.
LCCN:92-015281.
Audience: l,u,f. Choice, 1993.

Zane, Nolan W.   **E184.O6H36 1998**
Handbook of Asian American Psychology. Lee C. Lee (Editor).
Trade Cloth. SAGE Publications, Inc. Thousand Oaks, CA.
1998. 600p. ISBN:0-8039-4963-4, ISBN13: 978-0-8039-4963-8.
Dewey:155.8/4951073. LCCN:98-008967.
Audience: u,f. Choice, 1998.

Social Sciences > Race

Alba, Richard D. &   **JV6475.A433 2003**
  Nee, Victor
Remaking the American Mainstream: Assimilation and
Contemporary Immigration. Trade Cloth. Harvard University
Press. Cambridge, MA. 2003. 384p. ISBN:0-674-01040-X,
ISBN13: 978-0-674-01040-6. Dewey:303.48/273.
LCCN:2002-191300.
Audience: l,u,f. Choice, 2004.

Bayor, Ronald H.   **E184.A1R244 2003**
Race and Ethnicity in America: A Concise History. Trade Cloth.
Eastern European Monographs. Bradenton, FL. 2003. 288p.
ISBN:0-231-12940-8, ISBN13: 978-0-231-12940-4.
Dewey:305.8/00973. LCCN:2003-046164.
Audience: l,u,f. Choice, 2004.

Cha, Theresa Hak   **PS3566.L27**
  Kyung
Dictee. Trade Cloth. Tanam Press. New York, NY. 1982. 176p.
ISBN:0-934378-10-X, ISBN13: 978-0-934378-10-9.
Dewey:811/.54.
Audience: l,u,f.

Chen, Tina   PS153.A84C47 2005
Double Agency: Acts of Impersonation in Asian American
Literature and Culture. Trade Cloth. Stanford University Press.
Palo Alto, CA. 2005. 280p. ISBN:0-8047-5185-4, ISBN13:
978-0-8047-5185-8. Dewey:810.9/353. LCCN:2005-000563.
                              Audience: **l,u,f.** *Choice, 2006.*

Espiritu, Yen Le   E184.O6
Asian American Panethnicity: Bridging Institutions and
Identities. Trade Paper. Temple University Press. Philadelphia,
PA. 1993. 222p. Asian American History and Culture Ser.
ISBN:1-56639-096-6, ISBN13: 978-1-56639-096-5.
Dewey:305.895/073.
                              Audience: **l,u,f.** *Choice, 1993.*

Espiritu, Yen Le   E184.O6 E875
Asian American Women and Men. Trade Paper. SAGE
Publications, Inc. Thousand Oaks, CA. 1996.
ISBN:0-8080-3972-5, ISBN13: 978-0-8080-3972-3.
Dewey:305.895073.
                                        Audience: **l,u,f.**

Espiritu, Yen Le   E184.O6E875 1996
Asian American Women and Men: Labor, Laws and Love. Sage
Publications, Ltd. 1996. Gender Lens Ser. ISBN:0-8039-7254-7,
ISBN13: 978-0-8039-7254-4.
                                        Audience: **l,u,f.**

Gooding-Williams,   F869.L89A26 1993
Robert (Editor)
Reading Rodney King - Reading Urban Uprising. Paper over
Boards. Routledge. New York, NY. 1993. 256p.
ISBN:0-415-90734-9, ISBN13: 978-0-415-90734-7.
Dewey:305.896073079494. LCCN:92-043381.
                              Audience: **l,u,f.** *Choice, 1993.*

Gyory, Andrew   E184.C5G9 1998
Closing the Gate: Race, Politics and the Chinese Exclusion Act.
Trade Cloth. University of North Carolina Press. Chapel Hill,
NC. 1998. 368p. ISBN:0-8078-2432-1, ISBN13:
978-0-8078-2432-0. Dewey:325.73089951. LCCN:97-047746.
                              Audience: **l,u,f.** *Choice, 1999.*

Hall, Patricia Wong &   HV6250.5.E75A57 2001
Hwang, Victor M. (Editors)
Anti-Asian Violence in North America: Asian American and
Asian Canadian Reflections on Hate, Healing and Resistance.
Trade Cloth. AltaMira Press. Walnut Creek, CA. 2001. 224p.
Critical Perspectives on Asian Pacific Americans Ser.
ISBN:0-7425-0458-1, ISBN13: 978-0-7425-0458-5.
Dewey:364.1. LCCN:00-056931.
                              Audience: **l,u,f.** *Choice, 2001.*

Han, Arar & Hsu, John   E184.A75A8426 2004
Y. (Editors)
Asian American X: An Intersection of Twenty-First Century
Asian American Voices. Trade Cloth. University of Michigan
Press. Chicago, IL. 2004. 264p. ISBN:0-472-09874-8, ISBN13:
978-0-472-09874-3. Dewey:305.895/073. LCCN:2004-003463.
                                        Audience: **g,l.**

Joyce, Patrick D.   E185.615.J695 2003
No Fire Next Time: Black-Korean Conflicts and the Future of
America's Cities. Book, Other. Cornell University Press. Ithaca,
NY. 2003. 240p. ISBN:0-8014-3941-8, ISBN13:
978-0-8014-3941-4. Dewey:305.895/7073/091732.
LCCN:2003-002345.
                              Audience: **l,u,f.** *Choice, 2004.*

Kim, Claire Jean   F128.9.N4K56 2000
Bitter Fruit: The Politics of Black-Korean Conflict in New York
City. Cloth over Boards. Yale University Press. Cumberland, RI.
2000. 320p. The Renaissance in Europe Ser., :A Cultural
Enquiry ISBN:0-300-07406-9, ISBN13: 978-0-300-07406-2.
Dewey:323.1/1/957/07471. LCCN:00-035174.
                              Audience: **l,u,f.** *Choice, 2001.*

Kim, Kwang Chung   E184.K6K6555 1999
(Editor)
Koreans in the Hood: Conflict with African Americans. Trade
Cloth. Johns Hopkins University Press. Baltimore, MD. 1999.
264p. ISBN:0-8018-6103-9, ISBN13: 978-0-8018-6103-1.
Dewey:305.895/7073. LCCN:98-032012.
                              Audience: **l,u,f.** *Choice, 2000.*

Kondo, Dorinne K.   E184.O6K65 1997
About Face: Performing Race in Fashion and Theater. Paper
over Boards. Routledge. New York, NY. 1997. 288p.
ISBN:0-415-91140-0, ISBN13: 978-0-415-91140-5.
Dewey:391/.00952. LCCN:96-043837.
                                        Audience: **u,f.**

Koshy, Susan   PS374.M53K67 2004
Sexual Naturalization: Asian Americans and Miscegenation.
Trade Cloth. Stanford University Press. Palo Alto, CA. 2005.
224p. Asian America Ser. ISBN:0-8047-4728-8, ISBN13:
978-0-8047-4728-8. Dewey:813.009/3552. LCCN:2004-018764.
                              Audience: **l,u,f.** *Choice, 2005.*

Lee, Jennifer   F128.9.A1L44 2002
Civility in the City: Blacks, Jews, and Koreans in Urban
America. Trade Cloth. Harvard University Press. Cambridge,
MA. 2002. 288p. ISBN:0-674-00897-9, ISBN13:
978-0-674-00897-7. Dewey:305.8/0097471. LCCN:2002-024259.
                              Audience: **l,u,f.** *Choice, 2003.*

Lee, Jennifer & Zhou,   E184.A75A84264 2004
Min (Editors)
Asian American Youth: Culture, Identity and Ethnicity. Paper
over Boards. Routledge. New York, NY. 2004. 376p.
ISBN:0-415-94668-9, ISBN13: 978-0-415-94668-1.
Dewey:305.235/089/95073. LCCN:2004-007207.
                                        Audience: **g,l.**

Lee, Rachel C. & Wong,   T173.8.A815 2003
Sau-Ling Cynthia (Editors)
Asian America.Net: Ethnicity, Nationalism and Cyberspace.
Paper over Boards. Routledge. New York, NY. 2003. 336p.
ISBN:0-415-96559-4, ISBN13: 978-0-415-96559-0.
Dewey:303.483. LCCN:2002-153218.
                                        Audience: **l,u,f.**

Leonard, Karen I.   F870.P36L46 1992
Making Ethnic Choices: California's Punjabi Mexican
Americans. Trade Cloth. Temple University Press. Philadelphia,
PA. 1992. 368p. Asian American History and Culture Ser.
ISBN:0-87722-890-6, ISBN13: 978-0-87722-890-5.
Dewey:305.891/420794. LCCN:91-024482.
                              Audience: **g,l,u.** *Choice, 1993.*

Manalansan, Martin F.   E184.O6C85 2000
IV (Editor)
Cultural Compass: Ethnographic Explorations of Asian America.
Trade Cloth. Temple University Press. Philadelphia, PA. 2000.
241p. Asian American History and Culture Ser.
ISBN:1-56639-772-3, ISBN13: 978-1-56639-772-8.
Dewey:305.895073. LCCN:99-087506.
                                        Audience: **u,f.**

McIllwain, Jeffrey Scott   HV6452.N7
Organizing Crime In Chinatown: Race and Racketeering in New York City, 1890-1910. Paper Text. McFarland & Company, Incorporated Publishers. Jefferson, NC. 2004. 260p. ISBN:0-7864-1626-2, ISBN13: 978-0-7864-1626-4. Dewey:364.1/06/08995107471. LCCN:2003-021121.
Audience: **l,u,f.** *Choice, 2004.*

Min, Pyong Gap   E184
  (Editor)
Encyclopedia of Racism in the United States. Cloth Text. Greenwood Publishing Group, Inc. Portsmouth, NH. 2005. 1024p. ISBN:0-313-32688-6, ISBN13: 978-0-313-32688-2. Dewey:305.8/00973/03. LCCN:2005-008523.
Audience: **g,l,u,f.** *Choice, 2006.*

Min, Pyong Gap   E184.O6M57 2001
The Second Generation: Ethnic Identity among Asian Americans. Trade Cloth. AltaMira Press. Walnut Creek, CA. 2002. 280p. Critical Perspectives on Asian Pacific Americans Ser. ISBN:0-7591-0175-2, ISBN13: 978-0-7591-0175-3. Dewey:305.895073. LCCN:2001-022783.
Audience: **l,u,f.**

Ngai, Mae M.   KF4800.N485 2005
Impossible Subjects: Illegal Aliens and the Making of Modern America. Trade Paper. Princeton University Press. Princeton, NJ. 2005. 400p. Politics and Society in Twentieth Century America Ser. ISBN:0-691-12429-9, ISBN13: 978-0-691-12429-2. Dewey:342.73/083.
Audience: **l,u,f.** *Choice, 2004.*

Okihiro, Gary Y.   E175.9.O38 2001
Common Ground: Reimagining American History. Trade Cloth. Princeton University Press. Princeton, NJ. 2001. xvi, 158p. ISBN:0-691-07006-7, ISBN13: 978-0-691-07006-3. Dewey:973. LCCN:00-049112.
Audience: **l,u,f.** *Choice, 2002, 2001.*

Omi, Michael &   E184.A1O47 1994
  Winant, Howard A.
Racial Formation in the United States: 1960-1990. Ed. 2. Trade Paper. Routledge. New York, NY. 1994. 240p. Critical Social Thought Ser. ISBN:0-415-90864-7, ISBN13: 978-0-415-90864-1. Dewey:305.8/00973. LCCN:93-336254.
Audience: **l,u,f.**

Ong, Paul & Hee,   F869.L89K68 1993
  Suzanne
Losses in the Los Angeles Civil Unrest, April 29-May 1, 1992: Lists of the Damaged Properties and Korean Merchants and the L. A. Riot - Rebellion. Trade Paper. University of California, Los Angeles, Asia Institute. Los Angeles, CA. 1993. 138p. ISBN:1-883191-00-9, ISBN13: 978-1-883191-00-9. Dewey:929/.3/089957079494. LCCN:93-070183.
Audience: **l,u,f.**

Palumbo-Liu, David   E184.O6P26 1999
Asian/American: Historical Crossings of a Racial Frontier. Trade Cloth. Stanford University Press. Palo Alto, CA. 1999. 534p. ISBN:0-8047-3444-5, ISBN13: 978-0-8047-3444-8. Dewey:973/.0495073. LCCN:98-048250.
Audience: **u,f.** *Choice, 1999.*

Prashad, Vijay   E184.S69P73 2000
  (Contribution by)
The Karma of Brown Folk. Trade Cloth. University of Minnesota Press. Minneapolis, MN. 2000. xv, 253p.

ISBN:0-8166-3438-6, ISBN13: 978-0-8166-3438-5. Dewey:305.891/4073. LCCN:99-047918.
Audience: **g,l,u,f.**

Pulido, Laura   HN79.C23R336 2006
Black, Brown, Yellow, and Left: Radical Activism in Los Angeles. Trade Cloth. University of California Press. Berkeley, CA. 2006. 352p. American Crossroads Ser., Vol. 19 ISBN:0-520-24519-9, ISBN13: 978-0-520-24519-8. Dewey:305.8/009794/909047. LCCN:2005-002624.
Audience: **l,u,f.** *Choice, 2006.*

Root, Maria P. (Editor)   E184.A1M89 1996
The Multiracial Experience: Racial Borders as the New Frontier. Paper Text. SAGE Publications, Inc. Thousand Oaks, CA. 1995. 509p. ISBN:0-8039-7059-5, ISBN13: 978-0-8039-7059-5. Dewey:305.8. LCCN:95-034980.
Audience: **l,u,f.**

Said, Edward W.   DS5
Orientalism. Ed. 25. Trade Paper. Knopf Publishing Group. New York, NY. 1979. 432p. ISBN:0-394-74067-X, ISBN13: 978-0-394-74067-6. Dewey:950. LCCN:79-010497.
Audience: **g,l,u,f.**

San Juan, E.   E184.A1
Racial Formations/Critical Transformations: Articulations of Power in Ethnic and Racial Studies in the United States. Trade Cloth. Prometheus Books, Publishers. Amherst, NY. 1994. 172p. ISBN:1-57392-486-5, ISBN13: 978-1-57392-486-3. Dewey:305.8.
Audience: **l,u,f.**

San Juan, Epifanio, Jr.   E184.F4S258 2000
After Postcolonialism: Remapping Philippines - U. S. Confrontations. Rowman & Littlefield Publishers, Inc. 2000. ISBN:0-8476-9860-2, ISBN13: 978-0-8476-9860-8.
Audience: **l,u,f.**

Shankar, Lavina   E184.S69P37 1998
  Dhingra & Srikanth, Rajini (Editors)
A Part, Yet Apart: South Asians in Asian America. Paper Text. Temple University Press. Philadelphia, PA. 1998. 320p. Asian American History and Culture Ser. ISBN:1-56639-578-X, ISBN13: 978-1-56639-578-6. Dewey:973/.04914. LCCN:97-038354.
Audience: **l,u.**

Takagi, Dana Y.   LB2351.52.U6
The Retreat from Race: Asian Admissions and Racial Politics. Cloth Text. Rutgers University Press. Piscataway, NJ. 1993. 260p. ISBN:0-8135-1913-6, ISBN13: 978-0-8135-1913-5. Dewey:378.1/616. LCCN:92-013377.
Audience: **l,f.**

Tchen, John Kuo Wei   PR4148.P6
New York Before Chinatown: Orientalism and the Shaping of American Culture, 1776-1882. Trade Cloth. DIANE Publishing Company. Collingdale, PA. 2004. 385p. ISBN:0-7567-7146-3, ISBN13: 978-0-7567-7146-1. Dewey:821/.7.
Audience: **g,l,u,f.**

Tuan, Mia   E184.O6T8 1999
Forever Foreigners or Honorary Whites: The Asian Ethnic Experience Today. Cloth Text. Rutgers University Press. Piscataway, NJ. 1999. 192p. ISBN:0-8135-2623-X, ISBN13: 978-0-8135-2623-2. Dewey:305.895073. LCCN:98-036388.
Audience: **l,u,f.** *Choice, 1999.*

Ty, Eleanor Rose &   **PS153.A84A86 2004**
Goellnicht, Donald C. (Editors)
e Asian North American Identities: Beyond the Hyphen.
E-Book. Indiana University Press. Bloomington, IN. 2004. 212p.
ISBN:0-253-34380-1, ISBN13: 978-0-253-34380-2.
Dewey:810.9/895. LCCN:2003-017925.
Audience: **g,l.** *Choice, 2004.*

Vigil, James Diego   **HV6439.U7L788 2002**
A Rainbow of Gangs: Street Cultures in the Mega-City. Trade
Paper. University of Texas Press. Austin, TX. 2002. 231p.
ISBN:0-292-78749-9, ISBN13: 978-0-292-78749-0.
Dewey:364.1/06/60979494. LCCN:2002-001063.
Audience: **l,u,f.** *Choice, 2003.*

Volkman, Toby Alice   **HV875.5.C86 2005**
(Editor)
Cultures of Transnational Adoption. Trade Cloth. Duke
University Press. Durham, NC. 2005. 232p.
ISBN:0-8223-3576-X, ISBN13: 978-0-8223-3576-4.
Dewey:362.734. LCCN:2004-026187.
Audience: **l,u.**

Wallace, Kendra R.   **LC3731**
Relative/Outsider: The Art and Politics of Identity among Mixed
Heritage Students. Trade Cloth. Greenwood Publishing Group,
Inc. Portsmouth, NH. 2001. 200p. Contemporary Studies in
Social and Policy Issues in Education ISBN:1-56750-550-3,
ISBN13: 978-1-56750-550-4. Dewey:371.829/00973.
LCCN:00-049343.
Audience: **l,f.** *Choice, 2002.*

Williams-Leon, Teresa   **E184.O6.S86 2001**
& Nakashima, Cynthia L. (Editors)
The Sum of Our Parts: Mixed-Heritage Asian Americans.
Michael Omi (Foreword by). Trade Cloth. Temple University
Press. Philadelphia, PA. 2000. xiii, 279p. Asian American
History and Culture Ser. ISBN:1-56639-846-0, ISBN13:
978-1-56639-846-6. Dewey:305.895073. LCCN:00-055214.
Audience: **g,l,u,f.** *Choice, 2002.*

Wu, Frank   **E184.O6W84 2003**
Yellow: Race in America Beyond Black and White. Trade Paper.
Basic Books. New York, NY. 2003. 416p. ISBN:0-465-00640-X,
ISBN13: 978-0-465-00640-3. Dewey:305.8/95073.
Audience: **l,u,f.**

Yamamoto, Eric K.   **E184.A1Y36 1999**
Interracial Justice: Conflict and Reconciliation in Post-Civil
Rights America. Trade Cloth. New York University Press. New
York, NY. 1999. 352p. Critical America Ser.
ISBN:0-8147-9674-5, ISBN13: 978-0-8147-9674-0.
Dewey:305.8/00973. LCCN:98-039108.
Audience: **l,u,f.** *Choice, 1999.*

Yancey, George   **E184.A1Y37 2003**
Who Is White?: Latinos, Asians, and the New Black/Nonblack
Divide. Library Binding. Lynne Rienner Publishers, Inc.
Boulder, CO. 2003. 250p. ISBN:1-58826-123-9, ISBN13:
978-1-58826-123-6. Dewey:305.8/00973. LCCN:2002-190869.
Audience: **l,u,f.** *Choice, 2003.*

Yoon, In-Jin   **HD2346.U5Y66 1997**
On My Own: Korean Businesses and Race Relations in
America. Trade Cloth. University of Chicago Press. Chicago, IL.
1997. 276p. ISBN:0-226-95927-9, ISBN13: 978-0-226-95927-6.
Dewey:338.6/422/089957073. LCCN:96-039395.
Audience: **l,u,f.** *Choice, 1998.*

Yu, Eui-Young (Editor)   **F869.L89N319 1994**
Black-Korean Encounter: Toward Understanding and Alliance.
Trade Paper. Regina Books. Claremont, CA. 1994. viii, 160p.
ISBN:0-941690-60-1, ISBN13: 978-0-941690-60-7.
Dewey:979.4/9400496073. LCCN:94-019786.
Audience: **g,l,u,f.**

Yu, Henry   **E184.O6**
Thinking Orientals: Migration, Contact, and Exoticism in
Modern America. Trade Paper. Oxford University Press, Inc.
New York, NY. 2002. 288p. ISBN:0-19-515127-5, ISBN13:
978-0-19-515127-5. Dewey:305.8/95/073.
Audience: **u,f.** *Choice, 2001.*

Social Sciences > Sociology

Dorow, Sara K.   **HV875.58.C6D67 2006**
Transnational Adoption: A Cultural Economy of Race, Gender,
and Kinship. Trade Cloth. New York University Press. New
York, NY. 2006. 344p. Nation of Newcomers Ser.
ISBN:0-8147-1971-6, ISBN13: 978-0-8147-1971-8.
Dewey:362.7340951. LCCN:2005-034182.
Audience: **l,u.**

Franks, Joel S.   **GV583.F73 2000**
Crossing Sidelines, Crossing Cultures: Sport and Asian Pacific
American Cultural Citizenship. Trade Cloth. University Press of
America, Inc. Lanham, MD. 2000. 232p. ISBN:0-7618-1592-9,
ISBN13: 978-0-7618-1592-1. Dewey:796/.089/95073.
LCCN:99-056934.
Audience: **g,l.** *Choice, 2000.*

Rojewski, Jay W. &   **HV875**
Rojewski, Jacy L.
Intercountry Adoption from China: Examining Cultural-Heritage
and Other Postadoption Issues. Paper Text. Greenwood
Publishing Group, Inc. Portsmouth, NH. 2001. 232p.
ISBN:0-89789-812-5, ISBN13: 978-0-89789-812-6.
Dewey:362.73/4/0951. LCCN:2001-025176.
Audience: **g,l.** *Choice, 2002.*

Volkman, Toby Alice   **HV875.5.C86 2005**
(Editor)
Cultures of Transnational Adoption. Trade Cloth. Duke
University Press. Durham, NC. 2005. 232p.
ISBN:0-8223-3576-X, ISBN13: 978-0-8223-3576-4.
Dewey:362.734. LCCN:2004-026187.
Audience: **l,u.**

Social Sciences > Ethnic Groups

Alba, Richard D. &   **JV6475.A433 2003**
Nee, Victor
Remaking the American Mainstream: Assimilation and
Contemporary Immigration. Trade Cloth. Harvard University
Press. Cambridge, MA. 2003. 384p. ISBN:0-674-01040-X,
ISBN13: 978-0-674-01040-6. Dewey:303.48/273.
LCCN:2002-191300.
Audience: **l,u,f.** *Choice, 2004.*

Ngai, Mae M.   **KF4800.N485 2005**
Impossible Subjects: Illegal Aliens and the Making of Modern
America. Trade Paper. Princeton University Press. Princeton, NJ.
2005. 400p. Politics and Society in Twentieth Century America

Ser. ISBN:0-691-12429-9, ISBN13: 978-0-691-12429-2. Dewey:342.73/083.

Audience: **l,u,f.** *Choice, 2004.*

Talwar, Jennifer Parker **HD6300**
Fast Food, Fast Track: Immigrants, Big Business, and the American Dream. Trade Paper. Westview Press. Boulder, CO. 2003. 240p. ISBN:0-8133-4155-8, ISBN13: 978-0-8133-4155-2. Dewey:331.6/2/0973.

Audience: **g,l.** *Choice, 2002.*

Ty, Eleanor Rose & **PS153.A84A86 2004**
  Goellnicht, Donald C. (Editors)
🄴 Asian North American Identities: Beyond the Hyphen. E-Book. Indiana University Press. Bloomington, IN. 2004. 212p. ISBN:0-253-34380-1, ISBN13: 978-0-253-34380-2. Dewey:810.9/895. LCCN:2003-017925.

Audience: **g,l.** *Choice, 2004.*

Social Sciences > Ethnic Groups > Chinese Americans

Bao, Xiaolan **HD6073.C6U533 2001**
Holding up More Than Half the Sky: Chinese Women Garment Workers in New York City, 1948-92. Trade Cloth. University of Illinois Press. Champaign, IL. 2001. 360p. The Asian American Experience Ser. ISBN:0-252-02631-4, ISBN13: 978-0-252-02631-7. Dewey:331.48870899510747. LCCN:00-010607.

Audience: **l,u,f.** *Choice, 2002.*

Boggs, Grace L. **F574.D49C53 1998**
Living for Change: An Autobiography. Book, Other. University of Minnesota Press. Minneapolis, MN. 1998. 344p. ISBN:0-8166-2954-4, ISBN13: 978-0-8166-2954-1. Dewey:[B]. LCCN:97-027296.

Audience: **l,u.**

Chan, Sucheng **E184.C5C478 2005**
Chinese American Transnationalism: The Flow of People, Resources, and Ideas Between China and America During the Exclusion Era. Trade Cloth. Temple University Press. Philadelphia, PA. 2005. 312p. Asian American History and Cultu Ser. ISBN:1-59213-434-3, ISBN13: 978-1-59213-434-2. Dewey:973/.04951. LCCN:2005-041834.

Audience: **l,u.** *Choice, 2006.*

Chan, Sucheng **HD8039.F32**
This Bittersweet Soil: The Chinese in California Agriculture, 1860-1910. Trade Cloth. University of California Press. Berkeley, CA. 1987. ISBN:0-520-05376-1, ISBN13: 978-0-520-05376-2. Dewey:338.1/089951/0764.

Audience: **g,l.**

Chen, Yong **F869.S39C515 2000**
Chinese San Francisco, 1850-1943: A Trans-Pacific Community. Trade Cloth. Stanford University Press. Palo Alto, CA. 2000. xvi, 392p. Asian America Ser. ISBN:0-8047-3605-7, ISBN13: 978-0-8047-3605-3. Dewey:979.4/61004951073. LCCN:99-055529.

Audience: **l,u,f.** *Choice, 2001.*

Chin, Ko-lin **HV6439.U7**
Chinatown Gangs: Extortion, Enterprise, and Ethnicity. Trade Paper. Oxford University Press, Inc. New York, NY. 2000. 248p.

Studies in Crime and Public Policy ISBN:0-19-513627-6, ISBN13: 978-0-19-513627-2. Dewey:364.1/066/097471.

Audience: **l,u,f.**

Chin, Ko-lin **E184.C5C474 1999**
Smuggled Chinese: Clandestine Immigration to the United States. Douglas S. Massey (Foreword by). Trade Cloth. Temple University Press. Philadelphia, PA. 1999. 296p. Asian American History and Culture Ser. ISBN:1-56639-732-4, ISBN13: 978-1-56639-732-2. Dewey:304.873051. LCCN:99-036086.

Audience: **g,l,u,f.**

Chin, Tung Pok & **E184.C5P27 2000**
  Chin, Winifred C.
Paper Son: One Man's Story. K. Scott Wong (Introduction by). Trade Cloth. Temple University Press. Philadelphia, PA. 2000. xx, 147p. Asian American History and Culture Ser. ISBN:1-56639-800-2, ISBN13: 978-1-56639-800-8. Dewey:973.04/951. LCCN:00-034347.

Audience: **l,u,f.** *Choice, 2001.*

Chun, Gloria H. **E184.C5C56 2000**
Of Orphans and Warriors: Inventing Chinese-American Culture and Identity. Cloth Text. Rutgers University Press. Piscataway, NJ. 2000. ix, 198p. ISBN:0-8135-2708-2, ISBN13: 978-0-8135-2708-6. Dewey:305.895/1073/0904. LCCN:99-033563.

Audience: **l,u,f.** *Choice, 2000.*

Daniels, Roger **E184.O6**
Asian America: Chinese and Japanese in the United States Since 1850. Trade Cloth. University of Washington Press. Seattle, WA. 1990. 402p. ISBN:0-295-97018-9, ISBN13: 978-0-295-97018-9. Dewey:973/.0495. LCCN:88-005643.

Audience: **l,u,f.** *Choice, 1989.*

Dirlik, Arif & Yeung, **E184.C5C496 2001**
  Malcolm (Editors)
Chinese on the American Frontier. Book, Other. Rowman & Littlefield Publishers, Inc. Lanham, MD. 2001. 544p. Pacific Formation Ser., :Global Relations in Asian and Pacific Perspective ISBN:0-8476-8532-2, ISBN13: 978-0-8476-8532-5. Dewey:973.04/951. LCCN:00-034199.

Audience: **l,u,f.** *Choice, 2001.*

Fong, Timothy P. **F869.M7F68 1994**
The First Suburban Chinatown: The Remaking of Monterey Park, California. Trade Cloth. Temple University Press. Philadelphia, PA. 1994. 240p. Asian American History and Culture Ser. ISBN:1-56639-123-7, ISBN13: 978-1-56639-123-8. Dewey:979.4/93. LCCN:93-020562.

Audience: **l,u,f.**

Guest, Kenneth J. **BL2527.N7G84 2003**
God in Chinatown: Religion and Survival in New York's Evolving Immigrant Community. Trade Cloth. New York University Press. New York, NY. 2003. 237p. Religion, Race, and Ethnicity Ser. ISBN:0-8147-3153-8, ISBN13: 978-0-8147-3153-6. Dewey:200/.89/95107471. LCCN:2003-000761.

Audience: **l,u,f.** *Choice, 2004.*

Gyory, Andrew **E184.C5G9 1998**
Closing the Gate: Race, Politics and the Chinese Exclusion Act. Trade Cloth. University of North Carolina Press. Chapel Hill, NC. 1998. 368p. ISBN:0-8078-2432-1, ISBN13: 978-0-8078-2432-0. Dewey:325.73089951. LCCN:97-047746.

Audience: **l,u,f.** *Choice, 1999.*

Hsu, Madeline Y.   **E184.O6H78 2000**
Dreaming of Gold, Dreaming of Home: Transnationalism and
Migration Between the United States and South China,
1882-1943. Trade Cloth. Stanford University Press. Palo Alto,
CA. 2000. xx, 271p. Asian America Ser. ISBN:0-8047-3814-9,
ISBN13: 978-0-8047-3814-9. Dewey:973/.04951.
LCCN:00-056355.

Audience: **l,u.** *Choice, 2001.*

Kibria, Nazli   **E184.C5K45 2003**
Becoming Asian American: Second-Generation Chinese and
Korean American Identities. Trade Paper. Johns Hopkins
University Press. Baltimore, MD. 2003. 232p.
ISBN:0-8018-7744-X, ISBN13: 978-0-8018-7744-5.
Dewey:305.8951073. LCCN:2001-002795.

Audience: **l,u,f.** *Choice, 2003.*

Kwong, Peter   **HD8079**
Chinatown, N. Y.: Labor and Politics, 1930-1950. Trade Paper.
New Press, The. New York, NY. 2001. 208p.
ISBN:1-56584-640-0, ISBN13: 978-1-56584-640-1.
Dewey:331.6/251/07471. LCCN:79-002327.

Audience: **l,u,f.**

Kwong, Peter   **F128.64.C47K97 1996**
The New Chinatown. Trade Paper. Farrar, Straus & Giroux.
New York, NY. 1996. 210p. ISBN:0-8090-1585-4, ISBN13:
978-0-8090-1585-6. Dewey:330.9747/1. LCCN:95-047731.

Audience: **l,u,f.** *Choice, 1988.*

Lai, Him Mark   **E184.C5L355 2003**
On Becoming Chinese American: A History of Communities and
Institutions, Vol. 13. Trade Paper. AltaMira Press. Walnut Creek,
CA. 2004. 418p. Critical Perspectives on Asian Pacific
Americans Ser. ISBN:0-7591-0458-1, ISBN13:
978-0-7591-0458-7. Dewey:973/.04951. LCCN:2003-020363.

Audience: **g,l,u,f.**

Lai, Him Mark   **E184.O6A84265**
A History Reclaimed: An Annotated Bibliography of Chinese
Language Materials on the Chinese of America. Russell Leong
& Jean P. Yip (Editors). Cloth Text. University of California,
Los Angeles, Asian American Studies Center. Los Angeles, CA.
1986. 160p. ISBN:0-934052-32-8, ISBN13: 978-0-934052-32-0.
Dewey:973.0495.

Audience: **l,u,f.**

Lai, Him M., et al.   **PL3164.5.E5L35 1991**
Island: Poetry and History of Chinese Immigrants on Angel
Island, 1910 to 1949. Genny Lim & Judy Yung (Authors). Trade
Cloth. University of Washington Press. Seattle, WA. 2003. 174p.
ISBN:0-295-97109-6, ISBN13: 978-0-295-97109-4.
Dewey:895.1/15108. LCCN:91-008372.

Audience: **g,l,u,f.**

Lee, Anthony W.   **N8214.5.U6L43 2001**
Picturing Chinatown: Art and Orientalism in San Francisco.
Trade Cloth. University of California Press. Berkeley, CA. 2001.
362p. ISBN:0-520-22592-9, ISBN13: 978-0-520-22592-3.
Dewey:704.9/4997461. LCCN:2001-027087.

Audience: **g,l,u,f.** *Choice, 2002.*

Lee, Erika   **E184.C5L523 2003**
At America's Gates: Chinese Immigration During the Exclusion
Era, 1882-1943. Trade Paper. University of North Carolina
Press. Chapel Hill, NC. 2003. 352p. ISBN:0-8078-5448-4,
ISBN13: 978-0-8078-5448-8. Dewey:325/.251073.
LCCN:2002-013375.

Audience: **l,u,f.** *Choice, 2004.*

Liu, Eric   **E184.C5**
The Accidental Asian: Notes of a Native Speaker. Trade Paper.
Alfred A. Knopf Inc. New York, NY. 1999. 224p. Vintage Bks.
ISBN:0-375-70486-8, ISBN13: 978-0-375-70486-4.
Dewey:305.8951/073.

Audience: **g,l.**

Loo, Chalsa M.   **F869**
Chinatown: Most Time, Hard Time. Trade Cloth. Greenwood
Publishing Group, Inc. Portsmouth, NH. 1991. 384p.
ISBN:0-275-93893-X, ISBN13: 978-0-275-93893-2.
Dewey:979.4/61. LCCN:91-027984.

Audience: **l,u,f.**

Louie, Vivian S.   **E184.C5L685 2004**
Compelled to Excel: Immigration, Education, and Opportunity
among Chinese Americans. Trade Cloth. Stanford University
Press. Palo Alto, CA. 2004. 272p. ISBN:0-8047-4984-1,
ISBN13: 978-0-8047-4984-8. Dewey:305.895/1073.
LCCN:2004-011167.

Audience: **l,u,f.**

Ma, Laurence J. C. &   **DS732.C5563 2002**
Cartier, Carolyn L.
The Chinese Diaspora: Space, Place, Mobility and Identity.
Book, Other. Rowman & Littlefield Publishers, Inc. Lanham,
MD. 2003. 400p. Why of Where Ser. ISBN:0-7425-1755-1,
ISBN13: 978-0-7425-1755-4. Dewey:909/.04951.
LCCN:2002-151795.

Audience: **l,u,f.** *Choice, 2003.*

McIllwain, Jeffrey Scott   **HV6452.N7**
Organizing Crime In Chinatown: Race and Racketeering in New
York City, 1890-1910. Paper Text. McFarland & Company,
Incorporated Publishers. Jefferson, NC. 2004. 260p.
ISBN:0-7864-1626-2, ISBN13: 978-0-7864-1626-4.
Dewey:364.1/06/08995107471. LCCN:2003-021121.

Audience: **l,u,f.** *Choice, 2004.*

Muse, Erika A.   **BR563.C45M87 2005**
The Evangelical Church in Boston's Chinatown: A Discourse of
Language, Gender, and Identity. Paper over Boards. Routledge.
New York, NY. 2005. 226p. Asian Americans Ser.,
:Reconceptualizing Culture, History, Politics
ISBN:0-415-97406-2, ISBN13: 978-0-415-97406-6.
Dewey:289.9/5/089951074461. LCCN:2004-030687.

Audience: **l,u,f.**

Nee, Victor G. & De   **F869.S39C55 1986**
Bary Nee, Brett
Longtime Californ': A Documentary Study of an American
Chinatown. Trade Paper. Stanford University Press. Palo Alto,
CA. 1986. 451p. ISBN:0-8047-1336-7, ISBN13:
978-0-8047-1336-8. Dewey:979.4/61. LCCN:85-063406.

Audience: **l.**

Park, Lisa Sun-Hee   **E184.K6P365 2005**
Consuming Citizenship: Children of Asian Immigrant
Entrepreneurs. Trade Cloth. Stanford University Press. Palo
Alto, CA. 2005. 184p. Asian America Ser. ISBN:0-8047-5247-8,
ISBN13: 978-0-8047-5247-3. Dewey:305.895/7073.
LCCN:2005-013560.

Audience: **l,u.**

Rojewski, Jay W. &   **HV875**
Rojewski, Jacy L.
Intercountry Adoption from China: Examining Cultural Heritage
and Other Postadoption Issues. Paper Text. Greenwood
Publishing Group, Inc. Portsmouth, NH. 2001. 232p.

ISBN:0-89789-812-5, ISBN13: 978-0-89789-812-6. Dewey:362.73/4/0951. LCCN:2001-025176.

Audience: **g,l.** *Choice, 2002.*

Sabine, Maureen   **PS3561.I52Z87 2004**
Maxine Hong Kingston's Broken Book of Life: An Intertextual Study of the Woman Warrior and China Men. Trade Cloth. University of Hawaii Press. Honolulu, HI. 2004. 264p. ISBN:0-8248-2784-8, ISBN13: 978-0-8248-2784-7. Dewey:813/.54. LCCN:2003-018420.

Audience: **l,u,f.** *Choice, 2004.*

Saxton, Alexander   **HD8081.C5S3 1995**
The Indispensable Enemy: Labor and the Anti-Chinese Movement in California. Trade Paper. University of California Press. Berkeley, CA. 1975. 304p. ISBN:0-520-02905-4, ISBN13: 978-0-520-02905-7. Dewey:331.6/21510794. LCCN:72-115494.

Audience: **l,u.**

Shah, Nayan   **RA448.5.C45S53 2001**
Contagious Divides: Epidemics and Race in San Francisco's Chinatown. Trade Cloth. University of California Press. Berkeley, CA. 2001. 400p. American Crossroads Ser., Vol. 7 ISBN:0-520-22628-3, ISBN13: 978-0-520-22628-9. Dewey:614.4/9794. LCCN:2001-027615.

Audience: **l,u,f.**

Siu, Paul C.   **HD8081.C5**
The Chinese Laundryman: A Study of Social Isolation. Daniel J. Walkowitz & John Kuo Wei Tchen (Introduction by). Trade Paper. New York University Press. New York, NY. 1988. 351p. ISBN:0-8147-7874-7, ISBN13: 978-0-8147-7874-6. LCCN:87-005609.

Audience: **l,u,f.**

Tchen, John Kuo Wei   **PR4148.P6**
New York Before Chinatown: Orientalism and the Shaping of American Culture, 1776-1882. Trade Cloth. DIANE Publishing Company. Collingdale, PA. 2004. 385p. ISBN:0-7567-7146-3, ISBN13: 978-0-7567-7146-1. Dewey:821/.7.

Audience: **g,l,u,f.**

Tong, Benson   **E184.C5T63 2003**
The Chinese Americans. Trade Paper. University Press of Colorado. Boulder, CO. 2003. 307p. ISBN:0-87081-730-2, ISBN13: 978-0-87081-730-4. Dewey:973/.04951. LCCN:2003-006542.

Audience: **l,u,f.**

Tong, Benson   **HQ146.S4T66 1994**
Unsubmissive Women: Chinese Prostitutes in Nineteenth-Century San Francisco. Trade Cloth. University of Oklahoma Press. Norman, OK. 1994. 320p. ISBN:0-8061-2653-1, ISBN13: 978-0-8061-2653-1. Dewey:306.74/2/0979461. LCCN:94-016168.

Audience: **l,u,f.** *Choice, 1995.*

Tung, May Paomay   **E184.C5T85 2000**
Chinese Americans and Their Immigrant Parents: Conflict, Identity and Values. Trade Cloth. Haworth Press, Incorporated, The. Binghamton, NY. 2000. 112p. ISBN:0-7890-1055-0, ISBN13: 978-0-7890-1055-1. Dewey:305.8951073. LCCN:99-056008.

Audience: **l,u,f.** *Choice, 2001.*

Wong, K. Scott   **E184.C5W65 2005**
Americans First: Chinese Americans and the Second World War. Trade Cloth. Harvard University Press. Cambridge, MA. 2005.

272p. ISBN:0-674-01671-8, ISBN13: 978-0-674-01671-2. Dewey:940.54/089/951073. LCCN:2004-059790.

Audience: **l,u,f.** *Choice, 2006.*

Wong, K. Scott &   **E184.C5C57 1998**
 Chan, Sucheng (Editors)
Claiming America: Constructing Chinese American Identities During the Exclusion Era. Cloth Text. Temple University Press. Philadelphia, PA. 1998. 256p. Asian American History and Culture Ser. ISBN:1-56639-575-5, ISBN13: 978-1-56639-575-5. Dewey:973/.04951. LCCN:97-002539.

Audience: **l,u.** *Choice, 1998.*

Wu, William F.   **PS374.C46 W8**
The Yellow Peril: Chinese Americans in American Fiction, 1850-1940. Trade Cloth. Elliot's Books. Northford, CT. 1982. 241p. ISBN:0-208-01915-4, ISBN13: 978-0-208-01915-8. Dewey:813/.009/35203951. LCCN:81-012701.

Audience: **g,l,u,f.**

Yang, Fenggang   **BR563.C45Y36 1999**
Chinese Christians in America: Conversion, Assimilation and Adhesive Identities. Trade Cloth. Pennsylvania State University Press. University Park, PA. 1999. 272p. ISBN:0-271-01916-6, ISBN13: 978-0-271-01916-1. Dewey:280/.4/0899510753. LCCN:98-037365.

Audience: **l,u,f.** *Choice, 2000.*

Yin, Xiao-Huang   **PS153.C45Y56 2000**
Chinese American Literature since the 1850s. Trade Cloth. University of Illinois Press. Champaign, IL. 2000. 336p. The Asian American Experience Ser. ISBN:0-252-02524-5, ISBN13: 978-0-252-02524-2. Dewey:810.9/8951. LCCN:99-006512.

Audience: **l,u,f.** *Choice, 2000.*

Yu, Renqiu   **HD9999.L383U639 1992**
To Save China, to Save Ourselves: The Chinese Hand Laundry Alliance of New York. Trade Cloth. Temple University Press. Philadelphia, PA. 1992. 253p. Asian American History and Culture Ser. ISBN:0-87722-996-1, ISBN13: 978-0-87722-996-4. Dewey:338.4/76481/097471. LCCN:92-009205.

Audience: **l,u,f.** *Choice, 1993.*

Yung, Judy   **F869.S39C597 1999**
Unbound Voices: A Documentary History of Chinese Women in San Francisco. Trade Paper. University of California Press. Berkeley, CA. 1999. 560p. ISBN:0-520-21860-4, ISBN13: 978-0-520-21860-4. Dewey:979.4/61004951/00922. LCCN:99-031772.

Audience: **l,u,f.** *Choice, 2000.*

Yung, Judy, et al.   **E184.C5C479 2006**
Chinese American Voices: From the Gold Rush to the Present. Gordon H. Chang & H. Mark Lai (Authors). Trade Cloth. University of California Press. Berkeley, CA. 2006. 474p. ISBN:0-520-24309-9, ISBN13: 978-0-520-24309-5. Dewey:973/.04951. LCCN:2005-021227.

Audience: **l,u,f.** *Choice, 2006.*

Zhao, Xiaojian   **E184.C5Z43 2002**
Remaking Chinese America: Immigration, Family and Community, 1940-1965. Cloth Text. Rutgers University Press. Piscataway, NJ. 2002. 256p. ISBN:0-8135-3010-5, ISBN13: 978-0-8135-3010-9. Dewey:305.895/1073/0904. LCCN:2001-019844.

Audience: **l,u,f.** *Choice, 2002.*

Zhu, Liping   **E184.C5Z48 1997**
A Chinaman's Chance: The Chinese on the Rocky Mountain
Mining Frontier. Trade Cloth. University Press of Colorado.
Boulder, CO. 1997. 200p. ISBN:0-87081-467-2, ISBN13:
978-0-87081-467-9. Dewey:305.8/951078. LCCN:97-019879.

Audience: **l,u,f.** *Choice, 1998.*

Social Sciences > Ethnic Groups > Filipino Americans

Almirol, Edwin B.   **F869.S17A55 1985**
Ethnic Identity and Social Negotiation: A Study of a Filipino
Community in California. Trade Cloth. A M S Press, Inc. New
York, NY. 1985. Immigrant Communities and Ethnic Minorities
in the U. S. and Canada Ser., No. 10 ISBN:0-404-19401-X,
ISBN13: 978-0-404-19401-7. Dewey:305.8/9921/079476.
LCCN:83-045347.

Audience: **l.**

Bonus, Rick   **E184.F4B66 2000**
Locating Filipino Americans: Ethnicity and Cultural Politics of
Space. Trade Cloth. Temple University Press. Philadelphia, PA.
2000. xiii, 217p. Asian American History and Culture Ser.
ISBN:1-56639-778-2, ISBN13: 978-1-56639-778-0.
Dewey:305.89/921073. LCCN:99-462220.

Audience: **l,u.**

Bulosan, Carlos   **PS3503.U5627**
The Laughter of My Father. Trade Paper. Books on Demand.
Ann Arbor, MI. 201p. ISBN:0-598-44144-1, ISBN13:
978-0-598-44144-7. Dewey:617.52. LCCN:44-040087.

Audience: **g,l,u,f.**

Choy, Catherine Ceniza   **RT17.P6C48 2003**
Empire of Care: Nursing and Migration in Filipino American
History. Trade Cloth. Duke University Press. Durham, NC.
2003. 280p. American Encounters/Global Interactions Ser.
ISBN:0-8223-3052-0, ISBN13: 978-0-8223-3052-3.
Dewey:610.73/09599. LCCN:2002-012388.

Audience: **l,u,f.** *Choice, 2003.*

De Jesus, Melinda L.   **E184.F4P547 2004**
Pinay Power: Peminist Critical Theory. Paper over Boards.
Routledge. New York, NY. 2005. 416p. ISBN:0-415-94982-3,
ISBN13: 978-0-415-94982-8. Dewey:305.48/89921073.
LCCN:2004-021270.

Audience: **l,u,f.**

Espiritu, Yen Le   **F869.S22E9 1995**
Filipino American Lives. Library Binding. Temple University
Press. Philadelphia, PA. 1995. 256p. Asian American History
and Culture Ser. ISBN:1-56639-316-7, ISBN13:
978-1-56639-316-4. Dewey:305.89/921073/0922 B.
LCCN:94-048081.

Audience: **l.** *Choice, 1995.*

Espiritu, Yen Le   **E184.F4 E87 2003**
Home Bound: Filipino Lives Across Cultures, Communities, and
Countries. Trade Cloth. University of California Press. Berkeley,
CA. 2003. 292p. ISBN:0-520-22755-7, ISBN13:
978-0-520-22755-2. Dewey:306.8/089/9921073.
LCCN:2002-007139.

Audience: **l,u.** *Choice, 2003.*

Fujita-Rony, Dorothy B.   **F899.S49F85 2003**
American Workers, Colonial Power: Philippine Seattle and the
Transpacific West, 1919-1941. Trade Cloth. University of

California Press. Berkeley, CA. 2003. 320p.
ISBN:0-520-23094-9, ISBN13: 978-0-520-23094-1.
Dewey:979.7/7720049921. LCCN:2001-052279.

Audience: **l,u.** *Choice, 2003.*

Ignacio, Emily   **E184.F4I37 2005**
Building Diaspora: Filipino Community Formation on the
Internet. Trade Cloth. Rutgers University Press. Piscataway, NJ.
2005. 184p. ISBN:0-8135-3513-1, ISBN13: 978-0-8135-3513-5.
Dewey:305.89/921073/090511. LCCN:2004-011749.

Audience: **l,u,f.** *Choice, 2005.*

Juan, E. San Jr.   **PR9550.9.B8A6 1995**
On Becoming Filipino: Selected Writings of Carlos Bulosan.
Cloth Text. Temple University Press. Philadelphia, PA. 1995.
240p. Asian American History and Culture Ser.
ISBN:1-56639-309-4, ISBN13: 978-1-56639-309-6.
Dewey:818/.5209. LCCN:94-048937.

Audience: **l,u,f.**

Lasker, Bruno   **JV6891.F54**
Filipino Immigration to the Continental United States and to
Hawaii. J. Ishotwell (Foreword by). Trade Cloth. Ayer Company
Publishers, Inc. Manchester, NH. 1976. American Immigration
Collection, :Series 1 ISBN:0-405-00531-8, ISBN13:
978-0-405-00531-2. Dewey:325.2914. LCCN:69-018783.

Audience: **g,l.**

Manalansan, Martin F.   **HQ76.2.P6M36 2003**
Global Divas: Filipino Gay Men in the Diaspora. Trade Cloth.
Duke University Press. Durham, NC. 2003. 224p. Perverse
Modernities Ser. ISBN:0-8223-3204-3, ISBN13:
978-0-8223-3204-6. Dewey:305.38/9664/09599.
LCCN:2003-009459.

Audience: **l,u,f.**

Mendoza, Susanah L.   **E184.F4M46 2001**
Between Home and the Diaspora: The Politics of Theorizing
Filipino and Filipino American Identities. Paper over Boards.
Routledge. New York, NY. 2001. 176p. Asian-American Ser.,
:Reconceptualizing Culture, History and Politics
ISBN:0-415-93157-6, ISBN13: 978-0-415-93157-1.
Dewey:305.89/921073. LCCN:2001-034981.

Audience: **u.**

Okamura, Jonathan Y.   **E184.F4O36 1998**
Imagining the Filipino American Diaspora: Transnational
Relations, Identities, and Communities. Cloth Text. Garland
Publishing, Inc. New York, NY. 1998. 168p. Asian Americans
Ser., :Reconceptualizing Culture, History and Politics
ISBN:0-8153-3183-5, ISBN13: 978-0-8153-3183-4.
Dewey:305.89921073. LCCN:98-028383.

Audience: **g,l,u.**

Parrenas, Rhacel   **HQ792.P5P37 2005**
Salazar
Children of Global Migration: Transnational Families and
Gendered Woes. Trade Cloth. Stanford University Press. Palo
Alto, CA. 2005. 232p. ISBN:0-8047-4944-2, ISBN13:
978-0-8047-4944-2. Dewey:306.85/09599. LCCN:2004-016220.

Audience: **l,u.** *Choice, 2006.*

Parrenas, Rhacel   **HQ792.P5P37 2005**
Salazar
Children of Global Migration: Transnational Families and
Gender Woes. Stanford University Press. 2005.
ISBN:0-8047-4944-2, ISBN13: 978-0-8047-4944-2.

Audience: **l,u,f.**

Parrenas, Rhacel   **HD6072.P27 2001**
  Salazar
Servants of Globalization: Women, Migration, and Domestic
Work. Stanford University Press. 2001. ISBN:0-8047-3921-8,
ISBN13: 978-0-8047-3921-4.

Audience: **l,u.**

Posadas, Barbara M.   **E184**
The Filipino Americans. Cloth Text. Greenwood Publishing
Group, Inc. Portsmouth, NH. 1999. 208p. The New Americans
Ser. ISBN:0-313-29742-8, ISBN13: 978-0-313-29742-7.
Dewey:973/.049921. LCCN:99-010140.

Audience: **l.**

Roley, Brian Ascalon   **PS3568.O5333A84 2001**
The American Son: A Novel. Trade Paper. W. W. Norton &
Company, Inc. New York, NY. 2001. 256p.
ISBN:0-393-32154-1, ISBN13: 978-0-393-32154-8.
Dewey:813/.6. LCCN:00-053307.

Audience: **g,l.**

Root, Maria P. (Editor)   **E184.F4F385 1997**
Filipino Americans: Transformation and Identity. Trade Cloth.
SAGE Publications, Inc. Thousand Oaks, CA. 1997. 368p.
ISBN:0-7619-0578-2, ISBN13: 978-0-7619-0578-3.
Dewey:973/.049921. LCCN:97-004591.

Audience: **l.** *Choice, 1997.*

San Juan, E. Jr.   **PL5531.S25 1996**
The Philippine Temptation: Dialectics of Philippines - U. S.
Literary Relations. Library Binding. Temple University Press.
Philadelphia, PA. 1996. 256p. Asian American History and
Culture Ser. ISBN:1-56639-417-1, ISBN13: 978-1-56639-417-8.
Dewey:809/.89599. LCCN:95-047191.

Audience: **u,f.** *Choice, 1996.*

San Juan, E.   **E184.F4S26 1998**
From Exile to Diaspora: Versions of the Filipino Experience in
the United States. Harper Collins Publishers Canada, Ltd. 1998.
ISBN:0-8133-3169-2, ISBN13: 978-0-8133-3169-0.

Audience: **l,u.**

San Juan, E., Jr.   **PL5531.S25 1996**
The Philippine Temptation: Dialectics of Philippines - U. S.
Literary Relations. Temple University Press. 1996.
ISBN:1-56639-417-1, ISBN13: 978-1-56639-417-8.

Audience: **l,u.**

San Juan, Epifanio, Jr.   **E184.F4S258 2000**
After Postcolonialism: Remapping Philippines - U. S.
Confrontations. Rowman & Littlefield Publishers, Inc. 2000.
ISBN:0-8476-9860-2, ISBN13: 978-0-8476-9860-8.

Audience: **l,u,f.**

Scharlin, Craig &   **HD6515.A292U547 2000**
  Villanueva, Lilia V.
Philip Vera Cruz: A Personal History of Filipino Immigrants and
the Farmworkers Movement. Ed. 3. Trade Paper. University of
Washington Press. Seattle, WA. 2000. xxviii, 167p.
ISBN:0-295-97984-4, ISBN13: 978-0-295-97984-7.
Dewey:331.88/13/092 B. LCCN:00-029902.

Audience: **g,l,u.**

Tompar-Tiu, Aurora &   **RC451.5.F54T56 1995**
  Sustento-Severicher, Juliana
Depression and Other Mental Health Issues: The Filipino
American Experience. Trade Cloth. John Wiley & Sons, Inc.

Hoboken, NJ. 1994. 180p. Social and Behavioral Science Ser.
ISBN:0-7879-0041-9, ISBN13: 978-0-7879-0041-0.
Dewey:616.89/0089/9921073. LCCN:94-027879.

Audience: **l.**

Tyner, James A.   **HD6305.F55T94 2004**
Made in the Philippines: Gendered Discourses and the Making
of Migrants. Cloth Text. Routledge. New York, NY. 2004. 176p.
RoutledgeCurzon Pacific Rim Geographies Ser., Vol. 5
ISBN:0-415-70015-9, ISBN13: 978-0-415-70015-3.
Dewey:331.6/2599. LCCN:2003-010299.

Audience: **l,u.**

Villa, Jose G.   **PR9550.9.V48A6 1999**
The Anchored Angel: Selected Writings by Jose Garcia Villa.
Eileen Tabios (Editor). Paper Text. Kaya Production. New York,
NY. 1999. xv, 255p. ISBN:1-885030-28-2, ISBN13:
978-1-885030-28-3. Dewey:821/.912. LCCN:99-066355.

Audience: **g,l,u.**

Social Sciences > Ethnic Groups > Hawaiians and Pacific Islanders

Buck, Elizabeth   **DU624.65.B83**
Paradise Remade: The Politics of Culture and History in
Hawai'i. Trade Paper. Temple University Press. Philadelphia,
PA. 1994. 288p. ISBN:1-56639-200-4, ISBN13:
978-1-56639-200-6. Dewey:996.9.

Audience: **l,u.** *Choice, 1993.*

Bushnell, O. A.   **RA448.5.H38.B87 1993**
The Gifts of Civilization: Germs and Genocide in Hawai'I.
Paper Text. University of Hawaii Press. Honolulu, HI. 1993.
352p. ISBN:0-8248-1457-6, ISBN13: 978-0-8248-1457-1.
Dewey:362.1/089994. LCCN:92-040415.

Audience: **l,u.** *Choice, 1993.*

Coffman, Tom   **DU627.5.C64 2003**
The Island Edge of America: A Political History of Hawaii.
Trade Cloth. University of Hawaii Press. Honolulu, HI. 2003.
440p. ISBN:0-8248-2625-6, ISBN13: 978-0-8248-2625-3.
Dewey:996.9/03. LCCN:2002-074240.

Audience: **l,u.** *Choice, 2003.*

Denoon, Donald &   **DU28.3.C33 1997**
  Meleisea, Malama
The Cambridge History of the Pacific Islanders. Stewart Firth,
Jocelyn Linnekin & Karen Nero (As told tos). Trade Paper.
Cambridge University Press. New York, NY. 2004. 539p.
ISBN:0-521-00354-7, ISBN13: 978-0-521-00354-4. Dewey:990.

Audience: **g,l,u,f.** *Choice, 1998.*

Halualani, Rona Tamiko   **DU624.65.H345 2002**
In the Name of Hawaiians: Native Identities and Cultural
Politics. Trade Cloth. University of Minnesota Press.
Minneapolis, MN. 2002. 336p. ISBN:0-8166-3726-1, ISBN13:
978-0-8166-3726-3. Dewey:305.89942. LCCN:2002-005311.

Audience: **l,u.**

Merry, Sally Engle   **DU624.65.M47 2000**
Colonizing Hawai'i: The Cultural Power of Law. Cloth Text.
Princeton University Press. Princeton, NJ. 2000. 364p. Princeton
Studies in Culture/Power/History ISBN:0-691-00931-7, ISBN13:
978-0-691-00931-5. Dewey:996.9. LCCN:99-030345.

Audience: **l,u.**

Osorio, Jonathan K. K. DU624.6.O86 2002
Dismembering Lahui: A History of the Hawaiian Nation to 1887. Trade Cloth. University of Hawaii Press. Honolulu, HI. 2002. 320p. ISBN:0-8248-2432-6, ISBN13: 978-0-8248-2432-7. Dewey:996.9/02. LCCN:2001-058302.
Audience: **l,u.** *Choice, 2003.*

Silva, Noenoe K. DU625.S49 2004
Aloha Betrayed: Native Hawaiian Resistance to American Colonialism. Trade Cloth. Duke University Press. Durham, NC. 2004. 248p. American Encounters/Global Interactions Ser. ISBN:0-8223-3350-3, ISBN13: 978-0-8223-3350-0. Dewey:996.9/02. LCCN:2004-003304.
Audience: **l,u.**

Spickard, Paul (Editor), E184.P25.P34 2002
  et al.
Pacific Diaspora: Island Peoples in the United States and Across the Pacific. Joanne Rondilla & Debbie Hippolite Wright (Editors). Trade Cloth. University of Hawaii Press. Honolulu, HI. 2002. 392p. ISBN:0-8248-2562-4, ISBN13: 978-0-8248-2562-1. Dewey:304.8/0996. LCCN:2002-018080.
Audience: **l,u,f.**

Stannard, David E. GN875.H3S73 1989
Before the Horror: The Population of Hawai'i on the Eve of Western Contact. Trade Paper. University of Hawaii Press. Honolulu, HI. 1989. 168p. ISBN:0-8248-1232-8, ISBN13: 978-0-8248-1232-4. Dewey:304.6/09969. LCCN:88-032127.
Audience: **l,u.** *Choice, 1989.*

Sumida, Stephen H. PS283.H3S86 1991
And the View from the Shore: Literary Traditions of Hawaii. Cloth Text. University of Washington Press. Seattle, WA. 1991. 330p. Samuel and Althea Stroum Bks. ISBN:0-295-97078-2, ISBN13: 978-0-295-97078-3. Dewey:810.9/9969. LCCN:90-046127.
Audience: **g,l.**

Wilson, Rob DU18.W55 2000
Reimagining the American Pacific: From South Pacific to Bamboo Ridge. Trade Cloth. Duke University Press. Durham, NC. 2000. xix, 295p. New Americanists Ser. ISBN:0-8223-2500-4, ISBN13: 978-0-8223-2500-0. Dewey:909/.09823. LCCN:99-056924.
Audience: **u,f.** *Choice, 2001.*

Wood, Houston DU624.65.W66 1999
Displacing Natives: The Rhetorical Production of Hawaii. Book, Other. Rowman & Littlefield Publishers, Inc. Lanham, MD. 1999. 240p. Pacific Formations Ser., :Global Relations in Asian and Pacific Perspectives ISBN:0-8476-9140-3, ISBN13: 978-0-8476-9140-1. Dewey:996.9/007/2. LCCN:99-010343.
Audience: **l,u.**

Social Sciences > Ethnic Groups > Japanese Americans

Adler, Susan M. E184.J3A35 1998
Mothering, Education, and Ethnicity: The Transformation of Japanese American Culture. Cloth Text. Garland Publishing, Inc. New York, NY. 1998. 203p. Asian Americans Ser., :Reconceptualizing Culture, History and Politics ISBN:0-8153-3159-2, ISBN13: 978-0-8153-3159-9. Dewey:305.48/8956073. LCCN:98-008583.
Audience: **l,u,f.**

Azuma, Eiichiro F596.3.J3A98 2005
Between Two Empires: Race, History, and Transnationalism in Japanese America. Trade Cloth. Oxford University Press, Inc. New York, NY. 2005. 320p. ISBN:0-19-515940-3, ISBN13: 978-0-19-515940-0. Dewey:973/.04956. LCCN:2004-050145.
Audience: **l,u,f.** *Choice, 2006.*

Chin, Frank E184.J3S84 2002
Born in the U. S. A.: A Story of Japanese America: 1889-1947. Book, Other. Rowman & Littlefield Publishers, Inc. Lanham, MD. 2002. 432p. Pacific Formations Ser., :Global Relations in Asian and Pacific Perspectives ISBN:0-7425-1851-5, ISBN13: 978-0-7425-1851-3. Dewey:973/.04951. LCCN:2002-001878.
Audience: **l,u,f.** *Choice, 2003.*

Creef, Elena Tajima NX652.J37C74 2004
Imaging Japanese America: The Visual Construction of Citizenship, Nation, and the Body. Trade Cloth. New York University Press. New York, NY. 2004. 256p. ISBN:0-8147-1621-0, ISBN13: 978-0-8147-1621-2. Dewey:700/.4529956073. LCCN:2003-016328.
Audience: **l,u,f.**

Daniels, Roger E184.O6
Asian America: Chinese and Japanese in the United States Since 1850. Trade Cloth. University of Washington Press. Seattle, WA. 1990. 402p. ISBN:0-295-97018-9, ISBN13: 978-0-295-97018-9. Dewey:973/.0495. LCCN:88-005643.
Audience: **l,u,f.** *Choice, 1989.*

Fugita, Stephen S. & E184.J3
  O'Brien, David J.
Japanese American Ethnicity: The Persistence of Community. Paper Text. University of Washington Press. Seattle, WA. 1994. 218p. ISBN:0-295-97376-5, ISBN13: 978-0-295-97376-0. Dewey:305.895/6073. LCCN:90-256584.
Audience: **l,u,f.** *Choice, 1992.*

Fujino, Diane Carol E184.J3F8335 2005
Heartbeat of Struggle: The Revolutionary Life of Yuri Kochiyama. Trade Cloth. University of Minnesota Press. Minneapolis, MN. 2005. 432p. Critical American Studies ISBN:0-8166-4592-2, ISBN13: 978-0-8166-4592-3. Dewey:979.4/004956/0092 B. LCCN:2004-026943.
Audience: **g,l,u,f.**

Glenn, Evelyn N. HD6072.2.U52 C24
Issei, Nisei, War Bride: Three Generations of Japanese American Women in Domestic Service. Trade Paper. Temple University Press. Philadelphia, PA. 1988. 312p. ISBN:0-87722-564-8, ISBN13: 978-0-87722-564-5. Dewey:331.4/8164046/089956. LCCN:85-025107.
Audience: **l,u,f.**

Hirabayashi, Lane Ryo E29.J3N49 2002
  (Editor), et al.
New Worlds, New Lives: Globalization and People of Japanese Descent in the Americas and from Latin America in Japan. Akemi Kikumura-Yano & James A. Hirabayashi (Editors). Trade Cloth. Stanford University Press. Palo Alto, CA. 2003. 384p. Asian America Ser. ISBN:0-8047-4461-0, ISBN13: 978-0-8047-4461-4. Dewey:305.895/607. LCCN:2001-008166.
Audience: **l,u,f.**

Ichioka, Yuji E184.J3
The Issei: The World of the First-Generation Japanese Immigrants, 1885-1924. Trade Paper. Simon & Schuster. New

York, NY. 1990. 317p. ISBN:0-02-932435-1, ISBN13: 978-0-02-932435-6. Dewey:973/.04956. LCCN:88-003693.

Audience: **g,l,u.**

Kawakami, Barbara F.   **GT617.H3**
Japanese Immigrant Clothing in Hawaii, 1885-1941. Trade Paper. University of Hawaii Press. Honolulu, HI. 1993. 272p. ISBN:0-8248-1730-3, ISBN13: 978-0-8248-1730-5. Dewey:391/.0089/9560969. LCCN:92-042593.

Audience: **g,l.** *Choice, 1994.*

Kitano, Harry H.   **E184.J3K496 1993**
Generations and Identity: Japanese Americans. Trade Cloth. Pearson Custom Publishing. Boston, MA. 1993. 218p. ISBN:0-536-58370-6, ISBN13: 978-0-536-58370-3. Dewey:305.895/6073. LCCN:94-105226.

Audience: **g,l,u,f.**

Kitano, Harry H.   **E184.J3**
Japanese Americans: Evolution of a Subculture. Ed. 2. Trade Cloth. Prentice Hall PTR. Upper Saddle River, NJ. 1976. 224p. Ethnic Groups in American Life Ser. ISBN:0-13-509430-5, ISBN13: 978-0-13-509430-3. Dewey:301.45/19/56073.

Audience: **l,u.**

Kurashige, Lon   **F869.L89 J338 2002**
Japanese American Celebration and Conflict: A History of Ethnic Identity and Festival, 1934-1990. Trade Cloth. University of California Press. Berkeley, CA. 2002. 296p. American Crossroads Ser., Vol. 8 ISBN:0-520-22742-5, ISBN13: 978-0-520-22742-2. Dewey:979.4/94004956. LCCN:2001-006510.

Audience: **l,u,f.**

Matsumoto, Valerie J.   **F868.M55**
Farming the Home Place: A Japanese American Community in California, 1919-1982. Trade Paper. Cornell University Press. Ithaca, NY. 1993. 272p. ISBN:0-8014-8115-5, ISBN13: 978-0-8014-8115-4. Dewey:979.4/58. LCCN:92-056774.

Audience: **l,u,f.** *Choice, 1994.*

Mura, David   **E184.J3**
Where the Body Meets the Memory: An Odyssey of Race, Sexuality and Identity. Trade Paper. Doubleday Publishing. New York, NY. 1997. 288p. ISBN:0-385-47184-X, ISBN13: 978-0-385-47184-8. Dewey:305.895/6073.

Audience: **g,l,u,f.**

O'Brien, David J. &   **E184.J3O27 1991**
Fugita, Stephen S.
The Japanese American Experience. Trade Paper. Indiana University Press. Bloomington, IN. 1991. 188p. Minorities in Modern America Ser., MB-656 ISBN:0-253-20656-1, ISBN13: 978-0-253-20656-5. Dewey:973/.04956. LCCN:90-023961.

Audience: **g,l,u.** *Choice, 1992.*

Odo, Franklin S.   **D753.8**
No Sword to Bury: Japanese Americans in Hawaii During World War II. Trade Paper. Temple University Press. Philadelphia, PA. 2004. 344p. Asian American History and Culture Ser. ISBN:1-59213-270-7, ISBN13: 978-1-59213-270-6. Dewey:305.895/60969/09041.

Audience: **g,l,u,f.**

Okihiro, Gary Y.   **DU624.7.J3**
Cane Fires: The Anti-Japanese Movement in Hawaii, 1865-1945. Trade Paper. Temple University Press. Philadelphia, PA. 1992. 352p. Asian American History and Culture Ser.

ISBN:0-87722-945-7, ISBN13: 978-0-87722-945-2. Dewey:996.9/004956.

Audience: **l,u,f.** *Choice, 1991.*

Okihiro, Gary Y; Ito,   **D753.8.O38 1999**
Leslie A
Storied Lives: Japanese American Students and World War II. Leslie A. Ito (Contribution by). University of Washington Press. 1999. The Scott and Laurie Oki Series in Asian American Studies ISBN:0-295-97796-5, ISBN13: 978-0-295-97796-6.

Audience: **g,l,u,f.**

Roth, Joshua Hotaka   **DS832.7.B73R68 2002**
Brokered Homeland: Japanese Brazilian Migrants in Japan. Book, Other. Cornell University Press. Ithaca, NY. 2002. 192p. The Anthropology of Contemporary Issues Ser. ISBN:0-8014-4010-6, ISBN13: 978-0-8014-4010-6. Dewey:952/.004698. LCCN:2002-001539.

Audience: **l,u.**

Sakata, Yasuo   **Z1361.J2**
Fading Footsteps of the Issei: An Annotated Checklist of the Manuscript Holdings of the Japanese. Trade Paper. University of California, Los Angeles, Asian American Studies Center. Los Angeles, CA. 1992. 358p. ISBN:0-934052-20-4, ISBN13: 978-0-934052-20-7. Dewey:16.9173.

Audience: **l,u,f.**

Simpson, Caroline   **E184.J3S55 2001**
Chung
An Absent Presence: Japanese-Americans in Postwar American Culture, 1945-1960. Trade Cloth. Duke University Press. Durham, NC. 2001. 224p. New Americanists Ser. ISBN:0-8223-2756-2, ISBN13: 978-0-8223-2756-1. Dewey:305.895/6073. LCCN:2001-040213.

Audience: **l,u,f.**

Spickard, Paul R.   **E184.J3S7 1996**
Japanese Americans. Trade Cloth. Macmillan Publishing Company, Inc. Old Tappan, NJ. 1996. 223p. Twayne's Immigrant Heritage of America Ser. ISBN:0-8057-7841-1, ISBN13: 978-0-8057-7841-0. Dewey:973/.04956. LCCN:96-015111.

Audience: **g,l,u.** *Choice, 1997.*

Takahashi, Jere   **E184.J3**
Nisei/Sansei: Shifting Japanese American Identities and Politics. Paper Text. Temple University Press. Philadelphia, PA. 1998. 280p. Asian American History and Culture Ser. ISBN:1-56639-659-X, ISBN13: 978-1-56639-659-2. Dewey:305.895/6073.

Audience: **l,u,f.**

Tamura, Eileen H.   **DU624.7.J3.T36 1994**
Americanization, Acculturation, and Ethnic Identity: The Nisei Generation in Hawaii. Roger Daniels (Foreword by). Trade Cloth. University of Illinois Press. Champaign, IL. 1994. 360p. The Asian American Experience Ser. ISBN:0-252-02031-6, ISBN13: 978-0-252-02031-5. Dewey:996.9/004956. LCCN:93-018118.

Audience: **g,l,u.** *Choice, 1994.*

Tamura, Linda   **F882.H9**
The Hood River Issei: An Oral History of Japanese Settlers in Oregon's Hood River Valley. Roger Daniels (Foreword by). Trade Paper. University of Illinois Press. Champaign, IL. 1993. 384p. The Asian American Experience Ser.

ISBN:0-252-06359-7, ISBN13: 978-0-252-06359-6.
Dewey:979.5/61004956. LCCN:92-034546.
Audience: **l,u,f.** *Choice, 1994.*

Tomita, Mary Kimoto   **E184.J3T65 1995**
Dear Miye: Letters Home from Japan, 1939-1946. Robert G.
Lee (Editor). Trade Cloth. Stanford University Press. Palo Alto,
CA. 1995. 464p. Asian America Ser. ISBN:0-8047-2419-9,
ISBN13: 978-0-8047-2419-7. Dewey:940.5/3151/092.
LCCN:94-024110.
Audience: **l,u,f.** *Choice, 1996.*

Tsuda, Takeyuki   **DS832.7.B73T78 2003**
Strangers in the Ethnic Homeland: Japanese Brazilian Return
Migration in Transnational Perspective. Trade Cloth. Columbia
University Press. New York, NY. 2003. 432p.
ISBN:0-231-12838-X, ISBN13: 978-0-231-12838-4.
Dewey:305.8956081. LCCN:2002-067460.
Audience: **l,u,f.** *Choice, 2003.*

Van Sant, John E.   **E184.J3V3 2000**
Pacific Pioneers: Japanese Journeys to Hawaii and America,
1850-80. Trade Cloth. University of Illinois Press. Champaign,
IL. 2000. 208p. The Asian American Experience Ser.
ISBN:0-252-02560-1, ISBN13: 978-0-252-02560-0.
Dewey:304.8/73052/09034. LCCN:99-006829.
Audience: **l,u,f.** *Choice, 2000.*

Yamamoto, Traise   **PS153.J34Y36 1999**
Masking Selves, Making Subjects: Japanese American Women,
Identity, and the Body. Trade Paper. University of California
Press. Berkeley, CA. 1999. 320p. ISBN:0-520-21034-4, ISBN13:
978-0-520-21034-9. Dewey:810.9/9287/089956.
LCCN:98-014154.
Audience: **u,f.** *Choice, 1999.*

Yanagisako, Sylvia J.   **E184.J3**
Transforming the Past: Tradition and Kinship among Japanese
Americans. Trade Paper. Stanford University Press. Palo Alto,
CA. 1985. 312p. ISBN:0-8047-2017-7, ISBN13:
978-0-8047-2017-5. Dewey:306.8/089956073. LCCN:83-042541.
Audience: **l,u,f.** *Choice, 1986.*

Yoo, David K.   **F870.J3Y66 2000**
Growing up Nisei: Race, Generation and Culture among
Japanese Americans of California, 1924-49. Trade Paper.
University of Illinois Press. Champaign, IL. 1999. 264p. The
Asian American Experience Ser. ISBN:0-252-06822-X, ISBN13:
978-0-252-06822-5. Dewey:305.895/6073/0904.
LCCN:99-006263.
Audience: **l,u,f.** *Choice, 2000.*

Social Sciences > Ethnic Groups > Japanese Americans > Internment

Austin, Allan W.   **D769.8.A6A94 2004**
From Concentration Camp to Campus: Japanese American
Students and World War II. Trade Cloth. University of Illinois
Press. Champaign, IL. 2005. 256p. The Asian American
Experience Ser. ISBN:0-252-02933-X, ISBN13:
978-0-252-02933-2. Dewey:940.53/089/956073.
LCCN:2003-024507.
Audience: **l,u,f.** *Choice, 2005.*

Burton, Jeffrey F., et al.   **D769.8.A6C57 2001**
Confinement and Ethnicity: An Overview of World War II
Japanese American Relocation Sites. Mary M. Farrell, I.

F.lorence B. Lord & Richard W. Lord (Authors), Tetsuden
Kashima (Foreword by). Trade Cloth. University of Washington
Press. Seattle, WA. 2003. 472p. Scott and Laurie Oki Book Ser.
ISBN:0-295-98156-3, ISBN13: 978-0-295-98156-7.
Dewey:940.54/7273. LCCN:2001-033288.
Audience: **g,l,u,f.**

Chin, Frank   **E184.J3S84 2002**
Born in the U. S. A.: A Story of Japanese America: 1889-1947.
Book, Other. Rowman & Littlefield Publishers, Inc. Lanham,
MD. 2002. 432p. Pacific Formations Ser., :Global Relations in
Asian and Pacific Perspectives ISBN:0-7425-1851-5, ISBN13:
978-0-7425-1851-3. Dewey:973/.04951. LCCN:2002-001878.
Audience: **l,u,f.** *Choice, 2003.*

Daniels, Roger   **D769.8.A6**
Concentration Camps USA: Japanese Americans and World War
II. Trade Paper. Holt, Rinehart & Winston. Austin, TX. 1971.
xiv, 188p. ISBN:0-03-081869-9, ISBN13: 978-0-03-081869-1.
Dewey:940.547/2/73. LCCN:72-143320.
Audience: **l,u,f.**

Daniels, Roger   **D769.8.A6J364 1991**
Japanese Americans: From Relocation to Redress. Trade Paper.
University of Washington Press. Seattle, WA. 1992. 264p.
ISBN:0-295-97117-7, ISBN13: 978-0-295-97117-9.
Dewey:940.53/14. LCCN:91-002892.
Audience: **g,l,u,f.** *Choice, 1987.*

Fugita, Stephen &   **D769.8.A6F78 2003**
Fernandez, Marilyn
Altered Lives, Enduring Community: Japanese Americans
Remember Their World War II Incarceration. Trade Cloth.
University of Washington Press. Seattle, WA. 2004. 288p. The
Scott and Laurie Oki Series in Asian American Studies
ISBN:0-295-98380-9, ISBN13: 978-0-295-98380-6.
Dewey:940.53/17/089956073. LCCN:2003-065757.
Audience: **l,u,f.** *Choice, 2005.*

Gesensway, Deborah &   **D769.8.A6**
Roseman, Mindy
Beyond Words: Images from America's Concentration Camps.
Book, Other. Cornell University Press. Ithaca, NY. 1988. 192p.
ISBN:0-8014-9522-9, ISBN13: 978-0-8014-9522-9.
Dewey:940.54/72/73. LCCN:86-029088.
Audience: **g,l,u,f.** *Choice, 1987.*

Harth, Erica (Editor)   **D769.8.A6**
Last Witnesses: Reflections on the Wartime Internment of
Japanese Americans. Trade Paper. Palgrave Macmillan. New
York, NY. 2003. 320p. ISBN:1-4039-6230-8, ISBN13:
978-1-4039-6230-0. Dewey:940.54/7273.
Audience: **g,l,u.** *Choice, 2002.*

Hatamiya, Leslie T.   **D769.8.A6H38**
Righting a Wrong: Japanese Americans and the Passage of the
Civil Liberties Act of 1988. Trade Paper. Stanford University
Press. Palo Alto, CA. 1994. 283p. Asian America
ISBN:0-8047-2366-4, ISBN13: 978-0-8047-2366-4.
Dewey:940.53/1503956073. LCCN:92-040402.
Audience: **g,l,u,f.** *Choice, 1994.*

Hayashi, Brian Masaru   **D769.8.A6H39 2004**
Democratizing the Enemy: The Japanese American Internment.
Trade Cloth. Princeton University Press. Princeton, NJ. 2004.
328p. ISBN:0-691-00945-7, ISBN13: 978-0-691-00945-2.
Dewey:940.53/089/956073. LCCN:2003-057956.
Audience: **u,f.**

Houston, Jeanne   **D769.A6H68 2002**
  Wakatsuki & Houston, James D.
Farewell to Manzanar. Trade Cloth. Houghton Mifflin Company
Trade & Reference Division. Boston, MA. 2002. 208p.
ISBN:0-618-21620-0, ISBN13: 978-0-618-21620-8.
Dewey:940.54/72/7309794. LCCN:2002-727748.
Audience: **g,l,u,f.**

Ichioka, Yuji   **E184.J3I415 2006**
Before Internment: Essays in Prewar Japanese-American
History. Gordon H. Chang & Eiichiro Azuma (Editors). Trade
Cloth. Stanford University Press. Palo Alto, CA. 2006. 352p.
Asian America Ser. ISBN:0-8047-5147-1, ISBN13:
978-0-8047-5147-6. Dewey:973/.04956. LCCN:2005-032978.
Audience: **l,u.**

Inada, Lawson Fusao   **PS3559.N3.L43 1993**
Legends from Camp. Trade Paper. Coffee House Press.
Minneapolis, MN. 1993. 112p. ISBN:1-56689-004-7, ISBN13:
978-1-56689-004-5. Dewey:811/.54. LCCN:92-038871.
Audience: **g,l,u,f.** *Choice, 1993.*

Inada, Lawson Fusao   **D769.8.A6O55 2000**
  (Editor)
Only What We Could Carry: The Japanese American Internment
Experience. Trade Paper. Heyday Books. Berkeley, CA. 2001.
464p. ISBN:1-890771-30-9, ISBN13: 978-1-890771-30-0.
Dewey:940.53/089956073. LCCN:00-009182.
Audience: **g,l.**

Irons, Peter H.   **KF7224.5**
Justice at War: The Story of the Japanese-American Internment
Cases. Trade Paper. University of California Press. Berkeley,
CA. 1993. 432p. ISBN:0-520-08312-1, ISBN13:
978-0-520-08312-7. LCCN:92-037238.
Audience: **l,u,f.**

Irons, Peter H. (Editor)   **KF7224.5.J87 1989**
Justice Delayed: The Record of the Japanese American
Internment Cases. Trade Paper. Wesleyan University Press.
Middletown, CT. 1989. 458p. ISBN:0-8195-6175-4, ISBN13:
978-0-8195-6175-6. Dewey:342.73/083. LCCN:88-020880.
Audience: **g,l,u,f.** *Choice, 1990.*

James, Thomas   **D769.8.A6J345 1987**
Exile Within: The Schooling of Japanese Americans. Trade
Cloth. Harvard University Press. Cambridge, MA. 1987. 224p.
ISBN:0-674-27526-8, ISBN13: 978-0-674-27526-3.
Dewey:370/.89956/073. LCCN:86-025792.
Audience: **l,u,f.** *Choice, 1988.*

Kashima, Tetsuden   **D769.8.A6**
Judgment without Trial: Japanese American Imprisonment
during World War II. Trade Cloth. University of Washington
Press. Scattle, WA. 2004. 328p. The Scott and Laurie Oki Series
in Asian American Studies ISBN:0-295-98451-1, ISBN13:
978-0-295-98451-3. Dewey:940.53/17/089956073.
Audience: **g,l,u,f.**

Kashima, Tetsuden   **D769.8.A6U39 1997**
  (Editor)
Personal Justice Denied: Report of the Commission on Wartime
Relocation and Internment of Civilians. Trade Cloth. University
of Washington Press. Seattle, WA. 2003. 480p.
ISBN:0-295-97558-X, ISBN13: 978-0-295-97558-0.
Dewey:940.53/1503956073. LCCN:96-013689.
Audience: **g,l,u,f.**

Kessler, Lauren   **F885.J3**
Stubborn Twig: Three Generations in the Life of a Japanese
American Family. Trade Paper. Oregon Historical Society Press.
Portland, OR. 2005. 398p. ISBN:0-87595-296-8, ISBN13:
978-0-87595-296-3. Dewey:929/.2089956073.
LCCN:2005-024552.
Audience: **g,l,u,f.**

Maki, Mitchell T., et al.   **D769.8.A6M29 1999**
Achieving the Impossible Dream: How Japanese Americans
Obtained Redress. S. Megan Berthold & Harry M. Kitano
(Authors). Trade Cloth. University of Illinois Press. Champaign,
IL. 1999. 344p. The Asian American Experience Ser.
ISBN:0-252-02458-3, ISBN13: 978-0-252-02458-0.
Dewey:940.53/089/956073. LCCN:98-058016.
Audience: **g,l,u,f.** *Choice, 2000.*

Muller, Eric L.   **D810.C82M85 2001**
Free to Die for Their Country: The Story of the Japanese
American Draft Resisters in World War II. Trade Cloth.
University of Chicago Press. Chicago, IL. 2001. 250p. The
Chicago Series in Law and Society ISBN:0-226-54822-8,
ISBN13: 978-0-226-54822-7. Dewey:940.53/162.
LCCN:2001-027405.
Audience: **l,u,f.** *Choice, 2002.*

Murray, Alice Yang   **D769.8.A6W53 2000**
What Did the Internment of Japanese Americans Mean? Roger
Daniels (Contribution by). Trade Paper. Bedford/Saint Martin's.
New York, NY. 2000. 162p. Historians at Work Ser.
ISBN:0-312-20829-4, ISBN13: 978-0-312-20829-5.
Dewey:940.53/17/0973. LCCN:99-063689.
Audience: **g,l,u,f.**

Ng, Wendy L.   **D769**
Japanese American Internment During World War II: A History
and Reference Guide. Cloth Text. Greenwood Publishing Group,
Inc. Portsmouth, NH. 2001. 232p. ISBN:0-313-31375-X,
ISBN13: 978-0-313-31375-2. Dewey:940.53/17/0973.
LCCN:00-069128.
Audience: **l,u.** *Choice, 2002.*

Obata, Chiura   **N6537.O22A2 2000**
Topaz Moon: Chiura Obata's Art of the Internment. Kimi
Kodani Hill (Editor), Rutha Asawa (Foreword by), Timothy
Anglin Burgard (Introduction by). Trade Paper. Heyday Books.
Berkeley, CA. 2000. 168p. ISBN:1-890771-26-0, ISBN13:
978-1-890771-26-3. Dewey:760/.092 B. LCCN:99-089212.
Audience: **g,l,u.**

Okihiro, Gary Y.   **D769.8.A6O36 1996**
Whispered Silences: Japanese Americans and World War II.
Trade Paper. University of Washington Press. Seattle, WA. 1996.
256p. Samuel and Althea Stroum Bks. ISBN:0-295-97498-2,
ISBN13: 978-0-295-97498-9. Dewey:940.53/1503956073.
LCCN:95-021895.
Audience: **g,l,u,f.** *Choice, 1996.*

Robinson, Greg   **D769.8.A6R63 2001**
By Order of the President: FDR and the Internment of Japanese
Americans. Trade Cloth. Harvard University Press. Cambridge,
MA. 2001. 336p. ISBN:0-674-00639-9, ISBN13:
978-0-674-00639-3. Dewey:940.53/089956073.
LCCN:2001-024609.
Audience: **g,l,u,f.** *Choice, 2002.*

Shimabukuro, Robert   **D819.U6S45 2001**
  Sadamu
Born in Seattle: The Campaign for Japanese American Redress.

Trade Paper. University of Washington Press. Seattle, WA. 2001. 184p. The Scott and Laurie Oki Series in Asian American Studies ISBN:0-295-98142-3, ISBN13: 978-0-295-98142-0. Dewey:940.53/1422. LCCN:2001-027170.

Audience: **g,l,u,f.** *Choice, 2002.*

Takezawa, Yasuko I.   **F899.S49J38 1995**
Breaking the Silence: The Redress Movement in Seattle. Trade Paper. Cornell University Press. Ithaca, NY. 1995. 248p. The Anthropology of Contemporary Issues Ser. ISBN:0-8014-8181-3, ISBN13: 978-0-8014-8181-9. Dewey:305.895/60797772. LCCN:94-029600.

Audience: **g,l,u,f.** *Choice, 1995.*

Taylor, Sandra C.   **D769.8.A6T39 1993**
[e] Jewel of the Desert: Japanese American Internment at Topaz. E-Book. NetLibrary, Inc. Boulder, CO. 1993. ISBN:0-585-07933-1, ISBN13: 978-0-585-07933-2. Dewey:979.461004956.

Audience: **g,l,u,f.** *Choice, 1994.*

Uchida, Yoshiko   **D769.8.A6**
Desert Exile: The Uprooting of a Japanese-American Family. Trade Cloth. University of Washington Press. Seattle, WA. 2003. 160p. ISBN:0-295-96190-2, ISBN13: 978-0-295-96190-3. Dewey:940.5472. LCCN:81-016187.

Audience: **g,l,u,f.**

Social Sciences > Ethnic Groups > Korean Americans

Ablemann, Nancy &   **F869.L89**
Lie, John
Blue Dreams: Korean Americans and the Los Angeles Riots. Trade Paper. Harvard University Press. Cambridge, MA. 1997. 288p. ISBN:0-674-07705-9, ISBN13: 978-0-674-07705-8. Dewey:979.4/94004957. LCCN:94-023034.

Audience: **l,u,f.** *Choice, 1995.*

Danico, Mary Yu   **DU624.7.K67D36 2004**
The 1. 5 Generation: Becoming Korean American in Hawai'i. University of California Staff (Contribution by). Trade Paper. University of Hawaii Press. Honolulu, HI. 2004. 208p. Intersections: Asian and Pacific Transcultural Studies ISBN:0-8248-2695-7, ISBN13: 978-0-8248-2695-6. Dewey:305.895/70969. LCCN:2003-055275.

Audience: **l,u,f.** *Choice, 2004.*

Foster, Jenny Ryun   **PN771**
(Editor), et al.
Century of the Tiger: One Hundred Years of Korean Culture in America. Heinz Insu Fenkl & Frank Stewart (Editors). Trade Cloth. University of Hawaii Press. Honolulu, HI. 2003. 256p. Manoa Ser., 14:2:A Pacific Journal of International Writing ISBN:0-8248-2644-2, ISBN13: 978-0-8248-2644-4. Dewey:973.04957.

Audience: **g,l.**

Gooding-Williams,   **F869.L89A26 1993**
Robert (Editor)
Reading Rodney King - Reading Urban Uprising. Paper over Boards. Routledge. New York, NY. 1993. 256p. ISBN:0-415-90734-9, ISBN13: 978-0-415-90734-7. Dewey:305.896073079494. LCCN:92-043381.

Audience: **l,u,f.** *Choice, 1993.*

Joyce, Patrick D.   **E185.615.J695 2003**
No Fire Next Time: Black-Korean Conflicts and the Future of America's Cities. Book, Other. Cornell University Press. Ithaca, NY. 2003. 240p. ISBN:0-8014-3941-8, ISBN13: 978-0-8014-3941-4. Dewey:305.895/7073/091732. LCCN:2003-002345.

Audience: **l,u,f.** *Choice, 2004.*

Jung Ha Kim   **BR563.K67K52 1997**
Bridge-Makers and Cross-Bearers: Korean-American Women and the Church. Trade Cloth. Oxford University Press, Inc. New York, NY. 1996. 168p. AAR Academy Ser., No. 92 ISBN:0-7885-0165-8, ISBN13: 978-0-7885-0165-4. Dewey:306.6/73. LCCN:95-038598.

Audience: **l,u,f.**

Keller, Nora (Editor)   **PS508.K67**
Yobo: Korean American Writing in Hawai'i. Trade Paper. Bamboo Ridge Press. Honolulu, HI. 2003. 382p. ISBN:0-910043-65-5, ISBN13: 978-0-910043-65-6. Dewey:813.

Audience: **l,u,f.**

Kibria, Nazli   **E184.C5K45 2003**
Becoming Asian American: Second-Generation Chinese and Korean American Identities. Trade Paper. Johns Hopkins University Press. Baltimore, MD. 2003. 232p. ISBN:0-8018-7744-X, ISBN13: 978-0-8018-7744-5. Dewey:305.8951073. LCCN:2001-002795.

Audience: **l,u,f.** *Choice, 2003.*

Kim, Claire Jean   **F128.9.N4K56 2000**
Bitter Fruit: The Politics of Black-Korean Conflict in New York City. Cloth over Boards. Yale University Press. Cumberland, RI. 2000. 320p. The Renaissance in Europe Ser., :A Cultural Enquiry ISBN:0-300-07406-9, ISBN13: 978-0-300-07406-2. Dewey:323.1/1/957/07471. LCCN:00-035174.

Audience: **l,u,f.** *Choice, 2001.*

Kim, Elaine H. & Choi,   **HQ1765.5.D36 1998**
Chungmoo (Editors)
Dangerous Women: Gender and Korean Nationalism. Paper over Boards. Routledge. New York, NY. 1997. 250p. ISBN:0-415-91505-8, ISBN13: 978-0-415-91505-2. Dewey:305.420951. LCCN:96-049259.

Audience: **l,u,f.**

Kim, Elaine H. & Kang,   **PS508.K67**
Laura Hyun Yi (Editors)
Echoes upon Echoes: New Korean American Writings. Trade Cloth. Asian American Writers' Workshop. New York, NY. 2003. 288p. ISBN:1-889876-13-5, ISBN13: 978-1-889876-13-9. Dewey:810.8/08957073. LCCN:2002-113033.

Audience: **l,u,f.** *Choice, 2004.*

Kim, Elaine M. & Yu,   **E184.K6E27**
Eui-Young
East to America: Korean American Life Stories. Anna Deveare Smith (Foreword by). Trade Paper. DIANE Publishing Company. Collingdale, PA. 2004. 386p. ISBN:0-7567-9113-8, ISBN13: 978-0-7567-9113-1. Dewey:973/.04957.

Audience: **g,l,u,f.**

Kim, Kwang Chung   **E184.K6K6555 1999**
(Editor)
Koreans in the Hood: Conflict with African Americans. Trade Cloth. Johns Hopkins University Press. Baltimore, MD. 1999. 264p. ISBN:0-8018-6103-9, ISBN13: 978-0-8018-6103-1. Dewey:305.895/7073. LCCN:98-032012.

Audience: **l,u,f.** *Choice, 2000.*

Kim, Kwang Chung &   **BL2525.K67 2001**
Warner, R. Stephen
Korean Americans and Their Religions: Pilgrims and
Missionaries from a Different Shore. Ho Youn Kwon (Editor).
Trade Cloth. Pennsylvania State University Press. University
Park, PA. 2001. 307p. ISBN:0-271-02072-5, ISBN13:
978-0-271-02072-3. Dewey:200/.89/957073. LCCN:00-037452.

Audience: **l,u,f.** *Choice, 2001.*

Lee, Jennifer   **F128.9.A1L44 2002**
Civility in the City: Blacks, Jews, and Koreans in Urban
America. Trade Cloth. Harvard University Press. Cambridge,
MA. 2002. 288p. ISBN:0-674-00897-9, ISBN13:
978-0-674-00897-7. Dewey:305.8/0097471. LCCN:2002-024259.

Audience: **l,u,f.** *Choice, 2003.*

Lee, Mary P.   **E184.K6L445 1990**
Quiet Odyssey: A Pioneer Korean Woman in America. Sucheng
Chan (Introduction by). Trade Cloth. University of Washington
Press. Seattle, WA. 1990. 264p. Samuel and Althea Stroum Bks.
ISBN:0-295-96946-6, ISBN13: 978-0-295-96946-6.
Dewey:973.00495702 B. LCCN:89-028077.

Audience: **g,l,u,f.**

Lew, Jamie   **LC3501.K6L49 2006**
Asian Americans in Class: Charting the Achievement Gap
among Korean American Youth. Trade Cloth. Teachers College
Press, Teachers College, Columbia University. New York, NY.
2003. 144p. ISBN:0-8077-4694-0, ISBN13: 978-0-8077-4694-3.
Dewey:371.82995/7073. LCCN:2005-046747.

Audience: **l,f.**

Light, Ivan H. &   **HD2346.U52L64**
Bonacich, Edna
Immigrant Entrepreneurs: Koreans in Los Angeles, 1965-1982.
Trade Cloth. University of California Press. Berkeley, CA. 1991.
506p. ISBN:0-520-07656-7, ISBN13: 978-0-520-07656-3.
Dewey:338/.04/089957079493. LCCN:87-025541.

Audience: **l,u.** *Choice, 1989.*

Min, Pyong Gap   **F128.9.K6M56 1996**
Caught in the Middle: Korean Merchants in America's
Multiethnic Cities. Trade Paper. University of California Press.
Berkeley, CA. 1996. 274p. ISBN:0-520-20489-1, ISBN13:
978-0-520-20489-8. LCCN:95-047020.

Audience: **l,u,f.** *Choice, 1997.*

Min, Pyong Gap &   **F128.9.K6**
Foner, Nancy
Changes and Conflicts: Korean Immigrant Families in New
York. Trade Paper. Allyn & Bacon, Inc. Boston, MA. 1997.
133p. ISBN:0-205-27455-2, ISBN13: 978-0-205-27455-0.
Dewey:305.895/707471.

Audience: **g,l,u,f.**

Min, Pyong G. & Kim,   **BL2525.M56 2001**
Jung H. (Editors)
Religions in Asian America: Building Faith Communities. Trade
Cloth. AltaMira Press. Walnut Creek, CA. 2001. 224p. Critical
Perspectives on Asian Pacific Americans Ser.
ISBN:0-7591-0082-9, ISBN13: 978-0-7591-0082-4.
Dewey:200/.89/95073. LCCN:2001-022788.

Audience: **l,u,f.**

Min, Pyong G. & Kim,   **E184.O6S76 1999**
Rose
Struggle for Ethnic Identity: Narratives by Asian American
Professionals. Trade Cloth. AltaMira Press. Walnut Creek, CA.
1999. 240p. Critical Perspectives on Asian Pacific Americans

Ser., Vol. 4 ISBN:0-7619-9066-6, ISBN13: 978-0-7619-9066-6.
Dewey:305.8/95/073. LCCN:98-040171.

Audience: **l,u,f.**

Moon, Ailee & Song,   **E184**
Young I. (Editors)
Korean American Women: From Tradition to Modern Feminism.
Trade Cloth. Greenwood Publishing Group, Inc. Portsmouth,
NH. 1998. 312p. ISBN:0-275-95977-5, ISBN13:
978-0-275-95977-7. Dewey:305.42. LCCN:97-026184.

Audience: **l,u,f.**

Ong, Paul & Hee,   **F869.L89K68 1993**
Suzanne
Losses in the Los Angeles Civil Unrest, April 29-May 1, 1992:
Lists of the Damaged Properties and Korean Merchants and the
L. A. Riot - Rebellion. Trade Paper. University of California,
Los Angeles, Asia Institute. Los Angeles, CA. 1993. 138p.
ISBN:1-883191-00-9, ISBN13: 978-1-883191-00-9.
Dewey:929/.3/089957079494. LCCN:93-070183.

Audience: **l,u,f.**

Park, Kyeyoung   **HD2346.U52N547 1997**
The Korean American Dream: Immigrants and Small Business
in New York City. Book, Other. Cornell University Press. Ithaca,
NY. 1997. 224p. Anthropology of Contemporary Issues Ser.
ISBN:0-8014-3343-6, ISBN13: 978-0-8014-3343-6.
Dewey:338.6/422/0899570747. LCCN:97-003083.

Audience: **l,u,f.** *Choice, 1998.*

Park, Lisa Sun-Hee   **E184.K6P365 2005**
Consuming Citizenship: Children of Asian Immigrant
Entrepreneurs. Trade Cloth. Stanford University Press. Palo
Alto, CA. 2005. 184p. Asian America Ser. ISBN:0-8047-5247-8,
ISBN13: 978-0-8047-5247-3. Dewey:305.895/7073.
LCCN:2005-013560.

Audience: **l,u.**

Patterson, Wayne   **DU624.7.K67P36 2000**
The Ilse: First-Generation Korean Immigrants in Hawaii,
1903-1973. Trade Cloth. University of Hawaii Press. Honolulu,
HI. 2000. 288p. Hawai'i Studies on Korea ISBN:0-8248-2093-2,
ISBN13: 978-0-8248-2093-0. Dewey:996.9/00495.
LCCN:99-037153.

Audience: **l,u,f.** *Choice, 2000.*

Robinson, Katy   **E184.K6R63 2002**
A Single Square Picture: A Korean Adoptee's Search for Her
Roots. Trade Paper. Penguin Group (USA) Inc. New York, NY.
2002. 304p. ISBN:0-425-18496-X, ISBN13: 978-0-425-18496-7.
Dewey:973/.04957/0092. LCCN:2001-052922.

Audience: **g,l.**

Shin, Sarah J.   **P115.2.S5 2004**
Developing in Two Languages: Korean Children in America.
Trade Cloth. Multilingual Matters Ltd. Clevedon, 2004. 180p.
Child Language and Child Development Ser., Vol. 5
ISBN:1-85359-747-3, ISBN13: 978-1-85359-747-3.
Dewey:404/.2/08309073. LCCN:2004-002920.

Audience: **l,u,f.** *Choice, 2005.*

Suh, Sharon A.   **BQ6377.L672S84 2004**
Being Buddhist in a Christian World: Gender and Community in
a Korean American Temple. Trade Cloth. University of
Washington Press. Seattle, WA. 2004. 256p. American Ethnic
and Cultural Studies ISBN:0-295-98378-7, ISBN13:
978-0-295-98378-3. Dewey:294.3/089/95709494.
LCCN:2003-065751.

Audience: **l,u,f.** *Choice, 2005.*

Takaki, Ronald T.   **E184.K6T33 1994**
From the Land of Morning Calm: The Koreans in America.
Library Binding. Chelsea House Publishers. Langhorne, PA.
1994. 120p. The Asian American Experience Ser.
ISBN:0-7910-2181-5, ISBN13: 978-0-7910-2181-1.
Dewey:973/.04957. LCCN:93-043713.
                                        Audience: **g,l.**

Trenka, Jane Jeong   **E184.K6T74 2003**
The Language of Blood: A Memoir. Trade Paper. Minnesota
Historical Society Press. Saint Paul, MN. 2003. 226p.
ISBN:0-87351-466-1, ISBN13: 978-0-87351-466-8.
Dewey:977.6/004957/0092 B. LCCN:2003-005135.
                                        Audience: **g,l.**

Yoon, In-Jin   **HD2346.U5Y66 1997**
On My Own: Korean Businesses and Race Relations in
America. Trade Cloth. University of Chicago Press. Chicago, IL.
1997. 276p. ISBN:0-226-95927-9, ISBN13: 978-0-226-95927-6.
Dewey:338.6/422/089957073. LCCN:96-039395.
                            Audience: **l,u,f.**   *Choice, 1998.*

Yu, Eui-Young (Editor)   **F869.L89N319 1994**
Black-Korean Encounter: Toward Understanding and Alliance.
Trade Paper. Regina Books. Claremont, CA. 1994. viii, 160p.
ISBN:0-941690-60-1, ISBN13: 978-0-941690-60-7.
Dewey:979.4/9400496073. LCCN:94-019786.
                                        Audience: **g,l,u,f.**

Yuh, Ji-Yeon   **E184.K6Y85 2002**
Beyond the Shadow of Camptown: Korean Military Brides in
America. Trade Cloth. New York University Press. New York,
NY. 2002. 302p. Nation of Newcomers Ser., :Immigrant History
as American History ISBN:0-8147-9698-2, ISBN13:
978-0-8147-9698-6. Dewey:305.48/8957073.
LCCN:2002-002674.
                            Audience: **l,u,f.**   *Choice, 2003.*

Social Sciences > Ethnic Groups > South Asian Americans

Abraham, Margaret   **HV6626.2.A27 2000**
Speaking the Unspeakable: Marital Violence among South Asian
Immigrants in the United States. Trade Cloth. Rutgers
University Press. Piscataway, NJ. 2004. 256p.
ISBN:0-8135-2793-7, ISBN13: 978-0-8135-2793-2.
Dewey:362.84/914073. LCCN:99-045632.
                            Audience: **u,f.**   *Choice, 2000.*

Bahri, Deepika &   **E184.S69B48 1996**
  Vasudeva, Mary (Editors)
Between the Lines: South Asians and Postcoloniality. Library
Binding. Temple University Press. Philadelphia, PA. 1996. 400p.
Asian American History and Culture Ser. ISBN:1-56639-467-8,
ISBN13: 978-1-56639-467-3. Dewey:973/.04914.
LCCN:95-052972.
                                        Audience: **u,f.**

Bates, Crispin   **DS339.4.S66 2001**
🄴 Community, Empire and Migration: South Asians in
Diaspora. E-Book. Palgrave Macmillan. New York, NY.
ISBN:0-333-97729-7, ISBN13: 978-0-333-97729-3.
Dewey:305.8914.
                                        Audience: **l,u.**

Coward, Harold   **BL1055.S68 2000**
  (Editor), et al.
The South Asian Religious Diaspora in Britain, Canada, and the
United States. John R. Hinnells & Raymond Brady Williams
(Editors). Cloth Text. State University of New York Press.
Albany, NY. 2000. viii, 301p. SUNY Series in Religious Studies
ISBN:0-7914-4509-7, ISBN13: 978-0-7914-4509-9.
Dewey:200/.89/914. LCCN:99-039476.
                            Audience: **l,u,f.**   *Choice, 2000.*

DasGupta, Shamita D.   **E184.S69P38 1998**
  (Editor)
A Patchwork Shawl: Chronicles of South Asian Women in
America. Cloth Text. Rutgers University Press. Piscataway, NJ.
1998. 256p. ISBN:0-8135-2517-9, ISBN13: 978-0-8135-2517-4.
Dewey:305.48/8914073. LCCN:97-049650.
                            Audience: **g,l,u,f.**   *Choice, 1999.*

Fenton, John Y.   **BL1055**
South Asian Religions in the Americas: An Annotated
Bibliography of Immigrant Religious Traditions. Cloth Text.
Greenwood Publishing Group, Inc. Portsmouth, NH. 1995. 256p.
Bibliographies and Indexes in Religious Studies, Vol. 34
ISBN:0-313-27835-0, ISBN13: 978-0-313-27835-8.
Dewey:016.294/097. LCCN:94-039769.
                            Audience: **l,u,f.**   *Choice, 1995.*

Leonard, Karen I.   **F870.P36L46 1992**
Making Ethnic Choices: California's Punjabi Mexican
Americans. Trade Cloth. Temple University Press. Philadelphia,
PA. 1992. 368p. Asian American History and Culture Ser.
ISBN:0-87722-890-6, ISBN13: 978-0-87722-890-5.
Dewey:305.891/420794. LCCN:91-024482.
                            Audience: **g,l,u.**   *Choice, 1993.*

Leonard, Karen I.   **E184**
The South Asian Americans. Cloth Text. Greenwood Publishing
Group, Inc. Portsmouth, NH. 1997. 208p. The New Americans
Ser. ISBN:0-313-29788-6, ISBN13: 978-0-313-29788-5.
Dewey:305.891/4073. LCCN:97-002219.
                                        Audience: **l.**

Maira, Sunaina   **F128.9.E2M35 2002**
Desis in the House: Indian American Youth Culture in New
York City. Trade Cloth. Temple University Press. Philadelphia,
PA. 2002. 256p. Asian American History and Culture Ser.
ISBN:1-56639-927-0, ISBN13: 978-1-56639-927-2.
Dewey:305.89140747. LCCN:2001-034071.
                            Audience: **l,u.**   *Choice, 2003, 2002.*

Maira, Sunaina &   **E184.S69C66 1996**
  Srikanth, Rajini (Editors)
Contours of the Heart: South Asians Map North America. Trade
Paper. Asian American Writers' Workshop. New York, NY.
1996. 480p. ISBN:1-889876-00-3, ISBN13: 978-1-889876-00-9.
Dewey:305.891/4073. LCCN:96-078960.
                            Audience: **l,u,f.**   *Choice, 1997.*

Prashad, Vijay   **E184.S69P73 2000**
  (Contribution by)
The Karma of Brown Folk. Trade Cloth. University of
Minnesota Press. Minneapolis, MN. 2000. xv, 253p.
ISBN:0-8166-3438-6, ISBN13: 978-0-8166-3438-5.
Dewey:305.891/4073. LCCN:99-047918.
                            Audience: **g,l,u,f.**

Rajan, Gita & Sharma,   **E184.S69N49 2006**
  Shailja
New Cosmopolitanisms: South Asians in the US. Trade Cloth.

Stanford University Press. Palo Alto, CA. 2006. 192p. Asian America Ser. ISBN:0-8047-5280-X, ISBN13: 978-0-8047-5280-0. Dewey:305.891/4073. LCCN:2005-027366.

Audience: **l,u.**

Shankar, Lavina   **E184.S69P37 1998**
  Dhingra & Srikanth, Rajini (Editors)
A Part, Yet Apart: South Asians in Asian America. Cloth Text. Temple University Press. Philadelphia, PA. 1998. 320p. Asian American History and Culture Ser. ISBN:1-56639-577-1, ISBN13: 978-1-56639-577-9. Dewey:973/.04914. LCCN:97-038354.

Audience: **l,u,f.**

Shankar, Lavina   **E184.S69P37 1998**
  Dhingra & Srikanth, Rajini (Editors)
A Part, Yet Apart: South Asians in Asian America. Paper Text. Temple University Press. Philadelphia, PA. 1998. 320p. Asian American History and Culture Ser. ISBN:1-56639-578-X, ISBN13: 978-1-56639-578-6. Dewey:973/.04914. LCCN:97-038354.

Audience: **l,u.**

Singh, Jane (Editor,   **E49.2.S68**
  Preface by)
South Asians in North America: An Annotated and Selected Bibliography. Emily Hodges (Editor), Kenneth R. Logan (Editor, Introduction by), Bruce La Brack, Mark Juergensmeyer & N. Gerald Barrier (Editors). Trade Paper. University of California, Berkeley, Centers for South & Southeast Asia Studies. Berkeley, CA. 1988. 200p. Occasional Papers, No. 14 ISBN:0-944613-03-9, ISBN13: 978-0-944613-03-0. Dewey:016.97/0004914. LCCN:87-073457.

Audience: **g,l.**

Srikanth, Rajini   **PS153.S68S73 2004**
The World Next Door: South Asian American Literature and the Idea of America. Trade Cloth. Temple University Press. Philadelphia, PA. 2005. 304p. Asian American History and Culture Ser. ISBN:1-59213-080-1, ISBN13: 978-1-59213-080-1. Dewey:810.98914. LCCN:2003-070260.

Audience: **l,u,f.**   *Choice, 2005.*

Williams, Raymond B.   **BR563.E27W55 1996**
Christian Pluralism in the United States: The Indian Immigrant Experience. Trade Cloth. Cambridge University Press. New York, NY. 1996. 315p. Cambridge Studies in Religious Traditions, No. 9 ISBN:0-521-57016-6, ISBN13: 978-0-521-57016-9. Dewey:277.3/082. LCCN:95-051450.

Audience: **l,u,f.**   *Choice, 1997.*

Women of South Asian   **PS153.A84O97 1993**
  Descent Collective Staff (Editor)
Our Feet Walk the Sky: Women of the South Asian Diaspora. Trade Paper. Aunt Lute Books. San Francisco, CA. 1998. 380p. ISBN:1-879960-32-X, ISBN13: 978-1-879960-32-9. Dewey:810.8/09287/08995. LCCN:93-036354.

Audience: **g,l,u,f.**

Social Sciences > Ethnic Groups > South Asian Americans > Indian Americans

Alexander, Meena   **E184.E2A44 1996**
The Shock of Arrival: Reflections on Postcolonial Experience. Trade Cloth. South End Press. Cambridge, MA. 1996. 224p.

Literature Ser. ISBN:0-89608-546-5, ISBN13: 978-0-89608-546-6. Dewey:973.04914. LCCN:96-015058.

Audience: **l,u,f.**

Bacon, Jean   **F548.9.E2B33 1996**
Life Lines: Community, Family, and Assimilation among Asian Indian Immigrants. Cloth Text. Oxford University Press, Inc. New York, NY. 1997. 320p. ISBN:0-19-509972-9, ISBN13: 978-0-19-509972-0. Dewey:305.8/94/073. LCCN:95-049367.

Audience: **l,u,f.**   *Choice, 1997.*

Kumar, Amitava   **E184.E2**
Passport Photos. Trade Paper. University of California Press. Berkeley, CA. 2000. 290p. ISBN:0-520-21817-5, ISBN13: 978-0-520-21817-8. Dewey:305.8914073. LCCN:99-031257.

Audience: **l,u,f.**   *Choice, 2000.*

Social Sciences > Ethnic Groups > Southeast Asian Americans

Hein, Jeremy   **HV640.5.I5H44 1995**
From Migrants to Ethnic Minorities: The Settlement of Refugees from Vietnam, Laos, and Cambodia in the United States. Trade Cloth. Thomson Gale. Farmington Hills, MI. 1995. 193p. Twayne's Immigrant Heritage of America Ser. ISBN:0-8057-8432-2, ISBN13: 978-0-8057-8432-9. Dewey:362.87/089/959. LCCN:94-041960.

Audience: **g,l,u,f.**   *Choice, 1995.*

Tenhula, John   **E184.I43T46 1990**
Voices from Southeast Asia: The Refugee Experience in the United States. Liv Ullmann (Foreword by). Trade Cloth. Holmes & Meier Publishers, Inc. Teaneck, NJ. 1991. 270p. Ellis Island Ser. ISBN:0-8419-1110-X, ISBN13: 978-0-8419-1110-9. Dewey:305.895/9073. LCCN:90-040696.

Audience: **g,l,u,f.**

Social Sciences > Ethnic Groups > Southeast Asian Americans > Cambodian Americans

Canniff, Julie G.   **E184.K45.C36 2001**
Cambodian Refugees' Pathways to Success: Developing a Bi-Cultural Identity. Library Binding. LFB Scholarly Publishing LLC. New York, NY. 2001. 336p. The New Americans, :Recent Immigration and American Society ISBN:1-931202-15-X, ISBN13: 978-1-931202-15-2. Dewey:305.895/93073. LCCN:2001-003676.

Audience: **l,u,f.**

Chan, Sucheng   **E184.K45C48 2004**
Survivors: Cambodian Refugees in the United States. Trade Paper. University of Illinois Press. Champaign, IL. 2004. 376p. Asian American Experience Ser. ISBN:0-252-07179-4, ISBN13: 978-0-252-07179-9. Dewey:305.895/93073. LCCN:2003-021628.

Audience: **l,u.**   *Choice, 2005.*

Chan, Sucheng (Editor,   **E184.K45**
  Introduction by)
Not Just Victims: Conversations with Cambodian Community Leaders in the United States. Audrey U. Kim (Interviewed By). Trade Cloth. University of Illinois Press. Champaign, IL. 2003. 336p. The Asian American Experience Ser.

ISBN:0-252-02799-X, ISBN13: 978-0-252-02799-4. Dewey:973/.049593. LCCN:2002-007574.

Audience: **g,l,u,f.**

Haines, David W.   **HV640.5.I5R42 1987**
(Editor)
Refugees As Immigrants: Cambodians, Laotians and Vietnamese in America. Book, Other. Rowman & Littlefield Publishers, Inc. Lanham, MD. 1988. 256p. ISBN:0-8476-7553-X, ISBN13: 978-0-8476-7553-1. Dewey:362.8/7/089959. LCCN:87-026637.

Audience: **l,u.** *Choice, 1989.*

Hein, Jeremy   **E184.K45H45 2006**
Ethnic Origins: The Adaptation of Cambodian and Hmong Refugees in Four American Cities. Russell Sage Foundation. 2006. ISBN:0-87154-336-2, ISBN13: 978-0-87154-336-3.

Audience: **l,u,f.**

Hopkins, MaryCarol   **E184**
Braving a New World: Cambodian (Khmer) Refugees in an American City. Trade Cloth. Greenwood Publishing Group, Inc. Portsmouth, NH. 1996. 192p. Contemporary Urban Studies ISBN:0-89789-392-1, ISBN13: 978-0-89789-392-3. Dewey:305.895/93073. LCCN:96-015353.

Audience: **g,l,f.** *Choice, 1997.*

Smith-Hefner, Nancy   **F73.9.K45S65 1999**
   Joan
Khmer American: Identity and Moral Education in a Diasporic Community. Trade Paper. University of California Press. Berkeley, CA. 1999. 258p. ISBN:0-520-21349-1, ISBN13: 978-0-520-21349-4. Dewey:305.89593074461. LCCN:97-051812.

Audience: **l,u.** *Choice, 1999.*

Ung, Loung   **DS554.83.P65**
First They Killed My Father: A Daughter of Cambodia Remembers. Trade Cloth. Mainstream Publishing. Snohomish, WA. 2001. 224p. ISBN:1-84018-415-9, ISBN13: 978-1-84018-415-0. Dewey:959.6/042/092.

Audience: **g,l.**

Ung, Loung   **E184.K45U54 2005**
Lucky Child: A Daughter of Cambodia Reunites with the Sister She Left Behind. Trade Cloth. HarperCollins Publishers. New York, NY. 2005. 388p. ISBN:0-06-073394-2, ISBN13: 978-0-06-073394-0. Dewey:973/.049593/0092. LCCN:2004-054346.

Audience: **g,l.**

Welaratna, Usha   **DS554.8.W45**
Beyond the Killing Fields: Voices of Nine Cambodian Survivors in America. Trade Paper. Stanford University Press. Palo Alto, CA. 1994. 309p. Asian America ISBN:0-8047-2372-9, ISBN13: 978-0-8047-2372-5. Dewey:959.604.

Audience: **l,u.** *Choice, 1994.*

Social Sciences > Ethnic Groups > Southeast Asian Americans > Hmong Americans

Chan, Sucheng (Editor)   **DS558.8.H56 1994**
Hmong Means Free: Life in Laos and America. Trade Cloth. Temple University Press. Philadelphia, PA. 1994. 288p. Asian American History and Culture Ser. ISBN:1-56639-162-8,

ISBN13: 978-1-56639-162-7. Dewey:959.404/092/2. LCCN:93-011650.

Audience: **l,u.** *Choice, 1995.*

Donnelly, Nancy D   **E184.H55**
Changing Lives of Refugee Hmong Women. University of Washington Press. 1997. ISBN:0-295-97621-7, ISBN13: 978-0-295-97621-1.

Audience: **l,u,f.**

Faderman, Lillian &   **E184.H55**
   Xiong, Ghia
I Begin My Life All Over: The Hmong and the American Immigrant Experience. Trade Paper. Beacon Press. Boston, MA. 1999. 288p. ISBN:0-8070-7235-4, ISBN13: 978-0-8070-7235-6. Dewey:305.895/942073.

Audience: **g,l,u,f.**

Fadiman, Anne   **RA418.5.T73**
The Spirit Catches You and You Fall Down: A Hmong Child, Her American Doctors, and the Collision of Two Cultures. Trade Paper. Farrar, Straus & Giroux. New York, NY. 1998. 352p. ISBN:0-374-52564-1, ISBN13: 978-0-374-52564-4. Dewey:306.461. LCCN:97-005175.

Audience: **g,l,u,f.**

Hein, Jeremy   **E184.K45H45 2006**
Ethnic Origins: The Adaptation of Cambodian and Hmong Refugees in Four American Cities. Russell Sage Foundation. 2006. ISBN:0-87154-336-2, ISBN13: 978-0-87154-336-3.

Audience: **l,u,f.**

Hopkins, MaryCarol   **E184**
Braving a New World: Cambodian (Khmer) Refugees in an American City. Trade Cloth. Greenwood Publishing Group, Inc. Portsmouth, NH. 1996. 192p. Contemporary Urban Studies ISBN:0-89789-392-1, ISBN13: 978-0-89789-392-3. Dewey:305.895/93073. LCCN:96-015353.

Audience: **g,l,f.** *Choice, 1997.*

Koltyk, Jo A. & Foner,   **F589.W4K65 1998**
   Nancy
New Pioneers in the Heartland: Hmong Life in Wisconsin. Trade Paper. Allyn & Bacon, Inc. Boston, MA. 1997. 146p. New Immigrants Ser. ISBN:0-205-27412-9, ISBN13: 978-0-205-27412-3. Dewey:977.5/29. LCCN:97-227948.

Audience: **l,u.**

Miyares, Ines   **E184.H55M59 1998**
The Hmong Refugees Experience in the United States: Crossing the River. Cloth Text. Garland Publishing, Inc. New York, NY. 1998. 152p. Asian Americans Ser., :Reconceptualizing Culture, History and Politics ISBN:0-8153-3279-3, ISBN13: 978-0-8153-3279-4. Dewey:305.895942073. LCCN:98-039541.

Audience: **l,u.**

Moua, Mai Neng   **PS508.H63B36 2002**
   (Editor)
Bamboo among the Oaks: Contemporary Writing by Hmong Americans. Trade Cloth. Minnesota Historical Society Press. Saint Paul, MN. 2002. 215p. ISBN:0-87351-436-X, ISBN13: 978-0-87351-436-1. Dewey:810.9/895942. LCCN:2002-004320.

Audience: **g,l,u,f.**

Social Sciences > Ethnic Groups > Southeast Asian Americans > Laotian Americans

Caplan, Nathan, et al.   **E184.I43.C37 1989**
The Boat People and Achievement in America: A Study of
Economic and Educational Success. John K. Whitmore &
Marcella Trautmann (Authors). Trade Cloth. University of
Michigan Press. Chicago, IL. 1989. 256p. ISBN:0-472-09397-5,
ISBN13: 978-0-472-09397-7. Dewey:306/.0899922.
LCCN:89-030371.
    Audience: **g,l,u,f.** *Choice, 1990.*

Haines, David W.   **HV640.5.I5R42 1987**
(Editor)
Refugees As Immigrants: Cambodians, Laotians and Vietnamese
in America. Book, Other. Rowman & Littlefield Publishers, Inc.
Lanham, MD. 1988. 256p. ISBN:0-8476-7553-X, ISBN13:
978-0-8476-7553-1. Dewey:362.8/7/089959. LCCN:87-026637.
    Audience: **l,u.** *Choice, 1989.*

MacDonald, Jeffery L.   **F884.P89L275 1997**
Transnational Aspects of Iu-Mien Refugee Identity. Cloth Text.
Garland Publishing, Inc. New York, NY. 1997. 352p. Asian
Americans Ser., :Reconceptualizing Culture, History and Politics
ISBN:0-8153-2994-6, ISBN13: 978-0-8153-2994-7.
Dewey:305.891/91079549. LCCN:97-038689.
    Audience: **l,u,f.**

Social Sciences > Ethnic Groups > Southeast Asian Americans > Vietnamese Americans

Bass, Thomas A.   **DS556.45.A43B38 1996**
Vietnamerica: The War Comes Home. Trade Cloth. Soho Press,
Inc. New York, NY. 1996. 278p. ISBN:1-56947-050-2, ISBN13:
978-1-56947-050-3. Dewey:959.7/00413. LCCN:95-049994.
    Audience: **l,u.** *Choice, 1996.*

Caplan, Nathan, et al.   **E184.I43.C37 1989**
The Boat People and Achievement in America: A Study of
Economic and Educational Success. John K. Whitmore &
Marcella Trautmann (Authors). Trade Cloth. University of
Michigan Press. Chicago, IL. 1989. 256p. ISBN:0-472-09397-5,
ISBN13: 978-0-472-09397-7. Dewey:306/.0899922.
LCCN:89-030371.
    Audience: **g,l,u,f.** *Choice, 1990.*

Chan, Sucheng (Editor)   **E184.V53V55 2006**
The Vietnamese American 1.5 Generation: Stories of War,
Revolution, Flight and New Beginnings. Trade Cloth. Temple
University Press. Philadelphia, PA. 2006. 344p. Asian American
History and Culture Ser. ISBN:1-59213-500-5, ISBN13:
978-1-59213-500-4. Dewey:973/.04959200922 B.
LCCN:2005-055985.
    Audience: **l,u.**

Christopher, Renny   **PS228.V5C47 1995**
The Vietnam War - the American War: Images and
Representations in Euro-American and Vietnamese Exile
Narratives. Cloth Text. University of Massachusetts Press.
Amherst, MA. 1996. 360p. ISBN:1-55849-008-6, ISBN13:
978-1-55849-008-6. Dewey:813/.5409358. LCCN:95-019687.
    Audience: **l,u,f.** *Choice, 1996.*

DeBonis, Steven   **DS556.45.A43D43 1995**
Children of the Enemy: Oral Histories of Vietnamese
Amerasians and Their Mothers. Trade Cloth. McFarland &
Company, Incorporated Publishers. Jefferson, NC. 1994. 309p.
ISBN:0-89950-975-4, ISBN13: 978-0-89950-975-4.
Dewey:959.7/00413. LCCN:94-28735.
    Audience: **l,u.** *Choice, 1995.*

Do, Hien Duc   **E184**
The Vietnamese Americans. Cloth Text. Greenwood Publishing
Group, Inc. Portsmouth, NH. 1999. 168p. The New Americans
Ser. ISBN:0-313-29780-0, ISBN13: 978-0-313-29780-9.
Dewey:973/.049592. LCCN:99-022706.
    Audience: **l.**

Freeman, James M.   **E184.V53F74 1989**
Hearts of Sorrow: Vietnamese-American Lives. Trade Cloth.
Stanford University Press. Palo Alto, CA. 1989. 446p.
ISBN:0-8047-1585-8, ISBN13: 978-0-8047-1585-0.
Dewey:973/.049592. LCCN:89-032115.
    Audience: **g,l,u,f.** *Choice, 1990.*

Haines, David W.   **HV640.5.I5R42 1987**
(Editor)
Refugees As Immigrants: Cambodians, Laotians and Vietnamese
in America. Book, Other. Rowman & Littlefield Publishers, Inc.
Lanham, MD. 1988. 256p. ISBN:0-8476-7553-X, ISBN13:
978-0-8476-7553-1. Dewey:362.8/7/089959. LCCN:87-026637.
    Audience: **l,u.** *Choice, 1989.*

Hayslip, Le Ly   **E184.V53**
Child of War, Woman of Peace. Trade Paper. Doubleday
Publishing. New York, NY. 1999. ISBN:0-385-50006-8,
ISBN13: 978-0-385-50006-7. Dewey:959.704/38.
    Audience: **g,l,u.**

Hayslip, Le Ly &   **DS556.93.H39A3 2003**
Wurts, Jay
When Heaven and Earth Changed Places: A Vietnamese
Woman's Journey from War to Peace. Trade Paper. Penguin
Group (USA) Inc. New York, NY. 1993. 400p.
ISBN:0-452-27168-1, ISBN13: 978-0-452-27168-5.
Dewey:959.704/38 B. LCCN:89-013711.
    Audience: **g.**

Kibria, Nazli   **E184.V53.K53 1993**
Family Tightrope: The Changing Lives of Vietnamese
Americans. Trade Cloth. Princeton University Press. Princeton,
NJ. 1993. 200p. ISBN:0-691-03260-2, ISBN13:
978-0-691-03260-3. Dewey:305.89592073. LCCN:93-018777.
    Audience: **l,u,f.** *Choice, 1994.*

Lam, Andrew   **E184.V53L36 2005**
Perfume Dreams: Reflections on the Vietnamese Diaspora.
Richard Rodriguez (Foreword by). Trade Paper, Perfect. Heyday
Books. Berkeley, CA. 2005. 143p. ISBN:1-59714-020-1,
ISBN13: 978-1-59714-020-1. Dewey:305.895/92073/092 B.
LCCN:2005-012942.
    Audience: **l,u.**

Long, Patrick D. &   **HV6439.U5**
Ricard, Laura
The Dream Shattered: Vietnamese Gangs in America. Paper
Text. Northeastern University Press. Boston, MA. 1995. 256p.
ISBN:1-55553-314-0, ISBN13: 978-1-55553-314-4.
Dewey:364.1/066/0899592073. LCCN:95-020446.
    Audience: **l,u.** *Choice, 1996.*

Formats: Web: ☐ Ebook: 🄴 CD/DVD-ROM: 🍢 BCL3: 𝓑

Nguyen, Kien　　　　　　　　**E184.V53N36 2001**
The Unwanted: A Memoir. Trade Cloth. Little Brown &
Company. New York, NY. 2001. 352p. ISBN:0-316-28664-8,
ISBN13: 978-0-316-28664-0. Dewey:973/.049592.
LCCN:00-057997.
　　　　　　　　　　　　　Audience: **g,l,u.**

Pham, Andrew X.　　　　　　　　**DS556.39**
Catfish and Mandala: A Two-Wheeled Voyage Through the
Landscape and Memory of Vietnam. Trade Paper. Picador. New
York, NY. 2000. 352p. ISBN:0-312-26717-7, ISBN13:
978-0-312-26717-9. Dewey:915.9704/44. LCCN:99-022711.
　　　　　　　　　　　　　Audience: **g,l,u,f.**

Phan, Aimee　　　　　　　　**PS3616.H36W4 2004**
We Should Never Meet: Stories. Cloth over Boards. St. Martin's
Press. Gordonville, VA. 2004. 256p. ISBN:0-312-32266-6,
ISBN13: 978-0-312-32266-3. Dewey:813/.6.
LCCN:2004-051295.
　　　　　　　　　　　　　Audience: **g,l.**

Reyes, Adelaida　　　　　　　　**ML3560.V5R49 1999**
Songs of the Caged, Songs of the Free: Music and the
Vietnamese Refugee Experience. Trade Cloth. Temple
University Press. Philadelphia, PA. 1999. 248p.
ISBN:1-56639-685-9, ISBN13: 978-1-56639-685-1.
Dewey:780/.89/9592073. LCCN:98-054778.
　　　　　　　　Audience: **l,u.**　*Choice, 1999.*

Tran, Barbara (Editor),　　　　　　　　**PS508.V54**
　et al.
Watermark: Vietnamese American Poetry and Prose. Monique
Truong & Luu T. Khoi (Editors). Cloth Text. Asian American
Writers' Workshop. New York, NY. 1998. 225p.
ISBN:1-889876-05-4, ISBN13: 978-1-889876-05-4.
Dewey:810.8/089592. LCCN:97-078154.
　　　　　　　Audience: **g,l,u,f.**　*Choice, 1998.*

Zhou, Min & Bankston,　　　　　　　　**E184.V53Z48 1998**
　Carl L. III
Growing up American: How Vietnamese Children Must Adapt
to Life in the United States. Trade Cloth. Russell Sage
Foundation. New York, NY. 1998. 296p. ISBN:0-87154-994-8,
ISBN13: 978-0-87154-994-5. Dewey:305.23/0973.
LCCN:97-036932.
　　　　　　　Audience: **u,f.**　*Choice, 1998.*

Science, Health, and Technology > Science

Lee, Wen Ho & Zia,　　　　　　　　**QC774.L44 A3**
　Helen
My Country Versus Me: The First Hand Account by the Los
Alamos Scientist Who Was. Trade Paper. Hyperion Press. New
York, NY. 2003. 352p. ISBN:0-7868-8687-0, ISBN13:
978-0-7868-8687-6. Dewey:327.1251073/092.
　　　　　　　　　　　　　Audience: **g,l,u,f.**

Science, Health, and Technology > Health

Choy, Catherine Ceniza　　　　　　　　**RT17.P6C48 2003**
Empire of Care: Nursing and Migration in Filipino American
History. Trade Cloth. Duke University Press. Durham, NC.
2003. 280p. American Encounters/Global Interactions Ser.

ISBN:0-8223-3052-0, ISBN13: 978-0-8223-3052-3.
Dewey:610.73/09599. LCCN:2002-012388.
　　　　　　　Audience: **l,u,f.**　*Choice, 2003.*

Comas-Diaz, Lillian &　　　　　　　　**RC451.4.M58W66 1994**
　Greene, Beverly (Editors)
Women of Color: Integrating Ethnic and Gender Identities in
Psychotherapy. Cloth over Boards. Guilford Publications, Inc.
New York, NY. 1994. 518p. ISBN:0-89862-371-5, ISBN13:
978-0-89862-371-0. Dewey:616.89/14/08693. LCCN:94-010840.
　　　　　　　Audience: **l,u,f.**　*Choice, 1995.*

Fadiman, Anne　　　　　　　　**RA418.5.T73**
The Spirit Catches You and You Fall Down: A Hmong Child,
Her American Doctors, and the Collision of Two Cultures. Trade
Paper. Farrar, Straus & Giroux. New York, NY. 1998. 352p.
ISBN:0-374-52564-1, ISBN13: 978-0-374-52564-4.
Dewey:306.461. LCCN:97-005175.
　　　　　　　　　　　　　Audience: **g,l,u,f.**

Shah, Nayan　　　　　　　　**RA448.5.C45S53 2001**
Contagious Divides: Epidemics and Race in San Francisco's
Chinatown. Trade Cloth. University of California Press.
Berkeley, CA. 2001. 400p. American Crossroads Ser., Vol. 7
ISBN:0-520-22628-3, ISBN13: 978-0-520-22628-9.
Dewey:614.4/9794. LCCN:2001-027615.
　　　　　　　　　　　　　Audience: **l,u,f.**

Zhan, Lin　　　　　　　　**E184.O6A8446 2002**
Asian Americans: Vulnerable Populations, Model Interventions,
Clarifying Agendas. Paper Text. Jones & Bartlett Publishers,
Inc. Sudbury, MA. 2002. 330p. Other Nursing Titles of Interest
Ser. ISBN:0-7637-2241-3, ISBN13: 978-0-7637-2241-8.
Dewey:305.895/073. LCCN:2002-028642.
　　　　　　　　　　　　　Audience: **l,u.**

Zhan, Lin & National　　　　　　　　**RA448.5.A83A86 1997**
　League for Nursing Staff
Asian Voices: Asian and Asian American Health Educators
Speak Out. Trade Cloth. National League for Nursing Press (N
L N Press). New York, NY. 1998. 227p. ISBN:0-88737-741-6,
ISBN13: 978-0-88737-741-9. Dewey:362.1/089/95073.
LCCN:97-034603.
　　　　　　　　　　　　　Audience: **l,u.**

Science, Health, and Technology > Technology

Ignacio, Emily　　　　　　　　**E184.F4I37 2005**
Building Diaspora: Filipino Community Formation on the
Internet. Trade Cloth. Rutgers University Press. Piscataway, NJ.
2005. 184p. ISBN:0-8135-3513-1, ISBN13: 978-0-8135-3513-5.
Dewey:305.89/921073/090511. LCCN:2004-011749.
　　　　　　　Audience: **l,u,f.**　*Choice, 2005.*

Lee, Rachel C. & Wong,　　　　　　　　**T173.8.A815 2003**
　Sau-Ling Cynthia (Editors)
Asian America.Net: Ethnicity, Nationalism and Cyberspace.
Paper over Boards. Routledge. New York, NY. 2003. 336p.
ISBN:0-415-96559-4, ISBN13: 978-0-415-96559-0.
Dewey:303.483. LCCN:2002-153218.
　　　　　　　　　　　　　Audience: **l,u,f.**

ASIAN HISTORY, LANGUAGES, AND LITERATURES

Since the publication of BCL3, Asia itself has completely transformed; college course offerings, academic fields of study, and, consequently, demands on college libraries have changed even more. There are many more Asia-related topics and titles which are deemed essential. In order to have up-to-date, selective, but wide coverage, we started from standard current bibliographies, journal reviews, and college course syllabuses, not from BCL3 (though most titles listed there remain valuable). Acquisition policy should take our lists as starting points, not fixed answers. Some items not necessary for general users are essential for upper level course offerings. Others are accessible to readers at any level but deal with specialized topics. Some classic works are retained not because they are still definitive, but because there is no replacement for them as entry points. Primary sources, reference works, and standard series are given preference; even though expensive, they are likely to be lastingly valuable. We have not listed many books on current events since they are evanescent and covered elsewhere. On the same rationale, we list only a few Internet resources unless they obviously replace books.

— Charles Hayford

Abu-Lughod, Janet L.   HC41.A28 1989
Before European Hegemony: The World System A.D.
1250-1350. Trade Cloth. Oxford University Press, Inc. New
York, NY. 1989. 464p. ISBN:0-19-505886-0, ISBN13:
978-0-19-505886-4. Dewey:330.94/017. LCCN:88-025580.
Audience: **g,u,f.** *Choice, 1990.*

Johnson, Chalmers   E840.J63 2000
Blowback: The Costs and Consequences of American Empire.
Cloth over Boards. Henry Holt & Company. New York, NY.
2000. 288p. ISBN:0-8050-6238-6, ISBN13: 978-0-8050-6238-0.
Dewey:327.73. LCCN:99-047713.
Audience: **g,f.** *Choice, 2000.*

Kristof, Nicholas D. &   DS5.K66 2000
WuDunn, Sheryl
Thunder from the East: Portrait of a Rising Asia. Trade Cloth.
Alfred A. Knopf Inc. New York, NY. 2000. 400p.
ISBN:0-375-40325-6, ISBN13: 978-0-375-40325-5.
Dewey:950.4/29. LCCN:00-023046.
Audience: **g,f.**

Lach, Donald F.   CB203 .L32
Asia in the Making of Europe: A Century of Wonder: The
Literary Arts. Trade Paper. University of Chicago Press.
Chicago, IL. 1994. 432p. Asia in the Making of Europe Ser.,
Vol. II ISBN:0-226-46733-3, ISBN13: 978-0-226-46733-7.
Dewey:940.
Audience: **g,u,f.**

Lach, Donald F.   CB203 .L32
Asia in the Making of Europe: The Century of Discovery, vol.
1. Trade Paper. University of Chicago Press. Chicago, IL. 1994.
520p. ISBN:0-226-46731-7, ISBN13: 978-0-226-46731-3.
Dewey:940.
Audience: **g,u,f.**

Lach, Donald F.   CB203
Asia in the Making of Europe: The Century of Discovery. Trade
Paper. University of Chicago Press. Chicago, IL. 1994. 504p.
Asia in the Making of Europe Ser., Vol. I ISBN:0-226-46732-5,
ISBN13: 978-0-226-46732-0. Dewey:940.095.
Audience: **g,u,f.**

Lach, Donald F.   CB203 .L32
A Century of Wonder: The Scholarly Disciplines, Vol. 2. Trade
Paper. University of Chicago Press. Chicago, IL. 1994. 440p.
Asia in the Making of Europe Ser., Vol. II ISBN:0-226-46734-1,
ISBN13: 978-0-226-46734-4. Dewey:940.
Audience: **g,u,f.**

Lach, Donald F. & Van   CB203 .L32
Kley, Edwin J.
Asia in the Making of Europe: A Century of Advance: East
Asia. Trade Paper. University of Chicago Press. Chicago, IL.
1998. 752p. ISBN:0-226-46769-4, ISBN13: 978-0-226-46769-6.
Dewey:940.
Audience: **g,u,f.**

Lach, Donald F. & Van   CB203 .L32
Kley, Edwin J.
Asia in the Making of Europe: A Century of Advance, South
Asia. Trade Paper. University of Chicago Press. Chicago, IL.
1998. 662p. ISBN:0-226-46767-8, ISBN13: 978-0-226-46767-2.
Dewey:940.
Audience: **g,u,f.**

Lach, Donald F. & Van   CB203 .L32
Kley, Edwin J.
A Century of Advance: Trade, Missions, Literature. Trade Paper.
University of Chicago Press. Chicago, IL. 1998. 666p. Asia in
the Making of Europe Ser., III ISBN:0-226-46765-1, ISBN13:
978-0-226-46765-8. Dewey:940.
Audience: **g,u,f.**

Lach, Donald F. & Van   CB203 .L32
Kley, Edwin J.
A Century of Advance: Southeast Asia. Trade Paper. University
of Chicago Press. Chicago, IL. 1998. 578p. Asia in the Making
of Europe Vol. III Ser., Vol. 3 ISBN:0-226-46768-6, ISBN13:
978-0-226-46768-9. Dewey:940.
Audience: **g,u,f.**

Levinson, David &   DS4.L48 2002
Christensen, Karen
Encyclopedia of Modern Asia, Set. Ed. 2. Trade Cloth. Thomson
Gale. Farmington Hills, MI. 2002. 3600p. ISBN:0-684-80617-7,
ISBN13: 978-0-684-80617-4. Dewey:950/.03.
LCCN:2002-008712.
Audience: **g,l,u,f.** *Choice, 2003.*

Pomeranz, Kenneth &   HF352.P58W67 2006
Topik, Steven
The World That Trade Created: Society, Culture, and the World
Economy 1400 to the Present. Ed. 2. Saddle Stitched, Cloth
over Boards. M. E. Sharpe Inc. Armonk, NY. 2005. 287p.
Sources and Studies in World History Ser. ISBN:0-7656-1708-0,
ISBN13: 978-0-7656-1708-8. Dewey:382/.09.
LCCN:2005-018044.
Audience: **l,u,f.**

Trocki, Carl A.   HV5840.A74T76 1999
Opium, empire, and the global political economy : a study of
the Asian opium trade, 1750-1950. Routledge. 1999. Asia's
Transformations ISBN:0-415-19918-2, ISBN13:
978-0-415-19918-6.
Audience: **g,f.**

South Asia, General

Ali, Daud (Editor)   DS340.I69
Invoking the Past: The Uses of History in South Asia. Trade
Paper. Oxford University Press, Inc. New York, NY. 2002. 412p.
SOAS Studies on South Asia ISBN:0-19-565912-0, ISBN13:
978-0-19-565912-2. Dewey:954.
Audience: **u,f.**

Allchin, Raymond   DS338 .A45 1995
The Archaeology of Early Historic South Asia: The Emergence
of Cities and States. Trade Paper. Cambridge University Press.
New York, NY. 1995. 389p. ISBN:0-521-37695-5, ISBN13:
978-0-521-37695-2. Dewey:934. LCCN:94-023181.
Audience: **u,f.** *Choice, 1996.*

Assayag, Jackie &   DS339.9.U6A89 2003
Binio, Vironique (Editors)
At Home in Diaspora: South Asian Scholars and the West. Trade
Cloth. Indiana University Press. Bloomington, IN. 2003. 224p.
ISBN:0-253-34332-1, ISBN13: 978-0-253-34332-1.
Dewey:305.891/401821. LCCN:2003-014792.
Audience: **u,f.**

Barua, Pradeep P.   DS340.B37 2005
The State at War in South Asia. Trade Cloth. University of
Nebraska Press. Lincoln, NE. 2005. 640p. Studies in War,

Society, and the Military Ser. ISBN:0-8032-1344-1, ISBN13: 978-0-8032-1344-9. Dewey:355.02/0954. LCCN:2004-021050.

Audience: **l,u,f.** *Choice, 2006.*

Bayly, C. A.   **DS463**
Origins of Nationality in South Asia: Patriotism and Ethical Government in the Making of Modern India. Trade Paper. Oxford University Press, Inc. New York, NY. 2001. 352p. ISBN:0-19-565841-8, ISBN13: 978-0-19-565841-5. Dewey:320.5/4/0954/09033.

Audience: **u,f.**

Chakrabarty, Dipesh   **DS435.C46 2002**
Habitations of Modernity: Essays in the Wake of Subaltern Studies. Trade Cloth. University of Chicago Press. Chicago, IL. 2002. 180p. ISBN:0-226-10038-3, ISBN13: 978-0-226-10038-8. Dewey:954/.007/2. LCCN:2002-019210.

Audience: **u,f.**

Chatterjee, Partha &   **HQ1742**
  Jeganathan, Pradeep (Editors)
Community, Gender and Violence: Subaltern Studies XI. Trade Cloth. Columbia University Press. New York, NY. 2001. 192p. ISBN:0-231-12314-0, ISBN13: 978-0-231-12314-3. Dewey:954.

Audience: **u,f.**

Clarke, Colin, et al.   **DS339.4.S68 1990**
South Asians Overseas: Migration and Ethnicity. Ceri Peach & Steven Vertovec (Authors). Trade Cloth. Cambridge University Press. New York, NY. 1990. 395p. Comparative Ethnic and Race Relations Ser. ISBN:0-521-37543-6, ISBN13: 978-0-521-37543-6. Dewey:305.8/914. LCCN:89-034308.

Audience: **u,f.** *Choice, 1991.*

Claus, Peter (Editor), et   **GR302.S68 2002**
al.
South Asian Folklore: An Encyclopedia. Sarah Diamond & Margaret Mills (Editors). Paper over Boards. Routledge. New York, NY. 2002. 736p. ISBN:0-415-93919-4, ISBN13: 978-0-415-93919-5. Dewey:398/.0954/03. LCCN:2002-023695.

Audience: **g,l,u,f.** *Choice, 2003.*

Cohn, Bernard S.   **DS436.C65 1996**
Colonialism and Its Forms of Knowledge: The British in India. Trade Paper. Princeton University Press. Princeton, NJ. 1996. 210p. Princeton Studies in Culture/Power/History ISBN:0-691-00043-3, ISBN13: 978-0-691-00043-5. Dewey:954. LCCN:96-006448.

Audience: **u,f.** *Choice, 1997.*

Dube, Saurabh   **GN17.3.I4**
Postcolonial Passages: Handbook of Contemporary History-Writing on India. Trade Cloth. Oxford University Press, Inc. New York, NY. 2004. 256p. ISBN:0-19-566508-2, ISBN13: 978-0-19-566508-6. Dewey:954/.04. LCCN:2004-329530.

Audience: **g,l,u.**

Guha, Ranajit (Editor)   **DS436**
Subaltern Studies: Writings on South Asian History and Society, Vol. 3. Trade Paper. Oxford University Press, Inc. New York, NY. 1994. 338p. India Readings Ser. ISBN:0-19-563529-9, ISBN13: 978-0-19-563529-4. Dewey:954.

Audience: **l,u,f.**

Guha, Ranajit (Editor)   **DS436**
Subaltern Studies: Writings on South Asian History and Society, Vol. 1. Trade Paper. Oxford University Press, Inc. New York,

NY. 1994. 252p. Oxford India Paperbacks Ser. ISBN:0-19-563443-8, ISBN13: 978-0-19-563443-3. Dewey:954.

Audience: **l,u,f.**

Guha, Ranajit (Editor)   **DS436**
Subaltern Studies: Writings on South Asian History and Society, Vol. 2. Trade Paper. Oxford University Press, Inc. New York, NY. 1994. 370p. Oxford India Paperbacks Ser. ISBN:0-19-563365-2, ISBN13: 978-0-19-563365-8. Dewey:954.

Audience: **l,u,f.**

Guha, Ranajit (Editor)   **DS436**
Subaltern Studies: Writings on South Asian History and Society, Vol. 4. Trade Paper. Oxford University Press, Inc. New York, NY. 1994. 394p. India Readings Ser. ISBN:0-19-563530-2, ISBN13: 978-0-19-563530-0. Dewey:954.

Audience: **l,u,f.**

Guha, Ranajit (Editor)   **DS436**
Subaltern Studies: Writings on South Asian History and Society, Vol. 5. Trade Paper. Oxford University Press, Inc. New York, NY. 1996. 306p. Oxford India Paperbacks Ser. ISBN:0-19-563535-3, ISBN13: 978-0-19-563535-5. Dewey:954.

Audience: **l,u,f.**

Guha, Ranajit (Editor)   **DS436**
Subaltern Studies: Writings on South Asian History and Society, Vol. 6. Trade Paper. Oxford University Press, Inc. New York, NY. 1996. 346p. India Readings Ser. ISBN:0-19-563536-1, ISBN13: 978-0-19-563536-2. Dewey:954.

Audience: **l,u,f.**

Guha, Ranajit (Editor)   **DS463.S426 1988**
Selected Subaltern Studies. Gayatri Chakravorty Spivak (Editor, Introduction by), Edward W. Said (Foreword by). Trade Paper. Oxford University Press, Inc. New York, NY. 1988. 448p. ISBN:0-19-505289-7, ISBN13: 978-0-19-505289-3. Dewey:954.03. LCCN:87-034875.

Audience: **u,f.**

Hasan, Mushirul &   **HV9475.I32S824**
  Asaduddin, M. (Editors)
Image and Representation: Stories of Muslim Lives in India. Trade Paper. Oxford University Press, Inc. New York, NY. 2002. 360p. ISBN:0-19-566261-X, ISBN13: 978-0-19-566261-0. Dewey:823/.01/08/352/2971.

Audience: **g,l,u,f.**

Lal, Vinay   **DS435.L35 2003**
The History of History: Politics and Scholarship in Modern India. Trade Cloth. Oxford University Press, Inc. New York, NY. 2003. 324p. ISBN:0-19-566465-5, ISBN13: 978-0-19-566465-2. Dewey:954. LCCN:2003-321543.

Audience: **u,f.** *Choice, 2004.*

Mukherjee, Tutun   **PK5437**
  (Editor)
Acts of Resistance: Plays by Women, in Translation. Trade Cloth. Oxford University Press, Inc. New York, NY. 2005. 564p. ISBN:0-19-567008-6, ISBN13: 978-0-19-567008-0. Dewey:891.4. LCCN:2005-318196.

Audience: **u,f.**

Nayar, Baldev Raj &   **DS448.N354 2002**
  Paul, T. V.
India in the World Order: Searching for Major-Power Status. Cloth Text. Cambridge University Press. New York, NY. 2002. 302p. Contemporary South Asia Ser., Vol. 9

ISBN:0-521-82125-8, ISBN13: 978-0-521-82125-4.
Dewey:327.54/009/045. LCCN:2002-031163.
Audience: **u,f.** *Choice, 2004.*

Pearson, M. N.   **HC51.P43 1988**
Before Colonialism: Theories on Asian-European Relations,
1500-1750. Oxford University Press. 1988.
ISBN:0-19-562078-X, ISBN13: 978-0-19-562078-8.
Audience: **u,f.**

Pfaff-Czarnecka,   **DS340.E85 1999**
Joanna, et al.
Ethnic Futures: The State and Identity Politics in Asia. Darini
Rajasingham-Senanayake, Edmund Terence Gomez, Ashis
Nandy & Sagnik Nandy (Authors). Trade Paper. SAGE
Publications, Inc. Thousand Oaks, CA. 2000. 212p.
ISBN:0-7619-9360-6, ISBN13: 978-0-7619-9360-5.
Dewey:323.154. LCCN:99-016908.
Audience: **l,u,f.**

Rao, Velcheru Narayana   **PK2978.E5P64 1998**
& Shulman, David (Editors)
A Poem at the Right Moment: Remembered Verses from
Premodern South India. Trade Cloth. University of California
Press. Berkeley, CA. 1998. 195p. Voices from Asia Ser.
ISBN:0-520-20847-1, ISBN13: 978-0-520-20847-6.
Dewey:891.4. LCCN:96-029616.
Audience: **g,l,u,f.**

Southworth, Franklin C.   **PK223.S67 2004**
Linguistic Archaeology of South Asia. Paper over Boards.
Routledge. New York, NY. 2005. 384p. ISBN:0-415-33323-7,
ISBN13: 978-0-415-33323-8. Dewey:491/.1.
LCCN:2004-009693.
Audience: **u,f.**

Tharu, Susie J. &   **PK2978.E5W57 1990**
Lalita, K. (Editors)
Women Writing in India: 600 BC to the Present, Vol. I. Trade
Paper. Feminist Press at The City University of New York. New
York, NY. 1991. 576p. Women Writing in India Ser., Vol. 1
ISBN:1-55861-027-8, ISBN13: 978-1-55861-027-9.
Dewey:891/.1. LCCN:90-003788.
Audience: **g,l,u,f.**

South Asia, General > Languages and Literatures, General

                                        PK2902.E53
Encyclopaedia of Indian Literature, Vol. 2. Trade Cloth.
National Sahitya Akademi. 1988. ISBN:0-8364-2423-9, ISBN13:
978-0-8364-2423-2. Dewey:891/.1.
Audience: **g,l,u,f.** *Choice, 1989.*

                                        PK2902
International Encyclopaedia of Indian Literature, Vol. 2: Tamil.
Trade Cloth. Mittal Publishers Distributors. 1987. 204p.
ISBN:81-7099-029-7, ISBN13: 978-81-7099-029-1.
Dewey:894.811.
Audience: **g,l,u,f.**

☐ Sahitya Akademi.
http://www.sahitya-akademi.org/sahitya-akademi/home.htm
Audience: **g,l,u,f.**

Chandrasekhar, Indira   **PK85.T84 2003**
(ed.)
Twenty Stories from South Asia. Katha. 2003.
ISBN:81-87649-71-2, ISBN13: 978-81-87649-71-7.
Audience: **g,l,u,f.**

Claus, Peter (Editor), et   **GR302.S68 2002**
al.
South Asian Folklore: An Encyclopedia. Sarah Diamond &
Margaret Mills (Editors). Paper over Boards. Routledge. New
York, NY. 2002. 736p. ISBN:0-415-93919-4, ISBN13:
978-0-415-93919-5. Dewey:398/.0954/03. LCCN:2002-023695.
Audience: **g,l,u,f.** *Choice, 2003.*

Colleran, Jeanne &   **PN2049.S66 1998**
Spencer, Jenny S. (Editors)
Staging Resistance: Essays on Political Theater. Trade Paper.
University of Michigan Press. Chicago, IL. 1998. 320p. Theater
Ser., :Theory - Text - Performance ISBN:0-472-06671-4,
ISBN13: 978-0-472-06671-1. Dewey:792. LCCN:98-008958.
Audience: **u,f.** *Choice, 1999.*

Dutt, K. C. (Kartik   **PK2908.W495 1999**
Chandra) (Editor)
Who's Who of Indian Writers, 1999: End-Century Edition. Vol.
1, (A-M). Sahitya Akademi. 1999. ISBN:81-260-0873-3,
ISBN13: 978-81-260-0873-5.
Audience: **g,l,u,f.**

Dutt, K. C. (Kartik   **PK2908.W495 1999**
Chandra) (Editor)
Who's Who of Indian Writers, 1999: End-Century Edition. Vol.
2, (N-Z). Sahitya Akademi. 1999. ISBN:81-260-0874-1,
ISBN13: 978-81-260-0874-2.
Audience: **g,l,u,f.**

Dutt, K.C. (ed.)   **PK2908.W495 1999**
Who's Who of Indian Writers, 1999. Sahitya Akademi. 1999.
ISBN:81-260-0873-3, ISBN13: 978-81-260-0873-5.
Audience: **g,l,u,f.**

Garg, Ganga R.   **PK2902**
(Editor)
International Encyclopaedia of Indian Literature: Urdu. Trade
Cloth. Mittal Publishers Distributors. 1991.
ISBN:81-7099-279-6, ISBN13: 978-81-7099-279-0.
Dewey:891.439.
Audience: **g,l,u,f.**

Garg, Ganga R.   **PK2902**
International Encyclopaedia of Indian Literature, Vol. V. Trade
Cloth. Mittal Publishers Distributors. 1988.
ISBN:0-317-93107-5, ISBN13: 978-0-317-93107-5.
Dewey:894.811.
Audience: **g,l,u,f.**

Garg, Ganga R.   **PK2902**
International Encyclopaedia of Indian Literature: Kannada.
Trade Cloth. Mittal Publishers Distributors. 1987.
ISBN:81-7099-038-6, ISBN13: 978-81-7099-038-3.
Dewey:894.811.
Audience: **g,l,u,f.**

Garg, Ganga R.   **PK2902**
International Encyclopaedia of Indian Literature: Sindhi. Trade
Cloth. Mittal Publishers Distributors. 1991.
ISBN:81-7099-322-9, ISBN13: 978-81-7099-322-3.
Dewey:891.41.
Audience: **g,l,u,f.**

Garg, Ganga R.   **PK2902**
International Encyclopaedia of Indian Literature: Oriya. Trade
Cloth. Mittal Publishers Distributors. 1995.
ISBN:81-7099-572-8, ISBN13: 978-81-7099-572-2.
Dewey:894.811.

Audience: **g,l,u,f.**

Garg, Ganga R.   **PK2902**
International Encyclopaedia of Indian Literature: Assamese.
Trade Cloth. Mittal Publishers Distributors. 1987. 129p.
ISBN:81-7099-027-0, ISBN13: 978-81-7099-027-7.
Dewey:894.811.

Audience: **g,l,u,f.** *Choice, 1989.*

Garg, Ganga R.   **PK2902**
International Encyclopaedia of Indian Literature, Vol. VI. Trade
Cloth. Mittal Publishers Distributors. 1988.
ISBN:81-7099-061-0, ISBN13: 978-81-7099-061-1.
Dewey:894.811.

Audience: **g,l,u,f.**

Hasan, Mushirul &   **HV9475.I32S824**
  Asaduddin, M. (Editors)
Image and Representation: Stories of Muslim Lives in India.
Trade Paper. Oxford University Press, Inc. New York, NY. 2002.
360p. ISBN:0-19-566261-X, ISBN13: 978-0-19-566261-0.
Dewey:823/.01/08/352/2971.

Audience: **g,l,u,f.**

Library of Congress
☐ The South Asian Literary Recordings Project.
http://www.loc.gov/acq/ovop/delhi/salrp/

Audience: **g,l,u,f.**

Mee, Erin (Editor)   **PK5437**
Drama Contemporary: India. Trade Paper. Theatre
Communications Group, Inc. New York, NY. 2005. 362p.
ISBN:1-55554-064-3, ISBN13: 978-1-55554-064-7.
Dewey:808.82/00954/09045.

Audience: **l,u,f.**

Mukherjee, Tutun   **PK5437**
  (Editor)
Acts of Resistance: Plays by Women, in Translation. Trade
Cloth. Oxford University Press, Inc. New York, NY. 2005. 564p.
ISBN:0-19-567008-6, ISBN13: 978-0-19-567008-0.
Dewey:891.4. LCCN:2005-318196.

Audience: **u,f.**

Rao, Velcheru Narayana   **PK2978.E5P64 1998**
  & Shulman, David (Editors)
A Poem at the Right Moment: Remembered Verses from
Premodern South India. Trade Cloth. University of California
Press. Berkeley, CA. 1998. 195p. Voices from Asia Ser.
ISBN:0-520-20847-1, ISBN13: 978-0-520-20847-6.
Dewey:891.4. LCCN:96-029616.

Audience: **g,l,u,f.**

Satchidanandan, K.   **PK2908.W495 1993**
  (Editor)
Who's Who of Indian Writers: Supplementary Volume, 1990.
Trade Cloth. Indian Publishers. Delhi, 1993.
ISBN:81-7201-514-3, ISBN13: 978-81-7201-514-5.
Dewey:891/.1. LCCN:93-911500.

Audience: **g,l,u,f.**

Selby, Martha Ann   **PK2978.E5S44 2000**
Grow Long, Blessed Night: Love Poems from Classical India.
Cloth Text. Oxford University Press, Inc. New York, NY. 2001.

288p. ISBN:0-19-512733-1, ISBN13: 978-0-19-512733-1.
Dewey:891/.2100803543. LCCN:00-020193.

Audience: **g,l,u,f.**

Southworth, Franklin C.   **PK223.S67 2004**
Linguistic Archaeology of South Asia. Paper over Boards.
Routledge. New York, NY. 2005. 384p. ISBN:0-415-33323-7,
ISBN13: 978-0-415-33323-8. Dewey:491/.1.
LCCN:2004-009693.

Audience: **u,f.**

Tharu, Susie J. &   **PK2978.E5W57**
  Lalita, K. (Editors)
Women Writing in India: The Twentieth Century. Trade Paper.
Feminist Press at The City University of New York. New York,
NY. 1993. 688p. ISBN:1-55861-029-4, ISBN13:
978-1-55861-029-3. Dewey:891/.1. LCCN:90-003788.

Audience: **g,l,u,f.** *Choice, 1993.*

Tharu, Susie J. &   **PK2978.E5W57 1990**
  Lalita, K. (Editors)
Women Writing in India: 600 BC to the Present, Vol. I. Trade
Paper. Feminist Press at The City University of New York. New
York, NY. 1991. 576p. Women Writing in India Ser., Vol. 1
ISBN:1-55861-027-8, ISBN13: 978-1-55861-027-9.
Dewey:891/.1. LCCN:90-003788.

Audience: **g,l,u,f.**

Bangladesh

Ansari, Sarah F. D.   **DS392.S58A57 1992**
Sufi Saints and State Power: The Pirs of Sind, 1843-1947. Trade
Cloth. Cambridge University Press. New York, NY. 1992. 198p.
Cambridge Asian Studies, No. 50 ISBN:0-521-40530-0,
ISBN13: 978-0-521-40530-0. Dewey:954.9. LCCN:91-016242.

Audience: **u,f.** *Choice, 1992.*

Sisson, Richard & Rose,   **DS395.5 .S59**
  Leo E.
War and Secession: Pakistan, India, and the Creation of
Bangladesh. Trade Paper. University of California Press.
Berkeley, CA. 1991. 350p. ISBN:0-520-07665-6, ISBN13:
978-0-520-07665-5. Dewey:954.9205. LCCN:89-032545.

Audience: **u,f.**

Umar, Badruddin   **DS395.B895 2004**
The Emergence of Bangladesh: Class and Political Struggles in
East Pakistan, 1947-1958. Trade Cloth. Oxford University Press,
Inc. New York, NY. 2004. 402p. ISBN:0-19-579571-7, ISBN13:
978-0-19-579571-4. Dewey:954.9204. LCCN:2003-344711.

Audience: **u,f.** *Choice, 2005.*

Zaman, Niaz (Editor)   **PK1716.5.E5**
The Escape and Other Stories of 1947. University Press. 2000.
ISBN:984-05-1561-6, ISBN13: 978-984-05-1561-5.

Audience: **g,u,f.**

Zaman, Niaz (Editor)   **PK1717.B32**
Under the Krishnachura: Fifty Years of Bangladeshi Writing.
University Press. 2003. ISBN:984-05-1663-9, ISBN13:
978-984-05-1663-6.

Audience: **g,l,u,f.**

India > Social Life. Customs. Caste

Bandyopadhyay, Sekhar   **DS422.C3B3428 2004**
Caste, Culture and Hegemony: Social Dominance in Colonial
Bengal. Trade Cloth. SAGE Publications, Inc. Thousand Oaks,
CA. 2004. 256p. ISBN:0-7619-9849-7, ISBN13:
978-0-7619-9849-5. Dewey:305.5/122. LCCN:2003-028044.
     Audience: **u,f.**

Bayly, Susan   **DS436 .N47 1999 PT.**
Caste, Society and Politics in India from the Eighteenth Century
to the Modern Age. C. A. Bayly, Gordon Johnson & John F.
Richards (Contribution by). Cloth Text. Cambridge University
Press. New York, NY. 1999. 440p. History of India Ser., Vol.
IV:3 ISBN:0-521-26434-0, ISBN13: 978-0-521-26434-1.
Dewey:305.5/122/0954. LCCN:98-038434.
     Audience: **u,f.** *Choice, 2000.*

Beteille, Andre   **DS422**
Caste, Class and Power: Changing Patterns of Stratification in a
Tanjore Village. Ed. 2. Trade Paper. Oxford University Press,
Inc. New York, NY. 2004. 312p. Oxford India Paperbacks Ser.
ISBN:0-19-565834-5, ISBN13: 978-0-19-565834-7.
Dewey:305.5/095482.
     Audience: **u,f.** B

Brass, Paul R.   **DS422.C64B73 2003**
The Production of Hindu-Muslim Violence in Contemporary
India. Trade Cloth. University of Washington Press. Seattle, WA.
2003. 448p. Jackson School Publications in International Studies
ISBN:0-295-98258-6, ISBN13: 978-0-295-98258-8.
Dewey:954/.2. LCCN:2002-027192.
     Audience: **u,f.**

Dirks, Nicholas B.   **DS422.C3D58 2001**
Castes of Mind: Colonialism and the Making of Modern India.
Trade Paper. Princeton University Press. Princeton, NJ. 2001.
388p. ISBN:0-691-08895-0, ISBN13: 978-0-691-08895-2.
Dewey:305.5/122/0954. LCCN:2001-021236.
     Audience: **u,f.** *Choice, 2002.*

Fuller, C. J. (Editor)   **DS422.C3C3861996**
Caste Today. Trade Cloth. Oxford University Press, Inc. New
York, NY. 1996. 308p. SOAS Studies on South Asia
ISBN:0-19-563795-X, ISBN13: 978-0-19-563795-3.
Dewey:305.5/122/0954. LCCN:96-900194.
     Audience: **g,l,u.**

Jaffrelot, Christophe   **DS422.C3J325 2002**
India's Silent Revolution: The Rise of the Lower Castes in
North Indian Politics. Trade Cloth. Columbia University Press.
New York, NY. 2003. 500p. CERI Series in Comparative
Politics and International Studies ISBN:0-231-12786-3, ISBN13:
978-0-231-12786-8. Dewey:323.3/224. LCCN:2002-073707.
     Audience: **u,f.** *Choice, 2004.*

Kakar, Sudhir   **DS422.C64K35 1996**
The Colors of Violence: Cultural Identities, Religion, and
Conflict. Trade Cloth. University of Chicago Press. Chicago, IL.
1996. 232p. ISBN:0-226-42284-4, ISBN13: 978-0-226-42284-8.
Dewey:303.6/0954. LCCN:95-035971.
     Audience: **u,f.**

Ludden, David (Editor)   **DS422.C64C66 1996**
Contesting the Nation: Religion, Community, and the
Democracy in India. Book, Other. University of Pennsylvania

Press. Philadelphia, PA. 1996. 320p. ISBN:0-8122-3354-9,
ISBN13: 978-0-8122-3354-4. Dewey:320.954.
LCCN:95-052811.
     Audience: **u,f.**

Mendelsohn, Oliver &   **DS422.C3 M39 1998**
  Vicziany, Marika
The Untouchables: Subordination, Poverty and the State in
Modern India. Jan Breman, G. P. Hawthorn, Ayesha Jalal,
Patricia Jeffery, Atul Kohli & Dharma Kumar (Contribution by).
Cloth Text. Cambridge University Press. New York, NY. 1998.
307p. Contemporary South Asia Ser., No. 4
ISBN:0-521-55362-8, ISBN13: 978-0-521-55362-9.
Dewey:305.5/68. LCCN:97-027947.
     Audience: **u,f.** *Choice, 1999.*

O'Hanlon, Rosalind   **DS422.C3O35**
Caste, Conflict and Ideology: Mahatma Jotirao Phule and Low
Caste Protest in Nineteenth-Century Western India. Trade Paper.
Cambridge University Press. New York, NY. 2002. 340p.
Cambridge South Asian Studies ISBN:0-521-52308-7, ISBN13:
978-0-521-52308-0. Dewey:305.5/122/0954792.
     Audience: **u,f.**

Prashad, Vijay   **DS422.C3P728 2000**
Untouchable Freedom: A Social History of a Dalit Community.
Cloth Text. Oxford University Press, Inc. New York, NY. 2000.
196p. ISBN:0-19-565075-1, ISBN13: 978-0-19-565075-4.
Dewey:305.5/68. LCCN:99-952353.
     Audience: **u,f.** *Choice, 2001.*

Singh, K. S.   **GN635.I4**
People of India: National Series: The Scheduled Tribes. Paper
Text. Oxford University Press, Inc. New York, NY. 1998. 1278p.
ISBN:0-19-564253-8, ISBN13: 978-0-19-564253-7.
Dewey:307.7/72/0954.
     Audience: **g,l,u.**

Singh, K. S. (Editor)   **DS422.C3**
The Scheduled Castes. Trade Cloth. Oxford University Press,
Inc. New York, NY. 1994. 1400p. People of India Ser., Vol. II
ISBN:0-19-563254-0, ISBN13: 978-0-19-563254-5.
Dewey:305.51220954.
     Audience: **u,f.** *Choice, 1994.*

Valmiki, Omprakash &   **DS422.C3V275 2003**
  Mukherjee, Arun Prabha
Joothan: An Untouchable's Life. Trade Cloth. Columbia
University Press. New York, NY. 2003. 160p.
ISBN:0-231-12972-6, ISBN13: 978-0-231-12972-5.
Dewey:305.5/122/0954. LCCN:2002-041710.
     Audience: **l,u,f.**

Van Woerkens, Martine   **DS422.W6413 2002**
The Strangled Traveler: Colonial Imaginings and the Thugs of
India. Catherine Tihanyi (Translator). Trade Cloth. University of
Chicago Press. Chicago, IL. 2002. 375p. ISBN:0-226-85085-4,
ISBN13: 978-0-226-85085-6. Dewey:915.4.
LCCN:2002-007633.
     Audience: **u,f.**

Varshney, Ashutosh   **DS422.C64V37 2001**
Ethnic Conflict and Civic Life: Hindus and Muslims in India.
Cloth over Boards. Yale University Press. Cumberland, RI.
2002. 400p. ISBN:0-300-08530 3, ISBN13: 978-0-300-08530-3.
Dewey:954/.0088/2971. LCCN:2001-046526.
     Audience: **u,f.** *Choice, 2002.*

India > Civilization

Ali, Daud　　　　　　　　　　**DS425.A645 2004**
Courtly Culture and Political Life in Early Medieval India. C. A. Bayly, Rajnarayan Chandavarkar & Gordon Johnson (Contribution by). Trade Cloth. Cambridge University Press. New York, NY. 2004. 318p. Cambridge Studies in Indian History and Society, Vol. 10 ISBN:0-521-81627-0, ISBN13: 978-0-521-81627-4. Dewey:954.02/1. LCCN:2003-055901.

Audience: **u,f.**

Breckenridge, Carol A.　　　　　**DS423.C577 1995**
　(Editor)
Consuming Modernity: Public Culture in a South Asian World. Cloth Text. University of Minnesota Press. Minneapolis, MN. 1995. 224p. ISBN:0-8166-2305-8, ISBN13: 978-0-8166-2305-1. Dewey:306/.0954. LCCN:94-046772.

Audience: **u,f.**

Eaton, Richard M.　　　　　　　**DS427.I59 2003**
　(Editor)
India's Islamic Traditions: 711-1750. Trade Cloth. Oxford University Press, Inc. New York, NY. 2003. 448p. Oxford in India Readings Ser., :Themes in Indian History Ser. ISBN:0-19-565974-0, ISBN13: 978-0-19-565974-0. Dewey:954.02. LCCN:2003-306319.

Audience: **g,l,u.** *Choice, 2003.*

Gottlob, Michael　　　　　　　　　**DS339.8**
Historical Thinking in South Asia: A Handbook of Sources from Colonial Times to the Present. Trade Cloth. Oxford University Press, Inc. New York, NY. 2003. 334p. ISBN:0-19-566217-2, ISBN13: 978-0-19-566217-7. Dewey:954/.0072. LCCN:2003-321545.

Audience: **l,u.**

Kenoyer, Jonathan M.　　　　　**DS425.K43 1998**
Ancient Cities of the Indus Valley Civilization. Paper Text. Oxford University Press, Inc. New York, NY. 1998. 264p. ISBN:0-19-577940-1, ISBN13: 978-0-19-577940-0. Dewey:934. LCCN:98-930419.

Audience: **l,u,f.**

Lal, Vinay (Editor)　　　　　　**DS480.84.D572 2000**
Dissenting Knowledges, Open Futures: The Multiple Selves and Strange Destinations of Ashis Nandy. Trade Cloth. Oxford University Press, Inc. New York, NY. 2001. 366p. ISBN:0-19-565115-4, ISBN13: 978-0-19-565115-7. Dewey:306/.0954. LCCN:2001-270738.

Audience: **u,f.**

Mayo, Katherine　　　　　　　**DS428.M382 2000**
Mother India: Selections from the Controversial 1927 Text, Edited and with an Introduction by Mrinalini Sinha. Mrinalini Sinha (Editor). Trade Cloth. University of Michigan Press. Chicago, IL. 2000. 308p. ISBN:0-472-09715-6, ISBN13: 978-0-472-09715-9. Dewey:954.03. LCCN:99-058162.

Audience: **u,f.**

Nandy, Ashis　　　　　　　　　　**DS428.2**
Time Warps: Silent and Evasive Pasts in Indian Politics and Religion. Trade Cloth. Rutgers University Press. Piscataway, NJ. 2002. 240p. ISBN:0-8135-3118-7, ISBN13: 978-0-8135-3118-2. Dewey:322.10954.

Audience: **u,f.**

Pinney, Christopher　　　　　　　　**DS423**
Pleasure and the Nation: The History, Politics and Consumption of Popular Culture in India. Rachel Dwyer (Editor). Trade

Paper. Oxford University Press, Inc. New York, NY. 2003. 372p. SOAS Studies on South Asia Ser. ISBN:0-19-566332-2, ISBN13: 978-0-19-566332-7. Dewey:306/.0954.

Audience: **u,f.**

Procida, Mary A.　　　　　　　**DS428.P76 2002**
Married to the Empire: Gender, Politics and Imperialism in India, 1883-1947. Cloth over Boards. Manchester University Press. Manchester, 2002. 256p. Studies in Imperialism ISBN:0-7190-6073-7, ISBN13: 978-0-7190-6073-1. Dewey:954.03/5. LCCN:2001-057981.

Audience: **u,f.** *Choice, 2002.*

Renford, Raymond K.　　　　　　**DS428 .R37 1987**
The Non-Official British in India to 1920. Cloth Text. Oxford University Press, Inc. New York, NY. 1987. 490p. ISBN:0-19-561388-0, ISBN13: 978-0-19-561388-9. Dewey:954.03. LCCN:87-900003.

Audience: **u,f.**

Trautmann, Thomas R.　　　　　**DS425.T68 1997**
Aryans and British India. Trade Cloth. University of California Press. Berkeley, CA. 1997. 274p. ISBN:0-520-20546-4, ISBN13: 978-0-520-20546-8. Dewey:954.03/1. LCCN:96-034953.

Audience: **u,f.** *Choice, 1997.*

India > Languages and Literatures

Acokamittiran　　　　　　　　**PL4758.9.A28**
My Father's Friend and Other Stories. Sahitya Akademi. 2002. ISBN:81-260-1347-8, ISBN13: 978-81-260-1347-0.

Audience: **g,l,u,f.**

Acokamittiran　　　　　　　　**PL4758.9.A28**
Tannir. English / Water. Holmstrom, Lakshmi (Translator). Katha. 2001. ISBN:81-87649-13-5, ISBN13: 978-81-87649-13-7.

Audience: **g,l,u,f.**

Bachchan, Harivansh　　　　**PK2098.B22Z464 1998**
Rai
In the Afternoon of Time: An Autobiography. Rupert Snell (Translator). Trade Cloth. Penguin Group (USA) Inc. New York, NY. 1998. xi, 498p. ISBN:0-670-88158-9, ISBN13: 978-0-670-88158-1. Dewey:891.4316. LCCN:98-901300.

Audience: **l,u,f.**

Bandopadhyay,　　　　　　　　**PK1718.B298**
　Bibhutibhushan
The Mountain of the Moon. Santanu Sinha Chaudhuri (Translator). Trade Paper. Katha. New Delhi, 2002. 175p. Yuva Ser. ISBN:81-87649-30-5, ISBN13: 978-81-87649-30-4. Dewey:891.4. LCCN:2004-325860.

Audience: **u,f.**

Bandyopadhyaya,　　　　　　**PK1718.B298P313 1999**
　Bibhutibhushana
Pather Panchali: Song of the Road. HarperCollins Publishers. 2000. ISBN:81-7223-333-7, ISBN13: 978-81-7223-333-4.

Audience: **g,l,u,f.**

Bandyopadhyaya,　　　　　　　**PK1718.B298**
　Bibhutibhushana
Aparajito: the Unvanquished. HarperCollins. 1990. ISBN:81-7223-320-5, ISBN13: 978-81-7223-320-4.

Audience: **g,l,u,f.**

Bardhan, Kalpana   PK1716.O4 1990
  (Editor)
Of Women, Outcastes, Peasants, and Rebels: A Selection of
Bengali Short Stories. Trade Cloth. University of California
Press. Berkeley, CA. 1990. 344p. Voices from Asia Ser.
ISBN:0-520-06714-2, ISBN13: 978-0-520-06714-1.
Dewey:891/.4430108. LCCN:89-035749.

Audience: **g,u,f.**

Basir, Vaikkam   PL4718.9.B33
  Muhammad
Short Stories. Katha. 1996. ISBN:81-85586-51-9, ISBN13:
978-81-85586-51-9.

Audience: **g,l,u,f.**

Chatterji,   PK1718.C43A813 2005
  Bankimcandra
Anandamath, or the Sacred Brotherhood. Julius J. Lipner
(Translator). Trade Paper, Perfect. Oxford University Press, Inc.
New York, NY. 2005. 329p. ISBN:0-19-517858-0, ISBN13:
978-0-19-517858-6. Dewey:891.4/434. LCCN:2004-057598.

Audience: **u.**

Dehejia, Vidya   PL4758.9.A58T5313
Antal and Her Path of Love: Poems of a Woman Saint from
South India. Paper Text. State University of New York Press.
Albany, NY. 1990. 183p. SUNY Series in Hindu Studies
ISBN:0-7914-0396-3, ISBN13: 978-0-7914-0396-9.
Dewey:894/.81111. LCCN:89-048505.

Audience: **u,f.**

Dharwadker, Vinay   PK2095.K3
Kabir: the Weaver's Songs. Trade Paper, Perfect. Penguin Group
(USA) Inc. New York, NY. 2005. 304p. ISBN:0-14-302968-1,
ISBN13: 978-0-14-302968-7. Dewey:295. LCCN:2003-312656.

Audience: **g,l,u.**

Dyson, Ketaki Kushari   PK1718.B6
The Selected Poems of Buddhadeva Bose. Trade Cloth. Oxford
University Press, Inc. New York, NY. 2003. 292p.
ISBN:0-19-566335-7, ISBN13: 978-0-19-566335-8.
Dewey:891.441. LCCN:2003-331472.

Audience: **g,l,u,f.**

Faiz, Faiz Ahmad   PK2199.F255
Culture and Identity: Selected English Writings of Faiz Ahmad
Faiz. Oxford University Press. 2006.

Audience: **u,f.**

Faiz, Faiz Ahmed   PK2199.F255
The True Subject: Selected Poems of Faiz Ahmed Faiz.
Princeton Univeristy Press. 1987. ISBN:0-691-06704-X,
ISBN13: 978-0-691-06704-9.

Audience: **g,l,u,f.**

Faiz, Faiz Ahmed   PK2199.F255A23 1995
The Rebel's Silhouette: Selected Poems. Agha Shahid Ali
(Translator, Introduction by). Trade Paper. University of
Massachusetts Press. Amherst, MA. 1995. 128p.
ISBN:0-87023-975-9, ISBN13: 978-0-87023-975-5.
Dewey:891/.43917. LCCN:94-040502.

Audience: **l,u,f.**

Husain, Initzar &   PK2200.I57A6 1998
  Mcmon, Mohammad U.
The Seventh Door and Other Stories. Trade Cloth. Lynne
Rienner Publishers, Inc. Boulder, CO. 1998. 242p. Three

Continents Ser. ISBN:0-89410-821-2, ISBN13:
978-0-89410-821-1. Dewey:891/.43937. LCCN:95-049396.

Audience: **g,l,u,f.**

Hussain, Intizar   PK2211.E8
  (Editor)
Short Stories from Pakistan: Fifty Years of Pakistani Short
Stories. Farrukhi, Asif (Editor). Sahitya Akademi. 2004.
ISBN:81-260-1598-5, ISBN13: 978-81-260-1598-6.

Audience: **g,l,u,f.**

Hutt, Michael J.   PK2598.Z95E5 1990
Himalayan Voices: An Introduction to Modern Nepali Literature.
Trade Cloth. University of California Press. Berkeley, CA. 1991.
280p. Voices from Asia Ser., No. 2 ISBN:0-520-07046-1,
ISBN13: 978-0-520-07046-2. Dewey:891/.49. LCCN:90-011145.

Audience: **g,l,u.**

Kabir   PK2095.K3B4913 2002
The Bijak of Kabir. Linda Beth Hess (Translator, Notes by),
Shuk Deo Singh (Translator). Trade Paper. Oxford University
Press, Inc. New York, NY. 2002. 216p. ISBN:0-19-514876-2,
ISBN13: 978-0-19-514876-3. Dewey:891.4/312.
LCCN:2001-045168.

Audience: **u,f.** *B*

Kalidasa   PK3796.S4 J55 2001
The Recognition of Sakuntala: A Play in Seven Acts. W. J.
Johnson (Editor). Trade Paper. Oxford University Press, Inc.
New York, NY. 2001. 162p. Oxford World's Classics Ser.
ISBN:0-19-283911-X, ISBN13: 978-0-19-283911-4.
Dewey:891/.22. LCCN:2002-276601.

Audience: **u,f.**

Kalidasa   PK3796.K7S58 2005
Birth of Kumára. David Smith (Editor). Trade Cloth. New York
University Press. New York, NY. 2005. 360p. The Clay Sanskrit
Library ISBN:0-8147-4008-1, ISBN13: 978-0-8147-4008-8.
Dewey:891/.21. LCCN:2004-025441.

Audience: **u,f.**

Karnad, Girish   PL4659.K283
Three Plays: Naga-Mandala; Hayavadana; Tughlaq. Trade Paper.
Oxford University Press, Inc. New York, NY. 1996. 226p.
ISBN:0-19-563765-8, ISBN13: 978-0-19-563765-6.
Dewey:894/.81427.

Audience: **u,f.**

Kiernan, V.G.   PK2199.I65
Poems from Iqbal: Renderings in English Verse with
Comparative Urdu Text. Trade Cloth. Oxford University Press,
Inc. New York, NY. 2005. 306p. ISBN:0-19-579974-7, ISBN13:
978-0-19-579974-3. Dewey:891.4'3915. LCCN:2005-274165.

Audience: **u,f.**

Kumar, Shiv K.   PK2199.F255 A248 2001
The Best of Faiz. UBS Publishers. 2001. ISBN:81-7476-330-9,
ISBN13: 978-81-7476-330-3.

Audience: **u,f.**

Lorenzen, David N.   PK2040.2.L67 1996
Praises to a Formless God: Nirguni Texts from North India.
Cloth Text. State University of New York Press. Albany, NY.
1996. 303p. SUNY Series in Religious Studies
ISBN:0-7914-2805-2, ISBN13: 978-0-7914-2805-4.
Dewey:891/.4310080382. LCCN:95-020931.

Audience: **u,f.**

Macwan, Joseph **PK1858**
The Stepchild: Angaliyat. Rita Kothari (Translator). Trade Cloth. Oxford University Press, Inc. New York, NY. 2003. 272p. ISBN:0-19-566624-0, ISBN13: 978-0-19-566624-3. Dewey:891.4/7371. LCCN:2003-316076.

Audience: **g,l,u,f.**

Malik, Aditya **PK2708.2.M35 2004**
Nectar Gaze and Poison Breath: An Analysis and Translation of the Rajasthani Oral Narrative of Devnarayan. Trade Cloth. Oxford University Press, Inc. New York, NY. 2005. 576p. South Asia Research Ser. ISBN:0-19-515019-8, ISBN13: 978-0-19-515019-3. Dewey:398.2/0954/401. LCCN:2004-050140.

Audience: **u,f.**

Manjhan Shattari **PK2598.Z95**
  Rajgiri, Mir Sayyid
Madhumalati: An Indian Sufi Romance. Aditya Behl & Simon Weightman (Editors). Trade Paper. Oxford University Press, Inc. New York, NY. 2001. 336p. Oxford World's Classics Ser. ISBN:0-19-284037-1, ISBN13: 978-0-19-284037-0. Dewey:891.4/9.

Audience: **g,l,u,f.**

Manto, Sa'adat Hasan **PK2199**
Black Margins: Sa'adat Hasan Manto Stories. Katha. 2003. ISBN:81-87649-40-2, ISBN13: 978-81-87649-40-3.

Audience: **g,l,u,f.**

McDermott, Rachel Fell **PK1714.5.E5M33 2000**
Mother of My Heart, Daughter of My Dreams: Kali and Uma in the Devotional Poetry of Bengal. Trade Cloth. Oxford University Press, Inc. New York, NY. 2001. 456p. ISBN:0-19-513435-4, ISBN13: 978-0-19-513435-3. Dewey:891.4/41008. LCCN:99-089433.

Audience: **u,f.** *Choice, 2002.*

Miller, Barbara S. & **PK3794.J3.G53**
  Miller, Barbara Stoler (Translators)
Love Song of the Dark Lord: Jayadeva's Gitagovinda. John Stratton Hawley (Foreword by). Trade Paper. Columbia University Press. New York, NY. 1997. 254p. Translations from the Asian Classics ISBN:0-231-11097-9, ISBN13: 978-0-231-11097-6. Dewey:891.21. LCCN:76-013165.

Audience: **g,l,u,f.** *B*

Narayanaravu, Velceru **PL4780.65E**
Classical Telugu Poetry: An Anthology. David Dean Shulman (Editor, Translator). Trade Cloth. Oxford University Press, Inc. New York, NY. 2002. xii, 418p. ISBN:0-19-565300-9, ISBN13: 978-0-19-565300-7. Dewey:645. LCCN:2002-301097.

Audience: **l,u,f.**

Olivelle, Patrick **BL1124.54**
  (Editor)
Upanisads. Trade Paper. Oxford University Press, Inc. New York, NY. 1998. 512p. Oxford World's Classics Ser. ISBN:0-19-283576-9, ISBN13: 978-0-19-283576-5. Dewey:294.5/9218.

Audience: **g,l,u.**

Olivelle, Patrick **PK3741.P3**
  (Author, Translator)
Pancatantra: The Book of India's Folk Wisdom. Trade Paper. Oxford University Press, Inc. New York, NY. 2002. 256p. Oxford World's Classics ISBN:0-19-283988-8, ISBN13: 978-0-19-283988-6. Dewey:891/.23.

Audience: **g,l,u,f.**

Premchand, Munshi **PK2199.P76B3913 2003**
Courtesan's Quarter. Amina Azfar (Translator). Trade Paper. Oxford University Press, Inc. New York, NY. 2003. 272p. Classics from South Asia and the near East Ser. ISBN:0-19-597710-6, ISBN13: 978-0-19-597710-3. Dewey:891.4/335. LCCN:2004-556118.

Audience: **g,l,u,f.**

Premchand, Munshi **PK2098.S7**
Sevasadan. Snehal Shingavi (Translator). Trade Cloth. Oxford University Press, Inc. New York, NY. 2005. 320p. ISBN:0-19-566899-5, ISBN13: 978-0-19-566899-5. Dewey:891.4335. LCCN:2005-386491.

Audience: **g,l,u,f.**

Premchand **PK2098.S7G613 2002**
The Gift of a Cow: A Translation of the Hindi Novel, Godaan. Ed. 2. Gordon C. Roadarmel (Translator), Vasudha Dalmia (Introduction by). Trade Paper. Indiana University Press. Bloomington, IN. 2002. 480p. ISBN:0-253-21567-6, ISBN13: 978-0-253-21567-3. Dewey:891.4/335. LCCN:2002-023293.

Audience: **g,l,u,f.**

Premchand **PK2098.S7A2 2004**
The Oxford India Premchand. David Rubin, Alok Rai & Christopher R. King (Translators), Francesca Orsini (Introduction by). Trade Cloth. Oxford University Press, Inc. New York, NY. 2004. 1,000p. The Oxford India Collection ISBN:0-19-566501-5, ISBN13: 978-0-19-566501-7. Dewey:891.4371. LCCN:2004-401821.

Audience: **g,l,u,f.**

Ramanujan, A. K. **PL4780.65.E5 1994**
  (Editor, Translator)
When God Is a Customer: Telugu Courtesan Songs by Ksetrayya and Others. Trade Paper. University of California Press. Berkeley, CA. 1994. 166p. ISBN:0-520-08069-6, ISBN13: 978-0-520-08069-0. Dewey:894.82713. LCCN:93-028264.

Audience: **u,f.**

Richman, Paula **PL4758.65.E5E97 1997**
Extraordinary Child: Poems from a South Indian Devotional Genre. Trade Cloth. University of Hawaii Press. Honolulu, HI. 1997. 312p. Shaps Library of Translations ISBN:0-8248-1063-5, ISBN13: 978-0-8248-1063-4. Dewey:894.8/11100938294543. LCCN:96-040072.

Audience: **u,f.**

Russell, Ralph (Editor) **PK2198.G4**
The Oxford India Ghalib: Life, Letters, and Ghazals. Trade Cloth. Oxford University Press, Inc. New York, NY. 2003. 580p. The Oxford India Collection ISBN:0-19-566037-4, ISBN13: 978-0-19-566037-1. Dewey:891.43913. LCCN:2003-334753.

Audience: **g,l,u,f.** *Choice, 2004.*

Sarma, Ramacandra **PL4659.S526**
Home and Away: A Collection of Kannada Short Stories. Katha. 2001. ISBN:81-87649-15-1, ISBN13: 978-81-87649-15-1.

Audience: **g,l,u,f.**

Sheikh, Moazzam (ed.) **PK2190**
A Letter from India: Contemporary Short Stories from Pakistan. Penguin. 2004. ISBN:0-14-303049-3, ISBN13: 978-0-14-303049-2.

Audience: **g,l,u,f.**

Sultan Bahu   PK2656.5.E5 A6 1998
Death Before Dying: The Sufi Poems of Sultan Bahu. Jamal J.
Elias (Translator). Trade Paper. University of California Press.
Berkeley, CA. 1998. 156p. ISBN:0-520-21242-8, ISBN13:
978-0-520-21242-8. Dewey:891.4/213. LCCN:97-019194.
                                                    Audience: **u,f.**

Suranna, Pingali   PL4780.9.P49K313
The Sound of the Kiss, or the Story That Must Never Be Told.
Velcheru Narayana Rao & David Dean Shulman (Translators).
Trade Cloth. Columbia University Press. New York, NY. 2002.
248p. Translations from the Asian Classics Ser.
ISBN:0-231-12596-8, ISBN13: 978-0-231-12596-3.
Dewey:894.8/27371. LCCN:2002-025746.
                                              Audience: **g,l,u,f.**

Tagore, Rabindranath   PK1722.A2 2004
Selected Poems. Sukanta Chaudhuri & Sankha Ghosh (Editors).
Trade Cloth. Oxford University Press, Inc. New York, NY. 2004.
472p. Oxford Tagore Translations Ser. ISBN:0-19-566867-7,
ISBN13: 978-0-19-566867-4. Dewey:891.4/414.
LCCN:2004-327830.
                                                    Audience: **u,f.**

Tallapaka   PL4780.9.T25A24 2005
  Annamacharya & Narayanaravu, Velceru
God on the Hill: Temple Poems from Tirupati. David Dean
Shulman (Translator). Trade Cloth. Oxford University Press, Inc.
New York, NY. 2005. 156p. ISBN:0-19-518283-9, ISBN13:
978-0-19-518283-5. Dewey:894.8/2712. LCCN:2004-065419.
                                                    Audience: **u,f.**

Tendulkar, Vijay   PK5461
Collected Plays in Translation. Trade Paper. Oxford University
Press, Inc. New York, NY. 2004. 650p. Oxford India Paperbacks
Ser. ISBN:0-19-566913-4, ISBN13: 978-0-19-566913-8.
Dewey:891.4/6271.
                                                    Audience: **l,u,f.**

Valmiki, Omprakash &   DS422.C3V275 2003
  Mukherjee, Arun Prabha
Joothan: An Untouchable's Life. Trade Cloth. Columbia
University Press. New York, NY. 2003. 160p.
ISBN:0-231-12972-6, ISBN13: 978-0-231-12972-5.
Dewey:305.5/122/0954. LCCN:2002-041710.
                                                    Audience: **l,u,f.**

Vatsyayana, Mallanaga   HQ18.14
Kamasutra. Wendy Doniger & Sudhir Kakar (Translators). Trade
Paper. Oxford University Press, Inc. New York, NY. 2003. 302p.
Oxford World's Classics Ser. ISBN:0-19-283982-9, ISBN13:
978-0-19-283982-4. Dewey:613.960954.
                                              Audience: **g,l,u,f.**

Vaudeville, Charlotte   PK2095.K3
Kabir. Clarendon Press. 1974. ISBN:0-19-826526-3, ISBN13:
978-0-19-826526-9.
                                              Audience: **g,l,u,f.**

Venkatesa Iyengar,   PL4659.V419
  Masti
Short Stories. Katha. 1995. ISBN:81-85586-33-0, ISBN13:
978-81-85586-33-5.
                                              Audience: **g,l,u,f.**

India > Ethnography

Agrawal, Arun   DS432.R13A37 1999
Greener Pastures: Politics, Markets and Community Among a
Migrant Pastoral People. Cloth Text. Duke University Press.
Durham, NC. 1999. xvii, 219p. ISBN:0-8223-2233-1, ISBN13:
978-0-8223-2233-7. Dewey:305.9/0691. LCCN:98-021274.
                                       Audience: **u,f.** *Choice, 1999.*

Axel, Brian Keith   DS432.S5A94 2001
The Nation's Tortured Body: Violence, Representation and the
Formation of a Sikh "Diaspora". Library Binding. Duke
University Press. Durham, NC. 2000. 376p.
ISBN:0-8223-2607-8, ISBN13: 978-0-8223-2607-6.
Dewey:954/.5/00882946. LCCN:00-029399.
                                                    Audience: **u,f.**

Baviskar, Amita   GN635.I4B396 2004
In the Belly of the River: Tribal Conflicts over Development in
the Narmada Valley. Ed. 2. Trade Paper. Oxford University
Press, Inc. New York, NY. 2005. 324p. Studies in Social
Ecology and Environmental History Ser. ISBN:0-19-567136-8,
ISBN13: 978-0-19-567136-0. Dewey:306/.08/09543.
LCCN:2005-281620.
                                                    Audience: **u,f.**

Cohen, Lawrence   GN485.C64 1998
No Aging in India: Alzheimer's, Bad Families, and Other
Modern Things. Trade Cloth. University of California Press.
Berkeley, CA. 1998. 400p. ISBN:0-520-08396-2, ISBN13:
978-0-520-08396-7. Dewey:305.26. LCCN:97-038659.
                                       Audience: **u,f.** *Choice, 1999.*

Cohn, Bernard S
The Bernard Cohn Omnibus: An Anthropologist among the
Historians and Other Essays, Colonialism and Its Forms of
Knowledge, India: The Social Anthropology of a Civilization.
Oxford University Press India. 2004. ISBN:0-19-566871-5,
ISBN13: 978-0-19-566871-1.
                                                    Audience: **u,f.**

Daniel, E. Valentine   GN635.S72D36 1996
Charred Lullabies: Chapters in an Anthropography of Violence.
Trade Cloth. Princeton University Press. Princeton, NJ. 1996.
272p. Princeton Studies in Culture/Power/History
ISBN:0-691-02774-9, ISBN13: 978-0-691-02774-6.
Dewey:303.6/095493. LCCN:96-020275.
                                                    Audience: **u,f.**

Das, Suranjan   HV6485.I52B433 1991
Communal Riots in Bengal, 1905-1947. Trade Cloth. Oxford
University Press, Inc. New York, NY. 1992. 328p. South Asian
Studies ISBN:0-19-562840-3, ISBN13: 978-0-19-562840-1.
Dewey:954.14035. LCCN:91-900833.
                                                    Audience: **l,u.**

Deliege, Robert   DS432.P25D4513 1997
The World of the Untouchable: The Paraiyars of India. Trade
Cloth. Oxford University Press. Oxford, 1998. 324p.
ISBN:0-19-564230-9, ISBN13: 978-0-19-564230-8.
Dewey:305.5/68. LCCN:97-914029.
                                                    Audience: **u,f.**

Dube, Leela   HQ1742
Women and Kinship: Comparative Perspectives on Gender in
South and South-East Asia. Trade Cloth. United Nations
University Press. Tokyo, 2004. 212p. ISBN:92-808-0922-9,
ISBN13: 978-92-808-0922-0. Dewey:305.4/0954.
                                       Audience: **u,f.** *Choice, 1998.*

Gamburd, Michele Ruth   GN635.S72G36 2000

The Kitchen Spoon's Handle: Transnationalism and Sri Lanka's Migrant Households. Trade Cloth. Cornell University Press. Ithaca, NY. 2000. 272p. ISBN:0-8014-3738-5, ISBN13: 978-0-8014-3738-0. Dewey:306./095493. LCCN:00-008931.

Audience: **u,f.**

Glushkova, Irina   DS432.M2H65 1999

Home, Family and Kinship in Maharashtra. Trade Cloth. Oxford University Press, Inc. New York, NY. 2000. 248p. ISBN:0-19-564635-5, ISBN13: 978-0-19-564635-1. Dewey:954.792. LCCN:99-952768.

Audience: **u,f.**

Good, Anthony   GN635.I4G66 1991

The Female Bridegroom: A Comparative Study in Life-Crisis Rituals in South India and Sri Lanka. Trade Cloth. Oxford University Press, Inc. New York, NY. 1991. 300p. Oxford Studies in Social and Cultural Anthropology - Cultural Forms ISBN:0-19-827853-5, ISBN13: 978-0-19-827853-5. Dewey:392/.0954. LCCN:90-045585.

Audience: **u,f.**

Goonatilake, Susantha   GN635.S72G66 2001

e Anthropologizing Sri Lanka: A Eurocentric Misadventure. E-Book. Indiana University Press. Bloomington, IN. 2001. 300p. ISBN:0-253-33999-5, ISBN13: 978-0-253-33999-7. Dewey:305.8/0095493. LCCN:00-053538.

Audience: **u,f.** *Choice, 2002.*

Gottschalk, Peter   GN635

Beyond Hindu and Muslim: Multiple Identity in Narratives from Village India. Wendy Doniger (Contribution by). Trade Paper. Oxford University Press, Inc. New York, NY. 2005. 248p. ISBN:0-19-518915-9, ISBN13: 978-0-19-518915-5. Dewey:306.095412.

Audience: **u,f.**

Gupta, Dipankar   DS485.P2

The Context of Ethnicity: Sikh Identity in a Comparative Perspective. Trade Paper. Oxford University Press, Inc. New York, NY. 1998. 254p. Oxford India Paperbacks Ser. ISBN:0-19-564391-7, ISBN13: 978-0-19-564391-6. Dewey:954/.5.

Audience: **u,f.**

Harlan, Lindsey   DS432.R3H37 1991

Religion and Rajput Women: The Ethic of Protection in Contemporary Narratives. Trade Cloth. University of California Press. Berkeley, CA. 1991. 286p. ISBN:0-520-07339-8, ISBN13: 978-0-520-07339-5. Dewey:305.4/0954/4. LCCN:91-002389.

Audience: **u,f.**

Karlekar, Malavika   DS432.B4 K37 1991

Voices from Within: Early Personal Narratives of Bengali Women. Cloth Text. Oxford University Press, Inc. New York, NY. 1991. 264p. ISBN:0-19-562836-5, ISBN13: 978-0-19-562836-4. Dewey:305.420954. LCCN:92-191836.

Audience: **g,l,u,f.**

Kumar, Nita   GN21.K86.A3 1992

Friends, Brothers and Informants: Fieldwork Memoirs of Banaras. Trade Cloth. University of California Press. Berkeley, CA. 1992. 250p. ISBN:0-520-07138-7, ISBN13: 978-0-520-07138-4. LCCN:91-033815.

Audience: **u,f.** *Choice, 1993.*

Lynch, Owen M. (Editor)   GN635.I4D58 1990

Divine Passions: The Social Construction of Emotion in India. Trade Cloth. University of California Press. Berkeley, CA. 1990. 340p. ISBN:0-520-06647-2, ISBN13: 978-0-520-06647-2. Dewey:152.4. LCCN:89-004975.

Audience: **u,f.** *Choice, 1990.*

Madan, T. N. & Barnes, J. A.   DS432

Family and Kinship: A Study of the Pandits of Rural Kashmir. Ed. 2. Trade Paper. Oxford University Press, Inc. New York, NY. 2002. 358p. ISBN:0-19-565785-3, ISBN13: 978-0-19-565785-2. Dewey:306.8/09546.

Audience: **u,f.**

Mayaram, Shail   DS432.M35M38 2003

Against History, Against State: Counterperspectives from the Margins. Trade Cloth. Eastern European Monographs. Bradenton, FL. 2003. 344p. Cultures of History Ser. ISBN:0-231-12730-8, ISBN13: 978-0-231-12730-1. Dewey:305.6/9710544. LCCN:2003-051633.

Audience: **u,f.**

Mines, Diane P.   GN635.I4M553 2005

Fierce Gods: Inequality, Ritual, and the Politics of Dignity in a South Indian Village. Trade Cloth. Indiana University Press. Bloomington, IN. 2005. 240p. ISBN:0-253-34576-6, ISBN13: 978-0-253-34576-9. Dewey:306.4/0954/82. LCCN:2004-025823.

Audience: **u,f.**

Pinney, Christopher   GN635.I4P49 1997

Camera Indica: The Social Life of Indian Photographs. Trade Cloth. University of Chicago Press. Chicago, IL. 1998. 240p. ISBN:0-226-66865-7, ISBN13: 978-0-226-66865-9. Dewey:770.9/54. LCCN:97-023831.

Audience: **u,f.** *Choice, 1998.*

Raheja, Gloria G.   GN635.I6R34 1988

The Poison in the Gift: Ritual, Prestation, and the Dominant Caste in a North Indian Village. Trade Cloth. University of Chicago Press. Chicago, IL. 1988. 300p. ISBN:0-226-70728-8, ISBN13: 978-0-226-70728-0. Dewey:392/.0954/2. LCCN:87-028924.

Audience: **u,f.**

Rubiés, Joan-Pau   GN575 .R83 2000

Travel and Ethnology in the Renaissance: South India Through European Eyes, 1250-1625. Lyndal Roper (Contribution by). Trade Cloth. Cambridge University Press. New York, NY. 2000. 468p. Past and Present Publications ISBN:0-521-77055-6, ISBN13: 978-0-521-77055-2. Dewey:305.8/00954/0902. LCCN:2001-267152.

Audience: **u,f.** *Choice, 2001.*

Rudner, David W.   DS432.N38.R84 1994

Caste and Capitalism in Colonial India: The Nattukottai Chettiars. Trade Cloth. University of California Press. Berkeley, CA. 1994. 370p. ISBN:0-520-07236-7, ISBN13: 978-0-520-07236-7. Dewey:305.554095482. LCCN:92-038124.

Audience: **u,f.** *Choice, 1995.*

Sharma, Suresh   GN635.I4S4495 1994

Tribal Identity and the Modern World. Trade Cloth. SAGE Publications, Inc. Thousand Oaks, CA. 1994. 216p. ISBN:0-8039-9155-X, ISBN13: 978-0-8039-9155-2. Dewey:305.800954. LCCN:93-050134.

Audience: **g,l,u.**

Singh, K. S. (Editor)   **DS430**
India's Communities A-Z, Set. Cloth Text. Oxford University
Press, Inc. New York, NY. 1999. 4206p. People of India Ser.,
Vol. IV ISBN:0-19-563354-7, ISBN13: 978-0-19-563354-2.
Dewey:305.8/00954.

Audience: **g,l,u,f.**

Singh, K. S. (Editor), et al.   **DS485.B45 S56 1994**
The Biological Variation in Indian Populations. V. Bhalla &
Vinod Kaul (Editors). Cloth Text. Oxford University Press, Inc.
New York, NY. 1994. 778p. People of India Ser.
ISBN:0-19-563351-2, ISBN13: 978-0-19-563351-1.
Dewey:573.220954.

Audience: **u,f.**

von Furer-Haimendorf,   **GN21.F87.A3 1990**
Christoph
Life among Indian Tribes: The Autobiography of an
Anthropologist. Trade Cloth. Oxford University Press, Inc. New
York, NY. 1990. 214p. ISBN:0-19-562471-8, ISBN13:
978-0-19-562471-7. Dewey:301.092. LCCN:90-900149.

Audience: **g,l,u,f.** *Choice, 1991.*

Wadley, Susan S.   **GN635.I4W33 1994**
Struggling with Destiny in Karimpur, 1925-1984. Trade Paper.
University of California Press. Berkeley, CA. 1994. 330p.
ISBN:0-520-08407-1, ISBN13: 978-0-520-08407-0.
Dewey:306/.0954/2. LCCN:93-048297.

Audience: **u,f.**

Webster, John C. B.   **DS432.C55 W4 1992**
A History of the Dalit Christians in India. Trade Cloth. Edwin
Mellen Press, The. Lewiston, NY. 1992. 260p.
ISBN:0-7734-9867-2, ISBN13: 978-0-7734-9867-9.
Dewey:305.5/68. LCCN:92-024885.

Audience: **l,u.**

India > History

Arnold, David &   **CT1503.T45 2004**
Blackburn, Stuart (Editors)
Telling Lives in India: Biography, Autobiography, and Life
History. Trade Cloth. Indiana University Press. Bloomington,
IN. 2004. 288p. ISBN:0-253-34486-7, ISBN13:
978-0-253-34486-1. Dewey:954. LCCN:2005-270442.

Audience: **u,f.**

Dube, Saurabh   **DS341.D82 2004**
Stitches on Time: Colonial Textures and Postcolonial Tangles.
Trade Cloth. Duke University Press. Durham, NC. 2004. 304p.
ISBN:0-8223-3325-2, ISBN13: 978-0-8223-3325-8. Dewey:954.
LCCN:2003-021427.

Audience: **f.**

Frankel, Francine R. &   **DS450.C6I523 2004**
Harding, Harry
The India-China Relationship: What the United States Needs to
Know. Trade Paper. Columbia University Press. New York, NY.
2004. 352p. ISBN:0-231-13237-9, ISBN13: 978-0-231-13237-4.
Dewey:327.51054. LCCN:2003-062712.

Audience: **g,u,f.** *Choice, 2005.*

Pearson, M. N.   **DS436 .N47 1987 PT.**
The Portuguese in India. C. A. Bayly, Gordon Johnson & John
F. Richards (Contribution by). Trade Cloth. Cambridge
University Press. New York, NY. 1988. 202p. The New

Cambridge History of India Ser., Vol. 1 ISBN:0-521-25713-1,
ISBN13: 978-0-521-25713-8. Dewey:954. LCCN:86-017100.

Audience: **g,l,u.** *Choice, 1989.*

Rahman, A. (Editor)   **DS450.C6I55 2002**
India's Interaction with China, Central and West Asia. Trade
Cloth. Oxford University Press, Inc. New York, NY. 2002. 564p.
Project of History of Indian Science, Philosophy and Culture
Ser., Pt. 2 ISBN:0-19-565789-6, ISBN13: 978-0-19-565789-0.
Dewey:509.5/4. LCCN:2002-288926.

Audience: **g,u,f.**

Wolpert, Stanley   **DS436.W66 2003**
A New History of India. Ed. 7. Cloth Text. Oxford University
Press, Inc. New York, NY. 2003. 544p. ISBN:0-19-516677-9,
ISBN13: 978-0-19-516677-4. Dewey:954. LCCN:2003-053589.

Audience: **g,l,u.**

India > History > To 997

Asher, Catherine B. &   **DS452.A84 2005**
Talbot, Cynthia
India Before Europe. Cloth Text. Cambridge University Press.
New York, NY. 2006. 336p. ISBN:0-521-80904-5, ISBN13:
978-0-521-80904-7. Dewey:954/.02. LCCN:2005-024164.

Audience: **g,u,f.** *Choice, 2006.*

Habib, Irfan (Editor)   **DS452 .M42**
Medieval India: Researches in the History of India, 1200-1750.
Cloth Text. Oxford University Press, Inc. New York, NY. 1993.
234p. ISBN:0-19-562330-4, ISBN13: 978-0-19-562330-7.
Dewey:954.02.

Audience: **f.**

Thapar, Romila   **DS451.5**
Asoka and the Decline of the Mauryas: With a New Afterword
Bibliography and Index. Ed. 2. Trade Paper. Oxford University
Press, Inc. New York, NY. 1998. 356p. Oxford India Paperbacks
Ser. ISBN:0-19-564445-X, ISBN13: 978-0-19-564445-6.
Dewey:934/.045.

Audience: **g,u,f.**

Thapar, Romila   **DS451.T452 2000**
Cultural Pasts: Essays in Early Indian History. Cloth Text.
Oxford University Press, Inc. New York, NY. 2001. 1172p.
ISBN:0-19-564050-0, ISBN13: 978-0-19-564050-2. Dewey:934.
LCCN:00-440398.

Audience: **g,u,f.**

Thapar, Romilla   **DS451.T465 2000**
History and Beyond: Interpreting Early India, Time as a
Metaphor of History, Cultural Transaction and Early India and
from Lineage to State. Cloth Text. Oxford University Press, Inc.
New York, NY. 2000. 500p. ISBN:0-19-564708-4, ISBN13:
978-0-19-564708-2. Dewey:934. LCCN:99-952723.

Audience: **g,u,f.**

India > History > Muslim Rule (997-1761)

Das Gupta, Ashin &   **HF3788.I44 I53**
Pearson, M. N.
India and the Indian Ocean - 1500 to 1800. Trade Cloth. Asia
Book Corporation of America. Flushing, NY. 1987. 374p.
ISBN:0-318-36991-5, ISBN13: 978-0-318-36991-4.
Dewey:382/.0954/05.

Audience: **f.**

Habib, Irfan (Editor)   **DS461.3.A42 1997**
Akbar and His India. Cloth Text. Oxford University Press, Inc.
New York, NY. 1997. 328p. ISBN:0-19-563791-7, ISBN13:
978-0-19-563791-5. Dewey:954/.0254/092. LCCN:97-903276.
Audience: **f.**

Jackson, Peter   **DS459 .J27 1999**
The Delhi Sultanate: A Political and Military History. David
Morgan (Contribution by). Cloth Text. Cambridge University
Press. New York, NY. 1999. 388p. Studies in Islamic
Civilization ISBN:0-521-40477-0, ISBN13: 978-0-521-40477-8.
Dewey:954/.56023. LCCN:98-030080.
Audience: **f.** *Choice, 1999.*

Laine, James W.   **DS461.9.S5A4 2003**
Shivaji: Hindu King in Islamic India. Trade Cloth. Oxford
University Press, Inc. New York, NY. 2003. 138p.
ISBN:0-19-514126-1, ISBN13: 978-0-19-514126-9.
Dewey:954/.792. LCCN:2002-025810.
Audience: **g,u,f.**

Marshall, P. J. (Editor)   **DS462**
The Eighteenth Century in Indian History: Revolution or
Evolution? Trade Paper. Oxford University Press, Inc. New
York, NY. 2005. 464p. Oxford in India Readings Ser., :Themes
in Indian History Ser. ISBN:0-19-567814-1, ISBN13:
978-0-19-567814-7. Dewey:954.029.
Audience: **g,u,f.**

Pearson, Michael N.   **DT432 .P43**
Port Cities and Intruders: The Swahili Coast, India, and Portugal
in the Early Modern Era. Trade Paper. Johns Hopkins University
Press. Baltimore, MD. 2003. 216p. Johns Hopkins Symposia in
Comparative History Ser. ISBN:0-8018-7242-1, ISBN13:
978-0-8018-7242-6. Dewey:967.6/01.
Audience: **g,u,f.**

Richards, John F.   **DS436 .N47 1987 PT.**
(Author, Contribution by)
The Mughal Empire. C. A. Bayly & Gordon Johnson
(Contribution by). Cloth Text. Cambridge University Press. New
York, NY. 1993. 337p. The New Cambridge History of India
Ser., I: 5 ISBN:0-521-25119-2, ISBN13: 978-0-521-25119-8.
Dewey:954/.025. LCCN:92-003074.
Audience: **f.** *Choice, 1994.*

Subrahmanyam, Sanjay   **DS340**
Explorations in Connected History: Mughals and Franks. Trade
Cloth. Oxford University Press, Inc. New York, NY. 2005. 250p.
ISBN:0-19-566866-9, ISBN13: 978-0-19-566866-7. Dewey:954.
LCCN:2005-280596.
Audience: **f.**

Subrahmanyam, Sanjay   **DS498.S5 1998**
(Contribution by)
Sinners and Saints: The Successors of Vasco Da Gama. Trade
Cloth. Oxford University Press, Inc. New York, NY. 1998. 212p.
ISBN:0-19-564426-3, ISBN13: 978-0-19-564426-5.
Dewey:954/.004691. LCCN:98-903534.
Audience: **f.**

Thackston, Wheeler M.   **DS461.5.J28813 1999**
(Editor)
The Jahangirnama: Memoirs of Jahangir, Emperor of India.
Trade Cloth. Oxford University Press, Inc. New York, NY. 1999.
528p. ISBN:0-19-512718-8, ISBN13: 978-0-19-512718-8.
Dewey:954.02/56/092 b. LCCN:98-018798.
Audience: **g,u,f.** *Choice, 2000.*

Ziad, Zeenut (Editor)   **DS461.M26 2002**
The Magnificent Mughals. Trade Cloth. Oxford University
Press, Inc. New York, NY. 2002. 340p. ISBN:0-19-579444-3,
ISBN13: 978-0-19-579444-1. Dewey:954.02/5.
LCCN:2003-268675.
Audience: **g,u,f.** *Choice, 2003.*

India > History > British Rule

Aloysius, G.   **DS463.A565 1997**
Nationalism Without a Nation in India. Trade Cloth. Oxford
University Press, Inc. New York, NY. 1998. 280p.
ISBN:0-19-564104-3, ISBN13: 978-0-19-564104-2.
Dewey:322.4/2/0954. LCCN:97-903271.
Audience: **g,u,f.**

Alter, Joseph S.   **DS480.45.A782 2000**
Gandhi's Body: Sex, Diet and the Politics of Nationalism. Book,
Other. University of Pennsylvania Press. Philadelphia, PA. 2000.
216p. Critical Histories Ser. ISBN:0-8122-3556-8, ISBN13:
978-0-8122-3556-2. Dewey:954.03/5/092. LCCN:00-023421.
Audience: **g,u,f.** *Choice, 2001.*

Bayly, C. A. (Author,   **DS436 .N47 1987 PT.**
Contribution by)
Indian Society and the Making of the British Empire. Gordon
Johnson & John F. Richards (Contribution by). Trade Cloth.
Cambridge University Press. New York, NY. 1988. 248p. The
New Cambridge History of India Ser., II: 1
ISBN:0-521-25092-7, ISBN13: 978-0-521-25092-4. Dewey:954
s. LCCN:87-000704.
Audience: **f.** *Choice, 1989.*

Bose, Purnima   **DS480.45.B586 2003**
Organizing Empire: Individualism, Collective Agency, and India.
Trade Cloth. Duke University Press. Durham, NC. 2003. 280p.
ISBN:0-8223-2759-7, ISBN13: 978-0-8223-2759-2.
Dewey:954.03. LCCN:2003-002263.
Audience: **f.**

Brown, Judith M.   **DS475.B79 1994**
Modern India: The Origins of an Asian Democracy. Ed. 2. Paper
Text. Oxford University Press, Inc. New York, NY. 1994. 480p.
Short Oxford History of the Modern World Ser.
ISBN:0-19-873113-2, ISBN13: 978-0-19-873113-9. Dewey:954.
LCCN:93-031405.
Audience: **g,u,f.** *B Choice, 1985.*

Buettner, Elizabeth   **DS428**
Empire Families: Britons and Late Imperial India. Trade Cloth.
Oxford University Press, Inc. New York, NY. 2004. 328p.
ISBN:0-19-924907-5, ISBN13: 978-0-19-924907-7.
Dewey:306.85/089/21054. LCCN:2004-301766.
Audience: **g,u,f.** *Choice, 2005.*

Chatterjee, Partha   **DS468 .C47 1993**
The Nation and Its Fragments: Colonial and Postcolonial
Histories. Trade Paper. Princeton University Press. Princeton,
NJ. 1993. 296p. Princeton Studies in Culture/Power/History
ISBN:0-691-01943-6, ISBN13: 978-0-691-01943-7.
Dewey:954.03. LCCN:93-015536.
Audience: **g,u,f.** *Choice, 1994.*

Chatterjee, Partha   **DS463.C36 1999**
The Partha Chatterjee Omnibus: Nationalist Thought and the
Colonial World, the Nation and Its Fragments, a Possible India.
Trade Cloth. Oxford University Press, Inc. New York, NY. 2000.

314p. ISBN:0-19-565156-1, ISBN13: 978-0-19-565156-0.
Dewey:320.54/0954. LCCN:99-939183.

Audience: **g,u,f.**

Goswami, Manu　　　　　　**DS463.G687 2004**
Producing India: From Colonial Economy to National Space.
Trade Cloth. University of Chicago Press. Chicago, IL. 2004.
400p. Chicago Studies in Practices of Meaning
ISBN:0-226-30508-2, ISBN13: 978-0-226-30508-0.
Dewey:954.03/5. LCCN:2003-019956.

Audience: **f.**

Guha, Ranajit　　　　　　**DS463.S77 1997**
A Subaltern Studies Reader, 1986-1995. Cloth Text. University
of Minnesota Press. Minneapolis, MN. 1997. 320p.
ISBN:0-8166-2758-4, ISBN13: 978-0-8166-2758-5.
Dewey:954.03. LCCN:97-018632.

Audience: **g,u,f.**

Guha, Ranajit　　　　　　**DS463.G837 1997**
Dominance Without Hegemony: History and Power in Colonial
India. Edward W. Said (Contribution by). Trade Cloth. Harvard
University Press. Cambridge, MA. 1998. 268p. Convergences
Ser., :Inventories of the Present ISBN:0-674-21482-X, ISBN13:
978-0-674-21482-8. Dewey:954. LCCN:97-015888.

Audience: **g,u,f.**

Hardiman, David　　　　　　**DS432.A2 H34 1987**
The Coming of the Devi: Adivasi Assertion in Western India.
Trade Cloth. Oxford University Press, Inc. New York, NY. 1987.
260p. ISBN:0-19-561957-9, ISBN13: 978-0-19-561957-7.
Dewey:954/.75. LCCN:87-900016.

Audience: **g,u,f.**

Hardiman, David　　　　　　**DS479.P43 1992**
(Editor)
Peasants and Resistance in India, 1858-1914. Cloth Text. Oxford
University Press, Inc. New York, NY. 1992. 320p. Themes in
Indian History Ser. ISBN:0-19-562725-3, ISBN13:
978-0-19-562725-1. Dewey:322.420954. LCCN:92-905887.

Audience: **f.**

Harrison, Mark　　　　　　**DS463**
Climates and Constitutions: Health, Race, Environment and
British Imperialism in India, 1600-1850. Trade Paper. Oxford
University Press, Inc. New York, NY. 2003. 280p. Oxford India
Paperbacks Ser. ISBN:0-19-566128-1, ISBN13:
978-0-19-566128-6. Dewey:954/.03. LCCN:2003-536746.

Audience: **g,u,f.**

Hasan, Mushirul　　　　　　**DS480.842.I58 2000**
(Editor)
Inventing Boundaries: Gender, Politics and the Partition of
India. Cloth Text. Oxford University Press, Inc. New York, NY.
2001. 404p. ISBN:0-19-565103-0, ISBN13: 978-0-19-565103-4.
Dewey:954.04. LCCN:00-371225.

Audience: **f.**

Israel, Milton　　　　　　**DS480.45 .I84 1994**
Communications and Power: Propaganda and the Press in the
Indian National Struggle, 1920-1947. Trade Paper. Cambridge
University Press. New York, NY. 1994. 352p. South Asian
Studies, No. 56 ISBN:0-521-46763-2, ISBN13:
978-0-521-46763-6. Dewey:954.035. LCCN:93-005226.

Audience: **g,u,f.**

Jaffrelot, Christophe　　　　　　**DS480.45.J29813 1996**
The Hindu Nationalist Movement in India. Cloth Text.
Columbia University Press. New York, NY. 1995. xxiii, 592p.
ISBN:0-231-10334-4, ISBN13: 978-0-231-10334-3.
Dewey:324.254/082. LCCN:95-012330.

Audience: **f.**

Jalal, Ayesha　　　　　　**DS481.G3**
The Sole Spokesman: Jinnah, the Muslim League and the
Demand for Pakistan. Trade Paper. Cambridge University Press.
New York, NY. 1994. 334p. Cambridge South Asian Studies
ISBN:0-521-45850-1, ISBN13: 978-0-521-45850-4.
Dewey:954.03/5/0924.

Audience: **f.** *Choice, 1986.*

Kennedy, Dane　　　　　　**DS412.K46 1996**
The Magic Mountains: Hill Stations and the British Raj. Trade
Cloth. University of California Press. Berkeley, CA. 1996. 265p.
ISBN:0-520-20188-4, ISBN13: 978-0-520-20188-0.
Dewey:954/.00943. LCCN:95-014014.

Audience: **g,u,f.** *Choice, 1996.*

Krishnaswamy, Revathi　　　　　　**DS479.K75 1998**
Effeminism: The Economy of Colonial Desire. Trade Cloth.
University of Michigan Press. Chicago, IL. 1999. 208p.
ISBN:0-472-10975-8, ISBN13: 978-0-472-10975-3.
Dewey:954.03. LCCN:98-025517.

Audience: **f.** *Choice, 1999.*

Low, D. A.　　　　　　**DS480.45 .L68 1997**
Britain and Indian Nationalism: The Imprint of Ambiguity,
1929-1942. Trade Cloth. Cambridge University Press. New
York, NY. 1997. 374p. ISBN:0-521-55017-3, ISBN13:
978-0-521-55017-8. Dewey:954/.0358. LCCN:96-049356.

Audience: **g,u,f.** *Choice, 1998.*

Metcalf, Thomas R.　　　　　　**DS436.N47**
Ideologies of the Raj. C. A. Bayly, Gordon Johnson & John F.
Richards (Contribution by). Cloth Text. Cambridge University
Press. New York, NY. 1995. 224p. The New Cambridge History
of India Ser., Vol. III.4 ISBN:0-521-39547-X, ISBN13:
978-0-521-39547-2. Dewey:954/.03. LCCN:94-006117.

Audience: **g,u,f.** *Choice, 1995.*

Nanda, B. R.　　　　　　**DS479**
Gandhi: Pan-Islamism, Imperialism and Nationalism in India.
Trade Paper. Oxford University Press, Inc. New York, NY. 2002.
476p. ISBN:0-19-565827-2, ISBN13: 978-0-19-565827-9.
Dewey:320.5/5/0954/09041.

Audience: **f.**

Nandy, Ashis　　　　　　**DS475.N354 1998**
Exiled at Home: Comprising at the Edge of Psychology, the
Intimate Enemy and Creating a Nationality. Cloth Text. Oxford
University Press, Inc. New York, NY. 1998. 244p.
ISBN:0-19-564177-9, ISBN13: 978-0-19-564177-6. Dewey:954.
LCCN:98-902993.

Audience: **f.**

Nandy, Ashis　　　　　　**DS480.45.N25 1998**
Return from Exile: Alternative Sciences, Illegitimacy of
Nationalism, the Savage Freud. Cloth Text. Oxford University
Press, Inc. New York, NY. 1999. 560p. ISBN:0-19-564178-7,
ISBN13: 978-0-19-564178-3. Dewey:954. LCCN:99-933486.

Audience: **f.**

Paxton, Nancy L.　　　　　　**DS479.W75 1999**
Writing under the Raj: Gender, Race, and Rape in the British
Colonial Imagination, 1830-1947. Cloth Text. Rutgers University

Press. Piscataway, NJ. 1999. 304p. ISBN:0-8135-2600-0, ISBN13: 978-0-8135-2600-3. Dewey:954.03. LCCN:98-019522.
Audience: **f.** *Choice, 1999.*

Prakash, Gyan   **DS463.P67 1999**
Another Reason: Science and the Imagination of Modern India. Trade Paper. Princeton University Press. Princeton, NJ. 1999. 318p. ISBN:0-691-00453-6, ISBN13: 978-0-691-00453-2. Dewey:954. LCCN:99-017185.
Audience: **g,u,f.** *Choice, 2000.*

Roy, Raja Rammohun   **DS475.2.R18A25 1999**
The Essential Writings of Raja Rammohan Ray. Bruce Carlisle Robertson (Editor). Trade Cloth. Oxford University Press, Inc. New York, NY. 1999. 340p. ISBN:0-19-564731-9, ISBN13: 978-0-19-564731-0. Dewey:082. LCCN:99-932755.
Audience: **f.**

Shaikh, Farzana   **DS479.S52 1989**
Community and Consensus in Islam: Muslim Representation in Colonial India 1860-1947. Trade Cloth. Cambridge University Press. New York, NY. 1989. 272p. Cambridge South Asian Studies, No. 42 ISBN:0-521-36328-4, ISBN13: 978-0-521-36328-0. Dewey:954.03/5. LCCN:88-023472.
Audience: **f.** *Choice, 1990.*

Stern, Robert W.   **DS463.S73 2003**
Changing India: Bourgeois Revolution on the Subcontinent. Ed. 2. Cloth Text. Cambridge University Press. New York, NY. 2003. 268p. ISBN:0-521-81080-9, ISBN13: 978-0-521-81080-7. Dewey:954.03/5. LCCN:2003-043485.
Audience: **g,u,f.**

Stokes, Eric & Bayly, C. A.   **DS478.S85 1986**
The Peasant Armed: The Indian Revolt of 1857. Trade Cloth. Oxford University Press, Inc. New York, NY. 1986. 280p. ISBN:0-19-821570-3, ISBN13: 978-0-19-821570-7. Dewey:954.03/1. LCCN:85-021698.
Audience: **g,u,f.**

Sugata, Bose   **DS480.45 .N329 1998**
Nationalism, Democracy, and Development: State and Politics in India. Paper Text. Oxford University Press, Inc. New York, NY. 1999. 206p. Oxford India Paperbacks Ser. ISBN:0-19-564442-5, ISBN13: 978-0-19-564442-5. Dewey:320.954.
Audience: **f.**

Tytler, Harriet   **DS412.T98 1986**
An Englishwoman in India: The Memoirs of Harriet Tyler 1828-1858. Anthony Sattin (Editor), Philip Mason (Introduction by). Trade Cloth. Oxford University Press, Inc. New York, NY. 1986. 268p. ISBN:0-19-212244-4, ISBN13: 978-0-19-212244-5. Dewey:954.03/17. LCCN:85-015521.
Audience: **g,u,f.**

Visram, Rozina   **DS479 .V57 1992**
Women in India and Pakistan: The Struggle for Independence from British Rule. Trade Paper. Cambridge University Press. New York, NY. 1992. 64p. Women in History Ser. ISBN:0-521-38643-8, ISBN13: 978-0-521-38643-2. Dewey:305.42/0954. LCCN:91-026093.
Audience: **g,u,f.**

Zastoupil, Lynn   **DS463.Z37 1994**
John Stuart Mill and India. Trade Cloth. Stanford University Press. Palo Alto, CA. 1994. 296p. ISBN:0-8047-2256-0, ISBN13: 978-0-8047-2256-8. Dewey:954.03. LCCN:93-002225.
Audience: **g,u,f.** *Choice, 1994.*

Zavos, John (Editor), et al.   **DS480.45.P62 2004**
The Politics of Cultural Mobilization in India. Andrew Wyatt & Vernon Hewitt (Editors). Trade Cloth. Oxford University Press, Inc. New York, NY. 2004. 276p. ISBN:0-19-566801-4, ISBN13: 978-0-19-566801-8. Dewey:323.1/54/09045. LCCN:2004-301616.
Audience: **f.**

India > History > Independence (1947-)

Ambedkar, B. R.   **DS481.A525A7 2002**
The Essential Writings of B. R. Ambedkar. Valerian Rodrigues (Editor). Trade Cloth. Oxford University Press, Inc. New York, NY. 2002. 576p. ISBN:0-19-565608-3, ISBN13: 978-0-19-565608-4. Dewey:306.0954. LCCN:2003-306296.
Audience: **f.**

Blinkenberg, Lars   **DS450.P18B64 1998**
India-Pakistan: The History of Unsolved Conflicts. Trade Cloth. Syddansk Universitetsforlag/University Press of Southern Denmark. Odense M, 1998. ISBN:87-7838-286-6, ISBN13: 978-87-7838-286-3. Dewey:327.5405491. LCCN:98-178084.
Audience: **g,u,f.**

Bonner, Arthur, et al.   **DS480.84.D386 1994**
Democracy in India: A Hollow Shell. Kancha Ilaiah, Suranjit K. Saha, Asghar Ali Engineer & Gerard Hueze (Authors). Trade Cloth. American University. Washington, DC. 1994. 300p. ISBN:1-879383-25-X, ISBN13: 978-1-879383-25-8. Dewey:320.954. LCCN:94-019522.
Audience: **g,u,f.** *Choice, 1995.*

Bose, Sisir K. & Bose,   **DS481.G3**
  Sugata (Editors)
The Essential Writings of Netaji Subhas Chandra Bose. Trade Paper. Oxford University Press, Inc. New York, NY. 1999. 348p. ISBN:0-19-564854-4, ISBN13: 978-0-19-564854-6. Dewey:954.03/5/092.
Audience: **f.**

Brown, Judith   **DS481.G3**
Gandhi: Prisoner of Hope. Trade Paper. Yale University Press. Cumberland, RI. 1991. 440p. ISBN:0-300-05125-5, ISBN13: 978-0-300-05125-4. Dewey:954.03/5/092 B.
Audience: **g,u,f.** *Choice, 1990.*

Brown, Judith M.   **DS481.N35B762 2003**
Nehru: A Political Life. Cloth over Boards. Yale University Press. Cumberland, RI. 2003. 440p. ISBN:0-300-09279-2, ISBN13: 978-0-300-09279-0. Dewey:954.04092. LCCN:2003-005807.
Audience: **g,u,f.** *Choice, 2004.*

Chadda, Maya   **DS480.84.C45 1997**
Ethnicity, Security, and Separatism in India. Cloth Text. Columbia University Press. New York, NY. 1996. 304p. ISBN:0-231-10736-6, ISBN13: 978-0-231-10736-5. Dewey:327.54. LCCN:96-048962.
Audience: **f.** *Choice, 1997.*

Chatterjee, Partha   **DS480.84**
A Possible India: Essays in Political Criticism. Trade Paper. Oxford University Press, Inc. New York, NY. 1999. 316p. Oxford India Paperbacks Ser. ISBN:0-19-564766-1, ISBN13: 978-0-19-564766-2. Dewey:954.05.
Audience: **g,u,f.** *Choice, 1998.*

Corbridge, Stuart &   **DS480.84.C783 2000**
Harriss, John
Reinventing India: Liberalization, Hindu Nationalism and
Popular Democracy. Trade Cloth. Polity Press. Cambridge,
2000. 336p. ISBN:0-7456-2076-0, ISBN13: 978-0-7456-2076-3.
Dewey:954.04. LCCN:00-039986.

Audience: **f.** *Choice, 2001.*

De Silva, K. M.   **DS480.853.D384 1995**
Regional Powers and Small State Security: India and Sri Lanka,
1977-1990. Trade Cloth. Johns Hopkins University Press.
Baltimore, MD. 1966. 388p. ISBN:0-8018-5149-1, ISBN13:
978-0-8018-5149-0. Dewey:327.5405493/09/048.
LCCN:95-008097.

Audience: **f.** *Choice, 1996.*

Deschaumes, Ghislaine   **D841**
Glasson & Ivekovic, Rada
Divided Countries, Separated Cities. Trade Cloth. Oxford
University Press, Inc. New York, NY. 2004. 250p.
ISBN:0-19-566540-6, ISBN13: 978-0-19-566540-6.
Dewey:320.1/2/0904. LCCN:2003-334750.

Audience: **f.**

Ganguly, Sumit   **DS450.P18G36 2002**
Conflict Unending: India-Pakistan Tensions Since 1947. Trade
Cloth. Edinburgh University Press. Edinburgh, 2002. 200p.
ISBN:0-231-12368-X, ISBN13: 978-0-231-12368-6.
Dewey:954.04. LCCN:2002-019477.

Audience: **g,u,f.**

Ganguly, Sumit &   **DS450.P18G37 2005**
Hagerty, Devin T.
Fearful Symmetry: India-Pakistan Crises in the Shadow of
Nuclear Weapons. Trade Cloth. University of Washington Press.
Seattle, WA. 2005. 234p. ISBN:0-295-98525-9, ISBN13:
978-0-295-98525-1. Dewey:327.5405491/09/045.
LCCN:2005-002816.

Audience: **g,u,f.** *Choice, 2006.*

Hardiman, David   **DS481.G3H276 2003**
Gandhi in His Time and Ours: The Global Legacy of His Ideas.
Trade Cloth. Columbia University Press. New York, NY. 2004.
256p. ISBN:0-231-13114-3, ISBN13: 978-0-231-13114-8.
Dewey:954.03/5/092. LCCN:2003-051464.

Audience: **g,u,f.** *Choice, 2004.*

Harrison, Selig S.   **DS480.84 .I4854 1999**
(Editor), et al.
India and Pakistan: The First Fifty Years. Paul H. Kreisberg &
Dennis Kux (Editors), John Adams, Paul Brass, Stephen P.
Cohen, Sonalde Desai, Sumit Ganguly, Robert LaPorte & Lee
H. Hamilton (Contribution by). Trade Paper. Cambridge
University Press. New York, NY. 1998. 230p. Woodrow Wilson
Center Press Ser. ISBN:0-521-64585-9, ISBN13:
978-0-521-64585-0. Dewey:954.04. LCCN:98-036434.

Audience: **g,u,f.** *Choice, 1999.*

Hasan, Mushirul   **DS480.842.I53**
(Editor)
India's Partition: Process, Strategy and Mobilization. Trade
Paper. Oxford University Press, Inc. New York, NY. 1994. 444p.
India Readings Ser. ISBN:0-19-563504-3, ISBN13:
978-0-19-563504-1. Dewey:954.0359.

Audience: **f.**

Hoffmann, Steven A.   **DS480.85.H64 1990**
India and the China Crisis. Trade Cloth. University of California
Press. Berkeley, CA. 1990. 340p. International Crisis Behavior

Ser., Vol. 6 ISBN:0-520-06537-9, ISBN13: 978-0-520-06537-6.
Dewey:954.04. LCCN:89-004672.

Audience: **g,u,f.** *Choice, 1990.*

Jaffrelot, Christophe   **DS481.A6J18 2005**
Dr. Ambedkar and Untouchability: Fighting the Indian Caste
System. Trade Cloth. Columbia University Press. New York,
NY. 2004. 224p. ISBN:0-231-13602-1, ISBN13:
978-0-231-13602-0. Dewey:954.04/2/092 B.
LCCN:2004-057133.

Audience: **g,u,f.**

Majmudar, Uma   **DS481.G3M2735 2005**
Gandhi's Pilgrimage of Faith: From Darkness to Light.
Rajmohan Gandhi (Foreword by). Cloth Text. State University
of New York Press. Albany, NY. 2005. 304p.
ISBN:0-7914-6405-9, ISBN13: 978-0-7914-6405-2.
Dewey:954.03/5/092 B. LCCN:2004-014223.

Audience: **f.**

Menon, Ritu & Bhasin,   **DS480.842.M46 1998**
Kamla
Borders and Boundaries: Women in India's Partition. Trade
Cloth. Rutgers University Press. Piscataway, NJ. 1998. 276p.
ISBN:0-8135-2551-9, ISBN13: 978-0-8135-2551-8.
Dewey:954.04. LCCN:98-017638.

Audience: **l,u,f.**

Nanda, B. R.   **DS481.N35**
Jawaharlal Nehru: Rebel and Statesman. Trade Paper. Oxford
University Press, Inc. New York, NY. 1998. 322p. Oxford India
Paperbacks Ser. ISBN:0-19-564586-3, ISBN13:
978-0-19-564586-6. Dewey:954/.042/092.

Audience: **g,u,f.** *Choice, 1996.*

Nanda, B. R.   **DS481.G3**
Mahatma Gandhi: A Biography. Trade Paper. Oxford University
Press, Inc. New York, NY. 1996. 542p. Oxford India Paperbacks
Ser. ISBN:0-19-563855-7, ISBN13: 978-0-19-563855-4.
Dewey:954.03/5/0924.

Audience: **g,u,f.**

Nehru, Jawaharlal   **DS481.N35 A25 2003**
The Essential Writings of Jawaharlal Nehru, Vol. II. S. Gopal
(Editor). Trade Cloth. Oxford University Press, Inc. New York,
NY. 2003. 760p. ISBN:0-19-565324-6, ISBN13:
978-0-19-565324-3. Dewey:954.042. LCCN:2003-307522.

Audience: **g,u,f.** *Choice, 2004.*

Pandey, Gyanendra   **DS480.842 .P363 2001**
Remembering Partition: Violence, Nationalism and History in
India. Cloth Text. Cambridge University Press. New York, NY.
2001. 232p. Contemporary South Asia Ser.
ISBN:0-521-80759-X, ISBN13: 978-0-521-80759-3.
Dewey:954.035. LCCN:2001-025600.

Audience: **g,u,f.**

Parekh, Bhikhu   **DS481.G3P3465 1997**
Gandhi. Trade Paper. Oxford University Press, Inc. New York,
NY. 1997. 128p. Past Masters Ser. ISBN:0-19-287692-9,
ISBN13: 978-0-19-287692-8. Dewey:954.03/5/092.
LCCN:97-010822.

Audience: **g,u,f.**

Talbot, Ian   **DS480.84.T287 2000**
India and Pakistan. Cloth Text. Oxford University Press, Inc.
New York, NY. 2000. 336p. Inventing the Nation Ser.

ISBN:0-340-70632-5, ISBN13: 978-0-340-70632-9.
Dewey:954.04. LCCN:2001-269407.

Audience: **g,u,f.**

Tarlo, Emma   **DS480.852 .T37 2001**
Unsettling Memories: Narratives of the Emergency in Delhi.
Trade Cloth. University of California Press. Berkeley, CA. 2003.
268p. ISBN:0-520-23120-1, ISBN13: 978-0-520-23120-7.
Dewey:954.05. LCCN:2001-027447.

Audience: **g,u,f.** *Choice, 2004.*

Van Praagh, David   **DS480.853**
Greater Game: India's Race with Destiny and China. Trade
Cloth. McGill-Queen's University Press. Montreal, PQ. 2003.
464p. ISBN:0-7735-2639-0, ISBN13: 978-0-7735-2639-6.
Dewey:954/.05.

Audience: **g,f.**

Wolpert, Stanley   **DS481.G3**
Gandhi's Passion: The Life and Legacy of Mahatma Gandhi.
Trade Paper. Oxford University Press, Inc. New York, NY. 2002.
320p. ISBN:0-19-515634-X, ISBN13: 978-0-19-515634-8.
Dewey:954.03/5/092 B.

Audience: **g,u,f.**

India > History > Local History

Amin, Shahid   **DS486.C464A45 1995**
Event, Metaphor, Memory: Chauri Chaura, 1922-1992. Trade
Cloth. University of California Press. Berkeley, CA. 1995. 210p.
ISBN:0-520-08779-8, ISBN13: 978-0-520-08779-8.
Dewey:954/.2. LCCN:94-000737.

Audience: **f.** *Choice, 1996.*

Barauh, Sanjib   **DS485.A88B355 1999**
India Against Itself: Assam and the Politics of Nationality.
Book, Other. University of Pennsylvania Press. Philadelphia, PA.
1999. 280p. Critical Histories Ser. ISBN:0-8122-3491-X,
ISBN13: 978-0-8122-3491-6. Dewey:320.954/162/09045.
LCCN:99-012909.

Audience: **f.** *Choice, 1999.*

Bayly, Susan   **DS484.4 .B39 1989**
Saints, Goddesses and Kings: Muslims and Christians in South
Indian Society, 1700-1900. Trade Cloth. Cambridge University
Press. New York, NY. 1990. 520p. Cambridge South Asian
Studies, No. 43 ISBN:0-521-37201-1, ISBN13:
978-0-521-37201-5. Dewey:954/.8. LCCN:89-000543.

Audience: **f.** *Choice, 1990.*

Butalia, Urvashi   **DS480.45**
   (Contribution by)
The Other Side of Silence: Voices from the Partition of India.
Trade Cloth. Oxford University Press, Inc. New York, NY. 1999.
ISBN:0-19 579054-5, ISBN13: 978-0-19-579054-2.
Dewey:954/.0359. LCCN:99-921581.

Audience: **g,u,f.** *Choice, 2001.*

Chatterjee, Partha   **DS485.B493C485 1997**
The Present History of West Bengal: Essays in Political
Criticism. Cloth Text. Oxford University Press, Inc. New York,
NY. 1997. 240p. ISBN:0-19-563945-6, ISBN13:
978-0-19-563945-2. Dewey:954/.14. LCCN:96-912037.

Audience: **f.**

Chatterji, Joya   **DS485.B493 C49 1994**
Bengal Divided: Hindu Communalism and Partition, 1932-1947.
Trade Paper. Cambridge University Press. New York, NY. 2002.

323p. Cambridge South Asian Studies ISBN:0-521-52328-1,
ISBN13: 978-0-521-52328-8. Dewey:954/.140359.

Audience: **f.** *Choice, 1995.*

Dirks, Nicholas B.   **DS485.P12D57 1993**
The Hollow Crown: Ethnohistory of an Indian Kingdom. Ed. 2.
Trade Paper. University of Michigan Press. Chicago, IL. 1993.
488p. ISBN:0-472-08187-X, ISBN13: 978-0-472-08187-5.
Dewey:954/.82. LCCN:93-031920.

Audience: **g,u,f.**

Eaton, Richard M.   **DS485.B46.E16**
The Rise of Islam and the Bengal Frontier, 1204-1760. Trade
Paper. University of California Press. Berkeley, CA. 1996. 388p.
Comparative Studies on Muslim Societies, Vol. 17
ISBN:0-520-20507-3, ISBN13: 978-0-520-20507-9.
Dewey:954.1402. LCCN:92-034002.

Audience: **f.** *Choice, 1994.*

Fox, Richard G.   **DS485.P3**
Lions of the Punjab. Trade Cloth. Archives Publishers,
Distributors. 1986. ISBN:0-7855-1819-3, ISBN13:
978-0-7855-1819-8. Dewey:306/.0954/5.

Audience: **g,u,f.**

Freitag, Sandria B.   **DS475**
Collective Action and Community: Public Arenas and the
Emergence of Communalism in North India. Trade Cloth.
University of California Press. Berkeley, CA. 1989. xvii, 328p.
ISBN:0-520-06439-9, ISBN13: 978-0-520-06439-3. Dewey:954.
LCCN:88-036579.

Audience: **g,u,f.**

Freitag, Sandria B.   **DS486.B4C85 1989**
   (Editor)
Culture and Power in Banaras: Community, Performance, and
Environment, 1800-1980. Trade Cloth. University of California
Press. Berkeley, CA. 1989. 308p. ISBN:0-520-06367-8, ISBN13:
978-0-520-06367-9. Dewey:954/.2. LCCN:88-021092.

Audience: **g,u,f.** *Choice, 1990.*

Frykenberg, Robert E.   **DS486.D3D44 1986**
   (Editor)
Delhi Through the Ages: Essays in Urban History, Culture and
Society. Cloth Text. Oxford University Press, Inc. New York,
NY. 1988. 564p. ISBN:0-19-561728-2, ISBN13:
978-0-19-561728-3. Dewey:954/.56. LCCN:86-900004.

Audience: **l,u,f.** *Choice, 1989.*

Ganguly, Sumit   **DS485.K27 G37 1997**
The Crisis in Kashmir: Portents of War, Hopes of Peace. Lee H.
Hamilton (Contribution by). Cloth Text. Cambridge University
Press. New York, NY. 1997. 203p. Woodrow Wilson Center
Press Ser. ISBN:0-521-59066-3, ISBN13: 978-0-521-59066-2.
Dewey:954.6/05. LCCN:96-039401.

Audience: **g,u,f.** *Choice, 1997.*

Gilmartin, David   **DS485.P2G54 1988**
Empire and Islam: Punjab and the Making of Pakistan. Trade
Cloth. University of California Press. Berkeley, CA. 1988. 303p.
Comparative Studies on Muslim Societies, No. 7
ISBN:0-520-06249-3, ISBN13: 978-0-520-06249-8.
Dewey:954/.5. LCCN:88-008592.

Audience: **g,u,f.** *Choice, 1989.*

Gordon, Stewart   **DS436 .N47 1987 PT.**
The Marathas 1600-1818. C. A. Bayly, Gordon Johnson & John
F. Richards (Contribution by). Trade Cloth. Cambridge
University Press. New York, NY. 1993. 224p. The New

Cambridge History of India Ser., II: 4 ISBN:0-521-26883-4, ISBN13: 978-0-521-26883-7. Dewey:954.7025. LCCN:92-016525.

Audience: **f.**

Graff, Violette (Editor)   **DS486.B4**
Lucknow: Memories of a City. Trade Paper. Oxford University Press, Inc. New York, NY. 1999. 324p. ISBN:0-19-564887-0, ISBN13: 978-0-19-564887-4. Dewey:954/.2.

Audience: **g,u,f.**

Grewal, J. S.   **DS436 .N47 1987 PT.**
The Sikhs of the Punjab. C. A. Bayly, Gordon Johnson & John F. Richards (Contribution by). Trade Cloth. Cambridge University Press. New York, NY. 1991. 292p. The New Cambridge History of India Ser., II: 3 ISBN:0-521-26884-2, ISBN13: 978-0-521-26884-4. Dewey:954.500882946. LCCN:89-017348.

Audience: **g,u,f.** *Choice, 1992.*

Guha, Sumit   **DS485.M348 G84 1999**
Environment and Ethnicity in India, 1200-1991. C. A. Bayly, Rajnarayan Chandavarkar & Gordon Johnson (Contribution by). Trade Cloth. Cambridge University Press. New York, NY. 1999. 234p. Cambridge Studies in Indian History and Society, Vol. 4 ISBN:0-521-64078-4, ISBN13: 978-0-521-64078-7. Dewey:954/.792. LCCN:98-040358.

Audience: **u,f.** *Choice, 2000.*

Harlan, Lindsey   **DS485.R24.H38 2003**
The Goddesses' Henchmen: Gender in Indian Hero Worship. Trade Paper. Oxford University Press, Inc. New York, NY. 2003. 272p. ISBN:0-19-515426-6, ISBN13: 978-0-19-515426-9. Dewcy:306/.0954/4. LCCN:2002-071520.

Audience: **g,f.**

Huttenback, Robert A.   **DS485.K26H88 2004**
Kashmir and the British Raj 1847-1947. Trade Cloth. Oxford University Press, Inc. New York, NY. 2005. 200p. ISBN:0-19-579967-4, ISBN13: 978-0-19-579967-5. Dewey:954/.6. LCCN:2005-298364.

Audience: **g,u,f.**

Irschick, Eugene F.   **DS484.7 .I77 1994**
Dialogue and History: Constructing South India, 1795-1895. Trade Paper. University of California Press. Berkeley, CA. 1994. 278p. ISBN:0-520-08405-5, ISBN13: 978-0-520-08405-6. Dewey:954.8031. LCCN:93-010238.

Audience: **g,u,f.** *Choice, 1994.*

Jha, Prem Shankar   **DS385.9**
Kashmir 1947: Rival Versions of History. Trade Cloth. Pluto Press. London, 2003. 200p. ISBN:0-7453-2085-6, ISBN13: 978-0-7453-2085-4. Dewey:954/.042.

Audience: **f.**

Kanwar, Pamela   **DS486.S5K28 2003**
Imperial Simla: The Political Culture of the Raj. Ed. 2. Trade Paper. Oxford University Press, Inc. New York, NY. 2003. 372p. Oxford India Paperbacks Ser. ISBN:0-19-566721-2, ISBN13: 978-0-19-566721-9. Dewey:954/.6. LCCN:2004-295180.

Audience: **g,u,f.**

Kaul, H. K. (Editor)   **DS485.D3 H55 1985**
Historic Delhi: An Anthology. Cloth Text. Oxford University Press, Inc. New York, NY. 1986. 492p. ISBN:0-19-561484-4, ISBN13: 978-0-19-561484-8. Dewey:954/.56. LCCN:85-903946.

Audience: **f.**

Lecomte-Tilouine,   **DS485.H6E85 2003**
  Marie & Dollfus, Pascale (Editors)
Ethnic Revival And Religious Turmoil: Identities and Representatons in the Himalayas. Trade Cloth. Oxford University Press, Inc. New York, NY. 2003. 352p. ISBN:0-19-565592-3, ISBN13: 978-0-19-565592-6. Dewey:305.80095496. LCCN:2003-334754.

Audience: **f.**

Marshall, P. J.   **DS436 .N47 1987 PT.**
Bengal: The British Bridgehead: Eastern India 1740-1828. C. A. Bayly, Gordon Johnson & John F. Richards (Contribution by). Trade Cloth. Cambridge University Press. New York, NY. 1988. 222p. The New Cambridge History of India Ser., II: 2 ISBN:0-521-25330-6, ISBN13: 978-0-521-25330-7. Dewey:954/.1029. LCCN:86-009719.

Audience: **f.** *Choice, 1989.*

Menon, Dilip M.   **DS485.K48.M46 1994**
Caste, Nationalism, and Communism in South India: Malabar, 1900-1948. Trade Cloth. Cambridge University Press. New York, NY. 1994. 228p. Cambridge South Asian Studies, No. 55 ISBN:0-521-41879-8, ISBN13: 978-0-521-41879-9. Dewey:954.83035. LCCN:93-006609.

Audience: **f.** *Choice, 1994.*

Pandey, Gyanendra   **DS422**
The Construction of Communalism in Colonial North India. Ed. 2. Trade Paper. Oxford University Press, Inc. New York, NY. 2006. 348p. ISBN:0-19-567678-5, ISBN13: 978-0-19-567678-5. Dewey:302/.14. LCCN:2006-345278.

Audience: **g,u,f.** *Choice, 1991.*

Preston, Laurence W.   **DS485.M348P74 1989**
The Devs of Cincvad: A Lineage and State in Maharashtra. Trade Cloth. Cambridge University Press. New York, NY. 1989. 288p. Cambridge South Asian Studies ISBN:0-521-34633-9, ISBN13: 978-0-521-34633-7. Dewey:954/.792. LCCN:88-010857.

Audience: **f.** *Choice, 1990.*

Ramusack, Barbara N.   **DS436.R256 2003**
The Indian Princes and Their States. C. A. Bayly, Gordon Johnson & John F. Richards (Contribution by). Cloth Text. Cambridge University Press. New York, NY. 2003. 324p. The New Cambridge History of India Ser., Vol. 6 ISBN:0-521-26727-7, ISBN13: 978-0-521-26727-4. Dewey:954.03. LCCN:2003-055516.

Audience: **l,u,f.**

Raychaudhuri, Tapan   **DS485.B41**
Europe Reconsidered: Perceptions of the West in Nineteenth-Century Bengal. Ed. 2. Trade Paper. Oxford University Press, Inc. New York, NY. 2006. 420p. Oxford India Paperbacks Ser. ISBN:0-19-568002-2, ISBN13: 978-0-19-568002-7. Dewey:954.1/4/035.

Audience: **g,u,f.**

Rudolph, Susanne   **DS480.S63 2002**
  Hoeber, et al.
Reversing the Gaze: Amar Singh's Diary, a Colonial Subject's Narrative of Imperial India. Lloyd I. Rudolph & Mohan Singh Kanota (Authors). Trade Cloth. Westview Press. Boulder, CO. 2002. 656p. ISBN:0-8133-3626-0, ISBN13: 978-0-8133-3626-8. Dewey:954.03. LCCN:2002-003069.

Audience: **g,u,f.**

Singh, Upinder   **DS486.D3S58 1999**
Ancient Delhi. Cloth Text. Oxford University Press, Inc. New
York, NY. 2000. 130p. ISBN:0-19-564919-2, ISBN13:
978-0-19-564919-2. Dewey:954/.56. LCCN:99-952349.
Audience: **f.**

Stein, Burton   **DS484 .S74**
Peasant State and Society in Medieval South India. Trade Cloth.
Oxford University Press, Inc. New York, NY. 1980. 550p.
ISBN:0-19-561065-2, ISBN13: 978-0-19-561065-9.
Dewey:323.32.
Audience: **f.**

Stein, Burton   **DS436 .N47 1987 PT.**
The New Cambridge History of India: Vijayanagara. Gordon
Johnson, C. A. Bayly & John F. Richards (Contribution by).
Trade Paper. Cambridge University Press. New York, NY. 2005.
181p. The New Cambridge History of India Ser.
ISBN:0-521-61925-4, ISBN13: 978-0-521-61925-7. Dewey:954.
Audience: **f.**

Subrahmanyam, Sanjay   **DS484.65.S86 2001**
Penumbral Visions: Making Polities in Early Modern South
India. Trade Cloth. University of Michigan Press. Chicago, IL.
2001. 312p. ISBN:0-472-11216-3, ISBN13: 978-0-472-11216-6.
Dewey:954/.8025. LCCN:2001-034777.
Audience: **f.** *Choice, 2002.*

Talbot, Cynthia   **DS485.A55T35 2001**
Precolonial India in Practice: Society, Region, and Identity in
Medieval Andhra. Trade Cloth. Oxford University Press, Inc.
New York, NY. 2001. 322p. ISBN:0-19-513661-6, ISBN13:
978-0-19-513661-6. Dewey:954/.84. LCCN:99-049890.
Audience: **f.** *Choice, 2002.*

Wink, Andre   **DS485.M349W56 1986**
Land and Sovereignty in India: Agrarian Society and Politics
under the Eighteenth Century Maratha Svarajya. Trade Cloth.
Cambridge University Press. New York, NY. 1986. 418p.
University of Cambridge Oriental Publications, No. 36
ISBN:0-521-32064-X, ISBN13: 978-0-521-32064-1.
Dewey:954.03. LCCN:85-022333.
Audience: **f.**

Zurick, David & Karan,   **DS485.H6Z87 1999**
P. P.
Himalaya: Life on the Edge of the World. Trade Cloth. Johns
Hopkins University Press. Baltimore, MD. 1999. 376p.
ISBN:0-8018-6168-3, ISBN13: 978-0-8018-6168-0.
Dewey:954.96. LCCN:99-011037.
Audience: **g,u,f.** *Choice, 2000.*

Zutshi, Chitralekha   **DS485.K25Z88 2003**
Languages of Belonging: Islam, Regional Identity, and the
Making of Kashmir. Trade Cloth. Oxford University Press, Inc.
New York, NY. 2004. 320p. ISBN:0-19-521939-2, ISBN13:
978-0-19-521939-5. Dewey:954/.6. LCCN:2003-015966.
Audience: **f.** *Choice, 2005.*

Pakistan

Burke, S. M. &   **DS385.J5B87 1997**
Quraishi, Salim A.
Quaid-i-Azam Mohammad Ali Jinnah: His Personality and His
Politics. Cloth Text. Oxford University Press, Inc. New York,
NY. 1997. 428p. Jubilee Ser. ISBN:0-19-577783-2, ISBN13:
978-0-19-577783-3. Dewey:954.904/2/092. LCCN:98-107916.
Audience: **u,f.**

Burki, Shahid Javed   **DS384.B877 1986**
Pakistan: A Nation in the Making. Oxford University Press.
1986. ISBN:0-86531-353-9, ISBN13: 978-0-86531-353-8.
Audience: **g,l,u,f.**

Faiz, Faiz Ahmad;   **PK2199.F255**
Majeed, Sheema
Culture and Identity: Selected English Writings of Faiz Ahmad
Faiz. Oxford University Press, Inc. 2006. ISBN:0-19-597958-3,
ISBN13: 978-0-19-597958-9.
Audience: **u,f.**

Faiz, Faiz Ahmed   **PK2199.F255A23 1995**
The Rebel's Silhouette: Selected Poems. Agha Shahid Ali
(Translator, Introduction by). Trade Paper. University of
Massachusetts Press. Amherst, MA. 1995. 128p.
ISBN:0-87023-975-9, ISBN13: 978-0-87023-975-5.
Dewey:891/.43917. LCCN:94-040502.
Audience: **l,u,f.**

Jalal, Ayesha   **DS384.J36 1990**
The State of Martial Rule: The Origins of Pakistan's Political
Economy of Defence. Trade Cloth. Cambridge University Press.
New York, NY. 1990. 376p. Cambridge South Asian Studies,
No. 46 ISBN:0-521-37348-4, ISBN13: 978-0-521-37348-7.
Dewey:954.904. LCCN:89-007266.
Audience: **u.** *Choice, 1991.*

Kennedy, Charles H.   **DS389**
(Editor), et al.
Pakistan at the Millennium. Kathleen McNeil, Carl Ernst &
David Gilmartin (Editors). Trade Cloth. Oxford University
Press, Inc. New York, NY. 2003. 410p. ISBN:0-19-579776-0,
ISBN13: 978-0-19-579776-3. Dewey:954.9/105.
LCCN:2003-341173.
Audience: **u,f.**

Lazard, Naomi   **PK2199.F255**
The True Subject: Selected Poems of Faiz Ahmed Faiz. Cloth
Text. Princeton University Press. Princeton, NJ. 1987. 110p.
ISBN:0-691-06704-X, ISBN13: 978-0-691-06704-9.
Dewey:891/.43917.
Audience: **g,l,u,f.**

Mozzam, Sheikh   **PK2211.E8**
(Editor)
Letter from India: Contemporary Short Stories from Pakistan.
Trade Paper. Penguin Group (USA) Inc. New York, NY. 2004.
xvii, 168p. ISBN:0-14-303049-3, ISBN13: 978-0-14-303049-2.
Dewey:200. LCCN:2004-326597.
Audience: **g,l,u.**

Weiss, Anita M. &   **HN690.5.P6P68 2001**
Gilani, S. Zulfiger (Editors)
Power and Civil Society in Pakistan. Cloth Text. Oxford
University Press, Inc. New York, NY. 2001. 328p.
ISBN:0-19-579414-1, ISBN13: 978-0-19-579414-4.
Dewey:954.9105. LCCN:2001-300075.
Audience: **u,f.**

Wolpert, Stanley A.   **DS385.B45W65 1993**
Zulfi Bhutto of Pakistan: His Life and Times. Trade Cloth.
Oxford University Press, Inc. New York, NY. 1993. 400p.
ISBN:0-19-507661-3, ISBN13: 978-0-19-507661-5.
Dewey:954.9105/092.. LCCN:92-030044.
Audience: **u,f.**

Sri Lanka (Ceylon)

De Silva, K. M. &   **DS489.83.J3D4 1988**
   Wriggins, W. Howard
J. R. Jayewardene of Sri Lanka: A Political Biography: The First
Fifty Years. Trade Cloth. University of Hawaii Press. Honolulu,
HI. 1988. 336p. ISBN:0-8248-1183-6, ISBN13:
978-0-8248-1183-9. Dewey:954.9/3. LCCN:88-010828.
                              Audience: **l,u,f.** *Choice, 1989.*

De Silva, K. M. &   **DS489.83.J3**
   Wriggins, W. Howard
J. R. Jayewardene of Sri Lanka: A Political Biography: from
1956 to His Retirement, Vol. 2. Trade Cloth. University of
Hawaii Press. Honolulu, HI. 1995. 416p. ISBN:0-8248-1692-7,
ISBN13: 978-0-8248-1692-6. Dewey:954.9/3.
                              Audience: **l,u,f.**

DeVotta, Neil   **DS489.84.D48 2004**
Blowback: Linguistic Nationalism, Institutional Decay, and
Ethnic Conflict in Sri Lanka. Trade Cloth. Stanford University
Press. Palo Alto, CA. 2004. 304p. Contemporary Issues in Asia
and the Pacific Ser. ISBN:0-8047-4923-X, ISBN13:
978-0-8047-4923-7. Dewey:323.15493/09/045.
LCCN:2003-027044.
                              Audience: **u,f.**

Dharmadasa, K. N.   **DS489.7 .D52 1992**
Language, Religion, and Ethnic Assertiveness: The Growth of
Sinhalese Nationalism in Sri Lanka. Trade Cloth. University of
Michigan Press. Chicago, IL. 1993. 384p. ISBN:0-472-10288-5,
ISBN13: 978-0-472-10288-4. Dewey:305.8/0095493.
LCCN:92-031734.
                              Audience: **u,f.**

Ghosh, Partha S.   **DS489.84.G48 2003**
Ethnicity Versus Nationalism: The Devolution Discourse in Sri
Lanka. Trade Cloth. SAGE Publications, Inc. Thousand Oaks,
CA. 2003. 496p. ISBN:0-7619-9771-7, ISBN13:
978-0-7619-9771-9. Dewey:323.119481105493.
LCCN:2003-001029.
                              Audience: **u,f.**

Manogaran, Chelvadurai   **DS489.8.M36 1987**
Ethnic Conflict and Reconciliation in Sri Lanka. Cloth Text.
University of Hawaii Press. Honolulu, HI. 1987. 248p.
ISBN:0-8248-1116-X, ISBN13: 978-0-8248-1116-7.
Dewey:954.9/303. LCCN:87-016247.
                              Audience: **l,u,f.** *Choice, 1988.*

Manor, James   **DS489.83.B3M36 1989**
The Expedient Utopian: Bandaranaike and Ceylon. Trade Cloth.
Cambridge University Press. New York, NY. 1990. 352p.
ISBN:0-521-37191-0, ISBN13: 978-0-521-37191-9.
Dewey:954.9/303/0924 B. LCCN:89-000724.
                              Audience: **u,f.** *Choice, 1990.*

Peebles, Patrick   **DS489.25.T3P384 2001**
The Plantation Tamils of Ceylon. Trade Cloth. Continuum
International Publishing Group, Ltd. London, 2001. 256p. New
Historical Perspectives on Migration Ser. ISBN:0-7185-0154-3,
ISBN13: 978-0-7185-0154-9. Dewey:954.93/0049411.
LCCN:00-063736.
                              Audience: **u,f.**

Somasundaram, Daya   **DS489.25.T3S66 1998**
Scarred Minds: The Psychological Impact of War on Sri Lankan
Tamils. Trade Cloth. SAGE Publications, Inc. Thousand Oaks,
CA. 1998. 356p. ISBN:0-7619-9267-7, ISBN13:

978-0-7619-9267-7. Dewey:616.85/21/008994811.
LCCN:98-007050.
                              Audience: **l,u,f.**

Spencer, Jonathan   **HN670.8**
A Sinhala Village in a Time of Trouble: Politics and Change in
Rural Sri Lanka. Paper Text. Oxford University Press, Inc. New
York, NY. 2000. 308p. Oxford University South Asian Studies
ISBN:0-19-565080-8, ISBN13: 978-0-19-565080-8.
Dewey:320.9/5493. LCCN:90-900161.
                              Audience: **l,u,f.**

Tambiah, Stanley J.   **DS489.8.T34 1986**
Sri Lanka: Ethnic Fratricide and the Dismantling of Democracy.
Trade Cloth. University of Chicago Press. Chicago, IL. 1993.
xii, 198p. ISBN:0-226-78951-9, ISBN13: 978-0-226-78951-4.
Dewey:305.8/0095493. LCCN:85-024598.
                              Audience: **u,f.**

Nepal

Adams, Vincanne   **DS493.9.S5A33 1996**
Tigers of the Snow and Other Virtual Sherpas: An Ethnography
of Himalayan Encounters. Trade Paper. Princeton University
Press. Princeton, NJ. 1995. 320p. ISBN:0-691-00111-1, ISBN13:
978-0-691-00111-1. Dewey:305.8/0095496. LCCN:95-004618.
                              Audience: **u,f.** *Choice, 1996.*

Ahearn, Laura M.   **DS493.9.M3A54 2001**
Invitations to Love: Literacy, Love Letters, and Social Change
in Nepal. Trade Cloth. University of Michigan Press. Chicago,
IL. 2001. 312p. ISBN:0-472-09784-9, ISBN13:
978-0-472-09784-5. Dewey:306.81/089/954.
LCCN:2001-053049.
                              Audience: **l,u,f.**

Cameron, Mary M.   **DS495.8.B456C36 1998**
On the Edge of the Auspicious: Gender and Caste in Nepal.
Trade Paper. University of Illinois Press. Champaign, IL. 1998.
328p. ISBN:0-252-06716-9, ISBN13: 978-0-252-06716-7.
Dewey:305.48/9694. LCCN:97-045408.
                              Audience: **u,f.**

Fisher, James F.   **DS493.9.M3**
Himalayan Traders: Economy, Society, and Culture in Northwest
Nepal. Trade Cloth. University of California Press. Berkeley,
CA. 1986. 246p. ISBN:0-520-05375-3, ISBN13:
978-0-520-05375-5. Dewey:306/.09549/6. LCCN:85-005834.
                              Audience: **u,f.** *Choice, 1986.*

Fisher, James F.   **DS495.33 .A25**
Living Martyrs: Individuals and Revolution in Nepal. Tanka
Prasad Acharya & Rewanta Kumari Acharya (Contribution by).
Trade Paper. Oxford University Press, Inc. New York, NY. 2000.
336p. ISBN:0-19-564544-8, ISBN13: 978-0-19-564544-6.
Dewey:954.9/6/0099.
                              Audience: **u,f.**

Fisher, William F.   **DS493.9.T45F57 2001**
Fluid Boundaries: Forming and Transforming Identity in Nepal.
Trade Cloth. Columbia University Press. New York, NY. 2001.
256p. ISBN:0-231-11086-3, ISBN13: 978-0-231-11086-0.
Dewey:305.891/495. LCCN:2001-032461.
                              Audience: **u,f.** *Choice, 2002.*

Fricke, Tom   **DS493.9.T35F75 1994**
Himalayan Households: Tamang Demography and Domestic
Processes. Trade Paper. Columbia University Press. New York,
NY. 1994. 243p. ISBN:0-231-10007-8, ISBN13:
978-0-231-10007-6. Dewey:306.4/08991495. LCCN:93-037643.
Audience: **u,f.**

Gellner, David N. &   **DS493.9.N4C65 1995**
  Quigley, Declan (Editors)
Contested Hierarchies: A Collaborative Ethnography of Caste
among the Newars of the Kathmandu Valley, Nepal. Trade
Cloth. Oxford University Press, Inc. New York, NY. 1995. 378p.
Oxford Studies in Social and Cultural Anthropology - Cultural
Forms ISBN:0-19-827960-4, ISBN13: 978-0-19-827960-0.
Dewey:305.5/122/08995. LCCN:94-046776.
Audience: **f.**

Hutt, Michael J.   **PK2598.Z95E5 1990**
Himalayan Voices: An Introduction to Modern Nepali Literature.
Trade Cloth. University of California Press. Berkeley, CA. 1991.
280p. Voices from Asia Ser., No. 2 ISBN:0-520-07046-1,
ISBN13: 978-0-520-07046-2. Dewey:891/.49. LCCN:90-011145.
Audience: **g,l,u.**

Levine, Nancy E.   **DS493.9.N92L48 1988**
The Dynamics of Polyandry: Kinship, Domesticity, and
Population on the Tibetan Border. Paper Text. University of
Chicago Press. Chicago, IL. 1998. 344p. ISBN:0-226-47569-7,
ISBN13: 978-0-226-47569-1. Dewey:306.8/08991495.
LCCN:87-034478.
Audience: **u,f.** *Choice, 1989.*

March, Kathryn S.   **DS493.9.T35M64 2002**
If Each Comes Halfway: Meeting Tamang Women in Nepal.
Trade Cloth. Cornell University Press. Ithaca, NY. 2002. 336p.
ISBN:0-8014-4017-3, ISBN13: 978-0-8014-4017-5.
Dewey:305.48/8954. LCCN:2002-007945.
Audience: **u,f.**

Whelpton, John   **DS494.5.W43 2005**
A History of Nepal. Cloth Text. Cambridge University Press.
New York, NY. 2005. 320p. ISBN:0-521-80026-9, ISBN13:
978-0-521-80026-6. Dewey:954.96. LCCN:2004-051856.
Audience: **g,l,u,f.** *Choice, 2006.*

Southeast Asia, General

Bayly, Christopher &   **D767.B39 2005**
  Harper, Tim
Forgotten Armies: The Fall of British Asia, 1941-1945. Trade
Cloth. Harvard University Press. Cambridge, MA. 2005. 616p.
ISBN:0-674-01748-X, ISBN13: 978-0-674-01748-1.
Dewey:940.54/25. LCCN:2004-054300.
Audience: **g,u,f.** *Choice, 2005.*

Brissenden, Rosemary   **TX724**
South East Asian Food: Classic and Modern Dishes from
Thailand, Indonesia, Malaysia, Singapore, Laos, Cambodia and
Vietnam. Trade Paper. Hardie Grant Books. Prahran, VIC. 2004.
592p. ISBN:1-74066-013-7, ISBN13: 978-1-74066-013-6.
Dewey:973.
Audience: **g,u,f.**

Coedes, G.   **DS511**
The Indianized States of South-East Asia. Walter F. Vella
(Editor), Susan B. Cowing (Translator). Trade Cloth. University

of Hawaii Press. Honolulu, HI. 1975. 424p.
ISBN:0-8248-0368-X, ISBN13: 978-0-8248-0368-1. Dewey:959.
LCCN:67-029224.
Audience: **u,f.**

Cribb, Robert &   **DS524.4**
  Hoadley, Mason C.
The Palgrave Concise Historical Atlas of South East Asia. Trade
Cloth. Palgrave Macmillan. New York, NY. 2007. 128p.
ISBN:0-312-29625-8, ISBN13: 978-0-312-29625-4.
Dewey:911.59.
Audience: **g,l,u,f.**

Gullick, J. M.   **DS522.2.A38 1995**
  (Compiled by)
Adventures and Encounters: Europeans in South-East Asia.
Trade Paper. Oxford University Press, Inc. New York, NY. 1996.
334p. Oxford in Asia Paperbacks Ser. ISBN:967-65-3090-5,
ISBN13: 978-967-65-3090-5. Dewey:959. LCCN:95-001527.
Audience: **g,u,f.**

Hall, Daniel G.   **DS511 .H15 1981**
A History of South-East Asia. Ed. 4. Cloth Text. Palgrave
Macmillan. New York, NY. 1981. ISBN:0-312-38641-9,
ISBN13: 978-0-312-38641-2. Dewey:959.
Audience: **g,u,f.** *B*

Jue, Joyce & Williams,   **TX724.5.S68J84 2000**
  Chuck
Savoring Southeast Asia: Recipes and Reflections on Southeast
Asian Cooking. Marlene McLoughlin (Illustrator), Noel
Barnhurst (Photographer). Trade Cloth. Time-Life Inc. Fairfax,
VA. 2000. 256p. The Savoring Ser. ISBN:0-7370-2043-1,
ISBN13: 978-0-7370-2043-4. Dewey:641.5959.
LCCN:99-057164.
Audience: **g,u,f.**

Lamb, Margaret &   **D741.L32 2001**
  Tarling, Nicholas
From Versailles to Pearl Harbor: The Origins of the Second
World War in Europe and Asia. Trade Cloth. Palgrave
Macmillan. New York, NY. 2001. 238p. ISBN:0-333-73839-X,
ISBN13: 978-0-333-73839-9. Dewey:940.53/11.
LCCN:00-048341.
Audience: **u,f.** *Choice, 2002.*

Lieberman, Victor B.   **DS524.4.L54 2003**
Strange Parallels: Southeast Asia in Global Context, C.
800-1830. Michael Adas, Edmund Burke III & Philip D. Curtin
(Contribution by). Cloth Text. Cambridge University Press. New
York, NY. 2003. 508p. Studies in Comparative World History
ISBN:0-521-80086-2, ISBN13: 978-0-521-80086-0. Dewey:959.
LCCN:2002-071481.
Audience: **u,f.**

Matsuyama, Akira   **GT2853.J3**
The Traditional Dietary Culture of Southeast Asia: A Culinary
History. Trade Cloth. Kegan Paul International, Ltd. London,
2003. 350p. ISBN:0-7103-0729-2, ISBN13: 978-0-7103-0729-3.
Dewey:394.1/059.
Audience: **u,f.**

McCoy, Alfred W.   **HV5822.H4M33 1991**
The Politics of Heroin: CIA Complicity in the Global Drug
Trade. Trade Cloth. Chicago Review Press, Inc. Chicago, IL.
1991. 654p. ISBN:1-55652-126-X, ISBN13: 978-1-55652-126-3.
Dewey:363.4/5/0959. LCCN:90-047398.
Audience: **u,f.**

Owen, Norman G.   DS525.E44 2005
The Emergence of Modern Southeast Asia: A New History.
Trade Cloth. University of Hawaii Press. Honolulu, HI. 2005.
576p. ISBN:0-8248-2841-0, ISBN13: 978-0-8248-2841-7.
Dewey:959. LCCN:2004-007660.
Audience: g,u,f. Choice, 2005.

Parker, Geoffrey &   D246.G24 1997
  Smith, Lesley M.
The General Crisis of the Seventeenth Century. Ed. 2. Paper
over Boards. Routledge. New York, NY. 1997. 320p.
ISBN:0-415-16518-0, ISBN13: 978-0-415-16518-1.
Dewey:940.2/52. LCCN:96-045505.
Audience: g,u,f.

Reid, Anthony   DS526.4.R46 1988
Southeast Asia in the Age of Commerce, 1450-1680: Expansion
and Crisis. Trade Cloth. Yale University Press. Cumberland, RI.
1993. 392p. ISBN:0-300-05412-2, ISBN13: 978-0-300-05412-5.
Dewey:959. LCCN:87-020749.
Audience: g,u,f. Choice, 1994.

Reid, Anthony   DS526.4.R46 1988
Southeast Asia in the Age of Commerce, 1450-1680: The Lands
Below the Winds, Vol. 1. Trade Cloth. Yale University Press.
Cumberland, RI. 1988. 272p. ISBN:0-300-03921-2, ISBN13:
978-0-300-03921-4. Dewey:959. LCCN:87-020749.
Audience: g,u,f. Choice, 1989.

Steinberg, David J.   DS525.I48 1987
  (Editor)
In Search of Southeast Asia: A Modern History. Ed. 2. Trade
Cloth. University of Hawaii Press. Honolulu, HI. 1987. 608p.
ISBN:0-8248-1110-0, ISBN13: 978-0-8248-1110-5. Dewey:959.
LCCN:87-019233.
Audience: g,u,f. ℬ

Tarling, Nicholas   DS525 .C36
The Cambridge History of Southeast Asia Set. Trade Cloth.
Cambridge University Press. New York, NY.
ISBN:0-521-46678-4, ISBN13: 978-0-521-46678-3. Dewey:959.
Audience: g,u,f.

Tarling, Nicholas   DS526.4.T373 2001
Imperialism in Southeast Asia: A Fleeting Passing Phase. Paper
over Boards. Routledge. New York, NY. 2001. 336p. Asia's
Transformation Ser. ISBN:0-415-23289-9, ISBN13:
978-0-415-23289-0. Dewey:959/.04. LCCN:00-054370.
Audience: g,u,f. Choice, 2002.

Tarling, Nicholas   DS526.6.T37 2004
Nationalism in Southeast Asia. Paper over Boards. Routledge.
New York, NY. 2004. 288p. RoutledgeCurzon Studies in the
Modern History of Asia Ser., Vol. 26 ISBN:0-415-33476-4,
ISBN13: 978-0-415-33476-1. Dewey:320.54/0959.
LCCN:2004-006171.
Audience: g,u,f.

Tarling, Nicholas   DS525.T373 2001
South-East Asia: A Modern History. Trade Cloth. Oxford
University Press, Inc. New York, NY. 2001. 568p.
ISBN:0-19-558441-4, ISBN13: 978-0-19-558441-7. Dewey:959.
LCCN:2001-275214.
Audience: g,u,f. Choice, 2002.

Yen Ho, Alice   TX724.5.S68H63 1995
At the South-East Asian Table. Trade Cloth. Oxford University
Press, Inc. New York, NY. 1996. 96p. Images of Asia Ser.

ISBN:967-65-3107-3, ISBN13: 978-967-65-3107-0.
Dewey:641.5/959. LCCN:95-009419.
Audience: g,u,f.

Myanmar (Burma)

Myint-U, Thant   DS529.3 .T48 2001
The Making of Modern Burma. Trade Cloth. Cambridge
University Press. New York, NY. 2001. 292p.
ISBN:0-521-78021-7, ISBN13: 978-0-521-78021-6.
Dewey:959.103. LCCN:00-040372.
Audience: l,u.

Silverstein, Josef   DS530.4
Burma: Military Rule and the Politics of Stagnation. Book,
Other. Cornell University Press. Ithaca, NY. 1977. 224p. Politics
and International Relations of Southeast Asia Ser.
ISBN:0-8014-0911-X, ISBN13: 978-0-8014-0911-0.
Dewey:959.1/05. LCCN:77-003127.
Audience: u,f. ℬ

Skidmore, Monique   GN635.B8B87 2005
  (Editor)
Burma at the Turn of the Twenty-First Century. Perfect.
University of Hawaii Press. Honolulu, HI. 2005. 304p.
ISBN:0-8248-2857-7, ISBN13: 978-0-8248-2857-8.
Dewey:306/.09591. LCCN:2005-003440.
Audience: u,f. Choice, 2006.

Steinberg, David I.   DS530.65.S74 2001
Burma, the State of Myanmar. Trade Cloth. Georgetown
University Press. Washington, DC. 2000. xxxiii, 342p.
ISBN:0-87840-842-8, ISBN13: 978-0-87840-842-9.
Dewey:959.105. LCCN:00-061037.
Audience: u,f. Choice, 2002.

Taylor, Robert H.   JQ751.A58B87 2001
  (Editor)
Burma: Political Economy under Military Rule. Cloth over
Boards. Palgrave Macmillan. New York, NY. 2001. 168p.
ISBN:0-312-23568-2, ISBN13: 978-0-312-23568-0.
Dewey:959.1/05. LCCN:00-033349.
Audience: u,f.

Taylor, Robert H.   JQ442.T39 1988
The State in Burma. Cloth Text. University of Hawaii Press.
Honolulu, HI. 1988. 400p. ISBN:0-8248-1141-0, ISBN13:
978-0-8248-1141-9. Dewey:320.9591. LCCN:87-016200.
Audience: u,f. Choice, 1988.

Myanmar (Burma) > History

Cady, John F.   DS485.B86 C2
A History of Modern Burma. Book, Other. Cornell University
Press. Ithaca, NY. 1958. 729p. ISBN:0-8014-0059-7, ISBN13:
978-0-8014-0059-9. Dewey:959.1.
Audience: l,u.

Furnivall, J. S.   DS485.B89 F8
Colonial Policy and Practice: A Comparative Study of Burma
and Netherlands India. Paper Text. Textbook Publishers.
Temecula, CA. 2003. xii, 568p. ISBN:0-7581-7741-0, ISBN13:
978-0-7581-7741-4. Dewey:959.1.
Audience: u,f. ℬ

Koenig, William J.   **DS529.3.K64 1990**
The Burmese Polity, 1752-1819: Politics, Administration, and
Social Organization in the Early Kon-baung Period. Trade Cloth.
University of Michigan, Center for South & Southeast Asian
Studies. Ann Arbor, MI. 1990. 352p. Michigan Papers on South
and Southeast Asia, No. 34 ISBN:0-89148-056-0, ISBN13:
978-0-89148-056-3. Dewey:959.1/02. LCCN:88-063416.
                         Audience: **u,f.**   *Choice, 1990.*

Lintner, Bertil   **DS530.4 .L55 1999**
Burma in Revolt: Opium and Insurgency since 1948. Ed. 2.
Trade Cloth. Silk Worm Books. Bangkok, 2000. 604p.
ISBN:974-7100-78-9, ISBN13: 978-974-7100-78-5.
Dewey:959.105. LCCN:2001-398787.
                                        Audience: **l,u.**

Maung Maung, U.   **DS530.M37 1990**
Burmese Nationalist Movements, 1940-1949. Cloth Text.
University of Hawaii Press. Honolulu, HI. 1991. 416p.
ISBN:0-8248-1342-1, ISBN13: 978-0-8248-1342-0.
Dewey:959.1/04. LCCN:90-011053.
                         Audience: **l,u.**   *Choice, 1991.*

Myint-U, Thant   **DS529.3 .T48 2001**
The Making of Modern Burma. Trade Cloth. Cambridge
University Press. New York, NY. 2001. 292p.
ISBN:0-521-78021-7, ISBN13: 978-0-521-78021-6.
Dewey:959.103. LCCN:00-040372.
                                        Audience: **l,u.**

Nash, Manning   **DS485.B84.N3**
Golden Road to Modernity. Paper Text. University of Chicago
Press. Chicago, IL. 1993. viii, 333p. ISBN:0-226-56860-1,
ISBN13: 978-0-226-56860-7. Dewey:390.09591.
LCCN:65-021437.
                                        Audience: **u,f.**

Seekins, Donald M.   **DS528.34.S44 2006**
Historical Dictionary of Burma (Myanmar). Trade Cloth.
Scarecrow Press, Inc. Lanham, MD. 2006. 528p.
ISBN:0-8108-5476-7, ISBN13: 978-0-8108-5476-5.
Dewey:959.1003. LCCN:2006-001432.
                                        Audience: **g,l,u,f.**

Silverstein, Josef   **DS530.4**
Burma: Military Rule and the Politics of Stagnation. Book,
Other. Cornell University Press. Ithaca, NY. 1977. 224p. Politics
and International Relations of Southeast Asia Ser.
ISBN:0-8014-0911-X, ISBN13: 978-0-8014-0911-0.
Dewey:959.1/05. LCCN:77-003127.
                                        Audience: **u,f.** *B*

Singh, Balwant   **DS530.4**
Independence and Democracy in Burma, 1945-1952: The
Turbulent Years. Trade Cloth. University of Michigan, Center
for South & Southeast Asian Studies. Ann Arbor, MI. 1993.
180p. Michigan Papers on South and Southeast Asia, No. 40
ISBN:0-89148-068-4, ISBN13: 978-0-89148-068-6.
Dewey:320.9591. LCCN:92-073828.
                                        Audience: **u,f.**

Skidmore, Monique   **GN635.B8B87 2005**
   (Editor)
Burma at the Turn of the Twenty-First Century. Perfect.
University of Hawaii Press. Honolulu, HI. 2005. 304p.
ISBN:0-8248-2857-7, ISBN13: 978-0-8248-2857-8.
Dewey:306/.09591. LCCN:2005-003440.
                         Audience: **u,f.**   *Choice, 2006.*

Steinberg, David I.   **DS530.65.S74 2001**
Burma, the State of Myanmar. Trade Cloth. Georgetown
University Press. Washington, DC. 2000. xxxiii, 342p.
ISBN:0-87840-842-8, ISBN13: 978-0-87840-842-9.
Dewey:959.105. LCCN:00-061037.
                         Audience: **u,f.**   *Choice, 2002.*

Taylor, Robert H.   **JQ751.A58B87 2001**
   (Editor)
Burma: Political Economy under Military Rule. Cloth over
Boards. Palgrave Macmillan. New York, NY. 2001. 168p.
ISBN:0-312-23568-2, ISBN13: 978-0-312-23568-0.
Dewey:959.1/05. LCCN:00-033349.
                                        Audience: **u,f.**

Taylor, Robert H.   **JQ442.T39 1988**
The State in Burma. Cloth Text. University of Hawaii Press.
Honolulu, HI. 1988. 400p. ISBN:0-8248-1141-0, ISBN13:
978-0-8248-1141-9. Dewey:320.9591. LCCN:87-016200.
                         Audience: **u,f.**   *Choice, 1988.*

U Maung Maung   **DS530 .M38**
From Sangha to Laity: Nationalist Movements of Burma,
1920-1940. Trade Cloth. South Asia Books. Columbia, MO.
1981. ISBN:0-8364-0706-7, ISBN13: 978-0-8364-0706-8.
Dewey:959.1/04.
                                        Audience: **u,f.**

Vietnam

Castorina, Jan & Stais,   **TX724.5.S68C37 1996**
   Dimitra
A Taste of Indochina. Sue Ninham (Illustrator), Ashley
Mackevicius (Photographer), Marie H. Clauzon (Designed by).
Trade Cloth. Barron's Educational Series, Inc. Hauppauge, NY.
1996. 160p. ISBN:0-8120-6602-2, ISBN13: 978-0-8120-6602-9.
Dewey:641.5959. LCCN:96-000302.
                                        Audience: **g.**

Condominas, Georges &   **DS539.M58**
   Foulke, Adrienne
We Have Eaten the Forest: The Story of a Montagnard Village
in the Central Highlands of Vietnam. Trade Cloth. Farrar, Straus
& Giroux. New York, NY. 1977. xxii, 423p.
ISBN:0-8090-9672-2, ISBN13: 978-0-8090-9672-5.
Dewey:301.29/597. LCCN:77-000887.
                                        Audience: **g,u,f.** *B*

Ellington, Lucien   **DS556.3.W66 2002**
Vietnam: A Global Studies Handbook. ABC-Clio. 2002.
ISBN:1-57607-416-1, ISBN13: 978-1-57607-416-9.
                                        Audience: **g,u,f.**

Pelley, Patricia M.   **DS556.5.P45 2002**
Postcolonial Vietnam: New Histories of the National Past. Trade
Cloth. Duke University Press. Durham, NC. 2002. 328p.
Asia-Pacific Ser. ISBN:0-8223-2984-0, ISBN13:
978-0-8223-2984-8. Dewey:959.704/4. LCCN:2002-002593.
                         Audience: **f.**   *Choice, 2003.*

Templer, Robert   **DS559.912.T45 1999**
Shadows and Wind: A View of Modern Vietnam. Penguin. 1999.
ISBN:0-14-028597-0, ISBN13: 978-0-14-028597-0.
                                        Audience: **g,l,u,f.**

Vietnam > History

Duiker, William J.   DS556.5.D85 1995
Vietnam: Revolution in Transit. Ed. 2. Trade Paper. Westview
Press. Boulder, CO. 1995. xi, 250p. Profiles, Nations of
Contemporary Asia Ser. ISBN:0-8133-8588-1, ISBN13:
978-0-8133-8588-4. Dewey:959.7. LCCN:94-036485.
     Audience: **l,u.**

Lam, Truong B.   DS556.5
Resistance Rebellion Revolution: Popular Movements in
Vietnamese History. Paper Text. Ashgate Publishing Company.
Williston, VT. 1984. 64p. ISBN:9971-902-73-7, ISBN13:
978-9971-902-73-5. Dewey:322.4/2/09597. LCCN:84-941043.
     Audience: **l,u.**

Lockhart, Bruce   DS556.25.D85 2006
   McFarland & Duiker, William J.
Historical Dictionary of Vietnam. Ed. 3. Trade Cloth. Scarecrow
Press, Inc. Lanham, MD. 2006. 488p. Historical Dictionaries of
Asia, Oceania, and the Middle East Ser., No. 57
ISBN:0-8108-5053-2, ISBN13: 978-0-8108-5053-8.
Dewey:959.7/003. LCCN:2005-020145.
     Audience: **g,l,u,f.**

Tai, Hue-Tam H.   BQ9800.P452.T34 1983
Millenarianism and Peasant Politics in Vietnam. Trade Cloth.
Harvard University Press. Cambridge, MA. 1983. 240p. East
Asian Monographs, No. 99 ISBN:0-674-57555-5, ISBN13:
978-0-674-57555-4. Dewey:299/.592. LCCN:82-011798.
     Audience: **u,f.** *B*

Woodside, Alexander   JQ1510.W66 2006
Lost Modernities: China, Vietnam, Korea, and the Hazards of
World History. Trade Cloth. Harvard University Press.
Cambridge, MA. 2006. 160p. The Edwin O. Reischauer
Lectures ISBN:0-674-02217-3, ISBN13: 978-0-674-02217-1.
Dewey:320.951. LCCN:2005-056710.
     Audience: **u,f.**

Vietnam > History > to 19th Century

Dutton, George   DS556.7.D88 2006
The Tay Son Uprising: Society and Rebellion in
Eighteenth-Cenury Vietnam. Trade Cloth. University of Hawaii
Press. Honolulu, HI. 2006. 320p. Southeast Aisa Ser., :Politics,
Meaning, and Memory Ser. ISBN:0-8248-2984-0, ISBN13:
978-0-8248-2984-1. Dewey:959.7/03. LCCN:2006-000835.
     Audience: **l,u.**

Taylor, Keith W.   DS556.6
The Birth of Vietnam. Trade Cloth. University of California
Press. Berkeley, CA. 1983. 440p. ISBN:0-520-04428-2, ISBN13:
978-0-520-04428-9. Dewey:959.7/03. LCCN:81-011590.
     Audience: **l,u,f.** *B*

Woodside, Alexander B.   JQ811.W66 1988
Vietnam and the Chinese Model: A Comparative Study of
Vietnamese and Chinese Government in the First Half of the
Nineteenth Century. Trade Paper. Harvard University, Asia
Center. Cambridge, MA. 1988. 370p. East Asian Monographs,
No. 140 ISBN:0-674-93721-X, ISBN13: 978-0-674-93721-5.
Dewey:320.3. LCCN:88-022869.
     Audience: **u,f.**

Vietnam > History > French Indochina (to 1954)

Duiker, William J.   DS560.72.H6D85 2000
Ho Chi Minh: A Life. Trade Cloth. Hyperion Press. New York,
NY. 2000. 704p. ISBN:0-7868-6387-0, ISBN13:
978-0-7868-6387-7. Dewey:959.704/092 B. LCCN:00-026757.
     Audience: **g,u,f.**

Duiker, William J.   DS556.8.D84
The Rise of Nationalism in Vietnam, 1900-1941. Book, Other.
Cornell University Press. Ithaca, NY. 1976. 320p.
ISBN:0-8014-0951-9, ISBN13: 978-0-8014-0951-6.
Dewey:320.9/597/03. LCCN:75-018723.
     Audience: **u,f.** *B*

Long, Ngo Vinh   HD1536.I8
Before the Revolution: The Vietnamese Peasants under the
French. Trade Paper. Columbia University Press. New York, NY.
1991. 292p. A Morningside Book Ser. ISBN:0-231-07679-7,
ISBN13: 978-0-231-07679-1. Dewey:305.5/63.
     Audience: **l,u.** *B*

Marr, David G.   DS556.8.M36 1995
Vietnam, 1945: The Quest for Power. Cloth Text. University of
California Press. Berkeley, CA. 1995. 587p.
ISBN:0-520-07833-0, ISBN13: 978-0-520-07833-8.
Dewey:959.7/03. LCCN:95-015856.
     Audience: **l,u.** *Choice, 1996.*

Marr, David G.   DS556.8
Vietnamese Anticolonialism, 1885-1925. Trade Paper. University
of California Press. Berkeley, CA. 1980. Center for South and
Southeast Asia Studies, UC Berkeley, No. 33
ISBN:0-520-04277-8, ISBN13: 978-0-520-04277-3.
Dewey:959.7/03.
     Audience: **l,u.**

Marr, David G.   DS556.8.M37 1984
Vietnamese Tradition on Trial, 1920-1945. Trade Paper.
University of California Press. Berkeley, CA. 1984. 450p.
ISBN:0-520-05081-9, ISBN13: 978-0-520-05081-5.
Dewey:959.7/03.
     Audience: **l,u.** *B*

Osborne, Milton E.   DS557.C7
French Presence in Cochinchina and Cambodia: Rule and
Response 1859-1905. Trade Cloth. Cornell University Press.
Ithaca, NY. 1969. xvii, 379p. ISBN:0-8014-0512-2, ISBN13:
978-0-8014-0512-9. Dewey:325.3/44/09597. LCCN:78-087021.
     Audience: **l,u.** *B*

Vietnam > History > 1954-

Chanda, Nayan   DS550.C48 1986
Brother Enemy: The War after the War. Trade Cloth. Harcourt
Trade Publishers. New York, NY. 1986. 384p.
ISBN:0-15-114420-6, ISBN13: 978-0-15-114420-4.
Dewey:959/.053. LCCN:85-024745.
     Audience: **g,u,f.**

Duiker, William J.   DS556.8 .D83
The Communist Road to Power in Vietnam. Cloth Text.
Westview Press. Boulder, CO. 1981. 394p. Special Studies on
South and Southeast Asia ISBN:0-89158-794-2, ISBN13:
978-0-89158-794-1. Dewey:959.7. LCCN:80-022098.
     Audience: **u,f.** *B* *Choice, 1996.*

Duiker, William J.　　DS560.72.H6D85 2000
Ho Chi Minh: A Life. Trade Cloth. Hyperion Press. New York, NY. 2000. 704p. ISBN:0-7868-6387-0, ISBN13: 978-0-7868-6387-7. Dewey:959.704/092 B. LCCN:00-026757.
Audience: **g,u,f.**

Hickey, Gerald C.　　DS556.44
Free in the Forest: Ethnohistory of the Vietnamese Central Highlands, 1954-1976, Vol. 2. Trade Cloth. Yale University Press. Cumberland, RI. 1982. 320p. ISBN:0-300-02437-1, ISBN13: 978-0-300-02437-1. Dewey:305.8/009597. LCCN:81-011595.
Audience: **u,f.** *B*

Hood, Steven J.　　DS559.916.H66 1992
Dragons Entangled: Indochina and the China-Vietnam War. Cloth Text. M. E. Sharpe Inc. Armonk, NY. 1992. 208p. ISBN:0-87332-862-0, ISBN13: 978-0-87332-862-3. Dewey:959.704/4. LCCN:91-010743.
Audience: **g,u,f.** *Choice, 1993.*

Isaacs, Arnold R.　　DS557.7.I82 1999
Without Honor: Defeat in Vietnam and Cambodia. Trade Paper. Johns Hopkins University Press. Baltimore, MD. 1999. 576p. ISBN:0-8018-6107-1, ISBN13: 978-0-8018-6107-9. Dewey:959.704/3. LCCN:99-192603.
Audience: **g,l,u,f.** *B*

Morley, James W. & Nishihara, Masashi (Editors)　　DS559.912.V5427 1997
Vietnam Joins the World. Paper Text. M. E. Sharpe Inc. Armonk, NY. 1997. 260p. ISBN:1-56324-975-8, ISBN13: 978-1-56324-975-4. Dewey:327.597/009/049. LCCN:96-039809.
Audience: **g,u,f.**

Morris, Stephen J.　　DS556.8.M69 1999
Why Vietnam Invaded Cambodia: Political Culture and the Causes of War. Trade Cloth. Stanford University Press. Palo Alto, CA. 1999. 280p. ISBN:0-8047-3049-0, ISBN13: 978-0-8047-3049-5. Dewey:959.704. LCCN:98-053891.
Audience: **g,u,f.** *Choice, 1999.*

Steele, Philip　　DS560.72.H6S74 2003
Ho Chi Minh. Library Binding. Heinemann Library. Chicago, IL. 2003. 64p. Leading Lives Ser. ISBN:1-4034-0836-X, ISBN13: 978-1-4034-0836-5. Dewey:959.7/043/092. LCCN:2002-012044.
Audience: **g,u,f.**

Tai, Hue-Tam Ho　　DS556.8.T34 1992
Radicalism and the Origins of the Vietnamese Revolution. Trade Cloth. Harvard University Press. Cambridge, MA. 1992. 336p. ISBN:0-674-74612-0, ISBN13: 978-0-674-74612-1. Dewey:959.7/03. LCCN:91-016930.
Audience: **u,f.** *Choice, 1992.*

Westad　　DS554.84
Vietnam and the Third Indochina War. Trade Cloth. Routledge. New York, NY. 2006. 240p. ISBN:0-415-39058-3, ISBN13: 978-0-415-39058-3. Dewey:959.704/4. LCCN:2005-034237.
Audience: **g,u,f.**

Woodside, Alexander B.　　DS556.36 .W66
Community and Revolution in Modern Vietnam. Cloth Text. Houghton Mifflin Company. New York, NY. 1976. 418p. ISBN:0-395-20367-8, ISBN13: 978-0-395-20367-5. Dewey:322.4/2/09597. LCCN:75-018429.
Audience: **l,u.**

Vietnam > History > 1954- > Vietnam War

Becker, Elizabeth　　DS558 .B43 1992
America's Vietnam War: A Narrative History. Trade Cloth. Houghton Mifflin Company Trade & Reference Division. Boston, MA. 1992. 160p. ISBN:0-395-59094-9, ISBN13: 978-0-395-59094-2. Dewey:959.704/3373. LCCN:91-041144.
Audience: **g,l,u,f.**

Bradley, Mark Philip　　DS556.8.B73 2000
Imagining Vietnam and America: The Making of Postcolonial Vietnam, 1919-1950. John Lewis Gaddis (Foreword by). Trade Cloth. University of North Carolina Press. Chapel Hill, NC. 2000. 320p. The New Cold War History Ser. ISBN:0-8078-2549-2, ISBN13: 978-0-8078-2549-5. Dewey:959.7/03. LCCN:99-088185.
Audience: **g,u,f.** *Choice, 2001.*

Clymer, Kenton J. (Editor)　　DS557.3.V54 1998
The Vietnam War: Its History, Literature, and Music. Trade Paper. University of Texas Press. Austin, TX. 1999. 208p. Southwestern Studies ISBN:0-87404-277-1, ISBN13: 978-0-87404-277-1. Dewey:959.704/3. LCCN:97-062483.
Audience: **g,u,f.**

Havens, Thomas R.　　DS0558.6.J3H
Fire Across the Sea: The Vietnam War and Japan, 1965-1975. Trade Paper. Books on Demand. Ann Arbor, MI. 340p. ISBN:0-608-06377-0, ISBN13: 978-0-608-06377-5. Dewey:959.704/33/52. LCCN:86-022630.
Audience: **g,u,f.**

Herring, George C.　　DS558.H45 2002
America's Longest War: The United States and Vietnam, 1950-1975. Ed. 4. Trade Paper. McGraw-Hill Higher Education. Burr Ridge, IL. 2001. 416p. ISBN:0-07-241755-2, ISBN13: 978-0-07-241755-5. Dewey:959.7043373. LCCN:2001-052123.
Audience: **g,u,f.**

Hunt, Michael H.　　DS558.H85 1996
Lyndon Johnson's War: America's Cold War Crusade in Vietnam, 1945-1965: a Critical Issue. Eric Foner (Editor). Cloth over Boards. Farrar, Straus & Giroux. New York, NY. 1996. 146p. ISBN:0-8090-5023-4, ISBN13: 978-0-8090-5023-9. Dewey:959.704/3373. LCCN:95-026361.
Audience: **g,u,f.**

Kahin, George M.　　DS558.K34 1986
Intervention: How America Became Involved in Vietnam. Ashbel Green (Editor). Trade Cloth. Alfred A. Knopf Inc. New York, NY. 1986. 537p. ISBN:0-394-54367-X, ISBN13: 978-0-394-54367-3. Dewey:959.704/33/73. LCCN:85-040331.
Audience: **g,u,f.** *Choice, 1986.*

Karnow, Stanley　　DS558.K37 1997
Vietnam: A History. Ed. 2. Trade Paper. Penguin Group (USA) Inc. New York, NY. 1997. 784p. ISBN:0-14-026547-3, ISBN13: 978-0-14-026547-7. Dewey:959.7. LCCN:91-011088.
Audience: **g,l.** *B*

Kovic, Ron　　DS559.5
Born on the Fourth of July. Trade Paper. Akashic Books. New York, NY. 2005. 225p. ISBN:1-888451-78-5, ISBN13: 978-1-888451-78-8. Dewey:959.704/345/092 B. LCCN:2004-115734.
Audience: **g,l,u,f.** *B*

Kroll, Barry M.   **PS228.V5K7 1992**
Teaching Hearts and Minds: College Students Reflect on the
Vietnam War in Literature. Trade Cloth. Southern Illinois
University Press. Carbondale, IL. 1992. 215p.
ISBN:0-8093-1748-6, ISBN13: 978-0-8093-1748-6.
Dewey:810.9/358. LCCN:91-002868.
                                    Audience: **g,u,f.**

Lee, Steven H.   **DS33.3.L44 1995**
Outposts of Empire: Korea, Vietnam, and the Origins of the
Cold War in Asia, 1949-1954. Trade Cloth. McGill-Queen's
University Press. Montreal, PQ. 1995. 312p.
ISBN:0-7735-1326-4, ISBN13: 978-0-7735-1326-6.
Dewey:327.7305/09645. LCCN:97-135057.
                              Audience: **g,u,f.**   *Choice, 1996.*

Logevall, Fredrik   **DS557.6.L64 2001**
The Origins of the Vietnam War. Trade Paper. Longman
Publishing. Boston, MA. 2001. 168p. Seminar Studies in
History ISBN:0-582-31918-8, ISBN13: 978-0-582-31918-9.
Dewey:959.704/3. LCCN:2001-029311.
                                  Audience: **g,l,u,f.**

Lomperis, Timothy J.   **DS558.L64 1996**
From People's War to People's Rule: Insurgency, Intervention,
and the Lessons of Vietnam. Library Binding. University of
North Carolina Press. Chapel Hill, NC. 1996. 456p.
ISBN:0-8078-2273-6, ISBN13: 978-0-8078-2273-9.
Dewey:959.704/3373. LCCN:95-036667.
                              Audience: **g,u,f.**   *Choice, 1997.*

Nguyen, Dac B. &   **DS559.93.S66.L861992**
  Luong, Hy V.
Revolution in the Village: Tradition and Transformation in North
Vietnam, 1925-1988. Trade Cloth. University of Hawaii Press.
Honolulu, HI. 1992. 286p. ISBN:0-8248-1382-0, ISBN13:
978-0-8248-1382-6. Dewey:959.7. LCCN:91-040031.
                                    Audience: **g,u,f.**

Ross, Robert J.   **DS740.5.V5R67 1988**
The Indochina Tangle: China's Vietnam Policy, 1975-1979.
Trade Cloth. Columbia University Press. New York, NY. 1988.
361p. ISBN:0-231-06564-7, ISBN13: 978-0-231-06564-1.
Dewey:327.510597. LCCN:87-015819.
                              Audience: **g,u,f.**   *Choice, 1988.*

Steele, Philip   **DS560.72.H6S74 2003**
Ho Chi Minh. Library Binding. Heinemann Library. Chicago,
IL. 2003. 64p. Leading Lives Ser. ISBN:1-4034-0836-X,
ISBN13: 978-1-4034-0836-5. Dewey:959.7/043/092.
LCCN:2002-012044.
                                    Audience: **g,u,f.**

Taylor, Mark   **DS558.T27 2004**
The Vietnam War in History, Literature and Film. Trade Cloth.
University of Alabama Press. Tuscaloosa, AL. 2003. 176p.
ISBN:0-8173-1401-6, ISBN13: 978-0-8173-1401-9.
Dewey:959.7/043. LCCN:2003-018994.
                              Audience: **g,u,f.**   *Choice, 2004.*

Young, Marilyn   **DS557.7.Y678 1991**
The Vietnam Wars, 1945-1990. Trade Cloth. HarperCollins
Publishers. New York, NY. 1991. 352p. ISBN:0-06-016553-7,
ISBN13: 978-0-06-016553-6. Dewey:959.704/3.
LCCN:90-055560.
                              Audience: **g,u,f.**   *Choice, 1991.*

Zhai, Qiang   **DS777.8.Z388 2000**
China and the Vietnam Wars, 1950-1975. John L. Gaddis
(Foreword by). Trade Cloth. University of North Carolina Press.
Chapel Hill, NC. 2000. 320p. The New Cold War History Ser.
ISBN:0-8078-2532-8, ISBN13: 978-0-8078-2532-7.
Dewey:959.704. LCCN:99-016884.
                              Audience: **g,u,f.**   *Choice, 2000.*

Vietnam > Language and Literature

Bowen, Kevin (Editor,   **PL4378.6.M74 1998**
  Translator)
Mountain River: Vietnamese Poetry from the Wars, 1948-1993.
Nguyen Ba Chung (Editor, Translator, Introduction by), Bruce
Weigl (Editor, Translator). Trade Paper. University of
Massachusetts Press. Amherst, MA. 1998. 304p.
ISBN:1-55849-141-4, ISBN13: 978-1-55849-141-0.
Dewey:895.9/22134080358. LCCN:98-012598.
                              Audience: **g,u.**   *Choice, 1999.*

Huynh Sanh Thong   **PL4382.E3H47**
The Heritage of Vietnamese Poetry. Trade Paper. Books on
Demand. Ann Arbor, MI. 349p. ISBN:0-608-18081-5, ISBN13:
978-0-608-18081-6. Dewey:895.9/2/21008. LCCN:78-017092.
                                  Audience: **g,l,u,f.**

Huynh Sanh Thong   **PL4378.9.N5**
  (Translator)
The Tale of Kieu: A Bilingual Edition of Nguyen Du's Truyen
Kieu. Ed. 2. Yale University Press. 1987. ISBN:0-300-04051-2,
ISBN13: 978-0-300-04051-7.
                                  Audience: **g,l,u,f.**

Thong, Huynh Sanh   **PL4382.E3**
  (Editor, Translator)
An Anthology of Vietnamese Poems: From the Eleventh
Through the Twentieth Centuries. Trade Paper. Yale University
Press. Cumberland, RI. 2001. 448p. ISBN:0-300-09100-1,
ISBN13: 978-0-300-09100-7. Dewey:895.9/22/1/008.
                              Audience: **g,u,f.**   *Choice, 1997.*

Weigl, Bruce (Editor,   **PL4378.65.E5P64 1994**
  Translator)
Poems from Captured Documents: A Bilingual Edition: Selected
and Translated from the Vietnamese. Thanh T. Nguyen
(Translator, Selected by). Cloth Text. University of
Massachusetts Press. Amherst, MA. 1994. 80p.
ISBN:0-87023-921-X, ISBN13: 978-0-87023-921-2.
Dewey:895/.92213. LCCN:93-046189.
                              Audience: **g,u,f.**   *Choice, 1994.*

Kampuchea (Cambodia)

Chandler, David   **DS554.842**
The Killing Fields. Trade Cloth. Twin Palms Publishers. Santa
Fe, NM. 1996. 124p. ISBN:0-944092-39-X, ISBN13:
978-0-944092-39-2. Dewey:959.6.
                                    Audience: **g,u,f.**

Chandler, David P.   **DS554.5.C46 1992**
A History of Cambodia. Ed. 2. Trade Paper. Westview Press.
Boulder, CO. 1992. 320p. ISBN:0-8133-0926-3, ISBN13:
978-0-8133-0926-2. Dewey:959.6/03. LCCN:91-041680.
                                    Audience: **u,f.** *B*

Chandler, David P.   DS554.7.C46
The Tragedy of Cambodian History: Politics, War, and
Revolution Since 1945. Trade Paper. Yale University Press.
Cumberland, RI. 1993. 408p. ISBN:0-300-05752-0, ISBN13:
978-0-300-05752-2. Dewey:959.604. LCCN:91-017074.
Audience: **f.** *Choice, 1992.*

Chandler, David P.   HV8599.C16 C48 1999
Voices from S-21: Terror and History in Pol Pot's Secret Prison.
Trade Cloth. University of California Press. Berkeley, CA. 2000.
251p. ISBN:0-520-22005-6, ISBN13: 978-0-520-22005-8.
Dewey:303.609596. LCCN:99-013924.
Audience: **f.** *Choice, 2000.*

Clymer, Kenton J.   E183.8.C15C573 2004
The United States and Cambodia, 1969-2000: A Troubled
Relationship. Paper over Boards. Routledge. New York, NY.
2004. 240p. RoutledgeCurzon Studies in the Modern History of
Asia, Vol. 18 ISBN:0-415-32602-8, ISBN13:
978-0-415-32602-5. Dewey:327.730596/09/045.
LCCN:2003-018367.

Audience: **f.**

Corfield, Justin J. &   DS554.25.C67 2003
Summers, Laura
Historical Dictionary of Cambodia. Trade Cloth. Scarecrow
Press, Inc. Lanham, MD. 2002. 560p. Asian/Oceanian Historical
Dictionaries Ser., No. 42 ISBN:0-8108-4524-5, ISBN13:
978-0-8108-4524-4. Dewey:959.6/003. LCCN:2002-012023.
Audience: **g,f.** *Choice, 2004.*

Ebihara, May M.   DS554.8.C359 1994
(Editor), et al.
Cambodian Culture since Nineteen Seventy-Five: Homeland and
Exile. Carol A. Mortland & Judy Ledgerwood (Editors). Book,
Other. Cornell University Press. Ithaca, NY. 1994. 216p. Asia
East by South Ser. ISBN:0-8014-2967-6, ISBN13:
978-0-8014-2967-5. Dewey:959.604. LCCN:93-043741.
Audience: **f.**

Edwards, Penny   DS554.7.E39 2006
Cambodge: The Cultivation of a Nation, 1860-1945. Trade
Cloth. University of Hawaii Press. Honolulu, HI. 2006. 392p.
Southeast Aisa Ser., :Politics, Meaning, and Memory Ser.
ISBN:0-8248-2923-9, ISBN13: 978-0-8248-2923-0.
Dewey:959.6/03. LCCN:2006-000837.

Audience: **f.**

Freeman, Michael   DS554.8
Cambodia. Trade Paper. Reaktion Books, Ltd. London, 2004.
224p. Topographics Ser. ISBN:1-86189-186-5, ISBN13:
978-1-86189-186-0. Dewey:959.6/042.
Audience: **f.**

Freeman, Michael &   DS554.98.A5F73 1999
Jacques, Claude
Ancient Angkor. Trade Paper. River Books. 2006. 288p. River
Books Guide Ser. ISBN:974-8225-27-5, ISBN13:
978-974-8225-27-2. Dewey:959.6. LCCN:99-910363.
Audience: **g,f.**

Gottesman, Evan R.   DS554.8.G68 2002
Cambodia after the Khmer Rouge: Inside the Politics of Nation
Building. Cloth over Boards. Yale University Press.
Cumberland, RI. 2002. 464p. ISBN:0-300-08957-0, ISBN13:
978-0-300-08957-8. Dewey:959.604/2. LCCN:2002-005653.
Audience: **f.** *Choice, 2003.*

Groslier, B. P.   DS558
Angkor Cambodia 16th Cent. Trade Paper. Orchid Press
Publishing, Ltd. Chatuchak, Bangkok, 2005. 208p.
ISBN:974-524-053-2, ISBN13: 978-974-524-053-7.
Dewey:959.7043373.

Audience: **f.**

Harris, Ian   BQ466.H37 2005
Cambodian Buddhism: History and Practice. Trade Cloth.
University of Hawaii Press. Honolulu, HI. 2004. 402p.
ISBN:0-8248-2765-1, ISBN13: 978-0-8248-2765-6.
Dewey:294.3/09596. LCCN:2004-018492.
Audience: **f.** *Choice, 2005.*

Higham, Charles   DS554.6 .H54 2001
The Civilization of Angkor. Trade Cloth. University of
California Press. Berkeley, CA. 2002. 207p.
ISBN:0-520-23442-1, ISBN13: 978-0-520-23442-0.
Dewey:959.6/03. LCCN:2001-053047.
Audience: **g,u,f.** *Choice, 2002.*

Hinton, Alexander   DS554.8 .H56 2005
Laban
Why Did They Kill?: Cambodia in the Shadow of Genocide.
Trade Cloth. University of California Press. Berkeley, CA. 2004.
410p. California Series in Public Anthropology, Vol. 11
ISBN:0-520-24178-9, ISBN13: 978-0-520-24178-7.
Dewey:959.604/2. LCCN:2004-009189.
Audience: **g,u,f.** *Choice, 2005.*

Kiernan, Ben   DS554.8.K584 1996
The Pol Pot Regime: Race, Power, and Genocide in Cambodia
under the Khmer Rouge, 1975-79. Cloth over Boards. Yale
University Press. Cumberland, RI. 1996. 492p.
ISBN:0-300-06113-7, ISBN13: 978-0-300-06113-0.
Dewey:959.6/04. LCCN:95-018669.
Audience: **f.** *Choice, 1997.*

Osborne, Milton E.   DS557.C7
French Presence in Cochinchina and Cambodia: Rule and
Response 1859-1905. Trade Cloth. Cornell University Press.
Ithaca, NY. 1969. xvii, 379p. ISBN:0-8014-0512-2, ISBN13:
978-0-8014-0512-9. Dewey:325.3/44/09597. LCCN:78-087021.
Audience: **l,u.** *B*

Osborne, Milton E.   DS554.83.N6O84 1994
Sihanouk: Prince of Light, Prince of Darkness. Trade Cloth.
University of Hawaii Press. Honolulu, HI. 1994. 304p.
ISBN:0-8248-1639-0, ISBN13: 978-0-8248-1639-1.
Dewey:959.604/092 B. LCCN:93-048520.
Audience: **f.** *Choice, 1994.*

Schanberg, Sydney H.   DS554.8
Death and Life of Dith Pran. Trade Cloth. Penguin Group
(USA) Inc. New York, NY. 1985. ISBN:0-670-80857-1,
ISBN13: 978-0-670-80857-1. Dewey:959.6/04.
LCCN:85 006560.

Audience: **g,f.**

Shawcross, William   DS557.8.C3
Sideshow: Kissinger, Nixon, and the Destruction of Cambodia.
Trade Paper. Cooper Square Publishers, Inc. New York, NY.
2002. 544p. ISBN:0-8154-1224-X, ISBN13: 978-0-8154-1224-3.
Dewey:959.6042.

Audience: **g,u,f.**

Short, Philip   DS554.83.P65S53 2005
Pol Pot: Anatomy of a Nightmare. Cloth over Boards. Henry
Holt & Company. New York, NY. 2005. 560p.

Formats: Web: ☐   Ebook: **e**   CD/DVD-ROM: 🌐   BCL3: *B*

ISBN:0-8050-6662-4, ISBN13: 978-0-8050-6662-3.
Dewey:959.604/2. LCCN:2004-054080.

Audience: **g,f.** *Choice, 2006.*

Laos

Cranmer, Jeff &   **DS555.25**
  Martin, Steven
Laos. Ed. 2. Rough Guides Staff (Editor). Trade Paper. Rough
Guides, Ltd. London, 2002. 416p. Rough Guide Travel Guides
ISBN:1-85828-905-X, ISBN13: 978-1-85828-905-2.
Dewey:915.940405.

Audience: **g,l,u,f.**

Evans, Grant   **DS555.5**
A Short History of Laos: The Land in Between. Milton Osborne
(Editor). Trade Paper. Allen & Unwin Pty., Ltd. Crows Nest,
NSW. 2003. 272p. A Short History of Asia Ser.
ISBN:1-86448-997-9, ISBN13: 978-1-86448-997-2.
Dewey:959.4. LCCN:2003-269528.

Audience: **g,u,f.**

Quincy, Keith   **DS559.73.L28Q56 2000**
Harvesting Pa Chay's Wheat: The Hmong and America's Secret
War in Laos. Trade Cloth. Eastern Washington University Press.
Spokane, WA. 2000. xiii, 597p. ISBN:0-910055-61-0, ISBN13:
978-0-910055-61-1. Dewey:959.704/38. LCCN:99-059813.

Audience: **u,f.**

Stuart-Fox, Martin   **DS555.5.S78 2001**
Historical Dictionary of Laos. Ed. 2. Trade Cloth. Scarecrow
Press, Inc. Lanham, MD. 2001. 592p. Asian-Oceanian Historical
Dictionaries Ser., No. 35 ISBN:0-8108-3880-X, ISBN13:
978-0-8108-3880-2. Dewey:959.4/003. LCCN:00-041286.

Audience: **g,f.** *Choice, 2001, 1992.*

Thailand (Siam)

Akira, Suehiro   **HG5750.55.A3**
Capitol Accumulation in Thailand, 1855-1985. Paper Text.
University of Washington Press. Seattle, WA. 1998. 446p.
ISBN:974-390-005-5, ISBN13: 978-974-390-005-1.
Dewey:332.041509593.

Audience: **f.**

Baker, Chris &   **DS571.P26 2005**
  Phongpaichit, Pasuk
A History of Thailand. Cloth Text. Cambridge University Press.
New York, NY. 2005. 320p. ISBN:0-521-81615-7, ISBN13:
978-0-521-81615-1. Dewey:959.3. LCCN:2004-028435.

Audience: **g,f.**

Batson, Benjamin A.   **DS584.B36 1984**
The End of the Absolute Monarchy in Siam. Trade Cloth.
Oxford University Press, Inc. New York, NY. 1984. 372p.
ISBN:0-19-582612-4, ISBN13: 978-0-19-582612-8.
Dewey:959.3/042. LCCN:84-942085.

Audience: **f.** B

De Choisy, Abbe   **DS564.C5613 1993**
Journal of a Voyage to Siam, 1685-1686. Michael Smithies
(Translator). Cloth Text. Oxford University Press, Inc. New
York, NY. 1994. 316p. Oxford in Asia Hardback Reprints Ser.
ISBN:967-65-3026-3, ISBN13: 978-967-65-3026-4.
Dewey:915.930423. LCCN:93-017228.

Audience: **f.**

Fineman, Daniel M.   **DS586.F56 1997**
A Special Relationship: The United States and Military
Government in Thailand, 1947-1958. Trade Cloth. University of
Hawaii Press. Honolulu, HI. 1997. 376p. ISBN:0-8248-1818-0,
ISBN13: 978-0-8248-1818-0. Dewey:327.593073/09/045.
LCCN:96-025657.

Audience: **g,u,f.** *Choice, 1997.*

Hewison, Kevin   **HC445.Z9C35 1989**
Bankers and Bureaucrats: The Development of Capital and the
Role of the State in Thailand. Trade Cloth. Yale University
Southeast Asia Studies. New Haven, CT. 1989. xiv, 320p.
Monographs, No. 34 ISBN:0-938692-41-0, ISBN13:
978-0-938692-41-6. Dewey:330.9593. LCCN:89-051448.

Audience: **f.**

Hewison, Kevin   **JQ1740.P65 1997**
Political Change in Thailand: Democracy and Participation.
Trade Paper. Routledge. New York, NY. 1997. 320p. Politics in
Asia Ser. ISBN:0-415-17971-8, ISBN13: 978-0-415-17971-3.
Dewey:320.9593/09/049. LCCN:97-005094.

Audience: **f.**

Ingram, James C.   **HC497.S5 I5 1971**
Economic Change in Thailand, 1850-1970. Ed. 2. Trade Cloth.
Stanford University Press. Palo Alto, CA. 1971. xii, 352p.
ISBN:0-8047-0782-0, ISBN13: 978-0-8047-0782-4.
Dewey:330.9593. LCCN:70-150325.

Audience: **f.** B

Ishii, Yoneo   **BQ0554.I813**
Sangha, State, and Society: Thai Buddhism in History. Trade
Paper. Books on Demand. Ann Arbor, MI. 1986. 211p.
Monographs of the Center for Southeast Asian Studies, Kyoto
University; 15 [I. E. 16], No. 16 ISBN:0-608-04372-9, ISBN13:
978-0-608-04372-2. Dewey:294.3/377/09593. LCCN:86-673063.

Audience: **f.** *Choice, 1986.*

McVey, Ruth (Editor)   **HC445.M657 2000**
Money and Power in Provincial Thailand. Trade Cloth.
University of Hawaii Press. Honolulu, HI. 2000. 288p.
ISBN:0-8248-2273-0, ISBN13: 978-0-8248-2273-6.
Dewey:338.9593. LCCN:99-034360.

Audience: **u,f.**

Peleggi, Maurizio   **JQ1746.P4 2002**
Lords of Things: The Fashioning of the Siamese Monarchy's
Modern Image. Trade Cloth. University of Hawaii Press.
Honolulu, HI. 2002. 248p. ISBN:0-8248-2558-6, ISBN13:
978-0-8248-2558-4. Dewey:959.3. LCCN:2002-001546.

Audience: **u,f.**

Reynolds, Craig J.   **DS568 .R42 1987**
  (Author, Translator)
Thai Radical Discourse: The Real Face of Thai Feudalism
Today. Paper Text. Cornell University, Southeast Asia Program
Publications. Ithaca, NY. 1994. 186p. Studies on Southeast Asia,
No. 3 ISBN:0-87727-702-8, ISBN13: 978-0-87727-702-6.
Dewey:959.3. LCCN:87-404871.

Audience: **f.**

Reynolds, E. Bruce   **DS849.T5R49 1994**
Thailand and Japan's Southern Advance, 1940-1945. Cloth over
Boards. Palgrave Macmillan. New York, NY. 1994. 320p.
ISBN:0-312-10402-2, ISBN13: 978-0-312-10402-3.
Dewey:940.53/25593. LCCN:93-026125.

Audience: **u,f.**

Reynolds, E. Bruce   **D802.T5R49 2004**
Thailand's Secret War: OSS, SOE and the Free Thai Underground During World War II. Hew Strachan & Geoffrey Wawro (Contribution by). Trade Cloth. Cambridge University Press. New York, NY. 2005. 482p. Cambridge Military Histories Ser. ISBN:0-521-83601-8, ISBN13: 978-0-521-83601-2. Dewey:940.53/593. LCCN:2004-062105.

Audience: **g,u,f.**

Smithies, Michael   **DS561.5.D47 1995**
  (Compiled by)
Descriptions of Old Siam. Trade Paper. Oxford University Press, Inc. New York, NY. 1996. 320p. Oxford in Asia Paperbacks Ser. ISBN:967-65-3083-2, ISBN13: 978-967-65-3083-7. Dewey:915.9/3/04. LCCN:94-045559.

Audience: **g,u,f.**

Stowe, Judith A.   **DS584.S76 1991**
Siam Becomes Thailand. Trade Cloth. University of Hawaii Press. Honolulu, HI. 1991. 400p. ISBN:0-8248-1393-6, ISBN13: 978-0-8248-1393-2. Dewey:959.304. LCCN:90-023778.

Audience: **u,f.**

Thongchai, Winichakul   **DS563.9.T47**
Siam Mapped: A History of the Geo-Body of a Nation. Trade Cloth. University of Hawaii Press. Honolulu, HI. 1994. 280p. ISBN:0-8248-1974-8, ISBN13: 978-0-8248-1974-3. Dewey:911.593.

Audience: **g,u,f.**

Vella, Walter F.   **DS0583.V44**
Chaiyol, King Vajiravudh and the Development of Thai Nationalism. Trade Paper. Books on Demand. Ann Arbor, MI. 364p. ISBN:0-608-04378-8, ISBN13: 978-0-608-04378-4. Dewey:959.3/04/0924. LCCN:78-001060.

Audience: **f.**

Vella, Walter F.   **DS580 .V4**
Siam under Rama III 1824: 1851. Paper Text. Textbook Publishers. Temecula, CA. 2003. ix, 180p. ISBN:0-7581-5542-5, ISBN13: 978-0-7581-5542-9. Dewey:959.3.

Audience: **f.** ℬ

Vella, Walter F. & Vella,   **DS583.V44**
  Dorothy
Chaiyo! King Vajiravudh and the Development of Thai Nationalism. Cloth Text. University of Hawaii Press. Honolulu, HI. 1978. 364p. ISBN:0-8248-0493-7, ISBN13: 978-0-8248-0493-0. Dewey:959.3/04/0924. LCCN:78-001060.

Audience: **f.** ℬ

Wilson, Constance M.   **HA4600.55 .W54 1983**
Thailand: A Handbook of Historical Statistics. Trade Cloth. Macmillan Publishing Company, Inc. Old Tappan, NJ. 1983. 360p. ISBN:0-8161-8115-2, ISBN13: 978-0-8161-8115-5. Dewey:315.93. LCCN:82-021251.

Audience: **f.**

Wood, William A.   **DS577 .W66 1974**
A History of Siam, from the Earliest Times to the Year A. D. 1781. Trade Cloth. A M S Press, Inc. New York, NY. ISBN:0-404-54880-6, ISBN13: 978-0-404-54880-3. Dewey:959.3/02. LCCN:71-179254.

Audience: **f.** ℬ

Wyatt, David K.   **LA1221.W9**
The Politics of Reform in Thailand. Trade Cloth. Yale University Press. Cumberland, RI. 1970. xix, 425p. Southeast Asia Studies, No. 4 ISBN:0-300-01156-3, ISBN13: 978-0-300-01156-2. Dewey:370/.9593. LCCN:77-081435.

Audience: **u,f.**

Wyatt, David K.   **DS571.W92 1984**
Thailand: A Short History. Trade Cloth. Yale University Press. Cumberland, RI. 1984. 354p. ISBN:0-300-03054-1, ISBN13: 978-0-300-03054-9. Dewey:959.3. LCCN:83-025953.

Audience: **u,f.** ℬ

Malaysia

Andaya, Barbara   **DS596.A76 2001**
  Watson & Andaya, Leonard Y.
A History of Malaysia. Ed. 2. Trade Cloth. University of Hawaii Press. Honolulu, HI. 2001. 396p. ISBN:0-8248-2425-3, ISBN13: 978-0-8248-2425-9. Dewey:959.5. LCCN:00-060761.

Audience: **g,u,f.**

Burgess, Anthony   **PR6052.U638**
The Long Day Wanes: A Malayan Trilogy. Norton. 1965.

Audience: **g,l,u,f.**

Clutterbuck, Richard   **DS598.S775**
Conflict and Violence in Singapore and Malaysia 1945-1983. Cloth Text. Westview Press. Boulder, CO. 1985. 412p. ISBN:0-8133-0168-8, ISBN13: 978-0-8133-0168-6. Dewey:959.5104.

Audience: **u,f.** *Choice, 1985.*

Drabble, John H.   **HC445.5..D7298 2000**
An Economic History of Malaysia, C. 1800-1990: The Transition to Modern Economic Growth. Cloth over Boards. Palgrave Macmillan. New York, NY. 2000. 346p. Modern Economic History of Southeast Asia Ser. ISBN:0-312-23077-X, ISBN13: 978-0-312-23077-7. Dewey:330.9595. LCCN:99-053111.

Audience: **u,f.** *Choice, 2000.*

Kaur, Amarjit   **DS596.K36 1993**
Historical Dictionary of Malaysia. Trade Cloth. Scarecrow Press, Inc. Lanham, MD. 1993. 329p. Asian Historical Dictionaries Ser., No. 13 ISBN:0-8108-2629-1, ISBN13: 978-0-8108-2629-8. Dewey:959.5/003. LCCN:92-037427.

Audience: **f.** *Choice, 1993.*

Matheson Hooker,   **DS596**
  Virginia
A Short History of Malaysia: Linking East and West. Trade Paper. Allen & Unwin Pty., Ltd. Crows Nest, NSW. 2003. 372p. A Short History of Asia Ser. ISBN:1-86448-955-3, ISBN13: 978-1-86448-955-2. Dewey:959.5.

Audience: **g,u,f.**

Nonini, Donald M.   **DS596.6 .N66 1992**
British Colonial Rule and the Resistance of the Malay Peasantry, 1900-1957. Trade Cloth. Yale University Southeast Asia Studies. New Haven, CT. 1992. 350p. Monograph Ser. - Yale University Southeast Asia Studies, No. 38 ISBN:0-938692-48-8, ISBN13: 978-0-938692-48-5. Dewey:959.5/1. LCCN:92-053707.

Audience: **f.**

Roff, William R.　　　　　　　　　**DS596.5**
The Origins of Malay Nationalism. Ed. 2. Paper Text. Oxford
University Press, Inc. New York, NY. 1995. 352p.
ISBN:967-65-3059-X, ISBN13: 978-967-65-3059-2.
Dewey:959.503.
　　　　　　　　　　　　Audience: **u,f.** ℬ

Turnbull, C. Mary　　　　　　　**DS596.T84 1989**
A History of Malaysia, Singapore and Brunei. Paper Text. Allen
& Unwin Pty., Ltd. Crows Nest, NSW. 1989. 336p.
ISBN:0-04-364025-7, ISBN13: 978-0-04-364025-8.
Dewey:959.5. LCCN:88-083859.
　　　　　　　　　　　　Audience: **g,u,f.**

Singapore

Allen, Louis　　　　　　　　　**D767.25.H6**
Singapore, 1941-1942. Trade Paper. Taylor & Francis Group.
Abingdon, 2003. 360p. ISBN:0-7146-8198-9, ISBN13:
978-0-7146-8198-6. Dewey:940.54/25.
　　　　　　　　　　　　Audience: **g,u,f.**

Ambler, Eric　　　　　　　**PR6001.M48P37 2004**
Passage of Arms. Trade Paper. Knopf Publishing Group. New
York, NY. 2004. 256p. Vintage Crime/Black Lizard Ser.
ISBN:0-375-72678-0, ISBN13: 978-0-375-72678-1.
Dewey:823/.914. LCCN:2004-558966.
　　　　　　　　　　　　Audience: **g,l,u,f.**

Barber, Noel　　　　　　　　　**D767.55**
Sinister Twilight: The Fall of Singapore. Trade Paper. Cassell P
L C. London, 2003. 288p. Cassell Military Paperbacks Ser.
ISBN:0-304-36437-1, ISBN13: 978-0-304-36437-4.
Dewey:940.542/5. LCCN:2003-446791.
　　　　　　　　　　　　Audience: **g,u,f.**

Barr, Michael D.　　　　　　**DS610.73.L45B37 2000**
Lee Kuan Yew: The Beliefs Behind the Man. Trade Cloth.
Georgetown University Press. Washington, DC. 2000. xiv, 273p.
ISBN:0-87840-816-9, ISBN13: 978-0-87840-816-0.
Dewey:959.5/7/05/092. LCCN:00-039327.
　　　　　　　　　　　　Audience: **g,u,f.**

Corfield, Justin　　　　　　**DS610.4.C67 2006**
Encyclopedia of Singapore. Trade Cloth. Scarecrow Press, Inc.
Lanham, MD. 2006. 304p. ISBN:0-8108-5347-7, ISBN13:
978-0-8108-5347-8. Dewey:959.57003. LCCN:2005-031341.
　　　　　　　　　　　　Audience: **f.**

Eng, Lai A.　　　　　　　　　**DS610.L35 1995**
Meanings of Multiethnicity: A Case-Study of Ethnicity and
Ethnic Relations in Singapore. Cloth Text. Oxford University
Press, Inc. New York, NY. 1995. 240p. South-East Asian Social
Science Monographs ISBN:967-65-3087-5, ISBN13:
978-967-65-3087-5. Dewey:305.8/0095957. LCCN:94-046290.
　　　　　　　　　　　　Audience: **u,f.**

Milne, R. S. & Mauzy,　　　　**DS598.S7M53 1990**
　Diane K.
Singapore: The Legacy of Lee Kuan Yew. Cloth Text. Westview
Press. Boulder, CO. 1990. 217p. ISBN:0-8133-0407-5, ISBN13:
978-0-8133-0407-6. Dewey:959.57. LCCN:89-024756.
　　　　　　　Audience: **f.** *Choice, 1990.*

Peterson, William　　　　　**PN2960.S5P48 2001**
Theater and the Politics of Culture in Contemporary Singapore.
Library Binding. Wesleyan University Press. Middletown, CT.

2001. 297p. ISBN:0-8195-6471-0, ISBN13: 978-0-8195-6471-9.
Dewey:792/.095957. LCCN:00-069598.
　　　　　　　Audience: **u,f.** *Choice, 2002.*

Quah, Jon S.　　　　　　　**JQ745.S5 G68 1987**
Government and Politics of Singapore. Trade Paper. Oxford
University Press, Inc. New York, NY. 1989. 356p. South-East
Asian Studies Program ISBN:0-19-588855-3, ISBN13:
978-0-19-588855-3. Dewey:320.9595/7. LCCN:90-121452.
　　　　　　　　　　　　Audience: **f.** ℬ

Song Ong Siang　　　　　　**DS598.S742 S66 1984**
One Hundred Years' History of the Chinese in Singapore. Trade
Cloth. Oxford University Press, Inc. New York, NY. 1984. 624p.
ISBN:0-19-582603-5, ISBN13: 978-0-19-582603-6.
Dewey:959.5/7004951. LCCN:85-101646.
　　　　　　　　　　　　Audience: **f.**

Trocki, Carl A.　　　　　　**DS610.6.T76 2005**
Singapore Wealth Power and Culture. Paper over Boards.
Routledge. New York, NY. 2005. 224p. Asia's Great Cities Ser.
ISBN:0-415-26385-9, ISBN13: 978-0-415-26385-6.
Dewey:959.5705. LCCN:2005-003172.
　　　　　　　　　　　　Audience: **g,u,f.**

Trocki, Carl A.　　　　　　**HN700.67.A8T76 1990**
Opium and Empire: Chinese Society in Colonial Singapore,
1800-1910. Cornell University Press. 1990. Asia, east by south
ISBN:0-8014-2390-2, ISBN13: 978-0-8014-2390-1.
　　　　　　　　　　　　Audience: **u,f.**

Turnbull, C. M.　　　　　　**DS598.S75T87 1989**
A History of Singapore, Eighteen Nineteen to Nineteen
Eighty-Five. Ed. 2. Trade Cloth. Oxford University Press, Inc.
New York, NY. 1989. 416p. ISBN:0-19-588911-8, ISBN13:
978-0-19-588911-6. Dewey:959.57. LCCN:89-009307.
　　　　　　　　　　　　Audience: **f.**

Yew, Lee Kuan　　　　　　　**DS610.73.L45**
The Singapore Story: Memoirs of Lee Kuan Yew. Trade Cloth.
Prentice Hall PTR. Upper Saddle River, NJ. 1998. 680p.
ISBN:0-13-020803-5, ISBN13: 978-0-13-020803-3.
Dewey:959.5705/092 B.
　　　　　　　　　　　　Audience: **g,u,f.**

Indonesia

Anderson, Benedict R.　　　　**JQ776.A64 1990**
O'G.
Language and Power: Exploring Indonesian Political Culture.
David Laitin (Editor). Book, Other. Cornell University Press.
Ithaca, NY. 1990. 352p. The Wilder House Series in Politics,
History, and Culture ISBN:0-8014-2354-6, ISBN13:
978-0-8014-2354-3. Dewey:306.2/09598. LCCN:90-055126.
　　　　　　　Audience: **u,f.** *Choice, 1991.*

Belo, Jane (Selected by)　　　　　　**DS647.B2**
Traditional Balinese Culture: Essays. Trade Cloth. Columbia
University Press. New York, NY. 1970. xxvii, 421p.
ISBN:0-231-03084-3, ISBN13: 978-0-231-03084-7.
Dewey:915.98/6. LCCN:68-054454.
　　　　　　　　　　　　Audience: **u,f.** ℬ

Benda, Harry J.　　　　　　　**DS643.5 .B4**
The Crescent and the Rising Sun. Trade Cloth. Walter de
Gruyter GmbH & Co. KG. Berlin, 1958. ISBN:0-686-20916-8,
ISBN13: 978-0-686-20916-4. Dewey:991.
　　　　　　　　　　　　Audience: **l,u.**

Boon, James A.   GN635.I65
The Anthropological Romance of Bali 1597-1972. Trade Paper. Cambridge University Press. New York, NY. 1977. Cambridge Studies in Cultural Systems Ser. ISBN:0-521-29226-3, ISBN13: 978-0-521-29226-9. Dewey:301.29/598/6. LCCN:76-019626.
Audience: **u,f.**

Booth, Anne &   HC447.I5567 1990
Weidemann, Anna (Editors)
Indonesian Economic History of the Dutch Colonial Era. William J. O'Malley (Introduction by). Trade Cloth. Yale University Southeast Asia Studies. New Haven, CT. 1990. 367p. Monographs, No. 35 ISBN:0-938692-42-9, ISBN13: 978-0-938692-42-3. Dewey:330.9598. LCCN:89-051449.
Audience: **u,f.**

Cotton, James   DS649.6.C67 2004
East Timor, Australia and Regional Order: Intervention and Its Aftermath in Southeast Asia. Paper over Boards. Routledge. New York, NY. 2004. 208p. Politics in Asia Ser. ISBN:0-415-33580-9, ISBN13: 978-0-415-33580-5. Dewey:959.8704. LCCN:2003-023575.
Audience: **u,f.**

Cribb, Robert   G2401
Historical Atlas of Indonesia. Trade Cloth. University of Hawaii Press. Honolulu, HI. 2000. 240p. ISBN:0-8248-2111-4, ISBN13: 978-0-8248-2111-1. Dewey:911.5/98. LCCN:99-012717.
Audience: **u,f.** *Choice, 2001.*

Elson, R. E.   DS644.1.S56 E44 2001
Suharto: A Political Biography. Cloth Text. Cambridge University Press. New York, NY. 2001. 412p. ISBN:0-521-77326-1, ISBN13: 978-0-521-77326-3. Dewey:959.803/092 B. LCCN:2002-318969.
Audience: **l,u.** *Choice, 2002.*

Feith, Herbert   DS644.F4
The Decline of Constitutional Democracy in Indonesia. Book, Other. Cornell University Press. Ithaca, NY. 1962. 638p. ISBN:0-8014-0126-7, ISBN13: 978-0-8014-0126-8. Dewey:991.03.
Audience: **u,f.**

Feith, Herbert &   JA84.I45
Castles, Lance (Editors)
Indonesian Political Thinking, 1945-1965. Trade Cloth. Cornell University Press. Ithaca, NY. 1970. 520p. ISBN:0-8014-0531-9, ISBN13: 978-0-8014-0531-0. Dewey:320/.0991. LCCN:69-018357.
Audience: **u,f.**

Frederick, William H.   DS615 .I518
(Editor)
Indonesia: A Country Study. Ed. 4. Trade Cloth, Box or Slipcased. United States Government Printing Office. Washington, DC. 1994. 512p. Area Handbook Ser., DA Pam 550-39 ISBN:0-16-001599-5, ISBN13: 978-0-16-001599-1. Dewey:959.8. LCCN:93-028505.
Audience: **l,u,f.**

Friend, Theodore   DS644.F69 2003
Indonesian Destinies. Trade Cloth. Harvard University Press. Cambridge, MA. 2003. 640p. ISBN:0-674-01137-6, ISBN13: 978-0-674-01137-3. Dewey:959.803. LCCN:2002-043937.
Audience: **u,f.**

Furnivall, J. S.   DS485.B89 F8
Colonial Policy and Practice: A Comparative Study of Burma and Netherlands India. Paper Text. Textbook Publishers. Temecula, CA. 2003. xii, 568p. ISBN:0-7581-7741-0, ISBN13: 978-0-7581-7741-4. Dewey:959.1.
Audience: **u,f.** *B*

Geertz, Clifford   HC447.G4
Agricultural Involution: The Processes of Ecological Change in Indonesia. Trade Cloth. University of California Press. Berkeley, CA. 1963. ISBN:0-520-00458-2, ISBN13: 978-0-520-00458-0. Dewey:330.9598. LCCN:63-020356.
Audience: **u.**

Geertz, Clifford   BP63.I5
Islam Observed: Religious Development in Morocco and Indonesia. Trade Cloth. Yale University Press. Cumberland, RI. 1968. Terry Lectures ISBN:0-300-00483-4, ISBN13: 978-0-300-00483-0. Dewey:297/.09598. LCCN:68-027753.
Audience: **u,f.** *B*

Geertz, Clifford   BL2120.J3G42
The Religion of Java. Trade Paper. University of Chicago Press. Chicago, IL. 1976. 412p. ISBN:0-226-28510-3, ISBN13: 978-0-226-28510-8. Dewey:200.9/5982. LCCN:75-018746.
Audience: **u,f.** *B*

Gold, Lisa   ML345.I5G65 2004
Music in Bali: Experiencing Music, Expressing Culture. Trade Cloth. Oxford University Press, Inc. New York, NY. 2004. 208p. Global Music Ser. ISBN:0-19-514150-4, ISBN13: 978-0-19-514150-4. Dewey:780/.9598/6. LCCN:2004-041563.
Audience: **u,f.**

Hefner, Robert W.   BP63.I5H44 2000
Civil Islam: Muslims and Democratization in Indonesia. Cloth Text. Princeton University Press. Princeton, NJ. 2000. xxiv, 286p. ISBN:0-691-05046-5, ISBN13: 978-0-691-05046-1. Dewey:322/.1/09598. LCCN:00-020486.
Audience: **u,f.** *Choice, 2001.*

Herbst, Edward   ML3758.I53H47 1997
Voices in Bali: Energies and Perceptions in Vocal Music and Dance Theater. Judith Becker (Foreword by), Rene T. A. Lysloff (Afterword by). Library Binding. Wesleyan University Press. Middletown, CT. 1997. 218p. Music Culture Ser. ISBN:0-8195-6316-1, ISBN13: 978-0-8195-6316-3. Dewey:781.62/9922. LCCN:97-019855.
Audience: **u,f.** *Choice, 1998.*

Heryanto, Ariel   DS644.4.H487 2005
State Terrorism and Political Identity in Indonesia: Fatally Belonging. Paper over Boards. Routledge. New York, NY. 2005. 224p. Politics in Asia Ser. ISBN:0-415-37152-X, ISBN13: 978-0-415-37152-0. Dewey:323.4/9/0959809045. LCCN:2005-003602.
Audience: **u,f.**

Holt, Claire (Editor)   DS644.4
Culture and Politics in Indonesia. C. Geertz & L. Laundry (Introduction by). Trade Cloth. Cornell University Press. Ithaca, NY. 1972. 362p. ISBN:0-8014-0665-X, ISBN13: 978-0-8014-0665-2. Dewey:301.5/92/09598. LCCN:78-162538.
Audience: **u,f.**

Kingsbury, Damien   **JQ770**
The Politics of Indonesia. Ed. 3. Trade Paper. Oxford University
Press, Inc. New York, NY. 2005. 400p. ISBN:0-19-551742-3,
ISBN13: 978-0-19-551742-2. Dewey:959.803.
LCCN:2005-280632.

Audience: **u,f.**

Lev, Daniel S.   **KNW1588.4**
Islamic Courts in Indonesia: A Study in the Political Bases of
Legal Institutions. Trade Cloth. University of California Press.
Berkeley, CA. 1972. 304p. Center for South and Southeast Asia
Studies, UC Berkeley, No. 12 ISBN:0-520-02173-8, ISBN13:
978-0-520-02173-0. Dewey:347/.598. LCCN:78-182281.

Audience: **u,f.**

McIntyre, Angus   **DS644.M28 2005**
The Indonesian Presidency: The Shift from Personal Toward
Constitutional Rule. Book, Other. Rowman & Littlefield
Publishers, Inc. Lanham, MD. 2005. 312p.
Asia/Pacific/Perspectives Ser. ISBN:0-7425-3826-5, ISBN13:
978-0-7425-3826-9. Dewey:959.803. LCCN:2004-026496.

Audience: **u,f.** *Choice, 2006.*

McPhee, Colin   **DS646.59.T55**
A House in Bali. Trade Cloth. A M S Press, Inc. New York, NY.
ISBN:0-404-16766-7, ISBN13: 978-0-404-16766-0.
Dewey:959.8/6. LCCN:77-086965.

Audience: **u,f.**

Mintz, Jeanne S.   **DS615 .M5**
Indonesia: A Profile. Paper Text. Textbook Publishers. Temecula,
CA. 2003. 241p. ISBN:0-7581-1099-5, ISBN13:
978-0-7581-1099-2. Dewey:919.1.

Audience: **g,l.**

Nairn, Allan   **DS644**
Our Kind of Guys: The United States and the Indonesian
Military. Trade Cloth. Analytical Psychology Club of San
Francisco, Inc. San Francisco, CA. 1999. 160p.
ISBN:1-85984-735-8, ISBN13: 978-1-85984-735-0.
Dewey:327.5/98/073.

Audience: **u,f.**

Pemberton, John   **DS646.18.P4 1994**
On the Subject of "Java". Book, Other. Cornell University Press.
Ithaca, NY. 1994. 320p. ISBN:0-8014-2672-3, ISBN13:
978-0-8014-2672-8. Dewey:959.8/2. LCCN:94-025827.

Audience: **l,u.**

Philpott, Simon   **JQ776.P45 2000**
Rethinking Indonesia: Postcolonial Theory, Authoritarianism and
Identity. Cloth over Boards. Palgrave Macmillan. New York,
NY. 2000. 256p. ISBN:0-312-23642-5, ISBN13:
978-0-312-23642-7. Dewey:306.2/09598. LCCN:00-042069.

Audience: **u,f.**

Robinson, Geoffrey B.   **DS647.B2R63 1995**
The Dark Side of Paradise: Political Violence in Bali. Trade
Paper. Cornell University Press. Ithaca, NY. 1998. 376p.
ISBN:0-8014-8172-4, ISBN13: 978-0-8014-8172-7.
Dewey:959.8/6. LCCN:95-009754.

Audience: **u,f.** *Choice, 1996.*

Rodgers, Susan (Editor)   **DS643.T45 1995**
Telling Lives, Telling Histories: Autobiography and Historical
Imagination in Modern Indonesia. Trade Cloth. University of
California Press. Berkeley, CA. 1995. 348p.

ISBN:0-520-08546-9, ISBN13: 978-0-520-08546-6.
Dewey:959.803. LCCN:94-030282.

Audience: **u,f.** *Choice, 1995.*

Sen, Krishna   **PN1993.5.I84S46 1994**
Indonesian Cinema: Framing the New World Order. Cloth over
Boards. Zed Books, Ltd. London, 1994. 192p.
ISBN:1-85649-123-4, ISBN13: 978-1-85649-123-5.
Dewey:302.234309598. LCCN:94-035308.

Audience: **l,u.**

Shiraishi, Takashi   **HC447.A856 1994**
  (Editor)
Approaching Suharto's Indonesia from the Margins. Paper Text.
Cornell University, Southeast Asia Program Publications. Ithaca,
NY. 1995. Translation Ser., No. 4 ISBN:0-87727-403-7,
ISBN13: 978-0-87727-403-2. Dewey:331.7/598.
LCCN:95-142214.

Audience: **u,f.**

Siegel, James T.   **DS643.S54 1997**
Fetish, Recognition, Revolution. Trade Cloth. Princeton
University Press. Princeton, NJ. 1997. 286p.
ISBN:0-691-02653-X, ISBN13: 978-0-691-02653-4.
Dewey:959.8/022. LCCN:96-003204.

Audience: **u,f.** *Choice, 1997.*

Sievers, Allen M.   **DS634.S52**
The Mystical World of Indonesia: Culture and Economic
Development in Conflict. Trade Cloth. Johns Hopkins University
Press. Baltimore, MD. 1994. 448p. ISBN:0-8018-1591-6,
ISBN13: 978-0-8018-1591-1. Dewey:915.98/03.
LCCN:74-006838.

Audience: **u,f.** *B*

Sjahrir, Soetan   **DS644 .S513**
Out of Exile. Charles Wolf Jr. (Translator). Trade Cloth.
Greenwood Publishing Group, Inc. Portsmouth, NH. 1969.
ISBN:0-8371-1045-9, ISBN13: 978-0-8371-1045-5.
Dewey:991/.022.

Audience: **u,f.**

Vatikiotis, Michael R. J.   **DS644.4.V383 1998**
Indonesian Politics under Suharto: The Rise and Fall of the New
Order. Ed. 3. Cloth Text. Routledge. New York, NY. 1999. 272p.
Politics in Asia Ser. ISBN:0-415-20501-8, ISBN13:
978-0-415-20501-6. Dewey:959.803. LCCN:99-220281.

Audience: **u,f.**

Vickers, Adrian (Editor)   **DS647.B2B37 1996**
Being Modern in Bali: Image and Change. Library Binding.
Yale University Southeast Asia Studies. New Haven, CT. 1996.
246p. Southeast Asia Studies, Vol. 43 ISBN:0-938692-57-7,
ISBN13: 978-0-938692-57-7. Dewey:959.8/6. LCCN:95-061261.

Audience: **l,u.**

Indonesia > History

Anderson, Benedict R.   **DS644**
  O'G.
Java in a Time of Revolution. Trade Cloth. Cornell University
Press. Ithaca, NY. 1972. 503p. ISBN:0-8014-0687-0, ISBN13:
978-0-8014-0687-4. Dewey:959.8/2. LCCN:74-174891.

Audience: **l,u.** *B*

Anderson, Benedict R.   **JQ776.A64 1990**
  O'G.
Language and Power: Exploring Indonesian Political Culture.

David Laitin (Editor). Book, Other. Cornell University Press. Ithaca, NY. 1990. 352p. The Wilder House Series in Politics, History, and Culture ISBN:0-8014-2354-6, ISBN13: 978-0-8014-2354-3. Dewey:306.2/09598. LCCN:90-055126.

Audience: **u,f.** *Choice, 1991.*

Belo, Jane (Selected by)   **DS647.B2**
Traditional Balinese Culture: Essays. Trade Cloth. Columbia University Press. New York, NY. 1970. xxvii, 421p. ISBN:0-231-03084-3, ISBN13: 978-0-231-03084-7. Dewey:915.98/6. LCCN:68-054454.

Audience: **u,f.** *B*

Boon, James A.   **GN635.I65**
The Anthropological Romance of Bali 1597-1972. Trade Paper. Cambridge University Press. New York, NY. 1977. Cambridge Studies in Cultural Systems Ser. ISBN:0-521-29226-3, ISBN13: 978-0-521-29226-9. Dewey:301.29/598/6. LCCN:76-019626.

Audience: **u,f.**

Booth, Anne &   **HC447.I5567 1990**
 Weidemann, Anna (Editors)
Indonesian Economic History of the Dutch Colonial Era. William J. O'Malley (Introduction by). Trade Cloth. Yale University Southeast Asia Studies. New Haven, CT. 1990. 367p. Monographs, No. 35 ISBN:0-938692-42-9, ISBN13: 978-0-938692-42-3. Dewey:330.9598. LCCN:89-051449.

Audience: **u,f.**

Cotton, James   **DS649.6.C67 2004**
East Timor, Australia and Regional Order: Intervention and Its Aftermath in Southeast Asia. Paper over Boards. Routledge. New York, NY. 2004. 208p. Politics in Asia Ser. ISBN:0-415-33580-9, ISBN13: 978-0-415-33580-5. Dewey:959.8704. LCCN:2003-023575.

Audience: **u,f.**

Cribb, Robert   **G2401**
Historical Atlas of Indonesia. Trade Cloth. University of Hawaii Press. Honolulu, HI. 2000. 240p. ISBN:0-8248-2111-4, ISBN13: 978-0-8248-2111-1. Dewey:911.5/98. LCCN:99-012717.

Audience: **u,f.** *Choice, 2001.*

Cribb, Robert &   **DS644.C74 1995**
 Brown, Colin
Modern Indonesia: A History since 1945. Cloth Text. Longman Publishing. Boston, MA. 1995. 208p. The Post War World Ser. ISBN:0-582-05712-4, ISBN13: 978-0-582-05712-8. Dewey:959.8/03. LCCN:94-048236.

Audience: **u,f.**

Elson, R. E.   **DS644.1.S56 E44 2001**
Suharto: A Political Biography. Cloth Text. Cambridge University Press. New York, NY. 2001. 412p. ISBN:0-521-77326-1, ISBN13: 978-0-521-77326-3. Dewey:959.803/092 B. LCCN:2002-318969.

Audience: **l,u.** *Choice, 2002.*

Frederick, William H.   **DS646.29.S8F74 1989**
Visions and Heat: The Making of the Indonesian Revolution. Library Binding. Ohio University Press. Athens, OH. 1988. 380p. ISBN:0-8214-0905-0, ISBN13: 978-0-8214-0905-3. Dewey:959.8/2. LCCN:88-025339.

Audience: **l,u.** *Choice, 1989.*

Friend, Theodore   **DS644.F69 2003**
Indonesian Destinies. Trade Cloth. Harvard University Press. Cambridge, MA. 2003. 640p. ISBN:0-674-01137-6, ISBN13: 978-0-674-01137-3. Dewey:959.803. LCCN:2002-043937.

Audience: **u,f.**

Furnivall, J. S.   **DS485.B89 F8**
Colonial Policy and Practice: A Comparative Study of Burma and Netherlands India. Paper Text. Textbook Publishers. Temecula, CA. 2003. xii, 568p. ISBN:0-7581-7741-0, ISBN13: 978-0-7581-7741-4. Dewey:959.1.

Audience: **u,f.** *B*

Furnivall, John S.   **DS634 .F8 1983**
Netherlands India: A Study of Plural Economy. A. C. De Graeff (Introduction by). Trade Cloth. A M S Press, Inc. New York, NY. ISBN:0-404-16712-8, ISBN13: 978-0-404-16712-7. Dewey:959.8/022. LCCN:77-086961.

Audience: **u,f.**

Geertz, Clifford   **BP63.I5**
Islam Observed: Religious Development in Morocco and Indonesia. Trade Cloth. Yale University Press. Cumberland, RI. 1968. Terry Lectures ISBN:0-300-00483-4, ISBN13: 978-0-300-00483-0. Dewey:297/.09598. LCCN:68-027753.

Audience: **u,f.** *B*

Geertz, Clifford   **DS647.B2**
Negara: The Theatre State in 19th Century Bali. Trade Cloth. Princeton University Press. Princeton, NJ. 1981. 256p. ISBN:0-691-05316-2, ISBN13: 978-0-691-05316-5. Dewey:959.8/6. LCCN:80-007520.

Audience: **u,f.**

Geertz, Clifford   **BL2120.J3G42**
The Religion of Java. Trade Paper. University of Chicago Press. Chicago, IL. 1976. 412p. ISBN:0-226-28510-3, ISBN13: 978-0-226-28510-8. Dewey:200.9/5982. LCCN:75-018746.

Audience: **u,f.** *B*

Gold, Lisa   **ML345.I5G65 2004**
Music in Bali: Experiencing Music, Expressing Culture. Trade Cloth. Oxford University Press, Inc. New York, NY. 2004. 208p. Global Music Ser. ISBN:0-19-514150-4, ISBN13: 978-0-19-514150-4. Dewey:780/.9598/6. LCCN:2004-041563.

Audience: **u,f.**

Hefner, Robert W.   **BP63.I5H44 2000**
Civil Islam: Muslims and Democratization in Indonesia. Cloth Text. Princeton University Press. Princeton, NJ. 2000. xxiv, 286p. ISBN:0-691-05046-5, ISBN13: 978-0-691-05046-1. Dewey:322/.1/09598. LCCN:00-020486.

Audience: **u,f.** *Choice, 2001.*

Herbst, Edward   **ML3758.I53H47 1997**
Voices in Bali: Energies and Perceptions in Vocal Music and Dance Theater. Judith Becker (Foreword by), Rene T. A. Lysloff (Afterword by). Library Binding. Wesleyan University Press. Middletown, CT. 1997. 218p. Music Culture Ser. ISBN:0-8195-6316-1, ISBN13: 978-0-8195-6316-3. Dewey:781.62/9922. LCCN:97-019855.

Audience: **u,f.** *Choice, 1998.*

Heryanto, Ariel   **DS644.4.H487 2005**
State Terrorism and Political Identity in Indonesia: Fatally Belonging. Paper over Boards. Routledge. New York, NY. 2005.

224p. Politics in Asia Ser. ISBN:0-415-37152-X, ISBN13: 978-0-415-37152-0. Dewey:323.4/9/0959809045. LCCN:2005-003602.

Audience: **u,f.**

Kahin, George　　　　　　　　　**DS644.K32 2003**
　McTurnan
Nationalism and Revolution in Indonesia. Trade Paper. Cornell University, Southeast Asia Program Publications. Ithaca, NY. 2003. xxvii, 490p. Studies on Southeast Asia, No. 35 ISBN:0-87727-734-6, ISBN13: 978-0-87727-734-7. Dewey:959.803. LCCN:2004-266939.

Audience: **u,f.**

Kingsbury, Damien　　　　　　　　　**JQ770**
The Politics of Indonesia. Ed. 3. Trade Paper. Oxford University Press, Inc. New York, NY. 2005. 400p. ISBN:0-19-551742-3, ISBN13: 978-0-19-551742-2. Dewey:959.803. LCCN:2005-280632.

Audience: **u,f.**

McDonald, Hamish　　　　　　　　　**DS644.4**
Suharto's Indonesia. Paper Text. University of Hawaii Press. Honolulu, HI. 1981. 277p. ISBN:0-8248-0781-2, ISBN13: 978-0-8248-0781-8. Dewey:320.9598.

Audience: **u,f.**

McIntyre, Angus　　　　　　　　　**DS644.M28 2005**
The Indonesian Presidency: The Shift from Personal Toward Constitutional Rule. Book, Other. Rowman & Littlefield Publishers, Inc. Lanham, MD. 2005. 312p. Asia/Pacific/Perspectives Ser. ISBN:0-7425-3826-5, ISBN13: 978-0-7425-3826-9. Dewey:959.803. LCCN:2004-026496.

Audience: **u,f.** *Choice, 2006.*

McPhee, Colin　　　　　　　　　**DS646.59.T55**
A House in Bali. Trade Cloth. A M S Press, Inc. New York, NY. ISBN:0-404-16766-7, ISBN13: 978-0-404-16766-0. Dewey:959.8/6. LCCN:77-086965.

Audience: **u,f.**

Milton, Giles　　　　　　　　　**HD9211.N883I55 1999**
Nathaniel's Nutmeg: Or, the True and Incredible Adventures of the Spice Trader Who Changed the Course of History. Cloth over Boards. Farrar, Straus & Giroux. New York, NY. 1999. 256p. ISBN:0-374-21936-2, ISBN13: 978-0-374-21936-9. Dewey:338.1/7383. LCCN:98-041955.

Audience: **g,l,u.**

Nairn, Allan　　　　　　　　　**DS644**
Our Kind of Guys: The United States and the Indonesian Military. Trade Cloth. Analytical Psychology Club of San Francisco, Inc. San Francisco, CA. 1999. 160p. ISBN:1-85984-735-8, ISBN13: 978-1-85984-735-0. Dewey:327.5/98/073.

Audience: **u,f.**

Pemberton, John　　　　　　　　　**DS646.18.P4 1994**
On the Subject of "Java". Book, Other. Cornell University Press. Ithaca, NY. 1994. 320p. ISBN:0-8014-2672-3, ISBN13: 978-0-8014-2672-8. Dewey:959.8/2. LCCN:94-025827.

Audience: **l,u.**

Philpott, Simon　　　　　　　　　**JQ776.P45 2000**
Rethinking Indonesia: Postcolonial Theory, Authoritarianism and Identity. Cloth over Boards. Palgrave Macmillan. New York, NY. 2000. 256p. ISBN:0-312-23642-5, ISBN13: 978-0-312-23642-7. Dewey:306.2/09598. LCCN:00-042069.

Audience: **u,f.**

Raden, Adjeng K. &　　　　　　　　**HQ1752.K3713 1985**
　Geertz, Hildred
Letters of a Javanese Princess by Raden Adjeng Kartini. Agnes L. Symmers (Translator). Trade Paper. University Press of America, Inc. Lanham, MD. 1985. 246p. ISBN:0-8191-4758-3, ISBN13: 978-0-8191-4758-5. Dewey:305.4/2/095982. LCCN:85-011098.

Audience: **u,f.**

Raffles, Stamford　　　　　　　　　**DS646.27**
The History of Java. John Bastin (Introduction by). Trade Cloth. Oxford University Press, Inc. New York, NY. 1979. xlviiii, 479p. Asia Historical Reprints Ser. ISBN:0-19-580347-7, ISBN13: 978-0-19-580347-1. Dewey:959.8/201.

Audience: **u,f.**

Reid, Anthony　　　　　　　　　**DS644**
The Indonesian National Revolution 1945-1950. Trade Cloth. Greenwood Publishing Group, Inc. Portsmouth, NH. 1986. 205p. Studies in Contemporary Southeast Asia ISBN:0-313-25376-5, ISBN13: 978-0-313-25376-8. Dewey:959.8/035. LCCN:86-022768.

Audience: **u,f.**

Ricklefs, M. C.　　　　　　　　　**DS634.R53 2001**
A History of Modern Indonesia since c. 1200. Ed. 3. Trade Cloth. Stanford University Press. Palo Alto, CA. 2001. xviii, 495p. ISBN:0-8047-4479-3, ISBN13: 978-0-8047-4479-9. Dewey:959.8. LCCN:2001-090449.

Audience: **l,u.**

Ricklefs, M.C.　　　　　　　　　**DS646.27.R533 2006**
Mystic Synthesis in Java: A History of Islamization from the Fourteenth to the Early Nineteenth Centuries. Trade Cloth. EastBridge. Norwalk, CT. 2006. 256p. ISBN:1-891936-62-X, ISBN13: 978-1-891936-62-3. Dewey:959.8/201. LCCN:2005-029378.

Audience: **l,u.**

Ricklefs, Merle C.　　　　　　　　　**DS646.27.R536 1998**
The Seen and Unseen Worlds in Java, 1726-1749: History, Literature and Islam in the Court of Pakubuwana II. Trade Cloth. University of Hawaii Press. Honolulu, HI. 1998. 408p. ASAA Southeast Asia Publication Ser. ISBN:0-8248-2052-5, ISBN13: 978-0-8248-2052-7. Dewey:959.8/2021. LCCN:97-042719.

Audience: **f.** *Choice, 1999.*

Robinson, Geoffrey B.　　　　　　　　**DS647.B2R63 1995**
The Dark Side of Paradise: Political Violence in Bali. Trade Paper. Cornell University Press. Ithaca, NY. 1998. 376p. ISBN:0-8014-8172-4, ISBN13: 978-0-8014-8172-7. Dewey:959.8/6. LCCN:95-009754.

Audience: **u,f.** *Choice, 1996.*

Rodgers, Susan (Editor)　　　　　　　　**DS643.T45 1995**
Telling Lives, Telling Histories: Autobiography and Historical Imagination in Modern Indonesia. Trade Cloth. University of California Press. Berkeley, CA. 1995. 348p. ISBN:0-520-08546-9, ISBN13: 978-0-520-08546-6. Dewey:959.803. LCCN:94-030282.

Audience: **u,f.** *Choice, 1995.*

Rush, James R.　　　　　　　　　**HV5816.R87 1990**
Opium to Java: Revenue Farming and Chinese Enterprise in Colonial Indonesia, 1860-1910. Book, Other. Cornell University Press. Ithaca, NY. 1990. 280p. Asia East by South Ser.

ISBN:0-8014-2218-3, ISBN13: 978-0-8014-2218-8.
Dewey:363.4/5/095982. LCCN:89-045974.

Audience: **u,f.** *Choice, 1990.*

Sato, Shigeru   **DS646.27.S35 1994**
War, Nationalism and Peasants: Java under the Japanese
Occupation, 1942-1945. Cloth Text. M. E. Sharpe Inc. Armonk,
NY. 1994. 300p. Japan in the Modern World Ser.
ISBN:1-56324-544-2, ISBN13: 978-1-56324-544-2.
Dewey:959.8/2. LCCN:94-031953.

Audience: **l,u.** *Choice, 1995.*

Sears, Laurie J.   **PN1978.I53S43 1996**
Shadows of Empire: Colonial Discourse and Javanese Tales.
Cloth Text. Duke University Press. Durham, NC. 1996. 352p.
ISBN:0-8223-1685-4, ISBN13: 978-0-8223-1685-5.
Dewey:791.5/3. LCCN:95-030518.

Audience: **u,f.** *Choice, 1996.*

Shiraishi, Takashi   **DS646.27.S55 1990**
An Age in Motion: Popular Radicalism in Java, 1912-1926.
Book, Other. Cornell University Press. Ithaca, NY. 1990. 392p.
Asia East by South Ser. ISBN:0-8014-2188-8, ISBN13:
978-0-8014-2188-4. Dewey:959.8/2. LCCN:89-037476.

Audience: **u,f.** *Choice, 1990.*

Shiraishi, Takashi   **HC447.A856 1994**
  (Editor)
Approaching Suharto's Indonesia from the Margins. Paper Text.
Cornell University, Southeast Asia Program Publications. Ithaca,
NY. 1995. Translation Ser., No. 4 ISBN:0-87727-403-7,
ISBN13: 978-0-87727-403-2. Dewey:331.7/598.
LCCN:95-142214.

Audience: **u,f.**

Siegel, James T.   **DS643.S54 1997**
Fetish, Recognition, Revolution. Trade Cloth. Princeton
University Press. Princeton, NJ. 1997. 286p.
ISBN:0-691-02653-X, ISBN13: 978-0-691-02653-4.
Dewey:959.8/022. LCCN:96-003204.

Audience: **u,f.** *Choice, 1997.*

Sievers, Allen M.   **DS634.S52**
The Mystical World of Indonesia: Culture and Economic
Development in Conflict. Trade Cloth. Johns Hopkins University
Press. Baltimore, MD. 1994. 448p. ISBN:0-8018-1591-6,
ISBN13: 978-0-8018-1591-1. Dewey:915.98/03.
LCCN:74-006838.

Audience: **u,f.** *B*

Sjahrir, Soetan   **DS644 .S513**
Out of Exile. Charles Wolf Jr. (Translator). Trade Cloth.
Greenwood Publishing Group, Inc. Portsmouth, NH. 1969.
ISBN:0-8371-1045-9, ISBN13: 978-0-8371-1045-5.
Dewey:991/.022.

Audience: **u,f.**

Vatikiotis, Michael R. J.   **DS644.4.V383 1998**
Indonesian Politics under Suharto: The Rise and Fall of the New
Order. Ed. 3. Cloth Text. Routledge. New York, NY. 1999. 272p.
Politics in Asia Ser. ISBN:0-415-20501-8, ISBN13:
978-0-415-20501-6. Dewey:959.803. LCCN:99-220281.

Audience: **u,f.**

Vickers, Adrian (Editor)   **DS647.B2B37 1996**
Being Modern in Bali: Image and Change. Library Binding.
Yale University Southeast Asia Studies. New Haven, CT. 1996.
246p. Southeast Asia Studies, Vol. 43 ISBN:0-938692-57-7,
ISBN13: 978-0-938692-57-7. Dewey:959.8/6. LCCN:95-061261.

Audience: **l,u.**

Vickers, Adrian   **DS643**
A History of Modern Indonesia. Cloth Text. Cambridge
University Press. New York, NY. 2005. 306p.
ISBN:0-521-83493-7, ISBN13: 978-0-521-83493-3.
Dewey:959.803. LCCN:2006-296366.

Audience: **l,u.**

Indonesia > Language and Literature

Koch, C. J.   **PR6019.O9**
The Year of Living Dangerously. Trade Paper. Penguin Group
(USA) Inc. New York, NY. 1983. 288p. ISBN:0-14-006535-0,
ISBN13: 978-0-14-006535-0. Dewey:823/.9/1.
LCCN:82-012259.

Audience: **g,l,u,f.**

Toer, Pramoedya   **PL5089.T8J4513 1994**
  Ananta
Footsteps. Trade Cloth. HarperCollins Publishers. New York,
NY. 1995. 474p. ISBN:0-688-13748-2, ISBN13:
978-0-688-13748-9. Dewey:899.2/2132. LCCN:94-005130.

Audience: **g,l,u,f.**

Toer, Pramoedya   **PL5089.T8A25 1993**
  Ananta
Child of All Nations. Max Lane (Translator). Trade Cloth.
HarperCollins Publishers. New York, NY. 1993. 352p.
ISBN:0-688-12726-6, ISBN13: 978-0-688-12726-8.
Dewey:899.2/2132. LCCN:93-003516.

Audience: **g,u,f.**

Toer, Pramoedya   **PL5089.T8R8613 1996**
  Ananta
House of Glass: A Novel. Max Lane (Translator, Introduction
by). Trade Cloth. HarperCollins Publishers. New York, NY.
1996. 352p. ISBN:0-688-14594-9, ISBN13: 978-0-688-14594-1.
Dewey:899.22132. LCCN:95-046294.

Audience: **g,u,f.**

Toer, Pramoedya   **PL5089.T8G3313 2002**
  Ananta
The Girl from the Coast: A Novel. William Samuels
(Translator). Trade Cloth. Hyperion Press. New York, NY. 2002.
288p. ISBN:0-7868-6820-1, ISBN13: 978-0-7868-6820-9.
Dewey:899/.22132. LCCN:2002-069063.

Audience: **g,u,f.**

Philippines

Abueva, Jose V.   **DS668.A2M35 1998**
The Making of the Filipino Nation and Republic: From
Barangays, Tribes, Sultanates and Colony (Ang Pagbubuo Ng
Bansa at Republika Ng Pilipinas: Mula sa Mga Barangay, Tribu,
Sultanato at Kolonya. Trade Cloth. University of the Philippines
Press. Quezon City, 1999. 1,078p. Pamana Ser.
ISBN:971-542-215-2, ISBN13: 978-971-542-215-4.
Dewey:959.9. LCCN:98-947826.

Audience: **f.**

Agcaoili, T. D. (Editor)   PR9797.P65 A4 1971
Philippine Writing: An Anthology. Trade Cloth. Greenwood
Publishing Group, Inc. Portsmouth, NH. 1971. 351p.
ISBN:0-8371-3063-8, ISBN13: 978-0-8371-3063-7. Dewey:820.
LCCN:76-098742.

Audience: **g,u,f.**

Agoncillo, Teodoro A.   DS676
Malolos: The Crisis of the Republic. Trade Cloth. University of
the Philippines Press. Quezon City, 1997. xviii, 700p.
ISBN:971-542-096-6, ISBN13: 978-971-542-096-9.
Dewey:991.402. LCCN:97-947310.

Audience: **f.**

Aguino, Benigno S. Jr.   DS686.5 .A67
Testament from a Prison Cell. Consuelo Fernandez, Mark G.
Vera, Edmundo Leoncio & Art Palalay (Editors), Arnold Adao
& Charles Funk (Illustrators), Corazon C. Aquino (Foreword
by). Trade Cloth. Philippine Journal, Inc. Henderson, NV. 1989.
190p. ISBN:0-9621695-0-1, ISBN13: 978-0-9621695-0-2.
Dewey:959.9/046 19.

Audience: **g,u,f.**

Bell, Walter F.   Z3298
(Compiled by)
The Philippines in World War II, 1941-1945: A Chronology and
Select Annotated Bibliography of Books and Articles in English.
Cloth Text. Greenwood Publishing Group, Inc. Portsmouth, NH.
1999. 280p. Bibliographies and Indexes in Military Studies, No.
12 ISBN:0-313-30614-1, ISBN13: 978-0-313-30614-3.
Dewey:016.94053/599. LCCN:99-030327.

Audience: **f.**

Boudreau, Vincent   DS530.6.B68 2004
Resisting Dictatorship: Repression and Protest in Southeast Asia.
Cloth Text. Cambridge University Press. New York, NY. 2004.
306p. ISBN:0-521-83989-0, ISBN13: 978-0-521-83989-1.
Dewey:321.9/0959. LCCN:2004-041852.

Audience: **f.**

Cullather, Nick   HF1456.5.P6C85 1994
Illusions of Influence: The Political Economy of United
States-Philippines Relations, 1942-1960. Trade Cloth. Stanford
University Press. Palo Alto, CA. 1994. xiv, 264p. Modern
America ISBN:0-8047-2280-3, ISBN13: 978-0-8047-2280-3.
Dewey:337.730599. LCCN:93-036104.

Audience: **f.** *Choice, 1995.*

De Bevoise, Ken   RA650.7.P6D4 1995
Agents of Apocalypse: Epidemic Disease in the Colonial
Philippines. Cloth Text. Princeton University Press. Princeton,
NJ. 1995. 328p. ISBN:0-691-03486-9, ISBN13:
978-0-691-03486-7. Dewey:614.4/2599. LCCN:94-019328.

Audience: **g,u,f.** *Choice, 1995.*

Elliott, Charles B.   DS685
Philippines to the End of the Commission Government: A Study
in Tropical Democracy. Trade Cloth. Greenwood Publishing
Group, Inc. Portsmouth, NH. 1969. 541p. ISBN:0-8371-0406-8,
ISBN13: 978-0-8371-0406-5. Dewey:991.4/032.
LCCN:69-010088.

Audience: **f.** *B*

Francia, Luis H.   PR9550.5.B76 1993
(Introduction by)
Brown River, White Ocean: An Anthology of Twentieth-Century
Philippine Literature in English. Cloth Text. Rutgers University

Press. Piscataway, NJ. 1993. 279p. ISBN:0-8135-1989-6,
ISBN13: 978-0-8135-1989-0. Dewey:820.809.
LCCN:92-046381.

Audience: **u,f.**

Friend, Theodore   DS0685
Between Two Empires: The Ordeal of the Philippines,
1929-1946. Trade Paper. Books on Demand. Ann Arbor, MI.
344p. Yale Historical Publications, Studies, No. 22
ISBN:0-598-44164-6, ISBN13: 978-0-598-44164-5.
Dewey:991.403. LCCN:65-012541.

Audience: **g,u,f.** *B*

Gates, John M.   DS679
Schoolbooks and Krags: The United States Army in the
Philippines, 1898-1902. Trade Cloth. Greenwood Publishing
Group, Inc. Portsmouth, NH. 1973. 315p. Contributions in
Military History Ser., No. 3 ISBN:0-8371-5818-4, ISBN13:
978-0-8371-5818-1. Dewey:959.9/031. LCCN:77-140917.

Audience: **f.**

Gonzalez, N. V. M.   PR9550.9.G66 B7 1993
The Bread of Salt and Other Stories. Trade Cloth. University of
Washington Press. Seattle, WA. 1993. 224p.
ISBN:0-295-97246-7, ISBN13: 978-0-295-97246-6. Dewey:823.
LCCN:92-043922.

Audience: **g,l,u,f.**

Guillermo, Artemio R.   DS667.G85 2005
Historical Dictionary of the Philippines. Ed. 2. Trade Cloth.
Scarecrow Press, Inc. Lanham, MD. 2005. 616p. Historical
Dictionaries of Asia, Oceania, and the Middle East Ser., No. 54
ISBN:0-8108-5490-2, ISBN13: 978-0-8108-5490-1.
Dewey:959.9. LCCN:2004-030020.

Audience: **f.**

Hayden, Joseph R.   DS686 .H3 1972
The Philippines: A Study in National Development. Trade Cloth.
Ayer Company Publishers, Inc. Manchester, NH. 1972. 1050p.
World Affairs Ser., National & International Viewpoints
ISBN:0-405-04570-0, ISBN13: 978-0-405-04570-7.
Dewey:309.1/599/035. LCCN:72-004276.

Audience: **f.**

Hedman, Eva-Lotta E.   JQ1416.H43 2006
In the Name of Civil Society: From Free Election Movements to
People Power in the Philippines. Trade Cloth. University of
Hawaii Press. Honolulu, HI. 2005. 296p. ISBN:0-8248-2921-2,
ISBN13: 978-0-8248-2921-6. Dewey:320.9599.
LCCN:2005-021234.

Audience: **g,u,f.**

Holthe, Tess Uriza   PS3553.R7858
When the Elephants Dance: A Novel. Trade Paper. Penguin
Group (USA) Inc. New York, NY. 2003. 384p.
ISBN:0-14-200288-7, ISBN13: 978-0-14-200288-9.
Dewey:813/.6.

Audience: **g,l,u,f.**

Jose, F. Sionil   PR9550.9.J67S56 1996
Sins. Trade Cloth. Random House, Inc. New York, NY. 1996.
207p. ISBN:0-679-42018-5, ISBN13: 978-0-679-42018-7.
LCCN:95-039828.

Audience: **g,u,f.**

Kerkvliet, Benedict J.   DS686.5
The Huk Rebellion: A Study of Peasant Revolt in the
Philippines. Ed. 2. Book, Other. Rowman & Littlefield

Publishers, Inc. Lanham, MD. 2002. 338p. ISBN:0-7425-1867-1, ISBN13: 978-0-7425-1867-4. Dewey:322.4/2/09599.

Audience: **g,l,u,f.** ℬ

Kramer, Paul A.   **DS685.K73 2006**
The Blood of Government: Race, Empire, the United States, and the Philippines. Trade Cloth. University of North Carolina Press. Chapel Hill, NC. 2006. 552p. ISBN:0-8078-2985-4, ISBN13: 978-0-8078-2985-1. Dewey:959.9/03. LCCN:2005-031380.

Audience: **g,u,f.**

Larkin, John A.   **HD9116.P61L37 1993**
Sugar and the Origins of Modern Philippine Society. Trade Cloth. University of California Press. Berkeley, CA. 1993. 339p. ISBN:0-520-07956-6, ISBN13: 978-0-520-07956-4. Dewey:338.1736109599. LCCN:92-006325.

Audience: **u,f.** *Choice, 1993.*

Linn, Brian McAllister   **DS679**
The Philippine War, 1899-1902. Trade Cloth. University Press of Kansas. Lawrence, KS. 2004. xiv, 428p. Modern War Studies ISBN:0-7006-1225-4, ISBN13: 978-0-7006-1225-3. Dewey:959.9/031.

Audience: **g,l,u,f.** *Choice, 2000.*

May, Glenn A.   **DS685**
Social Engineering in the Philippines: The Aims, Execution and Impact of American Colonial Policy, 1900-1913. Trade Cloth. Greenwood Publishing Group, Inc. Portsmouth, NH. 1980. 268p. Contributions in Comparative Colonial Studies, No. 2 ISBN:0-313-20978-2, ISBN13: 978-0-313-20978-9. Dewey:309.1/599/032. LCCN:79-007467.

Audience: **f.** ℬ

Miller, Stuart C.   **DS679**
Benevolent Assimilation: The American Conquest of the Philippines, 1899-1903. Trade Paper. Yale University Press. Cumberland, RI. 1984. 342p. ISBN:0-300-03081-9, ISBN13: 978-0-300-03081-5. Dewey:959.9/031. LCCN:82-001957.

Audience: **l,u.** ℬ

Pomeroy, William J.   **DS685 .P63**
American Neo-Colonialism: Its Emergence in the Philippines and Asia. Trade Cloth. International Publishers Company, Inc. New York, NY. 1970. ISBN:0-7178-0251-5, ISBN13: 978-0-7178-0251-7. Dewey:327.730599. LCCN:71-108385.

Audience: **u,f.**

Rafael, Vicente L.   **DS675.R34 2005**
The Promise of the Foreign: Nationalism and the Technics of Translation in the Spanish Philippines. Trade Paper. Duke University Press. Durham, NC. 2005. 264p. ISBN:0-8223-3664-2, ISBN13: 978-0-8223-3664-8. Dewey:320.54/09599/09034. LCCN:2005-011388.

Audience: **f.**

Roosevelt, Nicholas   **DS685.R7 1970**
Philippines: A Treasure and a Problem. Trade Cloth. A M S Press, Inc. New York, NY. 1970. xii, 315p. ISBN:0-404-00618-3, ISBN13: 978-0-404-00618-1. Dewey:309.1/914. LCCN:71-100510.

Audience: **g,l,u,f.** ℬ

Rosaldo, Renato   **DS666.I4.R68**
Ilongot Headhunting, 1883-1974: A Study in Society and History. Trade Cloth. Stanford University Press. Palo Alto, CA. 1980. 325p. ISBN:0-8047-1046-5, ISBN13: 978-0-8047-1046-6. Dewey:959.9/1. LCCN:79-064218.

Audience: **u,f.** ℬ

Stanley, Peter W.   **DS0686.S75**
A Nation in the Making: The Philippines and the United States, 1899-1921. Trade Paper. Books on Demand. Ann Arbor, MI. 351p. Harvard Studies in American-East Asian Relations, Vol. 4 ISBN:0-7837-2337-7, ISBN13: 978-0-7837-2337-2. Dewey:959.9/03. LCCN:73-082342.

Audience: **g,u,f.** ℬ

Storey, Moorfield &   **DS685 .S7 1971**
  Lichauco, Marcial P.
The Conquest of the Philippines by the United States, 1898-1925. Trade Cloth. Ayer Company Publishers, Inc. Manchester, NH. 1977. Select Bibliographies Reprint Ser. ISBN:0-8369-6702-X, ISBN13: 978-0-8369-6702-9. Dewey:973.8/9. LCCN:70-037355.

Audience: **f.**

Sturtevant, David R.   **HD905**
Popular Uprisings in the Philippines, 1840-1940. Book, Other. Cornell University Press. Ithaca, NY. 1976. 344p. ISBN:0-8014-0877-6, ISBN13: 978-0-8014-0877-9. Dewey:301.6/333/09599. LCCN:75-036521.

Audience: **u,f.** ℬ

Thompson, Mark R.   **DS686.5.T49 1995**
The Anti-Marcos Struggle: Personalistic Rule and Democratic Transition in the Philippines. Cloth over Boards. Yale University Press. Cumberland, RI. 1995. 272p. ISBN:0-300-06243-5, ISBN13: 978-0-300-06243-4. Dewey:959.9/04/6. LCCN:95-018890.

Audience: **u,f.**

East Asia, General

Berger, Mark T. &   **DS504.5.R57 1997**
  Borer, Douglas A.
The Rise of East Asia: Critical Visions of the Pacific Century. Paper over Boards. Routledge. New York, NY. 1997. 320p. ISBN:0-415-16167-3, ISBN13: 978-0-415-16167-1. Dewey:950. LCCN:96-043154.

Audience: **g,l,u,f.**

Brook, Timothy &   **HV5840.C6 O65 2000**
  Wakabayashi, Bob Tadashi
Opium Regimes: China, Britain and Japan, 1839-1952. Trade Cloth. University of California Press. Berkeley, CA. 2000. 460p. ISBN:0-520-22236-9, ISBN13: 978-0-520-22236-6. Dewey:363.45/0951. LCCN:99-035149.

Audience: **u,f.**

Cohen, Warren I.   **DS511.C786 2000**
East Asia at the Center: Four Thousand Years of Engagement with the World. Trade Cloth. Columbia University Press. New York, NY. 2000. 528p. ISBN:0-231-10108-2, ISBN13: 978-0-231-10108-0. Dewey:303.48259. LCCN:00-031615.

Audience: **g,u,f.**

Cumings, Bruce   **DS518.8.C76 1999**
Parallax Visions: Making Sense of American-East Asian Relations at the End of the Century. Trade Cloth. Duke University Press. Durham, NC. 1999. 304p. Asia-Pacific, Culture, Politics, and Society Ser. ISBN:0-8223-2276-5, ISBN13: 978-0-8223-2276-4. Dewey:303.48/27305. LCCN:98-032017.

Audience: **g,u,f.** *Choice, 1999.*

Ebrey, Patricia Buckley,   **DS511**
et al.
East Asia: A Cultural, Social, and Political History. Anne
Walthall & James Palais (Authors). Paper Text. Houghton
Mifflin College Division. Boston, MA. 2005. 652p.
ISBN:0-618-13384-4, ISBN13: 978-0-618-13384-0. Dewey:950.
Audience: **g,l,u,f.**

Iriye, Akira   **DS518.8.I73 1992**
Across the Pacific: An Inner History of American-East Asian
Relations. Trade Cloth. Imprint Publications, Inc. Chicago, IL.
1992. 448p. ISBN:1-879176-08-4, ISBN13: 978-1-879176-08-9.
Dewey:305.295. LCCN:92-073114.
Audience: **u,f.**

Iriye, Akira   **DS849.C6I78 1992**
China and Japan in the Global Setting. Harvard University
Press. 1992. Edwin O Reischauer Lectures ISBN:0-674-11838-3,
ISBN13: 978-0-674-11838-6.
Audience: **g,u,f.**

King, F. H.   **S471.C6.K5 1973**
Farmers of Forty Centuries: Permanent Agriculture in China,
Korea and Japan. Trade Cloth. Rodale Press, Inc. Emmaus, PA.
1973. 456p. ISBN:0-87857-054-3, ISBN13: 978-0-87857-054-6.
Dewey:630/.951. LCCN:72-090823.
Audience: **g,u,f.**

Ko, Dorothy (Editor), et al.   **HQ1767 .W64 2003**
Women and Confucian Cultures in Premodern China, Korea,
and Japan. JaHyun Kim Haboush & Joan R. Piggott (Editors).
Trade Cloth. University of California Press. Berkeley, CA. 2003.
350p. ISBN:0-520-23105-8, ISBN13: 978-0-520-23105-4.
Dewey:305.4/0951. LCCN:2003-001855.
Audience: **g,f.**

Mostow, Joshua   **PL493.C55 2003**
(Editor)
The Columbia Companion to Modern East Asian Literature.
Trade Cloth. Columbia University Press. New York, NY. 2003.
700p. ISBN:0-231-11314-5, ISBN13: 978-0-231-11314-4.
Dewey:895. LCCN:2002-035141.
Audience: **g,u,f.** *Choice, 2004.*

Pomeranz, Kenneth   **IIC240.P5965 2000**
The Great Divergence: China, Europe and the Making of the
Modern World Economy. Trade Cloth. Princeton University
Press. Princeton, NJ. 2000. x, 382p. Princeton Economic History
of the Western World Ser. ISBN:0-691-00543-5, ISBN13:
978-0-691-00543-0. Dewey:337. LCCN:99-027681.
Audience: **g,u,f.** *Choice, 2000.*

Reynolds, E. Bruce   **DS849.T5R49 1994**
Thailand and Japan's Southern Advance, 1940-1945. Cloth over
Boards. Palgrave Macmillan. New York, NY. 1994. 320p.
ISBN:0-312-10402-2, ISBN13: 978-0-312-10402-3.
Dewey:940.53/25593. LCCN:93-026125.
Audience: **u,f.**

Schirokauer, Conrad, et   **DS721.S367 2006**
al.
A Brief History of Chinese and Japanese Civilizations. Ed. 3.
Suzanne Gay, David Lurie & Miranda Brown (Authors). Paper
Text. Thomson Wadsworth. Belmont, CA. 2005. 736p.
ISBN:0-534-64307-8, ISBN13: 978-0-534-64307-2. Dewey:951.
LCCN:2005-925208.
Audience: **g,l,u,f.**

Vogel, Ezra F.   **HC460.5.V64 1991**
The Four Little Dragons: The Spread of Industrialization in East
Asia. Trade Cloth. Harvard University Press. Cambridge, MA.
1991. x, 138p. The Edwin O. Reischauer Lectures
ISBN:0-674-31525-1, ISBN13: 978-0-674-31525-9.
Dewey:338.095. LCCN:91-016051.
Audience: **g,l,u,f.** *Choice, 1992.*

World Bank Staff   **HC460.5.E275 1993**
The East Asian Miracle: Economic Growth and Public Policy.
Cloth Text. World Bank Publications. Washington, DC. 1993.
408p. A World Bank Policy Research Report
ISBN:0-19-520993-1, ISBN13: 978-0-19-520993-8.
Dewey:338.95. LCCN:93-030466.
Audience: **g,u,f.** *Choice, 1994.*

China

Anderson, E. N.   **GT2853.C6A53 1988**
The Food of China. Cloth over Boards. Yale University Press.
Cumberland, RI. 1988. 288p. ISBN:0-300-03955-7, ISBN13:
978-0-300-03955-9. Dewey:641.3/00951. LCCN:87-029466.
Audience: **g,u,f.** *Choice, 1988.*

Bauer, Wolfgang   **DS721 .B3413**
China and the Search for Happiness: Recurring Themes in Four
Thousand Years of Chinese Cultural History. Michael Shaw
(Translator). Trade Cloth. Continuum International Publishing
Group, Ltd. London, 1976. ISBN:0-8264-0078-7, ISBN13:
978-0-8264-0078-9. Dewey:951. LCCN:76-010679.
Audience: **f.**

Becker, Jasper   **DS706.B393 2002**
The Chinese. Trade Paper. Oxford University Press, Inc. New
York, NY. 2002. 496p. ISBN:0-19-514940-8, ISBN13:
978-0-19-514940-1. Dewey:951. LCCN:2001-037037.
Audience: **g,l,u,f.**

Blum, Susan D. &   **HN733.5.M35 2002**
Jensen, Lionel M. (Editors)
China off Center: Mapping the Margins of the Middle Kingdom.
Prasenjit Duara (Foreword by). Trade Cloth. University of
Hawaii Press. Honolulu, HI. 2002. 424p. ISBN:0-8248-2335-4,
ISBN13: 978-0-8248-2335-1. Dewey:306/.0951.
LCCN:2002-002101.
Audience: **f.**

Blunden, Caroline &   **DS721.B56 1998**
Elvin, Mark
Cultural Atlas of China. Ed. 2. Trade Cloth. Facts On File, Inc.
New York, NY. 1998. 240p. Cultural Atlas Ser.
ISBN:0-8160-3814-7, ISBN13: 978-0-8160-3814-5. Dewey:951.
LCCN:98-034322.
Audience: **g,u,f.** *B Choice, 1999.*

Chang, K. C. (Editor)   **GT2853.C6**
Food in Chinese Culture: Anthropological and Historical
Perspectives. Trade Cloth. Yale University Press. Cumberland,
RI. 1977. 448p. ISBN:0-300-01938-6, ISBN13:
978-0-300-01938-4. Dewey:301.2/1. LCCN:75-043312.
Audience: **g,f.** *B*

Chao, Buwei Y.   **TS724.5.C5**
How to Cook and Eat in Chinese. Trade Paper. Random House,
Inc. New York, NY. 1972. 320p. ISBN:0-394-71703-1, ISBN13:
978-0-394-71703-6. Dewey:641.5/9/41.
Audience: **g,u,f.**

Cohen, Warren I.   DS511.C786 2000
East Asia at the Center: Four Thousand Years of Engagement with the World. Trade Cloth. Columbia University Press. New York, NY. 2000. 528p. ISBN:0-231-10108-2, ISBN13: 978-0-231-10108-0. Dewey:303.48259. LCCN:00-031615.

Audience: **g,u,f.**

De Bary, W. Theodore   DS721.D37 1999
  & Lufrano, Richard J.
Sources of Chinese Tradition: From 1600 Through the Twentieth Century. Ed. 2. Trade Cloth. Columbia University Press. New York, NY. 2000. 656p. Introduction to Asian Civilizations Ser. ISBN:0-231-11270-X, ISBN13: 978-0-231-11270-3. Dewey:951. LCCN:98-021762.

Audience: **g,l,u,f.**

DeBary, William T. &   DS721.D37 1999
  Bloom, Irene (Editors)
Sources of Chinese Tradition: From Earliest Times to 1600. Ed. 2. Trade Cloth. Columbia University Press. New York, NY. 1999. 944p. Sources of Chinese Tradition Ser., Vol. 1 ISBN:0-231-10938-5, ISBN13: 978-0-231-10938-3. Dewey:951. LCCN:98-021762.

Audience: **g,l,u,f.**

Donald, Stephanie   G2306.G1
  Hemelryk & Benewick, Robert
The State of China Atlas: Mapping the World's Fastest Growing Economy. Trade Paper, Saddle Stitched. University of California Press. Berkeley, CA. 2005. 128p. ISBN:0-520-24627-6, ISBN13: 978-0-520-24627-0. Dewey:912.51.

Audience: **g,l,u,f.**

Fung, Yu-Lan   B126 .F3413
History of Chinese Philosophy, Set. Derk Bodde (Translator). Trade Paper. Princeton University Press. Princeton, NJ. 1953. 1304p. Princeton Library of Asian Translations Ser. ISBN:0-691-02024-8, ISBN13: 978-0-691-02024-2. Dewey:181/.11.

Audience: **g,u,f.**

Hayford, Charles   Z3106.H39 1997
  Wishart
🄴 China. E-Book. ABC-CLIO, Inc. Santa Barbara, CA. 1999. World Bibliographical Ser. ISBN:0-585-03112-6, ISBN13: 978-0-585-03112-5. Dewey:16.951.

Audience: **g,l,u,f.**

Hsu, Francis L.   DS721 .H685 1981
Americans and Chinese: Passage to Differences. Ed. 3. Trade Cloth. University of Hawaii Press. Honolulu, HI. 1981. 562p. ISBN:0-8248-0757-X, ISBN13: 978-0-8248-0757-3. Dewey:951. LCCN:81-010461.

Audience: **g,u,f.**

Leffman, David, et al.   DS705
The Rough Guide to China. Ed. 4. Simon Lewis & Jeremy Atiyah (Authors). Trade Paper, Perfect. Rough Guides, Ltd. London, 2005. 1312p. Rough Guide Travel Guides ISBN:1-84353-479-7, ISBN13: 978-1-84353-479-2. Dewey:915.

Audience: **g,l,u,f.**

Mote, Frederick W.   DS721 .M73 1989
Intellectual Foundations of China. Ed. 2. Trade Cloth. Random House, Inc. New York, NY. 1989. xiii, 129p. Studies in World Civilization Ser. ISBN:0-394-38338-9, ISBN13: 978-0-394-38338-5. Dewey:931. LCCN:88-000560.

Audience: **g,l,u,f.**

Needham, Joseph   DS721.N39 2003
  (Author, Contribution by)
Science and Civilisation in China: The Social Background General Conclusions and Reflections. Kenneth Girdwood Robinson (Editor), C. Cullen (Contribution by), Mark Elvin (Introduction by), Ray Huang (Contribution by). Trade Cloth. Cambridge University Press. New York, NY. 2004. 336p. Science and Civilisation in China Ser., Vol. 7 ISBN:0-521-08732-5, ISBN13: 978-0-521-08732-2. Dewey:509.51.

Audience: **g,u,f.** *Choice, 2005.*

Newman, Jacqueline M.   GT2853
Food Culture in China. Cloth Text. Greenwood Publishing Group, Inc. Portsmouth, NH. 2004. 256p. Food Culture Around the World Ser. ISBN:0-313-32581-2, ISBN13: 978-0-313-32581-6. Dewey:394.1/2/0951. LCCN:2004-012484.

Audience: **g,u,f.**

Ropp, Paul S. (Editor)   DS721.H45 1990
The Heritage of China: Contemporary Perspectives on Chinese Civilization. Trade Cloth. University of California Press. Berkeley, CA. 1990. 390p. ISBN:0-520-06440-2, ISBN13: 978-0-520-06440-9. Dewey:951. LCCN:89-037365.

Audience: **g,l,u,f.** *Choice, 1990.*

Simonds, Nina   TX724.5.C5
Classic Chinese Cuisine. Trade Paper. Houghton Mifflin Company Trade & Reference Division. Boston, MA. 2003. 400p. ISBN:0-618-37965-7, ISBN13: 978-0-618-37965-1. Dewey:641.5951.

Audience: **g,l,u,f.**

Sivin, Nathan (Editor)   G2305.C986 1988
The Contemporary Atlas of China. Trade Cloth. Houghton Mifflin Company. New York, NY. 1988. 200p. ISBN:0-395-47329-2, ISBN13: 978-0-395-47329-0. Dewey:912/.51. LCCN:88-009452.

Audience: **g,l,u,f.** *Choice, 1989.*

Smith, Richard J.   G2305.S6 1996
Chinese Maps: Images of All under Heaven. Cloth Text. Oxford University Press, Inc. New York, NY. 1996. 112p. Images of Asia Ser. ISBN:0-19-585949-9, ISBN13: 978-0-19-585949-2. Dewey:526/.0951. LCCN:96-004390.

Audience: **g,l,u,f.**

Wilkinson, Endymion   DS735.W695 2000
  Porter
Chinese History: A Manual. Ed. 2. Trade Paper. Harvard University Press. Cambridge, MA. 2000. 1,100p. Harvard-Yenching Institute Monographs, Vol. 52 ISBN:0-674-00249-0, ISBN13: 978-0-674-00249-4. Dewey:951. LCCN:99-056876.

Audience: **u,f.**

Wittfogel, Karl August   JC414.W5
Oriental Despotism: A Comparative Study of Total Power. Paper Text. Textbook Publishers. Temecula, CA. 2003. xix, 556p. ISBN:0-7581-0052-3, ISBN13: 978-0-7581-0052-8. Dewey:321.6.

Audience: **f.** *B*

Wong, R. Bin   DS735.W79 1997
China Transformed: Historical Change and the Limits of European Experience. Book, Other. Cornell University Press. Ithaca, NY. 1997. 400p. ISBN:0-8014-3254-5, ISBN13: 978-0-8014-3254-5. Dewey:951. LCCN:97-023232.

Audience: **g,u,f.** *Choice, 1998.*

China > History

Adshead, Samuel   **DS740.4.A644 2000**
  Adrian M.
China in World History. Ed. 3. Trade Paper. Palgrave
Macmillan. New York, NY. 2000. 452p. ISBN:0-312-22565-2,
ISBN13: 978-0-312-22565-0. Dewey:327.51. LCCN:99-027935.
Audience: **u,f.**

Cohen, Paul A. &   **DS755**
  Townsend, Paul A.
Discovering History in China: American Historical Writing on
the Recent Chinese Past. Ed. 2. Trade Paper. Eastern European
Monographs. Bradenton, FL. 1997. 243p. Studies of the East
Asian Institute, Columbia University Ser. ISBN:0-231-05811-X,
ISBN13: 978-0-231-05811-7. Dewey:951/.0072073.
LCCN:83-020868.
Audience: **g,u,f.**

Ebrey, Patricia Buckley   **DS706**
The Cambridge Illustrated History of China. Kwang-Ching Liu
(Foreword by). Trade Cloth. Cambridge University Press. New
York, NY. 1996. 352p. Illustrated Histories Ser.
ISBN:0-521-43519-6, ISBN13: 978-0-521-43519-2. Dewey:951.
LCCN:95-038548.
Audience: **g,l,u,f.**

Fairbank, John King &   **DS735**
  Goldman, Merle
China: A New History. Ed. 2. Trade Paper. Harvard University
Press. Cambridge, MA. 2006. 640p. ISBN:0-674-01828-1,
ISBN13: 978-0-674-01828-0. Dewey:951. LCCN:2005-053695.
Audience: **g,l,u,f.**

Fairbank, John K. &   **DS740.4 .T43 1979**
  Teng, S. Y.
China's Response to the West: A Documentary Survey,
1839-1923. Trade Paper. Harvard University Press. Cambridge,
MA. 1979. 308p. ISBN:0-674-12025-6, ISBN13:
978-0-674-12025-9. Dewey:303.4/82/0951 19.
LCCN:53-005061.
Audience: **g,l,u,f.**

Fitzgerald, C. P.   **DS721.F55**
China: A Short Cultural History. Paper Text. Textbook
Publishers. Temecula, CA. 2003. xviii, 621p.
ISBN:0-7581-6253-7, ISBN13: 978-0-7581-6253-3. Dewey:951.
Audience: **g,l,u,f.** *B*

Gernet, Jacques   **DS721 .G3913 1996**
A History of Chinese Civilization. Ed. 2. J. R. Foster & Charles
Hartman (Translators). Trade Cloth. Cambridge University Press.
New York, NY. 1996. 780p. ISBN:0-521-49712-4, ISBN13:
978-0-521-49712-1. Dewey:951. LCCN:95-006047.
Audience: **g,u,f.**

Hook, Brian &   **DS705 .C35 1991**
  Twitchett, Denis C. (Editors)
The Cambridge Encyclopedia of China. Ed. 2. Trade Cloth.
Cambridge University Press. New York, NY. 1991. 506p.
Cambridge World Encyclopedias Ser. ISBN:0-521-35594-X,
ISBN13: 978-0-521-35594-0. Dewey:951/.003.
LCCN:91-018600.
Audience: **g,u,f.** *B*

Hsu, Immanuel C.   **DS754.H74 2000**
The Rise of Modern China. Ed. 6. Paper Text. Oxford
University Press, Inc. New York, NY. 1999. 1136p.

ISBN:0-19-512504-5, ISBN13: 978-0-19-512504-7.
Dewey:951/.03. LCCN:99-010876.
Audience: **g,f.** *B*

Huang, Ray   **DS735.H785 1997**
e China: A Macro History. E-Book. NetLibrary, Inc. Boulder,
CO. 1997. ISBN:0-585-19022-4, ISBN13: 978-0-585-19022-8.
Dewey:951.
Audience: **g,f.**

Lieberthal, Kenneth   **DS753.84.P47 1991**
  (Editor), et al.
Perspectives on Modern China: Four Anniversaries. Joyce
Kallgren, Roderick MacFarquhar & Frederic Wakeman Jr.
(Editors). Paper Text. M. E. Sharpe Inc. Armonk, NY. 1991.
448p. Studies on Modern China ISBN:0-87332-890-6, ISBN13:
978-0-87332-890-6. Dewey:951/.03. LCCN:91-013410.
Audience: **g,u,f.**

Schrecker, John E.   **DS735**
The Chinese Revolution in Historical Perspective. Ed. 2. Paper
Text. Greenwood Publishing Group, Inc. Portsmouth, NH. 2004.
344p. ISBN:0-275-97476-6, ISBN13: 978-0-275-97476-3.
Dewey:951. LCCN:2003-053029.
Audience: **f.** *Choice, 1991.*

Shouyi, Bai   **DS735**
An Outline History of China. Trade Cloth. Beijing Foreign
Languages Press. Beijing, 2002. 803p. ISBN:7-119-02347-0,
ISBN13: 978-7-119-02347-2. Dewey:951.
Audience: **g,f.**

Spence, Jonathan D.   **DS754**
The Search for Modern China. Trade Paper. W. W. Norton &
Company, Inc. New York, NY. 2001. 928p.
ISBN:0-393-30780-8, ISBN13: 978-0-393-30780-1.
Dewey:951/.03.
Audience: **g,l,u,f.** *Choice, 1990.*

China > History > to 221 BCE

Ames, Roger T.   **U101**
Sun-Tzu: The Art of War: New Translation Incorporating the
Recently Discovered Yin-Ch Ueh-Shan Texts. Trade Cloth.
Ballantine Books. New York, NY. 1993. 336p. Classics of
Ancient China Ser. ISBN:0-345-36239-X, ISBN13:
978-0-345-36239-1. Dewey:355.02. LCCN:92-052662.
Audience: **u,f.**

Barnes, Gina L.   **DS509.3.B37 1993**
China, Korea and Japan: The Rise of Civilization in East Asia.
Trade Cloth. Thames & Hudson. New York, NY. 1993. 304p.
ISBN:0-500-05071-6, ISBN13: 978-0-500-05071-2.
Dewey:950.1. LCCN:93-060205.
Audience: **g,u,f.**

Baynes, Cary F. &   **PL2478**
  Wilhelm, Richard (Translators)
The I Ching: Or Book of Changes. Ed. 3. Hellmut Wilhelm
(Produced by). Cloth Text. Princeton University Press.
Princeton, NJ. 1967. 806p. Bollingen Ser., No. 19
ISBN:0-691-09750-X, ISBN13: 978-0-691-09750-3.
Dewey:299.51. LCCN:67-024740.
Audience: **g,l,u,f.**

Cho-yun Hsu   **HN733**
Ancient China in Transition: An Analysis of Social Mobility,
722-222 B. C. Trade Paper. Stanford University Press. Palo

Alto, CA. 1965. viii, 240p. ISBN:0-8047-0224-1, ISBN13:
978-0-8047-0224-9. Dewey:305.5. LCCN:65-013110.

Audience: **g,u,f.**

Confucius   **PL2478.L8 2000**
The Analects. Arthur Waley (Editor, Translator), Sarah Allan
(Introduction by). Trade Cloth. Alfred A. Knopf Inc. New York,
NY. 2001. 304p. ISBN:0-375-41204-2, ISBN13:
978-0-375-41204-2. Dewey:181/.112. LCCN:00-053460.

Audience: **g,l,u,f.**

Creel, H. G.   **B128.C8 C65**
Confucius and the Chinese Way. Trade Cloth. Peter Smith
Publisher, Inc. Magnolia, MA. 1980. ISBN:0-8446-1918-3,
ISBN13: 978-0-8446-1918-7. Dewey:299/.5126/4.

Audience: **g,l,u,f.**

Guisso, Richard W., et   **DS747.9.C47G85 1989**
al.
The First Emperor of China. Catherine Pagani & David Miller
(Authors), Hillel Black (Editor). Trade Cloth. Carol Publishing
Group. Secaucus, NJ. 1989. 224p. ISBN:1-55972-016-6,
ISBN13: 978-1-55972-016-8. Dewey:931/.04/092 B.
LCCN:89-015742.

Audience: **g,u,f.**

Hao-Heyi-Suichu   **DS715.Q513**
Out of China's Earth. Trade Cloth. Harry N. Abrams, Inc. New
York, NY. 1981. 206p. ISBN:0-8109-0766-6, ISBN13:
978-0-8109-0766-9. Dewey:931. LCCN:81-002058.

Audience: **g,u,f.**

Keightley, David N.   **DS715**
The Origins of Chinese Civilization. Trade Cloth. University of
California Press. Berkeley, CA. 1983. 555p. Studies on China,
Vol. 1 ISBN:0-520-04229-8, ISBN13: 978-0-520-04229-2.
Dewey:931. LCCN:81-004595.

Audience: **f.**

Keightley, David N.   **DS723**
Sources of Shang History: The Oracle-Bone Inscriptions of
Bronze Age China. Trade Cloth. University of California Press.
Berkeley, CA. 1979. 300p. ISBN:0-520-02969-0, ISBN13:
978-0-520-02969-9. Dewey:931. LCCN:74-029806.

Audience: **u,f.**

Legge, James
(Translator)
The Chinese Classics: With a Translation, Critical and
Exegetical Notes, Prolegomena, and Copious Indexes, Set. Trade
Cloth. S M C Publishing, Inc. Taipei, 1991. 587p.
ISBN:957-638-038-3, ISBN13: 978-957-638-038-9.
Dewey:895.1082.

Audience: **g,l,u,f.**

Mote, Frederick W.   **DS721 .M73 1989**
Intellectual Foundations of China. Ed. 2. Trade Cloth. Random
House, Inc. New York, NY. 1989. xiii, 129p. Studies in World
Civilization Ser. ISBN:0-394-38338-9, ISBN13:
978-0-394-38338-5. Dewey:931. LCCN:88-000560.

Audience: **g,l,u,f.**

Sawyer, Ralph D.   **U43.C6**
Seven Military Classics of Ancient China. Trade Cloth.
Westview Press. Boulder, CO. 1993. 592p. History and Warfare
Ser. ISBN:0-8133-1228-0, ISBN13: 978-0-8133-1228-6.
Dewey:355.020951. LCCN:92-039146.

Audience: **g,u,f.**

Ssu-ma Chien   **DS741.3 .S6813 1994**
The Grand Scribe's Records: The Basic Annals of Pre-Han
China, Vol. 7. Trade Cloth. Indiana University Press.
Bloomington, IN. 1995. 396p. ISBN:0-253-34027-6, ISBN13:
978-0-253-34027-6. Dewey:931. LCCN:94-018408.

Audience: **f.**

Twitchett, Denis C.   **DS754**
(Editor, Contribution by)
Ch'in and Han Empires, 221 BC-AD 220, Vol. 1. Michael
Loewe (Editor), John K. Fairbank (Contribution by). Cloth Text.
Cambridge University Press. New York, NY. 1986. 1023p. The
Cambridge History of China Ser., Vol. 1 ISBN:0-521-24327-0,
ISBN13: 978-0-521-24327-8. Dewey:951. LCCN:76-029852.

Audience: **f.** *Choice, 1987.*

Watson, Burton   **B128.H66**
(Translator)
Hsun Tzu: Basic Writings. Ed. 2. Trade Paper. Columbia
University Press. New York, NY. 1996. 177p. Translations from
the Asian Classics ISBN:0-231-10689-0, ISBN13:
978-0-231-10689-4. Dewey:181.09512.

Audience: **g,l,u,f.**

Watson, Burton   **DS735.A2**
Records of the Historian: Chapters from the Shih Chi of Ssu-ma
Ch'ien. Trade Paper. Columbia University Press. New York, NY.
1969. 356p. ISBN:0-231-03321-4, ISBN13: 978-0-231-03321-3.
Dewey:931. LCCN:70-089860.

Audience: **u,f.**

Watson, Burton   **PL2470**
The Tso Chuan: Selections from China's Oldest Narrative
History. Trade Paper. Columbia University Press. New York,
NY. 1992. 232p. ISBN:0-231-06715-1, ISBN13:
978-0-231-06715-7. Dewey:931/.03.

Audience: **g,u,f.**

Wilhelm, Hellmut &   **PL2464.Z7W53 1995**
Wilhelm, Richard
Understanding the I Ching: The Wilhelm Lectures on the Book
of Changes. C. F. Baynes & Irene Eber (Translators). Trade
Paper. Princeton University Press. Princeton, NJ. 1995. 350p.
Bollingen Ser., Vol. 19 ISBN:0-691-00171-5, ISBN13:
978-0-691-00171-5. Dewey:299/.51282. LCCN:94-037282.

Audience: **f.**

China > History > Imperial China

Elvin, Mark   **DS721**
Pattern of the Chinese Past. Trade Cloth. Stanford University
Press. Palo Alto, CA. 1973. 346p. ISBN:0-8047-0826-6,
ISBN13: 978-0-8047-0826-5. Dewey:951. LCCN:72-078869.

Audience: **g,u,f.**

Elvin, Mark   **GF656.E48 2004**
Retreat of the Elephants: An Environmental History of China.
Cloth over Boards. Yale University Press. Cumberland, RI.
2004. 592p. ISBN:0-300-10111-2, ISBN13: 978-0-300-10111-9.
Dewey:304.2/0951. LCCN:2003-017378.

Audience: **g,f.** *Choice, 2004.*

Elvin, Mark & Liu,   **QH540.83.C6 S44 1998**
Ts'ui-jung
Sediments of Time: Environment and Society in Chinese
History. Alfred W. Crosby & Donald Worster (Contribution by).
Trade Cloth. Cambridge University Press. New York, NY. 1998.

842p. Studies in Environment and History ISBN:0-521-56381-X, ISBN13: 978-0-521-56381-9. Dewey:333.7/0951. LCCN:96-022662.

Audience: **f.**

Hinsch, Bret   **HQ76.2.C5H56 1990**
Passions of the Cut Sleeve: The Male Homosexual Tradition in China. Trade Cloth. University of California Press. Berkeley, CA. 1990. 256p. ISBN:0-520-06720-7, ISBN13: 978-0-520-06720-2. Dewey:306.76/62/0951. LCCN:89-049037.

Audience: **l,u,f.** *Choice, 1991.*

Mote, Frederick W.   **DS750.64.M67 1999**
Imperial China, 900-1800. Trade Cloth. Harvard University Press. Cambridge, MA. 2000. 1136p. ISBN:0-674-44515-5, ISBN13: 978-0-674-44515-4. Dewey:951/.02. LCCN:99-031840.

Audience: **g,u,f.** *Choice, 2000.*

Wright, Arthur F.   **BQ4055**
Buddhism in Chinese History. Trade Cloth. Stanford University Press. Palo Alto, CA. 1959. xiv, 144p. ISBN:0-8047-0546-1, ISBN13: 978-0-8047-0546-2. Dewey:294.3. LCCN:59-007432.

Audience: **g,l,u,f.**

China > History > Imperial China > Unification to 9th Century

Ch'u, T'ung-tsu   **HN673**
Han Social Structure. Jack L. Dull (Editor). Trade Cloth. University of Washington Press. Seattle, WA. 1972. 570p. Han Dynasty China Ser., Vol. 1 ISBN:0-295-95068-4, ISBN13: 978-0-295-95068-6. Dewey:309.1/31. LCCN:69-014206.

Audience: **u,f.** *B*

Graff, David   **DS747.43.G73 2002**
Medieval Chinese Warfare 300-900. Paper over Boards. Routledge. New York, NY. 2001. 304p. Warfare and History Ser. ISBN:0-415-23954-0, ISBN13: 978-0-415-23954-7. Dewey:951/.01. LCCN:2001-052022.

Audience: **u,f.** *Choice, 2002.*

Holcombe, Charles   **DS748.6.H65 1994**
In the Shadow of the Han: Literati Thought and Society at the Beginning of the Southern Dynasties. Trade Cloth. University of Hawaii Press. Honolulu, HI. 1994. 252p. ISBN:0-8248-1592-0, ISBN13: 978-0-8248-1592-9. Dewey:931/.03. LCCN:94-028355.

Audience: **u,f.**

Hung, William   **Q172.5.S96**
Tu Fu, China's Greatest Poet. Paper Text. Textbook Publishers. Temecula, CA. 2003. x, 300p. ISBN:0-7581-4322-2, ISBN13: 978-0-7581-4322-8. Dewey:3.7.

Audience: **g,u,f.**

Pirazzoli-t'Serstevens,   **DS748.P5713 1982**
  Michele
The Han Dynasty. Trade Cloth. Rizzoli International Publications, Inc. New York, NY. 1982. 240p. ISBN:0-8478-0438-0, ISBN13: 978-0-8478-0438-2. Dewey:931/.04. LCCN:82-050109.

Audience: **g,u,f.**

Reischauer, Edwin O.   **DS707 .E512**
  (Translator)
Ennin's Diary: The Record of a Pilgrimage to China in Search of the Law. Trade Cloth. John Wiley & Sons, Inc. Hoboken, NJ.

1955. ISBN:0-8260-7400-6, ISBN13: 978-0-8260-7400-3. Dewey:951.016.

Audience: **g,u,f.**

Reischauer, Edwin O.   **DS707 .R45**
Ennin's Travels in Tang China. Paper Text. Textbook Publishers. Temecula, CA. 2003. xii, 341p. ISBN:0-7581-4637-X, ISBN13: 978-0-7581-4637-3. Dewey:951.016.

Audience: **l,u,f.**

Schafer, Edward H.   **HE325**
The Golden Peaches of Samarkand. Trade Cloth. Kegan Paul International, Ltd. London, 2004. 410p. ISBN:0-7103-1014-5, ISBN13: 978-0-7103-1014-9. Dewey:382.5/0951/09021.

Audience: **g,u,f.**

Schafer, Edward H.   **DS749.3**
The Vermilion Bird: T'ang Images of the South. Trade Paper. University of California Press. Berkeley, CA. 1967. ISBN:0-520-05463-6, ISBN13: 978-0-520-05463-9. Dewey:951.017. LCCN:67-010463.

Audience: **f.**

Twitchett, Denis C.   **DS735**
  (Editor, Contribution by)
Sui and T'ang China, 589-906 AD. John K. Fairbank (Contribution by). Cloth Text. Cambridge University Press. New York, NY. 1979. 870p. The Cambridge History of China Ser. ISBN:0-521-21446-7, ISBN13: 978-0-521-21446-9. Dewey:951. LCCN:76-029852.

Audience: **f.**

Wriggins, Sally Hovey   **BQ8149.H787**
Xuanzang: A Buddhist Pilgrim on the Silk Road. Paper Text. Westview Press. Boulder, CO. 1997. 292p. ISBN:0-8133-3407-1, ISBN13: 978-0-8133-3407-3. Dewey:939.6/0099.

Audience: **g,u,f.**

Wright, Arthur F.   **DS749.3**
The Sui Dynasty. Paper Text. Random House Children's Books. New York, NY. 1979. ISBN:0-394-32332-7, ISBN13: 978-0-394-32332-9. Dewey:951/.01.

Audience: **g,u,f.**

Wright, Arthur F. &   **DS721**
  Twitchett, Denis Crispin (Editors)
Perspectives on the T'ang. Trade Cloth. Yale University Press. Cumberland, RI. 2004. viii, 458p. ISBN:0-300-01522-4, ISBN13: 978-0-300-01522-5. Dewey:951/.01. LCCN:72-091310.

Audience: **f.**

China > History > Imperial China > Early Modern (10th-15th Centuries)

Bol, Peter K.   **DS747.42.B64 1992**
This Culture of Ours: Intellectual Transitions in T'ang and Sung China. Trade Cloth. Stanford University Press. Palo Alto, CA. 1992. 532p. ISBN:0-8047-1920-9, ISBN13: 978-0-8047-1920-9. Dewey:951/.01. LCCN:91-016004.

Audience: **f.** *Choice, 1993.*

Brook, Timothy   **DS753 .B76 1998**
The Confusions of Pleasure: Commerce and Culture in Ming China. Trade Cloth. University of California Press. Berkeley, CA. 1998. 345p. ISBN:0-520-21091-3, ISBN13: 978-0-520-21091-2. Dewey:951/.026. LCCN:97-008838.

Audience: **u,f.** *Choice, 1998.*

Brook, Timothy   **BQ641.B7 1993**
Praying for Power: Buddhism and the Formation of Gentry
Society in Late-Ming China. Trade Cloth. Harvard University
Press. Cambridge, MA. 1994. 400p. Harvard-Yenching Institute
Monographs, No. 38 ISBN:0-674-69775-8, ISBN13:
978-0-674-69775-1. Dewey:306.69430951. LCCN:93-005407.
Audience: **f.** *Choice, 1994.*

Clunas, Craig   **SB466.C5C6 1996**
Fruitful Sites: Garden Culture in Ming Dynasty China. Cloth
Text. Duke University Press. Durham, NC. 1996. 240p.
ISBN:0-8223-1800-8, ISBN13: 978-0-8223-1800-2.
Dewey:712/.0951. LCCN:95-044802.
Audience: **u,f.**

Clunas, Craig   **HN740.Z9S6233 2004**
Superfluous Things: Material Culture and Social Status in Early
Modern China. Trade Paper. University of Hawaii Press.
Honolulu, HI. 2004. 240p. ISBN:0-8248-2820-8, ISBN13:
978-0-8248-2820-2. Dewey:305.50951. LCCN:2004-001199.
Audience: **f.**

de Bary, Wm. Theodore   **JQ1508.H7883**
(Translator)
Waiting for the Dawn: A Plan for the Prince. Trade Paper.
Columbia University Press. New York, NY. 1994. 340p.
ISBN:0-231-08097-2, ISBN13: 978-0-231-08097-2.
Dewey:321/.6/0951.
Audience: **g,u,f.**

Ebrey, Patricia B.   **HQ684.A25 1993**
The Inner Quarters: Marriage and the Lives of Chinese Women
in the Sung Period. Trade Cloth. University of California Press.
Berkeley, CA. 1993. 312p. ISBN:0-520-08156-0, ISBN13:
978-0-520-08156-7. Dewey:305.420951. LCCN:92-031376.
Audience: **u,f.** *Choice, 1994.*

Gernet, Jacques   **DS721 .G413**
Daily Life in China on the Eve of the Mongol Invasion,
1250-1276. Paper Text. Textbook Publishers. Temecula, CA.
2003. 254p. ISBN:0-7581-3531-9, ISBN13: 978-0-7581-3531-5.
Dewey:915.1/03/2.
Audience: **g,l,u,f.**

Goodrich, L.   **DS753.5**
Carrington & Fang, Chaoying (Editors)
Dictionary of Ming Biography, 1364-1644. Trade Cloth.
Columbia University Press. New York, NY. 1976. 1751p.
ISBN:0-231-03833-X, ISBN13: 978-0-231-03833-1.
Dewey:951/.026/0922. LCCN:75-026938.
Audience: **f.** *B*

Huang, Ray   **DS753**
Fifteen-Eighty-Seven, a Year of No Significance: The Ming
Dynasty in Decline. Trade Cloth. Yale University Press.
Cumberland, RI. 1981. 396p. ISBN:0-300-02518-1, ISBN13:
978-0-300-02518-7. Dewey:951/.026. LCCN:80-005392.
Audience: **g,u,f.**

Marks, Robert B.   **HC427.6 .M37 1997**
Tigers, Rice, Silk, and Silt: Environment and Economy in Late
Imperial South China. Alfred W. Crosby & Donald Worster
(Contribution by). Trade Cloth. Cambridge University Press.
New York, NY. 1998. 407p. Studies in Environment and History
ISBN:0-521-59177-5, ISBN13: 978-0-521-59177-5.
Dewey:951/.026. LCCN:96-053322.
Audience: **u,f.**

Mote, Frederick W. &   **DS753**
Twitchett, Denis C.
The Ming Dynasty: 1368-1644. Denis Twitchett & John K.
Fairbank (Contribution by). Cloth Text. Cambridge University
Press. New York, NY. 1998. 1231p. The Cambridge History of
China Ser. ISBN:0-521-24333-5, ISBN13: 978-0-521-24333-9.
Dewey:951/.026. LCCN:76-029852.
Audience: **f.** *Choice, 1998.*

Mote, Frederick W.   **DS735**
(Editor)
The Ming Dynasty, 1368-1644. Denis Twitchett (Editor,
Contribution by), John K. Fairbank (Contribution by). Trade
Cloth. Cambridge University Press. New York, NY. 1988.
1008p. The Cambridge History of China Ser., Vol. 7
ISBN:0-521-24332-7, ISBN13: 978-0-521-24332-2. Dewey:951.
Audience: **f.** *Choice, 1989.*

Mungello, David E.   **BV3417.M86 1989**
Curious Land: Jesuit Accommodation and the Origins of
Sinology. Trade Paper. University of Hawaii Press. Honolulu,
HI. 1989. 408p. ISBN:0-8248-1219-0, ISBN13:
978-0-8248-1219-5. Dewey:951.007. LCCN:88-027874.
Audience: **g,u,f.** *Choice, 1990.*

Polo, Marco   **G465**
The Travels of Marco Polo. Ronald Latham (Translator). Library
Binding. OPAL Publishing Corporation. Norwalk, CT. 1982.
318p. ISBN:0-89835-058-1, ISBN13: 978-0-89835-058-6.
Dewey:910.4.
Audience: **g,l,u,f.**

Polo, Marco, et al.   **G370.P9 P6713 1993**
The Travels of Marco Polo: The Complete Yule-Cordier Edition.
Henry Yule & Henri Cordier (Authors). Trade Paper. Dover
Publications, Inc. Mineola, NY. 1993. Extensive editorial
apparatus, nearly 200 illustrations (many double-page spreads)
and 32 maps and site plans augment the text. 855p. 0
ISBN:0-486-27587-6, ISBN13: 978-0-486-27587-1.
Dewey:915.10425092. LCCN:92-039066.
Audience: **g,l,u.**

Polo, Marco, et al.   **G370.P9 P6713 1993**
The Travels of Marco Polo: The Complete Yule-Cordier Edition.
Henry Yule & Henri Cordier (Authors). Trade Paper. Dover
Publications, Inc. Mineola, NY. 1993. 567p. 0
ISBN:0-486-27586-8, ISBN13: 978-0-486-27586-4.
Dewey:915.10425092. LCCN:92-039066.
Audience: **g.**

Rossabi, Morris   **DS752.6.K83.R67 1988**
Khubilai Khan: His Life and Times. Trade Paper. University of
California Press. Berkeley, CA. 1989. 344p.
ISBN:0-520-06740-1, ISBN13: 978-0-520-06740-0.
Dewey:950/.2/0924 B. LCCN:86-025031.
Audience: **g,u,f.** *Choice, 1989.*

Twitchett, Denis C. &   **DS751.72**
Franke, Herbert (Editors)
Alien Regimes and Border States, 907-1368. John K. Fairbank
& Denis Twitchett (Contribution by). Trade Cloth. Cambridge
University Press. New York, NY. 1994. 816p. The Cambridge
History of China Ser., Vol. 6 ISBN:0-521-24331-9, ISBN13:
978-0-521-24331-5. Dewey:951.02.
Audience: **f.**

Von Glahn, Richard   **DS793.S8V66 1987**
The Country of Streams and Grottoes: Expansion, Settlement,
and the Civilizing of the Sichuan Frontier in Song Times. Trade

Cloth. Harvard University Press. Cambridge, MA. 1988. 304p.
Harvard East Asian Monographs, Vol. 123 ISBN:0-674-17543-3,
ISBN13: 978-0-674-17543-3. Dewey:951/.38024.
LCCN:87-013526.

Audience: **f.**

China > History > Qing Dynasty (1617-1912)

Bays, Daniel H. (Editor)   **BR1287.C47 1996**
Christianity in China: From the Eighteenth Century to the
Present. Trade Cloth. Stanford University Press. Palo Alto, CA.
1996. xxii, 483p. ISBN:0-8047-2609-4, ISBN13:
978-0-8047-2609-2. Dewey:275.1/08. LCCN:95-053046.

Audience: **g,u,f.**

Esherick, Joseph &   **HN740.Z9E426 1990**
  Rankin, Mary Backus
🄴 Chinese Local Elites and Patterns of Dominance. E-Book.
NetLibrary, Inc. Boulder, CO. 1990. ISBN:0-585-10435-2,
ISBN13: 978-0-585-10435-5. Dewey:305.5/52/095109045.

Audience: **f.**

Hsiao, Kung-Chuan   **NE400.H66**
Rural China: Imperial Control in the Nineteenth Century. Paper
Text. Textbook Publishers. Temecula, CA. 2003. xiv, 783p.
ISBN:0-7581-1443-5, ISBN13: 978-0-7581-1443-3.
Dewey:765.09.

Audience: **f.**

Hummel, Arthur W.   **DS0734**
Eminent Chinese of the Ch'ing Period, 1644-1912. Library
Binding. Gordon Press Publishers. New York, NY. 1976.
ISBN:0-8490-1761-0, ISBN13: 978-0-8490-1761-2.
Dewey:920.051.

Audience: **f.**

Sakakida-Rawski,   **DS754 .R38 1998**
  Evelyn
The Last Emperors: A Social History of Qing Imperial
Institutions. Trade Cloth. University of California Press.
Berkeley, CA. 1998. 466p. Philip E. Lilienthal Bks.
ISBN:0-520-21289-4, ISBN13: 978-0-520-21289-3.
Dewey:951/.03. LCCN:97-038792.

Audience: **f.** *Choice, 1999.*

Smith, Arthur H.   **DS793.M234**
Village Life in China: A Study in Sociology. Library Binding.
Greenwood Publishing Group, Inc. Portsmouth, NH. 1986.
ISBN:0-8371-1167-6, ISBN13: 978-0-8371-1167-4.
Dewey:951/.009734.

Audience: **u,f.**

Smith, Arthur H.   **DS721.S642 2002**
Chinese Characteristics. Lydia Liu (Introduction by). Trade
Paper. EastBridge. Norwalk, CT. 2003. 342p.
ISBN:1-891936-26-3, ISBN13: 978-1-891936-26-5.
Dewey:950.3/092/2. LCCN:2002-016779.

Audience: **g,u,f.**

Smith, Richard J.   **DS754.14.S6 1994**
China's Cultural Heritage: The Qing Dynasty, 1644-1912. Ed. 2.
Trade Paper. Westview Press. Boulder, CO. 1994. 400p.
ISBN:0-8133-1347-3, ISBN13: 978-0-8133-1347-4.
Dewey:951/.03. LCCN:94-000948.

Audience: **g,l,u,f.**

Spence, Jonathan D.   **DS740.4**
To Change China: Western Advisors in China, 1620-1960. Trade
Paper. Penguin Group (USA) Inc. New York, NY. 1980. 352p.
ISBN:0-14-005528-2, ISBN13: 978-0-14-005528-3.
Dewey:301.29/51/01821.

Audience: **g,l,u,f.**

Teng Ssu-Yu   **DS740.4 .T43 1979**
China's Response to the West: A Documentary Survey,
1839-1923. Trade Cloth. Harvard University Press. Cambridge,
MA. 1954. ISBN:0-674-12000-0, ISBN13: 978-0-674-12000-6.
Dewey:303.4/82/0951. LCCN:80-118719.

Audience: **g,u,f.**

T'ung-tsu Ch'u   **JS7352.A3C5 1988**
Local Government in China under the Ch'ing. Trade Paper.
Harvard University, Asia Center. Cambridge, MA. 1989. 374p.
Harvard East Asian Monographs, No. 143 ISBN:0-674-53678-9,
ISBN13: 978-0-674-53678-4. Dewey:352.051.
LCCN:88-024669.

Audience: **f.**

China > History > Qing Dynasty (1617-1912) > 1617-1839

Fay, Peter W.   **DS757.5.F39 1997**
The Opium War, 1840-1842: Barbarians in the Celestial Empire
in the Early Part of the Nineteenth Century and the War by
Which They Forced Her Gates Ajar. Trade Paper. University of
North Carolina Press. Chapel Hill, NC. 1998. 440p.
ISBN:0-8078-4714-3, ISBN13: 978-0-8078-4714-5.
Dewey:951/.033. LCCN:97-035261.

Audience: **g,l,u,f.**

Kahn, Harold L.   **DS754.4.C5**
Monarchy in the Emperor's Eyes: Image and Reality in the
Chien-Lung Reign. Trade Cloth. Harvard University Press.
Cambridge, MA. 1971. xi, 314p. East Asian Monographs, No.
59 ISBN:0-674-58230-6, ISBN13: 978-0-674-58230-9.
Dewey:951/.03/0924. LCCN:75-135546.

Audience: **f.** *B*

Kuhn, Philip A.   **DS755.K77**
Rebellion and Its Enemies in Late Imperial China, Militarization
and Social Structure, 1796-1864. Trade Cloth. Harvard
University Press. Cambridge, MA. 1970. 254p.
ISBN:0-674-74951-0, ISBN13: 978-0-674-74951-1.
Dewey:951/.03. LCCN:75-115476.

Audience: **f.**

Kuhn, Philip A.   **DS754.8**
Soulstealers: The Chinese Sorcery Scare of 1768. Trade Paper.
Harvard University Press. Cambridge, MA. 1992. 320p.
ISBN:0-674-82152-1, ISBN13: 978-0-674-82152-1.
Dewey:951/.032.

Audience: **g,u,f.** *Choice, 1991.*

Naquin, Susan &   **DS754**
  Rawski, Evelyn S.
Chinese Society in the Eighteenth Century. Trade Paper. Yale
University Press. Cumberland, RI. 1989. 270p.
ISBN:0-300-04602-2, ISBN13: 978-0-300-04602-1.
Dewey:951/.03.

Audience: **u,f.** *Choice, 1988.*

Peterson, Willard J.   **DS721**
The Cambridge History of China. John K. Fairbank & Denis Twitchett (Contribution by). Trade Cloth. Cambridge University Press. New York, NY. 2002. 780p. The Cambridge History of China Ser., Vol. 9, Pt. 1 ISBN:0-521-24334-3, ISBN13: 978-0-521-24334-6. Dewey:951.

Audience: **f.**

Polachek, James M.   **DS757.55.P65 1991**
The Inner Opium War. Trade Cloth. Harvard University Press. Cambridge, MA. 1991. 420p. Harvard East Asian Monographs, No. 151 ISBN:0-674-45446-4, ISBN13: 978-0-674-45446-0. Dewey:951/.033. LCCN:91-030657.

Audience: **f.** *Choice, 1992.*

Spence, Jonathan D.   **DS754.4.C53.A33 1974**
Emperor of China. Trade Cloth. Random House, Inc. New York, NY. 1974. xxv, 217p. ISBN:0-394-48835-0, ISBN13: 978-0-394-48835-6. Dewey:951/.03/0924. LCCN:73-020743.

Audience: **g,u,f.** *B*

Spence, Jonathan D.   **DS754.74.T74S64 2001**
Treason by the Book. Trade Cloth. Penguin Group (USA) Inc. New York, NY. 2001. 336p. ISBN:0-670-89292-0, ISBN13: 978-0-670-89292-1. Dewey:951/.032/092 B. LCCN:00-043805.

Audience: **g,u,f.**

Struve, Lynn A. (Editor,   **DS753**
  Translator)
Voices from the Ming-Qing Cataclysm: China in Tigers' Jaws. Trade Paper. Yale University Press. Cumberland, RI. 1998. 312p. ISBN:0-300-07553-7, ISBN13: 978-0-300-07553-3. Dewey:951/.026.

Audience: **f.**

Waley, Arthur   **DS757.5 .W3**
The Opium War Through Chinese Eyes. Paper Text. Textbook Publishers. Temecula, CA. 2003. 256p. ISBN:0-7581-3509-2, ISBN13: 978-0-7581-3509-4. Dewey:951/.03.

Audience: **g,l,u,f.** *B*

Waley, Arthur   **PL2735.A5.Z94 1970**
Yuan Mei: Eighteenth Century Chinese Poet. Trade Cloth. Stanford University Press. Palo Alto, CA. 1956. 227p. ISBN:0-8047-0718-9, ISBN13: 978-0-8047-0718-3. Dewey:895.1/1/4. LCCN:70-107646.

Audience: **g,u,f.**

China > History > Qing Dynasty (1617-1912) > 1839-1912

Brandt, Nat   **BV3420.S43B73 1999**
Massacre in Shansi. Trade Paper. iUniverse, Inc. Lincoln, NE. 1999. 364p. ISBN:1-58348-347-0, ISBN13: 978-1-58348-347-3. Dewey:275. LCCN:99-063476.

Audience: **g,l,u,f.**

Cohen, Paul A.   **DS762 .C6**
China and Christianity: The Missionary Movement and the Growth of Chinese Anti-Foreignism, 1860-1870. Trade Cloth. Harvard University Press. Cambridge, MA. 1963. 406p. East Asian Monographs, No. 11 ISBN:0-674-11701-8, ISBN13: 978-0-674-11701-3. Dewey:266.009. LCCN:63-019135.

Audience: **g,u,f.** *B*

Cohen, Paul A. &   **DS771.C67 1997**
  Townsend, Paul A.
History in Three Keys: The Boxers as Event, Experience, and Myth. Trade Cloth. Columbia University Press. New York, NY. 1997. 428p. ISBN:0-231-10650-5, ISBN13: 978-0-231-10650-4. Dewey:951/.035. LCCN:96-027118.

Audience: **g,l,u,f.**

Crossley, Pamela K.   **DS754**
Orphan Warriors: Three Manchu Generations and the End of the Qing World. Trade Paper. Princeton University Press. Princeton, NJ. 1991. 328p. ISBN:0-691-00877-9, ISBN13: 978-0-691-00877-6. Dewey:951/.03. LCCN:89-034963.

Audience: **u,f.** *Choice, 1990.*

Esherick, Joseph W.   **DS754**
The Origins of the Boxer Uprising. Trade Cloth. University of California Press. Berkeley, CA. 1988. 410p. ISBN:0-520-06459-3, ISBN13: 978-0-520-06459-1. Dewey:951/.03.

Audience: **u,f.** *Choice, 1987.*

Fairbank, John K.   **DS735 .C3145**
  (Editor, Contribution by)
Late Ch'ing 1800-1911. Denis C. Twitchett (Contribution by). Cloth Text. Cambridge University Press. New York, NY. 1978. 725p. The Cambridge History of China Ser. ISBN:0-521-21447-5, ISBN13: 978-0-521-21447-6. Dewey:951.03. LCCN:76-029852.

Audience: **u,f.** *B Choice, 1995.*

Fairbank, John K.   **DS735**
  (Editor, Contribution by)
Late Ch'ing, 1800-1911. Kwang-Ching Liu (Editor), Denis C. Twitchett (Contribution by). Cloth Text. Cambridge University Press. New York, NY. 1980. 784p. The Cambridge History of China Ser., Vol. 11, Pt. 2 ISBN:0-521-22029-7, ISBN13: 978-0-521-22029-3. Dewey:951. LCCN:76-029852.

Audience: **u,f.**

Michael, Franz &   **DS759**
  Chang, Chung-Li
The Taiping Rebellion: Documents and Comments. Trade Cloth. University of Washington Press. Seattle, WA. 1971. Publications on Asia of the Institute for Comparative and Foreign Area Studies, No. 14, Pt. 2 ISBN:0-318-56165-4, ISBN13: 978-0-318-56165-3. Dewey:951/.03. LCCN:66-013538.

Audience: **f.**

Pu Yi, Aisin-Gioro   **DS773 .C51513**
From Emperor to Citizen. Ed. 2. Trade Cloth. China Books & Periodicals, Inc. South San Francisco, CA. 1980. ISBN:0-8351-0619-5, ISBN13: 978-0-8351-0619-1. Dewey:951/.03/0924 B.

Audience: **g,l,u,f.**

Reynolds, Douglas R.   **DS761.R47 1993**
China, 1898-1912: The Xinzheng Revolution and Japan. Trade Cloth. Harvard University Press. Cambridge, MA. 1993. 336p. Harvard East Asian Monographs, No. 160 ISBN:0-674-11660-7, ISBN13: 978-0-674-11660-3. Dewey:951.035. LCCN:92-041724.

Audience: **f.** *Choice, 1994.*

Rhoads, Edward J.   **DS793.K7 R48 1975**
China's Republican Revolution: The Case of Kwangtung, 1895-1913. Trade Cloth. Harvard University Press. Cambridge,

MA. 1975. 392p. Harvard East Asian Monographs, No. 81
ISBN:0-674-11980-0, ISBN13: 978-0-674-11980-2.
Dewey:951/.27/03. LCCN:74-084090.

Audience: **f.**

Schoppa, R. Keith JQ1519.C442
Chinese Elites and Political Change: Zheijang Province in the
Early Twentieth Century. Trade Cloth. Harvard University Press.
Cambridge, MA. 1982. 304p. East Asian Ser., No. 96
ISBN:0-674-12325-5, ISBN13: 978-0-674-12325-0.
Dewey:305.52. LCCN:81-007075.

Audience: **f.**

Spence, Jonathan D. DS758.23.H85 S64
God's Chinese Son: The Taiping Heavenly Kingdom of Hong
Xiaquan. Trade Cloth. DIANE Publishing Company.
Collingdale, PA. 2005. 400p. ISBN:0-7567-9680-6, ISBN13:
978-0-7567-9680-8. Dewey:951/.034/092.

Audience: **g,u,f.**

Warner, Marina DS763.63.T96W37 1986
The Dragon Empress. Trade Paper. Central Bureau voor
Schimmelcultures. 1986. 256p. ISBN:0-689-70714-2, ISBN13:
978-0-689-70714-8. Dewey:951/.03/0924 B. LCCN:86-007909.

Audience: **g,u,f.**

Wright, Mary C. DS773
China in Revolution: The First Phase, 1900-1913. Trade Paper.
Yale University Press. Cumberland, RI. 1971. 520p.
ISBN:0-300-01460-0, ISBN13: 978-0-300-01460-0.
Dewey:951/.03. LCCN:68-027770.

Audience: **u,f.** *B*

Wright, Mary C. DS762
The Last Stand of Chinese Conservatism: The T'ung-Chih
Restoration, 1862-1874. Trade Cloth. Stanford University Press.
Palo Alto, CA. 1957. xii, 426p. ISBN:0-8047-0475-9, ISBN13:
978-0-8047-0475-5. Dewey:951.038.

Audience: **u,f.**

China > History > Republican Period (1912-1949)

Arkush, R. David HM22.C62 F4329 1981
Fei Xiaotong and Sociology in Revolutionary China. Trade
Cloth. Harvard University Press. Cambridge, MA. 1981. 416p.
Harvard East Asian Monographs, No. 98 ISBN:0-674-29815-2,
ISBN13: 978-0-674-29815-6. Dewey:301/.092/4.
LCCN:81-001801.

Audience: **f.**

Barnett, Arthur Doak DS777.53
China on the Eve of Communist Takeover. Paper Text.
Westview Press. Boulder, CO. 1985. 371p. An Encore Reprint
Ser. ISBN:0-8133-0163-7, ISBN13: 978-0-8133-0163-1.
Dewey:951.055.

Audience: **g,u,f.**

Bays, Daniel H. (Editor) BR1287.C47 1996
Christianity in China: From the Eighteenth Century to the
Present. Trade Cloth. Stanford University Press. Palo Alto, CA.
1996. xxii, 483p. ISBN:0-8047-2609-4, ISBN13:
978-0-8047-2609-2. Dewey:275.1/08. LCCN:95-053046.

Audience: **g,u,f.**

Bergere, Marie-Claire DS777.B47 1998
Sun Yat-Sen. Janet Lloyd (Translator). Trade Cloth. Stanford
University Press. Palo Alto, CA. 1998. 480p.
ISBN:0-8047-3170-5, ISBN13: 978-0-8047-3170-6. Dewey:[B].
LCCN:97-035504.

Audience: **g,u,f.** *Choice, 1998.*

Boorman, Howard L. CT1823
Biographical Dictionary of Republican China, Vol. 3. Richard C.
Howard (Editor). Trade Cloth. Columbia University Press. New
York, NY. 1970. 471p. ISBN:0-231-08957-0, ISBN13:
978-0-231-08957-9. Dewey:920/.051. LCCN:67-012006.

Audience: **f.** *B*

Chang, Hao DS763.L67
Liang Ch'i-Ch'ao and Intellectual Transition in China,
1890-1907. Trade Cloth. Harvard University Press. Cambridge,
MA. 1971. 342p. East Asian Monographs, No. 64
ISBN:0-674-53009-8, ISBN13: 978-0-674-53009-6.
Dewey:915.1/03/30924. LCCN:75-162635.

Audience: **g,f.**

Chow Tse-Tsung DS775
The May Fourth Movement: Intellectual Revolution in Modern
China. Trade Paper. Harvard University Press. Cambridge, MA.
1960. 502p. Harvard East Asian Monographs, Vol. No. 6
ISBN:0-674-55751-4, ISBN13: 978-0-674-55751-2.
Dewey:951.041.

Audience: **g,f.** *B*

Chu, Samuel C. DS777.488.C5
Madame Chiang Kai-Shek and Her China. Trade Cloth.
EastBridge. Norwalk, CT. 2005. 288p. ISBN:1-891936-71-9,
ISBN13: 978-1-891936-71-5. Dewey:951.24/905/092 B.
LCCN:2004-026988.

Audience: **g,l,u,f.**

Coble, Parks M. DS775.7
The Shanghai Capitalists and the Nationalist Government,
1927-1937. Ed. 2. Trade Paper. Harvard University Press.
Cambridge, MA. 1986. 376p. Harvard East Asian Monographs,
No. 94 ISBN:0-674-80536-4, ISBN13: 978-0-674-80536-1.
Dewey:951/.132042. LCCN:86-013579.

Audience: **f.**

Cochran, Sherman HD9419.C42
Big Business in China: Sino-Foreign Rivalry in the Cigarette
Industry, 1890-1930. Trade Cloth. Harvard University Press.
Cambridge, MA. 1980. 342p. Harvard Studies in Business
History, No. 33 ISBN:0-674-07262-6, ISBN13:
978-0-674-07262-6. Dewey:380.1/45/679730951.
LCCN:79-023907.

Audience: **g,u,f.**

Cochran, Sherman DS777.5194
(Editor), et al.
One Day in China: May 21, 1936. Andrew C. K. Hsieh & Janis
Cochran (Editors). Trade Paper. Yale University Press.
Cumberland, RI. 1985. 304p. ISBN:0-300-03400-8, ISBN13:
978-0-300-03400-4. Dewey:951.04/2/0922. LCCN:82-048901.

Audience: **g,u,f.** *B*

Dikotter, Frank DS730 .D54 1992
The Discourse of Race in Modern China. Trade Cloth. Stanford
University Press. Palo Alto, CA. 1994. 259p.
ISBN:0-8047-1994-2, ISBN13: 978 0 8047-1994-0.
Dewey:305.8/00951. LCCN:91-065999.

Audience: **g,u,f.**

Dikotter, Frank　　　　　　　　HQ18.C6D55 1995
Sex, Culture and Modernity in China. Trade Cloth. University of
Hawaii Press. Honolulu, HI. 1995. 200p. ISBN:0-8248-1676-5,
ISBN13: 978-0-8248-1676-6. Dewey:306/.0951.
LCCN:94-046204.

Audience: **g,u,f.** *Choice, 1996.*

Dirlik, Arif　　　　　　　　　HX950.D57 1991
Anarchism in the Chinese Revolution. Trade Cloth. University
of California Press. Berkeley, CA. 1991. 336p.
ISBN:0-520-07297-9, ISBN13: 978-0-520-07297-8.
Dewey:320.5/7/09510904. LCCN:90-021407.

Audience: **f.**

Duara, Prasenjit　　　　　　　DS734.7.D83 1995
Rescuing History from the Nation: Questioning Narratives of
Modern China. Trade Cloth. University of Chicago Press.
Chicago, IL. 1995. 286p. ISBN:0-226-16721-6, ISBN13:
978-0-226-16721-3. Dewey:951/.072. LCCN:95-003205.

Audience: **f.** *Choice, 1996.*

Eastman, Lloyd E.　　　　　　DS777.47.E24 1990
The Abortive Revolution: China under Nationalist Rule,
1927-1937. Trade Paper. Harvard University Press. Cambridge,
MA. 1990. 415p. East Asian Monographs, No. 153
ISBN:0-674-00176-1, ISBN13: 978-0-674-00176-3.
Dewey:951.04/2. LCCN:90-002152.

Audience: **f.**

Eastman, Lloyd E.　　　　　　　　DS777.518
Seeds of Destruction: Nationalist China in War and Revolution,
1937-1949. Trade Cloth. Stanford University Press. Palo Alto,
CA. 1984. 328p. ISBN:0-8047-1191-7, ISBN13:
978-0-8047-1191-3. Dewey:951.04/2. LCCN:82-042861.

Audience: **f.** *B*

Eastman, Lloyd E., et al.　　　　　DS774.N38 1991
The Nationalist Era in China, 1927-1949. Jerome Ch'en,
Suzanne Pepper & Lyman P. Van Slyke (Authors). Trade Paper.
Cambridge University Press. New York, NY. 1991. 418p.
ISBN:0-521-38591-1, ISBN13: 978-0-521-38591-6.
Dewey:951.04. LCCN:90-030310.

Audience: **f.**

Fairbank, John K.　　　　　　　　　DS735
(Editor, Contribution by)
Republican China, 1912-1949. Albert Feuerwerker (Editor),
Denis C. Twitchett (Contribution by). Trade Cloth. Cambridge
University Press. New York, NY. 1986. 2012p. The Cambridge
History of China Ser., Vol. 13, Pt. 2 ISBN:0-521-24338-6,
ISBN13: 978-0-521-24338-4. Dewey:951.

Audience: **g,u,f.** *Choice, 1987.*

Fairbank, John K. &　　　　　　　　DS735
Twitchett, Denis C. (Editor, Contribution by)
Republican China, 1912-1949. Cloth Text. Cambridge University
Press. New York, NY. 1983. 1120p. The Cambridge History of
China Ser., Vol. 12, Pt. 1 ISBN:0-521-23541-3, ISBN13:
978-0-521-23541-9. Dewey:951. LCCN:76-029852.

Audience: **g,u,f.** *Choice, 1987.*

Fei, Hsiao-tung　　　　　　　　HD1513.C6.F44 1976
Peasant Life in China: A Field Study of Country Life in the
Yangtze Valley. Bronislaw Malinowski (Preface by). Trade
Cloth. A M S Press, Inc. New York, NY. 1976. xx, 300p.
ISBN:0-404-14539-6, ISBN13: 978-0-404-14539-2.
Dewey:951/.13. LCCN:75-041090.

Audience: **g,u,f.**

Fitzgerald, John　　　　　　　DS776.6.F58 1996
Awakening China: Politics, Culture, and Class in the Nationalist
Revolution. Trade Cloth. Stanford University Press. Palo Alto,
CA. 1996. xi, 461p. ISBN:0-8047-2659-0, ISBN13:
978-0-8047-2659-7. Dewey:951.04. LCCN:96-000565.

Audience: **u,f.** *Choice, 1997.*

Grieder, Jerome B.　　　　　　　　DS754.14
Intellectuals and the State in Modern China. Trade Paper. Simon
& Schuster. New York, NY. 1983. 416p. The Transformation of
Modern China Ser. ISBN:0-02-912670-3, ISBN13:
978-0-02-912670-7. Dewey:951. LCCN:81-066436.

Audience: **f.**

Harrison, Henrietta　　　　　　DS797.75.C45H374
Man Awakened from Dreams: One Man's Life in a North China
Village, 1857-1942. Trade Cloth. Stanford University Press. Palo
Alto, CA. 2004. 240p. ISBN:0-8047-5068-8, ISBN13:
978-0-8047-5068-4. Dewey:951/.17 B. LCCN:2004-018647.

Audience: **g,u,f.**

Hayford, Charles W.　　　　　　HN740.Z9C6378 1990
To the People: James Yen and Village China. Trade Cloth.
Columbia University Press. New York, NY. 1990. 304p.
ISBN:0-231-07204-X, ISBN13: 978-0-231-07204-5.
Dewey:307.1/412/0951. LCCN:90-031930.

Audience: **g,u,f.** *Choice, 1990.*

Lee, Leo Ou-fan　　　　　　　DS796.S25L43 1999
Shanghai Modern: The Flowering of a New Urban Culture in
China, 1930-1945. Trade Cloth. Harvard University Press.
Cambridge, MA. 1999. 436p. Interpretations of Asia Ser.
ISBN:0-674-80550-X, ISBN13: 978-0-674-80550-7.
Dewey:306/.0951/132. LCCN:98-032318.

Audience: **g,u,f.** *Choice, 2000.*

Levenson, Joseph　　　　　　　　DS721.L538
  Richmond
Confucian China and Its Modern Fate: The Problem of
Intellectual Continuity. Paper Text. Textbook Publishers.
Temecula, CA. 2003. 223p. ISBN:0-7581-2694-8, ISBN13:
978-0-7581-2694-8. Dewey:915.1/03.

Audience: **f.** *B*

MacKinnon, Stephen R.　　　　DS777.533.P825.U65
  & Friesen, Oris
China Reporting: An Oral History of American Journalism in
the 1930's and 1940's. Trade Cloth. University of California
Press. Berkeley, CA. 1987. 200p. ISBN:0-520-05843-7, ISBN13:
978-0-520-05843-9. Dewey:070.4/33/0924. LCCN:86-019193.

Audience: **g,u,f.** *Choice, 1988.*

McCord, Edward Allen　　　　　DS777.36.M33 1993
e The Power of the Gun: The Emergence of Modern Chinese
Warlordism. E-Book. NetLibrary, Inc. Boulder, CO. 1993.
ISBN:0-585-13121-X, ISBN13: 978-0-585-13121-4.
Dewcy:951.04/1.

Audience: **f.**

McKenna, Richard　　　　　　　　PS3568.O243
The Sand Pebbles. Trade Cloth. Naval Institute Press. Annapolis,
MD. 1984. 597p. Classics of Naval Literature Ser.
ISBN:0-87021-592-2, ISBN13: 978-0-87021-592-6.
Dewey:813/.54. LCCN:83-027007.

Audience: **g,l,u,f.**

Pepper, Suzanne　　　　　　　DS777.54.P44 1999
  (Editor)
Civil War in China: The Political Struggle, 1945-1949. Ed. 2.

Trade Cloth. Rowman & Littlefield Publishers, Inc. Lanham, MD. 1999. 544p. ISBN:0-8476-9133-0, ISBN13: 978-0-8476-9133-3. Dewey:951.04/2. LCCN:99-010885.

Audience: **g,u,f.** 𝓑

Pepper, Suzanne   **LA1131.82.P47 1996**
Radicalism and Education Reform in 20th-Century China: The Search for an Ideal Development Model. Cloth Text. Cambridge University Press. New York, NY. 1996. 622p. ISBN:0-521-49669-1, ISBN13: 978-0-521-49669-8. Dewey:370/.951/09047. LCCN:95-024843.

Audience: **u,f.** *Choice, 1997.*

Pu Yi, Aisin-Gioro   **DS773 .C51513**
From Emperor to Citizen. Ed. 2. Trade Cloth. China Books & Periodicals, Inc. South San Francisco, CA. 1980. ISBN:0-8351-0619-5, ISBN13: 978-0-8351-0619-1. Dewey:951/.03/0924 B.

Audience: **g,l,u,f.**

Pusey, James R.   **DS754.14**
China and Charles Darwin. Trade Cloth. Harvard University Press. Cambridge, MA. 1983. 572p. Harvard East Asian Monographs, No. 100 ISBN:0-674-11735-2, ISBN13: 978-0-674-11735-8. Dewey:951/.03. LCCN:82-023264.

Audience: **f.**

Rawski, Thomas G.   **HC427.8.R384 1989**
Economic Growth in Prewar China. Trade Cloth. University of California Press. Berkeley, CA. 1989. 481p. ISBN:0-520-06372-4, ISBN13: 978-0-520-06372-3. Dewey:338.951. LCCN:88-007834.

Audience: **f.** *Choice, 1990.*

Rhoads, Edward J. M.   **DS761.2.R49 2000**
Manchus and Han: Ethnic Relations and Political Power in Late Qing and Early Republican China, 1861-1928. Trade Cloth. University of Washington Press. Seattle, WA. 2000. x, 394p. Studies on Ethnic Groups in China ISBN:0-295-97938-0, ISBN13: 978-0-295-97938-0. Dewey:951/.035. LCCN:00-008470.

Audience: **u,f.** *Choice, 2001.*

Schoppa, R. Keith   **DS777.15.S53S36 1995**
Blood Road: The Mystery of Shen Dingyi in Revolutionary China. Trade Cloth. University of California Press. Berkeley, CA. 1995. 322p. ISBN:0-520-20015-2, ISBN13: 978-0-520-20015-9. Dewey:951.04/1/092 B. LCCN:94-022072.

Audience: **u,f.** *Choice, 1996.*

Schwartz, Benjamin I.   **JA83**
In Search of Wealth and Power: Yen Fu and the West. Trade Cloth. Harvard University Press. Cambridge, MA. 1964. 318p. East Asian Ser., No. 16 ISBN:0-674-44651-8, ISBN13: 978-0-674-44651-9. Dewey:190. LCCN:64-016069.

Audience: **u,f.**

Spence, Jonathan D.   **DS740.4**
To Change China: Western Advisors in China, 1620-1960. Trade Paper. Penguin Group (USA) Inc. New York, NY. 1980. 352p. ISBN:0-14-005528-2, ISBN13: 978-0-14-005528-3. Dewey:301.29/51/01821.

Audience: **g,l,u,f.**

Strand, David   **DS795.3.S82 1989**
🄴 Rickshaw Beijing: City People and Politics in the 1920s. E-Book. NetLibrary, Inc. Boulder, CO. 1989.

ISBN:0-585-10827-7, ISBN13: 978-0-585-10827-8. Dewey:951/.156041.

Audience: **g,u,f.** *Choice, 1990.*

Tawney, Richard H.   **HC427.8.T36**
Land and Labor in China. Trade Paper. M. E. Sharpe Inc. Armonk, NY. 1978. ISBN:0-87332-106-5, ISBN13: 978-0-87332-106-8. Dewey:330.951. LCCN:77-072070.

Audience: **g,u,f.**

Teng Ssu-Yu   **DS740.4 .T43 1979**
China's Response to the West: A Documentary Survey, 1839-1923. Trade Cloth. Harvard University Press. Cambridge, MA. 1954. ISBN:0-674-12000-0, ISBN13: 978-0-674-12000-6. Dewey:303.4/82/0951. LCCN:80-118719.

Audience: **g,u,f.**

Wakeman, Frederic Jr.   **DS796.S257**
Policing Shanghai, 1927-1937. Trade Paper. University of California Press. Berkeley, CA. 1996. 526p. Philip E. Lilienthal Bks. ISBN:0-520-20761-0, ISBN13: 978-0-520-20761-5. Dewey:951/.132.

Audience: **f.** *Choice, 1995.*

Wang, Ke-wen (Editor)   **DS755.2.M63 1998**
Modern China: An Encyclopedia of History, Culture, and Nationalism. Cloth Text. Garland Publishing, Inc. New York, NY. 1997. 480p. Reference Library of the Humanities ISBN:0-8153-0720-9, ISBN13: 978-0-8153-0720-4. Dewey:951.003. LCCN:97-019299.

Audience: **g,u,f.** *Choice, 1998.*

Wasserstrom, Jeffrey N.   **LA1134.S4W37 1991**
Student Protests in Twentieth-Century China: The View from Shanghai. Trade Cloth. Stanford University Press. Palo Alto, CA. 1991. 444p. ISBN:0-8047-1881-4, ISBN13: 978-0-8047-1881-3. Dewey:371.8/1/0951. LCCN:90-022307.

Audience: **f.** *Choice, 1992.*

White, Theodore H. &   **DS777.53**
  Jacoby, Annalee
Thunder Out of China. Harrison Salisbury (Foreword by). Trade Paper. Da Capo Press, Inc. Cambridge, MA. 1980. 352p. Quality Paperbacks Ser. ISBN:0-306-80128-0, ISBN13: 978-0-306-80128-0. Dewey:951.04/2.

Audience: **g,l,u,f.**

Yeh, Wen-hsin   **LC179.C6**
The Alienated Academy: Culture and Politics in Republican China, 1919-1937. Trade Paper. Harvard University Press. Cambridge, MA. 2000. 464p. Harvard East Asian Monographs ISBN:0-674-00284-9, ISBN13: 978-0-674-00284-5. Dewey:378.51. LCCN:90-030046.

Audience: **f.**

Young, Ernest P.   **DS777.2.Y68 1977**
The Presidency of Yuan Shih-K'ai: Liberalism and Dictatorship in Early Republican China. Trade Cloth. University of Michigan Press. Chicago, IL. 1977. 372p. Studies on China ISBN:0-472-08995-1, ISBN13: 978-0-472-08995-6. Dewey:951/.03/0924. LCCN:75-031057.

Audience: **f.** 𝓑

Zhao, Suisheng   **DS755.2.Z463 2005**
A Nation-State by Construction: Dynamics of Modern Chinese Nationalism. Trade Cloth. Stanford University Press. Palo Alto, CA. 2004. 416p. ISBN:0-8047-4897-7, ISBN13: 978-0-8047-4897-1. Dewey:320.54/0951. LCCN:2004-006013.

Audience: **g,u,f.** *Choice, 2005.*

China > History > Republican Period (1912-1949) > Rise of Communist Revolution (1912-1949)

Belden, Jack   DS777.53
China Shakes the World. Trade Paper. Monthly Review Press. New York, NY. 1970. ISBN:0-85345-159-1, ISBN13: 978-0-85345-159-4. Dewey:951.04/2. LCCN:77-105312.
Audience: **g,l,u,f.**

Benton, Gregor &   DS777.75.W54 1995
Hunter, Alan
🄮 Wild Lily, Prairie Fire: China's Road to Democracy, Yan'an to Tian'anmen, 1942-1989. E-Book. Princeton University Press. Princeton, NJ. ISBN:1-4008-1101-5, ISBN13: 978-1-4008-1101-4. Dewey:951.05.
Audience: **f.**

Bianco, Lucien   DS775.B513
Origins of the Chinese Revolution, 1915-1949. Muriel Bell (Translator). Trade Cloth. Stanford University Press. Palo Alto, CA. 1971. xvii, 220p. ISBN:0-8047-0746-4, ISBN13: 978-0-8047-0746-6. Dewey:951.04. LCCN:75-150321.
Audience: **g,u,f.** 𝓑

Cheek, Timothy   DS778.M3.C47 2002
(Editor)
Mao Zedong and China's Revolutions: A Brief History with Documents. Cloth over Boards. Palgrave Macmillan. New York, NY. 2002. 272p. ISBN:0-312-29429-8, ISBN13: 978-0-312-29429-8. Dewey:951.05092.
Audience: **g,u,f.**

Dirlik, Arif   HX418.5.D58 2005
Marxism in the Chinese Revolution. Book, Other. Rowman & Littlefield Publishers, Inc. Lanham, MD. 2005. 342p. Pacific Formations Ser. ISBN:0-7425-3069-8, ISBN13: 978-0-7425-3069-0. Dewey:335.43/45. LCCN:2005-003075.
Audience: **f.**

Dirlik, Arif   HX416.5.D57 1989
The Origins of Chinese Communism. Trade Paper. Oxford University Press, Inc. New York, NY. 1989. 330p. ISBN:0-19-505454-7, ISBN13: 978-0-19-505454-5. Dewey:335.43/0951. LCCN:88-017460.
Audience: **f.** *Choice, 1989.*

Feigon, Lee   DS777.15.C5
Chen Duxiu, Founder of the Chinese Communist Party. Trade Cloth. Princeton University Press. Princeton, NJ. 1983. 304p. ISBN:0-691-05393-6, ISBN13: 978-0-691-05393-6. Dewey:951.04/092/4. LCCN:83-042556.
Audience: **f.** 𝓑

Gilmartin, Christina K.   HX546.G54 1995
Engendering the Chinese Revolution: Radical Women, Communist Politics, and Mass Movements in the 1920s. Trade Cloth. University of California Press. Berkeley, CA. 1995. 302p. ISBN:0-520-08981-2, ISBN13: 978-0-520-08981-5. Dewey:335.43/082. LCCN:94-024723.
Audience: **u,f.** *Choice, 1996.*

Hinton, William   HD866 .H5
Fanshen: A Documentary of Revolution in a Chinese Village. Trade Cloth. Monthly Review Press. New York, NY. 1967.

ISBN:0-85345-046-3, ISBN13: 978-0-85345-046-7. Dewey:301.3509512. LCCN:66-023525.
Audience: **g,u,f.**

Isaacs, Harold Robert   DS774 .I7
The Tragedy of the Chinese Revolution. Paper Text. Textbook Publishers. Temecula, CA. 2003. 392p. ISBN:0-7581-3511-4, ISBN13: 978-0-7581-3511-7. Dewey:951.042.
Audience: **g,u,f.**

Johnson, Chalmers A.   DS777.53 .J58
Peasant Nationalism and Communist Power: The Emergence of Revolutionary China, 1937-1945. Trade Cloth. Stanford University Press. Palo Alto, CA. 1962. xii, 256p. ISBN:0-8047-0073-7, ISBN13: 978-0-8047-0073-3. Dewey:951.042.
Audience: **f.**

Levine, Steven I.   DS777.5425.M36L48
Anvil of Victory: The Communist Revolution in Manchuria. Cloth Text. Columbia University Press. New York, NY. 1987. 384p. ISBN:0-231-06436-5, ISBN13: 978-0-231-06436-1. Dewey:951/.8042. LCCN:86-019821.
Audience: **u,f.**

Malraux, André   PQ2625.A716C53 1984
Man's Fate. Trade Cloth. Random House, Inc. New York, NY. 1984. ISBN:0-394-54379-3, ISBN13: 978-0-394-54379-6. Dewey:843. LCCN:84-017944.
Audience: **g,l,u,f.**

Meisner, Maurice J.   HX0387.L48M4
Li Ta-Chao and the Origins of Chinese Marxism. Trade Paper. Books on Demand. Ann Arbor, MI. 345p. Harvard East Asian Ser., Vol. 27 ISBN:0-598-22887-X, ISBN13: 978-0-598-22887-1. Dewey:335.4/0951. LCCN:67-010904.
Audience: **u,f.** 𝓑

Saich, Tony & Van de   JQ1519.A5N42 1994
Ven, Hans (Editors)
New Perspectives on the Chinese Revolution. Cloth Text. M. E. Sharpe Inc. Armonk, NY. 1994. 436p. ISBN:1-56324-428-4, ISBN13: 978-1-56324-428-5. Dewey:951.04. LCCN:94-026985.
Audience: **u,f.** *Choice, 1995.*

Saich, Tony (Editor)   JQ1519.A5R57 1996
The Rise to Power of the Chinese Communist Party: Documents and Analysis. Benjamin Yang (Contribution by). Trade Cloth. M. E. Sharpe Inc. Armonk, NY. 1996. 1,504p. ISBN:1-56324-154-4, ISBN13: 978-1-56324-154-3. Dewey:951.04. LCCN:94-030009.
Audience: **g,u,f.**

Selden, Mark   HX420.S48S44 1995
China in Revolution: The Yenan Way Revisited. Ed. 2. Cloth Text. M. E. Sharpe Inc. Armonk, NY. 1995. 312p. Socialism and Social Movements Ser. ISBN:1-56324-554-X, ISBN13: 978-1-56324-554-1. Dewey:335.43/45/09514. LCCN:94-044357.
Audience: **u,f.** *Choice, 1995.*

Smedley, Agnes   DS778.C6 S5
The Great Road: The Life and Times of Chu Teh. Paper Text. Textbook Publishers. Temecula, CA. 2003. 461p. ISBN:0-7581-8047-0, ISBN13: 978-0-7581-8047-6. Dewey:923.551.
Audience: **g,u,f.** 𝓑

Snow, Edgar R.   DS775;
Red Star over China. John J. Fairbanks (Introduction by). Trade Paper. Grove/Atlantic, Inc. New York, NY. 1994. 544p.

ISBN:0-8021-5093-4, ISBN13: 978-0-8021-5093-6.
Dewey:951.04. LCCN:68-017724.

Audience: **g,l,u,f.**

Spence, Jonathan D.   **DS775.7**
The Gate of Heavenly Peace: The Chinese and Their
Revolution, 1895-1980. Trade Paper. Penguin Group (USA) Inc.
New York, NY. 1982. 560p. ISBN:0-14-006279-3, ISBN13:
978-0-14-006279-3. Dewey:951. LCCN:82-005245.

Audience: **g,l,u,f.** **B**

Trotsky, Len   **DS775 .T7**
Problems of the Chinese Revolution. Max Shachtman (Foreword
by). Trade Paper. University of Michigan Press. Chicago, IL.
1967. ISBN:0-472-06131-3, ISBN13: 978-0-472-06131-0.
Dewey:951.04.

Audience: **f.**

Wou, Odoric Y. K.   **DS793.H5W6 1994**
Mobilizing the Masses: Building Revolution in Henan. Trade
Cloth. Stanford University Press. Palo Alto, CA. 1994. xi, 478p.
ISBN:0-8047-2142-4, ISBN13: 978-0-8047-2142-4.
Dewey:951/.18042.220. LCCN:93-020624.

Audience: **f.** *Choice, 1994.*

China > History > Republican Period (1912-1949) > Sino-Japanese War (1939-1945)

Brook, Timothy   **DS777.533.C64B76**
Collaboration: Japanese Agents and Local Elites in Wartime
China. Trade Cloth. Harvard University Press. Cambridge, MA.
2005. 302p. ISBN:0-674-01563-0, ISBN13: 978-0-674-01563-0.
Dewey:940.53/163/0951. LCCN:2004-051130.

Audience: **f.** *Choice, 2005.*

Brook, Timothy (Editor)   **DS796.N2D63 1999**
Documents on the Rape of Nanking. Trade Cloth. University of
Michigan Press. Chicago, IL. 1999. 320p. Ann Arbor Paperback
Ser. ISBN:0-472-11134-5, ISBN13: 978-0-472-11134-3.
Dewey:940.53. LCCN:99-054728.

Audience: **g,l,u,f.**

Coble, Parks M.   **HC428.S5234 C635**
Chinese Capitalists in Japan's New Order: The Occupied Lower
Yangzi, 1937-1945. Trade Cloth. University of California Press.
Berkeley, CA. 2003. 310p. ISBN:0-520-23268-2, ISBN13:
978-0-520-23268-6. Dewey:330.951/132042.
LCCN:2002-012587.

Audience: **f.** *Choice, 2003.*

Coble, Parks M.   **DS777.47.C65 1991**
Facing Japan: Chinese Politics and Japanese Imperialism,
1931-1937. Trade Cloth. Harvard University Press. Cambridge,
MA. 1991. 475p. East Asian Monographs, Vol. 135
ISBN:0-674-29011-9, ISBN13: 978-0-674-29011-2.
Dewey:327.51052. LCCN:91-021271.

Audience: **f.** *Choice, 1992.*

Hsiung, James C. &   **DS777.53.C525**
  Levine, Steven I. (Editors)
China's Bitter Victory: The War with Japan, 1937-1945. Paper
Text. M. E. Sharpe Inc. Armonk, NY. 1993. 360p.
ISBN:1-56324-246-X, ISBN13: 978-1-56324-246-5.
Dewcy:940.53. LCCN:91-006961.

Audience: **u,f.**

Hu, Hua-ling   **BV3427.V38H813 2000**
American Goddess at the Rape of Nanking: The Courage of
Minnie Vautrin. Paul Simon (Foreword by). Trade Cloth.
Southern Illinois University Press. Carbondale, IL. 2000. 208p.
ISBN:0-8093-2303-6, ISBN13: 978-0-8093-2303-6.
Dewey:266/.0092 B. LCCN:99-030526.

Audience: **g,u,f.**

Hung, Chang-tai   **NX583.A1H86 1994**
ⓔ War and Popular Culture: Resistance in Modern China,
1937-1945. E-Book. NetLibrary, Inc. Boulder, CO. 1994.
ISBN:0-585-13079-5, ISBN13: 978-0-585-13079-8.
Dewey:306.40951.

Audience: **f.** *Choice, 1994.*

Stilwell, Joseph W.   **D811**
The Stilwell Papers. Theodore H. White (Editor). Trade Cloth. A
M S Press, Inc. New York, NY. ISBN:0-404-20247-0, ISBN13:
978-0-404-20247-7. Dewey:940.54. LCCN:83-045889.

Audience: **f.**

Sun, Youli   **D742.C5S85 1993**
China and the Origins of the Pacific War, 1931-1941. Cloth over
Boards. Palgrave Macmillan. New York, NY. 1993. 256p.
ISBN:0-312-09010-2, ISBN13: 978-0-312-09010-4.
Dewey:951/.042. LCCN:92-036305.

Audience: **g,u,f.** *Choice, 1994.*

Tuchman, Barbara W.   **D767.6**
Stilwell and the American Experience in China, 1911-45.
Library Binding. Buccaneer Books, Inc. Cutchogue, NY. 1995.
600p. ISBN:1-56849-604-4, ISBN13: 978-1-56849-604-7.
Dewey:940.54/25/0924.

Audience: **g,u,f.**

China > History > People's Republic of China (1949-)

Chan, Anita, et al.   **HN733.5.C423 1992**
Chen Village under Mao and Deng: The Recent History of a
Peasant Community in Mao's China. Ed. 2. Richard Madsen &
Jonathan Unger (Authors). Trade Cloth. University of California
Press. Berkeley, CA. 1992. 345p. ISBN:0-520-08108-0, ISBN13:
978-0-520-08108-6. Dewey:307.720951. LCCN:92-014342.

Audience: **g,l,u,f.**

Chang, Jung   **CT1828.C478 A3 1991**
Wild Swans: Three Daughters of China. Trade Paper. Simon &
Schuster. New York, NY. 2003. 544p. ISBN:0-7432-4698-5,
ISBN13: 978-0-7432-4698-9. Dewey:951.05'092 B.
LCCN:91-020696.

Audience: **g,l,u,f.**

Farquhar, Judith   **GT497.C6F37 2002**
Appetites: Food and Sex in Postsocialist China. Trade Cloth.
Duke University Press. Durham, NC. 2002. 360p. Body,
Commodity, Text Ser. ISBN:0-8223-2906-9, ISBN13:
978-0-8223-2906-0. Dewey:394.1/0951. LCCN:2001-054710.

Audience: **f.** *Choice, 2002.*

Friedman, Edward, et   **HN733.5**
  al.
Chinese Village, Socialist State. Paul G. Pickowicz, Mark
Selden & Kay A. Johnson (Authors). Trade Paper. Yale
University Press. Cumberland, RI. 1993. 360p.

ISBN:0-300-05428-9, ISBN13: 978-0-300-05428-6.
Dewey:307.72/0951/15. LCCN:90-071877.

Audience: **g,u,f.** *Choice, 1991.*

Friedman, Edward, et al.   **HN740.H66F74 2005**
Revolution, Resistance, and Reform in Village China. Paul
Pickowicz & Mark Selden (Authors). Saddle Stitched, Cloth
over Boards, Dust Jacket. Yale University Press. Cumberland,
RI. 2005. 368p. ISBN:0-300-10896-6, ISBN13:
978-0-300-10896-5. Dewey:307.72/0951/52.
LCCN:2005-043966.

Audience: **g,u,f.** *Choice, 2006.*

Goldman, Merle R.   **DS777.6**
China's Intellectuals: Advise and Dissent. Trade Cloth. Harvard
University Press. Cambridge, MA. 1981. 282p.
ISBN:0-674-11970-3, ISBN13: 978-0-674-11970-3.
Dewey:951.05. LCCN:81-002945.

Audience: **g,u,f.** *B*

Hinton, Harold C.   **DS777.547 .G68 1982**
  (Editor)
Government and Politics in Revolutionary China: Selected
Documents, 1949-1979. Book, Other. Rowman & Littlefield
Publishers, Inc. Lanham, MD. 1982. 505p. ISBN:0-8420-2190-6,
ISBN13: 978-0-8420-2190-6. Dewey:951.05. LCCN:81-086385.

Audience: **f.**

Hinton, Harold C.   **DS777.55.P4243**
  (Editor)
The People's Republic of China, Nineteen Forty-Nine to
Nineteen Seventy-Nine: A Documentary Survey. Library
Binding. Rowman & Littlefield Publishers, Inc. Lanham, MD.
1980. 3000p. ISBN:0-8420-2166-3, ISBN13:
978-0-8420-2166-1. Dewey:951.05. LCCN:80-005228.

Audience: **f.** *B*

Honig, Emily   **DS796.S29H66 1992**
Creating Chinese Ethnicity: Subei People in Shanghai,
1850-1980. Cloth over Boards. Yale University Press.
Cumberland, RI. 1992. 208p. ISBN:0-300-05105-0, ISBN13:
978-0-300-05105-6. Dewey:305.800951132. LCCN:92-006055.

Audience: **g,u,f.** *Choice, 1993.*

Klein, Donald & Clark,   **DS778.A1**
  Anne B.
Biographic Dictionary of Chinese Communism, 1921-1965:
Volume 1, Ai Szu-ch'i - lo I-nung; Volume 2, lo
Jui-ch'ing—Yun Tai-ying, Set. Trade Cloth. Harvard University
Press. Cambridge, MA. 1971. 1221p. Harvard East Asian
Monographs, No. 57 ISBN:0-674-07410-6, ISBN13:
978-0-674-07410-1. Dewey:951.04/0922. LCCN:69-012725.

Audience: **f.** *B*

Lu, Xiaobo & Perry,   **HX418.5.D38 1997**
  Elizabeth J. (Editors)
Danwei: The Changing Chinese Workplace in Historical and
Comparative Perspective. Cloth Text. M. E. Sharpe Inc.
Armonk, NY. 1997. 270p. Socialism and Social Movements Ser.
ISBN:0-7656-0075-7, ISBN13: 978-0-7656-0075-2.
Dewey:306.3/6/0951. LCCN:97-009979.

Audience: **g,u,f.**

MacFarquhar, Roderick   **DS735**
  (Editor)
The People's Republic: The Emergence of Revolutionary China,
1949-1965. John K. Fairbank (Editor, Contribution by), Denis C.
Twitchett (Contribution by). Cloth Text. Cambridge University
Press. New York, NY. 1987. 739p. The Cambridge History of

China Ser. ISBN:0-521-24336-X, ISBN13: 978-0-521-24336-0.
Dewey:951. LCCN:76-029852.

Audience: **g,u,f.** *Choice, 1988.*

MacFarquhar, Roderick   **DS735.C3145 1991**
  (Editor)
The People's Republic: Revolutions Within the Chinese
Revolution, 1966-1982. John K. Fairbank (Editor, Contribution
by), Denis C. Twitchett (Contribution by). Trade Cloth.
Cambridge University Press. New York, NY. 1991. 1134p. The
Cambridge History of China Ser. ISBN:0-521-24337-8, ISBN13:
978-0-521-24337-7. Dewey:951.05.

Audience: **g,u,f.** *Choice, 1992.*

McGregor, James H. S.   **HC427.95.M43 2006**
One Billion Customers: Lessons from the Front Lines of Doing
Business in China. Trade Cloth. Simon & Schuster. New York,
NY. 2005. 336p. A Wall Street Journal Book Ser.
ISBN:0-7432-5839-8, ISBN13: 978-0-7432-5839-5.
Dewey:658.1/8/0951. LCCN:2005-044398.

Audience: **g,u,f.** *Choice, 2006.*

Meisner, Maurice   **DS777.55.M455 1999**
Mao's China and After: A Histroy of the People's Republic. Ed.
3. Trade Paper. Simon & Schuster. New York, NY. 1999. 608p.
ISBN:0-684-85635-2, ISBN13: 978-0-684-85635-3.
Dewey:951.05. LCCN:98-031734.

Audience: **g,u,f.**

Morris, Andrew D.   **GV651 .M67 2004**
Marrow of the Nation: A History of Sport and Physical Culture
in Republican China. Trade Cloth. University of California
Press. Berkeley, CA. 2004. 368p. Asia-Local Studies/Global
Themes, Vol. 10 ISBN:0-520-24084-7, ISBN13:
978-0-520-24084-1. Dewey:796/.0951/09. LCCN:2004-001057.

Audience: **g,l,u,f.** *Choice, 2005.*

Nathan, Andrew J.   **JQ1516.N38 1986**
Chinese Democracy. Trade Cloth. University of California Press.
Berkeley, CA. 1986. 313p. ISBN:0-520-05933-6, ISBN13:
978-0-520-05933-7. Dewey:323/.042/0951. LCCN:86-011305.

Audience: **g,u,f.** *Choice, 1986.*

Pepper, Suzanne   **LA1131.82.P47 1996**
Radicalism and Education Reform in 20th-Century China: The
Search for an Ideal Development Model. Cloth Text. Cambridge
University Press. New York, NY. 1996. 622p.
ISBN:0-521-49669-1, ISBN13: 978-0-521-49669-8.
Dewey:370/.951/09047. LCCN:95-024843.

Audience: **u,f.** *Choice, 1997.*

Riordan, James &   **GV651.S655 1999**
  Jones, Robin
Sport and Physical Education in China. Paper over Boards.
Routledge. New York, NY. 1999. 280p. ISCPES Book Ser.
ISBN:0-419-24750-5, ISBN13: 978-0-419-24750-0.
Dewey:613.7/0951. LCCN:98-051481.

Audience: **u,f.** *Choice, 2000.*

Shapiro, Judith   **GE190.C6 S48 2001**
Mao's War Against Nature: Politics and the Environment in
Revolutionary China. Alfred W. Crosby & Donald Worster
(Contribution by). Cloth Text. Cambridge University Press. New
York, NY. 2001. 306p. Studies in Environment and History
ISBN:0-521-78150-7, ISBN13: 978-0-521-78150-3.
Dewey:363.7/00951/0904. LCCN:00-041420.

Audience: **g.**

Smil, Vaclav   **GE160.C6C63 2003**
China's Past, China's Future: Energy, Food, Environment. Paper over Boards. Routledge. New York, NY. 2003. 256p. Critical Asian Scholarship Ser. ISBN:0-415-31498-4, ISBN13: 978-0-415-31498-5. Dewey:304.2/8/0951. LCCN:2003-006064.
Audience: **g,u,f.**

Vogel, Ezra F.   **DS796.C2V6**
Canton under Communism: Programs and Politics in a Provincial Capital, 1949-1968. Trade Cloth. Harvard University Press. Cambridge, MA. 1969. 468p. East Asian Monographs, No. 41 ISBN:0-674-09475-1, ISBN13: 978-0-674-09475-8. Dewey:309.1/51/27. LCCN:70-091631.
Audience: **u,f.**

Walder, Andrew G.   **HD8736.5.W34 1986**
Communist Neo-Traditionalism: Work and Authority in Chinese Industry. Trade Cloth. University of California Press. Berkeley, CA. 1986. 250p. ISBN:0-520-05439-3, ISBN13: 978-0-520-05439-4. Dewey:306/.36/0951. LCCN:85-027093.
Audience: **f.** *ℬ*

Wang, Ke-wen (Editor)   **DS755.2.M63 1998**
Modern China: An Encyclopedia of History, Culture, and Nationalism. Cloth Text. Garland Publishing, Inc. New York, NY. 1997. 480p. Reference Library of the Humanities ISBN:0-8153-0720-9, ISBN13: 978-0-8153-0720-4. Dewey:951.003. LCCN:97-019299.
Audience: **g,u,f.** *Choice, 1998.*

Zhao, Suisheng   **DS755.2.Z463 2005**
A Nation-State by Construction: Dynamics of Modern Chinese Nationalism. Trade Cloth. Stanford University Press. Palo Alto, CA. 2004. 416p. ISBN:0-8047-4897-7, ISBN13: 978-0-8047-4897-1. Dewey:320.54/0951. LCCN:2004-006013.
Audience: **g,u,f.** *Choice, 2005.*

Zhong, Xueping   **HQ1767.S598 2001**
  (Editor), et al.
Some of Us: Chinese Women Growing up in the Mao Era. Wang Zheng & Bai Di (Editors). Cloth Text. Rutgers University Press. Piscataway, NJ. 2001. 224p. ISBN:0-8135-2968-9, ISBN13: 978-0-8135-2968-4. Dewey:305.4/0951. LCCN:00-068351.
Audience: **g,u,f.** *Choice, 2002.*

China > History > People's Republic of China (1949-) > Cultural Revolution (1966-1976)

Bennett, Gordon A. &   **DS778.D34**
  Montaperto, Ronald N.
Red Guard: The Political Biography of Dai Hsiao-Ai. Trade Cloth. Peter Smith Publisher, Inc. Magnolia, MA. 1981. ISBN:0-8446-4710-1, ISBN13: 978-0-8446-4710-4. Dewey:951.05/0924.
Audience: **g,u,f.**

Chang, Tony H.   **DS778**
  (Compiled by)
China During the Cultural Revolution, 1966-1976: A Selected Bibliography of English Language Works. Cloth Text. Greenwood Publishing Group, Inc. Portsmouth, NH. 1999. 216p. Bibliographies and Indexes in Asian Studies Ser., Vol. 3

ISBN:0-313-30905-1, ISBN13: 978-0-313-30905-2. Dewey:016.95105. LCCN:98-044393.
Audience: **f.** *Choice, 1999.*

Cheng, Nien   **DS778.7.C445 1995**
Life and Death in Shanghai. Trade Paper. HarperCollins Publishers. New York, NY. 1995. 496p. ISBN:0-00-654861-X, ISBN13: 978-0-00-654861-4. Dewey:365/.45/0924. LCCN:98-143622.
Audience: **g,u,f.**

Dittmer, Lowell   **DS778.L49D57 1998**
Liu Shaoqi and the Chinese Cultural Revolution. Cloth Text. M. E. Sharpe Inc. Armonk, NY. 1998. 400p. ISBN:1-56324-951-0, ISBN13: 978-1-56324-951-8. Dewey:951.056. LCCN:97-041292.
Audience: **f.**

Evans, Harriet &   **DS778.7.P535 1999**
  Donald, Stephanie (Editors)
Picturing Power in the People's Republic of China: Posters of the Cultural Revolution. Book, Other. Rowman & Littlefield Publishers, Inc. Lanham, MD. 1999. 208p. ISBN:0-8476-9510-7, ISBN13: 978-0-8476-9510-2. Dewey:951.05/6. LCCN:99-024279.
Audience: **u,f.**

Gao Yuan   **DS778.7.G36 1987**
Born Red: A Chronicle of the Cultural Revolution. William A. Joseph (Foreword by). Trade Cloth. Stanford University Press. Palo Alto, CA. 1987. 416p. ISBN:0-8047-1368-5, ISBN13: 978-0-8047-1368-9. Dewey:951.05/6. LCCN:86-023058.
Audience: **g,u,f.** *Choice, 1987.*

Gao, Mobo C. F.   **HN740.G36**
Gao Village. Trade Cloth. University of Hawaii Press. Honolulu, HI. 288p. ISBN:0-8248-2205-6, ISBN13: 978-0-8248-2205-7. Dewey:307.72/0951/222.
Audience: **f.**

Heng, Liang & Shapiro,   **DS778.7**
  Judith
Son of the Revolution. Jerome A. Cohen (Introduction by). Trade Cloth. Alfred A. Knopf Inc. New York, NY. 1983. xii, 301p. ISBN:0-394-52568-X, ISBN13: 978-0-394-52568-6. Dewey:951.05/6. LCCN:82-018704.
Audience: **g,l,u,f.**

Joseph, William A.   **DS778.7.N48 1991**
  (Editor), et al.
New Perspectives on the Cultural Revolution. Christine P. Wong & David Zweig (Editors). Trade Cloth. Harvard University Press. Cambridge, MA. 1991. 365p. Harvard Contemporary China Ser., No. 8 ISBN:0-674-61757-6, ISBN13: 978-0-674-61757-5. Dewey:951.05/6. LCCN:90-020970.
Audience: **f.** *Choice, 1992.*

Law, Kam-Yee (Editor)   **DS778.7.C4565 2003**
The Chinese Cultural Revolution Reconsidered: Beyond Purge and Holocaust. Cloth over Boards. Palgrave Macmillan. New York, NY. 2003. 352p. ISBN:0-333-73835-7, ISBN13: 978-0-333-73835-1. Dewey:951.05/6. LCCN:2002-026955.
Audience: **f.**

MacFarquhar, Roderick   **DS777.75.M32 1974**
The Origins of the Cultural Revolution: Contradictions among the People, 1956-1957. Cloth Text. Columbia University Press. New York, NY. 1974. 439p. Studies of the East Asian Institute

ISBN:0-231-03841-0, ISBN13: 978-0-231-03841-6.
Dewey:951.05. LCCN:73-015793.

Audience: **u,f.** *B*

MacFarquhar, Roderick   DS777.75.M32
The Origins of the Cultural Revolution: The Great Leap
Forward. Cloth Text. Columbia University Press. New York, NY.
1983. 480p. Studies of the East Asian Institute
ISBN:0-231-05716-4, ISBN13: 978-0-231-05716-5.
Dewey:951.05. LCCN:98-152853.

Audience: **g,f.**

Perry, Elizabeth & Li,   HD8738.P47 1997
Xun
Proletarian Power: Shanghai in the Cultural Revolution. Trade
Paper. Westview Press. Boulder, CO. 1997. 264p. Transitions
Ser., :Asia and Asian America ISBN:0-8133-2166-2, ISBN13:
978-0-8133-2166-0. Dewey:331.8/0951132. LCCN:96-042940.

Audience: **f.** *Choice, 1997.*

Schoenhals, Michael   DS778.7.C456 1996
(Editor)
China's Cultural Revolution, 1966-1969: Not a Dinner Party.
Cloth Text. M. E. Sharpe Inc. Armonk, NY. 1996. 420p. East
Gate Reader Ser. ISBN:1-56324-736-4, ISBN13:
978-1-56324-736-1. Dewey:951.05/6. LCCN:96-012785.

Audience: **g,u,f.**

Song, Yongyi & Sun,   Z3108.A5S86 1998
Dajin
The Cultural Revolution: A Bibliography, 1966-1996. Eugene W.
Wu (Editor). Cloth Text. Harvard-Yenching Library. Cambridge,
MA. 1998. xi, 521p. Bibliographical Ser., No. VI
ISBN:0-941128-06-7, ISBN13: 978-0-941128-06-3.
Dewey:016.306/0951. LCCN:98-072501.

Audience: **f.**

Witke, Roxanne   DS778.C5374.W57
Comrade Chiang Ch'ing. Trade Cloth. Little Brown &
Company. New York, NY. 1977. xxvi, 549p.
ISBN:0-316-94900-0, ISBN13: 978-0-316-94900-2.
Dewey:951.05/092/4. LCCN:77-000935.

Audience: **g,f.** *B*

Yang, Rae   DS778.7.Y42 1997
Spider Eaters: A Memoir. Trade Cloth. University of California
Press. Berkeley, CA. 1997. 318p. ISBN:0-520-20480-8, ISBN13:
978-0-520-20480-5. LCCN:96-031622.

Audience: **g,u,f.** *Choice, 1997.*

Ye, Weili & Xiadong, Ma   DS778.7.W445 2005
Growing up in the People's Republic: Conversations between
Two Daughters of China's Revolution. Cloth over Boards.
Palgrave Macmillan. New York, NY. 2005. 208p. Palgrave
Studies in Oral History Ser. ISBN:1-4039-6995-7, ISBN13:
978-1-4039-6995-8. Dewey:951.05/6. LCCN:2005-048676.

Audience: **g,u,f.**

China > History > People's Republic of China (1949-) > 1976-

Barme, Geremie   DS779.32.N48 1991
New Ghosts, Old Dreams: Chinese Rebel Voices. Trade Cloth.
Crown Publishing Group. New York, NY. 1992. 95p.
ISBN:0-8129-1927-0, ISBN13: 978-0-8129-1927-1.
Dewey:951.05. LCCN:90-071447.

Audience: **g,l,u,f.**

Barme, Geremie &   PL2658.E1S44 1988
Minford, John (Editors)
Seeds of Fire: Chinese Voices of Conscience. Trade Cloth.
Farrar, Straus & Giroux. New York, NY. 1988. 452p.
ISBN:0-8090-8521-6, ISBN13: 978-0-8090-8521-7.
Dewey:895.1/8508/08. LCCN:88-019861.

Audience: **g,l,u,f.**

Barmé, Geremie R.   DS777.6.B37 1999
In the Red: On Contemporary Chinese Culture. Trade Cloth.
Columbia University Press. New York, NY. 1999. 512p.
ISBN:0-231-10614-9, ISBN13: 978-0-231-10614-6.
Dewey:306/.0951/09045. LCCN:98-039734.

Audience: **g,u,f.** *Choice, 1999.*

Baum, Richard   DS779.26.B38 1994
Burying Mao: Chinese Politics in the Age of Deng Xiaoping.
Trade Cloth. Princeton University Press. Princeton, NJ. 1994.
500p. ISBN:0-691-03639-X, ISBN13: 978-0-691-03639-7.
Dewey:951.05/8. LCCN:94-009892.

Audience: **g,f.** *Choice, 1995.*

Becker, Jasper   DS706.B393 2002
The Chinese. Trade Paper. Oxford University Press, Inc. New
York, NY. 2002. 496p. ISBN:0-19-514940-8, ISBN13:
978-0-19-514940-1. Dewey:951. LCCN:2001-037037.

Audience: **g,l,u,f.**

Bernstein, Richard   DS779.23 .B47 1982
From the Center of the Earth: The Search for the Truth about
China. Trade Cloth. Little Brown & Company. New York, NY.
1982. ISBN:0-316-09194-4, ISBN13: 978-0-316-09194-7.
Dewey:951.05/7. LCCN:81-023647.

Audience: **g,u,f.**

Blum, Susan D. &   HN733.5.M35 2002
Jensen, Lionel M. (Editors)
China off Center: Mapping the Margins of the Middle Kingdom.
Prasenjit Duara (Foreword by). Trade Cloth. University of
Hawaii Press. Honolulu, HI. 2002. 424p. ISBN:0-8248-2335-4,
ISBN13: 978-0-8248-2335-1. Dewey:306/.0951.
LCCN:2002-002101.

Audience: **f.**

Brook, Timothy   DS779.32.B76 1992
Quelling the People: The Military Supression of the Beijing
Democracy Movement. Trade Cloth. Oxford University Press,
Inc. New York, NY. 1992. 288p. ISBN:0-19-507457-2, ISBN13:
978-0-19-507457-4. Dewey:951.05/8. LCCN:92-016396.

Audience: **g,l,u,f.** *Choice, 1993.*

Dutton, Michael   DS779.23 .S75 1998
(Editor)
Streetlife China. Cloth Text. Cambridge University Press. New
York, NY. 1999. 320p. Modern China Ser. ISBN:0-521-63141-6,
ISBN13: 978-0-521-63141-9. Dewey:951.05/7.
LCCN:98-008136.

Audience: **g,u,f.**

Economy, Elizabeth C.   HC430.E5E36 2004
The River Runs Black: The Environmental Challenge to China's
Future. Trade Cloth. Cornell University Press. Ithaca, NY. 2005.
368p. ISBN:0-8014-4220-6, ISBN13: 978-0-8014-4220-9.
Dewey:333.7/0951. LCCN:2003-024994.

Audience: **g,u,f.** *Choice, 2004.*

Fishman, Ted C.   HC427.95.F57 2005
China, Inc: How the Rise of the Next Superpower Challenges
America and the World. Trade Cloth. Simon & Schuster. New

York, NY. 2005. 352p. ISBN:0-7432-5752-9, ISBN13: 978-0-7432-5752-7. Dewey:338.951/009/051. LCCN:2004-065328.

Audience: **g,l,u,f.**

Goldman, Merle R.   JQ1510.G65 1994
Sowing the Seeds of Democracy in China: Political Reform in the Deng Xiaoping Era. Trade Cloth. Harvard University Press. Cambridge, MA. 1994. 444p. ISBN:0-674-83007-5, ISBN13: 978-0-674-83007-3. Dewey:320.951. LCCN:93-026965.

Audience: **g,u,f.** *Choice, 1994.*

Goodman, David S.   DS778.T39G66 1994
Deng Xiaoping and the Chinese Revolution: A Political Biography. Ed. 2. Paper over Boards. Routledge. New York, NY. 1995. 240p. Asia Ser. ISBN:0-415-11252-4, ISBN13: 978-0-415-11252-9. Dewey:951.05/8/092 B. LCCN:94-021699.

Audience: **g,u,f.**

Gries, Peter Hays   DS779.215 .G75 2004
China's New Nationalism: Pride, Politics, and Diplomacy. Trade Cloth. University of California Press. Berkeley, CA. 2004. 224p. ISBN:0-520-23297-6, ISBN13: 978-0-520-23297-6. Dewey:320.54/0951. LCCN:2003-008451.

Audience: **g,u,f.** *Choice, 2004.*

Hinton, Carma &   DS779.32
Gordon, Richard (Directed Bys)
The Gate of Heavenly Peace. Peter Kovler, Orville Schell, Lise Yasui & David Carnochan (Contribution by). Video, VHS Format. NAATA Distribution. San Francisco, CA. Dewey:951.058.

Audience: **g,l,u,f.**

Hinton, Harold C.   DS779.17.P46 1986
(Editor)
The People's Republic of China, 1979-1984: A Documentary Survey, Set. Trade Cloth. Rowman & Littlefield Publishers, Inc. Lanham, MD. 1986. 800p. ISBN:0-8420-2253-8, ISBN13: 978-0-8420-2253-8. Dewey:951.05/8. LCCN:85-030391.

Audience: **f.** *Choice, 1987.*

Jing, Jun   HN740.K365J56 1996
The Temple of Memories: History, Power, and Morality in a Chinese Village. Elizabeth J. Perry (Foreword by). Trade Cloth. Stanford University Press. Palo Alto, CA. 1996. 230p. ISBN:0-8047-2756-2, ISBN13: 978-0-8047-2756-3. Dewey:951.4/05. LCCN:96-015406.

Audience: **f.** *Choice, 1997.*

Kuhn, Robert Lawrence   DS779.29.J53K85 2004
The Man Who Changed China: The Life and Legacy of Jiang Zemin. Trade Cloth. Crown Publishing Group. New York, NY. 2005. 720p. ISBN:1-4000-5474-5, ISBN13: 978-1-4000-5474-9. Dewey:951.05/9/092 B. LCCN:2004-013162.

Audience: **g,u,f.**

Leffman, David, et al.   DS705
The Rough Guide to China. Ed. 4. Simon Lewis & Jeremy Atiyah (Authors). Trade Paper, Perfect. Rough Guides, Ltd. London, 2005. 1312p. Rough Guide Travel Guides ISBN:1-84353-479-7, ISBN13: 978-1-84353-479-2. Dewey:915.

Audience: **g,l,u,f.**

Liang, Zhang, et al.   DS779.32.L54 2001
The Tiananmen Papers. Andrew J. Nathan, Perry Link, Orville Schell & Liang Zhang (Authors). Trade Cloth. PublicAffairs.

New York, NY. 2000. 560p. ISBN:1-58648-012-X, ISBN13: 978-1-58648-012-7. Dewey:951.05/8. LCCN:00-045823.

Audience: **g,u,f.**

Mahoney, Rosemary   DS778.T39
The Early Arrival of Dreams: A Year in China. Trade Paper. Ballantine Books. New York, NY. 1992. 336p. ISBN:0-449-90655-8, ISBN13: 978-0-449-90655-2. Dewey:951.058092.

Audience: **g,u,f.**

McGregor, James H. S.   HC427.95.M43 2006
One Billion Customers: Lessons from the Front Lines of Doing Business in China. Trade Cloth. Simon & Schuster. New York, NY. 2005. 336p. A Wall Street Journal Book Ser. ISBN:0-7432-5839-8, ISBN13: 978-0-7432-5839-5. Dewey:658.1/8/0951. LCCN:2005-044398.

Audience: **g,u,f.** *Choice, 2006.*

Morath, Inge & Miller,   DS712
Arthur
Chinese Encounters. Trade Cloth. Farrar, Straus & Giroux. New York, NY. 1979. 255p. ISBN:0-374-12208-3, ISBN13: 978-0-374-12208-9. Dewey:915.1/0457.

Audience: **g,u,f.**

Mulvenon, James C.   DS779.15 .C48
(Editor)
China Facts and Figures Annual, Vol. 23. Trade Cloth. Academic International Press. Gulf Breeze, FL. 1998. 512p. ISBN:0-87569-202-8, ISBN13: 978-0-87569-202-9. Dewey:951/.005.

Audience: **f.**

Pei, Minxin   HX418.5.P43 1994
From Reform to Revolution: The Demise of Communism in China and the Soviet Union. Trade Cloth. Harvard University Press. Cambridge, MA. 1998. 264p. ISBN:0-674-32563-X, ISBN13: 978-0-674-32563-0. Dewey:321.9/2/0947. LCCN:93-050948.

Audience: **g,u,f.**

Salzman, Mark   DS712.S245 1986
Iron and Silk: In Which a Young American Encounters Swordsmen, Bureaucrats and Other Citizens of Contemporary China. Trade Cloth. Random House, Inc. New York, NY. 1986. 224p. ISBN:0-394-55156-7, ISBN13: 978-0-394-55156-2. Dewey:951.05/8. LCCN:86-011846.

Audience: **g,l,u,f.**

Shu-min, Huang   HN733.5.H84 1989
Spiral Road: Change in a Chinese Village Through the Eyes of a Communist Party Leader. Cloth Text. Westview Press. Boulder, CO. 1989. 222p. ISBN:0-8133-7637-8, ISBN13: 978-0-8133-7637-0. Dewey:307.7/62/0951. LCCN:88-017596.

Audience: **g,u,f.**

Smil, Vaclav   HC430.E5S55 1993
China's Environmental Crisis: An Inquiry into the Limits of National Development. Trade Cloth. M. E. Sharpe Inc. Armonk, NY. 1993. 280p. ISBN:1-56324-041-6, ISBN13: 978-1-56324-041-6. Dewey:363.7/0951. LCCN:91-020037.

Audience: **g,u,f.**

Vogel, Ezra F.   DS793.K7V64 1989
One Step Ahead in China: Guangdong under Reform. Trade Cloth. Harvard University Press. Cambridge, MA. 1989. 544p.

Interpretations of Asia Ser. ISBN:0-674-63910-3, ISBN13: 978-0-674-63910-2. Dewey:951.2/7/058. LCCN:89-031695.

Audience: **g,u,f.** *Choice, 1990.*

Wang, Jing   **DS779.23.W36 1996**
High Culture Fever: Politics, Aesthetics, and Ideology in Deng's China. Trade Cloth. University of California Press. Berkeley, CA. 1996. 399p. ISBN:0-520-20294-5, ISBN13: 978-0-520-20294-8. Dewey:001.1/0951. LCCN:96-005580.

Audience: **g,u,f.** *Choice, 1997.*

Yu, Guangyuan   **JQ1519.A5Y7764 2004**
Deng Xiaoping Shakes the World: An Eyewitness Account of China's Party Work Conference and the Third Plenum. Ezra F. Vogel (Editor, Introduction by), Steven I. Levine (Editor). Trade Cloth. EastBridge. Norwalk, CT. 2004. 252p. Voices of Asia Ser. ISBN:1-891936-54-9, ISBN13: 978-1-891936-54-8. Dewey:324.251/075. LCCN:2003-027826.

Audience: **f.**

China > Science and Technology

Elvin, Mark & Liu,   **QH540.83.C6 S44 1998**
  Ts'ui-jung
Sediments of Time: Environment and Society in Chinese History. Alfred W. Crosby & Donald Worster (Contribution by). Trade Cloth. Cambridge University Press. New York, NY. 1998. 842p. Studies in Environment and History ISBN:0-521-56381-X, ISBN13: 978-0-521-56381-9. Dewey:333.7/0951. LCCN:96-022662.

Audience: **f.**

King, F. H.   **S471.C6**
Farmers of Forty Centuries or Permanent Agriculture in China, Korea and Japan. Trade Paper. Kessinger Publishing, LLC. Whitefish, MT. 2004. ISBN:1-4191-1934-6, ISBN13: 978-1-4191-1934-7. Dewey:630/.951.

Audience: **l,u,f.**

Needham, Joseph   **Q127.C5 N42**
The Grand Titration. Trade Paper. University of Toronto Press. Toronto, ON. 1979. ISBN:0-8020-6359-4, ISBN13: 978-0-8020-6359-5. Dewey:301.2/4. LCCN:76-483302.

Audience: **g,u,f.**

Needham, Joseph   **DS721.N39 2003**
  (Author, Contribution by)
Science and Civilisation in China: The Social Background General Conclusions and Reflections. Kenneth Girdwood Robinson (Editor), C. Cullen (Contribution by), Mark Elvin (Introduction by), Ray Huang (Contribution by). Trade Cloth. Cambridge University Press. New York, NY. 2004. 336p. Science and Civilisation in China Ser., Vol. 7 ISBN:0-521-08732-5, ISBN13: 978-0-521-08732-2. Dewey:509.51.

Audience: **g,u,f.** *Choice, 2005.*

Ronan, Colin A.   **DS721.N392**
The Shorter Science and Civilisation in China, Vol. 1. Trade Cloth. Cambridge University Press. New York, NY. 1978. 347p. Shorter Science and Civilisation in China Ser. ISBN:0-521-21821-7, ISBN13: 978-0-521-21821-4. Dewey:509/.51. LCCN:77-082513.

Audience: **g.** *Choice, 1995, 1987.*

Ronan, Colin A.   **Q127.C5**
The Shorter Science and Civilisation in China, Vol. 3. Trade Cloth. Cambridge University Press. New York, NY. 1986. 320p.

Shorter Science and Civilisation in China Ser. ISBN:0-521-25272-5, ISBN13: 978-0-521-25272-0. Dewey:509/.51.

Audience: **g.** *Choice, 1995, 1987.*

Ronan, Colin A.   **DS721.N392**
The Shorter Science and Civilisation in China, Vol. 5. Trade Cloth. Cambridge University Press. New York, NY. 1995. 380p. Shorter Science and Civilisation in China Ser. ISBN:0-521-46214-2, ISBN13: 978-0-521-46214-3. Dewey:509/.51. LCCN:77-082513.

Audience: **g.** *Choice, 1995, 1987.*

Ronan, Colin A.   **DS721.N392**
The Shorter Science and Civilisation in China, Vol. 2. Trade Cloth. Cambridge University Press. New York, NY. 1981. 480p. Shorter Science and Civilisation in China Ser. ISBN:0-521-23582-0, ISBN13: 978-0-521-23582-2. Dewey:509/.51. LCCN:77-082513.

Audience: **g.** *Choice, 1995, 1987.*

Ronan, Colin A.   **Q127.C5**
The Shorter Science and Civilisation in China, Vol. 4. Trade Cloth. Cambridge University Press. New York, NY. 1994. 350p. Shorter Science and Civilisation in China Ser. ISBN:0-521-32995-7, ISBN13: 978-0-521-32995-8. Dewey:509/.51.

Audience: **g.** *Choice, 1995, 1987.*

Temple, Robert   **DS721.T46 1986**
The Genius of China: Three Thousand Years of Discovery, Invention and Science. Joseph Needham (Introduction by). Trade Cloth. Simon & Schuster. New York, NY. 1987. 256p. ISBN:0-671-62028-2, ISBN13: 978-0-671-62028-8. Dewey:509.51. LCCN:86-015620.

Audience: **g,l,u,f.** *Choice, 1987.*

Ying-Hsing, Sung   **T27.C5S9313 1996**
Chinese Technology in the 17th Century: T'Ien-Kung K'Ai-Wu. Shiou-Chuan Sun & E-Tu Zen Sun (Translators). Trade Paper. Dover Publications, Inc. Mineola, NY. 1997. 384p. ISBN:0-486-29593-1, ISBN13: 978-0-486-29593-0. Dewey:600. LCCN:96-053237.

Audience: **g,u,f.**

Yoke, Ho Peng   **Q127.C5H627 2000**
Li, Qi and Shu: An Introduction to Science and Civilization in China. Trade Paper. Dover Publications, Inc. Mineola, NY. 2000. 272p. ISBN:0-486-41445-0, ISBN13: 978-0-486-41445-4. Dewey:509.51. LCCN:00-043122.

Audience: **g,u,f.**

China > Biography, Memoirs

Boorman, Howard L.   **CT1823**
Biographical Dictionary of Republican China, Vol. 3. Richard C. Howard (Editor). Trade Cloth. Columbia University Press. New York, NY. 1970. 471p. ISBN:0-231-08957-0, ISBN13: 978-0-231-08957-9. Dewey:920/.051. LCCN:67-012006.

Audience: **f.** *B*

Goodrich, L.   **DS753.5**
  Carrington & Fang, Chaoying (Editors)
Dictionary of Ming Biography, 1364-1644. Trade Cloth. Columbia University Press. New York, NY. 1976. 1751p.

ISBN:0-231-03833-X, ISBN13: 978-0-231-03833-1. Dewey:951/.026/0922. LCCN:75-026938.

Audience: **f.** ℬ

Hummel, Arthur W.   **DS0734**
Eminent Chinese of the Ch'ing Period, 1644-1912. Library Binding. Gordon Press Publishers. New York, NY. 1976. ISBN:0-8490-1761-0, ISBN13: 978-0-8490-1761-2. Dewey:920.051.

Audience: **f.**

Klein, Donald & Clark,   **DS778.A1**
  Anne B.
Biographic Dictionary of Chinese Communism, 1921-1965: Volume 1, Ai Szu-ch'i - lo I-nung; Volume 2, lo Jui-ch'ing—Yun Tai-ying, Set. Trade Cloth. Harvard University Press. Cambridge, MA. 1971. 1221p. Harvard East Asian Monographs, No. 57 ISBN:0-674-07410-6, ISBN13: 978-0-674-07410-1. Dewey:951.04/0922. LCCN:69-012725.

Audience: **f.** ℬ

Leung, Edwin Pak-Wah   **DS755**
  (Editor)
Political Leaders of Modern China, 1840-2001: A Biographical Dictionary. Cloth Text. Greenwood Publishing Group, Inc. Portsmouth, NH. 2002. 296p. ISBN:0-313-30216-2, ISBN13: 978-0-313-30216-9. Dewey:951/.03/0922. LCCN:2002-016615.

Audience: **f.** *Choice, 2003.*

Li, Yu-ning (Editor)   **HQ1767.C454 1992**
Chinese Women Through Chinese Eyes. Trade Cloth. M. E. Sharpe Inc. Armonk, NY. 1992. 282p. ISBN:0-87332-596-6, ISBN13: 978-0-87332-596-7. Dewey:305.42/0951. LCCN:91-011313.

Audience: **u,f.**

Wills, John E.   **DS734.W63 1994**
ⓔ Mountain of Fame: Portraits in Chinese History. E-Book. Princeton University Press. Princeton, NJ. ISBN:1-4008-1385-9, ISBN13: 978-1-4008-1385-8. Dewey:920.051.

Audience: **g,u,f.**

China > Biography, Memoirs > A-M

Alitto, Guy S.   **BL1875.L/**
The Last Confucian: Liang Shu-ming and the Chinese Dilemma of Modernity. Trade Cloth. University of California Press. Berkeley, CA. 1979. xvii, 396p. Center for Chinese Studies, UC Berkeley, No. 20 ISBN:0-520-03123-7, ISBN13: 978-0-520-03123-4. Dewey:951.04092. LCCN:75-027920.

Audience: **g,u,f.** ℬ

Arkush, R. David   **HM22.C62 F4329 1981**
Fei Xiaotong and Sociology in Revolutionary China. Trade Cloth. Harvard University Press. Cambridge, MA. 1981. 416p. Harvard East Asian Monographs, No. 98 ISBN:0-674-29815-2, ISBN13: 978-0-674-29815-6. Dewey:301/.092/4. LCCN:81-001801.

Audience: **f.**

Barme, Geremie R.   **ND1049.F45B37 2002**
An Artistic Exile: A Life of Feng Zikai (1898-1975). Trade Cloth. University of California Press. Berkeley, CA. 2002. 558p. Asia Ser., No. 9:Local Studies/Global Themes ISBN:0-520-20832-3, ISBN13: 978-0-520-20832-2. Dewey:759.951. LCCN:2001-005019.

Audience: **g,l,u,f.** *Choice, 2003.*

Bennett, Gordon A. &   **DS778.D34**
  Montaperto, Ronald N.
Red Guard: The Political Biography of Dai Hsiao-Ai. Trade Cloth. Peter Smith Publisher, Inc. Magnolia, MA. 1981. ISBN:0-8446-4710-1, ISBN13: 978-0-8446-4710-4. Dewey:951.05/0924.

Audience: **g,u,f.**

Byron, John & Pack,   **DS778.K29 B97 1992**
  Robert
The Claws of the Dragon: Kang Sheng - the Evil Genius Behind Mao - and His Legacy of Terror in People's China. Trade Cloth. Simon & Schuster. New York, NY. 1992. 608p. ISBN:0-671-69537-1, ISBN13: 978-0-671-69537-8. Dewey:951.05/092 B. LCCN:91-032369.

Audience: **g,u,f.**

Chang, Hao   **DS763.L67**
Liang Ch'i-Ch'ao and Intellectual Transition in China, 1890-1907. Trade Cloth. Harvard University Press. Cambridge, MA. 1971. 342p. East Asian Monographs, No. 64 ISBN:0-674-53009-8, ISBN13: 978-0-674-53009-6. Dewey:915.1/03/30924. LCCN:75-162635.

Audience: **g,f.**

Chang, Jung   **CT1828.C478 A3 1991**
Wild Swans: Three Daughters of China. Trade Paper. Simon & Schuster. New York, NY. 2003. 544p. ISBN:0-7432-4698-5, ISBN13: 978-0-7432-4698-9. Dewey:951.05'092 B. LCCN:91-020696.

Audience: **g,l,u,f.**

Cheng, Nien   **DS778.7.C445 1995**
Life and Death in Shanghai. Trade Paper. HarperCollins Publishers. New York, NY. 1995. 496p. ISBN:0-00-654861-X, ISBN13: 978-0-00-654861-4. Dewey:365/.45/0924. LCCN:98-143622.

Audience: **g,u,f.**

Creel, H. G.   **B128.C8 C65**
Confucius and the Chinese Way. Trade Cloth. Peter Smith Publisher, Inc. Magnolia, MA. 1980. ISBN:0-8446-1918-3, ISBN13: 978-0-8446-1918-7. Dewey:299/.5126/4.

Audience: **g,l,u,f.**

Dittmer, Lowell   **DS778.L49D57 1998**
Liu Shaoqi and the Chinese Cultural Revolution. Cloth Text. M. E. Sharpe Inc. Armonk, NY. 1998. 400p. ISBN:1-56324-951-0, ISBN13: 978-1-56324-951-8. Dewey:951.056. LCCN:97-041292.

Audience: **f.**

Egan, Susan C.   **CT3990.H86E35 1987**
A Latter Day Confucian: Reminiscences of William Hung, 1893-1980. Trade Cloth. Harvard University Press. Cambridge, MA. 1988. 200p. Harvard East Asian Monographs, Vol. 131 ISBN:0-674-51297-9, ISBN13: 978-0-674-51297-9. Dewey:951.04/092/4 B. LCCN:87-020193.

Audience: **f.**

Fairbank, Wilma   **NA1549.L53F35 1994**
Liang and Lin: Partners in Exploring China's Architectural Past. Jonathan D. Spence (Introduction by). Book, Other. University of Pennsylvania Press. Philadelphia, PA. 1994. 256p. ISBN:0-8122-3278-X, ISBN13: 978-0-8122-3278 3. Dewey:720/.92/2 B. LCCN:94-016414.

Audience: **f.** *Choice, 1995.*

Feigon, Lee   DS777.15.C5
Chen Duxiu, Founder of the Chinese Communist Party. Trade
Cloth. Princeton University Press. Princeton, NJ. 1983. 304p.
ISBN:0-691-05393-6, ISBN13: 978-0-691-05393-6.
Dewey:951.04/092/4. LCCN:83-042556.

Audience: **f.** *B*

Feng, Youlan   B5234.F44A3713 2000
The Hall of Three Pines: An Account of My Life. Denis C.
Mair (Translator). Trade Cloth. University of Hawaii Press.
Honolulu, HI. 2000. 296p. SHAPS Library of Translations
ISBN:0-8248-2220-X, ISBN13: 978-0-8248-2220-0.
Dewey:181/.11 B. LCCN:99-035524.

Audience: **f.** *Choice, 2000.*

Gao Yuan   DS778.7.G36 1987
Born Red: A Chronicle of the Cultural Revolution. William A.
Joseph (Foreword by). Trade Cloth. Stanford University Press.
Palo Alto, CA. 1987. 416p. ISBN:0-8047-1368-5, ISBN13:
978-0-8047-1368-9. Dewey:951.05/6. LCCN:86-023058.

Audience: **g,u,f.** *Choice, 1987.*

Goodman, David S.   DS778.T39G66 1994
Deng Xiaoping and the Chinese Revolution: A Political
Biography. Ed. 2. Paper over Boards. Routledge. New York, NY.
1995. 240p. Asia Ser. ISBN:0-415-11252-4, ISBN13:
978-0-415-11252-9. Dewey:951.05/8/092 B. LCCN:94-021699.

Audience: **g,u,f.**

Harrison, Henrietta   DS797.75.C45H374
Man Awakened from Dreams: One Man's Life in a North China
Village, 1857-1942. Trade Cloth. Stanford University Press. Palo
Alto, CA. 2004. 240p. ISBN:0-8047-5068-8, ISBN13:
978-0-8047-5068-4. Dewey:951/.17 B. LCCN:2004-018647.

Audience: **g,u,f.**

Heng, Liang & Shapiro,   DS778.7
Judith
Son of the Revolution. Jerome A. Cohen (Introduction by).
Trade Cloth. Alfred A. Knopf Inc. New York, NY. 1983. xii,
301p. ISBN:0-394-52568-X, ISBN13: 978-0-394-52568-6.
Dewey:951.05/6. LCCN:82-018704.

Audience: **g,l,u,f.**

Hung, William   Q172.5.S96
Tu Fu, China's Greatest Poet. Paper Text. Textbook Publishers.
Temecula, CA. 2003. x, 300p. ISBN:0-7581-4322-2, ISBN13:
978-0-7581-4322-8. Dewey:3.7.

Audience: **g,u,f.**

Kahn, Harold L.   DS754.4.C5
Monarchy in the Emperor's Eyes: Image and Reality in the
Chien-Lung Reign. Trade Cloth. Harvard University Press.
Cambridge, MA. 1971. xi, 314p. East Asian Monographs, No.
59 ISBN:0-674-58230-6, ISBN13: 978-0-674-58230-9.
Dewey:951/.03/0924. LCCN:75-135546.

Audience: **f.** *B*

Kuhn, Robert Lawrence   DS779.29.J53K85 2004
The Man Who Changed China: The Life and Legacy of Jiang
Zemin. Trade Cloth. Crown Publishing Group. New York, NY.
2005. 720p. ISBN:1-4000-5474-5, ISBN13: 978-1-4000-5474-9.
Dewey:951.05/9/092 B. LCCN:2004-013162.

Audience: **g,u,f.**

Lee, Leo O. (Editor)   PL2754.S5Z/
Lu Xun and His Legacy. Trade Cloth. University of California
Press. Berkeley, CA. 1985. xix, 324p. ISBN:0-520-05158-0,

ISBN13: 978-0-520-05158-4. Dewey:895.1/35.
LCCN:83-018048.

Audience: **g,u,f.** *B*

Meisner, Maurice J.   HX0387.L48M4
Li Ta-Chao and the Origins of Chinese Marxism. Trade Paper.
Books on Demand. Ann Arbor, MI. 345p. Harvard East Asian
Ser., Vol. 27 ISBN:0-598-22887-X, ISBN13:
978-0-598-22887-1. Dewey:335.4/0951. LCCN:67-010904.

Audience: **u,f.** *B*

Pu Yi, Aisin-Gioro   DS773 .C51513
From Emperor to Citizen. Ed. 2. Trade Cloth. China Books &
Periodicals, Inc. South San Francisco, CA. 1980.
ISBN:0-8351-0619-5, ISBN13: 978-0-8351-0619-1.
Dewey:951/.03/0924 B.

Audience: **g,l,u,f.**

Spence, Jonathan D.   DS758.23.H85 S64
God's Chinese Son: The Taiping Heavenly Kingdom of Hong
Xiaquan. Trade Cloth. DIANE Publishing Company.
Collingdale, PA. 2005. 400p. ISBN:0-7567-9680-6, ISBN13:
978-0-7567-9680-8. Dewey:951/.034/092.

Audience: **g,u,f.**

Taylor, Jay   DS799.82.C437T39
The Generalissimo's Son: Chiang Ching-kuo and the
Revolutions in China and Taiwan. Trade Cloth. Harvard
University Press. Cambridge, MA. 2000. 544p.
ISBN:0-674-00287-3, ISBN13: 978-0-674-00287-6.
Dewey:951.24/905/092 B. LCCN:00-035053.

Audience: **g,u,f.** *Choice, 2001.*

Terrill, Ross   DS778.C5374T45 1999
Madame Mao: The White-Boned Demon. Trade Paper. Stanford
University Press. Palo Alto, CA. 2000. 424p.
ISBN:0-8047-2922-0, ISBN13: 978-0-8047-2922-2.
Dewey:951.05/092 B. LCCN:98-045872.

Audience: **g,u,f.**

Witke, Roxanne   DS778.C5374.W57
Comrade Chiang Ch'ing. Trade Cloth. Little Brown &
Company. New York, NY. 1977. xxvi, 549p.
ISBN:0-316-94900-0, ISBN13: 978-0-316-94900-2.
Dewey:951.05/092/4. LCCN:77-000935.

Audience: **g,f.** *B*

China > Biography, Memoirs > Foreigners in China

Buck, Pearl S.   BV3427.S852
The Exile. John Day. 1936.

Audience: **g,l,u,f.**

Buck, Pearl S.   PS3503.U198
Fighting Angel. John Day. 1936.

Audience: **g,l,u,f.**

Conn, Peter   PS3503.U198 Z624 19
Pearl S. Buck: A Cultural Biography. Cloth Text. Cambridge
University Press. New York, NY. 1996. 496p.
ISBN:0-521-56080-2, ISBN13: 978-0-521-56080-1.
Dewey:813.5/2. LCCN:95-043105.

Audience: **g,u,f.** *Choice, 1997.*

Dimbleby, Jonathan   **DS796.H757D56 1997**
The Last Governor: Chris Patten and the Handover of Hong
Kong. Trade Cloth. Little Brown & Company. New York, NY.
1997. xvi, 461p. ISBN:0-316-64018-2, ISBN13:
978-0-316-64018-3. Dewey:951.25. LCCN:98-115639.
> Audience: **g,u,f.**

Fairbank, John K.   **DS774**
Chinabound: A Fifty Year Memoir. Trade Cloth. HarperCollins
Publishers. New York, NY. 1982. 480p. ISBN:0-06-039005-0,
ISBN13: 978-0-06-039005-1. Dewey:951.05/092/4.
LCCN:81-047656.
> Audience: **g,u,f.** *B*

Hunter, Jane   **BV3415.2 .H86**
The Gospel of Gentility: American Women Missionaries in
Turn-of-the-Century China. Trade Paper. Yale University Press.
Cumberland, RI. 1989. 322p. ISBN:0-300-04603-0, ISBN13:
978-0-300-04603-8. Dewey:266/.023/73051088042.
> Audience: **g,u,f.**

Lord, Bette Bao   **DS779.23.L67**
Legacies: A Chinese Mosaic. Trade Paper. DIANE Publishing
Company. Collingdale, PA. 2001. 312p. ISBN:0-7881-9887-4,
ISBN13: 978-0-7881-9887-8. Dewey:951.05.
> Audience: **g,u,f.**

MacKinnon, Janice R.   **PS3537.M16Z77 1988**
   & MacKinnon, Stephen R.
Agnes Smedley: The Life and Times of an American Radical.
Trade Cloth. University of California Press. Berkeley, CA. 1987.
460p. ISBN:0-520-05966-2, ISBN13: 978-0-520-05966-5.
Dewey:818/.5209 B. LCCN:87-010853.
> Audience: **g,l,u,f.** *Choice, 1988.*

Newman, Robert P.   **E748.L34N48 1992**
Owen Lattimore and the "Loss" of China. Trade Cloth.
University of California Press. Berkeley, CA. 1992. 685p.
ISBN:0-520-07388-6, ISBN13: 978-0-520-07388-3.
Dewey:327.51073. LCCN:91-021888.
> Audience: **u,f.** *Choice, 1992.*

Rossabi, Morris   **DS752.6.K83.R67 1988**
Khubilai Khan: His Life and Times. Trade Paper. University of
California Press. Berkeley, CA. 1989. 344p.
ISBN:0-520-06740-1, ISBN13: 978-0-520-06740-0.
Dewey:950/.2/0924 B. LCCN:86-025031.
> Audience: **g,u,f.** *Choice, 1989.*

Spence, Jonathan D.   **DS740.4**
To Change China: Western Advisors in China, 1620-1960. Trade
Paper. Penguin Group (USA) Inc. New York, NY. 1980. 352p.
ISBN:0-14-005528-2, ISBN13: 978-0-14-005528-3.
Dewey:301.29/51/01821.
> Audience: **g,l,u,f.**

Stilwell, Joseph W.   **D811**
The Stilwell Papers. Theodore H. White (Editor). Trade Cloth. A
M S Press, Inc. New York, NY. ISBN:0-404-20247-0, ISBN13:
978-0-404-20247-7. Dewey:940.54. LCCN:83-045889.
> Audience: **f.**

Stuart, John Leighton   **DS775.S84**
My Fifty Years in China: The Memoirs of John Leighton Stuart,
Missionary and Ambassador. Paper Text. Textbook Publishers.
Temecula, CA. 2003. 346p. ISBN:0-7581-5022-9, ISBN13:
978-0-7581-5022-6. Dewcy:951.04.
> Audience: **g,u,f.**

Thomas, S. Bernard   **PN4874.S5715T46 1996**
Season of High Adventure: Edgar Snow in China. Trade Cloth.
University of California Press. Berkeley, CA. 1996. 587p.
ISBN:0-520-20276-7, ISBN13: 978-0-520-20276-4.
Dewey:070/.92 B. LCCN:95-021157.
> Audience: **g,u,f.**

Trevor-Roper, Hugh R.   **CT3990.L58**
The Hermit of Peking: The Hidden Life of Sir Edmund
Backhouse. Trade Cloth. Random House Children's Books. New
York, NY. 1977. ISBN:0-394-41104-8, ISBN13:
978-0-394-41104-0. Dewey:951.007202.
> Audience: **g,u,f.**

Tuchman, Barbara W.   **D767.6**
Stilwell and the American Experience in China, 1911-45.
Library Binding. Buccaneer Books, Inc. Cutchogue, NY. 1995.
600p. ISBN:1-56849-604-4, ISBN13: 978-1-56849-604-7.
Dewey:940.54/25/0924.
> Audience: **g,u,f.**

Yu-ming, Shaw   **BV3427.S828S5 1992**
John Leighton Stuart and Twentieth-Century Chinese-American
Relations. Trade Cloth. Harvard University Press. Cambridge,
MA. 1992. 350p. East Asian Monographs, No. 158
ISBN:0-674-47835-5, ISBN13: 978-0-674-47835-0.
Dewey:266/.51/092/. LCCN:92-032007.
> Audience: **f.**

China > Biography, Memoirs > Mao Zedong

Barme, Geremie R.   **DS778.M3B374 1996**
Shades of Mao: The Posthumous Cult of the Great Leader.
Cloth Text. M. E. Sharpe Inc. Armonk, NY. 1996. 334p.
ISBN:1-56324-678-3, ISBN13: 978-1-56324-678-4.
Dewey:951.05/092. LCCN:95-025979.
> Audience: **g,l,u,f.**

Chang, Jung &   **DS778.M3C38 2005**
   Halliday, Jon
Mao: The Unknown Story. Saddle Stitched, Cloth over Boards,
Dust Jacket. Alfred A. Knopf Inc. New York, NY. 2005. 814p.
ISBN:0-679-42271-4, ISBN13: 978-0-679-42271-6.
Dewey:951.05/092 B. LCCN:2004-063826.
> Audience: **g,l,u,f.** *Choice, 2006.*

Cheek, Timothy   **DS778.M3.C47 2002**
   (Editor)
Mao Zedong and China's Revolutions: A Brief History with
Documents. Cloth over Boards. Palgrave Macmillan. New York,
NY. 2002. 272p. ISBN:0-312-29429-8, ISBN13:
978-0-312-29429-8. Dewey:951.05092.
> Audience: **g,u,f.**

Feigon, Lee   **DS777.75**
Mao: A Reinterpretation. Trade Paper. Ivan R. Dee Publisher.
Blue Ridge Summit, PA. 2003. 240p. ISBN:1-56663-522-5,
ISBN13: 978-1-56663-522-6. Dewey:951.05.
> Audience: **g,f.** *Choice, 2003.*

Li, Zhisui   **DS778.M3L5164 1994**
The Private Life of Chairman Mao: The Memoirs of Mao's
Personal Physician. Trade Cloth. Random House, Inc. New
York, NY. 1994. 624p. ISBN:0-679-40035-4, ISBN13:
978-0-679-40035-6. Dewey:951.05. LCCN:94-029970.
> Audience: **g,l,u,f.** *Choice, 1995.*

Mao Zedong   DS778.M3
☐ Selected Works of Mao Tse-Tung.
http://www.marx2mao.com/

Audience: **g.**

Schram, Stuart R.   DS778.M3 A25 1992
(Editor)
Mao's Road to Power: Revolutionary Writings, 1912-1949 - The
Pre-Marxist Period, 1912-1920. Trade Cloth. M. E. Sharpe Inc.
Armonk, NY. 1992. 688p. An East Gate Book Ser., Vol. 1
ISBN:1-56324-049-1, ISBN13: 978-1-56324-049-2.
Dewey:951.05092. LCCN:92-026783.

Audience: **u,f.**

Schram, Stuart R.   DS778.M3A25
(Editor)
Mao's Road to Power - Revolutionary Writings, 1912-1949: The
Pre-Marxist Period, 1912-1920, Vol. I. Trade Cloth. M. E.
Sharpe Inc. Armonk, NY. 1992. 688p. ISBN:1-56324-457-8,
ISBN13: 978-1-56324-457-5. Dewey:951.04. LCCN:92-026783.

Audience: **u,f.**

Schram, Stuart R.   DS778.M3
(Editor)
Mao's Road to Power: Revolutionary Writings, 1912-1949: The
Rise and Fall of the Chinese Soviet Republic, 1931-1934. Trade
Cloth. M. E. Sharpe Inc. Armonk, NY. 1997. 1,110p. An East
Gate Book Ser. ISBN:1-56324-891-3, ISBN13:
978-1-56324-891-7. Dewey:951.04. LCCN:92-026783.

Audience: **u,f.**

Schram, Stuart R.   DS778.M3
(Editor)
Mao's Road to Power: Revolutionary Writings, 1912-1949:
From the Jinggangshan to the Establishment of the Jiangxi.
Trade Cloth. M. E. Sharpe Inc. Armonk, NY. 1995. 848p. An
East Gate Book Ser. ISBN:1-56324-439-X, ISBN13:
978-1-56324-439-1. Dewey:951.04. LCCN:92-026783.

Audience: **u,f.**

Schram, Stuart R.   DS778.M3
(Editor)
Mao's Road to Power: Revolutionary Writings, 1912-1949:
National Revolution and Social Revolution. Trade Cloth. M. E.
Sharpe Inc. Armonk, NY. 1995. 608p. An East Gate Book Ser.
ISBN:1-56324-430-6, ISBN13: 978-1-56324-430-8.
Dewey:951.04. LCCN:92-026783.

Audience: **u,f.**

Short, Philip   DS778.M3S548 2000
Mao: A Life. Cloth over Boards. Henry Holt & Company. New
York, NY. 2000. 768p. ISBN:0-8050-3115-4, ISBN13:
978-0-8050-3115-7. Dewey:951.05/092 B. LCCN:99-041839.
Audience: **g,l,u,f.**   *Choice, 2000.*

Spence, Jonathan D.   DS778.M3S685 1999
Mao Zedong: A Penguin Life. Trade Cloth. Penguin Group
(USA) Inc. New York, NY. 1999. 208p. Penguin Lives Ser.
ISBN:0-670-88669-6, ISBN13: 978-0-670-88669-2.
Dewey:951.05/092. LCCN:99-027739.

Audience: **g,l,u,f.**

Terrill, Ross   DS778.M3T45 1999
Mao: A Biography. Trade Paper. Stanford University Press. Palo
Alto, CA. 2000. 576p. ISBN:0-8047-2921-2, ISBN13:
978-0-8047-2921-5. Dewey:951.05/092/4. LCCN:99-017082.

Audience: **g.**

China > Biography, Memoirs > M-Z

Bergere, Marie-Claire   DS777.B47 1998
Sun Yat-Sen. Janet Lloyd (Translator). Trade Cloth. Stanford
University Press. Palo Alto, CA. 1998. 480p.
ISBN:0-8047-3170-5, ISBN13: 978-0-8047-3170-6. Dewey:[B].
LCCN:97-035504.

Audience: **g,u,f.**   *Choice, 1998.*

Bernstein, Richard   BQ8149.H787B47 2002
Ultimate Journey: Retracing the Path of an Ancient Buddhist
Monk Who Crossed Asia in Search of Enlightenment. UK-Trade
Paper. Alfred A. Knopf Inc. New York, NY. 2002. 368p.
ISBN:0-679-78157-9, ISBN13: 978-0-679-78157-8.
Dewey:294.3/92 B. LCCN:2001-045484.

Audience: **g,f.**   *Choice, 2001.*

Bingying, Xie   PL2765.I45Z5213 2001
A Woman Soldier's Own Story: The Autobiography of Xie
Bingying. Lily Chia Brissman & Barry Brissman (Translators).
Trade Cloth. Columbia University Press. New York, NY. 2001.
288p. ISBN:0-231-12250-0, ISBN13: 978-0-231-12250-4.
Dewey:895.1/85109. LCCN:2001-023514.

Audience: **g,u,f.**

Chu, Samuel C.   DS777.488.C5
Madame Chiang Kai-Shek and Her China. Trade Cloth.
EastBridge. Norwalk, CT. 2005. 288p. ISBN:1-891936-71-9,
ISBN13: 978-1-891936-71-5. Dewey:951.24/905/092 B.
LCCN:2004-026988.

Audience: **g,l,u,f.**

Guisso, Richard W., et al.   DS747.9.C47G85 1989
The First Emperor of China. Catherine Pagani & David Miller
(Authors), Hillel Black (Editor). Trade Cloth. Carol Publishing
Group. Secaucus, NJ. 1989. 224p. ISBN:1-55972-016-6,
ISBN13: 978-1-55972-016-8. Dewey:931/.04/092 B.
LCCN:89-015742.

Audience: **g,u,f.**

Hayford, Charles W.   HN740.Z9C6378 1990
To the People: James Yen and Village China. Trade Cloth.
Columbia University Press. New York, NY. 1990. 304p.
ISBN:0-231-07204-X, ISBN13: 978-0-231-07204-5.
Dewey:307.1/412/0951. LCCN:90-031930.
Audience: **g,u,f.**   *Choice, 1990.*

Hu, Hua-ling   BV3427.V38H813 2000
American Goddess at the Rape of Nanking: The Courage of
Minnie Vautrin. Paul Simon (Foreword by). Trade Cloth.
Southern Illinois University Press. Carbondale, IL. 2000. 208p.
ISBN:0-8093-2303-6, ISBN13: 978-0-8093-2303-6.
Dewey:266/.0092 B. LCCN:99-030526.

Audience: **g,u,f.**

Mahoney, Rosemary   DS778.T39
The Early Arrival of Dreams: A Year in China. Trade Paper.
Ballantine Books. New York, NY. 1992. 336p.
ISBN:0-449-90655-8, ISBN13: 978-0-449-90655-2.
Dewey:951.058092.

Audience: **g,u,f.**

Schoppa, R. Keith   DS777.15.S53S36 1995
Blood Road: The Mystery of Shen Dingyi in Revolutionary
China. Trade Cloth. University of California Press. Berkeley,
CA. 1995. 322p. ISBN:0-520-20015-2, ISBN13:
978-0-520-20015-9. Dewey:951.04/1/092 B. LCCN:94-022072.
Audience: **u,f.**   *Choice, 1996.*

Schwartz, Benjamin I.   **JA83**
In Search of Wealth and Power: Yen Fu and the West. Trade
Cloth. Harvard University Press. Cambridge, MA. 1964. 318p.
East Asian Ser., No. 16 ISBN:0-674-44651-8, ISBN13:
978-0-674-44651-9. Dewey:190. LCCN:64-016069.
Audience: **u,f.**

Smedley, Agnes   **DS778.C6 S5**
The Great Road: The Life and Times of Chu Teh. Paper Text.
Textbook Publishers. Temecula, CA. 2003. 461p.
ISBN:0-7581-8047-0, ISBN13: 978-0-7581-8047-6.
Dewey:923.551.
Audience: **g,u,f.** ℬ

Spence, Jonathan D.   **HQ1767.S63 1978**
The Death of Woman Wang. Trade Cloth. Penguin Group (USA)
Inc. New York, NY. 1978. xvii, 169p. ISBN:0-670-26232-3,
ISBN13: 978-0-670-26232-8. Dewey:951/.14. LCCN:77-029134.
Audience: **g,l,u,f.**

Spence, Jonathan D.   **DS754.4.C53.A33 1974**
Emperor of China. Trade Cloth. Random House, Inc. New York,
NY. 1974. xxv, 217p. ISBN:0-394-48835-0, ISBN13:
978-0-394-48835-6. Dewey:951/.03/0924. LCCN:73-020743.
Audience: **g,u,f.** ℬ

T'ai-t'ai, Ning L.   **CT1828.N5 A3**
A Daughter of Han: The Autobiography of a Chinese Working
Woman. Ida Pruitt (Editor). Trade Cloth. Stanford University
Press. Palo Alto, CA. 1945. viii, 254p. ISBN:0-8047-0605-0,
ISBN13: 978-0-8047-0605-6. Dewey:951.
Audience: **g,l,u,f.**

Thurston, Anne F.   **DS778.N53.T48 1991**
A Chinese Odyssey: The Life and Times of a Chinese Dissident.
Trade Cloth. Thomson Gale. Farmington Hills, MI. 1992. 384p.
ISBN:0-684-19219-5, ISBN13: 978-0-684-19219-2.
Dewey:951.05/092. LCCN:91-023216.
Audience: **g,u,f.** *Choice, 1992.*

Waley, Arthur   **PL2735.A5.Z94 1970**
Yuan Mei: Eighteenth Century Chinese Poet. Trade Cloth.
Stanford University Press. Palo Alto, CA. 1956. 227p.
ISBN:0-8047-0718-9, ISBN13: 978-0-8047-0718-3.
Dewcy:895.1/1/4. LCCN:70-107646.
Audience: **g,u,f.**

Warner, Marina   **DS763.63.T96W37 1986**
The Dragon Empress. Trade Paper. Central Bureau voor
Schimmelcultures. 1986. 256p. ISBN:0-689-70714-2, ISBN13:
978-0-689-70714-8. Dewey:951/.03/0924 B. LCCN:86-007909.
Audience: **g,u,f.**

Wriggins, Sally Hovey   **BQ8149.H787**
Xuanzang: A Buddhist Pilgrim on the Silk Road. Paper Text.
Westview Press. Boulder, CO. 1997. 292p. ISBN:0-8133-3407-1,
ISBN13: 978-0-8133-3407-3. Dewey:939.6/0099.
Audience: **g,u,f.**

Wu, Harry &   **DS777.75.W787**
Wakeman, Carolyn
Bitter Winds: A Memoir of My Years in China's Gulag. Trade
Paper. John Wiley & Sons, Inc. Hoboken, NJ. 1995. 304p.
ISBN:0-471-11425-1, ISBN13: 978-0-471-11425-3.
Dewey:365.45092. LCCN:93-015799.
Audience: **g,f.**

Ye, Weili & Xiadong,   **DS778.7.W445 2005**
Ma
Growing up in the People's Republic: Conversations between
Two Daughters of China's Revolution. Cloth over Boards.
Palgrave Macmillan. New York, NY. 2005. 208p. Palgrave
Studies in Oral History Ser. ISBN:1-4039-6995-7, ISBN13:
978-1-4039-6995-8. Dewey:951.05/6. LCCN:2005-048676.
Audience: **g,u,f.**

Young, Ernest P.   **DS777.2.Y68 1977**
The Presidency of Yuan Shih-K'ai: Liberalism and Dictatorship
in Early Republican China. Trade Cloth. University of Michigan
Press. Chicago, IL. 1977. 372p. Studies on China
ISBN:0-472-08995-1, ISBN13: 978-0-472-08995-6.
Dewey:951/.03/0924. LCCN:75-031057.
Audience: **f.** ℬ

China > Foreign Relations

Bickers, Robert A.   **DA47.9.C6B53 1999**
Britain in China: Community, Culture and Colonialism,
1900-49. Cloth over Boards. Manchester University Press.
Manchester, 1999. 256p. Studies in Imperialism
ISBN:0-7190-4697-1, ISBN13: 978-0-7190-4697-1.
Dewey:327.51041. LCCN:99-039760.
Audience: **g,u,f.** *Choice, 2000.*

Brady, Anne-Marie   **DS775.8.B73 2003**
Making the Foreign Serve China: Managing Foreigners in the
People's Republic. Book, Other. Rowman & Littlefield
Publishers, Inc. Lanham, MD. 2003. 320p.
Asia/Pacific/Perspectives Ser. ISBN:0-7425-1861-2, ISBN13:
978-0-7425-1861-2. Dewey:327.51. LCCN:2003-015562.
Audience: **g,u,f.** *Choice, 2004.*

Brandt, Nat   **BV3420.S43B73 1999**
Massacre in Shansi. Trade Paper. iUniverse, Inc. Lincoln, NE.
1999. 364p. ISBN:1-58348-347-0, ISBN13: 978-1-58348-347-3.
Dewey:275. LCCN:99-063476.
Audience: **g,l,u,f.**

Clifford, Nicholas R.   **DS796.S257**
Spoilt Children of Empire: Westerners in Shanghai and the
Chinese Revolution of the 1920s. Trade Paper. University Press
of New England. Lebanon, NH. 1992. 384p.
ISBN:0-87451-595-5, ISBN13: 978-0-87451-595-4.
Dewey:951/.132041. LCCN:90-050904.
Audience: **g,u,f.** *Choice, 1992.*

Cohen, Paul A.   **DS762 .C6**
China and Christianity: The Missionary Movement and the
Growth of Chinese Anti-Foreignism, 1860-1870. Trade Cloth.
Harvard University Press. Cambridge, MA. 1963. 406p. East
Asian Monographs, No. 11 ISBN:0-674-11701-8, ISBN13:
978-0-674-11701-3. Dewey:266.009. LCCN:63-019135.
Audience: **g,u,f.** ℬ

Cohen, Paul A. &   **DS771.C67 1997**
Townsend, Paul A.
History in Three Keys: The Boxers as Event, Experience, and
Myth. Trade Cloth. Columbia University Press. New York, NY.
1997. 428p. ISBN:0-231-10650-5, ISBN13: 978-0-231-10650-4.
Dewey:951/.035. LCCN:96-027118.
Audience: **g,l,u,f.**

Cohen, Warren I.   **E183.8.C5C62 2000**
America's Response to China: A History of Sino-American
Relations. Ed. 4. Trade Cloth. Columbia University Press. New

---

York, NY. 2000. 270p. ISBN:0-231-11928-3, ISBN13: 978-0-231-11928-3. Dewey:327.73051. LCCN:2001-524810.

Audience: **l,u,f.**

Fay, Peter W.　　　　DS757.5.F39 1997
The Opium War, 1840-1842: Barbarians in the Celestial Empire in the Early Part of the Nineteenth Century and the War by Which They Forced Her Gates Ajar. Trade Paper. University of North Carolina Press. Chapel Hill, NC. 1998. 440p. ISBN:0-8078-4714-3, ISBN13: 978-0-8078-4714-5. Dewey:951/.033. LCCN:97-035261.

Audience: **g,l,u,f.**

Gries, Peter Hays　　　　DS779.215 .G75 2004
China's New Nationalism: Pride, Politics, and Diplomacy. Trade Cloth. University of California Press. Berkeley, CA. 2004. 224p. ISBN:0-520-23297-6, ISBN13: 978-0-520-23297-6. Dewey:320.54/0951. LCCN:2003-008451.

Audience: **g,u,f.** *Choice, 2004.*

Hevia, James L.　　　　DS740.5.G5H48 1995
Cherishing Men from Afar: Qing Guest Ritual and the Macartney Embassy of 1793. Cloth Text. Duke University Press. Durham, NC. 1995. 296p. ISBN:0-8223-1625-0, ISBN13: 978-0-8223-1625-1. Dewey:327.51041/09/033. LCCN:94-043610.

Audience: **f.** *Choice, 1996.*

Hevia, James Louis　　　　DS740.5.G5H484 2003
English Lessons: The Pedagogy of Imperialism in Nineteenth-Century China. Trade Cloth. Duke University Press. Durham, NC. 2003. 392p. ISBN:0-8223-3151-9, ISBN13: 978-0-8223-3151-3. Dewey:951/.033. LCCN:2003-009460.

Audience: **f.** *Choice, 2004.*

Hopkirk, Peter　　　　DS793.S62H66 2001
Foreign Devils on the Silk Road: The Search for the Lost Treasures of Central Asia. Trade Paper. Oxford University Press, Inc. New York, NY. 2001. 264p. ISBN:0-19-280211-9, ISBN13: 978-0-19-280211-8. Dewey:931. LCCN:2001-280262.

Audience: **g,u,f.**

Jagchid, Sechin &　　　　DS329.4.J3413 1989
Symons, Van J.
Peace, War, and Trade along the Great Wall: Nomadic-Chinese Interaction Through Two Millennia. Trade Cloth. Indiana University Press. Bloomington, IN. 1989. 288p. ISBN:0-253-33187-0, ISBN13: 978-0-253-33187-8. Dewey:303.4/8258/051. LCCN:88-046020.

Audience: **g,u,f.** *Choice, 1990.*

Levathes, Louise　　　　DS753.6.C48L48 1996
When China Ruled the Seas: The Treasure Fleet of the Dragon Throne, 1405-1433. Trade Paper. Oxford University Press, Inc. New York, NY. 1997. 252p. ISBN:0-19-511207-5, ISBN13: 978-0-19-511207-8. Dewey:359/.00951. LCCN:96-024966.

Audience: **g,u,f.**

Liu, Lydia H.　　　　DS761.L58 2004
The Clash of Empires: The Invention of China in Modern World Making. Trade Cloth. Harvard University Press. Cambridge, MA. 2004. 334p. ISBN:0-674-01307-7, ISBN13: 978-0-674-01307-0. Dewey:951/.034. LCCN:2004-042218.

Audience: **f.** *Choice, 2005.*

Liu, Lydia He　　　　PL2302.L534 1995
Translingual Practice: Literature, National Culture, and Modernity - China, 1900-1937. Trade Cloth. Stanford University Press. Palo Alto, CA. 1995. 368p. ISBN:0-8047-2534-9,

ISBN13: 978-0-8047-2534-7. Dewey:895.109. LCCN:94-045961.

Audience: **f.** *Choice, 1996.*

Ong, Aihwa (Editor)　　　　DS732.U54 1997
Ungrounded Empires: The Cultural Politics of Modern Chinese Transnationalism. Paper over Boards. Routledge. New York, NY. 1996. 352p. ISBN:0-415-91542-2, ISBN13: 978-0-415-91542-7. Dewey:305.8/951/05. LCCN:96-030223.

Audience: **f.**

Rossabi, Morris　　　　DS750.82
(Editor)
China among Equals: The Middle Kingdom and Its Neighbors, 10th-14th Centuries. Trade Cloth. University of California Press. Berkeley, CA. 1983. 400p. ISBN:0-520-04383-9, ISBN13: 978-0-520-04383-1. Dewey:327.51. LCCN:81-011486.

Audience: **g,u,f.**

Schafer, Edward H.　　　　HE325
The Golden Peaches of Samarkand. Trade Cloth. Kegan Paul International, Ltd. London, 2004. 410p. ISBN:0-7103-1014-5, ISBN13: 978-0-7103-1014-9. Dewey:382.5/0951/09021.

Audience: **g,u,f.**

Sun, Youli　　　　D742.C5S85 1993
China and the Origins of the Pacific War, 1931-1941. Cloth over Boards. Palgrave Macmillan. New York, NY. 1993. 256p. ISBN:0-312-09010-2, ISBN13: 978-0-312-09010-4. Dewey:951/.042. LCCN:92-036305.

Audience: **g,u,f.** *Choice, 1994.*

Tsou, Tang　　　　DS777.53.T866
America's Failure in China, Nineteen Forty-One to Nineteen Fifty, Vol. II. Paper Text. University of Chicago Press. Chicago, IL. 1993. ISBN:0-226-81518-8, ISBN13: 978-0-226-81518-3. Dewey:327.730951. LCCN:63-013072.

Audience: **u,f.**

Twitchett, Denis C. &　　　　DS751.72
Franke, Herbert (Editors)
Alien Regimes and Border States, 907-1368. John K. Fairbank & Denis Twitchett (Contribution by). Trade Cloth. Cambridge University Press. New York, NY. 1994. 816p. The Cambridge History of China Ser., Vol. 6 ISBN:0-521-24331-9, ISBN13: 978-0-521-24331-5. Dewey:951.02.

Audience: **f.**

Waley, Arthur　　　　DS757.5 .W3
The Opium War Through Chinese Eyes. Paper Text. Textbook Publishers. Temecula, CA. 2003. 256p. ISBN:0-7581-3509-2, ISBN13: 978-0-7581-3509-4. Dewey:951/.03.

Audience: **g,l,u,f.** *Ɓ*

Wong, R. Bin　　　　DS735.W79 1997
China Transformed: Historical Change and the Limits of European Experience. Book, Other. Cornell University Press. Ithaca, NY. 1997. 400p. ISBN:0-8014-3254-5, ISBN13: 978-0-8014-3254-5. Dewey:951. LCCN:97-023232.

Audience: **g,u,f.** *Choice, 1998.*

Yu-ming, Shaw　　　　BV3427.S828S5 1992
John Leighton Stuart and Twentieth-Century Chinese-American Relations. Trade Cloth. Harvard University Press. Cambridge, MA. 1992. 350p. East Asian Monographs, No. 158 ISBN:0-674-47835-5, ISBN13: 978-0-674-47835-0. Dewey:266/.51/092/. LCCN:92-032007.

Audience: **f.**

Zi, Zhongyun   **E183.8.C5Z54 2002**
No Exit?: The Origin and Evolution of U. S. Policy Toward
China, 1945-1950. Ciyun Zhang & Yanli Jia (Translators),
Michael H. Hunt (Foreword by). Trade Cloth. EastBridge.
Norwalk, CT. 2003. 334p. Voices of Asia Ser.
ISBN:1-891936-23-9, ISBN13: 978-1-891936-23-4.
Dewey:327.73051/09/044. LCCN:2003-000168.
Audience: **u,f.**   *Choice, 2004.*

China > Regional History

Arlington, Lewis C. &   **DS795.A7 1987**
 Lewisohn, William
In Search of Old Peking. Geremie Barme (Introduction by).
Trade Cloth. Oxford University Press, Inc. New York, NY. 1988.
436p. ISBN:0-19-584226-X, ISBN13: 978-0-19-584226-5.
Dewey:915.1/1560458. LCCN:87-028218.
Audience: **g,u,f.**

Blofeld, John Eaton   **DS795**
 Calthorpe
City of Lingering Splendour: A Frank Account of Old Peking's
Exotic Pleasures. Trade Paper. Shambhala Publications, Inc.
Boston, MA. 2001. 280p. ISBN:1-57062-637-5, ISBN13:
978-1-57062-637-1. Dewey:951.156. LCCN:89-101139.
Audience: **u,f.**

Cameron, Nigel   **DS796.H757C36 1991**
An Illustrated History of Hong Kong. Trade Cloth. Oxford
University Press, Inc. New York, NY. 1991. 388p.
ISBN:0-19-584997-3, ISBN13: 978-0-19-584997-4.
Dewey:951.25. LCCN:90-048787.
Audience: **g,u,f.**   *Choice, 1991.*

Cameron, Nigel   **DS795.3**
Old Peking Revisited. Trade Cloth. Cheng & Tsui Company.
Boston, MA. 2004. 104p. ISBN:962-7283-69-X, ISBN13:
978-962-7283-69-0. Dewey:951.15609.
Audience: **g,l,u,f.**

Carroll, John M.   **DS796.H757C38 2005**
Edge of Empires: Chinese Elites and British Colonials in Hong
Kong. Trade Cloth. Harvard University Press. Cambridge, MA.
2005. 274p. ISBN:0-674-01701-3, ISBN13: 978-0-674-01701-6.
Dewey:951.25/04. LCCN:2004-059693.
Audience: **g,u,f.**   *Choice, 2006.*

Chan, Ming K. (Editor)   **DS796.H757P74 1994**
Precarious Balance: Hong Kong Between China and Britain,
1842-1992. Trade Cloth. M. E. Sharpe Inc. Armonk, NY. 1994.
235p. Hong Kong Becoming China Ser. ISBN:1-56324-380-6,
ISBN13: 978-1-56324-380-6. Dewey:951.25/04.
LCCN:93-032290.
Audience: **g,u,f.**

Chan, Ming K. & Lo,   **DS796.H757C428 2006**
 Shiu Hing
Historical Dictionary of the Hong Kong SAR and the Macao
SAR. Trade Cloth. Scarecrow Press, Inc. Lanham, MD. 2006.
328p. Historical Dictionaries of Asia, Oceania, and the Middle
East Ser., Vol. 60 ISBN:0-8108-5061-3, ISBN13:
978-0-8108-5061-3. Dewey:951.25003. LCCN:2006-003663.
Audience: **f.**

Chan, Ming K. & So,   **DS796.H757**
 Alvin Y. (Editors)
Crisis and Transformation in China's Hong Kong. Lynn T.
White (Foreword by). Trade Cloth. M. E. Sharpe Inc. Armonk,

NY. 2002. 415p. Hong Kong Becoming China: Beyond 1997
Ser. ISBN:0-7656-1001-9, ISBN13: 978-0-7656-1001-0.
Dewey:951.25/05. LCCN:2002-019092.
Audience: **g,u,f.**

Dimbleby, Jonathan   **DS796.H757D56 1997**
The Last Governor: Chris Patten and the Handover of Hong
Kong. Trade Cloth. Little Brown & Company. New York, NY.
1997. xvi, 461p. ISBN:0-316-64018-2, ISBN13:
978-0-316-64018-3. Dewey:951.25. LCCN:98-115639.
Audience: **g,u,f.**

Duara, Prasenjit   **JC311.D83 2003**
Sovereignty and Authenticity: Manchukuo and the East Asian
Modern. Book, Other. Rowman & Littlefield Publishers, Inc.
Lanham, MD. 2003. 320p. State and Society in East Asia Ser.
ISBN:0-7425-2577-5, ISBN13: 978-0-7425-2577-1.
Dewey:320.54/095. LCCN:2002-151157.
Audience: **u,f.**   *Choice, 2003.*

Faure, David (Editor)   **DS796.H74 S645 1997**
A Documentary History of Hong Kong: Society. Trade Paper.
Hong Kong University Press. Hong Kong, 1997. 388p.
ISBN:962-209-393-0, ISBN13: 978-962-209-393-5.
Dewey:951.25/04.
Audience: **f.**

Faure, David & Pui-tak,   **HC470.3**
 Lee (Editors)
Documentary History of Hong Kong: Economy. Trade Cloth.
Hong Kong University Press. Hong Kong, 2004. 380p.
ISBN:962-209-616-6, ISBN13: 978-962-209-616-5.
Dewey:330.9/5125.
Audience: **f.**

Hayes, James   **DS796.H7**
The Rural Communities of Hong Kong: Studies and Themes.
Trade Cloth. Oxford University Press, Inc. New York, NY. 1985.
318p. EASSM Ser. ISBN:0-19-581504-1, ISBN13:
978-0-19-581504-7. Dewey:307.72/0951/25.
Audience: **f.**

Johnson, Graham E. &   **DS796.C2J64 1999**
 Peterson, Glen D.
Historical Dictionary of Guangzhou (Canton) and Guangdong.
Trade Cloth. Scarecrow Press, Inc. Lanham, MD. 1999. 320p.
Historical Dictionaries of Cities of the World Ser., No. 6
ISBN:0-8108-3516-9, ISBN13: 978-0-8108-3516-0.
Dewey:951/.27/00202. LCCN:98-020324.
Audience: **u,f.**

Johnson, Linda C.   **DS796.S257J614 1995**
Shanghai: From Market Town to Treaty Port, 1074-1858. Trade
Cloth. Stanford University Press. Palo Alto, CA. 1995. xvi-440p.
ISBN:0-8047-2294-3, ISBN13: 978-0-8047-2294-0.
Dewey:951/.132. LCCN:94-025034.
Audience: **u,f.**

Lee, Leo Ou-fan   **DS796.S25L43 1999**
Shanghai Modern: The Flowering of a New Urban Culture in
China, 1930-1945. Trade Cloth. Harvard University Press.
Cambridge, MA. 1999. 436p. Interpretations of Asia Ser.
ISBN:0-674-80550-X, ISBN13: 978-0-674-80550-7.
Dewey:306/.0951/132. LCCN:98-032318.
Audience: **g,u,f.**   *Choice, 2000.*

Lethbridge, Henry J.   **DS793.Y8**
Hong Kong: Stability and Change: A Collection of Essays.
Trade Cloth. Oxford University Press, Inc. New York, NY. 1979.
275p. ISBN:0-19-580402-3, ISBN13: 978-0-19-580402-7.
Dewey:951/.2500421.

Audience: **f.**

Levine, Steven I.   **DS777.5425.M36L48**
Anvil of Victory: The Communist Revolution in Manchuria.
Cloth Text. Columbia University Press. New York, NY. 1987.
384p. ISBN:0-231-06436-5, ISBN13: 978-0-231-06436-1.
Dewey:951/.8042. LCCN:86-019821.

Audience: **u,f.**

Marks, Robert B.   **HC427.6 .M37 1997**
Tigers, Rice, Silk, and Silt: Environment and Economy in Late
Imperial South China. Alfred W. Crosby & Donald Worster
(Contribution by). Trade Cloth. Cambridge University Press.
New York, NY. 1998. 407p. Studies in Environment and History
ISBN:0-521-59177-5, ISBN13: 978-0-521-59177-5.
Dewey:951/.026. LCCN:96-053322.

Audience: **u,f.**

Morris, Jan   **DS796.H757M67 1988**
Hong Kong. Trade Cloth. Random House, Inc. New York, NY.
1988. 352p. ISBN:0-394-55097-8, ISBN13: 978-0-394-55097-8.
Dewey:951/.25. LCCN:88-042677.

Audience: **g,u,f.**

Perry, Elizabeth & Li, Xun   **HD8738.P47 1997**
Proletarian Power: Shanghai in the Cultural Revolution. Trade
Paper. Westview Press. Boulder, CO. 1997. 264p. Transitions
Ser., :Asia and Asian America ISBN:0-8133-2166-2, ISBN13:
978-0-8133-2166-0. Dewey:331.8/0951132. LCCN:96-042940.
Audience: **f.** *Choice, 1997.*

Rough Guides Staff &   **DS796.H73**
  Brown, Jules
The Rough Guide to Hong Kong and Macau. Ed. 6. Trade
Paper. Rough Guides, Ltd. London, 2006. 416p. Rough Guide
Travel Guides ISBN:1-84353-534-3, ISBN13:
978-1-84353-534-8. Dewey:915.1/25/046.

Audience: **g,l,u,f.**

Salaff, Janet W.   **HQ687**
Working Daughters of Hong Kong: Female Piety or Power in
the Family? Ernest Q. Campbell (Contribution by). Cloth Text.
Cambridge University Press. New York, NY. 1981. 337p.
American Sociological Association Rose Monographs
ISBN:0-521-23679-7, ISBN13: 978-0-521-23679-9.
Dewey:306.8/5/08995105125. LCCN:80-023909.

Audience: **f.**

Schoppa, R. Keith   **JQ1519.C442**
Chinese Elites and Political Change: Zhejiang Province in the
Early Twentieth Century. Trade Cloth. Harvard University Press.
Cambridge, MA. 1982. 304p. East Asian Ser., No. 96
ISBN:0-674-12325-5, ISBN13: 978-0-674-12325-0.
Dewey:305.52. LCCN:81-007075.

Audience: **f.**

Smith, Arthur H.   **DS793.M234**
Village Life in China: A Study in Sociology. Library Binding.
Greenwood Publishing Group, Inc. Portsmouth, NH. 1986.
ISBN:0-8371-1167-6, ISBN13: 978-0-8371-1167-4.
Dewey:951/.009734.

Audience: **u,f.**

Snow, Philip   **DS796.H74S64 2003**
The Fall of Hong Kong: Britain, China, and the Japanese
Occupation. Cloth over Boards. Yale University Press.
Cumberland, RI. 2003. 528p. ISBN:0-300-09352-7, ISBN13:
978-0-300-09352-0. Dewey:940.5425. LCCN:2002-155540.

Audience: **g,u,f.** *Choice, 2004.*

Strand, David   **DS795.3.S82 1989**
🄴 Rickshaw Beijing: City People and Politics in the 1920s.
E-Book. NetLibrary, Inc. Boulder, CO. 1989.
ISBN:0-585-10827-7, ISBN13: 978-0-585-10827-8.
Dewey:951/.156041.

Audience: **g,u,f.** *Choice, 1990.*

Tsang, Steve   **DS796.H757**
A Modern History of Hong Kong: 1841-1998. Cloth over
Boards. I. B. Tauris & Company, Ltd. London, 2004. 356p.
ISBN:1-86064-184-9, ISBN13: 978-1-86064-184-8.
Dewey:951.25/04. LCCN:2004-303820.

Audience: **g,l,u,f.** *Choice, 2004.*

Van Kemenade, Willem   **DS706.K464**
China, Hong Kong, Taiwan, Inc. Trade Cloth. Random House
Value Publishing. New York, NY. 1998. ISBN:0-517-28893-1,
ISBN13: 978-0-517-28893-1. Dewey:951.

Audience: **g,u,f.**

Vogel, Ezra F.   **DS796.C2V6**
Canton under Communism: Programs and Politics in a
Provincial Capital, 1949-1968. Trade Cloth. Harvard University
Press. Cambridge, MA. 1969. 468p. East Asian Monographs,
No. 41 ISBN:0-674-09475-1, ISBN13: 978-0-674-09475-8.
Dewey:309.1/51/27. LCCN:70-091631.

Audience: **u,f.**

Vogel, Ezra F.   **HC460.5.V64 1991**
The Four Little Dragons: The Spread of Industrialization in East
Asia. Trade Cloth. Harvard University Press. Cambridge, MA.
1991. x, 138p. The Edwin O. Reischauer Lectures
ISBN:0-674-31525-1, ISBN13: 978-0-674-31525-9.
Dewey:338.095. LCCN:91-016051.

Audience: **g,l,u,f.** *Choice, 1992.*

Von Glahn, Richard   **DS793.S8V66 1987**
The Country of Streams and Grottoes: Expansion, Settlement,
and the Civilizing of the Sichuan Frontier in Song Times. Trade
Cloth. Harvard University Press. Cambridge, MA. 1988. 304p.
Harvard East Asian Monographs, Vol. 123 ISBN:0-674-17543-3,
ISBN13: 978-0-674-17543-3. Dewey:951/.38024.
LCCN:87-013526.

Audience: **f.**

Wasserstrom, Jeff   **DS796.S257**
Shanghai: Global City. Trade Paper. Routledge. New York, NY.
2005. 224p. Asia's Global Cities Ser. ISBN:0-415-21328-2,
ISBN13: 978-0-415-21328-8. Dewey:951.132.

Audience: **u,f.**

Wasserstrom, Jeffrey N.   **LA1134.S4W37 1991**
Student Protests in Twentieth-Century China: The View from
Shanghai. Trade Cloth. Stanford University Press. Palo Alto,
CA. 1991. 444p. ISBN:0-8047-1881-4, ISBN13:
978-0-8047-1881-3. Dewey:371.8/1/0951. LCCN:90-022307.

Audience: **f.** *Choice, 1992.*

Welsh, Frank   **DS796.H757 W45 1993**
A Borrowed Place: The History of Hong Kong. Gordon Wise
(Editor). Trade Cloth. Kodansha America, Inc. New York, NY.

1993. 640p. ISBN:1-56836-002-9, ISBN13: 978-1-56836-002-7. Dewey:951.25. LCCN:93-005017.

Audience: **g,u,f.**

Wou, Odoric Y. K.   **DS793.H5W6 1994**
Mobilizing the Masses: Building Revolution in Henan. Trade Cloth. Stanford University Press. Palo Alto, CA. 1994. xi, 478p. ISBN:0-8047-2142-4, ISBN13: 978-0-8047-2142-4. Dewey:951/.18042.220. LCCN:93-020624.

Audience: **f.** *Choice, 1994.*

Xiaolong, Qiu   **PS3553.H537D43 2000**
Death of a Red Heroine: An Inspector Chen Investigation. Trade Cloth. Soho Press, Inc. New York, NY. 2000. 463p. ISBN:1-56947-193-2, ISBN13: 978-1-56947-193-7. Dewey:813/.6. LCCN:00-020362.

Audience: **g,l,u,f.**

China > Language

De Francis, John   **PL1171 .D4 1972**
Nationalism and Language Reform in China. Library Binding. Hippocrene Books, Inc. New York, NY. 1972. xii, 306p. ISBN:0-374-92095-8, ISBN13: 978-0-374-92095-1. Dewey:495.1/09/04. LCCN:74-187315.

Audience: **f.**

DeFrancis, John   **PL1455.A33 2003**
ABC Chinese-English Comprehensive Dictionary. Trade Cloth. University of Hawaii Press. Honolulu, HI. 2003. 1,464p. ABC Chinese Dictionary Ser. ISBN:0-8248-2766-X, ISBN13: 978-0-8248-2766-3. Dewey:495.1/321. LCCN:2003-040296.

Audience: **g,l,u,f.**

DeFrancis, John   **PL1171 .D83 1986**
The Chinese Language: Fact and Fantasy. Trade Cloth. University of Hawaii Press. Honolulu, HI. 1984. 342p. ISBN:0-8248-1068-6, ISBN13: 978-0-8248-1068-9. Dewey:495.1. LCCN:84-008546.

Audience: **g,u,f.**

Matthews, Stephen &   **PL1733.M38 1994**
  Yip, Virginia
Cantonese: A Comprehensive Grammar. Trade Paper. Routledge. New York, NY. 1994. 448p. Routledge Grammars Ser. ISBN:0-415-08945-X, ISBN13: 978-0-415-08945-6. Dewey:495.1/7. LCCN:93-036173.

Audience: **f.**

Norman, Jerry   **PL1075 .N67 1988**
Chinese. S. R. Anderson, J. Bresnan, B. Comrie, W. Dressler, C. Ewen & R. Lass (Contribution by). Cloth Text. Cambridge University Press. New York, NY. 1988. 304p. Cambridge Language Surveys Ser. ISBN:0-521-22809-3, ISBN13: 978-0-521-22809-1. Dewey:495.1/09. LCCN:87-006570.

Audience: **g,f.** *Choice, 1988.*

Ramsey, S. Robert   **PL1071.R34 1986**
The Languages of China. Trade Cloth. Princeton University Press. Princeton, NJ. 1987. 353p. ISBN:0-691-06694-9, ISBN13: 978-0-691-06694-3. Dewey:409/.51. LCCN:86-012212.

Audience: **f.**

China > Literature

Baynes, Cary F. &   **PL2478**
  Wilhelm, Richard (Translators)
The I Ching: Or Book of Changes. Ed. 3. Hellmut Wilhelm (Produced by). Cloth Text. Princeton University Press. Princeton, NJ. 1967. 806p. Bollingen Ser., No. 19 ISBN:0-691-09750-X, ISBN13: 978-0-691-09750-3. Dewey:299.51. LCCN:67-024740.

Audience: **g,l,u,f.**

Berry, Chris   **PN1993.5.C4B47 2004**
Postsocialist Cinema in Post-Mao China: The Cultural Revolution after the Cultural Revolution. Paper over Boards. Routledge. New York, NY. 2004. 272p. East Asia History, Politics, Sociology and Culture Ser. ISBN:0-415-94786-3, ISBN13: 978-0-415-94786-2. Dewey:791.43/0951. LCCN:2003-026390.

Audience: **u,f.**

Berry, Christopher J. &   **PN1993.5.C4B44 2006**
  Farquhar, Mary Ann
China on Screen: Cinema and Nation. Trade Cloth. Columbia University Press. New York, NY. 2006. 336p. ISBN:0-231-13706-0, ISBN13: 978-0-231-13706-5. Dewey:791.43/0951. LCCN:2005-053930.

Audience: **g,u,f.**

Birch, Cyril (Editor,   **PL2658.E1 B5**
  Translator)
Anthology of Chinese Literature: From the Fourteenth Century to the Present Day, Vol. 2. Trade Paper. Grove/Atlantic, Inc. New York, NY. 1988. 512p. ISBN:0-8021-5090-X, ISBN13: 978-0-8021-5090-5. Dewey:895.108. LCCN:65-014202.

Audience: **g,l,u,f.**

Birch, Cyril (Editor,   **PL2658.E1**
  Translator)
Anthology of Chinese Literature: From the Earliest Times to the Fourteenth Century. Donald Keene (Editor). Trade Paper. Grove/Atlantic, Inc. New York, NY. 1988. 528p. Anthology of Chinese Literature Ser., Vol. 1 ISBN:0-8021-5038-1, ISBN13: 978-0-8021-5038-7. Dewey:895.108. LCCN:65-014202.

Audience: **g,u,f.**

Chang, Kang-i Sun   **PL2278.W65 1999**
  (Editor), et al.
Women Writers of Traditional China: An Anthology of Poetry and Criticism. Haun Saussy & Charles Yim-tze Kwong (Editors). Trade Cloth. Stanford University Press. Palo Alto, CA. 1999. xxiv, 891p. ISBN:0-8047-3230-2, ISBN13: 978-0-8047-3230-7. Dewey:895.1/10809287. LCCN:99-019030.

Audience: **g,u,f.** *Choice, 2000.*

Clark, Paul   **PN1993.5.C4**
Reinventing China: A Generation and Its Films. Trade Cloth. Chinese University of Hong Kong, The. Hong Kong SAR, 2005. 280p. ISBN:962-996-207-1, ISBN13: 978-962-996-207-4. Dewey:791.430951.

Audience: **g,u,f.** *Choice, 2005.*

Confucius   **PL2478.L8 2000**
The Analects. Arthur Waley (Editor, Translator), Sarah Allan (Introduction by). Trade Cloth. Alfred A. Knopf Inc. New York, NY. 2001. 304p. ISBN:0-375-41204-2, ISBN13: 978-0-375-41204-2. Dewey:181/.112. LCCN:00-053460.

Audience: **g,l,u,f.**

Embree, Ainslie T. & de   **Z7046.G8 1989**
  Bary, Wm. Theodore
A Guide to the Oriental Classics. Ed. 3. William T. Debary &
Amy V. Heinrich (Editors). Trade Cloth. Columbia University
Press. New York, NY. 1989. 325p. ISBN:0-231-06674-0,
ISBN13: 978-0-231-06674-7. Dewey:016.89. LCCN:88-028538.
Audience: **g,u,f.**

Hsia, C. T.   **PL2443**
A History of Modern Chinese Fiction. Ed. 3. David
Der-Weiwang (Introduction by). Trade Paper. DIANE Publishing
Company. Collingdale, PA. 2004. 726p. ISBN:0-7567-7315-6,
ISBN13: 978-0-7567-7315-1. Dewey:895.1/3/509.
Audience: **u,f.**

Lau, Joseph S. M. &   **PL2658.E1C64 1995**
  Goldblatt, Howard (Editors)
The Columbia Anthology of Modern Chinese Literature. Trade
Cloth. Eastern European Monographs. Bradenton, FL. 1995.
726p. Modern Asian Literature Ser. ISBN:0-231-08002-6,
ISBN13: 978-0-231-08002-6. Dewey:895.1/08005.
LCCN:94-035304.
Audience: **g,u,f.** *Choice, 1995.*

Lee, Ou-Fan Leo   **PL2277.L4 1973**
The Romantic Generation of Modern Chinese Writers. Trade
Cloth. Harvard University Press. Cambridge, MA. 1973. 320p.
East Asian Monographs, No. 71 ISBN:0-674-77930-4, ISBN13:
978-0-674-77930-3. Dewey:895.1/0/914. LCCN:73-075058.
Audience: **g,u,f.** *B*

Legge, James
  (Translator)
The Chinese Classics: With a Translation, Critical and
Exegetical Notes, Prolegomena, and Copious Indexes, Set. Trade
Cloth. S M C Publishing, Inc. Taipei, 1991. 587p.
ISBN:957-638-038-3, ISBN13: 978-957-638-038-9.
Dewey:895.1082.
Audience: **g,l,u,f.**

Lin, Yutang   **BD431.L42 1996**
The Importance of Living. Trade Cloth. HarperCollins
Publishers. New York, NY. 1996. 448p. ISBN:0-688-14717-8,
ISBN13: 978-0-688-14717-4. Dewey:128. LCCN:95-042352.
Audience: **g,l,u,f.**

Link, Perry   **PL2658.E8**
Roses and Thorns: The Second Blooming of the Hundred
Flowers in Chinese Fiction, 1979-80. Trade Paper. University of
California Press. Berkeley, CA. 1986. 300p.
ISBN:0-520-04980-2, ISBN13: 978-0-520-04980-2.
Dewey:895.1/301/08. LCCN:83-009147.
Audience: **g,u,f.** *B*

Liu, James J.   **PL2307.L572 1982**
The Interlingual Critic: Interpreting Chinese Poetry. Trade Cloth.
Indiana University Press. Bloomington, IN. 1982. 160p.
ISBN:0-253-33030-0, ISBN13: 978-0-253-33030-7.
Dewey:895.1/1/009. LCCN:81-047010.
Audience: **g,u,f.** *B*

Mair, Victor H. (Editor)   **PL2658.E1C65 1994**
The Columbia Anthology of Traditional Chinese Literature.
Trade Cloth. Columbia University Press. New York, NY. 1995.
1372p. Translations from the Asian Classics
ISBN:0-231-07428-X, ISBN13: 978-0-231-07428-5.
Dewey:895.1/08. LCCN:93-048174.
Audience: **g,l,u,f.** *Choice, 1996.*

Mair, Victor H.   **PL2658.E1S53 2000**
The Shorter Columbia Anthology of Traditional Chinese
Literature. Trade Cloth. Columbia University Press. New York,
NY. 2000. 704p. Translations from the Asian Classics
ISBN:0-231-11998-4, ISBN13: 978-0-231-11998-6.
Dewey:895.1/08. LCCN:00-035878.
Audience: **g,u,f.**

Murck, Alfreda & Fong,   **NK3634.A2 W67 1991**
  Wen C.
Words and Images: Chinese Poetry, Calligraphy, and Painting.
Trade Cloth. Princeton University Press. Princeton, NJ. 1991.
616p. ISBN:0-691-04096-6, ISBN13: 978-0-691-04096-7.
Dewey:745.6/19951. LCCN:90-024239.
Audience: **g,u,f.** *Choice, 1992.*

Nienhauser, William H.   **Z3108.L5I53 1985**
  Jr. (Editor, Compiled by)
The Indiana Companion to Traditional Chinese Literature, Vol.
1. Charles O. Hartman, Y. W. Ma & Stephen H. West (Editors).
Trade Cloth. Indiana University Press. Bloomington, IN. 1986.
1096p. ISBN:0-253-32983-3, ISBN13: 978-0-253-32983-7.
Dewey:895.1/09. LCCN:83-049511.
Audience: **f.** *B Choice, 1999, 1986.*

Nienhauser, William H.   **PL2264**
  Jr. (Editor), et al.
The Indiana Companion to Traditional Chinese Literature, Vol.
2. Charles Hartman & Scott W. Galer (Editors). Trade Cloth.
DIANE Publishing Company. Collingdale, PA. 2004. 547p.
ISBN:0-7567-7318-0, ISBN13: 978-0-7567-7318-2.
Dewey:895.1/09.
Audience: **f.** *Choice, 1999, 1986.*

Owen, Stephen (Editor,   **PL2658.E1A814 1996**
  Translator)
An Anthology of Chinese Literature: Beginnings to 1911. Trade
Cloth. W. W. Norton & Company, Inc. New York, NY. 1996.
928p. ISBN:0-393-03823-8, ISBN13: 978-0-393-03823-1.
Dewey:895.1/08. LCCN:95-011409.
Audience: **g,l,u,f.** *Choice, 1996.*

Waley, Arthur   **PL3277.E3**
Translations from the Chinese. Trade Paper. Random House,
Inc. New York, NY. 1971. ISBN:0-394-71156-4, ISBN13:
978-0-394-71156-0. Dewey:895.110822. LCCN:41-004061.
Audience: **g,l,u,f.** *B*

Wang, Jing   **DS779.23.W36 1996**
High Culture Fever: Politics, Aesthetics, and Ideology in Deng's
China. Trade Cloth. University of California Press. Berkeley,
CA. 1996. 399p. ISBN:0-520-20294-5, ISBN13:
978-0-520-20294-8. Dewey:001.1/0951. LCCN:96-005580.
Audience: **g,u,f.** *Choice, 1997.*

Watson, Burton   **PL2280.W3**
Early Chinese Literature. Trade Paper. Columbia University
Press. New York, NY. 1962. 304p. ISBN:0-231-08671-7,
ISBN13: 978-0-231-08671-4. Dewey:895.109001.
LCCN:62-017552.
Audience: **g,u,f.** *B*

Watson, Burton   **B128.H66**
  (Translator)
Hsun Tzu: Basic Writings. Ed. 2. Trade Paper. Columbia
University Press. New York, NY. 1996. 177p. Translations from
the Asian Classics ISBN:0-231-10689-0, ISBN13:
978-0-231-10689-4. Dewey:181.09512.
Audience: **g,l,u,f.**

Watson, Burton   **DS735.A2**
Records of the Historian: Chapters from the Shih Chi of Ssu-ma
Ch'ien. Trade Paper. Columbia University Press. New York, NY.
1969. 356p. ISBN:0-231-03321-4, ISBN13: 978-0-231-03321-3.
Dewey:931. LCCN:70-089860.

Audience: **u,f.**

Watson, Burton   **PL2470**
The Tso Chuan: Selections from China's Oldest Narrative
History. Trade Paper. Columbia University Press. New York,
NY. 1992. 232p. ISBN:0-231-06715-1, ISBN13:
978-0-231-06715-7. Dewey:931/.03.

Audience: **g,u,f.**

Yue, Gang   **PL2303.Y83 1999**
The Mouth That Begs: Hunger, Cannibalism and the Politics of
Eating in Modern China. Trade Cloth. Duke University Press.
Durham, NC. 1999. viii, 447p. Post-Contemporary Interventions
Ser. ISBN:0-8223-2308-7, ISBN13: 978-0-8223-2308-2.
Dewey:895.1/09358. LCCN:98-045873.

Audience: **g,f.** *Choice, 2000.*

Zhen, Ni   **PN1993.5.C4N52 2002**
Memoirs from the Beijing Film Academy: The Genesis of
China's Fifth Generation. Chris Berry (Translator). Trade Cloth.
Duke University Press. Durham, NC. 2002. 240p. Asia-Pacific
Ser. ISBN:0-8223-2956-5, ISBN13: 978-0-8223-2956-5.
Dewey:791.43/0233/092251 B. LCCN:2002-005107.

Audience: **g,u,f.** *Choice, 2003.*

China > Literature > Drama

Broman, Sven   **PN1979.S5B68 1981**
Chinese Shadow Theatre. Trade Paper. Almqvist & Wiksell
International. Stockholm, 1981. 250p. Ethnographical Museum
of Sweden Monograph Ser. ISBN:91-85344-01-X, ISBN13:
978-91-85344-01-7. Dewey:791.5. LCCN:85-118648.

Audience: **u,f.**

Chen, Xiaomei (Editor,   **PL2658.E5R43 2003**
Introduction by)
Reading the Right Text: An Anthology of Contemporary
Chinese Drama. Trade Cloth. University of Hawaii Press.
Honolulu, HI. 2003. 480p. ISBN:0-8248-2505-5, ISBN13:
978-0-8248-2505-8. Dewey:895.1/2508. LCCN:2002-155363.

Audience: **l,u,f.**

Fei, Faye Chunfang   **PN2871.C535**
(Editor)
Chinese Theories of Theater and Performance from Confucius to
the Present. Trade Paper. University of Michigan Press. Chicago,
IL. 2002. 232p. ISBN:0-472-08923-4, ISBN13:
978-0-472-08923-9. Dewey:792.0951. LCCN:99-017404.

Audience: **u,f.**

Hsu, Tao-Ching   **PN2871**
The Chinese Conception of the Theatre. Cloth Text. University
of Washington Press. Seattle, WA. 1985. 676p.
ISBN:0-295-96034-5, ISBN13: 978-0-295-96034-0.
Dewey:792/.0951. LCCN:83-005964.

Audience: **u,f.**

Shangren, Kong   **PS1449.C85Z75**
The Peach Blossom Fan. Trade Cloth. New World Press.
Beijing, 2001. 234p. Classic Drama Ser. ISBN:7-80005-432-2,
ISBN13: 978-7-80005-432-7. Dewey:813/.4.

Audience: **f.**

Tang, Xianzu   **PL2695.M8E5 2002**
The Peony Pavilion. Ed. 2. Trade Paper. Indiana University
Press. Bloomington, IN. 2002. 400p. ISBN:0-253-21527-7,
ISBN13: 978-0-253-21527-7. Dewey:895.1/24.
LCCN:2002-068779.

Audience: **l,u,f.** *Choice, 2002.*

Tang, Xianzu   **PL2693.H76**
The Peony Pavilion. Cyril Birch (Translator). Trade Paper.
Cheng & Tsui Company. Boston, MA. 2000. 360p.
ISBN:0-88727-206-1, ISBN13: 978-0-88727-206-6.
Dewey:895.1/24. LCCN:79-009631.

Audience: **u,f.** *Choice, 2002.*

Tung Chieh-Yuan   **PL2687.T9H813 1994**
Master Tung's Western Chamber Romance: A Chinese
Chantefable. Li-Li Chen (Introduction by). Trade Paper.
Columbia University Press. New York, NY. 1994. 238p.
ISBN:0-231-10119-8, ISBN13: 978-0-231-10119-6.
Dewey:895.1/142. LCCN:94-018056.

Audience: **f.**

China > Literature > Traditional Poetry

Birrell, Anne M.   **ML3746**
Popular Songs and Ballads of Han China. Trade Cloth.
Routledge. New York, NY. 1988. 370p. ISBN:0-04-895028-9,
ISBN13: 978-0-04-895028-4. Dewey:784.4/951.

Audience: **f.**

Chaves, Jonathan   **PL2658.E3**
(Editor, Translator)
The Columbia Book of Later Chinese Poetry: Yuan, Ming, and
Ch'ing Dynasties (1279-1911). Cloth Text. Columbia University
Press. New York, NY. 1988. 520p. ISBN:0-231-06148-X,
ISBN13: 978-0-231-06148-3. Dewey:895.1/14/08.
LCCN:86-002302.

Audience: **g,u,f.** *Choice, 1987.*

Faurot, Jeannette L.   **PL2658.E3**
Drinking with the Moon: A Guide to Classical Chinese Poetry.
Jiang Yizhu (Editor). Trade Cloth. China Books & Periodicals,
Inc. South San Francisco, CA. 1998. 150p.
ISBN:0-8351-2641-2, ISBN13: 978-0-8351-2641-0.
Dewey:895.1/108.

Audience: **g,u,f.**

Hawkes, David   **PL2675**
A Little Primer of Tu Fu. Trade Paper. Chinese University of
Hong Kong - Research Centre for Translation, The. Shatin, N.T.,
1994. 246p. Renditions Paperbacks Ser. ISBN:962-7255-02-5,
ISBN13: 978-962-7255-02-4. Dewey:895.1/1/3.

Audience: **g,u,f.**

Hung, William   **Q172.5.S96**
Tu Fu, China's Greatest Poet. Paper Text. Textbook Publishers.
Temecula, CA. 2003. x, 300p. ISBN:0-7581-4322-2, ISBN13:
978-0-7581-4322-8. Dewey:3.7.

Audience: **g,u,f.**

Kojiro, Yoshikawa   **PL2323**
Five Hundred Years of Chinese Poetry, 1150-1650: The Chin,
Yuan, and Ming Dynasties. John T. Wixted (Translator). Trade
Paper. Princeton University Press. Princeton, NJ. 1992. 236p.
Library of Asian Translations ISBN:0-691-01522-8, ISBN13:
978-0-691-01522-4. Dewey:895.1/14/09.

Audience: **g,u,f.** *Choice, 1990.*

Kojiro, Yoshikawa   PL2322.5.Y6713 1989
Five Hundred Years of Chinese Poetry, 1150-1650: The Chin, Yuan, and Ming Dynasties. John T. Wixted (Translator). Trade Cloth. Princeton University Press. Princeton, NJ. 1989. 236p. Library of Asian Translations ISBN:0-691-06768-6, ISBN13: 978-0-691-06768-1. Dewey:895.1/14/09. LCCN:88-037432.

Audience: **f.** *Choice, 1990.*

Liu, James J.   PL2307.L57
The Art of Chinese Poetry. Trade Paper. University of Chicago Press. Chicago, IL. 1966. 171p. ISBN:0-226-48687-7, ISBN13: 978-0-226-48687-1. Dewey:895.1/1/009. LCCN:62-007475.

Audience: **g,l,u,f.**

Liu, Wu-Chi & Lo,   PL2658.E3S84 1990
Irving Y. (Editors)
Sunflower Splendor: Three Thousand Years of Chinese Poetry. Trade Cloth. Indiana University Press. Bloomington, IN. 1990. 696p. ISBN:0-253-35580-X, ISBN13: 978-0-253-35580-5. Dewey:895.1/1008. LCCN:90-039420.

Audience: **g,u,f.**

Lo, Irving Y. & Schultz,   PL2537.W28 1986
William (Editors)
Waiting for the Unicorn: Poems and Lyrics of China's Last Dynasty, 1644-1911. Trade Cloth. Indiana University Press. Bloomington, IN. 1986. 456p. Chinese Literature in Translation Ser. ISBN:0-253-36321-7, ISBN13: 978-0-253-36321-3. Dewey:895.1/14/08. LCCN:85-042816.

Audience: **g,u,f.** *Choice, 1987.*

Owen, Stephen   PL2291.O84 1996
The End of the Chinese 'Middle Ages': Essays in Mid-Tang Literary Culture. Trade Cloth. Stanford University Press. Palo Alto, CA. 1996. 209p. ISBN:0-8047-2666-3, ISBN13: 978-0-8047-2666-5. Dewey:895.1/09003. LCCN:95-025619.

Audience: **f.** *Choice, 1996.*

Owen, Stephen   PL2321
The Great Age of Chinese Poetry: The High T'ang. Trade Cloth. Yale University Press. Cumberland, RI. 1980. 456p. ISBN:0-300-02367-7, ISBN13: 978-0-300-02367-1. Dewey:895.1/13/09. LCCN:80-000141.

Audience: **f.** ℬ

Owen, Stephen   PL2307
The Poetry of the Early T'ang. Trade Cloth. Yale University Press. Cumberland, RI. 1977. xv, 455p. ISBN:0-300-02103-8, ISBN13: 978-0-300-02103-5. Dewey:895.1/12/09. LCCN:77-003884.

Audience: **f.** ℬ

Rexroth, Kenneth &   PL2658.E3
Ling Chung (Translators)
The Orchid Boat. Trade Paper. New Directions Publishing Corporation. New York, NY. 1984. 168p. ISBN:0-8164-9333-2, ISBN13: 978-0-8164-9333-3. Dewey:895.1/1/008. LCCN:72-006791.

Audience: **g,u,f.**

Waley, Arthur   PL2997.S452 W3
(Translator)
The Book of Songs. Trade Paper. Grove/Atlantic, Inc. New York, NY. 1960. ISBN:0-394-17331-7, ISBN13: 978-0-394-17331-3. Dewey:895.11082.

Audience: **g,l,u,f.**

Waley, Arthur D.   PL2658.E3 W26 1976
(Editor)
Chinese Poems. Trade Paper. Routledge. New York, NY. 1982. 213p. ISBN:0-04-895021-1, ISBN13: 978-0-04-895021-5. Dewey:895.1/1/008. LCCN:80-513947.

Audience: **g,l,u,f.**

Waley, Arthur   PL2478.F7 1987
(Translator)
The Books of Songs: The Ancient Chinese Classic of Poetry. Stephen Owen (Introduction by). Trade Paper. Grove/Atlantic, Inc. New York, NY. 1987. 368p. ISBN:0-8021-3021-6, ISBN13: 978-0-8021-3021-1. Dewey:895.1/11/08. LCCN:87-007440.

Audience: **g,u,f.**

Watson, Burton   PL2658.E3.W34
(Translator)
Chinese Rhyme-Prose: Poems in the Fu Form from the Han and Six Dynasties Period. Cloth Text. Columbia University Press. New York, NY. 1971. 128p. ISBN:0-231-03553-5, ISBN13: 978-0-231-03553-8. Dewey:895.1/1/2. LCCN:75-159674.

Audience: **f.** ℬ

Watson, Burton   PL2658.E3
The Columbia Book of Chinese Poetry: From Early Times to the Thirteenth Century. Trade Paper. Columbia University Press. New York, NY. 1986. 385p. Translations from the Oriental Classics Ser. ISBN:0-231-05683-4, ISBN13: 978-0-231-05683-0. Dewey:895.1/1/008. LCCN:83-026182.

Audience: **g,u,f.** ℬ

Watson, Burton   PL2687
The Old Man Who Does As He Pleases. Trade Paper. Columbia University Press. New York, NY. 1994. 0p. ISBN:0-231-10155-4, ISBN13: 978-0-231-10155-4. Dewey:895.1/1/4. LCCN:73-010278.

Audience: **f.**

Watson, Burton   PL2685 .A28
(Translator)
Su Tung-P'o: Selections from a Sung Dynasty Poet. Paper Text. Columbia University Press. New York, NY. 1977. ISBN:0-231-02799-0, ISBN13: 978-0-231-02799-1. Dewey:895.11. LCCN:65-013619.

Audience: **f.**

Weinberger, Eliot &   PL2676.A683W4 1987
Paz, Octavio
Nineteen Ways of Looking at Wang Wei: How a Chinese Poem is Translated. Trade Paper. Moyer Bell. Kingston, RI. 1987. 64p. ISBN:0-918825-14-8, ISBN13: 978-0-918825-14-8. Dewey:895.1/13. LCCN:85-021654.

Audience: **g,u,f.**

Yu, Pauline   PL2676.A285
The Poetry of Wang Wei. Trade Cloth. Indiana University Press. Bloomington, IN. 1980. 288p. Chinese Literature in Translation Ser. ISBN:0-253-17772-3, ISBN13: 978-0-253-17772-8. Dewey:895.1/13. LCCN:79-003623.

Audience: **g,u,f.** ℬ

Yuan, Qu   PL2521.C524 1985
The Songs of the South: An Anthology of Ancient Chinese Poems by Qu Yuan and Other Poets. David Hawks (Translator, Introduction by). Trade Paper. Penguin Group (USA) Inc. New York, NY. 1986. 352p. Penguin Classics Ser. ISBN:0-14-044375-4, ISBN13: 978-0-14-044375-2. Dewey:895.1/11. LCCN:86-110526.

Audience: **f.** ℬ

China > Literature > Modern Poetry

Cheung, Dominic   **PL2658.E3**
The Isle Full of Noises: Modern Chinese Poetry from Taiwan.
Trade Cloth. Columbia University Press. New York, NY. 1986.
265p. ISBN:0-231-06402-0, ISBN13: 978-0-231-06402-6.
Dewey:895.1/15/080951249. LCCN:86-013614.
Audience: f. Choice, 1987.

Haft, Lloyd (Editor)   **PL2302.S45**
A Selective Guide to Chinese Literature, 1900-1949: The Poem.
Trade Cloth. Brill Academic Publishers, Inc. Boston, MA. 1989.
xii, 301p. ISBN:90-04-08960-8, ISBN13: 978-90-04-08960-0.
Dewey:895.1/09/005. LCCN:87-017871.
Audience: f.

Hom, Marion K.   **PL2997.T3**
Songs of Gold Mountain: Cantonese Rhymes from San
Francisco Chinatown. Trade Paper. University of California
Press. Berkeley, CA. 1992. 332p. ISBN:0-520-08104-8, ISBN13:
978-0-520-08104-8. Dewey:895.1/1. LCCN:86-011234.
Audience: g,u,f. Choice, 1988.

Liu, Wu-Chi & Lo,   **PL2658.E3S84 1990**
  Irving Y. (Editors)
Sunflower Splendor: Three Thousand Years of Chinese Poetry.
Trade Cloth. Indiana University Press. Bloomington, IN. 1990.
696p. ISBN:0-253-35580-X, ISBN13: 978-0-253-35580-5.
Dewey:895.1/1008. LCCN:90-039420.
Audience: g,u,f.

Morin, Edward   **PL2658.E3R33 1990**
The Red Azalea: Chinese Poetry since the Cultural Revolution.
Trade Cloth. University of Hawaii Press. Honolulu, HI. 1990.
256p. ISBN:0-8248-1320-0, ISBN13: 978-0-8248-1320-8.
Dewey:895.1/15208. LCCN:90-041829.
Audience: g,u,f.

Yeh, Michelle   **PL2332.Y44 1991**
Modern Chinese Poetry: Theory and Practice since 1917. Trade
Cloth. Yale University Press. Cumberland, RI. 1991. 248p.
ISBN:0-300-04787-8, ISBN13: 978-0-300-04787-5.
Dewey:895.1/1509. LCCN:90-041707.
Audience: f. Choice, 1991.

China > Literature > Traditional Prose

Birch, Cyril (Editor,   **PL2658.E8**
  Translator)
Stories from a Ming Collection. Trade Paper. Grove/Atlantic,
Inc. New York, NY. 1968. 208p. UNESCO Collection of
Representative Works ISBN:0-8021-5031-4, ISBN13:
978-0-8021-5031-8. Dewey:895.13. LCCN:68-044187.
Audience: g,u,f.

Cao Xue Qin   **PL2727.S2**
The Story of the Stone: The Dreamer Awakes. Gao E (Editor),
John Minford (Translator). Trade Cloth. Indiana University
Press. Bloomington, IN. 1987. 384p. Chinese Literature in
Translation Ser. ISBN:0-253-19265-X, ISBN13:
978-0-253-19265-3. Dewey:895.1/34. LCCN:78-020279.
Audience: g,u,f.

Cao Xue Qin   **PL2727.S2**
The Story of the Stone: The Debt of Tears. E. Gao (Editor),
John Minford (Translator). Trade Cloth. Indiana University
Press. Bloomington, IN. 1983. 400p. Chinese Literature in

Translation Ser. ISBN:0-253-19264-1, ISBN13:
978-0-253-19264-6. Dewey:895.1/34. LCCN:78-020279.
Audience: g,u,f.

Cao Xue Qin   **PL2727.S2**
The Story of the Stone: The Golden Days. David Hawkes
(Translator). Trade Cloth. Indiana University Press.
Bloomington, IN. 1979. 544p. Chinese Literature in Translation
Ser. ISBN:0-253-19261-7, ISBN13: 978-0-253-19261-5.
Dewey:895.1/34. LCCN:78-020279.
Audience: g,u,f.

Cao Xue Qin   **PL2727.S2**
The Story of the Stone: The Warning Voice. David Hawkes
(Translator). Trade Cloth. Indiana University Press.
Bloomington, IN. 1981. 640p. Chinese Literature in Translation
Ser. ISBN:0-253-19263-3, ISBN13: 978-0-253-19263-9.
Dewey:895.134. LCCN:78-020279.
Audience: g,u,f.

Cao Xue Qin   **PL2727.S2**
The Story of the Stone: The Crab-Flower Club. David Hawkes
(Translator). Trade Cloth. Indiana University Press.
Bloomington, IN. 1979. 608p. Chinese Literature in Translation
Ser. ISBN:0-253-19262-5, ISBN13: 978-0-253-19262-2.
Dewey:895.1/34. LCCN:78-020279.
Audience: g,u,f.

Ching-tzu, Wu   **PL2727.S2**
The Scholars. Yang Hsien-Yi & Glagys Yang (Translators),
Cheng Shih-fa (Illustrator), C. T. Hsia (Foreword by). Cloth
Text. Columbia University Press. New York, NY. 1993. 448p.
ISBN:0-231-08152-9, ISBN13: 978-0-231-08152-8.
Dewey:895.1/348. LCCN:92-024471.
Audience: g,u,f.

Egan, Ronald C.   **PL2683.Z5E3 1984**
The Literary Works of Ou-Yang Hsiu (1007-72). Cloth Text.
Cambridge University Press. New York, NY. 1984. 276p.
Cambridge Studies in Chinese History, Literature and
Institutions ISBN:0-521-25888-X, ISBN13: 978-0-521-25888-3.
Dewey:895.1/14. LCCN:84-001740.
Audience: f. ℬ

Li Ju-chen   **PL2674**
Flowers in the Mirror. Tai-yi Lin (Editor, Illustrator). Trade
Cloth. University of California Press. Berkeley, CA. 1965.
ISBN:0-520-00747-6, ISBN13: 978-0-520-00747-5.
Dewey:895.13.
Audience: g,u,f.

Lo Kuan-Chung &   **PL2690.S3 E5325 1999**
  Roberts, Moss
Three Kingdoms: A Historical Novel. Trade Paper. University of
California Press. Berkeley, CA. 1999. 506p.
ISBN:0-520-21585-0, ISBN13: 978-0-520-21585-6.
Dewey:895.1/346. LCCN:98-039516.
Audience: g,u,f. ℬ Choice, 1993.

Mair, Victor H.   **PL2658.E1S53 2000**
The Shorter Columbia Anthology of Traditional Chinese
Literature. Trade Cloth. Columbia University Press. New York,
NY. 2000. 704p. Translations from the Asian Classics
ISBN:0-231-11998-4, ISBN13: 978-0-231-11998-6.
Dewey:895.1/08. LCCN:00-035878.
Audience: g,u,f.

Owen, Stephen　　　　PL2291.O84 1996
The End of the Chinese 'Middle Ages': Essays in Mid-Tang
Literary Culture. Trade Cloth. Stanford University Press. Palo
Alto, CA. 1996. 209p. ISBN:0-8047-2666-3, ISBN13:
978-0-8047-2666-5. Dewey:895.1/09003. LCCN:95-025619.
　　　　　　　　　　Audience: **f.** *Choice, 1996.*

Paper, Jordan D.　　　　PL2264
Guide to Chinese Prose. Ed. 2. Trade Cloth. Macmillan
Publishing Company, Inc. Old Tappan, NJ. 1984. Asian
Literature Bibliography Ser. ISBN:0-8161-8621-9, ISBN13:
978-0-8161-8621-1. Dewey:016.8951/008. LCCN:83-026473.
　　　　　　　　　　Audience: **f.**

Roy, David T.　　　　PL2698.H73.C4713
　(Translator)
The Plum in the Golden Vase: Chin P'ing Mei The Gathering,
Vol. 1. Cloth Text. Princeton University Press. Princeton, NJ.
1993. 544p. Library of Asian Translations ISBN:0-691-06932-8,
ISBN13: 978-0-691-06932-6. Dewey:895.1346.
LCCN:92-045054.
　　　　　Audience: **g,l,u,f.** *Choice, 1994.*

Roy, David Tod　　　　PL2698
　(Translator)
The Plum in the Golden Vase, Vol. 3. Trade Cloth. Princeton
University Press. Princeton, NJ. 2006. 776p.
ISBN:0-691-12534-1, ISBN13: 978-0-691-12534-3.
Dewey:895.1346.
　　　　　　　　　　Audience: **g,l,u,f.**

Roy, David Tod (Edited　　　　PL2698.H73
　and Translated by)
The Plum in the Golden Vase, or Chin P'ing Mei: The Rivals.
Trade Cloth. Princeton University Press. Princeton, NJ. 2001.
716p. Princeton Library of Asian Translations Ser.
ISBN:0-691-07077-6, ISBN13: 978-0-691-07077-3.
Dewey:895.1/346. LCCN:92-045054.
　　　　　　　　　　Audience: **g,l,u,f.**

Shi Nai'an &　　　　PL2727.S2
　Guanzhong, Luo
Outlaws of the Marsh. Sidney Shapiro (Translator). Trade Cloth.
Beijing Foreign Languages Press. Beijing, 1993. 2149p.
ISBN:7-119-01662-8, ISBN13: 978-7-119-01662-7.
Dewey:895.1/34.
　　　　　　Audience: **g,l,u,f.** *B*

Van Gulik, Robert H.　　　　PL2699.C4 1976
Celebrated Cases of Judge Dee: An Authentic Eighteenth
Century Chinese Detective Novel. Trade Paper. Dover
Publications, Inc. Mineola, NY. 1976. 237p.
ISBN:0-486-23337-5, ISBN13: 978-0-486-23337-6.
Dewey:895.1/3/4. LCCN:76-005059.
　　　　　　Audience: **g,l,u,f.** *B*

Waley, Arthur　　　　PL2735.A5.Z94 1970
Yuan Mei: Eighteenth Century Chinese Poet. Trade Cloth.
Stanford University Press. Palo Alto, CA. 1956. 227p.
ISBN:0-8047-0718-9, ISBN13: 978-0-8047-0718-3.
Dewey:895.1/1/4. LCCN:70-107646.
　　　　　　　　　　Audience: **g,u,f.**

Wu Ch'eng-en　　　　PL2697.H75E5 1961
Monkey. Arthur Waley (Translator, Introduction by). Trade
Paper. Penguin Group (USA) Inc. New York, NY. 1994. 352p.
ISBN:0-14-044111-5, ISBN13: 978-0-14-044111-6.
Dewey:895.1/346. LCCN:94-138187.
　　　　　　　　　　Audience: **l,u,f.**

Yu, Anthony C.　　　　PL2727.S2
　(Translator)
Journey to the West, Vol. 2. Trade Cloth. University of Chicago
Press. Chicago, IL. 1978. 448p. ISBN:0-226-97146-5, ISBN13:
978-0-226-97146-9. Dewey:895.1/34. LCCN:75-027896.
　　　　　　　　　　Audience: **g,u,f.**

Yu, Anthony C. (Editor)　　　　PL2697.H75.E596 1977
The Journey to the West, Vol. 1. Library Binding. University of
Chicago Press. Chicago, IL. 1977. xiv, 544p.
ISBN:0-226-97145-7, ISBN13: 978-0-226-97145-2.
Dewey:895.1/34. LCCN:75-027896.
　　　　　　　　　　Audience: **g,u,f.**

China > Literature > Modern Prose

Barme, Geremie &　　　　PL2658.E1S44 1988
　Minford, John (Editors)
Seeds of Fire: Chinese Voices of Conscience. Trade Cloth.
Farrar, Straus & Giroux. New York, NY. 1988. 452p.
ISBN:0-8090-8521-6, ISBN13: 978-0-8090-8521-7.
Dewey:895.1/8508/08. LCCN:88-019861.
　　　　　　　　　　Audience: **g,l,u,f.**

Chen, Ruoxi, et al.　　　　PL2840.J6A6 2004
e The Execution of Mayor Yin and Other Stories from the
Great Proletarian Cultural Revolution. Ed. 2. Nancy Ing &
Howard Goldblatt (Authors). E-Book. Indiana University Press.
Bloomington, IN. 2004. 272p. ISBN:0-253-34416-6, ISBN13:
978-0-253-34416-8. Dewey:895.1/352. LCCN:2004-000689.
　　　　　Audience: **g,u,f.** *Choice, 2005.*

Chin, Pa　　　　PL2780.L4
The Family. Trade Paper. University Press of the Pacific. Miami,
FL. 2001. 304p. ISBN:0-89875-213-2, ISBN13:
978-0-89875-213-7. Dewey:Fic.
　　　　　　　　　　Audience: **g,u,f.**

Goldblatt, Howard　　　　PL2658.E8C43 1995
　(Editor)
Chairman Mao Would Not Be Amused: Fiction from Today's
China. Cloth Text. Grove/Atlantic, Inc. New York, NY. 1995.
336p. ISBN:0-8021-1573-X, ISBN13: 978-0-8021-1573-7.
Dewey:895.1/35208. LCCN:95-001931.
　　　　　　　　　　Audience: **u,f.**

Hui, Wei　　　　PL2929.7.O58S464
Shanghai Baby: A Novel. Bruce Humes (Translator). Trade
Cloth. Simon & Schuster. New York, NY. 2001. 272p.
ISBN:0-7434-2156-6, ISBN13: 978-0-7434-2156-0.
Dewey:895.1/352. LCCN:2001-133033.
　　　　　　　　　　Audience: **u,f.**

Lao She　　　　PL2804.C5 L613 1979
Rickshaw: The Novel Lo-t'o Hsiang Tzu. University of Hawaii
Press. 1979. ISBN:0-8248-0616-6, ISBN13: 978-0-8248-0616-3.
　　　　　　　　　　Audience: **g,l,u,f.**

Lau, Joseph S. M. &　　　　PL2658.E1C64 1995
　Goldblatt, Howard (Editors)
The Columbia Anthology of Modern Chinese Literature. Trade
Cloth. Eastern European Monographs. Bradenton, FL. 1995.
726p. Modern Asian Literature Ser. ISBN:0-231-08002-6,
ISBN13: 978-0-231-08002-6. Dewey:895.1/08005.
LCCN:94-035304.
　　　　　Audience: **g,u,f.** *Choice, 1995.*

Lau, Joseph S. (Editor), PL2658.E8
et al.
Modern Chinese Stories and Novellas, 1919 to 1949. C. T. Hsia
& Leo O. Lee (Editors). Cloth Text. Columbia University Press.
New York, NY. 1981. 608p. Modern Asian Literature Ser.
ISBN:0-231-04202-7, ISBN13: 978-0-231-04202-4.
Dewey:895.1/301/08. LCCN:80-027572.
　　　　　　　　　　　　　　　Audience: **g,u,f.** *B*

Lee, Leo O. (Editor) PL2754.S5Z/
Lu Xun and His Legacy. Trade Cloth. University of California
Press. Berkeley, CA. 1985. xix, 324p. ISBN:0-520-05158-0,
ISBN13: 978-0-520-05158-4. Dewey:895.1/35.
LCCN:83-018048.
　　　　　　　　　　　　　　　Audience: **g,u,f.** *B*

Lee, Leo Ou-fan DS796.S25L43 1999
Shanghai Modern: The Flowering of a New Urban Culture in
China, 1930-1945. Trade Cloth. Harvard University Press.
Cambridge, MA. 1999. 436p. Interpretations of Asia Ser.
ISBN:0-674-80550-X, ISBN13: 978-0-674-80550-7.
Dewey:306/.0951/132. LCCN:98-032318.
　　　　　　　　　　　　Audience: **g,u,f.** *Choice, 2000.*

Link, Perry (Editor) PL2658.E1.S78 1983
Stubborn Weeds: Popular and Controversial Chinese Literature
after the Cultural Revolution. Trade Cloth. Indiana University
Press. Bloomington, IN. 1984. 304p. Chinese Literature in
Translation Ser. ISBN:0-253-35512-5, ISBN13:
978-0-253-35512-6. Dewey:895.1/08/005. LCCN:82-048268.
　　　　　　　　　　　　　　　Audience: **g,u,f.** *B*

Lu Xun PL2754.S5
Selected Stories of Lu Xun. Trade Cloth. Beijing Foreign
Languages Press. Beijing, 2001. ISBN:7-119-02698-4, ISBN13:
978-7-119-02698-5. Dewey:495.18.
　　　　　　　　　　　　　　　Audience: **u,f.**

Lu Xun PL2754.S5
Selected Stories of Lu Xun. Beijing Foreign Languages Press.
2001. ISBN:7-119-02698-4, ISBN13: 978-7-119-02698-5.
　　　　　　　　　　　　　　　Audience: **g,l,u,f.**

Nieh, Hualing (Editor) PL2658.E1
Literature of the Hundred Flowers, Vol. 1. Trade Cloth.
Columbia University Press. New York, NY. 1981. 279p.
ISBN:0-231-05074-7, ISBN13: 978-0-231-05074-6.
Dewey:895.1/08/005. LCCN:80-036748.
　　　　　　　　　　　　　　　Audience: **f.**

Nieh, Hualing PL2856.N4S213 1998
Mulberry and Peach: Two Women of China. Jane P. Young &
Linda Lappin (Translators), Sau-ling Wong (Afterword by).
Trade Paper. Feminist Press at The City University of New
York. New York, NY. 1997. 224p. ISBN:1-55861-182-7,
ISBN13: 978-1-55861-182-5. Dewey:895.1/352.
LCCN:98-012259.
　　　　　　　　　　　　　　　Audience: **g,l,u,f.**

Pai Hsien-yung (Author, PL2892.A345A24 1982
Translator)
Wandering in the Garden, Waking from a Dream: Tales of
Taipei Characters. George Kao (Editor), Patia Yasin (Translator).
Trade Cloth. Indiana University Press. Bloomington, IN. 1982.
224p. Chinese Literature in Translation Ser., No. 276
ISBN:0-253-19981-6, ISBN13: 978-0-253-19981-2.
Dewey:895.1/35. LCCN:81-047165.
　　　　　　　　　　　　　　　Audience: **g,u,f.**

Ruowang, Wang PL2919.J6C3813 1991
Hunger Trilogy. Kyna Rubin (Translator, Introduction by), Ira E.
Kasoff (Translator). Trade Cloth. M. E. Sharpe Inc. Armonk,
NY. 1991. 176p. ISBN:0-87332-739-X, ISBN13:
978-0-87332-739-8. Dewey:895.1/352. LCCN:91-009017.
　　　　　　　　　　　　　　　Audience: **g,u,f.**

Tun, Mao PZ3.S54723
Midnight. Trade Paper. Fredonia Books. Miami, FL. 2001. 588p.
ISBN:1-58963-568-X, ISBN13: 978-1-58963-568-5.
Dewey:895.1/3/5.
　　　　　　　　　　　　　　　Audience: **g,u,f.**

Wang, David & Tai, PL2658.E8R86 1994
Jeanne (Editors)
Running Wild: New Chinese Writers. Trade Cloth. Columbia
University Press. New York, NY. 1994. 264p.
ISBN:0-231-09648-8, ISBN13: 978-0-231-09648-5.
Dewey:895.1/35208. LCCN:93-037041.
　　　　　　　　　　　Audience: **g,u,f.** *Choice, 1995.*

Xiaolong, Qiu PS3553.H537D43 2000
Death of a Red Heroine: An Inspector Chen Investigation. Trade
Cloth. Soho Press, Inc. New York, NY. 2000. 463p.
ISBN:1-56947-193-2, ISBN13: 978-1-56947-193-7.
Dewey:813/.6. LCCN:00-020362.
　　　　　　　　　　　　　　　Audience: **g,l,u,f.**

Yan, Mo PL2886.O1684
Red Sorghum: A Novel of China. Howard Goldblatt
(Translator). Trade Paper. Penguin Group (USA) Inc. New York,
NY. 2003. 368p. ISBN:0-14-016854-0, ISBN13:
978-0-14-016854-9. Dewey:895.13.
　　　　　　　　　　　　　　　Audience: **g,u,f.**

China > Taiwan

Brown, Melissa J. DS799.42 .B76 2004
Is Taiwan Chinese?: The Impact of Culture, Power, and
Migration on Changing Identities. Trade Cloth. University of
California Press. Berkeley, CA. 2004. 330p. Berkeley Series in
Interdisciplinary Studies of China, Vol. 2 ISBN:0-520-23181-3,
ISBN13: 978-0-520-23181-8. Dewey:305.89/925.
LCCN:2003-012763.
　　　　　　　　　　　　Audience: **f.** *Choice, 2004.*

Cheung, Dominic PL2658.E3
The Isle Full of Noises: Modern Chinese Poetry from Taiwan.
Trade Cloth. Columbia University Press. New York, NY. 1986.
265p. ISBN:0-231-06402-0, ISBN13: 978-0-231-06402-6.
Dewey:895.1/15/080951249. LCCN:86-013614.
　　　　　　　　　　　　Audience: **f.** *Choice, 1987.*

Copper, John F. DS798.96.C67 2000
Historical Dictionary of Taiwan (Republic of China). Ed. 2. Jon
Woronoff (Editor). Trade Cloth. Scarecrow Press, Inc. Lanham,
MD. 2000. 320p. Asian Historical Dictionaries Ser., No. 34
ISBN:0-8108-3665-3, ISBN13: 978-0-8108-3665-5.
Dewey:951.24/9/003. LCCN:99-027946.
　　　　　　　　　　　　Audience: **g,u,f.** *Choice, 2000.*

Davidson, James West DS799.9.P4
The Island of Formosa: Past and Present. Trade Cloth. A M S
Press, Inc. New York, NY, ISBN:0-404-16704-7, ISBN13:
978-0-404-16704-2. Dewey:951.24902. LCCN:77-086949.
　　　　　　　　　　　　　　　Audience: **u,f.**

Gold, Thomas B.   HC430.5.G65 1986
State and Society in the Taiwan Miracle. Trade Cloth. M. E.
Sharpe Inc. Armonk, NY. 1986. 176p. Taiwan in the Modern
World Ser. ISBN:0-87332-349-1, ISBN13: 978-0-87332-349-9.
Dewey:338.951/249. LCCN:85-002350.

Audience: **g,u,f.**

Pai Hsien-yung (Author,   PL2892.A345A24 1982
Translator)
Wandering in the Garden, Waking from a Dream: Tales of
Taipei Characters. George Kao (Editor), Patia Yasin (Translator).
Trade Cloth. Indiana University Press. Bloomington, IN. 1982.
224p. Chinese Literature in Translation Ser., No. 276
ISBN:0-253-19981-6, ISBN13: 978-0-253-19981-2.
Dewey:895.1/35. LCCN:81-047165.

Audience: **g,u,f.**

Riggers, Shelley   DS799.816.R54 1999
Politics in Taiwan: Voting for Democracy. Trade Paper.
Routledge. New York, NY. 1999. 240p. ISBN:0-415-17209-8,
ISBN13: 978-0-415-17209-7. Dewey:320.95124/9/09045.
LCCN:99-022354.

Audience: **g,u,f.**

Roy, Denny   DS799.816.R69 2003
Taiwan: A Political History. Trade Cloth. Cornell University
Press. Ithaca, NY. 2003. xiii, 255p. ISBN:0-8014-4070-X,
ISBN13: 978-0-8014-4070-0. Dewey:320.95124/9/09045.
LCCN:2002-012235.

Audience: **g,u,f.** *Choice, 2004.*

Rubinstein, Murray A.   DS799.5.T3114 1999
(Editor)
Taiwan: A New History. Trade Cloth. M. E. Sharpe Inc.
Armonk, NY. 1999. 536p. Taiwan in the Modern World Ser.
ISBN:1-56324-815-8, ISBN13: 978-1-56324-815-3.
Dewey:951.24/905. LCCN:98-006043.

Audience: **g,l,u,f.**

Shepherd, John Robert   HC430.5.S38 1993
Statecraft and Political Economy on the Taiwan Frontier,
1600-1800. Trade Cloth. Stanford University Press. Palo Alto,
CA. 1993. 624p. ISBN:0-8047-2066-5, ISBN13:
978-0-8047-2066-3. Dewey:951.24/903. LCCN:91-046158.

Audience: **f.** *Choice, 1993.*

Taylor, Jay   DS799.82.C437T39
The Generalissimo's Son: Chiang Ching-kuo and the
Revolutions in China and Taiwan. Trade Cloth. Harvard
University Press. Cambridge, MA. 2000. 544p.
ISBN:0-674-00287-3, ISBN13: 978-0-674-00287-6.
Dewey:951.24/905/092 B. LCCN:00-035053.

Audience: **g,u,f.** *Choice, 2001.*

Tucker, Nancy Bernkopf   E183.8.C5D26 2005
Dangerous Strait: The U.S.—Taiwan—China Crisis. Trade
Cloth. University of Tokyo Press. 2005. 288p.
ISBN:0-231-13564-5, ISBN13: 978-0-231-13564-1.
Dewey:327.73051/09/045. LCCN:2004-059373.

Audience: **u,f.** *Choice, 2005.*

Wachman, Alan M.   DS799.847.W33 1994
Taiwan: National Identity and Democratization. Cloth Text. M.
E. Sharpe Inc. Armonk, NY. 1994. 312p. Taiwan in the Modern
World Ser. ISBN:1-56324-398-9, ISBN13: 978-1-56324-398-1.
Dewey:305.8/00951. LCCN:94-012659.

Audience: **f.**

Wolf, Margery   HQ668.95
The House of Lim: A Study of a Chinese Family. Trade Paper.
Prentice Hall PTR. Upper Saddle River, NJ. 1960. 147p.
ISBN:0-13-394973-7, ISBN13: 978-0-13-394973-5.
Dewey:301.420951249.

Audience: **g,u,f.**

China > Foreign Views of China

Ballard, J. G.   PR6015.I3
Empire of the Sun. Trade Paper. Simon & Schuster, Inc. New
York, NY. 2005. 288p. ISBN:0-7432-6523-8, ISBN13:
978-0-7432-6523-2. Dewey:823/.914.

Audience: **g,l,u,f.**

Belden, Jack   DS0777.53B38
China Shakes the World. Owen Lattimore (Introduction by).
Trade Paper. Books on Demand. Ann Arbor, MI. 544p.
ISBN:0-8357-6054-5, ISBN13: 978-0-8357-6054-6.
Dewey:951.04/2. LCCN:77-105312.

Audience: **g,u,f.**

Bickers, Robert A.   DA47.9.C6B53 1999
Britain in China: Community, Culture and Colonialism,
1900-49. Cloth over Boards. Manchester University Press.
Manchester, 1999. 256p. Studies in Imperialism
ISBN:0-7190-4697-1, ISBN13: 978-0-7190-4697-1.
Dewey:327.51041. LCCN:99-039760.

Audience: **g,u,f.** *Choice, 2000.*

Bird   DS709
Yangtze Valley and Beyond. Trade Cloth. Random House, Inc.
New York, NY. 1987. 560p. ISBN:0-86068-790-2, ISBN13:
978-0-86068-790-0. Dewey:915.1/043.

Audience: **g,u,f.**

Buck, Pearl S.   PS3511.A86
The Good Earth. Trade Cloth. Amereon, Ltd. Mattituck, NY.
ISBN:0-8488-1251-4, ISBN13: 978-0-8488-1251-5.
Dewey:813/.52.

Audience: **g,l,u,f.**

Conn, Peter   PS3503.U198 Z624 19
Pearl S. Buck: A Cultural Biography. Cloth Text. Cambridge
University Press. New York, NY. 1996. 496p.
ISBN:0-521-56080-2, ISBN13: 978-0-521-56080-1.
Dewey:813.5/2. LCCN:95-043105.

Audience: **g,u,f.** *Choice, 1997.*

Crow, Carl   DS775.2.C76 2002
Four Hundred Million Customers: The Experiences - Some
Happy, Some Sad - of an American in China and What They
Taught Him. G. Saponjnikoff (Illustrator), Ezra E. Vogel
(Introduction by). Trade Paper. EastBridge. Norwalk, CT. 2002.
318p. ISBN:1-891936-07-7, ISBN13: 978-1-891936-07-4.
Dewey:951.04/2. LCCN:2002-067557.

Audience: **g,u,f.**

Fairbank, John K.   DS774
Chinabound: A Fifty Year Memoir. Trade Cloth. HarperCollins
Publishers. New York, NY. 1982. 480p. ISBN:0-06-039005-0,
ISBN13: 978-0-06-039005-1. Dewey:951.05/092/4.
LCCN:81-047656.

Audience: **g,u,f.** *B*

Hessler, Peter   DS796.F855H47 2001
River Town: Two Years on the Yangtze. Trade Cloth.
HarperCollins Publishers. New York, NY. 2001. 416p.

ISBN:0-06-019544-4, ISBN13: 978-0-06-019544-1.
Dewey:915.1/38. LCCN:00-049872.

Audience: **g,l,u,f.**

Hilton, James   **PR9619.3.L376**
Lost Horizon. Trade Cloth. HarperCollins Publishers. New York,
NY. 1934. ISBN:0-688-02007-0, ISBN13: 978-0-688-02007-1.
Dewey:823/.92.

Audience: **g,l,u,f.**

Hobart, Alice Tisdale   **PS3515.O134O5 2002**
Oil for the Lamps of China. Sherman Cochran (Introduction by).
Trade Paper. EastBridge. Norwalk, CT. 2002. 432p.
ISBN:1-891936-08-5, ISBN13: 978-1-891936-08-1.
Dewey:813/.52. LCCN:2002-067559.

Audience: **g,l,u,f.**

Huc, Evariste Regis &   **DS709.H85 1987**
Gabet, Joseph
Travels in Tartary, Thibet and China, 1844-1846. Trade Paper.
Dover Publications, Inc. Mineola, NY. 1987. 864p.
ISBN:0-486-25438-0, ISBN13: 978-0-486-25438-8.
Dewey:915/.043/0922. LCCN:87-002978.

Audience: **g,l,u,f.**

Isaacs, Harold R.   **DS706**
Scratches on Our Minds: American Views of China and India.
Paper Text. M. E. Sharpe Inc. Armonk, NY. 1980. 452p.
ISBN:0-87332-161-8, ISBN13: 978-0-87332-161-7.
Dewey:327.73051. LCCN:80-000214.

Audience: **g,u,f.**

Isaacs, Harold Robert   **DS774 .I7**
The Tragedy of the Chinese Revolution. Paper Text. Textbook
Publishers. Temecula, CA. 2003. 392p. ISBN:0-7581-3511-4,
ISBN13: 978-0-7581-3511-7. Dewey:951.042.

Audience: **g,u,f.**

Jespersen, T.   **DS774.5.J47 1996**
Christopher
American Images of China, 1931-1949. Trade Cloth. Stanford
University Press. Palo Alto, CA. 1996. 306p.
ISBN:0-8047-2596-9, ISBN13: 978-0-8047-2596-5.
Dewey:327.7/3/051. LCCN:95-019565.

Audience: **g,u,f.**

Lach, Donald F.   **CB245**
Asia in the Making of Europe. Library Binding. University of
Chicago Press. Chicago, IL. 1993. xxiii, 764p.
ISBN:0-226-46751-1, ISBN13: 978-0-226-46751-1.
Dewey:909/.09/812. LCCN:64-019848.

Audience: **g,u,f.**

Lach, Donald F.   **CB203 .L32**
Asia in the Making of Europe: A Century of Wonder: The
Visual Arts. Trade Paper. University of Chicago Press. Chicago,
IL. 1994. 276p. Asia in the Making of Europe Ser., Vol. II
ISBN:0-226-46730-9, ISBN13: 978-0-226-46730-6. Dewey:940.

Audience: **g,l,u.**

Lach, Donald F.   **CB251**
A Century of Wonder: The Visual Arts. Trade Cloth. University
of Chicago Press. Chicago, IL. 1970. 276p. Asia in the Making
of Europe Ser., Vol. 2 ISBN:0-226-46750-3, ISBN13:
978-0-226-46750-4. Dewey:910/.031/812. LCCN:64 019848.

Audience: **g,l,u.**

Lach, Donald F. & Van   **CB203 .L32**
Kley, Edwin J.
Asia in the Making of Europe: A Century of Advance. Trade
Cloth. University of Chicago Press. Chicago, IL. 1993. 568p.
Asia in the Making of Europe Vol. III Ser., Vol. 2
ISBN:0-226-46754-6, ISBN13: 978-0-226-46754-2. Dewey:950.

Audience: **u,f.** *Choice, 1994.*

Lach, Donald F. & Van   **DS5**
Kley, Edwin J.
Asia in the Making of Europe: A Century of Advance: Trade,
Missions, Literature. Trade Cloth. University of Chicago Press.
Chicago, IL. 1993. 674p. Asia in the Making of Europe Vol. III
Ser., Vol. 1 ISBN:0-226-46753-8, ISBN13: 978-0-226-46753-5.
Dewey:950.

Audience: **u,f.**

Lach, Donald F. & Van   **CB203 .L32**
Kley, Edwin J.
Asia in the Making of Europe: A Century of Advance: East
Asia. Trade Cloth. University of Chicago Press. Chicago, IL.
1993. 627p. Asia in the Making of Europe Vol. III Ser., Vol. 4
ISBN:0-226-46756-2, ISBN13: 978-0-226-46756-6. Dewey:940.

Audience: **g,u,f.**

Lach, Donald F. & Van   **CB203 .L32**
Kley, Edwin J.
Asia in the Making of Europe: A Century of Advance. Trade
Cloth. University of Chicago Press. Chicago, IL. 1993. 504p.
ISBN:0-226-46755-4, ISBN13: 978-0-226-46755-9. Dewey:950.

Audience: **g,u,f.** *Choice, 1994.*

Larner, John   **G370.P9**
Marco Polo and the Discovery of the World. Trade Paper. Yale
University Press. Cumberland, RI. 2001. 266p.
ISBN:0-300-08900-7, ISBN13: 978-0-300-08900-4.
Dewey:915.04/2. LCCN:99-024887.

Audience: **g,u,f.** *Choice, 2000.*

Leong, Karen J.   **E183.8.C5**
The China Mystique: Pearl S. Buck, Anna May Wong, Mayling
Soong, and the Transformation of American Orientalism. Trade
Cloth. University of California Press. Berkeley, CA. 2005. 304p.
ISBN:0-520-24422-2, ISBN13: 978-0-520-24422-1.
Dewey:305.48/8951073/0922. LCCN:2004-024699.

Audience: **g,l,u,f.** *Choice, 2006, 2005.*

Levi, Jean   **PQ2672.E942G7313**
The Chinese Emperor. Barbara Bray (Translator). Trade Cloth.
Harcourt Trade Publishers. New York, NY. 1987.
ISBN:0-15-117649-3, ISBN13: 978-0-15-117649-6.
Dewey:843/.914. LCCN:86-031835.

Audience: **g,l,u,f.**

MacKinnon, Stephen R.   **DS777.53.P8U6 1987**
& Friesen, Oris
ⓔ China Reporting: An Oral History of American Journalism in
the 1930's and 1940's. E-Book. NetLibrary, Inc. Boulder, CO.
1987. ISBN:0-585-06988-3, ISBN13: 978-0-585-06988-3.
Dewey:070.4/33/0924.

Audience: **g,u,f.** *Choice, 1988.*

MacKinnon, Stephen R.   **DS777.533.P825.U65**
& Friesen, Oris
China Reporting: An Oral History of American Journalism in
the 1930's and 1940's. Trade Cloth. University of California
Press. Berkeley, CA. 1987. 200p. ISBN:0-520-05843-7, ISBN13:
978-0-520-05843-9. Dewey:070.4/33/0924. LCCN:86-019193.

Audience: **g,u,f.** *Choice, 1988.*

Mahoney, Rosemary   DS778.T39
The Early Arrival of Dreams: A Year in China. Trade Paper.
Ballantine Books. New York, NY. 1992. 336p.
ISBN:0-449-90655-8, ISBN13: 978-0-449-90655-2.
Dewey:951.058092.

Audience: **g,u,f.**

Malraux, Andre   PQ2625.A716C612 1992
The Conquerors. Stephen Becker (Translator), Herbert R.
Lottman (Foreword by). Trade Paper. University of Chicago
Press. Chicago, IL. 1992. 212p. Phoenix Fiction Ser.
ISBN:0-226-50290-2, ISBN13: 978-0-226-50290-8.
Dewey:843/.912. LCCN:72-091594.

Audience: **g,u,f.**

Malraux, André   PQ2625.A716C53 1984
Man's Fate. Trade Cloth. Random House, Inc. New York, NY.
1984. ISBN:0-394-54379-3, ISBN13: 978-0-394-54379-6.
Dewey:843. LCCN:84-017944.

Audience: **g,l,u,f.**

McKenna, Richard   PS3568.O243
The Sand Pebbles. Trade Cloth. Naval Institute Press. Annapolis,
MD. 1984. 597p. Classics of Naval Literature Ser.
ISBN:0-87021-592-2, ISBN13: 978-0-87021-592-6.
Dewey:813/.54. LCCN:83-027007.

Audience: **g,l,u,f.**

Miller, Arthur   PS3525.I5156.D4356
Salesman in Beijing. Trade Cloth. Penguin Group (USA) Inc.
New York, NY. 1984. 256p. ISBN:0-670-61601-X, ISBN13:
978-0-670-61601-5. Dewey:792.92. LCCN:83-047999.

Audience: **g,l,u,f.** *B*

Morath, Inge & Miller,   DS712
Arthur
Chinese Encounters. Trade Cloth. Farrar, Straus & Giroux. New
York, NY. 1979. 255p. ISBN:0-374-12208-3, ISBN13:
978-0-374-12208-9. Dewey:915.1/0457.

Audience: **g,u,f.**

Mungello, David E.   BV3417.M86 1989
Curious Land: Jesuit Accommodation and the Origins of
Sinology. Trade Paper. University of Hawaii Press. Honolulu,
HI. 1989. 408p. ISBN:0-8248-1219-0, ISBN13:
978-0-8248-1219-5. Dewey:951.007. LCCN:88-027874.

Audience: **g,u,f.** *Choice, 1990.*

Newman, Robert P.   E748.L34N48 1992
Owen Lattimore and the "Loss" of China. Trade Cloth.
University of California Press. Berkeley, CA. 1992. 685p.
ISBN:0-520-07388-6, ISBN13: 978-0-520-07388-3.
Dewey:327.51073. LCCN:91-021888.

Audience: **u,f.** *Choice, 1992.*

Polo, Marco   G465
The Travels of Marco Polo. Ronald Latham (Translator). Library
Binding. OPAL Publishing Corporation. Norwalk, CT. 1982.
318p. ISBN:0-89835-058-1, ISBN13: 978-0-89835-058-6.
Dewey:910.4.

Audience: **g,l,u,f.**

Polo, Marco, et al.   G370.P9 P6713 1993
The Travels of Marco Polo: The Complete Yule-Cordier Edition.
Henry Yule & Henri Cordier (Authors). Trade Paper. Dover
Publications, Inc. Mineola, NY. 1993. Extensive editorial
apparatus, nearly 200 illustrations (many double-page spreads)
and 32 maps and site plans augment the text. 855p. 0

ISBN:0-486-27587-6, ISBN13: 978-0-486-27587-1.
Dewey:915.10425092. LCCN:92-039066.

Audience: **g,l,u.**

Polo, Marco, et al.   G370.P9 P6713 1993
The Travels of Marco Polo: The Complete Yule-Cordier Edition.
Henry Yule & Henri Cordier (Authors). Trade Paper. Dover
Publications, Inc. Mineola, NY. 1993. 567p. 0
ISBN:0-486-27586-8, ISBN13: 978-0-486-27586-4.
Dewey:915.10425092. LCCN:92-039066.

Audience: **g.**

Reischauer, Edwin O.   DS707 .R45
Ennin's Travels in Tang China. Paper Text. Textbook Publishers.
Temecula, CA. 2003. xii, 341p. ISBN:0-7581-4637-X, ISBN13:
978-0-7581-4637-3. Dewey:951.016.

Audience: **l,u,f.**

Salzman, Mark   DS712.S245 1986
Iron and Silk: In Which a Young American Encounters
Swordsmen, Bureaucrats and Other Citizens of Contemporary
China. Trade Cloth. Random House, Inc. New York, NY. 1986.
224p. ISBN:0-394-55156-7, ISBN13: 978-0-394-55156-2.
Dewey:951.05/8. LCCN:86-011846.

Audience: **g,l,u,f.**

Smith, Arthur H.   DS721.S642 2002
Chinese Characteristics. Lydia Liu (Introduction by). Trade
Paper. EastBridge. Norwalk, CT. 2003. 342p.
ISBN:1-891936-26-3, ISBN13: 978-1-891936-26-5.
Dewey:950.3/092/2. LCCN:2002-016779.

Audience: **g,u,f.**

Spence, Jonathan   DS706.S62 1998
The Chan's Great Continent: China in Western Minds. Norton.
1998. ISBN:0-393-02747-3, ISBN13: 978-0-393-02747-1.

Audience: **g,l,u,f.**

Spence, Jonathan D.   DS740.4
To Change China: Western Advisors in China, 1620-1960. Trade
Paper. Penguin Group (USA) Inc. New York, NY. 1980. 352p.
ISBN:0-14-005528-2, ISBN13: 978-0-14-005528-3.
Dewey:301.29/51/01821.

Audience: **g,l,u,f.**

Stilwell, Joseph W.   D811
The Stilwell Papers. Theodore H. White (Editor). Trade Cloth. A
M S Press, Inc. New York, NY. ISBN:0-404-20247-0, ISBN13:
978-0-404-20247-7. Dewey:940.54. LCCN:83-045889.

Audience: **f.**

Trevor-Roper, Hugh R.   CT3990.L58
The Hermit of Peking: The Hidden Life of Sir Edmund
Backhouse. Trade Cloth. Random House Children's Books. New
York, NY. 1977. ISBN:0-394-41104-8, ISBN13:
978-0-394-41104-0. Dewey:951.007202.

Audience: **g,u,f.**

Trotsky, Len   DS775 .T7
Problems of the Chinese Revolution. Max Shachtman (Foreword
by). Trade Paper. University of Michigan Press. Chicago, IL.
1967. ISBN:0-472-06131-3, ISBN13: 978-0-472-06131-0.
Dewey:951.04.

Audience: **f.**

White, Theodore H. &   DS777.53
Jacoby, Annalee
Thunder Out of China. Harrison Salisbury (Foreword by). Trade
Paper. Da Capo Press, Inc. Cambridge, MA. 1980. 352p.

Quality Paperbacks Ser. ISBN:0-306-80128-0, ISBN13: 978-0-306-80128-0. Dewey:951.04/2.

Audience: **g,l,u,f.**

China > Women in China

Bingying, Xie   **PL2765.I45Z5213 2001**
A Woman Soldier's Own Story: The Autobiography of Xie Bingying. Lily Chia Brissman & Barry Brissman (Translators). Trade Cloth. Columbia University Press. New York, NY. 2001. 288p. ISBN:0-231-12250-0, ISBN13: 978-0-231-12250-4. Dewey:895.1/85109. LCCN:2001-023514.

Audience: **g,u,f.**

Chang, Jung   **CT1828.C478 A3 1991**
Wild Swans: Three Daughters of China. Trade Paper. Simon & Schuster. New York, NY. 2003. 544p. ISBN:0-7432-4698-5, ISBN13: 978-0-7432-4698-9. Dewey:951.05'092 B. LCCN:91-020696.

Audience: **g,l,u,f.**

Chu, Samuel C.   **DS777.488.C5**
Madame Chiang Kai-Shek and Her China. Trade Cloth. EastBridge. Norwalk, CT. 2005. 288p. ISBN:1-891936-71-9, ISBN13: 978-1-891936-71-5. Dewey:951.24/905/092 B. LCCN:2004-026988.

Audience: **g,l,u,f.**

Ebrey, Patricia B.   **HQ684.A25 1993**
The Inner Quarters: Marriage and the Lives of Chinese Women in the Sung Period. Trade Cloth. University of California Press. Berkeley, CA. 1993. 312p. ISBN:0-520-08156-0, ISBN13: 978-0-520-08156-7. Dewey:305.420951. LCCN:92-031376.

Audience: **u,f.** *Choice, 1994.*

Gilmartin, Christina K.   **HX546.G54 1995**
Engendering the Chinese Revolution: Radical Women, Communist Politics, and Mass Movements in the 1920s. Trade Cloth. University of California Press. Berkeley, CA. 1995. 302p. ISBN:0-520-08981-2, ISBN13: 978-0-520-08981-5. Dewey:335.43/082. LCCN:94-024723.

Audience: **u,f.** *Choice, 1996.*

Hershatter, Gail   **HQ250.S52H47 1997**
Dangerous Pleasures: Prostitution and Modernity in Twentieth-Century Shanghai. Trade Cloth. University of California Press. Berkeley, CA. 1997. 603p. ISBN:0-520-20438-7, ISBN13: 978-0-520-20438-6. Dewey:306.74/0951/132. LCCN:96-005357.

Audience: **u,f.** *Choice, 1997.*

Ko, Dorothy (Editor), et al.   **HQ1767 .W64 2003**
Women and Confucian Cultures in Premodern China, Korea, and Japan. JaHyun Kim Haboush & Joan R. Piggott (Editors). Trade Cloth. University of California Press. Berkeley, CA. 2003. 350p. ISBN:0-520-23105-8, ISBN13: 978-0-520-23105-4. Dewey:305.4/0951. LCCN:2003-001855.

Audience: **g,f.**

Li, Yu-ning (Editor)   **HQ1767.C454 1992**
Chinese Women Through Chinese Eyes. Trade Cloth. M. E. Sharpe Inc. Armonk, NY. 1992. 282p. ISBN:0-87332-596-6, ISBN13: 978-0-87332-596-7. Dewey:305.42/0951. LCCN:91-011313.

Audience: **u,f.**

Lord, Bette Bao   **DS779.23.L67**
Legacies: A Chinese Mosaic. Trade Paper. DIANE Publishing Company. Collingdale, PA. 2001. 312p. ISBN:0-7881-9887-4, ISBN13: 978-0-7881-9887-8. Dewey:951.05.

Audience: **g,u,f.**

Spence, Jonathan D.   **HQ1767.S63 1978**
The Death of Woman Wang. Trade Cloth. Penguin Group (USA) Inc. New York, NY. 1978. xvii, 169p. ISBN:0-670-26232-3, ISBN13: 978-0-670-26232-8. Dewey:951/.14. LCCN:77-029134.

Audience: **g,l,u,f.**

T'ai-t'ai, Ning L.   **CT1828.N5 A3**
A Daughter of Han: The Autobiography of a Chinese Working Woman. Ida Pruitt (Editor). Trade Cloth. Stanford University Press. Palo Alto, CA. 1945. viii, 254p. ISBN:0-8047-0605-0, ISBN13: 978-0-8047-0605-6. Dewey:951.

Audience: **g,l,u,f.**

Terrill, Ross   **DS778.C5374T45 1999**
Madame Mao: The White-Boned Demon. Trade Paper. Stanford University Press. Palo Alto, CA. 2000. 424p. ISBN:0-8047-2922-0, ISBN13: 978-0-8047-2922-2. Dewey:951.05/092 B. LCCN:98-045872.

Audience: **g,u,f.**

Warner, Marina   **DS763.63.T96W37 1986**
The Dragon Empress. Trade Paper. Central Bureau voor Schimmelcultures. 1986. 256p. ISBN:0-689-70714-2, ISBN13: 978-0-689-70714-8. Dewey:951/.03/0924 B. LCCN:86-007909.

Audience: **g,u,f.**

Witke, Roxanne   **DS778.C5374.W57**
Comrade Chiang Ch'ing. Trade Cloth. Little Brown & Company. New York, NY. 1977. xxvi, 549p. ISBN:0-316-94900-0, ISBN13: 978-0-316-94900-2. Dewey:951.05/092/4. LCCN:77-000935.

Audience: **g,f.** *B*

Ye, Weili & Xiadong, Ma   **DS778.7.W445 2005**
Growing up in the People's Republic: Conversations between Two Daughters of China's Revolution. Cloth over Boards. Palgrave Macmillan. New York, NY. 2005. 208p. Palgrave Studies in Oral History Ser. ISBN:1-4039-6995-7, ISBN13: 978-1-4039-6995-8. Dewey:951.05/6. LCCN:2005-048676.

Audience: **g,u,f.**

Zhong, Xueping (Editor), et al.   **HQ1767.S598 2001**
Some of Us: Chinese Women Growing up in the Mao Era. Wang Zheng & Bai Di (Editors). Cloth Text. Rutgers University Press. Piscataway, NJ. 2001. 224p. ISBN:0-8135-2968-9, ISBN13: 978-0-8135-2968-4. Dewey:305.4/0951. LCCN:00-068351.

Audience: **g,u,f.** *Choice, 2002.*

China > Foreign Presence in China (Missions, Business, Education)

Bickers, Robert A.   **DA47.9.C6B53 1999**
Britain in China: Community, Culture and Colonialism, 1900-49. Cloth over Boards. Manchester University Press. Manchester, 1999. 256p. Studies in Imperialism ISBN:0-7190-4697-1, ISBN13: 978-0-7190-4697-1. Dewey:327.51041. LCCN:99-039760.

Audience: **g,u,f.** *Choice, 2000.*

Cochran, Sherman   HD9419.C42
Big Business in China: Sino-Foreign Rivalry in the Cigarette Industry, 1890-1930. Trade Cloth. Harvard University Press. Cambridge, MA. 1980. 342p. Harvard Studies in Business History, No. 33 ISBN:0-674-07262-6, ISBN13: 978-0-674-07262-6. Dewey:380.1/45/679730951. LCCN:79-023907.

Audience: **g,u,f.**

Cohen, Paul A.   DS762 .C6
China and Christianity: The Missionary Movement and the Growth of Chinese Anti-Foreignism, 1860-1870. Trade Cloth. Harvard University Press. Cambridge, MA. 1963. 406p. East Asian Monographs, No. 11 ISBN:0-674-11701-8, ISBN13: 978-0-674-11701-3. Dewey:266.009. LCCN:63-019135.

Audience: **g,u,f.** *B*

Cohen, Warren I.   E183.8.C5C62 2000
America's Response to China: A History of Sino-American Relations. Ed. 4. Columbia University Press. 2000. ISBN:0-231-11928-3, ISBN13: 978-0-231-11928-3.

Audience: **g,u,f.**

Fairbank, John K.   BV3415.2 .F34
  (Editor)
The Missionary Enterprise in China and America. Trade Cloth. Harvard University Press. Cambridge, MA. 1974. 442p. Studies in American-East Asian Relations, No. 6 ISBN:0-674-57655-1, ISBN13: 978-0-674-57655-1. Dewey:266/.023/0951. LCCN:74-082191.

Audience: **f.** *B*

Hersey, John   PS3515.E7715C3 1985
The Call. Judith B. Jones (Editor). Trade Cloth. Alfred A. Knopf Inc. New York, NY. 1985. 704p. ISBN:0-394-54331-9, ISBN13: 978-0-394-54331-4. Dewey:813/.52. LCCN:84-048669.

Audience: **g,l,u,f.**

Hunter, Jane   BV3415.2 .H86
The Gospel of Gentility: American Women Missionaries in Turn-of-the-Century China. Trade Paper. Yale University Press. Cumberland, RI. 1989. 322p. ISBN:0-300-04603-0, ISBN13: 978-0-300-04603-8. Dewey:266/.023/73051088042.

Audience: **g,u,f.**

Mungello, David E.   BV3417.M86 1989
Curious Land: Jesuit Accommodation and the Origins of Sinology. Trade Paper. University of Hawaii Press. Honolulu, HI. 1989. 408p. ISBN:0-8248-1219-0, ISBN13: 978-0-8248-1219-5. Dewey:951.007. LCCN:88-027874.

Audience: **g,u,f.** *Choice, 1990.*

Reischauer, Edwin O.   DS707 .R45
Ennin's Travels in Tang China. Paper Text. Textbook Publishers. Temecula, CA. 2003. xii, 341p. ISBN:0-7581-4637-X, ISBN13: 978-0-7581-4637-3. Dewey:951.016.

Audience: **l,u,f.**

Spence, Jonathan D.   BV3427.R46 S66 1984
The Memory Palace of Matteo Ricci. Trade Cloth. Penguin Group (USA) Inc. New York, NY. 1984. 368p. ISBN:0-670-46830-4, ISBN13: 978-0-670-46830-0. Dewey:266/.2/0924. LCCN:83-040653.

Audience: **g,u,f.**

Stuart, John Leighton   DS775.S84
My Fifty Years in China: The Memoirs of John Leighton Stuart, Missionary and Ambassador. Paper Text. Textbook Publishers.

Temecula, CA. 2003. 346p. ISBN:0-7581-5022-9, ISBN13: 978-0-7581-5022-6. Dewey:951.04.

Audience: **g,u,f.**

Yu-ming, Shaw   BV3427.S828S5 1992
John Leighton Stuart and Twentieth-Century Chinese-American Relations. Trade Cloth. Harvard University Press. Cambridge, MA. 1992. 350p. East Asian Monographs, No. 158 ISBN:0-674-47835-5, ISBN13: 978-0-674-47835-0. Dewey:266/.51/092/. LCCN:92-032007.

Audience: **f.**

Japan

     HA4621
Japan Statistical Yearbook 2004. Ed. 53. Cloth Text. International Publications Service. Levittown, PA. 2004. ISBN:4-8223-2906-2, ISBN13: 978-4-8223-2906-8. Dewey:315.2.

Audience: **f.**

Allison, Anne   GT3415.J3A45 1994
Nightwork: Sexuality, Pleasure, and Corporate Masculinity in a Tokyo Hostess Club. Trade Paper. University of Chicago Press. Chicago, IL. 1994. 228p. ISBN:0-226-01487-8, ISBN13: 978-0-226-01487-6. Dewey:305.310952135. LCCN:93-034877.

Audience: **g,u,f.**

Aoki, Masahiko &   HG187.J3F555 2000
  Saxonhouse, Gary R. (Editors)
Finance, Governance, and Competitiveness in Japan. Trade Cloth. Oxford University Press, Inc. New York, NY. 2000. 298p. Japan Business and Economics Ser. ISBN:0-19-829721-1, ISBN13: 978-0-19-829721-5. Dewey:332/.0951. LCCN:99-059051.

Audience: **f.**

Atkins, E. Taylor   ML3509.J3A85 2001
Blue Nippon: Authenticating Jazz in Japan. Trade Cloth. Duke University Press. Durham, NC. 2001. 408p. ISBN:0-8223-2710-4, ISBN13: 978-0-8223-2710-3. Dewey:781.65/0952. LCCN:2001-023019.

Audience: **g,u,f.** *Choice, 2002.*

Bestor, Theodore C.   HN730.T65B47 1989
Neighborhood Tokyo. Trade Cloth. Stanford University Press. Palo Alto, CA. 1989. 368p. ISBN:0-8047-1439-8, ISBN13: 978-0-8047-1439-6. Dewey:307.3/362/0952135. LCCN:88-012383.

Audience: **g,u,f.** *Choice, 1989.*

Brinton, Mary C.   HD6197 .B75
Women and the Economic Miracle: Gender and Work in Postwar Japan. Trade Paper. University of California Press. Berkeley, CA. 1994. 318p. California Series on Social Choice and Political Economy Ser. ISBN:0-520-08920-0, ISBN13: 978-0-520-08920-4. Dewey:331.40952. LCCN:91-030670.

Audience: **g,u,f.**

Brinton, Mary C.   HD6196.W66 2001
  (Editor)
Women's Working Lives in East Asia. Trade Cloth. Stanford University Press. Palo Alto, CA. 2001. 400p. Studies in Social Inequality ISBN:0-8047-4149-2, ISBN13: 978-0-8047-4149-1. Dewey:331.4/095. LCCN:2001-020377.

Audience: **g,u,f.**

Buruma, Ian   **DS821.B796 1985**
Behind the Mask: On Sexual Demons, Sacred Mothers,
Transvestites, Gangsters and Other Japanese Cultural Heroes.
Trade Paper. Penguin Group (USA) Inc. New York, NY. 1985.
ISBN:0-452-00738-0, ISBN13: 978-0-452-00738-3.
Dewey:306/.0952. LCCN:85-002901.

Audience: **g,u,f.**

Carlile, Lonny E. &   **HD3616.J33I8 1998**
Tilton, Mark (Editors)
Is Japan Really Changing Its Ways?: Regulatory Reform and the
Japanese Economy. Trade Paper. Brookings Institution Press.
Washington, DC. 1998. 232p. ISBN:0-8157-1291-X, ISBN13:
978-0-8157-1291-6. Dewey:338.952. LCCN:98-025374.

Audience: **g,u,f.** *Choice, 1999.*

Chamberlain, Basil Hall   **DS821**
Japanese Things: Being Notes on Various Subjects Connected
with Japan. Ed. 5. Kegan Paul International, Ltd. 2005.
ISBN:0-7103-1007-2, ISBN13: 978-0-7103-1007-1.

Audience: **g,u,f.**

Christopher, Robert   **DS821 .C587 1983**
The Japanese Mind: The Goliath Explained. Trade Cloth. Simon
& Schuster. New York, NY. 1983. 352p. ISBN:0-671-44947-8,
ISBN13: 978-0-671-44947-6. Dewey:952.04. LCCN:82-025896.

Audience: **f.** *B*

Davis, Winston   **BL2203.D37 1992**
Japanese Religion and Society: Paradigms of Structure and
Change. Paper Text. State University of New York Press.
Albany, NY. 1992. 327p. ISBN:0-7914-0840-X, ISBN13:
978-0-7914-0840-7. Dewey:306.6/0952. LCCN:90-024745.

Audience: **u,f.** *Choice, 1992.*

Dobbins, James C.   **BQ8712.6..D63 2002**
Jodo Shinshu: Shin Buddhism in Medieval Japan. Trade Cloth.
University of Hawaii Press. Honolulu, HI. 2002. 264p. Pure
Land Buddhist Studies ISBN:0-8248-2620-5, ISBN13:
978-0-8248-2620-8. Dewey:294.3/926. LCCN:2002-018047.

Audience: **f.** *Choice, 1990.*

Dore, Ronald P.   **HD70**
Stock Market Capitalism: Japan and Germany versus the
Anglo-Saxons. Trade Cloth. Oxford University Press, Inc. New
York, NY. 2000. 278p. ISBN:0-19-924062-0, ISBN13:
978-0-19-924062-3. Dewey:330.12/2. LCCN:00-025534.

Audience: **g,u,f.**

Fowler, Edward   **HD4901**
San'ya Blues: Laboring Life in Contemporary Tokyo. Book,
Other. Cornell University Press. Ithaca, NY. 1998. 296p.
ISBN:0-8014-8570-3, ISBN13: 978-0-8014-8570-1.
Dewey:305.5/62.

Audience: **g,u,f.**

Gao, Bai   **HC462.95 .G36 2001**
Japan's Economic Dilemma: The Institutional Origins of
Prosperity and Stagnation. Trade Cloth. Cambridge University
Press. New York, NY. 2001. 312p. ISBN:0-521-79025-5,
ISBN13: 978-0-521-79025-3. Dewey:330.952.
LCCN:2001-025592.

Audience: **g,u,f.**

Gerlach, Michael L.   **HD69.S8.G47**
Alliance Capitalism: The Social Organization of Japanese
Business. Trade Paper. University of California Press. Berkeley,

CA. 1997. 374p. ISBN:0-520-20889-7, ISBN13:
978-0-520-20889-6. Dewey:338.80952. LCCN:92-016619.

Audience: **g,u,f.** *Choice, 1993.*

Gibney, Frank (Editor)   **HD4313.U55 1998**
Unlocking the Bureaucrat's Kingdom: Deregulation and the
Japanese Economy. Trade Cloth. Brookings Institution Press.
Washington, DC. 1998. 282p. ISBN:0-8157-3126-4, ISBN13:
978-0-8157-3126-9. Dewey:338.952. LCCN:97-033784.

Audience: **g,u,f.**

Haley, John O.   **KNX68**
Authority Without Power: Law and the Japanese Paradox. Trade
Paper. Oxford University Press, Inc. New York, NY. 1994. 268p.
Studies on Law and Social Control ISBN:0-19-509257-0,
ISBN13: 978-0-19-509257-8. Dewey:349.52.

Audience: **l,u.**

Kodansha International   **G2359.T7**
Staff
Tokyo City Atlas: A Bilingual Guide. Ed. 3. Trade Paper.
Kodansha International. Tokyo, 2005. 124p.
ISBN:4-7700-2503-3, ISBN13: 978-4-7700-2503-6.

Audience: **g,f.**

Kodansha Ltd. Staff   **DS805.K6323 1998**
Bilingual Encyclopedia of Japan. Trade Cloth, Box or Slipcased.
Kodansha International. Tokyo, 944p. ISBN:4-7700-2130-5,
ISBN13: 978-4-7700-2130-4. Dewey:952/.003.
LCCN:98-012322.

Audience: **f.**

LeBlanc, Robin M.   **HQ1236.5.J3 L43 1999**
Bicycle Citizens: The Political World of the Japanese
Housewife. Trade Paper. University of California Press.
Berkeley, CA. 1999. 266p. Asia Ser., :Local Studies/Global
Themes ISBN:0-520-21291-6, ISBN13: 978-0-520-21291-6.
Dewey:305.42/0952. LCCN:98-046632.

Audience: **g,u,f.** *Choice, 1999.*

LeTendre, Gerald K.   **LB1135.L47 2000**
Learning to Be Adolescent: Growing up in U. S. and Japanese
Middle Schools. Cloth over Boards. Yale University Press.
Cumberland, RI. 2000. 256p. ISBN:0-300-08438-2, ISBN13:
978-0-300-08438-2. Dewey:373.18. LCCN:00-036641.

Audience: **l,u,f.** *Choice, 2001.*

Lincoln, Edward J.   **HC462.95.L56 2001**
Arthritic Japan: The Slow Pace of Economic Reform. Trade
Paper. Brookings Institution Press. Washington, DC. 2001. 254p.
ISBN:0-8157-0073-3, ISBN13: 978-0-8157-0073-9.
Dewey:338.951. LCCN:2001-004200.

Audience: **g,u,f.**

Littlewood, Ian   **DS821.L58 1996**
The Idea of Japan: Western Images, Western Myths. Trade
Cloth. Ivan R. Dee Publisher. Blue Ridge Summit, PA. 1996.
264p. ISBN:1-56663-117-3, ISBN13: 978-1-56663-117-4.
Dewey:952. LCCN:96-024432.

Audience: **g,u,f.**

Mason, Penelope   **N7350.M26 2004**
History of Japanese Art. Ed. 2. Trade Cloth. Prentice Hall Art.
Upper Saddle River, NJ. 2004. 432p. ISBN:0-13-117602-1,
ISBN13: 978-0-13-117602-7. Dewey:709.52.
LCCN:2004-044653.

Audience: **g,l,u,f.** *Choice, 1993.*

McConnell, David L.　　　　**LB2285.J3M33 2000**
ⓔ Importing Diversity: Inside Japan's JET Program. E-Book.
NetLibrary, Inc. Boulder, CO. 2000. ISBN:0-585-28069-X,
ISBN13: 978-0-585-28069-1. Dewey:370.117/0952.
　　　　　　　　　　　　　　　Audience: **g,u,f.**

Milhaupt, Curtis J.　　　　**KNX74.J374 2001**
　(Editor), et al.
Japanese Law in Context: Readings in Society, the Economy,
and Politics. Michael K. Young & J. Mark Ramseyer (Editors).
Trade Cloth. Harvard University Press. Cambridge, MA. 2001.
672p. Harvard East Asian Monographs, Vol. 198
ISBN:0-674-00518-X, ISBN13: 978-0-674-00518-1.
Dewey:349.52. LCCN:00-054427.
　　　　　　　　　　　　　　　Audience: **g,u,f.**

Mulgan, Aurelia George　　　　**HD2093.M85 2000**
ⓔ The Politics of Agriculture in Japan. E-Book. NetLibrary,
Inc. Boulder, CO. 2000. ISBN:0-585-45337-3, ISBN13:
978-0-585-45337-8. Dewey:338.1/852.
　　　　　　　　　　　　　　　Audience: **g,u,f.**

Oda, Hiroshi　　　　**KNX68**
Japanese Law. Ed. 2. Trade Paper. Oxford University Press, Inc.
New York, NY. 2001. 494p. ISBN:0-19-924810-9, ISBN13:
978-0-19-924810-0. Dewey:349.52.
　　　　　　　　　　　　　　　Audience: **u,f.**

Okuno-Fujiwara,　　　　**HC462.8.G427 1999**
　Masahiro & Okazaki, Tetsuji (Editors)
The Japanese Economic System and Its Historical Origins.
Susan Herbert (Translator). Trade Cloth. Oxford University
Press, Inc. New York, NY. 1999. 304p. Japan Business and
Economics Ser. ISBN:0-19-828901-4, ISBN13:
978-0-19-828901-2. Dewey:330.952. LCCN:00-268902.
　　　　　　　　　　　　　　　Audience: **f.**

Patrick, Hugh T. &　　　　**HG3324.J363 1994**
　Aoki, M. (Editors)
The Japanese Main Bank System: Its Relevance for Developing
and Transforming Economies. Trade Cloth. Oxford University
Press, Inc. New York, NY. 1995. 684p. ISBN:0-19-828899-9,
ISBN13: 978-0-19-828899-2. Dewey:332.1/0952.
LCCN:94-029638.
　　　　　　　　　　　　　　　Audience: **f.**

Pempel, T. J.　　　　**HC462.9.P413 1998**
Regime Shift: Comparative Dynamics of the Japanese Political
Economy. Book, Other. Cornell University Press. Ithaca, NY.
1998. 288p. Studies in Political Economy ISBN:0-8014-3532-3,
ISBN13: 978-0-8014-3532-4. Dewey:338.952.
LCCN:98-030185.
　　　　　　　　　　　　　　　Audience: **f.**

Port, Kenneth L. &　　　　**KNX68.P67 2003**
　McAlinn, Gerald Paul
Comparative Law: The Role of Law and the Legal Process in
Japan. Ed. 2. Trade Cloth. Carolina Academic Press. Durham,
NC. 2003. 1136p. Carolina Academic Press Law Casebook Ser.
ISBN:0-89089-464-7, ISBN13: 978-0-89089-464-4.
Dewey:349.52. LCCN:2002-115661.
　　　　　　　　　　　　　　　Audience: **f.**

Porter, Michael, et al.　　　　**HF1601.P67 2000**
Can Japan Compete? Hirotaka Takeuchi & Mariko Sakakibara
(Authors). Trade Cloth. Basic Books. New York, NY. 2000.
224p. ISBN:0-465-05989-9, ISBN13: 978-0-465-05989-8.
Dewey:338.6/048/0952.
　　　　　　　　　　　Audience: **g,u,f.** *Choice, 2001.*

Reischauer, Edwin O.　　　　**DS821**
The Japanese. Paper Text. Harvard University Press. Cambridge,
MA. 1977. ISBN:0-674-47178-4, ISBN13: 978-0-674-47178-8.
Dewey:952.
　　　　　　　　　　　　Audience: **g,l,u,f.** 𝓑

Shulman, Frank Joseph　　　　**Z3301.S475 1989**
ⓔ Japan. E-Book. ABC-CLIO, Inc. Santa Barbara, CA. 1989.
World Bibliographical Ser. ISBN:0-585-05873-3, ISBN13:
978-0-585-05873-3.
　　　　　　　　　　　　　　　Audience: **f.**

Stockwin, J. A. A.　　　　**JQ1605.S86 2003**
Dictionary of the Modern Politics of Japan. Paper over Boards.
Routledge. New York, NY. 2003. 336p. Routledge in Asia Ser.
ISBN:0-415-15170-8, ISBN13: 978-0-415-15170-2.
Dewey:320.952/03. LCCN:2002-036778.
　　　　　　　　　　Audience: **g,u,f.** *Choice, 2003.*

Sugimoto, Yoshio　　　　**HN723.S7 2002**
　(Author, Contribution by)
An Introduction to Japanese Society. Ed. 2. Harumi Befu, Roger
Goodman, Michio Muramatsu, Wolfgang Seifert & Chizuko
Ueno (Contribution by). Cloth Text. Cambridge University
Press. New York, NY. 2002. 330p. Contemporary Japanese
Society Ser. ISBN:0-521-82193-2, ISBN13: 978-0-521-82193-3.
Dewey:306/.0952. LCCN:2002-074194.
　　　　　　　　　Audience: **g,l,u,f.** *Choice, 1997.*

Tanaka, Stefan　　　　**DS834.7.T355**
Japan's Orient: Rendering Pasts into History. Trade Paper.
University of California Press. Berkeley, CA. 1995. 318p.
ISBN:0-520-20170-1, ISBN13: 978-0-520-20170-5.
Dewey:951.0072. LCCN:92-020639.
　　　　　　　　　　Audience: **u,f.** *Choice, 1994.*

Upham, Frank K.　　　　**KNX465**
Law and Social Change in Postwar Japan. Trade Cloth. Harvard
University Press. Cambridge, MA. 1989. 288p.
ISBN:0-674-51787-3, ISBN13: 978-0-674-51787-5.
Dewey:347.52/009. LCCN:86-019472.
　　　　　　　　　　Audience: **f.** *Choice, 1987.*

Varley, Paul H.　　　　**DS821.V36 2000**
Japanese Culture. Ed. 4. Trade Cloth. University of Hawaii
Press. Honolulu, HI. 2000. 400p. ISBN:0-8248-2152-1, ISBN13:
978-0-8248-2152-4. Dewey:952. LCCN:99-057345.
　　　　　　　　　　　　　Audience: **g,l,u,f.**

Vogel, Ezra F.　　　　**HN723.5**
Japan As Number One: Lessons for America. Trade Cloth.
Harvard University Press. Cambridge, MA. 1979. 286p.
ISBN:0-674-47215-2, ISBN13: 978-0-674-47215-0.
Dewey:309.1/52/04. LCCN:78-024059.
　　　　　　　　　　　　Audience: **g,u,f.** 𝓑

Vogel, Steven K.　　　　**HC256.6**
Freer Markets, More Rules: Regulatory Reform in Advanced
Industrial Countries. Trade Paper. Cornell University Press.
Ithaca, NY. 1998. 312p. Cornell Studies in Political Economy
ISBN:0-8014-8534-7, ISBN13: 978-0-8014-8534-3.
Dewey:338.9/41.
　　　　　　　　　　　　　　　Audience: **f.**

Japan > Civilization

Benedict, Ruth   DS821.B46 2005
The Chrysanthemum and the Sword: Patterns of Japanese
Culture. Trade Paper. Houghton Mifflin Company Trade &
Reference Division. Boston, MA. 2006. 352p.
ISBN:0-618-61959-3, ISBN13: 978-0-618-61959-7. Dewey:952.
LCCN:2006-271282.

Audience: **g,u,f.** B

Bestor, Theodore   HF5475.J3
Tsukiji: The Fish Market at the Center of the World. University
of California Press. 2004. (California Studies in Food and
Culture) ISBN:0-520-22023-4, ISBN13: 978-0-520-22023-2.

Audience: **g,l,u,f.**

Coaldrake, William H.   TH5618.C63 1990
The Way of the Carpenter: Tools and Japanese Architecture.
Trade Cloth. Shambhala Publications, Inc. Boston, MA. 1990.
220p. ISBN:0-8348-0231-7, ISBN13: 978-0-8348-0231-5.
Dewey:694/.0952. LCCN:90-035137.

Audience: **f.**

Daishonin, Nichiren &   BQ8349.N573E5 1990
  Yampolsky, Philip B.
Selected Writings of Nichiren. Burton Watson (Translator).
Trade Cloth. Columbia University Press. New York, NY. 1990.
508p. Translations from the Oriental Classics Ser.
ISBN:0-231-07260-0, ISBN13: 978-0-231-07260-1.
Dewey:294.3/928. LCCN:90-001367.

Audience: **u,f.**

Doi, Takeo   BF108.J3
The Anatomy of Dependence. Trade Paper. Kodansha
International. Tokyo, 2002. 192p. ISBN:4-7700-2800-8, ISBN13:
978-4-7700-2800-6. Dewey:155.8/952.

Audience: **g,u,f.** B

Dore, Ronald P.   HN723.5.D67 1978
Shinohata: A Portrait of a Japanese Village. Trade Paper.
University of California Press. Berkeley, CA. 1994. 332p.
ISBN:0-520-08628-7, ISBN13: 978-0-520-08628-9.
Dewey:307.72/0952. LCCN:93-041319.

Audience: **g,l,u,f.**

Dresser, Christopher   N7350.D7 2001
Japan: Its Architecture, Art and Art Manufacturers. Trade Cloth.
Kegan Paul International, Ltd. London, 2001. 488p. The Kegan
Paul Japan Library ISBN:0-7103-0686-5, ISBN13:
978-0-7103-0686-9. Dewey:709.5/2/09034. LCCN:2002-319077.

Audience: **g,u,f.**

Hakeda, Yoshita S.   BQ8999.K853
  (Translator)
Kukai: Major Works, Translated with an Account of His Life
and a Study of His Thought. William T. DeBary (Introduction
by). Trade Paper. Columbia University Press. New York, NY.
1972. 303p. ISBN:0-231-05933-7, ISBN13: 978-0-231-05933-6.
Dewey:294.3/9. LCCN:72-003124.

Audience: **f.**

Hardacre, Helen   BL2202
Marketing the Menacing Fetus in Japan. Trade Paper. University
of California Press. Berkeley, CA. 1999. 332p. Twentieth
Century Japan: the Emergence of a World Power Ser.
ISBN:0-520-21654-7, ISBN13: 978-0-520-21654-9.
Dewey:291.3/8/0952.

Audience: **g,u,f.**

Hendry, Joy   HN723.5.H46 2003
Understanding Japanese Society. Ed. 3. Paper over Boards.
Routledge. New York, NY. 2003. 256p. The Nissan
Institute/Routledge Japanese Studies ISBN:0-415-26382-4,
ISBN13: 978-0-415-26382-5. Dewey:306/.0952.
LCCN:2002-153220.

Audience: **g,l,u,f.**

Honen   BQ8469.H664.S4413
Honen's Senchakushu: Passages on the Selection of the
Nembutsu in the Original Vow. Senchakushu (Editor,
Translator). Trade Cloth. University of Hawaii Press. Honolulu,
HI. 1998. 296p. Classics in East Asian Buddhism
ISBN:0-8248-2025-8, ISBN13: 978-0-8248-2025-1.
Dewey:294.3/42. LCCN:98-012263.

Audience: **f.**

Hudson, Mark J.   DS830.H83 1999
Ruins of Identity: Ethnogenesis in the Japanese Islands. Trade
Cloth. University of Hawaii Press. Honolulu, HI. 1999. 336p.
ISBN:0-8248-2156-4, ISBN13: 978-0-8248-2156-2. Dewey:952.
LCCN:99-011829.

Audience: **f.** *Choice, 2000.*

Itoh, Teiji   SB458
The Gardens of Japan. Ed. 2. Trade Cloth. Kodansha
International. Tokyo, 1998. 244p. ISBN:4-7700-2321-9, ISBN13:
978-4-7700-2321-6. Dewey:712/.0952.

Audience: **g,u,f.** B

Kashiwahara, Yusen   BQ683.N54513 1994
Shapers of Japanese Buddhism. Koyu Sonoda (Editor). Trade
Paper. Kosei Publishing Company. Tokyo, 1994. 392p.
ISBN:4-333-01630-4, ISBN13: 978-4-333-01630-3.
Dewey:294.3/092/252 B. LCCN:95-129805.

Audience: **f.**

Kato, Shuichi   N7350.K3713 1994
Japan: Spirit and Form. Trade Cloth. Tuttle Publishing. Boston,
MA. 1994. 260p. ISBN:0-8048-1969-6, ISBN13:
978-0-8048-1969-5. Dewey:709/.54. LCCN:94-060344.

Audience: **u,f.**

Kondo, Dorinne K.   HD6197.K658 1990
Crafting Selves: Power, Gender, and Discourses of Identity in a
Japanese Workplace. Trade Paper. University of Chicago Press.
Chicago, IL. 1990. 354p. ISBN:0-226-45044-9, ISBN13:
978-0-226-45044-5. Dewey:305.420952. LCCN:89-038547.

Audience: **g,u,f.**

Lebra, Takie S.   DS821 .L346
Japanese Patterns of Behavior. Trade Cloth. University of
Hawaii Press. Honolulu, HI. 1976. 320p. East-West Center Bk.
ISBN:0-8248-0460-0, ISBN13: 978-0-8248-0460-2.
Dewey:301.29/52. LCCN:76-110392.

Audience: **g,l,u,f.**

LeTendre, Gerald K.   LA1312.C64 1999
  (Editor)
Competitor or Ally?: Japan's Role in American Educational
Debates. Merry White, Ineko Tsuchida, Catherine C. Lewis,
David McConnell, Hidetada Shimizu, Hua Yang, Kangmin Zeng
& David Baker (Contribution by). Cloth Text. Garland
Publishing, Inc. New York, NY. 1999. 200p. Reference Books in
International Education, No. 45 ISBN:0-8153-3273-4, ISBN13:
978-0-8153-3273-2. Dewey:370/.952. LCCN:00-552170.

Audience: **l,u,f.**

Lock, Margaret M.　　　　QP89.L63 2002
e Twice Dead: Organ Transplants and the Reinvention of Death. E-Book. NetLibrary, Inc. Boulder, CO. 2002. ISBN:0-585-46634-3, ISBN13: 978-0-585-46634-7. Dewey:617.9/5/0952.

Audience: **g,u,f.**

Munroe, Alexandra　　　　N7355
Japanese Art after 1945: Scream Against the Sky. Trade Paper. Harry N. Abrams, Inc. New York, NY. 1996. 416p. ISBN:0-8109-2593-1, ISBN13: 978-0-8109-2593-9. Dewey:709/.52/09045.

Audience: **g,u,f.**

Ohnuki-Tierney, Emiko　　　　DS806
Rice As Self: Japanese Identities Through Time. Trade Paper. Princeton University Press. Princeton, NJ. 1994. 198p. ISBN:0-691-02110-4, ISBN13: 978-0-691-02110-2. Dewey:952.

Audience: **g,u,f.** *Choice, 1994.*

Okano, Kaori, et al.　　　　LA1312 .O426 1999
Education in Contemporary Japan: Inequality and Diversity. Robert Oprandy & Motonori Tsuchiya (Authors), Harumi Befu, Roger Goodman, Michio Muramatsu, Wolfgang Seifert, Yoshio Sugimoto & Chizuko Ueno (Contribution by). Trade Paper. Cambridge University Press. New York, NY. 1999. 286p. Contemporary Japanese Society Ser. ISBN:0-521-62686-2, ISBN13: 978-0-521-62686-6. Dewey:370/.952. LCCN:98-043666.

Audience: **f.** *Choice, 1999.*

Peak, Lois　　　　LB1140.25.J3
Learning to Go to School in Japan: The Transition from Home to Preschool Life. Trade Paper. University of California Press. Berkeley, CA. 1993. 228p. ISBN:0-520-08387-3, ISBN13: 978-0-520-08387-5. Dewey:372.21/0952. LCCN:91-013628.

Audience: **f.**

Philippi, Donald L.　　　　BL2224.25.O5
　(Translator)
Norito: A Translation of the Ancient Japanese Ritual Prayers. Joseph M. Kitagawa (Preface by). Paper Text. DIANE Publishing Company. Collingdale, PA. 1998. 95p. ISBN:0-7881-5459-1, ISBN13: 978-0-7881-5459-1. Dewey:299/.56138.

Audience: **f.**

Powers, Richard G.　　　　DS822
　(Editor), et al.
Handbook of Japanese Popular Culture. Hidetoshi Kato & Bruce Stronach (Editors). Cloth Text. Greenwood Publishing Group, Inc. Portsmouth, NH. 1989. 368p. ISBN:0-313-23922-3, ISBN13: 978-0-313-23922-9. Dewey:952.04/8. LCCN:87-007586.

Audience: **g,u,f.** *Choice, 1990.*

Robertson, Jennifer E.　　　　GN635.J2 R62 1998
Takarazuka: Sexual Politics and Popular Culture in Modern Japan. Trade Paper. University of California Press. Berkeley, CA. 1998. 296p. ISBN:0-520-21151-0, ISBN13: 978-0-520-21151-3. Dewey:306/.0952. LCCN:97-038671.

Audience: **g,u,f.** *Choice, 1999.*

Rohlen, Thomas P. &　　　　LB1025.3.R64 1996
　LeTendre, Gerald K. (Editors)
Teaching and Learning in Japan. Trade Paper. Cambridge

University Press. New York, NY. 1999. 410p. ISBN:0-521-65115-8, ISBN13: 978-0-521-65115-8. Dewey:371.3/0952.

Audience: **f.**

Schwade, Arcadio　　　　BL2220
Shinto-Bibliography in Western Languages: Bibliography on Shinto and Religious Sects, Intellectual Schools and Movements Influenced by Shintoism. Trade Paper. Brill Academic Publishers, Inc. Boston, MA. 1986. xiv, 126p. ISBN:90-04-08173-9, ISBN13: 978-90-04-08173-4. Dewey:016.299/561. LCCN:87-117957.

Audience: **f.**

Shields, James J. Jr.　　　　LC210.8.J3
　(Editor)
Japanese Schooling: Patterns of Socialization, Equality, and Political Control. Perfect. Pennsylvania State University Press. University Park, PA. 2004. 320p. ISBN:0-271-02340-6, ISBN13: 978-0-271-02340-3. Dewey:370.19/0952.

Audience: **f.** *Choice, 1989.*

Singleton, John (Editor)　　　　LB1059 .L33 1998
Learning in Likely Places: Varieties of Apprenticeship in Japan. John Seely Brown, Christian Heath & Roy Pea (Contribution by). Trade Cloth. Cambridge University Press. New York, NY. 1998. 392p. University of Cambridge Department of Applied Economics Occasional Paper Ser. ISBN:0-521-48012-4, ISBN13: 978-0-521-48012-3. Dewey:371.3/8. LCCN:97-025904.

Audience: **g,u,f.**

Skov, Lise & Moeran,　　　　P94.5.W652J38 1995
　Brian (Editors)
Women, Media, and Consumption in Japan. Trade Cloth. University of Hawaii Press. Honolulu, HI. 1995. 320p. Consumasian Book Ser. ISBN:0-8248-1775-3, ISBN13: 978-0-8248-1775-6. Dewey:305.4/0952. LCCN:95-019376.

Audience: **g,u,f.**

Smith, Robert J. &　　　　HQ1765.S93
　Wiswell, Ella L.
The Women of Suye Mura. Trade Paper. University of Chicago Press. Chicago, IL. 1982. 348p. ISBN:0-226-76345-5, ISBN13: 978-0-226-76345-3. Dewey:305.4/2/09522. LCCN:82-002708.

Audience: **g,l,u,f.**

Tsuchimochi, Gary H.　　　　LA1312.T7313 1993
　& Kawabe, Daito
Education Reform in Postwar Japan: The 1946 U. S. Educational Mission. Cloth Text. University of Tokyo Press. 1993. 350p. ISBN:0-86008-496-5, ISBN13: 978-0-86008-496-9. Dewey:370/.952/09044. LCCN:93-192546.

Audience: **f.**

Tsuneyoshi, Ryoko　　　　LA1312 .T77 2001
Japanese Model of Schooling: Comparisons with the U. S. Paper over Boards. Garland Publishing, Inc. New York, NY. 2001. 225p. Reference Bks in International Education Ser. ISBN:0-8153-3641-1, ISBN13: 978-0-8153-3641-9. Dewey:370.952. LCCN:00-059297.

Audience: **f.**

White, Merry I.　　　　HQ682 .W484 2002
Perfectly Japanese: Making Families in an Era of Upheaval. Trade Cloth. University of California Press. Berkeley, CA. 2002. 266p. Twentieth-Century Japan Ser., Vol. 14 ISBN:0-520-21754-3, ISBN13: 978-0-520-21754-6. Dewey:306.85/0952. LCCN:2002-005535.

Audience: **g,l,u,f.**

Wilson, Richard NK4167
Inside Japanese Ceramics. Trade Paper. Shambhala Publications, Inc. Boston, MA. 1999. 192p. ISBN:0-8348-0442-5, ISBN13: 978-0-8348-0442-5. Dewey:738.095.

Audience: **g,l,u,f.**

Yamada, Koun BQ9289.Y36 2004
Gateless Gate: The Classic Book of Zen Koans. Trade Paper. Publishers Group West. Berkeley, CA. 2005. 288p. ISBN:0-86171-382-6, ISBN13: 978-0-86171-382-0. Dewey:294.3/443. LCCN:2003-114197.

Audience: **g,u,f.**

Yoneyama, Shoko LA1316.Y67 1999
Japanese High School: Silence and Resistance. Paper over Boards. Routledge. New York, NY. 1999. 312p. Nissan Institute/Routledge Japanese Studies ISBN:0-415-15439-1, ISBN13: 978-0-415-15439-0. Dewey:373.52. LCCN:98-042020.

Audience: **f.** *Choice, 2000.*

Japan > History

Alcock, Rutherford DS809 .A65
Capital of the Tycoon: A Narrative of a Three Years' Residence in Japan. Library Binding. Greenwood Publishing Group, Inc. Portsmouth, NH. 1968. ISBN:0-8371-9938-7, ISBN13: 978-0-8371-9938-2. Dewey:915.2/04/3. LCCN:68-030995.

Audience: **g,u,f.** *B*

Aston, William G. DS851.A2.N53 1972
(Translator)
Nihongi: Chronicles of Japan from the Earliest Times to A.D. 697. Trade Paper. Princeton University Press. Princeton, NJ. 1989. 852p. ISBN:0-8048-0984-4, ISBN13: 978-0-8048-0984-9. Dewey:915.2/03/1. LCCN:70-152110.

Audience: **f.** *B*

Beer, Lawrence Ward & KNX2101.B44 2002
Maki, John M.
From Imperial Myth to Democracy: Japan's Two Constitutions, 1889-2001. Trade Cloth. University Press of Colorado. Boulder, CO. 2002. xiv, 234p. ISBN:0-87081-674-8, ISBN13: 978-0-87081-674-1. Dewey:342.52/029. LCCN:2002-005403.

Audience: **u,f.** *Choice, 2003.*

Black, John R. DS881
Young Japan: Yokohama and Yedo, a Narrative of the Settlement and the City from the Signing of the Treaties in 1858, to the Close of the Year 1879. with a Glance at the Progress of Japan During a Period of Twenty-One Years, Vol. 2. Trade Paper. Adamant Media. Chestnut Hill, MA. 2001. 538p. ISBN:1-4021-9374-2, ISBN13: 978-1-4021-9374-3. Dewey:952.031.

Audience: **f.**

Bowen, Roger W. DS882.5.B68
Rebellion and Democracy in Meiji Japan: A Study of Commoners in the Popular Rights Movement. Trade Cloth. University of California Press. Berkeley, CA. 1980. 450p. ISBN:0-520-03665-4, ISBN13: 978-0-520-03665-9. Dewey:952.03/1. LCCN:78-051755.

Audience: **u,f.** *B*

Butow, R. J. C. HC461.5.S48
Tojo and the Coming of the War. Trade Cloth. Stanford University Press. Palo Alto, CA. 1961. xii, 584p. ISBN:0-8047-0690-5, ISBN13: 978-0-8047-0690-2. Dewey:952.03092.

Audience: **u,f.**

Cook, Haruko Taya & D811.A2
Cook, Theodore F.
Japan at War: An Oral History. Trade Paper. DIANE Publishing Company. Collingdale, PA. 2005. 479p. ISBN:0-7567-9389-0, ISBN13: 978-0-7567-9389-0. Dewey:940.53/52/0922.

Audience: **g,l,u,f.** *Choice, 1993.*

Cooper, Michael DS808.T48 1995
(Editor)
They Came to Japan: An Anthology of European Reports on Japan, 1543-1640. Trade Paper. University of Michigan, Center for Japanese Studies. Ann Arbor, MI. 1995. xviii, 439p. Michigan Classics in Japanese Studies, No. 15 ISBN:0-939512-73-4, ISBN13: 978-0-939512-73-7. Dewey:952. LCCN:95-041563.

Audience: **u,f.** *B*

Craig, Albert M. DS894.79.Y349C4623
Choshu in the Meiji Restoration. Book, Other. Lexington Books. Lanham, MD. 2000. 456p. Studies of Modern Japan ISBN:0-7391-0193-5, ISBN13: 978-0-7391-0193-3. Dewey:952.025. LCCN:00-057402.

Audience: **f.**

Curtis, Gerald L. JQ1631.C87 1999
The Logic of Japanese Politics: Leaders, Institutions and the Limits of Change. Trade Paper. Columbia University Press. New York, NY. 2000. 336p. Studies of the East Asian Institute ISBN:0-231-10843-5, ISBN13: 978-0-231-10843-0. Dewey:320.952/09/049. LCCN:99-019910.

Audience: **l,u,f.**

Dower, J. W. PG3476.G326
Empire and Aftermath: Yoshida Shigeru and the Japanese Experience, 1878-1954. Trade Paper. Harvard University Press. Cambridge, MA. 1988. 618p. East Asian Monographs, No. 84 ISBN:0-674-25126-1, ISBN13: 978-0-674-25126-7. Dewey:952.04/092/4.

Audience: **f.** *B*

Dower, John D767.9.D69 1986
War Without Mercy: Race and Power in the Pacific War. Trade Cloth. Knopf Publishing Group. New York, NY. 1986. 416p. ISBN:0-394-50030-X, ISBN13: 978-0-394-50030-0. Dewey:940.53/1. LCCN:85-043462.

Audience: **g,u,f.** *Choice, 1986.*

Dower, John W. DS889.D69
Embracing Defeat: Japan in the Wake of World War II. Trade Cloth. DIANE Publishing Company. Collingdale, PA. 2003. 676p. ISBN:0-7567-6840-3, ISBN13: 978-0-7567-6840-9. Dewey:952.04.

Audience: **g,l,u,f.**

Ebrey, Patricia Buckley, DS511
et al.
Japan: East Asia: A Cultural, Social and Political History. Anne Walthall & James B. Palais (Authors). Paper Text. Houghton Mifflin College Division. Boston, MA. 2005. 224p. World History Ser., :Specialized Courses Ser. ISBN:0-618-13388-7, ISBN13: 978-0-618-13388-8. Dewey:950.

Audience: **g,l,u,f.**

Garon, Sheldon   **HD8726.5**
The State and Labor in Modern Japan. Trade Cloth. University
of California Press. Berkeley, CA. 1990. 326p.
ISBN:0-520-06838-6, ISBN13: 978-0-520-06838-4.
Dewey:331/.0952. LCCN:86-030890.

Audience: **u,f.**

Gluck, Carol   **DS882**
Japan's Modern Myths: Ideology in the Late Meiji Period. Trade
Paper. Princeton University Press. Princeton, NJ. 1987. 424p.
Columbia University, Studies of the East Asian Institute
ISBN:0-691-00812-4, ISBN13: 978-0-691-00812-7.
Dewey:952/.031.

Audience: **g,u,f.** *Choice, 1986.*

Gordon, Andrew   **HD8726.5**
The Wages of Affluence: Labor and Management in Postwar
Japan. Trade Paper. Harvard University Press. Cambridge, MA.
2001. 288p. ISBN:0-674-00706-9, ISBN13: 978-0-674-00706-2.
Dewey:331/.0952.

Audience: **u,f.**

Green, Michael   **DS889 .G64**
Japan's Reluctant Realism: Foreign Policy Challenges in an Era
of Uncertain Power. Trade Paper. Palgrave Macmillan. New
York, NY. 2003. 368p. ISBN:1-4039-6235-9, ISBN13:
978-1-4039-6235-5. Dewey:327.52.

Audience: **g,u,f.**

Hane, Mikiso   **DS881.H36 2001**
Modern Japan: A Historical Survey. Ed. 3. Trade Paper.
Westview Press. Boulder, CO. 2001. 568p. ISBN:0-8133-3756-9,
ISBN13: 978-0-8133-3756-2. Dewey:952.03. LCCN:00-049528.
Audience: **g,u,f.** *Choice, 1987.*

Hanes, Jeffrey E. &   **HB126.J4 S374 2002**
  Seki, Hajime
The City As Subject: Seki Hajime and the Reinvention of
Modern Osaka. Trade Cloth. University of California Press.
Berkeley, CA. 2002. 362p. Twentieth-Century Japan Ser.
ISBN:0-520-22849-9, ISBN13: 978-0-520-22849-8.
Dewey:307.1/26/092 B. LCCN:2001-027321.
Audience: **f.** *Choice, 2003.*

Harootunian, H. D.   **DS881.3**
Toward Restoration: The Growth of Political Consciousness in
Tokugawa Japan. Trade Cloth. University of California Press.
Berkeley, CA. 1970. xviii, 421p. Center for Japanese and
Korean Studies, UC Berkeley ISBN:0-520-01566-5, ISBN13:
978-0-520-01566-1. Dewey:952.025. LCCN:79-094993.
Audience: **f.** *B*

Harootunian, Harry D.   **DS822.2.H313 1988**
Things Seen and Unseen: Discourse and Ideology in Tokugawa
Nativism. Trade Paper. University of Chicago Press. Chicago,
IL. 1988. 508p. ISBN:0-226-31707-2, ISBN13:
978-0-226-31707-6. Dewey:001.1/0952. LCCN:87 019069.
Audience: **f.**

Havens, Thomas R.   **DS0558.6.J3H**
Fire Across the Sea: The Vietnam War and Japan, 1965-1975.
Trade Paper. Books on Demand. Ann Arbor, MI. 340p.
ISBN:0-608-06377-0, ISBN13: 978-0-608-06377-5.
Dewey:959.704/33/52. LCCN:86-022630.

Audience: **g,u,f.**

Hook, Glenn D. &   **KNX2101.J37 2000**
  McCormack, Gavan (Editors)
The Japanese Constitution: Documents and Analysis. Paper over

Boards. Routledge. New York, NY. 2001. 224p. Sheffield Centre
for Japanese Studies/routledge Ser. ISBN:0-415-24099-9,
ISBN13: 978-0-415-24099-4. Dewey:342.52/02.
LCCN:00-062797.

Audience: **f.**

Horio, Teruhisa   **LA1311 .H66**
Educational Thought and Ideology in Modern Japan: State
Authority and Individual Freedom. Stephen Platzer (Translator).
Trade Paper. University of Tokyo Press. 1995. 436p.
ISBN:0-86008-517-1, ISBN13: 978-0-86008-517-1.
Dewey:370/.952.

Audience: **f.**

Hoshi, Takeo &   **HG187.J3C67 2004**
  Kashyap, Anil
Corporate Financing and Governance in Japan: The Road to the
Future. Trade Paper. MIT Press. Cambridge, MA. 2004. 384p.
ISBN:0-262-58248-1, ISBN13: 978-0-262-58248-3.
Dewey:332.1/0952.

Audience: **f.**

Huber, Thomas M.   **DS894.79.Y349.C4637**
The Revolutionary Origins of Modern Japan. Trade Cloth.
Stanford University Press. Palo Alto, CA. 1990. 272p.
ISBN:0-8047-1048-1, ISBN13: 978-0-8047-1048-0.
Dewey:952.03/1/0922. LCCN:79-064214.
Audience: **u,f.** *B*

Hunter, Janet E.   **DS881.9**
Concise Dictionary of Modern Japanese History. Trade Cloth.
University of California Press. Berkeley, CA. 1984. 464p.
ISBN:0-520-04557-2, ISBN13: 978-0-520-04557-6.
Dewey:952.03. LCCN:82-017456.
Audience: **g,u,f.** *B*

Ikegami, Eiko   **DS827.S3I54 1995**
The Taming of the Samurai: Honorific Individualism and the
Making of Modern Japan. Trade Cloth. Harvard University
Press. Cambridge, MA. 1998. 448p. ISBN:0-674-86808-0,
ISBN13: 978-0-674-86808-3. Dewey:306/.0952.
LCCN:94-036784.
Audience: **f.** *Choice, 1995.*

Jansen, Marius B.   **DS871.J35 2002**
The Making of Modern Japan. Trade Paper. Harvard University
Press. Cambridge, MA. 2002. 936p. ISBN:0-674-00991-6,
ISBN13: 978-0-674-00991-2. Dewey:952/.025.
Audience: **g,u,f.** *Choice, 2001.*

Johnson, Chalmers A.   **HC462.9 .J63**
Japan: Who Governs?: The Rise of the Developmental State.
Trade Paper. W. W. Norton & Company, Inc. New York, NY.
1996. 384p. ISBN:0-393-31450-2, ISBN13: 978-0-393-31450-2.
Dewey:338.952.

Audience: **g,u,f.**

Kaempfer, Engelbert   **DS835.K2 1971**
The History of Japan, Together with a Description of the
Kingdom of Siam, 1690-92. Trade Cloth. A M S Press, Inc.
New York, NY. 1971. ISBN:0-404-03630-9, ISBN13:
978-0-404-03630-0. Dewey:915.2/03/25. LCCN:78-137313.
Audience: **f.** *B*

Kaempfer, Engelbert &   **DS822.2.K313 1999**
Beatrice, M. Bodart-Bailey
📖 Kaempfer's Japan: Tokugawa Culture Observed. E-Book.
NetLibrary, Inc. Boulder, CO. 1999. ISBN:0-585-37532-1,
ISBN13: 978-0-585-37532-8. Dewey:952/.025.

Audience: **f.**

Kornicki, Peter F.   **Z8.J3K67 2001**
The Book in Japan: A Cultural History from the Beginnings to
the Nineteenth Century. Trade Cloth. University of Hawaii
Press. Honolulu, HI. 2000. 520p. ISBN:0-8248-2337-0, ISBN13:
978-0-8248-2337-5. Dewey:002/.0952. LCCN:00-064896.

Audience: **f.**

Lu, David John   **DS835.J37 1997**
📖 Japan: A Documentary History. E-Book. NetLibrary, Inc.
Boulder, CO. 1997. ISBN:0-585-11109-X, ISBN13:
978-0-585-11109-4. Dewey:952.

Audience: **g,u,f.**

Maruyama, Masao   **DS889 .M34**
Thought and Behavior in Modern Japanese Politics. Ed. 2. Carol
Gluck (Preface by). Trade Paper. Columbia University Press.
New York, NY. 1995. 450p. A Morningside Bk.
ISBN:0-231-10141-4, ISBN13: 978-0-231-10141-7.
Dewey:320.9/52.

Audience: **u,f.** 𝓑

McCullough, Helen   **DS0861**
Craig
Taiheiki: A Chronicle of Medieval Japan. Trade Paper. Tuttle
Publishing. Boston, MA. 2003. 452p. ISBN:0-8048-3538-1,
ISBN13: 978-0-8048-3538-1. Dewey:895.6/3/2.

Audience: **u,f.**

Mulgan, Aurelia George   **HC462.95.M845 2002**
Japan's Failed Revolution: Koizumi and the Politics of
Economic Reform. Trade Paper. Asia Pacific Press. Canberra,
ACT. 2002. 260p. ISBN:0-7315-3693-2, ISBN13:
978-0-7315-3693-1. Dewey:338.952. LCCN:2003-386997.

Audience: **g,u,f.** *Choice, 2003.*

Nakane, Chie, et al.   **DS871 .T527**
Tokugawa Japan: The Social and Economic Antecedents of
Modern Japan. Shinsaburo Oishi & Saburo Okita (Authors),
Conrad Totman (Translator). Trade Paper. University of Tokyo
Press. 1992. 248p. ISBN:0-86008-490-6, ISBN13:
978-0-86008-490-7. Dewey:952/.025 20.

Audience: **f.** *Choice, 1991.*

Nishiyama,   **DS822.2.N558 1997**
Matsunosuke
Edo Culture: Daily Life and Diversions in Urban Japan,
1600-1868. Gerald Groemer (Translator). Trade Cloth.
University of Hawaii Press. Honolulu, HI. 1997. 320p.
ISBN:0-8248-1850-4, ISBN13: 978-0-8248-1850-0.
Dewey:952/.025. LCCN:96-009710.

Audience: **u,f.**

Norman, E. Herbert   **DS882**
Japan's Emergence as a Modern State: Political and Economic
Problems of the Meiji Period. Ed. 60. Lawrence T. Woods
(Editor). Trade Cloth. University of British Columbia Press.
Vancouver, BC. 2000. 336p. ISBN:0-7748-0823-3, ISBN13:
978-0-7748-0823-1. Dewey:952.03/1. LCCN:2001-431932.

Audience: **f.**

Notehelfer, F. G.   **DS884.K65**
Kotoku Shusui: Portrait of a Japanese Radical. Trade Cloth.
Cambridge University Press. Cambridge, 1971. 238p.
ISBN:0-521-07989-6, ISBN13: 978-0-521-07989-1.
Dewey:952/.03/10924. LCCN:76-134620.

Audience: **g,u,f.** 𝓑

Perrin, Noel   **DS868.2.P47**
Giving up the Gun: Japan's Reversion to the Sword, 1543-1879.
Trade Cloth. David R. Godine Publisher. Boston, MA. 1978.
96p. ISBN:0-87923-278-1, ISBN13: 978-0-87923-278-8.
Dewey:952/.02. LCCN:78-074252.

Audience: **g,u,f.** 𝓑

Philippi, Donald L.   **BL2220**
(Translator)
Kojiki. Trade Paper. University of Tokyo Press. 1982.
ISBN:0-86008-320-9, ISBN13: 978-0-86008-320-7.
Dewey:299.5.

Audience: **f.**

Ruoff, Kenneth J.   **JQ1640.R86 2001**
The People's Emperor: Democracy and the Japanese Monarchy,
1945-1995. Trade Cloth. Harvard University Press. Cambridge,
MA. 2002. 360p. Harvard East Asian Monographs, Vol. 211
ISBN:0-674-00840-5, ISBN13: 978-0-674-00840-3.
Dewey:952.04. LCCN:2001-039392.

Audience: **l,u,f.** *Choice, 2002.*

Samuels, Richard J.   **JN5345.S25 2003**
Machiavelli's Children: Leaders and Their Legacies in Italy and
Japan. Trade Cloth. Cornell University Press. Ithaca, NY. 2005.
480p. ISBN:0-8014-3492-0, ISBN13: 978-0-8014-3492-1.
Dewey:303.34094509034. LCCN:2002-015019.

Audience: **g,u,f.** *Choice, 2003.*

Sansom, George Bailey   **DS855**
Japan: A Short Cultural History. Ed. 3. Trade Paper. Stanford
University Press. Palo Alto, CA. 1952. 564p.
ISBN:0-8047-0954-8, ISBN13: 978-0-8047-0954-5.
Dewey:952/.01. LCCN:77-076152.

Audience: **g,l,u,f.** 𝓑

Sato, Hiroaki   **DS827.S3S36 1995**
Legends of the Samurai. Trade Cloth. Overlook Press, The. New
York, NY. 1995. 432p. ISBN:0-87951-619-4, ISBN13:
978-0-87951-619-2. Dewey:355.1/0952. LCCN:95-018058.

Audience: **g,u,f.**

Shillony, Ben-Ami   **DS888.5.S487**
Revolt in Japan: The Young Officers and the February 26, 1936
Incident. Trade Cloth. Princeton University Press. Princeton, NJ.
1973. 256p. ISBN:0-691-07548-4, ISBN13: 978-0-691-07548-8.
Dewey:952.03/3. LCCN:76-039793.

Audience: **f.** 𝓑

Shinoda, Minoru   **DS0859.S5**
The Founding of the Kamakura Shogunate, 1880-1885. with
Selected Translations from the Azuma Kagami. Trade Paper.
Books on Demand. Ann Arbor, MI. 399p. Records of
Civilization: Sources and Studies, No. 57 ISBN:0-598-37445-0,
ISBN13: 978-0-598-37445-5. Dewey:952.02. LCCN:59-010433.

Audience: **f.**

Steenstrup, Carl　　　　KNX120.S74 1996
A History of Law in Japan until 1868. Ed. 2. Trade Cloth. Brill
Academic Publishers. Leiden, 1996. xvi, 202p. Handbuch der
Orientalistik Ser., Vol. 5 ISBN:90-04-10453-4, ISBN13:
978-90-04-10453-2. Dewey:349.52. LCCN:95-025112.
Audience: **f.**

Streeck, Wolfgang &　　　　HC286.8.O76
Yamamura, Kozo
The Origins of Nonliberal Capitalism: Germany and Japan in
Comparison. Book, Other. Cornell University Press. Ithaca, NY.
2005. 288p. ISBN:0-8014-8983-0, ISBN13: 978-0-8014-8983-9.
Dewey:330.1220943. LCCN:2001-003219.
Audience: **f.**

Tonomura, Hitomi　　　　HQ1762.W625 1999
(Editor), et al.
Women and Class in Japanese History. Anne Walthall & Wakita
Haruko (Editors). Trade Cloth. University of Michigan, Center
for Japanese Studies. Ann Arbor, MI. 1999. ix, 330p. Michigan
Monograph Series in Japanese Studies, No. 25
ISBN:0-939512-91-2, ISBN13: 978-0-939512-91-1.
Dewey:305.4/0952. LCCN:99-011034.
Audience: **u,f.**

Totman, Conrad　　　　DS871
The Collapse of the Tokugawa Bakufu, 1862-1868: Eighteen
Sixty-Two to Eighteen Sixty-Eight. Trade Cloth. University of
Hawaii Press. Honolulu, HI. 1997. 616p. ISBN:0-8248-0614-X,
ISBN13: 978-0-8248-0614-9. Dewey:952/.025.
LCCN:79-022094.
Audience: **u,f.**

Totman, Conrad　　　　DS835.T57 2004
History of Japan. Ed. 2. Trade Paper. Blackwell Publishing, Inc.
Malden, MA. 2005. 720p. Blackwell History of the World Ser.
ISBN:1-4051-2359-1, ISBN13: 978-1-4051-2359-4. Dewey:952.
LCCN:2004-016236.
Audience: **g,l,u,f.**

Totman, Conrad　　　　DS835 .T58
Japan Before Perry: A Short History. Trade Cloth. University of
California Press. Berkeley, CA. 1982. 275p.
ISBN:0-520-04134-8, ISBN13: 978-0-520-04134-9. Dewey:952.
LCCN:80-014708.
Audience: **g,u,f.** 𝕭

Totman, Conrad　　　　DS871
Politics in the Tokugawa Bakufu, 1600-1843. Trade Paper.
University of California Press. Berkeley, CA. 1988. 368p.
ISBN:0-520-06313-9, ISBN13: 978-0-520-06313-6.
Dewey:952/.025. LCCN:88-015473.
Audience: **f.** 𝕭

Yonemoto, Marcia　　　　DS822.2 .Y665 2003
Mapping Early Modern Japan: Space, Place, and Culture in the
Tokugawa Period, 1603-1868. Trade Cloth. University of
California Press. Berkeley, CA. 2003. 240p. Asia-Local
Studies/Global Themes, Vol. 7 ISBN:0-520-23269-0, ISBN13:
978-0-520-23269-3. Dewey:915.204/25. LCCN:2002-013902.
Audience: **g,u,f.**

Japan > Biography, Memoirs

Bernstein, Gail L.　　　　HQ1764.E33 B47 1983
Haruko's World: A Japanese Farm Woman and Her Community.
Trade Cloth. Stanford University Press. Palo Alto, CA. 1983.

xviii, 199p. ISBN:0-8047-1174-7, ISBN13: 978-0-8047-1174-6.
Dewey:305.4/2/0952. LCCN:82-061783.
Audience: **g,l,u,f.**

Berry, Mary E.　　　　DS869.T6.B47 1982
Hideyoshi. Trade Cloth. Harvard University Press. Cambridge,
MA. 1982. 320p. East Asian Monographs, No. 97
ISBN:0-674-39025-3, ISBN13: 978-0-674-39025-6.
Dewey:952.023. LCCN:82-001056.
Audience: **g,u,f.** 𝕭

Bix, Herbert P.　　　　DS889.8.B59 2000
Hirohito and the Making of Modern Japan. Trade Cloth.
HarperCollins Publishers. New York, NY. 2000. 816p.
ISBN:0-06-019314-X, ISBN13: 978-0-06-019314-0.
Dewey:952/.033/092. LCCN:99-089427.
Audience: **g,u,f.**

Bowring, Richard J.　　　　PL811.O7Z/
Mori Ogai and the Modernization of Japanese Culture. Trade
Cloth. Cambridge University Press. New York, NY. 1979. 320p.
University of Cambridge Oriental Publications, No. 28
ISBN:0-521-21319-3, ISBN13: 978-0-521-21319-6.
Dewey:895.6/3/4. LCCN:76-011074.
Audience: **f.** 𝕭

Craig, Albert M. &　　　　DS871.75.P47 1995
Shively, Donald H. (Editors)
Personality in Japanese History. Trade Paper. University of
Michigan, Center for Japanese Studies. Ann Arbor, MI. 1995. x,
481p. Michigan Classics in Japanese Studies, No. 13
ISBN:0-939512-67-X, ISBN13: 978-0-939512-67-6.
Dewey:952/.025/0922 B. LCCN:94-043147.
Audience: **g,u,f.**

Dower, J. W.　　　　PG3476.G326
Empire and Aftermath: Yoshida Shigeru and the Japanese
Experience, 1878-1954. Trade Paper. Harvard University Press.
Cambridge, MA. 1988. 618p. East Asian Monographs, No. 84
ISBN:0-674-25126-1, ISBN13: 978-0-674-25126-7.
Dewey:952.04/092/4.
Audience: **f.** 𝕭

Fujitani, Takashi　　　　DS881.9.F847 1996
Splendid Monarchy: Power and Pageantry in Modern Japan.
Trade Cloth. University of California Press. Berkeley, CA. 1996.
320p. Twentieth-Century Japan Ser., Vol. 6:The Emergence of a
World Power ISBN:0-520-20237-6, ISBN13:
978-0-520-20237-5. Dewey:952.03. LCCN:95-038543.
Audience: **u,f.** *Choice, 1997.*

Galbraith, Stuart IV　　　　PN1998.3.K87G35 2001
Emperor and the Wolf: The Lives and Films of Akira Kurosawa
and Toshiro Mifune. Trade Cloth. Faber & Faber, Inc. New
York, NY. 2002. 544p. ISBN:0-571-19982-8, ISBN13:
978-0-571-19982-2. Dewey:791.43/0233/092 B.
LCCN:2001-023825.
Audience: **g,u,f.** *Choice, 2002.*

Gordon, Beate S.　　　　ML429.G673
Only Woman in the Room: A Memoir. Trade Cloth. Kodansha
International. Tokyo, 1998. 224p. ISBN:4-7700-2145-3, ISBN13:
978-4-7700-2145-8. Dewey:940.548673.
Audience: **g,u,f.**

Grew, Joseph C.　　　　E183.8.J3 G72 1973
Ten Years in Japan: A Contemporary Record Drawn from the
Diaries and Private and Official Papers of Joseph C. Grew,
United States Ambassador to Japan, 1932-1942. Library

Binding. Greenwood Publishing Group, Inc. Portsmouth, NH. 1973. 554p. ISBN:0-8371-6723-X, ISBN13: 978-0-8371-6723-7. Dewey:327.73/052. LCCN:72-012556.

Audience: **g.** *B*

Griffis, William Elliot   DS882 .G75
The Mikado: Institution and Person a Study of the Internal Political Forces of Japan. Trade Paper. Kessinger Publishing, LLC. Whitefish, MT. 2004. ISBN:1-4179-4860-4, ISBN13: 978-1-4179-4860-4. Dewey:288.41.

Audience: **g,u,f.**

Hakuseki, Arai   DS872.A7 A3
Told Round a Brushwood Fire: The Autobiography of Arai Hakuseki. Joyce Ackroyd (Translator). Trade Cloth. University of Tokyo Press. 1995. 360p. ISBN:0-86008-248-2, ISBN13: 978-0-86008-248-4. Dewey:952/.025/0924.

Audience: **g,u,f.**

Hane, Mikiso   HN726.R44 1990
Reflections on Way to Gallows. Trade Paper. Knopf Publishing Group. New York, NY. 1990. ISBN:0-679-72273-4, ISBN13: 978-0-679-72273-1. Dewey:303.48/4/0952. LCCN:89-043217.

Audience: **g,u,f.**

Howes, John F.   BR1317.U22H68 2005
Japan's Modern Prophet: Uchimura Kanzo, 1861-1930. Trade Cloth. University of British Columbia Press. Vancouver, BC. 2005. 464p. Asian Religions and Society Scr. ISBN:0-7748-1145-5, ISBN13: 978-0-7748-1145-3. Dewey:275.2/082092 B. LCCN:2006-372836.

Audience: **g,u,f.** *Choice, 2006.*

Hoyt, Edwin P.   DS885.5.Y3H68 1990
Yamamoto: The Man Who Planned Pearl Harbor. Trade Cloth. McGraw-Hill Companies, The. New York, NY. 1990. ISBN:0-07-030626-5, ISBN13: 978-0-07-030626-4. Dewey:952.03/3/092 B. LCCN:89-013169.

Audience: **g,u.**

Huffman, James L.   PN5406.F77 H8
Politics of the Meiji Press: The Life of Fukuchi Gen'ichiro. Cloth Text. University of Hawaii Press. Honolulu, HI. 1980. 282p. ISBN:0-8248-0679-4, ISBN13: 978-0-8248-0679-8. Dewey:070.4/092/4. LCCN:79-003879.

Audience: **g,u,f.**

Irokawa, Daikichi   DS888.2 .I758
The Age of Hirohito: In Search of Modern Japan. Mikiso Hane & John K. Urda (Translators). Trade Cloth. DIANE Publishing Company. Collingdale, PA. 1995. 163p. ISBN:0-7567-6067-4, ISBN13: 978-0-7567-6067-0. Dewey:952.03/3.

Audience: **g,u,f.**

Jansen, Marius B.   DS881.3.J28 1994
Sakamoto Ryoma and the Meiji Restoration. Trade Paper. Columbia University Press. New York, NY. 1995. 423p. ISBN:0-231-10173-2, ISBN13: 978-0-231-10173-8. Dewey:952/.025/092. LCCN:94-039075.

Audience: **f.**

Katsu Kokichi   DS881.5.K285A3 1988
Musui's Story: The Autobiography of a Tokugawa Samurai. Teruko Craig (Editor). Trade Cloth. University of Arizona Press. Tucson, AZ. 1988. 178p. ISBN:0-8165-1035-0, ISBN13: 978-0-8165-1035-1. Dewey:952/.025/0924. LCCN:87-036545.

Audience: **g,l,u,f.**

Keene, Donald   DS882.7.K44 2002
Emperor of Japan: Meiji and His World, 1852-1912. Trade Cloth. Columbia University Press. New York, NY. 2002. 928p. ISBN:0-231-12340-X, ISBN13: 978-0-231-12340-2. Dewey:952.03/1/092. LCCN:2001-028826.

Audience: **g,u,f.** *Choice, 2003.*

Keene, Donald   PL741.6
Modern Japanese Diaries: The Japanese at Home and Abroad as Revealed Through Their Diaries. Cloth Text. DIANE Publishing Company. Collingdale, PA. 1998. 534p. ISBN:0-7881-5521-0, ISBN13: 978-0-7881-5521-5. Dewey:895.6/840309.

Audience: **g,u,f.**

Keene, Donald   PL741.1
Travelers of a Hundred Ages: The Japanese As Revealed Through 1,000 Years of Diaries. Cloth Text. DIANE Publishing Company. Collingdale, PA. 1998. 468p. ISBN:0-7881-5520-2, ISBN13: 978-0-7881-5520-8. Dewey:895.6/803.

Audience: **g,u,f.** *Choice, 1990.*

Kuroyanagi, Tetsuko   PN1992.4.K87.A3713
Totto-Chan: The Little Girl at the Window. Dorothy Britton (Translator), Chihiro Iwasaki (Illustrator). Trade Cloth. Kodansha America, Inc. New York, NY. 1982. 195p. ISBN:0-87011-537-5, ISBN13: 978-0-87011-537-0. Dewey:372.92. LCCN:81-080735.

Audience: **g,u,f.**

Lyons, Phyllis I.   PL825.A8.Z74117 1985
The Saga of Dazai Osamu: A Critical Study with Translations. Trade Cloth. Stanford University Press. Palo Alto, CA. 1985. 432p. ISBN:0-8047-1197-6, ISBN13: 978-0-8047-1197-5. Dewey:895.6/34. LCCN:83-042542.

Audience: **f.** *B* *Choice, 1985.*

Makiko, Nakano   DS897.K85N3313 1995
(Translator)
Makiko's Diary: A Merchant Wife in 1910 Kyoto. Kazuko Smith (Introduction by, Notes by). Trade Paper. Stanford University Press. Palo Alto, CA. 1995. 278p. ISBN:0-8047-2441-5, ISBN13: 978-0-8047-2441-8. Dewey:952/.1864031/092 B. LCCN:94-039864.

Audience: **f.** *Choice, 1996.*

Masuda, Sayo   GT3412.7.M37A3 2003
Autobiography of a Geisha. G. G. Rowley (Translator). Trade Cloth. Columbia University Press. New York, NY. 2003. 216p. ISBN:0-231-12950-5, ISBN13: 978-0-231-12950-3. Dewey:792.7/028/092 B. LCCN:2002-041020.

Audience: **g,u,f.**

McClellan, Edwin   CT1838
Woman in the Crested Kimono: The Life of Shibue Io and Her Family Drawn from Mori Ogai's Shibue Chusai. Trade Paper. Yale University Press. Cumberland, RI. 1998. 208p. ISBN:0-300-04618-9, ISBN13: 978-0-300-04618-2. Dewey:952/.025/092. LCCN:85-005359.

Audience: **f.**

Miyazaki, Toten   DS0884.M5A31
My Thirty-Three Years' Dream: The Autobiography of Miyazaki Toten. Eto Shinkichi & Marius B. Jansen (Translator, Introduction by). Trade Paper. Books on Demand. Ann Arbor, MI. 1982. 327p. Princeton Library of Asian Translations ISBN:0-7837-9444-4, ISBN13: 978-0-7837-9444-0. Dewey:951/.03/0924. LCCN:81-047925.

Audience: **f.**

Morris, Ivan   **DS834 .M64**
The Nobility of Failure: Tragic Heroes in the History of Japan.
Trade Paper. Farrar, Straus & Giroux. New York, NY. 1988.
528p. Noonday Ser. ISBN:0-374-52120-4, ISBN13:
978-0-374-52120-2. Dewey:952/.00992.
                              Audience: **g,l,u,f.** $\mathcal{B}$

Notehelfer, F. G.   **DS884.K65**
Kotoku Shusui: Portrait of a Japanese Radical. Trade Cloth.
Cambridge University Press. Cambridge, 1971. 238p.
ISBN:0-521-07989-6, ISBN13: 978-0-521-07989-1.
Dewey:952/.03/10924. LCCN:76-134620.
                              Audience: **g,u,f.** $\mathcal{B}$

Oh, Sadaharu &   **GV865.O13**
 Falkner, David
Sadaharu Oh: A Zen Way of Baseball. Trade Cloth. Crown
Publishing Group. New York, NY. 1984. 279p.
ISBN:0-8129-1109-1, ISBN13: 978-0-8129-1109-1.
Dewey:796.357/092/4 B. LCCN:83-045922.
                              Audience: **g,l,u,f.**

Oka, Yoshitake   **DS885.5.K6.O3813**
Konoe Fumimaro: A Political Biography. Trade Paper.
University of Tokyo Press. 1983. 214p. ISBN:0-86008-304-7,
ISBN13: 978-0-86008-304-7. Dewey:952.03/3/0924.
LCCN:83-165058.
                              Audience: **f.** $\mathcal{B}$

Okamoto, Shiro   **DS890.B68O3313 2001**
The Man Who Saved Kabuki: Faubion Bowers and Theatre
Censorship in Occupied Japan. Samuel L. Leiter (Translator).
Trade Cloth. University of Hawaii Press. Honolulu, HI. 2001.
232p. ISBN:0-8248-2382-6, ISBN13: 978-0-8248-2382-5.
Dewey:952.04/092. LCCN:00-066591.
                              Audience: **f.**

Peattie, Mark R.   **DS885.5.I77**
Ishiwara Kanji and Japan's Confrontation with the West. Trade
Cloth. Princeton University Press. Princeton, NJ. 1975. 420p.
ISBN:0-691-03099-5, ISBN13: 978-0-691-03099-9.
Dewey:355.3/32/0924. LCCN:73-002489.
                              Audience: **f.** $\mathcal{B}$

Perez, Louis G.   **DS884.M87P476 2001**
Mutsu Munemitsu and Identity Formation of the Individual and
the State in Modern Japan. Trade Cloth. Edwin Mellen Press,
The. Lewiston, NY. 2001. 342p. Japanese Studies, Vol. 14
ISBN:0-7734-7366-1, ISBN13: 978-0-7734-7366-9.
Dewey:952.03/1/092 B. LCCN:2001-030019.
                              Audience: **f.**

Peterson, Susan   **NK4210.H32**
Shoji Hamada: A Potter's Way and Work. Trade Cloth.
Kodansha America, Inc. New York, NY. 1984. 240p.
ISBN:0-87011-228-7, ISBN13: 978-0-87011-228-7.
Dewey:738/.092 B. LCCN:74-077957.
                              Audience: **g,f.**

Ravina, Mark   **DS881.5.S2R35 2004**
The Last Samurai: The Life and Battles of Saigo Takamori.
Trade Cloth. John Wiley & Sons, Inc. Hoboken, NJ. 2003. 288p.
ISBN:0-471-08970-2, ISBN13: 978-0-471-08970-4.
Dewey:952.03/1/092 B. LCCN:2003-006646.
                              Audience: **g,l,u,f.**

Reischauer, Haru M.   **DS881.97.R44 1986**
Samurai and Silk: A Japanese and American Heritage. Trade
Cloth. Harvard University Press. Cambridge, MA. 1986. 400p.

ISBN:0-674-78800-1, ISBN13: 978-0-674-78800-8.
Dewey:952.03/092/4. LCCN:85-022006.
                         Audience: **g,l,u,f.** *Choice, 1986.*

Richie, Donald   **CT1836**
Geisha, Gangster, Neighbor, Nun: Scenes from Japanese Lives.
Trade Paper. Kodansha America, Inc. New York, NY. 1991.
212p. ISBN:4-7700-1526-7, ISBN13: 978-4-7700-1526-6.
Dewey:952.048.
                              Audience: **g,f.**

Rimer, J. Thomas   **PL811.O7.Z83**
Mori Ogai. Library Binding. Thomson Gale. Farmington Hills,
MI. 1975. 135p. World Authors Ser., No. 355
ISBN:0-8057-2636-5, ISBN13: 978-0-8057-2636-7.
Dewey:895.6/3/4. LCCN:74-028163.
                              Audience: **f.** $\mathcal{B}$

Satow, Ernest M.   **E748.G835**
A Diplomat in Japan. Trade Paper. Tuttle Publishing. Boston,
MA. 1983. 432p. ISBN:0-8048-1447-3, ISBN13:
978-0-8048-1447-8. Dewey:327.2/092/4. LCCN:82-050326.
                              Audience: **f.**

Schodt, Frederik L.   **F853.S38 2003**
Native American in the Land of the Shogun: Ranald MacDonald
and the Opening of Japan. Trade Cloth. Stone Bridge Press.
Berkeley, CA. 2003. 448p. ISBN:1-880656-78-7, ISBN13:
978-1-880656-78-5. Dewey:915.204/25/092 B.
LCCN:2003-003856.
                         Audience: **u,f.** *Choice, 2004.*

Seidensticker, Edward   **PL812.A4Z88 1990**
G.
Kafu the Scribbler: The Life and Writings of Nagai Kafu,
1879-1959. Trade Paper. University of Michigan, Center for
Japanese Studies. Ann Arbor, MI. 1990. viii, 360p. Michigan
Classics in Japanese Studies, No. 3 ISBN:0-939512-46-7,
ISBN13: 978-0-939512-46-1. Dewey:895.6/342.
LCCN:90-001385.
                              Audience: **g,u,f.**

Totman, Conrad   **DS871**
Tokugawa Ieyasu: Shogun. Trade Paper. Heian International
Publishing, Inc. Berkeley, CA. 1983. 205p.
ISBN:0-89346-210-1, ISBN13: 978-0-89346-210-9.
Dewey:952.02.
                              Audience: **g,u,f.** $\mathcal{B}$

Vining, Elizabeth G.   **DS889 .V5**
Windows for the Crown Prince: An American Woman's Four
Years as Private Tutor to the Crown Prince of Japan. Trade
Cloth. HarperCollins Publishers. New York, NY. 1952.
ISBN:0-397-00037-5, ISBN13: 978-0-397-00037-1.
Dewey:952.033.
                              Audience: **g,u,f.**

Walthall, Anne   **DS881.5.M323W35 1998**
The Weak Body of a Useless Woman: Matsuo Taseko and the
Meiji Restoration. Trade Cloth. University of Chicago Press.
Chicago, IL. 1998. 428p. Women in Culture and Society Ser.
ISBN:0-226-87235-1, ISBN13: 978-0-226-87235-3.
Dewey:952/.025. LCCN:98-016365.
                         Audience: **g,u,f.** *Choice, 1999.*

Wilson, George M.   **DS0885.5.K52**
Radical Nationalist in Japan: Kita Ikki, 1883-1937. Trade Cloth.
Harvard University Press. Cambridge, MA. 1969. East Asian

Monographs, No. 37 ISBN:0-674-74590-6, ISBN13: 978-0-674-74590-2. Dewey:952.030924. LCCN:69-012740.

Audience: **f.** ℬ

Yoshida, Shigeru   **DS889 .Y583 1973**
The Yoshida Memoirs: The Story of Japan in Crisis. Library Binding. Greenwood Publishing Group, Inc. Portsmouth, NH. 1973. 305p. ISBN:0-8371-6733-7, ISBN13: 978-0-8371-6733-6. Dewey:952.04. LCCN:72-012336.

Audience: **f.**

Yukichi, Fukuzawa   **LB775.F82A235 1992**
The Autobiography of Fukuzawa Yukichi. Kiyooka Eiichi (Translator). Trade Cloth. Madison Books, Inc. New York, NY. 1992. 448p. Library of Japan ISBN:0-8191-8295-8, ISBN13: 978-0-8191-8295-1. Dewey:952.03/1/0992. LCCN:92-008907.

Audience: **g,l,u,f.**

Japan > Japanese Literature

PL790.H413 1975
The Tale of the Heike. Trade Cloth. University of Tokyo Press. 1975. xli, 807p. ISBN:0-86008-128-1, ISBN13: 978-0-86008-128-9. Dewey:895.6/3/2. LCCN:75-325691.

Audience: **f.** ℬ

Akutagawa, Ryunosuke   **PL833.I7**
Rashomon and Other Stories. Ed. 2. Kojima Takashi (Translator), Howard Hibbet (Illustrator). Trade Paper. Tuttle Publishing. Boston, MA. 1989. 112p. ISBN:0-8048-1457-0, ISBN13: 978-0-8048-1457-7. Dewey:895.6/3/5. LCCN:83-050837.

Audience: **g,u,f.** ℬ

Arishima, Takeo   **PL801.R5**
A Certain Woman. Kenneth Strong (Translator, Introduction by). Trade Cloth. University of Tokyo Press. 1978. 382p. ISBN:0-86008-237-7, ISBN13: 978-0-86008-237-8. Dewey:895.6/3/4.

Audience: **f.** ℬ

Ariyoshi, Sawako   **PL845.R5.K613 1984**
The Twilight Years. Trade Cloth. Bow Historical Books. New Providence, NJ. 1984. 216p. ISBN:4-7700-1177-6, ISBN13: 978-4-7700-1177-0. Dewey:895.6/35. LCCN:84-047687.

Audience: **g,u,f.** ℬ

Basho, Matsuo   **PL794.Z5**
The Narrow Road to the Deep North and Other Travel Sketches. Noboyuki Yuasa (Translator). Trade Paper. Penguin Group (USA) Inc. New York, NY. 1967. 176p. Classics Ser. ISBN:0-14-044185-9, ISBN13: 978-0-14-044185-7. Dewey:895.6132.

Audience: **g,u,f.**

Brazell, Karen   **PL792.N3**
(Translator)
The Confessions of Lady Nijo. Trade Paper. Stanford University Press. Palo Alto, CA. 1973. 320p. ISBN:0-8047-0930-0, ISBN13: 978-0-8047-0930-9. Dewey:895.6/3/2.

Audience: **f.**

Danly, Robert Lyons   **PL808.I4**
In the Shade of Spring Leaves: The Life and Writings of Higuchi Ichiyo, with Nine of Her Best Short Stories. Trade

Paper. W. W. Norton & Company, Inc. New York, NY. 1992. 384p. ISBN:0-393-30913-4, ISBN13: 978-0-393-30913-3. Dewey:895.6342.

Audience: **f.**

Dazai, Osamu   **PL825.A8**
The Setting Sun. Donald Keene (Translator). Trade Paper. New Directions Publishing Corporation. New York, NY. 1968. ISBN:0-8112-0032-9, ISBN13: 978-0-8112-0032-5. Dewey:895.63. LCCN:56-013350.

Audience: **g,u,f.** ℬ

Dazai, Osamu   **PL825.A8**
No Longer Human. Donald Keene (Translator, Introduction by). Trade Paper. New Directions Publishing Corporation. New York, NY. 1973. 192p. ISBN:0-8112-0481-2, ISBN13: 978-0-8112-0481-1. Dewey:Fic. LCCN:58-009509.

Audience: **g,u,f.** ℬ

Doe, Paula   **PL785.4.Z5**
A Warbler's Song in the Dusk: The Life and Writings of Otomo Yakamochi (718-785). Trade Cloth. University of California Press. Berkeley, CA. 1982. 180p. ISBN:0-520-04346-4, ISBN13: 978-0-520-04346-6. Dewey:895.6/11. LCCN:80-029236.

Audience: **f.** ℬ

Doi, Takeo   **PL812.A8**
The Psychological World of Natsume Soseki. William J. Tyler (Translator, Introduction by). Trade Cloth. Harvard University Press. Cambridge, MA. 1976. 250p. East Asian Monographs, No. 68 ISBN:0-674-72116-0, ISBN13: 978-0-674-72116-6. Dewey:895.6/34. LCCN:76-006889.

Audience: **g,u,f.** ℬ

Enchi, Fumiko   **PL833.I7**
The Waiting Years. Shaw (Editor), John Bester (Translator). Trade Paper. Kodansha America, Inc. New York, NY. 1980. 208p. Japan Women Writers Ser. ISBN:0-87011-424-7, ISBN13: 978-0-87011-424-3. Dewey:895.6/3/5. LCCN:72-015864.

Audience: **f.** ℬ

Endo, Shusaku   **PL849.N4.C413 1980**
Silence. William Johnston (Translator). Trade Paper. Taplinger Publishing Company, Inc. Marlboro, NJ. 1997. 201p. ISBN:0-8008-7186-3, ISBN13: 978-0-8008-7186-4. Dewey:895.635. LCCN:78-027168.

Audience: **g,l,u.** ℬ

Hibbett, Howard   **PL740**
The Floating World in Japanese Fiction. Ed. 2. Trade Paper. DIANE Publishing Company. Collingdale, PA. 2005. 232p. ISBN:0-7567-9699-7, ISBN13: 978-0-7567-9699-0. Dewey:895.6/3/08.

Audience: **f.**

Ibuse, Masuji   **PL812.A8**
Black Rain. Shaw (Editor), John Bester (Translator). Trade Paper. Kodansha America, Inc. New York, NY. 1988. 304p. ISBN:0-87011-364-X, ISBN13: 978-0-87011-364-2. Dewey:895.6/34. LCCN:88-080297.

Audience: **g,u,f.** ℬ

Ihara, Saikaku   **PL2997.T8Z7**
The Japanese Family Storehouse, or, the Millionaire's Gospel Modernised = Nippon Eitai: Gura, or, Daifuku Shin Choja Kyo (1688). Paper Text. Textbook Publishers. Temecula, CA. 2003. xlix, 281p. ISBN:0-7581-1299-8, ISBN13: 978-0-7581-1299-6. Dewey:895.11.

Audience: **f.**

Ishikawa, Takuboku   PL809.S5Z47513 2001
Romaji Diary and Sad Toys. Sanford Goldstein & Seishi
Shinoda (Translators). Trade Paper. Tuttle Publishing. Boston,
MA. 2001. 280p. ISBN:0-8048-3253-6, ISBN13:
978-0-8048-3253-3. Dewey:895.6/142. LCCN:00-055237.
                                        Audience: **f.**

Itaya, Kikuo   PL830.T35.T413 1983
Tengu Child. John Gardner (Translator). Trade Cloth. Southern
Illinois University Press. Carbondale, IL. 1983. 243p.
ISBN:0-8093-1081-3, ISBN13: 978-0-8093-1081-4.
Dewey:895.6/35. LCCN:82-005876.
                                        Audience: **f.** *B*

Jippensha, Ikku   PL898.J5
Shank's Mare or Hizakurige: Japan's Great Comic Novel.
Thomas Satchell (Translator). Trade Paper. Princeton University
Press. Princeton, NJ. 1989. 416p. Unesco Collection of
Representative Works, Series of Translations from the Literature
of the Union of Soviet Socialist Republics ISBN:0-8048-1580-1,
ISBN13: 978-0-8048-1580-2. Dewey:895.634.
LCCN:60-014370.
                                        Audience: **g,u,f.**

Kamens, Edward   PL789.S43H635 1990
The Buddhist Poetry of the Great Kamo Priestess: Daisaiin
Senshi and "Hosshin Wakashu". Trade Cloth. University of
Michigan, Center for Japanese Studies. Ann Arbor, MI. 1990.
xiv, 171p. Michigan Monographs in Japanese Studies, No. 5
ISBN:0-939512-41-6, ISBN13: 978-0-939512-41-6.
Dewey:895.6/114. LCCN:89-071219.
                                        Audience: **f.**

Kamens, Edward   BQ4000.M563 K36 1988
The Three Jewels: A Study and Translation of Minamoto
Tamenori's Sanboe. Trade Cloth. University of Michigan, Center
for Japanese Studies. Ann Arbor, MI. 1988. xii, 446p. Michigan
Monographs in Japanese Studies, No. 2 ISBN:0-939512-34-3,
ISBN13: 978-0-939512-34-8. Dewey:294.3/92.
LCCN:87-030940.
                                        Audience: **f.**

Kankyusha   PL679
Kenkyusha's New Little English-Japanese Dictionary. Trade
Cloth. French & European Publications, Inc. New York, NY.
1982. 566p. ISBN:0-8288-1609-3, ISBN13: 978-0-8288-1609-0.
Dewey:495.6.
                                        Audience: **g,f.**

Kawabata, Yasunari   PL832.A9 L3
The Lake. Ed. 3. Trade Paper. Kodansha International. Tokyo,
2004. 168p. ISBN:4-7700-3001-0, ISBN13: 978-4-7700-3001-6.
Dewey:895.635.
                                        Audience: **f.** *B*

Kawabata, Yasunari   PL832.A9
The Master of Go. Trade Paper. Random House Value
Publishing. New York, NY. 1996. 208p. ISBN:0-679-76106-3,
ISBN13: 978-0-679-76106-8. Dewey:895.634.
                                        Audience: **g,u,f.** *B*

Kawabata, Yasunari   PL832.A9U813 1996
Beauty and Sadness. Ed. 1. Howard S. Hibbett Jr. (Translator).
UK-Trade Paper. Random House, Inc. New York, NY. 1996.
224p. ISBN:0-679-76105-5, ISBN13: 978-0-679-76105-1.
Dewey:895.6/344. LCCN:96-134201.
                                        Audience: **g,u,f.** *B*

Kawabata, Yasunari   PL832.A9Y813 1996
Snow Country. Edward G. Seidensticker (Translator). Trade
Paper. Alfred A. Knopf Inc. New York, NY. 1996. 192p.
ISBN:0-679-76104-7, ISBN13: 978-0-679-76104-4.
Dewey:895.6/344. LCCN:95-032725.
                                        Audience: **g,u,f.**

Kawabata, Yasunari   PL812.A8
The Sound of the Mountain. Edward G. Seidensticker
(Translator). Trade Paper. Alfred A. Knopf Inc. New York, NY.
1996. 288p. ISBN:0-679-76264-7, ISBN13: 978-0-679-76264-5.
Dewey:895.6/3/4.
                                        Audience: **g,u,f.** *B*

Kawabata, Yasunari   PL832.A9S413 1996
Thousand Cranes. Edward G. Seidensticker (Translator). Trade
Paper. Random House Value Publishing. New York, NY. 1996.
160p. ISBN:0-679-76265-5, ISBN13: 978-0-679-76265-2.
Dewey:895.6/344. LCCN:97-120691.
                                        Audience: **g,u,f.**

Keene, Donald   PL793.4
Chushingura: The Treasury of Loyal Retainers. Trade Paper.
Eastern European Monographs. Bradenton, FL. 1997. 183p.
Translations from the Asian Classics Ser. ISBN:0-231-03531-4,
ISBN13: 978-0-231-03531-6. Dewey:895.6/232.
LCCN:78-142283.
                                        Audience: **g,u,f.**

Keene, Donald   PL791.6.T7E48 1998
(Translator)
Essays in Idleness: The Tsurezuregusa of Kenko. Ed. 2. Trade
Paper. Columbia University Press. New York, NY. 1998. 235p.
Translations from the Asian Classics ISBN:0-231-11255-6,
ISBN13: 978-0-231-11255-0. Dewey:895.6/4/2.
LCCN:99-236124.
                                        Audience: **f.**

Keene, Donald   PL726.35.K4 1999
World Within Walls: Japanese Literature of the Pre-Modern Era,
1600-1867. Trade Paper. Columbia University Press. New York,
NY. 1999. 606p. ISBN:0-231-11467-2, ISBN13:
978-0-231-11467-7. Dewey:895.6/09003. LCCN:99-024626.
                                        Audience: **f.**

Kelsey, W. Michael   PL787.K63.K4 1982
Konjaku Monogatari-Shu. Library Binding. Thomson Gale.
Farmington Hills, MI. 1982. 174 p. :p. World Authors Ser.
ISBN:0-8057-6463-1, ISBN13: 978-0-8057-6463-5.
Dewey:895.6/31/08. LCCN:82-002914.
                                        Audience: **f.** *B*

Kimball, Arthur G.   PL747.65 .K5
Crisis in Identity and Contemporary Japanese Novels. Trade
Cloth. Tuttle Publishing. Boston, MA. 1972.
ISBN:0-8048-1090-7, ISBN13: 978-0-8048-1090-6.
Dewey:895.6/3/03. LCCN:72-091549.
                                        Audience: **f.** *B*

Kinoshita Junji   PL832.I5.K313
Between God and Man: A Judgment on War Crimes; a Play in
Two Parts. Eric J. Gangloff (Translator, Introduction by). Trade
Cloth. University of Washington Press. Seattle, WA. 1979. 180p.
ISBN:0-295-95670-4, ISBN13: 978-0-295-95670-1.
Dewey:895/.6/2/5. LCCN:79-084890.
                                        Audience: **f.** *B*

Kobayashi, Hideo   **PL832.O28A22**
Literature of the Lost Home: Kobayashi Hideo—Literary
Criticism, 1924-1939. Paul Anderer (Editor). Trade Paper.
Stanford University Press. Palo Alto, CA. 2000. 189p.
ISBN:0-8047-4115-8, ISBN13: 978-0-8047-4115-6. Dewey:809.
LCCN:94-049638.

Audience: **f.**

Koh, Masuda   **PL679.K4**
Kenkyusha's New Japanese-English Dictionary. Trade Cloth.
French & European Publications, Inc. New York, NY.
ISBN:0-7859-7128-9, ISBN13: 978-0-7859-7128-3.
Dewey:495.6/3/21.

Audience: **g,f.**

Koine, J.   **PL679.K388**
Kenkyusha's New English-Japanese Dictionary. Trade Cloth.
French & European Publications, Inc. New York, NY.
ISBN:0-7859-7127-0, ISBN13: 978-0-7859-7127-6.
Dewey:423/.956.

Audience: **g,f.**

Lyons, Phyllis I.   **PL825.A8.Z74117 1985**
The Saga of Dazai Osamu: A Critical Study with Translations.
Trade Cloth. Stanford University Press. Palo Alto, CA. 1985.
432p. ISBN:0-8047-1197-6, ISBN13: 978-0-8047-1197-5.
Dewey:895.6/34. LCCN:83-042542.

Audience: **f.** *Choice, 1985.*

McClellan, Edwin   **PL747.6**
Two Japanese Novelists. Trade Paper. Tuttle Publishing. Boston,
MA. 2004. 180p. Tuttle Classics of Japanese Literature Ser.
ISBN:0-8048-3340-0, ISBN13: 978-0-8048-3340-0.
Dewey:895.6/34209.

Audience: **f.**

McCullough, Helen   **PL787 .I813**
  Craig (Translator)
Tales of Ise: Lyrical Episodes from Tenth-Century Japan. Trade
Cloth. Stanford University Press. Palo Alto, CA. 1968. 277p.
ISBN:0-8047-0653-0, ISBN13: 978-0-8047-0653-7.
Dewey:895.6/1/1.

Audience: **f.**

Miner, Earl   **PL733.33.P38**
Japanese Linked Poetry. Trade Paper. Princeton University
Press. Princeton, NJ. 1980. 400p. ISBN:0-691-01368-3, ISBN13:
978-0-691-01368-8. Dewey:895.6/1/209. LCCN:78-051182.

Audience: **f.**

Miner, Earl, et al.   **PL717**
The Princeton Companion to Classical Japanese Literature.
Hiroko Odagiri & Robert E. Morrell (Authors). Trade Paper.
Princeton University Press. Princeton, NJ. 1988. 296p.
ISBN:0-691-00825-6, ISBN13: 978-0-691-00825-7.
Dewey:895.6/09. LCCN:83-024475.

Audience: **g,f.** *Choice, 1986.*

Mishima, Yukio   **PL833.I7H6613 1990**
Runaway Horses. Michael Gallagher (Translator). Trade Paper.
Knopf Publishing Group. New York, NY. 1990. 432p. Sea of
Fertility Ser. ISBN:0-679-72240-8, ISBN13: 978-0-679-72240-3.
Dewey:895.6/35. LCCN:89-040560.

Audience: **g,l,u,f.**

Mishima, Yukio   **PL833.I7H3613 1990**
Spring Snow. Michael Gallagher (Translator). Trade Paper.
Knopf Publishing Group. New York, NY. 1990. 400p. Sea of

Fertility Ser., Vol. 1 ISBN:0-679-72241-6, ISBN13:
978-0-679-72241-0. Dewey:895.6/35. LCCN:89-040565.

Audience: **g,l,u,f.**

Mishima, Yukio   **PL818.I7K513 1994**
The Temple of the Golden Pavilion. Ivan Morris (Translator),
Donald Keene (Introduction by). Trade Cloth. Random House,
Inc. New York, NY. 1995. 304p. Everyman's Library
ISBN:0-679-43315-5, ISBN13: 978-0-679-43315-6.
Dewey:895.6/35. LCCN:94-006237.

Audience: **g,l,u,f.**

Mishima, Yukio   **PL833.I7A727 1990**
The Temple of Dawn. E. Dale Saunders & Cecilia S. Seigle
(Translators). Trade Paper. Knopf Publishing Group. New York,
NY. 1990. 352p. Sea of Fertility Ser., Vol. 3
ISBN:0-679-72242-4, ISBN13: 978-0-679-72242-7.
Dewey:895.6/35. LCCN:89-040557.

Audience: **g,l,u,f.**

Mishima, Yukio   **PL833.I7T4613 1990**
The Decay of the Angel. Edward G. Seidensticker (Translator).
Trade Paper. Knopf Publishing Group. New York, NY. 1990.
256p. Sea of Fertility Ser., Vol. 4 ISBN:0-679-72243-2, ISBN13:
978-0-679-72243-4. Dewey:895.6/35. LCCN:89-040554.

Audience: **g,l,u,f.**

Mishima, Yukio   **PL833.I7**
Confessions of a Mask. Meredith Weatherby (Translator). Trade
Paper. New Directions Publishing Corporation. New York, NY.
1968. ISBN:0-8112-0118-X, ISBN13: 978-0-8112-0118-6.
Dewey:895.6/35. LCCN:58-012637.

Audience: **g,f.**

Mishima, Yukio   **PL833.I7S413 1994**
The Sound of Waves. Meredith Weatherby (Translator),
Yoshinori Kinoshita (Illustrator). Trade Paper. Alfred A. Knopf
Inc. New York, NY. 1994. 192p. ISBN:0-679-75268-4, ISBN13:
978-0-679-75268-4. Dewey:895.6/35. LCCN:94-019314.

Audience: **g,u,f.**

Miyoshi, Masao   **PL747.55.M5 1996**
Accomplices of Silence: The Modern Japanese Novel. Trade
Paper. University of Michigan, Center for Japanese Studies. Ann
Arbor, MI. 1996. xx, 194p. Michigan Classics in Japanese
Studies ISBN:0-939512-76-9, ISBN13: 978-0-939512-76-8.
Dewey:895.6/3/03. LCCN:96-042106.

Audience: **f.**

Molasky, Michael S.   **PL747.82.M54M65 1999**
The American Occupation of Japan and Okinawa: Literature and
Memory. Paper over Boards. Routledge. New York, NY. 1999.
256p. Asia's Transformation Ser. ISBN:0-415-19194-7, ISBN13:
978-0-415-19194-4. Dewey:895.6/3509358. LCCN:99-021088.

Audience: **g,u,f.**

Mori, Ogai   **PL812.A8**
Vita Sexualis. Sanford Goldstein & Kazuji Ninomiya
(Translators). Trade Paper. Tuttle Publishing. Boston, MA. 1989.
160p. ISBN:0-8048-1048-6, ISBN13: 978-0-8048-1048-7.
Dewey:895.6/34. LCCN:72-079020.

Audience: **f.**

Mori, Ogai   **PL811.O7.G33**
The Wild Geese. Sanford Goldstein & Kingo Ochiai
(Translators). Trade Paper. Tuttle Publishing. Boston, MA. 1989.
128p. Classics of Japanese Literature ISBN:0-8048-1070-2,

ISBN13: 978-0-8048-1070-8. Dewey:895.6/3/42. LCCN:59-014087.

Audience: **f.** *B*

Morris, Ivan   **PL788.6.M3E56 1991**
The Pillow Book of Sei Shonagon. Cloth Text. Columbia University Press. New York, NY. 1991. ISBN:0-231-07336-4, ISBN13: 978-0-231-07336-3. Dewey:823.9/14. LCCN:91-015757.

Audience: **g,u,f.**

Murakami, Haruki   **PL856.U673A2 2004**
Vintage Murakami. Trade Cloth. Knopf Publishing Group. New York, NY. 2004. 192p. ISBN:1-4000-3396-9, ISBN13: 978-1-4000-3396-6. Dewey:895.6/35. LCCN:2003-049700.

Audience: **g,u,f.**

Murakami, Haruki   **PL856.U673H5713 1989**
A Wild Sheep Chase. Alfred T. Birnbaum (Translator). Trade Cloth. Kodansha America, Inc. New York, NY. 1989. 272p. ISBN:0-87011-905-2, ISBN13: 978-0-87011-905-7. Dewey:895.6/35. LCCN:88-080299.

Audience: **g,u,f.** *Choice, 1990.*

Murakami, Haruki   **BP605.O88M8613 2001**
Underground: The Tokyo Gas Attack and the Japanese Psyche. Alfred Birnbaum & Philip Gabriel (Translators). Trade Paper. Knopf Publishing Group. New York, NY. 2001. 384p. ISBN:0-375-72580-6, ISBN13: 978-0-375-72580-7. Dewey:364.1/0952135. LCCN:00-069310.

Audience: **g,f.**

Murasaki, Shikibu   **PL788.4.G415 E5 1993**
The Tale of Genji. Arthur Waley (Translator). Trade Cloth. Random House, Inc. New York, NY. 1993. 1354p. ISBN:0-679-42467-9, ISBN13: 978-0-679-42467-3. Dewey:895.6/31. LCCN:92-051068.

Audience: **g,f.**

Natsume Soseki   **PL812.A8S5813 1997**
And Then: Natsume Soseki's Novel Sorekara. Norma M. Field (Translator). Trade Paper. University of Michigan, Center for Japanese Studies. Ann Arbor, MI. 1997. viii, 280p. Michigan Classics in Japanese Studies, Vol. 17 ISBN:0-939512-82-3, ISBN13: 978-0-939512-82-9. Dewey:895.6/342. LCCN:97-021881.

Audience: **g,f.**

Natsume Soseki   **PL812.A8**
Kokoro. Edwin McClellan (Translator). Trade Paper. Regnery Publishing, Incorporated, An Eagle Publishing Company. Washington, DC. 1957. 248p. ISBN:0-89526-715-2, ISBN13: 978-0-89526-715-3. Dewey:895.6/34. LCCN:85-007574.

Audience: **u,f.**

Natsume Soseki   **PL812.A8M513 1990**
Grass on the Wayside. Edwin McClellan (Translator, Introduction by). Paper Text. University of Michigan, Center for Japanese Studies. Ann Arbor, MI. 1990. xii, 169p. Michigan Classics in Japanese Studies, No. 2 ISBN:0-939512-45-9, ISBN13: 978-0-939512-45-4. Dewey:895.6/342. LCCN:90-001363.

Audience: **f.**

Natsume Soseki   **PL812.A8 M413 1982**
Light and Darkness. V. H. Viglielmo (Translator). Other. Penguin Group (USA) Inc. New York, NY. 1982. 397p. The Perigee Japanese Library ISBN:0-399-50610-1, ISBN13: 978-0-399-50610-9. Dewey:895.6/3/4. LCCN:81-015426.

Audience: **f.**

Nelson, Andrew N   **PL679**
Original Modern Reader's Japanese-English Character Dictionary. Trade Cloth. Tuttle Publishing. Boston, MA. 2004. 1112p. ISBN:0-8048-1965-3, ISBN13: 978-0-8048-1965-7. Dewey:495.6321.

Audience: **g,f.**

Oe, Kenzaburo   **PL858.E14.P4 1969**
A Personal Matter. John Nathan (Translator). Trade Paper. Grove/Atlantic, Inc. New York, NY. 1970. 176p. ISBN:0-8021-5061-6, ISBN13: 978-0-8021-5061-5. Dewey:895.635. LCCN:68-022007.

Audience: **g,u,f.** *B*

Oe, Kenzaburo   **PL858.E14**
Teach Us to Outgrow Our Madness: Four Short Novels. John Nathan (Translator). Trade Paper. Grove/Atlantic, Inc. New York, NY. 1977. 288p. ISBN:0-8021-5185-X, ISBN13: 978-0-8021-5185-8. Dewey:895.6/35. LCCN:76-054582.

Audience: **f.**

Ooka, Shohei   **PL835.O5**
Fires on the Plain. Ivan Morris (Translator). Trade Paper. Tuttle Publishing. Boston, MA. 1989. 256p. ISBN:0-8048-1379-5, ISBN13: 978-0-8048-1379-2. Dewey:895.63.

Audience: **g,u,f.** *B*

Osaragi, Jiro   **PL835.S3**
Homecoming. Brewster Horwitz (Translator), Harold Strauss (Introduction by). Library Binding. Greenwood Publishing Group, Inc. Portsmouth, NH. 1977. 303p. ISBN:0-8371-9369-9, ISBN13: 978-0-8371-9369-4. Dewey:895. LCCN:76-054833.

Audience: **f.** *B*

Powers, Richard G.   **DS822**
(Editor), et al.
Handbook of Japanese Popular Culture. Hidetoshi Kato & Bruce Stronach (Editors). Cloth Text. Greenwood Publishing Group, Inc. Portsmouth, NH. 1989. 368p. ISBN:0-313-23922-3, ISBN13: 978-0-313-23922-9. Dewey:952.04/8. LCCN:87-007586.

Audience: **g,u,f.** *Choice, 1990.*

Puette, William J.   **PL788.4**
Tale of Genji: A Reader's Guide. Trade Paper. Tuttle Publishing. Boston, MA. 2003. 196p. ISBN:0-8048-3331-1, ISBN13: 978-0-8048-3331-8. Dewey:895.6314.

Audience: **f.**

Rimer, J. Thomas   **PL747.55**
Modern Japanese Fiction and Its Traditions: An Introduction. Trade Paper. Princeton University Press. Princeton, NJ. 1987. 328p. ISBN:0-691-10225-2, ISBN13: 978-0-691-10225-2. Dewey:895.6/3/409. LCCN:68-051188.

Audience: **f.** *B*

Rimer, J. Thomas   **PL832.I8.Z85**
Toward a Modern Japanese Theatre: Kishida Kunio. Trade Cloth. Princeton University Press. Princeton, NJ. 1974. 428p. ISBN:0-691-06249-8, ISBN13: 978-0-691-06249-5. Dewey:895.6/2/4. LCCN:72-006521.

Audience: **f.** *B*

Rohlich, Thomas H.   **PL789.S8.H313 1983**
(Translator)
A Tale of Eleventh Century Japan: Hamamatsu Chunagon
Monogatari. Trade Cloth. Princeton University Press. Princeton,
NJ. 1983. 256p. Library of Asian Translations
ISBN:0-691-05377-4, ISBN13: 978-0-691-05377-6.
Dewey:895.6/31. LCCN:82-061380.

Audience: **f.**

Rubin, Jay   **PL726.63.C37.R8 1984**
Injurious to Public Morals: Writers and the Meiji State. Trade
Cloth. University of Washington Press. Seattle, WA. 1984. 400p.
ISBN:0-295-96043-4, ISBN13: 978-0-295-96043-2.
Dewey:895.6/4/09. LCCN:83-047976.

Audience: **f.**

Ryan, Marleigh G.   **PL817.S8.Z86**
The Development of Realism in the Fiction of Tsubouchi Shoyo.
Trade Cloth. University of Washington Press. Seattle, WA. 1975.
148p. Publications on Asia of the School of International
Studies, No. 26 ISBN:0-295-95382-9, ISBN13:
978-0-295-95382-3. Dewey:895.6/3/4. LCCN:75-001451.

Audience: **f.**

Saigyo   **PL758.15**
Mirror for the Moon. William R. LaFleur (Translator), Gary
Snyder (Foreword by). Trade Paper. New Directions Publishing
Corporation. New York, NY. 1978. ISBN:0-8112-0699-8,
ISBN13: 978-0-8112-0699-0. Dewey:895.6/1/1.
LCCN:78-005952.

Audience: **u,f.**

Saikaku, Ihara & De   **PL794.K613, PZ3.I235**
Bary, William T.
Five Women Who Loved Love. Trade Paper. Tuttle Publishing.
Boston, MA. 1989. 272p. ISBN:0-8048-0184-3, ISBN13:
978-0-8048-0184-3. Dewey:895.611408. LCCN:55-010619.

Audience: **g,f.**

Seidensticker, Edward   **PL788.4.G4**
G. (Translator)
The Gossamer Years: The Diary of a Noblewoman of Heian
Japan. Trade Paper. Tuttle Publishing. Boston, MA. 1989. 208p.
Classics of Japanese Literature ISBN:0-8048-1123-7, ISBN13:
978-0-8048-1123-1. Dewey:895.6/31. LCCN:64-022750.

Audience: **g,f.**

Shiga Naoya   **PL816.H5 A513**
A Dark Night's Passing. Shaw (Editor), Edwin McClellan
(Translator). Trade Paper. Kodansha America, Inc. New York,
NY. 1994. 408p. Japan's Modern Writers Ser.
ISBN:0-87011-362-3, ISBN13: 978-0-87011-362-8.
Dewey:895.634. LCCN:76-009351.

Audience: **f.**

Shikibu, Murasaki   **PL788.4.Z5A3513 1996**
The Diary of Lady Murasaki. Richard Bowring (Translator,
Introduction by, Notes by). Trade Paper. Penguin Group (USA)
Inc. New York, NY. 1996. 144p. Classics Ser.
ISBN:0-14-043576-X, ISBN13: 978-0-14-043576-4.
Dewey:895.6/81403. LCCN:96-217268.

Audience: **f.**

Shikibu, Murasaki   **PL788.4.G4.E5 1976**
The Tale of Genji. Edward Seidensticker (Translator,
Introduction by). Trade Cloth. Random House, Inc. New York,
NY. 1976. "xix, 1090"p. ISBN:0-394-48328-6, ISBN13:
978-0-394-48328-3. Dewey:895.6/314. LCCN:76-013680.

Audience: **g,u,f.**

Shikibu, Murasaki   **PL788.4.G4A6 2006**
The Tale of Genji. Royall Tyler (Editor, Translator, Abridged
by). Trade Paper. Penguin Group (USA) Inc. New York, NY.
2006. 400p. Penguin Classics Ser. ISBN:0-14-303949-0,
ISBN13: 978-0-14-303949-5. Dewey:895.6/314.
LCCN:2005-048742.

Audience: **g,u,f.**

Shimazaki, Toson   **PL816.H55.H33**
The Broken Commandment. Trade Cloth. University of Tokyo
Press. 1974. 249p. ISBN:0-86008-110-9, ISBN13:
978-0-86008-110-4. Dewey:895.6/3/4. LCCN:75-309384.

Audience: **f.**

Sibley, William F.   **PL816.H5.Z846**
The Shiga Hero. Trade Cloth. University of Chicago Press.
Chicago, IL. 1979. 230p. ISBN:0-226-75620-3, ISBN13:
978-0-226-75620-2. Dewey:895.6/3/4. LCCN:79-014120.

Audience: **f.**

Soseki, Natsume   **PZ0003.N216**
The Wayfarer. Beongcheon Yu (Translator, Introduction by).
Trade Paper. Books on Demand. Ann Arbor, MI. 326p.
ISBN:0-7837-3625-8, ISBN13: 978-0-7837-3625-9.
Dewey:895.634. LCCN:66-026974.

Audience: **f.**

Sugawara Takasue no   **PL789.S8.S2513**
Musume & Morris, Ivan
As I Crossed the Bridge of Dreams: Recollections of a Woman
in Eleventh-Century Japan. Trade Cloth. Oxford University
Press, Inc. New York, NY. 1971. 159p. ISBN:0-19-212553-2,
ISBN13: 978-0-19-212553-8. Dewey:952/.01/0924.
LCCN:79-144386.

Audience: **f.**

Tahara, Mildred   **PL787.Y3.E5 1980**
(Translator)
Tales of Yamato: A Tenth-Century Poem - Tale. Cloth Text.
University of Hawaii Press. Honolulu, HI. 1980. 334p.
ISBN:0-8248-0617-4, ISBN13: 978-0-8248-0617-0.
Dewey:895.6/1108. LCCN:79-028535.

Audience: **f.**

Tanizaki, Jun'ichiro   **PL839.A7S3713 1995**
The Makioka Sisters. Trade Paper. Random House, Inc. New
York, NY. 1995. 544p. ISBN:0-679-76164-0, ISBN13:
978-0-679-76164-8. Dewey:895.6/344. LCCN:95-013245.

Audience: **g,u,f.**

Tanizaki, Junichiro   **PL839.A7K313 2004**
The Key and Diary of a Mad Old Man. Howard Hibbett
(Translator). Trade Paper. Knopf Publishing Group. New York,
NY. 2004. 368p. ISBN:1-4000-7900-4, ISBN13:
978-1-4000-7900-1. Dewey:895.6/344. LCCN:2004-303252.

Audience: **g,u,f.**

Tanizaki, Jun'ichiro   **PL839.A7T313 1995**
Some Prefer Nettles. Edward G. Seidensticker (Translator).
Trade Paper. Random House, Inc. New York, NY. 1995. 224p.
ISBN:0-679-75269-2, ISBN13: 978-0-679-75269-1.
Dewey:895.6/344. LCCN:95-014182.

Audience: **g,u,f.**

Ueda, Akinari   **PZ3.U25UG5**
Ugetsu Monogatari: Tales of Moonlight and Rain : A Complete
English Version Of The Eighteenth-century Japanese Collection
Of Tales of the Supernatural. Trade Cloth. University of British
Columbia Press. Vancouver, BC. 1974. 280p. Unesco Collection

of Representative Works Ser. ISBN:0-7748-0026-7, ISBN13: 978-0-7748-0026-6. Dewey:895.6/3/3. LCCN:73-093888.

Audience: **f.** *B*

Ueda, Makoto   **PL733.55.U38 1983**
Modern Japanese Poets and the Nature of Literature. Trade Cloth. Stanford University Press. Palo Alto, CA. 1983. 462p. ISBN:0-8047-1166-6, ISBN13: 978-0-8047-1166-1. Dewey:895.6/14/09. LCCN:82-060487.

Audience: **f.** *B*

Uyeda, Akinari   **PL782.E8**
Tales of Moonlight and Rain: Japanese Gothic Tales. Kengi Hamada (Translator). Trade Cloth. Columbia University Press. New York, NY. 1972. xxix, 150p. ISBN:0-231-03631-0, ISBN13: 978-0-231-03631-3. Dewey:895.6/3/3. LCCN:79-175064.

Audience: **f.** *B*

Walker, Janet A.   **PL747.6.W34**
The Japanese Novel of the Meiji Period and the Ideal of Individualism. Trade Cloth. Princeton University Press. Princeton, NJ. 1979. 334p. ISBN:0-691-06400-8, ISBN13: 978-0-691-06400-0. Dewey:895.6/3/409353. LCCN:79-004501.

Audience: **f.** *B*

Watson, Burton   **PL797.6**
  (Translator)
Ryokan: Zen Monk-Poet of Japan. Trade Paper. Columbia University Press. New York, NY. 1992. 126p. Translations from the Asian Classics Ser. ISBN:0-231-04415-1, ISBN13: 978-0-231-04415-8. Dewey:895.1/14. LCCN:77-011140.

Audience: **g,u,f.** *B*

Yoshimoto, Banana   **PL865.O7138K5813**
Kitchen. Trade Cloth. Tusquests Editores Mexico, S.A. de C.V.. Mexico, D.F., ISBN:968-7723-13-0, ISBN13: 978-968-7723-13-6. Dewey:895.635.

Audience: **g,l,u,f.**

Japan > Japanese Literature > Special Forms

Basho, Matsuo   **PL794.4.Z5**
A Haiku Journey: Basho's Narrow Road to a Far Province. Trade Paper. Kodansha International. Tokyo, 2002. 128p. ISBN:4-7700-2858-X, ISBN13: 978-4-7700-2858-7. Dewey:895.6/132.

Audience: **g,u,f.**

Blyth, R. H.   **PL729**
A History of Haiku: From Issa up to the Present. Trade Paper. Hokuseido Press, The. Tokyo, 1998. 430p. ISBN:0-9647040-3-X, ISBN13: 978-0-9647040-3-9. Dewey:895.6109.

Audience: **g,u,f.**

Brandon, James R.   **PL782.E5K3 1992**
e Kabuki: Five Classic Plays. E-Book. NetLibrary, Inc. Boulder, CO. 1992. ISBN:0-585-34233-4, ISBN13: 978-0-585-34233-7. Dewey:895.6/2/308.

Audience: **f.** *B*

Brandon, James R. &   **PL782.E5K36 2002**
  Leiter, Samuel L. (Editors)
Kabuki Plays on Stage: Brilliance and Bravado, 1697-1766. Trade Cloth. University of Hawaii Press. Honolulu, HI. 2002.

408p. Kabuki Plays On-Stage Ser. ISBN:0-8248-2403-2, ISBN13: 978-0-8248-2403-7. Dewey:895.6/2008. LCCN:2001-027912.

Audience: **f.** *Choice, 2003.*

Brandon, James R. &   **PL782.E5K36 2002**
  Leiter, Samuel L. (Editors)
Kabuki Plays on Stage: Darkness and Desire, 1804-1864. Trade Cloth. University of Hawaii Press. Honolulu, HI. 2002. 416p. Kabuki Plays On-Stage Ser. ISBN:0-8248-2455-5, ISBN13: 978-0-8248-2455-6. Dewey:895.6. LCCN:2001-027912.

Audience: **f.** *Choice, 2003.*

Brandon, James R. &   **PL782.E5K36 2002**
  Leiter, Samuel L. (Editors)
Kabuki Plays on Stage: Restoration and Reform, 1872-1905, Vol. 4. Trade Cloth. University of Hawaii Press. Honolulu, HI. 2003. 448p. ISBN:0-8248-2574-8, ISBN13: 978-0-8248-2574-4. Dewey:895.62008. LCCN:2001-027912.

Audience: **f.** *Choice, 2004.*

Brandon, James R. &   **PL782.E5K36 2002**
  Leiter, Samuel L. (Editors)
Kabuki Plays on Stage: Villainy and Vengeance, 1773-1799. Trade Cloth. University of Hawaii Press. Honolulu, HI. 2002. 432p. Kabuki Plays On-Stage Ser. ISBN:0-8248-2413-X, ISBN13: 978-0-8248-2413-6. Dewey:895.6/2/008. LCCN:2001-027912.

Audience: **f.** *Choice, 2003.*

Brandon, James R. &   **PL782**
  Leiter, Samuel L. (Editors)
Masterpieces of Kabuki: Eighteen Plays on Stage. Trade Cloth. University of Hawaii Press. Honolulu, HI. 2004. 368p. ISBN:0-8248-2788-0, ISBN13: 978-0-8248-2788-5. Dewey:895.62008. LCCN:2004-553320.

Audience: **l,u,f.** *Choice, 2005.*

Brower, Robert H. &   **PL865 .B7**
  Miner, Earl
Japanese Court Poetry. Trade Cloth. Stanford University Press. Palo Alto, CA. 1961. xvi, 527p. ISBN:0-8047-0536-4, ISBN13: 978-0-8047-0536-3. Dewey:895.6109.

Audience: **f.**

Gerstle, C. Andrew   **PL793.4.A6 2001**
Chikamatsu: Five Late Plays. Trade Cloth. Columbia University Press. New York, NY. 2001. 376p. Translations from the Asian Classics ISBN:0-231-12166-0, ISBN13: 978-0-231-12166-8. Dewey:895.6/232. LCCN:00-052361.

Audience: **f.**

Keene, Donald   **PL793.4.A6 1990**
The Major Plays of Chikamatsu. Trade Paper. Columbia University Press. New York, NY. 1961. 485p. ISBN:0-231-07415-8, ISBN13: 978-0-231-07415-5. Dewey:895.6/23. LCCN:90-001850.

Audience: **f.**

Keene, Donald   **PR2894.G7**
The Battles of Coxinga: Chikamatsu's Puppet Play, Its Background and Importance. Mark Van Doren (Preface by). Trade Cloth. Cambridge University Press. New York, NY. 1951. 215p. Cambridge Oriental Ser. ISBN:0-521-05469-9, ISBN13: 978-0-521-05469-0. Dewey:822.33.

Audience: **u,f.**

Leiter, Samuel L.   **PN2924.5.K3A7 1999**
Art of Kabuki: Five Famous Plays. Ed. 2. Trade Paper. Dover
Publications, Inc. Mineola, NY. 1999. 300p.
ISBN:0-486-40872-8, ISBN13: 978-0-486-40872-9.
Dewey:895.6/2008. LCCN:99-046425.
                                                    Audience: **l,u,f.**

Leiter, Samuel L.   **PN2924**
New Kabuki Encyclopedia: A Revised Adaptation of Kabuki
Jiten. Ed. 2. Cloth Text. Greenwood Publishing Group, Inc.
Portsmouth, NH. 1997. 840p. ISBN:0-313-29288-4, ISBN13:
978-0-313-29288-0. Dewey:792/.9052. LCCN:96-036530.
                                    Audience: **f.** *Choice, 1998.*

Mishima, Yukio   **PL833.I7 A6**
Five Modern No Plays. Donald Keene (Translator). Trade Paper.
Tuttle Publishing. Boston, MA. 1989. 228p.
ISBN:0-8048-1380-9, ISBN13: 978-0-8048-1380-8.
Dewey:895.6/2/5.
                                                    Audience: **f.**

Pound, Ezra &   **PN2924.5.N6F46 2004**
  Fenollosa, Ernest
The Noh Theatre of Japan: With Complete Texts of 15 Classic
Plays. Trade Paper. Dover Publications, Inc. Mineola, NY. 2004.
288p. ISBN:0-486-43699-3, ISBN13: 978-0-486-43699-9.
Dewey:895.6/2008. LCCN:2004-050239.
                                                    Audience: **l,u,f.**

Sato, Hiroaki &   **PL782.E3**
Watson, Burton
From the Country of Eight Islands: An Anthology of Japanese
Poetry. Trade Paper. Columbia University Press. New York, NY.
1986. 652p. ISBN:0-231-06395-4, ISBN13: 978-0-231-06395-1.
Dewey:895.6/1/008. LCCN:86-007881.
                                                    Audience: **u,f.**

Yamada, Koun   **BQ9289.Y36 2004**
Gateless Gate: The Classic Book of Zen Koans. Trade Paper.
Publishers Group West. Berkeley, CA. 2005. 288p.
ISBN:0-86171-382-6, ISBN13: 978-0-86171-382-0.
Dewey:294.3/443. LCCN:2003-114197.
                                                    Audience: **g,u,f.**

Japan > Okinawa

Feifer, George   **D767.99.O45F45 1992**
Tennozan: The Battle of Okinawa and the Dropping of the Atom
Bomb. Trade Cloth. Houghton Mifflin Company. New York, NY.
1992. 512p. ISBN:0-395-59924-5, ISBN13: 978-0-395-59924-2.
Dewey:940.5425. LCCN:91-046913.
                                                    Audience: **g,u,f.**

Hein, Laura Elizabeth   **DS894.99.O374I85**
  & Selden, Mark (Editors)
Islands of Discontent: Okinawan Responses to Japanese and
American Power. Book, Other. Rowman & Littlefield Publishers,
Inc. Lanham, MD. 2003. 352p. Asian Voices Ser.
ISBN:0-7425-1865-5, ISBN13: 978-0-7425-1865-0.
Dewey:952/.29033. LCCN:2002-014944.
                                                    Audience: **g,u,f.**

Johnson, Chalmers   **DS894.99.O3785O3625**
Okinawa: Cold War Island. Trade Paper. Japan Policy Research
Institute. Cardiff, CA. 1999. 310p. ISBN:0-9673642-0-5,
ISBN13: 978-0-9673642-0-9. Dewey:952/.29404.
LCCN:00-269692.
                                                    Audience: **f.**

Kerr, George H.   **DS895.O4**
Okinawa: The History of an Island People. Trade Cloth. Tuttle
Publishing. Boston, MA. 1975. ISBN:0-8048-0437-0, ISBN13:
978-0-8048-0437-0. Dewey:952.81. LCCN:58-012283.
                                                    Audience: **g,u,f.**

Molasky, Michael S.   **PL747.82.M54M65 1999**
The American Occupation of Japan and Okinawa: Literature and
Memory. Paper over Boards. Routledge. New York, NY. 1999.
256p. Asia's Transformation Ser. ISBN:0-415-19194-7, ISBN13:
978-0-415-19194-4. Dewey:895.6/3509358. LCCN:99-021088.
                                                    Audience: **g,u,f.**

Molasky, Michael &   **PL886.O542S68 2000**
  Rabson, Steve (Editors)
Southern Exposure: Modern Japanese Literature from Okinawa.
Trade Cloth. University of Hawaii Press. Honolulu, HI. 2000.
376p. ISBN:0-8248-2300-1, ISBN13: 978-0-8248-2300-9.
Dewey:895.6/08095229. LCCN:00-024001.
                                    Audience: **f.** *Choice, 2001.*

Sarantakes, Nicholas   **DS889.16.S26 2001**
  Evan
Keystone: The American Occupation of Okinawa and U.
S.-Japanese Relations. Trade Cloth. Texas A&M University
Press. College Station, TX. 2001. xxiii, 264p. Foreign Relations
and the Presidency Ser., Vol. 6 ISBN:0-89096-969-8, ISBN13:
978-0-89096-969-4. Dewey:952/.29404. LCCN:00-044340.
                                    Audience: **f.** *Choice, 2001.*

Korea

Ch'oe, Yongho (Editor),   **DS904**
  et al.
Sources of Korean Tradition: From the Sixteenth to the
Twentieth Centuries. Peter H. Lee & William Theodore De Bary
(Editors). Trade Cloth. Columbia University Press. New York,
NY. 2001. 448p. ISBN:0-231-12030-3, ISBN13:
978-0-231-12030-2. Dewey:951.9. LCCN:96-017701.
                                                    Audience: **g,u,f.**

Kwak, Jenny & Fried,   **TX724.5.K65K83 1998**
  Liz
Dok Suni: Recipes from My Mother's Korean Kitchen. Cloth
over Boards. St. Martin's Press. Gordonville, VA. 1998. 144p.
ISBN:0-312-19261-4, ISBN13: 978-0-312-19261-7.
Dewey:641.59519. LCCN:98-018718.
                                                    Audience: **g.**

Lee, Cecilia Hae-Jin   **TX724.5.K65L44 2005**
Eating Korean: From Barbecue to Kimchi, Recipes from My
Home. Trade Cloth. John Wiley & Sons, Inc. Hoboken, NJ.
2005. 272p. ISBN:0-7645-4078-5, ISBN13: 978-0-7645-4078-3.
Dewey:641.59519. LCCN:2004-024092.
                                                    Audience: **g,f.**

Korea > History

                                                    DS918 .U5 1979
Military Situation in the Far East: U. S. Congress, Senate
Committee on Armed Services and the Committee on Foreign
Relations, Set. Library Binding. Ayer Company Publishers, Inc.
Manchester, NH. 1979. American Military Experience Ser.
ISBN:0-405-11878-3, ISBN13: 978-0-405-11878-4.
Dewey:951.9/042. LCCN:78-022402.
                                                    Audience: **f.**

Armstrong, Charles　　　　　　**DS902.A75 2006**
Koreas. Paper over Boards. Routledge. New York, NY. 2006.
224p. Globalizing Regions Ser., Vol. 4 ISBN:0-415-94852-5,
ISBN13: 978-0-415-94852-4. Dewey:951.9.
LCCN:2006-015186.
　　　　　　　　　　　　　　　　　Audience: **u,f.**

Armstrong, Charles K.　　　**JQ1499.A38R437 2005**
　(Editor), et al.
Korea at the Center: Dynamics of Regionalism in Northeast
Asia. Gilbert Rozman, Samuel S. Kim & Stephen Kotkin
(Editors). Cloth Text. M. E. Sharpe Inc. Armonk, NY. 2005.
344p. Northeast Asia Seminar Ser. ISBN:0-7656-1655-6,
ISBN13: 978-0-7656-1655-5. Dewey:327.51905.
LCCN:2005-000073.
　　　　　　　　　　　　　　　　Audience: **g,u,f.**

Clark, Donald N.　　　　　　**DS925.K86K88 1988**
　(Editor)
The Kwangju Uprising: Shadows over the Regime in South
Korea. Paper Text. Westview Press. Boulder, CO. 1987. 96p.
Special Studies on East Asia ISBN:0-8133-7523-1, ISBN13:
978-0-8133-7523-6. Dewey:951.9/5043. LCCN:87-027419.
　　　　　　　　　　　　　　　　　Audience: **u,f.**

Clark, Donald N.　　　　　　**DS916.55.C553 2003**
Living Dangerously in Korea: The Western Experience, 1900 -
1950. Trade Paper. EastBridge. Norwalk, CT. 2002. 455p. The
Missionary Enterprise in Asia Ser. ISBN:1-891936-11-5,
ISBN13: 978-1-891936-11-1. Dewey:951.9/03.
LCCN:2003-000169.
　　　　　　　　　　Audience: **g,l,u,f.**　*Choice, 2004.*

Conroy, Hilary　　　　　　　**DS915.C6 1960**
The Japanese Seizure of Korea, 1868-1910. Trade Paper.
University of Pennsylvania Press. Philadelphia, PA. 1974. 544p.
ISBN:0-8122-1074-3, ISBN13: 978-0-8122-1074-3.
Dewey:951.902. LCCN:60-006936.
　　　　　　　　　　　　　　　　　Audience: **f.**

Cumings, Bruce　　　　　　　**DS917.C86 1997**
Korea's Place in the Sun: A Modern History. Trade Cloth. W.
W. Norton & Company, Inc. New York, NY. 1997. 527p.
ISBN:0-393-04011-9, ISBN13: 978-0-393-04011-1.
Dewey:951.904. LCCN:96-015398.
　　　　　　　　　　Audience: **g,u,f.**　*Choice, 1997.*

Cumings, Bruce　　　　　　　**F1221.N3**
The Origins of the Korean War: Liberation and the Emergence
of Separate Regimes. Trade Cloth. Princeton University Press.
Princeton, NJ. 1981. 552p. ISBN:0-691-09383-0, ISBN13:
978-0-691-09383-3. Dewey:306.8/3/097247. LCCN:80-008543.
　　　　　　　　　　Audience: **l,u,f.**　*Choice, 1991.*

Cumings, Bruce　　　　　　　**DS918**
The Origins of the Korean War, 1947-1950: The Roaring of the
Cataract. Trade Cloth. Princeton University Press. Princeton, NJ.
1990. 986p. ISBN:0-691-07843-2, ISBN13: 978-0-691-07843-4.
Dewey:951.9042. LCCN:80-008543.
　　　　　　　　　　Audience: **g,l,u,f.**　*Choice, 1991.*

Deuchler, Martina　　　　　**DS915.D48 1977**
Confucian Gentlemen and Barbarian Envoys: The Opening of
Korea, 1875-1885. Trade Cloth. University of Washington Press.
Seattle, WA. 1978. 324p. Royal Asiatic Society Ser.
ISBN:0-295-95552-X, ISBN13: 978-0-295-95552-0.
Dewey:951.9/02. LCCN:76-057228.
　　　　　　　　　　　　　Audience: **f.** *B*

Duncan, John B.　　　　　　**JQ1725.A7D86 2000**
The Origins of the Chosŏn Dynasty. Trade Cloth. University of
Washington Press. Seattle, WA. 2000. xii, 395p. Korean Studies
of the Henry M. Jackson School of International Studies
ISBN:0-295-97985-2, ISBN13: 978-0-295-97985-4.
Dewey:951.9/02. LCCN:00-029876.
　　　　　　　　　　Audience: **l,u,f.**　*Choice, 2001.*

Duus, Peter　　　　　　　　**DS882.D88 1995**
The Abacus and the Sword: The Japanese Penetration of Korea,
1895-1910. Trade Cloth. University of California Press.
Berkeley, CA. 1995. 498p. Twentieth-Century Japan Ser., Vol. 4
ISBN:0-520-08614-7, ISBN13: 978-0-520-08614-2.
Dewey:951.9.02. LCCN:94-006118.
　　　　　　　　　　　Audience: **f.**　*Choice, 1996.*

Fehrenbach, T. R.　　　　　　　**DS918**
This Kind of War: The Classic Korean War History. Ed. 50.
Trade Paper. Potomac Books, Inc. Dulles, VA. 2001. 540p.
ISBN:1-57488-334-8, ISBN13: 978-1-57488-334-3.
Dewey:951.904/2. LCCN:94-010908.
　　　　　　　　　　　　　　　　Audience: **g,u,f.**

Foot, Rosemary　　　　　　　　**DS918**
A Substitute for Victory: The Politics of Peacemaking at the
Korean Armistice Talks. Trade Cloth. DIANE Publishing
Company. Collingdale, PA. 2000. 273p. ISBN:0-7881-6942-4,
ISBN13: 978-0-7881-6942-7. Dewey:951.904/2.
　　　　　　　　　　　　　　　　Audience: **g,u,f.**

Griffis, William Elliot　　　　　　**DS907**
Corea the Hermit Nation. Trade Paper. Kessinger Publishing,
LLC. Whitefish, MT. 2004. ISBN:1-4179-4866-3, ISBN13:
978-1-4179-4866-6. Dewey:951.9/01.
　　　　　　　　　　　　　　　　　Audience: **f.**

Haboush, JaHyun Kim　　　　　**DS913.392**
The Confucian Kingship in Korea: Yôngjo and the Politics of
Sagacity. Trade Paper. Columbia University Press. New York,
NY. 2001. 336p. ISBN:0-231-06657-0, ISBN13:
978-0-231-06657-0. Dewey:951.902. LCCN:87-031972.
　　　　　　　　　　　　　　　　　Audience: **f.**

Haboush, JaHyun Kim　　　　　**DS902.2**
　(Editor)
Culture and the State in Late Choson Korea. Trade Paper.
Harvard University Press. Cambridge, MA. 2002. 328p. Harvard
East Asian Monographs ISBN:0-674-00774-3, ISBN13:
978-0-674-00774-1. Dewey:951.9/02.
　　　　　　　　　　　　　　　　　Audience: **f.**

Harrison, Selig S.　　　　　**E183.8.K7H34 2002**
Korean Endgame: A Strategy for Reunification and U. S.
Disengagement. Cloth Text. Princeton University Press.
Princeton, NJ. 2002. 448p. ISBN:0-691-09604-X, ISBN13:
978-0-691-09604-9. Dewey:327.7305193. LCCN:2001-055186.
　　　　　　　　　　　　　　　　Audience: **g,u,f.**

Kim, Ilpyong J.　　　　　　**DS933.7.K55 2003**
Historical Dictionary of North Korea. Ed. 40. Trade Cloth.
Scarecrow Press, Inc. Lanham, MD. 2003. 280p. Asian/Oceanian
Historical Dictionaries Ser., No. 39 ISBN:0-8108-4331-5,
ISBN13: 978-0-8108-4331-8. Dewey:951.93/003.
LCCN:2002-012349.
　　　　　　　　　　　Audience: **g,f.**　*Choice, 2003.*

Lee, Steven H.　　　　　　**DS33.3.L44 1995**
Outposts of Empire: Korea, Vietnam, and the Origins of the
Cold War in Asia, 1949-1954. Trade Cloth. McGill-Queen's

University Press. Montreal, PQ. 1995. 312p.
ISBN:0-7735-1326-4, ISBN13: 978-0-7735-1326-6.
Dewey:327.7305/09645. LCCN:97-135057.

Audience: **g,u,f.** *Choice, 1996.*

Lowe, Peter   **DS918.L68 1997**
The Origins of the Korean War. Ed. 2. Trade Paper. Longman
Publishing Group. White Plains, NY. 1997. 280p. Origins of
Modern Wars Ser. ISBN:0-582-25147-8, ISBN13:
978-0-582-25147-2. Dewey:951.9/042. LCCN:96-039698.

Audience: **g,u,f.**

Marshall, Samuel L.   **DS918.2.C4**
The River and the Gauntlet. Ed. 14. Trade Cloth. Battery Press.
Nashville, TN. 1987. 400p. Combat Arms Ser.
ISBN:0-89839-097-4, ISBN13: 978-0-89839-097-1.
Dewey:951.9.

Audience: **g,u,f.**

Millett, Allan Reed   **DS916.M465 2005**
The War for Korea, 1945—1950: A House Burning. Trade
Cloth. University Press of Kansas. Lawrence, KS. 2005. 376p.
Modern War Studies ISBN:0-7006-1393-5, ISBN13:
978-0-7006-1393-9. Dewey:951.904/1. LCCN:2005-009166.

Audience: **f.** *Choice, 2006.*

Moon, Katherine H.   **E183.8.K6M664 1997**
Sex among Allies: Military Prostitution in U. S.-Korea
Relations. Trade Cloth. Columbia University Press. New York,
NY. 1997. 336p. ISBN:0-231-10642-4, ISBN13:
978-0-231-10642-9. Dewey:327.730519. LCCN:97-002641.

Audience: **f.** *Choice, 1998.*

Nahm, Andrew C. &   **DS904.8.N34 2004**
Hoare, James
Historical Dictionary of the Republic of Korea. Ed. 2. Trade
Cloth. Scarecrow Press, Inc. Lanham, MD. 2004. 448p.
Historical Dictionaries of Asia, Oceania, and the Middle East
Ser., Vol. 52 ISBN:0-8108-4949-6, ISBN13: 978-0-8108-4949-5.
Dewey:951.95/003. LCCN:2004-001624.

Audience: **g.** *Choice, 2004, 1993.*

Oberdorfer, Don   **DS922.2.O25 2001**
The Two Koreas: A Contemporary History. Trade Paper. Basic
Books. New York, NY. 2001. 544p. ISBN:0-465-05162-6,
ISBN13: 978-0-465-05162-5. Dewey:951.904.
LCCN:2001-043486.

Audience: **g,u,f.** *Choice, 1998.*

Pratt, Keith   **DS907.18**
Everlasting Flower: A History of Korea. Trade Cloth. Reaktion
Books, Ltd. London, 2006. 256p. ISBN:1-86189-273-X,
ISBN13: 978-1-86189-273-7. Dewey:951.9.

Audience: **g,u,f.**

Schmid, Andre   **DS915.25.S36 2002**
Korea Between Empires, 1895-1919. Trade Cloth. Edinburgh
University Press. Edinburgh, 2002. 480p. ISBN:0-231-12538-0,
ISBN13: 978-0-231-12538-3. Dewey:951.9/02.
LCCN:2001-058377.

Audience: **f.** *Choice, 2003.*

Shin, Gi-Wook &   **DS916.54.C65 1999**
Robinson, Michael E.
Colonial Modernity in Korea. Trade Cloth. Harvard University
Press. Cambridge, MA. 2000. 496p. East Asian Monographs,
Vol. 184 ISBN:0-674-14255-1, ISBN13: 978-0-674-14255-8.
Dewey:951.9/03. LCCN:99-037149.

Audience: **f.** *Choice, 2000.*

Spurr, Russell   **DS918**
Enter the Dragon: China's Undeclared War Against the U. S. in
Korea, 1950-51. Trade Cloth. Newmarket Press. New York, NY.
2004. 384p. ISBN:1-55704-249-7, ISBN13: 978-1-55704-249-1.
Dewey:951.9/042. LCCN:92-001163.

Audience: **u,f.**

Stone, I. F.   **DS919.S76 1988**
The Hidden History of the Korean War, 1950-1951. Trade Paper.
Little Brown & Company. New York, NY. 1988. 368p. A
Nonconformist History of Our Times Ser. ISBN:0-316-81770-8,
ISBN13: 978-0-316-81770-7. Dewey:951.9/042.
LCCN:88-012995.

Audience: **f.**

Stueck, William (Editor)   **DS918.K684 2004**
The Korean War in World History. Trade Cloth. University Press
of Kentucky. Lexington, KY. 2004. 232p. ISBN:0-8131-2306-2,
ISBN13: 978-0-8131-2306-6. Dewey:951.904/2.
LCCN:2003-024565.

Audience: **f.** *Choice, 2005.*

Stueck, William   **DS918.A555 2002**
Whitney
Rethinking the Korean War: A New Diplomatic and Strategic
History. Trade Cloth. Princeton University Press. Princeton, NJ.
2002. 304p. ISBN:0-691-08853-5, ISBN13: 978-0-691-08853-2.
Dewey:951.904/21. LCCN:2001-059167.

Audience: **f.** *Choice, 2003.*

West, Philip & Ji-Moon,   **PL957.5.K67R46 2001**
Suh (Editors)
Remembering the 'Forgotten War': The Korean War Through
Literature and Art. Trade Cloth. M. E. Sharpe Inc. Armonk, NY.
2000. xiii, 225p. Studies of the Maureen and Mike Mansfield
Center ISBN:0-7656-0696-8, ISBN13: 978-0-7656-0696-9.
Dewey:895.7/09358. LCCN:00-047003.

Audience: **g,l,u,f.** *Choice, 2001.*

Woodside, Alexander   **JQ1510.W66 2006**
Lost Modernities: China, Vietnam, Korea, and the Hazards of
World History. Trade Cloth. Harvard University Press.
Cambridge, MA. 2006. 160p. The Edwin O. Reischauer
Lectures ISBN:0-674-02217-3, ISBN13: 978-0-674-02217-1.
Dewey:320.951. LCCN:2005-056710.

Audience: **u,f.**

Yuh, Ji-Yeon Yuh   **E184.K6Y85 2004**
Beyond the Shadow of Camptown: Korean Military Brides in
America. Trade Paper. New York University Press. New York,
NY. 2004. 302p. ISBN:0-8147-9699-0, ISBN13:
978-0-8147-9699-3. Dewey:305.4/88957073.

Audience: **g,u,f.**

Korea > Language and Literature

Haboush, JaHyun Kim   **DS913.392.H94A3 1996**
(Editor, Translator, Annotations by, Introduction by)
The Memoirs of Lady Hyegyong: The Autobiographical
Writings of a Crown Princess of Eighteenth-Century Korea.
Trade Cloth. University of California Press. Berkeley, CA. 1996.
329p. ISBN:0-520-20054-3, ISBN13: 978-0-520-20054-8.
Dewey:951.9/02/092 B. LCCN:94-040457.

Audience: **f.**

Hyun, Theresa   **P306.8.K6H98 2003**
Writing Women in Korea: Translation and Feminism in the
Colonial Period. Trade Cloth. University of Hawaii Press.

Honolulu, HI. 2003. 192p. ISBN:0-8248-2677-9, ISBN13: 978-0-8248-2677-2. Dewey:418/.02/08209519. LCCN:2003-009995.

Audience: **u,f.** *Choice, 2004.*

Kim, Hunggyu　　　　**PL955.K4913 1997**
Understanding Korean Literature. Robert J. Fouser (Translator). Trade Cloth. M. E. Sharpe Inc. Armonk, NY. 1997. 246p. New Studies in Asian Culture ISBN:1-56324-773-9, ISBN13: 978-1-56324-773-6. Dewey:895.7/09. LCCN:97-011941.

Audience: **g,u,f.**

Kim, Kichung　　　　**PL956.K48 1996**
An Introduction to Classical Korean Literature: From Hyangga to P'ansori. Trade Cloth. M. E. Sharpe Inc. Armonk, NY. 1996. 244p. New Studies in Asian Culture ISBN:1-56324-785-2, ISBN13: 978-1-56324-785-9. Dewey:895.7/09. LCCN:96-011505.

Audience: **g,u,f.**

Kwon, Youngmin　　　　**PL984.E8F85 2005**
(Editor)
Modern Korean Fiction: An Anthology. Trade Cloth. Edinburgh University Press. Edinburgh, 2005. 408p. ISBN:0-231-13512-2, ISBN13: 978-0-231-13512-2. Dewey:895.7/30108/0904. LCCN:2005-041378.

Audience: **g,u,f.**

Lee, Peter H. (Editor)　　　　**PL984.E8F67 1986**
Flowers of Fire: Twentieth-Century Korean Stories. Trade Paper. University of Hawaii Press. Honolulu, HI. 1986. 512p. ISBN:0-8248-1036-8, ISBN13: 978-0-8248-1036-8. Dewey:895.7/301/08. LCCN:85-020968.

Audience: **f.**

Lee, Peter H. (Editor)　　　　**PL956.H57 2003**
A History of Korean Literature. Trade Cloth. Cambridge University Press. New York, NY. 2003. 654p. ISBN:0-521-82858-9, ISBN13: 978-0-521-82858-1. Dewey:895.7/09. LCCN:2002-041540.

Audience: **f.**

Lee, Peter H.　　　　**PL984.E3P56 1991**
(Translator)
Pine River and Lone Peak: An Anthology of 3 Choson Dynasty Poets. Trade Cloth. University of Hawaii Press. Honolulu, HI. 1991. 208p. ISBN:0-8248-1298-0, ISBN13: 978-0-8248-1298-0. Dewey:895.7/1208. LCCN:90-044433.

Audience: **u,f.**

Lee, Peter H. (Editor)　　　　**PL984.E3.L4 1974**
Poems from Korea: A Historical Anthology. Trade Cloth. University of Hawaii Press. Honolulu, HI. 1974. 196p. ISBN:0-8248-0263-2, ISBN13: 978-0-8248-0263-9. Dewey:895.7/1/008. LCCN:73-080209.

Audience: **f.** *B*

Lee, Peter H.　　　　**PL961.23.Y63.L4**
Songs of Flying Dragons: A Critical Reading. Trade Cloth. Harvard University Press. Cambridge, MA. 1975. 352p. Harvard-Yenching Institute Monographs, No. 22 ISBN:0-674-82075-4, ISBN13: 978-0-674-82075-3. Dewey:895.7/1/2. LCCN:73-092866.

Audience: **f.** *B*

McCann, David R.　　　　**PL984.E1E27 2000**
Early Korean Literature: Selections and Introductions. Trade Cloth. Columbia University Press. New York, NY. 2000. 192p. ISBN:0-231-11946-1, ISBN13: 978-0-231-11946-7. Dewey:895.7/08001. LCCN:99-053800.

Audience: **f.**

Myers, Brian　　　　**PL991.26.S6Z75 1994**
Han Sorya and North Korean Literature: The Failure of Socialist Realism in the DPRK. Trade Cloth. Cornell University East Asia Program. Ithaca, NY. 1994. 224p. Cornell East Asia Ser., No. 69 ISBN:0-939657-84-8, ISBN13: 978-0-939657-84-1. Dewey:895.734. LCCN:94-184777.

Audience: **f.**

O'Rourke, Kevin　　　　**PL984.E3B66 2002**
(Translator)
The Book of Korean Shijo. Trade Cloth. Harvard University Press. Cambridge, MA. 2002. 248p. Harvard East Asian Monographs, Vol. 215 ISBN:0-674-00857-X, ISBN13: 978-0-674-00857-1. Dewey:895.7/1008. LCCN:2002-017339.

Audience: **g,u,f.** *Choice, 2003.*

Yi, Nam-ho, et al.　　　　**PL958.6.T94 2005**
Twentieth Century Korean Literature. Ch'angje U, Kwangho Yi & Mi Hyun Kim (Authors), Brother Anthony of T'aise (Editor), Youngju Ryu (Translator). Trade Cloth. EastBridge. Norwalk, CT. 2003. 120p. ISBN:1-891936-46-8, ISBN13: 978-1-891936-46-3. Dewey:895.7/409. LCCN:2005-001721.

Audience: **g,u,f.**

Central Asia — General

Adshead, S. A. M.　　　　**DS329.4.A37 1993**
Central Asia in World History. Ed. 1. Cloth Text. Palgrave Macmillan. New York, NY. 1993. vii, 291p. ISBN:0-312-08547-8, ISBN13: 978-0-312-08547-6. Dewey:958. LCCN:92-015177.

Audience: **u,f.** *Choice, 1993.*

Allsen, Thomas T.　　　　**DS740.5.I7 A45 2001**
Culture and Conquest in Mongol Eurasia. David Morgan (Contribution by). Trade Paper. Cambridge University Press. New York, NY. 2004. 261p. Cambridge Studies in Islamic Civilization Ser. ISBN:0-521-60270-X, ISBN13: 978-0-521-60270-9. Dewey:303.4825505109022.

Audience: **u.** *Choice, 2003, 2002.*

Barfield, Thomas J.　　　　**DS329.4.B37 1989**
The Perilous Frontier: Nomadic Empires and China. Cloth Text. Blackwell Publishing, Inc. Malden, MA. 1989. 300p. ISBN:1-55786-043-2, ISBN13: 978-1-55786-043-9. Dewey:958. LCCN:88-007746.

Audience: **u,f.** *Choice, 1990.*

Boyle, John A.　　　　**D17**
(Translator)
The Successors of Genghis Khan. Trade Cloth. Columbia University Press. New York, NY. 1971. 372p. ISBN:0-231-03351-6, ISBN13: 978-0-231-03351-0. Dewey:950/.2. LCCN:70-135987.

Audience: **u,f.** *B*

Buell, Paul D.　　　　**DS19.B84 2003**
Historical Dictionary of the Mongol World Empire. Trade Cloth. Scarecrow Press, Inc. Lanham, MD. 2003. 388p. Historical Dictionaries of Ancient Civilizations and Historical Eras Ser.,

No. 8 ISBN:0-8108-4571-7, ISBN13: 978-0-8108-4571-8.
Dewey:909/.0494201/03. LCCN:2002-152655.
Audience: **g,u,f.** *Choice, 2003.*

Crossley, Pamela K.   **DS731.M35C75 1996**
The Manchus. Book, Other. Blackwell Publishing, Inc. Malden,
MA. 1997. 256p. The Peoples of Asia Ser. ISBN:1-55786-560-4,
ISBN13: 978-1-55786-560-1. Dewey:951/.03. LCCN:96-017702.
Audience: **g,u,f.**

Endicott-West, E., et al.   **HC412.M58 1991**
The Modernization of Inner Asia. E. Naby, A. Waldron, Cyril E.
Black, Daniel Matuszewski & Louis Dupree (Authors). Cloth
Text. M. E. Sharpe Inc. Armonk, NY. 1991. 424p.
ISBN:0-87332-778-0, ISBN13: 978-0-87332-778-7.
Dewey:338.958. LCCN:90-023385.
Audience: **u,f.** *Choice, 1992.*

Hopkirk, Peter   **DS786.H6177 1995**
Trespassers on the Roof of the World: The Secret Exploration of
Tibet. Trade Paper. Kodansha America, Inc. New York, NY.
1995. 288p. Kodansha Globe Ser. ISBN:1-56836-050-9,
ISBN13: 978-1-56836-050-8. Dewey:951/.5. LCCN:94-048629.
Audience: **g,l,u,f.**

Kahn, Paul   **PS3561.A38 S4 1998**
The Secret History of the Mongols: The Origin of Chingis
Khan. Trade Paper. Cheng & Tsui Company. Boston, MA. 2002.
240p. ISBN:0-88727-299 1, ISBN13: 978-0-88727-299-8.
Dewey:811/.54. LCCN:00-265509.
Audience: **g,u,f.**

Lattimore, Owen   **DS706.5.L3 1988**
Inner Asian Frontiers of China. Cloth Text. Oxford University
Press, Inc. New York, NY. 1989. 610p. ISBN:0-19-582781-3,
ISBN13: 978-0-19-582781-1. Dewey:911/.51. LCCN:88-025233.
Audience: **g,u,f.** *B*

Meyer, Karl E. &   **DS329.4**
Brysac, Shareen Blair
Tournament of Shadows: The Great Game and the Race for
Empire in Central Asia. Trade Paper. Basic Books. New York,
NY. 2000. 672p. ISBN:1-58243-106-X, ISBN13:
978-1-58243-106-2. Dewey:958.
Audience: **g,l,u.**

Morgan, David   **DS19.M67 1986**
The Mongols. Trade Cloth. Blackwell Publishing, Inc. Malden,
MA. 1987. 256p. ISBN:0-631-13556-1, ISBN13:
978-0-631-13556-2. Dewey:950/.2. LCCN:85-026700.
Audience: **g,l.** *Choice, 1987.*

Perdue, Peter C.   **DS754.P47 2005**
China Marches West: The Qing Conquest of Central Eurasia.
Trade Cloth. Harvard University Press. Cambridge, MA. 2005.
752p. ISBN:0-674-01684-X, ISBN13: 978-0-674-01684-2.
Dewey:951/.03. LCCN:2004-059472.
Audience: **g,u,f.** *Choice, 2006.*

Polo, Marco, et al.   **G370.P9 P6713 1993**
The Travels of Marco Polo: The Complete Yule-Cordier Edition.
Henry Yule & Henri Cordier (Authors). Trade Paper. Dover
Publications, Inc. Mineola, NY. 1993. Extensive editorial
apparatus, nearly 200 illustrations (many double-page spreads)
and 32 maps and site plans augment the text. 855p. 0
ISBN:0-486-27587-6, ISBN13: 978-0-486-27587-1.
Dewey:915.10425092. LCCN:92-039066.
Audience: **g,l,u.**

Polo, Marco, et al.   **G370.P9 P6713 1993**
The Travels of Marco Polo: The Complete Yule-Cordier Edition.
Henry Yule & Henri Cordier (Authors). Trade Paper. Dover
Publications, Inc. Mineola, NY. 1993. 567p. 0
ISBN:0-486-27586-8, ISBN13: 978-0-486-27586-4.
Dewey:915.10425092. LCCN:92-039066.
Audience: **g.**

Rossabi, Morris   **DS752.6.K83R67 1988**
Khubilai Khan: His Life and Times. Trade Cloth. University of
California Press. Berkeley, CA. 1988. 344p.
ISBN:0-520-05913-1, ISBN13: 978-0-520-05913-9.
Dewey:950/.2/0924 B. LCCN:86-025031.
Audience: **g,u.** *Choice, 1989.*

Sinor, Denis (Editor)   **DS329.4 .C35 1990**
The Cambridge History of Early Inner Asia: From Earliest
Times to the Rise of the Mongols. Trade Cloth. Cambridge
University Press. New York, NY. 1990. 504p.
ISBN:0-521-24304-1, ISBN13: 978-0-521-24304-9. Dewey:958.
LCCN:88-018887.
Audience: **f.** *Choice, 1990.*

Soucek, Svat   **DK856 .S66 2000**
A History of Inner Asia. Cloth Text. Cambridge University
Press. New York, NY. 2000. 384p. ISBN:0-521-65169-7,
ISBN13: 978-0-521-65169-1. Dewey:958. LCCN:99-031839.
Audience: **f.** *Choice, 2000.*

Weatherford, Jack   **DS22.G45W43 2004**
Genghis Khan and the Making of the Modern World. Trade
Cloth. Crown Publishing Group. New York, NY. 2005. 352p.
ISBN:0-609-80964-4, ISBN13: 978-0-609-80964-8.
Dewey:950/.21/092 B. LCCN:2003-020659.
Audience: **g,u,f.**

Wood, Frances   **DS33.1.W59 2002**
The Silk Road: Two Thousand Years in the Heart of Asia. Trade
Cloth. University of California Press. Berkeley, CA. 2003. 270p.
ISBN:0-520-23786-2, ISBN13: 978-0-520-23786-5.
Dewey:950.1. LCCN:2003-273631.
Audience: **g,u,f.** *Choice, 2004.*

Wriggins, Sally Hovey   **BQ8149.H787**
Xuanzang: A Buddhist Pilgrim on the Silk Road. Paper Text.
Westview Press. Boulder, CO. 1997. 292p. ISBN:0-8133-3407-1,
ISBN13: 978-0-8133-3407-3. Dewey:939.6/0099.
Audience: **g,u,f.**

Mongolia

Atwood, Christopher   **DS798.5**
Pratt
Encyclopedia of Mongolia and the Mongol Empire. Perfect,
Paper over Boards. Facts On File, Inc. New York, NY. 2004.
678p. Facts on File Library of World History
ISBN:0-8160-4671-9, ISBN13: 978-0-8160-4671-3.
Dewey:951.7/3/003. LCCN:2003-061696.
Audience: **u,f.** *Choice, 2004.*

Bawden, C. R.   **DS798 .B53**
Modern History of Mongolia. Trade Cloth. Kegan Paul
International, Ltd. London, 2002. 476p. ISBN:0-7103-0800-0,
ISBN13: 978-0-7103-0800-9. Dewey:951.7/3.
Audience: **u,f.**

Bulag, Uradyn E.   **DS19.B85 1998**
Nationalism and Hybridity in Mongolia. Trade Cloth. Oxford University Press, Inc. New York, NY. 1998. 318p. Oxford Studies in Social and Cultural Anthropology - Cultural Forms ISBN:0-19-823357-4, ISBN13: 978-0-19-823357-2. Dewey:306/.09517/3. LCCN:97-039268.
Audience: **f.** *Choice, 1998.*

Goldstein, Melvyn C. &   **DS798.4.G65 1994**
  Beall, Cynthia M.
The Changing World of Mongolia's Nomads. Trade Paper. University of California Press. Berkeley, CA. 1994. 176p. ISBN:0-520-08551-5, ISBN13: 978-0-520-08551-0. Dewey:951.7. LCCN:93-024004.
Audience: **g,u,f.**

Heissig, Walther   **BL1945**
The Religions of Mongolia. Ed. 3. Geoffrey Samuel (Translator). Trade Cloth. Kegan Paul International, Ltd. London, 2001. 146p. ISBN:0-7103-0685-7, ISBN13: 978-0-7103-0685-2. Dewey:299/.42.
Audience: **f.**

Kotkin, Stephen   **DS798.75.M653 1999**
  (Editor)
Mongolia in the Twentieth Century. Bruce A. Elleman (Editor, Contribution by), Lan Meihua, Elizabeth Endicott, Nakami Tatsuo, Yeshen-Khorlo Dugarova-Montgomery, Robert Montgomery, Elena Boikova, Christopher P. Atwood, T. Batbayar, A. Hurelbaatar, David Sneath, J. Boldbaatar, Tom Ginsburg & G. Tumurchulunn (Contribution by). Cloth Text. M. E. Sharpe Inc. Armonk, NY. 1999. 336p. ISBN:0-7656-0535-X, ISBN13: 978-0-7656-0535-1. Dewey:951/.705. LCCN:99-044518.
Audience: **f.**

Moses, Larry W.   **DS798.5**
Introduction to Mongolian History and Culture. Cloth Text. Taylor & Francis Group. Philadelphia, PA. 1997. 305p. ISBN:0-7007-0949-5, ISBN13: 978-0-7007-0949-6. Dewey:951/.7.
Audience: **u,f.**

Rossabi, Morris   **DS798.84 .R67 2005**
Modern Mongolia: From Khans to Commissars to Capitalists. Trade Cloth. University of California Press. Berkeley, CA. 2005. 428p. ISBN:0-520-24399-4, ISBN13: 978-0-520-24399-6. Dewey:951.7/3. LCCN:2004-017992.
Audience: **g,f.**

Sanders, Alan J. K.   **DS798.5.S36 2003**
Historical Dictionary of Mongolia. Ed. 2. Trade Cloth. Scarecrow Press, Inc. Lanham, MD. 2003. 512p. Asian/Oceanian Historical Dictionaries Ser., No. 41 ISBN:0-8108-4434-6, ISBN13: 978-0-8108-4434-6. Dewey:951.7/3/003. LCCN:2002-011391.
Audience: **g.** *Choice, 2003.*

Tibet

Barnett, Robert &   **DS785.A1R47 1994**
  Akiner, Shirin (Editors)
Resistance and Reform in Tibet. Trade Cloth. Indiana University Press. Bloomington, IN. 1994. xxx, 314p. ISBN:0-253-31131-4, ISBN13: 978-0-253-31131-3. Dewey:951/.5. LCCN:93-003072.
Audience: **g,u,f.** *Choice, 1995.*

Bishop, Peter   **DS786.B53 1989**
The Myth of Shangri-la: Tibet, Travel Writing and the Western Creation of Sacred Landscape. Trade Cloth. University of California Press. Berkeley, CA. 1989. 400p. ISBN:0-520-06686-3, ISBN13: 978-0-520-06686-1. Dewey:915.1/5. LCCN:89-040450.
Audience: **g,u,f.**

Conboy, Kenneth J. &   **E183.8.T55C66 2002**
  Morrison, James
The CIA's Secret War in Tibet. Trade Cloth. University Press of Kansas. Lawrence, KS. 2004. x, 302p. Modern War Studies ISBN:0-7006-1159-2, ISBN13: 978-0-7006-1159-1. Dewey:327.1273/0515/09045. LCCN:2001-005247.
Audience: **g,u,f.** *Choice, 2002.*

Dalai Lama XIV   **BQ7935.B777A3 1997**
My Land and My People: The Original Autobiography of His Holiness the Dalai Lama of Tibet. Melissa Mathison Ford (Foreword by). Trade Paper. Warner Books, Inc. New York, NY. 1997. 256p. ISBN:0-446-67421-4, ISBN13: 978-0-446-67421-8. Dewey:[B]. LCCN:97-023849.
Audience: **g,u,f.**

David-Neel, Alexandra   **DS785.D27813 1986**
My Journey to Lhasa. Library Binding. Beacon Press. Boston, MA. 1986. 320p. ISBN:0-8070-5900-5, ISBN13: 978-0-8070-5900-5. Dewey:915.1/5. LCCN:85-047947.
Audience: **g,u,f.**

Fleming, Peter   **DS785.F56 1986**
Bayonets to Lhasa. Brian Shaw (Introduction by). Trade Paper. Oxford University Press, Inc. New York, NY. 1986. 334p. Oxford Asia Paperbacks Ser. ISBN:0-19-583862-9, ISBN13: 978-0-19-583862-6. Dewey:951/.5. LCCN:86-171646.
Audience: **g,u,f.**

Goldstein, Melvyn C.   **DS786.G635 1989**
A History of Modern Tibet, 1913-1951: The Demise of the Lamaist State. Trade Cloth. University of California Press. Berkeley, CA. 1989. 898p. ISBN:0-520-06140-3, ISBN13: 978-0-520-06140-8. Dewey:951/.5. LCCN:87-034933.
Audience: **g,u,f.** *Choice, 1990.*

Goldstein, Melvyn C.   **DS786.G636 1997**
The Snow Lion and the Dragon: China, Tibet, and the Dalai Lama. Trade Cloth. University of California Press. Berkeley, CA. 1997. 165p. ISBN:0-520-21254-1, ISBN13: 978-0-520-21254-1. Dewey:951.5. LCCN:97-002562.
Audience: **g,u,f.** *Choice, 1998.*

Goldstein, Melvyn C. &   **GN635.C5G65 1990**
  Beall, Cynthia M.
Nomads of Western Tibet: The Survival of a Way of Life. Trade Cloth. University of California Press. Berkeley, CA. 1990. 200p. ISBN:0-520-07210-3, ISBN13: 978-0-520-07210-7. Dewey:305.9/0693. LCCN:90-010892.
Audience: **g,f.** *Choice, 1991.*

Goldstein, Melvyn C. &   **BQ7590 .B84 1998**
  Kapstein, Matthew T.
Buddhism in Contemporary Tibet: Religious Revival and Cultural Identity. Trade Cloth. University of California Press. Berkeley, CA. 1998. 235p. ISBN:0-520-21130-8, ISBN13: 978-0-520-21130-8. Dewey:294.3/923/0951509048. LCCN:97-026851.
Audience: **g,u,f.** *Choice, 1999.*

Goldstein, Melvyn C. &   PL3637.E5 N48 2001
Robillard, Pierre
The New Tibetan-English Dictionary of Modern Tibetan. Ed. 2.
T. N. Shelling & J. T. Surkhang (Editors). Trade Cloth.
University of California Press. Berkeley, CA. 2001. 1214p.
ISBN:0-520-20437-9, ISBN13: 978-0-520-20437-9.
Dewey:495/.4321. LCCN:00-047521.

Audience: **f.**

Grunfeld, A. Tom   DS786.G76 1996
The Making of Modern Tibet. Ed. 2. Trade Cloth. M. E. Sharpe
Inc. Armonk, NY. 1996. 370p. ISBN:1-56324-713-5, ISBN13:
978-1-56324-713-2. Dewey:951/.5. LCCN:96-011504.

Audience: **g,l,u,f.** *Choice, 1987.*

Gyatso, Janet   BQ966.I32965.A3 1998
Apparitions of the Self: The Secret Autobiographies of a Tibetan
Visionary. Trade Cloth. Princeton University Press. Princeton,
NJ. 1998. xxiv, 360p. ISBN:0-691-01110-9, ISBN13:
978-0-691-01110-3. Dewey:294.3923092. LCCN:97-010191.

Audience: **g,f.** *Choice, 1998.*

Gyatso, Janet &   HQ1769.T55W66 2004
Havnevik, Hanna
Women in Tibet: Past and Present. Trade Cloth. Columbia
University Press. New York, NY. 2006. 352p.
ISBN:0-231-13098-8, ISBN13: 978-0-231-13098-1.
Dewey:305.4/0951/5. LCCN:2003-055510.

Audience: **g,u.**

Harrer, Heinrich   DS786
Seven Years in Tibet. Trade Cloth. State Mutual Book &
Periodical Service, Ltd. Bridgehampton, NY. 1955.
ISBN:0-7855-2422-3, ISBN13: 978-0-7855-2422-9.
Dewey:951.5/042/092.

Audience: **g,u,f.**

Lopez Jr., Donald S.   BQ7455.D483L67 2005
The Madman's Middle Way: Reflections on Reality of a Tibetan
Monk Gendun Chopel. Trade Cloth. University of Chicago
Press. Chicago, IL. 2005. 264p. Buddhism and Modernity Ser.
ISBN:0-226-49316-4, ISBN13: 978-0-226-49316-9.
Dewey:294.3/923/092 B. LCCN:2005-011087.

Audience: **g,f.** *Choice, 2006.*

Lopez, Donald S.   BQ7620.R45 1997
Religions of Tibet in Practice. Cloth Text. Princeton University
Press. Princeton, NJ. 1997. 560p. Princeton Readings in
Religions Ser. ISBN:0-691-01184-2, ISBN13:
978-0-691-01184-4. Dewey:294.3/923. LCCN:96-031592.

Audience: **g,u,f.** *Choice, 1997.*

Lopez, Donald S. Jr.   BQ1967.L67 1988
The Heart Sutra Explained: Indian and Tibetan Commentaries.
Cloth Text. State University of New York Press. Albany, NY.
1988. 230p. SUNY Series in Buddhist Studies
ISBN:0-88706-589-9, ISBN13: 978-0-88706-589-7.
Dewey:294.3/85. LCCN:87-006479.

Audience: **f.**

Lopez, Donald S. Jr.   BQ7604.L66 1998
Prisoners of Shangri-La: Tibetan Buddhism and the West. Trade
Cloth. University of Chicago Press. Chicago, IL. 1998. 294p.
ISBN:0-226-49310-5, ISBN13: 978-0-226-49310-7.
Dewey:951.5/059. LCCN:97-041202.

Audience: **g,u,f.**

McGovern, William   DS785
Montgomery
To Lhasa in Disguise: an Account of a Secret Expedition
Through Mysterious Tibet. Trade Cloth. Kegan Paul
International, Ltd. London, 2004. 352p. ISBN:0-7103-1060-9,
ISBN13: 978-0-7103-1060-6. Dewey:915.1/5/044.

Audience: **f.**

Pattison, Eliot   PS3566.A82497S55
The Skull Mantra. Cloth over Boards. St. Martin's Press.
Gordonville, VA. 1999. 352p. ISBN:0-312-20478-7, ISBN13:
978-0-312-20478-5. Dewey:813.5/4. LCCN:99-023847.

Audience: **g,l,u,f.**

Rockhill, William W.   DS785
The Land of the Lamas: Notes of a Journey Through China,
Mongolia and Tibet. Trade Cloth. Asian Educational Services.
New Delhi, 1988. 397p. ISBN:81-206-0354-0, ISBN13:
978-81-206-0354-7. Dewey:915.1.

Audience: **f.**

Rowell, Galen   DS786
(Photographer, Introduction by)
My Tibet. Dalai Lama XIV (Text by). Trade Cloth. University
of California Press. Berkeley, CA. 1995. 168p.
ISBN:0-520-08948-0, ISBN13: 978-0-520-08948-8.
Dewey:951/.505.

Audience: **g,u,f.**

Schell, Orville   DS786.S295 2000
Virtual Tibet: Searching for Shangri-La from the Himalayans to
Hollywood. Cloth over Boards. Henry Holt & Company. New
York, NY. 2000. 368p. ISBN:0-8050-4381-0, ISBN13:
978-0-8050-4381-5. Dewey:951/.5. LCCN:99-088146.

Audience: **g,u,f.**

Schwartz, Ronald D.   DS786.S347 1994
Circle of Protest: Political Ritual in the Tibetan Uprising,
1987-1992. Trade Cloth. Columbia University Press. New York,
NY. 1995. 263p. ISBN:0-231-10094-9, ISBN13:
978-0-231-10094-6. Dewey:320.9515. LCCN:94-005522.

Audience: **f.**

Shakya, Tsering   DS786
The Dragon in the Land of Snows: A History of Modern Tibet
Since 1947. Trade Paper. Penguin Group (USA) Inc. New York,
NY. 2000. 608p. ISBN:0-14-019615-3, ISBN13:
978-0-14-019615-3. Dewey:951/.505.

Audience: **g,u,f.** *Choice, 2000.*

Thurman, Robert A. F.   BQ7604 .T496
Essential Tibetan Buddhism. Cloth Text. DIANE Publishing
Company. Collingdale, PA. 1999. 317p. ISBN:0-7881-6757-X,
ISBN13: 978-0-7881-6757-7. Dewey:294.3/923.

Audience: **g,u,f.**

Thurman, Robert A.   BQ4490.K3713 1993
(Translator)
The Tibetan Book of the Dead: The Great Book of Natural
Liberation Through Understanding in the Between. Padma
Sambhava (Compiled by), Dalia Lama (Foreword by). Trade
Paper. Bantam Books. New York, NY. 1993. 304p.
ISBN:0-553 37090-1, ISBN13: 978-0-553-37090-4.
Dewey:294.3/423. LCCN:93-002891.

Audience: **g,u,f.**

Trungpa, Chogyam   **BQ990.R867**
Born in Tibet. Book, Other. Shambhala Publications, Inc.
Boston, MA. 2000. 280p. ISBN:1-57062-714-2, ISBN13:
978-1-57062-714-9. Dewey:294.3/923/0924 B.

Audience: **g,u,f.**

Tsering, Tashi, et al.   **LA2383.C52T37**
The Struggle for Modern Tibet: The Autobiography of Tashi
Tsering. Melvyn Goldstein & William Siebenschuh (Authors).

Trade Cloth. M. E. Sharpe Inc. Armonk, NY. 1997. 220p.
ISBN:0-7656-0509-0, ISBN13: 978-0-7656-0509-2.
Dewey:365/.45/092 B. LCCN:97-004968.

Audience: **f.**

CRIMINAL JUSTICE

This section is organized to reflect the major subdivisions in the field of Criminal Justice: Criminal Justice Systems and Processes, Criminology, Law Enforcement, Law and Courts, and Corrections. The specific subjects included are based on undergraduate curricula at U.S. colleges and universities with well-respected criminal justice programs. In BCL3, Criminal Justice was presented largely as a sub-discipline of Sociology with criminology, law enforcement and corrections included there. Materials on administration of justice, criminal law and courts fell under Law. This reflects the history of the academic field of criminal justice which appeared as a distinctive field only in the 1960s. Criminal Justice continues to be interdisciplinary and materials from related subjects such as sociology, law, African American Studies, women's studies, social welfare, public administration and policy, and psychology have great impact on study and research.

Resources selected for this RCL section are suitable for undergraduate study, research, and teaching. Many high quality specialized resources are excluded as more appropriate for graduate level work. While the emphasis is on resources which focus on the United States, selected international and comparative materials are included. Also listed are a substantial number of general books published in other countries, particularly the United Kingdom. The field of Criminal Justice relies heavily upon journal literature and government documents at the international, national, state, and local level. Many of the government documents are freely available on the Internet. Two U.S. government websites are included — NCJRS Abstracts Database, which is a gateway to government reports in the field of criminal justice, and the Bureau of Justice Statistics website, which is similarly a gateway to U.S. statistics in criminal justice.

Some overarching issues such as administration of criminal justice, policy issues, legal issues, capital punishment, etc. do not fit within one subdivision of the field, and are therefore placed under Criminal Justice Systems and Processes. The Law Enforcement section includes only a limited selection of forensics materials suitable for general knowledge about law enforcement investigation. While there is necessary duplication between the Criminal Justice section and several other RCL sections on related topics, such overlap has been kept to a minimum.

— Mary Jane Brustman

Criminal Justice, Generally > History of Criminal Justice

Chapin, Bradley KF9223.C53 1983
Criminal Justice in Colonial America, 1606-1660. Cloth Text.
University of Georgia Press. Athens, GA. 1983. 224p.
ISBN:0-8203-0624-X, ISBN13: 978-0-8203-0624-7.
Dewey:345.73/05. LCCN:82-002753.

Audience: **l,u,f.**

Johnson, Herbert Alan HV7419.J64 2001
& Wolfe, Nancy Travis
History of Criminal Justice. Ed. 3. Trade Paper, Mixed Media,
Book, Other. Anderson Publishing Company. Miamisburg, OH.
2003. 384p. ISBN:1-58360-515-0, ISBN13: 978-1-58360-515-8.
Dewey:364.9. LCCN:2001-034110.

Audience: **l,u.**

Jones, David A. HV6021
History of Criminology: A Philosophical Perspective. Trade
Cloth. Greenwood Publishing Group, Inc. Portsmouth, NH.
1986. 255p. Contributions to Criminology and Penology Ser.,
No. 10 ISBN:0-313-23647-X, ISBN13: 978-0-313-23647-1.
Dewey:364/.9. LCCN:85-017724.

Audience: **l,u.** *Choice, 1987.*

Mannheim, Hermann HV6025.M322 1972
Pioneers in Criminology. Ed. 2. Trade Cloth. Patterson Smith
Publishing Corporation. Montclair, NJ. 1972. xv, 505p.
Criminology, Law Enforcement, and Social Problems Ser., No.
121 ISBN:0-87585-121-5, ISBN13: 978-0-87585-121-1.
Dewey:364/.092/2. LCCN:78-108238.

Audience: **l,u.**

Monkkonen, Eric H. HV6789.M63 2002
Crime, Justice, History. Trade Cloth. Ohio State University
Press. Columbus, OH. 2002. xi, 293p. History of Crime and
Criminal Justice Ser. ISBN:0-8142-0902-5, ISBN13:
978-0-8142-0902-8. Dewey:364.973. LCCN:2002-008374.

Audience: **u,f.**

Walker, Samuel HV8138.W342 1998
Popular Justice: A History of American Criminal Justice. Ed. 2.
Paper Text. Oxford University Press, Inc. New York, NY. 1997.
304p. ISBN:0-19-507451-3, ISBN13: 978-0-19-507451-2.
Dewey:364.973. LCCN:97-008994.

Audience: **l,u.**

Criminal Justice, Generally > Education, Teaching, and Careers

Anderson, James F., et al. HV9950.A54 2003
Criminal Justice and Criminology: A Career Guide to Local,
State, Federal, and Academic Positions. Nancie J. Mangels &
Laronistine Dyson (Authors). Trade Paper. University Press of
America, Inc. Lanham, MD. 2003. 322p. ISBN:0-7618-2761-7,
ISBN13: 978-0-7618-2761-0. Dewey:364.973/023.
LCCN:2003-112787.

Audience: **l,u.** *Choice, 2004.*

Harr, J. Scott & Hess, HV8143.H327 2006
Kären M.
Careers in Criminal Justice and Related Fields: From Internship
to Promotion. Ed. 5. Paper Text. Thomson Wadsworth. Belmont,

CA. 2005. 368p. ISBN:0-534-62620-3, ISBN13:
978-0-534-62620-4. Dewey:363.2023/73. LCCN:2004-115405.

Audience: **g,l,u.**

Kleinig, John & Smith, HV9950.T43 1997
Margaret L.
Teaching Criminal Justice Ethics: Strategic Issues. Trade Paper.
Anderson Publishing Company. Miamisburg, OH. 1997. 248p.
ISBN:0-87084-831-3, ISBN13: 978-0-87084-831-5.
Dewey:364.973. LCCN:97-072026.

Audience: **f.**

Solan, Lawrence M. & KF9223.S668 2005
Tiersma, Peter M.
Speaking of Crime: The Language of Criminal Justice. Trade
Cloth. University of Chicago Press. Chicago, IL. 2005. 264p.
Chicago Series in Law and Society ISBN:0-226-76792-2,
ISBN13: 978-0-226-76792-5. Dewey:345.73/05/014.
LCCN:2004-010382.

Audience: **l,u,f.**

Taylor, Dorothy L. HV9950.T38 2004
Jumpstarting Your Career: An Internship Guide for Criminal
Justice. Ed. 2. Trade Paper. Prentice Hall PTR. Upper Saddle
River, NJ. 2004. 160p. ISBN:0-13-117577-7, ISBN13:
978-0-13-117577-8. Dewey:364.973/071/55.
LCCN:2003-024816.

Audience: **l,u.**

Criminal Justice, Generally > Comprehensive Reference Sources > Encyclopedias

Dressler, Joshua HV6017.E52 2002
(Editor)
Encyclopedia of Crime and Justice, Set. Ed. 2. Thomson Gale
Staff (Contribution by). Trade Cloth. Thomson Gale. Farmington
Hills, MI. 2001. 1780p. ISBN:0-02-865319-X, ISBN13:
978-0-02-865319-8. Dewey:364/.03. LCCN:2001-042707.

Audience: **g,l,u.** *Choice, 2002.*

Levinson, David (Editor, HV6017.E524 2002
Compiled by)
Encyclopedia of Crime and Punishment, Set. Trade Cloth.
SAGE Publications, Inc. Thousand Oaks, CA. 2002. 2104p.
ISBN:0-7619-2258-X, ISBN13: 978-0-7619-2258-2.
Dewey:346/.03. LCCN:2002-001220.

Audience: **l,u.** *Choice, 2002.*

Criminal Justice, Generally > Comprehensive Reference Sources > Databases and Bibliographies

☐ Criminal Justice Abstracts (Database).
http://www.csa.com/
Sage Publications (on Internet via CSA).

Audience: **l,u,f.**

HV7231

☐ Criminal Justice Periodicals (Database).
http://proquest.umi.com/
ProQuest Company.

Audience: **l,u,f.**

Audience: g=general, l=lower division undergraduate, u=upper division undergraduate, f=faculty.

245

☐ NCJRS Abstracts Database.
http://www.ncjrs.gov/abstractdb/search.asp
United States Department of Justice, Office of Justice Programs,
National Criminal Justice Reference Service

Audience: **l,u,f.**

Criminal Justice, Generally > Comprehensive Reference Sources > Dictionaries and Thesauri

Z7164.P76

☐ NCJ (National Criminal Justice) Thesaurus.
http://www.ncjrs.gov/abstractdb/thesaurus/search.asp
United States Department of Justice, Office of Justice Programs,
National Criminal Justice Reference Service

Audience: **l,u,f.**

Champion, Dean John   **HV6017**
The American Dictionary of Criminal Justice: Key Terms and
Major Court Cases. Ed. 3. Trade Cloth. Scarecrow Press, Inc.
Lanham, MD. 2004. 456p. ISBN:0-8108-5406-6, ISBN13:
978-0-8108-5406-2. Dewey:364/.03. LCCN:2004-042836.

Audience: **g,l.**

McLaughlin, Eugene &   **HV6017**
Muncie, John (Editors)
The SAGE Dictionary of Criminology. Ed. 2. Cloth Text. SAGE
Publications, Ltd. London, 2005. 504p. ISBN:1-4129-1085-4,
ISBN13: 978-1-4129-1085-9. Dewey:364.03.

Audience: **l,u,f.**

Rush, George E.   **HV7411.R87 2003**
Dictionary of Criminal Justice. Ed. 6. Paper Text. McGraw-Hill
Higher Education. Burr Ridge, IL. 2004. 496p.
ISBN:0-07-295112-5, ISBN13: 978-0-07-295112-7.
Dewey:364/.03. LCCN:99-074549.

Audience: **l,u,f.**

Criminal Justice, Generally > Research > Methods and Design

Bachman, Ronet &   **HV6024.5.B33 2003**
Schutt, Russell K.
The Practice of Research in Criminology and Criminal Justice.
Ed. 2. Paper Text. SAGE Publications, Inc. Thousand Oaks, CA.
2003. 560p. ISBN:0-7619-2877-4, ISBN13: 978-0-7619-2877-5.
Dewey:364/.07/2. LCCN:2003-000231.

Audience: **l,u.**

Pepper, John V., et al.   **HV7419.5.M43 2003**
Measurement Problems in Criminal Justice Research: Workshop
Summary. National Research Council Staff & Carol V. Petrie
(Authors). Perfect. National Academies Press. Washington, DC.
2003. 112p. ISBN:0-309-08635-3, ISBN13: 978-0-309-08635-6.
Dewey:364/.072. LCCN:2002-115675.

Audience: **u,f.**

Pope, Carl E., et al.   **HV6024.5**
Voices from the Field: Readings in Criminal Justice Research
Methods and Research Methods in Criminal Justice. Rick Lovell

& Steven Gerard Brandl (Authors). Trade Cloth. Thomson
Wadsworth. Belmont, CA. 2001. ISBN:0-534-97578-X, ISBN13:
978-0-534-97578-4. Dewey:364/.07/2.

Audience: **l,u.**

Walters, Reece   **HV6024.5**
Deviant Knowledge: Criminology, Politics and Policy. Trade
Cloth. Willan Publishing. Devon, 2003. 218p.
ISBN:1-84392-030-1, ISBN13: 978-1-84392-030-4.
Dewey:364.072. LCCN:2004-555043.

Audience: **u,f.**

Criminal Justice, Generally > Research > Statistics

HV7248

☐ Bureau of Justice Statistics.
http://www.ojp.usdoj.gov/bjs/
United States Department of Justice, Office of Justice Programs,
Bureau of Justice Statistics.

Audience: **l,u,f.**

HV7245

☐ Sourcebook of Criminal Justice Statistics.
http://www.albany.edu/sourcebook/
United States Department of Justice, Bureau of Justice Statistics.

Audience: **l,u,f.**

HV6787

☐ Uniform Crime Reports.
http://www.fbi.gov/ucr/ucr.htm
United States Department of Justice, Federal Bureau of
Investigation.

Audience: **l,u,f.**

United Nations. Crime
and Justice Information Network
☐ Statistics and Research Sources.
http://www.uncjin.org/Statistics/statistics.html
United Nations. Crime and Justice Information Network.

Audience: **l,u,f.**

Criminal Justice Systems and Processes > Legal and Policy Issues

Benson, Bruce L.   **HV9950.B49 1998**
To Serve and Protect: Privatization and Community in Criminal
Justice. Trade Cloth. New York University Press. New York,
NY. 1998. 400p. Political Economy of the Austrian School Ser.
ISBN:0-8147-1327-0, ISBN13: 978-0-8147-1327-3.
Dewey:364.973. LCCN:98-019688.

Audience: **u,f.** *Choice, 1999.*

Carpenter, Ted Galen   **HV5825.C34 2003**
Bad Neighbor Policy: Washington's Futile War on Drugs in
Latin America. Cloth over Boards. Palgrave Macmillan. New
York, NY. 2003. 288p. ISBN:1-4039-6137-9, ISBN13:
978-1-4039-6137-2. Dewey:363.45/0973. LCCN:2002-032248.

Audience: **u,f.** *Choice, 2003.*

Cohen, Mark A.   **HV6171.C64 2005**
The Costs of Crime and Justice. Paper over Boards. Routledge.
New York, NY. 2005. 144p. Studies in Crime and Economics
Ser. ISBN:0-415-70072-8, ISBN13: 978-0-415-70072-6.
Dewey:364. LCCN:2004-050836.

Audience: **l,u.**

Gest, Ted   **HV6789.G47 2001**
Crime and Politics: Big Government's Erratic Campaign for
Law and Order. Trade Cloth. Oxford University Press, Inc. New
York, NY. 2001. 304p. ISBN:0-19-510343-2, ISBN13:
978-0-19-510343-4. Dewey:364.4/0973. LCCN:00-065214.

Audience: **l,u.**

Harris, Andrew J.   **HV6592.H38 2005**
Civil Commitment of Sexual Predators: A Study in Policy
Implementation. Trade Cloth. LFB Scholarly Publishing LLC.
New York, NY. 2005. 288p. Criminal Justice, :Recent
Scholarship ISBN:1-59332-095-7, ISBN13: 978-1-59332-095-9.
Dewey:364.15/3. LCCN:2005-012791.

Audience: **u,f.**

Newburn, Tim &   **HV7431**
  Sparks, Richard (Editors)
Criminal Justice and Political Culture: National and International
Dimensions of Crime Control. Trade Cloth. Willan Publishing.
Devon, 2004. 276p. ISBN:1-84392-026-3, ISBN13:
978-1-84392-026-7. Dewey:363.23. LCCN:2004-301623.

Audience: **l,u.**

Shichor, David &   **HV9469.P756 2001**
  Gilbert, Michael J.
Privatization in Criminal Justice: Past, Present and Future. Ed.
5. Mixed Media, Book, Other, Trade Paper. Anderson Publishing
Company. Miamisburg, OH. 2001. 376p. ISBN:1-58360-500-2,
ISBN13: 978-1-58360-500-4. Dewey:365/.973.
LCCN:00-036354.

Audience: **l,u.**

Stolz, Barbara Ann   **HV9950**
Criminal Justice Policy Making: Federal Roles and Processes.
Paper Text. Greenwood Publishing Group, Inc. Portsmouth, NH.
2001. 248p. ISBN:0-275-97324-7, ISBN13: 978-0-275-97324-7.
Dewey:364.973. LCCN:2001-034632.

Audience: **l,u.**

Valier, Claire   **HV6001**
Crime and Punishment in Contemporary Culture. Paper over
Boards. Routledge. New York, NY. 2003. 192p. International
Library of Sociology ISBN:0-415-28175-X, ISBN13:
978-0-415-28175-1. Dewey:364. LCCN:2003-006407.

Audience: **u.**

Walker, Samuel   **HV9950.W35 2006**
Sense and Nonsense about Crime and Drugs: A Policy Guide.
Ed. 6. Paper Text. Thomson Wadsworth. Belmont, CA. 2005.
360p. ISBN:0-534-61654-2, ISBN13: 978-0-534-61654-0.
Dewey:364.4/04560973. LCCN:2005-928204.

Audience: **l,u.**

Walters, Reece   **HV6024.5**
Deviant Knowledge: Criminology, Politics and Policy. Trade
Cloth. Willan Publishing. Devon, 2003. 218p.
ISBN:1-84392-030-1, ISBN13: 978-1-84392-030-4.
Dewey:364.072. LCCN:2004-555043.

Audience: **u,f.**

Criminal Justice Systems and Processes > Legal and Policy Issues > Capital Punishment

Acker, James R.   **HV8699.U5**
America's Experiment with Capital Punishment: Reflections on
the Past, Present, and Future of the Ultimate Penal Sanction. Ed.
2. Trade Paper. Carolina Academic Press. Durham, NC. 2003.
824p. ISBN:0-89089-064-1, ISBN13: 978-0-89089-064-6.
Dewey:364.66/0973.

Audience: **u,f.**

Banner, Stuart   **HV8699.U5B367 2002**
The Death Penalty: An American History. Trade Cloth. Harvard
University Press. Cambridge, MA. 2002. 408p.
ISBN:0-674-00751-4, ISBN13: 978-0-674-00751-2.
Dewey:364.66/0973. LCCN:2001-047047.

Audience: **l,u,f.** *Choice, 2003, 2002.*

Bedau, Hugo Adam   **HV8699.U5.B43 2004**
Killing As Punishment: Reflection on the Death Penalty in
America. Trade Cloth. Northeastern University Press. Boston,
MA. 2005. 256p. ISBN:1-55553-595-X, ISBN13:
978-1-55553-595-7. Dewey:364.66/0973. LCCN:2003-018649.

Audience: **u,f.**

Bohm, Robert M.   **HV8699.U5B65 2003**
Deathquest II: An Introduction to the Theory and Practice of
Capital Punishment in the United States. Ed. 2. Trade Paper,
Mixed Media, Book, Other. Anderson Publishing Company.
Miamisburg, OH. 2003. 323p. ISBN:1-58360-553-3, ISBN13:
978-1-58360-553-0. Dewey:364.66/0973. LCCN:2004-270067.

Audience: **l.**

Galliher, John F., et al.   **HV8699.U5G35 2002**
America Without the Death Penalty: States Leading the Way.
Larry W. Koch, David Patrick Keys & Teresa J. Guess
(Authors). Trade Cloth. Northeastern University Press. Boston,
MA. 2002. 320p. ISBN:1-55553-529-1, ISBN13:
978-1-55553-529-2. Dewey:364.66/0973. LCCN:2002-004923.

Audience: **u,f.** *Choice, 2003.*

Prejean, Helen   **HV8699.U5**
Dead Man Walking. Library Binding. Sagebrush Education
Resources. Caledonia, MN. 1994. ISBN:0-7857-5300-1,
ISBN13: 978-0-7857-5300-1. Dewey:364.660922.

Audience: **g,l,u.**

Schabas, William A.   **K5104**
The Abolition of the Death Penalty in International Law. Ed. 3.
Trade Cloth. Cambridge University Press. New York, NY. 2002.
506p. ISBN:0-521-81491-X, ISBN13: 978-0-521-81491-1.
Dewey:345/.0773. LCCN:96-029108.

Audience: **u,f.** *Choice, 1998.*

Simon, Rita J. &   **HV8694.S55 2002**
  Blaskovich, Dagny A.
A Comparative Analysis of Capital Punishment: Statutes,
Policies, Frequencies and Public Attitudes the World Over.
Trade Cloth. Lexington Books. Lanham, MD. 2002. 136p.
ISBN:0-7391-0382-2, ISBN13: 978-0-7391-0382-1.
Dewey:364.66. LCCN:2002-005659.

Audience: **u,f.**

Steelwater, Eliza   **HV8699.U5**
Hangman's Knot: Lynching, Legal Execution, and America's
Struggle with the Death Penalty. Trade Cloth. Westview Press.

Boulder, CO. 2003. 304p. ISBN:0-8133-4042-X, ISBN13: 978-0-8133-4042-5. Dewey:364.66/0973. LCCN:2003-010154.

Audience: l,u,f.

Zimring, Franklin E.   **HV8699.U5**
The Contradictions of American Capital Punishment. Trade Paper. Oxford University Press, Inc. New York, NY. 2004. 272p. Studies in Crime and Public Policy ISBN:0-19-517820-3, ISBN13: 978-0-19-517820-3. Dewey:364.33/0973. LCCN:2002-012490.

Audience: l,u.   *Choice, 2004.*

Criminal Justice Systems and Processes > Criminal Justice Administration

Garland, David   **HV9950.G36 2001**
The Culture of Control: Crime and Social Order in Contemporary Society. Trade Cloth. University of Chicago Press. Chicago, IL. 2001. 336p. ISBN:0-226-28383-6, ISBN13: 978-0-226-28383-8. Dewey:364.9/73. LCCN:00-051209.

Audience: u,f.   *Choice, 2002.*

Hawkins, Darnell Felix   **HV7431**
(Editor), et al.
Crime Control and Social Justice: The Delicate Balance. Samuel L. Myers & Randolph N. Stone (Editors). Trade Cloth. Greenwood Publishing Group, Inc. Portsmouth, NH. 2003. 504p. Contributions in Criminology and Penology Ser., No. 55 ISBN:0-313-30790-3, ISBN13: 978-0-313-30790-4. Dewey:364.4/0973. LCCN:2002-024479.

Audience: l,u,f.

Houston, James G.   **HV9950.H68 2001**
Crime, Policy and Criminal Behavior in America: Criminology Studies. Trade Cloth. Edwin Mellen Press, The. Lewiston, NY. 2001. 256p. Criminology Studies, Vol. 13 ISBN:0-7734-7661-X, ISBN13: 978-0-7734-7661-5. Dewey:364.973. LCCN:00-058244.

Audience: l,u.

Merlo, Alida V. &   **HV9950.M45 2000**
Benekos, Peter J.
What's Wrong with the Criminal Justice System: Ideology, Politics and the Media. Mixed Media, Book, Other, Trade Paper. Anderson Publishing Company. Miamisburg, OH. 2000. 207p. ISBN:0-87084-933-6, ISBN13: 978-0-87084-933-6. Dewey:364.973. LCCN:99-041038.

Audience: l,u.

Moriarty, Laura J.   **HV9950.C76 2005**
(Editor)
Criminal Justice Technology in the 21st Century. Ed. 2. Ryan Baggett, Marialina Bello, Christine E. Bryce, Pamela A. Collins, Gary Cordner, Jill A. Gordon, Janet Hutchinson, Janice O. Joseph, Robyn Diehl Lacks, James E. Mays, Larry J. Myers, Laura B. Myers, Samuel Nunn, Timothy J. Potts, Kathryn E. Scarborough, Eric Shepardson, Irina R. Soderstrom & Faye S. Taxman (Contribution by). Laminated. Charles C. Thomas Publisher, Ltd. Springfield, IL. 2005. 334p. ISBN:0-398-07559-X, ISBN13: 978-0-398-07559-0. Dewey:364.973. LCCN:2004-059825.

Audience: l,u.

Criminal Justice Systems and Processes > Criminal Justice Administration > Juvenile Justice

Guarino-Ghezzi, Susan   **HV9104**
& Loughran, Edward J.
Balancing Juvenile Justice. Ed. 2. Trade Paper. Transaction Publishers. Somerset, NJ. 2005. 233p. ISBN:1-4128-0504-X, ISBN13: 978-1-4128-0504-9. Dewey:364.36/0973.

Audience: l,u.   *Choice, 1996.*

Hawkins, Darnell Felix   **HV9104.O97 2005**
& Kempf-Leonard, Kimberly (Editors)
Our Children, Their Children: Confronting Racial and Ethnic Differences in American Juvenile Justice. Trade Cloth. University of Chicago Press. Chicago, IL. 2005. 440p. The John D. and Catherine T. MacArthur Foundation Series on Mental Health and Development ISBN:0-226-31988-1, ISBN13: 978-0-226-31988-9. Dewey:364.36/089/00973. LCCN:2004-030246.

Audience: u,f.

Heilbrun, Kirk, et al.   **HV9104.C799 2005**
Juvenile Delinquency: Prevention, Assessment, and Intervention. Naomi Goldstein & Richard E. Redding (Authors). Trade Cloth. Oxford University Press, Inc. New York, NY. 2005. 356p. ISBN:0-19-516007-X, ISBN13: 978-0-19-516007-9. Dewey:364.36/0973. LCCN:2004-011413.

Audience: l,f.

Katzmann, Gary S.   **HV9104.S37 2002**
(Editor)
Securing Our Children's Future: New Approaches to Juvenile Justice and Youth Violence. Trade Cloth. Brookings Institution Press. Washington, DC. 2002. 432p. ISBN:0-8157-0606-5, ISBN13: 978-0-8157-0606-9. Dewey:364.36. LCCN:2002-008637.

Audience: u,f.   *Choice, 2003.*

National Research   **HV9104.J832 2001**
Council Staff & Institute of Medicine Staff
Juvenile Crime, Juvenile Justice. Joan McCord, Cathy Spatz Widom & Nancy A. Crowell (Editors). Trade Cloth. National Academies Press. Washington, DC. 2000. 404p. ISBN:0-309-06842-8, ISBN13: 978-0-309-06842-0. Dewey:364.36/0973. LCCN:2001-001248.

Audience: u,f.

Parry, David L.   **KF9778.E84 2004**
Essential Readings in Juvenile Justice. Trade Paper. Prentice Hall PTR. Upper Saddle River, NJ. 2004. 432p. ISBN:0-13-098186-9, ISBN13: 978-0-13-098186-8. Dewey:345.73/08. LCCN:2004-000988.

Audience: l,u.

Roberts, Albert R.   **HV9104.R6 2004**
(Editor)
Juvenile Justice Sourcebook: Past, Present, and Future. Ed. 3. Trade Cloth. Oxford University Press, Inc. New York, NY. 2004. 648p. ISBN:0-19-516755-4, ISBN13: 978-0-19-516755-9. Dewey:364.36/0973. LCCN:2003-016989.

Audience: l,u.   *Choice, 2005.*

Tanenhaus, David S.   **KF9794.T36 2004**
Juvenile Justice in the Making. Trade Cloth. Oxford University
Press, Inc. New York, NY. 2004. 264p. Studies in Crime and
Public Policy ISBN:0-19-516045-2, ISBN13:
978-0-19-516045-1. Dewey:345.73/08. LCCN:2003-008470.
Audience: **u,f.**

Zimring, Franklin E.   **HV9104.Z575 2005**
American Juvenile Justice. Trade Paper, Perfect. Oxford
University Press, Inc. New York, NY. 2005. 258p.
ISBN:0-19-518117-4, ISBN13: 978-0-19-518117-3.
Dewey:364.36/0973. LCCN:2005-001816.
Audience: **l,u,f.**

Criminal Justice Systems and Processes > Ethical and Moral Issues

Mauer, Marc &   **HV9950.I59 2003**
  Chesney-Lind, Meda (Editors)
Invisible Punishment: The Collateral Consequences of Mass
Imprisonment. Trade Cloth. New Press, The. New York, NY.
2002. 368p. ISBN:1-56584-726-1, ISBN13: 978-1-56584-726-2.
Dewey:365.6/0973. LCCN:2002-141430.
Audience: **l,u,f.**

Smith, Christopher E.,   **KF9223.S574 2002**
  et al.
The Supreme Court, Crime, and the Ideal of Equal Justice.
Christina DeJong & John D. Burrow (Authors). Trade Paper.
Peter Lang Publishing, Inc. New York, NY. 2002. 248p. Studies
in Crime and Punishment, Vol. 14 ISBN:0-8204-6121-0,
ISBN13: 978-0-8204-6121-2. Dewey:347.73/26.
LCCN:2002-021408.
Audience: **l,u,f.**

Criminology > Criminology, Generally

Anderson, James F. &   **HV6022.U6**
  Dyson, Laronistine
Criminological Theories: Understanding Crime in America.
Trade Cloth. University Press of America, Inc. Lanham, MD.
2002. 364p. ISBN:0-7618-2335-2, ISBN13: 978-0-7618-2335-3.
Dewey:364.
Audience: **l,u.**

Arrigo, Bruce A. &   **HV6025.P494 2006**
  Williams, Christopher R. (Editors)
Philosophy, Crime, and Criminology. Trade Paper. University of
Illinois Press. Champaign, IL. 2006. 304p. Critical Perspectives
in Criminology (CPC) Ser. ISBN:0-252-07289-8, ISBN13:
978-0-252-07289-5. Dewey:364. LCCN:2005-017094.
Audience: **l,u,f.**

Beccaria, Cesare   **HV8661.B15213 1995**
Baccaria: On Crimes and Punishments and Other Writings.
Richard Bellamy (Editor), Richard Davies (Translator). Trade
Paper. Cambridge University Press. New York, NY. 1995. 229p.
Texts in the History of Political Thought ISBN:0-521-47982-7,
ISBN13: 978-0-521-47982-0. Dewey:364.6. LCCN:94-020983.
Audience: **u,f.**

Bryant, Clifton D.   **HV6017.E53 2001**
  (Editor)
Encyclopedia of Criminology and Deviant Behaviour, Set. Paper
over Boards. Brunner-Routledge. Philadelphia, PA. 2000. 3000p.

ISBN:1-56032-772-3, ISBN13: 978-1-56032-772-1.
Dewey:364/.03. LCCN:00-058558.
Audience: **g,l,u,f.**

Hillyard, Paddy   **HV6025**
  (Editor), et al.
Beyond Criminology: Taking Harm Seriously. Christina
Pantazis, Dave Gordon & Steve Tombs (Editors). Trade Cloth.
Pluto Press. London, 2004. 348p. ISBN:0-7453-1904-1,
ISBN13: 978-0-7453-1904-9. Dewey:361.1.
LCCN:2004-276468.
Audience: **l,u.**

Maguire, Mike (Editor),   **HV6025.O87 2002**
  et al.
The Oxford Handbook of Criminology. Ed. 3. Rod Morgan &
Robert Reiner (Editors). Cloth Text. Oxford University Press,
Inc. New York, NY. 2002. 1,246p. ISBN:0-19-925609-8,
ISBN13: 978-0-19-925609-9. Dewey:364. LCCN:2002-074282.
Audience: **u,f.**

Siegel, Larry J.   **HV6025**
Criminology: Theories, Patterns, and Typologies. Ed. 9. Cloth
Text. Thomson Wadsworth. Belmont, CA. 2006. 576p.
ISBN:0-495-00572-X, ISBN13: 978-0-495-00572-8. Dewey:364.
LCCN:2005-937991.
Audience: **l,u.**

Criminology > Criminology, Generally > Theories

Akers, Ronald L.   **HV6018.A38 2003**
Criminological Theories: Introduction, Evaluation, and
Application. Ed. 4. Trade Paper. Roxbury Publishing Company.
Los Angeles, CA. 2003. 368p. ISBN:1-931719-06-3, ISBN13:
978-1-931719-06-3. Dewey:364. LCCN:2002-067952.
Audience: **l,u.**

Beirne, Piers   **HV6021.B38 1993**
Inventing Criminology: Essays on the Rise of 'Homo
Criminalis'. Paper Text. State University of New York Press.
Albany, NY. 1993. 274p. SUNY Series in Deviance and Social
Control ISBN:0-7914-1276-8, ISBN13: 978-0-7914-1276-3.
Dewey:364. LCCN:91-046327.
Audience: **u,f.**

Bernard, Thomas J., et al.   **HV6035.B47 2001**
Theoretical Criminology. Ed. 5. George B. Vold & Jeffrey B.
Snipes (Authors). Cloth Text. Oxford University Press, Inc. New
York, NY. 2001. 352p. ISBN:0-19-514202-0, ISBN13:
978-0-19-514202-0. Dewey:364.2. LCCN:2001-039095.
Audience: **u.**

Burke, Roger Hopkins   **HV6001**
An Introduction to Criminological Theory. Ed. 2. Trade Cloth.
Willan Publishing. Devon, 2005. 300p. ISBN:1-84392-165-0,
ISBN13: 978-1-84392-165-3. Dewey:364. LCCN:2005-283380.
Audience: **l,u.** *Choice, 2002.*

Clarke, Ronald V. &   **HV6025**
  Felson, Marcus (Editors)
Routine Activity and Rational Choice. Trade Paper. Transaction
Publishers. Somerset, NJ. 2004. 428p. Advances in
Criminological Theory Ser., Vol. 5 ISBN:0-7658-0831-5,
ISBN13: 978-0-7658-0831-8. Dewey:364. LCCN:2004-557923.
Audience: **u,f.**

Moyer, Imogene   **HV6025.M69 2001**
Criminological Theories: Traditional and Non-Traditional Voices
and Themes. Cloth Text. SAGE Publications, Inc. Thousand
Oaks, CA. 2001. 392p. ISBN:0-8039-5850-1, ISBN13:
978-0-8039-5850-0. Dewey:364. LCCN:00-012750.
                                        Audience: **l,u.** *Choice, 2002.*

Ross, Jeffrey Ian   **HV6025**
  (Editor)
Cutting the Edge: Current Perspectives in Radical and Critical
Criminology and Criminal Justice. Trade Cloth. Greenwood
Publishing Group, Inc. Portsmouth, NH. 1998. 240p.
ISBN:0-275-95708-X, ISBN13: 978-0-275-95708-7. Dewey:364.
LCCN:98-011129.
                                        Audience: **u.**

Criminology > Criminology, Generally > History

Jones, David A.   **HV6021**
History of Criminology: A Philosophical Perspective. Trade
Cloth. Greenwood Publishing Group, Inc. Portsmouth, NH.
1986. 255p. Contributions to Criminology and Penology Ser.,
No. 10 ISBN:0-313-23647-X, ISBN13: 978-0-313-23647-1.
Dewey:364/.9. LCCN:85-017724.
                                        Audience: **l,u.** *Choice, 1987.*

Mannheim, Hermann   **HV6025.M322 1972**
Pioneers in Criminology. Ed. 2. Trade Cloth. Patterson Smith
Publishing Corporation. Montclair, NJ. 1972. xv, 505p.
Criminology, Law Enforcement, and Social Problems Ser., No.
121 ISBN:0-87585-121-5, ISBN13: 978-0-87585-121-1.
Dewey:364/.092/2. LCCN:78-108238.
                                        Audience: **l,u.**

Criminology > Criminology, Generally > Comparative

Kalunta-Crumpton,   **HV7138.5**
  Anita & Agozino, Biko (Editors)
Pan-African Issues in Crime and Justice. Trade Cloth. Ashgate
Publishing, Ltd. Aldershot, 2004. 276p. Interdisciplinary
Research Series in Ethnic, Gender, and Class Relations
ISBN:0-7546-1882-X, ISBN13: 978-0-7546-1882-9.
Dewey:364.96. LCCN:2003-058290.
                                        Audience: **u,f.**

Leonardsen, Dag   **HV7113.5.L46 2004**
Japan as a Low-Crime Nation. Cloth over Boards. Palgrave
Macmillan. New York, NY. 2005. 248p. ISBN:1-4039-4111-4,
ISBN13: 978-1-4039-4111-4. Dewey:364.952.
LCCN:2004-042840.
                                        Audience: **l,u,f.** *Choice, 2006.*

Pridemore, William   **HV9960.R9R85 2005**
  Alex
Ruling Russia: Law, Crime, and Justice in a Changing Society.
Saddle Stitched, Cloth over Boards. Rowman & Littlefield
Publishers, Inc. Lanham, MD. 2005. 325p. ISBN:0-7425-3675-0,
ISBN13: 978-0-7425-3675-3. Dewey:364.947.
LCCN:2005-008569.
                                        Audience: **l,u.** *Choice, 2006.*

Criminology > Crime

Law Commission of   **HV6025.W52 2004**
  Canada (Editor)
What Is a Crime?: Defining Criminal Conduct in Contemporary
Society. Trade Cloth. University of British Columbia Press.
Vancouver, BC. 2004. 224p. Legal Dimensions Ser.
ISBN:0-7748-1086-6, ISBN13: 978-0-7748-1086-9.
Dewey:364.971. LCCN:2004-445148.
                                        Audience: **l,u,f.** *Choice, 2005.*

McCord, Joan (Editor)   **HV6080.B45 2004**
Beyond Empiricism: Institutions and Intentions in the Study of
Crime. Trade Cloth. Transaction Publishers. Somerset, NJ. 2004.
188p. Advances in Criminological Theory Ser., Vol. 13
ISBN:0-7658-0251-1, ISBN13: 978-0-7658-0251-4.
Dewey:364.3. LCCN:2004-043970.
                                        Audience: **u,f.**

Radzinowicz, Leon   **HV6025.R37**
Ideology and Crime: A Study of Crime in Its Social and
Historical Context. Trade Cloth. Columbia University Press.
New York, NY. 1966. James S. Carpentier Lecture Ser
ISBN:0-231-02926-8, ISBN13: 978-0-231-02926-1. Dewey:364.
LCCN:66-015724.
                                        Audience: **l,u,f.**

Ruth, Henry S. & Reitz,   **HV9950.R88 2003**
  Kevin R.
The Challenge of Crime: Rethinking Our Response. Trade
Cloth. Harvard University Press. Cambridge, MA. 2003. 384p.
ISBN:0-674-00891-X, ISBN13: 978-0-674-00891-5.
Dewey:364.973. LCCN:2002-038731.
                                        Audience: **u,f.** *Choice, 2003.*

Tonry, Michael H.   **HV6025**
  (Editor)
The Handbook of Crime and Punishment. Trade Paper. Oxford
University Press, Inc. New York, NY. 2000. 832p.
ISBN:0-19-514060-5, ISBN13: 978-0-19-514060-6. Dewey:364.
                                        Audience: **u,f.** *Choice, 1999.*

Criminology > Crime > Causes of Crime

Akers, Ronald L. &   **HV6018.S67 2002**
  Jensen, Gary F. (Editors)
Social Learning Theory and the Explanation of Crime: A Guide
for the New Century. Trade Cloth. Transaction Publishers.
Somerset, NJ. 2002. 379p. Advances in Criminological Theory
Ser., Vol. 11 ISBN:0-7658-0133-7, ISBN13: 978-0-7658-0133-3.
Dewey:364. LCCN:2002-021139.
                                        Audience: **u,f.**

Walsh, Anthony & Ellis,   **HV6025.B534 2003**
  Lee (Editors)
Biosocial Criminology: Challenging Environmentalism's
Supremacy. Trade Cloth. Nova Science Publishers, Inc.
Hauppauge, NY. 2003. 267p. ISBN:1-59033-774-3, ISBN13:
978-1-59033-774-5. Dewey:364.2. LCCN:2003-012688.
                                        Audience: **u.**

Wilson, James Q.   **HV6789.W53 1985**
Thinking about Crime. Trade Paper. Knopf Publishing Group.
New York, NY. 1985. 293p. ISBN:0-394-72917-X, ISBN13:
978-0-394-72917-6. Dewey:364/.973. LCCN:84-040520.
                                        Audience: **u,f.**

Criminology > Crime > Crime Patterns. Crime Mapping

Ainsworth, Peter   **HV6080.A53 2001**
Offender Profiling and Crime Analysis. Trade Cloth. Willan Publishing. Devon, 2001. 208p. ISBN:1-903240-22-0, ISBN13: 978-1-903240-22-9. Dewey:364.3. LCCN:2001-273306.
Audience: **u,f.** *Choice, 2002.*

Blumstein, Alfred   **HV6791**
(Editor, Contribution by)
The Crime Drop in America. Ed. 2. Joel Wallman (Editor), David Farrington (Contribution by). Cloth Text. Cambridge University Press. New York, NY. 2005. 374p. Cambridge Studies in Criminology Ser. ISBN:0-521-86279-5, ISBN13: 978-0-521-86279-0. Dewey:364.973. LCCN:2005-055304.
Audience: **u,f.**

Chainey, Spencer &   **HV7936.C88C48 2005**
Ratcliffe, Jerry
GIS and Crime Mapping. Trade Cloth. John Wiley & Sons, Inc. Hoboken, NJ. 2005. 442p. Mastering GIS Ser., :Technol, Applications and Mgmnt Ser. ISBN:0-470-86098-7, ISBN13: 978-0-470-86098-4. Dewey:363.25. LCCN:2004-028500.
Audience: **u,f.**

Goldsmith, Victor   **HV7936.C88A53 2000**
(Editor), et al.
Analyzing Crime Patterns: Frontiers of Practice. Philip G. McGuire, John H. Mollenkopf & Timothy A. Ross (Editors). Cloth Text. SAGE Publications, Inc. Thousand Oaks, CA. 1999. 200p. ISBN:0-7619-1940-6, ISBN13: 978-0-7619-1940-7. Dewey:364/.042/0973. LCCN:99-006533.
Audience: **u,f.**

Criminology > Crime > Crime Statistics. Crime Reporting

Mosher, Clayton James,   **HV6018.M67 2002**
et al.
The Mismeasure of Crime. Terance D. Miethe & Dretha M. Phillips (Authors). Paper Text. SAGE Publications, Inc. Thousand Oaks, CA. 2002. 224p. Key Questions for Criminal Justice Ser. ISBN:0-7619-8711-8, ISBN13: 978-0-7619-8711-6. Dewey:362.88/0973. LCCN:2001-058137.
Audience: **u,f.**

Ménard, Kim S.   **HV8079.R35M46 2005**
Reporting Sexual Assault: A Social Ecology Perspective. Trade Cloth. LFB Scholarly Publishing LLC. New York, NY. 2005. 224p. Criminal Justice, :Recent Scholarship ISBN:1-59332-126-0, ISBN13: 978-1-59332-126-0. Dewey:362.883. LCCN:2005-022452.
Audience: **u,f.**

Criminology > Crime > Organized Crime

Block, Alan A. &   **HV6768**
Weaver, Constance A.
All Is Clouded by Desire: Global Banking, Money Laundering, and International Organized Crime. Trade Cloth. Greenwood Publishing Group, Inc. Portsmouth, NH. 2004. 288p. International and Comparative Criminology Ser.

ISBN:0-275-98330-7, ISBN13: 978-0-275-98330-7. Dewey:364.16/8. LCCN:2004-040892.
Audience: **l,u,f.** *Choice, 2005.*

Kaplan, David E. &   **HV6453.J33**
Dubro, Alec
Yakuza: Japan's Criminal Underworld. Trade Paper. University of California Press. Berkeley, CA. 2003. 422p. ISBN:0-520-21562-1, ISBN13: 978-0-520-21562-7. Dewey:364.1060952. LCCN:2002-007138.
Audience: **l,u,f.**

Kenney, Dennis Jay &   **HV6446.K46 1995**
Finckenauer, James O.
Organized Crime in America. Paper Text. Thomson Wadsworth. Belmont, CA. 1994. 416p. Criminal Justice Ser. ISBN:0-534-24702-4, ISBN13: 978-0-534-24702-7. Dewey:364.1/06/0973. LCCN:94-018081.
Audience: **l,u.**

Liddick, Donald R.   **HV6252**
The Global Underworld: Transnational Crime and the United States. Trade Cloth. Greenwood Publishing Group, Inc. Portsmouth, NH. 2004. 176p. International and Comparative Criminology Ser. ISBN:0-275-98074-X, ISBN13: 978-0-275-98074-0. Dewey:364.1/06/0973. LCCN:2004-044380.
Audience: **l,u.** *Choice, 2005.*

Reppetto, Thomas A.   **HV6446.R47 2003**
American Mafia: A History of Its Rise to Power. Cloth over Boards. Henry Holt & Company. New York, NY. 2004. 336p. ISBN:0-8050-7210-1, ISBN13: 978-0-8050-7210-5. Dewey:364.1/06/0973. LCCN:2003-056736.
Audience: **g,l,u.**

Schatzberg, Rufus &   **HV6446.S38 1996**
Kelly, Robert J.
African-American Organized Crime: A Social History. Paper over Boards. Garland Publishing, Inc. New York, NY. 1995. 288p. Current Issues in Criminal Justice Ser., Vol. 12 ISBN:0-8153-1573-2, ISBN13: 978-0-8153-1573-5. Dewey:364.1/06/08996073. LCCN:95-025097.
Audience: **l,u,f.**

Criminology > Crime > Terrorism

Bloom, Mia   **HV6431.B576 2005**
Dying to Kill: The Allure of Suicide Terror. Trade Cloth. Columbia University Press. New York, NY. 2005. 280p. ISBN:0-231-13320-0, ISBN13: 978-0-231-13320-3. Dewey:303.6/25. LCCN:2004-063474.
Audience: **u,f.**

Deflem, Mathieu   **HV6431**
(Editor)
Terrorism and Counter-Terrorism: Criminological Perspectives. Trade Cloth. Elsevier Science & Technology Books. Saint Louis, MO. 2004. 238p. Sociology of Crime,Law and Deviance Ser., Vol. 5 ISBN:0-7623-1040-5, ISBN13: 978-0-7623-1040-1. Dewey:364.1.
Audience: **u,f.**

Griset, Pamela L. &   **HV6431.T4667 2003**
Mahan, Sue
Terrorism in Perspective. Cloth Text. SAGE Publications, Inc.

Thousand Oaks, CA. 2002. 408p. ISBN:0-7619-2752-2, ISBN13: 978-0-7619-2752-5. Dewey:303.6/25. LCCN:2002-012736.

Audience: l,u.

Navarro, Joe   **HV6431.N387 2005**
Hunting Terrorists: A Look at the Psychopathology of Terror. Laminated. Charles C. Thomas Publisher, Ltd. Springfield, IL. 2005. 122p. ISBN:0-398-07593-X, ISBN13: 978-0-398-07593-4. Dewey:303.6/25/019. LCCN:2005-043961.

Audience: l,u.

Strathern, Andrew   **HV6431**
(Editor), et al.
Terror and Violence: Imagination and the Unimaginable. Pamela J. Stewart & Neil L. Whitehead (Editors). Trade Cloth. Pluto Press. London, 2005. 264p. Anthropology, Culture and Society Ser. ISBN:0-7453-2399-5, ISBN13: 978-0-7453-2399-2. Dewey:303.625. LCCN:2006-273454.

Audience: u,f.

Criminology > Crime > Violent Crime

Reamer, Frederic G.   **HV6791.R4 2004**
Heinous Crime: Cases, Causes, and Consequences. Trade Cloth. Columbia University Press. New York, NY. 2004. 272p. ISBN:0-231-13188-7, ISBN13: 978-0-231-13188-9. Dewey:364.150973. LCCN:2004-055136.

Audience: u,f.

Waldrep, Christopher   **HV6457.L95 2005**
(Editor)
Lynching in America: A History in Documents. Trade Cloth. New York University Press. New York, NY. 2006. 303p. ISBN:0-8147-9398-3, ISBN13: 978-0-8147-9398-5. Dewey:364.1/34. LCCN:2005-015600.

Audience: l,u,f.   *Choice, 2006.*

Criminology > Crime > Violent Crime > Homicide

Blom-Cooper, Louis &   **K5171**
Morris, Terence
With Malice Aforethought: A Study of the Crime and Punishment for Homicide. Trade Cloth. Hart Publishing Ltd. Oxford, 2004. 216p. ISBN:1-84113-485-6, ISBN13: 978-1-84113-485-7. Dewey:345.0252. LCCN:2005-273756.

Audience: l,u,f.

Brookman, Fiona   **HV6515**
Understanding Homicide. Cloth Text. SAGE Publications, Inc. Thousand Oaks, CA. 2005. 368p. ISBN:0-7619-4754-X, ISBN13: 978-0-7619-4754-7. Dewey:364.152. LCCN:2005-273821.

Audience: l,u.

Fox, James Alan, et al.   **HV6515.F69 2005**
The Will to Kill: Making Sense of Senseless Murder. Ed. 2. Jack Levin & Kenna D. Quinet (Authors). Trade Paper. Allyn & Bacon, Inc. Boston, MA. 2004. 240p. ISBN:0-205-41880-5, ISBN13: 978-0-205-41880-0. Dewey:364.152/3. LCCN:2004-044742.

Audience: l,u,f.

Wolfgang, Marvin E.   **HV6534.P5W6 1975**
Patterns in Criminal Homicide. Trade Cloth. Patterson Smith Publishing Corporation. Montclair, NJ. 1975. 413p. Criminology, Law Enforcement, and Social Problems Ser., No. 211 ISBN:0-87585-211-4, ISBN13: 978-0-87585-211-9. Dewey:364.1/52. LCCN:74-034157.

Audience: u,f.

Criminology > Crime > Violent Crime > Rape and Other Sexual Offenses

Brownmiller, Susan   **HV6558.B76 1993**
Against Our Will: Men, Women, and Rape. Trade Paper. Ballantine Books. New York, NY. 1993. 480p. ISBN:0-449-90820-8, ISBN13: 978-0-449-90820-4. Dewey:364.1/532. LCCN:92-097327.

Audience: l,u,f.

Cling, B. J. (Editor)   **HV6250.4.W65S49 2004**
Sexualized Violence Against Women and Children: A Psychology and Law Perspective. Cloth over Boards. Guilford Publications, Inc. New York, NY. 2004. 305p. ISBN:1-59385-061-1, ISBN13: 978-1-59385-061-6. Dewey:362.883/0973. LCCN:2004-012745.

Audience: l,u.   *Choice, 2005.*

Reddington, Frances P.   **HV6561.S475 2003**
& Kreisel, Betsy W.
Sexual Assault: The Victims, the Perpetrators, and the Criminal Justice System. Trade Paper. Carolina Academic Press. Durham, NC. 2004. xix, 353p. ISBN:0-89089-334-9, ISBN13: 978-0-89089-334-0. Dewey:364.15/32/0973. LCCN:2003-060583.

Audience: l,u,f.   *Choice, 2005.*

Criminology > Crime > Violent Crime > Hate Crimes

Jacobs, James B. &   **KF9345.J33 1998**
Potter, Kimberly
Hate Crimes: Criminal Law and Identity Politics. Trade Cloth. Oxford University Press, Inc. New York, NY. 1998. 222p. Studies in Crime and Public Policy ISBN:0-19-511448-5, ISBN13: 978-0-19-511448-5. Dewey:345.73/025. LCCN:97-037802.

Audience: u,f.

Levin, Jack &   **HV6773.5.L484 2004**
Rabrenovic, Gordana
Why We Hate. Trade Cloth. Prometheus Books, Publishers. Amherst, NY. 2004. 260p. ISBN:1-59102-191-X, ISBN13: 978-1-59102-191-9. Dewey:302.5/4. LCCN:2004-004496.

Audience: l,u.

Neiwert, David A.   **HV6534.O27**
Death on the Fourth of July: The Story of a Killing, a Trial, and Hate Crime in America. Trade Paper, Perfect. Palgrave Macmillan. New York, NY. 2005. 256p. ISBN:1-4039-6900-0, ISBN13: 978-1-4039-6900-2. Dewey:364.152/3/0979795.

Audience: l,u.

Criminology > Crime > Violent Crime > Other

Wright, Richard T. & Decker, Scott H.   HV6658.W75 1997
Armed Robbers in Action: Stickups and Street Culture. Paper Text. Northeastern University Press. Boston, MA. 1997. 128p. Series in Criminal Behavior ISBN:1-55553-323-X, ISBN13: 978-1-55553-323-6. Dewey:364.15/52/0973. LCCN:97-014230.
Audience: **l,u,f.**

Wright, Richard T. & Decker, Scott H.   HV6661.M8W75 1994
Burglars on the Job: Streetlife and Residential Break-Ins. Gilbert Geis (Foreword by). Cloth Text. Northeastern University Press. Boston, MA. 1994. 248p. ISBN:1-55553-185-7, ISBN13: 978-1-55553-185-0. Dewey:364.1/62. LCCN:93-044357.
Audience: **l,u.**

Criminology > Crime > Nonviolent Crime > White Collar Crime

Green, Penny & Ward, Tony   HV6254
State Crime: Governments, Violence and Corruption. Trade Cloth. Pluto Press. London, 2004. 264p. ISBN:0-7453-1785-5, ISBN13: 978-0-7453-1785-4. Dewey:364.13. LCCN:2004-271801.
Audience: **l,u.**

Masciandaro, Donato   HV6768.G56 2004
Global Financial Crime: Terrorism, Money Laundering, and Off Shore Centres. Trade Cloth. Ashgate Publishing, Ltd. Aldershot, 2004. 266p. Global Finance Ser. ISBN:0-7546-3707-7, ISBN13: 978-0-7546-3707-3. Dewey:364.16/8. LCCN:2003-025531.
Audience: **u,f.**

Weisburd, David, et al.   HV6768 .W44 2001
White-Collar Crime and Criminal Careers. Elin Waring & Ellen Chayet (Authors), David Farrington & Alfred Blumstein (Contribution by). Trade Cloth. Cambridge University Press. New York, NY. 2001. 208p. Cambridge Studies in Criminology ISBN:0-521-77162-5, ISBN13: 978-0-521-77162-7. Dewey:364.168. LCCN:00-031260.
Audience: **u,f.**

Criminology > Crime > Nonviolent Crime > Victimless Crime

Schwartz, David G.   KF9440.S39 2005
Cutting the Wire: Gambling Prohibition and the Internet. Trade Cloth. University of Nevada Press. Reno, NV. 2005. 296p. The Gambling Studies ISBN:0-87417-619-0, ISBN13: 978-0-87417-619-3. Dewey:345.73/0272/02854678. LCCN:2005-010632.
Audience: **u,f.**

Criminology > Crime > Nonviolent Crime > Technology and Crime

Newman, Graeme & Clarke, Ronald V.   HV6773
Superhighway Robbery: Preventing E-Commerce Crime. Trade

Cloth. Willan Publishing. Devon, 2003. 240p. Crime Science Ser. ISBN:1-84392-018-2, ISBN13: 978-1-84392-018-2. Dewey:364.168. LCCN:2004-297293.
Audience: **u,f.**

Savona, Ernesto U. (Editor)   HV6768
Crime and Technology: New Frontiers for Regulation, Law Enforcement and Research. Trade Cloth. Springer. New York, NY. 2005. xiii, 142p. ISBN:1-4020-2923-3, ISBN13: 978-1-4020-2923-3. Dewey:364.168.
Audience: **u,f.**

Schelle, Bernadette & Martin, Clemens   HV6773.S3547 2004
Cybercrime: A Reference Handbook. Mildred Vasan (Editor). Library Binding. ABC-CLIO, Inc. Santa Barbara, CA. 2004. 268p. Contemporary World Issues Ser. ISBN:1-85109-683-3, ISBN13: 978-1-85109-683-1. Dewey:364.16/8. LCCN:2004-013960.
Audience: **l,u.** *Choice, 2005.*

Schwartz, David G.   KF9440.S39 2005
Cutting the Wire: Gambling Prohibition and the Internet. Trade Cloth. University of Nevada Press. Reno, NV. 2005. 296p. The Gambling Studies ISBN:0-87417-619-0, ISBN13: 978-0-87417-619-3. Dewey:345.73/0272/02854678. LCCN:2005-010632.
Audience: **u,f.**

Taylor, Robert W., et al.   HV6773.D54 2006
Digital Crime and Digital Terrorism. Tory J. Caeti, Eric J. Fritsch, John Liederbach & Kall Loper (Authors). Trade Paper. Prentice Hall PTR. Upper Saddle River, NJ. 2005. 416p. ISBN:0-13-114137-6, ISBN13: 978-0-13-114137-7. Dewey:364.16/8. LCCN:2004-028224.
Audience: **l,u.**

Criminology > Crime > Nonviolent Crime > Drug Offenses

de Marneffe, Peter & Husak, Douglas N.   KF3890.H87 2005
The Legalization of Drugs. R. G. Frey (Contribution by). Trade Cloth. Cambridge University Press. New York, NY. 2005. 224p. For and Against Ser. ISBN:0-521-83786-3, ISBN13: 978-0-521-83786-6. Dewey:364.1/77/0973. LCCN:2004-027502.
Audience: **u,f.**

Gerber, Rudolph J.   HV5822
Legalizing Marijuana: Drug Policy Reform and Prohibition Politics. Trade Cloth. Greenwood Publishing Group, Inc. Portsmouth, NH. 2004. 208p. ISBN:0-275-97448-0, ISBN13: 978-0-275-97448-0. Dewey:364.1/77. LCCN:2003-068715.
Audience: **l,u.** *Choice, 2005.*

Jacobs, Bruce A.   HV5825.J3 1999
Dealing Crack: The Social World of Streetcorner Selling. James F. Short Jr. (Foreword by). Trade Paper. Northeastern University Press. Boston, MA. 1999. 163p. Series in Criminal Behavior ISBN:1-55553-387-6, ISBN13: 978-1-55553-387-8. Dewey:364.1/77/0973. LCCN:98-045390.
Audience: **u,f.**

Sommers, Ira Brant & Baskin, Deborah R.   HV5825.S5843 2004
The Social Consequences of Methamphetamine Use. Trade

Cloth. Edwin Mellen Press, The. Lewiston, NY. 2004. 112p. Interdisciplinary Studies in Alcohol and Drug Use and Abuse, Vol. 8 ISBN:0-7734-6569-3, ISBN13: 978-0-7734-6569-5. Dewey:362.29/9. LCCN:2003-064864.

Audience: **l,u.**

Criminology > Crime > Civil Disorder

Curtis, Lynn A. &   **HV6791.A72 1985**
  Moyers, Bill (Editors)
American Violence and Public Policy: An Update of the National Commission on the Causes and Prevention of Violence. Trade Cloth. Yale University Press. Cumberland, RI. 1985. 288p. ISBN:0-300-03231-5, ISBN13: 978-0-300-03231-4. Dewey:364.1. LCCN:84-040194.

Audience: **u,f.**

National Advisory   **HV6477.U54 1988**
  Commission Staff & Kerner, Otto
The Kerner Report: The 1968 Report of the National Advisory Commission on Civil Disorders. Trade Paper. Knopf Publishing Group. New York, NY. 1988. ISBN:0-679-72078-2, ISBN13: 978-0-679-72078-2. Dewey:303.6/23/0973. LCCN:89-187684.

Audience: **l,u,f.**

Criminology > Criminals and Criminal Behavior

Campbell, John H. &   **HV6080.P66 2004**
  DeNevi, Don (Editors)
Profilers: Leading Investigators Take You Inside the Criminal Mind. Trade Cloth. Prometheus Books, Publishers. Amherst, NY. 2004. 390p. ISBN:1-59102-266-5, ISBN13: 978-1-59102-266-4. Dewey:363.25. LCCN:2004-014513.

Audience: **l,u.**

Ellis, Havelock   **HV6035.E6 1973**
Criminal. Ed. 5. Trade Cloth. Patterson Smith Publishing Corporation. Montclair, NJ. 1973. Criminology, Law Enforcement, and Social Problems Ser., No. 200 ISBN:0-87585-200-9, ISBN13: 978-0-87585-200-3. Dewey:364.2. LCCN:74-172610.

Audience: **u,f.**

Criminology > Criminals and Criminal Behavior > Biology and Neurobiology of Criminal Behavior

Gibson, Mary   **HV6047**
Born to Crime: Cesare Lombroso and the Origins of Biological Criminology. Trade Cloth. Greenwood Publishing Group, Inc. Portsmouth, NH. 2002. 296p. Italian and Italian-American Studies ISBN:0-275-97062-0, ISBN13: 978-0-275-97062-8. Dewey:364.2/4. LCCN:2001-059152.

Audience: **l,u.**   *Choice, 2003.*

Lombroso-Ferrero,   **HV6045.L83 1972**
  Gina & Savitz, Leonard D.
Criminal Man: According to the Classification of Cesare Lombroso. Library Binding. Patterson Smith Publishing

Corporation. Montclair, NJ. 1972. 395p. Criminology, Law Enforcement, and Social Problems Ser., No. 134 ISBN:0-87585-134-7, ISBN13: 978-0-87585-134-1. Dewey:364.1. LCCN:70-129338.

Audience: **u,f.** 𝓑

Rafter, Nicole H.   **HV6047**
Creating Born Criminals. Trade Paper. University of Illinois Press. Champaign, IL. 1998. 320p. ISBN:0-252-06741-X, ISBN13: 978-0-252-06741-9. Dewey:364.2/4.

Audience: **l,u,f.**

Wasserman, David &   **RC455.4.G4 G437 2001**
  Wachbroit, Robert (Editors)
Genetics and Criminal Behavior. Douglas MacLean (Contribution by). Trade Paper. Cambridge University Press. New York, NY. 2001. 348p. Studies in Philosophy and Public Policy ISBN:0-521-62728-1, ISBN13: 978-0-521-62728-3. Dewey:616.89/042. LCCN:00-037821.

Audience: **u,f.**

Criminology > Criminals and Criminal Behavior > Criminal Behavior

Colvin, Mark   **HV6035.C65 2000**
Crime and Coercion: An Integrated Theory of Chronic Criminality. Cloth over Boards. Palgrave Macmillan. New York, NY. 2000. 224p. ISBN:0-312-23389-2, ISBN13: 978-0-312-23389-1. Dewey:364.3. LCCN:00-038237.

Audience: **l,u.**   *Choice, 2001.*

Farrington, David P.   **HV9069.I64 2005**
  (Editor)
Integrated Developmental and Life-Course Theories of Offending. Trade Cloth. Transaction Publishers. Somerset, NJ. 2005. 279p. Advances in Criminological Theory Ser., Vol. 14 ISBN:0-7658-0280-5, ISBN13: 978-0-7658-0280-4. Dewey:364.36/01/9. LCCN:2004-066079.

Audience: **u.**

Palermo, George B. &   **HV6080.P32 2004**
  Kocsis, Richard N.
Offender Profiling: An Introduction to the Sociopsychological Analysis of Violent Crime. Laminated. Charles C. Thomas Publisher, Ltd. Springfield, IL. 2005. 284p. American Series in Behavioral Science and Law ISBN:0-398-07548-4, ISBN13: 978-0-398-07548-4. Dewey:363.25/8. LCCN:2004-055371.

Audience: **l,u.**

Pogrebin, Mark   **HV6789.A3442 2004**
  (Editor)
About Criminals: A View of the Offender's World. Paper Text. SAGE Publications, Inc. Thousand Oaks, CA. 2004. 376p. ISBN:0-7619-2816-2, ISBN13: 978-0-7619-2816-4. Dewey:364.3/0973. LCCN:2003-025481.

Audience: **u,f.**

Wideman, John Edgar   **PS3573**
Brothers and Keepers: A Memoir. Trade Paper. Houghton Mifflin Company Trade & Reference Division. Boston, MA. 2005. 272p. ISBN:0-618-50963-1, ISBN13: 978-0-618-50963-8. Dewey:813/.54 B. LCCN:2005-272204.

Audience: **g,l,u.**

Criminology > Criminals and Criminal Behavior > Criminal Careers

Laub, John H. &   **HV9069.L28 2006**
  Sampson, Robert J.
Shared Beginnings, Divergent Lives: Delinquent Boys to Age 70. Trade Paper. Harvard University Press. Cambridge, MA. 2006. 352p. ISBN:0-674-01993-8, ISBN13: 978-0-674-01993-5. Dewey:364.36/0973.

Audience: **u,f.** *Choice, 2004.*

Weisburd, David, et al.   **HV6768 .W44 2001**
White-Collar Crime and Criminal Careers. Elin Waring & Ellen Chayet (Authors), David Farrington & Alfred Blumstein (Contribution by). Trade Cloth. Cambridge University Press. New York, NY. 2001. 208p. Cambridge Studies in Criminology ISBN:0-521-77162-5, ISBN13: 978-0-521-77162-7. Dewey:364.168. LCCN:00-031260.

Audience: **u,f.**

Criminology > Criminals and Criminal Behavior > Juvenile Offenders

Chesney-Lind, Meda &   **HV6046**
  Pasko, Lisa
The Female Offender: Girls, Women and Crime. Ed. 2. Cloth Text. SAGE Publications, Inc. Thousand Oaks, CA. 2003. 232p. Women in the Criminal Justice System Ser. ISBN:0-7619-2978-9, ISBN13: 978-0-7619-2978-9. Dewey:364.3/74/0973. LCCN:2003-006150.

Audience: **l,u.** *Choice, 1997.*

Chesney-Lind, Meda &   **HV9104.C39 2004**
  Shelden, Randall G.
Girls, Delinquency, and Juvenile Justice. Ed. 3. Paper Text. Thomson Wadsworth. Belmont, CA. 2003. 368p. ISBN:0-534-55774-0, ISBN13: 978-0-534-55774-4. Dewey:364.36/082. LCCN:2003-104975.

Audience: **u,f.**

Greenwood, Peter W.   **HV9104.G685 2006**
Changing Lives: Delinquency Prevention as Crime-Control Policy. Franklin E. Zimring (Foreword by). Trade Cloth. University of Chicago Press. Chicago, IL. 2005. 200p. Adolescent Development and Legal Policy Ser. ISBN:0-226-30719-0, ISBN13: 978-0-226-30719-0. Dewey:364.4. LCCN:2005-011954.

Audience: **u,f.** *Choice, 2006.*

Hagan, John &   **HV9110.T7H33 1997**
  McCarthy, Bill
Mean Streets: Youth Crime and Homelessness. Alfred Blumstein & David Farrington (Contribution by). Cloth Text. Cambridge University Press. New York, NY. 1997. 317p. Criminology Ser. ISBN:0-521-49743-4, ISBN13: 978-0-521-49743-5. Dewey:362.7/4/0971. LCCN:96-040359.

Audience: **u,f.**

Hindelang, Michael J.,   **HV9104.H53**
  et al.
Measuring Delinquency. Travis Hirschi & Joseph G. Weis (Authors). Trade Paper. Books on Demand. Ann Arbor, MI. 1981. 248p. Sage Library of Social Research, Vol. 123 ISBN:0-608-01175-4, ISBN13: 978-0-608-01175-2. Dewey:364.3/6/0973. LCCN:81-002522.

Audience: **u,f.**

Hirschi, Travis   **HV9069.H643 2001**
Causes of Delinquency. Trade Paper. Transaction Publishers. Somerset, NJ. 2001. 309p. ISBN:0-7658-0900-1, ISBN13: 978-0-7658-0900-1. Dewey:364.36. LCCN:2001-043719.

Audience: **u,f.**

May, David C.   **HV9069.M38 2001**
Adolescent Fear of Crime and Defensive Behaviors: An Alternative Explanation of Violent Delinquency. Trade Cloth. Edwin Mellen Press, The. Lewiston, NY. 2001. 204p. Criminology Studies, Vol. 15 ISBN:0-7734-7367-X, ISBN13: 978-0-7734-7367-6. Dewey:364.36. LCCN:2001-030532.

Audience: **l,u.**

Mennel, Robert M.   **HV9104**
Thorns and Thistles: Juvenile Delinquents in the United States, 1825-1940. Trade Paper. University Press of New England. Lebanon, NH. 1983. 259p. ISBN:0-87451-273-5, ISBN13: 978-0-87451-273-1. Dewey:364.36/0973. LCCN:72-095187.

Audience: **u,f.**

Wolfgang, Marvin E., et al.   **HV9106.P5**
Delinquency in a Birth Cohort. Robert M. Figlio & Thorsten D. Sellin (Authors), Norval Morris (Foreword by). Trade Paper. University of Chicago Press. Chicago, IL. 1987. 338p. Studies in Crime and Justice ISBN:0-226-90558-6, ISBN13: 978-0-226-90558-7. Dewey:364.36/09748/11. LCCN:75-187929.

Audience: **u,f.** *B*

Zimring, Franklin E.   **KF9802.Z56 2004**
  (Author, Foreword by)
An American Travesty: Legal Responses to Adolescent Sexual Offending. Trade Cloth. University of Chicago Press. Chicago, IL. 2004. 216p. Adolescent Development and Legal Policy Ser. ISBN:0-226-98357-9, ISBN13: 978-0-226-98357-8. Dewey:364.15/3/08350973. LCCN:2003-017512.

Audience: **u,f.**

Criminology > Criminals and Criminal Behavior > Substance Abuse and Crime

Brochu, Serge (Editor),   **HV5801**
  et al.
Drug and Crime Deviant Pathways. Candido da Agra & Marie-Marthe Cousineau (Editors). Trade Cloth. Ashgate Publishing, Ltd. Aldershot, 2002. 268p. ISBN:0-7546-3023-4, ISBN13: 978-0-7546-3023-4. Dewey:364.2/4. LCCN:2002-018202.

Audience: **u,f.**

Flowers, R. Barri   **HV5825.F62 1999**
Drugs, Alcohol and Criminality in American Society. Cloth Text. McFarland & Company, Incorporated Publishers. Jefferson, NC. 1999. 246p. ISBN:0-7864-0306-3, ISBN13: 978-0-7864-0306-6. Dewey:364.2/4. LCCN:99-12922.

Audience: **l,u.**

Criminology > Sociology of Crime > Class and crime

Crowther, Christy &   **HV4028.C76 2000**
  Campling, Jo
Policing Urban Poverty. Cloth over Boards. Palgrave Macmillan. New York, NY. 2000. 278p. ISBN:0-312-22846-5, ISBN13: 978-0-312-22846-0. Dewey:364.4. LCCN:99-040401.

Audience: **l,u,f.**

McNamara, Robert P.   HV4045.M36 1999
Beating the Odds: Crime, Poverty and Life in the Inner City.
Trade Cloth. Child Welfare League of America, Inc.
Washington, DC. 1999. 193p. ISBN:0-87868-765-3, ISBN13:
978-0-87868-765-7. Dewey:362.7/0973. LCCN:99-020811.

Audience: **l,u.**

Criminology > Sociology of Crime > Crime and mass media

Best, Joel   HV6789.B47 1998
Random Violence: Worrying about New Crimes and New
Victims. Trade Paper. University of California Press. Berkeley,
CA. 1999. 260p. ISBN:0-520-21572-9, ISBN13:
978-0-520-21572-6. Dewey:364.973. LCCN:98-006234.

Audience: **l,u,f.** *Choice, 1999.*

Brown, Sheila   P96.C74B76 2003
Crime and Law in Media Culture. Cloth Text. McGraw-Hill
Education. Maidenhead, 2003. 192p. ISBN:0-335-20549-6,
ISBN13: 978-0-335-20549-3. Dewey:364. LCCN:2002-074910.

Audience: **l,u,f.**

Cottle, Simon   HV6535
The Racist Murder of Stephen Lawrence: Media Performance
and Public Transformation. Trade Cloth. Greenwood Publishing
Group, Inc. Portsmouth, NH. 2004. 256p. ISBN:0-275-97941-5,
ISBN13: 978-0-275-97941-6. Dewey:364.152/3/09421.
LCCN:2004-050968.

Audience: **l,u,f.**

Jewkes, Yvonne   P96.C74
Media and Crime. Cloth Text. SAGE Publications, Inc.
Thousand Oaks, CA. 2004. 256p. Key Approaches to
Criminology Ser. ISBN:0-7619-4764-7, ISBN13:
978-0-7619-4764-6. Dewey:364. LCCN:2004-559813.

Audience: **l,u.**

Rome, Dennis   P94
Black Demons: The Media's Depiction of the African American
Male Criminal Stereotype. Trade Cloth. Greenwood Publishing
Group, Inc. Portsmouth, NH. 2004. 144p. Crime, Media, and
Popular Culture Ser. ISBN:0-275-97244-5, ISBN13:
978-0-275-97244-8. Dewey:302.23/089/96073.
LCCN:2004-044387.

Audience: **l,u.** *Choice, 2005.*

Schmid, David   HV6529.S32 2005
Natural Born Celebrities: Serial Killers in American Culture.
Trade Cloth. University of Chicago Press. Chicago, IL. 2005.
336p. ISBN:0-226-73867-1, ISBN13: 978-0-226-73867-3.
Dewey:364.152/3/0973. LCCN:2004-026467.

Audience: **l,u,f.** *Choice, 2006.*

Simon, David R. &   HN59.2.S576 2003
  Love, Tamar
Tony Soprano's America: The Criminal Side of the American
Dream. Cloth Text. Westview Press. Boulder, CO. 2002. 288p.
ISBN:0-8133-4036-5, ISBN13: 978-0-8133-4036-4.
Dewey:361.1/0973. LCCN:2002-012425.

Audience: **l,u.** *Choice, 2003.*

Van Deburg, William L.   HV6791.V36 2004
Hoodlums: Black Villains and Social Bandits in American Life.
Trade Cloth. University of Chicago Press. Chicago, IL. 2004.
304p. ISBN:0-226-84719-5, ISBN13: 978-0-226-84719-1.
Dewey:305.896/073. LCCN:2004-003549.

Audience: **g,l,u,f.** *Choice, 2005.*

Criminology > Sociology of Crime > Gangs

Chesney-Lind, Meda &   HV6439.U5F46 1999
  Hagedorn, John M. (Editors)
Female Gangs in America: Essays on Girls, Gangs and Gender.
Trade Cloth. Lake View Press. Chicago, IL. 1999. 364p.
ISBN:0-941702-48-0, ISBN13: 978-0-941702-48-5.
Dewey:364.1/06/60820973. LCCN:98-053160.

Audience: **l,u,f.**

Decker, Steve, et al.   HV6439.U7S723 1996
Life in the Gang: Family, Friends, and Violence. Barrik Van
Winkle & Scott H. Decker (Authors), Alfred Blumstein & David
Farrington (Contribution by). Trade Paper. Cambridge University
Press. New York, NY. 1996. 315p. Criminology Ser.
ISBN:0-521-56566-9, ISBN13: 978-0-521-56566-0.
Dewey:302.3/4. LCCN:96-007896.

Audience: **l,u,f.** *Choice, 1997.*

Klein, Malcolm W.   HM133
The American Street Gang: Its Nature, Prevalence, and Control.
Trade Paper. Oxford University Press, Inc. New York, NY. 1997.
284p. Studies in Crime and Public Policy ISBN:0-19-511573-2,
ISBN13: 978-0-19-511573-4. Dewey:302.3/4.

Audience: **u,f.**

Klein, Malcolm W.   HV6439
  (Editor), et al.
The Eurogang Paradox: Street Gangs and Youth Groups in the
U. S. and Europe. Hans-Jurgen Kerner, Cheryl L. Maxson &
Elmar G. M. Weitekamp (Editors). Trade Cloth. Springer. New
York, NY. 2000. 356p. ISBN:0-7923-6844-4, ISBN13:
978-0-7923-6844-1. Dewey:364.1/06/60835094.
LCCN:00-047806.

Audience: **u,f.**

Thornberry, Terence P.,   HV6439.U52N74 2003
  et al.
Gangs and Delinquency in Developmental Perspective. Marvin
D. Krohn, Alan J. Lizotte, Carolyn A. Smith & Kimberly Tobin
(Authors). Cloth Text. Cambridge University Press. New York,
NY. 2003. 262p. Cambridge Studies in Criminology Ser.
ISBN:0-521-81439-1, ISBN13: 978-0-521-81439-3.
Dewey:364.1/06/60974789. LCCN:2002-066520.

Audience: **l,u,f.**

Thrasher, Frederic M.   HV6439.U52C57 2000
The Gang: A Study of 1,313 Gangs in Chicago. Paper Text.
New Chicago School Press, Inc. Peotone, IL. 2000. 239p.
ISBN:0-9665155-5-2, ISBN13: 978-0-9665155-5-8.
Dewey:364.1/06/60977311. LCCN:00-133629.

Audience: **u,f.** *B*

Warr, Mark   HV6155 .W37 2002
Companions in Crime: The Social Aspects of Criminal Conduct.
Alfred Blumstein & David Farrington (Contribution by). Cloth
Text. Cambridge University Press. New York, NY. 2002. 190p.
Cambridge Studies in Criminology ISBN:0-521-81083-3,
ISBN13: 978-0-521-81083-8. Dewey:364.2/5.
LCCN:2001-037395.

Audience: **u,f.** *Choice, 2002.*

Formats: Web: ☐   Ebook: **e**   CD/DVD-ROM: 🌀   BCL3: *B*

Criminology > Sociology of Crime > Masculinities

Bowker, Lee H. (Editor)   **HQ1090.M379 1998**
Masculinities and Violence, Vol. 1. Trade Cloth. SAGE
Publications, Inc. Thousand Oaks, CA. 1997. 285p. Research on
Men and Masculinities Ser. ISBN:0-7619-0451-4, ISBN13:
978-0-7619-0451-9. Dewey:303.6/081. LCCN:97-033904.
                                        Audience: **u,f.**

Messerschmidt, James   **HV6025**
  W.
Masculinities and Crime: Critique and Reconceptualization of
Theory. Trade Cloth. Rowman & Littlefield Publishers, Inc.
Lanham, MD. 1993. 248p. ISBN:0-8476-7868-7, ISBN13:
978-0-8476-7868-6. Dewey:364. LCCN:93-007809.
                          Audience: **u,f.** *Choice, 1994.*

Criminology > Sociology of Crime > Minorities and crime

Bailey, Frankie Y. &   **E185**
  Green, Alice P.
"Law Never Here": A Social History of African American
Responses to Issues of Crime and Justice. Trade Cloth.
Greenwood Publishing Group, Inc. Portsmouth, NH. 1999. 264p.
ISBN:0-275-95303-3, ISBN13: 978-0-275-95303-4.
Dewey:973/.0496073. LCCN:98-038282.
                          Audience: **l,u,f.** *Choice, 1999.*

Russell-Brown, Kathryn   **HV9950.R873 2003**
Underground Codes: Race, Crime and Related Fires. Trade
Cloth. New York University Press. New York, NY. 2004. 208p.
ISBN:0-8147-7540-3, ISBN13: 978-0-8147-7540-0.
Dewey:364/.08/0973. LCCN:2003-017314.
                                        Audience: **l,u,f.**

Temple-Raston, Dina   **HV6534.J36T45 2002**
A Death in Texas: A Story of Race, Murder and a Small Town's
Struggle for Redemption. Cloth over Boards. Henry Holt &
Company. New York, NY. 2002. 336p. ISBN:0-8050-6652-7,
ISBN13: 978-0-8050-6652-4. Dewey:364.15/23/09764159.
LCCN:2001-039052.
                                        Audience: **l,u,f.**

Walker, Samuel, et al.   **HV9950.W33 2003**
The Color of Justice: Race, Ethnicity, and Crime in America.
Ed. 3. Cassia Spohn & Miriam DeLone (Authors). Paper Text.
Thomson Wadsworth. Belmont, CA. 2003. 408p.
ISBN:0-534-59499-9, ISBN13: 978-0-534-59499-2.
Dewey:364/.089/00973.
                                        Audience: **l,u.**

Walsh, Anthony   **HV6791.W35 2004**
Race and Crime: A Biosocial Analysis. Trade Cloth. Nova
Science Publishers, Inc. Hauppauge, NY. 2004. 160p.
ISBN:1-59033-970-3, ISBN13: 978-1-59033-970-1.
Dewey:364.973/089/96073. LCCN:2004-008188.
                                        Audience: **l,u,f.**

Wilson, David   **HV6789.W525 2005**
Inventing Black-on-Black Violence: Discourse, Space, and
Representation. Saddle Stitched, Cloth over Boards, Dust Jacket.

Syracuse University Press. Syracuse, NY. 2005. 193p. Space,
Place, and Society Ser. ISBN:0-8156-3080-8, ISBN13:
978-0-8156-3080-7. Dewey:364.3/496/073. LCCN:2004-028510.
                                        Audience: **u,f.**

Criminology > Sociology of Crime > War and crime

Chuter, David   **K5301.C485 2003**
War Crimes: Confronting Atrocity in the Modern World. Library
Binding. Lynne Rienner Publishers, Inc. Boulder, CO. 2003.
280p. IISS Studies in International Security
ISBN:1-58826-209-X, ISBN13: 978-1-58826-209-7.
Dewey:341.6/9. LCCN:2003-046722.
                          Audience: **u,f.** *Choice, 2004.*

Daly, Kathleen   **HV9956.N48**
Gender, Crime, and Punishment. Trade Paper. Yale University
Press. Cumberland, RI. 1996. 352p. ISBN:0-300-06866-2,
ISBN13: 978-0-300-06866-5. Dewey:364/.082.
                                        Audience: **u,f.**

Giles, Wenona Mary &   **HM886.S58 2004**
  Hyndman, Jennifer (Editors)
Sites of Violence: Gender and Conflict Zones. Trade Cloth.
University of California Press. Berkeley, CA. 2004. 357p.
ISBN:0-520-23072-8, ISBN13: 978-0-520-23072-9.
Dewey:303.6. LCCN:2003-008450.
                                        Audience: **u,f.**

Jones, Adam (Editor)   **HV6322.7.G458 2004**
Genocide, War Crimes and the West: History and Complicity.
Cloth over Boards. Zed Books, Ltd. London, 2004. 400p.
ISBN:1-84277-190-6, ISBN13: 978-1-84277-190-7.
LCCN:2003-047914.
                          Audience: **l,u,f.** *Choice, 2005.*

Maogoto, Jackson   **K5301.M36 2004**
  Nyamuya
War Crimes and Realpolitik: International Justice from World
War I to the 21st Century. Library Binding. Lynne Rienner
Publishers, Inc. Boulder, CO. 2004. 260p. ISBN:1-58826-276-6,
ISBN13: 978-1-58826-276-9. Dewey:341.6/9/09.
LCCN:2003-023330.
                          Audience: **u,f.** *Choice, 2005.*

Melvern, Linda   **DT450.435.M423 2004**
Conspiracy to Murder: The Rwanda Genocide. Trade Cloth.
Verso Books. London, 2004. 256p. ISBN:1-85984-588-6,
ISBN13: 978-1-85984-588-2. Dewey:967.57104/31.
LCCN:2004-000822.
                          Audience: **l,u,f.** *Choice, 2004.*

Valentino, Benjamin A.   **HV6322.7.V35 2004**
Final Solutions: Mass Killing and Genocide in the 20th Century.
Trade Cloth. Cornell University Press. Ithaca, NY. 2005. 336p.
Cornell Studies in Security Affairs Ser. ISBN:0-8014-3965-5,
ISBN13: 978-0-8014-3965-0. Dewey:364.15/1/0904.
LCCN:2003-019941.
                          Audience: **l,u,f.** *Choice, 2004.*

Waller, James   **HV6322.7.W35 2002**
Becoming Evil: How Ordinary People Commit Genocide and
Mass Killing. Christopher R. Browning (Foreword by). Trade
Cloth. Oxford University Press, Inc. New York, NY. 2002. 336p.
ISBN:0-19-514868-1, ISBN13: 978-0-19-514868-8.
Dewey:364.15/1019. LCCN:2002-070404.
                                        Audience: **u,f.**

Criminology > Sociology of Crime > Women and crime

Boyd, Susan C.   HV5824.W6B686 2003
From Witches to Crack Moms: Women, Drug Law, and Policy.
Trade Cloth. Carolina Academic Press. Durham, NC. 2003.
392p. ISBN:0-89089-127-3, ISBN13: 978-0-89089-127-8.
Dewey:362.29/082. LCCN:2003-065407.
Audience: **u,f.** *Choice, 2005.*

Chesney-Lind, Meda &   HV6046
Pasko, Lisa
The Female Offender: Girls, Women and Crime. Ed. 2. Cloth
Text. SAGE Publications, Inc. Thousand Oaks, CA. 2003. 232p.
Women in the Criminal Justice System Ser.
ISBN:0-7619-2978-9, ISBN13: 978-0-7619-2978-9.
Dewey:364.3/74/0973. LCCN:2003-006150.
Audience: **l,u.** *Choice, 1997.*

Chesney-Lind, Meda &   HV9104.C39 2004
Shelden, Randall G.
Girls, Delinquency, and Juvenile Justice. Ed. 3. Paper Text.
Thomson Wadsworth. Belmont, CA. 2003. 368p.
ISBN:0-534-55774-0, ISBN13: 978-0-534-55774-4.
Dewey:364.36/082. LCCN:2003-104975.
Audience: **u,f.**

Heimer, Karen &   HV6158.G457 2005
Kruttschnitt, Candace
Gender and Crime: Patterns in Victimization and Offending.
Trade Cloth. New York University Press. New York, NY. 2005.
352p. ISBN:0-8147-3674-2, ISBN13: 978-0-8147-3674-6.
Dewey:364.3/74. LCCN:2005-017343.
Audience: **u,f.**

Simon, Rita James &   HV6046.S54 2004
Heitfield, Heather
The Crimes Women Commit: The Punishments They Receive.
Ed. 2. Trade Cloth. Lexington Books. Lanham, MD. 2005. 208p.
ISBN:0-7391-1007-1, ISBN13: 978-0-7391-1007-2.
Dewey:364.3/74/0973. LCCN:2004-016988.
Audience: **l,u.**

Criminology > Victimology

Dignan, James   HV8688
Understanding Victims and Restorative Justice. Cloth Text.
McGraw-Hill Education. Maidenhead, 2004. 248p. Crime and
Justice Ser. ISBN:0-335-20980-7, ISBN13: 978-0-335-20980-4.
Dewey:364.6/8.
Audience: **u,f.**

Moriarty, Laura J.   HV6250.3.U5C56 2001
Controversies in Victimology. Ed. 2. Trade Paper, Mixed Media,
Book, Other. Anderson Publishing Company. Miamisburg, OH.
2003. 160p. Controversies in Crime and Justice Ser.
ISBN:1-58360-511-8, ISBN13: 978-1-58360-511-0.
Dewey:362.88. LCCN:00-054841.
Audience: **l,u.**

Strang, Heather   HV8688.S77 2004
Repair or Revenge?: Victims and Restorative Justice. Trade
Paper. Oxford University Press, Inc. New York, NY. 2004. 318p.
Clarendon Studies in Criminology ISBN:0-19-927429-0,
ISBN13: 978-0-19-927429-1. Dewey:344/.03288.
Audience: **u,f.**

Criminology > Victimology > Fear of crime

Best, Joel   HV6789.B47 1998
Random Violence: Worrying about New Crimes and New
Victims. Trade Paper. University of California Press. Berkeley,
CA. 1999. 260p. ISBN:0-520-21572-9, ISBN13:
978-0-520-21572-6. Dewey:364.973. LCCN:98-006234.
Audience: **l,u,f.** *Choice, 1999.*

Callanan, Valerie J.   HV6789.C35 2005
Feeding the Fear of Crime: Crime-Related Media and Support
for Three Strikes. Library Binding. LFB Scholarly Publishing
LLC. New York, NY. 2004. 236p. Criminal Justice Ser., :Recent
Scholarship ISBN:1-59332-062-0, ISBN13: 978-1-59332-062-1.
Dewey:364.973. LCCN:2004-019391.
Audience: **l,u.**

Scott, Yolanda M.   HV6250.4.E75S367
Fear of Crime among Inner-City African Americans. Library
Binding. LFB Scholarly Publishing LLC. New York, NY. 2001.
182p. Criminal Justice Ser., :Recent Scholarship
ISBN:1-931202-05-2, ISBN13: 978-1-931202-05-3.
Dewey:364.973/089/96073. LCCN:2001-004864.
Audience: **u,f.**

Snell, Clete   HT110.S64 2001
Neighborhood Structure, Crime and Fear of Crime: Testing
Bursik and Grasmick's Neighborhood Control Theory. Library
Binding. LFB Scholarly Publishing LLC. New York, NY. 2001.
viii, 160p. Criminal Justice Ser., :Recent Scholarship
ISBN:1-931202-07-9, ISBN13: 978-1-931202-07-7.
Dewey:307.76/072. LCCN:2001-002453.
Audience: **u,f.**

Criminology > Victimology > Victimization

Coston, Charisse Tia   HV6250
Maria (Editor)
Victimizing Vulnerable Groups: Images of Uniquely High-Risk
Crime Targets. Trade Cloth. Greenwood Publishing Group, Inc.
Portsmouth, NH. 2004. 408p. Praeger Series in Criminology and
Crime Control Policy Ser. ISBN:0-275-96614-3, ISBN13:
978-0-275-96614-0. Dewey:362.88. LCCN:2003-068983.
Audience: **u,f.**

Dubber, Markus Dirk   HV6250.3.U5D82 2002
Victims in the War on Crime: The Use and Abuse of Victims'
Rights. Trade Cloth. New York University Press. New York, NY.
2002. 412p. Critical America Ser. ISBN:0-8147-1928-7,
ISBN13: 978-0-8147-1928-2. Dewey:362.88/0973.
LCCN:2002-001436.
Audience: **u,f.** *Choice, 2003.*

Heimer, Karen &   HV6158.G457 2005
Kruttschnitt, Candace
Gender and Crime: Patterns in Victimization and Offending.
Trade Cloth. New York University Press. New York, NY. 2005.
352p. ISBN:0-8147-3674-2, ISBN13: 978-0-8147-3674-6.
Dewey:364.3/74. LCCN:2005-017343.
Audience: **u,f.**

Reddington, Frances P.   HV6561.S475 2003
  & Kreisel, Betsy W.
Sexual Assault: The Victims, the Perpetrators, and the Criminal
Justice System. Trade Paper. Carolina Academic Press. Durham,
NC. 2004. xix, 353p. ISBN:0-89089-334-9, ISBN13:
978-0-89089-334-0. Dewey:364.15/32/0973.
LCCN:2003-060583.

Audience: **l,u,f.** *Choice, 2005.*

Criminology > Victimology > Victimization > Domestic violence

Barnett, Ola W., et al.   HV6626.B315 2004
Family Violence Across the Lifespan: An Introduction. Ed. 2.
Cindy L. Miller-Perrin & Robin Perrin (Authors). Cloth Text.
SAGE Publications, Inc. Thousand Oaks, CA. 2004. 576p.
ISBN:0-7619-2755-7, ISBN13: 978-0-7619-2755-6.
Dewey:362.82/92. LCCN:2003-024429.

Audience: **l,u.**

Bui, Hoan N.   HV6626
In the Adopted Land: Abused Immigrant Women and the
Criminal Justice System. Trade Cloth. Greenwood Publishing
Group, Inc. Portsmouth, NH. 2004. 176p. Criminal Justice,
Delinquency, and Corrections Ser. ISBN:0-275-97708-0,
ISBN13: 978-0-275-97708-5. Dewey:362.82/92/0899592073.
LCCN:2003-062430.

Audience: **g,l,u.** *Choice, 2005.*

Hemmons, Willa Mae   KF9322.H46 2002
A Critical Legal Study of Solutions to Domestic Violence
among Black Male-Female Couples. Trade Cloth. Edwin Mellen
Press, The. Lewiston, NY. 2002. 160p. Criminology Studies,
Vol. 16 ISBN:0-7734-7282-7, ISBN13: 978-0-7734-7282-2.
Dewey:364.15/553/08996073. LCCN:2001-041003.

Audience: **u,f.**

Lutzker, John R.   HM1116.P738 2006
Preventing Violence: Research and Evidence-Based Intervention
Strategies. American Psychological Association Staff
(Contribution by). Trade Cloth. American Psychological
Association. Washington, DC. 2005. 320p.
ISBN:1-59147-342-X, ISBN13: 978-1-59147-342-8.
Dewey:303.6. LCCN:2005-015470.

Audience: **u,f.**

McKie, Linda   HQ728
Families, Violence and Social Change. Cloth Text. McGraw-Hill
Education. Maidenhead, 2005. 192p. ISBN:0-335-21159-3,
ISBN13: 978-0-335-21159-3. Dewey:306.8/5.

Audience: **l,u,f.**

Smeenk, Wilma &   HV6626
  Malsch, Marijke
Family Violence and Police Response: Learning from Research,
Policy and Practice in European Countries. Trade Cloth. Ashgate
Publishing, Ltd. Aldershot, 2005. 276p. Advances in
Criminology Ser. ISBN:0-7546-2506-0, ISBN13:
978-0-7546-2506-3. Dewey:362.82/92/094. LCCN:2005-005674.

Audience: **l,u.**

Wang, L. G. (Editor)   HV6594.S718 2004
Stalking and Domestic Violence: Current Issues. Trade Cloth.
Nova Science Publishers, Inc. Hauppauge, NY. 2004. 90p.
ISBN:1-59454-055-1, ISBN13: 978-1-59454-055-4.
Dewey:362.82/92. LCCN:2004-011417.

Audience: **l,u.**

Law Enforcement > Police and Law Enforcement Officers > Biographies

Bratton, William W. &   HV7911.B72A3 1998
  Knobler, Peter
The Turnaround: How America's Top Cop Reversed the Crime
Epidemic. Trade Cloth. Random House, Inc. New York, NY.
1998. 368p. ISBN:0-679-45251-6, ISBN13: 978-0-679-45251-5.
Dewey:363.2/092 B. LCCN:97-028105.

Audience: **l,u,f.** *Choice, 1998.*

Freeh, Louis J.   HV7911
My FBI: Bringing down the Mafia, Investigating Bill Clinton,
and Fighting the War on Terror. Cloth over Boards. St. Martin's
Press. Gordonville, VA. 2005. 352p. ISBN:0-312-32189-9,
ISBN13: 978-0-312-32189-5. Dewey:363.25092 B.

Audience: **l,u,f.**

Gallo, Gina   HV7911.H825
Armed and Dangerous: Memoirs of a Chicago Policewoman.
Trade Paper. Tom Doherty Associates, LLC. New York, NY.
2002. 336p. ISBN:0-312-87890-7, ISBN13: 978-0-312-87890-0.
Dewey:363.2/092 B.

Audience: **l,u,f.**

Griffin, Joe L. &   HV6446.G83 2002
  DeNevi, Don
Mob Nemesis: How the FBI Crippled Organized Crime. G.
Robert Blakey (Introduction by). Trade Cloth. Prometheus
Books, Publishers. Amherst, NY. 2002. 320p.
ISBN:1-57392-919-0, ISBN13: 978-1-57392-919-6.
Dewey:364.1/06/0973. LCCN:2001-048719.

Audience: **l,u.**

Powers, Richard G.   KF26
Secrecy and Power: The Life of J. Edgar Hoover. Trade Paper.
Simon & Schuster. New York, NY. 1988. 656p.
ISBN:0-02-925061-7, ISBN13: 978-0-02-925061-7.
Dewey:353.0074/092/4 B. LCCN:86-026926.

Audience: **l,u,f.** *Choice, 1987.*

Law Enforcement > Police and Law Enforcement Officers > Minority Officers

Bolton, Kenneth &   HV8138.B556 2004
  Feagin, Joe R.
Black in Blue: African American Police Officers and Racism.
Paper over Boards. Routledge. New York, NY. 2004. 296p.
ISBN:0-415-94518-6, ISBN13: 978-0-415-94518-9.
Dewey:363.2/089/96073. LCCN:2003-017150.

Audience: **l,u,f.**

Dulaney, W. Marvin   HV8138.D85 1996
Black Police in America. Trade Paper. Indiana University Press.
Bloomington, IN. 1996. 216p. Blacks in the Diaspora Ser.
ISBN:0-253-21040-2, ISBN13: 978-0-253-21040-1.
Dewey:363.2/089/96073. LCCN:95-019359.

Audience: **l,u,f.** *Choice, 1996.*

Thompson, R. Alan   HV8141.T48 2003
Career Experiences of African American Police Executives:
Black in Blue Revisited. Library Binding. LFB Scholarly
Publishing LLC. New York, NY. 2003. 188p. Criminal Justice

Ser., :Recent Scholarship ISBN:1-931202-57-5, ISBN13: 978-1-931202-57-2. Dewey:363.2/089/96073. LCCN:2003-000397.

Audience: **u,f.**

Law Enforcement > Police and Law Enforcement Officers > Women Officers

Belknap, Joanne   **HV9950.B45 2000**
The Invisible Woman: Gender, Crime, and Justice. Ed. 2. Paper Text. Thomson Wadsworth. Belmont, CA. 2000. 464p. Criminal Justice Ser. ISBN:0-534-54209-3, ISBN13: 978-0-534-54209-2. Dewey:364/.082/0973. LCCN:00-063333.

Audience: **l,u.**

Brown, Jennifer M. &   **HV8023.B76 2000**
  Heidensohn, Frances M.
Gender and Policing: Comparative Perspectives. Cloth over Boards. Palgrave Macmillan. New York, NY. 2000. 215p. ISBN:0-312-23308-6, ISBN13: 978-0-312-23308-2. Dewey:363.2/082. LCCN:99-086555.

Audience: **l,u,f.** *Choice, 2001.*

Collins, Pamela A. &   **HV8023.S27 2001**
  Scarborough, Kathryn E.
Women in Public and Private Law Enforcement. Paper Text. Elsevier Science & Technology Books. Saint Louis, MO. 2001. 166p. ISBN:0-7506-7115-7, ISBN13: 978-0-7506-7115-6. Dewey:363.2/3/0820973. LCCN:2001-037770.

Audience: **l,u,f.**

Gerber, Gwendolyn L.   **HV8009**
Women and Men Police Officers: Status, Gender, and Personality. Trade Cloth. Greenwood Publishing Group, Inc. Portsmouth, NH. 2001. 248p. ISBN:0-275-96749-2, ISBN13: 978-0-275-96749-9. Dewey:363.2/09747/1. LCCN:00-049170.

Audience: **l,u.**

Natarajan, Mangai   **HV8023**
Women Police. Ed. 2. Trade Cloth. Ashgate Publishing, Ltd. Aldershot, 2005. 578p. ISBN:0-7546-2445-5, ISBN13: 978-0-7546-2445-5. Dewey:363.2/082. LCCN:2004-053822.

Audience: **u,f.**

Schulz, Dorothy Moses   **HV8139**
Breaking the Brass Ceiling: Women Police Chiefs and Their Paths to the Top. Trade Cloth. Greenwood Publishing Group, Inc. Portsmouth, NH. 2004. 264p. ISBN:0-275-98180-0, ISBN13: 978-0-275-98180-8. Dewey:363.2/092/273. LCCN:2004-014775.

Audience: **u,f.** *Choice, 2005.*

Wells, Sandra K. & Alt,   **HV8023**
  Betty L.
Police Women: Life with the Badge. Trade Cloth. Greenwood Publishing Group, Inc. Portsmouth, NH. 2005. 176p. ISBN:0-275-98477-X, ISBN13: 978-0-275-98477-9. Dewey:363.2/082/0973. LCCN:2005-017187.

Audience: **l,u.**

Law Enforcement > Police Behavior

Donner, Frank   **HV8080.P2**
Protectors of Privilege: Red Squads and Police Repression in Urban America. Trade Paper. University of California Press.

Berkeley, CA. 1992. 518p. ISBN:0-520-08035-1, ISBN13: 978-0-520-08035-5. Dewey:363.2/32. LCCN:89-020290.

Audience: **u,f.** *Choice, 1991.*

Law Enforcement > Police Behavior > Police corruption

Bouza, Anthony V.   **HV8138.B596 2001**
Police Unbound: Corruption, Abuse and Heroism by the Boys in Blue. Trade Cloth. Prometheus Books, Publishers. Amherst, NY. 2001. 303p. ISBN:1-57392-877-1, ISBN13: 978-1-57392-877-9. Dewey:363.2/0973. LCCN:00-065316.

Audience: **l,u.**

Champion, Dean J.   **HV8141.C44 2001**
[e] Police Misconduct in America: A Reference Handbook. Mildred Vasan (Editor). E-Book. ABC-CLIO, Inc. Santa Barbara, CA. 2002. Contemporary World Issues Ser. ISBN:1-57607-538-9, ISBN13: 978-1-57607-538-8. Dewey:363.2/3.

Audience: **l,u.**

Kutnjak Ivkovic, Sanja   **HV7936.C85K88 2005**
Fallen Blue Knights: Controlling Police Corruption. Trade Cloth. Oxford University Press, Inc. New York, NY. 2005. 288p. Studies in Crime and Public Policy ISBN:0-19-516916-6, ISBN13: 978-0-19-516916-4. Dewey:363.25/9323. LCCN:2004-029057.

Audience: **u,f.**

McKetta, Frank   **HV8145.P4M43 2000**
Police, Politics and Corruption: The Mixture Dangerous to Freedom and Justice. Trade Cloth. McClain Printing Company. Parsons, WV. 2000. 202p. ISBN:0-87012-611-3, ISBN13: 978-0-87012-611-6. Dewey:363.2/09748. LCCN:00-090918.

Audience: **l,u.**

Palmiotto, Michael J.   **HV8141.P583 2001**
Police Misconduct: A Reader for the 21st Century. Trade Paper. Prentice Hall PTR. Upper Saddle River, NJ. 2000. 485p. ISBN:0-13-025604-8, ISBN13: 978-0-13-025604-1. Dewey:363.2/3. LCCN:00-059843.

Audience: **l,u.**

Law Enforcement > Police Behavior > Police use of force

Alpert, Geoffrey P. &   **HV8080.A6U53 2004**
  Dunham, Roger G.
Understanding Police Use of Force: Officers, Suspects, and Reciprocity. Alfred Blumstein & David Farrington (Contribution by). Cloth Text. Cambridge University Press. New York, NY. 2004. 202p. Cambridge Studies in Criminology ISBN:0-521-83773-1, ISBN13: 978-0-521-83773-6. Dewey:363.2/32. LCCN:2003-063883.

Audience: **u,f.**

Collins, Allyson   **HV8141.S53 1998**
Shielded from Justice: Police Brutality and Accountability in United States. Trade Paper. Human Rights Watch. New York, NY. 1998. 450p. ISBN:1-56432-183-5, ISBN13: 978-1-56432-183-1. Dewey:363.232. LCCN:98-086155.

Audience: **l,u,f.** *Choice, 1999.*

Cothran, Helen (Editor)   HV8141.P57 2001
Police Brutality: Opposing Viewpoints. Trade Cloth. Thomson
Gale. Farmington Hills, MI. 2001. 160p. ISBN:0-7377-0516-7,
ISBN13: 978-0-7377-0516-4. Dewey:363.2/32.
LCCN:00-032996.

Audience: **l.**

Geller, William A. &   HV8141.P595 1996
  Toch, Hans (Editors)
Police Violence: Understanding and Controlling Police Abuse of
Force. Cloth over Boards. Yale University Press. Cumberland,
RI. 1996. 392p. ISBN:0-300-06429-2, ISBN13:
978-0-300-06429-2. Dewey:363.2/0973. LCCN:96-033939.

Audience: **u,f.** *Choice, 1997.*

Johnson, Marilynn S.   HV8148.N52J63 2003
Street Justice: A History of Police Violence in New York City.
Trade Cloth, Trade Paper. Beacon Press. Boston, MA. 2003.
384p. ISBN:0-8070-5022-9, ISBN13: 978-0-8070-5022-4.
Dewey:363.2/32. LCCN:2003-014312.

Audience: **l,u,f.** *Choice, 2004.*

Kappeler, Victor E., et al.   HV7936.C56K36 1998
Forces of Deviance: Understanding the Dark Side of Policing.
Ed. 2. Richard D. Sluder & Geoffrey P. Alpert (Authors). Paper
Text. Waveland Press, Inc. Prospect Heights, IL. 1998. 314p.
ISBN:0-88133-983-0, ISBN13: 978-0-88133-983-3.
Dewey:363.2/0973. LCCN:00-267502.

Audience: **u,f.**

National Association for   HV8141.B49 1995
  the Advancement of Colored People Staff, et al.
Beyond the Rodney King Story: An Investigation of Police
Conduct in Minority Communities. Criminal Justice Institute of
Harvard Law School Staff & University of Massachusetts,
William Monroe Trotte (Authors), Charles J. Ogletree (Editor).
Cloth Text. Northeastern University Press. Boston, MA. 1994.
224p. ISBN:1-55553-202-0, ISBN13: 978-1-55553-202-4.
Dewey:363.2/32/0973. LCCN:94-030409.

Audience: **l,u,f.** *Choice, 1995.*

Rahtz, Howard   HV8142.R35 2003
Understanding Police Use of Force. Paper Text. Willow Tree
Press. Monsey, NY. 2003. 171p. ISBN:1-881798-42-9, ISBN13:
978-1-881798-42-2. Dewey:363.20715. LCCN:2003-536654.

Audience: **l,u,f.**

Skolnick, Jerome H., et al.   HV8141
Above the Law: Police and the Excessive Use of Force. James
Fyfe & Skolnick Fyfe (Authors). Trade Paper. Simon &
Schuster. New York, NY. 1994. 336p. ISBN:0-02-929153-4,
ISBN13: 978-0-02-929153-5. Dewey:363/.22. LCCN:92-038815.

Audience: **l,u,f.**

Terrill, William   HV7936.D54T47 2001
Police Coercion: Application of the Force Continuum. Library
Binding. LFB Scholarly Publishing LLC. New York, NY. 2001.
vii, 287p. Criminal Justice Ser., :Recent Scholarship
ISBN:1-931202-09-5, ISBN13: 978-1-931202-09-1.
Dewey:363.2/32. LCCN:2001-001150.

Audience: **u,f.**

Law Enforcement > Law Enforcement, generally

Brandl, Steven G. &   HV8141.P575 2004
  Barlow, David E.
The Police in America: Classic and Contemporary Readings.

Paper Text. Thomson Wadsworth. Belmont, CA. 2003. 352p.
The Wadsworth Professionalism in Policing Ser.
ISBN:0-534-62376-X, ISBN13: 978-0-534-62376-0.
Dewey:363.2/0973. LCCN:2003-105496.

Audience: **l,u,f.**

Grant, Heath, et al.   HV8139.G72 2004
Law Enforcement in the 21st Century. Karen J. Terry &
Benjamin J. Goold (Authors). Cloth Text. Allyn & Bacon, Inc.
Boston, MA. 2004. 464p. ISBN:0-205-33633-7, ISBN13:
978-0-205-33633-3. Dewey:363.2/0973. LCCN:2004-041489.

Audience: **l,u,f.**

Kraska, Peter B.   HV8138.M48 2001
  (Editor)
Militarizing the American Criminal Justice System: The
Changing Roles of the Armed Forces and the Police. Cloth Text.
Northeastern University Press. Boston, MA. 2001. 192p.
ISBN:1-55553-476-7, ISBN13: 978-1-55553-476-9.
Dewey:363.2/0973. LCCN:2001-031228.

Audience: **u,f.** *Choice, 2002.*

Sullivan, Larry E.   HV7921.E53 2004
  (Editor), et al.
Encyclopedia of Law Enforcement. Marie Simonetti Rosen, M.
R. Haberfeld & Schulz Dorothy M. (Moses) (Editors). Trade
Cloth. SAGE Publications, Inc. Thousand Oaks, CA. 2004.
1736p. ISBN:0-7619-2649-6, ISBN13: 978-0-7619-2649-8.
Dewey:363.2/0973/03. LCCN:2004-021803.

Audience: **l,u,f.** *Choice, 2005.*

Law Enforcement > Law Enforcement, generally > History

Lardner, James &   HV8148.N5N94 2000
  Reppetto, Thomas A.
NYPD: A City and Its Police. Cloth over Boards. Henry Holt &
Company. New York, NY. 2000. 384p. ISBN:0-8050-5578-9,
ISBN13: 978-0-8050-5578-8. Dewey:363.2/09747/1.
LCCN:00-023778.

Audience: **l,u,f.**

Roth, Mitchel   HV7903
Historical Dictionary of Law Enforcement. Cloth Text.
Greenwood Publishing Group, Inc. Portsmouth, NH. 2000. 496p.
ISBN:0-313-30560-9, ISBN13: 978-0-313-30560-3.
Dewey:363.2/03. LCCN:00-024646.

Audience: **l,u,f.** *Choice, 2001.*

Theoharis, Athan G.   HV8144.F43T49 2004
The FBI and American Democracy: A Brief Critical History.
Trade Cloth. University Press of Kansas. Lawrence, KS. 2004.
208p. ISBN:0-7006-1345-5, ISBN13: 978-0-7006-1345-8.
Dewey:363.25/0973. LCCN:2004-006077.

Audience: **l,u.** *Choice, 2005.*

Law Enforcement > Law Enforcement, generally > Comparative

Bakken, Børge   HV7118.5.C76 2005
Crime, Punishment, and Policing in China. Trade Cloth.
Rowman & Littlefield Publishers, Inc. Lanham, MD. 2005.
256p. Asia/Pacific/Perspectives Ser. ISBN:0-7425-3574-6,
ISBN13: 978-0-7425-3574-9. Dewey:364.951.
LCCN:2004-025864.

Audience: **u,f.**

Barak, Gregg (Editor)   **HV7431**
Crime and Crime Control: A Global View. Cloth Text.
Greenwood Publishing Group, Inc. Portsmouth, NH. 2000. 288p.
A World View of Social Issues Ser. ISBN:0-313-30681-8,
ISBN13: 978-0-313-30681-5. Dewey:364.4. LCCN:99-049044.
Audience: **l,u,f.**

Bessel, Richard &   **HV8055.P38 2000**
  Emsley, Clive
Patterns of Provocation: Police and Public Disorder. Trade
Cloth. Berghahn Books, Inc. New York, NY. 2000. 208p.
ISBN:1-57181-227-X, ISBN13: 978-1-57181-227-8.
Dewey:363.34/97. LCCN:99-086560.
Audience: **u,f.**

Cooley, Dennis   **HV8157**
Re-imagining Policing in Canada. Dust Jacket. University of
Toronto Press. Toronto, ON. 2005. 330p. ISBN:0-8020-3681-3,
ISBN13: 978-0-8020-3681-0. Dewey:363.2/0971.
LCCN:2005-278882.
Audience: **u,f.**

Hills, Alice   **HV8267.A3H55 2000**
Policing Africa: Internal Security and the Limits of
Liberalization. Trade Cloth. Lynne Rienner Publishers, Inc.
Boulder, CO. 2000. xii, 213p. ISBN:1-55587-715-X, ISBN13:
978-1-55587-715-6. Dewey:363.2/096. LCCN:99-037488.
Audience: **u,f.**

Hodgson, James F. &   **HV8139.P83 2005**
  Orban, Catherine (Editors)
Public Policing in the 21st Century: Issues and Dilemmas in the
U. S. and Canada. Perfect. Willow Tree Press. Monsey, NY.
2005. viii, 267p. ISBN:1-881798-56-9, ISBN13:
978-1-881798-56-9. Dewey:363.2/30973. LCCN:2005-282046.
Audience: **u,f.**

Parker, L. Craig Jr.   **HV8257.A2P36 2001**
The Japanese Police System Today: A Comparative Study. Cloth
Text. M. E. Sharpe Inc. Armonk, NY. 2001. 284p.
ISBN:0-7656-0761-1, ISBN13: 978-0-7656-0761-4.
Dewey:363.2/0952. LCCN:2001-020723.
Audience: **u,f.** *Choice, 2002.*

Law Enforcement > Law Enforcement, generally > Policy Issues

Bayley, David H.   **HV7921.B39 2005**
Changing the Guard: Developing Democratic Police Abroad.
Trade Cloth. Oxford University Press, Inc. New York, NY. 2006.
182p. Studies in Crime and Public Policy ISBN:0-19-518975-2,
ISBN13: 978-0-19-518975-9. Dewey:363.2/09172/4.
LCCN:2005-004301.
Audience: **u,f.**

Forst, Brian &   **HV9950.F67 1999**
  Manning, Peter K.
The Privatization of Policing: Two Views. Trade Cloth.
Georgetown University Press. Washington, DC. 1999. 166p.

Controversies in Public Policy Ser. ISBN:0-87840-734-0,
ISBN13: 978-0-87840-734-7. Dewey:363.2/0973.
LCCN:99-018789.
Audience: **u,f.**

Sewell, James D. &   **HV8141.C625 1999**
  Egger, Steven A.
Controversial Issues in Policing. Trade Paper. Allyn & Bacon,
Inc. Boston, MA. 1998. 247p. Controversial Issues Ser.
ISBN:0-205-27209-6, ISBN13: 978-0-205-27209-9.
Dewey:363.2/0973. LCCN:98-039662.
Audience: **l,u.**

Law Enforcement > Law Enforcement, generally > International and Cross-Border Law Enforcement

Carpenter, Ted Galen   **HV5825.C34 2003**
Bad Neighbor Policy: Washington's Futile War on Drugs in
Latin America. Cloth over Boards. Palgrave Macmillan. New
York, NY. 2003. 288p. ISBN:1-4039-6137-9, ISBN13:
978-1-4039-6137-2. Dewey:363.45/0973. LCCN:2002-032248.
Audience: **u,f.** *Choice, 2003.*

Eide, Espen Barth   **HV7921.P32 2000**
Peacebuilding and Police Reform. Tor Tanke Holm (Editor).
Trade Paper. Taylor & Francis Group. Abingdon, 2000. 240p.
Peacekeeping Ser., No. 7 ISBN:0-7146-8040-0, ISBN13:
978-0-7146-8040-8. Dewey:363.2. LCCN:99-086860.
Audience: **u,f.**

Huggins, Martha K.   **HV8160.A2.H84**
Political Policing: The United States and Latin America. Trade
Cloth. Duke University Press. Durham, NC. 1998. 256p.
ISBN:0-8223-2159-9, ISBN13: 978-0-8223-2159-0.
Dewey:363.2/0973. LCCN:97-052378.
Audience: **u,f.** *Choice, 1999.*

Koenig, Daniel J.   **HV7921.I55 2001**
International Police Cooperation: A World Perspective. Dilip K.
Das (Editor). Trade Cloth. Lexington Books. Lanham, MD.
2001. 208p. ISBN:0-7391-0226-5, ISBN13: 978-0-7391-0226-8.
Dewey:363.2. LCCN:00-048411.
Audience: **u,f.** *Choice, 2002.*

Occhipinti, John D.   **HV8194.5**
The Politics of EU Police Cooperation: Toward a European
FBI? Library Binding. Lynne Rienner Publishers, Inc. Boulder,
CO. 2003. 225p. ISBN:1-58826-118-2, ISBN13:
978-1-58826-118-2. Dewey:363.2/06/04. LCCN:2003-041369.
Audience: **u,f.**

Santiago, Michael   **HV8079.O73S36 2000**
Europol and Police Cooperation in Europe. Ed. 1. Trade Cloth.
Edwin Mellen Press, The. Lewiston, NY. 2000. 268p.
Criminology Studies, Vol. 11 ISBN:0-7734-7731-4, ISBN13:
978-0-7734-7731-5. Dewey:363.2/06/04. LCCN:00-035517.
Audience: **u,f.**

Sheptycki, James   HV7921.I77 2000
Issues in Transnational Policing. Trade Paper. Routledge. New York, NY. 2000. 256p. ISBN:0-415-19261-7, ISBN13: 978-0-415-19261-3. Dewey:363.2. LCCN:00-025484.
Audience: **l,u,f.**

Law Enforcement > Law Enforcement, generally > Teaching, Education, and Training

Haberfeld, M. R.   HV8142.H3 2002
Critical Issues in Police Training. Trade Paper. Prentice Hall PTR. Upper Saddle River, NJ. 2002. 320p. ISBN:0-13-083709-1, ISBN13: 978-0-13-083709-7. Dewey:363.2/068/3. LCCN:2001-058241.
Audience: **u,f.**

Trautman, Neal E.   HV8143.T725 2005
Police Work: A Career Survival Guide. Ed. 2. Trade Paper. Prentice Hall PTR. Upper Saddle River, NJ. 2004. 384p. ISBN:0-13-113311-X, ISBN13: 978-0-13-113311-2. Dewey:363.2/023/73. LCCN:2004-044654.
Audience: **l,u.**

Law Enforcement > Policing

Crank, John P.   HV7936.P75
Understanding Police Culture. Ed. 2. Trade Paper, Mixed Media, Book, Other. Anderson Publishing Company. Miamisburg, OH. 2004. 360p. ISBN:1-58360-545-2, ISBN13: 978-1-58360-545-5. Dewey:363.2/01/9.
Audience: **l,u,f.**

Miller, Seumas &   HV7924.M544 2004
  Blackler, John
Ethical Issues in Policing: Contemporary Problems and Perspectives: Contemporary Problems and Perspectives. Trade Cloth. Ashgate Publishing, Ltd. Aldershot, 2005. 178p. ISBN:0-7546-2244-4, ISBN13: 978-0-7546-2244-4. Dewey:174/.93632. LCCN:2004-023402.
Audience: **u,f.**

Waddington, P. A. J.   HV7921.W32 1999
Policing Citizens: Authority and Rights. Trade Paper. Taylor & Francis Group. Philadelphia, PA. 1999. 312p. ISBN:1-85728-693-6, ISBN13: 978-1-85728-693-9. Dewey:363.2/32. LCCN:00-506092.
Audience: **l.**

Law Enforcement > Policing > Policing Methods, Process, and Strategies

Bayley, David H.   HV7921.W48 1998
  (Editor)
What Works in Policing. Trade Paper. Oxford University Press, Inc. New York, NY. 1997. 256p. Readings in Crime and Punishment Ser. ISBN:0-19-510821-3, ISBN13: 978-0-19-510821-7. Dewey:363.2. LCCN:97-016779.
Audience: **l,u,f.**

Law Enforcement > Policing > Policing Methods, Process, and Strategies > Crime Prevention and Control

Gordon, Diana R.   HV7431.G67 1990
The Justice Juggernaut: Fighting Street Crime, Controlling Citizens. Trade Cloth. Rutgers University Press. Piscataway, NJ. 1990. 366p. Crime, Law, and Deviance Ser. ISBN:0-8135-1477-0, ISBN13: 978-0-8135-1477-2. Dewey:364.4/0973. LCCN:89-034882.
Audience: **u,f.** *Choice, 1990.*

Groeneveld, Richard F.   HV7936.D54G76 2005
Arrest Discretion of Police Officers: The Impact of Varying Organizational Structures. Trade Cloth. LFB Scholarly Publishing LLC. New York, NY. 2005. 170p. Criminal Justice, :Recent Scholarship ISBN:1-59332-125-2, ISBN13: 978-1-59332-125-3. Dewey:363.2/3. LCCN:2005-012790.
Audience: **u,f.**

Harcourt, Bernard E.   HV6025.H297 2001
Illusion of Order: The False Promise of Broken Windows Policing. Trade Cloth. Harvard University Press. Cambridge, MA. 2001. 304p. ISBN:0-674-00472-8, ISBN13: 978-0-674-00472-6. Dewey:364. LCCN:2001-016809.
Audience: **l,u,f.** *Choice, 2002.*

Harris, David A.   HV8139.H37 2004
Good Cops: The Case for Preventative Policing. Trade Cloth. New Press, The. New York, NY. 2005. 352p. ISBN:1-56584-923-X, ISBN13: 978-1-56584-923-5. Dewey:363.2/3/0973. LCCN:2004-053673.
Audience: **l,u,f.**

Hawkins, Darnell Felix   HV7431
  (Editor), et al.
Crime Control and Social Justice: The Delicate Balance. Samuel L. Myers & Randolph N. Stone (Editors). Trade Cloth. Greenwood Publishing Group, Inc. Portsmouth, NH. 2003. 504p. Contributions in Criminology and Penology Ser., No. 55 ISBN:0-313-30790-3, ISBN13: 978-0-313-30790-4. Dewey:364.4/0973. LCCN:2002-024479.
Audience: **l,u,f.**

Silverman, Eli B.   HV8148.N5S56 1999
NYPD Battles Crime: Innovative Strategies in Policing. Cloth Text. Northeastern University Press. Boston, MA. 1999. 256p. ISBN:1-55553-402-3, ISBN13: 978-1-55553-402-8. Dewey:363.2/09747. LCCN:99-017514.
Audience: **l,u,f.** *Choice, 1999.*

Wilson, James Q. &   HV9950.C743155 2001
  Petersilia, Joan (Editors)
Crime: Public Policies for Crime Control. Trade Paper. I C S Press. Oakland, CA. 2001. 715p. ISBN:1-55815-509-0, ISBN13: 978-1-55815-509-1. Dewey:364.973. LCCN:2001-024924.
Audience: **l,u,f.** *Choice, 2002.*

Law Enforcement > Policing > Policing Methods, Process, and Strategies > Community Policing

Bayley, David H.   HV7936.C83C43 1994
The Challenge of Community Policing: Testing the Promises. Dennis P. Rosenbaum (Editor). Trade Paper. SAGE Publications,

Inc. Thousand Oaks, CA. 1994. 320p. ISBN:0-8039-5444-1, ISBN13: 978-0-8039-5444-1. Dewey:363.2. LCCN:94-000811.
Audience: **l,u,f.** *Choice, 1994.*

Decker, Scott   **HV7936.C83P657 2003**
Policing Gangs and Youth Violence. Paper Text. Thomson Wadsworth. Belmont, CA. 2002. 368p. ISBN:0-534-59841-2, ISBN13: 978-0-534-59841-9. Dewey:364.4. LCCN:2002-110761.
Audience: **l,u,f.**

Herbert, Steven Kelly   **HN90.C6H47 2006**
Citizens, Cops, and Power: Recognizing the Limits of Community. Trade Cloth. University of Chicago Press. Chicago, IL. 2006. 168p. ISBN:0-226-32730-2, ISBN13: 978-0-226-32730-3. Dewey:363.2/3/0973. LCCN:2005-021525.
Audience: **u,f.**

Morash, Merry & Ford,   **HV7936.C83M69 2002**
J. Kevin (Editors)
The Move to Community Policing: Making Change Happen. Cloth Text. SAGE Publications, Inc. Thousand Oaks, CA. 2002. 320p. ISBN:0-7619-2472-8, ISBN13: 978-0-7619-2472-2. Dewey:363.2/3. LCCN:2001-004075.
Audience: **l,u,f.**

Rahtz, Howard   **HV7936.C83R35 2001**
Community Policing: A Handbook for Beat Cops and Supervisors. Paper Text. Willow Tree Press. Monsey, NY. 2001. 141pp. ISBN:1-881798-29-1, ISBN13: 978-1-881798-29-3. Dewey:363.2/3. LCCN:2001-275095.
Audience: **l,u,f.**

Robin, Gerald D.   **HV7936.C83R62 2000**
Community Policing-Origins, Elements, Implementation, Assessment. Trade Cloth. Edwin Mellen Press, The. Lewiston, NY. 2001. 148p. Criminology Studies, Vol. 12 ISBN:0-7734-7643-1, ISBN13: 978-0-7734-7643-1. Dewey:363.2/3. LCCN:00-060512.
Audience: **l,u,f.**

Skogan, Wesley G.   **HV7936.C83C6635 2004**
Community Policing: Can It Work? Paper Text. Thomson Wadsworth. Belmont, CA. 2003. 272p. The Wadsworth Professionalism in Policing Ser. ISBN:0-534-62505-3, ISBN13: 978-0-534-62505-4. Dewey:363.2/3/0973. LCCN:2003-102661.
Audience: **l,u.**

Stevens, Dennis J.   **HV7936.C83P654 2002**
Policing and Community Partnerships. Trade Paper. Prentice Hall PTR. Upper Saddle River, NJ. 2001. 194p. Prentice Hall's Policing and ... Ser. ISBN:0-13-028049-6, ISBN13: 978-0-13-028049-7. Dewey:363.2/3. LCCN:00-068203.
Audience: **l,u.**

Law Enforcement > Policing > Policing Methods, Process, and Strategies > Problem Oriented Policing

Braga, Anthony A.   **HV8141.B68 2002**
Problem-Oriented Policing and Crime Prevention. Trade Paper. Willow Tree Press. Monsey, NY. 2002. 182p. ISBN:1-881798-41-0, ISBN13: 978-1-881798-41-5. Dewey:363.23/0973. LCCN:2003-278145.
Audience: **u,f.**

Goldstein, Herman &   **HV9950.G65 1990**
McGraw-Hill Staff
Problem-Oriented Policing. Paper Text. McGraw-Hill Higher Education. Burr Ridge, IL. 1990. 256p. ISBN:0-07-023694-1, ISBN13: 978-0-07-023694-3. Dewey:363.2/0973. LCCN:89-013681.
Audience: **u,f.** *Choice, 1991.*

Knutsson, Johannes   **HV7936.C83P75 2003**
(Editor)
Problem-Oriented Policing: From Innovation to Mainstream. Trade Cloth. Willow Tree Press. Monsey, NY. 2003. 240p. Crime Prevention Studies, 15 ISBN:1-881798-37-2, ISBN13: 978-1-881798-37-8. Dewey:363.2/3. LCCN:2004-556385.
Audience: **l,u,f.**

Law Enforcement > Policing > Policing Methods, Process, and Strategies > Profiling

Bumgarner, Jeffrey B.   **HV6080**
Profiling and Criminal Justice in America: A Reference Handbook. Library Binding. ABC-CLIO, Inc. Santa Barbara, CA. 2004. 300p. Contemporary World Issues Ser. ISBN:1-85109-469-5, ISBN13: 978-1-85109-469-1. Dewey:363.2/3/08900973. LCCN:2004-014005.
Audience: **g,l,u.** *Choice, 2005.*

Harris, David A.   **HV8141.H298 2002**
Profiles in Injustice: Why Racial Profiling Cannot Work. Trade Cloth. New Press, The. New York, NY. 2002. 320p. ISBN:1-56584-696-6, ISBN13: 978-1-56584-696-8. Dewey:363.2/3/08900973. LCCN:2001-044177.
Audience: **g,l,u,f.** *Choice, 2002.*

Heumann, Milton &   **HV8141.C37 2003**
Cassak, Lance
Good Cop, Bad Cop: Racial Profiling and Competing Views of Justice. Trade Paper. Peter Lang Publishing, Inc. New York, NY. 2003. ix, 246p. Studies in Crime and Punishment Ser. ISBN:0-8204-5829-5, ISBN13: 978-0-8204-5829-8. Dewey:363.2/3/08900973. LCCN:2003-002788.
Audience: **l,u.** *Choice, 2004.*

Holbert, Steve & Rose,   **HV7936.R3.H65 2004**
Lisa
The Color of Guilt and Innocence: Racial Profiling and Police Practices in America. Trade Cloth. Page Marque Press. San Ramon, CA. 2004. 316p. ISBN:0-9746640-0-6, ISBN13: 978-0-9746640-0-2. Dewey:363.2/3/0890073. LCCN:2003-113959.
Audience: **l,u.** *Choice, 2005.*

Mac Donald, Heather   **HV8141.M23 2003**
Are Cops Racist?: How the War Against the Police Harms Black Americans. Trade Cloth. Ivan R. Dee Publisher. Blue Ridge Summit, PA. 2003. 192p. ISBN:1-56663-489-X, ISBN13: 978-1-56663-489-2. Dewey:363.2/32. LCCN:2002-031248.
Audience: **l,f.**

O'Reilly, James T.   **HV8141.O74 2002**
Police Traffic Stops and Racial Profiling: Resolving Management, Labor and Civil Rights Conflicts. Cloth Text. Charles C. Thomas Publisher, Ltd. Springfield, IL. 2002. 304p.

ISBN:0-398-07295-7, ISBN13: 978-0-398-07295-7.
Dewey:363.2/3/08900973. LCCN:2002-019784.
Audience: **l,u,f.**

Law Enforcement > Policing > Policing Methods, Process, and Strategies > Other Methods

Goold, Benjamin J.   **HV7936.T4**
CCTV and Policing: Public Area Surveillance and Police
Practices in Britain. Trade Cloth. Oxford University Press, Inc.
New York, NY. 2004. 260p. Clarendon Studies in Criminology
ISBN:0-19-926514-3, ISBN13: 978-0-19-926514-5.
Dewey:363.2320941. LCCN:2004-300918.
Audience: **u,f.**

Smeenk, Wilma &   **HV6626**
  Malsch, Marijke
Family Violence and Police Response: Learning from Research,
Policy and Practice in European Countries. Trade Cloth. Ashgate
Publishing, Ltd. Aldershot, 2005. 276p. Advances in
Criminology Ser. ISBN:0-7546-2506-0, ISBN13:
978-0-7546-2506-3. Dewey:362.82/92/094. LCCN:2005-005674.
Audience: **l,u.**

Law Enforcement > Policing > Juveniles and Police

Burns, Kate   **LB3013.3.S376 2005**
School Violence. Trade Cloth. Thomson Gale. Farmington Hills,
MI. 2004. 171p. Contemporary Issues Companion Ser.
ISBN:0-7377-3076-5, ISBN13: 978-0-7377-3076-0.
Dewey:371.7/82. LCCN:2004-047410.
Audience: **l,u.**

Egendorf, Laura K.   **LB3013.3.S36 2002**
  (Editor)
School Shootings. Library Binding. Thomson Gale. Farmington
Hills, MI. 2002. 80p. At Issue Ser. ISBN:0-7377-1276-7,
ISBN13: 978-0-7377-1276-6. Dewey:371.7/82.
LCCN:2001-042896.
Audience: **l,u,f.**

Newman, Katherine S.   **LB3013.3**
Rampage: The Social Roots of School Shootings. Trade Cloth.
DIANE Publishing Company. Collingdale, PA. 2004. 399p.
ISBN:0-7567-7609-0, ISBN13: 978-0-7567-7609-1.
Dewey:371.7/82.
Audience: **l,u,f.** *Choice, 2004.*

Law Enforcement > Policing > Minorities and Police

Barlow, David E. &   **HV8143.B27 2000**
  Barlow, Melissa Hickman
Police in a Multicultural Society: An American Story. Paper
Text. Waveland Press, Inc. Prospect Heights, IL. 2000. 313p.
ISBN:1-57766-129-X, ISBN13: 978-1-57766-129-0.
Dewey:363.202373. LCCN:00-712094.
Audience: **l,u,f.**

Carlson, Daniel P.   **HV7936.P8C327 2005**
When Cultures Clash: Strategies for Strengthened
Police-Community Relations. Ed. 2. Trade Paper. Prentice Hall
PTR. Upper Saddle River, NJ. 2004. 192p.
ISBN:0-13-113797-2, ISBN13: 978-0-13-113797-4.
Dewey:363.2/3. LCCN:2003-064681.
Audience: **l,u.**

Escobar, Edward J.   **HV8148.L55 E73 1999**
Race, Police, and the Making of a Political Identity: Mexican
Americans and the Los Angeles Police Department, 1900-1945.
Trade Cloth. University of California Press. Berkeley, CA. 1999.
372p. Latinos in American Society and Culture Ser., 7
ISBN:0-520-21334-3, ISBN13: 978-0-520-21334-0.
Dewey:365/.9794/93. LCCN:98-023322.
Audience: **u,f.** *Choice, 2000.*

Rowe, Michael   **HV8195**
Policing, Race and Racism. Les Johnston, Frank Leishman &
Tim Newburn (Editors). Trade Paper. Willan Publishing. Devon,
2004. 192p. Policing and Society Ser. ISBN:1-84392-044-1,
ISBN13: 978-1-84392-044-1. Dewey:363.208900941.
LCCN:2004-302532.
Audience: **g,l,u.**

Shusta, Robert M., et al.   **HV7936.P8M85 2005**
Multicultural Law Enforcement: Strategies for Peacekeeping in a
Diverse Society. Ed. 3. Deena R. Levine, Philip R. Harris &
Herbert Z. Wong (Authors). Trade Paper. Prentice Hall PTR.
Upper Saddle River, NJ. 2004. 560p. ISBN:0-13-113307-1,
ISBN13: 978-0-13-113307-5. Dewey:363.2/3.
LCCN:2004-012616.
Audience: **l,u.**

Law Enforcement > Policing > Police Administration

Beach, Raymond W. &   **HV7935**
  O'Leary, James S.
Defensible Policies: Developing, Writing and Implementing
Valid Policies for Problem Oriented Policing. Trade Cloth.
Charles C. Thomas Publisher, Ltd. Springfield, IL. 2001. 156p.
ISBN:0-398-07181-0, ISBN13: 978-0-398-07181-3.
Dewey:363.2/068.
Audience: **l,u,f.**

Jurkanin, Thomas J., et al.   **HV7935.E53 2001**
Enduring, Surviving and Thriving As a Law Enforcement
Executive. Larry T. Hoover, Jerry L. Dowling & Janice Ahmad
(Authors), Illinois Law Enforcement Training and Standards
Board (Editor). Trade Cloth. Charles C. Thomas Publisher, Ltd.
Springfield, IL. 2001. xix, 167p. ISBN:0-398-07116-0, ISBN13:
978-0-398-07116-5. Dewey:363.2/068. LCCN:00-057737.
Audience: **l,u.**

Smith, Jim   **HV7935.S57 2004**
A Practical Guide for the Law Enforcement and Security
Manager: A Theoretical and Experiential Approach. Trade Cloth.
Charles C. Thomas Publisher, Ltd. Springfield, IL. 2004. 208p.
ISBN:0-398-07462-3, ISBN13: 978-0-398-07462-3.
Dewey:363.2/068. LCCN:2003-061239.
Audience: **l,u.**

Law Enforcement > Firearms

Carter, Gregg Lee   **HV7436.G8783 2002**
(Editor)
🄴 Guns in American Society: An Encyclopedia of History,
Politics, Culture, and the Law. E-Book. ABC-CLIO, Inc. Santa
Barbara, CA. 2003. ISBN:1-57607-748-9, ISBN13:
978-1-57607-748-1. Dewey:363.3/3/097303.
Audience: **l,u.** *Choice, 2003.*

Harcourt, Bernard E.   **HV7436.G8775 2002**
(Editor)
Guns, Crime, and Punishment in America. Trade Cloth. New
York University Press. New York, NY. 2003. 432p.
ISBN:0-8147-3655-6, ISBN13: 978-0-8147-3655-5.
Dewey:363.3/3/0973. LCCN:2002-154636.
Audience: **u,f.**

Law Enforcement > Firearms > Gun Control

Crooker, Constance   **HV7436**
Emerson
Gun Control and Gun Rights. Cloth Text. Greenwood Publishing
Group, Inc. Portsmouth, NH. 2003. 200p. Historical Guides to
Controversial Issues in America Ser. ISBN:0-313-32174-4,
ISBN13: 978-0-313-32174-0. Dewey:363.3/3/0973.
LCCN:2002-035213.
Audience: **l,u,f.**

Harcourt, Bernard E.   **HV7436.G8775 2002**
(Editor)
Guns, Crime, and Punishment in America. Trade Cloth. New
York University Press. New York, NY. 2003. 432p.
ISBN:0-8147-3655-6, ISBN13: 978-0-8147-3655-5.
Dewey:363.3/3/0973. LCCN:2002-154636.
Audience: **u,f.**

Hemenway, David   **RD96.3.H45 2004**
Private Guns, Public Health. Trade Cloth. University of
Michigan Press. Chicago, IL. 2004. 344p. ISBN:0-472-11405-0,
ISBN13: 978-0-472-11405-4. Dewey:617.1/45/0973.
LCCN:2003-024583.
Audience: **u,f.** *Choice, 2004.*

Jacobs, James B.   **HV7436**
Can Gun Control Work? Trade Paper. Oxford University Press,
Inc. New York, NY. 2004. 304p. Studies in Crime and Public
Policy ISBN:0-19-517658-8, ISBN13: 978-0-19-517658-2.
Dewey:363.3/3/0973.
Audience: **l,u,f.**

Ludwig, Jens & Cook,   **HV7436.E9 2003**
Philip J. (Editors)
Evaluating Gun Policy: Effects on Crime and Violence. Trade
Cloth. Brookings Institution Press. Washington, DC. 2002. 456p.
ISBN:0-8157-5312-8, ISBN13: 978-0-8157-5312-4.
Dewey:364.15/0973. LCCN:2002-014696.
Audience: **u,f.**

Lytton, Timothy   **KF3941.S85 2005**
(Editor)
Suing the Gun Industry: A Battle at the Crossroads of Gun
Control and Mass Torts. Trade Cloth. University of Michigan
Press. Chicago, IL. 2005. 424p. Law, Meaning, and Violence

Ser. ISBN:0-472-11510-3, ISBN13: 978-0-472-11510-5.
Dewey:346.7303/8. LCCN:2004-030731.
Audience: **l,u.** *Choice, 2006.*

McClurg, Andrew J.   **HV7436.G84 2002**
(Editor), et al.
Gun Control and Gun Rights: A Reader and Guide. David B.
Kopel & Brannon P. Denning (Editors). Trade Cloth. New York
University Press. New York, NY. 2002. 384p.
ISBN:0-8147-4759-0, ISBN13: 978-0-8147-4759-9.
Dewey:363.3/3/0973. LCCN:2001-008620.
Audience: **l,u.**

Nisbet, Lee (Editor)   **HV7436.G866 2001**
The Gun Control Debate: You Decide. Ed. 2. Trade Paper.
Prometheus Books, Publishers. Amherst, NY. 2004. 380p.
Contemporary Issues Ser. ISBN:1-57392-861-5, ISBN13:
978-1-57392-861-8. Dewey:363.3/3/0973. LCCN:00-062576.
Audience: **l,u.**

Torr, James D.   **HV7436.G8677 2003**
Gun Violence: Opposing Viewpoints. Trade Cloth. Thomson
Gale. Farmington Hills, MI. 2002. 200p. Opposing Viewpoints
Ser. ISBN:0-7377-0747-X, ISBN13: 978-0-7377-0747-2.
Dewey:363.3/3/0973. LCCN:2002-023622.
Audience: **l.**

Law Enforcement > Investigation > Scientific Investigation of Crime

Craig, Emily A.   **HV8073.C65 2004**
Teasing Secrets from the Dead: My Investigations at America's
Most Infamous Crime Scenes. Kathy Reichs (Foreword by).
Trade Cloth. Crown Publishing Group. New York, NY. 2004.
304p. ISBN:1-4000-4922-9, ISBN13: 978-1-4000-4922-6.
Dewey:363.25/62. LCCN:2003-023410.
Audience: **l,u.**

Innes, Brian   **HV8073**
Body in Question: Exploring the Cutting Edge in Forensic
Science. Trade Cloth. Sterling Publishing Co., Inc. New York,
NY. 2005. 256p. ISBN:1-4027-2222-2, ISBN13:
978-1-4027-2222-6. Dewey:363.25.
Audience: **l,u.**

Lazer, David (Editor)   **KF9666.5.D63 2004**
DNA and the Criminal Justice System: The Technology of
Justice. Trade Cloth. MIT Press. Cambridge, MA. 2004. 424p.
Basic Bioethics Ser. ISBN:0-262-12265-0, ISBN13:
978-0-262-12265-8. Dewey:345.73/067. LCCN:2004-042847.
Audience: **u,f.**

Lee, Henry C. &   **HV8073.L44 2002**
O'Neill, Thomas W.
Cracking Cases: The Science of Solving Crimes. Trade Cloth.
Prometheus Books, Publishers. Amherst, NY. 2002. 316p.
ISBN:1-57392-985-9, ISBN13: 978-1-57392-985-1.
Dewey:363.25. LCCN:2002-020819.
Audience: **l,u.** *Choice, 2002.*

Nickell, Joe & Fischer,   **HV8073.N517 1999**
John F.
Crime Science: Methods of Forensic Detection. Trade Cloth.
University Press of Kentucky. Lexington, KY. 1998. 312p.
ISBN:0-8131-2091-8, ISBN13: 978-0-8131-2091-1.
Dewey:363.25. LCCN:98-030749.
Audience: **l,u.**

Zonderman, Jon   HV8073.Z66 1999
Beyond the Crime Lab: The New Science of Investigation. Ed.
2. Trade Cloth. John Wiley & Sons, Inc. Hoboken, NJ. 1998.
272p. ISBN:0-471-25466-5, ISBN13: 978-0-471-25466-9.
Dewey:363.25. LCCN:98-014283.

Audience: **l,u.**

Law Enforcement > Investigation > Investigative Procedure

Inbau, Fred Edward, et al.   HV8073.I43 2001
Criminal Interrogation and Confessions. Ed. 4. John E. Reid,
Joseph P. Buckley & Brian C. Jayne (Authors). Cloth Text.
Jones & Bartlett Publishers, Inc. Sudbury, MA. 2001. 639p.
Criminal Justice Ser. ISBN:0-8342-1775-9, ISBN13:
978-0-8342-1775-1. Dewey:363.25/4. LCCN:00-067634.

Audience: **u,f.**

Palermo, George B. & Kocsis, Richard N.   HV6080.P32 2004
Offender Profiling: An Introduction to the Sociopsychological
Analysis of Violent Crime. Laminated. Charles C. Thomas
Publisher, Ltd. Springfield, IL. 2005. 284p. American Series in
Behavioral Science and Law ISBN:0-398-07548-4, ISBN13:
978-0-398-07548-4. Dewey:363.25/8. LCCN:2004-055371.

Audience: **l,u.**

Pickett, K. H. Spencer & Pickett, Jennifer M.   HV6768.P53 2002
Financial Crime Investigation and Control. Trade Cloth. John
Wiley & Sons, Inc. Hoboken, NJ. 2002. 288p.
ISBN:0-471-20335-1, ISBN13: 978-0-471-20335-3.
Dewey:364.163. LCCN:2002-280953.

Audience: **l,u.** *Choice, 2003, 2002.*

Stuart, Gary L.   KF224.M54S78 2004
Miranda: The Story of America's Right to Remain Silent. Trade
Cloth. University of Arizona Press. Tucson, AZ. 2004. 210p.
ISBN:0-8165-2313-4, ISBN13: 978-0-8165-2313-9.
Dewey:345.73/056. LCCN:2004-008436.

Audience: **l,u,f.** *Choice, 2005.*

White, Welsh S.   KF9625.W48 2001
Miranda's Waning Protections: Police Interrogation Practices
after Dickerson. Trade Cloth. University of Michigan Press.
Chicago, IL. 2001. 240p. ISBN:0-472-11172-8, ISBN13:
978-0-472-11172-5. Dewey:345.73/056. LCCN:2001-002078.

Audience: **l,u,f.** *Choice, 2002.*

Yeschke, Charles L.   HV8073.Y467 2004
Interrogation: Achieving Confessions Using Permissible
Persuasion. Trade Cloth. Charles C. Thomas Publisher, Ltd.
Springfield, IL. 2004. 254p. ISBN:0-398-07494-1, ISBN13:
978-0-398-07494-4. Dewey:363.25/4. LCCN:2003-070325.

Audience: **l,u.**

Zulawski, David E. & Wicklander, Douglas E.   HV8073.Z85 2001
Practical Aspects of Interview and Interrogation. Ed. 2. CRC
Press. 2002. ISBN:0-8493-0101-7, ISBN13: 978-0-8493-0101-8.

Audience: **l,u.**

Law Enforcement > Investigation > Law Enforcement Intelligence

Fijnaut, Cyrille & Marx, Gary T. (Editors)   HV8080.U5U53 1995
Undercover-Police Surveillance in Comparative Perspective.
Trade Cloth. Kluwer Law International. Alphen a/d Rijn, 1995.
x, 337p. ISBN:90-411-0015-6, ISBN13: 978-90-411-0015-3.
Dewey:363.2/32. LCCN:95-018010.

Audience: **u,f.**

Madinger, John   HV8138.M33 2000
Confidential Informant: Law Enforcement's Most Valuable Tool.
CRC Press. 2000. ISBN:0-8493-0709-0, ISBN13:
978-0-8493-0709-6.

Audience: **l,u.**

Law Enforcement > Police and Terrorism

Hodgson, James F. & Orban, Catherine (Editors)   HV8139.P83 2005
Public Policing in the 21st Century: Issues and Dilemmas in the
U. S. and Canada. Perfect. Willow Tree Press. Monsey, NY.
2005. viii, 267p. ISBN:1-881798-56-9, ISBN13:
978-1-881798-56-9. Dewey:363.2/30973. LCCN:2005-282046.

Audience: **u,f.**

Law and Courts > Criminal Courts

Butts, Jeffrey A. & Roman, John   KF9794.J875 2004
Juvenile Drug Courts and Teen Substance Abuse. Trade Paper.
Urban Institute Press. Washington, DC. 2004. xx, 369p.
ISBN:0-87766-725-X, ISBN13: 978-0-87766-725-4.
Dewey:345.73/081. LCCN:2004-019669.

Audience: **u,f.**

Dripps, Donald A.   KF9619
About Guilt and Innocence: The Origins, Development, and
Future of Constitutional Criminal Procedure. Trade Cloth.
Greenwood Publishing Group, Inc. Portsmouth, NH. 2002. 320p.
ISBN:0-275-97730-7, ISBN13: 978-0-275-97730-6.
Dewey:345.73/05. LCCN:2002-068625.

Audience: **u,f.** *Choice, 2004.*

Eisenstein, James & Jacob, Herbert   KF9619.E5 1991
Felony Justice: An Organizational Analysis of Criminal Courts.
Trade Paper. University Press of America, Inc. Lanham, MD.
1991. 334p. ISBN:0-8191-8088-2, ISBN13: 978-0-8191-8088-9.
Dewey:345.73/05. LCCN:90-021249.

Audience: **u,f.**

Emmelman, Debra S.   KF9646.E47 2003
Justice for the Poor: A Study of Criminal Defense Work. Trade
Cloth. Ashgate Publishing, Ltd. Aldershot, 2003. 166p. Law,
Justice and Power Ser. ISBN:0-7546-2309-2, ISBN13:
978-0-7546-2309-0. Dewey:345.73/01. LCCN:2002-034534.

Audience: **u,f.**

Flemming, Roy B., et al.   KF9223.F43 1992
The Craft of Justice: Politics and Work in Criminal Court
Communities. Peter F. Nardulli & James Eisenstein (Authors).
Trade Cloth. University of Pennsylvania Press. Philadelphia, PA.

1992. 232p. Law in Social Context Ser. ISBN:0-8122-3187-2, ISBN13: 978-0-8122-3187-8. Dewey:345.73/01. LCCN:92-025106.

Audience: **l,u,f.** *Choice, 1993.*

Schabas, William A.   **KZ6310.S33 2004**
An Introduction to the International Criminal Court. Ed. 2. Cloth Text. Cambridge University Press. New York, NY. 2004. 494p. ISBN:0-521-83055-9, ISBN13: 978-0-521-83055-3. Dewey:341.77. LCCN:2003-055727.

Audience: **l,u,f.**

Law and Courts > Criminal Courts > Policy

Feeley, Malcolm M. &   **KF9730.F44 1998**
  Rubin, Edward L.
Judicial Policy Making and the Modern State: How the Courts Reformed America's Prisons. Alfred Blumstein & David Farrington (Contribution by). Trade Cloth. Cambridge University Press. New York, NY. 1998. 506p. Criminology Ser. ISBN:0-521-59353-0, ISBN13: 978-0-521-59353-3. Dewey:344.73/035. LCCN:97-025523.

Audience: **u,f.** *Choice, 1999.*

Foley, Michael A.   **KF9227**
Arbitrary and Capricious: The Supreme Court, the Constitution, and the Death Penalty. Trade Cloth. Greenwood Publishing Group, Inc. Portsmouth, NH. 2003. 264p. ISBN:0-275-97587-8, ISBN13: 978-0-275-97587-6. Dewey:345.73/0773. LCCN:2003-042853.

Audience: **u,f.** *Choice, 2004.*

Latzer, Barry   **KF9227.C2L38 2002**
Death Penalty Cases. Ed. 2. Paper Text. Elsevier Science & Technology Books. Saint Louis, MO. 2002. 348p. ISBN:0-7506-7594-2, ISBN13: 978-0-7506-7594-9. Dewey:345.73/0773. LCCN:2002-035612.

Audience: **l,u,f.**

McGoldrick, Dominic,   **KZ6310**
  et al.
The Permanent International Criminal Court: Legal and Policy Issues. Peter Rowe & Eric Donnelly (Authors). Trade Paper. Hart Publishing Ltd. Oxford, 2004. 514p. ISBN:1-84113-281-0, ISBN13: 978-1-84113-281-5. Dewey:345/.01. LCCN:2004-557994.

Audience: **u,f.**

Radelet, Michael L., et   **KF9756.R33 1992**
  al.
In Spite of Innocence: Erroneous Convictions in Capital Cases. Hugo Adam Bedau & Constance E. Putnam (Authors). Cloth Text. Northeastern University Press. Boston, MA. 1992. 400p. ISBN:1-55553-142-3, ISBN13: 978-1-55553-142-3. Dewey:347.73/12. LCCN:92-017899.

Audience: **l,u,f.** *Choice, 1993.*

Smith, Christopher E.,   **KF9223.S574 2002**
  et al.
The Supreme Court, Crime, and the Ideal of Equal Justice. Christina DeJong & John D. Burrow (Authors). Trade Paper. Peter Lang Publishing, Inc. New York, NY. 2002. 248p. Studies in Crime and Punishment, Vol. 14 ISBN:0-8204-6121-0,

ISBN13: 978-0-8204-6121-2. Dewey:347.73/26. LCCN:2002-021408.

Audience: **l,u,f.**

Law and Courts > Criminal Courts > Criminal Law

Allen, Francis A.   **KF9223.A934 1996**
The Habits of Legality: Criminal Justice and the Rule of the Law. Cloth Text. Oxford University Press, Inc. New York, NY. 1996. 168p. Studies in Crime and Public Policy ISBN:0-19-510088-3, ISBN13: 978-0-19-510088-4. Dewey:345.73/05. LCCN:95-015079.

Audience: **l,u,f.**

Brody, David C., et al.   **KF9219.B73 2001**
Criminal Law. Ed. 2. James R. Acker & Wayne A. Logan (Authors). Cloth Text. Jones & Bartlett Publishers, Inc. Sudbury, MA. 2000. 652p. Criminal Justice Ser. ISBN:0-8342-1083-5, ISBN13: 978-0-8342-1083-7. Dewey:345.73. LCCN:00-044220.

Audience: **l,u.**

Cassese, Antonio   **K5000**
International Criminal Law. Ed. 1. Paper Text. Oxford University Press, Inc. New York, NY. 2003. 528p. ISBN:0-19-925911-9, ISBN13: 978-0-19-925911-3. Dewey:345/.0235. LCCN:2003-267444.

Audience: **l,u,f.**

Fletcher, George P.   **KF9218**
Basic Concepts of Criminal Law. Paper Text. Oxford University Press, Inc. New York, NY. 1998. 236p. ISBN:0-19-512171-6, ISBN13: 978-0-19-512171-1. Dewey:345.7/3. LCCN:97-033550.

Audience: **l,u,f.**

Robinson, Paul H.   **KF9218.R634 1999**
Would You Convict?: 17 Cases That Challenged the Law. Trade Cloth. New York University Press. New York, NY. 1999. 256p. ISBN:0-8147-7530-6, ISBN13: 978-0-8147-7530-1. Dewey:345.73. LCCN:99-006451.

Audience: **l,u,f.** *Choice, 2000.*

Law and Courts > Criminal Courts > Criminal Law > Constitutional Issues

Amar, Akhil R.   **KF9619.A72196 1997**
Constitution and Criminal Procedure: First Principles. Cloth over Boards. Yale University Press. Cumberland, RI. 1997. 288p. ISBN:0-300-06678-3, ISBN13: 978-0-300-06678-4. Dewey:345.73/05. LCCN:96-021079.

Audience: **u,f.** *Choice, 1997.*

Dripps, Donald A.   **KF9619**
About Guilt and Innocence: The Origins, Development, and Future of Constitutional Criminal Procedure. Trade Cloth. Greenwood Publishing Group, Inc. Portsmouth, NH. 2002. 320p. ISBN:0-275-97730-7, ISBN13: 978-0-275-97730-6. Dewey:345.73/05. LCCN:2002-068625.

Audience: **u,f.** *Choice, 2004.*

Latzer, Barry   **KF9620**
State Constitutions and Criminal Justice, Vol. 65. Trade Cloth. Greenwood Publishing Group, Inc. Portsmouth, NH. 1991. 232p.

Contributions in Legal Studies Ser. ISBN:0-313-26112-1, ISBN13: 978-0-313-26112-1. Dewey:345.73/05. LCCN:91-003249.

Audience: **u,f.**

Law and Courts > Criminal Courts > Criminal Law > Reform

Berman, Greg & Feinblatt, John KF9223.B47 2004
Good Courts: The Case for Problem-Solving Justice. Sarah Glazer (As told to). Trade Cloth. New Press, The. New York, NY. 2005. 256p. ISBN:1-56584-973-6, ISBN13: 978-1-56584-973-0. Dewey:345.73. LCCN:2004-063176.

Audience: **l,u,f.**

Clarkson, C. M. & Morgan, Rod (Editors) K5121.P65 1995
The Politics of Sentencing Reform. Cloth Text. Oxford University Press, Inc. New York, NY. 1995. 296p. ISBN:0-19-825872-0, ISBN13: 978-0-19-825872-8. Dewey:345/.0772. LCCN:94-038332.

Audience: **u,f.**

Feld, Barry C. HV9104.F43 1999
Bad Kids: Race and the Transformation of the Juvenile Court. Trade Paper. Oxford University Press, Inc. New York, NY. 1999. 392p. Studies in Crime and Public Policy ISBN:0-19-509788-2, ISBN13: 978-0-19-509788-7. Dewey:364.36/0973. LCCN:98-007271.

Audience: **l,u,f.**

Pizzi, William T. KF9618
Trials Without Truth: Why Our System of Criminal Trials Has Become an Expensive Failure and What We Need to Do to Rebuild It. Trade Cloth. New York University Press. New York, NY. 1998. 257p. ISBN:0-8147-6649-8, ISBN13: 978-0-8147-6649-1. Dewey:345.7305. LCCN:98-025530.

Audience: **l,u,f.**

Smart, Carol K644.S63 1995
Law, Crime and Sexuality: Essays in Feminism. Paper Text. SAGE Publications, Ltd. London, 1995. 256p. ISBN:0-8039-8960-1, ISBN13: 978-0-8039-8960-3. Dewey:305.42. LCCN:94-069678.

Audience: **l,u,f.**

Szasz, Thomas KF9242.S937 1989
Law, Liberty, and Psychiatry: An Inquiry into the Social Uses of Mental Health Practices. Trade Paper. Syracuse University Press. Syracuse, NY. 1989. 296p. ISBN:0-8156-0242-1, ISBN13: 978-0-8156-0242-2. Dewey:345.73/04. LCCN:63-014187.

Audience: **u,f.**

Wicharaya, Tamasak KF9685.W53 1995
Simple Theory, Hard Reality: The Impact of Sentencing Reforms on Courts, Prisons, and Crime. Cloth Text. State University of New York Press. Albany, NY. 1995. 235p. Series in New Directions in Crime and Justice Studies ISBN:0-7914-2507-X, ISBN13: 978-0-7914-2507-7. Dewey:345.73/0772. LCCN:94-031688.

Audience: **l,u,f.** *Choice, 1996.*

Wilson, James Q. KF9235.W55
Moral Judgment: Does the Abuse Excuse Threaten Our Legal System? Trade Cloth. Basic Books. New York, NY. 1997.

ISBN:0-614-28007-9, ISBN13: 978-0-614-28007-4. Dewey:340/.112.

Audience: **l,u,f.**

Law and Courts > Law and Practice of Criminal Procedure

Acker, James R. & Brody, David C. KF9619.A72165 2004
Criminal Procedure: A Contemporary Perspective. Ed. 2. Cloth Text. Jones & Bartlett Publishers, Inc. Sudbury, MA. 2003. 634p. ISBN:0-7637-3169-2, ISBN13: 978-0-7637-3169-4. Dewey:345.73/05. LCCN:2003-019052.

Audience: **l,u.**

Crump, David & Jacobs, George KF9227.C2C78 2000
A Capital Case in America: How Today's Justice System Handles Death Penalty Cases, from Crime Scene to Ultimate Execution of Sentence. Trade Paper. Carolina Academic Press. Durham, NC. 2000. 288p. ISBN:0-89089-729-8, ISBN13: 978-0-89089-729-4. Dewey:345.73/0773. LCCN:99-069661.

Audience: **u,f.** *Choice, 2001.*

Fagan, Jeffrey & Zimring, Franklin E. (Editors) KF9779.C435 2000
The Changing Borders of Juvenile Justice: Transfer of Adolescents to the Criminal Court. Trade Cloth. University of Chicago Press. Chicago, IL. 2000. 408p. John D. and Catherine T. MacArthur Foundation Series on Mental Health and Development ISBN:0-226-23380-4, ISBN13: 978-0-226-23380-2. Dewey:364.36/0973. LCCN:99-045190.

Audience: **u,f.**

Lewis, Anthony KF228.G53L49 1989
Gideon's Trumpet. Trade Paper. Knopf Publishing Group. New York, NY. 1989. 288p. ISBN:0-679-72312-9, ISBN13: 978-0-679-72312-7. Dewey:345.73/056. LCCN:88-040504.

Audience: **l,u.**

McInnis, Thomas N. KF224
The Christian Burial Case: An Introduction to Criminal and Judicial Procedure. Paper Text. Greenwood Publishing Group, Inc. Portsmouth, NH. 2000. 256p. ISBN:0-275-97028-0, ISBN13: 978-0-275-97028-4. Dewey:345.73/02523. LCCN:00-032619.

Audience: **l,u.** *Choice, 2001.*

Vogler, Richard K5001.V65 2005
A World View of Criminal Justice: Hunger for Justice. Trade Cloth. Ashgate Publishing, Ltd. Aldershot, 2005. 338p. International and Comparative Criminal Justice Ser. ISBN:0-7546-2467-6, ISBN13: 978-0-7546-2467-7. Dewey:345/.05. LCCN:2005-017370.

Audience: **u,f.**

Law and Courts > Law and Practice of Criminal Procedure > Adjudication/trials

Campbell, Douglas G. KF9223
Free Press vs. Fair Trial: Supreme Court Decisions since 1807. Trade Cloth. Greenwood Publishing Group, Inc. Portsmouth, NH. 1993. 264p. ISBN:0-275-94277-5, ISBN13: 978-0-275-94277-9. Dewey:347.302853. LCCN:93-018241.

Audience: **u,f.**

Audience: g=general, l=lower division undergraduate, u=upper division undergraduate, f=faculty.

269

Fisher, George   **KF9654.F57 2004**
Plea Bargainings Triumph. Trade Paper. Stanford University
Press. Palo Alto, CA. 2004. 416p. ISBN:0-8047-5135-8,
ISBN13: 978-0-8047-5135-3. Dewey:347.7/372.
                                        Audience: **u,f.**

Fletcher, George P.   **KF9763.F58 1995**
With Justice for Some: Protecting Victims in Criminal Trials.
Trade Cloth. Perseus Books Group. New York, NY. 1994. 336p.
ISBN:0-201-62254-8, ISBN13: 978-0-201-62254-6.
Dewey:344.73/03288. LCCN:94-032263.
                            Audience: **u,f.** *Choice, 1995.*

Giles, Robert & Snyder,   **KF9223.5.C68 1999**
  Robert W. (Editors)
Covering the Courts: Free Press, Fair Trials and Journalistic
Performance. Trade Paper. Transaction Publishers. Somerset, NJ.
1999. 146p. ISBN:0-7658-0462-X, ISBN13: 978-0-7658-0462-4.
Dewey:347.73/12. LCCN:98-026638.
                                    Audience: **l,u,f.**

Goldfarb, Ronald   **KF8725.G65 1998**
TV or Not TV: Television, Justice, and the Courts. Trade Cloth.
New York University Press. New York, NY. 1998. 238p.
ISBN:0-8147-3112-0, ISBN13: 978-0-8147-3112-3.
Dewey:347.7/3/5. LCCN:97-045289.
                            Audience: **l,u,f.** *Choice, 1998.*

Langbein, John H.   **KD8364**
The Origins of Adversary Criminal Trial. Trade Cloth. Oxford
University Press, Inc. New York, NY. 2003. 376p. Oxford
Studies in Modern Legal History ISBN:0-19-925888-0, ISBN13:
978-0-19-925888-8. Dewey:345.4207509. LCCN:2002-035562.
                                    Audience: **l,u,f.**

Westervelt, Saundra D.   **KF220.W76 2001**
  & Humphrey, John A. (Editors)
Wrongly Convicted: Perspectives on Failed Justice. Michael L.
Radelet (Foreword by). Cloth Text. Rutgers University Press.
Piscataway, NJ. 2001. xiv, 301p. ISBN:0-8135-2951-4, ISBN13:
978-0-8135-2951-6. Dewey:364.973. LCCN:00-045748.
                            Audience: **l,u,f.** *Choice, 2001.*

White, Welsh S.   **KF9227.C2W453 2006**
Litigating in the Shadow of Death: Defense Attorneys in Capital
Cases. Trade Cloth. University of Michigan Press. Chicago, IL.
2005. 232p. ISBN:0-472-09911-6, ISBN13: 978-0-472-09911-5.
Dewey:345.73/0773. LCCN:2005-022349.
                                    Audience: **u,f.**

Law and Courts > Law and Practice of
Criminal Procedure > Evidence

Casey, Eoghan   **K5465**
Digital Evidence and Computer Crime. Ed. 2. Cloth Text.
Elsevier Science & Technology Books. Saint Louis, MO. 2004.
688p. ISBN:0-12-163104-4, ISBN13: 978-0-12-163104-8.
Dewey:363.25/968. LCCN:2003-063576.
                                    Audience: **u,f.**

Lazer, David (Editor)   **KF9666.5.D63 2004**
DNA and the Criminal Justice System: The Technology of
Justice. Trade Cloth. MIT Press. Cambridge, MA. 2004. 424p.
Basic Bioethics Ser. ISBN:0-262-12265-0, ISBN13:
978-0-262-12265-8. Dewey:345.73/067. LCCN:2004-042847.
                                    Audience: **u,f.**

Nemeth, Charles P.   **KF9660.N46 2001**
Law and Evidence: A Primer for Criminal Justice, Criminology,
Law, and Legal Studies. Cloth Text. Prentice Hall PTR. Upper
Saddle River, NJ. 2000. 295p. ISBN:0-13-030811-0, ISBN13:
978-0-13-030811-5. Dewey:345.73/06. LCCN:00-058868.
                                    Audience: **l,u.**

Rogers, Richard &   **KF8965.R64 2005**
  Shuman, Daniel W.
Fundamentals of Forensic Practice: Mental Health and Criminal
Law. Trade Cloth. Springer. New York, NY. 2005. viii, 445p.
ISBN:0-387-25227-4, ISBN13: 978-0-387-25227-8.
Dewey:347.7367. LCCN:2005-923617.
                                    Audience: **u,f.**

Shapiro, Barbara J.   **KD8371.S5 1991**
Beyond Reasonable Doubt and Probable Cause: Historical
Perspectives on the Anglo-American Law of Evidence. Trade
Cloth. University of California Press. Berkeley, CA. 1991. 352p.
ISBN:0-520-07286-3, ISBN13: 978-0-520-07286-2.
Dewey:345.41/06. LCCN:92-005314.
                            Audience: **u,f.** *Choice, 1992.*

Law and Courts > Law and Practice of
Criminal Procedure > Juries

Abramson, Jeffrey   **KF8972.A727 2000**
We, the Jury: The Jury System and the Ideal of Democracy.
Trade Paper. Harvard University Press. Cambridge, MA. 2000.
350p. ISBN:0-674-00430-2, ISBN13: 978-0-674-00430-6.
Dewey:347.730752. LCCN:00-040771.
                                    Audience: **l,u,f.**

Fleury-Steiner,   **HV8699.U5F54 2004**
  Benjamin D.
Jurors' Stories of Death: How America's Death Penalty Invests
in Inequality. Trade Cloth. University of Michigan Press.
Chicago, IL. 2004. 224p. Law, Meaning, and Violence Ser.
ISBN:0-472-09860-8, ISBN13: 978-0-472-09860-6.
Dewey:364.66/0973. LCCN:2003-017198.
                                    Audience: **u,f.**

Fukurai, Hiroshi &   **KF9680.F85 2003**
  Krooth, Richard
Race in the Jury Box: Affirmative Action in Jury Selection.
Paper Text. State University of New York Press. Albany, NY.
2003. 288p. SUNY Series in New Directions in Crime and
Justice Studies ISBN:0-7914-5838-5, ISBN13:
978-0-7914-5838-9. Dewey:347.73/752. LCCN:2002-042633.
                            Audience: **l,u,f.** *Choice, 2004.*

Jonakait, Randolph N.   **KF8972.J66 2003**
The American Jury System. Cloth over Boards. Yale University
Press. Cumberland, RI. 2003. 384p. Yale Contemporary Law
Ser. ISBN:0-300-09395-0, ISBN13: 978-0-300-09395-7.
Dewey:347.73/752. LCCN:2002-014241.
                            Audience: **u,f.** *Choice, 2003.*

Kressel, Neil J. &   **KF8979.K74 2004**
  Kressel, Dorit F.
Stack and Sway: The New Science of Jury Consulting. Trade
Paper. Westview Press. Boulder, CO. 2004. 310p.
ISBN:0-8133-4241-4, ISBN13: 978-0-8133-4241-2.
Dewey:347.73/752. LCCN:2004-556235.
                            Audience: **l,u,f.** *Choice, 2002.*

Levy, Leonard W.   **KD7505.Z9**
The Palladium of Justice: Origins of Trial by Jury. Trade Cloth.
Ivan R. Dee Publisher. Blue Ridge Summit, PA. 1999. 128p.
ISBN:1-56663-259-5, ISBN13: 978-1-56663-259-1.
Dewey:345.42/075. LCCN:99-012923.
Audience: **l,u.** *Choice, 2000.*

Posey, Amy J. &   **KF8915.P67 2005**
  Wrightsman, Lawrence S.
Trial Consulting. Trade Cloth. Oxford University Press, Inc.
New York, NY. 2005. 272p. American Psychology-Law Society
Ser. ISBN:0-19-518309-6, ISBN13: 978-0-19-518309-2.
Dewey:347.73/75. LCCN:2004-029052.
Audience: **u,f.**

Law and Courts > Law and Practice of Criminal Procedure > Rights of accused

Banaszak, Ronald Sr.   **KF9223**
  (Editor)
Fair Trial Rights of the Accused: A Documentary History. Cloth
Text. Greenwood Publishing Group, Inc. Portsmouth, NH. 2001.
264p. Primary Documents in American History and
Contemporary Issues Ser. ISBN:0-313-30525-0, ISBN13:
978-0-313-30525-2. Dewey:345.73/056. LCCN:2001-023304.
Audience: **l,u,f.** *Choice, 2002.*

Bodenhamer, David J.   **KF4765.B63 1992**
Fair Trial: Rights of the Accused in American History. Paper
Text. Oxford University Press, Inc. New York, NY. 1991. 192p.
Bicentennial Essays on the Bill of Rights Ser.
ISBN:0-19-505559-4, ISBN13: 978-0-19-505559-7.
Dewey:347.73/05. LCCN:90-019611.
Audience: **l,u,f.** *Choice, 1992.*

Feld, Barry C.   **HV9104.F44 1993**
Justice for Children: The Right to Counsel and the Juvenile
Court. Cloth Text. Northeastern University Press. Boston, MA.
1993. 384p. ISBN:1-55553-157-1, ISBN13: 978-1-55553-157-7.
Dewey:364.3/6/0973. LCCN:92-038429.
Audience: **u,f.** *Choice, 1993.*

Stuart, Gary L.   **KF224.M54S78 2004**
Miranda: The Story of America's Right to Remain Silent. Trade
Cloth. University of Arizona Press. Tucson, AZ. 2004. 210p.
ISBN:0-8165-2313-4, ISBN13: 978-0-8165-2313-9.
Dewey:345.73/056. LCCN:2004-008436.
Audience: **l,u,f.** *Choice, 2005.*

Taylor, John B. (Author,   **KF9646**
  Illustrator)
Right to Counsel and Privilege Against Self-Incrimination:
Rights and Liberties under the Law. Donald Grier Stephenson
(Editor). Library Binding. ABC-CLIO, Inc. Santa Barbara, CA.
2004. 399p. America's Freedoms Ser. ISBN:1-57607-618-0,
ISBN13: 978-1-57607-618-7. Dewey:345.73/056.
LCCN:2004-019641.
Audience: **l,u.**

White, Welsh S.   **KF9625.W48 2001**
Miranda's Waning Protections: Police Interrogation Practices
after Dickerson. Trade Cloth. University of Michigan Press.
Chicago, IL. 2001. 240p. ISBN:0-472-11172-8, ISBN13:
978-0-472-11172-5. Dewey:345.73/056. LCCN:2001-002078.
Audience: **l,u,f.** *Choice, 2002.*

Law and Courts > Law and Practice of Criminal Procedure > Witnesses

Earley, Pete & Shur,   **KF9672.E117 2002**
  Gerald
WITSEC: Inside the Federal Witness Protection Program. Trade
Cloth. Bantam Books. New York, NY. 2002. 368p.
ISBN:0-553-80145-7, ISBN13: 978-0-553-80145-3.
Dewey:345.73/066. LCCN:2001-043425.
Audience: **l,u.**

Loftus, Elizabeth F.   **KF9672.L65 1991**
Witness for the Defense: The Accused, the Eyewitness and the
Expert Who Puts Memory on Trial. Trade Cloth. St. Martin's
Press. Gordonville, VA. 1991. 288p. ISBN:0-312-05537-4,
ISBN13: 978-0-312-05537-0. Dewey:345.73/066.
LCCN:90-048523.
Audience: **l,u,f.**

Ross, David Frank   **K5483.A73 1994**
  (Editor), et al.
Adult Eyewitness Testimony: Current Trends and Developments.
J. Don Read & Michael P. Toglia (Editors). Trade Cloth.
Cambridge University Press. New York, NY. 1994. 448p.
ISBN:0-521-43255-3, ISBN13: 978-0-521-43255-9.
Dewey:363.2540973. LCCN:93-008004.
Audience: **u,f.**

Law and Courts > Sentencing

Forer, Lois G.   **KF9685.Z9F67 1994**
A Rage to Punish: The Unintended Consequences of Mandatory
Sentencing. Trade Cloth. W. W. Norton & Company, Inc. New
York, NY. 1994. 204p. ISBN:0-393-03641-3, ISBN13:
978-0-393-03641-1. Dewey:345.73/0772. LCCN:93-037329.
Audience: **l,u.** *Choice, 1994.*

Leiber, Michael J.   **HV9105.I8L45 2003**
The Contexts of Juvenile Justice Decision Making: When Race
Matters. Cloth Text. State University of New York Press.
Albany, NY. 2003. 240p. ISBN:0-7914-5767-2, ISBN13:
978-0-7914-5767-2. Dewey:364.36/089/009777.
LCCN:2003-057272.
Audience: **u,f.**

Morris, Norval &   **HV9304.M67 1990**
  Tonry, Michael H.
Between Prison and Probation: Intermediate Punishments in a
Rational Sentencing System. Trade Cloth. Oxford University
Press, Inc. New York, NY. 1990. 296p. ISBN:0-19-506108-X,
ISBN13: 978-0-19-506108-6. Dewey:364.6/5/0973.
LCCN:89-023230.
Audience: **l,u,f.** *Choice, 1990.*

Shichor, David &   **HV9950.S55 1996**
  Sechrest, Dale K. (Editors)
Three Strikes and You're Out: Vengeance as Social Policy.
Trade Paper. SAGE Publications, Inc. Thousand Oaks, CA.
1996. 303p. ISBN:0-7619-0005-5, ISBN13: 978-0-7619-0005-4.
Dewey:364.650973. LCCN:96-010039.
Audience: **l,u,f.**

Spohn, Cassia   **KF9685.S68 2002**
How Do Judges Decide?: The Search for Fairness and Justice in
Punishment. Paper Text. SAGE Publications, Inc. Thousand

Oaks, CA. 2002. 352p. Key Questions for Criminal Justice Ser. ISBN:0-7619-8760-6, ISBN13: 978-0-7619-8760-4. Dewey:345.73/077. LCCN:2001-005430.

Audience: **l,u.**

Stith, Kate & Cabranes,   **KF9685.S75 1998**
  Jose A.
Fear of Judging: Sentencing Guidelines in the Federal Courts. Trade Paper. University of Chicago Press. Chicago, IL. 1998. 290p. ISBN:0-226-77486-4, ISBN13: 978-0-226-77486-2. Dewey:345.73/0772. LCCN:98-013344.

Audience: **u,f.**

Tonry, Michael H.   **KF9685**
Sentencing Matters. Trade Paper. Oxford University Press, Inc. New York, NY. 1998. 232p. Studies in Crime and Public Policy ISBN:0-19-512293-3, ISBN13: 978-0-19-512293-0. Dewey:345.7/3/0772.

Audience: **u,f.** *Choice, 1996.*

Von Hirsch, Andrew &   **K5121**
  Ashworth, Andrew (Editors)
Principled Sentencing: Reading on Theory and Policy. Ed. 2. Trade Cloth. Hart Publishing Ltd. Oxford, 1998. 448p. ISBN:1-901362-12-4, ISBN13: 978-1-901362-12-1. Dewey:345/.0772.

Audience: **l,u.**

Law and Courts > Clemency/pardons

Burnett, Cathleen   **KFM8365.C2B87 2002**
Justice Denied: Clemency Appeals in Death Penalty Cases. Trade Paper. Northeastern University Press. Boston, MA. 2002. 320p. ISBN:1-55553-520-8, ISBN13: 978-1-55553-520-9. Dewey:345.778/0773. LCCN:2002-004922.

Audience: **u,f.** *Choice, 2003.*

Sarat, Austin   **KFI1785.S27 2005**
Mercy on Trial: What It Means to Stop an Execution. Trade Cloth. Princeton University Press. Princeton, NJ. 2005. 304p. ISBN:0-691-12140-0, ISBN13: 978-0-691-12140-6. Dewey:345.773/077. LCCN:2005-005904.

Audience: **l,u,f.** *Choice, 2006.*

Corrections > Corrections, Generally

     HV9463
Directory of Adult and Juvenile Correctional Departments, Institutions, Agencies and Probation and Parole. Ed. 67. American Correctional Association. 2006.

Audience: **l,u,f.**

Bosworth, Mary   **HV9471.B675 2005**
  (Editor)
Encyclopedia of Prisons and Correctional Facilities. Trade Cloth. SAGE Publications, Inc. Thousand Oaks, CA. 2004. 1400p. ISBN:0-7619-2731-X, ISBN13: 978-0-7619-2731-0. Dewey:365/.973/03. LCCN:2004-021802.

Audience: **l,u.** *Choice, 2005.*

Clear, Todd R., et al.   **HV9471**
American Corrections. Ed. 7. George F. Cole & Michael D. Reisig (Authors). Cloth Text. Thomson Wadsworth. Belmont, CA. 2005. 592p. ISBN:0-534-64652-2, ISBN13: 978-0-534-64652-3. Dewey:365/.973.

Audience: **l.**

Whitehead, John T.   **HV9304**
Exploring Corrections in America. Ed. 3. Trade Paper, Mixed Media, Book, Other. Anderson Publishing Company. Miamisburg, OH. 2003. 675p. ISBN:1-58360-516-9, ISBN13: 978-1-58360-516-5. Dewey:364.6.

Audience: **l.**

Corrections > Corrections, Generally > Theories

MacKenzie, Doris L.   **HV9304.M24 2006**
What Works in Corrections: Reducing the Criminal Activities of Offenders and Delinquents. Alfred Blumstein & David Farrington (Contribution by). Cloth Text. Cambridge University Press. New York, NY. 2006. 404p. Cambridge Studies in Criminology Ser. ISBN:0-521-80645-3, ISBN13: 978-0-521-80645-9. Dewey:364.3. LCCN:2006-000775.

Audience: **u,f.**

Pattillo, Mary E., et al.   **HV8705.I455 2004**
Imprisoning America: The Social Effects of Mass Incarceration. David F. Weiman & Bruce Western (Authors). Trade Cloth. Russell Sage Foundation. New York, NY. 2004. 277p. ISBN:0-87154-652-3, ISBN13: 978-0-87154-652-4. Dewey:365/.973. LCCN:2003-066871.

Audience: **l,u,f.** *Choice, 2005.*

Toch, Hans   **HV9471.T63 1997**
Corrections: A Humanistic Approach. Cloth Text. Willow Tree Press. Monsey, NY. 1997. 250p. ISBN:0-911577-41-6, ISBN13: 978-0-911577-41-9. Dewey:365/.973. LCCN:97-016295.

Audience: **l,u,f.**

Tonry, Michael H.   **HV9471.F88 2004**
The Future of Imprisonment. Trade Cloth. Oxford University Press, Inc. New York, NY. 2004. 272p. ISBN:0-19-516163-7, ISBN13: 978-0-19-516163-2. Dewey:365/.973. LCCN:2003-007644.

Audience: **l,u,f.** *Choice, 2005.*

Welch, Michael   **HV9471.W4594 2005**
Ironies of Imprisonment. Cloth Text. SAGE Publications, Inc. Thousand Oaks, CA. 2004. 256p. ISBN:1-4129-0480-3, ISBN13: 978-1-4129-0480-3. Dewey:364.6/0973. LCCN:2004-007913.

Audience: **l,u,f.**

Zimring, Franklin E. &   **HV 9471.Z55 1997**
  Hawkins, Gordon
Incapacitation: Penal Confinement and the Restraint of Crime. Trade Paper. Oxford University Press, Inc. New York, NY. 1997. 202p. Studies in Crime and Public Policy ISBN:0-19-511583-X, ISBN13: 978-0-19-511583-3. Dewey:364.6.

Audience: **l,u,f.**

Zimring, Franklin E. &   **HV9471**
  Hawkins, Gordon J.
The Scale of Imprisonment. Trade Paper. University of Chicago Press. Chicago, IL. 1993. 258p. Studies in Crime and Justice ISBN:0-226-98354-4, ISBN13: 978-0-226-98354-7. Dewey:365/.973. LCCN:90-044613.

Audience: **u,f.** *Choice, 1991.*

Corrections > Corrections, Generally > History

Bernault, Florence   **HV9837**
A History of Prison and Confinement in Africa. Trade Cloth. Heinemann. Portsmouth, NH. 2003. 304p. Social History of Africa Ser. ISBN:0-325-07119-5, ISBN13: 978-0-325-07119-0. Dewey:365/.96. LCCN:2002-027286.

                          Audience: **u,f.** *Choice, 2004.*

Blomberg, Thomas G.   **HV9466.B55 2000**
& Lucken, Karol
American Penology: A History of Control. Trade Cloth. Aldine Transaction. Somerset, NJ. 2000. 270p. New Lines in Criminology Ser. ISBN:0-202-30637-2, ISBN13: 978-0-202-30637-7. Dewey:365/.973. LCCN:00-043031.

                          Audience: **l,u,f.** *Choice, 2001.*

Christianson, Scott   **HV9471**
With Liberty for Some: 500 Years of Imprisonment in America. Trade Paper. Northeastern University Press. Boston, MA. 2000. 416p. ISBN:1-55553-468-6, ISBN13: 978-1-55553-468-4. Dewey:365/.973. LCCN:98-023541.

                          Audience: **l,u,f.** *Choice, 1999.*

Cummins, Eric   **HV9475.C3C83 1994**
The Rise and Fall of California's Radical Prison Movement. Trade Paper. Stanford University Press. Palo Alto, CA. 1993. 335p. ISBN:0-8047-2232-3, ISBN13: 978-0-8047-2232-2. Dewey:365/.9794. LCCN:93-017831.

                          Audience: **u,f.** *Choice, 1994.*

Jacobs, James B.   **HV8705**
Stateville: The Penitentiary in Mass Society. Morris Janowitz (Foreword by). Trade Paper. University of Chicago Press. Chicago, IL. 1978. 300p. Studies in Crime and Justice ISBN:0-226-38977-4, ISBN13: 978-0-226-38977-6. Dewey:365.977. LCCN:76-022957.

                          Audience: **l,u,f.**

Keve, Paul W.   **HV9466**
Prisons and the American Conscience: A History of U. S. Federal Corrections. Trade Cloth. Southern Illinois University Press. Carbondale, IL. 1995. 295p. ISBN:0-8093-2003-7, ISBN13: 978-0-8093-2003-5. Dewey:365/.32/0973.

                          Audience: **u,f.** *Choice, 1992.*

McKelvey, Blake   **HV9466.M3 1977**
American Prisons: A History of Good Intentions. Ed. 2. Trade Cloth. Patterson Smith Publishing Corporation. Montclair, NJ. 1977. xv, 408p. Criminology, Law Enforcement, and Social Problems Ser., No. 17 ISBN:0-87585-704-3, ISBN13: 978-0-87585-704-6. Dewey:365/.973. LCCN:75-014556.

                          Audience: **l,u,f.** ℬ

Morris, Norval   **HV8950.N84**
Maconochie's Gentlemen: The Story of Norfolk Island and the Roots of Modern Prison Reform. Trade Paper. Oxford University Press, Inc. New York, NY. 2003. 240p. Studies in Crime and Public Policy ISBN:0-19-516912-3, ISBN13: 978-0-19-516912-6. Dewey:365/.99482.

                          Audience: **l,u,f.**

Rothman, David J.   **HV91.R73 2002**
The Discovery of the Asylum: Social Order and Disorder in the New Republic. Ed. 2. Trade Paper. Aldine Transaction. Somerset, NJ. 2002. 380p. New Lines in Criminology Ser.

ISBN:0-202-30715-8, ISBN13: 978-0-202-30715-2. Dewey:306.2/0973. LCCN:2002-066560.

                          Audience: **l,u,f.**

Stanko, Stephen, et al.   **HV8705**
Living in Prison: A History of the Correctional System with an Insider's View. Gordon A. Crews & Wayne Gillespie (Authors). Cloth Text. Greenwood Publishing Group, Inc. Portsmouth, NH. 2004. 208p. ISBN:0-313-31856-5, ISBN13: 978-0-313-31856-6. Dewey:365. LCCN:2003-056801.

                          Audience: **l,u,f.** *Choice, 2005.*

Tonry, Michael H. &   **HV6001.C672 VOL.33**
Farrington, David P. (Editors)
Crime and Punishment in Western Countries, 1980/1999, Vol. 33. Trade Paper. University of Chicago Press. Chicago, IL. 2006. 424p. Crime and Justice Ser., :A Review of Research Ser. ISBN:0-226-80871-8, ISBN13: 978-0-226-80871-0. Dewey:364 s 364.9. LCCN:2005-024762.

                          Audience: **u,f.**

Corrections > Corrections, Generally > Law and Policy

Collins, William C.   **KF9728.Z9C654 2003**
Correctional Law for the Correctional Officer. Ed. 4. Trade Paper. American Correctional Association. Alexandria, VA. 2003. v, 247p. ISBN:1-56991-209-2, ISBN13: 978-1-56991-209-6. Dewey:344.7303/5. LCCN:2003-062958.

                          Audience: **l,u.**

DiIulio, John J. Jr.   **KF9728.Z9**
(Editor)
Courts, Corrections, and the Constitution: The Impact of Judicial Intervention on Prisons and Jails. Paper Text. Oxford University Press, Inc. New York, NY. 1992. 352p. ISBN:0-19-507905-1, ISBN13: 978-0-19-507905-0. Dewey:344.73/035. LCCN:89-070946.

                          Audience: **l,u,f.** *Choice, 1991.*

Feeley, Malcolm M. &   **KF9730.F44 1998**
Rubin, Edward L.
Judicial Policy Making and the Modern State: How the Courts Reformed America's Prisons. Alfred Blumstein & David Farrington (Contribution by). Trade Cloth. Cambridge University Press. New York, NY. 1998. 506p. Criminology Ser. ISBN:0-521-59353-0, ISBN13: 978-0-521-59353-3. Dewey:344.73/035. LCCN:97-025523.

                          Audience: **u,f.** *Choice, 1999.*

Flanagan, Timothy J.   **HV8708.L65 1995**
(Editor)
Long-Term Imprisonment: Policy, Science, and Correctional Practice. Trade Cloth. SAGE Publications, Inc. Thousand Oaks, CA. 1995. 280p. ISBN:0-8039-7032-3, ISBN13: 978-0-8039-7032-8. Dewey:364.650973. LCCN:95-001494.

                          Audience: **l,u,f.**

Fliter, John A.   **KF9731**
Prisoners' Rights: The Supreme Court and Evolving Standards of Decency, 96. Trade Cloth. Greenwood Publishing Group, Inc. Portsmouth, NH. 2000. 240p. Contributions in Legal Studies Ser., Vol. 96 ISBN:0-313-31475-6, ISBN13: 978-0-313-31475-9. Dewey:344.73/0356. LCCN:00-035373.

                          Audience: **u,f.** *Choice, 2001.*

Pisciotta, Alexander W.   HV9304.P57 1994
Benevolent Repression: Social Control and the American
Reformatory-Prison Movement. Trade Cloth. New York
University Press. New York, NY. 1994. 211p.
ISBN:0-8147-6623-4, ISBN13: 978-0-8147-6623-1.
Dewey:365/.7/0973. LCCN:93-041515.
Audience: l,u,f. *Choice, 1994.*

Smith, Christopher E.   KF9225.S64 1997
The Rehnquist Court and Criminal Punishment. Cloth Text.
Garland Publishing, Inc. New York, NY. 1997. 176p. Current
Issues in Criminal Justice Ser., No. 21 ISBN:0-8153-2573-8,
ISBN13: 978-0-8153-2573-4. Dewey:345.73/077.
LCCN:97-010778.
Audience: u,f. *Choice, 1998.*

Tonry, Michael H.   HV9471.T65 2004
Thinking about Crime: Sense and Sensibility in American Penal
Culture. Trade Cloth. Oxford University Press, Inc. New York,
NY. 2004. 272p. Studies in Crime and Public Policy
ISBN:0-19-514101-6, ISBN13: 978-0-19-514101-6.
Dewey:365/.973. LCCN:2003-004245.
Audience: u,f.

Corrections > Corrections, Generally > Correctional Reform

Austin, James & Irwin,   HV9471.A969 2001
John
It's about Time: America's Imprisonment Binge. Ed. 3. Paper
Text. Thomson Wadsworth. Belmont, CA. 2000. 280p. Criminal
Justice Ser. ISBN:0-534-51498-7, ISBN13: 978-0-534-51498-3.
Dewey:365/.973. LCCN:00-035940.
Audience: l,u,f.

Bakal, Yitzhak &   HV9105.M4.B34
Polsky, Howard W.
Reforming Corrections for Juvenile Offenders: Alternatives and
Strategies. Trade Cloth. Lexington Books. Lanham, MD. 1979.
xxii, 213p. ISBN:0-669-90209-8, ISBN13: 978-0-669-90209-9.
Dewey:364.6. LCCN:73-011680.
Audience: l,u. *B*

Carroll, Leo   HV9304.C365 1998
Lawful Order: A Case Study of Correctional Crisis and Reform.
Marilyn D. McShane & Frank P. Williams III (Editors). Cloth
Text. Garland Publishing, Inc. New York, NY. 1998. 376p.
Current Issues in Criminal Justice Ser., Vol. 23
ISBN:0-8153-1617-8, ISBN13: 978-0-8153-1617-6.
Dewey:365.70973. LCCN:97-039224.
Audience: l,u,f. *Choice, 1998.*

Eriksson, Torsten   HV8975.E74
The Reformers: An Historical Survey of Pioneer Experiments in
the Treatment of Criminals. Trade Cloth. Elsevier Science &
Technology Books. Saint Louis, MO. 1976. 310p.
ISBN:0-444-99030-5, ISBN13: 978-0-444-99030-3.
Dewey:364.6/09. LCCN:76-025049.
Audience: l,u,f. *B*

Haas, Kenneth C. &   HV9471.D575 2006
Alpert, Geoffrey P. (Editors)
The Dilemmas of Corrections: Multidisciplinary Perspectives.
Ed. 5. Paper Text. Waveland Press, Inc. Prospect Heights, IL.
2005. 571p. ISBN:1-57766-398-5, ISBN13: 978-1-57766-398-0.
Dewey:365/.973. LCCN:2006-275305.
Audience: l,u.

Jacobson, Michael   HV9471.J317 2005
Downsizing Prisons: How to Reduce Crime and End Mass
Incarceration. Trade Cloth. New York University Press. New
York, NY. 2005. 304p. ISBN:0-8147-4274-2, ISBN13:
978-0-8147-4274-7. Dewey:364.6/0973. LCCN:2004-020592.
Audience: l,u,f. *Choice, 2006.*

Johnson, Robert   HV9471.J64 2002
Hard Time: Understanding and Reforming the Prison. Ed. 3.
Paper Text. Thomson Wadsworth. Belmont, CA. 2001. 360p.
ISBN:0-534-50717-4, ISBN13: 978-0-534-50717-6.
Dewey:365/.7/0973. LCCN:2001-039121.
Audience: l,u,f.

MacKenzie, Doris L. &   HV9278.5.C683 2004
Armstrong, Gaylene S. (Editors)
Correctional Boot Camps: Military Basic Training or a Model
for Corrections? Cloth Text. SAGE Publications, Inc. Thousand
Oaks, CA. 2004. 344p. ISBN:0-7619-2938-X, ISBN13:
978-0-7619-2938-3. Dewey:365/.34. LCCN:2003-027810.
Audience: l,u,f.

Palmer, Ted   HV9304
A Profile of Correctional Effectiveness and New Directions for
Research. Cloth Text. State University of New York Press.
Albany, NY. 1994. 339p. Series in New Directions in Crime and
Justice Studies ISBN:0-7914-1909-6, ISBN13:
978-0-7914-1909-0. Dewey:364.6/0973. LCCN:93-024925.
Audience: l,u,f.

Wright, Paul & Herivel,   HV9471.W36 2003
Tara (Editors)
Prison Nation: The Warehousing of America's Poor. Paper over
Boards. Routledge. New York, NY. 2003. 256p.
ISBN:0-415-93537-7, ISBN13: 978-0-415-93537-1.
Dewey:365/.973. LCCN:2002-009260.
Audience: l,u,f.

Wright, Richard A.   HV9466
In Defense of Prisons. Trade Cloth. Greenwood Publishing
Group, Inc. Portsmouth, NH. 1993. 216p. Contributions in
Criminology and Penology Ser., Vol. 43 ISBN:0-313-27926-8,
ISBN13: 978-0-313-27926-3. Dewey:365.973.
LCCN:93-015839.
Audience: l,u,f. *Choice, 1994.*

Corrections > Corrections, Generally > Teaching, Education, and Training

    E185.97.W4

☐ Correctional Education Association.
http://www.ceanational.org
Correctional Education Association.
Audience: l,u.

Corrections > Punishment

Adler, Jacob   HV8675.A35 1991
The Urgings of Conscience: A Theory of Punishment. Trade
Cloth. Temple University Press. Philadelphia, PA. 1992. ix,
316p. ISBN:0-87722-826-4, ISBN13: 978-0-87722-826-4.
Dewey:364.6. LCCN:90-024041.
Audience: u,f. *Choice, 1992.*

Golash, Deirdre   HV8693.G65 2004
The Case Against Punishment: Retribution, Crime Prevention,
and the Law. Trade Cloth. New York University Press. New
York, NY. 2005. 220p. ISBN:0-8147-3158-9, ISBN13:
978-0-8147-3158-1. Dewey:364.6. LCCN:2004-015007.
                                    Audience: **l,u,f.** *Choice, 2005.*

Morris, Norval &   HV8708
  Tonry, Michael H.
Between Prison and Probation: Intermediate Punishments in a
Rational Sentencing System. Trade Paper. Oxford University
Press, Inc. New York, NY. 1991. 304p. ISBN:0-19-507138-7,
ISBN13: 978-0-19-507138-2. Dewey:364.6/5/0973.
                                    Audience: **u,f.** *Choice, 1990.*

Primoratz, Igor   HV8665
Justifying Legal Punishment. Ed. 2. Trade Cloth. Prometheus
Books, Publishers. Amherst, NY. 1999. 209p.
ISBN:1-57392-410-5, ISBN13: 978-1-57392-410-8.
Dewey:364.6.
                                    Audience: **l,u,f.** *Choice, 1990.*

Tunick, Mark   K5103.T86 1992
Punishment: Theory and Practice. Trade Cloth. University of
California Press. Berkeley, CA. 1992. 211p.
ISBN:0-520-07737-7, ISBN13: 978-0-520-07737-9.
Dewey:364.601. LCCN:91-032129.
                                    Audience: **u,f.** *Choice, 1993.*

Zimring, Franklin E., et   HV9305.C2Z58 2003
  al.
Punishment and Democracy: Three Strikes and You're Out in
California. Gordon Hawkins & Sam Kamin (Authors). Trade
Paper. Oxford University Press, Inc. New York, NY. 2003. 256p.
Studies in Crime and Public Policy ISBN:0-19-517117-9,
ISBN13: 978-0-19-517117-4. Dewey:364.6/5.
                                    Audience: **l,u,f.**

Corrections > Prisons and Jails

Dow, Mark   JV6483.D69 2004
American Gulag: Inside U. S. Immigration Prisons. Trade Cloth.
University of California Press. Berkeley, CA. 2004. 385p.
ISBN:0-520-23942-3, ISBN13: 978-0-520-23942-5.
Dewey:365/.4. LCCN:2003-026179.
                                    Audience: **l,u,f.** *Choice, 2004.*

Foucault, Michel   HV8666.F6813 1995
Discipline and Punish: The Birth of the Prison. Ed. 2. Trade
Paper. Alfred A. Knopf Inc. New York, NY. 1995. 352p.
ISBN:0-679-75255-2, ISBN13: 978-0-679-75255-4.
Dewey:365.6/43. LCCN:95-203580.
                                    Audience: **u,f.**

Irwin, John   HV9471.I786 2005
The Warehouse Prison: Disposal of the New Dangerous Class.
Trade Paper. Roxbury Publishing Company. Los Angeles, CA.
2005. xii, 318p. ISBN:1-931719-35-7, ISBN13:
978-1-931719-35-3. Dewey:365/.973. LCCN:2004-007917.
                                    Audience: **l,u,f.**

Jacobson-Hardy,   HV9471.J32 1998
  Michael (Photographer, Text by)
Behind the Razor Wire: Portrait of a Contemporary American
Prison System. Angela Y. Davis (Foreword by), John Edgar
Wideman, Marc Mauer & James Gilligan (Contribution by).
Trade Cloth. New York University Press. New York, NY. 1998.

152p. ISBN:0-8147-4240-8, ISBN13: 978-0-8147-4240-2.
Dewey:365/.973. LCCN:98-024771.
                                    Audience: **g,l,u,f.** *Choice, 1999.*

Tonry, Michael H. &   HV9471
  Petersilia, Joan (Editors)
Prisons: Crime and Justice. Trade Cloth. University of Chicago
Press. Chicago, IL. 1999. 558p. Crime and Justice Ser., :A
Review of Research Ser. ISBN:0-226-80849-1, ISBN13:
978-0-226-80849-9. Dewey:365.9/73.
                                    Audience: **l,u,f.**

Corrections > Prisons and Jails > Administration of Prisons and Jails

Bartollas, Clemens &   HV9470.B37 2003
  Wood, Frank W.
Becoming a Model Warden: Striving for Excellence. Trade
Cloth. American Correctional Association. Alexandria, VA.
2003. xviii, 180p. ISBN:1-56991-204-1, ISBN13:
978-1-56991-204-1. Dewey:364/.068/4. LCCN:2003-056321.
                                    Audience: **l,u,f.**

Diiulio, John J.   HV9469 .D54
Governing Prisons. Trade Paper. Simon & Schuster. New York,
NY. 1990. 364p. ISBN:0-02-907883-0, ISBN13:
978-0-02-907883-9. Dewey:365/.068. LCCN:87-008478.
                                    Audience: **l,u,f.**

Keve, Paul W.   HV9104.K48 1996
Measuring Excellence: The History of Correctional Standards
and Accreditation. Trade Paper. American Correctional
Association. Alexandria, VA. 1996. 225p. ISBN:1-56991-040-5,
ISBN13: 978-1-56991-040-5. Dewey:365/.973.
LCCN:95-052084.
                                    Audience: **u,f.**

Phillips, Richard &   HV9469.P47 2005
  McConnell, Charles
The Effective Corrections Manager: Correctional Supervision for
the Future. Ed. 2. Cloth Text. Jones & Bartlett Publishers, Inc.
Sudbury, MA. 2004. 500p. ISBN:0-7637-3311-3, ISBN13:
978-0-7637-3311-7. Dewey:365/.068. LCCN:2004-011541.
                                    Audience: **l,u,f.**

Stojkovic, Stan &   HV9471.S839 2003
  Farkas, Mary Ann
Correctional Leadership: A Cultural Perspective. Cloth Text.
Thomson Wadsworth. Belmont, CA. 2002. 168p. Criminal
Justice Ser. ISBN:0-534-57429-7, ISBN13: 978-0-534-57429-1.
Dewey:365/.973/0684. LCCN:2003-266895.
                                    Audience: **l,u,f.**

Wright, Kevin N.   HV9469.W75 1994
Effective Prison Leadership. Cloth Text. William Neil
Publishing. Binghamton, NY. 1994. 224p. ISBN:0-9642806-0-4,
ISBN13: 978-0-9642806-0-1. Dewey:365/.0068.
LCCN:94-092257.
                                    Audience: **l,u,f.**

Corrections > Prisons and Jails > Correctional Officers

Conover, Ted   HV8978.F7
Newjack: Guarding Sing Sing. Trade Cloth. Knopf Publishing
Group. New York, NY. 2001. 352p. Vintage Bks.

ISBN:0-375-72662-4, ISBN13: 978-0-375-72662-0.
Dewey:365/.9/2 B.
Audience: **g,l,u,f.** *Choice, 2000.*

Whitehead, John T.   **HV9304**
Burnout in Probation and Corrections. Trade Cloth. Greenwood
Publishing Group, Inc. Portsmouth, NH. 1989. 171p.
ISBN:0-275-92959-0, ISBN13: 978-0-275-92959-6.
Dewey:364.6/01/9. LCCN:88-028776.
Audience: **l,u,f.**

Corrections > Prisons and Jails > Privatization

Armstrong, Gaylene   **HV9104.A825 2001**
Styve
Private vs. Public Operation of Juvenile Correctional Facilities.
Library Binding. LFB Scholarly Publishing LLC. New York,
NY. 2001. 188p. Criminal Justice, :Recent Scholarship
ISBN:1-931202-00-1, ISBN13: 978-1-931202-00-8.
Dewey:365/.42/0973. LCCN:2001-001750.
Audience: **u,f.**

Coyle, Andrew (Editor),   **HV9469**
et al.
Capitalist Punishment: Prison Privatization and Human Rights.
Allison Campbell & Rodney Neufeld (Editors), Nigel S. Rodley
(Preface by). Trade Cloth. Clarity Press, Inc. Atlanta, GA. 2003.
246p. ISBN:0-932863-35-3, ISBN13: 978-0-932863-35-5.
Dewey:365/.06.
Audience: **l,u,f.** *Choice, 2003.*

Hallett, Michael A.   **HV9469.H256 2006**
Private Prisons in America: A Critical Race Perspective. Randall
Shelden (Foreword by). Trade Cloth. University of Illinois
Press. Champaign, IL. 2006. 208p. Critical Perspectives in
Criminology (CPC) Ser. ISBN:0-252-03069-9, ISBN13:
978-0-252-03069-7. Dewey:365/.973. LCCN:2005-017072.
Audience: **u,f.** *Choice, 2006.*

Logan, Charles H.   **HV9469.L64 1990**
Private Prisons: Cons and Pros. Trade Cloth. Oxford University
Press, Inc. New York, NY. 1990. 328p. ISBN:0-19-506353-8,
ISBN13: 978-0-19-506353-0. Dewey:365/.973.
LCCN:89-049028.
Audience: **u,f.**

Corrections > Prisoners

Abbott, Jack Henry   **HV9468.A22A37 1991**
In the Belly of the Beast: Letters from Prison. Trade Paper.
Knopf Publishing Group. New York, NY. 1991. 192p.
ISBN:0-679-73237-3, ISBN13: 978-0-679-73237-2.
Dewey:365/.44/092 B. LCCN:90-050214.
Audience: **g,l,u,f.** ℬ

Allen, Bud & Bosta,   **HV6241.A4**
Diana
Games Criminals Play: How You Can Profit by Knowing Them.
Trade Cloth. Rae John Publishers. Berkeley, CA. 1981. 228p.
ISBN:0-9605226-0-3, ISBN13: 978-0-9605226-0-6.
Dewey:365/.643. LCCN:80-054225.
Audience: **l,u.**

Braman, Donald   **HV9950.B7 2004**
Doing Time on the Outside: Incarceration and Family Life in
Urban America. Trade Cloth. University of Michigan Press.
Chicago, IL. 2004. 280p. ISBN:0-472-11381-X, ISBN13:
978-0-472-11381-1. Dewey:362.82/95/0973.
LCCN:2004-003467.
Audience: **l,u,f.** *Choice, 2005.*

Cordilia, Ann   **HV9471.C667 1983**
The Making of an Inmate. Trade Cloth. Schenkman Books, Inc.
Rochester, VT. 1983. 133p. ISBN:0-87073-722-8, ISBN13:
978-0-87073-722-0. Dewey:365/.6/019. LCCN:82-020447.
Audience: **l,u,f.** ℬ

Hassine, Victor   **HV9475.P2L54 2002**
Life Without Parole: Living in Prison Today. Ed. 3. Thomas J.
Bernarel, Richard McCleary & Richard A. Wright (Editors).
Trade Paper. Roxbury Publishing Company. Los Angeles, CA.
2004. 181p. ISBN:1-891487-86-8, ISBN13: 978-1-891487-86-6.
Dewey:365/.6/0922748. LCCN:2001-041937.
Audience: **l,u,f.**

Palmer, John W. &   **KF9731**
Palmer, Stephen E.
Constitutional Rights of Prisoners. Ed. 7. Trade Paper, Mixed
Media, Book, Other. Anderson Publishing Company.
Miamisburg, OH. 2003. 830p. ISBN:1-58360-555-X, ISBN13:
978-1-58360-555-4. Dewey:344.73/0356.
Audience: **u,f.**

Payne, Brian K.   **HV6768.P39 2002**
Incarcerating White-Collar Offenders: The Prison Experience
and Beyond. Cloth Text. Charles C. Thomas Publisher, Ltd.
Springfield, IL. 2003. 192p. ISBN:0-398-07344-9, ISBN13:
978-0-398-07344-2. Dewey:364.16/8. LCCN:2002-020461.
Audience: **l,u,f.**

Peterson, Mark A., et   **HV6793.C2.P48 1981**
al.
Who Commits Crimes?: A Survey of Prison Inmates. Harriet B.
Braiker & Suzanne M. Polich (Authors). Cloth Text.
Oelgeschlager, Gunn & Hain, Inc. Weston, MA. 1981. 298p.
ISBN:0-89946-103-4, ISBN13: 978-0-89946-103-8.
Dewey:364.3/09794. LCCN:81-009478.
Audience: **u,f.** ℬ

Ross, Jeffrey Ian &   **HB9469.R67 2003**
Richards, Stephen C.
Convict Criminology. Paper Text. Thomson Wadsworth.
Belmont, CA. 2002. 424p. ISBN:0-534-57433-5, ISBN13:
978-0-534-57433-8. Dewey:364. LCCN:2002-104945.
Audience: **l,u,f.** *Choice, 2003.*

Thomas, Jill   **KF9731.T48 1988**
Prisoner Litigation: The Paradox of the Jailhouse Lawyer. Trade
Cloth. Rowman & Littlefield Publishers, Inc. Lanham, MD.
1988. 288p. ISBN:0-8476-7477-0, ISBN13: 978-0-8476-7477-0.
Dewey:344.73/0356. LCCN:87-019870.
Audience: **l,u,f.** *Choice, 1989.*

Toch, Hans   **HV8665**
Living in Prison: The Ecology of Survival. Frank Porporino
(Foreword by). Paper Text. American Psychological Association.
Washington, DC. 1992. 403p. ISBN:1-55798-176-0, ISBN13:
978-1-55798-176-9. Dewey:365/.4/019. LCCN:92-030700.
Audience: **u,f.** ℬ

Corrections > Prisoners > Offender Rehabilitation and Treatment

Bernfeld, Betsy   HV9274.O33 2001
Offender Rehabilitation in Practice: Implementing and Evaluating Effective Programs. Gary A. Bernfeld, David P. Farrington & Alan W. Leschied (Editors). Trade Paper. John Wiley & Sons, Inc. Hoboken, NJ. 2001. 308p. Wiley Series in Forensic Clinical Psychology ISBN:0-471-72026-7, ISBN13: 978-0-471-72026-3. Dewey:365/.66. LCCN:2001-026497.
  Audience: **l,u,f.**

Cullen, Francis T. &   HV9275.O35 1997
  Applegate, Brandon K. (Editors)
Offender Rehabilitation: Effective Correctional Intervention. Trade Cloth. Ashgate Publishing, Ltd. Aldershot, 1997. 542p. International Library of Criminology, Criminal Justice, and Penology ISBN:1-85521-798-8, ISBN13: 978-1-85521-798-0. Dewey:365/.66. LCCN:97-007873.
  Audience: **l,u,f.**

Farabee, David   HV9304.F37 2005
Rethinking Rehabilitation: Why Can't We Reform Our Criminals? Trade Paper, Perfect. American Enterprise Institute for Public Policy Research. Washington, DC. 2005. 95p. ISBN:0-8447-7190-2, ISBN13: 978-0-8447-7190-8. Dewey:364.601. LCCN:2004-026949.
  Audience: **l,u,f.**

Corrections > Prisoners > Mental Health

Fagan, Thomas J. &   RC451.4.P68C6685
  Ax, Robert K. (Editors)
Correctional Mental Health Handbook. Trade Cloth. SAGE Publications, Inc. Thousand Oaks, CA. 2002. 376p. ISBN:0-7619-2753-0, ISBN13: 978-0-7619-2753-2. Dewey:365/.66. LCCN:2002-015734.
  Audience: **l,u,f.**

Hollin, Clive R. (Editor)   HV6080
The Essential Handbook of Offender Assessment and Treatment. Trade Paper. John Wiley & Sons, Inc. Hoboken, NJ. 2003. 304p. ISBN:0-470-85436-7, ISBN13: 978-0-470-85436-5. Dewey:364.3. LCCN:2003-013115.
  Audience: **u,f.**

Steadman, Henry J., et al.   RC451.4.P68S72 1989
The Mentally Ill in Jail: Planning for Essential Services. Dennis W. McCarty & Joseph P. Morrissey (Authors). Cloth over Boards. Guilford Publications, Inc. New York, NY. 1988. 242p. Law and Behavior Ser. ISBN:0-89862-279-4, ISBN13: 978-0-89862-279-9. Dewey:365/.66. LCCN:88-024157.
  Audience: **u,f.** *Choice, 1989.*

Toch, Hans, et al.   HV9475.N7T64 2002
Acting Out: Maladaptive Behavior in Confinement. Kenneth Adams & James Douglas Grant (Authors). Trade Paper. American Psychological Association. Washington, DC. 2002. xiv, 446p. ISBN:1-55798-880-3, ISBN13: 978-1-55798-880-5. Dewey:365/.6/019. LCCN:2002-001986.
  Audience: **u,f.** *Choice, 2003.*

Toch, Hans & Adams,   RC569.5.V55T62 1994
  Kenneth
The Disturbed Violent Offender. Ed. 2. Edwin I. Megargee (Foreword by). Paper Text. American Psychological Association.

Washington, DC. 1994. 252p. ISBN:1-55798-260-0, ISBN13: 978-1-55798-260-5. Dewey:364.3. LCCN:94-027951.
  Audience: **u,f.** *Choice, 1990.*

Toch, Hans   HV6089.T63 1992
Mosaic of Despair: Human Breakdowns in Prison. Julian Rappaport (Introduction by). Cloth Text. American Psychological Association. Washington, DC. 1992. 452p. ISBN:1-55798-177-9, ISBN13: 978-1-55798-177-6. Dewey:365/.6/019. LCCN:92-017878.
  Audience: **u,f.**

Corrections > Prisoners > Minorities in Prisons and Jails

Davis, Angela   HV9471 .D38
If They Come in the Morning: Voices of Resistance. Julian Bond (Foreword by). Trade Cloth. Okpaku Communications Corporation. New Rochelle, NY. 1971. 256p. ISBN:0-89388-022-1, ISBN13: 978-0-89388-022-4. Dewey:365/.45. LCCN:71-169154.
  Audience: **l,u,f.** *B*

Murty, Komanduri, et al.   HV9950.M87 2004
Voices from Prison: An Ethnographic Study of Black Male Prisoners. Angela M. Owens & Ashwin G. Vyas (Authors). Trade Paper, Perfect. University Press of America, Inc. Lanham, MD. 2004. 262p. ISBN:0-7618-2966-0, ISBN13: 978-0-7618-2966-9. Dewey:364.3496073. LCCN:2004-108503.
  Audience: **l,u,f.**

Tonry, Michael H.   HV9950.T66 1996
Malign Neglect: Race, Crime, and Punishment in America. Trade Paper. Oxford University Press, Inc. New York, NY. 1996. 256p. ISBN:0-19-510469-2, ISBN13: 978-0-19-510469-1. Dewey:364.973.
  Audience: **l,u,f.**

Corrections > Prisoners > Women in Prisons and Jails

Collins, Catherine   HV9471
  Fisher
Imprisonment of African American Women: Causes, Conditions and Future Implications. Paper Text. McFarland & Company, Incorporated Publishers. Jefferson, NC. 2005. 166p. ISBN:0-7864-2159-2, ISBN13: 978-0-7864-2159-6. Dewey:365.973.
  Audience: **g,l,u,f.**

Johnson, Paula C.   HV9468.J65 2002
Inner Lives: Profiles of African American Women in Prison. Trade Cloth. New York University Press. New York, NY. 2003. 368p. ISBN:0-8147-4254-8, ISBN13: 978-0-8147-4254-9. Dewey:349.51. LCCN:2002-014117.
  Audience: **l,u,f.** *Choice, 2003.*

Morton, Joann B.   HV9471.M68 2003
Working with Women Offenders in Correctional Institutions. Trade Paper. American Correctional Association. Alexandria, VA. 2004. xiii, 441p. ISBN:1-56991-211-4, ISBN13:

978-1-56991-211-9. Dewey:365/.6/0820973.
LCCN:2003-062832.

Audience: **l,u,f.**

Pollock, Joycelyn M.   **HV9471.P65 2002**
Women, Prison, and Crime. Ed. 2. Paper Text. Thomson
Wadsworth. Belmont, CA. 2001. 256p. ISBN:0-534-51689-0,
ISBN13: 978-0-534-51689-5. Dewey:365/.43/0973.
LCCN:2001-026220.

Audience: **l,u.**

Corrections > Prisoners > Juveniles in Prisons and Jails

Boesky, Lisa Melanie   **RJ506.J88B625 2002**
Juvenile Offenders with Mental Health Disorders: Who Are
They and What Do We Do with Them? Trade Paper. American
Correctional Association. Alexandria, VA. 2002. 300p.
ISBN:1-56991-154-1, ISBN13: 978-1-56991-154-9.
Dewey:364.36. LCCN:2003-268108.

Audience: **l,u,f.**

Glick, Barry &   **HV9104.G59 2001**
  Sturgeon, William
Recess Is Over: A Handbook for Managing Youthful Offenders
in Adult Systems. Trade Paper. American Correctional
Association. Alexandria, VA. 2001. 110p. ISBN:1-56991-143-6,
ISBN13: 978-1-56991-143-3. Dewey:365/.6/083.
LCCN:2001-034322.

Audience: **l,u.**

Corrections > Probation, Parole, and Community Corrections

☐ American Probation and Parole Association.
http://www.appa-net.org
American Probation and Parole Association.

Audience: **l,u.**

Champion, Dean J.   **HV9304**
Felony Probation: Problems and Prospects. Trade Cloth.
Greenwood Publishing Group, Inc. Portsmouth, NH. 1988. 185p.
ISBN:0-275-92993-0, ISBN13: 978-0-275-92993-0.
Dewey:364.6/3/0973. LCCN:88-009744.

Audience: **l,u.** *Choice, 1989.*

Champion, Dean John   **HV9304.C463 2005**
Probation, Parole and Community Corrections. Ed. 5. Trade
Cloth. Prentice Hall PTR. Upper Saddle River, NJ. 2004. 720p.
ISBN:0-13-182984-X, ISBN13: 978-0-13-182984-8.
Dewey:364.6/3/0973. LCCN:2004-011351.

Audience: **l,u.**

Clear, Todd R. &   **HV9279.C54 2002**
  Dammer, Harry R.
The Offender in the Community. Ed. 2. Cloth Text. Thomson
Wadsworth. Belmont, CA. 2002. 528p. ISBN:0-534-59526-X,
ISBN13: 978-0-534-59526-5. Dewey:364.6/8.
LCCN:2002-028633.

Audience: **l,u,f.**

McCleary, Richard   **HV9304.M363 1992**
Dangerous Men: The Sociology of Parole. Ed. 2. Todd Clear
(Preface by). Trade Paper. Willow Tree Press. Monsey, NY.
1992. 182p. ISBN:0-911577-24-6, ISBN13: 978-0-911577-24-2.
Dewey:364.6/2/0973. LCCN:92-022071.

Audience: **l,u,f.**

Petersilia, Joan   **HV9304.P46 2001**
Reforming Probation and Parole in the 21st Century. Trade
Paper. American Correctional Association. Alexandria, VA.
2002. 75p. ISBN:1-56991-144-4, ISBN13: 978-1-56991-144-0.
Dewey:364.6/2/0973. LCCN:2001-034324.

Audience: **l,u,f.**

Petersilia, Joan   **HV9304**
When Prisoners Come Home: Parole and Prisoner Reentry.
Trade Cloth. Oxford University Press, Inc. New York, NY. 2003.
288p. Studies in Crime and Public Policy ISBN:0-19-516086-X,
ISBN13: 978-0-19-516086-4. Dewey:364.8/0973.
LCCN:2002-011531.

Audience: **l,u,f.** *Choice, 2003.*

Sieh, Edward W.   **HV9304.S53 2005**
Community Corrections and Human Dignity. Cloth Text. Jones
& Bartlett Publishers, Inc. Sudbury, MA. 2005. 382p. Criminal
Justice Illuminated Ser. ISBN:0-7637-2905-1, ISBN13:
978-0-7637-2905-9. Dewey:364.680973. LCCN:2005-007149.

Audience: **l,u.**

Worrall, Anne & Hoy,   **HV9279**
  Claire
Punishment in the Community: Managing Offenders, Making
Choices. Ed. 2. Trade Paper. Willan Publishing. Devon, 2005.
274p. ISBN:1-84392-076-X, ISBN13: 978-1-84392-076-2.
Dewey:364.68094109049. LCCN:2005-282799.

Audience: **l,u,f.**

Corrections > Restorative Justice

Braithwaite, John   **HV8688.B73 2002**
Restorative Justice and Responsive Regulation. Trade Paper.
Oxford University Press, Inc. New York, NY. 2002. 328p.
Studies in Crime and Public Policy ISBN:0-19-515839-3,
ISBN13: 978-0-19-515839-7. Dewey:364.

Audience: **u,f.**

Clear, Todd R. & Karp,   **HV9304.W45 2002**
  David R. (Editors)
What Is Community Justice?: Case Studies of Restorative
Justice and Community Supervision. Paper Text. SAGE
Publications, Inc. Thousand Oaks, CA. 2002. 192p. Key
Questions for Criminal Justice Ser. ISBN:0-7619-8746-0,
ISBN13: 978-0-7619-8746-8. Dewey:365/.6/0973.
LCCN:2001-005423.

Audience: **l,u,f.**

Hirsch, Andrew Von   **K970**
  (Editor), et al.
Restorative Justice and Criminal Justice: Competing or
Reconcilable Paradigms? Julian Roberts & Anthony E. Bottoms
(Editors). Trade Paper. Hart Publishing Ltd. Oxford, 2004. 360p.
ISBN:1-84113-518-6, ISBN13: 978-1-84113-518-2.
Dewey:344/.03288.

Audience: **u,f.**

Johnstone, G.   **HV8688**
A Restorative Justice Reader. Wheeler (Editor). Trade Paper.
Willan Publishing. Devon, 2003. 524p. ISBN:1-903240-81-6,
ISBN13: 978-1-903240-81-6. Dewey:364.601.
LCCN:2004-298211.

Audience: **l,u.**

Strang, Heather   **HV8688.S77 2004**
Repair or Revenge?: Victims and Restorative Justice. Trade
Paper. Oxford University Press, Inc. New York, NY. 2004. 318p.
Clarendon Studies in Criminology ISBN:0-19-927429-0,
ISBN13: 978-0-19-927429-1. Dewey:344/.03288.

Audience: **u,f.**

Strickland, Ruth Ann   **HV8688.S78 2004**
   (Translator)
Restorative Justice. Trade Paper. Peter Lang Publishing, Inc.
New York, NY. 2004. vii, 143p. Studies in Crime and
Punishment, Vol. 5 ISBN:0-8204-5758-2, ISBN13:
978-0-8204-5758-1. Dewey:345/.001. LCCN:2003-006800.

Audience: **u,f.**

Zehr, Howard & Toews,   **HV8688**
   Barb (Editors)
Critical Issues in Restorative Justice. Trade Paper, Perfect.
Willan Publishing. Devon, 2004. 436p. ISBN:1-881798-51-8,
ISBN13: 978-1-881798-51-4. Dewey:364.68.
LCCN:2004-276647.

Audience: **l,u,f.**

Corrections > Post-incarceration

Maruna, Shadd   **HV9276.M37 2001**
Making Good: How Ex-Convicts Reform and Rebuild Their
Lives. Trade Cloth. American Psychological Association.

Washington, DC. 2001. xix, 211p. ISBN:1-55798-731-9,
ISBN13: 978-1-55798-731-0. Dewey:364.8/0973.
LCCN:00-058620.

Audience: **u,f.**

Maruna, Shadd &   **HV9275**
   Immarigeon, Russ (Editors)
After Crime and Punishment: Pathways to Offender
Reintegration. Trade Cloth. Willan Publishing. Devon, 2004.
302p. ISBN:1-84392-058-1, ISBN13: 978-1-84392-058-8.
Dewey:364.8. LCCN:2004-301561.

Audience: **u,f.**

Travis, Jeremy &   **HV9304.P74 2005**
   Visher, Christy (Editors)
Prisoner Reentry and Crime in America. Alfred Blumstein &
David Farrington (Contribution by). Cloth Text. Cambridge
University Press. New York, NY. 2005. 274p. Cambridge
Studies in Criminology Ser. ISBN:0-521-84916-0, ISBN13:
978-0-521-84916-6. Dewey:364.8/0973. LCCN:2005-008118.

Audience: **l,u,f.**

Travis, Jeremy & Waul,   **HV8886.U6P75 2003**
   Michelle (Editors)
Prisoners Once Removed: The Impact of Incarceration and
Reentry on Children, Families, and Communities. Trade Paper.
Urban Institute Press. Washington, DC. 2003. xiv, 396p.
ISBN:0-87766-715-2, ISBN13: 978-0-87766-715-5.
Dewey:362.82/95/0973. LCCN:2003-017077.

Audience: **l,u,f.**   *Choice, 2004.*

ENVIRONMENTAL STUDIES

Since the publication of BCL3 in 1988, a new bifurcated field of Environmental Studies and Environmental Science emerged as a college major/minor on many American campuses. The impetus for the new discipline arose from citizen action movements that lobbied to "protect the earth" during the 1960s and 1970s via traditional groups like The Nature Conservancy (founded in 1917) and more provocative ones as in Earth First! (founded in 1979). The advocacy efforts influenced both governmental policies and trends in higher education. Throughout the 1980s ES settled into academic respectability where the hard sciences dominated course offerings. By the 1990s, universities began recognizing the importance of the Social Sciences and the Humanities to ES. This more comprehensive approach and shift in emphasis informed many of the title choices in Literature, Philosophy, Religion, Economics, History, Political Science, and Sociology found listed here. The aim was to find titles providing appropriate historical background on many fronts with some approaching "classic" status, currency, and readability accessible to undergraduates. Please check under Environmental Science for substantive titles relating to Biology, Chemistry, Engineering, and Technology although some of those titles appear here as well.Where possible, works are recommended in their newest, most reliable, and often cost effective (issued in paperback only or e-book) editions.

— JoEllen Broome

American Geological   **TN9**
  Institute Staff (Compiled by)
Dictionary of Mining, Mineral, and Related Terms. Ed. 2. Trade
Cloth. Springer. New York, NY. 2003. x, 646p.
ISBN:3-540-01271-0, ISBN13: 978-3-540-01271-9.
Dewey:622/.03.

Audience: **g,l,u,f.**

Barker, Rocky   **SD421.32.Y45B37 2005**
Scorched Earth: How the Fires of Yellowstone Changed
America. Trade Cloth. Island Press. Washington, DC. 2005.
288p. ISBN:1-55963-735-8, ISBN13: 978-1-55963-735-0.
Dewey:634.9/618/0978752. LCCN:2005-017199.

Audience: **g,l.**

Coetzer, J. A. W. &   **SF781.I525 2004**
  Tustin, R. C.
Infectious Diseases of Livestock, Set. Ed. 2. Trade Cloth.
Oxford University Press, Inc. New York, NY. 2005. 650p.
ISBN:0-19-578202-X, ISBN13: 978-0-19-578202-8.
Dewey:636.0896. LCCN:2005-298502.

Audience: **g,l,u,f.**

Daniel, Pete   **RA1270.P4D36 2005**
Toxic Drift: Pesticides and Health in the Post-World War II
South. Saddle Stitched, Cloth over Boards, Dust Jacket.
Louisiana State University Press. Baton Rouge, LA. 2005. 209p.
The Walter Lynwood Fleming Lectures in Southern History
ISBN:0-8071-3098-2, ISBN13: 978-0-8071-3098-8.
Dewey:615.9/02/0975. LCCN:2005-002594.

Audience: **g,l,u,f.**

Deere, Carolyn L. &   **HF1746.G74 2002**
  Esty, Daniel C. (Editors)
Greening the Americas: NAFTA's Lessons for Hemispheric
Trade. Trade Paper. MIT Press. Cambridge, MA. 2002. 398p.
ISBN:0-262-54138-6, ISBN13: 978-0-262-54138-1.
Dewey:333.7. LCCN:2002-022921.

Audience: **u,f.** *Choice, 2003.*

Dessler, Andrew E. &   **QC981.8.C5**
  Parson, Edward A.
The Science and Politics of Global Climate Change: A Guide to
the Debate. Trade Paper. Cambridge University Press. New
York, NY. 2006. 200p. ISBN:0-521-53941-2, ISBN13:
978-0-521-53941-8. Dewey:363.73874. LCCN:2006-296170.

Audience: **g,l,u,f.**

Fascione, Nina (Editor),   **QL737.C2P36 2004**
  et al.
People and Predators: From Conflict to Coexistence. Aimee
Delach & Martin E. Smith (Editors). Trade Cloth. Island Press.
Washington, DC. 2004. 304p. ISBN:1-55963-083-3, ISBN13:
978-1-55963-083-2. Dewey:639.97/97. LCCN:2004-004597.

Audience: **g,l,u,f.**

Garrett, Laurie   **RA651**
The Coming Plague: Newly Emerging Diseases in a World Out
of Balance. Trade Paper. Penguin Group (USA) Inc. New York,
NY. 1995. 768p. ISBN:0-14-025091-3, ISBN13:
978-0-14-025091-6. Dewey:614.4.

Audience: **g,l.** *Choice, 1995.*

Hartemann, Frederic &   **GB500.5.H37 2005**
  Hauptman, Robert
The Mountain Encyclopedia: An A-Z Compendium of over
2,250 Terms, Concepts, Ideas, and People. Trade Cloth.
Scarecrow Press, Inc. Lanham, MD. 2005. 432p.

ISBN:0-8108-5056-7, ISBN13: 978-0-8108-5056-9.
Dewey:551.43/2/03. LCCN:2004-008539.

Audience: **g,l.** *Choice, 2005.*

Hayden, Corinne P.   **QK99.M498H38 2003**
When Nature Goes Public: The Making and Unmaking of
Bioprospecting in Mexico. Trade Cloth. Princeton University
Press. Princeton, NJ. 2003. 312p. In-Formation Ser.
ISBN:0-691-09556-6, ISBN13: 978-0-691-09556-1.
Dewey:333.95/3. LCCN:2003-043339.

Audience: **u,f.**

Hays, Samuel P.   **S930.H38 1999**
Conservation and the Gospel of Efficiency: The Progressive
Conservation Movement, 1890-1920. Trade Paper. University of
Pittsburgh Press. Pittsburgh, PA. 1999. 292p.
ISBN:0-8229-5702-7, ISBN13: 978-0-8229-5702-7.
Dewey:333.7/2/0973. LCCN:98-054700.

Audience: **g,l,u,f.** ℬ

Herschy, R. W. &   **GB655**
  Fairbridge, R. W. (Editors)
Encyclopedia of Hydrology and Water Resources. Mixed Media.
Springer. New York, NY. 2006. 832p. ISBN:1-4020-4867-X,
ISBN13: 978-1-4020-4867-8. Dewey:551.48/03.

Audience: **g,l,u.**

Higgs, Eric S.   **QH541.15.R45H54 2003**
Nature by Design: People, Natural Process, and Ecological
Restoration. Trade Cloth. MIT Press. Cambridge, MA. 2003.
357p. ISBN:0-262-08316-7, ISBN13: 978-0-262-08316-4.
Dewey:333.7153. LCCN:2002-040783.

Audience: **g,l,u,f.** *Choice, 2004.*

Hoffman, David J.   **RA1226.H36 2002**
Handbook of Ecotoxicology. Ed. 2. Paper over Boards. Lewis
Publishers. Boca Raton, FL. 2002. 1312p. ISBN:1-56670-546-0,
ISBN13: 978-1-56670-546-2. Dewey:615.9/02.
LCCN:2002-075228.

Audience: **u,f.** *Choice, 1995.*

Honey, Martha   **G156.5.E26H66 1999**
Ecotourism and Sustainable Development: Who Owns Paradise?
Trade Paper. Island Press. Washington, DC. 1998. 416p.
ISBN:1-55963-582-7, ISBN13: 978-1-55963-582-0.
Dewey:338.4/791. LCCN:98-048342.

Audience: **g,l,u,f.** *Choice, 1999.*

Jordan, William R.   **QH541.15.R45 J67**
The Sunflower Forest: Ecological Restoration and the New
Communion with Nature. Trade Cloth. University of California
Press. Berkeley, CA. 2003. 270p. ISBN:0-520-23320-4, ISBN13:
978-0-520-23320-1. Dewey:333.95/153. LCCN:2002-005538.

Audience: **g,l,u.** *Choice, 2004.*

Kay, Robert & Alder,   **HT391.K36 2003**
  Jackie
Coastal Planning and Management. Ed. 2. Paper over Boards.
Routledge. New York, NY. 2005. 400p. ISBN:0-415-31772-X,
ISBN13: 978-0-415-31772-6. Dewey:333.91/7.
LCCN:2004-014309.

Audience: **u,f.**

Long, John L.   **QL703.L66 2004**
Introduced Mammals of the World: Their History, Distribution
and Influence. Cloth Text. Oxford University Press, Inc. New
York, NY. 2004. 612p. CABI Publishing Ser.

ISBN:0-85199-736-8, ISBN13: 978-0-85199-736-0.
Dewey:599.16. LCCN:2003-051673.
Audience: **g,l,u,f.** *Choice, 2004.*

Lott, Dale F.   **QL737.U53**
American Bison: A Natural History. Harry W. Greene (Prologue by). Trade Paper. University of California Press. Berkeley, CA. 2003. 245p. Organisms and Environments Ser. ISBN:0-520-24062-6, ISBN13: 978-0-520-24062-9. Dewey:599.64/3. LCCN:2002-000243.
Audience: **g,l.** *Choice, 2003.*

Matthews, John A.   **GE149**
  (Editor)
The Encyclopaedic Dictionary of Environmental Change. Trade Paper. Oxford University Press, Inc. New York, NY. 2003. 704p. A Hodder Arnold Publication ISBN:0-340-80976-0, ISBN13: 978-0-340-80976-1. Dewey:333.7/03.
Audience: **g,l,u,f.**

McGraw-Hill   **QH302.5.M378 2004**
McGraw-Hill Concise Encyclopedia of Bioscience. Trade Paper. McGraw-Hill Professional Publishing. New York, NY. 2005. 972p. ISBN:0-07-143956-0, ISBN13: 978-0-07-143956-5. Dewey:570/.3. LCCN:2004-049947.
Audience: **g,l.** *Choice, 2005.*

Merchant, Carolyn   **QH540.5.M48 2005**
Radical Ecology: The Search for a Livable World. Ed. 2. Trade Paper. Routledge. New York, NY. 2005. 304p. Revolutionary Thought/Radical Movements Ser. ISBN:0-415-93577-6, ISBN13: 978-0-415-93577-7. Dewey:304.2. LCCN:2005-009520.
Audience: **g,l,u,f.** *Choice, 1993.*

Newton, David E.   **GB655**
Encyclopedia of Water. Cloth Text. Greenwood Publishing Group, Inc. Portsmouth, NH. 2003. 424p. ISBN:1-57356-304-8, ISBN13: 978-1-57356-304-8. Dewey:553.7/03. LCCN:2002-070031.
Audience: **g,l.** *Choice, 2003.*

Nottingham, Stephen   **QH442.6.N684 2002**
Genescapes: The Ecology of Genetic Engineering. Trade Paper. Zed Books, Ltd. London, 2002. 224p. ISBN:1-84277-037-3, ISBN13: 978-1-84277-037-5. Dewey:660.6/5. LCCN:2001-057365.
Audience: **g,l,u.** *Choice, 2003, 2002.*

Nuttall, Mark (Editor)   **G606**
Encyclopedia of the Arctic. Ed. 3. Cloth Text. Routledge. New York, NY. 2004. 2380p. ISBN:1-57958-436-5, ISBN13: 978-1-57958-436-8. Dewey:909/.0913/03. LCCN:2004-016694.
Audience: **g,l,u,f.** *Choice, 2005.*

Nybakken, James   **GC9.I58 2002**
  Willard (Editor), et al.
Interdisciplinary Encyclopedia of Marine Sciences. William W. Broenkow & T. L. Vallier (Editors). Trade Cloth. Scholastic Library Publishing. Danbury, CT. 2002. 1425p. ISBN:0-7172-5946-3, ISBN13: 978-0-7172-5946-5. Dewey:551.46/003. LCCN:2002-192707.
Audience: **g,l,u.** *Choice, 2003.*

Oliver, John E. (Editor)   **QC854**
The Encyclopedia of World Climatology. Mixed Media. Springer. New York, NY. 2006. 20p. ISBN:1-4020-4870-X, ISBN13: 978-1-4020-4870-8. Dewey:551.603.
Audience: **g,l,u,f.** *Choice, 2006.*

Perrow, Martin R. &   **QH541.15.R45H36 2002**
  Davy, Anthony J. (Editors)
Handbook of Ecological Restoration: Restoration in Practice, Vol. 2. Trade Cloth. Cambridge University Press. New York, NY. 2002. 618p. ISBN:0-521-79129-4, ISBN13: 978-0-521-79129-8. Dewey:333.95/153. LCCN:2001-043443.
Audience: **g,l,u.** *Choice, 2003.*

Pyne, Stephen J.   **SD421.3.P96 1997**
Fire in America: A Cultural History of Wildland and Rural Fire. Trade Paper. University of Washington Press. Seattle, WA. 1997. 680p. Weyerhaeuser Environmental Bks. ISBN:0-295-97592-X, ISBN13: 978-0-295-97592-4. Dewey:304.2. LCCN:96-049191.
Audience: **g,l,u,f.** *B*

Salyers, Abigail A. &   **QR177.S26 2005**
  Whitt, Dixie D.
Revenge of the Microbes: How Bacterial Resistance Is Undermining the Antibiotic Miracle. Trade Paper, Perfect. ASM Press. Washington, DC. 2005. 194p. ISBN:1-55581-298-8, ISBN13: 978-1-55581-298-0. Dewey:616.9201061. LCCN:2005-002847.
Audience: **g,l,u.** *Choice, 2005.*

Schwartz, M. (Editor)   **GB451.2**
Encyclopedia of Coastal Science. Mixed Media. Springer. New York, NY. 2006. XXXV, 1211p. ISBN:1-4020-4871-8, ISBN13: 978-1-4020-4871-5. Dewey:551.45/7.
Audience: **g,l,u,f.** *Choice, 2006.*

Soule, David C. (Editor)   **HT384**
Urban Sprawl: A Comprehensive Reference Guide. Cloth Text. Greenwood Publishing Group, Inc. Portsmouth, NH. 2005. 592p. ISBN:0-313-32038-1, ISBN13: 978-0-313-32038-5. Dewey:307.76/0973. LCCN:2005-019208.
Audience: **g,l,u,f.**

Turner, Jack   **F767.T3**
Teewinot: Climbing and Contemplating the Teton Range. Trade Paper. St. Martin's Press. Gordonville, VA. 2001. 272p. ISBN:0-312-28446-2, ISBN13: 978-0-312-28446-6. Dewey:508.7/8755.
Audience: **g,l,u,f.**

Westley, Frances R. &   **QL82.E86 2003**
  Miller, Philip S. (Editors)
Experiments in Consilience: Integrating Science and Social Process to Save Endangered Species. Trade Cloth. Island Press. Washington, DC. 2003. 328p. ISBN:1-55963-993-8, ISBN13: 978-1-55963-993-4. Dewey:333.95/22. LCCN:2003-007224.
Audience: **g,l,u,f.** *Choice, 2004.*

Whitney, Gordon G.   **GF503 .W53 1994**
From Coastal Wilderness to Fruited Plain: A History of Environmental Change in Temperate North America from 1500 to the Present. Trade Paper. Cambridge University Press. New York, NY. 1996. 485p. ISBN:0-521-57658-X, ISBN13: 978-0-521-57658-1. Dewey:3337.7/3/13/0973. LCCN:93-029701.
Audience: **g,l.** *Choice, 1995.*

Reference Works

                                                    HA202.S73 2004
Statistical Abstract of the United States: The National Data Book, 2004-2005. Ed. 124. Trade Cloth. Bernan Associates.

Lanham, MD. 2005. 1024p. ISBN:1-886222-23-1, ISBN13: 978-1-886222-23-6. Dewey:317.3.

Audience: **g,l,u,f.**

American Geological   **QE5.A48 1984**
Institute Staff
Dictionary of Geological Terms. Ed. 3. UK-Trade Paper. Doubleday Publishing. New York, NY. 1984. 576p. ISBN:0-385-18101-9, ISBN13: 978-0-385-18101-3. Dewey:550.3. LCCN:82-045315.

Audience: **g,l,u,f.**

Bailey, Ronald (Editor)   **GE140.E59 2000**
Earth Report 2000. Ed. 1. Book, Other. McGraw-Hill Trade. New York, NY. 1999. 400p. ISBN:0-07-134260-5, ISBN13: 978-0-07-134260-5. Dewey:363.7. LCCN:99-053268.

Audience: **g,l,u,f.**

Barry, John &   **GE170.I55 2001**
Frankland, E. Gene (Editors)
International Encyclopedia of Environmental Politics. Paper over Boards. Routledge. New York, NY. 2001. 544p. ISBN:0-415-20285-X, ISBN13: 978-0-415-20285-5. Dewey:363.7/056. LCCN:2001-019754.

Audience: **g,l,f.** *Choice, 2002.*

Becher, Anne   **GE55.B43 2000**
@ American Environmental Leaders: From Colonial Times to the Present. E-Book. ABC-CLIO, Inc. Santa Barbara, CA. 2001. ISBN:1-57607-385-8, ISBN13: 978-1-57607-385-8. Dewey:363.7/0092/273 B.

Audience: **g,l,u,f.** *Choice, 2001.*

Becher, Anne   **QH541.15.B56.B435**
@ Biodiversity: A Reference Handbook. Mildred Vasan (Editor). E-Book. ABC-CLIO, Inc. Santa Barbara, CA. 1999. Contemporary World Issues Ser. ISBN:0-585-05817-2, ISBN13: 978-0-585-05817-7. Dewey:333.95.

Audience: **g,l.** *Choice, 1998.*

Bekoff, Marc (Editor)   **QL750**
Encyclopedia of Animal Behavior. Jane Goodall (Foreword by). Cloth Text. Greenwood Publishing Group, Inc. Portsmouth, NH. 2004. 1424p. ISBN:0-313-32745-9, ISBN13: 978-0-313-32745-2. Dewey:591.5/03. LCCN:2004-056073.

Audience: **g,l,u,f.** *Choice, 2005.*

Canarache, A., et al.   **S592**
Elsevier's Dictionary of Soil Science: Definitions in English with French, German, and Spanish Word Translations. I. I. Vintila & I. Munteanu (Authors). Trade Cloth. Elsevier Science & Technology Books. Saint Louis, MO. 2006. 1355p. ISBN:0-444-82478-2, ISBN13: 978-0-444-82478-3. Dewey:631.403.

Audience: **l,u,f.**

Clark, John O. E. &   **QE5.F318 2006**
Stiegeler, Stella E.
The Facts on File Dictionary of Earth Science. Ed. 2. Trade Cloth. Facts On File, Inc. New York, NY. 2006. 400p. ISBN:0-8160-6000-2, ISBN13: 978-0-8160-6000-9. Dewey:550.3. LCCN:2006-042340.

Audience: **g,l.** *Choice, 2001.*

Daintith, John   **QD5.F33 2005**
Facts on File Dictionary of Chemistry. Ed. 4. Trade Cloth. Facts On File, Inc. New York, NY. 2005. 320p. Science Dictionary Ser. ISBN:0-8160-5649-8, ISBN13: 978-0-8160-5649-1. Dewey:540/.3. LCCN:2005-043785.

Audience: **g,l.**

D'Aleo, Joseph S.   **GC296**
The Oryx Resource Guide to el Nino and la Nina. Cloth Text. Greenwood Publishing Group, Inc. Portsmouth, NH. 2002. 248p. ISBN:1-57356-378-1, ISBN13: 978-1-57356-378-9. Dewey:551.6. LCCN:2001-050030.

Audience: **g,l.** *Choice, 2002.*

De Kerchove, Rene   **V23.K4**
International Maritime Dictionary. Ed. 2. Trade Cloth. French & European Publications, Inc. New York, NY. 1993. 1018p. ISBN:0-8288-0429-X, ISBN13: 978-0-8288-0429-5. Dewey:355/.0213. LCCN:92-013463.

Audience: **g,l.**

Gale Research Staff   **QL7.G7813 2004**
Grzimek's Animal Life Encyclopedia, Set. Ed. 2. Trade Cloth. Thomson Gale. Farmington Hills, MI. 2002. 9000p. ISBN:0-7876-5362-4, ISBN13: 978-0-7876-5362-0. Dewey:590/.3. LCCN:2002-003351.

Audience: **g,l,u,f.** *Choice, 2004, 2003.*

Geist, Helmut   **GF90.O87 2006**
Our Earth's Changing Land: An Encyclopedia of Land-Use and Land-Cover Change. Trade Cloth. Greenwood Publishing Group, Inc. Portsmouth, NH. 2005. xlviii, 715p. ISBN:0-313-32784-X, ISBN13: 978-0-313-32784-1. Dewey:333.7. LCCN:2005-019212.

Audience: **g,l,f.** *Choice, 2006.*

Geological Survey   **TN13**
(USGS) Staff
Minerals Yearbook, Area Reports: Domestic 2003. Perfect. United States Government Printing Office. Washington, DC. 2005. 388p. ISBN:0-16-072511-9, ISBN13: 978-0-16-072511-1. Dewey:338.2.

Audience: **l,u,f.**

Goldfarb, Theodore D.   **GE105.S67**
(Editor)
Sources: Notable Selections in Environmental Studies. Trade Cloth. McGraw-Hill Higher Education. Burr Ridge, IL. 1997. ISBN:0-697-33010-9, ISBN13: 978-0-697-33010-9. Dewey:363.7.

Audience: **l,u,f.**

Goldstein, Inge F. &   **RA566.27.G65 2002**
Goldstein, Martin
How Much Risk?: A Guide to Understanding Environmental Health Hazards. Trade Cloth. Oxford University Press, Inc. New York, NY. 2002. 352p. ISBN:0-19-513994-1, ISBN13: 978-0-19-513994-5. Dewey:615.9/02. LCCN:2001-021985.

Audience: **l,u,f.** *Choice, 2002.*

Goryshkina, T.   **QH540.6**
Terminological Dictionary of Ecology, Geobotany and Pedology. Trade Cloth. Collets. 1988. 248p. ISBN:0-7855-6482-9, ISBN13: 978-0-7855-6482-9. Dewey:574.503.

Audience: **g,l,u.**

Hildebrand, Sharon   **T55.3.H3**
(Editor)
NIOSH Pocket Guide to Chemical Hazards. Paper Text. DIANE

Publishing Company. Collingdale, PA. 2001. 500p.
ISBN:0-7567-0921-0, ISBN13: 978-0-7567-0921-1. Dewey:624.
Audience: g,l,u,f.

Kollin, Susan   **PS283.A4K65 2001**
Nature's State: Imagining Alaska As the Last Frontier. Trade
Cloth. University of North Carolina Press. Chapel Hill, NC.
2001. 248p. Cultural Studies of the United States
ISBN:0-8078-2645-6, ISBN13: 978-0-8078-2645-4.
Dewey:810.9/32798. LCCN:2001-027414.
Audience: l,u,f. *Choice, 2002.*

Little, Charles E. &   **TD9.A84 2001**
Ashworth, William
Encyclopedia of Environmental Studies. Ed. 2. Trade Cloth.
Facts On File, Inc. New York, NY. 2001. 608p. The Facts on
File Science Library ISBN:0-8160-4255-1, ISBN13:
978-0-8160-4255-5. Dewey:333.7/03. LCCN:00-051379.
Audience: l,u,f. *Choice, 2002.*

Matthews, John A.   **GE149**
(Editor)
The Encyclopaedic Dictionary of Environmental Change. Trade
Paper. Oxford University Press, Inc. New York, NY. 2003. 704p.
A Hodder Arnold Publication ISBN:0-340-80976-0, ISBN13:
978-0-340-80976-1. Dewey:333.7/03.
Audience: g,l,u,f.

McGraw-Hill Staff   **QE5**
Dictionary of Geology and Mineralogy. Ed. 2. Trade Paper.
McGraw-Hill Professional Publishing. New York, NY. 2003.
420p. ISBN:0-07-141044-9, ISBN13: 978-0-07-141044-1.
Dewey:550/.3. LCCN:2002-033173.
Audience: g,l,u,f. *Choice, 2003.*

Merchant, Carolyn   **GF501.M47 2005**
The Columbia Guide to American Environmental History. Trade
Paper, Perfect. Columbia University Press. New York, NY. 2005.
400p. ISBN:0-231-11233-5, ISBN13: 978-0-231-11233-8.
Dewey:304.2.
Audience: l,u,f. *Choice, 2002.*

Mirovitskaya, Natalia &   **HC79.E5G85 2001**
Ascher, William L. (Editors)
Guide to Sustainable Development and Environmental Policy.
Trade Cloth. Duke University Press. Durham, NC. 2002. 400p.
ISBN:0-8223-2735-X, ISBN13: 978-0-8223-2735-6.
Dewey:338.9/27. LCCN:2001-033688.
Audience: g,l,u,f. *Choice, 2002.*

Mittermeier, Russell A.,   **QH75.H675 2004**
et al.
Hotspots Revisited: Earth's Biologically Richest and Most
Endangered Terrestrial Ecoregions. Patricio Robles Gil, John
Pilgrim, Cristina Goettsch Mittermeier, Thomas Brooks, Michael
Hoffman, Gustavo A. B. da Fonseca & John Lamoreux
(Authors), Peter A. Seligmann (Preface by), Harrison Ford
(Foreword by). Trade Cloth. Conservation International.
Washington, DC. 2005. 392p. ISBN:968-6397-77-9, ISBN13:
978-968-6397-77-2. Dewey:577.
Audience: g,l,u,f. *Choice, 2006.*

Munn, Ted (Editor)   **GE149.E443 2002**
Encyclopedia of Global Environmental Change: A CBT
Workbook for Young People. Trade Cloth. John Wiley & Sons,
Inc. Hoboken, NJ. 2002. 3440p. ISBN:0-471-97796-9, ISBN13:
978-0-471-97796-4. Dewey:363.7/003. LCCN:2001-046740.
Audience: g,l,u,f. *Choice, 2003.*

National Wildlife   **S920.N3**
Federation Staff
Conservation Directory: The Guide to Worldwide Environmental
Organizations. Library Binding. Sagebrush Education Resources.
Caledonia, MN. 2003. ISBN:0-613-91697-2, ISBN13:
978-0-613-91697-4. Dewey:333.72.
Audience: g,l,u,f.

O'Neil, Maryadele J.   **RS51.M4 2001**
(Editor), et al.
The Merck Index: An Encyclopedia of Chemicals, Drugs, and
Biologicals. Ed. 13. Susan Budavari & Patricia Heckelman
(Editors), Ann Smith (Associate Editor). Trade Cloth. John
Wiley & Sons, Inc. Hoboken, NJ. 2001. 1741p.
ISBN:0-911910-13-1, ISBN13: 978-0-911910-13-1.
Dewey:615/.1/03. LCCN:2003-267062.
Audience: l,u,f.

Pohanish, Richard P. &   **T55.3.H3P647 2003**
Greene, Stanley A.
[e] Wiley Guide to Chemical Incompatibilities. Ed. 2. E-Book.
John Wiley & Sons, Inc. Hoboken, NJ. 2005.
ISBN:0-471-72162-X, ISBN13: 978-0-471-72162-8.
Dewey:660/.2804.
Audience: l,u,f.

Sigurdsson, Haraldur, et   **QE522.E53 2000**
al.
Encyclopedia of Volcanoes. Bruce Houghton, Steve McNutt,
Hazel Rymer & John Stix (Authors), Robert D. Ballard
(Foreword by). Trade Cloth. Elsevier Science & Technology
Books. Saint Louis, MO. 1999. 1417p. ISBN:0-12-643140-X,
ISBN13: 978-0-12-643140-7. Dewey:551.21/03.
LCCN:99-062781.
Audience: l,u,f. *Choice, 2000.*

Sittig, Marshall   **RA1215.S58 2002**
Handbook of Toxic and Hazardous Chemicals and Carcinogens.
Ed. 4. Richard P. Pohanish (Editor). Trade Cloth. Noyes Data
Corporation/Noyes Publications. Park Ridge, NJ. 2002. 2300p.
ISBN:0-8155-1459-X, ISBN13: 978-0-8155-1459-6.
Dewey:615.9/02. LCCN:2001-056289.
Audience: u,f. *Choice, 2003, 2002.*

Staudinger, Jeff   **TD171.S734 2002**
The Environmental Guidebook: A Selective Reference Guide to
Environmental Organizations and Related Entities. Perfect.
Environmental Frontlines. Menlo Pk., CA. 2002. 312p.
ISBN:0-9720685-0-3, ISBN13: 978-0-9720685-0-5.
Dewey:363.7. LCCN:2002-106011.
Audience: l,u,f. *Choice, 2003.*

Stein, Bruce A. (Editor),   **QH76.P69 2000**
et al.
Precious Heritage: The Status of Biodiversity in the United
States. Lynn S. Kutner & Jonathan S. Adams (Editors). Trade
Cloth. Oxford University Press, Inc. New York, NY. 2000. 426p.
ISBN:0-19-512519-3, ISBN13: 978-0-19-512519-1.
Dewey:333.95/16/0973. LCCN:99-030213.
Audience: g,l,u,f. *Choice, 2000.*

Vickers, Amy   **TD388.V53 2001**
Handbook of Water Use and Conservation: Homes, Landscapes,
Businesses, Industries, Farms. Trade Cloth. WaterPlow Press.
Amherst, MA. 2001. 460p. ISBN:1-931579-07-5, ISBN13:
978-1-931579-07-0. Dewey:333.91/16. LCCN:99-025179.
Audience: l,u,f. *Choice, 2001.*

Formats: Web: 🖵 Ebook: [e] CD/DVD-ROM: 🕮 BCL3: *B*

Weber, E.   **SB613.5**
Invasive Plant Species of the World: A Reference Guide to
Environmental Weeds. CAB International Staff (Contribution
by). Cloth Text. Oxford University Press, Inc. New York, NY.
2003. 560p. CABI Publishing Ser. ISBN:0-85199-695-7,
ISBN13: 978-0-85199-695-0. Dewey:632/.5.
LCCN:2003-010034.
     Audience: **g,l,u,f.** *Choice, 2004.*

Literature

Adamson, Joni   **PS153.I52A33 2001**
American Indian Literature, Environmental Justice, and
Ecocriticism: The Middle Place. Trade Cloth. University of
Arizona Press. Tucson, AZ. 2000. 213p. ISBN:0-8165-1791-6,
ISBN13: 978-0-8165-1791-6. Dewey:810.9/355.
LCCN:00-010360.
     Audience: **g,l,u,f.** *Choice, 2001.*

Adamson, Joni (Editor),   **GE220.E585 2002**
et al.
The Environmental Justice Reader Politics, Poetics, and
Pedagogy. Mei Mei Evans & Rachel Stein (Editors). Trade
Cloth. University of Arizona Press. Tucson, AZ. 2002. 385p.
ISBN:0-8165-2206-5, ISBN13: 978-0-8165-2206-4.
Dewey:363.7. LCCN:2002-003308.
     Audience: **l,f.** *Choice, 2003.*

Allister, Mark   **PS366.A88A4 2001**
Christopher
Refiguring the Map of Sorrow: Nature Writing and
Autobiography. Trade Cloth. University Press of Virginia.
Charlottesville, VA. 2001. viii, 199p. Under the Sign of Nature
Ser. ISBN:0-8139-2064-7, ISBN13: 978-0-8139-2064-1.
Dewey:818/.5409492. LCCN:2001-023547.
     Audience: **g,l,u,f.** *Choice, 2002.*

Berger, John   **PR6019.O9**
Pig Earth. Trade Paper. Knopf Publishing Group. New York,
NY. 1992. 208p. ISBN:0-679-73715-4, ISBN13:
978-0-679-73715-5. Dewey:823/.9/1. LCCN:92-050074.
     Audience: **g,l,f.**

Bryson, Michael A.   **PS169.E25B79 2002**
Visions of the Land: Science, Literature and the American
Environment from the Era of Exploration to the Age of Ecology.
Trade Cloth. University Press of Virginia. Charlottesville, VA.
2002. 240p. Under the Sign of Nature Ser. ISBN:0-8139-2106-6,
ISBN13: 978-0-8139-2106-8. Dewey:810.9/355.
LCCN:2001-007122.
     Audience: **g,l,f.** *Choice, 2003.*

Buell, Lawrence   **PS169.E25B84 2001**
Writing for an Endangered World: Literature, Culture, and
Environment in the U. S. and Beyond. Trade Cloth. Harvard
University Press. Cambridge, MA. 2001. 384p.
ISBN:0-674-00449-3, ISBN13: 978-0-674-00449-8.
Dewey:810.9/355. LCCN:00-049796.
     Audience: **g,l,f.** *Choice, 2001.*

Cassuto, David N.   **PS277.C37 2001**
Dripping Dry: Literature, Politics and Water in the Desert
Southwest. Trade Paper. University of Michigan Press. Chicago,
IL. 2001. 224p. Studies in Literature and Science
ISBN:0-472-06756-7, ISBN13: 978-0-472-06756-5.
Dewey:810.9/358. LCCN:00-010715.
     Audience: **g,l,f.** *Choice, 2002.*

Conlogue, William   **PS228.A52C66 2001**
Working the Garden: American Writers and the Industrialization
of Agriculture. Trade Cloth. University of North Carolina Press.
Chapel Hill, NC. 2002. 230p. Studies in Rural Culture
ISBN:0-8078-2668-5, ISBN13: 978-0-8078-2668-3.
Dewey:810.9/321734. LCCN:2001-027914.
     Audience: **g,l,f.** *Choice, 2002.*

Crawford, Rachel   **PR555.L27C73 2002**
Poetry, Enclosure, and the Vernacular Landscape, 1700-1830.
Trade Cloth. Cambridge University Press. New York, NY. 2002.
332p. ISBN:0-521-81531-2, ISBN13: 978-0-521-81531-4.
Dewey:821/.50932. LCCN:2002-067659.
     Audience: **g,l,f.** *Choice, 2003.*

Dorman, Robert L.   **GE55.D67 1998**
A Word for Nature: Four Pioneering Environmental Advocates,
1845-1913. Trade Cloth. University of North Carolina Press.
Chapel Hill, NC. 1998. 272p. ISBN:0-8078-2396-1, ISBN13:
978-0-8078-2396-5. Dewey:[B]. LCCN:97-023896.
     Audience: **g,l.** *Choice, 1998.*

Garrard, Greg   **PR143.G37 2004**
Ecocriticism. Paper over Boards. Routledge. New York, NY.
2004. 224p. New Critical Idiom Ser. ISBN:0-415-19691-4,
ISBN13: 978-0-415-19691-8. Dewey:820.9/36.
LCCN:2004-003429.
     Audience: **u,f.**

Kocks, Dorothee E.   **PS374.L28K63 2000**
Dream a Little: Land and Social Justice in Modern America.
Trade Paper. University of California Press. Berkeley, CA. 2000.
276p. ISBN:0-520-22280-6, ISBN13: 978-0-520-22280-9.
Dewey:813/.520932. LCCN:99-056435.
     Audience: **g,l,f.** *Choice, 2001.*

McKusick, James C.   **PR590**
Green Writing: Romanticism and Ecology. Cloth over Boards.
Palgrave Macmillan. New York, NY. 2000. 272p.
ISBN:0-312-23448-1, ISBN13: 978-0-312-23448-5.
Dewey:821.7/09.
     Audience: **l,u,f.** *Choice, 2001.*

Muir, John   **QH31.M9A3 1997**
John Muir: Nature Writings: The Story of My Boyhood and
Youth; My First Summer in the Sierra; The Mountains of
California; Stickeen; Essays. William Cronon (Editor). Trade
Cloth. Library of America, The. New York, NY. 1997. 928p.
Library of America ISBN:1-883011-24-8, ISBN13:
978-1-883011-24-6. Dewey:[B]. LCCN:96-009664.
     Audience: **g,l,u,f.**

Nicholsen, Shierry   **GF21.N53 2001**
Weber
The Love of Nature and the End of the World: The Unspoken
Dimensions of Environmental Concern. Trade Cloth. MIT Press.
Cambridge, MA. 2001. 226p. ISBN:0-262-14076-4, ISBN13:
978-0-262-14076-8. Dewey:179/.1. LCCN:2001-044329.
     Audience: **g,l,f.** *Choice, 2002.*

Quinn, Daniel   **PS3567.U338**
Ishmael: An Adventure of the Mind and Spirit. Library Binding.
Sagebrush Education Resources. Caledonia, MN. 1995.
ISBN:0-613-08093-9, ISBN13: 978-0-613-08093-4.
Dewey:813/.54.
     Audience: **g,l,f.**

Scheese, Don   SD421.375.S34 2001
Mountains of Memory: A Fire Lookout's Life in the River of
No Return Wilderness. Wayne Franklin (Contribution by). Trade
Cloth. University of Iowa Press. Iowa City, IA. 2001. 262p.
American Land and Life Ser. ISBN:0-87745-783-2, ISBN13:
978-0-87745-783-1. Dewey:634.9/3. LCCN:2001-033292.
                              Audience: **g,l,u,f.** *Choice, 2002.*

Schneider, Richard J.   PS3057.N3T46 2000
   (Editor)
Thoreau's Sense of Place: Essays in American Environmental
Writing. Lawrence Buell (Foreword by). Trade Cloth. University
of Iowa Press. Iowa City, IA. 2000. 324p. American Land and
Life Ser. ISBN:0-87745-708-5, ISBN13: 978-0-87745-708-4.
Dewey:818/.309. LCCN:99-058112.
                              Audience: **u,f.** *Choice, 2000.*

Sweet, Timothy   PS169.E25S94 2001
American Georgics: Economy and Environment in American
Literature, 1580-1864. Book, Other. University of Pennsylvania
Press. Philadelphia, PA. 2001. 232p. ISBN:0-8122-3637-8,
ISBN13: 978-0-8122-3637-8. Dewey:810.9/355.
LCCN:2001-037029.
                              Audience: **l,u,f.** *Choice, 2002.*

Tournier, Michel   PQ2680.O83V413 1997
Friday. Norman Denny (Translator). Trade Paper. Johns Hopkins
University Press. Baltimore, MD. 1997. 240p.
ISBN:0-8018-5592-6, ISBN13: 978-0-8018-5592-4.
Dewey:843/.914. LCCN:96-045295.
                              Audience: **g,l,u,f.**

Williams, Raymond   PR409.C5
   (Contribution by)
The Country and the City. Trade Cloth. Oxford University Press,
Inc. New York, NY. 1972. 335p. ISBN:0-19-519736-4, ISBN13:
978-0-19-519736-5. Dewey:820.9/32. LCCN:72-098128.
                              Audience: **l,u,f.** *B*

Zakin, Susan   HC110.E5
Coyotes and Town Dogs: Earth First! and the Environmental
Movement. Library Binding. Sagebrush Education Resources.
Caledonia, MN. 2002. ISBN:0-613-91795-2, ISBN13:
978-0-613-91795-7. Dewey:363.7/057/0973.
                              Audience: **g,l,u,f.**

Philosophy and Religion

Ashworth, William   GF21.A84 1999
The Left Hand of Eden: Meditations on Nature and Human
Nature. Trade Cloth. Oregon State University Press. Corvallis,
OR. 1999. 208p. ISBN:0-87071-460-0, ISBN13:
978-0-87071-460-3. Dewey:304.2. LCCN:98-054935.
                              Audience: **g,l,u,f.**

Barnhill, David Landis   GE195.D437 2001
   & Gottlieb, Roger S. (Editors)
Deep Ecology and World Religions: New Essays on Sacred
Ground. Paper Text. State University of New York Press.
Albany, NY. 2001. xiii, 291p. Suny Series, Radical Social and
Political Theory Ser. ISBN:0-7914-4884-3, ISBN13:
978-0-7914-4884-7. Dewey:179.1. LCCN:00-030081.
                              Audience: **g,l,u,f.** *Choice, 2001.*

Botkin, Daniel B.   QH31.T485B68 2001
No Man's Garden: Thoreau and a New Vision for Civilization
and Nature. Trade Cloth. Island Press. Washington, DC. 2000.

288p. ISBN:1-55963-465-0, ISBN13: 978-1-55963-465-6.
Dewey:304.2. LCCN:00-010445.
                              Audience: **g,l,u,f.** *Choice, 2001.*

Brooke, John Hedley   BL245 .B77 1991
   (Editor)
Science and Religion: Some Historical Perspectives. George
Basalla & Owen Hannaway (Contribution by). Trade Paper.
Cambridge University Press. New York, NY. 1991. 434p.
Cambridge History of Science Ser. ISBN:0-521-28374-4,
ISBN13: 978-0-521-28374-8. Dewey:291.1/75.
LCCN:90-048909.
                              Audience: **l,u,f.** *Choice, 1992.*

Capra, Fritjof   QH501.C375
Web of Life: A New Understanding of Living Systems. Library
Binding. Sagebrush Education Resources. Caledonia, MN. 1997.
ISBN:0-613-91162-8, ISBN13: 978-0-613-91162-7.
Dewey:574/.01.
                              Audience: **g,l,f.**

Cohen, Carl & Regan,   HV4711.C63 2001
   Tom
The Animal Rights Debate. Book, Other. Rowman & Littlefield
Publishers, Inc. Lanham, MD. 1955. 336p. Point - Counterpoint
Ser. ISBN:0-8476-9663-4, ISBN13: 978-0-8476-9663-5.
Dewey:179/.3. LCCN:00-069044.
                              Audience: **g,l,u,f.** *Choice, 2002.*

Harrod, Howard L.   E78.G73H353 2000
The Animals Came Dancing: Native American Sacred Ecology
and Animal Kinship. Trade Cloth. University of Arizona Press.
Tucson, AZ. 2000. 220p. ISBN:0-8165-2026-7, ISBN13:
978-0-8165-2026-8. Dewey:799.2978. LCCN:99-006771.
                              Audience: **g,l,u,f.** *Choice, 2000.*

Hessel, Dieter T.   BT695.5 .A37 1992
   (Editor)
After Nature's Revolt: Eco-Justice and Theology. Trade Paper.
Augsburg Fortress, Publishers. Minneapolis, MN. 1992. 240p.
ISBN:0-8006-2532-3, ISBN13: 978-0-8006-2532-0.
Dewey:261.8/3628. LCCN:91-044441.
                              Audience: **l,u,f.**

Kohak, Erazim V.   GE42.K64813 2000
Green Halo: A Bird's-Eye View of Ecological Ethics. Trade
Paper. Open Court Publishing Company. Chicago, IL. 1999.
256p. ISBN:0-8126-9411-2, ISBN13: 978-0-8126-9411-6.
Dewey:179/.1. LCCN:99-038665.
                              Audience: **g,l,f.** *Choice, 2000.*

Leopold, Aldo   QH81.L56 2001
A Sand County Almanac. Michael Sewell (Photographer),
Kenneth Brower (Introduction by). Trade Cloth. Oxford
University Press, Inc. New York, NY. 2001. 192p.
ISBN:0-19-514617-4, ISBN13: 978-0-19-514617-2.
Dewey:508.73. LCCN:2001-034038.
                              Audience: **g,l,u,f.**

MacIntyre, Alasdair   BJ1012
Dependent Rational Animals: Why Human Beings Need the
Virtues. Trade Paper. Cricket Books. Chicago, IL. 2001. 180p.
ISBN:0-8126-9452-X, ISBN13: 978-0-8126-9452-9. Dewey:170.
                              Audience: **l,u,f.** *Choice, 2000.*

Meyer, John M.   JA75.8.M49 2001
Political Nature: Environmentalism and the Interpretation of
Western Thought. Trade Cloth. MIT Press. Cambridge, MA.

2001. 224p. ISBN:0-262-13390-3, ISBN13: 978-0-262-13390-6. Dewey:320.5. LCCN:2001-030459.

Audience: **l,u,f.** *Choice, 2002.*

Minteer, Ben A.   **GE197.M57 2006**
The Landscape of Reform: Civic Pragmatism and Environmental Thought in America. Trade Cloth. MIT Press. Cambridge, MA. 2006. 272p. ISBN:0-262-13461-6, ISBN13: 978-0-262-13461-3. Dewey:333.72. LCCN:2005-053428.

Audience: **u,f.**

Nash, Roderick   **GE42**
The Rights of Nature: A History of Environmental Ethics. Trade Paper. University of Wisconsin Press. Chicago, IL. 1989. 304p. History of American Thought and Culture Ser. ISBN:0-299-11844-4, ISBN13: 978-0-299-11844-0. Dewey:179/.1. LCCN:88-017169.

Audience: **u,f.** *Choice, 1989.*

Nash, Roderick   **E169.1**
Wilderness and the American Mind. Ed. 4. Trade Paper. Yale University Press. Cumberland, RI. 2001. 432p. ISBN:0-300-09122-2, ISBN13: 978-0-300-09122-9. Dewey:333.78/2/0973.

Audience: **u,f.** *B*

Pimentel, David   **QH541.15.E245E36**
 (Editor), et al.
Ecological Integrity: Integrating Environment, Conservation and Health. Laura Westra & Reed F. Noss (Editors). Trade Cloth. Island Press. Washington, DC. 2000. 400p. ISBN:1-55963-807-9, ISBN13: 978-1-55963-807-4. Dewey:304.2. LCCN:00-008255.

Audience: **l,u,f.** *Choice, 2001.*

Postel, Sandra   **S618.P67 1999**
Pillar of Sand: Can the Irrigation Miracle Last? Trade Paper. W. W. Norton & Company, Inc. New York, NY. 1999. xv, 313p. ISBN:0-393-31937-7, ISBN13: 978-0-393-31937-8. Dewey:333.91/3. LCCN:00-501134.

Audience: **g,l,u,f.** *Choice, 2000.*

Singer, Peter (Editor)   **HV4711.I6 2005**
In Defense of Animals: The Second Wave. Ed. 2. Trade Cloth. Blackwell Publishing, Inc. Malden, MA. 2005. 264p. ISBN:1-4051-1940-3, ISBN13: 978-1-4051-1940-5. Dewey:179/.3. LCCN:2005-009479.

Audience: **g,l,u,f.**

Thompson, Paul B. &   **B832.A34 2000**
 Hilde, Thomas C. (Editors)
Agrarian Roots of Pragmatism. Trade Cloth. Vanderbilt University Press. Nashville, TN. 2000. ix, 342p. Vanderbilt Library of American Philosophy ISBN:0-8265-1339-5, ISBN13: 978-0-8265-1339-7. Dewey:144/.3/0973. LCCN:00-008775.

Audience: **u,f.** *Choice, 2001.*

Wenz, Peter S.   **GE42.W458 2001**
Environmental Ethics Today. Paper Text. Oxford University Press, Inc. New York, NY. 2000. 368p. ISBN:0-19-513384-6, ISBN13: 978-0-19-513384-4. Dewey:179/.1. LCCN:00-058895.

Audience: **l,u,f.** *Choice, 2001.*

Science and Technology

                    TD427.P4C665
Coping with an Oiled Sea: An Analysis of Oil Spill Response Technologies. Paper Text. DIANE Publishing Company. Collingdale, PA. 1994. 70p. ISBN:0-7881-0416-0, ISBN13: 978-0-7881-0416-9. Dewey:363.73/82/0973.

Audience: **u,f.**

Charbeneau, Randall J.   **TD426**
Groundwater Hydraulics and Pollutant Transport. Trade Cloth. Simon & Schuster. New York, NY. 2000. ISBN:0-13-016612-X, ISBN13: 978-0-13-016612-8. Dewey:628.1/68.

Audience: **u,f.** *Choice, 2000.*

Collman, James P.   **TX531.C58 2000**
Naturally Dangerous: Surprising Facts about Food, Health and the Environment. Trade Cloth. University Science Books. Sausalito, CA. 2001. 280p. ISBN:1-891389-09-2, ISBN13: 978-1-891389-09-2. Dewey:363.19/26. LCCN:00-049743.

Audience: **g,l.** *Choice, 2002.*

Dick, Warren A. &   **S596.7.S87 2001**
 Hatfield, Jerry L. (Editors)
Sustaining Soil Fertility in West Africa. Trade Paper. ASA-CSSA-SSSA. Madison, WI. 2001. 321p. Special Publications, No. 58 ISBN:0-89118-838-X, ISBN13: 978-0-89118-838-4. Dewey:631.4/22/0966. LCCN:2001-132918.

Audience: **l,u,f.** *Choice, 2002.*

Douglas, Scott L.   **TC223.D68 2002**
Saving America's Beaches: The Causes of and Solutions to Beach Erosion. Trade Paper. World Scientific Publishing Company, Inc. Hackensack, NJ. 2002. 104p. Advanced Series on Ocean Engineering, Vol. 19 ISBN:981-238-097-3, ISBN13: 978-981-238-097-5. Dewey:333.91/716/0973. LCCN:2002-726737.

Audience: **u,f.**

Lecomte, Paul   **TD878**
Polluted Sites: Remediation of Soils and Groundwater. Paper over Boards. Taylor & Francis Group. Abingdon, 1999. 220p. ISBN:90-5410-784-7, ISBN13: 978-90-5410-784-2. Dewey:628.5.

Audience: **u,f.** *Choice, 2000.*

Mosley, Stephen R.   **TD884.M67 2001**
The Chimney of the World: A History of Smoke Pollution in Victorian and Edwardian Manchester. Trade Cloth. White Horse Press. Cambridge, 2001. 250p. ISBN:1-874267-49-9, ISBN13: 978-1-874267-49-2. Dewey:363.7392094273309034. LCCN:2004-351051.

Audience: **g,l,u,f.** *Choice, 2002.*

Smith, A. C. (Editor)   **TK9152.17.T73 2004**
Transportation, Storage, and Disposal of Radioactive Materials. Trade Paper. American Society of Mechanical Engineers. Fairfield, NJ. 2004. 227p. ISBN:0-7918-4678-4, ISBN13: 978-0-7918-4678-0. Dewey:604.7. LCCN:2004-302152.

Audience: **u,f.**

Sterrett, Frances   **TD195.E49A44 1995**
 (Editor)
Alternative Fuels and the Environment. Paper over Boards.

Lewis Publishers. Boca Raton, FL. 1994. 288p.
ISBN:0-87371-978-6, ISBN13: 978-0-87371-978-0.
Dewey:621.042. LCCN:94-025419.

Audience: **l,u,f.** *Choice, 1995.*

Webb, R. H. &   **QH545.A43.E58 1983**
  Wilshire, H. G. (Editors)
Environmental Effects of Off-Road Vehicles: Impact and
Management in Arid Regions. Cloth Text. Springer. New York,
NY. 1983. 534p. Environmental Management Ser.
ISBN:0-387-90737-8, ISBN13: 978-0-387-90737-6.
Dewey:574.5/222. LCCN:82-010479.

Audience: **l,u,f.** ℬ

Wilson, Arthur   **TN15**
The Living Rock: The Story of Metals since Earliest Time and
Their Impact on Civilization. Trade Paper. Woodhead
Publishing, Ltd. Cambridge, 1996. 272p. ISBN:1-85573-301-3,
ISBN13: 978-1-85573-301-5. Dewey:622.34.

Audience: **l,u,f.**

Science and Technology > Biological Sciences and Ecology

Abell, Robin A., et al.   **QH77.N56F69 2000**
Freshwater Ecoregions of North America: A Conservation
Assessment. David M. Olson, Eric Dinerstein, Patrick T. Hurley,
James T. Diggs, William Eichbaum, Steven Walters, Wesley
Wettengel, Tom Allnutt, Colby J. Loucks & Prashant Hedao
(Authors). Trade Paper. Island Press. Washington, DC. 1999.
368p. ISBN:1-55963-734-X, ISBN13: 978-1-55963-734-3.
Dewey:577.6. LCCN:99-016796.

Audience: **g,l,u,f.** *Choice, 2000.*

Agrawal, Shashi B. &   **QK750.E58 2000**
  Agrawal, Madhoolika
Environmental Pollution and Plant Responses. Saddle Stitched.
Lewis Publishers. Boca Raton, FL. 1999. 408p.
ISBN:1-56670-341-7, ISBN13: 978-1-56670-341-3.
Dewey:581.7. LCCN:99-026504.

Audience: **l,u,f.** *Choice, 2000.*

Barbour, Michael G. &   **QK110 .N854 2000**
  Billings, William Dwight (Editors)
North American Terrestrial Vegetation. Ed. 2. Trade Paper.
Cambridge University Press. New York, NY. 1999. 720p.
ISBN:0-521-55986-3, ISBN13: 978-0-521-55986-7.
Dewey:581.7/22/097. LCCN:97-029061.

Audience: **l,u,f.** *Choice, 2000, 1988.*

Begon, Michael, et al.   **QH352.B43 1996**
Population Ecology: A Unified Study of Animals and Plants. Ed.
3. Martin Mortimer & D. J. Thompson (Authors). Trade Paper.
Blackwell Publishing, Inc. Malden, MA. 1996. 256p.
ISBN:0-632-03478-5, ISBN13: 978-0-632-03478-9.
Dewey:574.5/248. LCCN:95-023676.

Audience: **l,u,f.**

Bekoff, Marc (Editor)   **QL750**
Encyclopedia of Animal Behavior. Jane Goodall (Foreword by).
Cloth Text. Greenwood Publishing Group, Inc. Portsmouth, NH.
2004. 1424p. ISBN:0-313-32745-9, ISBN13:
978-0-313-32745-2. Dewey:591.5/03. LCCN:2004-056073.

Audience: **g,l,u,f.** *Choice, 2005.*

Blount   **GF49**
Environmental Anthropology: A Reader. Trade Cloth. Pearson
Custom Publishing. Boston, MA. 1997. 464p.
ISBN:0-536-00253-3, ISBN13: 978-0-536-00253-2.
Dewey:304.2.

Audience: **g,l.**

Carle, David &   **SD421**
  Kaufmann, Je
Burning Questions: America's Fight with Nature's Fire. Trade
Cloth. Greenwood Publishing Group, Inc. Portsmouth, NH.
2002. 312p. ISBN:0-275-97371-9, ISBN13: 978-0-275-97371-1.
Dewey:634.9/618/0973. LCCN:2001-059061.

Audience: **u,f.** *Choice, 2003, 2002.*

Carson, Rachel   **QH545**
Silent Spring. Ed. 40. Dust Jacket. Houghton Mifflin Company
Trade & Reference Division. Boston, MA. 2002. 400p.
ISBN:0-618-25305-X, ISBN13: 978-0-618-25305-0.
Dewey:363.738/4. LCCN:2002-726803.

Audience: **g,l,u,f.** ℬ

Centner, Terence J.   **S441.C45 2004**
Empty Pastures: Confined Animals and the Transformation of
the Rural Landscape. Trade Cloth. University of Illinois Press.
Champaign, IL. 2004. 208p. ISBN:0-252-02895-3, ISBN13:
978-0-252-02895-3. Dewey:636/.00973. LCCN:2003-012760.

Audience: **g,l,f.** *Choice, 2004.*

Clark, Timothy W.   **QL737.C25**
  (Editor)
Averting Extinction: Reconstructing Endangered Species
Recovery. Trade Paper. Yale University Press. Cumberland, RI.
2005. 288p. ISBN:0-300-11333-1, ISBN13: 978-0-300-11333-4.
Dewey:333.95/976629.

Audience: **u,f.** *Choice, 1997.*

Cokinos, Christopher   **QL676.8**
Hope Is the Thing with Feathers: A Personal Chronicle of
Vanished Birds. Trade Cloth. DIANE Publishing Company.
Collingdale, PA. 2000. 359p. ISBN:0-7567-6165-4, ISBN13:
978-0-7567-6165-3. Dewey:598.168/097.

Audience: **g,l.**

Cox, Donald D.   **QK115.C72 2002**
A Naturalist's Guide to Wetland Plants: An Ecology for Eastern
North America. Shirley A. Peron (Illustrator). Trade Paper.
Syracuse University Press. Syracuse, NY. 2002. 168p.
ISBN:0-8156-0740-7, ISBN13: 978-0-8156-0740-3.
Dewey:581.7/68/0974. LCCN:2002-004522.

Audience: **g,l,u,f.** *Choice, 2003.*

Cronk, Julie K. &   **QK938.M3C76 2001**
  Fennessy, M. Siobhan
Wetland Plants: Biology and Ecology. Paper over Boards. Lewis
Publishers. Boca Raton, FL. 2001. 488p. ISBN:1-56670-372-7,
ISBN13: 978-1-56670-372-7. Dewey:581.7/68.
LCCN:2001-020390.

Audience: **u,f.** *Choice, 2002.*

Cronk, Quentin C. B. &   **QK86.A1**
  Fuller, Janice L.
Plant Invaders: The Threat to Natural Ecosystems. Trade Paper.
Earthscan/James & James. London, 2001. 255p. People and
Plants Conservation Manual Ser. ISBN:1-85383-781-4, ISBN13:
978-1-85383-781-4. Dewey:639.9/9.

Audience: **l,u,f.** *Choice, 2002.*

Crosby, Alfred W.   **RA644.I6C76 2003**
America's Forgotten Pandemic: The Influenza of 1918. Ed. 2.
Cloth Text. Cambridge University Press. New York, NY. 2003.
352p. ISBN:0-521-83394-9, ISBN13: 978-0-521-83394-3.
Dewey:614.5/18/0973. LCCN:2003-053176.
Audience: **g,l,u,f.** *Choice, 2004.*

Darwin, Charles   **QH365.O2 2003**
The Origin of Species and the Voyage of the Beagle. Richard
Dawkins (Introduction by). Trade Cloth. Knopf Publishing
Group. New York, NY. 2003. 1024p. ISBN:1-4000-4127-9,
ISBN13: 978-1-4000-4127-5. Dewey:576.8/2.
LCCN:2003-049220.
Audience: **g,l,u,f.**

Elton, Charles S.   **QH541.E4 2000**
The Ecology of Invasions by Animals and Plants. Trade Paper.
University of Chicago Press. Chicago, IL. 2000. 186p.
ISBN:0-226-20638-6, ISBN13: 978-0-226-20638-7.
Dewey:577/.18. LCCN:99-052582.
Audience: **l,u,f.** **B** *Choice, 2000.*

Elton, Charles S.   **QH541.E398 2001**
Animal Ecology. Mathew A. Leibold & J. Timothy Wootton
(Introduction by). Trade Paper. University of Chicago Press.
Chicago, IL. 2001. 296p. ISBN:0-226-20639-4, ISBN13:
978-0-226-20639-4. Dewey:591.7. LCCN:00-069087.
Audience: **l,u,f.** **B** *Choice, 2001.*

Fimbel, Robert A.   **QL109.C66 2001**
  (Editor), et al.
The Cutting Edge: Conserving Wildlife in Logged Tropical
Forests. Alejandro Grajal & John G. Robinson (Editors). Trade
Cloth. Columbia University Press. New York, NY. 2001. 700p.
Biology and Resource Management Ser. ISBN:0-231-11454-0,
ISBN13: 978-0-231-11454-7. Dewey:333.95/416/0913.
LCCN:00-031782.
Audience: **l,u,f.** *Choice, 2002.*

Gale Research Staff   **QL7.G7813 2004**
Grzimek's Animal Life Encyclopedia, Set. Ed. 2. Trade Cloth.
Thomson Gale. Farmington Hills, MI. 2002. 9000p.
ISBN:0-7876-5362-4, ISBN13: 978-0-7876-5362-0.
Dewey:590/.3. LCCN:2002-003351.
Audience: **g,l,u,f.** *Choice, 2004, 2003.*

Goble, Dale D. (Editor),   **KF5640.E482 2005**
  et al.
The Endangered Species Act at Thirty: Renewing the
Conservation Promise. J. Michael Scott & Frank W. Davis
(Editors). Trade Cloth. Island Press. Washington, DC. 2005.
432p. ISBN:1-59726-008-8, ISBN13: 978-1-59726-008-4.
Dewey:346.7304/69522. LCCN:2005-026419.
Audience: **g,l,f.**

Gore, Albert   **GE170.G67 2000**
Earth in the Balance: Ecology and the Human Spirit. Trade
Cloth. Houghton Mifflin Company Trade & Reference Division.
Boston, MA. 2000. 416p. ISBN:0-618-05664-5, ISBN13:
978-0-618-05664-4. Dewey:363.7. LCCN:00-038311.
Audience: **l,u,f.**

Gosling, L. Morris &   **QH75 .B45 2000**
  Sutherland, William J. (Editors)
Behaviour and Conservation. Guy Cowlishaw, John L.
Gittleman, Rosie Woodroffe & Michael J. Samways
(Contribution by). Trade Paper. Cambridge University Press.
New York, NY. 2000. 450p. Conservation Biology Ser., No. 2

ISBN:0-521-66539-6, ISBN13: 978-0-521-66539-1.
Dewey:333.95/16. LCCN:99-026461.
Audience: **l,u,f.** *Choice, 2000.*

Graeub, Ralph   **RA596**
The Petkau Effect: The Devastating Effect of Nuclear Radiation
on Human Health and the Environment. Ernest J. Sternglass
(Introduction by). Trade Paper. Avalon Publishing Group. New
York, NY. 1994. 250p. ISBN:1-56858-019-3, ISBN13:
978-1-56858-019-7. Dewey:574.19/15. LCCN:91-026809.
Audience: **u,f.**

Griffin, Donald R.   **QL751.5**
Animal Minds. Trade Paper. University of Chicago Press.
Chicago, IL. 1994. 320p. ISBN:0-226-30864-2, ISBN13:
978-0-226-30864-7. Dewey:591.51. LCCN:92-006538.
Audience: **u,f.** *Choice, 1993.*

Ingegnoli, V.   **QH541.5.L35**
Landscape Ecology - A Widening Foundation: A Holistic
Unifying Approach. R. F. F. Forman (Preface by). Trade Cloth.
Springer. New York, NY. 2004. xxiiiI,357p.
ISBN:3-540-42743-0, ISBN13: 978-3-540-42743-8. Dewey:577.
LCCN:2003-275803.
Audience: **l,u,f.** *Choice, 2003.*

Jackson, Jerome A.   **QL696.P56J24 2004**
In Search of the Ivory-Billed Woodpecker. Trade Paper.
Smithsonian Institution Press. Washington, DC. 2004. 256p.
ISBN:1-58834-132-1, ISBN13: 978-1-58834-132-7.
Dewey:598.7/2. LCCN:2004-040944.
Audience: **g,l,u,f.**

John H. Heinz III   **QH104.S73 2002**
  Center for Science, Economics and the Environment
The State of the Nation's Ecosystems: Measuring the Lands,
Waters, and Living Resources of the United States. Trade Paper.
Cambridge University Press. New York, NY. 2002. 288p.
ISBN:0-521-52572-1, ISBN13: 978-0-521-52572-5.
Dewey:333.7/2. LCCN:2002-073890.
Audience: **l,u,f.** *Choice, 2003.*

Kurlansky, Mark   **PN6071.C66K87 1997**
Cod: A Biography of the Fish That Changed the World. Cloth
over Boards. Walker & Company. New York, NY. 1997. 304p.
ISBN:0-8027-1326-2, ISBN13: 978-0-8027-1326-1.
Dewey:333.9/56633. LCCN:97-012165.
Audience: **g,l,u,f.** *Choice, 1997.*

Linder, Greg (Editor),   **QL669.2.M85 2003**
  et al.
Multiple Stressor Effects in Relation to Declining Amphibian
Populations. Sherry Krest, D. W. Sparling & E. E. Little
(Editors), ASTM International Staff (Contribution by). Trade
Cloth. American Society for Testing & Materials. West
Conshohocken, PA. 2003. 292p. STP Ser., Vol. 1443
ISBN:0-8031-3464-9, ISBN13: 978-0-8031-3464-5.
Dewey:571.9/5178. LCCN:2003-045244.
Audience: **u,f.**

Lomborg, Bjorn   **GE149.L65 2001**
The Skeptical Environmentalist: Measuring the Real State of the
World. Cloth Text. Cambridge University Press. New York, NY.
2001. 540p. ISBN:0-521-80447-7, ISBN13: 978-0-521-80447-9.
Dewey:363.7. LCCN:00-068915.
Audience: **l,u,f.** *Choice, 2002.*

Mitchell, Alanna   **GF75.M58 2005**
Dancing at the Dead Sea: Tracking the World's Environmental Hot Spots. Trade Cloth. University of Chicago Press. Chicago, IL. 2005. 239p. ISBN:0-226-53200-3, ISBN13: 978-0-226-53200-4. Dewey:304.2/8. LCCN:2004-062123.
Audience: **g,l,u,f.**

Mittermeier, Russell A.,   **QH75.H675 2004**
et al.
Hotspots Revisited: Earth's Biologically Richest and Most Endangered Terrestrial Ecoregions. Patricio Robles Gil, John Pilgrim, Cristina Goettsch Mittermeier, Thomas Brooks, Michael Hoffman, Gustavo A. B. da Fonseca & John Lamoreux (Authors), Peter A. Seligmann (Preface by), Harrison Ford (Foreword by). Trade Cloth. Conservation International. Washington, DC. 2005. 392p. ISBN:968-6397-77-9, ISBN13: 978-968-6397-77-2. Dewey:577.
Audience: **g,l,u,f.** *Choice, 2006.*

Mooney, Harold A. &   **QH353.I59 2000**
Hobbs, Richard J. (Editors)
Invasive Species in a Changing World. Trade Paper. Island Press. Washington, DC. 2000. 384p. ISBN:1-55963-782-X, ISBN13: 978-1-55963-782-4. Dewey:577/.18. LCCN:00-008791.
Audience: **g,l,u,f.** *Choice, 2001.*

Oliveira, Paulo S. &   **QH117.C52 2002**
Marquis, Robert J.
The Cerrados of Brazil: Ecology and Natural History of a Neotropical Savanna. Trade Cloth. Columbia University Press. New York, NY. 2002. 424p. ISBN:0-231-12042-7, ISBN13: 978-0-231-12042-5. Dewey:577.4/8/0981. LCCN:2002-022739.
Audience: **l,u,f.** *Choice, 2003.*

Paddle, Robert   **QL737.M388P34 2002**
The Last Tasmanian Tiger: The History and Extinction of the Thylacine. Trade Paper. Cambridge University Press. New York, NY. 2002. 284p. ISBN:0-521-53154-3, ISBN13: 978-0-521-53154-2. Dewey:599.2/7.
Audience: **g,l,u,f.** *Choice, 2001.*

Pluschke, Peter (Editor)   **TD883.17**
Indoor Air Pollution. Mixed Media. Springer. New York, NY. 2004. xi, 270p. The Handbook of Environmental Chemistry Ser., Vol. 4:Air Pollution, Part F ISBN:3-540-21098-9, ISBN13: 978-3-540-21098-6. Dewey:363.7/392. LCCN:2004-104243.
Audience: **l,u,f.** *Choice, 2005.*

Riley, Glenda   **GE55.R55 1999**
Women and Nature: Saving the "Wild" West. Trade Cloth. University of Nebraska Press. Lincoln, NE. 1999. 368p. Women in the West Ser. ISBN:0-8032-3932-7, ISBN13: 978-0-8032-3932-6. Dewey:333.7/2/0820973. LCCN:98-035168.
Audience: **l,u,f.** *Choice, 1999.*

Satterfield, Terre   **SD387.O43S28 2003**
Anatomy of a Conflict: Identity, Knowledge, and Emotion in Old-Growth Forests. Trade Cloth. University of British Columbia Press. Vancouver, BC. 2003. x,198p. ISBN:0-7748-0892-6, ISBN13: 978-0-7748-0892-7. Dewey:333.75/16/09795. LCCN:2002-004897.
Audience: **l,u,f.** *Choice, 2003.*

Scott, J. Michael   **KF5640**
(Editor), et al.
The Endangered Species Act at Thirty: Conserving Biodiversity in Human-Dominated Landscapes. Dale D. Goble & Frank W. Davis (Editors). Trade Cloth. Island Press. Washington, DC.

2006. 450p. ISBN:1-59726-054-1, ISBN13: 978-1-59726-054-1. Dewey:346.7304/69522.
Audience: **l,u,f.**

Snyder, Noel F. &   **QL696.F33S69 2000**
Snyder, Helen
The California Condor: A Saga of Natural History and Conservation. Trade Cloth. Princeton University Press. Princeton, NJ. 2000. 432p. ISBN:0-12-654005-5, ISBN13: 978-0-12-654005-5. Dewey:598.9/2. LCCN:2002-319406.
Audience: **g,l,u,f.** *Choice, 2000.*

Stein, Bruce A. (Editor),   **QH76.P69 2000**
et al.
Precious Heritage: The Status of Biodiversity in the United States. Lynn S. Kutner & Jonathan S. Adams (Editors). Trade Cloth. Oxford University Press, Inc. New York, NY. 2000. 426p. ISBN:0-19-512519-3, ISBN13: 978-0-19-512519-1. Dewey:333.95/16/0973. LCCN:99-030213.
Audience: **g,l,u,f.** *Choice, 2000.*

Sunquist, Mel &   **QL737.C23S863 2002**
Sunquist, Fiona
Wild Cats of the World. Trade Cloth. University of Chicago Press. Chicago, IL. 2002. 462p. ISBN:0-226-77999-8, ISBN13: 978-0-226-77999-7. Dewey:599.75. LCCN:2001-052771.
Audience: **g,l,u,f.** *Choice, 2003.*

Todd, Kim   **QL86.T64 2001**
Tinkering with Eden: A Natural History of Exotics in America. Trade Cloth. W. W. Norton & Company, Inc. New York, NY. 2001. 288p. ISBN:0-393-04860-8, ISBN13: 978-0-393-04860-5. Dewey:591.6. LCCN:00-058740.
Audience: **g,l,u,f.** *Choice, 2001.*

Tomback, Diana F.   **QK494.5.P66W55 2001**
(Editor), et al.
Whitebark Pine Communities: Ecology and Restoration. Stephen F. Arno & Robert E. Keane (Editors). Trade Cloth. Island Press. Washington, DC. 2001. 328p. ISBN:1-55963-717-X, ISBN13: 978-1-55963-717-6. Dewey:585/.2. LCCN:00-011161.
Audience: **u,f.** *Choice, 2001.*

Wardle, David A.   **QH541.5.S6W37 2002**
Communities and Ecosystems: Linking the Aboveground and Belowground Components. Trade Cloth. Princeton University Press. Princeton, NJ. 2002. 400p. Monographs in Population Biology, Vol. 34 ISBN:0-691-07486-0, ISBN13: 978-0-691-07486-3. Dewey:577.5/7. LCCN:2001-055403.
Audience: **u,f.** *Choice, 2003.*

Weidensaul, Scott   **QL82.W45 2002**
The Ghost with Trembling Wings: Science, Wishful Thinking, and the Search for Lost Species. Cloth over Boards. Farrar, Straus & Giroux. New York, NY. 2002. 352p. ISBN:0-374-24664-5, ISBN13: 978-0-374-24664-8. Dewey:591.68. LCCN:2001-054605.
Audience: **g,l,u,f.** *Choice, 2003.*

Wilson, Edward O.   **QH75.W535 2002**
The Future of Life. Trade Cloth. Alfred A. Knopf Inc. New York, NY. 2002. 256p. ISBN:0-679-45078-5, ISBN13: 978-0-679-45078-8. Dewey:333.95/22. LCCN:2001-038316.
Audience: **g,l,u,f.** *Choice, 2002.*

Wolfe, David   **QH541.5.S6**
Tales from the Underground: A Natural History of Subterranean Life. Trade Paper. Perseus Books Group. New York, NY. 2002.

240p. ISBN:0-7382-0679-2, ISBN13: 978-0-7382-0679-0. Dewey:577.5/7.

Audience: **g,l,u,f.**

Science and Technology > General Science

American Geological   **QE5.A48 1984**
Institute Staff
Dictionary of Geological Terms. Ed. 3. UK-Trade Paper. Doubleday Publishing. New York, NY. 1984. 576p. ISBN:0-385-18101-9, ISBN13: 978-0-385-18101-3. Dewey:550.3. LCCN:82-045315.

Audience: **g,l,u,f.**

Bailey, Robert G.   **QH541.15.L35B35 2002**
Ecoregion-Based Design for Sustainability. L. Ropes (Drawings by). Trade Cloth. Springer. New York, NY. 2002. xiiiI,222p. ISBN:0-387-95429-5, ISBN13: 978-0-387-95429-5. Dewey:577. LCCN:2001-059796.

Audience: **l,u,f.** *Choice, 2003.*

Ballard, Robert D.   **GC65**
The Eternal Darkness: A Personal History of Deep-Sea Exploration. Trade Paper. Princeton University Press. Princeton, NJ. 2002. 400p. ISBN:0-691-09554-X, ISBN13: 978-0-691-09554-7. Dewey:551.46/07.09.

Audience: **g,l,u,f.** *Choice, 2000.*

Bates, Marston   **QH541.B3**
The Forest and the Sea: A Look at the Economy of Nature and the Ecology of Man. Paper Text. Textbook Publishers. Temecula, CA. 2003. 277p. ISBN:0-7581-4992-1, ISBN13: 978-0-7581-4992-3. Dewey:574.5.

Audience: **g,l,u,f.** *B*

Bohlen, Janet   **QH26.B63 1993**
Trowbridge
For the Wild Places: Profiles in Conservation. Al Gore (Foreword by). Trade Cloth. Island Press. Washington, DC. 1993. 228p. ISBN:1-55963-125-2, ISBN13: 978-1-55963-125-9. Dewey:333.95/16/0922. LCCN:92-038118.

Audience: **g,l,u,f.** *Choice, 1993.*

Bowen, Mark   **QC879.59.B69 2005**
Thin Ice: Unlocking the Secrets of Climate in the World's Highest Mountains. Saddle Stitched, Cloth over Boards, Dust Jacket. Henry Holt & Company. New York, NY. 2005. 320p. ISBN:0-8050-6443-5, ISBN13: 978-0-8050-6443-8. Dewey:551.51/4/072. LCCN:2005-040426.

Audience: **g,l,u,f.**

Bradstock, Ross A.   **QH197.F563 2002**
(Editor), et al.
Flammable Australia: The Fire Regimes and Biodiversity of a Continent. Jann E. Williams & Malcolm A. Gill (Editors). Trade Cloth. Cambridge University Press. New York, NY. 2001. 472p. ISBN:0-521-80591-0, ISBN13: 978-0-521-80591-9. Dewey:577.2. LCCN:2001-025479.

Audience: **u,f.** *Choice, 2002.*

Callenbach, Ernest   **QH541.13.C65 1998**
Ecology: A Pocket Guide. Trade Paper. University of California Press. Berkeley, CA. 1998. 168p. ISBN:0-520-21463-3, ISBN13: 978-0-520-21463-7. Dewey:577. LCCN:98-004728.

Audience: **g,l.**

Cousteau, Jacques &   **GC65.C68 2004**
Dumas, Frederic
The Silent World. UK-Trade Paper. National Geographic Society. Washington, DC. 2004. 220p. National Geographic Adventure Classics Ser. ISBN:0-7922-6796-6, ISBN13: 978-0-7922-6796-6. Dewey:551.46. LCCN:2004-044995.

Audience: **g,l,f.**

Dugan, Patrick (Editor)   **QH541.5.M3 2005**
Guide to Wetlands: A Comprehensive and Fascinating Guide to the Wetlands of the World. Trade Paper. Firefly Books, Ltd. Tonawanda, NY. 2005. 304p. Firefly Pocket Reference Ser. ISBN:1-55407-111-9, ISBN13: 978-1-55407-111-1. Dewey:578.768. LCCN:2006-276145.

Audience: **g,l.** *Choice, 2006.*

Ehrlich, Gretel   **G465.E46 2004**
The Future of Ice: A Journey into the Cold. Trade Cloth. Knopf Publishing Group. New York, NY. 2004. 224p. ISBN:0-375-42251-X, ISBN13: 978-0-375-42251-5. Dewey:818/.5403. LCCN:2004-044666.

Audience: **g,l,u,f.**

Gelbspan, Ross   **QC981.8.G56G45 1998**
The Heat Is On: The Climate Crisis, the Cover-Up, the Prescription. Trade Paper. Basic Books. New York, NY. 1998. 288p. ISBN:0-7382-0025-5, ISBN13: 978-0-7382-0025-5. Dewey:363.738/74. LCCN:98-086419.

Audience: **g,l,f.** *Choice, 1999.*

Gleick, Peter H.   **TD345**
The World's Water 2004-2005: The Biennial Report on Freshwater Resources. Trade Paper. Island Press. Washington, DC. 2004. 362p. ISBN:1-55963-536-3, ISBN13: 978-1-55963-536-3. Dewey:333.9/1.

Audience: **g,l,u,f.**

Graham, Frank Jr.   **QL671.G7 1992**
The Audubon Ark: A History of the National Audubon Society. Trade Paper. University of Texas Press. Austin, TX. 1992. 350p. ISBN:0-292-70440-2, ISBN13: 978-0-292-70440-4. Dewey:598/.06073. LCCN:91-043864.

Audience: **g,l,f.**

Jenny, Hans   **S592.2.J455 1994**
Factors of Soil Formation: A System of Quantitative Pedology. Trade Paper. Dover Publications, Inc. Mineola, NY. 1994. 288p. ISBN:0-486-68128-9, ISBN13: 978-0-486-68128-3. Dewey:551.3/05. LCCN:94-017606.

Audience: **u,f.**

Lamb, Hubert   **QC943.5.N75 L35 1991**
Historic Storms of the North Sea, British Isles and Northwest Europe. Knud Frydendahl (As told to). Trade Paper. Cambridge University Press. New York, NY. 2005. 224p. ISBN:0-521-61931-9, ISBN13: 978-0-521-61931-8. Dewey:551.55/0941. LCCN:2005-280543.

Audience: **l,u,f.**

Love, Rosaleen   **QH197.L68 2001**
Reefscape: Reflections on the Great Barrier Reef. Trade Cloth. National Academies Press. Washington, DC. 2001. v, 255p. ISBN:0-309-07260-3, ISBN13: 978-0-309-07260-1. Dewey:508.943. LCCN:2001-024281.

Audience: **g,l,u,f.** *Choice, 2001.*

Audience: g=general, l=lower division undergraduate, u=upper division undergraduate, f=faculty.

293

Maupin, Molly A. &   **TD493.M38 2005**
Barber, Nancy L.
Estimated Withdrawals from Principal Aquifers in the United
States, 2000. Trade Cloth. United States Geological Survey.
Denver, CO. 2005. v, 46p. U.S. Geological Survey Circular Ser.,
Vol. 1279 ISBN:0-607-96780-3, ISBN13: 978-0-607-96780-7.
Dewey:333.91/0413/0973. LCCN:2005-049174.
Audience: **l,u,f.**

Miller, Raymond W. &   **S591.M733**
Gardiner, Duane T.
Soils in Our Environment. Ed. 11. Cloth Text. Prentice Hall
PTR. Upper Saddle River, NJ. 2006. 750p.
ISBN:0-13-219104-0, ISBN13: 978-0-13-219104-3.
Dewey:631.4.
Audience: **u,f.**

Niamir-Fuller, Maryam   **GB618.82**
Managing Mobility in African Rangelands: The Legitimization
of Transhumance. Trade Paper. Intermediate Technology
Publications (ITDG). Rugby, 1999. 240p. ISBN:1-85339-473-4,
ISBN13: 978-1-85339-473-7. Dewey:333.7/36/096.
LCCN:00-303617.
Audience: **u,f.**

Page, Jake & Officer,   **QB631.O34 1994**
Charles B.
Tales of the Earth: Paroxysms and Perturbations of the Blue
Planet. Paper Text. Oxford University Press, Inc. New York, NY.
1994. 240p. ISBN:0-19-509048-9, ISBN13: 978-0-19-509048-2.
Dewey:550.
Audience: **g,l,u,f.** *Choice, 1994.*

Pence, Gregory E.   **TP248.65.F66P46 2002**
Designer Food: Mutant Harvest or Breadbasket of the World?
Trade Cloth. Rowman & Littlefield Publishers, Inc. Lanham,
MD. 2002. 256p. ISBN:0-7425-0839-0, ISBN13:
978-0-7425-0839-2. Dewey:363.19/29. LCCN:2001-041926.
Audience: **g,l,u,f.** *Choice, 2002.*

Pimm, Stuart L.   **GE140.P56 2001**
The World According to Pimm: A Scientist Audits the Earth.
Trade Cloth. McGraw-Hill Companies, The. New York, NY.
2001. 304p. ISBN:0-07-137490-6, ISBN13: 978-0-07-137490-3.
Dewey:333.7/2. LCCN:2001-030229.
Audience: **g,l,u,f.** *Choice, 2002.*

Powell, John Wesley   **HD1671.U5P68 2004**
The Arid Lands. Wallace Stegner (Editor), John Vernon
(Foreword by). Trade Cloth. University of Nebraska Press.
Lincoln, NE. 2005. 230p. ISBN:0-8032-8781-X, ISBN13:
978-0-8032-8781-5. Dewey:333.73/0978. LCCN:2004-015894.
Audience: **g,l,u,f.**

Seddon, George   **QH45.2.S434 1998**
Landprints: Reflections on Place and Landscape. Gustav J. V.
Nossal (Foreword by). Trade Cloth. Cambridge University Press.
New York, NY. 1997. 272p. ISBN:0-521-58501-5, ISBN13:
978-0-521-58501-9. Dewey:508. LCCN:97-027550.
Audience: **g,l,u,f.**

Ward, Peter D.   **QE721.2.E97W38 2000**
Rivers in Time: The Search for Clues to Earth's Mass
Extinctions. Trade Cloth. Columbia University Press. New York,
NY. 2000. 320p. ISBN:0-231-11862-7, ISBN13:
978-0-231-11862-0. Dewey:576.8/4. LCCN:00-056954.
Audience: **g,l,u,f.** *Choice, 2001.*

Science and Technology > Chemistry and Related Subjects

Andersen, Tom   **GC1212.N7A53 2002**
This Fine Piece of Water: An Environmental History of Long
Island Sound. Cloth over Boards. Yale University Press.
Cumberland, RI. 2002. 272p. ISBN:0-300-08250-9, ISBN13:
978-0-300-08250-0. Dewey:363.739/4/0916346.
LCCN:2001-006401.
Audience: **g,l,u,f.** *Choice, 2003, 2002.*

Drake, Frances   **QC981.8.G56D73 2000**
Global Warming: The Science of Climate Change. Cloth Text.
Oxford University Press, Inc. New York, NY. 2000. 288p. An
Arnold Publication Ser. ISBN:0-340-65301-9, ISBN13:
978-0-340-65301-2. Dewey:363.738/74. LCCN:00-711952.
Audience: **l,u,f.** *Choice, 2001.*

Stevens, E. S.   **TP1180.B55S74 2002**
Green Plastics: An Introduction to the New Science of
Biodegradable Plastics. Trade Cloth. Princeton University Press.
Princeton, NJ. 2001. 248p. ISBN:0-691-04967-X, ISBN13:
978-0-691-04967-0. Dewey:668.4. LCCN:2001-036257.
Audience: **l,u,f.** *Choice, 2002.*

Environmental History

Association of State and   **KF3790.C552 2004**
Interstate Water Pollution Control Administrators
Clean Water Act Thirty-Year Retrospective: History and
Documents Related to the Federal Statute. Brian Van Wye
(Editor). Perfect. Association of State & Interstate Water
Pollution Control Administrators. Washington, DC. 2004. 807p.
ISBN:0-615-12522-0, ISBN13: 978-0-615-12522-0.
Dewey:344.046343. LCCN:2005-276183.
Audience: **l,u,f.**

Bogue, Margaret   **SH219.6.B64 2000**
Beattie
Fishing the Great Lakes: An Environmental History, 1783-1933.
Trade Paper. University of Wisconsin Press. Chicago, IL. 2000.
464p. ISBN:0-299-16764-X, ISBN13: 978-0-299-16764-6.
Dewey:333.95/613/0977. LCCN:00-008601.
Audience: **l,u,f.** *Choice, 2001.*

Bulliet, Richard W.   **SF401.C2B84 1990**
The Camel and the Wheel. Trade Cloth. Columbia University
Press. New York, NY. 1990. 327p. ISBN:0-231-07234-1,
ISBN13: 978-0-231-07234-2. Dewey:636.2/95/09.
LCCN:89-025121.
Audience: **g,l,u,f.**

Carstensen, Vernon   **HD0216.C3**
(Editor)
The Public Lands: Studies in the History of the Public Domain.
Trade Paper. Books on Demand. Ann Arbor, MI. 538p.
ISBN:0-608-09848-5, ISBN13: 978-0-608-09848-7.
Dewey:333.10973. LCCN:62-021554.
Audience: **l,u,f.** *B*

Cronon, William   **GF504.N45C76 2003**
Changes in the Land: Indians, Colonists, and the Ecology of
New England. Ed. 20. Trade Paper. Farrar, Straus & Giroux.
New York, NY. 2003. 242p. ISBN:0-8090-1634-6, ISBN13:
978-0-8090-1634-1. Dewey:304.2/0974. LCCN:2003-042340.
Audience: **g,l.**

Cronon, William   **F548.4 .C85**
Nature's Metropolis: Chicago and the Great West. Trade Paper.
W. W. Norton & Company, Inc. New York, NY. 1992. 592p.
ISBN:0-393-30873-1, ISBN13: 978-0-393-30873-0.
Dewey:977.3/11/03.

Audience: **g,l,u,f.** *Choice, 1991.*

Crosby, Alfred W.   **GF50.C76 2004**
  (Author, Contribution by)
Ecological Imperialism: The Biological Expansion of Europe,
900-1900. Ed. 2. Donald Worster (Contribution by). Cloth Text.
Cambridge University Press. New York, NY. 2004. 390p.
Studies in Environment and History Ser. ISBN:0-521-83732-4,
ISBN13: 978-0-521-83732-3. Dewey:302.4.
LCCN:2004-040401.

Audience: **g,l,u,f.** *Choice, 1987.*

Drayton, Richard   **DA470.D73 2000**
Nature's Government: Science, British Imperialism and the
Improvement of the World. Cloth over Boards. Yale University
Press. Cumberland, RI. 2000. 368p. ISBN:0-300-05976-0,
ISBN13: 978-0-300-05976-2. Dewey:325/.341/009033.
LCCN:99-059158.

Audience: **l,u,f.** *Choice, 2001.*

Dunlap, Riley E. &   **HC110.E5A648 1992**
  Mertig, Angela G. (Editors)
American Environmentalism: The U. S. Environmental
Movement, 1970-1990. UK-B Format Paperback. Taylor &
Francis Group. Philadelphia, PA. 1992. 134p.
ISBN:0-8448-1730-9, ISBN13: 978-0-8448-1730-9.
Dewey:363.70570973. LCCN:92-007035.

Audience: **g,l,f.**

Fixico, Donald Lee   **E93.F515 1998**
[e] The Invasion of Indian Country in the Twentieth Century:
American Capitalism and Tribal Natural Resources. E-Book.
NetLibrary, Inc. Boulder, CO. 1998. ISBN:0-585-04247-0,
ISBN13: 978-0-585-04247-3. Dewey:333.2.

Audience: **g,l,f.**

Flannery, Tim   **QH102**
The Eternal Frontier: An Ecological History of North America
and Its Peoples. Trade Paper. Grove/Atlantic, Inc. New York,
NY. 2002. 432p. ISBN:0-8021-3888-8, ISBN13:
978-0-8021-3888-0. Dewey:508.7.

Audience: **g,l,f.** *Choice, 2001.*

Forlag, Albert B. &   **F722.M23 1999**
  Magoc, Christopher J.
Yellowstone: The Creation and Selling of an American
Landscape, 1870-1903. Trade Cloth. University of New Mexico
Press. Albuquerque, NM. 1999. 304p. ISBN:0-8263-2119-4,
ISBN13: 978-0-8263-2119-0. Dewey:978.7/52.
LCCN:98-058035.

Audience: **g,l,u,f.** *Choice, 2000.*

Goble, Dale D. (Editor),   **KF5640.E482 2005**
  et al.
The Endangered Species Act at Thirty: Renewing the
Conservation Promise. J. Michael Scott & Frank W. Davis
(Editors). Trade Cloth. Island Press. Washington, DC. 2005.
432p. ISBN:1-59726-008-8, ISBN13: 978-1-59726-008-4.
Dewey:346.7304/69522. LCCN:2005-026419.

Audience: **g,l,f.**

Graham, Frank Jr.   **QL671.G7 1992**
The Audubon Ark: A History of the National Audubon Society.
Trade Paper. University of Texas Press. Austin, TX. 1992. 350p.

ISBN:0-292-70440-2, ISBN13: 978-0-292-70440-4.
Dewey:598/.06073. LCCN:91-043864.

Audience: **g,l,f.**

Hurst, James W.   **KF9949.**
Law and Economic Growth: The Legal History of the Lumber
Industry in Wisconsin, 1836-1915. Trade Paper. Books on
Demand. Ann Arbor, MI. 980p. ISBN:0-608-20442-0, ISBN13:
978-0-608-20442-0. Dewey:343.775/078674/09.
LCCN:83-040287.

Audience: **l,u,f.**

King, F. H.   **S471.C6**
Farmers of Forty Centuries or Permanent Agriculture in China,
Korea and Japan. Trade Paper. Kessinger Publishing, LLC.
Whitefish, MT. 2004. ISBN:1-4191-1934-6, ISBN13:
978-1-4191-1934-7. Dewey:630/.951.

Audience: **l,u,f.**

Krech, Shepard   **E98.P5K74**
Ecological Indian: Myth and History. Library Binding.
Sagebrush Education Resources. Caledonia, MN. 2003.
ISBN:0-613-91414-7, ISBN13: 978-0-613-91414-7.
Dewey:333.7/089/97.

Audience: **g,l,u,f.**

Langston, Nancy &   **QH76.5.O7**
  Cronon, William
Where Land and Water Meet: A Western Landscape
Transformed. Trade Cloth. University of Washington Press.
Seattle, WA. 2005. 248p. ISBN:0-295-98499-6, ISBN13:
978-0-295-98499-5. Dewey:333.91/8/09795.

Audience: **l,u,f.** *Choice, 2003.*

Leonard, Barry (Editor)   **ML1751.C5**
25 Years of the Safe Drinking Water Act: History and Trends.
Paper Text. DIANE Publishing Company. Collingdale, PA. 2001.
54p. ISBN:0-7567-1071-5, ISBN13: 978-0-7567-1071-2.
Dewey:792.027.

Audience: **g,l,u,f.**

MacEachern, Alan   **SB484.C2M23 2001**
Natural Selections: National Parks in Atlantic Canada,
1935-1970. Trade Cloth. McGill-Queen's University Press.
Montreal, PQ. 2001. xiii, 328p. ISBN:0-7735-2157-7, ISBN13:
978-0-7735-2157-5. Dewey:333.78/3/09715.
LCCN:2002-421349.

Audience: **l,u,f.** *Choice, 2001.*

McClelland, Linda F.   **SB482.A4M3 1998**
Building the National Parks: The Historic Landscape Design and
Construction. John S. Reynolds (Foreword by). Trade Paper.
Johns Hopkins University Press. Baltimore, MD. 1997. 624p.
ISBN:0-8018-5583-7, ISBN13: 978-0-8018-5583-2.
Dewey:353.7/8. LCCN:97-012664.

Audience: **g,l,u,f.**

McCoy, Drew R.   **HC105**
The Elusive Republic: Political Economy in Jeffersonian
America. Trade Paper. University of North Carolina Press.
Chapel Hill, NC. 1996. 278p. Published for the Omohundro
Institute of Early American History and Culture, Williamsburg,
Virginia Ser. ISBN:0-8078-4616-3, ISBN13: 978-0-8078-4616-2.
Dewey:973.4. LCCN:79-020952.

Audience: **u,f.**

McIver, Stuart B.   **GE56.B73M35 2003**
Death in the Everglades: The Murder of Guy Bradley, America's
First Martyr to Environmentalism. Trade Cloth. University Press

---

of Florida. Gainesville, FL. 2003. 208p. The Florida History and Culture Ser. ISBN:0-8130-2671-7, ISBN13: 978-0-8130-2671-8. Dewey:333.95/83416/0975939. LCCN:2003-054080.

Audience: **g,l,u,f.**

McNeill, J. R.   **GF13**
Something New under the Sun: An Environmental History of the 20th-Century World. Trade Paper. W. W. Norton & Company, Inc. New York, NY. 2001. 416p. Global Century Ser. ISBN:0-393-32183-5, ISBN13: 978-0-393-32183-8. Dewey:304.2/8/0904.

Audience: **l,u,f.**

McNeill, William H.   **RA649**
Plagues and People. Trade Cloth. Peter Smith Publisher, Inc. Magnolia, MA. 1992. ISBN:0-8446-6492-8, ISBN13: 978-0-8446-6492-7. Dewey:614.4/9.

Audience: **g,l,u,f.**

Mosley, Stephen R.   **TD884.M67 2001**
The Chimney of the World: A History of Smoke Pollution in Victorian and Edwardian Manchester. Trade Cloth. White Horse Press. Cambridge, 2001. 250p. ISBN:1-874267-49-9, ISBN13: 978-1-874267-49-2. Dewey:363.7392094273309034. LCCN:2004-351051.

Audience: **g,l,u,f.** *Choice, 2002.*

Nelson, Gaylord, et al.   **GE195.N45 2002**
Beyond Earth Day: Fulfilling the Promise. Susan Campbell & Paul R. Wozniak (Authors). Trade Cloth. University of Wisconsin Press. Chicago, IL. 2002. 224p. ISBN:0-299-18040-9, ISBN13: 978-0-299-18040-9. Dewey:333.7/2. LCCN:2002-002806.

Audience: **g,l,u,f.** *Choice, 2003.*

Righter, Robert W.   **TD225.S25R54 2005**
🄴 The Battle over Hetch Hetchy: America's Most Controversial Dam and the Birth of Modern Environmentalism. E-Book. Oxford University Press, Inc. New York, NY. ISBN:1-4237-2010-5, ISBN13: 978-1-4237-2010-2. Dewey:363.6/1/0979447.

Audience: **g,l,u,f.**

Robinson, Glen O.   **SD0565.R6**
The Forest Service: A Study in Public Land Management. Trade Paper. Books on Demand. Ann Arbor, MI. 358p. ISBN:0-598-12042-4, ISBN13: 978-0-598-12042-7. Dewey:634.9/0973. LCCN:75-011352.

Audience: **u,f.** *B*

Runte, Alfred   **E160**
National Parks: The American Experience. Library Binding. Sagebrush Education Resources. Caledonia, MN. 1997. ISBN:0-613-91506-2, ISBN13: 978-0-613-91506-9. Dewey:719/.32/0973.

Audience: **g,l,u,f.**

Russell, Edmund   **QH545.C48 R87 2001**
War and Nature: Fighting Humans and Insects with Chemicals from World War I to Silent Spring. Alfred W. Crosby & Donald Worster (Contribution by). Trade Cloth. Cambridge University Press. New York, NY. 2001. 336p. Studies in Environment and History ISBN:0-521-79003-4, ISBN13: 978-0-521-79003-1. Dewey:577.27. LCCN:00-040323.

Audience: **g,l,u,f.** *Choice, 2001.*

Scott, J. Michael   **KF5640**
(Editor), et al.
The Endangered Species Act at Thirty: Conserving Biodiversity in Human-Dominated Landscapes. Dale D. Goble & Frank W. Davis (Editors). Trade Cloth. Island Press. Washington, DC. 2006. 450p. ISBN:1-59726-054-1, ISBN13: 978-1-59726-054-1. Dewey:346.7304/69522.

Audience: **l,u,f.**

Sellars, Richard W.   **HC103.7**
Preserving Nature in the National Parks: A History. Trade Paper. Yale University Press. Cumberland, RI. 1999. 394p. ISBN:0-300-07578-2, ISBN13: 978-0-300-07578-6. Dewey:333.7/0973.

Audience: **l,u,f.**

Smith, Duane A.   **TD195.T7**
Mining America: The Industry and the Environment, 1800-1980. Trade Paper. University Press of Colorado. Boulder, CO. 1994. 224p. ISBN:0-87081-306-4, ISBN13: 978-0-87081-306-1. Dewey:363.7/31. LCCN:93-013337.

Audience: **g,l,u,f.** *Choice, 1987.*

Steinberg, Ted   **GF27**
Down to Earth: Nature's Role in American History. Paper Text. Oxford University Press, Inc. New York, NY. 2002. 368p. ISBN:0-19-514010-9, ISBN13: 978-0-19-514010-1. Dewey:333.7/13/0973.

Audience: **g,l,u,f.**

Strasser, Susan   **KF27**
Waste and Want: A Social History of Trash. Trade Paper. Henry Holt & Company. New York, NY. 2000. 368p. ISBN:0-8050-6512-1, ISBN13: 978-0-8050-6512-1. Dewey:363.72/8. LCCN:99-017571.

Audience: **g,l,u,f.**

Sutter, Paul S.   **QH76.S86 2002**
Driven Wild: How the Fight Against Automobiles Launched the Modern Wilderness Movement. William Cronon (Introduction by). Trade Cloth. University of Washington Press. Seattle, WA. 2003. 360p. Weyerhaeuser Environmental Bks. ISBN:0-295-98219-5, ISBN13: 978-0-295-98219-9. Dewey:333.7/2/0973. LCCN:2002-024206.

Audience: **g,l,u,f.** *Choice, 2002.*

Warner, Sam Bass Jr.   **HN80.B7W3**
Streetcar Suburbs: The Process of Growth in Boston, 1870-1900. Ed. 2. Trade Cloth. Harvard University Press. Cambridge, MA. 1962. 236p. Joint Center for Urban Studies ISBN:0-674-84210-3, ISBN13: 978-0-674-84210-6. Dewey:711.4/5/0974461. LCCN:62-017228.

Audience: **l,u,f.** *B*

Williams, Michael   **SD131.W53 2002**
Deforesting the Earth: From Prehistory to Global Crisis. Trade Cloth. University of Chicago Press. Chicago, IL. 2002. 715p. ISBN:0-226-89926-8, ISBN13: 978-0-226-89926-8. Dewey:333.75/137. LCCN:2001-007754.

Audience: **l,u,f.**

Winter, James   **GF551.W56**
Secure from Rash Assault: Sustaining the Victorian Environment. Trade Paper. University of California Press. Berkeley, CA. 2002. 354p. ISBN:0-520-22930-4, ISBN13: 978-0-520-22930-3. Dewey:333.7/13/0941/09034. LCCN:98-043970.

Audience: **l,u,f.**

Worster, Donald   **F786.W87 2004**
Dust Bowl: The Southern Plains in the 1930s. Ed. 25. Trade
Cloth. Oxford University Press, Inc. New York, NY. 2004. 304p.
ISBN:0-19-517489-5, ISBN13: 978-0-19-517489-2.
Dewey:978/.032. LCCN:2004-054703.

Audience: **u,f.** ℬ

Social & Behavioral Sciences

Beuter, John H.   **SD565.C64 1989**
Community Stability in Forest-Based Economies. Dennis C.
LeMaster (Editor). Trade Cloth. Timber Press, Inc. Portland,
OR. 2003. 198p. ISBN:0-88192-129-7, ISBN13:
978-0-88192-129-8. Dewey:333.75/0973. LCCN:88-024831.

Audience: **l,u,f.**

Bolgiano, Chris   **F106.B673 1998**
The Appalachian Forest: A Search for Roots and Renewal. Trade
Cloth. Stackpole Books. Mechanicsburg, PA. 1998. 280p.
ISBN:0-8117-0126-3, ISBN13: 978-0-8117-0126-6.
Dewey:974/.00943. LCCN:98-017747.

Audience: **l,u,f.**

Bove, Jose & Dufour,   **HD1536.F813B774 2000**
Francois
The World Is Not for Sale: Farmers Against Junkfood. Trade
Cloth. Verso Books. London, 2002. 240p. ISBN:1-85984-614-9,
ISBN13: 978-1-85984-614-8. Dewey:338.1/7/0944.
LCCN:2001-523778.

Audience: **g,l,f.** *Choice, 2001.*

Fisher, Andy   **BF353.5.N37F57 2002**
Radical Ecopsychology: Psychology in the Service of Life.
David Abram (Foreword by). Cloth Text. State University of
New York Press. Albany, NY. 2002. 336p. SUNY Series in
Radical, Social, and Political Theory ISBN:0-7914-5303-0,
ISBN13: 978-0-7914-5303-2. Dewey:155.9/1.
LCCN:2001-059888.

Audience: **u,f.** *Choice, 2002.*

Fisher, William H.   **F2520.1.X5F57 2000**
Rain Forest Exchanges: Industry and Community on an
Amazonian Frontier. Trade Cloth. Smithsonian Institution Press.
Washington, DC. 2000. 240p. Series in Ethnographic Inquiry
ISBN:1-56098-958-0, ISBN13: 978-1-56098-958-5.
Dewey:981.004/984. LCCN:00-028516.

Audience: **l,u,f.** *Choice, 2001.*

Grusin, Richard   **SB484.A4G78 2003**
Culture, Technology, and the Creation of America's National
Parks. Albert Gelpi & Ross Posnock (Contribution by). Trade
Cloth. Cambridge University Press. New York, NY. 2004. 232p.
Cambridge Studies in American Literature and Culture Ser.
ISBN:0-521-82649-7, ISBN13: 978-0-521-82649-5.
Dewey:333.78/3/0973. LCCN:2003-043507.

Audience: **g,l,u,f.** *Choice, 2005.*

Head, Lesley   **GF801.H36 2000**
Second Nature: The History and Implications of Australia as
Aboriginal Landscape. Trade Cloth. Syracuse University Press.
Syracuse, NY. 1999. xiii, 272p. Space, Place and Society Ser.
ISBN:0-8156-0587-0, ISBN13: 978-0-8156-0587-4.
Dewey:306/.0899/915. LCCN:99-024394.

Audience: **l,u,f.** *Choice, 2000.*

Jacoby, Karl   **SB486.S65**
Crimes Against Nature: Squatters, Poachers, Thieves, and the
Hidden History of American Conservation. Trade Paper.

University of California Press. Berkeley, CA. 2003. 306p.
ISBN:0-520-23909-1, ISBN13: 978-0-520-23909-8.
Dewey:333.78/0973. LCCN:00-061521.

Audience: **l,u,f.**

Low, Setha, et al.   **HT153.L68 2005**
Rethinking Urban Parks: Public Space and Cultural Diversity.
Dana Taplin & Suzanne Scheld (Authors). Trade Cloth.
University of Texas Press. Austin, TX. 2005. 240p.
ISBN:0-292-70685-5, ISBN13: 978-0-292-70685-9.
Dewey:307.76. LCCN:2005-014161.

Audience: **l,u,f.**

Mandala, Elias C.   **HD1538.M3M36 1990**
Work and Control in a Peasant Economy: A History of the
Lower Tchiri Valley in Malawi, 1859-1960. Cloth Text.
University of Wisconsin Press. Chicago, IL. 1990. 480p.
ISBN:0-299-12490-8, ISBN13: 978-0-299-12490-8.
Dewey:305.5/633/096897. LCCN:90-050093.

Audience: **l,u,f.** *Choice, 1991.*

Moore, Keith M.   **HC1000.Z65C66 2004**
Conflict, Social Capital, and Managing Natural Resources: A
West African Case Study. SANREM Staff (Contribution by).
Cloth Text. CAB International. Wallingford, 2005. 278p. CABI
Publishing Ser. ISBN:0-85199-948-4, ISBN13:
978-0-85199-948-7. Dewey:333.7/0966. LCCN:2004-012409.

Audience: **u,f.**

Thomas, William L. Jr.   **G56.I63**
(Editor)
Man's Role in Changing the Face of the Earth. Trade Cloth.
University of Chicago Press. Chicago, IL. 1956. 1236p.
ISBN:0-226-79603-5, ISBN13: 978-0-226-79603-1.
Dewey:304.2. LCCN:56-005865.

Audience: **l,u,f.** ℬ

Warren, Christian   **RA1231.L4**
Brush with Death: A Social History of Lead Poisoning. Trade
Paper. Johns Hopkins University Press. Baltimore, MD. 2001.
384p. ISBN:0-8018-6820-3, ISBN13: 978-0-8018-6820-7.
Dewey:615.9/25688/0973.

Audience: **l,u,f.** *Choice, 2000.*

Yakovleva, Natalia   **HD60.Y34 2005**
Corporate Social Responsibility in the Mining Industries. Trade
Cloth. Ashgate Publishing, Ltd. Aldershot, 2005. 324p.
Corporate Social Responsibility Ser. ISBN:0-7546-4268-2,
ISBN13: 978-0-7546-4268-8. Dewey:622/.068/4.
LCCN:2005-009755.

Audience: **l,u,f.**

Economics and Development

Barnes, Pamela M. &   **GE190.E85B37 1999**
Barnes, Ian G.
Environmental Policy in the European Union. Trade Cloth.
Edward Elgar Publishing, Inc. Northampton, MA. 1999. 360p.
ISBN:1-85898-339-8, ISBN13: 978-1-85898-339-4.
Dewey:363.7/0094. LCCN:99-015403.

Audience: **l,u,f.** *Choice, 2000.*

Barringer, Mark Daniel   **F722.B27 2002**
Selling Yellowstone: Capitalism and the Construction of Nature.
Trade Cloth. University Press of Kansas. Lawrence, KS. 2002.
viii, 238p. Development of Western Resources Ser.

ISBN:0-7006-1167-3, ISBN13: 978-0-7006-1167-6.
Dewey:978.7/52. LCCN:2001-006732.

Audience: **g,l,u,f**. *Choice, 2003.*

Beattie, Andrew &   **QH541.15.B56B42 2001**
  Ehrlich, Paul R.
Wild Solutions: How Biodiversity Is Money in the Bank.
Christine Turnbull (Illustrator). Cloth over Boards. Yale
University Press. Cumberland, RI. 2001. 256p.
ISBN:0-300-07636-3, ISBN13: 978-0-300-07636-3.
Dewey:333.95/11. LCCN:00-043445.

Audience: **g,l,u,f**. *Choice, 2001.*

Beder, Sharon   **GE300.B43 2002**
Global Spin: The Corporate Assault on Environmentalism. Ed.
2. Trade Paper. Chelsea Green Publishing. White River Junction,
VT. 2004. 336p. ISBN:1-931498-08-3, ISBN13:
978-1-931498-08-1. Dewey:363.7. LCCN:2003-272268.

Audience: **g,l,u,f**. *Choice, 2003.*

Beuter, John H.   **SD565.C64 1989**
Community Stability in Forest-Based Economies. Dennis C.
LeMaster (Editor). Trade Cloth. Timber Press, Inc. Portland,
OR. 2003. 198p. ISBN:0-88192-129-7, ISBN13:
978-0-88192-129-8. Dewey:333.75/0973. LCCN:88-024831.

Audience: **l,u,f**.

Brewer, Richard   **HD205.B74 2003**
Conservancy. Trade Cloth. University Press of New England.
Lebanon, NH. 2003. 320p. ISBN:1-58465-350-7, ISBN13:
978-1-58465-350-9. Dewey:333.3/234. LCCN:2003-012938.

Audience: **u,f**. *Choice, 2004.*

Clements, Kendrick A.   **HC110.C6C53 2000**
Hoover, Conservation and Consumerism: Engineering the Good
Life. Trade Cloth. University Press of Kansas. Lawrence, KS.
2000. xiv,330p. ISBN:0-7006-1033-2, ISBN13:
978-0-7006-1033-4. Dewey:333.7/0973. LCCN:00-028316.

Audience: **l,u,f**. *Choice, 2001.*

Deere, Carolyn L. &   **HF1746.G74 2002**
  Esty, Daniel C. (Editors)
Greening the Americas: NAFTA's Lessons for Hemispheric
Trade. Trade Paper. MIT Press. Cambridge, MA. 2002. 398p.
ISBN:0-262-54138-6, ISBN13: 978-0-262-54138-1.
Dewey:333.7. LCCN:2002-022921.

Audience: **u,f**. *Choice, 2003.*

Gedicks, Al   **GN449.3.G43 2001**
Resource Rebels: Native Challenges to Mining and Oil
Corporations. Trade Cloth. South End Press. Cambridge, MA.
2001. 250p. Native American Studies ISBN:0-89608-641-0,
ISBN13: 978-0-89608-641-8. Dewey:333.8/517.
LCCN:2001-042687.

Audience: **g,l,u,f**. *Choice, 2002.*

Hoffman, Andrew J.   **HD30.255.H64 1997**
From Heresy to Dogma: An Institutional History of Corporate
Environmentalism. Trade Cloth. Lexington Books. Lanham,
MD. 1997. 256p. The New Lexington Press Management Ser.
ISBN:0-7879-0819-3, ISBN13: 978-0-7879-0819-5.
Dewey:658.4/08. LCCN:97-003694.

Audience: **l,u,f**. *Choice, 2002.*

Kantor, Shawn Everett   **HD241.K36 1998**
Politics and Property Rights: The Closing of the Open Range in
the Postbellum South. Trade Cloth. University of Chicago Press.
Chicago, IL. 1998. 198p. Studies in Law and Economics

ISBN:0-226-42375-1, ISBN13: 978-0-226-42375-3.
Dewey:333.33/5. LCCN:97-025887.

Audience: **l,u,f**.

McDaniel, Carl N. &   **HC682.25.Z9 M33 2000**
  Gowdy, John M.
Paradise for Sale: Back to Sustainability. Trade Paper.
University of California Press. Berkeley, CA. 2000. 240p.
ISBN:0-520-22229-6, ISBN13: 978-0-520-22229-8.
Dewey:333.7/099685. LCCN:99-012829.

Audience: **g,l,u,f**. *Choice, 2000.*

McDonough, William   **TD794.5.M395**
Cradle to Cradle: Remaking the Way We Make Things. Library
Binding. Sagebrush Education Resources. Caledonia, MN. 2002.
ISBN:0-613-91987-4, ISBN13: 978-0-613-91987-6.
Dewey:745.2.

Audience: **g,l,u,f**. *Choice, 2002.*

Ofiara, Douglas D. &   **HC110.W32O37 2001**
  Seneca, Joseph J.
Economic Losses from Marine Pollution: A Handbook for
Assessment. Trade Cloth. Island Press. Washington, DC. 2001.
203p. ISBN:1-55963-609-2, ISBN13: 978-1-55963-609-4.
Dewey:363.739/4/0973. LCCN:00-012385.

Audience: **u,f**. *Choice, 2002.*

Owen, Bruce M., et al.   **HC107**
The Economics of a Disaster: The Exxon Valdez Oil Spill.
David A. Argue & Harold W. Furchtgott-Roth (Authors). Trade
Cloth. Greenwood Publishing Group, Inc. Portsmouth, NH.
1995. 216p. ISBN:0-89930-987-9, ISBN13: 978-0-89930-987-3.
Dewey:338.3. LCCN:95-003782.

Audience: **l,u,f**.

Pearce, David &   **HD75.6.P428 2000**
  Barbier, Edward B.
Blueprint for a Sustainable Economy. Trade Cloth.
Earthscan/James & James. London, 2000. 240p. The Blueprint
Ser. ISBN:1-85383-682-6, ISBN13: 978-1-85383-682-4.
Dewey:333.7. LCCN:2003-270749.

Audience: **g,l,u,f**. *Choice, 2000.*

Roberts, Paul   **HD9650.6.R63 2004**
The End of Oil: On the Edge of a Perilous New World. Dust
Jacket. Houghton Mifflin Company Trade & Reference Division.
Boston, MA. 2004. 400p. ISBN:0-618-23977-4, ISBN13:
978-0-618-23977-1. Dewey:333.79. LCCN:2004-042718.

Audience: **g,l,u,f**. *Choice, 2004.*

Sampson, Gary P., et al.   **HF1379.T723 1999**
Trade, Environment and the Millennium. W. Bradnee Chambers,
Institute of Advanced Studies Staff & Environmental
Governance and Multilateralism Program Staff (Authors). Trade
Paper. United Nations Publications. New York, NY. 2005. 400p.
ISBN:92-808-1043-X, ISBN13: 978-92-808-1043-1.
Dewey:382/.92. LCCN:99-050491.

Audience: **l,u,f**.

Swanson, Timothy M.   **HC55.E355 1996**
  (Editor)
The Economics of Environmental Degradation: Tragedy for the
Commons? Trade Cloth. Edward Elgar Publishing, Inc.
Northampton, MA. 1997. 208p. ISBN:1-85898-486-6, ISBN13:
978-1-85898-486-5. Dewey:333.7. LCCN:96-006434.

Audience: **u,f**.

Tucker, Richard P.   **HD1417.T83 2000**
Insatiable Appetite: The U. S. and the Ecological Degradation of
the Tropical World. Trade Cloth. University of California Press.
Berkeley, CA. 2000. 566p. ISBN:0-520-22087-0, ISBN13:
978-0-520-22087-4. Dewey:333.7/0913. LCCN:00-037774.
                                        Audience: **l,u,f.** *Choice, 2001.*

Victor, David G.   **QC981.8.G56V53 2001**
The Collapse of the Kyoto Protocol and the Struggle to Slow
Global Warming. Trade Cloth. Princeton University Press.
Princeton, NJ. 2001. 192p. ISBN:0-691-08870-5, ISBN13:
978-0-691-08870-9. Dewey:363.738/74526. LCCN:00-051633.
                                        Audience: **l,u,f.** *Choice, 2001.*

Weinberg, Adam S., et   **HN49.C6W437 2000**
  al.
Urban Recycling and the Search for Sustainable Community
Development. David N. Pellow & Allan Schnaiberg (Authors).
Trade Cloth. Princeton University Press. Princeton, NJ. 2000.
236p. ISBN:0-691-05014-7, ISBN13: 978-0-691-05014-0.
Dewey:307.1/4. LCCN:00-021055.
                                        Audience: **l,u,f.** *Choice, 2001.*

World Resources   **HC85.W67 2005**
  Institute (Created by)
World Resources: The Wealth of the Poor: Managing
Ecosystems to Fight Poverty. Trade Paper, Perfect. World
Resources Institute. Washington, DC. 2005. 254p.
ISBN:1-56973-582-4, ISBN13: 978-1-56973-582-4.
Dewey:338.91724.
                                        Audience: **g,l,u,f.**

Political Science and Policy

Bacher, John C.   **HD9560.5.B23 2000**
Petrotyranny. Trade Paper. Science for Peace, University of
Toronto. Toronto, ON. 2004. 320p. ISBN:0-88866-956-9,
ISBN13: 978-0-88866-956-8. Dewey:333.8/232.
LCCN:2001-320532.
                                        Audience: **g,l,u,f.** *Choice, 2001.*

Barlow, Maude &   **TD345**
  Clarke, Tony
Blue Gold: The Fight to Stop the Corporate Theft of the
World's Water. Trade Paper. New Press, The. New York, NY.
2005. 304p. ISBN:1-56584-813-6, ISBN13: 978-1-56584-813-9.
Dewey:333.91.
                                        Audience: **g,l,u,f.** *Choice, 2002.*

Barnes, Pamela M. &   **GE190.E85B37 1999**
  Barnes, Ian G.
Environmental Policy in the European Union. Trade Cloth.
Edward Elgar Publishing, Inc. Northampton, MA. 1999. 360p.
ISBN:1-85898-339-8, ISBN13: 978-1-85898-339-4.
Dewey:363.7/0094. LCCN:99-015403.
                                        Audience: **l,u,f.** *Choice, 2000.*

Baron, Jill S. (Editor)   **GE160.R58R63 2002**
Rocky Mountain Futures: An Ecological Perspective. Paul R.
Ehrlich (Foreword by). Trade Cloth. Island Press. Washington,
DC. 2002. 352p. ISBN:1-55963-953-9, ISBN13:
978-1-55963-953-8. Dewey:333.73/0978. LCCN:2002-007978.
                                        Audience: **l,u,f.** *Choice, 2003.*

Burnham, Philip   **E98.L3B87 2000**
Indian Country, God's Country: Native Americans and the
National Parks. Trade Cloth. Island Press. Washington, DC.

2000. 384p. ISBN:1-55963-667-X, ISBN13: 978-1-55963-667-4.
Dewey:333.78/3/089973. LCCN:99-050934.
                                        Audience: **g,l,u,f.** *Choice, 2000.*

Carter, Neil   **JA75.8.C38 2001**
The Politics of the Environment: Ideas, Activism, Policy. Cloth
Text. Cambridge University Press. New York, NY. 2001. 382p.
ISBN:0-521-47037-4, ISBN13: 978-0-521-47037-7.
Dewey:320.5. LCCN:2001-035638.
                                        Audience: **g,l,f.** *Choice, 2002.*

Chasek, Pamela S.   **GE149.C42 2001**
Earth Negotiations: Analyzing Thirty Years of Environmental
Diplomacy. Trade Paper. United Nations University Press.
Tokyo, 2004. 314p. ISBN:92-808-1047-2, ISBN13:
978-92-808-1047-9. Dewey:363.7/0526. LCCN:00-012568.
                                        Audience: **l,u,f.** *Choice, 2002.*

Chasek, Pamela S.   **HC79.E5**
The Global Environment in the Twenty-First Century: Prospects
for International Co-operation. Trade Cloth. Manas Publications.
New Delhi, 2004. 465p. ISBN:81-7049-199-1, ISBN13:
978-81-7049-199-6. Dewey:363.7/0526.
                                        Audience: **g,l,u,f.**

Darst, Robert G.   **TD170.D37 2001**
Smokestack Diplomacy: Cooperation and Conflict in East-West
Environmental Politics. Trade Cloth. MIT Press. Cambridge,
MA. 2001. 330p. Global Environmental Accord Ser., :Strategies
for Sustainability and Institutional Innovation
ISBN:0-262-04183-9, ISBN13: 978-0-262-04183-6.
Dewey:363.7/0526. LCCN:00-056240.
                                        Audience: **l,u,f.** *Choice, 2001.*

De-Shalit, Avner   **GE170.D465 2000**
The Environment: Between Theory and Practice. Trade Paper.
Oxford University Press, Inc. New York, NY. 2000. 248p.
ISBN:0-19-924038-8, ISBN13: 978-0-19-924038-8.
Dewey:363.7. LCCN:99-057190.
                                        Audience: **l,u,f.** *Choice, 2001.*

DeSombre, Elizabeth R.   **GE170.D47 2000**
Domestic Sources of International Environmental Policy:
Industry, Environmentalists, and U. S. Power. Trade Paper. MIT
Press. Cambridge, MA. 2000. 316p. American and Comparative
Environmental Policy Ser. ISBN:0-262-54107-6, ISBN13:
978-0-262-54107-7. Dewey:363.7/0526. LCCN:99-041745.
                                        Audience: **u,f.** *Choice, 2001.*

Dewey, Scott Hamilton   **TD883.2.D48 2000**
Don't Breathe the Air: Air Pollution and U. S. Environmental
Politics, 1945-1970. Trade Cloth. Texas A&M University Press.
College Station, TX. 2000. 321p. Environmental History Ser.,
Vol. 16 ISBN:0-89096-914-0, ISBN13: 978-0-89096-914-4.
Dewey:363.739/2/0973. LCCN:99-088267.
                                        Audience: **g,l,u,f.** *Choice, 2001.*

Ellerman, A. Denny, et al.   **HC110.A4 M37 2000**
Markets for Clean Air: The U. S. Acid Rain Program. Paul L.
Joskow, Richard Schmalensee, Juan-Pablo Montero & Elizabeth
M. Bailey (Authors). Trade Cloth. Cambridge University Press.
New York, NY. 2000. 384p. ISBN:0-521-66083-1, ISBN13:
978-0-521-66083-9. Dewey:363.738/7. LCCN:99-016913.
                                        Audience: **u,f.** *Choice, 2001.*

Flippen, J. Brooks   **GE180.F55 2000**
Nixon and the Environment. Trade Cloth. University of New
Mexico Press. Albuquerque, NM. 2000. 308p.

ISBN:0-8263-1993-9, ISBN13: 978-0-8263-1993-7.
Dewey:363.7/056/097309047. LCCN:00-008607.

Audience: **u,f.** *Choice, 2001.*

French, Hilary   **HC79.E5F723 2000**
Vanishing Borders: Protecting the Planet in the Age of
Globalization. Trade Paper. W. W. Norton & Company, Inc.
New York, NY. 2000. 257p. ISBN:0-393-32004-9, ISBN13:
978-0-393-32004-6. Dewey:363.7/0526. LCCN:00-701466.

Audience: **g,l,f.** *Choice, 2000.*

Gorman, Hugh S.   **TD195.P4G67 2001**
Redefining Efficiency: Pollution Concerns, Regulatory
Mechanisms and Technological Change in the U. S. Petroleum
Industry. Trade Cloth. University of Akron Press, The. Akron,
OH. 2001. 451p. Technology and the Environment Ser.
ISBN:1-884836-75-5, ISBN13: 978-1-884836-75-6.
Dewey:363.73/5765. LCCN:2001-002140.

Audience: **u,f.**

Hall, G. Emlen   **KF2576.P43H35 2002**
High and Dry: The Texas-New Mexico Struggle for the Pecos
River. Trade Cloth. University of New Mexico Press.
Albuquerque, NM. 2002. 290p. ISBN:0-8263-2429-0, ISBN13:
978-0-8263-2429-0. Dewey:346.7304/32. LCCN:2001-006776.

Audience: **l,u,f.** *Choice, 2002.*

Haycox, Stephen W.   **F904.H26 2002**
Frigid Embrace: Politics, Economics, and Environment in
Alaska. Trade Paper. Oregon State University Press. Corvallis,
OR. 2002. 192p. Culture and Environment in the Pacific West
Ser. ISBN:0-87071-536-4, ISBN13: 978-0-87071-536-5.
Dewey:979.8. LCCN:2001-005633.

Audience: **g,l,u,f.** *Choice, 2003.*

Hays, Samuel P.   **GE180.H392 2000**
A History of Environmental Politics. Trade Cloth. University of
Pittsburgh Press. Pittsburgh, PA. 2000. ix, 256p.
ISBN:0-8229-4128-7, ISBN13: 978-0-8229-4128-6.
Dewey:363.7/05/0973. LCCN:00-009651.

Audience: **l,u,f.** *Choice, 2001.*

Ingram, David   **PN1993**
Green Screen: Environmentalism and Hollywood Cinema. Trade
Cloth. University of Exeter Press. Exeter, 2000. 256p.
Representing American Culture Ser. ISBN:0-85989-608-0,
ISBN13: 978-0-85989-608-5. Dewey:302.2/34/3/0973.
LCCN:2003-427261.

Audience: **g,l,f.** *Choice, 2001.*

Jamison, Andrew   **GE195 .J36 2001**
The Making of Green Knowledge: Environmental Politics and
Cultural Transformation. Cloth Text. Cambridge University
Press. New York, NY. 2001. 218p. ISBN:0-521-79252-5,
ISBN13: 978-0-521-79252-3. Dewey:363.705.
LCCN:2001-035300.

Audience: **g,l,u,f.** *Choice, 2002.*

Kemmis, Daniel   **HD243.W38K46 2001**
This Sovereign Land: A New Vision for Governing the West.
Trade Cloth. Island Press. Washington, DC. 2001. 224p.
ISBN:1-55963-842-7, ISBN13: 978-1-55963-842-5.
Dewey:333.1/0978. LCCN:2001-002093.

Audience: **g,l,u,f.**

Leggett, Jeremy   **QC981.8.C5L45 2001**
The Carbon War: Global Warming and the End of the Oil Era.
Paper over Boards. Routledge. New York, NY. 2001. 352p.

ISBN:0-415-93101-0, ISBN13: 978-0-415-93101-4.
Dewey:363.738/742. LCCN:2001-018158.

Audience: **g,l,u,f.**

Leonard, Barry (Editor)   **ML1751.C5**
25 Years of the Safe Drinking Water Act: History and Trends.
Paper Text. DIANE Publishing Company. Collingdale, PA. 2001.
54p. ISBN:0-7567-1071-5, ISBN13: 978-0-7567-1071-2.
Dewey:792.027.

Audience: **g,l,u,f.**

Lindstrom, Matthew J.   **GE180.L55 2001**
& Smith, Zachary A.
The National Environmental Policy Act: Judicial
Misconstruciton, Legislative Indifference, and Executive
Neglect. Lynton K. Caldwell (Foreword by). Cloth Text. Texas
A&M University Press. College Station, TX. 2001. 224p.
Environmental History Ser., Vol. 17 ISBN:1-58544-125-2,
ISBN13: 978-1-58544-125-9. Dewey:363.7/056/0973.
LCCN:2001-002410.

Audience: **l,u,f.** *Choice, 2002.*

Malone, Linda A.   **KF3775.Z9M352 2003**
Environmental Law. Paper Text. Aspen Publishers, Inc. New
York, NY. 2003. xiv, 63p. Emanuel Law Outlines Ser.
ISBN:0-7355-3439-X, ISBN13: 978-0-7355-3439-1.
Dewey:344.7304/6. LCCN:2003-619213.

Audience: **l,u,f.**

Martineau, Robert J. &   **KF3812.C554 1997**
Novello, David
Clean Air Act Handbook. Trade Cloth. American Bar
Association. Chicago, IL. 1997. ISBN:1-57073-503-4, ISBN13:
978-1-57073-503-5. Dewey:344.73/046342. LCCN:97-024110.

Audience: **u,f.**

Martineau, Robert J. &   **KF3812.C554 2004**
Novello, David P.
The Clean Air Act Handbook. Ed. 2. Trade Paper. American Bar
Association. Chicago, IL. 2005. 728p. ISBN:1-59031-289-9,
ISBN13: 978-1-59031-289-6. Dewey:344.7304/6342.
LCCN:2004-001471.

Audience: **u,f.**

McCutcheon, Chuck   **TD898.12.N6M38 2002**
Nuclear Reactions: The Politics of Opening a Radioactive Waste
Disposal Site. Trade Cloth. University of New Mexico Press.
Albuquerque, NM. 2002. 232p. ISBN:0-8263-2209-3, ISBN13:
978-0-8263-2209-8. Dewey:363.72/89/0973.
LCCN:2002-006711.

Audience: **g,l,u,f.** *Choice, 2003.*

McDonald, David A.   **GE240.S6E58 2001**
(Editor)
Environmental Justice in South Africa. Trade Cloth. Ohio
University Press. Athens, OH. 2002. 352p. ISBN:0-8214-1415-1,
ISBN13: 978-0-8214-1415-6. Dewey:363.7/056/0968.
LCCN:2001-036344.

Audience: **l,u,f.** *Choice, 2003.*

McMahon, Robert   **KF26**
The Environmental Protection Agency: Structuring Motivation in
a Green Bureaucracy: the Conflict Between Regulatory Style
and Cultural Identity. Trade Cloth. Sussex Academic Press.
Eastbourne, 2005. 220p. ISBN:1-903900-69-7, ISBN13:
978-1-903900-69-7. Dewey:354.3280973. LCCN:2005-031335.

Audience: **l,u,f.**

Nakamura, Robert T. &   HD3616.U46N27 2003
  Church, Thomas W.
Taming Regulation: Superfund and the Challenge of Regulatory
Reform. Trade Cloth. Brookings Institution Press. Washington,
DC. 2003. 192p. ISBN:0-8157-5942-8, ISBN13:
978-0-8157-5942-3. Dewey:363.738/4. LCCN:2003-018458.
                                      Audience: **g,l,u,f.**

Neimark, Peninah   GE197
  Rhodes & Mott, Peter (Editors)
The Environmental Debate: A Documentary History. Cloth Text.
Greenwood Publishing Group, Inc. Portsmouth, NH. 1999. 352p.
Primary Documents in American History and Contemporary
Issues Ser. ISBN:0-313-30020-8, ISBN13: 978-0-313-30020-2.
Dewey:363.7/05/0973. LCCN:99-017844.
                            Audience: **l,u,f.**   *Choice, 2000.*

O'Brien, Mary   GE145.O27 2000
Making Better Environmental Decisions: An Alternative to Risk
Assessment. Trade Cloth. MIT Press. Cambridge, MA. 2000.
352p. ISBN:0-262-15051-4, ISBN13: 978-0-262-15051-4.
Dewey:333.7/14. LCCN:99-056868.
                            Audience: **l,u,f.**   *Choice, 2001.*

Paterson, Matthew   GE170.P38 2000
Understanding Global Environmental Politics: Domination,
Accumulation, Resistance. Cloth over Boards. Palgrave
Macmillan. New York, NY. 2000. 210p. ISBN:0-312-23090-7,
ISBN13: 978-0-312-23090-6. Dewey:363.7. LCCN:99-053110.
                            Audience: **l,u,f.**   *Choice, 2000.*

Rahm, Dianne   TD1040.T687 2002
Toxic Waste and Environmental Policy in the 21st Century
United States. Paper Text. McFarland & Company, Incorporated
Publishers. Jefferson, NC. 2002. 190p. ISBN:0-7864-1202-X,
ISBN13: 978-0-7864-1202-0. Dewey:363.72/87.
LCCN:86-43090.
                            Audience: **g,l,u,f.**   *Choice, 2002.*

Ringius, Lasse   TD898.4.R56 2001
Radioactive Waste Disposal at Sea: Public Ideas, Transnational
Policy Entrepreneurs, and Environmental Regimes. Trade Cloth.
MIT Press. Cambridge, MA. 2000. 337p. Global Environmental
Accord Ser., :Strategies for Sustainability and Institutional
Innovation ISBN:0-262-18202-5, ISBN13: 978-0-262-18202-7.
Dewey:363.7289. LCCN:00-031879.
                            Audience: **l,u,f.**   *Choice, 2001.*

Ryan, Mark   KF3790.C545 2003
Clean Water Act Handbook. Ed. 2. American Bar Association,
Section of Environment, Energy, and Resources Staff
(Contribution by). Trade Paper. American Bar Association.
Chicago, IL. 2004. 336p. ISBN:1-59031-217-1, ISBN13:
978-1-59031-217-9. Dewey:344.73/046343. LCCN:2003-010677.
                                      Audience: **u,f.**

Schneider, Stephen H.   QC981.8.C5C511416
  (Editor), et al.
Climate Change Policy: A Survey. Armin Rosencranz & John O.
Niles (Editors). Cloth Text. Island Press. Washington, DC. 2002.
368p. ISBN:1-55963-880-X, ISBN13: 978-1-55963-880-7.
Dewey:363.738/745. LCCN:2002-005344.
                            Audience: **l,u,f.**   *Choice, 2003.*

Sproule-Jones, Mark   TD223.3.S67 2002
Restoration of the Great Lakes: Promises, Practices, and
Performances. Trade Cloth. Michigan State University Press.
East Lansing, MI. 2002. 144p. ISBN:0-87013-628-3, ISBN13:

978-0-87013-628-3. Dewey:333.91/63153/0977.
LCCN:2002-000076.
                            Audience: **u,f.**   *Choice, 2002.*

Susskind, Lawrence E.,   GE180.S855 2001
  et al.
Better Environmental Policy Studies: How to Design and
Conduct More Effective Analysis. Ravi K. Jain & Andrew O.
Martyniuk (Authors). Trade Cloth. Island Press. Washington,
DC. 2001. 256p. ISBN:1-55963-870-2, ISBN13:
978-1-55963-870-8. Dewey:363.7/056/0973.
LCCN:2001-003712.
                            Audience: **u,f.**   *Choice, 2002.*

Tschirhart, John &   QH76.P755 2001
  Shogren, Jason F. (Editors)
Protecting Endangered Species in the United States: Biological
Needs, Political Realities, Economic Choices. Norman Myers
(Foreword by). Trade Cloth. Cambridge University Press. New
York, NY. 2001. 438p. ISBN:0-521-66210-9, ISBN13:
978-0-521-66210-9. Dewey:333.95/22/0973. LCCN:00-059874.
                            Audience: **l,u,f.**   *Choice, 2002.*

Victor, David G.   QC981.8.G56V53 2001
The Collapse of the Kyoto Protocol and the Struggle to Slow
Global Warming. Trade Cloth. Princeton University Press.
Princeton, NJ. 2001. 192p. ISBN:0-691-08870-5, ISBN13:
978-0-691-08870-9. Dewey:363.738/74526. LCCN:00-051633.
                            Audience: **l,u,f.**   *Choice, 2001.*

Waterman, Richard W.,   JF1501.W37 2004
  et al.
Bureaucrats, Politics, and the Environment. Amelia A. Rouse &
Robert Wright (Authors). Trade Paper. University of Pittsburgh
Press. Pittsburgh, PA. 2004. 160p. ISBN:0-8229-5829-5,
ISBN13: 978-0-8229-5829-1. Dewey:351/.01.
LCCN:2003-015505.
                            Audience: **l,u,f.**   *Choice, 2005.*

Wildavsky, Aaron B. &   HJ2051.W483 2003
  Caiden, Naomi
The New Politics of the Budgetary Process. Ed. 5. Trade Paper.
Longman Publishing. Boston, MA. 2003. 288p. Longmand
Classics in Political Science Ser. ISBN:0-321-15967-5, ISBN13:
978-0-321-15967-0. Dewey:352.4/8/0973. LCCN:2003-045817.
                                      Audience: **u,f.**

Williams, Michael   SD131.W53 2002
Deforesting the Earth: From Prehistory to Global Crisis. Trade
Cloth. University of Chicago Press. Chicago, IL. 2002. 715p.
ISBN:0-226-89926-8, ISBN13: 978-0-226-89926-8.
Dewey:333.75/137. LCCN:2001-007754.
                                      Audience: **l,u,f.**

World Resources   HC85.W67 2005
  Institute (Created by)
World Resources: The Wealth of the Poor: Managing
Ecosystems to Fight Poverty. Trade Paper, Perfect. World
Resources Institute. Washington, DC. 2005. 254p.
ISBN:1-56973-582-4, ISBN13: 978-1-56973-582-4.
Dewey:338.91724.
                                      Audience: **g,l,u,f.**

Wurzel, Rudiger K.   GE190.G7W87 2002
Environmental Policy-Making in Britain, Germany and the
European Union: The Europeanisation of Air and Water
Pollution Control. Cloth over Boards. Manchester University
Press. Manchester, 2002. 304p. Issues in Environmental Politics

Ser. ISBN:0-7190-5997-6, ISBN13: 978-0-7190-5997-1.
Dewey:363.7/0094. LCCN:2002-072532.
                              Audience: **u,f.**   *Choice, 2003.*

FILM STUDIES

The Film Studies section is intended as a core collection for college students majoring in film, cinema, media, communications, or any discipline that makes use of film to teach. The main focus of the collection is on critical and theoretical writings, reference materials, and practical filmmaking guides.

Film Studies covers subjects of interest to film students, including analysis and criticism, theory, history, national cinema, society and politics, genre, the motion picture industry, filmmaking, and filmmakers. Filmmakers are limited to collective works with only the giants of cinema receiving individual attention. Reference materials include research guides, bibliographies and filmographies, indexes and abstracts, and dictionaries and encyclopedias. Individual films and DVDs are not listed.

Film Studies is international in scope, covering nearly 800 English-language books, databases, and web sites available early in 2006. The vast majority of the books listed are in-print, but a handful of seminal publications now out-of-print are included.

— Mark Emmons and Jane Sloan

General Reference

☐ Filmbug.
http://www.filmbug.com/

Audience: **g,l,u.**

PN1993.4

☐ Internet Movie Database: IMDb.
http://www.imdb.com/

Audience: **g,l,u,f.**

AMG: All Media Guide　　　　**PN1998.A1**
☐ All Movie Guide.
http://www.allmovie.com/

Audience: **g,l,u,f.**

General Reference > Guides to Resources

Corrigan, Timothy　　　　**PN1995.C66 2005**
A Short Guide to Writing about Film. Ed. 6. Trade Paper.
Longman Publishing. Boston, MA. 2005. 190p. The Short Guide
Ser. ISBN:0-321-41228-1, ISBN13: 978-0-321-41228-7.
Dewey:808/.066791. LCCN:2005-040194.

Audience: **g,l,u.**

Emmons, Mark　　　　**Z5784**
Film and Television: A Guide to the Reference Literature. Trade
Paper. Libraries Unlimited, Inc. Westport, CT. 2006. 384p.
Reference Sources in the Humanities Ser. ISBN:1-56308-914-9,
ISBN13: 978-1-56308-914-5. Dewey:016.79143.
LCCN:2005-034358.

Audience: **g,l,u,f.**

Ochoa, George &　　　　**PN1994.A599 2002**
　Corey, Melinda
American Film Institute Desk Reference: Complete Guide to
Everything You Need to Know about the Movies. Clint
Eastwood (Introduction by), Jean Picker Firstenberg (Preface
by). Trade Cloth. Dorling Kindersley Publishing, Inc. New York,
NY. 2002. 608p. ISBN:0-7894-8934-1, ISBN13:
978-0-7894-8934-0. Dewey:791.43. LCCN:2002-071408.

Audience: **g,l,u,f.**

General Reference > Indexes and Abstracts

Z5784.M9
Film Literature Index. Filmdex. 1973.

Audience: **g,l,u,f.**

LB1043.Z9
Media Review Digest. Pierian Press. 1974.

Audience: **g,l,u,f.**

International Federation　　　　**Z5784.M9**
　of Film Archives
International Index to Film Periodicals. New York: R.R.
Bowker. 1972.

Audience: **g,l,u,f.**

General Reference > Bibliographies

Z5784.M9 W75
Film Index: A Bibliography: The Film As Art, Vol. 1. Trade
Cloth. Ayer Company Publishers, Inc. Manchester, NH. 1979.
Museum of Modern Art Publications in Reprint
ISBN:0-405-01512-7, ISBN13: 978-0-405-01512-0.
Dewey:011/.37. LCCN:41-008716.

Audience: **g,l,u,f.**

Bowles, Stephen E.　　　　**Z5784.M9B637 1994**
The Film Anthologies Index. Trade Cloth. Scarecrow Press, Inc.
Lanham, MD. 1994. 482p. ISBN:0-8108-2896-0, ISBN13:
978-0-8108-2896-4. Dewey:086.79143/75. LCCN:94-013541.

Audience: **g,l,u,f.** *Choice, 1995.*

Ellis, Jack　　　　**Z5784.M9**
The Film Book Bibliography, 1940-1975. Trade Cloth.
Scarecrow Press, Inc. Lanham, MD. 1979. 764p.
ISBN:0-8108-1127-8, ISBN13: 978-0-8108-1127-0.
Dewey:016.79143. LCCN:78-004055.

Audience: **g,l,u,f.** ℬ

Hagener, Malte;　　　　**Z5784.M9H29 2002**
　Töteberg, Michael
Film, an International Bibliography. Stuttgart: Metzler. 2002.
ISBN:3-476-01523-8, ISBN13: 978-3-476-01523-5.

Audience: **g,l,u,f.**

Manchel, Frank　　　　**Z5784.M9M34**
Film Study: An Analytical Bibliography, Vol. 3. Trade Cloth.
Fairleigh Dickinson University Press. Cranbury, NJ. 1991. 976p.
ISBN:0-8386-3413-3, ISBN13: 978-0-8386-3413-4.
Dewey:016.79143. LCCN:85-045026.

Audience: **g,l,u,f.** *Choice, 1991.*

General Reference > Filmographies

PN1992.95
Video Source Book. Ed. 26. Trade Cloth. Thomson Gale.
Farmington Hills, MI. 2001. ISBN:0-7876-3698-3, ISBN13:
978-0-7876-3698-2. Dewey:791.437.

Audience: **g,l,u,f.**

Brown, Gene (Editor)　　　　**PN1993 .N465**
The New York Times Encyclopedia of Film, Set. Paper over
Boards. Garland Publishing, Inc. New York, NY. 1992.
ISBN:0-8153-0349-1, ISBN13: 978-0-8153-0349-7.
Dewey:791.43.

Audience: **g,l,u,f.**

Buehrer, Beverly B.　　　　**PN1993.5.J3B78 1990**
Japanese Films: A Filmography and Commentary, 1921-1989.
Library Binding. McFarland & Company, Incorporated
Publishers. Jefferson, NC. 1990. 344p. ISBN:0-89950-458-2,
ISBN13: 978-0-89950-458-2. Dewey:791.43/75/0952.
LCCN:89-043684.

Audience: **g,l,u,f.** *Choice, 1991.*

Fenton, Jill R., et al.　　　　**PN1997.85.W58 1990**
Women Writers, from Page to Screen: A Guide to Literary
Sources. Charles G. Waugh, Jane Russo & Martin H.
Greensberg (Authors). Paper over Boards. Garland Publishing,
Inc. New York, NY. 1990. 512p. ISBN:0-8240-8529-9, ISBN13:
978-0-8240-8529-2. Dewey:016.79143/75/082.
LCCN:89-023479.

Audience: **g,l,u,f.** *Choice, 1991.*

Magill, Frank N.   PN1995.9.F67
(Editor)
Magill's Survey of Cinema, Foreign Language Films, 8 vols.
Library Binding. Salem Press, Inc. Hackensack, NJ. 1985.
3743p. ISBN:0-89356-243-2, ISBN13: 978-0-89356-243-4.
Dewey:791.43/75. LCCN:85-018241.
Audience: **g,l,u.** *Choice, 1986.*

Magill, Frank N   PN1993.5.A1
Magill's Survey of Cinema: English Language Films, First
Series, Set. Frank N. Magill (Editor). Salem Press, Inc. 1980.
First Ser. ISBN:0-89356-225-4, ISBN13: 978-0-89356-225-0.
Audience: **g,l,u.** *B*

Magill, Frank N   PN1933.5.A1
Magill's Survey of Cinema: English Language Films, Second
Series, Set. Frank N. Magill (Editor). Salem Press, Inc. 1981.
Second Ser. ISBN:0-89356-230-0, ISBN13: 978-0-89356-230-4.
Audience: **g,u,f.**

Magill, Frank N   PN1993.5.A1
Magill's Survey of Cinema: Silent Films, Set. Frank N. Magill
(Editor). Salem Press, Inc. 1982. ISBN:0-89356-239-4, ISBN13:
978-0-89356-239-7.
Audience: **g,l,u.** *B*

Mes, Tom & Sharp,   PN1993.5.J3M47 2004
Jasper
Midnight Eye Guide to New Japanese Film. Hideo Nakata
(Foreword by). Trade Paper. Stone Bridge Press. Berkeley, CA.
2004. 376p. ISBN:1-880656-89-2, ISBN13: 978-1-880656-89-1.
Dewey:791.43/0952. LCCN:2004-022653.
Audience: **g,l,u,f.** *Choice, 2005.*

Nash, Jay R. & Ross,   PN1995
Stanley R.
The Motion Picture Guide, Vol. 110. Trade Cloth. CineBooks.
New York, NY. 1987. The Complete Film Resource Center Ser.
ISBN:0-933997-00-0, ISBN13: 978-0-933997-00-4.
Dewey:792.93. LCCN:85-071145.
Audience: **g,l,u,f.** *Choice, 1988.*

Schilling, Mark   PN1995.9.G3S33 2003
The Yakuza Movie Book: A Guide to Japanese Gangster Films.
Trade Paper. Stone Bridge Press. Berkeley, CA. 2003. 320p.
ISBN:1-880656-76-0, ISBN13: 978-1-880656-76-1.
Dewey:791.43/655. LCCN:2003-003855.
Audience: **g,l,u,f.** *Choice, 2004.*

Slide, Anthony (Editor)   PN1995
Selected Film Criticism: Foreign Films, 1930-1950. Trade Cloth.
Scarecrow Press, Inc. Lanham, MD. 1984. 207p.
ISBN:0-8108-1673-3, ISBN13: 978-0-8108-1673-2.
Dewey:791.43/75. LCCN:81-023344.
Audience: **u,f.**

Slide, Anthony (Editor)   PN1995
Selected Film Criticism, 1896-1911. Trade Cloth. Scarecrow
Press, Inc. Lanham, MD. 1982. 134p. ISBN:0-8108-1575-3,
ISBN13: 978-0-8108-1575-9. Dewey:791.43/75.
LCCN:82-010623.
Audience: **u,f.** *B*

Slide, Anthony (Editor)   PN1995
Selected Film Criticism, 1912-1920, Vol. 2. Trade Cloth.
Scarecrow Press, Inc. Lanham, MD. 1982. 325p.
ISBN:0-8108-1525-7, ISBN13: 978-0-8108-1525-4.
Dewey:791.43/75. LCCN:81-023344.
Audience: **u,f.**

Slide, Anthony (Editor)   PN1995
Selected Film Criticism, 1921-1930. Trade Cloth. Scarecrow
Press, Inc. Lanham, MD. 1982. 335p. ISBN:0-8108-1551-6,
ISBN13: 978-0-8108-1551-3. Dewey:791.43/75.
LCCN:81-023344.
Audience: **u,f.**

Slide, Anthony (Editor)   PN1995
Selected Film Criticism, 1931-1940. Trade Cloth. Scarecrow
Press, Inc. Lanham, MD. 1982. 292p. ISBN:0-8108-1570-2,
ISBN13: 978-0-8108-1570-4. Dewey:791.43/75.
LCCN:82-010642.
Audience: **u,f.**

Slide, Anthony (Editor)   PN1995
Selected Film Criticism, 1941-1950. Trade Cloth. Scarecrow
Press, Inc. Lanham, MD. 1983. 280p. ISBN:0-8108-1593-1,
ISBN13: 978-0-8108-1593-3. Dewey:791.43/75.
LCCN:81-023344.
Audience: **u,f.**

Slide, Anthony (Editor)   PN1995
Selected Film Criticism, 1951-1960, Vol. 7. Trade Cloth.
Scarecrow Press, Inc. Lanham, MD. 1985. 198p.
ISBN:0-8108-1763-2, ISBN13: 978-0-8108-1763-0.
Dewey:791.43/75. LCCN:81-023344.
Audience: **u,f.**

General Reference > Dictionaries and Encyclopedias

Beaver, Frank Eugene   PN1993.45.B33 2005
Dictionary of Film Terms: The Aesthetic Companion to Film
Art. Trade Cloth. Peter Lang Publishing, Inc. New York, NY.
2005. viii, 289p. ISBN:0-8204-7298-0, ISBN13:
978-0-8204-7298-0. Dewey:791.43/03. LCCN:2005-002249.
Audience: **g,l,u,f.**

Blandford, Steve   PN1993.45.B49 2001
(Editor), et al.
The Film Studies Dictionary. Barry K. Grant & Jim Hiller
(Editors). Trade Paper. Oxford University Press, Inc. New York,
NY. 2001. 296p. An Arnold Publication Ser.
ISBN:0-340-74191-0, ISBN13: 978-0-340-74191-7.
Dewey:791.43/03. LCCN:2001-269526.
Audience: **g,l,u,f.** *Choice, 2001.*

Bognar, Desi K.   PN1990.4.B64 2000
International Dictionary of Broadcasting and Film. Ed. 2. Trade
Paper. Elsevier Science & Technology Books. Saint Louis, MO.
1999. 328p. ISBN:0-240-80376-0, ISBN13: 978-0-240-80376-0.
Dewey:384.54/03. LCCN:99-027781.
Audience: **g,l,u,f.** *Choice, 1996.*

Fernett, Gene   PN1993.5.U6F45 2003
American Film Studios: An Historical Encyclopedia. Paper Text.
McFarland & Company, Incorporated Publishers. Jefferson, NC.
2001. 310p. ISBN:0-7864-1325-5, ISBN13: 978-0-7864-1325-6.
Dewey:791.4/3/0973. LCCN:88-42514.
Audience: **g,l,u,f.** *Choice, 1989.*

HAYWARD   PN1993.45H36 2006
Cinema Studies Key Concepts E3. Ed. 3. Paper over Boards.
Routledge. New York, NY. 2006. 576p. ISBN:0-415-36781-6,
ISBN13: 978-0-415-36781-3. Dewey:791.43/03.
LCCN:2005-020302.
Audience: **g,l,u.**

Jackson, Kevin PN1993.45.J23 1998
The Language of Cinema. Trade Paper. Routledge. New York, NY. 1998. 288p. ISBN:0-415-92049-3, ISBN13: 978-0-415-92049-0. Dewey:791.4/3/014. LCCN:97-038644.
Audience: **g,l,u,f.**

Katz, Ephraim PN1993.45.K34 2005
The Film Encyclopedia: The Most Comprehensive Encyclopedia of World Cinema in a Single Volume. Ed. 5. Trade Paper. HarperCollins Publishers. New York, NY. 2005. 1552p. ISBN:0-06-074214-3, ISBN13: 978-0-06-074214-0. Dewey:791.43/03. LCCN:2005-041393.
Audience: **g,l,u,f.**

Konigsberg, Ira TR850
Complete Film Dictionary. Ed. 2. Trade Paper. Penguin Group (USA) Inc. New York, NY. 1998. 480p. ISBN:0-14-051393-0, ISBN13: 978-0-14-051393-6. Dewey:778.5/3. LCCN:96-052953.
Audience: **g,l,u,f.** *Choice, 1999.*

Law, Jonathan; Wright, John PN1993.45.B74 1997
Cassell Companion to Cinema. Jonathan Law (Editor) ; John Wright (Contribution by). Continuum International Publishing Group, Ltd. 1997. ISBN:0-304-34992-5, ISBN13: 978-0-304-34992-0.
Audience: **g,l,u,f.**

Miller, Blair PN1995.9.C55M53 1995
American Silent Film Comedies: An Illustrated Encyclopedia of Persons, Studios and Terminology. Cloth Text. McFarland & Company, Incorporated Publishers. Jefferson, NC. 1995. 292p. ISBN:0-89950-929-0, ISBN13: 978-0-89950-929-7. Dewey:791.43/617/0973. LCCN:94-38777.
Audience: **g,l,u,f.** *Choice, 1996.*

Pearson, Roberta E. (Editor), et al. PN1993.45.C75 2000
Critical Dictionary of Film and Television Theory. Gill Branston, William Urricchio, Philip Simpson & David Black (Editors). Paper over Boards. Routledge. New York, NY. 2000. 528p. ISBN:0-415-16218-1, ISBN13: 978-0-415-16218-0. Dewey:791.43/01. LCCN:00-024897.
Audience: **g,l,u,f.** *Choice, 2001.*

Silver, Alain & Ward, Elizabeth (Editors) PN1995.9.F54F55 1992
Film Noir: An Encyclopedic Reference to the American Style. Ed. 3. Trade Paper. Overlook Press, The. New York, NY. 1993. 479p. ISBN:0-87951-479-5, ISBN13: 978-0-87951-479-2. Dewey:791.4/36/55. LCCN:93-236035.
Audience: **g,l,u,f.** ℬ *Choice, 1993.*

Film Analysis and Criticism

Clamen, Stewart M. PN1995
☐ MRQE: Review Query Engine.
http://www.mrqe.com/lookup
Audience: **g,l,u,f.**

Film Analysis and Criticism > Animation

Bendazzi, Giannalberto NC1765.B4213 1994
Cartoons: One Hundred Years of Cinema Animation. Anna Taraboletti-Segre (Translator). Trade Paper. Indiana University Press. Bloomington, IN. 1995. 434p. ISBN:0-253-20937-4,

ISBN13: 978-0-253-20937-5. Dewey:791.43/3. LCCN:94-029075.
Audience: **g,l,u,f.** *Choice, 1995.*

Brasch, Walter M. PN1997.5
Cartoon Monickers: An Insight Into the Animation Industry. Trade Paper. iUniverse, Inc. Lincoln, NE. 2000. 196p. ISBN:0-595-14501-9, ISBN13: 978-0-595-14501-0. Dewey:791.43/3/0973.
Audience: **u,f.**

Cohen, Karl F. NC1766.5.C45
Forbidden Animation: Censored Cartoons and Blacklisted Animators in America. Paper Text. McFarland & Company, Incorporated Publishers. Jefferson, NC. 2004. 238p. ISBN:0-7864-2032-4, ISBN13: 978-0-7864-2032-2. Dewey:791.4/33/0973.
Audience: **g,l,u,f.** *Choice, 1998.*

Crafton, Donald NC1765.C7 1993
Before Mickey: The Animated Film, 1898-1928. Trade Paper. University of Chicago Press. Chicago, IL. 1993. 436p. ISBN:0-226-11667-0, ISBN13: 978-0-226-11667-9. Dewey:791.433. LCCN:93-029048.
Audience: **u,f.**

Drazen, Patrick NC1766.J3 D73 2003
Anime Explosion!: The What? Why? and Wow! of Japanese Animation. Trade Paper. Stone Bridge Press. Berkeley, CA. 2002. 320p. ISBN:1-880656-72-8, ISBN13: 978-1-880656-72-3. Dewey:791.43/34. LCCN:2005-281368.
Audience: **l,u,f.** *Choice, 2003.*

Grant, John TR897.5.G73 2001
Masters of Animation. Trade Cloth. Watson-Guptill Publications, Inc. New York, NY. 2001. 192p. ISBN:0-8230-3041-5, ISBN13: 978-0-8230-3041-5. Dewey:791.43/3 B. LCCN:2001-091776.
Audience: **g,l,u,f.** *Choice, 2002.*

Klein, Norman M. NC1766.U5
Seven Minutes: The Life and Death of the American Animated Cartoon. Trade Paper. Analytical Psychology Club of San Francisco, Inc. San Francisco, CA. 1996. 284p. ISBN:1-85984-150-3, ISBN13: 978-1-85984-150-1. Dewey:791.4/33/0973.
Audience: **g,l,u,f.**

Koch, Dave NC1765
☐ Big Cartoon Database.
http://www.bcdb.com/
Audience: **g,l,u,f.**

Lawson, Tim & Persons, Alisa PN2285.L38 2004
The Magic Behind the Voices: A Who's Who of Cartoon Voice Actors. Trade Cloth. University Press of Mississippi. Jackson, MS. 2004. 356p. ISBN:1-57806-695-6, ISBN13: 978-1-57806-695-7. Dewey:791.4302/8/092273 B. LCCN:2004-006488.
Audience: **u,f.**

Lenburg, Jeff NC1766.U5L46 1999
The Encyclopedia of Animated Cartoons. Ed. 2. June Foray (Foreword by). Trade Paper. Facts On File, Inc. New York, NY. 1999. xv, 576p. ISBN:0-8160-3832-5, ISBN13: 978-0-8160-3832-9. Dewey:791.43/3. LCCN:98-046100.
Audience: **g,l,u,f.** *Choice, 2000, 1992.*

Lent, John A. (Editor)　　　　NC1765.A538 2001
Animation in Asia and the Pacific. Trade Cloth. Indiana
University Press. Bloomington, IN. 2001. 304p.
ISBN:0-253-34035-7, ISBN13: 978-0-253-34035-1.
Dewey:778.5/347. LCCN:2001-024780.
　　　　　　　　　　　Audience: **l,u,f.**

Maltin, Leonard　　　　　　　**NC1765**
Of Mice and Magic: A History of American Animated Cartoons.
Library Binding. Sagebrush Education Resources. Caledonia,
MN. 1987. ISBN:0-613-64753-X, ISBN13: 978-0-613-64753-3.
Dewey:791.43/3.
　　　　　　　　　　　Audience: **g,l.** *B*

Markstein, Donald D.
☐ Don Markstein's Toonopedia.
http://www.toonopedia.com/
　　　　　　　　　　　Audience: **g,l,u,f.**

Merritt, Russell　　　　　NC1766.U52.D548 1993
Walt in Wonderland: The Silent Films of Walt Disney. Trade
Cloth. Bow Historical Books. New Providence, NJ. 1993. 164p.
ISBN:88-86155-02-6, ISBN13: 978-88-86155-02-1.
Dewey:741.5/8. LCCN:94-073156.
　　　　　　　　　Audience: **u,f.** *Choice, 1994.*

Napier, Susan Jolliffe　　　　NC1766.J3N37 2001
Anime from Akira to Princess Mononoke: Experiencing
Contemporary Japanese Animation. Trade Cloth. Palgrave
Macmillan. New York, NY. 2001. 336p. ISBN:0-312-23862-2,
ISBN13: 978-0-312-23862-9. Dewey:791.43/3.
LCCN:00-051473.
　　　　　　　　　Audience: **u,f.** *Choice, 2001.*

Pettigrew, Neil　　　　　　TR897.5.P495 1999
The Stop Motion Filmography: A Critical Guide to over 325
Features Using Puppet Animation. Ray Harryhausen (Foreword
by). Cloth Text. McFarland & Company, Incorporated
Publishers. Jefferson, NC. 1999. 878p. ISBN:0-7864-0446-9,
ISBN13: 978-0-7864-0446-9. Dewey:791.43/3. LCCN:98-49799.
　　　　　　　Audience: **g,l,u,f.** *Choice, 2000.*

Sampson, Henry T.　　　　NC1766.5.A35S26 1997
That's Enough Folks: Black Images in Animated Cartoons,
1900-1960. Trade Cloth. Scarecrow Press, Inc. Lanham, MD.
1998. 288p. ISBN:0-8108-3250-X, ISBN13: 978-0-8108-3250-3.
Dewey:791.43/6520396073. LCCN:96-049987.
　　　　　　　Audience: **g,l,u,f.** *Choice, 1999.*

Shull, Michael S. &　　　　　　**D743.23**
Wilt, David E.
Doing Their Bit: Wartime American Animated Short Films,
1939-1945. Ed. 2. Paper Text. McFarland & Company,
Incorporated Publishers. Jefferson, NC. 2004. 256p.
ISBN:0-7864-1555-X, ISBN13: 978-0-7864-1555-7.
Dewey:741.5/0973/09044. LCCN:2003-024614.
　　　　　　　　　Audience: **u,f.** *Choice, 1987.*

Smoodin, Eric　　　　　　NC1766.U5S66 1993
Animating Culture: Hollywood Cartoons from the Sound Era.
Cloth Text. Rutgers University Press. Piscataway, NJ. 1993.
232p. Media, Culture, and Communication Ser.
ISBN:0-8135-1948-9, ISBN13: 978-0-8135-1948-7.
Dewey:791.433. LCCN:92-032891.
　　　　　　　　　Audience: **u,f.** *Choice, 1993.*

Smoodin, Eric (Editor)　　　　PN1999.W27D57 1994
Disney Discourse: Producing the Magic Kingdom. UK-B
Format Paperback. Routledge. New York, NY. 1994. 272p. AFI

Film Readers Ser. ISBN:0-415-90616-4, ISBN13:
978-0-415-90616-6. Dewey:384/.8/0979494. LCCN:93-032366.
　　　　　　　　　Audience: **u,f.** *Choice, 1995.*

Thomas, Frank &　　　　　NC1766.U52D58 1995
Johnston, Ollie A.
The Illusion of Life: Disney Animation. Trade Cloth. Disney
Press. New York, NY. 1995. 576p. ISBN:0-7868-6070-7,
ISBN13: 978-0-7868-6070-8. Dewey:741.5/8/0979494.
LCCN:95-019427.
　　　　　　　　　Audience: **g,l,u.**

Webb, Graham　　　　　　NC1765.W42 2000
The Animated Film Encyclopedia: A Complete Guide to
American Shorts, Features and Sequences, 1900-1979. Trade
Cloth. McFarland & Company, Incorporated Publishers.
Jefferson, NC. 2000. 640p. ISBN:0-7864-0728-X, ISBN13:
978-0-7864-0728-6. Dewey:791.4/33/03. LCCN:00-699089.
　　　　　　　Audience: **g,l,u,f.** *Choice, 2000.*

Wells, Paul　　　　　　　**PN1997.5**
Animation: Genre and Authorship. Trade Paper. Wallflower
Press. London, 2002. 148p. Short Cuts Ser.
ISBN:1-903364-20-5, ISBN13: 978-1-903364-20-8.
Dewey:791.4334.
　　　　　　　　　Audience: **l,u,f.**

Wells, Paul　　　　　　PN1997.5.W45 2002
Animation and America. Trade Cloth. Rutgers University Press.
Piscataway, NJ. 2002. 172p. ISBN:0-8135-3159-4, ISBN13:
978-0-8135-3159-5. Dewey:791.4334097309.
　　　　　　　Audience: **l,u,f.** *Choice, 2003.*

Film Analysis and Criticism >
Documentary Film

Aitken, Ian　　　　　　PN1995.9.D6D575 1998
The Documentary Film Movement: An Anthology. Trade Paper.
Edinburgh University Press. Edinburgh, 1998. 256p.
ISBN:0-7486-0948-2, ISBN13: 978-0-7486-0948-2.
Dewey:070.1/8. LCCN:98-226148.
　　　　　　　　　Audience: **u,f.**

Aitken, Ian (Editor)　　　　PN1995.9.D6E53 2005
Encyclopedia of the Documentary Film. Paper over Boards.
Routledge. New York, NY. 2005. 1968p. ISBN:1-57958-445-4,
ISBN13: 978-1-57958-445-0. Dewey:070.1/8.
LCCN:2005-046519.
　　　　　　　Audience: **l,u.** *Choice, 2006.*

Barnouw, Erik　　　　　PN1995.9.D6 B37 1993
Documentary: A History of the Non-Fiction Film. Ed. 3. Trade
Paper. Oxford University Press, Inc. New York, NY. 1993. 408p.
ISBN:0-19-507898-5, ISBN13: 978-0-19-507898-5.
Dewey:070.1/8. LCCN:92-034052.
　　　　　　　　　Audience: **l,u,f.**

Barsam, Richard M.　　　　PN1995.9.D6B38 1992
Nonfiction Film: A Critical History. Paper Text. Indiana
University Press. Bloomington, IN. 1992. 504p.
ISBN:0-253-20706-1, ISBN13: 978-0-253-20706-7.
Dewey:070.1/8/09. LCCN:91-026985.
　　　　　　　Audience: **g,l,u,f.**

Beattie, Keith　　　　　PN1995.9.D6B384 2004
Documentary Screens: Non-Fiction Film and Television. Cloth
over Boards. Palgrave Macmillan. New York, NY. 2004. 224p.

ISBN:0-333-74116-1, ISBN13: 978-0-333-74116-0.
Dewey:070.1/8. LCCN:2004-042736.

Audience: **l,u,f.**

Bernard, Sheila Curran   **PN1995.9.D6B394 2003**
Documentary Storytelling for Video and Filmmakers. Paper
Text. Elsevier Science & Technology Books. Saint Louis, MO.
2003. 297p. ISBN:0-240-80539-9, ISBN13: 978-0-240-80539-9.
Dewey:070.1/8. LCCN:2003-057748.

Audience: **u,f.**

Bruzzi, Stella   **PN1995.9.D6B78 2006**
New Documentary: A Critical Introduction. Ed. 2. Paper over
Boards. Routledge. New York, NY. 2006. 224p.
ISBN:0-415-38525-3, ISBN13: 978-0-415-38525-1.
Dewey:070.1/8. LCCN:2006-006456.

Audience: **g,l.**

Corner, John   **PN1995.9.D6C57 1996**
The Art of Record: A Critical Introduction to Documentary.
Trade Paper. Manchester University Press. Manchester, 1996.
240p. ISBN:0-7190-4687-4, ISBN13: 978-0-7190-4687-2.
Dewey:070.1/8. LCCN:95-047212.

Audience: **l,u.**

Cunningham, Megan   **PN1995.9.D6**
The Art of the Documentary: Ten Conversations with Leading
Directors, Cinematographers, Editors, and Producers. Trade
Paper, Perfect. New Riders Publishing. Berkeley, CA. 2005.
275p. Voices That Matter Ser. ISBN:0-321-31623-1, ISBN13:
978-0-321-31623-3. Dewey:070.1/8. LCCN:2005-541551.

Audience: **u,f.**

Ellis, Jack C.   **PN1998.3.G75E44 2000**
John Grierson: Life, Contributions, Influence. Trade Cloth.
Southern Illinois University Press. Carbondale, IL. 2000. 384p.
ISBN:0-8093-2242-0, ISBN13: 978-0-8093-2242-8.
Dewey:791.43/0232/092. LCCN:99-036971.

Audience: **u,f.** *Choice, 2000.*

Ellis, Jack C. &   **PN1995.9.D6E46 2005**
  McLane, Betsy
A New History of Documentary Film. Trade Cloth. Continuum
International Publishing Group, Ltd. London, 2005. 384p.
ISBN:0-8264-1750-7, ISBN13: 978-0-8264-1750-3.
Dewey:070.1/8. LCCN:2005-013290.

Audience: **g,l,u.** *Choice, 2006.*

Gaines, Jane & Renov,   **PN1995.9.D6C535 1999**
  Michael (Editors)
Collecting Visible Evidence. Book, Other. University of
Minnesota Press. Minneapolis, MN. 1999. ix, 339p. Visible
Evidence Ser., Vol. 6 ISBN:0-8166-3135-2, ISBN13:
978-0-8166-3135-3. Dewey:070.1/8. LCCN:99-014043.

Audience: **l,u,f.**

Girgus, Sam B.   **PN1995.9.U64G57 2002**
America on Film: Modernism, Documentary, and a Changing
America. Cloth Text. Cambridge University Press. New York,
NY. 2002. 238p. ISBN:0-521-81092-2, ISBN13:
978-0-521-81092-0. Dewey:791.43/6273. LCCN:2001-052853.

Audience: **u,f.** *Choice, 2003.*

Grant, Barry K. &   **PN1995.9.D6D58 1998**
  Sloniowski, Jeannette (Editors)
Documenting the Documentary: Close Readings of Documentary
Film and Video. Trade Cloth. Wayne State University Press.
Detroit, MI. 1998. 488p. Contemporary Film and Television Ser.

ISBN:0-8143-2639-0, ISBN13: 978-0-8143-2639-8.
Dewey:070.1/8. LCCN:97-051990.

Audience: **u,f.** *Choice, 1999.*

Hogarth, David   **PN1995.9.D6H56 2006**
Realer Than Reel: Global Directions in Documentary. Trade
Cloth. University of Texas Press. Austin, TX. 2006. 198p.
ISBN:0-292-71259-6, ISBN13: 978-0-292-71259-1.
Dewey:070.1/8. LCCN:2005-011657.

Audience: **u,f.**

Izod, John (Editor), et al.   **PN1995.9.D6F76 2000**
From Grierson to the Docu-Soap: Breaking the Boundaries.
Richard Kilborn & Matthew Hibberd (Editors). Trade Paper.
University of Luton Press. Luton, 2003. 240p.
ISBN:1-86020-577-1, ISBN13: 978-1-86020-577-4.
Dewey:070.1/8. LCCN:2001-339625.

Audience: **u,f.**

Nichols, Bill   **PN1995.9.D6N538 1994**
Blurred Boundaries: Questions of Meaning in Contemporary
Culture. Trade Paper. Indiana University Press. Bloomington,
IN. 1995. 208p. ISBN:0-253-20900-5, ISBN13:
978-0-253-20900-9. Dewey:070.1/8. LCCN:94-002205.

Audience: **u,f.** *Choice, 1995.*

Nichols, Bill   **PN1995.9.D6N539 2001**
Introduction to Documentary. Trade Paper. Indiana University
Press. Bloomington, IN. 2001. 404p. ISBN:0-253-21469-6,
ISBN13: 978-0-253-21469-0. Dewey:070.1/8. LCCN:00-054267.

Audience: **g,l.** *Choice, 2002.*

Nichols, Bill   **PN1995.9.D6N54 1991**
Representing Reality: Issues and Concepts in Documentary.
Trade Paper. Indiana University Press. Bloomington, IN. 1992.
336p. ISBN:0-253-20681-2, ISBN13: 978-0-253-20681-7.
Dewey:070.1/8. LCCN:91-002637.

Audience: **u,f.** *Choice, 1992.*

Nornes, Markus   **PN1995.9.D6N59 2003**
Japanese Documentary Films: The Meiji Era Through
Hiroshima. Trade Paper. University of Minnesota Press.
Minneapolis, MN. 2003. 248p. Visible Evidence Ser., Vol. 15
ISBN:0-8166-4046-7, ISBN13: 978-0-8166-4046-1.
Dewey:070.1/8. LCCN:2003-000796.

Audience: **u,f.**

O'Connell, P. J.   **PN1998.3.D73.O25**
Robert Drew and the Development of Cinema Verite in
America. Trade Cloth. Southern Illinois University Press.
Carbondale, IL. 1992. 312p. ISBN:0-8093-1779-6, ISBN13:
978-0-8093-1779-0. Dewey:070.1/8. LCCN:91-039992.

Audience: **u.** *Choice, 1993.*

Plantinga, Carl R.   **PN1995.9.D6 P56 1997**
Rhetoric and Representation in Nonfiction Film. Dudley Andrew
& William Rothman (Contribution by). Trade Cloth. Cambridge
University Press. New York, NY. 1997. 267p. Studies in Film
ISBN:0-521-57326-2, ISBN13: 978-0-521-57326-9.
Dewey:070.1/8. LCCN:96-045968.

Audience: **u,f.**

Rabiger, Michael   **PN1995.9.D6R33 2004**
Directing the Documentary. Ed. 4. Paper Text. Elsevier Science
& Technology Books. Saint Louis, MO. 2004. 627p.
ISBN:0-240-80608-5, ISBN13: 978-0-240-80608-2.
Dewey:070.1/8. LCCN:2004-043282.

Audience: **u,f.**

Renov, Michael   **PN1995.9.D6R44 2004**
The Subject of Documentary. Trade Cloth. University of
Minnesota Press. Minneapolis, MN. 2004. 264p. Visible
Evidence Ser., Vol. 16 ISBN:0-8166-3440-8, ISBN13:
978-0-8166-3440-8. Dewey:070.1/8. LCCN:2003-028176.
Audience: **l,u,f.**   *Choice, 2005.*

Renov, Michael (Editor)   **PN1995.9.D6T45 1993**
Theorizing Documentary. UK-B Format Paperback. Routledge.
New York, NY. 1993. 272p. AFI Film Readers Ser.
ISBN:0-415-90382-3, ISBN13: 978-0-415-90382-0.
Dewey:070.18. LCCN:92-033807.
Audience: **u,f.**   *Choice, 1993.*

Rosenthal, Alan &   **PN1995.9.D6**
  Corner, John (Editors)
New Challenges for Documentary. Ed. 2. Cloth over Boards.
Manchester University Press. Manchester, 2005. 512p.
ISBN:0-7190-6898-3, ISBN13: 978-0-7190-6898-0.
Dewey:070.1/8. LCCN:2005-272069.
Audience: **u,f.**   *Choice, 1989.*

Rothman, William   **PN1995.9.D6 R69 1997**
  (Author, Contribution by)
Documentary Film Classics. Dudley Andrew, J. Dudley Andrew
& Henry Breitrose (Contribution by). Trade Paper. Cambridge
University Press. New York, NY. 1997. 238p. Cambridge
Studies in Film ISBN:0-521-45681-9, ISBN13:
978-0-521-45681-4. Dewey:070.1/8. LCCN:96-014029.
Audience: **g,l,u,f.**

Sherman, Sharon R.   **PN1995.9.D6S494 1998**
Documenting Ourselves: Film, Video, and Culture. Paper Text.
University Press of Kentucky. Lexington, KY. 1998. 312p.
ISBN:0-8131-0934-5, ISBN13: 978-0-8131-0934-3.
Dewey:070.1/8. LCCN:97-023971.
Audience: **u,f.**   *Choice, 1998.*

Stubbs, Liz   **PN1995.9.D6S853 2002**
Documentary Filmmakers Speak. Trade Paper. Allworth Press.
New York, NY. 2002. 240p. ISBN:1-58115-236-1, ISBN13:
978-1-58115-236-4. Dewey:070.1/8. LCCN:2002-005830.
Audience: **l,u.**

Swann, Paul   **PN1995.9.D6S88 1989**
The British Documentary Film Movement, 1926-1946. Dudley
Andrew & William Rothman (Contribution by). Trade Cloth.
Cambridge University Press. New York, NY. 1989. 232p.
Cambridge Studies in Film ISBN:0-521-33479-9, ISBN13:
978-0-521-33479-2. Dewey:791.43/53/0941. LCCN:88-025693.
Audience: **u,f.**   *Choice, 1990.*

Waldman, Diane   **PN1995.9.W6F447 1999**
  (Author, Editor)
Feminism and Documentary. Book, Other. University of
Minnesota Press. Minneapolis, MN. 1999. 372p. Visible
Evidence Ser. ISBN:0-8166-3006-2, ISBN13:
978-0-8166-3006-6. Dewey:070.1/8. LCCN:98-045119.
Audience: **u,f.**

Warren, Charles   **PN1995.9.D6B48 1996**
  (Editor)
Beyond Document: Essays on Nonfiction Film. Trade Paper.
Wesleyan University Press. Middletown, CT. 1996. 396p.

ISBN:0-8195-6290-4, ISBN13: 978-0-8195-6290-6.
Dewey:070.1/8. LCCN:95-016674.
Audience: **u,f.**   *Choice, 1996.*

Film Analysis and Criticism >
Documentary Film > Ethnographic Film

Barbash, Ilisa & Taylor,   **GN347.B37 1997**
  Lucien
Cross-Cultural Filmmaking: A Handbook for Making
Documentary and Ethnographic Films and Videos. Trade Paper.
University of California Press. Berkeley, CA. 1997. 580p.
ISBN:0-520-08760-7, ISBN13: 978-0-520-08760-6.
Dewey:305.8/00208. LCCN:96-017662.
Audience: **u,f.**

Griffiths, Alison   **GN347.G73 2002**
Wondrous Difference: Cinema, Anthropology, and
Turn-of-the-Century Visual Culture. Trade Paper. Columbia
University Press. New York, NY. 2002. 528p. Film and Culture
Ser. ISBN:0-231-11697-7, ISBN13: 978-0-231-11697-8.
Dewey:305.8. LCCN:2001-047227.
Audience: **u,f.**   *Choice, 2003, 2002.*

Hockings, Paul   **GN347C**
Principles of Visual Anthropology. Ed. 3. Trade Paper. Walter
De Gruyter Inc. Ossining, NY. 2003. xix, 562p.
ISBN:3-11-017930-X, ISBN13: 978-3-11-017930-9.
Dewey:301/.078.
Audience: **u,f.**

Lewis, E. D. (Editor)   **GN21.A83T56 2004**
Timothy Asch and Ethnographic Film. Paper over Boards.
Routledge. New York, NY. 2003. 328p. Studies in Visual
Culture Ser. ISBN:0-415-32774-1, ISBN13: 978-0-415-32774-9.
Dewey:791.43/0233/092 B. LCCN:2003-046904.
Audience: **u,f.**

Loizos, Peter   **PN1995.9.D6**
Innovation in Ethnographic Film: From Innocence to
Self-Consciousness, 1955-1985. Trade Paper. University of
Chicago Press. Chicago, IL. 1993. 234p. ISBN:0-226-49227-3,
ISBN13: 978-0-226-49227-8. Dewey:070.1/8. LCCN:93-006877.
Audience: **u,f.**   *Choice, 1994.*

MacDougall, David   **GN347.M33 1998**
Transcultural Cinema. Lucien Taylor (Editor). Trade Paper.
Princeton University Press. Princeton, NJ. 1998. 328p.
ISBN:0-691-01234-2, ISBN13: 978-0-691-01234-6.
Dewey:305.8. LCCN:98-021197.
Audience: **u,f.**   *Choice, 1999.*

Rony, Fatimah T.   **GN347.R55 1996**
The Third Eye: Race, Cinema, and Ethnographic Spectacle.
Trade Paper. Duke University Press. Durham, NC. 1996. 320p.
ISBN:0-8223-1840-7, ISBN13: 978-0-8223-1840-8.
Dewey:305.8/00208. LCCN:96-013255.
Audience: **u,f.**

Russell, Catherine   **PN1995.9.D6R79 1999**
Experimental Ethnography: The Work of Film in the Age of
Video. Trade Paper. Duke University Press. Durham, NC. 1999.
xviii, 391p. ISBN:0-8223-2319-2, ISBN13: 978-0-8223-2319-8.
Dewey:070.1/8. LCCN:98-046549.

Audience: **u,f.**

Film Analysis and Criticism > Narrative Film and Genres

Altman, Rick   **PN1995.A383 1999**
Film/Genre. Trade Paper. BFI Publishing. London, 1999. 246p.
ISBN:0-85170-717-3, ISBN13: 978-0-85170-717-4.
Dewey:791.43/6. LCCN:99-229768.

Audience: **l,u,f.**

Armstrong, Richard B.   **PN1997.8**
& Armstrong, Mary Willems
Encyclopedia of Film Themes, Settings and Series. Cloth Text.
McFarland & Company, Incorporated Publishers. Jefferson, NC.
2000. 237p. ISBN:0-7864-0893-6, ISBN13: 978-0-7864-0893-1.
Dewey:791.4/3/0973. LCCN:00-64009.

Audience: **g,l,u,f.** *Choice, 2001.*

Browne, Nick (Editor)   **PN1993.5.U6R443 1998**
Refiguring American Film Genres: History and Theory. Trade
Paper. University of California Press. Berkeley, CA. 1998. 342p.
ISBN:0-520-20731-9, ISBN13: 978-0-520-20731-8.
Dewey:791.43/6. LCCN:97-042091.

Audience: **u,f.** *Choice, 1998.*

Case, Christopher   **PN1998.C323 1996**
The Ultimate Movie Thesaurus: The Only Book You'll Ever
Need to Find the Movie You Want. Trade Paper. Henry Holt &
Company. New York, NY. 1996. 1104p. ISBN:0-8050-3496-X,
ISBN13: 978-0-8050-3496-7. Dewey:016.79143/75.
LCCN:96-036427.

Audience: **g,l,u,f.**

Dixon, Wheeler Winston   **PN1995.F45787 2000**
(Editor)
Film Genre 2000: New Critical Essays. Cloth Text. State
University of New York Press. Albany, NY. 2000. vii, 266p.
ISBN:0-7914-4513-5, ISBN13: 978-0-7914-4513-6.
Dewey:791.43/6. LCCN:99-029901.

Audience: **u,f.** *Choice, 2000.*

Gehring, Wes D.   **PN1993**
(Editor)
Handbook of American Film Genres. Cloth Text. Greenwood
Publishing Group, Inc. Portsmouth, NH. 1988. 417p.
ISBN:0-313-24715-3, ISBN13: 978-0-313-24715-6.
Dewey:791.43/75/0973. LCCN:87-031784.

Audience: **g,l,u.** *Choice, 1989.*

Grant, Barry Keith   **PN1995.F45793 2003**
(Editor)
Film Genre Reader III. Trade Cloth. University of Texas Press.
Austin, TX. 2003. 656p. ISBN:0-292-70184-5, ISBN13:
978-0-292-70184-7. Dewey:791.43/6. LCCN:2003-002794.

Audience: **u,f.**

Kaminsky, Stuart M.   **PN1993.5.U6**
American Film Genres: Approaches to a Critical Theory of
Popular Film. Trade Paper. C E B C O Standard Publishing.
Fairfield, NJ. 1974. ISBN:0-8278-0277-3, ISBN13:
978-0-8278-0277-3. Dewey:791.43/0973. LCCN:74-080930.

Audience: **u,f.**

Lopez, Daniel   **PN1998.L63 1993**
Films by Genre: 775 Categories, Styles, Trends and Movements
Defined, with a Filmography for Each. Cloth Text. McFarland &
Company, Incorporated Publishers. Jefferson, NC. 1993. 519p.
ISBN:0-89950-780-8, ISBN13: 978-0-89950-780-4.
Dewey:791.4375. LCCN:92-56661.

Audience: **g,l,u,f.** *Choice, 1994.*

Neale, Steve (Editor)   **PN1993**
Genre and Contemporary Hollywood. Trade Cloth. BFI
Publishing. London, 2002. 264p. ISBN:0-85170-886-2, ISBN13:
978-0-85170-886-7. Dewey:791.43/0973. LCCN:2003-464610.

Audience: **l,u,f.**

Schatz, Thomas G.   **PN1993.5.U6**
Hollywood Genres: Formulas, Filmmaking, and the Studio
System. Paper Text. McGraw-Hill Higher Education. Burr
Ridge, IL. 1981. 300p. ISBN:0-07-553623-4, ISBN13:
978-0-07-553623-9. Dewey:791.4/36/0979494.

Audience: **g,l,u.**

Film Analysis and Criticism > Narrative Film and Genres > Action and Adventure

Silver, Alain   **PN1995.9.S24S5 1983**
The Samurai Film. Trade Cloth. Overlook Press, The. New
York, NY. 1984. 242p. ISBN:0-87951-175-3, ISBN13:
978-0-87951-175-3. Dewey:791.4309. LCCN:82-022288.

Audience: **g,l,u,f.** *Choice, 2006.*

Film Analysis and Criticism > Narrative Film and Genres > Children and Young Adults

Bazalgette, Cary   **HQ784.T4I5 1995**
In Front of the Children: Screen Entertainment and Young
Audiences. Trade Cloth. BFI Publishing. London, 1995. 224p.
ISBN:0-85170-452-2, ISBN13: 978-0-85170-452-4.
Dewey:302.2/34/083. LCCN:96-107535.

Audience: **u,f.** *Choice, 1996.*

Bell, Elizabeth (Editor),   **PN1999.W27F76 1995**
et al.
[e] From Mouse to Mermaid: The Politics of Film, Gender, and
Culture. Lynda Haas & Laura Sells (Editors). E-Book. Indiana
University Press. Bloomington, IN. 1995. 272p.
ISBN:0-253-20978-1, ISBN13: 978-0-253-20978-8.
Dewey:791.43/75/0973. LCCN:94-049374.

Audience: **u,f.** *Choice, 1996.*

Kids First Staff   **PN1998.N7327 1999**
The New York Times Guide to the Best Children's Videos.
LeVar Burton (Foreword by), Linda Ellerbee (Preface by). Trade
Paper. Simon & Schuster. New York, NY. 1999. 384p.
ISBN:0-671-03669-6, ISBN13: 978-0-671-03669-0.
Dewey:016.79143/75/083. LCCN:00-711527.

Audience: **g,l,u,f.**

Kinder, Marsha   **HQ784.T4**
Playing with Power in Movies, Television, and Video Games:
From Muppet Babies to Teenage Mutant Ninja Turtles. Trade
Paper. University of California Press. Berkeley, CA. 1993. 278p.
ISBN:0-520-07776-8, ISBN13: 978-0-520-07776-8.
Dewey:302.2/34/083. LCCN:91-011252.

Audience: **u,f.**

Smith, Sarah   **PN1995.9.C45**
Children, Cinema and Censorship: From Dracula to Dead End.
Cloth over Boards, Trade Cloth. I. B. Tauris & Company, Ltd.
London, 2005. 256p. ISBN:1-85043-812-9, ISBN13:
978-1-85043-812-0. Dewey:791.43083/0941.
LCCN:2006-295221.
                                    Audience: **g,l,u,f.**

Wojcik-Andrews, Ian   **PN1995.9.C45W59 2000**
Children's Films: History, Ideology, Pedagogy, Theory. Trade
Paper. Garland Publishing, Inc. New York, NY. 2000. 275p.
Children's Literature and Culture Ser., Vol. 12
ISBN:0-8153-3794-9, ISBN13: 978-0-8153-3794-2.
Dewey:791.43/75/083. LCCN:99-047804.
                                    Audience: **g,l,u,f.**

Film Analysis and Criticism > Narrative Film and Genres > Comedy

Beach, Christopher   **PN1995.9.C55 B43 20**
Class, Language, and American Film Comedy. Trade Paper.
Cambridge University Press. New York, NY. 2002. 250p.
ISBN:0-521-00209-5, ISBN13: 978-0-521-00209-7.
Dewey:791.43617. LCCN:2001-025935.
                                    Audience: **u,f.** *Choice, 2002.*

Byrge, Duane & Milton,   **PN1995.9**
 Robert G.
The Screwball Comedy Films: A History and Filmography,
1934-1942. Paper Text. McFarland & Company, Incorporated
Publishers. Jefferson, NC. 2001. 156p. ISBN:0-7864-1106-6,
ISBN13: 978-0-7864-1106-1. Dewey:791.4361709.
LCCN:90-52654.
                                    Audience: **g,l,u,f.**

Cavell, Stanley   **PN1995**
Pursuits of Happiness: The Hollywood Comedy of Remarriage.
Trade Paper. Harvard University Press. Cambridge, MA. 1981.
296p. Harvard Film Studies ISBN:0-674-73906-X, ISBN13:
978-0-674-73906-2. Dewey:791.43/75.
                                    Audience: **u,f.**

Dale, Alan S.   **PN1995.9.C55D35 2000**
Comedy Is a Man in Trouble: Slapstick in American Movies.
Trade Paper. University of Minnesota Press. Minneapolis, MN.
2000. xiv, 270p. ISBN:0-8166-3658-3, ISBN13:
978-0-8166-3658-7. Dewey:791.43/617. LCCN:00-009080.
                                    Audience: **u,f.** *Choice, 2001.*

DiBattista, Maria   **PN1995.9.W6D53 2001**
Fast-Talking Dames. Cloth over Boards. Yale University Press.
Cumberland, RI. 2001. 384p. ISBN:0-300-08815-9, ISBN13:
978-0-300-08815-1. Dewey:791.4/36/52042. LCCN:00-049946.
                                    Audience: **g,l,u,f.** *Choice, 2001.*

Everson, William K.   **PN1995.9.C55E9 1994**
Hollywood Bedlam: Classic Screwball Comedies. Trade Paper.
Carol Publishing Group. Secaucus, NJ. 1994. 256p.
ISBN:0-8065-1534-1, ISBN13: 978-0-8065-1534-2.
Dewey:791.43/617. LCCN:94-019231.
                                    Audience: **u,f.**

Gehring, Wes D.   **PN1995**
Parody As Film Genre: Never Give a Saga an Even Break.
Trade Cloth. Greenwood Publishing Group, Inc. Portsmouth,
NH. 1999. 248p. Contributions to the Study of Popular Culture

Ser., No. 69 ISBN:0-313-26186-5, ISBN13: 978-0-313-26186-2.
Dewey:791.43/617. LCCN:99-018592.
                                    Audience: **g,l,u.** *Choice, 2000.*

Gehring, Wes D.   **PN1995**
Personality Comedians As Genre: Selected Players. Trade Cloth.
Greenwood Publishing Group, Inc. Portsmouth, NH. 1997. 232p.
Contributions to the Study of Popular Culture Ser., Vol. 61
ISBN:0-313-26185-7, ISBN13: 978-0-313-26185-5.
Dewey:791.43/617. LCCN:96-047536.
                                    Audience: **l,u.** *Choice, 1997.*

Gehring, Wes D.   **PN1995.9.C55G428**
Romantic vs. Screwball Comedy: Charting the Difference. Trade
Cloth. Scarecrow Press, Inc. Lanham, MD. 2002. 224p. Studies
in Film Genres ISBN:0-8108-4424-9, ISBN13:
978-0-8108-4424-7. Dewey:791.43/617. LCCN:2002-006524.
                                    Audience: **l,u,f.** *Choice, 2003.*

Gehring, Wes D.   **PN1995**
Screwball Comedy: A Genre of Madcap Romance. Trade Cloth.
Greenwood Publishing Group, Inc. Portsmouth, NH. 1986. 228p.
Contributions to the Study of Popular Culture Ser., No. 13
ISBN:0-313-24650-5, ISBN13: 978-0-313-24650-0.
Dewey:791.43/09/0917. LCCN:85-012703.
                                    Audience: **g,l,u.** *Choice, 1986.*

Gehring, Wes D.   **PN1995**
American Dark Comedy: Beyond Satire. R. Karl Largent
(Foreword by). Trade Cloth. Greenwood Publishing Group, Inc.
Portsmouth, NH. 1996. 224p. Contributions to the Study of
Popular Culture Ser., No. 55 ISBN:0-313-26184-9, ISBN13:
978-0-313-26184-8. Dewey:791.43/617. LCCN:96-000154.
                                    Audience: **g,l,u.** *Choice, 1996.*

Horton, Andrew S.   **PN1995.9.C55**
 (Editor)
Comedy - Cinema - Theory. Trade Paper. University of
California Press. Berkeley, CA. 1991. 256p.
ISBN:0-520-07040-2, ISBN13: 978-0-520-07040-0.
Dewey:791.43/617. LCCN:90-042213.
                                    Audience: **u,f.** *Choice, 1992.*

Horton, Andrew S.   **PN1995.9.C55 I54 19**
 (Editor)
Inside Soviet Film Satire. Dudley Andrew & William Rothman
(Contribution by). Trade Cloth. Cambridge University Press.
New York, NY. 1993. 185p. Cambridge Studies in Film
ISBN:0-521-43016-X, ISBN13: 978-0-521-43016-6.
Dewey:791.43617. LCCN:96-031986.
                                    Audience: **u,f.**

Jenkins, Henry   **PN1995.9.C55J46 1992**
What Made Pistachio Nuts?: Early Sound Comedy and the
Vaudeville Aesthetic. Cloth Text. Columbia University Press.
New York, NY. 1992. 416p. Film and Culture Ser.
ISBN:0-231-07854-4, ISBN13: 978-0-231-07854-2.
Dewey:791.43617. LCCN:92-022094.
                                    Audience: **u.** *Choice, 1993.*

Karnick, Kristine B. &   **PN1995.9.C55**
 Jenkins, Henry (Editors)
Classical Hollywood Comedy. UK-B Format Paperback.
Routledge. New York, NY. 1994. 440p. AFI Film Readers Ser.
ISBN:0-415-90640-7, ISBN13: 978-0-415-90640-1.
Dewey:791.43/617. LCCN:94-003859.
                                    Audience: **g,l,u.** *Choice, 1996.*

Kendall, Elizabeth   **PN1995.9.C55K38 2002**
The Runaway Bride: Hollywood Romantic Comedy of the
1930s. Trade Paper. Cooper Square Publishers, Inc. New York,
NY. 2002. 312p. ISBN:0-8154-1199-5, ISBN13:
978-0-8154-1199-4. Dewey:791.43/617/097309043.
LCCN:2002-524042.

Audience: **u,f.**

Mast, Gerald   **PN1995.9.C55**
The Comic Mind: Comedy and the Movies. Ed. 2. Trade Paper.
University of Chicago Press. Chicago, IL. 1979. 377p.
ISBN:0-226-50978-8, ISBN13: 978-0-226-50978-5.
Dewey:791.43/0909/17. LCCN:78-068546.

Audience: **u,f.** *B*

Matthews, Nicole   **PN1995.9.C55**
Comic Politics: Gender in Hollywood Comedy after the New
Right. Trade Paper. Manchester University Press. Manchester,
2001. 192p. Inside Popular Film Ser. ISBN:0-7190-5503-2,
ISBN13: 978-0-7190-5503-4. Dewey:791.4/3617.

Audience: **u,f.** *Choice, 2001.*

McCaffrey, Donald W.   **PN1995.9.C55.M39**
Assault on Society: Satirical Literature to Film. Trade Cloth.
Scarecrow Press, Inc. Lanham, MD. 1992. 293p.
ISBN:0-8108-2507-4, ISBN13: 978-0-8108-2507-9.
Dewey:791.43617. LCCN:92-004040.

Audience: **g,l,u.** *Choice, 1992.*

Miller, Blair   **PN1995.9.C55M53 1995**
American Silent Film Comedies: An Illustrated Encyclopedia of
Persons, Studios and Terminology. Cloth Text. McFarland &
Company, Incorporated Publishers. Jefferson, NC. 1995. 292p.
ISBN:0-89950-929-0, ISBN13: 978-0-89950-929-7.
Dewey:791.43/617/0973. LCCN:94-38777.

Audience: **g,l,u,f.** *Choice, 1996.*

Neale, Steve & Krutnik,   **PN1995.9.C55N44 1990**
  Frank
Popular Film and Television Comedy. Trade Paper. Routledge.
New York, NY. 1990. 304p. Popular Fictions Ser.
ISBN:0-415-04692-0, ISBN13: 978-0-415-04692-3.
Dewey:791.43/617. LCCN:90-008494.

Audience: **g,l,u.** *Choice, 1990.*

Okuda, Ted & Watz,   **PN1995.9.C55**
  Edward
The Columbia Comedy Shorts: Two-Reel Hollywood Film
Comedies, 1933-1958. Paper Text. McFarland & Company,
Incorporated Publishers. Jefferson, NC. 1998. 272p.
ISBN:0-7864-0577-5, ISBN13: 978-0-7864-0577-0.
Dewey:791.4/3617. LCCN:84-43241.

Audience: **u,f.** *Choice, 1986.*

Paul, William   **PN1995.9.H6P35 1994**
Laughing Screaming: Modern Hollywood Horror and Comedy.
Trade Paper. Columbia University Press. New York, NY. 1995.
510p. ISBN:0-231-08465-X, ISBN13: 978-0-231-08465-9.
Dewey:791.436164.

Audience: **g,l,u,f.** *Choice, 1994.*

Rubinfeld, Mark D.   **PN1995**
Bound to Bond: Gender, Genre and the Hollywood Romantic
Comedy. Trade Cloth. Greenwood Publishing Group, Inc.
Portsmouth, NH. 2001. 248p. ISBN:0-275-97271-2, ISBN13:
978-0-275-97271-4. Dewey:791.43/617. LCCN:00-069899.

Audience: **g,l,u,f.** *Choice, 2002.*

Sikov, Ed   **PN1995.9.C55**
Laughing Hysterically: American Screen Comedy of the 1950s.
John Belton (Editor). Trade Paper. Columbia University Press.
New York, NY. 1996. 282p. Film and Culture Ser.
ISBN:0-231-07983-4, ISBN13: 978-0-231-07983-9.
Dewey:791.43/617.

Audience: **u,f.** *Choice, 1995.*

Silverman, Stephen M.   **PN2285.S533 1999**
Funny Ladies: 100 Years of Great Comediennes. Trade Cloth.
Harry N. Abrams, Inc. New York, NY. 1999. 160p.
ISBN:0-8109-3337-3, ISBN13: 978-0-8109-3337-8.
Dewey:792.7/028/0820973 B. LCCN:99-011058.

Audience: **g,l,u,f.**

Slide, Anthony   **PN2285.S542 1998**
Eccentrics of Comedy. Trade Cloth. Scarecrow Press, Inc.
Lanham, MD. 1998. 180p. ISBN:0-8108-3534-7, ISBN13:
978-0-8108-3534-4. Dewey:[B]. LCCN:98-025751.

Audience: **g,l,u.** *Choice, 1999.*

Vineberg, Steve   **PN1995.9.C55V56 2004**
High Comedy in American Movies: Class Humor from the
1920's to the Present. Book, Other. Rowman & Littlefield
Publishers, Inc. Lanham, MD. 2005. 224p. Genre and Beyond
Ser. ISBN:0-7425-2633-X, ISBN13: 978-0-7425-2633-4.
Dewey:791.43/617. LCCN:2004-013388.

Audience: **g,l,u.** *Choice, 2005.*

Wagg, Stephen   **PN1992.8.C66B43 1998**
Because I Tell a Joke or Two: Comedy, Politics and Social
Difference. Paper over Boards. Routledge. New York, NY. 1998.
336p. ISBN:0-415-12920-6, ISBN13: 978-0-415-12920-6.
Dewey:700/.417. LCCN:97-023653.

Audience: **l,u,f.**

Wilde, Larry (Author,   **F884.P88**
  Interviewed By)
Great Comedians Talk About Comedy. Woody Allen, Milton
Berle, Shelley Berman, Jack Benny, Joey Bishop, George Burns,
Johnny Carson, Maurice Chevalier, Phyllis Diller, Jimmy
Durante, Dick Gregory, Bob Hope, George Jessel, Jerry Lewis,
Jerry Seinfeld, Danny Thomas & Ed Wynn (Contribution by).
Trade Cloth. Executive Books. Mechanicsburg, PA. 2000. 404p.
ISBN:0-937539-51-1, ISBN13: 978-0-937539-51-4.
Dewey:791.0922.

Audience: **g,l,u,f.**

Film Analysis and Criticism > Narrative Film and Genres > Exploitation

Brottman, Mikita   **PN1995.9.H6B67 2005**
Offensive Films. Trade Paper, Perfect. Vanderbilt University
Press. Nashville, TN. 2005. 205p. ISBN:0-8265-1491-X,
ISBN13: 978-0-8265-1491-2. Dewey:791.43/6164.
LCCN:2005-005456.

Audience: **u,f.**

Jancovich, Mark   **PN1993.5.A1**
  (Editor), et al.
Defining Cult Movies: The Cultural Politics of Oppositional
Tastes. Antonio Lazaro Reboli, Julian Stringer & Andrew Willis
(Editors). Trade Paper. Manchester University Press.
Manchester, 2003. 256p. Inside Popular Film Ser.
ISBN:0-7190-6631-X, ISBN13: 978-0-7190-6631-3.
Dewey:791.43/653. LCCN:2003-056221.

Audience: **u,f.**

Mathijs, Ernest &   **PN1995.9.S284**
  Mendik, Xavier (Editors)
Alternative Europe: Eurotrash and Exploitation Cinema Since
1945. Trade Paper. Wallflower Press. London, 2004. 269p.
ISBN:1-903364-93-0, ISBN13: 978-1-903364-93-2.
Dewey:791.43611.
Audience: u,f.

McDonagh, Maitland   **PN1998.2.M43 1995**
Filmmaking on the Fringe: The Good, the Bad and the Deviant
Directors. Trade Paper. Carol Publishing Group. Secaucus, NJ.
1994. 256p. ISBN:0-8065-1557-0, ISBN13: 978-0-8065-1557-1.
Dewey:791.43/0233/092273. LCCN:94-020342.
Audience: u,f.

Pomerance, Murray   **PN1995.9.E93B33 2003**
  (Editor)
Bad: Infamy, Darkness, Evil, and Slime on Screen. Cloth Text.
State University of New York Press. Albany, NY. 2003. xviii,
357p. The SUNY Series, Cultural Studies in Cinema/Video
ISBN:0-7914-5939-X, ISBN13: 978-0-7914-5939-3.
Dewey:791.43/653. LCCN:2003-042556.
Audience: u,f.   Choice, 2004.

Quarles, Mike   **PN1998.A2**
Down and Dirty: Hollywoods Exploitation Filmmakers and
Their Movies. Paper Text. McFarland & Company, Incorporated
Publishers. Jefferson, NC. 2001. 208p. ISBN:0-7864-1142-2,
ISBN13: 978-0-7864-1142-9. Dewey:791.4/3/023/0973.
LCCN:92-56683.
Audience: g,l,u,f.

Schaefer, Eric   **PN1995.9.S284S33**
"Bold! Daring! Shocking! True!": A History of Exploitation
Films, 1919-1959. Trade Paper. Duke University Press. Durham,
NC. 1999. xii, 474p. ISBN:0-8223-2374-5, ISBN13:
978-0-8223-2374-7. Dewey:791.43/653. LCCN:99-012439.
Audience: g,l,u,f.

Vieira, Mark A.   **PN1995.62.V54 2003**
Sin in Soft Focus: Pre-Code Hollywood. Trade Cloth. Harry N.
Abrams, Inc. New York, NY. 2003. 240p. ISBN:0-8109-8228-5,
ISBN13: 978-0-8109-8228-4. Dewey:363.3/1/0973/09043.
Audience: g,l,u,f.   Choice, 2000.

Film Analysis and Criticism > Narrative Film and Genres > Film Noir

Krutnik, Frank   **PN1995.9.F54K78 1991**
In a Lonely Street: Film Noir, Genre and Masculinity. Trade
Paper. Routledge. New York, NY. 1991. 288p.
ISBN:0-415-02630-X, ISBN13: 978-0-415-02630-7.
Dewey:791.43/655. LCCN:90-023774.
Audience: u,f.   Choice, 1992.

Silver, Alain & Ward,   **PN1995.9.F54F55 1992**
  Elizabeth (Editors)
Film Noir: An Encyclopedic Reference to the American Style.
Ed. 3. Trade Paper. Overlook Press, The. New York, NY. 1993.
479p. ISBN:0-87951-479-5, ISBN13: 978-0-87951-479-2.
Dewey:791.4/36/55. LCCN:93-236035.
Audience: g,l,u,f.   𝐵   Choice, 1993.

Film Analysis and Criticism > Narrative Film and Genres > Historical Films

Barta, Tony (Editor)   **PN1995**
Screening the Past: Film and the Representation of History.
Trade Cloth. Greenwood Publishing Group, Inc. Portsmouth,
NH. 1998. 296p. ISBN:0-275-95402-1, ISBN13:
978-0-275-95402-4. Dewey:791.43/658. LCCN:97-037811.
Audience: g,l,u.   Choice, 1999.

Burgoyne, Robert   **PN1995.9.H5B87 1997**
Film Nation: Hollywood Looks at U. S. History. Book, Other.
University of Minnesota Press. Minneapolis, MN. 1997. 160p.
ISBN:0-8166-2070-9, ISBN13: 978-0-8166-2070-8.
Dewey:791.43/658. LCCN:97-005919.
Audience: u,f.   Choice, 1998.

Cameron, Kenneth M.   **PN1995.9.H5C36 1997**
America on Film: Hollywood and American History. Trade
Cloth. Continuum International Publishing Group, Ltd. London,
1997. 256p. ISBN:0-8264-1033-2, ISBN13: 978-0-8264-1033-7.
Dewey:791.43/658. LCCN:98-008470.
Audience: g,l,u,f.

Carnes, Mark C.   **PN1995.9.H5**
Past Imperfect: History According to the Movies. Trade Paper.
Henry Holt & Company. New York, NY. 1996. 320p.
ISBN:0-8050-3760-8, ISBN13: 978-0-8050-3760-9.
Dewey:791.4/36/58.
Audience: l,u,f.   Choice, 1996.

Custen, George F.   **PN1995.9.B55C87 1992**
Bio-Pics: How Hollywood Constructed Public History. Cloth
Text. Rutgers University Press. Piscataway, NJ. 1992. 300p.
ISBN:0-8135-1754-0, ISBN13: 978-0-8135-1754-4.
Dewey:791.43/658. LCCN:91-026427.
Audience: g,l,u,f.   Choice, 1992.

Grindon, Leger   **PN1995.9.H5G75 1994**
Shadows on the Past: Studies in the Historical Fiction Film.
Trade Cloth. Temple University Press. Philadelphia, PA. 1994.
256p. Culture and the Moving Image Ser. ISBN:1-56639-181-4,
ISBN13: 978-1-56639-181-8. Dewey:791.43/658.
LCCN:93-033042.
Audience: u,f.   Choice, 1995.

Harty, Kevin J.   **PN1995.9.M52H37 1999**
The Reel Middle Ages: American, Western and Eastern
European, Middle Eastern and Asian Films about Medieval
Europe. Cloth Text. McFarland & Company, Incorporated
Publishers. Jefferson, NC. 1999. 324p. ISBN:0-7864-0541-4,
ISBN13: 978-0-7864-0541-1. Dewey:791.43/658.
LCCN:98-29385.
Audience: g,l,u,f.   Choice, 1999.

Klossner, Michael   **PN1995.9.H5K59 2002**
The Europe of 1500-1815 on Film and Television: A Worldwide
Filmography of over 2550 Works, 1895 Through 2000. Cloth
Text. McFarland & Company, Incorporated Publishers. Jefferson,
NC. 2002. 520p. ISBN:0-7864-1223-2, ISBN13:
978-0-7864-1223-5. Dewey:016.79143/658. LCCN:2002-000734.
Audience: g,l,u,f.   Choice, 2002.

Landy, Marcia (Editor)   PN1995.9.H5H59 2001
The Historical Film: History and Memory in Media. Trade
Cloth. Rutgers University Press. Piscataway, NJ. 2000. 370p.
Rutgers Depth of Field Ser. ISBN:0-8135-2856-9, ISBN13:
978-0-8135-2856-4. Dewey:791.43/658. LCCN:00-028080.
Audience: **u,f.**

McCrisken, Trevor B. &   PN1995.9.H5M43 2005
Pepper, Andrew
American History and Contemporary Hollywood Film. Trade
Cloth. Rutgers University Press. Piscataway, NJ. 2005. 240p.
ISBN:0-8135-3620-0, ISBN13: 978-0-8135-3620-0.
Dewey:791.43/658. LCCN:2004-051365.
Audience: **u,f.** *Choice, 2005.*

Osterburg, Bertil O.   PN1995.9.U64O78 2001
Colonial America on Film and Television: A Filmography. Cloth
Text. McFarland & Company, Incorporated Publishers. Jefferson,
NC. 2000. 275p. ISBN:0-7864-0862-6, ISBN13:
978-0-7864-0862-7. Dewey:016.79143/658. LCCN:00-56835.
Audience: **g,l,u,f.**

Picart, Caroline Joan   Z6374
("Kay") (Editor)
The Holocaust Film Sourcebook. Trade Cloth. Greenwood
Publishing Group, Inc. Portsmouth, NH. 2004. 788p.
ISBN:0-275-97850-8, ISBN13: 978-0-275-97850-1.
Dewey:016.79143/658. LCCN:2003-064904.
Audience: **l,u,f.** *Choice, 2005.*

Rollins, Peter C.   PN1995.9.H5H64 1998
Hollywood As Historian: American Film in a Cultural Context.
Trade Paper. University Press of Kentucky. Lexington, KY.
1998. 304p. ISBN:0-8131-0951-5, ISBN13: 978-0-8131-0951-0.
Dewey:791.43/658. LCCN:97-046072.
Audience: **u,f.**

Rollins, Peter C. &   PN1995.9.U64H65 2005
O'Connor, John E. (Editors)
Hollywood's White House: The American Presidency in Film
and History. Trade Paper. University Press of Kentucky.
Lexington, KY. 2005. 464p. ISBN:0-8131-9126-2, ISBN13:
978-0-8131-9126-3. Dewey:791.43/658.
Audience: **u,f.**

Rosenstone, Robert A.   PN1995.2.R67 1995
Visions of the Past: The Challenge of Film to Our Idea of
History. Trade Paper. Harvard University Press. Cambridge,
MA. 1998. 288p. ISBN:0-674-94098-9, ISBN13:
978-0-674-94098-7. Dewey:791.4/3658. LCCN:95-006720.
Audience: **u,f.** *Choice, 1996.*

Smith, Gary A.   PN1995.9.H5S55 2003
Epic Films: Casts, Credits, and Commentary on over 300
Historical Spectacle Movies. Ed. 2. Cloth Text. McFarland &
Company, Incorporated Publishers. Jefferson, NC. 2004. 320p.
ISBN:0-7864-1530-4, ISBN13: 978-0-7864-1530-4.
Dewey:791.43/658. LCCN:2003-019131.
Audience: **g,l,u,f.**

Solomon, Jon   PN1995.9.H5S6 2001
The Ancient World in the Cinema. Ed. 2. Cloth over Boards.
Yale University Press. Cumberland, RI. 2001. 384p.
ISBN:0-300-08335-1, ISBN13: 978-0-300-08335-4.
Dewey:791.43/658. LCCN:00-044915.
Audience: **l,u,f.**

Toplin, Robert B.   PN1995.9.H5T66 1996
History by Hollywood: The Use and Abuse of the American
Past. Trade Paper. University of Illinois Press. Champaign, IL.
1996. 288p. ISBN:0-252-06536-0, ISBN13: 978-0-252-06536-1.
Dewey:791.43/658. LCCN:95-041734.
Audience: **u,f.** *Choice, 1997.*

Toplin, Robert Brent   PN1995.9.H5T67 2002
Reel History: In Defense of Hollywood. Trade Cloth. University
Press of Kansas. Lawrence, KS. 2002. viii, 232p.
CultureAmerica Ser. ISBN:0-7006-1199-1, ISBN13:
978-0-7006-1199-7. Dewey:791.43/658. LCCN:2002-005421.
Audience: **u,f.** *Choice, 2003.*

Tracey, Grant   PN1995
Filmography of American History. Cloth Text. Greenwood
Publishing Group, Inc. Portsmouth, NH. 2001. 352p.
ISBN:0-313-31300-8, ISBN13: 978-0-313-31300-4.
Dewey:791.43/658. LCCN:2001-033717.
Audience: **g,l,u,f.**

Wyke, Maria   PN1995.9.H5W95 1997
Projecting the Past: Ancient Rome, Cinema and History. UK-B
Format Paperback. Routledge. New York, NY. 1997. 248p.
ISBN:0-415-90614-8, ISBN13: 978-0-415-90614-2.
Dewey:791.43/658. LCCN:96-035995.
Audience: **g,l,u,f.**

Film Analysis and Criticism > Narrative Film and Genres > Music and Dance

Altman, Rick   PN1995.9.M86
The American Film Musical. Trade Paper. Indiana University
Press. Bloomington, IN. 1988. 400p. ISBN:0-253-20514-X,
ISBN13: 978-0-253-20514-8. Dewey:791.43/09/09357.
LCCN:86-045473.
Audience: **l,u,f.** *Choice, 1987.*

Barrios, Richard   PN1995.9.M86B37 1995
A Song in the Dark: The Birth of the Musical Film. Trade
Paper. Oxford University Press, Inc. New York, NY. 1995. 506p.
ISBN:0-19-508811-5, ISBN13: 978-0-19-508811-3.
Dewey:791.43/6. LCCN:94-027595.
Audience: **l,u,f.** *Choice, 1996.*

Bloom, Kenneth   ML128.M7B6 1995
Hollywood Song: The Complete Film and Musical Companion.
Trade Cloth. Facts On File, Inc. New York, NY. 1995.
ISBN:0-8160-3231-9, ISBN13: 978-0-8160-3231-0.
Dewey:016.7821/4/0973. LCCN:90-022261.
Audience: **g,l,u,f.**

Bradley, Edwin M.   PN1995.9.M86 B73
First Hollywood Musicals: A Critical Filmography of 171
Features, 1927 Through 1932. Paper Text. McFarland &
Company, Incorporated Publishers. Jefferson, NC. 2004. 400p.
ISBN:0-7864-2029-4, ISBN13: 978-0-7864-2029-2.
Dewey:791.4360973.
Audience: **g,l,u,f.**

Cohan, Steven (Editor)   ML2075.H65 2002
Hollywood Musicals, the Film Reader. Trade Paper. Routledge.
New York, NY. 2001. 224p. In Focus Ser. ISBN:0-415-23560-X,
ISBN13: 978-0-415-23560-0. Dewey:791.436.
LCCN:2001-058919.
Audience: **g,l,u.**

Craggs, Stewart R.   **ML102.M68C73 1998**
Soundtracks: An International Dictionary of Film Music
Composers. Trade Cloth. Ashgate Publishing, Ltd. Aldershot,
1998. 360p. ISBN:1-85928-189-3, ISBN13: 978-1-85928-189-5.
Dewey:781.5/42/0922 B. LCCN:97-019854.
Audience: **g,l,u,f.** *Choice, 1998.*

Dunne, Michael   **PN1995.9.M86**
American Film Musical Themes and Forms. Paper Text.
McFarland & Company, Incorporated Publishers. Jefferson, NC.
2004. 223p. ISBN:0-7864-1877-X, ISBN13: 978-0-7864-1877-0.
Dewey:791.43/6. LCCN:2004-012121.
Audience: **g,l,u.**

Fawkes, Richard   **MT955 .F385 2000**
Opera on Film. Trade Cloth. Gerald Duckworth & Company,
Ltd. London, 2000. 250p. ISBN:0-7156-2943-3, ISBN13:
978-0-7156-2943-7. Dewey:782.1.
Audience: **l,u.** *Choice, 2001.*

Feuer, Jane   **PN1995.9**
The Hollywood Musical. Ed. 2. Trade Paper. Indiana University
Press. Bloomington, IN. 1993. 176p. ISBN:0-253-20768-1,
ISBN13: 978-0-253-20768-5. Dewey:782.81/09794/94.
LCCN:92-016286.
Audience: **l,u,f.**

Gabbard, Krin   **ML2075.G33 1996**
Jammin' at the Margins: Jazz and the American Cinema. Trade
Cloth. University of Chicago Press. Chicago, IL. 1996. 357p.
ISBN:0-226-27788-7, ISBN13: 978-0-226-27788-2.
Dewey:791.43/657. LCCN:95-025337.
Audience: **u,f.** *Choice, 1996.*

Gallafent, Edward   **GV1785.A3G35 2002**
Astaire and Rogers. Trade Cloth. Columbia University Press.
New York, NY. 2002. 256p. Film and Culture Ser.
ISBN:0-231-12626-3, ISBN13: 978-0-231-12626-7.
Dewey:792.8/028/092. LCCN:2001-055262.
Audience: **g,l,u,f.** *Choice, 2002.*

Green, Stanley   **PN1995.25**
Hollywood Musicals Year by Year. Perfect. Hal Leonard
Corporation. Milwaukee, WI. 1990. 352p. ISBN:0-88188-610-6,
ISBN13: 978-0-88188-610-8. Dewey:791.43/657.
LCCN:90-053537.
Audience: **g,l,u,f.**

Hischak, Thomas   **PN1995**
Film It with Music: Encyclopedic Guide to the American Movie
Musical. Cloth Text. Greenwood Publishing Group, Inc.
Portsmouth, NH. 2001. 480p. ISBN:0-313-31538-8, ISBN13:
978-0-313-31538-1. Dewey:791.43/6. LCCN:00-061707.
Audience: **g,l,u,f.** *Choice, 2001.*

Hischak, Thomas S.   **ML102**
The American Musical Film Song Encyclopedia. Cloth Text.
Greenwood Publishing Group, Inc. Portsmouth, NH. 1999. 536p.
ISBN:0-313-30737-7, ISBN13: 978-0-313-30737-9.
Dewey:782.1/4/097303. LCCN:98-034723.
Audience: **g,l,u,f.** *Choice, 1999.*

Hischak, Thomas S.   **ML1711.H42 2004**
Through the Screen Door: What Happened to the Broadway
Musical When it Went to Hollywood. Trade Paper. Scarecrow
Press, Inc. Lanham, MD. 2004. 328p. ISBN:0-8108-5018-4,
ISBN13: 978-0-8108-5018-7. Dewey:791.43/6.
LCCN:2004-004067.
Audience: **l,u.** *Choice, 2005.*

Knight, Arthur   **PN1995.9.N4K59 2002**
Disintegrating the Musical: Black Performance and American
Musical Film. Trade Paper. Duke University Press. Durham,
NC. 2002. 352p. ISBN:0-8223-2963-8, ISBN13:
978-0-8223-2963-3. Dewey:791.43/6. LCCN:2002-002700.
Audience: **u,f.** *Choice, 2003.*

Lawson-Peebles, Robert   **ML1711**
(Editor)
Approaches to the American Musical. Trade Paper. University of
Exeter Press. Exeter, 1996. 192p. Cultural and Social Studies
ISBN:0-85989-405-3, ISBN13: 978-0-85989-405-0.
Dewey:782.1/4/0973.
Audience: **u,f.**

Parish, James Robert &   **ML400.P295 2003**
Pitts, Michael R.
Hollywood Songsters: Singers Who Act and Actors Who Sing,
Set. Ed. 2. Trade Cloth. Routledge. New York, NY. 2003. xv,
953p. ISBN:0-415-94332-9, ISBN13: 978-0-415-94332-1.
Dewey:782.42164/092/273 B. LCCN:2003-267579.
Audience: **g,l,u,f.**

Parish, James R. &   **PN1995.9.M86.P37**
Pitts, Michael R.
The Great Hollywood Musical Pictures. Trade Cloth. Scarecrow
Press, Inc. Lanham, MD. 1992. 816p. ISBN:0-8108-2529-5,
ISBN13: 978-0-8108-2529-1. Dewey:791.436.
LCCN:92-007483.
Audience: **g,l,u,f.** *Choice, 1993.*

Romney, Jonathan &   **ML2075.C45 1995**
Wootton, Adrian (Editors)
Celluloid Jukebox: Popular Music and the Movies since the 50s.
Trade Cloth. BFI Publishing. London, 1995. 175p.
ISBN:0-85170-506-5, ISBN13: 978-0-85170-506-4.
Dewey:781.542. LCCN:95-224068.
Audience: **u,f.**

Rubin, Martin   **PN1998.3.B475R8 1993**
Showstoppers: Busby Berkeley and the Tradition of Spectacle.
John Belton (Editor). Trade Cloth. Columbia University Press.
New York, NY. 1993. 249p. Film and Culture Ser.
ISBN:0-231-08054-9, ISBN13: 978-0-231-08054-5.
Dewey:791.430233092. LCCN:92-037956.
Audience: **u,f.**

Sackett, Susan   **ML128.M7 S33**
Hollywood Sings: An Inside Look at Sixty Years of Academy
Award-Nominated Songs. Paper Text. DIANE Publishing
Company. Collingdale, PA. 2000. 332p. ISBN:0-7881-6815-0,
ISBN13: 978-0-7881-6815-4. Dewey:782.42164/1542.
Audience: **g,l.**

Stanfield, Peter   **PN1995.9.J37S72 2005**
Body and Soul: Jazz, Blues, and Race in American Film,
1927-63. Trade Paper, Perfect. University of Illinois Press.
Champaign, IL. 2005. 232p. ISBN:0-252-07235-9, ISBN13:
978-0-252-07235-2. Dewey:791.43/657. LCCN:2004-029989.
Audience: **u,f.** *Choice, 2006.*

Wlaschin, Ken   **ML102.O6W55 2004**
Encyclopedia of Opera on Screen: A Guide to More Than 100
Years of Opera Films, Videos, and DVDs. Cloth over Boards.
Yale University Press. Cumberland, RI. 2004. 896p.
ISBN:0-300-10263-1, ISBN13: 978-0-300-10263-5.
Dewey:791.43/657. LCCN:2004-041519.
Audience: **g,l,u,f.** *Choice, 2004.*

Yanow, Scott   ML3508.Y39 2004
Jazz on Film: The Complete Story of the Musicians and Music
Onscreen. Trade Paper. Backbeat Books. San Francisco, CA.
2004. 320p. ISBN:0-87930-783-8, ISBN13: 978-0-87930-783-7.
Dewey:781.65/09. LCCN:2004-015615.
                                                Audience: **g,l,u.**

Film Analysis and Criticism > Narrative Film and Genres > Mystery, Crime, Detective

Schilling, Mark   PN1995.9.G3S33 2003
The Yakuza Movie Book: A Guide to Japanese Gangster Films.
Trade Paper. Stone Bridge Press. Berkeley, CA. 2003. 320p.
ISBN:1-880656-76-0, ISBN13: 978-1-880656-76-1.
Dewey:791.43/655. LCCN:2003-003855.
                                    Audience: **g,l,u,f.** *Choice, 2004.*

Film Analysis and Criticism > Narrative Film and Genres > Pornography

Gaffin, Harris   NX650.E7
Hollywood Blue: The Tinseltown Pornographers. Ed. 713. Paper
Text. Anova Books. London, 1998. 208p. ISBN:0-7134-7906-X,
ISBN13: 978-0-7134-7906-5. Dewey:338.4/779143/6538.
                                                Audience: **l,u,f.**

Limbacher, James L.   PN1995.9.S45
Sexuality in World Cinema, Set. Trade Cloth. Scarecrow Press,
Inc. Lanham, MD. 1983. 1535p. ISBN:0-8108-1609-1, ISBN13:
978-0-8108-1609-1. Dewey:016.79143/09/09353.
LCCN:83-003019.
                                                Audience: **l,u,f.**

McNeil, Legs &   PN1995.9.S45M36 2004
  Osborne, Jennifer
The Other Hollywood: The Uncensored Oral History of the Porn
Film Industry. Peter Pavia (Abridged by). Trade Cloth.
HarperCollins Publishers. New York, NY. 2005. 640p.
ISBN:0-06-009659-4, ISBN13: 978-0-06-009659-5.
Dewey:791.43/6538/0973. LCCN:2004-051048.
                                                Audience: **g,l,u.**

O'Toole, Laurence J.   HQ472.U6
Pornocopia: Porn, Sex, Technology and Desire. Ed. 2. Trade
Paper. Serpent's Tail Ltd. London, 2000. 420p.
ISBN:1-85242-720-5, ISBN13: 978-1-85242-720-7.
Dewey:338.4/7/36347. LCCN:99-063331.
                                                Audience: **u,f.**

Turan, Kenneth & Zito,   PN1995.9.S45
  Stephen F.
Sinema: American Pornographic Films and the People Who
Make Them. Trade Cloth. Greenwood Publishing Group, Inc.
Portsmouth, NH. 1974. xi, 244p. ISBN:0-275-50770-X, ISBN13:
978-0-275-50770-1. Dewey:791.43/0909/3538.
LCCN:73-018750.
                                                Audience: **g,l,u,f.**

Williams, Linda   PN1995.9.S45 W5 1999
Hard Core: Power, Pleasure, and the Frenzy of the Visible.
Trade Paper. University of California Press. Berkeley, CA. 1999.
398p. ISBN:0-520-21943-0, ISBN13: 978-0-520-21943-4.
Dewey:791.43/6538. LCCN:98-038977.
                                                Audience: **u,f.**

Williams, Linda   HQ471.P59 2004
Porn Studies. Trade Cloth. Duke University Press. Durham, NC.
2004. 520p. ISBN:0-8223-3300-7, ISBN13: 978-0-8223-3300-5.
Dewey:363.4/7. LCCN:2003-025389.
                                    Audience: **l,u,f.** *Choice, 2004.*

Film Analysis and Criticism > Narrative Film and Genres > Romance

Rubinfeld, Mark D.   PN1995
Bound to Bond: Gender, Genre and the Hollywood Romantic
Comedy. Trade Cloth. Greenwood Publishing Group, Inc.
Portsmouth, NH. 2001. 248p. ISBN:0-275-97271-2, ISBN13:
978-0-275-97271-4. Dewey:791.43/617. LCCN:00-069899.
                                    Audience: **g,l,u,f.** *Choice, 2002.*

Film Analysis and Criticism > Narrative Film and Genres > Science Fiction, Fantasy, and Horror

Benshoff, Harry M.   PN1995.9.H55 B457 1997
Monsters in the Closet: Homosexuality and the Horror Film.
Manchester University Press. 1997. Inside Popular Film
ISBN:0-7190-4473-1, ISBN13: 978-0-7190-4473-1.
                                                Audience: **g,l,u,f.**

Berenstein, Rhona J.   PN1995.9.H6B48 1996
Attack of the Leading Ladies: Gender, Sexuality and
Spectatorship in Classic Horror Cinema. Trade Cloth. Columbia
University Press. New York, NY. 1995. 292p. Film and Culture
Ser. ISBN:0-231-08462-5, ISBN13: 978-0-231-08462-8.
Dewey:791.43/616. LCCN:95-031390.
                                    Audience: **u,f.** *Choice, 1996.*

Carroll, Noel   PN56.H6C37 1990
The Philosophy of Horror: Paradoxes of the Heart. UK-B
Format Paperback. Routledge. New York, NY. 1990. 272p.
ISBN:0-415-90216-9, ISBN13: 978-0-415-90216-8.
Dewey:809/.916. LCCN:89-010469.
                                                Audience: **u,f.**

Clover, Carol J.   PN1995.9.H6
Men, Women, and Chain Saws: Gender in the Modern Horror
Film. Trade Paper. Princeton University Press. Princeton, NJ.
1993. 270p. ISBN:0-691-00620-2, ISBN13: 978-0-691-00620-8.
Dewey:791.43/616.
                                    Audience: **u,f.** *Choice, 1992.*

Crane, Jonathan L.   PN1995.9.H6C72 1994
Terror and Everyday Life: Singular Moments in the History of
the Horror Film. Trade Cloth. SAGE Publications, Inc.
Thousand Oaks, CA. 1994. 183p. ISBN:0-8039-5848-X,
ISBN13: 978-0-8039-5848-7. Dewey:791.43/616.
LCCN:94-029949.
                                    Audience: **l,u,f.** *Choice, 1995.*

Dika, Vera   PN1995.9.H6D48 1990
Games of Terror: Halloween, Friday the 13th and the Films of
the Stalker Cycle. Trade Cloth. Fairleigh Dickinson University
Press. Cranbury, NJ. 1990. 160p. ISBN:0-8386-3364-1, ISBN13:
978-0-8386-3364-9. Dewey:791.43/616. LCCN:88-046187.
                                    Audience: **u,f.** *Choice, 1991.*

Fischer, Dennis   PN1995.9.S26F54 2000
Science Fiction Directors, 1895-1998. Cloth Text. McFarland &
Company, Incorporated Publishers. Jefferson, NC. 2000. 767p.
ISBN:0-7864-0740-9, ISBN13: 978-0-7864-0740-8.
Dewey:791.43/615. LCCN:99-29838.
                                    Audience: **g,l,u,f.** *Choice, 2001.*

Freeland, Cynthia A.   PN1995.9.H6F755 2000
The Naked and the Undead: Evil and the Appeal of Horror.
Trade Paper. Westview Press. Boulder, CO. 2001. 336p.
Thinking Through Cinema Ser. ISBN:0-8133-6563-5, ISBN13:
978-0-8133-6563-3. Dewey:791.43/6164.
                                    Audience: **l,u,f.**

Gelder, Ken   PN56.V3G45 1994
Reading the Vampire. Trade Paper. Routledge. New York, NY.
1994. 176p. Popular Fictions Ser. ISBN:0-415-08013-4,
ISBN13: 978-0-415-08013-2. Dewey:809.3/9375.
LCCN:93-044485.
                                    Audience: **g,l,u,f.**

Grant, Barry K.   PN1995.9.H6D74 1996
(Editor)
The Dread of Difference: Gender and the Horror Film. Trade
Paper. University of Texas Press. Austin, TX. 1996. 476p. Texas
Film Studies Ser. ISBN:0-292-72794-1, ISBN13:
978-0-292-72794-6. Dewey:791.43/616. LCCN:96-011099.
                                    Audience: **u,f.** *Choice, 1997.*

Halberstam, Judith   PR830.T3H27 1995
Skin Shows: Gothic Horror and the Technology of Monsters.
Cloth Text. Duke University Press. Durham, NC. 1995. 240p.
ISBN:0-8223-1651-X, ISBN13: 978-0-8223-1651-0.
Dewey:823/.0872909. LCCN:95-000948.
                                    Audience: **u,f.** *Choice, 1996.*

Hantke, Steffen (Editor)   PN1995.9.H6H674 2004
Horror Film: Creating and Marketing Fear. Trade Cloth.
University Press of Mississippi. Jackson, MS. 2006. 272p.
ISBN:1-57806-692-1, ISBN13: 978-1-57806-692-6.
Dewey:791.43/6164. LCCN:2004-005373.
                                    Audience: **u,f.** *Choice, 2005.*

Hardy, Phil (Editor)   PN1995.9.G3 O83
The Overlook Film Encyclopedia: Science Fiction. Trade Paper.
Overlook Press, The. New York, NY. 1995. 512p.
ISBN:0-87951-626-7, ISBN13: 978-0-87951-626-0.
Dewey:791.43/6278.
                                    Audience: **g,l,u,f.**

Hawkins, Joan   PN1995.9.E96H38 2000
Cutting Edge: Art-Horror and the Horrific Avant-Garde. Trade
Cloth. University of Minnesota Press. Minneapolis, MN. 2000.
xiii, 326p. ISBN:0-8166-3413-0, ISBN13: 978-0-8166-3413-2.
Dewey:791.43/6164. LCCN:99-051008.
                                    Audience: **u,f.**

Henderson, C. J.   PN1995.9.S26H38 2001
The Encyclopedia of Science Fiction Movies: From 1897 to the
Present. William Shatner (Foreword by). Trade Paper. Facts On
File, Inc. New York, NY. 2001. xii, 516p. Facts on File Film
Reference Library ISBN:0-8160-4567-4, ISBN13:
978-0-8160-4567-9. Dewey:791.43/615. LCCN:00-061001.
                                    Audience: **g,l,u,f.**

Hogan, David J.   PN1995.9.H6
Dark Romance: Sexuality in the Horror Film. Paper Text.
McFarland & Company, Incorporated Publishers. Jefferson, NC.

1997. 350p. ISBN:0-7864-0474-4, ISBN13: 978-0-7864-0474-2.
Dewey:791.43/09/0916. LCCN:86-161.
                                    Audience: **l,u,f.** *Choice, 1987.*

Humphries, Reynold   PN1995.9.H6
The American Horror Film: An Introduction. Trade Paper.
Edinburgh University Press. Edinburgh, 2003. 224p.
ISBN:0-7486-1416-8, ISBN13: 978-0-7486-1416-5.
Dewey:791.4/36164/0973.
                                    Audience: **g,l.**

Iaccino, James F.   PN1995
Jungian Reflections Within the Cinema: A Psychological
Analysis of Sci-Fi and Fantasy Archetypes. Trade Cloth.
Greenwood Publishing Group, Inc. Portsmouth, NH. 1998. 240p.
ISBN:0-275-95048-4, ISBN13: 978-0-275-95048-4.
Dewey:791.43/65. LCCN:97-041705.
                                    Audience: **u,f.** *Choice, 1998.*

Jones, Darryl   PN3435
Horror: A Thematic History in Fiction and Film. Trade Paper.
Oxford University Press, Inc. New York, NY. 2003. 224p. A
Hodder Arnold Publication ISBN:0-340-76253-5, ISBN13:
978-0-340-76253-0. Dewey:823.0873809. LCCN:2003-271104.
                                    Audience: **g,l,u,f.**

Jones, Stephen   PN1995.9.M6J66 2000
The Essential Monster Movie Guide. Forrest J. Ackerman
(Introduction by). Trade Paper. Watson-Guptill Publications, Inc.
New York, NY. 2000. 448p. ISBN:0-8230-7936-8, ISBN13:
978-0-8230-7936-0. Dewey:791.43/67. LCCN:00-102974.
                                    Audience: **g,l,u,f.** *Choice, 2001.*

Kaveney, Roz   PN1995.9.S26
From Alien to the Matrix: Reading Science Fiction Film. Cloth
over Boards, Trade Cloth. I. B. Tauris & Company, Ltd.
London, 2005. 256p. ISBN:1-85043-805-6, ISBN13:
978-1-85043-805-2. Dewey:791.43/615. LCCN:2005-298493.
                                    Audience: **l,u,f.**

King, Geoff &   PN1995.9.S26.K5 2000
  Krzywinska, Tanya
Science Fiction Cinema: From Outerspace to Cyberspace. Trade
Paper. Wallflower Press. London, 2001. 128p. Short Cuts Ser.
ISBN:1-903364-03-5, ISBN13: 978-1-903364-03-1.
Dewey:791.43615.
                                    Audience: **g,l,u,f.**

Kinnard, Roy   PN1995.9.H6
Horror in Silent Films: A Filmography, 1896-1929. Paper Text.
McFarland & Company, Incorporated Publishers. Jefferson, NC.
1999. 284p. ISBN:0-7864-0751-4, ISBN13: 978-0-7864-0751-4.
Dewey:016.7/9143/616. LCCN:95-6727.
                                    Audience: **g,l,u,f.** *Choice, 1996.*

Kuhn, Annette   PN1995.9.S26A818
Alien Zone: Cultural Theory and Contemporary Science Fiction
Cinema. Trade Paper. Analytical Psychology Club of San
Francisco, Inc. San Francisco, CA. 1990. 256p.
ISBN:0-86091-993-5, ISBN13: 978-0-86091-993-3.
Dewey:791.43/656. LCCN:90-011934.
                                    Audience: **u,f.**

Kuhn, Annette   PN1995.9.S26A47 1999
Alien Zone 2: The Spaces of Science Fiction Cinema. Trade
Paper. Verso Books. London, 2000. 256p. ISBN:1-85984-259-3,
ISBN13: 978-1-85984-259-1. Dewey:791.43/615.
LCCN:99-042420.
                                    Audience: **u,f.**

Lentz, Harris M. III   PN1995.9.S26L46 2001
Science Fiction, Horror and Fantasy Film and Television
Credits, Vol. 1. Ed. 2. Cloth Text. McFarland & Company,
Incorporated Publishers. Jefferson, NC. 2000. 848p.
ISBN:0-7864-0950-9, ISBN13: 978-0-7864-0950-1.
Dewey:791.43/65. LCCN:00-38656.
                                        Audience: **g,l,u,f.**

McRoy, Jay (Editor)   PN19195.9.H6
Japanese Horror Cinema. Christopher Bolton, Phillip Brophy,
Ian Conrich, Gareth Evans, Ruth Goldberg, Richard Hand,
Steffen Hantke & Matt Hills (Contribution by). Trade Cloth.
University of Hawaii Press. Honolulu, HI. 2005. 238p.
ISBN:0-8248-2899-2, ISBN13: 978-0-8248-2899-8.
Dewey:791.4361640952.
                                        Audience: **g,l,u,f.**

Milne, Tom, et al.   PN1995.9.H6 M5 1994
The Overlook Film Encyclopedia: Horror. Paul Willemen, Julian
Petley, Tim Pulleine & Kim Newman (Authors), Phil Hardy
(Editor), Verina Glaessner (Contribution by). Trade Cloth.
Overlook Press, The. New York, NY. 1994. 496p.
ISBN:0-87951-518-X, ISBN13: 978-0-87951-518-8.
Dewey:791.43/616. LCCN:93-023387.
                    Audience: **g,l,u,f.** *Choice, 1995.*

Noonan, Bonnie   PN1995.9.S26N66 2005
Women Scientists in Fifties Science Fiction Films. Paper Text.
McFarland & Company, Incorporated Publishers. Jefferson, NC.
2005. 235p. ISBN:0-7864-2130-4, ISBN13: 978-0-7864-2130-5.
Dewey:791.43/615. LCCN:2005-011461.
                                        Audience: **u,f.**

Paul, William   PN1995.9.H6P35 1994
Laughing Screaming: Modern Hollywood Horror and Comedy.
Trade Cloth. Edinburgh University Press. Edinburgh, 1994.
524p. ISBN:0-231-08464-1, ISBN13: 978-0-231-08464-2.
Dewey:791.436164. LCCN:93-027388.
                    Audience: **u,f.** *Choice, 1994.*

Penley, Constance   PN1995.9.S26C57 1990
Close Encounters: Film, Feminism, and Science Fiction. Lynn
Speigel & Janet Bergstrom (Editors). Book, Other. University of
Minnesota Press. Minneapolis, MN. 1990. 313p. Camera
Obscura Book Ser. ISBN:0-8166-1912-3, ISBN13:
978-0-8166-1912-2. Dewey:791.43/656. LCCN:90-040163.
                                        Audience: **u,f.**

Phillips, Kendall R.   PN1995
Projected Fears: Horror Films and American Culture. Trade
Cloth. Greenwood Publishing Group, Inc. Portsmouth, NH.
2005. 240p. ISBN:0-275-98353-6, ISBN13: 978-0-275-98353-6.
Dewey:791.43/6164. LCCN:2004-028376.
                    Audience: **g,l,u.** *Choice, 2005.*

Pierson, Michele   PN1995.9.S26P54 2002
Special Effects: Still in Search of Wonder. Trade Cloth.
Columbia University Press. New York, NY. 2002. 256p. Film
and Culture Ser. ISBN:0-231-12562-3, ISBN13:
978-0-231-12562-8. Dewey:791.43/615. LCCN:2001-055263.
                    Audience: **u,f.** *Choice, 2002.*

Pinedo, Isabel Cristina   PN1995.9.H6P46 1997
Recreational Terror: Women and the Pleasures of Horror Film
Viewing. Trade Paper. State University of New York Press.
Albany, NY. 1997. 177p. SUNY Series, Interruptions, :Border
Testimony(ies) and Critical Discourse(s) ISBN:0-7914-3442-7,

ISBN13: 978-0-7914-3442-0. Dewey:791.43/616/082.
LCCN:97-008033.
                    Audience: **u,f.** *Choice, 1998.*

Prince, Stephen (Editor,   PN1995.9.H6H667 2004
  Translator, Introduction by)
The Horror Film. Trade Cloth. Rutgers University Press.
Piscataway, NJ. 2004. 256p. Rutgers Depth of Field Ser.
ISBN:0-8135-3362-7, ISBN13: 978-0-8135-3362-9.
Dewey:791.43/6164. LCCN:2003-009691.
                    Audience: **g,l,u.** *Choice, 2004.*

Rasmussen, Randy   PN1995.9.H6R37 1998
Children of the Night: The Six Archetypal Characters of Classic
Horror Films. Cloth Text. McFarland & Company, Incorporated
Publishers. Jefferson, NC. 1998. 277p. ISBN:0-7864-0337-3,
ISBN13: 978-0-7864-0337-0. Dewey:791.4/361/64.
LCCN:97-18383.
                                        Audience: **g,l,u,f.**

Redmond, Sean (Editor)   PN1995.9.S26
Liquid Metal: The Science Fiction Film Reader. Trade Cloth.
Wallflower Press. London, 2004. 352p. ISBN:1-903364-88-4,
ISBN13: 978-1-903364-88-8. Dewey:791.4/3615.
                                        Audience: **l,u,f.**

Rickman, Gregg   PN1995.9.S26R53 2003
The Science Fiction Film Reader. Trade Paper. Hal Leonard
Corporation. Milwaukee, WI. 2004. 432p. ISBN:0-87910-994-7,
ISBN13: 978-0-87910-994-3. Dewey:791.43/615.
LCCN:2003-020928.
                                        Audience: **g,l,u.**

Rockett, Will H.   PN1995
Devouring Whirlwind: Terror and Transcendence in the Cinema
of Cruelty, 21. Trade Cloth. Greenwood Publishing Group, Inc.
Portsmouth, NH. 1988. 221p. Contributions to the Study of
Popular Culture Ser., No. 21 ISBN:0-313-25998-4, ISBN13:
978-0-313-25998-2. Dewey:791.43/09/09353. LCCN:88-010254.
                    Audience: **l,u,f.** *Choice, 1989.*

Sardar, Ziauddin &   PN1995.9.S26A45 2002
  Cubitt, Sean (Editors)
Aliens R Us: The Other in Science Fiction Cinema. Trade Cloth.
Pluto Press. London, 2002. 200p. ISBN:0-7453-1544-5,
ISBN13: 978-0-7453-1544-7. Dewey:791.43/915.
LCCN:2001-003316.
                                        Audience: **u,f.**

Schelde, Per   PN1995.9.S26
Androids, Humanoids and Other Science Fiction Monsters:
Science and Soul in Science Fiction. Trade Paper. New York
University Press. New York, NY. 1994. 291p.
ISBN:0-8147-7995-6, ISBN13: 978-0-8147-7995-8.
Dewey:791.4/3/615.
                                        Audience: **u,f.**

Schneider, Steven Jay &   PN1995.9.H6D27 2003
  Shaw, Daniel (Editors)
Dark Thoughts: Philosophic Reflections on Cinematic Horror.
Trade Cloth. Scarecrow Press, Inc. Lanham, MD. 2003. 304p.
ISBN:0-8108-4792-2, ISBN13: 978-0-8108-4792-7.
Dewey:791.43/6164. LCCN:2003-008100.
                    Audience: **l,u,f.** *Choice, 2004.*

Seed, David   PS374.S35S44 1999
American Science Fiction and the Cold War: Literature and
Film. Trade Paper. Edinburgh University Press. Edinburgh,

2002. 224p. ISBN:1-85331-227-4, ISBN13: 978-1-85331-227-4. Dewey:813/.0876209358. LCCN:99-488045.

Audience: **u,f.** *Choice, 2000.*

Shapiro, Jerome F. PN1995.9.W3S53 2002
Atomic Bomb Cinema: Apocalyptic Imagination on Film. UK-B Format Paperback. Routledge. New York, NY. 2001. 288p. ISBN:0-415-93660-8, ISBN13: 978-0-415-93660-6. Dewey:791.43/658. LCCN:2002-277634.

Audience: **u,f.** *Choice, 2002.*

Sharrett, Christopher PN1995.9.H6P56 2004
Planks of Reason: Essays on the Horror Film. Barry Keith Grant (Editor). Trade Paper. Scarecrow Press, Inc. Lanham, MD. 2004. 432p. ISBN:0-8108-5013-3, ISBN13: 978-0-8108-5013-2. Dewey:791.43/6164. LCCN:2004-006623.

Audience: **g,l,u.** *Choice, 2005.*

Silver, Alain & Ursini, PN1995.9.H6H68 2000
James (Editors)
Horror Film Reader. Trade Paper. Hal Leonard Corporation. Milwaukee, WI. 2004. 320p. ISBN:0-87910-297-7, ISBN13: 978-0-87910-297-5. Dewey:791.43/6164. LCCN:00-044366.

Audience: **g,l,u.**

Silver, Alain & Ursini, PN1995.9.V3U77 1997
James
The Vampire Film: From Nosferatu to Interview with a Vampire. Ed. 3. Trade Paper. Hal Leonard Corporation. Milwaukee, WI. 1997. 342p. ISBN:0-87910-266-7, ISBN13: 978-0-87910-266-1. Dewey:791.43/675. LCCN:97-034919.

Audience: **g,l,u,f.**

Skal, David J. PN1995.9.H6 S57 2001
The Monster Show: A Cultural History of Horror. Trade Paper. Faber & Faber, Inc. New York, NY. 2001. 432p. ISBN:0-571-19996-8, ISBN13: 978-0-571-19996-9. Dewey:791.43/6164. LCCN:2002-278460.

Audience: **g,l,u,f.** *Choice, 1993.*

Sobchack, Vivian C. PN1995.9.S26S57 1997
Screening Space: The American Science Fiction Film. Ed. 2. Trade Cloth. Rutgers University Press. Piscataway, NJ. 1997. 345p. ISBN:0-8135-2492-X, ISBN13: 978-0-8135-2492-4. Dewey:791.43/615. LCCN:97-016074.

Audience: **u,f.**

Telotte, J. P. PN1995.9.S26T45
A Distant Technology: Science Fiction Film and the Machine Age. Library Binding. Wesleyan University Press. Middletown, CT. 1999. 230p. ISBN:0-8195-6345-5, ISBN13: 978-0-8195-6345-3. Dewey:791.4/3615/09041. LCCN:98-038718.

Audience: **u,f.**

Telotte, J. P. PN1995.9.S26T46 1995
Replications: A Robotic History of the Science Fiction Film. Trade Cloth. University of Illinois Press. Champaign, IL. 1995. 232p. ISBN:0-252-02177-0, ISBN13: 978-0-252-02177-0. Dewey:791.43/615. LCCN:95-006586.

Audience: **u,f.** *Choice, 1996.*

Tudor, Andrew PN1995.9.H6 T78 1989
Monsters and Mad Scientists: A Cultural History of the Horror Movie. Trade Paper. Blackwell Publishing, Inc. Malden, MA. 1989. 256p. ISBN:0-631-16992-X, ISBN13: 978-0-631-16992-5. Dewey:791.43/616. LCCN:89-032084.

Audience: **g,l,u,f.** *Choice, 1990.*

Vieth, Errol PN1995.9.V54 2001
Screening Science: Contexts, Texts and Science in Fifties Science Fiction Film. Trade Cloth. Scarecrow Press, Inc. Lanham, MD. 2001. 264p. ISBN:0-8108-4023-5, ISBN13: 978-0-8108-4023-2. Dewey:791.43/658. LCCN:2001-018879.

Audience: **l,u,f.** *Choice, 2002.*

Waller, Gregory A. PN1995.9.H6
(Editor)
American Horrors: Essays on the Modern American Horror Film. Trade Paper. University of Illinois Press. Champaign, IL. 1987. 248p. ISBN:0-252-01448-0, ISBN13: 978-0-252-01448-2. Dewey:791.43/09/0916. LCCN:87-005833.

Audience: **u,f.**

Weaver, Tom PN1995.9.S26W456
Return of the B Science Fiction and Horror Heroes: The Mutant Melding of Two Volumes of Classic Interviews. Paper Text. McFarland & Company, Incorporated Publishers. Jefferson, NC. 1999. 896p. ISBN:0-7864-0755-7, ISBN13: 978-0-7864-0755-2. Dewey:791.43/615. LCCN:99-48762.

Audience: **u,f.**

Williams, Tony PN1995.9.H6W46 1996
Hearths of Darkness: The Family in the American Horror Film. Trade Cloth. Fairleigh Dickinson University Press. Cranbury, NJ. 1996. 320p. ISBN:0-8386-3564-4, ISBN13: 978-0-8386-3564-3. Dewey:791.43/616. LCCN:95-041886.

Audience: **u,f.** *Choice, 1997.*

Young, R. G. PN1995.9.F36Y68 1997
The Encyclopedia of Fantastic Film: Ali Baba to Zombies. Trade Paper. Applause Theatre Book Publishers. New York, NY. 2000. 999p. ISBN:1-55783-269-2, ISBN13: 978-1-55783-269-6. Dewey:016.7/9143615. LCCN:96-037913.

Audience: **g,l,u,f.**

Film Analysis and Criticism > Narrative Film and Genres > Social Issues Films

Belton, John PN1995.9.S6M68 1996
Movies and Mass Culture. Trade Cloth. Rutgers University Press. Piscataway, NJ. 1995. 279p. Depth of Field Ser. ISBN:0-8135-2228-5, ISBN13: 978-0-8135-2228-9. Dewey:306.4/85/0973. LCCN:95-012438.

Audience: **u,f.** *Choice, 1996.*

Bouzereau, Laurent PN1995.9.V5B68 1998
Ultraviolent Movies: From Sam Peckinpah to Quentin Tarantino. Ed. 2. Trade Paper. Kensington Publishing Corporation. New York, NY. 2000. 272p. ISBN:0-8065-2045-0, ISBN13: 978-0-8065-2045-2. Dewey:791.4/36/55. LCCN:98-039469.

Audience: **l,u,f.**

Bromley, Roger PN3352.M34B76 2000
Narratives for a New Belonging: Diasporic Cultural Fictions. Trade Paper. Edinburgh University Press. Edinburgh, 2001. 182p. Tendencies Ser. ISBN:0-7486-0951-2, ISBN13: 978-0-7486-0951-2. Dewey:809/.93355. LCCN:2001-369168.

Audience: **u,f.** *Choice, 2001.*

Brownlow, Kevin PN1995.75.B68 1990
Behind the Mask of Innocence: Sex, Violence, Prejudice, Crime: Films of Social Conscience in the Silent Era. Trade Cloth. Alfred A. Knopf Inc. New York, NY. 1990. 579p.

Formats: Web: ☐ Ebook: 🄴 CD/DVD-ROM: 🗗 BCL3: 𝓑

ISBN:0-394-57747-7, ISBN13: 978-0-394-57747-0.
Dewey:791.43/655/09041. LCCN:89-071676.
Audience: **g,l,u,f.** *Choice, 1991.*

Campbell, Russell   **PN1995.9.P76C36 2005**
Marked Women: Prostitutes and Prostitution in the Cinema.
Trade Cloth. University of Wisconsin Press. Chicago, IL. 2006.
464p. Wisconsin Film Studies ISBN:0-299-21250-5, ISBN13:
978-0-299-21250-6. Dewey:791.43/6692. LCCN:2005-008259.
Audience: **u,f.**

Charney, Leo &   **PN1995.9.S6C47 1995**
  Schwartz, Vanessa R. (Editors)
Cinema and the Invention of Modern Life. Trade Paper.
University of California Press. Berkeley, CA. 1996. 418p.
ISBN:0-520-20112-4, ISBN13: 978-0-520-20112-5.
Dewey:302.23/43. LCCN:95-010821.
Audience: **u,f.**

Courtney, Susan   **PN1995.9.M57C38 2004**
Hollywood Fantasies of Miscegenation: Spectacular Narratives
of Gender and Race. Trade Paper. Princeton University Press.
Princeton, NJ. 2004. 376p. ISBN:0-691-11305-X, ISBN13:
978-0-691-11305-0. Dewey:791.43/6552. LCCN:2004-044320.
Audience: **u,f.**

Gerster, Carole &   **LC1099.3.T432 2005**
  Zlogar, Laura W. (Editors)
Teaching Ethnic Diversity with Film: Essays and Resources for
Educators in History, Social Studies, Literature and Film
Studies. Paper Text. McFarland & Company, Incorporated
Publishers. Jefferson, NC. 2006. 328p. ISBN:0-7864-2195-9,
ISBN13: 978-0-7864-2195-4. Dewey:370.117.
LCCN:2005-011457.
Audience: **u,f.**

Giovacchini, Saverio   **PN1993.5.U65G552**
Hollywood Modernism: Film and Politics in the Age of the New
Deal. Library Binding. Temple University Press. Philadelphia,
PA. 2001. x, 292p. Culture and the Moving Image Ser.
ISBN:1-56639-862-2, ISBN13: 978-1-56639-862-6.
Dewey:791.43/658. LCCN:00-053215.
Audience: **u,f.**

Gormley, Paul   **PN1995.9.V5G67 2005**
New-Brutality Film: Race and Affect in Contemporary American
Film. Trade Paper. Intellect, Ltd. Bristol, 2005. 256p.
ISBN:1-84150-119-0, ISBN13: 978-1-84150-119-2.
Dewey:791.43/6552. LCCN:2005-296704.
Audience: **u,f.**

Hoberman, J.   **PN1993.5.U6H56 2003**
The Dream Life: Movies, Media, and the Mythology of the
Sixties. Trade Cloth. New Press, The. New York, NY. 2003.
400p. ISBN:1-56584-763-6, ISBN13: 978-1-56584-763-7.
Dewey:791.43/658. LCCN:2003-045914.
Audience: **g,l,u.**

James, David E. &   **PN1995.9.P6H5 1996**
  Berg, Rick (Editors)
The Hidden Foundation: Cinema and the Question of Class.
Book, Other. University of Minnesota Press. Minneapolis, MN.
1996. 297p. ISBN:0-8166-2704-5, ISBN13: 978-0-8166-2704-2.
Dewey:791.43/652062. LCCN:95-022733.
Audience: **u,f.**

Lovell, John P. (Editor)   **PN1995**
Insights from Film into Violence and Oppression: Shattered
Dreams of the Good Life. Trade Cloth. Greenwood Publishing

Group, Inc. Portsmouth, NH. 1998. 184p. ISBN:0-275-95972-4,
ISBN13: 978-0-275-95972-2. Dewey:791.43/655.
LCCN:97-023878.
Audience: **u,f.**

McCaughey, Martha &   **PN1995.9.W6R454 2001**
  King, Neal (Editors)
Reel Knockouts: Violent Women in the Movies. Trade Paper.
University of Texas Press. Austin, TX. 2001. 291p.
ISBN:0-292-75251-2, ISBN13: 978-0-292-75251-1.
Dewey:791.43/652042. LCCN:00-047977.
Audience: **u,f.**

Medved, Michael   **PN1994**
Hollywood vs. America. Trade Paper. HarperCollins Publishers.
New York, NY. 1993. 416p. ISBN:0-06-092435-7, ISBN13:
978-0-06-092435-5. Dewey:302.23/43/0973. LCCN:92-052604.
Audience: **l,u,f.**

Mitchell, Charles P.   **PN1995**
Filmography of Social Issues: A Reference Guide. Book, Other.
Greenwood Publishing Group, Inc. Portsmouth, NH. 2004. 328p.
ISBN:0-313-32037-3, ISBN13: 978-0-313-32037-8.
Dewey:791.43/6556. LCCN:2004-017893.
Audience: **g,l,u,f.**

Naficy, Hamid   **PN1993.5.D44N34 2001**
An Accented Cinema: Exilic and Diasporic Filmmaking. Trade
Paper. Princeton University Press. Princeton, NJ. 2001. 390p.
ISBN:0-691-04391-4, ISBN13: 978-0-691-04391-3.
Dewey:791.43/09172/4. LCCN:00-057458.
Audience: **u,f.** *Choice, 2002.*

Prince, Stephen   **PN1995.9.V5P75 2003**
Classical Film Violence: Designing and Regulating Brutality in
Hollywood Cinema, 1930-1968. Trade Cloth. Rutgers University
Press. Piscataway, NJ. 2003. 320p. ISBN:0-8135-3280-9,
ISBN13: 978-0-8135-3280-6. Dewey:791.43/6.
LCCN:2002-015870.
Audience: **u.** *Choice, 2004.*

Williams, Alan (Editor)   **PN1994.F43817 2002**
Film and Nationalism. Trade Cloth. Rutgers University Press.
Piscataway, NJ. 2002. 290p. Rutgers Depth of Field Ser.
ISBN:0-8135-3039-3, ISBN13: 978-0-8135-3039-0.
Dewey:791.43. LCCN:2001-041685.
Audience: **u,f.** *Choice, 2002.*

Film Analysis and Criticism > Narrative Film and Genres > War

Anderegg, Michael   **DS557.73.A5 1991**
  (Editor)
Inventing Vietnam: The War in Film and Television. Trade
Cloth. Temple University Press. Philadelphia, PA. 1991. 315p.
Culture and the Moving Image Ser. ISBN:0-87722-861-2,
ISBN13: 978-0-87722-861-5. Dewey:791.43/658.
LCCN:91-011392.
Audience: **u,f.**

Auster, Albert & Quart,   **DS557**
  Leonard
How the War Was Remembered: Hollywood and Vietnam. Trade
Cloth. Greenwood Publishing Group, Inc. Portsmouth, NH.

1988. 186p. ISBN:0-275-92383-5, ISBN13: 978-0-275-92383-9. Dewey:959.704/3. LCCN:87-036125.

Audience: **g,l,u.** *Choice, 1989.*

Basinger, Jeanine   **D743.23.B36 2003**
The World War II Combat Film: Anatomy of a Genre. Ed. 2. Trade Paper. Wesleyan University Press. Middletown, CT. 2003. 400p. ISBN:0-8195-6623-3, ISBN13: 978-0-8195-6623-2. Dewey:791.43/658. LCCN:2003-000243.

Audience: **u,f.** *Choice, 1986.*

Bates, Milton J.   **PS228.V5B38 1996**
The Wars We Took to Vietnam: Cultural Conflict and Storytelling. Trade Paper. University of California Press. Berkeley, CA. 1996. 338p. ISBN:0-520-20433-6, ISBN13: 978-0-520-20433-1. Dewey:810.9/358. LCCN:95-046772.

Audience: **u,f.** *Choice, 1997.*

Chambers, John W. 2nd   **D743.23.W67 1996**
  & Culbert, David
World War II, Film, and History. Trade Paper. Oxford University Press, Inc. New York, NY. 1996. 202p. ISBN:0-19-509967-2, ISBN13: 978-0-19-509967-6. Dewey:791.4/36/58. LCCN:95-049890.

Audience: **u,f.** *Choice, 1997.*

Davenport, Robert   **PN1995.9.W3D38 2003**
  Ralsey
The Encyclopedia of War Movies: Wars 1900 to the Present. Trade Cloth. Facts On File, Inc. New York, NY. 2004. 464p. ISBN:0-8160-4478-3, ISBN13: 978-0-8160-4478-8. Dewey:791.43/658. LCCN:2002-045201.

Audience: **g,l,u,f.** *Choice, 2004.*

DeBauche, Leslie   **D522.23.D43 1997**
  Midkiff
Reel Patriotism: The Movies and World War I. Trade Paper. University of Wisconsin Press. Chicago, IL. 1997. 262p. Wisconsin Studies in Film ISBN:0-299-15404-1, ISBN13: 978-0-299-15404-2. Dewey:940.3. LCCN:96-045979.

Audience: **g,l,u,f.** *Choice, 1997.*

Devine, Jeremy M.   **DS557.73 .D48 1999**
Vietnam at 24 Frames a Second: A Critical and Thematic Analysis of over 400 Films about the Vietnam War. Thomas Schatz (Foreword by). Trade Paper. University of Texas Press. Austin, TX. 1999. 421p. Texas Film and Media Studies Ser. ISBN:0-292-71601-X, ISBN13: 978-0-292-71601-8. Dewey:959.704/3. LCCN:98-051732.

Audience: **u,f.**

Dick, Bernard F.   **D743.D44 1996**
The Star-Spangled Screen: The American World War II Film. Trade Paper. University Press of Kentucky. Lexington, KY. 1996. 304p. ISBN:0-8131-0885-3, ISBN13: 978-0-8131-0885-8. Dewey:791.43/09/09358. LCCN:96-024072.

Audience: **g,l,u,f.** *Choice, 1986.*

Dittmar, Linda &   **DS557.73.F76 1990**
  Michaud, Gene (Editors)
From Hanoi to Hollywood: The Vietnam War in American Film. Trade Paper. Rutgers University Press. Piscataway, NJ. 1990. 400p. ISBN:0-8135-1587-4, ISBN13: 978-0-8135-1587-8. Dewey:791.43/658. LCCN:90-032548.

Audience: **u,f.** *Choice, 1991.*

Eberwein, Robert T.   **PN1995.9.W3W36 2004**
  (Introduction by)
The War Film. Trade Cloth. Rutgers University Press.

Piscataway, NJ. 2004. 240p. Rutgers Depth of Field Ser. ISBN:0-8135-3496-8, ISBN13: 978-0-8135-3496-1. Dewey:791.43/658. LCCN:2004-003820.

Audience: **g,l,u.** *Choice, 2005.*

Edwards, Paul M.   **DS918**
A Guide to Films on the Korean War. Cloth Text. Greenwood Publishing Group, Inc. Portsmouth, NH. 1997. 168p. Bibliographies and Indexes in American History Ser., Vol. 35 ISBN:0-313-30316-9, ISBN13: 978-0-313-30316-6. Dewey:951.904/1. LCCN:96-037601.

Audience: **g,l,u,f.**

Evans, Alun   **PN1995..9.W3**
Brasseys' Guide to War Films. Trade Paper. Potomac Books, Inc. Dulles, VA. 2000. 256p. ISBN:1-57488-263-5, ISBN13: 978-1-57488-263-6. Dewey:791.43658.

Audience: **g,l,u,f.**

Freitas, Gary A.   **PN1995.9.W3F74 2004**
War Movies: The Belle and Blade Guide to Classic War Videos. Trade Paper. Robert D. Reed Publishers. Bandon, OR. 2004. 414p. ISBN:1-931741-38-7, ISBN13: 978-1-931741-38-5. Dewey:791.43/658. LCCN:2003-095796.

Audience: **g,l,u,f.**

Gruner, Elliott   **P96.V46 G78 1993**
Prisoners of Culture: Representing the Vietnam POW. Trade Paper. Rutgers University Press. Piscataway, NJ. 1993. 280p. Communications, Media, and Culture Ser. ISBN:0-8135-1931-4, ISBN13: 978-0-8135-1931-9. Dewey:303.6/6. LCCN:92-030903.

Audience: **u,f.**

Hirsch, Joshua Francis   **PN1995.9.H53H57 2004**
Afterimage: Film, Trauma, and the Holocaust. Trade Cloth. Temple University Press. Philadelphia, PA. 2003. 232p. Emerging Media Ser. ISBN:1-59213-209-X, ISBN13: 978-1-59213-209-6. Dewey:791.43/658. LCCN:2003-053131.

Audience: **u,f.** *Choice, 2004.*

Kelly, Andrew   **PN1995.9.H5**
Cinema and the Great War. Paper over Boards. Routledge. New York, NY. 1997. 240p. Cinema and Society Ser. ISBN:0-415-05203-3, ISBN13: 978-0-415-05203-0. Dewey:791.4/36/58. LCCN:98-162421.

Audience: **g,l,u,f.**

Kinnard, Roy   **E656.K56 1996**
Blue and the Gray on the Silver Screen: More Than 80 Years of Civil War Movies. Trade Cloth. Carol Publishing Group. Secaucus, NJ. 1996. 356p. ISBN:1-55972-383-1, ISBN13: 978-1-55972-383-1. Dewey:973.7. LCCN:96-031476.

Audience: **g,l,u,f.**

Lentz, Robert J.   **DS918.16.L46 2002**
Korean War Filmography: 93 English Language Features through 2000. Cloth Text. McFarland & Company, Incorporated Publishers. Jefferson, NC. 2003. 496p. ISBN:0-7864-1046-9, ISBN13: 978-0-7864-1046-0. Dewey:016.79143/658. LCCN:2002-015084.

Audience: **g,l,u,f.** *Choice, 2003.*

Lipschutz, Ronnie D.   **PN1995.9.W3L57 2001**
Cold War Fantasies: Film, Fiction and Foreign Policy. Book, Other. Rowman & Littlefield Publishers, Inc. Lanham, MD. 2001. 256p. ISBN:0-7425-1051-4, ISBN13: 978-0-7425-1051-7. Dewey:791.43/658. LCCN:2001-040422.

Audience: **u,f.** *Choice, 2002.*

Formats: Web: ▢   Ebook: 🄴   CD/DVD-ROM: 🎔   BCL3: *B*

Malo, Jean-Jacques &   DS557.73.V53 1994
  Williams, Tony (Editors)
Vietnam War Films: Over 600 Feature, Made-for-TV, Pilot and
Short Movies, 1939-1992, from the United States, Vietnam,
France, Belgium, Australia, Hong Kong, South Africa, Great
Britain and Other Countries. Cloth Text. McFarland &
Company, Incorporated Publishers. Jefferson, NC. 1994. 592p.
ISBN:0-89950-781-6, ISBN13: 978-0-89950-781-1.
Dewey:791.43658. LCCN:92-56662.
                         Audience: **g,l,u,f.** *Choice, 1994.*

Matelski, Marilyn J. &   PN1995.9.W3W35 2003
  Nancy, Lynch Street (Editor, Translators)
War and Film in America: Historical and Critical Essays. Paper
Text. McFarland & Company, Incorporated Publishers. Jefferson,
NC. 2003. 218p. ISBN:0-7864-1673-4, ISBN13:
978-0-7864-1673-8. Dewey:791.43/658. LCCN:2003-010999.
                         Audience: **l,u,f.** *Choice, 2004.*

Mayo, Mike (Editor)   PN1995.9.W3M39 1999
VideoHound's War Movies: Classic Conflict on Film. Paper
Text. Visible Ink Press. Canton, MI. 2000. 668p. VideoHound
Ser. ISBN:1-57859-089-2, ISBN13: 978-1-57859-089-6.
Dewey:016.79143/658. LCCN:99-040600.
                         Audience: **g,l,u,f.**

McAdams, Frank J.   PN1995.9.W3M395 2002
The American War Film: History and Hollywood. Trade Cloth.
Greenwood Publishing Group, Inc. Portsmouth, NH. 2002. 408p.
ISBN:0-275-96871-5, ISBN13: 978-0-275-96871-7.
Dewey:791.43/658. LCCN:2001-053086.
                         Audience: **g,l,u,f.** *Choice, 2003.*

Paris, Michael (Editor)   D522.23.F57
The First World War and Popular Cinema: 1914 to the Present.
Trade Paper. Rutgers University Press. Piscataway, NJ. 2000.
240p. ISBN:0-8135-2825-9, ISBN13: 978-0-8135-2825-0.
Dewey:940.4/8. LCCN:99-055762.
                         Audience: **u,f.** *Choice, 2000.*

Rollins, Peter C. &   D522.23.H65 1997
  O'Connor, John E. (Editors)
Hollywood's World War I: Motion Picture Images. Trade Paper.
University of Wisconsin Press. Chicago, IL. 1997. 304p.
ISBN:0-87972-756-X, ISBN13: 978-0-87972-756-7.
Dewey:791.43/658. LCCN:97-026062.
                         Audience: **u,f.** *Choice, 1998.*

Shull, Michael S. &   D743.23.S55 1996
  Wilt, David E.
Hollywood War Films, 1937-1945: An Exhaustive Filmography
of American Feature-Length Motion Pictures Relating to World
War II. Trade Cloth. McFarland & Company, Incorporated
Publishers. Jefferson, NC. 1996. 488p. ISBN:0-7864-0145-1,
ISBN13: 978-0-7864-0145-1. Dewey:940.53. LCCN:96-4799.
                         Audience: **g,l,u,f.** *Choice, 1996.*

Suid, Lawrence H.   PN1995.9
Guts and Glory: The Making of the American Military Image in
Film. Ed. 2. Trade Paper. University Press of Kentucky.
Lexington, KY. 2002. 672p. ISBN:0-8131-9018-5, ISBN13:
978-0-8131-9018-1. Dewey:791.43/658. LCCN:2001-007630.
                         Audience: **u,f.**

Virilio, Paul   PN1995.9.W3V58 1989
War and Cinema: The Logistics of Perception. Patrick Camiller
(Translator). Trade Paper. Analytical Psychology Club of San

Francisco, Inc. San Francisco, CA. 1989. 200p.
ISBN:0-86091-928-5, ISBN13: 978-0-86091-928-5.
Dewey:791.43/09/09358. LCCN:89-030059.
                         Audience: **u,f.**

Walker, Mark   PN1995.9.V44W35 1991
Vietnam Veteran Films. Trade Cloth. Scarecrow Press, Inc.
Lanham, MD. 1991. 238p. ISBN:0-8108-2475-2, ISBN13:
978-0-8108-2475-1. Dewey:791.43/658. LCCN:91-028813.
                         Audience: **g,l,u,f.** *Choice, 1992.*

Weber, Cynthia   PN1995.9.W3
Imagining America at War: Politics, War and Film. Trade Paper.
Routledge. New York, NY. 2005. VIII, 192p.
ISBN:0-415-37537-1, ISBN13: 978-0-415-37537-5.
Dewey:791.436580973. LCCN:2005-012064.
                         Audience: **l,u,f.** *Choice, 2006.*

Wetta, Frank J. &   PN1995
  Curley, Stephen J.
Celluloid Wars: A Guide to Film and the American Experience
of War. Cloth Text. Greenwood Publishing Group, Inc.
Portsmouth, NH. 1992. 320p. Research Guides in Military
Studies, No. 5 ISBN:0-313-26099-0, ISBN13:
978-0-313-26099-5. Dewey:791.43658. LCCN:92-008210.
                         Audience: **g,l,u,f.** *Choice, 1993.*

Film Analysis and Criticism > Narrative Film and Genres > Westerns

Aquila, Richard   F596.W28 1996
  (Editor)
Wanted Dead or Alive: The American West in Popular Culture.
Trade Paper. University of Illinois Press. Champaign, IL. 1998.
328p. ISBN:0-252-06527-1, ISBN13: 978-0-252-06527-9.
Dewey:306/.0978. LCCN:95-032476.
                         Audience: **u,f.**

Athearn, Robert G.   F595.A85 1986
The Mythic West in Twentieth-Century America. Elliott West
(Foreword by). Trade Cloth. University Press of Kansas.
Lawrence, KS. 1986. xii, 324p. ISBN:0-7006-0304-2, ISBN13:
978-0-7006-0304-6. Dewey:978/.03. LCCN:86-011106.
                         Audience: **g,l,u,f.** *Choice, 1987.*

Buscombe, Edward &   PN1995.9.W4B24 1998
  Pearson, Roberta E. (Editors)
Back in the Saddle Again: New Essays on the Western. Trade
Cloth. BFI Publishing. London, 1998. 218p.
ISBN:0-85170-660-6, ISBN13: 978-0-85170-660-3.
Dewey:791.43/6278. LCCN:98-210526.
                         Audience: **u,f.** *Choice, 1999.*

Cawelti, John G.   P96.W48C393 1999
The Six-Gun Mystique Sequel. Ed. 2. Trade Paper. Da Capo
Press, Inc. Cambridge, MA. 1999. 215p. ISBN:0-87972-786-1,
ISBN13: 978-0-87972-786-4. Dewey:700/.4278.
LCCN:98-047399.
                         Audience: **u,f.** *Choice, 1999.*

Corkin, Stanley   PN1995.9.W4C65 2004
Cowboys As Cold Warriors: The Western and U. S. History.
Trade Cloth. Temple University Press. Philadelphia, PA. 2004.
272p. Culture and the Moving Image Ser. ISBN:1-59213-253-7,

ISBN13: 978-1-59213-253-9. Dewey:791.43/6278.
LCCN:2003-067201.

Audience: **u,f.** *Choice, 2005.*

Coyne, Michael   **PN1995.9.W4**
The Crowded Prairie: American National Identity in the
Hollywood Western. Trade Paper. I. B. Tauris & Company, Ltd.
London, 1998. 264p. ISBN:1-86064-259-4, ISBN13:
978-1-86064-259-3. Dewey:791.4/36/278.

Audience: **u,f.**

Davis, Robert M.   **PS374.W4D38**
Playing Cowboys: Low Culture and High Art in the Western.
Trade Paper. University of Oklahoma Press. Norman, OK. 1994.
192p. ISBN:0-8061-2627-2, ISBN13: 978-0-8061-2627-2.
Dewey:813.087409. LCCN:91-034453.

Audience: **u,f.** *Choice, 1992.*

Fagen, Herb   **PN1995.9.W4F27 2002**
The Encyclopedia of Westerns. Trade Cloth. Facts On File, Inc.
New York, NY. 2003. 640p. ISBN:0-8160-4456-2, ISBN13:
978-0-8160-4456-6. Dewey:791.43/63278/03.
LCCN:2002-026355.

Audience: **g,l,u,f.** *Choice, 2004.*

Frantz, Joe Bertram   **F596 .F75**
The American Cowboy: The Myth and the Reality. Paper Text.
Textbook Publishers. Temecula, CA. 2003. 232p.
ISBN:0-7581-1749-3, ISBN13: 978-0-7581-1749-6. Dewey:978.

Audience: **g,l,u,f.**

Frayling, Christopher   **PN1995.9.W4**
Spaghetti Westerns: Cowboys and Europeans from Karl May to
Sergio Leone, Vol. 1. Ed. 2. Trade Paper. I. B. Tauris &
Company, Ltd. London, 1998. 320p. Cinema and Society Ser.
ISBN:1-86064-200-4, ISBN13: 978-1-86064-200-5.
Dewey:791.43/6278.

Audience: **l,u,f.**

Hardy, Phil (Editor)   **PN1995.9.W4**
The Overlook Film Encyclopedia: The Western. Trade Cloth.
Overlook Press, The. New York, NY. 1994. 416p. The Overlook
Film Encyclopedia Ser. ISBN:0-87951-517-1, ISBN13:
978-0-87951-517-1. Dewey:791.43/6278. LCCN:93-024439.
Audience: **g,l,u,f.** *Choice, 1996.*

Katchmer, George A.   **PN1995.9.W4K33 2000**
A Biographical Dictionary of Silent Film Western Actors and
Actresses. Diana Serra Cary (Foreword by). Cloth Text.
McFarland & Company, Incorporated Publishers. Jefferson, NC.
2002. 488p. ISBN:0-7864-0763-8, ISBN13: 978-0-7864-0763-7.
Dewey:791.43/6278/092273 B. LCCN:00-052196.

Audience: **g,l,u,f.**

Kitses, Jim   **PN1995.9.W4**
Horizons West: The Western from John Ford to Clint Eastwood.
Ed. 2. Trade Cloth. BFI Publishing. London, 2004. 342p.
ISBN:1-84457-019-3, ISBN13: 978-1-84457-019-5.
Dewey:791.4/36278.

Audience: **g,l,u,f.**

Langman, Larry   **PN1995**
A Guide to Silent Westerns. Cloth Text. Greenwood Publishing
Group, Inc. Portsmouth, NH. 1992. 616p. Bibliographies and
Indexes in the Performing Arts Ser., No. 13
ISBN:0-313-27858-X, ISBN13: 978-0-313-27858-7.
Dewey:016.791436278. LCCN:92-023783.
Audience: **g,l,u,f.** *Choice, 1993.*

Lenihan, John H.   **PN1995.9.W4**
Showdown: Confronting Modern America in the Western Film.
Trade Paper. University of Illinois Press. Champaign, IL. 1985.
224p. Illini Book Ser. ISBN:0-252-01254-2, ISBN13:
978-0-252-01254-9. Dewey:791.43/0909/32. LCCN:79-025271.
Audience: **u,f.**

Lentz, Harris M. III   **PN1995.9.W4L383 1996**
Western and Frontier Film and Television Credits: 1903-1995,
Vol. 1. Cloth Text. McFarland & Company, Incorporated
Publishers. Jefferson, NC. 1996. 1015p. ISBN:0-7864-0217-2,
ISBN13: 978-0-7864-0217-5. Dewey:791.4/36278/03.
LCCN:95-43360.

Audience: **g,l,u,f.** *Choice, 1997.*

McDonald, Archie P.   **PN1995.9.W4S**
  (Editor)
Shooting Stars: Heroes and Heroines of Western Film. Trade
Paper. Books on Demand. Ann Arbor, MI. 287p.
ISBN:0-8357-3957-0, ISBN13: 978-0-8357-3957-3.
Dewey:791.43/09/093278. LCCN:85-045988.

Audience: **l,u,f.** *Choice, 1987.*

Mitchell, Lee C.   **PS374.W4**
Westerns: Making the Man in Fiction and Film. Trade Paper.
University of Chicago Press. Chicago, IL. 1998. 348p.
ISBN:0-226-53235-6, ISBN13: 978-0-226-53235-6.
Dewey:813/.087409353.

Audience: **u,f.**

Philip, R.   **PN1995.9.W4L694 2004**
Westerns in a Changing America, 1955-2000. Paper Text.
McFarland & Company, Incorporated Publishers. Jefferson, NC.
2004. 328p. ISBN:0-7864-1871-0, ISBN13: 978-0-7864-1871-8.
Dewey:791.43/6278. LCCN:2004-009588.

Audience: **g,l,u.**

Phillips, R.   **PN1995.9.W4L69 2001**
Westerns and American Culture, 1930-1955. Paper Text.
McFarland & Company, Incorporated Publishers. Jefferson, NC.
2001. 280p. ISBN:0-7864-1076-0, ISBN13: 978-0-7864-1076-7.
Dewey:791.43/6278. LCCN:2001-031256.

Audience: **g,l,u.**

Pitts, Michael R.   **PN1995.9.W4**
Western Movies: A TV and Video Guide to 4200 Genre Films.
Paper Text. McFarland & Company, Incorporated Publishers.
Jefferson, NC. 1997. 635p. ISBN:0-7864-0421-3, ISBN13:
978-0-7864-0421-6. Dewey:791.4/36/278. LCCN:85-31014.
Audience: **g,l,u,f.** *Choice, 1987.*

Prats, A. J.   **PS374.W4P73 2002**
Invisible Natives: Myth and Identity in the American Western.
Trade Paper. Cornell University Press. Ithaca, NY. 2002. 344p.
ISBN:0-8014-8754-4, ISBN13: 978-0-8014-8754-5.
Dewey:791.43/6278. LCCN:2001-006863.

Audience: **u,f.** *Choice, 2003.*

Simmon, Scott   **PN1995.9.W4S53 2002**
The Invention of the Western Film: A Cultural History of the
Genre's First Half Century. Cloth Text. Cambridge University
Press. New York, NY. 2003. 410p. ISBN:0-521-55473-X,
ISBN13: 978-0-521-55473-2. Dewey:791.43/6278.
LCCN:2002-035117.

Audience: **u.** *Choice, 2004.*

Slotkin, Richard   **E169.12.S57 1998**
Gunfighter Nation: The Myth of the Frontier in
Twentieth-Century America. Trade Paper. University of

Oklahoma Press. Norman, OK. 1998. 864p.
ISBN:0-8061-3031-8, ISBN13: 978-0-8061-3031-6. Dewey:978.
LCCN:97-032043.

Audience: **u,f.**

Smith, Andrew Brodie   **PN1995.9.W4S63 2003**
Shooting Cowboys and Indians: Silent Western Films, American
Culture, and the Birth of Hollywood. Trade Cloth. University
Press of Colorado. Boulder, CO. 2003. 230p.
ISBN:0-87081-746-9, ISBN13: 978-0-87081-746-5.
Dewey:791.43/6278. LCCN:2003-014272.

Audience: **u,f.** *Choice, 2004.*

Tompkins, Jane P.   **PS374.W4T66 1993**
West of Everything: The Inner Life of Westerns. Trade Paper.
Oxford University Press, Inc. New York, NY. 1993. 272p.
ISBN:0-19-508268-0, ISBN13: 978-0-19-508268-5.
Dewey:813.087409.

Audience: **u,f.**

Walker, Janet   **PN1995.9.W4W44 2001**
Westerns: Films through History. UK-B Format Paperback.
Routledge. New York, NY. 2001. 296p. AFI Film Readers Ser.
ISBN:0-415-92424-3, ISBN13: 978-0-415-92424-5.
Dewey:791.43/6278. LCCN:00-051708.

Audience: **g,l,u,f.**

Wallmann, Jeffrey M.   **PS374.W4W27 1999**
The Western: Parables of the Western Dream. Trade Cloth.
Texas Tech University Press. Lubbock, TX. 1999. 231p.
ISBN:0-89672-423-9, ISBN13: 978-0-89672-423-5.
Dewey:813/.087409. LCCN:99-039869.

Audience: **u,f.** *Choice, 2000.*

Weisser, Thomas   **PN1995.9.W4 W32**
Spaghetti Westerns the Good, the Bad and the Violent: A
Comprehensive, Illustrated Filmography of 558 Eurowesterns
and Their Personnel, 1961-1977. Craig Ledbetter & Tom Betts
(Foreword by), William Connolly (Commentaries by). Paper
Text. McFarland & Company, Incorporated Publishers. Jefferson,
NC. 2005. 498p. ISBN:0-7864-2442-7, ISBN13:
978-0-7864-2442-9. Dewey:016.79143/6278. LCCN:92-050002.
Audience: **g,l,u,f.**

Wright, Will   **PN1995.9.W4**
Sixguns and Society: A Structural Study of the Western. Trade
Cloth. University of California Press. Berkeley, CA. 1977. 217p.
ISBN:0-520-03491-0, ISBN13: 978-0-520-03491-4.
Dewey:791.4/36278.

Audience: **u,f.**

Film Analysis and Criticism > Narrative Film and Genres > Adaptations

Aycock, Wendell M. &   **PN1995.3 .F5 1988**
  Schoenecke, Michael (Editors)
Film and Literature: A Comparative Approach to Adaptation.
Trade Paper. Texas Tech University Press. Lubbock, TX. 1998.
202p. Studies in Comparative Literature: No. 1, No. 19
ISBN:0-89672-169-8, ISBN13: 978-0-89672-169-2.
Dewey:791.43. LCCN:88-024965.

Audience: **u,f.**

Burt, Richard & Boose,   **PR3093.S543 2003**
  Lynda E. (Editors)
Shakespeare, the Movie II: Popularizing the Plays on Film, TV,
Video and DVD. Ed. 2. Trade Paper. Routledge. New York, NY.

2003. 352p. ISBN:0-415-28299-3, ISBN13: 978-0-415-28299-4.
Dewey:791.43/6. LCCN:2002-155445.

Audience: **g,l,u,f.**

Cahir, Linda Costanzo   **PN1997.85.C25 2006**
Literature into Film: Theory and Practical Approaches. Trade
Paper. McFarland & Company, Incorporated Publishers.
Jefferson, NC. 2006. 315p. ISBN:0-7864-2597-0, ISBN13:
978-0-7864-2597-6. Dewey:791.43/6. LCCN:2006-003234.

Audience: **u,f.** *Choice, 2006.*

Cartmell, Deborah   **PR3093.C37 2000**
Interpreting Shakespeare on Screen. Cloth over Boards. Palgrave
Macmillan. New York, NY. 2000. 186p. ISBN:0-312-23392-2,
ISBN13: 978-0-312-23392-1. Dewey:822.3/3. LCCN:00-025540.

Audience: **u,f.** *Choice, 2001.*

Davies, Anthony   **PR3093.D38 1988**
Filming Shakespeare's Plays: The Adaptations of Laurence
Olivier, Orson Welles, Peter Brook and Akira Kurosawa. Trade
Paper. Cambridge University Press. New York, NY. 1990. 233p.
ISBN:0-521-39913-0, ISBN13: 978-0-521-39913-5.
Dewey:791.43/75.

Audience: **u,f.** *Choice, 1989.*

Davies, Anthony &   **PR3093 .S53 1994**
  Wells, Stanley (Editors)
Shakespeare and the Moving Image: The Plays on Film and
Television. Trade Paper. Cambridge University Press. New York,
NY. 1994. 278p. ISBN:0-521-43573-0, ISBN13:
978-0-521-43573-4. Dewey:791.43/75. LCCN:93-042524.

Audience: **u,f.** *Choice, 1995.*

Elliott, Kamilla   **PN1997.85.E44 2003**
Rethinking the Novel/Film Debate. Trade Cloth. Cambridge
University Press. New York, NY. 2003. 314p.
ISBN:0-521-81844-3, ISBN13: 978-0-521-81844-5.
Dewey:791.43/6. LCCN:2002-034806.

Audience: **u,f.**

Enser, A. G. S.   **Z5784.M9B385 2002**
Enser's Filmed Books and Plays: A List of Books and Plays
from Which Films Have Been Made, 1928-2001. Ed. 6. Ellen
Baskin (Editor). Trade Cloth. Ashgate Publishing, Ltd.
Aldershot, 2003. 1216p. ISBN:0-7546-0878-6, ISBN13:
978-0-7546-0878-3. Dewey:016.79143/6. LCCN:2002-028174.
Audience: **g,l,u,f.** *Choice, 2004.*

Fenton, Jill R., et al.   **PN1997.85.W58 1990**
Women Writers, from Page to Screen: A Guide to Literary
Sources. Charles G. Waugh, Jane Russo & Martin H.
Greensberg (Authors). Paper over Boards. Garland Publishing,
Inc. New York, NY. 1990. 512p. ISBN:0-8240-8529-9, ISBN13:
978-0-8240-8529-2. Dewey:016.79143/75/082.
LCCN:89-023479.

Audience: **g,l,u,f.** *Choice, 1991.*

Giddings, Robert &   **PN1995**
  Sheen, Erica (Editors)
From Page to Screen: Adaptations of the Classic Novel. Trade
Paper. Manchester University Press. Manchester, 2000. 272p.
ISBN:0-7190-5231-9, ISBN13: 978-0-7190-5231-6.
Dewey:791.4/375.

Audience: **u,f.**

Glavin, John (Editor)   PR4575.D53 2003
Dickens on Screen. Trade Paper. Cambridge University Press.
New York, NY. 2003. 238p. On Screen Ser.
ISBN:0-521-00124-2, ISBN13: 978-0-521-00124-3.
Dewey:791.43/6. LCCN:2003-041205.
                                                Audience: **u,f.**

Griffin, Susan M.   PS2127.F55H45 2001
(Editor)
Henry James Goes to the Movies. Trade Cloth. University Press
of Kentucky. Lexington, KY. 2001. 320p. ISBN:0-8131-2191-4,
ISBN13: 978-0-8131-2191-8. Dewey:813/.4. LCCN:00-012274.
                                        Audience: **u,f.** *Choice, 2002.*

Hatchuel, Sarah   PR3093.H37 2004
Shakespeare, from Stage to Screen. Trade Cloth. Cambridge
University Press. New York, NY. 2004. 200p.
ISBN:0-521-83624-7, ISBN13: 978-0-521-83624-1.
Dewey:822.3/3. LCCN:2004-040791.
                                        Audience: **l,u,f.** *Choice, 2005.*

Haut, Woody   PS379
Heartbreak and Vine: Hardboiled Writers in Hollywood. Trade
Paper. Serpent's Tail Ltd. London, 2002. 256p.
ISBN:1-85242-678-0, ISBN13: 978-1-85242-678-1.
Dewey:813/.087209. LCCN:2002-101378.
                                                Audience: **u,f.**

Hischak, Thomas S.   PS338.M67H57 2005
American Plays and Musicals on Screen: 650 Stage Productions
and Their Film and Televison Adaptations. Cloth Text.
McFarland & Company, Incorporated Publishers. Jefferson, NC.
2004. 351p. ISBN:0-7864-2003-0, ISBN13: 978-0-7864-2003-2.
Dewey:791.43/6. LCCN:2004-022967.
                                        Audience: **g,l,u,f.** *Choice, 2005.*

Hopkins, Lisa   PR408.G68H67 2005
Screening the Gothic. Trade Cloth. University of Texas Press.
Austin, TX. 2005. 188p. ISBN:0-292-70645-6, ISBN13:
978-0-292-70645-3. Dewey:820.9/11. LCCN:2004-024535.
                                                Audience: **u,f.**

Howlett, Kathy M.   PR3093.H69 2000
Framing Shakespeare on Film. Trade Cloth. Ohio University
Press. Athens, OH. 2000. 275p. ISBN:0-8214-1247-7, ISBN13:
978-0-8214-1247-3. Dewey:791.43/6. LCCN:98-050057.
                                        Audience: **u,f.** *Choice, 2001.*

Jackson, Russell   PR3093 .C36 2000
(Editor)
The Cambridge Companion to Shakespeare on Film. Trade
Paper. Cambridge University Press. New York, NY. 2000. 354p.
Companions to Literature Ser. ISBN:0-521-63975-1, ISBN13:
978-0-521-63975-0. Dewey:791.43/6. LCCN:00-023195.
                                        Audience: **l,u,f.** *Choice, 2001.*

Keller, James R. &   PR3093.A46 2004
Stratyner, Leslie (Editors)
Almost Shakespeare: Reinventing His Works for Cinema and
Television. Paper Text. McFarland & Company, Incorporated
Publishers. Jefferson, NC. 2004. 203p. ISBN:0-7864-1909-1,
ISBN13: 978-0-7864-1909-8. Dewey:791.43/6.
LCCN:2004-017517.
                                        Audience: **g,l,u.** *Choice, 2005.*

Krevolin, Richard W.   PN1996.K718 2003
How to Adapt Anything into a Screenplay. Trade Paper. John
Wiley & Sons, Inc. Hoboken, NJ. 2003. 218p.
ISBN:0-471-22545-2, ISBN13: 978-0-471-22545-4.
Dewey:808.2/3. LCCN:2002-027001.
                                                Audience: **u,f.**

Lupack, Barbara T.   PN1997.85.V57 1996
(Editor)
Vision/Re-Vision: Adapting Contemporary American Fiction by
Women to Film. Trade Cloth. University of Wisconsin Press.
Chicago, IL. 1996. 250p. ISBN:0-87972-713-6, ISBN13:
978-0-87972-713-0. Dewey:791.43. LCCN:96-028222.
                                                Audience: **u,f.**

Lupack, Barbara Tepa   PN1995.9.N4L87 2002
Literary Adaptations in Black American Cinema: From
Micheaux to Morrison. Trade Cloth. University of Rochester
Press. Rochester, NY. 2002. 584p. ISBN:1-58046-103-4,
ISBN13: 978-1-58046-103-0. Dewey:791.43/6520396073.
LCCN:2002-022332.
                                        Audience: **u,f.** *Choice, 2003.*

Lupack, Barbara Tepa   PN1997.85.N56 1999
(Editor)
Nineteenth-Century Women at the Movies: Adapting Classic
Women's Fiction to Film. Trade Cloth. University of Wisconsin
Press. Chicago, IL. 1999. 321p. ISBN:0-87972-805-1, ISBN13:
978-0-87972-805-2. Dewey:791.43/6. LCCN:99-038681.
                                                Audience: **u,f.**

Mayer, Robert (Editor)   PN1997.85
Eighteenth-Century Fiction on Screen. Trade Paper. Cambridge
University Press. New York, NY. 2002. 240p.
ISBN:0-521-52910-7, ISBN13: 978-0-521-52910-5.
Dewey:791.43/6.
                                        Audience: **u,f.** *Choice, 2003.*

Moore, Gene M.   PR6005.O4 Z581165 1
(Editor)
Conrad on Film. Trade Paper. Cambridge University Press. New
York, NY. 2006. 278p. ISBN:0-521-02679-2, ISBN13:
978-0-521-02679-6. Dewey:791.43/6.
                                                Audience: **u,f.**

Niemeyer, Paul J.   PR4757.F55N54 2003
Seeing Hardy: Film and Television Adaptations of the Fiction of
Thomas Hardy. Paper Text. McFarland & Company,
Incorporated Publishers. Jefferson, NC. 2003. 308p.
ISBN:0-7864-1429-4, ISBN13: 978-0-7864-1429-1.
Dewey:791.43/6. LCCN:2002-152177.
                                                Audience: **u,f.**

Parrill, Sue   PR4038.F55P37 2002
Jane Austen on Film and Television: A Critical Study of the
Adaptations. Paper Text. McFarland & Company, Incorporated
Publishers. Jefferson, NC. 2002. 229p. ISBN:0-7864-1349-2,
ISBN13: 978-0-7864-1349-2. Dewey:791.43/6.
LCCN:2002-000752.
                                        Audience: **g,l,u,f.** *Choice, 2002.*

Reynolds, William &   PN1995.3.I87 1994
Trembley, Elizabeth (Editors)
It's a Print!: Detective Fiction from Page to Screen. Trade
Cloth. University of Wisconsin Press. Chicago, IL. 1994. 235p.
ISBN:0-87972-661-X, ISBN13: 978-0-87972-661-4.
Dewey:791.43/655. LCCN:94-070906.
                                        Audience: **g,l,u,f.** *Choice, 1995.*

Roberts, Jerry   PS338.M67R63 2003
The Great American Playwrights on the Screen: A Critical
Guide to Film, TV, Video and DVD. Trade Paper. Applause
Theatre Book Publishers. New York, NY. 2003. 576p.
ISBN:1-55783-512-8, ISBN13: 978-1-55783-512-3.
Dewey:791.43/6. LCCN:2003-000060.
                              Audience: **g,l,u,f.** *Choice, 2003.*

Rothwell, Kenneth S.   PR3093
A History of Shakespeare on Screen: A Century of Film and
Television. Ed. 2. Cloth Text. Cambridge University Press. New
York, NY. 2004. 398p. ISBN:0-521-83537-2, ISBN13:
978-0-521-83537-4. Dewey:791.43/6. LCCN:2005-272422.
                              Audience: **u,f.** *Choice, 2000.*

Stam, Robert   PN1997.85.S76 2004
Literature Through Film: Realism, Magic, and the Art of
Adaptation. Trade Paper. Blackwell Publishing, Inc. Malden,
MA. 2004. 408p. ISBN:1-4051-0288-8, ISBN13:
978-1-4051-0288-9. Dewey:791.43/6. LCCN:2004-011846.
                              Audience: **l,u,f.** *Choice, 2005.*

Stam, Robert &   PN1997.85.L515 2005
  Raengo, Alessandra (Editors)
Literature and Film: A Guide to the Theory and Practice of Film
Adaptation. Trade Paper. Blackwell Publishing, Inc. Malden,
MA. 2004. 376p. ISBN:0-631-23055-6, ISBN13:
978-0-631-23055-7. Dewey:791.43/6. LCCN:2004-015927.
                              Audience: **u,f.** *Choice, 2005.*

Tibbetts, John C. &   PN1997.85.T54 2005
  Welsh, James Michael
The Encyclopedia of Novels into Film. Ed. 2. Trade Cloth. Facts
On File, Inc. New York, NY. 2005. 608p. Facts on File Film
Reference Library ISBN:0-8160-5449-5, ISBN13:
978-0-8160-5449-7. Dewey:791.43/6. LCCN:2004-003317.
                              Audience: **g,l,u,f.** *Choice, 2005, 1998.*

Tibbetts, John C. &   PN1997.85.T544 2001
  Welsh, James M.
The Encyclopedia of Stage Plays into Film. Steve Allen
(Foreword by). Trade Cloth. Facts On File, Inc. New York, NY.
2001. 688p. Facts on File Film Reference Library
ISBN:0-8160-4155-5, ISBN13: 978-0-8160-4155-8.
Dewey:016.79143/6. LCCN:00-063622.
                              Audience: **g,l,u,f.** *Choice, 2001.*

Troost, Linda &   PR4038.F55J36 1998
  Greenfield, Sayre (Editors)
Jane Austen in Hollywood. Trade Cloth. University Press of
Kentucky. Lexington, KY. 1998. 240p. ISBN:0-8131-2084-5,
ISBN13: 978-0-8131-2084-3. Dewey:791.43/6.
LCCN:98-007882.
                              Audience: **g,l,u,f.** *Choice, 1999.*

Film Analysis and Criticism > Narrative Film and Genres > Melodrama

Singer, Ben   PN1995.9.M45S56 2001
🄴 Melodrama and Modernity: Early Sensational Cinema and Its
Contexts. E-Book. Columbia University Press. New York, NY.
ISBN:0-231-50507-8, ISBN13: 978-0-231-50507-9.
Dewey:791.43/653.
                              Audience: **u,f.** *Choice, 2001.*

Film Theory

Custen, George F.   PN1995.9.B55C87 1992
Bio-Pics: How Hollywood Constructed Public History. Cloth
Text. Rutgers University Press. Piscataway, NJ. 1992. 300p.
ISBN:0-8135-1754-0, ISBN13: 978-0-8135-1754-4.
Dewey:791.43/658. LCCN:91-026427.
                              Audience: **g,l,u,f.** *Choice, 1992.*

DeAngelis, Michael   PN1995.9.H55D43 2001
Gay Fandom and Crossover Stardom: James Dean, Mel Gibson,
and Keanu Reeves. Trade Cloth. Duke University Press.
Durham, NC. 2001. 296p. ISBN:0-8223-2728-7, ISBN13:
978-0-8223-2728-8. Dewey:791.43/086/642.
LCCN:2001-023153.
                              Audience: **u,f.** *Choice, 2002.*

Ehrlich, Linda C. &   N72.M6C55 1994
  Desser, David (Editors)
Cinematic Landscapes: Observations on the Visual Arts and
Cinema of China and Japan. Cloth Text. University of Texas
Press. Austin, TX. 1994. 384p. ISBN:0-292-72086-6, ISBN13:
978-0-292-72086-2. Dewey:791.43/01. LCCN:93-043041.
                              Audience: **u,f.**

Fenton, Jill R., et al.   PN1997.85.W58 1990
Women Writers, from Page to Screen: A Guide to Literary
Sources. Charles G. Waugh, Jane Russo & Martin H.
Greensberg (Authors). Paper over Boards. Garland Publishing,
Inc. New York, NY. 1990. 512p. ISBN:0-8240-8529-9, ISBN13:
978-0-8240-8529-2. Dewey:016.79143/75/082.
LCCN:89-023479.
                              Audience: **g,l,u,f.** *Choice, 1991.*

Hughes, Alex &   PN1993.5.F7H84 2001
  Williams, James S. (Editors)
Gender and French Cinema. Cloth over Boards. Berg Publishers.
Oxford, 2001. 256p. ISBN:1-85973-570-3, ISBN13:
978-1-85973-570-1. Dewey:791.43/652042/0944.
LCCN:2001-004389.
                              Audience: **g,l,u,f.**

McDonald, Keiko I.   PL747.55.M36 2000
From Book to Screen: Modern Japanese Literature in Films.
Trade Cloth. M. E. Sharpe Inc. Armonk, NY. 1999. 344p.
ISBN:0-7656-0387-X, ISBN13: 978-0-7656-0387-6.
Dewey:791.43/6. LCCN:99-010679.
                              Audience: **l,u,f.** *Choice, 2000.*

Mitry, Jean   PN1995.M54813 2000
Semiotics and the Analysis of Film. Christopher King
(Translator). Trade Cloth. Indiana University Press.
Bloomington, IN. 2000. xi, 277p. ISBN:0-253-33733-X,
ISBN13: 978-0-253-33733-7. Dewey:791.4/3/015.
LCCN:00-700028.
                              Audience: **u,f.** *Choice, 2000.*

Neale, Steve   PN1993.5.U6N43 2000
Genre and Hollywood. Paper over Boards. Routledge. New
York, NY. 2000. 344p. Sightlines Ser. ISBN:0-415-02605-9,
ISBN13: 978-0-415-02605-5. Dewey:791.43/6.
LCCN:00-698318.
                              Audience: **u,f.** *Choice, 2000.*

Nolletti, Arthur Jr. &   PN1993.5.J3.R44 1992
  Desser, David (Editors)
Reframing Japanese Cinema: Authorship, Genre, History. Trade
Cloth. Indiana University Press. Bloomington, IN. 1992. 384p.

ISBN:0-253-34108-6, ISBN13: 978-0-253-34108-2.
Dewey:791.43/0952. LCCN:91-033659.

Audience: **g,u,f.** *Choice, 1993.*

Rubinfeld, Mark D.   **PN1995**
Bound to Bond: Gender, Genre and the Hollywood Romantic
Comedy. Trade Cloth. Greenwood Publishing Group, Inc.
Portsmouth, NH. 2001. 248p. ISBN:0-275-97271-2, ISBN13:
978-0-275-97271-4. Dewey:791.43/617. LCCN:00-069899.

Audience: **g,l,u,f.** *Choice, 2002.*

Society, Politics, and Culture

Cazdyn, Eric   **PN1993.5.J3C39 2002**
The Flash of Capital: Film and Geopolitics in Japan. Trade
Cloth. Duke University Press. Durham, NC. 2002. 328p.
Asia-Pacific Ser. ISBN:0-8223-2912-3, ISBN13:
978-0-8223-2912-1. Dewey:791.43/0952. LCCN:2002-005423.

Audience: **u,f.** *Choice, 2003.*

Crowdus, Gary (Editor)   **PN1993.5.U6**
The Political Companion to American Film. Trade Cloth. Fitzroy
Dearborn Publishers, Inc. Chicago, IL. 1996. 525p.
ISBN:1-884964-53-2, ISBN13: 978-1-884964-53-4.
Dewey:791.4/3/0973. LCCN:93-041593.

Audience: **g,l,u,f.** *Choice, 1995.*

Society, Politics, and Culture > Film and the State: Censorship, Propaganda

Berry, Chris   **PN1993.5.C4B47 2004**
Postsocialist Cinema in Post-Mao China: The Cultural
Revolution after the Cultural Revolution. Paper over Boards.
Routledge. New York, NY. 2004. 272p. East Asia History,
Politics, Sociology and Culture Ser. ISBN:0-415-94786-3,
ISBN13: 978-0-415-94786-2. Dewey:791.43/0951.
LCCN:2003-026390.

Audience: **u,f.**

Skinner, James M.   **BX1407**
The Cross and the Cinema: The Legion of Decency and the
National Catholic Office for Motion Pictures, 1933-1970. Trade
Cloth. Greenwood Publishing Group, Inc. Portsmouth, NH.
1993. 248p. ISBN:0-275-94193-0, ISBN13: 978-0-275-94193-2.
Dewey:791.43. LCCN:92-043431.

Audience: **u,f.** *Choice, 1994.*

Society, Politics, and Culture > Class

Horne, Gerald   **PN1993.5.U65H67 2001**
Class Struggle in Hollywood, 1930-1950: Moguls, Mobsters,
Stars, Reds, and Trade Unionists. Trade Paper. University of
Texas Press. Austin, TX. 2001. 363p. ISBN:0-292-73138-8,
ISBN13: 978-0-292-73138-7. Dewey:331.88/1179143/09794.
LCCN:00-025950.

Audience: **u,f.** *Choice, 2001.*

Society, Politics, and Culture > Gender and Sexuality

Ascheid, Antje   **PN1995.9.N36A83 2002**
Hitler's Heroines: Stardom and Womanhood in Nazi Cinema.
Library Binding. Temple University Press. Philadelphia, PA.

2002. 240p. Culture and the Moving Image Ser.
ISBN:1-56639-983-1, ISBN13: 978-1-56639-983-8.
Dewey:791.43/658. LCCN:2002-071460.

Audience: **g,l,u,f.** *Choice, 2003.*

Bean, Jennifer M. &   **PN1995.9.W6F467 2002**
Negra, Diane (Editors)
A Feminist Reader in Early Cinema. Trade Cloth. Duke
University Press. Durham, NC. 2003. 592p. Camera Obscura
Ser. ISBN:0-8223-3025-3, ISBN13: 978-0-8223-3025-7.
Dewey:791.43/652042. LCCN:2002-007087.

Audience: **u,f.** *Choice, 2003.*

DeAngelis, Michael   **PN1995.9.H55D43 2001**
Gay Fandom and Crossover Stardom: James Dean, Mel Gibson,
and Keanu Reeves. Trade Cloth. Duke University Press.
Durham, NC. 2001. 296p. ISBN:0-8223-2728-7, ISBN13:
978-0-8223-2728-8. Dewey:791.43/086/642.
LCCN:2001-023153.

Audience: **u,f.** *Choice, 2002.*

DiBattista, Maria   **PN1995.9.W6D53 2001**
Fast-Talking Dames. Cloth over Boards. Yale University Press.
Cumberland, RI. 2001. 384p. ISBN:0-300-08815-9, ISBN13:
978-0-300-08815-1. Dewey:791.4/36/52042. LCCN:00-049946.

Audience: **g,l,u,f.** *Choice, 2001.*

Jeffords, Susan   **PN1995.9.M46J44 1993**
Hard Bodies: Hollywood Masculinity in the Reagan Era. Cloth
Text. Rutgers University Press. Piscataway, NJ. 1993. 240p.
ISBN:0-8135-2002-9, ISBN13: 978-0-8135-2002-5.
Dewey:791.43/652041/09048. LCCN:93-018282.

Audience: **u,f.** *Choice, 1994.*

Krutnik, Frank   **PN1995.9.F54K78 1991**
In a Lonely Street: Film Noir, Genre and Masculinity. Trade
Paper. Routledge. New York, NY. 1991. 288p.
ISBN:0-415-02630-X, ISBN13: 978-0-415-02630-7.
Dewey:791.43/655. LCCN:90-023774.

Audience: **u,f.** *Choice, 1992.*

Lane, Christina   **PN1998.2.L35 2000**
Feminist Hollywood: From Born in Flames to Point Break.
Trade Cloth. Wayne State University Press. Detroit, MI. 2000.
261p. Contemporary Film and Television Ser.
ISBN:0-8143-2799-0, ISBN13: 978-0-8143-2799-9.
Dewey:791.43/0233/0820973. LCCN:99-053522.

Audience: **g,l,u,f.** *Choice, 2001.*

LaSalle, Mick   **PN1995.9.W6**
Complicated Women: Sex and Power in Pre-Code Hollywood.
Trade Paper. St. Martin's Press. Gordonville, VA. 2001. 304p.
ISBN:0-312-28431-4, ISBN13: 978-0-312-28431-2.
Dewey:791.43/652042.

Audience: **u,f.** *Choice, 2001.*

Marchetti, Gina   **PN1995.9.A78M37 1993**
Romance and the "Yellow Peril": Race, Sex, and Discursive
Strategies in Hollywood Fiction. Trade Paper. University of
California Press. Berkeley, CA. 1994. 270p.
ISBN:0-520-08495-0, ISBN13: 978-0-520-08495-7.
Dewey:791.436520395. LCCN:92-010878.

Audience: **l,u,f.** *Choice, 1994.*

Rubinfeld, Mark D.   **PN1995**
Bound to Bond: Gender, Genre and the Hollywood Romantic
Comedy. Trade Cloth. Greenwood Publishing Group, Inc.

Portsmouth, NH. 2001. 248p. ISBN:0-275-97271-2, ISBN13: 978-0-275-97271-4. Dewey:791.43/617. LCCN:00-069899.
Audience: **g,l,u,f.** *Choice, 2002.*

Stamp, Shelley   **PN1995.9.W6S75 2000**
Movie-Struck Girls: Women and Motion Picture Culture after the Nickelodeon. Trade Paper. Princeton University Press. Princeton, NJ. 2000. 284p. ISBN:0-691-04457-0, ISBN13: 978-0-691-04457-6. Dewey:791.43/082. LCCN:99-046548.
Audience: **l,u,f.** *Choice, 2000.*

Tarr, Carrie & Rollet,   **PN1993.5.F7T27 2001**
Brigitte
Cinema and the Second Sex. Trade Cloth. Continuum International Publishing Group, Ltd. London, 2001. 320p. Women Make Cinema Ser. ISBN:0-8264-4741-4, ISBN13: 978-0-8264-4741-8. Dewey:791.43/0233/0820944. LCCN:2001-025333.
Audience: **g,l,u,f.**

Society, Politics, and Culture > Race and Ethnicity

Antonio, Sheril D.   **PN1995.9.N4A58 2001**
Contemporary African American Cinema. Trade Cloth. Peter Lang Publishing, Inc. New York, NY. 2002. 152p. Framing Film Ser., Vol. 4:The History and Art of Cinema
ISBN:0-8204-5517-2, ISBN13: 978-0-8204-5517-4. Dewey:384/.8/08996073. LCCN:00-067154.
Audience: **u,f.**

Bernstein, Matthew &   **PN1995.9.E95V57 1997**
Studlar, Gaylyn (Editors)
Visions of the East: Orientalism in Film. Cloth Text. Rutgers University Press. Piscataway, NJ. 1997. 325p.
ISBN:0-8135-2294-3, ISBN13: 978-0-8135-2294-4. Dewey:791.4/3/6/2/5. LCCN:96-018112.
Audience: **u,f.** *Choice, 1997.*

Bobo, Jacqueline   **PN1995.9.N4B57 1995**
Black Women As Cultural Leaders. Trade Paper. Columbia University Press. New York, NY. 1995. 224p. Film and Culture Ser. ISBN:0-231-08395-5, ISBN13: 978-0-231-08395-9. Dewey:791.4/36/52042. LCCN:94-025317.
Audience: **u,f.** *Choice, 1995.*

Bobo, Jacqueline   **PN1998.2.B57 1998**
Black Women Film and Video Artists. Paper over Boards. Routledge. New York, NY. 1998. 288p. AFI Film Readers Ser. ISBN:0-415-92041-8, ISBN13: 978-0-415-92041-4. Dewey:791.43/023/08996073. LCCN:97-032062.
Audience: **g,l,u,f.**

Bogle, Donald   **PN1995.9.N4B58 1988**
Blacks in American Film and Television: An Encyclopedia. Paper over Boards. Garland Publishing, Inc. New York, NY. 1988. 700p. ISBN:0-8240-8715-1, ISBN13: 978-0-8240-8715-9. Dewey:791.43/08996073. LCCN:87-029241.
Audience: **g,l,u,f.** *Choice, 1988.*

Bowser, Pearl (Editor),   **PN1998.3.M494O83**
et al.
Oscar Micheaux and His Circle: African-American Filmmaking and Race Cinema of the Silent Era. Jane Gaines & Charles Musser (Editors). Trade Cloth. Indiana University Press. Bloomington, IN. 2001. 384p. ISBN:0-253-33994-4, ISBN13:

978-0-253-33994-2. Dewey:791.43/0233/092. LCCN:2001-001386.
Audience: **l,u,f.**

Bowser, Pearl &   **PN1998.3.M494B69**
Spence, Louise
Writing Himself into History: Oscar Micheaux, His Silent Films and His Audiences. Thulani Davis (Foreword by). Trade Cloth. Rutgers University Press. Piscataway, NJ. 2000. 280p. ISBN:0-8135-2803-8, ISBN13: 978-0-8135-2803-8. Dewey:791.43/0233/092. LCCN:99-055380.
Audience: **u,f.** *Choice, 2001.*

Diawara, Manthia   **PN1995.9.N4.B45 1993**
(Editor)
Black American Cinema: Aesthetics and Spectatorship. Paper over Boards. Routledge. New York, NY. 1993. 256p. AFI Film Readers Ser. ISBN:0-415-90396-3, ISBN13: 978-0-415-90396-7. Dewey:791.4308996073. LCCN:92-032907.
Audience: **l,u,f.** *Choice, 1994.*

Donalson, Melvin   **PN1995.9.N4D66 2003**
Black Directors in Hollywood. Trade Paper. University of Texas Press. Austin, TX. 2003. 389p. ISBN:0-292-70179-9, ISBN13: 978-0-292-70179-3. Dewey:791.43/0233/092273 B. LCCN:2003-006770.
Audience: **g,l,u,f.**

Everett, Anna   **PN1995.9.N4E94 2001**
Returning the Gaze: A Genealogy of Black Film Criticism, 1909-1949. Trade Cloth. Duke University Press. Durham, NC. 2001. 384p. ISBN:0-8223-2606-X, ISBN13: 978-0-8223-2606-9. Dewey:791.43/01/508996073. LCCN:00-010758.
Audience: **u,f.** *Choice, 2001.*

Feng, Peter X.   **PN1995.9.A77F46 2002**
Identities in Motion: Asian American Film and Video. Trade Cloth. Duke University Press. Durham, NC. 2002. 304p. ISBN:0-8223-2983-2, ISBN13: 978-0-8223-2983-1. Dewey:791.43/6520395. LCCN:2002-003056.
Audience: **u,f.** *Choice, 2003.*

Friedman, Lester D.   **PN1995.9.M56U57 1991**
(Editor)
Unspeakable Images: Ethnicity and the American Cinema. Trade Paper. University of Illinois Press. Champaign, IL. 1991. 456p. ISBN:0-252-06152-7, ISBN13: 978-0-252-06152-3. Dewey:791.43/6520693. LCCN:90-039869.
Audience: **l,u,f.** *Choice, 1991.*

Gabbard, Krin   **PN1995.9.N4G33 2004**
Black Magic: White Hollywood and African American Culture. Trade Cloth. Rutgers University Press. Piscataway, NJ. 2004. 256p. ISBN:0-8135-3383-X, ISBN13: 978-0-8135-3383-4. Dewey:791.43/652996073. LCCN:2003-020083.
Audience: **u,f.**

Green, J. Ronald   **PN1998.3.M494G74**
Straight Lick: The Cinema of Oscar Micheaux. Trade Cloth. Indiana University Press. Bloomington, IN. 2000. xvi, 295p. ISBN:0-253-33753-4, ISBN13: 978-0-253-33753-5. Dewey:791.43/0233/092. LCCN:99-087110.
Audience: **u,f.** *Choice, 2001.*

Green, J. Ronald   **PN1998.3.M494G76**
With a Crooked Stick: The Films of Oscar Micheaux. Trade Paper. Indiana University Press. Bloomington, IN. 2004. 304p.

ISBN:0-253-21715-6, ISBN13: 978-0-253-21715-8.
Dewey:791.43/02/33092. LCCN:2003-015584.

Audience: **u,f.** *Choice, 2004.*

Hanke, Ken   **PN1995.9**
Charlie Chan at the Movies: History, Filmography, and
Criticism. Paper Text. McFarland & Company, Incorporated
Publishers. Jefferson, NC. 2004. 286p. ISBN:0-7864-1921-0,
ISBN13: 978-0-7864-1921-0. Dewey:791.43/75.

Audience: **g,l,u.**

hooks, bell   **PN1995.9.S6H66 1996**
Reel to Real: Race, Sex and Class at the Movies. UK-B Format
Paperback. Routledge. New York, NY. 1996. 256p.
ISBN:0-415-91824-3, ISBN13: 978-0-415-91824-4.
Dewey:302.23/43. LCCN:96-026474.

Audience: **l,u.**

Klotman, Phyllis R.   **PN1997.A1S36 1991**
  (Editor)
Screenplays of the African American Experience. Trade Cloth.
Indiana University Press. Bloomington, IN. 1991. 280p.
ISBN:0-253-33145-5, ISBN13: 978-0-253-33145-8.
Dewey:791.43/6520396073. LCCN:90-043511.

Audience: **g,l,u,f.** *Choice, 1991.*

Klotman, Phyllis Rauch   **PN1995.9.N4S77 1999**
& Cutler, Janet K.
Struggles for Representation: African American Documentary
Film and Video. Trade Cloth. Indiana University Press.
Bloomington, IN. 1999. 464p. ISBN:0-253-33595-7, ISBN13:
978-0-253-33595-1. Dewey:070.1/8. LCCN:99-029890.

Audience: **u,f.** *Choice, 2000.*

Klotman, Phyllis R. &   **PN1995.9.N4K58 1997**
Gibson, Gloria J.
Frame by Frame II: A Filmography of the African American
Image, 1978-1994. Trade Cloth. Indiana University Press.
Bloomington, IN. 1997. 944p. ISBN:0-253-33280-X, ISBN13:
978-0-253-33280-6. Dewey:791.43/08996073. LCCN:96-029770.

Audience: **g,l,u,f.** *Choice, 1998.*

Knight, Arthur   **PN1995.9.N4K59 2002**
Disintegrating the Musical: Black Performance and American
Musical Film. Trade Cloth. Duke University Press. Durham,
NC. 2002. 352p. ISBN:0-8223-2935-2, ISBN13:
978-0-8223-2935-0. Dewey:791.43/6. LCCN:2002-002700.

Audience: **u,f.** *Choice, 2003.*

Lee, Spike & Aftab,   **PN1998.3.L44A3 2005**
Kaleem
Spike Lee: That's My Story and I'm Sticking to It. Trade Cloth.
W. W. Norton & Company, Inc. New York, NY. 2005. 320p.
ISBN:0-393-06153-1, ISBN13: 978-0-393-06153-6.
Dewey:791.43/0233/092 B. LCCN:2005-014211.

Audience: **g,l,u,f.**

Lommel, Cookie   **PN1995.9.N4L66 2001**
Black Filmmakers. Trade Paper. Facts On File, Inc. New York,
NY. 2002. 144p. African American Achievers Ser.
ISBN:0-7910-5817-4, ISBN13: 978-0-7910-5817-6.
Dewey:791.43/089/96073. LCCN:00-052333.

Audience: **g,l,u.**

Lupack, Barbara Tepa   **PN1995.9.N4L87 2002**
Literary Adaptations in Black American Cinema: From
Micheaux to Morrison. Trade Cloth. University of Rochester
Press. Rochester, NY. 2002. 584p. ISBN:1-58046-103-4,

ISBN13: 978-1-58046-103-0. Dewey:791.43/6520396073.
LCCN:2002-022332.

Audience: **u,f.** *Choice, 2003.*

Marchetti, Gina   **PN1995.9.A78M37 1993**
Romance and the "Yellow Peril": Race, Sex, and Discursive
Strategies in Hollywood Fiction. Trade Paper. University of
California Press. Berkeley, CA. 1994. 270p.
ISBN:0-520-08495-0, ISBN13: 978-0-520-08495-7.
Dewey:791.436520395. LCCN:92-010878.

Audience: **l,u,f.** *Choice, 1994.*

Massood, Paula J.   **PN1995.9.N4M33 2003**
Black City Cinema: African American Urban Experiences in
Film. Library Binding. Temple University Press. Philadelphia,
PA. 2002. 296p. Culture and the Moving Image Ser.
ISBN:1-59213-002-X, ISBN13: 978-1-59213-002-3.
Dewey:791.43/6520396073. LCCN:2002-020421.

Audience: **u,f.** *Choice, 2003.*

Reid, Mark A.   **PN1995.9.N4R43 2005**
Black Lenses, Black Voices: African American Film Now. Book,
Other. Rowman & Littlefield Publishers, Inc. Lanham, MD.
2005. 136p. Genre and Beyond Ser. ISBN:0-7425-2641-0,
ISBN13: 978-0-7425-2641-9. Dewey:791.43750899.
LCCN:2004-026201.

Audience: **g,l,u,f.** *Choice, 2005.*

Rhines, Jesse A.   **PN1995.9.N4R52 1996**
Black Film, White Money. Trade Paper. Rutgers University
Press. Piscataway, NJ. 2003. 200p. ISBN:0-8135-2267-6,
ISBN13: 978-0-8135-2267-8. Dewey:384/.8/08996073.
LCCN:95-033932.

Audience: **u,f.** *Choice, 1996.*

Richard, Alfred C. Jr.   **PN1998**
The Hispanic Image on the Silver Screen: An Interpretive
Filmography from Silents into Sound, 1898-1935. Cloth Text.
Greenwood Publishing Group, Inc. Portsmouth, NH. 1992. 624p.
Bibliographies and Indexes in the Performing Arts Ser., No. 12
ISBN:0-313-27832-6, ISBN13: 978-0-313-27832-7.
Dewey:016.791436520368. LCCN:92-008917.

Audience: **g,l,u,f.** *Choice, 1992.*

Richards, Larry   **PN1995.9N4**
African American Films Through 1959: A Comprehensive,
Illustrated Filmography. Paper Text. McFarland & Company,
Incorporated Publishers. Jefferson, NC. 2005. 320p.
ISBN:0-7864-2274-2, ISBN13: 978-0-7864-2274-6.
Dewey:791.43'6520396073. LCCN:97-023730.

Audience: **g,l,u,f.** *Choice, 1998.*

Sampson, Henry T.   **PN1995.9.N4.S2 1995**
Blacks in Black and White: A Source Book on Black Films. Ed.
2. Trade Cloth. Scarecrow Press, Inc. Lanham, MD. 1995. 749p.
ISBN:0-8108-2605-4, ISBN13: 978-0-8108-2605-2.
Dewey:791.4308996073. LCCN:93-001965.

Audience: **g,l,u,f.** *Choice, 1995.*

Shaheen, Jack   **PN1995.9.A68S54 2001**
Reel Bad Arabs: How Hollywood Vilifies a People. Trade Cloth.
Interlink Publishing Group, Inc. Northampton, MA. 2004. 592p.
ISBN:1-56656-388-7, ISBN13: 978-1-56656-388-8.
Dewey:791.43/65203927. LCCN:2001-003040.

Audience: **g,l,u.** *Choice, 2002.*

Smith, Valerie (Editor)   **PN1995.9.N4R47 1997**
Representing Blackness: Issues in Film and Video. Trade Cloth.
Rutgers University Press. Piscataway, NJ. 2003. 250p. Depth of

Field Ser. ISBN:0-8135-2313-3, ISBN13: 978-0-8135-2313-2. Dewey:791.4/36/52/03/96073. LCCN:96-036075.
Audience: **u,f.** *Choice, 1997.*

Stewart, Jacqueline   **PN1995.9.N4S74 2005**
(Author, Illustrator)
Migrating to the Movies: Cinema and Black Urban Modernity. Trade Cloth. University of California Press. Berkeley, CA. 2005. 360p. ISBN:0-520-23350-6, ISBN13: 978-0-520-23350-8. Dewey:791.43/652996073. LCCN:2004-016541.
Audience: **g,l,u.** *Choice, 2005.*

Watkins, S. Craig   **PN1995.9.N4W38 1998**
Representing: Hip Hop Culture and the Production of Black Cinema. Trade Cloth. University of Chicago Press. Chicago, IL. 1998. 330p. ISBN:0-226-87488-5, ISBN13: 978-0-226-87488-3. Dewey:791.43/652396073. LCCN:97-043151.
Audience: **u,f.** *Choice, 1999.*

History

Chapman, James   **PN1995.9.S6**
Cinemas of the World: Film and Society from 1895 to the Present. Trade Cloth. Reaktion Books, Ltd. London, 2004. 256p. Globalities Ser. ISBN:1-86189-162-8, ISBN13: 978-1-86189-162-4. Dewey:302.2/343.
Audience: **g,l,u.** *Choice, 2003.*

Cook, David A.   **PN1993.5**
A History of Narrative Film. Ed. 4. Trade Paper. W. W. Norton & Company, Inc. New York, NY. 2003. 1000p. ISBN:0-393-97868-0, ISBN13: 978-0-393-97868-1. Dewey:791.43/09. LCCN:2003-061090.
Audience: **g,l,u.**

Fleishman, Avrom   **PN1995**
Narrated Films: Storytelling Situations in Cinema History. Trade Paper. Johns Hopkins University Press. Baltimore, MD. 2004. 264p. ISBN:0-8018-7865-9, ISBN13: 978-0-8018-7865-7. Dewey:791.43/015. LCCN:91-012350.
Audience: **u,f.** *Choice, 1992.*

Gledhill, Christine   **PN1995.S677 1990**
(Editor)
Stardom: Industry of Desire. Paper over Boards. Routledge. New York, NY. 1991. 344p. ISBN:0-415-05217-3, ISBN13: 978-0-415-05217-7. Dewey:791.43/028/0922. LCCN:90-033813.
Audience: **g,l,u,f.** *Choice, 1992.*

Hjort, Mette &   **PN1995.9.N33C56 2000**
MacKenzie, Scott (Editors)
Cinema and Nation. Paper over Boards. Routledge. New York, NY. 2000. 352p. ISBN:0-415-20862-9, ISBN13: 978-0-415-20862-8. Dewey:791.43/658. LCCN:00-036636.
Audience: **l,u,f.** *Choice, 2001.*

Landy, Marcia   **PN1995.9.H5L36 1996**
Cinematic Uses of the Past. Book, Other. University of Minnesota Press. Minneapolis, MN. 1996. 264p. ISBN:0-8166-2824-6, ISBN13: 978-0-8166-2824-7. Dewey:791.4/36/58. LCCN:96-022176.
Audience: **u,f.** *Choice, 1997.*

Mast, Gerald & Kawin,   **PN1993.5.A1**
Bruce F.
A Short History of the Movies. Ed. 8. Trade Paper. Longman Publishing Group. White Plains, NY. 2002. 752p.

ISBN:0-321-10603-2, ISBN13: 978-0-321-10603-2. Dewey:791.43/09.
Audience: **g,l.** *B*

McGreevey, Tom &   **TR886.3.M37 1997**
Yeck, Joanne L.
Our Movie Heritage. Leonard Maltin (Foreword by). Trade Cloth. Rutgers University Press. Piscataway, NJ. 1997. 208p. ISBN:0-8135-2431-8, ISBN13: 978-0-8135-2431-3. Dewey:778.5. LCCN:97-003737.
Audience: **g,l,u,f.** *Choice, 1998.*

Michaels, Lloyd   **PN1995.9.C36M53 1998**
The Phantom of the Cinema: Character in Modern Film. Cloth Text. State University of New York Press. Albany, NY. 1997. 191p. SUNY Series in Cultural Studies in Cinema/Video ISBN:0-7914-3567-9, ISBN13: 978-0-7914-3567-0. Dewey:791.43/6. LCCN:97-011383.
Audience: **u,f.** *Choice, 1998.*

Nollen, Scott A.   **PN1995.9.R65N66 1999**
Robin Hood: A Cinematic History of the English Outlaw and His Scottish Counterparts. Cloth Text. McFarland & Company, Incorporated Publishers. Jefferson, NC. 1999. 269p. ISBN:0-7864-0643-7, ISBN13: 978-0-7864-0643-2. Dewey:791.43/651. LCCN:99-26060.
Audience: **l,u.**

Picart, Caroline Joan S.   **PN1995.9.F8P54 2003**
Remaking the Frankenstein Myth on Film: Between Laughter and Horror. Cloth Text. State University of New York Press. Albany, NY. 2003. viii, 288p. SUNY Series in Psychoanalysis and Culture ISBN:0-7914-5769-9, ISBN13: 978-0-7914-5769-6. Dewey:791.43/651. LCCN:2002-045262.
Audience: **u,f.** *Choice, 2003.*

Rosenstone, Robert A.   **PN1995.2.R48 1995**
(Editor)
Revisioning History: Film and the Construction of a New Past. Trade Paper. Princeton University Press. Princeton, NJ. 1994. 264p. Princeton Studies in Culture/Power/History ISBN:0-691-02534-7, ISBN13: 978-0-691-02534-6. Dewey:791.43/658. LCCN:94-019563.
Audience: **u,f.** *Choice, 1995.*

Rossell, Deac   **TR848.R68 1998**
Living Pictures: The Origins of the Movies. Cloth Text. State University of New York Press. Albany, NY. 1998. 192p. SUNY Series in Cultural Studies in Cinema/Video ISBN:0-7914-3767-1, ISBN13: 978-0-7914-3767-4. Dewey:778.5/3/09. LCCN:94-027561.
Audience: **l,u,f.** *Choice, 1999.*

Stringer, Julian (Editor)   **PN1993.5**
Movie Blockbusters. Paper over Boards. Routledge. New York, NY. 2003. 288p. ISBN:0-415-25608-9, ISBN13: 978-0-415-25608-7. Dewey:791.43/75. LCCN:2005-363582.
Audience: **g,l,u.** *Choice, 2004.*

Wasson, Haidee   **PN1993.4 .W27 2005**
Museum Movies: The Museum of Modern Art and the Birth of Art Cinema. Trade Paper, Perfect. University of California Press. Berkeley, CA. 2005. 336p. ISBN:0-520-24131-2, ISBN13: 978-0-520-24131-2. Dewey:026/.79143/097471. LCCN:2004-024026.
Audience: **l,u,f.** *Choice, 2005.*

History > By Period

Abel, Richard (Editor)　　　　　**PN1995.7**
Encyclopedia of Early Cinema. Paper over Boards. Routledge.
New York, NY. 2005. 704p. ISBN:0-415-23440-9, ISBN13:
978-0-415-23440-5. Dewey:791.43/09/03. LCCN:2004-051460.
　　　　　　　　　　Audience: **g,l,u,f.**　*Choice, 2005.*

Bachman, Gregg　　　　　**PN1995.75.S59 2002**
　(Editor)
American Silent Film: Discovering Marginalized Voices. Trade
Cloth. Southern Illinois University Press. Carbondale, IL. 2002.
400p. ISBN:0-8093-2401-6, ISBN13: 978-0-8093-2401-9.
Dewey:791.43/0973. LCCN:2001-049352.
　　　　　　　　　Audience: **u,f.**　*Choice, 2003, 2002.*

Bean, Jennifer M. &　　　　　**PN1995.9.W6F467 2002**
　Negra, Diane (Editors)
A Feminist Reader in Early Cinema. Trade Cloth. Duke
University Press. Durham, NC. 2003. 592p. Camera Obscura
Ser. ISBN:0-8223-3025-3, ISBN13: 978-0-8223-3025-7.
Dewey:791.43/652042. LCCN:2002-007087.
　　　　　　　　　　　　Audience: **u,f.**　*Choice, 2003.*

Flom, Eric L.　　　　　**PN2287.C5F58 1997**
Chaplin in the Sound Era: An Analysis of the Seven Talkies.
Cloth Text. McFarland & Company, Incorporated Publishers.
Jefferson, NC. 1997. 336p. ISBN:0-7864-0325-X, ISBN13:
978-0-7864-0325-7. Dewey:791.43/028/092 B. LCCN:96-29890.
　　　　　　　　　　　　　　Audience: **l,u,f.**

Hanson, Peter　　　　　**PN1993.5.U6H34 2002**
The Cinema of Generation X: A Critical Study of Films and
Directors. Paper Text. McFarland & Company, Incorporated
Publishers. Jefferson, NC. 2002. 227p. ISBN:0-7864-1334-4,
ISBN13: 978-0-7864-1334-8. Dewey:791.43/75/097309049.
LCCN:2001-008469.
　　　　　　　　　　　Audience: **g,l,u.**　*Choice, 2002.*

Hunt, Marsha　　　　　**PN2287.H79 A3 1993**
The Way We Wore: Styles of the 1930s and '40s. Trade Cloth.
Fallbrook Publishing, Ltd. Fallbrook, CA. 1994. 460p.
ISBN:1-882747-00-3, ISBN13: 978-1-882747-00-9.
Dewey:391/.2/097309043. LCCN:92-083890.
　　　　　　　　　　　　　　Audience: **u,f.**

Klepper, Robert K.　　　　　**PN1995**
Silent Films, 1877-1996: A Critical Guide to 646 Movies. Paper
Text. McFarland & Company, Incorporated Publishers. Jefferson,
NC. 2005. 596p. ISBN:0-7864-2164-9, ISBN13:
978-0-7864-2164-0. Dewey:791.43/75.
　　　　　　　　　　　Audience: **g,l,u.**　*Choice, 1999.*

LaSalle, Mick　　　　　**PN1995.9.W6**
Complicated Women: Sex and Power in Pre-Code Hollywood.
Trade Paper. St. Martin's Press. Gordonville, VA. 2001. 304p.
ISBN:0-312-28431-4, ISBN13: 978-0-312-28431-2.
Dewey:791.43/652042.
　　　　　　　　　　　　Audience: **u,f.**　*Choice, 2001.*

Lisanti, Tom　　　　　**PN1995**
Fantasy Femmes of Sixties Cinema: Interviews with 20
Actresses from Biker, Beach, and Elvis Movies. Cloth Text.
McFarland & Company, Incorporated Publishers. Jefferson, NC.
2000. 320p. ISBN:0-7864-0868-5, ISBN13: 978-0-7864-0868-9.
Dewey:791.4/3/028/082. LCCN:00-64008.
　　　　　　　　　　　　　　Audience: **g,l,u.**

Lowe, Denise　　　　　**PN1998.2.L686 2004**
An Encyclopedic Dictionary of Women in Early American
Films: 1895-1930. Trade Cloth. Haworth Press, Incorporated,
The. Binghamton, NY. 2004. 623p. ISBN:0-7890-1842-X,
ISBN13: 978-0-7890-1842-7. Dewey:791.43/092/27309041.
LCCN:2003-025274.
　　　　　　　　　　　　Audience: **g,l,u.**　*Choice, 2005.*

McCaffrey, Donald W.　　　　　**PN1995**
　& Jacobs, Christopher P.
Guide to the Silent Years of American Cinema. Cloth Text.
Greenwood Publishing Group, Inc. Portsmouth, NH. 1999. 384p.
Reference Guides to the World's Cinema ISBN:0-313-30345-2,
ISBN13: 978-0-313-30345-6. Dewey:791.43/09.
LCCN:99-010111.
　　　　　　　　　　　Audience: **g,l,u,f.**　*Choice, 2000.*

Michael, Eugene　　　　　**PN1998.2.V38 2001**
Silent Film Necrology. Ed. 2. Cloth Text. McFarland &
Company, Incorporated Publishers. Jefferson, NC. 2001. 591p.
ISBN:0-7864-1059-0, ISBN13: 978-0-7864-1059-0.
Dewey:016.79143/028/092273. LCCN:2001-031608.
　　　　　　　　　　　　Audience: **u,f.**　*Choice, 2002.*

Miller, Blair　　　　　**PN1995.9.C55M53 1995**
American Silent Film Comedies: An Illustrated Encyclopedia of
Persons, Studios and Terminology. Cloth Text. McFarland &
Company, Incorporated Publishers. Jefferson, NC. 1995. 292p.
ISBN:0-89950-929-0, ISBN13: 978-0-89950-929-7.
Dewey:791.43/617/0973. LCCN:94-38777.
　　　　　　　　　　　Audience: **g,l,u,f.**　*Choice, 1996.*

Musser, Charles　　　　　**PN1993.5.U6.H55**
The Emergence of the Cinema: The American Screen to 1907,
Vol. 1. Charles H. Harpole (Editor). Trade Cloth. Thomson
Gale. Farmington Hills, MI. 1905. 613p. History of the
American Cinema Ser., Vol. 1 ISBN:0-684-18413-3, ISBN13:
978-0-684-18413-5. Dewey:791.430973. LCCN:90-048307.
　　　　　　　　　　　Audience: **g,l,u,f.**　*Choice, 1991.*

Natoli, Joseph　　　　　**PN1995.9.S6N375 2003**
Memory's Orbit: Film and Culture 1999-2000. Cloth Text. State
University of New York Press. Albany, NY. 2003. viii, 234p.
SUNY Series in Postmodern Culture ISBN:0-7914-5719-2,
ISBN13: 978-0-7914-5719-1. Dewey:302.23/43/0973.
LCCN:2002-029180.
　　　　　　　　　　　　Audience: **u,f.**　*Choice, 2003.*

Natoli, Joseph P.　　　　　**PN1995.N36 2001**
Postmodern Journeys: Film and Culture 1996-1998. Cloth Text.
State University of New York Press. Albany, NY. 2000. xiv,
287p. SUNY Series in Postmodern Culture
ISBN:0-7914-4771-5, ISBN13: 978-0-7914-4771-0.
Dewey:791.43/01. LCCN:00-020339.
　　　　　　　　　　　　Audience: **u,f.**　*Choice, 2001.*

Nowlan, Robert A. &　　　　　**PN1998.N784 2001**
　Nowlan, Gwendolyn L.
The Films of the Nineties: A Complete, Qualitative Filmography
to over 3000 Feature-Length English Language Films, Theatrical
and Video-Only, Released Between January 1, 1990, and
December 31, 1999. Cloth Text. McFarland & Company,
Incorporated Publishers. Jefferson, NC. 2001. 736p.
ISBN:0-7864-0974-6, ISBN13: 978-0-7864-0974-7.
Dewey:016.79143/75/09049. LCCN:2001-020241.
　　　　　　　　　　　Audience: **g,l,u,f.**　*Choice, 2001.*

Nowlan, Robert A. &   PN1998.N78 1991
  Nowlan, Gwendolyn W.
The Films of the Eighties: A Complete, Qualitative Filmography
to over 3400 Feature-Length English Language Films, Theatrical
and Video-Only, Released Between Janaury 1, 1980, and
December 31, 1989. Cloth Text. McFarland & Company,
Incorporated Publishers. Jefferson, NC. 1991. 868p.
ISBN:0-89950-560-0, ISBN13: 978-0-89950-560-2.
Dewey:016.79143/75. LCCN:90-53516.
                              Audience: **g,l,u,f.**

Shull, Michael S.   PN1995.75.S54 2000
Radicalism in American Silent Films, 1909-1929: A
Filmography and History. Cloth Text. McFarland & Company,
Incorporated Publishers. Jefferson, NC. 2000. 355p.
ISBN:0-7864-0692-5, ISBN13: 978-0-7864-0692-0.
Dewey:791.43/658. LCCN:99-43011.
                      Audience: **g,l,u,f.** *Choice, 2000.*

Sigoloff, Marc   PN1993.45
The Films of the Seventies: A Filmography of American, British
and Canadian Films 1970-1979. Paper Text. McFarland &
Company, Incorporated Publishers. Jefferson, NC. 2000. 432p.
ISBN:0-7864-0882-0, ISBN13: 978-0-7864-0882-5.
Dewey:791.4/3/09047. LCCN:83-42887.
                              Audience: **g,l,u,f.**

Singer, Ben   PN1995.9.M45S56 2001
ⓔ Melodrama and Modernity: Early Sensational Cinema and Its
Contexts. E-Book. Columbia University Press. New York, NY.
ISBN:0-231-50507-8, ISBN13: 978-0-231-50507-9.
Dewey:791.43/653.
                      Audience: **u,f.** *Choice, 2001.*

Vincent, Terrace   PN1992.8.P54T46 1997
Experimental Television, Test Films, Pilots and Trial Series,
1925 Through 1995: Seven Decades of Small Screen Almosts.
Cloth Text. McFarland & Company, Incorporated Publishers.
Jefferson, NC. 1997. 798p. ISBN:0-7864-0178-8, ISBN13:
978-0-7864-0178-9. Dewey:791.4/53/03. LCCN:96-17135.
                      Audience: **g,l,u.** *Choice, 1997.*

History > By Region and Country > Africa and the Middle East

Armes, Roy   PN1993.5.A35A76 2004
Postcolonial Images: Studies in North African Film. Trade
Cloth. Indiana University Press. Bloomington, IN. 2004. 272p.
ISBN:0-253-34444-1, ISBN13: 978-0-253-34444-1.
Dewey:791.43/0961. LCCN:2004-007896.
                      Audience: **u,f.** *Choice, 2005.*

Barlet, Olivier   PN1993.5.A35B3713
African Cinemas: Decolonizing the Gaze. Chris Turner
(Translator). Cloth over Boards. Zed Books, Ltd. London, 2001.
320p. ISBN:1-85649-742-9, ISBN13: 978-1-85649-742-8.
Dewey:791.43/096. LCCN:00-032001.
                      Audience: **u,f.** *Choice, 2001.*

Dabashi, Hamid   PN1993.5.I846D32
Close Up: Iranian Cinema, Past, Present and Future. Trade
Cloth. Verso Books. London, 2001. 300p. ISBN:1-85984-626-2,
ISBN13: 978-1-85984-626-1. Dewey:791.43/09555.
LCCN:2001-277765.
                      Audience: **l,u,f.** *Choice, 2002.*

Diawara, Manthia   PN1993.5.A35D5 1992
African Cinema: Politics and Culture. Cloth Text. Indiana
University Press. Bloomington, IN. 1992. 208p. Blacks in the
Diaspora Ser. ISBN:0-253-31704-5, ISBN13:
978-0-253-31704-9. Dewey:791.43/096. LCCN:91-024579.
                      Audience: **u,f.** *Choice, 1992.*

Egan, Eric   PN1993.5.I846
Films of Makhmalbaf: Cinema, Politics and Culture in Iran.
Trade Cloth. Mage Publishers, Inc. Washington, DC. 2005.
232p. ISBN:0-934211-94-9, ISBN13: 978-0-934211-94-9.
Dewey:791.4302/33/092. LCCN:2004-028534.
                              Audience: **u,f.**

Foster, Gwendolyn   PN1998.2.F672 1997
  Audrey
Women Filmmakers of the African and Asian Diaspora:
Decolonizing the Gaze, Locating Subjectivity. Trade Paper.
Southern Illinois University Press. Carbondale, IL. 1997. 160p.
ISBN:0-8093-2120-3, ISBN13: 978-0-8093-2120-9.
Dewey:791.43/0233/092273. LCCN:96-027635.
                      Audience: **u,f.** *Choice, 1998.*

Foster, Gwendolyn   PN1998.2.F672 1997
  Audrey
Women Filmmakers of the African and Asian Diaspora:
Decolonizing the Gaze, Locating Subjectivity. Trade Cloth.
Southern Illinois University Press. Carbondale, IL. 1997. 208p.
ISBN:0-8093-2119-X, ISBN13: 978-0-8093-2119-3.
Dewey:791.43/0233/092273. LCCN:96-027635.
                      Audience: **u.** *Choice, 1998.*

George, Terry (Editor,   PN1997.2.H66H68 2005
  Compiled by)
Hotel Rwanda: Bringing the True Story of an African Hero to
Film. Paul Rusesabagina & Don Cheadle (Afterword by). Trade
Cloth. Newmarket Press. New York, NY. 2005. 160p. Insider
Filmbooks Ser. ISBN:1-55704-671-9, ISBN13:
978-1-55704-671-0. Dewey:791.43/72. LCCN:2005-541281.
                              Audience: **g,l,u.**

Gugler, Josef   PN1993.5.A35G77 2003
African Film: Re-Imagining a Continent. Trade Cloth. Indiana
University Press. Bloomington, IN. 2003. 200p.
ISBN:0-253-34350-X, ISBN13: 978-0-253-34350-5.
Dewey:791.43/626. LCCN:2003-014797.
                      Audience: **u,f.** *Choice, 2004.*

Kronish, Amy &   PN1993
  Safirman, Costel
Israeli Film: A Reference Guide. Trade Cloth. Greenwood
Publishing Group, Inc. Portsmouth, NH. 2003. 280p. Reference
Guides to the World's Cinema Ser. ISBN:0-313-32144-2,
ISBN13: 978-0-313-32144-3. Dewey:791.43/095694.
LCCN:2002-028310.
                      Audience: **g,l,u,f.** *Choice, 2003.*

Leaman, Oliver (Editor)   PN1993.5.A65C66 2001
Companion Encyclopedia of Middle Eastern and North African
Film. Paper over Boards. Routledge. New York, NY. 2001.
624p. ISBN:0-415-18703-6, ISBN13: 978-0-415-18703-9.
Dewey:791.43/75/0956. LCCN:00-068390.
                      Audience: **g,l,u,f.** *Choice, 2002.*

Loshitzky, Yosefa   PN1993.5.I86L37 2001
Identity Politics on the Israeli Screen. Trade Cloth. University of
Texas Press. Austin, TX. 2002. 264p. ISBN:0-292-74723-3,

ISBN13: 978-0-292-74723-4. Dewey:791.43/095694.
LCCN:2001-017137.

Audience: **u,f.** *Choice, 2002.*

Pfaff, Francoise (Editor)   **PN1993.5.A35F63 2004**
Focus on African Films. Trade Paper. Indiana University Press.
Bloomington, IN. 2004. 312p. ISBN:0-253-21668-0, ISBN13:
978-0-253-21668-7. Dewey:791.43/096. LCCN:2003-021199.

Audience: **u,f.** *Choice, 2005.*

Pfaff, Francoise   **PN1998**
Twenty-Five Black African Filmmakers: A Critical Study, with
Filmography and Bio-Bibliography. Cloth Text. Greenwood
Publishing Group, Inc. Portsmouth, NH. 1988. 344p.
ISBN:0-313-24695-5, ISBN13: 978-0-313-24695-1.
Dewey:791.43/023/0922 B. LCCN:87-015024.

Audience: **l,u.** *Choice, 1988.*

Russell, Sharon A.   **PN1993**
A Guide to African Cinema. Cloth Text. Greenwood Publishing
Group, Inc. Portsmouth, NH. 1998. 208p. Reference Guides to
the World's Cinema ISBN:0-313-29621-9, ISBN13:
978-0-313-29621-5. Dewey:791.43/096. LCCN:97-027560.

Audience: **g,l.** *Choice, 1998.*

Schmidt, Nancy J.   **Z5784.M9S32 1994**
Sub-Saharan African Films and Filmmakers: An Annotated
Bibliography, 1987-1992. Trade Cloth. Hans Zell Publishers.
East Grinstead, 1994. 418p. ISBN:1-873836-21-X, ISBN13:
978-1-873836-21-7. Dewey:016.79143/75/0967.
LCCN:94-010101.

Audience: **g,l,u,f.** *Choice, 1995.*

Shiri, Keith (Editor)   **PN1993**
Directory of African Film-Makers and Films. Cloth Text.
Greenwood Publishing Group, Inc. Portsmouth, NH. 1992. 400p.
ISBN:0-313-28756-2, ISBN13: 978-0-313-28756-5.
Dewey:791.430233096. LCCN:92-022105.

Audience: **g,l,u,f.** *Choice, 1993.*

Shohat, Ella   **PN1993.5.I86S56 1989**
Israeli Cinema: East-West and the Politics of Representation.
Cloth Text. University of Texas Press. Austin, TX. 1989. 320p.
ISBN:0-292-73847-1, ISBN13: 978-0-292-73847-8.
Dewey:791.43/095694. LCCN:88-027758.

Audience: **u,f.** *Choice, 1990.*

Tapper, Richard   **PN1993.5.I846N49**
(Editor)
The New Iranian Cinema: Politics, Representation and Identity.
Cloth over Boards, Trade Cloth. I. B. Tauris & Company, Ltd.
London, 2002. 256p. ISBN:1-86064-803-7, ISBN13:
978-1-86064-803-8. Dewey:791.430955. LCCN:2002-726688.

Audience: **u,f.** *Choice, 2003.*

Ukadike, N. Frank   **PN1993.5.A35U4 1994**
Black African Cinema. Trade Paper. University of California
Press. Berkeley, CA. 1994. 382p. ISBN:0-520-07748-2, ISBN13:
978-0-520-07748-5. Dewey:791.430967. LCCN:92-029076.

Audience: **u,f.** *Choice, 1995.*

History > By Region and Country > Asia

Bowyer, Justin (Editor)   **PN1993.5.K6**
Cinema of Japan and Korea. Jinhee Choi (Foreword by). Trade
Cloth. Wallflower Press. London, 2004. 258p.

ISBN:1-904764-12-6, ISBN13: 978-1-904764-12-0.
Dewey:791.4/3/09519.

Audience: **g,l,u.**

Dissanayake, Wimal   **PN1993.5.A75C56 1988**
(Editor)
Cinema and Cultural Identity: Reflections on Films from Japan,
India and China. Trade Cloth. University Press of America, Inc.
Lanham, MD. 1988. 222p. ISBN:0-8191-6945-5, ISBN13:
978-0-8191-6945-7. Dewey:791.43/095. LCCN:88-005467.

Audience: **g,l,u,f.**

Ehrlich, Linda C. &   **N72.M6C55 1994**
Desser, David (Editors)
Cinematic Landscapes: Observations on the Visual Arts and
Cinema of China and Japan. Cloth Text. University of Texas
Press. Austin, TX. 1994. 384p. ISBN:0-292-72086-6, ISBN13:
978-0-292-72086-2. Dewey:791.43/01. LCCN:93-043041.

Audience: **u,f.**

Kim, Kyung Hyun   **PN1993.5.K6K524 2004**
The Remasculinization of Korean Cinema. Trade Cloth, Pictures
or Photographs. Duke University Press. Durham, NC. 2004.
368p. Asia-Pacific Ser. ISBN:0-8223-3278-7, ISBN13:
978-0-8223-3278-7. Dewey:791.43/6521/09519.
LCCN:2003-016644.

Audience: **u,f.** *Choice, 2004.*

Lau, Jenny Kwok Wah   **PN1993.5.E9M75 2002**
(Editor)
Multiple Modernities: Cinemas and Popular Media in
Transcultural East Asia. Library Binding. Temple University
Press. Philadelphia, PA. 2002. 304p. ISBN:1-56639-985-8,
ISBN13: 978-1-56639-985-2. Dewey:791.43/095.
LCCN:2002-020339.

Audience: **u,f.**

Nagappan, Ramu   **PK5410.S63N34 2005**
Speaking Havoc: Social Suffering and South Asian Narratives.
Trade Cloth. University of Washington Press. Seattle, WA. 2005.
256p. Literary Conjugations Ser. ISBN:0-295-98488-0, ISBN13:
978-0-295-98488-9. Dewey:809/.933556. LCCN:2004-029560.

Audience: **u,f.** *Choice, 2006.*

Vasudev, Aruna, et al.   **PN1993.5.A75B45 2002**
Being and Becoming, the Cinemas of Asia. Latika Padgaonkar
& Rashmi Doraiswamy (Authors). Trade Cloth. Macmillan
Publishing Company, Inc. Old Tappan, NJ. 2002. xii, 580p.
ISBN:0-333-93820-8, ISBN13: 978-0-333-93820-1.
Dewey:791.43095. LCCN:2002-294529.

Audience: **u,f.**

History > By Region and Country > Asia > China

Berry, Chris   **PN1993.5.C4B47 2004**
Postsocialist Cinema in Post-Mao China: The Cultural
Revolution after the Cultural Revolution. Paper over Boards.
Routledge. New York, NY. 2004. 272p. East Asia History,
Politics, Sociology and Culture Ser. ISBN:0-415-94786-3,
ISBN13: 978-0-415-94786-2. Dewey:791.43/0951.
LCCN:2003-026390.

Audience: **u,f.**

Shen, Vivian   **PN1993.5.C4S52 2004**
Origins of Leftwing Cinema in China, 1932-37. Paper over
Boards. Routledge. New York, NY. 2005. 228p. East Asia

History, Politics, Sociology and Culture Ser.
ISBN:0-415-97183-7, ISBN13: 978-0-415-97183-6.
Dewey:791.43/0951/09043. LCCN:2004-018132.

Audience: **u,f.**

Tam, Kwok-kan &   **PN1993.5.C4**
  Dissanayake, Wimal
New Chinese Cinema. Trade Cloth. Oxford University Press,
Inc. New York, NY. 1998. 104p. Images of Asia Ser.
ISBN:0-19-590607-1, ISBN13: 978-0-19-590607-3.
Dewey:791.4/3/0951. LCCN:97-051578.

Audience: **l,u.**

Wang, Jing & Barlow,   **PN1993.5.C4**
  Tani E. (Editors)
Cinema and Desire: Feminist Marxism and Cultural Politics in
the Works of Dai Jinhua. Trade Paper. Verso Books. London,
2005. 280p. ISBN:1-85984-264-X, ISBN13: 978-1-85984-264-5.
Dewey:306/.0951.

Audience: **u,f.** *Choice, 2003.*

Zhen, Ni   **PN1993.5.C4N52 2002**
Memoirs from the Beijing Film Academy: The Genesis of
China's Fifth Generation. Chris Berry (Translator). Trade Cloth.
Duke University Press. Durham, NC. 2002. 240p. Asia-Pacific
Ser. ISBN:0-8223-2956-5, ISBN13: 978-0-8223-2956-5.
Dewey:791.43/0233/092251 B. LCCN:2002-005107.

Audience: **g,u,f.** *Choice, 2003.*

History > By Region and Country > Asia > Hong Kong

Kar, Law & Bren,   **PN1993.5.C4K37 2004**
  Frank
Hong Kong Cinema: A Cross-Cultural View. Trade Cloth.
Scarecrow Press, Inc. Lanham, MD. 2004. 400p.
ISBN:0-8108-4986-0, ISBN13: 978-0-8108-4986-0.
Dewey:791.43/095125. LCCN:2003-024604.

Audience: **l,u,f.** *Choice, 2005.*

History > By Region and Country > Asia > Japan

Anderson, Joseph L. &   **PN1993.5.J3**
  Richie, Donald
The Japanese Film: Art and Industry. Akira Kurosawa
(Foreword by). Trade Cloth. Princeton University Press.
Princeton, NJ. 1983. 500p. ISBN:0-691-05351-0, ISBN13:
978-0-691-05351-6. Dewey:791.43/0952. LCCN:81-047985.

Audience: **u,f.**

Barrett, Gregory   **PN1993.5.J3B37 1989**
Archetypes in Japanese Film: The Sociopolitical and Religious
Significance of the Principal Heroes and Heroines. Trade Cloth.
Susquehanna University Press. Cranbury, NJ. 1989. 256p.
ISBN:0-941664-93-7, ISBN13: 978-0-941664-93-6.
Dewey:302.2/343/0952. LCCN:87-043126.

Audience: **u,f.** *Choice, 1989.*

Bock, Audie   **PN1998.2.B6 1985**
Japanese Film Directors. Trade Paper. Kodansha America, Inc.
New York, NY. 1985. 378p. ISBN:0-87011-714-9, ISBN13:
978-0-87011-714-5. Dewey:791.43/0233/092252.
LCCN:84-082294.

Audience: **g,l,u,f.**

Broderick, Mick   **PN1993.5.J3H53 1996**
  (Editor)
Hibakusha Cinema: Hiroshima, Nagasaki, and the Nuclear
Image in Japanese Film. Trade Cloth. Kegan Paul International,
Ltd. London, 1996. 256p. Japanese Studies
ISBN:0-7103-0529-X, ISBN13: 978-0-7103-0529-9.
Dewey:791.4/3/658/0952. LCCN:95-041180.

Audience: **u,f.** *Choice, 1997.*

Buehrer, Beverly B.   **PN1993.5.J3B78 1990**
Japanese Films: A Filmography and Commentary, 1921-1989.
Library Binding. McFarland & Company, Incorporated
Publishers. Jefferson, NC. 1990. 344p. ISBN:0-89950-458-2,
ISBN13: 978-0-89950-458-2. Dewey:791.43/75/0952.
LCCN:89-043684.

Audience: **g,l,u,f.** *Choice, 1991.*

Burch, Noel   **PN1993.5.J3 B8**
To the Distant Observer: Form and Meaning in Japanese
Cinema. Trade Cloth. University of California Press. Berkeley,
CA. 1979. ISBN:0-520-03605-0, ISBN13: 978-0-520-03605-5.
Dewey:791.43/0952. LCCN:79-111821.

Audience: **u,f.**

Cazdyn, Eric   **PN1993.5.J3C39 2002**
The Flash of Capital: Film and Geopolitics in Japan. Trade
Cloth. Duke University Press. Durham, NC. 2002. 328p.
Asia-Pacific Ser. ISBN:0-8223-2912-3, ISBN13:
978-0-8223-2912-1. Dewey:791.43/0952. LCCN:2002-005423.

Audience: **u,f.** *Choice, 2003.*

Davis, Darrell William   **PN1993.5.J3D38 1996**
Picturing Japaneseness: Monumental Style, National Identity,
Japanese Film. Trade Cloth. Columbia University Press. New
York, NY. 1996. 352p. Film and Culture Ser.
ISBN:0-231-10230-5, ISBN13: 978-0-231-10230-8.
Dewey:791.43095209043. LCCN:95-022747.

Audience: **u.** *Choice, 1996.*

Desjardins, Chris   **PN1993.5.J3**
Outlaw Masters of Japanese Film. Trade Cloth, Cloth over
Boards. I. B. Tauris & Company, Ltd. London, 2005. 320p.
ISBN:1-84511-090-0, ISBN13: 978-1-84511-090-1.
Dewey:791.43/652692. LCCN:2005-296178.

Audience: **u,f.**

Desser, David   **PN1993.5.J3D47 1988**
Eros Plus Massacre: An Introduction to the Japanese New Wave
Cinema. Trade Cloth. Indiana University Press. Bloomington,
IN. 1988. 250p. ISBN:0-253-31961-7, ISBN13:
978-0-253-31961-6. Dewey:791.4/3/0952/09046.
LCCN:87-045245.

Audience: **l,u,f.**

Desser, David (Editor)   **PN1997.T5953 O92 19**
Ozu's Tokyo Story. Horton Andrew (Contribution by). Cloth
Text. Cambridge University Press. New York, NY. 1997. 187p.
Cambridge Film Handbooks Ser. ISBN:0-521-48204-6, ISBN13:
978-0-521-48204-2. Dewey:791.43/72. LCCN:96-046113.

Audience: **u,f.**

Galbraith, Stuart IV   **PN1998.3.K87G35 2001**
Emperor and the Wolf: The Lives and Films of Akira Kurosawa
and Toshiro Mifune. Trade Cloth. Faber & Faber, Inc. New
York, NY. 2002. 544p. ISBN:0-571-19982-8, ISBN13:
978-0-571-19982-2. Dewey:791.43/0233/092 B.
LCCN:2001-023825.

Audience: **g,u,f.** *Choice, 2002.*

High, Peter B.   **PN2924.H4713 2003**
The Imperial Screen: Japanese Film Culture in the Fifteen Years
War of 1931-1945. Trade Cloth. University of Wisconsin Press.
Chicago, IL. 2003. xxx, 586p. Wisconsin Studies in Film
ISBN:0-299-18130-8, ISBN13: 978-0-299-18130-7.
Dewey:791.43/0952/09043. LCCN:2002-010191.
                                        Audience: **g,u,f.** *Choice, 2003.*

Hirano, Kyoko   **PN1993.5.J3H57 1992**
Mr. Smith Goes to Tokyo: Japanese Cinema under the American
Occupation, 1945-1952. Trade Cloth. Smithsonian Institution
Press. Washington, DC. 1992. 400p. Studies in the History of
Film and Television ISBN:1-56098-157-1, ISBN13:
978-1-56098-157-2. Dewey:791.4/3/0952/09044.
LCCN:92-007033.
                                        Audience: **g,l,u,f.** *Choice, 1993.*

Kirihara, Donald   **PN1998.3.M58K5 1992**
Patterns of Time: Mizoguchi and the 1930s. Library Binding.
University of Wisconsin Press. Chicago, IL. 1992. 240p.
Wisconsin Studies in Film ISBN:0-299-13240-4, ISBN13:
978-0-299-13240-8. Dewey:791.430233092. LCCN:91-040951.
                                        Audience: **g,u,f.**

McDonald, Keiko I.   **PN1993.5.J3 M35 1983**
Cinema East: A Critical Study of Major Japanese Films. Trade
Cloth. Fairleigh Dickinson University Press. Cranbury, NJ.
1983. 280p. ISBN:0-8386-3094-4, ISBN13: 978-0-8386-3094-5.
Dewey:791.43/0952. LCCN:81-065870.
                                        Audience: **g,l,u,f.**

McDonald, Keiko I.   **PL747.55.M36 2000**
From Book to Screen: Modern Japanese Literature in Films.
Trade Cloth. M. E. Sharpe Inc. Armonk, NY. 1999. 344p.
ISBN:0-7656-0387-X, ISBN13: 978-0-7656-0387-6.
Dewey:791.43/6. LCCN:99-010679.
                                        Audience: **l,u,f.** *Choice, 2000.*

McDonald, Keiko I.   **PN1993.5.J3M365 2006**
Reading a Japanese Film: Cinema in Context. Perfect, Paper
over Boards. University of Hawaii Press. Honolulu, HI. 2006.
292p. ISBN:0-8248-2939-5, ISBN13: 978-0-8248-2939-1.
Dewey:791.43/75/0952. LCCN:2005-013946.
                                        Audience: **g,l,u,f.** *Choice, 2006.*

McRoy, Jay (Editor)   **PN19195.9.H6**
Japanese Horror Cinema. Christopher Bolton, Phillip Brophy,
Ian Conrich, Gareth Evans, Ruth Goldberg, Richard Hand,
Steffen Hantke & Matt Hills (Contribution by). Trade Cloth.
University of Hawaii Press. Honolulu, HI. 2005. 238p.
ISBN:0-8248-2899-2, ISBN13: 978-0-8248-2899-8.
Dewey:791.4361640952.
                                        Audience: **g,l,u,f.**

Mellen, Joan   **PN1997**
Seven Samurai. Trade Paper. BFI Publishing. London, 2002.
96p. Film Classics ISBN:0-85170-915-X, ISBN13:
978-0-85170-915-4. Dewey:791.4/372.
                                        Audience: **g,l,u.**

Mellen, Joan   **PN1993.5.J3 M4**
The Waves at Genji's Door: Japan Through Its Cinema. Trade
Cloth. Knopf Publishing Group. New York, NY. 1976. 448p.
ISBN:0-394-49799-6, ISBN13: 978-0-394-49799-0.
Dewey:791.43/0952. LCCN:76-009592.
                                        Audience: **g,l,u,f.**

Mes, Tom & Sharp,   **PN1993.5.J3M47 2004**
  Jasper
Midnight Eye Guide to New Japanese Film. Hideo Nakata
(Foreword by). Trade Paper. Stone Bridge Press. Berkeley, CA.
2004. 376p. ISBN:1-880656-89-2, ISBN13: 978-1-880656-89-1.
Dewey:791.43/0952. LCCN:2004-022653.
                                        Audience: **g,l,u,f.** *Choice, 2005.*

Nolletti, Arthur Jr. &   **PN1993.5.J3.R44 1992**
  Desser, David (Editors)
Reframing Japanese Cinema: Authorship, Genre, History. Trade
Cloth. Indiana University Press. Bloomington, IN. 1992. 384p.
ISBN:0-253-34108-6, ISBN13: 978-0-253-34108-2.
Dewey:791.43/0952. LCCN:91-033659.
                                        Audience: **g,u,f.** *Choice, 1993.*

Prince, Stephen   **PN1998.3.K87P75 1991**
The Warrior's Camera: The Cinema of Akira Kurosawa. Trade
Cloth. Princeton University Press. Princeton, NJ. 1990. 370p.
ISBN:0-691-03160-6, ISBN13: 978-0-691-03160-6.
Dewey:791.43/0233/092. LCCN:90-036647.
                                        Audience: **g,l,u,f.** *Choice, 1991.*

Richie, Donald   **PN1998.3.K87R5 1996**
The Films of Akira Kurosawa. Ed. 3. Trade Paper. University of
California Press. Berkeley, CA. 1996. 275p.
ISBN:0-520-20026-8, ISBN13: 978-0-520-20026-5.
Dewey:791.43/0233/092. LCCN:95-047804.
                                        Audience: **g,l,u,f.** **ℬ**

Richie, Donald   **PN1993.5.J3R474 1990**
Japanese Cinema: An Introduction. Trade Cloth. Oxford
University Press, Inc. New York, NY. 1990. 112p. Images of
Asia Ser. ISBN:0-19-584950-7, ISBN13: 978-0-19-584950-9.
Dewey:791.43/0952. LCCN:89-029893.
                                        Audience: **g,l,u,f.**

Richie, Donald   **PN1993.5.J3**
A Hundred Years of Japanese Film: A Concise History, with a
Selective Guide to DVDs and Videos. Paul Schrader (Foreword
by). Trade Paper, Video, Other. Kodansha International. Tokyo,
2005. 336p. ISBN:4-7700-2995-0, ISBN13: 978-4-7700-2995-9.
Dewey:791.430952.
                                        Audience: **g,l,u,f.**

Ruh, Brian   **PN1998.3.O83R84 2004**
Stray Dog of Anime: The Films of Mamoru Oshii. Cloth over
Boards. Palgrave Macmillan. New York, NY. 2004. 240p.
ISBN:1-4039-6329-0, ISBN13: 978-1-4039-6329-1.
Dewey:791.43/34023/092. LCCN:2003-068903.
                                        Audience: **u,f.** *Choice, 2004.*

Schilling, Mark   **PN1993.5.J3S37 1999**
Contemporary Japanese Film. Trade Paper. Shambhala
Publications, Inc. Boston, MA. 1999. 400p.
ISBN:0-8348-0415-8, ISBN13: 978-0-8348-0415-9.
Dewey:791.43/0952. LCCN:99-052092.
                                        Audience: **g,l,u,f.** *Choice, 2000.*

Silver, Alain   **PN1995.9.S24S5 1983**
The Samurai Film. Trade Cloth. Overlook Press, The. New
York, NY. 1984. 242p. ISBN:0-87951-175-3, ISBN13:
978-0-87951-175-3. Dewey:791.4309. LCCN:82-022288.
                                        Audience: **g,l,u,f.** *Choice, 2006.*

Standish, Isolde   **PN1993.5.J3S72 2005**
A New History of Japanese Cinema: A Century of Narrative
Film. Trade Cloth. Continuum International Publishing Group,

Ltd. London, 2005. 452p. ISBN:0-8264-1709-4, ISBN13:
978-0-8264-1709-1. Dewey:791.43/0952. LCCN:2004-023894.

Audience: **g,l,u.** *Choice, 2005.*

Turim, Maureen   **PN1998.3.O84T87 1997**
The Films of Nagisa Oshima: Images of a Japanese Iconoclast.
Trade Cloth. University of California Press. Berkeley, CA. 1998.
317p. ISBN:0-520-20665-7, ISBN13: 978-0-520-20665-6.
Dewey:791.43/0233/092. LCCN:96-039466.

Audience: **g,u,f.** *Choice, 1999.*

Washburn, Dennis &   **PN1993.5.J3 W67 2001**
Cavanaugh, Carole (Editors)
Word and Image in Japanese Cinema. Trade Cloth. Cambridge
University Press. New York, NY. 2000. 384p.
ISBN:0-521-77182-X, ISBN13: 978-0-521-77182-5.
Dewey:791.43/0952. LCCN:00-711584.

Audience: **u,f.** *Choice, 2001.*

Yoshida, Yoshishige   **PN1998.3.O98Y6713**
Ozu's Anti-Cinema. Trade Paper. University of Michigan,
Center for Japanese Studies. Ann Arbor, MI. 2003. 198p.
Michigan Monograph Series in Japanese Studies, No. 49
ISBN:1-929280-27-0, ISBN13: 978-1-929280-27-8.
Dewey:791.4302/33/092. LCCN:2003-062525.

Audience: **g,u,f.** *Choice, 2004.*

History > By Region and Country > Australia and New Zealand

Bertrand, Ina (Editor)   **PN1993.5.A8C55 1989**
Cinema in Australia: A Documentary History. Trade Cloth.
University of New South Wales Press. Sydney, NSW. 1990.
448p. ISBN:0-86840-075-0, ISBN13: 978-0-86840-075-4.
Dewey:791.43/0994. LCCN:88-207418.

Audience: **u,f.** *Choice, 1990.*

McFarlane, Brian   **PN1993.5.A8O96 1999**
(Editor), et al.
The Oxford Companion to Australian Film. Geoff Mayer & Ina
Bertrand (Editors). Trade Cloth. Oxford University Press, Inc.
New York, NY. 2000. 606p. ISBN:0-19-553797-1, ISBN13:
978-0-19-553797-0. Dewey:791.43/0994/03. LCCN:00-300401.

Audience: **g,l,u.** *Choice, 2000.*

Moran, Albert & Vieth,   **PN1993.5.A8M66 2005**
Errol
Historical Dictionary of Australian and New Zealand Cinema.
Trade Cloth. Scarecrow Press, Inc. Lanham, MD. 2005. 432p.
Historical Dictionaries of Literature and the Arts Ser., Vol. 6
ISBN:0-8108-5459-7, ISBN13: 978-0-8108-5459-8.
Dewey:791.43/0994/03. LCCN:2005-015419.

Audience: **u,f.** *Choice, 2006.*

Rayner, Jonathan   **PN1993.5.A8**
Contemporary Australian Cinema: An Introduction. Cloth over
Boards. Manchester University Press. Manchester, 2001. 224p.
ISBN:0-7190-5326-9, ISBN13: 978-0-7190-5326-9.
Dewey:791.43/0994.

Audience: **l,u.** *Choice, 2001.*

Sheckels, Theodore F.   **PN1993**
Celluloid Heroes down Under: Australian Film, 1970-2000.
Trade Cloth. Greenwood Publishing Group, Inc. Portsmouth,
NH. 2002. 264p. ISBN:0-275-97677-7, ISBN13:
978-0-275-97677-4. Dewey:791.43/75/0994.
LCCN:2002-020586.

Audience: **l,u.**

History > By Region and Country > Europe

Mazierska, Ewa &   **PN1995.9.C513**
Rascaroli, Laura
From Moscow to Madrid: European Cities, Postmodern Cinema.
Cloth over Boards, Trade Cloth. I. B. Tauris & Company, Ltd.
London, 2003. 240p. Cinema and Society Ser.
ISBN:1-86064-850-9, ISBN13: 978-1-86064-850-2.
Dewey:791.4/3621732.

Audience: **u,f.** *Choice, 2003.*

History > By Region and Country > Europe > Eastern Europe

Cunningham, John   **PN1993.5.H8.C8 2004**
Hungarian Cinema: A Concise History. Trade Cloth. Wallflower
Press. London, 2004. 258p. ISBN:1-903364-80-9, ISBN13:
978-1-903364-80-2. Dewey:791.4309439.

Audience: **u,f.** *Choice, 2004.*

Ford, Charles &   **PN1993.5.P5F67 2002**
Hammond, Robert
Polish Film: A Twentieth Century History. Grazyna Kudy (As
told to). Cloth Text. McFarland & Company, Incorporated
Publishers. Jefferson, NC. 2005. 368p. ISBN:0-7864-1309-3,
ISBN13: 978-0-7864-1309-6. Dewey:791.436/09438.
LCCN:2002-011401.

Audience: **g,l,u.** *Choice, 2006.*

Hames, Peter   **PN1993.5.C9**
Czechoslovak New Wave. Trade Cloth. Wallflower Press.
London, 2005. 288p. ISBN:1-904764-43-6, ISBN13:
978-1-904764-43-4. Dewey:791.4/3/09437.

Audience: **u,f.** *Choice, 2006.*

History > By Region and Country > Europe > France

Andrew, Dudley   **PN1993.5.F7A745 1995**
Mists of Regret: Culture and Sensibility in Classic French Film.
Trade Paper. Princeton University Press. Princeton, NJ. 1995.
426p. ISBN:0-691-00883-3, ISBN13: 978-0-691-00883-7.
Dewey:791.43/0944. LCCN:94-015486.

Audience: **u,f.** *Choice, 1995.*

Bazin, Andre &   **PN1993.5.F7B3413**
Cardullo, Bert (Contribution by)
French Cinema from the Liberation to the New Wave,
1945-1958. Trade Cloth. Peter Lang Publishing, Inc. New York,
NY. 2000. ISBN:0-8204-4875-3, ISBN13: 978-0-8204-4875-6.
Dewey:791.43/0944/09045. LCCN:99-052919.

Audience: **g,l,f.**

Crisp, Colin   **PN1993.5.F7C78 1993**
The Classic French Cinema, 1930-1960. Trade Cloth. Indiana
University Press. Bloomington, IN. 1994. 516p.
ISBN:0-253-31550-6, ISBN13: 978-0-253-31550-2.
Dewey:791.4/3/0944. LCCN:92-021657.

Audience: **g,l,u,f.** *Choice, 1994.*

Greene, Naomi   PN1993.5.F7G72 1999
Landscapes of Loss: The National Past in Postwar French
Cinema. Cloth Text. Princeton University Press. Princeton, NJ.
1999. 240p. ISBN:0-691-02959-8, ISBN13: 978-0-691-02959-7.
Dewey:791.43/658. LCCN:98-035156.
Audience: **u,f.** *Choice, 1999.*

Hayward, Susan &   PN1993.5.F7F74 2000
Vincendeau, Ginette (Editors)
French Film: Text and Contexts. Ed. 2. Trade Paper. Routledge.
New York, NY. 2000. 368p. ISBN:0-415-16118-5, ISBN13:
978-0-415-16118-3. Dewey:791.43/0944. LCCN:00-029094.
Audience: **u,f.** *Choice, 2000, 1990.*

Hughes, Alex &   PN1993.5.F7H84 2001
Williams, James S. (Editors)
Gender and French Cinema. Cloth over Boards. Berg Publishers.
Oxford, 2001. 256p. ISBN:1-85973-570-3, ISBN13:
978-1-85973-570-1. Dewey:791.43/652042/0944.
LCCN:2001-004389.
Audience: **g,l,u,f.**

Neupert, Richard John   PN1993.5.F7N48 2002
A History of the French New Wave Cinema. Trade Cloth.
University of Wisconsin Press. Chicago, IL. 2002. 376p.
Wisconsin Studies in Film ISBN:0-299-18160-X, ISBN13:
978-0-299-18160-4. Dewey:791.43/611. LCCN:2002-002305.
Audience: **g,l,u,f.** *Choice, 2003.*

Powrie, Phil   PN1993.5.F7
French Cinema in the 1980s: Nostalgia and the Crisis of
Masculinity. Trade Cloth. Oxford University Press, Inc. New
York, NY. 1997. 218p. ISBN:0-19-871118-2, ISBN13:
978-0-19-871118-6. Dewey:791.4/3/0944/09048.
Audience: **u,f.** *Choice, 1998.*

Smith, Alison   PN1993.5
French Cinema in The 1970s: The Echoes of May. Trade Paper,
Perfect. Manchester University Press. Manchester, 2005. 304p.
ISBN:0-7190-6341-8, ISBN13: 978-0-7190-6341-1.
Dewey:791.430944/09047. LCCN:2005-296431.
Audience: **u,f.** *Choice, 2006.*

Wilson, Emma   PN1993.5.F7
French Cinema since 1950. Trade Cloth. Rowman & Littlefield
Publishers, Inc. Lanham, MD. ISBN:0-7425-0979-6, ISBN13:
978-0-7425-0979-5. Dewey:791.430944.
Audience: **g,l,u,f.**

History > By Region and Country > Europe > Germany

Alter, Nora M.   PN1995.9.D6A39 2002
Projecting History: German Nonfiction Cinema, 1967-2000.
Trade Paper. University of Michigan Press. Chicago, IL. 2002.
232p. Social History, Popular Culture, and Politics in Germany
Ser. ISBN:0-472-06812-1, ISBN13: 978-0-472-06812-8.
Dewey:070.1/8. LCCN:2002-002091.
Audience: **u,f.** *Choice, 2003.*

Ascheid, Antje   PN1995.9.N36A83 2002
Hitler's Heroines: Stardom and Womanhood in Nazi Cinema.
Library Binding. Temple University Press. Philadelphia, PA.
2002. 240p. Culture and the Moving Image Ser.

ISBN:1-56639-983-1, ISBN13: 978-1-56639-983-8.
Dewey:791.43/658. LCCN:2002-071460.
Audience: **g,l,u,f.** *Choice, 2003.*

Bergfelder, Tim   PN1993.5.G3
(Editor), et al.
The German Cinema Book. Erica Carter & Deniz Göktürk
(Editors). Trade Cloth. BFI Publishing. London, 2003. 288p.
ISBN:0-85170-945-1, ISBN13: 978-0-85170-945-1.
Dewey:791.4/3/0943.
Audience: **g,l,u.** *Choice, 2003.*

Berghahn, Daniela   PN1993.5.G3
Hollywood Behind the Wall: The Cinema of East Germany.
Cloth over Boards. Manchester University Press. Manchester,
2005. 288p. ISBN:0-7190-6171-7, ISBN13: 978-0-7190-6171-4.
Dewey:791.4309431. LCCN:2005-299882.
Audience: **u,f.** *Choice, 2005.*

Flinn, Caryl   PN1993.5.G3 F57 2004
The New German Cinema: Music, History, and the Matter of
Style. Trade Cloth. University of California Press. Berkeley, CA.
2003. 352p. ISBN:0-520-22895-2, ISBN13: 978-0-520-22895-5.
Dewey:791.43/657. LCCN:2003-005040.
Audience: **u,f.** *Choice, 2004.*

Giesen, Rolf   PN1995.9
Nazi Propaganda Films: A History and Filmography. Cloth Text.
McFarland & Company, Incorporated Publishers. Jefferson, NC.
2003. 295p. ISBN:0-7864-1556-8, ISBN13: 978-0-7864-1556-4.
Dewey:791.43/658. LCCN:2003-006853.
Audience: **g,l,u.**

Hake, Sabine   PN1993.5.G3H28 2001
German National Cinema. Paper over Boards. Routledge. New
York, NY. 2001. 240p. National Cinemas Ser.
ISBN:0-415-08901-8, ISBN13: 978-0-415-08901-2.
Dewey:791.43/0943. LCCN:2001-038711.
Audience: **g,l,u,f.** *Choice, 2002.*

McCormick, Richard   PN1993.5.G3M39 2002
W.
Gender and Sexuality in Weimar Modernity: Film, Literature
and New Objectivity. Trade Cloth. Palgrave Macmillan. New
York, NY. 2002. 256p. ISBN:0-312-29298-8, ISBN13:
978-0-312-29298-0. Dewey:791.43/653. LCCN:2001-046160.
Audience: **g,u,f.**

Naughton, Leonie   PN1993.5
That Was the Wild East: Film Culture, Unification, and the New
Germany. Trade Paper. University of Michigan Press. Chicago,
IL. 2002. 288p. Social History, Popular Culture, and Politics in
Germany Ser. ISBN:0-472-08888-2, ISBN13:
978-0-472-08888-1. Dewey:791.43/0943/1. LCCN:2001-003726.
Audience: **u,f.** *Choice, 2003.*

History > By Region and Country > Europe > Italy

McCallum, Lawrence   PN1995.9.H6
Italian Horror Films of the 1960s: A Critical Catalog of 62
Chillers. Paper Text. McFarland & Company, Incorporated
Publishers. Jefferson, NC. 2004. 288p. ISBN:0-7864-1968-7,
ISBN13: 978-0-7864-1968-5. Dewey:791.4/36164/0945.
LCCN:98-022473.
Audience: **g,l,u,f.**

Rumble, Patrick A.   PN1998.3.P367R86
Allegories of Contamination: Pier Paolo Pasolini's Trilogy of
Life. Trade Paper. University of Toronto Press. Toronto, ON.
1995. 207p. Italian Studies, : ISBN:0-8020-7219-4, ISBN13:
978-0-8020-7219-1. Dewey:791.43. LCCN:96-138021.
                                    Audience: **u,f**. *Choice, 1996.*

History > By Region and Country > Europe > Russia

Goodwin, James   PN1998.3.H58
Eisenstein, Cinema, and History. Trade Paper. University of
Illinois Press. Champaign, IL. 1993. 274p. ISBN:0-252-06269-8,
ISBN13: 978-0-252-06269-8. Dewey:791.43/0233/092.
LCCN:92-024035.
                                    Audience: **u,f**. *Choice, 1993.*

Taylor, Richard &   PN1993.5.R9F47 1994
  Christie, Ian
The Film Factory: New Approaches to Russian and Soviet
Cinema. Trade Paper. Routledge. New York, NY. 1994. 480p.
Soviet Cinema Ser. ISBN:0-415-05298-X, ISBN13:
978-0-415-05298-6. Dewey:791.43/0947. LCCN:95-113211.
                                    Audience: **u,f**.

Yuri, Tsivian   PN1993.5.R9T7713
Early Russian Cinema and Its Cultural Reception. Paper over
Boards. Routledge. New York, NY. 1994. 296p. Soviet Cinema
Ser. ISBN:0-415-07135-6, ISBN13: 978-0-415-07135-2.
Dewey:791.43/0947. LCCN:94-002200.
                                    Audience: **u,f**. *Choice, 1996.*

History > By Region and Country > Europe > Spain

Mira, Alberto   PN1993.5.S7
The Cinema of Spain and Portugal. Trade Cloth. Wallflower
Press. London, 2005. 268p. ISBN:1-904764-45-2, ISBN13:
978-1-904764-45-8. Dewey:791.430946.
                                    Audience: **l,u,f**. *Choice, 2006.*

Richardson, Nathan E.   PQ6140.R87R53 2002
Postmodern Paletos: Immigration, Democracy and Globalization
in Spanish Narrative and Film, 1950-2000. Trade Cloth.
Bucknell University Press. Cranbury, NJ. 2002. 264p.
ISBN:0-8387-5498-8, ISBN13: 978-0-8387-5498-6.
Dewey:791.43/0946. LCCN:2001-037544.
                                    Audience: **u,f**. *Choice, 2002.*

History > By Region and Country > Europe > United Kingdom

Friedman, Lester D.   PN1993.5.G7.F57 1992
  (Editor)
Fires Were Started: British Cinema and Thatcherism. Book,
Other. University of Minnesota Press. Minneapolis, MN. 1992.
352p. ISBN:0-8166-2079-2, ISBN13: 978-0-8166-2079-1.
Dewey:302.23430941. LCCN:92-014210.
                                    Audience: **u,f**. *Choice, 1993.*

Higson, Andrew   PN1993.5.G7
Waving the Flag: Constructing a National Cinema in Britain.
Trade Paper. Oxford University Press, Inc. New York, NY. 1997.
334p. ISBN:0-19-874229-0, ISBN13: 978-0-19-874229-6.
Dewey:791.4/3/0941.
                                    Audience: **u,f**. *Choice, 1995.*

Higson, Andrew   PN1993.5.G7
  (Editor)
Young and Innocent?: The Cinema in Britain, 1896-1930. Trade
Cloth. University of Exeter Press. Exeter, 2002. 432p.
ISBN:0-85989-659-5, ISBN13: 978-0-85989-659-7.
Dewey:791.4/3/0941.
                                    Audience: **u,f**. *Choice, 2003.*

MacKillop, Ian &   PN1993.5.G7
  Sinyard, Neil (Editors)
British Cinema in the 1950s: An Art in Peacetime. Cloth over
Boards. Manchester University Press. Manchester, 2003. 220p.
ISBN:0-7190-6488-0, ISBN13: 978-0-7190-6488-3.
Dewey:791.43/0941/09045. LCCN:2003-042120.
                                    Audience: **u,f**. *Choice, 2003.*

Murphy, Robert   PN1993.5.G7
The British Cinema Book. Ed. 2. Trade Cloth. University of
California Press. Berkeley, CA. 2002. 272p.
ISBN:0-85170-852-8, ISBN13: 978-0-85170-852-2.
Dewey:791.43/0941.
                                    Audience: **l,u,f**. *Choice, 1998.*

Petrie, Duncan   NX545
Contemporary Scottish Fictions—Film, Television, and the
Novel. Trade Paper. Edinburgh University Press. Edinburgh,
2004. 224p. ISBN:0-7486-1789-2, ISBN13: 978-0-7486-1789-0.
Dewey:700.941109049.
                                    Audience: **u,f**. *Choice, 2005.*

Smith, Gary A.   PN1995.9.H6S618 2000
Uneasy Dreams: The Golden Age of British Horror Films,
1956-1976. James Bernard (Foreword by). Cloth Text.
McFarland & Company, Incorporated Publishers. Jefferson, NC.
2000. 277p. ISBN:0-7864-0604-6, ISBN13: 978-0-7864-0604-3.
Dewey:791.43/6164/0941. LCCN:99-55753.
                                    Audience: **g,l,u**.

Williams, Tony   PN1993.5.G7W55 2000
Structures of Desire: British Cinema, 1939-1955. Cloth Text.
State University of New York Press. Albany, NY. 2000. 224p.
ISBN:0-7914-4643-3, ISBN13: 978-0-7914-4643-0.
Dewey:791.43/0941/09044. LCCN:00-023991.
                                    Audience: **u,f**.

History > By Region and Country > North America

Garcma, Alfonso J.   PN1993.5.C8G375 2003
The Cuban Filmography: 1897 Through 2001. Trade Cloth.
McFarland & Company, Incorporated Publishers. Jefferson, NC.
2003. 224p. ISBN:0-7864-1275-5, ISBN13: 978-0-7864-1275-4.
Dewey:791.43/75/097291. LCCN:2002-153760.
                                    Audience: **g,l,u,f**. *Choice, 2003.*

History > By Region and Country > North America > Mexico

Fregoso, Rosa Linda   **F790.M5 F75 2003**
Mexicana Encounters: The Making of Social Identities on the Borderlands. Trade Cloth. University of California Press. Berkeley, CA. 2003. 246p. American Crossroads Ser., Vol. 12 ISBN:0-520-22997-5, ISBN13: 978-0-520-22997-6. Dewey:305.48/868720721. LCCN:2003-000594.
Audience: **u,f.** *Choice, 2004.*

Rashkin, Elissa J.   **PN1993.5.M4R33 2001**
Women Filmmakers in Mexico: The Country of Which We Dream. Trade Cloth. University of Texas Press. Austin, TX. 2001. 310p. ISBN:0-292-77108-8, ISBN13: 978-0-292-77108-6. Dewey:791.43/082/0972. LCCN:00-041772.
Audience: **u,f.** *Choice, 2001.*

History > By Region and Country > North America > United States

Abel, Richard   **PN1993.5.F7**
French Cinema: The First Wave, 1915-1929. Trade Cloth. Princeton University Press. Princeton, NJ. 1984. 550p. ISBN:0-691-05408-8, ISBN13: 978-0-691-05408-7. Dewey:791.43/0944. LCCN:83-043057.
Audience: **g,u,f.** *B*

Antonio, Sheril D.   **PN1995.9.N4A58 2001**
Contemporary African American Cinema. Trade Cloth. Peter Lang Publishing, Inc. New York, NY. 2002. 152p. Framing Film Ser., Vol. 4:The History and Art of Cinema ISBN:0-8204-5517-2, ISBN13: 978-0-8204-5517-4. Dewey:384/.8/08996073. LCCN:00-067154.
Audience: **u,f.**

Auster, Albert & Quart, Leonard   **PN1995**
American Film and Society since 1945. Ed. 3. Paper Text. Greenwood Publishing Group, Inc. Portsmouth, NH. 2001. 248p. ISBN:0-275-96743-3, ISBN13: 978-0-275-96743-7. Dewey:302.23/43/0973. LCCN:2001-034630.
Audience: **g,l,u.**

Bernardoni, James   **PN1993.5.U6.B39**
The New Hollywood: What the Movies Did with the New Freedoms of the Seventies. Ed. 2. Paper Text. McFarland & Company, Incorporated Publishers. Jefferson, NC. 2001. 240p. ISBN:0-7864-1206-2, ISBN13: 978-0-7864-1206-8. Dewey:791.43. LCCN:91-52742.
Audience: **g,u.** *Choice, 1992.*

Beuka, Robert   **PS374.S82B48 2004**
SuburbiaNation: Reading Suburban Landscape in Twentieth-Century American Fiction and Film. Trade Paper. Palgrave Macmillan. New York, NY. 2004. 304p. ISBN:1-4039-6340-1, ISBN13: 978-1-4039-6340-6. Dewey:813/.509321733. LCCN:2003-054914.
Audience: **l,u,f.** *Choice, 2004.*

Beverly, William   **PS374.F83B48 2003**
On the Lam: Narratives of Flight in J. Edgar Hoover's America. Trade Cloth. University Press of Mississippi. Jackson, MS. 2006. 208p. ISBN:1-57806-537-2, ISBN13: 978-1-57806-537-0. Dewey:813/.509355. LCCN:2002-010799.
Audience: **u,f.** *Choice, 2003.*

Bobo, Jacqueline   **PN1995.9.N4B57 1995**
Black Women As Cultural Leaders. Trade Paper. Columbia University Press. New York, NY. 1995. 224p. Film and Culture Ser. ISBN:0-231-08395-5, ISBN13: 978-0-231-08395-9. Dewey:791.4/36/52042. LCCN:94-025317.
Audience: **u,f.** *Choice, 1995.*

Bobo, Jacqueline   **PN1998.2.B57 1998**
Black Women Film and Video Artists. Paper over Boards. Routledge. New York, NY. 1998. 288p. AFI Film Readers Ser. ISBN:0-415-92041-8, ISBN13: 978-0-415-92041-4. Dewey:791.43/023/08996073. LCCN:97-032062.
Audience: **g,l,u,f.**

Bogle, Donald   **PN1995.9.N4B58 1988**
Blacks in American Film and Television: An Encyclopedia. Paper over Boards. Garland Publishing, Inc. New York, NY. 1988. 700p. ISBN:0-8240-8715-1, ISBN13: 978-0-8240-8715-9. Dewey:791.43/08996073. LCCN:87-029241.
Audience: **g,l,u,f.** *Choice, 1988.*

Bowser, Pearl (Editor), et al.   **PN1998.3.M494O83**
Oscar Micheaux and His Circle: African-American Filmmaking and Race Cinema of the Silent Era. Jane Gaines & Charles Musser (Editors). Trade Cloth. Indiana University Press. Bloomington, IN. 2001. 384p. ISBN:0-253-33994-4, ISBN13: 978-0-253-33994-2. Dewey:791.43/0233/092. LCCN:2001-001386.
Audience: **l,u,f.**

Bowser, Pearl & Spence, Louise   **PN1998.3.M494B69**
Writing Himself into History: Oscar Micheaux, His Silent Films and His Audiences. Thulani Davis (Foreword by). Trade Cloth. Rutgers University Press. Piscataway, NJ. 2000. 280p. ISBN:0-8135-2803-8, ISBN13: 978-0-8135-2803-8. Dewey:791.43/0233/092. LCCN:99-055380.
Audience: **u,f.** *Choice, 2001.*

Burgoyne, Robert   **PN1995.9.H5B87 1997**
Film Nation: Hollywood Looks at U. S. History. Book, Other. University of Minnesota Press. Minneapolis, MN. 1997. 160p. ISBN:0-8166-2070-9, ISBN13: 978-0-8166-2070-8. Dewey:791.43/658. LCCN:97-005919.
Audience: **u,f.** *Choice, 1998.*

Crowdus, Gary (Editor)   **PN1993.5.U6**
The Political Companion to American Film. Trade Cloth. Fitzroy Dearborn Publishers, Inc. Chicago, IL. 1996. 525p. ISBN:1-884964-53-2, ISBN13: 978-1-884964-53-4. Dewey:791.4/3/0973. LCCN:93-041593.
Audience: **g,l,u,f.** *Choice, 1995.*

Davis, Ronald L.   **PN1993.5.U65.D34**
The Glamour Factory: Inside Hollywood's Big Studio System. Trade Cloth. Southern Methodist University Press. Dallas, TX. 1993. 464p. ISBN:0-87074-357-0, ISBN13: 978-0-87074-357-3. Dewey:384/.8/0979494. LCCN:93-008861.
Audience: **l,u.** *Choice, 1994.*

DeAngelis, Michael   **PN1995.9.H55D43 2001**
Gay Fandom and Crossover Stardom: James Dean, Mel Gibson, and Keanu Reeves. Trade Cloth. Duke University Press. Durham, NC. 2001. 296p. ISBN:0-8223-2728-7, ISBN13: 978-0-8223-2728-8. Dewey:791.43/086/642. LCCN:2001-023153.
Audience: **u,f.** *Choice, 2002.*

Diawara, Manthia   PN1995.9.N4.B45 1993
(Editor)
Black American Cinema: Aesthetics and Spectatorship. Paper
over Boards. Routledge. New York, NY. 1993. 256p. AFI Film
Readers Ser. ISBN:0-415-90396-3, ISBN13: 978-0-415-90396-7.
Dewey:791.4308996073. LCCN:92-032907.
Audience: **l,u,f.** *Choice, 1994.*

DiBattista, Maria   PN1995.9.W6D53 2001
Fast-Talking Dames. Cloth over Boards. Yale University Press.
Cumberland, RI. 2001. 384p. ISBN:0-300-08815-9, ISBN13:
978-0-300-08815-1. Dewey:791.4/36/52042. LCCN:00-049946.
Audience: **g,l,u,f.** *Choice, 2001.*

Donalson, Melvin   PN1995.9.N4D66 2003
Black Directors in Hollywood. Trade Paper. University of Texas
Press. Austin, TX. 2003. 389p. ISBN:0-292-70179-9, ISBN13:
978-0-292-70179-3. Dewey:791.43/0233/092273 B.
LCCN:2003-006770.

Audience: **g,l,u,f.**

Everett, Anna   PN1995.9.N4E94 2001
Returning the Gaze: A Genealogy of Black Film Criticism,
1909-1949. Trade Cloth. Duke University Press. Durham, NC.
2001. 384p. ISBN:0-8223-2606-X, ISBN13: 978-0-8223-2606-9.
Dewey:791.43/01/508996073. LCCN:00-010758.
Audience: **u,f.** *Choice, 2001.*

Feng, Peter X.   PN1995.9.A77F46 2002
Identities in Motion: Asian American Film and Video. Trade
Cloth. Duke University Press. Durham, NC. 2002. 304p.
ISBN:0-8223-2983-2, ISBN13: 978-0-8223-2983-1.
Dewey:791.43/6520395. LCCN:2002-003056.
Audience: **u,f.** *Choice, 2003.*

Fernett, Gene   PN1993.5.U6F45 2003
American Film Studios: An Historical Encyclopedia. Paper Text.
McFarland & Company, Incorporated Publishers. Jefferson, NC.
2001. 310p. ISBN:0-7864-1325-5, ISBN13: 978-0-7864-1325-6.
Dewey:791.4/3/0973. LCCN:88-42514.
Audience: **g,l,u,f.** *Choice, 1989.*

Fetrow, Alan G.   PN1993.5.U6.F457
Feature Films, 1950-1959: A United States Filmography. Cloth
Text. McFarland & Company, Incorporated Publishers. Jefferson,
NC. 1999. 718p. ISBN:0-7864-0427-2, ISBN13:
978-0-7864-0427-8. Dewey:791.4/3/0973/09045.
LCCN:98-16105.
Audience: **g,l,u.** *Choice, 1999.*

Friedman, Lester D.   PN1995.9.M56U57 1991
(Editor)
Unspeakable Images: Ethnicity and the American Cinema. Trade
Paper. University of Illinois Press. Champaign, IL. 1991. 456p.
ISBN:0-252-06152-7, ISBN13: 978-0-252-06152-3.
Dewey:791.43/6520693. LCCN:90-039869.
Audience: **l,u,f.** *Choice, 1991.*

Gabbard, Krin   PN1995.9.N4G33 2004
Black Magic: White Hollywood and African American Culture.
Trade Cloth. Rutgers University Press. Piscataway, NJ. 2004.
256p. ISBN:0-8135-3383-X, ISBN13: 978-0-8135-3383-4.
Dewey:791.43/652996073. LCCN:2003-020083.
Audience: **u,f.**

Girgus, Sam B.   PN1993.5.U6 G497 19
Hollywood Renaissance: The Cinema of Democracy in the Era
of Ford, Capra and Kazan. Trade Paper. Cambridge University
Press. New York, NY. 1998. 270p. ISBN:0-521-62552-1,

ISBN13: 978-0-521-62552-4. Dewey:791.43/0233/092273.
LCCN:97-047090.
Audience: **u,f.** *Choice, 1999.*

Green, J. Ronald   PN1998.3.M494G74
Straight Lick: The Cinema of Oscar Micheaux. Trade Cloth.
Indiana University Press. Bloomington, IN. 2000. xvi, 295p.
ISBN:0-253-33753-4, ISBN13: 978-0-253-33753-5.
Dewey:791.43/0233/092. LCCN:99-087110.
Audience: **u,f.** *Choice, 2001.*

Green, J. Ronald   PN1998.3.M494G76
With a Crooked Stick: The Films of Oscar Micheaux. Trade
Paper. Indiana University Press. Bloomington, IN. 2004. 304p.
ISBN:0-253-21715-6, ISBN13: 978-0-253-21715-8.
Dewey:791.43/02/33092. LCCN:2003-015584.
Audience: **u,f.** *Choice, 2004.*

Grieveson, Lee   PN1995.62 .G75 2004
Policing Cinema: Movies and Censorship in Early-Twentieth-
Century America. Trade Cloth. University of California Press.
Berkeley, CA. 2004. 352p. ISBN:0-520-23965-2, ISBN13:
978-0-520-23965-4. Dewey:363.31/0973. LCCN:2003-016038.
Audience: **u,f.** *Choice, 2004.*

Horne, Gerald   PN1993.5.U65H67 2001
Class Struggle in Hollywood, 1930-1950: Moguls, Mobsters,
Stars, Reds, and Trade Unionists. Trade Paper. University of
Texas Press. Austin, TX. 2001. 363p. ISBN:0-292-73138-8,
ISBN13: 978-0-292-73138-7. Dewey:331.88/1179143/09794.
LCCN:00-025950.
Audience: **u,f.** *Choice, 2001.*

Horwath, Alexander   PN1993.5.U6
(Editor), et al.
The Last Great American Picture Show: New Hollywood
Cinema in the 1970s. Noel King & Thomas Elsaesser (Editors).
Trade Cloth. Amsterdam University Press. Amsterdam, 2004.
348p. Amsterdam University Press - Film Culture in Transition
Ser. ISBN:90-5356-493-4, ISBN13: 978-90-5356-493-6.
Dewey:791.43097309047.
Audience: **u,f.** *Choice, 2004.*

Jarvie, Ian   PN1993.5.U6 J3 1992
Hollywood's Overseas Campaign: The North Atlantic Movie
Trade, 1920-1950. David Culbert, Garth Jowett & Kenneth
Short (Contribution by). Cloth Text. Cambridge University
Press. New York, NY. 1992. 493p. Cambridge Studies in the
History of Mass Communications ISBN:0-521-41566-7,
ISBN13: 978-0-521-41566-8. Dewey:384.80973.
LCCN:92-007723.
Audience: **u,f.** *Choice, 1993.*

Jeffords, Susan   PN1995.9.M46J44 1993
Hard Bodies: Hollywood Masculinity in the Reagan Era. Cloth
Text. Rutgers University Press. Piscataway, NJ. 1993. 240p.
ISBN:0-8135-2002-9, ISBN13: 978-0-8135-2002-5.
Dewey:791.43/652041/09048. LCCN:93-018282.
Audience: **u,f.** *Choice, 1994.*

Kalinak, Kathryn   ML2075
Settling the Score: Music and the Classical Hollywood Film.
Trade Paper. University of Wisconsin Press. Chicago, IL. 1992.
266p. Wisconsin Studies in Film ISBN:0-299-13364-8, ISBN13:
978-0-299-13364-1. Dewey:781.5/42/0973. LCCN:92-006853.
Audience: **u,f.**

Kelley, Beverly Merrill   PN1995.9.P6K43 2004
Reelpolitik II: Political Idelogies in '50s and '60s Films. Book,
Other. Rowman & Littlefield Publishers, Inc. Lanham, MD.
2004. 344p. Communication, Media, and Politics Ser.
ISBN:0-7425-3040-X, ISBN13: 978-0-7425-3040-9.
Dewey:791.43/658/0973. LCCN:2003-026860.
                              Audience: **l,u,f**. *Choice, 2004.*

Klotman, Phyllis R.   PN1997.A1S36 1991
   (Editor)
Screenplays of the African American Experience. Trade Cloth.
Indiana University Press. Bloomington, IN. 1991. 280p.
ISBN:0-253-33145-5, ISBN13: 978-0-253-33145-8.
Dewey:791.43/6520396073. LCCN:90-043511.
                              Audience: **g,l,u,f**. *Choice, 1991.*

Klotman, Phyllis Rauch   PN1995.9.N4S77 1999
   & Cutler, Janet K.
Struggles for Representation: African American Documentary
Film and Video. Trade Cloth. Indiana University Press.
Bloomington, IN. 1999. 464p. ISBN:0-253-33595-7, ISBN13:
978-0-253-33595-1. Dewey:070.1/8. LCCN:99-029890.
                              Audience: **u,f**. *Choice, 2000.*

Klotman, Phyllis R. &   PN1995.9.N4K58 1997
   Gibson, Gloria J.
Frame by Frame II: A Filmography of the African American
Image, 1978-1994. Trade Cloth. Indiana University Press.
Bloomington, IN. 1997. 944p. ISBN:0-253-33280-X, ISBN13:
978-0-253-33280-6. Dewey:791.43/08996073. LCCN:96-029770.
                              Audience: **g,l,u,f**. *Choice, 1998.*

Knight, Arthur   PN1995.9.N4K59 2002
Disintegrating the Musical: Black Performance and American
Musical Film. Trade Cloth. Duke University Press. Durham,
NC. 2002. 352p. ISBN:0-8223-2935-2, ISBN13:
978-0-8223-2935-0. Dewey:791.43/6. LCCN:2002-002700.
                              Audience: **u,f**. *Choice, 2003.*

Krutnik, Frank   PN1995.9.F54K78 1991
In a Lonely Street: Film Noir, Genre and Masculinity. Trade
Paper. Routledge. New York, NY. 1991. 288p.
ISBN:0-415-02630-X, ISBN13: 978-0-415-02630-7.
Dewey:791.43/655. LCCN:90-023774.
                              Audience: **u,f**. *Choice, 1992.*

Lane, Christina   PN1998.2.L35 2000
Feminist Hollywood: From Born in Flames to Point Break.
Trade Cloth. Wayne State University Press. Detroit, MI. 2000.
261p. Contemporary Film and Television Ser.
ISBN:0-8143-2799-0, ISBN13: 978-0-8143-2799-9.
Dewey:791.43/0233/0820973. LCCN:99-053522.
                              Audience: **g,l,u,f**. *Choice, 2001.*

Lee, Spike & Aftab,   PN1998.3.L44A3 2005
   Kaleem
Spike Lee: That's My Story and I'm Sticking to It. Trade Cloth.
W. W. Norton & Company, Inc. New York, NY. 2005. 320p.
ISBN:0-393-06153-1, ISBN13: 978-0-393-06153-6.
Dewey:791.43/0233/092 B. LCCN:2005-014211.
                              Audience: **g,l,u,f**.

Lev, Peter   PN1993.5.U6L44 2000
American Films of the 70s: Conflicting Visions. Trade Paper.
University of Texas Press. Austin, TX. 2000. 260p.
ISBN:0-292-74716-0, ISBN13: 978-0-292-74716-6.
Dewey:791.43/75/097309047. LCCN:99-053348.
                              Audience: **l,u,f**. *Choice, 2000.*

Lewis, Randolph   PN1998.3.D3846L48
Emile de Antonio: Radical Filmmaker in Cold War America.
Trade Cloth. University of Wisconsin Press. Chicago, IL. 2000.
344p. ISBN:0-299-16910-3, ISBN13: 978-0-299-16910-7.
Dewey:791.43/0233/092 B. LCCN:00-009309.
                              Audience: **u,f**. *Choice, 2001.*

Lisanti, Thomas   PN1995.9.B38L57 2005
Hollywood Surf and Beach Movies: The First Wave, 1959-1969.
Cloth Text. McFarland & Company, Incorporated Publishers.
Jefferson, NC. 2005. 456p. ISBN:0-7864-2104-5, ISBN13:
978-0-7864-2104-6. Dewey:791.43/657. LCCN:2004-029518.
                              Audience: **l,u**.

Lommel, Cookie   PN1995.9.N4L66 2001
Black Filmmakers. Trade Paper. Facts On File, Inc. New York,
NY. 2002. 144p. African American Achievers Ser.
ISBN:0-7910-5817-4, ISBN13: 978-0-7910-5817-6.
Dewey:791.43/089/96073. LCCN:00-052333.
                              Audience: **g,l,u**.

Lupack, Barbara Tepa   PN1995.9.N4L87 2002
Literary Adaptations in Black American Cinema: From
Micheaux to Morrison. Trade Cloth. University of Rochester
Press. Rochester, NY. 2002. 584p. ISBN:1-58046-103-4,
ISBN13: 978-1-58046-103-0. Dewey:791.43/6520396073.
LCCN:2002-022332.
                              Audience: **u,f**. *Choice, 2003.*

Marchetti, Gina   PN1995.9.A78M37 1993
Romance and the "Yellow Peril": Race, Sex, and Discursive
Strategies in Hollywood Fiction. Trade Paper. University of
California Press. Berkeley, CA. 1994. 270p.
ISBN:0-520-08495-0, ISBN13: 978-0-520-08495-7.
Dewey:791.436520395. LCCN:92-010878.
                              Audience: **l,u,f**. *Choice, 1994.*

Marmorstein, Gary   ML2075.M246 1997
Hollywood Rhapsody: The Story of Movie Music, 1900-1975.
Ed. 2. Cloth Text. Thomson Wadsworth. Belmont, CA. 1997.
456p. ISBN:0-02-864595-2, ISBN13: 978-0-02-864595-7.
Dewey:781.5/42/0973. LCCN:97-019891.
                              Audience: **g,l,u**. *Choice, 1998.*

Massood, Paula J.   PN1995.9.N4M33 2003
Black City Cinema: African American Urban Experiences in
Film. Library Binding. Temple University Press. Philadelphia,
PA. 2002. 296p. Culture and the Moving Image Ser.
ISBN:1-59213-002-X, ISBN13: 978-1-59213-002-3.
Dewey:791.43/6520396073. LCCN:2002-020421.
                              Audience: **u,f**. *Choice, 2003.*

McCrisken, Trevor B. &   PN1995.9.H5M43 2005
   Pepper, Andrew
American History and Contemporary Hollywood Film. Trade
Cloth. Rutgers University Press. Piscataway, NJ. 2005. 240p.
ISBN:0-8135-3620-0, ISBN13: 978-0-8135-3620-0.
Dewey:791.43/658. LCCN:2004-051365.
                              Audience: **u,f**. *Choice, 2005.*

Morreale, Joanne   JK2281
The Presidential Campaign Film: A Critical History. Paper Text.
Greenwood Publishing Group, Inc. Portsmouth, NH. 1996. 224p.
ISBN:0-275-95580-X, ISBN13: 978-0-275-95580-9.
Dewey:324.730973. LCCN:93-020129.
                              Audience: **l,u,f**. *Choice, 1994.*

Musico, Giuliana   PN1995.9.N47M87 1997
Hollywood's New Deal. Trade Cloth. Temple University Press.
Philadelphia, PA. 1997. 320p. Culture and the Moving Image
Ser. ISBN:1-56639-495-3, ISBN13: 978-1-56639-495-6.
Dewey:302.23/43/0973. LCCN:96-034525.
                            Audience: **u,f.** *Choice, 1997.*

Musser, Charles   PN1993.5.U6.H55
The Emergence of the Cinema: The American Screen to 1907,
Vol. 1. Charles H. Harpole (Editor). Trade Cloth. Thomson
Gale. Farmington Hills, MI. 1905. 613p. History of the
American Cinema Ser., Vol. 1 ISBN:0-684-18413-3, ISBN13:
978-0-684-18413-5. Dewey:791.430973. LCCN:90-048307.
                            Audience: **g,l,u,f.** *Choice, 1991.*

Nadel, Alan   PN1995.9.S6N33 1997
Flatlining on the Field of Dreams: Cultural Narratives in the
Films of President Reagan's America. Cloth Text. Rutgers
University Press. Piscataway, NJ. 1997. 224p.
ISBN:0-8135-2439-3, ISBN13: 978-0-8135-2439-9.
Dewey:302.23/43/097309048. LCCN:96-049062.
                            Audience: **u,f.** *Choice, 1997.*

Neale, Steve   PN1993.5.U6N43 2000
Genre and Hollywood. Paper over Boards. Routledge. New
York, NY. 2000. 344p. Sightlines Ser. ISBN:0-415-02605-9,
ISBN13: 978-0-415-02605-5. Dewey:791.43/6.
LCCN:00-698318.
                            Audience: **u,f.** *Choice, 2000.*

Neve, Brian   PN1995.9.S6.N46 1992
Film and Politics in America: A Social Tradition. Cloth Text.
Routledge. New York, NY. 1992. 192p. Studies in Film,
Television and the Media ISBN:0-415-02619-9, ISBN13:
978-0-415-02619-2. Dewey:302.23430973. LCCN:92-005196.
                            Audience: **l,u,f.** *Choice, 1993.*

Pribram, E. Deidre   PN2993.5.U6P75 2001
Cinema and Culture: Independent Film in the United States,
1980-2001. Trade Paper. Peter Lang Publishing, Inc. New York,
NY. 2002. 305p. Framing Film Ser., Vol. 2:The History and Art
of Cinema ISBN:0-8204-5217-3, ISBN13: 978-0-8204-5217-3.
Dewey:791.43/0973/09048. LCCN:2001-029270.
                            Audience: **u,f.**

Prince, Stephen (Editor)   PN1993.5.U6H55
A New Pot of Gold: Hollywood Under the Electric Rainbow,
1980-1989, Vol. 10. Trade Cloth. Thomson Gale. Farmington
Hills, MI. 1905. xxi, 564p. History of the American Cinema
Ser., Vol. 10 ISBN:0-684-80493-X, ISBN13:
978-0-684-80493-4. Dewey:384/.8/097309048.
LCCN:99-038369.
                            Audience: **g,l,u,f.** *Choice, 2000.*

Rabinovitz, Lauren   PN1995.9.W6R33 1998
For the Love of Pleasure: Women, Movies, and Culture in
Turn-of-the-Century Chicago. Cloth Text. Rutgers University
Press. Piscataway, NJ. 1998. 208p. ISBN:0-8135-2533-0,
ISBN13: 978-0-8135-2533-4. Dewey:791.43/082/0977311.
LCCN:97-045724.
                            Audience: **u,f.** *Choice, 1998.*

Reid, Mark A.   PN1995.9.N4R43 2005
Black Lenses, Black Voices: African American Film Now. Book,
Other. Rowman & Littlefield Publishers, Inc. Lanham, MD.
2005. 136p. Genre and Beyond Ser. ISBN:0-7425-2641-0,
ISBN13: 978-0-7425-2641-9. Dewey:791.43750899.
LCCN:2004-026201.
                            Audience: **g,l,u,f.** *Choice, 2005.*

Richards, Larry   PN1995.9N4
African American Films Through 1959: A Comprehensive,
Illustrated Filmography. Paper Text. McFarland & Company,
Incorporated Publishers. Jefferson, NC. 2005. 320p.
ISBN:0-7864-2274-2, ISBN13: 978-0-7864-2274-6.
Dewey:791.43'6520396073. LCCN:97-023730.
                            Audience: **g,l,u,f.** *Choice, 1998.*

Rothman, Stanley, et al.   PN1995.9.S6P67 1996
Hollywood's America: Social and Political Themes in Motion
Pictures. Stephen P. Powers & David J. Rothman (Authors).
Trade Paper. Westview Press. Boulder, CO. 1996. 320p.
ISBN:0-8133-2933-7, ISBN13: 978-0-8133-2933-8.
Dewey:791.4/3/0973. LCCN:96-015009.
                            Audience: **l,u.** *Choice, 1996.*

Rubinfeld, Mark D.   PN1995
Bound to Bond: Gender, Genre and the Hollywood Romantic
Comedy. Trade Cloth. Greenwood Publishing Group, Inc.
Portsmouth, NH. 2001. 248p. ISBN:0-275-97271-2, ISBN13:
978-0-275-97271-4. Dewey:791.43/617. LCCN:00-069899.
                            Audience: **g,l,u,f.** *Choice, 2002.*

Segrave, Kerry   PN1995.9.F67S44 2004
Foreign Films in America: A History. Paper Text. McFarland &
Company, Incorporated Publishers. Jefferson, NC. 2004. 259p.
ISBN:0-7864-1764-1, ISBN13: 978-0-7864-1764-3.
Dewey:791.43/75/0973. LCCN:2004-000958.
                            Audience: **g,l.**

Silver, Alain & Ward,   PN1995.9.F54F55 1992
  Elizabeth (Editors)
Film Noir: An Encyclopedic Reference to the American Style.
Ed. 3. Trade Paper. Overlook Press, The. New York, NY. 1993.
479p. ISBN:0-87951-479-5, ISBN13: 978-0-87951-479-2.
Dewey:791.4/36/55. LCCN:93-236035.
                            Audience: **g,l,u,f.** *B* *Choice, 1993.*

Singer, Ben   PN1995.9.M45S56 2001
e Melodrama and Modernity: Early Sensational Cinema and Its
Contexts. E-Book. Columbia University Press. New York, NY.
ISBN:0-231-50507-8, ISBN13: 978-0-231-50507-9.
Dewey:791.43/653.
                            Audience: **u,f.** *Choice, 2001.*

Skinner, James M.   BX1407
The Cross and the Cinema: The Legion of Decency and the
National Catholic Office for Motion Pictures, 1933-1970. Trade
Cloth. Greenwood Publishing Group, Inc. Portsmouth, NH.
1993. 248p. ISBN:0-275-94193-0, ISBN13: 978-0-275-94193-2.
Dewey:791.43. LCCN:92-043431.
                            Audience: **u,f.** *Choice, 1994.*

Staiger, Janet (Editor)   PN1993.5.U65S77 1995
The Studio System. Cloth Text. Rutgers University Press.
Piscataway, NJ. 1994. 275p. Depth of Field Ser.
ISBN:0-8135-2130-0, ISBN13: 978-0-8135-2130-5.
Dewey:791.4/3/0979494. LCCN:94-014489.
                            Audience: **g,l,u,f.**

Sterritt, David   PS228.B6S755 1998
Mad to Be Saved: The Beats, the '50s, and Film. Trade Cloth.
Southern Illinois University Press. Carbondale, IL. 1998. 320p.
ISBN:0-8093-2180-7, ISBN13: 978-0-8093-2180-3.
Dewey:810.9/0054. LCCN:97-043376.
                            Audience: **u,f.** *Choice, 1999.*

Taylor, Greg PN1995
Artists in the Audience: Cults, Camp, and American Film Criticism. Trade Paper. Princeton University Press. Princeton, NJ. 2001. 208p. ISBN:0-691-08955-8, ISBN13: 978-0-691-08955-3. Dewey:791.4/3/015/0973.
Audience: **u,f.** *Choice, 2000.*

Troost, Linda & PR4038.F55J36 1998
Greenfield, Sayre (Editors)
Jane Austen in Hollywood. Trade Cloth. University Press of Kentucky. Lexington, KY. 1998. 240p. ISBN:0-8131-2084-5, ISBN13: 978-0-8131-2084-3. Dewey:791.43/6. LCCN:98-007882.
Audience: **g,l,u,f.** *Choice, 1999.*

Verswijver, Leo PN1993.5.U65V47 2003
Movies Were Always Magical: Interviews with 13 Actors, Directors, and Producers from the Hollywood of the 1950s. Paper Text. McFarland & Company, Incorporated Publishers. Jefferson, NC. 2003. 264p. ISBN:0-7864-1129-5, ISBN13: 978-0-7864-1129-0. Dewey:384/.8/0979494. LCCN:2002-153189.
Audience: **g,l.**

History > By Region and Country > South America

Finkielman, Jorge PN1993.5
The Film Industry in Argentina: An Illustrated Cultural History. Paper Text. McFarland & Company, Incorporated Publishers. Jefferson, NC. 2003. 278p. ISBN:0-7864-1628-9, ISBN13: 978-0-7864-1628-8. Dewey:384/.8/0982. LCCN:2003-024611.
Audience: **g,l.**

Stock, Ann M. (Editor) PN1993.5.L3F73 1997
Framing Latin American Cinema: Contemporary Critical Perspectives. Book, Other. University of Minnesota Press. Minneapolis, MN. 1997. 240p. Hispanic Issues Ser., Vol. 15 ISBN:0-8166-2973-0, ISBN13: 978-0-8166-2973-2. Dewey:791.43/098. LCCN:96-051570.
Audience: **u,f.** *Choice, 1998.*

Individual Films: Analysis, Screenplays, Shooting Scripts

Desser, David (Editor) PN1997.T5953 O92 19
Ozu's Tokyo Story. Horton Andrew (Contribution by). Cloth Text. Cambridge University Press. New York, NY. 1997. 187p. Cambridge Film Handbooks Ser. ISBN:0-521-48204-6, ISBN13: 978-0-521-48204-2. Dewey:791.43/72. LCCN:96-046113.
Audience: **u,f.**

Internet Archive PN1993.4
Moving Image Archive.
http://www.archive.org/details/movies
Audience: **g,l,u,f.**

Kurosawa, Akira PN1997.A1 K8713 1992
The Seven Samurai: And Other Screenplays. Donald Richie (Translator). Trade Paper. Faber & Faber, Inc. New York, NY. 1992. 227p. Classic Screenplay Ser. ISBN:0-571-16224-X, ISBN13: 978-0-571-16224-6. Dewey:791.4375.
Audience: **g,l,u,f.**

McDonald, Keiko PN1997.U373 U34 1993
(Editor)
Ugetsu. Kenji Mizoguchi (Contribution by). Trade Cloth. Rutgers University Press. Piscataway, NJ. 1992. 200p. Films in Print Ser., Vol. 17 ISBN:0-8135-1861-X, ISBN13: 978-0-8135-1861-9. Dewey:791.43/72. LCCN:92-008419.
Audience: **g,l,u.**

Mellen, Joan PN1997
Seven Samurai. Trade Paper. BFI Publishing. London, 2002. 96p. Film Classics ISBN:0-85170-915-X, ISBN13: 978-0-85170-915-4. Dewey:791.4/372.
Audience: **g,l,u.**

Film Industry

Daniels, Bill, et al. PN1993.5.U6D25 2006
Movie Money: Understanding Hollywood's Creative Account Practices. Ed. 2. David Leedy & Steven D. Sills (Authors). Trade Paper. Silman-James Press. Los Angeles, CA. 2006. 297p. ISBN:1-879505-86-X, ISBN13: 978-1-879505-86-5. Dewey:384/.830973. LCCN:2005-035936.
Audience: **u,f.**

De Vany, Arthur S. PN1993.5.U6D34 2003
Hollywood Economics: How Extreme Uncertainty Shapes the Film Industry. Trade Paper. Routledge. New York, NY. 2003. 328p. Contemporary Political Economy Ser. ISBN:0-415-31261-2, ISBN13: 978-0-415-31261-5. Dewey:384/.83/0973. LCCN:2003-046987.
Audience: **u,f.**

Desser, David & Jowett, PN1995.9.S6H65 2000
Garth
Hollywood Goes Shopping. Trade Paper. University of Minnesota Press. Minneapolis, MN. 2000. xxi, 363p. Commerce and Mass Culture Ser., Vol. 3 ISBN:0-8166-3513-7, ISBN13: 978-0-8166-3513-9. Dewey:302.23/43/0973. LCCN:99-056290.
Audience: **g,l,u,f.**

Epstein, Edward Jay PN1993.5.U65
The Big Picture: The New Logic of Money and Power in Hollywood. E-Book. Random House Adult Trade Publishing Group. New York, NY. 2005. ISBN:1-58836-454-2, ISBN13: 978-1-58836-454-8. Dewey:384/.83/0979494.
Audience: **g,l,u,f.** *Choice, 2005.*

Harpole, Charles PN1993.5.U6
(Editor)
History of the American Cinema, Set. Trade Cloth. Thomson Gale. Farmington Hills, MI. 1997. ISBN:0-684-80539-1, ISBN13: 978-0-684-80539-9. Dewey:791.43/0973.
Audience: **g,l,u.**

Hayes, Dade & Bing, PN1993.5.U6H39 2004
Jonathan
Open Wide: How Hollywood Box Office Became a National Obsession. Trade Cloth. Miramax Books. New York, NY. 2004. 448p. ISBN:1-4013-5200-6, ISBN13: 978-1-4013-5200-4. Dewey:384/.83/0973. LCCN:2005-297510.
Audience: **g,l,u,f.**

Hoskins, Colin, et al. PN1993.5.A1H67 1997
Global Television and Film: An Introduction to the Economics of the Business. Stuart McFadyen & Adam Finn (Authors). Paper Text. Oxford University Press, Inc. New York, NY. 1998.

186p. ISBN:0-19-871147-6, ISBN13: 978-0-19-871147-6. Dewey:384.551. LCCN:97-019752.

Audience: **g,l,u.**

Kindem, Gorham A.   **PN1993.5.A1I54 2000**
  (Editor)
The International Movie Industry. Trade Cloth. Southern Illinois University Press. Carbondale, IL. 2000. 432p. ISBN:0-8093-2298-6, ISBN13: 978-0-8093-2298-5. Dewey:384.8. LCCN:99-052977.

Audience: **g,l,u,f.**

Lewis, Jon   **PN1993.5.U6N47 1998**
The New American Cinema. Trade Paper. Duke University Press. Durham, NC. 1998. 392p. ISBN:0-8223-2115-7, ISBN13: 978-0-8223-2115-6. Dewey:384/.83/0973. LCCN:97-035210.

Audience: **g,l,u,f.** *Choice, 1998.*

Moran, Albert (Editor)   **PN1993.5.A1F513 1996**
Film Policy: International, National, and Regional Perspectives. Trade Paper. Routledge. New York, NY. 1996. 304p. Culture, Policy, and Politics Ser. ISBN:0-415-09791-6, ISBN13: 978-0-415-09791-8. Dewey:791.4/3. LCCN:95-048260.

Audience: **g,l,u,f.**

Moul, Charles C.   **PN1993.5.U6**
  (Editor)
e A Concise Handbook of Movie Industry Economics. E-Book. Cambridge University Press. New York, NY. 2005. ISBN:0-511-11020-0, ISBN13: 978-0-511-11020-7. Dewey:384/.83/0973.

Audience: **g,l,u,f.**

Puttnam, David   **PN1993.5.U6P88 1998**
Movies and Money: Undeclared War Between Europe and America. Trade Paper. Knopf Publishing Group. New York, NY. 2000. 364p. ISBN:0-679-76741-X, ISBN13: 978-0-679-76741-1. Dewey:384/.83/0973. LCCN:97-031244.

Audience: **g,l,u,f.** *Choice, 1999.*

Scott, Allen John   **PN1993.5.U65S35 2005**
On Hollywood: The Place, the Industry. Trade Cloth. Princeton University Press. Princeton, NJ. 2004. 264p. ISBN:0-691-11683-0, ISBN13: 978-0-691-11683-9. Dewey:384/.8/0979494. LCCN:2004-044314.

Audience: **g,l,u,f.**

Sedgwick, John &   **PN1993.5.U6S46 2004**
  Pokorny, Michael (Editors)
An Economic History of Film. Paper over Boards. Routledge. New York, NY. 2004. 368p. Routledge Explorations in Economic History Ser., Vol. 26 ISBN:0-415-32492-0, ISBN13: 978-0-415-32492-2. Dewey:384/.83. LCCN:2004-046790.

Audience: **g,l,u.**

Waterman, David   **PN1993.5.U6W39 2005**
Hollywood's Road to Riches. Trade Cloth. Harvard University Press. Cambridge, MA. 2005. 416p. ISBN:0-674-01945-8, ISBN13: 978-0-674-01945-4. Dewey:384/.83/0973. LCCN:2005-046300.

Audience: **g,l,u,f.** *Choice, 2006.*

Film Industry > Production

Balio, Tino   **PN1993.5.U6B28 1995**
Grand Design: Hollywood As a Modern Business Enterprise, 1930-1939. Trade Paper. University of California Press.

Berkeley, CA. 1996. 496p. History of the American Cinema Ser., Vol. 5 ISBN:0-520-20334-8, ISBN13: 978-0-520-20334-1. Dewey:384/.8/0973. LCCN:95-030572.

Audience: **u,f.**

Bordwell, David, et al.   **PN1993.5.U6**
The Classical Hollywood Cinema: Film Style and Mode of Production to 1960. Janet Staiger & Kristin Thompson (Authors). Trade Paper. Columbia University Press. New York, NY. 1987. 506p. ISBN:0-231-06055-6, ISBN13: 978-0-231-06055-4. Dewey:791.43/0973. LCCN:85-000372.

Audience: **u,f.** β *Choice, 1985.*

Koster, Robert   **PN1995.9.P7**
The Budget Book for Film and Television. Ed. 2. Paper Text. Elsevier Science & Technology Books. Saint Louis, MO. 2004. 340p. ISBN:0-240-80620-4, ISBN13: 978-0-240-80620-4. Dewey:791.4302/32. LCCN:2004-556111.

Audience: **u,f.**

Moore, Schuyler M.   **KF4302.M66 2003**
The Biz: The Basic Business, Legal, and Financial Aspects of the Film Industry. Ed. 2. Trade Paper. Silman-James Press. Los Angeles, CA. 2003. 372p. ISBN:1-879505-69-X, ISBN13: 978-1-879505-69-8. Dewey:384/.8/0973. LCCN:2003-041510.

Audience: **l,u,f.**

Film Industry > Distribution, Marketing, Exhibition

Acland, Charles R.   **PN1995.9.A8A28 2003**
Screen Traffic: Movies, Multiplexes, and Global Culture. Trade Cloth. Duke University Press. Durham, NC. 2003. 320p. ISBN:0-8223-3175-6, ISBN13: 978-0-8223-3175-9. Dewey:302.23/43. LCCN:2003-005050.

Audience: **u,f.** *Choice, 2004.*

Bosko, Mark Steven   **PN1995.9.M29B67 2003**
The Complete Independent Movie Marketing Handbook: Promote, Distribute and Sell Your Film or Video. Trade Paper, Perfect. Michael Wiese Productions. Studio City, CA. 2003. 300p. ISBN:0-941188-76-0, ISBN13: 978-0-941188-76-0. Dewey:384/.8/0688. LCCN:2002-154125.

Audience: **u,f.**

Cones, John W.   **PN1993.5.U6C634 1997**
The Feature Film Distribution Deal: A Critical Analysis of the Single Most Important Film Industry Agreement. Trade Cloth. Southern Illinois University Press. Carbondale, IL. 1997. 380p. ISBN:0-8093-2081-9, ISBN13: 978-0-8093-2081-3. Dewey:384/.83/0973. LCCN:96-033733.

Audience: **u,f.**

Cones, John W.   **PN1993.5.U6C635 1992**
Film Finance and Distribution: A Dictionary of Terms. Trade Paper. Silman-James Press. Los Angeles, CA. 1992. 638p. ISBN:1-879505-12-6, ISBN13: 978-1-879505-12-4. Dewey:384/.83/0973. LCCN:92-023667.

Audience: **g,l,u,f.**

Lukk, Tiiu   **PN1995.9.M29L85 1997**
Movie Marketing: Opening the Picture and Giving It Legs. Trade Paper. Silman-James Press. Los Angeles, CA. 1998. 274p. ISBN:1-879505-38-X, ISBN13: 978-1-879505-38-4. Dewey:384/.8.0688. LCCN:97-031744.

Audience: **u,f.**

Marich, Robert PN1995.9.M29M37 2005
Marketing to Moviegoers: A Handbook of Strategies Used by
Major Studios and Independents. Paper Text. Elsevier Science &
Technology Books. Saint Louis, MO. 2005. 312p.
ISBN:0-240-80687-5, ISBN13: 978-0-240-80687-7.
Dewey:791.43/068/8. LCCN:2004-065952.
Audience: **u,f.**

Film Industry > Film Organizations

Houston, Penelope PN1993.4.H68 1994
Keepers of the Frame: The Film Archives. Trade Paper. BFI
Publishing. London, 1994. 176p. ISBN:0-85170-471-9, ISBN13:
978-0-85170-471-5. Dewey:026.791437. LCCN:94-197781.
Audience: **g,l,u,f.** *Choice, 1995.*

International Federation PN1993.I57
  of Film Archives
☐ FIAF Directory.
http://www.fiafnet.org/uk/members/directory.cfm
Audience: **u,f.**

Film Industry > Film Festivals

Bowser, Kathryn PN1993.4.B66 1996
The AIVF Guide to International Film and Video Festivals. Ed.
4. Trade Paper. Foundation for Independent Video & Film, Inc.
New York, NY. 1996. 223p. ISBN:0-9622448-2-1, ISBN13:
978-0-9622448-2-7. Dewey:791.43/079. LCCN:96-216507.
Audience: **g,l,u,f.**

Gore, Chris PN1993.4.G67 2004
The Ultimate Film Festival Survival Guide. Ed. 3. Trade Paper.
Watson-Guptill Publications, Inc. New York, NY. 2004. 477p.
ISBN:1-58065-057-0, ISBN13: 978-1-58065-057-1.
Dewey:791.43/079. LCCN:2004-048770.
Audience: **l,u,f.**

Langer, Adam & PN1993.4.L36 2000
  Barsanti, Chris
The Film Festival Guide: For Filmmakers, Film Buffs and
Industry Professionals. Trade Paper. Chicago Review Press, Inc.
Chicago, IL. 2000. 280p. ISBN:1-55652-415-3, ISBN13:
978-1-55652-415-8. Dewey:791.43/079. LCCN:00-035871.
Audience: **g,l,u,f.**

Nowlan, Robert A. & PN1998
  Nowlan, Gwendolyn W.
An Encyclopedia of Film Festivals. Trade Cloth. Elsevier
Science & Technology Books. Saint Louis, MO. 1989. 380p.
Foundations in Library and Information Science Ser., Vol. 23
ISBN:0-89232-734-0, ISBN13: 978-0-89232-734-8.
Dewey:011/.37. LCCN:88-013152.
Audience: **g,l,u,f.**

Turan, Kenneth PN1993.4 .T865 2002
Sundance to Sarajevo: Film Festivals and the World They Made.
Trade Cloth. University of California Press. Berkeley, CA. 2002.
192p. ISBN:0-520-21867-1, ISBN13: 978-0-520-21867-3.
Dewey:791.43/079. LCCN:2001-044418.
Audience: **u,f.**

Film Industry > Film Awards

Franks, Don PN2270.A93F68 2004
Entertainment Awards: A Music, Cinema, Theatre and
Broadcasting Guide, 1928 Through 2003. Ed. 3. Cloth Text.
McFarland & Company, Incorporated Publishers. Jefferson, NC.
2004. 623p. ISBN:0-7864-1798-6, ISBN13: 978-0-7864-1798-8.
Dewey:791/.079/73. LCCN:2003-026998.
Audience: **g,l,u,f.**

Mowrey, Peter C. PN1993.9.M68 1994
Award Winning Films: A Viewer's Reference to 2700 Acclaimed
Motion Pictures. Paper Text. McFarland & Company,
Incorporated Publishers. Jefferson, NC. 1993. 560p.
ISBN:0-89950-783-2, ISBN13: 978-0-89950-783-5.
Dewey:791.4375079. LCCN:92-56667.
Audience: **g,l,u,f.** *Choice, 1994.*

O'Neil, Tom PN1993.92.O53 2003
Movie Awards: The Ultimate, Unofficial Guide to the Oscars,
Golden Globes, Critica, Guild and Indie Honors. Ed. 13. Trade
Cloth. Penguin Group (USA) Inc. New York, NY. 2003. 880p.
ISBN:0-399-52922-5, ISBN13: 978-0-399-52922-1.
Dewey:791.43/079. LCCN:2003-062419.
Audience: **g,l.**

Osborne, Robert PN1993.92.O82 2003
75 Years of the Oscar: The Official History of the Academy
Awards. Trade Cloth. Abbeville Press, Inc. New York, NY. 2003.
408p. ISBN:0-7892-0787-7, ISBN13: 978-0-7892-0787-6.
Dewey:791.43/079/73. LCCN:2003-045311.
Audience: **g,l,u,f.**

Filmmaking > General Filmmaking Guides

Ascher, Steven & TR850.P54 1999
  Pincus, Edward
The Filmmaker's Handbook: A Comprehensive Guide for the
Digital Age. Ed. 2. Trade Paper. Penguin Group (USA) Inc.
New York, NY. 1999. 448p. ISBN:0-452-27957-7, ISBN13:
978-0-452-27957-5. Dewey:778.5/3. LCCN:98-041665.
Audience: **l,u,f.**

Collier, Maxie D. TR850.C55 2000
The IFILM Digital Video Filmmaker's Handbook. Trade Paper.
Watson-Guptill Publications, Inc. New York, NY. 2000. 325p.
ISBN:1-58065-031-7, ISBN13: 978-1-58065-031-1.
Dewey:778.5/3. LCCN:00-046488.
Audience: **l,u,f.**

Geuens, Jean-Pierre PN1995.9.P7G437 2000
Film Production Theory. Paper Text. State University of New
York Press. Albany, NY. 2000. ix, 308p. SUNY Series, Cultural
Studies in Cinema/Video ISBN:0-7914-4526-7, ISBN13:
978-0-7914-4526-6. Dewey:791.43/0232. LCCN:99-057804.
Audience: **l,u,f.** *Choice, 2000.*

Goodell, Gregory PN1995.9.P7G64 1998
Independent Feature Film Production: A Complete Guide from
Concept Through Distribution. Ed. 4. Trade Cloth. St. Martin's
Press. Gordonville, VA. 1998. 352p. ISBN:0-312-18117-5,
ISBN13: 978-0-312-18117-8. Dewey:791.43/068.
LCCN:82-005746.
Audience: **l,u,f.** *B*

Hines, William E. PN1995.9.P75H56 1999
Job Descriptions for Film, Video and CGI: Responsibilities and
Duties for the Cinematic Craft Categories and Classifications.
Ed. 5. Thomas C. Short (Foreword by). Trade Paper. Ed-Venture
Films/Books. Los Angeles, CA. 1999. 340p.
ISBN:0-935873-02-3, ISBN13: 978-0-935873-02-3.
Dewey:791.43. LCCN:98-093965.
Audience: **l,u.**

Honthaner, Eve Light PN1995.9.P7H66 2001
The Complete Film Production Handbook. Ed. 3. Paper Text.
Elsevier Science & Technology Books. Saint Louis, MO. 2001.
520p. ISBN:0-240-80419-8, ISBN13: 978-0-240-80419-4.
Dewey:791.43/0232. LCCN:00-063598.
Audience: **l,u,f.**

Jolliffe, Genevieve PN1995.9.D6
Guerilla Documentary Film Makers Handbook. Trade Paper.
Continuum International Publishing Group, Ltd. London, 2006.
432p. ISBN:0-8264-1665-9, ISBN13: 978-0-8264-1665-0.
Dewey:070.18.
Audience: **l,u,f.**

Jones, Chris & Jolliffe, PN1995.9.P7
Genevieve
Guerilla Film Makers. Trade Paper. Continuum International
Publishing Group, Ltd. London, 2003. 720p.
ISBN:0-8264-1464-8, ISBN13: 978-0-8264-1464-9.
Dewey:791.4302/3. LCCN:2004-100536.
Audience: **l,u,f.**

Katz, Steven PN1995.9.P7K38 1991
Film Directing Shot by Shot: Visualizing from Concept to
Screen. Paper Text. Michael Wiese Productions. Studio City,
CA. 1991. 366p. Michael Wiese Productions Ser.
ISBN:0-941188-10-8, ISBN13: 978-0-941188-10-4.
Dewey:791.43/0233. LCCN:90-070213.
Audience: **u,f.**

Lumet, Sidney PN1998.3.H58
Making Movies. Trade Paper. Random House, Inc. New York,
NY. 1996. 240p. ISBN:0-679-75660-4, ISBN13:
978-0-679-75660-6. Dewey:791.4/3/0233/092.
Audience: **g,l,u,f.** *Choice, 1995.*

Newton, Dale & PN1995.9.P7N47 2001
Gaspard, John
Digital Filmmaking 101: An Essential Guide to Producing
Low-Budget Movies. Trade Paper, Perfect. Michael Wiese
Productions. Studio City, CA. 2001. 300p. ISBN:0-941188-33-7,
ISBN13: 978-0-941188-33-3. Dewey:791.43/0232.
LCCN:00-068563.
Audience: **l,u.**

Polish, Mark, et al. PN1995.9.P7P57 2005
The Declaration of Independent Filmmaking: An Insider's Guide
to Making Movies Outside of Hollywood. Michael Polish &
Jonathan Sheldon (Authors). Trade Paper, Perfect. Harcourt
Trade Publishers. New York, NY. 2005. 336p.
ISBN:0-15-602952-9, ISBN13: 978-0-15-602952-0.
Dewey:791.4302/3/023. LCCN:2005-008056.
Audience: **l,u,f.**

Reed, Maxine K. & HE8700.4.R43 1999
Reed, Robert M.
Career Opportunities in Television, Cable, Video and
Multimedia: A Comprehensive Guide to More Than 100
Exciting Careers in Television, Video, and New Media. Ed. 4.
Lee Phenner (Editor). Trade Paper. Facts On File, Inc. New

York, NY. 1999. 288p. Career Opportunities Ser.
ISBN:0-8160-3941-0, ISBN13: 978-0-8160-3941-8.
Dewey:384.55/023/73. LCCN:98-051425.
Audience: **l,u.**

Seger, Linda PN1995.9.P7S38 2003
From Script to Screen: The Collaborative Art of Filmmaking.
Ed. 2. Trade Paper. Watson-Guptill Publications, Inc. New York,
NY. 2003. 236p. ISBN:1-58065-054-6, ISBN13:
978-1-58065-054-0. Dewey:791.43/028. LCCN:2003-054671.
Audience: **l,u.**

Simonelli, Rocco & PN1995.9.P7F77 2002
Frumkes, Roy
Shoot Me: Independent Filmmaking from Creative Concept to
Rousing Release. Trade Paper. Allworth Press. New York, NY.
2002. 240p. ISBN:1-58115-247-7, ISBN13: 978-1-58115-247-0.
Dewey:791.43/023. LCCN:2002-013795.
Audience: **l,u,f.**

Strock, Herbert L. PN1995.9.P7S77 2000
Picture Perfect. Trade Cloth. Scarecrow Press, Inc. Lanham,
MD. 2000. 304p. Filmmakers Ser., No. 80
ISBN:0-8108-3815-X, ISBN13: 978-0-8108-3815-4.
Dewey:791.43/023. LCCN:00-041987.
Audience: **u,f.** *Choice, 2001.*

Taub, Eric TR849.A1T38 1994
Gaffers, Grips and Best Boys: From Producer-Director to Gaffer
and Computer Special Effects Creator, a Behind-the-Scenes
Look at Who Does What in the Making of a Motion Picture.
Trade Paper. St. Martin's Press. Gordonville, VA. 1995. 272p.
ISBN:0-312-11276-9, ISBN13: 978-0-312-11276-9.
Dewey:791.43/092/2. LCCN:94-028113.
Audience: **l,u,f.**

Zettl, Herbert TR850
Sight Sound Motion: Applied Media Aesthetics. Ed. 4. Cloth
Text. Thomson Wadsworth. Belmont, CA. 2004. 448p.
ISBN:0-534-52723-X, ISBN13: 978-0-534-52723-5.
Dewey:778.5. LCCN:2004-106598.
Audience: **u,f.**

Filmmaking > Specialized Filmmaking Guides > Acting

Baron, Cynthia & PN1995.9.A26M67 2004
Carson, Diane (Editors)
More Than a Method: Trends and Traditions in Contemporary
Film Performance. Trade Paper. Wayne State University Press.
Detroit, MI. 2004. 424p. Contemporary Approaches to Film and
Television Ser. ISBN:0-8143-3079-7, ISBN13:
978-0-8143-3079-1. Dewey:791.4302/8. LCCN:2004-000534.
Audience: **u,f.**

Barr, Tony PN1995.9.A26B37 1997
Acting for the Camera. Ed. 2. Trade Paper. HarperCollins
Publishers. New York, NY. 1997. 384p. ISBN:0-06-092819-0,
ISBN13: 978-0-06-092819-3. Dewey:791.43/028.
LCCN:97-000993.
Audience: **l,u,f.**

Benedetti, Jean (Editor) PN2122
The Art of the Actor: The Essential History of Acting from
Classical Times to the Present Day. Paper over Boards.
Routledge. New York, NY. 2006. 256p. ISBN:0-87830-203-4,
ISBN13: 978-0-87830-203-1. Dewey:792.02809.
Audience: **l,u,f.**

Bernard, Ian   PN1995.9.A26B47 1998
Film and Television Acting: From Stage to Screen. Ed. 2. Trade
Paper. Elsevier Science & Technology Books. Saint Louis, MO.
1997. 176p. ISBN:0-240-80301-9, ISBN13: 978-0-240-80301-2.
Dewey:791.43/028. LCCN:97-024630.
Audience: **l,u,f.**

Cardullo, Bert (Editor),   PN1995.9.A26P63 1998
et al.
Playing to the Camera: Film Actors Discuss Their Craft. Harry
Geduld, Ronald Gottesman & Leigh Woods (Editors), Stanley
Kauffmann (Foreword by). Cloth over Boards. Yale University
Press. Cumberland, RI. 1998. 384p. ISBN:0-300-06983-9,
ISBN13: 978-0-300-06983-9. Dewey:791.43/028.
LCCN:97-001644.
Audience: **u,f.** *Choice, 1998.*

Comey, Jeremiah   PN1995.9.A26C65 2002
The Art of Film Acting: A Guide for Actors and Directors.
Paper Text. Elsevier Science & Technology Books. Saint Louis,
MO. 2002. 290p. ISBN:0-240-80507-0, ISBN13:
978-0-240-80507-8. Dewey:791.43/028. LCCN:2001-058628.
Audience: **u,f.**

Naremore, James   PN1995.9.A26N37 1988
Acting in the Cinema. Trade Cloth. University of California
Press. Berkeley, CA. 1988. 316p. ISBN:0-520-06228-0, ISBN13:
978-0-520-06228-3. Dewey:791.43/028. LCCN:87-030180.
Audience: **u,f.** *Choice, 1989.*

Stanislavski, Constantin   PN2061.S7 2004
An Actor's Handbook. Ed. 2. Trade Cloth. Routledge. New
York, NY. 2004. 160p. ISBN:0-87830-181-X, ISBN13:
978-0-87830-181-2. Dewey:792.02/8. LCCN:2004-002063.
Audience: **l,u.**

Tucker, Patrick   PN1995.9.A26T8 2003
(Translator)
Secrets of Screen Acting. Ed. 2. UK-B Format Paperback.
Routledge. New York, NY. 2003. 256p. ISBN:0-87830-177-1,
ISBN13: 978-0-87830-177-5. Dewey:791.43/028/023.
LCCN:2003-007434.
Audience: **l,u.**

Wojcik, Pamela   PN1995.9.A26
Robertson
Movie Acting, the Film Reader. Paper over Boards. Routledge.
New York, NY. 2004. 256p. In Focus Ser., :Film Readers
ISBN:0-415-31024-5, ISBN13: 978-0-415-31024-6.
Dewey:791.4/3028.
Audience: **l,u.**

Zucker, Carole (Editor)   PN1995.9.A26M35 1989
Making Visible the Invisible: An Anthology of Original Essays
on Film Acting. Trade Cloth. Scarecrow Press, Inc. Lanham,
MD. 1990. 438p. ISBN:0-8108-2220-2, ISBN13:
978-0-8108-2220-7. Dewey:791.43/028. LCCN:89-036466.
Audience: **u,f.** *Choice, 1991.*

Filmmaking > Specialized Filmmaking Guides > Animation

Anzovin, Steve &   TR897.5
Anzovin, Raf
3D Toons: Creative 3D Design for Cartoonists and Animators.
Trade Paper. Barron's Educational Series, Inc. Hauppauge, NY.

2005. 192p. ISBN:0-7641-2951-1, ISBN13: 978-0-7641-2951-3.
Dewey:741.58. LCCN:2004-107404.
Audience: **l,u,f.**

Beauchamp, Robin   PN1995.7
Designing Sound for Animation. Paper Text. Elsevier Science &
Technology Books. Saint Louis, MO. 2005. 216p.
ISBN:0-240-80733-2, ISBN13: 978-0-240-80733-1.
Dewey:778.5/344. LCCN:2005-279816.
Audience: **u,f.**

Beckerman, Howard S.   NC1765
Animation: The Whole Story. Trade Cloth. Allworth Press. New
York, NY. 2003. 336p. ISBN:1-58115-301-5, ISBN13:
978-1-58115-301-9. Dewey:778.5/347. LCCN:2003-022936.
Audience: **l,u,f.**

Hedgpeth, Kevin &   NC1765.H35 2003
Missal, Stephen
Exploring Drawing for Animation. Trade Paper. Thomson
Delmar Learning. Albany, NY. 2003. 260p. Design Exploration
Ser. ISBN:1-4018-2419-6, ISBN13: 978-1-4018-2419-8.
Dewey:741.5/8. LCCN:2003-008885.
Audience: **l,u,f.**

Wellins, Mike   TR897.7.W46 2005
Storytelling Through Animation. Trade Paper. Charles River
Media. Herndon, VA. 2005. 464p. ISBN:1-58450-394-7,
ISBN13: 978-1-58450-394-1. Dewey:791.43/34.
LCCN:2005-000314.
Audience: **u,f.**

Filmmaking > Specialized Filmmaking Guides > Art Direction and Set Design

Affron, Charles &   PN1995.9.A74A35 1995
Affron, Mirella
Sets in Motion: Art Direction and Film Narrative. Cloth Text.
Rutgers University Press. Piscataway, NJ. 1995. 300p.
ISBN:0-8135-2160-2, ISBN13: 978-0-8135-2160-2.
Dewey:791.43/0233. LCCN:94-039443.
Audience: **u,f.** *Choice, 1995.*

Barnwell, Janet   PN1995.9.S4
Production Design: Architects of the Screen. Trade Paper.
Wallflower Press. London, 2004. 135p. ISBN:1-903364-55-8,
ISBN13: 978-1-903364-55-0. Dewey:791.4/3/025.
Audience: **l,u,f.**

Ettedgui, Peter   PN1995.9.A74
Production Design and Art Direction. Trade Cloth. RotoVision
SA. Hove, 1999. 208p. ISBN:2-88046-364-5, ISBN13:
978-2-88046-364-9. Dewey:791.43/025/0922.
Audience: **u,f.**

Heisner, Beverly   PN1995.9.A74
Production Design in the Contemporary American Film: A
Critical Study of 23 Movies and Their Designers. Paper Text.
McFarland & Company, Incorporated Publishers. Jefferson, NC.
2004. 181p. ISBN:0-7864-1865-6, ISBN13: 978-0-7864-1865-7.
Dewey:791.4/302/0973. LCCN:94-030909.
Audience: **u,f.** *Choice, 1997.*

LoBrutto, Vincent   PN1995.9.A74L63 2002
The Filmmaker's Guide to Production Design. Trade Paper.
Allworth Press. New York, NY. 2002. 240p.

ISBN:1-58115-224-8, ISBN13: 978-1-58115-224-1.
Dewey:791.43/025. LCCN:2002-007998.

Audience: **l,u,f.** *Choice, 2003.*

Olson, Robert **PN1995.9.A74O48 1998**
Art Direction for Film and Video. Ed. 2. Trade Paper. Elsevier
Science & Technology Books. Saint Louis, MO. 1998. 160p.
ISBN:0-240-80338-8, ISBN13: 978-0-240-80338-8.
Dewey:791.4/3/025. LCCN:98-025752.

Audience: **u,f.**

Preston, Ward **PN1995.9.A74P74 1994**
What an Art Director Does: An Introduction to Motion Picture
Production Design. Trade Paper. Silman-James Press. Los
Angeles, CA. 1994. 190p. ISBN:1-879505-18-5, ISBN13:
978-1-879505-18-6. Dewey:791.43/0233. LCCN:94-030605.

Audience: **g,l,u.**

Tashiro, C. S. **PN1995.9.A74T37 1998**
Pretty Pictures: Production Design and the History Film. Trade
Paper. University of Texas Press. Austin, TX. 1998. 252p.
ISBN:0-292-78150-4, ISBN13: 978-0-292-78150-4.
Dewey:791.43/0233. LCCN:97-004762.

Audience: **u,f.**

Filmmaking > Specialized Filmmaking Guides > Cinematography and Lighting

Box, Harry C. **TR891.B68 2003**
Set Lighting Technician's Handbook: Film Lighting Equipment,
Practice, and Electrical Distribution. Ed. 3. Trade Paper. Elsevier
Science & Technology Books. Saint Louis, MO. 2003. 556p.
ISBN:0-240-80495-3, ISBN13: 978-0-240-80495-8.
Dewey:778.5/343. LCCN:2002-192744.

Audience: **u,f.** *Choice, 2004.*

Burum, Stephen H. **TR850**
(Editor)
American Cinematographer Manual. Ed. 9. Trade Cloth. A S C
Holding Corporation. Hollywood, CA. 2004. 887p.
ISBN:0-935578-24-2, ISBN13: 978-0-935578-24-9.
Dewey:778.53.

Audience: **u,f.**

Carlson, Sylvia E. & **TR850.C37 1994**
Carlson, Verne
The Professional Cameraman's Handbook. Ed. 4. Trade Cloth.
Elsevier Science & Technology Books. Saint Louis, MO. 1993.
576p. ISBN:0-240-80080-X, ISBN13: 978-0-240-80080-6.
Dewey:778.5/3. LCCN:93-031799.

Audience: **u,f.**

Malkiewicz, Kris & **TR850.M276 2005**
Mullen, M. David
Cinematography. Ed. 3. Jim Fletcher (Illustrator). Trade Paper.
Simon & Schuster. New York, NY. 2005. 272p.
ISBN:0-7432-6438-X, ISBN13: 978-0-7432-6438-9.
Dewey:778.5/3.

Audience: **g,l,u.**

Mascelli, Joseph V. **TR850.M33 1998**
The Five C's of Cinematography: Motion Picture Filming
Techniques. Trade Paper. Silman-James Press. Los Angeles, CA.
1998. 252p. ISBN:1-879505-41-X, ISBN13: 978-1-879505-41-4.
Dewey:778.5/3. LCCN:98-012705.

Audience: **l,u,f.**

Thompson, Roy **TR850.T377 1998**
Grammar of the Shot. Audio, Other. Elsevier Science &
Technology Books. Saint Louis, MO. 1998. 224p. Media
Manual Ser. ISBN:0-240-51398-3, ISBN13: 978-0-240-51398-0.
Dewey:778.5/3. LCCN:98-022217.

Audience: **u,f.**

Wheeler, Paul **TR845**
Practical Cinematography. Ed. 2. Paper Text. Elsevier Science &
Technology Books. Saint Louis, MO. 2005. 224p.
ISBN:0-240-51962-0, ISBN13: 978-0-240-51962-3.
Dewey:778.5/3. LCCN:2005-296432.

Audience: **l,u,f.**

Filmmaking > Specialized Filmmaking Guides > Costume Design

Bruzzi, Stella **PN1995.9.C56B78 1997**
Undressing Cinema: Clothing and Identity in the Movies. Trade
Paper. Routledge. New York, NY. 1997. 248p.
ISBN:0-415-13957-0, ISBN13: 978-0-415-13957-1.
Dewey:791.43/655. LCCN:97-007260.

Audience: **g,l,u,f.** *Choice, 1998.*

Ingham, Rosemary & **PN2067**
Covey, Liz
The Costume Designer's Handbook: A Complete Guide for
Amateur and Professional Costume Designers. Ed. 2. Trade
Paper. Heinemann. Portsmouth, NH. 1992. 296p.
ISBN:0-435-08607-3, ISBN13: 978-0-435-08607-7.
Dewey:792/.026. LCCN:92-15238.

Audience: **l,u.**

Ingham, Rosemary & **TT507.I47 2003**
Covey, Liz
The Costume Technician's Handbook. Ed. 3. Trade Paper.
Heinemann. Portsmouth, NH. 2003. 544p. ISBN:0-325-00477-3,
ISBN13: 978-0-325-00477-8. Dewey:646.4/78.
LCCN:2003-007797.

Audience: **l,u,f.**

Landis, Deborah **PN2067 .L33 2003**
Nadoolman
Costume Design. Paper Text. Elsevier Science & Technology
Books. Saint Louis, MO. 2003. 176p. Screencraft Ser.
ISBN:0-240-80590-9, ISBN13: 978-0-240-80590-0.
Dewey:791.4/3/026/092.

Audience: **l,u,f.**

Landis, Deborah **TT507**
Nadoolman & Makovsky, Judianna
50 Designers/50 Costumes: Concept to Character. Trade Paper,
Perfect. University of California Press. Berkeley, CA. 2005.
124p. ISBN:0-942102-46-0, ISBN13: 978-0-942102-46-8.
Dewey:791.43026.

Audience: **u,f.**

Leese, Elizabeth **TT507.L42 1990**
Costume Design in the Movies: An Illustrated Guide to the
Work of 157 Great Designers. Ed. 2. Trade Paper. Dover
Publications, Inc. Mineola, NY. 1991. 176p.
ISBN:0-486-26548-X, ISBN13: 978-0-486-26548-3.
Dewey:791.43/026/0922 B. LCCN:90-044762.

Audience: **l,u,f.**

Street, Sarah   **PN1995.9.C56**
Costume and Cinema: Dress Codes in Popular Film. Trade
Paper. Wallflower Press. London, 2002. 144p. Short Cuts Ser.
ISBN:1-903364-18-3, ISBN13: 978-1-903364-18-5.
Dewey:791.43026. LCCN:2002-107151.
                          Audience: **g,l,u,f.** *Choice, 2003.*

Filmmaking > Specialized Filmmaking Guides > Directing

Bordwell, David   **PN1995.9.P7 B635**
Figures Traced in Light: On Cinematic Staging. Trade Cloth.
University of California Press. Berkeley, CA. 2005. 330p.
ISBN:0-520-23226-7, ISBN13: 978-0-520-23226-6.
Dewey:791.4302/33. LCCN:2004-001354.
                          Audience: **u,f.** *Choice, 2006.*

Hart, John   **PN1995.9.P7H42 1998**
The Art of the Storyboard: Storyboarding for Film, TV, and
Animation. Paper Text. Elsevier Science & Technology Books.
Saint Louis, MO. 1998. 240p. ISBN:0-240-80329-9, ISBN13:
978-0-240-80329-6. Dewey:741.5/8. LCCN:98-036549.
                          Audience: **l,u,f.**

Mackendrick,   **PN1995.9.P7**
  Alexander
On Film-Making: An Introduction to the Craft of the Director.
Paul Cronin (Editor), Martin Scorsese (Foreword by). Cloth over
Boards. Faber & Faber, Inc. New York, NY. 2005. 336p.
ISBN:0-571-21561-0, ISBN13: 978-0-571-21561-4.
Dewey:791.4302/33. LCCN:2005-391464.
                          Audience: **l,u.**

Mamet, David   **PN1995.9.P7 M28 1992**
On Directing Film. Trade Paper. Penguin Group (USA) Inc.
New York, NY. 1992. 128p. ISBN:0-14-012722-4, ISBN13:
978-0-14-012722-5. Dewey:791.430233. LCCN:90-050428.
                          Audience: **g,l,u,f.**

Rabiger, Michael   **PN1995.9.P7**
Directing: Film Techniques and Aesthetics. Ed. 3. Paper Text.
Elsevier Science & Technology Books. Saint Louis, MO. 2003.
560p. ISBN:0-240-80517-8, ISBN13: 978-0-240-80517-7.
Dewey:791.43/0233/092. LCCN:2003-040846.
                          Audience: **u,f.**

Weston, Judith   **PN1995.9.P7W45 1996**
Directing Actors: Creating Memorable Performances for Film
and Television. Trade Paper, Perfect. Michael Wiese
Productions. Studio City, CA. 1996. 300p. ISBN:0-941188-24-8,
ISBN13: 978-0-941188-24-1. Dewey:791.43/0233.
LCCN:96-025539.
                          Audience: **u,f.**

Filmmaking > Specialized Filmmaking Guides > Editing

Browne, Steven E.   **TR899.B723 1998**
Nonlinear Editing Basics: A Primer on Electronic Film and
Video Editing. Paper Text. Elsevier Science & Technology
Books. Saint Louis, MO. 1998. 224p. ISBN:0-240-80282-9,
ISBN13: 978-0-240-80282-4. Dewey:778.5/238/0285.
LCCN:98-009166.
                          Audience: **u,f.**

Dancyger, Ken   **TR899.D26 2002**
The Technique of Film and Video Editing: History,Theory, and
Practice. Ed. 3. Paper Text. Elsevier Science & Technology
Books. Saint Louis, MO. 2002. 520p. ISBN:0-240-80420-1,
ISBN13: 978-0-240-80420-0. Dewey:778.5/235.
LCCN:2002-019446.
                          Audience: **u,f.**

Fairservice, Don   **TR899 .F35 2001**
Film Editing: History, Theory and Practice: Looking at the
Invisible. Trade Paper. Manchester University Press. Manchester,
2002. 368p. ISBN:0-7190-5777-9, ISBN13: 978-0-7190-5777-9.
Dewey:778.5/35. LCCN:2001-031223.
                          Audience: **u,f.**

Hollyn, Norman   **TR899**
Film Editing Room Handbook: How to Manage the near Chaos
of the Cutting Room. Ed. 3. Trade Paper. Watson-Guptill
Publications, Inc. New York, NY. 1999. 583p.
ISBN:1-58065-006-6, ISBN13: 978-1-58065-006-9.
Dewey:778.5/35. LCCN:98-030708.
                          Audience: **u,f.**

LoBrutto, Vincent   **TR899**
Selected Takes: Film Editors on Editing. Paper Text. Greenwood
Publishing Group, Inc. Portsmouth, NH. 1991. 264p.
ISBN:0-275-93395-4, ISBN13: 978-0-275-93395-1.
Dewey:778.5/35. LCCN:90-024262.
                          Audience: **u,f.** *Choice, 1991.*

McGrath, Declan   **TR899**
Editing and Postproduction. Audio, Other. Elsevier Science &
Technology Books. Saint Louis, MO. 2001. 176p. Screencraft
Ser. ISBN:0-240-80468-6, ISBN13: 978-0-240-80468-2.
Dewey:778.5/35.
                          Audience: **u,f.**

Murch, Walter (Author,   **TR899.M87 2001**
  Preface by)
In the Blink of an Eye: A Perspective on Film Editing. Ed. 2.
Francis Coppola (Foreword by). Trade Paper. Silman-James
Press. Los Angeles, CA. 2001. 120p. ISBN:1-879505-62-2,
ISBN13: 978-1-879505-62-9. Dewey:778.5/35.
LCCN:2001-042949.
                          Audience: **l,u,f.**

Oldham, Gabriella   **TR899.O43**
First Cut: Conversations with Film Editors. Trade Paper.
University of California Press. Berkeley, CA. 1995. 428p.
ISBN:0-520-07588-9, ISBN13: 978-0-520-07588-7.
Dewey:778.535. LCCN:91-047713.
                          Audience: **l,u,f.**

Orpen, Valerie   **TR899**
Film Editing: The Art of the Expressive. Trade Paper.
Wallflower Press. London, 2003. 144p. Short Cuts Ser.
ISBN:1-903364-53-1, ISBN13: 978-1-903364-53-6.
Dewey:778.5/35.
                          Audience: **l,u.**

Reisz, Karl & Millar,   **TR899**
  Gavin
Technique of Film Editing. Ed. 2. Trade Paper. Elsevier Science
& Technology Books. Saint Louis, MO. 1995. 416p.
ISBN:0-240-51437-8, ISBN13: 978-0-240-51437-6.
Dewey:778.5/35.
                          Audience: **l,u,f.**

Thompson, Roy   **TR899.T49 1993**
Grammar of the Edit. Paper Text. Elsevier Science &
Technology Books. Saint Louis, MO. 1993. 160p. Media
Manual Ser. ISBN:0-240-51340-1, ISBN13: 978-0-240-51340-9.
Dewey:778.5/235. LCCN:93-202020.

Audience: **u,f.**

Filmmaking > Specialized Filmmaking Guides > Makeup

Delamar, Penny   **PN2068**
The Complete Make-up Artist: Working in Film, Television, and
Theatre. Ed. 2. Trade Paper. Northwestern University Press.
Evanston, IL. 2002. 212p. ISBN:0-8101-1969-2, ISBN13:
978-0-8101-1969-7. Dewey:792.027.

Audience: **u,f.**

Kehoe, Vincent J.   **PN1995.9.M25K429**
Special Make-up Effects. Trade Paper. Elsevier Science &
Technology Books. Saint Louis, MO. 1991. 144p.
ISBN:0-240-80099-0, ISBN13: 978-0-240-80099-8.
Dewey:791.43/027. LCCN:90-003924.

Audience: **u,f.**

Musgrove, Jan   **PN1992.8.P4**
Make-up, Hair and Costume for Film and Television. Paper
Text. Elsevier Science & Technology Books. Saint Louis, MO.
2003. 208p. Media Manual Ser. ISBN:0-240-51660-5, ISBN13:
978-0-240-51660-8. Dewey:791.45/027. LCCN:2003-040832.

Audience: **g,l,u,f.**

Timpone, Anthony   **TR858.T56 1996**
Men, Makeup and Monsters: Hollywood's Masters of Illustion
and FX. Trade Paper. St. Martin's Press. Gordonville, VA. 1996.
240p. ISBN:0-312-14678-7, ISBN13: 978-0-312-14678-8.
Dewey:791.4/3/027. LCCN:96-008578.

Audience: **g,l,u,f.**

Vinther, Janus   **PN2068**
Special Effects Make-Up. Trade Cloth. Routledge. New York,
NY. 2003. 256p. ISBN:0-87830-178-X, ISBN13:
978-0-87830-178-2. Dewey:792.027.

Audience: **l,u,f.**

Filmmaking > Specialized Filmmaking Guides > Music

Adorno, Theodor W. &   **MT40.E35 1994**
Eisler, Hanns
Composing for the Films. Graham McCann (Introduction by).
Trade Cloth. Continuum International Publishing Group, Ltd.
London, 1994. 171p. ISBN:0-485-11454-2, ISBN13:
978-0-485-11454-6. Dewey:781.5/4213. LCCN:94-017469.

Audience: **u,f.**

Burt, George D.   **ML2075**
The Art of Film Music. Paper Text. Northeastern University
Press. Boston, MA. 1994. 280p. ISBN:1-55553-270-5, ISBN13:
978-1-55553-270-3. Dewey:781.5/42.

Audience: **u,f.** *Choice, 1995.*

Davis, Richard   **ML2075.D38 1999**
Complete Guide to Film Scoring: The Art and Business of
Writing Music for Movies and TV. Trade Paper. Hal Leonard

Corporation. Milwaukee, WI. 2000. 384p. Music Reference Ser.,
:Music Theory Ser. ISBN:0-634-00636-3, ISBN13:
978-0-634-00636-4. Dewey:781.5/4213. LCCN:00-268228.

Audience: **u,f.**

Karlin, Fred & Wright,   **MT64.M65K3 2003**
Doris
On the Track: A Guide to Contemporary Film Scoring. Ed. 2.
John Williams (Foreword by). UK-B Format Paperback.
Routledge. New York, NY. 2004. 560p. ISBN:0-415-94136-9,
ISBN13: 978-0-415-94136-5. Dewey:781.5/4213.
LCCN:2003-011579.

Audience: **u,f.**

Morgan, David   **ML2075.K58 2000**
Knowing the Score: Film Composers Talk about the Art, Craft,
Blood, Sweat, and Tears of Writing. Trade Paper. HarperCollins
Publishers. New York, NY. 2000. 336p. Masters in Film Ser.,
No. 3 ISBN:0-380-80482-4, ISBN13: 978-0-380-80482-5.
Dewey:781.5/42/0922. LCCN:00-038285.

Audience: **l,u,f.**

Rona, Jeff   **MT64.M65R66 2000**
The Reel World: Scoring for Pictures. Trade Paper. Backbeat
Books. San Francisco, CA. 2000. 272p. ISBN:0-87930-591-6,
ISBN13: 978-0-87930-591-8. Dewey:781.5/4213.
LCCN:00-056058.

Audience: **u,f.**

Filmmaking > Specialized Filmmaking Guides > Producing and Production Management

Houghton, Buck   **PN1995.9.P7 H68 1991**
What a Producer Does: The Art of Moviemaking (Not the
Business). Trade Paper. Silman-James Press. Los Angeles, CA.
1991. 200p. ISBN:1-879505-05-3, ISBN13: 978-1-879505-05-6.
Dewey:791.43/0232. LCCN:92-006748.

Audience: **g,l,u,f.**

Filmmaking > Specialized Filmmaking Guides > Sound

Altman, Rick   **PN1995.7.S69 1992**
Sound Theory - Sound Practice. UK-B Format Paperback.
Routledge. New York, NY. 1992. 304p. AFI Film Readers Ser.
ISBN:0-415-90457-9, ISBN13: 978-0-415-90457-5.
Dewey:791.43. LCCN:91-046026.

Audience: **u,f.** *Choice, 1993.*

Holman, Tomlinson   **TK7881.4 .H63 2002**
Sound for Film and Television. Ed. 2. Paper Text. Elsevier
Science & Technology Books. Saint Louis, MO. 2001. 368p.
ISBN:0-240-80453-8, ISBN13: 978-0-240-80453-8.
Dewey:778.5/344. LCCN:2002-282852.

Audience: **u,f.** *Choice, 1997.*

McGee, Marty   **TK7881.4.M47 2001**
The Encyclopedia of Motion Picture Sound. Cloth Text.
McFarland & Company, Incorporated Publishers. Jefferson, NC.
2001. 300p. ISBN:0-7864-1023-X, ISBN13: 978-0-7864-1023-1.
Dewey:778.5/344/03. LCCN:00-54803.

Audience: **g,l,u,f.** *Choice, 2001.*

Sonnenschein, David   TR897.S66 2001
(Editor)
Sound Design: The Expressive Power of Music, Voice and
Sound Effects in Cinema. Trade Paper, Perfect. Michael Wiese
Productions. Studio City, CA. 2001. 250p. ISBN:0-941188-26-4,
ISBN13: 978-0-941188-26-5. Dewey:778.5/344.
LCCN:2001-035804.

Audience: **u,f.**

Weis, Elisabeth &   PN1995.7.F53 1985
Belton, John (Editors)
Film Sound: Theory and Practice. Trade Paper. Columbia
University Press. New York, NY. 1985. 462p.
ISBN:0-231-05637-0, ISBN13: 978-0-231-05637-3.
Dewey:791.43/024. LCCN:84-023117.

Audience: **u,f.**

Filmmaking > Specialized Filmmaking Guides > Special Effects and Computer Graphics

Mitchell, Mitch   PN1992.8
Visual Effects for Film and Television. Paper Text. Elsevier
Science & Technology Books. Saint Louis, MO. 2004. 248p.
Media Manual Ser. ISBN:0-240-51675-3, ISBN13:
978-0-240-51675-2. Dewey:791.4/5/024.

Audience: **u,f.**

Netzley, Patricia D.   TR858.N48 2000
Encyclopedia of Movie Special Effects. Cloth Text. Greenwood
Publishing Group, Inc. Portsmouth, NH. 1999. 304p.
ISBN:1-57356-167-3, ISBN13: 978-1-57356-167-9.
Dewey:778.5/345. LCCN:99-047733.

Audience: **g,l,u,f.** *Choice, 2000.*

Perisic, Zoran   TR858.P474 2000
Visual Effects Cinematography. Trade Paper. Elsevier Science &
Technology Books. Saint Louis, MO. 1999. 290p.
ISBN:0-240-80351-5, ISBN13: 978-0-240-80351-7.
Dewey:778.5/345. LCCN:99-042963.

Audience: **u,f.**

Pierson, Michele   PN1995.9.S26P54 2002
Special Effects: Still in Search of Wonder. Trade Paper.
Columbia University Press. New York, NY. 2002. 256p. Film
and Culture Ser. ISBN:0-231-12563-1, ISBN13:
978-0-231-12563-5. Dewey:791.43/615. LCCN:2001-055263.

Audience: **u,f.** *Choice, 2002.*

Pinteau, Pascal   TR858.P5613 2004
Special Effects: An Oral History. Trade Cloth. Harry N. Abrams,
Inc. New York, NY. 2005. 568p. ISBN:0-8109-5591-1, ISBN13:
978-0-8109-5591-2. Dewey:778.5/345. LCCN:2004-007699.

Audience: **g,l,u.**

Rickitt, Richard   TR858.R53 2000
Special Effects: The History and the Technique. Trade Cloth.
Watson-Guptill Publications, Inc. New York, NY. 2000. 320p.
Film Reference Essentials Ser. ISBN:0-8230-7733-0, ISBN13:
978-0-8230-7733-5. Dewey:791.43024. LCCN:00-102955.

Audience: **g,l,u,f.** *Choice, 2001.*

Filmmaking > Specialized Filmmaking Guides > Writing

Ackerman, Hal   PN1996
Write Screenplays That Sell - The Ackerman Way: Revelations
of a Remarkable Teacher. Trade Cloth. Tallfellow Press. Los
Angeles, CA. 2003. 320p. ISBN:1-931290-52-0, ISBN13:
978-1-931290-52-4. Dewey:808.2/3.

Audience: **u,f.**

Cooper, Dona   PN1992.7
American Film Institute's Guide to Writing Great Screenplays
for Film and TV, Set. Ed. 2. Trade Cloth. Peterson's.
Lawrenceville, NJ. 1997. 208p. ISBN:0-02-861555-7, ISBN13:
978-0-02-861555-4. Dewey:808.2/25. LCCN:97-070076.

Audience: **l,u,f.**

Dancyger, Ken & Rush, Jeff   PN1996.D36 2001
Alternative Scriptwriting: Successfully Breaking the Rules. Ed.
3. Paper Text. Elsevier Science & Technology Books. Saint
Louis, MO. 2001. 382p. Scriptwriting Ser. ISBN:0-240-80477-5,
ISBN13: 978-0-240-80477-4. Dewey:808.2/3.
LCCN:2001-054538.

Audience: **u,f.**

Field, Syd   PN1996.F43 2005
Screenplay: The Foundations of Screenwriting. Trade Paper.
Dell Publishing. New York, NY. 2005. 336p.
ISBN:0-385-33903-8, ISBN13: 978-0-385-33903-2.
Dewey:808.2/3. LCCN:2005-048491.

Audience: **l,u,f.**

Haddad, Michael   PN1996.H255 2005
The Screenwriter's Sourcebook: A Comprehensive Marketing
Guide for Screen and Television Writers. Trade Paper. Chicago
Review Press, Inc. Chicago, IL. 2005. 384p.
ISBN:1-55652-550-8, ISBN13: 978-1-55652-550-6.
Dewey:808.2/3/0688. LCCN:2004-011483.

Audience: **u,f.**

Horton, Andrew   PN1996
Writing the Character-Centered Screenplay. Ed. 2. Trade Paper.
University of California Press. Berkeley, CA. 2000. 250p.
ISBN:0-520-22165-6, ISBN13: 978-0-520-22165-9.
Dewey:808.2/3. LCCN:93-037307.

Audience: **l,u,f.** *Choice, 1994.*

Howard, David   PN1996
How to Build a Great Screenplay: A Master Class in
Storytelling for Film. Trade Paper. St. Martin's Press.
Gordonville, VA. 2006. 464p. ISBN:0-312-35262-X, ISBN13:
978-0-312-35262-2. Dewey:808.2/3.

Audience: **u,f.**

Karetnikova, Inga   PN1996.K24 1990
How Scripts Are Made. Trade Cloth. Southern Illinois
University Press. Carbondale, IL. 1990. 188p.
ISBN:0-8093-1380-4, ISBN13: 978-0-8093-1380-8.
Dewey:808.2/3. LCCN:89-026186.

Audience: **l,u,f.**

Keane, Christopher   PN1996 .K34 1998
How to Write a Selling Screenplay. Julius Epstein (Foreword
by). Trade Cloth. Broadway Books. New York, NY. 1998. 320p.
ISBN:0-7679-0071-5, ISBN13: 978-0-7679-0071-3.
Dewey:808.2/3. LCCN:97-036109.

Audience: **u,f.**

MacDermott, Felim &   **PN1996**
McGrath, Declan
Screenwriting. Trade Paper. Elsevier Science & Technology
Books. Saint Louis, MO. 2003. 176p. Screencraft Ser.
ISBN:0-240-80512-7, ISBN13: 978-0-240-80512-2.
Dewey:808.2/3. LCCN:2002-007571.

Audience: **u,f.** *Choice, 2003.*

McKee, Robert   **PN1996.M465 1997**
Story: Style, Structure, Substance, and the Principles of
Screenwriting. Trade Cloth. HarperCollins Publishers. New
York, NY. 1997. 480p. ISBN:0-06-039168-5, ISBN13:
978-0-06-039168-3. Dewey:808.2/3. LCCN:97-024139.

Audience: **l,u.**

Mehring, Margaret   **PN1996.M47 1990**
The Screenplay: A Blend of Film Form and Content. Trade
Paper. Elsevier Science & Technology Books. Saint Louis, MO.
1989. 296p. ISBN:0-240-80007-9, ISBN13: 978-0-240-80007-3.
Dewey:808/.066791. LCCN:88-013880.

Audience: **u,f.**

Phillips, William H.   **PN1996.P58 1999**
Writing Short Scripts. Ed. 2. Trade Paper. Syracuse University
Press. Syracuse, NY. 1999. 256p. ISBN:0-8156-2802-1, ISBN13:
978-0-8156-2802-6. Dewey:808.2/3. LCCN:98-053790.

Audience: **l,u,f.**

Riley, Christopher   **PN1996.R48 2005**
The Hollywood Standard: The Complete and Authoritative
Guide to Script Format and Style. Trade Paper. Michael Wiese
Productions. Studio City, CA. 2005. 208p. ISBN:1-932907-01-7,
ISBN13: 978-1-932907-01-8. Dewey:808.2/3.
LCCN:2004-009132.

Audience: **l,u,f.**

Seger, Linda   **PN1997.85.S44 1992**
The Art of Adaptation: Turning Fact and Fiction into Film.
Trade Paper. Henry Holt & Company. New York, NY. 1992.

256p. ISBN:0-8050-1626-0, ISBN13: 978-0-8050-1626-0.
Dewey:808.2/3. LCCN:91-029095.

Audience: **g,l,u,f.**

Seger, Linda   **PN1689.S44 1990**
Creating Unforgettable Characters. Trade Paper. Henry Holt &
Company. New York, NY. 1990. 256p. ISBN:0-8050-1171-4,
ISBN13: 978-0-8050-1171-5. Dewey:808.2. LCCN:89-048877.

Audience: **u,f.**

Seger, Linda (Author,   **PN1996.S384 1994**
Preface by)
Making a Good Script Great. Ed. 2. Trade Cloth. Samuel French
Trade. Hollywood, CA. 1994. 240p. ISBN:0-573-69921-6,
ISBN13: 978-0-573-69921-4. Dewey:808.23. LCCN:94-032338.

Audience: **u,f.**

Straczynski, J. Michael   **PN1661.S75 1996**
The Complete Book of Scriptwriting. Trade Paper. F & W
Publications, Inc. Cincinnati, OH. 2002. 448p.
ISBN:1-58297-158-7, ISBN13: 978-1-58297-158-2.
Dewey:808.2. LCCN:96-030630.

Audience: **l,u.**

Thompson, Kristin   **PN1996.T46 1999**
Storytelling in the New Hollywood: Understanding Classical
Narrative Technique. Trade Paper. Harvard University Press.
Cambridge, MA. 1999. 416p. ISBN:0-674-83975-7, ISBN13:
978-0-674-83975-5. Dewey:808.2/3. LCCN:99-018427.

Audience: **u,f.** *Choice, 2000.*

Trottier, David   **PN1996.T76 2005**
The Screenwriter's Bible: A Complete Guide to Writing,
Formatting, and Selling Your Script. Ed. 4. Trade Paper.
Silman-James Press. Los Angeles, CA. 2005. 386p.
ISBN:1-879505-84-3, ISBN13: 978-1-879505-84-1.
Dewey:808.2/3. LCCN:2005-054119.

Audience: **l,u,f.**

GAY, LESBIAN, BISEXUAL, AND TRANSGENDERED STUDIES

The only subject access to gay, lesbian, bisexual, or transgendered (GLBT) materials in BCL3 was through the subject term "homosexuality," which referred users to Library of Congress classifications HQ75-76.8 and Z7164. This method resulted in only eighteen titles, or less than one percent of all BCL3 titles, clearly associated with GLBT issues.

Since the previous edition of BCL3, the availability of GLBT publications has greatly increased. The development of university-based GLBT studies programs legitimizes academic study of the community and necessitates the identification of a core collection and development of a unique subject taxonomy representing the interdisciplinary nature of the subject.

The entries are organized by subject in a broad taxonomy designed to reflect the interdisciplinary nature of GLBT studies. The resultant titles cross over large sections of the Library of Congress classification system.

The primary subject categories are: general and reference works, history, personal identity, religion, relationships, health, economics, sports, education, politics, creative production, science, and outside North America. Selected areas include subcategories unique to the larger subject area, although general and reference works and biography recur throughout the taxonomy. Occasionally, titles among the categories are duplicated to reflect the scope of each title.

— Ellen Bosman

Abelove, Henry   **HQ76.25.L48 1993**
  (Editor), et al.
Lesbian and Gay Studies Reader. Michele A. Barale & David
M. Halperin (Editors). Paper over Boards. Routledge. New York,
NY. 1993. 666p. ISBN:0-415-90518-4, ISBN13:
978-0-415-90518-3. Dewey:305.90664.

                                        Audience: **g.**

Duberman, Martin   **HQ76.Q44 1997**
  (Editor)
A Queer World: The Center for Lesbian and Gay Studies
Reader. Trade Cloth. New York University Press. New York,
NY. 1997. 719p. ISBN:0-8147-1874-4, ISBN13:
978-0-8147-1874-2. Dewey:306.76/6. LCCN:96-053390.

                                        Audience: **l,u.**

Morton, Donald   **HQ75.15.M37 1996**
  (Editor)
Material Queer: A Lesbigay Cultural Studies Reader. Trade
Paper. Westview Press. Boulder, CO. 1996. 416p. Queer
Critique Ser. ISBN:0-8133-1927-7, ISBN13: 978-0-8133-1927-8.
Dewey:306.7/66. LCCN:96-007423.

                                        Audience: **l,u.**

Robertson, Jennifer   **GN484.35.S36 2005**
  (Editor)
Same-Sex Cultures and Sexualities: An Anthropological Reader.
Trade Cloth. Blackwell Publishing, Inc. Malden, MA. 2004.
320p. Blackwell Readers in Anthropology Ser., Vol. 6
ISBN:0-631-23299-0, ISBN13: 978-0-631-23299-5.
Dewey:306.76/6. LCCN:2003-026674.

                                        Audience: **l,u.**

Sandfort, Theo (Editor),   **HQ75.15.L44 2000**
  et al.
Lesbian and Gay Studies: An Introductory, Interdisciplinary
Approach. Judith Schuyf, Jan Willem Duyvendak & Jeffrey
Weeks (Editors). Paper Text. SAGE Publications, Ltd. London,
2000. 256p. ISBN:0-7619-5418-X, ISBN13: 978-0-7619-5418-7.
Dewey:305.9/0664. LCCN:00-131533.

                                        Audience: **l,u.**

Valocchi, Stephen &   **HQ75.15.Q48 2003**
  Corber, Robert J. (Editors)
Queer Studies: An Interdisciplinary Reader. Trade Cloth.
Blackwell Publishing, Inc. Malden, MA. 2002. 272p.
ISBN:0-631-22916-7, ISBN13: 978-0-631-22916-2.
Dewey:305.9/0664/07. LCCN:2002-026250.

                                        Audience: **l,u.**

General and Reference Works

                                        HQ74
☐ Bisexual Resource Center.
http://www.biresource.org/

                                        Audience: **g.**

                                        HQ76.25
☐ Gay & Lesbian Alliance Against Defamation (GLAAD).
http://www.glaad.org/

                                        Audience: **g.**

                                        HQ76.8.U5
☐ Human Rights Campaign.
http://www.hrc.org/

                                        Audience: **g.**

                                        HQ75.5
☐ Lesbian Herstory Archives.
http://www.lesbianherstoryarchives.org/

                                        Audience: **g.**

                                        HQ76.8.U5
☐ National Gay and Lesbian Task Force.
http://www.thetaskforce.org/

                                        Audience: **g.**

                                        HQ76.8.U5
☐ NCLR: National Center for Lesbian Rights.
http://www.nclrights.org/

                                        Audience: **g.**

                                        HQ75.15
☐ ONE National Gay & Lesbian Archives.
http://www.oneinstitute.org/

                                        Audience: **g,l,u,f.**

                                        HQ75.15
☐ PLFAG (Parents, Families and Friends of Lesbians and
Gays).
http://www.pflag.org/

                                        Audience: **g.**

Adrich, Robert &   **HQ75.7.W488 2002**
  Wotherspoon, Garry (Editors)
Who's Who in Gay and Lesbian History: From Antiquity to
World War II. Ed. 2. Trade Paper. Routledge. New York, NY.
2003. 528p. Who's Who Ser. ISBN:0-415-15983-0, ISBN13:
978-0-415-15983-8. Dewey:306.76/6/0922 B.
LCCN:2002-031734.

                                        Audience: **g.**

Aldrich, Robert &   **HQ75.2**
  Wotherspoon, Garry (Editors)
Who's Who in Contemporary Gay and Lesbian History: From
World War II to the Present Day. Paper over Boards. Routledge.
New York, NY. 2000. 480p. Who's Who Ser.
ISBN:0-415-22974-X, ISBN13: 978-0-415-22974-6.
Dewey:306.76/6/0922 B.
                              Audience: **g.** *Choice, 2001.*

Cowan, Thomas   **HQ75.2.C69 1989**
Gay Men and Women Who Enriched the World. Trade Cloth.
William Mulvey Inc. New Canaan, CT. 1989. 257p.
ISBN:0-934791-16-3, ISBN13: 978-0-934791-16-8.
Dewey:306.7/66/0922. LCCN:88-043401.

                                        Audience: **g.**

Katz, Jonathan N.   **HQ76.3.U5 K37 1992**
Gay American History: Lesbians and Gay Men in the U.S.A.
Trade Paper. Penguin Group (USA) Inc. New York, NY. 1992.
720p. ISBN:0-452-01092-6, ISBN13: 978-0-452-01092-5.
Dewey:306.76/6/0973. LCCN:91-044504.

                                        Audience: **g,l,u,f.**

Murphy, Timothy   **HQ75.15.R43 2000**
  (Editor)
Reader's Guide to Lesbian and Gay Studies. Trade Cloth.
Fitzroy Dearborn Publishers, Inc. Chicago, IL. 2000. 748p.
ISBN:1-57958-142-0, ISBN13: 978-1-57958-142-8.
Dewey:305.9/0664. LCCN:00-698915.
                              Audience: **g.** *Choice, 2000.*

Russell, Paul   **HQ75.2**
The Gay 100: A Ranking of the Most Influential Gay Men and
Lesbians, Past and Present. Trade Paper. Kensington Publishing
Corporation. New York, NY. 2002. 386p. ISBN:0-7582-0100-1,
ISBN13: 978-0-7582-0100-3. Dewey:306.7/66/0922.

Audience: **g.**

General and Reference Works >
Encyclopedias

Blasius, Mark &   **HQ76.W33 1997**
  Phelan, Shane (Editors)
We Are Everywhere: A Historical Sourcebook of Gay and
Lesbian Politics. Paper over Boards. Routledge. New York, NY.
1997. 600p. ISBN:0-415-90858-2, ISBN13: 978-0-415-90858-0.
Dewey:323.3/264. LCCN:95-002434.

Audience: **g,l.**

Conner, Randy P., et al.   **BL795.H6C65 1998**
Cassell's Encyclopedia of Queer Myth, Symbol and Spirit: Gay,
Lesbian, Bisexual and Transgender Lore. David H. Sparks &
Mariya Sparks (Authors). Trade Paper. Continuum International
Publishing Group, Ltd. London, 1998. 400p. Cassell Sexual
Politics Ser. ISBN:0-304-70423-7, ISBN13: 978-0-304-70423-1.
Dewey:291.1/3/08664. LCCN:98-020180.

Audience: **g,l,u,f.**

Haggerty, George   **HQ75.13.G37 2000**
  (Editor)
Gay Histories and Cultures. Trade Cloth. Garland Publishing,
Inc. New York, NY. 1999. 800p. Special - Reference Ser.
ISBN:0-8153-1880-4, ISBN13: 978-0-8153-1880-4.
Dewey:306.76/6/03. LCCN:99-040905.

Audience: **g.** *Choice, 2000.*

Hogan, Steve   **HQ75.H63 1998**
Completely Queer: The Gay and Lesbian Encyclopedia. Trade
Cloth. Henry Holt & Company. New York, NY. 1998. 704p.
ISBN:0-8050-3629-6, ISBN13: 978-0-8050-3629-9.
Dewey:305.9/0664. LCCN:96-022676.

Audience: **g.** *Choice, 1998.*

Stein, Marc (Editor)   **HQ76.3.U5E53 2003**
Encyclopedia of Lesbian, Gay, Bisexual and Transgendered
History in America. Trade Cloth. Thomson Gale. Farmington
Hills, MI. 2003. 1200p. ISBN:0-684-31261-1, ISBN13:
978-0-684-31261-3. Dewey:306.76/6/097303.
LCCN:2003-017434.

Audience: **g.** *Choice, 2004.*

Summers, Claude J.,   **HQ75.13**
  editor
⬚ glbtq: The Online Encyclopedia of Gay, Lesbian, Bisexual,
Transgender, and Queer Culture.
http://www.glbtq.com/
glbtq, Inc.

Audience: **g,l,u,f.**

Zimmerman, Bonnie   **HQ75.5.L4395 2000**
  (Editor)
Lesbian Histories and Cultures. Trade Cloth. Garland
Publishing, Inc. New York, NY. 1999. 800p. Special - Reference
Ser., Vol. 1 ISBN:0-8153-1920-7, ISBN13: 978-0-8153-1920-7.
Dewey:306.76/63/03. LCCN:99-045010.

Audience: **g,l,u,f.** *Choice, 2000.*

General and Reference Works >
Dictionaries

Baker, Paul   **PE3727.G39B34 2002**
Fantabulosa: The Dictionary of Polari and Gay Slang. Trade
Cloth. Continuum International Publishing Group, Ltd. London,
2003. 240p. ISBN:0-8264-5961-7, ISBN13: 978-0-8264-5961-9.
Dewey:427/.0086/64. LCCN:2002-073324.

Audience: **g,l,u,f.**

Gale, Robert L.   **E169**
The Gay Nineties in America: A Cultural Dictionary of the
1890s. Cloth Text. Greenwood Publishing Group, Inc.
Portsmouth, NH. 1992. 488p. ISBN:0-313-27819-9, ISBN13:
978-0-313-27819-8. Dewey:973.8. LCCN:91-047061.

Audience: **g,l,u,f.** *Choice, 1993.*

Hunt, Ronald J.   **HQ76.5.H86 1999**
Historical Dictionary of the Gay Liberation Movement: Gay
Men and the Quest for Social Justice. Trade Cloth. Scarecrow
Press, Inc. Lanham, MD. 1999. 266p. Historical Dictionaries of
Religions, Philosophies, and Movements Ser., No. 22:
ISBN:0-8108-3587-8, ISBN13: 978-0-8108-3587-0.
Dewey:305.9/0664. LCCN:98-039383.

Audience: **g,l,u.** *Choice, 1999.*

Murray, Raymond   **PN1995.9.H55M87 199**
Images in the Dark: An Encyclopedia of Gay and Lesbian Film
and Video. T L A Video Management, Inc. 1994.
ISBN:1-880707-01-2, ISBN13: 978-1-880707-01-2.

Audience: **g,l.**

Myers, JoAnne   **HQ76.5.M94 2003**
Historical Dictionary of the Lesbian Liberation Movement: Still
the Rage. Trade Cloth. Scarecrow Press, Inc. Lanham, MD.
2003. 360p. Historical Dictionaries of Religions, Philosophies,
and Movements Ser., No. 45 ISBN:0-8108-4506-7, ISBN13:
978-0-8108-4506-0. Dewey:305.9/0664. LCCN:2002-156624.

Audience: **g,l.** *Choice, 2004.*

Rauch, Karen &   **HQ75.17.F47 1997**
  Fessler, Jeff
When Drag Is Not a Car Race: An Irreverent Dictionary of over
400 Gay and Lesbian Words and Phrases. Trade Paper. Simon &
Schuster. New York, NY. 1997. 128p. ISBN:0-684-83081-7,
ISBN13: 978-0-684-83081-0. Dewey:306.76/6/03.
LCCN:97-011165.

Audience: **g.**

Rodgens, Bruce   **HQ9.R63 1979**
Gay Talk: A (Sometimes Outrageous) Dictionary of Gay Slang.
Trade Paper, Other. Penguin Group (USA) Inc. New York, NY.
1979. ISBN:0-399-50392-7, ISBN13: 978-0-399-50392-4.
Dewey:301.41/57/03. LCCN:79-013972.

Audience: **g.**

Schanke, Robert A.   **PN2286.5.G38 2005**
  (Editor), et al.
The Gay and Lesbian Theatrical Legacy: A Biographical
Dictionary of Major Figures in American Stage History in the
Pre-Stonewall Era. Kimberley Bell Marra & Billy J. Harbin
(Editors). Trade Cloth. University of Michigan Press. Chicago,
IL. 2005. 440p. Triangulations Ser., :Lesbian/Gay/Queer
Theater/Drama/Performance Ser. ISBN:0-472-09858-6, ISBN13:
978-0-472-09858-3. Dewey:792/.092/273 B.
LCCN:2004-020338.

Audience: **g,l.** *Choice, 2005.*

General and Reference Works > Bibliographies

Bullough, Vern L., et al.   **Z7164.S42**
An Annotated Bibliography of Homosexuality. W. Dorr Legg &
Barrett W. Elcano (Authors). Library Binding. Garland
Publishing, Inc. New York, NY. 1976. 1000p. Reference Library
of Social Science ISBN:0-8240-9959-1, ISBN13:
978-0-8240-9959-6. Dewey:016.3067/66. LCCN:75-024106.
Audience: **g,l,u,f.**

Day, Frances Ann   **Z1037**
Lesbian and Gay Voices: An Annotated Bibliography and Guide
to Literature for Children and Young Adults. Nancy Garden
(Foreword by). Cloth Text. Greenwood Publishing Group, Inc.
Portsmouth, NH. 2000. 296p. Culture and Customs of Asia Ser.
ISBN:0-313-31162-5, ISBN13: 978-0-313-31162-8.
Dewey:951.9. LCCN:00-021047.
Audience: **g,l,u,f.** *Choice, 2000.*

Furtado, Ken &   **Z1229.G25.F87 1993**
Hellner, Nancy
Gay and Lesbian American Plays: An Annotated Bibliography.
Terry Helbing (Foreword by). Trade Cloth. Scarecrow Press,
Inc. Lanham, MD. 1993. 233p. ISBN:0-8108-2689-5, ISBN13:
978-0-8108-2689-2. Dewey:016.812009920664.
LCCN:93-017078.
Audience: **g,l,u,f.** *Choice, 1994.*

Garber, Linda   **Z5866.L44.G37 1993**
Lesbian Sources: A Bibliography of Periodical Articles,
1970-1990. Cloth Text. Garland Publishing, Inc. New York, NY.
1992. 736p. Gay and Lesbian Studies, Vol. 9
ISBN:0-8153-0782-9, ISBN13: 978-0-8153-0782-2.
Dewey:016.3067663. LCCN:92-021941.
Audience: **g,l,u,f.** *Choice, 1993.*

Grier, Barbara   **PN56.L45**
The Lesbian in Literature: A Bibliography. Ed. 3. Trade Paper.
Bella Books, Inc. Tallahassee, FL. 1981. 200p.
ISBN:0-930044-23-1, ISBN13: 978-0-930044-23-7.
Dewey:016.8088/0353. LCCN:81-082859.
Audience: **g.**

Horner, Tom   **BR115.H6**
Homosexuality and the Judeo-Christian Tradition: An Annotated
Bibliography. Trade Cloth. Scarecrow Press, Inc. Lanham, MD.
1981. 141p. American Theological Library Association
Monograph, No. 5 ISBN:0-8108-1412-9, ISBN13:
978-0-8108-1412-7. Dewey:016.2618/3576. LCCN:81-000899.
Audience: **g,l,u,f.**

Katz, Jonathan N.   **HQ76**
(Editor)
A Gay Bibliography: Eight Bibliographies on Lesbian and Male
Homosexuality: an Original Anthology. Trade Cloth. Ayer
Company Publishers, Inc. Manchester, NH. 1975.
Homosexuality Ser. ISBN:0-405-07349-6, ISBN13:
978-0-405-07349-6. Dewey:016.30141/57. LCCN:75-012317.
Audience: **g,l,u,f.**

Maggiore, Dolores J.   **Z7164.H74**
Lesbianism: An Annotated Bibliography and Guide to the
Literature, 1976-1986. Ed. 2. Trade Cloth. Scarecrow Press, Inc.
Lanham, MD. 1992. 271p. ISBN:0-8108-2617-8, ISBN13:
978-0-8108-2617-5. Dewey:016.3067/663. LCCN:92-034699.
Audience: **g.**

Nordquist, Joan   **HQ75.27**
(Editor)
Gay and Lesbian Families: A Bibliography. Trade Paper.
Reference & Research Services. Santa Cruz, CA. 2000. 72p.
Contemporary Social Issues, Vol. 57:A Bibliographic Series
ISBN:1-892068-12-5, ISBN13: 978-1-892068-12-5.
Dewey:306.85.
Audience: **g,l,u,f.**

Nordquist, Joan (Editor,   **HQ76.25**
Compiled by)
Queer Theory: A Bibliography. Trade Paper. Reference &
Research Services. Santa Cruz, CA. 1997. 72p. Social Theory,
Vol. 48:A Bibliographic Ser. ISBN:0-937855-95-2, ISBN13:
978-0-937855-95-9. Dewey:016.30676/6. LCCN:98-184500.
Audience: **l,u,f.**

Parker, William   **Z7164.S42 P35**
Homosexuality: A Selective Bibliography of Over Three
Thousand Items. Trade Cloth. Scarecrow Press, Inc. Lanham,
MD. 1971. ISBN:0-8108-0425-5, ISBN13: 978-0-8108-0425-8.
Dewey:016.30141/57. LCCN:71-163430.
Audience: **g.** *B*

Parker, William   **Z7164.S42**
Homosexuality Bibliography: Supplement, 1970-1975. Trade
Cloth. Scarecrow Press, Inc. Lanham, MD. 1977. 343p.
ISBN:0-8108-1050-6, ISBN13: 978-0-8108-1050-1.
Dewey:016.30141'57. LCCN:77-001114.
Audience: **g.**

Parker, William   **Z7164.S42P34 1985**
Homosexuality Bibliography: Second Supplement, 1976-1982.
Trade Paper. Scarecrow Press, Inc. Lanham, MD. 1985. 401p.
ISBN:0-8108-1753-5, ISBN13: 978-0-8108-1753-1.
Dewey:016.3067/66. LCCN:84-020299.
Audience: **g.**

Ridinger, Robert B.   **Z6174**
(Compiled by)
The Homosexual and Society: An Annotated Bibliography, 18.
Cloth Text. Greenwood Publishing Group, Inc. Portsmouth, NH.
1990. 456p. Bibliographies and Indexes in Sociology Ser., No.
18 ISBN:0-313-25357-9, ISBN13: 978-0-313-25357-7.
Dewey:016.30676/6. LCCN:90-031738.
Audience: **g.** *Choice, 1990.*

Watts, Tim J.   **Z7164.S42W38 1990**
Gay Couples and the Law: A Bibliography. Trade Cloth. Vance
Bibliographies. Monticello, IL. 1990. 13p. Public Administration
Ser., No. 2810 ISBN:0-7920-0430-2, ISBN13:
978-0-7920-0430-1. Dewey:16.3067. LCCN:90-197013.
Audience: **g,l,u,f.**

Weinberg, Martin &   **Z7164.S42W425**
Bell, Alan (Editors)
Homosexuality: An Annotated Bibliography. Trade Cloth.
HarperCollins Publishers. New York, NY. 1972.
ISBN:0-06-014541-2, ISBN13: 978-0-06-014541-5.
Dewey:016.30141/57. LCCN:70-160653.
Audience: **g.**

Young, Ian   **Z2014.H6**
The Male Homosexual in Literature: A Bibliography. Ed. 2.
Trade Cloth. Scarecrow Press, Inc. Lanham, MD. 1982. 360p.
ISBN:0-8108-1529-X, ISBN13: 978-0-8108-1529-2.
Dewey:016.8209/35206642. LCCN:82-000785.
Audience: **g.**

General and Reference Works > Quotations

Derus, Richard M.   **PN6084.L6I52 1996**
(Editor)
In Your Eyes: Quotations on Gay Love. Cloth over Boards. St.
Martin's Press. Gordonville, VA. 1996. 86p.
ISBN:0-312-14057-6, ISBN13: 978-0-312-14057-1.
Dewey:302.3. LCCN:95-042858.
    Audience: **g.**

Gould, Allan   **PN6084.G35W48 1995**
What Did They Say about Gays? Trade Cloth. ECW Press.
Toronto, ON. 1995. 108p. ISBN:1-55022-235-X, ISBN13:
978-1-55022-235-7. Dewey:082/.08/664. LCCN:95-193983.
    Audience: **g.**

Grahn, Judy Rae   **HQ76.25.U5G73 1990**
Another Mother Tongue: Gay Words, Gay Worlds. Trade Paper.
Beacon Press. Boston, MA. 1990. 354p. Gay, Lesbian, and
Gender Studies ISBN:0-8070-7911-1, ISBN13:
978-0-8070-7911-9. Dewey:306.76/6. LCCN:90-052597.
    Audience: **g,l,u,f.**

Rutledge, Leigh &   **PN6084.G35T66 2000**
Hancock, Gregory R. (Editors)
Too Much of a Good Thing...: Quotes You Can't Get Enough
Of. Trade Cloth. Alyson Publications. Los Angeles, CA. 2000.
259p. ISBN:1-55583-413-2, ISBN13: 978-1-55583-413-5.
Dewey:306.766. LCCN:00-045364.
    Audience: **g.**

Smith, Patricia Juliana   **PN6084.G35B66**
(Editor)
The Book of Gay and Lesbian Quotations: A Collection of
3,000 Thoughts, Insights, Views, and Perceptions from Antiquity
to the Present. Trade Paper. DIANE Publishing Company.
Collingdale, PA. 1999. 415p. ISBN:0-7567-6468-8, ISBN13:
978-0-7567-6468-5. Dewey:808.882.
    Audience: **g.**

Theophano, Teresa   **PN6084.G35Q45 2004**
Queer Quotes: On Coming Out and Culture, Love and Lust,
Politics and Pride, and Much More. Trade Cloth. Beacon Press.
Boston, MA. 2004. 192p. ISBN:0-8070-7906-5, ISBN13:
978-0-8070-7906-5. Dewey:306.76/6. LCCN:2004-004490.
    Audience: **g.**

Usukawa, Saejo   **HQ76.25**
The Little Lavender Book: Quotations on Gays and Lesbians.
Trade Paper. Arsenal Pulp Press. Vancouver, BC. 1994. 96p.
ISBN:1-55152-004-4, ISBN13: 978-1-55152-004-9.
Dewey:306.76/6.
    Audience: **g.**

General and Reference Works > Directories/Handbooks/Almanacs

Dynes, Wayne R.   **Z7164.S42D96 1987**
Homosexuality: A Research Guide. Paper over Boards. Garland
Publishing, Inc. New York, NY. 1987. 880p.
ISBN:0-8240-8692-9, ISBN13: 978-0-8240-8692-3.
Dewey:016.3067/66. LCCN:85-045109.
    Audience: **g.** *Choice, 1987.*

Ellis, Alan, et al.   **HQ76.25.H375 2002**
The Harvey Milk Institute Guide to Lesbian, Gay, Bisexual,
Transgender and Queer Internet Research. Liz Highley, Kevin
Schaub & Melissa White (Authors). Trade Cloth. Haworth Press,
Incorporated, The. Binghamton, NY. 2003. 180p. Gay and
Lesbian Studies ISBN:1-56023-353-2, ISBN13:
978-1-56023-353-4. Dewey:025.04/086/64. LCCN:2001-039707.
    Audience: **g.**

Essed, Philomenia &   **HQ1075.C656 2005**
Goldberg, David Theo (Editors)
Companion to Gender Studies. Trade Cloth. Blackwell
Publishing, Inc. Malden, MA. 2004. 576p. Blackwell
Companions in Cultural Studies, Vol. 8 ISBN:0-631-22109-3,
ISBN13: 978-0-631-22109-8. Dewey:305.3/072.
LCCN:2004-006865.
    Audience: **g,l,u,f.** *Choice, 2005.*

Katz, Jonathan N.   **HQ76.8.U5K37 1994**
Gay and Lesbian Almanac. Trade Paper. Avalon Publishing
Group. New York, NY. 1994. 724p. ISBN:0-7867-0148-X,
ISBN13: 978-0-7867-0148-3. Dewey:306.7/66/0973.
LCCN:94-025730.
    Audience: **g.**

Kranz, Rachel &   **HQ76.8.U5K73 2005**
Cusick, Tim
Gay Rights. Ed. 2. Trade Cloth. Facts On File, Inc. New York,
NY. 2005. 368p. Library in a Book ISBN:0-8160-5810-5,
ISBN13: 978-0-8160-5810-5. Dewey:323.3/264/0973.
LCCN:2005-009832.
    Audience: **g.** *Choice, 2006, 2001.*

National Museum and   **HQ76.3.U5G367 1996**
**Archive of Lesbian and Gay History & Program of the
Lesbian and Gay Community Services Staff**
The Gay Almanac: The Most Comprehensive Reference Source
of Its Kind. Trade Paper. Penguin Group (USA) Inc. New York,
NY. 1996. 544p. ISBN:0-425-15300-2, ISBN13:
978-0-425-15300-0. Dewey:305.90664. LCCN:96-162965.
    Audience: **g.** *Choice, 1996.*

Ochs, Robyn (Editor)   **HQ74**
Bisexual Resource Guide. Ed. 4. Trade Paper. Bisexual Resource
Center. Cambridge, MA. 2001. 296p. ISBN:0-9653881-3-1,
ISBN13: 978-0-9653881-3-9. Dewey:306.765.
    Audience: **g.**

Smith, Raymond A. &   **HQ76.3.U5S59 2002**
Haider-Markel, Donald P.
Gay and Lesbian Americans and Political Participation: A
Reference Handbook. E-Book. ABC-CLIO, Inc. Santa Barbara,
CA. 2003. Political Participation in America Ser.
ISBN:1-57607-731-4, ISBN13: 978-1-57607-731-3.
Dewey:305.9/0664/0973.
    Audience: **g.** *Choice, 2003.*

St. James Press Staff   **HQ76.3.U5S75 1998**
St. James Press Gay and Lesbian Almanac. Neil Schlager
(Editor). Trade Cloth. Thomson Gale. Farmington Hills, MI.
1998. 680p. ISBN:1-55862-358-2, ISBN13: 978-1-55862-358-3.
Dewey:305.906. LCCN:98-006156.
    Audience: **g.** *Choice, 1999.*

Summers, Claude J.   **PN56.H57G365 2002**
(Editor)
Gay and Lesbian Literary Heritage: A Reader's Companion to
the Writers and Their Works, from Antiquity to the Present. Ed.

Formats: Web: ☐   Ebook: **e**   CD/DVD-ROM: 🌣   BCL3: **B**

2. Paper over Boards. Routledge. New York, NY. 2002. 864p.
ISBN:0-415-92926-1, ISBN13: 978-0-415-92926-4.
Dewey:809/.8920664. LCCN:2002-022120.

Audience: **g.**

Witt, Lynn (Editor), et al.   **HQ76.3.U5**
Out in All Directions: The Almanac of Gay and Lesbian
America. Sherry Thomas & Eric Marcus (Editors). Trade Cloth.
DIANE Publishing Company. Collingdale, PA. 2004. 635p.
ISBN:0-7567-7552-3, ISBN13: 978-0-7567-7552-0.
Dewey:305.9/0664.

Audience: **g.**

General and Reference Works >
Indexes/Abstracts

HQ75
☐ Alternative Press Index.
http://www.altpress.org/
The Alternative Press Center (APC).

Audience: **g.**

HQ75.A38 SUPPL.
An Index to the Advocate: The National Gay Newsmagazine
1967-1982. Trade Cloth. Liberation Publications, Inc. Los
Angeles, CA. 1988. ISBN:0-917076-08-7, ISBN13:
978-0-917076-08-4. Dewey:305. LCCN:88-186989.

Audience: **g.**

Damon, Gene   **HQ76.3.U5**
Index to the Ladder, Vols I-XVI, 1956-1972. Arno (reprint).
1973.

Audience: **g.**

Malinowsky, H. Robert   **HQ76.25.M35 1987**
International Directory of Gay and Lesbian Periodicals. Trade
Paper. Greenwood Publishing Group, Inc. Portsmouth, NH.
1987. 240p. ISBN:0-89774-297-4, ISBN13: 978-0-89774-297-9.
Dewey:306.7/66/025. LCCN:86-043114.

Audience: **g,l,u,f.** *Choice, 1987.*

Potter, Clare (Compiled by)   **HQ75.6.U5P68 1986**
The Lesbian Periodicals Index. Joan Nestle & Deborah Edel
(Preface by). Trade Paper. Bella Books, Inc. Tallahassee, FL.
1986. 432p. ISBN:0-930044-74-6, ISBN13: 978-0-930044-74-9.
Dewey:016.3067/663. LCCN:85-021798.

Audience: **g,l,u,f.**

General and Reference Works >
Databases

HQ75
☐ Alternative Press Index.
http://www.altpress.org/
The Alternative Press Center (APC).

Audience: **g.**

HQ75
☐ GLBT Life with Full Text.
http://www.epnet.com/
EBSCO Publishing.

Audience: **g,l,u,f.**

HQ75
☐ Sexual Diversity Studies: Gay, Lesbian, Bisexual &
Transgender Abstracts.
http://www.nisc.com/
NISC.

Audience: **g,l,u,f.**

General and Reference Works >
Periodicals

HQ76.8.U5
The Advocate. L P I Media. 1967.

Audience: **g.**

HQ56
American Journal of Sexuality Education. Haworth Press. 1975.

Audience: **l,u,f.**

HQ75
Gay & Lesbian Review Worldwide. Gay & Lesbian Review,
Inc. 2000.

Audience: **g.**

HQ75.15.G57
GLQ: A Journal of Lesbian and Gay Studies. Duke University
Press. 1993.

Audience: **l,u,f.**

RC560.G45
International Journal of Transgenderism: The Official Journal of
the Harry Benjamin International Gender Dysphoria Association.
Haworth Press.

Audience: **l,u,f.**

HQ74
Journal of Bisexuality. Haworth Press. 2000.

Audience: **l,u,f.**

Journal of G L B T Family Studies. Haworth Press. 2005.

Audience: **l,u,f.**

Journal of G L B T Issues in Counseling. Haworth Press. 2006.

Audience: **l,u,f.**

RC558
Journal of Gay & Lesbian Issues in Education: An International
Quarterly Devoted to Research, Theory, and Practice. Haworth
Press. 2003.

Audience: **l,u,f.**

RC558
Journal of Gay & Lesbian Psychotherapy. Haworth Press. 1988.

Audience: **l,u,f.**

HV1449
Journal of Gay & Lesbian Social Services. Haworth Press. 1994.

Audience: **l,u,f.**

HQ75
Journal of Homosexuality. Harrington Park Press. 1974.

Audience: **l,u,f.**

Journal of L G B T Health Research. Haworth Press. 2006.

Audience: **l,u,f.**

HQ75

Journal of Lesbian Studies. Harrington Park Press. 1997.

Audience: **l,u,f.**

Journal of the History of Sexuality. The University of Texas.
1990.

Audience: **l,u,f.**

Lambda Book Report. Lambda Literary Foundation. 1987.

Audience: **g.**

History

Altman, Dennis   **HQ76.3.U5.A4 1982**
The Homosexualization of America: The Americanization of the
Homosexual. Trade Cloth. St. Martin's Press. Gordonville, VA.
1982. 252p. ISBN:0-312-38888-8, ISBN13: 978-0-312-38888-1.
Dewey:306.7/66/0973. LCCN:81-023193.

Audience: **g.** *B*

Angelides, Steven   **HQ74.A54 2001**
A History of Bisexuality. Trade Cloth. University of Chicago
Press. Chicago, IL. 2001. 296p. Chicago Series on Sexuality,
History and Society ISBN:0-226-02089-4, ISBN13:
978-0-226-02089-1. Dewey:306.76/5. LCCN:00-013141.

Audience: **g,l,u,f.**

Bailey, D. Sherwin   **HQ76.B3 1975**
Homosexuality and the Western Christian Tradition. Trade
Cloth. Shoe String Press, Inc. North Haven, CT. 1975. xii, 181p.
ISBN:0-208-01492-6, ISBN13: 978-0-208-01492-4.
Dewey:301.41/57. LCCN:74-034384.

Audience: **g,l.**

Bullough, Vern L.   **HQ76.25.B84**
Homosexuality: A History. Trade Paper. Penguin Group (USA)
Inc. New York, NY. 1979. ISBN:0-452-00725-9, ISBN13:
978-0-452-00725-3. Dewey:306.7/6/09.

Audience: **g,l,u.**

Bullough, Vern L.   **HQ71**
Sexual Variance in Society and History. Library Binding.
University of Chicago Press. Chicago, IL. 1980. xvii, 715p.
ISBN:0-226-07995-3, ISBN13: 978-0-226-07995-0.
Dewey:301.41/5/09. LCCN:79-026504.

Audience: **l,u,f.** *B*

Chauncey, George   **HQ76.2.U52**
Gay New York: Gender, Urban Culture, and the Making of the
Gay Male World 1890-1940. Trade Paper. Basic Books. New
York, NY. 1995. 496p. ISBN:0-465-02621-4, ISBN13:
978-0-465-02621-0. Dewey:305.9/06642/0973.

Audience: **g,l,u,f.** *Choice, 1994.*

Cory, Donald W.   **HQ76.3.U5C67 1975**
The Homosexual in America: A Subjective Approach. Trade
Cloth. Ayer Company Publishers, Inc. Manchester, NH. 1975.
Homosexuality Ser. ISBN:0-405-07365-8, ISBN13:
978-0-405-07365-6. Dewey:301.41/57/0973. LCCN:75-012310.

Audience: **g,l,f.**

D'Emilio, John &   **HQ18.U5D45 1997**
  Freedman, Estelle B.
Intimate Matters: A History of Sexuality in America. Ed. 2.
Trade Paper. University of Chicago Press. Chicago, IL. 1998.
466p. ISBN:0-226-14264-7, ISBN13: 978-0-226-14264-7.
Dewey:306.7/0973. LCCN:97-025238.

Audience: **u,f.** *Choice, 1988.*

Duberman, Martin B.   **HQ76.25.H527 1989**
  (Editor), et al.
Hidden from History: Reclaiming the Gay and Lesbian Past.
Martha Vicinus & George Chauncey Jr. (Editors). Trade Cloth.
Penguin Group (USA) Inc. New York, NY. 1989. 608p.
ISBN:0-453-00689-2, ISBN13: 978-0-453-00689-7.
Dewey:306.76/6/09. LCCN:89-009417.

Audience: **g,l,u.**

Edsall, Nicholas C.   **HQ76.3.E37 2003**
Toward Stonewall: Homosexuality and Society in the Modern
Western World. Trade Cloth. University Press of Virginia.
Charlottesville, VA. 2003. 384p. ISBN:0-8139-2211-9, ISBN13:
978-0-8139-2211-9. Dewey:306.76/6/094. LCCN:2002-155966.

Audience: **g,l,u,f.** *Choice, 2004.*

Faderman, Lillian &   **HQ75.6.G3L47 1990**
  Eriksson, Brigitte
Lesbians in Germany, 1890's-1920's. Ed. 2. Trade Paper. Bella
Books, Inc. Tallahassee, FL. 1990. 128p. ISBN:0-941483-62-2,
ISBN13: 978-0-941483-62-9. Dewey:306.76/63/0943.
LCCN:89-048962.

Audience: **l,u.**

Feinberg, Leslie   **HQ77.9.F44 1996**
Transgender Warriors: Making History from Joan of Arc to
Dennis Rodman. Trade Paper. Beacon Press. Boston, MA. 1997.
240p. ISBN:0-8070-7941-3, ISBN13: 978-0-8070-7941-6.
Dewey:305.3. LCCN:96-037682.

Audience: **g,l,u,f.** *Choice, 1996.*

Fone, Byrne   **HQ76.25.F7 2000**
Homophobia: A History. Cloth over Boards. Henry Holt &
Company. New York, NY. 2000. 480p. ISBN:0-8050-4559-7,
ISBN13: 978-0-8050-4559-8. Dewey:306.76/6/09.
LCCN:99-087004.

Audience: **g.** *Choice, 2001.*

Gide, Andre   **HQ76.25.G5213 2000**
Corydon. Richard Howard (Translator). Trade Paper. University
of Illinois Press. Champaign, IL. 2001. 160p.
ISBN:0-252-07006-2, ISBN13: 978-0-252-07006-8.
Dewey:306.76/6. LCCN:2001-027389.

Audience: **g,l,u,f.**

Goodich, Michael   **HQ76.2.E9 G66**
The Unmentionable Vice. Trade Cloth. ABC-CLIO, Inc. Santa
Barbara, CA. 1979. 164p. ISBN:0-87436-287-3, ISBN13:
978-0-87436-287-9. Dewey:301.41/57/0902. LCCN:78-013276.

Audience: **g.**

History Project Staff   **HQ76.3.U52**
Improper Bostonians: Lesbian and Gay History from the
Puritans to Playland. Barney Frank (Foreword by). Trade Paper.

Beacon Press. Boston, MA. 1999. 224p. ISBN:0-8070-7949-9, ISBN13: 978-0-8070-7949-2. Dewey:305.9/0664/0974461. LCCN:98-011928.

Audience: **g,l.**

Katz, Jonathan N.   **PS3501.C7**
(Editor)
Homosexuality: Lesbians and Gay Men in Society, History and Literature. Trade Cloth. Ayer Company Publishers, Inc. Manchester, NH. 1975. ISBN:0-405-07348-8, ISBN13: 978-0-405-07348-9. Dewey:928.1.

Audience: **g.**

Katz, Jonathan Ned   **HQ76.3.U5K375 2001**
Love Stories: Sex Between Men Before Homosexuality. Trade Cloth. University of Chicago Press. Chicago, IL. 2001. 440p. ISBN:0-226-42615-7, ISBN13: 978-0-226-42615-0. Dewey:306.76/62/0973. LCCN:2001-027753.

Audience: **g,l,u,f.** *Choice, 2002.*

Lesbian History Group   **HQ75.5**
Staff
Not a Passing Phase: Reclaiming Lesbians in History, 1840-1985. Trade Paper. Women's Press, Limited, The. London, 1997. 204p. ISBN:0-7043-4175-1, ISBN13: 978-0-7043-4175-3. Dewey:306.7/663/09.

Audience: **g,l.**

Meyerowitz, Joanne   **HQ77**
How Sex Changed: A History of Transsexuality in the United States. Trade Cloth. Harvard University Press. Cambridge, MA. 2002. 400p. ISBN:0-674-00925-8, ISBN13: 978-0-674-00925-7. Dewey:306.77. LCCN:2002-020536.

Audience: **g,l,u,f.** *Choice, 2003.*

Miller, Neil   **HQ75.15**
Out of the Past. Trade Paper. Alyson Publications. Los Angeles, CA. 2005. 408p. ISBN:1-55583-870-7, ISBN13: 978-1-55583-870-6. Dewey:306.76609.

Audience: **g.**

Weeks, Jeffrey   **HQ76.8.G7.W43 1977**
Coming Out: Homosexual Politics in Britain from the 19th Century to the Present. Trade Paper. Charles River Books. Carlisle, MA. 288p. ISBN:0-7043-3175-6, ISBN13: 978-0-7043-3175-4. Dewey:301.41/57/0941. LCCN:78-309964.

Audience: **l,u,f.**

Weeks, Jeffrey   **HQ18.G7W43 1989**
Sex, Politics and Society: The Regulation of Sexuality since 1800. Ed. 2. Trade Paper. Pearson Education. Boston, MA. 1989. 336p. Themes in British Social History Ser. ISBN:0-582-02383-1, ISBN13: 978-0-582-02383-3. Dewey:306.7/0941. LCCN:88-013197.

Audience: **l,u,f.**

Haggerty, George   **HQ75.13.G37 2000**
(Editor)
Gay Histories and Cultures. Trade Cloth. Garland Publishing, Inc. New York, NY. 1999. 800p. Special - Reference Ser. ISBN:0-8153-1880-4, ISBN13: 978-0-8153-1880-4. Dewey:306.76/6/03. LCCN:99-040905.

Audience: **g.** *Choice, 2000.*

Hunt, Ronald J.   **HQ76.5.H86 1999**
Historical Dictionary of the Gay Liberation Movement: Gay Men and the Quest for Social Justice. Trade Cloth. Scarecrow Press, Inc. Lanham, MD. 1999. 266p. Historical Dictionaries of Religions, Philosophies, and Movements Ser., No. 22: ISBN:0-8108-3587-8, ISBN13: 978-0-8108-3587-0. Dewey:305.9/0664. LCCN:98-039383.

Audience: **g,l,u.** *Choice, 1999.*

Myers, JoAnne   **HQ76.5.M94 2003**
Historical Dictionary of the Lesbian Liberation Movement: Still the Rage. Trade Cloth. Scarecrow Press, Inc. Lanham, MD. 2003. 360p. Historical Dictionaries of Religions, Philosophies, and Movements Ser., No. 45 ISBN:0-8108-4506-7, ISBN13: 978-0-8108-4506-0. Dewey:305.9/0664. LCCN:2002-156624.

Audience: **g,l.** *Choice, 2004.*

Ridinger, Robert B.   **HQ76.5.R53 1996**
The Gay and Lesbian Movement: References and Resources. Trade Cloth. Thomson Gale. Farmington Hills, MI. 1996. 487p. Reference Publications on American Social Movements Ser. ISBN:0-8161-7373-7, ISBN13: 978-0-8161-7373-0. Dewey:305.9/0664. LCCN:96-030352.

Audience: **g.** *Choice, 1997.*

Ridinger, Robert B.   **HQ75.16.U6S53 2004**
(Editor)
Speaking for Our Lives: Historic Speeches and Rhetoric for Gay and Lesbian Rights/1892-2000. Trade Paper. Haworth Press, Incorporated, The. Binghamton, NY. 2005. 845p. ISBN:1-56023-175-0, ISBN13: 978-1-56023-175-2. Dewey:306.7660973. LCCN:2003-006746.

Audience: **g,l,u,f.** *Choice, 2004.*

Stein, Marc (Editor)   **HQ76.3.U5E53 2003**
Encyclopedia of Lesbian, Gay, Bisexual and Transgendered History in America. Trade Cloth. Thomson Gale. Farmington Hills, MI. 2003. 1200p. ISBN:0-684-31261-1, ISBN13: 978-0-684-31261-3. Dewey:306.76/6/097303. LCCN:2003-017434.

Audience: **g.** *Choice, 2004.*

Zimmerman, Bonnie   **HQ75.5.L4395 2000**
(Editor)
Lesbian Histories and Cultures. Trade Cloth. Garland Publishing, Inc. New York, NY. 1999. 800p. Special - Reference Ser., Vol. 1 ISBN:0-8153-1920-7, ISBN13: 978-0-8153-1920-7. Dewey:306.76/63/03. LCCN:99-045010.

Audience: **g,l,u,f.** *Choice, 2000.*

History > General and Reference Works

Blasius, Mark &   **HQ76.W33 1997**
Phelan, Shane (Editors)
We Are Everywhere: A Historical Sourcebook of Gay and Lesbian Politics. Paper over Boards. Routledge. New York, NY. 1997. 600p. ISBN:0-415-90858-2, ISBN13: 978-0-415-90858-0. Dewey:323.3/264. LCCN:95-002434.

Audience: **g,l.**

History > Pre-20th Century

Boswell, John   **HQ76.3**
Christianity, Social Tolerance, and Homosexuality: Gay People in Western Europe from the Beginning of the Christian Era to the Fourteenth Century. Trade Paper. University of Chicago Press. Chicago, IL. 1981. 442p. ISBN:0-226-06711-4, ISBN13: 978-0-226-06711-7. Dewey:306.7/66/094. LCCN:79-011171.

Audience: **u,f.** *B*

Bray, Alan   HQ76.2.G7B69 1995
Homosexuality in Renaissance England. Ed. 2. Trade Cloth.
Columbia University Press. New York, NY. 1996. 165p.
Between Men, Between Women Ser. ISBN:0-231-10288-7,
ISBN13: 978-0-231-10288-9. Dewey:306.7/662/0942.
LCCN:95-031441.

Audience: **l,u,f.**

Brooten, Bernadette J.   BS2665.6.L47B76 1996
Love Between Women: Early Christian Responses to Female
Homoeroticism. Trade Cloth. University of Chicago Press.
Chicago, IL. 1996. 446p. The Chicago Series on Sexuality,
History, and Society Ser. ISBN:0-226-07591-5, ISBN13:
978-0-226-07591-4. Dewey:306.7/663/0901. LCCN:96-004727.
Audience: **g,l,u,f.** *Choice, 1997.*

Cantarella, Eva   HQ76.2.R6C3613 1992
Bisexuality in the Ancient World. Cormac O. Cuilleanain
(Translator). Cloth over Boards. Yale University Press.
Cumberland, RI. 1992. 296p. ISBN:0-300-04844-0, ISBN13:
978-0-300-04844-5. Dewey:306.7/65/0938. LCCN:92-011566.
Audience: **u,f.** *Choice, 1993.*

Crompton, Louis   HQ76.25.C76 2003
Homosexuality and Civilization. Trade Cloth. Harvard
University Press. Cambridge, MA. 2003. 648p.
ISBN:0-674-01197-X, ISBN13: 978-0-674-01197-7.
Dewey:306.76/6/09. LCCN:2003-045327.
Audience: **g,l,f.** *Choice, 2004.*

Dover, Kenneth J.   HQ76.3.G8D68 1989
Greek Homosexuality: Updated and with a New Postscript.
Trade Paper. Harvard University Press. Cambridge, MA. 1989.
256p. ISBN:0-674-36270-5, ISBN13: 978-0-674-36270-3.
Dewey:306.76/6/09495. LCCN:89-034289.

Audience: **l,u,f.**

Duberman, Martin B.   HQ76.25.D83 1991
About Time: Exploring the Gay Past. Trade Paper. Penguin
Group (USA) Inc. New York, NY. 1991. 528p.
ISBN:0-452-01081-0, ISBN13: 978-0-452-01081-9.
Dewey:305.9/0664. LCCN:91-016203.
Audience: **g,l,u,f.**

Faderman, Lillian   PN3401
   (Editor)
Chloe Plus Olivia: An Anthology of Lesbian Literature from the
Seventh Century to the Present. Trade Paper. Penguin Group
(USA) Inc. New York, NY. 1995. 848p. ISBN:0-14-017248-3,
ISBN13: 978-0-14-017248-5. Dewey:809.3/0082.
LCCN:93-045750.

Audience: **l,u.**

Faderman, Lillian   HQ75.5.F33 1998
Surpassing the Love of Men: Romantic Friendship and Love
Between Women from the Renaissance to the Present. Trade
Paper. HarperCollins Publishers. New York, NY. 1998. 496p.
ISBN:0-688-13330-4, ISBN13: 978-0-688-13330-6.
Dewey:306.76/63/09. LCCN:99-160164.
Audience: **g,l.** *B*

Foucault, Michel   HQ12.F6813 1980
The History of Sexuality: The Use of Pleasure, Vol. 2. Trade
Paper. Knopf Publishing Group. New York, NY. 1990. 304p.
ISBN:0-394-75122-1, ISBN13: 978-0-394-75122-1.
Dewey:306.7. LCCN:79-007460.
Audience: **u,f.**

Foucault, Michel   HQ12
The History of Sexuality: The Care of the Self, Vol. 3. Trade
Paper. Knopf Publishing Group. New York, NY. 1988. 288p.
ISBN:0-394-74155-2, ISBN13: 978-0-394-74155-0.
Dewey:306.7.

Audience: **u,f.**

Foucault, Michel   HQ16
A History of Sexuality: An Introduction, Vol. 1. Trade Paper.
Knopf Publishing Group. New York, NY. 1990. 176p.
ISBN:0-679-72469-9, ISBN13: 978-0-679-72469-8.
Dewey:306.7/091821. LCCN:79-007460.
Audience: **u,f.**

Gerard, Kent &   HQ76.2.E9.P87 1989
   Hekma, Gert
The Pursuit of Sodomy: Male Homosexuality in Renaissance
and Enlightenment Europe. Cloth Text. Haworth Press,
Incorporated, The. Binghamton, NY. 1989. 553p. Journal of
Homosexuality Ser., Vol. 16, Nos. 1-2 ISBN:0-86656-491-8,
ISBN13: 978-0-86656-491-5. Dewey:306.7/662/094.
LCCN:88-032231.

Audience: **u,f.**

Halperin, David M.   HQ76.2.G8H35 1990
One Hundred Years of Homosexuality: And Other Essays on
Greek Love. Trade Cloth. Routledge. New York, NY. 1989.
320p. ISBN:0-415-90096-4, ISBN13: 978-0-415-90096-6.
Dewey:306.76/62/09495. LCCN:89-033158.
Audience: **g,l,u,f.**

Robb, Graham   HQ76.3.E8R63 2004
Strangers: Homosexual Love in the Nineteenth Century. Trade
Cloth. W. W. Norton & Company, Inc. New York, NY. 2004.
352p. ISBN:0-393-02038-X, ISBN13: 978-0-393-02038-0.
Dewey:306.76/6/09409034. LCCN:2003-066239.
Audience: **g,l.** *Choice, 2004.*

Thornton, Bruce S.   HQ13
Eros: The Myth of Ancient Greek Sexuality. Trade Paper.
Westview Press. Boulder, CO. 1998. 304p. ISBN:0-8133-3226-5,
ISBN13: 978-0-8133-3226-0. Dewey:306.7/0938.
Audience: **l,u.** *Choice, 1997.*

Winkler, John J.   DF93.W56 1990
Constraints of Desire: The Anthropology of Sex and Gender in
Ancient Greece. Trade Cloth. Routledge. New York, NY. 1989.
288p. ISBN:0-415-90122-7, ISBN13: 978-0-415-90122-2.
Dewey:392.6/0938. LCCN:89-033156.
Audience: **g,l,u,f.**

History > Modern

Berenbaum, Michael   D804.G4
A Mosaic of Victims: Non-Jews Persecuted and Murdered by
the Nazis. Richard L. Rubenstein (Introduction by). Trade Paper.
New York University Press. New York, NY. 1992. 244p.
ISBN:0-8147-1175-8, ISBN13: 978-0-8147-1175-0.
Dewey:940.54/05.
Audience: **l,u,f.**

Berube, Allan   D769.2.B46 1990
Coming Out under Fire: The History of Gay Men and Women
in World War Two. Trade Cloth. Simon & Schuster. New York,
NY. 1990. 377p. ISBN:0-02-903100-1, ISBN13:

978-0-02-903100-1. Dewey:940.54/0973/08664.
LCCN:89-025653.

Audience: **g,l.** *Choice, 1990.*

Brown, Howard   **HQ76.2.U5**
Familiar Faces, Hidden Lives: The Story of Homosexual Men in
America Today. Trade Cloth. Harcourt Trade Publishers. New
York, NY. 1976. 246p. ISBN:0-15-130149-2, ISBN13:
978-0-15-130149-2. Dewey:306.376. LCCN:76-024910.

Audience: **g,l.**

Clendinen, Dudley &   **HQ76.8.U5C58 1999**
  Nagourney, Adam
Out for Good: The Struggle to Build a Gay Rights Movement in
America. Trade Cloth. Simon & Schuster. New York, NY. 1999.
720p. ISBN:0-684-81091-3, ISBN13: 978-0-684-81091-1.
Dewey:305.9/0664. LCCN:99-012523.

Audience: **g,l,u.**

D'Emilio, John   **HQ76.8.U5**
Sexual Politics, Sexual Communities. Ed. 2. Trade Paper.
University of Chicago Press. Chicago, IL. 1998. 286p.
ISBN:0-226-14267-1, ISBN13: 978-0-226-14267-8.
Dewey:305.9/0664. LCCN:98-024148.

Audience: **l,u,f.**

Duberman, Martin   **HQ75.8.D82A32 1996**
Midlife Queer: Autobiography of a Decade, 1971-1991. Trade
Cloth. Simon & Schuster. New York, NY. 1996. 240p.
ISBN:0-684-81836-1, ISBN13: 978-0-684-81836-8.
Dewey:305.38/9664/092 B. LCCN:95-052738.

Audience: **g,l.**

Duberman, Martin   **HQ76.8.U5 D85 1993**
Stonewall. Dutton. 1993. ISBN:0-525-93602-5, ISBN13:
978-0-525-93602-2.

Audience: **g,l,u.**

Duberman, Martin B.   **HQ76.25.D83 1991**
About Time: Exploring the Gay Past. Trade Paper. Penguin
Group (USA) Inc. New York, NY. 1991. 528p.
ISBN:0-452-01081-0, ISBN13: 978-0-452-01081-9.
Dewey:305.9/0664. LCCN:91-016203.

Audience: **g,l,u,f.**

Epstein, Rob &   **D804.5.G38**
  Friedman, Jeffrey (Directed Bys)
Paragraph 175. DVD. New Yorker Video. New York, NY. 2001.
ISBN:1-56730-254-8, ISBN13: 978-1-56730-254-7.
Dewey:940.53/18/08664.

Audience: **g.**

Grau, Gunter;
  Schoppmann, Claudia
A Hidden Holocaust: Lesbian and Gay Persecution in Germany,
1933-1945. Cassell P L C. 1994. Sexual Politics Ser.
ISBN:0-304-32958-4, ISBN13: 978-0-304-32958-8.

Audience: **l,u,f.**

Gustav-Wrathall, John   **BV1090.G88 1998**
  Donald
Take the Young Stranger by the Hand: Same-Sex Relations and
the YMCA. Trade Cloth. University of Chicago Press. Chicago,
IL. 1998. 288p. Chicago Series on Sexuality, History and
Society ISBN:0-226-90784-8, ISBN13: 978-0-226-90784-0.
Dewey:267/.3973. LCCN:98-009904.

Audience: **u,f.** *Choice, 1999.*

Harris, Daniel   **HQ76.2.U5H347 1997**
The Rise and Fall of Gay Culture. Trade Cloth. Hyperion Press.
New York, NY. 1997. 278p. ISBN:0-7868-6165-7, ISBN13:
978-0-7868-6165-1. Dewey:305.38/96642. LCCN:96-047822.

Audience: **g,l,u,f.**

Hay, Harry   **HQ75.8.H39A3 1996**
Radically Gay: Gay Liberation in the Words of Its Founder
Harry Hay. Will Roscoe (Editor). Trade Cloth. Beacon Press.
Boston, MA. 1996. 352p. ISBN:0-8070-7080-7, ISBN13:
978-0-8070-7080-2. Dewey:305.38/9664/092. LCCN:95-039290.

Audience: **l,u,f.**

Heger, Heinz   **HQ75.7.H4313 1994**
The Men with the Pink Triangle: The True Life and Death Story
of Homosexuals in the Nazi Death Camps. Ed. 2. Trade Paper.
Alyson Publications. Los Angeles, CA. 1994. 120p.
ISBN:1-55583-006-4, ISBN13: 978-1-55583-006-9.
Dewey:940.54/7243. LCCN:94-029646.

Audience: **g,l.**

Jay, Karla   **HQ1426**
Tales of the Lavender Menace: A Memoir of Liberation. Trade
Paper. Basic Books. New York, NY. 2000. 288p.
ISBN:0-465-08366-8, ISBN13: 978-0-465-08366-4.
Dewey:305.4/2/0973. LCCN:00-274554.

Audience: **g,l.**

John Scagliotti, director   **HQ76.8.U5.A384**
🎬 After Stonewall: From the Riots to the Millennium. Ed. 2.
Janet Baus and Dan Hunt, co-directors. First Run Features.
2005.

Audience: **g.**

Johnson, David K.   **JK723.H6J64 2003**
The Lavender Scare: The Cold War Persecution of Gays and
Lesbians in the Federal Government. Trade Cloth. University of
Chicago Press. Chicago, IL. 2004. 312p. ISBN:0-226-40481-1,
ISBN13: 978-0-226-40481-3. Dewey:352.6/086/640973.
LCCN:2003-009138.

Audience: **g,l,u,f.** *Choice, 2004.*

Kennedy, Elizabeth L.   **HQ75.6.U5K47 1994**
  & Davis, Madeline D.
Boots of Leather, Slippers of Gold: The History of a Lesbian
Community. Trade Paper. Penguin Group (USA) Inc. New York,
NY. 1994. 464p. ISBN:0-14-023550-7, ISBN13:
978-0-14-023550-0. Dewey:305.48/9664/0974797.
LCCN:94-142388.

Audience: **u,f.**

Marcus, Eric   **HQ76.8.U5M36 2002**
Making Gay History: The Half-Century Fight for Lesbian and
Gay Equal Rights. Trade Paper. HarperCollins Publishers. New
York, NY. 2002. 496p. ISBN:0-06-093391-7, ISBN13:
978-0-06-093391-3. Dewey:305.9/0664. LCCN:2001-051818.

Audience: **g.**

Marcus, Eric   **HQ76.8.U5M36 1992**
Making History: An Oral History of the Struggle for Gay and
Lesbian Civil Rights, 1945-1990. Trade Cloth. HarperCollins
Publishers. New York, NY. 1992. 384p. ISBN:0-06-016708-4,
ISBN13: 978-0-06-016708-0. Dewey:305.9/0664.
LCCN:90-056389.

Audience: **g,l.**

Marotta, Toby HQ76.8.U5
The Politics of Homosexuality. Trade Cloth. Houghton Mifflin
Company. New York, NY. 1981. 384p. ISBN:0-395-29477-0,
ISBN13: 978-0-395-29477-2. Dewey:306.7/2/0973.

Audience: **g,l.**

Miller, Neil HV6534.S53M55 2002
Sex-Crime Panic: A Journey to the Paranoid Heart of the 1950s.
Trade Paper. Alyson Publications. Los Angeles, CA. 2002. 240p.
ISBN:1-55583-659-3, ISBN13: 978-1-55583-659-7.
Dewey:364.15/23/0977741. LCCN:2001-045807.

Audience: **g,l.**

Plant, Richard HQ76.2.G4
The Pink Triangle: The Nazi War Against Homosexuals. Trade
Paper. Henry Holt & Company. New York, NY. 1988. 272p.
ISBN:0-8050-0600-1, ISBN13: 978-0-8050-0600-1.
Dewey:306.7/662/0943. LCCN:86-000346.

Audience: **g,l,u.** *Choice, 1987.*

Scagliotti, John, and HQ76.8.U5.B44
  Greta Schiller, directors
Before Stonewall: The Making of a Gay and Lesbian
Community. Ed. 2. First Run Features. 2004.

Audience: **g.**

Sears, James T. HQ75.6.U52S687 1997
Lonely Hunters: An Oral History of Lesbian and Gay Southern
Life, 1948-1968. Trade Cloth. Westview Press. Boulder, CO.
1997. 336p. ISBN:0-8133-2474-2, ISBN13: 978-0-8133-2474-6.
Dewey:305.9/0664/0975. LCCN:97-019782.

Audience: **g,l,u,f.**

Walters, Suzanna PN1992.8.H64W35 2001
  Danuta
All the Rage: The Story of Gay Visibility in America. Trade
Cloth. University of Chicago Press. Chicago, IL. 2001. 356p.
ISBN:0-226-87231-9, ISBN13: 978-0-226-87231-5.
Dewey:791.45/653. LCCN:2001-001665.

Audience: **g,l,u,f.** *Choice, 2002.*

Wat, Eric C. HQ76.2.U52C38 2002
Making of a Gay Asian Community: An Oral History of
Pre-AIDS Los Angeles. Book, Other. Rowman & Littlefield
Publishers, Inc. Lanham, MD. 2002. 224p. Pacific Formations
Ser., :Global Relations in Asian and Pacific Perspectives
ISBN:0-7425-1109-X, ISBN13: 978-0-7425-1109-5.
Dewey:305.8950794/94. LCCN:2001-041928.

Audience: **g,l,u,f.**

White, Edmund HQ76.2.U5W45 1980
States of Desire: Travels in Gay America. Trade Cloth. Penguin
Group (USA) Inc. New York, NY. 1980. ISBN:0-525-22235-9,
ISBN13: 978-0-525-22235-4. Dewey:301.41/57/0973.
LCCN:79-017693.

Audience: **g,l,u.**

Personal Identity

Atkins, Dawn (Editor) HQ75.6U5L66
Looking Queer: Body Image and Identity in Lesbian, Bisexual,
Gay, and Transgender Communities. Trade Cloth. Haworth
Press, Incorporated, The. Binghamton, NY. 1998. 467p. Winner
of the Lammy in the Transgender Category! Ser.
ISBN:1-56023-931-X, ISBN13: 978-1-56023-931-4.
Dewey:306.76/6. LCCN:98-014678.

Audience: **u,f.**

Beauvoir, Simone de HQ1154
The Second Sex. H. N. Pashley (Editor, Translator), Margaret
Crosland (Introduction by). Trade Cloth. Alfred A. Knopf Inc.
New York, NY. 1993. 848p. Everyman's Library
ISBN:0-679-42016-9, ISBN13: 978-0-679-42016-3.
Dewey:305.4/2. LCCN:92-054303.

Audience: **l,u,f.** *B*

Beemyn, Brett & HQ76.25.Q383 1996
  Eliason, Mickey (Editors)
Queer Studies: A Lesbian, Gay, Bisexual, and Transgender
Anthology. Trade Paper. New York University Press. New York,
NY. 1996. 368p. ISBN:0-8147-1258-4, ISBN13:
978-0-8147-1258-0. Dewey:306.76. LCCN:96-025709.

Audience: **l,u,f.**

Behling, Laura L. HQ1236.5.U6B45 2001
The Masculine Woman in America, 1890-1935. Trade Cloth.
University of Illinois Press. Champaign, IL. 2001. 224p.
ISBN:0-252-02627-6, ISBN13: 978-0-252-02627-0.
Dewey:305.42/0973. LCCN:00-009894.

Audience: **u,f.** *Choice, 2001.*

Boykin, Keith HQ76.3.U5
One More River to Cross: Black and Gay in America. Trade
Paper. Doubleday Publishing. New York, NY. 1997. 288p.
ISBN:0-385-47983-2, ISBN13: 978-0-385-47983-7.
Dewey:305.9/0664.

Audience: **g,l.**

D'Augelli, Anthony R. HQ76.25
  & Patterson, Charlotte J. (Editors)
Lesbian, Gay, and Bisexual Identities over the Lifespan:
Psychological Perspectives. Trade Paper. Oxford University
Press, Inc. New York, NY. 1996. 468p. ISBN:0-19-510899-X,
ISBN13: 978-0-19-510899-6. Dewey:155.34.

Audience: **u,f.**

DuBay, William H. HQ76.3.U5D82 1987
Gay Identity: The Self under Ban. Library Binding. McFarland
& Company, Incorporated Publishers. Jefferson, NC. 1987.
184p. ISBN:0-89950-269-5, ISBN13: 978-0-89950-269-4.
Dewey:306.7/66. LCCN:87-042505.

Audience: **u,f.** *Choice, 1988.*

Esterberg, Kristin G. HQ75.5.E85 1997
Lesbian and Bisexual Identities: Constructing Communities,
Constructing Selves. Trade Paper. Temple University Press.
Philadelphia, PA. 1997. 216p. ISBN:1-56639-510-0, ISBN13:
978-1-56639-510-6. Dewey:305.9/06643. LCCN:96-035409.

Audience: **l,u,f.** *Choice, 1997.*

Feinberg, Leslie HQ77.9
Trans Liberation: Beyond Pink or Blue. Trade Paper. Beacon
Press. Boston, MA. 1999. 160p. ISBN:0-8070-7951-0, ISBN13:
978-0-8070-7951-5. Dewey:305.9/066. LCCN:98-016476.

Audience: **g.**

Fisher, Peter HQ76.F55
The Gay Mystique: The Myth and Reality of Male
Homosexuality. Trade Cloth. Scarborough House. Chelsea, MI.
1972. 258p. ISBN:0-8128-1431-2, ISBN13: 978-0-8128-1431-6.
Dewey:301.41/57. LCCN:73-186149.

Audience: **g,l.**

Formats: Web: ☐ Ebook: *e* CD/DVD-ROM: 🐟 BCL3: *B*

Garber, Marjorie B.   HQ74.G37 1995
Vice Versa: Bisexuality and the Eroticism of Everyday Life.
Trade Cloth. Simon & Schuster. New York, NY. 1995. 608p.
ISBN:0-684-80308-9, ISBN13: 978-0-684-80308-1.
Dewey:306.7/65. LCCN:95-007083.

Audience: **g,l.**

Garcia, Bernardo C.   HQ76.2.U5 G35
The Development of a Gay Latino Identity. Cloth Text. Garland
Publishing, Inc. New York, NY. 1998. 136p. Latino
Communities: Emerging Voices - Political, Social, Cultural and
Legal Issues Ser. ISBN:0-8153-3285-8, ISBN13:
978-0-8153-3285-5. Dewey:305.38868073. LCCN:98-039178.

Audience: **l.**

Howey, Noelle &   HQ777.8.O87 2000
Samuels, Ellen
Out of the Ordinary: Essays on Growing up with Gay, Lesbian
and Transgender Parents. Dan Savage (Contribution by),
Margarethe Cammer-Meyer (Foreword by). Trade Paper. St.
Martin's Press. Gordonville, VA. 2000. 240p.
ISBN:0-312-24489-4, ISBN13: 978-0-312-24489-7.
Dewey:306.874. LCCN:00-025493.

Audience: **g,l,u,f.**

Hunter, D.   PS509.H57
Sojourner Black Gay Voice. Trade Paper. Other Countries -
Black Gay Men Writing. New York, NY. 1997.
ISBN:0-9638032-0-4, ISBN13: 978-0-9638032-0-7.
Dewey:810.8.

Audience: **g.**

Khan, Badruddin   HQ76.3.P18K47 1997
Sex, Longing and Not Belonging: A Gay Muslim's Quest for
Love and Meaning. Stephen O. Murray (Afterword by). Trade
Paper. Floating Lotus. Oakland, CA. 1997. 238p.
ISBN:0-942777-16-6, ISBN13: 978-0-942777-16-1.
Dewey:306.766094. LCCN:96-062080.

Audience: **g,l,u,f.**

Loughery, John   HQ76.2.U5L68 1998
The Other Side of Silence: Men's Lives and Gay Identities - a
Twentieth-Century History. Cloth over Boards. Henry Holt &
Company. New York, NY. 1998. 527p. ISBN:0-8050-3896-5,
ISBN13: 978-0-8050-3896-5. Dewey:305.38/9664.
LCCN:97-042575.

Audience: **l,u,f.** *Choice, 1998.*

Martin, Del   HQ76.3.U5.M37
Lesbian/Woman. Trade Cloth. Glide Word Press. San Francisco,
CA. 1972. 283p. ISBN:0-912078-20-0, ISBN13:
978-0-912078-20-5. Dewey:301.41/57. LCCN:72-076532.

Audience: **g.**

Murphy, Peter F.   HQ1090.F46 2004
(Editor)
Feminism and Masculinities. Trade Paper. Oxford University
Press, Inc. New York, NY. 2004. 304p. Oxford Readings in
Feminism Ser. ISBN:0-19-926724-3, ISBN13:
978-0-19-926724-8. Dewey:305.32. LCCN:2004-050074.

Audience: **g,u,f.**

Murray, Stephen O.   HQ76.3.N67M87 1996
American Gay. Trade Cloth. University of Chicago Press.
Chicago, IL. 1996. 345p. Worlds of Desire Ser.
ISBN:0-226-55191-1, ISBN13: 978-0-226-55191-3.
Dewey:306.76/6/097. LCCN:95 049388.

Audience: **u,f.** *Choice, 1996.*

Nestle, Joan (Editor)   PS509.L47P47 1992
The Persistent Desire: A Femme-Butch Reader. Trade Cloth.
Alyson Publications. Los Angeles, CA. 1992. 502p.
ISBN:1-55583-190-7, ISBN13: 978-1-55583-190-5.
Dewey:810.8. LCCN:92-006166.

Audience: **g.**

Queen, Carol   HQ76.25.P66 1997
PoMoSexuals: Challenging Assumptions about Gender and
Sexuality. Schimel Queen (Editor). Trade Paper. Cleis Press. San
Francisco, CA. 1997. 180p. ISBN:1-57344-074-4, ISBN13:
978-1-57344-074-5. Dewey:306.76/6. LCCN:97-037703.

Audience: **g,l,u.**

Reid-Pharr, Robert F.   HQ76.2.U5R45 2001
Black Gay Man. Trade Cloth. New York University Press. New
York, NY. 2001. 214p. Sexual Cultures Ser.
ISBN:0-8147-7502-0, ISBN13: 978-0-8147-7502-8.
Dewey:305.38/96642. LCCN:2001-000080.

Audience: **g,l,u.** *Choice, 2002.*

Rosenfeld, Dana   HQ76.3.U5R68 2003
The Changing of the Guard: Lesbian and Gay Elders, Identity,
and Social Change. Library Binding. Temple University Press.
Philadelphia, PA. 2003. 272p. ISBN:1-59213-030-5, ISBN13:
978-1-59213-030-6. Dewey:306.76/6. LCCN:2002-043552.

Audience: **l,u,f.**

Warren, Carol A.   HQ76.3.U5
Identity and Community in the Gay World. Ed. 99. Trade Cloth.
John Wiley & Sons, Inc. Hoboken, NJ. 1974. 191p.
ISBN:0-471-92112-2, ISBN13: 978-0-471-92112-7.
Dewey:301.41/57/0973. LCCN:73-001812.

Audience: **l.**

Wat, Eric C.   HQ76.2.U52C38 2002
Making of a Gay Asian Community: An Oral History of
Pre-AIDS Los Angeles. Book, Other. Rowman & Littlefield
Publishers, Inc. Lanham, MD. 2002. 224p. Pacific Formations
Ser., :Global Relations in Asian and Pacific Perspectives
ISBN:0-7425-1109-X, ISBN13: 978-0-7425-1109-5.
Dewey:305.8950794/94. LCCN:2001-041928.

Audience: **g,l,u,f.**

Weinberg, Martin S., et al.   HQ74.W44
Dual Attraction: Understanding Bisexuality. Colin J. Williams &
Douglas W. Pryor (Authors). Trade Paper. DIANE Publishing
Company. Collingdale, PA. 2003. 437p. ISBN:0-7567-9017-4,
ISBN13: 978-0-7567-9017-2. Dewey:306.7650973.

Audience: **u,f.**

Wheelwright, Julie   HQ77.W49 1989
(Author, Introduction by)
Amazons and Military Maids: Women Who Dressed as Men in
Pursuit of Life, Liberty and Happiness. Trade Paper. Rivers
Oram Press/Pandora. London, 1990. 224p. ISBN:0-04-440494-8,
ISBN13: 978-0-04-440494-1. Dewey:306.77. LCCN:90-106373.

Audience: **u,f.**

Wilchins, Riki A.   HQ77.8.W55A3 1997
Read My Lips: Sexual Subversion and the End of Gender. Trade
Paper. Firebrand Books. Ithaca, NY. 1997. 234p.
ISBN:1-56341-090-7, ISBN13: 978-1-56341-090-1.
Dewey:305.9/066 B. LCCN:97-030783.

Audience: **g.**

Williams, Walter L.   E98.S48
The Spirit and the Flesh: Sexual Diversity in American Indian
Culture. Trade Paper. Beacon Press. Boston, MA. 1992. 368p.

ISBN:0-8070-4615-9, ISBN13: 978-0-8070-4615-9.
Dewey:306.7/66/08997. LCCN:91-037980.
Audience: **g,l,u,f.** *Choice, 1987.*

Personal Identity > Sexual

Califia, Pat **HQ76.3.U5C354 2000**
Public Sex: The Culture of Radical Sex. Ed. 2. Trade Paper.
Cleis Press. San Francisco, CA. 2000. 250p.
ISBN:1-57344-096-5, ISBN13: 978-1-57344-096-7.
Dewey:306.7/0973. LCCN:2001-265464.
Audience: **g,l.**

Garber, Marjorie B. **HQ74.G37 1995**
Bisexuality and the Eroticism of Everyday Life. UK-B Format
Paperback. Routledge. New York, NY. 2000. 624p.
ISBN:0-415-92661-0, ISBN13: 978-0-415-92661-4.
Dewey:306.76/5. LCCN:00-266473.
Audience: **g,l,u,f.**

Halberstam, Judith **HQ75.5.H33 1998**
Female Masculinity. Trade Cloth. Duke University Press.
Durham, NC. 1998. 352p. ISBN:0-8223-2226-9, ISBN13:
978-0-8223-2226-9. Dewey:305.48/9664. LCCN:98-019527.
Audience: **u,f.** *Choice, 1999.*

Wittig, Monique **HQ1190.W58 1992**
The Straight Mind and Other Essays. Trade Paper. Beacon
Press. Boston, MA. 1992. 128p. ISBN:0-8070-7917-0, ISBN13:
978-0-8070-7917-1. Dewey:305.42. LCCN:91-018409.
Audience: **g,u,f.**

Personal Identity > Coming Out

Bauer, Marion Dane **PS648.H57**
Am I Blue?: Coming Out from the Silence. Beck Underwood
(Illustrator). Trade Paper. HarperCollins Publishers. New York,
NY. 1995. 288p. A Trophy Bk. ISBN:0-06-440587-7, ISBN13:
978-0-06-440587-4. Dewey:813/.01/08352/0664.
LCCN:93-029574.
Audience: **g,l.**

Borhek, Mary V. **HQ75.5.B68 1993**
Coming Out to Parents: A Two-Way Survival Guide for
Lesbians and Gay Men and Their Parents. Ed. 2. Trade Paper.
Pilgrim Press, The/United Church Press. Cleveland, OH. 1993.
320p. ISBN:0-8298-0957-0, ISBN13: 978-0-8298-0957-2.
Dewey:306.874. LCCN:93-023919.
Audience: **g,l.**

Boykin, Keith **HQ74.2.U5**
Beyond the Down Low: Sex, Lies, and Denial in Black
America. E. Lynn Harris (Foreword by). Trade Cloth. Avalon
Publishing Group. New York, NY. 2005. 256p.
ISBN:0-7867-1434-4, ISBN13: 978-0-7867-1434-6.
Dewey:305.38/896073.
Audience: **g,l.**

Brown, Rita Mae **PS3552.R698.R8**
Rubyfruit Jungle. Daughters, Inc. 1973. ISBN:0-913780-02-2,
ISBN13: 978-0-913780-02-2.
Audience: **g.**

Buxton, Amity Pierce **HQ74.B89 1994**
The Other Side of the Closet: The Coming-Out Crisis for
Straight Spouses and Families. Ed. 2. Trade Paper. John Wiley

& Sons, Inc. Hoboken, NJ. 1994. 352p. ISBN:0-471-02152-0,
ISBN13: 978-0-471-02152-0. Dewey:306.76/5.
LCCN:94-009325.
Audience: **g,l.**

Chvany, Pete **HQ74.B525 2005**
Bi Men: Coming Out Every Which Way. Ron Jackson Suresha
(Editor). Trade Cloth. Haworth Press, Incorporated, The.
Binghamton, NY. 2005. 213p. ISBN:1-56023-614-0, ISBN13:
978-1-56023-614-6. Dewey:306.76/5/081. LCCN:2005-008520.
Audience: **g,l.**

Dews, Carlos L. & Law, **HQ76.3.U52S276 2001**
Carolyn Leste (Editors)
Out in the South. Trade Cloth. Temple University Press.
Philadelphia, PA. 2001. vi, 243p. ISBN:1-56639-813-4, ISBN13:
978-1-56639-813-8. Dewey:306.76/6/0975. LCCN:00-037706.
Audience: **g,l.**

Doan, Laura **PS153.L46L45 1994**
The Lesbian Postmodern. Trade Cloth. Columbia University
Press. New York, NY. 1994. 267p. Between Men, Between
Women Ser. ISBN:0-231-08410-2, ISBN13: 978-0-231-08410-9.
Dewey:810.9/9206643. LCCN:94-187096.
Audience: **l,u,f.** *Choice, 1994.*

Gross, Larry **HQ76.8.U5G76 1993**
Contested Closets: The Politics and Ethics of Outing. Trade
Paper. University of Minnesota Press. Minneapolis, MN. 1993.
362p. ISBN:0-8166-2179-9, ISBN13: 978-0-8166-2179-8.
Dewey:305.9/0664. LCCN:93-000394.
Audience: **l,u,f.**

Isay, Richard A. **HQ76.2.U5I83 1996**
Becoming Gay: The Journey to Self-Acceptance. Trade Cloth.
Knopf Publishing Group. New York, NY. 1996. 224p.
ISBN:0-679-42159-9, ISBN13: 978-0-679-42159-7.
Dewey:155.3. LCCN:95-026209.
Audience: **g,l.**

Jensen, Karol L. **HQ75.6.U52M555 1999**
Lesbian Epiphanies: Women Coming Out in Later Life. Trade
Paper. Haworth Press, Incorporated, The. Binghamton, NY.
2003. 230p. Gay and Lesbian Studies ISBN:1-56023-964-6,
ISBN13: 978-1-56023-964-2. Dewey:305.244.
LCCN:99-013599.
Audience: **g,l.**

Johansson, Warren & **HQ76.8.U5.J64 1994**
Percy, William
Outing: Shattering the Conspiracy of Silence. Library Binding.
Haworth Press, Incorporated, The. Binghamton, NY. 1994. 322p.
Gay and Lesbian Studies ISBN:1-56024-419-4, ISBN13:
978-1-56024-419-6. Dewey:305.9/0664. LCCN:93-017368.
Audience: **g,l.** *Choice, 1994.*

Kaeser, Gigi **HQ76.13.K34 1999**
(Photographer)
Love Makes a Family: Portraits of Lesbian, Gay, Bisexual and
Transgendered Parents and Their Families. Peggy Gillespie
(Contribution by), Kath Weston (Introduction by), Minnie Bruce
Pratt (Foreword by). Trade Cloth. University of Massachusetts
Press. Amherst, MA. 1999. 280p. ISBN:1-55849-160-0,
ISBN13: 978-1-55849-160-1. Dewey:306.874.
LCCN:98-030266.
Audience: **g.**

King, J. L. & Hunter,　　　　HQ74.2.U5K56 2004
　Karen
On the down Low: A Journey into the Lives of "Straight" Black
Men Who Sleep with Men. Trade Paper. Broadway Books. New
York, NY. 2005. 208p. ISBN:0-7679-1399-X, ISBN13:
978-0-7679-1399-7. Dewey:305.38/896073. LCCN:2003-056006.
　　　　　　　　　　　　　　　　Audience: **g,l.**

Markowe, Laura　　　　　　HQ75.5.M37 1996
Redefining the Self: Coming Out As Lesbian. Trade Cloth.
Polity Press. Cambridge, 1996. 230p. ISBN:0-7456-1128-1,
ISBN13: 978-0-7456-1128-0. Dewey:305.48/9664.
LCCN:96-000798.
　　　　　　　　　Audience: **g,l.** *Choice, 1997.*

Mastoon, Adam　　　　　　HQ75.2.M37 2001
The Shared Heart: Portraits and Stories Celebrating Lesbian,
Gay, and Bisexual Young People. Trade Cloth. HarperCollins
Publishers. New York, NY. 2001. 192p. ISBN:0-06-029556-2,
ISBN13: 978-0-06-029556-1. Dewey:305.235/08664.
LCCN:00-061410.
　　　　　　　　　　　　　　　　Audience: **g.**

McNaught, Brian　　　　　HQ76.3.U5M395 1997
Now That I'm Out What Do I Do. Cloth over Boards. St.
Martin's Press. Gordonville, VA. 1997. 205p.
ISBN:0-312-15616-2, ISBN13: 978-0-312-15616-9.
Dewey:305.9/0664. LCCN:96-053513.
　　　　　　　　　　　　　　　Audience: **g,l.**

Moore, Lisa C. (Editor)　　　PS648.L47D64 1997
Does Your Mama Know?: An Anthology of Black Lesbian
Coming Out Stories. Trade Cloth. RedBone Press. Washington,
DC. 1997. 314p. ISBN:0-9656659-0-9, ISBN13:
978-0-9656659-0-2. Dewey:813/.01089206643.
LCCN:97-177620.
　　　　　　　　　　　　　　　　Audience: **g.**

Pollack, Rachel &　　　　　HQ76.3.U5P655 1995
　Schwartz, Cheryl
The Journey Out: A Guide for and about Lesbian, Gay, and
Bisexual Teens. Trade Cloth. Penguin Group (USA) Inc. New
York, NY. 1995. 160p. ISBN:0-670-85845-5, ISBN13:
978-0-670-85845-3. Dewey:305.2/35/0973. LCCN:95-014276.
　　　　　　　　　　　　　　　Audience: **g,l.**

Schimel, Lawrence　　　　HQ76.2.U5F68 2002
　(Editor)
Found Tribe: Jewish Coming Out Stories. Trade Paper. Sherman
Asher Publishing. Santa Fe, NM. 2002. 192p.
ISBN:1-890932-20-5, ISBN13: 978-1-890932-20-6.
Dewey:305.38/9664. LCCN:2002-018521.
　　　　　　　　　　　　　　　　Audience: **g.**

Signorile, Michelangelo　　　HQ76.3.U5S54 1995
Outing Yourself: How to Come Out to Your Family, Your
Friends, and Your Coworkers. Trade Cloth. Random House, Inc.
New York, NY. 1995. ISBN:0-679-43838-6, ISBN13:
978-0-679-43838-0. Dewey:305.9/0664. LCCN:95-018702.
　　　　　　　　　　　　　　　　Audience: **g.**

Walters, Suzanna　　　　　PN1992.8.H64W35 2001
　Danuta
All the Rage: The Story of Gay Visibility in America. Trade
Cloth. University of Chicago Press. Chicago, IL. 2001. 356p.
ISBN:0-226-87231-9, ISBN13: 978-0-226-87231-5.
Dewey:791.45/653. LCCN:2001-001665.
　　　　　　　Audience: **g,l,u,f.** *Choice, 2002.*

Personal Identity > Gender Identity

Adams, Rachel &　　　　　HQ1088.M377 2001
　Savran, David (Editors)
The Masculinity Studies Reader. Trade Paper. Blackwell
Publishing, Inc. Malden, MA. 2002. 432p. Keyworks in Cultural
Studies, Vol. 5 ISBN:0-631-22660-5, ISBN13:
978-0-631-22660-4. Dewey:305.31. LCCN:2001-043229.
　　　　　　　　　　　　　　　Audience: **g,l,u,f.**

Allen, J. J.　　　　　　　HQ77.A29 1996
The Man in the Red Velvet Dress: Inside the World of Cross
Dressing. Trade Cloth. Carol Publishing Group. Secaucus, NJ.
1996. 288p. ISBN:1-55972-338-6, ISBN13: 978-1-55972-338-1.
Dewey:306.77. LCCN:95-050096.
　　　　　　　　　　　　　　　Audience: **g,l,u,f.**

Backett-Milburn,　　　　　HQ1075.C665 2001
　Kathryn & McKie, Linda (Editors)
Constructing Gendered Bodies. Trade Paper. Palgrave
Macmillan. New York, NY. 2001. 273p. Explorations in
Sociology Ser., Vol. 59 ISBN:0-333-77462-0, ISBN13:
978-0-333-77462-5. Dewey:305.3. LCCN:00-053060.
　　　　　　　　　　　　　　　　Audience: **u,f.**

Bloom, Amy　　　　　　　HQ77.95.U6
Normal: Transexual CEOs, Crossdressing Cops and
Hermaphrodites with Attitude. Trade Paper. Knopf Publishing
Group. New York, NY. 2003. 176p. ISBN:1-4000-3244-X,
ISBN13: 978-1-4000-3244-0. Dewey:306.77.
　　　　　　　　　　　　　　　Audience: **g,l.**

Bordo, Susan　　　　　　　HQ1090
The Male Body: A New Look at Men in Public and in Private.
Trade Paper. Farrar, Straus & Giroux. New York, NY. 2000.
368p. ISBN:0-374-52732-6, ISBN13: 978-0-374-52732-7.
Dewey:305.31.
　　　　　　　　　　　　　　　Audience: **g,l,u,f.**

Bornstein, Kate　　　　　HQ77.9.B67 1994
Gender Outlaw: On Men, Women and the Rest of Us. Paper
over Boards. Routledge. New York, NY. 1994. 224p.
ISBN:0-415-90897-3, ISBN13: 978-0-415-90897-9.
Dewey:305.3. LCCN:93-046979.
　　　　　　　　　　　　　　　Audience: **g,l,u,f.**

Boyd, Helen　　　　　　　HQ77.B63 2003
My Husband Betty: Love, Sex, and Life with a Crossdresser.
Trade Paper. Avalon Publishing Group. New York, NY. 2003.
304p. ISBN:1-56025-515-3, ISBN13: 978-1-56025-515-4.
Dewey:306.778. LCCN:2003-055966.
　　　　　　　　　　　　　　　Audience: **g,l.**

Brod, Harry (Editor)　　　HQ1088.M35 1987
The Making of Masculinities: The New Men's Studies. Cloth
Text. Routledge. New York, NY. 1987. 304p.
ISBN:0-04-497035-8, ISBN13: 978-0-04-497035-4.
Dewey:305.3/1. LCCN:86-028796.
　　　　　Audience: **g,l,u,f.** *Choice, 1988.*

Brown, Mildred L. &　　　　HQ77.7
　Rounsley, Chloe Ann
True Selves: Understanding Transsexualism—for Families,
Friends, Coworkers, and Helping Professionals. Trade Paper.
John Wiley & Sons, Inc. Hoboken, NJ. 2003. 288p.
ISBN:0-7879-6702-5, ISBN13: 978-0-7879-6702-4.
Dewey:305.3. LCCN:2003-269583.
　　　　　　　　　　　　　　　Audience: **g,l.**

GLBT STUDIES   Volume 6 - Interdisciplinary and Area Studies

Brubach, Holly   HQ77.B7 1999
Girlfriend: Men, Women and Drag. Michael J. O'Brien
(Photographer). Trade Cloth. Random House, Inc. New York,
NY. 1999. xix, 178p. ISBN:0-679-41443-6, ISBN13:
978-0-679-41443-8. Dewey:306.77. LCCN:98-035604.
                                    Audience: **g,l,u,f.**

Bullough, Vern L. &   HQ77.B785 1993
  Bullough, Bonnie
Cross Dressing, Sex, and Gender. Book, Other. University of
Pennsylvania Press. Philadelphia, PA. 1993. 400p.
ISBN:0-8122-1431-5, ISBN13: 978-0-8122-1431-4.
Dewey:306.7/7. LCCN:92-032030.
                          Audience: **l,u,f.** *Choice, 1993.*

Butler, Judith   HQ1154.B88 1999
Gender Trouble: Feminism and the Subversion of Identity. Ed.
10. Trade Paper. Routledge. New York, NY. 1999. 256p.
ISBN:0-415-92499-5, ISBN13: 978-0-415-92499-3.
Dewey:305.3. LCCN:99-029349.
                          Audience: **u,f.** *Choice, 1990.*

Califia, Patrick   HQ77.9
Sex Changes: Transgender Politics. Trade Cloth. Cleis Press.
San Francisco, CA. 2003. 250p. ISBN:1-57344-164-3, ISBN13:
978-1-57344-164-3. Dewey:305.9/066.
                                       Audience: **g,l.**

Cameron, Loren   HQ77.95.U6C36 1996
Body Alchemy: Transsexual Portraits. Trade Paper. Cleis Press.
San Francisco, CA. 1996. 100p. ISBN:1-57344-062-0, ISBN13:
978-1-57344-062-2. Dewey:305.3. LCCN:96-025696.
                                    Audience: **g,l,u,f.**

Chiland, Colette   HQ77.9.C4813 2003
Transsexualism: Illusion and Reality. Philip Slotkin (Translator).
Library Binding. University Press of New England. Lebanon,
NH. 2003. 208p. Disseminations Ser. ISBN:0-8195-6657-8,
ISBN13: 978-0-8195-6657-7. Dewey:305.9/066.
LCCN:2004-270103.
                          Audience: **u,f.** *Choice, 2003.*

Cromwell, Jason   HQ77.9.C76 1999
Transmen and FTMs: Identities, Bodies, Genders, and
Sexualities. Trade Paper. University of Illinois Press.
Champaign, IL. 1999. 216p. ISBN:0-252-06825-4, ISBN13:
978-0-252-06825-6. Dewey:305.9/066. LCCN:99-006186.
                                       Audience: **u,f.**

Essed, Philomenia &   HQ1075.C656 2005
  Goldberg, David Theo (Editors)
Companion to Gender Studies. Trade Cloth. Blackwell
Publishing, Inc. Malden, MA. 2004. 576p. Blackwell
Companions in Cultural Studies, Vol. 8 ISBN:0-631-22109-3,
ISBN13: 978-0-631-22109-8. Dewey:305.3/072.
LCCN:2004-006865.
                          Audience: **g,l,u,f.** *Choice, 2005.*

Feinberg, Leslie   PS3556.E427S7 1993
Stone Butch Blues. Trade Paper. Firebrand Books. Ithaca, NY.
1993. 304p. ISBN:1-56341-029-X, ISBN13: 978-1-56341-029-1.
Dewey:813/.54. LCCN:93-016092.
                                       Audience: **g.**

Feinberg, Leslie   HQ77.9.F44 1996
Transgender Warriors: Making History from Joan of Arc to
Dennis Rodman. Trade Paper. Beacon Press. Boston, MA. 1997.

240p. ISBN:0-8070-7941-3, ISBN13: 978-0-8070-7941-6.
Dewey:305.3. LCCN:96-037682.
                          Audience: **g,l,u,f.** *Choice, 1996.*

Foucault, Michel   RC883.B3713
Herculine Barbin: Being the Recently Discovered Memoirs of a
Nineteenth-Century French Hermaphodite. Richard McDougall
(Translator). Trade Paper. Knopf Publishing Group. New York,
NY. 1980. 224p. ISBN:0-394-73862-4, ISBN13:
978-0-394-73862-8. Dewey:616.6940092.
                                    Audience: **g,l,u,f.**

Garber, Marjorie B.   HQ77.G37
Vested Interests: Cross-Dressing and Cultural Anxiety. UK-B
Format Paperback. Routledge. New York, NY. 1997. 456p.
ISBN:0-415-91951-7, ISBN13: 978-0-415-91951-7.
Dewey:306.77.
                                       Audience: **l,u,f.**

Haeberle, Erwin J. &   HQ74.B575 1998
  Gindorf, Rolf (Editors)
Bisexualities: The Ideology and Practice of Sexual Contact with
Both Males and Females. Trade Cloth. Continuum International
Publishing Group, Ltd. London, 1997. 266p.
ISBN:0-8264-0923-7, ISBN13: 978-0-8264-0923-2.
Dewey:306.76/5. LCCN:96-040051.
                                       Audience: **u,f.**

Halberstam, Judith   HQ75.5.H335 2004
In a Queer Time and Place: Transgender Bodies, Subcultural
Lives. Trade Cloth. New York University Press. New York, NY.
2005. 256p. Sexual Cultures Ser. ISBN:0-8147-3584-3, ISBN13:
978-0-8147-3584-8. Dewey:306.76/8. LCCN:2004-018151.
                                       Audience: **l,u,f.**

Haynes, Felicity &   HQ1075.U65 2001
  McKenna, Tarquam (Editors)
Unseen Genders: Beyond the Binaries. Paper Text. Peter Lang
Publishing, Inc. New York, NY. 2001. vi, 239p. Eruptions Ser.,
Vol. 12:New Thinking Across the Disciplines
ISBN:0-8204-5024-3, ISBN13: 978-0-8204-5024-7.
Dewey:305.3. LCCN:00-034803.
                                       Audience: **l,u,f.**

Hirschfeld, Magnus   HQ77.H57 1991
Transvestites: The Erotic Drive to Cross-Dress. Michael A.
Lombardi-Nash (Translator), Vern L. Bullough (Foreword by).
Trade Cloth. Prometheus Books, Publishers. Amherst, NY. 1991.
424p. ISBN:0-87975-665-9, ISBN13: 978-0-87975-665-9.
Dewey:306.77. LCCN:90-024827.
                                       Audience: **l,u,f.**

Jorgensen, Christine T.   HQ77.8.J67J67 2000
Christine Jorgensen: A Personal Autobiography. Ed. 2. Susan
Stryker (Introduction by). Trade Paper. Cleis Press. San
Francisco, CA. 2000. 340p. ISBN:1-57344-100-7, ISBN13:
978-1-57344-100-1. Dewey:305.9/066 B. LCCN:00-063904.
                                       Audience: **g,l.**

Lang, Sabine   E98.S48L3613 1998
Men as Women, Women as Men: Changing Gender in Native
American Cultures. John L. Vantine (Translator). Trade Cloth.
University of Texas Press. Austin, TX. 1998. 416p.
ISBN:0-292-74700-4, ISBN13: 978-0-292-74700-5.
Dewey:305.3/08997. LCCN:97-034759.
                          Audience: **l,u,f.** *Choice, 1999.*

Formats: Web: ☐ Ebook: ℮ CD/DVD-ROM: 🗲 BCL3: ℬ

Lester, Toni P. (Editor)   **HQ1075.G4645 2002**
Gender Nonconformity, Race, and Sexuality: Charting the
Connections. Trade Cloth. University of Wisconsin Press.
Chicago, IL. 2003. ix, 232p. ISBN:0-299-18140-5, ISBN13:
978-0-299-18140-6. Dewey:305.3. LCCN:2002-003997.
> Audience: **l,u,f.** *Choice, 2003.*

Meyerowitz, Joanne   **HQ77**
How Sex Changed: A History of Transsexuality in the United
States. Trade Cloth. Harvard University Press. Cambridge, MA.
2002. 400p. ISBN:0-674-00925-8, ISBN13: 978-0-674-00925-7.
Dewey:306.77. LCCN:2002-020536.
> Audience: **g,l,u,f.** *Choice, 2003.*

Middlebrook, Diane   **ML410.E44**
  Wood
Suits Me: The Double Life of Billy Tipton. Trade Paper.
Houghton Mifflin Company Trade & Reference Division.
Boston, MA. 1999. 356p. ISBN:0-395-95789-3, ISBN13:
978-0-395-95789-9. Dewey:781.6/5/092.
> Audience: **g,l,u,f.**

Morris, Jan   **HQ77.9**
Conundrum. Trade Paper. Henry Holt & Company. New York,
NY. 1987. 192p. ISBN:0-8050-0361-4, ISBN13:
978-0-8050-0361-1. Dewey:306.76/8. LCCN:87-008668.
> Audience: **g,l,u,f.**

Namaste, Viviane K.   **HQ77.95.C2N35 2000**
Invisible Lives: The Erasure of Transsexual and Transgendered
People in the Cultural and Institutional World. Trade Paper.
University of Chicago Press. Chicago, IL. 2000. 320p.
ISBN:0-226-56810-5, ISBN13: 978-0-226-56810-2.
Dewey:305.9/066. LCCN:00-024155.
> Audience: **g,l,u,f.**

Nestle, Joan, et al.   **HQ23**
GenderQueer: Voices from Beyond the Sexual Binary. Riki
Anne Wilchins & Clare Howell (Authors). Trade Paper. Alyson
Publications. Los Angeles, CA. 2002. 320p.
ISBN:1-55583-730-1, ISBN13: 978-1-55583-730-3.
Dewey:305.3.
> Audience: **g,l,u,f.**

Newton, Esther   **PN2270.I4**
Mother Camp: Female Impersonators in America. Trade Paper.
University of Chicago Press. Chicago, IL. 1979. 158p.
ISBN:0-226-57760-0, ISBN13: 978-0-226-57760-9.
Dewey:306/.484. LCCN:76-037634.
> Audience: **l,u,f.**

Pettiway, Leon E.   **HQ77.P44 1996**
Honey, Honey, Miss Thang: Being Black, Gay, and on the
Streets. Trade Cloth. Temple University Press. Philadelphia, PA.
1996. 320p. ISBN:1-56639-497-X, ISBN13: 978-1-56639-497-0.
Dewey:305.3. LCCN:96-020077.
> Audience: **g,l,u,f.**

Preves, Sharon E.   **RC883.P74 2003**
Intersex and Identity: The Contested Self. Trade Cloth. Rutgers
University Press. Piscataway, NJ. 2004. 240p.
ISBN:0-8135-3229-9, ISBN13: 978-0-8135-3229-5.
Dewey:616.6/94. LCCN:2002-012493.
> Audience: **u,f.**

Roscoe, Will (Editor)   **E98.S48R67 1998**
Changing Ones: Third and Fourth Genders in Native North
America. Trade Cloth. Palgrave Macmillan. New York, NY.

1998. 334p. ISBN:0-312-17539-6, ISBN13: 978-0-312-17539-9.
Dewey:305.308997. LCCN:97-041762.
> Audience: **g,l,u,f.** *Choice, 1998.*

Roscoe, Will   **E99.Z9R78 1991**
ⓔ The Zuni Man-Woman. E-Book. NetLibrary, Inc. Boulder,
CO. 1991. ISBN:0-585-28264-1, ISBN13: 978-0-585-28264-0.
Dewey:306.73/089974.
> Audience: **g,l,u,f.** *Choice, 1992.*

Wilton, Tamsin   **HQ29.W55 2004**
Sexual (Dis)Orientation: Gender, Sex, Desire and
Self-Fashioning. Cloth over Boards. Palgrave Macmillan. New
York, NY. 2004. 240p. ISBN:1-4039-0572-X, ISBN13:
978-1-4039-0572-7. Dewey:305.3. LCCN:2004-043790.
> Audience: **u,f.**

Personal Identity > Sexual Orientation

Angelides, Steven   **HQ74.A54 2001**
A History of Bisexuality. Trade Cloth. University of Chicago
Press. Chicago, IL. 2001. 296p. Chicago Series on Sexuality,
History and Society ISBN:0-226-02089-4, ISBN13:
978-0-226-02089-1. Dewey:306.76/5. LCCN:00-013141.
> Audience: **g,l,u,f.**

Bell, Alan P. &   **HQ76.2.U5.B45**
  Weinberg, Martin S.
Homosexualities: A Study of Diversity Among Men and
Women. Trade Cloth. Simon & Schuster. New York, NY. 1978.
505p. ISBN:0-671-24212-1, ISBN13: 978-0-671-24212-1.
Dewey:301.41/57/0973. LCCN:78-007398.
> Audience: **g.** *B*

Bell, Alan P., et al.   **HQ76.B438 1981**
Sexual Preference: Its Development in Men and Women. Martin
S. Weinberg & Sue K. Hammersmith (Authors). Trade Cloth.
Indiana University Press. Bloomington, IN. 1981. 336p.
ISBN:0-253-16674-8, ISBN13: 978-0-253-16674-6.
Dewey:306.7/6. LCCN:81-047006.
> Audience: **l,u.**

Blackwood, Evelyn &   **HQ75.5.F43 1999**
  Wieringa, Saskia
Female Desires: Same-Sex Relations and Transgender Practices
Across Cultures. Trade Cloth. Columbia University Press. New
York, NY. 1999. 352p. Between Men, Between Women Ser.
ISBN:0-231-11260-2, ISBN13: 978-0-231-11260-4.
Dewey:306.76/6. LCCN:98-037847.
> Audience: **u,f.**

Downs, Alan   **HQ76.D69 2005**
The Velvet Rage: Overcoming the Pain of Growing up Gay in a
Straight Man's World. Trade Cloth. Da Capo Press, Inc.
Cambridge, MA. 2005. 224p. ISBN:0-7382-1011-0, ISBN13:
978-0-7382-1011-7. Dewey:306.76620973. LCCN:2005-004606.
> Audience: **g,l,u.**

Firestein, Beth A.   **HQ74.2.U5B57 1996**
  (Editor)
Bisexuality: The Psychology and Politics of an Invisible
Minority. Trade Cloth. SAGE Publications, Inc. Thousand Oaks,
CA. 1996. 354p. ISBN:0-8039-7273-3, ISBN13:
978-0-8039-7273-5. Dewey:306.7/65. LCCN:96-009987.
> Audience: **g,l,u,f.**

Haeberle, Erwin J. & Gindorf, Rolf (Editors)　　　HQ74.B575 1998
Bisexualities: The Ideology and Practice of Sexual Contact with Both Males and Females. Trade Cloth. Continuum International Publishing Group, Ltd. London, 1997. 266p. ISBN:0-8264-0923-7, ISBN13: 978-0-8264-0923-2. Dewey:306.76/5. LCCN:96-040051.
Audience: **u,f.**

Hutchins, Loraine & Kaahumanu, Lani (Editors)　　　HQ74.B5 1990
Bi Any Other Name: Bisexual People Speak Out. Trade Paper. Alyson Publications. Los Angeles, CA. 1991. 408p. ISBN:1-55583-174-5, ISBN13: 978-1-55583-174-5. Dewey:306.7/65/0973. LCCN:90-045816.
Audience: **g.**

Kaeser, Gigi (Photographer)　　　HQ76.13.K34 1999
Love Makes a Family: Portraits of Lesbian, Gay, Bisexual and Transgendered Parents and Their Families. Peggy Gillespie (Contribution by), Kath Weston (Introduction by), Minnie Bruce Pratt (Foreword by). Trade Cloth. University of Massachusetts Press. Amherst, MA. 1999. 280p. ISBN:1-55849-160-0, ISBN13: 978-1-55849-160-1. Dewey:306.874. LCCN:98-030266.
Audience: **g.**

Katz, Jonathan N.　　　HQ23.K315 1995
The Invention of Heterosexuality. Gore Vidal (Foreword by). Trade Cloth. Penguin Group (USA) Inc. New York, NY. 1995. 320p. ISBN:0-525-93845-1, ISBN13: 978-0-525-93845-3. Dewey:306.7. LCCN:94-032650.
Audience: **g,l.**

Kitzinger, Celia　　　HQ75.5.K58 1987
The Social Construction of Lesbianism. Trade Cloth. SAGE Publications, Ltd. London, 1988. 240p. Inquiries in Social Construction Ser., Vol. 1 ISBN:0-8039-8116-3, ISBN13: 978-0-8039-8116-4. Dewey:306.7/663. LCCN:87-062029.
Audience: **u,f.** *Choice, 1988.*

Lorde, Audre Geraldine　　　PS3562.O75S5 1984
Sister Outsider: Essays and Speeches. Trade Cloth. Crossing Press, Incorporated, The. Berkeley, CA. 1984. 192p. Feminist Ser. ISBN:0-89594-141-4, ISBN13: 978-0-89594-141-1. Dewey:814/.54. LCCN:84-001844.
Audience: **g,l,u,f.**

Mondimore, Francis M.　　　HQ76.25.M649 1996
A Natural History of Homosexuality. Trade Paper. Johns Hopkins University Press. Baltimore, MD. 1996. 304p. ISBN:0-8018-5440-7, ISBN13: 978-0-8018-5440-8. Dewey:306.76/6. LCCN:96-016191.
Audience: **g,l,u,f.** *Choice, 1997.*

Murray, Stephen O.　　　HQ76.25
Homosexualities. Trade Paper. University of Chicago Press. Chicago, IL. 2002. 515p. Worlds of Desire Ser., :The Chicago Series on Sexuality, Gender, and Culture Ser. ISBN:0-226-55195-4, ISBN13: 978-0-226-55195-1. Dewey:306.76/62. LCCN:99-087502.
Audience: **g,l,u,f.** *Choice, 2001.*

Orndorff, Kata (Editor)　　　HQ74.B52 1999
Bi Lives: Bisexual Women Tell Their Stories. Trade Paper. See Sharp Press. Tucson, AZ. 1999. 252p. ISBN:1-884365-09-4, ISBN13: 978-1-884365-09-6. Dewey:305.48/9663. LCCN:00-698940.
Audience: **g,l.**

Roscoe, Will & Murray, Stephen O. (Editors)　　　HQ76.3.A35B69 1998
Boy-Wives and Female-Husbands: Studies in African Homosexualities. Cloth over Boards. Palgrave Macmillan. New York, NY. 1998. 336p. ISBN:0-312-21216-X, ISBN13: 978-0-312-21216-2. Dewey:306.76/6/096. LCCN:98-021464.
Audience: **g,l,u,f.**

Rust, Paula C.　　　HQ75.6.U5R87 1995
Bisexuality and the Challenge to Lesbian Politics: Sex, Loyalty, and Revolution. Trade Cloth. New York University Press. New York, NY. 1995. 387p. The Cutting Edge: Lesbian Life and Literature Ser. ISBN:0-8147-7444-X, ISBN13: 978-0-8147-7444-1. Dewey:305.48/9664. LCCN:95-031419.
Audience: **u,f.**

Signorile, Michelangelo　　　HQ76.2.U5.S54
Life Outside: The Signorile Report on Gay Men: Sex, Drugs, Muscles, and the Passages of Life. HarperCollins. 1997. ISBN:0-06-018761-1, ISBN13: 978-0-06-018761-3.
Audience: **g,l.**

Storr, Merl　　　HQ74.B577 1999
Bisexuality: A Critical Reader. Paper over Boards. Routledge. New York, NY. 1999. 256p. ISBN:0-415-16659-4, ISBN13: 978-0-415-16659-1. Dewey:306.76/5. LCCN:98-042140.
Audience: **g,u,f.**

Swan, Wallace (Editor)　　　HQ76.8.U5G358 1997
Gay, Lesbian, Bisexual and Transgender Public Policy Issues: A Citizen's and Administrator's Guide to the New Cultural Struggle. Trade Cloth. Haworth Press, Incorporated, The. Binghamton, NY. 1997. 148p. ISBN:0-7890-0250-7, ISBN13: 978-0-7890-0250-1. Dewey:305.9/066. LCCN:97-018836.
Audience: **g,l,u,f.**

Tejirian, Edward J.　　　HQ1090.T453 2000
Male to Male: Sexual Feelings Across the Boundaries of Identity. Trade Cloth. Haworth Press, Incorporated, The. Binghamton, NY. 2000. xix, 382p. ISBN:1-56023-975-1, ISBN13: 978-1-56023-975-8. Dewey:305.31. LCCN:00-027137.
Audience: **u,f.**

Religion

Besen, Wayne R. (Author, Editor)　　　BV4437.5.B47 2003
Anything but Straight: Unmasking the Scandals and Lies Behind the Ex-Gay Myth. Trade Cloth. Haworth Press, Incorporated, The. Binghamton, NY. 2003. 242p. ISBN:1-56023-445-8, ISBN13: 978-1-56023-445-6. Dewey:261.8/3577. LCCN:2002-013857.
Audience: **g.**

Conner, Randy P., et al.　　　BL795.H6C65 1998
Cassell's Encyclopedia of Queer Myth, Symbol and Spirit: Gay, Lesbian, Bisexual and Transgender Lore. David H. Sparks & Mariya Sparks (Authors). Trade Paper. Continuum International Publishing Group, Ltd. London, 1998. 400p. Cassell Sexual

Politics Ser. ISBN:0-304-70423-7, ISBN13: 978-0-304-70423-1.
Dewey:291.1/3/08664. LCCN:98-020180.

Audience: **g,l,u,f.**

Helminiak, Daniel A.   **BS680.H67**
What the Bible Really Says about Homosexuality: Millennium
Edition. Trade Paper. Alamo Square Press. Tajique, NM. 2000.
152p. ISBN:1-886360-09-X, ISBN13: 978-1-886360-09-9.
Dewey:261.835766. LCCN:94-070336.

Audience: **g.**

Horner, Tom   **BR115.H6**
Homosexuality and the Judeo-Christian Tradition: An Annotated
Bibliography. Trade Cloth. Scarecrow Press, Inc. Lanham, MD.
1981. 141p. American Theological Library Association
Monograph, No. 5 ISBN:0-8108-1412-9, ISBN13:
978-0-8108-1412-7. Dewey:016.2618/3576. LCCN:81-000899.

Audience: **g,l,u,f.**

Swidler, Arlene (Editor)   **BL65.H64 H65 1993**
Homosexuality and World Religions. Trade Paper. Continuum
International Publishing Group, Ltd. London, 1993. 240p.
ISBN:1-56338-051-X, ISBN13: 978-1-56338-051-8.
Dewey:291.1/7835766. LCCN:93-006848.

Audience: **g.**

Religion > Christianity

Bailey, D. Sherwin   **HQ76.B3 1975**
Homosexuality and the Western Christian Tradition. Trade
Cloth. Shoe String Press, Inc. North Haven, CT. 1975. xii, 181p.
ISBN:0-208-01492-6, ISBN13: 978-0-208-01492-4.
Dewey:301.41/57. LCCN:74-034384.

Audience: **g,l.**

Boswell, John   **HQ76.3**
Christianity, Social Tolerance, and Homosexuality: Gay People
in Western Europe from the Beginning of the Christian Era to
the Fourteenth Century. Trade Paper. University of Chicago
Press. Chicago, IL. 1981. 442p. ISBN:0-226-06711-4, ISBN13:
978-0-226-06711-7. Dewey:306.7/66/094. LCCN:79-011171.

Audience: **u,f.** ℬ

Boswell, John   **HQ76.3.E8**
Same-Sex Unions in Premodern Europe. UK-Trade Paper.
Knopf Publishing Group. New York, NY. 1995. 464p.
ISBN:0-679-75164-5, ISBN13: 978-0-679-75164-9.
Dewey:306.76/6/094.

Audience: **g,l,u,f.** *Choice, 1994.*

Brooten, Bernadette J.   **BS2665.6.L47B76 1996**
Love Between Women: Early Christian Responses to Female
Homoeroticism. Trade Cloth. University of Chicago Press.
Chicago, IL. 1996. 446p. The Chicago Series on Sexuality,
History, and Society Ser. ISBN:0-226-07591-5, ISBN13:
978-0-226-07591-4. Dewey:306.7/663/0901. LCCN:96-004727.

Audience: **g,l,u,f.** *Choice, 1997.*

Curb, Rosemary &   **BX4225**
Manahan, Nancy (Editors)
Lesbian Nuns: Breaking Silence. Trade Cloth. Bella Books, Inc.
Tallahassee, FL. 1985. 432p. ISBN:0-930044-63-0, ISBN13:
978-0-930044-63-3. Dewey:255/.9/008806643.
LCCN:84-029594.

Audience: **g,l.**

Gramick, Jeannine   **BX1795.H66H67 1989**
(Editor), et al.
Homosexuality in the Priesthood and Religious Life. John
Boswell, Daniel C. Maguire & Rosemary Radford Ruether
(Editors). Trade Paper. Crossroad Publishing Company. New
York, NY. 1989. ISBN:0-8245-0963-3, ISBN13:
978-0-8245-0963-7. Dewey:253/.2. LCCN:89-033997.

Audience: **g,l,u,f.**

Gross, Robert E. &   **BS680.H67.T35 2000**
West, Mona (Editors)
Take Back the Word: A Queer Reading of the Bible. Trade
Paper. Pilgrim Press, The/United Church Press. Cleveland, OH.
2000. xvi, 239p. ISBN:0-8298-1397-7, ISBN13:
978-0-8298-1397-5. Dewey:220.6/086/64. LCCN:00-048293.

Audience: **g.**

Herman, Didi   **BR115.H6H47 1997**
The Antigay Agenda: Orthodox Vision and the Christian Right.
Trade Cloth. University of Chicago Press. Chicago, IL. 1997.
252p. ISBN:0-226-32764-7, ISBN13: 978-0-226-32764-8.
Dewey:261.8/35766/0973. LCCN:96-030354.

Audience: **g,l.** *Choice, 1998.*

McNeill, John J.   **HQ76.25**
The Church and the Homosexual. Ed. 4. Trade Paper. Beacon
Press. Boston, MA. 1993. 256p. ISBN:0-8070-7931-6, ISBN13:
978-0-8070-7931-7. Dewey:261.8/34/157. LCCN:94-015723.

Audience: **g,l,u,f.**

Scanzoni, Letha D. &   **BR115.H6S3 1994**
Mollenkott, Virginia R.
Is the Homosexual My Neighbor?: A Positive Christian
Response. Trade Paper. HarperCollins Publishers. New York,
NY. 1994. 256p. ISBN:0-06-067078-9, ISBN13:
978-0-06-067078-8. Dewey:261.8/35766. LCCN:93-034182.

Audience: **g.**

White, Mel   **BX9896.Z8W45 1995**
Stranger at the Gate: To Be Gay and Christian in America.
Trade Paper. Penguin Group (USA) Inc. New York, NY. 1995.
352p. ISBN:0-452-27381-1, ISBN13: 978-0-452-27381-8.
Dewey:261.8/35766/092 B. LCCN:94-038810.

Audience: **g,l.**

Religion > Judaism

Alpert, Rebecca T.   **BM729.H65A47**
Like Bread on the Seder Plate: Jewish Lesbians and the
Transformation of Tradition. Trade Paper. Columbia University
Press. New York, NY. 1998. 224p. ISBN:0-231-09661-5,
ISBN13: 978-0-231-09661-4. Dewey:296.086643.
LCCN:96-043411.

Audience: **g.**

Balka, Christie & Rose,   **BM729.H65T85 1989**
Andy (Editors)
Twice Blessed: On Being Lesbian or Gay and Jewish. Trade
Cloth. Beacon Press. Boston, MA. 1989. 320p.
ISBN:0-8070-7908-1, ISBN13: 978-0-8070-7908-9.
Dewey:296/.08/664. LCCN:89-042598.

Audience: **g.**

Boyarin, Daniel, et al.   **HQ75.15.Q5 2003**
Queer Theory and the Jewish Question. Daniel Itzkovitz & Ann
Pellegrini (Authors). Trade Cloth. Edinburgh University Press.
Edinburgh, 2003. 464p. Between Men, Between Women Ser.

ISBN:0-231-11374-9, ISBN13: 978-0-231-11374-8. Dewey:305.892/4. LCCN:2003-048494.

Audience: **l,u,f.** *Choice, 2004.*

Elwell, Sue Levi   **BM753.L47 2001**
(Editor), et al.
Lesbian Rabbis: The First Generation. Rebecca Alpert & Shirley Idelson (Editors). Trade Cloth. Rutgers University Press. Piscataway, NJ. 2001. 224p. ISBN:0-8135-2916-6, ISBN13: 978-0-8135-2916-5. Dewey:296.6/1/086643. LCCN:00-045751.

Audience: **g.**

Greenberg, Steven   **BM729.H65G74 2004**
Wrestling with God and Men: Homosexuality in the Jewish Tradition. Trade Cloth. University of Wisconsin Press. Chicago, IL. 2004. 312p. ISBN:0-299-19090-0, ISBN13: 978-0-299-19090-3. Dewey:296.3/66. LCCN:2003-020568.

Audience: **l,u,f.** *Choice, 2004.*

Raphael, Lee   **HQ75.8.R36A3 1996**
Journeys and Arrivals: On Being Gay and Jewish. Trade Cloth. Faber & Faber, Inc. New York, NY. 1996. 156p. ISBN:0-571-19882-1, ISBN13: 978-0-571-19882-5. Dewey:305.38/9664/092 B. LCCN:95-039070.

Audience: **g.**

Schimel, Lawrence   **HQ76.2.U5F68 2002**
(Editor)
Found Tribe: Jewish Coming Out Stories. Trade Paper. Sherman Asher Publishing. Santa Fe, NM. 2002. 192p. ISBN:1-890932-20-5, ISBN13: 978-1-890932-20-6. Dewey:305.38/9664. LCCN:2002-018521.

Audience: **g.**

Shneer, David & Aviv,   **HQ75.16.U6Q44 2002**
Caryn (Editors)
Queer Jews. Trade Paper. Routledge. New York, NY. 2002. 304p. ISBN:0-415-93167-3, ISBN13: 978-0-415-93167-0. Dewey:305.9/0664. LCCN:2002-024902.

Audience: **g,l,u.**

Religion > Other religions

Conner, Randy P. &   **BL65.H64C67 2004**
Sparks, David Hatfield
Queering Creole Spiritual Traditions: Lesbian, Gay, Bisexual, and Transgender Participation in African-Inspired Traditions in the Americas. Joseph M. Murphy (Foreword by). Trade Paper. Haworth Press, Incorporated, The. Binghamton, NY. 2005. 392p. ISBN:1-56023-351-6, ISBN13: 978-1-56023-351-0. Dewey:299/.6/08664. LCCN:2003-011305.

Audience: **l,u,f.**

Harvey, Andrew   **BL625.E76 1997**
The Essential Gay Mystics: Shiva's Dancing Ground. Trade Paper. HarperCollins Publishers. New York, NY. 2000. 384p. ISBN:0-06-251524-1, ISBN13: 978-0-06-251524-7. Dewey:291.4/22/08663. LCCN:96-052873.

Audience: **g.**

Leyland, Winston   **BQ4570.H65**
(Editor)
Queer Dharma: Voices of Gay Buddhists. Trade Cloth. Gay Sunshine Press, Inc. San Francisco, CA. 2000. 224p. Queer Dharma Ser., Vol. 2 ISBN:0-940567-23-7, ISBN13: 978-0-940567-23-8. Dewey:294.3/086/64. LCCN:97-027590.

Audience: **g.**

Leyland, Winston   **BQ4570.H65Q84 1998**
(Editor)
Queer Dharma: Voices of Gay Buddhists. Trade Cloth. Gay Sunshine Press, Inc. San Francisco, CA. 2000. 416p. Queer Dharma Ser., Vol. 1 ISBN:0-940567-22-9, ISBN13: 978-0-940567-22-1. Dewey:294.3/086/64. LCCN:97-027590.

Audience: **g.**

Murray, Stephen O. &   **HQ76.3.I75M87 1997**
Roscoe, Will (Editors)
Islamic Homosexualities: Culture, History, and Literature. Trade Cloth. New York University Press. New York, NY. 1997. 392p. ISBN:0-8147-7467-9, ISBN13: 978-0-8147-7467-0. Dewey:306/.62/0917671. LCCN:96-035677.

Audience: **g,l,u,f.** *Choice, 1997.*

Nanda, Serena   **HQ449.N36 1998**
Neither Man nor Woman: The Hijras of India. Ed. 2. Paper Text. Thomson Wadsworth. Belmont, CA. 1998. 208p. Anthropology Ser. ISBN:0-534-50903-7, ISBN13: 978-0-534-50903-3. Dewey:305.3. LCCN:98-041187.

Audience: **l,u,f.** *Choice, 1990.*

Schmitt, Arno & Sofer,   **HQ76.2.I74**
Jehoeda
Sexuality and Eroticism among Males in Moslem Societies. Jeffrey Weeks (Introduction by). Library Binding. Haworth Press, Incorporated, The. Binghamton, NY. 1992. 210p. ISBN:1-56024-047-4, ISBN13: 978-1-56024-047-1. Dewey:306.76/62/0917671. LCCN:91-002316.

Audience: **g,l.**

Relationships

Adelman, Marcy R.   **HQ75.6.U5M53 2000**
(Editor)
Midlife Lesbian Relationships: Friends, Lovers, Children, and Parents. Trade Cloth. Haworth Press, Incorporated, The. Binghamton, NY. 2000. xvii, 162p. ISBN:1-56023-141-6, ISBN13: 978-1-56023-141-7. Dewey:305.244. LCCN:00-031966.

Audience: **l,u,f.**

Berzon, Betty   **HQ76.3.U5B467 1996**
The Intimacy Dance: A Guide to Long-Term Success in Gay and Lesbian Relationships. Trade Cloth. Penguin Group (USA) Inc. New York, NY. 1996. 304p. ISBN:0-525-94234-3, ISBN13: 978-0-525-94234-4. Dewey:306.76/6. LCCN:96-019392.

Audience: **g.**

Brown, Mildred L. &   **HQ77.7**
Rounsley, Chloe Ann
True Selves: Understanding Transsexualism—for Families, Friends, Coworkers, and Helping Professionals. Trade Paper. John Wiley & Sons, Inc. Hoboken, NJ. 2003. 288p. ISBN:0-7879-6702-5, ISBN13: 978-0-7879-6702-4. Dewey:305.3. LCCN:2003-269583.

Audience: **g,l.**

Esterberg, Kristin G.   **HQ75.5.E85 1997**
Lesbian and Bisexual Identities: Constructing Communities, Constructing Selves. Trade Paper. Temple University Press. Philadelphia, PA. 1997. 216p. ISBN:1-56639-510-0, ISBN13: 978-1-56639-510-6. Dewey:305.9/06643. LCCN:96-035409.

Audience: **l,u,f.** *Choice, 1997.*

Harry, Joseph & Devall,   **HQ76.3.U5**
  William B.
The Social Organization of Gay Males. Trade Cloth. Greenwood
Publishing Group, Inc. Portsmouth, NH. 1978. Praeger Special
Studies ISBN:0-275-90296-X, ISBN13: 978-0-275-90296-4.
Dewey:301.41/57/0973. LCCN:78-008381.
                                        Audience: **u,f.** ℬ

Howey, Noelle &   **HQ777.8.O87 2000**
  Samuels, Ellen
Out of the Ordinary: Essays on Growing up with Gay, Lesbian
and Transgender Parents. Dan Savage (Contribution by),
Margarethe Cammer-Meyer (Foreword by). Trade Paper. St.
Martin's Press. Gordonville, VA. 2000. 240p.
ISBN:0-312-24489-4, ISBN13: 978-0-312-24489-7.
Dewey:306.874. LCCN:00-025493.
                                        Audience: **g,l,u,f.**

Lewin, Ellen   **HQ75.53.L49 1993**
Lesbian Mothers: Accounts of Gender in American Culture.
Book, Other. Cornell University Press. Ithaca, NY. 1993. 256p.
The Anthropology of Contemporary Issues Ser.
ISBN:0-8014-2857-2, ISBN13: 978-0-8014-2857-9.
Dewey:306.874/3/086643. LCCN:92-054977.
                         Audience: **l,u,f.** *Choice, 1993.*

Nardi, Peter M.   **HQ76.2.U5N37 1999**
Gay Men's Friendships: Invincible Communities. Trade Cloth.
University of Chicago Press. Chicago, IL. 1999. 264p. Worlds
of Desire Ser. ISBN:0-226-56843-1, ISBN13:
978-0-226-56843-0. Dewey:302.3/4/086642. LCCN:98-049657.
                         Audience: **u,f.** *Choice, 1999.*

Nestle, Joan & Preston,   **HQ76.25**
  John (Editors)
Sister and Brother: Lesbians and Gay Men Write about Their
Lives Together. Trade Paper. Continuum International Publishing
Group, Ltd. London, 256p. ISBN:0-304-33483-9, ISBN13:
978-0-304-33483-4. Dewey:306.7/66.
                                        Audience: **g,l.**

Preston, John (Editor)   **HQ76.2.U5M46 1992**
A Member of the Family: Gay Men Write about Their Closest
Relations. Trade Cloth. Penguin Group (USA) Inc. New York,
NY. 1992. 320p. ISBN:0-525-93549-5, ISBN13:
978-0-525-93549-0. Dewey:306.874. LCCN:92-052867.
                                        Audience: **g.**

Preston, John &   **HQ76.2.U5F75 1995**
  Lowenthal, Michael (Editors)
Friends and Lovers: Gay Men Write about the Families They
Create. Trade Cloth. Penguin Group (USA) Inc. New York, NY.
1995. 320p. ISBN:0-525-93858-3, ISBN13: 978-0-525-93858-3.
Dewey:305.9/06/642. LCCN:94-041345.
                                        Audience: **g.**

Weston, Kath   **HQ76.3.U5W48**
Families We Choose: Lesbians, Gays, Kinship. Ed. 2. Trade
Paper. Columbia University Press. New York, NY. 1997. 288p.
Between Men, Between Women Ser. ISBN:0-231-11093-6,
ISBN13: 978-0-231-11093-8. Dewey:306.87. LCCN:90-049349.
                         Audience: **g,l,u,f.** *Choice, 1991.*

Relationships > Dating

Boykin, Keith   **HQ74.2.U5**
Beyond the Down Low: Sex, Lies, and Denial in Black
America. E. Lynn Harris (Foreword by). Trade Cloth. Avalon

Publishing Group. New York, NY. 2005. 256p.
ISBN:0-7867-1434-4, ISBN13: 978-0-7867-1434-6.
Dewey:305.38/896073.
                                        Audience: **g,l.**

King, J. L. & Hunter,   **HQ74.2.U5K56 2004**
  Karen
On the down Low: A Journey into the Lives of "Straight" Black
Men Who Sleep with Men. Trade Paper. Broadway Books. New
York, NY. 2005. 208p. ISBN:0-7679-1399-X, ISBN13:
978-0-7679-1399-7. Dewey:305.38/896073. LCCN:2003-056006.
                                        Audience: **g,l.**

Relationships > Sex

Blackwood, Evelyn &   **HQ75.5.F43 1999**
  Wieringa, Saskia
Female Desires: Same-Sex Relations and Transgender Practices
Across Cultures. Trade Cloth. Columbia University Press. New
York, NY. 1999. 352p. Between Men, Between Women Ser.
ISBN:0-231-11260-2, ISBN13: 978-0-231-11260-4.
Dewey:306.76/6. LCCN:98-037847.
                                        Audience: **u,f.**

Boykin, Keith   **HQ74.2.U5**
Beyond the Down Low: Sex, Lies, and Denial in Black
America. E. Lynn Harris (Foreword by). Trade Cloth. Avalon
Publishing Group. New York, NY. 2005. 256p.
ISBN:0-7867-1434-4, ISBN13: 978-0-7867-1434-6.
Dewey:305.38/896073.
                                        Audience: **g,l.**

Gerard, Kent &   **HQ76.2.E9.P87 1989**
  Hekma, Gert
The Pursuit of Sodomy: Male Homosexuality in Renaissance
and Enlightenment Europe. Cloth Text. Haworth Press,
Incorporated, The. Binghamton, NY. 1989. 553p. Journal of
Homosexuality Ser., Vol. 16, Nos. 1-2 ISBN:0-86656-491-8,
ISBN13: 978-0-86656-491-5. Dewey:306.7/662/094.
LCCN:88-032231.
                                        Audience: **u,f.**

King, J. L. & Hunter,   **HQ74.2.U5K56 2004**
  Karen
On the down Low: A Journey into the Lives of "Straight" Black
Men Who Sleep with Men. Trade Paper. Broadway Books. New
York, NY. 2005. 208p. ISBN:0-7679-1399-X, ISBN13:
978-0-7679-1399-7. Dewey:305.38/896073. LCCN:2003-056006.
                                        Audience: **g,l.**

Loughery, John   **HQ76.2.U5L68 1998**
The Other Side of Silence: Men's Lives and Gay Identities - a
Twentieth-Century History. Cloth over Boards. Henry Holt &
Company. New York, NY. 1998. 527p. ISBN:0-8050-3896-5,
ISBN13: 978-0-8050-3896-5. Dewey:305.38/9664.
LCCN:97-042575.
                         Audience: **l,u,f.** *Choice, 1998.*

Rust, Paula C.   **HQ75.6.U5R87 1995**
Bisexuality and the Challenge to Lesbian Politics: Sex, Loyalty,
and Revolution. Trade Cloth. New York University Press. New
York, NY. 1995. 387p. The Cutting Edge: Lesbian Life and
Literature Ser. ISBN:0-8147-7444-X, ISBN13:
978-0-8147-7444-1. Dewey:305.48/9664. LCCN:95-031419.
                                        Audience: **u,f.**

Relationships > Family Relationships

Carrington, Christopher   **HQ76.3.U53S253 1999**
No Place Like Home: Relationships and Family Life among
Lesbians and Gay Men. Trade Cloth. University of Chicago
Press. Chicago, IL. 2000. 285p. Worlds of Desire Ser.
ISBN:0-226-09485-5, ISBN13: 978-0-226-09485-4.
Dewey:306.8/48/0973. LCCN:99-019780.
                                        Audience: **l,u.** *Choice, 2000.*

D'Emilio, John   **PL888.N5**
What Our Families Need: Toward a Policy Agenda for Lesbian
and Gay Families. Paper Text. National Gay & Lesbian Task
Force Policy Institute. Washington, DC. 1997.
ISBN:0-9652779-3-3, ISBN13: 978-0-9652779-3-8.
Dewey:895.62082.
                                        Audience: **g,l,u.**

Downs, Alan   **HQ76.D69 2005**
The Velvet Rage: Overcoming the Pain of Growing up Gay in a
Straight Man's World. Trade Cloth. Da Capo Press, Inc.
Cambridge, MA. 2005. 224p. ISBN:0-7382-1011-0, ISBN13:
978-0-7382-1011-7. Dewey:306.76620973. LCCN:2005-004606.
                                        Audience: **g,l,u.**

Drucker, Jane   **HQ76.3.U5**
Lesbian and Gay Families Speak Out: Understanding the Joys
and Challenges of Diverse Family Life. Trade Paper. Basic
Books. New York, NY. 2001. 288p. ISBN:0-7382-0466-8,
ISBN13: 978-0-7382-0466-6. Dewey:306.8/5/08664.
                                        Audience: **g,l.**

Galluccio, Jon, et al.   **HV875.72.U6G35 2001**
An American Family. Michael Galluccio & David Groff
(Authors). Trade Cloth. St. Martin's Press. Gordonville, VA.
2001. x, 266p. ISBN:0-312-26123-3, ISBN13:
978-0-312-26123-8. Dewey:362.73/4/08664. LCCN:00-045764.
                                        Audience: **g,l.**

Garner, Abigail   **HQ777.8.G37 2004**
Families Like Mine: Children of Gay Parents Tell It Like It Is.
Trade Cloth. HarperCollins Publishers. New York, NY. 2004.
272p. ISBN:0-06-052757-9, ISBN13: 978-0-06-052757-0.
Dewey:306.874/086/64. LCCN:2003-056975.
                                        Audience: **g,l.**

Kaeser, Gigi   **HQ76.13.K34 1999**
(Photographer)
Love Makes a Family: Portraits of Lesbian, Gay, Bisexual and
Transgendered Parents and Their Families. Peggy Gillespie
(Contribution by), Kath Weston (Introduction by), Minnie Bruce
Pratt (Foreword by). Trade Cloth. University of Massachusetts
Press. Amherst, MA. 1999. 280p. ISBN:1-55849-160-0,
ISBN13: 978-1-55849-160-1. Dewey:306.874.
LCCN:98-030266.
                                        Audience: **g.**

Lehr, Valerie   **HQ76.3.U5L44 1999**
Queer Family Values: Debunking the Myth of the Nuclear
Family. Trade Cloth. Temple University Press. Philadelphia, PA.
1999. x, 212p. Queer Politics, Queer Theories Ser.
ISBN:1-56639-683-2, ISBN13: 978-1-56639-683-7.
Dewey:306.85/0973. LCCN:98-045411.
                                        Audience: **u.**

Loughery, John   **HQ76.2.U5L68 1998**
The Other Side of Silence: Men's Lives and Gay Identities - a
Twentieth-Century History. Cloth over Boards. Henry Holt &
Company. New York, NY. 1998. 527p. ISBN:0-8050-3896-5,

ISBN13: 978-0-8050-3896-5. Dewey:305.38/9664.
LCCN:97-042575.
                                        Audience: **l,u,f.** *Choice, 1998.*

Sears, R. Bradley, Gary   **HQ75.28.U6**
  Gates, & William B. Rubenstein
☐ Same-Sex Couples and Same-Sex Couples Raising Children
in the United States.
http://www.law.ucla.edu/williamsproj/publications/USReport.pdf
Williams Project on Sexual Orientation Law and Public Policy,
UCLA School of Law. Williams Project on Sexual Orientation
Law and Public Policy, UCLA School of Law.
                                        Audience: **g,l,u,f.**

Shanley, Mary L.   **HQ536**
Making Babies, Making Families: What Matters Most in an Age
of Reproductive Technologies, Surrogacy, Adoption, and
Same-Sex and Unwed Parents' Rights. Trade Paper. Beacon
Press. Boston, MA. 2002. 224p. ISBN:0-8070-4409-1, ISBN13:
978-0-8070-4409-4. Dewey:306.85/0973.
                                        Audience: **g,l,u,f.**

Shernoff, Michael   **HQ76.2.U5G398 1997**
  (Editor)
Gay Widowers: Life after the Death of a Partner. Trade Cloth.
Haworth Press, Incorporated, The. Binghamton, NY. 1997. 161p.
ISBN:0-7890-0355-4, ISBN13: 978-0-7890-0355-3.
Dewey:305.38/9664. LCCN:97-033478.
                                        Audience: **g,l.**

Tasker, Fiona L. &   **HQ759**
  Golombok, Susan
Growing up in a Lesbian Family: Effects on Child
Development. Trade Paper. Guilford Publications, Inc. New
York, NY. 1998. 194p. ISBN:1-57230-412-X, ISBN13:
978-1-57230-412-3. Dewey:306.874/3. LCCN:96-444471.
                                        Audience: **l,u,f.** *Choice, 1997.*

Woodson, Jacqueline   **PZ7.W868**
From the Notebooks of Melanin Sun. Library Binding.
Sagebrush Education Resources. Caledonia, MN. 1995.
ISBN:0-613-05026-6, ISBN13: 978-0-613-05026-5.
Dewey:[Fic].
                                        Audience: **g.**

Relationships > Parenting

Glazer, Deborah F. &   **HQ75.28.U6G39 2001**
  Drescher, Jack (Editors)
Gay and Lesbian Parenting. Trade Cloth. Haworth Press,
Incorporated, The. Binghamton, NY. 2000. 165p. Journal of Gay
and Lesbian Psychotherapy Monograph, Vol. 4, Nos. 3-4
ISBN:0-7890-1349-5, ISBN13: 978-0-7890-1349-1.
Dewey:306.874. LCCN:2001-039150.
                                        Audience: **l,u,f.**

Green, Jesse   **HQ76.13.G74 2000**
The Velveteen Father: An Unexpected Journey to Parenthood.
UK-Trade Paper. Ballantine Books. New York, NY. 2000. 256p.
ISBN:0-345-43709-8, ISBN13: 978-0-345-43709-9.
Dewey:306.874/2. LCCN:00-190373.
                                        Audience: **g.**

Kaeser, Gigi   **HQ76.13.K34 1999**
  (Photographer)
Love Makes a Family: Portraits of Lesbian, Gay, Bisexual and
Transgendered Parents and Their Families. Peggy Gillespie

(Contribution by), Kath Weston (Introduction by), Minnie Bruce Pratt (Foreword by). Trade Cloth. University of Massachusetts Press. Amherst, MA. 1999. 280p. ISBN:1-55849-160-0, ISBN13: 978-1-55849-160-1. Dewey:306.874. LCCN:98-030266.

Audience: **g.**

Lev, Arlene Istar   **HQ75.28.U6L48 2004**
The Complete Lesbian and Gay Parenting Guide. Trade Paper. Penguin Group (USA) Inc. New York, NY. 2004. 400p. ISBN:0-425-19197-4, ISBN13: 978-0-425-19197-2. Dewey:649/.1/08664. LCCN:2004-057080.

Audience: **g,l.**

Mallon, Gerald   **HV1449.M35 1998**
We Don't Exactly Get the Welcome Wagon: The Experiences of Gay and Lesbian Adolescents in Child Welfare Systems. Cloth Text. Columbia University Press. New York, NY. 1998. 208p. ISBN:0-231-10454-5, ISBN13: 978-0-231-10454-8. Dewey:362.7/083. LCCN:97-045545.

Audience: **u,f.** *Choice, 1998.*

Pollack, Jill S.   **HQ76.3.U5P65 1995**
Lesbian and Gay Families: Redefining Parenting in America. Trade Paper. Scholastic Library Publishing. Danbury, CT. 1995. 128p. The Changing Family Ser. ISBN:0-531-11207-1, ISBN13: 978-0-531-11207-6. Dewey:306.85. LCCN:94-023934.

Audience: **g,l.**

Sears, R. Bradley, Gary   **HQ75.28.U6**
  Gates, & William B. Rubenstein
▢ Same-Sex Couples and Same-Sex Couples Raising Children in the United States.
http://www.law.ucla.edu/williamsproj/publications/USReport.pdf
Williams Project on Sexual Orientation Law and Public Policy, UCLA School of Law. Williams Project on Sexual Orientation Law and Public Policy, UCLA School of Law.

Audience: **g,l,u,f.**

Shanley, Mary L.   **HQ536**
Making Babies, Making Families: What Matters Most in an Age of Reproductive Technologies, Surrogacy, Adoption, and Same-Sex and Unwed Parents' Rights. Trade Paper. Beacon Press. Boston, MA. 2002. 224p. ISBN:0-8070-4409-1, ISBN13: 978-0-8070-4409-4. Dewey:306.85/0973.

Audience: **g,l,u,f.**

Wells, Jess (Editor)   **HQ75.28.U6H65 2000**
Home Fronts: Controversies in Nontraditional Parenting. Trade Cloth. Alyson Publications. Los Angeles, CA. 2000. xvi, 237p. ISBN:1-55583-532-5, ISBN13: 978-1-55583-532-3. Dewey:306.874. LCCN:00-032767.

Audience: **g,l.**

Relationships > Abuse

Island, David &   **HQ76.2.U5.I85 1991**
  Letellier, Patrick
Men Who Beat the Men Who Love Them: Battered Gay Men and Domestic Violence. Lenore E. Walker & Tom L. Rhodus (Introduction by). Library Binding. Haworth Press, Incorporated, The. Binghamton, NY. 1991. 328p. Gay and Lesbian Studies ISBN:1-56024-112-8, ISBN13: 978-1-56024-112-6. Dewey:362.82/92. LCCN:91-004631.

Audience: **l,u.** *Choice, 1992.*

Renzetti, Claire M.   **HQ75.6.U5R46 1992**
Violent Betrayal: Partner Abuse in Lesbian Relationships. Trade Paper. SAGE Publications, Inc. Thousand Oaks, CA. 1992. 208p. ISBN:0-8039-3889-6, ISBN13: 978-0-8039-3889-2. Dewey:362.8292. LCCN:92-009359.

Audience: **l,u.**

Renzetti, Claire M. &   **HQ76.2.U5V58 1996**
  Miley, Charles H. (Editors)
Violence in Gay and Lesbian Domestic Partnerships. Trade Cloth. Haworth Press, Incorporated, The. Binghamton, NY. 1996. 144p. Journal of Gay and Lesbian Social Services Ser., Vol. 4, No. 1 ISBN:1-56024-753-3, ISBN13: 978-1-56024-753-1. Dewey:362.82/92. LCCN:95-052579.

Audience: **l,u.**

Ristock, Janice L.   **HQ75.5.R574 2002**
No More Secrets: Violence in Lesbian Relationships. Trade Paper. Routledge. New York, NY. 2002. 224p. ISBN:0-415-92946-6, ISBN13: 978-0-415-92946-2. Dewey:305.48/96643. LCCN:2001-041840.

Audience: **g,l,u.**

Health > General Health

Brownworth, Victoria   **RC281.W65C645 2000**
Coming Out of Cancer: Writings from the Lesbian Cancer Epidemic. Trade Paper. Avalon Publishing Group. New York, NY. 2000. xxiv, 235p. ISBN:1-58005-044-1, ISBN13: 978-1-58005-044-9. Dewey:362.1/96994/0082. LCCN:00-056288.

Audience: **g,l.**

Butler, Sandra &   **RC280.B8B85 1996**
  Rosenblum, Barbara
Cancer in Two Voices. Ed. 2. Trade Paper. Spinsters Ink Books. Midway, FL. 1996. 256p. ISBN:1-883523-16-8, ISBN13: 978-1-883523-16-9. Dewey:362.1/9699/449092 B. LCCN:91-018052.

Audience: **g.**

Dolan, Kathleen A.   **RA564.87.D654 2005**
Lesbian Women and Sexual Health: The Social Construction of Risk and Susceptibility. Trade Paper. Haworth Press, Incorporated, The. Binghamton, NY. 2005. 126p. ISBN:0-7890-2479-9, ISBN13: 978-0-7890-2479-4. Dewey:613.9/5/086643. LCCN:2004-021699.

Audience: **u,f.**

Eliason, Michele   **RA564.9.H65E45 1996**
Who Cares?: Institutional Barriers to Health Care for Lesbian, Gay and Bisexual Persons. Paper Text. Jones & Bartlett Publishers, Inc. Sudbury, MA. 1996. 220p. ISBN:0-88737-676-2, ISBN13: 978-0-88737-676-4. Dewey:362.1/08/664. LCCN:96-017319.

Audience: **g.**

Gruskin, Elisabeth Paige   **RA564.87.G78 1998**
Treating Lesbians and Bisexual Women: Challenges and Strategies for Health Professionals. Trade Paper. SAGE Publications, Inc. Thousand Oaks, CA. 1998. 207p. ISBN:0-7619-0045-4, ISBN13: 978-0-7619-0045-0. Dewey:362.1/086/643. LCCN:98-025343.

Audience: **u,f.**

Institute of Medicine   **RA564.87.L46 1999**
  Staff
Lesbian Health. Andrea L. Solarz (Editor). Trade Paper. National

---

Academies Press. Washington, DC. 1999. 200p.
ISBN:0-309-06567-4, ISBN13: 978-0-309-06567-2.
Dewey:613/.086/643. LCCN:99-006101.

Audience: **u,f.**

Scarce, Michael   **RA564.9.H65S28**
Smearing the Queer: Medical Bias in the Health Care of Gay
Men. Trade Cloth. Haworth Press, Incorporated, The.
Binghamton, NY. 2005. 200p. ISBN:1-56023-926-3, ISBN13:
978-1-56023-926-0. Dewey:362.1/086/64. LCCN:99-023095.

Audience: **l,u,f.**

Sontag, Susan   **RA644.A25S66 1989**
Illness As Metaphor and Aids and Its Metaphors. Cloth over
Boards. Farrar, Straus & Giroux. New York, NY. 1989. 128p.
ISBN:0-374-10257-0, ISBN13: 978-0-374-10257-9.
LCCN:88-021173.

Audience: **g,l,u,f.**

Health > AIDS

Altman, Dennis   **RC607.A26**
AIDS in the Mind of America: The Social, Political and
Psychological Impact of a New Epidemic. Trade Paper. Alfred
A. Knopf Inc. New York, NY. 1986. ISBN:0-385-19524-9,
ISBN13: 978-0-385-19524-9. Dewey:616.9792.

Audience: **g,l.**

Altman, Dennis   **RA644.A25A434 1994**
Power and Community: Organizational and Cultural Responses
to AIDS. Paper over Boards. Taylor & Francis Group.
Philadelphia, PA. 1994. 188p. ISBN:0-7484-0193-8, ISBN13:
978-0-7484-0193-2. Dewey:362.1/969792. LCCN:94-005754.

Audience: **l,u.**

Andriote, John-Manuel   **RA644.A25**
Victory Deferred: How AIDS Changed Gay Life in America.
Trade Cloth. University of Chicago Press. Chicago, IL. 1999.
494p. ISBN:0-226-02049-5, ISBN13: 978-0-226-02049-5.
Dewey:362.1/969792/00973. LCCN:98-046236.

Audience: **g,l,u,f.** *Choice, 1999.*

Boykin, Keith   **HQ74.2.U5**
Beyond the Down Low: Sex, Lies, and Denial in Black
America. E. Lynn Harris (Foreword by). Trade Cloth. Avalon
Publishing Group. New York, NY. 2005. 256p.
ISBN:0-7867-1434-4, ISBN13: 978-0-7867-1434-6.
Dewey:305.38/896073.

Audience: **g,l.**

Brown, Rebecca   **PS3568.O243**
The Gifts of the Body. Trade Paper. HarperCollins Publishers.
New York, NY. 1995. 180p. ISBN:0-06-092653-8, ISBN13:
978-0-06-092653-3. Dewey:813/.54.

Audience: **g.**

Burkett, Elinor   **RA644.A25B868 1995**
The Gravest Show on Earth: America in the Age of AIDS.
Trade Cloth. Houghton Mifflin Company. New York, NY. 1995.
375p. ISBN:0-395-74537-3, ISBN13: 978-0-395-74537-3.
Dewey:362.1/969792/00973. LCCN:95-009021.

Audience: **g,l,u,f.** *Choice, 1996.*

Crimp, Douglas   **RA643.8.C754 2002**
Melancholia and Moralism: Essays on AIDS and Queer Politics.
Trade Cloth. MIT Press. Cambridge, MA. 2002. 336p.
ISBN:0-262-03295-3, ISBN13: 978-0-262-03295-7.
Dewey:362.1/969792. LCCN:2001-044076.

Audience: **u,f.**

Diaz, Rafael M.   **RA644.A25D53 1998**
Latino Gay Men and HIV: Culture, Sexuality and Risk
Behavior. Trade Paper. Routledge. New York, NY. 1997. 208p.
ISBN:0-415-91388-8, ISBN13: 978-0-415-91388-1.
Dewey:362.1/969792/0089680. LCCN:97-023167.

Audience: **u,f.**

Doty, Mark   **RC607.A26**
Heaven's Coast: A Memoir. Trade Paper. HarperCollins
Publishers. New York, NY. 1997. 320p. ISBN:0-06-092805-0,
ISBN13: 978-0-06-092805-6. Dewey:362.1/9/69792/0092.
LCCN:95-053316.

Audience: **g,l.**

Epstein, Rob, and   **RC607.A26.C65**
  Jeffrey Friedman, producers
Common Threads: Stories from the Quilt. Ed. 2. New Yorker
Video. 2004.

Audience: **g.**

Epstein, Steven   **RA644.A25**
Impure Science: AIDS, Activism, and the Politics of
Knowledge. Trade Paper. University of California Press.
Berkeley, CA. 1998. 482p. Medicine and Society Ser., Vol. 7
ISBN:0-520-21445-5, ISBN13: 978-0-520-21445-3.
Dewey:362.1/969792/00973.

Audience: **u,f.** *Choice, 1997.*

Feinberg, David B.   **PS3556.E425E34 1990**
Eighty-Sixed. Trade Paper. Penguin Group (USA) Inc. New
York, NY. 1990. 336p. ISBN:0-14-011252-9, ISBN13:
978-0-14-011252-8. Dewey:813/.54. LCCN:89-036585.

Audience: **g.**

Feinberg, David B.   **RC607.A26**
Queer and Loathing: Rants and Raves of a Raging AIDS Clone.
Tony Kushner (Preface by). Trade Paper. Penguin Group (USA)
Inc. New York, NY. 1995. 288p. ISBN:0-14-024080-2, ISBN13:
978-0-14-024080-1. Dewey:362.1/969792. LCCN:94-005074.

Audience: **g,l.**

Green, Gill & Sobo, E. J.   **RC606.6.G74 2000**
Endangered Self: Identity and Social Risk. Trade Paper. Taylor
& Francis Group. Abingdon, 2000. 256p. Health, Risk and
Society Ser. ISBN:1-85728-910-2, ISBN13: 978-1-85728-910-7.
Dewey:362.1/69792. LCCN:00-710308.

Audience: **l,u.** *Choice, 2000.*

Gurganus, Allan   **PS3568.O243**
Plays Well with Others. Trade Paper. Knopf Publishing Group.
New York, NY. 1999. 368p. ISBN:0-375-70203-2, ISBN13:
978-0-375-70203-7. Dewey:813.5/4.

Audience: **g.**

Hoffman, William M.   **PS3545.I5365**
As Is. Trade Paper. Dramatists Play Service, Inc. New York, NY.
1985. ISBN:0-8222-0073-2, ISBN13: 978-0-8222-0073-4.
Dewey:812/.54.

Audience: **g,l,u.**

Johnson, Fenton   HQ75.8.R67J65 1996
Geography of the Heart: A Memoir. Trade Cloth. Simon &
Schuster. New York, NY. 1996. 240p. ISBN:0-684-81417-X,
ISBN13: 978-0-684-81417-9. Dewey:305.9/06/642/0922.
LCCN:95-053070.

Audience: **g,l.**

Jones, Cleve & Dawson,   RC607.A26J6573 2000
 Jeff
Stitching a Revolution: The Making of an AIDS Activist. Trade
Cloth. HarperCollins Publishers. New York, NY. 2000. 304p.
ISBN:0-06-251641-8, ISBN13: 978-0-06-251641-1.
Dewey:362.1/969792/0092 B. LCCN:99-052721.

Audience: **g,l.**

Kayal, Philip M.   HQ76.2.U5K39 1993
Bearing Witness: Gay Men's Health Crisis and the Politics of
AIDS. Trade Paper. Westview Press. Boulder, CO. 1993. 275p.
ISBN:0-8133-1729-0, ISBN13: 978-0-8133-1729-8.
Dewey:305.389664. LCCN:92-040293.

Audience: **g,l,f.**   *Choice, 1994.*

Kerr, M. E.   PZ7.K46825
Night Kites. Perfect. Sagebrush Education Resources. Caledonia,
MN. 1987. 245p. ISBN:0-8335-0968-3, ISBN13:
978-0-8335-0968-0. Dewey:FIC.

Audience: **g.**

Kinsella, James   RA644.A25
Covering the Plague: AIDS and the American Media. Trade
Paper. Rutgers University Press. Piscataway, NJ. 1992. 299p.
ISBN:0-8135-1482-7, ISBN13: 978-0-8135-1482-6.
Dewey:362.1/9697/9200973.

Audience: **g,l,u,f.**   *Choice, 1990.*

Klitzman, Robert &   RA643.8.K56 2003
 Bayer, Ronald
Mortal Secrets: Truth and Lies in the Age of AIDS. Trade Cloth.
Johns Hopkins University Press. Baltimore, MD. 2003. 232p.
ISBN:0-8018-7427-0, ISBN13: 978-0-8018-7427-7.
Dewey:362.1/969792. LCCN:2002-156771.

Audience: **u,f.**

Kramer, Larry   RA644.A25
Reports from the Holocaust: The Making of an AIDS Activist.
Trade Paper. St. Martin's Press. Gordonville, VA. 1989. 304p.
Stonewall Inn Editions Ser. ISBN:0-312-03921-2, ISBN13:
978-0-312-03921-9. Dewey:362.1/9697/9200973.

Audience: **g,l.**

Kramer, Larry   PS3561.R252N6 2000
The Normal Heart and the Destiny of Me. Tony Kushner
(Foreword by). Trade Paper. Grove/Atlantic, Inc. New York, NY.
2000. xxv, 252p. ISBN:0-8021-3692-3, ISBN13:
978-0-8021-3692-3. Dewey:812/.54. LCCN:00-024177.

Audience: **g,l,u.**

Monette, Paul   HQ75.8.M64A3 1992
Becoming a Man: Half a Life Story. Trade Cloth. Harcourt
Trade Publishers. New York, NY. 1992. 278p.
ISBN:0-15-111519-2, ISBN13: 978-0-15-111519-8.
Dewey:306.76/6/092. LCCN:91-039475.

Audience: **g,l.**

Monette, Paul   RC607.A26
Borrowed Time: An AIDS Memoir. Trade Paper. HarperCollins
Publishers. New York, NY. 1990. ISBN:0-380-70779-9, ISBN13:
978-0-380-70779-9. Dewey:362.1/969792/00922 B.

Audience: **g,l.**

Monette, Paul   PS3563.O523
Halfway Home. Trade Paper. Kensington Publishing
Corporation. New York, NY. 2002. 384p. ISBN:0-7582-0189-3,
ISBN13: 978-0-7582-0189-8. Dewey:813.5/4.

Audience: **g.**

Nelson, Theresa   PZ7.N4377EAR 1994
Earthshine. Trade Cloth. Scholastic, Inc. New York, NY. 1994.
192p. ISBN:0-531-08717-4, ISBN13: 978-0-531-08717-6.
Dewey:[Fic]. LCCN:94-008793.

Audience: **g.**

Patton, Cindy   RC607.A26
Inventing AIDS. Trade Paper. Routledge. New York, NY. 1990.
160p. ISBN:0-415-90257-6, ISBN13: 978-0-415-90257-1.
Dewey:362.1/969792.

Audience: **u,f.**   *Choice, 1991.*

Patton, Cindy   RA644.A25P38 1985
Sex and Germs: The Politics of AIDS. Trade Paper. South End
Press. Cambridge, MA. 1985. 182p. ISBN:0-89608-259-8,
ISBN13: 978-0-89608-259-5. Dewey:362.1/969792/00973.
LCCN:85-026240.

Audience: **u,f.**

Picano, Felice   PS3566.I25L5 1995
Like People in History: A Gay American Epic. Trade Cloth.
Penguin Group (USA) Inc. New York, NY. 1995. 528p.
ISBN:0-670-86047-6, ISBN13: 978-0-670-86047-0.
LCCN:94-038159.

Audience: **g.**

Price, Reynolds   PS3568.O243
The Promise of Rest. Trade Paper. Simon & Schuster. New
York, NY. 1996. 368p. ISBN:0-684-82510-4, ISBN13:
978-0-684-82510-6. Dewey:813.5/4.

Audience: **g.**

Shilts, Randy   RA644
And the Band Played On: Politics, People, and the AIDS
Epidemic. William Greider (Introduction by). Trade Paper. St.
Martin's Press. Gordonville, VA. 2000. 630p.
ISBN:0-312-24135-6, ISBN13: 978-0-312-24135-3.
Dewey:362.1/969792/00973.

Audience: **g,l,u.**

Smith, Raymond A.   RA644.A25E5276 1998
 (Editor)
Encyclopedia of AIDS: A Social, Political, Cultural, and
Scientific Record of the HIV Epidemic. Ed. 2. James W. Curran
(Foreword by). Trade Cloth. Fitzroy Dearborn Publishers, Inc.
Chicago, IL. 1998. 600p. ISBN:1-57958-007-6, ISBN13:
978-1-57958-007-0. Dewey:616.9792003. LCCN:98-200474.

Audience: **g.**   *Choice, 1999.*

Sontag, Susan   RA644.A25S66 1989
Illness As Metaphor and Aids and Its Metaphors. Cloth over
Boards. Farrar, Straus & Giroux. New York, NY. 1989. 128p.
ISBN:0-374-10257-0, ISBN13: 978-0-374-10257-9.
LCCN:88-021173.

Audience: **g,l,u,f.**

Turner, Dwayne   HQ76.2.U52W477 1997
Risky Sex?: Gay Men and HIV Prevention. Trade Cloth.
Columbia University Press. New York, NY. 1997. 208p.
Between Men, Between Women Ser. ISBN:0-231-10574-6,
ISBN13: 978-0-231-10574-3. Dewey:306.7/086/642.
LCCN:96-040290.

Audience: **u,f.**   *Choice, 1997.*

Weir, John   **PS3573.E39745I7 1999**
The Irreversible Decline of Eddie Socket: A Novel. Trade Cloth.
Alyson Publications. Los Angeles, CA. 1999. 304p.
ISBN:1-55583-472-8, ISBN13: 978-1-55583-472-2.
Dewey:813/.54. LCCN:99-045569.

Audience: **g.**

White, Edmund   **PS3573.H463**
The Married Man: A Novel. Trade Paper. Knopf Publishing
Group. New York, NY. 2001. 336p. ISBN:0-679-78144-7,
ISBN13: 978-0-679-78144-8. Dewey:813.5.

Audience: **g.**

Health > Aging

     F212.C7
◈ Beauty Before Age: Growing Older in Gay Culture. Video,
VHS Format. New Day Films. Harriman, NY. 2001.
ISBN:1-57448-050-2, ISBN13: 978-1-57448-050-4. Dewey:975.

Audience: **g,l,u,f.**

Berger, Raymond M.   **HQ76.B475 1996**
Gay and Gray: The Older Homosexual Man. Ed. 2. Cloth Text.
Haworth Press, Incorporated, The. Binghamton, NY. 1995. 340p.
ISBN:1-56024-986-2, ISBN13: 978-1-56024-986-3.
Dewey:305.26. LCCN:95-023223.

Audience: **l,u,f.**

Brown, Lester B., et al.   **HQ76.2.U5G385 1997**
Gay Men and Aging. Terry Cook, J. Geramy Quarto & Steven
Sarosy (Authors). Cloth Text. Garland Publishing, Inc. New
York, NY. 1997. 128p. Studies on the Elderly in America
ISBN:0-8153-2866-4, ISBN13: 978-0-8153-2866-7.
Dewey:306.76/62/0846. LCCN:97-013967.

Audience: **l,u,f.**

Cahill, Sean, Ken   **HQ76.U6**
   South, & Jane Spade
☐ Outing Age: Public Policy Issues Affecting Gay, Lesbian
Bisexual and Transgender Elders.
http://www.thetaskforce.org/downloads/outingage.pdf
Policy Institute of the National Gay and Lesbian Task Force
Foundation.

Audience: **g,l.**

Coleman, Penny   **HQ75.6.U52N73 2000**
Village Elders. Trade Cloth. University of Illinois Press.
Champaign, IL. 2000. 168p. ISBN:0-252-02552-0, ISBN13:
978-0-252-02552-5. Dewey:305.26. LCCN:99-050549.

Audience: **g,l.**

Cruz, J. Michael   **HQ76.14 .C78 2003**
Sociological Analysis of Aging: The Gay Male Perspective.
Harrington Park Press. 2003. ISBN:1-56023-454-7, ISBN13:
978-1-56023-454-8.

Audience: **u,f.**

Herdt, Gilbert H. & de   **HQ75.115.G39 2004**
   Vries, Brian (Editors)
Gay and Lesbian Aging: Research and Future Directions. Trade
Cloth. Springer Publishing Company, Inc. New York, NY. 2004.
320p. ISBN:0-8261-2234-5, ISBN13: 978-0-8261-2234-6.
Dewey:305.244. LCCN:2003-063324.

Audience: **l,u,f.**

Kooden, Harold &   **HQ76.14.K66 2000**
   Flowers, Charles
Golden Men: The Power of Gay Midlife. Trade Paper.

HarperCollins Publishers. New York, NY. 2000. 368p.
ISBN:0-380-80443-3, ISBN13: 978-0-380-80443-6.
Dewey:305.244. LCCN:99-055639.

Audience: **g,l.**

Lee, John A.   **HQ76.25.G42 1991**
Gay Midlife and Maturity. Franklin E. Kameny (Introduction
by). Cloth Text. Haworth Press, Incorporated, The. Binghamton,
NY. 1991. 246p. Journal of Homosexuality Ser.
ISBN:1-56024-028-8, ISBN13: 978-1-56024-028-0.
Dewey:305.24/4/08664. LCCN:90-005285.

Audience: **l,u,f.**

Macdonald, Barbara &   **HQ1061.M23 2001**
   Rich, Cynthia
Look Me in the Eye: Old Women, Aging, and Ageism. Trade
Cloth. Spinsters Ink Books. Midway, FL. 2002. 192p.
ISBN:1-883523-40-0, ISBN13: 978-1-883523-40-4.
Dewey:305.26. LCCN:2001-020831.

Audience: **g,l.**

Rosenfeld, Dana   **HQ76.3.U5R68 2003**
The Changing of the Guard: Lesbian and Gay Elders, Identity,
and Social Change. Library Binding. Temple University Press.
Philadelphia, PA. 2003. 272p. ISBN:1-59213-030-5, ISBN13:
978-1-59213-030-6. Dewey:306.76/6. LCCN:2002-043552.

Audience: **l,u,f.**

Snyder, Pat (Directed   **HQ76.25**
   By), et al.
◈ Silent Pioneers: Gay and Lesbian Elders. Lucy Winer,
Harvey Marks & Paula deKoenigsberg (Directed Bys). Video,
VHS Format. Filmakers Library. New York, NY. 1985.
Dewey:306.7.

Audience: **g,l,u,f.**

Vacha, Keith   **HQ75.7.V33 1985**
Quiet Fire: Memoirs of Older Gay Men. Don Clark
(Introduction by). Trade Cloth. Crossing Press, Incorporated,
The. Berkeley, CA. 1985. 160p. Gay Ser. ISBN:0-89594-158-9,
ISBN13: 978-0-89594-158-9. Dewey:306.7/662/0922.
LCCN:85-005699.

Audience: **g.** *Choice, 1985.*

Health > Mental Health and Psychology

Bailey, J. Michael   **HQ76.2.U5B35 2003**
The Man Who Would Be Queen: The Psychology of
Gender-Bending and Transsexualism. Trade Cloth. National
Academies Press. Washington, DC. 2003. 256p.
ISBN:0-309-08418-0, ISBN13: 978-0-309-08418-5.
Dewey:305.38/9664. LCCN:2002-154181.

Audience: **l,u,f.** *Choice, 2003.*

Bayer, Ronald   **RC558.B39 1987**
Homosexuality and American Psychiatry: The Politics of
Diagnosis. Trade Paper. Princeton University Press. Princeton,
NJ. 1987. 249p. ISBN:0-691-02837-0, ISBN13:
978-0-691-02837-8. Dewey:616.85/834. LCCN:86-043142.

Audience: **l,u,f.**

Boston Lesbian   **HQ75.5.L445 1987**
   Psychologies Collective Staff (Editor)
Lesbian Psychologies: Explorations and Challenges. Trade
Paper. University of Illinois Press. Champaign, IL. 1987. 384p.

ISBN:0-252-01404-9, ISBN13: 978-0-252-01404-8.
Dewey:306.7/663. LCCN:86-030736.

Audience: **l,u,f.** *Choice, 1988.*

Cory, Donald W.   **HQ76.3.U5C67 1975**
The Homosexual in America: A Subjective Approach. Trade
Cloth. Ayer Company Publishers, Inc. Manchester, NH. 1975.
Homosexuality Ser. ISBN:0-405-07365-8, ISBN13:
978-0-405-07365-6. Dewey:301.41/57/0973. LCCN:75-012310.

Audience: **g,l,f.**

Coyle, Adrian &   **HQ75.15.L46 2002**
  Kitzinger, Celia (Editors)
Lesbian and Gay Psychology: New Perspectives. Ed. 2. Trade
Paper. British Psychological Society. Leicester, 2002. 304p.
ISBN:1-4051-0222-5, ISBN13: 978-1-4051-0222-3.
Dewey:155.3/4. LCCN:2003-103274.

Audience: **l,u,f.** *Choice, 2002.*

Cruz, J. Michael   **HQ76.14 .C78 2003**
Sociological Analysis of Aging: The Gay Male Perspective.
Harrington Park Press. 2003. ISBN:1-56023-454-7, ISBN13:
978-1-56023-454-8.

Audience: **u,f.**

D'Augelli, Anthony R.   **HQ76.25**
  & Patterson, Charlotte J. (Editors)
Lesbian, Gay, and Bisexual Identities over the Lifespan:
Psychological Perspectives. Trade Paper. Oxford University
Press, Inc. New York, NY. 1996. 468p. ISBN:0-19-510899-X,
ISBN13: 978-0-19-510899-6. Dewey:155.34.

Audience: **u,f.**

Duberman, Martin B.   **HQ75.8.D82A3 1991**
Cures: A Gay Man's Odyssey. Trade Cloth. Penguin Group
(USA) Inc. New York, NY. 1991. 336p. ISBN:0-525-24955-9,
ISBN13: 978-0-525-24955-9. Dewey:305.38/9664/092.
LCCN:90-046658.

Audience: **g,l.**

Ellis, Havelock &   **RC558.E43 1975**
  Symonds, John Addington
Sexual Inversion. Trade Cloth. Ayer Company Publishers, Inc.
Manchester, NH. 1975. Homosexuality, :Lesbians and Gay Men
in Society, History and Literature Ser. ISBN:0-405-07363-1,
ISBN13: 978 0 405 07363 2. Dewey:155.3. LCCN:75-012312.

Audience: **u,f.**

Garnets, Linda &   **HQ76.3.U5P783 2002**
  Kimmel, Douglas C.
Psychological Perspectives on Lesbian, Gay, and Bisexual
Experiences. Ed. 2. Trade Paper. Columbia University Press.
New York, NY. 2003. 562p. ISBN:0-231-12413-9, ISBN13:
978-0-231-12413-3. Dewey:305.9/0664/0973.
LCCN:2002-025717.

Audience: **u,f.**

Greenan, David E. &   **RC558.G745 2003**
  Tunnell, Gil
Couple Therapy with Gay Men. Cloth over Boards. Guilford
Publications, Inc. New York, NY. 2002. 214p. Guilford Family
Therapy Ser. ISBN:1-57230-808-7, ISBN13: 978-1-57230-808-4.
Dewey:616.89/14/086642. LCCN:2002-012811.

Audience: **l,u,f.** *Choice, 2003.*

Hardin, Kimeron &   **HQ76.25.H367 2001**
  Hall, Marny
Queer Blues: The Lesbian and Gay Guide to Overcoming
Depression. Erin Corrigan (Editor), Betty Berzon (Foreword by).

Trade Paper. New Harbinger Publications. Oakland, CA. 2001.
260p. ISBN:1-57224-244-2, ISBN13: 978-1-57224-244-9.
Dewey:616.8/527/008664. LCCN:2003-545346.

Audience: **g.**

Hirschfeld, Magnus   **HQ76**
Sexual Anomalies: The Origin, Nature, and Treatment of Sexual
Disorders. Trade Cloth. Brown Book Company. Miami, FL.
1948. 538p. ISBN:0-317-39779-6, ISBN13: 978-0-317-39779-6.
Dewey:306.7/6.

Audience: **u,f.**

Hirschfeld, Magnus   **HQ76.25.H5813 2000**
The Homosexuality of Men and Women. Michael A.
Lombardi-Nash (Translator), Vern L. Bullough (Introduction by).
Trade Cloth. Prometheus Books, Publishers. Amherst, NY. 1999.
1200p. ISBN:1-57392-705-8, ISBN13: 978-1-57392-705-5.
Dewey:306.76/6. LCCN:99-026829.

Audience: **l,u,f.** *Choice, 2001.*

Hirschfeld, Magnus   **HQ77.H57 1991**
Transvestites: The Erotic Drive to Cross-Dress. Michael A.
Lombardi-Nash (Translator), Vern L. Bullough (Foreword by).
Trade Cloth. Prometheus Books, Publishers. Amherst, NY. 1991.
424p. ISBN:0-87975-665-9, ISBN13: 978-0-87975-665-9.
Dewey:306.77. LCCN:90-024827.

Audience: **l,u,f.**

Kitzinger, Celia   **HQ75.5.K58 1987**
The Social Construction of Lesbianism. Trade Cloth. SAGE
Publications, Ltd. London, 1988. 240p. Inquiries in Social
Construction Ser., Vol. 1 ISBN:0-8039-8116-3, ISBN13:
978-0-8039-8116-4. Dewey:306.7/663. LCCN:87-062029.

Audience: **u,f.** *Choice, 1988.*

Lev, Arlene Istar   **RC560.G45L48 2003**
Transgender Emergence: Therapeutic Guidelines for Working
with Gender-Variant People and Their Families. Trade Cloth.
Haworth Press, Incorporated, The. Binghamton, NY. 2003. 461p.
ISBN:0-7890-0708-8, ISBN13: 978-0-7890-0708-7.
Dewey:616.85/83. LCCN:2002-156666.

Audience: **u,f.**

Martell, Christopher R.,   **RC451.4.G39M37 2004**
  et al.
Cognitive-Behavioral Therapies with Lesbian, Gay and Bisexual
Clients. Steven A. Safren & Stacey E. Prince (Authors). Cloth
over Boards. Guilford Publications, Inc. New York, NY. 2003.
263p. ISBN:1-57230-954-7, ISBN13: 978-1-57230-954-8.
Dewey:616.89/142/08664. LCCN:2003-017548.

Audience: **u,f.** *Choice, 2004.*

Morrow, Deana F. &   **HV1449.S49 2006**
  Messinger, Lori
Sexual Orientation and Gender Expression in Social Work
Practice: Working with Gay, Lesbian, Bisexual, and Transgender
People. Trade Cloth. Columbia University Press. New York, NY.
2005. 536p. ISBN:0-231-12728-6, ISBN13: 978-0-231-12728-8.
Dewey:362.8. LCCN:2005-045564.

Audience: **u,f.**

Nimmons, David   **HQ75.8**
The Soul Beneath the Skin: The Unseen Hearts and Habits of
Gay Men. Trade Paper. St. Martin's Press. Gordonville, VA.
2003. 276p. ISBN:0-312-32040-X, ISBN13: 978-0-312-32040-9.
Dewey:305.38/9664/0973.

Audience: **g.**

Omoto, Allen Martin &   **RC451.4.G39S46 2005**
Kurtzman, Howard S.
Sexual Orientation and Mental Health: Examining Identity and
Development in Lesbian, Gay, and Bisexual People. Trade
Cloth. American Psychological Association. Washington, DC.
2005. 336p. The Division 44 Ser. ISBN:1-59147-232-6,
ISBN13: 978-1-59147-232-2. Dewey:616.89/17/08664.
LCCN:2005-002995.

Audience: **u.** *Choice, 2006.*

Quam, Jean K. (Editor)   **HV1449.S65 1997**
Social Services for Senior Gay Men and Lesbians. Trade Cloth.
Haworth Press, Incorporated, The. Binghamton, NY. 1997. 142p.
Journal of Gay and Lesbian Social Services Ser., Vol. 6, No. 1
ISBN:1-56024-808-4, ISBN13: 978-1-56024-808-8.
Dewey:362.6/086/64. LCCN:96-052129.

Audience: **l,u,f.**

Savin-Williams, Ritch   **HQ76.25.L59 1996**
C. (Author, Editor)
The Lives of Lesbians, Gays and Bisexuals: Children to Adults.
Kenneth M. Cohen (Editor). Paper Text. Thomson Wadsworth.
Belmont, CA. 1995. 512p. ISBN:0-15-501497-8, ISBN13:
978-0-15-501497-8. Dewey:306.76/6. LCCN:95-076861.

Audience: **l,u,f.**

Sears, James T. &   **HQ76.3.U5O994 1997**
Williams, Walter L.
Overcoming Heterosexism and Homophobia: Strategies That
Work. Trade Cloth. Columbia University Press. New York, NY.
1997. 470p. ISBN:0-231-10422-7, ISBN13: 978-0-231-10422-7.
Dewey:306.76/6. LCCN:96-050483.

Audience: **g.** *Choice, 1998.*

Shernoff, Michael   **HQ76.2.U5G398 1997**
(Editor)
Gay Widowers: Life after the Death of a Partner. Trade Cloth.
Haworth Press, Incorporated, The. Binghamton, NY. 1997. 161p.
ISBN:0-7890-0355-4, ISBN13: 978-0-7890-0355-3.
Dewey:305.38/9664. LCCN:97-033478.

Audience: **g,l.**

Shidlo, Ariel (Editor), et al.   **RC558.S494 2001**
Sexual Conversion Therapy: Ethical, Clincial, and Research
Perspectives. Michael Schroeder & Jack Drescher (Editors).
Trade Cloth. Haworth Press, Incorporated, The. Binghamton,
NY. 2002. 234p. ISBN:0-7890-1910-8, ISBN13:
978-0-7890-1910-3. Dewey:616.89/14/08664.
LCCN:2001-059452.

Audience: **l,u.**

Signorile, Michelangelo   **HQ76.2.U5.S54**
Life Outside: The Signorile Report on Gay Men: Sex, Drugs,
Muscles, and the Passages of Life. HarperCollins. 1997.
ISBN:0-06-018761-1, ISBN13: 978-0-06-018761-3.

Audience: **g,l.**

Economics and Business

Badgett, M. V. Lee   **HQ76.25.B33 2001**
Money, Myths, and Change: The Economic Lives of Lesbians
and Gay Men. Trade Cloth. University of Chicago Press.
Chicago, IL. 2001. 272p. Worlds of Desire Ser., :Series on
Sexuality, Gender and Culture ISBN:0-226-03400-3, ISBN13:
978-0-226-03400-3. Dewey:305.9/0664. LCCN:00-011126.
Audience: **l,u,f.** *Choice, 2002.*

Dunne, Gillian A.   **HQ75.5.D85 1997**
Lesbian Lifestyles: Women's Work and the Politics of Sexuality.
Cloth Text. University of Toronto Press. Toronto, ON. 1996.
440p. ISBN:0-8020-4104-3, ISBN13: 978-0-8020-4104-3.
Dewey:305.4/89664. LCCN:97-130146.

Audience: **u,f.** *Choice, 1997.*

Gluckman, Amy &   **HQ76.3.U5H63 1997**
Reed, Betsy (Editors)
Homo Economics: Capitalism, Community and Lesbian and Gay
Life. Paper over Boards. Routledge. New York, NY. 1997. 488p.
ISBN:0-415-91378-0, ISBN13: 978-0-415-91378-2.
Dewey:305.9/0664/0973. LCCN:96-016035.

Audience: **l,u.**

Raeburn, Nicole C.   **HD6285.5.U6R34 2004**
Changing Corporate America from Inside Out: Lesbian and Gay
Workplace Rights. Trade Paper. University of Minnesota Press.
Minneapolis, MN. 2004. 360p. Social Movements, Protest, and
Contention Ser., Vol. 20 ISBN:0-8166-3999-X, ISBN13:
978-0-8166-3999-1. Dewey:331.5/3/0973. LCCN:2004-008523.
Audience: **g,l,u,f.** *Choice, 2005.*

Snyder, Kirk   **HD6285.S693 2003**
Lavender Road to Success: The Career Guide for the Gay
Community. Trade Paper. Ten Speed Press. Berkeley, CA. 2004.
208p. ISBN:1-58008-496-6, ISBN13: 978-1-58008-496-3.
Dewey:650.1/086/6. LCCN:2003-011973.

Audience: **g,l,u,f.**

Winfeld, Liz &   **HD6285.W56 2001**
Spielman, Susan
Straight Talk about Gays in the Workplace. Ed. 2. Trade Cloth.
Haworth Press, Incorporated, The. Binghamton, NY. 2005. 185p.
Gay and Lesbian Studies ISBN:1-56023-171-8, ISBN13:
978-1-56023-171-4. Dewey:658.3/0086/64. LCCN:00-039712.
Audience: **g,l,u,f.** *Choice, 2001.*

Woods, James D. &   **HQ76.2.U5W66 1993**
Lucas, Jay H.
The Corporate Closet: The Professional Lives of Gay Men in
America. Children's Board Books. Simon & Schuster. New
York, NY. 1993. 330p. ISBN:0-02-935603-2, ISBN13:
978-0-02-935603-6. Dewey:305.38/9664. LCCN:93-019898.
Audience: **g,l,u.**

Economics and Business > Advertising and Marketing

HF5415.127
☐ Commercial Closet.
http://www.commercialcloset.org
Commercial Closet Association.

Audience: **g,l,u,f.**

Kates, Steven M.   **HF5415.33.U6K38 1998**
Twenty Million New Customers!: Understanding Gay Men's
Consumer Behavior. Trade Cloth. Haworth Press, Incorporated,
The. Binghamton, NY. 2005. 235p. Gay and Lesbian Studies
ISBN:1-56023-903-4, ISBN13: 978-1-56023-903-1.
Dewey:306.3/086/6420973. LCCN:97-017008.

Audience: **g,l.**

Lukenbill, Grant   **HC110.C6L852 1999**
Untold Millions: The Truth about Gay and Lesbian Consumers.
Ed. 2. Trade Cloth. Haworth Press, Incorporated, The.
Binghamton, NY. 2005. 200p. Gay and Lesbian Studies

ISBN:1-56023-948-4, ISBN13: 978-1-56023-948-2.
Dewey:658.8/34/086640973. LCCN:98-047911.
Audience: **l,u,f.** *Choice, 2000.*

Sender, Katherine   **HC110.C6S46 2004**
Business, Not Politics: The Making of the Gay Market. Trade
Paper. Columbia University Press. New York, NY. 2004. xii,
311p. Between Men, Between Women Ser.
ISBN:0-231-12735-9, ISBN13: 978-0-231-12735-6.
Dewey:658.8/0086/64. LCCN:2004-055119.
Audience: **g,l,u,f.** *Choice, 2005.*

Wardlow, Daniel L.   **HF5415.33.U6G38 1996**
  (Editor)
Gays, Lesbians and Consumer Behavior: Theory, Practice and
Research Issues in Marketing. Trade Cloth. Haworth Press,
Incorporated, The. Binghamton, NY. 1996. 261p. Journal of
Homosexuality Ser., Vol. 31, Nos. 1 & 2 ISBN:1-56024-761-4,
ISBN13: 978-1-56024-761-6. Dewey:658.8/348.
LCCN:96-004209.
Audience: **g,l,u.**

Economics and Business > Careers

Aarons, Leroy   **PN4784.T4**
☐ Lesbians and Gays in the Newsroom: 10 Years Later.
http://www.nlgja.org/publications/NLGJA_2000_Survey.pdf
Murphy, Sharon.
Audience: **g,l,u,f.**

Buttino, Frank &   **HV7911.B87 A3 1993**
  Buttino, Lou
A Special Agent: Gay and Inside the FBI. Trade Cloth.
HarperCollins Publishers. New York, NY. 1993.
ISBN:0-688-11958-1, ISBN13: 978-0-688-11958-4.
Dewey:363.2/092 B. LCCN:92-046238.
Audience: **g,l.**

Carmichael, James V.   **Z682**
  Jr. (Editor)
Daring to Find Our Names: The Search for Lesbigay Library
History. Trade Cloth. Greenwood Publishing Group, Inc.
Portsmouth, NH. 1998. 272p. Beta Phi Mu Monographs
ISBN:0-313-29963-3, ISBN13: 978-0-313-29963-6.
Dewey:020/.86/63. LCCN:97-048579.
Audience: **u,f.**

Gough, Cal &   **Z711.92.G37G37 1990**
  Greenblatt, Ellen (Editors)
Gay and Lesbian Library Service. Sanford Berman (Foreword
by). Library Binding. McFarland & Company, Incorporated
Publishers. Jefferson, NC. 1990. 379p. ISBN:0-89950-535-X,
ISBN13: 978-0-89950-535-0. Dewey:026.3059/0664.
LCCN:90-052641.
Audience: **u,f.** *Choice, 1991.*

Harbeck, Karen M.   **LC192.6.H37 1997**
Gay and Lesbian Educators: Personal Freedoms - Public
Constraints. Trade Cloth. Amethyst Press & Productions.
Malden, MA. 1997. 500p. ISBN:1-889393-48-7, ISBN13:
978-1-889393-48-3. Dewey:371.1/0086/64. LCCN:96-085545.
Audience: **g,l.** *Choice, 1997.*

Jennings, Kevin   **LB2844.1.G39O64 2005**
  (Editor)
One Teacher in 10. Ed. 2. Trade Paper. Alyson Publications. Los

Angeles, CA. 2005. 288p. ISBN:1-55583-869-3, ISBN13:
978-1-55583-869-0. Dewey:371.1/0086/64. LCCN:2004-062685.
Audience: **g,l,f.**

Johnson, David K.   **JK723.H6J64 2003**
The Lavender Scare: The Cold War Persecution of Gays and
Lesbians in the Federal Government. Trade Cloth. University of
Chicago Press. Chicago, IL. 2004. 312p. ISBN:0-226-40481-1,
ISBN13: 978-0-226-40481-3. Dewey:352.6/086/640973.
LCCN:2003-009138.
Audience: **g,l,u,f.** *Choice, 2004.*

Kester, Norman G.   **Z720.A4L48 1997**
  (Editor)
Liberating Minds: The Stories and Professional Lives of Gay,
Lesbian and Bisexual Librarians and Their Advocates. Cal
Gough (Foreword by). Cloth Text. McFarland & Company,
Incorporated Publishers. Jefferson, NC. 1997. 272p.
ISBN:0-7864-0363-2, ISBN13: 978-0-7864-0363-9.
Dewey:020/.86/63. LCCN:97-2117.
Audience: **g,l,u,f.**

Kissen, Rita M.   **LB2844.1.G39K57 1996**
The Last Closet: The Real Lives of Lesbian and Gay Teachers.
Trade Cloth. Heinemann. Portsmouth, NH. 1996. 198p.
ISBN:0-435-07005-3, ISBN13: 978-0-435-07005-2.
Dewey:371.1/008/664. LCCN:96-4128.
Audience: **g,l,u.** *Choice, 1997.*

Leinen, Stephen   **HV8138.L353 1993**
Gay Cops. Trade Cloth. Rutgers University Press. Piscataway,
NJ. 1993. 320p. ISBN:0-8135-2000-2, ISBN13:
978-0-8135-2000-1. Dewey:363.2/08/664. LCCN:93-009216.
Audience: **g,l.** *Choice, 1994.*

Sanlo, Ronni L.   **LB2844**
Unheard Voices: The Effects of Silence on Lesbian and Gay
Educators. Trade Cloth. Greenwood Publishing Group, Inc.
Portsmouth, NH. 1999. 176p. ISBN:0-89789-640-8, ISBN13:
978-0-89789-640-5. Dewey:371.1/008/664. LCCN:99-022082.
Audience: **g,l,f.**

Sports

Anderson, Eric   **GV708.8.A43 2005**
In the Game: Gay Athletes and the Cult of Masculinity. Paper
Text. State University of New York Press. Albany, NY. 2005.
208p. SUNY Series on Sport, Culture, and Social Relations
ISBN:0-7914-6534-9, ISBN13: 978-0-7914-6534-9.
Dewey:796.086/64. LCCN:2004-021367.
Audience: **l,u,f.** *Choice, 2005.*

Anderson, Eric   **GV697.O9**
Trailblazing: The True Story of America's First Openly Gay
Track Coach. Prebound. Turtleback Books. Madison, WI. 2000.
ISBN:0-606-20320-6, ISBN13: 978-0-606-20320-3.
Dewey:796.42/092 B.
Audience: **g,l.**

Bean, Billy & Bull,   **GV865.B336A3 2003**
Chris
Going the Other Way: Lessons from a Life in and out of Major
League Baseball. Trade Cloth. Avalon Publishing Group. New
York, NY. 2003. 240p. ISBN:1-56924-486-3, ISBN13:
978-1-56924-486-9. Dewey:796.357/092 B. LCCN:2003-041266.
Audience: **g,l,u,f.**

Griffin, Patricia J.   **GV708.8.G75 1998**
Strong Women, Deep Closets: Lesbians and Homophobia in
Sport. Donna A. Lopiano (Foreword by). Trade Paper. Human
Kinetics Publishers. Champaign, IL. 1998. 264p.
ISBN:0-88011-729-X, ISBN13: 978-0-88011-729-6.
Dewey:796/.086/643. LCCN:97-032363.
Audience: **g,l,u,f.** *Choice, 1998.*

Gustav-Wrathall, John   **BV1090.G88 1998**
  Donald
Take the Young Stranger by the Hand: Same-Sex Relations and
the YMCA. Trade Cloth. University of Chicago Press. Chicago,
IL. 1998. 288p. Chicago Series on Sexuality, History and
Society ISBN:0-226-90784-8, ISBN13: 978-0-226-90784-0.
Dewey:267/.3973. LCCN:98-009904.
Audience: **u,f.** *Choice, 1999.*

Kopay, David & Young,   **GV939.K6.A34 1977**
  Perry D.
David Kopay Story. Trade Cloth. HarperCollins Publishers. New
York, NY. 1977. xii, 247p. ISBN:0-87795-145-4, ISBN13:
978-0-87795-145-2. Dewey:796.33/2/0924. LCCN:76-029229.
Audience: **g,l,u,f.**

Miller, Toby   **GV706.2.M55 2001**
Sportsex. Library Binding. Temple University Press.
Philadelphia, PA. 2002. 224p. ISBN:1-56639-864-9, ISBN13:
978-1-56639-864-0. Dewey:306.4/83. LCCN:00-049098.
Audience: **u,f.** *Choice, 2002.*

Navratilova, Martina &   **GV994.N38**
  Vecsey, George
Martina: Autobiography. Trade Cloth. Alfred A. Knopf Inc. New
York, NY. 1985. 287p. ISBN:0-394-53640-1, ISBN13:
978-0-394-53640-8. Dewey:796.342/092/4 B. LCCN:84-048894.
Audience: **g.**

Pallone, Dave &   **GV865.P32**
  Steinberg, Alan
Behind the Mask: My Double Life in Baseball. Cloth Text.
Xlibris Corporation. Philadelphia, PA. 2002. 360p.
ISBN:1-4010-6745-X, ISBN13: 978-1-4010-6745-8.
Dewey:796.357/092 B. LCCN:2002-009334.
Audience: **g.**

Pronger, Brian   **GV706.5.P76 1991**
The Arena of Masculinity: Sports, Homosexuality, and the
Meaning of Sex. Trade Paper. St. Martin's Press. Gordonville,
VA. 1992. 320p. Stonewall Inn Editions Ser.
ISBN:0-312-06293-1, ISBN13: 978-0-312-06293-4.
Dewey:306.4/83. LCCN:91-029264.
Audience: **l,u,f.**

Waddell, Tom &   **GV697.W33A3 1996**
  Schaap, Dick
Gay Olympian: The Life and Death of Dr. Tom Waddell. Trade
Cloth. Random House, Inc. New York, NY. 1996. 240p.
ISBN:0-394-57223-8, ISBN13: 978-0-394-57223-9.
Dewey:796/.092 B. LCCN:95-031223.
Audience: **g.**

Woog, Dan   **GV697.A1W687 2002**
Jocks 2: Coming Out to Play. Trade Cloth. Alyson Publications.
Los Angeles, CA. 248p. ISBN:1-55583-726-3, ISBN13:
978-1-55583-726-6. Dewey:796/.086/642. LCCN:2002-071671.
Audience: **g,l.**

Woog, Dan   **GV697.A1W687 1998**
Jocks: True Stories of America's Gay Male Athletes. Kevin
Jennings (Editor). Trade Paper. Alyson Publications. Los
Angeles, CA. 1997. 256p. ISBN:1-55583-399-3, ISBN13:
978-1-55583-399-2. Dewey:796/.086/6420922 B.
LCCN:97-030488.
Audience: **g,l.**

Education

                                          LC192.6
⊡ Gay Lesbian Straight Education Network.
http://www.glsen.org/
Audience: **g,l,u,f.**

Besner, Hilda F. &   **LC192.6.B47 1995**
  Spungin, Charlotte I.
Gay and Lesbian Students: Understanding Their Needs. UK-B
Format Paperback. Taylor & Francis Group. Philadelphia, PA.
1995. 174p. ISBN:1-56032-338-8, ISBN13: 978-1-56032-338-9.
Dewey:370.19/345. LCCN:95-012727.
Audience: **g,l.** *Choice, 1996.*

Besner, Hilda F. &   **LC192.6.B49 1997**
  Spungin, Charlotte I.
Training for Professionals Who Work with Gay and Lesbian
Youth. UK-B Format Paperback. Hemisphere Publishing
Corporation. Philadelphia, PA. 1997. 236p.
ISBN:1-56032-566-6, ISBN13: 978-1-56032-566-6.
Dewey:378.1/2/0683. LCCN:97-020520.
Audience: **g,l.**

Birden, Susan   **LC192.6.B54 2004**
Rethinking Sexual Identity in Education. Book, Other. Rowman
& Littlefield Publishers, Inc. Lanham, MD. 2004. 224p.
Curriculum, Cultures, and (Homo)sexualities Ser.
ISBN:0-7425-4295-5, ISBN13: 978-0-7425-4295-2.
Dewey:371.826/64. LCCN:2004-010039.
Audience: **u,f.**

Blount, Jackie M.   **LC192.6.B56 2004**
Fit to Teach: Same-Sex Desire, Gender, and School Work in the
Twentieth Century. Cloth Text. State University of New York
Press. Albany, NY. 2004. 272p. ISBN:0-7914-6267-6, ISBN13:
978-0-7914-6267-6. Dewey:371.1/0086/64. LCCN:2004-041624.
Audience: **u.** *Choice, 2005.*

Bochenek, Michael &   **LC212.82.B63 2001**
  Brown, A. Widney
Hatred in the Hallways: Violence and Discrimination Against
Lesbian, Gay, Bisexual, and Transgender Students in U.S.
Schools. Human Rights Watch Staff (Contribution by). Trade
Paper. Human Rights Watch. New York, NY. 2001. 23p.
ISBN:1-56432-259-9, ISBN13: 978-1-56432-259-3.
Dewey:371.780973. LCCN:2001-089868.
Audience: **g.**

Cahill, Sean & Jason   **LC192.6**
  Cianciotto
⊡ Education Policy: Issues Affecting Lesbian, Gay, Bisexual
and Transgender Youth.
http://www.thetaskforce.org/downloads/EducationPolicy.pdf
Policy Institute of the National Gay and Lesbian Task Force.
Audience: **g,l,u,f.**

Campos, David   LC192.6.C265 2005
Understanding Gay and Lesbian Youth: Lessons for Straight
School Teachers, Counselors, and Administrators. Trade Paper.
Scarecrow Press, Inc. Lanham, MD. 2005. 410p.
ISBN:1-57886-290-6, ISBN13: 978-1-57886-290-0.
Dewey:371.826/64. LCCN:2005-004685.
                                                    Audience: **g,l.**

Campos, David   LC192.6.C26 2003
Diverse Sexuality and Schools: A Reference Handbook. Danny
Weil (Editor). Library Binding. ABC-CLIO, Inc. Santa Barbara,
CA. 2003. 289p. Contemporary Education Issues Ser.
ISBN:1-85109-545-4, ISBN13: 978-1-85109-545-2.
Dewey:371.826/6. LCCN:2003-003574.
                                                    Audience: **g,l.**

Dilley, Patrick   HQ76.2.U5D55 2002
Queer Man on Campus: A History of Non-Heterosexual College
Men 1945-2000. Paper over Boards. Routledge. New York, NY.
2002. 256p. ISBN:0-415-93336-6, ISBN13: 978-0-415-93336-0.
Dewey:378.1/9826/642. LCCN:2002-031728.
                                                    Audience: **g,l,u.**

Epstein, Debbie (Editor)   LC192.6.C43 1994
Challenging Lesbian and Gay Inequalities in Education. Book,
Other. McGraw-Hill Education. Maidenhead, 1994. 208p.
Gender and Education Ser. ISBN:0-335-19130-4, ISBN13:
978-0-335-19130-7. Dewey:371.8/2664. LCCN:93-038399.
                                                    Audience: **l,u,f.**

GLSEN Staff (Createdby)   LC192.6
The GLSEN Workbook: A Developmental Model for Assessing,
Describing and Improving Schools for Lesbian, Gay, Bisexual
and Transgender (LGBT) People. Stapled. Gay, Lesbian &
Straight Education Network. New York, NY. 2001. 48p.
ISBN:0-9722834-0-4, ISBN13: 978-0-9722834-0-3.
Dewey:370.43.
                                                    Audience: **g.**

Harbeck, Karen M.   LC192.6.H37 1997
Gay and Lesbian Educators: Personal Freedoms - Public
Constraints. Trade Cloth. Amethyst Press & Productions.
Malden, MA. 1997. 500p. ISBN:1-889393-48-7, ISBN13:
978-1-889393-48-3. Dewey:371.1/0086/64. LCCN:96-085545.
                                    Audience: **g,l.** *Choice, 1997.*

Howard, Kim &   LC2574.6.O87 2000
  Stevens, Annie (Editors)
Out and about Campus: Personal Accounts by Lesbian, Gay,
Bisexual and Transgendered College Students. Trade Cloth.
Alyson Publications. Los Angeles, CA. 2000. xiv, 304p.
ISBN:1-55583-480-9, ISBN13: 978-1-55583-480-7.
Dewey:378.1/9826/64. LCCN:99-059703.
                                                    Audience: **g,l.**

Human Relations Media   HQ75.15
  Staff (Produced by)
Dealing with Difference: Opening Dialogue about Lesbian, Gay
and Straight Issues. GLSEN Staff (Text by). Ringbound. Gay,
Lesbian & Straight Education Network. New York, NY. 2002.
82p. ISBN:0-9722834-3-9, ISBN13: 978-0-9722834-3-4.
Dewey:306.76.
                                                    Audience: **g.**

Jennings, Kevin   LB2844.1.G39O64 2005
  (Editor)
One Teacher in 10. Ed. 2. Trade Paper. Alyson Publications. Los

Angeles, CA. 2005. 288p. ISBN:1-55583-869-3, ISBN13:
978-1-55583-869-0. Dewey:371.1/0086/64. LCCN:2004-062685.
                                                    Audience: **g,l,f.**

Kissen, Rita M.   LB2844.1.G39K57 1996
The Last Closet: The Real Lives of Lesbian and Gay Teachers.
Trade Cloth. Heinemann. Portsmouth, NH. 1996. 198p.
ISBN:0-435-07005-3, ISBN13: 978-0-435-07005-2.
Dewey:371.1/008/664. LCCN:96-4128.
                                    Audience: **g,l,u.** *Choice, 1997.*

Letts, William J. IV &   LC192.6.Q85 1999
  Sears, James T. (Editors)
Queering Elementary Education: Advancing the Dialogue about
Sexualities and Schooling. Book, Other. Rowman & Littlefield
Publishers, Inc. Lanham, MD. 1999. 320p. Curriculum, Cultures,
and (Homo)sexualities Ser. ISBN:0-8476-9368-6, ISBN13:
978-0-8476-9368-9. Dewey:371/.01/1. LCCN:99-023762.
                                Audience: **g,l,u,f.** *Choice, 2000.*

Lipkin, Arthur   LC192.6.L56 2003
Beyond Diversity Day: A Q and A on Gay and Lesbian Issues in
Schools. Book, Other. Rowman & Littlefield Publishers, Inc.
Lanham, MD. 2003. 272p. Curriculum, Cultures, and
(Homo)sexualities Ser. ISBN:0-7425-2034-X, ISBN13:
978-0-7425-2034-9. Dewey:371.826/64. LCCN:2003-007672.
                                                    Audience: **g,l.**

Macgillivray, Ian K.   LC192.6.M33 2003
Sexual Orientation and School Policy: A Practical Guide for
Teachers, Administrators, and Community Activists. Book,
Other. Rowman & Littlefield Publishers, Inc. Lanham, MD.
2003. 224p. Curriculum, Cultures, and (Homo)sexualities Ser.
ISBN:0-7425-2508-2, ISBN13: 978-0-7425-2508-5.
Dewey:371.826/64. LCCN:2003-011932.
                                                    Audience: **l,u.**

McNaron, Toni A.   LC212.862.M35 1997
Poisoned Ivy: Lesbian and Gay Academics Confronting
Homophobia. Trade Paper. Temple University Press.
Philadelphia, PA. 1996. 256p. ISBN:1-56639-488-0, ISBN13:
978-1-56639-488-8. Dewey:378.1/2/08/664. LCCN:96-035334.
                                                    Audience: **l,u.**

Miceli, Melinda   HQ76.3.U5M49 2005
Standing Out, Standing Together: The Political and Social
Impact of Gay-Straight Alliances. Trade Paper. Routledge. New
York, NY. 2005. 272p. ISBN:0-415-95092-9, ISBN13:
978-0-415-95092-3. Dewey:306.76/6/0835. LCCN:2005-006116.
                                                    Audience: **l,u.**

Mitchell, Leif (Editor)   LC192.6
Tackling Gay Issues in School. Ringbound. Gay, Lesbian &
Straight Education Network. New York, NY. 1999. 230p.
ISBN:0-9722834-8-X, ISBN13: 978-0-9722834-8-9.
Dewey:371.82664.
                                                    Audience: **g.**

Rankin, Sue   LC2574
Our Place on Campus: Lesbian, Gay, Bisexual, Transgender
Services and Programs in Higher Education. Ronni L. Sanlo &
Robert Schoenberg (Editors). Cloth Text. Greenwood Publishing
Group, Inc. Portsmouth, NH. 2002. 296p. The Greenwood
Educators' Reference Collections ISBN:0-313-31406-3, ISBN13:
978-0-313-31406-3. Dewey:378.1/9826/64. LCCN:2001-058632.
                                                    Audience: **u,f.**

Rankin, Susan R.   HQ35.2
☐ Campus Climate for Gay, Lesbian, Bisexual, and
Transgender People: A National Perspective.
http://www.thetaskforce.org/downloads/CampusClimate.pdf
Policy Institute of the National Gay and Lesbian Task Force.
Audience: **g,l,u,f.**

Sanlo, Ronni L.   LB2844
Unheard Voices: The Effects of Silence on Lesbian and Gay
Educators. Trade Cloth. Greenwood Publishing Group, Inc.
Portsmouth, NH. 1999. 176p. ISBN:0-89789-640-8, ISBN13:
978-0-89789-640-5. Dewey:371.1/008/664. LCCN:99-022082.
Audience: **g,l,f.**

Sanlo, Ronni L. (Editor)   LC192
Working with Lesbian, Gay, Bisexual, and Transgender College
Students: A Handbook for Faculty and Administrators. Cloth
Text. Greenwood Publishing Group, Inc. Portsmouth, NH. 1998.
488p. Educators' Reference Collection ISBN:0-313-30227-8,
ISBN13: 978-0-313-30227-5. Dewey:378.1/98/0866.
LCCN:97-026182.
Audience: **u,f.**   *Choice, 1999.*

Sears, James T.   LC192.6.G38 2005
Gay, Lesbian, and Transgender Issues in Education: Programs,
Policies, and Practices. Trade Paper. Haworth Press,
Incorporated, The. Binghamton, NY. 2005. 200p.
ISBN:1-56023-524-1, ISBN13: 978-1-56023-524-8.
Dewey:371.8266. LCCN:2004-026628.
Audience: **u,f.**

Sears, James T.   LC192.6.Y68 2005
Youth, Education, and Sexualities: An International
Encyclopedia. Trade Cloth. Greenwood Publishing Group, Inc.
Portsmouth, NH. 2005. xxxviii, 981p. ISBN:0-313-32754-8,
ISBN13: 978-0-313-32754-4. Dewey:371.826/6/03.
LCCN:2005-018961.
Audience: **g.**

Talburt, Susan &   LC192.6.T55 2000
  Steinberg, Shirley R. (Editors)
Thinking Queer: Sexuality, Culture and Education. Paper Text.
Peter Lang Publishing, Inc. New York, NY. 2000. xvi, 235p.
Counterpoints of Education Ser., Vol. 118:Studies in the
Postmodern Theory of Education ISBN:0-8204-4521-5, ISBN13:
978-0-8204-4521-2. Dewey:306.76/6. LCCN:99-053017.
Audience: **u,f.**

Windmeyer, Shane L.   LJ51
  (Editor)
Brotherhood: Gay Life in College Fraternities. Trade Paper,
Perfect. Alyson Publications. Los Angeles, CA. 2005. 304p.
ISBN:1-55583-856-1, ISBN13: 978-1-55583-856-0.
Dewey:378.1/9855/0973. LCCN:2005-053062.
Audience: **g,l.**

Woog, Dan   LC192.6.W66 1995
School's Out: The Impact of Gay and Lesbian Issues on
America's Schools. Trade Cloth. Alyson Publications. Los
Angeles, CA. 1995. 383p. ISBN:1-55583-249-0, ISBN13:
978-1-55583-249-0. Dewey:371.8/2664. LCCN:95-005763.
Audience: **g,l.**

Politics

Altman, Dennis   HQ76.A585 1993
  (Author, Afterword by)
Homosexual: Oppression and Liberation. Jeffrey Weeks

(Introduction by). Trade Cloth. New York University Press. New
York, NY. 1993. 304p. ISBN:0-8147-0623-1, ISBN13:
978-0-8147-0623-7. Dewey:305.90664. LCCN:93-018284.
Audience: **u,f.**

Berrill, Kevin T.   HV6250.4.H66H38 1992
  (Author, Editor)
Hate Crimes: Confronting Violence Against Lesbians and Gay
Men. Gregory M. Herek (Editor). Trade Paper. SAGE
Publications, Inc. Thousand Oaks, CA. 1991. 328p.
ISBN:0-8039-4542-6, ISBN13: 978-0-8039-4542-5.
Dewey:364.15508664. LCCN:91-034912.
Audience: **l,u,f.**   *Choice, 1992.*

Blasius, Mark &   HQ76.W33 1997
  Phelan, Shane (Editors)
We Are Everywhere: A Historical Sourcebook of Gay and
Lesbian Politics. Paper over Boards. Routledge. New York, NY.
1997. 600p. ISBN:0-415-90858-2, ISBN13: 978-0-415-90858-0.
Dewey:323.3/264. LCCN:95-002434.
Audience: **g,l.**

Brandt, Eric (Editor)   HQ76.4.U6D35 1999
Dangerous Liaisons: Blacks, Gays and the Struggle for Equality.
Trade Cloth. New Press, The. New York, NY. 1999. 328p.
ISBN:1-56584-455-6, ISBN13: 978-1-56584-455-1.
Dewey:305.896/073. LCCN:98-056062.
Audience: **g,l,u.**

Clendinen, Dudley &   HQ76.8.U5C58 1999
  Nagourney, Adam
Out for Good: The Struggle to Build a Gay Rights Movement in
America. Trade Cloth. Simon & Schuster. New York, NY. 1999.
720p. ISBN:0-684-81091-3, ISBN13: 978-0-684-81091-1.
Dewey:305.9/0664. LCCN:99-012523.
Audience: **g,l,u.**

Comstock, Gary David   HV7431
Violence Against Lesbians and Gay Men. Trade Paper.
Columbia University Press. New York, NY. 1992. 220p.
Between Men, Between Women Ser. ISBN:0-231-07331-3,
ISBN13: 978-0-231-07331-8. Dewey:362.8/8.
Audience: **u,f.**   *Choice, 1991.*

Cruikshank, Margaret   HQ76.8.U5.C78 1992
The Gay and Lesbian Liberation Movement. Cloth Text.
Routledge. New York, NY. 1992. 240p. Revolutionary Thought
and Radical Movements Ser. ISBN:0-415-90647-4, ISBN13:
978-0-415-90647-0. Dewey:306.76. LCCN:92-008622.
Audience: **g,l.**   *Choice, 1993.*

D'Emilio, John   HQ76.8.U5D454 2002
The World Turned: Essays on Gay History, Politics, and Culture.
Trade Cloth. Duke University Press. Durham, NC. 2002. 328p.
ISBN:0-8223-2930-1, ISBN13: 978-0-8223-2930-5.
Dewey:305.9/0664/0973. LCCN:2002-001674.
Audience: **g,l.**

D'Emilio, John   HQ76.8.U5D447 1992
Making Trouble: Essays on Gay History, Politics, and the
University. Cloth Text. Routledge. New York, NY. 1992. 336p.
ISBN:0-415-90509-5, ISBN13: 978-0-415-90509-1.
Dewey:305.90664. LCCN:92-010049.
Audience: **l,u.**

Gross, Larry   HQ76.8.U5G76 1993
Contested Closets: The Politics and Ethics of Outing. Trade
Paper. University of Minnesota Press. Minneapolis, MN. 1993.

362p. ISBN:0-8166-2179-9, ISBN13: 978-0-8166-2179-8. Dewey:305.9/0664. LCCN:93-000394.

Audience: **l,u,f.**

Harris, Daniel   **HQ76.2.U5H347 1997**
The Rise and Fall of Gay Culture. Trade Cloth. Hyperion Press. New York, NY. 1997. 278p. ISBN:0-7868-6165-7, ISBN13: 978-0-7868-6165-1. Dewey:305.38/96642. LCCN:96-047822.

Audience: **g,l,u,f.**

Loffreda, Beth   **HV6250.4.H66**
Losing Matt Shepard: Life and Politics in the Aftermath of Anti-Gay Murder. Trade Paper. Columbia University Press. New York, NY. 2001. 160p. ISBN:0-231-11859-7, ISBN13: 978-0-231-11859-0. Dewey:306.76/6/0978795.

Audience: **g,l,u.**

Marcus, Eric   **HQ76.8.U5M36 2002**
Making Gay History: The Half-Century Fight for Lesbian and Gay Equal Rights. Trade Paper. HarperCollins Publishers. New York, NY. 2002. 496p. ISBN:0-06-093391-7, ISBN13: 978-0-06-093391-3. Dewey:305.9/0664. LCCN:2001-051818.

Audience: **g.**

Myers, JoAnne   **HQ76.5.M94 2003**
Historical Dictionary of the Lesbian Liberation Movement: Still the Rage. Trade Cloth. Scarecrow Press, Inc. Lanham, MD. 2003. 360p. Historical Dictionaries of Religions, Philosophies, and Movements Ser., No. 45 ISBN:0-8108-4506-7, ISBN13: 978-0-8108-4506-0. Dewey:305.9/0664. LCCN:2002-156624.

Audience: **g,l.** *Choice, 2004.*

Patton, Cindy   **RA644.A25P38 1985**
Sex and Germs: The Politics of AIDS. Trade Paper. South End Press. Cambridge, MA. 1985. 182p. ISBN:0-89608-259-8, ISBN13: 978-0-89608-259-5. Dewey:362.1/969792/00973. LCCN:85-026240.

Audience: **u,f.**

Rimmerman, Craig A.   **HQ76.8.U5R56 2002**
From Identity to Politics: The Lesbian and Gay Movements in the United States. Paper Text. Temple University Press. Philadelphia, PA. 2002. 272p. Queer Politics, Queer Theories Ser. ISBN:1-56639-905-X, ISBN13: 978-1-56639-905-0. Dewey:305.9/0664. LCCN:2001-027644.

Audience: **l,u,f.** *Choice, 2002.*

Robinson, Paul   **HQ76.85.R63 2005**
Queer Wars: The New Gay Right and Its Critics. Trade Cloth. University of Chicago Press. Chicago, IL. 2005. 192p. ISBN:0-226-72200-7, ISBN13: 978-0-226-72200-9. Dewey:306.76/6. LCCN:2004-005111.

Audience: **u,f.** *Choice, 2005.*

Rosenfeld, Dana   **HQ76.3.U5R68 2003**
The Changing of the Guard: Lesbian and Gay Elders, Identity, and Social Change. Library Binding. Temple University Press. Philadelphia, PA. 2003. 272p. ISBN:1-59213-030-5, ISBN13: 978-1-59213-030-6. Dewey:306.76/6. LCCN:2002-043552.

Audience: **l,u,f.**

Smith, Raymond A. &   **HQ76.3.U5S59 2002**
  Haider-Markel, Donald P.
🄴 Gay and Lesbian Americans and Political Participation: A Reference Handbook. E-Book. ABC-CLIO, Inc. Santa Barbara, CA. 2003. Political Participation in America Ser. ISBN:1-57607-731-4, ISBN13: 978-1-57607-731-3. Dewey:305.9/0664/0973.

Audience: **g.** *Choice, 2003.*

Stein, Arlene   **HQ76.8.U5**
The Stranger Next Door: The Story of a Small Community's Battle over Sex, Faith, and Civil Rights. Trade Paper. Beacon Press. Boston, MA. 2002. 280p. ISBN:0-8070-7953-7, ISBN13: 978-0-8070-7953-9. Dewey:305.9/0664/09795.

Audience: **g,l.** *Choice, 2001.*

Sullivan, Andrew   **HQ76.25**
Virtually Normal. Trade Paper. Alfred A. Knopf Inc. New York, NY. 1996. 240p. ISBN:0-679-74614-5, ISBN13: 978-0-679-74614-0. Dewey:306.76/6.

Audience: **g,l.**

Politics > History

Bullough, Vern L.   **HQ76.5.R56 2002**
  (Editor)
Before Stonewall: Activists for Gay and Lesbian Rights in Historical Context. Trade Paper. Haworth Press, Incorporated, The. Binghamton, NY. 2005. 467p. An Insightout Book Club Selection! Ser. ISBN:1-56023-193-9, ISBN13: 978-1-56023-193-6. Dewey:305.9/0664/0922 B. LCCN:2001-051858.

Audience: **g.** *Choice, 2003.*

Duberman, Martin   **HQ76.8.U5 D85 1993**
Stonewall. Dutton. 1993. ISBN:0-525-93602-5, ISBN13: 978-0-525-93602-2.

Audience: **g,l,u.**

Politics > Law/Civil Rights

                                          HQ75.8.U5
▢ Gay & Lesbian Alliance Against Defamation. http://www.glaad.org/

Audience: **g,l,u,f.**

                                          HQ76.8.U5
▢ Human Rights Campaign. http://www.hrc.org/

Audience: **g.**

                                          HQ76.8.U5
▢ Lambda Legal Defense. http://www.lambdalegal.org/

Audience: **g,l,u,f.**

Amnesty International   **HQ76.U5**
▢ Stonewalled: Police Abuse and Misconduct Against Lesbian, Gay, Bisexual and Transgender People in the U.S. http://web.amnesty.org/library/Index/ENGAMR511222005 Amnesty International.

Audience: **g.**

Button, James W., et al.   **HQ76.8.U5B87 1997**
Private Lives, Public Conflicts: Battles over Gay Rights in American Communities. Barbara A. Rienzo & Kenneth D. Wald (Authors). Trade Paper. CQ Press. Washington, DC. 1997. 223p. ISBN:1-56802-278-6, ISBN13: 978-1-56802-278-9. Dewey:323.3/264. LCCN:96-053442.

Audience: **u,f.** *Choice, 1997.*

D'Emilio, John   **PL888.N5**
What Our Families Need: Toward a Policy Agenda for Lesbian and Gay Families. Paper Text. National Gay & Lesbian Task Force Policy Institute. Washington, DC. 1997.

ISBN:0-9652779-3-3, ISBN13: 978-0-9652779-3-8.
Dewey:895.62082.

Audience: **g,l,u.**

D'Emilio, John (Editor),   **HQ76.8.U5C74 2000**
et al.
Creating Change: Public Policy, Civil Rights and Sexuality.
William B. Turner & Urvashi Vaid (Editors). Cloth over Boards.
St. Martin's Press. Gordonville, VA. 2000. 528p.
ISBN:0-312-24375-8, ISBN13: 978-0-312-24375-3.
Dewey:305.9/0664/0973. LCCN:00-031718.

Audience: **g,l.**

Duberman, Martin   **HQ76.8.U5 D85 1993**
Stonewall. Dutton. 1993. ISBN:0-525-93602-5, ISBN13:
978-0-525-93602-2.

Audience: **g,l,u.**

Epstein, Rob &   **D804.5.G38**
Friedman, Jeffrey (Directed Bys)
Paragraph 175. DVD. New Yorker Video. New York, NY. 2001.
ISBN:1-56730-254-8, ISBN13: 978-1-56730-254-7.
Dewey:940.53/18/08664.

Audience: **g.**

Eskridge, William N. Jr.   **KF4754.5.E84 1999**
Gaylaw: Challenging the Apartheid of the Closet. Trade Cloth.
Harvard University Press. Cambridge, MA. 1999. 480p.
ISBN:0-674-34161-9, ISBN13: 978-0-674-34161-6.
Dewey:342.73/087. LCCN:99-026321.

Audience: **u,f.** *Choice, 2000.*

Johnson, David K.   **JK723.H6J64 2003**
The Lavender Scare: The Cold War Persecution of Gays and
Lesbians in the Federal Government. Trade Cloth. University of
Chicago Press. Chicago, IL. 2004. 312p. ISBN:0-226-40481-1,
ISBN13: 978-0-226-40481-3. Dewey:352.6/086/640973.
LCCN:2003-009138.

Audience: **g,l,u,f.** *Choice, 2004.*

Kranz, Rachel &   **HQ76.8.U5K73 2005**
Cusick, Tim
Gay Rights. Ed. 2. Trade Cloth. Facts On File, Inc. New York,
NY. 2005. 368p. Library in a Book ISBN:0-8160-5810-5,
ISBN13: 978-0-8160-5810-5. Dewey:323.3/264/0973.
LCCN:2005-009832.

Audience: **g.** *Choice, 2006, 2001.*

Marotta, Toby   **HQ76.8.U5**
The Politics of Homosexuality. Trade Cloth. Houghton Mifflin
Company. New York, NY. 1981. 384p. ISBN:0-395-29477-0,
ISBN13: 978-0-395-29477-2. Dewey:306.7/2/0973.

Audience: **g,l.**

Murdoch, Joyce &   **HQ76.8.U5**
Price, Deb
Courting Justice: Gay Men and Lesbians vs. the Supreme Court.
Trade Paper. Basic Books. New York, NY. 2002. 592p.
ISBN:0-465-01514-X, ISBN13: 978-0-465-01514-6.
Dewey:305.906641.

Audience: **l,u,f.**

Ridinger, Robert B.   **HQ75.16.U6S53 2004**
(Editor)
Speaking for Our Lives: Historic Speeches and Rhetoric for Gay
and Lesbian Rights/1892-2000. Trade Paper. Haworth Press,
Incorporated, The. Binghamton, NY. 2005. 845p.

ISBN:1-56023-175-0, ISBN13: 978-1-56023-175-2.
Dewey:306.7660973. LCCN:2003-006746.

Audience: **g,l,u,f.** *Choice, 2004.*

Vaid, Urvashi   **HQ76.8.U5V35 1995**
Virtual Equality: The Mainstreaming of Gay and Lesbian
Liberation. Trade Cloth. Doubleday Publishing. New York, NY.
1995. 464p. ISBN:0-385-47298-6, ISBN13: 978-0-385-47298-2.
Dewey:305.9/0664. LCCN:95-016869.

Audience: **g,l,u,f.**

Walzer, Lee   **KF4754.5.W35 2001**
Gay Rights on Trial: A Handbook with Cases, Laws, and
Documents. Charles L. Zelden (Editor). Library Binding.
ABC-CLIO, Inc. Santa Barbara, CA. 2002. 323p. On Trial Ser.
ISBN:1-57607-254-1, ISBN13: 978-1-57607-254-7.
Dewey:305.9/0664. LCCN:2001-006905.

Audience: **g.**

Weeks, Jeffrey   **HQ18.G7W43 1989**
Sex, Politics and Society: The Regulation of Sexuality since
1800. Ed. 2. Trade Paper. Pearson Education. Boston, MA.
1989. 336p. Themes in British Social History Ser.
ISBN:0-582-02383-1, ISBN13: 978-0-582-02383-3.
Dewey:306.7/0941. LCCN:88-013197.

Audience: **l,u,f.**

Williams, Walter L. &   **HQ76**
Retter, Yolanda (Editors)
Gay and Lesbian Rights in the United States: A Documentary
History. Cloth Text. Greenwood Publishing Group, Inc.
Portsmouth, NH. 2003. 368p. Primary Documents in American
History and Contemporary Issues Ser. ISBN:0-313-30696-6,
ISBN13: 978-0-313-30696-9. Dewey:305.9/0664/0973.
LCCN:2002-035218.

Audience: **g,l,u,f.**

Politics > Marriage

Baird, Robert M. &   **HQ1034.U5S25 2004**
Rosenbaum, Stuart E.
Same-Sex Marriage: The Moral and Legal Debate. Ed. 2. Trade
Paper. Prometheus Books, Publishers. Amherst, NY. 2004. 317p.
ISBN:1-59102-274-6, ISBN13: 978-1-59102-274-9.
Dewey:306.84/8. LCCN:2004-016580.

Audience: **l,u,f.**

Cahill, Sean   **HQ1034.U5C34 2004**
Same-Sex Marriage in the United States: Focus on the Facts.
Trade Cloth. Lexington Books. Lanham, MD. 2004. 176p.
ISBN:0-7391-0881-6, ISBN13: 978-0-7391-0881-9.
Dewey:306.84/8/0973. LCCN:2004-013082.

Audience: **g,l.** *Choice, 2005.*

D'Emilio, John   **PL888.N5**
What Our Families Need: Toward a Policy Agenda for Lesbian
and Gay Families. Paper Text. National Gay & Lesbian Task
Force Policy Institute. Washington, DC. 1997.
ISBN:0-9652779-3-3, ISBN13: 978-0-9652779-3-8.
Dewey:895.62082.

Audience: **g,l,u.**

Eskridge, William N. Jr.   **KF538.E85**
The Case for Same-Sex Marriage: From Sexual Liberty to
Civilized Commitment. Trade Cloth. Simon & Schuster. New
York, NY. 1996. ISBN:0-02-874136-6, ISBN13:
978-0-02-874136-9. Dewey:306.84.

Audience: **u,f.** *Choice, 1996.*

Snyder, R. Claire   **HQ1034.U5S58 2005**
Gay Marriage and Democracy: Equality for All. Trade Cloth.
Rowman & Littlefield Publishers, Inc. Lanham, MD. 2006.
208p. ISBN:0-7425-2786-7, ISBN13: 978-0-7425-2786-7.
Dewey:306.84/8. LCCN:2005-018300.

Audience: **g.**

Strasser, Mark P.   **KF539**
The Challenge of Same-Sex Marriage: Federalist Principles and
Constitutional Protections. Trade Cloth. Greenwood Publishing
Group, Inc. Portsmouth, NH. 1999. 272p. ISBN:0-275-96624-0,
ISBN13: 978-0-275-96624-9. Dewey:346.7301/6.
LCCN:99-021589.

Audience: **u,f.**

Strasser, Mark P.   **KF539.S77 1997**
Legally Wed: Same-Sex Marriage and the Constitution. Book,
Other. Cornell University Press. Ithaca, NY. 1997. 256p.
ISBN:0-8014-3406-8, ISBN13: 978-0-8014-3406-8.
Dewey:346.7301/6. LCCN:96-050344.

Audience: **g,l,u,f.** *Choice, 1997.*

Strasser, Mark Philip   **KF539**
On Same-Sex Marriage, Civil Unions, and the Rule of Law:
Constitutional Interpretation at the Crossroads. Trade Cloth.
Greenwood Publishing Group, Inc. Portsmouth, NH. 2002. 208p.
Issues on Sexual Diversity and the Law Ser.
ISBN:0-275-97761-7, ISBN13: 978-0-275-97761-0.
Dewey:346.7301/6. LCCN:2002-025204.

Audience: **u,f.**

Sullivan, Andrew   **HQ1033.S26**
  (Editor)
For Better or Worse?: Same Sex Marriages, Pro and Con: A
Reader. Trade Paper. Knopf Publishing Group. New York, NY.
1997. ISBN:0-614-28079-6, ISBN13: 978-0-614-28079-1.
Dewey:306.84/8.

Audience: **g,l.**

Sullivan, Andrew   **HQ1033.S26 2004**
Same-Sex Marriage: Pro and Con. Trade Paper. Knopf
Publishing Group. New York, NY. 2004. 416p.
ISBN:1-4000-7866-0, ISBN13: 978-1-4000-7866-0.
Dewey:306.84/8. LCCN:2004-273579.

Audience: **g,l.**

Wardle, Lynn D.   **HQ1034**
  (Editor), et al.
Marriage and Same-Sex Unions: A Debate. David Orgon
Coolidge, William C. Duncan & Mark Strasser (Editors). Trade
Cloth. Greenwood Publishing Group, Inc. Portsmouth, NH.
2003. 408p. ISBN:0-275-97653-X, ISBN13: 978-0-275-97653-8.
Dewey:306.84/8/0973. LCCN:2002-031266.

Audience: **l,u,f.** *Choice, 2003.*

Warner, Michael   **HQ76.25**
The Trouble with Normal: Sex, Politics, and the Ethics of Queer
Life. Trade Paper. Harvard University Press. Cambridge, MA.
2000. 240p. ISBN:0-674-00441-8, ISBN13: 978-0-674-00441-2.
Dewey:306.76/6. LCCN:99-044356.

Audience: **g,l.** *Choice, 2000.*

Wolfson, Evan   **HQ1034.U5**
Why Marriage Matters: America, Equality, and Gay People's
Right to Marry. Trade Paper. Simon & Schuster, Inc. New York,
NY. 2005. 256p. ISBN:0-7432-6459-2, ISBN13:
978-0-7432-6459-4. Dewey:300.6.

Audience: **g,l.**

Politics > Military

                                        UB418.G38
⬚ Servicemembers Legal Defense Network (SLDN).
http://www.sldn.org

Audience: **g,l,u,f.**

Belkin, Aaron &   **UB418.G38D65 2003**
  Bateman, Geoffrey (Editors)
Don't Ask, Don't Tell: Debating the Gay Ban in the U. S.
Military. Paper Text. Lynne Rienner Publishers, Inc. Boulder,
CO. 2003. 190p. ISBN:1-58826-146-8, ISBN13:
978-1-58826-146-5. Dewey:355/.0086/640973.
LCCN:2002-031836.

Audience: **g,l,u,f.**

Berube, Allan   **D769.2.B46 1990**
Coming Out under Fire: The History of Gay Men and Women
in World War Two. Trade Cloth. Simon & Schuster. New York,
NY. 1990. 377p. ISBN:0-02-903100-1, ISBN13:
978-0-02-903100-1. Dewey:940.54/0973/08664.
LCCN:89-025653.

Audience: **g,l.** *Choice, 1990.*

Burg, B. R.   **UH630.G39 2001**
Gay Warriors: A Documentary History from the Ancient World
to the Present. Trade Cloth. New York University Press. New
York, NY. 2001. 310p. ISBN:0-8147-9885-3, ISBN13:
978-0-8147-9885-0. Dewey:355/.0086/642. LCCN:2001-004522.

Audience: **l,u.**

Cammermeyer,   **UB418.G38C36 1994**
  Margarethe & Fisher, Chris
Serving in Silence. Trade Cloth. Penguin Group (USA) Inc.
New York, NY. 1994. 320p. ISBN:0-670-85167-1, ISBN13:
978-0-670-85167-6. Dewey:305.48/9664/092 B.
LCCN:94-020825.

Audience: **g.**

Gershick, Zsa Zsa   **UB418.G38G47 2005**
Secret Service: Untold Stories of Lesbians in the Military. Trade
Paper, Perfect. Alyson Publications. Los Angeles, CA. 2005.
272p. ISBN:1-55583-748-4, ISBN13: 978-1-55583-748-8.
Dewey:355/.0092/273. LCCN:2004-062795.

Audience: **g,l,u,f.**

Halley, Janet E.   **UB418.G38H35 1999**
Don't: A Reader's Guide to the Military's Anti-Gay Policy.
Trade Paper. Duke University Press. Durham, NC. 1999. 176p.
Public Planet Bks. ISBN:0-8223-2317-6, ISBN13:
978-0-8223-2317-4. Dewey:355/.0086/6420973.
LCCN:98-038580.

Audience: **l,u,f.**

Hippler, Mike   **HQ75.8.M3 H56 1989**
Matlovich. Trade Paper. Alyson Publications. Los Angeles, CA.
1989. 172p. ISBN:1-55583-129-X, ISBN13: 978-1-55583-129-5.
Dewey:305.38/9664/092. LCCN:88-083332.

Audience: **g.**

Jobe, Jared B. (Editor),   **UB418.G38O93 1996**
  et al.
Out in Force: Sexual Orientation and the Military. Gregory M.
Herek & Ralph M. Carney (Editors). Trade Paper. University of
Chicago Press. Chicago, IL. 1996. 352p. Worlds of Desire Ser.
ISBN:0-226-40048-4, ISBN13: 978-0-226-40048-8.
Dewey:355/.008/664. LCCN:96-020110.

Audience: **l,u,f.**

Katzenstein, Mary F. &   **UB417.B48 1999**
  Reppy, Judith (Editors)
Beyond Zero Tolerance: Discrimination in Military Culture.
Book, Other. Rowman & Littlefield Publishers, Inc. Lanham,
MD. 1999. 308p. ISBN:0-8476-9315-5, ISBN13:
978-0-8476-9315-3. Dewey:355/.0089/00973. LCCN:98-041935.
                                        Audience: **g,l,u,f.**

Lehring, Gary L.   **UB418.G38L44 2003**
Officially Gay: The Political Construction of Sexuality in the U.
S. Military. Library Binding. Temple University Press.
Philadelphia, PA. 2003. 248p. Queer Politics, Queer Theories
Ser. ISBN:1-59213-034-8, ISBN13: 978-1-59213-034-4.
Dewey:355/.0086/640973. LCCN:2002-043554.
                                Audience: **u,f.** *Choice, 2004.*

Rimmerman, Craig A.   **UB418.G38G35 1996**
  (Editor)
Gay Rights, Military Wrongs: Political Perspectives on Lesbians
and Gays in the Military. Trade Paper. Garland Publishing, Inc.
New York, NY. 1996. 376p. Political Science Ser.
ISBN:0-8153-2580-0, ISBN13: 978-0-8153-2580-2.
Dewey:355/.008/664. LCCN:96-020929.
                                Audience: **l,u,f.** *Choice, 1996.*

Shilts, Randy   **UB418.G38**
Conduct Unbecoming: Gays and Lesbians in the U. S. Military.
Trade Paper, Perfect. St. Martin's Press. Gordonville, VA. 2005.
832p. ISBN:0-312-34264-0, ISBN13: 978-0-312-34264-7.
Dewey:355.0086/640973. LCCN:2005-280094.
                                        Audience: **g,l,u,f.**

University of California,   **UB418.G38**
  Santa Barbara
☐ Center for the Study of Sexual Minorities in the Military.
http://www.gaymilitary.ucsb.edu/index.htm
                                        Audience: **g,l,u,f.**

Politics > Biography

Cook, Blanche Wiesen   **E807.1.R48**
Eleanor Roosevelt: The Defining Years, 1933-1938. Trade Paper.
Penguin Group (USA) Inc. New York, NY. 2000. 704p. Eleanor
Roosevelt, 1933-1938 Ser., Vol. 2 ISBN:0-14-017894-5,
ISBN13: 978-0-14-017894-4. Dewey:92.
                                        Audience: **u,f.**

Cook, Blanche Wiesen   **E807**
Eleanor Roosevelt: 1884-1933. Trade Paper. Penguin Group
(USA) Inc. New York, NY. 1993. 608p. ISBN:0-14-009460-1,
ISBN13: 978-0-14-009460-2. Dewey:973.9/17/092.
LCCN:87-040632.
                                        Audience: **u,f.**

D'Emilio, John   **E185.97.R93D46 2003**
Lost Prophet: The Life and Times of Bayard Rustin. Trade
Cloth. Simon & Schuster. New York, NY. 2003. 576p.
ISBN:0-684-82780-8, ISBN13: 978-0-684-82780-3.
Dewey:323/.092 B. LCCN:2003-052771.
                                Audience: **g,l,u,f.** *Choice, 2004.*

Duberman, Martin   **HN57.D83 1999**
Left Out: A Political Journey. Trade Cloth. Basic Books. New
York, NY. 1999. 496p. ISBN:0-465-01744-4, ISBN13:
978-0-465-01744-7. Dewey:302.5/0973/09045.
LCCN:00-268116.
                                        Audience: **g,l.**

Hay, Harry   **HQ75.8.H39A3 1996**
Radically Gay: Gay Liberation in the Words of Its Founder
Harry Hay. Will Roscoe (Editor). Trade Cloth. Beacon Press.
Boston, MA. 1996. 352p. ISBN:0-8070-7080-7, ISBN13:
978-0-8070-7080-2. Dewey:305.38/9664/092. LCCN:95-039290.
                                        Audience: **l,u,f.**

Jay, Karla   **HQ1426**
Tales of the Lavender Menace: A Memoir of Liberation. Trade
Paper. Basic Books. New York, NY. 2000. 288p.
ISBN:0-465-08366-8, ISBN13: 978-0-465-08366-4.
Dewey:305.4/2/0973. LCCN:00-274554.
                                        Audience: **g,l.**

Shilts, Randy   **E184.A1F39**
The Mayor of Castro Street: The Life and Times of Harvey
Milk. Trade Paper. St. Martin's Press. Gordonville, VA. 1983.
388p. ISBN:0-312-52331-9, ISBN13: 978-0-312-52331-2.
Dewey:305.90664092.
                                        Audience: **g,l.**

Tripp, C. A.   **E457.2.T75 2004**
The Intimate World of Abraham Lincoln. Lewis Gannett
(Editor), Jean Baker (Introduction by). Trade Cloth. Simon &
Schuster, Inc. New York, NY. 2005. 384p. ISBN:0-7432-6639-0,
ISBN13: 978-0-7432-6639-0. Dewey:973.7/092.
LCCN:2004-057605.
                                        Audience: **g.**

Creative Production

Alwood, Edward   **P96.S45**
Straight News: Gays, Lesbians, and the News Media. Trade
Paper. Columbia University Press. New York, NY. 1998. 368p.
ISBN:0-231-08437-4, ISBN13: 978-0-231-08437-6.
Dewey:302.2/3/08664.
                                Audience: **g,l.** *Choice, 1997.*

Doty, Alexander   **PN1992.8.H64D68 1993**
Making Things Perfectly Queer: Interpreting Mass Culture.
Book, Other. University of Minnesota Press. Minneapolis, MN.
1993. 168p. ISBN:0-8166-2244-2, ISBN13: 978-0-8166-2244-3.
Dewey:306.766. LCCN:92-040036.
                                        Audience: **g.**

Gross, Larry P.   **P94.5.G38G76 2001**
Up from Invisibility: Lesbians, Gay Men, and the Media in
America. Trade Cloth. Columbia University Press. New York,
NY. 2001. 320p. Between Men, Between Women Ser.
ISBN:0-231-11952-6, ISBN13: 978-0-231-11952-8.
Dewey:305.9/0664/0973. LCCN:2001-042140.
                                        Audience: **g,u,f.**

Signorile, Michelangelo   **HQ76.8.U5S57 2003**
Queer in America: Sex, the Media and the Closets of Power. Ed.
3. Trade Paper. University of Wisconsin Press. Chicago, IL.
2003. 472p. ISBN:0-299-19374-8, ISBN13: 978-0-299-19374-4.
Dewey:305.9/0664. LCCN:2003-050114.
                                        Audience: **u,f.**

White, Edmund   **NX180.A36L67 2001**
  (Editor)
Loss Within Loss: Artists in the Age of AIDS. Trade Cloth.
University of Wisconsin Press. Chicago, IL. 2001. vi, 303p.
Living Out Ser. ISBN:0-299-17070-5, ISBN13:
978-0-299-17070-7. Dewey:700/.87. LCCN:00-011012.
                                        Audience: **g,l,u,f.**

Creative Production > Literature > General and Reference Works

Day, Frances Ann   **Z1037**
Lesbian and Gay Voices: An Annotated Bibliography and Guide to Literature for Children and Young Adults. Nancy Garden (Foreword by). Cloth Text. Greenwood Publishing Group, Inc. Portsmouth, NH. 2000. 296p. Culture and Customs of Asia Ser. ISBN:0-313-31162-5, ISBN13: 978-0-313-31162-8. Dewey:951.9. LCCN:00-021047.
         Audience: **g,l,u,f.** *Choice, 2000.*

Giard, Robert   **PS153.G38G515 1997**
Particular Voices: Portraits of Gay and Lesbian Writers. Trade Cloth. MIT Press. Cambridge, MA. 1997. 332p. ISBN:0-262-07180-0, ISBN13: 978-0-262-07180-2. Dewey:[B]. LCCN:96-047002.
         Audience: **g,l,u,f.**

Grier, Barbara   **PN56.L45**
The Lesbian in Literature: A Bibliography. Ed. 3. Trade Paper. Bella Books, Inc. Tallahassee, FL. 1981. 200p. ISBN:0-930044-23-1, ISBN13: 978-0-930044-23-7. Dewey:016.8088/0353. LCCN:81-082859.
         Audience: **g.**

Malinowski, Sharon   **PN56.H57.G36 1994**
(Editor)
Gay and Lesbian Literature, Vol. 1. Trade Cloth. Thomson Gale. Farmington Hills, MI. 1993. 488p. Gay and Lesbian Literature Ser., Vol. 1 ISBN:1-55862-174-1, ISBN13: 978-1-55862-174-9. Dewey:016.80993353. LCCN:93-047362.
         Audience: **g,l,u,f.** *Choice, 1994.*

Markowitz, Judith A.   **PS374.H63M37 2004**
The Gay Detective Novel: Lesbian and Gay Main Characters and Themes in Mystery Fiction. Katherine V. Forrest (Foreword by). Paper Text. McFarland & Company, Incorporated Publishers. Jefferson, NC. 2004. 312p. ISBN:0-7864-1957-1, ISBN13: 978-0-7864-1957-9. Dewey:813/.087209352664. LCCN:2004-019458.
         Audience: **g,l,u,f.** *Choice, 2005.*

Nelson, Emmanuel S.   **PS374**
(Editor)
Contemporary Gay American Novelists: A Bio-Bibliographical Critical Sourcebook. Cloth Text. Greenwood Publishing Group, Inc. Portsmouth, NH. 1993. 456p. ISBN:0-313-28019-3, ISBN13: 978-0-313-28019-1. Dewey:813.54099206642. LCCN:92-025762.
         Audience: **g.** *Choice, 1993.*

Nelson, Emmanuel S.   **PS325**
(Editor)
Contemporary Gay American Poets and Playwrights: An A-to-Z Guide. Cloth Text. Greenwood Publishing Group, Inc. Portsmouth, NH. 2003. 496p. ISBN:0-313-32232-5, ISBN13: 978-0-313-32232-7. Dewey:812/.54099206642. LCCN:2002-192771.
         Audience: **g,l,u,f.** *Choice, 2004.*

Pollack, Sandra &   **PS153**
Knight, Denise D. (Editors)
Contemporary Lesbian Writers of the United States: A Bio-Bibliographical Critical Sourcebook. Cloth Text. Greenwood Publishing Group, Inc. Portsmouth, NH. 1993. 688p.

ISBN:0-313-28215-3, ISBN13: 978-0-313-28215-7. Dewey:810.99206643. LCCN:92-039468.
         Audience: **g.** *Choice, 1994.*

Slide, Anthony   **PS374.H63S65 2003**
Lost Gay Novels: A Reference Guide to Fifty Works from the First Half of the Twentieth Century. Trade Paper. Haworth Press, Incorporated, The. Binghamton, NY. 2003. 204p. ISBN:1-56023-414-8, ISBN13: 978-1-56023-414-2. Dewey:813/.52099206642. LCCN:2002-027292.
         Audience: **g,l,u,f.**

St. James Press Staff   **PN56.H57G36 1994**
Gay and Lesbian Literature, Vol. 2. Ed. 2. Trade Cloth. Thomson Gale. Farmington Hills, MI. 1997. 500p. Gay and Lesbian Literature Ser., Vol. 2 ISBN:1-55862-350-7, ISBN13: 978-1-55862-350-7. Dewey:809.93353. LCCN:93-047362.
         Audience: **g.** *Choice, 1998.*

Summers, Claude J.   **PN56.H57G365 2002**
(Editor)
Gay and Lesbian Literary Heritage: A Reader's Companion to the Writers and Their Works, from Antiquity to the Present. Ed. 2. Paper over Boards. Routledge. New York, NY. 2002. 864p. ISBN:0-415-92926-1, ISBN13: 978-0-415-92926-4. Dewey:809/.8920664. LCCN:2002-022120.
         Audience: **g.**

Young, Ian   **Z2014.H6**
The Male Homosexual in Literature: A Bibliography. Ed. 2. Trade Cloth. Scarecrow Press, Inc. Lanham, MD. 1982. 360p. ISBN:0-8108-1529-X, ISBN13: 978-0-8108-1529-2. Dewey:016.8209/35206642. LCCN:82-000785.
         Audience: **g.**

Creative Production > Literature > Literary Criticism and Review

Ackerman, Susan   **PJ3771.G6A25 2005**
When Heroes Love: The Ambiguity of Eros in the Stories of Gilgamesh and David. E-Book. Columbia University Press. New York, NY. 2005. 336p. Religion and Gender Ser. ISBN:0-231-50725-9, ISBN13: 978-0-231-50725-7. Dewey:809/.93353.
         Audience: **u,f.**

Aldrich, Robert   **PN721.A43**
The Seduction of the Mediterranean: Writing, Art and Homosexual Fantasy. Trade Cloth. Routledge. New York, NY. 1993. ISBN:0-415-03277-6, ISBN13: 978-0-415-03277-3. Dewey:809.93321822. LCCN:92-040812.
         Audience: **l,u,f.**

Andreadis, Harriette   **PR428.H66A54 2001**
Sappho in Early Modern England: Female Same-Sex Literary Erotics, 1550-1714. Trade Paper. University of Chicago Press. Chicago, IL. 2001. 240p. Chicago Series on Sexuality, History and Society ISBN:0-226-02009-6, ISBN13: 978-0-226-02009-9. Dewey:820.9/3538/086643. LCCN:00-012562.
         Audience: **l,u,f.**

Austen, Roger   **PS374.H63.A9**
Playing the Game: The Homosexual Novel in America. Trade Cloth. Macmillan Publishing Company, Inc. Old Tappan, NJ. 1977. xv, 240 p. ;p. ISBN:0-672-52287-X, ISBN13: 978-0-672-52287-1. Dewey:813/.5/09352. LCCN:76-046228.
         Audience: **g.** *B*

Bergman, David   **PS153.G38.B4 1991**
Gaiety Transfigured: Gay Self-Representation in American
Literature. Trade Cloth. University of Wisconsin Press. Chicago,
IL. 1991. 259p. Wisconsin Project on American Writers Ser.
ISBN:0-299-13050-9, ISBN13: 978-0-299-13050-3.
Dewey:810.99206642. LCCN:91-050321.

Audience: **l,u.** *Choice, 1992.*

Bergman, David   **PS374.H63**
The Violet Hour: The Violet Quill and the Making of Gay
Culture. Trade Paper. Edinburgh University Press. Edinburgh,
2004. 368p. Between Men, Between Women Ser.
ISBN:0-231-13051-1, ISBN13: 978-0-231-13051-6.
Dewey:810.9/9206642. LCCN:2003-064645.

Audience: **l,u,f.**

Butters, Ronald R.   **PS169.H65D56 1989**
(Editor), et al.
Displacing Homophobia: Gay Male Perspectives in Literature
and Culture. John M. Clum & Michael Moon (Editors). Cloth
Text. Duke University Press. Durham, NC. 1989. 315p.
ISBN:0-8223-0962-9, ISBN13: 978-0-8223-0962-8.
Dewey:810.9/353. LCCN:89-027584.

Audience: **l,u.** *Choice, 1990.*

Canning, Richard   **PS374.H63C36 2000**
Gay Fiction Speaks: Conversations with Gay Novelists. Cloth
Text. Columbia University Press. New York, NY. 2001. xxvii,
439p. Between Men, Between Women Ser.
ISBN:0-231-11694-2, ISBN13: 978-0-231-11694-7.
Dewey:813/54099206642. LCCN:00-060143.

Audience: **g,l,u,f.**

Castle, Terry   **PN56.P92**
The Apparitional Lesbian: Female Homosexuality and Modern
Culture. Trade Paper. Columbia University Press. New York,
NY. 1995. 307p. Gender and Culture Series, Carolyn G.
Heilbrun and Nancy K. Miller, Editors Ser.
ISBN:0-231-07653-3, ISBN13: 978-0-231-07653-1.
Dewey:809.9/3353.

Audience: **l,u.** *Choice, 1994.*

Castle, Terry   **PN6071.L47L58 2003**
The Literature of Lesbianism: A Historical Anthology from
Ariosto to Stonewall. Trade Cloth. Columbia University Press.
New York, NY. 2003. 1110p. ISBN:0-231-12510-0, ISBN13:
978-0-231-12510-9. Dewey:808.8/0353. LCCN:2002-041491.

Audience: **l,u.** *Choice, 2004.*

Collecott, Diana   **PS3507.O726 Z615 19**
H. D. and Sapphic Modernism 1910-1950. Trade Cloth.
Cambridge University Press. New York, NY. 1999. 364p.
ISBN:0-521-55078-5, ISBN13: 978-0-521-55078-9.
Dewey:811.5/2. LCCN:98-038426.

Audience: **u,f.** *Choice, 2000.*

Doan, Laura   **HQ75.6.G7D63 2001**
Fashioning Sapphism: The Origins of a Modern English Lesbian
Culture. Trade Paper. Columbia University Press. New York,
NY. 2000. 288p. Between Men, Between Women Ser.
ISBN:0-231-11007-3, ISBN13: 978-0-231-11007-5.
Dewey:306.76/63/0941. LCCN:00-043161.

Audience: **l,u,f.** *Choice, 2001.*

Duberman, Martin   **NX650.H6Q43 1997**
(Editor)
Queer Representations: Reading Lives, Reading Cultures. Trade

Cloth. New York University Press. New York, NY. 1997. 456p.
ISBN:0-8147-1884-1, ISBN13: 978-0-8147-1884-1.
Dewey:700/.453. LCCN:96-053042.

Audience: **l,u.**

Dynes, Wayne R. &   **PN56.H57H65 1992**
Donaldson, Stephen (Editors)
Homosexual Themes in Literary Studies, 8. Library Binding.
Garland Publishing, Inc. New York, NY. 1992. 416p. Studies in
Homosexuality, Vol. 8 ISBN:0-8153-0553-2, ISBN13:
978-0-8153-0553-8. Dewey:809.93353. LCCN:92-013897.

Audience: **l,u.**

El-Rouayheb, Khaled   **HQ76.3.A65E576 2005**
Before Homosexuality in the Arab-Islamic World, 1500-1800.
Trade Cloth. University of Chicago Press. Chicago, IL. 2005.
208p. ISBN:0-226-72988-5, ISBN13: 978-0-226-72988-6.
Dewey:306.76/6/09174927. LCCN:2005-008022.

Audience: **l,u,f.**

Esquibel, Catrióna   **PS153.L46E85 2006**
Rueda
With Her Machete in Her Hand: Reading Chicana Lesbians.
Trade Paper. University of Texas Press. Austin, TX. 2006. 280p.
Chicana Matters Ser. ISBN:0-292-71275-8, ISBN13:
978-0-292-71275-1. Dewey:810.99206643. LCCN:2005-009217.

Audience: **u,f.**

Fone, Byrne R. S.   **PR408.H65F66 1994**
Road to Stonewall. Trade Cloth. Thomson Gale. Farmington
Hills, MI. 1994. 275p. Twayne's Literature and Society Ser., No.
14 ISBN:0-8057-8856-5, ISBN13: 978-0-8057-8856-3.
Dewey:820.9/35206642. LCCN:94-017118.

Audience: **u,f.** *Choice, 1995.*

Foster, David W.   **PQ7081**
(Editor)
Latin American Writers on Gay and Lesbian Themes: A
Bio-Critical Sourcebook. Cloth Text. Greenwood Publishing
Group, Inc. Portsmouth, NH. 1994. 544p. ISBN:0-313-28479-2,
ISBN13: 978-0-313-28479-3. Dewey:860.9/353.
LCCN:94-002191.

Audience: **l,u.** *Choice, 1995.*

Foster, Jeannette H.   **PN56.L45F6 1985**
Sex Variant Women in Literature. Trade Paper. Bella Books, Inc.
Tallahassee, FL. 1985. 432p. ISBN:0-930044-65-7, ISBN13:
978-0-930044-65-7. Dewey:809/.9335206643. LCCN:85-183446.

Audience: **g,l,u.**

Frantzen, Allen J.   **PR179.H66**
Before the Closet: Same-Sex Love from Beowulf to Angels in
America. Trade Paper. University of Chicago Press. Chicago, IL.
2000. 380p. ISBN:0-226-26092-5, ISBN13: 978-0-226-26092-1.
Dewey:829/.09353. LCCN:98-014935.

Audience: **l,u,f.** *Choice, 1999.*

Galvin, Mary E.   **PS153**
Queer Poetics: Five Modernist Women Writers, 161. Trade
Cloth. Greenwood Publishing Group, Inc. Portsmouth, NH.
1999. 160p. Contributions in Women's Studies, 161
ISBN:0-313-29810-6, ISBN13: 978-0-313-29810-3.
Dewey:810.9/9206643. LCCN:97-021449.

Audience: **u,f.** *Choice, 2000.*

Grahn, Judy Rae   **PS151.G7 1985**
The Highest Apple: Sappho and the Lesbian Poetic Tradition.
Trade Paper. Spinsters Ink Books. Midway, FL. 1985. 160p.
ISBN:0-933216-12-2, ISBN13: 978-0-933216-12-9.
Dewey:811/.009/9287. LCCN:84-051941.
                                        Audience: **l,u.**

Hobby, Elaine & White,   **PR120.L45W48 1991**
  Chris (Editors)
What Lesbians Do in Books: Lesbians as Writers, Readers and
Characters in Literature. Trade Paper. Women's Press, Limited,
The. London, 226p. ISBN:0-7043-4288-X, ISBN13:
978-0-7043-4288-0. Dewey:820.9/9206643. LCCN:92-215708.
                                        Audience: **l,u.**

Koponen, Wilfrid R.   **PS374**
Embracing a Gay Identity: Gay Novels As Guides. Trade Cloth.
Greenwood Publishing Group, Inc. Portsmouth, NH. 1993. 200p.
ISBN:0-89789-336-0, ISBN13: 978-0-89789-336-7.
Dewey:813.0099206642. LCCN:92-042090.
                             Audience: **u,f.** *Choice, 1993.*

Levin, James   **PS374.H63L4 1983**
The Gay Novel: The Male Homosexual Image in America.
Trade Cloth. Irvington Publishers. New York, NY. 1983. 350p.
ISBN:0-8290-1065-3, ISBN13: 978-0-8290-1065-7.
Dewey:813.009/353. LCCN:83-000119.
                                        Audience: **g,l,u.**

Martin, Robert A.   **PS3545.I5365.Z615**
Critical Essays on Tennessee Williams. Trade Cloth. Thomson
Gale. Farmington Hills, MI. 1997. 350p. Critical Essays on
American Literature Ser. ISBN:0-7838-0042-8, ISBN13:
978-0-7838-0042-4. Dewey:812/.54. LCCN:97-021446.
                                        Audience: **l,u,f.**

Martin, Robert K.   **PS310.H66M3 1998**
  (Editor)
The Homosexual Tradition in American Poetry. Ed. 2. Trade
Paper. University of Iowa Press. Iowa City, IA. 1998. 280p.
ISBN:0-87745-648-8, ISBN13: 978-0-87745-648-3.
Dewey:811/.4/09352. LCCN:98-020571.
                     Audience: **l,u.** *B* *Choice, 1999.*

McRue, Robert   **PS153.G38M38 1997**
The Queer Renaissance: Contemporary American Literature and
the Reinvention of Lesbian and Gay Identities. Trade Cloth.
New York University Press. New York, NY. 1997. 256p.
ISBN:0-8147-5554-2, ISBN13: 978-0-8147-5554-9.
Dewey:810.9/920664. LCCN:96-051220.
                             Audience: **l,u,f.** *Choice, 1997.*

Murphy, Timothy F. &   **PS153.G38W74 1993**
  Poirier, Suzanne
Writing AIDS: Gay Literature, Language, and Analysis. Trade
Cloth. Columbia University Press. New York, NY. 1993. 352p.
ISBN:0-231-07864-1, ISBN13: 978-0-231-07864-1.
Dewey:810.9/356. LCCN:92-020373.
                                        Audience: **l,u.**

Nelson, Emmanuel S.   **PS374**
  (Editor)
Contemporary Gay American Novelists: A Bio-Bibliographical
Critical Sourcebook. Cloth Text. Greenwood Publishing Group,
Inc. Portsmouth, NH. 1993. 456p. ISBN:0-313-28019-3,
ISBN13: 978 0 313 28019-1. Dewey:813.54099206642.
LCCN:92-025762.
                             Audience: **g.** *Choice, 1993.*

Palmer, Paulina   **PR888.T3P35 1999**
Lesbian Gothic: Transgressive Fictions. Trade Cloth. Continuum
International Publishing Group, Ltd. London, 1999. 160p.
ISBN:0-304-70153-X, ISBN13: 978-0-304-70153-7.
Dewey:823/.08729099206643. LCCN:99-012385.
                             Audience: **l,u,f.** *Choice, 2000.*

Perpetusa-Seva,   **PQ7081.5.T68 2003**
  Inmaculada & Torres, Lourdes (Editors)
Tortilleras: Hispanic and U. S. Latina Lesbian Expression. Paper
Text. Temple University Press. Philadelphia, PA. 2003. 256p.
ISBN:1-59213-007-0, ISBN13: 978-1-59213-007-8.
Dewey:860.9/9206643/098. LCCN:2002-073203.
                                        Audience: **l,u,f.**

Robinson, Paul   **HQ75.2.R63 1999**
Gay Lives: Homosexual Autobiography from John Addington
Symonds to Paul Monette. Trade Cloth. University of Chicago
Press. Chicago, IL. 1999. 456p. ISBN:0-226-72180-9, ISBN13:
978-0-226-72180-4. Dewey:306.76/62/0922 B.
LCCN:98-024460.
                             Audience: **u,f.** *Choice, 1999.*

Rohy, Valerie   **PS153.L46R64 2000**
Impossible Women: Lesbian Figures and American Literature.
Book, Other. Cornell University Press. Ithaca, NY. 2000. 208p.
ISBN:0-8014-3728-8, ISBN13: 978-0-8014-3728-1.
Dewey:810.9/9206643. LCCN:99-087706.
                                        Audience: **l,u,f.**

Rule, Jane   **PR449.S4**
Lesbian Images. Trade Cloth. Crossing Press, Incorporated, The.
Berkeley, CA. 1982. 246p. ISBN:0-89594-089-2, ISBN13:
978-0-89594-089-6. Dewey:820/.9/353.
                                        Audience: **g,l.**

Schwarz, A. B. Christa   **PS153.G38S39 2003**
Gay Voices of the Harlem Renaissance. Trade Paper. Indiana
University Press. Bloomington, IN. 2003. 264p. Blacks in the
Diaspora Ser. ISBN:0-253-21607-9, ISBN13:
978-0-253-21607-6. Dewey:810.9/9206642. LCCN:2002-153777.
                             Audience: **l,u,f.** *Choice, 2004.*

Sedgwick, Eve K.   **PN3352.A38**
Epistemology of the Closet. Trade Cloth. University of
California Press. Berkeley, CA. 1991. 220p.
ISBN:0-520-07874-8, ISBN13: 978-0-520-07874-1.
Dewey:809.3/9353.
                                        Audience: **u,f.**

Smith, Hazel   **PS3529.H28Z87 2000**
Hyperscapes in the Poetry of Frank O'Hara: Difference,
Homosexuality, Topography. Trade Cloth. Liverpool University
Press. Liverpool, 2000. 242p. ISBN:0-85323-994-0, ISBN13:
978-0-85323-994-9. Dewey:811/.54. LCCN:2001-431768.
                                        Audience: **u,f.**

Snyder, Jane M.   **PA4409.S64 1997**
Lesbian Desire in the Lyrics of Sappho. Trade Cloth. Columbia
University Press. New York, NY. 1997. 278p. Between Men,
Between Women Ser. ISBN:0-231-09994-0, ISBN13:
978-0-231-09994-3. Dewey:884/.01. LCCN:96-031981.
                             Audience: **u,f.** *Choice, 1997.*

Summers, Claude J.   **PR888.G34S86 1990**
Gay Fictions: Studies in a Male Homosexual Literary Tradition.
Trade Cloth. Continuum International Publishing Group, Ltd.
London, 1980. 271p. ISBN:0-8264-0466-9, ISBN13:

978-0-8264-0466-4. Dewey:823/.9109353/086642. LCCN:90-001461.

Audience: **l,u.** *Choice, 1991.*

Toibin, Colm PN56.H57
Love in a Dark Time: And Other Explorations of Gay Lives and Literature. Trade Paper. Simon & Schuster. New York, NY. 2004. 272p. ISBN:0-7432-4467-2, ISBN13: 978-0-7432-4467-1. Dewey:809/.8920664.

Audience: **g,l,u,f.**

Woodhouse, Reed PS374.H63 W66 1998
Unlimited Embrace: A Canon of Gay Fiction, 1945-1995. Trade Paper. University of Massachusetts Press. Amherst, MA. 2000. 392p. ISBN:1-55849-259-3, ISBN13: 978-1-55849-259-2. Dewey:813.54099206642. LCCN:97-048588.

Audience: **l,u,f.**

Yingling, Thomas E. PS3505.R272Z93 1990
Hart Crane and the Homosexual Text: New Thresholds, New Anatomies. Trade Cloth. University of Chicago Press. Chicago, IL. 1990. 282p. ISBN:0-226-95634-2, ISBN13: 978-0-226-95634-3. Dewey:811/.52. LCCN:89-048053.

Audience: **u,f.** *Choice, 1991.*

Zimmerman, Bonnie PS153.L46Z56 1990
The Safe Sea of Women: Lesbian Fiction, 1969-1989. Trade Cloth. Beacon Press. Boston, MA. 1990. 356p. ISBN:0-8070-7904-9, ISBN13: 978-0-8070-7904-1. Dewey:813/.54099287. LCCN:89-046057.

Audience: **l,u.**

Creative Production > Literature > Fiction

Allison, Dorothy PS3551.L453B37 1993
Bastard Out of Carolina. Trade Paper. Penguin Group (USA) Inc. New York, NY. 1993. 320p. Plume Contemporary Fiction Ser. ISBN:0-452-26957-1, ISBN13: 978-0-452-26957-6. Dewey:813/.54. LCCN:91-034607.

Audience: **g.**

Allison, Dorothy PS3551.L453T7 1988
Trash: Stories and Poems. Library Binding. Firebrand Books. Ithaca, NY. 1988. 176p. ISBN:0-932379-52-4, ISBN13: 978-0-932379-52-8. Dewey:813/.54. LCCN:88-030175.

Audience: **g.**

Allison, Dorothy PS3568.O243
Two or Three Things I Know for Sure. Trade Paper. Penguin Group (USA) Inc. New York, NY. 1996. 112p. ISBN:0-452-27340-4, ISBN13: 978-0-452-27340-5. Dewey:813.5/4.

Audience: **g.**

Alumit, Noel PS3601.L86L47 2002
Letters to Montgomery Clift. Trade Cloth. MacAdam/Cage Publishing, Inc. San Francisco, CA. 2003. 244p. ISBN:1-931561-02-8, ISBN13: 978-1-931561-02-0. Dewey:813/.6. LCCN:2001-058663.

Audience: **g.**

Anshaw, Carol PS3551.N7147L83 2002
Lucky in the Corner: A Novel. Trade Cloth. Houghton Mifflin Company Trade & Reference Division. Boston, MA. 2002. 256p. ISBN:0-395-94040-0, ISBN13: 978-0-395-94040-2. Dewey:813/.54. LCCN:2001-051891.

Audience: **g.**

Arnold, June PR6019.O9
Sister Gin. Jane Marcus (Afterword by). Trade Paper. Feminist Press at The City University of New York. New York, NY. 1989. 240p. ISBN:1-55861-010-3, ISBN13: 978-1-55861-010-1. Dewey:823/.9/1. LCCN:89-007926.

Audience: **g.**

Baldwin, James PS3568.O243
Giovanni's Room. Trade Paper. Dell Publishing. New York, NY. 2000. 176p. ISBN:0-385-33458-3, ISBN13: 978-0-385-33458-7. Dewey:813/.54.

Audience: **g.**

Bannon, Ann PS3552.A495O33 2001
Odd Girl Out. Trade Paper. Cleis Press. San Francisco, CA. 2001. 212p. Paperback Classics Ser. ISBN:1-57344-128-7, ISBN13: 978-1-57344-128-5. Dewey:813/.54. LCCN:2003-265524.

Audience: **g.**

Barnes, Djuna PS3503.A614L3 1992
Ladies Almanack. Trade Cloth. Dalkey Archive Press. Normal, IL. 1992. 96p. ISBN:0-916583-88-0, ISBN13: 978-0-916583-88-0. Dewey:818/.5207. LCCN:91-014515.

Audience: **u,f.**

Barnes, Djuna PS3503.A614N5 1995
Nightwood: The Original Version and Related Drafts. Cheryl J. Plumb (Editor). Trade Cloth. Dalkey Archive Press. Normal, IL. 1995. 319p. ISBN:1-56478-080-5, ISBN13: 978-1-56478-080-5. Dewey:813/.52. LCCN:94-036949.

Audience: **l,u,f.**

Barr, James PS3568.O243
Quatrefoil. Samuel M. Stewart (Introduction by). Trade Paper. Alyson Publications. Los Angeles, CA. 1982. 375p. ISBN:0-932870-16-3, ISBN13: 978-0-932870-16-2. Dewey:813/.54.

Audience: **g.**

Block, Francesca Lia PZ7.B61945
Baby Be-Bop. Library Binding. Sagebrush Education Resources. Caledonia, MN. 1997. ISBN:0-613-02103-7, ISBN13: 978-0-613-02103-6. Dewey:[Fic].

Audience: **g.**

Bowles, Jane PS3568.O243
Two Serious Ladies. Trade Paper. Peter Owen Ltd. London, 1996. 200p. ISBN:0-7206-1006-0, ISBN13: 978-0-7206-1006-2. Dewey:813.5/4.

Audience: **g.**

Boyd, Blanche M. PS3568.O243
The Revolution of Little Girls. Trade Paper. Knopf Publishing Group. New York, NY. 1992. 224p. Vintage Contemporaries Ser. ISBN:0-679-73812-6, ISBN13: 978-0-679-73812-1. Dewey:813.5/4. LCCN:91-050739.

Audience: **g.**

Bram, Christopher PS3568.O243
The Father of Frankenstein. Trade Paper. Penguin Group (USA) Inc. New York, NY. 1996. 288p. ISBN:0-452-27337-4, ISBN13: 978-0-452-27337-5. Dewey:813.5/4. LCCN:94-013192.

Audience: **g.**

Brown, Forman   PS3503.R812B48 2000
Better Angel: A Novel. Ed. 4. Trade Paper. Alyson Publications.
Los Angeles, CA. 2000. 224p. ISBN:1-55583-573-2, ISBN13:
978-1-55583-573-6. Dewey:813/.52. LCCN:99-088591.

Audience: **g.**

Brown, Rebecca   PS3568.O243
The Gifts of the Body. Trade Paper. HarperCollins Publishers.
New York, NY. 1995. 180p. ISBN:0-06-092653-8, ISBN13:
978-0-06-092653-3. Dewey:813/.54.

Audience: **g.**

Brown, Rita Mae   PS3552.R698.R8
Rubyfruit Jungle. Daughters, Inc. 1973. ISBN:0-913780-02-2,
ISBN13: 978-0-913780-02-2.

Audience: **g.**

Burns, John Horne   PS3503.U6385G3 2004
The Gallery. Trade Paper. New York Review of Books,
Incorporated, The. New York, NY. 2004. 368p. New York
Review Books Classics Ser. ISBN:1-59017-080-6, ISBN13:
978-1-59017-080-9. Dewey:813/.54. LCCN:2004-000089.

Audience: **g.**

Burroughs, William S.   PS3552.U75N3 2001
Naked Lunch: The Restored Text. James Grauerholz & Barry
Miles (Editors). Trade Cloth. Grove/Atlantic, Inc. New York,
NY. 2003. 304p. ISBN:0-8021-1639-6, ISBN13:
978-0-8021-1639-0. Dewey:813/.54. LCCN:2001-023190.

Audience: **g,l,u,f.**

Capote, Truman   PS3505.A59O7 2004
Other Voices, Other Rooms. John Berendt (Introduction by).
Trade Cloth. Random House, Inc. New York, NY. 2004. 224p.
ISBN:0-679-64322-2, ISBN13: 978-0-679-64322-7.
Dewey:813/.54. LCCN:2004-046666.

Audience: **g,l,u,f.** *B*

Chabon, Michael   PS3553.H15A82 2000
The Amazing Adventures of Kavalier and Clay. Trade Cloth.
Random House, Inc. New York, NY. 2000. 656p.
ISBN:0-679-45004-1, ISBN13: 978-0-679-45004-7.
LCCN:00-029063.

Audience: **g,l,u,f.**

Cheever, John   PS3505.H6428
Falconer. Ed. 2. Vintage Books. 1992. Vintage International
Edition

Audience: **g,l.**

Cocteau, Jean   PQ2605.O15
The Impostor. Dorothy Williams (Translator). Trade Paper. Peter
Owen Ltd. London, 1993. 132p. ISBN:0-7206-0843-0, ISBN13:
978-0-7206-0843-4. Dewey:843.9.

Audience: **g.**

Colette,   PQ2605.O28P813 2000
   Sidonie-Gabrielle
The Pure and the Impure. Herma Briffault (Translator), Judith
Thurman (Introduction by). Trade Paper. New York Review of
Books, Incorporated, The. New York, NY. 2000. 208p. New
York Review Books Classics Ser. ISBN:0-940322-48-X,
ISBN13: 978-0-940322-48-6. Dewey:843/.912.
LCCN:00-009532.

Audience: **g.**

Colette, Sidonie-Gabrielle   PQ2605.O28A287 2001
The Complete Claudine: Claudine at School - Claudine in Paris
- Claudine Married - Claudine and Annie. Ed. 2. Antonia White

(Translator), Judith Thurman (Introduction by). Trade Paper.
Farrar, Straus & Giroux. New York, NY. 2001. 660p.
ISBN:0-374-52803-9, ISBN13: 978-0-374-52803-4.
Dewey:843/.912. LCCN:2001-033699.

Audience: **g.**

Cooper, Dennis   PS3568.O243
Closer. Trade Paper. Grove/Atlantic, Inc. New York, NY. 1994.
144p. ISBN:0-8021-3212-X, ISBN13: 978-0-8021-3212-3.
Dewey:813/.54. LCCN:82-027396.

Audience: **g.**

Cruse, Howard   PN6728.B36
Stuck Rubber Baby. B. Taggart (Editor). Trade Paper. DC
Comics. New York, NY. 2000. 216p. ISBN:1-56389-255-3,
ISBN13: 978-1-56389-255-4. Dewey:741.5/973.

Audience: **g.**

Cunningham, Michael   PS3553.U484F57 1996
Flesh and Blood. Trade Paper. Simon & Schuster. New York,
NY. 1996. 480p. ISBN:0-684-87431-8, ISBN13:
978-0-684-87431-9. Dewey:813.5/4. LCCN:96-001899.

Audience: **g.**

Cunningham, Michael   PS3553.U484H68 1998
The Hours: A Novel. Cloth over Boards. Farrar, Straus &
Giroux. New York, NY. 1998. 230p. ISBN:0-374-17289-7,
ISBN13: 978-0-374-17289-3. Dewey:813/.54. LCCN:99-041903.

Audience: **g,l,u,f.**

Dawesar, Abha   PS3554.A9423B33 2004
Babyji. Trade Paper. Knopf Publishing Group. New York, NY.
2005. 368p. ISBN:1-4000-3456-6, ISBN13: 978-1-4000-3456-7.
Dewey:813/.6. LCCN:2004-048615.

Audience: **g.**

Delany, Samuel R.   PS3554.E437S7 2004
Stars in My Pocket Like Grains of Sand. Ed. 20. Trade Paper.
Wesleyan University Press. Middletown, CT. 2004. 376p.
ISBN:0-8195-6714-0, ISBN13: 978-0-8195-6714-7.
Dewey:813/.54. LCCN:2004-013614.

Audience: **g.**

D'Erasmo, Stacey   PS3554.E666S43 2004
A Seahorse Year: A Novel. Trade Cloth. Houghton Mifflin
Company Trade & Reference Division. Boston, MA. 2004.
368p. ISBN:0-618-43923-4, ISBN13: 978-0-618-43923-2.
Dewey:813/.54. LCCN:2004-042724.

Audience: **g.**

Dixon, Melvin   PS3568.O243
Vanishing Rooms. Trade Paper. Cleis Press. San Francisco, CA.
2001. 211p. ISBN:1-57344-123-6, ISBN13: 978-1-57344-123-0.
Dewey:813/.54.

Audience: **g.**

Donoghue, Emma   PR6054.O547H66 1995
Hood. Trade Cloth. HarperCollins Publishers. New York, NY.
1996. 320p. ISBN:0-06-017110-3, ISBN13: 978-0-06-017110-0.
Dewey:823.9/14. LCCN:95-048437.

Audience: **g.**

Donoghue, Emma   PZ8.D733KI 1997
Kissing the Witch: Old Tales in New Skins. Trade Cloth.
HarperCollins Publishers. New York, NY. 1997. 240p. Joanna
Cotler Bks. ISBN:0-06-027575-8, ISBN13: 978-0-06-027575-4.
Dewey:[Fic]. LCCN:96-043465.

Audience: **g.**

Donovan, John　　　　　　　　**PZ7.D7228 IL**
I'll Get There: It Better Be Worth the Trip. Trade Cloth.
HarperCollins Publishers. New York, NY. 1969.
ISBN:0-06-021718-9, ISBN13: 978-0-06-021718-1.
Dewey:[Fic]. LCCN:69-015539.

Audience: **g.**

Ebershoff, David　　　　　　　**PS3555.B4824**
The Danish Girl. Trade Paper. Penguin Group (USA) Inc. New
York, NY. 2001. 288p. ISBN:0-14-029848-7, ISBN13:
978-0-14-029848-2. Dewey:813.

Audience: **g.**

Eugenides, Jeffrey　　　　　　**PS3555.U4M53 2002**
Middlesex: A Novel. Cloth over Boards. Farrar, Straus &
Giroux. New York, NY. 2002. 544p. ISBN:0-374-19969-8,
ISBN13: 978-0-374-19969-2. Dewey:813/.54.
LCCN:2002-019921.

Audience: **g,l,u,f.**

Feinberg, David B.　　　　　　**PS3556.E425E34 1990**
Eighty-Sixed. Trade Paper. Penguin Group (USA) Inc. New
York, NY. 1990. 336p. ISBN:0-14-011252-9, ISBN13:
978-0-14-011252-8. Dewey:813/.54. LCCN:89-036585.

Audience: **g.**

Feinberg, Leslie　　　　　　　**PS3556.E427S7 1993**
Stone Butch Blues. Trade Paper. Firebrand Books. Ithaca, NY.
1993. 304p. ISBN:1-56341-029-X, ISBN13: 978-1-56341-029-1.
Dewey:813/.54. LCCN:93-016092.

Audience: **g.**

Firbank, Ronald　　　　　　　**PR6011.I7**
Five Novels of Ronald Firbank: Valmouth, Artificial Princess,
Flower Beneath the Foot, Prancing Nigger and Cardinal Pirelli.
Trade Paper. New Directions Publishing Corporation. New York,
NY. 1969. 482p. ISBN:0-8112-0799-4, ISBN13:
978-0-8112-0799-7. Dewey:823/.9/12. LCCN:49-048966.

Audience: **g.**

Ford, Charles Henri &　　　　**PS3511.O392**
Tyler, Parker
The Young and Evil. Trade Cloth. Ayer Company Publishers,
Inc. Manchester, NH. 1975. ISBN:0-405-07392-5, ISBN13:
978-0-405-07392-2. Dewey:813/.5/2. LCCN:75-012351.

Audience: **g.**

Forrest, Katherine V.　　　　**PS3556.O737C8 2002**
Curious Wine. Trade Paper. Alyson Publications. Los Angeles,
CA. 2002. 200p. ISBN:1-55583-661-5, ISBN13:
978-1-55583-661-0. Dewey:813.5/4. LCCN:2002-025568.

Audience: **g.**

Forster, E. M.　　　　　　　　**PR6019.O9**
Maurice. Trade Paper, Perfect. W. W. Norton & Company, Inc.
New York, NY. 1993. 256p. ISBN:0-393-31032-9, ISBN13:
978-0-393-31032-0. Dewey:823.9/12. LCCN:92-041161.

Audience: **g,l,u,f.** *B*

García Lorca, Federico　　　**PQ6613.A763.A17**
Poet in New York. Greg Simon & Steven White (Translators),
Christopher Maurer (Introduction by, Notes by). Trade Cloth.
Farrar, Straus & Giroux. New York, NY. 1988. 320p.
ISBN:0-374-23539-2, ISBN13: 978-0-374-23539-0.
Dewey:861.6/2. LCCN:87-033154.

Audience: **g,l,u,f.** *Choice, 1988.*

Garden, Nancy　　　　　　　**PZ7.G165**
Annie on My Mind. Library Binding. Sagebrush Education
Resources. Caledonia, MN. 1984. ISBN:0-8085-8756-0,
ISBN13: 978-0-8085-8756-9. Dewey:813.54.

Audience: **g.**

Genet, Jean　　　　　　　　　**PQ2613G285 F9**
Funeral Rites. Bernard Frechtman (Translator). Trade Paper.
Grove/Atlantic, Inc. New York, NY. 1987. 272p.
ISBN:0-8021-3087-9, ISBN13: 978-0-8021-3087-7.
Dewey:843/.9/12. LCCN:68-058157.

Audience: **g,l,u,f.**

Genet, Jean　　　　　　　　　**PQ2613.E53N613 1991**
Our Lady of the Flowers. Bernard Frechtman (Translator),
Jean-Paul Sartre (Introduction by). Trade Paper. Grove/Atlantic,
Inc. New York, NY. 1987. 320p. ISBN:0-8021-3013-5, ISBN13:
978-0-8021-3013-6. Dewey:843.9/12. LCCN:87-000414.

Audience: **g,l,u,f.** *B*

Genet, Jean　　　　　　　　　**PQ2613.E53J613 1987**
The Thief's Journal. Bernard Frechtman (Translator), Jean-Paul
Sartre (Foreword by). Trade Paper. Grove/Atlantic, Inc. New
York, NY. 1987. 272p. ISBN:0-8021-3014-3, ISBN13:
978-0-8021-3014-3. Dewey:843/.912. LCCN:87-012095.

Audience: **g,l,u,f.** *B*

Genet, Jean　　　　　　　　　**PQ2613.E53**
Querelle. Anselm Hollo (Translator). Trade Paper.
Grove/Atlantic, Inc. New York, NY. 1994. 288p.
ISBN:0-8021-5157-4, ISBN13: 978-0-8021-5157-5.
Dewey:843/.9/12. LCCN:73-017693.

Audience: **g.**

Gide, Andre　　　　　　　　　**PQ2613.I2**
The Counterfeiters. Trade Paper. Knopf Publishing Group. New
York, NY. 1973. 480p. ISBN:0-394-71842-9, ISBN13:
978-0-394-71842-2. Dewey:843/.9/12. LCCN:72-008064.

Audience: **g,l,u,f.** *B*

Gide, Andre　　　　　　　　　**PQ2613.I2I4813 2001**
The Immoralist. David Watson (Translator), Alan Sheridan
(Introduction by). Trade Paper. Penguin Group (USA) Inc. New
York, NY. 2001. 144p. Twentieth Century Classics Ser.
ISBN:0-14-218002-5, ISBN13: 978-0-14-218002-0.
Dewey:843/.912. LCCN:2001-032721.

Audience: **g.** *B*

Gomez, Jewelle　　　　　　　**PS3557.O457G5 1991**
The Gilda Stories. Trade Paper. Firebrand Books. Ithaca, NY.
2005. 250p. ISBN:1-56341-140-7, ISBN13: 978-1-56341-140-3.
Dewey:813/.54.

Audience: **g.**

Grimsley, Jim　　　　　　　　**PS3557.R4949D74 1995**
Dream Boy: A Novel. Trade Cloth. Algonquin Books of Chapel
Hill. Chapel Hill, NC. 1995. 195p. ISBN:1-56512-106-6,
ISBN13: 978-1-56512-106-5. Dewey:813/.54. LCCN:95-015005.

Audience: **g.**

Gurganus, Allan　　　　　　　**PS3568.O243**
Plays Well with Others. Trade Paper. Knopf Publishing Group.
New York, NY. 1999. 368p. ISBN:0-375-70203-2, ISBN13:
978-0-375-70203-7. Dewey:813.5/4.

Audience: **g.**

Hall, Radclyffe   PR6019.O9
The Unlit Lamp: A Novel. Trade Cloth. Scholarly Press, Inc.
Saint Clair Shores, MI. 1972. 343p. ISBN:0-403-01010-1,
ISBN13: 978-0-403-01010-3. Dewey:823/.912.
LCCN:74-145067.

Audience: **g.**

Hall, Radclyffe   PR6015.A33.W43
The Well of Loneliness: A 1920s Classic of Lesbian Fiction. Ed.
2. Anchor Books. 1990. ISBN:0-385-41609-1, ISBN13:
978-0-385-41609-2.

Audience: **g.**

Hardy, James Earl   PS3558.A62375
Love the One You're With: A B-Boy Blues Novel. Trade Paper.
HarperCollins Publishers. New York, NY. 2003. 272p. B-Boy
Blues Ser. ISBN:0-06-051239-3, ISBN13: 978-0-06-051239-2.
Dewey:813/.54.

Audience: **g.**

Harris, Bertha   PS3568.O243
Lover. Trade Cloth. New York University Press. New York, NY.
1993. 304p. The Cutting Edge: Lesbian Life and Literature Ser.
ISBN:0-8147-3504-5, ISBN13: 978-0-8147-3504-6.
Dewey:813/.54. LCCN:93-017716.

Audience: **g.**

Harris, E. Lynn   PS3558.A64438
Not a Day Goes By. Trade Paper. Knopf Publishing Group. New
York, NY. 2004. 288p. ISBN:1-4000-7578-5, ISBN13:
978-1-4000-7578-2. Dewey:813.5/4. LCCN:00-038368.

Audience: **g.**

Heim, Scott   PS3558.E4527.M87
Mysterious Skin. HarperCollins. 1995. ISBN:0-06-017175-8,
ISBN13: 978-0-06-017175-9.

Audience: **g.**

Hemphill, Essex   PS3558.E47925
Ceremonies: Prose and Poetry. Ed. 2. Charles Nero (Introduction
by). Trade Paper. Cleis Press. San Francisco, CA. 2000. 200p.
ISBN:1-57344-101-5, ISBN13: 978-1-57344-101-8. Dewey:810.

Audience: **g.**

Highsmith, Patricia   PS3558.I366
The Price of Salt. Trade Paper. W. W. Norton & Company, Inc.
New York, NY. 2004. 288p. ISBN:0-393-32599-7, ISBN13:
978-0-393-32599-7. Dewey:813/.54.

Audience: **g,l,u,f.**

Holleran, Andrew   PS3558.O3496D3 2001
Dancer from the Dance: A Novel. Trade Paper. HarperCollins
Publishers. New York, NY. 2001. 256p. ISBN:0-06-093706-8,
ISBN13: 978-0-06-093706-5. Dewey:813/.54.
LCCN:2001-036213.

Audience: **g.**

Holleran, Andrew   PS3568.O243
In September, the Light Changes: The Stories of Andrew
Holleran. Trade Cloth. Hyperion Press. New York, NY. 1999.
304p. ISBN:0-7868-6518-0, ISBN13: 978-0-7868-6518-5.
Dewey:813/.54.

Audience: **g.**

Hollinghurst, Alan   PR6058.O4467
Folding Star. UK-B Format Paperback. Knopf Publishing Group.
New York, NY. 1995. 432p. ISBN:0-09-947691-6, ISBN13:
978-0-09-947691-7. Dewey:823.9/14.

Audience: **g.**

Hollinghurst, Alan   PR6058.O4467L56 2004
The Line of Beauty: A Novel. Cloth over Boards. Bloomsbury
Publishing. New York, NY. 2004. 400p. ISBN:1-58234-508-2,
ISBN13: 978-1-58234-508-6. Dewey:823/.914.
LCCN:2004-047660.

Audience: **g,l,u,f.**

Hollinghurst, Alan   PR6058.O4467S9 1989
The Swimming-Pool Library. Trade Paper. Knopf Publishing
Group. New York, NY. 1989. 352p. Vintage International Ser.
ISBN:0-679-72256-4, ISBN13: 978-0-679-72256-4.
Dewey:823.9/14. LCCN:89-040113.

Audience: **g.**

Isherwood, Christopher   PR6017.S5S5 2001
A Single Man. Trade Cloth. University of Minnesota Press.
Minneapolis, MN. 2001. 192p. ISBN:0-8166-3862-4, ISBN13:
978-0-8166-3862-8. Dewey:823/.912. LCCN:00-054389.

Audience: **g,l,u,f.**

James, Henry   PS3511.A86
The Bostonians. R. D. Gooder (Editor, Introduction by, Notes
by). Trade Paper. Oxford University Press, Inc. New York, NY.
1998. 512p. Oxford World's Classics Ser. ISBN:0-19-283442-8,
ISBN13: 978-0-19-283442-3. Dewey:813/.52. LCCN:84-007884.

Audience: **g,l,u,f.**

Kerr, M. E.   PZ7.K46825
Night Kites. Perfect. Sagebrush Education Resources. Caledonia,
MN. 1987. 245p. ISBN:0-8335-0968-3, ISBN13:
978-0-8335-0968-0. Dewey:FIC.

Audience: **g.**

Kramer, Larry   PS3561.R252 F3 2000
Faggots. Ed. 2. Grove Press. 2000. ISBN:0-8021-3691-5,
ISBN13: 978-0-8021-3691-6.

Audience: **g.**

Leavitt, David   PS3562.E2618 L6 2005
The Lost Language of Cranes: A Novel. Ed. 2. Bloomsbury.
2005. ISBN:1-58234-573-2, ISBN13: 978-1-58234-573-4.

Audience: **g,l.**

Leduc, Violette   PQ2623.E3657B313
La Batarde. Derek Coltman (Translator), Simone de Beauvoir
(Foreword by), Rene de Ceccatty (Afterword by). Trade Paper.
Dalkey Archive Press. Normal, IL. 2003. 427p. French
Literature Ser. ISBN:1-56478-289-1, ISBN13:
978-1-56478-289-2. Dewey:843/.9814. LCCN:2002-041532.

Audience: **g.**

Mann, Thomas   PT2625.A44T62 2004
Death in Venice. Trade Cloth. HarperCollins Publishers. New
York, NY. 2004. 160p. ISBN:0-06-057605-7, ISBN13:
978-0-06-057605-9. Dewey:833/.912. LCCN:2003-063111.

Audience: **g.**

Maupin, Armistead   PS3568.O243
Tales of the City. Trade Paper. HarperCollins Publishers. New
York, NY. 1994. 384p. ISBN:0-06-092493-4, ISBN13:
978-0-06-092493-5. Dewey:813.5/4.

Audience: **g.**

Merrick, Gordon   PS3525.E6413 L6
The Lord Won't Mind. Trade Cloth. Alyson Publications. Los
Angeles, CA. 1996. 256p. ISBN:1-55583-290-3, ISBN13:
978-1-55583-290-2. Dewey:813/.5/2.

Audience: **g.**

Merrill, James   PS3525.E6645A6 2002
Collected Novels and Plays: James Merrill. J. D. McClatchy &
Stephen Yenser (Editors). Trade Cloth. Random House, Inc.
New York, NY. 2002. 688p. ISBN:0-375-41137-2, ISBN13:
978-0-375-41137-3. Dewey:818/.5408. LCCN:2002-020953.
Audience: **l,u,f.**

Miller, Isabel   PS3563.I39 P53
Patience & Sarah. Ed. 2. Arsenal Pulp Press. 2005. Little
Sister's Classics; No. 3 ISBN:1-55152-191-1, ISBN13:
978-1-55152-191-6.
Audience: **g.**

Mishima, Yukio   PL833.I7
Confessions of a Mask. Meredith Weatherby (Translator). Trade
Paper. New Directions Publishing Corporation. New York, NY.
1968. ISBN:0-8112-0118-X, ISBN13: 978-0-8112-0118-6.
Dewey:895.6/35. LCCN:58-012637.
Audience: **g,f.** *B*

Monette, Paul   PS3568.O243
Afterlife. Trade Paper. Kensington Publishing Corporation. New
York, NY. 2002. 264p. ISBN:0-7582-0188-5, ISBN13:
978-0-7582-0188-1. Dewey:813.5/4.
Audience: **g.**

Monette, Paul   PS3563.O523
Halfway Home. Trade Paper. Kensington Publishing
Corporation. New York, NY. 2002. 384p. ISBN:0-7582-0189-3,
ISBN13: 978-0-7582-0189-8. Dewey:813.5/4.
Audience: **g.**

Mordden, Ethan   PS3563.O7717I9 1996
I've a Feeling We're Not in Kansas Anymore. Trade Paper. St.
Martin's Press. Gordonville, VA. 1996. 208p. Stonewall Inn
Editions Ser., Vol. 1 ISBN:0-312-14112-2, ISBN13:
978-0-312-14112-7. Dewey:813.5/4. LCCN:95-045091.
Audience: **g.**

Muhanji, Cherry   PS3568.O243
Her. Trade Cloth. Aunt Lute Books. San Francisco, CA. 1990.
220p. ISBN:1-879960-03-6, ISBN13: 978-1-879960-03-9.
Dewey:813/.54. LCCN:90-047570.
Audience: **g.**

Nelson, Theresa   PZ7.N4377EAR 1994
Earthshine. Trade Cloth. Scholastic, Inc. New York, NY. 1994.
192p. ISBN:0-531-08717-4, ISBN13: 978-0-531-08717-6.
Dewey:[Fic]. LCCN:94-008793.
Audience: **g.**

Newman, Leslea   PZ7.N47988
Heather Has Two Mommies. Library Binding. Sagebrush
Education Resources. Caledonia, MN. 2000.
ISBN:0-613-78719-6, ISBN13: 978-0-613-78719-2.
Dewey:[Fic].
Audience: **g.**

Obejas, Achy   PS3565.B34M4 1996
Memory Mambo. Trade Paper. Cleis Press. San Francisco, CA.
1996. 250p. Fiction and Graphic Novels Ser.
ISBN:1-57344-017-5, ISBN13: 978-1-57344-017-2.
Dewey:813/.54. LCCN:96-016120.
Audience: **g,l,u.**

O'Neill, Jamie   PR6065.N4194A92 2001
At Swim, Two Boys. Trade Cloth. Simon & Schuster. New
York, NY. 2001. 643p. ISBN:0-7432-0712-2, ISBN13:
978-0-7432-0712-6. Dewey:823/.914. LCCN:2002-327505.
Audience: **g.**

Peters, Julie Anne   PZ7.P44158LU 2003
Luna. Trade Cloth. Little Brown & Company. New York, NY.
2004. 256p. ISBN:0-316-73369-5, ISBN13: 978-0-316-73369-4.
Dewey:[Fic]. LCCN:2003-058913.
Audience: **g.**

Picano, Felice   PS3566.I25L5 1995
Like People in History: A Gay American Epic. Trade Cloth.
Penguin Group (USA) Inc. New York, NY. 1995. 528p.
ISBN:0-670-86047-6, ISBN13: 978-0-670-86047-0.
LCCN:94-038159.
Audience: **g.**

Price, Reynolds   PS3568.O243
The Promise of Rest. Trade Paper. Simon & Schuster. New
York, NY. 1996. 368p. ISBN:0-684-82510-4, ISBN13:
978-0-684-82510-6. Dewey:813.5/4.
Audience: **g.**

Puig, Manuel   PQ7798.26.U4B413
Kiss of the Spider Woman. Thomas Colchie (Translator). Trade
Paper. Knopf Publishing Group. New York, NY. 1991. 288p.
ISBN:0-679-72449-4, ISBN13: 978-0-679-72449-0. Dewey:863.
LCCN:90-050626.
Audience: **g.** *B*

Purdy, James   PS3531.U426M34 1994
Malcolm. Trade Paper. Serpent's Tail Ltd. London, 1994. 196p.
ISBN:1-85242-368-4, ISBN13: 978-1-85242-368-1.
Dewey:813.5/4. LCCN:94-028945.
Audience: **g,l,u,f.**

Rechy, John   PS3568
City of Night. Trade Paper. Grove/Atlantic, Inc. New York, NY.
1988. 400p. ISBN:0-8021-3083-6, ISBN13: 978-0-8021-3083-9.
Dewey:813.5. LCCN:83-049451.
Audience: **g,l,u.**

Renault, Mary   PR6035.E55
The Charioteer. Trade Paper. Knopf Publishing Group. New
York, NY. 2003. 352p. ISBN:0-375-71418-9, ISBN13:
978-0-375-71418-4. Dewey:823.91. LCCN:2003-270072.
Audience: **g.**

Renault, Mary   PR6035.E55P4 1988
The Persian Boy. Trade Paper. Knopf Publishing Group. New
York, NY. 1988. 432p. ISBN:0-394-75101-9, ISBN13:
978-0-394-75101-6. Dewey:823/.9/1. LCCN:86-046179.
Audience: **g.** *B*

Rule, Jane   PS3568.O243
Desert of the Heart. Trade Paper. Bella Books, Inc. Tallahassee,
FL. 2005. 224p. ISBN:1-59493-035-X, ISBN13:
978-1-59493-035-5. Dewey:813/.54.
Audience: **g.**

Russell, Paul   PS3568.U7684C65 1999
The Coming Storm: A Novel. Trade Cloth. St. Martin's Press.
Gordonville, VA. 1999. 368p. ISBN:0-312-20514-7, ISBN13:
978-0-312-20514-0. Dewey:813/.54. LCCN:99-032207.
Audience: **g.**

Sanchez, Alex   PZ7.S19475RAI 2001
Rainbow Boys. Trade Cloth. Simon & Schuster Children's
Publishing. New York, NY. 2001. 256p. ISBN:0-689-84100-0,
ISBN13: 978-0-689-84100-2. Dewey:[Fic]. LCCN:2001-020952.

Audience: **g.**

Sarton, May   PS3511.A86
Mrs. Stevens Hears the Mermaids Singing. Trade Paper. W. W.
Norton & Company, Inc. New York, NY. 1993. 240p.
ISBN:0-393-30929-0, ISBN13: 978-0-393-30929-4.
Dewey:813.5/2.

Audience: **g,l,u,f.**

Schulman, Sarah   PS3569.C5393A69 1988
After Delores. Trade Cloth. Penguin Group (USA) Inc. New
York, NY. 1988. 176p. ISBN:0-525-24641-X, ISBN13:
978-0-525-24641-1. Dewey:813/.54. LCCN:87-025196.

Audience: **g.**

Schulman, Sarah   PS3568.O243
People in Trouble. Trade Cloth. Penguin Group (USA) Inc. New
York, NY. 1990. ISBN:0-525-24835-8, ISBN13:
978-0-525-24835-4. Dewey:813/.54. LCCN:89-017130.

Audience: **g.**

Schulman, Sarah   PS3569.C5393R37 1995
Rat Bohemia. Trade Cloth. Penguin Group (USA) Inc. New
York, NY. 1995. 240p. ISBN:0-525-93790-0, ISBN13:
978-0-525-93790-6. Dewey:813.5/4. LCCN:95-015475.

Audience: **g.**

Scoppettone, Sandra   PZ7.S4136TR 1996
Trying Hard to Hear You. Ed. 2. Trade Paper. Alyson
Publications. Los Angeles, CA. 1996. 256p.
ISBN:1-55583-367-5, ISBN13: 978-1-55583-367-1.
Dewey:[Fic]. LCCN:96-001252.

Audience: **g.**

Selvadurai, Shyam   PR9440.9.S42F86 1997
Funny Boy: A Novel in Six Stories. Trade Paper. Harcourt Trade
Publishers. New York, NY. 1997. 320p. Harvest Book Ser.
ISBN:0-15-600500-X, ISBN13: 978-0-15-600500-5. Dewey:813.
LCCN:97-006782.

Audience: **g,l,u,f.**

Shockley, Ann A.   PS3569.H568L68 1997
Loving Her. Trade Paper. Northeastern University Press. Boston,
MA. 1997. 208p. Library of Black Literature
ISBN:1-55553-329-9, ISBN13: 978-1-55553-329-8.
Dewey:813/.54. LCCN:97-018233.

Audience: **g.**

Toibin, Colm   PR6070.O455M37 2004
The Master. Trade Cloth. Simon & Schuster. New York, NY.
2004. 352p. ISBN:0-7432-5040-0, ISBN13: 978-0-7432-5040-5.
Dewey:823/.914. LCCN:2003-067376.

Audience: **g.**

Toibin, Colm   PR6070.O455S76 2005
The Story of the Night: A Novel. Trade Paper. Simon &
Schuster. New York, NY. 2005. 336p. ISBN:0-7432-7271-4,
ISBN13: 978-0-7432-7271-1. Dewey:823/.914.
LCCN:2005-042492.

Audience: **g.**

Truong, Monique   PS3620.R86B66 2003
The Book of Salt: A Novel. Dust Jacket. Houghton Mifflin
Company Trade & Reference Division. Boston, MA. 2003.
272p. ISBN:0-618-30400-2, ISBN13: 978-0-618-30400-4.
Dewey:813/.6. LCCN:2002-192152.

Audience: **g,l.**

Vidal, Gore   PS3568.O243
The City and the Pillar. Trade Paper. Knopf Publishing Group.
New York, NY. 2003. 240p. ISBN:1-4000-3037-4, ISBN13:
978-1-4000-3037-8. Dewey:813.5/4.

Audience: **g,l,u,f.** ℬ

Vidal, Gore   PS3543.I26M9 1987
Myra Breckinridge and Myron. Trade Paper. Penguin Group
(USA) Inc. New York, NY. 1997. 432p. Twentieth Century
Classics Ser. ISBN:0-14-118028-5, ISBN13: 978-0-14-118028-1.
Dewey:813/.54. LCCN:87-040002.

Audience: **g,l,u,f.**

Vivien, Renee   PQ2643.I9D3513 1983
The Woman of the Wolf and Other Stories. Karla Jay & Yvonne
Klein (Translators). Trade Cloth. Gay Presses of New York.
New York, NY. 1983. 122p. ISBN:0-9604724-5-2, ISBN13:
978-0-9604724-5-1. Dewey:843/.914. LCCN:83-080806.

Audience: **g.**

Walker, Alice   PS3568.O243
The Color Purple. Ed. 10. Cloth over Boards. Harcourt Trade
Publishers. New York, NY. 1992. 304p. ISBN:0-15-119154-9,
ISBN13: 978-0-15-119154-3. Dewey:813/.54. LCCN:91-047202.

Audience: **g,l,u,f.** ℬ

Warren, Patricia N.   PS3573.A776F7 1974
The Front Runner: 20th Anniversary Edition. Trade Cloth.
Wildcat Press. Beverly Hills, CA. 1995. 328p.
ISBN:0-9641099-1-3, ISBN13: 978-0-9641099-1-9.
Dewey:813/.54. LCCN:95-060336.

Audience: **g.**

Waters, Sarah   PR6073.A828 A69 2000
Affinity. Trade Paper. Penguin Group (USA) Inc. New York,
NY. 2002. 368p. ISBN:1-57322-873-7, ISBN13:
978-1-57322-873-2. Dewey:823.9/14. LCCN:99-087554.

Audience: **g.**

Waters, Sarah   PR6015.I3
Fingersmith. Trade Paper. Penguin Group (USA) Inc. New York,
NY. 2002. 592p. ISBN:1-57322-972-5, ISBN13:
978-1-57322-972-2. Dewey:823.9/14.

Audience: **g.**

Waters, Sarah   PR6073.A828
Tipping the Velvet: A Novel. Trade Paper. Penguin Group
(USA) Inc. New York, NY. 2000. 480p. ISBN:1-57322-788-9,
ISBN13: 978-1-57322-788-9. Dewey:823.92. LCCN:98-043836.

Audience: **g.**

Waugh, Evelyn   PR6019.O9
Brideshead Revisited. Frank Kermode (Introduction by). Trade
Cloth. Alfred A. Knopf Inc. New York, NY. 1993. 368p.
Everyman's Library, Vol. 172 ISBN:0-679-42300-1, ISBN13:
978-0-679-42300-3. Dewey:823/.912. LCCN:93-001854.

Audience: **g.**

Weir, John   PS3573.E39745I7 1999
The Irreversible Decline of Eddie Socket: A Novel. Trade Cloth.
Alyson Publications. Los Angeles, CA. 1999. 304p.
ISBN:1-55583-472-8, ISBN13: 978-1-55583-472-2.
Dewey:813/.54. LCCN:99-045569.

Audience: **g.**

White, Edmund   PS3568.O243
The Beautiful Room Is Empty. Trade Paper. Knopf Publishing
Group. New York, NY. 1994. 240p. ISBN:0-679-75540-3,
ISBN13: 978-0-679-75540-1. Dewey:813/.54.

Audience: **g.**

White, Edmund   PS3573.H463F37 1998
The Farewell Symphony. Trade Paper. Knopf Publishing Group.
New York, NY. 1998. 432p. ISBN:0-679-75476-8, ISBN13:
978-0-679-75476-3. Dewey:813.54. LCCN:98-026443.

Audience: **g.**

White, Edmund   PS3573.H463
The Married Man: A Novel. Trade Paper. Knopf Publishing
Group. New York, NY. 2001. 336p. ISBN:0-679-78144-7,
ISBN13: 978-0-679-78144-8. Dewey:813.5.

Audience: **g.**

White, Edmund   PS3573.H463N64 1988
Nocturnes for the King of Naples. Trade Paper. St. Martin's
Press. Gordonville, VA. 1988. 160p. Stonewall Inn Editions Ser.
ISBN:0-312-02263-8, ISBN13: 978-0-312-02263-1.
Dewey:823/.9/1. LCCN:88-011538.

Audience: **g.** *B*

White, Patrick   PR9619.3.W5
The Twyborn Affair. Trade Paper. Penguin Group (USA) Inc.
New York, NY. 1993. 432p. ISBN:0-14-018606-9, ISBN13:
978-0-14-018606-2. Dewey:823.

Audience: **g,l,u,f.** *B*

Wilde, Oscar   PR5812
The Complete Works of Oscar Wilde. Ed. 5. Trade Cloth.
HarperCollins Publishers Ltd. London, 2003. 1216p.
ISBN:0-00-714435-0, ISBN13: 978-0-00-714435-8.
Dewey:828.8/09.

Audience: **g,l,u,f.**

Willhoite, Michael   PZ7.W655485
Daddy's Roommate. Library Binding. Sagebrush Education
Resources. Caledonia, MN. 1991. ISBN:0-613-78713-7,
ISBN13: 978-0-613-78713-0. Dewey:[E].

Audience: **g.**

Williams, Tennessee   PS3568.O243
Collected Stories. Gore Vidal (Introduction by). Trade Paper.
New Directions Publishing Corporation. New York, NY. 1994.
602p. ISBN:0-8112-1269-6, ISBN13: 978-0-8112-1269-4.
Dewey:813.5/4. LCCN:85-010642.

Audience: **g,l,u.** *Choice, 1986.*

Wilson, Angus   PR6045.I577H43 1997
Hemlock and After. Trade Paper. St. Martin's Press.
Gordonville, VA. 1997. 352p. ISBN:0-312-15544-1, ISBN13:
978-0-312-15544-5. Dewey:823.9/14. LCCN:97-005836.

Audience: **g.** *B*

Winterson, Jeanette   PR6073.I55807 1987
Oranges Are Not the Only Fruit. Trade Paper. Grove/Atlantic,
Inc. New York, NY. 1997. 192p. ISBN:0-8021-3516-1, ISBN13:
978-0-8021-3516-2. Dewey:823.9/14. LCCN:87-014412.

Audience: **g,l,u,f.**

Winterson, Jeanette   PR6015.I3
Written on the Body. Trade Paper. Random House of Canada,
Ltd. Mississauga, ON. 1993. 192p. ISBN:0-394-28014-8,
ISBN13: 978-0-394-28014-1. Dewey:823.9/14.

Audience: **g,l,u,f.**

Wittig, Monique   PQ2683.I8
Les Guerilleres. Trade Cloth. Penguin Group (USA) Inc. New
York, NY. 1971. ISBN:0-670-42463-3, ISBN13:
978-0-670-42463-4. Dewey:843/.914. LCCN:70-158421.

Audience: **g,l,u,f.** *B*

Woodson, Jacqueline   PS3573.O64524A94
Autobiography of a Family Photo. Trade Cloth. Penguin Group
(USA) Inc. New York, NY. 1995. 128p. ISBN:0-525-93721-8,
ISBN13: 978-0-525-93721-0. Dewey:813/.54. LCCN:94-003639.

Audience: **g.**

Woodson, Jacqueline   PZ7.W868
From the Notebooks of Melanin Sun. Library Binding.
Sagebrush Education Resources. Caledonia, MN. 1995.
ISBN:0-613-05026-6, ISBN13: 978-0-613-05026-5.
Dewey:[Fic].

Audience: **g.**

Woodson, Jacqueline   PZ7.W868HO 2003
The House You Pass on the Way. Trade Cloth. Penguin Group
(USA) Inc. New York, NY. 2003. 112p. ISBN:0-399-23969-3,
ISBN13: 978-0-399-23969-4. Dewey:[Fic]. LCCN:2003-001277.

Audience: **g.**

Woolf, Virginia   PZ3.W8840R23
Orlando: A Biography. Trade Paper. Harcourt Trade Publishers.
New York, NY. 1973. 352p. Harvest Book Ser.
ISBN:0-15-670160-X, ISBN13: 978-0-15-670160-0.
Dewey:823/.9/12. LCCN:73-005729.

Audience: **g.** *B*

Yourcenar, Marguerite   PQ2631.R63
Alexis. Trade Paper. French & European Publications, Inc. New
York, NY. 1978. ISBN:0-8288-3803-8, ISBN13:
978-0-8288-3803-0. Dewey:843/.912.

Audience: **g.**

Yourcenar, Marguerite   PQ2649.O8
Memoirs of Hadrian. Grace Frick (Translator). Trade Paper.
Farrar, Straus & Giroux. New York, NY. 2005. 408p.
ISBN:0-374-52926-4, ISBN13: 978-0-374-52926-0.
Dewey:843/.912.

Audience: **g.**

Creative Production > Literature > Biography/Memoirs

Anzaldúa, Gloria   PS3551.N95Z464 2000
Interviews/Entrevistas. AnaLouise Keating (Editor). Paper over
Boards. Routledge. New York, NY. 2000. 320p.
ISBN:0-415-92503-7, ISBN13: 978-0-415-92503-7.
Dewey:818/.5409 B. LCCN:99-055530.

Audience: **l,u,f.**

Arenas, Reinaldo   PQ7390
Before Night Falls: A Memoir. Dolores M. Koch (Translator).
Trade Paper. Penguin Group (USA) Inc. New York, NY. 1994.
336p. ISBN:0-14-015765-4, ISBN13: 978-0-14-015765-9.
Dewey:863. LCCN:92-046264.

Audience: **g,l,u,f.**

Beauman, Nicola   PR6011.O58Z62 1994
E. M. Forster: A Biography of the Novelist E. M. Forster. Trade
Cloth. Alfred A. Knopf Inc. New York, NY. 1994. x, 404p.
ISBN:0-394-58381-7, ISBN13: 978-0-394-58381-5.
Dewey:823/.912. LCCN:92-044378.

       Audience: **g,l,u,f.** *Choice, 1994.*

Blum, Louise A.   HQ75.4.B55A3 2001
You're Not from Around Here, Are You?: A Lesbian in
Small-Town America. Trade Cloth. University of Wisconsin
Press. Chicago, IL. 2001. x, 271p. Living Out Ser.
ISBN:0-299-17090-X, ISBN13: 978-0-299-17090-5.
Dewey:305.9/0664 B. LCCN:00-011980.

       Audience: **g,l.**

Brownworth, Victoria A.   HQ75.5.B766 1996
Too Queer: Essays from a Radical Life. Trade Paper. Firebrand
Books. Ithaca, NY. 1996. 256p. ISBN:1-56341-074-5, ISBN13:
978-1-56341-074-1. Dewey:306.76/63. LCCN:96-002701.

       Audience: **g,l.**

Caveney, Graham   PS3552.U75Z58 1998
Gentleman Junkie: The Life and Legacy of William S.
Burroughs. Trade Cloth. Little Brown & Company. New York,
NY. 1998. 224p. ISBN:0-316-13725-1, ISBN13:
978-0-316-13725-6. Dewey:813/.54 B. LCCN:97-076356.

       Audience: **u,f.**

Clarke, Gerald   PS3551.N464
Capote: A Biography. Trade Paper. Avalon Publishing Group.
New York, NY. 2005. 636p. ISBN:0-7867-1661-4, ISBN13:
978-0-7867-1661-6. Dewey:818.5/4/09.

       Audience: **l,u.**

Cline, Sally   PR6015.A33Z62 1998
Radclyffe Hall: A Woman Called John. Trade Cloth. Overlook
Press, The. New York, NY. 1998. 304p. ISBN:0-87951-831-6,
ISBN13: 978-0-87951-831-8. Dewey:823/.912 B.
LCCN:97-024200.

       Audience: **u,f.** *Choice, 1998.*

Crisp, Quentin   HQ75.8
The Naked Civil Servant. Michael Holroyd (Preface by). Trade
Paper. Penguin Group (USA) Inc. New York, NY. 1997. 224p.
Twentieth Century Classics Ser. ISBN:0-14-118053-6, ISBN13:
978-0-14-118053-3. Dewey:306.7/662/092.

       Audience: **l.**

DeVeaux, Alexis   PS3562.O75Z66 2004
Warrior Poet: A Biography of Audre Lorde. Trade Cloth. W. W.
Norton & Company, Inc. New York, NY. 2004. 512p.
ISBN:0-393-01954-3, ISBN13: 978-0-393-01954-4.
Dewey:811/.54 B. LCCN:2003-023349.

       Audience: **g,l,u.** *Choice, 2004.*

Donaldson, Scott   PS3511.A86
John Cheever: A Biography. Trade Paper. iUniverse, Inc.
Lincoln, NE. 2002. 450p. ISBN:0-595-21138-0, ISBN13:
978-0-595-21138-8. Dewey:813/.52 B.

       Audience: **g,l,u,f.**

Doty, Mark   RC607.A26
Heaven's Coast: A Memoir. Trade Paper. HarperCollins
Publishers. New York, NY. 1997. 320p. ISBN:0-06-092805-0,
ISBN13: 978-0-06-092805-6. Dewey:362.1/9/69792/0092.
LCCN:95-053316.

       Audience: **g,l.**

Douglas, Alfred Bruce   PR6007.O8625
My Friendship with Oscar Wilde, Being the Autobiography of
Lord Alfred Douglas. Trade Paper. Books on Demand. Ann
Arbor, MI. 318p. ISBN:0-598-79751-3, ISBN13:
978-0-598-79751-3. Dewey:821.912. LCCN:34-004243.

       Audience: **g,l,u,f.**

Duberman, Martin   HQ75.8.D82A32 1996
Midlife Queer: Autobiography of a Decade, 1971-1991. Trade
Cloth. Simon & Schuster. New York, NY. 1996. 240p.
ISBN:0-684-81836-1, ISBN13: 978-0-684-81836-8.
Dewey:305.38/9664/092 B. LCCN:95-052738.

       Audience: **g,l.**

Duberman, Martin B.   HQ75.8.D82A3 1991
Cures: A Gay Man's Odyssey. Trade Cloth. Penguin Group
(USA) Inc. New York, NY. 1991. 336p. ISBN:0-525-24955-9,
ISBN13: 978-0-525-24955-9. Dewey:305.38/9664/092.
LCCN:90-046658.

       Audience: **g,l.**

Ellmann, Richard   PR5823.E38 1988
Oscar Wilde. Trade Cloth. Alfred A. Knopf Inc. New York, NY.
1988. 576p. ISBN:0-394-55484-1, ISBN13: 978-0-394-55484-6.
Dewey:828/.809 B. LCCN:87-045354.

       Audience: **g.** *Choice, 1988.*

Faderman, Lillian   CT3990.F33A3 2003
Naked in the Promised Land: A Memoir. Trade Cloth. Houghton
Mifflin Company Trade & Reference Division. Boston, MA.
2003. 368p. ISBN:0-618-12875-1, ISBN13: 978-0-618-12875-4.
Dewey:305.48/8924073/092 B. LCCN:2002-032233.

       Audience: **g,l.**

Faderman, Lillian   HQ75.6.U5F33 1991
Odd Girls and Twilight Lovers: A History of Lesbian Life in
Twentieth-Century America. Trade Cloth. Columbia University
Press. New York, NY. 1991. 373p. ISBN:0-231-07488-3,
ISBN13: 978-0-231-07488-9. Dewey:306.76/63/0973.
LCCN:90-026327.

       Audience: **l,u.**

Feinberg, David B.   RC607.A26
Queer and Loathing: Rants and Raves of a Raging AIDS Clone.
Tony Kushner (Preface by). Trade Paper. Penguin Group (USA)
Inc. New York, NY. 1995. 288p. ISBN:0-14-024080-2, ISBN13:
978-0-14-024080-1. Dewey:362.1/969792. LCCN:94-005074.

       Audience: **g,l.**

Fricke, Aaron   HQ76.3.U5
Reflections of a Rock Lobster: A Story about Growing up Gay.
Trade Cloth. Alyson Publications. Los Angeles, CA. 1995. 120p.
ISBN:1-55583-607-0, ISBN13: 978-1-55583-607-8.
Dewey:301.424.

       Audience: **g.**

Gooch, Brad   PS3529.H28Z687 1993
City Poet: The Life and Times of Frank O'Hara. Trade Cloth.
Alfred A. Knopf Inc. New York, NY. 1993. xiv, 532p. Borzoi
Reader Ser. ISBN:0-394-57118-5, ISBN13: 978-0-394-57118-8.
Dewey:811/.54 B. LCCN:92-056766.

       Audience: **g.** *Choice, 1993.*

Harris, E. Lynn   PS3558.A64438Z468
What Becomes of the Brokenhearted: A Memoir. Trade Cloth.
Doubleday Publishing. New York, NY. 2003. 288p.
ISBN:0-385-50264-8, ISBN13: 978-0-385-50264-1.
Dewey:813/.54 B. LCCN:2003-053209.

       Audience: **g.**

Heilbut, Anthony   PT2625.A44Z54415
Thomas Mann: Eros and Literature. Trade Cloth. Alfred A.
Knopf Inc. New York, NY. 1996. 688p. ISBN:0-394-55633-X,
ISBN13: 978-0-394-55633-8. Dewey:833.9/12.
LCCN:94-037034.
Audience: **u,f.**

Herring, Phillip F.   PS3503.A614 Z68 1995
Djuna: The Life and Work of Djuna Barnes. Viking. 1995.
ISBN:0-670-84969-3, ISBN13: 978-0-670-84969-7.
Audience: **g,l,u,f.**

Isherwood, Christopher   PR6017.S5Z498 2001
Christopher and His Kind. Trade Paper. University of Minnesota
Press. Minneapolis, MN. 2001. 352p. ISBN:0-8166-3863-2,
ISBN13: 978-0-8166-3863-5. Dewey:823/.912 B.
LCCN:2001-037031.
Audience: **u,f.**

Jay, Karla   PQ3939.B3Z72 1988
The Amazon and the Page: Natalie Clifford Barney and Renee
Vivien. Trade Paper. Indiana University Press. Bloomington, IN.
1988. 168p. ISBN:0-253-20476-3, ISBN13: 978-0-253-20476-9.
Dewey:840/.9/9287. LCCN:87-045405.
Audience: **u,f.** *Choice, 1988.*

Johnson, Fenton   HQ75.8.R67J65 1996
Geography of the Heart: A Memoir. Trade Cloth. Simon &
Schuster. New York, NY. 1996. 240p. ISBN:0-684-81417-X,
ISBN13: 978-0-684-81417-9. Dewey:305.9/06/642/0922.
LCCN:95-053070.
Audience: **g,l.**

Jones, Cleve & Dawson,   RC607.A26J6573 2000
Jeff
Stitching a Revolution: The Making of an AIDS Activist. Trade
Cloth. HarperCollins Publishers. New York, NY. 2000. 304p.
ISBN:0-06-251641-8, ISBN13: 978-0-06-251641-1.
Dewey:362.1/969792/0092 B. LCCN:99-052721.
Audience: **g,l.**

Jorgensen, Christine T.   HQ77.8.J67J67 2000
Christine Jorgensen: A Personal Autobiography. Ed. 2. Susan
Stryker (Introduction by). Trade Paper. Cleis Press. San
Francisco, CA. 2000. 340p. ISBN:1-57344-100-7, ISBN13:
978-1-57344-100-1. Dewey:305.9/066 B. LCCN:00-063904.
Audience: **g,l.**

Kaplan, Fred   PS3543.I26Z73 1999
Gore Vidal: A Biography. Trade Cloth. Doubleday Publishing.
New York, NY. 1999. 864p. ISBN:0-385-47703-1, ISBN13:
978-0-385-47703-1. Dewey:813.5/4. LCCN:99-014828.
Audience: **g,l,u,f.**

Kaplan, Fred   PS3568.O243
Gore Vidal: A Biography. Trade Paper. Knopf Publishing Group.
New York, NY. 2000. 896p. ISBN:0-385-47704-X, ISBN13:
978-0-385-47704-8. Dewey:813.5/4.
Audience: **g,l,u,f.**

Kennedy, Hubert   HQ75.8.U47 K46 1988
Ulrichs: The Life and Works of Karl Heinrich Ulrichs, Pioneer
of the Modern Gay Movement. Trade Paper. Alyson
Publications. Los Angeles, CA. 1988. 200p.
ISBN:1-55583-109-5, ISBN13: 978-1-55583-109-7.
Dewey:305.9/0664/092 B. LCCN:89-109922.
Audience: **u,f.**

Kramer, Larry   RA644.A25
Reports from the Holocaust: The Making of an AIDS Activist.
Trade Paper. St. Martin's Press. Gordonville, VA. 1989. 304p.
Stonewall Inn Editions Ser. ISBN:0-312-03921-2, ISBN13:
978-0-312-03921-9. Dewey:362.1/9697/9200973.
Audience: **g,l.**

Leeming, David   PS3552.A45Z77 1994
James Baldwin: A Biography. Trade Cloth. Alfred A. Knopf Inc.
New York, NY. 1994. 442p. ISBN:0-394-57708-6, ISBN13:
978-0-394-57708-1. Dewey:818/.5409 B. LCCN:93-030847.
Audience: **g.** *Choice, 1994.*

Leverich, Lyle   PS3545.I5365
Tom: The Unknown Tennessee Williams. Trade Paper. W. W.
Norton & Company, Inc. New York, NY. 1997. 644p.
ISBN:0-393-31663-7, ISBN13: 978-0-393-31663-6.
Dewey:812.5/4.
Audience: **l,u,f.** *Choice, 1996.*

Lorde, Audre Geraldine   PS3562.O75Z23 1982
Zami: A New Spelling of My Name: A Biomythography. Trade
Cloth. Crossing Press, Incorporated, The. Berkeley, CA. 1983.
256p. Feminist Ser. ISBN:0-89594-122-8, ISBN13:
978-0-89594-122-0. Dewey:813.5. LCCN:88-153779.
Audience: **g,l.**

Lurie, Alison   PS325
Familiar Spirits: A Memoir of James Merrill and David Jackson.
Trade Paper. Penguin Group (USA) Inc. New York, NY. 2002.
192p. ISBN:0-14-200045-0, ISBN13: 978-0-14-200045-8.
Dewey:811/.5409 B.
Audience: **u,f.**

Macey, David   B2430.F724M327 1993
The Lives of Michel Foucault. Trade Cloth. Knopf Publishing
Group. New York, NY. 1994. 624p. ISBN:0-679-43074-1,
ISBN13: 978-0-679-43074-2. Dewey:194. LCCN:93-028220.
Audience: **g.** *Choice, 1994.*

Manrique, Jaime   PQ8180.23.A52Z74
Eminent Maricones: Arenas, Lorca, Puig, and Me. Trade Cloth.
University of Wisconsin Press. Chicago, IL. 1999. ix, 116p.
Living Out Ser. ISBN:0-299-16180-3, ISBN13:
978-0-299-16180-4. Dewey:868. LCCN:98-049022.
Audience: **l,u,f.** *Choice, 2000.*

Mass, Lawrence D.   PS3561.R252Z99 1997
(Editor)
We Must Love One Another or Die: The Life and Legacies of
Larry Kramer. Cloth over Boards. Palgrave Macmillan. New
York, NY. 1997. 420p. ISBN:0-312-17704-6, ISBN13:
978-0-312-17704-1. Dewey:[B]. LCCN:97-030306.
Audience: **g,l,u.**

McCloskey, Deirdre N.   HQ77.8.M39A3 1999
Crossing: A Memoir. Trade Cloth. University of Chicago Press.
Chicago, IL. 1999. 282p. ISBN:0-226-55668-9, ISBN13:
978-0-226-55668-0. Dewey:305.9/066. LCCN:99-019450.
Audience: **g,l.** *Choice, 2000.*

McKenna, Neil   PR5823.M36 2005
The Secret Life of Oscar Wilde: An Intimate Biography. Trade
Cloth. Basic Books. New York, NY. 2005. 576p.
ISBN:0-465-04438-7, ISBN13: 978-0-465-04438-2.
Dewey:828/.809 B. LCCN:2005-040951.
Audience: **g,l,u,f.** *Choice, 2005.*

Millett, Kate   HQ75.4.M54 A3 2000
Sita. Ed. 2. University of Illinois Press. 2000.
ISBN:0-252-06887-4, ISBN13: 978-0-252-06887-4.
Audience: **g,l.**

Monette, Paul   HQ75.8.M64A3 1992
Becoming a Man: Half a Life Story. Trade Cloth. Harcourt
Trade Publishers. New York, NY. 1992. 278p.
ISBN:0-15-111519-2, ISBN13: 978-0-15-111519-8.
Dewey:306.76/6/092. LCCN:91-039475.
Audience: **g,l.**

Monette, Paul   RC607.A26
Borrowed Time: An AIDS Memoir. Trade Paper. HarperCollins
Publishers. New York, NY. 1990. ISBN:0-380-70779-9, ISBN13:
978-0-380-70779-9. Dewey:362.1/969792/00922 B.
Audience: **g,l.**

Morris, Jan   HQ77.9
Conundrum. Trade Paper. Henry Holt & Company. New York,
NY. 1987. 192p. ISBN:0-8050-0361-4, ISBN13:
978-0-8050-0361-1. Dewey:306.76/8. LCCN:87-008668.
Audience: **g,l,u,f.**

Nestle, Joan   HQ75.3
A Restricted Country. Ed. 2. Trade Paper. Cleis Press. San
Francisco, CA. 2003. 200p. ISBN:1-57344-152-X, ISBN13:
978-1-57344-152-0. Dewey:306.76/6/092 B.
LCCN:2004-304035.
Audience: **g,l,u.**

Nugent, Richard Bruce   PS3527.U34G39 2002
Gay Rebel of the Harlem Renaissance: Selections from the
Work of Richard Bruce Nugent. Thomas H. Wirth (Editor,
Introduction by). Trade Cloth. Duke University Press. Durham,
NC. 2002. 304p. ISBN:0-8223-2886-0, ISBN13:
978-0-8223-2886-5. Dewey:818/.5209 B. LCCN:2001-008587.
Audience: **g.** *Choice, 2002.*

Oliveira, Carmen L.   PQ9698.25.L4816F513
Rare and Commonplace Flowers: The Story of Elizabeth Bishop
and Lota de Macedo Soares. Neil K. Besner (Translator), Lloyd
Schwartz (Foreword by). Trade Cloth. Rutgers University Press.
Piscataway, NJ. 2002. 200p. ISBN:0-8135-3033-4, ISBN13:
978-0-8135-3033-8. Dewey:863.3/42. LCCN:2001-019838.
Audience: **g,l,u.** *Choice, 2002.*

Page, Norman   PR6001.U4Z765 1997
Auden and Isherwood: The Berlin Years. Cloth over Boards.
Palgrave Macmillan. New York, NY. 1998. 220p.
ISBN:0-312-21173-2, ISBN13: 978-0-312-21173-8.
Dewey:820.9/00912. LCCN:97-035010.
Audience: **g,l,u,f.** *Choice, 1999.*

Parker, Peter   PR6017.S5Z79 2004
Isherwood: A Life Revealed. Trade Cloth. Random House Adult
Trade Publishing Group. New York, NY. 2004. 832p.
ISBN:1-4000-6249-7, ISBN13: 978-1-4000-6249-2.
Dewey:823/.912 B. LCCN:2004-053185.
Audience: **g,l,u,f.**

Peters, Margot   PS3531.O82
May Sarton: Biography. Trade Paper. Ballantine Books. New
York, NY. 1998. 496p. ISBN:0-449-90798-8, ISBN13:
978-0-449-90798-6. Dewey:811/.52 B.
Audience: **l,u.**

Pratt, Minnie Bruce   HQ75.4.P7A3 2005
S/He. Trade Paper. Alyson Publications. Los Angeles, CA. 2005.
192p. Ser. ISBN:1-55583-888-X, ISBN13: 978-1-55583-888-1.
Dewey:306.76/63/092 B. LCCN:2004-062686.
Audience: **g.**

Reid, John & Tobias, Andrew   PS3568.O243
The Best Little Boy in the World. Ed. 25. Trade Paper.
Ballantine Books. New York, NY. 1993. 256p.
ISBN:0-345-38176-9, ISBN13: 978-0-345-38176-7.
Dewey:813.5/4. LCCN:92-090410.
Audience: **g.**

Rodriguez, Suzanne   PQ3939.B3
Wild Heart: A Life: Natalie Clifford Barney and the Decadence
of Literary Paris. Trade Paper. HarperCollins Publishers. New
York, NY. 2003. 448p. ISBN:0-06-093780-7, ISBN13:
978-0-06-093780-5. Dewey:305.48/9664.
Audience: **u,f.**

Rosco, Jerry   PS3545.E827Z84 2002
Glenway Wescott Personally: A Biography. Trade Cloth.
University of Wisconsin Press. Chicago, IL. 2002. 320p.
ISBN:0-299-17730-0, ISBN13: 978-0-299-17730-0.
Dewey:813/.52 B. LCCN:2001-005410.
Audience: **g,l.**

Savigneau, Josyane   PQ2649.O8Z8713 1993
Marguerite Yourcenar: Inventing a Life. Joan E. Howard
(Translator). Trade Cloth. University of Chicago Press. Chicago,
IL. 1993. 546p. ISBN:0-226-73544-3, ISBN13:
978-0-226-73544-3. Dewey:848.91209. LCCN:93-000449.
Audience: **u,f.**

Schanke, Robert A.   PS3501.C7Z87 2003
That Furious Lesbian: The Story of Mercedes de Acosta.
Edward Schiappa (Contribution by). Trade Cloth. Southern
Illinois University Press. Carbondale, IL. 2003. 272p. Theater in
the Americas Ser. ISBN:0-8093-2511-X, ISBN13:
978-0-8093-2511-5. Dewey:818/.5209 B. LCCN:2002-011762.
Audience: **u,f.** *Choice, 2004.*

Schmidgall, Gary   PS3232.S36 1997
Walt Whitman: A Gay Life. Trade Cloth. Penguin Group (USA)
Inc. New York, NY. 1997. 464p. ISBN:0-525-94373-0, ISBN13:
978-0-525-94373-0. Dewey:811.3. LCCN:97-014311.
Audience: **u,f.**

Schumacher, Michael   PS3513.I74Z86 1994
Dharma Lion: A Biography of Allen Ginsberg. Trade Cloth. St.
Martin's Press. Gordonville, VA. 1994. 784p.
ISBN:0-312-11263-7, ISBN13: 978-0-312-11263-9.
Dewey:811/.54. LCCN:94-018378.
Audience: **u,f.**

Souhami, Diana   PS3537.T323Z824
Gertrude and Alice. Ed. 2. Sterling Publishing Co., Inc. 2000.
Phoenix Press Ser. ISBN:1-84212-033-6, ISBN13:
978-1-84212-033-0.
Audience: **u,f.**

Stainton, Leslie   PQ6613.A763Z8856
Lorca: A Dream of Life. Trade Cloth. Farrar, Straus & Giroux.
New York, NY. 1999. 496p. ISBN:0-374-19097-6, ISBN13:
978-0-374-19097-2. Dewey:868.6/2/09. LCCN:98-051194.
Audience: **g,l,u,f.** *Choice, 2000.*

Stein, Gertrude   PS3537.T323A6 1998
Stein, 1903-1932: Q. E. D.; Three Lives; Autobiography of
Alice B. Toklas; Portraits. Catharine Stimpson & Harriet
Chessman (Editors). Trade Cloth. Library of America, The. New
York, NY. 1998. 960p. Library of America, Vol. 99
ISBN:1-883011-40-X, ISBN13: 978-1-883011-40-6.
Dewey:818/.5209. LCCN:97-028915.

Audience: **g,l,u,f.**

Streitmatter, Rodger   E807.1.R48A3
🄴 Empty Without You: The Intimate Letters of Eleanor
Roosevelt and Lorena Hickok. E-Book. Simon & Schuster. New
York, NY. 2000. ISBN:0-684-86766-4, ISBN13:
978-0-684-86766-3. Dewey:973.917/092/2 B.

Audience: **g,l.**

Sweetman, David   PR6035.E55Z87 1993
Mary Renault: A Biography. Trade Cloth. Harcourt Trade
Publishers. New York, NY. 1993. xiv, 322p.
ISBN:0-15-193110-0, ISBN13: 978-0-15-193110-1.
Dewey:823/.912 B. LCCN:93-016391.

Audience: **l,u.**

Timmons, Stuart   HQ75.8.H39
The Trouble with Harry Hay: Founder of the Modern Gay
Movement. Trade Paper. Alyson Publications. Los Angeles, CA.
1991. 350p. ISBN:1-55583-111-7, ISBN13: 978-1-55583-111-0.
Dewey:306.76/62/092 B.

Audience: **g,l.**   *Choice, 1991.*

Vidal, Gore   PS3568.O243
Palimpsest: A Memoir. Trade Paper. Penguin Group (USA) Inc.
New York, NY. 1996. 480p. ISBN:0-14-026089-7, ISBN13:
978-0-14-026089-2. Dewey:813.5/4.

Audience: **g,l,u.**   *Choice, 1996.*

Wagner-Martin, Linda   PS3537.T323Z87 1995
Favored Strangers: Gertrude Stein and Her Family. Trade Cloth.
Rutgers University Press. Piscataway, NJ. 1997. 400p.
ISBN:0-8135-2169-6, ISBN13: 978-0-8135-2169-5.
Dewey:818/.5209 B. LCCN:94-023700.

Audience: **u,f.**   *Choice, 1996.*

Werth, Barry   QC20
The Scarlet Professor: Newton Arvin: A Literary Life Shattered
by Scandal. Trade Paper. Knopf Publishing Group. New York,
NY. 2002. 352p. ISBN:0-385-49469-6, ISBN13:
978-0-385-49469-4. Dewey:530.1/01/13.

Audience: **g,l,u.**   *Choice, 2001.*

White, Edmund   PQ2613.E53.Z9 1993
Genet: A Biography. Trade Cloth. Alfred A. Knopf Inc. New
York, NY. 1993. xlii, 728p. ISBN:0-394-57171-1, ISBN13:
978-0-394-57171-3. Dewey:848/.91209 B. LCCN:93-018234.

Audience: **l,u.**   *Choice, 1994.*

Wilson, Andrew   PS3568.O243
Beautiful Shadow: A Life of Patricia Highsmith. Cloth over
Boards. Bloomsbury Publishing. New York, NY. 2003. 534p.
ISBN:1-58234-198-2, ISBN13: 978-1-58234-198-9.
Dewey:813/.54 B.

Audience: **g,l,u,f.**   *Choice, 2004.*

Wolff, Charlotte   HQ18.32.H57W64 1986
Magnus Hirschfeld: A Portrait of a Pioneer in Sexology. Trade
Cloth. Salem House Publishers. Scranton, PA. 1987. 496p.
ISBN:0-7043-2569-1, ISBN13: 978-0-7043-2569-2.
Dewey:306.7/092/4. LCCN:86-190523.

Audience: **u,f.**

Zilboorg, Caroline   PR6035.E55Z99 2001
The Masks of Mary Renault: A Literary Biography. Trade Paper.
University of Missouri Press. Columbia, MO. 2001. 296p.
ISBN:0-8262-1322-7, ISBN13: 978-0-8262-1322-8.
Dewey:823/.912 B. LCCN:00-066602.

Audience: **u,f.**   *Choice, 2002.*

Creative Production > Literature > Poetry

Broumas, Olga   PS3566.L27
Beginning with O. Stanley Kunitz (Foreword by). Trade Paper.
Yale University Press. Cumberland, RI. 1977. 87p. Younger
Poets Ser., Vol. 72 ISBN:0-300-02111-9, ISBN13:
978-0-300-02111-0. Dewey:811/.54. LCCN:76-049697.

Audience: **g,l,u,f.** *B*

Campo, Rafael   PS3553.A4883D58 1999
Diva. Trade Cloth. Duke University Press. Durham, NC. 1999.
104p. ISBN:0-8223-2383-4, ISBN13: 978-0-8223-2383-9.
Dewey:811/.54. LCCN:99-018342.

Audience: **g.**

Campo, Rafael   PS3553.A4883L36 2002
Landscape with Human Figure. Trade Paper. Duke University
Press. Durham, NC. 2002. 112p. ISBN:0-8223-2890-9, ISBN13:
978-0-8223-2890-2. Dewey:811/.54. LCCN:2001-047057.

Audience: **g.**

Coote, Stephen (Editor)   PN6110.H65P46 1986
The Penguin Book of Homosexual Verse. Trade Paper. Penguin
Group (USA) Inc. New York, NY. 1987. 416p.
ISBN:0-14-058551-6, ISBN13: 978-0-14-058551-3.
Dewey:808.81/9353. LCCN:88-108228.

Audience: **g.** *B*

Donoghue, Emma   PR1177
Poems Between Women: Four Centuries of Love, Romantic
Friendship, and Desire. Trade Paper. Columbia University Press.
New York, NY. 1999. 256p. Between Men, Between Women
Ser. ISBN:0-231-10925-3, ISBN13: 978-0-231-10925-3.
Dewey:821.008/09287.

Audience: **g.**

Doty, Mark   PS3554.O798S68 2001
Source: Poems. Trade Cloth. HarperCollins Publishers. New
York, NY. 2001. 96p. ISBN:0-06-621013-5, ISBN13:
978-0-06-621013-1. Dewey:811/.54. LCCN:2002-284316.

Audience: **g.**

Ginsberg, Allen   PS3513.I74 A17 1984
Collected Poems 1947-1980. Harper & Row. 1984.
ISBN:0-06-015341-5, ISBN13: 978-0-06-015341-0.

Audience: **g,l,u,f.**

Gunn, Thom   PR6013.U65A17
Collected Poems. Trade Paper. Farrar, Straus & Giroux. New
York, NY. 1995. 496p. ISBN:0-374-52433-5, ISBN13:
978-0-374-52433-3. Dewey:821.914. LCCN:93-074183.

Audience: **g.**

Hacker, Marilyn   PS3558.A28D47 2003
Desesperanto: Poems, 1999-2002. Trade Cloth. W. W. Norton &
Company, Inc. New York, NY. 2003. 128p.
ISBN:0-393-05418-7, ISBN13: 978-0-393-05418-7.
Dewey:811/.54. LCCN:2002-154390.

Audience: **g,l,u,f.**

Hacker, Marilyn   PS3558.A28A6 1994
Selected Poems of Marilyn Hacker, 1965-1990. Trade Cloth. W.
W. Norton & Company, Inc. New York, NY. 1994. 288p.
ISBN:0-393-03675-8, ISBN13: 978-0-393-03675-6.
Dewey:811/.54. LCCN:94-027507.

Audience: **g,l,u,f.**

Hemphill, Essex   PS3558.E47925
Ceremonies: Prose and Poetry. Ed. 2. Charles Nero (Introduction
by). Trade Paper. Cleis Press. San Francisco, CA. 2000. 200p.
ISBN:1-57344-101-5, ISBN13: 978-1-57344-101-8. Dewey:810.

Audience: **g.**

Klawitter, George   PR2209.B8 1990
(Editor)
Richard Barnfield: The Complete Poems. Trade Cloth.
Susquehanna University Press. Cranbury, NJ. 1991. 256p.
ISBN:0-945636-15-6, ISBN13: 978-0-945636-15-1.
Dewey:821/.3. LCCN:89-040776.

Audience: **g.**

Lorde, Audre Geraldine   PS3562.O75A17 1997
The Collected Poems of Audre Lorde. Trade Cloth. W. W.
Norton & Company, Inc. New York, NY. 1997. 500p.
ISBN:0-393-04090-9, ISBN13: 978-0-393-04090-6.
Dewey:811/.54. LCCN:97-010878.

Audience: **g,l,u,f.** *Choice, 1998.*

McClatchy, J. D.   PS3563.A26123H39
Hazmat. Trade Paper. Alfred A. Knopf Inc. New York, NY.
2004. 96p. ISBN:0-375-70991-6, ISBN13: 978-0-375-70991-3.
Dewey:813/.54. LCCN:2002-020529.

Audience: **g,l,u,f.**

McClatchy, J. D. (Editor)   PN6110.H65L68 2001
Love Speaks Its Name: Gay and Lesbian Love Poems. Trade
Cloth. Knopf Publishing Group. New York, NY. 2001. 256p.
Pocket Poets Ser. ISBN:0-375-41170-4, ISBN13:
978-0-375-41170-0. Dewey:808.81/9353. LCCN:2001-269713.

Audience: **g.**

Merrill, James   PS3525.E6645
The Changing Light at Sandover: A Poem. Ed. 2. Alfred A.
Knopf, Inc. 1993. ISBN:0-679-74736-2, ISBN13:
978-0-679-74736-9.

Audience: **g.**

Merrill, James   PS3525.E6645A17 2001
Collected Poems. Stephen Yenser & J. D. McClatchy (Editors).
Trade Cloth. Alfred A. Knopf Inc. New York, NY. 2001. 912p.
ISBN:0-375-41139-9, ISBN13: 978-0-375-41139-7.
Dewey:811/.54. LCCN:00-040542.

Audience: **g,l,u,f.**

Morse, Carl & Larkin,   PS595.H65G39 1988
Joan (Editors)
Gay and Lesbian Poetry in Our Time: An Anthology. Trade
Cloth. St. Martin's Press. Gordonville, VA. 1988. 448p.
ISBN:0-312-02213-1, ISBN13: 978-0-312-02213-6.
Dewey:811/.54/080353. LCCN:88-011546.

Audience: **g.**

O'Hara, Frank   PS3529.H28
The Collected Poems of Frank O'Hara. Donald Merriam Allen
(Editor). University of California Press. 1995.
ISBN:0-520-20166-3, ISBN13: 978-0-520-20166-8.

Audience: **g,l,u,f.**

Patrick, Robert   PS3566.A786U5 1988
Untold Decades. Harvey Fierstein (Introduction by), William M.
Hoffman (Preface by). Trade Cloth. St. Martin's Press.
Gordonville, VA. 1988. 160p. ISBN:0-312-02307-3, ISBN13:
978-0-312-02307-2. Dewey:812/.54. LCCN:88-017667.

Audience: **g.**

Phillips, Carl   PS3566.H476P3 2000
Pastoral. Trade Paper. Graywolf Press. St. Paul, MN. 2002. 96p.
ISBN:1-55597-298-5, ISBN13: 978-1-55597-298-1.
Dewey:811/.54. LCCN:99-060738.

Audience: **g.**

Powell, Neil (Editor,   PN6110.L6G39 1997
Introduction by)
Gay Love Poetry. Trade Paper. Avalon Publishing Group. New
York, NY. 1997. 254p. ISBN:0-7867-0469-1, ISBN13:
978-0-7867-0469-9. Dewey:808.81/93543. LCCN:97-029717.

Audience: **g.**

Pratt, Minnie B.   PS3566.R35C75 1990
Crime Against Nature. Trade Cloth. Firebrand Books. Ithaca,
NY. 1990. 128p. ISBN:0-932379-73-7, ISBN13:
978-0-932379-73-3. Dewey:811/.54. LCCN:90-002778.

Audience: **g.**

Pratt, Minnie Bruce   PS3566.R35
The Dirt She Ate: Selected and New Poems. Trade Paper.
University of Pittsburgh Press. Pittsburgh, PA. 2003. 127p. Pitt
Poetry Ser. ISBN:0-8229-5826-0, ISBN13: 978-0-8229-5826-0.
Dewey:811/.54. LCCN:2004-274340.

Audience: **g.**

Rich, Adrienne   PS3535.I233.A
The Fact of a Doorframe: Selected Poems, 1950-2001. Norton.
2002. ISBN:0-393-32395-1, ISBN13: 978-0-393-32395-5.

Audience: **g,l,u,f.**

Saint, Assoto (Editor)   PS595.H65R6 1991
The Road Before Us (One Hundred Gay Black Poets). Trade
Paper. Galiens Press. New York, NY. 1991.
ISBN:0-9621675-1-7, ISBN13: 978-0-9621675-1-5.
Dewey:811/.54080353. LCCN:91-030117.

Audience: **g.**

Saslow, James M.   PQ4656
The Poetry of Michelangelo: An Annotated Translation. Trade
Paper. Yale University Press. Cumberland, RI. 1993. 571p.
ISBN:0-300-05509-9, ISBN13: 978-0-300-05509-2.
Dewey:851/.4. LCCN:90-048480.

Audience: **g.** *Choice, 1991.*

Silvera, Makeda   PR9194.5.L47
(Editor)
Piece of My Heart: A Lesbian of Colour Anthology. Trade
Paper. Sister Vision Press. Toronto, ON. 1995. 620p.
ISBN:0-920813-65-8, ISBN13: 978-0-920813-65-2.
Dewey:C810.8/0353.

Audience: **g.**

Creative Production > Literature > Anthologies/Collections

Bao, Quang &   PS508.A8.T35
Yanagihara, Hanya (Editors)
Take Out: Queer Writing from Asian Pacific America. With
Timothy Liu. Asian American Writers' Workshop; Temple

University Press. 2001. ISBN:1-889876-12-7, ISBN13: 978-1-889876-12-2.

Audience: **g,l,u,f.**

Beam, Joseph (Editor) **PS509.H57I5 1986**
In the Life: A Black Gay Anthology. Trade Cloth. Alyson Publications. Los Angeles, CA. 1986. 255p. ISBN:0-932870-73-2, ISBN13: 978-0-932870-73-5. Dewey:810/.8/0353. LCCN:86-017283.

Audience: **g.**

Bouldrey, Brian (Editor) **PS648.H57 B45**
The Best American Gay Fiction. Mass Market. Little Brown & Company. New York, NY. 1998. ISBN:0-316-19078-0, ISBN13: 978-0-316-19078-7. Dewey:813.008/09206642/05.

Audience: **g,l.**

Cashorali, Peter **PS3553.A79393 F35 1995**
Fairy Tales: Traditional Stories Retold for Gay Men. HarperCollins. 1995. ISBN:0-06-251308-7, ISBN13: 978-0-06-251308-3.

Audience: **g.**

Faderman, Lillian (Editor) **PN3401**
Chloe Plus Olivia: An Anthology of Lesbian Literature from the Seventh Century to the Present. Trade Paper. Penguin Group (USA) Inc. New York, NY. 1995. 848p. ISBN:0-14-017248-3, ISBN13: 978-0-14-017248-5. Dewey:809.3/0082. LCCN:93-045750.

Audience: **l,u.**

Fone, Byrne R. S. **PN6071.H724**
The Columbia Anthology of Gay Literature: Readings from Western Antiquity to the Present Day. Trade Paper. Columbia University Press. New York, NY. 2001. 912p. Between Men, Between Women Ser. ISBN:0-231-09671-2, ISBN13: 978-0-231-09671-3. Dewey:808.8/0353. LCCN:97-039727.

Audience: **g.** *Choice, 1998.*

Galloway, David & Sabisch, Christian (Editors) **PN6071.H724 C3 1982B**
Calamus: Male Homosexuality in Twentieth Century Literature: An International Anthology. Trade Paper. HarperCollins Publishers. New York, NY. 1982. 480p. ISBN:0-688-00606-X, ISBN13: 978-0-688-00606-8. Dewey:808.8/0353. LCCN:81-013790.

Audience: **g.** *B*

Griffith, Nicola **PS648.F3F354 2004**
Bending the Landscape: Fantasy. Stephen Pagel (Editor). Trade Paper. Overlook Press, The. New York, NY. 2004. 362p. Bending the Landscape Ser., Vol. 3 ISBN:1-58567-576-8, ISBN13: 978-1-58567-576-0. Dewey:813/.0876608920664. LCCN:2004-053101.

Audience: **g.**

Griffith, Nicola & Pagel, Stephen (Editors) **PS3557.R48935B46**
Bending the Landscape: Horror. Trade Cloth. Overlook Press, The. New York, NY. 2001. 384p. ISBN:1-58567-116-9, ISBN13: 978-1-58567-116-8. Dewey:813/.54. LCCN:00-051514.

Audience: **g.**

Griffith, Nicola & Pagel, Stephen **PS648.S3S265 1998**
Original Gay and Lesbian Writing: Science Fiction. Trade Cloth. Overlook Press, The. New York, NY. 1998. 384p. Bending the

Landscape Ser. ISBN:0-87951-856-1, ISBN13: 978-0-87951-856-1. Dewey:813/.0876208920664. LCCN:98-009855.

Audience: **g.**

Harris, E. Lynn **PS509.H57**
Freedom in This Village: Twenty-Five Years of Black Gay Men's Writing. Trade Paper. Avalon Publishing Group. New York, NY. 2004. 352p. ISBN:0-7867-1387-9, ISBN13: 978-0-7867-1387-5. Dewey:810.8.

Audience: **g.**

Hemphill, Essex (Editor) **PS509.H57B76 1991**
Brother to Brother: New Writings by Black Gay Men. Trade Cloth. Alyson Publications. Los Angeles, CA. 1991. 275p. ISBN:1-55583-146-X, ISBN13: 978-1-55583-146-2. Dewey:818.5408. LCCN:91-071186.

Audience: **g.**

Heron, Ann (Editor) **HQ76.3.U5O54 1983**
One Teenager in Ten: Writings by Gay and Lesbian Youth. Trade Cloth. Alyson Publications. Los Angeles, CA. 1983. 120p. ISBN:0-932870-26-0, ISBN13: 978-0-932870-26-1. Dewey:306.76/6. LCCN:89-190732.

Audience: **g,l.**

Higgins, Patrick (Editor) **PN6071.H724**
A Queer Reader: 2500 Years of Male Homosexuality. Trade Cloth. New Press, The. New York, NY. 1994. 384p. ISBN:1-56584-210-3, ISBN13: 978-1-56584-210-6. Dewey:808.80353. LCCN:94-067359.

Audience: **g.**

Holleran, Andrew **PS3558.O3496B43 1996**
The Beauty of Men, Vol. 1. Trade Cloth. HarperCollins Publishers. New York, NY. 1996. 272p. ISBN:0-688-04857-9, ISBN13: 978-0-688-04857-0. Dewey:813/.54. LCCN:96-002035.

Audience: **g.**

Hunter, D. **PS509.H57**
Sojourner Black Gay Voice. Trade Paper. Other Countries - Black Gay Men Writing. New York, NY. 1997. ISBN:0-9638032-0-4, ISBN13: 978-0-9638032-0-7. Dewey:810.8.

Audience: **g.**

Leyland, Winston (Editor) **PQ7087.E5M9 1983**
My Deep Dark Pain Is Love: A Collection of Latin American Gay Fiction. E. A. Lacey (Translator), Jorge G. Maier (Illustrator). Trade Cloth. Gay Sunshine Press, Inc. San Francisco, CA. 1983. 384p. ISBN:0-917342-03-8, ISBN13: 978-0-917342-03-5. Dewey:863/.009/353. LCCN:83-014214.

Audience: **g.**

Leyland, Winston (Editor) **PQ9637.E5**
Now the Volcano: An Anthology of Latin American Gay Literature. Erskine Lane (Translator). Trade Paper. Gay Sunshine Press, Inc. San Francisco, CA. 1979. 288p. ISBN:0-917342-67-4, ISBN13: 978-0-917342-67-7. Dewey:869.

Audience: **g.**

McKinley, Catherine E.   **PS509.L47A38 1995**
Afrekete: An Anthology of Black Lesbian Writing. Joyce
Delaney (Editor). Trade Paper. Doubleday Publishing. New
York, NY. 1995. 336p. ISBN:0-385-47355-9, ISBN13:
978-0-385-47355-2. Dewey:810.8/09206643. LCCN:94-039560.
Audience: **g.**

Moore, Lisa C. (Editor)   **PS648.L47D64 1997**
Does Your Mama Know?: An Anthology of Black Lesbian
Coming Out Stories. Trade Cloth. RedBone Press. Washington,
DC. 1997. 314p. ISBN:0-9656659-0-9, ISBN13:
978-0-9656659-0-2. Dewey:813/.01089206643.
LCCN:97-177620.
Audience: **g.**

Quinn, Jay (Editor)   **PS647.G39R43 2001**
Rebel Yell: Stories by Contemporary Southern Gay Authors.
Trade Cloth. Haworth Press, Incorporated, The. Binghamton,
NY. 2001. xiii, 168p. Gay Men's Fiction Ser.
ISBN:1-56023-160-2, ISBN13: 978-1-56023-160-8.
Dewey:813/.0108920642. LCCN:00-063370.
Audience: **g,l,u.**

Ruff, Shawn S.   **PS648.H57G6 1996**
Go the Way Your Blood Beats. Trade Cloth. Henry Holt &
Company. New York, NY. 1996. 480p. ISBN:0-8050-4736-0,
ISBN13: 978-0-8050-4736-3. Dewey:813.008/0920664.
LCCN:96-004905.
Audience: **g.**

Singer, Bennett L.   **PS509.H57G76 1993**
(Editor)
Growing Up Gay/Growing Up Lesbian: A Literary Anthology.
Trade Cloth. New Press, The. New York, NY. 1993. 336p.
ISBN:1-56584-102-6, ISBN13: 978-1-56584-102-4.
Dewey:810.8/080353. LCCN:93-083622.
Audience: **g.**

Zahava, Irene   **PS648.H57L38 1994**
Lavender Mansions: 40 Contemporary Lesbian and Gay Short
Stories. Trade Paper. Westview Press. Boulder, CO. 1994. 430p.
ISBN:0-8133-2031-3, ISBN13: 978-0-8133-2031-1.
Dewey:813/.01083520664. LCCN:94-007858.
Audience: **g,l.**

Creative Production > Art

Cameron, Loren   **HQ77.95.U6C36 1996**
Body Alchemy: Transsexual Portraits. Trade Paper. Cleis Press.
San Francisco, CA. 1996. 100p. ISBN:1-57344-062-0, ISBN13:
978-1-57344-062-2. Dewey:305.3. LCCN:96-025696.
Audience: **g,l,u,f.**

Cooper, Emmanuel   **N72.H64C66 1994**
The Sexual Perspective: Homosexuality and Art in the Last 100
Years in the West. Ed. 2. Paper over Boards. Routledge. New
York, NY. 1994. 400p. ISBN:0-415-11100-5, ISBN13:
978-0-415-11100-3. Dewey:704.9/49306766. LCCN:93-041921.
Audience: **l,u.**

Miller, James   **NX65**
Fluid Exchanges: Artists and Critics in the AIDS Crisis. Trade
Cloth. University of Toronto Press. Toronto, ON. 1992. 810p.
ISBN:0-8020-5892-2, ISBN13: 978-0-8020-5892-8. Dewey:700.
Audience: **u,f.**

Weinberg, Jonathan   **N72.H64W45 2004**
Male Desire: The Homoerotic in American Art. Harry N.
Abrams. 2004. ISBN:0-8109-5894-5, ISBN13:
978-0-8109-5894-4.
Audience: **g,l,u,f.**

Creative Production > Art > General and Reference Works

Triptow, Robert   **PN6725.G39 1989**
(Editor)
Gay Comics. Trade Paper. Penguin Group (USA) Inc. New
York, NY. 1989. 12p. ISBN:0-452-26229-1, ISBN13:
978-0-452-26229-4. Dewey:741.5/973. LCCN:89-002851.
Audience: **g.**

Creative Production > Art > Criticism and Review

Casillo, Charles   **PS3568.E28.Z623**
Outlaw: The Lives and Careers of John Rechy. Advocate Books.
2002. Advocate Books: Life Stories ISBN:1-55583-734-4,
ISBN13: 978-1-55583-734-1.
Audience: **g.**

Saslow, James M.   **NX650.H6S27 1986**
Ganymede in the Renaissance: Homosexuality in Art and
Society. Cloth over Boards. Yale University Press. Cumberland,
RI. 1986. 320p. ISBN:0-300-03423-7, ISBN13:
978-0-300-03423-3. Dewey:700/.94. LCCN:85-002357.
Audience: **g.** *Choice, 1986.*

Creative Production > Art > Biography/Memoirs

Ashton, Dore & Hare,   **ND553.B6.A9**
Denise B.
Rosa Bonheur: A Life and a Legend. Trade Cloth. Penguin
Group (USA) Inc. New York, NY. 1981. 192p.
ISBN:0-670-60813-0, ISBN13: 978-0-670-60813-3.
Dewey:759.4. LCCN:80-036749.
Audience: **u,f.** *B*

Casillo, Charles   **PS3568.E28.Z623**
Outlaw: The Lives and Careers of John Rechy. Advocate Books.
2002. Advocate Books: Life Stories ISBN:1-55583-734-4,
ISBN13: 978-1-55583-734-1.
Audience: **g.**

Gruen, John   **N6537.H348G7 1991**
Keith Haring: The Authorized Biography. Trade Cloth. Prentice
Hall PTR. Upper Saddle River, NJ. 1991. 272p.
ISBN:0-13-516113-4, ISBN13: 978-0-13-516113-5.
Dewey:709/.2 B. LCCN:90-040600.
Audience: **g.**

Morrisroe, Patricia   **TR140.M347M67 1995**
Mapplethorpe: A Biography. Random House. 1995.
ISBN:0-394-57650-0, ISBN13: 978-0-394-57650-3.
Audience: **g,l,u,f.**

Wojnarowicz, David   RC607.A26W63 1991
Close to the Knives: A Memoir of Disintegration. Trade Paper.
Knopf Publishing Group. New York, NY. 1991. 288p.
ISBN:0-679-73227-6, ISBN13: 978-0-679-73227-3.
Dewey:362.1/969792/0092 B. LCCN:90-050210.
                                        Audience: **g,l.**

Wojnarowicz, David   RC607.A26W64 1992
David Wojnarowicz: Memories That Smell Like Gasoline. Trade
Cloth. Artspace Books. Sausalito, CA. 1992. 64p.
ISBN:0-9631095-0-2, ISBN13: 978-0-9631095-0-7.
Dewey:362.1/969792/0092. LCCN:91-038492.
                                        Audience: **g,l,u.**

Creative Production > Music

Brett, Philip (Editor), et al.   ML55.Q44 1993
Queering the Pitch: The New Gay and Lesbian Musicology.
Gary Thomas & Elizabeth Wood (Editors). Cloth Text.
Routledge. New York, NY. 1994. 440p. ISBN:0-415-90752-7,
ISBN13: 978-0-415-90752-1. Dewey:780.8664.
LCCN:93-015025.
                          Audience: **l,u,f.**   *Choice, 1995.*

Fuller, Sophie &   ML63.Q44 2002
  Whitesell, Lloyd (Editors)
Queer Episodes in Music and Modern Identity. Trade Cloth.
University of Illinois Press. Champaign, IL. 2002. 336p.
ISBN:0-252-02740-X, ISBN13: 978-0-252-02740-6.
Dewey:780/.86/64. LCCN:2001-005639.
                          Audience: **l,u,f.**   *Choice, 2003.*

Gill, John   ML63.G49 1995
Queer Noises: Male and Female Homosexuality in
Twentieth-Century Music. Cloth Text. University of Minnesota
Press. Minneapolis, MN. 1995. ISBN:0-8166-2718-5, ISBN13:
978-0-8166-2718-9. Dewey:780/.8/664. LCCN:94-043922.
                          Audience: **l,u,f.**

Hadleigh, Boze   ML385.H14 1997
Sing Out!: Gays and Lesbians in the Music World. Trade Cloth.
Barricade Books, Inc. Fort Lee, NJ. 1998. 336p.
ISBN:1-56980-116-9, ISBN13: 978-1-56980-116-1.
Dewey:782.4/2/166/08664. LCCN:97-033026.
                          Audience: **g,l,u,f.**

Harris, Ellen T.   ML410.H13H283 2001
Handel As Orpheus: Voice and Desire in the Chamber Cantatas.
Trade Cloth. Harvard University Press. Cambridge, MA. 2002.
448p. ISBN:0-674-00617-8, ISBN13: 978-0-674-00617-1.
Dewey:782.4/8/092. LCCN:2001-039075.
                          Audience: **l,u,f.**   *Choice, 2002.*

Hubbs, Nadine   ML200.5.H83 2004
The Queer Composition of America's Sound: Gay Modernists,
American Music, and National Identity. Trade Cloth. University
of California Press. Berkeley, CA. 2004. 288p.
ISBN:0-520-24184-3, ISBN13: 978-0-520-24184-8.
Dewey:780/.86/640973. LCCN:2004-003478.
                          Audience: **l,u,f.**   *Choice, 2005.*

Koestenbaum, Wayne   ML410.V4
The Queen's Throat: Opera, Homosexuality, and the Mystery of
Desire. Trade Paper. Da Capo Press, Inc. Cambridge, MA. 2001.
280p. ISBN:0-306-81008-5, ISBN13: 978-0-306-81008-4.
Dewey:782.1/092 B.
                          Audience: **g,l,u,f.**

Kostelanetz, Richard   ML410.M9
  (Editor)
Virgil Thomson Reader: Selected Writings, 1924-1984. Paper
over Boards. Routledge. New York, NY. 2002. 304p.
ISBN:0-415-93795-7, ISBN13: 978-0-415-93795-5.
Dewey:780.9/2.
                          Audience: **l,u,f.**

La Laurencie, Lionel D.   ML410.L95L2 1978
Lully. Ed. 2. Trade Cloth. A M S Press, Inc. New York, NY.
Music and Theatre in France in the 17th and 18th Centuries Ser.
ISBN:0-404-60167-7, ISBN13: 978-0-404-60167-6.
Dewey:780/.92/4. LCCN:76-043923.
                          Audience: **l,u,f.**

Nicholls, David (Editor)   ML410.C24C36 2002
The Cambridge Companion to John Cage. Jonathan Cross
(Contribution by). Trade Paper. Cambridge University Press.
New York, NY. 2002. 302p. Cambridge Companions to Music
Ser. ISBN:0-521-78968-0, ISBN13: 978-0-521-78968-4.
Dewey:780/.92 B. LCCN:2001-052401.
                          Audience: **l,u,f.**   *Choice, 2003.*

Peraino, Judith Ann   ML3838.P365 2006
Listening to the Sirens: Musical Technologies of Queer Identity
from Homer to Hedwig. Trade Cloth. University of California
Press. Berkeley, CA. 2005. 358p. ISBN:0-520-21587-7, ISBN13:
978-0-520-21587-0. Dewey:780/.86/64. LCCN:2005-006234.
                          Audience: **l,u,f.**   *Choice, 2006.*

Shapiro, Peter   ML3526.S5 2005
Turn the Beat Around: The Secret History of Disco. Saddle
Stitched, Cloth over Boards, Dust Jacket. Faber & Faber, Inc.
New York, NY. 2005. 384p. ISBN:0-571-21194-1, ISBN13:
978-0-571-21194-4. Dewey:306.4/8424/0973.
LCCN:2004-024211.
                          Audience: **g,l,u,f.**

Smith, Richard   ML3470
The Other Voices: A History of Homosexuality and Popular
Music. Trade Cloth. Cassell P L C. London, 1997. 224p.
Lesbian and Gay Studies Ser. ISBN:0-304-32860-X, ISBN13:
978-0-304-32860-4. Dewey:781.6409.
                          Audience: **l,u,f.**

Smith, Richard   ML63.S64 1995
Seduced and Abandoned: Essays on Gay Men and Popular
Music. Trade Cloth. Continuum International Publishing Group,
Ltd. London, 1997. 288p. Lesbian and Gay Studies
ISBN:0-304-33343-3, ISBN13: 978-0-304-33343-1.
Dewey:782.4216408664.
                          Audience: **l,u,f.**

Creative Production > Music > Biography

Albertson, Chris   ML420.S667A7 2003
Bessie. Ed. 2. Cloth over Boards. Yale University Press.
Cumberland, RI. 2003. 336p. ISBN:0-300-09902-9, ISBN13:
978-0-300-09902-7. Dewey:784/.092/4. LCCN:2002-155414.
                          Audience: **g,l,u,f.**   *Choice, 2004.*

Blackburn, Philip &   ML410.P176H37 1997
  Partch, Harry
Enclosure Three: Harry Partch. Trade Cloth. American
Composers Forum. Saint Paul, MN. 1997. 528p. Enclosures Ser.

ISBN:0-9656569-0-X, ISBN13: 978-0-9656569-0-0.
Dewey:780/.92 B. LCCN:97-014032.

Audience: **u,f.** *Choice, 1998.*

Brett, David   **ML420**
Morrissey: Scandal and Passion. Trade Paper. Anova Books.
London, 2005. 192p. ISBN:1-86105-787-3, ISBN13:
978-1-86105-787-7. Dewey:782.4/2166/092.

Audience: **g,l,u.**

Carpenter, Humphrey   **ML410.B853C37 1993**
Benjamin Britten: A Biography. Scribner. 1993.
ISBN:0-684-19569-0, ISBN13: 978-0-684-19569-8.

Audience: **g,l,u,f.**

Carr, Virginia   **PS3552.O874Z625 2004**
Paul Bowles: A Life. Trade Cloth. Simon & Schuster. New
York, NY. 2004. 432p. ISBN:0-684-19657-3, ISBN13:
978-0-684-19657-2. Dewey:813/.54 B. LCCN:2004-054748.

Audience: **g,l,u,f.**

Cheney, Margaret   **LB1131**
Midnight at Mabel's: The Mabel Mercer Story. Trade Cloth.
New Voyage Publishing. Washington, DC. 2000. 291p.
ISBN:0-615-11345-1, ISBN13: 978-0-615-11345-6.
Dewey:371.262. LCCN:00-132562.

Audience: **g,l,u,f.**

Feinstein, Michael   **ML420.F332A3 1995**
Nice Work If You Can Get It: My Life in Rhythm and Rhyme.
Trade Cloth. Hyperion Press. New York, NY. 1995. 416p.
ISBN:0-7868-6093-6, ISBN13: 978-0-7868-6093-7.
Dewey:782.42164/092 B. LCCN:95-002165.

Audience: **g,l,u.**

Gamson, Joshua   **ML420.S9815G36 2005**
The Fabulous Sylvester: The Legend, the Music, the 70s in San
Francisco. Cloth over Boards. Henry Holt & Company. New
York, NY. 2005. 320p. ISBN:0-8050-7250-0, ISBN13:
978-0-8050-7250-1. Dewey:782.42164/092 B.
LCCN:2004-042380.

Audience: **g,l,u,f.**

Gordon, Eric A.   **ML410.B6515**
Mark the Music: The Life and Work of Marc Blitzstein. Trade
Cloth. Boulevard Books. Topanga, CA. 1989. 605p.
ISBN:0-910278-61-X, ISBN13: 978-0-910278-61-4.
Dewey:780/.92/4 B. LCCN:88-029891.

Audience: **l,u,f.**

Greer, Jim   **ML421.R22**
R. E. M.: Behind the Mask. Trade Paper. Little Brown &
Company. New York, NY. 1994. ISBN:0-316-32732-8, ISBN13:
978-0-316-32732-9. Dewey:782.4216609.

Audience: **g,l,u,f.**

Hajdu, David   **ML410.S9325H35**
Lush Life: A Biography of Billy Strayhorn. Trade Paper. Farrar,
Straus & Giroux. New York, NY. 1997. 305p.
ISBN:0-86547-512-1, ISBN13: 978-0-86547-512-0.
Dewey:781.6/55/092.

Audience: **g.** *Choice, 1996.*

Heyman, Barbara B.   **ML410.M9**
Samuel Barber: The Composer and His Music. Trade Paper.
Oxford University Press, Inc. New York, NY. 1994. 608p.
ISBN:0-19-509058-6, ISBN13: 978-0-19-509058-1.
Dewey:780/.92. LCCN:91-002454.

Audience: **l,u,f.** *Choice, 1993.*

Hicks, Michael   **ML410.C859H53 2002**
Henry Cowell, Bohemian. Trade Cloth. University of Illinois
Press. Champaign, IL. 2002. 240p. Music in American Life Ser.
ISBN:0-252-02751-5, ISBN13: 978-0-252-02751-2.
Dewey:780/.92 B. LCCN:2001-007064.

Audience: **g,l,u,f.** *Choice, 2003.*

Holden, Anthony   **ML410.M9**
Tchaikovsky: A Biography. Trade Cloth. Random House Value
Publishing. New York, NY. 1998. ISBN:0-517-31769-9,
ISBN13: 978-0-517-31769-3. Dewey:780/.92 B.

Audience: **g,l,u,f.**

Jablonski, Edward   **ML410.A76J33 1996**
Harold Arlen: Rhythm, Rainbows, and Blues. Cloth Text.
Northeastern University Press. Boston, MA. 1996. 490p.
ISBN:1-55553-263-2, ISBN13: 978-1-55553-263-5.
Dewey:782.42164/092 B. LCCN:95-044708.

Audience: **g,l,u,f.** *Choice, 1996.*

Maisel, Edward   **ML410.G9134M2**
Charles T. Griffes: The Life of an American Composer. Library
Binding. Reprint Services Company. Temecula, CA. 1992. 347p.
Music Book Index Ser. ISBN:0-7812-9464-9, ISBN13:
978-0-7812-9464-5. Dewey:780/.92/4 B.

Audience: **l,u,f.**

McBrien, William   **ML410.S6872**
Cole Porter: A Biography. Trade Paper. Alfred A. Knopf Inc.
New York, NY. 2000. 480p. ISBN:0-679-72792-2, ISBN13:
978-0-679-72792-7. Dewey:782.1/4/092 B.

Audience: **g,l,u,f.** *Choice, 1999.*

Mellers, Wilfrid   **ML410.M9**
Francis Poulenc. Paper Text. Oxford University Press, Inc. New
York, NY. 1995. 204p. Oxford Studies of Composers
ISBN:0-19-816338-X, ISBN13: 978-0-19-816338-1.
Dewey:780/.92.

Audience: **l,u,f.** *Choice, 1994.*

Middlebrook, Diane   **ML410.E44**
Wood
Suits Me: The Double Life of Billy Tipton. Trade Paper.
Houghton Mifflin Company Trade & Reference Division.
Boston, MA. 1999. 356p. ISBN:0-395-95789-3, ISBN13:
978-0-395-95789-9. Dewey:781.6/5/092.

Audience: **g,l,u,f.**

Mungo, Ray   **ML3930.L45M86 1995**
Liberace. Martin Duberman (Editor). Trade Paper. Chelsea
House Publishers. Langhorne, PA. 1995. 140p. Lives of Notable
Gay Men and Lesbians Ser. ISBN:0-7910-2885-2, ISBN13:
978-0-7910-2885-8. Dewey:786.2/092 B. LCCN:94-010201.

Audience: **g,l.**

Near, Holly   **ML420.N375 A3**
Fire in the Rain...Singer in the Storm: An Autobiography. Trade
Paper. Hereford Publishing. Ukiah, CA. 1990. 288p.
ISBN:0-688-10964-0, ISBN13: 978-0-688-10964-6.
Dewey:782.42164/092.

Audience: **g,l,u,f.**

Nolan, Fredrick   **ML410.S6872**
Lorenz Hart: A Poet on Broadway. Trade Paper. Oxford
University Press, Inc. New York, NY. 1995. 416p.
ISBN:0-19-510289-4, ISBN13: 978-0-19-510289-5.
Dewey:782.1/4/092.

Audience: **u,f.**

Audience: g=general, l=lower division undergraduate, u=upper division undergraduate, f=faculty.

409

Pears, Peter   ML420.P37A3 1995
The Travel Diaries of Peter Pears, 1936-1978. Philip Reed
(Editor). Trade Cloth. Boydell & Brewer, Inc. Rochester, NY.
1995. 272p. Aldeburgh Studies in Music, No. 2
ISBN:0-85115-364-X, ISBN13: 978-0-85115-364-3.
Dewey:782.1/092. LCCN:95-003357.

Audience: **g,l,u,f.**

Pollack, Howard   ML410.C756P6 1999
Aaron Copland: The Life and Work of an Uncommon Man.
Cloth over Boards. Henry Holt & Company. New York, NY.
1999. 702p. ISBN:0-8050-4909-6, ISBN13: 978-0-8050-4909-1.
Dewey:780.92. LCCN:98-029179.

Audience: **g,l,u,f.** *Choice, 1999.*

Poznansky, Alexander   ML410.C4P85
Tchaikovsky: The Quest for the Inner Man. Trade Paper. Music
Sales Corporation. New York, NY. 1995. 679p.
ISBN:0-8256-7232-5, ISBN13: 978-0-8256-7232-3.
Dewey:780.92.

Audience: **g,l,u,f.**

Pyron, Darden Asbury   ML417.L67P97 2000
Liberace: An American Boy. Trade Cloth. University of Chicago
Press. Chicago, IL. 2000. 512p. ISBN:0-226-68667-1, ISBN13:
978-0-226-68667-7. Dewey:786.2/092 B. LCCN:99-089031.

Audience: **g,l,u,f.** *Choice, 2000.*

Rorem, Ned   ML410.R693A27 2000
Later Diaries of Ned Rorem: 1961-1972. Trade Paper. Da Capo
Press, Inc. Cambridge, MA. 2000. 456p. ISBN:0-306-80964-8,
ISBN13: 978-0-306-80964-4. Dewey:780/.92 B.
LCCN:00-060223.

Audience: **g,l,u,f.**

Rorem, Ned   CT275.R67
Lies: A Diary 1986-1999. Trade Paper. Da Capo Press, Inc.
Cambridge, MA. 2002. 448p. ISBN:0-306-81106-5, ISBN13:
978-0-306-81106-7. Dewey:780.92.

Audience: **g,l,u,f.**

Rorem, Ned   ML60.R78425 2001
A Ned Rorem Reader. Cloth over Boards. Yale University Press.
Cumberland, RI. 2001. 320p. ISBN:0-300-08984-8, ISBN13:
978-0-300-08984-4. Dewey:780. LCCN:2001-033334.

Audience: **g,l,u,f.**

Rorem, Ned   ML410.R693A3 1998
The Paris Diary and the New York Diary, 1951-1961. Richard
Howard (Introduction by). Trade Paper. Da Capo Press, Inc.
Cambridge, MA. 1998. 432p. ISBN:0-306-80838-2, ISBN13:
978-0-306-80838-8. Dewey:780/.92 B. LCCN:97-046200.

Audience: **g,l,u,f.**

Rosenstiel, Leonie   ML410.B4
Nadia Boulanger: A Life in Music. Trade Paper. W. W. Norton
& Company, Inc. New York, NY. 1998. 440p.
ISBN:0-393-31713-7, ISBN13: 978-0-393-31713-8.
Dewey:780/.92/4. LCCN:81-018811.

Audience: **l,u,f.**

Rosenthal, Elizabeth J.   ML410.J64R67 2004
His Song: The Musical Journey of Elton John. Trade Cloth.
Watson-Guptill Publications, Inc. New York, NY. 2004. 544p.
ISBN:0-8230-8892-8, ISBN13: 978-0-8230-8892-8.
Dewey:782.4/2166/092.

Audience: **g,l,u,f.** *Choice, 2002.*

Secrest, Meryle   ML410.B566
Leonard Bernstein: A Life. Random House. 1996.
ISBN:0-517-17008-6, ISBN13: 978-0-517-17008-3.

Audience: **g,l,u.**

Secrest, Meryle   ML410.S6872S42 1999
Stephen Sondheim: A Life. Trade Paper. Dell Publishing. New
York, NY. 1999. 480p. ISBN:0-385-33412-5, ISBN13:
978-0-385-33412-9. Dewey:780.9/2.

Audience: **g,l,u,f.** *Choice, 1999.*

Smith, Carolyn J.   ML134
Peter Maxwell Davies: A Bio-Bibliography. Cloth Text.
Greenwood Publishing Group, Inc. Portsmouth, NH. 1995. 360p.
Bio-Bibliographies in Music Ser., Vol. 57 ISBN:0-313-26831-2,
ISBN13: 978-0-313-26831-1. Dewey:780/.92 B.
LCCN:95-021757.

Audience: **l,u,f.** *Choice, 1996.*

Studd, Stephen   ML410.S15S78 1999
Saint-Saens: A Critical Biography. Trade Cloth. Fairleigh
Dickinson University Press. Cranbury, NJ. 1999. 320p.
ISBN:0-8386-3842-2, ISBN13: 978-0-8386-3842-2.
Dewey:780.9/2. LCCN:99-025256.

Audience: **l,u,f.** *Choice, 2000.*

Trotter, William R.   ML422.M59T76 1995
Priest of Music: The Life of Dimitri Mitropoulos. Trade Cloth.
Hal Leonard Corporation. Milwaukee, WI. 1995. 532p.
ISBN:0-931340-81-0, ISBN13: 978-0-931340-81-9.
Dewey:780/.92 B. LCCN:94-023928.

Audience: **g,l,u,f.** *Choice, 1996.*

Valentine, Penny &   ML420.S765V35 2001
Wickham, Vicki
Dancing with Demons: The Authorized Biography of Dusty
Springfield. Cloth over Boards. St. Martin's Press. Gordonville,
VA. 2001. 320p. ISBN:0-312-28202-8, ISBN13:
978-0-312-28202-8. Dewey:782.42164/092 B.
LCCN:2002-037070.

Audience: **g,l,u,f.**

Vargo, Marc E.   HQ75.7.V37 2005
Noble Lives: Biographical Portraits of Three Remarkable Gay
Men—Glenway Wescott, Aaron Copland, and Dag
Hammarskjöld. Harrington Park Press. 2005.
ISBN:1-56023-294-3, ISBN13: 978-1-56023-294-0.

Audience: **g,l,u,f.**

Creative Production > Drama

Barnes, Noreen C. &   PS627.H67T68 1992
Deutsch, Nicholas (Editors)
Tough Acts to Follow: One-Act Plays on the Gay-Lesbian
Experience. Trade Paper. Alamo Square Press. Tajique, NM.
1992. 160p. ISBN:0-9624751-6-5, ISBN13: 978-0-9624751-6-0.
Dewey:812/.04108920664. LCCN:92-070651.

Audience: **g.**

Clum, John C.   PS338.H66C58 1994
Acting Gay: Male Homosexuality in Modern Drama. Trade
Cloth. Columbia University Press. New York, NY. 1992. 393p.
ISBN:0-231-07510-3, ISBN13: 978-0-231-07510-7.
Dewey:812/.509353. LCCN:91-045663.

Audience: **u,f.**

Clum, John M.   **PS627.H67A85**
Asking and Telling. Trade Paper. Applause Theatre Book
Publishers. New York, NY. 2002. 458p. ISBN:1-55783-558-6,
ISBN13: 978-1-55783-558-1. Dewey:812.540809206642.

         Audience: **g.**

Clum, John M.   **ML1700.C58**
Something for the Boys: Musical Theater and Gay Culture.
Trade Paper. Palgrave Macmillan. New York, NY. 2001. 336p.
ISBN:0-312-23832-0, ISBN13: 978-0-312-23832-2.
Dewey:782.1/4/086642.

         Audience: **u,f.** *Choice, 2000.*

Clum, John M.   **PS338.H66C58 2000**
Still Acting Gay: Male Homosexuality in Modern Drama. Ed. 2.
Trade Paper. Palgrave Macmillan. New York, NY. 2000. 336p.
ISBN:0-312-22384-6, ISBN13: 978-0-312-22384-7.
Dewey:812/.509353. LCCN:00-021499.

         Audience: **u,f.**

Clum, John M. (Editor)   **PS627.H67S73 1995**
Staging Gay Lives: An Anthology of Contemporary Gay
Theater. Tony Kushner (Foreword by). Trade Paper. Westview
Press. Boulder, CO. 1996. 496p. ISBN:0-8133-2505-6, ISBN13:
978-0-8133-2505-7. Dewey:812/.540809206642.
LCCN:95-023652.

         Audience: **g,l,u,f.** *Choice, 1996.*

Crowley, Mart   **PS3553.R6B36 2003**
The Band Plays. Trade Paper. Alyson Publications. Los Angeles,
CA. 2003. 232p. ISBN:1-55583-831-6, ISBN13:
978-1-55583-831-7. Dewey:812/.54. LCCN:2003-052084.

         Audience: **g,l,u.**

De Jongh, Nicholas   **PN1861.D43 1991**
Not in Front of the Audience: Homosexuality on Stage. Trade
Paper. Routledge. New York, NY. 1992. 236p.
ISBN:0-415-03363-2, ISBN13: 978-0-415-03363-3.
Dewey:822/.9109353. LCCN:91-016819.

         Audience: **g,l,u,f.** *Choice, 1992.*

DiGangi, Mario   **PR658.H58D54 1997**
The Homoerotics of Early Modern Drama. Trade Cloth.
Cambridge University Press. New York, NY. 1997. 230p.
Studies in Renaissance Literature and Culture, Vol. 21
ISBN:0-521-58341-1, ISBN13: 978-0-521-58341-1.
Dewey:822/.309353. LCCN:96-037398.

         Audience: **l,u,f.** *Choice, 1998.*

Fierstein, Harvey   **PS3556.I4213H37 1987**
Safe Sex. Children's Board Books. Simon & Schuster. New
York, NY. 1987. 160p. ISBN:0-689-11953-4, ISBN13:
978-0-689-11953-8. Dewey:812.54. LCCN:87-011507.

         Audience: **g.**

Fierstein, Harvey   **PS3556.I4213.T6**
Torch Song Trilogy: Three Plays. Ed. 2. Villard Books. 1983.
ISBN:0-394-53428-X, ISBN13: 978-0-394-53428-2.

         Audience: **g.**

Franceschina, John C.   **PR635**
Homosexualities in the English Theatre: From Lyly to Wilde,
79. Trade Cloth. Greenwood Publishing Group, Inc. Portsmouth,
NH. 1997. 360p. Contributions in Drama and Theatre Studies
Ser., Vol. 79 ISBN:0-313-30034-8, ISBN13: 978-0-313-30034-9.
Dewey:822.009/353. LCCN:97-012289.

         Audience: **l,u,f.** *Choice, 1998.*

Freeman, Sandra   **PN2270.L47F74 1997**
Putting Your Daughters on the Stage: British Lesbian Theatre
from the 1960s to the Present. Trade Paper. Continuum
International Publishing Group, Ltd. London, 1996. 256p.
Sexual Politics Ser. ISBN:0-304-33309-3, ISBN13:
978-0-304-33309-7. Dewey:792/.086643. LCCN:97-176609.

         Audience: **l,u.**

Furtado, Ken &   **Z1229.G25.F87 1993**
  Hellner, Nancy
Gay and Lesbian American Plays: An Annotated Bibliography.
Terry Helbing (Foreword by). Trade Cloth. Scarecrow Press,
Inc. Lanham, MD. 1993. 233p. ISBN:0-8108-2689-5, ISBN13:
978-0-8108-2689-2. Dewey:016.812009920664.
LCCN:93-017078.

         Audience: **g,l,u,f.** *Choice, 1994.*

Gage, Carolyn   **PN2270.L47G34 1997**
Take Stage!: How to Direct and Produce a Lesbian Play. Trade
Paper. Scarecrow Press, Inc. Lanham, MD. 1997. 216p.
ISBN:0-8108-3208-9, ISBN13: 978-0-8108-3208-4.
Dewey:792/.023/086643. LCCN:96-044777.

         Audience: **g,l,u.**

Geis, Deborah R. &   **PS3561.U778A8532**
  Kruger, Steven F. (Editors)
Approaching the Millennium: Essays on Angels in America.
Trade Paper. University of Michigan Press. Chicago, IL. 1998.
320p. Theater Ser., :Theory - Text - Performance
ISBN:0-472-06623-4, ISBN13: 978-0-472-06623-0.
Dewey:812/.54. LCCN:97-033750.

         Audience: **l,u,f.**

Greenberg, Richard   **PS3557.R3789T35 2003**
Take Me Out: A Play. Trade Paper. Faber & Faber, Inc. New
York, NY. 2003. 128p. ISBN:0-571-21118-6, ISBN13:
978-0-571-21118-0. Dewey:812/.54. LCCN:2002-112791.

         Audience: **g,l,u.**

Helbing, Terry (Selected by)   **PS627.H67G38 1993**
Gay and Lesbian Plays Today. Trade Paper. Heinemann.
Portsmouth, NH. 1993. 288p. ISBN:0-435-08618-9, ISBN13:
978-0-435-08618-3. Dewey:812/.54080355. LCCN:92-021957.

         Audience: **g,l,u,f.**

Hellman, Lillian   **PS3515.E343**
The Children's Hour. Trade Paper. Kessinger Publishing, LLC.
Whitefish, MT. 2005. ISBN:1-4191-2392-0, ISBN13:
978-1-4191-2392-4. Dewey:812.52.

         Audience: **g,l,u.**

Herman, Jerry   **M1503.H54**
  (Composed by)
La Cage aux Folles. Trade Paper. Hal Leonard Corporation.
Milwaukee, WI. 1995. 256p. ISBN:0-7935-4005-4, ISBN13:
978-0-7935-4005-1. Dewey:782.13.

         Audience: **g,l,u,f.**

Hodges, Ben   **PN6120.G43F67 2003**
Forbidden Acts: Pioneering Gay and Lesbian Plays of the
Twentieth Century. Trade Paper. Applause Theatre Book
Publishers. New York, NY. 2003. 741p. ISBN:1-55783-587-X,
ISBN13: 978-1-55783-587-1. Dewey:808.82/0086/640904.
LCCN:2003-014043.

         Audience: **g,l,u,f.**

Hoffman, William M.   PS3545.I5365
As Is. Trade Paper. Dramatists Play Service, Inc. New York, NY.
1985. ISBN:0-8222-0073-2, ISBN13: 978-0-8222-0073-4.
Dewey:812/.54.

Audience: **g,l,u.**

Hoffman, William M., et al.   PS627.A53W38 1990
The Way We Live Now: American Plays and the AIDS Crisis.
Harry Kondoleon, Susan Sontag, Terrence McNally, Lanford
Wilson, David Greenspan, Tony Kushner, Christopher Durang &
Paula Vogel (Authors), M. Elizabeth Osborn (Editor). Trade
Cloth. Theatre Communications Group, Inc. New York, NY.
1990. 304p. ISBN:1-55936-005-4, ISBN13: 978-1-55936-005-0.
Dewey:812/.54080356. LCCN:90-010829.

Audience: **g.**

Hughes, Holly &   PS627.H67O2 1998
   Roman, David (Editors)
O Solo Homo: The New Queer Performance. Trade Paper.
Grove/Atlantic, Inc. New York, NY. 1998. 496p.
ISBN:0-8021-3570-6, ISBN13: 978-0-8021-3570-4.
Dewey:810.8/0920664. LCCN:98-005203.

Audience: **g,l,u.**

Kander, John, et al.   ML410.R6315
Colored Lights: Forty Years of Words and Music, Show Biz,
Collaboration, and All That Jazz. Fred Ebb & Greg Lawrence
(Authors). Trade Paper. Faber & Faber, Inc. New York, NY.
2004. 256p. ISBN:0-571-21169-0, ISBN13: 978-0-571-21169-2.
Dewey:782.1/4/0922 B.

Audience: **g,l,u,f.**

Kramer, Larry   PS3561.R252N6 2000
The Normal Heart and the Destiny of Me. Tony Kushner
(Foreword by). Trade Paper. Grove/Atlantic, Inc. New York, NY.
2000. xxv, 252p. ISBN:0-8021-3692-3, ISBN13:
978-0-8021-3692-3. Dewey:812/.54. LCCN:00-024177.

Audience: **g,l,u.**

Kushner, Tony   PS3561.U778A85 2003
Angels in America: A Gay Fantasia on National Themes. Trade
Paper. Theatre Communications Group, Inc. New York, NY.
2003. 304p. ISBN:1-55936-231-6, ISBN13: 978-1-55936-231-3.
Dewey:812/.54. LCCN:2003-017904.

Audience: **g,l,u.**

La Laurencie, Lionel D.   ML410.L95L2 1978
Lully. Ed. 2. Trade Cloth. A M S Press, Inc. New York, NY.
Music and Theatre in France in the 17th and 18th Centuries Ser.
ISBN:0-404-60167-7, ISBN13: 978-0-404-60167-6.
Dewey:780/.92/4. LCCN:76-043923.

Audience: **l,u,f.**

Lane, Eric & Shengold,   PS627.H67A28 1995
   Nina
The Actor's Book of Gay and Lesbian Plays. Trade Paper.
Penguin Group (USA) Inc. New York, NY. 1995. 560p.
ISBN:0-14-024552-9, ISBN13: 978-0-14-024552-3.
Dewey:812/.54080352064. LCCN:95-000339.

Audience: **g,l,u,f.**

Mass, Lawrence D.   PS3561.R252Z99 1997
   (Editor)
We Must Love One Another or Die: The Life and Legacies of
Larry Kramer. Cloth over Boards. Palgrave Macmillan. New
York, NY. 1997. 420p. ISBN:0-312-17704-6, ISBN13:
978-0-312-17704-1. Dewey:[B]. LCCN:97-030306.

Audience: **g,l,u.**

McNally, Terrence   PS3563.A323.L6 1995
Love! Valour! Compassion!. Trade Paper. Dramatists Play
Service, Inc. New York, NY. 1995. 104p. ISBN:0-8222-1467-9,
ISBN13: 978-0-8222-1467-0. Dewey:812/.54. LCCN:95-180772.

Audience: **g.**

McNally, Terrence   PS3563.A323.R5
The Ritz and Other Plays. Dodd, Mead. 1976.
ISBN:0-396-07315-8, ISBN13: 978-0-396-07315-4.

Audience: **g.**

Merrill, James   PS3525.E6645A6 2002
Collected Novels and Plays: James Merrill. J. D. McClatchy &
Stephen Yenser (Editors). Trade Cloth. Random House, Inc.
New York, NY. 2002. 688p. ISBN:0-375-41137-2, ISBN13:
978-0-375-41137-3. Dewey:818/.5408. LCCN:2002-020953.

Audience: **l,u,f.**

Miller, Carl   PR635.H65
Stages of Desire: Male and Female Homosexuality in British
and American Theatre. Trade Paper. Cassell P L C. London,
1996. 256p. ISBN:0-304-32817-0, ISBN13: 978-0-304-32817-8.
Dewey:822.009/353.

Audience: **g,l,u,f.**

Miller, D. A.   ML1711.M58 1998
Place for Us: Essay on the Broadway Musical. Trade Cloth.
Harvard University Press. Cambridge, MA. 1998. 160p.
ISBN:0-674-66990-8, ISBN13: 978-0-674-66990-1.
Dewey:782.1/4/0973. LCCN:98-015685.

Audience: **g,l,u,f.**

Miller, Tim   PS3613.I56B63 2002
Body Blows: Six Performances. Dona Ann McAdams
(Photographer), Tony Kushner (Foreword by). Trade Cloth.
University of Wisconsin Press. Chicago, IL. 2002. 272p. Living
Out Ser. ISBN:0-299-17680-0, ISBN13: 978-0-299-17680-8.
Dewey:812/.54. LCCN:2001-005418.

Audience: **g,l,u.**

O'Connor, Sean   PR635.H65O28 1998
Straight-Acting: Popular Gay Drama from Wilde to Rattigan.
Trade Paper. Continuum International Publishing Group, Ltd.
London, 1997. 256p. ISBN:0-304-32864-2, ISBN13:
978-0-304-32864-2. Dewey:822/.91099206642.
LCCN:97-013548.

Audience: **l,u,f.**

Paller, Michael   PS3545.I5365Z799
Gentlemen Callers: Tennessee Williams, Homosexuality, and
Mid-Twentieth-Century Drama. Cloth over Boards. Palgrave
Macmillan. New York, NY. 2005. 288p. ISBN:1-4039-6775-X,
ISBN13: 978-1-4039-6775-6. Dewey:812/.54.
LCCN:2004-054129.

Audience: **l,u,f.** *Choice, 2006.*

Reinhart, Robert C.   PS3568.E4924T45 1994
Telling Moments: Fifteen Gay Monologues. Trade Paper.
Applause Theatre Book Publishers. New York, NY. 1994. 80p.
Applause Acting Ser. ISBN:1-55783-163-7, ISBN13:
978-1-55783-163-7. Dewey:812/.54. LCCN:93-045366.

Audience: **g,l,u.**

Roman, David   PN2266.R66 1998
Acts of Intervention, Performance, Gay Culture and AIDS,
Unnatural Acts: Theorizing the Performative. Trade Cloth.
Indiana University Press. Bloomington, IN. 1998. 376p.
Unnatural Acts, :Theorizing the Performative Ser.

ISBN:0-253-33370-9, ISBN13: 978-0-253-33370-4.
Dewey:792/.086/640973. LCCN:97-035808.

Audience: **g,l,u,f.**

Savran, David   **PN2270.G39S28 2003**
A Queer Sort of Materialism: Recontextualizing American
Theater. Trade Cloth. University of Michigan Press. Chicago,
IL. 2003. 246p. Triangulations Ser., :Lesbian - Gay - Queer
Theater - Drama - Performance ISBN:0-472-09836-5, ISBN13:
978-0-472-09836-1. Dewey:791/.086/640973.
LCCN:2002-153618.

Audience: **l,u,f.**

Schanke, Robert A. &   **PS338.H66S73 2001**
  Marra, Kimberley B. (Editors)
Staging Desire: Queer Readings of American Theater History.
Trade Paper. University of Michigan Press. Chicago, IL. 2002.
416p. Triangulations Ser., :Lesbian - Gay - Queer Theater -
Drama - Performance ISBN:0-472-06749-4, ISBN13:
978-0-472-06749-7. Dewey:812.009/353. LCCN:2001-006446.

Audience: **g,l,u,f.** *Choice, 2003.*

Schanke, Robert A. &   **PN2286.5.P37 1998**
  Marra, Kimberley Bell (Editors)
Passing Performances: Queer Readings of Leading Players in
American Theater History. Trade Cloth. University of Michigan
Press. Chicago, IL. 1998. 352p. Triangulations Ser., :Lesbian -
Gay - Queer Theater - Drama - Performance
ISBN:0-472-09681-8, ISBN13: 978-0-472-09681-7.
Dewey:792/.028/08664 B. LCCN:98-019710.

Audience: **g,l,u,f.** *Choice, 1999.*

Schanke, Robert A.   **PN2286.5.G38 2005**
  (Editor), et al.
The Gay and Lesbian Theatrical Legacy: A Biographical
Dictionary of Major Figures in American Stage History in the
Pre-Stonewall Era. Kimberley Bell Marra & Billy J. Harbin
(Editors). Trade Cloth. University of Michigan Press. Chicago,
IL. 2005. 440p. Triangulations Ser., :Lesbian/Gay/Queer
Theater/Drama/Performance Ser. ISBN:0-472-09858-6, ISBN13:
978-0-472-09858-3. Dewey:792/.092/273 B.
LCCN:2004-020338.

Audience: **g,l.** *Choice, 2005.*

Schulman, Sarah   **ML410.L2857S38 1998**
Stagestruck: Theater, AIDS and Marketing of Gay America.
Trade Cloth. Duke University Press. Durham, NC. 1998. 152p.
ISBN:0-8223-2132-7, ISBN13: 978-0-8223-2132-3.
LCCN:98-012053.

Audience: **g,l,u,f.** *Choice, 1999.*

Senelick, Laurence   **PN6112.L595 1998**
Lovesick: Modernist Plays of Same-Sex Love, 1894-1925. Paper
over Boards. Routledge. New York, NY. 1999. 216p.
ISBN:0-415-18556-4, ISBN13: 978-0-415-18556-1.
Dewey:808.82/9353. LCCN:98-027240.

Audience: **g,l,u,f.** *Choice, 2000.*

Sherman, Martin   **PS3545.I5365**
Bent: The Play. Trade Paper. Applause Theatre Book Publishers.
New York, NY. 2000. 80p. ISBN:1-55783-336-2, ISBN13:
978-1-55783-336-5. Dewey:812/.54.

Audience: **g.**

Shewey, Don (Editor)   **PS627.H67O9 1988**
Out Front: Contemporary Gay and Lesbian Plays. Trade Paper.
Grove/Atlantic, Inc. New York, NY. 1988. 564p.

ISBN:0-8021-3025-9, ISBN13: 978-0-8021-3025-9.
Dewey:812/.52/080353. LCCN:88-001257.

Audience: **g,l,u,f.**

Wolf, Stacy   **ML2054.W65 2002**
A Problem Like Maria: Gender and Sexuality in the American
Musical. Trade Cloth. University of Michigan Press. Chicago,
IL. 2002. 312p. Triangulations Ser., :Lesbian - Gay - Queer
Theater - Drama - Performance ISBN:0-472-09772-5, ISBN13:
978-0-472-09772-2. Dewey:782.1/4/0820973.
LCCN:2001-008273.

Audience: **l,u,f.** *Choice, 2003.*

Wright, Doug &   **PS3573.R53252I3 2004**
  Mahlsdorf, Charlotte von
I Am My Own Wife: A Play. Trade Paper. Faber & Faber, Inc.
New York, NY. 2004. 112p. ISBN:0-571-21174-7, ISBN13:
978-0-571-21174-6. Dewey:812/.54. LCCN:2003-021583.

Audience: **g,l,u,f.**

Creative Production > Drama > Biography

Barranger, Milly S.   **PN2287.W4555A3 2004**
Margaret Webster: A Life in the Theater. Trade Cloth. University
of Michigan Press. Chicago, IL. 2004. 400p. Triangulations:
Lesbian/Gay/Queer Theater/Drama/Performance Ser.
ISBN:0-472-11390-9, ISBN13: 978-0-472-11390-3.
Dewey:792.02/33/092 B. LCCN:2003-024582.

Audience: **g,l,u,f.** *Choice, 2004.*

Citron, Stephen   **ML410.H5624C58 2004**
Jerry Herman: Poet of the Showtune. Cloth over Boards. Yale
University Press. Cumberland, RI. 2004. 352p.
ISBN:0-300-10082-5, ISBN13: 978-0-300-10082-2.
Dewey:782.1/4/092 B. LCCN:2003-027632.

Audience: **g,l,u,f.**

Kaufman, David   **PS3562.U258Z74 2005**
Ridiculous!: The Theatrical Life and Times of Charles Ludlam.
Trade Paper. Applause Theatre Book Publishers. New York, NY.
2005. 500p. ISBN:1-55783-637-X, ISBN13: 978-1-55783-637-3.
Dewey:812/.54 B. LCCN:2006-271090.

Audience: **g,l,u.** *Choice, 2003.*

Lahr, John   **PR6066.I53**
Prick Up Your Ears: The Biography of Joe Orton. Trade Paper.
University of California Press. Berkeley, CA. 2000. 315p.
ISBN:0-520-22666-6, ISBN13: 978-0-520-22666-1.
Dewey:822.9/14. LCCN:00-028691.

Audience: **g,l,u,f.**

Merrill, Lisa   **PN2287.C8.M47**
When Romeo Was a Woman: Charlotte Cushman and Her Circle
of Female Spectators. Trade Paper. University of Michigan
Press. Chicago, IL. 2000. 344p. Triangulations Ser.
ISBN:0-472-08749-5, ISBN13: 978-0-472-08749-5.
Dewey:792.028092. LCCN:98-041314.

Audience: **g,l,u.** *Choice, 1999.*

Creative Production > Dance

Banes, Sally GV1785.A1A78 1998
(Introduction by), et al.
Art Performs Life: Merce Cunningham, Meredith Monk, Bill T.
Jones. Philippe Vergne, Siri Engberg & Kellie Jones
(Introduction by), Philip Bither (Foreword by). Trade Paper.
Walker Art Center. Minneapolis, MN. 1998. 176p.
ISBN:0-935640-56-8, ISBN13: 978-0-935640-56-4.
Dewey:792.8/092/273. LCCN:98-007401.
Audience: l,u,f.

Desmond, Jane C. GV1588.6.D395 2001
(Editor)
Dancing Desires: Choreographing Sexualities on and off the
Stage. Trade Cloth. University of Wisconsin Press. Chicago, IL.
2001. x, 475p. Studies in Dance History ISBN:0-299-17050-0,
ISBN13: 978-0-299-17050-9. Dewey:792.8. LCCN:00-010661.
Audience: l,u,f. Choice, 2002.

Gere, David GV1588.6.G47 2004
How to Make Dances in an Epidemic: Tracking Choreography
in the Age of AIDS. Trade Cloth. University of Wisconsin Press.
Chicago, IL. 2004. 352p. ISBN:0-299-20080-9, ISBN13:
978-0-299-20080-0. Dewey:306.4/84. LCCN:2004-005184.
Audience: l,u,f. Choice, 2005.

Kirstein, Lincoln NX456.K56 2005
By with to and From: A Lincoln Kirstein Reader. Nicholas
Jenkins (Editor). Trade Paper, Perfect. University Press of
Florida. Gainesville, FL. 2006. 423p. ISBN:0-8130-2954-6,
ISBN13: 978-0-8130-2954-2. Dewey:709.04.
LCCN:2005-052923.
Audience: g,l,u,f.

Leddick, David NX504.L44 2000
Intimate Companions: A Triography of George Platt Lynes, Paul
Cadmus, Lincoln Kirstein, and Their Circle. Cloth over Boards.
St. Martin's Press. Gordonville, VA. 2000. 288p.
ISBN:0-312-20898-7, ISBN13: 978-0-312-20898-1.
Dewey:700/.92/273 B. LCCN:99-034004.
Audience: g,l,u,f.

Lewis, Lynette & Ross, HQ76.2.A82
Michael
A Select Body: The Gay Dance Party Subculture and the
HIV/AIDS Pandemic. Trade Cloth. Continuum International
Publishing Group, Ltd. London, 1997. 320p. AIDS Awareness
Ser. ISBN:0-304-33510-X, ISBN13: 978-0-304-33510-7.
Dewey:305.90664.
Audience: l,u,f.

Magriel, Paul GV1785.A1N54 1977B
Nijinsky, Pavlova, Duncan: Three Lives in Dance. Trade Paper.
Da Capo Press, Inc. Cambridge, MA. 1977. 276p. Series in
Dance ISBN:0-306-80035-7, ISBN13: 978-0-306-80035-1.
Dewey:792.8/092/4. LCCN:76-030403.
Audience: g,l,u,f.

Rudnick, Paul PS3568.U334J44 1994
Jeffrey. Trade Paper. Penguin Group (USA) Inc. New York, NY.
1994. 112p. ISBN:0-452-27120-7, ISBN13: 978-0-452-27120-3.
Dewey:812/.54. LCCN:93-021034.
Audience: g.

Creative Production > Dance > Biography

Acocella, Joan GV1785
Mark Morris. Trade Paper. Wesleyan University Press.
Middletown, CT. 2004. 320p. ISBN:0-8195-6731-0, ISBN13:
978-0-8195-6731-4. Dewey:792.8/2/092 B. LCCN:2004-110388.
Audience: g,l,u.

Ailey, Alvin Jr. & GV1785.A38A3 1994
Bailey, A. Peter
Revelations: The Autobiography of Alvin Ailey. Trade Cloth.
Carol Publishing Group. Secaucus, NJ. 1994. 256p.
ISBN:1-55972-255-X, ISBN13: 978-1-55972-255-1.
Dewey:792.8/2/092. LCCN:94-016684.
Audience: g,l,u,f. Choice, 1995.

Anawalt, Sasha GV1786.J64A53 1997
The Joffrey Ballet: Robert Joffrey and the Making of an
American Dance Company. Trade Paper. University of Chicago
Press. Chicago, IL. 1998. 466p. ISBN:0-226-01755-9, ISBN13:
978-0-226-01755-6. Dewey:792.8/0973. LCCN:97-023161.
Audience: l,u,f.

Desti, Mary GV1785.D8
The Untold Story: The Life of Isadora Duncan 1921 To 1927.
Trade Paper. Kessinger Publishing, LLC. Whitefish, MT. 2004.
ISBN:1-4179-1219-7, ISBN13: 978-1-4179-1219-3.
Dewey:792.8028.
Audience: g,l,u,f.

Dunning, Jennifer GV1785.A38D85 1998
Alvin Ailey: A Life in Dance. Trade Paper. Da Capo Press, Inc.
Cambridge, MA. 1998. 496p. ISBN:0-306-80825-0, ISBN13:
978-0-306-80825-8. Dewey:792.8/028/092 B. LCCN:97-042644.
Audience: g,l,u,f. Choice, 1997.

Jowitt, Deborah GV1785
Jerome Robbins: His Life, His Theater, His Dance. Trade Paper.
Simon & Schuster, Inc. New York, NY. 2005. 640p.
ISBN:0-684-86986-1, ISBN13: 978-0-684-86986-5.
Dewey:792.8/2/092 B.
Audience: g,l,u,f. Choice, 2005.

Kavanagh, Julie GV1785.A8K38 1996
Secret Muses: The Life of Frederick Ashton. Trade Cloth. Knopf
Publishing Group. New York, NY. 1997. 647p.
ISBN:0-679-44269-3, ISBN13: 978-0-679-44269-1.
Dewey:792.8/2/092 B. LCCN:96-029524.
Audience: g,l,u,f.

Kelly, Kevin GV1785.B38K45 1990
One Singular Sensation: The Michael Bennett Story. Trade
Cloth. Doubleday Publishing. New York, NY. 1989. 352p.
ISBN:0-385-26125-X, ISBN13: 978-0-385-26125-8.
Dewey:792.8/2/092 B. LCCN:89-035025.
Audience: g,l,u,f. Choice, 1990.

Kurth, Peter GV1785.K3
Isadora: A Sensational Life. Trade Paper. Little Brown &
Company. New York, NY. 2002. 704p. ISBN:0-316-05713-4,
ISBN13: 978-0-316-05713-4. Dewey:792.8/092.
Audience: g,l,u,f. Choice, 2002.

Lifar, Serge GV1785.D5L48 1976
Serge Diaghilev: His Life, His Work, His Legend. Paper Text.
Da Capo Press, Inc. Cambridge, MA. 1976. Series in Dance

ISBN:0-306-70839-6, ISBN13: 978-0-306-70839-8.
Dewey:792.8/092/4. LCCN:76-025041.

Audience: **g,l,u,f.**

Loney, Glenn   **GV1785.C63L66 1984**
Unsung Genius: The Passion of Dancer-Choreographer Jack
Cole. Trade Cloth. Scholastic Library Publishing. Danbury, CT.
1984. 384p. ISBN:0-531-09765-X, ISBN13: 978-0-531-09765-6.
Dewey:793.3/2/0924 B. LCCN:84-007447.

Audience: **g,l,u,f.**

Ostwald, Peter F.   **GV1785.K3**
Vaslav Nijinsky: A Leap into Madness. Trade Paper. Carol
Publishing Group. Secaucus, NJ. 1996. 400p.
ISBN:0-8065-1681-X, ISBN13: 978-0-8065-1681-3.
Dewey:792.8/092 B. LCCN:95-009381.

Audience: **g,l,u,f.** *Choice, 1991.*

Solway, Diane   **GV1785.N8S66 1998**
Nureyev: His Life. Trade Cloth. HarperCollins Publishers. New
York, NY. 1999. 625p. ISBN:0-688-12873-4, ISBN13:
978-0-688-12873-9. Dewey:792.8/092. LCCN:98-013483.

Audience: **g,l,u,f.** *Choice, 1999.*

Terry, Walter   **GV1785.S5.T47**
Ted Shawn, Father of American Dance: A Biography. Trade
Cloth. Dell Distributing. Toronto, ON. 1976. 186p.
ISBN:0-8037-8557-7, ISBN13: 978-0-8037-8557-1.
Dewey:793.3/2/0924. LCCN:76-013200.

Audience: **g,l,u,f.** ℬ

Tune, Tommy   **GV1785.T86A3 1997**
Footnotes: A Memoir. Trade Cloth. Simon & Schuster. New
York, NY. 1997. 240p. ISBN:0-684-84182-7, ISBN13:
978-0-684-84182-3. Dewey:792.8/028/092. LCCN:97-024763.

Audience: **g,l,u,f.**

Turnbaugh, Douglas   **GV1785.D5**
Sergei Diaghilev. Martin Duberman (Editor). Trade Paper.
Chelsea House Publishers. Langhorne, PA. 1995. 168p. Lives of
Notable Gay Men and Lesbians Ser. ISBN:0-7910-2887-9,
ISBN13: 978-0-7910-2887-2. Dewey:792.80924.

Audience: **g,l,u,f.**

Creative Production > Film

Aaron, Michele   **PN1995.9.H55N48 2004**
New Queer Cinema: A Critical Reader. Paper Text, Library
Binding. Rutgers University Press. Piscataway, NJ. 2004. 224p.
ISBN:0-8135-3485-2, ISBN13: 978-0-8135-3485-5.
Dewey:791.43/653. LCCN:2004-041863.

Audience: **g,l,u,f.**

Bad Object-Choices   **PN1995.9.H55**
Staff (Editor)
How Do I Look?: Queer Film and Video. Trade Paper. Bay
Press, Inc. Seattle, WA. 1991. 296p. ISBN:0-941920-20-8,
ISBN13: 978-0-941920-20-9. Dewey:791.43/653.
LCCN:91-017052.

Audience: **g,l,u.**

Barrios, Richard   **PN1995.9.H55B37 2002**
Screened Out: Playing Gay in Hollywood from Edison to
Stonewall. UK-B Format Paperback. Routledge. New York, NY.
2005. 416p. ISBN:0-415-92329-8, ISBN13: 978-0-415-92329-3.
Dewey:791.43/653. LCCN:2002-004760.

Audience: **g,l,u.**

Bell-Metereau, Rebecca   **PN1995.9.A26**
Louise
Hollywood Androgyny. Ed. 2. Trade Paper. Columbia University
Press. New York, NY. 1993. 345p. ISBN:0-231-08467-6,
ISBN13: 978-0-231-08467-3. Dewey:791.43/028.
LCCN:93-008321.

Audience: **g.** *Choice, 1985.*

Benshoff, Harry M.   **PN1995.9.H55 B457 1997**
Monsters in the Closet: Homosexuality and the Horror Film.
Manchester University Press. 1997. Inside Popular Film
ISBN:0-7190-4473-1, ISBN13: 978-0-7190-4473-1.

Audience: **g,l,u,f.**

Benshoff, Harry M. &   **PN1995.9.M56**
Griffin, Sean
America on Film: Representing Race, Class, Gender, and
Sexuality at the Movies. Trade Cloth. Blackwell Publishing, Inc.
Malden, MA. 2003. 396p. ISBN:0-631-22582-X, ISBN13:
978-0-631-22582-9. Dewey:791.43/6520693.
LCCN:2003-004935.

Audience: **u,f.**

Benshoff, Harry M. &   **PN1995.9.H55Q397**
Griffin, Sean
Queer Cinema: The Film Reader. Paper over Boards. Routledge.
New York, NY. 2004. 256p. In Focus—Routledge Film Readers
Ser. ISBN:0-415-31986-2, ISBN13: 978-0-415-31986-7.
Dewey:791.43/653. LCCN:2003-024424.

Audience: **u,f.**

Benshoff, Harry M. &   **PN1995.9.H55B44 2005**
Griffin, Sean
Queer Images: A History of Gay and Lesbian Film in America.
Trade Cloth. Rowman & Littlefield Publishers, Inc. Lanham,
MD. 2005. 336p. Genre and Beyond Ser. ISBN:0-7425-1971-6,
ISBN13: 978-0-7425-1971-8. Dewey:791.43/653.
LCCN:2005-012348.

Audience: **g.** *Choice, 2006.*

Bourne, Stephen   **PN1995.9.H55B68 1996**
Brief Encounters: Lesbians and Gays in British Cinema,
1930-1971. Trade Cloth. Continuum International Publishing
Group, Ltd. London, 1996. 256p. Film Studies
ISBN:0-304-33283-6, ISBN13: 978-0-304-33283-0.
Dewey:791.4/3/653. LCCN:96-013881.

Audience: **u,f.**

Braun, Eric   **PN1995.9.H55**
Frightening the Horses: The Rise and Rise of Gay Cinema.
Trade Paper. Reynolds & Hearn. Richmond, 2002. 192p.
ISBN:1-903111-10-2, ISBN13: 978-1-903111-10-9.
Dewey:791.4/3653.

Audience: **g.**

Bryant, Wayne M.   **PN1995.9.B57B78 1997**
Bisexual Characters in Film: From Anais to Zee. Trade Cloth.
Haworth Press, Incorporated, The. Binghamton, NY. 2005. 187p.
ISBN:1-56023-894-1, ISBN13: 978-1-56023-894-2.
Dewey:791.43/6538. LCCN:96-025868.

Audience: **g.**

Cestaro, Gary P.   **PQ4028.Q44 2004**
(Editor)
Queer Italia: Same-Sex Desire in Italian Literature and Film.
Cloth over Boards. Palgrave Macmillan. New York, NY. 2004.
256p. Italian and Italian American Studies ISBN:0-312-24024-4,

ISBN13: 978-0-312-24024-0. Dewey:850.9/353.
LCCN:2003-066427.

Audience: **g,u,f.** *Choice, 2005.*

Daniel, Lisa & Jackson,   **PN1995.9.H55B45 2003**
Claire (Editors)
The Bent Lens: A World Guide to Gay and Lesbian Film. Ed. 2.
Trade Paper. Alyson Publications. Los Angeles, CA. 2003. 424p.
ISBN:1-55583-806-5, ISBN13: 978-1-55583-806-5.
Dewey:791.43/653. LCCN:2002-190757.

Audience: **g.**

DeAngelis, Michael   **PN1995.9.H55D43 2001**
Gay Fandom and Crossover Stardom: James Dean, Mel Gibson,
and Keanu Reeves. Trade Cloth. Duke University Press.
Durham, NC. 2001. 296p. ISBN:0-8223-2728-7, ISBN13:
978-0-8223-2728-8. Dewey:791.43/086/642.
LCCN:2001-023153.

Audience: **u,f.** *Choice, 2002.*

Doty, Alexander   **PN1995.9.H55D68 2000**
Flaming Classics: Queering the Film Canon. Paper over Boards.
Routledge. New York, NY. 2000. 256p. ISBN:0-415-92344-1,
ISBN13: 978-0-415-92344-6. Dewey:791.43/653.
LCCN:00-031136.

Audience: **u,f.** *Choice, 2001.*

Dyer, Richard   **HQ76.D9 2002**
The Culture of Queers. Paper over Boards. Routledge. New
York, NY. 2002. 256p. ISBN:0-415-22375-X, ISBN13:
978-0-415-22375-1. Dewey:306.76/6. LCCN:2001-048303.

Audience: **g,l,u.**

Dyer, Richard   **PN1995.9.H55**
Now You See It: Studies on Lesbian and Gay Film. Ed. 2.
Juliane Pidduck (Introduction by). Paper over Boards.
Routledge. New York, NY. 2002. 352p. ISBN:0-415-25498-1,
ISBN13: 978-0-415-25498-4. Dewey:791.4/3653.

Audience: **g,l,u.**

Ehrenstein, David   **PN2286.5.E37 2000**
Open Secret: Gay Hollywood, 1928-2000. Trade Paper.
HarperCollins Publishers. New York, NY. 2000. 416p.
ISBN:0-688-17585-6, ISBN13: 978-0-688-17585-6.
Dewey:791.43/028/086640973. LCCN:00-697965.

Audience: **g.**

Grossman, Andrew   **PN1995.9.H55Q39 2000**
David (Editor)
Queer Asian Cinema: Shadows in the Shade. Trade Cloth.
Haworth Press, Incorporated, The. Binghamton, NY. 2000. xx,
346p. Journal of Homosexuality Ser., Vol. 39, Nos. 3, 4
ISBN:1-56023-139-4, ISBN13: 978-1-56023-139-4.
Dewey:791.43/653. LCCN:00-063369.

Audience: **u,f.**

Hadleigh, Boze   **HQ75.7.H33 2002**
Celluloid Gaze. Trade Paper. Hal Leonard Corporation.
Milwaukee, WI. 2004. 219p. ISBN:0-87910-971-8, ISBN13:
978-0-87910-971-4. Dewey:306.76/62/0922.
LCCN:2002-066060.

Audience: **g.**

Hadleigh, Boze   **PN1995.9.H55H33 1996**
Hollywood Gays. Trade Cloth. Barricade Books, Inc. Fort Lee,
NJ. 1996. 384p. ISBN:1-56980-083-9, ISBN13:
978-1-56980-083-6. Dewey:305.3/89/664/0979494.
LCCN:96-020453.

Audience: **g.**

Hadleigh, Boze   **PN1995.9.L48H23 1994**
Hollywood Lesbians. Trade Cloth. Barricade Books, Inc. Fort
Lee, NJ. 1994. 304p. ISBN:1-56980-014-6, ISBN13:
978-1-56980-014-0. Dewey:791.43/028/092273.
LCCN:94-025584.

Audience: **g.**

Hadleigh, Boze   **HQ76.3.U5 H33**
In or Out: Hollywood Gays and Straights Talk about
Themselves and Each Other. Trade Cloth. Barricade Books, Inc.
Fort Lee, NJ. 2000. 320p. ISBN:1-56980-156-8, ISBN13:
978-1-56980-156-7. Dewey:305.38/9664.

Audience: **g,l.**

Hadleigh, Boze   **PN1995.9.H55**
The Lavender Screen: The Gay and Lesbian Films - Their Stars,
Directors, Characters and Critics. Ed. 3. Samson DeBrier
(Introduction by). Trade Paper. Kensington Publishing
Corporation. New York, NY. 2001. 288p. ISBN:0-8065-2199-6,
ISBN13: 978-0-8065-2199-2. Dewey:791.43/653.
LCCN:2003-283521.

Audience: **g.**

Hanson, Ellis   **PN1995.9.H55O88 1999**
Out Takes: Essays on Queer Theory and Film. Trade Cloth.
Duke University Press. Durham, NC. 1999. vi, 364p. Series Q
ISBN:0-8223-2309-5, ISBN13: 978-0-8223-2309-9.
Dewey:791.43/653. LCCN:98-037161.

Audience: **g,l,u.**

Holmlund, Chris &   **P96.D622U63 1997**
Fuchs, Cynthia
Between the Sheets, in the Streets: Queer, Lesbian and Gay
Documentary. Trade Paper. University of Minnesota Press.
Minneapolis, MN. 1997. 304p. Visible Evidence Ser., Vol. 1
ISBN:0-8166-2775-4, ISBN13: 978-0-8166-2775-2.
Dewey:306.76/6. LCCN:96-047751.

Audience: **u,f.**

Hunter, Jack (Editor)   **PN1998.3.H58**
Moonchild: The Films of Kenneth Anger. Trade Cloth. Creation
Books. New York, NY. 2002. 128p. ISBN:1-84068-029-6,
ISBN13: 978-1-84068-029-4. Dewey:791.4/3/0233/092.

Audience: **g,l,u,f.**

Kuzniar, Alice A.   **PN1995.9.H55K89 2000**
The Queer German Cinema. Trade Cloth. Stanford University
Press. Palo Alto, CA. 2000. x, 314p. ISBN:0-8047-3748-7,
ISBN13: 978-0-8047-3748-7. Dewey:791.43/653.
LCCN:00-020494.

Audience: **g,l,u.**

Long, Robert Emmet   **PN1998.3.I89A3 2005**
James Ivory in Conversation: How Merchant Ivory Makes Its
Movies. Janet Maslin (Foreword by). Trade Cloth. University of
California Press. Berkeley, CA. 2005. 350p.
ISBN:0-520-23415-4, ISBN13: 978-0-520-23415-4.
Dewey:791.4302/33/092. LCCN:2004-022679.

Audience: **g,l,u,f.**

Madsen, Axel   **PN1995.9.L48**
The Sewing Circle: Sappho's Leading Ladies. Trade Paper.
Kensington Publishing Corporation. New York, NY. 2002. 256p.
ISBN:0-7582-0101-X, ISBN13: 978-0-7582-0101-0.
Dewey:791.4308.

Audience: **g,l,u.**

Mann, William   **PN2286.5.M36**
Behind the Screen: How Gays and Lesbians Shaped Hollywood, 1910-1969. Trade Paper. Penguin Group (USA) Inc. New York, NY. 2002. 448p. ISBN:0-14-200114-7, ISBN13: 978-0-14-200114-1. Dewey:791.43028.
                                        Audience: **g.**

Murray, Raymond   **PN1995.9.H55M87 199**
Images in the Dark: An Encyclopedia of Gay and Lesbian Film and Video. T L A Video Management, Inc. 1994. ISBN:1-880707-01-2, ISBN13: 978-1-880707-01-2.
                                      Audience: **g,l.**

Pencak, William   **PN1998.3.J3P46 2002**
The Films of Derek Jarman. Paper Text. McFarland & Company, Incorporated Publishers. Jefferson, NC. 2002. 213p. ISBN:0-7864-1430-8, ISBN13: 978-0-7864-1430-7. Dewey:791.43/023/092. LCCN:2002-013831.
                        Audience: **g,l,u,f.** *Choice, 2003.*

Rumble, Patrick &   **PQ4835.A48Z8626 1994**
 Testa, Bart (Editors)
Pier Paolo Pasolini: Contemporary Perspectives. Trade Cloth. University of Toronto Press. Toronto, ON. 1993. 530p. Toronto Italian Studies ISBN:0-8020-2966-3, ISBN13: 978-0-8020-2966-9. Dewey:858/.91409. LCCN:95-120658.
                                     Audience: **l,u,f.**

Russo, Vito   **PN1995.9.H55R8 1987**
The Celluloid Closet: Homosexuality in the Movies. Trade Paper. HarperCollins Publishers. New York, NY. 1987. 384p. ISBN:0-06-096132-5, ISBN13: 978-0-06-096132-9. Dewey:791.43/09/09353. LCCN:86-045684.
                                  Audience: **g.** *B*

Saunders, Michael W.   **PN1995**
Imps of the Perverse: Gay Monsters in Film. Trade Cloth. Greenwood Publishing Group, Inc. Portsmouth, NH. 1998. 160p. ISBN:0-275-95761-6, ISBN13: 978-0-275-95761-2. Dewey:791.43/653. LCCN:97-033242.
                                   Audience: **g,l,u.**

Stewart, Steve   **PN1995.9.H55**
Gay Hollywood Film & Video Guide: Over 75 Years of Male Homosexuality in the Movies. Companion Publications. 1993. ISBN:0-9625277-4-2, ISBN13: 978-0-9625277-4-6.
                                      Audience: **g,l.**

Straayer, Chris   **PN1995.9.H55S77 1996**
Deviant Eyes, Deviant Bodies: Sexual Re-Orientation in Film and Video. Trade Cloth. Columbia University Press. New York, NY. 1996. 364p. Film and Culture Ser. ISBN:0-231-07978-8, ISBN13: 978-0-231-07978-5. Dewey:791.43/653. LCCN:96-000169.
                        Audience: **g,l,u.** *Choice, 1997.*

Suarez, Juan A.   **PN1995.9.E96S82 1996**
Bike Boys, Drag Queens and Superstars: Avant-Garde, Mass Culture and Gay Identities in the 1960s Underground Cinema. Trade Cloth. Indiana University Press. Bloomington, IN. 1996. 77352642077352p. ISBN:0-253-32971-X, ISBN13: 978-0-253-32971-4. Dewey:791.43/653. LCCN:95-019742.
                        Audience: **l,u.** *Choice, 1996.*

Summers, Claude J.   **PN1590.G39Q44 2005**
 (Editor)
The Queer Encyclopedia of Film and Television. Trade Paper. Cleis Press. San Francisco, CA. 2005. 376p.

ISBN:1-57344-209-7, ISBN13: 978-1-57344-209-1. Dewey:790.2/086/64. LCCN:2005-015928.
                                     Audience: **g,l,u,f.**

Tomlin, Lily (Narrated by)   **PN1995.9.H55**
The Celluloid Closet. Jeffrey Friedman & Robert Epstein (Directed Bys), Shirley MacLaine, Tony Curtis, Susan Sarandon, Tom Hanks & Whoopi Goldberg (Contribution by). DVD. Columbia Tristar Home Entertainment. Culver City, CA. 2001. Dewey:791.43/653.
                                        Audience: **g.**

Tyler   **PN1995.9.H55T9**
Screening the Sexes. Trade Cloth. Henry Holt & Company. New York, NY. 1996. ISBN:0-8058-6583-7, ISBN13: 978-0-8058-6583-7. Dewey:791.43/09/09353.
                                        Audience: **g.**

Waters, John   **PN1998.3.W38**
Shock Value: A Tasteful Book about Bad Taste. Trade Paper. Avalon Publishing Group. New York, NY. 2005. 272p. ISBN:1-56025-698-2, ISBN13: 978-1-56025-698-4. Dewey:791.430233092. LCCN:2005-281152.
                                     Audience: **g,l,u,f.**

Waugh, Thomas   **PN1995.9.H55W38 2000**
The Fruit Machine: Twenty Years of Writings on Queer Cinema. John Greyson (Foreword by). Trade Cloth. Duke University Press. Durham, NC. 2000. 288p. ISBN:0-8223-2433-4, ISBN13: 978-0-8223-2433-1. Dewey:791.43/653. LCCN:99-027252.
                                       Audience: **u,f.**

Weiss, Andrea   **PN1995.9.L48**
Vampires and Violets: Lesbians in Film. Trade Paper. Penguin Group (USA) Inc. New York, NY. 1993. 192p. ISBN:0-14-023100-5, ISBN13: 978-0-14-023100-7. Dewey:791.43/65206643. LCCN:93-008634.
                                     Audience: **g,l,u,f.**

White, Patricia   **PN1995.9.L48W54 1999**
Uninvited: Classical Hollywood Cinema and Lesbian Representation. Trade Cloth. Indiana University Press. Bloomington, IN. 1999. 270p. ISBN:0-253-33641-4, ISBN13: 978-0-253-33641-5. Dewey:791.43/653. LCCN:99-035744.
                        Audience: **g,l,u.** *Choice, 2000.*

Yosef, Raz   **PN1993.5.I86Y67 2004**
Beyond Flesh: Queer Masculinities and Nationalism in Israeli Cinema. Trade Cloth. Rutgers University Press. Piscataway, NJ. 2004. 224p. ISBN:0-8135-3375-9, ISBN13: 978-0-8135-3375-9. Dewey:791.43/653. LCCN:2003-009390.
                        Audience: **g,l,u.** *Choice, 2005.*

Creative Production > Film > Biography

Almodóvar, Pedro   **PN1998.3.A46A5 2004**
Pedro Almodovar: Interviews. Paula Willoquet-Maricondi (Editor). Trade Cloth. University Press of Mississippi. Jackson, MS. 2004. 208p. Conversations with Filmmakers Ser. ISBN:1-57806-569-0, ISBN13: 978-1-57806-569-1. Dewey:791.43/0233/092. LCCN:2003-049711.
                                     Audience: **g,l,u,f.**

Bosworth, Patricia   **PN2287.C545B6 1990**
Montgomery Clift: A Biography. Trade Paper. Hal Leonard Corporation. Milwaukee, WI. 1990. 438p. ISBN:0-87910-135-0,

---

ISBN13: 978-0-87910-135-0. Dewey:791.43/028/0924. LCCN:89-049725.

Audience: **g,l,u.**

Braad Thomsen,   **PN1998.3.F37B73 2004**
Christian
Fassbinder: The Life and Work of a Provocative Genius. Trade Paper. University of Minnesota Press. Minneapolis, MN. 2004. 358p. ISBN:0-8166-4364-4, ISBN13: 978-0-8166-4364-6. Dewey:791.4302/33/092. LCCN:2004-041222.

Audience: **g,l,u.**

Callow, Simon   **PN2598.L27.C35 1987**
Charles Laughton, a Difficult Actor. Trade Cloth. Methuen & Company, Ltd. London, 1987. x, 318 p., [8p. ISBN:0-413-58770-3, ISBN13: 978-0-413-58770-1. Dewey:792/.028/0924. LCCN:87-025453.

Audience: **g,l,u.**

Chierichetti, David   **TT505.H4C455 2002**
Edith Head: The Life and Times of Hollywood's Celebrated Costume Designer. Trade Cloth. HarperCollins Publishers. New York, NY. 2003. 272p. ISBN:0-06-019428-6, ISBN13: 978-0-06-019428-4. Dewey:746.9/2/092 B. LCCN:2002-024677.

Audience: **g,l,u.**

Chierichetti, David   **PN1998.3.L45C47**
Mitchell Leisen, Hollywood Director. Trade Paper. Riverwood Press. Burbank, CA. 1994. ISBN:1-880756-07-2, ISBN13: 978-1-880756-07-2. Dewey:791.43/0233/0924.

Audience: **l,u,f.**

Curtis, James   **PN1998.3.W5C87 2003**
James Whale: A New World of Gods and Monsters. Trade Paper. University of Minnesota Press. Minneapolis, MN. 2003. 480p. ISBN:0-8166-4386-5, ISBN13: 978-0-8166-4386-8. Dewey:791.4302/33/092 B. LCCN:2003-018987.

Audience: **g,l,u.**

Gielgud, John   **PN2598.G45**
Sir John Gielgud: A Life in Letters. Trade Paper. Arcade Publishing, Inc. New York, NY. 2005. 576p. ISBN:1-55970-755-0, ISBN13: 978-1-55970-755-8. Dewey:792.02/8/092.

Audience: **g,l,u.**

Hastie, Amelie (Editor),   **PS3558.A8627**
et al.
Todd Haynes: A Magnificent Obsession. Lynne Joyrich, Constance Penley, Sasha Torres, Patricia White & Sharon Willis (Editors), Laura Christian, Mary Desjardins & Mary Ann Doane (Contribution by). Trade Paper. Duke University Press. Durham, NC. 2005. 220p. Camera Obscura Ser. ISBN:0-8223-6629-0, ISBN13: 978-0-8223-6629-4. Dewey:791.43082.

Audience: **g,l,u,f.**

Hunter, Tab   **PN2287.H82A3 2005**
Tab Hunter Confidential: The Making of a Movie Star. Trade Cloth. Algonquin Books of Chapel Hill. Chapel Hill, NC. 2005. 408p. ISBN:1-56512-466-9, ISBN13: 978-1-56512-466-0. Dewey:791.4302/8/092 B. LCCN:2005-045335.

Audience: **g,l,u.** *Choice, 2006.*

Jeffers, H. Paul   **PN2287.M6437J44 2001**
Sal Mineo: His Life, Murder, and Mystery. Trade Cloth. Thorndike Press. Waterville, ME. 2001. 447p. Thorndike Biography Ser. ISBN:0-7862-3167-X, ISBN13:

978-0-7862-3167-6. Dewey:791.43/028/092 B. LCCN:00-066622.

Audience: **g,l,u.**

King, Thomas R.   **PN1998.3.G42K56 2001**
The Operator: David Geffen Builds, Buys, and Sells the New Hollywood. UK-Trade Paper. Broadway Books. New York, NY. 2001. 688p. ISBN:0-7679-0757-4, ISBN13: 978-0-7679-0757-6. Dewey:791.43/0232/092 B. LCCN:2001-020214.

Audience: **g,l,u,f.**

Laurents, Arthur   **PS3525.I5156**
Original Story by Arthur Laurents: A Memoir of Broadway and Hollywood. Trade Paper. Applause Theatre Book Publishers. New York, NY. 2001. 448p. ISBN:1-55783-467-9, ISBN13: 978-1-55783-467-6. Dewey:812.5/2.

Audience: **g,l,u,f.**

Leider, Emily Wortis   **PN2287.V3L45 2003**
Dark Lover: The Life and Death of Rudolph Valentino. Cloth over Boards. Farrar, Straus & Giroux. New York, NY. 2003. 592p. ISBN:0-374-28239-0, ISBN13: 978-0-374-28239-4. Dewey:791.43/028/092 B. LCCN:2002-029779.

Audience: **g,l,u.** *Choice, 2003.*

Lobenthal, Joel   **PN2287.B17L63 2004**
Tallulah!: The Life and Times of a Leading Lady. Trade Cloth. HarperCollins Publishers. New York, NY. 2004. 592p. ISBN:0-06-039435-8, ISBN13: 978-0-06-039435-6. Dewey:792.028092. LCCN:2004-050915.

Audience: **g,l,u.**

Madsen, Axel   **PN2287.S67M34 1994**
Stanwyck. Trade Cloth. HarperCollins Publishers. New York, NY. 1994. 384p. ISBN:0-06-017997-X, ISBN13: 978-0-06-017997-7. Dewey:791.43/028/092 B. LCCN:93-047984.

Audience: **g,l,u,f.**

Mann, William J.   **PN1998.3.S35M36 2005**
Edge of Midnight: The Life of John Schlesinger: The Authorized Biography. Trade Cloth. Watson-Guptill Publications, Inc. New York, NY. 2006. 656p. ISBN:0-8230-8366-7, ISBN13: 978-0-8230-8366-4. Dewey:791.4/30233/092. LCCN:2004-226432.

Audience: **g,l,u,f.** *Choice, 2005.*

Mann, William J.   **PN2287.H172M36 1998**
Wisecracker: The Life and Times of William Haines, Hollywood's First Openly Gay Star. Trade Cloth. Penguin Group (USA) Inc. New York, NY. 1998. 480p. ISBN:0-670-87155-9, ISBN13: 978-0-670-87155-1. Dewey:791.43/028/092 B. LCCN:97-039665.

Audience: **g.**

Mann, William J.   **PN1998.3.S35.M366**
Edge of Midnight: The Life of John Schlesinger. Billboard Books. 2005. ISBN:0-8230-8366-7, ISBN13: 978-0-8230-8366-4.

Audience: **g.**

Mayne, Judith   **PN1998.3.A763M39**
Directed by Dorothy Arzner. Trade Cloth. Indiana University Press. Bloomington, IN. 1995. 240p. ISBN:0-253-33716-X, ISBN13: 978-0-253-33716-0. Dewey:791.43/0233/092. LCCN:93-051496.

Audience: **g,l,u,f.** *Choice, 1995.*

McGilligan, Patrick   PN1998.3.C8M34 1991
George Cukor: A Double Life: A Biography of the Gentleman
Director. St. Martin's Press. 1991. ISBN:0-312-05419-X,
ISBN13: 978-0-312-05419-9.
Audience: **g,l,u.**

Nowell-Smith, Geoffrey   **PN1998.3**
Luchino Visconti. Ed. 3. Trade Cloth. BFI Publishing. London,
2003. 25p. ISBN:0-85170-960-5, ISBN13: 978-0-85170-960-4.
Dewey:791.43/0233/0924.
Audience: **g,l,u,f.** *Choice, 2004.*

Parish, James Robert   **PN1998.3.V363P37**
Gus Van Sant: An Unauthorized Biography. Trade Cloth. Avalon
Publishing Group. New York, NY. 2001. 333p.
ISBN:1-56025-337-1, ISBN13: 978-1-56025-337-2.
Dewey:791.43/0233/092 B. LCCN:2001-048039.
Audience: **g,l,u.**

Radovich, Don   **PN1998**
Tony Richardson: A Bio-Bibliography. Cloth Text. Greenwood
Publishing Group, Inc. Portsmouth, NH. 1995. 304p.
Bio-Bibliographies in the Performing Arts Ser., No. 69
ISBN:0-313-28981-6, ISBN13: 978-0-313-28981-1.
Dewey:791.43/0233/092 B. LCCN:95-032990.
Audience: **l,u,f.** *Choice, 1996.*

Riva, Maria E.   **PN2658.D5 R58**
Marlene Dietrich. UK-Trade Paper. Ballantine Books. New
York, NY. 1994. 800p. ISBN:0-345-38645-0, ISBN13:
978-0-345-38645-8. Dewey:791.4302809.
Audience: **g,l,u,f.**

Soares, Andre   **PN2287.N6S66 2002**
Beyond Paradise: The Life of Ramon Novarro. Cloth over
Boards. St. Martin's Press. Gordonville, VA. 2002. 368p.
ISBN:0-312-28231-1, ISBN13: 978-0-312-28231-8.
Dewey:791.43/028/092 B. LCCN:2002-068125.
Audience: **g,l,u.**

Steegmuller, Francis   **PQ2605.O15Z86 1986**
Cocteau: A Biography. Trade Paper. David R. Godine Publisher.
Boston, MA. 1986. 608p. Nonpareil Bks., Vol. 40
ISBN:0-87923-606-X, ISBN13: 978-0-87923-606-9.
Dewey:848/.9/1209. LCCN:76-117039.
Audience: **g,l,u.** *B*

Williams, Michael   **PN2598**
Ivor Novello: Screen Idol. Trade Cloth. BFI Publishing. London,
2003. 193p. ISBN:0-85170-982-6, ISBN13: 978-0-85170-982-6.
Dewey:791/.092. LCCN:2003-501171.
Audience: **l,u,f.**

Winecoff, Charles   **PN2287.M69**
Split Image: The Life of Anthony Perkins. Trade Paper. DIANE
Publishing Company. Collingdale, PA. 2001. 482p.
ISBN:0-7881-9870-X, ISBN13: 978-0-7881-9870-0.
Dewey:791.4/3/028/092.
Audience: **g,l,u.**

Wymer, Rowland   **PN1998.3.J3**
Derek Jarman. Trade Paper. Manchester University Press.
Manchester, 2006. 240p. British Film Makers Ser.
ISBN:0-7190-5691-8, ISBN13: 978-0-7190-5691-8.
Dewey:791.430233092.
Audience: **g,l,u,f.**

Zeffirelli, Franco   **PN1998.A3Z4326 1986**
Zeffirelli: An Autobiography. Trade Cloth. Grove/Atlantic, Inc.
New York, NY. 1986. 376p. ISBN:1-55584-022-1, ISBN13:
978-1-55584-022-8. Dewey:791.43/0233/0924.
LCCN:86-015760.
Audience: **g,l,u,f.** *Choice, 1987.*

Creative Production > Television

DeGeneres, Betty   **HQ75.4.D44D44 1999**
Love, Ellen: A Mother/Daughter Journey. Trade Cloth.
HarperCollins Publishers. New York, NY. 1999. 384p.
ISBN:0-688-16274-6, ISBN13: 978-0-688-16274-0.
Dewey:306.874/3. LCCN:98-050367.
Audience: **g.**

Johnson, Phylis &   **PN1990.9.H64J64 2001**
  Keith, Michael C.
Queer Airwaves: The Story of Gay and Lesbian Broadcasting.
Cloth Text. M. E. Sharpe Inc. Armonk, NY. 2001. 314p. Media,
Communication, and Culture in America Ser.
ISBN:0-7656-0400-0, ISBN13: 978-0-7656-0400-2.
Dewey:791.44/028/08664. LCCN:00-049652.
Audience: **u,f.**

Keller, James R.   **PN1995.9.H55K45 2002**
Queer (Un)Friendly Film and Television. Paper Text. McFarland
& Company, Incorporated Publishers. Jefferson, NC. 2002.
221p. ISBN:0-7864-1246-1, ISBN13: 978-0-7864-1246-4.
Dewey:791.43/653. LCCN:2001-008124.
Audience: **u,f.** *Choice, 2002.*

Keller, James R. &   **PN1992.8.H64N49 2005**
  Stratyner, Leslie (Editors)
The New Queer Aesthetic on Television: Essays on Recent
Programming. Trade Paper, Perfect. McFarland & Company,
Incorporated Publishers. Jefferson, NC. 2005. 222p.
ISBN:0-7864-2390-0, ISBN13: 978-0-7864-2390-3.
Dewey:791.45/653. LCCN:2005-029556.
Audience: **f.**

Summers, Claude J.   **PN1590.G39Q44 2005**
  (Editor)
The Queer Encyclopedia of Film and Television. Trade Paper.
Cleis Press. San Francisco, CA. 2005. 376p.
ISBN:1-57344-209-7, ISBN13: 978-1-57344-209-1.
Dewey:790.2/086/64. LCCN:2005-015928.
Audience: **g,l,u,f.**

Tropiano, Stephen   **PN1992.8.H64T76 2002**
The Prime Time Closet: A History of Gays and Lesbians on TV.
Trade Paper. Applause Theatre Book Publishers. New York, NY.
2002. 304p. ISBN:1-55783-557-8, ISBN13: 978-1-55783-557-4.
Dewey:791.45/653. LCCN:2002-003220.
Audience: **g.**

Science

Bagemihl, Bruce   **QL761.B24 2000**
Biological Exuberance: Animal Homosexuality and Natural
Diversity. Trade Paper. St. Martin's Press. Gordonville, VA.
2000. 768p. ISBN:0-312-25377-X, ISBN13: 978-0-312-25377-6.
Dewey:591.5/62.
Audience: **g,l,u,f.**

Burr, Chandler   **QP81.6.B87 1996**
A Separate Creation: The Search for the Biological Origins of Sexual Orientation. Trade Cloth. Hyperion Press. New York, NY. 1996. 288p. ISBN:0-7868-6081-2, ISBN13: 978-0-7868-6081-4. Dewey:155.7. LCCN:95-050776.
Audience: **u,f.** *Choice, 1996.*

Corvino, John   **HQ76.25.S24 1997**
Same Sex: Debating the Ethics, Science, and Culture of Homosexuality. Trade Cloth. Rowman & Littlefield Publishers, Inc. Lanham, MD. 1997. 320p. Studies in Social, Political, and Legal Philosophy, Vol. 70 ISBN:0-8476-8482-2, ISBN13: 978-0-8476-8482-3. Dewey:306.7/66. LCCN:97-022315.
Audience: **l,u.**

Hamer, Dean &   **HQ76.25**
  Copeland, Peter
Science of Desire: The Gay Gene and the Biology of Behavior. Trade Paper. Simon & Schuster. New York, NY. 1995. 272p. ISBN:0-684-80446-8, ISBN13: 978-0-684-80446-0. Dewey:304.5. LCCN:94-022260.
Audience: **g,l.**

Hirschfeld, Magnus   **HQ76**
Sexual Anomalies: The Origin, Nature, and Treatment of Sexual Disorders. Trade Cloth. Brown Book Company. Miami, FL. 1948. 538p. ISBN:0-317-39779-6, ISBN13: 978-0-317-39779-6. Dewey:306.7/6.
Audience: **u,f.**

Hirschfeld, Magnus   **HQ76.25.H5813 2000**
The Homosexuality of Men and Women. Michael A. Lombardi-Nash (Translator), Vern L. Bullough (Introduction by). Trade Cloth. Prometheus Books, Publishers. Amherst, NY. 1999. 1200p. ISBN:1-57392-705-8, ISBN13: 978-1-57392-705-5. Dewey:306.76/6. LCCN:99-026829.
Audience: **l,u,f.** *Choice, 2001.*

Hirschfeld, Magnus   **HQ77.H57 1991**
Transvestites: The Erotic Drive to Cross-Dress. Michael A. Lombardi-Nash (Translator), Vern L. Bullough (Foreword by). Trade Cloth. Prometheus Books, Publishers. Amherst, NY. 1991. 424p. ISBN:0-87975-665-9, ISBN13: 978-0-87975-665-9. Dewey:306.77. LCCN:90-024827.
Audience: **l,u,f.**

Institute for Sex   **HQ29.S487 1998**
  Research Staff, et al.
Sexual Behavior in the Human Female. Alfred C. Kinsey, Wardell B. Pomeroy, Clyde E. Martin & Paul H. Gebhard (Authors). Trade Cloth. Indiana University Press. Bloomington, IN. 1998. 872p. ISBN:0-253-33411-X, ISBN13: 978-0-253-33411-4. Dewey:306.7/082. LCCN:98-017888.
Audience: **g,l,u,f.**

Kinsey, Alfred C., et al.   **HQ28.K55 1998**
Sexual Behavior in the Human Male. Wardell B. Pomeroy & Clyde E. Martin (Authors). Trade Cloth. Indiana University Press. Bloomington, IN. 1998. 830p. ISBN:0-253-33412-8, ISBN13: 978-0-253-33412-1. Dewey:306.7/081. LCCN:98-017912.
Audience: **g,l,u,f.** *B*

LeVay, Simon   **HQ76.25**
Queer Science: The Use and Abuse of Research into Homosexuality. Trade Paper. MIT Press. Cambridge, MA. 1997. 368p. ISBN:0-262-62119-3, ISBN13: 978-0-262-62119-9. Dewey:306.7/6/072.
Audience: **u,f.** *Choice, 1996.*

LeVay, Simon   **QP360**
The Sexual Brain. Trade Paper. MIT Press. Cambridge, MA. 1994. 190p. Bradford Bks. ISBN:0-262-62093-6, ISBN13: 978-0-262-62093-2. Dewey:155.33.
Audience: **l,u,f.** *Choice, 1993.*

Mondimore, Francis M.   **HQ76.25.M649 1996**
A Natural History of Homosexuality. Trade Paper. Johns Hopkins University Press. Baltimore, MD. 1996. 304p. ISBN:0-8018-5440-7, ISBN13: 978-0-8018-5440-8. Dewey:306.76/6. LCCN:96-016191.
Audience: **g,l,u,f.** *Choice, 1997.*

Murphy, Timothy F.   **E184.7**
Gay Science: The Ethics of Sexual Orientation Research. Trade Paper. Columbia University Press. New York, NY. 1999. 272p. Between Men, Between Women Ser. ISBN:0-231-10849-4, ISBN13: 978-0-231-10849-2. Dewey:306.76/6/072.
Audience: **l,u,f.** *Choice, 1998.*

Parker, David A. & De   **QP81.6.S48 1995**
  Cecco, John P. (Editors)
Sex, Cells, and Same-Sex Desire: The Biology of Sexual Preference. Trade Cloth. Haworth Press, Incorporated, The. Binghamton, NY. 1995. ISBN:1-56024-700-2, ISBN13: 978-1-56024-700-5. Dewey:306.76/6. LCCN:95-006140.
Audience: **u,f.**

Rogers, Lesley J.   **QP360.R628 2001**
Sexing the Brain. Trade Cloth. Columbia University Press. New York, NY. 2001. 152p. Maps of the Mind Ser. ISBN:0-231-12010-9, ISBN13: 978-0-231-12010-4. Dewey:612.8/2. LCCN:00-060255.
Audience: **l.** *Choice, 2001.*

Roughgarden, Joan   **QH541.15.B56 R68**
Evolution's Rainbow: Diversity, Gender, and Sexuality in Nature and People. Trade Cloth. University of California Press. Berkeley, CA. 2004. 472p. ISBN:0-520-24073-1, ISBN13: 978-0-520-24073-5. Dewey:305.3. LCCN:2003-024512.
Audience: **g,l,u,f.** *Choice, 2004.*

Von Krafft-Ebing,   **HQ71.K91213 1999**
  Richard
Psychopathia Sexualis: A Clinical-Forensic Study. Brian King (Editor). Trade Paper. Bloat. Burbank, CA. 1998. xlv, 683p. ISBN:0-9650324-1-8, ISBN13: 978-0-9650324-1-4. Dewey:616.85/83. LCCN:00-265138.
Audience: **u,f.**

Outside North America

Blackwood, Evelyn &   **HQ75.5.F43 1999**
  Wieringa, Saskia
Female Desires: Same-Sex Relations and Transgender Practices Across Cultures. Trade Cloth. Columbia University Press. New York, NY. 1999. 352p. Between Men, Between Women Ser. ISBN:0-231-11260-2, ISBN13: 978-0-231-11260-4. Dewey:306.76/6. LCCN:98-037847.
Audience: **u,f.**

Boswell, John   **HQ76.3.E8**
Same-Sex Unions in Premodern Europe. UK-Trade Paper. Knopf Publishing Group. New York, NY. 1995. 464p. ISBN:0-679-75164-5, ISBN13: 978-0-679-75164-9. Dewey:306.76/6/094.
Audience: **g,l,u,f.** *Choice, 1994.*

Bray, Alan   **HQ76.2.G7B69 1995**
Homosexuality in Renaissance England. Ed. 2. Trade Cloth.
Columbia University Press. New York, NY. 1996. 165p.
Between Men, Between Women Ser. ISBN:0-231-10288-7,
ISBN13: 978-0-231-10288-9. Dewey:306.7/662/0942.
LCCN:95-031441.
                                                Audience: **l,u,f.**

Carrier, Joseph   **HQ76.2.M62G813 1995**
De los Otros: Intimacy and Homosexuality among Mexican
Men. Trade Cloth. Columbia University Press. New York, NY.
1995. 288p. ISBN:0-231-09692-5, ISBN13: 978-0-231-09692-8.
Dewey:305.38/9664/0972. LCCN:95-006244.
                                        Audience: **u,f.** *Choice, 1996.*

Dasgupta, Romit &   **HQ1075.5.J3G46 2005**
McLelland, Mark
Genders and Sexualities in Japan. Paper over Boards. Routledge.
New York, NY. 2005. XVI, 224p. Asia's Transformations Ser.
ISBN:0-415-35370-X, ISBN13: 978-0-415-35370-0.
Dewey:305.3/0952. LCCN:2004-030609.
                                                Audience: **u,f.**

Dover, Kenneth J.   **HQ76.3.G8D68 1989**
Greek Homosexuality: Updated and with a New Postscript.
Trade Paper. Harvard University Press. Cambridge, MA. 1989.
256p. ISBN:0-674-36270-5, ISBN13: 978-0-674-36270-3.
Dewey:306.76/6/09495. LCCN:89-034289.
                                                Audience: **l,u,f.**

Epstein, Rob &   **D804.5.G38**
Friedman, Jeffrey (Directed Bys)
Paragraph 175. DVD. New Yorker Video. New York, NY. 2001.
ISBN:1-56730-254-8, ISBN13: 978-1-56730-254-7.
Dewey:940.53/18/08664.
                                                Audience: **g.**

Faderman, Lillian &   **HQ75.6.G3L47 1990**
Eriksson, Brigitte
Lesbians in Germany, 1890's-1920's. Ed. 2. Trade Paper. Bella
Books, Inc. Tallahassee, FL. 1990. 128p. ISBN:0-941483-62-2,
ISBN13: 978-0-941483-62-9. Dewey:306.76/63/0943.
LCCN:89-048962.
                                                Audience: **l,u.**

Gerard, Kent &   **HQ76.2.E9.P87 1989**
Hekma, Gert
The Pursuit of Sodomy: Male Homosexuality in Renaissance
and Enlightenment Europe. Cloth Text. Haworth Press,
Incorporated, The. Binghamton, NY. 1989. 553p. Journal of
Homosexuality Ser., Vol. 16, Nos. 1-2 ISBN:0-86656-491-8,
ISBN13: 978-0-86656-491-5. Dewey:306.7/662/094.
LCCN:88-032231.
                                                Audience: **u,f.**

Graupner, Helmut &   **HQ76.5.I57 2000**
Tahmindjis, Phillip (Editors)
Sexuality and Human Rights: A Global Overview. International
Bar Association, Conference Staff (Contribution by). Trade
Cloth. Haworth Press, Incorporated, The. Binghamton, NY.
2005. xviii, 244p. A Monograph Published Simultaneously As
the Journal of Homosexuality, Vol. 48, Nos. 3/4 Ser.
ISBN:1-56023-554-3, ISBN13: 978-1-56023-554-5.
Dewey:306.76/6. LCCN:2004-022790.
                                                Audience: **u,f.**

Hinsch, Bret   **HQ76.2.C5H56 1990**
Passions of the Cut Sleeve: The Male Homosexual Tradition in
China. Trade Cloth. University of California Press. Berkeley,

CA. 1990. 256p. ISBN:0-520-06720-7, ISBN13:
978-0-520-06720-2. Dewey:306.76/62/0951. LCCN:89-049037.
                                        Audience: **l,u,f.** *Choice, 1991.*

Lumsden, Ian   **HQ75.6.C9L85 1996**
Machos, Maricones, and Gays: Cuba and Homosexuality.
Library Binding. Temple University Press. Philadelphia, PA.
1996. 288p. ISBN:1-56639-370-1, ISBN13: 978-1-56639-370-6.
Dewey:306.7/66/097291/0904. LCCN:95-044233.
                                        Audience: **l,u,f.** *Choice, 1996.*

Merrick, Jeffrey W. &   **HQ76.3.F8**
Sebalis, Michael (Editors)
Homosexuality in French History and Culture. Harrington Park.
2002. ISBN:1-56023-263-3, ISBN13: 978-1-56023-263-6.
                                                Audience: **l,u,f.**

Miller, Neil   **HQ76.25.M55 1993**
Out in the World: Gay and Lesbian Life from Buenos Aires to
Bangkok. Trade Paper. Knopf Publishing Group. New York, NY.
1993. 384p. Vintage Departures Ser. ISBN:0-679-74551-3,
ISBN13: 978-0-679-74551-8. Dewey:305.90664.
LCCN:93-001300.
                                        Audience: **g.** *Choice, 1993.*

Murray, Stephen O.   **HQ76.3.A78O26 1992**
Oceanic Homosexualities. Trade Cloth. Garland Publishing, Inc.
New York, NY. 1992. 300p. Garland Gay and Lesbian Studies,
Vol. 7 ISBN:0-8240-7227-8, ISBN13: 978-0-8240-7227-8.
Dewey:306.76/6. LCCN:91-004780.
                                                Audience: **l,u,f.**

Murray, Stephen O. &   **HQ76.3.I75M87 1997**
Roscoe, Will (Editors)
Islamic Homosexualities: Culture, History, and Literature. Trade
Cloth. New York University Press. New York, NY. 1997. 392p.
ISBN:0-8147-7467-9, ISBN13: 978-0-8147-7467-0.
Dewey:306/.62/0917671. LCCN:96-035677.
                                        Audience: **g,l,u,f.** *Choice, 1997.*

Nanda, Serena   **HQ449.N36 1998**
Neither Man nor Woman: The Hijras of India. Ed. 2. Paper Text.
Thomson Wadsworth. Belmont, CA. 1998. 208p. Anthropology
Ser. ISBN:0-534-50903-7, ISBN13: 978-0-534-50903-3.
Dewey:305.3. LCCN:98-041187.
                                        Audience: **l,u,f.** *Choice, 1990.*

Robb, Graham   **HQ76.3.E8R63 2004**
Strangers: Homosexual Love in the Nineteenth Century. Trade
Cloth. W. W. Norton & Company, Inc. New York, NY. 2004.
352p. ISBN:0-393-02038-X, ISBN13: 978-0-393-02038-0.
Dewey:306.76/6/09409034. LCCN:2003-066239.
                                        Audience: **g,l.** *Choice, 2004.*

Roscoe, Will & Murray,   **HQ76.3.A35B69 1998**
Stephen O. (Editors)
Boy-Wives and Female-Husbands: Studies in African
Homosexualities. Cloth over Boards. Palgrave Macmillan. New
York, NY. 1998. 336p. ISBN:0-312-21216-X, ISBN13:
978-0-312-21216-2. Dewey:306.76/6/096. LCCN:98-021464.
                                                Audience: **g,l,u,f.**

Talmagne, Florence   **HQ76.3.E8**
A History of Homosexuality in Europe, 1919-1939. Trade Paper.
Algora Publishing. New York, NY. 2004. 596p.
ISBN:0-87586-355-8, ISBN13: 978-0-87586-355-9.
Dewey:306.76/6/0940904.
                                        Audience: **g,l,u,f.** *Choice, 2005.*

Thornton, Bruce S.   **HQ13**
Eros: The Myth of Ancient Greek Sexuality. Trade Paper.
Westview Press. Boulder, CO. 1998. 304p. ISBN:0-8133-3226-5,
ISBN13: 978-0-8133-3226-0. Dewey:306.7/0938.

Audience: **l,u.**   *Choice, 1997.*

Vanita, Ruth (Editor)   **HQ76.2.I4Q84 2001**
Queering India: Same-Sex Love and Eroticism in Indian Culture
and Society. Paper over Boards. Routledge. New York, NY.
2001. 256p. ISBN:0-415-92949-0, ISBN13: 978-0-415-92949-3.
Dewey:306.76/6/0954. LCCN:2001-019111.

Audience: **u,f.**

Weeks, Jeffrey   **HQ76.8.G7.W43 1977**
Coming Out: Homosexual Politics in Britain from the 19th
Century to the Present. Trade Paper. Charles River Books.
Carlisle, MA. 288p. ISBN:0-7043-3175-6, ISBN13:
978-0-7043-3175-4. Dewey:301.41/57/0941. LCCN:78-309964.

Audience: **l,u,f.**

Winkler, John J.   **DF93.W56 1990**
Constraints of Desire: The Anthropology of Sex and Gender in
Ancient Greece. Trade Cloth. Routledge. New York, NY. 1989.
288p. ISBN:0-415-90122-7, ISBN13: 978-0-415-90122-2.
Dewey:392.6/0938. LCCN:89-033156.

Audience: **g,l,u,f.**

Formats: Web: ☐   Ebook: 🅮   CD/DVD-ROM: 🏵   BCL3: 𝓑

GENDER STUDIES

The Gender Studies section is composed of approximately one thousand texts, culled from required or recommended reading for undergraduate courses in Gender Studies or Women's Studies. Major subject divisions within the section are feminism, sex/gender roles in society, feminist and gender theory, and history, as well as related areas crucial to the study of gender such as literary criticism, psychology, social issues, activism, politics, and the arts. Incorporated within each of these divisions are titles that speak to the prominence of race and class in Gender Studies, as well as contemporary issues that have arisen in the discipline, such as globalization and international development.

In BCL3, works on men and masculinity were only nominally represented; in this edition, current scholarship in men's studies is much more evident, reflecting the increased interest of the subject in the academy, and are interfiled within the section.

Since the nature of Gender Studies is interdisciplinary, many other relevant titles can be located in GLBT Studies and Sociology. Additional titles of interest can be found in nearly every section of RCL.

The Gender Studies section is focused on English-language titles, with some English translations; a selection of classics in the field from the previous edition; and online resources.

— Kim Clarke

Reference Works

HQ1150

Statistical Record of Women Worldwide 3. Trade Cloth.
Thomson Gale. Farmington Hills, MI. 1999.
ISBN:0-7876-7367-6, ISBN13: 978-0-7876-7367-3.
Dewey:305.4/021.

Audience: **g,l,u.**

☐ WIDNET: Women In Development Network Database.
http://www.focusintl.com/statangl.htm

Audience: **g,l,u.**

Adamson, Lynda G.   **Z7963**
Notable Women in World History: A Guide to Recommended
Biographies and Autobiographies. Cloth Text. Greenwood
Publishing Group, Inc. Portsmouth, NH. 1998. 416p.
ISBN:0-313-29818-1, ISBN13: 978-0-313-29818-9.
Dewey:016.92072. LCCN:97-033136.

Audience: **g,l,u,f.** *Choice, 1998.*

Amico, Eleanor (Editor)   **Z7961.R43 1998**
Reader's Guide to Women's Studies. Trade Cloth. Fitzroy
Dearborn Publishers, Inc. Chicago, IL. 1998. 750p.
ISBN:1-884964-77-X, ISBN13: 978-1-884964-77-0.
Dewey:016.3054/07. LCCN:98-138939.

Audience: **g,l,u.** *Choice, 1998.*

Bataille, Gretchen M. &   **E98.W8B38 2001**
Lisa, Laurie (Editors)
Native American Women: A Biographical Dictionary. Ed. 2.
Paper over Boards. Routledge. New York, NY. 2001. 384p.
Biographical Dictionaries of Minority Women Ser.
ISBN:0-415-93020-0, ISBN13: 978-0-415-93020-8.
Dewey:920.72/08997. LCCN:2001-019749.

Audience: **l,u,f.** *Choice, 2001, 1993.*

Brakeman, Lynne   **HQ1121.C617 1996**
Chronology of Women Worldwide: People, Places, and Events
That Shaped Women's History. Trade Cloth. Thomson Gale.
Farmington Hills, MI. 1996. 600p. ISBN:0-7876-0154-3,
ISBN13: 978-0-7876-0154-6. Dewey:305.4/09.
LCCN:96-023915.

Audience: **g.** *Choice, 1997.*

Commire, Anne &   **HQ1115.W6 1999**
Klezmer, Deborah (Editors)
Women in World History: A Biographical Encyclopedia, Set.
Trade Cloth, Box or Slipcased. Thomson Gale. Farmington
Hills, MI. 1999. 850p. ISBN:0-7876-3736-X, ISBN13:
978-0-7876-3736-1. Dewey:920.72/03. LCCN:99-024692.

Audience: **g,l,u,f.** *Choice, 2000.*

Davis, Kathy (Editor),   **HQ1180**
et al.
Handbook of Gender and Women's Studies. Mary Evans &
Judith Lorber (Editors). Trade Cloth. SAGE Publications, Inc.
Thousand Oaks, CA. 2006. 512p. ISBN:0-7619-4390-0,
ISBN13: 978-0-7619-4390-7. Dewey:305.4071.
LCCN:2005-927695.

Audience: **g,l,u.**

Essed, Philomenia &   **HQ1075.C656 2005**
Goldberg, David Theo (Editors)
Companion to Gender Studies. Trade Cloth. Blackwell
Publishing, Inc. Malden, MA. 2004. 576p. Blackwell
Companions in Cultural Studies, Vol. 8 ISBN:0-631-22109-3,

ISBN13: 978-0-631-22109-8. Dewey:305.3/072.
LCCN:2004-006865.

Audience: **g,l,u,f.** *Choice, 2005.*

Fast, Timothy H. &   **G1201.E1G5 1995**
Fast, Cathy C.
The Women's Atlas of the United States. Trade Cloth. Facts On
File, Inc. New York, NY. 1995. 256p. ISBN:0-8160-2970-9,
ISBN13: 978-0-8160-2970-9. Dewey:305.4/0973/022.
LCCN:94-029084.

Audience: **g,l,u.** *Choice, 1995.*

Flood, Michael   **HQ1088**
☐ The Men's Bibliography.
http://mensbiblio.xyonline.net/
Ed. 14. ISBN:0-646-18088-6, ISBN13: 978-0-646-18088-5.

Audience: **g,l,u,f.**

Greenfield, Lesley   **HQ1883.E53 1993**
Ripley
Encyclopedia of Women's Associations Worldwide. Trade Cloth.
Thomson Gale. Farmington Hills, MI. 1993. 550p.
ISBN:1-873477-25-2, ISBN13: 978-1-873477-25-0.
Dewey:305.406. LCCN:93-013702.

Audience: **g,l,u,f.** *Choice, 1994.*

Huls, Mary E.   **HQ1410**
United States Government Documents on Women, 1800-1990: A
Comprehensive Bibliography, Labor. Cloth Text. Greenwood
Publishing Group, Inc. Portsmouth, NH. 1993. 500p.
Bibliographies and Indexes in Women's Studies, No. 18
ISBN:0-313-28157-2, ISBN13: 978-0-313-28157-0.
Dewey:016.3054. LCCN:92-038990.

Audience: **g,l,u.**

Huls, Mary E.   **HQ1410**
United States Government Documents on Women, 1800-1990: A
Comprehensive Bibliography - Social Issues, Vol. 1. Cloth Text.
Greenwood Publishing Group, Inc. Portsmouth, NH. 1993. 520p.
Bibliographies and Indexes in Women's Studies, No. 17
ISBN:0-313-26712-X, ISBN13: 978-0-313-26712-3.
Dewey:016.3054. LCCN:92-038990.

Audience: **g,l,u.** *Choice, 1993.*

Kelly, Gail, et al.   **HQ1870.9.W6548 1998**
Women in the Third World: An Encyclopedia of Contemporary
Issues. Edith H. Altbach & Eva Rathgeber (Authors), Nelly P.
Stomquist (Editor). Library Binding. Garland Publishing, Inc.
New York, NY. 1998. 720p. Garland Reference Library of
Social Science, Vol. 760 ISBN:0-8153-0150-2, ISBN13:
978-0-8153-0150-9. Dewey:305.42/09172/4. LCCN:98-014689.

Audience: **g,l,u.** *Choice, 1998.*

Kimmel, Michael S. &   **HQ1090**
Aronson, Amy
Men and Masculinities: A Social, Cultural, and Historical
Encyclopedia. Library Binding. ABC-CLIO, Inc. Santa Barbara,
CA. 2003. 800p. ISBN:1-57607-774-8, ISBN13:
978-1-57607-774-0. Dewey:305.31/03. LCCN:2003-020729.

Audience: **l,u,f.** *Choice, 2004.*

Kramarae, Cheris &   **HQ1115.R69 2000**
Spender, Dale (Editors)
Routledge International Encyclopedia of Women: Global
Women's Issues and Knowledge, Set. Paper over Boards.
Routledge. New York, NY. 2000. 2050p. ISBN:0-415-92088-4,
ISBN13. 978-0-415-92088-9. Dewey:305.4/03.
LCCN:00-045792.

Audience: **g,l,u.** *Choice, 2001.*

Krikos, Linda & Ingold, Cindy   Z7963.F44K75 2004
Women's Studies: A Recommended Bibliography. Ed. 3. Trade
Cloth. Libraries Unlimited, Inc. Westport, CT. 2004. 848p.
ISBN:1-56308-566-6, ISBN13: 978-1-56308-566-6.
Dewey:016.30542. LCCN:2004-040918.
Audience: **g,l,u,f.** *Choice, 2005.*

Lind, Amy, et al.   HQ1588
The Greenwood Encyclopedia of Women's Issues Worldwide.
Manisha Desai, Cheryl Toronto Kalny, Bahira Sherif-Trask &
Aili Mari Tripp (Authors), Lynn Walter (Editor-In-Chief). Cloth
Text. Greenwood Publishing Group, Inc. Portsmouth, NH. 2003.
2500p. ISBN:0-313-32787-4, ISBN13: 978-0-313-32787-2.
Dewey:305.42/095. LCCN:2004-695024.
Audience: **g,l,u.** *Choice, 2004.*

Olsen, Kirstin   HQ1121
Chronology of Women's History. Cloth Text. Greenwood
Publishing Group, Inc. Portsmouth, NH. 1994. 532p.
ISBN:0-313-28803-8, ISBN13: 978-0-313-28803-6.
Dewey:305.4/09. LCCN:93-050542.
Audience: **g,l,u,f.** *Choice, 1994.*

Opdycke, Sandra   HQ1410.P68 2000
The Routledge Historical Atlas of Women in America. Paper
over Boards. Routledge. New York, NY. 2000. 144p. Routledge
Atlases of American History Ser. ISBN:0-415-92132-5, ISBN13:
978-0-415-92132-9. Dewey:973/.082. LCCN:99-053346.
Audience: **g,l,u.**

Pilcher, Jane & Whelehan, Imelda   HQ1180
50 Key Concepts in Gender Studies. Cloth Text. SAGE
Publications, Inc. Thousand Oaks, CA. 2004. 216p. SAGE Key
Concepts Ser. ISBN:0-7619-7035-5, ISBN13:
978-0-7619-7035-4. Dewey:305.42. LCCN:2003-108068.
Audience: **g,l,u,f.** *Choice, 2004.*

Reinharz, Shulamit & Davidman, Lynn   HQ1180.R448 1992
Feminist Methods in Social Research. Trade Paper. Oxford
University Press, Inc. New York, NY. 1992. 422p.
ISBN:0-19-507386-X, ISBN13: 978-0-19-507386-7.
Dewey:301/.072. LCCN:91-027838.
Audience: **l,u,f.** *Choice, 1992.*

Sadik, Nafis   HB848
The State of World Population (2000): Lives Together, Worlds
Apart - Men and Women in a Time of Change. Trade Paper.
United Nations Publications. New York, NY. 2000. 76p.
ISBN:0-89714-582-8, ISBN13: 978-0-89714-582-4.
Dewey:304.6/05.
Audience: **g,l,u,f.**

Scager, Joni   G1046.E1
The Penguin Atlas of Women in the World. Ed. 3. Trade Paper.
Penguin Group (USA) Inc. New York, NY. 2003. 128p.
ISBN:0-14-200241-0, ISBN13: 978-0-14-200241-4.
Dewey:305.42/022/3.
Audience: **g,l,u.**

Snyder, Paula   HQ1587.S69 1992
The European Women's Almanac. Juliet Lodge (Foreword by).
Trade Cloth. Columbia University Press. New York, NY. 1992.
399p. ISBN:0-231-08064-6, ISBN13: 978-0-231-08064-4.
Dewey:305.4/094. LCCN:92-013451.
Audience: **u,f.** *Choice, 1993.*

Taeuber, Cynthia M. (Editor)   HQ1420.T34 1996
Statistical Handbook on Women in America. Ed. 2. Cloth Text.
Greenwood Publishing Group, Inc. Portsmouth, NH. 1996. 384p.
Oryx Statistical Handbooks Ser. ISBN:1-57356-005-7, ISBN13:
978-1-57356-005-4. Dewey:305.4/0973/021. LCCN:96-001521.
Audience: **l,u.** *Choice, 1996.*

Tierney, Helen (Editor)   HQ1115
Women's Studies Encyclopedia. Cloth Text. Greenwood
Publishing Group, Inc. Portsmouth, NH. 1999. 1640p.
ISBN:0-313-29620-0, ISBN13: 978-0-313-29620-8.
Dewey:305.403. LCCN:98-014236.
Audience: **g,l,u,f.** *Choice, 2000.*

Vrato, Elizabeth & Running Press Staff   PN60815 .N49
The New Quotable Woman. Trade Cloth. Running Press Book
Publishers. Philadelphia, PA. 2003. 128p. Irresistible Miniature
Editionstm Ser., :Little Books to Treasure Ser.
ISBN:0-7624-1619-X, ISBN13: 978-0-7624-1619-6.
Dewey:082/.082.
Audience: **g,l,u,f.**

Ware, Susan & Braukman, Stacy (Editors)   CT3260.N5725 2004
Notable American Women: A Biographical Dictionary:
Completing the Twentieth Century. Trade Cloth. Harvard
University Press. Cambridge, MA. 2005. 768p. Notable
American Women Ser. ISBN:0-674-01488-X, ISBN13:
978-0-674-01488-6. Dewey:920.72/0973 B. LCCN:2004-048859.
Audience: **g,l,u,f.** *Choice, 2005.*

Weatherford, Doris (Editor)   HQ1410.H58 2003
A History of Women in the United States: State-By-State
Reference. Trade Cloth. Scholastic Library Publishing. Danbury,
CT. 2003. ISBN:0-7172-5805-X, ISBN13: 978-0-7172-5805-5.
Dewey:305.4/0973. LCCN:2003-049299.
Audience: **g,l,u.** *Choice, 2004.*

Worell, Judith (Editor)   HQ1115.E43 2001
Encyclopedia of Women and Gender: Sex Similarities and
Differences and the Impact of Society on Gender. Trade Cloth.
Elsevier Science & Technology Books. Saint Louis, MO. 2001.
1256p. ISBN:0-12-227245-5, ISBN13: 978-0-12-227245-5.
Dewey:305.4/03. LCCN:2001-088812.
Audience: **l,u,f.** *Choice, 2002.*

Feminist and Gender Theory

                                                      HQ1190
☐ Feminist Theory.
http://www.cddc.vt.edu/feminism/
Audience: **g,l,u.**

Alcoff, Linda & Potter, Elizabeth (Editors)   HQ1190.F45 1993
Feminist Epistemologies. UK-B Format Paperback. Routledge.
New York, NY. 1992. 320p. Thinking Gender Ser.
ISBN:0-415-90451-X, ISBN13: 978-0-415-90451-3.
Dewey:305.4201. LCCN:92-011309.
Audience: **l,u.**

Andermahr, Sonya, et al.   HQ1115.L68 1997
A Concise Glossary of Feminist Theory. Terry Lovell & Carol
Wolkowitz (Authors). Paper Text. Oxford University Press, Inc.
New York, NY. 1997. 296p. An Arnold Publication Ser.

ISBN:0-340-59663-5, ISBN13: 978-0-340-59663-0.
Dewey:305.42/01. LCCN:97-013574.

Audience: **l,u.** *Choice, 1998.*

Andermahr, Sonya, et al.   **HQ1190.A53 1997**
A Glossary of Feminist Theory. Terry Lovell & Carol
Wolkowitz (Authors). Cloth Text. Oxford University Press, Inc.
New York, NY. 1997. 356p. An Arnold Publication Ser.
ISBN:0-340-59662-7, ISBN13: 978-0-340-59662-3.
Dewey:305.42/01. LCCN:97-003800.

Audience: **g,l.**

Beauvoir, Simone de   **HQ1154**
The Second Sex. H. N. Pashley (Editor, Translator), Margaret
Crosland (Introduction by). Trade Cloth. Alfred A. Knopf Inc.
New York, NY. 1993. 848p. Everyman's Library
ISBN:0-679-42016-9, ISBN13: 978-0-679-42016-3.
Dewey:305.4/2. LCCN:92-054303.

Audience: **l,u,f.** *B*

Chodorow, Nancy Julia   **HQ759.C56 1999**
The Reproduction of Mothering: Psychoanalysis and the
Sociology of Gender. Ed. 2. Trade Paper. University of
California Press. Berkeley, CA. 1999. 284p.
ISBN:0-520-22155-9, ISBN13: 978-0-520-22155-0.
Dewey:306.874/3. LCCN:2001-266933.

Audience: **l,u,f.** *B*

Code, Lorraine (Editor)   **HQ1190**
Encyclopedia of Feminist Theories. Trade Paper. Routledge.
New York, NY. 2003. 560p. World Reference Ser.
ISBN:0-415-30885-2, ISBN13: 978-0-415-30885-4.
Dewey:305.4/2/03.

Audience: **l,u.** *Choice, 2001.*

Collins, Patricia Hill   **HQ1426.C633 2000**
[e] Black Feminist Thought: Knowledge, Consciousness, and the
Politics of Empowerment. Ed. 10. E-Book. Routledge. New
York, NY. 2000. ISBN:0-203-90005-7, ISBN13:
978-0-203-90005-5. Dewey:305.42/08996073.

Audience: **l,u.**

Echols, Alice   **HQ1421.E25 1989**
Daring to Be Bad: Radical Feminism in America, 1967-1975.
Trade Paper. University of Minnesota Press. Minneapolis, MN.
1989. 430p. ISBN:0-8166-1787-2, ISBN13: 978-0-8166-1787-6.
Dewey:305.4/2/097309047. LCCN:89-005058.

Audience: **u,f.** *Choice, 1990.*

England, Paula (Editor)   **HQ1190.T48 1993**
Theory on Gender: Feminism on Theory. Trade Cloth. Aldine
Transaction. Somerset, NJ. 1993. 377p. Social Institutions and
Social Change Ser. ISBN:0-202-30437-X, ISBN13:
978-0-202-30437-3. Dewey:305.42/01. LCCN:92-027886.

Audience: **u,f.** *Choice, 1993.*

Fraser, Nancy   **HM24.F732 1989**
Unruly Practices: Power, Discourse and Gender in
Contemporary Social Theory. Trade Paper. University of
Minnesota Press. Minneapolis, MN. 1989. 208p.
ISBN:0-8166-1778-3, ISBN13: 978-0-8166-1778-4.
Dewey:305.4201. LCCN:89-032093.

Audience: **l,u.**

Fraser, Nancy &   **HQ1190.R48 1992**
  Bartky, Sandra L. (Editors)
Revaluing French Feminism: Critical Essays on Difference,
Agency, and Culture. Trade Paper. Indiana University Press.

Bloomington, IN. 1992. 208p. ISBN:0-253-20682-0, ISBN13:
978-0-253-20682-4. Dewey:305.42/01. LCCN:91-008415.

Audience: **l,u,f.**

Freeman, Jo   **HQ1426.W62 1995**
Women: A Feminist Perspective. Ed. 5. Paper Text.
McGraw-Hill Higher Education. Burr Ridge, IL. 1994. 704p.
ISBN:1-55934-111-4, ISBN13: 978-1-55934-111-0.
Dewey:305.42/0973. LCCN:94-016032.

Audience: **l,u,f.** *B*

Garcia, Mario &   **HQ1421.C52 1997**
  Garcia, Alma (Editors)
Chicana Feminist Thought: The Basic Historical Writings. Paper
over Boards. Routledge. New York, NY. 1997. 416p.
ISBN:0-415-91800-6, ISBN13: 978-0-415-91800-8.
Dewey:305.48/868/72073. LCCN:96-049916.

Audience: **g,l,u,f.**

Gottfried, Heidi   **HQ1181.U5F449 1996**
  (Editor)
Feminism and Social Change: Bridging Theory and Practice.
Trade Paper. University of Illinois Press. Champaign, IL. 1995.
296p. ISBN:0-252-06495-X, ISBN13: 978-0-252-06495-1.
Dewey:305.42/01. LCCN:95-005922.

Audience: **l,u,f.** *Choice, 1996.*

Guy-Sheftall, Beverly   **E185.86.W927 1995**
  (Editor)
Words of Fire: An Anthology of African-American Feminist
Thought. Johnnetta B. Cole (Epilogue by). Trade Paper. New
Press, The. New York, NY. 1995. 608p. ISBN:1-56584-256-1,
ISBN13: 978-1-56584-256-4. Dewey:818/.08. LCCN:95-069570.

Audience: **l,u.**

Hirsch, Marianne &   **HQ1426.C634 1990**
  Keller, Evelyn F. (Editors)
Conflicts in Feminism. UK-B Format Paperback. Routledge.
New York, NY. 1990. 410p. ISBN:0-415-90178-2, ISBN13:
978-0-415-90178-9. Dewey:305.42/0973. LCCN:90-034999.

Audience: **u,f.** *Choice, 1991.*

hooks, bell   **E185.86**
Ain't I a Woman: Black Women and Feminism. Trade Cloth.
South End Press. Cambridge, MA. 1981. 205p.
ISBN:0-89608-130-3, ISBN13: 978-0-89608-130-7.
Dewey:305.4/8/896073. LCCN:81-051392.

Audience: **g,l,u.**

hooks, bell   **E185.86**
Talking Back: Thinking Feminist, Thinking Black. Trade Cloth.
South End Press. Cambridge, MA. 1989. 186p.
ISBN:0-89608-353-5, ISBN13: 978-0-89608-353-0.
Dewey:305.4/8896/073. LCCN:88-042874.

Audience: **l,u.**

hooks, bell   **HQ1426.H675 2000**
Feminist Theory: From Margin to Center. Ed. 2. Manning
Marable (Contribution by). Trade Cloth. South End Press.
Cambridge, MA. 2000. 179p. Classics Ser., No. 5
ISBN:0-89608-614-3, ISBN13: 978-0-89608-614-2.
Dewey:305.42/0973. LCCN:99-053683.

Audience: **l,u,f.** *B*

Humm, Maggie   **HQ1115.H86 1995**
The Dictionary of Feminist Theory. Ed. 2. Trade Cloth. Ohio
State University Press. Columbus, OH. 1995. 376p.

ISBN:0-8142-0666-2, ISBN13: 978-0-8142-0666-9.
Dewey:305.4/2/01. LCCN:94-048253.
Audience: **l,u.** *Choice, 1995, 1990.*

James, Stanlie M. &   **HQ1190.T47 1993**
  Busia, Abena P. (Editors)
Theorizing Black Feminisms: The Visionary Pragmatism of
Black Women. Johnnetta B. Cole (Foreword by). Paper over
Boards. Routledge. New York, NY. 1993. 312p.
ISBN:0-415-07336-7, ISBN13: 978-0-415-07336-3.
Dewey:305.4208996. LCCN:92-047346.
Audience: **g,l,u.**

Lancaster, Roger & Di   **GN479.65.G475 1997**
  Leonardo, Micaela (Editors)
The Gender/Sexuality Reader: Culture, History, Political
Economy. UK-B Format Paperback. Routledge. New York, NY.
1997. 584p. ISBN:0-415-91005-6, ISBN13: 978-0-415-91005-7.
Dewey:305.3. LCCN:96-039187.
Audience: **l,u,f.**

Lewis, Reina & Mills,   **HQ1150**
  Sara (Editors)
Feminist Postcolonial Theory: A Reader. Cloth Text. Routledge.
New York, NY. 2003. 768p. ISBN:0-415-94274-8, ISBN13:
978-0-415-94274-4. Dewey:305.42.
Audience: **l,u,f.**

McCann, Carole R. &   **HQ1190.F46346 2002**
  Kim, Seung-Kyung (Editors)
Feminist Theory Reader: Local and Global Perspectives. Paper
over Boards. Routledge. New York, NY. 2002. 520p.
ISBN:0-415-93152-5, ISBN13: 978-0-415-93152-6.
Dewey:305.42/01. LCCN:2002-005200.
Audience: **l,u,f.**

Mohanty, Chandra   **HQ1870.9.M64 2003**
  Talpade
Feminism Without Borders: Decolonizing Theory, Practicing
Solidarity. Trade Cloth. Duke University Press. Durham, NC.
2003. 320p. ISBN:0-8223-3010-5, ISBN13: 978-0-8223-3010-3.
Dewey:305.42. LCCN:2002-013266.
Audience: **u,f.**

Nicholson, Linda J.   **HQ1206.F453 1990**
  (Editor, Introduction by)
Feminism - Postmodernism. Trade Cloth. Routledge. New York,
NY. 1989. 352p. ISBN:0-415-90058-1, ISBN13:
978-0-415-90058-4. Dewey:305.42/01. LCCN:89-006432.
Audience: **u,f.**

Smith, Bonnie G.   **HQ1154.G56 2000**
  (Editor)
Global Feminisms: A Survey of Issues and Controversies. Paper
over Boards. Routledge. New York, NY. 2000. 336p. Rewriting
Histories Ser. ISBN:0-415-18490-8, ISBN13:
978-0-415-18490-8. Dewey:305.42. LCCN:99-089441.
Audience: **g,l,u,f.** *Choice, 2001.*

Tong, Rosemarie   **HQ1206.T65 1998**
  Putnam
Feminist Thought: A More Comprehensive Introduction. Ed. 2.
Trade Paper. Westview Press. Boulder, CO. 1998. 368p.
ISBN:0-8133-3295-8, ISBN13: 978-0-8133-3295-6.
Dewey:305.4201. LCCN:97-046430.
Audience: **l,u.**

Trujillo, Carla   **E184.M5L58 1998**
Living Chicana Theory. Trade Cloth. Third Woman Press.
Oakland, CA. 1997. ISBN:0-943219-15-9, ISBN13:
978-0-943219-15-8. Dewey:305.48/868/72073.
LCCN:97-038523.
Audience: **u,f.**

Walker, Rebecca Edby   **HQ1426.T623 1995**
To Be Real: Telling the Truth and Changing the Face of
Feminism. Trade Paper. Doubleday Publishing. New York, NY.
1995. 336p. ISBN:0-385-47262-5, ISBN13: 978-0-385-47262-3.
Dewey:305.42. LCCN:95-014412.
Audience: **g,l,u.**

Walters, Suzanna D.   **HM101.W225 1995**
Material Girls: Making Sense of Feminist Cultural Theory.
Trade Paper. University of California Press. Berkeley, CA. 1995.
232p. ISBN:0-520-08978-2, ISBN13: 978-0-520-08978-5.
Dewey:305.42/01. LCCN:94-029007.
Audience: **g,l,u,f.** *Choice, 1995.*

Gender Roles. Femininity. Masculinity

Adams, Rachel &   **HQ1088.M377 2001**
  Savran, David (Editors)
The Masculinity Studies Reader. Trade Paper. Blackwell
Publishing, Inc. Malden, MA. 2002. 432p. Keyworks in Cultural
Studies, Vol. 5 ISBN:0-631-22660-5, ISBN13:
978-0-631-22660-4. Dewey:305.31. LCCN:2001-043229.
Audience: **g,l,u,f.**

August, Eugene R.   **Z7164.M49A84 1994**
The New Men's Studies: A Selected and Annotated
Interdisciplinary Bibliography. Ed. 2. Book, Other. Libraries
Unlimited, Inc. Westport, CT. 1995. 440p. ISBN:1-56308-084-2,
ISBN13: 978-1-56308-084-5. Dewey:016.30531.
LCCN:94-032454.
Audience: **l,u,f.** *Choice, 1995.*

Barker-Benfield, G. J.   **HQ18.U5.B3**
The Horrors of the Half-Known Life: Male Attitudes Toward
Women and Sexuality in Nineteenth-Century America. Trade
Cloth. Harper & Row Ltd. London, 1976. xiv, 352p.
ISBN:0-06-010224-1, ISBN13: 978-0-06-010224-1.
Dewey:301.41/0973. LCCN:75-006327.
Audience: **l,u,f.** *B*

Berger, Maurice   **HQ1090.C66 1995**
  (Editor), et al.
Constructing Masculinity. Brian Wallis & Simon Watson
(Editors). Paper over Boards. Routledge. New York, NY. 1995.
320p. ISBN:0-415-91052-8, ISBN13: 978-0-415-91052-1.
Dewey:305.3. LCCN:95-022214.
Audience: **g,l,u,f.**

Bordo, Susan   **HQ1090**
The Male Body: A New Look at Men in Public and in Private.
Trade Paper. Farrar, Straus & Giroux. New York, NY. 2000.
368p. ISBN:0-374-52732-6, ISBN13: 978-0-374-52732-7.
Dewey:305.31.
Audience: **g,l,u,f.**

Brod, Harry (Editor)   **HQ1088.M35 1987**
The Making of Masculinities: The New Men's Studies. Cloth
Text. Routledge. New York, NY. 1987. 304p.
ISBN:0-04-497035-8, ISBN13: 978-0-04-497035-4.
Dewey:305.3/1. LCCN:86-028796.
Audience: **g,l,u,f.** *Choice, 1988.*

Chant, Sylvia & Craske,   HQ1075.5.L29C48 2003
  Nikki
Gender in Latin America. Trade Cloth. Rutgers University Press.
Piscataway, NJ. 2004. 320p. ISBN:0-8135-3196-9, ISBN13:
978-0-8135-3196-0. Dewey:305.3/098. LCCN:2003-266100.
                                Audience: **u,f.** *Choice, 2003.*

Connell, R. W.   HQ1075.C658 2002
Gender. Trade Paper. Polity Press. Cambridge, 2002. 184p. Short
Introductions Ser. ISBN:0-7456-2716-1, ISBN13:
978-0-7456-2716-8. Dewey:305.3/07/2. LCCN:2001-004496.
                                Audience: **g,l,u,f.**

Connell, R. W.   HQ1088 .C66 2005
Masculinities. Ed. 2. Trade Paper. University of California Press.
Berkeley, CA. 2005. 349p. ISBN:0-520-24698-5, ISBN13:
978-0-520-24698-0. Dewey:305.3. LCCN:2005-050590.
                                Audience: **g,l,u,f.**

Essed, Philomenia &   HQ1075.C656 2005
  Goldberg, David Theo (Editors)
Companion to Gender Studies. Trade Cloth. Blackwell
Publishing, Inc. Malden, MA. 2004. 576p. Blackwell
Companions in Cultural Studies, Vol. 8 ISBN:0-631-22109-3,
ISBN13: 978-0-631-22109-8. Dewey:305.3/072.
LCCN:2004-006865.
                        Audience: **g,l,u,f.** *Choice, 2005.*

Faludi, Susan   HQ1090.3.F35 1999
Stiffed: The Betrayal of the American Man. Trade Cloth.
HarperCollins Publishers. New York, NY. 1999. 662p.
ISBN:0-688-12299-X, ISBN13: 978-0-688-12299-7.
Dewey:305.31/0973. LCCN:99-035504.
                        Audience: **g,l,u,f.** *Choice, 2000.*

Flood, Michael   HQ1088
  ▢ The Men's Bibliography.
http://mensbiblio.xyonline.net/
Ed. 14. ISBN:0-646-18088-6, ISBN13: 978-0-646-18088-5.
                                Audience: **g,l,u,f.**

Foucault, Michel   HQ16
A History of Sexuality: An Introduction, Vol. 1. Trade Paper.
Knopf Publishing Group. New York, NY. 1990. 176p.
ISBN:0-679-72469-9, ISBN13: 978-0-679-72469-8.
Dewey:306.7/091821. LCCN:79-007460.
                                Audience: **u,f.**

Gardiner, Judith Kegan   HQ1088.M375 2001
Masculinity Studies and Feminist Theory. Trade Cloth.
Columbia University Press. New York, NY. 2001. 336p.
ISBN:0-231-12278-0, ISBN13: 978-0-231-12278-8.
Dewey:305.31/07. LCCN:2001-047017.
                        Audience: **u,f.** *Choice, 2002.*

Halberstam, Judith   HQ75.5.H33 1998
Female Masculinity. Trade Cloth. Duke University Press.
Durham, NC. 1998. 352p. ISBN:0-8223-2226-9, ISBN13:
978-0-8223-2226-9. Dewey:305.48/9664. LCCN:98-019527.
                        Audience: **u,f.** *Choice, 1999.*

Johnson, Allan G.   HQ1075.J64 2005
The Gender Knot: Unraveling Our Patriarchal Legacy. Ed. 2.
Trade Cloth. Temple University Press. Philadelphia, PA. 2005.
320p. ISBN:1-59213-382-7, ISBN13: 978-1-59213-382-6.
Dewey:305.3. LCCN:2004-062081.
                        Audience: **g,l,u.** *Choice, 1997.*

Kimmel, Michael S.   HQ1075
The Gendered Society: Identities, Behaviors, and Society. Ed. 2.
Paper Text. Oxford University Press, Inc. New York, NY. 2005.
ISBN:0-19-522145-1, ISBN13: 978-0-19-522145-9.
Dewey:305.3.
                                Audience: **l,u,f.**

Kimmel, Michael S.   HQ1090.3.K552 2005
The History of Men: Essays on the History of American and
British Masculinities. Cloth Text. State University of New York
Press. Albany, NY. 2005. 276p. ISBN:0-7914-6339-7, ISBN13:
978-0-7914-6339-0. Dewey:305.31/0973. LCCN:2004-060670.
                                Audience: **u,f.**

Kimmel, Michael S.   HQ1090.3.K553 2005
Manhood in America. Ed. 2. Trade Paper. Oxford University
Press, Inc. New York, NY. 2005. 352p. ISBN:0-19-518113-1,
ISBN13: 978-0-19-518113-5. Dewey:305.31/0973.
LCCN:2005-047346.
                                Audience: **g,l,u,f.**

Lorber, Judith   HQ1075.L667
Paradoxes of Gender. Trade Paper. Yale University Press.
Cumberland, RI. 1995. 435p. ISBN:0-300-06497-7, ISBN13:
978-0-300-06497-1. Dewey:305.3. LCCN:93-023459.
                        Audience: **l,u,f.** *Choice, 1994.*

Moghadam, Valentine   HQ1233.I34 1993
  M. (Editor)
Identity Politics and Women: Cultural Reassertions and
Feminisms in International Perspective. Trade Paper. Westview
Press. Boulder, CO. 1993. 458p. ISBN:0-8133-8691-8, ISBN13:
978-0-8133-8691-1. Dewey:305.42. LCCN:93-028018.
                        Audience: **l,u,f.** *Choice, 1994.*

Murphy, Peter F.   HQ1090.F46 2004
  (Editor)
Feminism and Masculinities. Trade Paper. Oxford University
Press, Inc. New York, NY. 2004. 304p. Oxford Readings in
Feminism Ser. ISBN:0-19-926724-3, ISBN13:
978-0-19-926724-8. Dewey:305.32. LCCN:2004-050074.
                                Audience: **g,u,f.**

Noble, Jean Bobby   PN56.G45N63 2004
Masculinities Without Men?: Female Masculinity in
Twentieth-Century Fictions. Trade Paper. University of British
Columbia Press. Vancouver, BC. 2004. 222p. Sexuality Studies
Ser. ISBN:0-7748-0997-3, ISBN13: 978-0-7748-0997-9.
Dewey:809/.93353. LCCN:2004-401596.
                                Audience: **g,l,u,f.**

O'Leary, Virginia   HQ1206.W875 1985
  (Editor), et al.
Women, Gender and Social Psychology. Rhoda K. Unger &
Barbara S. Wallston (Editors). Cloth Text. Lawrence Erlbaum
Associates, Inc. Mahwah, NJ. 1985. 400p. ISBN:0-89859-447-2,
ISBN13: 978-0-89859-447-8. Dewey:305.4. LCCN:84-023114.
                        Audience: **l,u,f.** 𝓑 *Choice, 1985.*

Oyewumi, Oyeronke   HQ1075.5.A35A376
  (Editor)
African Gender Studies. Cloth over Boards. Palgrave
Macmillan. New York, NY. 2005. 448p. ISBN:1-4039-6282-0,
ISBN13: 978-1-4039-6282-9. Dewey:305.3/096.
LCCN:2004-054696.
                                Audience: **l,u,f.**

Pease, Bob & Pringle,   HQ1090.D42 2001
Keith (Editors)
A Man's World?: Changing Men's Practices in a Globalized
World. Cloth over Boards. Zed Books, Ltd. London, 2002. 304p.
Global Masculinities Ser. ISBN:1-85649-911-1, ISBN13:
978-1-85649-911-8. Dewey:305.31. LCCN:2001-026236.
Audience: **l,u,f.** *Choice, 2003, 2002.*

Rotundo, E. Anthony   HQ1090.3
American Manhood: Transformations in Masculinity from the
Revolution to the Modern Era. Trade Paper. Basic Books. New
York, NY. 1994. 396p. ISBN:0-465-00169-6, ISBN13:
978-0-465-00169-9. Dewey:305.32/0973. LCCN:92-053247.
Audience: **l,u,f.** *Choice, 1993.*

Sanday, Peggy Reeves   HQ1075 .S26
Female Power and Male Dominance: On the Origins of Sexual
Inequality. Trade Paper. Cambridge University Press. New York,
NY. 1981. 368p. ISBN:0-521-28075-3, ISBN13:
978-0-521-28075-4. Dewey:305.3/0880633. LCCN:80-018461.
Audience: **u,f.**

Segal, Lynne   HQ1090.S43 1990
Slow Motion: Changing Masculinities, Changing Men. Trade
Paper. Rutgers University Press. Piscataway, NJ. 1990. 396p.
ISBN:0-8135-1620-X, ISBN13: 978-0-8135-1620-2.
Dewey:305.31. LCCN:90-041862.
Audience: **g,l,u,f.** *Choice, 1991.*

Seidler, Victor J.   HQ1090.S444 2005
Transforming Masculinities. Trade Paper. Routledge. New York,
NY. 2005. CLXXX, 28p. ISBN:0-415-37074-4, ISBN13:
978-0-415-37074-5. Dewey:305.31. LCCN:2005-002733.
Audience: **g,u,f.**

Sigel, Roberta S.   HQ1075.5.U6S56 1996
Ambition and Accommodation: How Women View Gender
Relations. Trade Cloth. University of Chicago Press. Chicago,
IL. 1996. 250p. ISBN:0-226-75695-5, ISBN13:
978-0-226-75695-0. Dewey:305.3. LCCN:95-039468.
Audience: **l,u,f.** *Choice, 1996.*

Walsh, Mary R.   HQ1206.W8748 1997
(Editor)
Women, Men and Gender: Ongoing Debates. Trade Paper. Yale
University Press. Cumberland, RI. 1996. 472p.
ISBN:0-300-06938-3, ISBN13: 978-0-300-06938-9.
Dewey:305.3. LCCN:96-016540.
Audience: **l,u.**

Activism and Social Movements. Suffrage

Agosín, Marjorie   HQ1236.W5852 2001
(Editor)
Women, Gender and Human Rights: A Global Perspective. Cloth
Text. Rutgers University Press. Piscataway, NJ. 2001. 320p.
ISBN:0-8135-2982-4, ISBN13: 978-0-8135-2982-0.
Dewey:305.42. LCCN:2001-019296.
Audience: **l,u.**

Anderson, Bonnie S.   HQ1154
Joyous Greetings: The First International Women's Movement,
1830-1860. Trade Cloth. HarperCollins Publishers. New York,
NY. 1999. 256p. ISBN:0-06-017072-7, ISBN13:
978-0-06-017072-1. Dewey:305.42/09/034.
Audience: **u,f.** *Choice, 2000.*

Baker, Jean H. (Editor)   JK1896.V67 2002
Votes for Women: The Struggle for Suffrage Revisited. Trade
Paper. Oxford University Press, Inc. New York, NY. 2002. 214p.
Viewpoints on American Culture Ser. ISBN:0-19-513017-0,
ISBN13: 978-0-19-513017-1. Dewey:324.6/23/0973.
LCCN:2001-036768.
Audience: **g,l,u,f.** *Choice, 2003, 2002.*

Basu, Amrita   HQ1101.C46 1995
Challenge of Local Feminisms: Women's Movements in Global
Perspective. C. Elizabeth McGrory (Contribution by). Trade
Paper. Westview Press. Boulder, CO. 1995. 510p. Social Change
in Global Perspective Ser. ISBN:0-8133-2628-1, ISBN13:
978-0-8133-2628-3. Dewey:305.42. LCCN:95-007664.
Audience: **l,u.**

Berkeley, Kathleen   HQ1421
The Women's Liberation Movement in America. Cloth Text.
Greenwood Publishing Group, Inc. Portsmouth, NH. 1999. 256p.
Guides to Historic Events of the Twentieth Century Ser.
ISBN:0-313-29875-0, ISBN13: 978-0-313-29875-2.
Dewey:305.42/0973. LCCN:99-025007.
Audience: **l,u.** *Choice, 2001.*

Bouvard, Marguerite G.   HV6322.3.A7B68 1994
Revolutionizing Motherhood: The Mothers of the Plaza De
Mayo. Book, Other. Rowman & Littlefield Publishers, Inc.
Lanham, MD. 1994. 278p. Latin American Silhouettes Ser.
ISBN:0-8420-2486-7, ISBN13: 978-0-8420-2486-0.
Dewey:323.4/9/0982. LCCN:93-041428.
Audience: **g,l,u.** *Choice, 1994.*

Chafetz, Janet S. &   HQ1121 .C45
Dworkin, Anthony G.
Female Revolt: Women's Movements in World and Historical
Perspective. Trade Paper. Rowman & Littlefield Publishers, Inc.
Lanham, MD. 1986. 272p. ISBN:0-8476-7393-6, ISBN13:
978-0-8476-7393-3. Dewey:305.4/2/09.
Audience: **l,u.**

Collier-Thomas, Betty   E185.61.S615 2001
& Franklin, V. P. (Editors)
Sisters in the Struggle: African-American Women in the Civil
Rights and Black Power Movements. Trade Cloth. New York
University Press. New York, NY. 2001. 376p.
ISBN:0-8147-1602-4, ISBN13: 978-0-8147-1602-1.
Dewey:323.1/196073/0922. LCCN:2001-001550.
Audience: **g,l,u.** *Choice, 2002.*

D'Ltri, Patricia W.   HQ1154.D55 1999
Cross Currents in the International Women's Movement,
1848-1948. Trade Cloth. University of Wisconsin Press.
Chicago, IL. 1999. xii, 267p. ISBN:0-87972-781-0, ISBN13:
978-0-87972-781-9. Dewey:305.42/09. LCCN:98-040947.
Audience: **u,f.** *Choice, 1999.*

Flexner, Eleanor &   HQ1410.F6 1996
Fitzpatrick, Ellen
Century of Struggle: The Woman's Rights Movement in the
United States. Ed. 3. Trade Paper. Harvard University Press.
Cambridge, MA. 1996. 432p. ISBN:0-674-10653-9, ISBN13:
978-0-674-10653-6. Dewey:305.42/0973. LCCN:96-005651.
Audience: **g,l,u,f.** *B*

Frost-Knappman,   JK1896.F77 2005
Elizabeth & Cullen-DuPont, Kathryn
Women's Suffrage in America: An Eyewitness History. Ed. 2.
Trade Cloth. Facts On File, Inc. New York, NY. 2005. 512p.

Eyewitness History Ser. ISBN:0-8160-5693-5, ISBN13: 978-0-8160-5693-4. Dewey:324.6/23/0973. LCCN:2004-043339.

Audience: **g,l,u.**

Gordon, Ann D., et al.   **JK1924.A47 1997**
African American Women and the Vote, 1837-1965. Betty Collier-Thomas & John H. Bracey (Authors), Arlene Voski Avakian & Joyce Avrech Berkman (Editors). Trade Paper. University of Massachusetts Press. Amherst, MA. 1997. 232p. ISBN:1-55849-059-0, ISBN13: 978-1-55849-059-8. Dewey:324.6/23/08996073. LCCN:96-014881.

Audience: **g,l,u.**

Green, Elna C.   **JK1896.G695 1997**
Southern Strategies: Southern Women and the Woman Suffrage Question. Trade Paper. University of North Carolina Press. Chapel Hill, NC. 1997. 312p. ISBN:0-8078-4641-4, ISBN13: 978-0-8078-4641-4. Dewey:324.6/23/0975. LCCN:96-036992.

Audience: **l,u,f.** *Choice, 1997.*

Hannam, June   **JF851.H28 2000**
International Encyclopedia of Women's Suffrage. Katherine Holden & Mitzi Auchterlonie (Editors). Library Binding. ABC-CLIO, Inc. Santa Barbara, CA. 2000. 0380p. ISBN:1-57607-064-6, ISBN13: 978-1-57607-064-2. Dewey:324.6/23/03. LCCN:00-011032.

Audience: **l,u.** *Choice, 2001.*

Hardy, Gayle J.   **JC599.U5.H273 1993**
American Women Civil Rights Activists: Biobibliographies of 68 Leaders, 1825-1992. Trade Cloth. McFarland & Company, Incorporated Publishers. Jefferson, NC. 1993. 503p. ISBN:0-89950-773-5, ISBN13: 978-0-89950-773-6. Dewey:323.34092273. LCCN:92-56649.

Audience: **g,l,u.** *Choice, 1994.*

Jordan, Ellen R.   **HD6135.J667 1999**
Women's Movement and Women's Employment in Nineteenth Century Britain. Paper over Boards. Routledge. New York, NY. 1999. 288p. Research in Gender and History Ser. ISBN:0-415-18951-9, ISBN13: 978-0-415-18951-4. Dewey:331.4/0941/09034. LCCN:98-051633.

Audience: **u,f.** *Choice, 2000.*

Kallen, Stuart A.   **E185.61.K3385 2005**
Women of the Civil Rights Movement. Library Binding, Paper over Boards. Thomson Gale. Farmington Hills, MI. 2005. 112p. Women in History Ser. ISBN:1-59018-569-2, ISBN13: 978-1-59018-569-8. Dewey:323.0973. LCCN:2004-023822.

Audience: **g,l,u,f.**

Katzenstein, Mary F.   **HQ1421.K27 1998**
Faithful and Fearless: Moving Feminist Protest Inside the Church and Military. Trade Cloth. Princeton University Press. Princeton, NJ. 1998. 284p. Princeton Studies in American Politics ISBN:0-691-05852-0, ISBN13: 978-0-691-05852-8. Dewey:305.42/0973. LCCN:98-005516.

Audience: **l,u,f.** *Choice, 1999.*

Kern, Kathi   **HQ1413**
Mrs. Stanton's Bible: Elizabeth Cady Stanton and the Woman's Bible. Book, Other. Cornell University Press. Ithaca, NY. 2001. 304p. ISBN:0-8014-3191-3, ISBN13: 978-0-8014-3191-3. Dewey:305.42/092. LCCN:00-010756.

Audience: **g,l,u,f.** *Choice, 2001.*

Kumar, Radha   **HQ1743.K85 1993**
The History of Doing: The Women's Movement in India. Trade Paper. Analytical Psychology Club of San Francisco, Inc. San

Francisco, CA. 1994. 203p. ISBN:0-86091-665-0, ISBN13: 978-0-86091-665-9. Dewey:305.42/0954. LCCN:93-036715.

Audience: **u,f.** *Choice, 1994.*

Lumsden, Linda J.   **JK1896.L86 1997**
Rampant Women: Suffragists and the Right of Assembly. Cloth Text. University of Tennessee Press. Knoxville, TN. 1997. 320p. ISBN:0-87049-986-6, ISBN13: 978-0-87049-986-9. Dewey:324.6/23/0973. LCCN:97-004627.

Audience: **l,u,f.** *Choice, 1998.*

Marilley, Suzanne M.   **JK1896.M37 1996**
Woman Suffrage and the Origins of Liberal Feminism in the United States, 1820-1920. Trade Cloth. Harvard University Press. Cambridge, MA. 1997. 304p. ISBN:0-674-95465-3, ISBN13: 978-0-674-95465-6. Dewey:324.6/23/0973. LCCN:96-026328.

Audience: **l,u,f.** *Choice, 1997.*

Mattingly, Carol   **HV5229.M37 1998**
Well-Tempered Women: Nineteenth-Century Temperance Rhetoric. Trade Cloth. Southern Illinois University Press. Carbondale, IL. 1999. 272p. ISBN:0-8093-2209-9, ISBN13: 978-0-8093-2209-1. Dewey:363.4/1/097309034. LCCN:98-016297.

Audience: **l,u,f.** *Choice, 1999.*

Molyneux, Maxine   **HQ1120.L29**
Women's Movements in International Perspective: Latin America and Beyond. Trade Paper. Institute of Latin American Studies. London, 2004. 244p. ISBN:1-900039-58-3, ISBN13: 978-1-900039-58-1. Dewey:305.42/098.

Audience: **l,u.** *Choice, 2001.*

Morgan, Robin (Editor)   **HQ1154.S54 1996**
Sisterhood Is Global: The International Women's Movement Anthology. Trade Paper. Feminist Press at The City University of New York. New York, NY. 1996. 832p. ISBN:1-55861-160-6, ISBN13: 978-1-55861-160-3. Dewey:305.42. LCCN:96-038456.

Audience: **g,l,u.**

Morgan, Robin (Editor,   **HQ1154.S539 2003**
Compiled by)
Sisterhood Is Forever: The Women's Anthology for a New Millennium. Trade Paper. Simon & Schuster. New York, NY. 2003. 640p. ISBN:0-7434-6627-6, ISBN13: 978-0-7434-6627-1. Dewey:305.42/0973. LCCN:2003-271791.

Audience: **g,l,u.**

Pardo, Mary   **HN80.M66P37 1998**
Mexican American Women Activists: Identity and Resistance in Two Los Angeles Communities. Trade Cloth. Temple University Press. Philadelphia, PA. 1998. 256p. ISBN:1-56639-572-0, ISBN13: 978-1-56639-572-4. Dewey:305.42/08968/7207949. LCCN:97-013960.

Audience: **u,f.** *Choice, 1998.*

Rhodes, Jane   **E185.97.C32R48 1998**
Mary Ann Shadd Cary: The Black Press and Protest in the Nineteenth Century. Library Binding. Indiana University Press. Bloomington, IN. 1998. 304p. ISBN:0-253-33446-2, ISBN13: 978-0-253-33446-6. Dewey:[B]. LCCN:98-019997.

Audience: **l,u,f.** *Choice, 1999.*

Rupp, Leila J.   HQ1154.R86 1997
Worlds of Women: The Making of an International Women's Movement. Cloth Text. Princeton University Press. Princeton, NJ. 1997. 328p. ISBN:0-691-01676-3, ISBN13: 978-0-691-01676-4. Dewey:305.42/09. LCCN:97-014449.
Audience: **l,u.**

Schultz, Debra L.   E185.61.S364 2001
Going South: Jewish Women in the Civil Rights Movement. Trade Cloth. New York University Press. New York, NY. 2001. 252p. ISBN:0-8147-9774-1, ISBN13: 978-0-8147-9774-7. Dewey:323.1/196073. LCCN:00-012211.
Audience: **u,f.**

Smith, Barbara   E185.86.S635 1999
The Truth That Never Hurts: Writings on Race, Gender and Freedom. Trade Cloth. Rutgers University Press. Piscataway, NJ. 2003. 232p. Lesbian and Gay Studies ISBN:0-8135-2573-X, ISBN13: 978-0-8135-2573-0. Dewey:305.4/8/8. LCCN:98-018668.
Audience: **l,u,f.** *Choice, 1999.*

Soto, Shirlene A.   HQ1236.5.M6S67 1990
Emergence of the Modern Mexican Woman, 1910-1940: Her Participation in Revolution and Struggle for Equality. Trade Cloth. Arden Press, Inc. Denver, CO. 1990. 200p. Women and Modern Revolution Ser. ISBN:0-912869-11-9, ISBN13: 978-0-912869-11-7. Dewey:305.42/0972. LCCN:89-077883.
Audience: **l,u.** *Choice, 1991.*

Special Collections,   HQ1421
  Duke University
☐ Documents from the Women's Liberation Movement: An On-line Archival Collection.
http://scriptorium.lib.duke.edu/wlm/
Audience: **g,l,u.**

Stephen, Lynn   HQ1240.5.L29S74 1997
Women and Social Movements in Latin America: Power from Below. Trade Cloth. University of Texas Press. Austin, TX. 1997. 352p. ISBN:0-292-77715-9, ISBN13: 978-0-292-77715-6. Dewey:305.42/098. LCCN:96-045788.
Audience: **u,f.** *Choice, 1998.*

Walter, Lynn (Editor)   HQ1236
Women's Rights: A Global View. Cloth Text. Greenwood Publishing Group, Inc. Portsmouth, NH. 2000. 288p. A World View of Social Issues Ser. ISBN:0-313-30890-X, ISBN13: 978-0-313-30890-1. Dewey:305.42. LCCN:00-027632.
Audience: **l,u,f.** *Choice, 2001.*

Wollstonecraft, Mary   HQ1597
A Vindication of the Rights of Woman. Library Binding. Sagebrush Education Resources. Caledonia, MN. 2001. ISBN:0-613-70758-3, ISBN13: 978-0-613-70758-9. Dewey:305.420941.
Audience: **l,u.**

Feminism

☐ African Women's Bibliographical Database.
http://www.africabib.org/women.html
Audience: **g,l,u.**

       HQ1410
☐ American Women: Library of Congress Guide for the Study of Women's History and Culture in the United States.
http://lcweb2.loc.gov/ammem/awhhtml/
Audience: **g,l,u.**

       HQ1101
☐ Contemporary Women's Issues.
http://www.gale.com/servlet/ItemDetailServlet?region=9&imprint=000&titleCode=GAL68&type=4&id=173259
Audience: **g,l,u.**

       HQ1148
☐ Early Modern Women Database.
http://www.lib.umd.edu/ETC/LOCAL/emw/emw.php3
Audience: **g,l,u.**

       HQ1154
☐ Feminist Majority Foundation.
http://feminist.org/
Audience: **g,l,u.**

       HQ1111
☐ GenderWatch.
http://www.proquest.com/products_pq/descriptions/genderwatch.shtml
Audience: **g,l,u.**

☐ H-Net Women: Internet Links.
http://www.h-net.org/%7Ewomen/links/
Audience: **g,l,u.**

       HQ1180
☐ National Council for Research on Women.
http://www.ncrw.org/
Audience: **g,l,u.**

       HQ1154
Women Go Global. CD-ROM. United Nations Publications. New York, NY. 2005. ISBN:92-1-130211-0, ISBN13: 978-92-1-130211-0. Dewey:305.42.
Audience: **g,l,u,f.**

       HQ1180
☐ Women's Studies International.
http://www.nisc.com/Frame/NISC_products-f.htm
Audience: **g,l,u.**

International   HQ1180
Information Centre and Archives for the Women's Movement
☐ Mapping the World of Women's Information Services.
http://www.iiav.nl/mapping-the-world/
Audience: **g,l,u.**

Agosín, Marjorie   HQ1236.W5852 2001
  (Editor)
Women, Gender and Human Rights: A Global Perspective. Cloth Text. Rutgers University Press. Piscataway, NJ. 2001. 320p. ISBN:0-8135-2982-4, ISBN13: 978-0-8135-2982-0. Dewey:305.42. LCCN:2001-019296.
Audience: **l,u.**

Alexander, M. Jacqui   HM671.S567 2002
Sing, Whisper, Shout, Pray!: Feminist Visions for a Just World. Trade Paper. EdgeWork Books. Fort Bragg, CA. 2002. xxviii,

737p. ISBN:1-931223-07-6, ISBN13: 978-1-931223-07-2.
Dewey:305.42. LCCN:2002-151596.

Audience: **g,l,u.**

Allen, Prudence   **BD450.A4725 1996**
The Concept of Woman: The Aristotelian Revolution, 750 B. C.
-A. D. 1250. Trade Paper. William B. Eerdmans Publishing
Company. Grand Rapids, MI. 1997. 607p. ISBN:0-8028-4270-4,
ISBN13: 978-0-8028-4270-1. Dewey:305.4/01.
LCCN:96-009102.

Audience: **l,u.**

Andersen, Margaret   **HQ1426.A6825 2005**
Thinking about Women: Sociological Perspectives on Sex and
Gender. Ed. 7. Trade Paper. Allyn & Bacon, Inc. Boston, MA.
2005. 480p. ISBN:0-205-45647-2, ISBN13: 978-0-205-45647-5.
Dewey:305.42/0973 2. LCCN:2005-046479.

Audience: **l,u,f.**

Andors, Phyllis   **HQ1768.A52**
The Unfinished Liberation of Chinese Women, 1949-1980.
Trade Paper. Books on Demand. Ann Arbor, MI. 224p.
ISBN:0-8357-3963-5, ISBN13: 978-0-8357-3963-4.
Dewey:305.420951. LCCN:81-048323.

Audience: **l,u.**

**Association of College
& Research Libraries: Women's Studies Section**
▢ WSSLINKS: Women and Gender Studies Websites.
http://libr.org/wss/WSSLinks/index.html

Audience: **g,l,u.**

Baxandall, Rosalyn   **HQ1421**
  Fraad & Gordon, Linda
Dear Sisters: Dispatches from the Women's Liberation
Movement. Trade Paper. Basic Books. New York, NY. 2001.
336p. ISBN:0-465-01707-X, ISBN13: 978-0-465-01707-2.
Dewey:305.420973.

Audience: **l,u,f.**

Boles, Janet K. &   **HQ1115.B65 2004**
  Hoeveler, Diane Long
Historical Dictionary of Feminism. Ed. 2. Trade Cloth.
Scarecrow Press, Inc. Lanham, MD. 2004. 488p. Historical
Dictionaries of Religions, Philosophies, and Movements Ser.,
No. 52 ISBN:0-8108-4946-1, ISBN13: 978-0-8108-4946-4.
Dewey:305.42/03. LCCN:2004-000060.

Audience: **g,l,u.** *Choice, 2005, 1997.*

Cantarow, Ellen   **HQ1412.C36**
Moving the Mountain: Women Working for Social Change.
Trade Cloth. Bow Historical Books. New Providence, NJ. 1980.
xli, 166p. ISBN:0-07-020443-8, ISBN13: 978-0-07-020443-0.
Dewey:301.24/2/0922. LCCN:79-011840.

Audience: **g,l,u.** ℬ

Cantú, Norma Elia &   **E184.M5C4 2002**
  Nájera-Ramírez, Olga (Editors)
Chicana Traditions: Continuity and Change. Trade Paper.
University of Illinois Press. Champaign, IL. 2002. 280p.
ISBN:0-252-07012-7, ISBN13: 978-0-252-07012-9.
Dewey:305.48/868/72073. LCCN:2001-002644.

Audience: **u,f.** *Choice, 2002.*

Celestin, Roger, et al.   **HQ1613**
Beyond French Feminisms: Debates on Women, Politics, and
Culture in France, 1981-2001. Eliane DalMolin & Isabelle De

Courtivron (Authors). Cloth over Boards. Palgrave Macmillan.
New York, NY. 2003. 324p. ISBN:0-312-24019-8, ISBN13:
978-0-312-24019-6. Dewey:305.42/0944.

Audience: **u,f.**

Cott, Nancy F.   **HQ1420.C67 1987**
The Grounding of Modern Feminism. Cloth over Boards. Yale
University Press. Cumberland, RI. 1987. 378p.
ISBN:0-300-03892-5, ISBN13: 978-0-300-03892-7.
Dewey:305.4/2/0973/0904. LCCN:87-010642.

Audience: **l,u.** *Choice, 1988.*

Duchen, Claire   **HQ1613.D8 1986**
Feminism in France: From May '68 to Mitterand. Trade Paper.
Routledge. New York, NY. 1986. 192p. ISBN:0-7102-0455-8,
ISBN13: 978-0-7102-0455-4. Dewey:305.4/2/0944.
LCCN:85-010705.

Audience: **l,u.** ℬ *Choice, 1986.*

Echols, Alice   **HQ1421.E25 1989**
Daring to Be Bad: Radical Feminism in America, 1967-1975.
Trade Paper. University of Minnesota Press. Minneapolis, MN.
1989. 430p. ISBN:0-8166-1787-2, ISBN13: 978-0-8166-1787-6.
Dewey:305.4/2/097309047. LCCN:89-005058.

Audience: **u,f.** *Choice, 1990.*

Faludi, Susan   **HQ1426.F35 2006**
Backlash: The Undeclared War Against American Women. Trade
Paper. Bantam Books. New York, NY. 2006. 592p.
ISBN:0-307-34542-4, ISBN13: 978-0-307-34542-4.
Dewey:305.420973. LCCN:2006-009331.

Audience: **g,l,u,f.**

Findlen, Barbara   **HQ1426.L57 2001**
  (Editor)
Listen Up: Voices from the Next Feminist Generation. Ed. 2.
Trade Paper. Avalon Publishing Group. New York, NY. 2001.
310p. ISBN:1-58005-054-9, ISBN13: 978-1-58005-054-8.
Dewey:305.42/0973. LCCN:2001-041081.

Audience: **g.**

Freedman, Estelle B.   **HQ1154**
No Turning Back: The History of Feminism and the Future of
Women. Trade Paper. Ballantine Books. New York, NY. 2003.
464p. ISBN:0-345-45053-1, ISBN13: 978-0-345-45053-1.
Dewey:305.42.

Audience: **g,l,u.** *Choice, 2002.*

Friedan, Betty   **HQ1426.F844 2001**
The Feminine Mystique. Anna Quindlen (Introduction by). Trade
Paper. W. W. Norton & Company, Inc. New York, NY. 2001.
512p. ISBN:0-393-32257-2, ISBN13: 978-0-393-32257-6.
Dewey:305.42/0973. LCCN:2001-044231.

Audience: **g,l,u,f.**

Friedman, Susan S.   **HQ1190.F77 1998**
Mappings: Feminism and the Cultural Geographies of
Encounter. Trade Cloth. Princeton University Press. Princeton,
NJ. 1998. 328p. ISBN:0-691-05803-2, ISBN13:
978-0-691-05803-0. Dewey:305.42/01. LCCN:98-011525.

Audience: **u,f.** *Choice, 1999.*

Gaard, Greta (Editor)   **HQ1233.E26 1993**
Ecofeminism: Women, Animals, Nature. Trade Cloth. Temple
University Press. Philadelphia, PA. 1993. 304p. Ethics and
Action Ser. ISBN:0-87722-988-0, ISBN13: 978-0-87722-988-9.
Dewey:304.2. LCCN:92-006598.

Audience: **l,u,f.** *Choice, 1993.*

Goldrick-Jones,   HQ1236
  Amanda
Men Who Believe in Feminism: Dismantling the Master's
House? Trade Cloth. Greenwood Publishing Group, Inc.
Portsmouth, NH. 2002. 224p. ISBN:0-275-96822-7, ISBN13:
978-0-275-96822-9. Dewey:305.42. LCCN:2001-054589.

         Audience: **g,l,u,f.** *Choice, 2003.*

Grossman, Avraham   BM729.W6G7613 2004
Pious and Rebellious: Jewish Women in Medieval Europe. Trade
Cloth. University Press of New England. Lebanon, NH. 2004.
352p. Tauber Institute for the Study of European Jewry Ser.
ISBN:1-58465-391-4, ISBN13: 978-1-58465-391-2.
Dewey:305.48/892404/0902. LCCN:2004-003029.

         Audience: **u,f.** *Choice, 2005.*

Hall, Catherine   HQ1597
White, Male and Middle Class: Explorations in Feminism and
History. UK-B Format Paperback. Routledge. New York, NY.
1992. 320p. ISBN:0-415-90663-6, ISBN13: 978-0-415-90663-0.
Dewey:305.420941.

         Audience: **l,u,f.** *Choice, 1993.*

Halsaa, Beatrice   HQ1161.C763 2004
  (Editor), et al.
Crossing Borders: Re-mapping Women's Movements at the Turn
of the 21st Century. Hilda Romer Christensen & Aino Saarinen
(Editors). Trade Paper. University Press of Southern Denmark.
Odense M, 2004. 371p. University of Southern Denmark Studies
in History and Social Sciences, Vol. 280 ISBN:87-7838-859-7,
ISBN13: 978-87-7838-859-9. Dewey:305.42.
LCCN:2004-304079.

         Audience: **u,f.** *Choice, 2005.*

Herrmann, Claudine   PN98.W64
The Tongue Snatchers. Nancy Kline (Translator, Introduction by,
Notes by). Trade Cloth. University of Nebraska Press. Lincoln,
NE. 1989. 145p. European Women Writers Ser.
ISBN:0-8032-7252-9, ISBN13: 978-0-8032-7252-1.
Dewey:809/.89287. LCCN:89-031136.

         Audience: **l,u,f.** *Choice, 1991.*

Hine, Darlene Clark   E185.86.B542 2005
Black Women in America, Set. Ed. 2. Trade Cloth. Oxford
University Press, Inc. New York, NY. 2005. 1696p.
ISBN:0-19-515677-3, ISBN13: 978-0-19-515677-5.
Dewey:305.48/896073. LCCN:2005-001532.

         Audience: **g,l,u,f.** *Choice, 2005.*

Howard, Judith A. &   HQ1190.F44234 2000
  Allen, Carolyn (Editors)
Feminisms at a Millennium. Trade Cloth. University of Chicago
Press. Chicago, IL. 2001. 318p. ISBN:0-226-01443-6, ISBN13:
978-0-226-01443-2. Dewey:305.42/01. LCCN:00-046719.

         Audience: **l,u.**

Hurtado, Aida   HQ1421.H87 1996
The Color of Privilege: Three Blasphemies on Race and
Feminism. Trade Paper. University of Michigan Press. Chicago,
IL. 1997. 216p. Critical Perspectives on Women and Gender Ser.
ISBN:0-472-06531-9, ISBN13: 978-0-472-06531-8.
Dewey:305.4/2/0973/0904. LCCN:96-021187.

         Audience: **u,f.** *Choice, 1997.*

Irigaray, Luce   HQ1154.I7413 1985
Speculum of the Other Woman. Gillian C. Gill (Translator).
Trade Paper. Cornell University Press. Ithaca, NY. 1985. 416p.
ISBN:0-8014-9330-7, ISBN13: 978-0-8014-9330-0.
Dewey:155.3/33. LCCN:84-045151.

         Audience: **u,f.**

James, Joy   E185.86
Shadowboxing: Representations of Black Feminist Politics.
Trade Paper. Palgrave Macmillan. New York, NY. 2002. 240p.
ISBN:0-312-29449-2, ISBN13: 978-0-312-29449-6.
Dewey:305.48/896073.

         Audience: **l,u.**

Jones, Charisse &   E185.625.J657 2003
  Shorter-Gooden, Kumea
Shifting: The Double Lives of Black Women in America. Trade
Cloth. HarperCollins Publishers. New York, NY. 2003. 352p.
ISBN:0-06-009054-5, ISBN13: 978-0-06-009054-8.
Dewey:306.7/089/96073. LCCN:2003-040728.

         Audience: **g,l,u,f.**

Lerner, Gerda   HQ1121
The Creation of Feminist Consciousness: From the Middle Ages
to Eighteen-Seventy. Trade Paper. Oxford University Press, Inc.
New York, NY. 1994. 416p. ISBN:0-19-509060-8, ISBN13:
978-0-19-509060-4. Dewey:305.4/09. LCCN:92-020411.

         Audience: **g,l,u,f.** *Choice, 1993.*

Lewis, Reina & Mills,   HQ1150
  Sara (Editors)
Feminist Postcolonial Theory: A Reader. Cloth Text. Routledge.
New York, NY. 2003. 768p. ISBN:0-415-94274-8, ISBN13:
978-0-415-94274-4. Dewey:305.42.

         Audience: **l,u,f.**

Lorde, Audre Geraldine   PS3562.O75S5 1984
Sister Outsider: Essays and Speeches. Trade Cloth. Crossing
Press, Incorporated, The. Berkeley, CA. 1984. 192p. Feminist
Ser. ISBN:0-89594-141-4, ISBN13: 978-0-89594-141-1.
Dewey:814/.54. LCCN:84-001844.

         Audience: **g,l,u,f.**

Mackie, Vera   HQ1762.M326 2003
Feminism in Modern Japan: Citizenship, Embodiment and
Sexuality. Harumi Befu, Roger Goodman, Michio Muramatsu,
Wolfgang Seifert, Yoshio Sugimoto & Chizuko Ueno
(Contribution by). Cloth Text. Cambridge University Press. New
York, NY. 2003. 308p. Contemporary Japanese Society Ser.
ISBN:0-521-82018-9, ISBN13: 978-0-521-82018-9.
Dewey:305.42/0952. LCCN:2002-038858.

         Audience: **u,f.** *Choice, 2003.*

Marcus, Jacob R.   HQ1172.M37 SUPPL
The American Jewish Woman: A Documentary History. Trade
Cloth. Ktav Publishing House, Inc. Jersey City, NJ. 1981.
1047p. ISBN:0-87068-752-2, ISBN13: 978-0-87068-752-5.
Dewey:205.4/8. LCCN:81-001966.

         Audience: **g,l,u.** *B*

Marcus, Jacob R.   HQ1172.M37
  (Editor)
The American Jewish Woman: 1654-1980. Trade Cloth. Ktav
Publishing House, Inc. Jersey City, NJ. 1981. xiv, 231p.
ISBN:0-87068-751-4, ISBN13: 978-0-87068-751-8.
Dewey:305.4/8. LCCN:81-001720.

         Audience: **u,f.** *B*

McClaurin, Irma   **GN33.8.B53 2001**
(Editor)
Black Feminist Anthropology: Theory, Politics, Praxis and
Poetics. Johnnetta B. Cole (Foreword by). Cloth Text. Rutgers
University Press. Piscataway, NJ. 2001. 272p.
ISBN:0-8135-2925-5, ISBN13: 978-0-8135-2925-7.
Dewey:305.42. LCCN:00-045686.

Audience: **g,l,u,f.** *Choice, 2002.*

Medina, Lara   **BX810.H57M43 2004**
Las Hermanas: Chicana/Latina Religious-Political Activism in
the U. S. Catholic Church. Trade Cloth. Temple University
Press. Philadelphia, PA. 2004. 232p. ISBN:1-59213-250-2,
ISBN13: 978-1-59213-250-8. Dewey:267.4/4273.
LCCN:2003-064591.

Audience: **u,f.** *Choice, 2005.*

Mikell, Gwendolyn   **HQ1240.5.A357.A36**
(Editor)
African Feminism: The Politics of Survival in Sub-Saharan
Africa. Trade Cloth. University of Pennsylvania Press.
Philadelphia, PA. 1997. 392p. ISBN:0-8122-3349-2, ISBN13:
978-0-8122-3349-0. Dewey:305.42/0967. LCCN:97-006260.

Audience: **l,u.** *Choice, 1998.*

Minesuah, Devon   **E98.W8M54 2003**
Abbott
Indigenous American Women: Decolonization, Empowerment,
Activism. Cloth Text. University of Nebraska Press. Lincoln,
NE. 2003. 288p. Contemporary Indigenous Issues Ser.
ISBN:0-8032-3227-6, ISBN13: 978-0-8032-3227-3.
Dewey:305.48/897073. LCCN:2002-028767.

Audience: **u,f.**

Moghadam, Valentine   **HQ1233.I34 1993**
M. (Editor)
Identity Politics and Women: Cultural Reassertions and
Feminisms in International Perspective. Trade Paper. Westview
Press. Boulder, CO. 1993. 458p. ISBN:0-8133-8691-8, ISBN13:
978-0-8133-8691-1. Dewey:305.42. LCCN:93-028018.

Audience: **l,u,f.** *Choice, 1994.*

Moghissi, Hiadeh   **HQ1170.M64 1999**
Feminism and Islamic Fundamentalism: The Limits of
Postmodern Analysis. Cloth over Boards. Zed Books, Ltd.
London, 1999. 128p. ISBN:1-85649-589-2, ISBN13:
978-1-85649-589-9. Dewey:305.48/6971. LCCN:99-022771.

Audience: **l,u,f.** *Choice, 2000.*

Montagu, Ashley   **HQ1206.M65 1999**
The Natural Superiority of Women. Ed. 5. Trade Cloth. AltaMira
Press. Walnut Creek, CA. 1999. 300p. ISBN:0-7619-8981-1,
ISBN13: 978-0-7619-8981-3. Dewey:305.4. LCCN:98-040173.

Audience: **g,l,u,f.**

Narayan, Uma   **HQ1870.9.N37 1997**
Dislocating Cultures: Identities, Traditions and Third World
Feminism. Paper over Boards. Routledge. New York, NY. 1997.
240p. Thinking Gender Ser. ISBN:0-415-91418-3, ISBN13:
978-0-415-91418-5. Dewey:305.42/09172/4. LCCN:97-012405.

Audience: **l,u,f.**

Nashat, Guity & Beck,   **HQ1735.2.W656 2003**
Lois (Editors)
Women in Iran from the Rise of Islam to 1800. Trade Cloth.
University of Illinois Press. Champaign, IL. 2003. 272p.
ISBN:0 252 02839-2, ISBN13: 978-0-252-02839-7.
Dewey:305.42/0955. LCCN:2002-152213.

Audience: **l,u,f.** *Choice, 2004.*

Newman, Louise   **HQ1410.N475 1999**
White Women's Rights: The Racial Origins of Feminism in the
United States. Trade Cloth. Oxford University Press, Inc. New
York, NY. 1999. 272p. ISBN:0-19-508692-9, ISBN13:
978-0-19-508692-8. Dewey:305.420973. LCCN:97-053286.

Audience: **u,f.** *Choice, 1999.*

Rhodes, Jane   **E185.97.C32R48 1998**
Mary Ann Shadd Cary: The Black Press and Protest in the
Nineteenth Century. Library Binding. Indiana University Press.
Bloomington, IN. 1998. 304p. ISBN:0-253-33446-2, ISBN13:
978-0-253-33446-6. Dewey:[B]. LCCN:98-019997.

Audience: **l,u,f.** *Choice, 1999.*

Riley, Denise   **HQ1154**
Am I That Name?: Feminism and the Category of Women in
History. Trade Paper. University of Minnesota Press.
Minneapolis, MN. 2003. 136p. ISBN:0-8166-4269-9, ISBN13:
978-0-8166-4269-4. Dewey:305.4/2/09.

Audience: **l,u.**

Rowland, Susan   **BF175.4.F45R69 2002**
(Editor)
Jung: A Feminist Revision. Trade Cloth. Polity Press.
Cambridge, 2002. 200p. ISBN:0-7456-2516-9, ISBN13:
978-0-7456-2516-4. Dewey:150.1/954. LCCN:2001-002545.

Audience: **u,f.** *Choice, 2002.*

Scanlon, Jennifer   **HQ1412**
Significant Contemporary American Feminists: A Biographical
Sourcebook. Cloth Text. Greenwood Publishing Group, Inc.
Portsmouth, NH. 1999. 384p. ISBN:0-313-30125-5, ISBN13:
978-0-313-30125-4. Dewey:305.42/0973. LCCN:98-022899.

Audience: **l,u.** *Choice, 1999.*

Segal, Lynne &   **HQ471 .S47 1993**
McIntosh, Mary (Editors)
Sex Exposed: Sexuality and the Pornography Debate. Trade
Paper. Rutgers University Press. Piscataway, NJ. 1993. 344p.
ISBN:0-8135-1938-1, ISBN13: 978-0-8135-1938-8.
Dewey:363.4/7. LCCN:92-029843.

Audience: **u,f.**

Shah, Sonia (Editor)   **HQ1426.D845 1997**
Dragon Ladies: Asian American Feminists Breathe Fire. Yuri
Kochiyama (Preface by), Karin Aguilar-San Juan (Foreword by).
Trade Paper. South End Press. Cambridge, MA. 1997. 241p.
Asian-American Studies ISBN:0-89608-575-9, ISBN13:
978-0-89608-575-6. Dewey:305.48/895073. LCCN:97-022918.

Audience: **g,l,u.**

Sharma, Arvind &   **BL458.F455 1998**
Young, Katherine K. (Editors)
Feminism and World Religions. Paper Text. State University of
New York Press. Albany, NY. 1998. 352p. SUNY Series, McGill
Studies in the History of Religions ISBN:0-7914-4024-9,
ISBN13: 978-0-7914-4024-7. Dewey:2913.1/783442.
LCCN:98-010509.

Audience: **u,f.** *Choice, 1999.*

Smith, Bonnie G.   **HQ1154.G56 2000**
(Editor)
Global Feminisms: A Survey of Issues and Controversies. Paper
over Boards. Routledge. New York, NY. 2000. 336p. Rewriting
Histories Ser. ISBN:0-415-18490-8, ISBN13:
978-0-415-18490-8. Dewey:305.42. LCCN:99-089441.

Audience: **g,l,u,f.** *Choice, 2001.*

Soble, Alan   HQ471.S635 2002
Pornography, Sex and Feminism. Trade Cloth. Prometheus
Books, Publishers. Amherst, NY. 2001. 210p.
ISBN:1-57392-944-1, ISBN13: 978-1-57392-944-8.
Dewey:363.4/7. LCCN:2002-019176.
Audience: **g,l,u,f.** *Choice, 2002.*

Soto, Shirlene A.   HQ1236.5.M6S67 1990
Emergence of the Modern Mexican Woman, 1910-1940: Her
Participation in Revolution and Struggle for Equality. Trade
Cloth. Arden Press, Inc. Denver, CO. 1990. 200p. Women and
Modern Revolution Ser. ISBN:0-912869-11-9, ISBN13:
978-0-912869-11-7. Dewey:305.42/0972. LCCN:89-077883.
Audience: **l,u.** *Choice, 1991.*

Stanford University
🔲 African Women on the Internet.
http://www-sul.stanford.edu/depts/ssrg/africa/women.html
Audience: **g,l,u.**

Taylor, Verta, et al.   HQ1426.T397 2007
Feminist Frontiers. Ed. 7. Nancy Whittier & Leila J. Rupp
(Authors). Paper Text. McGraw-Hill Higher Education. Burr
Ridge, IL. 2006. 576p. ISBN:0-07-319608-8, ISBN13:
978-0-07-319608-4. Dewey:305.420973. LCCN:2006-041926.
Audience: **l,u.**

Tsomo, Karma Lekshe   BQ4570.W6K34 1999
   (Editor)
Buddhist Women Across Cultures: Realizations. Cloth Text.
State University of New York Press. Albany, NY. 1999. 320p.
SUNY Series in Feminist Philosophy ISBN:0-7914-4137-7,
ISBN13: 978-0-7914-4137-4. Dewey:294.3/082.
LCCN:98-034325.
Audience: **l,u.**

United Nations   HQ1236
🔲 WomenWatch: UN Information and Resources on Gender
Equality and the Empowerment of Women.
http://www.un.org/womenwatch/
Audience: **g,l,u.**

University of California,
   Berkeley
🔲 International Gender Studies Resources.
http://globetrotter.berkeley.edu/GlobalGender/
Audience: **g,l,u.**

Walker, Rebecca Edby   HQ1426.T623 1995
To Be Real: Telling the Truth and Changing the Face of
Feminism. Trade Paper. Doubleday Publishing. New York, NY.
1995. 336p. ISBN:0-385-47262-5, ISBN13: 978-0-385-47262-3.
Dewey:305.42. LCCN:95-014412.
Audience: **g,l,u.**

Walters, Suzanna D.   HQ759.W332
Lives Together - Worlds Apart: Mothers and Daughters in
Popular Culture. Trade Paper. University of California Press.
Berkeley, CA. 1994. 310p. ISBN:0-520-08656-2, ISBN13:
978-0-520-08656-2. Dewey:306.8743. LCCN:91-032331.
Audience: **l,u,f.** *Choice, 1993.*

Wing, Adrien Katherine   HQ1154.C75 2003
   (Editor)
Critical Race Feminism: A Reader. Ed. 2. Trade Cloth. New
York University Press. New York, NY. 2003. 480p. Critical
America Ser. ISBN:0-8147-9393-2, ISBN13:

978-0-8147-9393-0. Dewey:305.48/8/00973.
LCCN:2003-008960.
Audience: **u,f.** *Choice, 2004.*

Wolf, Naomi   HQ1154
The Beauty Myth: How Images of Beauty are Used Against
Women. Trade Paper. Random House of Canada, Ltd.
Mississauga, ON. 1997. 348p. ISBN:0-679-30870-9, ISBN13:
978-0-679-30870-6. Dewey:305.42.
Audience: **l,u,f.** *Choice, 1992.*

Zinsser, Judith P.   HQ1181.U5Z56 1992
History and Feminism: A Glass Half Full. Cloth Text.
Macmillan Publishing Company, Inc. Old Tappan, NJ. 1992.
200p. The Feminist Impact on the Arts and Sciences Ser.
ISBN:0-8057-9751-3, ISBN13: 978-0-8057-9751-0.
Dewey:305.4/07/073. LCCN:92-028707.
Audience: **g,l,u,f.** *Choice, 1993.*

Body and Representation. Performativity

Bordo, Susan   HQ1220.U5 B67 2004
Unbearable Weight: Feminism, Western Culture, and the Body.
Ed. 2. Leslie Heywood (Prologue by). Trade Paper. University
of California Press. Berkeley, CA. 2004. 370p.
ISBN:0-520-24054-5, ISBN13: 978-0-520-24054-4.
Dewey:305.42. LCCN:2003-055221.
Audience: **l,u,f.**

Conboy, Katie, et al.   PN98.W64W687 1997
Writing on the Body: Female Embodiment and Feminist Theory.
Nadia Medina & Sarah Stanbury (Authors). Trade Cloth.
Columbia University Press. New York, NY. 1997. 384p. Gender
and Culture Ser. ISBN:0-231-10544-4, ISBN13:
978-0-231-10544-6. Dewey:305.4. LCCN:96-048177.
Audience: **u,f.**

Gimlin, Debra L.   HQ1220.U5 G56 2001
Body Work: Beauty and Self-Image in American Culture. Trade
Cloth. University of California Press. Berkeley, CA. 2002. 182p.
ISBN:0-520-21051-4, ISBN13: 978-0-520-21051-6.
Dewey:306.4. LCCN:2001-027242.
Audience: **g,l,u,f.** *Choice, 2003, 2002.*

Grosz, Elizabeth   HQ1190.G76 1994
Volatile Bodies: Toward a Corporeal Feminism. Trade Cloth.
Indiana University Press. Bloomington, IN. 1994. 272p.
Theories of Representation and Difference Ser.
ISBN:0-253-32686-9, ISBN13: 978-0-253-32686-7.
Dewey:305.4/2/01. LCCN:93-028611.
Audience: **l,u,f.** *Choice, 1995.*

Lancaster, Roger & Di   GN479.65.G475 1997
   Leonardo, Micaela (Editors)
The Gender/Sexuality Reader: Culture, History, Political
Economy. UK-B Format Paperback. Routledge. New York, NY.
1997. 584p. ISBN:0-415-91005-6, ISBN13: 978-0-415-91005-7.
Dewey:305.3. LCCN:96-039187.
Audience: **l,u,f.**

Price, Janet   HQ1190
Feminist Theory and the Body: A Reader. Trade Paper.
Routledge. New York, NY. 1999. 504p. ISBN:0-415-92566-5,
ISBN13: 978-0-415-92566-2. Dewey:305.4/2/01.
Audience: **l,u,f.**

Suleiman, Susan Rubin   **NX652.W6F46 1986**
  (Editor)
The Female Body in Western Culture: Contemporary
Perspectives. Trade Paper. Harvard University Press. Cambridge,
MA. 1986. 400p. ISBN:0-674-29871-3, ISBN13:
978-0-674-29871-2. Dewey:305.4. LCCN:85-027255.
                  Audience: **l,u,f.**

Tuana, Nancy (Editor),   **HQ1090.R455 2001**
  et al.
e Revealing Male Bodies. William Cowling, Maurice
Hamington, Greg Johnson & Terrance MacMullan (Editors).
E-Book. Indiana University Press. Bloomington, IN. 2002. 352p.
ISBN:0-253-33991-X, ISBN13: 978-0-253-33991-1.
Dewey:305.31. LCCN:2001-004647.
          Audience: **l,u,f.** *Choice, 2003.*

Wallace-Sanders,   **E185.625.S55 2003**
  Kimberly (Editor)
Skin Deep, Spirit Strong: The Black Female Body in American
Culture. Trade Cloth. University of Michigan Press. Chicago,
IL. 2002. 368p. ISBN:0-472-09707-5, ISBN13:
978-0-472-09707-4. Dewey:305.48/896073. LCCN:2002-075016.
                  Audience: **l,u,f.**

Weitz, Rose (Editor)   **HQ1206.P56 2003**
The Politics of Women's Bodies: Sexuality, Appearance, and
Behavior. Ed. 2. Paper Text. Oxford University Press, Inc. New
York, NY. 2002. 314p. ISBN:0-19-514977-7, ISBN13:
978-0-19-514977-7. Dewey:305.42. LCCN:2002-066287.
                  Audience: **l,u,f.**

Sports. Recreation

Birrell, Susan & Cole,   **GV709.W577 1994**
  Cheryl L. (Editors)
Women, Sport, and Culture. Trade Cloth. Human Kinetics
Publishers. Champaign, IL. 1994. 416p. ISBN:0-87322-650-X,
ISBN13: 978-0-87322-650-9. Dewey:796/.0194.
LCCN:93-038013.
          Audience: **u,f.** *Choice, 1995.*

Cahn, Susan K.   **GV709**
Coming on Strong: Gender and Sexuality in Twentieth-Century
Women's Sports. Trade Paper. Harvard University Press.
Cambridge, MA. 1998. 39p. ISBN:0-674-14434-1, ISBN13:
978-0-674-14434-7. Dewey:796/.0194.
               Audience: **g,l,u,f.**

Christensen, Karen   **GV709.I58 2000**
  (Editor), et al.
International Encyclopedia of Women and Sports, Set. Allen
Guttmann & Gertrude Pfister (Editors). Trade Cloth. Thomson
Gale. Farmington Hills, MI. 1999. 1428p. ISBN:0-02-864954-0,
ISBN13: 978-0-02-864954-2. Dewey:796/.082.
LCCN:00-062518.
          Audience: **g,l,u.** *Choice, 2001.*

Costa, D. Margaret &   **GV709.W56 1994**
  Guthrie, Sharon R. (Editors)
Women and Sport: Interdisciplinary Perspectives. Trade Cloth.
Human Kinetics Publishers. Champaign, IL. 1994. 416p.
ISBN:0 87322-686-0, ISBN13: 978-0-87322-686-8.
Dewey:796/.0194. LCCN:93-050167.
            Audience: **g,l,f.**

Edelson, Paula   **GV697.A1E28 2002**
A to Z of American Women in Sports. Trade Cloth. Facts On
File, Inc. New York, NY. 2002. 288p. A to Z of Women Ser.
ISBN:0-8160-4565-8, ISBN13: 978-0-8160-4565-5.
Dewey:796/.082/092273 B. LCCN:2001-054735.
          Audience: **g,l,u.** *Choice, 2003.*

Fields, Sarah K.   **GV709.18.U6F54 2004**
Female Gladiators: Gender, Law, and Contact Sport in America.
Trade Cloth. University of Illinois Press. Champaign, IL. 2004.
232p. Sport and Society Ser. ISBN:0-252-02958-5, ISBN13:
978-0-252-02958-5. Dewey:796/.082/0973. LCCN:2004-008913.
          Audience: **u,f.** *Choice, 2005.*

Gavora, Jessica   **GV709.18.U6G38 2002**
Tilting the Playing Field: Schools, Sports, Sex and Title IX.
Trade Cloth. National Book Network. Lanham, MD. 2001.
181p. ISBN:1-893554-35-X, ISBN13: 978-1-893554-35-1.
Dewey:796/.082. LCCN:2001-055597.
         Audience: **u,f.** *Choice, 2003, 2002.*

Guttmann, Allen   **GV709**
Women's Sports: A History. Trade Paper. Columbia University
Press. New York, NY. 1992. 339p. ISBN:0-231-06957-X,
ISBN13: 978-0-231-06957-1. Dewey:796/.0194.
         Audience: **g,l,u,f.** *Choice, 1991.*

Hall, M. Ann   **GV709.H32 1996**
Feminism and Sporting Bodies: Essays on Theory and Practice.
Trade Paper. Human Kinetics Publishers. Champaign, IL. 1996.
144p. ISBN:0-87322-969-X, ISBN13: 978-0-87322-969-2.
Dewey:796/.0194. LCCN:95-044480.
         Audience: **u,f.** *Choice, 1996.*

Hargreaves, Jennifer   **GV709.18.G7H37 1994**
Sporting Females: Critical Issues in the History and Sociology
of Women's Sports. Trade Paper. Routledge. New York, NY.
1994. 344p. ISBN:0-415-07028-7, ISBN13: 978-0-415-07028-7.
Dewey:796.0194. LCCN:93-024575.
                Audience: **u,f.**

Hartmann-Tews, Ilse   **GV709.S66 2003**
Sport and Women: Social Issues in International Perspective.
Gertrud Pfister (Editor). Paper over Boards. Routledge. New
York, NY. 2002. 304p. ISBN:0-415-24627-X, ISBN13:
978 0 415-24627-9. Dewey:796/.082. LCCN:2002-073982.
         Audience: **g,l,u,f.** *Choice, 2003.*

Hong, Fan & Mangan,   **GV944.5**
  J. A. (Editors)
Soccer, Women, Sexual Liberation: Kicking off a New Era.
Paper over Boards. Taylor & Francis Group. Abingdon, 2003.
272p. Sport in the Global Society Ser. ISBN:0-7146-5509-0,
ISBN13: 978-0-7146-5509-3. Dewey:796.334082.
LCCN:2004-298586.
         Audience: **g,l,u,f.** *Choice, 2004.*

Messner, Michael A.   **GV706.32.M47 2003**
Taking the Field: Women, Men and Sports. Trade Paper.
University of Minnesota Press. Minneapolis, MN. 2002. 280p.
Sport and Culture Ser., Vol. 4 ISBN:0-8166-3449-1, ISBN13:
978-0-8166-3449-1. Dewey:796/.082. LCCN:2001-008548.
         Audience: **g,l,u,f.** *Choice, 2003.*

Miller, Toby   **GV706.2.M55 2001**
Sportsex. Library Binding. Temple University Press.
Philadelphia, PA. 2002. 224p. ISBN:1-56639-864-9, ISBN13:
978-1-56639-864-0. Dewey:306.4/83. LCCN:00-049098.
         Audience: **u,f.** *Choice, 2002.*

Nelson, Mariah B.   GV706.4.N45 1993
The Stronger Women Get, the More Men Love Football: Sex
and Sports in America. Trade Cloth. Harcourt Trade Publishers.
New York, NY. 1994. x, 304p. ISBN:0-15-181393-0, ISBN13:
978-0-15-181393-3. Dewey:796/.01. LCCN:93-044358.
Audience: **g,l,f.**

Oglesby, Carole A.   GV709.E53 1998
 (Editor), et al.
Encyclopedia of Women and Sport in America. Doreen L.
Greenberg, Ruth L. Hall, Karen L. Hill, Frances Johnston &
Sheila E. Esterby (Editors), Marilyn Oshman & Mariah B.
Nelson (Foreword by). Cloth Text. Greenwood Publishing
Group, Inc. Portsmouth, NH. 1998. 384p. ISBN:0-89774-993-6,
ISBN13: 978-0-89774-993-0. Dewey:796/.082.
LCCN:97-052787.
Audience: **g,l,u.** *Choice, 1998.*

Park, Roberta J. &   GV709.F66 1987
 Mangan, James A. (Editors)
From "Fair Sex" to Feminism: Sport and the Socialization of
Women in the Industrial and Post-Industrial Eras. Paper over
Boards. Taylor & Francis Group. Philadelphia, PA. 1987. 336p.
ISBN:0-7146-3288-0, ISBN13: 978-0-7146-3288-9.
Dewey:306.4/83. LCCN:86-017529.
Audience: **g,l,u,f.** *Choice, 1988.*

Suggs, Welch   GV709.18.U6S86 2005
A Place on the Team: The Triumph and Tragedy of Title IX.
Trade Cloth. Princeton University Press. Princeton, NJ. 2005.
288p. ISBN:0-691-11769-1, ISBN13: 978-0-691-11769-0.
Dewey:796/.082. LCCN:2004-048902.
Audience: **u,f.** *Choice, 2005.*

Theberge, Nancy   GV848.6.W65T54 2000
Higher Goals: Women's Ice Hockey and the Politics of Gender.
Cloth Text. State University of New York Press. Albany, NY.
2000. xiii, 182p. SUNY Series on Sport, Culture, and Social
Relations ISBN:0-7914-4641-7, ISBN13: 978-0-7914-4641-6.
Dewey:796.962/082/0971. LCCN:99-057333.
Audience: **u,f.** *Choice, 2001.*

Tricard, Louise Mead   GV1060.8.T75 1996
American Women's Track and Field: A History, 1895 Through
1980. Cloth Text. McFarland & Company, Incorporated
Publishers. Jefferson, NC. 1996. 760p. ISBN:0-7864-0219-9,
ISBN13: 978-0-7864-0219-9. Dewey:796.4/2/082.
LCCN:96-13463.
Audience: **l,u,f.** *Choice, 1997.*

Wushanley, Ying   GV709.18.U6W87 2004
Playing Nice and Losing: The Struggle for Control of Women's
Intercollegiate Athletics, 1960-2000. Trade Cloth. Syracuse
University Press. Syracuse, NY. 2004. xviii, 225p. Sports and
Entertainment Ser. ISBN:0-8156-3045-X, ISBN13:
978-0-8156-3045-6. Dewey:796/.082. LCCN:2003-024656.
Audience: **g,l,u,f.** *Choice, 2004.*

Science and Technology

                                          Q130
☐ 4000 Years of Women in Science.
http://www.astr.ua.edu/4000WS/4000WS.html
Audience: **g,l,u.**

Ambrose, Susan A., et   Q130.J68 1997
 al.
Journeys of Women in Science and Engineering: No Universal
Constants. Kristin L. Dunkle, Barbara B. Lazarus, Indira Nair &
Deborah A. Harkus (Authors). Trade Cloth. Temple University
Press. Philadelphia, PA. 2000. 512p. Labor and Social Change
Ser. ISBN:1-56639-527-5, ISBN13: 978-1-56639-527-4.
Dewey:508.2. LCCN:96-050415.
Audience: **l,u.** *Choice, 1998.*

Balsamo, Anne   HQ1190.B35 1996
Technologies of the Gendered Body: Reading Cyborg Women.
Cloth Text. Duke University Press. Durham, NC. 1995. 232p.
ISBN:0-8223-1686-2, ISBN13: 978-0-8223-1686-2.
Dewey:305.42/01. LCCN:95-022648.
Audience: **u,f.**

Cassell, Justine &   GV1469.17.S63.F76
 Jenkins, Henry (Editors)
From Barbie to Mortal Kombat: Gender and Computer Games.
Trade Cloth. MIT Press. Cambridge, MA. 1998. 382p.
ISBN:0-262-03258-9, ISBN13: 978-0-262-03258-2.
Dewey:306.4/87/0285. LCCN:98-023562.
Audience: **l,u,f.**

Creager, Angela N. H.   Q130.F46 2001
 (Editor), et al.
Feminism in Twentieth-Century Science, Technology, and
Medicine. Elizabeth Lunbeck & Londa Schiebinger (Editors).
Trade Cloth. University of Chicago Press. Chicago, IL. 2001.
272p. Women in Culture and Society Ser. ISBN:0-226-12023-6,
ISBN13: 978-0-226-12023-2. Dewey:500/.82.
LCCN:2001-027410.
Audience: **l,u.**

Creese, Mary R. S. &   Q141.C693 2004
 Creese, Thomas M. (Contribution by)
Ladies in the Laboratory II: West European Women in Science,
1800-1900: A Survey of Their Contributions to Research. Trade
Cloth. Scarecrow Press, Inc. Lanham, MD. 2004. 304p.
ISBN:0-8108-4979-8, ISBN13: 978-0-8108-4979-2.
Dewey:500/.82/09409034. LCCN:2003-020846.
Audience: **g.** *Choice, 2004.*

Creese, Mary R.   Q141.C69 1998
Ladies in the Laboratory? American and British Women in
Science, 1800-1900: A Survey of Their Contributions to
Research. Thomas M. Creese (Contribution by). Trade Cloth.
Scarecrow Press, Inc. Lanham, MD. 1998. 452p.
ISBN:0-8108-3287-9, ISBN13: 978-0-8108-3287-9.
Dewey:500.8/2. LCCN:97-001125.
Audience: **g.** *Choice, 1998.*

Flanagan, Mary &   PS151.R45 2002
 Booth, Austin (Editors)
Reload: Rethinking Women + Cyberculture. Trade Cloth. MIT
Press. Cambridge, MA. 2002. 595p. ISBN:0-262-06227-5,
ISBN13: 978-0-262-06227-5. Dewey:813/.50809287.
LCCN:2001-056235.
Audience: **g,l,u,f.** *Choice, 2002.*

Furger, Roberta   HQ777.F87 1998
Does Jane Compute?: Preserving Our Daughters' Place in the
Cyber Revolution. Trade Paper. Warner Books, Inc. New York,
NY. 1998. 224p. ISBN:0-446-67311-0, ISBN13:
978-0-446-67311-2. Dewey:004/.083/42. LCCN:97-020837.
Audience: **l,u.**

Haraway, Donna Jeanne   GN365.9.H37 1991
Simians, Cyborgs, and Women: The Reinvention of Nature.
Trade Cloth. Routledge. New York, NY. 1990. 288p.
ISBN:0-415-90387-4, ISBN13: 978-0-415-90387-5.
Dewey:304.5. LCCN:90-008762.
                    Audience: **u,f.** *Choice, 1991.*

Harding, Sandra   Q130.H37 1991
Whose Science? Whose Knowledge?: Thinking from Women's
Lives. Book, Other. Cornell University Press. Ithaca, NY. 1991.
336p. ISBN:0-8014-9746-9, ISBN13: 978-0-8014-9746-9.
Dewey:305.43/5. LCCN:90-055724.
                    Audience: **l,u,f.** *Choice, 1992.*

Henrion, Claudia   QA27.5.H46 1997
Women in Mathematics: The Addition of Difference. Trade
Cloth. Indiana University Press. Bloomington, IN. 1997. 328p.
ISBN:0-253-33279-6, ISBN13: 978-0-253-33279-0.
Dewey:305.43/51. LCCN:97-002546.
                    Audience: **l,u,f.** *Choice, 1998.*

Keller, Evelyn F. &   Q175.5.F455 1996
  Longino, Helen E. (Editors)
Feminism and Science. Ed. 2. Paper Text. Oxford University
Press, Inc. New York, NY. 1996. 298p. Reading in Feminism
Ser. ISBN:0-19-875146-X, ISBN13: 978-0-19-875146-5.
Dewey:306.4/5. LCCN:95-045299.
                    Audience: **g,l,u.**

Lederman, Muriel &   Q130.G43 2000
  Bartsch, Ingrid (Editors)
The Gender and Science Reader. Paper over Boards. Routledge.
New York, NY. 2000. 528p. ISBN:0-415-21357-6, ISBN13:
978-0-415-21357-8. Dewey:500/.82. LCCN:00-044646.
                    Audience: **l,u,f.** *Choice, 2001.*

More, Ellen S.   R692.M645 1999
Restoring the Balance: Women Physicians and the Profession of
Medicine, 1850-1995. Trade Cloth. Harvard University Press.
Cambridge, MA. 2000. 352p. ISBN:0-674-76661-X, ISBN13:
978-0-674-76661-7. Dewey:610.69/52/0820973.
LCCN:99-038185.
                    Audience: **g,l,u,f.** *Choice, 2000.*

Ogilvie, Marilyn &   Q141.B5285 2000
  Harvey, Joy (Editors)
The Biographical Dictionary of Women in Science: Pioneering
Lives from Ancient Times to the Mid-20th Century, Set.
Margaret Rossiter (Introduction by). Paper over Boards.
Routledge. New York, NY. 2000. 1500p. ISBN:0-415-92038-8,
ISBN13: 978-0-415-92038-4. Dewey:509.2/2 B.
LCCN:99-017668.
                    Audience: **g,l,u,f.** *Choice, 2001.*

Sonnert, Gerhard &   Q149.U5S56 1995
Holton, Gerald
Gender Differences in Science Careers: The Project Access
Study. Robert K. Merton (Foreword by). Cloth Text. Rutgers
University Press. Piscataway, NJ. 1995. 200p. Arnold and
Caroline Rose Series of the American Sociological Association
ISBN:0-8135-2174-2, ISBN13: 978-0-8135-2174-9.
Dewey:502.3/73. LCCN:94-025219.
                    Audience: **l,u,f.** *Choice, 1995.*

Tuana, Nancy (Editor)   Q175.5.F45 1989
📵 Feminism and Science. E-Book. Indiana University Press.
Bloomington, IN. 1989. 272p. Race, Gender and Science Ser.

ISBN:0-253-20525-5, ISBN13: 978-0-253-20525-4.
Dewey:305.4/35. LCCN:88-046044.
                    Audience: **l,u,f.** *Choice, 1990.*

Weise, Elizabeth R. &   HQ1180.W57 1996
  Cherny, Lynn (Editors)
Wired Women: Gender and New Realities in Cyberspace. Trade
Paper. Avalon Publishing Group. New York, NY. 1996. 304p.
ISBN:1-878067-73-7, ISBN13: 978-1-878067-73-9.
Dewey:305.4/0285/467. LCCN:95-051742.
                    Audience: **l,u,f.**

Wyer, Mary (Editor), et al.   Q130.W672 2001
Women, Science and Technology: A Reader in Feminist Science
Studies. Donna Cookmeyer, Mary Barbercheck, Hatice Ozturk
& Marta Wayne (Editors). Paper over Boards. Routledge. New
York, NY. 2000. 400p. ISBN:0-415-92606-8, ISBN13:
978-0-415-92606-5. Dewey:500/.82. LCCN:00-046452.
                    Audience: **g,l.** *Choice, 2001.*

Xie, Yu & Shauman,   Q130.Z54 2003
  Kimberlee A.
Women in Science: Career Processes and Outcomes. Trade
Cloth. Harvard University Press. Cambridge, MA. 2003. 336p.
ISBN:0-674-01034-5, ISBN13: 978-0-674-01034-5.
Dewey:305.43/5. LCCN:2003-045274.
                    Audience: **g,l,u,f.** *Choice, 2004.*

Politics. International Relations. War. Peace

                                        HQ1236.5.U6
▢ CAWP: Center for American Women and Politics.
http://www.rci.rutgers.edu/~cawp/
                    Audience: **g,l,u.**

Alexander, M. Jacqui &   HQ1870.9.F45 1997
  Mohanty, Chandra T. (Editors)
Feminist Genealogies, Colonial Legacies, Democratic Futures.
Paper over Boards. Routledge. New York, NY. 1996. 352p.
Thinking Gender Ser. ISBN:0-415-91211-3, ISBN13:
978-0-415-91211-2. Dewey:323.3/4. LCCN:95-036341.
                    Audience: **u,f.**

Alonso, Harriet H.   JX1965.A45 1993
Peace As a Women's Issue: A History of the U. S. Movement
for World Peace and Women's Rights. Trade Paper. Syracuse
University Press. Syracuse, NY. 1993. 360p. Peace and Conflict
Resolution Ser. ISBN:0-8156-0269-3, ISBN13:
978-0-8156-0269-9. Dewey:327.1/72/082. LCCN:92-009719.
                    Audience: **g,l,u.** *Choice, 1993.*

Alvarez, Sonia E.   HQ1236.5.B6A44 1990
Engendering Democracy in Brazil: Women's Movements in
Transition Politics. Trade Paper. Princeton University Press.
Princeton, NJ. 1990. 320p. ISBN:0-691-02325-5, ISBN13:
978-0-691-02325-0. Dewey:305.42/0981. LCCN:90-033837.
                    Audience: **u,f.** *Choice, 1991.*

Ashfar, Haleh (Editor)   HQ1236.5.D44W665
Women and Politics in the Third World. Trade Paper. Routledge.
New York, NY. 1996. 224p. Women in Politics Ser.
ISBN:0-415-13861-2, ISBN13: 978-0-415-13861-1.
Dewey:322.4/082. LCCN:95-034526.
                    Audience: **u,f.**

Baker, Jean H. (Editor)   **JK1896.V67 2002**
Votes for Women: The Struggle for Suffrage Revisited. Trade
Paper. Oxford University Press, Inc. New York, NY. 2002. 214p.
Viewpoints on American Culture Ser. ISBN:0-19-513017-0,
ISBN13: 978-0-19-513017-1. Dewey:324.6/23/0973.
LCCN:2001-036768.
                Audience: **g,l,u,f.** *Choice, 2003, 2002.*

Baxandall, Rosalyn   **HQ1421**
   Fraad & Gordon, Linda
Dear Sisters: Dispatches from the Women's Liberation
Movement. Trade Paper. Basic Books. New York, NY. 2001.
336p. ISBN:0-465-01707-X, ISBN13: 978-0-465-01707-2.
Dewey:305.420973.
                       Audience: **l,u,f.**

Benedek, Wolfgang   **K644.A35**
   (Editor), et al.
The Human Rights of Women: International Instruments and
African Experiences. Esther Mayambala Kisaakye & Gerd
Oberleitner (Editors). Cloth over Boards. Zed Books, Ltd.
London, 2002. 352p. ISBN:1-84277-044-6, ISBN13:
978-1-84277-044-3. Dewey:341.4/81/082.
                       Audience: **l,u,f.**

Bookman, Ann &   **HQ1236.5.U6**
   Morgen, Sandra (Editors)
Women and the Politics of Empowerment. Trade Paper. Temple
University Press. Philadelphia, PA. 1987. 352p. Women in the
Political Economy Ser. ISBN:0-87722-525-7, ISBN13:
978-0-87722-525-6. Dewey:320/.088042. LCCN:87-006504.
             Audience: **l,u.** *Choice, 1988.*

Braudy, Leo   **HQ1090**
From Chivalry to Terrorism: War and the Changing Nature of
Masculinity. Trade Paper, Perfect. Alfred A. Knopf Inc. New
York, NY. 1999. 656p. ISBN:0-679-76830-0, ISBN13:
978-0-679-76830-2. Dewey:305.31. LCCN:2003-044600.
           Audience: **g,l,u,f.** *Choice, 2004.*

Brown, Wendy   **JA74.B724 1995**
States of Injury: Power and Freedom in Late Modernity. Trade
Paper. Princeton University Press. Princeton, NJ. 1995. 216p.
ISBN:0-691-02989-X, ISBN13: 978-0-691-02989-4.
Dewey:303.3. LCCN:94-024068.
            Audience: **u,f.** *Choice, 1996.*

Burns, Nancy, et al.   **JK1764.B87 2001**
The Private Roots of Public Action: Gender, Equality, and
Political Participation. Kay Lehman Schlozman & Sidney Verba
(Authors). Trade Cloth. Harvard University Press. Cambridge,
MA. 2001. 480p. ISBN:0-674-00601-1, ISBN13:
978-0-674-00601-0. Dewey:323/.042/0973. LCCN:2001-024928.
           Audience: **l,u,f.** *Choice, 2002.*

Carbert, Louise I.   **HQ1459.O57C37 1995**
Agrarian Feminism: The Politics of Ontario Farm Women. Trade
Cloth. University of Toronto Press. Toronto, ON. 1995. 530p.
ISBN:0-8020-2931-0, ISBN13: 978-0-8020-2931-7.
Dewey:305.4/09713. LCCN:95-178422.
           Audience: **u,f.** *Choice, 1996.*

Carroll, Susan J.   **HQ1236.5.U6I524 2001**
   (Editor)
The Impact of Women in Public Office. Trade Cloth. Indiana
University Press. Bloomington, IN. 2001. 256p.
ISBN:0-253-34008-X, ISBN13: 978-0-253-34008-5.
Dewey:320/.082/0973. LCCN:2001-001680.
           Audience: **l,u.** *Choice, 2002.*

Chappell, Louise   **HQ1236.5.C2C55 2002**
Gendering Government: Feminist Engagement with the State in
Australia and Canada. Trade Cloth. University of British
Columbia Press. Vancouver, BC. 2002. 224p.
ISBN:0-7748-0965-5, ISBN13: 978-0-7748-0965-8.
Dewey:320.9/0082/0971. LCCN:2003-446778.
           Audience: **g,l,u,f.** *Choice, 2003.*

Charrad, Mounira M.   **HQ1236.5.A355 C43**
States and Women's Rights: The Making of Postcolonial
Tunisia, Algeria, and Morocco. Trade Cloth. University of
California Press. Berkeley, CA. 2001. 362p.
ISBN:0-520-07323-1, ISBN13: 978-0-520-07323-4.
Dewey:323.3/4/0961. LCCN:00-051172.
           Audience: **u,f.** *Choice, 2002.*

Clements, Barbara   **HX313.7 .C64 1997**
   Evans
Bolshevik Women. Trade Cloth. Cambridge University Press.
New York, NY. 1997. 352p. ISBN:0-521-45403-4, ISBN13:
978-0-521-45403-2. Dewey:947/.084/082. LCCN:96-050036.
           Audience: **g,l,u,f.** *Choice, 1998.*

Cook, Rebecca J.   **K644.H86 1994**
   (Editor)
Human Rights of Women: National and International
Perspectives. Trade Paper. University of Pennsylvania Press.
Philadelphia, PA. 1994. 634p. Pennsylvania Studies in Human
Rights ISBN:0-8122-1538-9, ISBN13: 978-0-8122-1538-0.
Dewey:342/.0878. LCCN:94-020682.
           Audience: **g,l,u,f.** *Choice, 1995.*

Dobrowolsky, Alexandra   **HQ1236.W63863 2003**
   Z. & Hart, Vivien (Editors)
Women Making Constitutions: New Politics and Comparative
Perspectives. Cloth over Boards. Palgrave Macmillan. New
York, NY. 2004. 288p. ISBN:1-4039-0361-1, ISBN13:
978-1-4039-0361-7. Dewey:320/.082. LCCN:2003-049811.
           Audience: **l,u,f.** *Choice, 2004.*

Elshtain, Jean Bethke   **JA74.5**
Meditations on Modern Political Thought: Masculine - Feminine
Themes from Luther to Arendt. Trade Cloth. Pennsylvania State
University Press. University Park, PA. 1992. 142p.
ISBN:0-271-00864-4, ISBN13: 978-0-271-00864-6.
Dewey:320/.01/9. LCCN:91-046357.
           Audience: **l,u.** *Choice, 1986.*

Elshtain, Jean Bethke   **HQ1236.E47 1993**
Public Man, Private Woman: Women in Social and Political
Thought. Ed. 2. Trade Paper. Princeton University Press.
Princeton, NJ. 1993. 408p. ISBN:0-691-02476-6, ISBN13:
978-0-691-02476-9. Dewey:305.4/2. LCCN:92-029726.
           Audience: **l,u.** *B*

Enloe, Cynthia   **HQ1236**
Bananas, Beaches and Bases: Making Feminist Sense of
International Politics. Ed. 2. Trade Paper. University of
California Press. Berkeley, CA. 2001. 264p.
ISBN:0-520-22912-6, ISBN13: 978-0-520-22912-9.
Dewey:327/.082. LCCN:90-120472.
                 Audience: **g,l,u,f.**

Enloe, Cynthia H.   **HQ1233.E55 1993**
The Morning After: Sexual Politics at the End of the Cold War.
Trade Cloth. University of California Press. Berkeley, CA. 1993.
293p. ISBN:0-520-08335-0, ISBN13: 978-0-520-08335-6.
Dewey:305.3. LCCN:92-043416.
           Audience: **l,u,f.** *Choice, 1994.*

Geisler, Gisela   HQ1236.5.A356G45
A Women Remaking Politic South. Trade Paper. Nordic Africa
Institute, The. Uppsala, 2004. 241p. ISBN:91-7106-515-6,
ISBN13: 978-91-7106-515-5. LCCN:2004-471083.
                    Audience: **u,f.** *Choice, 2005.*

Gill, LaVerne M.   E840.6.G55 1997
African American Women in Congress. Cloth Text. Rutgers
University Press. Piscataway, NJ. 1997. 256p.
ISBN:0-8135-2352-4, ISBN13: 978-0-8135-2352-1.
Dewey:328.73/092/2 B. LCCN:96-029294.
                    Audience: **g,l,u.**

Goldstein, Joshua S.   U21.5 .G63 2001
War and Gender: How Gender Shapes the War System and Vice
Versa. Cloth Text. Cambridge University Press. New York, NY.
2001. 540p. ISBN:0-521-80716-6, ISBN13: 978-0-521-80716-6.
Dewey:303.6/6/082. LCCN:2001-277554.
                    Audience: **g,l,u.** *Choice, 2002.*

Grant, Rebecca &   JX1391.G46 1991
  Newland, Kathleen (Editors)
Gender and International Relations. Trade Cloth. Indiana
University Press. Bloomington, IN. 1991. 188p.
ISBN:0-253-32613-3, ISBN13: 978-0-253-32613-3.
Dewey:327/.082. LCCN:91-014471.
                    Audience: **g,l,u.** *Choice, 1992.*

Hooper, Charlotte   HQ1090.H66 2001
Manly States: Masculinities, International Relations, and Gender
Politics. Trade Cloth. Columbia University Press. New York,
NY. 2001. 224p. ISBN:0-231-12074-5, ISBN13:
978-0-231-12074-6. Dewey:305.31. LCCN:00-060142.
                    Audience: **u,f.** *Choice, 2002.*

Inglehart, Ronald &   HQ1075.I53 2003
  Norris, Pippa
Rising Tide: Gender Equality and Cultural Change Around the
World. Trade Cloth. Cambridge University Press. New York,
NY. 2003. 240p. ISBN:0-521-82203-3, ISBN13:
978-0-521-82203-9. Dewey:305.3. LCCN:2002-031077.
                    Audience: **u,f.** *Choice, 2004.*

Jaggar, Alison M.   HX546
Feminist Politics and Human Nature. Trade Cloth. Rowman &
Littlefield Publishers, Inc. Lanham, MD. 1983. 416p. Philosophy
and Society Ser. ISBN:0-8476-7181-X, ISBN13:
978-0-8476-7181-6. Dewey:305.4/2. LCCN:83-003402.
                    Audience: **u,f.** *B*

James, Joy   E185.86
Shadowboxing: Representations of Black Feminist Politics.
Trade Paper. Palgrave Macmillan. New York, NY. 2002. 240p.
ISBN:0-312-29449-2, ISBN13: 978-0-312-29449-6.
Dewey:305.48/896073.
                    Audience: **l,u.**

Jaquette, Jane S. &   HQ1236.W586 1998
  Wolchik, Sharon L. (Editors)
Women and Democracy: Latin America and Central and Eastern
Europe. Trade Paper. Johns Hopkins University Press.
Baltimore, MD. 1998. 264p. ISBN:0-8018-5838-0, ISBN13:
978-0-8018-5838-3. Dewey:305.42/098. LCCN:98-005120.
                    Audience: **l,u,f.** *Choice, 1999.*

Kerber, Linda K.   HQ1236.5.U6K47 1998
No Constitutional Right to Be Ladies: Women and the
Obligations of Citizenship. Cloth over Boards. Farrar, Straus &
Giroux. New York, NY. 1998. 352p. ISBN:0-8090-7383-8,

ISBN13: 978-0-8090-7383-2. Dewey:305.42/0973.
LCCN:98-021393.
                    Audience: **u,f.** *Choice, 1999.*

LeBlanc, Robin M.   HQ1236.5.J3 L43 1999
Bicycle Citizens: The Political World of the Japanese
Housewife. Trade Paper. University of California Press.
Berkeley, CA. 1999. 266p. Asia Ser., :Local Studies/Global
Themes ISBN:0-520-21291-6, ISBN13: 978-0-520-21291-6.
Dewey:305.42/0952. LCCN:98-046632.
                    Audience: **g,u,f.** *Choice, 1999.*

MacKay, Fiona   HQ1236.5.G7M3 2001
Love and Politics: Women Politicans and the Ethics of Care.
Trade Cloth. Continuum International Publishing Group, Ltd.
London, 2001. 254p. Political Theory and Contemporary Politics
Ser. ISBN:0-8264-4782-1, ISBN13: 978-0-8264-4782-1.
Dewey:320/.082/0941. LCCN:00-069376.
                    Audience: **u,f.** *Choice, 2002.*

MacKinnon, Catharine   K644
  A.
Toward a Feminist Theory of the State. Trade Paper. Harvard
University Press. Cambridge, MA. 1991. 350 dgtp.
ISBN:0-674-89646-7, ISBN13: 978-0-674-89646-8.
Dewey:305.42. LCCN:89-007540.
                    Audience: **g,l.** *Choice, 1990.*

Marshall, Barbara   HQ1075.M369 2000
Configuring Gender: Explorations in Theory and Politics. Trade
Paper. Broadview Press. Peterborough, ON. 2000. 191p.
ISBN:1-55111-094-6, ISBN13: 978-1-55111-094-3.
Dewey:305.3. LCCN:00-343488.
                    Audience: **u,f.** *Choice, 2000.*

Mink, Gwendolyn   HV700.5.M56 1998
Welfare's End. Book, Other. Cornell University Press. Ithaca,
NY. 1998. 192p. ISBN:0-8014-3347-9, ISBN13:
978-0-8014-3347-4. Dewey:362.83/928/0973. LCCN:97-038838.
                    Audience: **l,u.** *Choice, 1998.*

Nelson, Barbara J. &   HQ1236.5.U6
  Chowdhury, Najma (Editors)
Women and Politics Worldwide. Trade Paper. Yale University
Press. Cumberland, RI. 1994. 832p. ISBN:0-300-05408-4,
ISBN13: 978-0-300-05408-8. Dewey:320.082.
LCCN:93-028668.
                    Audience: **l,u,f.** *Choice, 1994.*

Nijeholt, Geertje A. &   HQ1236.W6523 1998
  Wieringa, Saskia
Women's Movements and Public Policy in Europe, Latin
America, and the Caribbean: The Triangle of Empowerment.
Virginia Vargas & Chandra Mohanty (Editors). Cloth Text.
Garland Publishing, Inc. New York, NY. 1997. 196p. Gender,
Culture, and Global Politics Ser., No. 2 ISBN:0-8153-2479-0,
ISBN13: 978-0-8153-2479-9. Dewey:305.42. LCCN:97-013518.
                    Audience: **l,u,f.** *Choice, 1998.*

Okin, Susan Moller   HQ1122
Women in Western Political Thought. Trade Paper. Princeton
University Press. Princeton, NJ. 1979. 384p.
ISBN:0-691-02191-0, ISBN13: 978-0-691-02191-1.
Dewey:305.4/2/01. LCCN:79-084004.
                    Audience: **l,u,f.**

Peters, J. S. & Wolper, 　　K644.Z9W665 1995
Andrea (Editors)
Women's Rights, Human Rights: International Feminist
Perspectives. Trade Paper. Routledge. New York, NY. 1994.
384p. ISBN:0-415-90995-3, ISBN13: 978-0-415-90995-2.
Dewey:323.3/4. LCCN:94-015775.
　　　　　　　　　Audience: **l,u,f.** *Choice, 1995.*

Pollitt, Katha 　　PS3566.O533S83 2001
Subject to Debate: Sense and Dissents on Women, Politics, and
Culture. Trade Paper. Random House Adult Trade Publishing
Group. New York, NY. 2001. 368p. ISBN:0-679-78343-1,
ISBN13: 978-0-679-78343-5. Dewey:814/.54. LCCN:00-056109.
　　　　　　　　　Audience: **g,l,u,f.**

Reardon, Betty A. 　　JX1965
Women and Peace: Feminist Visions of Global Security. Paper
Text. State University of New York Press. Albany, NY. 1993.
209p. SUNY Series in Global Conflict and Peace Education
ISBN:0-7914-1400-0, ISBN13: 978-0-7914-1400-2.
Dewey:327.1/72/082. LCCN:92-009682.
　　　　　　　　　Audience: **u,f.** *Choice, 1993.*

Reddock, Rhoda 　　HQ1525.7.R43 1994
Women, Labour and Politics in Trinidad and Tobago: A History.
Cloth over Boards. Zed Books, Ltd. London, 1994. 320p.
ISBN:1-85649-153-6, ISBN13: 978-1-85649-153-2.
Dewey:305.42/0972983. LCCN:94-024809.
　　　　　　　　　Audience: **l,u,f.** *Choice, 1995.*

Rodriguez, Victoria 　　HQ1236.5.M6W65 1998
Women's Participation in Mexican Political Life. Trade Paper.
Westview Press. Boulder, CO. 1998. 280p. ISBN:0-8133-3529-9,
ISBN13: 978-0-8133-3529-2. Dewey:320.0820972.
LCCN:98-020771.
　　　　　　　　　Audience: **u,f.** *Choice, 1999.*

Rodríguez, Victoria E. 　　HQ1236.5.M6R63 2003
Women in Contemporary Mexican Politics. Trade Cloth.
University of Texas Press. Austin, TX. 2003. 344p.
ISBN:0-292-77125-8, ISBN13: 978-0-292-77125-3.
Dewey:306/.2/0820972. LCCN:2002-013122.
　　　　　　　　　Audience: **g,l,u,f.** *Choice, 2003.*

Sapiro, Virginia 　　HQ1236
The Political Integration of Women: Roles, Socialization, and
Politics. Trade Paper. University of Illinois Press. Champaign,
IL. 1984. 216p. Illini Book Ser. ISBN:0-252-01141-4, ISBN13:
978-0-252-01141-2. Dewey:323.3/4. LCCN:82-002672.
　　　　　　　　　Audience: **l,u,f.** *B*

Sapiro, Virginia 　　JC176.W65S27 1992
A Vindication of Political Virtue: The Political Theory of Mary
Wollstonecraft. Trade Paper. University of Chicago Press.
Chicago, IL. 1992. 394p. ISBN:0-226-73491-9, ISBN13:
978-0-226-73491-0. Dewey:323.34092. LCCN:91-038426.
　　　　　　　　　Audience: **l,u,f.** *Choice, 1993.*

Sapiro, Virginia 　　GN0365.9.W65
(Editor)
Women, Biology and Public Policy. Trade Paper. Books on
Demand. Ann Arbor, MI. 1985. 272p. Sage Yearbooks in
Women's Policy Studies, Vol. 10 ISBN:0-608-01524-5, ISBN13:
978-0-608-01524-8. Dewey:304.5. LCCN:85-001935.
　　　　　　　　　Audience: **l,u,f.**

Schatzberg, Michael G. 　　JQ1879.A15S32 2001
🄴 Political Legitimacy in Middle Africa: Father, Family, Food.
E-Book. Indiana University Press. Bloomington, IN. 2001. xi,

292p. ISBN:0-253-33992-8, ISBN13: 978-0-253-33992-8.
Dewey:306.2/0967. LCCN:2001-002060.
　　　　　　　　　Audience: **l,u,f.** *Choice, 2002.*

Seltzer, Richard A., et al. 　　HQ1236.5.U6S45 1997
Sex As a Political Variable: Women As Candidates and Voters in
U. S. Elections. Jody Newman & Melissa V. Leighton
(Authors). Trade Paper. Lynne Rienner Publishers, Inc. Boulder,
CO. 1997. 189p. ISBN:1-55587-736-2, ISBN13:
978-1-55587-736-1. Dewey:306.2/0973. LCCN:97-009105.
　　　　　　　　　Audience: **g,l,u,f.** *Choice, 1998.*

Shanley, Mary L. & 　　HQ1190.F46 1991
Pateman, Carole (Editors)
Feminist Interpretations and Political Theory. Trade Paper.
Pennsylvania State University Press. University Park, PA. 1991.
442p. ISBN:0-271-00742-7, ISBN13: 978-0-271-00742-7.
Dewey:305.42/01. LCCN:90-043290.
　　　　　　　　　Audience: **l,u,f.**

Smith, J. Clay Jr. 　　KF299.A35
(Editor)
Rebels in Law: Voices in History of Black Women Lawyers.
Trade Paper. University of Michigan Press. Chicago, IL. 2000.
360p. ISBN:0-472-08646-4, ISBN13: 978-0-472-08646-7.
Dewey:340/.0896/073.
　　　　　　　　　Audience: **l,u,f.** *Choice, 1999.*

Steans, Jill 　　JZ1253.2.S74 1998
Gender and International Relations. Cloth Text. Rutgers
University Press. Piscataway, NJ. 1998. 232p.
ISBN:0-8135-2512-8, ISBN13: 978-0-8135-2512-9.
Dewey:327/.082. LCCN:97-041156.
　　　　　　　　　Audience: **l,u.** *Choice, 1998.*

Sunstein, Cass R. 　　HQ1206.F447 1990
Feminism and Political Theory. Trade Cloth. University of
Chicago Press. Chicago, IL. 1990. 304p. ISBN:0-226-78008-2,
ISBN13: 978-0-226-78008-5. Dewey:305.42. LCCN:90-030656.
　　　　　　　　　Audience: **l,u.**

Sylvester, Christine 　　HQ1190 .S95 1994
Feminist Theory and International Relations in a Postmodern
Era. Thomas Biersteker, Chris Brown, Phil Cerny, Joseph
Grieco, A. J. R. Groom, Steve Smith, Richard Higgott, G. John
Ikenberry, Caroline Kennedy-Pipe & Steve Lamy (Contribution
by). Trade Paper. Cambridge University Press. New York, NY.
1994. 280p. Studies in International Relations, No. 32
ISBN:0-521-45984-2, ISBN13: 978-0-521-45984-6.
Dewey:305.4201. LCCN:93-010251.
　　　　　　　　　Audience: **l,u,f.** *Choice, 1994.*

Taylor, Barbara 　　HQ1154
Eve and the New Jerusalem: Socialism and Feminism in the
Nineteenth Century. Trade Paper. Harvard University Press.
Cambridge, MA. 1993. 402p. ISBN:0-674-27023-1, ISBN13:
978-0-674-27023-7. Dewey:305.4/2/09034. LCCN:92-031980.
　　　　　　　　　Audience: **u,f.** *B*

Tetreault, Mary A. 　　HQ1236.W6364 1994
(Editor)
Women and Revolution in Africa, Asia, and the New World.
Cloth Text. University of South Carolina Press. Columbia, SC.
1994. 472p. ISBN:1-57003-016-2, ISBN13: 978-1-57003-016-1.
Dewey:305.42. LCCN:94-018706.
　　　　　　　　　Audience: **g,l,u.** *Choice, 1995.*

Thomas, Sue & Wilcox,   **HQ1391.U5W63 2005**
  Clyde
Women and Elective Office: Past, Present, and Future. Ed. 2.
Trade Cloth. Oxford University Press, Inc. New York, NY. 2005.
344p. ISBN:0-19-518082-8, ISBN13: 978-0-19-518082-4.
Dewey:320/.082. LCCN:2004-027124.
> Audience: **l,u,f.** *Choice, 1998.*

Tickner, J. Ann   **HQ1154.T53 2001**
Gendering World Politics: Issues and Approaches in the
Post-Cold War Era. Trade Cloth. Columbia University Press.
New York, NY. 2001. 262p. ISBN:0-231-11366-8, ISBN13:
978-0-231-11366-3. Dewey:305.42. LCCN:00-047503.
> Audience: **u,f.** *Choice, 2001.*

Tripp, Aili Mari   **HQ1236.5.U33T75 2000**
Women and Politics in Uganda: The Challenge of Associational
Autonomy. Cloth Text. University of Wisconsin Press. Chicago,
IL. 2000. xxvii, 277p. ISBN:0-299-16480-2, ISBN13:
978-0-299-16480-5. Dewey:305.42/096761. LCCN:99-028158.
> Audience: **l,u,f.** *Choice, 2000.*

Wood, Elizabeth A.   **HX546.W67 1997**
ⓔ The Baba and the Comrade: Gender and Politics in
Revolutionary Russia. E-Book. Indiana University Press.
Bloomington, IN. 1997. 336p. Indiana-Michigan Series in
Russian and East European Studies ISBN:0-253-33311-3,
ISBN13: 978-0-253-33311-7. Dewey:321.9/2/0820947.
LCCN:97-002290.
> Audience: **g,u,f.** *Choice, 1998.*

Health > General Health

Bair, Barbara &   **RA564.86.W55 1993**
  Cayleff, Susan E. (Editors)
Wings of Gauze: Women of Color and the Experience of Health
and Illness. Paper Text. Wayne State University Press. Detroit,
MI. 1993. 394p. ISBN:0-8143-2302-2, ISBN13:
978-0-8143-2302-1. Dewey:362.1/08/693. LCCN:92-046308.
> Audience: **g,l,u,f.** *Choice, 1994.*

Boston Women's Health   **RA778**
  Book Collective Staff
Our Bodies, Ourselves for the New Century: A Book by and for
Women. Library Binding. Sagebrush Education Resources.
Caledonia, MN. 1998. ISBN:0-7857-8072-6, ISBN13:
978-0-7857-8072-4. Dewey:613/.04244.
> Audience: **g,l,u,f.**

Davis, Kathy   **RD119.D385 1995**
Reshaping the Female Body: The Dilemma of Cosmetic
Surgery. UK-B Format Paperback. Routledge. New York, NY.
1994. 224p. ISBN:0-415-90632-6, ISBN13: 978-0-415-90632-6.
Dewey:617.9/5/0082. LCCN:94-019290.
> Audience: **l,u,f.**

Doyal, Lesley   **RA564.85.D69 1995**
What Makes Women Sick: Gender and the Political Economy of
Health. Cloth Text. Rutgers University Press. Piscataway, NJ.
1995. 320p. ISBN:0-8135-2206-4, ISBN13: 978-0-8135-2206-7.
Dewey:362.1/082. LCCN:94-047498.
> Audience: **u,f.** *Choice, 1995.*

Engel, June   **RC280.B8**
The Complete Breast Book: Everything You Need to Know
about Breast Disease. Trade Paper. Firefly Books, Ltd.
Tonawanda, NY. 1996. 276p. Your Personal Health Ser.

ISBN:1-55013-748-4, ISBN13: 978-1-55013-748-4.
Dewey:618.1/9.
> Audience: **g,l,u,f.** *Choice, 1996.*

Ferguson, Susan J. &   **RC280.B8**
  Kasper, Anne S.
Breast Cancer: Society Shapes an Epidemic: The Social
Construction of an Illness. Cloth over Boards. Palgrave
Macmillan. New York, NY. 2000. 320p. ISBN:0-312-21710-2,
ISBN13: 978-0-312-21710-5. Dewey:362.1969945.
> Audience: **g,l,u,f.** *Choice, 2001.*

Gorna, Robin   **RA644.A25G66 1996**
Vamps, Virgins and Victims: How Can Women Fight AIDS?
Trade Cloth. Cassell P L C. London, 1994. 288p. Women on
Women Ser. ISBN:0-304-32807-3, ISBN13: 978-0-304-32807-9.
Dewey:616.97/92/0082. LCCN:95-163136.
> Audience: **u,f.** *Choice, 1996.*

Haiken, Elizabeth   **RD119.H35 1997**
Venus Envy: A History of Cosmetic Surgery. Trade Cloth. Johns
Hopkins University Press. Baltimore, MD. 1999. 384p.
ISBN:0-8018-5763-5, ISBN13: 978-0-8018-5763-8.
Dewey:617.9/5. LCCN:97-019823.
> Audience: **g,l.** *Choice, 1998.*

Hillyer, Barbara   **HV1569.3.W65H55 1993**
ⓔ Feminism and Disability. E-Book. University of Oklahoma
Press. Norman, OK. 1993. ISBN:0-8061-7247-9, ISBN13:
978-0-8061-7247-7. Dewey:362.4082.
> Audience: **g,l,u,f.** *Choice, 1993.*

Inhorn, Marcia Claire   **RC889 .I5613 2002**
  & van Balen, Frank (Editors)
Infertility Around the Globe: New Thinking on Childlessness,
Gender, and Reproductive Technologies. Trade Cloth. University
of California Press. Berkeley, CA. 2002. 358p.
ISBN:0-520-23108-2, ISBN13: 978-0-520-23108-5.
Dewey:616.6/92. LCCN:2001-007069.
> Audience: **u,f.**

Kane, Penny   **HQ1206**
Women's Health from Womb to Tomb. Ed. 2. Trade Paper.
Palgrave Macmillan. New York, NY. 1994. xxiii, 209p.
ISBN:0-312-10623-8, ISBN13: 978-0-312-10623-2.
Dewey:305.4.
> Audience: **g,l,u,f.** *Choice, 1991.*

Lather, Patricia A. &   **RC607.A26L377 1997**
  Smithies, Chris
Troubling the Angels: Women Living with HIV/AIDS. Trade
Paper. Westview Press. Boulder, CO. 1997. 288p.
ISBN:0-8133-9016-8, ISBN13: 978-0-8133-9016-1.
Dewey:362.1/969792/0082. LCCN:97-003989.
> Audience: **u,f.** *Choice, 1998.*

Long, Lynellen D.   **RC607.A26W653 1996**
Women's Experiences with HIV/AIDS: An International
Perspective. E. Maxine Ankrah (Editor). Trade Paper. Columbia
University Press. New York, NY. 1996. 352p.
ISBN:0-231-10605-X, ISBN13: 978-0-231-10605-4.
Dewey:362.1/969792. LCCN:96-031322.
> Audience: **u,f.** *Choice, 1997.*

Lorber, Judith &   **RA418.L67 2002**
  Moore, Lisa Jean
Gender and the Social Construction of Illness. Ed. 2. Trade
Cloth. AltaMira Press. Walnut Creek, CA. 2002. 208p.

ISBN:0-7591-0237-6, ISBN13: 978-0-7591-0237-8.
Dewey:306.461. LCCN:2002-003798.

Audience: **l,u,f.**

Mahowald, Mary   **RB155.M3135 2000**
  Briody
Genes, Women, Equality. Trade Cloth. Oxford University Press,
Inc. New York, NY. 1999. 336p. ISBN:0-19-512110-4, ISBN13:
978-0-19-512110-0. Dewey:616/.042/082. LCCN:99-014296.

Audience: **l,u,f.**

Martin, Emily   **RG103.5.M37 2001**
The Woman in the Body: A Cultural Analysis of Reproduction.
Trade Paper. Beacon Press. Boston, MA. 2001. 320p.
ISBN:0-8070-4645-0, ISBN13: 978-0-8070-4645-6.
Dewey:155.3/33. LCCN:2001-029523.

Audience: **l,u,f.**

Messing, Karen   **RC963.6.W65M47 1998**
One-Eyed Science: Occupational Health and Women Workers.
Trade Cloth. Temple University Press. Philadelphia, PA. 1998.
264p. Labor and Social Change Ser. ISBN:1-56639-597-6,
ISBN13: 978-1-56639-597-7. Dewey:616.9/803*/082.
LCCN:97-026885.

Audience: **u,f.**   *Choice, 1998.*

Minkin, Mary Jane &   **RG121.M667 2003**
  Wright, Carol V.
The Yale Guide to Women's Reproductive Health: From
Menarche to Menopause. Cloth over Boards. Yale University
Press. Cumberland, RI. 2003. 464p. ISBN:0-300-09820-0,
ISBN13: 978-0-300-09820-4. Dewey:618.1.
LCCN:2002-035738.

Audience: **g,l,u,f.**   *Choice, 2003.*

Moss, Kary L. (Editor)   **RA564.85.M36 1996**
Man-Made Medicine: Women's Health, Public Policy and
Reform. Trade Cloth. Duke University Press. Durham, NC.
1996. 304p. ISBN:0-8223-1811-3, ISBN13: 978-0-8223-1811-8.
Dewey:362.1/082. LCCN:96-021855.

Audience: **u,f.**   *Choice, 1997.*

Purdy, Laura M.   **RG133.5.P87 1996**
Reproducing Persons: Issues in Feminist Bioethics. Book, Other.
Cornell University Press. Ithaca, NY. 1996. 304p.
ISBN:0-8014-3243-X, ISBN13: 978-0-8014-3243-9. Dewey:176.
LCCN:95-052019.

Audience: **g,l,u,f.**   *Choice, 1996.*

Rahman, Anika &   **K5304.F46 2000**
  Toubia, Nahid
Female Genital Mutilation: A Practical Guide to Worldwide
Laws and Policies. Trade Paper. Zed Books, Ltd. London, 2000.
192p. ISBN:1-85649-773-9, ISBN13: 978-1-85649-773-2.
Dewey:392.1. LCCN:00-043614.

Audience: **l,u,f.**   *Choice, 2001.*

Rosenfeld, Jo Ann   **RA778 .H225 2001**
  (Editor)
Handbook of Women's Health: An Evidence-Based Approach.
Trade Paper. Cambridge University Press. New York, NY. 2004.
628p. ISBN:0-521-54595-1, ISBN13: 978-0-521-54595-2.
Dewey:613/.04244. LCCN:2003-065267.

Audience: **g,l,u,f.**   *Choice, 2002.*

Ruzek, Sheryl B., et al.   **RA564.85W66686 1997**
Women's Health: Complexities and Differences. Virginia L.
Olesen & Adele E. Clarke (Authors). Cloth Text. Ohio State
University Press. Columbus, OH. 1997. 689p. Women and

Health Ser. ISBN:0-8142-0704-9, ISBN13: 978-0-8142-0704-8.
Dewey:613/.04244. LCCN:96-034047.

Audience: **l,u,f.**   *Choice, 1997.*

Scrivener, Laurie &   **R692**
  Barnes, J. Suzanne
A Biographical Dictionary of Women Healers: Midwives,
Nurses and Physicians. Cloth Text. Greenwood Publishing
Group, Inc. Portsmouth, NH. 2002. 352p. ISBN:1-57356-219-X,
ISBN13: 978-1-57356-219-5. Dewey:610/.82/0922 B.
LCCN:2001-058031.

Audience: **g.**   *Choice, 2003, 2002.*

Sen, Gita (Editor), et al.   **RA441.E544 2002**
Engendering International Health: The Challenge of Equity.
Asha George & Piroska Östlin (Editors). Trade Cloth. MIT
Press. Cambridge, MA. 2002. 467p. Basic Bioethics Ser.
ISBN:0-262-19469-4, ISBN13: 978-0-262-19469-3.
Dewey:362.1. LCCN:2001-055808.

Audience: **l,u,f.**

Sherwin, Susan   **R724**
No Longer Patient: Feminist Ethics and Health Care. Trade
Paper. Temple University Press. Philadelphia, PA. 1992. 280p.
ISBN:1-56639-061-3, ISBN13: 978-1-56639-061-3.
Dewey:174.2.

Audience: **l,u,f.**   *Choice, 1992.*

Smith, Susan L.   **RA448.5.N4S65 1995**
Sick and Tired of Being Sick and Tired: Black Women's Health
Activism in America, 1890-1950. Trade Cloth. University of
Pennsylvania Press. Philadelphia, PA. 1995. 288p. Studies in
Health, Illness, and Caregiving ISBN:0-8122-3237-2, ISBN13:
978-0-8122-3237-0. Dewey:362.1. LCCN:95-011310.

Audience: **g,l,u.**   *Choice, 1996.*

Wendell, Susan   **HV1568.W433 1996**
The Rejected Body: Feminist Philosophical Reflections on
Disability. Paper over Boards. Routledge. New York, NY. 1996.
316p. ISBN:0-415-91046-3, ISBN13: 978-0-415-91046-0.
Dewey:305.9/0816. LCCN:95-051391.

Audience: **u,f.**

Health > Aging

Allen, Jessie & Pifer,   **HQ1064.U5W617 1993**
  Alan (Editors)
Women on the Front Lines: Meeting the Challenge of an Aging
America. Trade Cloth. University Press of America, Inc.
Lanham, MD. 1993. 280p. ISBN:0-87766-574-5, ISBN13:
978-0-87766-574-8. Dewey:305.26. LCCN:92-034290.

Audience: **g,l,u,f.**   *Choice, 1993.*

Browne, Collette V.   **HQ1064.U5B765 1998**
Women, Feminism, and Aging: A New Look at Theory and
Practice. Trade Cloth. Springer Publishing Company, Inc. New
York, NY. 1998. 360p. Springer Series, Focus on Women Ser.
ISBN:0-8261-1200-5, ISBN13: 978-0-8261-1200-2.
Dewey:305.26/0973. LCCN:98-010304.

Audience: **l,u,f.**   *Choice, 1999.*

Calasanti, Toni M. &   **HQ1061.C28 2001**
  Slevin, Kathleen F.
Gender, Social Inequalities and Aging. Trade Cloth. AltaMira
Press. Walnut Creek, CA. 2001. 248p. Gender Lens Ser.

ISBN:0-7591-0185-X, ISBN13: 978-0-7591-0185-2.
Dewey:305.26. LCCN:2001-022919.
Audience: **g,l,u.** *Choice, 2002.*

Cruikshank, Margaret   **BF724.55.A35C78 2002**
Learning to Be Old: Gender, Culture, and Aging. Book, Other.
Rowman & Littlefield Publishers, Inc. Lanham, MD. 2002.
256p. ISBN:0-8476-9848-3, ISBN13: 978-0-8476-9848-6.
Dewey:305.26. LCCN:2002-005352.
Audience: **l,u,f.** *Choice, 2003.*

Day, Alice T.   **HQ1064.U5D388 1991**
Remarkable Survivors: Insights into Successful Aging among
Women. Trade Paper. University Press of America, Inc. Lanham,
MD. 1991. 340p. ISBN:0-87766-491-9, ISBN13:
978-0-87766-491-8. Dewey:305.4. LCCN:90-026598.
Audience: **l,u,f.** *Choice, 1992.*

Doress-Worters, Paula   **HQ1206**
B. & Siegal, Diana L.
The New Ourselves, Growing Older. Trade Cloth. Peter Smith
Publisher, Inc. Magnolia, MA. 1996. ISBN:0-8446-6844-3,
ISBN13: 978-0-8446-6844-4. Dewey:305.4.
Audience: **g.**

Farrell, Michael P. &   **HA1059**
Rosenberg, Stanley
Men at Midlife. Paper Text. Greenwood Publishing Group, Inc.
Portsmouth, NH. 1981. 256p. ISBN:0-86569-062-6, ISBN13:
978-0-86569-062-2. Dewey:305.2/44/088041. LCCN:81-003624.
Audience: **g,l,u,f.** *B*

Friedan, Betty   **HQ1061**
The Fountain of Age. Trade Paper. Simon & Schuster. New
York, NY. 2006. 672p. ISBN:0-7432-9987-6, ISBN13:
978-0-7432-9987-9. Dewey:305.26.
Audience: **g.**

Thompson, Edward H.   **Z7164**
Jr. (Compiled by)
Men and Aging: A Selected, Annotated Bibliography. Cloth
Text. Greenwood Publishing Group, Inc. Portsmouth, NH. 1996.
256p. Bibliographies and Indexes in Gerontology Ser., Vol. 32
ISBN:0-313-29106-3, ISBN13: 978-0-313-29106-7.
Dewey:016.30526 s. LCCN:95-025580.
Audience: **u,f.** *Choice, 1996.*

Wheeler, Helen R.   **Z7963.A4W54 1997**
Women and Aging: A Guide to the Literature. Library Binding.
Lynne Rienner Publishers, Inc. Boulder, CO. 1997. 259p.
ISBN:1-55587-661-7, ISBN13: 978-1-55587-661-6.
Dewey:016.30526. LCCN:96-041175.
Audience: **l,u,f.** *Choice, 1997.*

Health > Psychology

Braziel, Jana Evans &   **RC552.O25 B63 2001**
LeBesco, Kathleen (Editors)
Bodies Out of Bounds: Fatness and Transgression. Trade Cloth.
University of California Press. Berkeley, CA. 2001. 368p.
ISBN:0-520-21746-2, ISBN13: 978-0-520-21746-1.
Dewey:616.3/98/0019. LCCN:2001-027446.
Audience: **g,l,u,f.**

Brody, Leslie   **RC455.4.E46B76 1999**
Gender, Emotion, and the Family. Trade Cloth. Harvard
University Press. Cambridge, MA. 1999. 368p.

ISBN:0-674-34186-4, ISBN13: 978-0-674-34186-9.
Dewey:152.4. LCCN:98-032351.
Audience: **l,u,f.** *Choice, 1999.*

Chodorow, Nancy   **HQ1206.C52 1989**
e Feminism and Psychoanalytic Theory. E-Book. NetLibrary,
Inc. Boulder, CO. 1989. ISBN:0-585-34998-3, ISBN13:
978-0-585-34998-5. Dewey:305.42.
Audience: **l,u,f.**

Chodorow, Nancy Julia   **HQ759.C56 1999**
The Reproduction of Mothering: Psychoanalysis and the
Sociology of Gender. Ed. 2. Trade Paper. University of
California Press. Berkeley, CA. 1999. 284p.
ISBN:0-520-22155-9, ISBN13: 978-0-520-22155-0.
Dewey:306.874/3. LCCN:2001-266933.
Audience: **l,u,f.** *B*

Comas-Diaz, Lillian &   **RC451.4.M58W66 1994**
Greene, Beverly (Editors)
Women of Color: Integrating Ethnic and Gender Identities in
Psychotherapy. Cloth over Boards. Guilford Publications, Inc.
New York, NY. 1994. 518p. ISBN:0-89862-371-5, ISBN13:
978-0-89862-371-0. Dewey:616.89/14/08693. LCCN:94-010840.
Audience: **l,u,f.** *Choice, 1995.*

Davidman, Lynn   **BF575.G7**
Motherloss. Trade Paper. University of California Press.
Berkeley, CA. 2002. 308p. ISBN:0-520-23200-3, ISBN13:
978-0-520-23200-6. Dewey:155.937. LCCN:99-053072.
Audience: **l,u,f.** *Choice, 2000.*

Denmark, Florence L.   **HQ1206**
& Paludi, Michele A. (Editors)
Psychology of Women: A Handbook of Issues and Theories.
Cloth Text. Greenwood Publishing Group, Inc. Portsmouth, NH.
1993. 784p. ISBN:0-313-26295-0, ISBN13: 978-0-313-26295-1.
Dewey:155.333. LCCN:92-008642.
Audience: **g,l,u,f.** *Choice, 1994.*

Gilligan, Carol   **HQ1206.G58 1993**
In a Different Voice: Psychological Theory and Women's
Development. Trade Paper. Harvard University Press.
Cambridge, MA. 1993. 216p. ISBN:0-674-44544-9, ISBN13:
978-0-674-44544-4. Dewey:305.4/2. LCCN:81-013478.
Audience: **g,l,u,f.** *B*

Hesse-Biber, Sharlene   **BF697.5.B63H47**
Am I Thin Enough Yet?: The Cult of Thinness and the
Commercialization of Identity. Paper Text. Oxford University
Press, Inc. New York, NY. 1997. 200p. ISBN:0-19-511791-3,
ISBN13: 978-0-19-511791-2. Dewey:306.4.
Audience: **g,l,u,f.** *Choice, 1996.*

Horney, Karen   **HQ1206**
Feminine Psychology. Trade Paper. W. W. Norton & Company,
Inc. New York, NY. 1993. 272p. ISBN:0-393-31080-9, ISBN13:
978-0-393-31080-1. Dewey:155.633.
Audience: **l,u,f.**

Irigaray, Luce   **HQ1154.I7413 1985**
Speculum of the Other Woman. Gillian C. Gill (Translator).
Trade Paper. Cornell University Press. Ithaca, NY. 1985. 416p.
ISBN:0-8014-9330-7, ISBN13: 978-0-8014-9330-0.
Dewey:155.3/33. LCCN:84-045151.
Audience: **u,f.**

Kaschak, Ellyn   HQ1206.K37 1992
Engendered Lives: A New Psychology of Women's Experience.
Trade Cloth. Basic Books. New York, NY. 1992. 288p.
ISBN:0-465-01347-3, ISBN13: 978-0-465-01347-0.
Dewey:155.6/33. LCCN:91-058602.

     Audience: **u,f.** *Choice, 1993.*

Kaschak, Ellyn   HQ1206 .K37
Engendered Lives: A New Psychology of Women's Lives. Trade
Paper. Basic Books. New York, NY. 1993. 288p.
ISBN:0-465-01349-X, ISBN13: 978-0-465-01349-4.
Dewey:155.6/33. LCCN:91-058602.

     Audience: **l,u,f.**

Koss, Mary P., et al.   HV6626.2.N62 1994
No Safe Haven: Male Violence Against Women at Home, at
Work, and in the Community. Lisa A. Goodman, Angela
Browne, Louise Fitzgerald, Gwendolyn P. Keita & Nancy F.
Russo (Authors). Paper Text. American Psychological
Association. Washington, DC. 1994. 344p. ISBN:1-55798-244-9,
ISBN13: 978-1-55798-244-5. Dewey:364.1/5553/0973.
LCCN:94-015637.

     Audience: **u,f.** *Choice, 1995.*

Lowe, Margaret A.   HQ1220.U5L693 2006
Looking Good: College Women and Body Image, 1875-1930.
Trade Paper. Johns Hopkins University Press. Baltimore, MD.
2005. 222p. Gender Relations in the American Experience Ser.
ISBN:0-8018-8274-5, ISBN13: 978-0-8018-8274-6.
Dewey:306.4.

     Audience: **u,f.** *Choice, 2004.*

Luciano, Lynne   HM636
Looking Good: Male Body Image in Modern America. Library
Binding. Sagebrush Education Resources. Caledonia, MN. 2002.
ISBN:0-613-91534-8, ISBN13: 978-0-613-91534-2.
Dewey:306.4.

     Audience: **l,u,f.** *Choice, 2001.*

Manton, Catherine   HQ1410
Fed Up: Women and Food in America. Trade Cloth. Greenwood
Publishing Group, Inc. Portsmouth, NH. 1999. 184p.
ISBN:0-89789-448-0, ISBN13: 978-0-89789-448-7.
Dewey:305.4/0973. LCCN:98-019215.

     Audience: **l,u,f.** *Choice, 1999.*

McMahon, Anthony   HQ1090.3 .M383 1999
Taking Care of Men: Sexual Politics in the Public Mind. Trade
Cloth. Cambridge University Press. New York, NY. 1999. 240p.
ISBN:0-521-58204-0, ISBN13: 978-0-521-58204-9.
Dewey:305.31/0973. LCCN:99-025156.

     Audience: **u,f.** *Choice, 2000.*

Meyers, Diana Tietjens   HQ1075.M494 2002
Gender in the Mirror: Cultural Imagery and Women's Agency.
Trade Cloth. Oxford University Press, Inc. New York, NY. 2002.
241p. Studies in Feminist Philosophy ISBN:0-19-514040-0,
ISBN13: 978-0-19-514040-8. Dewey:305.42.
LCCN:2001-036805.

     Audience: **u,f.** *Choice, 2003.*

Newberger, Eli H.   HQ775
The Men They Will Become: The Nature and Nurture of the
Male Character. Trade Paper. Basic Books. New York, NY.
2000. 384p. A Merloyd Lawrence Book Ser.
ISBN:0-7382-0363-7, ISBN13: 978-0-7382-0363-8.
Dewey:155.432.

     Audience: **g,l,u.**

O'Leary, Virginia   HQ1206.W875 1985
(Editor), et al.
Women, Gender and Social Psychology. Rhoda K. Unger &
Barbara S. Wallston (Editors). Cloth Text. Lawrence Erlbaum
Associates, Inc. Mahwah, NJ. 1985. 400p. ISBN:0-89859-447-2,
ISBN13: 978-0-89859-447-8. Dewey:305.4. LCCN:84-023114.

     Audience: **l,u,f.** *B* *Choice, 1985.*

Rosenberger, Nancy R.   HQ1762.R68 2001
Gambling with Virtue: Japanese Women and the Search for Self
in a Changing Nation. Trade Cloth. University of Hawaii Press.
Honolulu, HI. 2000. 288p. ISBN:0-8248-2388-5, ISBN13:
978-0-8248-2388-7. Dewey:155.8/952. LCCN:00-055936.

     Audience: **u,f.** *Choice, 2001.*

Rowland, Susan   BF175.4.F45R69 2002
(Editor)
Jung: A Feminist Revision. Trade Cloth. Polity Press.
Cambridge, 2002. 200p. ISBN:0-7456-2516-9, ISBN13:
978-0-7456-2516-4. Dewey:150.1/954. LCCN:2001-002545.

     Audience: **u,f.** *Choice, 2002.*

Russell, Denise   RC451.4.W6
Women, Madness and Medicine. Trade Paper. Blackwell
Publishing, Inc. Malden, MA. 1995. 208p.
ISBN:0-7456-1261-X, ISBN13: 978-0-7456-1261-4.
Dewey:616.89/0082. LCCN:94-038395.

     Audience: **l,u,f.**

Schur, Edwin M.   HQ1206
Labeling Women Devlant. Trade Paper. Random House, Inc.
New York, NY. 2004. ISBN:0-394-33246-6, ISBN13:
978-0-394-33246-8. Dewey:302.542.

     Audience: **l,u,f.**

Segal, Lynne   HQ1090.S43 1990
Slow Motion: Changing Masculinities, Changing Men. Trade
Paper. Rutgers University Press. Piscataway, NJ. 1990. 396p.
ISBN:0-8135-1620-X, ISBN13: 978-0-8135-1620-2.
Dewey:305.31. LCCN:90-041862.

     Audience: **g,l,u,f.** *Choice, 1991.*

Unger, Rhoda K.   HQ1206
(Editor)
Handbook of the Psychology of Women and Gender. Trade
Paper. John Wiley & Sons, Inc. Hoboken, NJ. 2004. 576p.
ISBN:0-471-65357-8, ISBN13: 978-0-471-65357-8.
Dewey:155.3/3.

     Audience: **l,u,f.** *Choice, 2002.*

Walsh, Mary R.   HQ1206.W8748 1997
(Editor)
Women, Men and Gender: Ongoing Debates. Trade Paper. Yale
University Press. Cumberland, RI. 1996. 472p.
ISBN:0-300-06938-3, ISBN13: 978-0-300-06938-9.
Dewey:305.3. LCCN:96-016540.

     Audience: **l,u.**

Whalen, Mollie   HV1445.W43 1996
Counseling to End Violence Against Women: A Subversive
Model. Trade Cloth. SAGE Publications, Inc. Thousand Oaks,
CA. 1996. 184p. ISBN:0-8039-7379-9, ISBN13:
978-0-8039-7379-4. Dewey:361.3/23. LCCN:95-050177.

     Audience: **l,u.** *Choice, 1996.*

Williams, Juanita H.   HQ1206.W72 1987
Psychology of Women: Behavior in a Biosocial Context. Ed. 3.
Trade Paper. W. W. Norton & Company, Inc. New York, NY.

1987. 470p. ISBN:0-393-95567-2, ISBN13: 978-0-393-95567-5. Dewey:155.6/33. LCCN:86-231655.

Audience: **u,f.** *B*

Health > Sexuality

☐ SEXBIBLIO: Bibliography of the History of Western Sexuality.
http://wirtges.univie.ac.at/Sexbibl/about.html

Audience: **g,l,u.**

Dworkin, Andrea   **HQ471**
Pornography: Men Possessing Women. Trade Paper. Penguin Group (USA) Inc. New York, NY. 1991. 336p. ISBN:0-452-26793-5, ISBN13: 978-0-452-26793-0. Dewey:363.4/7.

Audience: **l,u,f.** *B*

Fausto-Sterling, Anne   **HQ1075.F39 2000**
Sexing the Body: Gender Politics and the Construction of Sexuality. Trade Paper. Basic Books. New York, NY. 2000. 496p. ISBN:0-465-07714-5, ISBN13: 978-0-465-07714-4. Dewey:305.3. LCCN:00-703212.

Audience: **u,f.** *Choice, 2000.*

Foucault, Michel   **HQ16**
A History of Sexuality: An Introduction, Vol. 1. Trade Paper. Knopf Publishing Group. New York, NY. 1990. 176p. ISBN:0-679-72469-9, ISBN13: 978-0-679-72469-8. Dewey:306.7/091821. LCCN:79-007460.

Audience: **u,f.**

Hartmann, Betsy   **HQ766.H38 1995**
Reproductive Rights and Wrongs: The Global Politics of Population Control. Trade Cloth. South End Press. Cambridge, MA. 1995. 388p. Women's Studies ISBN:0-89608-492-2, ISBN13: 978-0-89608-492-6. Dewey:363.9. LCCN:94-003626.

Audience: **g,l,u.**

Jejeebhoy, Shireen J.   **LC2607.J45 1995**
ⓔ Women's Education, Autonomy, and Reproductive Behaviour: Experience from Developing Countries. E-Book. NetLibrary, Inc. Boulder, CO. 1995. ISBN:0-585-22994-5, ISBN13: 978-0-585-22994-2. Dewey:305.4/091724.

Audience: **u,f.**

Roberts, Dorothy   **HQ766.5.U5**
Killing the Black Body: Race, Reproduction, and the Meaning of Liberty. Trade Paper. Knopf Publishing Group. New York, NY. 1998. 384p. ISBN:0-679-75869-0, ISBN13: 978-0-679-75869-3. Dewey:363.9/6/0973.

Audience: **g,l,u.**

Segal, Lynne &   **HQ471 .S47 1993**
  McIntosh, Mary (Editors)
Sex Exposed: Sexuality and the Pornography Debate. Trade Paper. Rutgers University Press. Piscataway, NJ. 1993. 344p. ISBN:0-8135-1938-1, ISBN13: 978-0-8135-1938-8. Dewey:363.4/7. LCCN:92-029843.

Audience: **u,f.**

Solinger, Rickie (Editor)   **HQ767.5.U5A2825 1998**
Abortion Wars: A Half Century of Struggle, 1950-2000. Trade Paper. University of California Press. Berkeley, CA. 1998. 430p. ISBN:0-520-20952-4, ISBN13: 978 0 520-20952-7. Dewey:363.46/0973. LCCN:97-012261.

Audience: **g,l,u.**

Vance, Carole S.   **BV4817 .W413 1979**
Pleasure and Danger: Exploring Female Sexuality. Trade Paper. Routledge. New York, NY. 1990. xix, 169p. ISBN:0-7100-0248-3, ISBN13: 978-0-7100-0248-8. Dewey:248. LCCN:79-314678.

Audience: **l,u,f.** *B*

Viney, Ethna   **HQ1075.V55 1996**
Dancing to Different Tunes: Sexuality and Its Misconceptions. Trade Cloth. Blackstaff Press, The. 1997. 318p. ISBN:0-85640-570-1, ISBN13: 978-0-85640-570-9. Dewey:305.3. LCCN:97-102970.

Audience: **u,f.** *Choice, 1997.*

Communications. Media. Popular Culture. Cultural Studies

Adams, Carol J.   **HM636.A33 2003**
The Pornography of Meat. Trade Cloth. Continuum International Publishing Group, Ltd. London, 2003. 208p. ISBN:0-8264-1448-6, ISBN13: 978-0-8264-1448-9. Dewey:306.4. LCCN:2002-155480.

Audience: **l,u,f.**

Beasley, Maurine H. &   **PN4784.W7**
  Gibbons, Sheila J.
Taking Their Place: A Documentary of Women in Journalism. Trade Paper. American University. Washington, DC. 1993. 300p. ISBN:1-879383-10-1, ISBN13: 978-1-879383-10-4. Dewey:070.4/082. LCCN:92-041011.

Audience: **u,f.** *Choice, 1994.*

Berns, Nancy   **HN59.2.B468 2004**
Framing the Victim: Domestic Violence, Media, and Social Problems. Trade Cloth. Aldine Transaction. Somerset, NJ. 2004. 194p. Social Problems and Social Issues Ser. ISBN:0-202-30740-9, ISBN13: 978-0-202-30740-4. Dewey:361.1/0973. LCCN:2004-001465.

Audience: **l,u,f.** *Choice, 2005.*

Blyth, Myrna   **PN4879.B58 2005**
Spin Sisters: How the Women of the Media Sell Unhappiness — and Liberalism — to the Women of America. Trade Paper. St. Martin's Press. Gordonville, VA. 2005. 352p. ISBN:0-312-33607-1, ISBN13: 978 0 312-33607-3. Dewey:302.23/082. LCCN:2004-051441.

Audience: **l,u,f.** *Choice, 2004.*

Bordo, Susan   **HQ1090**
The Male Body: A New Look at Men in Public and in Private. Trade Paper. Farrar, Straus & Giroux. New York, NY. 2000. 368p. ISBN:0-374-52732-6, ISBN13: 978-0-374-52732-7. Dewey:305.31.

Audience: **g,l,u,f.**

Brunsdon, Charlotte   **PN1992.8.S4B78 2000**
The Feminist, the Housewife, and the Soap Opera. Cloth Text. Oxford University Press, Inc. New York, NY. 2000. 220p. Oxford Television Studies ISBN:0-19-815980-3, ISBN13: 978-0-19-815980-3. Dewey:791.45/6. LCCN:00-269565.

Audience: **u,f.** *Choice, 2000.*

Caputi, Jane   **HQ1190.C368 2004**
Goddesses and Monsters: Women, Myth, Power, and Popular Culture. Trade Cloth. University of Wisconsin Press. Chicago, IL. 2004. 448p. ISBN:0-299-19620-8, ISBN13: 978-0-299-19620-2. Dewey:306. LCCN:2003-020572.

Audience: **l,u,f.**

Cortese, Anthony J.   HF5823.C5977 1999
Provocateur: Images of Women and Minorities in Advertising.
Book, Other. Rowman & Littlefield Publishers, Inc. Lanham,
MD. 1999. 176p. ISBN:0-8476-9174-8, ISBN13:
978-0-8476-9174-6. Dewey:659.1/042. LCCN:99-014501.
Audience: **u,f.** *Choice, 2000.*

Currie, Dawn H.   PN4878.C87 1999
Girl Talk: Adolescent Magazines and Their Readers. Trade
Paper. University of Toronto Press. Toronto, ON. 1999. 552p.
ISBN:0-8020-8217-3, ISBN13: 978-0-8020-8217-6.
Dewey:051/.0835/2. LCCN:00-550914.
Audience: **l,u,f.** *Choice, 1999.*

Douglas, Susan J.   P94.5.W65
Where the Girls Are: Growing up Female with the Mass Media.
Trade Paper. Crown Publishing Group. New York, NY. 1995.
368p. ISBN:0-8129-2530-0, ISBN13: 978-0-8129-2530-2.
Dewey:302.2/3/082.
Audience: **u,f.** *Choice, 1995.*

Dow, Bonnie J.   PN1992.8.W65D69 1996
Prime-Time Feminism: Television, Media Culture, and the
Women's Movement Since 1970. Trade Cloth. University of
Pennsylvania Press. Philadelphia, PA. 1996. 296p. Feminist
Cultural Studies, the Media, and Political Culture
ISBN:0-8122-3315-8, ISBN13: 978-0-8122-3315-5.
Dewey:305.4/0973. LCCN:96-005604.
Audience: **u,f.** *Choice, 1997.*

Kelsky, Karen   HQ1762.K45 2001
Women on the Verge: Japanese Women, Western Dreams. Trade
Cloth. Duke University Press. Durham, NC. 2001. 272p.
Asia-Pacific Ser. ISBN:0-8223-2805-4, ISBN13:
978-0-8223-2805-6. Dewey:305.42/0952. LCCN:2001-033378.
Audience: **g,l,u,f.** *Choice, 2002.*

Lent, John A.   P94
  (Compiled by)
Women and Mass Communications in the 1990s: An
International, Annotated Bibliography. Cloth Text. Greenwood
Publishing Group, Inc. Portsmouth, NH. 1999. 528p.
Bibliographies and Indexes in Women's Studies, No. 29
ISBN:0-313-30209-X, ISBN13: 978-0-313-30209-1.
Dewey:016.30223/082. LCCN:99-021787.
Audience: **l,u,f.**

Mankekar, Purnima   HE8700.9.I5M36 1999
Screening Culture, Viewing Politics: An Ethnography of
Television, Womanhood, and Nation in Post-Colonial India.
Trade Cloth. Duke University Press. Durham, NC. 1999. 432p.
ISBN:0-8223-2357-5, ISBN13: 978-0-8223-2357-0.
Dewey:302.23/45/0954. LCCN:99-021159.
Audience: **l,u,f.** *Choice, 2000.*

Mattingly, Carol   HV5229.M37 1998
Well-Tempered Women: Nineteenth-Century Temperance
Rhetoric. Trade Cloth. Southern Illinois University Press.
Carbondale, IL. 1999. 272p. ISBN:0-8093-2209-9, ISBN13:
978-0-8093-2209-1. Dewey:363.4/1/097309034.
LCCN:98-016297.
Audience: **l,u,f.** *Choice, 1999.*

Meyers, Marian &   HQ1421.M43 1999
  Paletz, David L. (Editors)
Mediated Women: Representations in Popular Culture. Cloth
Text. Hampton Press, Inc. Cresskill, NJ. 1999. xiv, 428p.

Communication Ser., :Political Communication
ISBN:1-57273-239-3, ISBN13: 978-1-57273-239-1.
Dewey:305.4/0973. LCCN:99-029090.
Audience: **u,f.**

Miller, Toby   GV706.2.M55 2001
Sportsex. Library Binding. Temple University Press.
Philadelphia, PA. 2002. 224p. ISBN:1-56639-864-9, ISBN13:
978-1-56639-864-0. Dewey:306.4/83. LCCN:00-049098.
Audience: **u,f.** *Choice, 2002.*

Norris, Pippa (Editor)   HQ1236.5.U6W6665
Women, Media and Politics. Trade Paper. Oxford University
Press, Inc. New York, NY. 1996. 286p. ISBN:0-19-510567-2,
ISBN13: 978-0-19-510567-4. Dewey:302.2/3/082.
LCCN:95-052162.
Audience: **l,u,f.** *Choice, 1997.*

Onslow, Barbara   PN5124.W58O59 2000
Women of the Press in Nineteenth-Century Britain. Cloth over
Boards. Palgrave Macmillan. New York, NY. 2001. 311p.
ISBN:0-312-23602-6, ISBN13: 978-0-312-23602-1.
Dewey:070.9/22. LCCN:00-033333.
Audience: **g,l,u,f.** *Choice, 2001.*

Rhodes, Jane   E185.97.C32R48 1998
Mary Ann Shadd Cary: The Black Press and Protest in the
Nineteenth Century. Library Binding. Indiana University Press.
Bloomington, IN. 1998. 304p. ISBN:0-253-33446-2, ISBN13:
978-0-253-33446-6. Dewey:[B]. LCCN:98-019997.
Audience: **l,u,f.** *Choice, 1999.*

Robertson, Jennifer E.   GN635.J2 R62 1998
Takarazuka: Sexual Politics and Popular Culture in Modern
Japan. Trade Paper. University of California Press. Berkeley,
CA. 1998. 296p. ISBN:0-520-21151-0, ISBN13:
978-0-520-21151-3. Dewey:306/.0952. LCCN:97-038671.
Audience: **g,u,f.** *Choice, 1999.*

Rooks, Noliwe M.   TT972.R66 1996
Hair Raising: Beauty, Culture, and African American Women.
Cloth Text. Rutgers University Press. Piscataway, NJ. 1996.
210p. ISBN:0-8135-2311-7, ISBN13: 978-0-8135-2311-8.
Dewey:391/.5/08996073. LCCN:95-051395.
Audience: **l,u,f.** *Choice, 1997.*

Smith-Shomade, Beretta E.   PN1992.8.A34S48 2002
Shaded Lives: African American Women and Television. Trade
Cloth. Rutgers University Press. Piscataway, NJ. 2002. 256p.
ISBN:0-8135-3104-7, ISBN13: 978-0-8135-3104-5.
Dewey:791.45/652042. LCCN:2001-048840.
Audience: **g,l,u.**

Spigel, Lynn   PN1992.6.S663 2001
Welcome to the Dreamhouse: Popular Media and Postwar
Suburbs. Trade Cloth. Duke University Press. Durham, NC.
2001. 408p. Console-Ing Passions Ser. ISBN:0-8223-2687-6,
ISBN13: 978-0-8223-2687-8. Dewey:302.23/45/0973.
LCCN:00-045186.
Audience: **u,f.** *Choice, 2001.*

Valdivia, Angharad N.   P94.5.W65F45 1995
  (Editor)
Feminism, Multiculturalism, and the Media: Global Diversities.
Trade Paper. SAGE Publications, Inc. Thousand Oaks, CA.
1995. 340p. ISBN:0-8039-5775-0, ISBN13: 978-0-8039-5775-6.
Dewey:302.23082. LCCN:95-008204.
Audience: **u,f.**

Valdivia, Angharad N.   **HQ1421.V35 2000**
A Latina in the Land of Hollywood and Other Essays on Media
Culture. Trade Cloth. University of Arizona Press. Tucson, AZ.
2000. 206p. ISBN:0-8165-1933-1, ISBN13: 978-0-8165-1933-0.
Dewey:305.48/868073. LCCN:99-006622.
                              Audience: **u,f.** *Choice, 2000.*

Wallace-Sanders,   **E185.625.S55 2003**
  Kimberly (Editor)
Skin Deep, Spirit Strong: The Black Female Body in American
Culture. Trade Cloth. University of Michigan Press. Chicago,
IL. 2002. 368p. ISBN:0-472-09707-5, ISBN13:
978-0-472-09707-4. Dewey:305.48/896073. LCCN:2002-075016.
                              Audience: **l,u,f.**

Walters, Suzanna D.   **HQ759.W332**
Lives Together - Worlds Apart: Mothers and Daughters in
Popular Culture. Trade Paper. University of California Press.
Berkeley, CA. 1994. 310p. ISBN:0-520-08656-2, ISBN13:
978-0-520-08656-2. Dewey:306.8743. LCCN:91-032331.
                              Audience: **l,u,f.** *Choice, 1993.*

Walters, Suzanna D.   **HM101.W225 1995**
Material Girls: Making Sense of Feminist Cultural Theory.
Trade Paper. University of California Press. Berkeley, CA. 1995.
232p. ISBN:0-520-08978-2, ISBN13: 978-0-520-08978-5.
Dewey:305.42/01. LCCN:94-029007.
                              Audience: **g,l,u,f.** *Choice, 1995.*

Watson, Elwood &   **HQ1220.U5T48 2004**
  Martin, Darcy (Editors)
There She Is, Miss America: The Politics of Sex, Beauty, and
Race in America's Most Famous Pageant. Cloth over Boards.
Palgrave Macmillan. New York, NY. 2004. 224p.
ISBN:1-4039-6301-0, ISBN13: 978-1-4039-6301-7.
Dewey:791.6/2. LCCN:2004-040002.
                              Audience: **l,u,f.** *Choice, 2005.*

History > General History

                                        HQ1121
☐ Internet Women's History Sourcebook.
http://www.fordham.edu/HALSALL/women/womensbook.html
                              Audience: **g,l,u.**

                                        Z7961
☐ ViVa: A Bibliography of Women's History.
http://www.iisg.nl/~womhist/vivahome.php
                              Audience: **g,l,u.**

                                        HQ1410
☐ Women and Social Movements in the United States,
1600-2000.
http://womhist.binghamton.edu/
                              Audience: **g,l,u,f.**

Ahmed, Leila   **HQ1170**
Women and Gender in Islam: Historical Roots of a Modern
Debate. Trade Paper. Yale University Press. Cumberland, RI.
1993. 304p. ISBN:0-300-05583-8, ISBN13: 978-0-300-05583-2.
Dewey:305.4/86971.
                              Audience: **l,u,f.** *Choice, 1992.*

Anderson, Bonnie S. &   **HQ1587.A53 1988**
  Zinsser, Judith P.
A History of Their Own: Women in Europe from Prehistory to
the Present, Vol. 1. Trade Cloth. HarperCollins Publishers. New

York, NY. 1988. 640p. History of Women's Studies
ISBN:0-06-015850-6, ISBN13: 978-0-06-015850-7.
Dewey:305.4/094. LCCN:87-011933.
                              Audience: **g,l,u.** *Choice, 1989.*

Anderson, Bonnie S. &   **HQ1587.A53 2000**
  Zinsser, Judith P.
A History of Their Own: Women in Europe from Prehistory to
the Present. Paper Text. Oxford University Press, Inc. New
York, NY. 1999. 601p. ISBN:0-19-512839-7, ISBN13:
978-0-19-512839-0. Dewey:305.4/094. LCCN:98-046743.
                              Audience: **g,l,u,f.** *Choice, 1989.*

Booker, Christopher B.   **E185**
I Will Wear No Chain!: A Social History of African American
Males. Trade Cloth. Greenwood Publishing Group, Inc.
Portsmouth, NH. 2000. 272p. ISBN:0-275-95637-7, ISBN13:
978-0-275-95637-0. Dewey:305.38/896073/09.
LCCN:99-086221.
                              Audience: **l,u,f.** *Choice, 2001.*

Bridenthal, Renate, et al.   **HQ1588.B43 1998**
Becoming Visible: Women in European History. Ed. 3. Susan
Mosher Stuard & Merry E. Wiesner (Authors). Paper Text.
Houghton Mifflin College Division. Boston, MA. 1997. 594p.
ISBN:0-395-79625-3, ISBN13: 978-0-395-79625-2.
Dewey:305.4/094. LCCN:97-072450.
                              Audience: **g,l,u,f.**

Coquery-Vidrovitch,   **HQ1787.C6613 1997**
  Catherine
African Women: A Modern History. Beth G. Raps (Translator).
Trade Paper. Westview Press. Boulder, CO. 1997. 336p. Social
Change in Global Perspective Ser. ISBN:0-8133-2360-6,
ISBN13: 978-0-8133-2360-2. Dewey:305.4/0967.
LCCN:96-047847.
                              Audience: **g,l,u,f.** *Choice, 1997.*

Cott, Nancy F. (Editor),   **HQ1410.R65 1996**
  et al.
Root of Bitterness: Documents on the Social History of
American Women. Ed. 2. Jeanne Boydston, Ann Braude, Lori D.
Ginzberg & Molly Ladd-Taylor (Editors). Paper Text.
Northeastern University Press. Boston, MA. 1996. 448p.
ISBN:1-55553-256-X, ISBN13: 978-1-55553-256-7.
Dewey:305.4/0973. LCCN:95-044965.
                              Audience: **l,u.**

Evans, Sara   **HQ1410**
Born for Liberty. Trade Paper. Simon & Schuster. New York,
NY. 1997. 448p. ISBN:0-684-83498-7, ISBN13:
978-0-684-83498-6. Dewey:305.4/0973.
                              Audience: **g,l,u.**

Gluck, Sherna B. &   **HQ1121.W886 1991**
  Patai, Daphne (Editors)
Women's Words: The Feminist Practice of Oral History. Cloth
Text. Routledge. New York, NY. 1991. 240p.
ISBN:0-415-90371-8, ISBN13: 978-0-415-90371-4.
Dewey:305.4/0722. LCCN:90-048234.
                              Audience: **u,f.**

Hine, Darlene Clark   **E185.86.B542 2005**
Black Women in America, Set. Ed. 2. Trade Cloth. Oxford
University Press, Inc. New York, NY. 2005. 1696p.
ISBN:0-19-515677-3, ISBN13: 978-0-19-515677-5.
Dewey:305.48/896073. LCCN:2005-001532.
                              Audience: **g,l,u,f.** *Choice, 2005.*

Howard, Angela &   HQ1410.H36 2000
  Kavenik, Frances M. (Editors)
Handbook of American Women's History. Ed. 2. Trade Cloth.
SAGE Publications, Inc. Thousand Oaks, CA. 2000. 744p.
ISBN:0-7619-1635-0, ISBN13: 978-0-7619-1635-2.
Dewey:305.4/0973. LCCN:99-050812.
                              Audience: **l,u,f.**

Kerber, Linda K.   HQ1410
Toward an Intellectual History of Women: Essays by Linda K.
Kerber. Trade Paper. DIANE Publishing Company. Collingdale,
PA. 1997. 333p. ISBN:0-7567-6006-2, ISBN13:
978-0-7567-6006-9. Dewey:305.4/0973.
                              Audience: **l,u,f.**

Kerber, Linda K.   HQ1426.W663 2003
  (Author, Editor)
Women's America: Refocusing the Past. Ed. 6. Jane Sherron
DeHart (Author), Jane Sherron De Hart (Editor). Paper Text.
Oxford University Press, Inc. New York, NY. 2003. 768p.
ISBN:0-19-515982-9, ISBN13: 978-0-19-515982-0.
Dewey:305.4/0973. LCCN:2003-042971.
                              Audience: **l,u.**

Kerber, Linda K. &   HQ1410.U17 1995
  Kessler-Harris, Alice (Editors)
U. S. History As Women's History: Knowledge, Power, and
State Formation. Trade Paper. University of North Carolina
Press. Chapel Hill, NC. 1995. 488p. Gender and American
Culture Ser. ISBN:0-8078-4495-0, ISBN13: 978-0-8078-4495-3.
Dewey:305.4/0973. LCCN:94-027192.
                              Audience: **g,l,u.**

Lerner, Gerda   E185.86.L4
  (Compiled by)
Black Women in White America: A Documentary History. Trade
Cloth. Random House, Inc. New York, NY. 1972. xxxvi, 630p.
ISBN:0-394-47540-2, ISBN13: 978-0-394-47540-0.
Dewey:301.41/2/0973. LCCN:77-173892.
                  Audience: **g,l,u,f.** 𝓑

Lerner, Gerda   HQ1121
The Creation of Feminist Consciousness: From the Middle Ages
to Eighteen-Seventy. Trade Paper. Oxford University Press, Inc.
New York, NY. 1994. 416p. ISBN:0-19-509060-8, ISBN13:
978-0-19-509060-4. Dewey:305.4/09. LCCN:92-020411.
               Audience: **g,l,u,f.** *Choice, 1993.*

Mankiller, Wilma   HQ1410.R43 1998
  (Editor), et al.
The Reader's Companion to U. S. Women's History. Gwendolyn
Mink, Marysa Navarro, Barbara Smith & Gloria Steinem
(Editors). Trade Cloth. Houghton Mifflin Company Trade &
Reference Division. Boston, MA. 1998. 720p.
ISBN:0-395-67173-6, ISBN13: 978-0-395-67173-3.
Dewey:305.4/0973. LCCN:97-039923.
             Audience: **g.** *Choice, 1998.*

Mernissi, Fatima   HQ1170.M46 1987
Beyond the Veil: Male-Female Dynamics in Modern Muslim
Society. Trade Paper. Indiana University Press. Bloomington,
IN. 1987. 224p. ISBN:0-253-20423-2, ISBN13:
978-0-253-20423-3. Dewey:305.4/862971. LCCN:86-046034.
                      Audience: **u,f.** 𝓑

Middleton, Frank   HQ1410
☐ American Women's History: A Research Guide.
http://www.mtsu.edu/~kmiddlet/history/women.html
                        Audience: **g,l,u,f.**

Ruiz, Vicki L.   E184.M5
From Out of the Shadows: Mexican Women in
Twentieth-Century America. Trade Paper. Oxford University
Press, Inc. New York, NY. 1999. 272p. ISBN:0-19-513099-5,
ISBN13: 978-0-19-513099-7. Dewey:305.4886872.
                              Audience: **l,u.**

Ruiz, Vicki L.   HQ1410.U54 2000
Unequal Sisters: A Multicultural Reader in U. S. Women's
History. Ed. 3. Ellen Carol DuBois (Editor). Paper over Boards.
Routledge. New York, NY. 1999. 696p. ISBN:0-415-92516-9,
ISBN13: 978-0-415-92516-7. LCCN:99-016825.
                            Audience: **g,l,u.**

Scott, Joan Wallach   HQ1154.S335 1999
Gender and the Politics of History. Ed. 2. Trade Paper.
Columbia University Press. New York, NY. 1999. 242p. Gender
and Culture Ser. ISBN:0-231-11857-0, ISBN13:
978-0-231-11857-6. Dewey:305.4/09. LCCN:99-028686.
                              Audience: **u,f.**

Vaz, Kim M. (Editor)   E185.86.B5418 1995
Black Women in America: Confronting Gender, Race, and Class.
Trade Cloth. SAGE Publications, Inc. Thousand Oaks, CA.
1994. 406p. ISBN:0-8039-5454-9, ISBN13: 978-0-8039-5454-0.
Dewey:305.48/896073. LCCN:94-031761.
                Audience: **l,u,f.** *Choice, 1995.*

Wiesner-Hanks,   HQ1075.W526 2001
  Merry E.
Gender in History. Trade Paper. Blackwell Publishing, Inc.
Malden, MA. 2001. 256p. New Perspectives on the Past Ser.
ISBN:0-631-21036-9, ISBN13: 978-0-631-21036-8.
Dewey:305.3/09. LCCN:00-013063.
               Audience: **g,l,u,f.** *Choice, 2002.*

Zinsser, Judith P.   HQ1181.U5Z56 1992
History and Feminism: A Glass Half Full. Cloth Text.
Macmillan Publishing Company, Inc. Old Tappan, NJ. 1992.
200p. The Feminist Impact on the Arts and Sciences Ser.
ISBN:0-8057-9751-3, ISBN13: 978-0-8057-9751-0.
Dewey:305.4/07/073. LCCN:92-028707.
               Audience: **g,l,u,f.** *Choice, 1993.*

History > Pre-Historic to Classical

                                         HQ1127
☐ Diotima: Materials for the Study of Women and Gender in
the Ancient World.
http://www.stoa.org/diotima/
                              Audience: **g,l,u.**

Brosius, Maria   HQ1130.B76 1998
🄴 Women in Ancient Persia, 559-331 B. C. E-Book.
NetLibrary, Inc. Boulder, CO. 1998. ISBN:0-585-24485-5,
ISBN13: 978-0-585-24485-3. Dewey:305.4/0935.
                              Audience: **u,f.**

Conkey, Margaret W.   HQ1127
Engendering Archaeology: Women and Prehistory. Joan M. Gero
(Editor). Trade Paper. Blackwell Publishing, Inc. Malden, MA.
1991. 432p. ISBN:0-631-17501-6, ISBN13: 978-0-631-17501-8.
Dewey:305.4/09/01. LCCN:90-035335.
                              Audience: **l,u.**

Foley, Helene P.   HQ1134
Reflections of Women in Antiquity. Cloth Text. Gordon &
Breach Publishing Group. New York, NY. 1982. xviii, 420p.

ISBN:0-677-16370-3, ISBN13: 978-0-677-16370-3.
Dewey:305.4/2/0938. LCCN:81-013352.

Audience: **l,u.** ℬ

Hemelrijk, Emily Ann   **HQ1136.H45 1999**
Matrona Docta: Educated Women in the Roman Elite from
Cornelia to Julia Domna. Paper over Boards. Routledge. New
York, NY. 1999. 400p. Classical Monographs
ISBN:0-415-19693-0, ISBN13: 978-0-415-19693-2.
Dewey:305.4/89631/09376. LCCN:98-053036.

Audience: **l,u,f.** *Choice, 2000.*

Lefkowitz, Mary R. &   **HQ1127.W653 2005**
  Fant, Maureen Brown
Women's Life in Greece and Rome: A Source Book in
Translation. Ed. 3. Trade Cloth. Johns Hopkins University Press.
Baltimore, MD. 2005. 464p. ISBN:0-8018-8309-1, ISBN13:
978-0-8018-8309-5. Dewey:305.40938. LCCN:2005-928766.

Audience: **g,l,u,f.**

Pomeroy, Sarah B.   **HQ1134.P64 1995**
Goddesses, Whores, Wives and Slaves: Women in Classical
Antiquity. Trade Paper. Knopf Publishing Group. New York,
NY. 1995. 304p. ISBN:0-8052-1030-X, ISBN13:
978-0-8052-1030-9. Dewey:305.4/2/0938. LCCN:95-109446.

Audience: **g,l,u,f.** ℬ

Pomeroy, Sarah B.   **HQ1137.E3P65 1984**
Women in Hellenistic Egypt: From Alexander to Cleopatra.
Trade Cloth. Knopf Publishing Group. New York, NY. 1984.
266p. ISBN:0-8052-3911-1, ISBN13: 978-0-8052-3911-9.
Dewey:305.4/0932. LCCN:84-003122.

Audience: **g,l,u,f.** ℬ

Pomeroy, Sarah B.   **HQ1127.W6525 1991**
  (Editor)
Women's History and Ancient History. Trade Cloth. University
of North Carolina Press. Chapel Hill, NC. 1991. 336p.
ISBN:0-8078-1949-2, ISBN13: 978-0-8078-1949-4.
Dewey:305.4/09. LCCN:90-024488.

Audience: **l,u,f.** *Choice, 1992.*

Van Bremen, Riet   **HQ1134.B74 1996**
The Limits of Participation: Women and the Civic Life in the
Greek East in the Hellenistic and Roman Periods. Library
Binding. J. C. Gieben Publisher. Amsterdam, 1996. 417p. Dutch
Monographs on Ancient History and Archaeology, No. XV
ISBN:90-5063-567-9, ISBN13: 978-90-5063-567-7.
Dewey:305.4/0938. LCCN:96-176186.

Audience: **u,f.** *Choice, 1997.*

History > Medieval

                                  HQ1143
☐ Feminae: Medieval Women and Gender Index.
http://www.haverford.edu/library/reference/mschaus/mfi/mfi.html
Audience: **g,l,u.**

Bolton, Brenda &   **HQ1143.W64**
  Stuard, Susan Mosher
ⓔ Women in Medieval Society. E-Book. NetLibrary, Inc.
Boulder, CO. 1976. ISBN:0-585-12738-7, ISBN13:
978-0-585-12738-5. Dewey:301.41/2/0902.

Audience: **l,u.**

Gold, Penny S.   **HQ1147.F7**
The Lady and the Virgin: Image, Attitude, and Experience in
Twelfth-Century France. Catherine R. Stimpson (Foreword by).

Trade Paper. University of Chicago Press. Chicago, IL. 1987.
206p. Women in Culture and Society Ser. ISBN:0-226-30088-9,
ISBN13: 978-0-226-30088-7. Dewey:305.42. LCCN:84-023701.

Audience: **u,f.**

Lawler, Jennifer   **HQ1143.L38 2001**
Encyclopedia of Women in the Middle Ages. Cloth Text.
McFarland & Company, Incorporated Publishers. Jefferson, NC.
2001. 287p. ISBN:0-7864-1119-8, ISBN13: 978-0-7864-1119-1.
Dewey:305.4/09/02. LCCN:2001-126809.

Audience: **g.** *Choice, 2002.*

Power, Eileen   **HQ1143 .P68 1997**
Medieval Women. M. M. Postan (Editor), Maxine Berg
(Foreword by). Trade Paper. Cambridge University Press. New
York, NY. 1997. 132p. A Canto Book Ser. ISBN:0-521-59556-8,
ISBN13: 978-0-521-59556-8. Dewey:305.4/2/0941/0902.
LCCN:97-219610.

Audience: **g,l,u,f.**

Wiesner, Merry E.   **HQ1149.G3.W54 1986**
Working Women in Renaissance Germany. Cloth Text. Rutgers
University Press. Piscataway, NJ. 1986. 250p. The Douglass
Series on Women's Lives and the Meaning of Gender
ISBN:0-8135-1138-0, ISBN13: 978-0-8135-1138-2.
Dewey:305.4/3/00943. LCCN:85-014451.

Audience: **l,u,f.** ℬ *Choice, 1986.*

History > Pre-Modern

Berkin, Carol   **E276.B47 2004**
Revolutionary Mothers: Women in the Struggle for America's
Independence. Trade Cloth. Alfred A. Knopf Inc. New York,
NY. 2005. 224p. ISBN:1-4000-4163-5, ISBN13:
978-1-4000-4163-3. Dewey:973.3/082. LCCN:2004-045406.

Audience: **g,l,u,f.** *Choice, 2006.*

Berkin, Carol &   **HQ1416.W67 1998**
  Horowitz, Leslie (Editors)
Women's Voices, Women's Lives: Documents in Early
American History. Cloth Text. Northeastern University Press.
Boston, MA. 1998. 224p. ISBN:1-55553-351-5, ISBN13:
978-1-55553-351-9. Dewey:305.4/0973. LCCN:98-011255.

Audience: **g,l,u.**

Boxer, Marilyn J. &   **HQ1150.B63 2000**
  Quataert, Jean H.
Connecting Spheres: European Women in a Globalizing World,
1500 to the Present. Ed. 2. Joan Scott (Foreword by). Paper
Text. Oxford University Press, Inc. New York, NY. 1999. 352p.
ISBN:0-19-510951-1, ISBN13: 978-0-19-510951-1.
Dewey:305.4/094. LCCN:99-019863.

Audience: **u,f.**

Brownell, Susan   **HQ1075.5.C6 C47 2002**
Chinese Femininities/Chinese Masculinities. Jeffrey N.
Wasserstrom & Thomas Laqueur (Editors). Trade Cloth.
University of California Press. Berkeley, CA. 2002. 474p. Asian
Studies, Vol. 4 ISBN:0-520-21103-0, ISBN13:
978-0-520-21103-2. Dewey:305.3/0951. LCCN:2001-005079.

Audience: **l,u,f.** *Choice, 2002.*

Bynum, Victoria E.   **HQ1438.N6B96 1992**
Unruly Women: The Politics of Social and Sexual Control in the
Old South. Trade Cloth. University of North Carolina Press.
Chapel Hill, NC. 1992. 250p. Gender and American Culture Ser.

ISBN:0-8078-2016-4, ISBN13: 978-0-8078-2016-2.
Dewey:305.409756. LCCN:91-033851.
Audience: l,u,f. Choice, 1992.

Ebrey, Patricia B.   **HQ684.A25 1993**
The Inner Quarters: Marriage and the Lives of Chinese Women
in the Sung Period. Trade Cloth. University of California Press.
Berkeley, CA. 1993. 312p. ISBN:0-520-08156-0, ISBN13:
978-0-520-08156-7. Dewey:305.420951. LCCN:92-031376.
Audience: u,f. Choice, 1994.

Edwards, Laura F.   **HQ1438.S63E35 1997**
Gendered Strife and Confusion: The Political Culture of
Reconstruction. Trade Paper. University of Illinois Press.
Champaign, IL. 1997. 400p. Women in American History Ser.
ISBN:0-252-06600-6, ISBN13: 978-0-252-06600-9.
Dewey:305.3/0973/09034. LCCN:96-025317.
Audience: l,u,f. Choice, 1997.

Farnham, Christie Anne   **HQ1438.S63**
  (Editor)
Women of the American South. Trade Cloth. New York
University Press. New York, NY. 1997. 319p.
ISBN:0-8147-2654-2, ISBN13: 978-0-8147-2654-9.
Dewey:305.40975. LCCN:97-033778.
Audience: l,u,f.

Fox-Genovese, Elizabeth   **HQ1438.A13F69 1988**
Within the Plantation Household: Black and White Women of
the Old South. Trade Paper. University of North Carolina Press.
Chapel Hill, NC. 1988. 563p. Gender and American Culture Ser.
ISBN:0-8078-4232-X, ISBN13: 978-0-8078-4232-4.
Dewey:305.4/0975. LCCN:88-040139.
Audience: l,u,f. Choice, 1989.

Gundersen, Joan R.   **E276.G86 1996**
To Be Useful to the World: Women in Revolutionary America,
1740-1790. Trade Cloth. Thomson Gale. Farmington Hills, MI.
1996. xv, 273p. ISBN:0-8057-9916-8, ISBN13:
978-0-8057-9916-3. Dewey:973.3082. LCCN:96-036313.
Audience: l,u,f. Choice, 1997.

Harper, Judith E.   **E628.H37 2003**
Women During the Civil War: An Encyclopedia. Paper over
Boards. Routledge. New York, NY. 2003. 368p.
ISBN:0-415-93723-X, ISBN13: 978-0-415-93723-8.
Dewey:973.7/082. LCCN:2003-007181.
Audience: g,l,u,f. Choice, 2004.

Ko, Dorothy   **HQ1767.K6 1994**
Teachers of the Inner Chambers: Women and Culture in
Seventeenth-Century China. Trade Cloth. Stanford University
Press. Palo Alto, CA. 1994. xviii, 396p. ISBN:0-8047-2358-3,
ISBN13: 978-0-8047-2358-9. Dewey:305.4/0951/09032.
LCCN:94-001166.
Audience: u,f. Choice, 1995.

Marcus, Jacob R.   **HQ1172.M37**
  (Editor)
The American Jewish Woman: 1654-1980. Trade Cloth. Ktav
Publishing House, Inc. Jersey City, NJ. 1981. xiv, 231p.
ISBN:0-87068-751-4, ISBN13: 978-0-87068-751-8.
Dewey:305.4/8. LCCN:81-001720.
Audience: u.f. B

Marrese, Michelle   **HQ1662.M367 2002**
  Lamarche
A Woman's Kingdom: Noblewomen and the Control of Property
in Russia, 1700-1861. Trade Cloth. Cornell University Press.

Ithaca, NY. 2002. 336p. ISBN:0-8014-3911-6, ISBN13:
978-0-8014-3911-7. Dewey:305.4/0947. LCCN:2001-007531.
Audience: u,f. Choice, 2003.

Mendelson, Sara &   **HQ1599.E5M46 1998**
  Crawford, Patricia
Women in Early Modern England 1550-1720. Trade Cloth.
Oxford University Press, Inc. New York, NY. 1998. 480p.
ISBN:0-19-820124-9, ISBN13: 978-0-19-820124-3.
Dewey:305.4/0942. LCCN:97-033337.
Audience: u,f. Choice, 1999.

Mill, John Stuart &   **HQ1154**
  Mill, Harriet Taylor
Essays on Sex Equality. Alice S. Rossi (Editor). Trade Paper.
University of Chicago Press. Chicago, IL. 1970. 252p.
ISBN:0-226-52546-5, ISBN13: 978-0-226-52546-4.
Dewey:301.41/2. LCCN:78-133381.
Audience: l,u. B

Nashat, Guity & Beck,   **HQ1735.2.W656 2003**
  Lois (Editors)
Women in Iran from the Rise of Islam to 1800. Trade Cloth.
University of Illinois Press. Champaign, IL. 2003. 272p.
ISBN:0-252-02839-2, ISBN13: 978-0-252-02839-7.
Dewey:305.42/0955. LCCN:2002-152213.
Audience: l,u,f. Choice, 2004.

Rotundo, E. Anthony   **HQ1090.3**
American Manhood: Transformations in Masculinity from the
Revolution to the Modern Era. Trade Paper. Basic Books. New
York, NY. 1994. 396p. ISBN:0-465-00169-6, ISBN13:
978-0-465-00169-9. Dewey:305.32/0973. LCCN:92-053247.
Audience: l,u,f. Choice, 1993.

Stern, Steve J.   **F1434.2.S63**
The Secret History of Gender: Women, Men, and Power in Late
Colonial Mexico. Trade Paper. University of North Carolina
Press. Chapel Hill, NC. 1997. 496p. ISBN:0-8078-4643-0,
ISBN13: 978-0-8078-4643-8. Dewey:305.3/0972.
LCCN:94-039349.
Audience: u,f. Choice, 1996.

Sturtz, Linda   **HQ1438.V8S78 2002**
Within Her Power: Propertied Women in Colonial Virginia.
Paper over Boards. Routledge. New York, NY. 2002. 304p. The
New World in the Atlantic World Ser. ISBN:0-415-92855-9,
ISBN13: 978-0-415-92855-7. Dewey:305.4/09755.
LCCN:2001-048677.
Audience: g,l,u,f. Choice, 2003.

Taylor, Quintard &   **E185.925.A45 2003**
  Moore, Shirley Ann Wilson (Editors)
African American Women Confront the West: 1600-2000. Trade
Cloth. University of Oklahoma Press. Norman, OK. 2003. 352p.
ISBN:0-8061-3524-7, ISBN13: 978-0-8061-3524-3.
Dewey:978/.00496073/0082. LCCN:2002-032479.
Audience: g,l,u,f. Choice, 2004.

White, Deborah Gray   **E443 .W58**
Ar'n't I a Woman?: Female Slaves in the Plantation South.
Trade Cloth. Peter Smith Publisher, Inc. Magnolia, MA. 1999.
ISBN:0-8446-7022-7, ISBN13: 978-0-8446-7022-5.
Dewey:305.5/67/082/0975.
Audience: l,u,f. Choice, 1986.

Wiesner, Merry E.   **HQ1587 .W54 2000**
Women and Gender in Early Modern Europe. Ed. 2. William
Beik, T. C. W. Blanning & Brendan Simms (Contribution by).

Cloth Text. Cambridge University Press. New York, NY. 2000.
342p. New Approaches to European History Ser., No. 20
ISBN:0-521-77105-6, ISBN13: 978-0-521-77105-4.
Dewey:305.4/094. LCCN:00-022070.

Audience: **g,l,u,f.** *Choice, 1994.*

History > Modern

Andors, Phyllis   **HQ1768.A52**
The Unfinished Liberation of Chinese Women, 1949-1980.
Trade Paper. Books on Demand. Ann Arbor, MI. 224p.
ISBN:0-8357-3963-5, ISBN13: 978-0-8357-3963-4.
Dewey:305.420951. LCCN:81-048323.

Audience: **l,u.**

Arrom, Silvia M.   **HQ1465.M6 A77 1985**
The Women of Mexico City, 1790-1857. Trade Cloth. Stanford
University Press. Palo Alto, CA. 1985. 400p.
ISBN:0-8047-1233-6, ISBN13: 978-0-8047-1233-0.
Dewey:305.4/2/097253/09034. LCCN:83-051324.

Audience: **l,u,f.** *Choice, 1986.*

Bay, Edna G.   **JQ3376.A91B39 1998**
Wives of the Leopard: Gender, Politics, and Culture in the
Kingdom of Dahomey. Cloth Text. University Press of Virginia.
Charlottesville, VA. 1998. 392p. ISBN:0-8139-1791-3, ISBN13:
978-0-8139-1791-7. Dewey:320/.082/096683. LCCN:97-045943.

Audience: **l,u,f.** *Choice, 2000.*

Bercaw, Nancy   **F347.M6B47 2003**
Gendered Freedoms: Race, Rights, and the Politics of
Household in the Delta, 1861-1875. Trade Cloth. University
Press of Florida. Gainesville, FL. 2003. xviii, 279p. Southern
Dissent Ser. ISBN:0-8130-2591-5, ISBN13: 978-0-8130-2591-9.
Dewey:305.896/07307624. LCCN:2002-040906.

Audience: **u,f.** *Choice, 2003.*

Berkin, Carol   **HQ1410**
Women of America. Paper Text. Houghton Mifflin Company.
New York, NY. 1995. ISBN:0-395-74155-6, ISBN13:
978-0-395-74155-9. Dewey:301.41/2/0973.

Audience: **l,u.**

Boxer, Marilyn J. &   **HQ1150.B63 2000**
Quataert, Jean H.
Connecting Spheres: European Women in a Globalizing World,
1500 to the Present. Ed. 2. Joan Scott (Foreword by). Paper
Text. Oxford University Press, Inc. New York, NY. 1999. 352p.
ISBN:0-19-510951-1, ISBN13: 978-0-19-510951-1.
Dewey:305.4/094. LCCN:99-019863.

Audience: **u,f.**

Brownell, Susan   **HQ1075.5.C6 C47 2002**
Chinese Femininities/Chinese Masculinities. Jeffrey N.
Wasserstrom & Thomas Laqueur (Editors). Trade Cloth.
University of California Press. Berkeley, CA. 2002. 474p. Asian
Studies, Vol. 4 ISBN:0-520-21103-0, ISBN13:
978-0-520-21103-2. Dewey:305.3/0951. LCCN:2001-005079.

Audience: **l,u,f.** *Choice, 2002.*

Celestin, Roger, et al.   **HQ1613**
Beyond French Feminisms: Debates on Women, Politics, and
Culture in France, 1981-2001. Eliane DalMolin & Isabelle De
Courtivron (Authors). Cloth over Boards. Palgrave Macmillan.
New York, NY. 2003. 324p. ISBN:0-312-24019-8, ISBN13:
978-0-312-24019-6. Dewey:305.42/0944.

Audience: **u,f.**

Charrad, Mounira M.   **HQ1236.5.A355 C43**
States and Women's Rights: The Making of Postcolonial
Tunisia, Algeria, and Morocco. Trade Cloth. University of
California Press. Berkeley, CA. 2001. 362p.
ISBN:0-520-07323-1, ISBN13: 978-0-520-07323-4.
Dewey:323.3/4/0961. LCCN:00-051172.

Audience: **u,f.** *Choice, 2002.*

Clements, Barbara   **HX313.7 .C64 1997**
Evans
Bolshevik Women. Trade Cloth. Cambridge University Press.
New York, NY. 1997. 352p. ISBN:0-521-45403-4, ISBN13:
978-0-521-45403-2. Dewey:947/.084/082. LCCN:96-050036.

Audience: **g,l,u,f.** *Choice, 1998.*

Clinton, Catherine   **HQ1410.C44 1999**
The Other Civil War: American Women in the Nineteenth
Century. Trade Paper. Farrar, Straus & Giroux. New York, NY.
1999. 12p. ISBN:0-8090-1622-2, ISBN13: 978-0-8090-1622-8.
Dewey:305.4/0973/09034. LCCN:98-052075.

Audience: **u,f.**

Conway, Jill Ker, et al.   **HQ1410.C66 1985**
The Female Experience in Eighteenth and Nineteenth-Century
America: A Guide to the History of American Women. Linda
Kealey & Janet E. Schulte (Authors). Trade Paper. Princeton
University Press. Princeton, NJ. 1985. 314p.
ISBN:0-691-00599-0, ISBN13: 978-0-691-00599-7.
Dewey:016.3054/0973. LCCN:85-042665.

Audience: **l,u.** *B*

Cook, Sharon Anne   **HQ1453.F73 2001**
(Editor), et al.
Framing Our Past: Constructing Canadian Women's History in
the Twentieth Century. Lorna McLean & Kate O'Rourke
(Editors). Trade Cloth. McGill-Queen's University Press.
Montreal, PQ. 2001. xxix, 495p. ISBN:0-7735-2172-0, ISBN13:
978-0-7735-2172-8. Dewey:305.4/0971/0904.
LCCN:2002-437728.

Audience: **g,l,u,f.** *Choice, 2002.*

Cott, Nancy F. (Editor),   **HQ1410.R65 1996**
et al.
Root of Bitterness: Documents of the Social History of
American Women. Ed. 2. Jeanne Boydston, Ann Braude, Lori D.
Ginzberg & Molly Ladd-Taylor (Editors). Cloth Text.
Northeastern University Press. Boston, MA. 1996. 448p.
ISBN:1-55553-255-1, ISBN13: 978-1-55553-255-0.
Dewey:305.4/0973. LCCN:95-044965.

Audience: **g,l,u.**

Duchen, Claire   **HQ1613.D8 1986**
Feminism in France: From May '68 to Mitterand. Trade Paper.
Routledge. New York, NY. 1986. 192p. ISBN:0-7102-0455-8,
ISBN13: 978-0-7102-0455-4. Dewey:305.4/2/0944.
LCCN:85-010705.

Audience: **l,u.** *B Choice, 1986.*

Echols, Alice   **HQ1421.E25 1989**
Daring to Be Bad: Radical Feminism in America, 1967-1975.
Trade Paper. University of Minnesota Press. Minneapolis, MN.
1989. 430p. ISBN:0-8166-1787-2, ISBN13: 978-0-8166-1787-6.
Dewey:305.4/2/097309047. LCCN:89-005058.

Audience: **u,f.** *Choice, 1990.*

Elson-Roessler, Shirley   **DC158.8**
Out of the Shadows: Women and Politics in the French
Revolution, 1789-95. Trade Paper. Peter Lang Publishing, Inc.
New York, NY. 1998. 275p. Studies in Modern European

History, Vol. 14 ISBN:0-8204-4012-4, ISBN13: 978-0-8204-4012-5. Dewey:944.04082. LCCN:94-040970.

Audience: **g,l,u.**

Engel, Barbara Alpern   **HV1662.E54 2003**
Women in Russia, 1700-2000. Cloth Text. Cambridge University Press. New York, NY. 2003. 304p. ISBN:0-521-80270-9, ISBN13: 978-0-521-80270-3. Dewey:305.4/0947. LCCN:2003-043017.

Audience: **g,l,u,f.**   *Choice, 2004.*

Flanagan, Maureen A.   **HQ1439.C47F53 2002**
Seeing with Their Hearts: Chicago Women and the Vision of the Good City, 1871-1933. Trade Cloth. Princeton University Press. Princeton, NJ. 2002. 328p. ISBN:0-691-09539-6, ISBN13: 978-0-691-09539-4. Dewey:305.4/09773/11. LCCN:2001-058005.

Audience: **g,l,u,f.**   *Choice, 2003.*

Fowler-Salamini,   **HQ1462.W66 1994**
  Heather & Vaughan, Mary K. (Editors)
Women of the Mexican Countryside, 1850-1990: Creating Spaces, Shaping Transitions. Library Binding. University of Arizona Press. Tucson, AZ. 1994. 253p. ISBN:0-8165-1415-1, ISBN13: 978-0-8165-1415-1. Dewey:305.42/0972. LCCN:94-010179.

Audience: **l,u,f.**   *Choice, 1995.*

Godson, Susan H.   **VB324.W65G63 2001**
Serving Proudly: A History of Women in the U. S. Navy. Trade Cloth. Naval Institute Press. Annapolis, MD. 2001. 480p. ISBN:1-55750-317-6, ISBN13: 978-1-55750-317-6. Dewey:359/.0082/0973. LCCN:2001-031279.

Audience: **g,l,u,f.**   *Choice, 2002.*

Goldman, Wendy Z.   **KLA540 .G65 1993**
Women, the State and Revolution: Soviet Family Policy and Social Life, 1917-1936. Trade Paper. Cambridge University Press. New York, NY. 1993. 363p. Cambridge Russian, Soviet and Post-Soviet Studies, No. 90 ISBN:0-521-45816-1, ISBN13: 978-0-521-45816-0. Dewey:305.420947. LCCN:92-047481.

Audience: **u,f.**   *Choice, 1994.*

Green, Elna C.   **JK1896.G695 1997**
Southern Strategies: Southern Women and the Woman Suffrage Question. Trade Paper. University of North Carolina Press. Chapel Hill, NC. 1997. 312p. ISBN:0-8078-4641-4, ISBN13: 978-0-8078-4641-4. Dewey:324.6/23/0975. LCCN:96-036992.

Audience: **l,u,f.**   *Choice, 1997.*

Higonnet, Margaret R.   **D639.W7**
Behind the Lines: Gender and the Two World Wars. Jane Jenson, Sonya Michel & Margaret C. Weitz (Editors). Trade Paper. Yale University Press. Cumberland, RI. 1989. 310p. ISBN:0-300-04429-1, ISBN13: 978-0-300-04429-4. Dewey:940.3/082. LCCN:86-028102.

Audience: **l,u,f.**   *Choice, 1987.*

Hiltermann, Joost R.   **DS110.W47H55 1991**
Behind the Intifada: Labor and Women's Movements in the Occupied Territories. Trade Cloth. Princeton University Press. Princeton, NJ. 1991. 283p. ISBN:0-691-07869-6, ISBN13: 978-0-691-07869-4. Dewey:322.4/4/095694. LCCN:91-014181.

Audience: **l,u,f.**   *Choice, 1992.*

Hyman, Paula E.   **DS148.H93 1995**
Gender and Assimilation in Modern Jewish History: The Roles and Representations of Women. Trade Cloth. University of Washington Press. Seattle, WA. 1995. 208p. Samuel and Althea

Stroum Lectures in Jewish Studies ISBN:0-295-97425-7, ISBN13: 978-0-295-97425-5. Dewey:305.48/696. LCCN:94-037932.

Audience: **g,l,u,f.**   *Choice, 1996.*

Ireson, Carol J.   **DS555.45.M5I74 1996**
Fields, Forest, and Family: Women's Work and Power in Rural Laos. Trade Paper. Westview Press. Boulder, CO. 1999. 312p. ISBN:0-8133-3730-5, ISBN13: 978-0-8133-3730-2. Dewey:305.4/09594. LCCN:96-027143.

Audience: **u,f.**

Jeffrey, Julie R.   **E449.J46 1998**
The Great Silent Army of Abolitionism: Ordinary Women in the Antislavery Movement. Trade Paper. University of North Carolina Press. Chapel Hill, NC. 1998. 328p. ISBN:0-8078-4741-0, ISBN13: 978-0-8078-4741-1. Dewey:326/.8/0820973. LCCN:98-013550.

Audience: **u,f.**   *Choice, 1999.*

Kazuko, Ono   **HQ1767.O5613 1989**
Chinese Women in a Century of Revolution, 1850-1950. Joshua A. Fogel (Editor). Trade Cloth. Stanford University Press. Palo Alto, CA. 1989. 288p. ISBN:0-8047-1496-7, ISBN13: 978-0-8047-1496-9. Dewey:305.4/2/0951. LCCN:88-008630.

Audience: **u,f.**   *Choice, 1989.*

Keddie, Nikki R. &   **HQ1726.5**
  Baron, Beth (Editors)
Women in Middle Eastern History: Shifting Boundaries in Sex and Gender. Cloth over Boards. Yale University Press. Cumberland, RI. 1992. 352p. ISBN:0-300-05005-4, ISBN13: 978-0-300-05005-9. Dewey:305.4/2/0956.

Audience: **l,u,f.**

Kelsky, Karen   **HQ1762.K45 2001**
Women on the Verge: Japanese Women, Western Dreams. Trade Cloth. Duke University Press. Durham, NC. 2001. 272p. Asia-Pacific Ser. ISBN:0-8223-2805-4, ISBN13: 978-0-8223-2805-6. Dewey:305.42/0952. LCCN:2001-033378.

Audience: **g,l,u,f.**   *Choice, 2002.*

Kennedy, Susan E.   **HQ1410.K45**
If All We Did Was to Weep at Home: A History of White Working-Class Women in America. Trade Cloth. Indiana University Press. Bloomington, IN. 1979. 352p. Minorities in Modern America Ser., No. 267 ISBN:0-253-19154-8, ISBN13: 978-0-253-19154-0. Dewey:301.41/2/0973. LCCN:78-020431.

Audience: **u,f.** *B*

Marcus, Jacob R.   **HQ1172.M37**
  (Editor)
The American Jewish Woman: 1654-1980. Trade Cloth. Ktav Publishing House, Inc. Jersey City, NJ. 1981. xiv, 231p. ISBN:0-87068-751-4, ISBN13: 978-0-87068-751-8. Dewey:305.4/8. LCCN:81-001720.

Audience: **u,f.** *B*

Menon, Ritu & Bhasin,   **DS480.842.M46 1998**
  Kamla
Borders and Boundaries: Women in India's Partition. Trade Cloth. Rutgers University Press. Piscataway, NJ. 1998. 276p. ISBN:0-8135-2551-9, ISBN13: 978-0-8135-2551-8. Dewey:954.04. LCCN:98-017638.

Audience: **l,u,f.**

Meyerowitz, Joanne   HQ1420.N68 1994
  (Editor)
Not June Cleaver: Women and Gender in the Postwar America,
1945-1960. Cloth Text. Temple University Press. Philadelphia,
PA. 1994. 368p. Critical Perspectives on the Past Ser.
ISBN:1-56639-170-9, ISBN13: 978-1-56639-170-2.
Dewey:305.42/0973/09045. LCCN:93-026987.
                              Audience: **u,f.** *Choice, 1995.*

Myres, Sandra L.   HQ1438.W45
Westering Women and the Frontier Experience, 1800-1915.
Trade Paper. University of New Mexico Press. Albuquerque,
NM. 1982. 387p. Histories of the American Frontier Ser.
ISBN:0-8263-0626-8, ISBN13: 978-0-8263-0626-5.
Dewey:305.4/2/0978. LCCN:82-006956.
                              Audience: **g.** 𝓑

Peteet, Julie M.   DS80.55.P34P47 1991
Gender in Crisis: Women and the Palestinian Resistance
Movement. Trade Cloth. Eastern European Monographs.
Bradenton, FL. 1991. 245p. ISBN:0-231-07446-8, ISBN13:
978-0-231-07446-9. Dewey:305.4/095692. LCCN:90-025824.
                              Audience: **u,f.** *Choice, 1992.*

Reagan, Leslie J.   HQ767.5.U5
When Abortion Was a Crime: Women, Medicine and Law in the
United States, 1867-1973. Trade Paper. University of California
Press. Berkeley, CA. 1998. 402p. ISBN:0-520-21657-1, ISBN13:
978-0-520-21657-0. Dewey:363.4/6/0973.
                              Audience: **g,l,u,f.** *Choice, 1997.*

Rhodes, Jane   E185.97.C32R48 1998
Mary Ann Shadd Cary: The Black Press and Protest in the
Nineteenth Century. Library Binding. Indiana University Press.
Bloomington, IN. 1998. 304p. ISBN:0-253-33446-2, ISBN13:
978-0-253-33446-6. Dewey:[B]. LCCN:98-019997.
                              Audience: **l,u,f.** *Choice, 1999.*

Rosen, Ruth   HQ1426
The World Split Open: How the Modern Women's Movement
Changed America. Trade Paper. Penguin Group (USA) Inc. New
York, NY. 2001. 496p. ISBN:0-14-009719-8, ISBN13:
978-0-14-009719-1. Dewey:305.42/0973. LCCN:99-054439.
                              Audience: **l,u.**

Rotundo, E. Anthony   HQ1090.3
American Manhood: Transformations in Masculinity from the
Revolution to the Modern Era. Trade Paper. Basic Books. New
York, NY. 1994. 396p. ISBN:0-465-00169-6, ISBN13:
978-0-465-00169-9. Dewey:305.32/0973. LCCN:92-053247.
                              Audience: **l,u,f.** *Choice, 1993.*

Ruiz, Vicki L.   E184.M5
From Out of the Shadows: Mexican Women in
Twentieth-Century America. Trade Paper. Oxford University
Press, Inc. New York, NY. 1999. 272p. ISBN:0-19-513099-5,
ISBN13: 978-0-19-513099-7. Dewey:305.4886872.
                              Audience: **l,u.**

Slaughter, Jane   D802.I8S53 1997
Women and the Italian Resistance, 1943-45. Trade Cloth. Arden
Press, Inc. Denver, CO. 1997. 201p. Women and Modern
Revolution Ser. ISBN:0-912869-13-5, ISBN13:
978-0-912869-13-1. Dewey:940.53/45. LCCN:97-004937.
                              Audience: **g,l,u,f.** *Choice, 1998.*

Tanaka, Yuki   D810.C698T36 2001
Japan's Comfort Women: The Military and Involuntary
Prostitution During War and Occupation. Paper over Boards.

Routledge. New York, NY. 2001. 232p. Asia's Transformation
Ser. ISBN:0-415-19400-8, ISBN13: 978-0-415-19400-6.
Dewey:940.54/05/0922519. LCCN:2001-048307.
                              Audience: **g,l,u,f.** *Choice, 2002.*

Taylor, Quintard &   E185.925.A45 2003
  Moore, Shirley Ann Wilson (Editors)
African American Women Confront the West: 1600-2000. Trade
Cloth. University of Oklahoma Press. Norman, OK. 2003. 352p.
ISBN:0-8061-3524-7, ISBN13: 978-0-8061-3524-3.
Dewey:978/.00496073/0082. LCCN:2002-032479.
                              Audience: **g,l,u,f.** *Choice, 2004.*

White, Luise   HQ260.5.N35W45 1990
The Comforts of Home: Prostitution in Colonial Nairobi. Trade
Cloth. University of Chicago Press. Chicago, IL. 1990. 300p.
ISBN:0-226-89506-8, ISBN13: 978-0-226-89506-2.
Dewey:306.74/2/0967625. LCCN:90-034266.
                              Audience: **l,u,f.** *Choice, 1991.*

Zweiniger-Bargielowska,   HQ1593.P65 1990
  Ina
Women in Twentieth-Century Britain: Social, Cultural and
Political Change. Trade Paper. Longman Publishing Group.
White Plains, NY. 2001. 392p. ISBN:0-582-40480-0, ISBN13:
978-0-582-40480-9. Dewey:305.4/2/0941/0904.
                              Audience: **g,l,u,f.** *Choice, 2001.*

Business and Economics. Employment. Development

▢ Women working, 1870-1930.
http://ocp.hul.harvard.edu/ww/
                              Audience: **g,l,u.**

Albelda, Randy P. &   HV95.A5988 1997
  Tilly, Chris
Glass Ceilings and Bottomless Pits: Women's Work, Women's
Poverty. Trade Cloth. South End Press. Cambridge, MA. 1997.
221p. Women's Studies ISBN:0-89608-566-X, ISBN13:
978-0-89608-566-4. Dewcy:362.83/086/942. LCCN:97-017419.
                              Audience: **l,u,f.** *Choice, 1998.*

Barker, Drucilla K. &   HQ1381.B365 2004
  Feiner, Susan F.
Liberating Economics: Feminist Perspectives on Families, Work,
and Globalization. Trade Cloth. University of Michigan Press.
Chicago, IL. 2004. 208p. ISBN:0-472-09843-8, ISBN13:
978-0-472-09843-9. Dewey:330/.082. LCCN:2004-015058.
                              Audience: **l,u,f.** *Choice, 2005.*

Blackwelder, Julia Kirk   HD6095.B57 1997
Now Hiring: The Feminization of Work in the United States,
1900-1995. Trade Cloth. Texas A&M University Press. College
Station, TX. 1997. 320p. ISBN:0-89096-776-8, ISBN13:
978-0-89096-776-8. Dewey:331.4/0973/0904. LCCN:97-015922.
                              Audience: **l,u,f.** *Choice, 1998.*

Browne, Irene (Editor)   HD6057.5.U5L37 1999
African American and Latina Women at Work: Race, Gender
and Economic Inequality. Book, Other. Russell Sage Foundation.
New York, NY. 1998. 356p. ISBN:0-87154-147-5, ISBN13:
978-0-87154-147-5. Dewey:331.4/089/96073. LCCN:98-019536.
                              Audience: **u,f.** *Choice, 1999.*

Burstyn, Varda (Editor)　　HQ471.W66 1985
Women Against Censorship. Trade Paper. Salem House
Publishers. Scranton, PA. 1985. 210p. ISBN:0-88894-455-1,
ISBN13: 978-0-88894-455-9. Dewey:363.4/7. LCCN:85-098057.
Audience: **l,u,f.** ℬ *Choice, 1985.*

Celestin, Roger, et al.　　HQ1613
Beyond French Feminisms: Debates on Women, Politics, and
Culture in France, 1981-2001. Eliane DalMolin & Isabelle De
Courtivron (Authors). Cloth over Boards. Palgrave Macmillan.
New York, NY. 2003. 324p. ISBN:0-312-24019-8, ISBN13:
978-0-312-24019-6. Dewey:305.42/0944.
Audience: **u,f.**

Chang, Grace　　HD6095.C48 2000
Disposable Domestics: Immigrant Women Workers in the Global
Economy. Mimi Abramovitz (Foreword by). Trade Cloth. South
End Press. Cambridge, MA. 2000. 256p. Women's Studies
ISBN:0-89608-618-6, ISBN13: 978-0-89608-618-0.
Dewey:331.4/8164046. LCCN:99-462383.
Audience: **g,l,u,f.**

Clark, Anna　　HD8390
Struggle for the Breeches: Gender and the Making of the British
Working Class. Trade Paper. University of California Press.
Berkeley, CA. 1997. 432p. Studies on the History of Society
and Culture, Vol. 23 ISBN:0-520-20883-8, ISBN13:
978-0-520-20883-4. Dewey:305.5/62/0941. LCCN:93-050835.
Audience: **u,f.**

Dailey, Nancy　　HQ1063
When Baby Boom Women Retire. Trade Cloth. Greenwood
Publishing Group, Inc. Portsmouth, NH. 1998. 168p.
ISBN:0-275-96070-6, ISBN13: 978-0-275-96070-4.
Dewey:306.3/8/082. LCCN:97-027003.
Audience: **l,u,f.** *Choice, 1998.*

Davidson, Marilyn J. &　　HD6054.3
Burke, Ronald J. (Editors)
Women in Management Worldwide: Facts, Figures and Analysis.
Trade Cloth. Ashgate Publishing, Ltd. Aldershot, 2004. 370p.
ISBN:0-7546-0837-9, ISBN13: 978-0-7546-0837-0.
Dewey:331.4. LCCN:2003-058297.
Audience: **l,u,f.** *Choice, 2004.*

Delacoste, Frederique &　　HQ144
Alexander, Priscilla (Editors)
Sex Work: Writings by Women in the Sex Industry. Ed. 2. Trade
Paper. Cleis Press. San Francisco, CA. 1998. 380p.
ISBN:1-57344-042-6, ISBN13: 978-1-57344-042-4.
Dewey:306.7/42/0973. LCCN:00-708785.
Audience: **l,u,f.**

Doyal, Lesley　　RA564.85.D69 1995
What Makes Women Sick: Gender and the Political Economy of
Health. Cloth Text. Rutgers University Press. Piscataway, NJ.
1995. 320p. ISBN:0-8135-2206-4, ISBN13: 978-0-8135-2206-7.
Dewey:362.1/082. LCCN:94-047498.
Audience: **u,f.** *Choice, 1995.*

Drachman, Virginia G.　　HC102.5.D73 2002
Enterprising Women: 250 Years of American Business. Trade
Cloth. University of North Carolina Press. Chapel Hill, NC.
2002. 208p. ISBN:0-8078-2762-2, ISBN13: 978-0-8078-2762-8.
Dewey:338.7/092/273. LCCN:2002-006428.
Audience: **g,l,u,f.** *Choice, 2003.*

Ehrenreich, Barbara &　　HD6072
Hochschild, Arlie Russell (Editors)
Global Woman: Nannies, Maids, and Sex Workers in the New
Economy. Trade Paper. Henry Holt & Company. New York, NY.
2004. 336p. ISBN:0-8050-7509-7, ISBN13: 978-0-8050-7509-0.
Dewey:331.4/8164046/08691.
Audience: **g,l,u.**

Elson, Diane & Keklik,　　HQ1240
Hanse
Progress of the World's Women: Gender Equality and the
Millennium Development Goals. Noeleen Heyzer (Preface by).
Paper Text. DIANE Publishing Company. Collingdale, PA. 2003.
68p. ISBN:0-7567-3646-3, ISBN13: 978-0-7567-3646-0.
Dewey:305.4209172.
Audience: **g,l,u,f.**

England, Paula &　　HQ536.E54 1986
Farkas, George
Households, Employment and Gender: A Social, Economic and
Demographic View. Trade Cloth. Aldine Transaction. Somerset,
NJ. 1986. 237p. Social Institutions and Social Change Ser.
ISBN:0-202-30322-5, ISBN13: 978-0-202-30322-2.
Dewey:304.6. LCCN:85-018628.
Audience: **g,l,u,f.** ℬ *Choice, 1986.*

French, John D. &　　HD6100.5.G46 1997
James, Daniel
The Gendered Worlds of Latin American Women Workers: From
Household and Factory to the Union Hall and Ballot Box. Trade
Cloth. Duke University Press. Durham, NC. 1997. 336p.
ISBN:0-8223-2000-2, ISBN13: 978-0-8223-2000-5.
Dewey:331.4/098. LCCN:97-020053.
Audience: **u,f.** *Choice, 1998.*

Ghorayshi, Parvin　　HD6223
(Compiled by)
Women and Work in Developing Countries: An Annotated
Bibliopgraphy. Cloth Text. Greenwood Publishing Group, Inc.
Portsmouth, NH. 1994. 248p. Bibliographies and Indexes in
Women's Studies, No. 20 ISBN:0-313-28834-8, ISBN13:
978-0-313-28834-0. Dewey:016.3314/09172/4.
LCCN:93-038803.
Audience: **u,f.** *Choice, 1994.*

Hart, Vivien　　K1781.H37 1994
ⓔ Bound by Our Constitution: Women, Workers, and the
Minimum Wage. E-Book. Princeton University Press. Princeton,
NJ. ISBN:1-4008-1201-1, ISBN13: 978-1-4008-1201-1.
Dewey:344/.0121.
Audience: **u,f.**

Hoodfar, Homa　　HC830.Z7C343 1997
Between Marriage and the Market: Intimate Politics and
Survival in Cairo. Trade Paper. University of California Press.
Berkeley, CA. 1997. 265p. Comparative Studies on Muslim
Societies ISBN:0-520-20825-0, ISBN13: 978-0-520-20825-4.
Dewey:339.2/2. LCCN:96-037296.
Audience: **l,u,f.** *Choice, 1998.*

Ireson, Carol J.　　DS555.45.M5I74 1996
Fields, Forest, and Family: Women's Work and Power in Rural
Laos. Trade Paper. Westview Press. Boulder, CO. 1999. 312p.
ISBN:0-8133-3730-5, ISBN13: 978-0-8133-3730-2.
Dewey:305.4/09594. LCCN:96-027143.
Audience: **u,f.**

Jahan, Rounaq　　　　　　　　　**HQ1240.J34 1995**
The Elusive Agenda: Mainstreaming Women in Development.
Trade Cloth. Zed Books, Ltd. London, 1995. 160p.
ISBN:1-85649-273-7, ISBN13: 978-1-85649-273-7.
Dewey:338.9/0082. LCCN:95-013689.
　　　　　　　　　　　　Audience: **u,f.**　*Choice, 1995.*

Jones, Jacqueline　　　　　　**HD6057.5.U5J66 1986**
Labor of Love, Labor of Sorrow: Black Women, Work and the
Family from Slavery to the Present. Trade Paper. Knopf
Publishing Group. New York, NY. 1986. 464p.
ISBN:0-394-74536-1, ISBN13: 978-0-394-74536-7.
Dewey:305.4/8896073. LCCN:85-040860.
　　　　　　　　Audience: **g,l,u.**　*ℬ　Choice, 1985.*

Jordan, Ellen R.　　　　　　　**HD6135.J667 1999**
Women's Movement and Women's Employment in Nineteenth
Century Britain. Paper over Boards. Routledge. New York, NY.
1999. 288p. Research in Gender and History Ser.
ISBN:0-415-18951-9, ISBN13: 978-0-415-18951-4.
Dewey:331.4/0941/09034. LCCN:98-051633.
　　　　　　　　　　　　Audience: **u,f.**　*Choice, 2000.*

Kanter, Rosabeth Moss　　　　　**H31.S67 NO. 9**
Work and Family in the United States: A Critical Review and
Agenda for Research and Policy. Trade Paper. Russell Sage
Foundation. New York, NY. 1977. 120p. Social Science
Frontiers Ser. ISBN:0-87154-433-4, ISBN13:
978-0-87154-433-9. Dewey:300/.8. LCCN:76-046870.
　　　　　　　　　　　Audience: **l,u,f.**　*ℬ*

Kempadoo, Kamala &　　　　　　**HQ111.G56 1998**
　Doezema, Jo
Global Sex Workers: Rights, Resistance and Redefinition. Paper
over Boards. Routledge. New York, NY. 1998. 304p.
ISBN:0-415-91828-6, ISBN13: 978-0-415-91828-2.
Dewey:306.74. LCCN:97-045759.
　　　　　　　　　　　　Audience: **g,l,u,f.**

Leacock, Eleanor Burke　　　　　　**HD6060**
　& Safa, Helen I.
Women's Work: Development and the Division of Labor by
Gender. Trade Cloth. Greenwood Publishing Group, Inc.
Portsmouth, NH. 1986. 311p. ISBN:0-89789-035-3, ISBN13:
978-0-89789-035-9. Dewey:305.4/3. LCCN:85-026674.
　　　　　　　　　　　　Audience: **l,u,f.**

Louie, Miriam Ching　　　　　**HD6057.5.U5L68 2001**
　Yoon
Sweatshop Warriors: Immigrant Women Workers Take on the
Global Factory. Trade Cloth. South End Press. Cambridge, MA.
2001. 256p. Women's Studies ISBN:0-89608-639-9, ISBN13:
978-0-89608-639-5. Dewey:331.4/086/24. LCCN:00-051577.
　　　　　　　　　　　　Audience: **l,u.**　*Choice, 2002.*

Matthaei, Julie A.　　　　　　　　**HQ1410**
An Economic History of Women in America: Women's Work,
the Sexual Division of Labor and the Development of
Capitalism. Trade Paper. Knopf Publishing Group. New York,
NY. 1982. 384p. ISBN:0-8052-0744-9, ISBN13:
978-0-8052-0744-6. Dewey:330.973/0088042. LCCN:81-084111.
　　　　　　　　Audience: **g,l,u,f.**　*ℬ*

Messing, Karen　　　　　　**RC963.6.W65M47 1998**
One-Eyed Science: Occupational Health and Women Workers.
Trade Cloth. Temple University Press. Philadelphia, PA. 1998.
264p. Labor and Social Change Ser. ISBN:1-56639-597-6,

ISBN13: 978-1-56639-597-7. Dewey:616.9/803*/082.
LCCN:97-026885.
　　　　　　　　　　　　Audience: **u,f.**　*Choice, 1998.*

Mies, Maria　　　　　　　　　　**HQ1154**
Patriarchy and Accumulation on a World Scale: Women in the
International Division of Labour. Ed. 2. Cloth over Boards. Zed
Books, Ltd. London, 1999. 256p. ISBN:1-85649-734-8, ISBN13:
978-1-85649-734-3. Dewey:305.4/2.
　　　　　　　　　　　　Audience: **l,u.**

Mies, Maria　　　　　　　　**HQ1870.9.M54 1988**
Women: The Last Colony. Trade Cloth. Zed Books, Ltd.
London, 1988. 185p. ISBN:0-86232-455-6, ISBN13:
978-0-86232-455-1. Dewey:305.4/2/091724. LCCN:88-014255.
　　　　　　　　　　　　Audience: **u,f.**　*Choice, 1988.*

Mikell, Gwendolyn　　　　　**HQ1240.5.A357.A36**
　(Editor)
African Feminism: The Politics of Survival in Sub-Saharan
Africa. Trade Cloth. University of Pennsylvania Press.
Philadelphia, PA. 1997. 392p. ISBN:0-8122-3349-2, ISBN13:
978-0-8122-3349-0. Dewey:305.42/0967. LCCN:97-006260.
　　　　　　　　　　　　Audience: **l,u.**　*Choice, 1998.*

Mohanty, Chandra　　　　　　**HQ1870.9.M64 2003**
　Talpade
Feminism Without Borders: Decolonizing Theory, Practicing
Solidarity. Trade Cloth. Duke University Press. Durham, NC.
2003. 320p. ISBN:0-8223-3010-5, ISBN13: 978-0-8223-3010-3.
Dewey:305.42. LCCN:2002-013266.
　　　　　　　　　　　　Audience: **u,f.**

Mohanty, Chandra T.　　　　　**HQ1870.9.T49 1991**
　(Editor), et al.
Third World Women and the Politics of Feminism. Ann Russo
& Lourdes Torres (Editors). Trade Cloth. Indiana University
Press. Bloomington, IN. 1991. 352p. ISBN:0-253-33873-5,
ISBN13: 978-0-253-33873-0. Dewey:305.42/09172/4.
LCCN:90-043510.
　　　　　　　　　　　　Audience: **u,f.**　*Choice, 1991.*

Momsen, Janet H.　　　　　　**HQ1240.5.C27.W66**
　(Editor)
Women and Change in the Caribbean. Trade Cloth. Indiana
University Press. Bloomington, IN. 1993. 320p.
ISBN:0-253-33897-2, ISBN13: 978-0-253-33897-6.
Dewey:305.4209729. LCCN:93-000422.
　　　　　　　　　　　　Audience: **u,f.**　*Choice, 1994.*

Overholt, Catherine　　　　　　**HQ1075.5.D44**
　(Editor)
Gender Roles in Development Projects: A Case Book. Trade
Paper. Books on Demand. Ann Arbor, MI. 1994. 340p.
Kumarian Press Case Studies Ser. ISBN:0-7837-7574-1,
ISBN13: 978-0-7837-7574-6. Dewey:305.3. LCCN:84-023325.
　　　　　　　　　　　　Audience: **u,f.**

Peterson, Janice &　　　　　　**HQ1381.E44 1999**
　Lewis, Margaret (Editors)
The Elgar Companion to Feminist Economics. Trade Cloth.
Edward Elgar Publishing, Inc. Northampton, MA. 2000. 832p.
ISBN:1-85898-453-X, ISBN13: 978-1-85898-453-7.
Dewey:330/.082. LCCN:99-033956.
　　　　　　　　　　　　Audience: **u,f.**　*Choice, 2001.*

Powell, Gary N. &　　　　　　**HD6054.3.P69 2003**
　Graves, Laura M.
Women and Men in Management. Ed. 3. Cloth Text. SAGE

Publications, Inc. Thousand Oaks, CA. 2002. 288p.
ISBN:0-7619-2195-8, ISBN13: 978-0-7619-2195-0.
Dewey:658.4/095. LCCN:2002-010312.
Audience: **g,l,u.** *Choice, 2003.*

Reddock, Rhoda   **HQ1525.7.R43 1994**
Women, Labour and Politics in Trinidad and Tobago: A History.
Cloth over Boards. Zed Books, Ltd. London, 1994. 320p.
ISBN:1-85649-153-6, ISBN13: 978-1-85649-153-2.
Dewey:305.42/0972983. LCCN:94-024809.
Audience: **l,u,f.** *Choice, 1995.*

Sachs, Carolyn E.   **HQ1240.S28 1996**
Gendered Fields: Rural Women, Agriculture, and Environment.
Trade Paper. Westview Press. Boulder, CO. 1996. 224p. Rural
Studies ISBN:0-8133-2520-X, ISBN13: 978-0-8133-2520-0.
Dewey:338.9/0082. LCCN:95-043943.
Audience: **u,f.** *Choice, 1996.*

Scanlon, Jennifer   **HC110.C6G457 2000**
Gender and Consumer Culture Reader. Trade Cloth. New York
University Press. New York, NY. 2000. 392p.
ISBN:0-8147-8131-4, ISBN13: 978-0-8147-8131-9.
Dewey:339.4/7/0820973. LCCN:00-039448.
Audience: **u,f.**

Sidel, Ruth   **HV1445.S49 1992**
Women and Children Last: The Plight of Poor Women in
Affluent America. Trade Paper. Penguin Group (USA) Inc. New
York, NY. 1992. 288p. ISBN:0-14-016766-8, ISBN13:
978-0-14-016766-5. Dewey:362.8/3/0973. LCCN:91-021102.
Audience: **l,u,f.**

Snyder, Margaret C.   **HD6210.7 .S69 2000**
Women in African Economies: From Burning Sun to
Boardroom. Trade Cloth. Fountain Publishers Ltd. Kampala,
2000. xx, 360p. ISBN:9970-02-187-7, ISBN13:
978-9970-02-187-1. Dewey:331.409676. LCCN:00-284961.
Audience: **l,u,f.** *Choice, 2001.*

Snyder, Margaret C. &   **HQ1240.5.A35S69 1995**
  Tadesse, Mary
African Women and Development: A History. Gertrude
Mongella (Preface by). Trade Cloth. Zed Books, Ltd. London,
1995. 256p. ISBN:1-85649-299-0, ISBN13: 978-1-85649-299-7.
Dewey:305.42/096. LCCN:94-040205.
Audience: **g,l,u,f.** *Choice, 1995.*

Sparr, Pamela (Editor)   **HD6223.M67 1994**
Mortgaging Women's Lives: Feminist Critiques of Structural
Adjustment. Trade Paper. Zed Books, Ltd. London, 1994. 224p.
ISBN:1-85649-102-1, ISBN13: 978-1-85649-102-0.
Dewey:331.4/09172/4. LCCN:94-041464.
Audience: **l,u,f.** *Choice, 1995.*

Stephen, Lynn   **HQ1240.5.L29S74 1997**
Women and Social Movements in Latin America: Power from
Below. Trade Cloth. University of Texas Press. Austin, TX.
1997. 352p. ISBN:0-292-77715-9, ISBN13: 978-0-292-77715-6.
Dewey:305.42/098. LCCN:96-045788.
Audience: **u,f.** *Choice, 1998.*

Tilly, Louise & Scott,   **HD6145**
  Joan W.
Women, Work and Family. Trade Cloth. Holt, Rinehart &
Winston. Austin, TX. 1978. xiv, 274p. ISBN:0-03-033326-1,
ISBN13: 978-0-03-033326-2. Dewey:301.5/5. LCCN:74-019821.
Audience: **u,f.**

Visvanathan, Nalini   **HQ1240.W6568 1996**
The Women, Gender and Development Reader. Lynne Duggan,
Laurie Nisonoff, Brenda Wyss & Nan Wiegersma (Editors).
Trade Paper. Zed Books, Ltd. London, 1997. 384p.
ISBN:1-85649-142-0, ISBN13: 978-1-85649-142-6.
Dewey:305.4/2/091724. LCCN:96-047238.
Audience: **l,u,f.**

Webster, Juliet   **HD6060.6.W43 1996**
Shaping Women's Work: Gender, Employment and Information
Technology. Trade Cloth. Longman Publishing Group. White
Plains, NY. 1996. 224p. Sociology Ser. ISBN:0-582-21810-1,
ISBN13: 978-0-582-21810-9. Dewey:306.3/615.
LCCN:96-000459.
Audience: **l,u,f.** *Choice, 1997.*

Williams, Christine L.   **HD6060.6 .D65 1993**
  (Editor)
Doing Women's Work: Men in Nontraditional Occupations.
Trade Paper. SAGE Publications, Inc. Thousand Oaks, CA.
1993. 205p. Research on Men and Masculinities Ser., Vol. 3
ISBN:0-8039-5305-4, ISBN13: 978-0-8039-5305-5.
Dewey:305.33. LCCN:93-025055.
Audience: **l,u,f.**

Young, Kate   **HQ1240.Y68 1993**
Planning Development with Women: Making a World of
Difference. Trade Cloth. Palgrave Macmillan. New York, NY.
1993. 200p. ISBN:0-312-09090-0, ISBN13: 978-0-312-09090-6.
Dewey:305.42. LCCN:92-029477.
Audience: **g,l,u,f.** *Choice, 1993.*

Religion and Spirituality

Ahmed, Leila   **HQ1170**
Women and Gender in Islam: Historical Roots of a Modern
Debate. Trade Paper. Yale University Press. Cumberland, RI.
1993. 304p. ISBN:0-300-05583-8, ISBN13: 978-0-300-05583-2.
Dewey:305.4/86971.
Audience: **l,u,f.** *Choice, 1992.*

Beck, Lois & Keddie,   **HQ1170**
  Nikki R. (Editors)
Women in the Muslim World. Trade Cloth. Harvard University
Press. Cambridge, MA. 1978. 712p. ISBN:0-674-95480-7,
ISBN13: 978-0-674-95480-9. Dewey:301.41/2/0917671.
LCCN:78-003633.
Audience: **u,f.** B

Benowitz, June Melby   **BL458**
ⓔ Encyclopedia of American Women and Religion. E-Book.
ABC-CLIO, Inc. Santa Barbara, CA. 2002.
ISBN:1-57607-496-X, ISBN13: 978-1-57607-496-1.
Dewey:200/.82/0973.
Audience: **g,l,u.**

Brink, Judy &   **BL238.M59 1997**
  Mencher, Joan (Editors)
Mixed Blessings: Gender and Religious Fundamentalism Cross
Culturally. UK-B Format Paperback. Routledge. New York, NY.
1996. 264p. ISBN:0-415-91186-9, ISBN13: 978-0-415-91186-3.
Dewey:291/.082. LCCN:96-028341.
Audience: **u,f.**

Caputi, Jane   **HQ1190.C368 2004**
Goddesses and Monsters: Women, Myth, Power, and Popular
Culture. Trade Cloth. University of Wisconsin Press. Chicago,

IL. 2004. 448p. ISBN:0-299-19620-8, ISBN13:
978-0-299-19620-2. Dewey:306. LCCN:2003-020572.

Audience: **l,u,f.**

Daly, Mary   **HQ1394.D28 1985**
The Church and the Second Sex. Trade Paper. Beacon Press.
Boston, MA. 1986. 240p. ISBN:0-8070-1101-0, ISBN13:
978-0-8070-1101-0. Dewey:261.8/344. LCCN:85-047519.

Audience: **l,u.** 𝔅

Falk, Nancy Auer &   **BL458.U57 2001**
 Gross, Rita M.
Unspoken Worlds: Women's Religious Lives. Ed. 3. Paper Text.
Thomson Wadsworth. Belmont, CA. 2000. 336p. Philosophy
Ser. ISBN:0-534-51570-3, ISBN13: 978-0-534-51570-6.
Dewey:200/.82. LCCN:00-033410.

Audience: **g,l,u,f.**

Gross, Rita M.   **BQ4570.W6**
Buddhism after Patriarchy: A Feminist History, Analysis, and
Reconstruction of Buddhism. Paper Text. State University of
New York Press. Albany, NY. 1992. 365p. ISBN:0-7914-1404-3,
ISBN13: 978-0-7914-1404-0. Dewey:294.3/082.
LCCN:92-009133.

Audience: **u,f.** *Choice, 1993.*

Grossman, Avraham   **BM729.W6G7613 2004**
Pious and Rebellious: Jewish Women in Medieval Europe. Trade
Cloth. University Press of New England. Lebanon, NH. 2004.
352p. Tauber Institute for the Study of European Jewry Ser.
ISBN:1-58465-391-4, ISBN13: 978-1-58465-391-2.
Dewey:305.48/892404/0902. LCCN:2004-003029.

Audience: **u,f.** *Choice, 2005.*

Holman Weisbard,   **QL666.O6**
 Phyllis
▢ Annotated Bibliography and Guide to Archival Resources on
the History of Jewish Women in America.
http://www.library.wisc.edu/libraries/WomensStudies/jewwom/
jwmain.htm

Audience: **g,l,u.**

Hyman, Paula E.   **DS148.H93 1995**
Gender and Assimilation in Modern Jewish History: The Roles
and Representations of Women. Trade Cloth. University of
Washington Press. Seattle, WA. 1995. 208p. Samuel and Althea
Stroum Lectures in Jewish Studies ISBN:0-295-97425-7,
ISBN13: 978-0-295-97425-5. Dewey:305.48/696.
LCCN:94-037932.

Audience: **g,l,u,f.** *Choice, 1996.*

Hyman, Paula E. &   **DS115.2.J49 1997**
 Moore, Deborah Dash (Editors)
Jewish Women in America: An Historical Encyclopedia, Set.
Paper over Boards. Routledge. New York, NY. 1997. 1800p.
ISBN:0-415-91936-3, ISBN13: 978-0-415-91936-4.
Dewey:920.72/089/924073 B. LCCN:97-026842.

Audience: **g,l,u,f.** *Choice, 1998.*

Jantzen, Grace M.   **BV5083 .J36 1995**
Power, Gender and Christian Mysticism. Trade Cloth.
Cambridge University Press. New York, NY. 1995. 403p.
Studies in Ideology and Religion, No. 8 ISBN:0-521-47376-4,
ISBN13: 978-0-521-47376-7. Dewey:248.2/2. LCCN:94-044562.

Audience: **u,f.** *Choice, 1996.*

Jantzen, Grace M.   **BV5083 .J36 1995**
Power, Gender and Christian Mysticism. Duncan Forrester &
Alistair Kee (Contribution by). Trade Paper. Cambridge

University Press. New York, NY. 1995. 403p. Studies in
Ideology and Religion, No. 8 ISBN:0-521-47926-6, ISBN13:
978-0-521-47926-4. Dewey:248.2/2. LCCN:94-044562.

Audience: **u,f.** *Choice, 1996.*

Joseph, Suad (Editor)   **HQ1170.E53 2003**
The Encyclopaedia of Women and Islamic Cultures. Trade
Cloth. Brill Academic Publishers. Leiden, 2004.
ISBN:90-04-13247-3, ISBN13: 978-90-04-13247-4.
Dewey:305.48/697/03. LCCN:2004-269368.

Audience: **g,l,u,f.**

Kent, Eliza F.   **BV3280.T3K46 2004**
Converting Women: Gender and Protestant Christianity in
Colonial South India. Trade Cloth. Oxford University Press, Inc.
New York, NY. 2004. 330p. ISBN:0-19-516507-1, ISBN13:
978-0-19-516507-4. Dewey:305.48/6204/09548.
LCCN:2003-049854.

Audience: **u,f.** *Choice, 2004.*

Kern, Kathi   **HQ1413**
Mrs. Stanton's Bible: Elizabeth Cady Stanton and the Woman's
Bible. Book, Other. Cornell University Press. Ithaca, NY. 2001.
304p. ISBN:0-8014-3191-3, ISBN13: 978-0-8014-3191-3.
Dewey:305.42/092. LCCN:00-010756.

Audience: **g,l,u,f.** *Choice, 2001.*

Kimball, Michelle &   **Z7963.I74K56 1996**
 Von Schlegell, Barbara R.
Muslim Women Throughout the World: A Bibliography with
Selected Annotations. Library Binding. Lynne Rienner
Publishers, Inc. Boulder, CO. 1997. 285p. ISBN:1-55587-680-3,
ISBN13: 978-1-55587-680-7. Dewey:016.30548/6971.
LCCN:96-025718.

Audience: **l,u,f.**

Marcus, Jacob R.   **HQ1172.M37 SUPPL**
The American Jewish Woman: A Documentary History. Trade
Cloth. Ktav Publishing House, Inc. Jersey City, NJ. 1981.
1047p. ISBN:0-87068-752-2, ISBN13: 978-0-87068-752-5.
Dewey:205.4/8. LCCN:81-001966.

Audience: **g,l,u.** 𝔅

Marcus, Jacob R.   **HQ1172.M37**
 (Editor)
The American Jewish Woman: 1654-1980. Trade Cloth. Ktav
Publishing House, Inc. Jersey City, NJ. 1981. xiv, 231p.
ISBN:0-87068-751-4, ISBN13: 978-0-87068-751-8.
Dewey:305.4/8. LCCN:81-001720.

Audience: **u,f.** 𝔅

Matory, J. Lorand   **DT515.45.Y67**
Sex and the Empire That Is No More: Gender and the Politics
of Metaphor in Oyo Yoruba Religion. Ed. 2. Trade Cloth.
Berghahn Books, Inc. New York, NY. 2004. 320p. Studies in
Applied Anthropology Ser. ISBN:1-57181-307-1, ISBN13:
978-1-57181-307-7. Dewey:306.6/9968333. LCCN:2004-046221.

Audience: **u,f.** *Choice, 1994.*

Medina, Lara   **BX810.H57M43 2004**
Las Hermanas: Chicana/Latina Religious-Political Activism in
the U. S. Catholic Church. Trade Cloth. Temple University
Press. Philadelphia, PA. 2004. 232p. ISBN:1-59213-250-2,
ISBN13: 978-1-59213-250-8. Dewey:267.4/4273.
LCCN:2003-064591.

Audience: **u,f.** *Choice, 2005.*

Moghissi, Hiadeh   HQ1170.M64 1999
Feminism and Islamic Fundamentalism: The Limits of
Postmodern Analysis. Cloth over Boards. Zed Books, Ltd.
London, 1999. 128p. ISBN:1-85649-589-2, ISBN13:
978-1-85649-589-9. Dewey:305.48/6971. LCCN:99-022771.
Audience: **l,u,f.** *Choice, 2000.*

Pratt, Annis   PR508.A66.P73 1994
Dancing with Goddesses: Archetypes, Poetry, and
Empowerment. Trade Cloth. Indiana University Press.
Bloomington, IN. 1994. 432p. ISBN:0-253-34586-3, ISBN13:
978-0-253-34586-8. Dewey:821.009/353. LCCN:93-028442.
Audience: **u,f.** *Choice, 1995.*

Ruether, Rosemary   BT704.R835 1998
  Radford
Women and Redemption: A Theological History. Trade Cloth.
Augsburg Fortress, Publishers. Minneapolis, MN. 2003. 384p.
ISBN:0-8006-2947-7, ISBN13: 978-0-8006-2947-2.
Dewey:261.8/3/44. LCCN:98-011783.
Audience: **u,f.** *Choice, 1999.*

Russell, Letty M. &   BT83.55.D53 1996
  Clarkson, J. Shannon (Editors)
Dictionary of Feminist Theologies. Trade Cloth. Westminster
John Knox Press. Louisville, KY. 1996. 351p.
ISBN:0-664-22058-4, ISBN13: 978-0-664-22058-7.
Dewey:261.8/34/42. LCCN:95-049454.
Audience: **g,l,u,f.** *Choice, 1997.*

Saliba, Therese (Editor),   HQ1170.G43 2002
  et al.
Gender, Politics, and Islam. Carolyn Allen & Judith A. Howard
(Editors). Trade Cloth. University of Chicago Press. Chicago,
IL. 2002. 292p. ISBN:0-226-73428-5, ISBN13:
978-0-226-73428-6. Dewey:305.48/6971017671.
LCCN:2002-067318.
Audience: **l,u,f.**

Sharma, Arvind &   BL458.F455 1998
  Young, Katherine K. (Editors)
Feminism and World Religions. Paper Text. State University of
New York Press. Albany, NY. 1998. 352p. SUNY Series, McGill
Studies in the History of Religions ISBN:0-7914-4024-9,
ISBN13: 978-0-7914-4024-7. Dewey:2913.1/783442.
LCCN:98-010509.
Audience: **u,f.** *Choice, 1999.*

Stowasser, Barbara   BP134.W6S76 1994
  Freyer
[e] Women in the Qur'an, Traditions, and Interpretation. E-Book.
NetLibrary, Inc. Boulder, CO. 1994. ISBN:0-585-32820-X,
ISBN13: 978-0-585-32820-1. Dewey:297.1228.
Audience: **g,l,u,f.**

Tsomo, Karma Lekshe   BQ4570.W6K34 1999
  (Editor)
Buddhist Women Across Cultures: Realizations. Cloth Text.
State University of New York Press. Albany, NY. 1999. 320p.
SUNY Series in Feminist Philosophy ISBN:0-7914-4137-7,
ISBN13: 978-0-7914-4137-4. Dewey:294.3/082.
LCCN:98-034325.
Audience: **l,u.**

Ulanov, Ann Belford   HQ1206
The Feminine: In Jungian Psychology and in Christian
Theology. Trade Paper. Northwestern University Press.
Evanston, IL. 1971. 347p. ISBN:0-8101-0608-6, ISBN13:
978-0-8101-0608-6. Dewey:136.15.
Audience: **l,u.**

Walsh, Mary-Paula   Z7963
Feminism and Christian Tradition: An Annotated Bibliography
and Critical Introduction to the Literature. Cloth Text.
Greenwood Publishing Group, Inc. Portsmouth, NH. 1999. 472p.
Bibliographies and Indexes in Religious Studies, Vol. 51
ISBN:0-313-26419-8, ISBN13: 978-0-313-26419-1.
Dewey:016.2618/344. LCCN:98-033137.
Audience: **l,u.** *Choice, 1999.*

Weinberger-Thomas,   GT3370.W5613 1999
  Catherine
Ashes of Immortality: Widow-Burning in India. Jeffrey
Mehlman & David Gordon White (Translators). Trade Paper.
University of Chicago Press. Chicago, IL. 2000. 329p.
ISBN:0-226-88569-0, ISBN13: 978-0-226-88569-8.
Dewey:393/.9. LCCN:99-037258.
Audience: **g,l,u,f.** *Choice, 2000.*

Young, Serinity   BL458.E53 1999
Encyclopedia of Women and World Religion, Vol. 2. Trade
Cloth. Simon & Schuster. New York, NY. 1998. xxxi, 1152p.
ISBN:0-02-864860-9, ISBN13: 978-0-02-864860-6.
Dewey:200/.82. LCCN:98-039292.
Audience: **g,l,u.**

Young, Serinity   BL458.E53 1999
Encyclopedia of Women and World Religion, Vol. 1. Trade
Cloth. Simon & Schuster. New York, NY. 1998. xxxi, 1152p.
ISBN:0-02-864859-5, ISBN13: 978-0-02-864859-0.
Dewey:200/.82. LCCN:98-039292.
Audience: **g,l,u.**

Philosophy and Ethics

Alcoff, Linda & Potter,   HQ1190.F45 1993
  Elizabeth (Editors)
Feminist Epistemologies. UK-B Format Paperback. Routledge.
New York, NY. 1992. 320p. Thinking Gender Ser.
ISBN:0-415-90451-X, ISBN13: 978-0-415-90451-3.
Dewey:305.4201. LCCN:92-011309.
Audience: **l,u.**

Allen, Prudence   BD450.A4725 1996
The Concept of Woman: The Aristotelian Revolution, 750 B. C.
-A. D. 1250. Trade Paper. William B. Eerdmans Publishing
Company. Grand Rapids, MI. 1997. 607p. ISBN:0-8028-4270-4,
ISBN13: 978-0-8028-4270-1. Dewey:305.4/01.
LCCN:96-009102.
Audience: **l,u.**

Card, Claudia (Editor)   BD450.F43 1991
Feminist Ethics. Trade Cloth. University Press of Kansas.
Lawrence, KS. 1991. viii, 304p. ISBN:0-7006-0482-0, ISBN13:
978-0-7006-0482-1. Dewey:170/.82. LCCN:91-006753.
Audience: **g,l,u,f.** *Choice, 1992.*

Code, Lorraine   HQ1190.C64 1991
What Can She Know?: Feminist Theory and the Construction of
Knowledge. Book, Other. Cornell University Press. Ithaca, NY.

1991. 384p. ISBN:0-8014-2476-3, ISBN13: 978-0-8014-2476-2. Dewey:305.42/01. LCCN:90-055755.

Audience: **l,u,f.** *Choice, 1991.*

Daly, Mary   **HQ1154.D312 1990**
Gyn/Ecology: The Metaethics of Radical Feminism. Trade Paper. Beacon Press. Boston, MA. 1990. 517p. ISBN:0-8070-1413-3, ISBN13: 978-0-8070-1413-4. Dewey:305.4/2. LCCN:90-052596.

Audience: **l,u.**

DesAutels, Peggy &   **BJ1395.D47 2001**
  Waugh, Joanne
Feminists Doing Ethics. Book, Other. Rowman & Littlefield Publishers, Inc. Lanham, MD. 2001. 280p. New Feminist Perspectives Ser. ISBN:0-7425-1210-X, ISBN13: 978-0-7425-1210-8. Dewey:170/.82. LCCN:2001-019407.

Audience: **g,u.** *Choice, 2002.*

Fricker, Miranda &   **HQ1154 .C25 2000**
  Hornsby, Jennifer (Editors)
The Cambridge Companion to Feminism in Philosophy. Cloth Text. Cambridge University Press. New York, NY. 2000. 294p. Cambridge Companions to Philosophy Ser. ISBN:0-521-62451-7, ISBN13: 978-0-521-62451-0. Dewey:305.42/01. LCCN:99-021117.

Audience: **g,l,u.** *Choice, 2000.*

Garry, Ann & Pearsall,   **HQ1190.W688 1996**
  Marilyn (Editors)
Women, Knowledge, and Reality: Explorations in Feminist Philosophy. Ed. 2. Paper over Boards. Routledge. New York, NY. 1996. 448p. ISBN:0-415-91796-4, ISBN13: 978-0-415-91796-4. Dewey:108.2. LCCN:96-025166.

Audience: **l,u.** *Choice, 1990.*

Gould, Carol (Editor)   **HQ1154**
Beyond Domination: New Perspectives on Women and Philosophy. Trade Paper. Rowman & Littlefield Publishers, Inc. Lanham, MD. 1983. 344p. New Feminist Perspectives Ser. ISBN:0-8476-7236-0, ISBN13: 978-0-8476-7236-3. Dewey:305.4/2. LCCN:83-010894.

Audience: **l,u.** *B*

Gould, Carol C. &   **HQ1154**
  Wartofsky, Marx W.
Women and Philosophy: Toward a Theory of Liberation. Other. Penguin Group (USA) Inc. New York, NY. 1976. ISBN:0-399-50362-5, ISBN13: 978-0-399-50362-7. Dewey:301.41/2/09.

Audience: **l,u.** *B*

Harding, Sandra &   **HQ1154.D538 2003**
  Hintikka, Merrill B. (Editors)
Discovering Reality: Feminist Perspectives on Epistemology, Metaphysics, Methodology, and Philosophy of Science. Ed. 2. Trade Paper. Springer. New York, NY. 1899. 372p. ISBN:1-4020-1319-1, ISBN13: 978-1-4020-1319-5. Dewey:305.4/2.

Audience: **u,f.**

Irigaray, Luce   **HQ1154.I7413 1985**
Speculum of the Other Woman. Gillian C. Gill (Translator). Trade Paper. Cornell University Press. Ithaca, NY. 1985. 416p. ISBN:0-8014-9330-7, ISBN13: 978-0-8014-9330-0. Dewey:155.3/33. LCCN:84-045151.

Audience: **u,f.**

Jaggar, Alison M.   **BJ1395**
  (Editor)
Living with Contradictions: Controversies in Feminist Social Ethics. Trade Paper. Westview Press. Boulder, CO. 1994. 698p. ISBN:0-8133-1776-2, ISBN13: 978-0-8133-1776-2. Dewey:170.82. LCCN:93-029466.

Audience: **l,u.**

Meyers, Diana Tietjens   **HQ1190.F4644 1997**
  (Editor)
Feminists Rethink the Self. Trade Paper. Westview Press. Boulder, CO. 1996. 288p. Feminist Theory and Politics Ser. ISBN:0-8133-2083-6, ISBN13: 978-0-8133-2083-0. Dewey:126. LCCN:96-043121.

Audience: **l,u.**

Meyers, Diana Tietjens   **HQ1075.M494 2002**
Gender in the Mirror: Cultural Imagery and Women's Agency. Trade Cloth. Oxford University Press, Inc. New York, NY. 2002. 241p. Studies in Feminist Philosophy ISBN:0-19-514040-0, ISBN13: 978-0-19-514040-8. Dewey:305.42. LCCN:2001-036805.

Audience: **u,f.** *Choice, 2003.*

Montagu, Ashley   **HQ1206.M65 1999**
The Natural Superiority of Women. Ed. 5. Trade Cloth. AltaMira Press. Walnut Creek, CA. 1999. 300p. ISBN:0-7619-8981-1, ISBN13: 978-0-7619-8981-3. Dewey:305.4. LCCN:98-040173.

Audience: **g,l,u,f.**

Nelson, Lynn H.   **Q175.N387 1990**
Who Knows: From Quine to a Feminist Empiricism. Trade Cloth. Temple University Press. Philadelphia, PA. 1990. 336p. ISBN:0-87722-647-4, ISBN13: 978-0-87722-647-5. Dewey:501. LCCN:89-005173.

Audience: **u,f.**

Nicholson, Linda J.   **HQ1206.F453 1990**
  (Editor, Introduction by)
Feminism - Postmodernism. Trade Cloth. Routledge. New York, NY. 1989. 352p. ISBN:0-415-90058-1, ISBN13: 978-0-415-90058-4. Dewey:305.42/01. LCCN:89-006432.

Audience: **u,f.**

Prokhovnik, Raia   **B812.P77 1999**
Rational Woman: A Feminist Critique of Dualism. Paper over Boards. Routledge. New York, NY. 1999. 208p. Routledge Innovations in Political Theory Ser. ISBN:0-415-14618-6, ISBN13: 978-0-415-14618-0. Dewey:305.4/01. LCCN:98-047963.

Audience: **g,l,u.** *Choice, 2000.*

Purdy, Laura M.   **RG133.5.P87 1996**
Reproducing Persons: Issues in Feminist Bioethics. Book, Other. Cornell University Press. Ithaca, NY. 1996. 304p. ISBN:0-8014-3243-X, ISBN13: 978-0-8014-3243-9. Dewey:176. LCCN:95-052019.

Audience: **g,l,u,f.** *Choice, 1996.*

Sawicki, Jana   **HQ1190.S28 1991**
Disciplining Foucault: Feminism, Power and the Body. UK-B Format Paperback. Routledge. New York, NY. 1991. 144p. Thinking Gender Ser. ISBN:0-415-90188-X, ISBN13: 978-0-415-90188-8. Dewey:305.42/01. LCCN:91-000142.

Audience: **u,f.** *Choice, 1992.*

Sherwin, Susan   **R724**
No Longer Patient: Feminist Ethics and Health Care. Trade Paper. Temple University Press. Philadelphia, PA. 1992. 280p.

ISBN:1-56639-061-3, ISBN13: 978-1-56639-061-3.
Dewey:174.2.
Audience: **l,u,f.** *Choice, 1992.*

Soble, Alan   **HQ471.S635 2002**
Pornography, Sex and Feminism. Trade Cloth. Prometheus
Books, Publishers. Amherst, NY. 2001. 210p.
ISBN:1-57392-944-1, ISBN13: 978-1-57392-944-8.
Dewey:363.4/7. LCCN:2002-019176.
Audience: **g,l,u,f.** *Choice, 2002.*

Weiss, Penny A.   **HQ1075.W437 1993**
Gendered Community: Rousseau, Sex and Politics. Trade Cloth.
New York University Press. New York, NY. 1993. 256p.
ISBN:0-8147-9263-4, ISBN13: 978-0-8147-9263-6.
Dewey:305.3. LCCN:93-023909.
Audience: **g,l,u,f.** *Choice, 1994.*

Education and Epistemologies

    HQ1186.U6
☐ NWSA: National Women's Studies Association.
http://www.nwsa.org/
Audience: **g,l,u.**

Alcoff, Linda & Potter,   **HQ1190.F45 1993**
Elizabeth (Editors)
Feminist Epistemologies. UK-B Format Paperback. Routledge.
New York, NY. 1992. 320p. Thinking Gender Ser.
ISBN:0-415-90451-X, ISBN13: 978-0-415-90451-3.
Dewey:305.4201. LCCN:92-011309.
Audience: **l,u.**

Barton, Angela C.   **Q183.3.A1B37 1998**
Feminist Science Education. Trade Cloth. Teachers College
Press, Teachers College, Columbia University. New York, NY.
1998. 168p. Athena Ser. ISBN:0-8077-6294-6, ISBN13:
978-0-8077-6294-3. Dewey:507/.1/1073. LCCN:97-049819.
Audience: **l,u,f.** *Choice, 1998.*

Bowles, Gloria   **HQ1180**
Theories of Women's Studies. Trade Paper. Routledge. New
York, NY. 1983. xiv, 277p. ISBN:0-7100-9488-4, ISBN13:
978-0-7100-9488-9. Dewey:305.4/07. LCCN:82-019512.
Audience: **l,u.** *B*

Brodie, Laura Fairchild   **LC212.862.B75 2000**
Breaking Out: VMI and the Coming of Women. Trade Cloth.
Knopf Publishing Group. New York, NY. 2000. 368p.
ISBN:0-375-40614-X, ISBN13: 978-0-375-40614-0.
Dewey:379.2/6. LCCN:99-049937.
Audience: **g,l,u,f.** *Choice, 2000.*

Code, Lorraine   **HQ1190.C64 1991**
What Can She Know?: Feminist Theory and the Construction of
Knowledge. Book, Other. Cornell University Press. Ithaca, NY.
1991. 384p. ISBN:0-8014-2476-3, ISBN13: 978-0-8014-2476-2.
Dewey:305.42/01. LCCN:90-055755.
Audience: **l,u,f.** *Choice, 1991.*

DiGeorgio-Lutz, JoAnn   **LC1567**
(Editor)
Women in Higher Education: Empowering Change. Trade Cloth.
Greenwood Publishing Group, Inc. Portsmouth, NH. 2002. 192p.
ISBN:0-89789-887-7, ISBN13: 978-0-89789-887-4.
Dewey:378/.0082. LCCN:2002-067945.
Audience: **u,f.**

Duran, Jane   **HQ1190.D89 2001**
Worlds of Knowing: Global Feminist Epistemologies. Paper
over Boards. Routledge. New York, NY. 2001. 320p.
ISBN:0-415-92739-0, ISBN13: 978-0-415-92739-0.
Dewey:305.42/01. LCCN:00-062806.
Audience: **l,u.**

Edwards, June   **LC1757**
Women in American Education, 1820-1955: The Female Force
and Educational Reform. Trade Cloth. Greenwood Publishing
Group, Inc. Portsmouth, NH. 2001. 176p. Contributions to the
Study of Education Ser., Vol. 81 ISBN:0-313-31947-2, ISBN13:
978-0-313-31947-1. Dewey:370/.82. LCCN:2001-045122.
Audience: **g,l,u.** *Choice, 2002.*

Eisenmann, Linda   **LC1752**
(Editor)
Historical Dictionary of Women's Education in the United
States. Cloth Text. Greenwood Publishing Group, Inc.
Portsmouth, NH. 1998. 552p. ISBN:0-313-29323-6, ISBN13:
978-0-313-29323-8. Dewey:371.822. LCCN:97-032966.
Audience: **l,u.** *Choice, 1998.*

Friedman, Susan S.   **HQ1190.F77 1998**
Mappings: Feminism and the Cultural Geographies of
Encounter. Trade Cloth. Princeton University Press. Princeton,
NJ. 1998. 328p. ISBN:0-691-05803-2, ISBN13:
978-0-691-05803-0. Dewey:305.42/01. LCCN:98-011525.
Audience: **u,f.** *Choice, 1999.*

Goodman, Joyce &   **LA5.G46 2002**
Martin, Jane
Gender, Colonialism and Education: The Politics of Experience.
Trade Paper. Routledge. New York, NY. 2005. 272p. Education
Ser. ISBN:0-7130-4046-7, ISBN13: 978-0-7130-4046-3.
Dewey:370.9. LCCN:2003-542834.
Audience: **u,f.**

Gore, Joan Elias   **LB2376.G68 2005**
Dominant Beliefs and Alternative Voices: Discourse, Belief and
Gender in American Study Abroad. Paper over Boards.
Routledge. New York, NY. 2005. 278p. Studies in Higher
Education ISBN:0-415-97457-7, ISBN13: 978-0-415-97457-8.
Dewey:378/.016. LCCN:2005-009582.
Audience: **u,f.**

Gumport, Patricia J.   **LB2332.3.G86 2002**
Academic Pathfinders: Knowledge Creation and Feminist
Scholarship. Trade Cloth. Greenwood Publishing Group, Inc.
Portsmouth, NH. 2002. 224p. Greenwood Studies in Higher
Education ISBN:0-313-32096-9, ISBN13: 978-0-313-32096-5.
Dewey:378/.0082. LCCN:2001-040583.
Audience: **l,u.** *Choice, 2003.*

Harding, Sandra   **Q130.H37 1991**
Whose Science? Whose Knowledge?: Thinking from Women's
Lives. Book, Other. Cornell University Press. Ithaca, NY. 1991.
336p. ISBN:0-8014-9746-9, ISBN13: 978-0-8014-9746-9.
Dewey:305.43/5. LCCN:90-055724.
Audience: **l,u,f.** *Choice, 1992.*

Harding, Sandra &   **HQ1154.D538 2003**
Hintikka, Merrill B. (Editors)
Discovering Reality: Feminist Perspectives on Epistemology,
Metaphysics, Methodology, and Philosophy of Science. Ed. 2.
Trade Paper. Springer. New York, NY. 1899. 372p.
ISBN:1-4020-1319-1, ISBN13: 978-1-4020-1319-5.
Dewey:305.4/2.
Audience: **u,f.**

Hartman, Joan E. &   HQ1190.E64 1991
  Messer-Davidow, Ellen (Editors)
(En)Gendering Knowledge: Feminists in Academe. Paper Text.
University of Tennessee Press. Knoxville, TN. 1991. 320p.
ISBN:0-87049-701-4, ISBN13: 978-0-87049-701-8.
Dewey:305.42/01. LCCN:90-026492.
                               Audience: **u,f.**

Hemelrijk, Emily Ann   HQ1136.H45 1999
Matrona Docta: Educated Women in the Roman Elite from
Cornelia to Julia Domna. Paper over Boards. Routledge. New
York, NY. 1999. 400p. Classical Monographs
ISBN:0-415-19693-0, ISBN13: 978-0-415-19693-2.
Dewey:305.4/89631/09376. LCCN:98-053036.
                     Audience: **l,u,f.** *Choice, 2000.*

Henry, Mary E.   LC225.3.H468 1996
ⓔ Parent-School Collaboration: Feminist Organizational
Structures and School Leadership. E-Book. NetLibrary, Inc.
Boulder, CO. 1996. ISBN:0-585-04300-0, ISBN13:
978-0-585-04300-5. Dewey:371.192.
                             Audience: **l,u,f.**

Howe, Florence (Editor)   HQ1181.U5P65 2000
The Politics of Women's Studies: Testimony from Thirty
Founding Mothers. Mari Jo Buhle (Introduction by). Trade
Cloth. Feminist Press at The City University of New York. New
York, NY. 2000. 440p. The Women's Studies History Ser., Vol.
1 ISBN:1-55861-240-8, ISBN13: 978-1-55861-240-2.
Dewey:305.4/071/173. LCCN:00-044251.
                               Audience: **l,u.**

Hull, Gloria T. (Editor),   E185.86.A4 1982
  et al.
All the Women Are White, All the Blacks are Men, but Some of
Us Are Brave: Black Women's Studies. Patricia Bell Scott &
Barbara Smith (Editors). Trade Cloth. Feminist Press at The
City University of New York. New York, NY. 1982. xxxiv,
401p. ISBN:0-912670-92-4, ISBN13: 978-0-912670-92-8.
Dewey:305.4/8896073 19. LCCN:81-068918.
                       Audience: **g,l,u,f.** 𝓑

Jaggar, Alison M. &   BD450.G4455 1989
  Bordo, Susan R. (Editors)
Gender - Body - Knowledge: Feminist Reconstruction of Being
and Knowing. Cloth Text. Rutgers University Press. Piscataway,
NJ. 1989. 384p. ISBN:0-8135-1378-2, ISBN13:
978-0-8135-1378-2. Dewey:110. LCCN:88-018370.
                     Audience: **u,f.** *Choice, 1990.*

Korenman, Joan   HQ1236
▢ Women's Studies Programs, Departments, & Research
Centers.
http://research.umbc.edu/~korenman/wmst/programs.html
                               Audience: **g,l,u.**

LANIC: Latin
  American Network Information Center
▢ Women and Gender Studies in Latin America.
http://www1.lanic.utexas.edu/la/region/women/
                               Audience: **g,l,u.**

Lingard, Bob &   LC212.9.L53 1999
  Douglas, Peter
Men Engaging Feminisms: Pro-Feminism, Backlashes and
Schooling. Library Binding. Taylor & Francis Group.

Philadelphia, PA. 1999. xvi, 192p. Feminist Educational
Thinking Ser. ISBN:0-335-19818-X, ISBN13:
978-0-335-19818-4. Dewey:306.43/2. LCCN:98-041548.
                               Audience: **u,f.**

Lowe, Margaret A.   HQ1220.U5L693 2006
Looking Good: College Women and Body Image, 1875-1930.
Trade Paper. Johns Hopkins University Press. Baltimore, MD.
2005. 222p. Gender Relations in the American Experience Ser.
ISBN:0-8018-8274-5, ISBN13: 978-0-8018-8274-6.
Dewey:306.4.
                     Audience: **u,f.** *Choice, 2004.*

MacNabb, Elizabeth L.   HQ1180.T73 2001
  (Editor), et al.
Transforming the Disciplines: A Women's Studies Primer. Mary
Jane Cherry, Susan Popham & Rene Perri Prys (Editors). Trade
Cloth. Haworth Press, Incorporated, The. Binghamton, NY.
2005. 262p. Haworth Innovations in Feminist Studies
ISBN:1-56023-960-3, ISBN13: 978-1-56023-960-4.
Dewey:305.4/07. LCCN:00-040739.
                     Audience: **l,u,f.** *Choice, 2002.*

Maher, Frances A. &   LC197.M35 2001
  Thompson Tetreault, Mary Kay
The Feminist Classroom: Dynamics of Gender, Race and
Privilege. Ed. 2. Book, Other. Rowman & Littlefield Publishers,
Inc. Lanham, MD. 2001. 336p. ISBN:0-7425-0996-6, ISBN13:
978-0-7425-0996-2. Dewey:378.1/9822. LCCN:00-054438.
                             Audience: **l,u,f.**

McManus, Barbara F.   PA78.U6M38 1997
Classics and Feminism: Gendering the Classics. Trade Cloth.
Thomson Gale. Farmington Hills, MI. 1997. xv, 201p. Impact of
Feminism on the Arts and Sciences Ser. ISBN:0-8057-9757-2,
ISBN13: 978-0-8057-9757-2. Dewey:480/.07/073.
LCCN:96-036021.
                     Audience: **u,f.** *Choice, 1997.*

Nash, Margaret A.   LC1752.N37 2005
Women's Education in the United States, 1780-1840. Cloth over
Boards. Palgrave Macmillan. New York, NY. 2005. 224p.
ISBN:1-4039-6937-X, ISBN13: 978-1-4039-6937-8.
Dewey:371.822/0973/09034. LCCN:2005-043028.
                             Audience: **l,u,f.**

Nelson, Lynn H.   Q175.N387 1990
Who Knows: From Quine to a Feminist Empiricism. Trade
Cloth. Temple University Press. Philadelphia, PA. 1990. 336p.
ISBN:0-87722-647-4, ISBN13: 978-0-87722-647-5. Dewey:501.
LCCN:89-005173.
                               Audience: **u,f.**

Polakow, Valerie   HV699.S523 2004
  (Editor), et al.
Shut Out: Low Income Mothers and Higher Education in
Post-Welfare America. Sandra S. Butler, Luisa Stormer Deprez
& Peggy Kahn (Editors). Cloth Text. State University of New
York Press. Albany, NY. 2004. 288p. ISBN:0-7914-6125-4,
ISBN13: 978-0-7914-6125-9. Dewey:378.1/9826941.
LCCN:2004-041675.
                     Audience: **l,u.** *Choice, 2005.*

Sadovnik, Alan R. &   LA2311.F69 2002
  Semel, Susan F. (Editors)
Founding Mothers and Others: Women Educational Leaders
During the Progressive Era. Cloth over Boards. Palgrave
Macmillan. New York, NY. 2002. 288p. ISBN:0-312-23297-7,

ISBN13: 978-0-312-23297-9. Dewey:370/.82/0973 B.
LCCN:2001-052311.

Audience: **g,l,u,f.** *Choice, 2003.*

Sanchez-Casal, Susan &   **LC197.T94 2002**
  MacDonald, Amie A. (Editors)
Twenty-First-Century Feminist Classrooms: Pedagogies of
Identity and Difference. Cloth over Boards. Palgrave Macmillan.
New York, NY. 2002. 352p. Comparative Feminist Studies
ISBN:0-312-29533-2, ISBN13: 978-0-312-29533-2.
Dewey:370.11/5. LCCN:2002-020725.

Audience: **l,u,f.** *Choice, 2003.*

Spender, Dale (Editor)   **LB2361**
Men's Studies Modified: The Impact of Feminism on the
Academic Disciplines. Cloth Text. Elsevier Science &
Technology Books. Saint Louis, MO. 1981. 350p. Athene Ser.,
Vol. 1 ISBN:0-08-026770-X, ISBN13: 978-0-08-026770-8.
Dewey:378/.199. LCCN:80-041818.

Audience: **u,f.** *B*

Streitmatter, Janice L.   **LB3067.4.S87 1999**
For Girls Only: Making a Case for Single-Sex Schooling. Paper
Text. State University of New York Press. Albany, NY. 1999.
192p. ISBN:0-7914-4094-X, ISBN13: 978-0-7914-4094-0.
Dewey:372.183/42. LCCN:98-026847.

Audience: **l,u.** *Choice, 1999.*

Thorne, Barrie   **LC212.92.T46 1993**
Gender Play: Girls and Boys in School. Trade Cloth. Rutgers
University Press. Piscataway, NJ. 1993. 247p.
ISBN:0-8135-1922-5, ISBN13: 978-0-8135-1922-7.
Dewey:370.19345. LCCN:92-022062.

Audience: **g,l,u,f.** *Choice, 1993.*

Society

Blood, Robert O. &   **HQ536 .B55 1978**
  Wolfe, Donald M.
Husbands and Wives: The Dynamics of Married Living. Trade
Cloth. Greenwood Publishing Group, Inc. Portsmouth, NH.
1978. 293p. ISBN:0-313-20453-5, ISBN13: 978-0-313-20453-1.
Dewey:301.42. LCCN:78-005734.

Audience: **g,l.**

Callahan, Sidney &   **HQ767.5.U5A28 1984**
  Callahan, Daniel (Editors)
Abortion: Understanding Differences. Cloth Text. Springer. New
York, NY. 1984. 360p. The Hastings Center Series in Ethics
ISBN:0-306-41640-9, ISBN13: 978-0-306-41640-8.
Dewey:363.4/6. LCCN:84-009965.

Audience: **g,l,u.** *B*

Colker, Ruth   **KF3771 .C65 1992**
e Abortion and Dialogue: Pro-Choice, Pro-Life, and American
Law. E-Book. Indiana University Press. Bloomington, IN. 1992.
200p. ISBN:0-253-20738-X, ISBN13: 978-0-253-20738-8.
Dewey:344.73/0546. LCCN:91-046603.

Audience: **g,l,u,f.** *Choice, 1993.*

Craig, Barbara H. &   **HQ767.5.U5**
  O'Brien, David M.
Abortion and American Politics. Paper Text. CQ Press.
Washington, DC. 1993. 398p. American Politics Ser.
ISBN:0-934540-89-6, ISBN13: 978-0-934540-89-6.
Dewey:363.4/6/0973. LCCN:92-041395.

Audience: **g,l,u,f.** *Choice, 1993.*

Ehrenreich, Barbara   **HD4918.E375 2001**
Nickel and Dimed: On (Not) Getting by in America. Cloth over
Boards. Henry Holt & Company. New York, NY. 2001. 224p.
ISBN:0-8050-6388-9, ISBN13: 978-0-8050-6388-2.
Dewey:305.569092. LCCN:00-052514.

Audience: **g,l,u,f.**

Elshtain, Jean Bethke   **JA74.5**
Meditations on Modern Political Thought: Masculine - Feminine
Themes from Luther to Arendt. Trade Cloth. Pennsylvania State
University Press. University Park, PA. 1992. 142p.
ISBN:0-271-00864-4, ISBN13: 978-0-271-00864-6.
Dewey:320/.01/9. LCCN:91-046357.

Audience: **l,u.** *Choice, 1986.*

Elshtain, Jean Bethke   **HQ1236.E47 1993**
Public Man, Private Woman: Women in Social and Political
Thought. Ed. 2. Trade Paper. Princeton University Press.
Princeton, NJ. 1993. 408p. ISBN:0-691-02476-6, ISBN13:
978-0-691-02476-9. Dewey:305.4/2. LCCN:92-029726.

Audience: **l,u.** *B*

Elshtain, Jean Bethke   **U21.5.E45 1995**
Women and War. Trade Paper. University of Chicago Press.
Chicago, IL. 1995. 318p. ISBN:0-226-20626-2, ISBN13:
978-0-226-20626-4. Dewey:303.6/6/088042. LCCN:95-000755.

Audience: **g,l,u,f.** *Choice, 1987.*

Enloe, Cynthia   **U21.75 .E5524 2000**
Maneuvers: The International Politics of Militarizing Women's
Lives. Trade Paper. University of California Press. Berkeley,
CA. 2000. 440p. ISBN:0-520-22071-4, ISBN13:
978-0-520-22071-3. Dewey:355/.0082. LCCN:99-028136.

Audience: **l,u.** *Choice, 2000.*

Finkelhor, David   **HQ809.3.U5**
  (Editor), et al.
The Dark Side of Families: Current Family Violence Research.
Richard J. Gelles, Gerald T. Hotaling & Murray A. Straus
(Editors). Trade Paper. SAGE Publications, Inc. Thousand Oaks,
CA. 1983. 376p. ISBN:0-8039-1935-2, ISBN13:
978-0-8039-1935-8. Dewey:306.8/7. LCCN:82-021496.

Audience: **u,f.** *B*

Fleisher, Mark S.   **HV9106.K2F54 1998**
Dead End Kids: Gang Girls and the Boys They Know. Trade
Cloth. University of Wisconsin Press. Chicago, IL. 2000. 336p.
ISBN:0-299-15880-2, ISBN13: 978-0-299-15880-4.
Dewey:364.36/082/09778411. LCCN:98-015537.

Audience: **l,u,f.** *Choice, 1999.*

Goldman, Wendy Z.   **KLA540 .G65 1993**
Women, the State and Revolution: Soviet Family Policy and
Social Life, 1917-1936. Trade Paper. Cambridge University
Press. New York, NY. 1993. 363p. Cambridge Russian, Soviet
and Post-Soviet Studies, No. 90 ISBN:0-521-45816-1, ISBN13:
978-0-521-45816-0. Dewey:305.420947. LCCN:92-047481.

Audience: **u,f.** *Choice, 1994.*

Gordon, Linda   **HQ766.5.U5G66 2002**
The Moral Property of Women: A History of Birth Control
Politics in America. Ed. 3. Trade Cloth. University of Illinois
Press. Champaign, IL. 2002. 464p. ISBN:0-252-02764-7,
ISBN13: 978-0-252-02764-2. Dewey:363.9/6/0973.
LCCN:2002-001551.

Audience: **l,u,f.** *Choice, 2003.*

Grossman, Avraham   BM729.W6G7613 2004
Pious and Rebellious: Jewish Women in Medieval Europe. Trade
Cloth. University Press of New England. Lebanon, NH. 2004.
352p. Tauber Institute for the Study of European Jewry Ser.
ISBN:1-58465-391-4, ISBN13: 978-1-58465-391-2.
Dewey:305.48/892404/0902. LCCN:2004-003029.

Audience: **u,f.** *Choice, 2005.*

Haas, Linda (Editor), et   HD58.8.O7289 2000
al.
Organizational Change and Gender Equity: International
Perspectives on Fathers and Mothers at the Workplace. Philip O.
Hwang & Graeme Russell (Editors). Trade Cloth. SAGE
Publications, Inc. Thousand Oaks, CA. 1999. 296p. Families and
Work Ser. ISBN:0-7619-1044-1, ISBN13: 978-0-7619-1044-2.
Dewey:331.25. LCCN:99-006398.

Audience: **g,l,u,f.** *Choice, 2000.*

Harrison, Beverly   HQ767.3.H37 1983
Wildung
Our Right to Choose: Toward a New Ethic of Abortion. Trade
Cloth. Beacon Press. Boston, MA. 1983. xi, 334p.
ISBN:0-8070-1508-3, ISBN13: 978-0-8070-1508-7.
Dewey:179/.76. LCCN:81-070488.

Audience: **g,l,u.** *ℬ*

Kamerman, Sheila B. &   HQ759
Kahn, Alfred J.
Mothers Alone: Strategies for a Time of Change. Trade Cloth.
Greenwood Publishing Group, Inc. Portsmouth, NH. 1988. 255p.
ISBN:0-86569-183-5, ISBN13: 978-0-86569-183-4.
Dewey:362.8/2. LCCN:88-006195.

Audience: **u,f.** *Choice, 1988.*

Langford, Wendy   BF575.L8L266 1999
Revolutions of the Heart: Gender, Power and the Delusions of
Love. Paper over Boards. Routledge. New York, NY. 1999.
192p. ISBN:0-415-16297-1, ISBN13: 978-0-415-16297-5.
Dewey:306.7. LCCN:98-050255.

Audience: **l,u.** *Choice, 2000.*

Lopata, Helena   HQ1058.L66
Znaniecka
Women As Widows: Support Systems. Trade Cloth. Elsevier.
New York, NY. 1979. 485p. ISBN:0-444-99053-4, ISBN13:
978-0-444-99053-2. Dewey:301.42/86. LCCN:78-021255.

Audience: **l,u,f.** *ℬ*

Lorentzen, Lois A. &   D810.W7 W656 1998
Turpin, Jennifer (Editors)
The Women and War Reader. Trade Cloth. New York University
Press. New York, NY. 1998. 296p. ISBN:0-8147-5144-X,
ISBN13: 978-0-8147-5144-2. Dewey:940.53082.
LCCN:98-018165.

Audience: **l,u.**

Luker, Kristin   HQ767.5.U5
Abortion and the Politics of Motherhood. Trade Cloth.
University of California Press. Berkeley, CA. 1985. 350p.
California Series on Social Choice and Political Economy, Vol.
3 ISBN:0-520-05597-7, ISBN13: 978-0-520-05597-1.
Dewey:363.4/6/0973. LCCN:83-047849.

Audience: **g,l,u,f.** *ℬ*

Luker, Kristin   HQ766.5.U5
Taking Chances: Abortion and the Decision Not to Contracept.
Trade Cloth. University of California Press. Berkeley, CA. 1975.

xii, 207p. ISBN:0-520-02872-4, ISBN13: 978-0-520-02872-2.
Dewey:301.5. LCCN:74-022965.

Audience: **l,u,f.** *ℬ*

Marcus, Jacob R.   HQ1172.M37 SUPPL
The American Jewish Woman: A Documentary History. Trade
Cloth. Ktav Publishing House, Inc. Jersey City, NJ. 1981.
1047p. ISBN:0-87068-752-2, ISBN13: 978-0-87068-752-5.
Dewey:205.4/8. LCCN:81-001966.

Audience: **g,l,u.** *ℬ*

Marcus, Jacob R.   HQ1172.M37
(Editor)
The American Jewish Woman: 1654-1980. Trade Cloth. Ktav
Publishing House, Inc. Jersey City, NJ. 1981. xiv, 231p.
ISBN:0-87068-751-4, ISBN13: 978-0-87068-751-8.
Dewey:305.4/8. LCCN:81-001720.

Audience: **u,f.** *ℬ*

Medina, Lara   BX810.H57M43 2004
Las Hermanas: Chicana/Latina Religious-Political Activism in
the U. S. Catholic Church. Trade Cloth. Temple University
Press. Philadelphia, PA. 2004. 232p. ISBN:1-59213-250-2,
ISBN13: 978-1-59213-250-8. Dewey:267.4/4273.
LCCN:2003-064591.

Audience: **u,f.** *Choice, 2005.*

Meyer, Leisa D.   UA565.W6M48 1996
Creating G. I. Jane: Sexuality and Power in the Women's Army
Corps During World War II. Trade Cloth. Columbia University
Press. New York, NY. 1996. 288p. ISBN:0-231-10144-9,
ISBN13: 978-0-231-10144-8. Dewey:940.54/0973/082.
LCCN:96-013858.

Audience: **l,u.** *Choice, 1997.*

Moghissi, Hiadeh   HQ1170.M64 1999
Feminism and Islamic Fundamentalism: The Limits of
Postmodern Analysis. Cloth over Boards. Zed Books, Ltd.
London, 1999. 128p. ISBN:1-85649-589-2, ISBN13:
978-1-85649-589-9. Dewey:305.48/6971. LCCN:99-022771.

Audience: **l,u,f.** *Choice, 2000.*

Mulroy, Elizabeth A.   HQ759
(Editor)
Women As Single Parents: Confronting Institutional Barriers in
the Courts, the Workplace, and the Housing Market. Trade
Cloth. Greenwood Publishing Group, Inc. Portsmouth, NH.
1988. 328p. ISBN:0-86569-176-2, ISBN13: 978-0-86569-176-6.
Dewey:306.8/56. LCCN:88-011920.

Audience: **u,f.** *Choice, 1989.*

Pleck, Joseph H.   HQ0536.P59
Working Wives, Working Husbands. Trade Paper. Books on
Demand. Ann Arbor, MI. 1985. 168p. New Perspectives on
Family Ser. ISBN:0-608-01525-3, ISBN13: 978-0-608-01525-5.
Dewey:306.8/7. LCCN:85-011974.

Audience: **g,l,u,f.**

Rainwater, Lee   HQ766
And the Poor Get Children: Sex, Contraception, and Family
Planning in the Working Class. Trade Cloth. Greenwood
Publishing Group, Inc. Portsmouth, NH. 1984. 202p.
ISBN:0-313-24452-9, ISBN13: 978-0-313-24452-0.
Dewey:304.6/6/0973. LCCN:84-012770.

Audience: **g,l,u,f.** *ℬ*

Rich, Adrienne   HQ759
Of Woman Born: Motherhood as Experience and Institution.
Trade Paper. W. W. Norton & Company, Inc. New York, NY.

1995. 352p. ISBN:0-393-31284-4, ISBN13: 978-0-393-31284-3. Dewey:306.8/743.

Audience: **g,l,u.**

Sharma, Arvind &   **BL458.F455 1998**
  Young, Katherine K. (Editors)
Feminism and World Religions. Paper Text. State University of New York Press. Albany, NY. 1998. 352p. SUNY Series, McGill Studies in the History of Religions ISBN:0-7914-4024-9, ISBN13: 978-0-7914-4024-7. Dewey:2913.1/783442. LCCN:98-010509.

Audience: **u,f.** *Choice, 1999.*

Staples, Robert   **HQ800**
The World of Black Singles: Changing Patterns of Male-Female Relations. Trade Cloth. Greenwood Publishing Group, Inc. Portsmouth, NH. 1981. 259p. Contributions in Afro-American and African Studies Ser., No. 57 ISBN:0-313-22478-1, ISBN13: 978-0-313-22478-2. Dewey:305. LCCN:80-001025.

Audience: **l,u,f.** *B*

Thorne, Barrie &   **HQ536**
  Yalom, Marilyn (Editors)
Rethinking the Family: Some Feminist Questions. Ed. 2. Cloth Text. Northeastern University Press. Boston, MA. 1992. 272p. ISBN:1-55553-144-X, ISBN13: 978-1-55553-144-7. Dewey:306.85/0973.

Audience: **u,f.** *B*

Vicinus, Martha   **HQ800.2**
Independent Women: Work and Community for Single Women, 1850-1920. Trade Paper. University of Chicago Press. Chicago, IL. 1992. 412p. Women in Culture and Society Ser. ISBN:0-226-85568-6, ISBN13: 978-0-226-85568-4. Dewey:305.4/89/652/0942. LCCN:84-016158.

Audience: **u,f.** *B Choice, 1985.*

Society > Marriage. Relationships. Life Cycle

Aldous, Joan (Editor)   **HQ0536.T85**
Two Paychecks: Life in Dual Earner Families. Trade Paper. Books on Demand. Ann Arbor, MI. 247p. Sage Focus Editions Ser., Vol. 56 ISBN:0-8357-4739-5, ISBN13: 978-0-8357-4739-4. Dewey:306.8/7. LCCN:82-010538.

Audience: **l,u.** *B*

Andre, Rae   **HQ0759.A5**
Homemakers, the Forgotten Workers. Trade Paper. Books on Demand. Ann Arbor, MI. 311p. ISBN:0-608-08042-X, ISBN13: 978-0-608-08042-0. Dewey:305.4/3. LCCN:80-021258.

Audience: **l,u,f.**

Blood, Robert O. &   **HQ536 .B55 1978**
  Wolfe, Donald M.
Husbands and Wives: The Dynamics of Married Living. Trade Cloth. Greenwood Publishing Group, Inc. Portsmouth, NH. 1978. 293p. ISBN:0-313-20453-5, ISBN13: 978-0-313-20453-1. Dewey:301.42. LCCN:78-005734.

Audience: **g,l.**

Blumstein, Philip   **HQ734.B659 1983**
American Couples: Money, Work, Sex. Trade Cloth. HarperCollins Publishers. New York, NY. 1983. 656p. ISBN:0-688-03772-0, ISBN13: 978-0-688-03772-7. Dewey:306.8/0973. LCCN:83-062066.

Audience: **l,u.** *B*

Brody, Leslie   **RC455.4.E46B76 1999**
Gender, Emotion, and the Family. Trade Cloth. Harvard University Press. Cambridge, MA. 1999. 368p. ISBN:0-674-34186-4, ISBN13: 978-0-674-34186-9. Dewey:152.4. LCCN:98-032351.

Audience: **l,u,f.** *Choice, 1999.*

Brumberg, Joan Jacobs   **HQ796**
The Body Project: An Intimate History of American Girls. Library Binding. Sagebrush Education Resources. Caledonia, MN. 1998. ISBN:0-613-18067-4, ISBN13: 978-0-613-18067-2. Dewey:305.235.

Audience: **g,l,u,f.** *Choice, 1998.*

Cott, Nancy F.   **HQ536**
Public Vows: A History of Marriage and the Nation. Trade Paper. Harvard University Press. Cambridge, MA. 2002. 304p. ISBN:0-674-00875-8, ISBN13: 978-0-674-00875-5. Dewey:306.8/0973.

Audience: **l,u,f.** *Choice, 2001.*

Edin, Kathryn & Lein,   **HQ759.915.E34 1997**
  Laura
Making Ends Meet: How Single Mothers Survive Welfare and Low-Wage Work. Cloth Text. Russell Sage Foundation. New York, NY. 1997. 320p. ISBN:0-87154-229-3, ISBN13: 978-0-87154-229-8. Dewey:306.85/6. LCCN:96-040379.

Audience: **u,f.** *Choice, 1997.*

Fleisher, Mark S.   **HV9106.K2F54 1998**
Dead End Kids: Gang Girls and the Boys They Know. Trade Cloth. University of Wisconsin Press. Chicago, IL. 2000. 336p. ISBN:0-299-15880-2, ISBN13: 978-0-299-15880-4. Dewey:364.36/082/09778411. LCCN:98-015537.

Audience: **l,u,f.** *Choice, 1999.*

Gilman, Charlotte   **HQ734.G5 2002**
  Perkins
The Home: Its Work and Influence. Trade Cloth. AltaMira Press. Walnut Creek, CA. 2002. 368p. Classics in Gender Studies ISBN:0-7591-0305-4, ISBN13: 978-0-7591-0305-4. Dewey:640. LCCN:2002-066632.

Audience: **g,l,u,f.** *B*

Goldman, Wendy Z.   **KLA540 .G65 1993**
Women, the State and Revolution: Soviet Family Policy and Social Life, 1917-1936. Trade Paper. Cambridge University Press. New York, NY. 1993. 363p. Cambridge Russian, Soviet and Post-Soviet Studies, No. 90 ISBN:0-521-45816-1, ISBN13: 978-0-521-45816-0. Dewey:305.420947. LCCN:92-047481.

Audience: **u,f.** *Choice, 1994.*

Haas, Linda (Editor), et   **HD58.8.O7289 2000**
  al.
Organizational Change and Gender Equity: International Perspectives on Fathers and Mothers at the Workplace. Philip O. Hwang & Graeme Russell (Editors). Trade Cloth. SAGE Publications, Inc. Thousand Oaks, CA. 1999. 296p. Families and Work Ser. ISBN:0-7619-1044-1, ISBN13: 978-0-7619-1044-2. Dewey:331.25. LCCN:99-006398.

Audience: **g,l,u,f.** *Choice, 2000.*

Hays, Sharon   **HV95.H36 2003**
Flat Broke with Children: Women in the Age of Welfare Reform. Trade Cloth. Oxford University Press, Inc. New York, NY. 2003. 304p. ISBN:0-19-513288-2, ISBN13: 978-0-19-513288-5. Dewey:362.83/92/0973. LCCN:2002-009841.

Audience: **g,l,u,f.**

Hochschild, Arlie   HQ536.H633 1997
  Russell
The Time Bind: When Work Becomes Home and Home
Becomes Work. Cloth over Boards. Henry Holt & Company.
New York, NY. 1997. 336p. ISBN:0-8050-4470-1, ISBN13:
978-0-8050-4470-6. Dewey:306.3/6. LCCN:97-003411.
                Audience: **g,l,u,f.** *Choice, 1997.*

Hochschild, Arlie   HQ536.H63 2003
  Russell & Machung, Anne
The Second Shift. Trade Paper. Penguin Group (USA) Inc. New
York, NY. 2003. 352p. ISBN:0-14-200292-5, ISBN13:
978-0-14-200292-6. Dewey:306.85. LCCN:2003-043384.
                          Audience: **l,u,f.**

Kamerman, Sheila B. &   HQ759
  Kahn, Alfred J.
Mothers Alone: Strategies for a Time of Change. Trade Cloth.
Greenwood Publishing Group, Inc. Portsmouth, NH. 1988. 255p.
ISBN:0-86569-183-5, ISBN13: 978-0-86569-183-4.
Dewey:362.8/2. LCCN:88-006195.
                  Audience: **u,f.** *Choice, 1988.*

Langford, Wendy   BF575.L8L266 1999
Revolutions of the Heart: Gender, Power and the Delusions of
Love. Paper over Boards. Routledge. New York, NY. 1999.
192p. ISBN:0-415-16297-1, ISBN13: 978-0-415-16297-5.
Dewey:306.7. LCCN:98-050255.
                Audience: **l,u.** *Choice, 2000.*

Larossa, Ralph   HQ756.L37 1997
The Modernization of Fatherhood: A Social and Political
History. Trade Paper. University of Chicago Press. Chicago, IL.
1996. 295p. ISBN:0-226-46904-2, ISBN13: 978-0-226-46904-1.
Dewey:306.874/2. LCCN:96-025634.
             Audience: **l,u,f.** *Choice, 1997.*

Lerner, Gerda   HQ1121
The Creation of Patriarchy. Trade Paper. Oxford University
Press, Inc. New York, NY. 1987. 344p. Women and History Ser.
ISBN:0-19-505185-8, ISBN13: 978-0-19-505185-8.
Dewey:305.4/09. LCCN:85-021578.
           Audience: **g,l,u,f.** *Choice, 1986.*

Lopata, Helena   HQ1058.L66
  Znaniecka
Women As Widows: Support Systems. Trade Cloth. Elsevier.
New York, NY. 1979. 485p. ISBN:0-444-99053-4, ISBN13:
978-0-444-99053-2. Dewey:301.42/86. LCCN:78-021255.
               Audience: **l,u,f.** ℬ

Mason, Mary A.   KF547.M37 1994
From Father's Property to Children's Rights: The History of
Child Custody in the United States. Trade Cloth. Columbia
University Press. New York, NY. 1994. 256p.
ISBN:0-231-08046-8, ISBN13: 978-0-231-08046-0.
Dewey:346.7301/7. LCCN:93-034524.
             Audience: **u,f.** *Choice, 1994.*

Mulroy, Elizabeth A.   HQ759
  (Editor)
Women As Single Parents: Confronting Institutional Barriers in
the Courts, the Workplace, and the Housing Market. Trade
Cloth. Greenwood Publishing Group, Inc. Portsmouth, NH.
1988. 328p. ISBN:0-86569-176-2, ISBN13: 978-0-86569-176-6.
Dewey:306.8/56. LCCN:88-011920.
             Audience: **u,f.** *Choice, 1989.*

Odem, Mary E.   HQ27.5.O34 1995
Delinquent Daughters: Protecting and Policing Adolescent
Female Sexuality in the United States, 1885-1920. Trade Paper.
University of North Carolina Press. Chapel Hill, NC. 1995.
288p. Gender and American Culture Ser. ISBN:0-8078-4528-0,
ISBN13: 978-0-8078-4528-8. Dewey:306.7/0835.
LCCN:95-013185.
                 Audience: **l,u,f.** *Choice, 1996.*

O'Leary, Virginia   HQ1206.W875 1985
  (Editor), et al.
Women, Gender and Social Psychology. Rhoda K. Unger &
Barbara S. Wallston (Editors). Cloth Text. Lawrence Erlbaum
Associates, Inc. Mahwah, NJ. 1985. 400p. ISBN:0-89859-447-2,
ISBN13: 978-0-89859-447-8. Dewey:305.4. LCCN:84-023114.
         Audience: **l,u,f.** ℬ *Choice, 1985.*

Pleck, Joseph H.   HQ0536.P59
Working Wives, Working Husbands. Trade Paper. Books on
Demand. Ann Arbor, MI. 1985. 168p. New Perspectives on
Family Ser. ISBN:0-608-01525-3, ISBN13: 978-0-608-01525-5.
Dewey:306.8/7. LCCN:85-011974.
               Audience: **g,l,u,f.**

Potuchek, Jean L.   HQ536.P668 1997
Who Supports the Family: Gender and Breadwinning in
Dual-Earner Marriages. Trade Cloth. Stanford University Press.
Palo Alto, CA. 1997. 280p. ISBN:0-8047-2835-6, ISBN13:
978-0-8047-2835-5. Dewey:306.872. LCCN:96-034115.
            Audience: **u,f.** *Choice, 1998.*

Rich, Adrienne   HQ759
Of Woman Born: Motherhood as Experience and Institution.
Trade Paper. W. W. Norton & Company, Inc. New York, NY.
1995. 352p. ISBN:0-393-31284-4, ISBN13: 978-0-393-31284-3.
Dewey:306.8/743.
                 Audience: **g,l,u.**

Riessman, Catherine K.   HQ834.R54 1990
Divorce Talk: Women and Men Make Sense of Personal
Relationships. Paper Text. Rutgers University Press. Piscataway,
NJ. 1990. 264p. ISBN:0-8135-1503-3, ISBN13:
978-0-8135-1503-8. Dewey:306.89. LCCN:89-036065.
            Audience: **g,l,u.** *Choice, 1991.*

Risman, Barbara J.   HQ535.R57 1998
Gender Vertigo: American Families in Transition. Cloth over
Boards. Yale University Press. Cumberland, RI. 1998. 208p.
ISBN:0-300-07215-5, ISBN13: 978-0-300-07215-0.
Dewey:306.85/0973. LCCN:97-028857.
            Audience: **u,f.** *Choice, 1998.*

Staples, Robert   HQ800
The World of Black Singles: Changing Patterns of Male-Female
Relations. Trade Cloth. Greenwood Publishing Group, Inc.
Portsmouth, NH. 1981. 259p. Contributions in Afro-American
and African Studies Ser., No. 57 ISBN:0-313-22478-1, ISBN13:
978-0-313-22478-2. Dewey:305. LCCN:80-001025.
              Audience: **l,u,f.** ℬ

Thorne, Barrie &   HQ536
  Yalom, Marilyn (Editors)
Rethinking the Family: Some Feminist Questions. Ed. 2. Cloth
Text. Northeastern University Press. Boston, MA. 1992. 272p.
ISBN:1-55553-144-X, ISBN13: 978-1-55553-144-7.
Dewey:306.85/0973.
                 Audience: **u,f.** ℬ

Vicinus, Martha   **HQ800.2**
Independent Women: Work and Community for Single Women,
1850-1920. Trade Paper. University of Chicago Press. Chicago,
IL. 1992. 412p. Women in Culture and Society Ser.
ISBN:0-226-85568-6, ISBN13: 978-0-226-85568-4.
Dewey:305.4/89/652/0942. LCCN:84-016158.
                               Audience: **u,f.** *ℬ* *Choice, 1985.*

Walters, Suzanna D.   **HQ759.W332**
Lives Together - Worlds Apart: Mothers and Daughters in
Popular Culture. Trade Paper. University of California Press.
Berkeley, CA. 1994. 310p. ISBN:0-520-08656-2, ISBN13:
978-0-520-08656-2. Dewey:306.8743. LCCN:91-032331.
                               Audience: **l,u,f.** *Choice, 1993.*

Society > Legal Issues. Social Issues

                                                     BF637.C6
☐ National Domestic Violence Hotline.
http://www.ndvh.org/educate/index.html
                                        Audience: **g,l,u.**

☐ National Sexual Violence Resource Center.
http://www.nsvrc.org/
                                        Audience: **g,l,u.**

☐ Office of Violence Against Women.
http://www.usdoj.gov/ovw/
                                        Audience: **g,l,u.**

Alexander, Ruth M.   **HV9105.N7A67 1995**
The Girl Problem: Female Sexual Delinquency in New York,
1900-1930. Book, Other. Cornell University Press. Ithaca, NY.
1995. 232p. ISBN:0-8014-2821-1, ISBN13: 978-0-8014-2821-0.
Dewey:364.3/6/082. LCCN:94-047525.
                               Audience: **u,f.** *Choice, 1996.*

Barry, Kathleen L.   **HQ117.B37**
The Prostitution of Sexuality. Trade Paper. New York University
Press. New York, NY. 1996. 504p. ISBN:0-8147-1277-0,
ISBN13: 978-0-8147-1277-1. Dewey:306.74. LCCN:94-027897.
                               Audience: **u,f.** *Choice, 1995.*

Beck, Lois & Keddie,   **HQ1170**
Nikki R. (Editors)
Women in the Muslim World. Trade Cloth. Harvard University
Press. Cambridge, MA. 1978. 712p. ISBN:0-674-95480-7,
ISBN13: 978-0-674-95480-9. Dewey:301.41/2/0917671.
LCCN:78-003633.
                               Audience: **u,f.** *ℬ*

Bergen, Raquel K.   **HV6250.4.W65S68 2001**
Sourcebook on Violence Against Women. Claire M. Renzetti &
Jeffrey L. Edleson (Editors). Trade Paper. SAGE Publications,
Inc. Thousand Oaks, CA. 2000. 552p. ISBN:0-7619-2005-6,
ISBN13: 978-0-7619-2005-2. Dewey:362.8292.
LCCN:00-010215.
                               Audience: **g,l,u,f.** *Choice, 2001.*

Berns, Nancy   **HN59.2.B468 2004**
Framing the Victim: Domestic Violence, Media, and Social
Problems. Trade Cloth. Aldine Transaction. Somerset, NJ. 2004.
194p. Social Problems and Social Issues Ser.

ISBN:0-202-30740-9, ISBN13: 978-0-202-30740-4.
Dewey:361.1/0973. LCCN:2004-001465.
                               Audience: **l,u,f.** *Choice, 2005.*

Bevacqua, Maria   **HV6561.B49 2000**
Rape on the Public Agenda: Feminism and the Politics of
Sexual Assault. Cloth Text. Northeastern University Press.
Boston, MA. 2000. xiii, 280p. ISBN:1-55553-447-3, ISBN13:
978-1-55553-447-9. Dewey:364.15/32/0973. LCCN:00-020542.
                               Audience: **u,f.** *Choice, 2001.*

Bredbenner, Candice   **KF4720.W6B74 1998**
Lewis
ℯ A Nationality of Her Own: Women, Marriage, and the Law
of Citizenship. E-Book. NetLibrary, Inc. Boulder, CO. 1998.
ISBN:0-585-11810-8, ISBN13: 978-0-585-11810-9.
Dewey:342.73/083.
                               Audience: **l,u,f.**

Brownmiller, Susan   **HV6558**
Against Our Will: Men, Women and Rape. Trade Cloth. Martin
Secker & Warburg, Ltd. London, 1975. 480p.
ISBN:0-436-07108-8, ISBN13: 978-0-436-07108-9.
Dewey:364.1/53.
                               Audience: **g,l.**

Burstyn, Varda (Editor)   **HQ471.W66 1985**
Women Against Censorship. Trade Paper. Salem House
Publishers. Scranton, PA. 1985. 210p. ISBN:0-88894-455-1,
ISBN13: 978-0-88894-455-9. Dewey:363.4/7. LCCN:85-098057.
                               Audience: **l,u,f.** *ℬ* *Choice, 1985.*

Callahan, Sidney &   **HQ767.5.U5A28 1984**
Callahan, Daniel (Editors)
Abortion: Understanding Differences. Cloth Text. Springer. New
York, NY. 1984. 360p. The Hastings Center Series in Ethics
ISBN:0-306-41640-9, ISBN13: 978-0-306-41640-8.
Dewey:363.4/6. LCCN:84-009965.
                               Audience: **g,l,u.** *ℬ*

Chesney-Lind, Meda &   **HV6439.U5F46 1999**
Hagedorn, John M. (Editors)
Female Gangs in America: Essays on Girls, Gangs and Gender.
Trade Cloth. Lake View Press. Chicago, IL. 1999. 364p.
ISBN:0-941702-48-0, ISBN13: 978-0-941702-48-5.
Dewey:364.1/06/60820973. LCCN:98-053160.
                               Audience: **l,u,f.**

Chesney-Lind, Meda &   **HV6046**
Pasko, Lisa
The Female Offender: Girls, Women and Crime. Ed. 2. Cloth
Text. SAGE Publications, Inc. Thousand Oaks, CA. 2003. 232p.
Women in the Criminal Justice System Ser.
ISBN:0-7619-2978-9, ISBN13: 978-0-7619-2978-9.
Dewey:364.3/74/0973. LCCN:2003-006150.
                               Audience: **l,u.** *Choice, 1997.*

Colker, Ruth   **KF3771 .C65 1992**
ℯ Abortion and Dialogue: Pro-Choice, Pro-Life, and American
Law. E-Book. Indiana University Press. Bloomington, IN. 1992.
200p. ISBN:0-253-20738-X, ISBN13: 978-0-253-20738-8.
Dewey:344.73/0546. LCCN:91-046603.
                               Audience: **g,l,u,f.** *Choice, 1993.*

Colker, Ruth   **HQ1190.C655 1994**
Pregnant Men: Practice, Theory, and Law. Paper Text. Indiana
University Press. Bloomington, IN. 1994. ISBN:0-253-20898-X,

ISBN13: 978-0-253-20898-9. Dewey:305.42/01.
LCCN:94-003922.

Audience: **u,f.** *Choice, 1995.*

Collins, Catherine   **HV9471**
  Fisher
Imprisonment of African American Women: Causes, Conditions
and Future Implications. Paper Text. McFarland & Company,
Incorporated Publishers. Jefferson, NC. 2005. 166p.
ISBN:0-7864-2159-2, ISBN13: 978-0-7864-2159-6.
Dewey:365.973.

Audience: **g,l,u,f.**

Corrin, Chris (Editor)   **HV6250.5.W65.W655**
Women in a Violent World: Feminist Analyses and Resistance
Across Europe. Trade Paper. Edinburgh University Press.
Edinburgh, 1997. 272p. ISBN:0-7486-0804-4, ISBN13:
978-0-7486-0804-1. Dewey:362.88/082. LCCN:97-165767.

Audience: **l,u,f.**

Craig, Barbara H. &   **HQ767.5.U5**
  O'Brien, David M.
Abortion and American Politics. Paper Text. CQ Press.
Washington, DC. 1993. 398p. American Politics Ser.
ISBN:0-934540-89-6, ISBN13: 978-0-934540-89-6.
Dewey:363.4/6/0973. LCCN:92-041395.

Audience: **g,l,u,f.** *Choice, 1993.*

Delacoste, Frederique &   **HQ144**
  Alexander, Priscilla (Editors)
Sex Work: Writings by Women in the Sex Industry. Ed. 2. Trade
Paper. Cleis Press. San Francisco, CA. 1998. 380p.
ISBN:1-57344-042-6, ISBN13: 978-1-57344-042-4.
Dewey:306.7/42/0973. LCCN:00-708785.

Audience: **l,u,f.**

Dixon-Mueller, Ruth   **HQ767.D59 2002**
Abortion and Common Sense. Trade Paper. Xlibris Corporation.
Philadelphia, PA. 2002. 298p. ISBN:1-4010-5954-6, ISBN13:
978-1-4010-5954-5. Dewey:363.46. LCCN:2002-092236.

Audience: **l,u.** *Choice, 2003.*

Dodson, Lisa   **HV1445**
Don't Call Us Out of Name: The Untold Lives of Women and
Girls in Poor America. Trade Paper. Beacon Press. Boston, MA.
1999. 272p. ISBN:0-8070-4209-9, ISBN13: 978-0-8070-4209-0.
Dewey:305.42/086/942. LCCN:98-016520.

Audience: **g,l,u,f.**

Downs, Donald A.   **KF9444.D69 1989**
The New Politics of Pornography. Trade Cloth. University of
Chicago Press. Chicago, IL. 1989. 290p. ISBN:0-226-16162-5,
ISBN13: 978-0-226-16162-4. Dewey:344.73/0547.
LCCN:89-034968.

Audience: **g,l,u,f.** *Choice, 1990.*

Dworkin, Andrea   **HQ471**
Pornography: Men Possessing Women. Trade Paper. Penguin
Group (USA) Inc. New York, NY. 1991. 336p.
ISBN:0-452-26793-5, ISBN13: 978-0-452-26793-0.
Dewey:363.4/7.

Audience: **l,u,f.** *B*

Díaz-Cotto, Juanita   **HV9305.C2D53 2006**
Chicana Lives and Criminal Justice: Voices from el Barrio.
Trade Cloth. University of Texas Press. Austin, TX. 2006. 368p.
ISBN:0-292-71272-3, ISBN13: 978-0-292-71272-0.
Dewey:365/.43092368720794. LCCN:2005-029912.

Audience: **u,f.**

Faludi, Susan   **HQ1090.3.F35 1999**
Stiffed: The Betrayal of the American Man. Trade Cloth.
HarperCollins Publishers. New York, NY. 1999. 662p.
ISBN:0-688-12299-X, ISBN13: 978-0-688-12299-7.
Dewey:305.31/0973. LCCN:99-035504.

Audience: **g,l,u,f.** *Choice, 2000.*

Finkelhor, David   **HQ809.3.U5**
  (Editor), et al.
The Dark Side of Families: Current Family Violence Research.
Richard J. Gelles, Gerald T. Hotaling & Murray A. Straus
(Editors). Trade Paper. SAGE Publications, Inc. Thousand Oaks,
CA. 1983. 376p. ISBN:0-8039-1935-2, ISBN13:
978-0-8039-1935-8. Dewey:306.8/7. LCCN:82-021496.

Audience: **u,f.** *B*

Gerstmann, Evan   **KF4754.5.G47 1999**
The Constitutional Underclass: Gays, Lesbians, and the Failure
of Class-Based Equal Protection. Trade Cloth. University of
Chicago Press. Chicago, IL. 1999. 206p. ISBN:0-226-28859-5,
ISBN13: 978-0-226-28859-8. Dewey:342.73/087.
LCCN:98-011679.

Audience: **u,f.** *Choice, 1999.*

Gordon, Linda   **HQ766.5.U5G66 2002**
The Moral Property of Women: A History of Birth Control
Politics in America. Ed. 3. Trade Cloth. University of Illinois
Press. Champaign, IL. 2002. 464p. ISBN:0-252-02764-7,
ISBN13: 978-0-252-02764-2. Dewey:363.9/6/0973.
LCCN:2002-001551.

Audience: **l,u,f.** *Choice, 2003.*

Gordon, Linda   **HV699**
Pitied but Not Entitled: Single Mothers and the History of
Welfare. Trade Paper. Harvard University Press. Cambridge,
MA. 1998. 448p. ISBN:0-674-66982-7, ISBN13:
978-0-674-66982-6. Dewey:362.8/294/8/0973.

Audience: **l,u.** *Choice, 1995.*

Harrison, Beverly   **HQ767.3.H37 1983**
  Wildung
Our Right to Choose: Toward a New Ethic of Abortion. Trade
Cloth. Beacon Press. Boston, MA. 1983. xi, 334p.
ISBN:0-8070-1508-3, ISBN13: 978-0-8070-1508-7.
Dewey:179/.76. LCCN:81-070488.

Audience: **g,l,u.** *B*

Hart, Vivien   **K1781.H37 1994**
|e| Bound by Our Constitution: Women, Workers, and the
Minimum Wage. E-Book. Princeton University Press. Princeton,
NJ. ISBN:1-4008-1201-1, ISBN13: 978-1-4008-1201-1.
Dewey:344/.0121.

Audience: **u,f.**

Hauser, Barbara R.   **KF478.W674 1996**
  (Editor)
Women's Legal Guide: A Comprehensive Guide to Legal Issues
Affecting Every Woman. Roberta C. Ramo (Foreword by).
Trade Paper. Fulcrum Publishing. Golden, CO. 1996. 544p.
ISBN:1-55591-303-2, ISBN13: 978-1-55591-303-8.
Dewey:346.7301/34. LCCN:95-046893.

Audience: **g.** *Choice, 1996.*

Hays, Sharon   **HV95.H36 2003**
Flat Broke with Children: Women in the Age of Welfare
Reform. Trade Cloth. Oxford University Press, Inc. New York,
NY. 2003. 304p. ISBN:0-19-513288-2, ISBN13:

978-0-19-513288-5. Dewey:362.83/92/0973. LCCN:2002-009841.

Audience: **g,l,u,f.**

Hofstetter, Eleanore O.   **JV6347**
☐ Women Immigrants, 1945 to the Present. http://www.towson.edu/~hofstet/

Audience: **l,u.**

Jaggar, Alison M. &   **HQ1426 .F47**
  Rothenberg, Paula S.
Feminist Frameworks: Alternative Theoretical Accounts of the Relations Between Women and Men. Ed. 4. Trade Cloth. McGraw-Hill Companies, The. New York, NY. 2001. ISBN:0-07-231498-2, ISBN13: 978-0-07-231498-4. Dewey:305.420973.

Audience: **l,u.**

Kempadoo, Kamala &   **HQ111.G56 1998**
  Doezema, Jo
Global Sex Workers: Rights, Resistance and Redefinition. Paper over Boards. Routledge. New York, NY. 1998. 304p. ISBN:0-415-91828-6, ISBN13: 978-0-415-91828-2. Dewey:306.74. LCCN:97-045759.

Audience: **g,l,u,f.**

Koss, Mary P., et al.   **HV6626.2.N62 1994**
No Safe Haven: Male Violence Against Women at Home, at Work, and in the Community. Lisa A. Goodman, Angela Browne, Louise Fitzgerald, Gwendolyn P. Keita & Nancy F. Russo (Authors). Paper Text. American Psychological Association. Washington, DC. 1994. 344p. ISBN:1-55798-244-9, ISBN13: 978-1-55798-244-5. Dewey:364.1/5553/0973. LCCN:94-015637.

Audience: **u,f.** *Choice, 1995.*

Lader, Lawrence   **HQ767.5.U5L33 1991**
RU 486: The Pill That Could End the Abortion Wars and Why American Women Don't Have It. Trade Cloth. Addison-Wesley Longman, Inc. Boston, MA. 1991. 172p. ISBN:0-201-57069-6, ISBN13: 978-0-201-57069-4. Dewey:363.4/6. LCCN:90-024451.

Audience: **g,l,u,f.**

Levit, Nancy   **KF475.L48 1998**
The Gender Line: Men, Women, and the Law. Trade Cloth. New York University Press. New York, NY. 1998. 320p. Critical America Ser. ISBN:0-8147-5121-0, ISBN13: 978-0-8147-5121-3. Dewey:305.3. LCCN:97-045398.

Audience: **g,l,u,f.** *Choice, 1998.*

Luker, Kristin   **HQ767.5.U5**
Abortion and the Politics of Motherhood. Trade Cloth. University of California Press. Berkeley, CA. 1985. 350p. California Series on Social Choice and Political Economy, Vol. 3 ISBN:0-520-05597-7, ISBN13: 978-0-520-05597-1. Dewey:363.4/6/0973. LCCN:83-047849.

Audience: **g,l,u,f.** *B*

Luker, Kristin   **HQ766.5.U5**
Taking Chances: Abortion and the Decision Not to Contracept. Trade Cloth. University of California Press. Berkeley, CA. 1975. xii, 207p. ISBN:0-520-02872-4, ISBN13: 978-0-520-02872-2. Dewey:301.5. LCCN:74-022965.

Audience: **l,u,f.** *B*

Mansbridge, Jane J.   **HQ1236.5.U6M37 1986**
Why We Lost the ERA. Trade Paper. University of Chicago Press. Chicago, IL. 1986. 335p. ISBN:0-226-50358-5, ISBN13: 978-0-226-50358-5. Dewey:347.302/87. LCCN:86-006954.

Audience: **l,u.**

Marsh, Margaret &   **RC889**
  Ronner, Wanda
The Empty Cradle: Infertility in America from Colonial Times to the Present. Trade Paper. DIANE Publishing Company. Collingdale, PA. 2004. 326p. ISBN:0-7567-7162-5, ISBN13: 978-0-7567-7162-1. Dewey:616.6/92/00973.

Audience: **g,l,u,f.** *Choice, 1996.*

Mink, Gwendolyn   **HV700.5.M56 1998**
Welfare's End. Book, Other. Cornell University Press. Ithaca, NY. 1998. 192p. ISBN:0-8014-3347-9, ISBN13: 978-0-8014-3347-4. Dewey:362.83/928/0973. LCCN:97-038838.

Audience: **l,u.** *Choice, 1998.*

Morrison, Toni   **KF8745.T48.R33 1992**
Race-Ing Justice, En-Gendering Power: Essays on Anita Hill, Clarence Thomas and the Construction of Social Reality. Trade Paper. Knopf Publishing Group. New York, NY. 1992. 512p. ISBN:0-679-74145-3, ISBN13: 978-0-679-74145-9. Dewey:347.3073534. LCCN:92-054119.

Audience: **g,l,u,f.** *Choice, 1993.*

Mullings, Leith   **E185.86.M945 1996**
On Our Own Terms: Race, Class and Gender in the Lives of African-American Women. Paper over Boards. Routledge. New York, NY. 1996. 224p. ISBN:0-415-91285-7, ISBN13: 978-0-415-91285-3. Dewey:305.48/896073. LCCN:96-028853.

Audience: **g,l,u.**

Murdock, Catherine   **HV5292**
  Gilbert
Domesticating Drink: Women, Men, and Alcohol in America, 1870-1940. Trade Paper. Johns Hopkins University Press. Baltimore, MD. 2002. 264p. Gender Relations in the American Experience Ser. ISBN:0-8018-6870-X, ISBN13: 978-0-8018-6870-2. Dewey:394.1/3/0973.

Audience: **l,u.**

O'Leary, Virginia   **HQ1206.W875 1985**
  (Editor), et al.
Women, Gender and Social Psychology. Rhoda K. Unger & Barbara S. Wallston (Editors). Cloth Text. Lawrence Erlbaum Associates, Inc. Mahwah, NJ. 1985. 400p. ISBN:0-89859-447-2, ISBN13: 978-0-89859-447-8. Dewey:305.4. LCCN:84-023114.

Audience: **l,u,f.** *B* *Choice, 1985.*

Pincus, Fred L.   **JC599.U5P478 2003**
Reverse Discrimination: Dismantling a Myth. Library Binding. Lynne Rienner Publishers, Inc. Boulder, CO. 2003. 175p. ISBN:1-58826-101-8, ISBN13: 978-1-58826-101-4. Dewey:305/.0973. LCCN:2003-041425.

Audience: **g,l,u.** *Choice, 2004.*

Pringle, Keith   **HQ1088.P75 1995**
Men, Masculinities and Social Welfare. Paper over Boards. Taylor & Francis Group. Abingdon, 1995. 224p. ISBN:1-85728-401-1, ISBN13: 978-1-85728-401-0. Dewey:305.32. LCCN:95-009566.

Audience: **u,f.** *Choice, 1996.*

Pulera, Dominic   **HQ1090.3**
Sharing the Dream: White Men in Multicultural America. Trade Paper. Continuum International Publishing Group, Ltd. London,

Formats: Web: ☐   Ebook: **e**   CD/DVD-ROM: 🏅   BCL3: *B*

2006. 456p. ISBN:0-8264-1829-5, ISBN13: 978-0-8264-1829-6.
Dewey:305.38090973.

Audience: **g,l,u,f.**

Rainwater, Lee   **HQ766**
And the Poor Get Children: Sex, Contraception, and Family
Planning in the Working Class. Trade Cloth. Greenwood
Publishing Group, Inc. Portsmouth, NH. 1984. 202p.
ISBN:0-313-24452-9, ISBN13: 978-0-313-24452-0.
Dewey:304.6/6/0973. LCCN:84-012770.
Audience: **g,l,u,f.** *B*

Reagan, Leslie J.   **HQ767.5.U5**
When Abortion Was a Crime: Women, Medicine and Law in the
United States, 1867-1973. Trade Paper. University of California
Press. Berkeley, CA. 1998. 402p. ISBN:0-520-21657-1, ISBN13:
978-0-520-21657-0. Dewey:363.4/6/0973.
Audience: **g,l,u,f.** *Choice, 1997.*

Renaud, Michelle L.   **RA643.86.A35**
Women at Crossroads: A Prostitute Community's Response to
AIDS in Urban Senegal. Cloth Text. Gordon & Breach
Publishing Group. New York, NY. 1997. 192p.
ISBN:90-5699-530-8, ISBN13: 978-90-5699-530-0.
Dewey:362.1/969792/0082096. LCCN:00-278355.
Audience: **g,l,u,f.** *Choice, 1998.*

Roberts, Dorothy   **HQ766.5.U5**
Killing the Black Body: Race, Reproduction, and the Meaning
of Liberty. Trade Paper. Knopf Publishing Group. New York,
NY. 1998. 384p. ISBN:0-679-75869-0, ISBN13:
978-0-679-75869-3. Dewey:363.9/6/0973.
Audience: **g,l,u.**

Roth, Rachel   **KF481.R67 2000**
Making Women Pay: The Hidden Costs of Fetal Rights. Book,
Other. Cornell University Press. Ithaca, NY. 1999. 264p.
ISBN:0-8014-3607-9, ISBN13: 978-0-8014-3607-9.
Dewey:342.73/085. LCCN:99-044982.
Audience: **g,l,u,f.** *Choice, 2000.*

Rothenberg, Paula S.   **HT1521.R335 2004**
Race, Class and Gender in the United States: An Integrated
Study. Ed. 6. Trade Paper. Worth Publishers, Inc. New York,
NY. 2003. 650p. ISBN:0-7167-5515-7, ISBN13:
978-0-7167-5515-9. Dewey:305.8/00973. LCCN:2003-105073.
Audience: **l,u,f.**

Schroedel, Jean Reith   **KF481.S37 2000**
Is the Fetus a Person?: A Comparison of Policies Across the
Fifty States. Trade Cloth. Cornell University Press. Ithaca, NY.
2000. 256p. ISBN:0-8014-3707-5, ISBN13: 978-0-8014-3707-6.
Dewey:342.73/085. LCCN:00-025087.
Audience: **g,l,u,f.** *Choice, 2001.*

Segal, Lynne &   **HQ471 .S47 1993**
McIntosh, Mary (Editors)
Sex Exposed: Sexuality and the Pornography Debate. Trade
Paper. Rutgers University Press. Piscataway, NJ. 1993. 344p.
ISBN:0-8135-1938-1, ISBN13: 978-0-8135-1938-8.
Dewey:363.4/7. LCCN:92-029843.
Audience: **u,f.**

Shapiro, Ann-Louise   **HV6046.S46 1996**
Breaking the Codes: Female Criminality in Fin-de-Siecle Paris.
Trade Cloth. Stanford University Press. Palo Alto, CA. 1996.
296p. ISBN:0-8047-1663-3, ISBN13: 978-0-8047-1663-5.
Dewey:364.3/74/0944. LCCN:95-037867.
Audience: **u,f.** *Choice, 1996.*

Simon, Rita James &   **HV6046.S54 2004**
Heitfield, Heather
The Crimes Women Commit: The Punishments They Receive.
Ed. 2. Trade Cloth. Lexington Books. Lanham, MD. 2005. 208p.
ISBN:0-7391-1007-1, ISBN13: 978-0-7391-1007-2.
Dewey:364.3/74/0973. LCCN:2004-016988.
Audience: **l,u.**

Solinger, Rickie (Editor)   **HQ767.5.U5A2825 1998**
Abortion Wars: A Half Century of Struggle, 1950-2000. Trade
Paper. University of California Press. Berkeley, CA. 1998. 430p.
ISBN:0-520-20952-4, ISBN13: 978-0-520-20952-7.
Dewey:363.46/0973. LCCN:97-012261.
Audience: **g,l,u.**

Solinger, Rickie   **HQ767.5.U5S73265**
Beggars and Choosers: How the Politics of Choice Shapes
Adoption, Abortion, and Welfare in the United States. Cloth
over Boards. Farrar, Straus & Giroux. New York, NY. 2001.
320p. ISBN:0-8090-9702-8, ISBN13: 978-0-8090-9702-9.
Dewey:363.46. LCCN:2001-016652.
Audience: **l,u,f.** *Choice, 2002.*

Stan, Adele M.   **HQ1237.5.U6 D43 1995**
Debating Sexual Correctness: Pornography, Sexual Harassment,
Date Rape and the Politics of Sexual Equality. Trade Paper. Dell
Publishing. New York, NY. 1995. 340p. ISBN:0-385-31384-5,
ISBN13: 978-0-385-31384-1. Dewey:305.42. LCCN:94-030568.
Audience: **g,l,u,f.**

Strossen, Nadine   **HQ472.U6S87 2000**
Defending Pornography. Ed. 2. Trade Paper. New York
University Press. New York, NY. 2000. 384p.
ISBN:0-8147-8149-7, ISBN13: 978-0-8147-8149-4.
Dewey:363.4/7. LCCN:00-036067.
Audience: **g,l,u.**

Walkowitz, Judith R.   **HQ185.A5**
Prostitution and Victorian Society: Women, Class, and the State.
Trade Paper. Cambridge University Press. New York, NY. 1982.
368p. ISBN:0-521-27064-2, ISBN13: 978-0-521-27064-9.
Dewey:301.4154. LCCN:79-021050.
Audience: **u,f.** *B*

Warren, Karen S. &   **JX1965.B75 1996**
Cady, Duane L. (Editors)
Bringing Peace Home: Feminism, Violence, and Nature. Cloth
Text. Indiana University Press. Bloomington, IN. 1996. 248p.
Hypatia Bk. ISBN:0-253-33086-6, ISBN13: 978-0-253-33086-4.
Dewey:327.1/72/082. LCCN:95-049791.
Audience: **u,f.** *Choice, 1997.*

Weinberger-Thomas,   **GT3370.W5613 1999**
Catherine
Ashes of Immortality: Widow-Burning in India. Jeffrey
Mehlman & David Gordon White (Translators). Trade Paper.
University of Chicago Press. Chicago, IL. 2000. 329p.
ISBN:0-226-88569-0, ISBN13: 978-0-226-88569-8.
Dewey:393/.9. LCCN:99-037258.
Audience: **g,l,u,f.** *Choice, 2000.*

Whalen, Mollie   **HV1445.W43 1996**
Counseling to End Violence Against Women: A Subversive
Model. Trade Cloth. SAGE Publications, Inc. Thousand Oaks,
CA. 1996. 184p. ISBN:0-8039 7379-9, ISBN13:
978-0-8039-7379-4. Dewey:361.3/23. LCCN:95-050177.
Audience: **l,u.** *Choice, 1996.*

Wing, Adrien Katherine　　　　　HQ1154.C75 2003
　(Editor)
Critical Race Feminism: A Reader. Ed. 2. Trade Cloth. New York University Press. New York, NY. 2003. 480p. Critical America Ser. ISBN:0-8147-9393-2, ISBN13: 978-0-8147-9393-0. Dewey:305.48/8/00973. LCCN:2003-008960.
　　　　　　　　　Audience: **u,f.** *Choice, 2004.*

Arts and Literature > Fine Arts

Borzello, Frances　　　　　　　N8354.B67 2000
A World of Our Own: Women as Artists since the Renaissance. Trade Cloth. Watson-Guptill Publications, Inc. New York, NY. 2000. 224p. ISBN:0-8230-5874-3, ISBN13: 978-0-8230-5874-7. Dewey:700.8/2. LCCN:00-103117.
　　　　　　　　　Audience: **g,l,u,f.** *Choice, 2001.*

Broude, Norma &　　　　　　N72.F45E96 1992
　Garrard, Mary D. (Editors)
Expanding Discourse: Feminism and Art History. Trade Paper. Westview Press. Boulder, CO. 1992. 528p. ISBN:0-06-430207-5, ISBN13: 978-0-06-430207-4. Dewey:704/.042. LCCN:91-058341.
　　　　　　　　　Audience: **g,l,u,f.**

Broude, Norma &　　　　　　　　N72.S6
　Garrard, Mary D. (Editors)
Feminism and Art History: Questioning the Litany. Trade Paper. Westview Press. Boulder, CO. 1982. 368p. Icon Editions Ser. ISBN:0-06-430117-6, ISBN13: 978-0-06-430117-6. Dewey:701/.03. LCCN:81-048062.
　　　　　　　　　Audience: **l,u,f.** *B*

Broude, Norma &　　　　　　　　N72.F45
　Garrard, Mary D.
Power of Feminist Art: The American Movement of the 1970s, History and Impact. Trade Paper. Harry N. Abrams, Inc. New York, NY. 1996. 320p. ISBN:0-8109-2659-8, ISBN13: 978-0-8109-2659-2. Dewey:701.03.
　　　　　　　　　Audience: **g,l,u.**

Chadwick, Whitney　　　　　　　　N8354
Women, Art, and Society. Ed. 3. Trade Paper. Thames & Hudson. New York, NY. 2002. 496p. World of Art Ser. ISBN:0-500-20354-7, ISBN13: 978-0-500-20354-5. Dewey:704/.042. LCCN:2001-092911.
　　　　　　　　　Audience: **g,l,u,f.**

Chiarmonte, Paula　　　　　Z7963.A75W65 1990
Women Artists in the U. S.: Guide on the Fine and Decorative Arts, 1750-1986. Trade Cloth. Macmillan Publishing Company, Inc. Old Tappan, NJ. 1990. 1080p. Reference Ser. ISBN:0-8161-8917-X, ISBN13: 978-0-8161-8917-5. Dewey:016.704/042/0973. LCCN:89-027932.
　　　　　　　　　Audience: **l,u,f.** *Choice, 1990.*

Clement, Clara E.　　　　　　　　N43
Women in the Fine Arts: From the Seventh Century B. C. to the Twentieth Century A. D. Trade Cloth. Corner House Historical Publications. Gansevoort, NY. 1977. 395p. ISBN:0-87928-079-4, ISBN13: 978-0-87928-079-6. Dewey:709/.2/2.
　　　　　　　　　Audience: **g,l,u.**

Coleman, Debra　　　　　　NA2543.F45A73 1996
　(Editor), et al.
Architecture and Feminism: Yale Publications on Architecture. Elizabeth Danze, Carol Henderson & Courtney Mercer (Editors).

Trade Paper. Princeton Architectural Press. New York, NY. 1997. 368p. ISBN:1-56898-043-4, ISBN13: 978-1-56898-043-0. Dewey:720/.82. LCCN:96-034510.
　　　　　　　　　Audience: **u,f.**

Collins, Lisa Gail　　　　　　N6538.N5C65 2002
The Art of History: African American Women Artists Engage the Past. Trade Paper. Rutgers University Press. Piscataway, NJ. 2002. 224p. ISBN:0-8135-3022-9, ISBN13: 978-0-8135-3022-2. Dewey:704/.042/08996073. LCCN:2001-048402.
　　　　　　　　　Audience: **g,u,f.** *Choice, 2002.*

Dysart, Dinah & Fink,　　　　　N7260 .A818
　Hannah
Asian Women Artists. Cloth Text. Craftsman House, B V I. Road Town, Tortola, 1996. 132p. ISBN:976-641-077-1, ISBN13: 978-976-641-077-3. Dewey:704.042095.
　　　　　　　　　Audience: **l,u,f.**

Farrington, Lisa E.　　　　　N6538.N5F27 2004
Creating Their Own Image: The History of African-American Women Artists. Trade Cloth. Oxford University Press, Inc. New York, NY. 2004. 368p. ISBN:0-19-516721-X, ISBN13: 978-0-19-516721-4. Dewey:704/.042/08996073. LCCN:2003-066171.
　　　　　　　　　Audience: **g,l,u,f.** *Choice, 2005.*

Farris, Phoebe M.　　　　　　　　N8354
　(Editor)
Women Artists of Color: A Bio-Critical Sourcebook to 20th Century Artists in the Americas. Cloth Text. Greenwood Publishing Group, Inc. Portsmouth, NH. 1999. 520p. ISBN:0-313-30374-6, ISBN13: 978-0-313-30374-6. Dewey:709/.2/39 B. LCCN:98-047134.
　　　　　　　　　Audience: **l,u,f.**

Frueh, Joanna (Editor),　　　　　　N72.F45
　et al.
New Feminist Criticism: Art, Identity, Action. Cassandra L. Langer & Arlene Raven (Editors). Cloth Text. Basic Books. New York, NY. 1969. 368p. ISBN:0-465-00420-2, ISBN13: 978-0-465-00420-1. Dewey:704/.042.
　　　　　　　　　Audience: **u,f.**

Gaze, Delia (Editor)　　　　　　N8354.D53 1997
Dictionary of Women Artists, Set. Trade Cloth. Fitzroy Dearborn Publishers, Inc. Chicago, IL. 1997. 1512p. ISBN:1-884964-21-4, ISBN13: 978-1-884964-21-3. Dewey:709.2/2. LCCN:97-206872.
　　　　　　　　　Audience: **g,l,u,f.** *Choice, 1998.*

Heller, Jules & Heller,　　　　　　　N40
　Nancy G. (Editors)
North American Women Artists of the Twentieth Century: A Biographical Dictionary. Trade Paper. Garland Publishing, Inc. New York, NY. 1997. 736p. Reference Library of the Humanities, Vol. 1219 ISBN:0-8153-2584-3, ISBN13: 978-0-8153-2584-0. Dewey:709/.2/2 B. LCCN:94-049710.
　　　　　　　　　Audience: **g,l,u,f.** *Choice, 1995.*

Heller, Nancy G.　　　　　　　　　N40
Women Artists: An Illustrated History. Ed. 4. Trade Cloth. Abbeville Press, Inc. New York, NY. 2003. 300p. ISBN:0-7892-0768-0, ISBN13: 978-0-7892-0768-5. Dewey:704/.042. LCCN:2004-269241.
　　　　　　　　　Audience: **g,l,u,f.** *Choice, 1992, 1988.*

Hill, Sarah H.　　　　　　　　E99.C5H68 1997
Weaving New Worlds: Southeastern Cherokee Women and Their Basketry. Trade Cloth. University of North Carolina Press.

Chapel Hill, NC. 1997. 440p. ISBN:0-8078-2345-7, ISBN13: 978-0-8078-2345-3. Dewey:746.41/2/0899755. LCCN:96-047882.

Audience: **g,l,u,f.** *Choice, 1997.*

Hillstrom, Laurie   **N8354.C66 1999**
  Collier & Hillstrom, Kevin
Contemporary Women Artists. Trade Cloth. Thomson Gale. Farmington Hills, MI. 1999. xx, 760p. ISBN:1-55862-372-8, ISBN13: 978-1-55862-372-9. Dewey:709/.2/2 B. LCCN:99-010053.

Audience: **g,l,u,f.** *Choice, 1999.*

Mostow, Joshua S.   **NX180.F4**
  (Editor), et al.
Gender and Power in the Japanese Visual Field. Norman Bryson & Maribeth Graybill (Editors). Trade Cloth. DIANE Publishing Company. Collingdale, PA. 2004. 291p. ISBN:0-7567-8154-X, ISBN13: 978-0-7567-8154-5. Dewey:700/.452042/0952.

Audience: **g,l,u.**

Mulvey, Laura   **PN1995.9.W6M84 1989**
Visual and Other Pleasures. Trade Cloth. Indiana University Press. Bloomington, IN. 1989. 218p. Theories of Representation and Difference Ser. ISBN:0-253-36226-1, ISBN13: 978-0-253-36226-1. Dewey:791.43/09/09352042. LCCN:88-009627.

Audience: **l,u.**

Nochlin, Linda   **N72.S6**
Women, Art, and Power and Other Essays. Trade Paper. Westview Press. Boulder, CO. 1989. 208p. ISBN:0-06-430183-4, ISBN13: 978-0-06-430183-1. Dewey:701/.03. LCCN:88-045118.

Audience: **g,l,u,f.** *Choice, 1989.*

Parker, Rozsika &   **N8354**
  Pollock, Griselda (Editors)
Framing Feminism: Art and the Women's Movement, 1970-1985. Trade Paper. Rivers Oram Press/Pandora. London, 1987. 360p. ISBN:0-86358-179-X, ISBN13: 978-0-86358-179-3. Dewey:700.82.

Audience: **l,u,f.**

Piland, Sherry   **Z7963.A75B32 1994**
Women Artists: A Historical, Contemporary and Feminist Bibliography. Ed. 2. Trade Cloth. Scarecrow Press, Inc. Lanham, MD. 1985. 497p. ISBN:0-8108-2559-7, ISBN13: 978-0-8108-2559-8. Dewey:016.7/092/2. LCCN:93-027248.

Audience: **g,l.** *Choice, 1995.*

Pollock, Griselda   **N72.F45G46 1996**
  (Editor)
Generations and Geographies in the Visual Arts: Feminist Readings. Paper over Boards. Routledge. New York, NY. 1996. 320p. ISBN:0-415-14127-3, ISBN13: 978-0-415-14127-7. Dewey:701.1/8/082. LCCN:95-025914.

Audience: **l,u,f.**

Pollock, Griselda   **N8354**
Vision and Difference: Femininity, Feminism, and Histories of Art. Trade Cloth. Routledge. New York, NY. 1988. 239p. ISBN:0-415-00721-6, ISBN13: 978-0-415-00721-4. Dewey:704/.042 19. LCCN:87-030783.

Audience: **l,u,f.** *Choice, 1989.*

Puerto, Cecilia   **Z7963**
Latin American Women Artists, Kahlo and Look Who Else: A Selective, Annotated Bibliography. Cloth Text. Greenwood Publishing Group, Inc. Portsmouth, NH. 1996. 260p. Art

Reference Collection Ser., Vol. 21 ISBN:0-313-28934-4, ISBN13: 978-0-313-28934-7. Dewey:016.7/092/28. LCCN:96-007150.

Audience: **g,l,u,f.** *Choice, 1997.*

Rosenblum, Naomi   **TR139.R67 2000**
A History of Women Photographers. Ed. 2. Trade Cloth. Abbeville Press, Inc. New York, NY. 2000. 400p. ISBN:0-7892-0658-7, ISBN13: 978-0-7892-0658-9. Dewey:770/.82. LCCN:00-036249.

Audience: **g,l,u,f.** *Choice, 1995.*

Schor, Mira &   **N72.F45S36 1997**
Wet: On Painting, Feminism and Art Culture. Library Binding. Duke University Press. Durham, NC. 1997. 280p. ISBN:0-8223-1910-1, ISBN13: 978-0-8223-1910-8. Dewey:704/.042/0973. LCCN:96-029410.

Audience: **l,u,f.**

Slatkin, Wendy   **N43.S57 2001**
Women Artists in History: From Antiquity to the Present. Ed. 4. Trade Paper. Prentice Hall PTR. Upper Saddle River, NJ. 2000. 306p. ISBN:0-13-027319-8, ISBN13: 978-0-13-027319-2. Dewey:704/.042. LCCN:00-026345.

Audience: **g,l,u,f.**

Suleiman, Susan Rubin   **NX652.W6F46 1986**
  (Editor)
The Female Body in Western Culture: Contemporary Perspectives. Trade Paper. Harvard University Press. Cambridge, MA. 1986. 400p. ISBN:0-674-29871-3, ISBN13: 978-0-674-29871-2. Dewey:305.4. LCCN:85-027255.

Audience: **l,u,f.**

Weidner, Marsha   **ND1040.F58 1990**
  (Editor)
Flowering in the Shadows: Women in the History of Chinese and Japanese Painting. Trade Cloth. University of Hawaii Press. Honolulu, HI. 1990. 328p. ISBN:0-8248-1149-6, ISBN13: 978-0-8248-1149-5. Dewey:759.951/082. LCCN:90-011001.

Audience: **l,u,f.** *Choice, 1991.*

Weisman, Leslie K.   **NA2543.W65**
Discrimination by Design: A Feminist Critique of the Man-Made Environment. Trade Paper. University of Illinois Press. Champaign, IL. 1994. 200p. ISBN:0-252-06399-6, ISBN13: 978-0-252-06399-2. Dewey:720/.82.

Audience: **u,f.** *Choice, 1992.*

Arts and Literature > Performing Arts

Ammer, Christine   **ML82.A45 2001**
Unsung: A History of Women in American Music. Ed. 2. Trade Paper. Hal Leonard Corporation. Milwaukee, WI. 2003. 382p. ISBN:1-57467-061-1, ISBN13: 978-1-57467-061-5. Dewey:780/.82/0973. LCCN:00-042017.

Audience: **u,f.** *B*

Banes, Sally   **GV1799.4.B35 1998**
Dancing Women: Female Bodies on Stage. Trade Paper. Routledge. New York, NY. 1998. 296p. ISBN:0-415-11162-5, ISBN13: 978-0-415-11162-1. Dewey:792.8/082. LCCN:97-024496.

Audience: **u,f.** *Choice, 1998.*

Bernstein, Jane A.   **ML82.W697 2003**
  (Editor)
Women's Voices Across Musical Worlds. Trade Paper.

Northeastern University Press. Boston, MA. 2005. 344p.
ISBN:1-55553-588-7, ISBN13: 978-1-55553-588-9.
Dewey:780/.82. LCCN:2003-008327.
Audience: **g,l,u,f.** *Choice, 2004.*

Bowers, Jane & Tick,   **ML82**
  Judith (Editors)
Women Making Music: The Western Art Tradition, 1150-1950.
Trade Paper. University of Illinois Press. Champaign, IL. 1987.
424p. ISBN:0-252-01470-7, ISBN13: 978-0-252-01470-3.
Dewey:780/.88042. LCCN:85-008642.
Audience: **g,l,u,f.** *Choice, 1986.*

Burns, Kristine H.   **ML82**
  (Editor)
Women and Music in America since 1900: An Encyclopedia.
Cloth Text. Greenwood Publishing Group, Inc. Portsmouth, NH.
2002. 808p. ISBN:1-57356-267-X, ISBN13: 978-1-57356-267-6.
Dewey:780/.82/0973. LCCN:2001-054570.
Audience: **g,l,u,f.** *Choice, 2003.*

Carson, Diane (Editor),   **PN1995.9.W6**
  et al.
Multiple Voices in Feminist Film Criticism. Linda Dittmar &
Janice R. Welsch (Editors). Trade Paper. University of
Minnesota Press. Minneapolis, MN. 1994. 560p.
ISBN:0-8166-2273-6, ISBN13: 978-0-8166-2273-3.
Dewey:791.43/015/082. LCCN:93-013743.
Audience: **g,u,f.** *Choice, 1994.*

Cook, Susan C. & Tsou,   **ML82 .C42 1994**
  Judy S. (Editors)
Cecilia Reclaimed: Feminist Perspectives on Gender and Music.
Susan McClary (Foreword by). Trade Paper. University of
Illinois Press. Champaign, IL. 1993. 256p. ISBN:0-252-06341-4,
ISBN13: 978-0-252-06341-1. Dewey:780/.82. LCCN:93-018463.
Audience: **u,f.** *Choice, 1994.*

Dahl, Linda   **ML82.D3 1984**
Stormy Weather: The Music and Lives of a Century of
Jazzwomen. Trade Cloth. Pantheon Books. New York, NY.
1984. xii, 371p. ISBN:0-03-945355-3, ISBN13:
978-0-03-945355-8. Dewey:785.42/092/2. LCCN:83-019456.
Audience: **l,u,f.**

Davis, Angela Y.   **ML3521**
Blues Legacies and Black Feminism: Gertrude "Ma" Rainey,
Bessie Smith, and Billie Holiday. UK-Trade Paper. Alfred A.
Knopf Inc. New York, NY. 1999. 464p. ISBN:0-679-77126-3,
ISBN13: 978-0-679-77126-5. Dewey:782.4/2/1643/082.
Audience: **g,l,u.**

De Lauretis, Teresa   **PN1995.9.W6**
Alice Doesn't: Feminism, Semiotics, Cinema. Trade Cloth.
Indiana University Press. Bloomington, IN. 1984. 232p.
ISBN:0-253-30467-9, ISBN13: 978-0-253-30467-4.
Dewey:791.43/09/09352042. LCCN:83-048189.
Audience: **u,f.**

Ericson, Margaret   **ML128.W7E75 1995**
Women and Music: A Selective Annotated Bibliography on
Women and Gender Issues in Music, 1987-1992. Trade Cloth.
Thomson Gale. Farmington Hills, MI. 1996. 350p.
ISBN:0-8161-0580-4, ISBN13: 978-0-8161-0580-9.
Dewey:016.7/8/082. LCCN:94-045222.
Audience: **l,u,f.** *Choice, 1996.*

Foster, Gwendolyn   **PN1998**
  Audrey
Women Film Directors: An International Bio-Critical Dictionary.
Cloth Text. Greenwood Publishing Group, Inc. Portsmouth, NH.
1995. 488p. ISBN:0-313-28972-7, ISBN13: 978-0-313-28972-9.
Dewey:791.43/0233/0922 B. LCCN:95-007395.
Audience: **g,l,u,f.** *Choice, 1996.*

Gaar, Gillian G.   **ML394**
She's a Rebel: The History of Women in Rock and Roll. Ed. 2.
Yoko Ono (Preface by). Trade Paper. Avalon Publishing Group.
New York, NY. 2002. 496p. ISBN:1-58005-078-6, ISBN13:
978-1-58005-078-4. Dewey:781.66/092/2 B.
LCCN:2003-267936.
Audience: **g,l,u,f.** *Choice, 1993.*

Hanna, Judith L.   **GV1595.H33 1988**
Dance, Sex, and Gender: Signs of Identity, Dominance,
Defiance, and Desire. Trade Paper. University of Chicago Press.
Chicago, IL. 1988. 233p. ISBN:0-226-31551-7, ISBN13:
978-0-226-31551-5. Dewey:793.3/2. LCCN:87-023784.
Audience: **u.** *Choice, 1988.*

Haskell, Molly   **PN1995.9.W6H3 1987**
From Reverence to Rape: The Treatment of Women in the
Movies. Ed. 2. Trade Paper. University of Chicago Press.
Chicago, IL. 1987. 444p. ISBN:0-226-31885-0, ISBN13:
978-0-226-31885-1. Dewey:791.43/0909/352. LCCN:87-014354.
Audience: **g,l,u.** *B*

Hixon, Don L. &   **ML105.H6 1993**
  Hennessee, Don A.
Women in Music: An Encyclopedic Biobibliography. Ed. 2.
Trade Cloth. Scarecrow Press, Inc. Lanham, MD. 1993. 772p.
ISBN:0-8108-2769-7, ISBN13: 978-0-8108-2769-1.
Dewey:016.78/0922. LCCN:93-034731.
Audience: **g,l,u,f.**

Jeffords, Susan   **PN1995.9.M46J44 1993**
Hard Bodies: Hollywood Masculinity in the Reagan Era. Cloth
Text. Rutgers University Press. Piscataway, NJ. 1993. 240p.
ISBN:0-8135-2002-9, ISBN13: 978-0-8135-2002-5.
Dewey:791.43/652041/09048. LCCN:93-018282.
Audience: **u,f.** *Choice, 1994.*

Kaplan, Ann E.   **PN1995.9.W6K25 1997**
Looking for the Other: Feminism, Film and the Imperial Gaze.
UK-B Format Paperback. Routledge. New York, NY. 1997.
256p. ISBN:0-415-91017-X, ISBN13: 978-0-415-91017-0.
Dewey:791.43/652042. LCCN:96-031257.
Audience: **l,u.**

Koskoff, Ellen (Editor)   **ML82.W63 1989**
Women and Music in Cross-Cultural Perspective. Trade Paper.
University of Illinois Press. Champaign, IL. 1989. 280p.
ISBN:0-252-06057-1, ISBN13: 978-0-252-06057-1.
Dewey:780/.88042. LCCN:88-023578.
Audience: **g,l,u.** *Choice, 1988.*

Kuhn, Annette   **PN1995.9.W6K8 1994**
Women's Pictures: Feminism and Cinema. Ed. 2. Trade Paper.
Analytical Psychology Club of San Francisco, Inc. San
Francisco, CA. 1994. 224p. ISBN:1-85984-010-8, ISBN13:
978-1-85984-010-8. Dewey:791.43/652042. LCCN:94-011624.
Audience: **l,u.**

Manatu, Norma   **PN1995.9.N4M28 2002**
African American Women and Sexuality in the Cinema. Paper
Text. McFarland & Company, Incorporated Publishers. Jefferson,

NC. 2002. 245p. ISBN:0-7864-1431-6, ISBN13:
978-0-7864-1431-4. Dewey:791.43/652042. LCCN:2002-015421.
Audience: **g,l,u.** *Choice, 2003.*

McClary, Susan   **ML82.M38 2002**
Feminine Endings: Music, Gender, and Sexuality. Trade Paper.
University of Minnesota Press. Minneapolis, MN. 2002. 240p.
ISBN:0-8166-4189-7, ISBN13: 978-0-8166-4189-5.
Dewey:780/.82. LCCN:2002-072791.
Audience: **g,l,u,f.**

McClary, Susan   **M2**
New Historical Anthology of Music by Women. James R.
Briscoe (Editor). Trade Paper. Indiana University Press.
Bloomington, IN. 2004. 524p. ISBN:0-253-21683-4, ISBN13:
978-0-253-21683-0. Dewey:780.8/2.
Audience: **g.**

Modleski, Tania   **PN1995.9.W6M55 1991**
Feminism Without Women: Culture and Criticism in a
"Postfeminist" Age. UK-B Format Paperback. Routledge. New
York, NY. 1991. 416p. ISBN:0-415-90417-X, ISBN13:
978-0-415-90417-9. Dewey:302.23/082. LCCN:91-013126.
Audience: **u,f.** *Choice, 1992.*

Nochlin, Linda   **N72.S6**
Women, Art, and Power and Other Essays. Trade Paper.
Westview Press. Boulder, CO. 1989. 208p. ISBN:0-06-430183-4,
ISBN13: 978-0-06-430183-1. Dewey:701/.03. LCCN:88-045118.
Audience: **g,l,u,f.** *Choice, 1989.*

Pendle, Karin (Editor)   **ML82.W6 2001**
Women and Music: A History. Ed. 2. Trade Cloth. Indiana
University Press. Bloomington, IN. 2000. x, 516p.
ISBN:0-253-33819-0, ISBN13: 978-0-253-33819-8.
Dewey:780/.82. LCCN:00-044886.
Audience: **g,l,u,f.** *Choice, 2001, 1992.*

Penley, Constance   **PN1995.9.W6**
Feminism and Film Theory. Routledge/BFI. 1988.
ISBN:0-415-90107-3, ISBN13: 978-0-415-90107-9.
Audience: **u,f.**

Puerto, Cecilia   **Z7963**
Latin American Women Artists, Kahlo and Look Who Else: A
Selective, Annotated Bibliography. Cloth Text. Greenwood
Publishing Group, Inc. Portsmouth, NH. 1996. 260p. Art
Reference Collection Ser., Vol. 21 ISBN:0-313-28934-4,
ISBN13: 978-0-313-28934-7. Dewey:016.7/092/28.
LCCN:96-007150.
Audience: **g,l,u,f.** *Choice, 1997.*

Reynolds, Simon &   **ML82.R53 1995**
 Press, Joy
The Sex Revolts: Gender, Rebellion, and Rock 'n' Roll. Trade
Cloth. Harvard University Press. Cambridge, MA. 1995. 432p.
ISBN:0-674-80272-1, ISBN13: 978-0-674-80272-8.
Dewey:781.66/082. LCCN:94-030683.
Audience: **g,l,u.** *Choice, 1995.*

Robinson, Alice M.;   **PN2285**
 Roberts, Vera Mowry; & Barranger, Milly S.
Notable Women in the American Theatre: A Biographical
Dictionary. Greenwood. 1989. ISBN:0-313-27217-4, ISBN13:
978-0-313-27217-2.
Audience: **g,l,u,f.**

Senelick, Laurence   **PN2037**
 (Editor)
Gender in Performance: The Presentation of Difference in the
Performing Arts. Trade Paper. University Press of New England.
Lebanon, NH. 1992. 372p. ISBN:0-87451-604-8, ISBN13:
978-0-87451-604-3. Dewey:792. LCCN:92-011968.
Audience: **l,u.** *Choice, 1993.*

Smelik, Anneke M.   **QC770 .W643 1985**
And the Mirror Cracked: Feminist Cinema and Film Theory.
Trade Paper. Palgrave Macmillan. New York, NY. 2001. 227p.
ISBN:0-333-92041-4, ISBN13: 978-0-333-92041-1.
Dewey:539.7. LCCN:92-902099.
Audience: **u,f.**

Solie, Ruth A. (Editor)   **ML82**
Musicology and Difference: Gender and Sexuality in Music
Scholarship. Trade Paper. University of California Press.
Berkeley, CA. 1995. 368p. ISBN:0-520-20146-9, ISBN13:
978-0-520-20146-0. Dewey:780.82.
Audience: **u,f.** *Choice, 1994.*

Stamp, Shelley   **PN1995.9.W6S75 2000**
Movie-Struck Girls: Women and Motion Picture Culture after
the Nickelodeon. Trade Paper. Princeton University Press.
Princeton, NJ. 2000. 284p. ISBN:0-691-04457-0, ISBN13:
978-0-691-04457-6. Dewey:791.43/082. LCCN:99-046548.
Audience: **l,u,f.** *Choice, 2000.*

Tasker, Yvonne   **PN1995.9.W6T36 1998**
Working Girls: Gender and Sexuality in Popular Cinema. Paper
over Boards. Routledge. New York, NY. 1998. 256p.
ISBN:0-415-14004-8, ISBN13: 978-0-415-14004-1.
Dewey:791.43652042. LCCN:97-038918.
Audience: **g,l,u.** *Choice, 1999.*

Thornham, Sue   **PN1995.9.W6F465 1999**
Feminist Film Theory: A Classical Reader. Trade Paper. New
York University Press. New York, NY. 1999. 320p.
ISBN:0-8147-8244-2, ISBN13: 978-0-8147-8244-6.
Dewey:791.43/082. LCCN:98-032118.
Audience: **g,l,u.** *Choice, 2000.*

Whiteley, Sheila   **ML3470.S46 1997**
Sexing the Groove: Popular Music and Gender. Paper over
Boards. Routledge. New York, NY. 1997. 400p.
ISBN:0-415-14670-4, ISBN13: 978-0-415-14670-8.
Dewey:306.4/84. LCCN:97-005416.
Audience: **l,u.**

Xing, Jun &   **PN1995.9.M56X56 2003**
 Hirabayashi, Ryo (Editors)
Reversing the Lens: Ethnicity, Race, Gender, and Sexuality
Through Film. Trade Cloth. University Press of Colorado.
Boulder, CO. 2003. 270p. ISBN:0-87081-724-8, ISBN13:
978-0-87081-724-3. Dewey:791.43/655. LCCN:2003-002123.
Audience: **u.** *Choice, 2003.*

Arts and Literature > Language and Literature

                    TK5105.5
▢ A Celebration of Women Writers.
http://digital.library.upenn.edu/women/
Audience: **l,u,f.**

PR1110.W6

☐ Emory Women Writers Resource Project.
http://chaucer.library.emory.edu/wwrp/index.html
Audience: **g,l,u.**

HQ1154

☐ Feminist Science Fiction, Fantasy and Utopia.
http://feministsf.org/femsf/index.html
Audience: **g,l,u.**

☐ GenderInn.
http://www.uni-koeln.de/phil-fak/englisch/datenbank/e_index.htm
Audience: **g,l,u.**

PL8010

☐ Reading Women Writers and African Literature.
http://www.arts.uwa.edu.au/AFLIT/FEMEChomeEN.html
Audience: **g,l,u.**

PR1110.W6

☐ Victorian Women Writers Project.
http://www.indiana.edu/%7Eletrs/vwwp/
Audience: **g,l,u.**

☐ Voices from the Gaps: Women Artists and Writers of Color.
http://voices.cla.umn.edu/
Audience: **g,l,u.**

☐ Women Writers Project.
http://www.wwp.brown.edu/
Audience: **g,l,u.**

Blain, Virginia;   **PR111**
Clements, Patricia; Grundy, Isobel
The Feminist Companion to Literature in English: Women
Writers from the Middle Ages to the Present. Yale University
Press. 1990. ISBN:0-300-04854-8, ISBN13: 978-0-300-04854-4.
Audience: **g,l,u.**

Coates, Jennifer   **P120.S48L338 1998**
(Editor)
Language and Gender: A Reader. Trade Paper. Blackwell
Publishing, Inc. Malden, MA. 1997. 544p. ISBN:0-631-19595-5,
ISBN13: 978-0-631-19595-5. Dewey:306.44. LCCN:97-018909.
Audience: **u,f.**

Schomburg Center for
Research in Black Culture
☐ African American Women Writers of the 19thCentury.
http://digital.nypl.org/schomburg/writers_aa19/toc.html
Audience: **g,l,u.**

Arts and Literature > Language and Literature > Autobiography. Biography. Memoirs

Bataille, Gretchen M. &   **PS366.A35**
Sands, Kathleen M.
American Indian Women: Telling Their Lives. Trade Paper.
University of Nebraska Press. Lincoln, NE. 1984. 209p.

ISBN:0-8032-6082-2, ISBN13: 978-0-8032-6082-5.
Dewey:818/.08. LCCN:83-010234.
Audience: **u,f.** 𝓑

Boynton, Victoria &   **HQ1185.E63 2005**
Malin, Jo
Encyclopedia of Women's Autobiography. Trade Cloth.
Greenwood Publishing Group, Inc. Portsmouth, NH. 2005.
ISBN:0-313-32738-6, ISBN13: 978-0-313-32738-4.
Dewey:305.4/092/2 B. LCCN:2005-008526.
Audience: **l,u.**

Boynton, Victoria &   **HQ1185.E63 2005**
Malin, Jo
Encyclopedia of Women's Autobiography. Trade Cloth.
Greenwood Publishing Group, Inc. Portsmouth, NH. 2005.
ISBN:0-313-32739-4, ISBN13: 978-0-313-32739-1.
Dewey:305.4/092/2 B. LCCN:2005-008526.
Audience: **g,l,u,f.**

Braxton, Joanne M.   **PS366.A35B73 1989**
Black Women Writing Autobiography: A Tradition Within a
Tradition. Trade Cloth. Temple University Press. Philadelphia,
PA. 1989. 240p. ISBN:0-87722-639-3, ISBN13:
978-0-87722-639-0. Dewey:818/.08. LCCN:89-030066.
Audience: **g,l,u,f.** *Choice, 1990.*

Culley, Margo (Editor,   **PS366.A88**
Introduction by)
American Women's Autobiography: Fea(s)ts of Memory. Trade
Paper. University of Wisconsin Press. Chicago, IL. 1992. 352p.
Studies in American Autobiography ISBN:0-299-13294-3,
ISBN13: 978-0-299-13294-1. Dewey:810.9492072.
LCCN:91-046700.
Audience: **l,u,f.** *Choice, 1993.*

Feracho, Lesley   **PQ7081.5.F47 2005**
Linking the Americas: Race, Hybrid Discourses, and the
Reformulation of Feminine Identity. Cloth Text. State University
of New York Press. Albany, NY. 2005. 256p. SUNY Series in
Latin American and Iberian Thought and Culture
ISBN:0-7914-6403-2, ISBN13: 978-0-7914-6403-8.
Dewey:860.9/9287/098. LCCN:2004-052138.
Audience: **u,f.** *Choice, 2005.*

Gallagher, Jean   **D570.9**
World Wars Through the Female Gaze. Trade Cloth. Southern
Illinois University Press. Carbondale, IL. 1999. 208p.
ISBN:0-8093-2318-4, ISBN13: 978-0-8093-2318-0.
Dewey:940.48173. LCCN:97-048874.
Audience: **g,l,u,f.**

Gluck, Sherna B. &   **HQ1121.W886 1991**
Patai, Daphne (Editors)
Women's Words: The Feminist Practice of Oral History. Cloth
Text. Routledge. New York, NY. 1991. 240p.
ISBN:0-415-90371-8, ISBN13: 978-0-415-90371-4.
Dewey:305.4/0722. LCCN:90-048234.
Audience: **u,f.**

Kanner, Barbara   **Z7963.B6K35 1997**
British Women's Autobiographics: A Comprehensive Guide to
Research. Trade Cloth. Thomson Gale. Farmington Hills, MI.
1997. 1049p. ISBN:0-8161-7346-X, ISBN13:
978-0-8161-7346-4. Dewey:016.3054/0942. LCCN:96-029645.
Audience: **g,l,u.** *Choice, 1998.*

Lionnet, Francoise   CT21
Autobiographical Voices: Race, Gender, Self-Portraiture. Trade Paper. Cornell University Press. Ithaca, NY. 1991. 280p. Reading Women Writing Ser. ISBN:0-8014-9927-5, ISBN13: 978-0-8014-9927-2. Dewey:809.9/3592. LCCN:88-043236.
            Audience: **u,f.** *Choice, 1990.*

Loftus, Ronald P.   CT25.T45 2004
  (Editor, Translator)
Telling Lives: Women's Self-Writing in Modern Japan. Trade Cloth. University of Hawaii Press. Honolulu, HI. 2004. 296p. ISBN:0-8248-2753-8, ISBN13: 978-0-8248-2753-3. Dewey:920.72/0951. LCCN:2003-023277.
            Audience: **u,f.** *Choice, 2005.*

Malin, Jo & Boynton,   HQ1185
  Victoria (Editors)
Encyclopedia of Women's Autobiography, Vol. 1. Cloth Text. Greenwood Publishing Group, Inc. Portsmouth, NH. 2005. 664p. ISBN:0-313-32737-8, ISBN13: 978-0-313-32737-7. Dewey:305.4/092/2 B. LCCN:2005-008526.
            Audience: **g,l,u,f.** *Choice, 2006.*

Personal Narratives   HQ1185.I58 1989
  Group Staff
Interpreting Women's Lives: Feminist Theory and Personal Narratives. Trade Cloth. Indiana University Press. Bloomington, IN. 1989. 286p. ISBN:0-253-33070-X, ISBN13: 978-0-253-33070-3. Dewey:305.4/2. LCCN:88-045445.
            Audience: **l,u.** *Choice, 1990.*

Smith, Sidonie &   PS366.A88W636 1998
  Watson, Julia (Editors)
Women, Autobiography, Theory: A Reader. Trade Cloth. University of Wisconsin Press. Chicago, IL. 1998. 544p. Wisconsin Studies in American Autobiography ISBN:0-299-15840-3, ISBN13: 978-0-299-15840-8. Dewey:818/.540809492072. LCCN:97-039731.
            Audience: **l,u,f.** *Choice, 1999.*

Arts and Literature > Language and Literature > Literary Criticism

Adams, James E.   PR468.M38A33 1995
Dandies and Desert Saints: Styles of Victorian Masculinity. Trade Paper. Cornell University Press. Ithaca, NY. 1995. 264p. ISBN:0-8014-8208-9, ISBN13: 978-0-8014-8208-3. Dewey:820.9/353. LCCN:95-011320.
            Audience: **u,f.** *Choice, 1996.*

Allen, Paula Gunn   E98.W8
The Sacred Hoop: Recovering the Feminine in American Indian Traditions. Ed. 2. Trade Paper. Beacon Press. Boston, MA. 1992. 336p. ISBN:0-8070-4617-5, ISBN13: 978-0-8070-4617-3. Dewey:970.004/97/0088042. LCCN:92-006332.
            Audience: **u,f.** *Choice, 1986.*

Anzaldúa, Gloria   PS3551.N95B6 1999
Borderlands - La Frontera: The New Mestiza. Ed. 2. Trade Cloth. Aunt Lute Books. San Francisco, CA. 1999. 260p. ISBN:1-879960-57-5, ISBN13: 978-1-879960-57-2. Dewey:811/.54. LCCN:99-022546.
            Audience: **u,f.** *Choice, 1988.*

Anzaldúa, Gloria   PS3561.A888M9 1990
  (Editor)
Making Face, Making Soul - Haciendo Caras: Creative and Critical Perspectives by Feminists of Color. Trade Cloth. Spinsters Ink Books. Midway, FL. 1990. 400p. ISBN:0-933216-74-2, ISBN13: 978-0-933216-74-7. Dewey:813/.54. LCCN:90-009428.
            Audience: **g,l,u,f.**

Barker, Adele Marie &   PG2997 .H56 2001
  Gheith, Jehanne M. (Editors)
A History of Women's Writing in Russia. Cloth Text. Cambridge University Press. New York, NY. 2002. 410p. ISBN:0-521-57280-0, ISBN13: 978-0-521-57280-4. Dewey:891.7099287. LCCN:2001-035693.
            Audience: **g,l,u,f.** *Choice, 2003.*

Baym, Nina   PS374.H5B39 1995
American Women Writers and the Work of History, 1790-1860. Paper Text. Rutgers University Press. Piscataway, NJ. 1995. 325p. ISBN:0-8135-2143-2, ISBN13: 978-0-8135-2143-5. Dewey:813/.081099287. LCCN:94-011283.
            Audience: **u,f.** *Choice, 1995.*

Benstock, Shari   PR111.H36 2002
  (Author, Editor), et al.
A Handbook of Literary Feminisms. Suzanne Ferriss & Susanne Woods (Author, Editors). Paper Text. Oxford University Press, Inc. New York, NY. 2002. 304p. ISBN:0-19-510206-1, ISBN13: 978-0-19-510206-2. Dewey:820.9/9287. LCCN:2001-036415.
            Audience: **g,l,u,f.**

Bohls, Elizabeth A.   PR778.T72 B64 1995
Women Travel Writers and the Language of Aesthetics, 1716-1818. Marilyn Butler & James Chandler (Contribution by). Trade Paper. Cambridge University Press. New York, NY. 2004. 320p. Cambridge Studies in Romanticism Ser. ISBN:0-521-60710-8, ISBN13: 978-0-521-60710-0. Dewey:910.4/082.
            Audience: **u,f.** *Choice, 1996.*

Bowers, Toni   PR448.M66 B69 1996
The Politics of Motherhood: British Writing and Culture, 1680-1760. Trade Paper. Cambridge University Press. New York, NY. 2005. 278p. ISBN:0-521-02033-6, ISBN13: 978-0-521-02033-6. Dewey:820.9/355.
            Audience: **l,u,f.** *Choice, 1997.*

Bristow, Joe   PR830.A38B75 1991
Empire Boys: Adventures in a Man's World. Trade Paper. Routledge. New York, NY. 1991. 240p. ISBN:0-04-445630-1, ISBN13: 978-0-04-445630-8. Dewey:823/.809352054. LCCN:90-021815.
            Audience: **g,l,u,f.**

Brody, Jennifer D.   PR468.B53B76 1998
Impossible Purities: Blackness, Femininity and Victorian Culture. Trade Cloth. Duke University Press. Durham, NC. 1998. 232p. ISBN:0-8223-2105-X, ISBN13: 978-0-8223-2105-7. Dewey:820.9/358. LCCN:98-023196.
            Audience: **u,f.** *Choice, 1999.*

Caminero-Santangelo,   PS374.M44C36 1998
  Marta
The Madwoman Can't Speak: or Why Insanity Is Not Subversive. Book, Other. Cornell University Press. Ithaca, NY. 1998. 224p. Reading Women Writing Ser. ISBN:0-8014-3514-5,

ISBN13: 978-0-8014-3514-0. Dewey:813/.5409353.
LCCN:98-004027.

Audience: **l,u,f.** *Choice, 1999.*

Cardinal, Agnes   **PN6071.E8W66 1999**
(Editor), et al.
Women's Writing on the First World War. Dorothy Goldman &
Judith Hattaway (Editors). Trade Cloth. Oxford University Press,
Inc. New York, NY. 2000. 388p. ISBN:0-19-812280-2, ISBN13:
978-0-19-812280-7. Dewey:808.8/0358. LCCN:99-015282.

Audience: **g,l,u,f.** *Choice, 2000.*

Chancy, Myriam J.   **PR9205.O5.C48 1997**
Searching for Safe Spaces: Afro-Caribbean Women Writers in
Exile. Trade Cloth. Temple University Press. Philadelphia, PA.
1997. 272p. ISBN:1-56639-539-9, ISBN13: 978-1-56639-539-7.
Dewey:820.9/9287/089960729. LCCN:96-046236.

Audience: **u,f.** *Choice, 1998.*

Chang, Kang-i Sun   **PL2278.W65 1999**
(Editor), et al.
Women Writers of Traditional China: An Anthology of Poetry
and Criticism. Haun Saussy & Charles Yim-tze Kwong
(Editors). Trade Cloth. Stanford University Press. Palo Alto, CA.
1999. xxiv, 891p. ISBN:0-8047-3230-2, ISBN13:
978-0-8047-3230-7. Dewey:895.1/10809287. LCCN:99-019030.

Audience: **g,u,f.** *Choice, 2000.*

Christian, Barbara   **PS153.N5C47 1985**
Black Feminist Criticism: Perspectives on Black Women
Writers. Cloth Text. Elsevier Science & Technology Books.
Saint Louis, MO. 1985. 350p. Athene Ser. ISBN:0-08-031956-4,
ISBN13: 978-0-08-031956-8. Dewey:810.9/9287/08996073.
LCCN:84-022805.

Audience: **l,u,f.** ℬ *Choice, 1985.*

Clyman, Toby W. &   **PG2997**
Greene, Diana (Editors)
Women Writers in Russian Literature. Trade Cloth. Greenwood
Publishing Group, Inc. Portsmouth, NH. 1994. 312p.
Contributions to the Study of World Literature Ser., No. 53
ISBN:0-313-27521-1, ISBN13: 978-0-313-27521-0.
Dewey:891.7099287. LCCN:93-021143.

Audience: **g,l,u,f.** *Choice, 1994.*

Conboy, Katie, et al.   **PN98.W64W687 1997**
Writing on the Body: Female Embodiment and Feminist Theory.
Nadia Medina & Sarah Stanbury (Authors). Trade Cloth.
Columbia University Press. New York, NY. 1997. 384p. Gender
and Culture Ser. ISBN:0-231-10544-4, ISBN13:
978-0-231-10544-6. Dewey:305.4. LCCN:96-048177.

Audience: **u,f.**

Cooke, Miriam   **PN3448.W3C66 1996**
Women and the War Story. Trade Paper. University of California
Press. Berkeley, CA. 1997. 378p. ISBN:0-520-20613-4, ISBN13:
978-0-520-20613-7. Dewey:892/.73609358. LCCN:96-011601.

Audience: **u,f.** *Choice, 1997.*

David, Deirdre   **PR468.I49 D38**
Rule Britannia: Women, Empire and Victorian Writing. Trade
Paper. Cornell University Press. Ithaca, NY. 1996. 256p.
ISBN:0-8014-8277-1, ISBN13: 978-0-8014-8277-9.
Dewey:823/.80932171241. LCCN:95-032733.

Audience: **g,l,u,f.**

Davidson, Michael   **PS310.C6D387 2004**
Guys Like Us: Citing Masculinity in Cold War Poetics. Trade
Cloth. University of Chicago Press. Chicago, IL. 2003. 296p.

ISBN:0-226-13739-2, ISBN13: 978-0-226-13739-1.
Dewey:811/.5409358. LCCN:2003-012948.

Audience: **g,l,u,f.** *Choice, 2004.*

Derounian-Stodola,   **E85.W85 1998**
Kathryn Zabelle (Editor, Introduction by, Notes by)
Women's Indian Captivity Narratives. Trade Paper. Penguin
Group (USA) Inc. New York, NY. 1998. 432p. Classics Ser.
ISBN:0-14-043671-5, ISBN13: 978-0-14-043671-6.
Dewey:305.48/969. LCCN:98-021291.

Audience: **u,f.**

Feracho, Lesley   **PQ7081.5.F47 2005**
Linking the Americas: Race, Hybrid Discourses, and the
Reformulation of Feminine Identity. Cloth Text. State University
of New York Press. Albany, NY. 2005. 256p. SUNY Series in
Latin American and Iberian Thought and Culture
ISBN:0-7914-6403-2, ISBN13: 978-0-7914-6403-8.
Dewey:860.9/9287/098. LCCN:2004-052138.

Audience: **u,f.** *Choice, 2005.*

Frawley, Maria H.   **PR778.T72F7 1994**
A Wider Range: Travel Writing by Women in Victorian
England. Trade Cloth. Fairleigh Dickinson University Press.
Cranbury, NJ. 1994. 237p. ISBN:0-8386-3544-X, ISBN13:
978-0-8386-3544-5. Dewey:820.9/355. LCCN:92-055127.

Audience: **g,l,u,f.** *Choice, 1995.*

Gilbert, Sandra M. &   **PR115.G5 2000**
Gubar, Susan
The Madwoman in the Attic: The Woman Writer and the
Nineteenth-Century Literary Imagination. Ed. 2. Trade Paper.
Yale University Press. Cumberland, RI. 2000. 768p.
ISBN:0-300-08458-7, ISBN13: 978-0-300-08458-0.
Dewey:820.9/9287/09034. LCCN:99-086038.

Audience: **g,l,u,f.**

Goscilo, Helena   **PG3213.L58 1995**
(Introduction by)
Lives in Transit: A Collection of Recent Russian Women's
Writing. Trade Cloth. Ardis Publishers. Woodstock, NY. 1995.
327p. ISBN:0-87501-100-4, ISBN13: 978-0-87501-100-4.
Dewey:891.708/09287. LCCN:93-022986.

Audience: **g,l,u,f.** *Choice, 1995.*

Greene, Gayle   **PR888.F45G7 1991**
Changing the Story: Feminist Fiction and the Tradition. Trade
Cloth. Indiana University Press. Bloomington, IN. 1992. 320p.
ISBN:0-253-32606-0, ISBN13: 978-0-253-32606-5.
Dewey:820.9/9287. LCCN:91-006849.

Audience: **l,u,f.** *Choice, 1992.*

Gwin, Minrose C.   **PS0261.G85**
Black and White Women of the Old South: The Peculiar
Sisterhood in American Literature. Trade Paper. Books on
Demand. Ann Arbor, MI. 240p. ISBN:0-608-09834-5, ISBN13:
978-0-608-09834-0. Dewey:810/.9/975. LCCN:85-003238.

Audience: **l,u.** *Choice, 1986.*

Hall, Kim F.   **PR449.S4**
Things of Darkness: Economies of Race and Gender in Early
Modern England. Trade Paper. Cornell University Press. Ithaca,
NY. 1996. 312p. ISBN:0-8014-8249-6, ISBN13:
978-0-8014-8249-6. Dewey:820.9/353. LCCN:95-036592.

Audience: **u,f.** *Choice, 1996.*

Hawkesworth, Celia   **PG1404.9.W65H39 2000**
Voices in the Shadows. Trade Cloth. Central European
University Press. Herndon, VA. 2000. 292p.

ISBN:963-9116-62-9, ISBN13: 978-963-9116-62-7.
Dewey:891.8/2099287. LCCN:00-022648.
Audience: **g,l,u,f.** *Choice, 2000.*

Holloway, Karla F. **PS153.N5H65 1992**
Moorings and Metaphors: Figures of Culture and Gender in
Black Women's Literature. Trade Paper. Rutgers University
Press. Piscataway, NJ. 2003. 207p. ISBN:0-8135-1746-X,
ISBN13: 978-0-8135-1746-9. Dewey:810.9/9287.
LCCN:91-016803.
Audience: **u,f.** *Choice, 1992.*

Joannou, Maroula **PR808.W65J63 1995**
Ladies, Please Don't Smash These Windows: Women's Writing,
Feminist Consciousness and Social Change 1918-1938. Trade
Paper. Berg Publishers. Oxford, 1995. 236p. Cross-Cultural
Perspectives on Women Ser. ISBN:1-85973-022-1, ISBN13:
978-1-85973-022-5. Dewey:828.91208099287.
LCCN:94-034792.
Audience: **u,f.** *Choice, 1995.*

Kaminsky, Amy K. **PQ7081.A1**
Reading the Body Politic: Feminist Criticism and Latin
American Women Writers. Trade Paper. University of Minnesota
Press. Minneapolis, MN. 1992. 192p. ISBN:0-8166-1948-4,
ISBN13: 978-0-8166-1948-1. Dewey:860.9/9287/098.
LCCN:92-016023.
Audience: **u,f.** *Choice, 1993.*

Keating, AnaLouise **PS151.K43 1996**
Women Reading Women Writing: Self-Invention in Paula Gunn
Allen, Gloria Anzaldua, and Audre Lorde. Trade Cloth. Temple
University Press. Philadelphia, PA. 1996. 240p.
ISBN:1-56639-419-8, ISBN13: 978-1-56639-419-2.
Dewey:810.9/9287. LCCN:95-039871.
Audience: **l,u,f.** *Choice, 1996.*

Keating, AnaLouise & **PS509.L47T48 2002**
 Anzaldúa, Gloria (Editors)
This Bridge We Call Home: Radical Visions for Transformation.
Paper over Boards. Routledge. New York, NY. 2002. 624p.
ISBN:0-415-93681-0, ISBN13: 978-0-415-93681-1.
Dewey:810.8/09206643. LCCN:2002-012821.
Audience: **g,l,u,f.**

Kelsky, Karen **HQ1762.K45 2001**
Women on the Verge: Japanese Women, Western Dreams. Trade
Cloth. Duke University Press. Durham, NC. 2001. 272p.
Asia-Pacific Ser. ISBN:0-8223-2805-4, ISBN13:
978-0-8223-2805-6. Dewey:305.42/0952. LCCN:2001-033378.
Audience: **g,l,u,f.** *Choice, 2002.*

Kester-Shelton, Pamela **PN451**
Feminist Writers. Trade Cloth. Thomson Gale. Farmington Hills,
MI. 1996. 641p. ISBN:1-55862-217-9, ISBN13:
978-1-55862-217-3. Dewey:016.30542. LCCN:96-025679.
Audience: **l,u,f.** *Choice, 1997.*

Knight, Denise D. **PS217**
 (Editor)
Nineteenth-Century American Women Writers: A
Bio-Bibliographical Critical Sourcebook. Cloth Text. Greenwood
Publishing Group, Inc. Portsmouth, NH. 1997. 552p.
ISBN:0-313-29713-4, ISBN13: 978-0-313-29713-7.
Dewey:810.9/9287/09034 B. LCCN:96-035351.
Audience: **g,l,u.** *Choice, 1997.*

London, Bette Lynn **PR111.L66 1999**
Writing Double: Women's Literary Partnerships. Book, Other.
Cornell University Press. Ithaca, NY. 1999. 256p. Reading
Women Writing Ser. ISBN:0-8014-3563-3, ISBN13:
978-0-8014-3563-8. Dewey:820.9/9287. LCCN:99-037635.
Audience: **u,f.** *Choice, 2000.*

Madsen, Deborah L. **PS153.M4M33 2000**
Understanding Contemporary Chicana Literature. Trade Cloth.
University of South Carolina Press. Columbia, SC. 2001. 283p.
Understanding Contemporary American Literature Ser.
ISBN:1-57003-379-X, ISBN13: 978-1-57003-379-7.
Dewey:810.9/9287/0896872. LCCN:00-011471.
Audience: **u,f.** *Choice, 2001.*

McDowell, Deborah E. **PS374.N4M37 1995**
The Changing Same: Black Women's Literature, Criticism, and
Theory. Trade Cloth. Indiana University Press. Bloomington, IN.
1995. 224p. ISBN:0-253-33629-5, ISBN13: 978-0-253-33629-3.
Dewey:813.009/896073. LCCN:94-010663.
Audience: **g,l,u.** *Choice, 1995.*

Mikhail, Mona H. **PJ7538.M554 2003**
Seen and Heard: A Century of Arab Women in Literature and
Culture. Trade Cloth. Interlink Publishing Group, Inc.
Northampton, MA. 2004. 184p. Bestselling History and Politics
Ser. ISBN:1-56656-463-8, ISBN13: 978-1-56656-463-2.
Dewey:892.7/09352042/0904. LCCN:2003-014171.
Audience: **l,u,f.** *Choice, 2004.*

Millett, Kate **HQ1154.M5 2000**
Sexual Politics. Trade Paper. University of Illinois Press.
Champaign, IL. 2000. 424p. ISBN:0-252-06889-0, ISBN13:
978-0-252-06889-8. Dewey:301.41/2. LCCN:99-086827.
Audience: **l,u,f.** *B*

Minh-ha, Trinh T. **PN471.T75 1989**
Woman, Native, Other: Writing Postcoloniality and Feminism.
Trade Cloth. Indiana University Press. Bloomington, IN. 1989.
184p. ISBN:0-253-36603-8, ISBN13: 978-0-253-36603-0.
Dewey:809/.89287. LCCN:88-045455.
Audience: **l,u,f.**

Mitchell, Sally **PR468.G5M58 1995**
The New Girl: Girls' Culture in England, 1880-1915. Trade
Cloth. Columbia University Press. New York, NY. 1995. 270p.
ISBN:0-231-10246-1, ISBN13: 978-0-231-10246-9.
Dewey:820.9/352042. LCCN:95-010929.
Audience: **l,u,f.** *Choice, 1996.*

Moi, Toril **PN98.W64M65 2002**
Sexual/Textual Politics: Feminist Literary Theory. Ed. 2. UK-B
Format Paperback. Routledge. New York, NY. 2002. 248p. New
Accents Ser. ISBN:0-415-28012-5, ISBN13: 978-0-415-28012-9.
Dewey:801.95082. LCCN:2002-074319.
Audience: **u,f.**

Moraga, Cherríe & **PS509.F44T5 2001**
 Anzaldúa, Gloria (Editors)
This Bridge Called My Back: Writings by Radical Women of
Color. Ed. 3. Trade Paper. Third Woman Press. Oakland, CA.
2002. 370p. ISBN:0-943219-22-1, ISBN13: 978-0-943219-22-6.
Dewey:810.8/09287. LCCN:2001-053486.
Audience: **g,l,u,f.** *B*

Nfah-Abbenyi, Juliana **PL8010.N467 1997**
 M.
[e] Gender in African Women's Writing: Identity, Sexuality and
Difference. E-Book. Indiana University Press. Bloomington, IN.

1997. 224p. ISBN:0-253-21149-2, ISBN13: 978-0-253-21149-1. Dewey:809/.89287/096. LCCN:97-013083.

Audience: **u,f.** *Choice, 1998.*

Noble, Jean Bobby   **PN56.G45N63 2004**
Masculinities Without Men?: Female Masculinity in Twentieth-Century Fictions. Trade Paper. University of British Columbia Press. Vancouver, BC. 2004. 222p. Sexuality Studies Ser. ISBN:0-7748-0997-3, ISBN13: 978-0-7748-0997-9. Dewey:809/.93353. LCCN:2004-401596.

Audience: **g,l,u,f.**

Peterson, Linda H.   **PR788.W65P47 1999**
Traditions of Victorian Women's Autobiography: The Poetics and Politics of Life Writing. Trade Cloth. University Press of Virginia. Charlottesville, VA. 1999. 272p. Victorian Literature and Culture Ser. ISBN:0-8139-1883-9, ISBN13: 978-0-8139-1883-9. Dewey:828/.80809492072. LCCN:99-019832.

Audience: **g,l,u,f.** *Choice, 2000.*

Quintana, Alvina E.   **PS153.M4Q56 1996**
Home Girls: Chicana Literary Voices. Library Binding. Temple University Press. Philadelphia, PA. 1996. 208p. ISBN:1-56639-372-8, ISBN13: 978-1-56639-372-0. Dewey:810.9/9287/896872. LCCN:95-039751.

Audience: **l,u,f.**

Rebolledo, Tey D.   **PS153.M4R43 1995**
Women Singing in the Snow: A Cultural Analysis of Chicana Literature. Library Binding. University of Arizona Press. Tucson, AZ. 1995. 250p. ISBN:0-8165-1520-4, ISBN13: 978-0-8165-1520-2. Dewey:810.9/9287/0896872. LCCN:94-018740.

Audience: **u,f.** *Choice, 1995.*

Reyes, Angelita Dianne   **PN56.3.B55R49 2001**
Mothering Across Cultures: Postcolonial Representations. Trade Paper. University of Minnesota Press. Minneapolis, MN. 2001. 256p. ISBN:0-8166-2353-8, ISBN13: 978-0-8166-2353-2. Dewey:809/.933520396. LCCN:2001-003296.

Audience: **u,f.** *Choice, 2003.*

Saldivar-Hull, Sonia   **PS374.M4837 S25 2000**
Feminism on the Border: Chicana Gender Politics and Literature. Trade Cloth. University of California Press. Berkeley, CA. 2000. 226p. ISBN:0-520-20732-7, ISBN13: 978-0-520-20732-5. Dewey:813/.54099287. LCCN:99-053297.

Audience: **u,f.** *Choice, 2000.*

Schriber, Mary S.   **PS366.T73S37 1997**
Writing Home: American Women Abroad, 1830-1920. Trade Cloth. University Press of Virginia. Charlottesville, VA. 1997. 302p. ISBN:0-8139-1730-1, ISBN13: 978-0-8139-1730-6. Dewey:810.9/355. LCCN:96-053086.

Audience: **g,l,u,f.** *Choice, 1998.*

Smith, Barbara   **E185.86.S635 1999**
The Truth That Never Hurts: Writings on Race, Gender and Freedom. Trade Cloth. Rutgers University Press. Piscataway, NJ. 2003. 232p. Lesbian and Gay Studies ISBN:0-8135-2573-X, ISBN13: 978-0-8135-2573-0. Dewey:305.4/8/8. LCCN:98-018668.

Audience: **l,u,f.** *Choice, 1999.*

Sánchez, Marta Ester   **PS153.M4.S26 1985**
ⓔ Contemporary Chicana Poetry: A Critical Approach to an Emerging Literature. E-Book. NetLibrary, Inc. Boulder, CO. 1985. ISBN:0-585-34175-3, ISBN13: 978-0-585-34175-0. Dewey:811/.54/0986872073.

Audience: **u,f.**

Trites, Roberta   **PN3426.C5T75 1997**
Seelinger
ⓔ Waking Sleeping Beauty: Feminist Voices in Children's Novels. E-Book. University of Iowa Press. Iowa City, IA. 1997. ISBN:1-58729-239-4, ISBN13: 978-1-58729-239-2. Dewey:809/.89282/082.

Audience: **g,l,u,f.**

Vorlicky, Robert   **PS338.M37V67 1995**
Act Like a Man: Challenging Masculinities in American Drama. Trade Paper. University of Michigan Press. Chicago, IL. 1994. 400p. ISBN:0-472-06572-6, ISBN13: 978-0-472-06572-1. Dewey:812/.5409353. LCCN:94-038076.

Audience: **l,u,f.** *Choice, 1995.*

Warhol, Robyn R. &   **PN98.W64F366 1997**
Herndl, Diane P. (Editors)
Feminisms: An Anthology of Literary Theory and Criticism. Ed. 2. Trade Cloth. Rutgers University Press. Piscataway, NJ. 1997. 1,150p. ISBN:0-8135-2389-3, ISBN13: 978-0-8135-2389-7. Dewey:809.8/9/287. LCCN:96-031072.

Audience: **u,f.** *Choice, 1998.*

Whitson, Kathy J.   **PN471.W455 2004**
Encyclopedia of Feminist Literature. Cloth Text. Greenwood Publishing Group, Inc. Portsmouth, NH. 2004. 312p. ISBN:0-313-32731-9, ISBN13: 978-0-313-32731-5. Dewey:809/.89287. LCCN:2004-042478.

Audience: **g,l,u,f.** *Choice, 2005.*

Wilcox, Helen (Editor)   **PR113 .W65 1996**
Women and Literature in Britain, 1500-1700. Trade Paper. Cambridge University Press. New York, NY. 1996. 329p. ISBN:0-521-46777-2, ISBN13: 978-0-521-46777-3. Dewey:820.9/9287/09031. LCCN:95-051404.

Audience: **l,u,f.** *Choice, 1997.*

Wilcox, John C.   **PQ6055.W55 1997**
Women Poets of Spain, 1860-1990: Toward a Gynocentric Vision. Trade Paper. University of Illinois Press. Champaign, IL. 1997. 392p. ISBN:0-252-06559-X, ISBN13: 978-0-252-06559-0. Dewey:861.009/9287. LCCN:96-009948.

Audience: **l,u,f.** *Choice, 1997.*

Williamson, Margaret   **PA4409.W55 1995**
Sappho's Immortal Daughters. Trade Cloth. Harvard University Press. Cambridge, MA. 1995. 208p. ISBN:0-674-78912-1, ISBN13: 978-0-674-78912-8. Dewey:884/.01. LCCN:95-020124.

Audience: **g,l,u,f.** *Choice, 1996.*

Wilson, Carol Shiner &   **PR457.R4556 1994**
Haefner, Joel (Editors)
Re-Visioning Romanticism: British Women Writers, 1776-1837. Book, Other. University of Pennsylvania Press. Philadelphia, PA. 1994. 344p. ISBN:0-8122-1421-8, ISBN13: 978-0-8122-1421-5. Dewey:820.9/9287/09034. LCCN:94-027188.

Audience: **u,f.** *Choice, 1995.*

Woolf, Virginia   **PR6045.O72Z474 1991**
A Room of One's Own. Cloth over Boards. Harcourt Trade Publishers. New York, NY. 1991. 132p. HBJ Book Ser.

ISBN:0-15-178733-6, ISBN13: 978-0-15-178733-3.
Dewey:823/.912. LCCN:91-017953.

Audience: **g,l,u,f.**

Wu, Qingyun   **PN56.W6F46 1995**
Female Rule in Chinese and English Literary Utopias. Cloth
Text. Syracuse University Press. Syracuse, NY. 1995. 288p.
Utopianism and Communitarianism Ser. ISBN:0-8156-2623-1,
ISBN13: 978-0-8156-2623-7. Dewey:820.9/352/042.
LCCN:94-024666.

Audience: **l,u,f.** *Choice, 1996.*

Yamamoto, Traise   **PS153.J34Y36 1999**
Masking Selves, Making Subjects: Japanese American Women,
Identity, and the Body. Trade Paper. University of California
Press. Berkeley, CA. 1999. 320p. ISBN:0-520-21034-4, ISBN13:
978-0-520-21034-9. Dewey:810.9/9287/089956.
LCCN:98-014154.

Audience: **u,f.** *Choice, 1999.*

Young, Elizabeth   **PS217.C58Y68 1999**
Disarming the Nation: Women's Writing and the American Civil
War. Trade Cloth. University of Chicago Press. Chicago, IL.

1999. 405p. Women in Culture and Society Ser.
ISBN:0-226-96087-0, ISBN13: 978-0-226-96087-6.
Dewey:810.9/358. LCCN:99-031518.

Audience: **u,f.** *Choice, 2000.*

Zeidan, Joseph T.   **PJ7525.2.Z45 1995**
Arab Women Novelists: The Formative Years and Beyond.
Paper Text. State University of New York Press. Albany, NY.
1995. 363p. SUNY Series in Middle Eastern Studies
ISBN:0-7914-2172-4, ISBN13: 978-0-7914-2172-7.
Dewey:892/.736099287. LCCN:94-001007.

Audience: **l,u,f.** *Choice, 1995.*

Zlotnick, Susan   **PR111**
Women, Writing, and the Industrial Revolution. Trade Paper.
Johns Hopkins University Press. Baltimore, MD. 2001. 336p.
ISBN:0-8018-6649-9, ISBN13: 978-0-8018-6649-4.
Dewey:820/.9/9287.

Audience: **u,f.** *Choice, 1999.*

LATINO STUDIES

The materials identified here are approrpiate for the undergradaute study of the history and culture of Chicanos, Mexican-Americans, Puerto Ricans, Cuban-Americans, and other Latinos in the United States. The section is broadly interdisciplinary in approach, and attempts to collect those titles which might be neglected by other, related disciplines (e.g., American Literature or Scoiology), a marked problem in BCL3.

While selections are primarily of recent publication, this section does include a limited number of classic works (in and out of print). Even though a significant percentage of resources pertain to the Chicano/a experience in the U.S., the every effort was made to strive for balance among the groups.

— Ana Maria Cobos and Rafaella Castr

General Works > Reference Works

E184.S75

The Hispanic Databook: Statistics for All U.S. Counties and Cities with over 10,000 Population. Ed. 2. Trade Cloth, CD-ROM. Grey House Publishing. Millerton, NY. 2004. 800p. ISBN:1-59237-008-X, ISBN13: 978-1-59237-008-5. Dewey:305.868.

Audience: **u,f.**　*Choice, 2004.*

Chabrán, Richard &　　　　**E184.S75L357 1996**
Chabrán, Rafael (Editors)
The Latino Encyclopedia, Set. Trade Cloth. Marshall Cavendish Corporation. Tarrytown, NY. 1996. 1,900p. ISBN:0-7614-0125-3, ISBN13: 978-0-7614-0125-4. Dewey:973/.0468/003. LCCN:95-013144.

Audience: **g,l.**　*Choice, 1996.*

Glasrud, Bruce A. & De　　　**Z1361.M4G57 2003**
Leon, Arnoldo
Bibliophiling Tejano Scholarship: Secondary Sources on Hispanic Texas. Trade Cloth. Sul Ross State University, Center for Big Bend Studies. Alpine, TX. 2004. 472p. Center for Big Bend Studies Occasional Papers, Vol. 8 ISBN:0-9707709-1-X, ISBN13: 978-0-9707709-1-2. Dewey:379. LCCN:2004-555362.

Audience: **u,f.**　*Choice, 2004.*

Graham, Joe S. (Compiled by)　　　　　**E184**
Hispanic-American Material Culture: A Directory of Collections, Sites, Archives and Festivals in the United States and Canada. Cloth Text. Greenwood Publishing Group, Inc. Portsmouth, NH. 1989. 281p. Material Culture Directories Ser., No. 2 ISBN:0-313-24789-7, ISBN13: 978-0-313-24789-7. Dewey:306/.4/0896872073. LCCN:89-001922.

Audience: **u,f.**　*Choice, 1989.*

Kanellos, Nicolás (Editor)　　　**E184.S75H557 2003**
The Hispanic American Almanac: A Reference Work on Hispanics in the United States. Ed. 3. Trade Cloth. Thomson Gale. Farmington Hills, MI. 2002. xxvii, 886p. ISBN:0-7876-2518-3, ISBN13: 978-0-7876-2518-4. Dewey:973/.0468. LCCN:2002-010070.

Audience: **g.**　*Choice, 2003.*

Kanellos, Nicolás　　　　**E184.S75.K36 1997**
Hispanic American Firsts: 500 Years of Extraordinary Achievement. Trade Cloth. Thomson Gale. Farmington Hills, MI. 1997. 372p. ISBN:0-7876-0517-4, ISBN13: 978-0-7876-0517-9. Dewey:973/.0468073. LCCN:97-010499.

Audience: **g.**　*Choice, 1998.*

Kanellos, Nicolás &　　　　**E184.S75H365**
Fabregat, Claudio E. (Editors)
Handbook of Hispanic Cultures of the U. S., Set. Trade Cloth. Arte Publico Press. Houston, TX. 1994. ISBN:1-55885-103-8, ISBN13: 978-1-55885-103-0. Dewey:973/.0468.

Audience: **g,l.**

Kanellos, Nicolás &　　　　**Z6953.5.S66K36 2000**
Martell, Helvetia
Hispanic Periodicals in the U. S., Origins To 1960: A Brief History and Comprehensive Bibliography. Trade Cloth. Arte Publico Press. Houston, TX. 2000. 368p. Recovering the U.S.-Hispanic Literary Heritage Ser. ISBN:1-55885-253-0, ISBN13: 978-1-55885-253-2. Dewey:015.73/034/08968. LCCN:98-028341.

Audience: **u,f.**　*Choice, 2001.*

Meier, Matt S. &　　　　　　**E184**
Gutierrez, Margo
The Mexican American Experience: An Encyclopedia. Cloth Text. Greenwood Publishing Group, Inc. Portsmouth, NH. 2003. 488p. ISBN:0-313-31643-0, ISBN13: 978-0-313-31643-2. Dewey:973/.046872/003. LCCN:2003-052845.

Audience: **g,l.**　*Choice, 2004.*

Meier, Matt S., et al.　　　　　　**E184**
Notable Latino Americans: A Biographical Dictionary. Conchita F. Serri & Richard A. Garcia (Authors). Cloth Text. Greenwood Publishing Group, Inc. Portsmouth, NH. 1997. 448p. ISBN:0-313-29105-5, ISBN13: 978-0-313-29105-0. Dewey:920/.009268. LCCN:96-027392.

Audience: **g,l.**　*Choice, 1997.*

Meyer, Nicholas E.　　　　　**E184.S75M49 2001**
The Biographical Dictionary of Hispanic Americans. Ed. 2. Trade Cloth. Facts On File, Inc. New York, NY. 2001. 336p. Facts on File Library of American History ISBN:0-8160-4330-2, ISBN13: 978-0-8160-4330-9. Dewey:920/.009268073 B. LCCN:00-049046.

Audience: **g,l.**　*Choice, 2002.*

Méndez-Méndez,　　　　　　**CT329**
Serafin, et al.
Notable Caribbeans and Caribbean Americans: A Biographical Dictionary. Gail A. Cueto & Neysa Rodríguez-Deynes (Authors). Cloth Text. Greenwood Publishing Group, Inc. Portsmouth, NH. 2003. 488p. ISBN:0-313-31443-8, ISBN13: 978-0-313-31443-8. Dewey:920.0729. LCCN:2001-033695.

Audience: **g,l.**　*Choice, 2004.*

Oboler, Suzanne &　　　　　**E184.S75**
González, Deena J. (Editors)
Encyclopedia of Latinos and Latinas in the United States. Trade Cloth. Oxford University Press, Inc. New York, NY. 2005. 2344p. ISBN:0-19-515600-5, ISBN13: 978-0-19-515600-3. Dewey:973/.0468/003. LCCN:2005-007764.

Audience: **g,l.**　*Choice, 2006.*

Stavans, Ilan &　　　　　**E184.S75E587 2005**
Augenbraum, Harold
Encyclopedia Latina: History, Culture, and Society in the United States. Trade Cloth. Scholastic Library Publishing. Danbury, CT. 2005. ISBN:0-7172-5815-7, ISBN13: 978-0-7172-5815-4. Dewey:973/.0468/003. LCCN:2004-023603.

Audience: **g,l.**　*Choice, 2005.*

General Works > Discipline and Borderland Studies

E1

☐ Centro de Estudios Puertorriqueños.
http://www.centropr.org/
Hunter College, City University of New York.

Audience: **l,u,f.**

F1776

☐ CHC Digital: Online Resources for Cuban and Cuban-American Studies from the Cuban Heritage Collection. http://digital.library.miami.edu/chcdigital/ University of Miami Libraries.

Audience: **g,l,u,f.**

E184.M5

☐ Chicano Research Collection.
http://www.asu.edu/lib/archives/chicano.htm
Arizona State University Libraries.

Audience: **l,u,f.**

LB2300

☐ CS: UCLA Chicano Studies Research Center.
http://www.chicano.ucla.edu/
UCLA Chicano Studies Research Center.

Audience: **l,u,f.**

☐ Cuban Research Institute.
http://lacc.fiu.edu/centers_institutes/?body=centers_cri&
rightbody=centers_cri

Audience: **l,u,f.**

F1934

☐ Dominican Studies Institute.
http://www.ccny.cuny.edu/dsi/index.html
The City College of New York.

Audience: **l,u,f.**

F1408

☐ IUPLR: Inter-University Program for Latino Research.
http://www.nd.edu/~iuplr/
Inter-University Program for Latino Research.

Audience: **l,u,f.**

Andreas, Peter   **HJ6690.A7 2000**
Border Games: Policing the U.S.- Mexico Divide. Book, Other.
Cornell University Press. Ithaca, NY. 2000. 192p. Studies in
Political Economy ISBN:0-8014-3796-2, ISBN13:
978-0-8014-3796-0. Dewey:363.45/0972/1. LCCN:00-024022.

Audience: **u,f.** *Choice, 2001.*

Barraza, Santa C. &   **N6537.B2245S26 2001**
  Herrera-Sobek, María
Santa Barraza, Artist of the Borderlands. Trade Cloth. Texas
A&M University Press. College Station, TX. 2000. xx, 114p.
Rio Grande/Rio Bravo Ser., Vol. 5 ISBN:0-89096-906-X,
ISBN13: 978-0-89096-906-9. Dewey:759.13. LCCN:00-010359.

Audience: **l,u.** *Choice, 2001.*

Chabram-Dernersesian,   **E184.M5C385 2005**
  Angie (Editor)
Chicana/o Cultural Studies Reader. Ed. 2. Trade Cloth.
Routledge. New York, NY. 2006. 552p. ISBN:0-415-23515-4,
ISBN13: 978-0-415-23515-0. Dewey:305.868/72073.
LCCN:2005-001402.

Audience: **u,f.**

Darder, Antonia &   **E184.S75L3627 1998**
  Torres, Rodolfo D. (Editors)
The Latino Studies Reader: Culture, Politics and Society. Trade
Paper. Blackwell Publishing, Inc. Malden, MA. 1998. 320p.
ISBN:1-55786-987-1, ISBN13: 978-1-55786-987-6.
Dewey:305.868073. LCCN:97-014134.

Audience: **l,u,f.**

Davidson, Miriam &   **HN120.N64D38 2000**
  Scott, Jeffry
Lives on the Line: Dispatches from the U. S.-Mexican Border.
Trade Cloth. University of Arizona Press. Tucson, AZ. 2000.
211p. ISBN:0-8165-1998-6, ISBN13: 978-0-8165-1998-9.
Dewey:306/.0972/62. LCCN:00-008566.

Audience: **u,f.** *Choice, 2001.*

De La Torre, Adela &   **E184.M5.T67 1993**
  Pesquera, Beatriz M. (Editors)
Building with Our Hands: Directions in Chicana Studies. Trade
Cloth. University of California Press. Berkeley, CA. 1993. 246p.
ISBN:0-520-07089-5, ISBN13: 978-0-520-07089-9.
Dewey:305.4886872073. LCCN:91-039227.

Audience: **u,f.** *Choice, 1993.*

Dunn, Timothy J.   **F787.D46 1996**
The Militarization of the U. S.-Mexico Border, 1978-1992:
Low-Intensity Conflict Doctrine Comes Home. Trade Cloth.
University of Texas Press. Austin, TX. 1996. 323p. CMAS
Border and Migration Studies Ser. ISBN:0-292-71579-X,
ISBN13: 978-0-292-71579-0. Dewey:972/.1. LCCN:94-042964.

Audience: **u,f.** *Choice, 1996.*

Fregoso, Rosa Linda   **F790.M5 F75 2003**
Mexicana Encounters: The Making of Social Identities on the
Borderlands. Trade Cloth. University of California Press.
Berkeley, CA. 2003. 246p. American Crossroads Ser., Vol. 12
ISBN:0-520-22997-5, ISBN13: 978-0-520-22997-6.
Dewey:305.48/868720721. LCCN:2003-000594.

Audience: **u,f.** *Choice, 2004.*

Garcia, Alma (Editor)   **HQ1421.C52 1997**
Chicana Feminist Thought: The Basic Historical Writings. UK-B
Format Paperback. Routledge. New York, NY. 1997. 344p.
ISBN:0-415-91801-4, ISBN13: 978-0-415-91801-5.
Dewey:305.48/868/72073. LCCN:96-049916.

Audience: **u,f.**

Garcia, Juan R.   **E184.M5**
Emerging Themes in Mexican American Research. Trade Paper.
University of Arizona, Mexican American Studies & Research
Center. Tucson, AZ. 1994. ISBN:0-939363-04-6, ISBN13:
978-0-939363-04-9. Dewey:305.86872073.

Audience: **u,f.**

García, Mario T.   **E184.M5B7 2000**
  (Editor)
Bridging Cultures: An Introduction to Chicano/Latino Studies.
Perfect. Kendall/Hunt Publishing Company. Dubuque, IA. 2000.
xv, 234p. ISBN:0-7872-7077-6, ISBN13: 978-0-7872-7077-3.
Dewey:973/.046872. LCCN:00-105534.

Audience: **l,f.**

Griffith, James S.   **F815 .G75**
A Shared Space: Folklife in the Arizona-Sonora Borderlands.
Trade Cloth. Utah State University Press. Logan, UT. 1995.
224p. ISBN:0-87421-198-0, ISBN13: 978-0-87421-198-6.
Dewey:306/.09791/7.

Audience: **u,f.**

Kaup, Monika   **PS366.M49K38 2001**
Rewriting North American Borders in Chicano and Chicana
Narrative. Trade Cloth. Peter Lang Publishing, Inc. New York,
NY. 2001. 368p. ISBN:0-8204-4956-3, ISBN13:
978-0-8204-4956-2. Dewey:818/.508098687. LCCN:00-039076.

Audience: **u,f.**

Kearney, Milo &   **F787.K435 2001**
  Medrano, Manuel
Medieval Culture and the Mexican American Borderlands. Cloth
Text. Texas A&M University Press. College Station, TX. 2002.
256p. Rio Grande/Rio Bravo Ser., Vol. 6 ISBN:1-58544-132-5,
ISBN13: 978-1-58544-132-7. Dewey:972/.1.
LCCN:2001-002736.

Audience: **u,f.** *Choice, 2002.*

León, Luis D.   BX1407.M48 L46 2004
La Llorona's Children: Religion, Life, and Death in the U.
S.-Mexican Borderlands. Trade Cloth. University of California
Press. Berkeley, CA. 2004. 296p. ISBN:0-520-22350-0, ISBN13:
978-0-520-22350-9. Dewey:277.3/083/0896872.
LCCN:2002-019426.

Audience: **u,f.** *Choice, 2005.*

Maril, Robert Lee   JV6483.M298 2004
Patrolling Chaos: The United States Border Patrol in Deep
South Texas. Trade Cloth. Texas Tech University Press.
Lubbock, TX. 2004. x, 368p. ISBN:0-89672-537-5, ISBN13:
978-0-89672-537-9. Dewey:363.28/5/097644.
LCCN:2004-009454.

Audience: **u,f.** *Choice, 2005.*

Martínez, Oscar J.   F787.M36 1994
Border People: Life and Society in the U.S.-Mexico
Borderlands. Trade Paper. University of Arizona Press. Tucson,
AZ. 1994. 352p. ISBN:0-8165-1414-3, ISBN13:
978-0-8165-1414-4. Dewey:972/.1. LCCN:93-045298.

Audience: **l,u.**

Martínez, Oscar J.   F787
Troublesome Border. Trade Paper. University of Arizona Press.
Tucson, AZ. 1989. 177p. Profmex Ser. ISBN:0-8165-1104-7,
ISBN13: 978-0-8165-1104-4. Dewey:972/.1. LCCN:87-034294.

Audience: **u,f.** *Choice, 1988.*

Nevins, Joseph   JV6483.N47 2002
Operation Gatekeeper: The Rise of the 'Illegal Alien' and
Remaking of U. S. - Mexico Boundary. Paper over Boards.
Routledge. New York, NY. 2001. 256p. ISBN:0-415-93104-5,
ISBN13: 978-0-415-93104-5. Dewey:363.28/5/0973.
LCCN:2001-034989.

Audience: **u,f.** *Choice, 2002.*

Noriega, Chon A.   E184.M5C458 2001
 (Editor)
The Chicano Studies Reader: An Anthology of Aztlan
1970-2000. Trade Paper. UCLA Chicano Studies Research
Center Press. Los Angeles, CA. 2001. 320p. Aztlan Anthology
Ser., Vol. 2 ISBN:0-89551-097-9, ISBN13: 978-0-89551-097-6.
Dewey:973/.046872. LCCN:2001-055643.

Audience: **l,u,f.**

Paredes, Americo   GR110.T5P28 1993
Folklore and Culture on the Texas-Mexican Border. Richard
Bauman (Editor). Trade Cloth. University of Texas Press.
Austin, TX. 1993. 288p. ISBN:0-292-72472-1, ISBN13:
978-0-292-72472-3. Dewey:398/.09764. LCCN:91-043059.

Audience: **l,u.**

Paredes, Américo   M1668.4
A Texas-Mexican Cancionero: Folksongs of the Lower Border.
Manuel Peña (Foreword by). Trade Paper. University of Texas
Press. Austin, TX. 1995. 226p. ISBN:0-292-76558-4, ISBN13:
978-0-292-76558-0. Dewey:976.4. LCCN:94-033615.

Audience: **u,f.**

Peña, Devon G.   HD8119.M49P46 1997
🅔 The Terror of the Machine: Technology, Work, Gender, and
Ecology on the U.S.-Mexico Border. E-Book. NetLibrary, Inc.
Boulder, CO. 1997. ISBN:0-585-23437-X, ISBN13:
978-0-585-23437-3. Dewey:331.4/87042/09721.

Audience: **u,f.**

Quinonez, Naomi   E184.M5D34 2001
 Helena
🅔 Decolonial Voices: Chicana and Chicano Cultural Studies in
the 21st Century. Arturo J. Aldama (Editor). E-Book. Indiana
University Press. Bloomington, IN. 2002. 413p.
ISBN:0-253-34014-4, ISBN13: 978-0-253-34014-6.
Dewey:305.868/72073. LCCN:2001-039495.

Audience: **u,f.** *Choice, 2003, 2002.*

Rebert, Paula   F786.R43 2001
La Gran Linea: Mapping the United States - Mexico Boundary,
1849-1857. Trade Cloth. University of Texas Press. Austin, TX.
2001. 279p. ISBN:0-292-77110-X, ISBN13: 978-0-292-77110-9.
Dewey:911/.721. LCCN:00-041771.

Audience: **l,u.** *Choice, 2001.*

Saldívar, Jose D.   F787.S19 1997
Border Matters: Remapping American Cultural Studies. Trade
Paper. University of California Press. Berkeley, CA. 1997. 266p.
American Crossroads Ser. ISBN:0-520-20682-7, ISBN13:
978-0-520-20682-3. Dewey:306/.0972/1. LCCN:96-049209.

Audience: **u,f.**

Schroer, Craig
🖵 Border Cultures: Conjunto Music.
http://www.lib.utexas.edu/benson/border/index.html
Benson Latin American Collection, University of Texas.

Audience: **g,l,u,f.**

Spener, David & Staudt,   F787.U66 1998
 Kathleen (Editors)
The U.S.-Mexico Border: Transcending Divisions, Contesting
Identities. Library Binding. Lynne Rienner Publishers, Inc.
Boulder, CO. 1998. 264p. ISBN:1-55587-796-6, ISBN13:
978-1-55587-796-5. Dewey:303.48/2730721. LCCN:98-029810.

Audience: **u,f.**

Staudt, Kathleen   HD2346.U52M497 1998
Free Trade?: Informal Economies at the U.S.-Mexican Border.
Trade Cloth. Temple University Press. Philadelphia, PA. 1998.
256p. ISBN:1-56639-567-4, ISBN13: 978-1-56639-567-0.
Dewey:338.0972/1. LCCN:97-012414.

Audience: **u,f.** *Choice, 1998.*

Staudt, Kathleen A. &   HM671.S73 2002
 Coronado, Irasema
Fronteras No Mas: Toward Social Justice at the U. S.-Mexico
Border. Cloth over Boards. Palgrave Macmillan. New York, NY.
2002. 224p. ISBN:0-312-23939-4, ISBN13: 978-0-312-23939-8.
Dewey:303.3/72/09721. LCCN:2002-068413.

Audience: **u,f.** *Choice, 2003.*

Stevens-Arroyo,   F1970.8.T68 1987
 Anthony M. & Sanchez, Maria E.
Toward a Renaissance of Puerto Rican Studies in University
Education. Trade Cloth. Eastern European Monographs.
Bradenton, FL. 1987. 165p. ISBN:0-88033-956-X, ISBN13:
978-0-88033-956-8. Dewey:972.95/007/1173. LCCN:87-060629.

Audience: **u,f.** *Choice, 1988.*

Torrans, Thomas   F786.T68 2000
Forging the Tortilla Curtain: Cultural Drift and Change along
the United States-Mexico Boarderlands from the Spanish
Conquest to the Present. Trade Cloth. Texas Christian University
Press. Fort Worth, TX. 2000. xi, 424p. ISBN:0-87565-231-X,
ISBN13: 978-0-87565-231-3. Dewey:972/.1. LCCN:00-030245.

Audience: **u,f.** *Choice, 2001.*

Torrans, Thomas   PS277 .T67 2002
The Magic Curtain: The Mexican-American Border in Fiction,
Film, and Song. Barbara Mathews Whitehead (Illustrator). Trade
Cloth. Texas Christian University Press. Fort Worth, TX. 2002.
312p. ISBN:0-87565-257-3, ISBN13: 978-0-87565-257-3.
Dewey:810.9327. LCCN:2002-002298.
Audience: **u,f.** *Choice, 2003, 2002.*

Velez-Ibanez, Carlos G.   F790.M5V45 1996
Border Visions: Mexican Cultures of the Southwest United
States. Trade Cloth. University of Arizona Press. Tucson, AZ.
1996. xii, 360p. ISBN:0-8165-1422-4, ISBN13:
978-0-8165-1422-9. Dewey:305.868/72073. LCCN:96-010100.
Audience: **l,u,f.** *Choice, 1997.*

Vila, Pablo   HN120.C48V54 2000
Crossing Borders, Reinforcing Borders: Social Categories,
Metaphors, and Narrative Identities on the U.S.-Mexico Frontier.
Trade Cloth. University of Texas Press. Austin, TX. 2000. 304p.
Inter-America Ser. ISBN:0-292-78739-1, ISBN13:
978-0-292-78739-1. Dewey:306/.0972/16. LCCN:99-046270.
Audience: **u,f.**

Webster, Grady L. &   QK142.C53 2001
  Bahre, Conrad J.
Changing Plant Life of la Frontera: Observations on Vegetation
in the United States/Mexico Borderlands. Trade Cloth.
University of New Mexico Press. Albuquerque, NM. 2001.
260p. ISBN:0-8263-2239-5, ISBN13: 978-0-8263-2239-5.
Dewey:581.972/1. LCCN:00-010451.
Audience: **u,f.** *Choice, 2001.*

Young, Elliott   F786.C67 2004
Continental Crossroads: Remapping U. S.-Mexico Borderlands
History. Samuel Truett (Editor). Trade Cloth. Duke University
Press. Durham, NC. 2004. 336p. American Encounters/Global
Interactions Ser. ISBN:0-8223-3353-8, ISBN13:
978-0-8223-3353-1. LCCN:2004-004074.
Audience: **u,f.** *Choice, 2005.*

General Works > Biography

Acosta, Oscar Z.   CT275.A186A3 1989
The Autobiography of a Brown Buffalo. Trade Paper. Knopf
Publishing Group. New York, NY. 1989. 208p.
ISBN:0-679-72213-0, ISBN13: 978-0-679-72213-7.
Dewey:978/.0046872073 B. LCCN:88-040356.
Audience: **l,u.**

Acosta, Oscar Z.   CT275.A186A3 1989
The Revolt of the Cockroach People. Trade Paper. Knopf
Publishing Group. New York, NY. 1989. 272p.
ISBN:0-679-72212-2, ISBN13: 978-0-679-72212-0.
Dewey:979.4/9405/0924 B. LCCN:88-040355.
Audience: **l,u.**

Aldama   PS3559.S44 Z54 2005
Dancing with Ghosts: A Critical Biography of Arturo Islas.
Trade Cloth. University of California Press. Berkeley, CA. 2004.
242p. ISBN:0-520-23188-0, ISBN13: 978-0-520-23188-7.
Dewey:818/.5409 B. LCCN:2004-011381.
Audience: **u,f.**

Benmayor, Rina, et al.   HQ1522 .S76 1987
Stories to Live By: Continuity and Change in Three Generations
of Puerto Rican Women. Ana Juarbe, Celia Alvarez & Blanca
Vazuqez (Authors). Library Binding. Hunter College, Centro de

Estudios Puertorriquenos. New York, NY. 1987. 67p.
ISBN:1-878483-02-1, ISBN13: 978-1-878483-02-7.
Dewey:305.4/097295.
Audience: **l,u.**

Cofer, Judith Ortiz   PS3565.R7737Z477
Silent Dancing: A Partial Remembrance of a Puerto Rican
Childhood. Ed. 2. Trade Paper. Arte Publico Press. Houston,
TX. 1991. 168p. ISBN:1-55885-015-5, ISBN13:
978-1-55885-015-6. Dewey:818/.5403 B. LCCN:89-077428.
Audience: **l,u.**

De La Campa, Roman   E184.C97D4 2001
Cuba on My Mind: Journeys to a Severed Nation. Trade Cloth.
Verso Books. London, 2002. 192p. ISBN:1-85984-790-0,
ISBN13: 978-1-85984-790-9. Dewey:973/.04687291/0092 B.
LCCN:00-054999.
Audience: **l,u.**

Ferriss, Susan &   HD6509.C68 F47 1997
  Sandoval, Ricardo
The Fight in the Fields: Cesar Chavez and the Farmworkers
Movement. Trade Paper. Harcourt Trade Publishers. New York,
NY. 1998. 352p. ISBN:0-15-600598-0, ISBN13:
978-0-15-600598-2. Dewey:331.8813092.
Audience: **l,u.**

Fischkin, Barbara   E184.D6F57 1997
Muddy Cup: A Dominican Family Comes of Age in a New
America. Trade Cloth. Simon & Schuster. New York, NY. 1997.
368p. ISBN:0-684-80704-1, ISBN13: 978-0-684-80704-1.
Dewey:974.7/1004687293. LCCN:97-003196.
Audience: **l,u.**

Galarza, Ernesto   E184.M5G3 2000
Barrio Boy. Trade Cloth. Holt, Rinehart & Winston. Austin, TX.
2000. 321p. HRW Library ISBN:0-03-055987-1, ISBN13:
978-0-03-055987-7. Dewey:301.45/16. LCCN:2001-271307.
Audience: **g,l,u.**

Garcia, Nasario   F804.L3G37 2005
Old Las Vegas: Hispanic Memories from the New Mexico
Meadowlands. Trade Cloth. Texas Tech University Press.
Lubbock, TX. 2005. xiv, 302p. ISBN:0-89672-539-1, ISBN13:
978-0-89672-539-3. Dewey:305.868/073/0978955.
LCCN:2004-014193.
Audience: **l,u.** *Choice, 2005.*

García, Mario T.   PQ7109.5.L43G37 2000
Luis Leal: An Auto/Biography. Trade Cloth. University of Texas
Press. Austin, TX. 2000. 230p. ISBN:0-292-72828-X, ISBN13:
978-0-292-72828-8. Dewey:860.9 B. LCCN:99-052635.
Audience: **u,f.**

García, Mario T.   HD8073.C67.G37
Memories of Chicano History: The Life and Narrative of Bert
Corona. David Montgomery (Foreword by). Trade Paper.
University of California Press. Berkeley, CA. 1995. 388p.
Latinos in American Society and Culture Ser., Vol. 2
ISBN:0-520-20152-3, ISBN13: 978-0-520-20152-1.
Dewey:323.116872.
Audience: **l,u.** *Choice, 1994.*

Glasser, Ruth   ML3481
My Music Is My Flag: Puerto Rican Musicians and Their New
York Communities, 1917-1940. Trade Paper. University of
California Press. Berkeley, CA. 1997. 278p. Latinos in
American Society and Culture Ser., Vol. 3 ISBN:0-520-20890-0,

ISBN13: 978-0-520-20890-2. Dewey:780/.8968729507471.
LCCN:94-009015.

Audience: **l,u.** *Choice, 1995.*

Grillo, Evelio **E184.C97G73 2000**
Black Cuban, Black American: A Memoir. Kenya
Dworkin-Mendez (Introduction by). Trade Paper. Arte Publico
Press. Houston, TX. 2000. 152p. Hispanic Civil Rights Ser.
ISBN:1-55885-293-X, ISBN13: 978-1-55885-293-8.
Dewey:973/.04687291. LCCN:00-020774.

Audience: **l,u.** *Choice, 2001.*

Griswold del Castillo, **HD6509.C48G75 1995**
Richard & Garcia, Richard A.
Cesar Chávez: A Triumph of Spirit. Trade Cloth. University of
Oklahoma Press. Norman, OK. 1995. 224p. Oklahoma Western
Biographies Ser., Vol. 11 ISBN:0-8061-2758-9, ISBN13:
978-0-8061-2758-3. Dewey:331.88. LCCN:95-015230.

Audience: **g,l,u.** *Choice, 1996.*

Gutierrez, Jose Angel **F394.C83G88 1998**
The Making of a Chicano Militant: Lessons from Cristal. Trade
Paper. University of Wisconsin Press. Chicago, IL. 1999. 352p.
Wisconsin Studies in American Autobiography
ISBN:0-299-15984-1, ISBN13: 978-0-299-15984-9.
Dewey:976.4/437 B. LCCN:98-013866.

Audience: **u,f.** *Choice, 1999.*

Hammerback, John C. **HD6509.C48H36 1998**
& Jensen, Richard J.
The Rhetorical Career of Cesar Chavez. Trade Cloth. Texas
A&M University Press. College Station, TX. 1998. 320p.
ISBN:0-89096-808-X, ISBN13: 978-0-89096-808-6.
Dewey:331.88/13/092. LCCN:97-032794.

Audience: **l,u.** *Choice, 1998.*

Hart, Dianne W. **F869.L89N53 1997**
Undocumented in L. A.: An Immigrant's Story. Trade Cloth.
Rowman & Littlefield Publishers, Inc. Lanham, MD. 1997.
136p. Latin American Silhouettes Ser. ISBN:0-8420-2648-7,
ISBN13: 978-0-8420-2648-2. Dewey:306.85/08968/7285079.
LCCN:96-050993.

Audience: **l,u.** *Choice, 1997.*

Herrera, Andrea **E184.C97R39 2001**
O'Reilly
ReMembering Cuba: Legacy of a Diaspora. Trade Cloth.
University of Texas Press. Austin, TX. 2001. 376p.
ISBN:0-292-73146-9, ISBN13: 978-0-292-73146-2.
Dewey:305.868/7291073. LCCN:00-061606.

Audience: **l,u.** *Choice, 2002.*

Johnson, Kevin R. **E184.M5J58 1998**
How Did You Get to Be Mexican?: A White/Brown Man's
Search for Identity. Trade Cloth. Temple University Press.
Philadelphia, PA. 1999. 256p. ISBN:1-56639-650-6, ISBN13:
978-1-56639-650-9. Dewey:[B]. LCCN:98-011811.

Audience: **l,u.**

Keller, Gary D. **PN1995.9.H47K46 1997**
A Biographical Handbook of Hispanics and United States Film.
Trade Cloth. Bilingual Press/Editorial Bilingue. Tempe, AZ.
1997. 336p. Cinema and Theater Studies ISBN:0-927534-56-8,
ISBN13: 978-0-927534-56-7. Dewey:791.43/08968073.
LCCN:96-041117.

Audience: **g,u,f.** *Choice, 1998.*

Landis, Jacquelyn **E184.C97C845 2006**
The Cubans. Trade Paper. Thomson Gale. Farmington Hills, MI.
2006. 208p. ISBN:0-7377-2764-0, ISBN13: 978-0-7377-2764-7.
Dewey:973/.04687291. LCCN:2004-060583.

Audience: **g,l.**

Loza, Steven J. **ML419.P82L6 1999**
Tito Puente and the Making of Latin Music. Trade Paper.
University of Illinois Press. Champaign, IL. 1999. 312p. Music
in American Life Ser. ISBN:0-252-06778-9, ISBN13:
978-0-252-06778-5. Dewey:784.4/81888/092 B.
LCCN:98-025507.

Audience: **l,u,f.** *Choice, 2000.*

Lucero, Helen R. & **F805.S75L83 1999**
Baizerman, Suzanne
Chimayo Weaving: The Transformation of a Tradition. Trade
Cloth. University of New Mexico Press. Albuquerque, NM.
1998. 232p. ISBN:0-8263-1975-0, ISBN13: 978-0-8263-1975-3.
Dewey:746.1/4/097895. LCCN:98-023210.

Audience: **u,f.** *Choice, 1999.*

López-Stafford, Gloria **E394.E4**
A Place in El Paso: A Mexican-American Childhood. Trade
Paper. University of New Mexico Press. Albuquerque, NM.
1996. 222p. ISBN:0-8263-1709-X, ISBN13: 978-0-8263-1709-4.
Dewey:976.4/96 B.

Audience: **l,u.** *Choice, 1996.*

Martin, Patricia **F820.M5R36 2004**
Preciado (Editor, Translator)
Beloved Land: Mexican American Oral Histories from Southern
Arizona. Jose Galvez (Photographer). Trade Cloth. University of
Arizona Press. Tucson, AZ. 2004. 173p. ISBN:0-8165-2382-7,
ISBN13: 978-0-8165-2382-5. Dewey:979.1/70046872/00922.
LCCN:2003-015503.

Audience: **l,u.**

Matthiessen, Peter **HD6509.C48 M38 2000**
Sal Si Puedes (Escape If You Can): Cesar Chavez and the New
American Revolution. Ilan Stavans (Foreword by). Trade Paper.
University of California Press. Berkeley, CA. 2000. 386p.
ISBN:0-520-22584-8, ISBN13: 978-0-520-22584-8.
Dewey:331.5/44/092 B. LCCN:00-055580.

Audience: **g,l,u.**

McMurtrey, Martin **BX4705.F6099.M37**
Mariachi Bishop: The Life of Patrick Flores, First
Mexican-American Bishop in the U. S. Trade Paper. Corona
Publishing Company. San Antonio, TX. 1987. 181p.
ISBN:0-931722-56-X, ISBN13: 978-0-931722-56-1.
Dewey:282/.092. LCCN:87-070378.

Audience: **u,f.**

Medina, Pablo **PS3566.L27**
Exiled Memories: A Cuban Childhood. Trade Paper. Persea
Books, Inc. New York, NY. 2002. 144p. ISBN:0-89255-280-8,
ISBN13: 978-0-89255-280-1. Dewey:811/.54 B.

Audience: **l,u.**

Meier, Matt S., et al. **E184**
Notable Latino Americans: A Biographical Dictionary. Conchita
F. Serri & Richard A. Garcia (Authors). Cloth Text. Greenwood
Publishing Group, Inc. Portsmouth, NH. 1997. 448p.
ISBN:0-313-29105-5, ISBN13: 978-0-313-29105-0.
Dewey:920/.009268. LCCN:96-027392.

Audience: **g,l.** *Choice, 1997.*

Meyer, Nicholas E.   E184.S75M49 2001
The Biographical Dictionary of Hispanic Americans. Ed. 2.
Trade Cloth. Facts On File, Inc. New York, NY. 2001. 336p.
Facts on File Library of American History ISBN:0-8160-4330-2,
ISBN13: 978-0-8160-4330-9. Dewey:920/.009268073 B.
LCCN:00-049046.
                    Audience: **g,l.** *Choice, 2002.*

Murguìa, Alejandro   F870.M5M87 2002
The Medicine of Memory: A Mexica Clan in California. Trade
Cloth. University of Texas Press. Austin, TX. 2002. 296p.
ISBN:0-292-75265-2, ISBN13: 978-0-292-75265-8.
Dewey:929/.2/0973. LCCN:2002-010187.
                    Audience: **l,u.** *Choice, 2003.*

Méndez-Méndez,   CT329
  Serafìn, et al.
Notable Caribbeans and Caribbean Americans: A Biographical
Dictionary. Gail A. Cueto & Neysa Rodríguez-Deynes
(Authors). Cloth Text. Greenwood Publishing Group, Inc.
Portsmouth, NH. 2003. 488p. ISBN:0-313-31443-8, ISBN13:
978-0-313-31443-8. Dewey:920.0729. LCCN:2001-033695.
                    Audience: **g,l.** *Choice, 2004.*

Noriega, Chon A. &   E184.M5I15 2004
  Belcher, Wendy L. (Editors)
I Am Aztlan: The Personal Essay in Chicano Studies. Perfect.
UCLA Chicano Studies Research Center Press. Los Angeles,
CA. 2004. 300p. ISBN:0-89551-099-5, ISBN13:
978-0-89551-099-0. Dewey:305.868/073. LCCN:2004-048035.
                    Audience: **u,f.** *Choice, 2005.*

Pacheco, Ferdie   F319.T2P33 1994
Ybor City Chronicles: A Memoir. Trade Cloth. University Press
of Florida. Gainesville, FL. 1994. 315p. ISBN:0-8130-1296-1,
ISBN13: 978-0-8130-1296-4. Dewey:975.9/65 B.
LCCN:94-000822.
                    Audience: **l,u.**

Padilla, Genaro M.   E184.M5.P28 1993
My History, Not Yours: The Formation of Mexican American
Autobiography. Trade Cloth. University of Wisconsin Press.
Chicago, IL. 1994. 224p. Studies in American Autobiography
ISBN:0-299-13970-0, ISBN13: 978-0-299-13970-4.
Dewey:920.00926872. LCCN:93-003457.
                    Audience: **u,f.** *Choice, 1994.*

Paris, Margaret L.   E184.C97B667 2002
Embracing America: A Cuban Exile Comes of Age. Trade Cloth.
University Press of Florida. Gainesville, FL. 2002. 224p.
ISBN:0-8130-2545-1, ISBN13: 978-0-8130-2545-2.
Dewey:973/.04687291/0092 B. LCCN:2002-027137.
                    Audience: **u,f.**

Patoski, Joe N.   ML420.S458P37 1996
Selena: Como la Flor. Trade Cloth. Little Brown & Company.
New York, NY. 1996. 304p. ISBN:0-316-69378-2, ISBN13:
978-0-316-69378-3. Dewey:782.4/2/163/092. LCCN:95-051815.
                    Audience: **l,u.**

Pérez Firmat, Gustavo   PS3566.E69138Z47
Next Year in Cuba: A Cubano's Coming-Of-Age in America.
Trade Paper. Arte Publico Press. Houston, TX. 2005. 272p.
ISBN:1-55885-461-4, ISBN13: 978-1-55885-461-1.
Dewey:81/.54 B. LCCN:2005-040991.
                    Audience: **l,u.**

Reyes, Luis & Rubie,   PN1995.9.H47R49 1994
  Peter (Editors)
Hispanics in Hollywood: An Encyclopedia of Film and
Television. Paper over Boards. Garland Publishing, Inc. New
York, NY. 1994. 592p. ISBN:0-8153-0827-2, ISBN13:
978-0-8153-0827-0. Dewey:791.43/08968. LCCN:93-040607.
                    Audience: **g,l,u.** *Choice, 1995.*

Riggs, Thomas (Editor)   N6538.H58S7 2002
St. James Guide to Hispanic Artists: Profiles of Latino and Latin
American Artists. Association of Hispanic Arts Staff &
Association for Latin American Art Staff (Contribution by).
Trade Cloth. Thomson Gale. Farmington Hills, MI. 2002. 700p.
ISBN:1-55862-470-8, ISBN13: 978-1-55862-470-2.
Dewey:704/.0368/00904 B. LCCN:2001-041935.
                    Audience: **g,l,u.**

Rodriguez, Luis J.   HV6439.U7L77 2005
Always Running: La Vida Loca: Gang Days in L. A. Trade
Paper. Simon & Schuster. New York, NY. 2005. 288p.
ISBN:0-7432-7691-4, ISBN13: 978-0-7432-7691-7.
Dewey:364.1092 B. LCCN:2005-281606.
                    Audience: **g,l,u.**

Roguez, Richard   F870.M5 R62
Hunger of Memory: The Education of Richard Rodriguez.
Library Binding. Sagebrush Education Resources. Caledonia,
MN. 1983. ISBN:0-7857-7698-2, ISBN13: 978-0-7857-7698-7.
Dewey:420/.4261.
                    Audience: **g,l,u.**

Ruiz, Vicki L. &   E184.S75L36245 2005
  Korrol, Virginia Sanchez
Latina Legacies: Identity, Biography, and Community. Trade
Cloth. Oxford University Press, Inc. New York, NY. 2005. 272p.
Viewpoints on American Culture Ser. ISBN:0-19-515398-7,
ISBN13: 978-0-19-515398-9. Dewey:920.72/089/68 B.
LCCN:2004-050131.
                    Audience: **l,u.**

Santiago, Esmeralda   F128.9.P85S267 1999
Almost a Woman. Trade Paper. Knopf Publishing Group. New
York, NY. 1999. 336p. ISBN:0-375-70521-X, ISBN13:
978-0-375-70521-2. Dewey:974.7/1004687295.
LCCN:99-025592.
                    Audience: **l,u.**

Santiago, Esmeralda   F128.9.P85
When I Was Puerto Rican. Trade Paper. Da Capo Press, Inc.
Cambridge, MA. 2006. 288p. ISBN:0-306-81452-8, ISBN13:
978-0-306-81452-5. Dewey:974.7/1004687295/009.
                    Audience: **g,l,u.**

Sepulveda, Juan A.   E184.M5V4 2003
The Life and Times of Willie Velasquez: Su Voto Es Su Voz.
Trade Cloth. Arte Publico Press. Houston, TX. 2004. 384p. The
Hispanic Civil Rights Ser. ISBN:1-55885-419-3, ISBN13:
978-1-55885-419-2. Dewey:323/.092 B. LCCN:2003-050044.
                    Audience: **l,u.**

Shorris, Earl   E184.S75
Latinos: A Biography of the People. Trade Paper. W. W. Norton
& Company, Inc. New York, NY. 2001. 544p.
ISBN:0-393-32190-8, ISBN13: 978-0-393-32190-6.
Dewey:973/.0468.
                    Audience: **g,l.**

Stavans, Ilan (Editor)   CT275.A186A25 1996
Oscar Zeta Acosta: The Uncollected Works. Trade Paper. Arte
Publico Press. Houston, TX. 1996. 368p. ISBN:1-55885-099-6,
ISBN13: 978-1-55885-099-6. Dewey:973/.046872/0092 B.
LCCN:95-033398.
                                        Audience: **u,f.** *Choice, 1996.*

Thomas, Piri   F128.9.P8
Down These Mean Streets. Library Binding. Sagebrush
Education Resources. Caledonia, MN. 1997.
ISBN:0-613-81057-0, ISBN13: 978-0-613-81057-9.
Dewey:301.451/67/97471.
                                        Audience: **l,u.**

Vega, Bernardo   F128.9.P85V4313 1984
Memoirs of Bernardo Vega: A Contribution to the History of the
Puerto Rican Community in New York. Cesar A. Iglesias
(Editor), Juan Flores (Translator). Trade Paper. Monthly Review
Press. New York, NY. 1984. 288p. ISBN:0-85345-656-9,
ISBN13: 978-0-85345-656-8. Dewey:974.7/104.
LCCN:84-009128.
                                        Audience: **l,u.**

Vega, Marta Moreno   F128.9.P85V438 2004
When the Spirits Dance Mambo: Growing up Nuyorican in el
Barrio. Trade Paper. Crown Publishing Group. New York, NY.
2004. 288p. ISBN:1-4000-4924-5, ISBN13: 978-1-4000-4924-0.
Dewey:974.7/004687295/0922. LCCN:2003-027912.
                                        Audience: **l,u.**

Wilson, Nick C.   GV865.A1.W545 2005
Early Latino Ballplayers in the United States: Major, Minor and
Negro Leagues, 1901-1949. Cloth Text. McFarland & Company,
Incorporated Publishers. Jefferson, NC. 2005. 208p.
ISBN:0-7864-2012-X, ISBN13: 978-0-7864-2012-4.
Dewey:796.357/092/368073 B. LCCN:2005-004471.
                                        Audience: **g,l.**

Humanities

Balido, Giselle   E184.C97B34 2001
CubanTime: A Celebration of Cuban Life in America. Cloth
over Boards. Sterling Publishing Co., Inc. New York, NY. 2001.
240p. ISBN:0-7607-2690-6, ISBN13: 978-0-7607-2690-7.
Dewey:305.868/7291073. LCCN:2001-281469.
                                        Audience: **l.**

Braschi, Giannina   PQ7440.B67I6613 1994
Empire of Dreams. Tess O'Dwyer (Translator). Cloth over
Boards. Yale University Press. Cumberland, RI. 1994. 244p.
ISBN:0-300-05795-4, ISBN13: 978-0-300-05795-9. Dewey:863.
LCCN:94-000648.
                                        Audience: **u.**

Chabram-Dernersesian,   E184.M5C385 2005
  Angie (Editor)
Chicana/o Cultural Studies Reader. Ed. 2. Trade Cloth.
Routledge. New York, NY. 2006. 552p. ISBN:0-415-23515-4,
ISBN13: 978-0-415-23515-0. Dewey:305.868/72073.
LCCN:2005-001402.
                                        Audience: **u,f.**

Habell-Pallan, Michelle   PS153.H56H33 2005
Loca Motion: The Travels of Chicana and Latina Popular
Culture. Trade Cloth. New York University Press. New York,
NY. 2005. 320p. ISBN:0-8147-3662-9, ISBN13:
978-0-8147-3662-3. Dewey:791/.082/0973. LCCN:2004-023712.
                                        Audience: **u,f.** *Choice, 2005.*

Maciel, David R.   E184.M5C453 2000
  (Editor), et al.
The Chicano Renaissance: Contemporary Cultural Trends. Isidro
D. Ortiz & María Herrera-Sobek (Editors). Trade Paper.
University of Arizona Press. Tucson, AZ. 2000. 330p.
ISBN:0-8165-2021-6, ISBN13: 978-0-8165-2021-3.
Dewey:704.0368. LCCN:00-008073.
                                        Audience: **u,f.** *Choice, 2001.*

McCracken, Ellen   PS3505.H625Z66 2000
  (Editor)
Fray Angelico Chavez: Poet, Priest, and Artist. Trade Cloth.
University of New Mexico Press. Albuquerque, NM. 2004.
168p. Paso Por Aqui: Series on the Nuevo Mexicano Literary
Heritag Ser. ISBN:0-8263-2007-4, ISBN13: 978-0-8263-2007-0.
Dewey:818/.5209. LCCN:99-050726.
                                        Audience: **u,f.** *Choice, 2000.*

Saldívar, Jose D.   F787.S19 1997
Border Matters: Remapping American Cultural Studies. Trade
Paper. University of California Press. Berkeley, CA. 1997. 266p.
American Crossroads Ser. ISBN:0-520-20682-7, ISBN13:
978-0-520-20682-3. Dewey:306/.0972/1. LCCN:96-049209.
                                        Audience: **u,f.**

Tatum, Charles M.   E184.M5T38 2001
Chicano Popular Culture: Que Hable el Pueblo. Trade Paper.
University of Arizona Press. Tucson, AZ. 2001. 230p. The
Mexican American Experience Ser. ISBN:0-8165-1983-8,
ISBN13: 978-0-8165-1983-5. Dewey:973/.046872.
LCCN:2001-001220.
                                        Audience: **l,u.**

Torrans, Thomas   PS277 .T67 2002
The Magic Curtain: The Mexican-American Border in Fiction,
Film, and Song. Barbara Mathews Whitehead (Illustrator). Trade
Cloth. Texas Christian University Press. Fort Worth, TX. 2002.
312p. ISBN:0-87565-257-3, ISBN13: 978-0-87565-257-3.
Dewey:810.9327. LCCN:2002-002298.
                                        Audience: **u,f.** *Choice, 2003, 2002.*

Humanities > Art

Barraza, Santa C. &   N6537.B2245S26 2001
  Herrera-Sobek, María
Santa Barraza, Artist of the Borderlands. Trade Cloth. Texas
A&M University Press. College Station, TX. 2000. xx, 114p.
Rio Grande/Rio Bravo Ser., Vol. 5 ISBN:0-89096-906-X,
ISBN13: 978-0-89096-906-9. Dewey:759.13. LCCN:00-010359.
                                        Audience: **l,u.** *Choice, 2001.*

Bosch, Lynette M. F.   N6538.C83
Cuban-American Art in Miami: Exile, Trauma, Postmodernism
and the Neo-Baroque. Trade Cloth. Ashgate Publishing, Ltd.
Aldershot, 2004. 184p. ISBN:0-85331-907-3, ISBN13:
978-0-85331-907-8. Dewey:704.03/6872910759381.
LCCN:2004-107984.
                                        Audience: **u,f.** *Choice, 2005.*

Boyd, E.   N7910.N6B69 1998
Saints and Saint Makers of New Mexico. Robin F. Gavin
(Revised by), Donna Pierce (Foreword by), Charles M. Carrillo
(Contribution by). Trade Paper. Western Edge Press. Sante Fe,
NM. 1997. 144p. ISBN:1-889921-02-5, ISBN13:
978-1-889921-02-0. Dewey:704.9/482/09789. LCCN:98-060248.
                                        Audience: **u,f.**

Durand, Jorge &   **ND1432.M46D87 1995**
Massey, Douglas S.
Miracles on the Border: Retablos of Mexican Migrants to the
United States. Library Binding. University of Arizona Press.
Tucson, AZ. 1995. 216p. ISBN:0-8165-1471-2, ISBN13:
978-0-8165-1471-7. Dewey:755/.2. LCCN:94-032080.
> Audience: **u,f.** *Choice, 1995.*

Fields, Virginia &   **F1219.3.C6F54 2001**
Zamudio-Taylor, Victor
The Road to Aztlan: Art from a Mythic Homeland. Los Angeles
County Museum of Art Staff (Contribution by). Trade Cloth.
University of New Mexico Press. Albuquerque, NM. 2001.
424p. ISBN:0-8263-2426-6, ISBN13: 978-0-8263-2426-9.
Dewey:979/.0074/79493. LCCN:2001-000245.
> Audience: **l,u.** *Choice, 2002.*

Fusco, Coco   **E169.04.F867 1995**
English Is Broken Here: Notes on Cultural Fusion in the
Americas. Trade Paper. New Press, The. New York, NY. 1995.
232p. ISBN:1-56584-245-6, ISBN13: 978-1-56584-245-8.
Dewey:306/.097. LCCN:95-067818.
> Audience: **u,f.**

Gaspar de Alba, Alicia   **N6538.M4G37 1998**
Chicano Art Inside/Outside the Master's House: Cultural Politics
and the CARA Exhibition. Trade Cloth. University of Texas
Press. Austin, TX. 1998. 332p. ISBN:0-292-72801-8, ISBN13:
978-0-292-72801-1. Dewey:704/.0368/72073. LCCN:97-011398.
> Audience: **u,f.**

Gomez-Pena, Guillermo   **N6853.P5**
Dangerous Border Crossers: Artist Talks Back. Paper over
Boards. Routledge. New York, NY. 2000. 304p.
ISBN:0-415-18236-0, ISBN13: 978-0-415-18236-2.
Dewey:709/.2. LCCN:99-052962.
> Audience: **u,f.** *Choice, 2001.*

Graham, Joe S. (Editor)   **GR1**
Hecho en Tejas: Texas-Mexican Folk Arts and Crafts. Trade
Paper. University of North Texas Press. Denton, TX. 1997.
358p. Texas Folklore Society Publications, Vol. 50
ISBN:1-57441-038-5, ISBN13: 978-1-57441-038-9.
Dewey:680.89/68720764. LCCN:91-037628.
> Audience: **l,u.**

Griffith, James   **NK839.3.M4G75 2000**
Hecho a Mano: The Traditional Arts of Tucson's Mexican
American Community. Patricia Preciado Martin (Foreword by).
Trade Cloth. University of Arizona Press. Tucson, AZ. 2000.
104p. ISBN:0-8165-1877-7, ISBN13: 978-0-8165-1877-7.
Dewey:704.03/68720791776. LCCN:00-008565.
> Audience: **u,f.**

Griswold del Castillo,   **N6538.M4C45 1991**
Richard (Editor), et al.
Chicano Art: Resistance and Affirmation, 1965-1985. Teresa
McKenna & Yvonne M. Yarbro-Bejarano (Editors). Trade Cloth.
Frederick S. Wight Art Galleries. Los Angeles, CA. 1993. 373p.
ISBN:0-943739-16-0, ISBN13: 978-0-943739-16-8.
Dewey:704/.0368/7207307479. LCCN:90-025188.
> Audience: **l,u.**

Guzman, Kristin   **NC999.4.S45A4 2005**
Self Help Graphics and Art: Chicano Art in the Heart of East
Los Angeles. Colin Gunckel (Editor). Perfect. UCLA Chicano
Studies Research Center Press. Los Angeles, CA. 2005. 200p.

The Chicano Archives Ser., Vol. 1 ISBN:0-89551-100-2,
ISBN13: 978-0-89551-100-3. Dewey:760/.092/3680794.
LCCN:2005-023237.
> Audience: **u,f.**

Güereña, Salvador
☐ Chicano Art Digital Image Collection.
http://cemaweb.library.ucsb.edu/digitalArchives.html
California Ethnic and Multicultural Archives, University of
California.
> Audience: **l,u,f.**

Keller, Gary D., et al.   **N6538.M4 C664**
Contemporary Chicana and Chicano Art: Artists, Works, Culture,
and Education. Joaquin Alvarado, Kaytie Johnson & Mary
Erickson (Authors). Trade Cloth. Bilingual Press/Editorial
Bilingue. Tempe, AZ. 2003. 360p. ISBN:1-931010-22-6,
ISBN13: 978-1-931010-22-1. Dewey:704.03/6872073.
> Audience: **u,f.**

Keller, Gary D., et al.   **N6538.M4K45 2004**
Chicano Art for Our Millennium: Collected Works from the
Arizona State University Community. Mary Erickson & Pat
Villeneuve (Authors), Marilyn Szabo & Craig Smith
(Photographers), Mesa Southwest Museum Staff (Contribution
by). Trade Cloth. Bilingual Press/Editorial Bilingue. Tempe, AZ.
2004. 160p. ISBN:1-931010-25-0, ISBN13: 978-1-931010-25-2.
Dewey:704.03/6872. LCCN:2004-041061.
> Audience: **u,f.**

Keller, Gary, et al.   **N6538.M4C664 2002**
Contemporary Chicano and Chicana Art: Artists, Works, Culture,
and Education, Vol. 2. Joaquin Alvarado, Kaytie Johnson &
Mary Erickson (Authors). Trade Cloth. Bilingual Press/Editorial
Bilingue. Tempe, AZ. 2002. ISBN:1-931010-10-2, ISBN13:
978-1-931010-10-8. Dewey:704.03/6872073.
LCCN:2002-066523.
> Audience: **l,u.**

Lipsitz, George, et al.   **F870.M5J87 2001**
Just Another Poster?: Chicano Graphic Arts in California. Tere
Romo, Raphael Perez-Torres & Carol Wells (Authors), Chon A.
Noriega (Editor). Trade Paper. University of California, Santa
Barbara, Art Museum. Santa Barbara, CA. 2002. 220p.
ISBN:0-942006-71-2, ISBN13: 978-0-942006-71-1.
Dewey:741.6/74/08968720794. LCCN:00-053238.
> Audience: **u,f.** *Choice, 2002.*

Lucero, Helen R. &   **F805.S75L83 1999**
Baizerman, Suzanne
Chimayo Weaving: The Transformation of a Tradition. Trade
Cloth. University of New Mexico Press. Albuquerque, NM.
1998. 232p. ISBN:0-8263-1975-0, ISBN13: 978-0-8263-1975-3.
Dewey:746.1/4/097895. LCCN:98-023210.
> Audience: **u,f.** *Choice, 1999.*

Marin, Cheech (Editor)   **ND212 .C455**
Chicano Visions: American Painters on the Verge. Trade Paper.
DIANE Publishing Company. Collingdale, PA. 2004. 160p.
ISBN:0-7567-8165-5, ISBN13: 978-0-7567-8165-1.
Dewey:759.13/089/6872.
> Audience: **u,f.**

Montano, Mary &   **NX510.N43M66 2001**
Montaano, Mary Caroline
Tradiciones Nuevomexicanas: Hispano Arts and Culture of New
Mexico. Trade Cloth. University of New Mexico Press.

Albuquerque, NM. 2001. 384p. ISBN:0-8263-2136-4, ISBN13: 978-0-8263-2136-7. Dewey:700/.9789. LCCN:00-011474.
Audience: **l,u.** *Choice, 2001.*

Riggs, Thomas (Editor)   **N6538.H58S7 2002**
St. James Guide to Hispanic Artists: Profiles of Latino and Latin American Artists. Association of Hispanic Arts Staff & Association for Latin American Art Staff (Contribution by). Trade Cloth. Thomson Gale. Farmington Hills, MI. 2002. 700p. ISBN:1-55862-470-8, ISBN13: 978-1-55862-470-2. Dewey:704/.0368/00904 B. LCCN:2001-041935.
Audience: **g,l,u.**

Humanities > Cinema

Fregoso, Rosa Linda   **PN1998.3.P675L68**
(Editor)
Lourdes Portillo: The Devil Never Sleeps and Other Films. Trade Cloth. University of Texas Press. Austin, TX. 2001. 328p. Chicano Matters Ser. ISBN:0-292-72524-8, ISBN13: 978-0-292-72524-9. Dewey:791.43/0233/092. LCCN:00-061516.
Audience: **l,u.**

Keller, Gary D.   **PN1995.9.H47K46 1997**
A Biographical Handbook of Hispanics and United States Film. Trade Cloth. Bilingual Press/Editorial Bilingue. Tempe, AZ. 1997. 336p. Cinema and Theater Studies ISBN:0-927534-56-8, ISBN13: 978-0-927534-56-7. Dewey:791.43/08968073. LCCN:96-041117.
Audience: **g,u,f.** *Choice, 1998.*

Noriega, Chon A.   **PN1995.9.M49N67 1991**
(Editor)
Chicanos and Film: Essays on Chicano Representation and Resistance. Trade Cloth. Garland Publishing, Inc. New York, NY. 1991. 394p. ISBN:0-8240-7439-4, ISBN13: 978-0-8240-7439-5. Dewey:791.43/652036872. LCCN:91-027763.
Audience: **u,f.** *Choice, 1992.*

Noriega, Chon A.   **PN1995.9.M49N69 2000**
Shot in America: Television, the State and the Rise of Chicano Cinema. Book, Other. University of Minnesota Press. Minneapolis, MN. 2000. xxxiii, 305p. ISBN:0-8166-2930-7, ISBN13: 978-0-8166-2930-5. Dewey:791.43/652036872073. LCCN:99-088112.
Audience: **u,f.**

Noriega, Chon A. &   **PN1995.9.L37E84 1996**
Lopez, Ana M. (Editors)
The Ethnic Eye: Latino Media Arts. Cloth Text. University of Minnesota Press. Minneapolis, MN. 1996. xxii, 289p. ISBN:0-8166-2674-X, ISBN13: 978-0-8166-2674-8. Dewey:791.43/6520368. LCCN:95-044107.
Audience: **u,f.** *Choice, 1996.*

Reyes, Luis & Rubie,   **PN1995.9.H47R49 1994**
Peter (Editors)
Hispanics in Hollywood: An Encyclopedia of Film and Television. Paper over Boards. Garland Publishing, Inc. New York, NY. 1994. 592p. ISBN:0-8153-0827-2, ISBN13: 978-0-8153-0827-0. Dewey:791.43/08968. LCCN:93-040607.
Audience: **g,l,u.** *Choice, 1995.*

Rodriguez, Clara E.   **P94.5.H582U65 1997**
(Editor)
Latin Looks: Images of Latinas and Latinos in the U.S. Media. Trade Paper. Westview Press. Boulder, CO. 1997. 320p.

ISBN:0-8133-2766-0, ISBN13: 978-0-8133-2766-2. Dewey:305.868/073. LCCN:97-001840.
Audience: **u,f.** *Choice, 1998.*

Sandoval-Sanchez,   **PN2270.H57S26 1999**
Alberto
Jose, Can You See?: Latinos on and off Broadway. Trade Cloth. University of Wisconsin Press. Chicago, IL. 1999. 288p. ISBN:0-299-16204-4, ISBN13: 978-0-299-16204-7. Dewey:792/.089/68073. LCCN:98-047441.
Audience: **u,f.** *Choice, 2000.*

Humanities > Communication and Mass Media

Gutierrez, Felix F. &   **PN1991.3.U6**
Schement, Jorge Reina
Spanish-Language Radio in the Southwestern United States. Trade Paper. University of Texas Press. Austin, TX. 1979. 130p. Mexican American Monographs, No. 5 ISBN:0-292-77550-4, ISBN13: 978-0-292-77550-3. Dewey:384.54097.
Audience: **u,f.**

Habell-Pall'an, Michelle   **E184.S75L3554 2002**
& Romero, Mary (Editors)
Latino/a Popular Culture. Trade Cloth. New York University Press. New York, NY. 2002. 280p. ISBN:0-8147-3624-6, ISBN13: 978-0-8147-3624-1. Dewey:305.868/073. LCCN:2001-007962.
Audience: **l,u.** *Choice, 2002.*

Hugenberger, Charles   **HE8690.S45**
E.
Spanish Speaking Radio and TV: Emisoras de Radio y Television en Español. Trade Paper. Charles E. Hugenberger. Cleveland, TN. 1994. 8p. ISBN:1-885057-06-7, ISBN13: 978-1-885057-06-8. Dewey:384.5405.
Audience: **u,f.**

Maciel, David R. &   **E184.M5C85 1998**
Herrera-Sobek, María
Culture Across Borders: Mexican Immigration and Popular Culture. Trade Cloth. University of Arizona Press. Tucson, AZ. 1998. 312p. ISBN:0-8165-1832-7, ISBN13: 978-0-8165-1832-6. Dewey:305.868/72073. LCCN:97-033899.
Audience: **u,f.**

Negron-Muntaner,   **E169.12**
Frances
Boricua Pop: Puerto Ricans and American Culture from West Side Story to Jennifer Lopez. Trade Cloth. New York University Press. New York, NY. 2004. 368p. Sexual Cultures Ser. ISBN:0-8147-5817-7, ISBN13: 978-0-8147-5817-5. Dewey:305.868/7295073. LCCN:2003-025217.
Audience: **u,f.** *Choice, 2004.*

Perez Firmat, Gustavo   **E184.C97P47 1994**
Life on the Hyphen: The Cuban-American Way. Cloth Text. University of Texas Press. Austin, TX. 1994. 231p. ISBN:0-292-71153-0, ISBN13: 978-0-292-71153-2. Dewey:973/.04687291. LCCN:93-033590.
Audience: **l,u.** *Choice, 1994.*

Quinonez, Naomi   **E184.M5D34 2001**
Helena
🄴 Decolonial Voices: Chicana and Chicano Cultural Studies in the 21st Century. Arturo J. Aldama (Editor). E-Book. Indiana

University Press. Bloomington, IN. 2002. 413p.
ISBN:0-253-34014-4, ISBN13: 978-0-253-34014-6.
Dewey:305.868/72073. LCCN:2001-039495.
Audience: **u,f.** *Choice, 2003, 2002.*

Rodriguez, America   **PN4888.H57R63 1999**
(Contribution by)
Making Latino News: Race, Language, Class. Trade Cloth.
SAGE Publications, Inc. Thousand Oaks, CA. 1999. 300p.
Intercultural Communication Ser. ISBN:0-7619-1551-6, ISBN13:
978-0-7619-1551-5. Dewey:070.4/84. LCCN:99-006306.
Audience: **u,f.**

Rodriguez, Clara E.   **P94.5.H582U65 1997**
(Editor)
Latin Looks: Images of Latinas and Latinos in the U.S. Media.
Trade Paper. Westview Press. Boulder, CO. 1997. 320p.
ISBN:0-8133-2766-0, ISBN13: 978-0-8133-2766-2.
Dewey:305.868/073. LCCN:97-001840.
Audience: **u,f.** *Choice, 1998.*

Salazar, Ruben   **F787.S18 1995**
Border Correspondent: Selected Writings, 1955-1970. Mario T.
García (Editor, Introduction by). Trade Cloth. University of
California Press. Berkeley, CA. 1995. 304p. Latinos in
American Society and Culture Ser., Vol. 6 ISBN:0-520-20125-6,
ISBN13: 978-0-520-20125-5. Dewey:972/.1. LCCN:94-040809.
Audience: **l,u.**

Santa Ana, Otto   **E184.S75S268 2002**
Brown Tide Rising: Metaphors of Latinos in Contemporary
American Public Discourse. Trade Paper. University of Texas
Press. Austin, TX. 2002. 424p. ISBN:0-292-77767-1, ISBN13:
978-0-292-77767-5. Dewey:305.868073. LCCN:2001-052227.
Audience: **u,f.** *Choice, 2003.*

Tatum, Charles M.   **E184.M5T38 2001**
Chicano Popular Culture: Que Hable el Pueblo. Trade Paper.
University of Arizona Press. Tucson, AZ. 2001. 230p. The
Mexican American Experience Ser. ISBN:0-8165-1983-8,
ISBN13: 978-0-8165-1983-5. Dewey:973/.046872.
LCCN:2001-001220.
Audience: **l,u.**

Valdivia, Angharad N.   **HQ1421.V35 2000**
A Latina in the Land of Hollywood and Other Essays on Media
Culture. Trade Cloth. University of Arizona Press. Tucson, AZ.
2000. 206p. ISBN:0-8165-1933-1, ISBN13: 978-0-8165-1933-0.
Dewey:305.48/868073. LCCN:99-006622.
Audience: **u,f.** *Choice, 2000.*

Humanities > Language

Bailey, Benjamin H.   **E184.D6B35 2002**
Language, Race, and Negotiation of Identity: A Study of
Dominican Americans. Library Binding. LFB Scholarly
Publishing LLC. New York, NY. 2002. 304p. The New
Americans, :Recent Immigration and American Society
ISBN:1-931202-24-9, ISBN13: 978-1-931202-24-4.
Dewey:305.868/72930745. LCCN:2002-003270.
Audience: **u,f.**

Farr, Marcia (Editor)   **P35.5.U6L38 2004**
Latino Language and Literacy in Ethnolinguistic Chicago. Elias
D. Barajas, Ralph Cintron & Jennifer L. Cohen (Contribution
by). Cloth over Boards. Lawrence Erlbaum Associates, Inc.

Mahwah, NJ. 2004. 416p. ISBN:0-8058-4347-7, ISBN13:
978-0-8058-4347-7. Dewey:306.44. LCCN:2004-047232.
Audience: **u,f.** *Choice, 2005.*

Fought, Carmen   **PE3102.M4F68 2002**
Chicano English in Context. Trade Paper. Palgrave Macmillan.
New York, NY. 2003. 288p. ISBN:0-333-98638-5, ISBN13:
978-0-333-98638-7. Dewey:427/.973/0896872.
LCCN:2002-074837.
Audience: **u,f.**

Lamboy, Edwin M.   **PC4829.N44L36 2004**
Caribbean Spanish in the Metropolis: Spanish Language among
Cubans, Dominicans and Puerto Ricans in the New York City
Area. Paper over Boards. Routledge. New York, NY. 2004.
142p. Latino Communities: Emerging Voices - Political, Social,
Cultural and Legal Issues Ser. ISBN:0-415-94925-4, ISBN13:
978-0-415-94925-5. Dewey:467/.97471. LCCN:2004-005120.
Audience: **u,f.**

Ortega, Adolfo   **PC4829.S6O78 1991**
Calo Orbis: Semiotic Aspects of a Chicano Language Variety.
Cloth Text. Peter Lang Publishing, Inc. New York, NY. 1991.
XXXI, 264p. American University Studies, Ser. XIII, Vol.
21:Linguistics ISBN:0-8204-1542-1, ISBN13:
978-0-8204-1542-0. Dewey:467/.09. LCCN:90-025441.
Audience: **u,f.**

Perez, Bertha   **LC2688.S2P47 2003**
Becoming Biliterate: A Study of Two-Way Bilingual Immersion
Education. Cloth over Boards. Lawrence Erlbaum Associates,
Inc. Mahwah, NJ. 2003. 256p. ISBN:0-8058-4678-6, ISBN13:
978-0-8058-4678-2. Dewey:370.117/09764/351.
LCCN:2003-046230.
Audience: **u,f.** *Choice, 2004.*

Sanchez, Rosaura   **P115.5.U5S26 1994**
Chicano Discourse: Socio-Historic Perspectives. Trade Paper.
Arte Publico Press. Houston, TX. 1994. 184p.
ISBN:1-55885-117-8, ISBN13: 978-1-55885-117-7.
Dewey:420/.4261. LCCN:94-008662.
Audience: **u,f.**

Schecter, Sandra R. &   **P40.45.U5S34 2002**
Bayley, Robert
Language As Cultural Practice: Mexicanos en el Norte. Ana
Celia Zentella (Contribution by). Cloth over Boards. Lawrence
Erlbaum Associates, Inc. Mahwah, NJ. 2002. 240p.
ISBN:0-8058-3533-4, ISBN13: 978-0-8058-3533-5.
Dewey:306.44/0973. LCCN:2001-040464.
Audience: **u,f.** *Choice, 2003, 2002.*

Urciuoli, Bonnie   **F128.9.P85U73 1996**
Exposing Prejudice: Puerto Rican Experiences of Language,
Race, and Class. Trade Paper. Westview Press. Boulder, CO.
1996. 240p. Institutional Structures of Feeling Ser.
ISBN:0-8133-2967-1, ISBN13: 978-0-8133-2967-3.
Dewey:305.8/687295/07471. LCCN:96-010325.
Audience: **u,f.** *Choice, 1996.*

Walsh, Catherine E.   **LC2693**
Pedagogy and the Struggle for Voice: Issues of Language,
Power, and Schooling for Puerto Ricans. Trade Cloth.
Greenwood Publishing Group, Inc. Portsmouth, NH. 1990. 192p.
Critical Studies in Education ISBN:0-89789-234-8, ISBN13:
978-0-89789-234-6. Dewey:370.19/34. LCCN:90-000719.
Audience: **u,f.**

Humanities > Literature

Brown, Monica   **HV6439.U5B76 2002**
Gang Nation: Delinquent Citizens in Puerto Rican, Chicano, and Chicana Narratives. Trade Paper. University of Minnesota Press. Minneapolis, MN. 2002. 256p. ISBN:0-8166-3479-3, ISBN13: 978-0-8166-3479-8. Dewey:364.1/06/608968073. LCCN:2001-008249.

Audience: **u,f.**

Humanities > Literature > Anthologies

Agüeros, Jack   **PS3551.G845.D66 1993**
Dominoes and Other Stories from the Puerto Rican. Trade Cloth. Curbstone Press. Willimantic, CT. 1993. 149p. ISBN:1-880684-11-X, ISBN13: 978-1-880684-11-5. Dewey:813/.54. LCCN:93-004849.
Audience: **g,l,u.**   *Choice, 1994.*

Algarin, Miguel &   **PS591.P8**
Pinero, Miguel
Nuyorican Poetry: An Anthology of Puerto Rican Words and Feelings. Trade Paper. HarperCollins Publishers. New York, NY. 1975. ISBN:0-688-07966-0, ISBN13: 978-0-688-07966-6. Dewey:811/.5/408.

Audience: **l,u.**

Antush, John (Editor)   **PS628.P84C66 1991**
Recent Puerto Rican Theatre: Five Plays from New York. Trade Paper. Arte Publico Press. Houston, TX. 2003. 256p. Latin-American Play Anthologies Ser. ISBN:1-55885-019-8, ISBN13: 978-1-55885-019-4. Dewey:812/.5408097295. LCCN:90-032908.

Audience: **l,u.**

Antush, John V.   **PS628.P84N84 1994**
(Editor)
Nuestro New York: An Anthology of Puerto Rican Plays. Mass Market. Penguin Group (USA) Inc. New York, NY. 1994. 608p. ISBN:0-451-62868-3, ISBN13: 978-0-451-62868-8. Dewey:812/.5408097295. LCCN:93-080398.

Audience: **l,u.**

Augenbraum, Harold &   **PS508.H57L4 1997**
Olmos, Margarite Fernández (Editors)
The Latino Reader: An American Literary Tradition from 1542 to the Present. Trade Paper. Houghton Mifflin Company Trade & Reference Division. Boston, MA. 1997. 528p. ISBN:0-395-76528-5, ISBN13: 978-0-395-76528-9. Dewey:810.8/0868. LCCN:96-042277.

Audience: **l,u,f.**

Behar, Ruth (Editor)   **PS508.C83B75 1995**
Bridges to Cuba/Puentes a Cuba. Trade Paper. University of Michigan Press. Chicago, IL. 1996. 448p. ISBN:0-472-06611-0, ISBN13: 978-0-472-06611-7. Dewey:810.8/08687291. LCCN:95-034522.
Audience: **l,u.**   *Choice, 1996.*

Christie, John S. &   **PS508.H57L39 2005**
Gonzalez, Jose B.
Latino Boom: An Anthology of U.S. Latino Literature. Trade Paper, Perfect. Longman Publishing Group. White Plains, NY. 2005. 567p. ISBN:0-321-09383-6, ISBN13: 978-0-321-09383-7. Dewey:810.8/0868. LCCN:2005-015977.

Audience: **g,l,u.**

Cocco de Filippis, Daisy   **PQ7408**
& Gutierrez, Franklin (Editors)
Stories from Washington Heights and Other Corners of the World - Historias de Washington Heights y Otros Rincones del Mundo. Trade Paper. Latino Press. Bronx, NY. 1994. 204p. ISBN:1-884912-02-8, ISBN13: 978-1-884912-02-3. Dewey:860.8097293.

Audience: **l,u.**

Cortina, Rodolfo   **PS628.C82C83 1991**
Cuban American Theater. Miguel Pando (Editor). Trade Paper. Arte Publico Press. Houston, TX. 1992. 280p. Latin-American Play Anthologies Ser. ISBN:1-55885-020-1, ISBN13: 978-1-55885-020-0. Dewey:812/.5408097291. LCCN:91-009898.
Audience: **l,u.**

De Hoyos, Angela &   **PS591.H58F58 1998**
Milligan, Mary G.
Floricanto Si!: A Collection of Latina Poetry. Bryce Milligan (Editor). Trade Paper. Penguin Group (USA) Inc. New York, NY. 1998. 304p. ISBN:0-14-058893-0, ISBN13: 978-0-14-058893-4. Dewey:811/.54080868. LCCN:97-034445.
Audience: **l,u.**

De Jesus, Joy L.   **PS508.P84G76 1997**
(Editor)
Growing up Puerto Rican: 20 Puerto Rican Authors Write in Fiction and Essay about Childhood. Trade Cloth. HarperCollins Publishers. New York, NY. 1997. 352p. ISBN:0-688-13740-7, ISBN13: 978-0-688-13740-3. Dewey:813. LCCN:96-043864.
Audience: **l,u.**

De Jesús   **PS508.M4.L58 1997**
Hernández-Gutiérrez, Manuel & Foster, David (Editors)
Literatura Chicana, 1965-1995: An Anthology in Spanish, English, and Calo. Library Binding. Garland Publishing, Inc. New York, NY. 1997. 520p. Reference Library of the Humanities, Vol. 1912 ISBN:0-8153-2077-9, ISBN13: 978-0-8153-2077-7. Dewey:810.8086872. LCCN:96-024202.
Audience: **l,u.**   *Choice, 1997.*

Fernández, Roberto   **PS508.H57I5 1994**
(Editor)
In Other Words: Literatures of Latinas of the United States. Trade Paper. Arte Publico Press. Houston, TX. 1994. 592p. ISBN:1-55885-110-0, ISBN13: 978-1-55885-110-8. Dewey:810.8/0868. LCCN:94-009206.

Audience: **l,u,f.**

García, Cristina (Editor,   **PQ7383.5.E5C83 2003**
Introduction by)
Cubanisimo!: The Vintage Book of Contemporary Cuban Literature. Trade Paper. Knopf Publishing Group. New York, NY. 2003. 400p. ISBN:0-385-72137-4, ISBN13: 978-0-385-72137-0. Dewey:860.8/097291. LCCN:2002-038076.
Audience: **g,l,u,f.**

Gaspar de Alba, Alicia,   **PS3557.A842**
et al.
Three Times a Woman: Chicana Poetry. María Herrera-Sobek & Demetria Martinez (Authors). Trade Cloth. Bilingual Press/Editorial Bilingue. Tempe, AZ. 1990. 168p. Anthologies and Collections ISBN:0-916950-91-3, ISBN13: 978-0-916950-91-0. Dewey:811.54. LCCN:88-064101.
Audience: **l,u.**

Gomez, Alma (Editor),   **PN6120.92.H56**
et al.
Cuentos: Stories by Latinas. Cherríe Moraga & Mariana

Romo-Carmona (Editors). Trade Cloth. Kitchen Table: Women of Color Press. Brooklyn, NY. 1983. 241p. ISBN:0-913175-20-X, ISBN13: 978-0-913175-20-0. Dewey:813/.01/089287.

Audience: **l,u.**

Gonzalez-Cruz, Luis F.   PS628.C82 C834 1992
  & Colecchia, Francesca M. (Editor, Translators)
Cuban Theater in the United States: A Critical Anthology. Trade Cloth. Bilingual Press/Editorial Bilingue. Tempe, AZ. 1992. 192p. ISBN:0-927534-27-4, ISBN13: 978-0-927534-27-7. Dewey:862. LCCN:92-000308.

Audience: **l,u.**

Hospital, Carolina &   PS508.C83C46 1996
  Cantera, Jorge (Editors)
A Century of Cuban Writers in Florida: Selected Prose and Poetry. Trade Paper. Pineapple Press, Inc. Sarasota, FL. 1996. 238p. ISBN:1-56164-104-9, ISBN13: 978-1-56164-104-8. Dewey:810.8/8687291. LCCN:96-020647.

Audience: **l,u.**

Huerta, Jorge A.   PS628.M4N4 1989
  (Editor)
Necessary Theatre: Six Plays about the Chicano Experience. Trade Paper. Arte Publico Press. Houston, TX. 2003. 368p. Latin-American Play Anthologies Ser. ISBN:0-934770-95-6, ISBN13: 978-0-934770-95-8. Dewey:812/.54/080352036872. LCCN:89-000283.

Audience: **l,u.**

Kanellos, Nicolás   PS508.H57
  (Editor)
Herencia: The Anthology of Hispanic Literature of the United States. Paper Text. Oxford University Press, Inc. New York, NY. 2003. 656p. ISBN:0-19-513825-2, ISBN13: 978-0-19-513825-2. Dewey:810.8/0868.

Audience: **l,u,f.**

Kanellos, Nicolás   PS647.H58.S48 1993
  (Editor)
Short Fiction by Hispanic Writers of the United States. Trade Paper. Arte Publico Press. Houston, TX. 1993. 228p. ISBN:1-55885-044-9, ISBN13: 978-1-55885-044-6. Dewey:813/.0108868. LCCN:92-020826.

Audience: **l,u.** *Choice, 1993.*

Manrique, Jaime   PS648.H57B43 1999
Besame Mucho: An Anthology of Gay Latino Fiction. Paper Text. Painted Leaf Press. New York, NY. 1999. 256p. New Gay Latino Fiction Ser. ISBN:1-891305-06-9, ISBN13: 978-1-891305-06-1. Dewey:813/.54080920664. LCCN:98-050721.

Audience: **l,u.**

Morales, Aurora L. &   PS508.P84M67 1986
  Morales, Rosario
Getting Home Alive. Trade Paper. Firebrand Books. Ithaca, NY. 1986. 216p. ISBN:0-932379-19-2, ISBN13: 978-0-932379-19-1. Dewey:810.8/08687295. LCCN:86-022769.

Audience: **l,u.**

Osborn, M. Elizabeth   PS628.H57O5 1987
  (Editor)
On New Ground: Contemporary Hispanic-American Plays. Trade Paper. Theatre Communications Group, Inc. New York, NY. 1987. 288p. ISBN:0-930452-68-2, ISBN13:

978-0-930452-68-1. Dewey:812/.54/0803520368. LCCN:87-026734.

Audience: **l,u.** *Choice, 1988.*

Pietri, Pedro   PS3566.I424I44 1992
Illusions of a Revolving Door. Alfredo Matilla Rivas (Editor). Trade Cloth. University of Puerto Rico Press. Rio Piedras, PR. 1993. 260p. ISBN:0-8477-3665-2, ISBN13: 978-0-8477-3665-2. Dewey:812/.54. LCCN:91-016785.

Audience: **l,u.**

Poey, Delia   PS647.H58I38 1992
Iguana Dreams: New Latino Fiction. Virgil Suarez (Editor), Óscar Hijuelos (Preface by). Trade Paper. HarperCollins Publishers. New York, NY. 1992. 400p. ISBN:0-06-096917-2, ISBN13: 978-0-06-096917-2. Dewey:813/.54080868. LCCN:92-052628.

Audience: **l,u.**

Ramos, Juanita   PS509.L47C65 1994
  (Compiled by)
Companeras: Latina Lesbians: An Anthology. Paper over Boards. Routledge. New York, NY. 1994. 288p. ISBN:0-415-90925-2, ISBN13: 978-0-415-90925-9. Dewey:810.8/09206643. LCCN:94-004288.

Audience: **l,u.**

Rebolledo, Tey D. &   F805.M5W66 2000
  Marquez, Maria T. (Editors)
La Diabla a Pie: Women's Tales from the New Mexico WPA. Trade Paper. Arte Publico Press. Houston, TX. 2000. 512p. Recovering the U.S.-Hispanic Literary Heritage Ser. ISBN:1-55885-312-X, ISBN13: 978-1-55885-312-6. Dewey:305.868/72073. LCCN:00-056589.

Audience: **u,f.** *Choice, 2001.*

Rebolledo, Tey D. &   PS508.W7
  Rivero, Eliana S. (Editors)
Infinite Divisions: An Anthology of Chicana Literature. Trade Paper. University of Arizona Press. Tucson, AZ. 1993. 387p. ISBN:0-8165-1384-8, ISBN13: 978-0-8165-1384-0. Dewey:810.8/09287. LCCN:92-045101.

Audience: **l,u,f.** *Choice, 1994.*

Santiago, Roberto   PS508.P84B67 1995
Boricuas: Influential Puerto Rican Writings - An Anthology. Trade Paper. Ballantine Books. New York, NY. 1995. 400p. ISBN:0-345-39502-6, ISBN13: 978-0-345-39502-3. Dewey:810.8/097295. LCCN:95-094411.

Audience: **g,l,u,f.**

Suarez, Virgil & Poey,   PS508.C83L58 1996
  Delia (Editors)
Little Havana Blues: A Cuban-American Literature Anthology. Trade Paper. Arte Publico Press. Houston, TX. 1996. 448p. ISBN:1-55885-160-7, ISBN13: 978-1-55885-160-3. Dewey:810.8/0687291. LCCN:96-014242.

Audience: **l,u.** *Choice, 1997.*

Tatum, Charles M.   QA10.5
  (Editor)
New Chicana/Chicano Writing, Set. Trade Paper. University of Arizona Press. Tucson, AZ. 1992. 600p. ISBN:0-8165-1307-4, ISBN13: 978-0-8165-1307-9. Dewey:510.92. LCCN:92-642671.

Audience: **l,u.**

Turner, Faythe   PS508.P84P8 1991
  (Introduction by)
Puerto Rican Writers at Home in the U.S.A.: An Anthology.

Formats: Web: ☐   Ebook: 🅮   CD/DVD-ROM: 🥏   BCL3: 𝓑

Trade Paper. Open Hand Publishing, LLC. Greensboro, NC. 1991. 352p. ISBN:0-940880-31-8, ISBN13: 978-0-940880-31-3. Dewey:810.8/08687295. LCCN:91-002141.

Audience: **l,u.**

Ventura, Gabriela   **PS508.H57U8 2005**
Baeza
U.S. Latino Literature Today. Trade Paper. Longman Publishing Group. White Plains, NY. 2004. 352p. ISBN:0-321-19843-3, ISBN13: 978-0-321-19843-3. Dewey:810.9/868. LCCN:2004-008654.

Audience: **l,u.**

Humanities > Literature > Chicano/a Literature

Acosta, Oscar Z.   **CT275.A186A3 1989**
The Autobiography of a Brown Buffalo. Trade Paper. Knopf Publishing Group. New York, NY. 1989. 208p. ISBN:0-679-72213-0, ISBN13: 978-0-679-72213-7. Dewey:978/.0046872073 B. LCCN:88-040356.

Audience: **l,u.**

Acosta, Oscar Z.   **CT275.A186A3 1989**
The Revolt of the Cockroach People. Trade Paper. Knopf Publishing Group. New York, NY. 1989. 272p. ISBN:0-679-72212-2, ISBN13: 978-0-679-72212-0. Dewey:979.4/9405/0924 B. LCCN:88-040355.

Audience: **l,u.**

Alarcón, Norma   **PS153.M4 C45 1993**
(Editor), et al.
Chicana Critical Issues. Rafaela Castro, Emma Perez, Beatriz Pesquera, Ada S. Riddell & Patricia Zavella (Editors), Juana Alicia, Judith Baca & Catalina Govea (Illustrators), Margarita Melville (Introduction by). Trade Paper. Third Woman Press. Oakland, CA. 1993. 304p. Chicana-Latina Studies ISBN:0-943219-09-4, ISBN13: 978-0-943219-09-7. Dewey:810.9/86872. LCCN:93-003097.

Audience: **u,f.**

Alcalá, Kathleen   **PS3551.L287**
Mrs. Vargas and the Dead Naturalist. Trade Cloth. Calyx Books. Corvallis, OR. 1992. 192p. ISBN:0-934971-26-9, ISBN13: 978-0-934971-26-3. Dewey:813/.54. LCCN:92-004469.

Audience: **g,l,u.**

Aldama   **PS3559.S44 Z54 2005**
Dancing with Ghosts: A Critical Biography of Arturo Islas. Trade Cloth. University of California Press. Berkeley, CA. 2004. 242p. ISBN:0-520-23188-0, ISBN13: 978-0-520-23188-7. Dewey:818/.5409 B. LCCN:2004-011381.

Audience: **u,f.**

Aldama, Frederick Luis   **PS3559.S44A6 2003**
Arturo Islas: The Uncollected Works. Trade Paper. Arte Publico Press. Houston, TX. 2003. 288p. ISBN:1-55885-368-5, ISBN13: 978-1-55885-368-3. Dewey:818/.5409. LCCN:2003-044432.

Audience: **u,f.**

Aldama, Frederick Luis   **PS3559.S44Z53 2004**
Critical Mappings of Arturo Islas's Fictions. Trade Cloth. Bilingual Press/Editorial Bilingue. Tempe, AZ. 2005. ISBN:1-931010-31-5, ISBN13: 978-1-931010-31-3. Dewey:813/.54. LCCN:2004-054545.

Audience: **u,f.**

Alurista   **PS3551.L84**
As Our Barrio Turns... Who the Yoke B On? Sal Barajas (Designed by). Trade Paper. Calaca Press. National City, CA. 2000. 122p. ISBN:0-9660773-3-4, ISBN13: 978-0-9660773-3-9. Dewey:811.54.

Audience: **l,u.**

Anaya, Rudolfo   **PS3551.N27M36 2006**
The Man Who Could Fly and Other Stories. Trade Cloth. University of Oklahoma Press. Norman, OK. 2006. 199p. Chicana & Chicano Visions of the Américas Ser., Vol. 5 ISBN:0-8061-3738-X, ISBN13: 978-0-8061-3738-4. Dewey:813/.54. LCCN:2005-051426.

Audience: **g,l,u.**

Anaya, Rudolfo A.   **PS3568.O243**
Bless Me, Ultima. Trade Cloth. Novel Units, Inc. Bulverde, TX. 1999. ISBN:1-56137-807-0, ISBN13: 978-1-56137-807-4. Dewey:813/.54.

Audience: **g,l,u.**

Anaya, Rudolfo A. &   **E184.M5**
Lomelí, Francisco A.
Aztlan: Essays on the Chicano Homeland. Trade Paper. University of New Mexico Press. Albuquerque, NM. 2001. 264p. ISBN:0-8263-1261-6, ISBN13: 978-0-8263-1261-7. Dewey:972.018. LCCN:89-083942.

Audience: **u,f.**

Arias, Ron   **PS3551.R427R6 1987**
The Road to Tamazunchale. Jose A. Burciaga (Illustrator), Eliud Martinez (Contribution by). Trade Cloth. Bilingual Press/Editorial Bilingue. Tempe, AZ. 1997. 134p. Chicano Classics - Clasicos Chicanos Ser., No. 3 ISBN:0-916950-70-0, ISBN13: 978-0-916950-70-5. Dewey:813/.54. LCCN:86-070700.

Audience: **g,l,u.**

Barrio, Raymond   **PS3552.A7365**
The Plum Plum Pickers. Ed. 2. Trade Cloth. Bilingual Press/Editorial Bilingue. Tempe, AZ. 1984. 232p. Clasicos Chicanos Ser. ISBN:0-916950-51-4, ISBN13: 978-0-916950-51-4. Dewey:813/.54. LCCN:84-070568.

Audience: **g,l,u.**

Brady, Mary Pat   **PS153.M4.B69 2002**
Extinct Lands, Temporal Geographies: Chicana Literature and the Urgency of Space. Trade Cloth. Duke University Press. Durham, NC. 2003. 272p. Latin America Otherwise Ser. ISBN:0-8223-3005-9, ISBN13: 978-0-8223-3005-9. Dewey:810.9/9287/0896872. LCCN:2002-006333.

Audience: **u,f.** *Choice, 2003.*

Bruce-Novoa, Juan   **PS153.M4**
Chicano Poetry: A Response to Chaos. Trade Paper. University of Texas Press. Austin, TX. 1982. 246p. ISBN:0-292-71092-5, ISBN13: 978-0-292-71092-4. Dewey:811.09. LCCN:81-023129.

Audience: **l,u.**

Burciaga, José Antonio   **E184.S75 B85 1993**
Drink Cultura: Chicanismo. Trade Paper. Joshua Odell Editions. Santa Barbara, CA. 1993. 140p. ISBN:1-877741-07-8, ISBN13: 978-1-877741-07-4. Dewey:305.868/72073. LCCN:92-032614.

Audience: **l,u.**

Calderon, Hector &   **PS153.M4C7 1991**
Saldivar, Jose D. (Editors)
Criticism in the Borderlands: Studies in Chicano Literature, Culture, and Ideology. Cloth Text. Duke University Press. Durham, NC. 1991. 312p. Post-Contemporary Interventions Ser.

ISBN:0-8223-1137-2, ISBN13: 978-0-8223-1137-9.
Dewey:810.9/86872. LCCN:90-025853.

Audience: **u,f.** *Choice, 1992.*

Calderón, Héctor   **PS153.M4C248 2004**
Narratives of Greater Mexico: Essays on Chicano Literary
History, Genre, and Borders. Trade Cloth. University of Texas
Press. Austin, TX. 2005. 304p. CMAS History, Culture, &
Society Ser. ISBN:0-292-70560-3, ISBN13: 978-0-292-70560-9.
Dewey:810.9/86872. LCCN:2004-008744.

Audience: **u,f.**

Castillo, Ana   **PS3553.A8135L68 1996**
Loverboys. Trade Cloth. W. W. Norton & Company, Inc. New
York, NY. 1996. 100p. ISBN:0-393-03959-5, ISBN13:
978-0-393-03959-7. Dewey:813/.54. LCCN:95-052048.

Audience: **l,u.**

Castillo, Ana   **PS3553.A8135**
The Mixquiahuala Letters. Trade Paper. Knopf Publishing
Group. New York, NY. 1992. 144p. ISBN:0-385-42013-7,
ISBN13: 978-0-385-42013-6. Dewey:813/.54.

Audience: **l,u.** *Choice, 1987.*

Castillo, Ana   **PS3553.A8135M9 2004**
My Father Was a Toltec. Trade Paper. Knopf Publishing Group.
New York, NY. 2004. 192p. ISBN:1-4000-3499-X, ISBN13:
978-1-4000-3499-4. Dewey:811/.54. LCCN:2003-062897.

Audience: **l,u.**

Cervantes, Lorna Dee   **PS3553.E79 E47**
Emplumada. Trade Paper. University of Pittsburgh Press.
Pittsburgh, PA. 1981. 80p. Pitt Poetry Ser. ISBN:0-8229-5327-7,
ISBN13: 978-0-8229-5327-2. Dewey:811/.54. LCCN:80-054063.

Audience: **l,u.**

Cervantes, Lorna Dee   **PS3553.E79F7 1991**
From the Cables of Genocide: Poems on Love and Hunger.
Trade Paper. Arte Publico Press. Houston, TX. 1991. 78p.
ISBN:1-55885-033-3, ISBN13: 978-1-55885-033-0.
Dewey:811/.54. LCCN:91-008721.

Audience: **g,l,u,f.**

Chavez, Denise   **PS3553.H346F34 1994**
Face of an Angel. Trade Cloth. Farrar, Straus & Giroux. New
York, NY. 1994. 356p. ISBN:0-374-15204-7, ISBN13:
978-0-374-15204-8. Dewey:813/.54. LCCN:94-004792.

Audience: **l,u.**

Chavez, Denise   **PS3553.H346L3 1986**
The Last of the Menu Girls. Trade Paper. Arte Publico Press.
Houston, TX. 1986. 192p. ISBN:0-934770-46-8, ISBN13:
978-0-934770-46-0. Dewey:813/.54. LCCN:84-072304.

Audience: **l,u.** *Choice, 1986.*

Chavez, Denise   **PS3568.O243**
Loving Pedro Infante. Trade Paper. Simon & Schuster. New
York, NY. 2002. 352p. ISBN:0-7434-4573-2, ISBN13:
978-0-7434-4573-3. Dewey:813/.54.

Audience: **l,u.**

Cisneros, Sandra   **PS3553.I78C37 2002**
Caramelo. Trade Cloth. Knopf Publishing Group. New York,
NY. 2003. 464p. ISBN:1-4000-4150-3, ISBN13:
978-1-4000-4150-3. Dewey:813/.54. LCCN:2002-025488.

Audience: **g,l,u.**

Cisneros, Sandra   **PS3553.I78H6 1994**
The House on Mango Street. Trade Cloth. Random House, Inc.
New York, NY. 1994. 160p. ISBN:0-679-43335-X, ISBN13:
978-0-679-43335-4. Dewey:FIC. LCCN:93-043564.

Audience: **g,l,u.**

Corpi, Lucha   **PS3553.O693 E93 1992**
Eulogy for a Brown Angel: A Mystery Novel. Trade Cloth. Arte
Publico Press. Houston, TX. 1992. 200p. ISBN:1-55885-050-3,
ISBN13: 978-1-55885-050-7. Dewey:813/.54. LCCN:91-048072.

Audience: **l,u.**

Cota-Cardenas,   **PQ7079.2.C69P8613**
Margarita
Puppet: A Chicano Novella. Trino Sandoval & Barbara D. Riess
(Translators), Tey Diana Rebolledo (Introduction by). Trade
Cloth. University of New Mexico Press. Albuquerque, NM.
2004. 284p. ISBN:0-8263-2228-X, ISBN13: 978-0-8263-2228-9.
Dewey:863/.64. LCCN:00-008469.

Audience: **l,u.** *Choice, 2001.*

De Jesús   **PS508.M4.L58 1997**
Hernández-Gutiérrez, Manuel & Foster, David (Editors)
Literatura Chicana, 1965-1995: An Anthology in Spanish,
English, and Calo. Library Binding. Garland Publishing, Inc.
New York, NY. 1997. 520p. Reference Library of the
Humanities, Vol. 1912 ISBN:0-8153-2077-9, ISBN13:
978-0-8153-2077-7. Dewey:810.8086872. LCCN:96-024202.

Audience: **l,u.** *Choice, 1997.*

Esquibel, Catrióna   **PS153.L46E85 2006**
Rueda
With Her Machete in Her Hand: Reading Chicana Lesbians.
Trade Paper. University of Texas Press. Austin, TX. 2006. 280p.
Chicana Matters Ser. ISBN:0-292-71275-8, ISBN13:
978-0-292-71275-1. Dewey:810.99206643. LCCN:2005-009217.

Audience: **u,f.**

Foster, David W.   **PS153.G38C48 1999**
Chicano/Latino Homoerotic Identities. Cloth Text. Garland
Publishing, Inc. New York, NY. 1999. 384p. Reference Library
of the Humanities, Vol. 16 ISBN:0-8153-3228-9, ISBN13:
978-0-8153-3228-2. Dewey:810.8/03538/08664.
LCCN:99-015048.

Audience: **u,f.**

Foster, David William   **PS153.M4 F64 2004**
El Ambiente Nuestro: Chicano/Latino Homoerotic Writing.
Trade Cloth. Bilingual Press/Editorial Bilingue. Tempe, AZ.
2005. 200p. ISBN:1-931010-23-4, ISBN13: 978-1-931010-23-8.
LCCN:2003-058298.

Audience: **u,f.**

Garcia, Lionel G.   **PS3557.A71115T6 1994**
To a Widow with Children. Trade Cloth. Arte Publico Press.
Houston, TX. 1994. 238p. ISBN:1-55885-069-4, ISBN13:
978-1-55885-069-9. Dewey:813/.54. LCCN:93-036397.

Audience: **l,u.**

Garcia, Nasario   **PS283.N6G37 2000**
Platicas: Conversations with Hispano Writers of New Mexico.
Trade Cloth. Texas Tech University Press. Lubbock, TX. 2000.
xii, 210p. ISBN:0-89672-428-X, ISBN13: 978-0-89672-428-0.
Dewey:810.9/8680789. LCCN:99-047064.

Audience: **l,u.** *Choice, 2000.*

Gaspar de Alba, Alicia,   **PS3557.A842**
et al.
Three Times a Woman: Chicana Poetry. María Herrera-Sobek &

Demetria Martinez (Authors). Trade Cloth. Bilingual Press/Editorial Bilingue. Tempe, AZ. 1990. 168p. Anthologies and Collections ISBN:0-916950-91-3, ISBN13: 978-0-916950-91-0. Dewey:811.54. LCCN:88-064101.

Audience: **l,u.**

Gilb, Dagoberto   **PS3557.I296M3 1994**
The Magic of Blood. Trade Paper. Grove/Atlantic, Inc. New York, NY. 1994. 304p. ISBN:0-8021-3399-1, ISBN13: 978-0-8021-3399-1. Dewey:813.5/4. LCCN:94-004315.

Audience: **l,u.**

Gilb, Dagoberto   **PS3557.I296**
Woodcuts of Women: Stories. Trade Paper. Grove/Atlantic, Inc. New York, NY. 2002. 192p. ISBN:0-8021-3874-8, ISBN13: 978-0-8021-3874-3. Dewey:813.54.

Audience: **l,u.**

Gomez-Pena, Guillermo   **PS3557.O459.W37 1993**
Warrior for Gringostroika: Essays, Performance Texts, and Poetry. Roger Bartra (Introduction by). Trade Paper. Graywolf Press. St. Paul, MN. 1993. 176p. ISBN:1-55597-199-7, ISBN13: 978-1-55597-199-1. Dewey:814/.54. LCCN:93-014529.

Audience: **u,f.** *Choice, 1994.*

Gonzales, Rodolfo   **PS3557.O47M4 2001**
Message to Aztlan: Selected Readings. Antonio Esquibel (Editor, Introduction by), Rodolfo F. Acuna (Foreword by). Trade Paper. Arte Publico Press. Houston, TX. 2001. 256p. Hispanic Civil Rights Ser. ISBN:1-55885-331-6, ISBN13: 978-1-55885-331-7. Dewey:818/.5409. LCCN:2001-022314.

Audience: **l,u.** *Choice, 2002.*

Gonzales-Berry, Erlinda   **PS283.N6P37 1989**
(Editor)
Paso Por Aqui: Critical Essays on the New Mexican Literary Tradition, 1542-1988. Trade Cloth. University of New Mexico Press. Albuquerque, NM. 1989. 325p. ISBN:0-8263-1158-X, ISBN13: 978-0-8263-1158-0. Dewey:860.9/9789. LCCN:89-033819.

Audience: **u,f.** *Choice, 1990.*

Gonzalez, Jovita   **PS3563.I6947D48 1997**
Dew on the Thorn. Jose E. Limon (Editor, Introduction by). Trade Paper. Arte Publico Press. Houston, TX. 1997. 181p. Recovering the U.S. Hispanic Literary Heritage Project Publi Ser. ISBN:1-55885-175-5, ISBN13: 978-1-55885-175-7. Dewey:813/.54. LCCN:96-014240.

Audience: **u,f.**

Gonzalez, Rigoberto   **PS3557.O4695C7 2003**
Crossing Vines: A Novel. Trade Cloth. University of Oklahoma Press. Norman, OK. 2003. 224p. Chicana and Chicano Visions of the Americas Ser., Vol. 2 ISBN:0-8061-3528-X, ISBN13: 978-0-8061-3528-1. Dewey:813/.54. LCCN:2002-075019.

Audience: **l,u.**

González, Jovita &   **PS3563.I6947C33 1996**
Raleigh, Eve
Caballero: A Historical Novel. Jose E. Limon & Maria Cotera (Editors), Thomas H. Kreneck (Foreword by). Trade Paper. Texas A&M University Press. College Station, TX. 1996. 392p. ISBN:0-89096-700-8, ISBN13: 978-0-89096-700-3. Dewey:813/.54. LCCN:95-045525.

Audience: **u,f.**

Guajardo, Paul   **PS153.M4G83 2002**
Chicano Controversy: Oscar Acosta and Richard Rodriguez. Trade Cloth. Peter Lang Publishing, Inc. New York, NY. 2002.

144p. Modern American Literature: New Approaches Ser. ISBN:0-8204-5706-X, ISBN13: 978-0-8204-5706-2. Dewey:810.9/86872. LCCN:2001-034693.

Audience: **u,f.**

Hernandez, Guillermo   **PS153.M4H47 1991**
E.
Chicano Satire: A Study in Literary Culture. Cloth Text. University of Texas Press. Austin, TX. 1991. 166p. Mexican American Monographs, No. 14 ISBN:0-292-71123-9, ISBN13: 978-0-292-71123-5. Dewey:817/.540986872. LCCN:90-043757.

Audience: **u,f.** *Choice, 1991.*

Herrara-Sobek, Maria   **BF108.U5**
(Editor)
Chicana Literary and Artistic Expressions: Culture and Society in Dialogue. Trade Paper. Center For Chicano Studies/UCSB. Santa Barbara, CA. 2000. 229p. ISBN:0-9700384-0-2, ISBN13: 978-0-9700384-0-1. Dewey:150.973.

Audience: **u,f.**

Herrera-Sobek, María   **PS153.M4 B49 1985**
(Editor)
Beyond Stereotypes: The Critical Analysis of Chicana Literature. Trade Cloth. Bilingual Press/Editorial Bilingue. Tempe, AZ. 1985. 152p. Feminism and Women's Studies ISBN:0-916950-54-9, ISBN13: 978-0-916950-54-5. Dewey:810/.9/86872073. LCCN:84-073316.

Audience: **u,f.**

Herrera-Sobek, María   **PQ7081.A1R315**
(Editor)
Reconstructing a Chicano/a Literary Heritage: Hispanic Colonial Literature of the Southwest. Trade Paper. DIANE Publishing Company. Collingdale, PA. 2005. 213p. ISBN:0-7567-9236-3, ISBN13: 978-0-7567-9236-7. Dewey:860.9/868.

Audience: **u,f.** *Choice, 1993.*

Herrera-Sobek, María   **PS508.M4C52 1996**
& Viramontes, Helena Maria (Editors)
Chicana Creativity and Criticism: New Frontiers in American Literature. Ed. 2. Trade Paper. University of New Mexico Press. Albuquerque, NM. 1996. 224p. ISBN:0-8263-1712-X, ISBN13: 978-0-8263-1712-4. Dewey:810.9/86872. LCCN:96-009940.

Audience: **u,f.**

Hinojosa, Rolando   **PS3558.I545B43 1990**
Becky and Her Friends. Trade Paper. Arte Publico Press. Houston, TX. 1989. 160p. Klail City Death Trip Ser. ISBN:1-55885-006-6, ISBN13: 978-1-55885-006-4. Dewey:813/.54. LCCN:89-035418.

Audience: **l,u.**

Hinojosa, Rolando   **PQ7082.N7**
Klail City. Trade Paper. Arte Publico Press. Houston, TX. 1987. 144p. Klail City Death Trip Ser. ISBN:0-934770-54-9, ISBN13: 978-0-934770-54-5. Dewey:863. LCCN:85-073353.

Audience: **l,u.**

Hinojosa, Rolando   **PS3558.I545 V3 1983**
The Valley. Trade Cloth. Bilingual Press/Editorial Bilingue. Tempe, AZ. 1983. 112p. Klail City Death Trip Ser. ISBN:0-916950-37-9, ISBN13: 978-0-916950-37-8. Dewey:813/.54. LCCN:83-070275.

Audience: **l,u.**

Hinojosa, Rolando   **PS3558.I545 C5 1986**
Claros Varones de Belken: Fair Gentlemen of Belken County, Bilingual Edition. Julia Cruz (Translator). Trade Cloth. Bilingual

Press/Editorial Bilingue. Tempe, AZ. 1986. 223p. United States Hispanic Creative Literature Ser. ISBN:0-916950-64-6, ISBN13: 978-0-916950-64-4. Dewey:863. LCCN:85-073395.

Audience: **g,l,u.**

Hinojosa, Rolando   **PQ7079.2.H5M513 2005**
Dear Rafe/Mi Querido Rafa. Manuel Martin Rodriguez (Introduction by). Trade Paper. Arte Publico Press. Houston, TX. 2005. 255p. ISBN:1-55885-456-8, ISBN13: 978-1-55885-456-7. Dewey:863/.64. LCCN:2004-055424.

Audience: **l,u.**

Hinojosa, Rolando   **PS3558.I545 Z87 1985**
The Rolando Hinojosa Reader. Jose D. Saldivar (Editor). Trade Paper. Arte Publico Press. Houston, TX. 1985. 190p. ISBN:0-934770-30-1, ISBN13: 978-0-934770-30-9. Dewey:813/.54. LCCN:83-072578.

Audience: **u,f.**

Horno Delgado,   **PS153.H56B74 1989**
  Asunción (Editor), et al.
Breaking Boundaries: Latina Writing and Critical Readings. Eliana Ortega, Nina M. Scott & Nancy S. Sternbach (Editors). Cloth Text. University of Massachusetts Press. Amherst, MA. 1989. 288p. ISBN:0-87023-635-0, ISBN13: 978-0-87023-635-8. Dewey:810/.9/9287. LCCN:88-017141.

Audience: **u,f.** *Choice, 1989.*

Ikas, Karin Rosa   **PS153.M4C455 2001**
Chicana Ways: Conversations with Ten Chicana Writers. Paper Text. University of Nevada Press. Reno, NV. 2001. 216p. ISBN:0-87417-493-7, ISBN13: 978-0-87417-493-9. Dewey:810.9/9287/0896872. LCCN:2001-002289.

Audience: **u,f.** *Choice, 2002.*

Islas, Arturo   **PS3559.S44**
Rain God. Trade Paper. HarperCollins Publishers. New York, NY. 1991. 192p. ISBN:0-380-76393-1, ISBN13: 978-0-380-76393-1. Dewey:813/.54. LCCN:84-012323.

Audience: **g,l,u.**

Islas, Arturo   **PS3559.S44M65 1996**
La Mollie and the King of Tears. Paul Skenazy (Afterword by). Trade Paper. University of New Mexico Press. Albuquerque, NM. 1996. 208p. ISBN:0-8263-1732-4, ISBN13: 978-0-8263-1732-2. Dewey:813/.54. LCCN:96-004423.

Audience: **l,u.**

Jiménez, Francisco   **PS153.M4 I33 1979**
  (Editor)
The Identification and Analysis of Chicano Literature. Trade Cloth. Bilingual Press/Editorial Bilingue. Tempe, AZ. 1979. 424p. Studies in the Language and Literature of United States Hispanos ISBN:0-916950-12-3, ISBN13: 978-0-916950-12-5. Dewey:860/.9/86872073. LCCN:78-067287.

Audience: **l,u,f.**

Kafka, Phillipa   **PS153**
Saddling la Gringa: Gatekeeping in Literature by Contemporary Latina Writers. Trade Cloth. Greenwood Publishing Group, Inc. Portsmouth, NH. 2000. 192p. Contributions in Women's Studies, Vol. 183 ISBN:0-313-31122-6, ISBN13: 978-0-313-31122-2. Dewey:813/.5099287/08968. LCCN:00-023957.

Audience: **u,f.** *Choice, 2001.*

Kanellos, Nicolas   **PS153**
Hispanic Literature of the United States: A Comprehensive Reference. Cloth Text. Greenwood Publishing Group, Inc.

Portsmouth, NH. 2003. 328p. ISBN:1-57356-558-X, ISBN13: 978-1-57356-558-5. Dewey:810.9/868. LCCN:2003-048542.

Audience: **g,l,u.** *Choice, 2004.*

Kanellos, Nicolás   **PQ7420**
  (Editor)
Biographical Dictionary of Hispanic Literature in the United States: The Literature of Puerto Ricans, Puerto Rican Americans, Cuban Americans, and Other Hispanic Writers. Cloth Text. Greenwood Publishing Group, Inc. Portsmouth, NH. 1989. 374p. ISBN:0-313-24465-0, ISBN13: 978-0-313-24465-0. Dewey:016.86/09/973. LCCN:88-037288.

Audience: **g,l,u.** *Choice, 1990.*

Kaup, Monika   **PS366.M49K38 2001**
Rewriting North American Borders in Chicano and Chicana Narrative. Trade Cloth. Peter Lang Publishing, Inc. New York, NY. 2001. 368p. ISBN:0-8204-4956-3, ISBN13: 978-0-8204-4956-2. Dewey:818/.508098687. LCCN:00-039076.

Audience: **u,f.**

Keller, Gary D. (Editor)   **PQ7079.2.M46Z75 1995**
Miguel Mendez in Aztlan: Two Decades of Literary Production. Trade Cloth. Bilingual Press/Editorial Bilingue. Tempe, AZ. 1995. 104p. ISBN:0-927534-53-3, ISBN13: 978-0-927534-53-6. Dewey:863. LCCN:94-043636.

Audience: **u,f.**

Lattin, Vernon E.   **PQ7079.2.R5 Z88 1988**
  (Editor), et al.
Tomas Rivera, 1935-1984: The Man and His Work. Rolando Hinojosa & Gary D. Keller (Editors). Trade Cloth. Bilingual Press/Editorial Bilingue. Tempe, AZ. 1988. 158p. ISBN:0-916950-89-1, ISBN13: 978-0-916950-89-7. Dewey:863. LCCN:88-071440.

Audience: **u,f.**

Lattin, Vernon E.   **PS153.M4C66 1986**
  (Editor, Introduction by)
Contemporary Chicano Fiction: A Critical Survey. Trade Cloth. Bilingual Press/Editorial Bilingue. Tempe, AZ. 1986. 336p. Studies in the Language and Literature of United States Hispanos ISBN:0-916950-56-5, ISBN13: 978-0-916950-56-9. Dewey:813/.54/00986872073. LCCN:85-071528.

Audience: **u,f.**

Lee, Joyce G.   **PS3558.I545Z76 1997**
Rolando Hinojosa and the American Dream. Trade Cloth. University of North Texas Press. Denton, TX. 1997. 221p. Texas Writers Ser., Vol. 5 ISBN:1-57441-023-7, ISBN13: 978-1-57441-023-5. Dewey:813/.54. LCCN:96-050027.

Audience: **u,f.** *Choice, 1998.*

Leonard, Kathy S.   **Z1229.M48L46 2002**
Bibliographic Guide to Chicana and Latina Narrative. Cloth Text. Greenwood Publishing Group, Inc. Portsmouth, NH. 2003. 290p. Bibliographies and Indexes in Women's Studies, No. 31 ISBN:0-313-31987-1, ISBN13: 978-0-313-31987-7. Dewey:016.8109/9287/08968. LCCN:2002-069607.

Audience: **u,f.** *Choice, 2004.*

Limon, Graciela   **PS3562.I464M46 1994**
The Memories of Ana Calderon. Trade Cloth. Arte Publico Press. Houston, TX. 1994. 200p. ISBN:1-55885-116-X, ISBN13: 978-1-55885-116-0. Dewey:813/.54. LCCN:94-008663.

Audience: **l,u.**

Limon, Graciela   PS3562.I464S66 1996
Song of the Hummingbird. Trade Paper. Arte Publico Press.
Houston, TX. 1996. 224p. ISBN:1-55885-091-0, ISBN13:
978-1-55885-091-0. Dewey:813/.54. LCCN:95-037666.
                                   Audience: **l,u.** *Choice, 1996.*

Lomelí, Francisco A. &   PS153.M4C485 1999
  Shirley, Carl R.
Chicano Writers. Cloth Text. Thomson Gale. Farmington Hills,
MI. 1999. 400p. Dictionary of Literary Biography Ser., Vol. 209
ISBN:0-7876-3103-5, ISBN13: 978-0-7876-3103-1.
Dewey:810.9/86872/03 B. LCCN:99-027671.
                                   Audience: **g,l,u.** *Choice, 2000.*

Luz Montes, Amelia   PS2736.R53 Z74 2004
  María de la & Goldman, Anne Elizabeth (Editors)
Maria Amparo Ruiz de Burton: Critical and Pedagogical
Perspectives. Cloth Text. University of Nebraska Press. Lincoln,
NE. 2004. x, 303p. Postwestern Horizons Ser.
ISBN:0-8032-3234-9, ISBN13: 978-0-8032-3234-1.
Dewey:813/.4. LCCN:2003-061289.
                                   Audience: **u,f.** *Choice, 2004.*

López, Miguel R.   PS3569.A4677Z76 2001
Chicano Timespace: The Poetry and Politics of Ricardo
Sanchez. Trade Cloth. Texas A&M University Press. College
Station, TX. 2001. xi, 199p. Rio Grande/Rio Bravo Ser., Vol. 3
ISBN:0-89096-962-0, ISBN13: 978-0-89096-962-5.
Dewey:811/.54. LCCN:00-031661.
                                   Audience: **u,f.** *Choice, 2001.*

López-Stafford, Gloria   E394.E4
A Place in El Paso: A Mexican-American Childhood. Trade
Paper. University of New Mexico Press. Albuquerque, NM.
1996. 222p. ISBN:0-8263-1709-X, ISBN13: 978-0-8263-1709-4.
Dewey:976.4/96 B.
                                   Audience: **l,u.** *Choice, 1996.*

Madsen, Deborah L.   PS153.M4M33 2000
Understanding Contemporary Chicana Literature. Trade Cloth.
University of South Carolina Press. Columbia, SC. 2001. 283p.
Understanding Contemporary American Literature Ser.
ISBN:1-57003-379-X, ISBN13: 978-1-57003-379-7.
Dewey:810.9/9287/0896872. LCCN:00-011471.
                                   Audience: **u,f.** *Choice, 2001.*

Martín-Rodríguez,   PS153.M4M365 2003
  Manuel M.
Life in Search of Readers: Reading in Chicano: A Literature.
Trade Cloth. University of New Mexico Press. Albuquerque,
NM. 2003. 232p. ISBN:0-8263-3360-5, ISBN13:
978-0-8263-3360-5. Dewey:810.9/86872. LCCN:2003-012773.
                                   Audience: **u,f.** *Choice, 2004.*

Martínez, Demetria   PS3568.O243
Mother Tongue. Trade Paper. Ballantine Books. New York, NY.
1997. 208p. ISBN:0-345-41656-2, ISBN13: 978-0-345-41656-8.
Dewey:813/.54.
                                   Audience: **l,u.**

Martínez, Julio A. &   PS153
  Lomelí, Francisco A. (Editors)
Chicano Literature: A Reference Guide. Cloth Text. Greenwood
Publishing Group, Inc. Portsmouth, NH. 1985. 492p.
ISBN:0-313-23691-7, ISBN13: 978-0-313-23691-4.
Dewey:809/.86872. LCCN:83-022583.
                                   Audience: **g,l,u.** *B Choice, 1985.*

Martínez, Manuel Luis   PS228.B6M37 2003
Countering the Counterculture: Rereading Postwar American
Dissent from Jack Kerouac to Tomás Rivera. Trade Cloth.
University of Wisconsin Press. Chicago, IL. 2003.
ISBN:0-299-19280-6, ISBN13: 978-0-299-19280-8.
Dewey:810.9/358. LCCN:2003-005654.
                                   Audience: **u,f.** *Choice, 2004.*

McKenna, Teresa   PS153.M4M55 1997
Migrant Song: Politics and Process in Contemporary Chicano
Literature. Trade Cloth. University of Texas Press. Austin, TX.
1997. 170p. ISBN:0-292-76518-5, ISBN13: 978-0-292-76518-4.
Dewey:810.9/86872/09045. LCCN:96-025379.
                                   Audience: **u,f.** *Choice, 1998.*

Mena, Maria C.   E184.M5 M66 1997
The Collected Stories of Maria Cristina Mena. Amy Doherty
(Editor). Trade Paper. Arte Publico Press. Houston, TX. 1997.
208p. Recovering the U.S.-Hispanic Literary Heritage Ser.
ISBN:1-55885-211-5, ISBN13: 978-1-55885-211-2.
Dewey:973/.046872/0092. LCCN:97-022160.
                                   Audience: **l,u.**

Mendez, Miguel   PQ7079.2.M46
Pilgrims in Aztlan. David W. Foster (Translator). Trade Cloth.
Bilingual Press/Editorial Bilingue. Tempe, AZ. 1992. 184p.
ISBN:0-927534-23-1, ISBN13: 978-0-927534-23-9. Dewey:863.
LCCN:92-023636.
                                   Audience: **l,u.**

Metzger, Linda (Editor)   PQ7081.3.H58 1991
Hispanic Writers: A Selection of Sketches from Contemporary
Authors. Trade Cloth. Thomson Gale. Farmington Hills, MI.
1990. 514p. ISBN:0-8103-7688-1, ISBN13: 978-0-8103-7688-5.
Dewey:860.998. LCCN:90-083635.
                                   Audience: **g,l,u.** *Choice, 1991.*

Metzger, Linda & Ryan,   PQ7081.3 .H58 1999
  Alan
Hispanic Writers: A Selection of Sketches from Contemporary
Authors. Ed. 2. Trade Cloth. Thomson Gale. Farmington Hills,
MI. 1999. 551p. ISBN:0-8103-8377-2, ISBN13:
978-0-8103-8377-7. Dewey:860.998.
                                   Audience: **g,l,u.** *Choice, 1991.*

Mora, Pat   PS3563.O73B67 1986
Borders. Ed. 2. Trade Paper. Arte Publico Press. Houston, TX.
1986. 88p. ISBN:0-934770-57-3, ISBN13: 978-0-934770-57-6.
Dewey:811.54. LCCN:85-073352.
                                   Audience: **g,l,u,f.**

Mora, Pat   PS3563.O73 C48 1984
Chants. Ed. 2. Trade Paper. Arte Publico Press. Houston, TX.
1985. 52p. ISBN:0-934770-24-7, ISBN13: 978-0-934770-24-8.
Dewey:811/.54. LCCN:83-070677.
                                   Audience: **g,l,u,f.**

Mora, Pat   PS3563.O73C6 1991
Communion. Trade Paper. Arte Publico Press. Houston, TX.
1991. 92p. ISBN:1-55885-035-X, ISBN13: 978-1-55885-035-4.
Dewey:811/.54. LCCN:91-000305.
                                   Audience: **g,l,u,f.**

Moraga, Cherríe   PS3563.O753L6 2000
Loving in the War Years: Lo Que Nunca Paso por Sus Labios.
Ed. 2. Trade Cloth. South End Press. Cambridge, MA. 2000.
208p. Classics Ser., Vol. 6 ISBN:0-89608-627-5, ISBN13:
978-0-89608-627-2. Dewey:818/.5409. LCCN:00-057344.
                                   Audience: **l,u.**

Morales, Alejandro   PS3563.O759B7 1988
The Brick People. Ed. 2. Trade Paper. Arte Publico Press.
Houston, TX. 1992. 320p. ISBN:0-934770-91-3, ISBN13:
978-0-934770-91-0. Dewey:863. LCCN:88-010409.

Audience: **g,l,u,f.** *Choice, 1989.*

Morales, Alejandro   PS3563.O759R34 1991
The Rag Doll Plagues. Trade Cloth. Arte Publico Press.
Houston, TX. 1992. 200p. ISBN:1-55885-036-8, ISBN13:
978-1-55885-036-1. Dewey:863. LCCN:91-002381.

Audience: **l,u.**

Morton, Carlos   PS3563.O88194D74
Dreaming on a Sunday in the Alameda and Other Plays. Trade
Cloth. University of Oklahoma Press. Norman, OK. 2004. 192p.
Chicana & Chicano Visions of the Americas Ser., Vol. 3
ISBN:0-8061-3626-X, ISBN13: 978-0-8061-3626-4.
Dewey:812/.54. LCCN:2004-045870.

Audience: **l,u.**

Nava, Michael   PS3564
The Little Death: A Henry Rios Mystery. Trade Paper. Alyson
Publications. Los Angeles, CA. 2003. 168p.
ISBN:1-55583-830-8, ISBN13: 978-1-55583-830-0.
Dewey:813.5/4.

Audience: **l,u.**

Paredes, Americo   PS3531.A525H36 1994
The Hammon and the Beans and Other Stories. Trade Paper.
Arte Publico Press. Houston, TX. 1994. 230p.
ISBN:1-55885-071-6, ISBN13: 978-1-55885-071-2.
Dewey:813/.54. LCCN:93-045644.

Audience: **g,l,u,f.**

Parédes, Americo   PS3531.A525G4 1990
George Washington Gómez. Trade Paper. Arte Publico Press.
Houston, TX. 1990. 302p. ISBN:1-55885-012-0, ISBN13:
978-1-55885-012-5. Dewey:813/.54. LCCN:89-048145.

Audience: **l,u.**

Poey, Delia   PS153.H56.P64 2002
Latino Literature in the Classroom: The Politics of
Transformation. Trade Cloth. University Press of Florida.
Gainesville, FL. 2002. 144p. ISBN:0-8130-2477-3, ISBN13:
978-0-8130-2477-6. Dewey:810.9/868073071.
LCCN:2002-016570.

Audience: **f.** *Choice, 2002.*

Pèrez-Torres, Rafael   PS153.M4 P47 1995
Movements in Chicano Poetry: Against Myths, Against Margins.
Albert Gelpi & Ross Posnock (Contribution by). Trade Paper.
Cambridge University Press. New York, NY. 1995. 348p.
Studies in American Literature and Culture, No. 88
ISBN:0-521-47803-0, ISBN13: 978-0-521-47803-8.
Dewey:811.009/86872. LCCN:94-022380.

Audience: **u,f.**

Quintana, Alvina E.   PQ7081.A1
Reading U. S. Latina Writers: Remapping American Literature.
Trade Paper, Perfect. Palgrave Macmillan. New York, NY. 2005.
224p. ISBN:1-4039-6945-0, ISBN13: 978-1-4039-6945-3.
Dewey:860.9/9287/098.

Audience: **u,f.** *Choice, 2004.*

Quintana, Leroy V.   PS3567.U365P76 2002
La Promesa and Other Stories. Trade Cloth. University of
Oklahoma Press. Norman, OK. 2002. 192p. Chicana and

Chicano Visions of the Americas Ser., Vol. 1
ISBN:0-8061-3449-6, ISBN13: 978-0-8061-3449-9.
Dewey:813/.54. LCCN:2002-017307.

Audience: **l,u.**

Ramos, Manuel   PS3568.A4468
The Ballad of Rocky Ruiz. Ilan Stavans (Introduction by), Gary
Phillips (Foreword by). Trade Paper. Northwestern University
Press. Evanston, IL. 2004. 212p. Latino Voices Ser.
ISBN:0-8101-2090-9, ISBN13: 978-0-8101-2090-7.
Dewey:813/.54. LCCN:2003-060960.

Audience: **l,u.**

Rebolledo, Tey D.   PS153.M4R43 1995
Women Singing in the Snow: A Cultural Analysis of Chicana
Literature. Library Binding. University of Arizona Press.
Tucson, AZ. 1995. 250p. ISBN:0-8165-1520-4, ISBN13:
978-0-8165-1520-2. Dewey:810.9/9287/0896872.
LCCN:94-018740.

Audience: **u,f.** *Choice, 1995.*

Rebolledo, Tey Diana   PS153.M4R427 2005
The Chronicles of Panchita Villa and Other Guerrilleras: Essays
on Chicana/Latina Literature and Criticism. Trade Cloth.
University of Texas Press. Austin, TX. 2006. 280p. Chicana
Matters Ser. ISBN:0-292-70692-8, ISBN13: 978-0-292-70692-7.
Dewey:810.9/9287. LCCN:2005-007620.

Audience: **u,f.** *Choice, 2006.*

Rebolledo, Tey D. &   F805.M5W66 2000
  Marquez, Maria T. (Editors)
La Diabla a Pie: Women's Tales from the New Mexico WPA.
Trade Paper. Arte Publico Press. Houston, TX. 2000. 512p.
Recovering the U.S.-Hispanic Literary Heritage Ser.
ISBN:1-55885-312-X, ISBN13: 978-1-55885-312-6.
Dewey:305.868/72073. LCCN:00-056589.

Audience: **u,f.** *Choice, 2001.*

Rebolledo, Tey D. &   PS508.W7
  Rivero, Eliana S. (Editors)
Infinite Divisions: An Anthology of Chicana Literature. Trade
Paper. University of Arizona Press. Tucson, AZ. 1993. 387p.
ISBN:0-8165-1384-8, ISBN13: 978-0-8165-1384-0.
Dewey:810.8/09287. LCCN:92-045101.

Audience: **l,u,f.** *Choice, 1994.*

Rechy, John   PS3568
City of Night. Trade Paper. Grove/Atlantic, Inc. New York, NY.
1988. 400p. ISBN:0-8021-3083-6, ISBN13: 978-0-8021-3083-9.
Dewey:813.5. LCCN:83-049451.

Audience: **g,l,u.**

Rechy, John   PS3568.E28M5 2001
The Miraculous Day of Amalia Gómez: A Novel. Trade Paper.
Grove/Atlantic, Inc. New York, NY. 2001. 224p.
ISBN:0-8021-3847-0, ISBN13: 978-0-8021-3847-7.
Dewey:813/.54. LCCN:2001-040159.

Audience: **g,l,u,f.**

Rios, Alberto   PS3568.I587 W5 1982
Whispering to Fool the Wind: Poems. Trade Paper. Sheep
Meadow Press, The. Riverdale-on-Hudson, NY. 1982. 82p.
ISBN:0-935296-31-X, ISBN13: 978-0-935296-31-0.
Dewey:811/.54. LCCN:82-003269.

Audience: **l,u.**

Formats: Web: ☐   Ebook: **ℯ**   CD/DVD-ROM: **✇**   BCL3: **ℬ**

Rivera, Tomás   **PQ7079.2.R5Y2 1996**
Y No Se lo Trago la Tierra. Trade Paper. Arte Publico Press.
Houston, TX. 1996. 115p. ISBN:1-55885-151-8, ISBN13:
978-1-55885-151-1. Dewey:863. LCCN:95-038284.

Audience: **g,l,u.**

Rivera, Tomás   **PQ7079.2.R5H37 1989**
The Harvest - La Cosecha. Julian Olivares (Editor, Translator).
Trade Paper. Arte Publico Press. Houston, TX. 1989. 136p.
ISBN:0-934770-94-8, ISBN13: 978-0-934770-94-1. Dewey:863.
LCCN:88-037945.

Audience: **l,u.**

Robinson, Cecil   **PS277.R6 1992**
No Short Journeys: The Interplay of Cultures in the History and
Literature of the Borderlands. Reed W. Dasenbrook
(Introduction by). Trade Cloth. University of Arizona Press.
Tucson, AZ. 1992. 148p. ISBN:0-8165-1270-1, ISBN13:
978-0-8165-1270-6. Dewey:810.9/86872. LCCN:91-028170.

Audience: **u,f.** *Choice, 1992.*

Rocard, Marcienne   **PS173.M39R613 1989**
The Children of the Sun: Mexican-Americans in the Literature
of the United States. Edward G. Brown Jr. (Translator). Trade
Cloth. University of Arizona Press. Tucson, AZ. 1989. 393p.
ISBN:0-8165-0992-1, ISBN13: 978-0-8165-0992-8.
Dewey:810/.9/352036872. LCCN:88-039772.

Audience: **u,f.** *Choice, 1990.*

Rodriguez, Luis J.   **HV6439.U7L77 2005**
Always Running: La Vida Loca: Gang Days in L. A. Trade
Paper. Simon & Schuster. New York, NY. 2005. 288p.
ISBN:0-7432-7691-4, ISBN13: 978-0-7432-7691-7.
Dewey:364.1092 B. LCCN:2005-281606.

Audience: **g,l,u.**

Ruiz de Burton, Maria   **PS2736.R53S658 2004**
Amparo
The Squatter and the Don. Ana Castillo (Introduction by). Trade
Paper. Random House, Inc. New York, NY. 2004. 432p.
ISBN:0-8129-7289-9, ISBN13: 978-0-8129-7289-4.
Dewey:813/.4. LCCN:2004-054689.

Audience: **l,u.**

Ruiz de Burton,   **PS2736.R53W48 1995**
Maria A.
Who Would Have Thought It? Rosaura Sanchez & Beatrice Pita
(Editor, Introduction by). Trade Paper. Arte Publico Press.
Houston, TX. 1995. 298p. Recovering the U.S.-Hispanic
Literary Heritage Ser. ISBN:1-55885-081-3, ISBN13:
978-1-55885-081-1. Dewey:813/.4. LCCN:95-011585.

Audience: **l,u.** *Choice, 1996.*

Salas, Floyd   **PS3569.A459**
Buffalo Nickel. Trade Cloth. Arte Publico Press. Houston, TX.
1992. 250p. ISBN:1-55885-049-X, ISBN13: 978-1-55885-049-1.
Dewey:813/.54 B. LCCN:91-048217.

Audience: **l,u.**

Saldivar, Ramon   **PS153.M4S24 1990**
Chicano Narrative: The Dialectics of Difference. Cloth Text.
University of Wisconsin Press. Chicago, IL. 1990. 256p.
Wisconsin Project on American Writers Ser.
ISBN:0-299-12470-3, ISBN13: 978-0-299-12470-0.
Dewey:810.9/6872. LCCN:89-040535.

Audience: **u,f.** *Choice, 1991.*

Saldivar-Hull, Sonia   **PS374.M4837 S25 2000**
Feminism on the Border: Chicana Gender Politics and
Literature. Trade Cloth. University of California Press. Berkeley,
CA. 2000. 226p. ISBN:0-520-20732-7, ISBN13:
978-0-520-20732-5. Dewey:813/.54099287. LCCN:99-053297.

Audience: **u,f.** *Choice, 2000.*

Smith, Leonora   **E184.M5V53 1994**
The Rebel. Clara Lomas (Editor). Trade Paper. Arte Publico
Press. Houston, TX. 1994. 297p. Recovering the U.S.-Hispanic
Literary Heritage Ser. ISBN:1-55885-056-2, ISBN13:
978-1-55885-056-9. Dewey:973/.046872/0092 B.
LCCN:93-003607.

Audience: **l,u.** *Choice, 1995.*

Sotelo, Susan Baker   **PS374.D4S69 2005**
Chicano Detective Fiction: A Critical Study of Five Novelists.
Paper Text. McFarland & Company, Incorporated Publishers.
Jefferson, NC. 2005. 235p. ISBN:0-7864-2185-1, ISBN13:
978-0-7864-2185-5. Dewey:813.08720908. LCCN:2005-007357.

Audience: **u,f.**

Soto, Gary   **PS3566.L27**
The Elements of San Joaquin. Trade Paper. University of
Pittsburgh Press. Pittsburgh, PA. 1977. 56p. Pitt Poetry Ser.
ISBN:0-8229-5279-3, ISBN13: 978-0-8229-5279-4.
Dewey:811/.54. LCCN:76-026104.

Audience: **l,u.**

Stavans, Ilan   **CT275.A186S73 2003**
Bandido: The Death and Resurrection of Oscar Zeta Acosta.
Trade Paper. Northwestern University Press. Evanston, IL. 2003.
152p. Latino Voices Ser. ISBN:0-8101-2028-3, ISBN13:
978-0-8101-2028-0. Dewey:978/.0046872/0092 B.
LCCN:2003-044173.

Audience: **u,f.**

Stavans, Ilan (Editor)   **CT275.A186A25 1996**
Oscar Zeta Acosta: The Uncollected Works. Trade Paper. Arte
Publico Press. Houston, TX. 1996. 368p. ISBN:1-55885-099-6,
ISBN13: 978-1-55885-099-6. Dewey:973/.046872/0092 B.
LCCN:95-033398.

Audience: **u,f.** *Choice, 1996.*

Suárez, Mario, et al.   **PS3569.U155C48 2004**
Chicano Sketches: Short Stories. Francisco A. Lomelí, Cecilia
Felicia Cota-Robles Suarez & Juan Casillas-Núñez (Authors).
Trade Cloth. University of Arizona Press. Tucson, AZ. 2004.
190p. ISBN:0-8165-2404-1, ISBN13: 978-0-8165-2404-4.
Dewey:813/.54. LCCN:2004-006903.

Audience: **l,u.**

Sánchez, Marta Ester   **PS153.M4.S26 1985**
ⓔ Contemporary Chicana Poetry: A Critical Approach to an
Emerging Literature. E-Book. NetLibrary, Inc. Boulder, CO.
1985. ISBN:0-585-34175-3, ISBN13: 978-0-585-34175-0.
Dewey:811/.54/0986872073.

Audience: **u,f.**

Tatum, Charles M.   **PS508.M4**
(Editor)
New Chicana - Chicano Writing. Library Binding. University of
Arizona Press. Tucson, AZ. 1993. 165p. ISBN:0-8165-1425-9,
ISBN13: 978-0-8165-1425-0. Dewey:808.

Audience: **l,u.**

Tatum, Charles M.   QA10.5
(Editor)
New Chicana/Chicano Writing, Set. Trade Paper. University of Arizona Press. Tucson, AZ. 1992. 600p. ISBN:0-8165-1307-4, ISBN13: 978-0-8165-1307-9. Dewey:510.92. LCCN:92-642671.
Audience: **l,u.**

Trambley, Estela P.   PS3570.R3342
Rain of Scorpions and Other Stories. Trade Cloth. Bilingual Press/Editorial Bilingue. Tempe, AZ. 1993. 184p. Clasicos Chicanos Ser., No. 9 ISBN:0-927534-28-2, ISBN13: 978-0-927534-28-4. Dewey:813/.54. LCCN:92-025450.
Audience: **l,u.**

Ulibarrí, Sabine R.   PQ7079.2.U4 M5
Mi Abuela Fumaba Puros. Trade Paper. T Q S Publications, Eclectic Chicano Literature. Berkeley, CA. 1977. 167p. ISBN:0-88412-105-4, ISBN13: 978-0-88412-105-3. Dewey:863. LCCN:77-085179.
Audience: **l,u.**

Ulibarrí, Sabine R.   PQ7079.2.U4.T5131993
Tierra Amarilla: Stories of New Mexico/Cuentos de Nuevo Mexico. Trade Cloth. University of New Mexico Press. Albuquerque, NM. 1993. 167p. Paso Por Aqui: Series on the Nuevomexicano Literary Heritage Ser. ISBN:0-8263-1438-4, ISBN13: 978-0-8263-1438-3. Dewey:863. LCCN:93-001882.
Audience: **l,u.**

Urrea, Luis Alberto   PS3571.R74H86 2005
The Hummingbird's Daughter: A Novel. Trade Cloth. Little Brown & Company. New York, NY. 2005. 512p. ISBN:0-316-74546-4, ISBN13: 978-0-316-74546-8. Dewey:813/.54. LCCN:2004-027849.
Audience: **l,u.**

Valdez, Luis   PS3572.A387A6 1990
Luis Valdez - Early Works: Actos, Bernabe and Pensamiento Serpentino. Trade Paper. Arte Publico Press. Houston, TX. 1990. 189p. Latin-American Play Anthologies Ser. ISBN:1-55885-003-1, ISBN13: 978-1-55885-003-3. Dewey:812/.54. LCCN:89-035438.
Audience: **l,u.**

Valdez, Luis   PS3572.A387Z6 1992
Zoot Suit and Other Plays. Trade Paper. Arte Publico Press. Houston, TX. 2003. 216p. Latin-American Play Anthologies Ser. ISBN:1-55885-048-1, ISBN13: 978-1-55885-048-4. Dewey:812/.54. LCCN:91-041789.
Audience: **g,l,u.**

Vasquez, Richard   PS3572.A85
Chicano: A Novel. Trade Paper. HarperCollins Publishers. New York, NY. 2005. 464p. ISBN:0-06-082104-3, ISBN13: 978-0-06-082104-3. Dewey:811.54.
Audience: **g,l,u.**

Venegas, Daniel &   PQ7079.2.V34A9413
Brammer, Ethriam C.
The Adventures of Don Chipote: Or When Parrots Breast-Feed. Trade Paper. Arte Publico Press. Houston, TX. 2000. 168p. Recovering the U.S.-Hispanic Literary Heritage Ser. ISBN:1-55885-297-2, ISBN13: 978-1-55885-297-6. Dewey:863/.64. LCCN:00-023987.
Audience: **l,u.**

Vigil, Evangelina   PS3572.I34 T55 1985
Thirty an' Seen a Lot. Trade Paper. Arte Publico Press. Houston, TX. 1982. 72p. ISBN:0-934770-13-1, ISBN13: 978-0-934770-13-2. Dewey:811.54. LCCN:81-068073.
Audience: **l,u.**

Villa, Raúl Homero   PS153.M4V55 2000
Barrio-Logos: Space and Place in Urban Chicano Literature and Culture. Trade Cloth. University of Texas Press. Austin, TX. 2000. 286p. Center for Mexican American Studies ISBN:0-292-78741-3, ISBN13: 978-0-292-78741-4. Dewey:810.9/86872. LCCN:99-030871.
Audience: **u,f.** *Choice, 2000.*

Villarreal, Jose A.   PS3568.O243
Pocho. Trade Paper. Alfred A. Knopf Inc. New York, NY. 1994. 272p. ISBN:0-385-47407-5, ISBN13: 978-0-385-47407-8. Dewey:813/.54. LCCN:71-011196.
Audience: **g,l,u.**

Villaseñor, Victor   PS3572.I384R35 1991
Rain of Gold. Trade Cloth. Arte Publico Press. Houston, TX. 1991. 552p. ISBN:1-55885-030-9, ISBN13: 978-1-55885-030-9. Dewey:[B]. LCCN:91-007587.
Audience: **g,l,u.**

Viramontes, Helena M.   PS3572.I63M6 1995
The Moths and Other Stories. Ed. 2. Trade Paper. Arte Publico Press. Houston, TX. 1995. 200p. ISBN:1-55885-138-0, ISBN13: 978-1-55885-138-2. Dewey:813/.54. LCCN:84-072308.
Audience: **l,u.**

Vázquez, Diego   PS3572.A987G7 1997
Growing Through the Ugly. Trade Cloth. W. W. Norton & Company, Inc. New York, NY. 1997. 224p. ISBN:0-393-03963-3, ISBN13: 978-0-393-03963-4. Dewey:813/.54. LCCN:96-025904.
Audience: **l,u.** *Choice, 1997.*

West, Alan (Editor)   PS153.H56L39 2004
Latino and Latina Writers. Trade Cloth. Thomson Gale. Farmington Hills, MI. 2004. 1100p. Scribner Writers Ser. ISBN:0-684-31293-X, ISBN13: 978-0-684-31293-4. Dewey:810.9/868. LCCN:2003-015728.
Audience: **l,u.** *Choice, 2004.*

Yarbro-Bejarano,   PS3563.O753Z96 2001
Yvonne
The Wounded Heart: Writing on Cherríe Moraga. Trade Cloth. University of Texas Press. Austin, TX. 2001. 217p. Chicano Matters Ser. ISBN:0-292-79607-2, ISBN13: 978-0-292-79607-2. Dewey:818/.5409. LCCN:2001-017139.
Audience: **u,f.** *Choice, 2002.*

Zilles, Klaus   PS3558.I545Z94 2001
Rolando Hinojosa: A Reader's Guide. Trade Cloth. University of New Mexico Press. Albuquerque, NM. 2004. 233p. ISBN:0-8263-2275-1, ISBN13: 978-0-8263-2275-3. Dewey:813/.54. LCCN:2001-002287.
Audience: **u,f.**

Humanities > Literature > Other Latino/a Literatures

Agüeros, Jack   PS3551.G845.D66 1993
Dominoes and Other Stories from the Puerto Rican. Trade Cloth. Curbstone Press. Willimantic, CT. 1993. 149p.

ISBN:1-880684-11-X, ISBN13: 978-1-880684-11-5.
Dewey:813/.54. LCCN:93-004849.

                        Audience: **g,l,u.** *Choice, 1994.*

Algarin, Miguel   **PS3551.L359L6 1997**
Love Is Hard Work: Memorias de Loisaida/Poems. Trade Paper.
Simon & Schuster. New York, NY. 1997. 160p.
ISBN:0-684-82517-1, ISBN13: 978-0-684-82517-5.
Dewey:811/.54. LCCN:97-002093.

                                Audience: **l,u.**

Algarin, Miguel &   **PS591.P8A46 1994**
  Holman, Bob (Editors)
Aloud!: Voices from the Nuyorican Poets Cafe. Trade Paper.
Henry Holt & Company. New York, NY. 1994. 544p.
ISBN:0-8050-3257-6, ISBN13: 978-0-8050-3257-4.
Dewey:811/.540808687295. LCCN:94-001240.

                                 Audience: **l,u.**

Alvarez, Julia   **PS3551.L845H66 1991**
How the Garcia Girls Lost Their Accents. Trade Cloth.
Algonquin Books of Chapel Hill. Chapel Hill, NC. 1999. 308p.
ISBN:0-945575-57-2, ISBN13: 978-0-945575-57-3. Dewey:FIC.
LCCN:90-048575.

                              Audience: **g,l,u.**

Alvarez, Julia   **PS3551.L845I45 2000**
In the Name of Salome. Trade Cloth. Algonquin Books of
Chapel Hill. Chapel Hill, NC. 2000. 368p. ISBN:1-56512-276-3,
ISBN13: 978-1-56512-276-5. Dewey:813/.54. LCCN:00-025818.

                                 Audience: **l,u.**

Alvarez, Julia   **PS3551.L845Y6 1997**
Yo!: A Novel. Trade Cloth. Algonquin Books of Chapel Hill.
Chapel Hill, NC. 2004. 350p. ISBN:1-56512-157-0, ISBN13:
978-1-56512-157-7. Dewey:813/.54. LCCN:96-024611.

                                 Audience: **l,u.**

Ambert, Alba N.   **PS3551.M23P47 1995**
A Perfect Silence. Trade Cloth. Arte Publico Press. Houston,
TX. 1995. 199p. ISBN:1-55885-125-9, ISBN13:
978-1-55885-125-2. Dewey:813/.54. LCCN:94-029360.

                     Audience: **l,u.** *Choice, 1995.*

Antush, John V.   **PS628.P84N84 1994**
  (Editor)
Nuestro New York: An Anthology of Puerto Rican Plays. Mass
Market. Penguin Group (USA) Inc. New York, NY. 1994. 608p.
ISBN:0-451-62868-3, ISBN13: 978-0-451-62868-8.
Dewey:812/.5408097295. LCCN:93-080398.

                                 Audience: **l,u.**

Arenas, Reinaldo   **PQ7390.A72**
The Doorman. Trade Paper. Grove/Atlantic, Inc. New York, NY.
1994. 208p. ISBN:0-8021-3405-X, ISBN13: 978-0-8021-3405-9.
Dewey:863.6. LCCN:90-028775.

                                 Audience: **l,u.**

Behar, Ruth (Editor)   **PS508.C83B75 1995**
Bridges to Cuba/Puentes a Cuba. Trade Paper. University of
Michigan Press. Chicago, IL. 1996. 448p. ISBN:0-472-06611-0,
ISBN13: 978-0-472-06611-7. Dewey:810.8/08687291.
LCCN:95-034522.

                     Audience: **l,u.** *Choice, 1996.*

Borland, Isabel A.   **PS153.C83A58 1998**
Cuban-American Literature of Exile: From Person to Persona.
Trade Paper. University Press of Virginia. Charlottesville, VA.
1998. 190p. New World Studies, : ISBN:0-8139-1813-8,

ISBN13: 978-0-8139-1813-6. Dewey:810.98687291073.
LCCN:98-015446.

                     Audience: **u,f.** *Choice, 1999.*

Campo, Rafael   **PS3553.A4883L36 2002**
Landscape with Human Figure. Trade Cloth. Duke University
Press. Durham, NC. 2002. 112p. ISBN:0-8223-2875-5, ISBN13:
978-0-8223-2875-9. Dewey:811/.54. LCCN:2001-047057.

                                 Audience: **l,u.**

Carlito, M. Delores   **Z1231.F4C365 2005**
Cuban American Fiction in English: An Annotated Bibliography
of Primary and Secondary Sources. Trade Paper. Scarecrow
Press, Inc. Lanham, MD. 2005. 138p. ISBN:0-8108-5680-8,
ISBN13: 978-0-8108-5680-6. Dewey:016.813008/08687291.
LCCN:2005-007603.

                                 Audience: **u,f.**

Cocco de Filippis, Daisy   **PQ7408**
  & Gutierrez, Franklin (Editors)
Stories from Washington Heights and Other Corners of the
World - Historias de Washington Heights y Otros Rincones del
Mundo. Trade Paper. Latino Press. Bronx, NY. 1994. 204p.
ISBN:1-884912-02-8, ISBN13: 978-1-884912-02-3.
Dewey:860.8097293.

                                 Audience: **l,u.**

Cofer, Judith Ortiz   **PS3565.R7737Z477**
Silent Dancing: A Partial Remembrance of a Puerto Rican
Childhood. Ed. 2. Trade Paper. Arte Publico Press. Houston,
TX. 1991. 168p. ISBN:1-55885-015-5, ISBN13:
978-1-55885-015-6. Dewey:818/.5403 B. LCCN:89-077428.

                                 Audience: **l,u.**

Cofer, Judith Ortiz   **PS3566.L27**
Terms of Survival. Ed. 2. Trade Paper. Arte Publico Press.
Houston, TX. 1995. 64p. ISBN:1-55885-079-1, ISBN13:
978-1-55885-079-8. Dewey:811/.54. LCCN:87-070270.

                                 Audience: **l,u.**

Cortina, Rodolfo   **PS628.C82C83 1991**
Cuban American Theater. Miguel Pando (Editor). Trade Paper.
Arte Publico Press. Houston, TX. 1992. 280p. Latin-American
Play Anthologies Ser. ISBN:1-55885-020-1, ISBN13:
978-1-55885-020-0. Dewey:812/.5408097291. LCCN:91-009898.

                                 Audience: **l,u.**

Cruz, Angie   **PS3553.R7858**
Let It Rain Coffee. Trade Paper. Simon & Schuster. New York,
NY. 2006. 304p. ISBN:0-7432-1204-5, ISBN13:
978-0-7432-1204-5.

                                 Audience: **l,u.**

De Burgos, Julia   **PQ7439.B9A17 1997**
Song of the Simple Truth: The Complete Poems of Julia de
Burgos, Obra Completa Poetica. Jack Agüeros (Translator).
Trade Paper. Curbstone Press. Willimantic, CT. 1995. 524p.
ISBN:1-880684-24-1, ISBN13: 978-1-880684-24-5. Dewey:861.
LCCN:94-039149.

                     Audience: **l,u.** *Choice, 1997.*

De Jesus, Joy L.   **PS508.P84G76 1997**
  (Editor)
Growing up Puerto Rican: 20 Puerto Rican Authors Write in
Fiction and Essay about Childhood. Trade Cloth. HarperCollins
Publishers. New York, NY. 1997. 352p. ISBN:0-688-13740-7,
ISBN13: 978-0-688-13740-3. Dewey:813. LCCN:96-043864.

                                 Audience: **l,u.**

De Laguna, Asela R.   PQ7420.15.I43 1985
 (Editor)
Images and Identities: The Puerto Rican in Two World Contexts.
Trade Paper. Transaction Publishers. Somerset, NJ. 1987. 288p.
ISBN:0-88738-617-2, ISBN13: 978-0-88738-617-6.
Dewey:860/.9/97295. LCCN:85-009930.

                                    Audience: **u.** *Choice, 1987.*

Diaz, Junot   PS3568.O243
Drown. Trade Paper. Penguin Group (USA) Inc. New York, NY.
1997. 224p. ISBN:1-57322-606-8, ISBN13: 978-1-57322-606-6.
Dewey:813.5/4. LCCN:96-018362.

                                                 Audience: **l,u.**

Engle, Margarita M.   PS3555.N4254S57 1993
Singing to Cuba. Trade Paper. Arte Publico Press. Houston, TX.
1993. 164p. ISBN:1-55885-070-8, ISBN13: 978-1-55885-070-5.
Dewey:813/.54. LCCN:93-013446.

                                                 Audience: **l,u.**

Espada, Martin   PS3555.S53T78 1994
Trumpets from the Islands of Their Eviction. Robert Creeley
(Foreword by). Trade Cloth. Bilingual Press/Editorial Bilingue.
Tempe, AZ. 1994. 96p. ISBN:0-927534-51-7, ISBN13:
978-0-927534-51-2. Dewey:811/.54. LCCN:94-035250.

                                                 Audience: **l,u.**

Esteves, Sandra M.   PS3555.S825B55 1990
Bluestown Mockingbird Mambo. Trade Paper. Arte Publico
Press. Houston, TX. 1990. 88p. ISBN:1-55885-017-1, ISBN13:
978-1-55885-017-0. Dewey:811/.54. LCCN:90-000193.

                                                 Audience: **l,u.**

Fernandez, Roberto G.   PS3556.E7243H64 1995
Holy Radishes. Trade Cloth. Arte Publico Press. Houston, TX.
1995. 298p. ISBN:1-55885-075-9, ISBN13: 978-1-55885-075-0.
Dewey:813/.54. LCCN:95-009767.

                                                 Audience: **l,u.**

Fernandez, Roberto G.   PS3568.O243
Raining Backwards. Ed. 2. Trade Paper. Arte Publico Press.
Houston, TX. 1998. 224p. ISBN:1-55885-223-9, ISBN13:
978-1-55885-223-5. Dewey:813/.54.

                                                 Audience: **l,u.**

Foster, David W.   PS153.G38C48 1999
Chicano/Latino Homoerotic Identities. Cloth Text. Garland
Publishing, Inc. New York, NY. 1999. 384p. Reference Library
of the Humanities, Vol. 16 ISBN:0-8153-3228-9, ISBN13:
978-0-8153-3228-2. Dewey:810.8/03538/08664.
LCCN:99-015048.

                                                 Audience: **u,f.**

Foster, David William   PS153.M4 F64 2004
El Ambiente Nuestro: Chicano/Latino Homoerotic Writing.
Trade Cloth. Bilingual Press/Editorial Bilingue. Tempe, AZ.
2005. 200p. ISBN:1-931010-23-4, ISBN13: 978-1-931010-23-8.
LCCN:2003-058298.

                                                 Audience: **u,f.**

García, Cristina   PS3557.A66A73 1997
The Aguero Sisters. Trade Cloth. Alfred A. Knopf Inc. New
York, NY. 1997. 288p. ISBN:0-679-45090-4, ISBN13:
978-0-679-45090-0. Dewey:813.5/4. LCCN:96-052204.

                                                 Audience: **l,u.**

García, Cristina   PS3557.A66D73 1992
Dreaming in Cuban. Trade Cloth. Alfred A. Knopf Inc. New
York, NY. 1992. ISBN:0-679-40883-5, ISBN13:
978-0-679-40883-3. Dewey:813/.54. LCCN:91-020755.

                                                 Audience: **g,l,u.**

García, Cristina (Editor,   PQ7383.5.E5C83 2003
 Introduction by)
Cubanisimo!: The Vintage Book of Contemporary Cuban
Literature. Trade Paper. Knopf Publishing Group. New York,
NY. 2003. 400p. ISBN:0-385-72137-4, ISBN13:
978-0-385-72137-0. Dewey:860.8/097291. LCCN:2002-038076.

                                                 Audience: **g,l,u,f.**

Gonzalez, Lisa Sanchez   PS153.P83S18 2001
Boricua Literature: A Literary History of the Puerto Rican
Diaspora. Trade Cloth. New York University Press. New York,
NY. 2001. 256p. ISBN:0-8147-3146-5, ISBN13:
978-0-8147-3146-8. Dewey:810.9/97295. LCCN:2001-001774.

                                    Audience: **u,f.** *Choice, 2002.*

Griffith, Lois   PS628.P84A28 1997
Action. Miguel Algarin (As told to). Trade Paper. Simon &
Schuster. New York, NY. 1997. 576p. ISBN:0-684-82611-9,
ISBN13: 978-0-684-82611-0. Dewey:812/.5408097295.
LCCN:97-027602.

                                                 Audience: **l,u.**

Hernández Cruz, Victor   PS3553.R8M37 2001
Panoramas: Poems. Trade Paper. Coffee House Press.
Minneapolis, MN. 1997. 192p. ISBN:1-56689-066-7, ISBN13:
978-1-56689-066-3. Dewey:811/.54. LCCN:2001-032479.

                                                 Audience: **l,u.**

Hernández Cruz, Victor   PS3553.R8 R44 1991
Red Beans. Trade Paper. Coffee House Press. Minneapolis, MN.
1991. 160p. ISBN:0-918273-91-9, ISBN13: 978-0-918273-91-8.
Dewey:811/.54. LCCN:91-025377.

                                                 Audience: **l,u.**

Hernández, Carmen D.   PS153
Puerto Rican Voices in English: Interviews with Writers. Trade
Cloth. Greenwood Publishing Group, Inc. Portsmouth, NH.
1997. 264p. ISBN:0-275-95809-4, ISBN13: 978-0-275-95809-1.
Dewey:810.9/8687295. LCCN:96-053924.

                                                 Audience: **l,u,f.**

Hijuelos, Óscar   PS3558.I376M36
The Mambo Kings Play Songs of Love. Trade Paper.
HarperCollins Publishers. New York, NY. 2005. 480p. P. S. Ser.
ISBN:0-06-084530-9, ISBN13: 978-0-06-084530-8.
Dewey:813/.54.

                                                 Audience: **g,l,u.**

Horno Delgado,   PS153.H56B74 1989
 Asunción (Editor), et al.
Breaking Boundaries: Latina Writing and Critical Readings.
Eliana Ortega, Nina M. Scott & Nancy S. Sternbach (Editors).
Cloth Text. University of Massachusetts Press. Amherst, MA.
1989. 288p. ISBN:0-87023-635-0, ISBN13: 978-0-87023-635-8.
Dewey:810/.9/9287. LCCN:88-017141.

                                    Audience: **u,f.** *Choice, 1989.*

Hospital, Carolina   PS3608.O8C48 2004
The Child of Exile: A Poetry Memoir. Trade Paper. Arte Publico
Press. Houston, TX. 2004. 96p. ISBN:1-55885-411-8, ISBN13:
978-1-55885-411-6. Dewey:811/.54. LCCN:2004-041087.

                                                 Audience: **l,u.**

Hospital, Carolina & Cantera, Jorge (Editors)   PS508.C83C46 1996
A Century of Cuban Writers in Florida: Selected Prose and Poetry. Trade Paper. Pineapple Press, Inc. Sarasota, FL. 1996. 238p. ISBN:1-56164-104-9, ISBN13: 978-1-56164-104-8. Dewey:810.8/8687291. LCCN:96-020647.
Audience: **l,u.**

Johnson, Kelli Lyon   PS3551.L845Z74 2005
Julia Alvarez: Writing a New Place on the Map. Saddle Stitched, Cloth over Boards, Dust Jacket. University of New Mexico Press. Albuquerque, NM. 2005. 180p. ISBN:0-8263-3651-5, ISBN13: 978-0-8263-3651-4. Dewey:818/.5409. LCCN:2005-011097.
Audience: **l,u.** *Choice, 2006.*

Kafka, Phillipa   PS153
Saddling la Gringa: Gatekeeping in Literature by Contemporary Latina Writers. Trade Cloth. Greenwood Publishing Group, Inc. Portsmouth, NH. 2000. 192p. Contributions in Women's Studies, Vol. 183 ISBN:0-313-31122-6, ISBN13: 978-0-313-31122-2. Dewey:813/.5099287/08968. LCCN:00-023957.
Audience: **u,f.** *Choice, 2001.*

Kanellos, Nicolas   PS153
Hispanic Literature of the United States: A Comprehensive Reference. Cloth Text. Greenwood Publishing Group, Inc. Portsmouth, NH. 2003. 328p. ISBN:1-57356-558-X, ISBN13: 978-1-57356-558-5. Dewey:810.9/868. LCCN:2003-048542.
Audience: **g,l,u.** *Choice, 2004.*

Kanellos, Nicolás (Editor)   PQ7420
Biographical Dictionary of Hispanic Literature in the United States: The Literature of Puerto Ricans, Puerto Rican Americans, Cuban Americans, and Other Hispanic Writers. Cloth Text. Greenwood Publishing Group, Inc. Portsmouth, NH. 1989. 374p. ISBN:0-313-24465-0, ISBN13: 978-0-313-24465-0. Dewey:016.86/09/973. LCCN:88-037288.
Audience: **g,l,u.** *Choice, 1990.*

Laviera, Tato   PS3562.A849A44 2003
AmeRícan. Trade Paper. Arte Publico Press. Houston, TX. 2003. 96p. ISBN:1-55885-395-2, ISBN13: 978-1-55885-395-9. Dewey:811/.54. LCCN:2003-044427.
Audience: **g,l,u.**

Laviera, Tato   PS3562.A849 E5 1985
Enclave. Juan Flores (Introduction by). Trade Paper. Arte Publico Press. Houston, TX. 1981. 72p. ISBN:0-934770-11-5, ISBN13: 978-0-934770-11-8. Dewey:811.54. LCCN:81-068067.
Audience: **l,u.**

Leonard, Kathy S.   Z1229.M48L46 2002
Bibliographic Guide to Chicana and Latina Narrative. Cloth Text. Greenwood Publishing Group, Inc. Portsmouth, NH. 2003. 290p. Bibliographies and Indexes in Women's Studies, No. 31 ISBN:0-313-31987-1, ISBN13: 978-0-313-31987-7. Dewey:016.8109/9287/08968. LCCN:2002-069607.
Audience: **u,f.** *Choice, 2004.*

Luis, William   PS153.C27L85 1997
Dance Between Two Cultures: Latino Caribbean Literature Written in the United States. Trade Cloth. Vanderbilt University Press. Nashville, TN. 1997. 376p. ISBN:0-8265-1302-6, ISBN13: 978-0-8265-1302-1. Dewey:810.9/868729. LCCN:97-021192.
Audience: **u,f.** *Choice, 1998.*

Manrique, Jaime   PS3563.A573L38 2003
Latin Moon in Manhattan: A Novel. Trade Paper. University of Wisconsin Press. Chicago, IL. 2003. 212p. ISBN:0-299-18754-3, ISBN13: 978-0-299-18754-5. Dewey:813/.54. LCCN:2002-075666.
Audience: **l,u.**

Manrique, Jaime   PS3563.A573T85 2003
Twilight at the Equator: A Novel. Trade Paper. University of Wisconsin Press. Chicago, IL. 2003. 198p. ISBN:0-299-18774-8, ISBN13: 978-0-299-18774-3. Dewey:813/.54. LCCN:2002-075663.
Audience: **l,u.**

Martínez, Julio A. (Editor)   PQ7378
Dictionary of Twentieth-Century Cuban Literature. Cloth Text. Greenwood Publishing Group, Inc. Portsmouth, NH. 1990. 549p. ISBN:0-313-25185-1, ISBN13: 978-0-313-25185-6. Dewey:860/.9/97291. LCCN:88-035805.
Audience: **g,l,u.** *Choice, 1990.*

Medina, Pablo   PS3563.E24C54 2005
The Cigar Roller: A Novel. Trade Cloth. Grove/Atlantic, Inc. New York, NY. 2005. 176p. ISBN:0-8021-1792-9, ISBN13: 978-0-8021-1792-2. Dewey:813/.54. LCCN:2004-054141.
Audience: **l,u.**

Metzger, Linda (Editor)   PQ7081.3.H58 1991
Hispanic Writers: A Selection of Sketches from Contemporary Authors. Trade Cloth. Thomson Gale. Farmington Hills, MI. 1990. 514p. ISBN:0-8103-7688-1, ISBN13: 978-0-8103-7688-5. Dewey:860.998. LCCN:90-083635.
Audience: **g,l,u.** *Choice, 1991.*

Metzger, Linda & Ryan, Alan   PQ7081.3 .H58 1999
Hispanic Writers: A Selection of Sketches from Contemporary Authors. Ed. 2. Trade Cloth. Thomson Gale. Farmington Hills, MI. 1999. 551p. ISBN:0-8103-8377-2, ISBN13: 978-0-8103-8377-7. Dewey:860.998.
Audience: **g,l,u.** *Choice, 1991.*

Mohr, Nicholasa   PS3563.O36
El Bronx Remembered. Trade Cloth. Peter Smith Publisher, Inc. Magnolia, MA. 1994. ISBN:0-8446-6779-X, ISBN13: 978-0-8446-6779-9. Dewey:813/.5/4.
Audience: **g,l.**

Mohr, Nicholasa   PZ7.M7276
Nilda. Ed. 2. Trade Paper. Arte Publico Press. Houston, TX. 1986. 292p. ISBN:0-934770-61-1, ISBN13: 978-0-934770-61-3. Dewey:813.5. LCCN:87-070274.
Audience: **g,l.**

Morales, Aurora L. & Morales, Rosario   PS508.P84M67 1986
Getting Home Alive. Trade Paper. Firebrand Books. Ithaca, NY. 1986. 216p. ISBN:0-932379-19-2, ISBN13: 978-0-932379-19-1. Dewey:810.8/08687295. LCCN:86-022769.
Audience: **l,u.**

Munoz, Elias M.   PS3563.U494B7 1998
Brand New Memory. Trade Paper. Arte Publico Press. Houston, TX. 1998. 224p. ISBN:1-55885-227-1, ISBN13: 978-1-55885-227-3. Dewey:813/.54. LCCN:98-012855.
Audience: **l,u.**

Munoz, Elias M.   PS3563.U494C7 1989
Crazy Love. Trade Paper. Arte Publico Press. Houston, TX.
1988. 160p. ISBN:0-934770-83-2, ISBN13: 978-0-934770-83-5.
Dewey:863. LCCN:88-006394.
                               Audience: **l,u.**

Obejas, Achy   PS3565.B34M4 1996
Memory Mambo. Trade Paper. Cleis Press. San Francisco, CA.
1996. 250p. Fiction and Graphic Novels Ser.
ISBN:1-57344-017-5, ISBN13: 978-1-57344-017-2.
Dewey:813/.54. LCCN:96-016120.
                               Audience: **g,l,u.**

Obejas, Achy   PS3565.B34W4 1994
We Came All the Way from Cuba So You Could Dress Like
This?: Stories. Trade Paper. Cleis Press. San Francisco, CA.
1994. 160p. ISBN:0-939416-93-X, ISBN13: 978-0-939416-93-6.
Dewey:813/.54. LCCN:94-018194.
                               Audience: **l,u.**

Paris, Margaret L.   E184.C97B667 2002
Embracing America: A Cuban Exile Comes of Age. Trade Cloth.
University Press of Florida. Gainesville, FL. 2002. 224p.
ISBN:0-8130-2545-1, ISBN13: 978-0-8130-2545-2.
Dewey:973/.04687291/0092 B. LCCN:2002-027137.
                               Audience: **u,f.**

Perez, Loida Maritza   PS3568.O243
Geographies of Home. Trade Paper. Penguin Group (USA) Inc.
New York, NY. 2000. 336p. ISBN:0-14-025371-8, ISBN13:
978-0-14-025371-9. Dewey:813/.54.
                               Audience: **l,u.**

Pietri, Pedro   PS3566.I424I44 1992
Illusions of a Revolving Door. Alfredo Matilla Rivas (Editor).
Trade Cloth. University of Puerto Rico Press. Rio Piedras, PR.
1993. 260p. ISBN:0-8477-3665-2, ISBN13: 978-0-8477-3665-2.
Dewey:812/.54. LCCN:91-016785.
                               Audience: **l,u.**

Pinero, Miguel   PS3566.I5216
Short Eyes. Trade Paper. Farrar, Straus & Giroux. New York,
NY. 1975. ISBN:0-8090-1232-4, ISBN13: 978-0-8090-1232-9.
Dewey:812/.5/4.
                               Audience: **l,u.**

Pinero, Miguel   PS3566.I5216 S8 1984
The Sun Always Shines for the Cool/Midnight Moon at the
Greasy Spoon: Eulogy for a Small Time Thief. Ed. 2. Trade
Paper. Arte Publico Press. Houston, TX. 2003. 128p.
Latin-American Play Anthologies Ser. ISBN:0-934770-25-5,
ISBN13: 978-0-934770-25-5. Dewey:812/.54. LCCN:83-072582.
                               Audience: **l,u.**

Poey, Delia   PS153.H56.P64 2002
Latino Literature in the Classroom: The Politics of
Transformation. Trade Cloth. University Press of Florida.
Gainesville, FL. 2002. 144p. ISBN:0-8130-2477-3, ISBN13:
978-0-8130-2477-6. Dewey:810.9/868073071.
LCCN:2002-016570.
                         Audience: **f.** *Choice, 2002.*

Prida, Dolores   PS3566.R558B4 1991
Beautiful Senoritas and Other Plays. Judith Weiss (Editor).
Trade Paper. Arte Publico Press. Houston, TX. 1991. 180p.
Latin-American Play Anthologies Ser. ISBN:1-55885-026-0,
ISBN13: 978-1-55885-026-2. Dewey:812/.54. LCCN:90-001239.
                               Audience: **l,u.**

Quesada, Roberto   PQ7509.2.Q44B54 1999
The Big Banana. Walter Krochmal (Translator). Trade Paper.
Arte Publico Press. Houston, TX. 1999. 256p.
ISBN:1-55885-255-7, ISBN13: 978-1-55885-255-6. Dewey:863.
LCCN:98-028333.
                               Audience: **l,u.**

Quintana, Alvina E.   PQ7081.A1
Reading U. S. Latina Writers: Remapping American Literature.
Trade Paper, Perfect. Palgrave Macmillan. New York, NY. 2005.
224p. ISBN:1-4039-6945-0, ISBN13: 978-1-4039-6945-3.
Dewey:860.9/9287/098.
                       Audience: **u,f.** *Choice, 2004.*

Rebolledo, Tey Diana   PS153.M4R427 2005
The Chronicles of Panchita Villa and Other Guerrilleras: Essays
on Chicana/Latina Literature and Criticism. Trade Cloth.
University of Texas Press. Austin, TX. 2006. 280p. Chicana
Matters Ser. ISBN:0-292-70692-8, ISBN13: 978-0-292-70692-7.
Dewey:810.9/9287. LCCN:2005-007620.
                       Audience: **u,f.** *Choice, 2006.*

Rivera, Beatriz   PS3568.I8287A69 1995
African Passions: And Other Stories. Trade Paper. Arte Publico
Press. Houston, TX. 1995. 168p. ISBN:1-55885-135-6, ISBN13:
978-1-55885-135-1. Dewey:813/.54. LCCN:94-036017.
                       Audience: **l,u.** *Choice, 1995.*

Rivera, Carmen S.   PS153.P83R48 2002
Kissing the Mango Tree: Puerto Rican Women Rewriting
American Literature. Trade Paper. Arte Publico Press. Houston,
TX. 2002. 208p. ISBN:1-55885-377-4, ISBN13:
978-1-55885-377-5. Dewey:810.9/9287/097295.
LCCN:2002-066675.
                               Audience: **u,f.**

Rivero Marín, Rosanna   PS3556.E7243R35 2004
Janus Identities and Forked Tongues: Two Caribbean Writers in
the United States. Trade Cloth. Peter Lang Publishing, Inc. New
York, NY. 2004. 161p. Caribbean Studies, Vol. 12
ISBN:0-8204-6736-7, ISBN13: 978-0-8204-6736-8.
Dewey:810.9/353. LCCN:2003-018752.
                               Audience: **u,f.**

Rodriguez, Abraham Jr.   PS3568.O34876
The Boy Without a Flag: Tales of the South Bronx. Ed. 2. Trade
Paper. Milkweed Editions. Minneapolis, MN. 1999. 120p.
ISBN:1-57131-028-2, ISBN13: 978-1-57131-028-6.
Dewey:813/.54.
                               Audience: **l,u.**

Rosario, Nelly   PS3553.R7858
Song of the Water Saints. Trade Paper. Knopf Publishing Group.
New York, NY. 2003. 256p. ISBN:0-375-72549-0, ISBN13:
978-0-375-72549-4.
                               Audience: **l,u.**

Sandin, Lyn Di Iorio   PS153.H56.S36 2004
Killing Spanish: Literary Essays on Ambivalent U. S. Latino/a
Identity. Cloth over Boards. Palgrave Macmillan. New York,
NY. 2004. 192p. ISBN:1-4039-6394-0, ISBN13:
978-1-4039-6394-9. Dewey:860.9/868. LCCN:2004-040120.
                       Audience: **u,f.** *Choice, 2005.*

Santiago, Esmeralda   F128.9.P85
When I Was Puerto Rican. Trade Paper. Da Capo Press, Inc.
Cambridge, MA. 2006. 288p. ISBN:0-306-81452-8, ISBN13:
978-0-306-81452-5. Dewey:974.7/1004687295/009.
                               Audience: **g,l,u.**

Santiago, Roberto   PS508.P84B67 1995
Boricuas: Influential Puerto Rican Writings - An Anthology.
Trade Paper. Ballantine Books. New York, NY. 1995. 400p.
ISBN:0-345-39502-6, ISBN13: 978-0-345-39502-3.
Dewey:810.8/097295. LCCN:95-094411.
Audience: **g,l,u,f.**

Sapia, Yvonne V.   PS3569.A586
Valentino's Hair. Trade Paper. Fiction Collective Two, Inc.
Tallahassee, FL. 1991. 157p. ISBN:0-932511-46-5, ISBN13:
978-0-932511-46-1.
Audience: **l,u.**

Sirias, Silvio   PS3551
Julia Alvarez: A Critical Companion. Cloth Text. Greenwood
Publishing Group, Inc. Portsmouth, NH. 2001. 184p. Critical
Companions to Popular Contemporary Writers Ser.
ISBN:0-313-30993-0, ISBN13: 978-0-313-30993-9.
Dewey:818/.5409. LCCN:2001-033482.
Audience: **l,u.**

Smorkaloff, Pamela   PQ7382.S66 1999
Maria
Contemporary Cuban Writers. Trade Cloth. Thomson Gale.
Farmington Hills, MI. 1999. xxiii, 100p. ISBN:0-8057-1617-3,
ISBN13: 978-0-8057-1617-7. Dewey:863. LCCN:99-027604.
Audience: **l,u.** *Choice, 2000.*

Soto, Pedro Juan   PQ6140.N3
Spiks. Victoria Ortiz (Translator, Introduction by). Trade Cloth.
Monthly Review Press. New York, NY. 1974. 96p.
ISBN:0-85345-299-7, ISBN13: 978-0-85345-299-7.
Dewey:863/.6. LCCN:73-008057.
Audience: **l,u.**

Suarez, Virgil   PS3569.U18G6 1996
Going Under. Trade Cloth. Arte Publico Press. Houston, TX.
1996. 159p. ISBN:1-55885-159-3, ISBN13: 978-1-55885-159-7.
Dewey:813/.54. LCCN:96-013699.
Audience: **l,u.**

Suarez, Virgil   PS3569.U18L38 2002
Latin Jazz. Trade Paper. Louisiana State University Press. Baton
Rouge, LA. 2002. 290p. Voices of the South Ser.
ISBN:0-8071-2790-6, ISBN13: 978-0-8071-2790-2.
Dewey:813/.54. LCCN:2001-054902.
Audience: **l,u.**

Suarez, Virgil & Poey,   PS508.C83L58 1996
Delia (Editors)
Little Havana Blues: A Cuban-American Literature Anthology.
Trade Paper. Arte Publico Press. Houston, TX. 1996. 448p.
ISBN:1-55885-160-7, ISBN13: 978-1-55885-160-3.
Dewey:810.8/0687291. LCCN:96-014242.
Audience: **l,u.** *Choice, 1997.*

Thomas, Piri   F128.9.P8
Down These Mean Streets. Library Binding. Sagebrush
Education Resources. Caledonia, MN. 1997.
ISBN:0-613-81057-0, ISBN13: 978-0-613-81057-9.
Dewey:301.451/67/97471.
Audience: **l,u.**

Tobar, Hector   PS3570.O22 T38
Tattooed Soldier. Trade Paper. Penguin Group (USA) Inc. New
York, NY. 2000. 320p. ISBN:0-14-028861-9, ISBN13:
978-0-14-028861-2. Dewey:813/.54.
Audience: **l,u.**

Turner, Faythe   PS508.P84P8 1991
(Introduction by)
Puerto Rican Writers at Home in the U.S.A.: An Anthology.
Trade Paper. Open Hand Publishing, LLC. Greensboro, NC.
1991. 352p. ISBN:0-940880-31-8, ISBN13: 978-0-940880-31-3.
Dewey:810.8/08687295. LCCN:91-002141.
Audience: **l,u.**

Vando, Gloria   PS3572.A67
Promesas: Geography of the Impossible. Trade Cloth. Arte
Publico Press. Houston, TX. 1993. 96p. ISBN:1-55885-061-9,
ISBN13: 978-1-55885-061-3. Dewey:811/.54. LCCN:92-028053.
Audience: **l,u.**

Vega, Ed   PS3572.E34C37 1991
Casualty Report. Trade Paper. Arte Publico Press. Houston, TX.
1991. 176p. ISBN:1-55885-034-1, ISBN13: 978-1-55885-034-7.
Dewey:813/.54. LCCN:91-007868.
Audience: **l,u.**

West, Alan (Editor)   PS153.H56L39 2004
Latino and Latina Writers. Trade Cloth. Thomson Gale.
Farmington Hills, MI. 2004. 1100p. Scribner Writers Ser.
ISBN:0-684-31293-X, ISBN13: 978-0-684-31293-4.
Dewey:810.9/868. LCCN:2003-015728.
Audience: **l,u.** *Choice, 2004.*

Yglesias, José   PS3575.G5 W3 1980
A Wake in Ybor City. Trade Cloth. Ayer Company Publishers,
Inc. Manchester, NH. 1981. ISBN:0-405-13172-0, ISBN13:
978-0-405-13172-1. Dewey:813/.54. LCCN:79-006225.
Audience: **l,u.**

Humanities > Literature > Poetry

Algarin, Miguel   PS3551.L359L6 1997
Love Is Hard Work: Memorias de Loisaida/Poems. Trade Paper.
Simon & Schuster. New York, NY. 1997. 160p.
ISBN:0-684-82517-1, ISBN13: 978-0-684-82517-5.
Dewey:811/.54. LCCN:97-002093.
Audience: **l,u.**

Algarin, Miguel &   PS591.P8A46 1994
Holman, Bob (Editors)
Aloud!: Voices from the Nuyorican Poets Cafe. Trade Paper.
Henry Holt & Company. New York, NY. 1994. 544p.
ISBN:0-8050-3257-6, ISBN13: 978-0-8050-3257-4.
Dewey:811/.540808687295. LCCN:94-001240.
Audience: **l,u.**

Algarin, Miguel &   PS591.P8
Pinero, Miguel
Nuyorican Poetry: An Anthology of Puerto Rican Words and
Feelings. Trade Paper. HarperCollins Publishers. New York, NY.
1975. ISBN:0-688-07966-0, ISBN13: 978-0-688-07966-6.
Dewey:811/.5/408.
Audience: **l,u.**

Bruce-Novoa, Juan   PS153.M4
Chicano Poetry: A Response to Chaos. Trade Paper. University
of Texas Press. Austin, TX. 1982. 246p. ISBN:0-292-71092-5,
ISBN13: 978-0-292-71092-4. Dewey:811.09. LCCN:81-023129.
Audience: **l,u.**

Campo, Rafael   PS3553.A4883L36 2002
Landscape with Human Figure. Trade Cloth. Duke University
Press. Durham, NC. 2002. 112p. ISBN:0-8223-2875-5, ISBN13:
978-0-8223-2875-9. Dewey:811/.54. LCCN:2001-047057.
Audience: **l,u.**

Castillo, Ana   PS3553.A8135M9 2004
My Father Was a Toltec. Trade Paper. Knopf Publishing Group.
New York, NY. 2004. 192p. ISBN:1-4000-3499-X, ISBN13:
978-1-4000-3499-4. Dewey:811/.54. LCCN:2003-062897.
Audience: **l,u.**

Cervantes, Lorna Dee   PS3553.E79 E47
Emplumada. Trade Paper. University of Pittsburgh Press.
Pittsburgh, PA. 1981. 80p. Pitt Poetry Ser. ISBN:0-8229-5327-7,
ISBN13: 978-0-8229-5327-2. Dewey:811/.54. LCCN:80-054063.
Audience: **l,u.**

Cervantes, Lorna Dee   PS3553.E79F7 1991
From the Cables of Genocide: Poems on Love and Hunger.
Trade Paper. Arte Publico Press. Houston, TX. 1991. 78p.
ISBN:1-55885-033-3, ISBN13: 978-1-55885-033-0.
Dewey:811/.54. LCCN:91-008721.
Audience: **g,l,u,f.**

Cofer, Judith Ortiz   PS3566.L27
Terms of Survival. Ed. 2. Trade Paper. Arte Publico Press.
Houston, TX. 1995. 64p. ISBN:1-55885-079-1, ISBN13:
978-1-55885-079-8. Dewey:811/.54. LCCN:87-070270.
Audience: **l,u.**

De Burgos, Julia   PQ7439.B9A17 1997
Song of the Simple Truth: The Complete Poems of Julia de
Burgos, Obra Completa Poetica. Jack Agüeros (Translator).
Trade Paper. Curbstone Press. Willimantic, CT. 1995. 524p.
ISBN:1-880684-24-1, ISBN13: 978-1-880684-24-5. Dewey:861.
LCCN:94-039149.
Audience: **l,u.** *Choice, 1997.*

De Hoyos, Angela &   PS591.H58F58 1998
Milligan, Mary G.
Floricanto Si!: A Collection of Latina Poetry. Bryce Milligan
(Editor). Trade Paper. Penguin Group (USA) Inc. New York,
NY. 1998. 304p. ISBN:0-14-058893-0, ISBN13:
978-0-14-058893-4. Dewey:811/.54080868. LCCN:97-034445.
Audience: **l,u.**

de Villagra, Gaspar   PQ7296.V54.H5713
Perez
Historia de la Nueva Mexico, 1610: A Critical and Annotated
Spanish/English Edition. Trade Cloth. University of New
Mexico Press. Albuquerque, NM. 1992. 367p.
ISBN:0-8263-1392-2, ISBN13: 978-0-8263-1392-8. Dewey:861.
LCCN:92-028780.
Audience: **u,f.** *Choice, 1994.*

Esteves, Sandra M.   PS3555.S825B55 1990
Bluestown Mockingbird Mambo. Trade Paper. Arte Publico
Press. Houston, TX. 1990. 88p. ISBN:1-55885-017-1, ISBN13:
978-1-55885-017-0. Dewey:811/.54. LCCN:90-000193.
Audience: **l,u.**

Gaspar de Alba, Alicia,   PS3557.A842
et al.
Three Times a Woman: Chicana Poetry. María Herrera-Sobek &
Demetria Martinez (Authors). Trade Cloth. Bilingual

Press/Editorial Bilingue. Tempe, AZ. 1990. 168p. Anthologies
and Collections ISBN:0-916950-91-3, ISBN13:
978-0-916950-91-0. Dewey:811.54. LCCN:88-064101.
Audience: **l,u.**

Hernández Cruz, Victor   PS3553.R8M37 2001
Panoramas: Poems. Trade Paper. Coffee House Press.
Minneapolis, MN. 1997. 192p. ISBN:1-56689-066-7, ISBN13:
978-1-56689-066-3. Dewey:811/.54. LCCN:2001-032479.
Audience: **l,u.**

Hernández Cruz, Victor   PS3553.R8 R44 1991
Red Beans. Trade Paper. Coffee House Press. Minneapolis, MN.
1991. 160p. ISBN:0-918273-91-9, ISBN13: 978-0-918273-91-8.
Dewey:811/.54. LCCN:91-025377.
Audience: **l,u.**

Hospital, Carolina   PS3608.O8C48 2004
The Child of Exile: A Poetry Memoir. Trade Paper. Arte Publico
Press. Houston, TX. 2004. 96p. ISBN:1-55885-411-8, ISBN13:
978-1-55885-411-6. Dewey:811/.54. LCCN:2004-041087.
Audience: **l,u.**

Laviera, Tato   PS3562.A849A44 2003
AmeRícan. Trade Paper. Arte Publico Press. Houston, TX. 2003.
96p. ISBN:1-55885-395-2, ISBN13: 978-1-55885-395-9.
Dewey:811/.54. LCCN:2003-044427.
Audience: **g,l,u.**

Laviera, Tato   PS3562.A849 E5 1985
Enclave. Juan Flores (Introduction by). Trade Paper. Arte
Publico Press. Houston, TX. 1981. 72p. ISBN:0-934770-11-5,
ISBN13: 978-0-934770-11-8. Dewey:811.54. LCCN:81-068067.
Audience: **l,u.**

Mora, Pat   PS3563.O73B67 1986
Borders. Ed. 2. Trade Paper. Arte Publico Press. Houston, TX.
1986. 88p. ISBN:0-934770-57-3, ISBN13: 978-0-934770-57-6.
Dewey:811.54. LCCN:85-073352.
Audience: **g,l,u,f.**

Mora, Pat   PS3563.O73 C48 1984
Chants. Ed. 2. Trade Paper. Arte Publico Press. Houston, TX.
1985. 52p. ISBN:0-934770-24-7, ISBN13: 978-0-934770-24-8.
Dewey:811/.54. LCCN:83-070677.
Audience: **g,l,u,f.**

Mora, Pat   PS3563.O73C6 1991
Communion. Trade Paper. Arte Publico Press. Houston, TX.
1991. 92p. ISBN:1-55885-035-X, ISBN13: 978-1-55885-035-4.
Dewey:811/.54. LCCN:91-000305.
Audience: **g,l,u,f.**

Moraga, Cherríe   PS3563.O753L6 2000
Loving in the War Years: Lo Que Nunca Paso por Sus Labios.
Ed. 2. Trade Cloth. South End Press. Cambridge, MA. 2000.
208p. Classics Ser., Vol. 6 ISBN:0-89608-627-5, ISBN13:
978-0-89608-627-2. Dewey:818/.5409. LCCN:00-057344.
Audience: **l,u.**

Pèrez-Torres, Rafael   PS153.M4 P47 1995
Movements in Chicano Poetry: Against Myths, Against Margins.
Albert Gelpi & Ross Posnock (Contribution by). Trade Paper.
Cambridge University Press. New York, NY. 1995. 348p.
Studies in American Literature and Culture, No. 88
ISBN:0-521-47803-0, ISBN13: 978-0-521-47803-8.
Dewey:811.009/86872. LCCN:94-022380.
Audience: **u,f.**

Rios, Alberto   **PS3568.I587 W5 1982**
Whispering to Fool the Wind: Poems. Trade Paper. Sheep
Meadow Press, The. Riverdale-on-Hudson, NY. 1982. 82p.
ISBN:0-935296-31-X, ISBN13: 978-0-935296-31-0.
Dewey:811/.54. LCCN:82-003269.
Audience: **l,u.**

Soto, Gary   **PS3566.L27**
The Elements of San Joaquin. Trade Paper. University of
Pittsburgh Press. Pittsburgh, PA. 1977. 56p. Pitt Poetry Ser.
ISBN:0-8229-5279-3, ISBN13: 978-0-8229-5279-4.
Dewey:811/.54. LCCN:76-026104.
Audience: **l,u.**

Sánchez, Marta Ester   **PS153.M4.S26 1985**
e Contemporary Chicana Poetry: A Critical Approach to an
Emerging Literature. E-Book. NetLibrary, Inc. Boulder, CO.
1985. ISBN:0-585-34175-3, ISBN13: 978-0-585-34175-0.
Dewey:811/.54/0986872073.
Audience: **u,f.**

Vando, Gloria   **PS3572.A67**
Promesas: Geography of the Impossible. Trade Cloth. Arte
Publico Press. Houston, TX. 1993. 96p. ISBN:1-55885-061-9,
ISBN13: 978-1-55885-061-3. Dewey:811/.54. LCCN:92-028053.
Audience: **l,u.**

Vigil, Evangelina   **PS3572.I34 T55 1985**
Thirty an' Seen a Lot. Trade Paper. Arte Publico Press. Houston,
TX. 1982. 72p. ISBN:0-934770-13-1, ISBN13:
978-0-934770-13-2. Dewey:811.54. LCCN:81-068073.
Audience: **l,u.**

Humanities > Literature > Literary Criticism

Alarcón, Norma   **PS153.M4 C45 1993**
(Editor), et al.
Chicana Critical Issues. Rafaela Castro, Emma Perez, Beatriz
Pesquera, Ada S. Riddell & Patricia Zavella (Editors), Juana
Alicia, Judith Baca & Catalina Govea (Illustrators), Margarita
Melville (Introduction by). Trade Paper. Third Woman Press.
Oakland, CA. 1993. 304p. Chicana-Latina Studies
ISBN:0-943219-09-4, ISBN13: 978-0-943219-09-7.
Dewey:810.9/86872. LCCN:93-003097.
Audience: **u,f.**

Aldama   **PS3559.S44 Z54 2005**
Dancing with Ghosts: A Critical Biography of Arturo Islas.
Trade Cloth. University of California Press. Berkeley, CA. 2004.
242p. ISBN:0-520-23188-0, ISBN13: 978-0-520-23188-7.
Dewey:818/.5409 B. LCCN:2004-011381.
Audience: **u,f.**

Aldama, Frederick Luis   **PS3559.S44Z53 2004**
Critical Mappings of Arturo Islas's Fictions. Trade Cloth.
Bilingual Press/Editorial Bilingue. Tempe, AZ. 2005.
ISBN:1-931010-31-5, ISBN13: 978-1-931010-31-3.
Dewey:813/.54. LCCN:2004-054545.
Audience: **u,f.**

Anaya, Rudolfo A. &   **E184.M5**
Lomelí, Francisco A.
Aztlan: Essays on the Chicano Homeland. Trade Paper.

University of New Mexico Press. Albuquerque, NM. 2001.
264p. ISBN:0-8263-1261-6, ISBN13: 978-0-8263-1261-7.
Dewey:972.018. LCCN:89-083942.
Audience: **u,f.**

Augenbraum, Harold   **PS153**
Fernandez & Olmos, Margarite Fernandez (Editors)
U. S. Latino Literature: A Critical Guide for Students and
Teachers. Cloth Text. Greenwood Publishing Group, Inc.
Portsmouth, NH. 2000. 232p. ISBN:0-313-31137-4, ISBN13:
978-0-313-31137-6. Dewey:810.9/868. LCCN:99-462065.
Audience: **l,u,f.**   *Choice, 2001.*

Borland, Isabel A.   **PS153.C83A58 1998**
Cuban-American Literature of Exile: From Person to Persona.
Trade Paper. University Press of Virginia. Charlottesville, VA.
1998. 190p. New World Studies, : ISBN:0-8139-1813-8,
ISBN13: 978-0-8139-1813-6. Dewey:810.98687291073.
LCCN:98-015446.
Audience: **u,f.**   *Choice, 1999.*

Brady, Mary Pat   **PS153.M4.B69 2002**
Extinct Lands, Temporal Geographies: Chicana Literature and
the Urgency of Space. Trade Cloth. Duke University Press.
Durham, NC. 2003. 272p. Latin America Otherwise Ser.
ISBN:0-8223-3005-9, ISBN13: 978-0-8223-3005-9.
Dewey:810.9/9287/0896872. LCCN:2002-006333.
Audience: **u,f.**   *Choice, 2003.*

Brown, Monica   **HV6439.U5B76 2002**
Gang Nation: Delinquent Citizens in Puerto Rican, Chicano, and
Chicana Narratives. Trade Paper. University of Minnesota Press.
Minneapolis, MN. 2002. 256p. ISBN:0-8166-3479-3, ISBN13:
978-0-8166-3479-8. Dewey:364.1/06/608968073.
LCCN:2001-008249.
Audience: **u,f.**

Bruce-Novoa, Juan   **PS153.M4**
Chicano Poetry: A Response to Chaos. Trade Paper. University
of Texas Press. Austin, TX. 1982. 246p. ISBN:0-292-71092-5,
ISBN13: 978-0-292-71092-4. Dewey:811.09. LCCN:81-023129.
Audience: **l,u.**

Calderon, Hector &   **PS153.M4C7 1991**
Saldivar, Jose D. (Editors)
Criticism in the Borderlands: Studies in Chicano Literature,
Culture, and Ideology. Cloth Text. Duke University Press.
Durham, NC. 1991. 312p. Post-Contemporary Interventions Ser.
ISBN:0-8223-1137-2, ISBN13: 978-0-8223-1137-9.
Dewey:810.9/86872. LCCN:90-025853.
Audience: **u,f.**   *Choice, 1992.*

Calderón, Héctor   **PS153.M4C248 2004**
Narratives of Greater Mexico: Essays on Chicano Literary
History, Genre, and Borders. Trade Cloth. University of Texas
Press. Austin, TX. 2005. 304p. CMAS History, Culture, &
Society Ser. ISBN:0-292-70560-3, ISBN13: 978-0-292-70560-9.
Dewey:810.9/86872. LCCN:2004-008744.
Audience: **u,f.**

Carlito, M. Delores   **Z1231.F4C365 2005**
Cuban American Fiction in English: An Annotated Bibliography
of Primary and Secondary Sources. Trade Paper. Scarecrow
Press, Inc. Lanham, MD. 2005. 138p. ISBN:0-8108-5680-8,
ISBN13: 978-0-8108-5680-6. Dewey:016.813008/08687291.
LCCN:2005-007603.
Audience: **u,f.**

Christie, John S. PS153.H56
Latino Fiction and the Modernist Imagination: Literature of the Borderlands. Cloth Text. Garland Publishing, Inc. New York, NY. 1998. 224p. Latino Communities: Emerging Voices - Political, Social, Cultural and Legal Issues Ser. ISBN:0-8153-3246-7, ISBN13: 978-0-8153-3246-6. Dewey:813/.5409868. LCCN:98-031294.
Audience: **u,f.**

De Laguna, Asela R. PQ7420.15.I43 1985
(Editor)
Images and Identities: The Puerto Rican in Two World Contexts. Trade Paper. Transaction Publishers. Somerset, NJ. 1987. 288p. ISBN:0-88738-617-2, ISBN13: 978-0-88738-617-6. Dewey:860/.9/97295. LCCN:85-009930.
Audience: **u.** *Choice, 1987.*

Elam, Harry J. Jr. PN3307.U6E4 1997
Taking It to the Streets: The Social Protest Theater of Luis Valdez and Amiri Baraka. Trade Cloth. University of Michigan Press. Chicago, IL. 1997. 208p. Theater Ser., :Theory - Text - Performance ISBN:0-472-10793-3, ISBN13: 978-0-472-10793-3. Dewey:792/.0973. LCCN:96-045790.
Audience: **u,f.** *Choice, 1998.*

Espada, Martin PS3555.S53T78 1994
Trumpets from the Islands of Their Eviction. Robert Creeley (Foreword by). Trade Cloth. Bilingual Press/Editorial Bilingue. Tempe, AZ. 1994. 96p. ISBN:0-927534-51-7, ISBN13: 978-0-927534-51-2. Dewey:811/.54. LCCN:94-035250.
Audience: **l,u.**

Esquibel, Catrióna PS153.L46E85 2006
Rueda
With Her Machete in Her Hand: Reading Chicana Lesbians. Trade Paper. University of Texas Press. Austin, TX. 2006. 280p. Chicana Matters Ser. ISBN:0-292-71275-8, ISBN13: 978-0-292-71275-1. Dewey:810.99206643. LCCN:2005-009217.
Audience: **u,f.**

Foster, David W. PS153.G38C48 1999
Chicano/Latino Homoerotic Identities. Cloth Text. Garland Publishing, Inc. New York, NY. 1999. 384p. Reference Library of the Humanities, Vol. 16 ISBN:0-8153-3228-9, ISBN13: 978-0-8153-3228-2. Dewey:810.8/03538/08664. LCCN:99-015048.
Audience: **u,f.**

Foster, David William PS153.M4 F64 2004
El Ambiente Nuestro: Chicano/Latino Homoerotic Writing. Trade Cloth. Bilingual Press/Editorial Bilingue. Tempe, AZ. 2005. 200p. ISBN:1-931010-23-4, ISBN13: 978-1-931010-23-8. LCCN:2003-058298.
Audience: **u,f.**

Garcia, Nasario PS283.N6G37 2000
Platicas: Conversations with Hispano Writers of New Mexico. Trade Cloth. Texas Tech University Press. Lubbock, TX. 2000. xii, 210p. ISBN:0-89672-428-X, ISBN13: 978-0-89672-428-0. Dewey:810.9/8680789. LCCN:99-047064.
Audience: **l,u.** *Choice, 2000.*

García, Mario T. PQ7109.5.L43G37 2000
Luis Leal: An Auto/Biography. Trade Cloth. University of Texas Press. Austin, TX. 2000. 230p. ISBN:0-292-72828-X, ISBN13: 978-0-292-72828-8. Dewey:860.9 B. LCCN:99-052635.
Audience: **u,f.**

Gonzales-Berry, Erlinda PS283.N6P37 1989
(Editor)
Paso Por Aqui: Critical Essays on the New Mexican Literary Tradition, 1542-1988. Trade Cloth. University of New Mexico Press. Albuquerque, NM. 1989. 325p. ISBN:0-8263-1158-X, ISBN13: 978-0-8263-1158-0. Dewey:860.9/9789. LCCN:89-033819.
Audience: **u,f.** *Choice, 1990.*

Gonzalez, Lisa Sanchez PS153.P83S18 2001
Boricua Literature: A Literary History of the Puerto Rican Diaspora. Trade Cloth. New York University Press. New York, NY. 2001. 256p. ISBN:0-8147-3146-5, ISBN13: 978-0-8147-3146-8. Dewey:810.9/97295. LCCN:2001-001774.
Audience: **u,f.** *Choice, 2002.*

Gonzalez-Cruz, Luis F. PS628.C82 C834 1992
& Colecchia, Francesca M. (Editor, Translators)
Cuban Theater in the United States: A Critical Anthology. Trade Cloth. Bilingual Press/Editorial Bilingue. Tempe, AZ. 1992. 192p. ISBN:0-927534-27-4, ISBN13: 978-0-927534-27-7. Dewey:862. LCCN:92-000308.
Audience: **l,u.**

Guajardo, Paul PS153.M4G83 2002
Chicano Controversy: Oscar Acosta and Richard Rodriguez. Trade Cloth. Peter Lang Publishing, Inc. New York, NY. 2002. 144p. Modern American Literature: New Approaches Ser. ISBN:0-8204-5706-X, ISBN13: 978-0-8204-5706-2. Dewey:810.9/86872. LCCN:2001-034693.
Audience: **u,f.**

Habell-Pallan, Michelle PS153.H56H33 2005
Loca Motion: The Travels of Chicana and Latina Popular Culture. Trade Cloth. New York University Press. New York, NY. 2005. 320p. ISBN:0-8147-3662-9, ISBN13: 978-0-8147-3662-3. Dewey:791/.082/0973. LCCN:2004-023712.
Audience: **u,f.** *Choice, 2005.*

Hernandez, Guillermo E. PS153.M4H47 1991
Chicano Satire: A Study in Literary Culture. Cloth Text. University of Texas Press. Austin, TX. 1991. 166p. Mexican American Monographs, No. 14 ISBN:0-292-71123-9, ISBN13: 978-0-292-71123-5. Dewey:817/.540986872. LCCN:90-043757.
Audience: **u,f.** *Choice, 1991.*

Hernández, Carmen D. PS153
Puerto Rican Voices in English: Interviews with Writers. Trade Cloth. Greenwood Publishing Group, Inc. Portsmouth, NH. 1997. 264p. ISBN:0-275-95809-4, ISBN13: 978-0-275-95809-1. Dewey:810.9/8687295. LCCN:96-053924.
Audience: **l,u,f.**

Herrara-Sobek, Maria BF108.U5
(Editor)
Chicana Literary and Artistic Expressions: Culture and Society in Dialogue. Trade Paper. Center For Chicano Studies/UCSB. Santa Barbara, CA. 2000. 229p. ISBN:0-9700384-0-2, ISBN13: 978-0-9700384-0-1. Dewey:150.973.
Audience: **u,f.**

Herrera-Sobek, María PS153.M4 B49 1985
(Editor)
Beyond Stereotypes: The Critical Analysis of Chicana Literature. Trade Cloth. Bilingual Press/Editorial Bilingue. Tempe, AZ.

1985. 152p. Feminism and Women's Studies
ISBN:0-916950-54-9, ISBN13: 978-0-916950-54-5.
Dewey:810/.9/86872073. LCCN:84-073316.

Audience: **u,f.**

Herrera-Sobek, María   **PQ7180.H4 1990**
The Mexican Corrido: A Feminist Analysis. Trade Cloth. Indiana
University Press. Bloomington, IN. 1990. 174p.
ISBN:0-253-32739-3, ISBN13: 978-0-253-32739-0.
Dewey:782.42/1626872. LCCN:89-045568.
Audience: **u,f.** *Choice, 1990.*

Herrera-Sobek, María   **PQ7081.A1R315**
(Editor)
Reconstructing a Chicano/a Literary Heritage: Hispanic Colonial
Literature of the Southwest. Trade Paper. DIANE Publishing
Company. Collingdale, PA. 2005. 213p. ISBN:0-7567-9236-3,
ISBN13: 978-0-7567-9236-7. Dewey:860.9/868.
Audience: **u,f.** *Choice, 1993.*

Herrera-Sobek, María   **PS508.M4C52 1996**
& Viramontes, Helena Maria (Editors)
Chicana Creativity and Criticism: New Frontiers in American
Literature. Ed. 2. Trade Paper. University of New Mexico Press.
Albuquerque, NM. 1996. 224p. ISBN:0-8263-1712-X, ISBN13:
978-0-8263-1712-4. Dewey:810.9/86872. LCCN:96-009940.
Audience: **u,f.**

Hinojosa, Rolando   **PS3558.I545 Z87 1985**
The Rolando Hinojosa Reader. Jose D. Saldivar (Editor). Trade
Paper. Arte Publico Press. Houston, TX. 1985. 190p.
ISBN:0-934770-30-1, ISBN13: 978-0-934770-30-9.
Dewey:813/.54. LCCN:83-072578.
Audience: **u,f.**

Horno Delgado,   **PS153.H56B74 1989**
Asunción (Editor), et al.
Breaking Boundaries: Latina Writing and Critical Readings.
Eliana Ortega, Nina M. Scott & Nancy S. Sternbach (Editors).
Cloth Text. University of Massachusetts Press. Amherst, MA.
1989. 288p. ISBN:0-87023-635-0, ISBN13: 978-0-87023-635-8.
Dewey:810/.9/9287. LCCN:88-017141.
Audience: **u,f.** *Choice, 1989.*

Huerta, Jorge   **PS153.M4 H84 2000**
Chicano Drama: Performance, Society and Myth. Don B.
Wilmeth (Contribution by). Cloth Text. Cambridge University
Press. New York, NY. 2000. 224p. Studies in American Theatre
and Drama, No. 12 ISBN:0-521-77119-6, ISBN13:
978-0-521-77119-1. Dewey:812.009/86872. LCCN:00-036300.
Audience: **u,f.** *Choice, 2001.*

Ikas, Karin Rosa   **PS153.M4C455 2001**
Chicana Ways: Conversations with Ten Chicana Writers. Paper
Text. University of Nevada Press. Reno, NV. 2001. 216p.
ISBN:0-87417-493-7, ISBN13: 978-0-87417-493-9.
Dewey:810.9/9287/0896872. LCCN:2001-002289.
Audience: **u,f.** *Choice, 2002.*

Jiménez, Francisco   **PS153.M4 I33 1979**
(Editor)
The Identification and Analysis of Chicano Literature. Trade
Cloth. Bilingual Press/Editorial Bilingue. Tempe, AZ. 1979.
424p. Studies in the Language and Literature of United States
Hispanos ISBN:0-916950-12-3, ISBN13: 978-0-916950-12-5.
Dewey:860/.9/86872073. LCCN:78-067287.
Audience: **l,u,f.**

Johnson, Kelli Lyon   **PS3551.L845Z74 2005**
Julia Alvarez: Writing a New Place on the Map. Saddle
Stitched, Cloth over Boards, Dust Jacket. University of New
Mexico Press. Albuquerque, NM. 2005. 180p.
ISBN:0-8263-3651-5, ISBN13: 978-0-8263-3651-4.
Dewey:818/.5409. LCCN:2005-011097.
Audience: **l,u.** *Choice, 2006.*

Kafka, Phillipa   **PS153**
Saddling la Gringa: Gatekeeping in Literature by Contemporary
Latina Writers. Trade Cloth. Greenwood Publishing Group, Inc.
Portsmouth, NH. 2000. 192p. Contributions in Women's Studies,
Vol. 183 ISBN:0-313-31122-6, ISBN13: 978-0-313-31122-2.
Dewey:813/.5099287/08968. LCCN:00-023957.
Audience: **u,f.** *Choice, 2001.*

Kanellos, Nicolas   **PS153**
Hispanic Literature of the United States: A Comprehensive
Reference. Cloth Text. Greenwood Publishing Group, Inc.
Portsmouth, NH. 2003. 328p. ISBN:1-57356-558-X, ISBN13:
978-1-57356-558-5. Dewey:810.9/868. LCCN:2003-048542.
Audience: **g,l,u.** *Choice, 2004.*

Kanellos, Nicolás   **PQ7420**
(Editor)
Biographical Dictionary of Hispanic Literature in the United
States: The Literature of Puerto Ricans, Puerto Rican
Americans, Cuban Americans, and Other Hispanic Writers.
Cloth Text. Greenwood Publishing Group, Inc. Portsmouth, NH.
1989. 374p. ISBN:0-313-24465-0, ISBN13: 978-0-313-24465-0.
Dewey:016.86/09/973. LCCN:88-037288.
Audience: **g,l,u.** *Choice, 1990.*

Kanellos, Nicolás   **PN2270.H57K36 1990**
A History of Hispanic Theatre in the United States: Origins to
1940. Cloth Text. University of Texas Press. Austin, TX. 1990.
288p. ISBN:0-292-73049-7, ISBN13: 978-0-292-73049-6.
Dewey:792/.08968073. LCCN:89-014645.
Audience: **l,u.** *Choice, 1990.*

Kanellos, Nicolás   **PN2270.M48M49 1989**
Mexican American Theatre: Then and Now. Trade Paper. Arte
Publico Press. Houston, TX. 2003. 120p. Latin-American Play
Anthologies Ser. ISBN:0-934770-22-0, ISBN13:
978-0-934770-22-4. Dewey:792/.0896872073. LCCN:83-070675.
Audience: **l,u.**

Kaup, Monika   **PS366.M49K38 2001**
Rewriting North American Borders in Chicano and Chicana
Narrative. Trade Cloth. Peter Lang Publishing, Inc. New York,
NY. 2001. 368p. ISBN:0-8204-4956-3, ISBN13:
978-0-8204-4956-2. Dewey:818/.508098687. LCCN:00-039076.
Audience: **u,f.**

Keller, Gary D. (Editor)   **PQ7079.2.M46Z75 1995**
Miguel Mendez in Aztlan: Two Decades of Literary Production.
Trade Cloth. Bilingual Press/Editorial Bilingue. Tempe, AZ.
1995. 104p. ISBN:0-927534-53-3, ISBN13: 978-0-927534-53-6.
Dewey:863. LCCN:94-043636.
Audience: **u,f.**

Lattin, Vernon E.   **PQ7079.2.R5 Z88 1988**
(Editor), et al.
Tomas Rivera, 1935-1984: The Man and His Work. Rolando
Hinojosa & Gary D. Keller (Editors). Trade Cloth. Bilingual
Press/Editorial Bilingue. Tempe, AZ. 1988. 158p.
ISBN:0-916950-89-1, ISBN13: 978-0-916950-89-7. Dewey:863.
LCCN:88-071440.
Audience: **u,f.**

Lattin, Vernon E.   PS153.M4C66 1986
  (Editor, Introduction by)
Contemporary Chicano Fiction: A Critical Survey. Trade Cloth.
Bilingual Press/Editorial Bilingue. Tempe, AZ. 1986. 336p.
Studies in the Language and Literature of United States
Hispanos ISBN:0-916950-56-5, ISBN13: 978-0-916950-56-9.
Dewey:813/.54/00986872073. LCCN:85-071528.
                                        Audience: **u,f.**

Lee, Joyce G.   PS3558.I545Z76 1997
Rolando Hinojosa and the American Dream. Trade Cloth.
University of North Texas Press. Denton, TX. 1997. 221p. Texas
Writers Ser., Vol. 5 ISBN:1-57441-023-7, ISBN13:
978-1-57441-023-5. Dewey:813/.54. LCCN:96-050027.
                        Audience: **u,f.** *Choice, 1998.*

Leonard, Kathy S.   Z1229.M48L46 2002
Bibliographic Guide to Chicana and Latina Narrative. Cloth
Text. Greenwood Publishing Group, Inc. Portsmouth, NH. 2003.
290p. Bibliographies and Indexes in Women's Studies, No. 31
ISBN:0-313-31987-1, ISBN13: 978-0-313-31987-7.
Dewey:016.8109/9287/08968. LCCN:2002-069607.
                        Audience: **u,f.** *Choice, 2004.*

Lomelí, Francisco A. &   PS153.M4C485 1999
  Shirley, Carl R.
Chicano Writers. Cloth Text. Thomson Gale. Farmington Hills,
MI. 1999. 400p. Dictionary of Literary Biography Ser., Vol. 209
ISBN:0-7876-3103-5, ISBN13: 978-0-7876-3103-1.
Dewey:810.9/86872/03 B. LCCN:99-027671.
                        Audience: **g,l,u.** *Choice, 2000.*

Luis, William   PS153.C27L85 1997
Dance Between Two Cultures: Latino Caribbean Literature
Written in the United States. Trade Cloth. Vanderbilt University
Press. Nashville, TN. 1997. 376p. ISBN:0-8265-1302-6,
ISBN13: 978-0-8265-1302-1. Dewey:810.9/868729.
LCCN:97-021192.
                        Audience: **u,f.** *Choice, 1998.*

Luz Montes, Amelia   PS2736.R53 Z74 2004
  María de la & Goldman, Anne Elizabeth (Editors)
Maria Amparo Ruiz de Burton: Critical and Pedagogical
Perspectives. Cloth Text. University of Nebraska Press. Lincoln,
NE. 2004. x, 303p. Postwestern Horizons Ser.
ISBN:0-8032-3234-9, ISBN13: 978-0-8032-3234-1.
Dewey:813/.4. LCCN:2003-061289.
                        Audience: **u,f.** *Choice, 2004.*

López, Miguel R.   PS3569.A4677Z76 2001
Chicano Timespace: The Poetry and Politics of Ricardo
Sanchez. Trade Cloth. Texas A&M University Press. College
Station, TX. 2001. xi, 199p. Rio Grande/Rio Bravo Ser., Vol. 3
ISBN:0-89096-962-0, ISBN13: 978-0-89096-962-5.
Dewey:811/.54. LCCN:00-031661.
                        Audience: **u,f.** *Choice, 2001.*

Madsen, Deborah L.   PS153.M4M33 2000
Understanding Contemporary Chicana Literature. Trade Cloth.
University of South Carolina Press. Columbia, SC. 2001. 283p.
Understanding Contemporary American Literature Ser.
ISBN:1-57003-379-X, ISBN13: 978-1-57003-379-7.
Dewey:810.9/9287/0896872. LCCN:00-011471.
                        Audience: **u,f.** *Choice, 2001.*

Martín-Rodríguez,   PS153.M4M365 2003
  Manuel M.
Life in Search of Readers: Reading in Chicano: A Literature.
Trade Cloth. University of New Mexico Press. Albuquerque,

NM. 2003. 232p. ISBN:0-8263-3360-5, ISBN13:
978-0-8263-3360-5. Dewey:810.9/86872. LCCN:2003-012773.
                        Audience: **u,f.** *Choice, 2004.*

Martínez, Julio A.   PQ7378
  (Editor)
Dictionary of Twentieth-Century Cuban Literature. Cloth Text.
Greenwood Publishing Group, Inc. Portsmouth, NH. 1990. 549p.
ISBN:0-313-25185-1, ISBN13: 978-0-313-25185-6.
Dewey:860/.9/97291. LCCN:88-035805.
                        Audience: **g,l,u.** *Choice, 1990.*

Martínez, Julio A. &   PS153
  Lomelí, Francisco A. (Editors)
Chicano Literature: A Reference Guide. Cloth Text. Greenwood
Publishing Group, Inc. Portsmouth, NH. 1985. 492p.
ISBN:0-313-23691-7, ISBN13: 978-0-313-23691-4.
Dewey:809/.86872. LCCN:83-022583.
                Audience: **g,l,u.** *B Choice, 1985.*

Martínez, Manuel Luis   PS228.B6M37 2003
Countering the Counterculture: Rereading Postwar American
Dissent from Jack Kerouac to Tomás Rivera. Trade Cloth.
University of Wisconsin Press. Chicago, IL. 2003.
ISBN:0-299-19280-6, ISBN13: 978-0-299-19280-8.
Dewey:810.9/358. LCCN:2003-005654.
                        Audience: **u,f.** *Choice, 2004.*

McCracken, Ellen   PS3505.H625Z66 2000
  (Editor)
Fray Angelico Chavez: Poet, Priest, and Artist. Trade Cloth.
University of New Mexico Press. Albuquerque, NM. 2004.
168p. Paso Por Aqui: Series on the Nuevo Mexicano Literary
Heritag Ser. ISBN:0-8263-2007-4, ISBN13: 978-0-8263-2007-0.
Dewey:818/.5209. LCCN:99-050726.
                        Audience: **u,f.** *Choice, 2000.*

McKenna, Teresa   PS153.M4M55 1997
Migrant Song: Politics and Process in Contemporary Chicano
Literature. Trade Cloth. University of Texas Press. Austin, TX.
1997. 170p. ISBN:0-292-76518-5, ISBN13: 978-0-292-76518-4.
Dewey:810.9/86872/09045. LCCN:96-025379.
                        Audience: **u,f.** *Choice, 1998.*

Mendoza, Louis Gerard   E184.M5
Historia: The Literary Making of Chicana and Chicano History.
Trade Paper. Texas A&M University Press. College Station, TX.
2004. 376p. Rio Grande/Rio Bravo Ser., Vol. 7
ISBN:1-58544-179-1, ISBN13: 978-1-58544-179-2.
Dewey:305.868/72073.
                        Audience: **u,f.** *Choice, 2002.*

Metzger, Linda (Editor)   PQ7081.3.H58 1991
Hispanic Writers: A Selection of Sketches from Contemporary
Authors. Trade Cloth. Thomson Gale. Farmington Hills, MI.
1990. 514p. ISBN:0-8103-7688-1, ISBN13: 978-0-8103-7688-5.
Dewey:860.998. LCCN:90-083635.
                        Audience: **g,l,u.** *Choice, 1991.*

Metzger, Linda & Ryan,   PQ7081.3 .H58 1999
  Alan
Hispanic Writers: A Selection of Sketches from Contemporary
Authors. Ed. 2. Trade Cloth. Thomson Gale. Farmington Hills,
MI. 1999. 551p. ISBN:0-8103-8377-2, ISBN13:
978-0-8103-8377-7. Dewey:860.998.
                        Audience: **g,l,u.** *Choice, 1991.*

Moraga, Cherríe &   **PS508.H57S49**
  Castillo, Ana (Editors)
The Sexuality of Latinas. Norma Alarcón (Introduction by).
Trade Paper. Third Woman Press. Oakland, CA. 1991. 192p.
ISBN:0-943219-07-8, ISBN13: 978-0-943219-07-3.
Dewey:810.8/03520643.

                   Audience: **u,f.**

Poey, Delia   **PS153.H56.P64 2002**
Latino Literature in the Classroom: The Politics of
Transformation. Trade Cloth. University Press of Florida.
Gainesville, FL. 2002. 144p. ISBN:0-8130-2477-3, ISBN13:
978-0-8130-2477-6. Dewey:810.9/868073071.
LCCN:2002-016570.

            Audience: **f.** *Choice, 2002.*

Pèrez-Torres, Rafael   **PS153.M4 P47 1995**
Movements in Chicano Poetry: Against Myths, Against Margins.
Albert Gelpi & Ross Posnock (Contribution by). Trade Paper.
Cambridge University Press. New York, NY. 1995. 348p.
Studies in American Literature and Culture, No. 88
ISBN:0-521-47803-0, ISBN13: 978-0-521-47803-8.
Dewey:811.009/86872. LCCN:94-022380.

                  Audience: **u,f.**

Quintana, Alvina E.   **PQ7081.A1**
Reading U. S. Latina Writers: Remapping American Literature.
Trade Paper, Perfect. Palgrave Macmillan. New York, NY. 2005.
224p. ISBN:1-4039-6945-0, ISBN13: 978-1-4039-6945-3.
Dewey:860.9/9287/098.

            Audience: **u,f.** *Choice, 2004.*

Ramirez, Arturo   **PS153.M4**
Aztlan: Chicano Culture and Folklore. Trade Paper.
McGraw-Hill Primis Custom Publishing. Hightstown, NJ. 1997.
ISBN:0-07-014381-1, ISBN13: 978-0-07-014381-4.
Dewey:810.986872073.

                   Audience: **l.**

Ramos-Garcia, Luis   **PN2270.H57R36 2002**
  (Editor)
The State of Latino Theater in the U. S.: Hybridity,
Transculturation and Identity. Paper over Boards. Routledge.
New York, NY. 2002. 256p. Hispanic Issues Ser.
ISBN:0-8153-3880-5, ISBN13: 978-0-8153-3880-2.
Dewey:792/.089/68073. LCCN:2002-024916.

                   Audience: **u,f.**

Rebolledo, Tey D.   **PS153.M4R43 1995**
Women Singing in the Snow: A Cultural Analysis of Chicana
Literature. Library Binding. University of Arizona Press.
Tucson, AZ. 1995. 250p. ISBN:0-8165-1520-4, ISBN13:
978-0-8165-1520-2. Dewey:810.9/9287/0896872.
LCCN:94-018740.

            Audience: **u,f.** *Choice, 1995.*

Rebolledo, Tey Diana   **PS153.M4R427 2005**
The Chronicles of Panchita Villa and Other Guerrilleras: Essays
on Chicana/Latina Literature and Criticism. Trade Cloth.
University of Texas Press. Austin, TX. 2006. 280p. Chicana
Matters Ser. ISBN:0-292-70692-8, ISBN13: 978-0-292-70692-7.
Dewey:810.9/9287. LCCN:2005-007620.

            Audience: **u,f.** *Choice, 2006.*

Rivera, Carmen S.   **PS153.P83R48 2002**
Kissing the Mango Tree: Puerto Rican Women Rewriting
American Literature. Trade Paper. Arte Publico Press. Houston,

TX. 2002. 208p. ISBN:1-55885-377-4, ISBN13:
978-1-55885-377-5. Dewey:810.9/9287/097295.
LCCN:2002-066675.

                   Audience: **u,f.**

Rivero Marín, Rosanna   **PS3556.E7243R35 2004**
Janus Identities and Forked Tongues: Two Caribbean Writers in
the United States. Trade Cloth. Peter Lang Publishing, Inc. New
York, NY. 2004. 161p. Caribbean Studies, Vol. 12
ISBN:0-8204-6736-7, ISBN13: 978-0-8204-6736-8.
Dewey:810.9/353. LCCN:2003-018752.

                   Audience: **u,f.**

Robinson, Cecil   **PS173.M4 R6 1977**
Mexico and the Hispanic Southwest in American Literature.
Trade Paper. University of Arizona Press. Tucson, AZ. 1977.
391p. ISBN:0-8165-0593-4, ISBN13: 978-0-8165-0593-7.
Dewey:810/.9/32. LCCN:76-024082.

                   Audience: **u,f.**

Robinson, Cecil   **PS277.R6 1992**
No Short Journeys: The Interplay of Cultures in the History and
Literature of the Borderlands. Reed W. Dasenbrook
(Introduction by). Trade Cloth. University of Arizona Press.
Tucson, AZ. 1992. 148p. ISBN:0-8165-1270-1, ISBN13:
978-0-8165-1270-6. Dewey:810.9/86872. LCCN:91-028170.
            Audience: **u,f.** *Choice, 1992.*

Rocard, Marcienne   **PS173.M39R613 1989**
The Children of the Sun: Mexican-Americans in the Literature
of the United States. Edward G. Brown Jr. (Translator). Trade
Cloth. University of Arizona Press. Tucson, AZ. 1989. 393p.
ISBN:0-8165-0992-1, ISBN13: 978-0-8165-0992-8.
Dewey:810/.9/352036872. LCCN:88-039772.
            Audience: **u,f.** *Choice, 1990.*

Saldivar, Ramon   **PS153.M4S24 1990**
Chicano Narrative: The Dialectics of Difference. Cloth Text.
University of Wisconsin Press. Chicago, IL. 1990. 256p.
Wisconsin Project on American Writers Ser.
ISBN:0-299-12470-3, ISBN13: 978-0-299-12470-0.
Dewey:810.9/6872. LCCN:89-040535.
            Audience: **u,f.** *Choice, 1991.*

Saldivar-Hull, Sonia   **PS374.M4837 S25 2000**
Feminism on the Border: Chicana Gender Politics and
Literature. Trade Cloth. University of California Press. Berkeley,
CA. 2000. 226p. ISBN:0-520-20732-7, ISBN13:
978-0-520-20732-5. Dewey:813/.54099287. LCCN:99-053297.
            Audience: **u,f.** *Choice, 2000.*

Saldívar, Jose D.   **F787.S19 1997**
Border Matters: Remapping American Cultural Studies. Trade
Paper. University of California Press. Berkeley, CA. 1997. 266p.
American Crossroads Ser. ISBN:0-520-20682-7, ISBN13:
978-0-520-20682-3. Dewey:306/.0972/1. LCCN:96-049209.
                   Audience: **u,f.**

Sandin, Lyn Di Iorio   **PS153.H56.S36 2004**
Killing Spanish: Literary Essays on Ambivalent U. S. Latino/a
Identity. Cloth over Boards. Palgrave Macmillan. New York,
NY. 2004. 192p. ISBN:1-4039-6394-0, ISBN13:
978-1-4039-6394-9. Dewey:860.9/868. LCCN:2004-040120.
            Audience: **u,f.** *Choice, 2005.*

Sandoval-Sanchez,   **PN2270.H57S26 1999**
  Alberto
Jose, Can You See?: Latinos on and off Broadway. Trade Cloth.
University of Wisconsin Press. Chicago, IL. 1999. 288p.

ISBN:0-299-16204-4, ISBN13: 978-0-299-16204-7.
Dewey:792/.089/68073. LCCN:98-047441.
Audience: u,f. Choice, 2000.

Sirias, Silvio   **PS3551**
Julia Alvarez: A Critical Companion. Cloth Text. Greenwood
Publishing Group, Inc. Portsmouth, NH. 2001. 184p. Critical
Companions to Popular Contemporary Writers Ser.
ISBN:0-313-30993-0, ISBN13: 978-0-313-30993-9.
Dewey:818/.5409. LCCN:2001-033482.
Audience: l,u.

Smorkaloff, Pamela   **PQ7382.S66 1999**
** Maria**
Contemporary Cuban Writers. Trade Cloth. Thomson Gale.
Farmington Hills, MI. 1999. xxiii, 100p. ISBN:0-8057-1617-3,
ISBN13: 978-0-8057-1617-7. Dewey:863. LCCN:99-027604.
Audience: l,u. Choice, 2000.

Sotelo, Susan Baker   **PS374.D4S69 2005**
Chicano Detective Fiction: A Critical Study of Five Novelists.
Paper Text. McFarland & Company, Incorporated Publishers.
Jefferson, NC. 2005. 235p. ISBN:0-7864-2185-1, ISBN13:
978-0-7864-2185-5. Dewey:813.08720908. LCCN:2005-007357.
Audience: u,f.

Stavans, Ilan   **CT275.A186S73 2003**
Bandido: The Death and Resurrection of Oscar Zeta Acosta.
Trade Paper. Northwestern University Press. Evanston, IL. 2003.
152p. Latino Voices Ser. ISBN:0-8101-2028-3, ISBN13:
978-0-8101-2028-0. Dewey:978/.0046872/0092 B.
LCCN:2003-044173.
Audience: u,f.

Stavans, Ilan (Editor)   **CT275.A186A25 1996**
Oscar Zeta Acosta: The Uncollected Works. Trade Paper. Arte
Publico Press. Houston, TX. 1996. 368p. ISBN:1-55885-099-6,
ISBN13: 978-1-55885-099-6. Dewey:973/.046872/0092 B.
LCCN:95-033398.
Audience: u,f. Choice, 1996.

Svich, Caridad &   **PS628.H57O78 2000**
** Marrero, Maria Teresa (Editors)**
Out of the Fringe: Contemporary Latina/o Theatre and
Performance. Trade Paper. Theatre Communications Group, Inc.
New York, NY. 1999. 400p. ISBN:1-55936-171-9, ISBN13:
978-1-55936-171-2. Dewey:812/.54080868. LCCN:99-044193.
Audience: l,u. Choice, 2001.

Sánchez, Marta Ester   **PS153.M4.S26 1985**
e Contemporary Chicana Poetry: A Critical Approach to an
Emerging Literature. E-Book. NetLibrary, Inc. Boulder, CO.
1985. ISBN:0-585-34175-3, ISBN13: 978-0-585-34175-0.
Dewey:811/.54/0986872073.
Audience: u,f.

Tatum, Charles M.   **PS508.M4**
** (Editor)**
New Chicana - Chicano Writing. Library Binding. University of
Arizona Press. Tucson, AZ. 1993. 165p. ISBN:0-8165-1425-9,
ISBN13: 978-0-8165-1425-0. Dewey:808.
Audience: l,u.

Taylor, Diana &   **PN2309.N45 1994**
** Villegas, Juan (Editors)**
Negotiating Performance: Gender, Sexuality, and Theatricality in
Latin-o America. Cloth Text. Duke University Press. Durham,

NC. 1994. 368p. ISBN:0-8223-1504-1, ISBN13:
978-0-8223-1504-9. Dewey:792/.098. LCCN:94-027647.
Audience: u,f. Choice, 1995.

Villa, Raúl Homero   **PS153.M4V55 2000**
Barrio-Logos: Space and Place in Urban Chicano Literature and
Culture. Trade Cloth. University of Texas Press. Austin, TX.
2000. 286p. Center for Mexican American Studies
ISBN:0-292-78741-3, ISBN13: 978-0-292-78741-4.
Dewey:810.9/86872. LCCN:99-030871.
Audience: u,f. Choice, 2000.

West, Alan (Editor)   **PS153.H56L39 2004**
Latino and Latina Writers. Trade Cloth. Thomson Gale.
Farmington Hills, MI. 2004. 1100p. Scribner Writers Ser.
ISBN:0-684-31293-X, ISBN13: 978-0-684-31293-4.
Dewey:810.9/868. LCCN:2003-015728.
Audience: l,u. Choice, 2004.

Yarbro-Bejarano,   **PS3563.O753Z96 2001**
** Yvonne**
The Wounded Heart: Writing on Cherríe Moraga. Trade Cloth.
University of Texas Press. Austin, TX. 2001. 217p. Chicano
Matters Ser. ISBN:0-292-79607-2, ISBN13: 978-0-292-79607-2.
Dewey:818/.5409. LCCN:2001-017139.
Audience: u,f. Choice, 2002.

Zilles, Klaus   **PS3558.I545Z94 2001**
Rolando Hinojosa: A Reader's Guide. Trade Cloth. University of
New Mexico Press. Albuquerque, NM. 2004. 233p.
ISBN:0-8263-2275-1, ISBN13: 978-0-8263-2275-3.
Dewey:813/.54. LCCN:2001-002287.
Audience: u,f.

Humanities > Literature > Drama

Acosta, Ivan   **PQ7390.A264S8 1982**
El Super: (Tragi-Comdeia). Julio E. Hernandez-Miyares (Editor).
Trade Cloth. Ediciones Universal. Miami, FL. 2001. 72p.
Coleccion Teatro ISBN:0-89729-271-5, ISBN13:
978-0-89729-271-9. Dewey:862. LCCN:80-068858.
Audience: l,u.

Antush, John (Editor)   **PS628.P84C66 1991**
Recent Puerto Rican Theatre: Five Plays from New York. Trade
Paper. Arte Publico Press. Houston, TX. 2003. 256p.
Latin-American Play Anthologies Ser. ISBN:1-55885-019-8,
ISBN13: 978-1-55885-019-4. Dewey:812/.5408097295.
LCCN:90-032908.
Audience: l,u.

Antush, John V.   **PS628.P84N84 1994**
** (Editor)**
Nuestro New York: An Anthology of Puerto Rican Plays. Mass
Market. Penguin Group (USA) Inc. New York, NY. 1994. 608p.
ISBN:0-451-62868-3, ISBN13: 978-0-451-62868-8.
Dewey:812/.5408097295. LCCN:93-080398.
Audience: l,u.

Arrizon, Alicia   **PN2270.M48A77 1999**
Latina Performance: Traversing the Stage. Cloth Text. Indiana
University Press. Bloomington, IN. 1999. 272p.
ISBN:0-253-33508-6, ISBN13: 978-0-253-33508-1.
Dewey:792/.089/68073. LCCN:99-011577.
Audience: l,u. Choice, 2000.

Broyles-González,   PN3307.U6B76 1994
  Yolanda
El Teatro Campesino: Theater in the Chicano Movement. Trade
Paper. University of Texas Press. Austin, TX. 1994. 304p.
ISBN:0-292-70801-7, ISBN13: 978-0-292-70801-3.
Dewey:792/.022. LCCN:94-000935.

                              Audience: **l,u.** *Choice, 1995.*

Chavez, Denise &   PS628.H57S5 1992
  Feyder, Linda (Editors)
Shattering the Myth: Plays by Hispanic Women. Trade Paper.
Arte Publico Press. Houston, TX. 2003. 256p. Latin-American
Play Anthologies Ser. ISBN:1-55885-041-4, ISBN13:
978-1-55885-041-5. Dewey:812/.540809287. LCCN:91-040997.

                              Audience: **g,l,u.**

Cortina, Rodolfo   PS628.C82C83 1991
Cuban American Theater. Miguel Pando (Editor). Trade Paper.
Arte Publico Press. Houston, TX. 1992. 280p. Latin-American
Play Anthologies Ser. ISBN:1-55885-020-1, ISBN13:
978-1-55885-020-0. Dewey:812/.5408097291. LCCN:91-009898.

                              Audience: **l,u.**

Culture Clash   PS572.S33C85 2003
Culture Clash in America. Trade Paper. Theatre Communications
Group, Inc. New York, NY. 2003. 224p. ISBN:1-55936-216-2,
ISBN13: 978-1-55936-216-0. Dewey:812/.6080979461.
LCCN:2003-000819.

                              Audience: **l,u.**

De La Roche, Elisa   PN2277.N5D4 1995
Teatro Hispano!: Three Major New York Companies. Cloth
Text. Garland Publishing, Inc. New York, NY. 1995. 224p.
Studies in American Popular History and Culture
ISBN:0-8153-1986-X, ISBN13: 978-0-8153-1986-3.
Dewey:792/.0896807471. LCCN:95-014987.

                              Audience: **l,u.**

Elam, Harry J. Jr.   PN3307.U6E4 1997
Taking It to the Streets: The Social Protest Theater of Luis
Valdez and Amiri Baraka. Trade Cloth. University of Michigan
Press. Chicago, IL. 1997. 208p. Theater Ser., :Theory - Text -
Performance ISBN:0-472-10793-3, ISBN13: 978-0-472-10793-3.
Dewey:792/.0973. LCCN:96-045790.

                              Audience: **u,f.** *Choice, 1998.*

Flores, Richard R.   PN3211.S27 F66
Los Pastores: History and Performance in the Mexican
Shepherd's Play of South Texas. Trade Paper. Smithsonian
Institution Press. Washington, DC. 1995. 216p.
ISBN:1-56098-519-4, ISBN13: 978-1-56098-519-8.
Dewey:394/.2/66309764351.

                              Audience: **u,f.** *Choice, 1996.*

Gonzalez-Cruz, Luis F.   PS628.C82 C834 1992
  & Colecchia, Francesca M. (Editor, Translators)
Cuban Theater in the United States: A Critical Anthology. Trade
Cloth. Bilingual Press/Editorial Bilingue. Tempe, AZ. 1992.
192p. ISBN:0-927534-27-4, ISBN13: 978-0-927534-27-7.
Dewey:862. LCCN:92-000308.

                              Audience: **l,u.**

Griffith, Lois   PS628.P84A28 1997
Action. Miguel Algarin (As told to). Trade Paper. Simon &
Schuster. New York, NY. 1997. 576p. ISBN:0-684-82611-9,
ISBN13: 978-0-684-82611-0. Dewey:812/.5408097295.
LCCN:97-027602.

                              Audience: **l,u.**

Huerta, Jorge A.   PS628.M4N4 1989
  (Editor)
Necessary Theatre: Six Plays about the Chicano Experience.
Trade Paper. Arte Publico Press. Houston, TX. 2003. 368p.
Latin-American Play Anthologies Ser. ISBN:0-934770-95-6,
ISBN13: 978-0-934770-95-8. Dewey:812/.54/080352036872.
LCCN:89-000283.

                              Audience: **l,u.**

Huerta, Jorge   PS153.M4 H84 2000
Chicano Drama: Performance, Society and Myth. Don B.
Wilmeth (Contribution by). Cloth Text. Cambridge University
Press. New York, NY. 2000. 224p. Studies in American Theatre
and Drama, No. 12 ISBN:0-521-77119-6, ISBN13:
978-0-521-77119-1. Dewey:812.009/86872. LCCN:00-036300.

                              Audience: **u,f.** *Choice, 2001.*

Kanellos, Nicolás   PN2270.H57K36 1990
A History of Hispanic Theatre in the United States: Origins to
1940. Cloth Text. University of Texas Press. Austin, TX. 1990.
288p. ISBN:0-292-73049-7, ISBN13: 978-0-292-73049-6.
Dewey:792/.08968073. LCCN:89-014645.

                              Audience: **l,u.** *Choice, 1990.*

Kanellos, Nicolás   PN2270.M48M49 1989
Mexican American Theatre: Then and Now. Trade Paper. Arte
Publico Press. Houston, TX. 2003. 120p. Latin-American Play
Anthologies Ser. ISBN:0-934770-22-0, ISBN13:
978-0-934770-22-4. Dewey:792/.0896872073. LCCN:83-070675.

                              Audience: **l,u.**

Montoya, Richard   PS3563.O5459C85 1998
Culture Clash: Life, Death and Revolutionary Comedy. Herbert
Siguenza & Ricardo Salinas (Contribution by). Trade Paper.
Theatre Communications Group, Inc. New York, NY. 1997.
260p. ISBN:1-55936-139-5, ISBN13: 978-1-55936-139-2.
Dewey:812.54. LCCN:97-040168.

                              Audience: **u,f.**

Morton, Carlos   PS3563.O88194D74
Dreaming on a Sunday in the Alameda and Other Plays. Trade
Cloth. University of Oklahoma Press. Norman, OK. 2004. 192p.
Chicana & Chicano Visions of the Americas Ser., Vol. 3
ISBN:0-8061-3626-X, ISBN13: 978-0-8061-3626-4.
Dewey:812/.54. LCCN:2004-045870.

                              Audience: **l,u.**

Osborn, M. Elizabeth   PS628.H57O5 1987
  (Editor)
On New Ground: Contemporary Hispanic-American Plays.
Trade Paper. Theatre Communications Group, Inc. New York,
NY. 1987. 288p. ISBN:0-930452-68-2, ISBN13:
978-0-930452-68-1. Dewey:812/.54/0803520368.
LCCN:87-026734.

                              Audience: **l,u.** *Choice, 1988.*

Pietri, Pedro   PS3566.I424I44 1992
Illusions of a Revolving Door. Alfredo Matilla Rivas (Editor).
Trade Cloth. University of Puerto Rico Press. Rio Piedras, PR.
1993. 260p. ISBN:0-8477-3665-2, ISBN13: 978-0-8477-3665-2.
Dewey:812/.54. LCCN:91-016785.

                              Audience: **l,u.**

Pinero, Miguel   PS3566.I5216
Short Eyes. Trade Paper. Farrar, Straus & Giroux. New York,
NY. 1975. ISBN:0-8090-1232-4, ISBN13: 978-0-8090-1232-9.
Dewey:812/.5/4.

                              Audience: **l,u.**

Pinero, Miguel   **PS3566.I5216 S8 1984**
The Sun Always Shines for the Cool/Midnight Moon at the Greasy Spoon: Eulogy for a Small Time Thief. Ed. 2. Trade Paper. Arte Publico Press. Houston, TX. 2003. 128p. Latin-American Play Anthologies Ser. ISBN:0-934770-25-5, ISBN13: 978-0-934770-25-5. Dewey:812/.54. LCCN:83-072582.
Audience: **l,u.**

Prida, Dolores   **PS3566.R558B4 1991**
Beautiful Senoritas and Other Plays. Judith Weiss (Editor). Trade Paper. Arte Publico Press. Houston, TX. 1991. 180p. Latin-American Play Anthologies Ser. ISBN:1-55885-026-0, ISBN13: 978-1-55885-026-2. Dewey:812/.54. LCCN:90-001239.
Audience: **l,u.**

Ramirez, Elizabeth C.   **PN2270.M48R36 1990**
Footlights Across the Border: A History of Spanish-Language Professional Theatre on the Texas Stage. Cloth Text. Peter Lang Publishing, Inc. New York, NY. 1990. 206p. American University Studies, Ser. XXVI, Vol. 1:Theatre Arts ISBN:0-8204-1035-7, ISBN13: 978-0-8204-1035-7. Dewey:792/.09764. LCCN:88-028585.
Audience: **u,f.** *Choice, 1990.*

Ramos-Garcia, Luis   **PN2270.H57R36 2002**
  (Editor)
The State of Latino Theater in the U. S.: Hybridity, Transculturation and Identity. Paper over Boards. Routledge. New York, NY. 2002. 256p. Hispanic Issues Ser. ISBN:0-8153-3880-5, ISBN13: 978-0-8153-3880-2. Dewey:792/.089/68073. LCCN:2002-024916.
Audience: **u,f.**

Sandoval-Sanchez,   **PN2270.H57S26 1999**
  Alberto
Jose, Can You See?: Latinos on and off Broadway. Trade Cloth. University of Wisconsin Press. Chicago, IL. 1999. 288p. ISBN:0-299-16204-4, ISBN13: 978-0-299-16204-7. Dewey:792/.089/68073. LCCN:98-047441.
Audience: **u,f.** *Choice, 2000.*

Svich, Caridad &   **PS628.H57O78 2000**
  Marrero, Maria Teresa (Editors)
Out of the Fringe: Contemporary Latina/o Theatre and Performance. Trade Paper. Theatre Communications Group, Inc. New York, NY. 1999. 400p. ISBN:1-55936-171-9, ISBN13: 978-1-55936-171-2. Dewey:812/.54080868. LCCN:99-044193.
Audience: **l,u.** *Choice, 2001.*

Taylor, Diana &   **PN2309.N45 1994**
  Villegas, Juan (Editors)
Negotiating Performance: Gender, Sexuality, and Theatricality in Latin-o America. Cloth Text. Duke University Press. Durham, NC. 1994. 368p. ISBN:0-8223-1504-1, ISBN13: 978-0-8223-1504-9. Dewey:792/.098. LCCN:94-027647.
Audience: **u,f.** *Choice, 1995.*

Valdez, Luis   **PS3572.A387A6 1990**
Luis Valdez - Early Works: Actos, Bernabe and Pensamiento Serpentino. Trade Paper. Arte Publico Press. Houston, TX. 1990. 189p. Latin-American Play Anthologies Ser. ISBN:1-55885-003-1, ISBN13: 978-1-55885-003-3. Dewey:812/.54. LCCN:89-035438.
Audience: **l,u.**

Valdez, Luis   **PS3572.A387Z6 1992**
Zoot Suit and Other Plays. Trade Paper. Arte Publico Press. Houston, TX. 2003. 216p. Latin-American Play Anthologies Ser.

ISBN:1-55885-048-1, ISBN13: 978-1-55885-048-4. Dewey:812/.54. LCCN:91-041789.
Audience: **g,l,u.**

Humanities > Music and Dance

Burr, Ramiro   **ML102.T45B87 1999**
The Billboard Guide to Tejano and Regional Mexican Music. Trade Paper. Watson-Guptill Publications, Inc. New York, NY. 1999. 288p. ISBN:0-8230-7691-1, ISBN13: 978-0-8230-7691-8. Dewey:781.64/089/68720764. LCCN:98-051910.
Audience: **g,l.**

Gerard, Charley   **ML394**
Music from Cuba: Mongo Santamaria, Chocolate Armenteros and Other Stateside Cuban Musicians. Trade Cloth. Greenwood Publishing Group, Inc. Portsmouth, NH. 2001. 168p. ISBN:0-275-96682-8, ISBN13: 978-0-275-96682-9. Dewey:780/.89/687291. LCCN:00-045148.
Audience: **g,l,u.** *Choice, 2001.*

Gerard, Charley &   **ML3475.G47 1989**
  Sheller, Marty
Salsa!: The Rhythm of Latin Music. Larry W. Smith (Editor). Trade Cloth. White Cliffs Media, Inc. Reno, NV. 1992. 154p. Performance in World Music Ser., No. 3 ISBN:0-941677-11-7, ISBN13: 978-0-941677-11-0. Dewey:781.64. LCCN:88-017164.
Audience: **g,l,u.** *Choice, 1989.*

Glasser, Ruth   **ML3481**
My Music Is My Flag: Puerto Rican Musicians and Their New York Communities, 1917-1940. Trade Paper. University of California Press. Berkeley, CA. 1997. 278p. Latinos in American Society and Culture Ser., Vol. 3 ISBN:0-520-20890-0, ISBN13: 978-0-520-20890-2. Dewey:780/.8968729507471. LCCN:94-009015.
Audience: **l,u.** *Choice, 1995.*

Leymarie, Isabelle   **ML3486.C8L38 2002**
Cuban Fire: The Saga of Salsa and Latin Jazz. Trade Cloth. Continuum International Publishing Group, Ltd. London, 2002. 352p. ISBN:0-8264-5586-7, ISBN13: 978-0-8264-5586-4. Dewey:781.64/097291. LCCN:2001-047160.
Audience: **u,f.**

Loza, Steven   **ML3558.L69 1992**
Barrio Rhythm: Mexican American Music in Los Angeles. Trade Paper. University of Illinois Press. Champaign, IL. 1993. 392p. Music in American Life Ser. ISBN:0-252-06288-4, ISBN13: 978-0-252-06288-9. Dewey:781.62/6872079494. LCCN:91-035181.
Audience: **u,f.** *Choice, 1994.*

Loza, Steven J.   **ML419.P82L6 1999**
Tito Puente and the Making of Latin Music. Trade Paper. University of Illinois Press. Champaign, IL. 1999. 312p. Music in American Life Ser. ISBN:0-252-06778-9, ISBN13: 978-0-252-06778-5. Dewey:784.4/81888/092 B. LCCN:98-025507.
Audience: **l,u,f.** *Choice, 2000.*

López-Santamaría,   **ML3481.L67 1999**
  Maya
Musica de la Raza: Mexican and Chicano Music in Minnesota. Compact Disc, Mixed Media, Trade Cloth. Minnesota Historical

Society Press. Saint Paul, MN. 1999. 76p. Minnesota Musical Traditions Ser. ISBN:0-87351-366-5, ISBN13: 978-0-87351-366-1. Dewey:781.62/68720776. LCCN:98-043709.

Audience: **u,f.**

Paredes, Américo   **M1668.4**
A Texas-Mexican Cancionero: Folksongs of the Lower Border. Manuel Peña (Foreword by). Trade Paper. University of Texas Press. Austin, TX. 1995. 226p. ISBN:0-292-76558-4, ISBN13: 978-0-292-76558-0. Dewey:976.4. LCCN:94-033615.

Audience: **u,f.**

Patoski, Joe N.   **ML420.S458P37 1996**
Selena: Como la Flor. Trade Cloth. Little Brown & Company. New York, NY. 1996. 304p. ISBN:0-316-69378-2, ISBN13: 978-0-316-69378-3. Dewey:782.4/2/163/092. LCCN:95-051815.

Audience: **l,u.**

Peña, Manuel   **ML3481.P44 1999**
The Mexican American Orquesta: Music, Culture, and the Dialectic of Conflict. Trade Cloth. University of Texas Press. Austin, TX. 1999. 364p. ISBN:0-292-76586-X, ISBN13: 978-0-292-76586-3. Dewey:781.64/089/6872079. LCCN:99-006098.

Audience: **l,u.** *Choice, 2000.*

Peña, Manuel   **ML3481.P45 1999**
Musica Tejana: The Cultural Economy of Artistic Transformation. Trade Cloth. Texas A&M University Press. College Station, TX. 2004. xii, 239p. University of Houston Series in Mexican American Studies, Vol. 1 ISBN:0-89096-877-2, ISBN13: 978-0-89096-877-2. Dewey:781.64/089/68720764. LCCN:98-047951.

Audience: **u,f.**

Peña, Manuel   **ML3481.P46 1985**
The Texas-Mexican Conjunto: History of a Working-Class Music. Trade Paper. University of Texas Press. Austin, TX. 1985. 234p. Mexican American Monographs, No. 9 ISBN:0-292-78080-X, ISBN13: 978-0-292-78080-4. Dewey:781.7/268720764. LCCN:84-027127.

Audience: **l,u.** *Choice, 1985.*

Reyes, David &   **ML3534.R388 1998**
Waldman, Tom
Land of a Thousand Dances: Chicano Rock 'n' Roll from Southern California. Trade Cloth. University of New Mexico Press. Albuquerque, NM. 1998. 178p. ISBN:0-8263-1929-7, ISBN13: 978-0-8263-1929-6. Dewey:781.66/089/687207949. LCCN:97-050573.

Audience: **u,f.**

Rivera, Raquel Z.   **F128.9.P85R585 2003**
New York Ricans from the Hip Hop Zone. Trade Paper. Palgrave Macmillan. New York, NY. 2003. 288p. New Directions in Latino American Culture Ser. ISBN:1-4039-6044-5, ISBN13: 978-1-4039-6044-3. Dewey:782.421649. LCCN:2004-351505.

Audience: **l,u.**

Robb, John D.   **M1668.4.H52**
Hispanic Folk Music of New Mexico and the Southwest: A Self-Portrait of the People. Trade Cloth. University of Oklahoma Press. Norman, OK. 1980. 910p. ISBN:0-8061-1492-4, ISBN13: 978-0-8061-1492-7. Dewey:784.7/5. LCCN:78-021392.

Audience: **u,f.** *ℬ*

Roberts, John S.   **ML3506 .R63**
Latin Jazz: The First of the Fusions, 1900-Today. Trade Cloth. Music Sales Corporation. New York, NY. 1998. 400p. ISBN:0-8256-7192-2, ISBN13: 978-0-8256-7192-0. Dewey:781.65/16268. LCCN:98-042730.

Audience: **l,u,f.**

Salazar, Max   **ML3411.8.N48**
Mambo Kingdom: Latin Music in New York, 1926-1990. Trade Cloth. Music Sales Corporation. New York, NY. 2002. 350p. ISBN:0-8256-7277-5, ISBN13: 978-0-8256-7277-4. Dewey:784.18/88/097471.

Audience: **g,l,u,f.**

Schroer, Craig
□ Border Cultures: Conjunto Music.
http://www.lib.utexas.edu/benson/border/index.html
Benson Latin American Collection, University of Texas.

Audience: **g,l,u,f.**

Sheehy, Daniel   **ML3485.S54 2005**
Mariachi Music in America: Experiencing Music, Expressing Culture. Trade Cloth, Compact Disc. Oxford University Press, Inc. New York, NY. 2005. 110p. Global Music Ser. ISBN:0-19-514145-8, ISBN13: 978-0-19-514145-0. Dewey:781.64/089/6872073. LCCN:2004-065663.

Audience: **u,f.**

Villarino, Jose Pepe   **ML210**
Mexican Chicano Music. Ed. 2. Paper Text. McGraw-Hill Primis Custom Publishing. Hightstown, NJ. 1999. 315p. ISBN:0-07-240199-0, ISBN13: 978-0-07-240199-8. Dewey:780.972.

Audience: **l,u.**

Humanities > Religion

Avalos, Hector   **BR563.H57I57 2004**
Introduction to the U. S. Latina and Latino Religious Experience. Trade Cloth. Brill Academic Publishers, Inc. Boston, MA. 2004. xiv, 322p. Religion in the Americas Ser., Vol. 2 ISBN:0-391-04149-5, ISBN13: 978-0-391-04149-3. Dewey:200/.89/6872073. LCCN:2003-069591.

Audience: **l,u.** *Choice, 2005.*

Cortes, Carlos E.   **BR563.H57 P76 1980**
(Editor)
Protestantism and Latinos in the United States: An Original Anthology. Library Binding. Ayer Company Publishers, Inc. Manchester, NH. 1981. Hispanics in the United States Ser. ISBN:0-405-13173-9, ISBN13: 978-0-405-13173-8. Dewey:280/.4/0896873. LCCN:79-006266.

Audience: **l,u.**

Cunningham, Hilary   **BV4466.C86 1995**
God and Caesar at the Rio Grande: Sanctuary and the Politicization of Religion in the United States. Trade Paper. University of Minnesota Press. Minneapolis, MN. 1995. 264p. ISBN:0-8166-2457-7, ISBN13: 978-0-8166-2457-7. Dewey:261.8/32. LCCN:94-031786.

Audience: **u,f.** *Choice, 1996.*

De La Torre, Miguel A.   **F319.M6 D4 2003**
La Lucha for Cuba: Religion and Politics on the Streets of Miami. Trade Cloth. University of California Press. Berkeley, CA. 2003. 200p. ISBN:0-520-23526-6, ISBN13:

978-0-520-23526-7. Dewey:305.868/72910759381.
LCCN:2002-015443.

Audience: **u,f.** *Choice, 2004.*

De La Torre, Miguel A.   **BL2532.S3D4 2004**
Santería: The Beliefs and Rituals of a Growing Religion in
America. Trade Paper. William B. Eerdmans Publishing
Company. Grand Rapids, MI. 2004. 264p. ISBN:0-8028-4973-3,
ISBN13: 978-0-8028-4973-1. Dewey:299.6/74.
LCCN:2004-050601.

Audience: **l,u.** *Choice, 2005.*

De La Torre, Miguel A.   **BT83.575.D4 2001**
 & Aponte, Edwin D.
Introducing Latino/a Theologies. Trade Paper. Orbis Books.
Maryknoll, NY. 2001. 208p. ISBN:1-57075-400-4, ISBN13:
978-1-57075-400-5. Dewey:230/.089/68073.
LCCN:2001-036717.

Audience: **u,f.** *Choice, 2002.*

Diaz-Stevens, Ana   **BR563.H57D53 1998**
 Maria & Stevens-Arroyo, Anthony M.
Recognizing the Latino Resurgence in U. S. Religion: The
Emmaus Paradigm. Trade Paper. Westview Press. Boulder, CO.
1997. 296p. Explorations Ser., :Contemporary Perspectives on
Religion ISBN:0-8133-2510-2, ISBN13: 978-0-8133-2510-1.
Dewey:277.3/082/08968073. LCCN:97-035173.

Audience: **u,f.** *Choice, 1998.*

León, Luis D.   **BX1407.M48 L46 2004**
La Llorona's Children: Religion, Life, and Death in the U.
S.-Mexican Borderlands. Trade Cloth. University of California
Press. Berkeley, CA. 2004. 296p. ISBN:0-520-22350-0, ISBN13:
978-0-520-22350-9. Dewey:277.3/083/0896872.
LCCN:2002-019426.

Audience: **u,f.** *Choice, 2005.*

Martínez, Richard   **E184.M5M387 2005**
 Edward
Padres: The National Chicano Priest Movement. Trade Paper,
Perfect. University of Texas Press. Austin, TX. 2005. 205p.
ISBN:0-292-70678-2, ISBN13: 978-0-292-70678-1.
Dewey:267/.24273/0896872. LCCN:2004-026227.

Audience: **u,f.**

Matovina, Timothy M.   **F394.S2M39 1995**
Tejano Religion and Ethnicity: San Antonio, 1821-1860. Trade
Cloth. University of Texas Press. Austin, TX. 1995. 182p.
ISBN:0-292-75170-2, ISBN13: 978-0-292-75170-5.
Dewey:976.4/3510046872073. LCCN:94-010617.

Audience: **u,f.** *Choice, 1995.*

McMurtrey, Martin   **BX4705.F6099.M37**
Mariachi Bishop: The Life of Patrick Flores, First
Mexican-American Bishop in the U. S. Trade Paper. Corona
Publishing Company. San Antonio, TX. 1987. 181p.
ISBN:0-931722-56-X, ISBN13: 978-0-931722-56-1.
Dewey:282/.092. LCCN:87-070378.

Audience: **u,f.**

McNally, Michael J.   **BX1415.F55M33 1984**
Catholicism in South Florida, 1868-1968. Philip Gleason
(Foreword by). Trade Paper. University Press of Florida.
Gainesville, FL. 1984. 334p. ISBN:0-8130-0788-7, ISBN13:
978-0-8130-0788-5. Dewey:282/.759. LCCN:84-007389.

Audience: **l,u.**

Medina, Lara   **BX810.H57M43 2004**
Las Hermanas: Chicana/Latina Religious-Political Activism in
the U. S. Catholic Church. Trade Cloth. Temple University
Press. Philadelphia, PA. 2004. 232p. ISBN:1-59213-250-2,
ISBN13: 978-1-59213-250-8. Dewey:267.4/4273.
LCCN:2003-064591.

Audience: **u,f.** *Choice, 2005.*

Stevens-Arroyo,   **Z7757.U5D57 1995**
 Anthony M. & Pantoja, Segundo (Editors)
Discovering Latino Religion: A Comprehensive Social Science
Bibliography. Robert Wuthnow (Foreword by). Trade Cloth.
City University of New York, Bildner Center. New York, NY.
1995. 142p. Paral Studies, Vol. IV ISBN:0-929972-13-9,
ISBN13: 978-0-929972-13-8. Dewey:016.2/0089/68073.
LCCN:95-011518.

Audience: **u,f.** *Choice, 1996.*

Social and Behavioral Sciences

                                      E184.M5
☐ Chicano Research Collection.
http://www.asu.edu/lib/archives/chicano.htm
Arizona State University Libraries.

Audience: **l,u,f.**

                                      LB2300
☐ CS: UCLA Chicano Studies Research Center.
http://www.chicano.ucla.edu/
UCLA Chicano Studies Research Center.

Audience: **l,u,f.**

                              E184.S75 J85
☐ The Julian Samora Research Institute.
http://www.jsri.msu.edu/
Michigan State University.

Audience: **l,u,f.**

☐ Pew Hispanic Center, Chronicling Latinos Diverse
Experience in a Changing America.
http://www.pewhispanic.org/
Pew Research Center.

Audience: **g,u,f.**

                                      E184.S75
☐ TRPI: Tomás Rivera Policy Institute.
http://www.trpi.org/
University of Southern California, School Policy, Planning,
Policy and Development.

Audience: **l,u,f.**

Acosta-Belén, Edna, et   **E184.P85 A35**
 al.
Aidios, Borinquen Querida: The Puerto Rican Diaspora, Its
History and Contributions. Marguarita Benitez, Jose E. Cruz,
Yvonne Gonzalez-Rodriguez, Clara E. Rodriguez, Carlos E.
Santiago, Azara Santiago-Rivera & Barbara R. Sjostrom
(Authors). Trade Cloth. Center for Latino, Latin American, &
Caribbean Studies. Albany, NY. 2000. 178p.
ISBN:0-9709644-0-4, ISBN13: 978-0-9709644-0-3.
Dewey:305.868/7295073.

Audience: **l,u.**

Acosta-Belén, Edna &   **E184.P85A23 2006**
 Santiago, Carlos E.
Puerto Ricans in the United States: A Contemporary Portrait.
Library Binding. Lynne Rienner Publishers, Inc. Boulder, CO.

2006. 215p. Latinos, Exploring Diversity and Change Ser. ISBN:1-58826-399-1, ISBN13: 978-1-58826-399-5. Dewey:973/.04687295. LCCN:2006-002396.

Audience: **l.**

Acuna, Rodolfo F.   **E184**
U. S. Latino Issues. Cloth Text. Greenwood Publishing Group, Inc. Portsmouth, NH. 2003. 224p. Contemporary American Ethnic Issues Ser. ISBN:0-313-32211-2, ISBN13: 978-0-313-32211-2. Dewey:305.868/073. LCCN:2003-040844.

Audience: **l,u.**

Balido, Giselle   **E184.C97B34 2001**
CubanTime: A Celebration of Cuban Life in America. Cloth over Boards. Sterling Publishing Co., Inc. New York, NY. 2001. 240p. ISBN:0-7607-2690-6, ISBN13: 978-0-7607-2690-7. Dewey:305.868/7291073. LCCN:2001-281469.

Audience: **l.**

Bonilla, Frank (Editor),   **E184.S75B674 1998**
et al.
Borderless Borders: U. S. Latinos, Latin Americans, and the Paradox of Interdependence. Edwin Melendez, Rebecca Morales & María De Los Angeles Torres (Editors). Cloth Text. Temple University Press. Philadelphia, PA. 1998. 336p. ISBN:1-56639-619-0, ISBN13: 978-1-56639-619-6. Dewey:305.868073. LCCN:97-041270.

Audience: **u,f.**

Cortes, Carlos E.   **E184.S75 L37**
(Editor)
Latinos in the United States: An Original Anthology. Library Binding. Ayer Company Publishers, Inc. Manchester, NH. 1981. Hispanics in the United States Ser. ISBN:0-405-13179-8, ISBN13: 978-0-405-13179-0. Dewey:973/.0468. LCCN:79-006232.

Audience: **g,l,u.**

Davidson, Miriam &   **HN120.N64D38 2000**
Scott, Jeffry
Lives on the Line: Dispatches from the U. S.-Mexican Border. Trade Cloth. University of Arizona Press. Tucson, AZ. 2000. 211p. ISBN:0-8165-1998-6, ISBN13: 978-0-8165-1998-9. Dewey:306/.0972/62. LCCN:00-008566.

Audience: **u,f.** *Choice, 2001.*

Delgado, Richard &   **E184.S75L355 1998**
Stefancic, Jean (Editors)
The Latino/a Condition: A Critical Reader. Trade Paper. New York University Press. New York, NY. 1998. 736p. ISBN:0-8147-1895-7, ISBN13: 978-0-8147-1895-7. Dewey:305.868. LCCN:98-013514.

Audience: **u,f.**

Gamboa, Erasmo &   **F885.S75N67 1995**
Buan, Carolyn M. (Editors)
Nosotros: The Hispanic People of Oregon, Essays and Recollections. Trade Paper. Oregon Council for the Humanities. Portland, OR. 1995. 180p. ISBN:1-880377-01-2, ISBN13: 978-1-880377-01-7. Dewey:979.5/00468. LCCN:95-079043.

Audience: **l.**

Garcia, Alma M.   **E184**
The Mexican Americans. Cloth Text. Greenwood Publishing Group, Inc. Portsmouth, NH. 2002. 240p. The New Americans Ser. ISBN:0-313-31499-3, ISBN13: 978-0-313-31499-5. Dewey:973/.046872. LCCN:2001-054549.

Audience: **g,l.**

Garcia, Juan R.   **E184.M5**
(Editor)
Perspectives in Mexican American Studies, Vol. 7. Trade Paper. University of Arizona Press. Tucson, AZ. 2001. 154p. ISBN:0-939363-07-0, ISBN13: 978-0-939363-07-0. Dewey:973.046872.

Audience: **l,u.**

Garcia, Juan (Editor),   **E184.M5I5 1988**
et al.
In Times of Challenge: Chicanos and Chicanas in American Society. Julia C. Rodriguez & Clara Lomas (Editors). Paper Text. University of Houston, Mexican American Studies Program. Houston, TX. 1988. 95p. Mexican American Studies, No. VI ISBN:0-939709-05-8, ISBN13: 978-0-939709-05-2. Dewey:305.8/6872073. LCCN:88-060483.

Audience: **u,f.**

Gonzales, Patrisia &   **E184.S75G645 1997**
Rodriguez, Roberto
Gonzales/Rodriguez: Uncut and Uncensored. Trade Paper. Ethnic Studies Library, University of California, Berkeley. Berkeley, CA. 1997. 208p. Ethnic Studies Library Publications, No. 19 ISBN:0-918520-22-3, ISBN13: 978-0-918520-22-7. Dewey:973/.0468073. LCCN:97-218422.

Audience: **l,u.**

Gonzalez-Pando, Miguel   **E184**
The Cuban Americans. Cloth Text. Greenwood Publishing Group, Inc. Portsmouth, NH. 1998. 224p. The New Americans Ser. ISBN:0-313-29824-6, ISBN13: 978-0-313-29824-0. Dewey:975.9/3004687291. LCCN:97-021448.

Audience: **g,l.**

Gutiérrez, David G.   **E184.S75C644 2004**
The Columbia History of Latinos in the United States Since 1960. Trade Cloth. Kegan Paul International, Ltd. London, 2004. 512p. ISBN:0-231-11808-2, ISBN13: 978-0-231-11808-8. Dewey:973/.0468. LCCN:2004-041310.

Audience: **g,l.** *Choice, 2005.*

Hayes-Bautista, David   **F870.S75 H385 2004**
E.
La Nueva California: Latinos in the Golden State. Trade Cloth. University of California Press. Berkeley, CA. 2004. 280p. ISBN:0-520-24145-2, ISBN13: 978-0-520-24145-9. Dewey:979.4/00468073. LCCN:2004-006949.

Audience: **l,u.** *Choice, 2005.*

Maciel, David & Ortiz,   **E184.M5C425 1996**
Isidro D. (Editors)
Chicanas - Chicanos at the Crossroads: Social, Economic, and Political Change. Trade Cloth. University of Arizona Press. Tucson, AZ. 1996. 258p. ISBN:0-8165-1343-0, ISBN13: 978-0-8165-1343-7. Dewey:973/.046872. LCCN:95-041767.

Audience: **u,f.** *Choice, 1996.*

Maldonado, Carlos &   **PN6112**
Garcia, Gilbert
The Chicano Experience in the Northwest. Perfect. Kendall/Hunt Publishing Company. Dubuque, IA. 2000. ISBN:0-7872-7664-2, ISBN13: 978-0-7872-7664-5. Dewey:812.508.

Audience: **l,u.**

Martinez, Ruben   **F869.L89 S756 1993**
The Other Side: The Fault Lines, Guerrilla Saints and True Heart of Rock 'n' Roll. Trade Paper. Knopf Publishing Group.

New York, NY. 1993. 192p. Vintage Departures Ser.
ISBN:0-679-74591-2, ISBN13: 978-0-679-74591-4.
Dewey:979.4/9400468. LCCN:92-050704.

Audience: **l,u.**

Martínez, Oscar J.   **F787.M36 1994**
Border People: Life and Society in the U.S.-Mexico
Borderlands. Trade Paper. University of Arizona Press. Tucson,
AZ. 1994. 352p. ISBN:0-8165-1414-3, ISBN13:
978-0-8165-1414-4. Dewey:972/.1. LCCN:93-045298.

Audience: **l,u.**

Melendez, Edwin &   **F1976 .C6 1993**
  Melendez, Edgardo (Editors)
Colonial Dilemma: Critical Perspectives on Contemporary
Puerto Rico. Trade Paper. South End Press. Cambridge, MA.
1993. 254p. Latina/O and Latin American Studies
ISBN:0-89608-441-8, ISBN13: 978-0-89608-441-4.
Dewey:320.97295. LCCN:92-023475.

Audience: **l,u.**

Mirandé, Alfredo   **E184.M5M553 1985**
The Chicano Experience: An Alternative Perspective. Trade
Cloth. University of Notre Dame Press. Notre Dame, IN. 1985.
281p. ISBN:0-268-00749-7, ISBN13: 978-0-268-00749-2.
Dewey:305.8/6872073. LCCN:84-040292.

Audience: **l,u.** *Choice, 1985.*

Moore, Joan W. &   **E184.S75M66 1985**
  Pachon, Harry
Hispanics in the United States. Ed. 1. Trade Paper. Prentice Hall
PTR. Upper Saddle River, NJ. 1985. 208p.
ISBN:0-13-388984-X, ISBN13: 978-0-13-388984-0.
Dewey:305.8/68/073. LCCN:84-026290.

Audience: **g,l.**

Moore, Joan &   **E184.S75I5 1993**
  Pinderhughes, Raquel (Editors)
In the Barrios: Latinos and the Underclass Debate. Trade Cloth.
Russell Sage Foundation. New York, NY. 1993. 352p.
ISBN:0-87154-612-4, ISBN13: 978-0-87154-612-8.
Dewey:305.868. LCCN:93-017668.

Audience: **u,f.** *Choice, 1994.*

Peña, Devon G.   **E184.M5P395 2005**
Mexican Americans and the Environment: Tierra y Vida. Trade
Paper. University of Arizona Press. Tucson, AZ. 2005. 232p.
The Mexican American Experience Ser. ISBN:0-8165-2211-1,
ISBN13: 978-0-8165-2211-8. Dewey:304.2/089/6872073.
LCCN:2004-023856.

Audience: **u,f.**

Rivera, José A.   **HD1694.A3 1998**
Acequia Culture: Water, Land and Community in the Southwest.
Trade Cloth. University of New Mexico Press. Albuquerque,
NM. 1998. 244p. ISBN:0-8263-1858-4, ISBN13:
978-0-8263-1858-9. Dewey:333.91/15/097644.
LCCN:98-023877.

Audience: **u,f.** *Choice, 1999.*

Santa Ana, Otto   **E184.S75S268 2002**
Brown Tide Rising: Metaphors of Latinos in Contemporary
American Public Discourse. Trade Paper. University of Texas
Press. Austin, TX. 2002. 424p. ISBN:0-292-77767-1, ISBN13:
978-0-292-77767-5. Dewey:305.868073. LCCN:2001-052227.

Audience: **u,f.** *Choice, 2003.*

Spener, David & Staudt,   **F787.U66 1998**
  Kathleen (Editors)
The U.S.-Mexico Border: Transcending Divisions, Contesting
Identities. Library Binding. Lynne Rienner Publishers, Inc.
Boulder, CO. 1998. 264p. ISBN:1-55587-796-6, ISBN13:
978-1-55587-796-5. Dewey:303.48/2730721. LCCN:98-029810.

Audience: **u,f.**

Stavans, Ilan   **E184.S75 S75**
The Hispanic Condition: Reflections on Culture and Identity in
America. Trade Paper. HarperCollins Publishers. New York, NY.
1996. 176p. ISBN:0-06-092693-7, ISBN13: 978-0-06-092693-9.
Dewey:305.868/073.

Audience: **l,u.**

Suárez-Orozco, Marcelo   **E184.S75 L37 2002**
  M. & Paez, Mariela (Editors)
Latinos: Remaking America. David Rockefeller Center for Latin
American Studies Staff (Contribution by). Trade Paper.
University of California Press. Berkeley, CA. 2002. 504p.
ISBN:0-520-23487-1, ISBN13: 978-0-520-23487-1.
Dewey:305.868073. LCCN:2001-053492.

Audience: **l,u.** *Choice, 2003.*

Torres-Saillant, Silvio &   **E184**
  Hernandez, Ramona
The Dominican Americans. Cloth Text. Greenwood Publishing
Group, Inc. Portsmouth, NH. 1998. 208p. The New Americans
Ser. ISBN:0-313-29839-4, ISBN13: 978-0-313-29839-4.
Dewey:973/.04687293. LCCN:97-037491.

Audience: **g,l.**

Vazquez, Francisco H.   **E184.S75L35545 2002**
  & Torres, Rodolfo D.
Latino/a Thought: Culture, Politics and Society. Book, Other.
Rowman & Littlefield Publishers, Inc. Lanham, MD. 2002.
496p. ISBN:0-8476-9940-4, ISBN13: 978-0-8476-9940-7.
Dewey:973/.04968073. LCCN:2002-004905.

Audience: **u,f.**

Vila, Pablo   **HN120.C48V54 2000**
Crossing Borders, Reinforcing Borders: Social Categories,
Metaphors, and Narrative Identities on the U.S.-Mexico Frontier.
Trade Cloth. University of Texas Press. Austin, TX. 2000. 304p.
Inter-America Ser. ISBN:0-292-78739-1, ISBN13:
978-0-292-78739-1. Dewey:306/.0972/16. LCCN:99-046270.

Audience: **u,f.**

Social and Behavioral Sciences > Folklore

Bauman, Richard   **GR0110.T5A52**
  (Author, Editor)
And Other Neighborly Names: Social Process and Cultural
Image in Texas Folklore. Roger D. Abrahams (Editor). Trade
Paper. Books on Demand. Ann Arbor, MI. 333p. The Dan
Danciger Publication Ser. ISBN:0-598-03044-1, ISBN13:
978-0-598-03044-3. Dewey:398/.09764. LCCN:80-023697.

Audience: **u,f.**

Boyd, E.   **N7910.N6B69 1998**
Saints and Saint Makers of New Mexico. Robin F. Gavin
(Revised by), Donna Pierce (Foreword by), Charles M. Carrillo
(Contribution by). Trade Paper. Western Edge Press. Sante Fe,
NM. 1997. 144p. ISBN:1-889921-02-5, ISBN13:
978-1-889921-02-0. Dewey:704.9/482/09789. LCCN:98-060248.

Audience: **u,f.**

Castro, Rafaela G.   GR111.M49C37 2001
Chicano Folklore: A Guide to the Folktales, Traditions, Rituals
and Religious Practices of Mexican Americans. Trade Paper.
Oxford University Press, Inc. New York, NY. 2001. 336p.
ISBN:0-19-514639-5, ISBN13: 978-0-19-514639-4.
Dewey:398/.089/6873. LCCN:2001-018550.

Audience: **g,l,u.**

Durand, Jorge &   ND1432.M46D87 1995
  Massey, Douglas S.
Miracles on the Border: Retablos of Mexican Migrants to the
United States. Library Binding. University of Arizona Press.
Tucson, AZ. 1995. 216p. ISBN:0-8165-1471-2, ISBN13:
978-0-8165-1471-7. Dewey:755/.2. LCCN:94-032080.

Audience: **u,f.** *Choice, 1995.*

Espinosa, Aurelio M.   GR111.S65 E87
The Folklore of Spain in the American Southwest: Traditional
Spanish Folk Literature in Northern New Mexico and Southern
Colorado. J. Manuel Espinosa (Editor, Introduction by). Trade
Paper. University of Oklahoma Press. Norman, OK. 1990. 324p.
ISBN:0-8061-2249-8, ISBN13: 978-0-8061-2249-6.
Dewey:398/.09788. LCCN:85-040473.

Audience: **u,f.** ℬ *Choice, 1986.*

Flores, Richard R.   PN3211.S27 F66
Los Pastores: History and Performance in the Mexican
Shepherd's Play of South Texas. Trade Paper. Smithsonian
Institution Press. Washington, DC. 1995. 216p.
ISBN:1-56098-519-4, ISBN13: 978-1-56098-519-8.
Dewey:394/.2/66309764351.

Audience: **u,f.** *Choice, 1996.*

Garcia, Nasario   F804.L3G37 2005
Old Las Vegas: Hispanic Memories from the New Mexico
Meadowlands. Trade Cloth. Texas Tech University Press.
Lubbock, TX. 2005. xiv, 302p. ISBN:0-89672-539-1, ISBN13:
978-0-89672-539-3. Dewey:305.868/073/0978955.
LCCN:2004-014193.

Audience: **l,u.** *Choice, 2005.*

Graham, Joe S. (Editor)   GR1
Hecho en Tejas: Texas-Mexican Folk Arts and Crafts. Trade
Paper. University of North Texas Press. Denton, TX. 1997.
358p. Texas Folklore Society Publications, Vol. 50
ISBN:1-57441-038-5, ISBN13: 978-1-57441-038-9.
Dewey:680.89/68720764. LCCN:91-037628.

Audience: **l,u.**

Griffith, James S.   F815 .G75
A Shared Space: Folklife in the Arizona-Sonora Borderlands.
Trade Cloth. Utah State University Press. Logan, UT. 1995.
224p. ISBN:0-87421-198-0, ISBN13: 978-0-87421-198-6.
Dewey:306/.09791/7.

Audience: **u,f.**

Griffith, James   NK839.3.M4G75 2000
Hecho a Mano: The Traditional Arts of Tucson's Mexican
American Community. Patricia Preciado Martin (Foreword by).
Trade Cloth. University of Arizona Press. Tucson, AZ. 2000.
104p. ISBN:0-8165-1877-7, ISBN13: 978-0-8165-1877-7.
Dewey:704.03/68720791776. LCCN:00-008565.

Audience: **u,f.**

Herrera-Sobek, María   PQ7203 .H47 1987
The Bracero Experience: Elitelore vs. Folklore. Trade Paper.
University of California, Latin American Center. Los Angeles,
CA. 1987. ISBN:0-87903-066-6, ISBN13: 978-0-87903-066-7.
Dewey:863. LCCN:87-019194.

Audience: **u,f.**

Herrera-Sobek, María   PQ7180.H4 1990
The Mexican Corrido: A Feminist Analysis. Trade Cloth. Indiana
University Press. Bloomington, IN. 1990. 174p.
ISBN:0-253-32739-3, ISBN13: 978-0-253-32739-0.
Dewey:782.42/1626872. LCCN:89-045568.

Audience: **u,f.** *Choice, 1990.*

Kiev, Ari   GN477.1.K5
Curanderismo: Mexican-American Folk Psychiatry. Trade Paper.
Simon & Schuster. New York, NY. 1972. ISBN:0-02-917260-8,
ISBN13: 978-0-02-917260-5. Dewey:615/.882.
LCCN:67-025331.

Audience: **u,f.**

Lamadrid, Enrique R.   E99.C85L35 2003
  & Gandert, Miguel A.
Hermanitos Comanchitos: Indo-Hispano Rituals of Captivity and
Redemption. Trade Cloth. University of New Mexico Press.
Albuquerque, NM. 2003. 264p. Paso Por Aqui Ser.
ISBN:0-8263-2877-6, ISBN13: 978-0-8263-2877-9.
Dewey:305.8. LCCN:2003-018068.

Audience: **u,f.** *Choice, 2004.*

Limon, Jose E.   F395.M5L56 1994
Dancing with the Devil: Society and Cultural Poetics in
Mexican-American South Texas. Trade Paper. University of
Wisconsin Press. Chicago, IL. 1994. 256p. New Directions in
Anthropological Writing Ser. ISBN:0-299-14224-8, ISBN13:
978-0-299-14224-7. Dewey:976.4/0046872073.
LCCN:93-039968.

Audience: **u,f.** *Choice, 1995.*

Lucero, Helen R. &   F805.S75L83 1999
  Baizerman, Suzanne
Chimayo Weaving: The Transformation of a Tradition. Trade
Cloth. University of New Mexico Press. Albuquerque, NM.
1998. 232p. ISBN:0-8263-1975-0, ISBN13: 978-0-8263-1975-3.
Dewey:746.1/4/097895. LCCN:98-023210.

Audience: **u,f.** *Choice, 1999.*

Martin, Patricia   F820.M5R36 2004
  Preciado (Editor, Translator)
Beloved Land: Mexican American Oral Histories from Southern
Arizona. Jose Galvez (Photographer). Trade Cloth. University of
Arizona Press. Tucson, AZ. 2004. 173p. ISBN:0-8165-2382-7,
ISBN13: 978-0-8165-2382-5. Dewey:979.1/70046872/00922.
LCCN:2003-015503.

Audience: **l,u.**

Montano, Mary &   NX510.N43M66 2001
  Montaano, Mary Caroline
Tradiciones Nuevomexicanas: Hispano Arts and Culture of New
Mexico. Trade Cloth. University of New Mexico Press.
Albuquerque, NM. 2001. 384p. ISBN:0-8263-2136-4, ISBN13:
978-0-8263-2136-7. Dewey:700/.9789. LCCN:00-011474.

Audience: **l,u.** *Choice, 2001.*

Paredes, Americo   PQ7297.A1C63
With His Pistol in His Hand, a Border Ballad and Its Hero.
Paper Text. Textbook Publishers. Temecula, CA. 2003. 262p.

ISBN:0-7581-1572-5, ISBN13: 978-0-7581-1572-0.
Dewey:398.22.

Audience: **g,l,u.**

Paredes, Americo   **GR110.T5P28 1993**
Folklore and Culture on the Texas-Mexican Border. Richard
Bauman (Editor). Trade Cloth. University of Texas Press.
Austin, TX. 1993. 288p. ISBN:0-292-72472-1, ISBN13:
978-0-292-72472-3. Dewey:398/.09764. LCCN:91-043059.

Audience: **l,u.**

Paredes, Américo   **M1668.4**
A Texas-Mexican Cancionero: Folksongs of the Lower Border.
Manuel Peña (Foreword by). Trade Paper. University of Texas
Press. Austin, TX. 1995. 226p. ISBN:0-292-76558-4, ISBN13:
978-0-292-76558-0. Dewey:976.4. LCCN:94-033615.

Audience: **u,f.**

Ramirez, Arturo   **PS153.M4**
Aztlan: Chicano Culture and Folklore. Trade Paper.
McGraw-Hill Primis Custom Publishing. Hightstown, NJ. 1997.
ISBN:0-07-014381-1, ISBN13: 978-0-07-014381-4.
Dewey:810.986872073.

Audience: **l.**

Rebolledo, Tey D. &   **F805.M5W66 2000**
  Marquez, Maria T. (Editors)
La Diabla a Pie: Women's Tales from the New Mexico WPA.
Trade Paper. Arte Publico Press. Houston, TX. 2000. 512p.
Recovering the U.S.-Hispanic Literary Heritage Ser.
ISBN:1-55885-312-X, ISBN13: 978-1-55885-312-6.
Dewey:305.868/72073. LCCN:00-056589.

Audience: **u,f.** *Choice, 2001.*

Robb, John D.   **M1668.4.H52**
Hispanic Folk Music of New Mexico and the Southwest: A
Self-Portrait of the People. Trade Cloth. University of Oklahoma
Press. Norman, OK. 1980. 910p. ISBN:0-8061-1492-4, ISBN13:
978-0-8061-1492-7. Dewey:784.7/5. LCCN:78-021392.

Audience: **u,f.** *B*

Torres, Eliseo   **GR111.M49 T6**
The Folk Healer: The Mexican-American Tradition of
Curanderismo. Carolyn Banks & Clark Magruder (Editors).
Trade Paper. Nieves Press. Albuquerque, NM. 1984. 64p.
ISBN:0-9612008-1-2, ISBN13: 978-0-9612008-1-7.
Dewey:615.882.

Audience: **l,u.**

Torres, Eliseo &   **RZ407.T67 2004**
  Sawyer, Tim
Curandero: A Life in Mexican Folk Healing. Trade Paper.
University of New Mexico Press. Albuquerque, NM. 2005.
184p. ISBN:0-8263-3640-X, ISBN13: 978-0-8263-3640-8.
Dewey:615.8/8/0972. LCCN:2004-020692.

Audience: **l,u.**

Trotter, Robert T. 2nd   **GR111.M49T76 1997**
  & Chavira, Juan A.
Curanderismo: Mexican American Folk Healing. Ed. 2. Luis D.
León (Foreword by). Paper Text. University of Georgia Press.
Athens, GA. 1997. 224p. ISBN:0-8203-1962-7, ISBN13:
978-0-8203-1962-9. Dewey:615.8/82/0896872073.
LCCN:97-015784.

Audience: **l,u.**

Social and Behavioral Sciences > Economics and Business

Baker, Susan S.   **E184.P85B35 2002**
Understanding Mainland Puerto Rican Poverty. Library Binding.
Temple University Press. Philadelphia, PA. 2002. 224p.
ISBN:1-56639-969-6, ISBN13: 978-1-56639-969-2.
Dewey:339.4/6/097295. LCCN:2002-020513.

Audience: **u,f.**

Calafate Boyle, Susan   **HF3161.N6B69 1997**
Los Capitalistas: Hispano Merchants on the Santa Fe Trade.
Trade Cloth. University of New Mexico Press. Albuquerque,
NM. 1997. 236p. ISBN:0-8263-1789-8, ISBN13:
978-0-8263-1789-6. Dewey:380.1/09789/0903.
LCCN:96-035705.

Audience: **u,f.** *Choice, 1997.*

Chong, Nilda & Baez,   **HD8081.H7C46 2005**
  Francia
Latino Culture: A Dynamic Force in the Changing American
Workplace. Trade Paper, Perfect. Intercultural Press, Inc.
Yarmouth, ME. 2005. 225p. ISBN:1-931930-13-9, ISBN13:
978-1-931930-13-0. Dewey:658.3/0089/68073.
LCCN:2005-009299.

Audience: **u,f.** *Choice, 2005.*

DeFreitas, Gregory   **HD8081.H7D44 1991**
Inequality at Work: Hispanics in the U. S. Labor Force. Trade
Cloth. Oxford University Press, Inc. New York, NY. 1991. 300p.
ISBN:0-19-506421-6, ISBN13: 978-0-19-506421-6.
Dewey:331.6/368073. LCCN:91-007283.

Audience: **l,u.** *Choice, 1992.*

Dohan, Daniel   **F869.S394 D64 2003**
The Price of Poverty: Money, Work, and Culture in the
Mexican-American Barrio. Trade Cloth. University of California
Press. Berkeley, CA. 2003. 304p. ISBN:0-520-22756-5, ISBN13:
978-0-520-22756-9. Dewey:330.9794/74/00896872.
LCCN:2003-002460.

Audience: **u,f.** *Choice, 2004.*

Frank, Ross   **HC107.N6 F73 2000**
From Settler to Citizen: New Mexican Economic Development
and the Creation of Vecino Society, 1750-1820. Trade Cloth.
University of California Press. Berkeley, CA. 2001. 354p.
ISBN:0-520-22206-7, ISBN13: 978-0-520-22206-9.
Dewey:338.9789/009/033. LCCN:00-034381.

Audience: **u,f.** *Choice, 2001.*

Hernandez, Ramona   **HD8081.D65H47 2002**
The Mobility of Workers under Advanced Capitalism:
Dominican Migration to the United States. Trade Cloth.
Columbia University Press. New York, NY. 2002. 200p.
ISBN:0-231-11622-5, ISBN13: 978-0-231-11622-0.
Dewey:331.12/791. LCCN:2001-047537.

Audience: **u,f.** *Choice, 2003, 2002.*

Hondagneu-Sotelo,   **HD6072.2.U52 L674**
  Pierrette
Doméstica: Immigrant Workers Cleaning and Caring in the
Shadows of Affluence. Trade Paper. University of California
Press. Berkeley, CA. 2001. 312p. ISBN:0-520-22643-7, ISBN13:
978-0-520-22643-2. Dewey:331.4/8164046. LCCN:00-051171.

Audience: **u,f.** *Choice, 2001.*

Massey, Douglas S., et al.   JV6483.M33 2002
Beyond Smoke and Mirrors: Mexican Immigration in an Era of Free Trade. Jorge Durand & Nolan J. Malone (Authors). Trade Cloth. Russell Sage Foundation. New York, NY. 2002. ix, 199p. ISBN:0-87154-589-6, ISBN13: 978-0-87154-589-3. Dewey:325/.272073. LCCN:2001-055712.
                                    Audience: **u,f.** *Choice, 2002.*

Moore, Joan & Pinderhughes, Raquel (Editors)   E184.S75I5 1993
In the Barrios: Latinos and the Underclass Debate. Trade Cloth. Russell Sage Foundation. New York, NY. 1993. 352p. ISBN:0-87154-612-4, ISBN13: 978-0-87154-612-8. Dewey:305.868. LCCN:93-017668.
                                    Audience: **u,f.** *Choice, 1994.*

Morales, Rebecca & Bonilla, Frank (Editors)   E184.S75L369 1993
Latinos in a Changing U. S. Economy: Comparative Perspectives on Growing Inequality. Trade Paper. SAGE Publications, Inc. Thousand Oaks, CA. 1993. 272p. Series on Race and Ethnic Relations, Vol. 7 ISBN:0-8039-4924-3, ISBN13: 978-0-8039-4924-9. Dewey:330.973008968. LCCN:92-040081.
                                    Audience: **u,f.** *Choice, 1993.*

Peña, Devon G.   HD8119.M49P46 1997
[e] The Terror of the Machine: Technology, Work, Gender, and Ecology on the U.S.-Mexico Border. E-Book. NetLibrary, Inc. Boulder, CO. 1997. ISBN:0-585-23437-X, ISBN13: 978-0-585-23437-3. Dewey:331.4/87042/09721.
                                    Audience: **u,f.**

Pulido, Laura   GE198.S86P85 1996
Environmentalism and Economic Justice: Two Chicano Struggles in the Southwest. Trade Cloth. University of Arizona Press. Tucson, AZ. 1996. 282p. Society, Environment and Place Ser. ISBN:0-8165-1424-0, ISBN13: 978-0-8165-1424-3. Dewey:363.7/0089/6872073. LCCN:95-032449.
                                    Audience: **u,f.**

Staudt, Kathleen   HD2346.U52M497 1998
Free Trade?: Informal Economies at the U.S.-Mexican Border. Trade Cloth. Temple University Press. Philadelphia, PA. 1998. 256p. ISBN:1-56639-567-4, ISBN13: 978-1-56639-567-0. Dewey:338.0972/1. LCCN:97-012414.
                                    Audience: **u,f.** *Choice, 1998.*

Social and Behavioral Sciences > Economics and Business > Agricultural Workers

Calavita, Kitty   JV6493.C35 1992
Inside the State: The Bracero Program, Illegal Immigrants, and the INS. Cloth Text. Routledge. New York, NY. 1992. 256p. After the Law Ser. ISBN:0-415-90537-0, ISBN13: 978-0-415-90537-4. Dewey:353.00817. LCCN:92-012340.
                                    Audience: **u,f.**

Daniel, Cletus E.   HD1527.C2
Bitter Harvest: A History of California Farmworkers, 1870-1941. Book, Other. Cornell University Press. Ithaca, NY. 1981. 368p. ISBN:0-8014-1284-6, ISBN13: 978-0-8014-1284-4. Dewey:305.5/63/09794. LCCN:80-025664.
                                    Audience: **l,u.**

Gamboa, Erasmo   HD1527.A19G36 2000
Mexican Labor and World War II: Braceros in the Pacific Northwest, 1942-1947. Trade Paper. University of Washington Press. Seattle, WA. 1999. xx, 178p. Columbia Classics Ser. ISBN:0-295-97849-X, ISBN13: 978-0-295-97849-9. Dewey:331.5/44/0896872079. LCCN:99-042805.
                                    Audience: **u,f.**

Gonzalez, Gilbert G.   HD9259.C53C254 1994
Labor and Community: Mexican Citrus Worker Villages in a Southern California County, 1900-1950. Trade Paper. University of Illinois Press. Champaign, IL. 1994. 280p. ISBN:0-252-06388-0, ISBN13: 978-0-252-06388-6. Dewey:307.7/66. LCCN:93-036584.
                                    Audience: **u,f.** *Choice, 1995.*

Guerin-Gonzales, Camille   HD1527.C2.G84 1994
Mexican Workers and American Dreams: Immigration, Repatriation, and California Farm Labor, 1900-1939. Cloth Text. Rutgers University Press. Piscataway, NJ. 1994. 190p. Class and Culture Ser. ISBN:0-8135-2047-9, ISBN13: 978-0-8135-2047-6. Dewey:331.54/4/0979409041. LCCN:93-024223.
                                    Audience: **u,f.** *Choice, 1995.*

Rios-Bustamante, Antonio   HD8081.M6 M37
Mexican Immigrant Workers in the United States. Paper Text. UCLA Chicano Studies Research Center Press. Los Angeles, CA. 1981. 190p. Anthology Ser., No. 2 ISBN:0-89551-051-0, ISBN13: 978-0-89551-051-8. Dewey:331.6/2/72073. LCCN:81-010155.
                                    Audience: **l,u.**

Valdes, Dennis N.   HD1527.A14V35 1991
Al Norte: Agricultural Workers in the Great Lakes Region, 1917-1970. Cloth Text. University of Texas Press. Austin, TX. 1991. 315p. Mexican American Monographs, No. 13 ISBN:0-292-70413-5, ISBN13: 978-0-292-70413-8. Dewey:331.5/44/0977. LCCN:90-021831.
                                    Audience: **u,f.**

Weber, Devra   HD8039.C662U68 1994
Dark Sweat, White Gold: California Farm Workers, Cotton, and the New Deal. Trade Cloth. University of California Press. Berkeley, CA. 1994. 344p. ISBN:0-520-08489-6, ISBN13: 978-0-520-08489-6. Dewey:331.6/2720794. LCCN:93-036933.
                                    Audience: **u,f.** *Choice, 1995.*

Social and Behavioral Sciences > Economics and Business > Labor Movement

Daniel, Clete   HD8081.M6D36 1991
Chicano Workers and the Politics of Fairness: The FEPC in the Southwest, 1941-1945. Cloth Text. University of Texas Press. Austin, TX. 1991. 248p. ISBN:0-292-76521-5, ISBN13: 978-0-292-76521-4. Dewey:331.6/36872079. LCCN:90-012707.
                                    Audience: **u,f.** *Choice, 1991.*

González, Gilbert G.   HD8081.M6G665 1999
Mexican Consuls and Labor Organizing: Imperial Politics in the American Southwest. Trade Cloth. University of Texas Press. Austin, TX. 1999. 304p. Center for Mexican American Studies

ISBN:0-292-72823-9, ISBN13: 978-0-292-72823-3.
Dewey:331.6/272076. LCCN:99-020648.
Audience: **u,f.** *Choice, 2000.*

Griswold del Castillo,   HD6509.C48G75 1995
 Richard & Garcia, Richard A.
Cesar Chávez: A Triumph of Spirit. Trade Cloth. University of
Oklahoma Press. Norman, OK. 1995. 224p. Oklahoma Western
Biographies Ser., Vol. 11 ISBN:0-8061-2758-9, ISBN13:
978-0-8061-2758-3. Dewey:331.88. LCCN:95-015230.
Audience: **g,l,u.** *Choice, 1996.*

Hammerback, John C.   HD6509.C48H36 1998
 & Jensen, Richard J.
The Rhetorical Career of Cesar Chavez. Trade Cloth. Texas
A&M University Press. College Station, TX. 1998. 320p.
ISBN:0-89096-808-X, ISBN13: 978-0-89096-808-6.
Dewey:331.88/13/092. LCCN:97-032794.
Audience: **l,u.** *Choice, 1998.*

Matthiessen, Peter   HD6509.C48 M38 2000
Sal Si Puedes (Escape If You Can): Cesar Chavez and the New
American Revolution. Ilan Stavans (Foreword by). Trade Paper.
University of California Press. Berkeley, CA. 2000. 386p.
ISBN:0-520-22584-8, ISBN13: 978-0-520-22584-8.
Dewey:331.5/44/092 B. LCCN:00-055580.

Audience: **g,l,u.**

Ruiz, Vicki L.   HD6515.F72U547 1987
Cannery Women, Cannery Lives: Mexican Women,
Unionization, and the California Food Processing Industry,
1930-1950. Trade Paper. University of New Mexico Press.
Albuquerque, NM. 1987. 194p. ISBN:0-8263-0988-7, ISBN13:
978-0-8263-0988-4. Dewey:331.88/1640282/09794.
LCCN:87-013878.
Audience: **u,f.** *Choice, 1988.*

Social and Behavioral Sciences > Economics and Business > Marketing

Davila, Arlene M.   HF5415.33.U6 D38
Latinos, Inc: The Marketing and Making of a People. Trade
Cloth. University of California Press. Berkeley, CA. 2001. 302p.
ISBN:0-520-22669-0, ISBN13: 978-0-520-22669-2.
Dewey:658.8/34/08968073. LCCN:2001-016206.
Audience: **u,f.** *Choice, 2002.*

Faura, Juan   HF5415.32.F38 2004
The Whole Enchilada: Hispanic Marketing 101. Cloth Text.
Paramount Market Publishing, Inc. Ithaca, NY. 2004. 140p.
ISBN:0-9725290-5-5, ISBN13: 978-0-9725290-5-1.
Dewey:658.8/3468/073. LCCN:2005-278873.
Audience: **u,f.** *Choice, 2005.*

Nevaer, Louis E. V.   HF5415.33.U6N47 2004
The Rise of the Hispanic Market in the United States:
Challenges, Dilemmas, and Opportunities for Corporate
Management. Trade Cloth. M. E. Sharpe Inc. Armonk, NY.
2004. 264p. ISBN:0-7656-1290-9, ISBN13: 978-0-7656-1290-8.
Dewey:658.8/34/08968073. LCCN:2003-050503.
Audience: **u,f.** *Choice, 2004.*

Valdes, Isabel   HC110.C6V348 2000
Marketing to American Latinos: A Guide to the In-Culture
Approach. Trade Cloth. Paramount Market Publishing, Inc.
Ithaca, NY. 2000. 190p. ISBN:0-9671439-3-4, ISBN13:
978-0-9671439-3-4. Dewey:658.83. LCCN:00-711774.
Audience: **u,f.** *Choice, 2000.*

Valdes, M. Isabel   HC110.C6 V348 2000
Marketing to American Latinos: A Guide to the In-Culture
Approach. Trade Cloth. Paramount Market Publishing, Inc.
Ithaca, NY. 2002. 250p. ISBN:0-9671439-2-6, ISBN13:
978-0-9671439-2-7. Dewey:658.8.
Audience: **u,f.** *Choice, 2003.*

Social and Behavioral Sciences > Education

Ambert, Alba N. &   LC2693.3.P84 1991
 Alvarez, Maria D.
Puerto Rican Children on the Mainland: Interdisciplinary
Perspectives. Trade Cloth. Garland Publishing, Inc. New York,
NY. 1991. 392p. Studies in Education and Culture, Vol. 4
ISBN:0-8240-4499-1, ISBN13: 978-0-8240-4499-2.
Dewey:305.23/089687295073. LCCN:91-014209.
Audience: **u,f.** *Choice, 1992.*

Blanton, Carlos Kevin   LC3732.T4B53 2004
The Strange Career of Bilingual Education in Texas, 1836-1981.
Trade Cloth. Texas A&M University Press. College Station, TX.
2004. 224p. Fronteras Ser., 2 ISBN:1-58544-310-7, ISBN13:
978-1-58544-310-9. Dewey:370.117/09764. LCCN:2003-016351.
Audience: **u,f.** *Choice, 2004.*

Cordasco, Francesco &   E184.P85
 Bucchioni, Eugene
The Puerto Rican Community and Its Children on the Mainland:
A Source Book for Teachers, Social Workers and Other
Professionals. Ed. 3. Trade Cloth. Scarecrow Press, Inc.
Lanham, MD. 1982. 469p. ISBN:0-8108-1506-0, ISBN13:
978-0-8108-1506-3. Dewey:305.8/687295/073.
LCCN:81-021250.

Audience: **g,l,u,f.** *B*

Darder, Antonia   LC2669.L39 1997
 (Editor)
Latinos and Education: Critical Reader. Paper over Boards.
Routledge. New York, NY. 1997. 485p. ISBN:0-415-91181-8,
ISBN13: 978-0-415-91181-8. Dewey:371.8/2968073.
LCCN:96-009686.
Audience: **u,f.**

Fine, Michelle   LC146.7.N7F56 1991
Framing Dropouts: Notes on the Politics of an Urban High
School. Cloth Text. State University of New York Press. Albany,
NY. 1991. 313p. SUNY Series in Teacher Empowerment and
School Reform ISBN:0-7914-0403-X, ISBN13:
978-0-7914-0403-4. Dewey:373.12/913/097471.
LCCN:90-032135.
Audience: **u,f.** *Choice, 1991.*

Fishman, Joshua A. &   LC2669 .B54
 Keller, Gary D. (Editors)
Bilingual Education for Hispanic Students in the United States.
Trade Cloth. Teachers College Press, Teachers College,
Columbia University. New York, NY. 1981. Bilingual Education
Ser. ISBN:0-8077-2655-9, ISBN13: 978-0-8077-2655-6.
Dewey:371.97/68/073. LCCN:80-027776.
Audience: **u,f.**

Flores-Gonzalez, Nilda   LC2670.F56 2002
School Kids/Street Kids: Identity Development in Latino
Students. Trade Cloth. Teachers College Press, Teachers College,
Columbia University. New York, NY. 2002. 216p.

ISBN:0-8077-4224-4, ISBN13: 978-0-8077-4224-2.
Dewey:371.829/68073. LCCN:2001-058537.

Audience: **u,f.** *Choice, 2002.*

Garcia, Eugene E.   **LC2669.G37 2001**
Hispanic Education in the United States: Raices y Alas. Trade
Cloth. Rowman & Littlefield Publishers, Inc. Lanham, MD.
2001. 320p. Critical Issues in Contemporary American
Education Ser. ISBN:0-7425-1076-X, ISBN13:
978-0-7425-1076-0. Dewey:371.829/68073. LCCN:00-054434.

Audience: **l,u.** *Choice, 2002.*

Gelsinon, Thomas   **E184.M5 P42**
(Editor)
Perspectives in Mexican American Studies: Community, Identity
and Education. Juan R. Garcia (Introduction by). Trade Paper.
University of Arizona, Mexican American Studies & Research
Center. Tucson, AZ. 1992. 210p. ISBN:0-939363-03-8, ISBN13:
978-0-939363-03-2. Dewey:909.

Audience: **l,u.**

Gonzalez, Gilbert G.   **LC2683.3.G66 1990**
Chicano Education in the Era of Segregation. Trade Cloth.
Balch Institute Press. Philadelphia, PA. 1990. 208p.
ISBN:0-944190-06-5, ISBN13: 978-0-944190-06-7.
Dewey:371.97/6872073/079. LCCN:88-043411.

Audience: **u,f.** *Choice, 1990.*

Gonzalez, Maria Luisa,   **LC2669.E37 1998**
et al.
Educating Latino Students: A Guide to Successful Practice. Ana
Huerta-Macias & Josefina Villamil Tinajero (Authors). Trade
Cloth. Scarecrow Press, Inc. Lanham, MD. 1997. 395p.
ISBN:1-56676-568-4, ISBN13: 978-1-56676-568-8.
Dewey:371.82968. LCCN:97-060883.

Audience: **u,f.** *Choice, 1998.*

Gray, Dulce Maria   **LC3746.G73 2001**
High Literacy and Ethnic Identity: Dominican American
Schooling in Transition. Book, Other. Rowman & Littlefield
Publishers, Inc. Lanham, MD. 2001. 256p. ISBN:0-7425-0005-5,
ISBN13: 978-0-7425-0005-1. Dewey:371.829/68/7293073.
LCCN:2001-019885.

Audience: **u.** *Choice, 2002.*

Huerta-Macias, Ana   **LC149**
Workforce Education for Latinos: Politics, Programs, and
Practices. Trade Cloth. Greenwood Publishing Group, Inc.
Portsmouth, NH. 2002. 160p. ISBN:0-89789-808-7, ISBN13:
978-0-89789-808-9. Dewey:374.1829/68073.
LCCN:2001-037912.

Audience: **u,f.** *Choice, 2002.*

Maldonado, Carlos S.   **LD1061.C79M24 2000**
Colegio Cesar Chavez, 1973-1983: A Chicano Struggle for
Educational Self-Determination. Cloth Text. Garland Publishing,
Inc. New York, NY. 2000. 180p. Latino Communities: Emerging
Voices - Political, Social, Cultural and Legal Issues Ser.
ISBN:0-8153-3631-4, ISBN13: 978-0-8153-3631-0.
Dewey:378.795/37. LCCN:00-027245.

Audience: **u,f.**

Meier, Kenneth J. &   **LC2670.M45 1991**
Stewart, Joseph Jr.
The Politics of Hispanic Education: Un Paso Pa'lante y Dos
Pa'tras. Cloth Text. State University of New York Press. Albany,
NY. 1991. 275p. SUNY Series, United States Hispanic Studies

ISBN:0-7914-0507-9, ISBN13: 978-0-7914-0507-9.
Dewey:370/.8968073. LCCN:90-033101.

Audience: **u,f.** *Choice, 1991.*

Nieto, Sonia (Editor)   **LC2692.P82 2000**
Puerto Rican Students in U. S. Schools. Alicia Nieto, Hipolito
Baez & Diana Caballero (Contribution by). Cloth over Boards.
Lawrence Erlbaum Associates, Inc. Mahwah, NJ. 2000. 368p.
Sociocultural, Political, and Historical Studies in Education
ISBN:0-8058-2764-1, ISBN13: 978-0-8058-2764-4.
Dewey:371.82968/7295. LCCN:99-047154.

Audience: **u,f.** *Choice, 2000.*

Olivas, Michael A.   **LC2670.4.L37**
(Editor)
Latino College Students. Trade Paper. Books on Demand. Ann
Arbor, MI. 384p. Bilingual Education Ser. ISBN:0-608-08642-8,
ISBN13: 978-0-608-08642-2. Dewey:378/.1982.
LCCN:86-005697.

Audience: **u,f.** *Choice, 1987.*

Perez, Bertha   **LC2688.S2P47 2003**
Becoming Biliterate: A Study of Two-Way Bilingual Immersion
Education. Cloth over Boards. Lawrence Erlbaum Associates,
Inc. Mahwah, NJ. 2003. 256p. ISBN:0-8058-4678-6, ISBN13:
978-0-8058-4678-2. Dewey:370.117/09764/351.
LCCN:2003-046230.

Audience: **u,f.** *Choice, 2004.*

Rodriguez, Camille &   **LC2693.6 .P84 1994**
Perez, Ramon B. (Editors)
Puerto Ricans and Higher Education Policies: Issues of
Scholarship, Fiscal Policies and Admissions. Trade Paper.
Hunter College, Centro de Estudios Puertorriquenos. New York,
NY. 1994. 68p. ISBN:1-878483-52-8, ISBN13:
978-1-878483-52-2. Dewey:378.1/9829687295.
LCCN:00-273715.

Audience: **f.**

Rodriguez-Fraticelli,   **LC2693.6.R63**
Carlos
Education and Imperialism: The Puerto Rican Experience in
Higher Education, 1898-1986. Library Binding. Hunter College,
Centro de Estudios Puertorriquenos. New York, NY. 1986. 51p.
ISBN:1-878483-07-2, ISBN13: 978-1-878483-07-2.
Dewey:378.7295.

Audience: **u,f.**

Roguez, Richard   **F870.M5 R62**
Hunger of Memory: The Education of Richard Rodriguez.
Library Binding. Sagebrush Education Resources. Caledonia,
MN. 1983. ISBN:0-7857-7698-2, ISBN13: 978-0-7857-7698-7.
Dewey:420/.4261.

Audience: **g,l,u.**

Rubal-Lopez, Alma &   **LC2698.N48R83 2004**
Anselmo, Angela
On Becoming Nuyorican. Trade Paper. Peter Lang Publishing,
Inc. New York, NY. 2004. xvii, 172p. ISBN:0-8204-5520-2,
ISBN13: 978-0-8204-5520-4. Dewey:371.82968/7295.
LCCN:2003-008142.

Audience: **u,f.**

San Miguel, Guadalupe   **LC2688.H8S26 2001**
Brown, Not White: School Integration and the Chicano
Movement in Houston. Trade Cloth. Texas A&M University
Press. College Station, TX. 2001. xiii, 283p. University of

Houston Series in Mexican American Studies, No. 3
ISBN:1-58544-115-5, ISBN13: 978-1-58544-115-0.
Dewey:379.2/63/097641411. LCCN:00-011204.

Audience: **u,f.**

San Miguel,   **LC2683.S36 2003**
  Guadalupe Jr.
Contested Policy: The Rise and Fall of Federal Bilingual
Education in the United States, 1960-2001. Trade Cloth.
University of North Texas Press. Denton, TX. 2004. 176p. Al
Filo Ser., No. 1 ISBN:1-57441-171-3, ISBN13:
978-1-57441-171-3. Dewey:370.117/0973. LCCN:2003-020875.

Audience: **l,u.** *Choice, 2005.*

Stanton-Salazar,   **HQ796.S822 2001**
  Richard D.
Manufacturing Hope and Despair: The School and Kin Support
Networks of U. S.-Mexican Youth. Trade Paper. Teachers
College Press, Teachers College, Columbia University. New
York, NY. 2001. xvi, 332p. Sociology of Education Ser.
ISBN:0-8077-4108-6, ISBN13: 978-0-8077-4108-5.
Dewey:305.235. LCCN:2001-027493.

Audience: **u,f.** *Choice, 2002.*

Suárez-Orozco,   **LC2670.4.S82 1989**
  Marcelo M.
Central American Refugees and U. S. High Schools: A
Psychosocial Study of Motivation and Achievement. Trade
Cloth. Stanford University Press. Palo Alto, CA. 1989. 200p.
ISBN:0-8047-1498-3, ISBN13: 978-0-8047-1498-3.
Dewey:373.18/08968073. LCCN:88-029315.

Audience: **u,f.** *Choice, 1989.*

Trumbull, Elise   **LC1099.3.B74 2001**
Bridging Cultures Between Home and School: A Guide for
Teachers with Special Focus on Immigrant Latino Families.
Trade Paper. Lawrence Erlbaum Associates, Inc. Mahwah, NJ.
2001. 184p. ISBN:0-8058-3519-9, ISBN13: 978-0-8058-3519-9.
Dewey:370.117/0973. LCCN:00-051404.

Audience: **u,f.** *Choice, 2002.*

Valdés, Guadalupe   **PE1129.S8V26 2001**
Learning and Not Learning English: Latino Students in
American Schools. Trade Cloth. Teachers College Press,
Teachers College, Columbia University. New York, NY. 2001.
xiv, 177p. ISBN:0-8077-4106-X, ISBN13: 978-0-8077-4106-1.
Dewey:428/.0071/073. LCCN:00-054495.

Audience: **u,f.** *Choice, 2001.*

Valencia, Richard R.   **LC2683.C47 2002**
  (Editor)
Chicano School Failure and Success: Past, Present, and Future.
Ed. 2. Trade Paper. Routledge. New York, NY. 2002. 416p.
ISBN:0-415-25774-3, ISBN13: 978-0-415-25774-9.
Dewey:373.1/2913089/68. LCCN:2002-021959.

Audience: **l,u.** *Choice, 2003.*

Walsh, Catherine E.   **LC2693**
Pedagogy and the Struggle for Voice: Issues of Language,
Power, and Schooling for Puerto Ricans. Trade Cloth.
Greenwood Publishing Group, Inc. Portsmouth, NH. 1990. 192p.
Critical Studies in Education ISBN:0-89789-234-8, ISBN13:
978-0-89789-234-6. Dewey:370.19/34. LCCN:90-000719.

Audience: **u,f.**

Yosso, Tara   **LC212.23.C4Y67 2005**
Critical Race Counterstories along the Chicana/Chicano
Educational Pipeline. Trade Paper. Routledge. New York, NY.

2005. 280p. Teaching/Learning Social Justice Ser.
ISBN:0-415-95196-8, ISBN13: 978-0-415-95196-8.
Dewey:71.829/680773/11. LCCN:2005-010409.

Audience: **u,f.**

Social and Behavioral Sciences > Migration

                         E184.S75

▢ constructing the new.
http://www.nclr.org/
NCLR.

Audience: **l,u,f.**

                         F1408

▢ LULAC: League of United Latin American Citizens.
http://www.lulac.org/
LULAC.

Audience: **g,l,u,f.**

Alvarez, Robert R. Jr.   **F870.M5**
Familia: Migration and Adaptation in Baja and Alta California,
1880-1975. Renato Rosaldo (Foreword by). Trade Paper.
University of California Press. Berkeley, CA. 1991. 230p.
ISBN:0-520-07389-4, ISBN13: 978-0-520-07389-0.
Dewey:979.4/980046872073. LCCN:85-023217.

Audience: **u,f.**

Baker-Cristales, Beth   **F867.B294 2004**
Salvadoran Migration to Southern California: Redefining el
Hermano Lejano. Trade Cloth. University Press of Florida.
Gainesville, FL. 2004. 200p. ISBN:0-8130-2761-6, ISBN13:
978-0-8130-2761-6. Dewey:305.868/728407949.
LCCN:2004-049334.

Audience: **u.**

Balderrama, Francisco   **E184.M5B35 2006**
  E. & Rodriguez, Raymond
Decade of Betrayal: Mexican Repatriation in the 1930s. Trade
Paper. University of New Mexico Press. Albuquerque, NM.
2006. 427p. ISBN:0-8263-3973-5, ISBN13: 978-0-8263-3973-7.
Dewey:323.1168/7207309043. LCCN:2005-024861.

Audience: **l,u.** *Choice, 1996.*

Browning, Harley L.   **E184.M5M523 1986**
Mexican Immigrants and Mexican Americans: An Evolving
Relation. Rudolfo O. De la Garza (Editor). Trade Paper.
University of Texas Press. Austin, TX. 1986. 264p.
ISBN:0-292-75094-3, ISBN13: 978-0-292-75094-4.
Dewey:305.8/6872/073. LCCN:85-073572.

Audience: **u,f.** *Choice, 1986.*

Burgos, William, et al.   **JV7381.C66 1994**
The Commuter Nation: Perspectives on Puerto Rican Migration.
Hugo R. Vecchini & Carlos A. Torres (Authors). Trade Cloth.
University of Puerto Rico Press. Rio Piedras, PR. 1994. 402p.
ISBN:0-8477-2498-0, ISBN13: 978-0-8477-2498-7.
Dewey:325.7295. LCCN:91-027083.

Audience: **l,u.**

Calavita, Kitty   **JV6493.C35 1992**
Inside the State: The Bracero Program, Illegal Immigrants, and
the INS. Cloth Text. Routledge. New York, NY. 1992. 256p.
After the Law Ser. ISBN:0-415-90537-0, ISBN13:
978-0-415-90537-4. Dewey:353.00817. LCCN:92-012340.

Audience: **u,f.**

Cordova, Carlos B.   E184.S15C67 2005
The Salvadoran Americans. Trade Cloth. Greenwood Publishing
Group, Inc. Portsmouth, NH. 2005. 196p. The New Americans
Ser. ISBN:0-313-32306-2, ISBN13: 978-0-313-32306-5.
Dewey:305.868/7284073. LCCN:2005-020463.
                                          Audience: **g,l.**

Dunn, Timothy J.   F787.D46 1996
The Militarization of the U. S.-Mexico Border, 1978-1992:
Low-Intensity Conflict Doctrine Comes Home. Trade Cloth.
University of Texas Press. Austin, TX. 1996. 323p. CMAS
Border and Migration Studies Ser. ISBN:0-292-71579-X,
ISBN13: 978-0-292-71579-0. Dewey:972/.1. LCCN:94-042964.
                                    Audience: **u,f.** *Choice, 1996.*

Durand, Jorge &   E184.M5B43 2004
  Massey, Douglas S.
Behind the Smoke and Mirrors: Research from the Mexican
Migration Project. Mexican Migration Project Staff
(Contribution by). Trade Cloth. Russell Sage Foundation. New
York, NY. 2004. 345p. ISBN:0-87154-288-9, ISBN13:
978-0-87154-288-5. Dewey:305.868/72073. LCCN:2004-042837.
                                    Audience: **u,f.** *Choice, 2005.*

Fitzpatrick, Joseph P.   F128.9.P85F57 1987
Puerto Rican Americans: The Meaning of Migration to the
Mainland. Ed. 2. Paper Text. Prentice Hall PTR. Upper Saddle
River, NJ. 1986. 224p. ISBN:0-13-740135-3, ISBN13:
978-0-13-740135-2. Dewey:305.8/687295/07471.
LCCN:86-022590.

                                    Audience: **l,u.** *B*

Fletcher, Peri L.   JV7409.Z6N364 1999
La Casa de Mis Suenos: Dreams of Home in a Transnational
Migrant Community. Trade Paper. Westview Press. Boulder, CO.
1999. 184p. ISBN:0-8133-2499-8, ISBN13: 978-0-8133-2499-9.
Dewey:304.8/730723. LCCN:99-015568.
                                    Audience: **u,f.** *Choice, 2000.*

Flores, Juan (Editor,   F128.9.P85
  Introduction by)
Puerto Rican Arrival in New York: Narrative of the Migration,
1920-150. Trade Paper. Markus Wiener Publishers, Inc.
Princeton, NJ. 2004. 168p. ISBN:1-55876-362-7, ISBN13:
978-1-55876-362-3. Dewey:305.8687. LCCN:2003-047905.
                                          Audience: **u,f.**

Flores, Juan (Editor,   F128.9.P85D58 2003
  Translator, Introduction by)
Divided Arrival: Narratives of the Puerto Rican Migration,
1920-1950. Trade Cloth. Markus Wiener Publishers, Inc.
Princeton, NJ. 2003. ISBN:1-55876-319-8, ISBN13:
978-1-55876-319-7. Dewey:305.868/729507471.
LCCN:2003-047905.
                                          Audience: **u,f.**

Grasmuck, Sherri &   JV7395.G7 1991
  Pessar, Patricia R.
Between Two Islands: Dominican International Migration. Trade
Cloth. University of California Press. Berkeley, CA. 1991. 280p.
ISBN:0-520-07149-2, ISBN13: 978-0-520-07149-0.
Dewey:304.8/097293. LCCN:90-050924.
                                    Audience: **u,f.** *Choice, 1992.*

Grosfoguel, Ramon   E184.P85 G68 2003
Colonial Subjects: Puerto Ricans in a Global Perspective. Trade
Paper. University of California Press. Berkeley, CA. 2003. 272p.

ISBN:0-520-23021-3, ISBN13: 978-0-520-23021-7.
Dewey:304.8/7307295/09043. LCCN:2003-047327.
                                    Audience: **u,f.** *Choice, 2004.*

Guerin-Gonzales,   HD1527.C2.G84 1994
  Camille
Mexican Workers and American Dreams: Immigration,
Repatriation, and California Farm Labor, 1900-1939. Cloth Text.
Rutgers University Press. Piscataway, NJ. 1994. 190p. Class and
Culture Ser. ISBN:0-8135-2047-9, ISBN13: 978-0-8135-2047-6.
Dewey:331.54/4/0979409041. LCCN:93-024223.
                                    Audience: **u,f.** *Choice, 1995.*

Gutiérrez, David G.   E184.M5G86 1995
Walls and Mirrors: Mexican Americans, Mexican Immigrants,
and the Politics of Ethnicity. Trade Paper. University of
California Press. Berkeley, CA. 1995. 334p.
ISBN:0-520-20219-8, ISBN13: 978-0-520-20219-1.
Dewey:323.1/168073. LCCN:94-001892.
                                    Audience: **u,f.** *Choice, 1995.*

Hart, Dianne W.   F869.L89N53 1997
Undocumented in L. A.: An Immigrant's Story. Trade Cloth.
Rowman & Littlefield Publishers, Inc. Lanham, MD. 1997.
136p. Latin American Silhouettes Ser. ISBN:0-8420-2648-7,
ISBN13: 978-0-8420-2648-2. Dewey:306.85/08968/7285079.
LCCN:96-050993.
                                    Audience: **l,u.** *Choice, 1997.*

Heer, David M.   E184.M5 H376 1990
Undocumented Mexicans in the U. S. A. Ernest Q. Campbell
(Contribution by). Cloth Text. Cambridge University Press. New
York, NY. 1990. 242p. American Sociological Association Rose
Monographs ISBN:0-521-38247-5, ISBN13: 978-0-521-38247-2.
Dewey:305.8/6872073. LCCN:89-049074.
                                    Audience: **l,u.** *Choice, 1991.*

Hendricks, Glenn   F128.9.D6H
The Dominican Diaspora: From the Dominican Republic to New
York City, Villagers in Transition. Trade Paper. Books on
Demand. Ann Arbor, MI. 183p. Publications of the Center for
Education in Africa ISBN:0-608-18800-X, ISBN13:
978-0-608-18800-3. Dewey:917.47/1/06687293.
LCCN:74-004203.
                                          Audience: **u,f.**

Hernandez, Ramona   HD8081.D65H47 2002
The Mobility of Workers under Advanced Capitalism:
Dominican Migration to the United States. Trade Cloth.
Columbia University Press. New York, NY. 2002. 200p.
ISBN:0-231-11622-5, ISBN13: 978-0-231-11622-0.
Dewey:331.12/791. LCCN:2001-047537.
                                    Audience: **u,f.** *Choice, 2003, 2002.*

Maciel, David R. &   E184.M5C85 1998
  Herrera-Sobek, María
Culture Across Borders: Mexican Immigration and Popular
Culture. Trade Cloth. University of Arizona Press. Tucson, AZ.
1998. 312p. ISBN:0-8165-1832-7, ISBN13: 978-0-8165-1832-6.
Dewey:305.868/72073. LCCN:97-033899.
                                          Audience: **u,f.**

Massey, Douglas S., et   JV7401.R47 1987
  al.
Return to Aztlan: The Social Process of International Migration
from Western Mexico. Rafeal Alarcon & Jorge Durand
(Authors). Trade Cloth. University of California Press. Berkeley,
CA. 1987. 354p. Studies in Demography, Vol. 1

ISBN:0-520-06079-2, ISBN13: 978-0-520-06079-1.
Dewey:325.72/0926. LCCN:87-005913.
Audience: **u,f.** *Choice, 1988.*

Massey, Douglas S., et al.   **JV6483.M33 2002**
Beyond Smoke and Mirrors: Mexican Immigration in an Era of Free Trade. Jorge Durand & Nolan J. Malone (Authors). Trade Cloth. Russell Sage Foundation. New York, NY. 2002. ix, 199p. ISBN:0-87154-589-6, ISBN13: 978-0-87154-589-3. Dewey:325/.272073. LCCN:2001-055712.
Audience: **u,f.** *Choice, 2002.*

Menjivar, Cecilia   **F869.S39 S155 2000**
Fragmented Ties: Salvadoran Immigrant Networks in America. Trade Paper. University of California Press. Berkeley, CA. 2000. 320p. ISBN:0-520-22211-3, ISBN13: 978-0-520-22211-3. Dewey:305.868/7284073. LCCN:00-020171.
Audience: **u,f.** *Choice, 2001.*

Nevins, Joseph   **JV6483.N47 2002**
Operation Gatekeeper: The Rise of the 'Illegal Alien' and Remaking of U. S. - Mexico Boundary. Paper over Boards. Routledge. New York, NY. 2001. 256p. ISBN:0-415-93104-5, ISBN13: 978-0-415-93104-5. Dewey:363.28/5/0973. LCCN:2001-034989.
Audience: **u,f.** *Choice, 2002.*

Pedraza-Bailey, Silvia   **JV6895.M48P43 1985**
Political and Economic Migrants in America: Cubans and Mexicans. Cloth Text. University of Texas Press. Austin, TX. 1985. 252p. ISBN:0-292-76492-8, ISBN13: 978-0-292-76492-7. Dewey:325.2/72/0973. LCCN:84-019648.
Audience: **l,u.**

Perez, Gina M.   **F548.9.P85 P47 2004**
The Near Northwest Side Story: Migration, Displacement, and Puerto Rican Families. Trade Paper. University of California Press. Berkeley, CA. 2004. 282p. ISBN:0-520-23368-9, ISBN13: 978-0-520-23368-3. Dewey:305.868/7295077311. LCCN:2004-048010.
Audience: **u,f.** *Choice, 2005.*

Pessar, Patricia R. & Foner, Nancy   **F128.9.D6P47 1995**
A Visa for a Dream: Dominicans in the United States. Trade Paper. Allyn & Bacon, Inc. Boston, MA. 1996. 100p. Immigrants Ser. ISBN:0-205-16675-X, ISBN13: 978-0-205-16675-6. Dewey:974.7/1004687293. LCCN:96-185888.
Audience: **l,u.**

Portes, Alejandro & Bach, Robert L.   **E184.C97**
Latin Journey: Cuban and Mexican Immigrants in the United States. Trade Cloth. University of California Press. Berkeley, CA. 1985. 432p. ISBN:0-520-05004-5, ISBN13: 978-0-520-05004-4. Dewey:305.8/687291/073. LCCN:83-009292.
Audience: **l,u.**

Suro, Roberto   **E184.S75S86 1998**
Strangers among Us: How Latino Immigration Is Transforming America. Trade Cloth. Alfred A. Knopf Inc. New York, NY. 1998. 352p. ISBN:0-679-42092-4, ISBN13: 978-0-679-42092-7. Dewey:305.868073. LCCN:97-036676.
Audience: **l,u.** *Choice, 1998.*

Suárez-Orozco, Carola & Suárez-Orozco, Marcelo M.   **F870.M5S83 1995**
Transformations: Migration, Family Life, and Achievement Motivation among Latino Adolescents. Trade Cloth. Stanford University Press. Palo Alto, CA. 1995. 334p. ISBN:0-8047-2550-0, ISBN13: 978-0-8047-2550-7. Dewey:305.23/5/0972. LCCN:95-016448.
Audience: **u,f.** *Choice, 1996.*

Urrea, Luis Alberto   **JV6475.U77 2004**
The Devil's Highway: A True Story. Trade Cloth. Little Brown & Company. New York, NY. 2004. 256p. ISBN:0-316-74671-1, ISBN13: 978-0-316-74671-7. Dewey:304.8/73072. LCCN:2003-058930.
Audience: **g,l,u.**

Whalen, Carmen Teresa & Vazquez-Hernandez, Victor (Editors)   **E184.P85P76 2005**
The Puerto Rican Diaspora: Historical Perspectives. Trade Cloth. Temple University Press. Philadelphia, PA. 2005. 304p. ISBN:1-59213-412-2, ISBN13: 978-1-59213-412-0. Dewey:305.868/7295073/09. LCCN:2004-063703.
Audience: **u,f.** *Choice, 2006.*

Social and Behavioral Sciences > History

Acuna, Rodolfo   **E184.M5A63 2003**
Occupied America: A History of Chicanos. Ed. 5. Trade Paper. Longman Publishing. Boston, MA. 2003. 536p. ISBN:0-321-10330-0, ISBN13: 978-0-321-10330-7. Dewey:973/.046872. LCCN:2003-046641.
Audience: **l,u.**

Arreola, Daniel D.   **F395.M5A77 2002**
Tejano South Texas: A Mexican American Cultural Province. Trade Cloth. University of Texas Press. Austin, TX. 2002. 288p. Jack and Doris Smothers Series in Texas History, Life, and Culture, No. 5 ISBN:0-292-70510-7, ISBN13: 978-0-292-70510-4. Dewey:976.4/40046872. LCCN:2001-044294.
Audience: **l,u.** *Choice, 2003, 2002.*

Camarillo, Albert   **F869.S45C25 2005**
Chicanos in a Changing Society: From Mexican Pueblos to American Barrios in Santa Barbara and Southern California, 1848-1930. Trade Paper. Southern Methodist University Press. Dallas, TX. 2005. 352p. ISBN:0-87074-497-6, ISBN13: 978-0-87074-497-6. Dewey:979.4/9/0046872073. LCCN:2004-065346.
Audience: **l,u.**

Campa, Arthur L.   **F 0786.C22**
Hispanic Culture in the Southwest. Trade Paper. University of Oklahoma Press. Norman, OK. 1993. 328p. ISBN:0-8061-2569-1, ISBN13: 978-0-8061-2569-5. Dewey:979.00468. LCCN:78-058135.
Audience: **g,l.**

Carlson, Alvar W.   **F802.R4C37 1990**
Spanish-American Homeland: Four Centuries in New Mexico's Rio Arriba. Trade Cloth. Johns Hopkins University Press. Baltimore, MD. 1982. 312p. Creating the North American Landscape Ser. ISBN:0-8018-3990-4, ISBN13: 978-0-8018-3990-0. Dewey:978.9/52. LCCN:90-004345.
Audience: **l,u.** *Choice, 1991.*

Chavez, John R. &   **E184.M5**
Platts-Mills, John
The Lost Land: The Chicano Image of the Southwest. Trade
Paper. University of New Mexico Press. Albuquerque, NM.
1984. 207p. ISBN:0-8263-0750-7, ISBN13: 978-0-8263-0750-7.
Dewey:979/.0046872. LCCN:84-011950.

Audience: **u,f.** *B*

De Leon, Arnoldo   **F394.H89 M512**
Ethnicity in the Sunbelt: A History of Mexican Americans in
Houston. Trade Cloth. University of Houston, Mexican
American Studies Program. Houston, TX. 1989. 255p. Mexican
American Studies ISBN:0-939709-06-6, ISBN13:
978-0-939709-06-9. Dewey:976.4/14110046872.

Audience: **l,u.** *Choice, 1990.*

Del Castillo, Richard G.   **F790.M5G75 1984**
La Familia: Chicano Families in the Urban Southwest, 1848 to
the Present. Paper Text. University of Notre Dame Press. Notre
Dame, IN. 1984. 224p. ISBN:0-268-01273-3, ISBN13:
978-0-268-01273-1. Dewey:306.8/50896872073.
LCCN:84-040356.

Audience: **u,f.** *B*

Duignan, Peter J. &   **E184.S75D85 1998**
Gann, Lewis H.
The Spanish Speakers in the United States: A History. Trade
Paper. University Press of America, Inc. Lanham, MD. 1998.
496p. ISBN:0-7618-1258-X, ISBN13: 978-0-7618-1258-6.
Dewey:973/.0468. LCCN:98-039212.

Audience: **l,u.**

Frank, Ross   **HC107.N6 F73 2000**
From Settler to Citizen: New Mexican Economic Development
and the Creation of Vecino Society, 1750-1820. Trade Cloth.
University of California Press. Berkeley, CA. 2001. 354p.
ISBN:0-520-22206-7, ISBN13: 978-0-520-22206-9.
Dewey:338.9789/009/033. LCCN:00-034381.

Audience: **u,f.** *Choice, 2001.*

Galarza, Ernesto   **F790.M5 G3**
Mexican-Americans in the Southwest. Paper Text. McNally &
Loftin, Publishers. Santa Barbara, CA. 1970.
ISBN:0-87461-020-6, ISBN13: 978-0-87461-020-8.
Dewey:917.91/09/746. LCCN:77-010039.

Audience: **g,l,u.**

Garcia, Juan R.   **E184.M5**
Emerging Themes in Mexican American Research. Trade Paper.
University of Arizona, Mexican American Studies & Research
Center. Tucson, AZ. 1994. ISBN:0-939363-04-6, ISBN13:
978-0-939363-04-9. Dewey:305.86872073.

Audience: **u,f.**

García, Mario T.   **F394.E4**
Desert Immigrants: The Mexican of el Paso, 1880-1920. Trade
Paper. Yale University Press. Cumberland, RI. 1982. 318p.
Western Americana Ser., No. 32 ISBN:0-300-02883-0, ISBN13:
978-0-300-02883-6. Dewey:976.4. LCCN:80-036862.

Audience: **u,f.**

Gonzales, Manuel G.   **E184.M5G638 2000**
Mexicanos: A History of Mexicans in the U. S. Trade Paper.
Indiana University Press. Bloomington, IN. 2000. 352p.
ISBN:0-253-21400-9, ISBN13: 978-0-253-21400-3.
Dewey:973/.046872.

Audience: **l,u.** *Choice, 1999.*

Gonzales-Berry, Erlinda   **F805.M5C66 2000**
& Maciel, David (Editors)
The Contested Homeland: A Chicano History of New Mexico.
Trade Paper. University of New Mexico Press. Albuquerque,
NM. 2000. 314p. ISBN:0-8263-2199-2, ISBN13:
978-0-8263-2199-2. Dewey:978.9/0046872. LCCN:99-050412.

Audience: **l,u.** *Choice, 2001.*

Gonzalez, Gilbert G. &   **E184.M5G645 2003**
Fernandez, Raul E.
A Century of Chicano History: Empire, Nations and Migration.
Paper over Boards. Routledge. New York, NY. 2003. 256p.
ISBN:0-415-94392-2, ISBN13: 978-0-415-94392-5.
Dewey:973/.046872. LCCN:2002-037050.

Audience: **l,u.**

Gonzalez, Juan   **E184.S75**
Harvest of Empire: A History of Latinos in America. Trade
Paper. Penguin Group (USA) Inc. New York, NY. 2001. 368p.
ISBN:0-14-025539-7, ISBN13: 978-0-14-025539-3.
Dewey:973/.0468. LCCN:99-033526.

Audience: **g,l.**

Gonzalez, Nancie L.   **F805.M5**
Spanish-Americans of New Mexico: A Heritage of Pride. Trade
Cloth. University of New Mexico Press. Albuquerque, NM.
1969. ISBN:0-8263-0137-1, ISBN13: 978-0-8263-0137-6.
Dewey:917.89/0974/6. LCCN:75-089517.

Audience: **l,u.**

González, Deena J.   **F804.S29 M54 1999**
Refusing the Favor: The Spanish-Mexican Women of Santa Fe,
1820-1880. Trade Cloth. Oxford University Press, Inc. New
York, NY. 1999. 206p. ISBN:0-19-507890-X, ISBN13:
978-0-19-507890-9. Dewey:978.9/560046872073.
LCCN:98-049560.

Audience: **u,f.** *Choice, 2000.*

Griswold del Castillo,   **E184.M5G74 1996**
Richard & De Leon, Arnoldo
North to Aztlan: A History of Mexican Americans in the United
States. Trade Cloth. Thomson Gale. Farmington Hills, MI. 1996.
xiv, 237p. ISBN:0-8057-4586-6, ISBN13: 978-0-8057-4586-3.
Dewey:973/.046872. LCCN:96-011777.

Audience: **l,u.** *Choice, 1997.*

Haas, Lisbeth   **F869.S395H33 1995**
Conquests and Historical Identities in California, 1769-1936.
Trade Cloth. University of California Press. Berkeley, CA. 1995.
284p. ISBN:0-520-08380-6, ISBN13: 978-0-520-08380-6.
Dewey:979.4/96. LCCN:94-044519.

Audience: **u,f.** *Choice, 1995.*

Landis, Jacquelyn   **E184.C97C845 2006**
The Cubans. Trade Paper. Thomson Gale. Farmington Hills, MI.
2006. 208p. ISBN:0-7377-2764-0, ISBN13: 978-0-7377-2764-7.
Dewey:973/.04687291. LCCN:2004-060583.

Audience: **g,l.**

Lopez, Adalberto   **F1972 .P83 1980**
(Editor)
The Puerto Ricans: Their History, Culture and Society. Paper
Text. Schenkman Books, Inc. Rochester, VT. 1981. 490p.
ISBN:0-87073-845-3, ISBN13: 978-0-87073-845-6.
Dewey:972.95. LCCN:79-028298.

Audience: **g,l.**

Martínez, Oscar J.   **F790.M5M37 2001**
Mexican-Origin People in the United States: A Topical History.
Trade Cloth. University of Arizona Press. Tucson, AZ. 2001.
244p. Modern American West Ser. ISBN:0-8165-1179-9,
ISBN13: 978-0-8165-1179-2. Dewey:305.868/079.
LCCN:00-010291.
           Audience: **g,l.** *Choice, 2001.*

Martínez, Oscar J.   **F787**
Troublesome Border. Trade Paper. University of Arizona Press.
Tucson, AZ. 1989. 177p. Profmex Ser. ISBN:0-8165-1104-7,
ISBN13: 978-0-8165-1104-4. Dewey:972/.1. LCCN:87-034294.
           Audience: **u,f.** *Choice, 1988.*

Matovina, Timothy M.   **F394.S2M39 1995**
Tejano Religion and Ethnicity: San Antonio, 1821-1860. Trade
Cloth. University of Texas Press. Austin, TX. 1995. 182p.
ISBN:0-292-75170-2, ISBN13: 978-0-292-75170-5.
Dewey:976.4/3510046872073. LCCN:94-010617.
           Audience: **u,f.** *Choice, 1995.*

McKenzie, Phyllis   **F395.M5M38 2004**
The Mexican Texans. University of Texas Institute of Texan
Cultures at San Antonio Staff (Contribution by). Trade Cloth.
Texas A&M University Press. College Station, TX. 2004. 160p.
Texans All Ser. ISBN:1-58544-306-9, ISBN13:
978-1-58544-306-2. Dewey:976.4/0046872. LCCN:2003-016356.
           Audience: **l,u.**

McNally, Michael J.   **BX1415.F55M33 1984**
Catholicism in South Florida, 1868-1968. Philip Gleason
(Foreword by). Trade Paper. University Press of Florida.
Gainesville, FL. 1984. 334p. ISBN:0-8130-0788-7, ISBN13:
978-0-8130-0788-5. Dewey:282/.759. LCCN:84-007389.
           Audience: **l,u.**

McWilliams, Carey &   **E184**
   Meier, Matt S.
North from Mexico: The Spanish-Speaking People of the United
States. Trade Cloth. Greenwood Publishing Group, Inc.
Portsmouth, NH. 1990. 376p. Contributions in American History
Ser. ISBN:0-313-26631-X, ISBN13: 978-0-313-26631-7.
Dewey:973.046872. LCCN:89-017031.
           Audience: **g,l,u.**

Meier, Matt S. &   **E184**
   Rivera, Feliciano
Dictionary of Mexican American History. Cloth Text.
Greenwood Publishing Group, Inc. Portsmouth, NH. 1981. 498p.
ISBN:0-313-21203-1, ISBN13: 978-0-313-21203-1.
Dewey:973/.046872. LCCN:80-024750.
           Audience: **g,l,u.**

Menchaca, Martha   **E184.M5M46 2001**
Recovering History, Constructing Race: The Indian, Black, and
White Roots of Mexican Americans. Trade Paper. University of
Texas Press. Austin, TX. 2002. 389p. Joe R. and Teresa Lozano
Long Series in Latin American and Latino Art and Culture
ISBN:0-292-75254-7, ISBN13: 978-0-292-75254-2.
Dewey:973/.046872. LCCN:2001-033309.
           Audience: **u,f.** *Choice, 2002.*

Mendoza, Louis Gerard   **E184.M5**
Historia: The Literary Making of Chicana and Chicano History.
Trade Paper. Texas A&M University Press. College Station, TX.
2004. 376p. Rio Grande/Rio Bravo Ser., Vol. 7
ISBN:1-58544-179-1, ISBN13: 978-1-58544-179-2.
Dewey:305.868/72073.
           Audience: **u,f.** *Choice, 2002.*

Miranda, Malvin   **F850.S75M57 1997**
A History of Hispanics in Southern Nevada. Trade Cloth.
University of Nevada Press. Reno, NV. 1997. 240p. History and
Humanities Ser. ISBN:0-87417-291-8, ISBN13:
978-0-87417-291-1. Dewey:979.3/1300468073.
LCCN:97-022015.
           Audience: **l,u.** *Choice, 1998.*

Montejano, David   **F395.M5M66 1987**
Anglos and Mexicans in the Making of Texas, 1836-1986. Trade
Paper. University of Texas Press. Austin, TX. 1987. 397p.
ISBN:0-292-77596-2, ISBN13: 978-0-292-77596-1.
Dewey:976.4. LCCN:86-027249.
           Audience: **l,u.**

Nostrand, Richard L.   **F805.M5**
The Hispano Homeland. Trade Paper. University of Oklahoma
Press. Norman, OK. 1996. 296p. ISBN:0-8061-2889-5, ISBN13:
978-0-8061-2889-4. Dewey:978.9/0046872073.
LCCN:91-050867.
           Audience: **l,u.** *Choice, 1993.*

Padilla, Felix M.   **F548.9.P85P33 1987**
Puerto Rican Chicago. Trade Cloth. University of Notre Dame
Press. Notre Dame, IN. 1988. 256p. ISBN:0-268-01564-3,
ISBN13: 978-0-268-01564-0. Dewey:977.3/11004687295.
LCCN:86-040244.
           Audience: **l,u.** *Choice, 1987.*

Padilla, Genaro M.   **E184.M5.P28 1993**
My History, Not Yours: The Formation of Mexican American
Autobiography. Trade Cloth. University of Wisconsin Press.
Chicago, IL. 1994. 224p. Studies in American Autobiography
ISBN:0-299-13970-0, ISBN13: 978-0-299-13970-4.
Dewey:920.00926872. LCCN:93-003457.
           Audience: **u,f.** *Choice, 1994.*

Pérez y González,   **E184.P85 P47 2000**
   María E.
Puerto Ricans in the United States. Greenwood Press. 2000.
ISBN:0-313-29748-7, ISBN13: 978-0-313-29748-9.
           Audience: **g,l.**

Rochin, Refugio &   **E184.M5V65 2000**
   Valdés, Dennis (Editors)
Voices of a New Chicana/o History. Trade Paper. Michigan State
University Press. East Lansing, MI. 2000. 275p.
ISBN:0-87013-523-6, ISBN13: 978-0-87013-523-1.
Dewey:305.48/86872073. LCCN:00-008064.
           Audience: **u,f.**

Samora, Julian, et al.   **E184.M5S25 1993**
ⓔ A History of the Mexican-American People. Patricia Vandel
Simon, Cordelia Candelaria & Alberto L. Pulido (Authors).
E-Book. NetLibrary, Inc. Boulder, CO. 1993.
ISBN:0-585-33332-7, ISBN13: 978-0-585-33332-8.
Dewey:973.046872.
           Audience: **l.**

Sanchez Korrol,   **E184.P85 S26 1999**
   Virginia
Teaching U. S. Puerto Rican History. Nell I. Painter & Antonio
Rios-Bustamante (Editors). Trade Paper. American Historical
Association. Washington, DC. 1999. 72p. Teaching Diversity
Ser., :People of Color ISBN:0-87229-098-0, ISBN13:
978-0-87229-098-3. Dewey:973/.04687295. LCCN:98-038956.
           Audience: **f.**

Sheridan, Thomas E.   **F819.T99**
Los Tucsonenses: The Mexican Community in Tucson, 1854-1941. Trade Paper. University of Arizona Press. Tucson, AZ. 1992. 327p. ISBN:0-8165-1298-1, ISBN13: 978-0-8165-1298-0. Dewey:979.1/77. LCCN:86-011404.
Audience: **l,u.**

Shorris, Earl   **E184.S75**
Latinos: A Biography of the People. Trade Paper. W. W. Norton & Company, Inc. New York, NY. 2001. 544p. ISBN:0-393-32190-8, ISBN13: 978-0-393-32190-6. Dewey:973/.0468.
Audience: **g,l.**

Sánchez Korrol,   **F128.9.P85S26 1994**
  Virginia
[e] From Colonia to Community: The History of Puerto Ricans in New York City. E-Book. NetLibrary, Inc. Boulder, CO. 1994. ISBN:0-585-07894-7, ISBN13: 978-0-585-07894-6. Dewey:974.7/1004687295.
Audience: **l,u.**

Sánchez, George Isidore   **F805.M5S355 1996**
[e] Forgotten People: A Study of New Mexicans. E-Book. NetLibrary, Inc. Boulder, CO. 1996. ISBN:0-585-18749-5, ISBN13: 978-0-585-18749-5. Dewey:978.9/5300461.
Audience: **l,u.**

Torrans, Thomas   **F786.T68 2000**
Forging the Tortilla Curtain: Cultural Drift and Change along the United States-Mexico Boarderlands from the Spanish Conquest to the Present. Trade Cloth. Texas Christian University Press. Fort Worth, TX. 2000. xi, 424p. ISBN:0-87565-231-X, ISBN13: 978-0-87565-231-3. Dewey:972/.1. LCCN:00-030245.
Audience: **u,f.** *Choice, 2001.*

Velez-Ibanez, Carlos G.   **F790.M5V45 1996**
Border Visions: Mexican Cultures of the Southwest United States. Trade Cloth. University of Arizona Press. Tucson, AZ. 1996. xii, 360p. ISBN:0-8165-1422-4, ISBN13: 978-0-8165-1422-9. Dewey:305.868/72073. LCCN:96-010100.
Audience: **l,u,f.** *Choice, 1997.*

Wagenheim, Kal & De   **F1971.P79 1994**
  Wagenheim, Olga Jimenez (Editors)
Puerto Ricans: A Documentary History. Ed. 2. Trade Paper. Markus Wiener Publishers, Inc. Princeton, NJ. 2002. 355p. ISBN:1-55876-077-6, ISBN13: 978-1-55876-077-6. Dewey:972.95. LCCN:93-020849.
Audience: **l,u.**

Weber, David J.   **E184.M5W42 2003**
Foreigners in Their Native Land: Historical Roots of the Mexican Americans. Ed. 13. Trade Paper. University of New Mexico Press. Albuquerque, NM. 2004. 292p. ISBN:0-8263-3510-1, ISBN13: 978-0-8263-3510-4. Dewey:973/.0468072. LCCN:2003-020529.
Audience: **l,u.**

Weber, David J.   **F786**
Myth and the History of the Hispanic Southwest: Essays. Trade Paper. University of New Mexico Press. Albuquerque, NM. 2002. 180p. Calvin P. Horn Lectures in Western History and Culture ISBN:0-8263-1194-6, ISBN13: 978-0-8263-1194-8. Dewey:972/.1. LCCN:88-012035.
Audience: **u,f.**

Whalen, Carmen Teresa   **E184.P85P76 2005**
  & Vazquez-Hernandez, Victor (Editors)
The Puerto Rican Diaspora: Historical Perspectives. Trade Cloth. Temple University Press. Philadelphia, PA. 2005. 304p. ISBN:1-59213-412-2, ISBN13: 978-1-59213-412-0. Dewey:305.868/7295073/09. LCCN:2004-063703.
Audience: **u,f.** *Choice, 2006.*

Wilson, Chris   **F804.S25W55 1997**
The Myth of Santa Fe: Creating a Modern Regional Tradition. Trade Paper. University of New Mexico Press. Albuquerque, NM. 1996. 418p. ISBN:0-8263-1746-4, ISBN13: 978-0-8263-1746-9. Dewey:978.9/5605. LCCN:95-050222.
Audience: **u,f.** *Choice, 1997.*

Young, Elliott   **F786.C67 2004**
Continental Crossroads: Remapping U. S.-Mexico Borderlands History. Samuel Truett (Editor). Trade Cloth. Duke University Press. Durham, NC. 2004. 336p. American Encounters/Global Interactions Ser. ISBN:0-8223-3353-8, ISBN13: 978-0-8223-3353-1. LCCN:2004-004074.
Audience: **u,f.** *Choice, 2005.*

Social and Behavioral Sciences > History > Mexican Period (to1848)

Briggs, Charles L. &   **HD0243.N5L36**
  Van Ness, John R. (Editors)
Land, Water, and Culture: New Perspectives on Hispanic Land Grants. Trade Paper. Books on Demand. Ann Arbor, MI. 432p. New Mexico Land Grant Ser. ISBN:0-7837-5860-X, ISBN13: 978-0-7837-5860-2. Dewey:333.1/6/09788. LCCN:87-010957.
Audience: **u,f.** *Choice, 1988.*

Calafate Boyle, Susan   **HF3161.N6B69 1997**
Los Capitalistas: Hispano Merchants on the Santa Fe Trade. Trade Cloth. University of New Mexico Press. Albuquerque, NM. 1997. 236p. ISBN:0-8263-1789-8, ISBN13: 978-0-8263-1789-6. Dewey:380.1/09789/0903. LCCN:96-035705.
Audience: **u,f.** *Choice, 1997.*

Connor, Seymour V.   **E404.C8**
North America Divided; the Mexican War, 1846-1848. Trade Cloth. Oxford University Press, Inc. New York, NY. 1971. viii, 300p. ISBN:0-19-501448-0, ISBN13: 978-0-19-501448-8. Dewey:973.6/2. LCCN:77-161885.
Audience: **g,l,u.** *B*

de Villagra, Gaspar   **PQ7296.V54.H5713**
  Perez
Historia de la Nueva Mexico, 1610: A Critical and Annotated Spanish/English Edition. Trade Cloth. University of New Mexico Press. Albuquerque, NM. 1992. 367p. ISBN:0-8263-1392-2, ISBN13: 978-0-8263-1392-8. Dewey:861. LCCN:92-028780.
Audience: **u,f.** *Choice, 1994.*

del Castillo, Richard   **E408.G75 1990**
  Griswold
The Treaty of Guadalupe Hidalgo: A Legacy of Conflict. Trade Cloth. University of Oklahoma Press. Norman, OK. 1990. 272p. ISBN:0-8061-2240-4, ISBN13: 978-0-8061-2240-3. Dewey:973.6/2. LCCN:89-038642.
Audience: **l,u.** *Choice, 1990.*

Eisenhower, John S. D.   E405.E37 1989
So Far from God: The U. S. War with Mexico, 1846-1848.
Trade Cloth. Random House, Inc. New York, NY. 1989. 704p.
ISBN:0-394-56051-5, ISBN13: 978-0-394-56051-9.
Dewey:973.6/2. LCCN:88-042675.
                              Audience: l,u.   *Choice, 1989.*

Gutierrez, Ramon A.   HQ835.N6G88 1991
When Jesus Came, the Corn Mothers Went Away: Marriage,
Sexuality and Power in New Mexico, 1500-1846. Trade Cloth.
Stanford University Press. Palo Alto, CA. 1991. 456p.
ISBN:0-8047-1816-4, ISBN13: 978-0-8047-1816-5.
Dewey:306.85/09789. LCCN:90-009512.
                              Audience: u,f.   *Choice, 1991.*

Johannsen, Robert W.   E404
To the Halls of the Montezumas: The Mexican War in the
American Imagination. Paper Text. Oxford University Press, Inc.
New York, NY. 1988. 384p. ISBN:0-19-504981-0, ISBN13:
978-0-19-504981-7. Dewey:973.6/2. LCCN:84-020696.
                              Audience: u,f. *B*

Johnson, Benjamin   F391.J64 2003
Heber
Revolution in Texas: How a Forgotten Rebellion and Its Bloody
Suppression Turned Mexicans into Americans. Cloth over
Boards. Yale University Press. Cumberland, RI. 2003. 272p.
Western American Ser. ISBN:0-300-09425-6, ISBN13:
978-0-300-09425-1. Dewey:976.4/4061. LCCN:2003-009133.
                              Audience: u,f.   *Choice, 2004.*

Kearney, Milo &   F787.K435 2001
Medrano, Manuel
Medieval Culture and the Mexican American Borderlands. Cloth
Text. Texas A&M University Press. College Station, TX. 2002.
256p. Rio Grande/Rio Bravo Ser., Vol. 6 ISBN:1-58544-132-5,
ISBN13: 978-1-58544-132-7. Dewey:972/.1.
LCCN:2001-002736.
                              Audience: u,f.   *Choice, 2002.*

Krieger, Alex D., et al.   E125.N9K75 2003
We Came Naked and Barefoot: The Journey of Cabeza de Vaca
across North America. Alvar Nunez Cabeza de Vaca & Gonzalo
Fernandez de Oviedo y Valdes (Authors), Margery H. Krieger
(Editor), Thomas R. Hester (Afterword by, Foreword by). Trade
Cloth. University of Texas Press. Austin, TX. 2002. 336p. Texas
Archaeology and Ethnohistory Ser. ISBN:0-292-74350-5,
ISBN13: 978-0-292-74350-2. Dewey:970.01/6.
LCCN:2002-004973.
                              Audience: l,u.   *Choice, 2003.*

Lovato, Andrew   F804.S29S75 2004
Santa Fe Hispanic Culture: Preserving Identity in a Tourist
Town. Trade Cloth. University of New Mexico Press.
Albuquerque, NM. 2004. 140p. ISBN:0-8263-3225-0, ISBN13:
978-0-8263-3225-7. Dewey:305.868/073/0978956.
LCCN:2004-015735.
                              Audience: l,u.   *Choice, 2005.*

Montgomery, Charles H.   F805.S75 M66 2002
The Spanish Redemption: Heritage, Power, and Loss on New
Mexico's Upper Rio Grande. Trade Cloth. University of
California Press. Berkeley, CA. 2002. 356p.
ISBN:0-520-22971-1, ISBN13: 978-0-520-22971-6.
Dewey:978.9/00468. LCCN:2001-005649.
                              Audience: u,f.   *Choice, 2003, 2002.*

Poyo, Gerald E. &   F394.S2T43 1991
Hinojosa, Gilberto M. (Editors)
Tejano Origins in Eighteenth-Century San Antonio. Jose
Cisneros (Illustrator). Trade Cloth. University of Texas Press.
Austin, TX. 1991. 222p. ISBN:0-292-71138-7, ISBN13:
978-0-292-71138-9. Dewey:976.4/3510046872.
LCCN:90-047345.
                              Audience: l,u.   *Choice, 1992.*

Reséndez, Andrés   F390.R46 2004
Changing National Identities at the Frontier: Texas and New
Mexico, 1800-1850. Cloth Text. Cambridge University Press.
New York, NY. 2004. 326p. ISBN:0-521-83555-0, ISBN13:
978-0-521-83555-8. Dewey:976.4/05. LCCN:2004-040651.
                              Audience: u,f.   *Choice, 2005.*

Seguin, Juan N.   F390.S465 2002
A Revolution Remembered: The Memoirs and Selected
Correspondence of Juan N. Seguin. Jesus F. de la Teja (Editor).
Trade Cloth. Texas State Historical Association. Austin, TX.
2002. 0p. The Fred H. and Ella Mae Moore Texas History
Reprint Ser. ISBN:0-87611-185-1, ISBN13: 978-0-87611-185-7.
Dewey:976.4/03. LCCN:2002-073576.
                              Audience: u,f.   *Choice, 1992.*

Social and Behavioral Sciences > History > 1849-1900

De Leon, Arnoldo   F395.M5.D43 1983
They Called Them Greasers: Anglo Attitudes toward Mexicans
in Texas, 1821-1900. Trade Cloth. University of Texas Press.
Austin, TX. 1983. 167p. ISBN:0-292-70363-5, ISBN13:
978-0-292-70363-6. Dewey:976.4/0046872. LCCN:82-024850.
                              Audience: l,u. *B*

De Leon, Arnoldo   F395.M5D4 1997
The Tejano Community, 1836-1900. Richard G. Del Castillo
(Foreword by). Trade Paper. Southern Methodist University
Press. Dallas, TX. 1997. 310p. ISBN:0-87074-419-4, ISBN13:
978-0-87074-419-8. Dewey:305.868/720764. LCCN:97-016564.
                              Audience: u,f.

Griswold del Castillo,   HE8700.8
Richard
The Los Angeles Barrio, 1850-1890: A Social History. Trade
Cloth. University of California Press. Berkeley, CA. 1980. 232p.
ISBN:0-520-03816-9, ISBN13: 978-0-520-03816-5.
Dewey:301.45/16/872079494. LCCN:78-065460.
                              Audience: l,u.

Keller, Gary D. &   E415.L44 1999
Candelaria, Cordelia (Editors)
The Legacy of the Mexican and Spanish-American Wars: Legal,
Literacy, and Historical Perspectives. Trade Cloth. Bilingual
Press/Editorial Bilingue. Tempe, AZ. 2000. 128p.
ISBN:0-927534-90-8, ISBN13: 978-0-927534-90-1.
Dewey:973.6/2. LCCN:99-058432.
                              Audience: l,u.

Monroy, Douglas   F867.M69 1990
Thrown among Strangers: The Making of Mexican Culture in
Frontier California. Trade Cloth. University of California Press.
Berkeley, CA. 1990. 288p. ISBN:0-520-06914-5, ISBN13:
978-0-520-06914-5. Dewey:979.40046872. LCCN:89-049035.
                              Audience: l,u.   *Choice, 1991.*

Pitt, Leonard   **F870.S75P58 1998**
The Decline of the Californios: A Social History of the
Spanish-Speaking Californians, 1846-1890. Ramon A. Gutierrez
(Foreword by). Trade Paper. University of California Press.
Berkeley, CA. 1999. 340p. ISBN:0-520-21958-9, ISBN13:
978-0-520-21958-8. Dewey:979.4/00468. LCCN:99-229612.
                                        Audience: **l,u.**

Rebert, Paula   **F786.R43 2001**
La Gran Linea: Mapping the United States - Mexico Boundary,
1849-1857. Trade Cloth. University of Texas Press. Austin, TX.
2001. 279p. ISBN:0-292-77110-X, ISBN13: 978-0-292-77110-9.
Dewey:911/.721. LCCN:00-041771.
                              Audience: **l,u.** *Choice, 2001.*

Rosenbaum, Robert J.   **F790.M5R67 1998**
  (Author, Afterword by)
Mexicano Resistance in the Southwest. John Chavez (Foreword
by). Trade Paper. Southern Methodist University Press. Dallas,
TX. 1998. 264p. ISBN:0-87074-429-1, ISBN13:
978-0-87074-429-7. Dewey:979/.0046872073. LCCN:98-003839.
                                        Audience: **l,u.**

Social and Behavioral Sciences > History > 1900 to the present

Acuna, Rodolfo F.   **F869.L89M5 1996**
Anything but Mexican: Chicanos in Contemporary Los Angeles.
Trade Cloth. Verso Books. London, 1996. 320p. Haymarket Ser.
ISBN:1-85984-936-9, ISBN13: 978-1-85984-936-1.
Dewey:979.4/053/0046872. LCCN:96-005040.
                              Audience: **l,u.** *Choice, 1996.*

Acuna, Rodolfo F.   **F869.E18 A28 1984**
A Community under Siege: A Chronicle of Chicanos East of the
Los Angeles River, 1945-1975. Trade Paper. UCLA Chicano
Studies Research Center Press. Los Angeles, CA. 1984. 540p.
Monographs, No. 11 ISBN:0-89551-066-9, ISBN13:
978-0-89551-066-2. Dewey:979.4/93. LCCN:83-026197.
                                        Audience: **l,u.**

Avila, Eric   **F869.L85 A95 2004**
Popular Culture in the Age of White Flight: Fear and Fantasy in
Suburban Los Angeles. Trade Cloth. University of California
Press. Berkeley, CA. 2004. 345p. American Crossroads Ser., Vol.
13 ISBN:0-520-24121-5, ISBN13: 978-0-520-24121-3.
Dewey:979.4/94. LCCN:2003-019072.
                              Audience: **u,f.** *Choice, 2005.*

Balderrama, Francisco   **E184.M5B35 2006**
  E. & Rodriguez, Raymond
Decade of Betrayal: Mexican Repatriation in the 1930s. Trade
Paper. University of New Mexico Press. Albuquerque, NM.
2006. 427p. ISBN:0-8263-3973-5, ISBN13: 978-0-8263-3973-7.
Dewey:323.1168/7207309043. LCCN:2005-024861.
                              Audience: **l,u.** *Choice, 1996.*

Cardona, Luis A.   **E184.P85 C36 1991**
A History of Puerto Ricans in the United States of America,
Vol. I. Ed. 2. Trade Paper. Carreta Press. Silver Spring, MD.
1995. 525p. ISBN:0-914199-09-9, ISBN13: 978-0-914199-09-0.
Dewey:973/.04687295. LCCN:91-070631.
                                        Audience: **l,u.**

Cardona, Luis A.   **E184.P85C373 1998**
A History of the Puerto Ricans in the United States of America,
Vol. II. Trade Paper. Carreta Press. Silver Spring, MD. 1998.
500p. ISBN:0-914199-10-2, ISBN13: 978-0-914199-10-6.
Dewey:973/.004687295. LCCN:98-071230.
                                        Audience: **l,u.**

Colón, Jesus   **F128.9.P85 C65 1993**
The Way It Was and Other Writings. Edna Acosta-Belén &
Virginia A. Korrol (Editors). Trade Paper. Arte Publico Press.
Houston, TX. 1993. 128p. ISBN:1-55885-057-0, ISBN13:
978-1-55885-057-6. Dewey:305.868/729507471.
LCCN:92-042443.
                                        Audience: **l,u.**

Colón, Jesús   **F128.9.P85 C64 1975**
A Puerto Rican in New York and Other Sketches. Trade Cloth.
Ayer Company Publishers, Inc. Manchester, NH. 1979. 206p. A
Puerto Rican Experience Ser. ISBN:0-405-06218-4, ISBN13:
978-0-405-06218-6. Dewey:305.8/687295/07471.
LCCN:74-014229.
                                        Audience: **l,u.**

Forrest, Suzanne   **F805.S75F67 1998**
The Preservation of the Village: New Mexico's Hispanics and
the New Deal. Trade Cloth. University of New Mexico Press.
Albuquerque, NM. 1989. 271p. New Mexico Land Grant Ser.
ISBN:0-8263-1973-4, ISBN13: 978-0-8263-1973-9.
Dewey:978.9/052. LCCN:98-022906.
                              Audience: **u,f.** *Choice, 1990.*

Galarza, Ernesto   **E184.M5G3 2000**
Barrio Boy. Trade Cloth. Holt, Rinehart & Winston. Austin, TX.
2000. 321p. HRW Library ISBN:0-03-055987-1, ISBN13:
978-0-03-055987-7. Dewey:301.45/16. LCCN:2001-271307.
                                        Audience: **g,l,u.**

Garcia, Juan R.   **F358.2.M5G37 1996**
Mexicans in the Midwest, 1900-1932. Trade Cloth. University
of Arizona Press. Tucson, AZ. 1996. 293p. ISBN:0-8165-1560-3,
ISBN13: 978-0-8165-1560-8. Dewey:977/.046872073.
LCCN:96-010098.
                              Audience: **l,u.** *Choice, 1997.*

Garcia, Matthew   **F869.L89A253 2002**
A World of Its Own: Race, Labor, and Citrus in the Making of
Greater Los Angeles, 1900-1970. Trade Cloth. University of
North Carolina Press. Chapel Hill, NC. 2002. 352p. Studies in
Rural Culture ISBN:0-8078-2658-8, ISBN13:
978-0-8078-2658-4. Dewey:305.8/009794/94.
LCCN:2001-035879.
                              Audience: **u,f.** *Choice, 2002.*

Garcia, Richard A.   **F394.S2G37 1991**
Rise of the Mexican American Middle Class: San Antonio,
1929-1941. Henry C. Schmidt (Foreword by). Trade Cloth.
Texas A&M University Press. College Station, TX. 1991. 416p.
Centennial Series of the Association of Former Students, No. 36
ISBN:0-89096-368-1, ISBN13: 978-0-89096-368-5.
Dewey:976.4/3510046872073. LCCN:90-038788.
                              Audience: **u,f.** *Choice, 1991.*

García, Mario T.   **HD8073.C67.G37**
Memories of Chicano History: The Life and Narrative of Bert
Corona. David Montgomery (Foreword by). Trade Paper.
University of California Press. Berkeley, CA. 1995. 388p.
Latinos in American Society and Culture Ser., Vol. 2

ISBN:0-520-20152-3, ISBN13: 978-0-520-20152-1.
Dewey:323.116872.

Audience: **l,u.** *Choice, 1994.*

Grosfoguel, Ramon   **E184.P85 G68 2003**
Colonial Subjects: Puerto Ricans in a Global Perspective. Trade
Paper. University of California Press. Berkeley, CA. 2003. 272p.
ISBN:0-520-23021-3, ISBN13: 978-0-520-23021-7.
Dewey:304.8/7307295/09043. LCCN:2003-047327.

Audience: **u,f.** *Choice, 2004.*

Gutiérrez, David G.   **E184.S75C644 2004**
The Columbia History of Latinos in the United States Since
1960. Trade Cloth. Kegan Paul International, Ltd. London, 2004.
512p. ISBN:0-231-11808-2, ISBN13: 978-0-231-11808-8.
Dewey:973/.0468. LCCN:2004-041310.

Audience: **g,l.** *Choice, 2005.*

Harris, Charles H. &   **F391.H28 2004**
Sadler, Louis R.
The Texas Rangers and the Mexican Revolution: The Bloodiest
Decade, 1910-1920. Trade Cloth. University of New Mexico
Press. Albuquerque, NM. 2004. 673p. ISBN:0-8263-3483-0,
ISBN13: 978-0-8263-3483-1. Dewey:972.08/16.
LCCN:2004-009059.

Audience: **l,u.** *Choice, 2005.*

Iber, Jorge   **F835.S75I24 2000**
Hispanics in the Mormon Zion, 1912-1999. Trade Cloth. Texas
A&M University Press. College Station, TX. 2000. xvi, 196p.
Elma Dill Russell Spencer Series in the West and Southwest,
Vol. 21 ISBN:0-89096-933-7, ISBN13: 978-0-89096-933-5.
Dewey:305.8680792. LCCN:99-054608.

Audience: **l,u,f.** *Choice, 2000.*

Lane, James B. &   **F535.S75F67 1987**
Escobar, Edward J. (Editors)
Forging a Community: The Latino Experience in Northwest
Indiana, 1919-1975. Trade Cloth. Indiana University Press.
Bloomington, IN. 1987. 306p. ISBN:0-253-32382-7, ISBN13:
978-0-253-32382-8. Dewey:977.2/00468. LCCN:87-010292.

Audience: **u,f.** *Choice, 1987.*

Lopez Tijerina, Reies   **F805.M5T5413 2000**
They Called Me King Tiger: My Struggle for the Land and Our
Rights. Jose Angel Gutierrez (Translator). Trade Paper. Arte
Publico Press. Houston, TX. 2000. 256p. Hispanic Civil Rights
Ser. ISBN:1-55885-302-2, ISBN13: 978-1-55885-302-7.
Dewey:978.9/0046873. LCCN:00-059426.

Audience: **l,u.**

MacLachlan, Colin M.   **F1234.F663M33 1991**
Anarchism and the Mexican Revolution: The Political Trials of
Ricardo Flores Magón in the United States. John M. Hart
(Foreword by). Trade Cloth. University of California Press.
Berkeley, CA. 1991. 201p. ISBN:0-520-06928-5, ISBN13:
978-0-520-06928-2. Dewey:322.4/2/092. LCCN:90-042212.

Audience: **u,f.** *Choice, 1991.*

Mazón, Mauricio   **F869.L89M56 1985**
The Zoot-Suit Riots: The Psychology of Symbolic Annihilation.
Trade Cloth. University of Texas Press. Austin, TX. 1984. 179p.
Mexican American Monographs, No. 8 ISBN:0-292-79801-6,
ISBN13: 978-0-292-79801-4. Dewey:979.4/940046872.
LCCN:84-005656.

Audience: **u,f.**

Monroy, Douglas   **F869.L89 M455 1999**
Rebirth: Mexican Los Angeles from the Great Migration to the
Great Depression. Trade Paper. University of California Press.
Berkeley, CA. 1999. 334p. ISBN:0-520-21333-5, ISBN13:
978-0-520-21333-3. Dewey:979.4/940046872073.
LCCN:98-050013.

Audience: **l,u.** *Choice, 1999.*

Murguìa, Alejandro   **F870.M5M87 2002**
The Medicine of Memory: A Mexica Clan in California. Trade
Cloth. University of Texas Press. Austin, TX. 2002. 296p.
ISBN:0-292-75265-2, ISBN13: 978-0-292-75265-8.
Dewey:929/.2/0973. LCCN:2002-010187.

Audience: **l,u.** *Choice, 2003.*

Pacheco, Ferdie   **F319.T2P33 1994**
Ybor City Chronicles: A Memoir. Trade Cloth. University Press
of Florida. Gainesville, FL. 1994. 315p. ISBN:0-8130-1296-1,
ISBN13: 978-0-8130-1296-4. Dewey:975.9/65 B.
LCCN:94-000822.

Audience: **l,u.**

Pagan, Eduardo   **F869.L89 M566 2003**
Obregon
Murder at the Sleepy Lagoon: Zoot Suits, Race, and Riot in
Wartime L.A. Trade Cloth. University of North Carolina Press.
Chapel Hill, NC. 2003. 312p. ISBN:0-8078-2826-2, ISBN13:
978-0-8078-2826-7. Dewey:979.4/94052. LCCN:2003-048891.

Audience: **l,u.** *Choice, 2004.*

Romo, Ricardo   **F869.E18 R65 1983**
East Los Angeles: History of a Barrio. Trade Paper. University
of Texas Press. Austin, TX. 1983. 232p. ISBN:0-292-72041-6,
ISBN13: 978-0-292-72041-1. Dewey:305.8/6872/079494.
LCCN:82-010891.

Audience: **l,u.** 𝓑

Rosales, Francisco A.   **E184.M5R637 1999**
🄴 Pobre Raza!: Violence, Justice, and Mobilization among
Mexico Lindo Immigrants, 1900-1936. E-Book. University of
Texas Press. Austin, TX. 1999. ISBN:0-292-79935-7, ISBN13:
978-0-292-79935-6. Dewey:323.1/16872073.

Audience: **l,u.**

Valdés, Dionicio Nodín   **F614.S4V35 2000**
Barrios Norteños: St. Paul and Midwestern Mexican
Communities in the Twentieth Century. Trade Cloth. University
of Texas Press. Austin, TX. 2000. 406p. Pike Subsidy Ser.
ISBN:0-292-78743-X, ISBN13: 978-0-292-78743-8.
Dewey:977.6/5810046872073. LCCN:99-036269.

Audience: **l,u.** *Choice, 2000.*

Vega, Bernardo   **F128.9.P85V4313 1984**
Memoirs of Bernardo Vega: A Contribution to the History of the
Puerto Rican Community in New York. Cesar A. Iglesias
(Editor), Juan Flores (Translator). Trade Paper. Monthly Review
Press. New York, NY. 1984. 288p. ISBN:0-85345-656-9,
ISBN13: 978-0-85345-656-8. Dewey:974.7/104.
LCCN:84-009128.

Audience: **l,u.**

Social and Behavioral Sciences > Politics, Government, and Law

                                              E184.S75
🖵 constructing the new.

http://www.nclr.org/
NCLR.

Audience: **l,u,f.**

F130.S75

Constructing the New York Area Hispanic Mosiac: A Demographic Portrait of Colombians and Dominicans in New York. Tomás Rivera Policy Institute and NALEO Educational Fund. 1977.

Audience: **f.**

F867

Diversifying the Los Angeles Area Latino Mosiac: Salvadoran and Guatemalan Leaders' Assessments of Community Public Policy Needs. Tomás Rivera Policy Institute and NALEO Educational Fund. 1997.

Audience: **f.**

F130.S75

Diversifying the New York Area Hispanic Mosiac: Colombian and Dominican Leaders' Assessments of Community Public Policy Needs. Tomás Rivera Policy Institute and NALEO Educational Fund. 1977.

Audience: **f.**

F1408

□ LULAC: League of United Latin American Citizens. http://www.lulac.org/
LULAC.

Audience: **g,l,u,f.**

Andreas, Peter   **HJ6690.A7 2000**
Border Games: Policing the U.S.- Mexico Divide. Book, Other. Cornell University Press. Ithaca, NY. 2000. 192p. Studies in Political Economy ISBN:0-8014-3796-2, ISBN13: 978-0-8014-3796-0. Dewey:363.45/0972/1. LCCN:00-024022.

Audience: **u,f.** *Choice, 2001.*

Burke, John Francis   **E184.A1B8985 2002**
Mestizo Democracy: The Politics of Crossing Borders. Trade Cloth. Texas A&M University Press. College Station, TX. 2002. xv, 304p. Rio Grande/Rio Bravo Ser., No. 8 ISBN:1-58544-208-9, ISBN13: 978-1-58544-208-9. Dewey:305.8/00973/090511. LCCN:2002-006061.

Audience: **u,f.** *Choice, 2003.*

Croucher, Sheila L.   **F319.M6C76 1997**
Imagining Miami: Ethnic Politics in a Postmodern World. Cloth Text. University Press of Virginia. Charlottesville, VA. 1997. 250p. Race, Ethnicity and Politics Ser. ISBN:0-8139-1704-2, ISBN13: 978-0-8139-1704-7. Dewey:305.8/009759/381. LCCN:96-041357.

Audience: **u,f.**

De la Garza, Rodolfo O.   **E184.S75.L365 1992**
Latino Voices: Mexican, Puerto Rican, and Cuban Perspectives on American Politics. Trade Paper. Westview Press. Boulder, CO. 1992. 232p. ISBN:0-8133-8724-8, ISBN13: 978-0-8133-8724-6. Dewey:323.1168. LCCN:92-035856.

Audience: **l,u.** *Choice, 1993.*

De la Garza, Rodolfo O.   **E184.S75M88 2004**
& DeSipio, Louis (Editors)
Muted Voices: Latinos and the 2000 Election. Robert Y. Shapiro (Introduction by). Book, Other. Rowman & Littlefield Publishers, Inc. Lanham, MD. 2004. 240p. Spectrum Ser., :Race and Ethnicity in National and Global Politics

ISBN:0-7425-3590-8, ISBN13: 978-0-7425-3590-9. Dewey:324.973/0929/08968. LCCN:2004-006817.

Audience: **l,u,f.** *Choice, 2005.*

De La Garza, Rodolfo   **E184.S75L3685 2000**
O. & Pachon, Harry (Editors)
Latinos and U. S. Foreign Policy: Representing the Homeland? Trade Cloth. Rowman & Littlefield Publishers, Inc. Lanham, MD. 2000. 192p. ISBN:0-7425-0136-1, ISBN13: 978-0-7425-0136-2. Dewey:327.7308. LCCN:00-042560.

Audience: **u,f.** *Choice, 2001.*

De la Isla, José   **E184.S75D376 2003**
The Rise of Hispanic Power. Trade Cloth. Archer Books. Santa Maria, CA. 2003. 340p. ISBN:1-931122-04-0, ISBN13: 978-1-931122-04-7. Dewey:320.973/089/68. LCCN:2002-026081.

Audience: **l,u.** *Choice, 2003.*

De La Torre, Miguel A.   **F319.M6 D4 2003**
La Lucha for Cuba: Religion and Politics on the Streets of Miami. Trade Cloth. University of California Press. Berkeley, CA. 2003. 200p. ISBN:0-520-23526-6, ISBN13: 978-0-520-23526-7. Dewey:305.868/72910759381. LCCN:2002-015443.

Audience: **u,f.** *Choice, 2004.*

Dunn, Timothy J.   **F787.D46 1996**
The Militarization of the U. S.-Mexico Border, 1978-1992: Low-Intensity Conflict Doctrine Comes Home. Trade Cloth. University of Texas Press. Austin, TX. 1996. 323p. CMAS Border and Migration Studies Ser. ISBN:0-292-71579-X, ISBN13: 978-0-292-71579-0. Dewey:972/.1. LCCN:94-042964.

Audience: **u,f.** *Choice, 1996.*

Escobar, Edward J.   **HV8148.L55 E73 1999**
Race, Police, and the Making of a Political Identity: Mexican Americans and the Los Angeles Police Department, 1900-1945. Trade Cloth. University of California Press. Berkeley, CA. 1999. 372p. Latinos in American Society and Culture Ser., 7 ISBN:0-520-21334-3, ISBN13: 978-0-520-21334-0. Dewey:365/.9794/93. LCCN:98-023322.

Audience: **u,f.** *Choice, 2000.*

Flores, Henry   **E184.M5F58 2003**
The Evolution of the Liberal Democratic State with a Case Study of Latinos in San Antonio, Texas. Trade Cloth. Edwin Mellen Press, The. Lewiston, NY. 2003. 248p. Studies in Political Science, Vol. 9 ISBN:0-7734-6674-6, ISBN13: 978-0-7734-6674-6. Dewey:320.9764/351. LCCN:2003-046480.
Audience: **u,f.** *Choice, 2004.*

Fox, Geoffrey E.   **E184.S75F69 1997**
Hispanic Nation: Culture, Politics and the Constructing of Identity. Trade Cloth. University of Arizona Press. Tucson, AZ. 1997. 264p. ISBN:0-8165-1799-1, ISBN13: 978-0-8165-1799-2. Dewey:305.868. LCCN:97-018533.

Audience: **u,f.**

Garcia, F. Chris   **E184.S75P87 1997**
(Editor)
Pursuing Power: Latinos and the Political System. Trade Paper. University of Notre Dame Press. Notre Dame, IN. 1997. 480p. ISBN:0-268-01313-6, ISBN13: 978-0-268-01313-4. Dewey:327/.042/08968073. LCCN:96-026440.

Audience: **l,u.** *Choice, 1997.*

Garcia, John A.   **E184.S75G367 2003**
Latino Politics in America: Community, Culture, and Interests.
Book, Other. Rowman & Littlefield Publishers, Inc. Lanham,
MD. 2003. 304p. Spectrum Ser., :Race and Ethnicity in National
and Global Politics ISBN:0-8476-9164-0, ISBN13:
978-0-8476-9164-7. Dewey:305.868/073. LCCN:2002-152244.
Audience: **l,u.** *Choice, 2003.*

Garcia, Juan R.   **E185.M5**
Mexican Americans in the 1990s: Politics, Policies, and
Perceptions. Trade Paper. University of Arizona, Mexican
American Studies & Research Center. Tucson, AZ. 1997. 228p.
Perspectives in Mexican American Studies, No. 6
ISBN:0-939363-06-2, ISBN13: 978-0-939363-06-3.
Dewey:973.046872.

Audience: **l,u.**

García Bedolla, Lisa   **F869.L89 S753 2005**
Fluid Borders: Latino Power, Identity, and Politics in Los
Angeles. Trade Cloth. University of California Press. Berkeley,
CA. 2005. 280p. ISBN:0-520-24368-4, ISBN13:
978-0-520-24368-2. Dewey:979.4/9400468. LCCN:2004-065937.
Audience: **u,f.** *Choice, 2006.*

García, Ignacio M.   **E184.M5G367 2000**
Viva Kennedy: Mexican Americans in Search of Camelot. Trade
Cloth. Texas A&M University Press. College Station, TX. 2000.
248p. Texas A&M Southwestern Studies, Vol. 12
ISBN:0-89096-917-5, ISBN13: 978-0-89096-917-5.
Dewey:324.973/0926/0896872. LCCN:99-037706.
Audience: **u,f.** *Choice, 2000.*

García, Mario T.   **E184.M5**
Mexican Americans: Leadership, Ideology, and Identity,
1930-1960. Trade Paper. Yale University Press. Cumberland, RI.
1991. 275p. Yale Western Americana Ser. ISBN:0-300-04984-6,
ISBN13: 978-0-300-04984-8. Dewey:303.3/4/0896872.
Audience: **u,f.**

Grenier, Guillermo J.,   **E184.C97G65 2003**
et al.
The Legacy of Exile: Cubans in the United States. Lisandro
Pérez & Nancy Foner (Authors). Trade Paper. Allyn & Bacon,
Inc. Boston, MA. 2002. 144p. New Immigrants Ser.
ISBN:0-205-34090-3, ISBN13: 978-0-205-34090-3.
Dewey:304.8/7307291. LCCN:2003-271769.
Audience: **l,u.**

Gutierrez, Jose Angel   **F394.C83G88 1998**
The Making of a Chicano Militant: Lessons from Cristal. Trade
Paper. University of Wisconsin Press. Chicago, IL. 1999. 352p.
Wisconsin Studies in American Autobiography
ISBN:0-299-15984-1, ISBN13: 978-0-299-15984-9.
Dewey:976.4/437 B. LCCN:98-013866.
Audience: **u,f.** *Choice, 1999.*

Gutiérrez, David G.   **E184.M5G86 1995**
Walls and Mirrors: Mexican Americans, Mexican Immigrants,
and the Politics of Ethnicity. Trade Paper. University of
California Press. Berkeley, CA. 1995. 334p.
ISBN:0-520-20219-8, ISBN13: 978-0-520-20219-1.
Dewey:323.1/168073. LCCN:94-001892.
Audience: **u,f.** *Choice, 1995.*

Gómez-Quiñones, Juan   **E184.M5G634 1990**
Chicano Politics: Reality and Promise, 1940-1990. Trade Paper.
University of New Mexico Press. Albuquerque, NM. 1990.
265p. Calvin P. Horn Lectures in Western History and Culture

ISBN:0-8263-1213-6, ISBN13: 978-0-8263-1213-6.
Dewey:973/.046872073. LCCN:90-031486.
Audience: **l,u.** *Choice, 1991.*

Gómez-Quiñones, Juan   **F790.M5G65 1994**
Roots of Chicano Politics, 1600-1940. Trade Paper. University
of New Mexico Press. Albuquerque, NM. 1994. 540p.
ISBN:0-8263-1431-7, ISBN13: 978-0-8263-1431-4.
Dewey:979/.0046872073. LCCN:93-031940.
Audience: **l,u,f.** *Choice, 1995.*

Hardy-Fanta, Carol &   **F75.S75L37 2001**
Gerson, Jeffrey
Latino Politics in Massachusetts: Struggles, Strategies and
Prospects. Cloth Text. Garland Publishing, Inc. New York, NY.
2001. 352p. Race and Politics Ser., 4 ISBN:0-8153-3142-8,
ISBN13: 978-0-8153-3142-1. Dewey:323.1/1680744.
LCCN:2001-016009.
Audience: **f.** *Choice, 2002.*

Hero, Rodney E.   **E184.S75H48 1992**
Latinos and the U. S. Political System: Two-Tiered Pluralism.
Trade Paper. Temple University Press. Philadelphia, PA. 1992.
256p. ISBN:0-87722-910-4, ISBN13: 978-0-87722-910-0.
Dewey:323.1/168078883. LCCN:91-020104.
Audience: **l,u.** *Choice, 1992.*

Jones-Correa, Michael   **F130.S75J66 1998**
Between Two Nations: The Political Predicament of Latinos in
New York City. Book, Other. Cornell University Press. Ithaca,
NY. 1998. 272p. ISBN:0-8014-3292-8, ISBN13:
978-0-8014-3292-7. Dewey:305.868/07471. LCCN:97-049415.
Audience: **u,f.** *Choice, 1999.*

Malavet, Pedro A.   **F1975.M23 2004**
America's Colony: The Political and Cultural Conflict Between
the United States and Puerto Rico. Trade Cloth. New York
University Press. New York, NY. 2004. 352p. Critical America
Ser. ISBN:0-8147-5680-8, ISBN13: 978-0-8147-5680-5.
Dewey:325.7295. LCCN:2004-006087.
Audience: **u,f.** *Choice, 2005.*

Maril, Robert Lee   **JV6483.M298 2004**
Patrolling Chaos: The United States Border Patrol in Deep
South Texas. Trade Cloth. Texas Tech University Press.
Lubbock, TX. 2004. x, 368p. ISBN:0-89672-537-5, ISBN13:
978-0-89672-537-9. Dewey:363.28/5/097644.
LCCN:2004-009454.
Audience: **u,f.** *Choice, 2005.*

Melendez, Edgardo   **JL1056**
Puerto Rico's Statehood Movement. Trade Cloth. Greenwood
Publishing Group, Inc. Portsmouth, NH. 1988. 212p.
Contributions in Political Science Ser., No. 220
ISBN:0-313-26131-8, ISBN13: 978-0-313-26131-2.
Dewey:324.27295. LCCN:88-010249.
Audience: **l,u.** *Choice, 1989.*

Montejano, David   **E184.M5C447 1999**
(Editor)
Chicano Politics and Society in the Late Twentieth Century.
Trade Cloth. University of Texas Press. Austin, TX. 1999. 293p.
ISBN:0-292-75214-8, ISBN13: 978-0-292-75214-6.
Dewey:973/.046872. LCCN:98-015617.
Audience: **l,u.** *Choice, 1999.*

Munoz, Carlos   **E184.M5**
Sixties Chicano Movement: Youth, Identity, Power. Ed. 2. Trade
Paper. Analytical Psychology Club of San Francisco, Inc. San

Francisco, CA. 2000. 300p. Haymarket Ser.
ISBN:1-85984-219-4, ISBN13: 978-1-85984-219-5.
Dewey:323.1/16872/073.

Audience: **l,u.**

Munoz, Carlos   **E184.M5M85 1989**
Youth, Identity, Power: The Chicano Movement. Trade Cloth.
Analytical Psychology Club of San Francisco, Inc. San
Francisco, CA. 1989. 320p. Haymarket Ser.
ISBN:0-86091-197-7, ISBN13: 978-0-86091-197-5.
Dewey:973/.046872. LCCN:89-032906.

Audience: **l,u.** *Choice, 1990.*

Navarro, Armando   **JK2391.R39N38 2000**
La Raza Unida Party: A Chicano Challenge to the U. S.
Two-Party Dictatorship. Trade Paper. Temple University Press.
Philadelphia, PA. 2000. xiv, 360p. Asian American History and
Culture Ser. ISBN:1-56639-771-5, ISBN13: 978-1-56639-771-1.
Dewey:324.273/8. LCCN:99-054861.

Audience: **u,f.**

Navarro, Sharon Ann &   **E184.S75L3557 2004**
  Mejia, Armando Xavier
Latino Americans and Political Participation: A Reference
Handbook. Raymond A. Smith (Editor). Library Binding.
ABC-CLIO, Inc. Santa Barbara, CA. 2004. 359p. Political
Participation in America Ser. ISBN:1-85109-523-3, ISBN13:
978-1-85109-523-0. Dewey:323/.042/08968073.
LCCN:2004-021063.

Audience: **g,l,u.** *Choice, 2005.*

Oboler, Suzanne   **E184.S75O27 1995**
Ethnic Labels, Latino Lives: Identity and the Politics of (Re)
Presentation. Trade Paper. University of Minnesota Press.
Minneapolis, MN. 1995. 226p. ISBN:0-8166-2286-8, ISBN13:
978-0-8166-2286-3. Dewey:305.868/073. LCCN:94-022751.

Audience: **u,f.** *Choice, 1995.*

Oropeza, Lorena   **E184.M5 O77 2005**
ÁRaza Sí! ÁGuerra No!: Chicano Protest and Patriotism during
the Viet Nam War Era. Trade Paper. University of California
Press. Berkeley, CA. 2005. 292p. ISBN:0-520-24195-9, ISBN13:
978-0-520-24195-4. Dewey:323.1168/72073/09046.
LCCN:2004-057996.

Audience: **l,u.** *Choice, 2006.*

Ramos-Zayas, Ana Y.   **F548.9.P85R36 2003**
National Performances: The Politics of Class, Race, and Space
in Puerto Rican Chicago. Trade Paper. University of Chicago
Press. Chicago, IL. 2003. 303p. ISBN:0-226-70359-2, ISBN13:
978-0-226-70359-6. Dewey:305.868/7295077311.
LCCN:2002-154906.

Audience: **u,f.** *Choice, 2004.*

Stepick, Alex   **F319.M6 T48 2003**
This Land Is Our Land: Immigrants and Power in Miami. Trade
Cloth. University of California Press. Berkeley, CA. 2003. 196p.
ISBN:0-520-23397-2, ISBN13: 978-0-520-23397-3.
Dewey:305.8/009759/381. LCCN:2002-011201.

Audience: **u,f.** *Choice, 2003.*

Torre, Adela de la   **F870.M5T67 2002**
Moving from the Margins: A Chicana Voice on Public Policy.
Trade Cloth. University of Arizona Press. Tucson, AZ. 2002.
xviii, 141p. ISBN:0-8165-1990-0, ISBN13: 978-0-8165-1990-3.
Dewey:320/.6/09794. LCCN:2001-004399.

Audience: **u,f.**

Torres, Andrés &   **E184.P85P77 1998**
  Velázquez, José E. (Editors)
The Puerto Rican Movement: Voices from the Diaspora. Cloth
Text. Temple University Press. Philadelphia, PA. 1998. 432p.
Puerto Rican Studies ISBN:1-56639-617-4, ISBN13:
978-1-56639-617-2. Dewey:973/.04687295. LCCN:97-045189.

Audience: **l,u.** *Choice, 1999.*

Torres, Maria de los   **E184.C97 T67 1999**
  Angeles
In the Land of Mirrors: Cuban Exile Politics in the United
States. Trade Paper. University of Michigan Press. Chicago, IL.
2001. 256p. ISBN:0-472-08788-6, ISBN13: 978-0-472-08788-4.
Dewey:324.089687294073. LCCN:99-036965.

Audience: **u,f.**

Torres, Maria de los   **HV640.5.C9**
  Angeles
The Lost Apple: Operation Pedro Pan, Cuban Children in the U.
S., and the Promise of a Better Future. Trade Paper. Beacon
Press. Boston, MA. 2004. 344p. ISBN:0-8070-0233-X, ISBN13:
978-0-8070-0233-9. Dewey:325/.21/083097291.

Audience: **u,f.**

Torres, Rodolfo D.   **E184.S75L3636 1999**
Latino Social Movements: Historical and Theoretical
Perspectives. Trade Paper. Routledge. New York, NY. 1999.
216p. New Political Science Reader Ser. ISBN:0-415-92299-2,
ISBN13: 978-0-415-92299-9. Dewey:305.868.
LCCN:98-033289.

Audience: **u,f.**

Vigil, Maurilio E.   **E184.S75V543 1996**
Hispanics in Congress: A Historical and Political Survey. Trade
Cloth. University Press of America, Inc. Lanham, MD. 1996.
140p. ISBN:0-7618-0474-9, ISBN13: 978-0-7618-0474-1.
Dewey:324/.089/68073. LCCN:96-032335.

Audience: **l,u.**

Social and Behavioral Sciences > Civil Rights Movement, Affirmative Action, Citizenship

E184.S75
☐ constructing the new.
http://www.nclr.org/
NCLR.

Audience: **l,u,f.**

F1408
☐ LULAC: League of United Latin American Citizens.
http://www.lulac.org/
LULAC.

Audience: **g,l,u,f.**

Acuna, Rodolfo   **E184.S75A66 1998**
Sometimes There Is No Other Side: Chicanos and the Myth of
Equality. Trade Cloth. University of Notre Dame Press. Notre
Dame, IN. 1998. 312p. ISBN:0-268-01762-X, ISBN13:
978-0-268-01762-0. Dewey:305.868073. LCCN:97-046840.

Audience: **u,f.** *Choice, 1998.*

Cardenas, Gilberto   **F358.2.S75C38 2004**
  (Editor)
La Causa: Civil Rights, Social Justice and the Struggle for
Equality in the Midwest. Trade Cloth. Arte Publico Press.

Houston, TX. 2004. 176p. The Hispanic Civil Rights Ser.
ISBN:1-55885-425-8, ISBN13: 978-1-55885-425-3.
Dewey:323.1168/073077. LCCN:2004-041078.

Audience: **u,f.** *Choice, 2005.*

Chavez, Ernesto   **F869.L89 M514 2002**
Mi Raza Primero! (My People First!): Nationalism, Identity, and
Insurgency in the Chicano Movement in Los Angeles,
1966-1978. Trade Cloth. University of California Press.
Berkeley, CA. 2002. 256p. ISBN:0-520-23017-5, ISBN13:
978-0-520-23017-0. Dewey:979.4/940046872.
LCCN:2002-018880.

Audience: **u,f.**

Chavez, Linda   **E184.S75.C48 1991**
Out of the Barrio: Toward a New Politics of Hispanic
Assimilation. Trade Cloth. Basic Books. New York, NY. 1991.
304p. ISBN:0-465-05430-7, ISBN13: 978-0-465-05430-5.
Dewey:305.868. LCCN:91-070060.

Audience: **u,f.** *Choice, 1992.*

Cunningham, Hilary   **BV4466.C86 1995**
God and Caesar at the Rio Grande: Sanctuary and the
Politicization of Religion in the United States. Trade Paper.
University of Minnesota Press. Minneapolis, MN. 1995. 264p.
ISBN:0-8166-2457-7, ISBN13: 978-0-8166-2457-7.
Dewey:261.8/32. LCCN:94-031786.

Audience: **u,f.** *Choice, 1996.*

Delgado, Richard &   **E184.S75L355 1998**
  Stefancic, Jean (Editors)
The Latino/a Condition: A Critical Reader. Trade Paper. New
York University Press. New York, NY. 1998. 736p.
ISBN:0-8147-1895-7, ISBN13: 978-0-8147-1895-7.
Dewey:305.868. LCCN:98-013514.

Audience: **u,f.**

Ferriss, Susan &   **HD6509.C68 F47 1997**
  Sandoval, Ricardo
The Fight in the Fields: Cesar Chavez and the Farmworkers
Movement. Trade Paper. Harcourt Trade Publishers. New York,
NY. 1998. 352p. ISBN:0-15-600598-0, ISBN13:
978-0-15-600598-2. Dewey:331.8813092.

Audience: **l,u.**

Flores, William &   **E184.S75**
  Benmayor, Rina (Editors)
Latino Cultural Citizenship: Claiming Identity, Space and
Rights. Trade Paper. Beacon Press. Boston, MA. 1998. 336p.
ISBN:0-8070-4635-3, ISBN13: 978-0-8070-4635-7.
Dewey:305.868. LCCN:97-005518.

Audience: **u,f.** *Choice, 1998.*

Galarza, Ernesto   **KF0228.D5G3**
Spiders in the House and Workers in the Field. Trade Paper.
Books on Demand. Ann Arbor, MI. 1970. 320p.
ISBN:0-608-00885-0, ISBN13: 978-0-608-00885-1.
Dewey:331.88/13/09794. LCCN:77-105730.

Audience: **l,u.**

Gonzales, Rodolfo   **PS3557.O47M4 2001**
Message to Aztlan: Selected Readings. Antonio Esquibel (Editor,
Introduction by), Rodolfo F. Acuna (Foreword by). Trade Paper.
Arte Publico Press. Houston, TX. 2001. 256p. Hispanic Civil
Rights Ser. ISBN:1-55885-331-6, ISBN13: 978-1-55885-331-7.
Dewey:818/.5409. LCCN:2001-022314.

Audience: **l,u.** *Choice, 2002.*

Gracia, Jorge J. & De   **E184.S75H627 2000**
  Greiff, Pablo
Hispanics/Latinos in the United States: Ethnicity, Race, and
Rights. UK-B Format Paperback. Routledge. New York, NY.
2000. 288p. ISBN:0-415-92620-3, ISBN13: 978-0-415-92620-1.
Dewey:305.8/68073. LCCN:99-048696.

Audience: **l,u.** *Choice, 2001.*

Gutierrez, Jose Angel   **E184.M5G868 2003**
A Chicano Manual on How to Handle Gringos. Trade Paper.
Arte Publico Press. Houston, TX. 2003. 240p. The Hispanic
Civil Rights Ser. ISBN:1-55885-396-0, ISBN13:
978-1-55885-396-6. Dewey:323.1/16872073.
LCCN:2003-044429.

Audience: **u,f.**

Gutierrez, Margo   **E184**
  (Author, Contribution by)
Encyclopedia of the Mexican American Civil Rights Movement.
Matt S. Meier (Author). Cloth Text. Greenwood Publishing
Group, Inc. Portsmouth, NH. 2000. 312p. ISBN:0-313-30425-4,
ISBN13: 978-0-313-30425-5. Dewey:305.86872073/03.
LCCN:99-016143.

Audience: **g,l,u.** *Choice, 2000.*

Haney-López, Ian   **F869.E18H36 2004**
Racism on Trial: The Chicano Fight for Justice. Trade Paper.
Harvard University Press. Cambridge, MA. 2004. 336p.
ISBN:0-674-01629-7, ISBN13: 978-0-674-01629-3.
Dewey:305.8/6872079493.

Audience: **u,f.**

Lopez Tijerina, Reies   **F805.M5T5413 2000**
They Called Me King Tiger: My Struggle for the Land and Our
Rights. Jose Angel Gutierrez (Translator). Trade Paper. Arte
Publico Press. Houston, TX. 2000. 256p. Hispanic Civil Rights
Ser. ISBN:1-55885-302-2, ISBN13: 978-1-55885-302-7.
Dewey:978.9/0046873. LCCN:00-059426.

Audience: **l,u.**

Mazón, Mauricio   **F869.L89M56 1985**
The Zoot-Suit Riots: The Psychology of Symbolic Annihilation.
Trade Cloth. University of Texas Press. Austin, TX. 1984. 179p.
Mexican American Monographs, No. 8 ISBN:0-292-79801-6,
ISBN13: 978-0-292-79801-4. Dewey:979.4/940046872.
LCCN:84-005656.

Audience: **u,f.**

Melendez, Miguel   **F128.9.P85M455 2005**
We Took the Streets: Fighting for Latino Rights with the Young
Lords. Trade Paper. Rutgers University Press. Piscataway, NJ.
2005. 272p. ISBN:0-8135-3559-X, ISBN13: 978-0-8135-3559-3.
Dewey:323.1/168729507471. LCCN:2004-050954.

Audience: **l,u.**

Menchaca, Martha   **F869.S53M46 1995**
The Mexican Outsiders: A Community History of
Marginalization and Discrimination in California. Trade Paper.
University of Texas Press. Austin, TX. 1995. 270p.
ISBN:0-292-75174-5, ISBN13: 978-0-292-75174-3.
Dewey:305.868/72079492. LCCN:94-046190.

Audience: **u,f.** *Choice, 1996.*

Morín, José Luis   **E184.S75M675 2004**
Latino/a Rights and Justice in the United States: Perspectives
and Approaches. Trade Paper. Carolina Academic Press.
Durham, NC. 2005. 308p. ISBN:1-59460-086-4, ISBN13:
978-1-59460-086-9. Dewey:323.1168/073. LCCN:2004-021706.

Audience: **u,f.** *Choice, 2006.*

Munoz, Carlos   **E184.M5**
Sixties Chicano Movement: Youth, Identity, Power. Ed. 2. Trade
Paper. Analytical Psychology Club of San Francisco, Inc. San
Francisco, CA. 2000. 300p. Haymarket Ser.
ISBN:1-85984-219-4, ISBN13: 978-1-85984-219-5.
Dewey:323.1/16872/073.

Audience: **l,u.**

Munoz, Carlos   **E184.M5M85 1989**
Youth, Identity, Power: The Chicano Movement. Trade Cloth.
Analytical Psychology Club of San Francisco, Inc. San
Francisco, CA. 1989. 320p. Haymarket Ser.
ISBN:0-86091-197-7, ISBN13: 978-0-86091-197-5.
Dewey:973/.046872. LCCN:89-032906.

Audience: **l,u.** *Choice, 1990.*

Navarro, Armando   **F395.M5N39 1995**
🖻 Mexican American Youth Organization: Avant-Garde of the
Chicano Movement in Texas. E-Book. NetLibrary, Inc. Boulder,
CO. 1995. ISBN:0-585-26503-8, ISBN13: 978-0-585-26503-2.
Dewey:323.3/52/08968720764.

Audience: **u,f.** *Choice, 1996.*

Oropeza, Lorena   **E184.M5 O77 2005**
ÁRaza Sí! ÁGuerra No!: Chicano Protest and Patriotism during
the Viet Nam War Era. Trade Paper. University of California
Press. Berkeley, CA. 2005. 292p. ISBN:0-520-24195-9, ISBN13:
978-0-520-24195-4. Dewey:323.1168/72073/09046.
LCCN:2004-057996.

Audience: **l,u.** *Choice, 2006.*

Pagan, Eduardo   **F869.L89 M566 2003**
Obregon
Murder at the Sleepy Lagoon: Zoot Suits, Race, and Riot in
Wartime L.A. Trade Cloth. University of North Carolina Press.
Chapel Hill, NC. 2003. 312p. ISBN:0-8078-2826-2, ISBN13:
978-0-8078-2826-7. Dewey:979.4/94052. LCCN:2003-048891.

Audience: **l,u.** *Choice, 2004.*

Ramos, Henry A. J.   **E184.M5R33 1998**
The American GI Forum: In Pursuit of the Dream, 1948-1983.
Trade Cloth. Arte Publico Press. Houston, TX. 1998. 224p.
Hispanic Civil Rights Ser. ISBN:1-55885-261-1, ISBN13:
978-1-55885-261-7. Dewey:323.1/16872073/06073.
LCCN:98-008679.

Audience: **l,u.** *Choice, 1999.*

Rosales, F. Arturo   **E184.M5R634 1997**
Chicano!: The History of the Mexican American Civil Rights
Movement. Trade Paper. Arte Publico Press. Houston, TX. 1997.
304p. Hispanic Civil Rights Ser. ISBN:1-55885-201-8, ISBN13:
978-1-55885-201-3. Dewey:973/.0496073. LCCN:97-227451.

Audience: **l,u.**

Rosales, Francisco A.   **E184.M5R637 1999**
🖻 Pobre Raza!: Violence, Justice, and Mobilization among
Mexico Lindo Immigrants, 1900-1936. E-Book. University of
Texas Press. Austin, TX. 1999. ISBN:0-292-79935-7, ISBN13:
978-0-292-79935-6. Dewey:323.1/16872073.

Audience: **l,u.**

Sepulveda, Juan A.   **E184.M5V4 2003**
The Life and Times of Willie Velasquez: Su Voto Es Su Voz.
Trade Cloth. Arte Publico Press. Houston, TX. 2004. 384p. The
Hispanic Civil Rights Ser. ISBN:1-55885-419-3, ISBN13:
978-1-55885-419-2. Dewey:323/.092 B. LCCN:2003-050044.

Audience: **l,u.**

Staudt, Kathleen A. &   **HM671.S73 2002**
Coronado, Irasema
Fronteras No Mas: Toward Social Justice at the U. S.-Mexico
Border. Cloth over Boards. Palgrave Macmillan. New York, NY.
2002. 224p. ISBN:0-312-23939-4, ISBN13: 978-0-312-23939-8.
Dewey:303.3/72/09721. LCCN:2002-068413.

Audience: **u,f.** *Choice, 2003.*

Trevino, Jesus Salvador   **E184.M5T74 2001**
Eyewitness: A Filmmaker's Memoir of the Chicano Movement.
Trade Paper. Arte Publico Press. Houston, TX. 2001. 400p.
Hispanic Civil Rights Ser. ISBN:1-55885-349-9, ISBN13:
978-1-55885-349-2. Dewey:973.046872. LCCN:2001-035545.

Audience: **l,u.**

Valencia, Reynaldo   **KF4757.5.M4M49 2004**
Anaya
Mexican Americans and the Law: El Pueblo Unido Jamás Ser
Vencido!. Trade Cloth. University of Arizona Press. Tucson, AZ.
2004. 197p. The Mexican American Experience Ser.
ISBN:0-8165-2279-0, ISBN13: 978-0-8165-2279-8.
Dewey:342.73/0873. LCCN:2003-015701.

Audience: **u,f.** *Choice, 2005.*

Vigil, Ernesto B.   **F790.M5V54 1999**
The Crusade for Justice: Chicano Militancy and the
Government's War on Dissent. Trade Cloth. University of
Wisconsin Press. Chicago, IL. 1999. 552p. ISBN:0-299-16220-6,
ISBN13: 978-0-299-16220-7. Dewey:323.1/16872079.
LCCN:98-051514.

Audience: **u,f.** *Choice, 1999.*

Social and Behavioral Sciences > Psychology

De Rios, Marlene D.   **RC451.5.H57D63 2001**
(Editor)
Brief Psychotherapy with the Latino Immigrant Client. Trade
Cloth. Haworth Press, Incorporated, The. Binghamton, NY.
2001. 191p. ISBN:0-7890-1089-5, ISBN13: 978-0-7890-1089-6.
Dewey:616.89/14/08968073. LCCN:00-033531.

Audience: **u,f.**

Martinez, Joe L. Jr. &   **E184.M5**
Mendoza, Richard H. (Editors)
Chicano Psychology. Ed. 2. Trade Cloth. Elsevier Science &
Technology Books. Saint Louis, MO. 1984. 456p.
ISBN:0-12-475660-3, ISBN13: 978-0-12-475660-1.
Dewey:155.8/46872. LCCN:83-026636.

Audience: **l,u.**

Velasquez, Roberto   **RC451.5.M48H36 2004**
(Editor), et al.
The Handbook of Chicana/o Psychology and Mental Health.
Leticia M. Arellano & Brian McNeill (Editors), Christina
Ayala-Alcantar, Louise Baca & Manuel Barrera Jr. (Contribution
by). Cloth over Boards. Lawrence Erlbaum Associates, Inc.
Mahwah, NJ. 2004. 544p. ISBN:0-8058-4158-X, ISBN13:
978-0-8058-4158-9. Dewey:362.2/089/68073.
LCCN:2003-045646.

Audience: **u,f.** *Choice, 2004.*

Social and Behavioral Sciences > Sociology

Blea, Irene I.   **F782.P9 B55**
Bessemer: A Sociological Perspective of a Chicano Barrio.
Trade Cloth. A M S Press, Inc. New York, NY. 1991. 207p.
Immigrant Communities and Ethnic Minorities in the U. S. and
Canada Ser., No. 13 ISBN:0-404-19423-0, ISBN13:
978-0-404-19423-9. Dewey:305.86872. LCCN:87-045778.
Audience: **u,f.**

Browning, Harley L.   **E184.M5M523 1986**
Mexican Immigrants and Mexican Americans: An Evolving
Relation. Rudolfo O. De la Garza (Editor). Trade Paper.
University of Texas Press. Austin, TX. 1986. 264p.
ISBN:0-292-75094-3, ISBN13: 978-0-292-75094-4.
Dewey:305.8/6872/073. LCCN:85-073572.
Audience: **u,f.** *Choice, 1986.*

Cordova, Carlos B.   **E184.S15C67 2005**
The Salvadoran Americans. Trade Cloth. Greenwood Publishing
Group, Inc. Portsmouth, NH. 2005. 196p. The New Americans
Ser. ISBN:0-313-32306-2, ISBN13: 978-0-313-32306-5.
Dewey:305.868/7284073. LCCN:2005-020463.
Audience: **g,l.**

de Genova, Nicholas &   **F548.9.M5D44 2003**
Zayas, Ana Ramos
Latino Crossings: Mexicans, Puerto Ricans and the Politics of
Race and Citizenship. Paper over Boards. Routledge. New York,
NY. 2003. 288p. ISBN:0-415-93456-7, ISBN13:
978-0-415-93456-5. Dewey:305.868/7207731.
LCCN:2003-005104.
Audience: **u,f.**

Grillo, Evelio   **E184.C97G73 2000**
Black Cuban, Black American: A Memoir. Kenya
Dworkin-Mendez (Introduction by). Trade Paper. Arte Publico
Press. Houston, TX. 2000. 152p. Hispanic Civil Rights Ser.
ISBN:1-55885-293-X, ISBN13: 978-1-55885-293-8.
Dewey:973/.04687291. LCCN:00-020774.
Audience: **l,u.** *Choice, 2001.*

Hamilton, Nora &   **F869.L89G824 2001**
Chinchilla, Norma Stoltz
Seeking Community in a Global City: Guatemalans and
Salvadorans in Los Angeles. Library Binding. Temple University
Press. Philadelphia, PA. 2001. xii, 292p. ISBN:1-56639-867-3,
ISBN13: 978-1-56639-867-1. Dewey:305.868/7281079494.
LCCN:00-048897.
Audience: **u,f.**

Haslip-Viera (Editor), et   **F128.9.S75 L37**
al.
Latinos in New York: Communities in Transition. Gabriel Baver
& Sherrie L. Baver (Editors). Paper Text. University of Notre
Dame Press. Notre Dame, IN. 1997. 400p. ISBN:0-268-01315-2,
ISBN13: 978-0-268-01315-8. Dewey:974.7/100468.
Audience: **l,u.**

Herrera, Andrea   **E184.C97R39 2001**
O'Reilly
ReMembering Cuba: Legacy of a Diaspora. Trade Cloth.
University of Texas Press. Austin, TX. 2001. 376p.
ISBN:0-292-73146-9, ISBN13: 978-0-292-73146-2.
Dewey:305.868/7291073. LCCN:00-061606.
Audience: **l,u.** *Choice, 2002.*

Lao-Montes, Agustin &   **F128.9.S75M36 2001**
Davila, Arlene M. (Editors)
Mambo Montage: The Latinization of New York City. Trade
Cloth. Kegan Paul International, Ltd. London, 2001. 448p.
ISBN:0-231-11274-2, ISBN13: 978-0-231-11274-1.
Dewey:974.7/100468073. LCCN:00-047548.
Audience: **l,u.** *Choice, 2002.*

Mindiola, Tatcho Jr., et   **F394.H89N47 2003**
al.
Black-Brown Relations and Stereotypes. Yolanda Flores
Niemann & Nestor Rodriguez (Authors). Trade Cloth.
University of Texas Press. Austin, TX. 2003. 165p.
ISBN:0-292-75264-4, ISBN13: 978-0-292-75264-1.
Dewey:305.868/07641411. LCCN:2002-003439.
Audience: **u,f.** *Choice, 2003.*

Pérez Firmat, Gustavo   **PS3566.E69138Z47**
Next Year in Cuba: A Cubano's Coming-Of-Age in America.
Trade Paper. Arte Publico Press. Houston, TX. 2005. 272p.
ISBN:1-55885-461-4, ISBN13: 978-1-55885-461-1.
Dewey:81/.54 B. LCCN:2005-040991.
Audience: **l,u.**

Rieff, David   **F319.M6R537 1993**
The Exile: Cuba in the Heart of Miami. Trade Cloth. Simon &
Schuster. New York, NY. 1993. 240p. ISBN:0-671-77604-5,
ISBN13: 978-0-671-77604-6. Dewey:975.9/004687291.
LCCN:93-012141.
Audience: **l,u.** *Choice, 1994.*

Rodriguez, Clara E.   **E184.P85P82 1984**
(Editor), et al.
The Puerto Rican Struggle: Essays on Survival in the U. S. Ed.
2. Virginia Sanchez-Korrel & Jose O. Alers (Editors). Trade
Cloth. Waterfront Press. Maplewood, NJ. 1984. 151p.
ISBN:0-943862-20-5, ISBN13: 978-0-943862-20-0.
Dewey:973/.04687295. LCCN:96-131721.
Audience: **l,u.**

Sutton, Constance R. &   **F128.9.C27 C37 1987**
Chaney, Elsa M. (Editors)
Caribbean Life in New York City: Sociocultural Dimensions.
Trade Paper. Center for Migration Studies. Staten Island, NY.
1993. 250p. CMS Migration and Ethnicity Ser.
ISBN:0-913256-92-7, ISBN13: 978-0-913256-92-3.
Dewey:305.8/68729/07471.
Audience: **u,f.**

Urciuoli, Bonnie   **F128.9.P85U73 1996**
Exposing Prejudice: Puerto Rican Experiences of Language,
Race, and Class. Trade Paper. Westview Press. Boulder, CO.
1996. 240p. Institutional Structures of Feeling Ser.
ISBN:0-8133-2967-1, ISBN13: 978-0-8133-2967-3.
Dewey:305.8/687295/07471. LCCN:96-010325.
Audience: **u,f.** *Choice, 1996.*

Social and Behavioral Sciences > Sociology > Elderly

Freidenberg, Judith   **HQ1064.U6N463 2000**
Growing Old in El Barrio. Trade Cloth. New York University
Press. New York, NY. 2000. 320p. ISBN:0-8147-2702-6,
ISBN13: 978-0-8147-2702-7. Dewey:305.26/09747.
LCCN:00-056001.
Audience: **u,f.** *Choice, 2001.*

Formats: Web: ☐   Ebook: 🄴   CD/DVD-ROM: 🕮   BCL3: 𝓑

Social and Behavioral Sciences > Sociology > Ethnicity (Group Identity)

Anzaldúa, Gloria   **PS3551.N95B6 1999**
Borderlands - La Frontera: The New Mestiza. Ed. 2. Trade
Cloth. Aunt Lute Books. San Francisco, CA. 1999. 260p.
ISBN:1-879960-57-5, ISBN13: 978-1-879960-57-2.
Dewey:811/.54. LCCN:99-022546.
                            Audience: **u,f.** *Choice, 1988.*

Arreola, Daniel D.   **F395.M5A77 2002**
Tejano South Texas: A Mexican American Cultural Province.
Trade Cloth. University of Texas Press. Austin, TX. 2002. 288p.
Jack and Doris Smothers Series in Texas History, Life, and
Culture, No. 5 ISBN:0-292-70510-7, ISBN13:
978-0-292-70510-4. Dewey:976.4/40046872.
LCCN:2001-044294.
                            Audience: **l,u.** *Choice, 2003, 2002.*

Bailey, Benjamin H.   **E184.D6B35 2002**
Language, Race, and Negotiation of Identity: A Study of
Dominican Americans. Library Binding. LFB Scholarly
Publishing LLC. New York, NY. 2002. 304p. The New
Americans, :Recent Immigration and American Society
ISBN:1-931202-24-9, ISBN13: 978-1-931202-24-4.
Dewey:305.868/72930745. LCCN:2002-003270.
                            Audience: **u,f.**

Baker-Cristales, Beth   **F867.B294 2004**
Salvadoran Migration to Southern California: Redefining el
Hermano Lejano. Trade Cloth. University Press of Florida.
Gainesville, FL. 2004. 200p. ISBN:0-8130-2761-6, ISBN13:
978-0-8130-2761-6. Dewey:305.868/728407949.
LCCN:2004-049334.
                            Audience: **u.**

Boswell, Thomas D. &   **E184.C97.B67 1984**
Curtis, James R.
The Cuban-American Experience: Culture, Images and
Perspectives. Trade Cloth. Rowman & Littlefield Publishers, Inc.
Lanham, MD. 1984. 214p. ISBN:0-86598-116-7, ISBN13:
978-0-86598-116-4. Dewey:305.8/687291/073.
LCCN:83-016042.
                            Audience: **l,u.** ℬ

Colón, Jesus   **F128.9.P85 C65 1993**
The Way It Was and Other Writings. Edna Acosta-Belén &
Virginia A. Korrol (Editors). Trade Paper. Arte Publico Press.
Houston, TX. 1993. 128p. ISBN:1-55885-057-0, ISBN13:
978-1-55885-057-6. Dewey:305.868/729507471.
LCCN:92-042443.
                            Audience: **l,u.**

Colón, Jesús   **F128.9.P85 C64 1975**
A Puerto Rican in New York and Other Sketches. Trade Cloth.
Ayer Company Publishers, Inc. Manchester, NH. 1979. 206p. A
Puerto Rican Experience Ser. ISBN:0-405-06218-4, ISBN13:
978-0-405-06218-6. Dewey:305.8/687295/07471.
LCCN:74-014229.
                            Audience: **l,u.**

De La Campa, Roman   **E184.C97D4 2001**
Cuba on My Mind: Journeys to a Severed Nation. Trade Cloth.
Verso Books. London, 2002. 192p. ISBN:1-85984-790-0,
ISBN13: 978-1-85984-790-9. Dewey:973/.04687291/0092 B.
LCCN:00-054999.
                            Audience: **l,u.**

Duany, Jorge   **F1975.D83 2002**
The Puerto Rican Nation on the Move: Identities on the Island
and in the United States. Trade Cloth. University of North
Carolina Press. Chapel Hill, NC. 2002. 360p.
ISBN:0-8078-2704-5, ISBN13: 978-0-8078-2704-8.
Dewey:972.9505. LCCN:2001-057826.
                            Audience: **u,f.** *Choice, 2003.*

Duany, Jorge   **F128.9.D6**
Quisqueya on the Hudson: The Transnational Identity of
Domincans in Washington. CUNY Dominican Studies Institute.
1994.
                            Audience: **u.**

Fischkin, Barbara   **E184.D6F57 1997**
Muddy Cup: A Dominican Family Comes of Age in a New
America. Trade Cloth. Simon & Schuster. New York, NY. 1997.
368p. ISBN:0-684-80704-1, ISBN13: 978-0-684-80704-1.
Dewey:974.7/1004687293. LCCN:97-003196.
                            Audience: **l,u.**

Flores, Juan   **E184.P85F58 2000**
From Bomba to Hip-Hop: Puerto Rican Culture and Latino
Identity. Trade Cloth. Columbia University Press. New York,
NY. 2000. 272p. Popular Culture, Everyday Lives Ser.
ISBN:0-231-11076-6, ISBN13: 978-0-231-11076-1.
Dewey:305.868/7295073. LCCN:99-049285.
                            Audience: **l,u.** *Choice, 2000.*

Flores, Juan   **E184.P85 F57 1993**
Divided Borders: Essays on Puerto Rican Identity. Jean Franco
(Introduction by). Trade Paper. Arte Publico Press. Houston, TX.
1993. 96p. ISBN:1-55885-046-5, ISBN13: 978-1-55885-046-0.
Dewey:305.8/687295073. LCCN:91-037313.
                            Audience: **l,u.**

Flores, William &   **E184.S75**
Benmayor, Rina (Editors)
Latino Cultural Citizenship: Claiming Identity, Space and
Rights. Trade Paper. Beacon Press. Boston, MA. 1998. 336p.
ISBN:0-8070-4635-3, ISBN13: 978-0-8070-4635-7.
Dewey:305.868. LCCN:97-005518.
                            Audience: **u,f.** *Choice, 1998.*

Flores-Gonzalez, Nilda   **LC2670.F56 2002**
School Kids/Street Kids: Identity Development in Latino
Students. Trade Cloth. Teachers College Press, Teachers College,
Columbia University. New York, NY. 2002. 216p.
ISBN:0-8077-4224-4, ISBN13: 978-0-8077-4224-2.
Dewey:371.829/68073. LCCN:2001-058537.
                            Audience: **u,f.** *Choice, 2002.*

Fox, Geoffrey E.   **E184.S75F69 1997**
Hispanic Nation: Culture, Politics and the Constructing of
Identity. Trade Cloth. University of Arizona Press. Tucson, AZ.
1997. 264p. ISBN:0-8165-1799-1, ISBN13: 978-0-8165-1799-2.
Dewey:305.868. LCCN:97-018533.
                            Audience: **u,f.**

Garcia, Maria C.   **F320.C97G37 1996**
Havana U. S. A.: Cuban Exiles and Cuban Americans in South
Florida, 1959-1994. Trade Cloth. University of California Press.
Berkeley, CA. 1996. 239p. ISBN:0-520-20131-0, ISBN13:
978-0-520-20131-6. Dewey:973/.04687291. LCCN:94-046401.
                            Audience: **l,u.** *Choice, 1996.*

García, Mario T.　　　　　　　　**E184.M5**
Mexican Americans: Leadership, Ideology, and Identity, 1930-1960. Trade Paper. Yale University Press. Cumberland, RI. 1991. 275p. Yale Western Americana Ser. ISBN:0-300-04984-6, ISBN13: 978-0-300-04984-8. Dewey:303.3/4/0896872.
Audience: **u,f.**

Gelsinon, Thomas　　　　　　　　**E184.M5 P42**
(Editor)
Perspectives in Mexican American Studies: Community, Identity and Education. Juan R. Garcia (Introduction by). Trade Paper. University of Arizona, Mexican American Studies & Research Center. Tucson, AZ. 1992. 210p. ISBN:0-939363-03-8, ISBN13: 978-0-939363-03-2. Dewey:909.
Audience: **l,u.**

Gracia, Jorge J.　　　　　　　　**E184.S75G67 1999**
Hispanic/Latino Identity: A Philosophical Perspective. Trade Cloth. Blackwell Publishing, Inc. Malden, MA. 1999. 256p. ISBN:0-631-21763-0, ISBN13: 978-0-631-21763-3. Dewey:305.868. LCCN:99-030908.
Audience: **u,f.** *Choice, 2000.*

Gracia, Jorge J. & De　　　　　　**E184.S75H627 2000**
Greiff, Pablo
Hispanics/Latinos in the United States: Ethnicity, Race, and Rights. UK-B Format Paperback. Routledge. New York, NY. 2000. 288p. ISBN:0-415-92620-3, ISBN13: 978-0-415-92620-1. Dewey:305.8/68073. LCCN:99-048696.
Audience: **l,u.** *Choice, 2001.*

Greenbaum, Susan D.　　　　　　**F319.T2G69 2002**
More Than Black: Afro-Cubans in Tampa. Trade Cloth. University Press of Florida. Gainesville, FL. 2002. 384p. New World Diaspora Ser. ISBN:0-8130-2466-8, ISBN13: 978-0-8130-2466-0. Dewey:305.868/7291075965. LCCN:2001-043726.
Audience: **u,f.** *Choice, 2003.*

Grenier, Guillermo J.,　　　　　**E184.C97G65 2003**
et al.
The Legacy of Exile: Cubans in the United States. Lisandro Pérez & Nancy Foner (Authors). Trade Paper. Allyn & Bacon, Inc. Boston, MA. 2002. 144p. New Immigrants Ser. ISBN:0-205-34090-3, ISBN13: 978-0-205-34090-3. Dewey:304.8/7307291. LCCN:2003-271769.
Audience: **l,u.**

Grenier, Guillermo &　　　　　　**F319.M6.M639 1992**
Stepick, Alex III (Editors)
Miami Now: Immigration, Ethnicity, and Social Change. Trade Cloth. University Press of Florida. Gainesville, FL. 1992. 256p. ISBN:0-8130-1154-X, ISBN13: 978-0-8130-1154-7. Dewey:305.8/009759/381. LCCN:92-010100.
Audience: **u,f.** *Choice, 1993.*

Haslip-Viera, Gabriel &　　　　　**F128.9.P85B67 2004**
Falcon, Angelo (Author, Editors)
Boricuas in Gotham: Puerto Ricans in the Making of New York City. Felix V. Matos Rodriguez & Antonia Pantoja (Editors). Trade Cloth. Markus Wiener Publishers, Inc. Princeton, NJ. 2004. 286p. ISBN:1-55876-355-4, ISBN13: 978-1-55876-355-5. Dewey:9747/.1004687295. LCCN:2004-016684.
Audience: **l,u.**

Hayes-Bautista,　　　　　　　　**F870.S75 H385 2004**
David E.
La Nueva California: Latinos in the Golden State. Trade Cloth. University of California Press. Berkeley, CA. 2004. 280p.

ISBN:0-520-24145-2, ISBN13: 978-0-520-24145-9. Dewey:979.4/00468073. LCCN:2004-006949.
Audience: **l,u.** *Choice, 2005.*

Johnson, Kevin R.　　　　　　　　**E184.M5J58 1998**
How Did You Get to Be Mexican?: A White/Brown Man's Search for Identity. Trade Cloth. Temple University Press. Philadelphia, PA. 1999. 256p. ISBN:1-56639-650-6, ISBN13: 978-1-56639-650-9. Dewey:[B]. LCCN:98-011811.
Audience: **l,u.**

Keefe, Susan E. &　　　　　　　　**E184.M5 K43 1987**
Padilla, Amado M.
Chicano Ethnicity. Trade Paper. University of New Mexico Press. Albuquerque, NM. 1987. 239p. ISBN:0-8263-0993-3, ISBN13: 978-0-8263-0993-8. Dewey:305.8/6872/073. LCCN:87-009217.
Audience: **l,u.**

Menchaca, Martha　　　　　　　　**E184.M5M46 2001**
Recovering History, Constructing Race: The Indian, Black, and White Roots of Mexican Americans. Trade Paper. University of Texas Press. Austin, TX. 2002. 389p. Joe R. and Teresa Lozano Long Series in Latin American and Latino Art and Culture ISBN:0-292-75254-7, ISBN13: 978-0-292-75254-2. Dewey:973/.046872. LCCN:2001-033309.
Audience: **u,f.** *Choice, 2002.*

Noriega, Chon A. &　　　　　　　**E184.M5I15 2004**
Belcher, Wendy L. (Editors)
I Am Aztlan: The Personal Essay in Chicano Studies. Perfect. UCLA Chicano Studies Research Center Press. Los Angeles, CA. 2004. 300p. ISBN:0-89551-099-5, ISBN13: 978-0-89551-099-0. Dewey:305.868/073. LCCN:2004-048035.
Audience: **u,f.** *Choice, 2005.*

Oboler, Suzanne　　　　　　　　**E184.S75O27 1995**
Ethnic Labels, Latino Lives: Identity and the Politics of (Re) Presentation. Trade Paper. University of Minnesota Press. Minneapolis, MN. 1995. 226p. ISBN:0-8166-2286-8, ISBN13: 978-0-8166-2286-3. Dewey:305.868/073. LCCN:94-022751.
Audience: **u,f.** *Choice, 1995.*

Ochoa, Enrique &　　　　　　　　**F869.L89S7537 2005**
Ochoa, Gilda L.
Latino Los Angeles: Transformations, Communities, and Activism. Trade Paper. University of Arizona Press. Tucson, AZ. 2005. 304p. ISBN:0-8165-2468-8, ISBN13: 978-0-8165-2468-6. Dewey:979.4/9400468. LCCN:2005-017394.
Audience: **u,f.**

Padilla, Felix M.　　　　　　　　**F548.9.M5P32 1985**
Latino Ethnic Consciousness: The Case of Mexican Americans and Puerto Ricans in Chicago. Cloth Text. University of Notre Dame Press. Notre Dame, IN. 1986. 196p. ISBN:0-268-01274-1, ISBN13: 978-0-268-01274-8. Dewey:305.8/68077311. LCCN:85-008576.
Audience: **u,f.** *Choice, 1986.*

Perez-Torres, Rafael　　　　　　　**E184.M5P425 2006**
Mestizaje: Critical Uses of Race in Chicano Culture. Trade Paper. University of Minnesota Press. Minneapolis, MN. 2006. 272p. Critical American Studies ISBN:0-8166-4595-7, ISBN13: 978-0-8166-4595-4. Dewey:305.868/72073. LCCN:2006-000239.
Audience: **u,f.**

Ricourt, Milagros　　　　　　　　**F128.9**
Power from Margins: Incorporation of Dominicans in New York City. Paper over Boards. Routledge. New York, NY. 2002. 152p.

Latino Communities: Emerging Voices - Political, Social, Cultural and Legal Issues Ser. ISBN:0-415-93330-7, ISBN13: 978-0-415-93330-8. Dewey:305.8/687293/07471.

Audience: **u,f.**

Ricourt, Milagros &   **F128.9.S75R53 2003**
  Danta, Ruby
Hispanas de Queens: Latino Panethnicity in a New York City Neighborhood. Trade Paper. Cornell University Press. Ithaca, NY. 2005. 224p. The Anthropology of Contemporary Issues Ser. ISBN:0-8014-8795-1, ISBN13: 978-0-8014-8795-8. Dewey:305.868/0747. LCCN:2002-007458.

Audience: **u,f.**

Rodriguez, Clara   **E184.S75R64 2000**
Changing Race: Latinos, the Census, and the History of Ethnicity in the United States. Trade Paper. New York University Press. New York, NY. 2000. 283p. Critical America Ser. ISBN:0-8147-7547-0, ISBN13: 978-0-8147-7547-9. Dewey:305.8/00973. LCCN:00-008629.

Audience: **u,f.**

Rodriguez, Clara E.   **E184.P85R59 1989**
Puerto Rican: Born in the USA. Trade Cloth. Routledge. New York, NY. 1989. 256p. ISBN:0-04-497041-2, ISBN13: 978-0-04-497041-5. Dewey:305.8/687295/073. LCCN:88-031430.

Audience: **l.** *Choice, 1990.*

Rodriguez, Juana Maria   **HQ76.3.U5R63 2003**
Queer Latinidad: Identity Practices, Discursive Spaces. Trade Cloth. New York University Press. New York, NY. 2003. 239p. Sexual Cultures Ser. ISBN:0-8147-7549-7, ISBN13: 978-0-8147-7549-3. Dewey:305.868073. LCCN:2002-008752.

Audience: **u,f.** *Choice, 2003.*

Stavans, Ilan   **E184.S75 S75**
The Hispanic Condition: Reflections on Culture and Identity in America. Trade Paper. HarperCollins Publishers. New York, NY. 1996. 176p. ISBN:0-06-092693-7, ISBN13: 978-0-06-092693-9. Dewey:305.868/073.

Audience: **l,u.**

Tobar, Hector   **E184.S75.T63 2005**
Translation Nation: Defining a New American Identity in the Spanish-Speaking United States. Perfect, Paper over Boards, Dust Jacket. Penguin Group (USA) Inc. New York, NY. 2005. 307p. ISBN:1-57322-305-0, ISBN13: 978-1-57322-305-8. Dewey:305.868073. LCCN:2004-051478.

Audience: **l,u.**

Trejo, Arnulfo D.   **E184.M5 C47**
  (Editor)
The Chicanos: As We See Ourselves. Trade Cloth. University of Arizona Press. Tucson, AZ. 1979. 221p. ISBN:0-8165-0675-2, ISBN13: 978-0-8165-0675-0. Dewey:301.45/16/872073. LCCN:78-023693.

Audience: **l,u.**

Trueba, Enrique T.   **E184.S75T78 1998**
Latinos Unidos: From Cultural Diversity to the Politics of Solidarity. George Spindler (Foreword by). Trade Cloth. Rowman & Littlefield Publishers, Inc. Lanham, MD. 1999. 216p. Critical Perspectives Ser., Vol. 110 ISBN:0-8476-8596-9, ISBN13: 978-0-8476-8596-7. Dewey:305.868. LCCN:98-008617.

Audience: **l,u.** *Choice, 1999.*

Vega, Marta Moreno   **F128.9.P85V438 2004**
When the Spirits Dance Mambo: Growing up Nuyorican in el Barrio. Trade Paper. Crown Publishing Group. New York, NY. 2004. 288p. ISBN:1-4000-4924-5, ISBN13: 978-1-4000-4924-0. Dewey:974.7/004687295/0922. LCCN:2003-027912.

Audience: **l,u.**

Social and Behavioral Sciences > Sociology > Family

Abalos, David T.   **E184**
The Latino Family and the Politics of Transformation. Trade Cloth. Greenwood Publishing Group, Inc. Portsmouth, NH. 1993. 192p. Praeger Series in Transformational Politics and Political Science ISBN:0-275-94527-8, ISBN13: 978-0-275-94527-5. Dewey:306.8508968. LCCN:93-019612.

Audience: **u,f.** *Choice, 1994.*

Alvarez, Robert R. Jr.   **F870.M5**
Familia: Migration and Adaptation in Baja and Alta California, 1880-1975. Renato Rosaldo (Foreword by). Trade Paper. University of California Press. Berkeley, CA. 1991. 230p. ISBN:0-520-07389-4, ISBN13: 978-0-520-07389-0. Dewey:979.4/980046872073. LCCN:85-023217.

Audience: **u,f.**

Del Castillo, Richard G.   **F790.M5G75 1984**
La Familia: Chicano Families in the Urban Southwest, 1848 to the Present. Paper Text. University of Notre Dame Press. Notre Dame, IN. 1984. 224p. ISBN:0-268-01273-3, ISBN13: 978-0-268-01273-1. Dewey:306.8/50896872073. LCCN:84-040356.

Audience: **u,f.** *B*

Williams, Norma   **E184.M5W53 1990**
The Mexican American Family: Tradition and Change. Trade Cloth. AltaMira Press. Walnut Creek, CA. 1990. 184p. The Reynolds Series in Sociology ISBN:0-930390-26-1, ISBN13: 978-0-930390-26-6. Dewey:306.8/0896872073. LCCN:89-082581.

Audience: **l,u.** *Choice, 1991.*

Social and Behavioral Sciences > Sociology > Women

Alarcón, Norma   **PS153.M4 C45 1993**
  (Editor), et al.
Chicana Critical Issues. Rafaela Castro, Emma Perez, Beatriz Pesquera, Ada S. Riddell & Patricia Zavella (Editors), Juana Alicia, Judith Baca & Catalina Govea (Illustrators), Margarita Melville (Introduction by). Trade Paper. Third Woman Press. Oakland, CA. 1993. 304p. Chicana-Latina Studies ISBN:0-943219-09-4, ISBN13: 978-0-943219-09-7. Dewey:810.9/86872. LCCN:93-003097.

Audience: **u,f.**

Anzaldúa, Gloria   **PS3551.N95B6 1999**
Borderlands - La Frontera: The New Mestiza. Ed. 2. Trade Cloth. Aunt Lute Books. San Francisco, CA. 1999. 260p. ISBN:1-879960-57-5, ISBN13: 978-1-879960-57-2. Dewey:811/.54. LCCN:99-022546.

Audience: **u,f.** *Choice, 1988.*

Arredondo, Gabriela F.   HQ1421.C492 2003
(Editor)
Chicana Feminisms: A Critical Reader. Trade Cloth. Duke
University Press. Durham, NC. 2003. 416p. Latin America
Otherwise Ser. ISBN:0-8223-3105-5, ISBN13:
978-0-8223-3105-6. Dewey:305.42/0973. LCCN:2002-154970.
Audience: l,u. *Choice, 2004.*

Blea, Irene I.   E184
La Chicana and the Intersection of Race, Class and Gender.
Trade Cloth. Greenwood Publishing Group, Inc. Portsmouth,
NH. 1991. 192p. ISBN:0-275-93980-4, ISBN13:
978-0-275-93980-9. Dewey:305.48/86872073. LCCN:90-028075.
Audience: u,f. *Choice, 1992.*

Cantú, Norma Elia &   E184.M5C4 2002
Nájera-Ramírez, Olga (Editors)
Chicana Traditions: Continuity and Change. Trade Paper.
University of Illinois Press. Champaign, IL. 2002. 280p.
ISBN:0-252-07012-7, ISBN13: 978-0-252-07012-9.
Dewey:305.48/868/72073. LCCN:2001-002644.
Audience: u,f. *Choice, 2002.*

Cordova, Teresa   E184.M5 C42 1993
(Editor), et al.
Chicana Voices: Intersections of Class, Race, and Gender.
Norma Elia Cantú, Gilberto Cardenas, Juan Garcia & Christine
M. Sierra (Editors). Trade Paper. University of New Mexico
Press. Albuquerque, NM. 1993. 247p. ISBN:0-8263-1404-X,
ISBN13: 978-0-8263-1404-8. Dewey:305.4/886872/073.
LCCN:93-021784.

Audience: u,f.

Cotera, Martha P.   E184.M5 C67
The Chicana Feminist. Trade Paper. Information Systems
Development. Tucson, AZ. 1977. 68p. ISBN:0-931738-01-6,
ISBN13: 978-0-931738-01-2. Dewey:305.4/886872/073 19.
Audience: l,u.

De La Torre, Adela &   E184.M5.T67 1993
Pesquera, Beatriz M. (Editors)
Building with Our Hands: Directions in Chicana Studies. Trade
Cloth. University of California Press. Berkeley, CA. 1993. 246p.
ISBN:0-520-07089-5, ISBN13: 978-0-520-07089-9.
Dewey:305.4886872073. LCCN:91-039227.
Audience: u,f. *Choice, 1993.*

Fregoso, Rosa Linda   F790.M5 F75 2003
Mexicana Encounters: The Making of Social Identities on the
Borderlands. Trade Cloth. University of California Press.
Berkeley, CA. 2003. 246p. American Crossroads Ser., Vol. 12
ISBN:0-520-22997-5, ISBN13: 978-0-520-22997-6.
Dewey:305.48/868720721. LCCN:2003-000594.
Audience: u,f. *Choice, 2004.*

Garcia, Alma (Editor)   HQ1421.C52 1997
Chicana Feminist Thought: The Basic Historical Writings. UK-B
Format Paperback. Routledge. New York, NY. 1997. 344p.
ISBN:0-415-91801-4, ISBN13: 978-0-415-91801-5.
Dewey:305.48/868/72073. LCCN:96-049916.
Audience: u,f.

Garcia, Juan R.   E184.M5
Mexican American Women: Changing Images. Paper Text.
University of Arizona Press. Tucson, AZ. 1996. 195p.
Persepctives in Mexican American Studies, Vol. 5
ISBN:0-939363-05-4, ISBN13: 978-0-939363-05-6.
Dewey:973.046872.
Audience: l,u.

González, Deena J.   F804.S29 M54 1999
Refusing the Favor: The Spanish-Mexican Women of Santa Fe,
1820-1880. Trade Cloth. Oxford University Press, Inc. New
York, NY. 1999. 206p. ISBN:0-19-507890-X, ISBN13:
978-0-19-507890-9. Dewey:978.9/560046872073.
LCCN:98-049560.
Audience: u,f. *Choice, 2000.*

Hondagneu-Sotelo,   HD6072.2.U52 L674
Pierrette
Doméstica: Immigrant Workers Cleaning and Caring in the
Shadows of Affluence. Trade Paper. University of California
Press. Berkeley, CA. 2001. 312p. ISBN:0-520-22643-7, ISBN13:
978-0-520-22643-2. Dewey:331.4/8164046. LCCN:00-051171.
Audience: u,f. *Choice, 2001.*

Medina, Lara   BX810.H57M43 2004
Las Hermanas: Chicana/Latina Religious-Political Activism in
the U. S. Catholic Church. Trade Cloth. Temple University
Press. Philadelphia, PA. 2004. 232p. ISBN:1-59213-250-2,
ISBN13: 978-1-59213-250-8. Dewey:267.4/4273.
LCCN:2003-064591.
Audience: u,f. *Choice, 2005.*

Mirandé, Alfredo &   E184.M5.M55
Enriquez, Evangelina
La Chicana: The Mexican-American Woman. Trade Cloth.
University of Chicago Press. Chicago, IL. 1979. x, 283p.
ISBN:0-226-53159-7, ISBN13: 978-0-226-53159-5.
Dewey:301.41/2/0973. LCCN:79-013536.
Audience: l,u. *B*

Moraga, Cherríe &   PS508.H57S49
Castillo, Ana (Editors)
The Sexuality of Latinas. Norma Alarcón (Introduction by).
Trade Paper. Third Woman Press. Oakland, CA. 1991. 192p.
ISBN:0-943219-07-8, ISBN13: 978-0-943219-07-3.
Dewey:810.8/03520643.
Audience: u,f.

Pardo, Mary   HN80.M66P37 1998
Mexican American Women Activists: Identity and Resistance in
Two Los Angeles Communities. Trade Cloth. Temple University
Press. Philadelphia, PA. 1998. 256p. ISBN:1-56639-572-0,
ISBN13: 978-1-56639-572-4. Dewey:305.42/08968/7207949.
LCCN:97-013960.
Audience: u,f. *Choice, 1998.*

Perez, Emma   E184.M5P418 1999
The Decolonial Imaginary: Writing Chicanas into History. Cloth
Text. Indiana University Press. Bloomington, IN. 1999. 240p.
Theories of Representation and Difference Ser.
ISBN:0-253-33504-3, ISBN13: 978-0-253-33504-3.
Dewey:305.4/886872073. LCCN:98-051190.
Audience: u,f.

Ruiz, Vicki L.   HD6515.F72U547 1987
Cannery Women, Cannery Lives: Mexican Women,
Unionization, and the California Food Processing Industry,
1930-1950. Trade Paper. University of New Mexico Press.
Albuquerque, NM. 1987. 194p. ISBN:0-8263-0988-7, ISBN13:
978-0-8263-0988-4. Dewey:331.88/1640282/09794.
LCCN:87-013878.
Audience: u,f. *Choice, 1988.*

Ruiz, Vicki L.   E184.M5
From Out of the Shadows: Mexican Women in
Twentieth-Century America. Trade Paper. Oxford University
Press, Inc. New York, NY. 1999. 272p. ISBN:0-19-513099-5,
ISBN13: 978-0-19-513099-7. Dewey:305.4886872.

         Audience: **l,u.**

Ruiz, Vicki L. (Editor)   E184.M5O27 2000
Las Obreras: Chicana Politics of Work and Family. Trade Paper.
UCLA Chicano Studies Research Center Press. Los Angeles,
CA. 2000. 320p. Aztlan Anthology Ser., Vol. 1
ISBN:0-89551-094-4, ISBN13: 978-0-89551-094-5.
Dewey:305.48/86872073. LCCN:00-022132.

         Audience: **l,u.**

Ruiz, Vicki L. &   E184.S75L36245 2005
   Korrol, Virginia Sanchez
Latina Legacies: Identity, Biography, and Community. Trade
Cloth. Oxford University Press, Inc. New York, NY. 2005. 272p.
Viewpoints on American Culture Ser. ISBN:0-19-515398-7,
ISBN13: 978-0-19-515398-9. Dewey:920.72/089/68 B.
LCCN:2004-050131.

         Audience: **l,u.**

Sanchez, Rosaura &   E184.M5 E87
   Cruz, Rosa M. (Editors)
Essays on la Mujer. Trade Paper. UCLA Chicano Studies
Research Center Press. Los Angeles, CA. 1977. 194p.
Anthology Ser., No. 1 ISBN:0-89551-020-0, ISBN13:
978-0-89551-020-4. Dewey:973/.04/6872.

         Audience: **u,f.**

Stoner, K. Lynn &   Z7964.C85S76 2000
   Perez, Luis Hipolito Serrano (Editor, Compiled by)
Cuban and Cuban-American Women: An Annotated
Bibliography. Book, Other. Rowman & Littlefield Publishers,
Inc. Lanham, MD. 2000. 189p. Latin American Silhouettes Ser.
ISBN:0-8420-2643-6, ISBN13: 978-0-8420-2643-7.
Dewey:016.3054/097291. LCCN:98-022317.

         Audience: **u,f.** *Choice, 2000.*

Trujillo, Carla   HQ75.6.U5C53 1991
   (Introduction by)
Chicana Lesbians: The Girls Our Mothers Warned Us About.
Trade Paper. Third Woman Press. Oakland, CA. 1991. 216p.
ISBN:0-943219-06-X, ISBN13: 978-0-943219-06-6.
Dewey:306.76/63/0896872073. LCCN:90-026885.

         Audience: **l,u.**

Trujillo, Carla   E184.M5L58 1998
Living Chicana Theory. Trade Cloth. Third Woman Press.
Oakland, CA. 1997. ISBN:0-943219-15-9, ISBN13:
978-0-943219-15-8. Dewey:305.48/868/72073.
LCCN:97-038523.

         Audience: **u,f.**

Social and Behavioral Sciences > Sociology > Gangs

Brotherton, David &   HV6439.U7N432 2003
   Barrios, Luis
The Almighty Latin King and Queen Nation: Street Politics and
the Transformation of a New York City Gang. Trade Cloth.
Chinese University of Hong Kong, The. Hong Kong SAR, 2004.

464p. ISBN:0-231-11418-4, ISBN13: 978-0-231-11418-9.
Dewey:364.1/066/097471. LCCN:2003-061751.

         Audience: **u,f.** *Choice, 2004.*

Brown, Monica   HV6439.U5B76 2002
Gang Nation: Delinquent Citizens in Puerto Rican, Chicano, and
Chicana Narratives. Trade Paper. University of Minnesota Press.
Minneapolis, MN. 2002. 256p. ISBN:0-8166-3479-3, ISBN13:
978-0-8166-3479-8. Dewey:364.1/06/608968073.
LCCN:2001-008249.

         Audience: **u,f.**

Moore, Joan W.   HV6439.U5M66 1991
Going down to the Barrio: Homeboys and Homegirls in Change.
Trade Cloth. Temple University Press. Philadelphia, PA. 1991.
176p. ISBN:0-87722-854-X, ISBN13: 978-0-87722-854-7.
Dewey:364.1/06/60979494. LCCN:91-002276.

         Audience: **u,f.**

Rodriguez, Luis J.   HV6439.U7L77 2005
Always Running: La Vida Loca: Gang Days in L. A. Trade
Paper. Simon & Schuster. New York, NY. 2005. 288p.
ISBN:0-7432-7691-4, ISBN13: 978-0-7432-7691-7.
Dewey:364.1092 B. LCCN:2005-281606.

         Audience: **g,l,u.**

Vigil, James Diego   HV6439.U7
Barrio Gangs: Street Life and Identity in Southern California.
Trade Paper. University of Texas Press. Austin, TX. 1988. 220p.
Mexican American Monographs, No. 12 ISBN:0-292-71119-0,
ISBN13: 978-0-292-71119-8. Dewey:364.1/066/0979494.
LCCN:88-023386.

         Audience: **u,f.** *Choice, 1989.*

Vigil, James Diego   HV6439.U7L788 2002
A Rainbow of Gangs: Street Cultures in the Mega-City. Trade
Paper. University of Texas Press. Austin, TX. 2002. 231p.
ISBN:0-292-78749-9, ISBN13: 978-0-292-78749-0.
Dewey:364.1/06/60979494. LCCN:2002-001063.

         Audience: **l,u,f.** *Choice, 2003.*

Social and Behavioral Sciences > Urban Studies

         F130.S75
Constructing the New York Area Hispanic Mosiac: A
Demographic Portrait of Colombians and Dominicans in New
York. Tomás Rivera Policy Institute and NALEO Educational
Fund. 1977.

         Audience: **f.**

         F867
Diversifying the Los Angeles Area Latino Mosiac: Salvadoran
and Guatemalan Leaders' Assessments of Community Public
Policy Needs. Tomás Rivera Policy Institute and NALEO
Educational Fund. 1997.

         Audience: **f.**

         F130.S75
Diversifying the New York Area Hispanic Mosiac: Colombian
and Dominican Leaders' Assessments of Community Public
Policy Needs. Tomás Rivera Policy Institute and NALEO
Educational Fund. 1977.

         Audience: **f.**

Acuna, Rodolfo F.   **F869.L89M5 1996**
Anything but Mexican: Chicanos in Contemporary Los Angeles.
Trade Cloth. Verso Books. London, 1996. 320p. Haymarket Ser.
ISBN:1-85984-936-9, ISBN13: 978-1-85984-936-1.
Dewey:979.4/053/0046872. LCCN:96-005040.
Audience: **l,u.** *Choice, 1996.*

Acuna, Rodolfo F.   **F869.E18 A28 1984**
A Community under Siege: A Chronicle of Chicanos East of the
Los Angeles River, 1945-1975. Trade Paper. UCLA Chicano
Studies Research Center Press. Los Angeles, CA. 1984. 540p.
Monographs, No. 11 ISBN:0-89551-066-9, ISBN13:
978-0-89551-066-2. Dewey:979.4/93. LCCN:83-026197.
Audience: **l,u.**

Avila, Eric   **F869.L85 A95 2004**
Popular Culture in the Age of White Flight: Fear and Fantasy in
Suburban Los Angeles. Trade Cloth. University of California
Press. Berkeley, CA. 2004. 345p. American Crossroads Ser., Vol.
13 ISBN:0-520-24121-5, ISBN13: 978-0-520-24121-3.
Dewey:979.4/94. LCCN:2003-019072.
Audience: **u,f.** *Choice, 2005.*

Blea, Irene I.   **F782.P9 B55**
Bessemer: A Sociological Perspective of a Chicano Barrio.
Trade Cloth. A M S Press, Inc. New York, NY. 1991. 207p.
Immigrant Communities and Ethnic Minorities in the U. S. and
Canada Ser., No. 13 ISBN:0-404-19423-0, ISBN13:
978-0-404-19423-9. Dewey:305.86872. LCCN:87-045778.
Audience: **u,f.**

Camarillo, Albert   **F869.S45C25 2005**
Chicanos in a Changing Society: From Mexican Pueblos to
American Barrios in Santa Barbara and Southern California,
1848-1930. Trade Paper. Southern Methodist University Press.
Dallas, TX. 2005. 352p. ISBN:0-87074-497-6, ISBN13:
978-0-87074-497-6. Dewey:979.4/9/0046872073.
LCCN:2004-065346.
Audience: **l,u.**

Croucher, Sheila L.   **F319.M6C76 1997**
Imagining Miami: Ethnic Politics in a Postmodern World. Cloth
Text. University Press of Virginia. Charlottesville, VA. 1997.
250p. Race, Ethnicity and Politics Ser. ISBN:0-8139-1704-2,
ISBN13: 978-0-8139-1704-7. Dewey:305.8/009759/381.
LCCN:96-041357.
Audience: **u,f.**

Davila, Arlene M.   **HT178.N5 D38 2004**
Barrio Dreams: Puerto Ricans, Latinos, and the Neoliberal City.
Trade Cloth. University of California Press. Berkeley, CA. 2004.
256p. ISBN:0-520-24092-8, ISBN13: 978-0-520-24092-6.
Dewey:307.1/416/097471. LCCN:2003-064572.
Audience: **u,f.** *Choice, 2005.*

Davis, Mike   **E184.S75D36 2000**
Magical Urbanism: Latinos Reinvent the U. S. Big City. Trade
Cloth. Analytical Psychology Club of San Francisco, Inc. San
Francisco, CA. 2000. 192p. Haymarket Ser.
ISBN:1-85984-771-4, ISBN13: 978-1-85984-771-8.
Dewey:305.868/073. LCCN:00-698296.
Audience: **u,f.** *Choice, 2001.*

De Leon, Arnoldo   **F394.H89 M512**
Ethnicity in the Sunbelt: A History of Mexican Americans in
Houston. Trade Cloth. University of Houston, Mexican
American Studies Program. Houston, TX. 1989. 255p. Mexican

American Studies ISBN:0-939709-06-6, ISBN13:
978-0-939709-06-9. Dewey:976.4/14110046872.
Audience: **l,u.** *Choice, 1990.*

Dohan, Daniel   **F869.S394 D64 2003**
The Price of Poverty: Money, Work, and Culture in the
Mexican-American Barrio. Trade Cloth. University of California
Press. Berkeley, CA. 2003. 304p. ISBN:0-520-22756-5, ISBN13:
978-0-520-22756-9. Dewey:330.9794/74/00896872.
LCCN:2003-002460.
Audience: **u,f.** *Choice, 2004.*

Duany, Jorge   **F128.9.D6**
Quisqueya on the Hudson: The Transnational Identity of
Domincans in Washington. CUNY Dominican Studies Institute.
1994.
Audience: **u.**

Escobar, Edward J.   **HV8148.L55 E73 1999**
Race, Police, and the Making of a Political Identity: Mexican
Americans and the Los Angeles Police Department, 1900-1945.
Trade Cloth. University of California Press. Berkeley, CA. 1999.
372p. Latinos in American Society and Culture Ser., 7
ISBN:0-520-21334-3, ISBN13: 978-0-520-21334-0.
Dewey:365/.9794/93. LCCN:98-023322.
Audience: **u,f.** *Choice, 2000.*

Farr, Marcia (Editor)   **P35.5.U6L38 2004**
Latino Language and Literacy in Ethnolinguistic Chicago. Elias
D. Barajas, Ralph Cintron & Jennifer L. Cohen (Contribution
by). Cloth over Boards. Lawrence Erlbaum Associates, Inc.
Mahwah, NJ. 2004. 416p. ISBN:0-8058-4347-7, ISBN13:
978-0-8058-4347-7. Dewey:306.44. LCCN:2004-047232.
Audience: **u,f.** *Choice, 2005.*

Fine, Michelle   **LC146.7.N7F56 1991**
Framing Dropouts: Notes on the Politics of an Urban High
School. Cloth Text. State University of New York Press. Albany,
NY. 1991. 313p. SUNY Series in Teacher Empowerment and
School Reform ISBN:0-7914-0403-X, ISBN13:
978-0-7914-0403-4. Dewey:373.12/913/097471.
LCCN:90-032135.
Audience: **u,f.** *Choice, 1991.*

Flores, Henry   **E184.M5F58 2003**
The Evolution of the Liberal Democratic State with a Case
Study of Latinos in San Antonio, Texas. Trade Cloth. Edwin
Mellen Press, The. Lewiston, NY. 2003. 248p. Studies in
Political Science, Vol. 9 ISBN:0-7734-6674-6, ISBN13:
978-0-7734-6674-6. Dewey:320.9764/351. LCCN:2003-046480.
Audience: **u,f.** *Choice, 2004.*

Freidenberg, Judith   **HQ1064.U6N463 2000**
Growing Old in El Barrio. Trade Cloth. New York University
Press. New York, NY. 2000. 320p. ISBN:0-8147-2702-6,
ISBN13: 978-0-8147-2702-7. Dewey:305.26/09747.
LCCN:00-056001.
Audience: **u,f.** *Choice, 2001.*

Gamboa, Erasmo &   **F885.S75N67 1995**
Buan, Carolyn M. (Editors)
Nosotros: The Hispanic People of Oregon, Essays and
Recollections. Trade Paper. Oregon Council for the Humanities.
Portland, OR. 1995. 180p. ISBN:1-880377-01-2, ISBN13:
978-1-880377-01-7. Dewey:979.5/00468. LCCN:95-079043.
Audience: **l.**

Formats: Web: ☐   Ebook: 🄴   CD/DVD-ROM: 🌐   BCL3: *B*

Garcia, Matthew   **F869.L89A253 2002**
A World of Its Own: Race, Labor, and Citrus in the Making of
Greater Los Angeles, 1900-1970. Trade Cloth. University of
North Carolina Press. Chapel Hill, NC. 2002. 352p. Studies in
Rural Culture ISBN:0-8078-2658-8, ISBN13:
978-0-8078-2658-4. Dewey:305.8/009794/94.
LCCN:2001-035879.
                              Audience: **u,f.** *Choice, 2002.*

Garcia, Richard A.   **F394.S2G37 1991**
Rise of the Mexican American Middle Class: San Antonio,
1929-1941. Henry C. Schmidt (Foreword by). Trade Cloth.
Texas A&M University Press. College Station, TX. 1991. 416p.
Centennial Series of the Association of Former Students, No. 36
ISBN:0-89096-368-1, ISBN13: 978-0-89096-368-5.
Dewey:976.4/3510046872073. LCCN:90-038788.
                              Audience: **u,f.** *Choice, 1991.*

García Bedolla, Lisa   **F869.L89 S753 2005**
Fluid Borders: Latino Power, Identity, and Politics in Los
Angeles. Trade Cloth. University of California Press. Berkeley,
CA. 2005. 280p. ISBN:0-520-24368-4, ISBN13:
978-0-520-24368-2. Dewey:979.4/9400468. LCCN:2004-065937.
                              Audience: **u,f.** *Choice, 2006.*

García, Mario T.   **F394.E4**
Desert Immigrants: The Mexican of el Paso, 1880-1920. Trade
Paper. Yale University Press. Cumberland, RI. 1982. 318p.
Western Americana Ser., No. 32 ISBN:0-300-02883-0, ISBN13:
978-0-300-02883-6. Dewey:976.4. LCCN:80-036862.
                              Audience: **u,f.**

Greenbaum, Susan D.   **F319.T2G69 2002**
More Than Black: Afro-Cubans in Tampa. Trade Cloth.
University Press of Florida. Gainesville, FL. 2002. 384p. New
World Diaspora Ser. ISBN:0-8130-2466-8, ISBN13:
978-0-8130-2466-0. Dewey:305.868/7291075965.
LCCN:2001-043726.
                              Audience: **u,f.** *Choice, 2003.*

Grenier, Guillermo &   **F319.M6.M639 1992**
Stepick, Alex III (Editors)
Miami Now: Immigration, Ethnicity, and Social Change. Trade
Cloth. University Press of Florida. Gainesville, FL. 1992. 256p.
ISBN:0-8130-1154-X, ISBN13: 978-0-8130-1154-7.
Dewey:305.8/009759/381. LCCN:92-010100.
                              Audience: **u,f.** *Choice, 1993.*

Griswold del Castillo,   **HE8700.8**
Richard
The Los Angeles Barrio, 1850-1890: A Social History. Trade
Cloth. University of California Press. Berkeley, CA. 1980. 232p.
ISBN:0-520-03816-9, ISBN13: 978-0-520-03816-5.
Dewey:301.45/16/872079494. LCCN:78-065460.
                              Audience: **l,u.**

Hamilton, Nora &   **F869.L89G824 2001**
Chinchilla, Norma Stoltz
Seeking Community in a Global City: Guatemalans and
Salvadorans in Los Angeles. Library Binding. Temple University
Press. Philadelphia, PA. 2001. xii, 292p. ISBN:1-56639-867-3,
ISBN13: 978-1-56639-867-1. Dewey:305.868/7281079494.
LCCN:00-048897.
                              Audience: **u,f.**

Haslip-Viera, Gabriel &   **F128.9.P85B67 2004**
Falcon, Angelo (Author, Editors)
Boricuas in Gotham: Puerto Ricans in the Making of New York
City. Felix V. Matos Rodriguez & Antonia Pantoja (Editors).

Trade Cloth. Markus Wiener Publishers, Inc. Princeton, NJ.
2004. 286p. ISBN:1-55876-355-4, ISBN13: 978-1-55876-355-5.
Dewey:9747/.1004687295. LCCN:2004-016684.
                              Audience: **l,u.**

Haslip-Viera (Editor), et   **F128.9.S75 L37**
al.
Latinos in New York: Communities in Transition. Gabriel Baver
& Sherrie L. Baver (Editors). Paper Text. University of Notre
Dame Press. Notre Dame, IN. 1997. 400p. ISBN:0-268-01315-2,
ISBN13: 978-0-268-01315-8. Dewey:974.7/100468.
                              Audience: **l,u.**

Hendricks, Glenn   **F128.9.D6H**
The Dominican Diaspora: From the Dominican Republic to New
York City, Villagers in Transition. Trade Paper. Books on
Demand. Ann Arbor, MI. 183p. Publications of the Center for
Education in Africa ISBN:0-608-18800-X, ISBN13:
978-0-608-18800-3. Dewey:917.47/1/06687293.
LCCN:74-004203.
                              Audience: **u,f.**

Jones-Correa, Michael   **F130.S75J66 1998**
Between Two Nations: The Political Predicament of Latinos in
New York City. Book, Other. Cornell University Press. Ithaca,
NY. 1998. 272p. ISBN:0-8014-3292-8, ISBN13:
978-0-8014-3292-7. Dewey:305.868/07471. LCCN:97-049415.
                              Audience: **u,f.** *Choice, 1999.*

Lao-Montes, Agustin &   **F128.9.S75M36 2001**
Davila, Arlene M. (Editors)
Mambo Montage: The Latinization of New York City. Trade
Cloth. Kegan Paul International, Ltd. London, 2001. 448p.
ISBN:0-231-11274-2, ISBN13: 978-0-231-11274-1.
Dewey:974.7/100468073. LCCN:00-047548.
                              Audience: **l,u.** *Choice, 2002.*

Loza, Steven   **ML3558.L69 1992**
Barrio Rhythm: Mexican American Music in Los Angeles. Trade
Paper. University of Illinois Press. Champaign, IL. 1993. 392p.
Music in American Life Ser. ISBN:0-252-06288-4, ISBN13:
978-0-252-06288-9. Dewey:781.62/6872079494.
LCCN:91-035181.
                              Audience: **u,f.** *Choice, 1994.*

Matovina, Timothy M.   **F394.S2M39 1995**
Tejano Religion and Ethnicity: San Antonio, 1821-1860. Trade
Cloth. University of Texas Press. Austin, TX. 1995. 182p.
ISBN:0-292-75170-2, ISBN13: 978-0-292-75170-5.
Dewey:976.4/3510046872073. LCCN:94-010617.
                              Audience: **u,f.** *Choice, 1995.*

Monroy, Douglas   **F869.L89 M455 1999**
Rebirth: Mexican Los Angeles from the Great Migration to the
Great Depression. Trade Paper. University of California Press.
Berkeley, CA. 1999. 334p. ISBN:0-520-21333-5, ISBN13:
978-0-520-21333-3. Dewey:979.4/940046872073.
LCCN:98-050013.
                              Audience: **l,u.** *Choice, 1999.*

Moore, Joan W.   **HV6439.U5M66 1991**
Going down to the Barrio: Homeboys and Homegirls in Change.
Trade Cloth. Temple University Press. Philadelphia, PA. 1991.
176p. ISBN:0-87722-854-X, ISBN13: 978-0-87722-854-7.
Dewey:364.1/06/60979494. LCCN:91-002276.
                              Audience: **u,f.**

Ochoa, Enrique &   F869.L89S7537 2005
Ochoa, Gilda L.
Latino Los Angeles: Transformations, Communities, and
Activism. Trade Paper. University of Arizona Press. Tucson, AZ.
2005. 304p. ISBN:0-8165-2468-8, ISBN13: 978-0-8165-2468-6.
Dewey:979.4/9400468. LCCN:2005-017394.

Audience: **u,f.**

Padilla, Felix M.   F548.9.P85P33 1987
Puerto Rican Chicago. Trade Cloth. University of Notre Dame
Press. Notre Dame, IN. 1988. 256p. ISBN:0-268-01564-3,
ISBN13: 978-0-268-01564-0. Dewey:977.3/11004687295.
LCCN:86-040244.

Audience: **l,u.** *Choice, 1987.*

Pagan, Eduardo   F869.L89 M566 2003
Obregon
Murder at the Sleepy Lagoon: Zoot Suits, Race, and Riot in
Wartime L.A. Trade Cloth. University of North Carolina Press.
Chapel Hill, NC. 2003. 312p. ISBN:0-8078-2826-2, ISBN13:
978-0-8078-2826-7. Dewey:979.4/94052. LCCN:2003-048891.

Audience: **l,u.** *Choice, 2004.*

Pardo, Mary   HN80.M66P37 1998
Mexican American Women Activists: Identity and Resistance in
Two Los Angeles Communities. Trade Cloth. Temple University
Press. Philadelphia, PA. 1998. 256p. ISBN:1-56639-572-0,
ISBN13: 978-1-56639-572-4. Dewey:305.42/08968/7207949.
LCCN:97-013960.

Audience: **u,f.** *Choice, 1998.*

Perez, Gina M.   F548.9.P85 P47 2004
The Near Northwest Side Story: Migration, Displacement, and
Puerto Rican Families. Trade Paper. University of California
Press. Berkeley, CA. 2004. 282p. ISBN:0-520-23368-9, ISBN13:
978-0-520-23368-3. Dewey:305.868/7295077311.
LCCN:2004-048010.

Audience: **u,f.** *Choice, 2005.*

Poyo, Gerald E. &   F394.S2T43 1991
Hinojosa, Gilberto M. (Editors)
Tejano Origins in Eighteenth-Century San Antonio. Jose
Cisneros (Illustrator). Trade Cloth. University of Texas Press.
Austin, TX. 1991. 222p. ISBN:0-292-71138-7, ISBN13:
978-0-292-71138-9. Dewey:976.4/3510046872.
LCCN:90-047345.

Audience: **l,u.** *Choice, 1992.*

Ramos-Zayas, Ana Y.   F548.9.P85R36 2003
National Performances: The Politics of Class, Race, and Space
in Puerto Rican Chicago. Trade Paper. University of Chicago
Press. Chicago, IL. 2003. 303p. ISBN:0-226-70359-2, ISBN13:
978-0-226-70359-6. Dewey:305.868/7295077311.
LCCN:2002-154906.

Audience: **u,f.** *Choice, 2004.*

Ricourt, Milagros   F128.9
Power from Margins: Incorporation of Dominicans in New York
City. Paper over Boards. Routledge. New York, NY. 2002. 152p.
Latino Communities: Emerging Voices - Political, Social,
Cultural and Legal Issues Ser. ISBN:0-415-93330-7, ISBN13:
978-0-415-93330-8. Dewey:305.8/687293/07471.

Audience: **u,f.**

Ricourt, Milagros &   F128.9.S75R53 2003
Danta, Ruby
Hispanas de Queens: Latino Panethnicity in a New York City
Neighborhood. Trade Paper. Cornell University Press. Ithaca,

NY. 2005. 224p. The Anthropology of Contemporary Issues Ser.
ISBN:0-8014-8795-1, ISBN13: 978-0-8014-8795-8.
Dewey:305.868/0747. LCCN:2002-007458.

Audience: **u,f.**

Romo, Ricardo   F869.E18 R65 1983
East Los Angeles: History of a Barrio. Trade Paper. University
of Texas Press. Austin, TX. 1983. 232p. ISBN:0-292-72041-6,
ISBN13: 978-0-292-72041-1. Dewey:305.8/6872/079494.
LCCN:82-010891.

Audience: **l,u.** 𝓑

San Miguel, Guadalupe   LC2688.H8S26 2001
Brown, Not White: School Integration and the Chicano
Movement in Houston. Trade Cloth. Texas A&M University
Press. College Station, TX. 2001. xiii, 283p. University of
Houston Series in Mexican American Studies, No. 3
ISBN:1-58544-115-5, ISBN13: 978-1-58544-115-0.
Dewey:379.2/63/097641411. LCCN:00-011204.

Audience: **u,f.**

Sheridan, Thomas E.   F819.T99
Los Tucsonenses: The Mexican Community in Tucson,
1854-1941. Trade Paper. University of Arizona Press. Tucson,
AZ. 1992. 327p. ISBN:0-8165-1298-1, ISBN13:
978-0-8165-1298-0. Dewey:979.1/77. LCCN:86-011404.

Audience: **l,u.**

Stepick, Alex   F319.M6 T48 2003
This Land Is Our Land: Immigrants and Power in Miami. Trade
Cloth. University of California Press. Berkeley, CA. 2003. 196p.
ISBN:0-520-23397-2, ISBN13: 978-0-520-23397-3.
Dewey:305.8/009759/381. LCCN:2002-011201.

Audience: **u,f.** *Choice, 2003.*

Sutton, Constance R. &   F128.9.C27 C37 1987
Chaney, Elsa M. (Editors)
Caribbean Life in New York City: Sociocultural Dimensions.
Trade Paper. Center for Migration Studies. Staten Island, NY.
1993. 250p. CMS Migration and Ethnicity Ser.
ISBN:0-913256-92-7, ISBN13: 978-0-913256-92-3.
Dewey:305.8/68729/07471.

Audience: **u,f.**

Sánchez Korrol,   F128.9.P85S26 1994
Virginia
ⓔ From Colonia to Community: The History of Puerto Ricans
in New York City. E-Book. NetLibrary, Inc. Boulder, CO. 1994.
ISBN:0-585-07894-7, ISBN13: 978-0-585-07894-6.
Dewey:974.7/1004687295.

Audience: **l,u.**

Valdés, Dionicio Nodín   F614.S4V35 2000
Barrios Norteños: St. Paul and Midwestern Mexican
Communities in the Twentieth Century. Trade Cloth. University
of Texas Press. Austin, TX. 2000. 406p. Pike Subsidy Ser.
ISBN:0-292-78743-X, ISBN13: 978-0-292-78743-8.
Dewey:977.6/5810046872073. LCCN:99-036269.

Audience: **l,u.** *Choice, 2000.*

Vigil, James Diego   HV6439.U7
Barrio Gangs: Street Life and Identity in Southern California.
Trade Paper. University of Texas Press. Austin, TX. 1988. 220p.
Mexican American Monographs, No. 12 ISBN:0-292-71119-0,
ISBN13: 978-0-292-71119-8. Dewey:364.1/066/0979494.
LCCN:88-023386.

Audience: **u,f.** *Choice, 1989.*

Vigil, James Diego   HV6439.U7L788 2002
A Rainbow of Gangs: Street Cultures in the Mega-City. Trade
Paper. University of Texas Press. Austin, TX. 2002. 231p.
ISBN:0-292-78749-9, ISBN13: 978-0-292-78749-0.
Dewey:364.1/06/60979494. LCCN:2002-001063.
         Audience: **l,u,f.** *Choice, 2003.*

Ward, Peter M.   HV4045.5.T4W37 1999
Colonias and Public Policy in Texas and Mexico: Urbanization
by Stealth. Trade Cloth. University of Texas Press. Austin, TX.
1999. 307p. ISBN:0-292-79124-0, ISBN13: 978-0-292-79124-4.
Dewey:307.3/36416/09721. LCCN:98-025402.
         Audience: **u,f.** *Choice, 1999.*

Wilson, Chris   F804.S25W55 1997
The Myth of Santa Fe: Creating a Modern Regional Tradition.
Trade Paper. University of New Mexico Press. Albuquerque,
NM. 1996. 418p. ISBN:0-8263-1746-4, ISBN13:
978-0-8263-1746-9. Dewey:978.9/5605. LCCN:95-050222.
         Audience: **u,f.** *Choice, 1997.*

Science and Technology > Environmental Studies

Peña, Devon G.   E184.M5P395 2005
Mexican Americans and the Environment: Tierra y Vida. Trade
Paper. University of Arizona Press. Tucson, AZ. 2005. 232p.
The Mexican American Experience Ser. ISBN:0-8165-2211-1,
ISBN13: 978-0-8165-2211-8. Dewey:304.2/089/6872073.
LCCN:2004-023856.
         Audience: **u,f.**

Pulido, Laura   GE198.S86P85 1996
Environmentalism and Economic Justice: Two Chicano
Struggles in the Southwest. Trade Cloth. University of Arizona
Press. Tucson, AZ. 1996. 282p. Society, Environment and Place
Ser. ISBN:0-8165-1424-0, ISBN13: 978-0-8165-1424-3.
Dewey:363.7/0089/6872073. LCCN:95-032449.
         Audience: **u,f.**

Rivera, José A.   HD1694.A3 1998
Acequia Culture: Water, Land and Community in the Southwest.
Trade Cloth. University of New Mexico Press. Albuquerque,
NM. 1998. 244p. ISBN:0-8263-1858-4, ISBN13:
978-0-8263-1858-9. Dewey:333.91/15/097644.
LCCN:98-023877.
         Audience: **u,f.** *Choice, 1999.*

Science and Technology > Botany and Ethnobotany

Webster, Grady L. &   QK142.C53 2001
   Bahre, Conrad J.
Changing Plant Life of la Frontera: Observations on Vegetation
in the United States/Mexico Borderlands. Trade Cloth.
University of New Mexico Press. Albuquerque, NM. 2001.
260p. ISBN:0-8263-2239-5, ISBN13: 978-0-8263-2239-5.
Dewey:581.972/1. LCCN:00-010451.
         Audience: **u,f.** *Choice, 2001.*

Science and Technology > Medicine and Public Health

De La Torre, Adela &   RA448.5.M4T67 2001
   Estrada, Antonio L.
Mexican Americans and Health: Sana! Sana!. Trade Cloth.
University of Arizona Press. Tucson, AZ. 2001. 156p. Mexican
American Studies ISBN:0-8165-1976-5, ISBN13:
978-0-8165-1976-7. Dewey:362.1/089/6872073.
LCCN:00-012932.
         Audience: **l,u.**

De Rios, Marlene D.   RC451.5.H57D63 2001
   (Editor)
Brief Psychotherapy with the Latino Immigrant Client. Trade
Cloth. Haworth Press, Incorporated, The. Binghamton, NY.
2001. 191p. ISBN:0-7890-1089-5, ISBN13: 978-0-7890-1089-6.
Dewey:616.89/14/08968073. LCCN:00-033531.
         Audience: **u,f.**

Hayes-Bautista, David   RA448.5.H57
E.
The Health Status of Latinos in California. Trade Paper.
California HealthCare Foundation. Oakland, CA. 1997. 48p.
Health Status Ser. ISBN:1-929008-12-0, ISBN13:
978-1-929008-12-4. Dewey:614.42794.
         Audience: **u,f.**

Kiev, Ari   GN477.1.K5
Curanderismo: Mexican-American Folk Psychiatry. Trade Paper.
Simon & Schuster. New York, NY. 1972. ISBN:0-02-917260-8,
ISBN13: 978-0-02-917260-5. Dewey:615/.882.
LCCN:67-025331.
         Audience: **u,f.**

Rosenwaike, Ira   HB1335
   (Editor)
Mortality of Hispanic Populations: Mexicans, Puerto Ricans, and
Cubans in the United States and in the Home Country. Trade
Cloth. Greenwood Publishing Group, Inc. Portsmouth, NH.
1991. 240p. Studies in Population and Urban Demography Ser.,
No. 6 ISBN:0-313-27500-9, ISBN13: 978-0-313-27500-5.
Dewey:304.6/4/08968. LCCN:91-000002.
         Audience: **u,f.** *Choice, 1992.*

Torres, Eliseo   GR111.M49 T6
The Folk Healer: The Mexican-American Tradition of
Curanderismo. Carolyn Banks & Clark Magruder (Editors).
Trade Paper. Nieves Press. Albuquerque, NM. 1984. 64p.
ISBN:0-9612008-1-2, ISBN13: 978-0-9612008-1-7.
Dewey:615.882.
         Audience: **l,u.**

Torres, Eliseo &   RZ407.T67 2004
   Sawyer, Tim
Curandero: A Life in Mexican Folk Healing. Trade Paper.
University of New Mexico Press. Albuquerque, NM. 2005.
184p. ISBN:0-8263-3640-X, ISBN13: 978-0-8263-3640-8.
Dewey:615.8/8/0972. LCCN:2004-020692.
         Audience: **l,u.**

Trotter, Robert T. 2nd   GR111.M49T76 1997
   & Chavira, Juan A.
Curanderismo: Mexican American Folk Healing. Ed. 2. Luis D.
León (Foreword by). Paper Text. University of Georgia Press.

Athens, GA. 1997. 224p. ISBN:0-8203-1962-7, ISBN13: 978-0-8203-1962-9. Dewey:615.8/82/0896872073. LCCN:97-015784.

Audience: **l,u.**

Science and Technology > Sports

Fainaru, Steve &   **GV863.25.A1**
  Sanchez, Ray
The Duke of Havana: Baseball, Cuba, and the Search for the American Dream. Trade Cloth. DIANE Publishing Company.

Collingdale, PA. 2001. 338p. ISBN:0-7567-5550-6, ISBN13: 978-0-7567-5550-8. Dewey:796.357/097291.

Audience: **l.** *Choice, 2002.*

Wilson, Nick C.   **GV865.A1.W545 2005**
Early Latino Ballplayers in the United States: Major, Minor and Negro Leagues, 1901-1949. Cloth Text. McFarland & Company, Incorporated Publishers. Jefferson, NC. 2005. 208p. ISBN:0-7864-2012-X, ISBN13: 978-0-7864-2012-4. Dewey:796.357/092/368073 B. LCCN:2005-004471.

Audience: **g,l.**

Formats: Web: ☐ Ebook: 🄴 CD/DVD-ROM: 💨 BCL3: 𝓑

MEDIEVAL STUDIES

The scope of medieval studies was limited geographically to Europe and the Near East. The time period used was the traditional one of the fall of the Roman Empire to the beginning of the Renaissance or Early Modern period. Major fields explored included history, religion, archaeology, economics, politics, literature, and philosophy, among others.

Books were selected with the lower division undergraduate in mind. More advanced works were selected for key topics where no work specific to undergraduates was available. While this section highlights interdisciplinary approaches, books written from a specific disciplinary perspective were included when appropriate. Effort was made to select recent publications, especially in covering topics that have grown in prominence in the last twenty years, but, as with many historical topics, older titles are often still classics in the field.

— Heather Ward

Crosby, Everett U.   **Z6203**
Medieval Studies: A Bibliographical Guide. Trade Cloth.
Garland Publishing, Inc. New York, NY. 1985. 1156p. Reference
Library of the Humanities, Vol. 427 ISBN:0-8240-9107-8,
ISBN13: 978-0-8240-9107-1. Dewey:016.9401.
LCCN:83-048259.

Audience: **u,f.**

Jones, Malcolm   **N6763**
The Secret Middle Ages: Discovering the Real Medieval World.
Trade Cloth. Greenwood Publishing Group, Inc. Portsmouth,
NH. 2003. 288p. ISBN:0-275-97980-6, ISBN13:
978-0-275-97980-5. Dewey:709/.02. LCCN:2002-193139.
Audience: **g,l,u,f.** *Choice, 2003.*

Jordan, William C.   **D114.D5 2004**
Dictionary of the Middle Ages: Supplement I. Trade Cloth.
Thomson Gale. Farmington Hills, MI. 1905. 600p.
ISBN:0-684-80642-8, ISBN13: 978-0-684-80642-6.
Dewey:909.07. LCCN:2004-540989.
Audience: **g,l,u,f.** *Choice, 2004.*

Linehan, Peter &   **CB351**
  Nelson, Janet L. (Editors)
The Medieval World. Trade Paper. Routledge. New York, NY.
2003. 768p. ISBN:0-415-30234-X, ISBN13: 978-0-415-30234-0.
Dewey:909/.07.

Audience: **l,u,f.**

Powell, James M.   **D116.M4 1992**
  (Editor)
Medieval Studies: An Introduction. Ed. 2. Cloth Text. Syracuse
University Press. Syracuse, NY. 1992. 500p.
ISBN:0-8156-2555-3, ISBN13: 978-0-8156-2555-1.
Dewey:940.1/072. LCCN:91-031160.

Audience: **l,u,f.**

Ross, James B. &   **PN6014**
  McLaughlin, Mary M. (Editors)
Portable Medieval Reader. Trade Paper. Penguin Group (USA)
Inc. New York, NY. 1977. 704p. Portable Library, No. 46
ISBN:0-14-015046-3, ISBN13: 978-0-14-015046-9.
Dewey:808.8/032. LCCN:77-001658.

Audience: **g,l,u,f.**

Strayer, Joseph R.   **D114.D5 1982**
  (Editor)
Dictionary of the Middle Ages, Set. American Council of
Learned Societies Staff (Contribution by). Trade Cloth. Thomson
Gale. Farmington Hills, MI. 1989. 8725p. ISBN:0-684-19073-7,
ISBN13: 978-0-684-19073-0. Dewey:909.07. LCCN:82-005904.
Audience: **g,l,u,f.** *B* *Choice, 1989.*

Vauchez, Andre (Editor)   **CB351.D5413 2000**
Encyclopedia of Middle Ages, Set. Paper over Boards. Fitzroy
Dearborn Publishers, Inc. Chicago, IL. 2001. 1642p.
ISBN:1-57958-282-6, ISBN13: 978-1-57958-282-1.
Dewey:909.07/03. LCCN:2002-728269.
Audience: **l,u,f.** *Choice, 2001.*

Archaeology

Austin, David & Alcock,   **DJK23.F76 1990**
  Leslie (Editors)
From the Baltic to the Black Sea: Studies in Medieval
Archaelogy. Paper over Boards. Routledge. New York, NY.

1990. 344p. One World Archaeology Ser., No. 18
ISBN:0-04-445119-9, ISBN13: 978-0-04-445119-8. Dewey:947.
LCCN:90-030809.

Audience: **u,f.**

Bischoff, Bernhard &   **Z114 .B5713 1990**
  Cóinín, Dáibhí Ó
Latin Palaeography: Antiquity and the Middle Ages. David Ganz
(Translator). Trade Paper. Cambridge University Press. New
York, NY. 1990. 303p. ISBN:0-521-36726-3, ISBN13:
978-0-521-36726-4. Dewey:417/.7. LCCN:88-034649.
Audience: **u,f.**

Boas, Adrian   **D183.B63 1999**
Crusader Archaeology: The Material Culture of the Latin East.
Paper over Boards. Routledge. New York, NY. 1999. 296p.
ISBN:0-415-17361-2, ISBN13: 978-0-415-17361-2.
Dewey:956/.014. LCCN:98-041042.
Audience: **g,l,u,f.** *Choice, 2000.*

Carver, Martin   **DA155.C38 1998**
Sutton Hoo: Burial Ground of Kings. Trade Cloth. University of
Pennsylvania Press. Philadelphia, PA. 1998. 224p.
ISBN:0-8122-3455-3, ISBN13: 978-0-8122-3455-8.
Dewey:936.2/646. LCCN:98-016434.
Audience: **g,l,u,f.** *Choice, 1999.*

Clarke, Helen   **DA175 .C58 1984**
The Archaeology of Medieval England. Trade Cloth. British
Museum Press. London, 1984. 224p. ISBN:0-7141-8058-0,
ISBN13: 978-0-7141-8058-8. Dewey:942. LCCN:84-213298.
Audience: **g,u,f.**

Crabtree, Pamela   **D125.M42 2001**
  (Editor)
Medieval Archaeology: An Encyclopedia. Trade Cloth. Garland
Publishing, Inc. New York, NY. 2000. 608p. Encyclopedias of
the Middle Ages Ser., Vol. 4 ISBN:0-8153-1286-5, ISBN13:
978-0-8153-1286-4. Dewey:936. LCCN:00-056156.
Audience: **g,l,u,f.**

Gerrard, Christopher   **DA90.G46 2002**
Medieval Archaeology: Understanding Traditions and
Contemporary Approaches. Paper over Boards. Routledge. New
York, NY. 2002. 320p. ISBN:0-415-23462-X, ISBN13:
978-0-415-23462-7. Dewey:941. LCCN:2002-075165.
Audience: **u,f.**

Architecture

Bony, Jean   **NA5543**
French Gothic Architecture of the Twelfth and Thirteenth
Centuries. Trade Paper. University of California Press. Berkeley,
CA. 1985. 640p. California Studies in the History of Art, No.
XX ISBN:0-520-05586-1, ISBN13: 978-0-520-05586-5.
Dewey:726/.5/0944. LCCN:74-082842.
Audience: **l,u.** *B*

Prache, Anne   **NA4830.P6813 2000**
Cathedrals of Europe. Trade Cloth. Cornell University Press.
Ithaca, NY. 2000. 290p. ISBN:0-8014-3781-4, ISBN13:
978-0-8014-3781-6. Dewey:726.6/094. LCCN:00-029507.
Audience: **g,l,u.** *Choice, 2001.*

Schultz, Juergen   **NA7514.623.V46S33**
The New Palaces of Medieval Venice. Trade Cloth.
Pennsylvania State University Press. University Park, PA. 2004.

412p. ISBN:0-271-02351-1, ISBN13: 978-0-271-02351-9.
Dewey:728.8/0945/310902. LCCN:2003-026259.
Audience: **l,u,f.** *Choice, 2005.*

Stoddard, Whitney S.   **N6843 .S7 1972**
Art and Architecture in Medieval France: Medieval Architecture,
Sculpture, Stained Glass, Manuscripts, the Art of the Church
Treasuries. Trade Paper. Westview Press. Boulder, CO. 1972.
432p. Icon Editions Ser. ISBN:0-06-430022-6, ISBN13:
978-0-06-430022-3. Dewey:726/.0944. LCCN:72-186590.
Audience: **g,l,u,f.**

Webb, Geoffrey   **F491.R76**
  Fairbank
Architecture in Britain: The Middle Ages. Paper Text. Textbook
Publishers. Temecula, CA. 2003. xxi, 234p.
ISBN:0-7581-6621-4, ISBN13: 978-0-7581-6621-0.
Dewey:917.71.
Audience: **l,u.** *B*

Art History

Norman, Diana   **ND621.S6N67 2003**
Painting in Late Medieval and Renaissance Siena (1260-1555).
Cloth over Boards. Yale University Press. Cumberland, RI.
2003. 352p. ISBN:0-300-09933-9, ISBN13: 978-0-300-09933-1.
Dewey:759/.558. LCCN:2002-155490.
Audience: **g,l,u,f.** *Choice, 2004.*

Olson, Mary C.   **PR179.T48O47 2002**
Fair and Varied Forms: Visual Textuality in Medieval
Illuminated Manuscripts. Paper over Boards. Routledge. New
York, NY. 2002. 260p. Studies in Medieval History and Culture,
Vol. 15 ISBN:0-415-94267-5, ISBN13: 978-0-415-94267-6.
Dewey:829.09. LCCN:2002-006359.
Audience: **u,f.**

Stoddard, Whitney S.   **N6843 .S7 1972**
Art and Architecture in Medieval France: Medieval Architecture,
Sculpture, Stained Glass, Manuscripts, the Art of the Church
Treasuries. Trade Paper. Westview Press. Boulder, CO. 1972.
432p. Icon Editions Ser. ISBN:0-06-430022-6, ISBN13:
978-0-06-430022-3. Dewey:726/.0944. LCCN:72-186590.
Audience: **g,l,u,f.**

Stokstad, Marilyn   **N5970.S75 2004**
Medieval Art. Ed. 2. Trade Paper. Westview Press. Boulder, CO.
2004. 432p. ISBN:0-8133-4114-0, ISBN13: 978-0-8133-4114-9.
Dewey:709/.02 19. LCCN:2003-006643.
Audience: **g,l,u,f.**

Chivalry

Duby, Georges   **DA228.M7**
William Marshal: The Flower of Chivalry. Richard Howard
(Translator). Trade Paper. Knopf Publishing Group. New York,
NY. 1987. 160p. ISBN:0-394-75154-X, ISBN13:
978-0-394-75154-2. Dewey:942.03/4/0924 B. LCCN:85-042837.
Audience: **g.** *B*

Duby, Georges   **HN11**
The Chivalrous Society. Cynthia Postan (Translator). Trade
Cloth. University of California Press. Berkeley, CA. 1981. 254p.
ISBN:0-520-04271-9, ISBN13: 978-0-520-04271-1.
Dewey:309.1/4/01. LCCN:74-081431.
Audience: **g,l,u.** *B*

Jaeger, C. Stephen   **GT3520.J34 1985**
The Origins of Courtliness: Civilizing Trends and the Formation
of Courtly Ideals, 939-1210. Book, Other. University of
Pennsylvania Press. Philadelphia, PA. 1985. 340p. Middle Ages
Ser. ISBN:0-8122-1307-6, ISBN13: 978-0-8122-1307-2.
Dewey:940.1. LCCN:84-015276.
Audience: **u,f.** *Choice, 1985.*

Keen, Maurice   **CR4513.K44 2005**
Chivalry. Trade Paper. Yale University Press. Cumberland, RI.
2005. 352p. ISBN:0-300-10767-6, ISBN13: 978-0-300-10767-8.
Dewey:394.7094.
Audience: **g,l,u.**

Mathew, Gervase   **DA235**
Court of Richard II. Norton. 1969.
Audience: **l,u.**

Crusades

Boas, Adrian   **D183.B63 1999**
Crusader Archaeology: The Material Culture of the Latin East.
Paper over Boards. Routledge. New York, NY. 1999. 296p.
ISBN:0-415-17361-2, ISBN13: 978-0-415-17361-2.
Dewey:956/.014. LCCN:98-041042.
Audience: **g,l,u,f.** *Choice, 2000.*

France, John   **D160.F73 1999**
Western Warfare in the Age of the Crusades, 1000-1300. Trade
Cloth. Cornell University Press. Ithaca, NY. 1999. 344p.
ISBN:0-8014-3671-0, ISBN13: 978-0-8014-3671-0.
Dewey:940.1/8. LCCN:98-048997.
Audience: **l,u,f.** *Choice, 1999.*

Housley, Norman   **D202.H68 1992**
The Later Crusades, 1274-1580: From Lyons to Alcazar. Paper
Text. Oxford University Press, Inc. New York, NY. 1992. 538p.
ISBN:0-19-822136-3, ISBN13: 978-0-19-822136-4.
Dewey:940.1. LCCN:91-022260.
Audience: **u,f.** *Choice, 1993.*

Kedar, Benjamin Z.   **BV2625.K43 1984**
Crusade and Mission. Trade Cloth. Princeton University Press.
Princeton, NJ. 1984. 259p. ISBN:0-691-05424-X, ISBN13:
978-0-691-05424-7. Dewey:266/.2/0917671. LCCN:84-003403.
Audience: **u,f.**

Maalouf, Amin   **D157**
The Crusades Through Arab Eyes. UK-Trade Paper. Knopf
Publishing Group. New York, NY. 1989. 352p.
ISBN:0-8052-0898-4, ISBN13: 978-0-8052-0898-6.
Dewey:909.07.
Audience: **g,l,u.**

Madden, Thomas   **D157.C775 2004**
  (Editor)
Crusades: The Illustrated History. Trade Cloth. University of
Michigan Press. Chicago, IL. 2004. 224p. ISBN:0-472-11463-8,
ISBN13: 978-0-472-11463-4. Dewey:909.07.
LCCN:2004-304592.
Audience: **g,l.** *Choice, 2005.*

Mayer, Hans E.   **D157.M3813 1988**
The Crusades. Ed. 2. John Gillingham (Translator). Paper Text.
Oxford University Press, Inc. New York, NY. 1988. 368p.
ISBN:0-19-873097-7, ISBN13: 978-0-19-873097-2.
Dewey:940.1/8. LCCN:87-024795.
Audience: **l,u.**

Setton, Kenneth M.   D157.S482 1989
   (Editor), et al.
A History of the Crusades: The Impact of the Crusades on
Europe. Harry W. Hazard & Norman P. Zacour (Editors). Trade
Paper. University of Wisconsin Press. Chicago, IL. 1990. 728p.
ISBN:0-299-10744-2, ISBN13: 978-0-299-10744-4.
Dewey:940.1/8.

Audience: **u,f.**

Setton, Kenneth M.   D157.S482 1985
   (Editor), et al.
A History of the Crusades: The Impact of the Crusades on the
near East. Norman P. Zacour & Harry W. Hazard (Editors).
Trade Paper. University of Wisconsin Press. Chicago, IL. 1985.
624p. ISBN:0-299-09144-9, ISBN13: 978-0-299-09144-6.
Dewey:909.07.

Audience: **u,f.**

Daily Life

Adamson, Melitta Weiss   TX641
Food in Medieval Times. Cloth Text. Greenwood Publishing
Group, Inc. Portsmouth, NH. 2004. 288p. Food through History
Ser. ISBN:0-313-32147-7, ISBN13: 978-0-313-32147-4.
Dewey:641.3/0094/0902. LCCN:2004-014054.
                         Audience: **g,l,u,f.** *Choice, 2005.*

Aries, Philippe (Editor),   GT2400
   et al.
A History of Private Life: From Pagan Rome to Byzantium, Vol.
I. Georges Duby & Paul Veyne (Editors), Arthur Goldhammer
(Translator). Trade Paper. Harvard University Press. Cambridge,
MA. 1992. 704p. History of Private Life Ser.
ISBN:0-674-39974-9, ISBN13: 978-0-674-39974-7.
Dewey:390/.009.

Audience: **g.**

Duby, Georges & Aries,   CB245
   Philippe (Editors)
A History of Private Life: Revelations of the Medieval World,
Vol. 2. Arthur Goldhammer (Translator). Trade Cloth. Harvard
University Press. Cambridge, MA. 1988. 688p. History of
Private Life Ser., Vol. 2 ISBN:0-674-39976-5, ISBN13:
978-0-674-39976-1. Dewey:909/.09821. LCCN:86-018286.

Audience: **l,u,f.**

Duckett, Eleanor S.   D123.D8
Death and Life in the Tenth Century. Trade Paper. University of
Michigan Press. Chicago, IL. 1989. 376p. Ann Arbor Paperback
Ser. ISBN:0-472-06172-0, ISBN13: 978-0-472-06172-3.
Dewey:940.14.

Audience: **l,u.**

Goody, Jack   HQ611 .G66 1983
The Development of the Family and Marriage in Europe. Lyndal
Roper (Contribution by). Trade Paper. Cambridge University
Press. New York, NY. 1983. 320p. Past and Present Publications
ISBN:0-521-28925-4, ISBN13: 978-0-521-28925-2.
Dewey:306.8/1/094. LCCN:82-023465.

Audience: **u,f.**

Herlihy, David   HQ611.H46 1985
Medieval Households. Trade Cloth. Harvard University Press.
Cambridge, MA. 1985. 272p. Studies in Cultural History, No. 2
ISBN:0-674-56375-1, ISBN13: 978-0-674-56375-9.
Dewey:306.8/5/094. LCCN:85-005439.
                         Audience: **l,u.** *Choice, 1986.*

Holmes, Urban T. Jr. &   GT120 .H64 1980
   Neckam, Alexander
Daily Living in the Twelfth Century: Based on the Observations
of Alexander Neckam in London and Paris. Trade Cloth.
Greenwood Publishing Group, Inc. Portsmouth, NH. 1980. 337p.
ISBN:0-313-22796-9, ISBN13: 978-0-313-22796-7.
Dewey:940.1/82. LCCN:80-019991.

Audience: **l,u.**

Marques, A. H. de   DP532.3 .M3413
   Oliveira
Daily Life in Portugal in the Late Middle Ages. S. S. Wyatt
(Translator), Vitor Andre (Illustrator). Trade Paper. University of
Wisconsin Press. Chicago, IL. 1971. 372p. ISBN:0-299-05584-1,
ISBN13: 978-0-299-05584-4. Dewey:914.690.
LCCN:78-106040.

Audience: **l,u,f.**

Riche, Pierre   DC33.2.R5413
Daily Life in the World of Charlemagne. Ed. 2. Jo Ann
McNamara (Translator). Book, Other. University of
Pennsylvania Press. Philadelphia, PA. 1978. 352p. Middle Ages
Ser. ISBN:0-8122-1096-4, ISBN13: 978-0-8122-1096-5.
Dewey:944/.01. LCCN:78-053330.
                         Audience: **g,l,u,f.** *B*

Sheehan, Michael M. &   HQ572
   Murray, Jacqueline (Editors)
Domestic Society in Medieval Europe: A Select Bibliography.
Trade Paper. Pontifical Institute of Mediaeval Studies,
Department of Publications. Toronto, ON. 1990. vi, 58p.
ISBN:0-88844-413-3, ISBN13: 978-0-88844-413-4.
Dewey:016.3068/094/0902. LCCN:91-132438.

Audience: **l,u,f.**

Economics

De Roover, Raymond A.   HG3110.B7 D4
Money, Banking and Credit in Mediaeval Bruges. Trade Cloth.
Medieval Academy of America. Cambridge, MA. 1983.
Medieval Academy Bks., No. 51 ISBN:0-910956-25-1, ISBN13:
978-0-910956-25-3. Dewey:332.1.

Audience: **g,l,u,f.**

Duby, Georges   HC240
The Early Growth of the European Economy: Warriors and
Peasants from the Seventh to the Twelfth Century. Howard B.
Clarke (Translator). Trade Paper. Cornell University Press.
Ithaca, NY. 1978. 292p. World Economic History Ser.
ISBN:0-8014-9169-X, ISBN13: 978-0-8014-9169-6.
Dewey:330.9/4/01. LCCN:73-016955.

Audience: **u,f.**

Duby, Georges   HD1917.D813
Rural Economy and Country Life in the Medieval West. Cynthia
Postan (Translator). Paper Text. University of South Carolina
Press. Columbia, SC. 1981. xvi, 615p. ISBN:0-87249-347-4,
ISBN13: 978-0-87249-347-6. Dewey:338.1. LCCN:68-020530.
                         Audience: **u,f.** *B*

Dyer, Christopher   HC254
Making a Living in the Middle Ages: The People of Britain
850-1520. Trade Paper. Yale University Press. Cumberland, RI.
2003. 424p. The New Economic History of Britain Seri Ser.
ISBN:0-300-10191-0, ISBN13: 978-0-300-10191-1.
Dewey:330.941/03.
                         Audience: **g,l,u,f.** *Choice, 2002.*

Favier, Jean   **HF3495.F3813 1998**
Gold and Spices: The Rise of Commerce in the Middle Ages.
Caroline Higgitt (Translator). Trade Cloth. Holmes & Meier
Publishers, Inc. Teaneck, NJ. 1998. 390p. ISBN:0-8419-1232-7,
ISBN13: 978-0-8419-1232-8. Dewey:382/.094/00902.
LCCN:98-014166.
         Audience: **l,u.** *Choice, 1999.*

Gilchrist, J. T.   **BR115.E3.G5 1969**
The Church and Economic Activity in the Middle Ages. Trade
Cloth. Macmillan Publishing Company, Inc. Old Tappan, NJ.
1969. xi, 328p. ISBN:0-333-05496-2, ISBN13:
978-0-333-05496-3. Dewey:261.8/5/0902. LCCN:69-013685.
         Audience: **u,f.**

Kowaleski, Maryanne   **HF3520.E95 K68 1995**
Local Markets and Regional Trade in Medieval Exeter. Trade
Cloth. Cambridge University Press. New York, NY. 1995. 458p.
ISBN:0-521-33371-7, ISBN13: 978-0-521-33371-9.
Dewey:381.1/8/0942356. LCCN:94-008396.
         Audience: **u,f.** *Choice, 1996.*

Le Goff, Jacques   **HC41.L4313 1988**
Your Money or Your Life: Economy and Religion in the Middle
Ages. Patricia M. Ranum (Translator). Trade Cloth. Zone Books.
Brooklyn, NY. 1988. 127p. ISBN:0-942299-14-0, ISBN13:
978-0-942299-14-4. Dewey:330.94/01. LCCN:87-025248.
         Audience: **u,f.**

Lopez, Robert S. &   **HF395.M43 2001**
  Raymond, Irving W. (Translators)
Medieval Trade in the Mediterranean World: Illustrative
Documents. Ed. 2. Olivia Remie Constable (Foreword by).
Trade Cloth. Columbia University Press. New York, NY. 2001.
496p. Records of Western Civilization Ser. ISBN:0-231-12356-6,
ISBN13: 978-0-231-12356-3. Dewey:382/.09182/2.
LCCN:2002-278336.
         Audience: **l,u,f.**

Masschaele, James   **HF3515.M37 1997**
Peasants, Merchants and Markets: Inland Trade in Medieval
England, 1150-1350. Cloth over Boards. Palgrave Macmillan.
New York, NY. 1997. 288p. ISBN:0-312-16035-6, ISBN13:
978-0-312-16035-7. Dewey:381/.0942. LCCN:96-052279.
         Audience: **l,u,f.** *Choice, 1998.*

Postan, M. M. (Editor)   **HD1917**
The Cambridge Economic History of Europe from the Decline
of the Roman Empire: The Agrarian Life of the Middle Ages.
Ed. 2. Cloth Text. Cambridge University Press. New York, NY.
1966. 888p. The Cambridge Economic History of Europe Ser.,
Vol. 1 ISBN:0-521-04505-3, ISBN13: 978-0-521-04505-6.
Dewey:338.1/094/0902.
         Audience: **l,u.**

Postan, M. M. & Miller,   **HC240**
  E (Editors)
The Cambridge Economic History of Europe: Trade and
Industry in the Middle Ages. Ed. 2. Cloth Text. Cambridge
University Press. New York, NY. 1987. 1024p. The Cambridge
Economic History of Europe Ser. ISBN:0-521-08709-0, ISBN13:
978-0-521-08709-4. Dewey:330.94.
         Audience: **l,u.**

Postan, M. M. (Editor),   **HC240**
  et al.
The Cambridge Economic History of Europe from the Decline
of the Roman Empire: Economic Organisation and Policies in
the Middle Ages. E. E. Rich & E Miller (Editors). Trade Cloth.

Cambridge University Press. New York, NY. 1963. 712p. The
Cambridge Economic History of Europe Ser.
ISBN:0-521-04506-1, ISBN13: 978-0-521-04506-3.
Dewey:338.1/094/0902.
         Audience: **l,u.**

Spufford, Peter   **HG925**
Money and Its Use in Medieval Europe. Trade Paper.
Cambridge University Press. New York, NY. 1989. 488p.
ISBN:0-521-37590-8, ISBN13: 978-0-521-37590-0.
Dewey:332.4/94.
         Audience: **l,u,f.** *Choice, 1989.*

Spufford, Peter   **HF3505.15**
Power and Profit: The Merchant in Medieval Europe. Trade
Cloth. Thames & Hudson. New York, NY. 2003. 432p.
ISBN:0-500-25118-5, ISBN13: 978-0-500-25118-8.
Dewey:382/.094. LCCN:2002-103867.
         Audience: **g,l,u,f.** *Choice, 2003.*

Education

De Ridder-Symoens,   **LA177 .U53 1991**
  Hilde (Editor)
A History of the University in Europe: Universities in the
Middle Ages. Trade Cloth. Cambridge University Press. New
York, NY. 1991. 534p. A History of the University in Europe
Ser. ISBN:0-521-36105-2, ISBN13: 978-0-521-36105-7.
Dewey:378.4/09/02. LCCN:90-033558.
         Audience: **u,f.**

Ferruolo, Stephen C.   **LF2165.F47 1985**
The Origins of the University: The Schools of Paris and Their
Critics, 1100-1215. Trade Cloth. Stanford University Press. Palo
Alto, CA. 1985. 392p. ISBN:0-8047-1266-2, ISBN13:
978-0-8047-1266-8. Dewey:378.44/361. LCCN:84-040445.
         Audience: **u,f.** *Choice, 1986.*

Haskins, Charles   **LA177.H3 2002**
  Homer
The Rise of Universities. Trade Paper. Transaction Publishers.
Somerset, NJ. 2001. 134p. Foundations of Higher Education Ser.
ISBN:0-7658-0895-1, ISBN13: 978-0-7658-0895-0.
Dewey:378/.009. LCCN:2001-048078.
         Audience: **l,u.**

Murphy, James J.   **PN173.M8 2001**
Rhetoric in the Middle Ages: A History of Rhetorical Theory
from Saint Augustine to the Renaissance. Trade Cloth. M R T S.
Tempe, AZ. 2000. xiv, 399p. ISBN:0-86698-269-8, ISBN13:
978-0-86698-269-6. Dewey:808/.0094/0902.
LCCN:2001-268760.
         Audience: **u,f.**

Orme, Nicholas   **LA631.3**
Medieval Schools: Roman Britain to Renaissance England.
Cloth over Boards. Yale University Press. Cumberland, RI.
2006. 432p. ISBN:0-300-11102-9, ISBN13: 978-0-300-11102-6.
Dewey:370.942/09031. LCCN:2006-004516.
         Audience: **u,f.**

Rashdall, Hastings;   **LA177.R25 1987**
  Powicke, Frederick M; Emden, A B
The Universities of Europe in the Middle Ages, Vol. I:
Salerno-Bologna-Paris. Ed. 2. Frederick M. Powicke (Editor) ;
A. B. Emden (Editor). Oxford University Press, Inc. 1987.
ISBN:0-19-822981-X, ISBN13: 978-0-19-822981-0.
         Audience: **u,f.**

Rashdall, Hastings;   **LA177.R25 1987**
  Powicke, Frederick M; Emden, A B
The Universities of Europe in the Middle Ages, Vol. II:
Italy-Spain-France-Germany-Scotland, etc. Frederick M.
Powicke (Editor) ; A. B. Emden (Editor). Oxford University
Press, Inc. 1987. ISBN:0-19-822982-8, ISBN13:
978-0-19-822982-7.

Audience: **u,f.**

Rashdall, Hastings;   **LA177.R25 1987**
  Powicke, Frederick M; Emden, A B
The Universities of Europe in the Middle Ages, Vol. III: English
Universities - Student Life. Frederick M. Powicke (Editor) ; A.
B. Emden (Editor). Oxford University Press, Inc. 1987.
ISBN:0-19-822983-6, ISBN13: 978-0-19-822983-4.

Audience: **u,f.**

Riche, Pierre   **LA96**
Education and Culture in the Barbarian West: Sixth Through
Eighth Centuries. J. J. Contreni (Translator). Paper Text.
University of South Carolina Press. Columbia, SC. 1978. 594p.
ISBN:0-87249-376-8, ISBN13: 978-0-87249-376-6.
Dewey:370.94. LCCN:76-025249.

Audience: **u,f.**

Gender

Amt, Emilie (Editor)   **HQ1143.W65 1993**
Women's Lives in Medieval Europe: A Sourcebook. UK-B
Format Paperback. Routledge. New York, NY. 1992. 360p.
ISBN:0-415-90628-8, ISBN13: 978-0-415-90628-9.
Dewey:305.42094. LCCN:92-012815.

Audience: **g,l,u,f.**

Anderson, Bonnie S. &   **HQ1587.A53 2000**
  Zinsser, Judith P.
A History of Their Own: Women in Europe from Prehistory to
the Present. Paper Text. Oxford University Press, Inc. New
York, NY. 1999. 601p. ISBN:0-19-512839-7, ISBN13:
978-0-19-512839-0. Dewey:305.4/094. LCCN:98-046743.

Audience: **g,l,u,f.** *Choice, 1989.*

Atkinson, Clarissa W.   **HQ759.A84 1991**
The Oldest Vocation: Christian Motherhood in the Middle Ages.
Book, Other. Cornell University Press. Ithaca, NY. 1991. 288p.
ISBN:0-8014-2071-7, ISBN13: 978-0-8014-2071-9.
Dewey:306.874/3. LCCN:91-055071.

Audience: **g.** *Choice, 1992.*

Bitel, Lisa M.   **HQ1143**
Women in Early Medieval Europe, 400-1100. Cloth Text.
Cambridge University Press. New York, NY. 2002. 344p.
Cambridge Medieval Textbooks Ser. ISBN:0-521-59207-0,
ISBN13: 978-0-521-59207-9. Dewey:305.42/094/0902.
LCCN:2003-544740.

Audience: **u,f.**

Blamires, Alcuin   **PR1912.A2 W65 1992**
  (Editor)
Woman Defamed and Woman Defended: An Anthology of
Medieval Texts. Karen Pratt & C. W. Marx (Contribution by).
Trade Paper. Oxford University Press, Inc. New York, NY. 1992.
342p. ISBN:0-19-871039-9, ISBN13: 978-0-19-871039-4.
Dewey:808. LCCN:92-003338.

Audience: **u,f.**

Bullough, Vern L. &   **HQ14.H35 1996**
  Brundage, James A. (Editors)
Handbook of Medieval Sexuality: A Book of Essays. Cloth Text.
Garland Publishing, Inc. New York, NY. 1996. 464p. Reference
Library of the Humanities, Vol. 1696 ISBN:0-8153-1287-3,
ISBN13: 978-0-8153-1287-1. Dewey:306.7/09/02.
LCCN:95-052021.

Audience: **u,f.**

Chibnall, Marjorie   **DA198.6**
The Empress Matilda: Queen Consort, Queen Mother and Lady
of the English. Trade Paper. Blackwell Publishing, Inc. Malden,
MA. 1993. 256p. ISBN:0-631-19028-7, ISBN13:
978-0-631-19028-8. Dewey:942.04/5/092 B. LCCN:91-012692.

Audience: **u,f.** *Choice, 1992.*

Dronke, Peter   **PN671 .D7 1984**
Women Writers of the Middle Ages: A Critical Study of Texts
from Perpetua to Marguerite Porete. Trade Paper. Cambridge
University Press. New York, NY. 1984. 348p.
ISBN:0-521-27573-3, ISBN13: 978-0-521-27573-6.
Dewey:809/.89287. LCCN:83-007456.

Audience: **l,u,f.** *B*

Duby, Georges   **HQ513.D8 1991**
Medieval Marriage: Two Models from Twelfth-Century France.
Elborg Forster (Translator). Trade Paper. Johns Hopkins
University Press. Baltimore, MD. 1986. 160p. Johns Hopkins
Symposia in Comparative History Ser., Vol. 11
ISBN:0-8018-4319-7, ISBN13: 978-0-8018-4319-8.
Dewey:306.810944. LCCN:77-017255.

Audience: **u,f.**

Duby, Georges (Editor),   **HQ1121**
  et al.
A History of Women: From Ancient Goddesses to Christian
Saints. Michelle Perrott & Pauline S. Pantel (Editors), Arthur
Goldhammer (Translator). Trade Paper. Harvard University
Press. Cambridge, MA. 1994. 600p. History of Women in the
West Ser. ISBN:0-674-40369-X, ISBN13: 978-0-674-40369-7.
Dewey:305.4094. LCCN:91-034134.

Audience: **g,l,u.**

Erler, Mary Carpenter   **HQ1143.G46 2003**
  & Kowaleski, Maryanne (Editors)
Gendering the Master Narrative: Women and Power in the
Middle Ages. Trade Cloth. Cornell University Press. Ithaca, NY.
2003. 288p. ISBN:0-8014-4112-9, ISBN13: 978-0-8014-4112-7.
Dewey:305.4/09/02. LCCN:2002-151956.

Audience: **u,f.**

Fell, Christine   **HQ1147.G7F44 1987**
Women in Anglo-Saxon England. Paper Text. Blackwell
Publishing, Inc. Malden, MA. 1987. 208p. ISBN:0-631-14924-4,
ISBN13: 978-0-631-14924-8. Dewey:305.4/2/0942.
LCCN:85-030625.

Audience: **u,f.**

Ferrante, Joan M.   **PN682.W6F39 1997**
To the Glory of Her Sex: Women's Roles in the Composition of
Medieval Texts. Trade Cloth. Indiana University Press.
Bloomington, IN. 1997. 310p. Women of Letters Ser.
ISBN:0-253-33254-0, ISBN13: 978-0-253-33254-7.
Dewey:809/.89287/0902. LCCN:96-043546.

Audience: **u,f.** *Choice, 1998.*

Gies, Joseph   HQ1143
Women in the Middle Ages. Trade Paper. HarperCollins
Publishers. New York, NY. 1991. 272p. ISBN:0-06-092304-0,
ISBN13: 978-0-06-092304-4. Dewey:301.41/2/0902.
                                    Audience: **g,l.**

Gold, Penny S.   HQ1147.F7
The Lady and the Virgin: Image, Attitude, and Experience in
Twelfth-Century France. Catherine R. Stimpson (Foreword by).
Trade Paper. University of Chicago Press. Chicago, IL. 1987.
206p. Women in Culture and Society Ser. ISBN:0-226-30088-9,
ISBN13: 978-0-226-30088-7. Dewey:305.42. LCCN:84-023701.
                                    Audience: **u,f.**

Grossman, Avraham   BM729.W6G7613 2004
Pious and Rebellious: Jewish Women in Medieval Europe. Trade
Cloth. University Press of New England. Lebanon, NH. 2004.
352p. Tauber Institute for the Study of European Jewry Ser.
ISBN:1-58465-391-4, ISBN13: 978-1-58465-391-2.
Dewey:305.48/892404/0902. LCCN:2004-003029.
                          Audience: **u,f.** *Choice, 2005.*

Jantzen, Grace M.   BV5083 .J36 1995
Power, Gender and Christian Mysticism. Trade Cloth.
Cambridge University Press. New York, NY. 1995. 403p.
Studies in Ideology and Religion, No. 8 ISBN:0-521-47376-4,
ISBN13: 978-0-521-47376-7. Dewey:248.2/2. LCCN:94-044562.
                          Audience: **u,f.** *Choice, 1996.*

Jochens, Jenny   HQ1147.N8J63 1995
Women in Old Norse Society. Book, Other. Cornell University
Press. Ithaca, NY. 1996. 328p. ISBN:0-8014-3165-4, ISBN13:
978-0-8014-3165-4. Dewey:305.4/09/02. LCCN:95-031506.
                       Audience: **g,l,u,f.** *Choice, 1996.*

Klapisch-Zuber,   HQ1121.S79513 1992
  Christiane (Editor), et al.
A History of Women in the West: Silences of the Middle Ages.
Georges Duby & Michelle Perrot (Editors). Trade Cloth.
Harvard University Press. Cambridge, MA. 1992. 592p. Women
in the West Ser. ISBN:0-674-40371-1, ISBN13:
978-0-674-40371-0. Dewey:305.4094. LCCN:91-034134.
                                    Audience: **g,l,u.**

Leyser, Henrietta   HQ1147.G7L49 1995
Medieval Women: A Social History of Women in England,
450-1500. Cloth Text. Palgrave Macmillan. New York, NY.
1995. 352p. ISBN:0-312-12934-3, ISBN13: 978-0-312-12934-7.
Dewey:305.4/0942/0902. LCCN:95-221665.
                       Audience: **g,l,u.** *Choice, 1996.*

Mate, Mavis E.   HQ1599.E5 M38 1999
Women in Medieval English Society. Maurice Kirby
(Contribution by). Cloth Text. Cambridge University Press. New
York, NY. 1999. 126p. New Studies in Economic and Social
History, No. 39 ISBN:0-521-58322-5, ISBN13:
978-0-521-58322-0. Dewey:305.42/0942/0902.
LCCN:98-043628.
                                    Audience: **l,u.**

Matter, E. Ann &   BV639.W7C69 1994
  Coakley, John (Editors)
Creative Women in Medieval and Early Modern Italy: A
Religious and Artistic Renaissance. Trade Cloth. University of
Pennsylvania Press. Philadelphia, PA. 1994. 376p. Middle Ages
Ser. ISBN:0-8122-3236-4, ISBN13: 978-0-8122-3236-3.
Dewey:274.5/05/082. LCCN:94-027864.
                          Audience: **u,f.** *Choice, 1995.*

Meale, Carol M.   PR113 .W64 1993
  (Editor)
Women and Literature in Britain, 1150-1500. Trade Cloth.
Cambridge University Press. New York, NY. 1993. 233p.
Cambridge Studies in Medieval Literature, Vol. 17
ISBN:0-521-40018-X, ISBN13: 978-0-521-40018-3.
Dewey:820.9001. LCCN:92-011691.
                                    Audience: **u,f.**

Meek, Christine &   HQ1143
  Lawless, Catherine (Editors)
Pawns or Players?: Studies on Medieval and Early Modern
Women. Trade Paper. Four Courts Press. Dublin 8, 2003. 224p.
ISBN:1-85182-775-7, ISBN13: 978-1-85182-775-6.
Dewey:305.42/094/0902. LCCN:2004-297733.
                                    Audience: **u,f.**

Nicholas, David   HQ0633.N53
The Domestic Life of a Medieval City: Women, Children and
the Family in Fourteenth-Century Ghent. Trade Paper. Books on
Demand. Ann Arbor, MI. 1985. 271p. ISBN:0-608-02037-0,
ISBN13: 978-0-608-02037-2. Dewey:306.8/5/094931.
LCCN:84-022011.
                                    Audience: **g.**

Nichols, John A. &   BX4210
  Shank, M. Thomas (Editors)
Hidden Springs (Medieval Religious Women), Set. Trade Paper.
Cistercian Publications, Inc. Kalamazoo, MI. 1995. 300p.
Cistercian Studies, Vol. III ISBN:0-87907-913-4, ISBN13:
978-0-87907-913-0. Dewey:271/.9/000902.
                                    Audience: **u,f.**

Nichols, John A. &   BX4210
  Shank, M. Thomas (Editors)
Medieval Religious Women I: Distant Echoes. Trade Paper.
Cistercian Publications, Inc. Kalamazoo, MI. 1984. 299p.
Cistercian Studies, No. 71 ISBN:0-87907-971-1, ISBN13:
978-0-87907-971-0. Dewey:271/.9/000902.
                                    Audience: **u,f.**

Parsons, John C.   DA229
Eleanor of Castile: Queen and Society in Thirteenth Century
England. Trade Paper. Palgrave Macmillan. New York, NY.
1997. 384p. ISBN:0-312-17297-4, ISBN13: 978-0-312-17297-8.
Dewey:942.03/5/092 B.
                         Audience: **l,u,f.** *Choice, 1995.*

Power, Eileen   HQ1143 .P68 1997
Medieval Women. M. M. Postan (Editor), Maxine Berg
(Foreword by). Trade Paper. Cambridge University Press. New
York, NY. 1997. 132p. A Canto Book Ser. ISBN:0-521-59556-8,
ISBN13: 978-0-521-59556-8. Dewey:305.4/2/0941/0902.
LCCN:97-219610.
                                    Audience: **g,l,u,f.**

Roberts, Anna (Editor)   PN682.V55V55 1998
Violence Against Women in Medieval Texts. Trade Cloth.
University Press of Florida. Gainesville, FL. 1998. 304p.
ISBN:0-8130-1566-9, ISBN13: 978-0-8130-1566-8.
Dewey:809/.93355. LCCN:97-048732.
                          Audience: **u,f.** *Choice, 1998.*

Rosen, Tova   PJ5016.R67 2003
Unveiling Eve: Reading Gender in Medieval Hebrew Literature.
Book, Other. University of Pennsylvania Press. Philadelphia, PA.
2003. 280p. Jewish Culture and Contexts Ser.

ISBN:0-8122-3710-2, ISBN13: 978-0-8122-3710-8.
Dewey:892.4/09352042. LCCN:2002-042988.
Audience: **u,f.** *Choice, 2003.*

Rosenthal, Joel Thomas   **HQ1143.M44 1990**
  (Editor)
Medieval Women and the Sources of Medieval History. Trade
Cloth. University of Georgia Press. Athens, GA. 1990. 456p.
ISBN:0-8203-1214-2, ISBN13: 978-0-8203-1214-9.
Dewey:305.4/09/02. LCCN:89-020296.
Audience: **u,f.** *Choice, 1991.*

Simons, Walter   **BX4272.S56 2001**
Cities of Ladies. Trade Cloth. University of Pennsylvania Press.
Philadelphia, PA. 2001. 328p. Middle Ages Ser.
ISBN:0-8122-3604-1, ISBN13: 978-0-8122-3604-0.
Dewey:274.92/05/082. LCCN:2001-027487.
Audience: **l,u,f.** *Choice, 2002.*

Stuard, Susan M.   **HQ1143**
  (Editor)
Women in Medieval History and Historiography. Trade Paper.
University of Pennsylvania Press. Philadelphia, PA. 1987. 222p.
Middle Ages Ser. ISBN:0-8122-1290-8, ISBN13:
978-0-8122-1290-7. Dewey:305.4/09/02. LCCN:89-005287.
Audience: **u,f.**

Stuard, Susan M.   **HQ1143**
  (Editor)
Women in Medieval Society. Book, Other. University of
Pennsylvania Press. Philadelphia, PA. 1976. 224p. Middle Ages
Ser. ISBN:0-8122-1088-3, ISBN13: 978-0-8122-1088-0.
Dewey:301.41/2/0902. LCCN:75-041617.
Audience: **g,l,u,f.** ℬ

Wemple, Suzanne F.   **HQ1147.F7**
Women in Frankish Society: Marriage and the Cloister, 500-900.
Book, Other. University of Pennsylvania Press. Philadelphia, PA.
1985. 368p. Middle Ages Ser. ISBN:0-8122-1209-6, ISBN13:
978-0-8122-1209-9. Dewey:305.409. LCCN:80-054051.
Audience: **u,f.**

Wilson, Katharina M.   **PN667.M43 1984**
  (Editor)
Medieval Women Writers. Paper Text. University of Georgia
Press. Athens, GA. 1984. 384p. ISBN:0-8203-0641-X, ISBN13:
978-0-8203-0641-4. Dewey:808.8/99287. LCCN:82-013380.
Audience: **l,u,f.**

Wilson, Katharina M.   **HQ1143.W643 2004**
  & Margolis, Nadia
Women in the Middle Ages: An Encyclopedia. Trade Cloth.
Greenwood Publishing Group, Inc. Portsmouth, NH. 2004. 997p.
ISBN:0-313-33017-4, ISBN13: 978-0-313-33017-9.
Dewey:305.4/09/0203. LCCN:2004-053042.
Audience: **g,l,u,f.** *Choice, 2005.*

History. Historiography

☐ Domesday Book Online.
http://www.nationalarchives.gov.uk/domesday/
Audience: **g,l,u,f.**

Benson, Robert L. &   **CB354.6**
  Constable, Giles (Editors)
Renaissance and Renewal in the Twelfth Century. Trade Paper.
University of Toronto Press. Toronto, ON. 1991. 781p. Medieval

Academy Reprints for Teaching Ser., No. 26
ISBN:0-8020-6850-2, ISBN13: 978-0-8020-6850-7.
Dewey:940.1/82.
Audience: **g,u.**

Bloch, Marc   **D131.B513**
Feudal Society, Vol. 2. L. A. Manyon (Translator). Trade Paper.
University of Chicago Press. Chicago, IL. 1964. 229p.
ISBN:0-226-05979-0, ISBN13: 978-0-226-05979-2.
Dewey:940.14. LCCN:61-004322.
Audience: **l,u,f.**

Bloch, Marc   **D131.B513 1961**
Feudal Society, Vol. 1. L. A. Manyon (Translator). Trade Paper.
University of Chicago Press. Chicago, IL. 1964. 287p.
ISBN:0-226-05978-2, ISBN13: 978-0-226-05978-5.
Dewey:940.14. LCCN:61-004322.
Audience: **l,u.**

Blomquist, Thomas W.   **CB351.S83 VOL. 34**
  & Mazzaoui, Maureen F. (Editors)
The "Other Tuscany": Essays in the History of Lucca, Pisa, and
Siena During the Thirteenth, Fourteenth and Fifteenth Centuries.
Trade Cloth, Box or Slipcased. Medieval Institute Publications.
Kalamazoo, MI. 1994. vi + 233p. Studies in Medieval Culture,
Vol. 34 ISBN:1-879288-41-9, ISBN13: 978-1-879288-41-6.
Dewey:940.1 s. LCCN:94-004664.
Audience: **g,l,u,f.**

Brooke, Christopher N.   **D123.B76 2000**
  L.
Europe in the Central Middle Ages, 962-1154. Ed. 3. Trade
Paper. Pearson Education. Boston, MA. 2000. 488p.
ISBN:0-582-36904-5, ISBN13: 978-0-582-36904-7.
Dewey:940.1/4. LCCN:00-024717.
Audience: **l,u.**

Campbell, James   **DA152 .C28 1991**
  (Editor), et al.
The Anglo-Saxons. Eric John & Patrick Wormald (Editors).
Trade Paper. Penguin Group (USA) Inc. New York, NY. 1991.
272p. Penguin History Ser. ISBN:0-14-014395-5, ISBN13:
978-0-14-014395-9. Dewey:942.01. LCCN:91-204926.
Audience: **l,u.** ℬ

Cantor, Norman F.   **CB351**
Civilization of the Middle Ages. Trade Paper. HarperCollins
Publishers. New York, NY. 1994. 624p. ISBN:0-06-092553-1,
ISBN13: 978-0-06-092553-6. Dewey:940.1. LCCN:92-056237.
Audience: **g,l.**

Cantor, Norman F.   **DA247.J6**
The Last Knight: The Twilight of the Middle Ages and the Birth
of the Modern Era. Trade Cloth. Simon & Schuster. New York,
NY. 2004. 272p. ISBN:0-7432-2688-7, ISBN13:
978-0-7432-2688-2. Dewey:940.1/92/092 B.
LCCN:2003-069700.
Audience: **g,l,u.** *Choice, 2005.*

Chibnall, Marjorie   **DA195.C47 1987**
Anglo-Norman England, 1066-1166. Trade Paper. Blackwell
Publishing, Inc. Malden, MA. 1987. 256p. ISBN:0-631-15439-6,
ISBN13: 978-0-631-15439-6. Dewey:942.02. LCCN:85-011255.
Audience: **l,u.** ℬ *Choice, 1986.*

Collins, Roger   **DP99**
Arab Conquest of Spain: 710-797. Trade Paper. Blackwell
Publishing, Inc. Malden, MA. 1995. 256p. ISBN:0-631-19405-3,
ISBN13: 978-0-631-19405-7. Dewey:946/.02. LCCN:88-033356.
                          Audience: **g,u,f.** *Choice, 1990.*

Collins, Roger   **D121.C65 1999**
Early Medieval Europe, 300-1000. Ed. 2. Cloth over Boards.
Palgrave Macmillan. New York, NY. 1999. 560p. History of
Europe Ser. ISBN:0-312-21885-0, ISBN13: 978-0-312-21885-0.
Dewey:940.1. LCCN:98-038110.

                                            Audience: **u.**

Collins, Roger   **DP96.C649 1995**
Early Medieval Spain: Unity in Diversity, 400-1000. Ed. 2.
Trade Paper. Palgrave Macmillan. New York, NY. 1995. 344p.
New Studies in Medieval History ISBN:0-312-12662-X,
ISBN13: 978-0-312-12662-9. Dewey:946/.01. LCCN:95-004155.
                                       Audience: **g,l,u,f.**

Cosgrove, Art (Editor)   **DA912**
A New History of Ireland: Medieval Ireland, 1169-1534. Ed. 2.
Trade Cloth. Oxford University Press, Inc. New York, NY. 1993.
1,064p. New History of Ireland Ser., Vol. 2
ISBN:0-19-821755-2, ISBN13: 978-0-19-821755-8.
Dewey:941.5. LCCN:76-376168.
                          Audience: **g,l,u,f.** *Choice, 1993.*

Dales, Richard C.   **CB351 .D27 1992**
The Intellectual Life of Western Europe in the Middle Ages. Ed.
2. Trade Paper. Brill Academic Publishers, Inc. Boston, MA.
1992. 322p. ISBN:90-04-09622-1, ISBN13: 978-90-04-09622-6.
Dewey:940.1. LCCN:92-010587.

                                 Audience: **u,f.** *B*

Davies, R. R.   **DA715.D374 2000**
The Age of Conquest: Wales 1063-1415. Paper Text. Oxford
University Press, Inc. New York, NY. 2000. 544p. Oxford
History of Wales Ser., Vol. 2 ISBN:0-19-820878-2, ISBN13:
978-0-19-820878-5. Dewey:942.9. LCCN:2001-268270.
                                            Audience: **u,f.**

Davies, R. R.   **DA716.G5D5 1995**
The Revolt of Owain Glyn Dwr. Trade Cloth. Oxford University
Press, Inc. New York, NY. 1996. 414p. ISBN:0-19-820508-2,
ISBN13: 978-0-19-820508-1. Dewey:942.9/041/092.
LCCN:95-010826.
                          Audience: **g,l,u,f.** *Choice, 1996.*

Drees, Clayton J.   **CB353**
(Editor)
The Late Medieval Age of Crisis and Renewal, 1300-1500: A
Biographical Dictionary. Cloth Text. Greenwood Publishing
Group, Inc. Portsmouth, NH. 2000. 568p. The Great Cultural
Eras of the Western World Ser. ISBN:0-313-30588-9, ISBN13:
978-0-313-30588-7. Dewey:940.1. LCCN:00-022335.
                          Audience: **l,u,f.** *Choice, 2001.*

Driver, Martha W. &   **PN1995.9.H44M44 2004**
Ray, Sid (Editors)
The Medieval Hero on Screen: Representations from Beowulf to
Buffy. Paper Text. McFarland & Company, Incorporated
Publishers. Jefferson, NC. 2004. 276p. ISBN:0-7864-1926-1,
ISBN13: 978-0-7864-1926-5. Dewey:791.43/652.
LCCN:2004-014708.
                          Audience: **l,u,f.** *Choice, 2005.*

Duby, Georges   **HN425.D78313 1997**
The Three Orders: Feudal Society Imagined. Arthur
Goldhammer (Translator), Thomas N. Bisson (Foreword by).
Trade Paper. University of Chicago Press. Chicago, IL. 1982.
392p. ISBN:0-226-16772-0, ISBN13: 978-0-226-16772-5.
Dewey:321.3/0944. LCCN:80-013158.
                             Audience: **g,l,u,f.** *B*

Duby, Georges   **DC33.2**
France in the Middle Ages, 987-1460: From Hugh Capet to Joan
of Arc. Juliet Vale (Translator). Trade Paper. Blackwell
Publishing, Inc. Malden, MA. 1993. 360p. History of France
Ser. ISBN:0-631-18945-9, ISBN13: 978-0-631-18945-9.
Dewey:944/.02. LCCN:91-007753.
                          Audience: **g,l,u,f.** *Choice, 1992.*

Durham, Thomas   **DR1978**
Serbia: The Rise and Fall of a Medieval Empire. Trade Paper.
William Sessions Ltd. York, 1989. 152p. ISBN:1-85072-060-6,
ISBN13: 978-1-85072-060-7. Dewey:914.971.
                                          Audience: **l,u.**

Einhard   **DC73.32**
Life of Charlemagne. Sidney Painter (Foreword by). Trade
Paper. University of Michigan Press. Chicago, IL. 1960. 80p.
Ann Arbor Paperbacks Ser. ISBN:0-472-06035-X, ISBN13:
978-0-472-06035-1. Dewey:944.014092.
                                       Audience: **g,l,u,f.**

Engel, Pal   **DB929.E545 2001**
Realm of St. Stephen: A History of Medieval Hungary,
895-1526. Andrew Ayton (Editor), Tamas Palosfalvi (Translator).
Cloth over Boards. I. B. Tauris & Company, Ltd. London, 2001.
416p. International Library of Historical Studies
ISBN:1-86064-061-3, ISBN13: 978-1-86064-061-2.
Dewey:943.9/02. LCCN:95-062314.
                          Audience: **g,l,u,f.** *Choice, 2002.*

Epstein, Steven A.   **DG637.E67 1996**
Genoa and the Genoese, 958-1528. Trade Cloth. University of
North Carolina Press. Chapel Hill, NC. 1996. 416p.
ISBN:0-8078-2291-4, ISBN13: 978-0-8078-2291-3.
Dewey:945/.182. LCCN:95-026585.
                          Audience: **g,l,u,f.** *Choice, 1997.*

Erickson, Carolly   **CB351.E76**
The Medieval Vision: Essays in History and Perception. Paper
Text. Oxford University Press, Inc. New York, NY. 1976. 256p.
ISBN:0-19-501963-6, ISBN13: 978-0-19-501963-6.
Dewey:940.1. LCCN:75-010179.
                             Audience: **g,l,u,f.** *B*

Fossier, Robert (Editor)   **CB351 .M7813 1986**
The Cambridge Illustrated History of the Middle Ages, Set.
Cloth Text. Cambridge University Press. New York, NY. 1997.
575p. ISBN:0-521-59078-7, ISBN13: 978-0-521-59078-5.
Dewey:909/.07. LCCN:85-021268.
                                          Audience: **l,u.**

Fouracre, Paul (Editor)   **D117**
The New Cambridge Medieval History, Set. Rosamond
McKitterick (Editor, Contribution by), Timothy Reuter, David
Luscombe & Jonathan Riley-Smith (Editors), David Abulafia
(Editor, Contribution by), Michael Jones & Christopher Allmand
(Editors), Martin Brett, Edward Powell, Simon Keynes, Jonathan
Shepard, Peter Linehan & Peter Spufford (Contribution by).
Quantity Pack, Trade Cloth. Cambridge University Press. New
York, NY. 2005. 8186p. The New Cambridge Medieval History

Ser. ISBN:0-521-85360-5, ISBN13: 978-0-521-85360-6.
Dewey:909.07. LCCN:93-039643.

Audience: **g,l,u,f.**

Fuhrmann, Horst   **DD141 .F8313 1986**
Germany in the High Middle Ages: C. 1050-1200. Timothy
Reuter (Translator). Trade Paper. Cambridge University Press.
New York, NY. 1986. 195p. Cambridge Medieval Textbooks
ISBN:0-521-31980-3, ISBN13: 978-0-521-31980-5.
Dewey:943/.02. LCCN:85-029988.

Audience: **g,l,u,f.**

Geary, Patrick J.   **DC65.G43 1988**
Before France and Germany: The Creation and Transformation
of the Merovingian World. Paper Text. Oxford University Press,
Inc. New York, NY. 1988. 272p. ISBN:0-19-504458-4, ISBN13:
978-0-19-504458-4. Dewey:943/.01. LCCN:87-007927.

Audience: **g,l,u,f.** *Choice, 1988.*

Gerli, Michael (Editor)   **DP99.M33 2002**
Medieval Iberia: An Encyclopedia. Paper over Boards.
Routledge. New York, NY. 2002. 952p. The Routledge
Encyclopedias of the Middle Ages Ser., Vol. 8
ISBN:0-415-93918-6, ISBN13: 978-0-415-93918-8.
Dewey:946/.02/03. LCCN:2002-012828.

Audience: **g,l,u,f.** *Choice, 2003.*

Gurevich, A. J.   **CB351.G8713 1985**
Categories of Medieval Culture. Trade Cloth. Routledge. New
York, NY. 1985. 224p. ISBN:0-7100-9578-3, ISBN13:
978-0-7100-9578-7. Dewey:909/.07. LCCN:84-009906.

Audience: **u,f.**

Haskins, Charles H.   **PA8035**
The Renaissance of the Twelfth Century. Trade Paper. Harvard
University Press. Cambridge, MA. 1927. 439p.
ISBN:0-674-76075-1, ISBN13: 978-0-674-76075-2.
Dewey:879.09.

Audience: **u,f.**

Herrin, Judith   **BR232.H47X 1989**
The Formation of Christendom. Trade Paper. Princeton
University Press. Princeton, NJ. 1989. 544p.
ISBN:0-691-00831-0, ISBN13: 978-0-691-00831-8.
Dewey:209/.4. LCCN:89-185411.

Audience: **g,l,u,f.** *Choice, 1987.*

Hughes, Kathleen   **DA908**
Early Christian Ireland: Introduction to the Sources. Trade
Paper. Books on Demand. Ann Arbor, MI. 320p.
ISBN:0-608-14566-1, ISBN13: 978-0-608-14566-2.
Dewey:914.15/03/1.

Audience: **l,u,f.**

Huizinga, Johan   **DC96**
The Waning of the Middle Ages. Trade Cloth. Peter Smith
Publisher, Inc. Magnolia, MA. 1999. ISBN:0-8446-6984-9,
ISBN13: 978-0-8446-6984-7. Dewey:944/.025.

Audience: **g,l,u,f.**

Jacob, Ernest F.   **DA250**
The Fifteenth Century, 1399-1485. Trade Cloth. Oxford
University Press, Inc. New York, NY. 1961. 794p. Oxford
History of England Ser., Vol. 6 ISBN:0-19-821714-5, ISBN13:
978-0-19-821714-5. Dewey:942/.04.

Audience: **l,f.**

Jarrett, Bede   **CB351 .J3**
Social Theories in the Middle Ages, 1200-1500. Cloth Text.
Taylor & Francis Group. Abingdon, 1968. 280p.
ISBN:0-7146-1327-4, ISBN13: 978-0-7146-1327-7.
Dewey:300/.9/02.

Audience: **u,f.**

Kleinhenz, Christopher   **DG443.M43 2003**
  (Editor)
Medieval Italy: An Encyclopedia. Paper over Boards. Routledge.
New York, NY. 2003. 2160p. The Routledge Encyclopedias of
the Middle Ages Ser. ISBN:0-415-93929-1, ISBN13:
978-0-415-93929-4. Dewey:945/.03/03. LCCN:2003-007183.

Audience: **l,u,f.** *Choice, 2004.*

Kreutz, Barbara M.   **DG827**
Before the Normans: Southern Italy in the Ninth and Tenth
Centuries. Book, Other. University of Pennsylvania Press.
Philadelphia, PA. 1996. 268p. Middle Ages Ser.
ISBN:0-8122-1587-7, ISBN13: 978-0-8122-1587-8.
Dewey:945/.702. LCCN:91-029118.

Audience: **u,f.** *Choice, 1992.*

Larner, John   **G370.P9L27 1999**
Marco Polo and the Discovery of the World. Cloth over Boards.
Yale University Press. Cumberland, RI. 1999. 264p.
ISBN:0-300-07971-0, ISBN13: 978-0-300-07971-5.
Dewey:915.04/2. LCCN:99-024887.

Audience: **g,l,u,f.** *Choice, 2000.*

Le Goff, Jacques   **D117.L42 2005**
Birth of Europe. Trade Cloth. Blackwell Publishing, Inc.
Malden, MA. 2005. 288p. The Making of Europe Ser.
ISBN:0-631-22888-8, ISBN13: 978-0-631-22888-2.
Dewey:940.1. LCCN:2004-011509.

Audience: **u,f.** *Choice, 2005.*

Le Goff, Jacques   **CB351.L413 1988**
The Civilization of Medieval Europe. Julia Barrow (Translator).
Trade Cloth. Blackwell Publishing, Inc. Malden, MA. 1988.
350p. ISBN:0-631-15512-0, ISBN13: 978-0-631-15512-6.
Dewey:940.1. LCCN:87-036064.

Audience: **l,u.** *Choice, 1989.*

Le Goff, Jacques   **CB351.L413**
Medieval Civilization, 400-1500. Julia Barrow (Translator).
Trade Paper. Blackwell Publishing, Inc. Malden, MA. 1991.
416p. ISBN:0-631-17566-0, ISBN13: 978-0-631-17566-7.
Dewey:940.1.

Audience: **l,u.**

Le Goff, Jacques   **PQ295.S9**
The Medieval Imagination. Arthur Goldhammer (Translator).
Trade Paper. University of Chicago Press. Chicago, IL. 1992.
302p. ISBN:0-226-47085-7, ISBN13: 978-0-226-47085-6.
Dewey:840/.9/15. LCCN:88-004787.

Audience: **u,f.** *Choice, 1989.*

Leeper, Alexander W.   **DB51 .L4 1978**
A History of Medieval Austria. Robert W. Seton-Watson
(Editor). Trade Cloth. A M S Press, Inc. New York, NY.
ISBN:0-404-15347-X, ISBN13: 978-0-404-15347-2.
Dewey:943.6/02. LCCN:76-029416.

Audience: **l,u,f.**

MacKay, Angus   **DP99 .M23**
Spain in the Middle Ages: From Frontier to Empire, 1000-1500.
Trade Cloth. Macmillan Publishers Ltd. London, 1977. xii,

245p. ISBN:0-333-12816-8, ISBN13: 978-0-333-12816-9.
Dewey:946/.02. LCCN:77-376063.

Audience: **g,l,u.** *B*

Mundy, John H.   **D200.M86 1991**
Europe in the High Middle Ages, 1150-1309. Ed. 2. Cloth Text.
Addison-Wesley Longman, Ltd. Harlow, 1991. 467p. General
History of Europe Ser. ISBN:0-582-08016-9, ISBN13:
978-0-582-08016-4. Dewey:914. LCCN:90-042973.

Audience: **g,l.**

Nicholas, David   **DH801.F462 N53 1992**
Medieval Flanders. Trade Paper. Longman Publishing Group.
White Plains, NY. 1995. 463p. ISBN:0-582-01678-9, ISBN13:
978-0-582-01678-1. Dewey:949.3101. LCCN:91-045256.

Audience: **l,u.**

Rosenwein, Barbara H.   **D117.R67 2002**
A Short History of the Middle Ages. Trade Paper. Broadview
Press. Peterborough, ON. 2002. 220p. ISBN:1-55111-290-6,
ISBN13: 978-1-55111-290-9. Dewey:940.1.
LCCN:2002-282702.

Audience: **l,u.** *Choice, 2002.*

Southern, Richard W.   **CB351 .S6 1992**
The Making of the Middle Ages. Trade Paper. Yale University
Press. Cumberland, RI. 1961. 288p. ISBN:0-300-00230-0,
ISBN13: 978-0-300-00230-0. Dewey:940.1. LCCN:92-018978.

Audience: **l,u.**

Watt, William M. &   **DP99**
  Cachia, Pierre A.
A Short History of Islamic Spain. Trade Paper. Edinburgh
University Press. Edinburgh, 1979. ISBN:0-85224-332-4,
ISBN13: 978-0-85224-332-9. Dewey:946.02.

Audience: **l,u.**

Literature

Beadle, Richard   **PN2587.C36 1994**
  (Editor)
The Cambridge Companion to Medieval English Theatre. Trade
Paper. Cambridge University Press. New York, NY. 1994. 394p.
Companions to Literature Ser. ISBN:0-521-45916-8, ISBN13:
978-0-521-45916-7. Dewey:792.0942. LCCN:93-004397.

Audience: **g,u,f.**

Benson, C. David   **PR2015.B4 2003**
Public Piers Plowman: Modern Scholarship and Late Medieval
English Culture. Trade Cloth. Pennsylvania State University
Press. University Park, PA. 2005. 304p. ISBN:0-271-02315-5,
ISBN13: 978-0-271-02315-1. Dewey:821/.1.
LCCN:2003-009908.

Audience: **u,f.** *Choice, 2004.*

Bergin, Thomas G.   **PQ4335**
Dante. Trade Cloth. Greenwood Publishing Group, Inc.
Portsmouth, NH. 1976. 326p. ISBN:0-8371-7973-4, ISBN13:
978-0-8371-7973-5. Dewey:851/.1. LCCN:76-010974.

Audience: **g,l,u.**

Bisson, Lillian M.   **PR1933.S59**
Chaucer and the Late Medieval World. Trade Paper. Macmillan
Publishers Ltd. London, 2000. 304p. ISBN:0-333-80036-2,
ISBN13: 978-0-333-80036-2. Dewey:821.1.

Audience: **u,f.**

Boitani, Piero & Mann,   **PR1924.C28 2003**
  Jill (Editors)
The Cambridge Companion to Chaucer. Ed. 2. Cloth Text.
Cambridge University Press. New York, NY. 2004. 334p.
Cambridge Companions to Literature Ser. ISBN:0-521-81556-8,
ISBN13: 978-0-521-81556-7. Dewey:821/.1.
LCCN:2003-051485.

Audience: **u,f.** *Choice, 2004, 1987.*

Burrow, J. A.   **PR281**
Medieval Writers and Their Work: Middle English Literature
and Its Background, 1100-1500. Paper Text. Oxford University
Press, Inc. New York, NY. 1982. 158p. ISBN:0-19-289122-7,
ISBN13: 978-0-19-289122-8. Dewey:820.9/001.
LCCN:81-016967.

Audience: **g,l,u.**

Calin, William   **PR128.C35 1994**
The French Tradition and the Literature of Medieval England.
Trade Paper. University of Toronto Press. Toronto, ON. 1994.
604p. Romance Ser. ISBN:0-8020-7202-X, ISBN13:
978-0-8020-7202-3. Dewey:820.9/001. LCCN:95-165484.

Audience: **f.** *Choice, 1995.*

Cerquiglini-Toulet,   **PQ155.M52C4713 1997**
  Jacqueline
The Color of Melancholy: The Uses of Books in the Fourteenth
Century. Lydia Cochrane (Translator), Roger Chartier (Foreword
by). Trade Cloth. Johns Hopkins University Press. Baltimore,
MD. 1997. 224p. Parallax Ser., :Re-Visions of Culture and
Society ISBN:0-8018-5381-8, ISBN13: 978-0-8018-5381-4.
Dewey:840.9/353. LCCN:97-005043.

Audience: **u,f.** *Choice, 1998.*

Cogan, Marc   **PQ4390.C68 1999**
The Design in the Wax: The Structure of the Divine Comedy
and Its Meaning. Trade Paper. University of Notre Dame Press.
Notre Dame, IN. 1999. 432p. William and Katherine Devers
Series in Dante Studies, Vol. 3 ISBN:0-268-00887-6, ISBN13:
978-0-268-00887-1. Dewey:851/.1. LCCN:98-054915.

Audience: **u,f.** *Choice, 1999.*

Cornish, Alison   **PQ4401.C67 2000**
Reading Dante's Stars. Cloth over Boards. Yale University
Press. Cumberland, RI. 2000. 240p. ISBN:0-300-07679-7,
ISBN13: 978-0-300-07679-0. Dewey:851/.1. LCCN:99-039103.

Audience: **g,l,u,f.** *Choice, 2000.*

Dinshaw, Carolyn &   **PN671**
  Wallace, David (Editors)
The Cambridge Companion to Medieval Women's Writing.
Cloth Text. Cambridge University Press. New York, NY. 2003.
312p. Cambridge Companions to Literature Ser.
ISBN:0-521-79188-X, ISBN13: 978-0-521-79188-5.
Dewey:809/.89287/0902. LCCN:2003-273212.

Audience: **u,f.** *Choice, 2004.*

Duncan, Thomas G.   **PR313.C66 2005**
  (Editor)
A Companion to the Middle English Lyric. Trade Cloth. Boydell
& Brewer, Ltd. Woodbridge, 2005. 328p. ISBN:1-84384-065-0,
ISBN13: 978-1-84384-065-7. Dewey:821/.1093823.
LCCN:2006-295904.

Audience: **u,f.** *Choice, 2006.*

Fisher, John H.   **PR1924.F57 1992**
The Importance of Chaucer. Trade Cloth. Southern Illinois
University Press. Carbondale, IL. 1991. 192p.

ISBN:0-8093-1741-9, ISBN13: 978-0-8093-1741-7.
Dewey:821/.1. LCCN:91-012626.

Audience: **l,u.** *Choice, 1992.*

Fletcher, Richard   **DP99.F57 1991**
The Quest for El Cid. Trade Paper. Oxford University Press,
Inc. New York, NY. 1991. 240p. ISBN:0-19-506955-2, ISBN13:
978-0-19-506955-6. Dewey:946/.02/092 B. LCCN:90-022382.

Audience: **g,l,u.** *Choice, 1990.*

Forni, Pier M.   **PQ4295.F67 1996**
Adventures in Speech: Rhetoric and Narration in Boccaccio's
Decameron. Trade Cloth. University of Pennsylvania Press.
Philadelphia, PA. 1996. 176p. Middle Ages Ser.
ISBN:0-8122-3338-7, ISBN13: 978-0-8122-3338-4.
Dewey:853/.1. LCCN:95-043882.

Audience: **u,f.** *Choice, 1996.*

Fulk, R. D., et al.   **PR173.F85 2002**
A History of Old English Literature. Christopher M. Cain &
Rachel S. Anderson (Authors). Trade Cloth. Blackwell
Publishing, Inc. Malden, MA. 2002. 360p. Blackwell Histories
of Literature Ser. ISBN:0-631-22397-5, ISBN13:
978-0-631-22397-9. Dewey:829.09. LCCN:2002-020896.

Audience: **l,u.** *Choice, 2003.*

Gellrich, Jesse M.   **Z6.G44 1985**
The Idea of the Book in the Middle Ages: Language Theory,
Mythology, and Fiction. Book, Other. Cornell University Press.
Ithaca, NY. 1985. 296p. ISBN:0-8014-1722-8, ISBN13:
978-0-8014-1722-1. Dewey:002. LCCN:84-023814.

Audience: **u,f.**

Godden, Malcolm R. &   **PR173 .C36 1991**
  Lapidge, Michael (Editors)
The Cambridge Companion to Old English Literature. Trade
Paper. Cambridge University Press. New York, NY. 1991. 314p.
Companions to Literature Ser. ISBN:0-521-37794-3, ISBN13:
978-0-521-37794-2. Dewey:829/.09. LCCN:90-002673.

Audience: **u,f.** *Choice, 1992.*

Greenfield, Stanley B.   **PR173**
A New Critical History of Old English Literature. Trade Paper.
New York University Press. New York, NY. 1996. 372p.
ISBN:0-8147-3088-4, ISBN13: 978-0-8147-3088-1.
Dewey:829/.09.

Audience: **u,f.**

Holt, James C.   **PR2129.H64 1989**
Robin Hood. Ed. 2. Trade Paper. Thames & Hudson. New York,
NY. 1989. 223p. ISBN:0-500-27541-6, ISBN13:
978-0-500-27541-2. Dewey:398.352. LCCN:88-051137.

Audience: **g,l,u.**

Jacoff, Rachel (Editor)   **PQ4335.C36 1993**
The Cambridge Companion to Dante. Trade Paper. Cambridge
University Press. New York, NY. 1993. 290p. Companions to
Literature Ser. ISBN:0-521-42742-8, ISBN13:
978-0-521-42742-5. Dewey:851.1. LCCN:92-017126.

Audience: **u,f.**

Jaeger, C. Stephen   **GT3520.J34 1985**
The Origins of Courtliness: Civilizing Trends and the Formation
of Courtly Ideals, 939-1210. Book, Other. University of
Pennsylvania Press. Philadelphia, PA. 1985. 340p. Middle Ages
Ser. ISBN:0-8122-1307-6, ISBN13: 978-0-8122-1307-2.
Dewey:940.1. LCCN:84-015276.

Audience: **u,f.** *Choice, 1985.*

Kaske, R. E., et al.   **PN671.Z99K37X 1988**
Medieval Christian Literary Imagery: A Guide to Interpretation.
Arthur Groos & Michael W. Twomney (Authors). Trade Paper.
University of Toronto Press. Toronto, ON. 1988. 340p.
ISBN:0-8020-6663-1, ISBN13: 978-0-8020-6663-3.
Dewey:809.9352. LCCN:89-127528.

Audience: **u,f.**

Krueger, Roberta L.   **PN671 .C36 2000**
  (Editor)
The Cambridge Companion to Medieval Romance. Cloth Text.
Cambridge University Press. New York, NY. 2000. 310p.
Companions to Literature Ser. ISBN:0-521-55342-3, ISBN13:
978-0-521-55342-1. Dewey:809/.02. LCCN:99-034240.

Audience: **u,f.** *Choice, 2001.*

Lambdin, Robert T. &   **PN669**
  Lambdin, Laura C. (Editors)
Encyclopedia of Medieval Literature. Cloth Text. Greenwood
Publishing Group, Inc. Portsmouth, NH. 2000. 560p.
ISBN:0-313-30054-2, ISBN13: 978-0-313-30054-7.
Dewey:809/.02. LCCN:97-013713.

Audience: **l,u,f.** *Choice, 2001.*

Lewis, C. S.   **PN671 .L4 1994**
The Discarded Image: An Introduction to Medieval and
Renaissance Literature. Trade Paper. Cambridge University
Press. New York, NY. 1994. 242p. A Canto Book Ser.
ISBN:0-521-47735-2, ISBN13: 978-0-521-47735-2.
Dewey:809/.02. LCCN:94-213150.

Audience: **l,u.** *B*

Martinez, Nancy C. &   **Z2014.P7M34 1991**
  Martinez, Joseph G.
Guide to British Poetry Explication: Old English - Medieval.
Trade Cloth. Macmillan Publishing Company, Inc. Old Tappan,
NJ. 1991. 225p. Reference Publication in Literature Ser., Vol. 1
ISBN:0-8161-8921-8, ISBN13: 978-0-8161-8921-2.
Dewey:016.821009. LCCN:90-049129.

Audience: **l,u,f.** *Choice, 1991.*

McDonald, Nicola   **PR321**
  (Editor)
Pulp Fictions of Medieval England: Essays in Popular Romance.
Trade Paper. Manchester University Press. Manchester, 2004.
272p. ISBN:0-7190-6319-1, ISBN13: 978-0-7190-6319-0.
Dewey:821/.03309. LCCN:2003-068870.

Audience: **u,f.** *Choice, 2005.*

Meale, Carol M.   **PR113 .W64 1993**
  (Editor)
Women and Literature in Britain, 1150-1500. Trade Cloth.
Cambridge University Press. New York, NY. 1993. 233p.
Cambridge Studies in Medieval Literature, Vol. 17
ISBN:0-521-40018-X, ISBN13: 978-0-521-40018-3.
Dewey:820.9001. LCCN:92-011691.

Audience: **u,f.**

Merwin, W. S.   **PN6110.E6M4 1998**
Medieval Epics: Beowulf, the Song of Roland, the
Nibelungenlied, and the Cid. William Alfred & Helen M.
Mustard (Translators). Trade Cloth. Random House, Inc. New
York, NY. 1998. 640p. Modern Library Ser.
ISBN:0-679-60301-8, ISBN13: 978-0-679-60301-6.
Dewey:808.81/32. LCCN:98-004488.

Audience: **g,l,u,f.**

Mohl, Ruth   E210.A15
The Three Estates in Medieval and Renaissance Literature.
Paper Text. Textbook Publishers. Temecula, CA. 2003. xi, 425p.
ISBN:0-7581-2939-4, ISBN13: 978-0-7581-2939-0.
Dewey:973.311.

Audience: **u,f.**

Nemoy, Leon   BM175.K3.N37
Karaite Anthology: Excerpts from the Early Literature. Trade
Paper. Yale University Press. Cumberland, RI. 1987. 438p. Yale
Judaica Ser. ISBN:0-300-03929-8, ISBN13: 978-0-300-03929-0.
Dewey:296. LCCN:52-005367.

Audience: **g,l,u,f.**

Over, Kristen Lee   PB2221.O95 2005
Kingship, Conquest, and Patria. Paper over Boards. Routledge.
New York, NY. 2005. 244p. Studies in Medieval History and
Culture Ser., Vol. 35 ISBN:0-415-97271-X, ISBN13:
978-0-415-97271-0. Dewey:891.6/6109358. LCCN:2005-013144.

Audience: **u,f.**

Raby, F. J. E.   PA8056.R3 1953
🄴 A History of Christian-Latin Poetry from the Beginnings to
the Close of the Middle Ages. Ed. 1997. E-Book. NetLibrary,
Inc. Boulder, CO. 1997. ISBN:0-585-30457-2, ISBN13:
978-0-585-30457-1. Dewey:879.109.

Audience: **g,u,f.**

Raby, F. J. E.   PA8051.R3 1997
🄴 A History of Secular Latin Poetry in the Middle Ages.
E-Book. NetLibrary, Inc. Boulder, CO. 1997.
ISBN:0-585-33863-9, ISBN13: 978-0-585-33863-7.
Dewey:879.109.

Audience: **g,u,f.**

Rosen, Tova   PJ5016.R67 2003
Unveiling Eve: Reading Gender in Medieval Hebrew Literature.
Book, Other. University of Pennsylvania Press. Philadelphia, PA.
2003. 280p. Jewish Culture and Contexts Ser.
ISBN:0-8122-3710-2, ISBN13: 978-0-8122-3710-8.
Dewey:892.4/09352042. LCCN:2002-042988.

Audience: **u,f.** *Choice, 2003.*

Scheindlin, Raymond P.   PJ5059.E3G3913 1999
The Gazelle: Medieval Hebrew Poems on God, Israel and the
Soul. Trade Paper. Oxford University Press, Inc. New York, NY.
1999. 286p. ISBN:0-19-512988-1, ISBN13: 978-0-19-512988-5.
Dewey:892.4/1208. LCCN:99-011841.

Audience: **u,f.**

Scheindlin, Raymond P.   PJ5059.E3W5613 1999
Wine, Women and Death: Medieval Hebrew Poems on the Good
Life. Trade Paper. Oxford University Press, Inc. New York, NY.
1999. 214p. ISBN:0-19-512987-3, ISBN13: 978-0-19-512987-8.
Dewey:892.4/1208. LCCN:99-011842.

Audience: **u,f.**

Tanner, Roland   DA783.5 .T36 2001
The Late Medieval Scottish Parliament: Politics and the Three
Estates, 1424-1488. Trade Paper. Birlinn, Ltd. Edinburgh, 2001.
316p. Scottish Historical Review Monograph Ser.
ISBN:1-86232-174-4, ISBN13: 978-1-86232-174-8.
Dewey:941.1/04. LCCN:2003-501713.

Audience: **f.**

Wallace, David (Editor)   PR255 .C35 1999
The Cambridge History of Medieval English Literature. Trade
Paper. Cambridge University Press. New York, NY. 2002.

1070p. The New Cambridge History of English Literature Ser.
ISBN:0-521-89046-2, ISBN13: 978-0-521-89046-5.
Dewey:820.9/001.

Audience: **u,f.**

Wilson, Katharina M.   PN667.M43 1984
  (Editor)
Medieval Women Writers. Paper Text. University of Georgia
Press. Athens, GA. 1984. 384p. ISBN:0-8203-0641-X, ISBN13:
978-0-8203-0641-4. Dewey:808.8/99287. LCCN:82-013380.

Audience: **l,u,f.**

Zinberg, Israel &   PJ5008
  Martin, Bernard
A History of Jewish Literature. Trade Cloth. Press of Case
Western Reserve University. Cleveland, OH. 1972. xxxi, 231p.
ISBN:0-8295-0228-9, ISBN13: 978-0-8295-0228-2.
Dewey:809/.889/24. LCCN:72-183310.

Audience: **g,l,u,f.** 𝓑

Military history

Allmand, Christopher   DC96.A44 1988
The Hundred Years War: England and France at War c.1300 -
c.1450. Trade Paper. Cambridge University Press. New York,
NY. 1988. 224p. Cambridge Medieval Textbooks
ISBN:0-521-31923-4, ISBN13: 978-0-521-31923-2.
Dewey:944/.025. LCCN:87-013251.

Audience: **g,l,u,f.**

Boas, Adrian   D183.B63 1999
Crusader Archaeology: The Material Culture of the Latin East.
Paper over Boards. Routledge. New York, NY. 1999. 296p.
ISBN:0-415-17361-2, ISBN13: 978-0-415-17361-2.
Dewey:956/.014. LCCN:98-041042.

Audience: **g,l,u,f.** *Choice, 2000.*

Contamine, Philippe   U37.C6513 1984
War in the Middle Ages. M. Jones (Translator). Trade Cloth.
Blackwell Publishing Ltd. Oxford, 1984. 402p.
ISBN:0-631-13142-6, ISBN13: 978-0-631-13142-7.
Dewey:355/.0094. LCCN:84-014647.

Audience: **g,l,u,f.** 𝓑

Contamine, Philippe   UA646
War in the Middle Ages. Michael Jones (Translator). Trade
Paper. Blackwell Publishing, Inc. Malden, MA. 1992. 424p.
ISBN:0-631-14469-2, ISBN13: 978-0-631-14469-4.
Dewey:355/.0094.

Audience: **g,l,u,f.** 𝓑

Devries, Kelly   Z6721.D48 2002
A Cumulative Bibliography of Medieval Military History and
Technology. Trade Cloth. Brill Academic Publishers. Leiden,
2002. xx, 1112p. History of Warfare Ser., No. 8
ISBN:90-04-12227-3, ISBN13: 978-90-04-12227-7.
Dewey:016.355/0094/0902. LCCN:2002-280204.

Audience: **l,u,f.** *Choice, 2002.*

Forey, Alan   CR4701.F67 1992
The Military Orders: From the Twelfth to the Early Fourteenth
Centuries. Cloth Text. University of Toronto Press. Toronto, ON.
1992. 280p. ISBN:0-8020-2805-5, ISBN13: 978-0-8020-2805-1.
Dewey:271.0500902. LCCN:92-135261.

Audience: **u.** *Choice, 1992.*

France, John   D160.F73 1999
Western Warfare in the Age of the Crusades, 1000-1300. Trade
Cloth. Cornell University Press. Ithaca, NY. 1999. 344p.
ISBN:0-8014-3671-0, ISBN13: 978-0-8014-3671-0.
Dewey:940.1/8. LCCN:98-048997.

Audience: **l,u,f.** *Choice, 1999.*

Keegan, John   D25.K43
The Face of Battle. Trade Cloth. Peter Smith Publisher, Inc.
Magnolia, MA. 2000. ISBN:0-8446-7126-6, ISBN13:
978-0-8446-7126-0. Dewey:909.08.

Audience: **g,l,u.** 𝐵

Lewis, Archibald Ross   VK0055.L48
European Naval and Maritime History, 300-1500: Archibald R.
Lewis and Timothy J. Runyan. Trade Paper. Books on Demand.
Ann Arbor, MI. 205p. ISBN:0-608-21041-2, ISBN13:
978-0-608-21041-4. Dewey:387.5/094. LCCN:84-048485.

Audience: **g,l.**

Lochrie, Karma   PR275.W6L63 1999
Covert Operations: Medieval Uses of Secrecy. Book, Other.
University of Pennsylvania Press. Philadelphia, PA. 1998. 304p.
Middle Ages Ser. ISBN:0-8122-3473-1, ISBN13:
978-0-8122-3473-2. Dewey:820.9/001. LCCN:98-011694.

Audience: **u,f.** *Choice, 1999.*

Mott, Lawrence V.   DG867.3.M68 2003
Sea Power in Medieval Mediterranean: The Catalan Aragonese
Fleet in the War of the Sicilian Vespers. Trade Cloth. University
Press of Florida. Gainesville, FL. 2003. 384p. New Perspectives
on Maritime History and Nautical Archaeology Ser.
ISBN:0-8130-2662-8, ISBN13: 978-0-8130-2662-6.
Dewey:945/.804. LCCN:2003-042634.

Audience: **u,f.** *Choice, 2004.*

Prestwich, Michael   DA60.P74 1996
Armies and Warfare in the Middle Ages: The English
Experience. Cloth over Boards. Yale University Press.
Cumberland, RI. 1996. 406p. ISBN:0-300-06452-7, ISBN13:
978-0-300-06452-0. Dewey:355.3/0942/0902. LCCN:95-036142.

Audience: **g,l,u,f.** *Choice, 1996.*

Sumption, Jonathan   DC96
Trial by Battle. Book, Other. University of Pennsylvania Press.
Philadelphia, PA. 1999. 672p. Hundred Years War Ser., Vol. 1
ISBN:0-8122-1655-5, ISBN13: 978-0-8122-1655-4. Dewey:944.

Audience: **g,l,u,f.**

Sumption, Jonathan   DC96
Trial by Fire. Trade Cloth. University of Pennsylvania Press.
Philadelphia, PA. 1999. 630p. Hundred Years War Ser., Vol. 2
ISBN:0-8122-3527-4, ISBN13: 978-0-8122-3527-2.
Dewey:944.025.

Audience: **u,f.** *Choice, 2000.*

Music

Hughes, Andrew S.   ML114 .H8 1980
Medieval Music: The Sixth Liberal Art. Ed. 2. Trade Cloth.
University of Toronto Press. Toronto, ON. 1980. 360p. Medieval
Bibliographics Scr. ISBN:0-8020-2358-4, ISBN13:
978-0-8020-2358-2. Dewey:016.78/0902. LCCN:79-018770.

Audience: **g,l,u,f.**

Reese, Gustave   ML172 .R4
Music in the Middle Ages. Paper Text. W. W. Norton &
Company, Inc. New York, NY. 2000. 520p.
ISBN:0-393-97713-7, ISBN13: 978-0-393-97713-4.
Dewey:780.902.

Audience: **u,f.**

Seay, Albert   ML172
Music in the Medieval World. Ed. 2. Paper Text. Waveland
Press, Inc. Prospect Heights, IL. 1991. 182p.
ISBN:0-88133-635-1, ISBN13: 978-0-88133-635-1.
Dewey:780/.902.

Audience: **g,l,u,f.** 𝐵

Philosophy

Bohner, Philotheus   BC34 .B6 1979
Medieval Logic: An Outline of Its Development from 1250 to c.
1400. Trade Cloth. Hyperion Press, Inc. Westport, CT. 1988.
ISBN:0-88355-682-0, ISBN13: 978-0-88355-682-5. Dewey:160.
LCCN:78-059007.

Audience: **f.** 𝐵

Chadwick, Henry   B659.Z7C45
🄴 Boethius, the Consolations of Music, Logic, Theology, and
Philosophy. E-Book. NetLibrary, Inc. Boulder, CO. 1981.
ISBN:0-585-25951-8, ISBN13: 978-0-585-25951-2. Dewey:189.

Audience: **l,u.**

Gilson, Etienne   B765.T54G5 1994
The Christian Philosophy of St. Thomas Aquinas: Philosophy.
Trade Paper. University of Notre Dame Press. Notre Dame, IN.
1994. 502p. ISBN:0-268-00801-9, ISBN13: 978-0-268-00801-7.
LCCN:94-010241.

Audience: **u,f.**

Gilson, Etienne   B72.G48
History of Christian Philosophy in the Middle Ages. Paper Text.
Textbook Publishers. Temecula, CA. 2003. 829p.
ISBN:0-7581-5033-4, ISBN13: 978-0-7581-5033-2. Dewey:189.

Audience: **g,u.** 𝐵

Gilson, Etienne   B765.B74 G52
The Philosophy of St. Bonaventure. Trade Cloth. Franciscan
Press. Quincy, IL. 1965. 499p. ISBN:0-8199-0526-7, ISBN13:
978-0-8199-0526-0. Dewey:189.4.

Audience: **l,u,f.** 𝐵

Haren, Michael   B721.H34 1992
Medieval Thought: The Western Intellectual Tradition from
Antiquity to the Thirteenth Century. Ed. 2. Cloth Text.
University of Toronto Press. Toronto, ON. 1992. 530p.
ISBN:0-8020-2868-3, ISBN13: 978-0-8020-2868-6. Dewey:189.
LCCN:92-094449.

Audience: **g,u,f.** 𝐵 *Choice, 1985.*

Inglis, John (Editor)   B721.M457 2003
Medieval Philosophy and the Classical Tradition: In Islam,
Judaism and Christianity. Paper over Boards. Taylor & Francis
Group. Abingdon, 2001. 328p. ISBN:0-7007-1469-3, ISBN13:
978-0-7007-1469-8. Dewey:189. LCCN:2003-467178.

Audience: **g,l,u.** *Choice, 2003.*

Laistner, Max L.   CB351 .L27
Thought and Letters in Western Europe, A. D. 500-900. Trade
Cloth. Gordon Press Publishers. New York, NY. 1972.

ISBN:0-8490-1207-4, ISBN13: 978-0-8490-1207-5.
Dewey:809.4.

Audience: **g,l,u,f.**

Sirat, Colette   **MLCM 91/04530 (B)**
A History of Jewish Philosophy in the Middle Ages. Trade
Paper. Cambridge University Press. New York, NY. 1990. 495p.
ISBN:0-521-39727-8, ISBN13: 978-0-521-39727-8.
Dewey:181/.06.

Audience: **u,f.**

Steneck, Nicholas H.   **Q127.E/**
Science and Creation in the Middle Ages: Henry of Langenstein
(D. 1397) on Genesis. Trade Paper. University of Notre Dame
Press. Notre Dame, IN. 1977. 227p. ISBN:0-268-01691-7,
ISBN13: 978-0-268-01691-3. Dewey:509/.2/4.
LCCN:75-019881.

Audience: **u,f.**

Weinberg, Julius Rudolf   **B721**
A Short History of Medieval Philosophy. Trade Paper. Princeton
University Press. Princeton, NJ. 1967. 316p.
ISBN:0-691-01956-8, ISBN13: 978-0-691-01956-7. Dewey:189.
Audience: **g,l,u.** ℬ

Politics and Law

Barraclough, Geoffrey   **DD89.B27 1984**
The Origins of Modern Germany. Trade Paper. W. W. Norton &
Company, Inc. New York, NY. 1984. 504p.
ISBN:0-393-30153-2, ISBN13: 978-0-393-30153-3. Dewey:943.
LCCN:84-001624.

Audience: **g,l,u,f.** ℬ

Blythe, James M.   **JA82.B59 1992**
Ideal Government and the Mixed Constitution in the Middle
Ages. Trade Cloth. Princeton University Press. Princeton, NJ.
1992. 365p. ISBN:0-691-03167-3, ISBN13: 978-0-691-03167-5.
Dewey:320/.09/02. LCCN:91-021104.
Audience: **l,u,f.** *Choice, 1992.*

Brundage, James A.   **KJ985.S48**
Law, Sex, and Christian Society in Medieval Europe. Trade
Paper. University of Chicago Press. Chicago, IL. 1990. 698p.
ISBN:0-226-07784-5, ISBN13: 978-0-226-07784-0.
Dewey:344.4054. LCCN:87-010759.

Audience: **u,f.**

Chibnall, Marjorie   **DA198.6**
The Empress Matilda: Queen Consort, Queen Mother and Lady
of the English. Trade Paper. Blackwell Publishing, Inc. Malden,
MA. 1993. 256p. ISBN:0-631-19028-7, ISBN13:
978-0-631-19028-8. Dewey:942.04/5/092 B. LCCN:91-012692.
Audience: **u,f.** *Choice, 1992.*

Gillingham, John   **DA205.G55 2001**
The Angevin Empire. Ed. 2. Trade Paper. Oxford University
Press, Inc. New York, NY. 2001. 160p. A Hodder Arnold
Publication ISBN:0-340-74115-5, ISBN13: 978-0-340-74115-3.
Dewey:940.1/8. LCCN:2001-268753.

Audience: **l,u.**

Hallam, Elizabeth M. &   **DC82.H34 2001**
Everard, Judith
Capetian France 987-1328. Ed. 2. Trade Paper. Longman

Publishing Group. White Plains, NY. 2001. 496p.
ISBN:0-582-40428-2, ISBN13: 978-0-582-40428-1.
Dewey:944/.021. LCCN:00-061499.

Audience: **u,f.**

Keen, Maurice H.   **DA225.K4 2003**
England in the Later Middle Ages. Ed. 2. Trade Paper.
Routledge. New York, NY. 2003. 504p. ISBN:0-415-27293-9,
ISBN13: 978-0-415-27293-3. Dewey:942.03.
LCCN:2003-011016.

Audience: **l,u.** ℬ

Le Patourel, John   **DC611.N862L46**
ⓔ The Norman Empire. E-Book. NetLibrary, Inc. Boulder, CO.
1976. ISBN:0-585-25957-7, ISBN13: 978-0-585-25957-4.
Dewey:940/.04/41.

Audience: **u,f.** ℬ

Morrall, John B.   **JA82**
Political Thought in Medieval Times. Trade Paper. University of
Toronto Press. Toronto, ON. 1980. 152p. Mediaeval Academy
Reprints for Teaching Ser., Vol. 7 ISBN:0-8020-6413-2,
ISBN13: 978-0-8020-6413-4. Dewey:320/.09/02.
Audience: **l,u.** ℬ

Post, Gaines   **KW0300**
Studies in Medieval Legal Thought: Public Law and the State,
1100-1322. Trade Paper. Books on Demand. Ann Arbor, MI.
649p. ISBN:0-598-27255-0, ISBN13: 978-0-598-27255-3.
Dewey:340.0902. LCCN:63-016237.

Audience: **u,f.**

Sanders, Paula   **DT146.S26 1994**
Ritual, Politics, and the City in Fatimid Cairo. Paper Text. State
University of New York Press. Albany, NY. 1994. 231p. SUNY
Series in Medieval Middle East History ISBN:0-7914-1782-4,
ISBN13: 978-0-7914-1782-9. Dewey:962/.16. LCCN:93-022317.
Audience: **u,f.** *Choice, 1994.*

Sayers, Jane   **BX1236.S38 1994**
Innocent III. Cloth Text. Addison-Wesley Longman, Ltd.
Harlow, 1994. 240p. The Medieval World Ser.
ISBN:0-582-08342-7, ISBN13: 978-0-582-08342-4.
Dewey:282.092. LCCN:92-046028.

Audience: **u,f.**

Tuck, Anthony   **DA175.T75 1999**
Crown and Nobility: England, 1272-1461. Ed. 2. Trade Cloth.
Blackwell Publishing, Inc. Malden, MA. 1999. 376p. Classic
Histories of Europe and England Ser. ISBN:0-631-21461-5,
ISBN13: 978-0-631-21461-8. Dewey:942.03. LCCN:99-033571.
Audience: **l,u.**

Reading and Literacy

Amodio, Mark C.   **PR311**
Writing the Oral Tradition: Oral Poetics and Literate Culture in
Medieval England. Trade Cloth. University of Notre Dame
Press. Notre Dame, IN. 2004. 336p. Poetics of Orality and
Literacy Ser. ISBN:0-268-02023-X, ISBN13:
978-0-268-02023-1. Dewey:821/.109. LCCN:2004-023679.
Audience: **u,f.** *Choice, 2005.*

Cerquiglini-Toulet,   **PQ155.M52C4713 1997**
Jacqueline
The Color of Melancholy: The Uses of Books in the Fourteenth
Century. Lydia Cochrane (Translator), Roger Chartier (Foreword

by). Trade Cloth. Johns Hopkins University Press. Baltimore, MD. 1997. 224p. Parallax Ser., :Re-Visions of Culture and Society ISBN:0-8018-5381-8, ISBN13: 978-0-8018-5381-4. Dewey:840.9/353. LCCN:97-005043.

Audience: **u,f.** *Choice, 1998.*

Clanchy, M. T.   **DA176 .C54 1993**
From Memory to Written Record: England 1066-1307. Ed. 2. Trade Paper. Blackwell Publishing, Inc. Malden, MA. 1993. 432p. ISBN:0-631-16857-5, ISBN13: 978-0-631-16857-7. Dewey:942.02. LCCN:92-020180.

Audience: **g,l,u,f.**

Gellrich, Jesse M.   **Z6.G44 1985**
The Idea of the Book in the Middle Ages: Language Theory, Mythology, and Fiction. Book, Other. Cornell University Press. Ithaca, NY. 1985. 296p. ISBN:0-8014-1722-8, ISBN13: 978-0-8014-1722-1. Dewey:002. LCCN:84-023814.

Audience: **u,f.**

Mayer, Lauryn S.   **PR275.H5M395 2004**
Worlds Made Flesh: Reading Medieval Manuscript Culture. Paper over Boards. Routledge. New York, NY. 2004. 192p. Studies in Medieval History and Culture, Vol. 28 ISBN:0-415-97060-1, ISBN13: 978-0-415-97060-0. Dewey:820.9/358. LCCN:2003-024474.

Audience: **u,f.**

McKitterick, Rosamond   **LC149**
(Editor)
The Uses of Literacy in Early Medieval Europe. Trade Paper. Cambridge University Press. New York, NY. 1992. 361p. ISBN:0-521-42896-3, ISBN13: 978-0-521-42896-5. Dewey:302.2/244. LCCN:89-034283.

Audience: **u,f.**

Murphy, James J.   **PN173.M8 2001**
Rhetoric in the Middle Ages: A History of Rhetorical Theory from Saint Augustine to the Renaissance. Trade Cloth. M R T S. Tempe, AZ. 2000. xiv, 399p. ISBN:0-86698-269-8, ISBN13: 978-0-86698-269-6. Dewey:808/.0094/0902. LCCN:2001-268760.

Audience: **u,f.**

Petrucci, Armando   **Z1003.5.I8P48 1995**
Writers and Readers in Medieval Italy: Studies in the History of Written Culture. Charles M. Radding (Editor, Translator). Cloth over Boards. Yale University Press. Cumberland, RI. 1995. 272p. ISBN:0-300-06089-0, ISBN13: 978-0-300-06089-8. Dewey:302.2/244. LCCN:94-041633.

Audience: **u,f.** *Choice, 1996.*

Saenger, Paul H.   **Z1003.S13 1997**
Space Between Words: The Origins of Silent Reading. Trade Cloth. Stanford University Press. Palo Alto, CA. 1997. 494p. Figurae - Reading Medieval Culture Ser. ISBN:0-8047-2653-1, ISBN13: 978-0-8047-2653-5. Dewey:028. LCCN:96-035088.

Audience: **u,f.** *Choice, 1998.*

Religion

Rudy, Gordon   **BT767.7.R83 2002**
The Mystical Language of Sensation in the Later Middle Ages. Paper over Boards. Routledge. New York, NY. 2002. 192p. Studies in Medieval History and Culture, Vol. 14 ISBN:0-415-94070-2, ISBN13: 978-0-415-94070-2. Dewey:248.2/2/0902. LCCN:2002-004216.

Audience: **u,f.**

Religion > Paganism, Magic and Witchcraft

Dowden, Ken   **BL689**
European Paganism: Realities of Cult from Antiquity to Middle Ages. Paper over Boards. Routledge. New York, NY. 1999. 392p. ISBN:0-415-12034-9, ISBN13: 978-0-415-12034-0. Dewey:299/.094. LCCN:99-028007.

Audience: **g,l,u.** *Choice, 2000.*

Flint, Valerie I.   **BF1593**
The Rise of Magic in Early Medieval Europe. Trade Paper. Princeton University Press. Princeton, NJ. 1994. 466p. ISBN:0-691-00110-3, ISBN13: 978-0-691-00110-4. Dewey:133.4/3/0940902.

Audience: **u,f.** *Choice, 1991.*

Kieckhefer, Richard   **BF1593 .K53 2000**
Magic in the Middle Ages. Ed. 2. Trade Paper. Cambridge University Press. New York, NY. 2000. 236p. A Canto Book Ser. ISBN:0-521-78576-6, ISBN13: 978-0-521-78576-1. Dewey:133.4/3/0940902. LCCN:00-269048.

Audience: **l,u,f.** *Choice, 1990.*

Kors, Alan C.   **BF1566.W739 2001**
Witchcraft in Europe, 400-1700: A Documentary History. Ed. 2. Trade Paper. University of Pennsylvania Press. Philadelphia, PA. 2000. 480p. Middle Ages Scr. ISBN:0-8122-1751-9, ISBN13: 978-0-8122-1751-3. Dewey:133.4/3/094. LCCN:00-064934.

Audience: **g,l,u,f.** *Choice, 2001.*

Levack, Brian P.   **BF1566.L475 2003**
(Editor)
The Witchcraft Sourcebook. Paper over Boards. Routledge. New York, NY. 2003. 368p. ISBN:0-415-19505-5, ISBN13: 978-0-415-19505-8. Dewey:133.4/3/09. LCCN:2003-008535.

Audience: **l,u,f.**

Page, Sophie   **BF1593.P34 2004**
Magic in Medieval Manuscripts. Trade Paper. University of Toronto Press. Toronto, ON. 2004. 65p. Medieval Life in Manuscripts ISBN:0-8020-3797-6, ISBN13: 978-0-8020-3797-8. Dewey:133.4/3/0902. LCCN:2005-434436.

Audience: **u,f.**

Russell, Jeffrey B.   **BF1593**
Witchcraft in the Middle Ages. Book, Other. Cornell University Press. Ithaca, NY. 1984. 394p. ISBN:0-8014-9289-0, ISBN13: 978-0-8014-9289-1. Dewey:133.4/3/094/0902. LCCN:72-037755.

Audience: **u,f.** *B*

Stephens, Walter   **BF1572.S4S74 2002**
Demon Lovers: Witchcraft, Sex, and the Crisis of Belief. Trade Cloth. University of Chicago Press. Chicago, IL. 2002. 478p. ISBN:0-226-77261-6, ISBN13: 978-0-226-77261-5. Dewey:133.4/09. LCCN:2001-043393.

Audience: **u.** *Choice, 2002.*

Religion > Christianity

Benedict, Kimberley M.   **BV5077.E85B46 2004**
Empowering Collaborations: Writing Partnerships Between Religious Women and Scribes in the Middle Ages. Paper over Boards. Routledge. New York, NY. 2004. 156p. Studies in

---

Medieval History and Culture, Vol. 27 ISBN:0-415-97059-8, ISBN13: 978-0-415-97059-4. Dewey:270.5/082. LCCN:2003-027558.
Audience: **u,f.**

Bowman, Mary A.   **Z7819.B68**
Western Mysticism: A Guide to the Basic Works. Trade Paper. Books on Demand. Ann Arbor, MI. 1978. 121p. ISBN:0-7837-7318-8, ISBN13: 978-0-7837-7318-6. Dewey:016.2914/2. LCCN:78-018311.
Audience: **g,l,u.**

Brooke, Rosalind B.   **BX3606**
The Coming of the Friars. Trade Cloth. Allen & Unwin, Ltd. London, 1975. ISBN:0-04-942045-3, ISBN13: 978-0-04-942045-8. Dewey:271/.2.
Audience: **u.**

Brooke, Rosalind B. &   **BR738.2**
Brooke, Christopher N. L.
Popular Religion in the Middle Ages. Trade Paper. Thames & Hudson. New York, NY. 1985. 176p. ISBN:0-500-27381-2, ISBN13: 978-0-500-27381-4. Dewey:274.04.
Audience: **g,l,u.**

Brown, Andrew   **BR744.B76 2003**
Church and Society in England, 1000-1500. Cloth over Boards. Palgrave Macmillan. New York, NY. 2003. 256p. Social History in Perspective Ser. ISBN:0-333-69144-X, ISBN13: 978-0-333-69144-1. Dewey:274.2/04. LCCN:2003-049832.
Audience: **u,f.**

Brown, George H.   **PA8260.B76 1987**
Bede the Venerable. Trade Cloth. Thomson Gale. Farmington Hills, MI. 1987. 144p. Twayne's English Authors Ser. ISBN:0-8057-6940-4, ISBN13: 978-0-8057-6940-1. Dewey:878/.0209 B. LCCN:86-025834.
Audience: **f.** *Choice, 1987.*

Brown, Peter   **BR1720.A9**
Augustine of Hippo. Trade Cloth. Dorset Press. New York, NY. 1987. 463p. ISBN:0-88029-098-6, ISBN13: 978-0-88029-098-2. Dewey:270.2/092.
Audience: **u,f.**

Brown, Peter   **BX2333 .B74**
The Cult of the Saints: Its Rise and Function in Latin Christianity. Trade Paper. University of Chicago Press. Chicago, IL. 1982. 204p. The Haskell Lectures, Vol. 2 ISBN:0-226-07622-9, ISBN13: 978-0-226-07622-5. Dewey:270.2. LCCN:80-011210.
Audience: **u,f.**

Brundage, James A.   **KJ985.S48**
Law, Sex, and Christian Society in Medieval Europe. Trade Paper. University of Chicago Press. Chicago, IL. 1990. 698p. ISBN:0-226-07784-5, ISBN13: 978-0-226-07784-0. Dewey:344.4054. LCCN:87-010759.
Audience: **u,f.**

Bynum, Caroline   **BT872.B96 1995**
Walker
Possible Lives. Trade Cloth. Columbia University Press. New York, NY. 1995. 384p. Lectures on the History of Religions Ser., No. 15 ISBN:0-231-08126-X, ISBN13: 978-0-231-08126-9. Dewey:236/.8/09. LCCN:94-017299.
Audience: **g,u,f.** *Choice, 1995.*

Caciola, Nancy   **BR253.C33 2003**
Discerning Spirits: Divine and Demonic Possession in the Middle Ages. Book, Other. Cornell University Press. Ithaca, NY. 2003. 352p. Conjunctions of Religion and Power in the Medieval Past Ser. ISBN:0-8014-4084-X, ISBN13: 978-0-8014-4084-7. Dewey:235/.2/082. LCCN:2003-005454.
Audience: **u,f.** *Choice, 2004.*

Chadwick, Henry   **B655.Z7 C46 2001**
Augustine: A Very Short Introduction. Trade Paper. Oxford University Press, Inc. New York, NY. 2001. 144p. Very Short Introductions Ser. ISBN:0-19-285452-6, ISBN13: 978-0-19-285452-0. Dewey:189/.2. LCCN:2001-278810.
Audience: **g,l,u.**

Chenu,   **BT0026.C5213**
Marie-Dominique
Nature, Man, and Society in the Twelfth Century: Essays on New Theological Perspectives in the Latin West. with a Preface by Etienne Gilson. Jerome Taylor & Lester K. Little (Translators). Trade Paper. Books on Demand. Ann Arbor, MI. 382p. Midway Reprint Ser. ISBN:0-598-05670-X, ISBN13: 978-0-598-05670-2. Dewey:230. LCCN:84-673564.
Audience: **u,f.**

Clark, James Midgley   **BV5077.G3C58**
The Great German Mystics: Eckhart, Tauler and Suso. Trade Paper. Books on Demand. Ann Arbor, MI. 129p. Modern Language Studies, Vol. 5 ISBN:0-598-89305-9, ISBN13: 978-0-598-89305-5. Dewey:248.2/2. LCCN:49-049375.
Audience: **u,f.**

Constable, Giles   **BV4490 .C65 1995**
Three Studies in Medieval Religious and Social Thought: The Interpretation of Mary and Martha, the Ideal of the Imitation of Christ, the Orders of Society. Cloth Text. Cambridge University Press. New York, NY. 1995. 443p. ISBN:0-521-30515-2, ISBN13: 978-0-521-30515-0. Dewey:274/.04. LCCN:94-008854.
Audience: **g,u,f.** *Choice, 1996.*

Dickinson, J. C.   **BR743.2.E32 VOL. 2**
The Later Middle Ages: From the Norman Conquest to the Eve of the Reformation. Trade Cloth. A & C Black. London, 1979. viii, 487p. ISBN:0-7136-1948-1, ISBN13: 978-0-7136-1948-5. Dewey:274.1. LCCN:79-321691.
Audience: **u,f.**

Fichtenau, Heinrich   **BT1319.F5313 1998**
Heretics and Scholars in the High Middle Ages, 1000-1200. Denise A. Kaiser (Translator). Trade Cloth. Pennsylvania State University Press. University Park, PA. 1998. 732p. ISBN:0-271-01765-1, ISBN13: 978-0-271-01765-5. Dewey:272/.6. LCCN:97-033622.
Audience: **u,f.** *Choice, 1999.*

Finucane, Ronald C.   **BR747.F56**
Miracles and Pilgrims: Popular Beliefs in Medieval England. Trade Paper. DIANE Publishing Company. Collingdale, PA. 2000. 248p. ISBN:0-7881-9342-2, ISBN13: 978-0-7881-9342-2. Dewey:274.2.
Audience: **g,l,u,f.**

Flanagan, Sabina   **BX4700.J7**
Hildegard of Bingen: A Visionary Life. Ed. 2. Trade Paper. Routledge. New York, NY. 1998. 244p. ISBN:0-415-18551-3, ISBN13: 978-0-415-18551-6. Dewey:248.2/2/092. LCCN:98-012847.
Audience: **u,f.**

Forey, Alan   **CR4701.F67 1992**
The Military Orders: From the Twelfth to the Early Fourteenth
Centuries. Cloth Text. University of Toronto Press. Toronto, ON.
1992. 280p. ISBN:0-8020-2805-5, ISBN13: 978-0-8020-2805-1.
Dewey:271.0500902. LCCN:92-135261.
                                    Audience: **u.** *Choice, 1992.*

Gilchrist, J. T.   **BR115.E3.G5 1969**
The Church and Economic Activity in the Middle Ages. Trade
Cloth. Macmillan Publishing Company, Inc. Old Tappan, NJ.
1969. xi, 328p. ISBN:0-333-05496-2, ISBN13:
978-0-333-05496-3. Dewey:261.8/5/0902. LCCN:69-013685.
                                    Audience: **u,f.**

Gilson, Etienne   **B765.T54G5 1994**
The Christian Philosophy of St. Thomas Aquinas: Philosophy.
Trade Paper. University of Notre Dame Press. Notre Dame, IN.
1994. 502p. ISBN:0-268-00801-9, ISBN13: 978-0-268-00801-7.
LCCN:94-010241.
                                    Audience: **u,f.**

Gilson, Etienne   **B765.B74 G52**
The Philosophy of St. Bonaventure. Trade Cloth. Franciscan
Press. Quincy, IL. 1965. 499p. ISBN:0-8199-0526-7, ISBN13:
978-0-8199-0526-0. Dewey:189.4.
                                    Audience: **l,u,f.**

Godfrey, John   **BR749 .G6**
The Church in Anglo-Saxon England. Paper Text. Textbook
Publishers. Temecula, CA. 2003. 529p. ISBN:0-7581-1261-0,
ISBN13: 978-0-7581-1261-3.
                                    Audience: **u,f.**

Grayzel, Solomon   **BM0535.G7**
The Church and the Jews in the Thirteenth Century: 1254-1314.
Kenneth R. Stow (Editor). Trade Paper. Books on Demand. Ann
Arbor, MI. 381p. ISBN:0-608-10542-2, ISBN13:
978-0-608-10542-0. Dewey:261.2/6/09022. LCCN:89-008941.
                                    Audience: **u,f.**

Grossman, Avraham   **BM729.W6G7613 2004**
Pious and Rebellious: Jewish Women in Medieval Europe. Trade
Cloth. University Press of New England. Lebanon, NH. 2004.
352p. Tauber Institute for the Study of European Jewry Ser.
ISBN:1-58465-391-4, ISBN13: 978-1-58465-391-2.
Dewey:305.48/892404/0902. LCCN:2004-003029.
                                    Audience: **u,f.** *Choice, 2005.*

Gurevich, Aron I.   **CB353.G8713 1990**
Medieval Popular Culture: Problems of Belief and Perception.
Janos M. Bak & Paul A. Hollingsworth (Translators). Trade
Paper. Cambridge University Press. New York, NY. 1990. 295p.
Cambridge Studies in Oral and Literate Culture, No. 14
ISBN:0-521-38658-6, ISBN13: 978-0-521-38658-6.
Dewey:940.1.
                                    Audience: **u,f.**

Hayes, Dawn Marie   **BV896.E85H39 2003**
Body and Sacred Place in Medieval Europe, 1100-1389. Paper
over Boards. Routledge. New York, NY. 2003. 218p. Studies in
Medieval History and Culture, Vol. 18 ISBN:0-415-98838-1,
ISBN13: 978-0-415-98838-4. Dewey:263/.0424/0902.
LCCN:2002-151625.
                                    Audience: **u,f.**

Head, Thomas   **BX4659.F8**
Hagiography and the Cult of Saints: The Diocese of Orléans,
800-1200. Rosamond McKitterick, Christine Carpenter &
Jonathan Shepard (Contribution by). Trade Paper. Cambridge
University Press. New York, NY. 2005. 360p. Cambridge
Studies in Medieval Life and Thought Ser., Vol. 14:Fourth Ser.
ISBN:0-521-02342-4, ISBN13: 978-0-521-02342-9.
Dewey:235/.2/0944509021.
                                    Audience: **l,u,f.**

Inglis, John (Editor)   **B721.M457 2003**
Medieval Philosophy and the Classical Tradition: In Islam,
Judaism and Christianity. Paper over Boards. Taylor & Francis
Group. Abingdon, 2001. 328p. ISBN:0-7007-1469-3, ISBN13:
978-0-7007-1469-8. Dewey:189. LCCN:2003-467178.
                                    Audience: **g,l,u.** *Choice, 2003.*

Jansen, Katherine   **BR270**
  Ludwig
The Making of the Magdalen: Preaching and Popular Devotion
in the Later Middle Ages. Trade Paper. Princeton University
Press. Princeton, NJ. 2001. 408p. ISBN:0-691-08987-6, ISBN13:
978-0-691-08987-4. Dewey:274/.05.
                                    Audience: **g,u,f.** *Choice, 2000.*

Jantzen, Grace M.   **BV5083 .J36 1995**
Power, Gender and Christian Mysticism. Trade Cloth.
Cambridge University Press. New York, NY. 1995. 403p.
Studies in Ideology and Religion, No. 8 ISBN:0-521-47376-4,
ISBN13: 978-0-521-47376-7. Dewey:248.2/2. LCCN:94-044562.
                                    Audience: **u,f.** *Choice, 1996.*

Kaske, R. E., et al.   **PN671.Z99K37X 1988**
Medieval Christian Literary Imagery: A Guide to Interpretation.
Arthur Groos & Michael W. Twomney (Authors). Trade Paper.
University of Toronto Press. Toronto, ON. 1988. 340p.
ISBN:0-8020-6663-1, ISBN13: 978-0-8020-6663-3.
Dewey:809.9352. LCCN:89-127528.
                                    Audience: **u,f.**

Kelly, J. N.   **BR60**
Jerome: His Life Writings and Controversies. Trade Paper.
Hendrickson Publishers, Inc. Peabody, MA. 1998. 368p.
ISBN:1-56563-084-X, ISBN13: 978-1-56563-084-0.
Dewey:281.3.
                                    Audience: **l,u,f.**

Kleinberg, Aviad M.   **BX4659.E85K54 1992**
Prophets in Their Own Country: Living Saints and the Making
of Sainthood in the Later Middle Ages. Trade Cloth. University
of Chicago Press. Chicago, IL. 1992. 200p.
ISBN:0-226-43971-2, ISBN13: 978-0-226-43971-6.
Dewey:235.20902. LCCN:91-038561.
                                    Audience: **u,f.**

Knowles, David   **BX2592**
Religious Orders, Vol. 2. Trade Paper. Cambridge University
Press. New York, NY. 1979. 419p. ISBN:0-521-29567-X,
ISBN13: 978-0-521-29567-3. Dewey:271.00942.
                                    Audience: **u,f.**

Knowles, David   **BX2592**
Religious Orders, Vol. 1. Trade Paper. Cambridge University
Press. New York, NY. 1979. 366p. ISBN:0-521-29566-1,
ISBN13: 978-0-521-29566-6. Dewey:271.00942.
                                    Audience: **u,f.**

Knowles, Dom David   BX2592
The Monastic Order in England: A History of Its Development
from the Times of St. Dunstan to the Fourth Lateran Council,
940-1216. Trade Paper. Cambridge University Press. New York,
NY. 2004. 804p. ISBN:0-521-54808-X, ISBN13:
978-0-521-54808-3. Dewey:271/.00942/0902.

Audience: **u,f.**

Lambert, Malcolm   BT1319.L35 2002
Medieval Heresy: Popular Movements from the Gregorian
Reform to the Reformation. Ed. 3. Trade Cloth. Blackwell
Publishing, Inc. Malden, MA. 2002. 504p. ISBN:0-631-22275-8,
ISBN13: 978-0-631-22275-0. Dewey:273/.6.
LCCN:2001-043102.

Audience: **g,u,f.**

Lawrence, C. H.   BX2470.L39 2001
Medieval Monasticism: Forms of Religious Life in Western
Europe in the Middle Ages. Ed. 3. Trade Paper. Longman
Publishing. Boston, MA. 2000. 336p. ISBN:0-582-40427-4,
ISBN13: 978-0-582-40427-4. Dewey:271/.0094/0902.
LCCN:2001-268236.

Audience: **g,l,u,f.**

Le Goff, Jacques   HC41.L4313 1988
Your Money or Your Life: Economy and Religion in the Middle
Ages. Patricia M. Ranum (Translator). Trade Cloth. Zone Books.
Brooklyn, NY. 1988. 127p. ISBN:0-942299-14-0, ISBN13:
978-0-942299-14-4. Dewey:330.94/01. LCCN:87-025248.

Audience: **u,f.**

Leclercq, Jean &   BX2470 .L413X 1978
  Misrahi, Catharine
The Love of Learning and the Desire for God: A Study of
Monastic Culture. Ed. 2. Trade Paper. Colin Smythe Ltd.
Gerrards Cross Bucks., 1978. ix, 397p. ISBN:0-281-03599-7,
ISBN13: 978-0-281-03599-1. Dewey:271/.0094.
LCCN:84-673662.

Audience: **u,f.**

Lekai, Louis J.   BX3402.2 .L44
The Cistercians: Ideals and Reality. Trade Cloth. Kent State
University Press. Kent, OH. 1977. 534p. ISBN:0-87338-201-3,
ISBN13: 978-0-87338-201-4. Dewey:271/.12. LCCN:77-003692.

Audience: **u,f.**

Little, Lester K.   BX808.5.I8 L58 1988
Liberty, Charity, Fraternity: Lay Religious Confraternities at
Bergamo in the Age of the Commune. Trade Paper. Smith
College Publications. Northampton, MA. 1989. 228p. Studies in
History, Vol. 51 ISBN:0-87391-040-0, ISBN13:
978-0-87391-040-8. Dewey:267/.1824524/0902.
LCCN:89-154929.

Audience: **l,u,f.**

Mayr-Harting, Henry   BR749.M42
The Coming of Christianity to Anglo-Saxon England. Ed. 3.
Cloth Text. Pennsylvania State University Press. University
Park, PA. 1991. 336p. ISBN:0-271-00806-7, ISBN13:
978-0-271-00806-6. Dewey:274.2.

Audience: **l,u.**

McFarlane, K. B.   BX4905 .M2
John Wycliffe and the Beginnings of English Nonconformity.
Paper Text. Textbook Publishers. Temecula, CA. 2003. 197p.
ISBN:0-7581-8912-5, ISBN13: 978-0-7581-8912-7.
Dewey:270.5/092/4.

Audience: **u,f.**

Milis, Ludo J. R.   BX2470.M52 1992
Angelic Monks and Earthly Men: Monasticism and Its Meaning
to Medieval Society. Trade Cloth. Boydell & Brewer, Inc.
Rochester, NY. 1992. 184p. ISBN:0-85115-303-8, ISBN13:
978-0-85115-303-2. Dewey:271/.0094. LCCN:91-045505.

Audience: **g,l,u,f.** *Choice, 1993.*

Moorman, John R. H.   BX3606.2.M6 1988
History of the Franciscan Order: From Its Origins to the Year
1517. Trade Cloth. Franciscan Press. Quincy, IL. 1988. 641p.
ISBN:0-8199-0921-1, ISBN13: 978-0-8199-0921-3.
Dewey:271/.3/00902. LCCN:88-016565.

Audience: **l,u.**

Nichols, John A. &   BX4210
  Shank, M. Thomas (Editors)
Hidden Springs (Medieval Religious Women), Set. Trade Paper.
Cistercian Publications, Inc. Kalamazoo, MI. 1995. 300p.
Cistercian Studies, Vol. III ISBN:0-87907-913-4, ISBN13:
978-0-87907-913-0. Dewey:271/.9/000902.

Audience: **u,f.**

Nichols, John A. &   BX4210
  Shank, M. Thomas (Editors)
Medieval Religious Women I: Distant Echoes. Trade Paper.
Cistercian Publications, Inc. Kalamazoo, MI. 1984. 299p.
Cistercian Studies, No. 71 ISBN:0-87907-971-1, ISBN13:
978-0-87907-971-0. Dewey:271/.9/000902.

Audience: **u,f.**

Oakley, Francis   BR252.O15 1985
The Western Church in the Later Middle Ages. Book, Other.
Cornell University Press. Ithaca, NY. 1979. 346p.
ISBN:0-8014-1208-0, ISBN13: 978-0-8014-1208-0.
Dewey:282/.09/023. LCCN:79-007621.

Audience: **f.** **B**

Pick, Lucy K.   BR1024
Conflict and Coexistence: Archbishop Rodrigo and the Muslims
and Jews of Medieval Spain. Trade Cloth. University of
Michigan Press. Chicago, IL. 2004. 264p. History, Languages,
and Cultures of the Spanish and Portuguese Worlds Ser.
ISBN:0-472-11387-9, ISBN13: 978-0-472-11387-3.
Dewey:22/.092 B. LCCN:2004-051644.

Audience: **u,f.** *Choice, 2005.*

Prache, Anne   NA4830.P6813 2000
Cathedrals of Europe. Trade Cloth. Cornell University Press.
Ithaca, NY. 2000. 290p. ISBN:0-8014-3781-4, ISBN13:
978-0-8014-3781-6. Dewey:726.6/094. LCCN:00-029507.

Audience: **g,l,u.** *Choice, 2001.*

Raitt, Jill, et al.   BV4490 .C48 1987
Christian Spirituality: High MiddleAges and Reformation. John
Meyendorff & Bernard McGinn (Authors). Trade Cloth.
Crossroad Publishing Company. New York, NY. 1987. 504p.
World Spirituality Ser., Vol. 17 ISBN:0-8245-0765-7, ISBN13:
978-0-8245-0765-7. Dewey:248/.09/02. LCCN:86-029212.

Audience: **u,f.** *Choice, 1987.*

Robinson, I. S.   BX1210.R63 1990
The Papacy, 1073-1198: Continuity and Innovation. Trade Paper.
Cambridge University Press. New York, NY. 1990. 571p.
Cambridge Medieval Textbooks ISBN:0-521-31922-6, ISBN13:
978-0-521-31922-5. Dewey:261/.13/0902. LCCN:89-034126.

Audience: **l,u.** *Choice, 1991.*

Russell, Jeffrey B.   **BT1319 .R87 1982**
Dissent and Reform in the Early Middle Ages. Trade Cloth. A
M S Press, Inc. New York, NY. 344p. Heresies of the Early
Christian and Medieval Era Ser., Second Ser.
ISBN:0-404-16196-0, ISBN13: 978-0-404-16196-5.
Dewey:273/.6. LCCN:78-063178.

Audience: **u.**

Sayers, Jane   **BX1236.S38 1994**
Innocent III. Cloth Text. Addison-Wesley Longman, Ltd.
Harlow, 1994. 240p. The Medieval World Ser.
ISBN:0-582-08342-7, ISBN13: 978-0-582-08342-4.
Dewey:282.092. LCCN:92-046028.

Audience: **u,f.**

Simons, Walter   **BX4272.S56 2001**
Cities of Ladies. Trade Cloth. University of Pennsylvania Press.
Philadelphia, PA. 2001. 328p. Middle Ages Ser.
ISBN:0-8122-3604-1, ISBN13: 978-0-8122-3604-0.
Dewey:274.92/05/082. LCCN:2001-027487.

Audience: **l,u,f.**   *Choice, 2002.*

Tolan, John Victor   **BP172.T62 2002**
Saracens: Islam in the Medieval European Imagination. Trade
Cloth. Columbia University Press. New York, NY. 2002. 400p.
ISBN:0-231-12332-9, ISBN13: 978-0-231-12332-7.
Dewey:261.2/7. LCCN:2001-047706.

Audience: **l,u,f.**   *Choice, 2002.*

Ward, Benedicta   **BT97.2 .W36 1987**
Miracles and the Medieval Mind: Theory, Record, and Event,
1000 to 1215. Trade Paper. University of Pennsylvania Press.
Philadelphia, PA. 1982. 300p. Middle Ages Ser.
ISBN:0-8122-1228-2, ISBN13: 978-0-8122-1228-0.
Dewey:231.7/3/09021. LCCN:86-027271.

Audience: **g,l,u,f.**

Warner, Marina   **BT602 .W37 1983**
Alone of All Her Sex: The Myth and the Cult of the Virgin
Mary. Trade Cloth. Alfred A. Knopf Inc. New York, NY. 1983.
480p. ISBN:0-394-71155-6, ISBN13: 978-0-394-71155-3.
Dewey:232.91. LCCN:82-004880.

Audience: **u,f.** ℬ

Weber, Elka   **DS105.W43 2005**
Traveling Through Text: Message and Method in Late Medieval
Pilgrimage Accounts. Saddle Stitched, Cloth over Boards.
Routledge. New York, NY. 2005. 204p. Studies in Medieval
History and Culture ISBN:0-415-97577-8, ISBN13:
978-0-415-97577-3. Dewey:203/.5/0956940902.
LCCN:2005-013485.

Audience: **u,f.**

Weinstein, Donald &   **BX4659.E85**
  Bell, Rudolph M.
Saints and Society: The Two Worlds of Western Christendom,
1000-1700. Trade Paper. University of Chicago Press. Chicago,
IL. 1986. 321p. ISBN:0-226-89056-2, ISBN13:
978-0-226-89056-2. Dewey:235.2. LCCN:82-007972.

Audience: **g,l,u,f.**

Weis, Rene   **BX4891.2.W45 2001**
The Yellow Cross: The Story of the Last Cathars. Trade Cloth.
Alfred A. Knopf Inc. New York, NY. 2001. 464p.
ISBN:0-375-40490-2, ISBN13: 978-0-375-40490-0.
Dewey:272/.3. LCCN:2001-088078.

Audience: **g.**   *Choice, 2001.*

Religion > Judaism

Bango, Isidro G.   **DS135.S7B36 2003**
Remembering Sepharad: Jewish Culture in Medieval Spain.
Trade Paper. Sociedad Estatal para la Accion Cultural Exterior,
S.A.. Madrid, 2003. 232p. ISBN:84-96008-27-4, ISBN13:
978-84-96008-27-4. Dewey:946/.004924. LCCN:2005-437222.

Audience: **g.**   *Choice, 2004.*

Beinart, Haim   **G1030**
Atlas of Medieval Jewish History. Cloth Text. Carta, The Israel
Map & Publishing Company Limited, Israel. Jerusalem, 1992.
144p. ISBN:965-220-188-X, ISBN13: 978-965-220-188-1.
Dewey:909/.04924/00223.

Audience: **g,l,u.**   *Choice, 1993.*

Brody, Robert   **BM501.5.B76 1998**
The Geonim of Babylonia and the Shaping of Medieval Jewish
Culture. Cloth over Boards. Yale University Press. Cumberland,
RI. 1998. 408p. ISBN:0-300-07047-0, ISBN13:
978-0-300-07047-7. Dewey:296/.09567/09021.
LCCN:97-002879.

Audience: **u,f.**   *Choice, 1998.*

Cohen, Mark R.   **BM535.C6125 1994**
Under Crescent and Cross: The Jews in the Middle Ages. Cloth
Text. Princeton University Press. Princeton, NJ. 1994. 304p.
ISBN:0-691-03378-1, ISBN13: 978-0-691-03378-5.
Dewey:909/.04924. LCCN:93-042865.

Audience: **l,u,f.**   *Choice, 1994.*

Gil, Moshe   **DS135.L4G545 2004**
Jews in Islamic Countries in the Middle Ages. Trade Cloth. Brill
Academic Publishers. Leiden, 2004. 864p. Etudes Sur le
Judaisme Medieval Ser., Vol. 28 ISBN:90-04-13882-X, ISBN13:
978-90-04-13882-7. Dewey:305.892/401767/0902.
LCCN:2004-045105.

Audience: **l,u,f.**   *Choice, 2004.*

Grayzel, Solomon   **BM0535.G7**
The Church and the Jews in the Thirteenth Century: 1254-1314.
Kenneth R. Stow (Editor). Trade Paper. Books on Demand. Ann
Arbor, MI. 381p. ISBN:0-608-10542-2, ISBN13:
978-0-608-10542-0. Dewey:261.2/6/09022. LCCN:89-008941.

Audience: **u,f.**

Hughes, Aaron W. &   **BP190.5.I57H84 2004**
  Ibn Ezra, Abraham ben Meir
🄴 The Texture of the Divine: Imagination in Medieval Islamic
and Jewish Thought. E-Book. Indiana University Press.
Bloomington, IN. 2004. 240p. ISBN:0-253-34353-4, ISBN13:
978-0-253-34353-6. Dewey:181/.07. LCCN:2003-013824.

Audience: **l,u,f.**   *Choice, 2004.*

Lewis, Bernard   **BP172**
The Jews of Islam. Trade Paper. Princeton University Press.
Princeton, NJ. 1987. 262p. ISBN:0-691-00807-8, ISBN13:
978-0-691-00807-3. Dewey:297/.1972. LCCN:84-042575.

Audience: **l,u,f.** ℬ

Nemoy, Leon   **BM175.K3.N37**
Karaite Anthology: Excerpts from the Early Literature. Trade
Paper. Yale University Press. Cumberland, RI. 1987. 438p. Yale
Judaica Ser. ISBN:0-300-03929-8, ISBN13: 978-0-300-03929-0.
Dewey:296. LCCN:52-005367.

Audience: **g,l,u,f.**

Pick, Lucy K.   **BR1024**
Conflict and Coexistence: Archbishop Rodrigo and the Muslims and Jews of Medieval Spain. Trade Cloth. University of Michigan Press. Chicago, IL. 2004. 264p. History, Languages, and Cultures of the Spanish and Portuguese Worlds Ser. ISBN:0-472-11387-9, ISBN13: 978-0-472-11387-3. Dewey:22/.092 B. LCCN:2004-051644.
Audience: **u,f.** *Choice, 2005.*

Rosen, Tova   **PJ5016.R67 2003**
Unveiling Eve: Reading Gender in Medieval Hebrew Literature. Book, Other. University of Pennsylvania Press. Philadelphia, PA. 2003. 280p. Jewish Culture and Contexts Ser. ISBN:0-8122-3710-2, ISBN13: 978-0-8122-3710-8. Dewey:892.4/09352042. LCCN:2002-042988.
Audience: **u,f.** *Choice, 2003.*

Roth, Cecil   **DS0135.E5R62**
A History of the Jews in England. Trade Paper. Books on Demand. Ann Arbor, MI. 318p. ISBN:0-598-39070-7, ISBN13: 978-0-598-39070-7. Dewey:942/.004924. LCCN:42-011942.
Audience: **u,f.** *B*

Scheindlin, Raymond P.   **PJ5059.E3G3913 1999**
The Gazelle: Medieval Hebrew Poems on God, Israel and the Soul. Trade Paper. Oxford University Press, Inc. New York, NY. 1999. 286p. ISBN:0-19-512988-1, ISBN13: 978-0-19-512988-5. Dewey:892.4/1208. LCCN:99-011841.
Audience: **u,f.**

Scheindlin, Raymond P.   **PJ5059.E3W5613 1999**
Wine, Women and Death: Medieval Hebrew Poems on the Good Life. Trade Paper. Oxford University Press, Inc. New York, NY. 1999. 214p. ISBN:0-19-512987-3, ISBN13: 978-0-19-512987-8. Dewey:892.4/1208. LCCN:99-011842.
Audience: **u,f.**

Sirat, Colette   **MLCM 91/04530 (B)**
A History of Jewish Philosophy in the Middle Ages. Trade Paper. Cambridge University Press. New York, NY. 1990. 495p. ISBN:0-521-39727-8, ISBN13: 978-0-521-39727-8. Dewey:181/.06.
Audience: **u,f.**

Stow, Kenneth   **DS124.S79 1992**
Alienated Minority: The Jews of Medieval Latin Europe. Trade Cloth. Harvard University Press. Cambridge, MA. 1993. 360p. ISBN:0-674-01592-4, ISBN13: 978-0-674-01592-0. Dewey:940/.04924. LCCN:91-045067.
Audience: **l,u,f.** *Choice, 1993.*

Trachtenberg, Joshua   **DS145 .T7 1993**
The Devil and the Jews: The Medieval Conception of the Jew and Its Relation to Modern Anti-Semitism. Marc Saperstein (Foreword by). Trade Paper. Jewish Publication Society. Dulles, VA. 2003. 278p. ISBN:0-8276-0227-8, ISBN13: 978-0-8276-0227-4. Dewey:305.892/404/0902. LCCN:92-044393.
Audience: **g,l,u,f.**

Weber, Elka   **DS105.W43 2005**
Traveling Through Text: Message and Method in Late Medieval Pilgrimage Accounts. Saddle Stitched, Cloth over Boards. Routledge. New York, NY. 2005. 204p. Studies in Medieval History and Culture ISBN:0-415-97577-8, ISBN13: 978-0-415-97577-3. Dewey:203/.5/0956940902. LCCN:2005-013485.
Audience: **u,f.**

Wolfson, Elliot R.   **BM526**
Through a Speculum That Shines: Vision and Imagination in Medieval Jewish Mysticism. Trade Paper. Princeton University Press. Princeton, NJ. 1997. 462p. ISBN:0-691-01722-0, ISBN13: 978-0-691-01722-8. Dewey:296.7/12/0902. LCCN:94-018186.
Audience: **u,f.** *Choice, 1995.*

Zinberg, Israel &   **PJ5008**
  Martin, Bernard
A History of Jewish Literature. Trade Cloth. Press of Case Western Reserve University. Cleveland, OH. 1972. xxxi, 231p. ISBN:0-8295-0228-9, ISBN13: 978-0-8295-0228-2. Dewey:809/.889/24. LCCN:72-183310.
Audience: **g,l,u,f.** *B*

Religion > Islam

Gil, Moshe   **DS135.L4G545 2004**
Jews in Islamic Countries in the Middle Ages. Trade Cloth. Brill Academic Publishers. Leiden, 2004. 864p. Etudes Sur le Judaisme Medieval Ser., Vol. 28 ISBN:90-04-13882-X, ISBN13: 978-90-04-13882-7. Dewey:305.892/401767/0902. LCCN:2004-045105.
Audience: **l,u,f.** *Choice, 2004.*

Grabar, Oleg   **DS109.916.G73 1996**
The Shape of the Holy: Early Islamic Jerusalem. Mohammad Al-Asad, Abeer Audeh & Said Nuseibeh (Contribution by). Trade Cloth. Princeton University Press. Princeton, NJ. 1996. 248p. ISBN:0-691-03653-5, ISBN13: 978-0-691-03653-3. Dewey:956.94/4203. LCCN:95-050443.
Audience: **g,l,u,f.** *Choice, 1997.*

Hughes, Aaron W. &   **BP190.5.I57H84 2004**
  Ibn Ezra, Abraham ben Meir
The Texture of the Divine: Imagination in Medieval Islamic and Jewish Thought. E-Book. Indiana University Press. Bloomington, IN. 2004. 240p. ISBN:0-253-34353-4, ISBN13: 978-0-253-34353-6. Dewey:181/.07. LCCN:2003-013824.
Audience: **l,u,f.** *Choice, 2004.*

Lewis, Bernard   **BP172**
The Jews of Islam. Trade Paper. Princeton University Press. Princeton, NJ. 1987. 262p. ISBN:0-691-00807-8, ISBN13: 978-0-691-00807-3. Dewey:297/.1972. LCCN:84-042575.
Audience: **l,u,f.** *B*

Meri, Josef W. (Editor)   **DS36.85**
Medieval Islamic Civilization: An Encyclopedia. Paper over Boards. Routledge. New York, NY. 2005. 1088p. The Routledge Encyclopedias of the Middle Ages Ser. ISBN:0-415-96690-6, ISBN13: 978-0-415-96690-0. Dewey:909/.09767/003. LCCN:2005-044229.
Audience: **g,l,u.** *Choice, 2006.*

Pick, Lucy K.   **BR1024**
Conflict and Coexistence: Archbishop Rodrigo and the Muslims and Jews of Medieval Spain. Trade Cloth. University of Michigan Press. Chicago, IL. 2004. 264p. History, Languages, and Cultures of the Spanish and Portuguese Worlds Ser. ISBN:0-472-11387-9, ISBN13: 978-0-472-11387-3. Dewey:22/.092 B. LCCN:2004-051644.
Audience: **u,f.** *Choice, 2005.*

Robinson, Chase F.   **BP49.R63 2002**
Islamic Historiography. Patricia Crone (Contribution by). Cloth Text. Cambridge University Press. New York, NY. 2002. 264p.

Themes in Islamic History Ser. ISBN:0-521-62081-3, ISBN13: 978-0-521-62081-9. Dewey:297/.07/22. LCCN:2002-031427.
Audience: **l,u,f.** *Choice, 2003.*

Sanders, Paula   DT146.S26 1994
Ritual, Politics, and the City in Fatimid Cairo. Paper Text. State University of New York Press. Albany, NY. 1994. 231p. SUNY Series in Medieval Middle East History ISBN:0-7914-1782-4, ISBN13: 978-0-7914-1782-9. Dewey:962/.16. LCCN:93-022317.
Audience: **u,f.** *Choice, 1994.*

Tolan, John Victor   BP172.T62 2002
Saracens: Islam in the Medieval European Imagination. Trade Cloth. Columbia University Press. New York, NY. 2002. 400p. ISBN:0-231-12332-9, ISBN13: 978-0-231-12332-7. Dewey:261.2/7. LCCN:2001-047706.
Audience: **l,u,f.** *Choice, 2002.*

Watt, W. Montgomery   D199.3
The Influence of Islam on Medieval Europe. Trade Cloth. Edinburgh University Press. Edinburgh, 1972. viii, 125p. Islamic Surveys Ser., Vol. 9 ISBN:0-85224-218-2, ISBN13: 978-0-85224-218-6. Dewey:914/.03/1. LCCN:70-182902.
Audience: **g,l,u,f.** *B*

Weber, Elka   DS105.W43 2005
Traveling Through Text: Message and Method in Late Medieval Pilgrimage Accounts. Saddle Stitched, Cloth over Boards. Routledge. New York, NY. 2005. 204p. Studies in Medieval History and Culture ISBN:0-415-97577-8, ISBN13: 978-0-415-97577-3. Dewey:203/.5/0956940902. LCCN:2005-013485.
Audience: **u,f.**

Rural World

Duby, Georges   HD1917.D813 1998
Rural Economy and Country Life in the Medieval West. Book, Other. University of Pennsylvania Press. Philadelphia, PA. 1998. 632p. Middle Ages Ser. ISBN:0-8122-1674-1, ISBN13: 978-0-8122-1674-5. Dewey:338.1. LCCN:98-020958.
Audience: **l,u.** *B*

Duby, Georges   HD1917.D813
Rural Economy and Country Life in the Medieval West. Cynthia Postan (Translator). Paper Text. University of South Carolina Press. Columbia, SC. 1981. xvi, 615p. ISBN:0-87249-347-4, ISBN13: 978-0-87249-347-6. Dewey:338.1. LCCN:68-020530.
Audience: **u,f.** *B*

Fossier, Robert   HD1531.5.F6713 1988
Peasant Life in the Medieval West. Juliet Vale (Translator). Cloth Text. Blackwell Publishing, Inc. Malden, MA. 1988. 224p. ISBN:0-631-14363-7, ISBN13: 978-0-631-14363-5. Dewey:305.5/63. LCCN:88-005094.
Audience: **l,u,f.** *Choice, 1989.*

Freedman, Paul   PN682.P35F74 1999
The Image of the Medieval Peasant as Alien and Exemplary. Trade Paper. Stanford University Press. Palo Alto, CA. 1998. 481p. Figurae - Reading Medieval Culture Ser. ISBN:0-8047-3373-2, ISBN13: 978-0-8047-3373-1. Dewey:809/.9335208863. LCCN:98-036596.
Audience: **u,f.** *Choice, 1999.*

Freedman, Paul   HT815.S8 F74 1991
The Origins of Peasant Servitude in Medieval Catalonia. A. R. D. Pagden, Enrique Pupo-Walker, P. E. Russell & Herbert S.

Klein (Contribution by). Trade Cloth. Cambridge University Press. New York, NY. 1991. 283p. Cambridge Iberian and Latin American Studies ISBN:0-521-39327-2, ISBN13: 978-0-521-39327-0. Dewey:305.5/63/09467. LCCN:90-044421.
Audience: **u,f.** *Choice, 1992.*

Genicot, Léopold   HN373.G45 1990
Rural Communities in the Medieval West. Trade Cloth. Johns Hopkins University Press. Baltimore, MD. 1990. 200p. Johns Hopkins Symposia in Comparative History Ser. ISBN:0-8018-3870-3, ISBN13: 978-0-8018-3870-5. Dewey:307.72/094/0902. LCCN:89-037340.
Audience: **l,u.**

Hoskins, W. G.   DA600
The Making of the English Landscape. Ed. 3. Trade Paper. Hodder General Publishing Division. London, 1993. 256p. ISBN:0-340-56648-5, ISBN13: 978-0-340-56648-0. Dewey:911/.42.
Audience: **g,l,u,f.**

Hoskins, W. G.   DA600
Making of the English Landscape. Trade Paper. Penguin Books, Ltd. London, 1992. 328p. ISBN:0-14-015410-8, ISBN13: 978-0-14-015410-8. Dewey:911.4/2.
Audience: **g,l,u,f.**

Postan, M. M. (Editor)   HD1917
The Cambridge Economic History of Europe from the Decline of the Roman Empire: The Agrarian Life of the Middle Ages. Ed. 2. Cloth Text. Cambridge University Press. New York, NY. 1966. 888p. The Cambridge Economic History of Europe Ser., Vol. 1 ISBN:0-521-04505-3, ISBN13: 978-0-521-04505-6. Dewey:338.1/094/0902.
Audience: **l,u.**

Rackham, Oliver   SD179.R33 2001
Trees and Woodland in the British Landscape: The Complete History of Britain's Trees, Woods and Hedgerows. Sterling Publishing Co., Inc. 2001. Phoenix Press Ser. ISBN:1-84212-469-2, ISBN13: 978-1-84212-469-7.
Audience: **g,l,u,f.**

Rosener, Werner   HD1531.5
Peasants in the Middle Ages. Alexander Stutzer (Translator). Trade Paper. Polity Press. Cambridge, 1996. 352p. ISBN:0-7456-1835-9, ISBN13: 978-0-7456-1835-7. Dewey:305.5/633/0940902.
Audience: **l,u,f.** *Choice, 1993.*

Science and Medicine

Cornish, Alison   PQ4401.C67 2000
Reading Dante's Stars. Cloth over Boards. Yale University Press. Cumberland, RI. 2000. 240p. ISBN:0-300-07679-7, ISBN13: 978-0-300-07679-0. Dewey:851/.1. LCCN:99-039103.
Audience: **g,l,u,f.** *Choice, 2000.*

Crombie, A. C.   Q125.C68 1961
Augustine to Galileo. Trade Cloth. Harvard University Press. Cambridge, MA. 1980. 728p. ISBN:0-674-05273-0, ISBN13: 978-0-674-05273-4. Dewey:509. LCCN:61-016151.
Audience: **g,l,u,f.**

Krebs, Robert E.   Q124.97.K73 2004
Groundbreaking Scientific Experiments, Inventions, and Discoveries of the Middle Ages and the Renaissance. Cloth Text. Greenwood Publishing Group, Inc. Portsmouth, NH. 2004.

344p. Groundbreaking Scientific Experiments, Inventions, and Discoveries Through the Ages Ser. ISBN:0-313-32433-6, ISBN13: 978-0-313-32433-8. Dewey:509.4/0902. LCCN:2003-060075.

Audience: **g,l,u.** *Choice, 2004.*

Lindberg, David C.   **Q124.97**
  (Editor)
Science in the Middle Ages. Trade Paper. University of Chicago Press. Chicago, IL. 1980. 596p. Chicago History of Science and Medicine Ser. ISBN:0-226-48233-2, ISBN13: 978-0-226-48233-0. Dewey:509/.02. LCCN:78-005367.

Audience: **u,f.** ℬ

Murdock, John E. &   **Q174.B67**
  Sylla, Edith D. (Editors)
The Cultural Context of Medieval Learning: Proceedings of the 1st International Colloquium on Philosophy, Science and Theology in the Middle Ages, Boston, Sept. 1973, No.76. Trade Cloth. Springer. New York, NY. 1975. 576p. Synthese Library, No. 26 ISBN:90-277-0587-9, ISBN13: 978-90-277-0587-7. Dewey:501 s 189.

Audience: **f.**

North, J. D.   **QB981.N773 1989**
Stars, Minds and Fate: Essays on Ancient and Medieval Cosmology. Trade Cloth. Continuum International Publishing Group, Ltd. London, 2003. 440p. ISBN:0-907628-94-X, ISBN13: 978-0-907628-94-1. Dewey:523.1. LCCN:88-035243.

Audience: **g,l,u,f.**

Steneck, Nicholas H.   **Q127.E/**
Science and Creation in the Middle Ages: Henry of Langenstein (D. 1397) on Genesis. Trade Paper. University of Notre Dame Press. Notre Dame, IN. 1977. 227p. ISBN:0-268-01691-7, ISBN13: 978-0-268-01691-3. Dewey:509/.2/4. LCCN:75-019881.

Audience: **u,f.**

Ziegler, Philip   **RC178.A1Z5 1997**
Black Death. Trade Paper. Sutton Publishing. New York, NY. 1997. 256p. ISBN:0-7509-1703-2, ISBN13: 978-0-7509-1703-2. Dewey:940.1/92. LCCN:98-112826.

Audience: **g.** ℬ

Social History

Artz, Frederick B.   **CB351.A56 1980**
The Mind of the Middle Ages: An Historical Survey. Ed. 3. Trade Paper. University of Chicago Press. Chicago, IL. 1980. 600p. ISBN:0-226-02840-2, ISBN13: 978-0-226-02840-8. Dewey:909.07. LCCN:79-016259.

Audience: **l,f.**

Fichtenau, Heinrich   **BR735.F5313 1993**
Living in the Tenth Century: Mentalities and Social Orders. Patrick J. Geary (Translator). Trade Paper. University of Chicago Press. Chicago, IL. 1993. 494p. ISBN:0-226-24621-3, ISBN13: 978-0-226-24621-5. Dewey:943/.022. LCCN:90-011134.

Audience: **g,l,u,f.** *Choice, 1992.*

Given-Wilson, Chris   **HT653.G7**
English Nobility in the Late Middle Ages. Trade Paper. Routledge. New York, NY. 1996. 240p. ISBN:0-415-14883-9, ISBN13: 978-0-415-14883-2. Dewey:942/.037/08621. LCCN:86-033862.

Audience: **l,u,f.**

Herlihy, David (Editor)   **CB351**
Medieval Culture and Society. Paper Text. Waveland Press, Inc. Prospect Heights, IL. 1993. 410p. ISBN:0-88133-747-1, ISBN13: 978-0-88133-747-1. Dewey:914.03/1.

Audience: **l,u,f.** ℬ

James, Edwin O.   **GT3930 .J3 1993**
Seasonal Feasts and Festivals. Library Binding. Omnigraphics, Inc. Detroit, MI. 1993. 336p. ISBN:0-7808-0001-X, ISBN13: 978-0-7808-0001-4. Dewey:394.2/6. LCCN:93-008917.

Audience: **g,l,u,f.**

Le Goff, Jacques   **CB351**
Time, Work, and Culture in the Middle Ages. Arthur Goldhammer (Translator). Trade Paper. University of Chicago Press. Chicago, IL. 1982. 400p. ISBN:0-226-47081-4, ISBN13: 978-0-226-47081-8. Dewey:940.1. LCCN:79-025400.

Audience: **g,l,u,f.**

Low, Anthony   **PR438.S45L69 2003**
Aspects of Subjectivity: Society and Individuality from the Middle Ages to Shakespeare and Milton. Trade Cloth. Duquesne University Press. Pittsburgh, PA. 2003. 275p. Medieval and Renaissance Literary Studies ISBN:0-8207-0337-0, ISBN13: 978-0-8207-0337-4. Dewey:820.9/353. LCCN:2002-151237.

Audience: **u,f.** *Choice, 2004.*

McFarlane, Kenneth   **DA176**
  Bruce
The Nobility of Later Medieval England: The Ford Lectures for 1953 and Related Studies. Trade Cloth. Oxford University Press, Inc. New York, NY. 1973. xlii, 315p. ISBN:0-19-822362-5, ISBN13: 978-0-19-822362-7. Dewey:301.44/2. LCCN:73-157237.

Audience: **u,f.** ℬ

Mollat, Michel   **HN11.M6413 1986**
The Poor in the Middle Ages: An Essay in Social History. Arthur Goldhammer (Translator). Cloth over Boards. Yale University Press. Cumberland, RI. 1986. 336p. ISBN:0-300-02789-3, ISBN13: 978-0-300-02789-1. Dewey:305.5/69/09. LCCN:86-001686.

Audience: **g,l.** *Choice, 1987.*

Painter, Sidney   **CB351 .P3**
Medieval Society. Book, Other. Cornell University Press. Ithaca, NY. 1951. 109p. ISBN:0-8014-9850-3, ISBN13: 978-0-8014-9850-3. Dewey:940.1.

Audience: **l,u.** ℬ

Richmond, Colin   **CS439**
The Paston Family in the Fifteenth Century: The First Phase. Trade Paper. Cambridge University Press. New York, NY. 2002. 291p. ISBN:0-521-52027-4, ISBN13: 978-0-521-52027-0. Dewey:929.2/0942.

Audience: **u,f.**

Richmond, Colin   **CS439**
The Paston Family in the Fifteenth Century: Endings. Cloth over Boards. Manchester University Press. Manchester, 2001. 340p. ISBN:0-7190-5990-9, ISBN13: 978-0-7190-5990-2. Dewey:929.2/0942.

Audience: **u,f.**

Richmond, Colin   DA247.F35 R53 1996
The Paston Family in the Fifteenth Century: Fastolf's Will.
Trade Paper. Cambridge University Press. New York, NY. 2002.
292p. ISBN:0-521-52028-2, ISBN13: 978-0-521-52028-7.
Dewey:929.2/0942.

Audience: **u,f.**

Urban World

Agus, Irving A.   CB354
Urban Civilization in Pre-Crusade Europe: A Study of
Organized Town-Life in Northwestern Europe During the Tenth
and Eleventh Centuries Based on the Responsa Literature.
Yeshiva University Press. 1965.

Audience: **f.**

Bensch, Stephen P.   HC388.B3 B3 1995
Barcelona and Its Rulers, 1096-1291. Christine Carpenter,
Rosamond McKitterick & Jonathan Shepard (Contribution by).
Trade Cloth. Cambridge University Press. New York, NY. 1995.
477p. Studies in Medieval Life and Thought, No. 26
ISBN:0-521-43511-0, ISBN13: 978-0-521-43511-6.
Dewey:946.7/202. LCCN:93-004251.

Audience: **u,f.** *Choice, 1995.*

Brentano, Robert   DG811 .B73 1974B
Rome Before Avignon: A Social History of Thirteenth-Century
Rome. Trade Cloth. Longman Group (Far East), Ltd. Hong
Kong, 1974. xiv, 340p. ISBN:0-582-50125-3, ISBN13:
978-0-582-50125-6. Dewey:945/.632/04. LCCN:75-312109.

Audience: **u,f.**

Ewan, Elizabeth   HT133.E94 1990
Townlife in Fourteenth Century Scotland. Trade Cloth.
Edinburgh University Press. Edinburgh, 1991. 208p.
ISBN:0-7486-0128-7, ISBN13: 978-0-7486-0128-8.
Dewey:307.76/2/0941109023. LCCN:90-185950.

Audience: **u,f.** *Choice, 1991.*

Foote, David   BX1547.O78F66 2004
Lordship, Reform, and the Development of Civil Society in
Medieval Italy: The Bishopric of Orvieto, 1100-1250. Trade
Cloth. University of Notre Dame Press. Notre Dame, IN. 2004.
272p. ISBN:0-268-02871-0, ISBN13: 978-0-268-02871-8.
Dewey:282/.45652/09021. LCCN:2004-011375.

Audience: **u,f.** *Choice, 2005.*

Frugoni, Chiara   N5975.F7813 1991
A Distant City: Images of Urban Experience in the Medieval
World. William McCuaig (Translator). Trade Cloth. Princeton
University Press. Princeton, NJ. 1991. 250p.
ISBN:0-691-04083-4, ISBN13: 978-0-691-04083-7.
Dewey:709/.02. LCCN:90-008876.

Audience: **u,f.** *Choice, 1991.*

Frugoni, Chiara   D134.F7913 2005
A Day in a Medieval City. William McCuaig (Translator),
Arsenio Frugoni (Introduction by). Trade Cloth. University of
Chicago Press. Chicago, IL. 2005. 224p. ISBN:0-226-26634-6,
ISBN13: 978-0-226-26634-3. Dewey:940.1.
LCCN:2004-025903.

Audience: **g,l,u,f.** *Choice, 2006.*

Holmes, Urban T. Jr. &   GT120 .H64 1980
  Neckam, Alexander
Daily Living in the Twelfth Century: Based on the Observations
of Alexander Neckam in London and Paris. Trade Cloth.
Greenwood Publishing Group, Inc. Portsmouth, NH. 1980. 337p.
ISBN:0-313-22796-9, ISBN13: 978-0-313-22796-7.
Dewey:940.1/82. LCCN:80-019991.

Audience: **l,u.**

Holt, Richard & Rosser,   HT115.E54 1990
  Gervase (Editors)
The Medieval Town: A Reader in English Urban History,
1200-1540. Paper Text. Longman Publishing Group. White
Plains, NY. 1990. 352p. Readers in Urban History Ser.
ISBN:0-582-05128-2, ISBN13: 978-0-582-05128-7.
Dewey:307.76/0942/0902. LCCN:89-049706.

Audience: **l,u,f.**

Kowaleski, Maryanne   HF3520.E95 K68 1995
Local Markets and Regional Trade in Medieval Exeter. Trade
Cloth. Cambridge University Press. New York, NY. 1995. 458p.
ISBN:0-521-33371-7, ISBN13: 978-0-521-33371-9.
Dewey:381.1/8/0942356. LCCN:94-008396.

Audience: **u,f.** *Choice, 1996.*

Krautheimer, Richard   DG811.K7 2000
Rome: Profile of a City, 312-1308. Marvin Trachtenberg
(Foreword by). Trade Paper. Princeton University Press.
Princeton, NJ. 2000. 418p. ISBN:0-691-04961-0, ISBN13:
978-0-691-04961-8. Dewey:945/.632. LCCN:99-053723.

Audience: **g,l,u,f.** **B**

Myers, A. R.   DA680
London in the Age of Chaucer. Trade Paper. University of
Oklahoma Press. Norman, OK. 1988. 248p. Centers of
Civilization Ser., Vol. 31 ISBN:0-8061-2111-4, ISBN13:
978-0-8061-2111-6. Dewey:942.103/7. LCCN:73-177342.

Audience: **g,l,u,f.** **B**

Nicholas, David   HQ0633.N53
The Domestic Life of a Medieval City: Women, Children and
the Family in Fourteenth-Century Ghent. Trade Paper. Books on
Demand. Ann Arbor, MI. 1985. 271p. ISBN:0-608-02037-0,
ISBN13: 978-0-608-02037-2. Dewey:306.8/5/094931.
LCCN:84-022011.

Audience: **g.**

Pirenne, Henri   JS61
Medieval Cities: Their Origins and the Revival of Trade. Frank
D. Halsey (Translator). Trade Cloth. Princeton University Press.
Princeton, NJ. 1969. 253p. ISBN:0-691-00760-8, ISBN13:
978-0-691-00760-1. Dewey:913.

Audience: **u,f.** **B**

Reynolds, Susan   HT133
An Introduction to the History of English Medieval Towns.
Trade Cloth. Oxford University Press, Inc. New York, NY. 1977.
248p. ISBN:0-19-822455-9, ISBN13: 978-0-19-822455-6.
Dewey:942/.009/732. LCCN:77-030146.

Audience: **g,l,u,f.**

Schultz, Juergen   NA7514.623.V46S33
The New Palaces of Medieval Venice. Trade Cloth.
Pennsylvania State University Press. University Park, PA. 2004.
412p. ISBN:0-271-02351-1, ISBN13: 978-0-271-02351-9.
Dewey:728.8/0945/310902. LCCN:2003-026259.

Audience: **l,u,f.** *Choice, 2005.*

MIDDLE EASTERN HISTORY, LANGUAGES, AND LITERATURES

This section covers the geographic area from Morocco to Afghanistan and Armenia. The history section surveys the period immediately preceding the rise of Islam to the contemporary era. It also includes politics, social issues, and popular culture. The languages and literatures section covers those languages associated with the region, both ancient and modern.

The field continues to be quite dependent on the traditional book. Therefore, they comprise the majority of entries. Currency of materials was considered important. Given the plethora of available good sources, we often opted for currency when making choices for inclusion. However, much of the earlier corpus includes standard works which are still widely used. These are included.

There is a vast amount of appropriate material dealing with current history, politics and social issues. Decisions for inclusion were often favored only by the availability of a positive review. An attempt was made with many areas to include not only what appears on syllabuses, but also a representation of various schools of thought.

Works dealing primarily with Islam as a religion are not included, but Islamic history and women in Muslim societies are. Works about the diverse ethnic and religious groups of the region are also included. Major regional social critics, philosophers, ideologues, politicians, statesmen, historians, and literary authors have been considered primary resources. If their works have been translated they are included. There has been a tremendous increase since 1988 of translations of modern literature, especially Arabic and Hebrew. Ideally, all of it should be included, certainly the works of the major authors. Almost all of it is used in undergraduate courses both for its universal literary value and as a mirror of the cultures. Because of space constraints, it was a matter of choosing a representation. Sometimes choices were arbitrary, but hopefully the seminal works are included.

— Meryle Gaston

Byzantine Empire 330-1453

Cameron, Averil &   **DS62.25**
  Conrad, Lawrence I. (Editors)
The Byzantine and Early Islamic near East: Problems in the
Literary Source Material. Trade Cloth. Darwin Press, Inc.
Princeton, NJ. 1992. 442p. Studies in Late Antiquity and Early
Islam, No. 1, Vol. I ISBN:0-87850-080-4, ISBN13:
978-0-87850-080-2. Dewey:939.4/0072. LCCN:92-000352.

                                        Audience: **u,f.**

Cheikh, Nadia Maria El   **DF504.5**
Byzantium Viewed by the Arabs. Trade Cloth. Harvard
University Press. Cambridge, MA. 2004. 254p. Harvard Middle
Eastern Monographs, No. XXXVI ISBN:0-932885-30-6,
ISBN13: 978-0-932885-30-2. Dewey:949.5/02.
LCCN:2003-116904.

                                        Audience: **u,f.**

Kaegi, Walter E.   **DF553.K34 1997**
Byzantium and the Early Islamic Conquests. Trade Paper.
Cambridge University Press. New York, NY. 1995. 327p.
ISBN:0-521-48455-3, ISBN13: 978-0-521-48455-8.
Dewey:949.5.

                                        Audience: **u,f.**

Runciman, Steven   **DR502 .R86 1990**
The Fall of Constantinople 1453. Trade Paper. Cambridge
University Press. New York, NY. 1990. 270p. A Canto Book
Ser. ISBN:0-521-39832-0, ISBN13: 978-0-521-39832-9.
Dewey:949.5/04. LCCN:90-033079.

                                        Audience: **g,l,u,f.**

Shahid, Irfan   **DS62.25.S512 1989**
Byzantium and the Arabs in the Fifth Century. Trade Cloth.
Dumbarton Oaks. Washington, DC. 1989. 620p.
ISBN:0-88402-152-1, ISBN13: 978-0-88402-152-0.
Dewey:327.495017/671. LCCN:88-013098.

                              Audience: **u,f.** *Choice, 1990.*

Shahid, Irfan   **DS62.25**
Byzantium and the Arabs in the Fourth Century. Dumbarton
Oaks. 1984. ISBN:0-88402-116-5, ISBN13: 978-0-88402-116-2.
                                        Audience: **u,f.**

Shahid, Irfan   **DS62.25.S515 1995**
Byzantium and the Arabs in the Sixth Century. Dumbarton
Oaks. 1995. ISBN:0-88402-214-5, ISBN13: 978-0-88402-214-5.
                                        Audience: **u,f.**

Islamic Middle East

Berkey, Jonathan P.   **BP63.A35B47 2002**
The Formation of Islam: Religion and Society in the near East,
600-1800. Patricia Crone (Contribution by). Cloth Text.
Cambridge University Press. New York, NY. 2002. 302p.
Themes in Islamic History Ser., Vol. 2 ISBN:0-521-58214-8,
ISBN13: 978-0-521-58214-8. Dewey:297/.09.
LCCN:2002-031470.

                              Audience: **l,u,f.** *Choice, 2003.*

Bianquis, Th. (Editor),   **DS35.53.E533 .D66**
  et al.
Encyclopaedia of Islam: Historical Atlas of Islam, and Index of
Subjects, Set. C. E. Bosworth, E. Van Donzel & W. P. Heinrichs
(Editors). Trade Cloth. Brill Academic Publishers. Leiden, 2003.

ISBN:90-04-12874-3, ISBN13: 978-90-04-12874-3.
Dewey:909/.097671.

                                        Audience: **g,l,u,f.**

Bosworth, Clifford   **DS35.627.B67 1996**
  Edmund
The New Islamic Dynasties: a Chronological and Genealogical
Manual. Columbia University Press. 1996. ISBN:0-231-10714-5,
ISBN13: 978-0-231-10714-3.

                                        Audience: **g,l,u,f.**

Brockelmann, Carl   **DS38.B72 2000**
History of the Islamic Peoples: Orientalism. Library Binding.
Routledge. New York, NY. 2000. 476p. Orientalism Ser., Vol. 11
ISBN:0-415-20909-9, ISBN13: 978-0-415-20909-0.
Dewey:909/.097671. LCCN:99-053540.

                                        Audience: **l,u,f.**

Eickelman, Dale F.   **GN635.N42E39 2001**
The Middle East and Central Asia: an Anthropological
Approach. Ed. 4. Prentice Hall. 2001. ISBN:0-13-033678-5,
ISBN13: 978-0-13-033678-1.

                                        Audience: **l,u,f.**

Falah, Ghazi-Walid &   **HQ1170.G44 2005**
  Nagel, Caroline (Editors)
Geographies of Muslim Women: Gender, Religion, and Space.
Paper over Boards. Guilford Publications, Inc. New York, NY.
2005. 337p. ISBN:1-59385-183-9, ISBN13: 978-1-59385-183-5.
Dewey:305.48/697. LCCN:2004-028841.
                              Audience: **u,f.** *Choice, 2006.*

Fisher, Sydney Nettleton   **DS62.F5 2003**
  & Ochsenwald, William
The Middle East: A History. Ed. 6. Paper Text. McGraw-Hill
Higher Education. Burr Ridge, IL. 2003. 768p.
ISBN:0-07-244233-6, ISBN13: 978-0-07-244233-5.
Dewey:915.6. LCCN:2003-041213.

                              Audience: **g,l,u,f.** *B*

Freeman-Grenville, G.   **G2206.S1**
  S. P.
Historical Atlas of the Middle East. Lorraine Kessel (Illustrator).
Trade Cloth. Carta, The Israel Map & Publishing Company
Limited, Israel. Jerusalem, 1993. 144p. ISBN:0-13-390915-8,
ISBN13: 978-0-13-390915-9. Dewey:911/.56. LCCN:93-009294.
                                        Audience: **g,l,u,f.**

Goldschmidt, Arthur Jr.   **DS62.G64 2001**
Concise History of the Middle East. Ed. 7. Trade Paper.
Westview Press. Boulder, CO. 2001. 520p. ISBN:0-8133-3885-9,
ISBN13: 978-0-8133-3885-9. Dewey:956. LCCN:2001-045326.
                                        Audience: **g,l,u,f.**

Hodgson, Marshall G.   **DS36.85.H63**
The Venture of Islam. Paper Text. University of Chicago Press.
Chicago, IL. 1977. 716p. ISBN:0-318-56082-8, ISBN13:
978-0-318-56082-3. Dewey:909/.09/7671. LCCN:73-087243.
                                        Audience: **l,u,f.**

Holt, P. M. (Editor)   **DS35.6**
The Cambridge History of Islam. Cambridge University Press.
1970.
                                        Audience: **l,u,f.**

Hurewitz, J. C. (Editor, Translator)   DS42
The Middle East and North Africa in World Politics: A Documentary Record. Yale University Press. 1975.
Audience: **u,f.**

Issawi, Charles   DS57.I85 1998
Cross-Cultural Encounters and Conflicts. Trade Cloth. Oxford University Press, Inc. New York, NY. 1998. 160p. Studies in Middle Eastern History ISBN:0-19-511813-8, ISBN13: 978-0-19-511813-1. Dewey:956. LCCN:97-034739.
Audience: **g,l,u,f.**

Issawi, Charles   HC415.15.I84 1982
An Economic History of the Middle East and North Africa. Columbia University Press. 1982. ISBN:0-231-03443-1, ISBN13: 978-0-231-03443-2.
Audience: **u,f.**

Joseph, Suad (Editor)   HQ1170.E53 2003
Encyclopedia of Women & Islamic Cultures. Afsanaeh (Assoc. Editor). Brill. 2003. ISBN:90-04-13247-3, ISBN13: 978-90-04-13247-4.
Audience: **g,l,u,f.**

Lewis, Bernard   D228.L49
Cultures in Conflict: Christians, Muslims, and Jews in the Age of Discovery. Trade Paper. Oxford University Press, Inc. New York, NY. 1996. 126p. ISBN:0-19-510283-5, ISBN13: 978-0-19-510283-3. Dewey:940.2/1.
Audience: **g,l,u,f.**

Lewis, Bernard   BP52 .L46 1993
Islam in History: Ideas, People and Events in the Middle East. Ed. 2. Trade Cloth. Open Court Publishing Company. Chicago, IL. 1993. 492p. ISBN:0-8126-9216-0, ISBN13: 978-0-8126-9216-7. Dewey:909.0917671. LCCN:92-046218.
Audience: **g,l,u,f.**

Lewis, Bernard   DS63.2.E8
The Muslim Discovery of Europe. W.W. Norton. 1982.
Audience: **l,u,f.**

Lewis, Bernard   HT1316
Race and Slavery in the Middle East: An Historical Enquiry. Trade Paper. Oxford University Press, Inc. New York, NY. 1992. 224p. ISBN:0-19-505326-5, ISBN13: 978-0-19-505326-5. Dewey:306.3/62/0956. LCCN:89-022913.
Audience: **l,u,f.** *Choice, 1991.*

Library of Congress
☐ A Country Study [Afghanistan, Algeria, Bahrein, Egypt, Iran, Iraq, Israel, Jordan, Kuwait, Lebanon, Libya, Oman, Qatar, Saudi Arabia, Sudan, Syria, UAE, and Turkey]. http://lcweb2.loc.gov/frd/cs/
Audience: **g,l,u,f.**

Mansfield, Peter & Pelham, Nicolas   DS62.4.M36 2004
A History of the Middle East. Ed. 2. Trade Paper. Penguin Group (USA) Inc. New York, NY. 2004. 448p. ISBN:0-14-303433-2, ISBN13: 978-0-14-303433-9. Dewey:956. LCCN:2004-044679.
Audience: **g,l,u,f.** *Choice, 1991.*

Robinson, Francis   DS35.6.R6 1982
Atlas of the Islamic World since 1500. Trade Cloth. Facts On File, Inc. New York, NY. 1982. 240p. Cultural Atlas Ser.

ISBN:0-87196-629-8, ISBN13: 978-0-87196-629-2. Dewey:909/.097/671. LCCN:82-675002.
Audience: **g,l,u,f.** *B*

Sonbol, Amira El-Azhary (Editor)   HQ1170
Beyond the Exotic: Women's Histories in Islamic Societies. Ed. 1. Syracuse University Press. 2005. ISBN:0-8156-3055-7, ISBN13: 978-0-8156-3055-5.
Audience: **l,u,f.**

Young, Theodore Cuyler   PJ0025.P7
Near Eastern Culture and Society: A Symposium on the Meeting of East and West. Paper Text. Textbook Publishers. Temecula, CA. 2003. x, 250p. ISBN:0-7581-5793-2, ISBN13: 978-0-7581-5793-5. Dewey:915.
Audience: **u,f.**

Islamic Middle East > Arab Countries in General

Ajami, Fouad   DS63.1 .A35 1992
The Arab Predicament: Arab Political Thought and Practice since 1967. Ed. 2. Trade Cloth. Cambridge University Press. New York, NY. 1992. 299p. ISBN:0-521-43243-X, ISBN13: 978-0-521-43243-6. Dewey:320.9174927. LCCN:92-008321.
Audience: **l,u,f.**

Ajami, Fouad   DS36.88
The Dream Palace of the Arabs: A Generation's Odyssey. Trade Paper. Knopf Publishing Group. New York, NY. 1999. 368p. Vintage International Ser. ISBN:0-375-70474-4, ISBN13: 978-0-375-70474-1. Dewey:956.04.
Audience: **g,l,u,f.**

Antonius, George   DS63
The Arab Awakening: The Story of the Arab National Movement. G.P. Putnam. 1979.
Audience: **l,u,f.**

Choueiri, Youssef M.   DS62.7.C46 2000
Arab Nationalism: A History:Nation and State in the Arab World. Trade Paper. Blackwell Publishing, Inc. Malden, MA. 2001. 288p. ISBN:0-631-21729-0, ISBN13: 978-0-631-21729-9. Dewey:320.54/089927. LCCN:00-009406.
Audience: **l,u,f.** *Choice, 2001.*

Cleveland, William L.   DS61.52.H87 C55
The Making of an Arab Nationalist: Ottomanism and Arabism in the Life and Thought of Sati' al-Husri. Princeton University Press. 1971. Princeton Studies on the Near East ISBN:0-691-03088-X, ISBN13: 978-0-691-03088-3.
Audience: **u,f.**

Dawisha, A. I.   DS63.6.D38 2003
Arab Nationalism in the Twentieth Century: From Triumph to Despair. Trade Cloth. Princeton University Press. Princeton, NJ. 2002. 352p. ISBN:0-691-10273-2, ISBN13: 978-0-691-10273-3. Dewey:320.54/089/927. LCCN:2002-070389.
Audience: **l,u,f.** *Choice, 2003.*

Doumato, Eleanor Abdella & Posusney, Marsha Pripstein (Editors)   HQ1240.5.M628W67
Women and Globalization in the Arab Middle East: Gender, Economy and Society. Library Binding. Lynne Rienner

Publishers, Inc. Boulder, CO. 2003. 275p. ISBN:1-58826-110-7, ISBN13: 978-1-58826-110-6. Dewey:305.42/0956. LCCN:2002-073941.

Audience: **u,f.**

El Saadawi, Nawal   **HQ1784**
The Hidden Face of Eve: Women in the Arab World. Trade Cloth. Zed Books, Ltd. London, 1980. 224p. ISBN:0-905762-50-9, ISBN13: 978-0-905762-50-0. Dewey:305.4/2/09174927.

Audience: **g,l,u,f.**

Fernea, Robert A. &   **DS36.7.F47 1997**
  Fernea, Elizabeth Warnock
The Arab World: 40 Years of Change. Trade Paper. Doubleday Publishing. New York, NY. 1997. 576p. ISBN:0-385-48520-4, ISBN13: 978-0-385-48520-3. Dewey:909/.09749270825. LCCN:96-049257.

Audience: **g,l,u,f.**

Harris, William   **DS62.H37 2002**
The Levant: A Fractured Mosaic. Trade Cloth. Markus Wiener Publishers, Inc. Princeton, NJ. 2003. 296p. Princeton Series on the Middle East ISBN:1-55876-264-7, ISBN13: 978-1-55876-264-0. Dewey:956. LCCN:2002-069007.

Audience: **l,u,f.** *Choice, 2004.*

Hitti, Philip K.   **DS223.H5 2002**
History of the Arabs. Ed. 10. Palgrave Macmillan. 2002. ISBN:0-333-63142-0, ISBN13: 978-0-333-63142-3.

Audience: **l,u,f.**

Holt, Peter M.   **DS63**
Egypt and the Fertile Crescent, 1516-1922: A Political History. Book, Other. Cornell University Press. Ithaca, NY. 1969. 349p. ISBN:0-8014-9079-0, ISBN13: 978-0-8014-9079-8. Dewey:956. LCCN:66-018429.

Audience: **g,l,u,f.**

Hourani, Albert H. &   **DS37.7**
  Ruthven, Malise
A History of the Arab Peoples. Ed. 2. Trade Cloth. Harvard University Press. Cambridge, MA. 2003. 624p. ISBN:0-674-01017-5, ISBN13: 978-0-674-01017-8. Dewey:909/.0974927. LCCN:2003-269357.

Audience: **g,l,u,f.** *Choice, 1991.*

Hudson, Michael   **DS39.M53 1999**
The Middle East Dilemma: The Politics and Economics of Arab Integration. Trade Cloth. Columbia University Press. New York, NY. 1998. 368p. ISBN:0-231-11138-X, ISBN13: 978-0-231-11138-6. Dewey:320.956/09/048. LCCN:98-023052.

Audience: **l,u,f.** *Choice, 1999.*

Khalidi, Rashid   **DS63.6**
  (Editor), et al.
The Origins of Arab Nationalism. Lisa Anderson, Muhammad Muslih & Reeva S. Simon (Editors). Cloth Text. DIANE Publishing Company. Collingdale, PA. 1998. 325p. ISBN:0-7881-5504-0, ISBN13: 978-0-7881-5504-8. Dewey:320.5/4/09174927.

Audience: **l,u,f.**

Lewis, Bernard   **DS37.7**
The Arabs in History. Library Binding. Millefleurs. San Bernardino, CA. 1991. 200p. ISBN:0-8095-9079-4, ISBN13: 978-0-8095-9079-7. Dewey:909.04927.

Audience: **g,l,u,f.**

Rugh, William A.   **P95**
Arab Mass Media: Newspapers, Radio, and Television in Arab Politics. Praeger. 2004. ISBN:0-275-98212-2, ISBN13: 978-0-275-98212-6.

Audience: **l,u,f.**

Shaaban, Bouthaina   **HQ1784.S47 1991**
Both Right and Left Handed: Arab Women Talk about Their Lives. Cloth Text. Indiana University Press. Bloomington, IN. 1991. 252p. ISBN:0-253-35189-8, ISBN13: 978-0-253-35189-0. Dewey:305.48/6971. LCCN:91-010866.

Audience: **g,l,u,f.** *Choice, 1992.*

Shami, Seteney, et al.   **HD6206.W67 1990**
Women in Arab Society: Work Patterns and Gender Relations in Egypt, Jordan and Sudan. Lucine Taminian, Soheir A. Morsey, Zeinab B. El-Bakri & El-Wathig M. Kameir (Authors). Trade Cloth. Berg Publishers. Oxford, 1991. 236p. Comparative Studies Ser. ISBN:0-85496-724-9, ISBN13: 978-0-85496-724-7. Dewey:305.4209174927. LCCN:90-039662.

Audience: **u,f.** *Choice, 1991.*

Suleiman, Yasir   **PJ6074.S85 2004**
A War of Words: Language and Conflict in the Middle East. Charles Tripp, Julia A. Clancy-Smith, Israel Gershoni, Roger Owen, Yezid Sayigh & Judith E. Tucker (Contribution by). Cloth Text. Cambridge University Press. New York, NY. 2004. 286p. Cambridge Middle East Studies, Vol. 19 ISBN:0-521-83743-X, ISBN13: 978-0-521-83743-9. Dewcy:306.44/09175927. LCCN:2003-065266.

Audience: **l,u,f.**

Tibi, Bassam   **DS63.6.T513 1990**
Arab Nationalism: A Critical Enquiry. Ed. 2. Marion F. Sluglett & Peter Sluglett (Translators). Cloth Text. Palgrave Macmillan. New York, NY. 1990. 334p. ISBN:0-312-04234-5, ISBN13: 978-0-312-04234-9. Dewey:320.5/4/09174927. LCCN:89-024392.

Audience: **l,u,f.**

Zeine, Zeine N.   **LA210.S4**
The Emergence of Arab Nationalism: With a Background Study of Arab-Turkish Relations in the Near East. Trade Cloth. Khayat Publications International. Stamford, CT. 2003. 203p. ISBN:1-932441-00-X, ISBN13: 978-1-932441-00-0. Dewey:371.96.

Audience: **u,f.**

Islamic Middle East > By Period > Pre-Islamic to 622

Crone, Patricia   **HF3763.Z9M43 1986**
Meccan Trade and the Rise of Islam. Princeton University Press. 1987. ISBN:0-691-05480-0, ISBN13: 978-0-691-05480-3.

Audience: **l,u,f.**

Shahid, Irfan   **DS62.25**
Byzantium and the Arabs in the Fourth Century. Dumbarton Oaks. 1984. ISBN:0-88402-116-5, ISBN13: 978-0-88402-116-2.

Audience: **u,f.**

Shahid, Irfan   **DS62.25.S515 1995**
Byzantium and the Arabs in the Sixth Century. Dumbarton Oaks. 1995. ISBN:0-88402-214-5, ISBN13: 978-0-88402-214-5.

Audience: **u,f.**

Sicker, Martin DS62
The Pre-Islamic Middle East. Trade Cloth. Greenwood Publishing Group, Inc. Portsmouth, NH. 2000. 240p. ISBN:0-275-96890-1, ISBN13: 978-0-275-96890-8. Dewey:939/.4. LCCN:99-054421.
Audience: **g,l,u,f.** *Choice, 2000.*

Trimingham, J. Spencer BR1070 .T73
Christianity among the Arabs in Pre-Islamic Times. Trade Cloth. International Book Centre, Inc. Troy, MI. 1990. 342p. ISBN:0-86685-533-5, ISBN13: 978-0-86685-533-4. Dewey:209/.56.
Audience: **u,f.**

Islamic Middle East > By Period > Medieval Period 622-1517

Al-Baladuri, Ahmad Ibn Yahya DS38.2 .B313
Origins of the Islamic State. Trade Cloth. A M S Press, Inc. New York, NY. Columbia University, Studies in the Social Sciences, No. 163 & No. 163a ISBN:0-404-51163-5, ISBN13: 978-0-404-51163-0. Dewey:909/.0974/927. LCCN:76-082247.
Audience: **l,u,f.**

Al-Maqrizi
al-Maqrizi's Book of Contention and Strife Concerning the Relations between the Banu Umayya and the Banu Hashim. Bosworth, Clifford Edmond (Translator; Editor). University of Manchester. 1980.
Audience: **u,f.**

Al-Muqaddasi DS44.95
The Best Divisions for Knowledge of the Regions. Trade Paper. Garnet Publishing, Ltd. Reading, 2001. 498p. ISBN:1-85964-136-9, ISBN13: 978-1-85964-136-1. Dewey:910.9/17671.
Audience: **u,f.**

Ashtor, Eliyahu DS135.S7
The Jews of Moslem Spain. Jewish Publication Society of America. 1974.
Audience: **u,f.**

Cameron, Averil & Conrad, Lawrence I. (Editors) DS62.25
The Byzantine and Early Islamic near East: Problems in the Literary Source Material. Trade Cloth. Darwin Press, Inc. Princeton, NJ. 1992. 442p. Studies in Late Antiquity and Early Islam, No. 1, Vol. I ISBN:0-87850-080-4, ISBN13: 978-0-87850-080-2. Dewey:939.4/0072. LCCN:92-000352.
Audience: **u,f.**

Cheikh, Nadia Maria El DF504.5
Byzantium Viewed by the Arabs. Trade Cloth. Harvard University Press. Cambridge, MA. 2004. 254p. Harvard Middle Eastern Monographs, No. XXXVI ISBN:0-932885-30-6, ISBN13: 978-0-932885-30-2. Dewey:949.5/02. LCCN:2003-116904.
Audience: **u,f.**

Cooperson, Michael DS38.4
Al-Ma'mun. Saddle Stitched, Cloth over Boards. Oneworld Publications. Oxford, 2005. 144p. ISBN:1-85168-386-0, ISBN13: 978-1-85168-386-4. Dewey:909.097670092.
Audience: **g,l,u,f.**

Crone, Patricia DS38.2.C76 2003
God's Rule: Government and Islam, Six Centuries of Medieval Islamic Political Thought. Trade Cloth. Columbia University Press. New York, NY. 2004. 472p. ISBN:0-231-13290-5, ISBN13: 978-0-231-13290-9. Dewey:320.5/5. LCCN:2003-062537.
Audience: **l,u,f.**

Crone, Patricia DF547.I742
Slaves on Horses: The Evolution of the Islamic Polity. Trade Paper. Cambridge University Press. New York, NY. 2003. 312p. ISBN:0-521-52940-9, ISBN13: 978-0-521-52940-2. Dewey:956/.013.
Audience: **l,u,f.**

Dols, Michael W. RC179.I6
The Black Death in the Middle East. Trade Cloth. Princeton University Press. Princeton, NJ. 1977. 408p. ISBN:0-691-03107-X, ISBN13: 978-0-691-03107-1. Dewey:616.9/232/00956. LCCN:76-003254.
Audience: **l,u,f.**

Donner, Fred DS38.1
The Early Islamic Conquests. Princeton University Press. 1981.
Audience: **l,u,f.**

Fierro, Maribel DP107
'Abd Al Rahman III: The First Cordoban Caliph, Vol. 3. Saddle Stitched, Cloth over Boards. Oneworld Publications. Oxford, 2005. 150p. ISBN:1-85168-384-4, ISBN13: 978-1-85168-384-0. Dewey:946.02092.
Audience: **g,l,u,f.** *Choice, 2006.*

Harvey, L. P. DP99
Islamic Spain, 1250 to 1500. Trade Paper. University of Chicago Press. Chicago, IL. 1992. 386p. ISBN:0-226-31962-8, ISBN13: 978-0-226-31962-9. Dewey:946/.02. LCCN:90-030225.
Audience: **g,l,u,f.** *Choice, 1991.*

Hawting, Gerald R. DS38.2
The First Dynasty of Islam: The Umayyad Caliphate, AD 661-750. Ed. 2. Paper over Boards. Routledge. New York, NY. 2000. 176p. ISBN:0-415-24072-7, ISBN13: 978-0-415-24072-7. Dewey:909/.09767101.
Audience: **l,u,f.**

Holt, P. M. DS38.6
The Age of the Crusades: The Near East from 11th C-1517. Paper Text. Longman Publishing. Boston, MA. 1989. 250p. History of the Near East Ser. ISBN:0-582-49302-1, ISBN13: 978-0-582-49302-5. Dewey:956/.01. LCCN:84-027801.
Audience: **l,u,f.**

Humphreys, R. Stephen Z3014.H55H85 1991
Islamic History: A Framework for Inquiry. Trade Cloth. Princeton University Press. Princeton, NJ. 1991. 401p. ISBN:0-691-03145-2, ISBN13: 978-0-691-03145-3. Dewey:909/.097671. LCCN:90-021268.
Audience: **g,l,u,f.** *Choice, 1992.*

Ibn Battuta G161
Travels of Ibn Battuta. Gibb, H. A. R. (ed.). Cambridge University Press for the Hakluyt Society. 1958.
Audience: **g,l,u,f.**

Ibn'Abd, Al-Hakam PJ817.I2
The History of the Conquest of Egypt, North Africa and Spain Known As the Futuh Misr of Ibn'abd Al-Hakan. Charles C.

Torrey (Editor). Trade Cloth. A M S Press, Inc. New York, NY. Yale Oriental Ser., No. 3:Researches ISBN:0-404-60273-8, ISBN13: 978-0-404-60273-4. Dewey:962/.02. LCCN:78-063545.

Audience: **u,f.**

Jubayr, ibn   **DS46**
The Travels of Ibn Jubayr: Arabic Text of the Rihla. Ed. 2. William Wright (Editor), M. J. De Goeje (Contribution by). Trade Cloth. Gibb Memorial Trust, The. Cambridge, 2002. 416p. ISBN:0-906094-45-3, ISBN13: 978-0-906094-45-7. Dewey:910/.031/767.

Audience: **g,l,u,f.**

Kaegi, Walter E.   **DF553.K34 1997**
Byzantium and the Early Islamic Conquests. Trade Paper. Cambridge University Press. New York, NY. 1995. 327p. ISBN:0-521-48455-3, ISBN13: 978-0-521-48455-8. Dewey:949.5.

Audience: **u,f.**

Kennedy, Hugh   **DS35.687.K46 2001**
The Armies of the Caliphs: Military and Society in the Early Islamic State. Paper over Boards. Routledge. New York, NY. 2001. 256p. Warfare and History Ser. ISBN:0-415-25092-7, ISBN13: 978-0-415-25092-4. Dewey:355/.00917/671. LCCN:2001-019109.

Audience: **g,l,u,f.**   *Choice, 2002.*

Kennedy, Hugh
The Early Abbasid Caliphate: A Political History. Croom Helm. 1981.

Audience: **g,l,u,f.**

Kennedy, Hugh   **DP102.K46 1996**
Muslim Spain and Portugal: A Political History of Al-Andalus. Trade Paper. Longman Publishing Group. White Plains, NY. 1997. 360p. ISBN:0-582-49515-6, ISBN13: 978-0-582-49515-9. Dewey:946/.02. LCCN:96-022764.

Audience: **g,l,u,f.**   *Choice, 1997.*

Kennedy, Hugh N.   **DS38.6**
When Baghdad Ruled the Muslim World. Ed. 1. DaCapo Press. 2005. ISBN:0-306-81435-8, ISBN13: 978-0-306-81435-8.

Audience: **g,l,u,f.**

Kennedy, Hugh &   **DS38.6**
  Barbir, Karl
The Prophet and the Age of the Caliphates: The Islamic Near East from the 6th to the 11th Century. Ed. 2. Trade Paper. Longman Publishing. Boston, MA. 2004. 440p. ISBN:0-582-40525-4, ISBN13: 978-0-582-40525-7. Dewey:956/.013.

Audience: **g,l,u,f.**

Khaldun, Ibn   **D16.7.I2413**
The Muqaddimah: An Introduction to History. Abridged ed. Dawood, N. J. (Editor); Rosenthal, Franz (Translator). Princeton University Press. 1981. ISBN:0-691-09946-4, ISBN13: 978-0-691-09946-0.

Audience: **l,u,f.**

Khalidi, Tarif   **DS38.16.K445 1994**
Arabic Historical Thought in the Classical Period. David Morgan (Contribution by). Trade Cloth. Cambridge University Press. New York, NY. 1994. 264p. Cambridge Studies in Islamic Civilization ISBN:0-521-46554-0, ISBN13: 978-0-521-46554-0. Dewey:909/.097671. LCCN:93-051021.

Audience: **u,f.**   *Choice, 1995.*

Le Strange, Guy   **DS44.9.L6 1976**
The Lands of the Eastern Caliphate. Trade Cloth. A M S Press, Inc. New York, NY. Cambridge Geographical Ser. ISBN:0-404-56287-6, ISBN13: 978-0-404-56287-8. Dewey:911/.56. LCCN:77-180355.

Audience: **l,u,f.**

Le Strange, Guy   **DS289**
Mesopotamia and Persia Under the Mongols in the Fourteenth Century A.D. Library Binding. Porcupine Press, Inc. Cedarburg, WI. 1985. 104p. Studies in Islamic History, No. 18 ISBN:0-87991-108-5, ISBN13: 978-0-87991-108-9. Dewey:955.02.

Audience: **l,u,f.**

Lyons, Malcolm C. &   **DS38.4.S2L93**
  Jackson, D. E. P.
Saladin: The Politics of the Holy War. Trade Paper. Cambridge University Press. New York, NY. 1997. 463p. Canto Original Ser. ISBN:0-521-58562-7, ISBN13: 978-0-521-58562-0. Dewey:956/.014/092. LCCN:79-013078.

Audience: **l,u,f.**

Masudi   **DS38.6.M3813 1989**
The Meadows of Gold. Paul Lunde & Catherine Stone (Translators). Trade Cloth. Kegan Paul International, Ltd. London, 1989. 320p. ISBN:0-7103-0246-0, ISBN13: 978-0-7103-0246-5. Dewey:909/.097671. LCCN:89-140337.

Audience: **l,u,f.**

Mottahedeh, Roy P.   **HN656.A8M67 2001**
Loyalty and Leadership in an Early Islamic Society. Ed. 2. Trade Paper, Perfect. I. B. Tauris & Company, Ltd. London, 2001. 239p. ISBN:1-86064-181-4, ISBN13: 978-1-86064-181-7. Dewey:301.4/009567. LCCN:2001-268502.

Audience: **u,f.**

Muir, William   **DS38.3 .M84 1975**
The Caliphate, Its Rise, Decline, and Fall: From Original Sources. Trade Cloth. A M S Press, Inc. New York, NY. ISBN:0-404-56305-8, ISBN13: 978-0-404-56305-9. Dewey:909/.09/7671. LCCN:74-180365.

Audience: **u,f.**

Robinson, Chase F.   **DS38.4**
'Abd Al-Malik. Saddle Stitched, Cloth over Boards. Oneworld Publications. Oxford, 2005. 139p. ISBN:1-85168-361-5, ISBN13: 978-1-85168-361-1. Dewey:909.097670092.

Audience: **g,l,u,f.**   *Choice, 2006.*

Robinson, Chase F.   **BP49.R63 2002**
Islamic Historiography. Patricia Crone (Contribution by). Cloth Text. Cambridge University Press. New York, NY. 2002. 264p. Themes in Islamic History Ser. ISBN:0-521-62081-3, ISBN13: 978-0-521-62081-9. Dewey:297/.07/22. LCCN:2002-031427.

Audience: **l,u,f.**   *Choice, 2003.*

Shaban, M. A.   **DS236**
The Abbasid Revolution. Trade Cloth. Cambridge University Press. New York, NY. 1979. 208p. ISBN:0-521-07849-0, ISBN13: 978-0-521-07849-8. Dewey:955/.92/02. LCCN:75-112474.

Audience: **u,f.**

Shaban, M. A. DS38.6.S48
Islamic History: A New Interpretation: AD 750-1055 (Ah 132-448). Trade Paper. Cambridge University Press. New York, NY. 1978. 230p. ISBN:0-521-29453-3, ISBN13: 978-0-521-29453-9. Dewey:909/.09/767101. LCCN:75-039390.
Audience: **u,f.**

Shaban, M. A. DS38.5
Islamic History: A. D. 600 - 750 (Ah 132). Trade Paper. Cambridge University Press. New York, NY. 1976. 206p. ISBN:0-521-29131-3, ISBN13: 978-0-521-29131-6. Dewey:231. LCCN:79-145604.
Audience: **u,f.**

Shahid, Irfan DS62.25.S512 1989
Byzantium and the Arabs in the Fifth Century. Trade Cloth. Dumbarton Oaks. Washington, DC. 1989. 620p. ISBN:0-88402-152-1, ISBN13: 978-0-88402-152-0. Dewey:327.495017/671. LCCN:88-013098.
Audience: **u,f.** *Choice, 1990.*

Shatzmiller, Maya DT313.S33 1999
The Berbers and the Islamic State: The Marinid Experience. Paper Text. Markus Wiener Publishers, Inc. Princeton, NJ. 2000. 280p. ISBN:1-55876-224-8, ISBN13: 978-1-55876-224-4. Dewey:964/.02. LCCN:99-049827.
Audience: **u,f.**

Smith, G. Rex
 (Translator)
The History of Al-Tabari: The Conquest of Iran, A. D. 641-643/A. H. 21-23. Paper Text. State University of New York Press. Albany, NY. 1994. 190p. SUNY Series in Near Eastern Studies ISBN:0-7914-1294-6, ISBN13: 978-0-7914-1294-7. LCCN:92-025776.
Audience: **l,u,f.**

Tabari DS38.2.T313
The History of Al-Tabari: The End of Expansion: The Caliphate of Hisham, A. D. 724-738/A. H. 105-120. Khalid Yahya Blankinship (Translator). Cloth Text. State University of New York Press. Albany, NY. 1989. 219p. SUNY Series in Near Eastern Studies ISBN:0-88706-569-4, ISBN13: 978-0-88706-569 9. Dewey:909/.1 s. LCCN:87-007125.
Audience: **l,u,f.**

Tabari DS38.2.T313
The History of Al-Tabari: The Challenge to the Empires, A. D. 633-635/A. H. 12-13. Khalid Yahya Blankinship (Translator). Cloth Text. State University of New York Press. Albany, NY. 1993. 261p. SUNY Series in Near Eastern Studies ISBN:0-7914-0851-5, ISBN13: 978-0-7914-0851-3. Dewey:909/.1 s. LCCN:90-028420.
Audience: **l,u,f.**

Tabari DS38.2.T313
The History of Al-Tabari: The Sasanids, the Lakhmids and Yemen. C. E. Bosworth (Translator). Cloth Text. State University of New York Press. Albany, NY. 1999. xxiv, 458p. SUNY Series in Near Eastern Studies ISBN:0-7914-4355-8, ISBN13: 978-0-7914-4355-2. Dewey:955.02. LCCN:99-038279.
Audience: **l,u,f.**

Tabari DS38.2.T313
The History of Al-Tabari: The Reunification of the 'Abbasid Caliphate: The Caliphate of Al-Ma'Mun, A. D. 813-833/A. H. 198-218. C. E. Bosworth (Translator). Cloth Text. State University of New York Press. Albany, NY. 1987. 281p. SUNY

Series in Near Eastern Studies ISBN:0-88706-058-7, ISBN13: 978-0-88706-058-8. Dewey:909/.097671. LCCN:84-016311.
Audience: **l,u,f.**

Tabari DS38.2.T313 VOL. 33
The History of Al-Tabari: Storm and Stress along the Northern Frontiers of the 'Abbasid Caliphate: The Caliphate of Al-Mu'Tasim A. D. 833-842/A. H. 218-227. C. E. Bosworth (Translator). Cloth Text. State University of New York Press. Albany, NY. 1991. 261p. SUNY Series in Near Eastern Studies ISBN:0-7914-0493-5, ISBN13: 978-0-7914-0493-5. Dewey:909/.1 s. LCCN:90-033516.
Audience: **l,u,f.**

Tabari DS38.2.T313
The History of Al-Tabari: The 'Abbasid Caliphate in Equilibrium: The Caliphates of Musa Al-Hadi and Harun Al-Rashid, A. D. 785-809/A. H. 169-193. C. E. Bosworth (Editor, Translator). Cloth Text. State University of New York Press. Albany, NY. 1989. 365p. SUNY Series in Near Eastern Studies ISBN:0-88706-564-3, ISBN13: 978-0-88706-564-4. Dewey:909/.1 s. LCCN:87-007124.
Audience: **l,u,f.**

Tabari DS38.2.T313
The History of Al-Tabari: The Children of Israel. William M. Brinner (Translator). Cloth Text. State University of New York Press. Albany, NY. 1991. 180p. SUNY Series in Near Eastern Studies ISBN:0-7914-0687-3, ISBN13: 978-0-7914-0687-8. Dewey:909/.1. LCCN:90-010264.
Audience: **l,u,f.**

Tabari DS38.2.T313
The History of Al-Tabari: Prophets and Patriarchs. William M. Brinner (Translator). Cloth Text. State University of New York Press. Albany, NY. 1986. 207p. SUNY Series in Near Eastern Studies ISBN:0-87395-921-3, ISBN13: 978-0-87395-921-6. Dewey:930. LCCN:84-000097.
Audience: **l,u,f.**

Tabari DS38.1
The History of Al-Tabari: The Community Divided: The Caliphate of 'Ali I, A. D. 656-657/A. H. 35-36. Adrian Brockett (Translator). Cloth Text. State University of New York Press. Albany, NY. 1997. 288p. SUNY Series in Near Eastern Studies ISBN:0-7914-2391-3, ISBN13: 978-0-7914-2391-2. Dewey:909/.1 s. LCCN:96-017177.
Audience: **l,u,f.**

Tabari
The History of Al-Tabari: The Conquest of Arabia: The Riddah Wars, A. D. 632-633/A. H. 11. Fred M. Donner (Translator). Cloth Text. State University of New York Press. Albany, NY. 1993. 216p. SUNY Series in Near Eastern Studies ISBN:0-7914-1071-4, ISBN13: 978-0-7914-1071-4. LCCN:91-035989.
Audience: **l,u,f.**

Tabari
The History of Al-Tabari: The 'Abbasid Recovery: The War Against the Zanj Ends, A. D. 879-893/A. H. 266-279. Philip M. Fields (Translator), Jacob Lassner (Annotations by). Cloth Text. State University of New York Press. Albany, NY. 1987. 195p. SUNY Series in Near Eastern Studies ISBN:0-88706-054-4, ISBN13: 978-0-88706-054-0. LCCN:83-024249.
Audience: **l,u,f.**

Tabari
The History of Al-Tabari: The War Between Brothers: The Caliphate of Muhammad al-Amin A. D. 809-813/A. H. 193-198. Michael Fishbein (Translator). Cloth Text. State University of New York Press. Albany, NY. 1992. 268p. SUNY Series in Near Eastern Studies ISBN:0-7914-1085-4, ISBN13: 978-0-7914-1085-1. LCCN:91-038852.

Audience: **l,u,f.**

Tabari   **DS38.2.T313**
The History of Al-Tabari: The Victory of the Marwanids, A. D. 685-693/A. H. 66-73. Michael Fishbein (Translator). Cloth Text. State University of New York Press. Albany, NY. 1990. 260p. SUNY Series in Near Eastern Studies ISBN:0-7914-0221-5, ISBN13: 978-0-7914-0221-4. Dewey:909/.097671. LCCN:89-004518.

Audience: **l,u,f.**

Tabari   **BP55**
The History of Al-Tabari: The Victory of Islam: Muhammad at Medina, A. D. 626-630/A. H. 5-8. Michael Fishbein (Translator). Cloth Text. State University of New York Press. Albany, NY. 1997. 224p. SUNY Series in Near Eastern Studies ISBN:0-7914-3149-5, ISBN13: 978-0-7914-3149-8. Dewey:909/.097671. LCCN:96-030872.

Audience: **l,u,f.**

Tabari   **DS38.2.T313**
The History of Al-Tabari: The Battle of Al-Qadisiyyah and the Conquest of Syria and Palestine, A. D. 635-637/A. H. 14-15. Yohanan Friedmann (Translator). Cloth Text. State University of New York Press. Albany, NY. 1992. 237p. SUNY Series in Near Eastern Studies ISBN:0-7914-0733-0, ISBN13: 978-0-7914-0733-2. Dewey:909/.1. LCCN:90-010326.

Audience: **l,u,f.**

Tabari   **DS38.2.T313**
The History of Al-Tabari: The First Civil War: From the Battle of Siffin to the Death of 'Ali, A. D. 656-661/A. H. 36-40. Gerald R. Hawting (Translator). Cloth Text. State University of New York Press. Albany, NY. 1996. 250p. SUNY Series in Near Eastern Studies ISBN:0-7914-2393-X, ISBN13: 978-0-7914-2393-6. Dewey:962/.02. LCCN:95-047957.

Audience: **l,u,f.**

Tabari   **DS38.2.T313**
The History of Al-Tabari: The Collapse of Sufyanid Authority and the Coming of the Marwanids: The Caliphates of Mu'Awiyah II and Marwan I and the Beginning of the Caliphate of 'Abd Al-Malik, A. D. 683-685/A.H. 64-66. Gerald R. Hawting (Translator). Cloth Text. State University of New York Press. Albany, NY. 1989. 246p. SUNY Series in Near Eastern Studies ISBN:0-88706-855-3, ISBN13: 978-0-88706-855-3. Dewey:909/.1 s. LCCN:88-024983.

Audience: **l,u,f.**

Tabari   **DS38.2.T313**
The History of Al-Tabari: The Waning of the Umayyad Caliphate: Prelude to Revolution, A. D. 738-745/A. H. 121-127. Carole Hillenbrand (Translator). Cloth Text. State University of New York Press. Albany, NY. 1989. 300p. SUNY Series in Near Eastern Studies ISBN:0-88706-810-3, ISBN13: 978-0-88706-810-2. Dewey:909/.097671 s. LCCN:87-033505.

Audience: **l,u,f.**

Tabari   **DS38.2.T313**
The History of Al-Tabari: The Zenith of the Marwanid House: The Last Years of 'Abd Al-Malik and the Caliphate of Al-Walid A. D. 700-715/A. H. 81-96. Martin Hinds (Translator). Cloth

Text. State University of New York Press. Albany, NY. 1990. 254p. SUNY Series in Near Eastern Studies ISBN:0-88706-721-2, ISBN13: 978-0-88706-721-1. Dewey:909/.1 s. LCCN:87-017997.

Audience: **l,u,f.**

Tabari   **DS38.2.T313**
The History of Al-Tabari: The Caliphate of Yazid B. Mu'awiyah, A. D. 680-683/A. H. 60-64. I. K. A. Howard (Translator). Cloth Text. State University of New York Press. Albany, NY. 1991. 248p. SUNY Series in Near Eastern Studies ISBN:0-7914-0040-9, ISBN13: 978-0-7914-0040-1. LCCN:88-039753.

Audience: **l,u,f.**

Tabari   **DS38.2.T313**
The History of Al-Tabari: The Crisis of the Early Caliphate: The Reign of 'Uthman, A. D. 644-656/A. H. 24-35. R. Stephen Humphreys (Translator). Cloth Text. State University of New York Press. Albany, NY. 1990. 285p. SUNY Series in Near Eastern Studies ISBN:0-7914-0154-5, ISBN13: 978-0-7914-0154-5. Dewey:909/.1 s. LCCN:88-035555.

Audience: **l,u,f.**

Tabari   **DS38.2.T313**
The History of Al-Tabari: The Conquest of Iraq, Southwestern Persia, and Egypt: The Middle Years of 'Umar's Caliphate, A .D. 636-642/A. H. 15-21. Gautier H. A. Juynboll (Translator). Cloth Text. State University of New York Press. Albany, NY. 1989. 251p. SUNY Series in Near Eastern Studies ISBN:0-88706-876-6, ISBN13: 978-0-88706-876-8. Dewey:909/.1 s. LCCN:88-002262.

Audience: **l,u,f.**

Tabari   **DS38.2.T313**
The History of Al-Tabari: Al-Mansur and Al-Mahdi, A. D. 763-786/A. H. 146-169. Hugh Kennedy (Translator). Cloth Text. State University of New York Press. Albany, NY. 1990. 281p. SUNY Series in Near Eastern Studies ISBN:0-7914-0142-1, ISBN13: 978-0-7914-0142-2. Dewey:909/.1 s. LCCN:88-035573.

Audience: **l,u,f.**

Tabari   **DS38.2.T313**
The History of Al-Tabari: Incipient Decline: The Caliphates of Al-Wathiq, Al-Mutawakkil, and Al-Muntasir, A.D. 841-863/A. H. 227-248. Joel L. Kraemer (Translator). Cloth Text. State University of New York Press. Albany, NY. 1989. 249p. SUNY Series in Near Eastern Studies ISBN:0-88706-874-X, ISBN13: 978-0-88706-874-4. Dewey:909/.1 s. LCCN:88-002261.

Audience: **l,u,f.**

Tabari   **DS38.2.T313 1985**
The History of Al-Tabari: Biographies of the Prophet's Companions and Their Successors: Al-Tabari's Supplement to His History. Ella Landau-Tasseron (Translator). Trade Cloth. State University of New York Press. Albany, NY. 1998. 320p. SUNY Series in Near Eastern Studies ISBN:0-7914-2819-2, ISBN13: 978-0-7914-2819-1. Dewey:297.6/48 B. LCCN:97-045138.

Audience: **l,u,f.**

Tabari   **DS38.6**
The History of Al-Tabari: 'Abbasid Authority Affirmed: The Early Years of Al-Mansur A. D. 753-763/A. H. 136-145. Jane Dammen McAuliffe (Translator). Cloth Text. State University of New York Press. Albany, NY. 1995. 326p. SUNY Series in Near

Eastern Studies ISBN:0-7914-1895-2, ISBN13: 978-0-7914-1895-6. Dewey:909/.1 s. LCCN:93-044496.

Audience: l,u,f.

Tabari   **DS38.2.T313**
The History of Al-Tabari: The Foundation of the Community: Muhammad at Al-Madina, A. D. 622-626/ijrah-4 A. H. M. V. McDonald (Translator), W. Montgomery Watt (Annotations by). Cloth Text. State University of New York Press. Albany, NY. 1987. 182p. SUNY Series in Near Eastern Studies ISBN:0-88706-344-6, ISBN13: 978-0-88706-344-2. Dewey:909/.097671. LCCN:87-012940.

Audience: l,u,f.

Tabari   **DS38.2.T313**
The History of Al-Tabari: Between Civil Wars: the Caliphate of Mu'Awiyah, A. D. 661-680/A. H. 40-60. Michael G. Morony (Translator). Cloth Text. State University of New York Press. Albany, NY. 1986. 261p. SUNY Series in Near Eastern Studies ISBN:0-87395-933-7, ISBN13: 978-0-87395-933-9. Dewey:909/.097671. LCCN:85-002823.

Audience: l,u,f.

Tabari   **DS38.2.T313**
The History of Al-Tabari: The Ancient Kingdoms. Moshe Perlmann (Editor, Translator). Cloth Text. State University of New York Press. Albany, NY. 1987. 205p. SUNY Series in Near Eastern Studies ISBN:0-88706-181-8, ISBN13: 978-0-88706-181-3. Dewey:935. LCCN:85-017282.

Audience: l,u,f.

Tabari   **DS38.2.T313**
The History of Al-Tabari: The Last Years of the Prophet: the Formation of the State, A. D. 630-632/A. H. 8-11. Ismail K. Poonawala (Editor, Translator). Cloth Text. State University of New York Press. Albany, NY. 1990. 250p. SUNY Series in Near Eastern Studies ISBN:0-88706-691-7, ISBN13: 978-0-88706-691-7. LCCN:87-007129.

Audience: l,u,f.

Tabari   **DS38.2.T313**
The History of Al-Tabari: The Empire in Transition: The Caliphates of Sulayman, 'Umar, and Yazid, A. D. 715-724/A. H. 97-105. David Stephan Powers (Translator). Cloth Text. State University of New York Press. Albany, NY. 1989. 218p. SUNY Series in Near Eastern Studies ISBN:0-7914-0072-7, ISBN13: 978-0-7914-0072-2. Dewey:909/.1 s. LCCN:88-039752.

Audience: l,u,f.

Tabari   **DS38.2**
The History of Al-Tabari: General Introduction and from the Creation to the Flood. Franz Rosenthal (Translator). Cloth Text. State University of New York Press. Albany, NY. 1989. 413p. SUNY Series in the History of Al-Tabari, Vol. 1 ISBN:0-88706-562-7, ISBN13: 978-0-88706-562-0. Dewey:909/.1 s. LCCN:87-033532.

Audience: l,u,f.

Tabari
The History of Al-Tabari: The Return of the Caliphate to Baghdad: The Caliphate of Al-Mu'Tadid, Al-Muktafi and Al-Muqtadir, A. D. 892-915/A. H. 279-302. Franz Rosenthal (Editor, Translator). Cloth Text. State University of New York Press. Albany, NY. 1985. 239p. SUNY Series in Near Eastern Studies ISBN:0-87395-876-4, ISBN13: 978-0-87395-876-9. LCCN:83-018115.

Audience: l,u,f.

Tabari   **DS38.2.T313**
The History of Al-Tabari: The Marwanid Restoration: the Caliphate of 'Abd Al-Malik: A. D. 693-701/A. H. 74-81. Everett K. Rowson (Translator). Cloth Text. State University of New York Press. Albany, NY. 1989. 228p. SUNY Series in Near Eastern Studies ISBN:0-88706-975-4, ISBN13: 978-0-88706-975-8. LCCN:88-016086.

Audience: l,u,f.

Tabari
The History of Al-Tabari: The Crisis of the 'Abbasid Caliphate -The Caliphates of Al-Musta'In and Al-Mu'Tazz, A. D. 862-869/A. H. 24-255. George Saliba (Translator). Cloth Text. State University of New York Press. Albany, NY. 1985. 187p. SUNY Series in Near Eastern Studies ISBN:0-87395-883-7, ISBN13: 978-0-87395-883-7. LCCN:83-024247.

Audience: l,u,f.

Tabari   **DS38.2.T313**
The History of Al-Tabari: The Revolt of the Zanj, A. D. 869-879/A. D. 255-265. David Waines (Translator). Cloth Text. State University of New York Press. Albany, NY. 1991. 250p. SUNY Series in Near Eastern Studies ISBN:0-7914-0763-2, ISBN13: 978-0-7914-0763-9. Dewey:956.7/02. LCCN:90-010324.

Audience: l,u,f.

Tabari   **DS38.2.T313**
The History of Al-Tabari: Muhammad at Mecca. W. Montgomery Watt & M. V. McDonald (Translators). Cloth Text. State University of New York Press. Albany, NY. 1989. 178p. SUNY Series in Near Eastern Studies ISBN:0-88706-706-9, ISBN13: 978-0-88706-706-8. Dewey:909/.1 s. LCCN:87-017949.

Audience: l,u,f.

Tabari
The History of Al-Tabari: The 'Abbasid Revolution, A. D. 743-750/A. H. 126-132. John A. Williams (Editor, Translator). Cloth Text. State University of New York Press. Albany, NY. 1985. 248p. SUNY Series in Near Eastern Studies ISBN:0-87395-884-5, ISBN13: 978-0-87395-884-4. LCCN:83-024249.

Audience: l,u,f.

Vryonis, Speros   **DF545.V78**
The Decline of Medieval Hellenism in Asia Minor and the Process of Islamization from the Eleventh Through the Fifteenth Century. Trade Cloth. University of California Press. Berkeley, CA. 1971. xvii, 532p. ISBN:0-520-01597-5, ISBN13: 978-0-520-01597-5. Dewey:913.3/95/03. LCCN:75-094984.

Audience: u,f.

Walker, E. Paul   **DT96**
Exploring an Islamic Empire: Fatimid History and Its Sources. Cloth over Boards. I. B. Tauris & Company, Ltd. London, 2002. 160p. ISBN:1-86064-692-1, ISBN13: 978-1-86064-692-8. Dewey:962/.02.

Audience: u,f.

Watt, W. Montgomery   **D199.3**
A History of Islamic Spain. Edinburgh University Press. 1965.

Audience: g,l,u,f.

Watt, William M.   **DS36.85.W37 1990**
The Majesty That Was Islam: The Islamic World, 661-1100. Cloth Text. Palgrave Macmillan. New York, NY. 1990. 288p.

Great Civilizations Ser. ISBN:0-312-04714-2, ISBN13: 978-0-312-04714-6. Dewey:909/.097671. LCCN:90-032496.

Audience: **g,l,u,f.**

Wellhausen, Julius　　　　**DS38.5.W4513 2000**
The Arab Kingdom and Its Fall. Routledge. 2000.
ISBN:0-415-20904-8, ISBN13: 978-0-415-20904-5.

Audience: **u,f.**

Islamic Middle East > By Period > Ottomans 1517-1918

Abou-El-Haj, Rifa'at　　　　**DR511**
'Ali
Formation of the Modern State: The Ottoman Empire, Sixteenth to Eighteenth Centuries. Cloth Text. State University of New York Press. Albany, NY. 1992. 155p. SUNY Series in the Social and Economic History of the Middle East ISBN:0-7914-0893-0, ISBN13: 978-0-7914-0893-3. Dewey:956/.0152. LCCN:91-002049.

Audience: **u,f.**

Babinger, Franz　　　　**DR501**
Mehmed the Conqueror and His Time. William C. Hickman (Editor). Trade Paper. Princeton University Press. Princeton, NJ. 1992. 570p. Bollingen Ser., No. XCVI ISBN:0-691-01078-1, ISBN13: 978-0-691-01078-6. Dewey:956.1/01/0924.

Audience: **u,f.** *B*

Braude, Benjamin &　　　　**DS58**
Lewis, Bernard (Editors)
Christians and Jews in the Ottoman Empire: The Functioning of a Plural Society. Holmes & Meier. 1982.

Audience: **u,f.**

Bromley, J. S., et al.　　　　**DR486**
History of the Ottoman Empire to 1730. H. Inalcik, A. N. Kurat & V. J. Parry (Authors), M. A. Cook (Editor). Trade Paper. Cambridge University Press. New York, NY. 1976. 232p. ISBN:0-521-09991-9, ISBN13: 978-0-521-09991-2. Dewey:956. LCCN:75-038188.

Audience: **g,l,u,f.**

Brown, L. Carl (Editor)　　　　**DS62.4.B679 1996**
The Imperial Legacy: The Ottoman Imprint on the Balkans and the Middle East. Trade Cloth. Columbia University Press. New York, NY. 1996. 320p. ISBN:0-231-10304-2, ISBN13: 978-0-231-10304-6. Dewey:909/.09712561. LCCN:95-015506.

Audience: **g,l,u,f.** *Choice, 1996.*

Clot, Andre　　　　**DR506.C5713 1992**
Suleiman the Magnificent: The Man, His Life, His Epoch. Matthew Reisz & John Howe (Translators). Cloth over Boards. I. B. Tauris & Company, Ltd. London, 1992. 360p. ISBN:0-86356-126-8, ISBN13: 978-0-86356-126-9. Dewey:956.1/01/0924. LCCN:93-165067.

Audience: **l,u,f.**

Creasy, Edward　　　　**DR440 .C91**
Shepherd
History of the Ottoman Turks: From the Beginning of Their Empire to the Present Time. Zeine N. Zeine (Introduction by). Trade Cloth. Khayat Publications International. Stamford, CT. 2003. 596p. ISBN:1-932441-09-3, ISBN13: 978-1-932441-09-3. Dewey:956.1.

Audience: **u,f.**

Davison, Roderic H.　　　　**DR569.D3**
Reform in the Ottoman Empire, 1856-1876. Trade Cloth. Gordian Press, Inc. Staten Island, NY. 1973. 503p. ISBN:0-87752-135-2, ISBN13: 978-0-87752-135-8. Dewey:956.101. LCCN:73-148618.

Audience: **u,f.** *B*

Evliya Celebi　　　　**QE475.A2**
Narrative of Travels in Europe, Asia and Africa in the 17th Century. Johnson Reprint Corporation. 1987. ISBN:0-384-14895-6, ISBN13: 978-0-384-14895-6.

Audience: **l,u,f.**

Faroqhi, Suraiya　　　　**DR486**
The Ottoman Empire and the World Around It. Trade Paper. I. B. Tauris & Company, Ltd. London, 2006. 304p. Library of Ottoman Studies ISBN:1-84511-122-2, ISBN13: 978-1-84511-122-9. Dewey:956.1/015.

Audience: **u,f.** *Choice, 2005.*

Faroqhi, Suraiya　　　　**DR432.F2313 2000**
Subjects of the Sultan: Culture and Daily Life in the Ottoman Empire. Cloth over Boards. I. B. Tauris & Company, Ltd. London, 2000. 287p. ISBN:1-86064-289-6, ISBN13: 978-1-86064-289-0. Dewey:956.1015. LCCN:00-711675.

Audience: **l,u,f.** *Choice, 2001.*

Findley, Carter V.　　　　**JQ1806.Z1**
Bureaucratic Reform in the Ottoman Empire: The Sublime Porte, 1789-1922. Trade Cloth. Princeton University Press. Princeton, NJ. 1980. 496p. Near East Studies ISBN:0-691-05288-3, ISBN13: 978-0-691-05288-5. Dewey:354/.496. LCCN:79-083987.

Audience: **u,f.** *B*

Frazee, C. A.　　　　**BX1490 .F7**
Catholics and Sultans: The Church and the Ottoman Empire 1453-1923. Trade Paper. Cambridge University Press. New York, NY. 2006. 396p. ISBN:0-521-02700-4, ISBN13: 978-0-521-02700-7. Dewey:282/.09/03.

Audience: **u,f.**

Gibb, H. A. R. &　　　　**DS38**
Bowen, Harold
Islamic Society and the West: A Study of the Impact of Western Civilization on Moslem Culture in the Near East. Oxford University Press. 1950.

Audience: **l,u,f.**

Gocek, Fatma M.　　　　**HN656.5.A8G63 1996**
Rise of the Bourgeoisie, Demise of Empire: Ottoman Westernization and Social Change. Trade Cloth. Oxford University Press, Inc. New York, NY. 1996. 228p. ISBN:0-19-509925-7, ISBN13: 978-0-19-509925-6. Dewey:306/.09561. LCCN:95-010331.

Audience: **u,f.** *Choice, 1996.*

Goffman, Daniel　　　　**DR486 .G62 2002**
The Ottoman Empire and Early Modern Europe. William Beik, T. C. W. Blanning & Brendan Simms (Contribution by). Cloth Text. Cambridge University Press. New York, NY. 2002. 300p. New Approaches to European History Ser., Vol. 24 ISBN:0-521-45280-5, ISBN13: 978-0-521-45280-9. Dewey:956.1015. LCCN:2001-043336.

Audience: **u,f.** *Choice, 2003.*

Haddad, William W. &   DS62.4 .N36
Ochsenwald, William L. (Editors)
Nationalism in a Non-National State: The Dissolution of the
Ottoman Empire. Trade Cloth. Ohio State University Press.
Columbus, OH. 1977. 307p. ISBN:0-8142-0191-1, ISBN13:
978-0-8142-0191-6. Dewey:320.9/56. LCCN:77-001253.
Audience: **u,f.**

Inalcik, Halil   DR486 .I477
From Empire to Republic: Essays on Ottoman and Turkish
Social History. Trade Paper. Evergreen Book Distributors. Los
Angeles, CA. 1996. 179p. ISBN:0-614-24318-1, ISBN13:
978-0-614-24318-5. Dewey:956/.015.
Audience: **u,f.**

Inalcik, Halil   DR486
The Ottoman Empire: The Classical Age, 1300-1600. Phoenix
Press. 2000.
Audience: **u,f.**

Inalcik, Halil   HC492 .E295 1994
An Economic and Social History of the Ottoman Empire,
1300-1914, Set. Donald Quataert (Preface by). Cloth Text.
Cambridge University Press. New York, NY. 1994. 1066p.
ISBN:0-521-34315-1, ISBN13: 978-0-521-34315-2.
Dewey:956.015. LCCN:93-014763.
Audience: **u,f.** *Choice, 1995.*

Itzkowitz, Norman   DR486.I89 1980
Ottoman Empire and Islamic Tradition. Trade Paper. University
of Chicago Press. Chicago, IL. 1980. 128p. Phoenix Book Ser.
ISBN:0-226-38806-9, ISBN13: 978-0-226-38806-9.
Dewey:956.1/01. LCCN:79-023386.
Audience: **l,u,f.** *B*

Kafadar, Cemal   DR486.K34
Between Two Worlds: The Construction of the Ottoman State.
Trade Paper. University of California Press. Berkeley, CA. 1996.
242p. ISBN:0-520-20600-2, ISBN13: 978-0-520-20600-7.
Dewey:956.1/0072.
Audience: **l,u,f.** *Choice, 1995.*

Karpat, Kemal H.   DR572.K28 2001
The Politicization of Islam: Reconstructing Identity, State, Faith,
and Community in the Late Ottoman State. Cloth Text. Oxford
University Press, Inc. New York, NY. 2001. 544p. Studies in
Middle Eastern History ISBN:0-19-513618-7, ISBN13:
978-0-19-513618-0. Dewey:320.54/09561/09034.
LCCN:99-053429.
Audience: **l,u,f.** *Choice, 2002.*

Karpat, Kemal H.   DR445.O77 2003
(Editor)
Ottoman Borderlands: Issues, Personalities, and Political
Changes. Robert Zens (Contribution by). Trade Paper.
University of Wisconsin Press. Chicago, IL. 2004. 352p.
Distributed for the International Journal of Turkish Studies, No.
2 ISBN:0-299-20024-8, ISBN13: 978-0-299-20024-4.
Dewey:911/.56. LCCN:2004-299384.
Audience: **u,f.**

Kasaba, Resat   HC492.K37 1988
The Ottoman Empire and the World Economy: The Nineteenth
Century. Cloth Text. State University of New York Press.
Albany, NY. 1988. 191p. SUNY Series in Middle Eastern
Studies ISBN:0-88706-804-9, ISBN13: 978-0-88706-804-1.
Dewey:330.9561/038. LCCN:88-003039.
Audience: **u,f.** *Choice, 1989.*

Koprulu, Mehmed Fuad   DR486.K6313 1991
The Origins of the Ottoman Empire. Gary Leiser (Editor,
Translator). Cloth Text. State University of New York Press.
Albany, NY. 1992. 155p. SUNY Series in the Social and
Economic History of the Middle East ISBN:0-7914-0819-1,
ISBN13: 978-0-7914-0819-3. Dewey:949.61. LCCN:90-022723.
Audience: **l,u,f.**

Levy, Avigdor (Editor)   DS135.T8J53 2002
Jews, Turks, and Ottomans: A Shared History, Fifteenth to
Twentieth Centuries. Trade Cloth. Syracuse University Press.
Syracuse, NY. 2002. 301p. Modern Jewish History Ser.
ISBN:0-8156-2941-9, ISBN13: 978-0-8156-2941-2.
Dewey:956/.004924. LCCN:2002-011481.
Audience: **u,f.** *Choice, 2003.*

Lewis, Raphaela   DR38
Everyday Life in Ottoman Turkey. Trade Cloth. Hippocrene
Books, Inc. New York, NY. 1988. 206p. Dorset Press Reprints
Ser. ISBN:0-88029-175-3, ISBN13: 978-0-88029-175-0.
Dewey:914.96/03.
Audience: **g,l,u,f.**

Lybyer, Albert Howe   DR507 .L8
The Government of the Ottoman Empire in the Time of
Suleiman the Magnificent. Trade Cloth. Library Reprints, Inc.
Temecula, CA. 349p. ISBN:0-7222-7300-2, ISBN13:
978-0-7222-7300-5. Dewey:320.9/561/01.
Audience: **u,f.** *B*

Masters, Bruce Alan   DS59.C48M37 2001
e Christians and Jews in the Ottoman Arab World: The Roots
of Sectarianism. E-Book. Cambridge University Press. New
York, NY. ISBN:0-511-01781-2, ISBN13: 978-0-511-01781-0.
Dewey:305.6/09569.
Audience: **u,f.** *Choice, 2002.*

McCarthy, Justin   DR568.M33 2001
The Ottoman Peoples and the End of Empire. Cloth Text.
Oxford University Press, Inc. New York, NY. 2001. 248p. An
Arnold Publication Ser. ISBN:0-340-70656-2, ISBN13:
978-0-340-70656-5. Dewey:956.1/015. LCCN:2001-273284.
Audience: **u,f.** *Choice, 2002.*

McCarthy, Justin   DR486.M33 1996
The Ottoman Turks: An Introductory History to 1923. Trade
Paper. Longman Publishing Group. White Plains, NY. 1997.
424p. ISBN:0-582-25655-0, ISBN13: 978-0-582-25655-2.
Dewey:956/.015. LCCN:96-016824.
Audience: **l,u,f.**

Mehmed, Pasha   JN9718 .M4 1971
Ottoman Statecraft: The Book of Council for Vezirs and
Governors (Nasaih Ul-Vuzera Ve' Lumera) of Sari Mehmed
Pasha, the Defterdar. Walter L. Wright (Translator). Library
Binding. Greenwood Publishing Group, Inc. Portsmouth, NH.
1971. ISBN:0-8371-5825-7, ISBN13: 978-0-8371-5825-9.
Dewey:320.9/561/01. LCCN:79-141262.
Audience: **u,f.**

Merriman, Roger B.   DR506
Suleiman the Magnificent, 1520-1566. Trade Cloth. Cooper
Square Publishers, Inc. New York, NY. 1966.
ISBN:0-8154-0152-3, ISBN13: 978-0-8154-0152-0.
Dewey:956.1/01/0924. LCCN:65-025497.
Audience: **l,u,f.**

Naima   **DR485 .N3132**
Annals of the Turkish Empire from 1591 to 1659 of the
Christian Era. Charles Fraser (Translator). Trade Cloth. Ayer
Company Publishers, Inc. Manchester, NH. 1973. The Middle
East Ser. ISBN:0-405-05352-5, ISBN13: 978-0-405-05352-8.
Dewey:956.1/01. LCCN:73-006294.

Audience: **u,f.**

Peirce, Leslie P.   **HQ1240.5.T87P45 1993**
The Imperial Harem: Women and Sovereignty in the Ottoman
Empire. Trade Cloth. Oxford University Press, Inc. New York,
NY. 1993. 400p. Studies in Middle Eastern History
ISBN:0-19-507673-7, ISBN13: 978-0-19-507673-8.
Dewey:305.420956. LCCN:93-018967.

Audience: **g,l,u,f.**

Piterberg, Gabriel   **DR438.8 .P58 2003**
An Ottoman Tragedy: History and Historiography at Play. Trade
Cloth. University of California Press. Berkeley, CA. 2003. 209p.
Studies on the History of Society and Culture, Vol. 50
ISBN:0-520-23836-2, ISBN13: 978-0-520-23836-7.
Dewey:956/.015. LCCN:2002-152983.

Audience: **l,u,f.**   *Choice, 2004.*

Quataert, Donald   **DR485 .Q37 2000**
The Ottoman Empire, 1700-1922. William Beik & T. C. W.
Blanning (Contribution by). Cloth Text. Cambridge University
Press. New York, NY. 2000. 230p. New Approaches to
European History Ser., No. 17 ISBN:0-521-63328-1, ISBN13:
978-0-521-63328-4. Dewey:956.1/015. LCCN:99-053406.

Audience: **u,f.**

Quataert, Donald   **HD9866.T92Q38 1993**
Ottoman Manufacturing in the Age of the Industrial Revolution.
Edmund Burke, Michael C. Hudson, Walid Kazziha, Rashid
Khalidi, Serif Mardin, Roger Owen, Basim Musallam, Avi
Shlaim & Malcolm Yapp (Contribution by). Trade Cloth.
Cambridge University Press. New York, NY. 1993. 244p.
Middle East Library ISBN:0-521-42017-2, ISBN13:
978-0-521-42017-4. Dewey:338.4/7/677/0956.
LCCN:94-136812.

Audience: **u,f.**

Quataert, Donald &   **HD8656.5.W67 1995**
Zurcher, Eric J. (Editors)
Workers and Working Class in the Ottoman Empire and the
Turkish Republic, 1839-1950. Cloth over Boards. I. B. Tauris &
Company, Ltd. London, 1995. 224p. Library of Modern Middle
East Studies ISBN:1-85043-875-7, ISBN13: 978-1-85043-875-5.
Dewey:305.5/9561. LCCN:94-061511.

Audience: **u,f.**

Shaw, Stanford J.   **DR440**
History of the Ottoman Empire and Modern Turkey. Cambridge
University Press. 1976. ISBN:0-521-21280-4, ISBN13:
978-0-521-21280-9.

Audience: **l,u,f.**

Somel, Selcuk Aksin   **DR436.S66 2003**
Historical Dictionary of the Ottoman Empire. Trade Cloth.
Scarecrow Press, Inc. Lanham, MD. 2003. 512p. Historical
Dictionaries of Ancient Civilizations and Historical Eras Ser.
ISBN:0-8108-4332-3, ISBN13: 978-0-8108-4332-5.
Dewey:956/.015/03. LCCN:2002-012346.

Audience: **g,l,u,f.**   *Choice, 2003.*

Wittek, Paul   **DR485**
The Rise of the Ottoman Empire: Studies on the History of
Turkey, 13th-15th Centuries. Trade Cloth. Routledge. New York,

NY. 2005. 260p. Royal Asiatic Society Bks Ser.
ISBN:0-7007-1500-2, ISBN13: 978-0-7007-1500-8.
Dewey:956.1/015.

Audience: **l,u,f.**

Islamic Middle East > By Period > Modern Middle East/Nation States 1918-

Abu Khaldun Sati Al   **DS98 .H813**
Husri
The Day of Maysalun: A Page from the Modern History of the
Arabs. Sidney Glazer (Translator). Trade Paper. Middle East
Institute. Washington, DC. 1966. ISBN:0-916808-06-8, ISBN13:
978-0-916808-06-8. Dewey:956.9104. LCCN:66-029228.

Audience: **u,f.**

Abu-Lughod, Lila   **HQ1726.5.R45 1998**
(Editor)
Remaking Women: Feminism and Modernity in the Middle East.
Trade Cloth. Princeton University Press. Princeton, NJ. 1998.
314p. Princeton Studies in Culture/Power/History
ISBN:0-691-05791-5, ISBN13: 978-0-691-05791-0.
Dewey:305.42/0956. LCCN:97-046125.

Audience: **g,l,u,f.**   *Choice, 1999.*

Afkhami, Mahnaz   **HQ1170.F35 1995**
(Editor, Introduction by)
Faith and Freedom: Women's Human Rights in the Middle East.
Trade Cloth. Syracuse University Press. Syracuse, NY. 1995.
184p. Gender, Culture, and Politics in the Middle East Ser.
ISBN:0-8156-2667-3, ISBN13: 978-0-8156-2667-1.
Dewey:305.48/6971. LCCN:95-021150.

Audience: **g,l,u,f.**

Al-Hakim, Tawfiq   **DT107.83.H334413**
The Return of Consciousness. Bayly Winder (Translator). Cloth
Text. New York University Press. New York, NY. 1985. 192p.
Studies in Near Eastern Civilization ISBN:0-8147-9202-2,
ISBN13: 978-0-8147-9202-5. Dewey:962/.05. LCCN:84-016670.

Audience: **l,u,f.**

Amirahmadi, Hooshang   **DS318.825.R44 1992**
& Entessar, Nader
Reconstruction and Regional Diplomacy in the Persian Gulf.
Paper over Boards. Routledge. New York, NY. 1992. 320p.
ISBN:0-415-06485-6, ISBN13: 978-0-415-06485-9.
Dewey:953.605. LCCN:92-009290.

Audience: **u,f.**   *Choice, 1993.*

Barakat, Halim I.   **DS36.88.B36 1993**
The Arab World: Society, Culture, and State. Trade Cloth.
University of California Press. Berkeley, CA. 1993. xiii, 348p.
ISBN:0-520-07907-8, ISBN13: 978-0-520-07907-6.
Dewey:909/.0974927. LCCN:92-023342.

Audience: **g,l,u,f.**   *Choice, 1993.*

Brand, Laurie A.   **HQ1236.5.M8B73 1998**
Women, the State, and Political Liberalization: Middle Eastern
and North African Experiences. Trade Cloth. Columbia
University Press. New York, NY. 1998. 320p.
ISBN:0-231-11266-1, ISBN13: 978-0-231-11266-6.
Dewey:305.42/095695. LCCN:98-004431.

Audience: **l,u,f.**   *Choice, 1999.*

Bulliet, Richard W.   **DS43.E53 1996**
(Editor)
Encyclopedia of the Modern Middle East. Trade Cloth.

Macmillan Publishing Company, Inc. Old Tappan, NJ. 1996. ISBN:0-02-897061-6, ISBN13: 978-0-02-897061-5. Dewey:956/.003. LCCN:96-011800.

Audience: **g,l,u,f.** *Choice, 1997.*

Caesar, Judith　　　　　　　**CT275.C15A3 1997**
Crossing Borders: An American Woman in the Middle East. Trade Cloth. Syracuse University Press. Syracuse, NY. 1997. 280p. Contemporary Issues in the Middle East Ser. ISBN:0-8156-2735-1, ISBN13: 978-0-8156-2735-7. Dewey:956/.00413. LCCN:97-003686.

Audience: **g,l,u,f.**

Carter, Mia　　　　　　　　**DS33.7.I45 1999**
Imperialism and Orientalism: A Documentary Sourcebook. Barbara Harlow (Editor). Trade Paper. Blackwell Publishing, Inc. Malden, MA. 1999. 416p. ISBN:1-55786-711-9, ISBN13: 978-1-55786-711-7. Dewey:950/.3. LCCN:98-028671.

Audience: **l,u,f.**

Chatty, Dawn & Rabo,　　　　**HQ1991.9.O74 1997**
Annika (Editors)
Organizing Women: Formal and Informal Women's Groups in the Middle East. Cloth over Boards. Berg Publishers. Oxford, 1997. 224p. Cross-Cultural Perspectives on Women Ser. ISBN:1-85973-910-5, ISBN13: 978-1-85973-910-5. Dewey:305.406056. LCCN:97-204030.

Audience: **l,u,f.**

Cleveland, William L.　　　　**DS62.4.C53 2004**
A History of the Modern Middle East. Ed. 3. Trade Paper. Westview Press. Boulder, CO. 2004. 608p. ISBN:0-8133-4048-9, ISBN13: 978-0-8133-4048-7. Dewey:956. LCCN:2004-001669.
Audience: **g,l,u,f.** *Choice, 2005, 1994.*

Davis, Uri　　　　　　　　　**JQ1758.A92**
Citizenship and the State: A Comparative Study of Citizenship Legislation in Israel, Jordan, Palestine, Syria and Lebanon. Trade Cloth. Garnet Publishing, Ltd. Reading, 2001. 252p. ISBN:0-86372-218-0, ISBN13: 978-0-86372-218-9. Dewey:323.6/0956.

Audience: **u,f.**

Doumani, Beshara　　　　　　**HQ663.3.F36 2003**
(Editor)
Family History in the Middle East: Household, Property, and Gender. Cloth Text. State University of New York Press. Albany, NY. 2003. xii, 341p. SUNY Series in the Social and Economic History of the Middle East ISBN:0-7914-5679-X, ISBN13: 978-0-7914-5679-8. Dewey:306.85/0956. LCCN:2002-067043.
Audience: **l,u,f.** *Choice, 2003.*

Fasi, Allal　　　　　　　　　**DT204**
The Independence Movements in Arab North Africa. Paper Text. Textbook Publishers. Temecula, CA. 2003. xi, 414p. ISBN:0-7581-7424-1, ISBN13: 978-0-7581-7424-6. Dewey:320.1/59/61.

Audience: **g,l,u,f.** *B*

Fernea, Elizabeth W.　　　　**HQ1784.W65 1985**
(Editor)
Women and the Family in the Middle East: New Voices of Change. Trade Cloth. University of Texas Press. Austin, TX. 1985. 368p. ISBN:0-292-75528-7, ISBN13: 978-0-292-75528-4. Dewey:305.4/2/09174927. LCCN:84-011944.

Audience: **g,l,u,f.** *B*

Fernea, Elizabeth　　　　　　**DS61.5.R46 2002**
Warnock (Editor, Introduction by)
Remembering Childhood in the Middle East: Memoirs from a Century of Change. Robert A. Fernea (Introduction by). Trade Cloth. University of Texas Press. Austin, TX. 2002. 398p. ISBN:0-292-72546-9, ISBN13: 978-0-292-72546-1. Dewey:920.056. LCCN:2002-004651.

Audience: **l,u,f.** *Choice, 2003.*

Freedman, Robert O.　　　　**DS63.2.S65F72 1991**
Moscow and the Middle East: Soviet Policy since the Invasion of Afghanistan. Cambridge University Press. 1991. ISBN:0-521-35184-7, ISBN13: 978-0-521-35184-3.

Audience: **g,l,u,f.**

Freedman, Robert　　　　　　**DS62.8.M54 2002**
Owen (Editor)
The Middle East Enters the Twenty-First Century. Baltimore Hebrew University, Center for the Study of Israel and the Contemporary Middle East Staff (Contribution by). Trade Paper. University Press of Florida. Gainesville, FL. 2002. 384p. ISBN:0-8130-2575-3, ISBN13: 978-0-8130-2575-9. Dewey:956.04. LCCN:2002-071464.

Audience: **u,f.** *Choice, 2003.*

Friedman, Thomas L.　　　　**DS119.7 .F736 1990B**
From Beirut to Jerusalem. Cloth over Boards. Farrar, Straus & Giroux. New York, NY. 1991. 576p. ISBN:0-374-15895-9, ISBN13: 978-0-374-15895-8. Dewey:956.04. LCCN:92-148666.
Audience: **g,l,u,f.**

Fromkin, David　　　　　　　**DS63.2.G7F76 1989**
A Peace to End All Peace: The Fall of the Ottoman Empire and the Creation of the Modern Middle East. Trade Cloth. Henry Holt & Company. New York, NY. 1989. 624p. ISBN:0-8050-0857-8, ISBN13: 978-0-8050-0857-9. Dewey:327.41056. LCCN:88-034727.

Audience: **g,l,u,f.**

Gelvin, James L. &　　　　　**DS62.4.G37 2004**
Gelvin, James
The Modern Middle East: A History. Cloth Text. Oxford University Press, Inc. New York, NY. 2004. 368p. ISBN:0-19-516788-0, ISBN13: 978-0-19-516788-7. Dewey:956. LCCN:2003-066230.

Audience: **g,l,u,f.**

Gocek, Fatma Muge &　　　　**HQ1726.5.R43 1994**
Shiva, Balaghi
Reconstructing Gender in the Middle East: Tradition, Identity, and Power. Shiva Balachi (Editor). Trade Cloth. Columbia University Press. New York, NY. 1995. 233p. ISBN:0-231-10122-8, ISBN13: 978-0-231-10122-6. Dewey:305.42/0956. LCCN:94-003733.

Audience: **u,f.**

Haddad, Yvonne　　　　　　**BP173.4.I73 1998**
Yazbeck & Esposito, John L. (Editors)
Islam, Gender, and Social Change. Paper Text. Oxford University Press, Inc. New York, NY. 1997. 288p. ISBN:0-19-511357-8, ISBN13: 978-0-19-511357-0. Dewey:305.486971. LCCN:97-002845.
Audience: **g,l,u,f.** *Choice, 1998.*

Halliday, Fred　　　　　　　**DS63.H282 1996**
Islam and the Myth of Confrontation: Religion and Politics in the Middle East. Trade Paper. I. B. Tauris & Company, Ltd.

London, 1996. 256p. ISBN:1-85043-959-1, ISBN13:
978-1-85043-959-2. Dewey:322/.1/0956. LCCN:95-061524.

Audience: **g,l,u,f.** *Choice, 1996.*

Halliday, Fred   **DS63.18.H35 2000**
Nation and Religion in the Middle East. Library Binding. Lynne
Rienner Publishers, Inc. Boulder, CO. 2000. 251p.
ISBN:1-55587-910-1, ISBN13: 978-1-55587-910-5.
Dewey:322/.1/0956. LCCN:00-025490.

Audience: **g,l,u,f.** *Choice, 2000.*

Hammond World Atlas   **G2205**
  Corporation Staff
Atlas of the Middle East. Trade Paper. Langenscheidt Publishers
Inc. Long Island City, NY. 2002. 48p. Atlas Ser.
ISBN:0-8437-1830-7, ISBN13: 978-0-8437-1830-0.
Dewey:912.56.

Audience: **g,l,u,f.**

Herzog, Chaim   **DS119.2**
The Arab-Israeli Wars: War and Peace in the Middle East from
the 1948 War of Independence to the Present. Ed. 2. Vintage
Books. 2005. ISBN:1-4000-7963-2, ISBN13:
978-1-4000-7963-6.

Audience: **l,u,f.**

Hinnebusch, Raymond   **DS631**
The International Politics of the Middle East. Cloth over Boards.
Manchester University Press. Manchester, 2003. 272p. Regional
International Politics Ser. ISBN:0-7190-5345 5, ISBN13:
978-0-7190-5345-0. Dewey:327/.0956. LCCN:2003-046321.

Audience: **l,u,f.** *Choice, 2004.*

Hourani, Albert H.   **JA84.A6 H6 1983**
Arabic Thought in the Liberal Age, 1798-1939. Trade Cloth.
Cambridge University Press. New York, NY. 1983. 416p.
ISBN:0-521-25837-5, ISBN13: 978-0-521-25837-1.
Dewey:181/.9. LCCN:83-001788.

Audience: **l,u,f.**

Hourani, Albert H.   **DS62.4**
  (Editor), et al.
The Modern Middle East: A Reader. Philip S. Khoury & Mary
C. Wilson (Editors). Trade Cloth. University of California Press.
Berkeley, CA. 1994. 600p. ISBN:0-520-08240-0, ISBN13:
978-0-520-08240-3. Dewey:956. LCCN:93-028464.

Audience: **g,l,u,f.**

Humphreys, R. Stephen   **DS63.1 .H856 1999**
Between Memory and Desire: The Middle East in a Troubled
Age. Trade Cloth. University of California Press. Berkeley, CA.
1999. 319p. ISBN:0-520-21411-0, ISBN13: 978-0-520-21411-8.
Dewey:956.04. LCCN:98-030576.

Audience: **g,l,u,f.** *Choice, 2000.*

Hurewitz, J. C.   **DS63.2.U5 H87**
Middle East Dilemmas: The Background of United States
Policy. Paper Text. Textbook Publishers. Temecula, CA. 2003.
xiv, 273p. ISBN:0-7581-5448-8, ISBN13: 978-0-7581-5448-4.
Dewey:327.73/056.

Audience: **g,l,u,f.**

Ismael, Tareq Y.   **DS63.1.I5986 2000**
  (Editor)
The International Relations of the Middle East in the 21st
Century: Patterns of Continuity and Change. Trade Cloth.
Ashgate Publishing, Ltd. Aldershot, 2000. 418p.

ISBN:0-7546-1506-5, ISBN13: 978-0-7546-1506-4.
Dewey:327/.0956. LCCN:00-134006.

Audience: **g,l,u,f.**

Ismael, Tareq Y.   **JQ1758.A58I86 2001**
Middle East Politics Today: Government and Civil Society.
Trade Cloth. University Press of Florida. Gainesville, FL. 2001.
528p. ISBN:0-8130-2098-0, ISBN13: 978-0-8130-2098-3.
Dewey:320.3/0956. LCCN:2001-034075.

Audience: **l,u,f.** *Choice, 2002.*

Joseph, Suad (Editor)   **JQ1758.A92G45 2000**
Gender and Citizenship in the Middle East. Trade Cloth.
Syracuse University Press. Syracuse, NY. 2000. xxxi, 400p.
Contemporary Issues in the Middle East Ser.
ISBN:0-8156-2864-1, ISBN13: 978-0-8156-2864-4.
Dewey:323.6/0956. LCCN:00-037015.

Audience: **l,u,f.** *Choice, 2001.*

Joseph, Suad   **HQ1726.5.W659 2001**
Women and Power in the Middle East. Trade Cloth. University
of Pennsylvania Press. Philadelphia, PA. 2000. 240p.
ISBN:0-8122-3579-7, ISBN13: 978-0-8122-3579-1.
Dewey:305.42/0956. LCCN:00-060200.

Audience: **l,u,f.**

Karsh, Efraim &   **DS62.4**
  Karsh, Inari
Empires of the Sand: The Struggle for Mastery in the Middle
East, 1789-1923. Trade Paper. Harvard University Press.
Cambridge, MA. 2001. 426p. ISBN:0-674-00541-4, ISBN13:
978-0-674-00541-9. Dewey:956/.015.

Audience: **u,f.**

Kayali, Hasan   **DS63.2.T8K39 1997**
Arabs and Young Turks: Ottomanism, Arabism, and Islamism in
the Ottoman Empire, 1908-1918. Trade Cloth. University of
California Press. Berkeley, CA. 1997. 266p.
ISBN:0-520-20444-1, ISBN13: 978-0-520-20444-7.
Dewey:327.56017/4927. LCCN:96-011474.

Audience: **u,f.** *Choice, 1998.*

Keddie, Nikki R. &   **HQ1726.5**
  Baron, Beth (Editors)
Women in Middle Eastern History: Shifting Boundaries in Sex
and Gender. Cloth over Boards. Yale University Press.
Cumberland, RI. 1992. 352p. ISBN:0-300-05005-4, ISBN13:
978-0-300-05005-9. Dewey:305.4/2/0956.

Audience: **l,u,f.**

Kepel, Gilles   **BP173.7.K453 2002**
Jihad: The Trail of Political Islam. Anthony Roberts (Translator).
Trade Cloth. Harvard University Press. Cambridge, MA. 2002.
464p. ISBN:0-674-00877-4, ISBN13: 978-0-674-00877-9.
Dewey:320.5/5/0917671. LCCN:2002-017181.

Audience: **l,u,f.** *Choice, 2003, 2002.*

Khoury, Philip S. &   **JQ1758.A2T75 1990**
  Kostiner, Joseph (Editors)
Tribes and State Formation in the Middle East. Trade Cloth.
University of California Press. Berkeley, CA. 1991. 400p.
ISBN:0-520-07079-8, ISBN13: 978-0-520-07079-0.
Dewey:306.2/0956. LCCN:90-035640.

Audience: **u,f.** *Choice, 1991.*

Kostiner, Joseph   **JQ1758.A58M53 2000**
  (Editor)
Middle East Monarchies: The Challenge of Modernity. Library
Binding. Lynne Rienner Publishers, Inc. Boulder, CO. 2000. vii,

---

344p. ISBN:1-55587-862-8, ISBN13: 978-1-55587-862-7.
Dewey:321/.6/0956. LCCN:99-051384.

Audience: **l,u,f.** *Choice, 2001.*

Lewis, Bernard　　　　　　　　**DS62.4 .L48 1994**
The Shaping of the Modern Middle East. Ed. 2. Cloth Text.
Oxford University Press, Inc. New York, NY. 1994. 200p.
ISBN:0-19-507281-2, ISBN13: 978-0-19-507281-5. Dewey:956.
LCCN:93-003283.

Audience: **g,l,u,f.**

Long, David E. &　　　　　　　**DS62.8.G68**
　Reich, Bernard
Government and Politics of the Middle East and North Africa.
Ed. 4. Trade Paper. Westview Press. Boulder, CO. 2002. 528p.
ISBN:0-8133-3972-3, ISBN13: 978-0-8133-3972-6. Dewey:956.

Audience: **l,u,f.**

Lustick, Ian S. (Editor)　　　　**DS119.7.R383 1994**
Religion, Culture, and Psychology in Arab-Israeli Relations.
Library Binding. Garland Publishing, Inc. New York, NY. 1994.
416p. Arab-Israeli Relations Ser., Vol. 5 ISBN:0-8153-1585-6,
ISBN13: 978-0-8153-1585-8. Dewey:303.48/25605694.
LCCN:93-048221.

Audience: **u,f.**

Lynch, Marc　　　　　　　　　**JQ1850.A91L93 2006**
Voices of the New Arab Public: Iraq, Al-Jazeera and Middle
East Politics Today. Trade Cloth. Columbia University Press.
New York, NY. 2005. 320p. ISBN:0-231-13448-7, ISBN13:
978-0-231-13448-4. Dewey:306.2/0917/492709051.
LCCN:2005-049677.

Audience: **l,u,f.** *Choice, 2006.*

Meriwether, Margaret　　　　　**HQ1726.5.S63 1999**
　Lee & Tucker, Judith (Editors)
Social History Of Women and the Family in the Middle East.
Trade Paper. Westview Press. Boulder, CO. 1999. 232p. Social
History of the Modern Middle East Ser. ISBN:0-8133-2100-X,
ISBN13: 978-0-8133-2100-4. Dewey:305.4/0956.
LCCN:99-017105.

Audience: **l,u,f.**

Mernissi, Fatema　　　　　　　**HQ1170.M467 2001**
Scheherazade Goes West: Different Cultures, Different Harems.
Trade Cloth. Simon & Schuster. New York, NY. 2001. 240p.
ISBN:0-7434-1242-7, ISBN13: 978-0-7434-1242-1.
Dewey:305.42. LCCN:2001-023608.

Audience: **g,l,u,f.**

Moore, Pete W.　　　　　　　　**HC415.39.M66 2004**
Doing Business in the Middle East: Politics and Economic
Crisis in Jordan and Kuwait. Charles Tripp, Julia A.
Clancy-Smith, Israel Gershoni, Roger Owen, Yezid Sayigh &
Judith E. Tucker (Contribution by). Trade Cloth. Cambridge
University Press. New York, NY. 2004. 228p. Cambridge
Middle East Studies, Vol. 20 ISBN:0-521-83955-6, ISBN13:
978-0-521-83955-6. Dewey:330.95367. LCCN:2003-069748.

Audience: **u,f.**

National Geographic　　　　　　**GA150**
　Society
Atlas of the Middle East. National Geographic Society. 2003.
ISBN:0-7922-5066-4, ISBN13: 978-0-7922-5066-1.

Audience: **g,l,u,f.**

Niblock, Tim　　　　　　　　　**JZ6373.N53 2001**
"Pariah States" and Sanctions in the Middle East: Iraq, LIbya,
Sudan. Library Binding. Lynne Rienner Publishers, Inc. Boulder,

CO. 2001. ix, 241p. The Middle East in the International
System Ser. ISBN:1-55587-962-4, ISBN13: 978-1-55587-962-4.
Dewey:341.5/82/0956. LCCN:00-045981.

Audience: **g,l,u,f.** *Choice, 2001.*

Ovendale, Ritchie　　　　　　　**DS119.7**
Modern Middle East: An Introductory and International History
since 1945. Trade Cloth. Pearson Education. Boston, MA. 2000.
ISBN:0-582-27318-8, ISBN13: 978-0-582-27318-4. Dewey:956.

Audience: **g,l,u,f.**

Palmer, Monte　　　　　　　　**DS62.8.P35 2002**
Politics of the Middle East. Paper Text. Thomson Wadsworth.
Belmont, CA. 2001. 448p. ISBN:0-87581-442-5, ISBN13:
978-0-87581-442-1. Dewey:20.956. LCCN:2001-135279.

Audience: **g,l,u,f.**

Parker, Richard B.　　　　　　　**DS63.1**
The Politics of Miscalculation in the Middle East. Trade Cloth.
Indiana University Press. Bloomington, IN. 1993. 320p. Indiana
University Series in Middle East Studies ISBN:0-253-34298-8,
ISBN13: 978-0-253-34298-0. Dewey:956.04. LCCN:92-023947.

Audience: **u,f.** *Choice, 1994.*

Peres, Shimon　　　　　　　　**DS119.76**
The New Middle East. Trade Paper. Henry Holt & Company.
New York, NY. 1995. 240p. ISBN:0-8050-3811-6, ISBN13:
978-0-8050-3811-8. Dewey:956.05/3.

Audience: **g,l,u,f.**

Peretz, Don　　　　　　　　　**DS62**
The Middle East Today. Ed. 6. Praeger. 1994.
ISBN:0-275-94575-8, ISBN13: 978-0-275-94575-6.

Audience: **g,l,u,f.**

Polk, William R. &　　　　　　　**DS119.7**
　Chambers, Richard L. (Editors)
Beginnings of Modernization in the Middle East: The
Nineteenth Century. Library Binding. University of Chicago
Press. Chicago, IL. 1968. x, 427p. Publications of the Center for
Middle Eastern Studies ISBN:0-226-67425-8, ISBN13:
978-0-226-67425-4. Dewey:956. LCCN:68-016712.

Audience: **l,u,f.**

Posusney, Marsha　　　　　　　**JC381**
　Pripstein & Angrist, Michele Penner (Editors)
Authoritarianism in the Middle East: Regimes and Resistance.
Trade Cloth. Lynne Rienner Publishers, Inc. Boulder, CO. 2005.
245p. ISBN:1-58826-317-7, ISBN13: 978-1-58826-317-9.
Dewey:909/.0974927083. LCCN:2005-011302.

Audience: **l,u,f.**

Quandt, William B.　　　　　　　**DS128.183**
Camp David: Peacemaking and Politics. Brookings Institution.
1986. ISBN:0-8157-7290-4, ISBN13: 978-0-8157-7290-3.

Audience: **u,f.**

Reich, Bernard　　　　　　　　**JQ1758**
Handbook of Political Science Research on the Middle East and
North Africa. Cloth Text. Greenwood Publishing Group, Inc.
Portsmouth, NH. 1998. 400p. ISBN:0-313-27372-3, ISBN13:
978-0-313-27372-8. Dewey:956/.007/2. LCCN:97-037549.

Audience: **g,l,u,f.** *Choice, 1998.*

Rubin, Barry　　　　　　　　　**JQ1758.A91R83 2006**
The Long War for Freedom: The Arab Struggle for Democracy
in the Middle East. Trade Cloth. John Wiley & Sons, Inc.

Hoboken, NJ. 2005. 304p. ISBN:0-471-73901-4, ISBN13: 978-0-471-73901-2. Dewey:320.956. LCCN:2005-020231.

Audience: **g,l,u,f.** *Choice, 2006.*

Rubin, Barry (Editor)   **BP60.R46 2003**
Revolutionaries and Reformers: Contemporary Islamist Movements in the Middle East. Cloth Text. State University of New York Press. Albany, NY. 2003. xi, 231p. ISBN:0-7914-5617-X, ISBN13: 978-0-7914-5617-0. Dewey:322.4/0917/671. LCCN:2002-075876.

Audience: **l,u,f.** *Choice, 2003.*

Rubin, Barry   **DS63.1.R835 2002**
The Tragedy of the Middle East. Cloth Text. Cambridge University Press. New York, NY. 2002. 296p. ISBN:0-521-80623-2, ISBN13: 978-0-521-80623-7. Dewey:956.04. LCCN:2002-023794.

Audience: **l,u,f.** *Choice, 2003.*

Said, Edward W.   **DS32.8**
Orientalism: Western Concepts of the Orient. Trade Cloth. Routledge. New York, NY. 1979. 384p. ISBN:0-7100-0040-5, ISBN13: 978-0-7100-0040-8. Dewey:950/.07. LCCN:78-040534.

Audience: **g,l,u,f.**

Schwedler, Jillian   **JQ1758.A5T68 1995**
(Editor)
Toward Civil Society in the Middle East?: A Primer. Library Binding. Lynne Rienner Publishers, Inc. Boulder, CO. 1995. 124p. ISBN:1-55587-588-2, ISBN13: 978-1-55587-588-6. Dewey:306.2/0956. LCCN:95-004613.

Audience: **g,l,u,f.**

Sela, Avraham (Editor)   **DS62.8.P64 2002**
Continuum Political Encyclopedia of the Middle East. Ed. 2. Trade Cloth. Continuum International Publishing Group, Ltd. London, 2002. 945p. ISBN:0-8264-1413-3, ISBN13: 978-0-8264-1413-7. Dewey:956.04/03. LCCN:2001-008542.

Audience: **l,u,f.** *Choice, 2003.*

Shlaim, Avi   **DS62.8.S53 1995**
War and Peace in the Middle East: A Critique of American Policy. Trade Paper. Penguin Group (USA) Inc. New York, NY. 1995. 160p. ISBN:0-14-024564-2, ISBN13: 978-0-14-024564-6. Dewey:956. LCCN:95-219561.

Audience: **g,l,u,f.**

Sicker, Martin   **DS62**
The Middle East in the Twentieth Century. Trade Cloth. Greenwood Publishing Group, Inc. Portsmouth, NH. 2001. 304p. ISBN:0-275-96893-6, ISBN13: 978-0-275-96893-9. Dewey:956.04. LCCN:00-064943.

Audience: **g,l,u,f.** *Choice, 2001.*

Sivan, Emmanuel &   **BP63.A4M537 1990**
Friedman, Menachem (Editors)
Religious Radicalism and Politics in the Middle East. Cloth Text. State University of New York Press. Albany, NY. 1990. 244p. SUNY Series in Near Eastern Studies ISBN:0-7914-0158-8, ISBN13: 978-0-7914-0158-3. Dewey:296.3/87. LCCN:89-004235.

Audience: **l,u,f.**

Sonn, Tamara   **DS38.9.S58 1990**
Between Qur'an and Crown: The Challenge of Political Legitimacy in the Arab World. Trade Paper. Westview Press. Boulder, CO. 1990. 266p. ISBN:0-8133-7579-7, ISBN13: 978-0-8133-7579-3. Dewey:320.956. LCCN:90-012048.

Audience: **l,u,f.** *Choice, 1991.*

Spencer, William   **DS624**
Global Studies: The Middle East. Ed. 10. Paper Text. McGraw-Hill Higher Education. Burr Ridge, IL. 2004. 272p. ISBN:0-07-286159-2, ISBN13: 978-0-07-286159-4. Dewey:956.05.

Audience: **g,l,u,f.**

Springborg, Robert &   **HC415.15 .H463 2001**
Henry, Clement M.
Globalization and the Politics of Development in the Middle East. Eugene L. Rogan (Contribution by). Cloth Text. Cambridge University Press. New York, NY. 2001. 280p. Contemporary Middle East Ser., Vol. 1 ISBN:0-521-62312-X, ISBN13: 978-0-521-62312-4. Dewey:338.956. LCCN:00-067452.

Audience: **u,f.** *Choice, 2002.*

Tessler, Mark (Editor),   **H62.A6626 1999**
et al.
Area Studies and Social Science: Strategies for Understanding Middle East Politics. Jodi Nachtwey & Anne Banda (Editors). Cloth Text. Indiana University Press. Bloomington, IN. 1999. 200p. Indiana University Series in Middle East Studies ISBN:0-253-33502-7, ISBN13: 978-0-253-33502-9. Dewey:300/.7/2. LCCN:98-033866.

Audience: **g,l,u,f.**

The Center for Middle
Eastern Studies at the University of Texas at Austin
☐ MENIC: The Middle East Information Center - Countries & Regions.
http://menic.utexas.edu/menic/Countries_and_Regions/

Audience: **g,l,u,f.**

Tibi, Bassam   **DS63.1.T5313 1998**
Conflict and War in the Middle East: From Interstate War to New Security. Ed. 2. Cloth over Boards. Palgrave Macmillan. New York, NY. 1998. 336p. ISBN:0-312-21150-3, ISBN13: 978-0-312-21150-9. Dewey:956.04. LCCN:97-040137.

Audience: **l,u,f.**

Vatikiotis, P. J.   **DS62.8.V37 1997**
Middle East: From the End of Empire to the End of the Cold War. Paper over Boards. Routledge. New York, NY. 1997. 296p. ISBN:0-415-15849-4, ISBN13: 978-0-415-15849-7. Dewey:956. LCCN:97-181171.

Audience: **l,u,f.**

Yaqub, Salim   **DS63.2.U5**
(Instructed by)
The United States and the Middle East, 1900 to 9/11, Parts I-II. Perfect. Teaching Company Limited Partnership. Chantilly, VA. 2003. ISBN:1-56585-686-4, ISBN13: 978-1-56585-686-8. Dewey:327.73056.

Audience: **g,l,u,f.**

Yegenoglu, Meyda   **PN98.W64 Y45 1998**
Colonial Fantasies: Towards a Feminist Reading of Orientalism. Jeffrey C. Alexander & Steven Seidman (Contribution by). Trade Cloth. Cambridge University Press. New York, NY. 1998. 192p. Cultural Social Studies ISBN:0-521-48233-X, ISBN13: 978-0-521-48233-2. Dewey:809/.89287. LCCN:97-025638.

Audience: **u,f.**

Ethnography (Including Ethno-Religious Groups) > Bedouins

Abu-Lughod, Lila   **DT72**
Veiled Sentiments: Honor and Poetry in a Bedouin Society.
Trade Paper. University of California Press. Berkeley, CA. 2000.
358p. ISBN:0-520-22473-6, ISBN13: 978-0-520-22473-5.
Dewey:306/.089927. LCCN:86-006948.
Audience: **g,l,u,f.** *Choice, 1987.*

Abu-Lughod, Lila   **HQ1793.A68 1993**
Writing Women's Worlds: Bedouin Stories. University of
California Press. 1993. ISBN:0-520-07946-9, ISBN13:
978-0-520-07946-5.
Audience: **g,l,u,f.**

Bailey, Clinton   **PN6519.A7B28 2004**
A Culture of Desert Survival: Bedouin Proverbs from Sinai and
the Negev. Cloth over Boards. Yale University Press.
Cumberland, RI. 2004. 512p. ISBN:0-300-09844-8, ISBN13:
978-0-300-09844-0. Dewey:398.9/927. LCCN:2003-065812.
Audience: **u,f.**

Cole, Donald Powell   **DS219.B4.C67**
Nomads of the Nomads: the Al Murrah Bedouin of the Empty
Quarter. Aldine Publishing CO.. 1975. ISBN:0-202-01117-8,
ISBN13: 978-0-202-01117-2.
Audience: **g,l,u,f.**

Ginat, Joseph   **DS113.7.G55 1997**
Blood Revenge: Family, Honor, Mediation and Outcasting.
Sussex Academic Press. 1997. ISBN:1-898723-18-4, ISBN13:
978-1-898723-18-9.
Audience: **u,f.**

Kressel, Gideon   **GN635.N42K74 2003**
Let Shepherding Endure: Applied Anthropology and the
Preservation of a Cultural Tradition in Israel and the Middle
East. State University of New York Press. 2003.
ISBN:0-7914-5805-9, ISBN13: 978-0-7914-5805-1.
Audience: **l,u,f.**

Lancaster, William   **DS219.R8**
The Rwala Bedouin Today. Cambridge University Press. 1981.
ISBN:0-521-23877-3, ISBN13: 978-0-521-23877-9.
Audience: **g,l,u,f.**

Marx, Emanuel   **DS113.7**
Bedouin of the Negev. Praeger. 1967.
Audience: **l,u,f.**

Marx, Emanuel (Editor)   **DS113.7**
The Changing Bedouin. Avshalom Shmueli (Editor). Transaction
Books. 1984. ISBN:0-87855-492-0, ISBN13:
978-0-87855-492-8.
Audience: **u,f.**

Meir, Avinoam   **DS110.N4 M38**
As Nomadism Ends: The Israeli Bedouin of the Negev. Paper
Text. Westview Press. Boulder, CO. 1998. 272p.
ISBN:0-8133-3556-6, ISBN13: 978-0-8133-3556-8.
Dewey:306/.089/924/056949.
Audience: **l,u,f.** *Choice, 1997.*

Mundy, Martha   **DS36.9.B4 T73 2000**
The Transforamtion of Nomadic Society in the Arab East.
Cambridge University Press. 2000. ISBN:0-521-77057-2,
ISBN13: 978-0-521-77057-6.
Audience: **l,u,f.**

Stewart, Frank   **DS36.9.B4S765 1994**
  Henderson
Honor. University of Chicago Press. 1994. ISBN:0-226-77407-4,
ISBN13: 978-0-226-77407-7.
Audience: **u,f.**

Ethnography (Including Ethno-Religious Groups) > Jews (of the Middle East)

Ahroni, Reuben   **DS135.Y4A46 1986**
Yemenite Jewry: Origins, Culture, and Literature. Trade Cloth.
Indiana University Press. Bloomington, IN. 1986. 240p. Jewish
Literature and Culture Ser. ISBN:0-253-36807-3, ISBN13:
978-0-253-36807-2. Dewey:953/.32004924. LCCN:84-048649.
Audience: **u,f.** *Choice, 1986.*

Alcalay, Ammiel   **DS113.A398 1993**
After Jews and Arabs: Remaking Levantine Culture. Trade
Cloth. University of Minnesota Press. Minneapolis, MN. 1992.
288p. ISBN:0-8166-2154-3, ISBN13: 978-0-8166-2154-5.
Dewey:305.892/4. LCCN:92-019124.
Audience: **u,f.** *Choice, 1993.*

Ashtor, Eliyahu   **DS135.S7**
The Jews of Moslem Spain. Jewish Publication Society of
America. 1974.
Audience: **u,f.**

Beinin, Joel   **DS135.E4B45 1998**
The Dispersion of Egyptian Jewry: Culture, Politics, and the
Formation of a Modern Diaspora. Trade Cloth. University of
California Press. Berkeley, CA. 1998. 344p. Contraversions Ser.,
Vol. 11:Critical Studies in Jewish Literature, Culture, and
Society ISBN:0-520-21175-8, ISBN13: 978-0-520-21175-9.
Dewey:962/.004924. LCCN:97-028043.
Audience: **l,u,f.** *Choice, 1998.*

Braude, Benjamin &   **DS58**
  Lewis, Bernard (Editors)
Christians and Jews in the Ottoman Empire: The Functioning of
a Plural Society. Holmes & Meier. 1982.
Audience: **u,f.**

Cohen, Hayyim J.   **DS135.L4 C6413**
Jews of the Middle East (1860-1972). Trade Cloth. Transaction
Publishers. Somerset, NJ. 1973. 224p. ISBN:0-87855-169-7,
ISBN13: 978-0-87855-169-9. Dewey:301.45/19/24056.
Audience: **l,u,f.**

Cohen, Mark R.   **HV17.C65 2005**
Poverty and Charity in the Jewish Community of Medieval
Egypt. Trade Cloth. Princeton University Press. Princeton, NJ.
2005. 312p. Jews, Christians, and Muslims from the Ancient to
the Modern World Ser. ISBN:0-691-09272-9, ISBN13:
978-0-691-09272-0. Dewey:362.5/089/924062.
LCCN:2004-062446.
Audience: **u,f.** *Choice, 2006.*

Cohen, Mark R.   **HV17.V65 2005**
The Voice of the Poor in the Middle Ages: An Anthology of
Documents from the Cairo Geniza. Trade Cloth. Princeton

University Press. Princeton, NJ. 2005. 224p.
ISBN:0-691-09262-1, ISBN13: 978-0-691-09262-1.
Dewey:363.5/089/924062. LCCN:2004-062827.

Audience: **u,f**. *Choice, 2006.*

De Felice, Renzo   **DS135.L44 D413 1985**
Jews in an Arab Land: Libya, 1835-1970. Judith Romani
(Translator). University of Texas Press. 1985.
ISBN:0-292-74016-6, ISBN13: 978-0-292-74016-7.

Audience: **l,u,f**.

Deshen, Shlomo &   **DS135.A68J47 1996**
Zenner, Walter P. (Editors)
Jews among Muslims: Communities in the Precolonial Middle
East. Trade Cloth. New York University Press. New York, NY.
1996. 336p. ISBN:0-8147-9675-3, ISBN13: 978-0-8147-9675-7.
Dewey:305.6/96/056. LCCN:96-030595.

Audience: **u,f**. *Choice, 1997.*

Eidelberg, Shlomo   **DS135.G31J48 1996**
(Editor, Translator)
The Jews and the Crusaders: The Hebrew Chronicles of the
First and Second Crusades. Trade Paper. Ktav Publishing House,
Inc. Jersey City, NJ. 1996. xi, 186p. ISBN:0-88125-541-6,
ISBN13: 978-0-88125-541-6. Dewey:943/.09424.
LCCN:96-000253.

Audience: **g,l,u,f**.

Goitein, S. D. (Editor)   **DS135.Y4**
From the Land of Sheba: Tales of the Jews of Yemen. Trade
Paper. Knopf Publishing Group. New York, NY. 1976. 160p.
ISBN:0-8052-0543-8, ISBN13: 978-0-8052-0543-5.
Dewey:915.3/32/06924. LCCN:73-081342.

Audience: **g,l,u,f**.

Goitein, S. D.   **DS119 .G58**
Jews and Arabs, Their Contacts Through the Ages. Paper Text.
Textbook Publishers. Temecula, CA. 2003. 257p.
ISBN:0-7581-4143-2, ISBN13: 978-0-7581-4143-9.
Dewey:956.94.

Audience: **g,l,u,f**.

Goitein, S. D. &   **D199.3 .G58 1999**
Lassner, Jacob
A Mediterranean Society. Trade Cloth. University of California
Press. Berkeley, CA. 2000. 526p. ISBN:0-520-21734-9, ISBN13:
978-0-520-21734-8. Dewey:956/.004924. LCCN:98-054216.

Audience: **g,l,u,f**.

Goldberg, Harvey E.   **DS135.L44G65 1990**
Jewish Life in Muslim Libya: Rivals and Relatives. Trade Cloth.
University of Chicago Press. Chicago, IL. 1997. 202p.
ISBN:0-226-30091-9, ISBN13: 978-0-226-30091-7.
Dewey:961.2/004924. LCCN:89-020593.

Audience: **u,f**. *Choice, 1991.*

Goldberg, Harvey E.   **DS135.M43S46 1996**
(Editor)
Sephardi and Middle Eastern Jewries: History and Culture.
Trade Cloth. Indiana University Press. Bloomington, IN. 1996.
360p. ISBN:0-253-33013-0, ISBN13: 978-0-253-33013-0.
Dewey:956/.004924. LCCN:95-031525.

Audience: **l,u,f**.

Kramer, Gudrun   **DS135.E4K68 1989**
The Jews in Modern Egypt, 1914-1952. Trade Cloth. University
of Washington Press. Seattle, WA. 1989. 310p.

ISBN:0-295-96795-1, ISBN13: 978-0-295-96795-0.
Dewey:962/.004924. LCCN:88-027805.

Audience: **u,f**. *Choice, 1990.*

Landau, Jacob M.   **DS135.E4**
Jews in Nineteenth Century Egypt. Trade Cloth. New York
University Press. New York, NY. 1969. Studies in Near Eastern
Civilization, No. 2 ISBN:0-8147-0248-1, ISBN13:
978-0-8147-0248-2. Dewey:301.451/924/062. LCCN:69-018282.

Audience: **u,f**.

Laskier, Michael M.   **DS135.M85**
The Alliance Israelite Universelle and the Jewish Communities
of Morocco, 1862-1962. Cloth Text. State University of New
York Press. Albany, NY. 1984. 384p. SUNY Series in Modern
Jewish History ISBN:0-87395-656-7, ISBN13:
978-0-87395-656-7. Dewey:305.8/924/064. LCCN:82-005892.

Audience: **u,f**.

Laskier, Michael M.   **DS135.E4L35 1991**
The Jews of Egypt, 1920-1970: In the Midst of Zionism,
Anti-Semitism, and the Middle East Conflict. Cloth Text. New
York University Press. New York, NY. 1991. 350p.
ISBN:0-8147-5058-3, ISBN13: 978-0-8147-5058-2.
Dewey:305.892/4062/0904. LCCN:91-031182.

Audience: **l,u,f**. *Choice, 1992.*

Levy, Avigdor (Editor)   **DS135.T8J53 2002**
Jews, Turks, and Ottomans: A Shared History, Fifteenth to
Twentieth Centuries. Trade Cloth. Syracuse University Press.
Syracuse, NY. 2002. 301p. Modern Jewish History Ser.
ISBN:0-8156-2941-9, ISBN13: 978-0-8156-2941-2.
Dewey:956/.004924. LCCN:2002-011481.

Audience: **u,f**. *Choice, 2003.*

Lewis, Bernard   **BP172**
The Jews of Islam. Trade Paper. Princeton University Press.
Princeton, NJ. 1987. 262p. ISBN:0-691-00807-8, ISBN13:
978-0-691-00807-3. Dewey:297/.1972. LCCN:84-042575.

Audience: **l,u,f**. ℬ

Malka, Eli S.   **DS135.S85M35 1997**
Jacob's Children in the Land of the Mahdi: Jews of the Sudan.
Trade Cloth. Syracuse University Press. Syracuse, NY. 1997.
250p. ISBN:0-8156-8122-4, ISBN13: 978-0-8156-8122-9.
Dewey:962.4/004924. LCCN:96-072628.

Audience: **u,f**.

Mann, Jacob   **DS124**
The Jews in Egypt and in Palestine Under the Fatimid Caliphs.
Trade Cloth. Ktav Publishing House, Inc. Jersey City, NJ. 1970.
Library of Jewish Classics Ser ISBN:0-87068-024-2, ISBN13:
978-0-87068-024-3. Dewey:909.04924.

Audience: **l,u,f**.

Masters, Bruce Alan   **DS59.C48M37 2001**
ⓔ Christians and Jews in the Ottoman Arab World: The Roots
of Sectarianism. E-Book. Cambridge University Press. New
York, NY. ISBN:0-511-01781-2, ISBN13: 978-0-511-01781-0.
Dewey:305.6/09569.

Audience: **u,f**. *Choice, 2002.*

Moreen, Vera Basch   **DS135.I65 M67**
Iranian Jewry's Hour of Peril and Heroism. Cloth Text.
Columbia University Press. New York, NY. 1987. 247p. A Study
of the American Academy for Jewish Research
ISBN:0-231-06578-7, ISBN13: 978-0-231-06578-8.
Dewey:955/.004924.

Audience: **l,u,f**.

Reguer, Sara   DS135.L4J49 2002
The Jews of the Middle East and North Africa in Modern
Times. Reeva S. Simon & Michael M. Laskier (Editors). Trade
Cloth. Columbia University Press. New York, NY. 2003. 432p.
ISBN:0-231-10796-X, ISBN13: 978-0-231-10796-9.
Dewey:956/.004924. LCCN:2002-073451.
                                        Audience: **l,u,f.**

Rejwan, Nissim   DS135.I713R447 2004
The Last Jews in Baghdad: Remembering a Lost Homeland.
Joel Beinin (Foreword by). Trade Cloth. University of Texas
Press. Austin, TX. 2004. 268p. ISBN:0-292-70293-0, ISBN13:
978-0-292-70293-6. Dewey:956.7/47004924/092 B.
LCCN:2004-004110.
                                        Audience: **l,u,f.**

Rodrigue, Aron   DS135.L4R63 2003
Jews and Muslims: Images of Sephardi and Easter Jewries in
Modern Times. University of Washington Press. 2003.
ISBN:0-295-98314-0, ISBN13: 978-0-295-98314-1.
                                        Audience: **u,f.**

Sachar, Howard Morley   DS135.S7S23 1994
Farewell Espana: The World of the Sephardim Remembered.
Trade Cloth. Alfred A. Knopf Inc. New York, NY. 1994. 448p.
ISBN:0-679-40960-2, ISBN13: 978-0-679-40960-1.
Dewey:946/.0004924. LCCN:93-039501.
                                        Audience: **l,u,f.**

Sassoon, David S.   DS135.I712 B337 1982
A History of the Jews in Baghdad. Trade Cloth. A M S Press,
Inc. New York, NY. 264p. ISBN:0-404-16427-7, ISBN13:
978-0-404-16427-0. Dewey:956.7/4. LCCN:77-087645.
                                        Audience: **u,f.**

Schroeter, Daniel J.   DS135.M8S37 2002
The Sultan's Jew: Morocco and the Sephardi World. Trade
Cloth. Stanford University Press. Palo Alto, CA. 2002. 292p.
Stanford Studies in Jewish History and Culture
ISBN:0-8047-3777-0, ISBN13: 978-0-8047-3777-7.
Dewey:964/.6. LCCN:2002-009241.
                                Audience: **u,f.** *Choice, 2003.*

Shaw, Stanford J.   DS135.T8S46 1991
The Jews of the Ottoman Empire and the Turkish Republic.
Trade Cloth. New York University Press. New York, NY. 1991.
384p. ISBN:0-8147-7924-7, ISBN13: 978-0-8147-7924-8.
Dewey:956.1/015. LCCN:91-006927.
                                Audience: **u,f.** *Choice, 1992.*

Shiblak, Abbas   DS135.I7
Iraqi Jews: A History of the Mass Exodus. Saqi. 2005.
ISBN:0-86356-504-2, ISBN13: 978-0-86356-504-5.
                                        Audience: **l,u,f.**

Stillman, Norman A.   DS135.A68
The Jews of Arab Lands in Modern Times. Trade Paper. Jewish
Publication Society. Dulles, VA. 2003. 604p.
ISBN:0-8276-0765-2, ISBN13: 978-0-8276-0765-1.
Dewey:304.8089924.
                                        Audience: **g,l,u,f.**

Zafrani, Haim   DS135.M8Z37 2002
Two Thousand Years of Jewish Life in Morocco. Trade Cloth.
Ktav Publishing House, Inc. Jersey City, NJ. 2002. x, 327p.
ISBN:0-88125-748-6, ISBN13: 978-0-88125-748-9.
Dewey:964/.004924. LCCN:2002-070238.
                                        Audience: **g,l,u,f.**

Ethnography (Including Ethno-Religious Groups) > Kurds

Allison, Christine &   DS59.K86K85434 1996
  Kreyenbroek, Philip (Editors)
Kurdish Culture and Identity. Cloth over Boards. Zed Books,
Ltd. London, 1996. 192p. ISBN:1-85649-329-6, ISBN13:
978-1-85649-329-1. Dewey:306/.0899159. LCCN:96-004697.
                                        Audience: **g,l,u,f.**

Bruinessen, Martin van   DS59.K86 B783 2000
Kurdish Ethno-Nationalism Versus Nation-Building States:
Collected Articles. Trade Cloth. Isis. Sturgeon Bay, WI. 2000.
301p. Analecta Isisiana Ser., Vol. 47 ISBN:975-428-177-7,
ISBN13: 978-975-428-177-4. Dewey:956.0049159.
LCCN:2001-302192.
                                        Audience: **u,f.**

Chaliand, Gerard   DS59.K86C4813 1994
The Kurdish Tragedy. Trade Cloth. Zed Books, Ltd. London,
1994. 128p. ISBN:1-85649-099-8, ISBN13: 978-1-85649-099-3.
Dewey:305.89159. LCCN:94-142896.
                                Audience: **g,l,u,f.** *Choice, 1995.*

Fuccaro, Nelida   BL1595
The Other Kurds: Yazidis in Colonial Iraq. Cloth over Boards. I.
B. Tauris & Company, Ltd. London, 1999. 256p. Library of
Modern Middle East Studies ISBN:1-86064-170-9, ISBN13:
978-1-86064-170-1. Dewey:305.8/91597/0567.
                                Audience: **u,f.** *Choice, 1999.*

Ghareeb, Edmund   DS70.8.K8 G48
The Kurdish Question in Iraq. Syracuse University Press. 1981.
ISBN:0-8156-0164-6, ISBN13: 978-0-8156-0164-7.
                                        Audience: **g,l,u,f.**

Ghassemlou, A. R.   DS59.K86
A People Without a Country: The Kurds and Kurdistan. Gerard
Chaliand (Editor), Michael Pallis (Translator). Trade Cloth.
Interlink Publishing Group, Inc. Northampton, MA. 1993. 320p.
ISBN:1-56656-114-0, ISBN13: 978-1-56656-114-3.
Dewey:956/.0049159. LCCN:92-014618.
                                Audience: **g,l,u,f.** *Choice, 1994.*

Gunter, Michael M.   DS59.K86G86 2003
Historical Dictionary of the Kurds. Trade Cloth. Scarecrow
Press, Inc. Lanham, MD. 2003. 320p. Historical Dictionaries of
People and Cultures Ser., No. 1 ISBN:0-8108-4870-8, ISBN13:
978-0-8108-4870-2. Dewey:956.6/7/003. LCCN:2003-011652.
                                Audience: **g,l,u,f.** *Choice, 2004.*

Hansen, Henny H.   HQ1779.K8
The Kurdish Woman's Life. Paper Text. Brill Academic
Publishers, Inc. Boston, MA. 1961. Ethnographical Ser., No. 7
ISBN:87-480-6231-6, ISBN13: 978-87-480-6231-3.
                                        Audience: **l,u,f.**

Houston, Christopher   DS59.K86.H68 2001
Islam, Kurds and the Turkish Nation State. Cloth over Boards.
Berg Publishers. Oxford, 2001. 224p. ISBN:1-85973-472-3,
ISBN13: 978-1-85973-472-8. Dewey:956.103.
                                Audience: **l,u,f.** *Choice, 2001.*

Human Rights Watch,   DS70.8.K8I37 1995
  Middle East Staff (Editor)
Iraq's Crime of Genocide: The Anfal Campaign Against the
Kurds. Trade Paper. Yale University Press. Cumberland, RI.
1995. 126p. Human Rights Watch Bks. ISBN:0-300-05757-1,

ISBN13: 978-0-300-05757-7. Dewey:305.89159.
LCCN:94-034779.

Audience: **g,l,u,f.**

Ibrahim, Ferhad &   **DR435.K87K86 2000**
  Gurbey, Gulistan (Editors)
The Kurdish Conflict in Turkey: Obstacles and Chances for
Peace and Democracy. Cloth over Boards. Palgrave Macmillan.
New York, NY. 2001. 206p. ISBN:0-312-23629-8, ISBN13:
978-0-312-23629-8. Dewey:956.6/7038. LCCN:00-042182.

Audience: **u,f.**

Izady, Mehrdad   **DS59.K86**
The Kurds: A Concise Handbook. Paper over Boards. Taylor &
Francis Group. Philadelphia, PA. 1992. 184p.
ISBN:0-8448-1729-5, ISBN13: 978-0-8448-1729-3.
Dewey:956.0049159. LCCN:92-008174.

Audience: **g,l,u,f.**

Jwaideh, Wadie   **DS59.K86J87 2006**
The Kurdish National Movement: Its Origins and Development.
Trade Paper. Syracuse University Press. Syracuse, NY. 2006.
360p. Contemporary Issues in the Middle East Ser.
ISBN:0-8156-3093-X, ISBN13: 978-0-8156-3093-7.
Dewey:320.5409566/7. LCCN:2006-001871.

Audience: **l,u,f.**

Koohi-Kamali, Farideh   **DS269.K87K66 2003**
The Political Development of the Kurds in Iran: Pastoral
Nationalism. Cloth over Boards. Palgrave Macmillan. New
York, NY. 2004. 256p. ISBN:0-333-73169-7, ISBN13:
978-0-333-73169-7. Dewey:955/.00491597. LCCN:2003-053648.

Audience: **u,f.**

Kreyenbroek, Philip G.   **DS59.K86**
  & Sperl, Stefan (Editors)
The Kurds: A Contemporary Overview. Paper over Boards.
Routledge. New York, NY. 1991. 272p. SOAS Series on
Contemporary Politics and Culture in the Middle East
ISBN:0-415-07265-4, ISBN13: 978-0-415-07265-6.
Dewey:305.89159. LCCN:91-027258.

Audience: **l,u,f.**

Manafy, A.   **DS59.K86**
The Kurdish Political Struggle in Iran, Iraq, and Turkey: A
Critical Analysis. University Press of America. 2005.
ISBN:0-7618-3003-0, ISBN13: 978-0-7618-3003-0.

Audience: **u,f.**

McDowall, David   **DS59.K86**
A Modern History of the Kurds. Trade Cloth. DIANE
Publishing Company. Collingdale, PA. 2004. 472p.
ISBN:0-7567-9117-0, ISBN13: 978-0-7567-9117-9.
Dewey:956/.00491597.

Audience: **g,l,u,f.**

McKiernan, Kevin   **DS59.K86M427 2006**
The Kurds: A People in Search of Their Homeland. Cloth over
Boards. St. Martin's Press. Gordonville, VA. 2006. 400p.
ISBN:0-312-32546-0, ISBN13: 978-0-312-32546-6.
Dewey:956/.00491597. LCCN:2005-044673.

Audience: **g,l,u,f.**

Meho, Lokman I.   **E183**
The Kurdish Question in U. S. Foreign Policy: A Documentary
Sourcebook. Trade Cloth. Greenwood Publishing Group, Inc.
Portsmouth, NH. 2003. 720p. Documentary Reference

Collections ISBN:0-313-31435-7, ISBN13: 978-0-313-31435-3.
Dewey:327.730566/7. LCCN:2003-057996.

Audience: **l,u,f.** *Choice, 2004.*

Meho, Lokman I. &   **Z3014**
  Maglaughlin, Kelly L. (Compiled by)
Kurdish Culture and Society: An Annotated Bibliography. Cloth
Text. Greenwood Publishing Group, Inc. Portsmouth, NH. 2001.
384p. Bibliographies and Indexes in Ethnic Studies, No. 9
ISBN:0-313-31543-4, ISBN13: 978-0-313-31543-5.
Dewey:016.305891/597. LCCN:00-063654.

Audience: **l,u,f.** *Choice, 2001.*

Natali, Denise   **DS59.K86N38 2005**
The Kurds and the State: Evolving National Identity in Iraq,
Turkey, and Iran. Saddle Stitched, Cloth over Boards, Dust
Jacket. Syracuse University Press. Syracuse, NY. 2005. 238p.
Contemporary Issues in the Middle East Ser.
ISBN:0-8156-3084-0, ISBN13: 978-0-8156-3084-5.
Dewey:320.54/089/91597. LCCN:2005-019612.

Audience: **u,f.** *Choice, 2006.*

Olson, Robert   **DS59.K86O47 2005**
Goat and the Butcher: Turkey, Kurdistan-Iraq, and Iraq
Relations. Cloth Text. Mazda Publishers, Inc. Costa Mesa, CA.
2005. 298p. Kurdish Studies Ser., Vol. 6 ISBN:1-56859-186-1,
ISBN13: 978-1-56859-186-5. Dewey:320.54/09567/2090511.
LCCN:2005-050853.

Audience: **u,f.** *Choice, 2006.*

Olson, Robert W.   **DS63.2.T8O47 2001**
Turkey's Relations with Iran, Syria, Israel and Russia,
1991-2000: The Kurdish and Islamist Question. Trade Paper.
Mazda Publishers, Inc. Costa Mesa, CA. 2001. 240p. Kurdish
Studies, No. 2 ISBN:1-56859-133-0, ISBN13:
978-1-56859-133-9. Dewey:327.561/009/049. LCCN:00-054895.

Audience: **u,f.** *Choice, 2001.*

O'Shea, Maria Theresa   **DS59.K86O84 2003**
Trapped Between the Map and Reality: Geography and
Perceptions of Kurdistan. Paper over Boards. Routledge. New
York, NY. 2004. 280p. Middle East Studies, :History, Politics
and Law Ser. ISBN:0-415-94766-9, ISBN13:
978-0-415-94766-4. Dewey:956.6/7. LCCN:2003-017039.

Audience: **l,u,f.**

Physicians for Human   **DS70.8.K8 W56**
  Rights Staff
Winds of Death: Iraq's Use of Poison Gas Against Its Kurdish
Population. Trade Paper. Physicians for Human Rights.
Cambridge, MA. 1989. 39p. ISBN:0-614-14420-5, ISBN13:
978-0-614-14420-8. Dewey:956.70049159.

Audience: **g,l,u,f.**

Romano, David   **DS59.K86**
The Kurdish Nationalist Movement: Opportunity, Mobilization
and Identity. Charles Tripp, Julia A. Clancy-Smith, Israel
Gershoni, Roger Owen, Yezid Sayigh & Judith E. Tucker
(Contribution by). Trade Paper. Cambridge University Press.
New York, NY. 2006. 290p. Cambridge Middle East Studies,
Vol. 22 ISBN:0-521-68426-9, ISBN13: 978-0-521-68426-2.
Dewey:956.67. LCCN:2006-297211.

Audience: **u,f.** *Choice, 2006.*

Taspinar, Omer   **BP173.7.T37 2004**
Kurdish Nationalism and Political Islam in Turkey: Kemalist
Identity in Transition. Paper over Boards. Routledge. New York,

NY. 2004. 293p. Middle East Studies, :History, Politics and Law Ser. ISBN:0-415-94998-X, ISBN13: 978-0-415-94998-9. Dewey:320.54/09561. LCCN:2004-009238.

Audience: **u,f.**

Vali, Abbas (Editor)   **DS59.K86E83 2003**
Essays on the Origins of Kurdish Nationalism. Trade Paper. Mazda Publishers, Inc. Costa Mesa, CA. 2003. 230p. Kurdish Studies, Vol. 4 ISBN:1-56859-142-X, ISBN13: 978-1-56859-142-1. Dewey:320.54/089/91597. LCCN:2003-044924.

Audience: **u,f.** *Choice, 2003.*

Vali, Abbas   **DS59.K86**
Kurds and Ethnicity in Iran. Trade Cloth. I. B. Tauris & Company, Ltd. London, 2003. 256p. ISBN:1-86064-050-8, ISBN13: 978-1-86064-050-6. Dewey:323.1/19159.

Audience: **l,u,f.**

Van Bruinessen, Martin   **DS59.K86B78 1992**
Agha, Shaikh and State: The Social and Political Structures of Kurdistan. Cloth over Boards. Zed Books, Ltd. London, 1992. 384p. ISBN:1-85649-018-1, ISBN13: 978-1-85649-018-4. Dewey:956/.0049159. LCCN:91-023906.

Audience: **g,l,u,f.** *Choice, 1992.*

Van Bruinessen, Martin   **DR432.B25 2000**
Mullas, Sufis and Heretics: The Role of Religion in Kurdish Society. Trade Paper. Isis Press. Istanbul, 2000. 322p. Analecta Isisana Ser., Vol. 44 ISBN:975-428-162-9, ISBN13: 978-975-428-162-0. Dewey:297/.09566/7. LCCN:99-905820.

Audience: **u,f.**

Wagner, Heather Lehr   **DS59.K86W335 2002**
The Kurds. Trade Cloth. Facts On File, Inc. New York, NY. 2002. 125p. Creation of the Modern Middle East Ser. ISBN:0-7910-6505-7, ISBN13: 978-0-7910-6505-1. Dewey:956/.00491597. LCCN:2002-009420.

Audience: **g,l,u,f.**

Yildiz, Kerim & Blass, Tom   **DS70.8.K8**
The Kurds in Iraq: The Past, Present and Future. Trade Cloth. Pluto Press. London, 2004. 216p. ISBN:0-7453-2229-8, ISBN13: 978-0-7453-2229-2. Dewey:305.8915970567. LCCN:2004-304682.

Audience: **g,l,u,f.**

Yildiz, Kerim   **DR435.K87**
The Kurds in Turkey: EU Accession and Human Rights. Noam Chomsky (Foreword by). Trade Cloth. Pluto Press. London, 2005. 216p. ISBN:0-7453-2489-4, ISBN13: 978-0-7453-2489-0. Dewey:323.1191/5970561. LCCN:2005-283932.

Audience: **l,u,f.** *Choice, 2006.*

Ethnography (Including Ethno-Religious Groups) > All Others

Abu-Izzedin, Nejla M.   **DS94.8.D8A24 1993**
The Druzes: A New Study of Their History, Faith and Society. Brill Academic Publishers, Inc. 1993. ISBN:90-04-09705-8, ISBN13: 978-90-04-09705-6.

Audience: **l,u,f.**

Braude, Benjamin & Lewis, Bernard (Editors)   **DS58**
Christians and Jews in the Ottoman Empire: The Functioning of a Plural Society. Holmes & Meier. 1982.

Audience: **u,f.**

Carter, Barbara L.   **DT72.C7C37 1986**
The Copts in Egyptian Politics 1918 - 1952. Trade Cloth. Croom Helm, Ltd. London, 1985. 256p. ISBN:0-7099-3417-3, ISBN13: 978-0-7099-3417-2. Dewey:323.1/1932/062. LCCN:85-032005.

Audience: **l,u,f.**

Dana, Nissim   **DS113.72.D364 2003**
The Druze in the Middle East: Their Faith, Leadership, Identity and Status. Sussex Academic Press. 2003. ISBN:1-903900-36-0, ISBN13: 978-1-903900-36-9.

Audience: **l,u,f.**

Gellner, Ernest & Micaud, Charles Antoine   **DT313.2 .A7 1973**
Arabs and Berbers: From Tribe to Nation in North Africa. Trade Cloth. Gerald Duckworth & Company, Ltd. London, 1973. 448p. ISBN:0-7156-0639-5, ISBN13: 978-0-7156-0639-1. Dewey:301.29/64. LCCN:73-165872.

Audience: **u,f.**

Goodman, Jane E.   **DT283.2.G66 2005**
Berber Culture on the World Stage: From Village to Video. Trade Cloth. Indiana University Press. Bloomington, IN. 2005. 256p. ISBN:0-253-34629-0, ISBN13: 978-0-253-34629-2. Dewey:305.89/33065. LCCN:2005-006229.

Audience: **l,u,f.**

Haddad, Robert M   **BR110**
Syrian Christians in Muslim Society: An Interpretation. Trade Cloth. Greenwood Publishing Group, Inc. Portsmouth, NH. 1981. 118p. Princeton Studies on the Near East ISBN:0-313-23054-4, ISBN13: 978-0-313-23054-7. Dewey:305.6/15/05691. LCCN:81-006202.

Audience: **g,l,u,f.**

Hitti, Philip K.   **DS94.8.D8**
Origins of the Druze People and Religion: With Extracts from Their Sacred Writings. A M S Press, Inc. 1966. ISBN:0-404-50518-X, ISBN13: 978-0-404-50518-9.

Audience: **l,u,f.**

Ilahiane, Hsain   **DT193.5.B45I447 2006**
Historical Dictionary of the Berbers (Iimazighen). Trade Cloth. Scarecrow Press, Inc. Lanham, MD. 2006. 400p. ISBN:0-8108-5452-X, ISBN13: 978-0-8108-5452-9. Dewey:961/.004933003. LCCN:2006-005071.

Audience: **g,l,u,f.**

Joseph, John   **DS59.J25 J67 1983**
Muslim-Christian Relations and Inter-Christian Rivalries in the Middle East: The Case of the Jacobites in an Age of Transition. State University of New York Press. 1983. ISBN:0-87395-611-7, ISBN13: 978-0-87395-611-6.

Audience: **u,f.**

Keohane, Alan   **DT310.3**
The Berbers of Morocco. Nicholas Shakespeare (Introduction by). Trade Cloth. Penguin Group (USA) Inc. New York, NY. 1991. 144p. ISBN:0-241-12966-4, ISBN13: 978-0-241-12966-1. Dewey:779.9964. LCCN:90-085831.

Audience: **g,l,u,f.**

Masters, Bruce Alan   **DS59.C48M37 2001**
🄴 Christians and Jews in the Ottoman Arab World: The Roots of Sectarianism. E-Book. Cambridge University Press. New York, NY. ISBN:0-511-01781-2, ISBN13: 978-0-511-01781-0. Dewey:305.6/09569.

Audience: **u,f.** *Choice, 2002.*

Miller, James Andrew   **DT329.I56.M54 1984**
Imlil, a Moroccan Mountain Community in Change. Trade Cloth. Westview Press. Boulder, CO. 1984. xxvii, 285p. ISBN:0-86531-980-4, ISBN13: 978-0-86531-980-6. Dewey:306/.0964/4. LCCN:83-014742.

Audience: **l,u,f.** 𝒷

Shatzmiller, Maya   **DT313.S33 1999**
The Berbers and the Islamic State: The Marinid Experience. Paper Text. Markus Wiener Publishers, Inc. Princeton, NJ. 2000. 280p. ISBN:1-55876-224-8, ISBN13: 978-1-55876-224-4. Dewey:964/.02. LCCN:99-049827.

Audience: **u,f.**

Swayd, Samy S.   **BL1695.S93 2006**
Historical Dictionary of the Druzes. Trade Cloth. Scarecrow Press, Inc. Lanham, MD. 2006. 264p. Historical Dictionaries of People and Cultures Ser., No. 3 ISBN:0-8108-5332-9, ISBN13: 978-0-8108-5332-4. Dewey:297.8/5/09. LCCN:2005-022963.

Audience: **g,l,u,f.**

Trimingham, J. Spencer   **BR1070 .T73**
Christianity among the Arabs in Pre-Islamic Times. Trade Cloth. International Book Centre, Inc. Troy, MI. 1990. 342p. ISBN:0-86685-533-5, ISBN13: 978-0-86685-533-4. Dewey:209/.56.

Audience: **u,f.**

History of Specific Countries > Cyprus > General

Calotychos, Vangelis   **DS54.5.C97 1998**
(Editor)
Cyprus and Its People: Nation, Identity, and Experience in an Unimaginable Community, 1955-1997. Trade Cloth. Westview Press. Boulder, CO. 1998. 344p. ISBN:0-8133-3515-9, ISBN13: 978-0-8133-3515-5. Dewey:956.9304. LCCN:98-019812.

Audience: **u,f.** *Choice, 1999.*

Panteli, Stavros   **DS54.S28P36 1994**
Historical Dictionary of Cyprus. Trade Cloth. Scarecrow Press, Inc. Lanham, MD. 1995. 258p. European Historical Dictionaries Ser., No. 6 ISBN:0-8108-2912-6, ISBN13: 978-0-8108-2912-1. Dewey:956.45/003. LCCN:94-018869.

Audience: **g,l,u,f.**

History of Specific Countries > Cyprus > Medieval

Edbury, Peter W.   **DS54.6.E33 1991**
The Kingdom of Cyprus and the Crusades, 1191-1374. Trade Cloth. Cambridge University Press. New York, NY. 1991. 260p. ISBN:0-521-26876-1, ISBN13: 978-0-521-26876-9. Dewey:956.45. LCCN:90-040488.

Audience: **u,f.** *Choice, 1992.*

History of Specific Countries > Cyprus > Modern

Jennings, Ronald C.   **DS54.7.J46 1993**
Christians and Muslims in Ottoman Cyprus and the Mediterranean World, 1571-1640. Trade Cloth. New York University Press. New York, NY. 1992. 429p. Studies in Near Eastern Civilization, No. 16 ISBN:0-8147-4181-9, ISBN13: 978-0-8147-4181-8. Dewey:956.4502. LCCN:92-003108.

Audience: **u,f.** *Choice, 1993.*

Mallinson, William   **DS54.9**
Cyprus: A Modern History. Alan Sked (Foreword by). Cloth over Boards. I. B. Tauris & Company, Ltd. London, 2005. 256p. ISBN:1-85043-580-4, ISBN13: 978-1-85043-580-8. Dewey:956.9303. LCCN:2005-280096.

Audience: **l,u,f.** *Choice, 2006.*

Orr, C. W.   **DS54.8**
Cyprus under British Rule. Cloth Text. Brill Academic Publishers, Inc. Boston, MA. 1972. 192p. Bibliotheca Historica Cyprica Ser. ISBN:0-900834-19-6, ISBN13: 978-0-900834-19-6. Dewey:325/.342/095645. LCCN:70-180478.

Audience: **u,f.**

Papadakis, Yiannis   **GN635.C9D58 2006**
(Editor), et al.
Divided Cyprus: Modernity, History, and an Island in Conflict. Nicos Peristianis & Gisela Welz (Editors). Trade Cloth. Indiana University Press. Bloomington, IN. 2006. 232p. ISBN:0-253-34751-3, ISBN13: 978-0-253-34751-0. Dewey:305.8005693. LCCN:2006-001258.

Audience: **l,u,f.**

Salih, Halil I.   **DS54.5.S24**
Cyprus: The Impact of Diverse Nationalism on a State. Cloth Text. University of Alabama Press. Tuscaloosa, AL. 1978. 224p. ISBN:0-8173-5706-8, ISBN13: 978-0-8173-5706-1. Dewey:956.4/5. LCCN:76-021743.

Audience: **u,f.**

Stefanidis, Yiannis D.   **DS54.8.S74 1999**
Isle of Discord: Nationalism, Imperialism, and the Making of the Cyprus Problem. Trade Cloth. New York University Press. New York, NY. 1999. 288p. ISBN:0-8147-8118-7, ISBN13: 978-0-8147-8118-0. Dewey:956.93/03. LCCN:98-045025.

Audience: **u,f.**

History of Specific Countries > Iraq > General

Ghareeb, Edmund   **DS70.9.G47 2004**
Historical Dictionary of Iraq. Trade Cloth. Scarecrow Press, Inc. Lanham, MD. 2004. 536p. Asian/Oceanian Historical Dictionaries Ser., No. 44 ISBN:0-8108-4330-7, ISBN13: 978-0-8108-4330-1. Dewey:956.7. LCCN:2003-011526.

Audience: **g,l,u,f.** *Choice, 2004.*

Ghareeb, Edmund   **DS70.8.K8 G48**
The Kurdish Question in Iraq. Syracuse University Press. 1981. ISBN:0-8156-0164-6, ISBN13: 978-0-8156-0164-7.

Audience: **g,l,u,f.**

Nakash, Yitzhak   DS70.8.S55N35 1994
The Shiis of Iraq. Cloth Text. Princeton University Press.
Princeton, NJ. 1994. 340p. ISBN:0-691-03431-1, ISBN13:
978-0-691-03431-7. Dewey:297/.82/09567. LCCN:93-031786.
   Audience: **l,u,f.** *Choice, 1995.*

Phillips, Larissa   G2251.S1
A Historical Atlas of Iraq. Rosen Publishing Group. 2003.
ISBN:0-8239-3865-4, ISBN13: 978-0-8239-3865-0.
   Audience: **l,u,f.**

Polk, William R.   DS70.9
Understanding Iraq: The Whole Sweep of Iraqi History, from
Genghis Khan's Mongols to the Ottoman Turks to the British
Mandate to the American Occupation. Trade Cloth.
HarperCollins Publishers. New York, NY. 2005. 240p.
ISBN:0-06-076468-6, ISBN13: 978-0-06-076468-5.
Dewey:956.7.
   Audience: **g,l,u,f.** *Choice, 2006.*

Sassoon, David S.   DS135.I712 B337 1982
A History of the Jews in Baghdad. Trade Cloth. A M S Press,
Inc. New York, NY. 264p. ISBN:0-404-16427-7, ISBN13:
978-0-404-16427-0. Dewey:956.7/4. LCCN:77-087645.
   Audience: **u,f.**

Yildiz, Kerim & Blass,   DS70.8.K8
   Tom
The Kurds in Iraq: The Past, Present and Future. Trade Cloth.
Pluto Press. London, 2004. 216p. ISBN:0-7453-2229-8,
ISBN13: 978-0-7453-2229-2. Dewey:305.8915970567.
LCCN:2004-304682.
   Audience: **g,l,u,f.**

History of Specific Countries > Iraq > Medieval

Morony, Michael G.   DS76
Iraq after the Muslim Conquest. Trade Cloth. Princeton
University Press. Princeton, NJ. 1984. 768p. Near East Studies
ISBN:0-691-05395-2, ISBN13: 978-0-691-05395-0.
Dewey:956.7/02. LCCN:83-042569.
   Audience: **l,u,f.** *B*

Robinson, Chase F.   HN768.Z9 E47 2000
Empire and Elites after the Muslim Conquest: The
Transformation of Northern Mesopotamia. David Morgan
(Contribution by). Trade Cloth. Cambridge University Press.
New York, NY. 2000. 222p. Studies in Islamic Civilization
ISBN:0-521-78115-9, ISBN13: 978-0-521-78115-2.
Dewey:956.74. LCCN:00-023710.
   Audience: **l,u,f.**

Wiet, Gaston   DS51.B3.W5
Baghdad, Metropolis of the Abbasid Caliphate. Ed. 1. University
of Okalahoma Press. 1971. ISBN:0-8061-0922-X, ISBN13:
978-0-8061-0922-0.
   Audience: **l,u,f.**

History of Specific Countries > Iraq > Modern

Baram, Amatzia   DS79.65.B36 1991
Culture, History and Ideology in the Formation of Ba'thist Iraq,
1968-1989. Trade Cloth. Palgrave Macmillan. New York, NY.
1991. 214p. ISBN:0-312-04805-X, ISBN13: 978-0-312-04805-1.
Dewey:956.7. LCCN:90-043870.
   Audience: **u,f.**

Batatu, Hanna   DS63 .B35 1984
The Egyptian, Syrian, and Iraqi Revolutions: Some Observations
on Their Underlying Causes and Social Character. Cloth Text.
Georgetown University, Center for Contemporary Arab Studies.
Washington, DC. 1984. 29p. ISBN:0-932568-10-6, ISBN13:
978-0-932568-10-6. Dewey:909/.0974927. LCCN:84-005862.
   Audience: **l,u,f.**

Batatu, John   JQ1825.I773.S493
The Old Social Classes and the Revolutionary Movements of
Iraq: A Study of Iraq's Old Landed and Commercial Classes and
of Its Communists, Ba'thists and Free Officers. Trade Cloth.
Princeton University Press. Princeton, NJ. 1979. 1312p. Near
East Studies ISBN:0-691-05241-7, ISBN13: 978-0-691-05241-0.
Dewey:329.9/567. LCCN:78-051157.
   Audience: **u,f.** *B*

Dodge, Toby   DS70.96.G7D633
Inventing Iraq: The Failure of Nation-Building and a History
Denied. Trade Cloth. Columbia University Press. New York,
NY. 2003. 288p. ISBN:0-231-13166-6, ISBN13:
978-0-231-13166-7. Dewey:956.704/1. LCCN:2003-051453.
   Audience: **l,u,f.** *Choice, 2004.*

Eppel, Michael   DS79.E67 2004
Iraq from Monarchy to Tyranny: from the Hashemites to the
Rise of Saddam. University Press of Florida. 2004.
ISBN:0-8130-2736-5, ISBN13: 978-0-8130-2736-4.
   Audience: **u,f.**

Farouk-Sluglett, Marion   DS79.65.F37 1990
   & Sluglett, Peter
Iraq since 1958: From Revolution to Dictatorship. Ed. 2. Cloth
Text. I. B. Tauris & Company, Ltd. London, 1991. 336p.
ISBN:1-85043-317-8, ISBN13: 978-1-85043-317-0.
Dewey:956.704/3. LCCN:90-063393.
   Audience: **l,u,f.** *Choice, 1988.*

Fernea, Elizabeth W.   HQ1735.Z9
Guests of the Sheik: An Ethnography of an Iraqi Village.
Doubldeday. 1965.
   Audience: **g,l,u,f.**

Fernea, Robert A. &   DS79.65.I74 1991
   Louis, William Roger (Editors)
Iraqi Revolution of 1958: The Old Social Classes Revisited.
Cloth Text. I. B. Tauris & Company, Ltd. London, 1991. 224p.
ISBN:1-85043-318-6, ISBN13: 978-1-85043-318-7.
Dewey:956.7043. LCCN:90-063392.
   Audience: **l,u,f.** *Choice, 1992.*

Fuccaro, Nelida   BL1595
The Other Kurds: Yazidis in Colonial Iraq. Cloth over Boards. I.
B. Tauris & Company, Ltd. London, 1999. 256p. Library of
Modern Middle East Studies ISBN:1-86064-170-9, ISBN13:
978-1-86064-170-1. Dewey:305.8/91597/0567.
   Audience: **u,f.** *Choice, 1999.*

Gregory, Derek   DS63.2.U5G74 2004
The Colonial Present: Afghanistan, Palestine, and Iraq.
Blackwell Pub.. 2004. ISBN:1-57718-089-5, ISBN13:
978-1-57718-089-0.

Audience: **u,f.**

Hiro, Dilip   DS318.85.H57 1991
The Longest War: The Iran-Iraq Military Conflict. Trade Paper.
Routledge. New York, NY. 1990. 323p. ISBN:0-415-90407-2,
ISBN13: 978-0-415-90407-0. Dewey:955/.054.
LCCN:90-045641.

Audience: **g,l,u,f.** *Choice, 1991.*

Hiro, Dilip   DS79.75.H57 2001
Neighbours, Not Friends: Iraq and Iran after the Gulf Wars.
Paper over Boards. Routledge. New York, NY. 2001. 432p.
ISBN:0-415-25411-6, ISBN13: 978-0-415-25411-3.
Dewey:956.7044/3. LCCN:2001-020487.

Audience: **l,u,f.**

Human Rights Watch,   JC599.I6552
Helsinki Staff
Bureaucracy of Repression: The Iraqi Government in Its Own
Words. Trade Paper. Human Rights Watch. New York, NY.
1994. 166p. ISBN:1-56432-127-4, ISBN13: 978-1-56432-127-5.
Dewey:323.4. LCCN:94-075191.

Audience: **g,l,u,f.**

Human Rights Watch,   DS70.8.K8I37 1995
Middle East Staff (Editor)
Iraq's Crime of Genocide: The Anfal Campaign Against the
Kurds. Trade Paper. Yale University Press. Cumberland, RI.
1995. 126p. Human Rights Watch Bks. ISBN:0-300-05757-1,
ISBN13: 978-0-300-05757-7. Dewey:305.89159.
LCCN:94-034779.

Audience: **g,l,u,f.**

Kelidar, Abbas R.   DS79.65 .I57 1979
(Editor)
Integration of Modern Iraq. Cloth Text. Palgrave Macmillan.
New York, NY. 1979. ISBN:0-312-41891-4, ISBN13:
978-0-312-41891-5. Dewey:956.7/04. LCCN:78-023322.

Audience: **u,f.**

Khadduri, Majid   DS79 .K43
Independent Iraq, Nineteen Thirty-Two to Nineteen Fifty-Eight:
A Study in Iraqi Politics. Ed. 2. Trade Cloth. A M S Press, Inc.
New York, NY. ISBN:0-404-18972-5, ISBN13:
978-0-404-18972-3. Dewey:956.7. LCCN:80-001919.

Audience: **u,f.**

Khadduri, Majid   DS79.65
Republican Iraq: A Study in Iraqi Politics Since the Revolution
of 1958. Trade Cloth. A M S Press, Inc. New York, NY.
ISBN:0-404-18973-3, ISBN13: 978-0-404-18973-0.
Dewey:320.9/55. LCCN:80-001923.

Audience: **u,f.** *B*

Khadduri, Majid   DS79.65.K49
Socialist Iraq: A Study in Iraqi Politics since 1968. Trade Cloth.
Middle East Institute. Washington, DC. 1978. 265p.
ISBN:0-916808-16-5, ISBN13: 978-0-916808-16-7.
Dewey:320.9/567/04. LCCN:78-051916.

Audience: **u,f.** *B*

Krasno, Jean E. &   UG447
Sutterlin, James S.
The United Nations and Iraq: Defanging the Viper. Paper Text.
Greenwood Publishing Group, Inc. Portsmouth, NH. 2003. 264p.

ISBN:0-275-97839-7, ISBN13: 978-0-275-97839-6.
Dewey:341.7/35/09567. LCCN:2002-068627.

Audience: **u,f.** *Choice, 2004.*

Longrigg, Stephen   DS70.9
Hemsley
Four Centuries of Modern Iraq. Trade Cloth. Garnet Publishing,
Ltd. Reading, 2002. 392p. ISBN:1-85964-169-5, ISBN13:
978-1-85964-169-9. Dewey:956.7.

Audience: **l,u,f.**

Marr, Phebe   DS79.65.M33 2003
The Modern History of Iraq. Ed. 2. Westview Press. 2004.
ISBN:0-8133-8214-9, ISBN13: 978-0-8133-8214-2.

Audience: **g,l,u,f.**

Nieuwenhuis, Tom   HN670.A8
Politics and Society in Early Modern Iraq. Trade Cloth.
Springer. New York, NY. 1982. 248p. ISBN:90-247-2576-3,
ISBN13: 978-90-247-2576-2. Dewey:956.7/03.
LCCN:81-022391.

Audience: **u,f.**

Rejwan, Nissim   DS135.I713R447 2004
The Last Jews in Baghdad: Remembering a Lost Homeland.
Joel Beinin (Foreword by). Trade Cloth. University of Texas
Press. Austin, TX. 2004. 268p. ISBN:0-292-70293-0, ISBN13:
978-0-292-70293-6. Dewey:956.7/47004924/092 B.
LCCN:2004-004110.

Audience: **l,u,f.**

Salih, Khaled (Editor)   DS70.8.K8F88 2005
The Future of Kurdistan in Iraq. Perfect, Paper over Boards,
Dust Jacket. University of Pennsylvania Press. Philadelphia, PA.
2005. 355p. ISBN:0-8122-3870-2, ISBN13: 978-0-8122-3870-9.
Dewey:956.7/20443. LCCN:2004-061229.

Audience: **u,f.** *Choice, 2005.*

Salucci, Ilario   JQ1849.A98S49613
A People's History of Iraq: The Iraqi Communist Party,
Workers Movements, and the Left 1923-2004. Trade Paper.
Haymarket Books. Chicago, IL. 2005. 208p.
ISBN:1-931859-14-0, ISBN13: 978-1-931859-14-1.
Dewey:324.2567/075. LCCN:2004-024314.

Audience: **u,f.**

Shiblak, Abbas   DS135.I7
Iraqi Jews: A History of the Mass Exodus. Saqi. 2005.
ISBN:0-86356-504-2, ISBN13: 978-0-86356-504-5.

Audience: **l,u,f.**

Silverfarb, Daniel   DA47.9.I72S56 1994
The Twilight of British Ascendancy in the Middle East: A Case
Study of Iraq, 1941-1950. St. Martin's Press. 1994.
ISBN:0-312-12090-7, ISBN13: 978-0-312-12090-0.

Audience: **u,f.**

Silverfarb, Daniel   DA47.9.I72S55 1986
Britain's Informal Empire in the Middle East: A Case Study of
Iraq 1929-1941. Majid Khadduri (Foreword by). Trade Cloth.
Oxford University Press, Inc. New York, NY. 1986. 210p.
ISBN:0-19-503997-1, ISBN13: 978-0-19-503997-9.
Dewey:327.410567. LCCN:85-025830.

Audience: **u,f.** *Choice, 1986.*

Simon, Reeva Spector   DS79.S57 2004
Iraq Between the Two World Wars: The Militarist Origins of
Tyranny. Ed. 2. Trade Cloth. Kegan Paul International, Ltd.

London, 2004. 256p. ISBN:0-231-13214-X, ISBN13: 978-0-231-13214-5. Dewey:956.704. LCCN:2003-070003.

Audience: **l,u,f.**

Simon, Reeva S. &   **DS77.C74 2004**
  Tejirian, Eleanor Harvey
The Creation of Iraq, 1914-1921. Gary Sick (Foreword by). Trade Cloth. Edinburgh University Press. Edinburgh, 2004. 200p. ISBN:0-231-13292-1, ISBN13: 978-0-231-13292-3. Dewey:956.7/03. LCCN:2004-045639.

Audience: **u,f.**   *Choice, 2005.*

Stansfield, Gareth R. V.   **JQ1849.A99K87 2003**
Iraqi Kurdistan: Political Development and Emergent Democracy. Cloth Text. Routledge. New York, NY. 2003. 224p. RoutledgeCurzon Advances in Middle East and Islamic Studies ISBN:0-415-30278-1, ISBN13: 978-0-415-30278-4. Dewey:320.9567/2. LCCN:2002-152242.

Audience: **u,f.**

History of Specific Countries > Iraq > Modern > Persian Gulf War 1990-1991

Atkinson, Rick   **DS79.724.U6**
Crusade: The Untold Story of the Persian Gulf War. Cloth Text. DIANE Publishing Company. Collingdale, PA. 1997. 575p. ISBN:0-7881-5133-9, ISBN13: 978-0-7881-5133-0. Dewey:956.7044/2373.

Audience: **g,l,u,f.**   *Choice, 1994.*

Baram, Amatzia &   **DS79.7.I73 1993**
  Rubin, Barry (Editors)
Iraq's Road to War. Trade Cloth. Palgrave Macmillan. New York, NY. 1994. 320p. ISBN:0-312-10171-6, ISBN13: 978-0-312-10171-8. Dewey:956.7044. LCCN:93-024709.

Audience: **l,u,f.**   *Choice, 1994.*

Cordesman, Anthony H.   **DS79.7.C67 1997**
  & Hashim, Ahmed S.
Iraq: Sanctions and Beyond. Trade Paper. Westview Press. Boulder, CO. 1997. 416p. CSIS Middle East Dynamic Net Assessment Ser. ISBN:0-8133-3236-2, ISBN13: 978-0-8133-3236-9. Dewey:956.704/3. LCCN:96-046046.

Audience: **u,f.**   *Choice, 1997.*

Physicians for Human   **DS70.8.K8 W56**
  Rights Staff
Winds of Death: Iraq's Use of Poison Gas Against Its Kurdish Population. Trade Paper. Physicians for Human Rights. Cambridge, MA. 1989. 39p. ISBN:0-614-14420-5, ISBN13: 978-0-614-14420-8. Dewey:956.70049159.

Audience: **g,l,u,f.**

History of Specific Countries > Iraq > Modern > U.S. Occupation 2002-

Israeli, Raphael   **DS63.1**
The Iraq War: Hidden Agendas and Babylonian Intrigue: The Regional Impact on Shi'ites, Kurds, Sunnis and Arabs. Sussex Academic Press. 2004. ISBN:1-903900-89-1, ISBN13: 978-1-903900-89-5.

Audience: **l,u,f.**

Record, Jeffrey   **DS79.76.R43 2004**
Dark Victory: America's Second War Against Iraq. Trade Cloth. Naval Institute Press. Annapolis, MD. 2004. 224p. ISBN:1-59114-711-5, ISBN13: 978-1-59114-711-4. Dewey:956.7044/3. LCCN:2003-026154.

Audience: **u,f.**   *Choice, 2004.*

History of Specific Countries > Lebanon > General

Abukhalil, Asad   **DS80.9.A28 1998**
Historical Dictionary of Lebanon. Scarecrow Press, Inc. 1998. ISBN:0-8108-3395-6, ISBN13: 978-0-8108-3395-1.

Audience: **g,l,u,f.**

Harris, William   **DS87.H3723 1997**
Faces of Lebanon: Sects, Wars and Global Expansion. Cloth Text. Markus Wiener Publishers, Inc. Princeton, NJ. 1997. 368p. Princeton Series on the Middle East ISBN:1-55876-115-2, ISBN13: 978-1-55876-115-5. Dewey:956.9204/4. LCCN:96-008855.

Audience: **l,u,f.**   *Choice, 1997.*

Hitti, Philip Khuri   **DS80.9.H5 1967**
Lebanon in History: From the Earliest Times to the Present. Ed. 3. St. Martin's Press. 1967.

Audience: **l,u,f.**

Hitti, Phillip K.   **DS95**
History of Syria, Including Lebanon and Palestine. Trade Cloth. Gorgias Press, LLC. Piscataway, NJ. 2004. ISBN:1-59333-119-3, ISBN13: 978-1-59333-119-1. Dewey:956.91.

Audience: **g,l,u,f.**

Salibi, Kamal S.   **DS80.9.S26 1988**
A House of Many Mansions: The History of Lebanon Reconsidered. Trade Cloth. University of California Press. Berkeley, CA. 1989. 254p. ISBN:0-520-06517-4, ISBN13: 978-0-520-06517-8. Dewey:952.9/2. LCCN:88-020679.

Audience: **g,l,u,f.**   *Choice, 1989.*

History of Specific Countries > Lebanon > Modern

Abkariyus, Iskandar   **DS84 .I7813 1980**
The Lebanon in Turmoil: Syria and the Powers in 1860. J. F. Scheltema (Translator). Trade Cloth. A M S Press, Inc. New York, NY. 1979. Yale Oriental Ser., No. 7:Researches ISBN:0-404-60277-0, ISBN13: 978-0-404-60277-2. Dewey:956.92/034. LCCN:78-063551.

Audience: **l,u,f.**

Akarli, Engin D.   **DS84.A35 1993**
The Long Peace: Ottoman Lebanon, 1861-1920. Trade Cloth. University of California Press. Berkeley, CA. 1993. 306p. ISBN:0-520-08014-9, ISBN13: 978-0-520-08014-0. Dewey:956.92/034. LCCN:92-018987.

Audience: **u,f.**   *Choice, 1994.*

Chalabi, Tamara   **DS80.55.S54C48 2006**
The Shi'is of Jabal 'Amal and the New Lebanon: Community and Nation State, 1918-1943. Palgrave Macmillan. 2006. ISBN:1-4039-7028-9, ISBN13: 978-1-4039-7028-2.

Audience: **u,f.**

Cobban, Helena　　　　　**DS80.9.C62X 1985**
The Making of Modern Lebanon. Trade Cloth. Random House.
London, 1985. 248p. ISBN:0-09-160791-4, ISBN13:
978-0-09-160791-3. Dewey:956.92. LCCN:86-673515.
　　　　　Audience: **g,l,u,f.**　**B**　*Choice, 1986.*

Deeb, Lara　　　　　**BP192.7.L4D44 2006**
An Enchanted Modern: Gender and Public Piety in Shi'i
Lebanon. Trade Cloth. Princeton University Press. Princeton,
NJ. 2006. 304p. Princeton Studies in Muslim Politics
ISBN:0-691-12420-5, ISBN13: 978-0-691-12420-9.
Dewey:305.48/69782/0956925. LCCN:2005-048753.
　　　　　Audience: **u,f.**

Fawaz, Leila T.　　　　　**DS89.B4**
Merchants and Migrants in Nineteenth Century Beirut. Trade
Cloth. Harvard University Press. Cambridge, MA. 1990. 196p.
Harvard Middle Eastern Studies, No. 18 ISBN:0-674-56925-3,
ISBN13: 978-0-674-56925-6. Dewey:956.92. LCCN:83-004396.
　　　　　Audience: **l,u,f.**

Fawaz, Leila T.　　　　　**DS84.F38 1994**
An Occasion for War: Ethnic Conflict in Lebanon and Damascus
in 1860. Trade Cloth. University of California Press. Berkeley,
CA. 1995. 300p. ISBN:0-520-08782-8, ISBN13:
978-0-520-08782-8. Dewey:956.9204/3. LCCN:94-001941.
　　　　　Audience: **l,u,f.**　*Choice, 1995.*

Gilsenan, Michael　　　　　**JC330**
Lords of the Lebanese Marches: Violence and Narrative in an
Arab Society. Cloth over Boards. I. B. Tauris & Company, Ltd.
London, 2003. 388p. ISBN:1-85043-085-3, ISBN13:
978-1-85043-085-8. Dewey:303.36095692.
　　　　　Audience: **l,u,f.**

Harik, Iliya F.　　　　　**DS84 .H3**
Politics and Change in a Traditional Society: Lebanon,
1711-1845. Trade Cloth. Princeton University Press. Princeton,
NJ. 1968. ISBN:0-691-03049-9, ISBN13: 978-0-691-03049-4.
Dewey:915.6/92/03/3. LCCN:67-021024.
　　　　　Audience: **l,u,f.**

Hourani, Albert H. &　　　　　**DS80.6.H68 1992**
　Shehadi, Nadim (Editors)
The Lebanese and the World: A Century of Emigration. Cloth
over Boards. I. B. Tauris & Company, Ltd. London, 1993. 250p.
ISBN:1-85043-303-8, ISBN13: 978-1-85043-303-3.
Dewey:304.8095692. LCCN:93-138207.
　　　　　Audience: **u,f.**　*Choice, 1993.*

Hudson, Michael C.　　　　　**DS87**
The Precarious Republic: Political Modernization in Lebanon.
Westview Press. 1985. ISBN:0-8133-0105-X, ISBN13:
978-0-8133-0105-1.
　　　　　Audience: **l,u,f.**

Khalaf, Samir　　　　　**DS87.K393 2002**
Civil and Uncivil Violence in Lebanon: A History of the
Internationalization of Communal Conflict. Trade Cloth. Kegan
Paul International, Ltd. London, 2002. 224p. History and
Society of the Modern Middle East Ser. ISBN:0-231-12476-7,
ISBN13: 978-0-231-12476-8. Dewey:956.9204.
LCCN:2001-058253.
　　　　　Audience: **u,f.**

Khater, Akram Fouad　　　　　**JV8748 .K53 2001**
Inventing Home: Emigration, Gender, and the Middle Class in
Lebanon, 1870-1920. Trade Cloth. University of California
Press. Berkeley, CA. 2001. 272p. ISBN:0-520-22739-5, ISBN13:

978-0-520-22739-2. Dewey:305.5/965692/09034.
LCCN:00-046709.
　　　　　Audience: **l,u,f.**　*Choice, 2002.*

Longrigg, Stephen H.　　　　　**DS98 .L6**
Syria and Lebanon under French Mandate, 1968. Trade Cloth.
International Book Centre, Inc. Troy, MI. 1967. Arab
Background Ser. ISBN:0-86685-021-X, ISBN13:
978-0-86685-021-6. Dewey:956.91.
　　　　　Audience: **u,f.**

Makdisi, Ussama S.　　　　　**DS84 .M35 2000**
The Culture of Sectarianism: Community, History, and Violence
in Nineteenth-Century Ottoman Lebanon. Trade Paper.
University of California Press. Berkeley, CA. 2000. 276p.
ISBN:0-520-21846-9, ISBN13: 978-0-520-21846-8.
Dewey:956.92/034. LCCN:99-047861.
　　　　　Audience: **l,u,f.**　*Choice, 2001.*

Mishaqah, Mikhail　　　　　**DS84.M5613 1988**
Murder, Mayhem, Pillage, and Plunder: The History of the
Lebanon in the 18th and 19th Centuries by Mikhayil Mishaqa
(1800-1873). Wheeler M. Thackston Jr. (Translator). Cloth Text.
State University of New York Press. Albany, NY. 1988. 309p.
ISBN:0-88706-712-3, ISBN13: 978-0-88706-712-9.
Dewey:956.92. LCCN:87-018034.
　　　　　Audience: **l,u,f.**　*Choice, 1989.*

Picard, Elizabeth　　　　　**DS87.P5213 1996**
Lebanon: A Shattered Country. Franklin Philip (Translator).
Trade Cloth. Holmes & Meier Publishers, Inc. Teaneck, NJ.
1996. 216p. ISBN:0-8419-1233-5, ISBN13: 978-0-8419-1233-5.
Dewey:956.92. LCCN:94-030521.
　　　　　Audience: **g,l,u,f.**　*Choice, 1996.*

Salibi, Kamal S.　　　　　**DS84 .S25 1976**
The Modern History of Lebanon. Trade Cloth. Greenwood
Publishing Group, Inc. Portsmouth, NH. 1976. 227p.
ISBN:0-8371-8230-1, ISBN13: 978-0-8371-8230-8.
Dewey:956.92. LCCN:75-014703.
　　　　　Audience: **g,l,u,f.**

Tibawi, A. L.　　　　　**DS95 .T5**
A Modern History of Syria: Including Lebanon and Palestine.
Paper Text. St. Martin's Press. Gordonville, VA. 1970.
ISBN:0-312-54005-1, ISBN13: 978-0-312-54005-0.
Dewey:956.91.
　　　　　Audience: **l,u,f.**

History of Specific Countries > Lebanon > Modern > Civil War 1975-1990

Accad, Evelyne　　　　　**PJ8082.A23 1990**
Sexuality and War: Literary Masks of the Middle East. Cloth
Text. New York University Press. New York, NY. 1990. 224p.
Feminist Crosscurrents Ser. ISBN:0-8147-0595-2, ISBN13:
978-0-8147-0595-7. Dewey:892/.736093538. LCCN:89-014278.
　　　　　Audience: **g,l,u,f.**　*Choice, 1991.*

Avi-Ran, Reuven　　　　　**DS80.96.S9A8513 1991**
The Syrian Involvement in Lebanon since 1975. Trade Paper.
Westview Press. Boulder, CO. 1991. 241p. ISBN:0-8133-7935-0,
ISBN13: 978-0-8133-7935-7. Dewey:956.9204/4.
LCCN:90-028789.
　　　　　Audience: **l,u,f.**

Barakat, Halim I.   **LA1463.7**
Lebanon in Strife: Student Preludes to the Civil War. Cloth Text.
University of Texas Press. Austin, TX. 1977. 256p. Modern
Middle East Ser., No. 2 ISBN:0-292-70322-8, ISBN13:
978-0-292-70322-3. Dewey:378.1/98/1095969.
LCCN:76-050046.

Audience: **g,l,u,f.**

Darwish, Mahmoud   **DS87.53.D36513 1995**
Memory for Forgetfulness: August, Beirut, 1982. Ibrahim
Muhawi (Translator). Trade Cloth. University of California
Press. Berkeley, CA. 1995. 182p. Literature of the Middle East
Ser. ISBN:0-520-08767-4, ISBN13: 978-0-520-08767-5.
Dewey:956.9204/4. LCCN:94-026351.

Audience: **g,l,u,f.**

Deeb, Marius K.   **DS87.5**
The Lebanese Civil War. Trade Cloth. Greenwood Publishing
Group, Inc. Portsmouth, NH. 1980. 176p. Praeger Special
Studies ISBN:0-275-90468-7, ISBN13: 978-0-275-90468-5.
Dewey:956.92/04. LCCN:79-019833.

Audience: **l,u,f.**

Deeb, Marius K.   **DS95.6.L4D44 2003**
Syria's Terrorist War on Lebanon and the Peace Process. Cloth
over Boards. Palgrave Macmillan. New York, NY. 2003. 288p.
ISBN:1-4039-6248-0, ISBN13: 978-1-4039-6248-5.
Dewey:327.569105692/09/045. LCCN:2003-041301.
Audience: **l,u,f.** *Choice, 2004.*

Fisk, Robert   **DS87.F55 1990**
Pity the Nation: Lebanon's Abduction. Trade Cloth. Simon &
Schuster. New York, NY. 1990. 704p. ISBN:0-689-12105-9,
ISBN13: 978-0-689-12105-0. Dewey:956.9204/4.
LCCN:90-000868.

Audience: **g,l,u,f.**

Kahan, Yitzhak, et al.   **DS87.53 .I85 1983**
The Beirut Massacre: The Complete Kahan Commission Report.
Aharon Barak & Yona Efrat (Authors), Bezalel Gordon
(Translator), Abba Eban (Introduction by). Trade Cloth.
Karz-Cohl Publishers, Inc. Walled Lake, MI. 1983. 155p.
ISBN:0-943828-55-4, ISBN13: 978-0-943828-55-8.
Dewey:956.92/044. LCCN:83-008385.

Audience: **g,l,u,f.** *B*

Oz, Amos   **DS102.95.O913 1989**
The Slopes of Lebanon. Maurie Goldberg-Bartura (Translator).
Trade Cloth. Harcourt Trade Publishers. New York, NY. 1989.
ISBN:0-15-183090-8, ISBN13: 978-0-15-183090-9.
Dewey:956.92/044. LCCN:89-002090.

Audience: **g,l,u,f.**

Petran, Tabitha   **DS87.P49 1987**
The Struggle over Lebanon. Trade Cloth. Monthly Review
Press. New York, NY. 1987. 320p. ISBN:0-85345-651-8,
ISBN13: 978-0-85345-651-3. Dewey:956.92/044.
LCCN:86-018284.

Audience: **g,l,u,f.** *Choice, 1988.*

Rabinovich, Itamar   **DS87.R332 1985**
The War for Lebanon: 1970-1985. Book, Other. Cornell
University Press. Ithaca, NY. 1984. 243p. ISBN:0-8014-1870-4,
ISBN13: 978-0-8014-1870-9. Dewey:956.92/04.
LCCN:83-045935.

Audience: **l,u,f.** *B*

Randal, Jonathan C.   **DS87.5 .R36 1984**
Going All the Way: Christian Warlords, Israeli Adventurers and
the War in Lebanon. Trade Paper. Knopf Publishing Group. New
York, NY. 1984. ISBN:0-394-72359-7, ISBN13:
978-0-394-72359-4. Dewey:956.92/044. LCCN:83-021574.

Audience: **g,l,u,f.**

Schiff, Ze'ev & Ya'ari,   **DS87**
Ehud
Israel's Lebanon War. Trade Paper. Simon & Schuster. New
York, NY. 1985. 320p. ISBN:0-671-60216-0, ISBN13:
978-0-671-60216-1. Dewey:956.92/044.

Audience: **g,l,u,f.**

Shehadeh, Lamia R.   **HQ1728.W63 1999**
Women and War in Lebanon. Trade Cloth. University Press of
Florida. Gainesville, FL. 1999. xvi, 363p. ISBN:0-8130-1707-6,
ISBN13: 978-0-8130-1707-5. Dewey:305.4/095692/5.
LCCN:99-017516.

Audience: **l,u,f.**

Timerman, Jacobo   **DS119.8.L4T5513 1982**
The Longest War: Israel in Lebanon. Miguel Acoca (Translator).
Trade Cloth. Alfred A. Knopf Inc. New York, NY. 1982. 167p.
ISBN:0-394-53022-5, ISBN13: 978-0-394-53022-2.
Dewey:956/.04. LCCN:82-020208.

Audience: **g,l,u,f.**

Weinberger, Naomi   **DS87.5.W45 1986**
Syrian Intervention in Lebanon. Cloth Text. Oxford University
Press, Inc. New York, NY. 1986. 377p. ISBN:0-19-504010-4,
ISBN13: 978-0-19-504010-4. Dewey:956.92/044.
LCCN:86-008353.

Audience: **g,l,u,f.** *Choice, 1987.*

History of Specific Countries > Syria > General

Commins, David Dean   **DS94.9.C66 1996**
Historical Dictionary of Syria. Scarecrow Press. 1996.
ISBN:0-8108-3176-7, ISBN13: 978-0-8108-3176-6.
Audience: **g,l,u,f.**

Haddad, Robert M   **BR110**
Syrian Christians in Muslim Society: An Interpretation. Trade
Cloth. Greenwood Publishing Group, Inc. Portsmouth, NH.
1981. 118p. Princeton Studies on the Near East
ISBN:0-313-23054-4, ISBN13: 978-0-313-23054-7.
Dewey:305.6/15/05691. LCCN:81-006202.

Audience: **g,l,u,f.**

Hitti, Phillip K.   **DS95**
History of Syria, Including Lebanon and Palestine. Trade Cloth.
Gorgias Press, LLC. Piscataway, NJ. 2004.
ISBN:1-59333-119-3, ISBN13: 978-1-59333-119-1.
Dewey:956.91.

Audience: **g,l,u,f.**

Joseph, John   **DS59.J25 J67 1983**
Muslim-Christian Relations and Inter-Christian Rivalries in the
Middle East: The Case of the Jacobites in an Age of Transition.
State University of New York Press. 1983. ISBN:0-87395-611-7,
ISBN13: 978-0-87395-611-6.

Audience: **u,f.**

Formats: Web: ☐   Ebook: 🅔   CD/DVD-ROM: 🍥   BCL3: *B*

History of Specific Countries > Syria > Medieval

Chamberlain, Michael   **DS99.D3**
Knowledge and Social Practice in Medieval Damascus, 1190-1350. David Morgan (Contribution by). Trade Paper. Cambridge University Press. New York, NY. 2002. 215p. Cambridge Studies in Islamic Civilization Ser. ISBN:0-521-52594-2, ISBN13: 978-0-521-52594-7. Dewey:956.9/14402.
                         Audience: **u,f.** *Choice, 1995.*

Muhamad, Ibn Sasra   **DS99.D3 I24**
A Chronicle of Damascus, 1389-1397: The Unique Bodleian Library Manuscript Al-Durra Al Mudi a Fi L-Dawla Al-Zahiriya. William M. Brinner (Editor). Trade Cloth. University of California Press. Berkeley, CA. 1963. ISBN:0-318-56001-1, ISBN13: 978-0-318-56001-4. Dewey:956.91.
                                   Audience: **u,f.**

Popper, William & Ibn   **DT96.7**
  Taghribirdi, Abu al-Mahasin Yusuf
Egypt and Syria under the Circassian Sultans, 1382-1468 A.D.: Systematic Notes to Ibn Taghri Birdi's Chronicles of Egypt. AMS Press, Inc. 1977. Publications in Semitic Philology, Nos. 15-16 ISBN:0-404-58815-8, ISBN13: 978-0-404-58815-1.
                                   Audience: **l,u,f.**

Ziadeh, Nicola   **DS99.D3 Z5**
Damascus under the Mamluks. University of Oklahoma Press. 1964. Centers of Civilization Series
                                   Audience: **g,l,u,f.**

History of Specific Countries > Syria > Modern

Batatu, Hanna   **DS63 .B35 1984**
The Egyptian, Syrian, and Iraqi Revolutions: Some Observations on Their Underlying Causes and Social Character. Cloth Text. Georgetown University, Center for Contemporary Arab Studies. Washington, DC. 1984. 29p. ISBN:0-932568-10-6, ISBN13: 978-0-932568-10-6. Dewey:909/.0974927. LCCN:84-005862.
                                   Audience: **l,u,f.**

Batatu, Hanna   **DS98.2B386 1999**
Syria's Peasantry, the Descendants of Its Lesser Rural Notables, and Their Politics. Trade Cloth. Princeton University Press. Princeton, NJ. 1999. 432p. ISBN:0-691-00254-1, ISBN13: 978-0-691-00254-5. Dewey:956.9104/088/63. LCCN:98-021289.
                         Audience: **u,f.** *Choice, 2000.*

Deeb, Marius K.   **DS95.6.L4D44 2003**
Syria's Terrorist War on Lebanon and the Peace Process. Cloth over Boards. Palgrave Macmillan. New York, NY. 2003. 288p. ISBN:1-4039-6248-0, ISBN13: 978-1-4039-6248-5. Dewey:327.569105692/09/045. LCCN:2003-041301.
                         Audience: **l,u,f.** *Choice, 2004.*

Fawaz, Leila T.   **DS84.F38 1994**
An Occasion for War: Ethnic Conflict in Lebanon and Damascus in 1860. Trade Cloth. University of California Press. Berkeley, CA. 1995. 300p. ISBN:0-520-08782-8, ISBN13: 978-0-520-08782-8. Dewey:956.9204/3. LCCN:94-001941.
                         Audience: **l,u,f.** *Choice, 1995.*

Gelvin, James L.   **DS98**
Divided Loyalties: Nationalism and Mass Politics in Syria at the Close of Empire. University of California Press. 1998. ISBN:0-520-21069-7, ISBN13: 978-0-520-21069-1.
                                   Audience: **l,u,f.**

Hinnebusch, Raymond   **DS98.2**
Syria: Revolution from Above. Trade Cloth. Gordon & Breach Publishing Group. New York, NY. 2000. 157p. The Contemporary Middle East Ser., Vol. 2 ISBN:90-5823-145-3, ISBN13: 978-90-5823-145-1. Dewey:956.91042.
                         Audience: **u,f.** *Choice, 2002.*

Hopwood, Derek   **JQ1825.S8H66 1988**
Syria, 1945-1986: Politics and Society. Trade Cloth. Routledge. New York, NY. 1988. 176p. ISBN:0-04-445039-7, ISBN13: 978-0-04-445039-9. Dewey:956.91/042. LCCN:87-032433.
                                   Audience: **u,f.**

Khoury, Philip S.   **DS98.K46 1987**
Syria and the French Mandate: The Politics of Arab Nationalism, 1920-1945. Cloth Text. Princeton University Press. Princeton, NJ. 1987. 720p. Middle Eastern History Ser. ISBN:0-691-05486-X, ISBN13: 978-0-691-05486-5. Dewey:946.08. LCCN:86-042859.
                         Audience: **l,u,f.** *Choice, 1987.*

Lewis, Norman N.   **DS94.7.L48 1987**
Nomads and Settlers in Syria and Jordan, 1800-1980. Edmund Burke, Michael C. Hudson & Walid Kazziha (Contribution by). Trade Cloth. Cambridge University Press. New York, NY. 1987. 270p. Cambridge Middle East Library ISBN:0-521-26548-7, ISBN13: 978-0-521-26548-5. Dewey:956.91/03. LCCN:86-017202.
                         Audience: **l,u,f.** *Choice, 1987.*

Longrigg, Stephen H.   **DS98 .L6**
Syria and Lebanon under French Mandate, 1968. Trade Cloth. International Book Centre, Inc. Troy, MI. 1967. Arab Background Ser. ISBN:0-86685-021-X, ISBN13: 978-0-86685-021-6. Dewey:956.91.
                                   Audience: **u,f.**

Marcus, Abraham   **DS99.A56M37 1989**
The Middle East on the Eve of Modernity: Aleppo in the 18th Century. Trade Cloth. Columbia University Press. New York, NY. 1989. 418p. ISBN:0-231-06594-9, ISBN13: 978-0-231-06594-8. Dewey:956.91/3. LCCN:88-036599.
                         Audience: **u,f.** *Choice, 1990.*

Meriwether, Margaret Lee   **HQ518**
The Kin Who Count: Family and Society in Ottoman Aleppo, 1770-1840. Trade Cloth. University of Texas Press. Austin, TX. 1999. 288p. ISBN:0-292-75223-7, ISBN13: 978-0-292-75223-8. Dewey:306./850. LCCN:98-041120.
                         Audience: **u,f.** *Choice, 2000.*

Moubayed, Sami M.   **DS98.2.M68 2000**
Damascus Between Democracy and Dictatorship. Trade Cloth. University Press of America, Inc. Lanham, MD. 2000. 248p. ISBN:0-7618-1744-1, ISBN13: 978-0-7618-1744-4. Dewey:956.9104/2. LCCN:00-034332.
                         Audience: **u,f.** *Choice, 2001.*

Moubayed, Sami M.   **CT1916**
Steel & Silk: Men & Women Who Shaped Syria, 1900-2000. Cune. 2005. ISBN:1-885942-40-0, ISBN13: 978-1-885942-40-1.
                                   Audience: **l,u,f.**

Sanjian, Avedis K.   DS97.5 .S2
Armenian Communities in Syria Under Ottoman Dominion.
Trade Cloth. Harvard University Press. Cambridge, MA. 1965.
402p. Middle Eastern Studies, No. 10 ISBN:0-674-04600-5,
ISBN13: 978-0-674-04600-9. Dewey:956.1093.
LCCN:65-019827.

Audience: **l,u,f.**

Seale, Patrick   DS98.3.A8S42
Asad of Syria: The Struggle for the Middle East. Trade Paper.
University of California Press. Berkeley, CA. 1996. 562p.
ISBN:0-520-06976-5, ISBN13: 978-0-520-06976-3.
Dewey:956.91042092.

Audience: **l,u,f.** *Choice, 1989.*

Seale, Patrick   DS98.2
The Struggle for Syria: A Study of Post-War Arab Politics,
1945-1958. I.B. Tauris. 1965. ISBN:1-85043-028-4, ISBN13:
978-1-85043-028-5.

Audience: **u,f.**

Tibawi, A. L.   DS95 .T5
A Modern History of Syria: Including Lebanon and Palestine.
Paper Text. St. Martin's Press. Gordonville, VA. 1970.
ISBN:0-312-54005-1, ISBN13: 978-0-312-54005-0.
Dewey:956.91.

Audience: **l,u,f.**

Tucker, Judith E.   KMC145.W64 T83 1998
In the House of the Law: Gender and Islamic Law in Ottoman
Syria and Palestine. Trade Cloth. University of California Press.
Berkeley, CA. 1998. 232p. ISBN:0-520-21039-5, ISBN13:
978-0-520-21039-4. Dewey:305.42/095691. LCCN:97-027168.
Audience: **l,u,f.** *Choice, 1998.*

Van Dam, Nikolaos   DS98.2
The Struggle for Power in Syria: Politics and Society under
Asad and the Ba'th Party. I.B. Tauris. 1996.
ISBN:1-86064-024-9, ISBN13: 978-1-86064-024-7.

Audience: **u,f.**

Wedeen, Lisa   DS98.4.W43 1999
Ambiguities of Domination: Politics, Rhetoric, and Symbols in
Contemporary Syria. Trade Cloth. University of Chicago Press.
Chicago, IL. 1999. 251p. ISBN:0-226-87787-6, ISBN13:
978-0-226-87787-7. Dewey:320.95691. LCCN:98-046430.

Audience: **u,f.**

Weinberger, Naomi   DS87.5.W45 1986
Syrian Intervention in Lebanon. Cloth Text. Oxford University
Press, Inc. New York, NY. 1986. 377p. ISBN:0-19-504010-4,
ISBN13: 978-0-19-504010-4. Dewey:956.92/044.
LCCN:86-008353.

Audience: **g,l,u,f.** *Choice, 1987.*

History of Specific Countries > Israel/Palestine > General

Avi-Yonah, Michael   DS117.H552 2001
A History of Israel and the Holy Land. Shimon Peres (Foreword
by). Trade Cloth. Continuum International Publishing Group,
Ltd. London, 2001. 375p. ISBN:0-8264-1322-6, ISBN13:
978-0-8264-1322-2. Dewey:956.94. LCCN:2001-017463.

Audience: **g,l,u,f.**

Gilbert, Martin   G2236.S1
The Atlas of Jewish History. Trade Cloth. HarperCollins
Publishers. New York, NY. 1993. 152p. ISBN:0-688-12264-7,
ISBN13: 978-0-688-12264-5. Dewey:911/.56. LCCN:92-018050.

Audience: **g,l,u,f.**

Hitti, Phillip K.   DS95
History of Syria, Including Lebanon and Palestine. Trade Cloth.
Gorgias Press, LLC. Piscataway, NJ. 2004.
ISBN:1-59333-119-3, ISBN13: 978-1-59333-119-1.
Dewey:956.91.

Audience: **g,l,u,f.**

Mattar, Philip   DS113.6.E53 2005
Encyclopedia of the Palestinians. Ed. 2. Trade Cloth. Facts On
File, Inc. New York, NY. 2005. 704p. ISBN:0-8160-5764-8,
ISBN13: 978-0-8160-5764-1. Dewey:909/.049274/003.
LCCN:2004-057673.

Audience: **l,u,f.** *Choice, 2006.*

Nazzal, Nafez & Nazzal,   DS102.8.N397 1997
Laila A.
Historical Dictionary of Palestine. Trade Cloth. Scarecrow Press,
Inc. Lanham, MD. 1997. 320p. Asian Historical Dictionaries
Ser., Vol. 23 ISBN:0-8108-3239-9, ISBN13: 978-0-8108-3239-8.
Dewey:956.94/003. LCCN:96-030594.

Audience: **g,l,u,f.** *Choice, 1997.*

Reich, Bernard   DS126.5.R38 1992
Historical Dictionary of Israel. Trade Cloth. Scarecrow Press,
Inc. Lanham, MD. 1992. 421p. Asian Historical Dictionaries
Ser., No. 8 ISBN:0-8108-2535-X, ISBN13: 978-0-8108-2535-2.
Dewey:956.94003. LCCN:92-005324.

Audience: **g,l,u,f.** *Choice, 1993.*

Torstrick, Rebecca L.   GN635
Culture and Customs of Israel. Cloth Text. Greenwood
Publishing Group, Inc. Portsmouth, NH. 2004. 208p. Culture
and Customs of the Middle East Ser. ISBN:0-313-32091-8,
ISBN13: 978-0-313-32091-0. Dewey:306/.095694.
LCCN:2004-004577.

Audience: **g,l,u,f.**

History of Specific Countries > Israel/Palestine > Early to 637

Hunt, Edward D.   BR205 .H84 1982
Holy Land Pilgrimage in the Later Roman Empire: AD 312-460.
Trade Cloth. Oxford University Press, Inc. New York, NY. 1982.
x, 269p. ISBN:0-19-826438-0, ISBN13: 978-0-19-826438-5.
Dewey:248.4/63/095694. LCCN:82-186936.

Audience: **l,u,f.**

History of Specific Countries > Israel/Palestine > Medieval

Gil, Moshe   DS124 .G5513 1992
A History of Palestine, 634-1099. Ethel Broido (Translator).
Trade Cloth. Cambridge University Press. New York, NY. 1992.
994p. ISBN:0-521-40437-1, ISBN13: 978-0-521-40437-2.
Dewey:956.9/4/03. LCCN:90-020807.

Audience: **l,u,f.** *Choice, 1992.*

Ibn Al-Firkah &   **BP187.5.P19**
Ibrahim ibn Abd Al-Rahman
Palestine: Mohammedan Holy Land. Charles Matthews (Editor). Trade Cloth. A M S Press, Inc. New York, NY. Yale Oriental Ser., No. 24:Researches ISBN:0-404-60324-6, ISBN13: 978-0-404-60324-3. Dewey:297/.095694. LCCN:78-063568.

Audience: **u,f.**

Mann, Jacob   **DS124**
The Jews in Egypt and in Palestine Under the Fatimid Caliphs. Trade Cloth. Ktav Publishing House, Inc. Jersey City, NJ. 1970. Library of Jewish Classics Ser ISBN:0-87068-024-2, ISBN13: 978-0-87068-024-3. Dewey:909.04924.

Audience: **l,u,f.**

Prawer, Joshua (Editor)   **DS109.916S4413 1996**
The History of Jerusalem: The Early Muslim Period, 638-1099. Trade Cloth. New York University Press. New York, NY. 1996. 400p. ISBN:0-8147-6639-0, ISBN13: 978-0-8147-6639-2. Dewey:956.94/42. LCCN:95-042754.

Audience: **u,f.** *Choice, 1997.*

History of Specific Countries > Israel/Palestine > Medieval > The Crusades 1099-1249

al-Umari, Ibn Fadl   **D163**
Allah
Saladin and the Crusaders: Selected Annals from Masalik Al-absar Fi Mamalik Al Amsar. Eva R. Lundquist (Editor). Paper Text. Krieger Publishing Company. Melbourne, FL. 1992. 132p. ISBN:91-7966-186-6, ISBN13: 978-91-7966-186-1. Dewey:909.07.

Audience: **u,f.**

Ehrenkreutz, Andrew S.   **DS38.4.S2**
Saladin. State University of New York Press. 1972. ISBN:0-87395-095-X, ISBN13: 978-0-87395-095-4.

Audience: **g,l,u,f.**

Eidelberg, Shlomo   **DS135.G31J48 1996**
(Editor, Translator)
The Jews and the Crusaders: The Hebrew Chronicles of the First and Second Crusades. Trade Paper. Ktav Publishing House, Inc. Jersey City, NJ. 1996. xi, 186p. ISBN:0-88125-541-6, ISBN13: 978-0-88125-541-6. Dewey:943/.09424. LCCN:96-000253.

Audience: **g,l,u,f.**

Gabrieli, Francesco   **D151**
Arab Historians of the Crusades. Trade Cloth. University of California Press. Berkeley, CA. 1978. 398p. ISBN:0-520-05224-2, ISBN13: 978-0-520-05224-6. Dewey:909.07. LCCN:68-023783.

Audience: **g,l,u,f.**

Holt, P. M.   **D157**
The Crusader States and their Neighbours: 1098-1291. Trade Paper. Longman Publishing. Boston, MA. 2004. 120p. ISBN:0-582-36931-2, ISBN13: 978-0-582-36931-3. Dewey:909/.07.

Audience: **u,f.**

Ibn Al-Qalanisi   **D152 .I25213 1980**
The Damascus Chronicle of the Crusades. Hamilton A. Gibb (Translator). Trade Cloth. A M S Press, Inc. New York, NY. The

Crusades and Military Orders Ser., Second Series ISBN:0-404-17019-6, ISBN13: 978-0-404-17019-6. Dewey:940.1/8. LCCN:78-063342.

Audience: **u,f.**

Ibn Munqidh, Usamah   **DS97.3.U813 2000**
Arab-Syrian Gentleman and Warrior in the Period of the Crusades: Memoirs of Usamah Ibn-Munqidh. Philip K. Hitti (Translator), Richard W. Bulliett (Foreword by). Trade Cloth. Columbia University Press. New York, NY. 2000. 265p. Records of Western Civilization Ser. ISBN:0-231-12124-5, ISBN13: 978-0-231-12124-8. Dewey:956.91/02. LCCN:00-022724.

Audience: **g,l,u,f.**

History of Specific Countries > Israel/Palestine > Modern

Arens, Moshe   **E183.8.I7A74 1995**
Broken Covenant. Trade Cloth. Simon & Schuster. New York, NY. 1995. 320p. ISBN:0-671-86964-7, ISBN13: 978-0-671-86964-9. Dewey:327.7305694. LCCN:94-045241.

Audience: **u,f.**

Begin, Menachem   **DS126.B375 1977**
The Revolt. Trade Cloth. Nash Publishing Corporation. New York, NY. 1977. xxvii, 386p. ISBN:0-8402-1370-0, ISBN13: 978-0-8402-1370-9. Dewey:956.94/04/0924. LCCN:77-010806.

Audience: **l,u,f.**

Bell, J. Bowyer   **DS126.B384 1996**
(Introduction by)
Terror Out of Zion: The Fight for Israeli Independence. Moshe Arens (Foreword by). Trade Paper. Transaction Publishers. Somerset, NJ. 1996. 374p. ISBN:1-56000-870-9, ISBN13: 978-1-56000-870-5. Dewey:956.94/04. LCCN:95-049992.

Audience: **g,l,u,f.**

Ben-Arieh, Yehoshua   **DS125**
The Rediscovery of the Holy Land in the Nineteenth Century. Trade Cloth. Wayne State University Press. Detroit, MI. 1980. 266p. ISBN:0-8143-1654-9, ISBN13: 978-0-8143-1654-2. Dewey:915.694. LCCN:79-067619.

Audience: **l,u,f.**

Ben-Arieh, Yehoshua &   **DS109**
Davis, Moshe (Editors)
Jerusalem in the Mind of the Western World, 1800-1948, V. Trade Cloth. Greenwood Publishing Group, Inc. Portsmouth, NH. 1997. 296p. With Eyes Toward Zion Ser., Vol. V ISBN:0-275-95405-6, ISBN13: 978-0-275-95405-5. Dewey:915.694/420454. LCCN:96-020171.

Audience: **u,f.**

Benvenisti, Meron   **DS119.7.B385813 1995**
Intimate Enemies: Jews and Arabs in a Shared Land. Thomas L. Friedman (Foreword by). Trade Cloth. University of California Press. Berkeley, CA. 1995. 274p. ISBN:0-520-08567-1, ISBN13: 978-0-520-08567-1. Dewey:956.9405/4. LCCN:95-001933.

Audience: **l,u,f.**

Blumberg, Arnold B.   **DS125.B58 1985**
Zion Before Zionism: Eighteen Thirty-Eight to Eighteen Eighty. Cloth Text. Syracuse University Press. Syracuse, NY. 1985. 240p. ISBN:0-8156-2336-4, ISBN13: 978-0-8156-2336-6. Dewey:956.94/004924. LCCN:85-017287.

Audience: **l,u,f.** *Choice, 1986.*

Buber, Martin (Editor),   **DS119.7**
  et al.
Towards Union in Palestine: Essays on Zionism and
Jewish-Arab Cooperation. Judah L. Magnes & E. Simon
(Editors). Trade Cloth. Greenwood Publishing Group, Inc.
Portsmouth, NH. 1972. 124p. Judaica Ser. ISBN:0-8371-2564-2,
ISBN13: 978-0-8371-2564-0. Dewey:956.94/001.
LCCN:76-097272.

                            Audience: **l,u,f.**

David, Abraham   **DS124.D3813 1999**
To Come to the Land: Immigration and Settlement in
Sixteenth-Century Eretz-Israel. Trade Cloth. University of
Alabama Press. Tuscaloosa, AL. 1999. 360p. Judaic Studies
ISBN:0-8173-0935-7, ISBN13: 978-0-8173-0935-0.
Dewey:305.892/4056944/0903. LCCN:98-025424.
                  Audience: **u,f.** *Choice, 1999.*

Davis, Moshe   **BM729**
America and the Holy Land: With Eyes Toward Zion, IV. Trade
Cloth. Greenwood Publishing Group, Inc. Portsmouth, NH.
1995. 208p. With Eyes Toward Zion Ser. ISBN:0-275-94621-5,
ISBN13: 978-0-275-94621-0. Dewey:296.3. LCCN:94-028005.
                  Audience: **u,f.** *Choice, 1995.*

Davis, Moshe (Editor)
With Eyes Toward Zion: Scholars Colloquium on America-Holy
Land Studies. Library Binding. Ayer Company Publishers, Inc.
Manchester, NH. 1977. America and the Holy Land Ser.
ISBN:0-405-10312-3, ISBN13: 978-0-405-10312-4.
LCCN:77-002493.

                            Audience: **u,f.**

Davis, Moshe (Editor)   **E183**
With Eyes Toward Zion: Themes and Sources in the Archives of
the United States, Breat Britain, Turkey and Israel, 2. Trade
Cloth. Greenwood Publishing Group, Inc. Portsmouth, NH.
1986. 434p. With Eyes Toward Zion Ser. ISBN:0-275-92090-9,
ISBN13: 978-0-275-92090-6. Dewey:303.4/8273/05694.
LCCN:85-028288.

                            Audience: **u,f.**

Davis, Moshe &   **DS101**
  Ben-Arieh, Yehoshua (Editors)
Eyes Toward Zion: Western Societies and the Holy Land. Trade
Cloth. Greenwood Publishing Group, Inc. Portsmouth, NH.
1991. 296p. With Eyes Toward Zion Ser. ISBN:0-275-93793-3,
ISBN13: 978-0-275-93793-5. Dewey:956.94/007.
LCCN:90-014310.

                            Audience: **u,f.**

Doumani, Beshara   **HC415.25.D68 1995**
Rediscovering Palestine: Merchants and Peasants of Jabal
Nablus, 1700-1900. Trade Cloth. University of California Press.
Berkeley, CA. 1995. 340p. ISBN:0-520-08895-6, ISBN13:
978-0-520-08895-5. Dewey:330.95695/3. LCCN:94-030401.
                  Audience: **l,u,f.** *Choice, 1996.*

Elon, Amos   **DS126.5.E41948 1997**
A Blood-Dimmed Tide: Dispatches from the Middle East. Trade
Cloth. Columbia University Press. New York, NY. 1997. 264p.
ISBN:0-231-10742-0, ISBN13: 978-0-231-10742-6.
Dewey:956.9/4/05. LCCN:96-048966.
                        Audience: **l,u,f.**

Frankel, Glenn   **DS126.5.F716 1996**
Beyond the Promised Land: Jews and Arabs on the Hard Road
to a New Israel. Trade Paper. Simon & Schuster. New York, NY.
1996. 432p. A Touchstone Book Ser. ISBN:0-684-82347-0,

ISBN13: 978-0-684-82347-8. Dewey:320.9/5694.
LCCN:96-010604.

                            Audience: **g,l,u,f.**

Gilbert, Martin   **DS109.93.G55 1996**
Jerusalem in the Twentieth Century. Trade Cloth. John Wiley &
Sons, Inc. Hoboken, NJ. 1996. 412p. ISBN:0-471-16308-2,
ISBN13: 978-0-471-16308-4. Dewey:956.9/442/05.
LCCN:96-018458.

                            Audience: **g,l,u,f.**

Gregory, Derek   **DS63.2.U5G74 2004**
The Colonial Present: Afghanistan, Palestine, and Iraq.
Blackwell Pub.. 2004. ISBN:1-57718-089-5, ISBN13:
978-1-57718-089-0.

                            Audience: **u,f.**

Halper, Jeff   **DS109.925.H35 1990**
Between Redemption and Revival: The Jewish Yishuv of
Jerusalem in the Nineteenth Century. Trade Paper. Westview
Press. Boulder, CO. 1990. 290p. ISBN:0-8133-7855-9, ISBN13:
978-0-8133-7855-8. Dewey:956.94/42. LCCN:90-046092.
                  Audience: **l,u,f.** *Choice, 1991.*

Katz, Sheila H.   **HQ1236.5.I75K38 2003**
Women and Gender in Early Jewish and Palestinian
Nationalism. Trade Cloth. University Press of Florida.
Gainesville, FL. 2003. xvi, 224p. ISBN:0-8130-2618-0, ISBN13:
978-0-8130-2618-3. Dewey:305.42/095694. LCCN:2003-040245.
                  Audience: **l,u,f.** *Choice, 2003.*

Kedourie, Elie & Haim,   **DS125 .P294 1982**
  Sylvia G. (Editors)
Palestine and Israel in the 19th and 20th Centuries. Trade Paper.
Taylor & Francis Group. Abingdon, 1982. 288p.
ISBN:0-7146-3121-3, ISBN13: 978-0-7146-3121-9.
Dewey:956.94/04. LCCN:82-193747.

                            Audience: **l,u,f.**

LeVine, Mark   **DS110.T357 L42 2005**
Overthrowing Geography: Jaffa, Tel Aviv, and the Struggle for
Palestine, 1880-1948. Trade Cloth. University of California
Press. Berkeley, CA. 2005. 512p. ISBN:0-520-23994-6, ISBN13:
978-0-520-23994-4. Dewey:956.94/8. LCCN:2004-008779.
                            Audience: **u,f.**

Lieber, Sherman   **DS125.L53 1992**
Mystics and Missionaries: The Jews in Palestine, 1799-1840.
Trade Cloth. University of Utah Press. Salt Lake City, UT.
1992. 544p. ISBN:0-87480-391-8, ISBN13: 978-0-87480-391-4.
Dewey:956.94/03. LCCN:92-053605.
                  Audience: **u,f.** *Choice, 1993.*

Louis, William Roger &   **DS126.4.E63 1986**
  Stookey, Robert W. (Editors)
The End of the Palestine Mandate. Cloth Text. University of
Texas Press. Austin, TX. 1986. 197p. Center for Middle Eastern
Studies, Modern Middle East, No. 12 ISBN:0-292-72052-1,
ISBN13: 978-0-292-72052-7. Dewey:956.94/05.
LCCN:85-015109.

                            Audience: **l,u,f.**

McCarthy, Justin   **HA4560.M35 1990**
The Population of Palestine: Population Statistics of the Late
Ottoman Period and the Mandate. Trade Cloth. Columbia
University Press. New York, NY. 1990. 242p. Institute for
Palestine Studies Ser. ISBN:0-231-07110-8, ISBN13:
978-0-231-07110-9. Dewey:304.6/095694. LCCN:90-001641.
                  Audience: **u,f.** *Choice, 1991.*

Morris, Benny   **DS126.954.M67 1990**
1948 and After: Israel and the Palestinians. Trade Cloth. Oxford
University Press, Inc. New York, NY. 1991. 304p.
ISBN:0-19-828784-4, ISBN13: 978-0-19-828784-1.
Dewey:956.04/2. LCCN:90-007469.

Audience: **g,l,u,f.**

Ovendale, Ritchie   **DS119.7.O931999**
The Origins of the Arab-Israeli Wars. Ed. 3. Trade Paper.
Longman Publishing. Boston, MA. 1999. 360p. Origins of
Modern Wars Ser. ISBN:0-582-36895-2, ISBN13:
978-0-582-36895-8. Dewey:956. LCCN:99-012400.

Audience: **l,u,f.**

Owen, Roger (Editor)   **HC415.25**
Studies in the Economic and Social History of Palestine in the
19th and 20th Centuries. Trade Cloth. Southern Illinois
University Press. Carbondale, IL. 1982. 271p.
ISBN:0-8093-1089-9, ISBN13: 978-0-8093-1089-0.
Dewey:330.95694. LCCN:82-080662.

Audience: **u,f.**

Oz, Amos   **DS119.7.O96 1995**
Israel, Palestine and Peace: Essays. Trade Paper. Harcourt Trade
Publishers. New York, NY. 1995. 162p. ISBN:0-15-600192-6,
ISBN13: 978-0-15-600192-2. Dewey:956.9405.
LCCN:95-005777.

Audience: **g,l,u,f.**

Oz, Amos   **DS126.7 .O95 1995**
Under This Blazing Light. Nicholas R. M. De Lange
(Translator). Trade Cloth. Cambridge University Press. New
York, NY. 1995. 219p. ISBN:0-521-44367-9, ISBN13:
978-0-521-44367-8. Dewey:956.9/4/054. LCCN:94-017040.

Audience: **g,l,u,f.**

Pappe, Ilan   **DS118**
A History of Modern Palestine: One Land, Two Peoples. Cloth
Text. Cambridge University Press. New York, NY. 2003. 356p.
ISBN:0-521-55406-3, ISBN13: 978-0-521-55406-0.
Dewey:956.9405. LCCN:2003-067430.

Audience: **l,u,f.**

Parfitt, Tudor   **DS125.P33 1987**
The Jews in Palestine, 1800-1882. Trade Cloth. Royal Historical
Society. London, 1987. 255p. Royal Historical Society Studies
in History ISBN:0-86193-209-9, ISBN13: 978-0-86193-209-2.
Dewey:956.94/004924. LCCN:87-005150.

Audience: **u,f.**

Rejwan, Nissim   **DS119.7.R374 1998**
Israel's Place in the Middle East: A Pluralist Perspective. Trade
Cloth. University Press of Florida. Gainesville, FL. 1998. 224p.
ISBN:0-8130-1601-0, ISBN13: 978-0-8130-1601-6.
Dewey:327.5605694. LCCN:98-006104.

Audience: **u,f.** *Choice, 1999.*

Rogan, Eugene (Editor)   **DS126.9 .R49 2001**
The War for Palestine: Rewriting the History of 1948. Shlaim,
Avi (Editor). Cambridge University Press. 2001.
ISBN:0-521-79139-1, ISBN13: 978-0-521-79139-7.

Audience: **u,f.**

Sachar, Howard Morley   **DS126.5**
A History of Israel: From the Rise of Zionism to Our Time. Ed.
2. Trade Paper. Random House, Inc. New York, NY. 1996.
1184p. ISBN:0-679-76563-8, ISBN13: 978-0-679-76563-9.
Dewey:956.94.

Audience: **g,l,u,f.**

Shapira, Anita   **DS149**
Land and Power: The Zionist Resort to Force, 1881-1948. Trade
Paper. Stanford University Press. Palo Alto, CA. 1999. 468p.
ISBN:0-8047-3776-2, ISBN13: 978-0-8047-3776-0.
Dewey:320.5/4/095694.

Audience: **u,f.** *Choice, 1993.*

Shavit, Jacob & Naor,   **DS113.S425 2004**
  Chaya
Staging and Stagers in Modern Jewish Palestine: The Creation
of Festive Lore in a New Culture, 1882-1948. Trade Cloth.
Wayne State University Press. Detroit, MI. 2004. 214p. Raphael
Patai Series in Jewish Folklore and Anthropology
ISBN:0-8143-2845-8, ISBN13: 978-0-8143-2845-3.
Dewey:394.2695694. LCCN:2004-000536.

Audience: **u,f.** *Choice, 2005.*

Shepherd, Naomi   **DS107.S54 1987**
The Zealous Intruders. Trade Cloth. HarperCollins Publishers.
New York, NY. 1988. 288p. ISBN:0-06-067271-4, ISBN13:
978-0-06-067271-3. Dewey:956.94/03. LCCN:87-017605.

Audience: **g,l,u,f.**

Singer, Amy   **HD1537.J4 S56 1994**
Palestinian Peasants and Ottoman Officials: Rural Administration
Around Sixteenth-Century Jerusalem. David Morgan
(Contribution by). Trade Paper. Cambridge University Press.
New York, NY. 1994. 219p. Cambridge Studies in Islamic
Civilization Ser. ISBN:0-521-47679-8, ISBN13:
978-0-521-47679-9. Dewey:305.5/633/09569442.
LCCN:93-038441.

Audience: **u,f.**

Slyomovics, Susan   **DS110.E645S59 1998**
The Object of Memory: Arab and Jew Narrate the Palestinian
Village. Trade Cloth. University of Pennsylvania Press.
Philadelphia, PA. 1998. 296p. ISBN:0-8122-3215-1, ISBN13:
978-0-8122-3215-8. Dewey:956.94. LCCN:98-005346.

Audience: **u,f.** *Choice, 1999.*

Thomas, Baylis   **DS126.5.T495 1999**
How Israel Was Won: A Concise History of the Arab-Israeli
Conflict. Trade Cloth. Lexington Books. Lanham, MD. 1999.
352p. ISBN:0-7391-0063-7, ISBN13: 978-0-7391-0063-9.
Dewey:956.94. LCCN:99-010673.

Audience: **l,u,f.** *Choice, 2000.*

Tibawi, A. L.   **DS95 .T5**
A Modern History of Syria: Including Lebanon and Palestine.
Paper Text. St. Martin's Press. Gordonville, VA. 1970.
ISBN:0-312-54005-1, ISBN13: 978-0-312-54005-0.
Dewey:956.91.

Audience: **l,u,f.**

Tucker, Judith E.   **KMC145.W64 T83 1998**
In the House of the Law: Gender and Islamic Law in Ottoman
Syria and Palestine. Trade Cloth. University of California Press.

Berkeley, CA. 1998. 232p. ISBN:0-520-21039-5, ISBN13: 978-0-520-21039-4. Dewey:305.42/095691. LCCN:97-027168.

Audience: **l,u,f.** *Choice, 1998.*

History of Specific Countries > Israel/Palestine > Modern > British Mandate Period 1917-1948

Bentwich, Norman D.   **DS126 .B413 1976**
Fulfillment in the Promised Land, 1917-1937. Trade Cloth. Hyperion Press, Inc. Westport, CT. 1976. 246p. The Rise of Jewish Nationalism and the Middle East Ser.
ISBN:0-88355-310-4, ISBN13: 978-0-88355-310-7. Dewey:956.94/04. LCCN:75-006423.

Audience: **l,u,f.**

Bernstein, Deborah S.   **HD5812.2.A7H35 2000**
Constructing Boundaries: Jewish and Arab Workers in Mandatory Palestine. Cloth Text. State University of New York Press. Albany, NY. 2000. xvi, 277p. SUNY Series in Israeli Studies ISBN:0-7914-4539-9, ISBN13: 978-0-7914-4539-6. Dewey:331.12/095694/6. LCCN:99-037759.

Audience: **u,f.** *Choice, 2000.*

Bernstein, Deborah S.   **HQ1728.5.P56 1992**
(Editor)
Pioneers and Homemakers: Jewish Women in Pre-State Israel. Cloth Text. State University of New York Press. Albany, NY. 1992. 312p. ISBN:0-7914-0905-8, ISBN13: 978-0-7914-0905-3. Dewey:305.48/696. LCCN:91-021247.

Audience: **l,u,f.**

Fleischman, Ellen   **HQ1728.5 .F57 2003**
The Nation and Its New Women: Feminism, Nationalism, Colonialism, and the Palestinian Women's Movement, 1920-1948. Trade Cloth. University of California Press. Berkeley, CA. 2003. 368p. ISBN:0-520-23789-7, ISBN13: 978-0-520-23789-6. Dewey:305.48/892/75. LCCN:2002-009719.

Audience: **l,u,f.**

Friedman, Isaiah   **DS125.5.F73 1992**
The Question of Palestine: British-Jewish-Arab Relations, 1914-1918. Ed. 2. Transaction Publishers. 1992.
ISBN:0-88738-214-2, ISBN13: 978-0-88738-214-7.

Audience: **u,f.**

Horowitz, Dan &   **DS126**
Lissak, Moshe
Origins of the Israeli Polity: Palestine under the Mandate. Charles Hoffman (Translator). Library Binding. University of Chicago Press. Chicago, IL. 1994. 320p. ISBN:0-226-35366-4, ISBN13: 978-0-226-35366-1. Dewey:323.1/19/2405694. LCCN:78-003175.

Audience: **l,u,f.**

Klieman, Aaron (Editor,   **DS119.7.R54 1987**
Introduction by)
Arab-Jewish Relations, 1921-1936. Howard M. Sachar (Editor). Library Binding. Garland Publishing, Inc. New York, NY. 1988. 340p. The Rise of Israel Ser. ISBN:0-8240-4916-0, ISBN13: 978-0-8240-4916-4. Dewey:956.94/001. LCCN:87-011922.

Audience: **u,f.**

Likhovski, Assaf   **KMQ1012.L57 2006**
Law and Identity in Mandate Palestine. Trade Cloth. University of North Carolina Press. Chapel Hill, NC. 2006. 376p. Studies in Legal History ISBN:0-8078-3017-8, ISBN13: 978-0-8078-3017-8. Dewey:349.5694. LCCN:2005-034983.

Audience: **u,f.**

Porath, Yehoshua   **DS126 .P6313**
The Emergence of the Palestinian Arab National Movement, 1918-1929. Trade Paper. Taylor & Francis Group. Abingdon, 1974. 406p. ISBN:0-7146-4181-2, ISBN13: 978-0-7146-4181-2. Dewey:956.94/04.

Audience: **u,f.**

Porath, Yehoshua   **DS126 .P636**
The Palestinian Arab National Movement, 1929-1939: From Riots to Rebellion. Trade Paper. Taylor & Francis Group. Abingdon, 1977. 414p. ISBN:0-7146-4197-9, ISBN13: 978-0-7146-4197-3. Dewey:956.94/04.

Audience: **u,f.**

Rubashow-Katznelson,   **HQ1781.P2 K3713 1976**
Rachel (Editor)
The Plough Women: Records of the Pioneer Women of Palestine. Trade Cloth. Hyperion Press, Inc. Westport, CT. 1975. 306p. The Rise of Jewish Nationalism and the Middle East Ser. ISBN:0-88355-328-7, ISBN13: 978-0-88355-328-2. Dewey:301.41/2/095694. LCCN:75-006441.

Audience: **l,u,f.**

Segev, Tom   **DS126**
One Palestine, Complete: Jews and Arabs under the British Mandate. Haim Watzman (Translator). Trade Cloth. DIANE Publishing Company. Collingdale, PA. 2000. 612p. ISBN:0-7567-6109-3, ISBN13: 978-0-7567-6109-7. Dewey:956.9/4/04.

Audience: **g,l,u,f.**

Sherman, A. J.   **DS126.S447 2001**
Mandate Days: British Lives in Palestine, 1918-1948. Trade Paper. Johns Hopkins University Press. Baltimore, MD. 2001. 264p. ISBN:0-8018-6620-0, ISBN13: 978-0-8018-6620-3. Dewey:956.94/04. LCCN:00-051984.

Audience: **u,f.** *Choice, 1998.*

Sicker, Martin   **DS125**
Reshaping Palestine: From Muhammad Ali to the British Mandate, 1831-1922. Trade Cloth. Greenwood Publishing Group, Inc. Portsmouth, NH. 1999. 200p. ISBN:0-275-96639-9, ISBN13: 978-0-275-96639-3. Dewey:956.94/03. LCCN:99-021191.

Audience: **g,l,u,f.**

Swedenburg, Ted   **DS126.S88 1995**
Memories of Revolt: The 1936-39 Rebellion and the Palestinian National Past. Book, Other. University of Minnesota Press. Minneapolis, MN. 1995. 288p. ISBN:0-8166-2164-0, ISBN13: 978-0-8166-2164-4. Dewey:956.94/04. LCCN:95-019977.

Audience: **u,f.**

Sykes, Christopher   **DS125 .S86 1973**
Crossroads to Israel 1917-1948. Trade Paper. Indiana University Press. Bloomington, IN. 1973. 416p. ISBN:0-253-20165-9, ISBN13: 978-0-253-20165-2. Dewey:956.94/04. LCCN:72-093912.

Audience: **u,f.**

Wasserstein, Bernard   **DS126.W34 1990**
The British in Palestine: The Mandatory Government and the
Arab-Jewish Conflict 1917-1929. Ed. 2. Cloth Text. Blackwell
Publishing, Inc. Malden, MA. 1991. 232p. ISBN:0-631-17574-1,
ISBN13: 978-0-631-17574-2. Dewey:956.94/04.
LCCN:90-039270.
Audience: u,f.

History of Specific Countries > Israel/Palestine > Modern > State of Israel 1948-

Bar-Joseph, Uri   **JK468.I6B37 1995**
Intelligence Intervention in the Politics of Democratic States:
The United States, Israel, and Britain. Pennsylvannia State
University Press. 1995. ISBN:0-271-01331-1, ISBN13:
978-0-271-01331-2.
Audience: l,u,f.

Bar-Joseph, Uri   **UA853.I8I89 2001**
Israel's National Security Towards the 21st Century. Paper over
Boards. Taylor & Francis Group. Abingdon, 2001. 224p.
ISBN:0-7146-5169-9, ISBN13: 978-0-7146-5169-9.
Dewey:355/.03305694. LCCN:2001-028963.
Audience: u,f.

Bar-Joseph, Uri   **DS128.1.B36613 2005**
The Watchman Fell Asleep: The Surprise of Yom Kippur and Its
Sources. Cloth Text. State University of New York Press.
Albany, NY. 2005. 306p. SUNY Series in Israeli Studies
ISBN:0-7914-6481-4, ISBN13: 978-0-7914-6481-6.
Dewey:956.04/8. LCCN:2004-016830.
Audience: u,f.

Bar-On, Mordechai   **DS119.7.B2832 1996**
In Pursuit of Peace: A History of the Israeli Peace Movement.
Trade Cloth. United States Institute of Peace Press (USIP Press).
Washington, DC. 1996. xix, 470p. ISBN:1-878379-54-2,
ISBN13: 978-1-878379-54-2. Dewey:956.9405.
LCCN:96-004787.
Audience: g,l,u,f.   Choice, 1997.

Barzilai, Gad   **DS119.2.B36 1996**
Wars, Internal Conflicts, and Political Order: A Jewish
Democracy in the Middle East. Cloth Text. State University of
New York Press. Albany, NY. 1996. 311p. SUNY Series in
Israeli Studies ISBN:0-7914-2943-1, ISBN13:
978-0-7914-2943-3. Dewey:956.9405. LCCN:92-037349.
Audience: u,f.   Choice, 1996.

Ben-Gurion, David   **DS126 .B3933 1973**
My Talks with Arab Leaders. Trade Cloth. Okpaku
Communications Corporation. New Rochelle, NY. 1973. 342p.
ISBN:0-89388-076-0, ISBN13: 978-0-89388-076-7.
Dewey:301.29/5694/0174927. LCCN:72-094298.
Audience: l,u,f.

Ben-Gurion, David   **DS126.3**
Rebirth and Destiny of Israel. Library Binding. Porcupine Press,
Inc. Cedarburg, WI. 1985. 539p. Return to Zion Ser.
ISBN:0-87991-139-5, ISBN13: 978-0-87991-139-3.
Dewey:956.94004.
Audience: u,f.

Benvenisti, Meron   **DS126.954 .B46 2000**
Sacred Landscape: The Buried History of the Holy Land Since
1948. Maxine Kaufman-Lacusta (Translator). Trade Cloth.
University of California Press. Berkeley, CA. 2000. 382p.
ISBN:0-520-21154-5, ISBN13: 978-0-520-21154-4.
Dewey:956.04/2. LCCN:99-037874.
Audience: g,l,u,f.   Choice, 2000.

Cordesman, Anthony H.   **UA853.I8C67 1996**
Perilous Prospects: The Peace Process and the Arab-Israeli
Military Balance. Trade Cloth. Westview Press. Boulder, CO.
1996. 336p. ISBN:0-8133-2939-6, ISBN13: 978-0-8133-2939-0.
Dewey:956.9/4/054. LCCN:96-007426.
Audience: u,f.   Choice, 1996.

Dayan, Moshe   **DS110.5**
Diary of the Sinai Campaign. Ed. 1. Harper & Row. 1966.
Audience: u,f.

Eban, Abba   **DS119.7**
My Country. Trade Cloth. Random House, Inc. New York, NY.
1972. ISBN:0-394-46314-5, ISBN13: 978-0-394-46314-8.
Dewey:956.94/05. LCCN:72-002725.
Audience: l,u,f.

Eban, Abba Solomon   **DS126.6.E2**
Personal Witness. Trade Cloth. Penguin Group (USA) Inc. New
York, NY. ISBN:0-399-19097-X, ISBN13: 978-0-399-19097-1.
Dewey:956.94/04/092.
Audience: g,l,u,f.

Elon, Amos   **DS126.5**
Israelis: Founders and Sons. Trade Paper. Penguin Group (USA)
Inc. New York, NY. 1983. 384p. ISBN:0-14-016969-5, ISBN13:
978-0-14-016969-0. Dewey:956.94.
Audience: g,l,u,f.

Evron, Boas   **DS149.E9313 1995**
ⓔ Jewish State or Israeli Nation? E-Book. Indiana University
Press. Bloomington, IN. 1995. 288p. ISBN:0-253-31963-3,
ISBN13: 978-0-253-31963-0. Dewey:320.5/4/095694.
LCCN:94-024878.
Audience: u,f.   Choice, 1995.

Flamhaft, Ziva   **DS119.7.F595 1996**
Israel on the Road to Peace: Accepting the Unacceptable. Cloth
Text. Westview Press. Boulder, CO. 1996. 272p.
ISBN:0-8133-2414-9, ISBN13: 978-0-8133-2414-2.
Dewey:320.9/5694. LCCN:96-018527.
Audience: l,u,f.   Choice, 1996.

Freedman, Robert Owen   **JQ1825.P3**
Israel in the Begin Era. Trade Cloth. Greenwood Publishing
Group, Inc. Portsmouth, NH. 1982. 280p. ISBN:0-275-90795-3,
ISBN13: 978-0-275-90795-2. Dewey:956.94054.
LCCN:82-013329.
Audience: u,f.

Freedman, Robert Owen (Editor)   **DS119.6.I778 2000**
Israel's First Fifty Years. Trade Paper. University Press of
Florida. Gainesville, FL. 2000. xix, 290p. ISBN:0-8130-1819-6,
ISBN13: 978-0-8130-1819-5. Dewey:956.9405.
LCCN:00-024427.
Audience: g,l,u,f.

Grossman, David DS113.7.G7613 1993
Sleeping on a Wire. Chaim Watzman (Translator). Trade Cloth.
Farrar, Straus & Giroux. New York, NY. 1993. 326p.
ISBN:0-374-17788-0, ISBN13: 978-0-374-17788-1.
Dewey:305.8/0095694. LCCN:92-028721.
Audience: **g,l,u,f.**

Grossman, David DS119.76.G77 2003
Death As a Way of Life: Israel Ten Years after Oslo. Haim
Watzman (Translator). Cloth over Boards. Farrar, Straus &
Giroux. New York, NY. 2003. 192p. ISBN:0-374-10211-2,
ISBN13: 978-0-374-10211-1. Dewey:956.9405/4.
LCCN:2002-044766.
Audience: **g,l,u,f.**

Grossman, David DS110.W47G7613 1988
The Yellow Wind. Haim Watzman (Translator). Cloth over
Boards. Farrar, Straus & Giroux. New York, NY. 1988. 224p.
ISBN:0-374-29345-7, ISBN13: 978-0-374-29345-1.
Dewey:956.94. LCCN:87-037527.
Audience: **g,l,u,f.**

Halperin-Kaddari, Ruth HQ1728.5.H35 2004
Women in Israel: A State of Their Own. Trade Cloth. University
of Pennsylvania Press. Philadelphia, PA. 2003. 320p.
Pennsylvania Studies in Human Rights ISBN:0-8122-3752-8,
ISBN13: 978-0-8122-3752-8. Dewey:305.42/095694.
LCCN:2003-061077.
Audience: **l,u,f.** *Choice, 2004.*

Herzog, Chaim DS126.6.R32
Living History: A Memoir. Trade Cloth. DIANE Publishing
Company. Collingdale, PA. 2000. 448p. ISBN:0-7881-9543-3,
ISBN13: 978-0-7881-9543-3. Dewey:956.9/4/05/092.
Audience: **l,u,f.**

Herzog, Chaim DS128.1
The War of Atonement, October 1973. Little, Brown. 1975.
Audience: **u,f.**

Herzog, Hanna HQ1236.5.I75H46 1999
Gendering Politics: Women in Israel. Trade Cloth. University of
Michigan Press. Chicago, IL. 1999. 312p. Interests, Identities,
and Institutions in Comparative Politics Ser.
ISBN:0-472-10945-6, ISBN13: 978-0-472-10945-6.
Dewey:320/.082/095694. LCCN:98-053596.
Audience: **l,u,f.** *Choice, 2000.*

Horovitz, David DS128.2.H675 2004
Still Life with Bombers: Israel in the Age of Terrorism. Trade
Cloth. Knopf Publishing Group. New York, NY. 2004. 288p.
ISBN:1-4000-4067-1, ISBN13: 978-1-4000-4067-4.
Dewey:956.9405/4. LCCN:2004-299012.
Audience: **g,l,u,f.**

Inbar, Efraim DS126.6.R32I63 1999
Rabin and Israel's National Security. Trade Cloth. Johns
Hopkins University Press. Baltimore, MD. 1999. 296p.
ISBN:0-8018-6217-5, ISBN13: 978-0-8018-6217-5.
Dewey:956.9405/092. LCCN:99-022113.
Audience: **u,f.** *Choice, 2000.*

Inbar, Efraim JQ1825.P373A952 1991
War and Peace in Israeli Politics: Labor Party Positions on
National Security. Library Binding. Lynne Rienner Publishers,
Inc. Boulder, CO. 1991. 180p. ISBN:1-55587-236-0, ISBN13:
978-1-55587-236-6. Dewey:324.25694/074. LCCN:90-043019.
Audience: **l,u,f.** *Choice, 1991.*

Jacobsohn, Gary J. K3165.J33 1993
Apple of God: Constitutionalism in Israel and the United States.
Trade Cloth. Princeton University Press. Princeton, NJ. 1992.
294p. ISBN:0-691-08622-2, ISBN13: 978-0-691-08622-4.
Dewey:345.69402. LCCN:92-015743.
Audience: **u,f.** *Choice, 1993.*

Jones, Clive & Murphy, DS126.5.J66 2002
Emma C.
Israel: Challenges to Identity, Democracy, and the State. Trade
Paper. Routledge. New York, NY. 2001. 176p. The
Contemporary Middle East Ser. ISBN:0-415-27088-X, ISBN13:
978-0-415-27088-5. Dewey:956.9405. LCCN:2001-041990.
Audience: **u,f.** *Choice, 2003.*

Karsh, Efraim DS115.5.K37 1997
Fabricating Israeli History: The "New Historians". Trade Cloth.
Taylor & Francis Group. Abingdon, 1997. 232p.
ISBN:0-7146-4725-X, ISBN13: 978-0-7146-4725-8.
Dewey:956.94/04. LCCN:98-126688.
Audience: **u,f.**

Karsh, Efraim (Editor) DS125.I75
Israel in the Next Century. Trade Cloth. Taylor & Francis
Group. Abingdon, 2000. 288p. Israeli History, Politics and
Society Ser., Vol. 5 ISBN:0-7146-4959-7, ISBN13:
978-0-7146-4959-7. Dewey:956.9405.
Audience: **u,f.**

Kaufman, Ilana (Editor) JQ1830.A98M545 1997
Arab National Communism in the Jewish State. Trade Cloth.
University Press of Florida. Gainesville, FL. 1997. 216p.
ISBN:0-8130-1478-6, ISBN13: 978-0-8130-1478-4.
Dewey:327.5/495694. LCCN:96-002138.
Audience: **u,f.** *Choice, 1998.*

Levy, Andre & DS134.H65 2004
Weingrod, Alex
Homelands and Diasporas: Holy Lands and Other Places. Trade
Paper. Stanford University Press. Palo Alto, CA. 2004. 376p.
ISBN:0-8047-5079-3, ISBN13: 978-0-8047-5079-0.
Dewey:956.9405. LCCN:2004-011640.
Audience: **u,f.**

Mahler, Gregory S. JQ1825.P3A176 1990
🄴 Israel after Begin. E-Book. NetLibrary, Inc. Boulder, CO.
1990. ISBN:0-585-05507-6, ISBN13: 978-0-585-05507-7.
Dewey:956.9405/4.
Audience: **l,u,f.** *Choice, 1991.*

Migdal, Joel S. JQ1830.A91M54 2001
Through the Lens of Israel: Explorations in State and Society.
Cloth Text. State University of New York Press. Albany, NY.
2001. ix, 237p. Suny Series, Israeli Studies
ISBN:0-7914-4985-8, ISBN13: 978-0-7914-4985-1.
Dewey:301/.095694. LCCN:00-058764.
Audience: **u,f.**

Morris, Benny DS115.5
Making Israel. Trade Cloth. I. B. Tauris & Company, Ltd.
London, 2004. 224p. ISBN:1-85043-441-7, ISBN13:
978-1-85043-441-2. Dewey:956.9/40072.
Audience: **l,u,f.**

Naveh, Hannah (Editor) HQ1728.5.I874 2003
Israeli Family and Community: Women's Time. Trade Cloth.
Vallentine Mitchell Publishers. Middlesex, 2003. 198p.

ISBN:0-85303-506-7, ISBN13: 978-0-85303-506-0.
Dewey:305.42/095694. LCCN:2003-014724.

Audience: **l,u,f.**

Oz, Amos   **PK5054.H2**
In the Land of Israel. Maurie Goldberg-Bartura (Translator).
Trade Cloth. Harcourt Trade Publishers. New York, NY. 1983.
272p. A Helen and Kurt Wolff Bk. ISBN:0-15-144644-X,
ISBN13: 978-0-15-144644-5. Dewey:892.4/8608.
LCCN:83-012940.

Audience: **g,l,u,f.**

Oz, Amos   **DS119.76**
How to Cure a Fanatic. Nadine Gordimer (Foreword by). Trade
Cloth. Princeton University Press. Princeton, NJ. 2006. 80p.
ISBN:0-691-12669-0, ISBN13: 978-0-691-12669-2.
Dewey:956.05/3. LCCN:2005-056559.

Audience: **g,l,u,f.**

Peres, Shimon   **DS126.5.P3913 1999**
The Imaginary Voyage: With Theodor Herzl in Israel. Trade
Cloth. Arcade Publishing, Inc. New York, NY. 1999. 256p.
ISBN:1-55970-468-3, ISBN13: 978-1-55970-468-7.
Dewey:320.54/095694. LCCN:99-024365.

Audience: **u,f.**

Peres, Shimon   **DS126.6.P47A3 1995**
Battling for Peace: A Memoir. David Landau (Editor). Trade
Cloth. Random House, Inc. New York, NY. 1995. 350p.
ISBN:0-679-43617-0, ISBN13: 978-0-679-43617-1.
Dewey:956.9405/4/092 B. LCCN:94-041950.

Audience: **g,l,u,f.** *Choice, 1995.*

Peres, Shimon, et al.   **DS126.6.P47A5 1998**
For the Future of Israel. Robert Littell & Avi Gil (Authors).
Trade Cloth. Johns Hopkins University Press. Baltimore, MD.
1998. 240p. ISBN:0-8018-5928-X, ISBN13: 978-0-8018-5928-1.
Dewey:956.9405/092. LCCN:97-047041.

Audience: **g,l,u,f.** *Choice, 1998.*

Peretz, Don & Doron,   **JQ1830.A58P47 1997**
Gideon
The Government and Politics of Israel. Ed. 3. Trade Paper.
Westview Press. Boulder, CO. 1997. 320p. ISBN:0-8133-2408-4,
ISBN13: 978-0-8133-2408-1. Dewey:320.95694.
LCCN:96-035240.

Audience: **l,u,f.** *Choice, 1997.*

Rabin, Yitzak   **DS126.6.R32A3613**
The Rabin Memoirs: With Recent Speeches, New Photographs,
and an Afterword. Yoram Peri (Afterword by). Trade Cloth.
University of California Press. Berkeley, CA. 1996. 416p.
ISBN:0-520-20776-9, ISBN13: 978-0-520-20776-9.
Dewey:956.9405/092 B. LCCN:96-025055.

Audience: **l,u,f.**

Rabinowitz, Dan   **DS110.N28 R33 1997**
Overlooking Nazareth: The Ethnography of Exclusion in
Galilee, Vol. 105. Cloth Text. Cambridge University Press. New
York, NY. 1997. 240p. Cambridge Studies in Social and Cultural
Anthropology, No. 105 ISBN:0-521-56361-5, ISBN13:
978-0-521-56361-1. Dewey:305.8/9275694. LCCN:96-011922.

Audience: **g,l,u,f.** *Choice, 1997.*

Reich, Bernard &   **DS126.5.R385 2000**
Goldberg, David H.
Political Dictionary of Israel. Trade Cloth. Scarecrow Press, Inc.

Lanham, MD. 2000. 560p. ISBN:0-8108-3778-1, ISBN13:
978-0-8108-3778-2. Dewey:956.94/003. LCCN:00-021979.

Audience: **g,l,u,f.** *Choice, 2001.*

Reich, Bernard &   **DS102.95.R45 1993**
Kieval, Gershon R.
Israel: Land of Tradition and Conflict. Ed. 2. Trade Paper.
Westview Press. Boulder, CO. 1993. 236p. Profiles - Nations of
Contemporary Middle East Ser. ISBN:0-8133-8222-X, ISBN13:
978-0-8133-8222-7. Dewey:956.94/054. LCCN:93-016314.

Audience: **u,f.**

Rejwan, Nissim   **DS143.R35 1999**
Israel in Search of Identity: Reading The Formative Years. Trade
Cloth. University Press of Florida. Gainesville, FL. 1999. 192p.
ISBN:0-8130-1664-9, ISBN13: 978-0-8130-1664-1.
Dewey:305.892/4/05694. LCCN:98-053889.

Audience: **u,f.**

Schiff, Ze'ev & Ya'ari,   **DS87**
Ehud
Israel's Lebanon War. Trade Paper. Simon & Schuster. New
York, NY. 1985. 320p. ISBN:0-671-60216-0, ISBN13:
978-0-671-60216-1. Dewey:956.92/044.

Audience: **g,l,u,f.**

Segev, Tom   **DS126.5.S41513 1986**
1949, the First Israelis. Trade Cloth. Simon & Schuster. New
York, NY. 1986. 384p. ISBN:0-02-929180-1, ISBN13:
978-0-02-929180-1. Dewey:956.94/05. LCCN:85-020472.

Audience: **g,l,u,f.** *Choice, 1986.*

Segev, Tom & Lewis,   **DS128.3.O84 2002**
Anthony
The Other Israel: Voices of Refusal and Dissent. Roane Carey &
Jonathan Shainin (Introduction by). Trade Cloth. New Press,
The. New York, NY. 2002. 224p. ISBN:1-56584-789-X,
ISBN13: 978-1-56584-789-7. Dewey:956.9405/4.
LCCN:2002-026496.

Audience: **g,l,u,f.**

Segev, Tom &   **DS126.5**
Watzman, Haim
Elvis in Jerusalem: Post-Zionism and the Americanization of
Israel. Trade Paper. Henry Holt & Company. New York, NY.
2003. 180p. ISBN:0-8050-7288-8, ISBN13: 978-0-8050-7288-4.
Dewey:956.94.

Audience: **g,l,u,f.**

Segev, Tom   **D804.3.S44513 1993**
The Seventh Million: Israel Confronts the Holocaust. Haim
Watzman (Translator). Cloth over Boards. Farrar, Straus &
Giroux. New York, NY. 1993. 593p. ISBN:0-8090-8563-1,
ISBN13: 978-0-8090-8563-7. Dewey:940.53/18.
LCCN:92-007372.

Audience: **g,l,u,f.**

Shafir, Gershon &   **HC415.25.N485 2000**
Peled, Yoav (Editors)
The New Israel: Peacemaking and Liberalization. Trade Paper.
Westview Press. Boulder, CO. 1999. 304p. ISBN:0-8133-3567-1,
ISBN13: 978-0-8133-3567-4. Dewey:338.95694.
LCCN:99-041453.

Audience: **u,f.**

Shafir, Gershon &   **JQ1830.A91 S53 2002**
Peled, Yoav
Being Israeli: The Dynamics of Multiple Citizenship. Julia A.
Clancy-Smith, Israel Gershoni, Roger Owen, Yezid Sayigh,

Charles Tripp & Judith E. Tucker (Contribution by). Cloth Text. Cambridge University Press. New York, NY. 2002. 412p. Middle East Studies, Vol. 16 ISBN:0-521-79224-X, ISBN13: 978-0-521-79224-0. Dewey:323.6095694. LCCN:2001-037490.

Audience: **g,l,u,f.** *Choice, 2002.*

Shamir, Yitzhak DS126.6.S355 A3
Summing Up: An Autobiography. Cloth Text. DIANE Publishing Company. Collingdale, PA. 1998. 276p. ISBN:0-7881-5736-1, ISBN13: 978-0-7881-5736-3. Dewey:956.9405/4/092.

Audience: **l,u,f.**

Sharkansky, Ira DS126.5.S4437 2005
Governing Israel: The Chosen People, the Promised Land, and the Prophetic Tradition. Trade Cloth. Transaction Publishers. Somerset, NJ. 2005. 216p. ISBN:0-7658-0277-5, ISBN13: 978-0-7658-0277-4. Dewey:320.6/095694. LCCN:2004-058004.
Audience: **l,u,f.**

Shlaim, Avi DS119.7
The Iron Wall: Israel and the Arab World. W.W. Norton. 2001. ISBN:0-393-32112-6, ISBN13: 978-0-393-32112-8.
Audience: **g,l,u,f.**

Shlaim, Avi DS119.8.J67S552 1998
The Politics of Partition: King Abdullah, the Zionists, and Palestine, 1921-1951. Oxford University Press. 1998. ISBN:0-19-829459-X, ISBN13: 978-0-19-829459-7.
Audience: **l,u,f.**

Tiger, Lionel & HQ1781.P2
Shepher, Joseph
Women in the Kibbutz. Trade Paper. Harcourt Trade Publishers. New York, NY. 1976. ISBN:0-15-698300-1, ISBN13: 978-0-15-698300-6. Dewey:301.41/2/095694. LCCN:76-013603.
Audience: **g,l,u,f.**

Timerman, Jacobo DS119.8.L4T5513 1982
The Longest War: Israel in Lebanon. Miguel Acoca (Translator). Trade Cloth. Alfred A. Knopf Inc. New York, NY. 1982. 167p. ISBN:0-394-53022-5, ISBN13: 978-0-394-53022-2. Dewey:956/.04. LCCN:82-020208.
Audience: **g,l,u,f.**

Weizman, Ezer DS128.183 .W44
The Battle for Peace. Trade Cloth. Bantam Books. New York, NY. 1981. 408p. ISBN:0-553-05002-8, ISBN13: 978-0-553-05002-8. Dewey:956/.048. LCCN:80-071057.
Audience: **l,u,f.**

Weizmann, Chaim DS125.3.W45
Trial and Error: the Autobiography of Chaim Weizmann. Harper. 1948.
Audience: **g,l,u,f.**

Yanlv, Avner (Editor) UA853.I8.N368 1993
National Security and Democracy in Israel. Library Binding. Lynne Rienner Publishers, Inc. Boulder, CO. 1993. 257p. An Israel Democracy Institute Policy Study Ser. ISBN:1-55587-324-3, ISBN13: 978-1-55587-324-0. Dewey:354.5694. LCCN:92-021085.
Audience: **u,f.** *Choice, 1993.*

Yishai, Yael HQ1236.5.I75Y57 1997
Between the Flag and the Banner: Women in Israeli Politics. Cloth Text. State University of New York Press. Albany, NY. 1996. 292p. SUNY Series in Israeli Studies

ISBN:0-7914-3127-4, ISBN13: 978-0-7914-3127-6. Dewey:320.9/0082. LCCN:97-001515.
Audience: **l,u,f.**

Zertal, Idith D804.3
Israel's Holocaust and the Politics of Nationhood. Charles Tripp, Julia A. Clancy-Smith, Israel Gershoni, Roger Owen, Yezid Sayigh & Judith E. Tucker (Contribution by). Cloth Text. Cambridge University Press. New York, NY. 2005. 248p. Cambridge Middle East Studies, Vol. 21 ISBN:0-521-85096-7, ISBN13: 978-0-521-85096-4. Dewey:940.53/18. LCCN:2005-044299.
Audience: **l,u,f.** *Choice, 2006.*

History of Specific Countries > Israel/Palestine > Modern > Israeli/Palestinian Conflict

Abu-Amr, Ziad BP63.P32
Islamic Fundamentalism in the West Bank and Gaza: Muslim Brotherhood and Islamic Jihad. Trade Cloth. Indiana University Press. Bloomington, IN. 1994. 192p. Indiana University Series in Middle East Studies ISBN:0-253-30121-1, ISBN13: 978-0-253-30121-5. Dewey:322.4/2/0956953. LCCN:93-028504.
Audience: **l,u,f.** *Choice, 1994.*

Abu-Lughod, Ibrahim DS119.7 .T7
The Transformation of Palestine: Essays on the Origin and Development of the Arab-Israeli Conflict. Ed. 2. Arnold J. Toynbee (Foreword by). Trade Paper. Northwestern University Press. Evanston, IL. 1971. 335p. ISBN:0-8101-0744-9, ISBN13: 978-0-8101-0744-1. Dewey:956.
Audience: **l,u,f.**

Alexander, Yonah JQ1830.A98H373 2002
Palestinian Religious Terrorism: Hamas and Islamic Jihad. Trade Paper. Transnational Publishers, Inc. Ardsley, NY. 2002. 426p. ISBN:1-57105-247-X, ISBN13: 978-1-57105-247-6. Dewey:322.4/2/095694. LCCN:2002-190388.
Audience: **l,u,f.** *Choice, 2003.*

Ashrawi, Hanan DS119.7.A68938 1995
This Side of Peace: A Personal Account. Trade Cloth. Simon & Schuster. New York, NY. 1995. 320p. ISBN:0-684-80294-5, ISBN13: 978-0-684-80294-7. Dewey:956.9/4/054/092. LCCN:95-001793.
Audience: **g,l,u,f.**

Beinin, Joel DS126.5.B359 1990
Was the Red Flag Flying There?: Marxist Politics and the Arab-Israeli Conflict in Egypt and Israel, 1948-1965. Trade Cloth. University of California Press. Berkeley, CA. 1990. 328p. ISBN:0-520-07035-6, ISBN13: 978-0-520-07035-6. Dewey:956.9405/2. LCCN:89-049036.
Audience: **l,u,f.**

Benvenisti, Meron DS110.W47
The West Bank Handbook: A Political Lexicon. Trade Cloth. Bow Historical Books. New Providence, NJ. 1986. 228 p., [15] p.p. ISBN:965-310-001-7, ISBN13: 978-965-310-001-5. Dewey:956.95/3. LCCN:87-404461.
Audience: **l,u,f.** *Choice, 1987.*

Bickerton, Ian J. & DS119.7.B49 2004
Klausner, Carla L.
A Concise History of the Arab-Israeli Conflict. Ed. 4. Trade Paper. Prentice Hall PTR. Upper Saddle River, NJ. 2004. 416p.

ISBN:0-13-190004-8, ISBN13: 978-0-13-190004-2.
Dewey:956.04. LCCN:2004-044495.

Audience: **g,l,u,f.**

Bowker, Robert   **HV640.5.P36B69 2003**
Palestinian Refugees: Mythology, Identity, and the Search for
Peace. Library Binding. Lynne Rienner Publishers, Inc. Boulder,
CO. 2003. 225p. ISBN:1-58826-202-2, ISBN13:
978-1-58826-202-8. Dewey:956.04. LCCN:2003-046719.

Audience: **u,f.** *Choice, 2004.*

Brand, Laurie A.   **DS113.6.B73 1988**
Palestinians in the Arab World: Institution Building and the
Search for State. Trade Cloth. Columbia University Press. New
York, NY. 1988. 286p. ISBN:0-231-06722-4, ISBN13:
978-0-231-06722-5. Dewey:909/.049275694. LCCN:88-006101.

Audience: **l,u,f.** *Choice, 1989.*

Bucaille, Laetitia   **DS119.76**
Growing up Palestinian: Israeli Occupation and the Intifada
Generation. Trade Paper. Princeton University Press. Princeton,
NJ. 2006. 208p. ISBN:0-691-12611-9, ISBN13:
978-0-691-12611-1. Dewey:956.95/3044.

Audience: **u,f.**

Chomsky, Noam   **E183.8.I7C48 1999**
Fateful Triangle: The United States, Israel, and the Palestinians.
Ed. 2. Edward W. Said (Foreword by). Trade Cloth. South End
Press. Cambridge, MA. 1999. 600p. South End Press Classics
Ser., Vol. 3 ISBN:0-89608-602-X, ISBN13: 978-0-89608-602-9.
Dewey:327.7/3/05694. LCCN:98-055140.

Audience: **l,u,f.**

Emmett, Ayala H.   **DS119.7.E565 1996**
Our Sisters' Promised Land: Women, Politics, and
Israeli-Palestinian Coexistence. Trade Cloth. University of
Michigan Press. Chicago, IL. 1996. 288p. Women and Culture
Ser. ISBN:0-472-10733-X, ISBN13: 978-0-472-10733-9.
Dewey:327.1/72/095694. LCCN:96-009949.

Audience: **u,f.** *Choice, 1997.*

Farsoun, Samih K. &   **DS119.76**
 Zacharia, Christina E.
Palestine and the Palestinians. Trade Paper. Westview Press.
Boulder, CO. 1998. 396p. ISBN:0-8133-2773-3, ISBN13:
978-0-8133-2773-0. Dewey:956.9405/4. LCCN:97-021954.

Audience: **l,u,f.** *Choice, 1998.*

Finkelstein, Norman G.   **DS119.75.F55 1996**
The Rise and Fall of Palestine: A Personal Account of the
Intifada Years. Book, Other. University of Minnesota Press.
Minneapolis, MN. 1996. 192p. ISBN:0-8166-2858-0, ISBN13:
978-0-8166-2858-2. Dewey:956.9/4/054. LCCN:96-017955.

Audience: **g,l,u,f.**

Finklestein, Norman G.   **DS119.7**
Image and Reality of the Israel-Palestine Conflict. Ed. 2. Trade
Paper. Verso Books. London, 2003. 256p. ISBN:1-85984-442-1,
ISBN13: 978-1-85984-442-7. Dewey:956.9/405.

Audience: **g,l,u,f.**

Freedman, Robert   **DS63.1.M4847 1998**
 Owen
The Middle East and the Peace Process: The Impact of the Oslo
Accords. Trade Paper. University Press of Florida. Gainesville,
FL. 1998. 435p. ISBN:0-8130-1554-5, ISBN13:
978-0-8130-1554-5. Dewey:956.05. LCCN:97-020336.

Audience: **g,l,u,f.**

Friedman, Isaiah   **DS126.F76 2000**
Palestine - A Twice-Promised Land?: The British, the Arabs, and
Zionism. Trade Cloth. Transaction Publishers. Somerset, NJ.
2000. 411p. ISBN:1-56000-391-X, ISBN13: 978-1-56000-391-5.
Dewey:327.41056/09/041. LCCN:99-030396.

Audience: **g,l,u,f.** *Choice, 2000.*

Galnoor, Itzhak   **DS126.G32 1995**
The Partition of Palestine: Decision Crossroads in the Zionist
Movement. Cloth Text. State University of New York Press.
Albany, NY. 1994. 379p. SUNY Series in Israeli Studies
ISBN:0-7914-2193-7, ISBN13: 978-0-7914-2193-2.
Dewey:956.94/04. LCCN:93-051016.

Audience: **u,f.** *Choice, 1995.*

Gelvin, James L.   **DS119.7.G3**
The Israel-Palestine Conflict: One Hundred Years of War. Trade
Paper. Cambridge University Press. New York, NY. 2005. 304p.
ISBN:0-521-61804-5, ISBN13: 978-0-521-61804-5.
Dewey:956.04/2. LCCN:2005-012022.

Audience: **g,l,u,f.** *Choice, 2006.*

Gerner, Deborah J.   **DS119.7.G425 1991**
One Land, Two Peoples: The Conflict over Palestine. Cloth
Text. Westview Press. Boulder, CO. 1990. 220p.
ISBN:0-8133-0908-5, ISBN13: 978-0-8133-0908-8.
Dewey:956.94/05. LCCN:90-043497.

Audience: **l,u,f.** *Choice, 1991.*

Gilbert, Martin   **G2236**
 (Author, Author)
The Routledge Atlas of the Arab-Israeli Conflict. Ed. 8. Trade
Paper, Perfect. Routledge. New York, NY. 2005. 187p.
Routledge Historical Atlases Ser. ISBN:0-415-35900-7, ISBN13:
978-0-415-35900-9. Dewey:911.56.

Audience: **g,l,u,f.**

Ginat, Joseph &   **DS199.76**
 Winckler, Onn (Editors)
The Jordanian - Palestinian - Israeli Triangle: Smoothing the
Path to Peace. Trade Cloth. Sussex Academic Press. Eastbourne,
1998. 232p. ISBN:1-898723-82-6, ISBN13: 978-1-898723-82-0.
Dewey:956.05/3. LCCN:98-014129.

Audience: **l,u,f.**

Gordon, Haim   **DS119**
Beyond Intifada: Narratives of Freedom Fighters in the Gaza
Strip. Praeger. 2003. ISBN:0-275-97129-5, ISBN13:
978-0-275-97129-8.

Audience: **g,l,u,f.**

Hiltermann, Joost R.   **DS110.W47H55 1991**
Behind the Intifada: Labor and Women's Movements in the
Occupied Territories. Trade Cloth. Princeton University Press.
Princeton, NJ. 1991. 283p. ISBN:0-691-07869-6, ISBN13:
978-0-691-07869-4. Dewey:322.4/4/095694. LCCN:91-014181.

Audience: **l,u,f.** *Choice, 1992.*

Hirst, David   **DS119.7.H545 2003**
The Gun and the Olive Branch: The Roots of Violence in the
Middle East. Trade Paper. Avalon Publishing Group. New York,
NY. 2003. 400p. Nation Bks. ISBN:1-56025-483-1, ISBN13:
978-1-56025-483-6. Dewey:322.4/2. LCCN:2003-047310.

Audience: **g,l,u,f.**

Hurewitz, Jacob C.   **DS126**
The Struggle for Palestine. Trade Cloth. Greenwood Publishing
Group, Inc. Portsmouth, NH. 1968. ISBN:0-8371-0111-5,

ISBN13: 978-0-8371-0111-8. Dewey:956.94/04.
LCCN:68-028594.

Audience: **g,l,u,f.**

Kanaaneh, Rhoda Ann   **HQ766.5.I75 K363**
Birthing the Nation: Strategies of Palestinian Women in Israel.
Trade Cloth. University of California Press. Berkeley, CA. 2002.
300p. California Series in Public Anthropology, Vol. 2
ISBN:0-520-22379-9, ISBN13: 978-0-520-22379-0.
Dewey:363.9/6/095694. LCCN:2002-001244.

Audience: **l,u,f.** *Choice, 2003.*

Khalidi, Rashid   **DS113.7.K53 1997**
Palestinian Identity: The Construction of Modern National
Consciousness. Trade Paper. Columbia University Press. New
York, NY. 1998. 304p. ISBN:0-231-10515-0, ISBN13:
978-0-231-10515-6. Dewey:305.8/92740569442.
LCCN:96-045757.

Audience: **l,u,f.** *Choice, 1997.*

Khalidi, Walid   **DS119.7 .K429 1992**
Palestine Reborn. Albert H. Hourani (Foreword by). Cloth Text.
I. B. Tauris & Company, Ltd. London, 1992. 200p.
ISBN:1-85043-559-6, ISBN13: 978-1-85043-559-4.
Dewey:956.9405. LCCN:92-246089.

Audience: **l,u,f.**

Khalidi, Walid &   **DS125**
 Khalidi, Muhammad A. (Editors)
All That Remains: The Palestinian Villages Occupied and
Depopulated by Israel in 1948. Sharif S. Elmusa (Introduction
by). Trade Cloth. Institute for Palestine Studies. Washington,
DC. 1992. 638p. ISBN:0-88728-224-5, ISBN13:
978-0-88728-224-9. Dewey:956.94. LCCN:92-010109.

Audience: **l,u,f.**

Kimmerling, Baruch   **DS119.7**
Politicide: Ariel Sharon's War Against the Palestinians. Trade
Cloth. Verso Books. London, 2003. 240p. ISBN:1-85984-517-7,
ISBN13: 978-1-85984-517-2. Dewey:956.9405/4/092 B.
LCCN:2003-053506.

Audience: **g,l,u,f.** *Choice, 2004.*

Kimmerling, Baruch &   **DS119.7.K4943 2003**
 Migdal, Joel S.
The Palestinian People: A History. Trade Cloth. Harvard
University Press. Cambridge, MA. 2003. 608p. Simultaneous
Editions Ser. ISBN:0-674-01131-7, ISBN13: 978-0-674-01131-1.
Dewey:956.94/0049274. LCCN:2002-191281.

Audience: **g,l,u,f.** *Choice, 2003.*

Klieman, Aaron   **DS149.A716 VOL. 13**
 (Editor)
Recognition of Israel: An End and a New Beginning. Cloth
Text. Garland Publishing, Inc. New York, NY. 1991. 576p.
American Zionism Ser., Vol. 13 ISBN:0-8240-7361-4, ISBN13:
978-0-8240-7361-9. Dewey:320.5/4/0956940973 s.
LCCN:90-048173.

Audience: **l,u,f.**

Laqueur, Walter &   **DS119.7.I8256 2001**
 Rubin, Barry (Editors)
The Israel-Arab Reader: A Documentary History of the Middle
East Conflict. Ed. 6. Trade Paper. Penguin Group (USA) Inc.
New York, NY. 2001. 448p. ISBN:0-14-029713-8, ISBN13:
978-0-14-029713-3. Dewey:956. LCCN:2001-276105.

Audience: **g,l,u,f.**

Lesch, Ann Mosely &   **DS119.7.L466 1989**
 Tessler,Mark
Israel, Egypt, and the Palestinians: From Camp David to
Intifada. RIchard B. Parker (Foreword). Indiana University
Press. 1989. Indiana Series in Arab and Islamic Studies
ISBN:0-253-33320-2, ISBN13: 978-0-253-33320-9.

Audience: **l,u,f.**

Lustick, Ian (Editor)   **DS119.7.C6525 1994**
The Conflict with the Arabs in Israeli Politics and Society. Paper
over Boards. Garland Publishing, Inc. New York, NY. 1994.
384p. Arab-Israeli Relations Ser., Vol. 7 ISBN:0-8153-1587-2,
ISBN13: 978-0-8153-1587-2. Dewey:306.2/095694.
LCCN:93-051015.

Audience: **u,f.**

Lustick, Ian S. (Editor)   **DS119.7.A67266 1994**
Arab-Israeli Relations in World Politics. Paper over Boards.
Garland Publishing, Inc. New York, NY. 1994. 360p.
ISBN:0-8153-1590-2, ISBN13: 978-0-8153-1590-2.
Dewey:956.04. LCCN:93-049876.

Audience: **u,f.**

Masalha, Nur (Editor)   **HV640.5.P36C38 2005**
Catastrophe Remembered: Palestine, Israel and the Internal
Refugees. Trade Paper, Perfect. Zed Books, Ltd. London, 2005.
288p. ISBN:1-84277-623-1, ISBN13: 978-1-84277-623-0.
Dewey:362.87/095694. LCCN:2004-066299.

Audience: **g,l,u,f.** *Choice, 2006.*

Masalha, Nur   **DS119.7.M31395 2000**
Imperial Israel and the Palestinians: The Politics of Expansion,
1967-2000. Trade Cloth. Pluto Press. London, 2000. 288p.
ISBN:0-7453-1620-4, ISBN13: 978-0-7453-1620-8.
Dewey:956.04. LCCN:00-027698.

Audience: **u,f.**

Masalha, Nur   **DS113.7.M32 2003**
The Politics of Denial: Israel and the Palestinian Refugee
Problem. Trade Cloth. Pluto Press. London, 2003. 304p.
ISBN:0-7453-2121-6, ISBN13: 978-0-7453-2121-9.
Dewey:325/.21/0899274. LCCN:2003-007464.

Audience: **g,l,u,f.**

Mayer, Tamar   **HQ1728.5.W66 1994**
Women and the Israeli Occupation: The Politics of Change.
Paper over Boards. Routledge. New York, NY. 1994. 224p.
International Studies of Women and Places
ISBN:0-415-09545-X, ISBN13: 978-0-415-09545-7.
Dewey:305.42/095694. LCCN:94-003886.

Audience: **l,u,f.**

Meital, Yoram   **DS119.76.M444 2005**
Peace in Tatters: Israel, Palestine, and the Middle East. Library
Binding. Lynne Rienner Publishers, Inc. Boulder, CO. 2005.
230p. ISBN:1-58826-362-2, ISBN13: 978-1-58826-362-9.
Dewey:956.05/4. LCCN:2005-011009.

Audience: **u,f.** *Choice, 2006.*

Mishal, Shaul & Sela,   **DS119.76.M57 2000**
 Avraham
The Palestinian Hamas: Vision, Violence and Coexistence. Trade
Cloth. Columbia University Press. New York, NY. 2000. 272p.
ISBN:0-231-11674-8, ISBN13: 978-0-231-11674-9.
Dewey:956.05/3. LCCN:99-047268.

Audience: **l,u,f.**

Morris, Benny   **HV640.5.A6M67 2003**
The Birth of the Palestinian Refugee Problem Revisited. Ed. 2.
Cambridge University Pess. 2004. ISBN:0-521-81120-1,
ISBN13: 978-0-521-81120-0.

Audience: **l,u,f.**

Morris, Benny   **DS119.7.M3132 2002**
The Road to Jerusalem: Glubb Pasha, Palestine and the Jews.
Cloth over Boards. I. B. Tauris & Company, Ltd. London, 2002.
320p. The Library of Middle East History, Vol. 1
ISBN:1-86064-812-6, ISBN13: 978-1-86064-812-0.
Dewey:956.9404092. LCCN:2002-512137.

Audience: **g,l,u,f.**

Najjar, Orayb A.   **HQ1728.5 .N35 1992**
Portraits of Palestinian Women. Rosemary Sayigh (Introduction
by). Trade Cloth. University of Utah Press. Salt Lake City, UT.
1992. 304p. ISBN:0-87480-385-3, ISBN13: 978-0-87480-385-3.
Dewey:305.42/095694. LCCN:91-051099.

Audience: **l,u,f.**

Pappe, Illan   **DS119.7.I82619 1999**
The Israel Palestine Question. Paper over Boards. Routledge.
New York, NY. 1999. 288p. Rewriting Histories Ser.
ISBN:0-415-16947-X, ISBN13: 978-0-415-16947-9.
Dewey:956.04/2. LCCN:98-036351.

Audience: **g,l,u,f.**

Peleg, Ilan   **JC599.W47P45 1995**
Human Rights in the West Bank and Gaza: Legacy and Politics.
Syracuse University Press. 1995. ISBN:0-8156-2682-7, ISBN13:
978-0-8156-2682-4.

Audience: **u,f.**

Peretz, Don   **DS110.W47P46 1990**
Intifada: The Palestinian Uprising. Westview Press. 1990.
ISBN:0-8133-0859-3, ISBN13: 978-0-8133-0859-3.

Audience: **u,f.**

Peteet, Julie M.   **DS80.55.P34P47 1991**
Gender in Crisis: Women and the Palestinian Resistance
Movement. Trade Cloth. Eastern European Monographs.
Bradenton, FL. 1991. 245p. ISBN:0-231-07446-8, ISBN13:
978-0-231-07446-9. Dewey:305.4/095692. LCCN:90-025824.

Audience: **u,f.** *Choice, 1992.*

Quandt, William B.   **DS119.7 .Q69 2001**
Peace Process: American Diplomacy and the Arab-Israeli
Conflict since 1967. Ed. 3. Trade Cloth. University of California
Press. Berkeley, CA. 2001. 500p. ISBN:0-520-22374-8, ISBN13:
978-0-520-22374-5. Dewey:327.73056/09/045.
LCCN:00-012148.

Audience: **l,u,f.** *Choice, 2002, 1993.*

Rabinowitz, Dan &   **DS113.7 .R3413 2005**
  Abu-Baker, Khawla
Coffins on Our Shoulders: The Experience of the Palestinian.
Trade Cloth. University of California Press. Berkeley, CA. 2005.
232p. ISBN:0-520-24441-9, ISBN13: 978-0-520-24441-2.
Dewey:305.892/7405694. LCCN:2004-022691.

Audience: **g,l,u,f.**

Reporters Without   **DS119.76.I8725 2003**
  Borders Staff (Editor)
Israel/Palestine: The Black Book. Reporters Sans Frontieres
Association Staff (Contribution by). Trade Cloth. Pluto Press.
London, 2003. 224p. ISBN:0-7453-2142-9, ISBN13:

978-0-7453-2142-4. Dewey:323.4/9/095694.
LCCN:2003-006658.

Audience: **g,l,u,f.**

Robinson, Glenn E.   **HN660.Z9E46 1997**
Building a Palestinian State: The Incomplete Revolution. Trade
Cloth. Indiana University Press. Bloomington, IN. 1997. 248p.
Indiana University Series in Middle East Studies
ISBN:0-253-33217-6, ISBN13: 978-0-253-33217-2.
Dewey:305.52/095694. LCCN:96-024708.

Audience: **u,f.** *Choice, 1997.*

Rubenberg, Cheryl A.   **HQ1728.7.R8 2001**
Palestinian Women: Patriarchy and Resistance in the West Bank.
Trade Cloth. Lynne Rienner Publishers, Inc. Boulder, CO. 2001.
ix, 318p. ISBN:1-55587-956-X, ISBN13: 978-1-55587-956-3.
Dewey:305.38/89274056953. LCCN:00-046002.

Audience: **u,f.** *Choice, 2001.*

Rubenberg, Cheryl A.   **DS119.76.R794 2003**
The Palestinians: In Search of a Just Peace. Trade Cloth. Lynne
Rienner Publishers, Inc. Boulder, CO. 2003. 504p.
ISBN:1-58826-225-1, ISBN13: 978-1-58826-225-7.
Dewey:956.05/3. LCCN:2003-041422.

Audience: **g,l,u,f.** *Choice, 2004.*

Rubin, Barry   **DS119.7.R754 1994**
Revolution until Victory?: The Politics and History of the PLO.
Trade Cloth. Harvard University Press. Cambridge, MA. 1994.
288p. ISBN:0-674-76803-5, ISBN13: 978-0-674-76803-1.
Dewey:322.4/2/095694. LCCN:93-031651.

Audience: **l,u,f.** *Choice, 1994.*

Rubinstein, Alvin Z.   **DS119.7.A6723 1990**
The Arab-Israeli Conflict. Paper Text. Addison-Wesley
Educational Publishers, Inc. Boston, MA. 1997.
ISBN:0-673-46405-9, ISBN13: 978-0-673-46405-7. Dewey:956.
LCCN:90-045243.

Audience: **g,l,u,f.**

Sabbagh, Suha   **HQ1728.8.P35 1998**
Palestinian Women of Gaza and the West Bank. Trade Cloth.
Indiana University Press. Bloomington, IN. 1998. 304p.
ISBN:0-253-33377-6, ISBN13: 978-0-253-33377-3.
Dewey:305.48/892740531. LCCN:97-040148.

Audience: **l,u,f.** *Choice, 1998.*

Said, Edward   **DS119.7**
Blaming the Victims. Ed. 2. Trade Paper. W. W. Norton &
Company, Inc. New York, NY. 2001. 304p.
ISBN:1-85984-340-9, ISBN13: 978-1-85984-340-6.
Dewey:956/.04.

Audience: **g,l,u,f.**

Said, Edward W.   **DS119.76.S245 2000**
The End of the Peace Process: Oslo and After. Trade Cloth.
Knopf Publishing Group. New York, NY. 2000. 368p.
ISBN:0-375-40930-0, ISBN13: 978-0-375-40930-1.
Dewey:956/.053. LCCN:99-044765.

Audience: **g,l,u,f.**

Said, Edward W.   **E885.S25 2004**
From Oslo to Iraq and the Road Map: Essays. Trade Cloth.
Knopf Publishing Group. New York, NY. 2004. 352p.
ISBN:0-375-42287-0, ISBN13: 978-0-375-42287-4.
Dewey:327.73056/09/049. LCCN:2003-070700.

Audience: **l,u,f.**

Said, Edward W. DS119.7.S3324 1995
Peace and Its Discontents: Essays on Palestine in the Middle
East Peace Process. Christopher Hitchens (Preface by). Trade
Paper. Knopf Publishing Group. New York, NY. 1996. 224p.
ISBN:0-679-76725-8, ISBN13: 978-0-679-76725-1.
Dewey:956.04. LCCN:95-034226.

Audience: **l,u,f.**

Sayigh, Yezid DS119.7.S3738 1997
Armed Struggle and the Search for State: The Palestinian
National Movement, 1949-1993. Trade Cloth. Oxford University
Press, Inc. New York, NY. 1998. 990p. ISBN:0-19-829265-1,
ISBN13: 978-0-19-829265-4. Dewey:956.9405.
LCCN:97-023852.

Audience: **l,u,f.** *Choice, 1998.*

Schiff, Zeev DS110.W47S34 1990
Intifada: The Palestinian Uprising - Israel's Third Front. Simon
and Schuster. 1990. ISBN:0-671-67530-3, ISBN13:
978-0-671-67530-1.

Audience: **g,l,u,f.**

Sharoni, Simona HQ1728.5.Z8W4773
Gender and the Israeli-Palestinian Conflict: The Politics of
Women's Resistance. Trade Cloth. Syracuse University Press.
Syracuse, NY. 1994. 192p. Peace and Conflict Resolution
Studies ISBN:0-8156-2643-6, ISBN13: 978-0-8156-2643-5.
Dewey:305.42/095695/3. LCCN:94-032264.

Audience: **l,u,f.** *Choice, 1995.*

Shehadeh, Raja KMM511.S53
Strangers in the House: Coming of Age in Occupied Palestine.
Anthony Lewis (Foreword by). Trade Paper. Penguin Group
(USA) Inc. New York, NY. 2003. 272p. ISBN:0-14-200293-3,
ISBN13: 978-0-14-200293-3. Dewey:956.95/30049274/0092.

Audience: **g,l,u,f.**

Talhami, Ghada H. DT107
Palestine and the Egyptian National Identity. Trade Cloth.
Greenwood Publishing Group, Inc. Portsmouth, NH. 1992. 192p.
ISBN:0-275-94124-8, ISBN13: 978-0-275-94124-6.
Dewey:320.5/4/0962. LCCN:91-027807.

Audience: **l,u,f.** *Choice, 1992.*

Tawil, Raymonda H. DS113.7
My Home, My Prison. Trade Cloth. Zed Books, Ltd. London,
1980. 272p. ISBN:0-86232-202-2, ISBN13: 978-0-86232-202-1.
Dewey:322.4/2/0924.

Audience: **g,l,u,f.**

Tessler, Mark A. DS119.7.T443 1994
A History of the Israeli-Palestinian Conflict. Indiana University
Press. 1994. ISBN:0-253-35848-5, ISBN13: 978-0-253-35848-6.

Audience: **l,u,f.**

History of Specific Countries > Jordan > General

Layne, Linda L. DS153.55.B43.L39
Home and Homeland: The Dialectics of Tribal and National
Identities in Jordan. Princeton University Press. 1994.
ISBN:0-691-09478-0, ISBN13: 978-0-691-09478-6.

Audience: **l,u,f.**

Rogan, Eugene & Tell, DS153.2.V55 1994
Tariq (Editors)
Village, Steppe, and State: The Social Origins of Modern
Jordan. Cloth over Boards. I. B. Tauris & Company, Ltd.
London, 1995. 256p. ISBN:1-85043-829-3, ISBN13:
978-1-85043-829-8. Dewey:956.95. LCCN:94-060699.

Audience: **u,f.**

Salibi, Kamal S. DS154.5.S25 1993
The Modern History of Jordan. Cloth over Boards. I. B. Tauris
& Company, Ltd. London, 1993. 305p. ISBN:1-85043-610-X,
ISBN13: 978-1-85043-610-2. Dewey:956.9504.
LCCN:93-183090.

Audience: **g,l,u,f.**

Shryock, Andrew DS153.55.B43S57 1997
Nationalism and the Genealogical Imagination: Oral History and
Textual Authority in Tribal Jordan. University of California
Press. 1997. ISBN:0-520-20101-9, ISBN13: 978-0-520-20101-9.

Audience: **l,u,f.**

Sonbol, Amira El HQ1729.S66 2002
Azhary
Women of Jordan: Islam, Labor, and the Law. Trade Cloth.
Syracuse University Press. Syracuse, NY. 2002. xi, 300p.
Gender, Culture, and Politics in the Middle East Ser.
ISBN:0-8156-2964-8, ISBN13: 978-0-8156-2964-1.
Dewey:305.42/095695. LCCN:2002-012942.

Audience: **u,f.**

History of Specific Countries > Jordan > Modern

Abdullah, King of DS154.52.A3
Jordan
Memoirs of King Abdullah of Transjordan. Cape. 1951.

Audience: **u,f.**

Abdullah, King of DS154.53
Jordan
My Memories Completed: al-Takmilah. Glidden, Harold W.
(Translator). Longman. 1978. ISBN:0-582-78082-9, ISBN13:
978-0-582-78082-8.

Audience: **u,f.**

Abu Nowar, Maan DS154.5
Development of Transjordan 1929-1939: A History of the
Hashemite Kingdom of Jordan. Trade Cloth. Garnet Publishing,
Ltd. Reading, 2006. 392p. ISBN:0-86372-303-9, ISBN13:
978-0-86372-303-2. Dewey:956.95042.

Audience: **u,f.**

Abu Nowar, Maan DS143.53.N68 2002
The Jordanian-Israeli War 1948-1951: A History of the
Hashemite Kingdom of Jordan. Trade Cloth. Garnet Publishing,
Ltd. Reading, 2002. 528p. ISBN:0-86372-286-5, ISBN13:
978-0-86372-286-8. Dewey:956.04/2. LCCN:2003-447960.

Audience: **u,f.** *Choice, 2003.*

Al-Rahman Munif, Abd PJ7850.U514S76 1996
Story of a City: A Childhood in Amman. Samira Kawar
(Translator). Trade Paper. Quartet Books, Ltd. London, 1998.
320p. Literature Ser. ISBN:0-7043-8023-4, ISBN13:
978-0-7043-8023-3. Dewey:892.7/36 B. LCCN:97-154894.

Audience: **g,l,u,f.**

Boulby, Marion **BP63.J6B68 1999**
The Muslim Brotherhood and the Kings of Jordan, 1945-1993.
John O. Voll (Foreword by). Trade Cloth. Scholars Press.
Atlanta, GA. 1999. 256p. South Florida-Rochester-Saint Louis
Studies on Religion and the Social Order ISBN:0-7885-0553-X,
ISBN13: 978-0-7885-0553-9. Dewey:322/.1/095695.
LCCN:99-020109.

Audience: **l,u,f.**

Dann, Uriel **DS154.5.D36 1984**
Studies in the History of Transjordan. Paper Text. Westview
Press. Boulder, CO. 1984. 130p. Special Studies on the Middle
East ISBN:0-86531-793-3, ISBN13: 978-0-86531-793-2.
Dewey:956.95/04. LCCN:84-003539.

Audience: **l,u,f.**

Droeber, Julia **HQ1729.D76 2005**
Dreaming of Change: Young Middle-Class Women and Social
Transformation in Jordan. Trade Cloth. Brill Academic
Publishers. Leiden, 2005. xii, 340p. Women and Gender : The
Middle East and the Islamic World Ser., Vol. 3
ISBN:90-04-14634-2, ISBN13: 978-90-04-14634-1.
Dewey:305.242/2. LCCN:2005-047220.

Audience: **u,f.**

Hussein, King of Jordan **DS154.55.H8**
Uneasy Lies the Head: The Autobiography of King Hussein I of
Jordan. Bernard Geis Associates. 1962.

Audience: **l,u,f.**

Lewis, Norman N. **DS94.7.L48 1987**
Nomads and Settlers in Syria and Jordan, 1800-1980. Edmund
Burke, Michael C. Hudson & Walid Kazziha (Contribution by).
Trade Cloth. Cambridge University Press. New York, NY. 1987.
270p. Cambridge Middle East Library ISBN:0-521-26548-7,
ISBN13: 978-0-521-26548-5. Dewey:956.91/03.
LCCN:86-017202.

Audience: **l,u,f.** *Choice, 1987.*

Lunt, J. **UA853.J6**
The Arab Legion, 1923-1957. Trade Cloth. Random House.
London, xviii, 178p. ISBN:0-09-477640-7, ISBN13:
978-0-09-477640-1. Dewey:355.3/095695.

Audience: **u,f.**

Mishal, Shaul **DS153.55.P34**
West Bank/East Bank: The Palestinians in Jordan, 1949-1967.
Yale University Press. 1978. ISBN:0-300-02191-7, ISBN13:
978-0-300-02191-2.

Audience: **l,u,f.**

Munif, Abd al-Rahma **PJ7850.U514 S76**
Story of a City: A Childhood in Amman. Samira Kawar
(Translator). Quartet Books. 1998. ISBN:0-7043-8023-4,
ISBN13: 978-0-7043-8023-3.

Audience: **g,l,u,f.**

Mutawi, Samir A. **DS127.9.J6 M88 1987**
Jordan in the 1967 War. Trade Cloth. Cambridge University
Press. New York, NY. 1987. 256p. Cambridge Middle East
Library, No. 10 ISBN:0-521-34352-6, ISBN13:
978-0-521-34352-7. Dewey:956/.046. LCCN:86-033451.

Audience: **l,u,f.** *Choice, 1987.*

Robins, Philip **DS154**
A History of Jordan. Cloth Text. Cambridge University Press.
New York, NY. 2004. 262p. ISBN:0-521-59117-1, ISBN13:
978-0-521-59117-1. Dewey:956.9504. LCCN:2004-043519.

Audience: **l,u,f.**

Rogan, Eugene L. **DS154.4 .R64 1999**
Frontiers of the State in the Late Ottoman Empire: Transjordan,
1850-1921. Julia A. Clancy-Smith, Israel Gershoni, Roger
Owen, Yezid Sayigh, Charles Tripp & Judith E. Tucker
(Contribution by). Trade Cloth. Cambridge University Press.
New York, NY. 1999. 291p. Middle East Studies, No. 12
ISBN:0-521-66312-1, ISBN13: 978-0-521-66312-0.
Dewey:956.95. LCCN:99-011032.

Audience: **u,f.** *Choice, 2000.*

Shlaim, Avi **DS119.8.J67S552 1998**
The Politics of Partition: King Abdullah, the Zionists, and
Palestine, 1921-1951. Oxford University Press. 1998.
ISBN:0-19-829459-X, ISBN13: 978-0-19-829459-7.

Audience: **l,u,f.**

Wilson, Mary Christina **DS154.5.W54 1987**
King Abdullah, Britain and the Making of Jordan. Trade Cloth.
Cambridge University Press. New York, NY. 1988. 320p.
Cambridge Middle East Library, No. 13 ISBN:0-521-32421-1,
ISBN13: 978-0-521-32421-2. Dewey:956.94. LCCN:87-006649.

Audience: **u,f.** *Choice, 1988.*

Wilson, Rodney (Editor) **HC415.26.P65 1990**
Politics and the Economy in Jordan. Paper over Boards.
Routledge. New York, NY. 1991. 256p. Routledge/SOAS Series
on Contemporary Politics and Culture in the Middle East Ser.
ISBN:0-415-05304-8, ISBN13: 978-0-415-05304-4.
Dewey:338.95695. LCCN:90-008155.

Audience: **g,l,u,f.** *Choice, 1991.*

History of Specific Countries > Turkey > General

Davidson, Roderic H **DR441.D24 1988**
Turkey: A Short History. Ed. 3. Cloth over Boards. Eothen
Press. Huntingdon, 1988. 205p. ISBN:0-906719-13-5, ISBN13:
978-0-906719-13-8. Dewey:956.1. LCCN:97-175733.

Audience: **g,l,u,f.**

Delaney, Carol L. **GR450.D45 1992**
The Seed and the Soil: Gender and Cosmology in Turkish
Village Society. Trade Cloth. University of California Press.
Berkeley, CA. 1991. 393p. Comparative Studies on Muslim
Societies, No. 11 ISBN:0-520-07314-2, ISBN13:
978-0-520-07314-2. Dewey:302/.12. LCCN:90-028545.

Audience: **u,f.** *Choice, 1992.*

Hale, William **DR474.H35 2000**
Turkish Foreign Policy, 1774-2000. Frank Cass Publishers.
2002. ISBN:0-7146-5071-4, ISBN13: 978-0-7146-5071-5.

Audience: **g,l,u,f.**

Heper, Metin **DR436.H47 2002**
Historical Dictionary of Turkey. Ed. 2. Trade Cloth. Scarecrow
Press, Inc. Lanham, MD. 2002. 611p. European Historical
Dictionaries Ser., No. 38 ISBN:0-8108-4133-9, ISBN13:
978-0-8108-4133-8. Dewey:956.1/003. LCCN:2001-057615.

Audience: **g,l,u,f.** *Choice, 2003, 2002, 1995.*

Houston, Christopher **DS59.K86.H68 2001**
Islam, Kurds and the Turkish Nation State. Cloth over Boards.
Berg Publishers. Oxford, 2001. 224p. ISBN:1-85973-472-3,
ISBN13: 978-1-85973-472-8. Dewey:956.103.

Audience: **l,u,f.** *Choice, 2001.*

Ibrahim, Ferhad & DR435.K87K86 2000
  Gurbey, Gulistan (Editors)
The Kurdish Conflict in Turkey: Obstacles and Chances for
Peace and Democracy. Cloth over Boards. Palgrave Macmillan.
New York, NY. 2001. 206p. ISBN:0-312-23629-8, ISBN13:
978-0-312-23629-8. Dewey:956.6/7038. LCCN:00-042182.
Audience: **u,f.**

Quataert, Donald & HD8656.5.W67 1995
  Zurcher, Eric J. (Editors)
Workers and Working Class in the Ottoman Empire and the
Turkish Republic, 1839-1950. Cloth over Boards. I. B. Tauris &
Company, Ltd. London, 1995. 224p. Library of Modern Middle
East Studies ISBN:1-85043-875-7, ISBN13: 978-1-85043-875-5.
Dewey:305.5/9561. LCCN:94-061511.
Audience: **u,f.**

Shaw, Stanford J. DS135.T8S46 1991
The Jews of the Ottoman Empire and the Turkish Republic.
Trade Cloth. New York University Press. New York, NY. 1991.
384p. ISBN:0-8147-7924-7, ISBN13: 978-0-8147-7924-8.
Dewey:956.1/015. LCCN:91-006927.
Audience: **u,f.** *Choice, 1992.*

Turfan, Naim DR486
Rise of the Young Turks: Politics, the Military, and Ottoman
Collapse. Cloth over Boards. I. B. Tauris & Company, Ltd.
London, 2000. 512p. ISBN:1-86064-533-X, ISBN13:
978-1-86064-533-4. Dewey:956.1/015. LCCN:00-271744.
Audience: **u,f.** *Choice, 2000.*

Vryonis, Speros Jr. DR440.V79 1991
The Turkish State and History: Clio Meets the Gray Wolf. Cloth
Text. Aristide D. Caratzas Publisher. Athens, 1993. 160p.
ISBN:0-89241-532-0, ISBN13: 978-0-89241-532-8.
Dewey:949.61. LCCN:91-046834.
Audience: **u,f.** *Choice, 1993.*

Yildiz, Kerim DR435.K87
The Kurds in Turkey: EU Accession and Human Rights. Noam
Chomsky (Foreword by). Trade Cloth. Pluto Press. London,
2005. 216p. ISBN:0-7453-2489-4, ISBN13: 978-0-7453-2489-0.
Dewey:323.1191/5970561. LCCN:2005-283932.
Audience: **l,u,f.** *Choice, 2006.*

History of Specific Countries > Turkey > Earliest to 1281/1453

Bosworth, Edmund D161.2
  (Editor)
History of the Seljuq Turks: The Saljuq-Nama of Zahir Al-Din
Nishapuri. Kenneth Allin Luther & University of Michigan Staff
(Translators). Paper over Boards. Taylor & Francis Group.
Abingdon, 2000. 189p. Studies in the History of Iran and
Turkey ISBN:0-7007-1342-5, ISBN13: 978-0-7007-1342-4.
Dewey:956/.014.
Audience: **u,f.**

Cahen, Claude DR481 .C3313
Pre-Ottoman Turkey: A General Survey of the Material and
Spiritual Culture and History, 1071-1330. Trade Cloth. Taplinger
Publishing Company, Inc. Marlboro, NJ. 1968.
ISBN:0-8008-6500-6, ISBN13: 978-0-8008-6500-9.
Dewey:915.61/03/1. LCCN:68-024744.
Audience: **u,f.**

Cameron, A. & Herrin, DR729 .P3713 1984
  J. (Editors)
Constantinople in the Early Eighth Century. Trade Cloth. Brill
Academic Publishers, Inc. Boston, MA. 1984.
ISBN:90-04-07010-9, ISBN13: 978-90-04-07010-3.
Dewey:956.3. LCCN:84-251023.
Audience: **u,f.**

History of Specific Countries > Turkey > Medieval

Cahen, Claude & Holt, DR481.C3313 2001
  P. M.
The Formation of Turkey: The Seljukid Sultanate of Reum:
Eleventh to Fourteenth Century. Trade Cloth. Longman
Publishing Group. White Plains, NY. 2001. 464p. A History of
the Near East Ser. ISBN:0-582-41492-X, ISBN13:
978-0-582-41492-1. Dewey:956.1/015. LCCN:00-069015.
Audience: **u,f.**

Mansel, Philip DR730.M25 1996
Constantinople: City of the World's Desire, 1453-1924. Trade
Cloth. St. Martin's Press. Gordonville, VA. 1996. 544p.
Constantinople Ser., Vol. 1 ISBN:0-312-14574-8, ISBN13:
978-0-312-14574-3. Dewey:949.6/18. LCCN:96-019951.
Audience: **u,f.**

History of Specific Countries > Turkey > Medieval > Ottomans 1281/1453-1918

Babinger, Franz DR501
Mehmed the Conqueror and His Time. William C. Hickman
(Editor). Trade Paper. Princeton University Press. Princeton, NJ.
1992. 570p. Bollingen Ser., No. XCVI ISBN:0-691-01078-1,
ISBN13: 978-0-691-01078-6. Dewey:956.1/01/0924.
Audience: **u,f.** *B*

Babinger, Franz DR501.B313
Mehmed the Conqueror and His Time. William C. Hickman
(Editor), Ralph Manheim (Translator). Trade Cloth. Princeton
University Press. Princeton, NJ. 1978. 572p. Bollingen Ser., No.
96 ISBN:0-691-09900-6, ISBN13: 978-0-691-09900-2.
Dewey:956.1/01/0924. LCCN:77-071972.
Audience: **l,u,f.** *B*

Evliya, Efendi QE475.A2
Narrative of Travels in Europe, Asia and Africa in the 17th
Century. Trade Cloth. Johnson Reprint Corporation. New York,
NY. 1987. Oriental Translation Fund Ser., No. 32
ISBN:0-384-14895-6, ISBN13: 978-0-384-14895-6.
Dewey:552/.4.
Audience: **l,u,f.**

Inalcik, Halil DR486 .I477
From Empire to Republic: Essays on Ottoman and Turkish
Social History. Trade Paper. Evergreen Book Distributors. Los
Angeles, CA. 1996. 179p. ISBN:0-614-24318-1, ISBN13:
978-0-614-24318-5. Dewey:956/.015.
Audience: **u,f.**

Lewis, Bernard DR726
Istanbul and the Civilization of the Ottoman Empire. Ed. 1.
University of Oklahoma Press. 1963.
Audience: **g,l,u,f.**

Lindner, Rudi Paul   **DR434**
Nomads and Ottomans in Medieval Anatolia. Cloth Text. Taylor
& Francis Group. Philadelphia, PA. 1997. 167p.
ISBN:0-7007-0944-4, ISBN13: 978-0-7007-0944-1.
Dewey:956.1/01.

Audience: **u,f.**

Ubicini, M. A.   **DR566 .U2413 1973**
Letters on Turkey. Lady Easthope (Translator). Trade Cloth.
Ayer Company Publishers, Inc. Manchester, NH. 1973. The
Middle East Ser. ISBN:0-405-05367-3, ISBN13:
978-0-405-05367-2. Dewey:915.61/03/1. LCCN:73-006306.

Audience: **u,f.**

Valensi, Lucette   **DR479.I8 V3513 1993**
The Birth of the Despot: Venice and the Sublime Porte. Arthur
Denner (Translator). Book, Other. Cornell University Press.
Ithaca, NY. 1993. 160p. ISBN:0-8014-2480-1, ISBN13:
978-0-8014-2480-9. Dewey:949.61/015. LCCN:93-001352.

Audience: **l,u,f.**

History of Specific Countries > Turkey > Modern

Adivar, Halide E.   **DR592.A4 A35 1981**
The Turkish Ordeal. Trade Cloth. Hyperion Press, Inc. Westport,
CT. 1981. 407p. ISBN:0-8305-0057-X, ISBN13:
978-0-8305-0057-4. Dewey:956.1/02/0924. LCCN:79-003081.

Audience: **l,u,f.**

Adivar, Halide Edib   **DR592.A4A3 2003**
House with Wisteria: Memoirs of Halide Edib. Ed. 2. Perfect.
Leopolis Press. Kensington, CA. 2003. 407p.
ISBN:0-9679960-3-1, ISBN13: 978-0-9679960-3-5.
Dewey:956.1/02/092 B. LCCN:2003-107612.

Audience: **g,l,u,f.**

Adivar, Halide Edib   **DR441 .A37 1973**
Turkey Faces West. Trade Cloth. Ayer Company Publishers, Inc.
Manchester, NH. 1973. The Middle East Ser.
ISBN:0-405-05320-7, ISBN13: 978-0-405-05320-7.
Dewey:956.1. LCCN:73-006266.

Audience: **l,u,f.**

Ahmad, Feroz   **DR576**
The Making of Modern Turkey. Trade Cloth. Routledge. New
York, NY. 1993. 240p. Making of the Modern Middle East Ser.
ISBN:0-415-07835-0, ISBN13: 978-0-415-07835-1.
Dewey:956.102. LCCN:93-020425.

Audience: **l,u,f.**

Altinay, Ayse Gul   **JF195.A48 2004**
The Myth of the Military-Nation: Militarism, Gender, and
Education in Turkey. Cloth over Boards. Palgrave Macmillan.
New York, NY. 2004. 224p. ISBN:1-4039-6281-2, ISBN13:
978-1-4039-6281-2. Dewey:355.02/13/09561.
LCCN:2004-044798.

Audience: **u,f.** *Choice, 2005.*

Aydin, Mustafa   **DR603**
Turkish Foreign Policy During the Gulf War of 1990-91. Trade
Paper. American University in Cairo Press. New York, NY.
1999. 92p. Cairo Papers in Social Science, Vol. 21, No. 1
ISBN:977-424-506-7, ISBN13: 978-977-424-506-0.
Dewey:327.561.

Audience: **u,f.**

Berkes, Niyazi   **DR557.B4 1998**
Development of Secularism in Turkey. Paper over Boards.
Routledge. New York, NY. 1999. 537p. ISBN:0-415-91983-5,
ISBN13: 978-0-415-91983-8. Dewey:956.1/015.
LCCN:99-200292.

Audience: **u,f.**

Davison, Andrew   **BL2747.8.D28 1998**
Secularism and Revivalism in Turkey: A Hermeneutic
Reconsideration. Cloth over Boards. Yale University Press.
Cumberland, RI. 1998. 280p. Yale Studies in Hermeneutics
ISBN:0-300-06936-7, ISBN13: 978-0-300-06936-5.
Dewey:322/.1/09561. LCCN:97-049379.

Audience: **u,f.** *Choice, 1999.*

Davison, Roderic H.   **DR555.D38 1990**
Essays in Ottoman and Turkish History, 1774-1923: The Impact
of the West. Cloth Text. University of Texas Press. Austin, TX.
1990. 299p. Modern Middle East Ser., No. 16
ISBN:0-292-72064-5, ISBN13: 978-0-292-72064-0.
Dewey:956.1/015. LCCN:89-070774.

Audience: **u,f.**

Gokalp, Ziya   **DR432**
Turkish Nationalism and Western Civilization: Selected Essays.
Berkes, Niyazi (Editor; Translator). Columbia University Press.
1959.

Audience: **u,f.**

Gole, Nilufer   **HQ1726.7.G65 1996**
The Forbidden Modern: Civilization and Veiling. Trade Paper.
University of Michigan Press. Chicago, IL. 1997. 184p. Critical
Perspectives on Women and Gender Ser. ISBN:0-472-06630-7,
ISBN13: 978-0-472-06630-8. Dewey:305.42/09561.
LCCN:96-018179.

Audience: **l,u,f.** *Choice, 1997.*

Heper, Metin & Evin,   **JQ1802.P66 1994**
  Ahmet O.
Politics in the Third Turkish Republic. Trade Paper. Westview
Press. Boulder, CO. 1994. 288p. ISBN:0-8133-8674-8, ISBN13:
978-0-8133-8674-4. Dewey:320.9561/09/048. LCCN:94-009567.

Audience: **l,u,f.** *Choice, 1995.*

Heper, Metin (Editor),   **DR432.T848 1993**
  et al.
Turkey and the West: Changing Political and Cultural Identities.
Heinz Kramer & Ayse Oncu (Editors). Cloth over Boards. I. B.
Tauris & Company, Ltd. London, 1993. 264p.
ISBN:1-85043-611-8, ISBN13: 978-1-85043-611-9.
Dewey:949.61. LCCN:93-170385.

Audience: **u,f.**

Heper, Metin & Sayari,   **DR593.P65 2002**
  Sabri (Editors)
Political Leaders and Democracy in Turkey. Trade Cloth.
Lexington Books. Lanham, MD. 2002. 270p.
ISBN:0-7391-0352-0, ISBN13: 978-0-7391-0352-4.
Dewey:956.1/02/0922 B. LCCN:2002-003585.

Audience: **l,u,f.** *Choice, 2003.*

Hovannisian, Richard   **DS195.5.L66 2003**
  G. (Editor)
Looking Backward, Moving Forward: Confronting the Armenian
Genocide. Trade Cloth. Transaction Publishers. Somerset, NJ.
2003. 301p. ISBN:0-7658-0196-5, ISBN13: 978-0-7658-0196-8.
Dewey:956.6/2015. LCCN:2002-073266.

Audience: **g,l,u,f.**

Hovannisian, Richard G.   **DS195.5R46 1999**
Remembrance and Denial: The Case of the Armenian Genocide.
Trade Cloth. Wayne State University Press. Detroit, MI. 1999.
304p. ISBN:0-8143-2777-X, ISBN13: 978-0-8143-2777-7.
Dewey:956.6/2015. LCCN:98-028282.
                                        Audience: **l,u,f.**

Kandiyoti, Deniz &   **DR432.F73 2002**
   Saktanber, Ayse (Editors)
Fragments of Culture: The Everyday of Modern Turkey. Trade
Cloth. Rutgers University Press. Piscataway, NJ. 2002. 368p.
ISBN:0-8135-3081-4, ISBN13: 978-0-8135-3081-9.
Dewey:956.1/02. LCCN:2001-058691.
                      Audience: **g,l,u,f.**   *Choice, 2003, 2002.*

Kedourie, Sylvia   **DR590.S48 2000**
   (Editor)
75 Years of the Turkish Republic. Paper over Boards. Taylor &
Francis Group. Abingdon, 2000. 248p. ISBN:0-7146-5042-0,
ISBN13: 978-0-7146-5042-5. Dewey:956.1/02.
LCCN:99-040497.
                                        Audience: **l,u,f.**

Kinross, Lord   **DR592.K4 K43 1992**
Ataturk: A Biography of Mustafa Kemal, Father of Modern
Turkey. Trade Paper. HarperCollins Publishers. New York, NY.
1992. 640p. ISBN:0-688-11283-8, ISBN13: 978-0-688-11283-7.
Dewey:956.1024092. LCCN:91-041211.
                                      Audience: **g,l,u,f.**

Lewis, Bernard   **DR583.L48 2002**
The Emergence of Modern Turkey. Ed. 3. Cloth Text. Oxford
University Press, Inc. New York, NY. 2001. 568p. Studies in
Middle Eastern History ISBN:0-19-513459-1, ISBN13:
978-0-19-513459-9. Dewey:956.1. LCCN:2001-031411.
                                      Audience: **g,l,u,f.**

Lewy, Guenter   **DS195.5.L49 2005**
The Armenian Massacres in Ottoman Turkey: A Disputed
Genocide. Trade Cloth. University of Utah Press. Salt Lake City,
UT. 2005. 416p. ISBN:0-87480-849-9, ISBN13:
978-0-87480-849-0. Dewey:956.6/20154. LCCN:2005-023322.
                      Audience: **l,u,f.**   *Choice, 2006.*

Mango, Andrew   **DR592.K4M36 2000**
Ataturk: The Biography of the Founder of Modern Turkey.
Trade Cloth. Overlook Press, The. New York, NY. 2000. 539p.
ISBN:1-58567-011-1, ISBN13: 978-1-58567-011-6.
Dewey:956.1/024/092 B. LCCN:99-086845.
                                      Audience: **g,l,u,f.**

Mango, Andrew   **DR576.M356 2004**
The Turks Today. Trade Cloth. Overlook Press, The. New York,
NY. 2004. 288p. ISBN:1-58567-615-2, ISBN13:
978-1-58567-615-6. Dewey:956.103. LCCN:2004-058339.
                                      Audience: **g,l,u,f.**

Martin, Lenore &   **DR477.F68 2002**
   Keridis, Dimitris (Editors)
The Future of Turkish Foreign Policy. Trade Cloth. MIT Press.
Cambridge, MA. 2004. 300p. BCSIA Studies in International
Security ISBN:0-262-13402-0, ISBN13: 978-0-262-13402-6.
Dewey:327.561. LCCN:2001-054628.
                      Audience: **u,f.**   *Choice, 2004.*

Olson, Robert W.   **DS63.2.T8O47 2001**
Turkey's Relations with Iran, Syria, Israel and Russia,
1991-2000: The Kurdish and Islamist Question. Trade Paper.
Mazda Publishers, Inc. Costa Mesa, CA. 2001. 240p. Kurdish

Studies, No. 2 ISBN:1-56859-133-0, ISBN13:
978-1-56859-133-9. Dewey:327.561/009/049. LCCN:00-054895.
                      Audience: **u,f.**   *Choice, 2001.*

Olson, Robert W.   **DR479.I7O47 2003**
Turkey-Iran Relations, 1979-2004: Revolution, War, Ideology,
Coups, and Geopolitics. Trade Paper. Mazda Publishers, Inc.
Costa Mesa, CA. 2003. 342p. ISBN:1-56859-114-4, ISBN13:
978-1-56859-114-8. Dewey:327.561055/09/045.
LCCN:2003-060610.
                                        Audience: **l,u,f.**

Ozbudun, Ergun   **JQ1805.A7O92 2000**
Contemporary Turkish Politics: Challenges to Democratic
Consolidation. Trade Cloth. Lynne Rienner Publishers, Inc.
Boulder, CO. 1999. ix, 171p. ISBN:1-55587-735-4, ISBN13:
978-1-55587-735-4. Dewey:320.9561/09/045. LCCN:99-038717.
                      Audience: **l,u.**   *Choice, 2000.*

Ozyegin, Gul   **HD8039.D52T926 2001**
Untidy Gender: Domestic Service in Turkey. Trade Cloth.
Temple University Press. Philadelphia, PA. 2000. xi, 276p.
Women in the Political Economy Ser. ISBN:1-56639-807-X,
ISBN13: 978-1-56639-807-7. Dewey:331.4/8164046/09563.
LCCN:00-036423.
                                        Audience: **u,f.**

Pamuk, Orhan   **DR723.P36 2005**
Istanbul: Memories and the City. Maureen Freely (Translator).
Trade Cloth. Knopf Publishing Group. New York, NY. 2005.
400p. ISBN:1-4000-4095-7, ISBN13: 978-1-4000-4095-7.
Dewey:949.61/803/092. LCCN:2004-061537.
                                      Audience: **g,l,u,f.**

Pamuk, Sevket   **HF1583.4.P36 1987**
The Ottoman Empire and European Capitalism, 1820-1913:
Trade, Investment and Production. Trade Cloth. Cambridge
University Press. New York, NY. 1987. 292p. Cambridge
Middle East Library ISBN:0-521-33194-3, ISBN13:
978-0-521-33194-4. Dewey:330.956/01. LCCN:86-028386.
                      Audience: **u,f.**   *Choice, 1988.*

Parla, Taha & Davison,   **HD3616.T872P37 2004**
   Andrew
Corporatist Ideology in Kemalist Turkey. Trade Cloth. Syracuse
University Press. Syracuse, NY. 2004. 320p. Modern Intellectual
and Political History of the Middle East Ser.
ISBN:0-8156-3054-9, ISBN13: 978-0-8156-3054-8.
Dewey:322/.3/09561. LCCN:2004-017122.
                      Audience: **u,f.**   *Choice, 2005.*

Roy, Olivier (Editor)   **DR603**
Turkey Today. Trade Cloth. Wimbledon Publishing Company.
London, 2005. 21p. ISBN:1-84331-172-0, ISBN13:
978-1-84331-172-0. Dewey:943.
                      Audience: **g,l,u,f.**   *Choice, 2006.*

Rubin, Barry M. &   **JQ1809.A795P654 2002**
   Heper, Metin (Editors)
Political Parties in Turkey. Paper over Boards. Taylor & Francis
Group. Abingdon, 2002. 160p. ISBN:0-7146-5274-1, ISBN13:
978-0-7146-5274-0. Dewey:324.2561. LCCN:2001-007614.
                      Audience: **g,l,u,f.**   *Choice, 2003.*

Rubin, Barry & Kirisci,   **DR477.T795 2001**
   Kemal (Editors)
Turkey in World Politics: An Emerging Multiregional Power.
Trade Cloth. Lynne Rienner Publishers, Inc. Boulder, CO. 2001.

ix, 270p. ISBN:1-55587-954-3, ISBN13: 978-1-55587-954-9. Dewey:327.561. LCCN:00-045983.

Audience: **l,u,f.** *Choice, 2001.*

Shaw, Stanford J.   **DR440**
History of the Ottoman Empire and Modern Turkey. Cambridge University Press. 1976. ISBN:0-521-21280-4, ISBN13: 978-0-521-21280-9.

Audience: **l,u,f.**

Taspinar, Omer   **BP173.7.T37 2004**
Kurdish Nationalism and Political Islam in Turkey: Kemalist Identity in Transition. Paper over Boards. Routledge. New York, NY. 2004. 293p. Middle East Studies, :History, Politics and Law Ser. ISBN:0-415-94998-X, ISBN13: 978-0-415-94998-9. Dewey:320.54/09561. LCCN:2004-009238.

Audience: **u,f.**

VanderLippe, John M.   **DR592.I5V36 2005**
The Politics of Turkish Democracy: Ismet Inonu and the Formation of the Multi-Party System, 1938-1950. Trade Cloth. State University of New York Press. Albany, NY. 2005. 288p. SUNY Series in the Social and Economic History of the Middle East ISBN:0-7914-6435-0, ISBN13: 978-0-7914-6435-9. Dewey:320.9561/09/044. LCCN:2004-014224.

Audience: **g,l,u,f.** *Choice, 2005.*

Webster, Donald E.   **DR590 .W37 1973**
The Turkey of Ataturk: Social Process in the Turkish Reformation. Trade Cloth. A M S Press, Inc. New York, NY. ISBN:0-404-56333-3, ISBN13: 978-0-404-56333-2. Dewey:956.1/02. LCCN:71-180308.

Audience: **l,u,f.**

Yavuz, M. Hakan &   **BP173.7.T875 2003**
Esposito, John L. (Editors)
Turkish Islam and the Secular State: The Gulen Movement. Trade Cloth. Syracuse University Press. Syracuse, NY. 2004. 256p. Contemporary Issues in the Middle East Ser. ISBN:0-8156-3015-8, ISBN13: 978-0-8156-3015-9. Dewey:322/.1/09561. LCCN:2003-060641.

Audience: **g,l,u,f.** *Choice, 2004.*

Zurcher, Erik J.   **JQ1809.A8T479 1991**
Political Opposition in the Early Turkish Republic: The Progressive Republican Party, 1924-1925. Trade Cloth. Brill Academic Publishers, Inc. Boston, MA. 1991. ix, 177p. Social, Economic, and Political Studies of the Middle East, No. 44 ISBN:90-04-09341-9, ISBN13: 978-90-04-09341-6. Dewey:324.2561/02. LCCN:90-024331.

Audience: **u,f.**

Zurcher, Erik J.   **DR557**
Turkey: A Modern History. Ed. 3. Cloth over Boards. I. B. Tauris & Company, Ltd. London, 2004. 424p. ISBN:1-85043-399-2, ISBN13: 978-1-85043-399-6. Dewey:956.102. LCCN:2004-303600.

Audience: **l,u,f.** *Choice, 1994.*

History of Specific Countries > Saudi Arabia > General

Al-Rasheed, Madawi   **DS244.52 .A43 2002**
A History of Saudi Arabia. Cloth Text. Cambridge University Press. New York, NY. 2002. 274p. ISBN:0-521-64335-X, ISBN13: 978-0-521-64335-1. Dewey:953.805/. LCCN:2001-043609.

Audience: **u,f.**

Doumato, Eleanor   **HQ1730.D68 2000**
Abdella
Getting God's Ear: Women, Islam and Healing in Saudi Arabia and the Gulf. Ed. 2. Trade Cloth. Columbia University Press. New York, NY. 1999. 498p. ISBN:0-231-11666-7, ISBN13: 978-0-231-11666-4. Dewey:305.4209538. LCCN:99-035113.

Audience: **g,l,u,f.** *Choice, 2000.*

Peters, F. E.   **DS248.M4P48 1994**
Mecca: A Literary History of the Muslim Holy Land. Trade Cloth. Princeton University Press. Princeton, NJ. 1994. 502p. ISBN:0-691-03267-X, ISBN13: 978-0-691-03267-2. Dewey:953.8. LCCN:94-020923.

Audience: **g,l,u,f.**

Peterson, J. E.   **DS221.P48 1993**
Historical Dictionary of Saudi Arabia. Trade Cloth. Scarecrow Press, Inc. Lanham, MD. 1993. 267p. Asian Historical Dictionaries Ser., No. 14 ISBN:0-8108-2780-8, ISBN13: 978-0-8108-2780-6. Dewey:953.8/003. LCCN:93-036808.

Audience: **g,l,u,f.** *Choice, 1994.*

Vassiliev, Alexei   **DS223**
The History of Saudi Arabia. Cloth over Boards. I. B. Tauris & Company, Ltd. London, 1997. 580p. ISBN:0-86356-935-8, ISBN13: 978-0-86356-935-7. Dewey:953.8. LCCN:98-148795.

Audience: **u,f.** *Choice, 1999.*

History of Specific Countries > Saudi Arabia > Early to 622

O'Leary, De Lacy E.   **DS231 .O5 1973**
Arabia Before Muhammad. Trade Cloth. A M S Press, Inc. New York, NY. ISBN:0-404-56313-9, ISBN13: 978-0-404-56313-4. Dewey:913.39/4. LCCN:74-180373.

Audience: **g,l,u,f.**

History of Specific Countries > Saudi Arabia > Medieval > Early Islamic Period

Watt, W. Montgomery   **BP75**
Muhammad's Mecca: History in the Qur'an. Edinburgh University Press. 1988. ISBN:0-85224-565-3, ISBN13: 978-0-85224-565-1.

Audience: **g,l,u,f.**

History of Specific Countries > Saudi Arabia > Medieval > Wahhabiyah

                    BP195.W2
Wahhabism: A Critical Essay. Cloth Text. Islamic Publications International. North Haledon, NY. 2002. 100p. ISBN:1-889999-31-8, ISBN13: 978-1-889999-31-9. Dewey:297.8/14.

Audience: **u,f.**

DeLong-Bas, Natana J.   **BP195.W2D45 2004**
Wahhabi Islam: From Revival and Reform to Global Jihad. Oxford Unviersity Press. 2004. ISBN:0-19-516991-3, ISBN13: 978-0-19-516991-1.

Audience: **u,f.**

History of Specific Countries > Saudi Arabia > Modern

Abu-Hakima, Ahmad M.   **DS326 .A27**
History of Eastern Arabia: Rise and Development of Bahrain, Kuwait and Wahhabi Saudi Arabia. Trade Cloth. International Book Centre, Inc. Troy, MI. 1988. ISBN:0-86685-473-8, ISBN13: 978-0-86685-473-3. Dewey:953.604.
Audience: **l,u,f.**

AbuKhalil, Asad   **DS228.U6**
The Battle for Saudi Arabia: Royalty, Fundamentalism, and Global Power. Trade Paper. Seven Stories Press. New York, NY. 2003. 176p. An Open Media Book Ser. ISBN:1-58322-610-9, ISBN13: 978-1-58322-610-0. Dewey:327.5/380/73.
Audience: **g,l,u,f.**

Baker, P. Randall   **DS247.H47 B34**
King Husain and the Kingdom of Hejaz. John Glubb (Introduction by). Trade Cloth. Oleander Press, The. Cambridge, 1979. 257p. Arabia Past and Present Ser., Vol. 10 ISBN:0-900891-48-3, ISBN13: 978-0-900891-48-9. Dewey:953/.8. LCCN:79-320408.
Audience: **g,l,u,f.**

Commins, David   **BP195.W2**
The Wahhabi Mission and Saudi Arabia. Cloth over Boards, Trade Cloth. I. B. Tauris & Company, Ltd. London, 2006. 288p. Library of Modern Middle East Studies ISBN:1-84511-080-3, ISBN13: 978-1-84511-080-2. Dewey:297.81409538. LCCN:2006-295872.
Audience: **l,u,f.**

Cordesman, Anthony H.   **DS244**
Saudi Arabia Enters the Twenty-First Century: The Political, Foreign Policy, Economic, and Energy Dimensions. Trade Cloth. Greenwood Publishing Group, Inc. Portsmouth, NH. 2003. 608p. ISBN:0-275-97998-9, ISBN13: 978-0-275-97998-0. Dewey:953.805/3. LCCN:2002-044974.
Audience: **u,f.**

Cordesman, Anthony H.   **UA853**
& Obaid, Nawaf
National Security in Saudi Arabia: Threats, Responses, and Challenges. Trade Cloth. Greenwood Publishing Group, Inc. Portsmouth, NH. 2005. 452p. ISBN:0-275-98811-2, ISBN13: 978-0-275-98811-1. Dewey:355/.0330538. LCCN:2005-016847.
Audience: **u,f.** *Choice, 2006.*

Helms, Christine M.   **DS244.H44 1981**
The Cohesion of Saudi Arabia: Evolution of Political Identity. Trade Cloth. Johns Hopkins University Press. Baltimore, MD. 1993. 315p. ISBN:0-8018-2475-3, ISBN13: 978-0-8018-2475-3. Dewey:953/.8. LCCN:80-008026.
Audience: **l,u,f.** 𝐵

Kechichian, Joseph A.   **DS244.52.K44 2001**
Succession in Saudi Arabia. Cloth over Boards. Palgrave Macmillan. New York, NY. 2001. 304p. ISBN:0-312-23880-0, ISBN13: 978-0-312-23880-3. Dewey:953.8. LCCN:00-062607.
Audience: **u,f.** *Choice, 2002.*

Kostiner, Joseph   **DS244.K68 1993**
The Making of Saudi Arabia, 1916-1936: From Chieftancy to Monarchical State. Trade Cloth. Oxford University Press, Inc. New York, NY. 1993. 272p. Studies in Middle Eastern History

ISBN:0-19-507440-8, ISBN13: 978-0-19-507440-6. Dewey:953.8. LCCN:92-017948.
Audience: **l,u,f.** *Choice, 1994.*

Long, David E.   **DS204.L65 1997**
The Kingdom of Saudi Arabia. Trade Cloth. University Press of Florida. Gainesville, FL. 1997. 192p. ISBN:0-8130-1471-9, ISBN13: 978-0-8130-1471-5. Dewey:953.8. LCCN:96-045618.
Audience: **g,l,u,f.** *Choice, 1997.*

Niblock, Timothy   **DS244.63**
Saudi Arabia: Power, Legitimacy and Survival. Paper over Boards. Routledge. New York, NY. 2006. XVIII, 206p. Contemporary Middle East Ser. ISBN:0-415-27419-2, ISBN13: 978-0-415-27419-7. Dewey:953.8053.
Audience: **u,f.**

Quandt, William B.   **DS227**
Saudi Arabia in the 1980's: Foreign Policy, Security, and Oil. Trade Cloth. Brookings Institution Press. Washington, DC. 1981. 190p. ISBN:0-8157-7286-6, ISBN13: 978-0-8157-7286-6. Dewey:327.538. LCCN:82-018086.
Audience: **u,f.**

Teitelbaum, Joshua   **DS247.9.H45T45 2001**
The Rise and Fall of the Hashemite Kingdom of the Hijaz. Trade Cloth. New York University Press. New York, NY. 2001. xviii, 310p. ISBN:0-8147-8271-X, ISBN13: 978-0-8147-8271-2. Dewey:953.8. LCCN:00-051978.
Audience: **l,u,f.** *Choice, 2002.*

Wilson, Rodney, et al.   **HC415.33.W55 2004**
Economic Development in Saudi Arabia. Monica Malik, Abdullah Al Salamah & Ahmed Al Rajhi (Authors), University of Durham, Institute for Middle Eastern and Islamic Studies Staff (Contribution by). Paper over Boards. Taylor & Francis Group. Abingdon, 2004. 208p. RoutledgeCurzon Durham Modern Middle East and Islamic World Ser. ISBN:0-7007-1729-3, ISBN13: 978-0-7007-1729-3. Dewey:330.9538. LCCN:2003-007645.
Audience: **u,f.**

Winder, R. Bayly   **DS242 .W56 1980**
Saudi Arabia in the Nineteenth Century. Library Binding. Hippocrene Books, Inc. New York, NY. 1980. xiv, 312p. ISBN:0-374-98676-2, ISBN13: 978-0-374-98676-6. Dewey:953/.804. LCCN:80-013191.
Audience: **u,f.**

History of Specific Countries > Bahrain

Abu-Hakima, Ahmad M.   **DS326 .A27**
History of Eastern Arabia: Rise and Development of Bahrain, Kuwait and Wahhabi Saudi Arabia. Trade Cloth. International Book Centre, Inc. Troy, MI. 1988. ISBN:0-86685-473-8, ISBN13: 978-0-86685-473-3. Dewey:953.604.
Audience: **l,u,f.**

Zahlan, Rosemarie Said   **DS326**
Making of the Modern Gulf States: Kuwait, Bahrain, Qatar, the United Arab Emirates and Oman. Trade Paper. Garnet Publishing, Ltd. Reading, 1998. 212p. ISBN:0-86372-229-6, ISBN13: 978-0-86372-229-5. Dewey:953.6.
Audience: **l,u,f.**

History of Specific Countries > Kuwait

Abu-Hakima, Ahmad M.   **DS326 .A27**
History of Eastern Arabia: Rise and Development of Bahrain,
Kuwait and Wahhabi Saudi Arabia. Trade Cloth. International
Book Centre, Inc. Troy, MI. 1988. ISBN:0-86685-473-8,
ISBN13: 978-0-86685-473-3. Dewey:953.604.
Audience: **l,u,f.**

Abu-Hakima, Ahmad M.   **DS247.K85**
The Modern History of Kuwait, 1750-1965. Trade Cloth.
International Book Centre, Inc. Troy, MI. 1983.
ISBN:0-7189-0259-9, ISBN13: 978-0-7189-0259-9.
Dewey:953.67.
Audience: **l,u,f.**

Al-Mughni, Haya   **HQ1734**
Women in Kuwait: The Politics of Gender. Ed. 2. Trade Paper.
Saqi Books. London, 2001. 220p. ISBN:0-86356-358-9,
ISBN13: 978-0-86356-358-4. Dewey:305.42/095367.
Audience: **u,f.** *Choice, 2001.*

Cordesman, Anthony H.   **DS247.K88C67 1997**
Kuwait: Recovery and Security after the Gulf War. Trade Paper.
Westview Press. Boulder, CO. 1997. 176p. ISBN:0-8133-3243-5,
ISBN13: 978-0-8133-3243-7. Dewey:953.6705/3.
LCCN:96-044401.
Audience: **l,u,f.** *Choice, 1997.*

Crystal, Jill   **DS247.K88 C79 1995**
Oil and Politics in the Gulf: Rulers and Merchants in Kuwait
and Qatar. Edmund Burke, Michael C. Hudson, Walid Kazziha,
Rashid Khalidi, Serif Mardin, Roger Owen, Basim Musallam,
Avi Shlaim, Malcolm Yapp, Steven Rosenberg & J. W. Bruce
(Contribution by). Trade Paper. Cambridge University Press.
New York, NY. 1995. 256p. Middle East Library, No. 24
ISBN:0-521-46635-0, ISBN13: 978-0-521-46635-6.
Dewey:953.67. LCCN:95-129737.
Audience: **u,f.** *Choice, 1991.*

Finnie, David H.   **DS70.96.K9F56 1992**
Shifting Lines in the Sand: Kuwait's Elusive Frontier with Iraq.
Trade Cloth. Harvard University Press. Cambridge, MA. 1992.
256p. ISBN:0-674-80639-5, ISBN13: 978-0-674-80639-9.
Dewey:341.42026656705367. LCCN:92-008938.
Audience: **l,u,f.** *Choice, 1993.*

Ismael, J. S.   **HN669.A8.I82**
Kuwait: Social Change in Historical Perspective. Trade Cloth.
Syracuse University Press. Syracuse, NY. 1982. 214p.
ISBN:0-8156-2254-6, ISBN13: 978-0-8156-2254-3.
Dewey:953/.67. LCCN:81-021244.
Audience: **l,u,f.** ₿

Ismael, Jacqueline S.   **HN669.A8 I82 1993**
Kuwait: Dependency and Class in a Rentier State. Ed. 2. Trade
Paper. University Press of Florida. Gainesville, FL. 1993. 256p.
ISBN:0-8130-1186-8, ISBN13: 978-0-8130-1186-8.
Dewey:306/.095367. LCCN:92-037002.
Audience: **u,f.**

Longva, Anh Nga   **JV8750.8.A3L66 1997**
Walls Built on Sand: Migration, Exclusion and Society in
Kuwait. Trade Paper. Westview Press. Boulder, CO. 1997. 280p.
ISBN:0-8133-2758-X, ISBN13: 978-0-8133-2758-7.
Dewey:304.8/5367. LCCN:96-049172.
Audience: **u,f.** *Choice, 1997.*

Tétreault, Mary Ann   **DS247.K88T48 2000**
Stories of Democracy: Politics and Society in Contemporary
Kuwait. Trade Cloth. Columbia University Press. New York,
NY. 2000. 326p. ISBN:0-231-11488-5, ISBN13:
978-0-231-11488-2. Dewey:953.67. LCCN:99-047271.
Audience: **l,u,f.**

Zahlan, Rosemarie Said   **DS326**
Making of the Modern Gulf States: Kuwait, Bahrain, Qatar, the
United Arab Emirates and Oman. Trade Paper. Garnet
Publishing, Ltd. Reading, 1998. 212p. ISBN:0-86372-229-6,
ISBN13: 978-0-86372-229-5. Dewey:953.6.
Audience: **l,u,f.**

History of Specific Countries > Oman

Eickelman, Christine   **HQ1731**
Women and Community in Oman. Trade Cloth. New York
University Press. New York, NY. 1984. 251p.
ISBN:0-8147-2165-6, ISBN13: 978-0-8147-2165-0.
Dewey:305.4/2/095353. LCCN:84-000974.
Audience: **l,u,f.**

Kechichian, Joseph A.   **DS247.O68K43 1995**
Oman and the World: The Emergence of an Independent
Foreign Policy. Trade Paper. RAND Corporation, The. Santa
Monica, CA. 1995. 409p. ISBN:0-8330-2332-2, ISBN13:
978-0-8330-2332-2. Dewey:953.53. LCCN:96-131215.
Audience: **l,u,f.**

Owtram, Francis   **DS247.O68.O98 2004**
A Modern History of Oman: Formation of the State since 1920.
Cloth over Boards. I. B. Tauris & Company, Ltd. London, 2004.
224p. Library of Modern Middle East Studies, Vol. 30
ISBN:1-86064-617-4, ISBN13: 978-1-86064-617-1.
Dewey:953.53. LCCN:2004-304780.
Audience: **l,u,f.**

Phillips, Wendel   **DS247.O65 P5**
Oman: A History. Trade Cloth. Librairie du Liban Publications.
1971. 246p. ISBN:0-86685-024-4, ISBN13: 978-0-86685-024-7.
Dewey:953/.5.
Audience: **g,l,u,f.**

Pridham, Brian R.   **HC415.35.O53 1987**
(Editor)
Oman: Economic, Social and Strategic Developments. Trade
Cloth. Croom Helm, Ltd. London, 272p. ISBN:0-7099-4056-4,
ISBN13: 978-0-7099-4056-2. Dewey:953/.53. LCCN:86-016823.
Audience: **l,u,f.**

Ruzaik, Ibn   **DS247.O65**
History of the Imams and Seyyids of Oman: From A.D. 661 to
1856. George P. Badger (Introduction by). Trade Cloth. Burt
Franklin Publisher. New York, NY. 1970. Hakluyt Society First
Ser., No. 44 ISBN:0-8337-3121-1, ISBN13: 978-0-8337-3121-0.
Dewey:953/.53. LCCN:70-131410.
Audience: **u,f.**

Skeet, Ian   **DS247.O62 S5**
Muscat and Oman: The End of an Era. Trade Cloth.
Transatlantic Arts, Inc. Albuquerque, NM. 1974.
ISBN:0-571-10476-2, ISBN13: 978-0-571-10476-5.
Dewey:915.3/5/045. LCCN:74-171461.
Audience: **g,l,u,f.**

Wikan, Unni &   HQ1731
  Wiggins, Peter
Behind the Veil in Arabia: Women in Oman. Trade Cloth. Johns
Hopkins University Press. Baltimore, MD. 1989. 336p.
ISBN:0-8018-2729-9, ISBN13: 978-0-8018-2729-7.
Dewey:305.42/0953. LCCN:81-018622.
Audience: **g,l,u,f.** *B*

Wilkinson, John C.   **DS247.O68W55 1987**
The Imamate Tradition of Oman. Trade Cloth. Cambridge
University Press. New York, NY. 1987. 432p. Cambridge
Middle East Library, No. 11 ISBN:0-521-32713-X, ISBN13:
978-0-521-32713-8. Dewey:953/.53. LCCN:86-018398.
Audience: **u,f.** *Choice, 1988.*

History of Specific Countries > Yemen

Burrowes, Robert D.   **DS247.Y45B87 1995**
Historical Dictionary of Yemen. Trade Cloth. Scarecrow Press,
Inc. Lanham, MD. 1995. 528p. Asian Historical Dictionaries
Ser., No. 17 ISBN:0-8108-2987-8, ISBN13: 978-0-8108-2987-9.
Dewey:953/.3/003. LCCN:94-046534.
Audience: **g,l,u,f.**

Carapico, Sheila   **JQ1842.A91 C37 1998**
Civil Society in the Yemen: The Political Economy of Activism
in Modern Arabia. Julia A. Clancy-Smith, Israel Gershoni,
Roger Owen, Yezid Sayigh, Charles Tripp & Judith E. Tucker
(Contribution by). Trade Cloth. Cambridge University Press.
New York, NY. 1998. 272p. Middle East Studies, No. 9
ISBN:0-521-59098-1, ISBN13: 978-0-521-59098-3.
Dewey:306.2. LCCN:97-023259.
Audience: **l,u,f.** *Choice, 1998.*

Dresch, Paul   **DS247.Y48 D74 2000**
A History of Modern Yemen. Cloth Text. Cambridge University
Press. New York, NY. 2000. 304p. ISBN:0-521-79092-1,
ISBN13: 978-0-521-79092-5. Dewey:953.305.
LCCN:00-029266.
Audience: **l,u,f.**

Dresch, Paul   **DS247.Y44D74 1989**
Tribes, Government, and History in Yemen. Trade Cloth. Oxford
University Press, Inc. New York, NY. 1990. 480p.
ISBN:0-19-827331-2, ISBN13: 978-0-19-827331-8.
Dewey:953.3/2. LCCN:89-009368.
Audience: **l,u,f.** *Choice, 1991.*

Goitein, S. D. (Editor)   **DS135.Y4**
From the Land of Sheba: Tales of the Jews of Yemen. Trade
Paper. Knopf Publishing Group. New York, NY. 1976. 160p.
ISBN:0-8052-0543-8, ISBN13: 978-0-8052-0543-5.
Dewey:915.3/32/06924. LCCN:73-081342.
Audience: **g,l,u,f.**

Halliday, Fred   **DS247.A28H35 1990**
Revolution and Foreign Policy: The Case of South Yemen,
1967-1987. Trade Cloth. Cambridge University Press. New
York, NY. 1990. 331p. Cambridge Middle East Library, No. 21
ISBN:0-521-32856-X, ISBN13: 978-0-521-32856-2.
Dewey:327.53/35. LCCN:89-000583.
Audience: **u,f.** *Choice, 1990.*

Hathaway, Jane   **DT97.H38 2003**
A Tale of Two Factions: Myth, Memory, and Identity in
Ottoman Egypt and Yemen. Cloth Text. State University of New
York Press. Albany, NY. 2003. 288p. SUNY Series in the Social

and Economic History of the Middle East ISBN:0-7914-5883-0,
ISBN13: 978-0-7914-5883-9. Dewey:962/.03.
LCCN:2003-055622.
Audience: **u,f.**

Mundy, Martha   **HN664.A8M85 1995**
Domestic Government: Kinship, Community, and Polity in
North Yemen. Cloth Text. I. B. Tauris & Company, Ltd.
London, 1995. 256p. Society and Culture in the Modern Middle
East Ser. ISBN:1-85043-918-4, ISBN13: 978-1-85043-918-9.
Dewey:306/.09533/2. LCCN:94-061502.
Audience: **l,u,f.**

Peterson, John E. &   **DS247.Y48 P47 1982**
  Peters, Ronald M.
Yemen: The Search for a Modern State. Trade Cloth. Johns
Hopkins University Press. Baltimore, MD. 1994. 224p.
ISBN:0-8018-2784-1, ISBN13: 978-0-8018-2784-6.
Dewey:953/.3205. LCCN:81-048187.
Audience: **g,l,u,f.**

Swagman, Charles F.   **HN664.Z9C678 1988**
Development and Change in Highland Yemen. Trade Cloth.
University of Utah Press. Salt Lake City, UT. 1988. 224p.
ISBN:0-87480-295-4, ISBN13: 978-0-87480-295-5.
Dewey:307.1/4/095332. LCCN:88-017082.
Audience: **l,u,f.** *Choice, 1989.*

Wenner, Manfred W.   **H31 .J6**
Modern Yemen, 1918-1966. Trade Cloth. Johns Hopkins
University Press. Baltimore, MD. 1984. 256p. Studies in
Historical and Political Science, 85th Series No. 1 (1967)
ISBN:0-8018-0668-2, ISBN13: 978-0-8018-0668-1.
Dewey:953/.3/205.
Audience: **l,u,f.**

Wenner, Manfred W.   **DS247.Y4W44 1991**
The Yemen Arab Republic: Development and Change in an
Ancient Land. Cloth Text. Westview Press. Boulder, CO. 1991.
194p. ISBN:0-89158-774-8, ISBN13: 978-0-89158-774-3.
Dewey:953.32. LCCN:90-024033.
Audience: **l,u,f.** *Choice, 1991.*

History of Specific Countries > United Arab Emirates

Heard-Bey, Frauke   **DS247.T8**
From Trucial States to United Arab Emirates: A Society in
Transisition. Ed. 2. Longman. 1996. ISBN:0-582-27728-0,
ISBN13: 978-0-582-27728-1.
Audience: **l,u,f.**

Zahlan, Rosemarie Said   **DS326**
Making of the Modern Gulf States: Kuwait, Bahrain, Qatar, the
United Arab Emirates and Oman. Trade Paper. Garnet
Publishing, Ltd. Reading, 1998. 212p. ISBN:0-86372-229-6,
ISBN13: 978-0-86372-229-5. Dewey:953.6.
Audience: **l,u,f.**

History of Specific Countries > Iran > General

Arjomand, Said A.   **DS292.A75**
The Shadow of God and the Hidden Inam: Religion, Political Order, and Societal Change in Shi'ite Iran from the Beginning to 1890. Paper Text. University of Chicago Press. Chicago, IL. 1997. xii, 368p. Publications of the Center for Middle Eastern Studies, No. 17 ISBN:0-226-02784-8, ISBN13: 978-0-226-02784-5. Dewey:322/.1/0955. LCCN:83-027196.
Audience: **l,u,f.** *B*

Avery, Peter (Editor), et al.   **DS288**
The Cambridge History of Iran. Stanley I. Grossman, Gavin R. G. Hambly & C. P. Melville (Editors). Trade Cloth. Cambridge University Press. New York, NY. 1991. 1096p. The Cambridge History of Iran Ser., Vol. 7 ISBN:0-521-20095-4, ISBN13: 978-0-521-20095-0. Dewey:955. LCCN:67-012845.
Audience: **l,u,f.** *Choice, 1992.*

Bailey, Harold (Editor)   **DS272 .C34**
The Cambridge History of Iran, Set. Quantity Pack, Trade Cloth. Cambridge University Press. New York, NY. 1993. The Cambridge History of Iran Ser. ISBN:0-521-45148-5, ISBN13: 978-0-521-45148-2. Dewey:955.
Audience: **l,u,f.**

Barthold, W.   **DS254.8**
An Historical Geography of Iran. Soucek, Svat (Translator); Bosworth, C.E. (Editor). Princeton University Press. 1984. ISBN:0-691-05418-5, ISBN13: 978-0-691-05418-6.
Audience: **u,f.**

Beck, Lois & Nashat,   **HQ1735.2.W655 2004**
Guity (Editors)
Women in Iran from 1800 to the Islamic Republic. Trade Cloth. University of Illinois Press. Champaign, IL. 2004. 304p. ISBN:0-252-02937-2, ISBN13: 978-0-252-02937-0. Dewey:305.4/0955. LCCN:2003-024078.
Audience: **l,u,f.** *Choice, 2005.*

Boyle, J. A. &
Grossman, Stanley I. (Editors)
The Saljuq and Mongol Periods. Trade Cloth. Cambridge University Press. New York, NY. 1968. 778p. The Cambridge History of Iran Ser., Vol. 5 ISBN:0-521-06936-X, ISBN13: 978-0-521-06936-6. Dewey:955. LCCN:67-012845.
Audience: **l,u,f.**

Ebadi, Shirin   **KMH2460.I2313 2000**
History and Documentation of Human Rights in Iran. Bibliotheca Persica. 2000. ISBN:0-933273-40-1, ISBN13: 978-0-933273-40-5.
Audience: **u,f.**

Fisher, W. B. &
Grossman, Stanley I. (Editors)
The Land of Iran. Trade Cloth. Cambridge University Press. New York, NY. 1968. 804p. The Cambridge History of Iran Ser., Vol. 1 ISBN:0-521-06935-1, ISBN13: 978-0-521-06935-9. Dewey:955. LCCN:67-012845.
Audience: **l,u,f.**

Friedl, Erika   **HQ1735.2.F75 1989**
Women of Deh Koh: Lives in an Iranian Village. Trade Cloth. Smithsonian Institution Press. Washington, DC. 1989. 251p.

ISBN:0-87474-400-8, ISBN13: 978-0-87474-400-2. Dewey:305.4/2/0955. LCCN:88-015613.
Audience: **l,u,f.**

Frye, R. N. &   **DS272**
Grossman, Stanley I. (Editors)
The Period from the Arab Invasion to the Salj. Trade Cloth. Cambridge University Press. New York, NY. 1975. 747p. The Cambridge History of Iran Ser., Vol. 4 ISBN:0-521-20093-8, ISBN13: 978-0-521-20093-6. Dewey:955. LCCN:67-012845.
Audience: **l,u,f.**

Frye, Richard N.   **DS275.F7 1993**
The Heritage of Persia. Paper Text. Mazda Publishers, Inc. Costa Mesa, CA. 1993. xiv, 330p. Bibliotheca Iranica Ser., No. 1 ISBN:1-56859-008-3, ISBN13: 978-1-56859-008-0. Dewey:935. LCCN:93-034039.
Audience: **g,l,u,f.**

Gershevitch, Ilya &   **DS272 1985**
Grossman, Stanley I. (Editors)
The Median and Archaemenian Periods. Trade Cloth. Cambridge University Press. New York, NY. 1985. 964p. The Cambridge History of Iran Ser., Vol. 2 ISBN:0-521-20091-1, ISBN13: 978-0-521-20091-2. Dewey:955. LCCN:67-012845.
Audience: **l,u,f.**

Jackson, Peter (Editor),   **DS272 1986**
et al.
The Timurid and Safavid Periods. Lawrence Lockhart & Stanley I. Grossman (Editors). Trade Cloth. Cambridge University Press. New York, NY. 1986. 1120p. The Cambridge History of Iran Ser., Vol. 6 ISBN:0-521-20094-6, ISBN13: 978-0-521-20094-3. Dewey:955. LCCN:67-012845.
Audience: **l,u,f.** *Choice, 1986.*

Katouzian, Homa   **DS315.K38 2003**
Iranian History and Politics: State and Society in Perpetual Conflict. Paper over Boards. Taylor & Francis Group. Philadelphia, PA. 2003. 304p. RoutledgeCurzon/BIPS Persian Studies ISBN:0-415-29754-0, ISBN13: 978-0-415-29754-7. Dewey:955.05. LCCN:2002-068278.
Audience: **l,u,f.** *Choice, 2003.*

Lorentz, John H.   **DS270.L67 1995**
Historical Dictionary of Iran. Trade Cloth. Scarecrow Press, Inc. Lanham, MD. 1995. 352p. Asian Historical Dictionaries Ser., No. 16 ISBN:0-8108-2994-0, ISBN13: 978-0-8108-2994-7. Dewey:955/.003. LCCN:94-045843.
Audience: **g,l,u,f.**

Moreen, Vera Basch   **DS135.I65 M67**
Iranian Jewry's Hour of Peril and Heroism. Cloth Text. Columbia University Press. New York, NY. 1987. 247p. A Study of the American Academy for Jewish Research ISBN:0-231-06578-7, ISBN13: 978-0-231-06578-8. Dewey:955/.004924.
Audience: **l,u,f.**

Najmabadi, Afsaneh   **HQ1735.2.Z9Q36 1998**
The Story of the Daughters of Quchan: Gender and National Memory in Iranian History. Trade Paper. Syracuse University Press. Syracuse, NY. 1998. 232p. Modern Intellectual and Political History of the Middle East Ser. ISBN:0-8156-2791-2, ISBN13: 978-0-8156-2791-3. Dewey:305.4/0955. LCCN:98-026381.
Audience: **l,u,f.** *Choice, 1999.*

Najmabadi, Afsaneh   HQ1735.2 .N35 2005
Women with Mustaches and Men Without Beards: Gender and
Sexual Anxieties of Iranian Modernity. Trade Cloth. University
of California Press. Berkeley, CA. 2005. 366p.
ISBN:0-520-24262-9, ISBN13: 978-0-520-24262-3.
Dewey:305.42/0955/09034. LCCN:2004-017984.
                       Audience: **l,u,f.** *Choice, 2006.*

Nashat, Guity & Beck,   HQ1735.2.W656 2003
Lois (Editors)
Women in Iran from the Rise of Islam to 1800. Trade Cloth.
University of Illinois Press. Champaign, IL. 2003. 272p.
ISBN:0-252-02839-2, ISBN13: 978-0-252-02839-7.
Dewey:305.42/0955. LCCN:2002-152213.
                       Audience: **l,u,f.** *Choice, 2004.*

Sanasarian, Eliz   BL2270 .S26 2000
Religious Minorities in Iran. Julia A. Clancy-Smith, Israel
Gershoni, Roger Owen, Yezid Sayigh, Charles Tripp & Judith E.
Tucker (Contribution by). Cloth Text. Cambridge University
Press. New York, NY. 2000. 249p. Middle East Studies, Vol. 13
ISBN:0-521-77073-4, ISBN13: 978-0-521-77073-6.
Dewey:305.60955. LCCN:99-032293.
                       Audience: **l,u,f.** *Choice, 2001.*

Sykes, Percy   DS272
A History of Persia. Ed. 3. Macmillan. 1963.
                       Audience: **u,f.**

Vali, Abbas   DS59.K86
Kurds and Ethnicity in Iran. Trade Cloth. I. B. Tauris &
Company, Ltd. London, 2003. 256p. ISBN:1-86064-050-8,
ISBN13: 978-1-86064-050-6. Dewey:323.1/19159.
                       Audience: **l,u,f.**

Yarshater, E. (Editor)   DS272
The Cambridge History of Iran: The Seleucid, Parthian and
Sasanid Periods. Trade Cloth. Cambridge University Press. New
York, NY. 1983. 883p. The Cambridge History of Iran Ser., Vol.
3 ISBN:0-521-24693-8, ISBN13: 978-0-521-24693-4.
Dewey:955. LCCN:67-012845.
                       Audience: **l,u,f.**

Yarshater, Ehsan   DS253
(Editor)
Encyclopedia Iranica: Ab-Abd-Al-Hamid. Trade Paper.
Bibliotheca Persica Press. New York, NY. 1982. 112p.
ISBN:0-7100-9090-0, ISBN13: 978-0-7100-9090-4.
Dewey:955/.003/21.
                       Audience: **l,u,f.**

History of Specific Countries > Iran > Early to 651

Olmstead, Arthur T.   DS281
History of the Persian Empire. Trade Paper. University of
Chicago Press. Chicago, IL. 1959. 600p. ISBN:0-226-62777-2,
ISBN13: 978-0-226-62777-9. Dewey:935.05. LCCN:48-007317.
                       Audience: **g,l,u,f.**

History of Specific Countries > Iran > Medieval

Bosworth, Clifford   DS288.7
Edmund
The Ghaznavids: Their Empire in Afghanistan and Eastern Iran,
994-1040. Ed. 2. Librairie du Liban. 1973.
                       Audience: **l,u,f.**

Lambton, Ann K. S.   DS288.L36 1988
Continuity and Change in Medieval Persia: Aspects of
Administrative, Economic and Social History, 11th-144th
Century. Cloth Text. State University of New York Press.
Albany, NY. 1988. 425p. ISBN:0-88706-133-8, ISBN13:
978-0-88706-133-2. Dewey:955/.02. LCCN:87-016192.
                       Audience: **l,u,f.** *Choice, 1988.*

Meisami, Julie S.   BP188.3.K55B3413
(Editor, Translator)
The Sea of Precious Virtues: A Medieval Islamic Mirror for
Princes. Trade Cloth. University of Utah Press. Salt Lake City,
UT. 1990. 468p. ISBN:0-87480-313-6, ISBN13:
978-0-87480-313-6. Dewey:297/.5. LCCN:88-027858.
                       Audience: **u,f.** *Choice, 1991.*

Melville, Charles   DS292.S24 1996
Safavid Persia: The History and Politics of an Islamic Society.
I.B. Tauris. 1996. ISBN:1-86064-023-0, ISBN13:
978-1-86064-023-0.
                       Audience: **u,f.**

History of Specific Countries > Iran > Modern

Abrahamian, Ervand   DS258
Iran Between Two Revolutions. Trade Paper. Princeton
University Press. Princeton, NJ. 1982. 561p. Princeton Studies
on the Near East ISBN:0-691-10134-5, ISBN13:
978-0-691-10134-7. Dewey:955/.04. LCCN:81-047905.
                       Audience: **l,u,f.** ℬ

Afary, Janet   JQ1782.A35 1996
The Iranian Constitutional Revolution, 1906-1911: Grassroots
Democracy, Social Democracy, and the Origins of Feminism.
Trade Cloth. Columbia University Press. New York, NY. 1996.
448p. History and Society of the Modern Middle East Ser.
ISBN:0-231-10350-6, ISBN13: 978-0-231-10350-3.
Dewey:320.955. LCCN:95-050433.
                       Audience: **l,u,f.** *Choice, 1997.*

Algar, Hamid   DS299
Religion and State in Iran, 1785-1906: The Role of the 'Ulama
in the Qajar Period. Trade Cloth. University of California Press.
Berkeley, CA. 1980. Near Eastern Center Series, UCLA, No. 17
ISBN:0-520-04100-3, ISBN13: 978-0-520-04100-4.
Dewey:297/.197/7. LCCN:72-079959.
                       Audience: **l,u,f.**

Babayan, Kathryn   BF188.8.I7
Mystics, Monarchs and Messiahs: Cultural Landscapes of Early
Modern Iran. Trade Paper. Harvard University Press. Cambridge,
MA. 2003. 270p. Harvard Middle Eastern Monographs, Vol. 35
ISBN:0-932885-28-4, ISBN13: 978-0-932885-28-9.
Dewey:297/.0955. LCCN:2002-105220.
                       Audience: **u,f.** *Choice, 2004.*

Bill, James A.   **E183.8.I7B5 1988**
The Eagle and the Lion: The Tragedy of American-Iranian
Relations. Trade Paper. Yale University Press. Cumberland, RI.
1989. 520p. ISBN:0-300-04412-7, ISBN13: 978-0-300-04412-6.
Dewey:327.73055.

Audience: **l,u,f.** *Choice, 1988.*

Farmaian, Sattareh F.   **CT1888.F37A3 1992**
Daughter of Persia: A Woman's Journey from Her Father's
Harem Through the Islamic Revolution. Dona Munker
(Contribution by). Trade Cloth. Crown Publishing Group. New
York, NY. 1992. 448p. ISBN:0-517-58697-5, ISBN13:
978-0-517-58697-6. Dewey:955.05/092 B. LCCN:91-023916.

Audience: **g,l,u,f.**

Fischer, Michael M. J.   **BP192.7.I68F57 2003**
Iran: From Religious Dispute to Revolution. Ed. 2. Trade Paper.
University of Wisconsin Press. Chicago, IL. 2003. 360p.
ISBN:0-299-18474-9, ISBN13: 978-0-299-18474-2.
Dewey:306.6/97/0955. LCCN:2002-074034.

Audience: **u,f.**

Ghani, Cyrus   **DS317.G47 2000**
Iran and the Rise of Reza Shah: From Qajar Collapse to Pahlavi
Power. Trade Paper. I. B. Tauris & Company, Ltd. London,
2001. 304p. ISBN:1-86064-629-8, ISBN13: 978-1-86064-629-4.
Dewey:955.05/2/092. LCCN:2001-268172.

Audience: **l,u,f.**

Guppy, Shusha   **DS316.F36**
The Blindfold Horse: Memories of a Persian Childhood. Trade
Cloth. Beacon Press. Boston, MA. 1989. 256p.
ISBN:0-8070-7042-4, ISBN13: 978-0-8070-7042-0.
Dewey:955.05/092 B. LCCN:88-047883.

Audience: **g,l,u,f.**

Hiro, Dilip   **DS79.75.H57 2001**
Neighbours, Not Friends: Iraq and Iran after the Gulf Wars.
Paper over Boards. Routledge. New York, NY. 2001. 432p.
ISBN:0-415-25411-6, ISBN13: 978-0-415-25411-3.
Dewey:956.7044/3. LCCN:2001-020487.

Audience: **l,u,f.**

Keddie, Nikki R. &   **DS316.3.K42 2003**
  Richard, Yann
Modern Iran: Roots and Results of Revolution. Trade Paper.
Yale University Press. Cumberland, RI. 2003. 406p.
ISBN:0-300-09856-1, ISBN13: 978-0-300-09856-3.
Dewey:955.05. LCCN:2003-052543.

Audience: **l,u,f.** *Choice, 2004.*

Koohi-Kamali, Farideh   **DS269.K87K66 2003**
The Political Development of the Kurds in Iran: Pastoral
Nationalism. Cloth over Boards. Palgrave Macmillan. New
York, NY. 2004. 256p. ISBN:0-333-73169-7, ISBN13:
978-0-333-73169-7. Dewey:955/.00491597. LCCN:2003-053648.

Audience: **u,f.**

Milani, Mohsen M.   **DS318.M495 1994**
The Making of Iran's Islamic Revolution: From Monarchy to
Islamic Republic. Ed. 2. Trade Paper. Westview Press. Boulder,
CO. 1994. xxv, 268p. ISBN:0-8133-8475-3, ISBN13:
978-0-8133-8475-7. Dewey:955/.053. LCCN:94-014600.

Audience: **l,u,f.** *Choice, 1989.*

Paidar, Parvin   **HQ1236.5.I7 P35 1995**
Women and the Political Process in Twentieth-Century Iran.
Charles Tripp (Editor, Contribution by), Julia A. Clancy-Smith,
Israel Gershoni, Roger Owen, Yezid Sayigh & Judith E. Tucker

(Contribution by). Trade Paper. Cambridge University Press.
New York, NY. 1997. 420p. Cambridge Middle East Studies
ISBN:0-521-59572-X, ISBN13: 978-0-521-59572-8.
Dewey:305.4/2/0955.

Audience: **u,f.** *Choice, 1996.*

Sanasarian, Eliz   **HQ1735**
  (Editor)
The Women's Rights Movement in Iran: Mutiny, Appeasement,
and Repression from 1900 to Khomeini. Trade Cloth.
Greenwood Publishing Group, Inc. Portsmouth, NH. 1982. 172p.
ISBN:0-275-90894-1, ISBN13: 978-0-275-90894-2.
Dewey:305.409567. LCCN:82-007714.

Audience: **l,u,f.**

History of Specific Countries > Iran > Modern > Pahlavi Dynasty

Banani, Amin   **DS317.B3**
The Modernization of Iran, 1921-1941. Stanford University
Press. 1961.

Audience: **u,f.**

Baraheni, Reza   **DS318 .B335**
The Crowned Cannibals. Trade Paper. Random House, Inc. New
York, NY. 1977. ISBN:0-394-72357-0, ISBN13:
978-0-394-72357-0. Dewey:320.9/55/05. LCCN:76-062496.

Audience: **g,l,u,f.**

Gasiorowski, Mark J. &   **DS316.6.M64 2004**
  Byrne, Malcolm
Mohammad Mosaddeq and the 1953 Coup in Iran. Trade Cloth.
Syracuse University Press. Syracuse, NY. 2004. 408p. Modern
Intellectual and Political History of the Middle East Ser.
ISBN:0-8156-3018-2, ISBN13: 978-0-8156-3018-0.
Dewey:955.05/3. LCCN:2004-001922.

Audience: **l,u,f.** *Choice, 2005.*

Katouzian, Homa   **DS316.9.M67K38 1990**
Musaddiq and the Struggle for Power in Iran. Cloth Text. I. B.
Tauris & Company, Ltd. London, 1991. 288p.
ISBN:1-85043-210-4, ISBN13: 978-1-85043-210-4.
Dewey:955.05/3/092 B. LCCN:90-206904.

Audience: **u,f.** *Choice, 2000, 1991.*

Pahlavi, Mohammad R.   **DS318**
Answer to History. Trade Cloth. Henry Holt & Company. New
York, NY. 1982. 204p. ISBN:0-8128-6138-8, ISBN13:
978-0-8128-6138-9. Dewey:955/.053/0924. LCCN:80-052039.

Audience: **g,l,u,f.** *B*

History of Specific Countries > Iran > Modern > Islamic Republic 1979-

Afkhami, Mahnaz &   **HQ1735.2.I49 1994**
  Friedl, Erika (Editors)
In the Eye of the Storm: Women in Postrevolutionary Iran.
Robin Morgon (Introduction by). Cloth Text. Syracuse
University Press. Syracuse, NY. 1994. 300p. Contemporary
Issues in the Middle East Ser. ISBN:0-8156-2633-9, ISBN13:
978-0-8156-2633-6. Dewey:305.4/0955/09048.
LCCN:93-049077.

Audience: **g,l,u,f.**

Algar, Hamid JX5486
(Translator)
Constitution of the Islamic Republic of Iran. Trade Cloth. Mizan
Press. Oneonta, NY. 1980. 94p. ISBN:0-933782-07-1, ISBN13:
978-0-933782-07-5. Dewey:342.55/023. LCCN:80-019896.
Audience: l,u,f.

Bakhash, Shaul DS318.8
The Reign of the Ayatollash: Iran and the Islamic Revolution.
Ed. 2. Basic Books. 1990. ISBN:0-465-06890-1, ISBN13:
978-0-465-06890-6.
Audience: l,u,f.

Buchta, Wilfried DS318.9.B83 2000
Who Rules Iran? the Structure of Power in the Islamic
Republic. WINEP and Konrad Adenauer Stiftung. 2000.
ISBN:0-944029-39-6, ISBN13: 978-0-944029-39-8.
Audience: u,f.

Chelkowski, Peter J. & DS318.825.C44 1999
Dabashi, Hamid
Staging a Revolution: The Art of Persuasion in the Islamic
Republic of Iran. Trade Cloth. New York University Press. New
York, NY. 1999. 320p. ISBN:0-8147-1597-4, ISBN13:
978-0-8147-1597-0. Dewey:955.05/42. LCCN:99-020633.
Audience: l,u,f.

Dabashi, Hamid BP63.I68D33 1993
Theology of Discontent: The Ideological Foundation of the
Islamic Revolution in Iran. Trade Cloth. New York University
Press. New York, NY. 1992. 644p. ISBN:0-8147-1839-6,
ISBN13: 978-0-8147-1839-1. Dewey:320.5/57/0955.
LCCN:92-025276.
Audience: l,u,f. *Choice, 1993.*

Esfandiari, Haleh HQ1735.2.I75 1997
Reconstructed Lives: Women and Iran's Islamic Revolution.
Trade Cloth. Johns Hopkins University Press. Baltimore, MD.
1997. 248p. ISBN:0-8018-5618-3, ISBN13: 978-0-8018-5618-1.
Dewey:305.48/6971055. LCCN:97-003080.
Audience: l,u,f. *Choice, 1997.*

Esposito, John L. DS35.74.I7I73 1990
(Editor)
The Iranian Revolution: Its Global Impact. Trade Cloth.
University Press of Florida. Gainesville, FL. 1990. 320p.
ISBN:0-8130-0998-7, ISBN13: 978-0-8130-0998-8.
Dewey:327.55017671. LCCN:90-003083.
Audience: g,l,u,f. *Choice, 1991.*

Hanaway, William, et al. HQ1186.I7W66 1990
Women's Autobiographies in Contemporary Iran. Michael
Hillman, Farzaneh Milani & Afsaneh Najmabadi (Authors).
Trade Paper. Harvard University Press. Cambridge, MA. 1991.
86p. Harvard Middle Eastern Monographs, Vol. No. 25
ISBN:0-932885-05-5, ISBN13: 978-0-932885-05-0.
Dewey:955.05/082. LCCN:90-081298.
Audience: u,f.

Hiro, Dilip DS318.85.H57 1991
The Longest War: The Iran-Iraq Military Conflict. Trade Paper.
Routledge. New York, NY. 1990. 323p. ISBN:0-415-90407-2,
ISBN13: 978-0-415-90407-0. Dewey:955/.054.
LCCN:90-045641.
Audience: g,l,u,f. *Choice, 1991.*

Jalal Al-e, Ahmad DS316.4.A4713 1997
Gharbzadegi: Weststruckness. John Green & Ahmad Alizadeh
(Translators), Ardeshir Mohassess (Illustrator). Paper Text.

Mazda Publishers, Inc. Costa Mesa, CA. 1982. 204p. Iran-e
Literary Collection ISBN:0-939214-07-5, ISBN13:
978-0-939214-07-5. Dewey:955. LCCN:82-061280.
Audience: g,l,u,f.

Khomeini, Iman DS318.K394 2002
Islam in Revolution. Trade Cloth. Kegan Paul International, Ltd.
London, 2002. 460p. Kegan Paul Library of Central Asia
ISBN:0-7103-0805-1, ISBN13: 978-0-7103-0805-4.
Dewey:955.05/42/092. LCCN:2002-032115.
Audience: l,u,f.

Kousha, Mahnaz HQ1735.2.K68 2002
Voices from Iran: The Changing Lives of Iranian Women. Trade
Cloth. Syracuse University Press. Syracuse, NY. 2002. x, 244p.
Gender, Culture, and Politics in the Middle East Ser.
ISBN:0-8156-2962-1, ISBN13: 978-0-8156-2962-7.
Dewey:305.4/0955. LCCN:2002-013874.
Audience: l,u,f.

Kurzman, Charles DS318.8.K87 2004
The Unthinkable Revolution in Iran. Trade Cloth. Harvard
University Press. Cambridge, MA. 2004. 304p.
ISBN:0-674-01328-X, ISBN13: 978-0-674-01328-5.
Dewey:955.05/42. LCCN:2003-056907.
Audience: u,f. *Choice, 2004.*

Mir-Hosseini, Ziba HQ1735.2.M55 1999
Islam and Gender: The Religious Debate in Contemporary Iran.
Cloth Text. Princeton University Press. Princeton, NJ. 1999.
304p. Princeton Studies in Muslim Politics
ISBN:0-691-05815-6, ISBN13: 978-0-691-05815-3.
Dewey:305.4/0955. LCCN:99-022786.
Audience: l,u,f. *Choice, 2000.*

Moallem, Minoo HQ1735.2 .M62 2005
Between Warrior Brother and Veiled Sister: Islamic
Fundamentalism and the Cultural Politics of Patriarchy in Iran.
Trade Cloth. University of California Press. Berkeley, CA. 2005.
256p. ISBN:0-520-24344-7, ISBN13: 978-0-520-24344-6.
Dewey:305.42/0955. LCCN:2004-012262.
Audience: l,u,f.

Mottahedeh, Roy DS266
The Mantle of the Prophet: Religion and Politics in Iran. Trade
Paper. Oneworld Publications. Oxford, 2000. 384p. Oneworld of
Wisdom Ser. ISBN:1-85168-234-1, ISBN13: 978-1-85168-234-8.
Dewey:955/.05.
Audience: g,l,u,f.

Nafisi, Azar PE64.N34A3 2003
Reading Lolita in Tehran: A Memoir in Books. Trade Cloth.
Random House, Inc. New York, NY. 2003. 368p.
ISBN:0-375-50490-7, ISBN13: 978-0-375-50490-7.
Dewey:820.9 B. LCCN:2002-036724.
Audience: g,l,u,f. *Choice, 2003.*

Nashat, Guity HQ1735.2
Women and Revolution in Iran. Paper Text. Westview Press.
Boulder, CO. 1983. 250p. A Replica Edition Ser.
ISBN:0-86531-931-6, ISBN13: 978-0-86531-931-8.
Dewey:305.4/2/0955. LCCN:83-010286.
Audience: l,u,f.

Ramazani, Rouhollah K. DS63.2.I68
Revolutionary Iran: Challenge and Response in the Middle East.
Johns Hopkins University Press. 1986.
Audience: u,f.

Schirazi, Asghar   **DS259.2**
The Constitution of Iran: Politics and the State in the Islamic
Republic. Trade Paper. I. B. Tauris & Company, Ltd. London,
1998. 336p. ISBN:1-86064-253-5, ISBN13: 978-1-86064-253-1.
Dewey:955/.0543.
Audience: **u,f.** *Choice, 1997.*

History of Specific Countries > Armenia > General

Adalian, Rouben Paul   **DS173.A33 2002**
Historical Dictionary of Armenia. Trade Cloth. Scarecrow Press,
Inc. Lanham, MD. 2002. 552p. European Historical Dictionaries
Ser., No. 39 ISBN:0-8108-4337-4, ISBN13: 978-0-8108-4337-0.
Dewey:956.6/2003. LCCN:2002-075844.
Audience: **g,l,u,f.** *Choice, 2003.*

Bournoutian, George A.   **DS175.B65 2002**
A Concise History of the Armenian People. Paper Text. Mazda
Publishers, Inc. Costa Mesa, CA. 2002. 510p.
ISBN:1-56859-141-1, ISBN13: 978-1-56859-141-4.
Dewey:909/.0491992. LCCN:2002-021898.
Audience: **l,u,f.** *Choice, 2003.*

Hovannisian, Richard   **DS175**
G. (Editor)
Armenian People from Ancient to Modern Times, Set. Quantity
Pack, Box or Slipcased. Palgrave Macmillan. New York, NY.
2004. 336p. ISBN:1-4039-6636-2, ISBN13: 978-1-4039-6636-0.
Dewey:947.5/6. LCCN:2004-273378.
Audience: **l,u,f.**

Hovannisian, Richard G.   **DS195.5**
From Versailles to London, 1919-1920, Vol. 2. Trade Cloth.
University of California Press. Berkeley, CA. 1982. 620p. Near
Eastern Center Series, UCLA, Vol. 8 ISBN:0-520-04186-0,
ISBN13: 978-0-520-04186-8. Dewey:956.6/202.
LCCN:72-129613.
Audience: **u,f.**

Hovannisian, Richard G.
The Republic of Armenia: Between Crescent and Sickle:
Partition and Sovietization. Trade Cloth. University of California
Press. Berkeley, CA. 1996. 345p. Near Eastern Center, UCLA
Ser. ISBN:0-520-08804-2, ISBN13: 978-0-520-08804-7.
Dewey:956.62. LCCN:72-129613.
Audience: **u,f.**

Hovannisian, Richard G.
The Republic of Armenia: From London to Sevres, February -
August 1920. Trade Cloth. University of California Press.
Berkeley, CA. 1996. 528p. Near Eastern Center, UCLA Ser.
ISBN:0-520-08803-4, ISBN13: 978-0-520-08803-0.
Dewey:956.62. LCCN:72-129613.
Audience: **u,f.**

Hovannisian, Richard G.
The Republic of Armenia: The First Year, 1918-1919. Trade
Cloth. University of California Press. Berkeley, CA. 1971. 547p.
Near Eastern Center Series, UCLA, Vol. 8 ISBN:0-520-01984-9,
ISBN13: 978-0-520-01984-3. LCCN:72-129613.
Audience: **u,f.**

History of Specific Countries > Armenia > Modern

Libaridian, Gerard J.   **DS195.L52 2004**
Modern Armenia: People, Nation, State. Trade Cloth.
Transaction Publishers. Somerset, NJ. 2004. 296p.
ISBN:0-7658-0205-8, ISBN13: 978-0-7658-0205-7.
Dewey:947.5608. LCCN:2003-054129.
Audience: **l,u,f.** *Choice, 2004.*

Miller, Donald E. &   **DK687 .M59 2003**
Miller, Lorna Touryan
Armenia: Portraits of Survival and Hope. Jerry Berndt
(Photographer). Trade Cloth. University of California Press.
Berkeley, CA. 2003. 256p. ISBN:0-520-23492-8, ISBN13:
978-0-520-23492-5. Dewey:947.56/08. LCCN:2003-000596.
Audience: **g,l,u,f.** *Choice, 2004.*

History of Specific Countries > Afghanistan > General

Adamec, Ludwig W.   **DS356.A27 2003**
Historical Dictionary of Afghanistan. Ed. 3. Trade Cloth.
Scarecrow Press, Inc. Lanham, MD. 2003. 616p. Asian/Oceanian
Historical Dictionaries Ser., No. 47 ISBN:0-8108-4852-X,
ISBN13: 978-0-8108-4852-8. Dewey:958,1/003.
LCCN:2003-010163.
Audience: **g,l,u,f.** *Choice, 2004, 1998, 1992.*

Dupree, Louis   **DS351.5**
Afghanistan. Trade Paper. Oxford University Press, Inc. New
York, NY. 2002. 804p. ISBN:0-19-577634-8, ISBN13:
978-0-19-577634-8. Dewey:958.1.
Audience: **l,u,f.**

Ewans, Martin   **DS356.E95 2002**
Afghanistan: A Short History of Its People and Politics. Trade
Paper. HarperCollins Publishers. New York, NY. 2002. 368p.
ISBN:0-06-050508-7, ISBN13: 978-0-06-050508-0.
Dewey:958.1. LCCN:2002-024954.
Audience: **g,l,u,f.**

Sykes, Percy &   **DS356.S8 2005**
McLane, Charles B.
A History of Afghanistan. Trade Cloth. Kegan Paul
International, Ltd. London, 2005. 912p. Library of Central Asia
Ser. ISBN:0-7103-1174-5, ISBN13: 978-0-7103-1174-0.
Dewey:958.1.
Audience: **u,f.**

Vogelsang, Willem   **DS358.V64 2001**
The Afghans. Trade Cloth. Blackwell Publishing, Inc. Malden,
MA. 2001. 392p. The Peoples of Asia Ser. ISBN:0-631-19841-5,
ISBN13: 978-0-631-19841-3. Dewey:958.1.
LCCN:2001-000332.
Audience: **l,u,f.** *Choice, 2002.*

History of Specific Countries > Afghanistan > Early to 1747

Adamec, Ludwig W.   **DS356.A26 2005**
Historical Dictionary of Afghan Wars, Revolutions and
Insurgencies. Ed. 2. Saddle Stitched, Cloth over Boards.

Scarecrow Press, Inc. Lanham, MD. 2005. 403p. Historical Dictionaries of War, Revolution, and Civil Unrest Ser., No. 30 ISBN:0-8108-4948-8, ISBN13: 978-0-8108-4948-8. Dewey:958.1/003. LCCN:2005-014338.

Audience: l,u,f.

Bosworth, Clifford Edmund   DS288.7
The Ghaznavids: Their Empire in Afghanistan and Eastern Iran, 994-1040. Ed. 2. Librairie du Liban. 1973.

Audience: l,u,f.

Bosworth, Clifford Edmund   DS358.B63 1977
The Later Ghaznavids: Splendour and Decay: The Dynasty in Afghanistan and Norther India, 1040-1186. Columbia University Press. 1977. ISBN:0-231-04428-3, ISBN13: 978-0-231-04428-8.

Audience: l,u,f.

History of Specific Countries > Afghanistan > Modern

Clements, Frank A.   DS356
Conflict in Afghanistan: An Encyclopedia. Library Binding. ABC-CLIO, Inc. Santa Barbara, CA. 2003. 425p. Roots of Modern Conflict Ser. ISBN:1-85109-402-4, ISBN13: 978-1-85109-402-8. Dewey:958.1/003. LCCN:2003-021334.

Audience: l,u,f. *Choice, 2004.*

Gregory, Derek   DS63.2.U5G74 2004
The Colonial Present: Afghanistan, Palestine, and Iraq. Blackwell Pub.. 2004. ISBN:1-57718-089-5, ISBN13: 978-1-57718-089-0.

Audience: u,f.

Grima, Benedicte   GR302.2.P85G75 1992
The Performance of Emotion among Paxtun Women: "The Misfortunes Which Have Befallen Me". Cloth Text. University of Texas Press. Austin, TX. 1992. 255p. Modern Middle East Ser., No. 17 ISBN:0-292-75145-1, ISBN13: 978-0-292-75145-3. Dewey:398.2/08991593. LCCN:91-046493.

Audience: u,f.

Kakar, Mohammad Hassan   DS364.K35 2006
A Political and Diplomatic History of Afghanistan, 1863-1901. Trade Cloth. Brill Academic Publishers, Inc. Boston, MA. 2006. 266p. Brill's Inner Asian Library, Vol. 17 ISBN:90-04-15185-0, ISBN13: 978-90-04-15185-7. Dewey:958.1/03. LCCN:2006-043934.

Audience: u,f.

Maley, William   DS371.2.M342 2002
The Afghanistan Wars. Cloth over Boards. Palgrave Macmillan. New York, NY. 2002. 352p. ISBN:0-333-80290-X, ISBN13: 978-0-333-80290-8. Dewey:958.104/5. LCCN:2002-070642.

Audience: u,f.

Rashid, Ahmed   DS371.2
Taliban: Militant Islam, Oil and Fundamentalism in Central Asia. Trade Cloth. DIANE Publishing Company. Collingdale, PA. 2004. 274p. ISBN:0-7567-7294-X, ISBN13: 978-0-7567-7294-9. Dewey:958.104.

Audience: l,u,f.

Roy, Olivier   BP63.A54 R6813 1990
Islam and Resistance in Afghanistan. Ed. 2. Edmund Burke, Michael C. Hudson, Walid Kazziha, Rashid Khalidi, Serif Mardin, Roger Owen, Basim Musallam, Avi Shlaim & Malcolm Yapp (Contribution by). Trade Paper. Cambridge University Press. New York, NY. 1990. 282p. Cambridge Middle East Library, No. 8 ISBN:0-521-39700-6, ISBN13: 978-0-521-39700-1. Dewey:322/.1/09581. LCCN:90-001709.

Audience: l,u,f. *Choice, 1987.*

Rubin, Barnett R.   DS371.2
The Fragmentation of Afghanistan: State Formation and Collapse in the International System. Ed. 2. Trade Paper. DIANE Publishing Company. Collingdale, PA. 2005. 378p. ISBN:0-7567-9234-7, ISBN13: 978-0-7567-9234-3. Dewey:958.104/5.

Audience: l,u,f. *Choice, 1995.*

Saikal, Amin   DS356
Modern Afghanistan: A History of Struggle and Survival. Cloth over Boards. I. B. Tauris & Company, Ltd. London, 2004. 352p. ISBN:1-85043-437-9, ISBN13: 978-1-85043-437-5. Dewey:958.1.

Audience: l,u,f. *Choice, 2005.*

History of Specific Countries > Egypt > General

Abu-Lughod, Janet L.   DT143.A26
Cairo: One Thousand-One Years of the City Victorious. Cloth Text. Princeton University Press. Princeton, NJ. 1971. 304p. Near East Studies ISBN:0-691-03085-5, ISBN13: 978-0-691-03085-2. Dewey:962/.16. LCCN:73-112992.

Audience: g,l,u,f. *B*

Asante, Molefi Kete   DT70
Culture and Customs of Egypt. Cloth Text. Greenwood Publishing Group, Inc. Portsmouth, NH. 2002. 184p. Culture and Customs of Africa Ser. ISBN:0-313-31740-2, ISBN13: 978-0-313-31740-8. Dewey:962. LCCN:2002-021620.

Audience: g,l,u,f.

Atiya, Nayra   HQ1793
Khul-Khaal: Five Egyptian Women Tell Their Stories. Andrea Rugh (Foreword by). Cloth Text. Syracuse University Press. Syracuse, NY. 1982. 216p. Contemporary Issues in the Middle East Ser. ISBN:0-8156-0177-8, ISBN13: 978-0-8156-0177-7. Dewey:305.4/0962. LCCN:82-005773.

Audience: g,l,u,f.

Badran, Margot   HQ1793.B33 1995
Feminists, Islam and Nation: Gender and the Making of Modern Egypt. Trade Cloth. Princeton University Press. Princeton, NJ. 1994. 368p. ISBN:0-691-03706-X, ISBN13: 978-0-691-03706-6. Dewey:305.4/2/0962. LCCN:94-019055.

Audience: l,u,f. *Choice, 1995.*

Baron, Beth   HQ1793 .B368 2005
Egypt As a Woman: Nationalism, Gender, and Politics. Trade Cloth. University of California Press. Berkeley, CA. 2005. 292p. ISBN:0-520-23857-5, ISBN13: 978-0-520-23857-2. Dewey:305.4/0962. LCCN:2004-008294.

Audience: l,u,f.

Beinin, Joel   DS135.E4B45 1998
The Dispersion of Egyptian Jewry: Culture, Politics, and the Formation of a Modern Diaspora. Trade Cloth. University of

California Press. Berkeley, CA. 1998. 344p. Contraversions Ser., Vol. 11:Critical Studies in Jewish Literature, Culture, and Society ISBN:0-520-21175-8, ISBN13: 978-0-520-21175-9. Dewey:962/.004924. LCCN:97-028043.

Audience: **l,u,f.** *Choice, 1998.*

Bell, Harold I.   **DT92**
Egypt from Alexander the Great to the Arab Conquest. Trade Paper. Ares Publishers, Inc. Golden, CO. 1980. xi, 168p. ISBN:0-89005-354-5, ISBN13: 978-0-89005-354-6. Dewey:932.02.

Audience: **g,l,u,f.**

Fahim, Hussein M.   **DT133.N79 F33 1983**
Egyptian Nubians: Resettlement and Years of Coping. Trade Cloth. University of Utah Press. Salt Lake City, UT. 1983. xiv, 197p. ISBN:0-87480-215-6, ISBN13: 978-0-87480-215-3. Dewey:305.8/931. LCCN:82-024723.

Audience: **u,f.** *B*

Fernea, Robert A. &   **DT135.N8**
  Gerster, Georg
Nubians in Egypt: Peaceful People. Trade Cloth. University of Texas Press. Austin, TX. 1973. 160p. ISBN:0-292-75504-X, ISBN13: 978-0-292-75504-8. Dewey:962/.3. LCCN:73-003078.

Audience: **g,l,u,f.** *B*

Goldschmidt, Arthur &   **DT75.G65 2003**
  Johnston, Robert
Historical Dictionary of Egypt. Ed. 3. Trade Cloth. Scarecrow Press, Inc. Lanham, MD. 2003. 552p. African Historical Dictionaries Ser., No. 89 ISBN:0-8108-4856-2, ISBN13: 978-0-8108-4856-6. Dewey:962/.003. LCCN:2003-010959.

Audience: **g,l,u,f.**

Perry, Glenn E.   **DT100**
The History of Egypt. Cloth Text. Greenwood Publishing Group, Inc. Portsmouth, NH. 2004. 216p. The Greenwood Histories of the Modern Nations Ser. ISBN:0-313-32264-3, ISBN13: 978-0-313-32264-8. Dewey:962. LCCN:2004-004719.

Audience: **g,l,u,f.**

Petry, Carl F. (Editor)   **DT94**
The Cambridge History of Egypt. 2 vols. Daly, M. W. (Editor). Cambridge University Press. 1998.

Audience: **l,u,f.**

Raymond, Andre   **DT143**
Cairo. Trade Cloth. Universe Publishing. New York, NY. 2003. 496p. ISBN:0-7893-1022-8, ISBN13: 978-0-7893-1022-4. Dewey:962/.16.

Audience: **u,f.** *Choice, 2001.*

History of Specific Countries > Egypt > Early to 638

Bagnall, Roger S.   **DT93**
Egypt in Late Antiquity. Trade Paper. Princeton University Press. Princeton, NJ. 1995. 382p. ISBN:0-691-01096-X, ISBN13: 978-0-691-01096-0. Dewey:932/.022.

Audience: **u,f.** *Choice, 1994.*

Butler, Alfred J.   **DT95.55 .B87 1978**
The Arab Conquest of Egypt and the Last Thirty Years of the Roman Dominion. Ed. 2. P. M. Fraser (Editor). Trade Cloth. Oxford University Press, Inc. New York, NY. 1978. 716p.

ISBN:0-19-821678-5, ISBN13: 978-0-19-821678-0. Dewey:932/.02. LCCN:78-324267.

Audience: **l,u,f.**

Pomeroy, Sarah B.   **HQ1137.E3P65 1984**
Women in Hellenistic Egypt: From Alexander to Cleopatra. Trade Cloth. Knopf Publishing Group. New York, NY. 1984. 266p. ISBN:0-8052-3911-1, ISBN13: 978-0-8052-3911-9. Dewey:305.4/0932. LCCN:84-003122.

Audience: **g,l,u,f.** *B*

History of Specific Countries > Egypt > Medieval

Cohen, Mark R.   **HV17.C65 2005**
Poverty and Charity in the Jewish Community of Medieval Egypt. Trade Cloth. Princeton University Press. Princeton, NJ. 2005. 312p. Jews, Christians, and Muslims from the Ancient to the Modern World Ser. ISBN:0-691-09272-9, ISBN13: 978-0-691-09272-0. Dewey:362.5/089/924062. LCCN:2004-062446.

Audience: **u,f.** *Choice, 2006.*

Iyas, Ibn   **DT96.7 .I2313 1981**
An Account of the Ottoman Conquest of Egypt in the Year A. H. 922 (A. D. 1516). W. H. Salmon (Translator). Trade Cloth. Hyperion Press, Inc. Westport, CT. 1980. 117p. ISBN:0-8305-0040-5, ISBN13: 978-0-8305-0040-6. Dewey:962/.02. LCCN:79-002867.

Audience: **u,f.**

Kindi   **PJ709**
The governors and judges of Egypt. AMS Press. 1966.

Audience: **u,f.**

Maqrizi   **DT95.8**
A History of the Ayyubid Sultans of Egypt. Broadhurst, R. J. C. (Translator). Twayne. 1980. ISBN:0-8057-8168-4, ISBN13: 978-0-8057-8168-7.

Audience: **u,f.**

Petry, Carl F.   **HN786.C3**
The Civilian Elite of Cairo in the Later Middle Ages. Trade Cloth. Princeton University Press. Princeton, NJ. 1982. 450p. ISBN:0-691-05329-4, ISBN13: 978-0-691-05329-5. Dewey:305.5/2/096216. LCCN:80-008570.

Audience: **l,u,f.**

Sengers, Gerda   **BF1275.F3S463 2002**
Women and Demons: Cultic Healing in Islamic Egypt. Trade Cloth. Brill Academic Publishers. Leiden, 2003. x, 302p. International Studies in Sociology and Social Anthropology Ser., Vol. 86 ISBN:90-04-12771-2, ISBN13: 978-90-04-12771-5. Dewey:297.3/9. LCCN:2002-028201.

Audience: **u,f.**

Shoshan, Boaz   **DT146.S54 1993**
Popular Culture in Medieval Cairo. David Morgan (Contribution by). Trade Cloth. Cambridge University Press. New York, NY. 1993. 164p. Studies in Islamic Civilization ISBN:0-521-43209-X, ISBN13: 978-0-521-43209-2. Dewey:962.1/6/02. LCCN:92-034084.

Audience: **l,u,f.**

History of Specific Countries > Egypt > Medieval > Fatimids

Halm, Heinz   **BP195.I8**
The Fatimids and Their Traditions of Learning. I.B. Tauris.
1997. ISBN:1-85043-920-6, ISBN13: 978-1-85043-920-2.
Audience: **u,f.**

Mann, Jacob   **DS124**
The Jews in Egypt and in Palestine Under the Fatimid Caliphs.
Trade Cloth. Ktav Publishing House, Inc. Jersey City, NJ. 1970.
Library of Jewish Classics Ser ISBN:0-87068-024-2, ISBN13:
978-0-87068-024-3. Dewey:909.04924.
Audience: **l,u,f.**

Sanders, Paula   **DT146.S26 1994**
Ritual, Politics, and the City in Fatimid Cairo. Cloth Text. State
University of New York Press. Albany, NY. 1994. 231p. SUNY
Series in Medieval Middle East History ISBN:0-7914-1781-6,
ISBN13: 978-0-7914-1781-2. Dewey:962/.16. LCCN:93-022317.
Audience: **u,f.** *Choice, 1994.*

History of Specific Countries > Egypt > Medieval > Mamluks

Ibn Taghribirdi, Abu   **DT96.7 .I2613 1976**
History of Egypt, 1382-1469 A. D. Trade Cloth. A M S Press,
Inc. New York, NY. University of California, Publications in
Semitic Philology ISBN:0-404-58800-X, ISBN13:
978-0-404-58800-7. Dewey:962/.02. LCCN:75-023924.
Audience: **l,u,f.**

Petry, Carl F.   **DT96.7.P47 1994**
Protectors or Praetorians?: The Last Mamluk Sultans and
Egypt's Waning as a Great Power. Cloth Text. State University
of New York Press. Albany, NY. 1994. 280p. SUNY Series in
Medieval Middle East History ISBN:0-7914-2139-2, ISBN13:
978-0-7914-2139-0. Dewey:962/.02. LCCN:94-002925.
Audience: **l,u,f.** *Choice, 1995.*

Philipp, Thomas &   **DT96 .M2156 1998**
Haarmann, Ulrich (Editor, Contribution by)
The Mamluks in Egyptian Politics and Society. P. M. Holt, A.
Levanoni, D. S. Richards, M. Winter, J. Hathaway & David
Morgan (Contribution by). Trade Cloth. Cambridge University
Press. New York, NY. 1998. 320p. Studies in Islamic
Civilization ISBN:0-521-59115-5, ISBN13: 978-0-521-59115-7.
Dewey:962/.02/088355. LCCN:97-009821.
Audience: **u,f.**

Popper, William & Ibn   **DT96.7**
Taghribirdi, Abu al-Mahasin Yusuf
Egypt and Syria under the Circassian Sultans, 1382-1468 A.D.:
Systematic Notes to Ibn Taghri Birdi's Chronicles of Egypt.
AMS Press, Inc. 1977. Publications in Semitic Philology, Nos.
15-16 ISBN:0-404-58815-8, ISBN13: 978-0-404-58815-1.
Audience: **l,u,f.**

Sabra, Adam   **HC830.Z9 P625 2000**
Abdelhamid
Poverty and Charity in Medieval Islam: Mamluk Egypt,
1250-1517. David Morgan (Contribution by). Trade Cloth.
Cambridge University Press. New York, NY. 2000. 208p.
Studies in Islamic Civilization ISBN:0-521-77291-5, ISBN13:
978-0-521-77291-4. Dewey:362.5/57/0962. LCCN:00-023607.
Audience: **u,f.**

History of Specific Countries > Egypt > Modern

Abdel Kader, Soha   **HQ1793.A67 1987**
Egyptian Women in a Changing Society, 1899-1987. Library
Binding. Lynne Rienner Publishers, Inc. Boulder, CO. 1987.
150p. ISBN:0-931477-47-6, ISBN13: 978-0-931477-47-8.
Dewey:305.4/2/0962. LCCN:87-013234.
Audience: **u,f.** *Choice, 1988.*

Al-Ali, Nadje   **HQ1793 .A75 2000**
Secularism, Gender and the State in the Middle East: The
Egyptian Women's Movement. Julia A. Clancy-Smith, Israel
Gershoni, Roger Owen, Yezid Sayigh, Charles Tripp & Judith E.
Tucker (Contribution by). Trade Cloth. Cambridge University
Press. New York, NY. 2000. 282p. Middle East Studies, No. 14
ISBN:0-521-78022-5, ISBN13: 978-0-521-78022-3. Dewey:na.
Audience: **l,u,f.** *Choice, 2001.*

Al-Jabarti, Abd   **DC225**
Al-Rahman
Napoleon in Egypt: Al-Jabartai's Chronicle of the French
Occupation 1798 Expanded Edition for the 250th Anniversary of
Al-Jabarti's Birth. Shmuel Moreh (Author, Translator), Robert
Tignor (Introduction by), Edward Said (Contribution by). Cloth
Text. Markus Wiener Publishers, Inc. Princeton, NJ. 2005.
ISBN:1-55876-338-4, ISBN13: 978-1-55876-338-8.
Dewey:940.2/74/0962. LCCN:2004-053426.
Audience: **l,u,f.**

Al-Sayyid-Marsot, Afaf   **JQ3811**
L.
Egypt's Liberal Experiment, 1922-1936. Trade Cloth. University
of California Press. Berkeley, CA. 1977. xii, 276p.
ISBN:0-520-03109-1, ISBN13: 978-0-520-03109-8.
Dewey:320.9/62/05. LCCN:75-022659.
Audience: **u,f.** *B*

Amin, Qasim   **HQ1793.Q313 1992**
The Liberation of Women: A Document in the History of
Egyptian Feminism. Samiha S. Peterson (Translator). Trade
Cloth. American University in Cairo Press. New York, NY.
1993. 120p. ISBN:977-424-280-7, ISBN13: 978-977-424-280-9.
Dewey:305.42/0962. LCCN:93-210094.
Audience: **l,u,f.**

Baron, Beth   **HQ1793.B37 1994**
The Women's Awakening in Egypt: Culture, Society, and the
Press. Cloth over Boards. Yale University Press. Cumberland,
RI. 1994. 272p. ISBN:0-300-05563-3, ISBN13:
978-0-300-05563-4. Dewey:059.9/27/082. LCCN:93-027067.
Audience: **u,f.** *Choice, 1994.*

Beinin, Joel &   **HD8786.B45**
Lockman, Zachary
Workers on the Nile: Nationalism, Communism, Islam, and the
Egyptian Working Class, 1882-1954. Paper Text. Princeton
University Press. Princeton, NJ. 1989. 512p.
ISBN:0-691-00845-0, ISBN13: 978-0-691-00845-5.
Dewey:305.5/62/0962.
Audience: **u,f.**

Berger, Morroe   **JQ3847**
Bureaucracy and Society in Modern Egypt: A Study of the
Higher Civil Service. Paper Text. Textbook Publishers.
Temecula, CA. 2003. xiii, 231p. ISBN:0-7581-5715-0, ISBN13:
978-0-7581-5715-7. Dewey:351.1.
Audience: **l,u,f.**

Bierman, Irene A.   DC225.N334 2003
  (Editor)
Napoleon in Egypt. Afaf Lufti Al-Sayyid Marsot (Introduction
by). Trade Cloth. Garnet Publishing, Ltd. Reading, 2003. In
association with the Gustav E. von Grunebaum Center for Near
Eastern Studies, University of California, Los Angeles 196p.
ISBN:0-86372-299-7, ISBN13: 978-0-86372-299-8.
Dewey:962/.03. LCCN:2004-272771.

Audience: **u,f.**

Carter, Barbara L.   DT72.C7C37 1986
The Copts in Egyptian Politics 1918 - 1952. Trade Cloth.
Croom Helm, Ltd. London, 1985. 256p. ISBN:0-7099-3417-3,
ISBN13: 978-0-7099-3417-2. Dewey:323.1/1932/062.
LCCN:85-032005.

Audience: **l,u,f.**

Cole, Juan R.I.   DT107.4
Colonialism and Revolution in the Middle East: Social and
Cultural Origins of Egypt's 'Urabi Movement. Princeton
University Press. 1993. ISBN:0-691-05683-8, ISBN13:
978-0-691-05683-8.

Audience: **l,u,f.**

Crabbs, Jack A. Jr.   DT100.C73 1984
The Writing of History in Nineteenth Century Egypt: A Study in
National Transformation. Trade Paper. Wayne State University
Press. Detroit, MI. 1984. 230p. ISBN:0-8143-1761-8, ISBN13:
978-0-8143-1761-7. Dewey:962/.03. LCCN:84-002176.

Audience: **u,f.** B

Cromer, Evelyn Baring   DT107.C88 2000
Modern Egypt: Orientalism. Library Binding. Routledge. New
York, NY. 2004. 476p. Orientalism Ser., Vols. 5-6
ISBN:0-415-20903-X, ISBN13: 978-0-415-20903-8.
Dewey:297.4/8. LCCN:99-046558.

Audience: **u,f.**

Cuno, Kenneth M.   HD1538.E3.C86 1992
The Pasha's Peasants: Society and Economy in Lower Egypt,
1740-1858. Cloth Text. Cambridge University Press. New York,
NY. 1993. 295p. Cambridge Middle East Library, No. 27
ISBN:0-521-40478-9, ISBN13: 978-0-521-40478-5.
Dewey:305.563309621. LCCN:91-038433.

Audience: **u,f.** *Choice, 1994.*

Danielson, Virginia   ML420.U46D36 1997
The Voice of Egypt: Umm Kulthum, Arabic Song, and Egyptian
Society in the Twentieth Century. Trade Paper. University of
Chicago Press. Chicago, IL. 1998. 288p. Chicago Studies in
Ethnomusicology ISBN:0-226-13612-4, ISBN13:
978-0-226-13612-7. Dewey:[B]. LCCN:96-045394.

Audience: **g,l,u,f.**

Early, Evelyn A.   GR355.2.C35
Baladi Women of Cairo: Playing with an Egg and a Stone.
Library Binding. Lynne Rienner Publishers, Inc. Boulder, CO.
1992. 218p. ISBN:1-55587-277-8, ISBN13: 978-1-55587-277-9.
Dewey:398.096216. LCCN:92-010682.

Audience: **l,u,f.**

Ener, Mine   HC830.Z9P614 2003
Managing Egypt's Poor and the Politics of Benevolence,
1800-1952. Trade Cloth. Princeton University Press. Princeton,
NJ. 2003. 240p. ISBN:0-691-11378-5, ISBN13:
978-0-691-11378-4. Dewey:362.5/8/096209034.
LCCN:2002-035479.

Audience: **u,f.** *Choice, 2004.*

Erlich, Haggai   LA1648.7.E75 1989
🄴 Students and University in 20th Century Egyptian Politics.
E-Book. Taylor & Francis Group. Philadelphia, PA.
ISBN:0-203-98853-1, ISBN13: 978-0-203-98853-4.
Dewey:378/.198/1.

Audience: **u,f.**

Gershoni, Israel &   DT107.8.G37 1987
  Jankowski, James P.
Egypt, Islam, and the Arabs: The Search for Egyptian
Nationhood, 1900-1930. Cloth Text. Oxford University Press,
Inc. New York, NY. 1987. 346p. Studies in Middle Eastern
History ISBN:0-19-504096-1, ISBN13: 978-0-19-504096-8.
Dewey:320.5/4/0962. LCCN:86-005221.

Audience: **u,f.** *Choice, 1987.*

Ghannam, Farha   HT384.E32 C3444 2002
Remaking the Modern: Space, Relocation, and the Politics of
Identity in a Global Cairo. Trade Cloth. University of California
Press. Berkeley, CA. 2002. 240p. ISBN:0-520-23045-0, ISBN13:
978-0-520-23045-3. Dewey:307.76/0962/16.
LCCN:2001-006438.

Audience: **u,f.**

Goldschmidt, Arthur Jr.   DT97.G65 1999
Biographical Dictionary of Modern Egypt. Library Binding.
Lynne Rienner Publishers, Inc. Boulder, CO. 2000. x, 300p.
ISBN:1-55587-229-8, ISBN13: 978-1-55587-229-8.
Dewey:920.062. LCCN:99-033550.

Audience: **g,l,u,f.** *Choice, 2000.*

Goldschmidt, Arthur Jr.   DT100.G65 2004
Modern Egypt: The Formation of a Nation-State. Ed. 2. Trade
Paper. Westview Press. Boulder, CO. 2004. 256p.
ISBN:0-8133-3886-7, ISBN13: 978-0-8133-3886-6. Dewey:962.
LCCN:2004-004728.

Audience: **g,l,u,f.** *Choice, 1989.*

Goldschmidt, Arthur   DT107
  (Editor), et al.
Re-Envisioning Egypt, 1919-1952. Amy J. Johnson & Barak A.
Salmoni (Editors). Saddle Stitched, Cloth over Boards, Dust
Jacket. American University in Cairo Press. New York, NY.
2005. 510p. ISBN:977-424-900-3, ISBN13: 978-977-424-900-6.
Dewey:962.03.

Audience: **l,u,f.** *Choice, 2006.*

Haeri, Niloofar   PJ6773.H34 2002
Sacred Language, Ordinary People: Dilemmas of Culture and
Politics in Egypt. Cloth over Boards. Palgrave Macmillan. New
York, NY. 2003. 192p. ISBN:0-312-23898-3, ISBN13:
978-0-312-23898-8. Dewey:492.7/70962. LCCN:2002-074880.

Audience: **u,f.**

Hanna, Nelly   HT690.E3I5 2003
In Praise of Books: A Cultural History of Cairo's Middle Class,
Sixteenth to the Eighteenth Century. Trade Cloth. Syracuse
University Press. Syracuse, NY. 2003. 224p. Middle East
Studies Beyond Dominant Paradigms ISBN:0-8156-3012-3,
ISBN13: 978-0-8156-3012-8. Dewey:305.5/5/0962.
LCCN:2003-013954.

Audience: **l,u,f.**

Hasan, Sana   BX133.2.H37 2002
Christians Versus Muslims in Modern Egypt: The Century-Long
Struggle for Coptic Equality. Trade Cloth. Oxford University
Press, Inc. New York, NY. 2003. 336p. ISBN:0-19-513868-6,

ISBN13: 978-0-19-513868-9. Dewey:281/.72/0962.
LCCN:2002-022039.

Audience: **l,u,f.** *Choice, 2004.*

Hathaway, Jane   DT97.H38 2003
A Tale of Two Factions: Myth, Memory, and Identity in
Ottoman Egypt and Yemen. Cloth Text. State University of New
York Press. Albany, NY. 2003. 288p. SUNY Series in the Social
and Economic History of the Middle East ISBN:0-7914-5883-0,
ISBN13: 978-0-7914-5883-9. Dewey:962/.03.
LCCN:2003-055622.

Audience: **u,f.**

Hinnebusch, Raymond A.   DT107.85 .H56 1988
Egyptian Politics under Sadat: The Post-Populist Development
of an Authoritarian-Modernizing State. Paper Text. Lynne
Rienner Publishers, Inc. Boulder, CO. 1988. 324p.
ISBN:1-55587-124-0, ISBN13: 978-1-55587-124-6.
Dewey:962/.054. LCCN:88-011447.

Audience: **u,f.**

Hoodfar, Homa   HC830.Z7C343 1997
Between Marriage and the Market: Intimate Politics and
Survival in Cairo. Trade Paper. University of California Press.
Berkeley, CA. 1997. 265p. Comparative Studies on Muslim
Societies ISBN:0-520-20825-0, ISBN13: 978-0-520-20825-4.
Dewey:339.2/2. LCCN:96-037296.

Audience: **l,u,f.** *Choice, 1998.*

Ismael, Tareq Y. &   HX443.A6I86 1990
 El-Sa'id, Rifa'at
The Communist Movement in Egpyt, 1920-1988. Cloth Text.
Syracuse University Press. Syracuse, NY. 1990. 280p.
Contemporary Issues in the Middle East Ser.
ISBN:0-8156-2497-2, ISBN13: 978-0-8156-2497-4.
Dewey:335.43/0962. LCCN:90-032961.

Audience: **l,u,f.** *Choice, 1991.*

Kepel, Gilles   BP64.E3 K4413 2003
Muslim Extremism in Egypt: The Prophet and Pharaoh. Ed. 2.
Trade Paper. University of California Press. Berkeley, CA. 2003.
290p. ISBN:0-520-23934-2, ISBN13: 978-0-520-23934-0.
Dewey:322/.1/096209048. LCCN:2003-042607.

Audience: **g,l,u,f.** *Choice, 1986.*

Kramer, Gudrun   DS135.E4K68 1989
The Jews in Modern Egypt, 1914-1952. Trade Cloth. University
of Washington Press. Seattle, WA. 1989. 310p.
ISBN:0-295-96795-1, ISBN13: 978-0-295-96795-0.
Dewey:962/.004924. LCCN:88-027805.

Audience: **u,f.** *Choice, 1990.*

Landau, Jacob M.   DS135.E4
Jews in Nineteenth Century Egypt. Trade Cloth. New York
University Press. New York, NY. 1969. Studies in Near Eastern
Civilization, No. 2 ISBN:0-8147-0248-1, ISBN13:
978-0-8147-0248-2. Dewey:301.451/924/062. LCCN:69-018282.

Audience: **u,f.**

Lane, Edward William   DT70
An Account of the Manners and Customs of the Modern
Egyptians: The Definitve 1860 Edition. Ed. 5. American

University in Cairo Press. 2003. ISBN:977-424-784-1, ISBN13:
978-977-424-784-2.

Audience: **l,u,f.**

Laskier, Michael M.   DS135.E4L35 1991
The Jews of Egypt, 1920-1970: In the Midst of Zionism,
Anti-Semitism, and the Middle East Conflict. Cloth Text. New
York University Press. New York, NY. 1991. 350p.
ISBN:0-8147-5058-3, ISBN13: 978-0-8147-5058-2.
Dewey:305.892/4062/0904. LCCN:91-031182.

Audience: **l,u,f.** *Choice, 1992.*

Leeder, S. H.   DT70 .L4 1973
Modern Sons of the Pharaohs. Trade Cloth. Ayer Company
Publishers, Inc. Manchester, NH. 1973. The Middle East Ser.
ISBN:0-405-05346-0, ISBN13: 978-0-405-05346-7.
Dewey:916.2/03/4. LCCN:73-006288.

Audience: **g,l,u,f.**

Mitchell, Timothy   DT100.M57 1988
Colonising Egypt. Trade Cloth. Cambridge University Press.
New York, NY. 1988. 228p. Cambridge Middle East Library,
No. 17 ISBN:0-521-33448-9, ISBN13: 978-0-521-33448-8.
Dewey:303.4/8262/04. LCCN:87-018761.

Audience: **l,u,f.** *Choice, 1989.*

Sengers, Gerda   BF1275.F3S463 2002
Women and Demons: Cultic Healing in Islamic Egypt. Trade
Cloth. Brill Academic Publishers. Leiden, 2003. x, 302p.
International Studies in Sociology and Social Anthropology Ser.,
Vol. 86 ISBN:90-04-12771-2, ISBN13: 978-90-04-12771-5.
Dewey:297.3/9. LCCN:2002-028201.

Audience: **u,f.**

Singerman, Diane &   HC830.D48 1996
 Hoodfar, Homa (Editors)
e Development, Change, and Gender in Cairo: A View from
the Household. E-Book. Indiana University Press. Bloomington,
IN. 1996. 240p. Indiana University Series in Middle East
Studies ISBN:0-253-21049-6, ISBN13: 978-0-253-21049-4.
Dewey:339.2/2. LCCN:95-034930.

Audience: **l,u,f.**

Talhami, Ghada H.   HQ1793.T35 1996
The Mobilizaiton of Muslim Women in Egypt. Trade Cloth.
University Press of Florida. Gainesville, FL. 1996. 192p.
ISBN:0-8130-1429-8, ISBN13: 978-0-8130-1429-6.
Dewey:305.42/0962. LCCN:95-042757.

Audience: **l,u,f.** *Choice, 1997.*

Tucker, Judith E.   HQ1793 .T83 1985
Women in Nineteenth Century Egypt. Trade Cloth. Cambridge
University Press. New York, NY. 1985. 263p. Cambridge
Middle East Library, No. 7 ISBN:0-521-30338-9, ISBN13:
978-0-521-30338-5. Dewey:305.4/2/0962/09034.
LCCN:85-005735.

Audience: **u,f.** *Choice, 1986.*

Vatikiotis, P. J.   DT107.V38 1991
The History of Modern Egypt: From Muhammad Ali to
Mubarak. Ed. 4. Trade Cloth. Johns Hopkins University Press.

Baltimore, MD. 1991. 560p. ISBN:0-8018-4214-X, ISBN13: 978-0-8018-4214-6. Dewey:962. LCCN:90-023160.

Audience: **l,u,f.** *B*

History of Specific Countries > Egypt > Modern > Muhammad Ali

Dodwell, Henry H.   **DT104 .D58 1977**
The Founder of Modern Egypt. Trade Cloth. A M S Press, Inc. New York, NY. BCL Ser. II ISBN:0-404-12036-9, ISBN13: 978-0-404-12036-8. Dewey:962/.03/0924. LCCN:74-015029.

Audience: **g,l,u,f.**

Fahmy, Khaled   **UA865**
All the Pasha's Men: Mehmed Ali, His Army and the Making of Modern Egypt. Ed. 2. Trade Paper. American University in Cairo Press. New York, NY. 2002. 352p. ISBN:977-424-696-9, ISBN13: 978-977-424-696-8. Dewey:355/.00962/09034.

Audience: **l,u,f.** *Choice, 1998.*

Marsot, Afaf Lutfi   **DT104 .S38 1984**
  al-Sayyid
Egypt in the Reign of Muhammad Ali. Edmund Burke, Michael C. Hudson, Walid Kazziha, Rashid Khalidi, Serif Mardin, Roger Owen, Basim Musallam, Avi Shlaim & Malcolm Yapp (Contribution by). Trade Paper. Cambridge University Press. New York, NY. 1984. 320p. Cambridge Middle East Library, No. 4 ISBN:0-521-28968-8, ISBN13: 978-0-521-28968-9. Dewey:962/.03. LCCN:83-005241.

Audience: **g,l,u,f.**

History of Specific Countries > Egypt > Modern > Egyptian Revolution and Republic

Abu-Lughod, Lila   **HE8700.9.E3A28 2005**
Dramas of Nationhood: The Politics of Television in Egypt. Anthony T. Carter (Foreword by). Trade Cloth. University of Chicago Press. Chicago, IL. 2004. 324p. The Lewis Henry Morgan Lectures, Vol. 2001 ISBN:0-226-00196-2, ISBN13: 978-0-226-00196-8. Dewey:302.23/45/0962. LCCN:2004-001470.

Audience: **l,u,f.**

Batatu, Hanna   **DS63 .B35 1984**
The Egyptian, Syrian, and Iraqi Revolutions: Some Observations on Their Underlying Causes and Social Character. Cloth Text. Georgetown University, Center for Contemporary Arab Studies. Washington, DC. 1984. 29p. ISBN:0-932568-10-6, ISBN13: 978-0-932568-10-6. Dewey:909/.0974927. LCCN:84-005862.

Audience: **l,u,f.**

Beinin, Joel   **DS126.5.B359 1990**
Was the Red Flag Flying There?: Marxist Politics and the Arab-Israeli Conflict in Egypt and Israel, 1948-1965. Trade Cloth. University of California Press. Berkeley, CA. 1990. 328p. ISBN:0-520-07035-6, ISBN13: 978-0-520-07035-6. Dewey:956.9405/2. LCCN:89-049036.

Audience: **l,u,f.**

El-Sadat, Anwar   **DT107.828.S12**
In Search of Identity. Library Binding. Buccaneer Books, Inc. Cutchogue, NY. 1994. 360p. ISBN:1-56849-277-4, ISBN13: 978-1-56849-277-3. Dewey:962.05.

Audience: **g,l,u,f.**

Gordon, Joel   **DT107.83.G67 1991**
Nasser's Blessed Movement: Egypt's Free Officers and the July Revolution. Trade Cloth. Oxford University Press, Inc. New York, NY. 1992. 268p. Studies in Middle Eastern History ISBN:0-19-506935-8, ISBN13: 978-0-19-506935-8. Dewey:962. LCCN:91-016836.

Audience: **l,u,f.** *Choice, 1992.*

Harik, Iliya F.   **HC830.H37 1997**
Economic Policy Reform in Egypt. Trade Cloth. University Press of Florida. Gainesville, FL. 1997. 344p. ISBN:0-8130-1483-2, ISBN13: 978-0-8130-1483-8. Dewey:338.962. LCCN:96-038520.

Audience: **g,l,u,f.** *Choice, 1998.*

Haykal, Muhammad   **DT107.83**
  Hasanayan
The Road to Ramadan. Collins. 1975. ISBN:0-00-211653-7, ISBN13: 978-0-00-211653-4.

Audience: **u,f.**

Heikal, Mohamed H.   **DT107.83.H3665 1987**
Cutting the Lion's Tail: Suez Through Egyptian Eyes. Trade Cloth. HarperCollins Publishers. New York, NY. 1987. 256p. ISBN:0-87795-919-6, ISBN13: 978-0-87795-919-9. Dewey:962/.053. LCCN:87-001031.

Audience: **g,l,u,f.**

Hopkins, Nicholas &   **HN786.A8+**
  Westergaard, Kirsten
Directions of Change in Rural Egypt. Trade Cloth. American University in Cairo Press. New York, NY. 1998. 352p. ISBN:977-424-483-4, ISBN13: 978-977-424-483-4. Dewey:363.7/00962. LCCN:98-961219.

Audience: **l,u,f.**

Ibrahim, Saad Eddin   **DT107.87.I27 2002**
Egypt, Islam and Democracy: Critical Essays. Trade Paper. American University in Cairo Press. New York, NY. 2002. 284p. ISBN:977-424-664-0, ISBN13: 978-977-424-664-7. Dewey:962.05/5. LCCN:2002-334543.

Audience: **l,u,f.**

Inhorn, Marcia C.   **HB1071.7.A3I55 1996**
Infertility and Patriarchy: The Cultural Politics of Gender and Family Life in Egypt. Trade Cloth. University of Pennsylvania Press. Philadelphia, PA. 1996. 312p. ISBN:0-8122-3235-6, ISBN13: 978-0-8122-3235-6. Dewey:304.6/32/0962. LCCN:95-031951.

Audience: **l,u,f.** *Choice, 1996.*

Lesch, Ann Mosely &   **DS119.7.L466 1989**
  Tessler,Mark
Israel, Egypt, and the Palestinians: From Camp David to Intifada. RIchard B. Parker (Foreword). Indiana University Press. 1989. Indiana Series in Arab and Islamic Studies ISBN:0-253-33320-2, ISBN13: 978-0-253-33320-9.

Audience: **l,u,f.**

Mitchell, Timothy   **HC830 .M587 2002**
Rule of Experts: Egypt, Techno-Politics, Modernity. Trade Cloth. University of California Press. Berkeley, CA. 2002. 376p. ISBN:0-520-23261-5, ISBN13: 978-0-520-23261-7. Dewey:338.962. LCCN:2002-012705.

Audience: **u,f.** *Choice, 2003.*

Podeh, Elie & Winckler, Onn   DT107.83.R45 2004
Rethinking Nasserism: Revolution and Historical Memory in
Modern Egypt. Trade Cloth. University Press of Florida.
Gainesville, FL. 2004. 520p. ISBN:0-8130-2704-7, ISBN13:
978-0-8130-2704-3. Dewey:962.05/2. LCCN:2003-070525.
                                        Audience: **u,f.**

Sonbol, Amira El-Azhary   DT100.S66 2000
The New Mamluks: Egyptian Society and Modern Feudalism.
Syracuse University Press. 2000. ISBN:0-8156-2844-7, ISBN13:
978-0-8156-2844-6.
                                        Audience: **u,f.**

Waterbury, John   HC830.W37 1983
The Egypt of Nasser and Sadat: the Political Economy of Two
Regimes. Princeton University Press. 1983. Princeton Studies on
the Near East ISBN:0-691-07650-2, ISBN13:
978-0-691-07650-8.
                                        Audience: **l,u,f.**

Zuhur, Sherifa   HQ1793.Z67 1992
Revealing Reveiling: Islamist Gender Ideology in Contemporary
Egypt. Cloth Text. State University of New York Press. Albany,
NY. 1992. 207p. SUNY Series in Middle Eastern Studies
ISBN:0-7914-0927-9, ISBN13: 978-0-7914-0927-5.
Dewey:305.42/0962/16. LCCN:91-003408.
                                Audience: **l,u,f.** *Choice, 1993.*

History of Specific Countries > Sudan > General

Holt, P. M.   DT156.4.H64 2000
A History of the Sudan: From the Coming of Islam to the
Present Day. Ed. 5. Longman. 2000. ISBN:0-582-36886-3,
ISBN13: 978-0-582-36886-6.
                                        Audience: **l,u,f.**

Hunwick, John O.   BP64.S8 R45 1992
Religion and National Integration in Africa: Islam, Christianity
and Politics in the Sudan and Nigeria. Trade Cloth.
Northwestern University Press. Evanston, IL. 1992. 176p. Series
in Islam and Society in Africa Ser. ISBN:0-8101-1037-7,
ISBN13: 978-0-8101-1037-3. Dewey:322/.1/09624.
LCCN:91-045253.
                                        Audience: **u,f.**

Malka, Eli S.   DS135.S85M35 1997
Jacob's Children in the Land of the Mahdi: Jews of the Sudan.
Trade Cloth. Syracuse University Press. Syracuse, NY. 1997.
250p. ISBN:0-8156-8122-4, ISBN13: 978-0-8156-8122-9.
Dewey:962.4/004924. LCCN:96-072628.
                                        Audience: **u,f.**

History of Specific Countries > Sudan > Modern

Niblock, Tim   DT156.7.N53 1987
Class and Power in Sudan: The Dynamics of Sudanese Politics,
1898-1985. Cloth Text. State University of New York Press.
Albany, NY. 1987. 370p. ISBN:0-88706-480-9, ISBN13:
978-0-88706-480-7. Dewey:962.4/05. LCCN:86-023059.
                                Audience: **u,f.** *Choice, 1988.*

Petterson, Donald   DT157.5.P47 2003
Inside Sudan: Political Islam, Conflict, and Catastrophe. Trade
Paper. Westview Press. Boulder, CO. 2003. 288p.
ISBN:0-8133-4111-6, ISBN13: 978-0-8133-4111-8.
Dewey:327.730624/09/049. LCCN:2003-015153.
                                        Audience: **u,f.**

Warburg, Gabriel   DT156.4.W375 2002
Sudan: Islam, Sectarianism, and Politics since the Mahdiyya.
Trade Cloth. University of Wisconsin Press. Chicago, IL. 2002.
xv, 252p. ISBN:0-299-18290-8, ISBN13: 978-0-299-18290-8.
Dewey:962.404. LCCN:2002-067595.
                                Audience: **u,f.** *Choice, 2004.*

History of Specific Countries > Libya > General

Abun-Nasr, Jamil M.   DT194
A History of the Maghrib in the Islamic Period. Cambridge
University Press. 1987. ISBN:0-521-33767-4, ISBN13:
978-0-521-33767-0.
                                        Audience: **u,f.**

De Felice, Renzo   DS135.L44 D413 1985
Jews in an Arab Land: Libya, 1835-1970. Judith Romani
(Translator). University of Texas Press. 1985.
ISBN:0-292-74016-6, ISBN13: 978-0-292-74016-7.
                                        Audience: **l,u,f.**

Goldberg, Harvey E.   DS135.L44G65 1990
Jewish Life in Muslim Libya: Rivals and Relatives. Trade Cloth.
University of Chicago Press. Chicago, IL. 1997. 202p.
ISBN:0-226-30091-9, ISBN13: 978-0-226-30091-7.
Dewey:961.2/004924. LCCN:89-020593.
                                Audience: **u,f.** *Choice, 1991.*

St. John, Ronald Bruce   DT223.3.S7 1991
Historical Dictionary of Libya. Ed. 2. Trade Cloth. Scarecrow
Press, Inc. Lanham, MD. 1992. 214p. African Historical
Dictionaries Ser., No. 33 ISBN:0-8108-2451-5, ISBN13:
978-0-8108-2451-5. Dewey:961.2003. LCCN:91-027764.
                                Audience: **g,l,u,f.** *Choice, 1999, 1992.*

History of Specific Countries > Libya > Modern

Ahmida, Ali Abdullatif   DT218
The Making of Modern Libya: State Formation, Colonization,
and Resistance, 1830-1932. Cloth Text. State University of New
York Press. Albany, NY. 1994. 222p. SUNY Series in the Social
and Economic History of the Middle East ISBN:0-7914-1761-1,
ISBN13: 978-0-7914-1761-4. Dewey:961.2/02.
LCCN:93-018526.
                                Audience: **u,f.** *Choice, 1994.*

El Kikhia, Mansour O.   DT236.E45 1997
Libya's Qaddafi: The Politics of Contradiction. University Press
of Florida. 1997. ISBN:0-8130-1488-3, ISBN13:
978-0-8130-1488-3.
                                        Audience: **l,u,f.**

Khadduri, Majid   **DT236 .K5**
Modern Libya: A Study in Political Development. Trade Cloth.
Johns Hopkins University Press. Baltimore, MD. 1970. 404p.
ISBN:0-8018-0335-7, ISBN13: 978-0-8018-0335-2.
Dewey:961.204.

Audience: **u,f.**

Pennell, C. R. (Editor)   **DT231.B35 1989**
Piracy and Diplomacy in 17th Century North Africa: The
Journal of Thomas Baker, English Consul in Tripoli, 1677-1685.
Trade Cloth. Fairleigh Dickinson University Press. Cranbury,
NJ. 1989. 264p. ISBN:0-8386-3302-1, ISBN13:
978-0-8386-3302-1. Dewey:961/.202. LCCN:86-045999.

Audience: **u,f.** *Choice, 1989.*

Vandewalle, Dirk   **DT236**
A History of Modern Libya. Cloth Text. Cambridge University
Press. New York, NY. 2006. 274p. ISBN:0-521-85048-7,
ISBN13: 978-0-521-85048-3. Dewey:961.2042.
LCCN:2006-296140.

Audience: **l,u,f.**

Vandewalle, Dirk   **DT235.5.V36 1998**
Libya since Independence: Oil and State-Building. Trade Cloth.
Cornell University Press. Ithaca, NY. 1998. 232p.
ISBN:0-8014-3472-6, ISBN13: 978-0-8014-3472-3.
Dewey:961.204/1. LCCN:98-003461.

Audience: **l,u,f.**

Wright, John & Wright,   **DT236 .W74 1982**
Richardson
Libya: A Modern History. Trade Cloth. Johns Hopkins
University Press. Baltimore, MD. 1992. 304p.
ISBN:0-8018-2767-1, ISBN13: 978-0-8018-2767-9.
Dewey:961/.2. LCCN:81-048183.

Audience: **g,l,u,f.**

History of Specific Countries > Tunisia > General

Abun-Nasr, Jamil M.   **DT194**
A History of the Maghrib in the Islamic Period. Cambridge
University Press. 1987. ISBN:0-521-33767-4, ISBN13:
978-0-521-33767-0.

Audience: **u,f.**

Holmes-Eber, Paula   **HQ1792.Z9T855 2002**
Daughters of Tunis: Women, Family, and Networks in a Muslim
City. Trade Paper. Westview Press. Boulder, CO. 2002. 192p.
Westview Case Studies in Anthropology ISBN:0-8133-3943-X,
ISBN13: 978-0-8133-3943-6. Dewey:306/.099611.
LCCN:2002-006168.

Audience: **l,u,f.**

Laroui, Abdallah   **DT194**
The History of the Maghrib: An Interpretive Essay. Princeton
University Press. 1977. ISBN:0-691-03109-6, ISBN13:
978-0-691-03109-5.

Audience: **u,f.**

Perkins, Kenneth J.   **DT244.P47 1997**
Historical Dictionary of Tunisia. Ed. 2. Trade Cloth. Scarecrow
Press, Inc. Lanham, MD. 1997. 448p. African Historical
Dictionaries Ser., No. 45 ISBN:0-8108-3286-0, ISBN13:
978-0-8108-3286-2. Dewey:961.1/003. LCCN:96-051075.

Audience: **g,l,u,f.** *Choice, 1990.*

Powers, David S.   **LAW**
Law, Society and Culture in the Maghrib, 1300-1500. Cloth
Text. Cambridge University Press. New York, NY. 2002. 280p.
Cambridge Studies in Islamic Civilization ISBN:0-521-81691-2,
ISBN13: 978-0-521-81691-5. Dewey:340.5/9/0964.
LCCN:2002-073812.

Audience: **u,f.**

History of Specific Countries > Tunisia > Modern

Brown, L. Carl   **DT264 .B76**
The Tunisia of Ahmad Bey, 1837 to 1855. Trade Cloth.
Princeton University Press. Princeton, NJ. 1975. 408p. Near
East Studies ISBN:0-691-03100-2, ISBN13: 978-0-691-03100-2.
Dewey:961/.1/03. LCCN:73-016770.

Audience: **l,u,f.**

Charrad, Mounira M.   **HQ1236.5.A355 C43**
States and Women's Rights: The Making of Postcolonial
Tunisia, Algeria, and Morocco. Trade Cloth. University of
California Press. Berkeley, CA. 2001. 362p.
ISBN:0-520-07323-1, ISBN13: 978-0-520-07323-4.
Dewey:323.3/4/0961. LCCN:00-051172.

Audience: **u,f.** *Choice, 2002.*

Clancy-Smith, Julia A.   **DT294 .C56 1994**
Rebel and Saint: Muslim Notables, Populist Protest, and
Colonial Encounters - Algeria and Tunisia, 1800-1904. Trade
Cloth. University of California Press. Berkeley, CA. 1994. 373p.
Comparative Studies on Muslim Societies, Vol. 18
ISBN:0-520-08242-7, ISBN13: 978-0-520-08242-7.
Dewey:965.03. LCCN:93-017223.

Audience: **u,f.**

Gallagher, Nancy E.   **RA650.8.T8**
Medicine and Power in Tunisia, 1780-1900. Trade Cloth.
Cambridge University Press. New York, NY. 1983. 160p.
Cambridge Middle East Library, No. 2 ISBN:0-521-25124-9,
ISBN13: 978-0-521-25124-2. Dewey:614.4/9611.
LCCN:82-022163.

Audience: **u,f.**

Hamdi, Mohamed E.   **BP64.T7**
Politicisation of Islam: A Case Study of Tunisia. Trade Paper.
Westview Press. Boulder, CO. 2000. 220p. ISBN:0-8133-3888-3,
ISBN13: 978-0-8133-3888-0. Dewey:322.4/2/09611.

Audience: **u,f.**

King, Stephen J.   **JQ3336.K56 2003**
Liberalization Against Democracy: The Local Politics of
Economic Reform in Tunisia. Trade Cloth. Indiana University
Press. Bloomington, IN. 2003. 168p. Indiana Series in Middle
East Studies ISBN:0-253-21583-8, ISBN13: 978-0-253-21583-3.
Dewey:320.9611. LCCN:2002-014600.

Audience: **l,u,f.** *Choice, 2004.*

Murphy, Emma C.   **HC820.M87 1999**
Economic and Political Change in Tunisia: From Bourguiba to
Ben Ali. St. Martin's Press. 1999. ISBN:0-312-22142-8,
ISBN13: 978-0-312-22142-3.

Audience: **u,f.**

Perkins, Kenneth J.   **DT263.P47 2004**
A History of Modern Tunisia. Cloth Text. Cambridge University
Press. New York, NY. 2004. 270p. ISBN:0-521-81124-4,

ISBN13: 978-0-521-81124-8. Dewey:961.1/04.
LCCN:2004-045812.

Audience: l,u,f.

Salem, Norma   **DT264.3.B6S24 1984**
Habib Bourguiba, Islam and the Creation of Tunisia. Trade
Cloth. Croom Helm, Ltd. London, 1984. 256p.
ISBN:0-7099-3319-3, ISBN13: 978-0-7099-3319-9.
Dewey:961/.105/0924 B. LCCN:84-045235.

Audience: u,f.

Valensi, Lucette   **HN784.A8**
Tunisian Peasants in the Eighteenth and Nineteenth Centuries.
Beth Archer (Translator). Trade Cloth. Cambridge University
Press. New York, NY. 1985. 277p. Studies in Modern
Capitalism ISBN:0-521-25558-9, ISBN13: 978-0-521-25558-5.
Dewey:305.5/63. LCCN:84-029206.

Audience: l,u,f.

History of Specific Countries > Algeria > General

Abun-Nasr, Jamil M.   **DT194**
A History of the Maghrib in the Islamic Period. Cambridge
University Press. 1987. ISBN:0-521-33767-4, ISBN13:
978-0-521-33767-0.

Audience: u,f.

Djebar, Assia   **PQ3989.2.D57V3713**
So Vast the Prison. Betsy Wing (Translator). Trade Cloth. Seven
Stories Press. New York, NY. 2004. ISBN:1-58322-009-7,
ISBN13: 978-1-58322-009-2. Dewey:965/.046.
LCCN:99-041329.

Audience: g,l,u,f.

Laroui, Abdallah   **DT194**
The History of the Maghrib: An Interpretive Essay. Princeton
University Press. 1977. ISBN:0-691-03109-6, ISBN13:
978-0-691-03109-5.

Audience: u,f.

Naylor, Phillip C. &   **DT283.7.N39 1994**
  Heggoy, Alf A.
The Historical Dictionary of Algeria. Ed. 2. Trade Cloth.
Scarecrow Press, Inc. Lanham, MD. 1994. 488p. African
Historical Dictionaries Ser., No. 59 ISBN:0-8108-2748-4,
ISBN13: 978-0-8108-2748-6. Dewey:965/.003.
LCCN:93-026302.

Audience: g,l,u,f. Choice, 1995.

Powers, David S.   **LAW**
Law, Society and Culture in the Maghrib, 1300-1500. Cloth
Text. Cambridge University Press. New York, NY. 2002. 280p.
Cambridge Studies in Islamic Civilization ISBN:0-521-81691-2,
ISBN13: 978-0-521-81691-5. Dewey:340.5/9/0964.
LCCN:2002-073812.

Audience: u,f.

History of Specific Countries > Algeria > Medieval

Spencer, William   **DT299.A5**
Algiers in the Age of the Corsairs. Ed. 1. University of
Okalahoma Press. 1976.

Audience: g,l,u,f.

History of Specific Countries > Algeria > Modern

Fanon, Frantz   **DT295**
A Dying Colonialism. Haakon Chevalier (Translator). Trade
Paper. Grove/Atlantic, Inc. New York, NY. 1988. 192p.
ISBN:0-8021-5027-6, ISBN13: 978-0-8021-5027-1.
Dewey:965/.046.

Audience: g,l,u,f.

Naylor, Phillip C.   **DT287.5.F8N39 2000**
France and Algeria: A History of Decolonization and
Transformation. Trade Cloth. University Press of Florida.
Gainesville, FL. 2000. xviii, 457p. ISBN:0-8130-1801-3,
ISBN13: 978-0-8130-1801-0. Dewey:965/.04. LCCN:00-048884.
Audience: l,u. Choice, 2001.

Quandt, William B.   **JQ3231.Q36 1998**
Between Ballots and Bullets: Algeria's Transition from
Authoritarianism. Trade Cloth. Brookings Institution Press.
Washington, DC. 1998. 199p. ISBN:0-8157-7302-1, ISBN13:
978-0-8157-7302-3. Dewey:320.965/09/049. LCCN:98-019668.

Audience: u,f.

Roberts, Hugh   **DT295.5.R628 2003**
The Battlefield: Algeria 1988-2002: Studies in a Broken Polity.
Trade Cloth. Verso Books. London, 2002. 320p.
ISBN:1-85984-684-X, ISBN13: 978-1-85984-684-1.
Dewey:965.05. LCCN:2003-374190.

Audience: g,l,u,f. Choice, 2004.

Ruedy, John   **DT294.5.R84 2005**
Modern Algeria: The Origins and Development of a Nation. Ed.
2. Trade Cloth. Indiana University Press. Bloomington, IN.
2005. 344p. ISBN:0-253-21782-2, ISBN13: 978-0-253-21782-0.
Dewey:965. LCCN:2005-281197.

Audience: l,u,f. Choice, 1993.

History of Specific Countries > Algeria > Modern > French Colony

Clancy-Smith, Julia A.   **DT294 .C56 1994**
Rebel and Saint: Muslim Notables, Populist Protest, and
Colonial Encounters - Algeria and Tunisia, 1800-1904. Trade
Cloth. University of California Press. Berkeley, CA. 1994. 373p.
Comparative Studies on Muslim Societies, Vol. 18
ISBN:0-520-08242-7, ISBN13: 978-0-520-08242-7.
Dewey:965.03. LCCN:93-017223.

Audience: u,f.

Fanon, Frantz   **DT33.F313 2004**
The Wretched of the Earth. Trade Paper. Grove/Atlantic, Inc.
New York, NY. 2004. 256p. ISBN:0-8021-4132-3, ISBN13:
978-0-8021-4132-3. Dewey:960/.0971244. LCCN:2004-042476.
Audience: g,l,u,f. **B**

History of Specific Countries > Algeria > Modern > Algerian Revolution

Djebar, Assia   **DT295.5**
Algerian White. David Kelley & Marjolijn de Jager
(Translators). Trade Paper. Seven Stories Press. New York, NY.
2004. 0p. ISBN:1-58322-516-1, ISBN13: 978-1-58322-516-5.
Dewey:965/.04.

Audience: g,l,u,f.

Horne, Alistair   DT295.H64 2006
A Savage War of Peace: Algeria 1954-1962. Trade Paper. New York Review of Books, Incorporated, The. New York, NY. 2006. 600p. New York Review Books Classics ISBN:1-59017-218-3, ISBN13: 978-1-59017-218-6. Dewey:965/.046. LCCN:2006-003506.

Audience: **g,u,f.**

History of Specific Countries > Morocco > General

Abun-Nasr, Jamil M.   DT194
A History of the Maghrib in the Islamic Period. Cambridge University Press. 1987. ISBN:0-521-33767-4, ISBN13: 978-0-521-33767-0.

Audience: **u,f.**

Laroui, Abdallah   DT194
The History of the Maghrib: An Interpretive Essay. Princeton University Press. 1977. ISBN:0-691-03109-6, ISBN13: 978-0-691-03109-5.

Audience: **u,f.**

Mernissi, Fatima   HQ1791
Women in Emergent Morocco: Changes and Continuities. Trade Cloth. Flame International, Inc. Springfield, VA. 1982. ISBN:0-933184-40-9, ISBN13: 978-0-933184-40-4. Dewey:305.40964.

Audience: **l,u,f.**

Mernissi, Fatima   HQ1791.M3713 1989
Doing Daily Battle: Interviews with Moroccan Women. Jo Lakeland (Translator). Cloth Text. Rutgers University Press. Piscataway, NJ. 1989. 224p. ISBN:0-8135-1417-7, ISBN13: 978-0-8135-1417-8. Dewey:305.4/2/0964. LCCN:88-034211.

Audience: **l,u,f.**

Miller, James Andrew   DT329.I56.M54 1984
Imlil, a Moroccan Mountain Community in Change. Trade Cloth. Westview Press. Boulder, CO. 1984. xxvii, 285p. ISBN:0-86531-980-4, ISBN13: 978-0-86531-980-6. Dewey:306/.0964/4. LCCN:83-014742.

Audience: **l,u,f.** *B*

Park, Thomas K.   DT313.7P37 2006
Historical Dictionary of Morocco. Ed. 2. Trade Cloth. Scarecrow Press, Inc. Lanham, MD. 2006. 752p. Historical Dictionaries of Africa, No. 95 Ser., No. 95 ISBN:0-8108-5341-8, ISBN13: 978-0-8108-5341-6. Dewey:964/.003. LCCN:2005-020694.

Audience: **g,l,u,f.**

Powers, David S.   LAW
Law, Society and Culture in the Maghrib, 1300-1500. Cloth Text. Cambridge University Press. New York, NY. 2002. 280p. Cambridge Studies in Islamic Civilization ISBN:0-521-81691-2, ISBN13: 978-0-521-81691-5. Dewey:340.5/9/0964. LCCN:2002-073812.

Audience: **u,f.**

Rabinow, Paul   DT329.Z36
Symbolic Domination: Cultural Symbols and Historical Change in Morocco. Paper Text. University of Chicago Press. Chicago, IL. 1978. Midway Reprint Ser. ISBN:0-226-70149-2, ISBN13: 978-0-226-70149-3. Dewey:301.29/64. LCCN:74-007565.

Audience: **u,f.**

Zafrani, Haim   DS135.M8Z37 2002
Two Thousand Years of Jewish Life in Morocco. Trade Cloth. Ktav Publishing House, Inc. Jersey City, NJ. 2002. x, 327p. ISBN:0-88125-748-6, ISBN13: 978-0-88125-748-9. Dewey:964/.004924. LCCN:2002-070238.

Audience: **g,l,u,f.**

History of Specific Countries > Morocco > Modern

Al Qadiri, Muhammad   DT321
Muhammad Al-Qadiri's Nashr Al-Mathani: The Chronicles. Norman Cigar (Editor, Translator). Trade Cloth. Oxford University Press, Inc. New York, NY. 1981. lxxi, 320p. Fontes Historiae Africanae Ser., Vol. VI ISBN:0-19-725994-4, ISBN13: 978-0-19-725994-8. Dewey:964/.02/0202.

Audience: **u,f.**

Baker, Alison   HQ1791.B35 1998
Voices of Resistance: Oral Histories of Moroccan Women. Cloth Text. State University of New York Press. Albany, NY. 1998. 352p. SUNY Series in Oral and Public History ISBN:0-7914-3621-7, ISBN13: 978-0-7914-3621-9. Dewey:305.4/0964. LCCN:97-002649.

Audience: **l,u,f.** *Choice, 1998.*

Burke, Edmund   DT324 .B844 1976
Prelude to Protectorate in Morocco: Precolonial Protest and Resistance, 1860-1912. Library Binding. University of Chicago Press. Chicago, IL. 1996. 328p. ISBN:0-226-08075-7, ISBN13: 978-0-226-08075-8. Dewey:964/.03. LCCN:75-043228.

Audience: **u,f.**

Howe, Marvine   DT305.H69 2005
Morocco: The Islamist Awakening and Other Challenges. Trade Cloth. Oxford University Press, Inc. New York, NY. 2005. 448p. ISBN:0-19-516963-8, ISBN13: 978-0-19-516963-8. Dewey:964.05. LCCN:2004-018891.

Audience: **u,f.** *Choice, 2005.*

Hughes, Stephen H.   DT325.7.H84 2001
Morocco Under King Hassan. Trade Cloth. Garnet Publishing, Ltd. Reading, 2001. 385p. ISBN:0-86372-285-7, ISBN13: 978-0-86372-285-1. Dewey:964.05. LCCN:2001-391467.

Audience: **u,f.**

Laskier, Michael M.   DS135.M85
The Alliance Israelite Universelle and the Jewish Communities of Morocco, 1862-1962. Cloth Text. State University of New York Press. Albany, NY. 1984. 384p. SUNY Series in Modern Jewish History ISBN:0-87395-656-7, ISBN13: 978-0-87395-656-7. Dewey:305.8/924/064. LCCN:82-005892.

Audience: **u,f.**

Mernissi, Fatima   CT2678.M47A3 1994
Dreams of Trespass: Tales of a Harem Girlhood. Ruth V. Ward (Photographer). Trade Cloth. Addison-Wesley Longman, Inc. Boston, MA. 1994. 242p. ISBN:0-201-62649-7, ISBN13: 978-0-201-62649-0. Dewey:964/.0082. LCCN:93-039523.

Audience: **g,l,u,f.**

Munson, Henry Jr.   DT313.6.F73
The House of Si Abd Allah: The Oral History of a Moroccan Family. Trade Paper. Yale University Press. Cumberland, RI. 1991. 280p. ISBN:0-300-05029-1, ISBN13: 978-0-300-05029-5. Dewey:929/.2/0964.

Audience: **u,f.**

Pennell, C. R.   DT324.P386 2000
Morocco Since 1830: A History. Trade Cloth. New York
University Press. New York, NY. 2001. 400p.
ISBN:0-8147-6676-5, ISBN13: 978-0-8147-6676-7.
Dewey:964/.03. LCCN:99-033567.
                                    Audience: l,u,f.

Pennell, Richard   DT314
Morocco: From Empire to Independence. Trade Cloth. Oneworld
Publications. Oxford, 2004. 224p. ISBN:1-85168-303-8,
ISBN13: 978-1-85168-303-1. Dewey:964.
                                    Audience: u,f.

Schade-Poulsen, Marc   ML3503.A4S33 1999
Men and Popular Music in Algeria: The Social Significance of
Raï. Trade Cloth. University of Texas Press. Austin, TX. 1999.
260p. Modern Middle East Ser., Vol. 20 ISBN:0-292-77739-6,
ISBN13: 978-0-292-77739-2. Dewey:781.63/0965.
LCCN:98-029603.
                                    Audience: g,l,u,f.

Schroeter, Daniel J.   DS135.M8S37 2002
The Sultan's Jew: Morocco and the Sephardi World. Trade
Cloth. Stanford University Press. Palo Alto, CA. 2002. 292p.
Stanford Studies in Jewish History and Culture
ISBN:0-8047-3777-0, ISBN13: 978-0-8047-3777-7.
Dewey:964/.6. LCCN:2002-009241.
                            Audience: u,f.   Choice, 2003.

History of Specific Countries > Muslims in India

Babur, Emperor of   DS461.1.B23213 1995
Hindustan
The Baburnama: Memoirs of Babur, Prince and Emperor.
Wheeler M. Thackston (Translator; Editor). Smithsonian
Institution. 1996. ISBN:0-19-509671-1, ISBN13:
978-0-19-509671-2.
                                    Audience: u,f.

Bosworth, Clifford   DS358.B63 1977
Edmund
The Later Ghaznavids: Splendour and Decay: The Dynasty in
Afghanistan and Norther India, 1040-1186. Columbia University
Press. 1977. ISBN:0-231-04428-3, ISBN13: 978-0-231-04428-8.
                                    Audience: l,u,f.

Middle Eastern Languages and Literatures > Hamitic Languages and Literatures > Egyptian (Egyptology)

Budge, E. A. Wallis   PJ1949.B83 2002
Egyptian Tales and Legends: Pagan, Christian, and Muslim.
Trade Paper. Dover Publications, Inc. Mineola, NY. 2002. 448p.
ISBN:0-486-42235-6, ISBN13: 978-0-486-42235-0.
Dewey:893/.13008. LCCN:2002-019207.
                                    Audience: u,f.

Middle Eastern Languages and Literatures > Hamitic Languages and Literatures > Egyptian (Egyptology) > Literature

Budge, E. A. Wallis   PJ1555
The Book of the Dead: Egyptian Literature. Trade Cloth. Carol
Publishing Group. Secaucus, NJ. 1960. ISBN:0-8216-0021-4,
ISBN13: 978-0-8216-0021-4. Dewey:299/.3/1.
                                    Audience: l,u,f.

Foster, John L.   PJ1943.A53 2001
(Translator)
Ancient Egyptian Literature: An Anthology. Trade Cloth.
University of Texas Press. Austin, TX. 2001. 298p.
ISBN:0-292-72526-4, ISBN13: 978-0-292-72526-3.
Dewey:893/.108. LCCN:00-061607.
                            Audience: u,f.   Choice, 2002.

Hollis, Susan T.   GR75.T93H65 1990
The Ancient Egyptian "Tale of Two Brothers": The Oldest Fairy
Tale in the World. Ronald J. Leprohon (Introduction by). Trade
Cloth. University of Oklahoma Press. Norman, OK. 1990. 288p.
Oklahoma Series in Classical Culture, Vol. 7
ISBN:0-8061-2269-2, ISBN13: 978-0-8061-2269-4.
Dewey:398.21/0932. LCCN:90-050236.
                                    Audience: l,u,f.

Lichtheim, Miriam   PJ1943
Ancient Egyptian Literature: The Old and the Middle Kingdoms.
Trade Paper. University of California Press. Berkeley, CA. 1975.
272p. Ancient Egyptian Literature, a Book of Readings Ser., No.
12 ISBN:0-520-02899-6, ISBN13: 978-0-520-02899-9.
Dewey:893.1/08. LCCN:75-189225.
                                    Audience: g,l,u,f.

Lichtheim, Miriam   PJ1943
Ancient Egyptian Literature: A Book of Readings: The New
Kingdom. Trade Paper. University of California Press. Berkeley,
CA. 1978. 256p. Near Eastern Center Series, UCLA, No. 12
ISBN:0-520-03615-8, ISBN13: 978-0-520-03615-4.
Dewey:893.1/08. LCCN:75-189225.
                                    Audience: g,l,u,f.

Lichtheim, Miriam   PJ1943 .L5 2006
Ancient Egyptian Literature: Late Period. Ed. 2. Trade Paper.
University of California Press. Berkeley, CA. 2006. 260p.
ISBN:0-520-24844-9, ISBN13: 978-0-520-24844-1.
Dewey:893/.108. LCCN:2005-046681.
                                    Audience: g,l,u,f.

Parkinson, R. B.   PJ1945.T35 1999
(Translator)
The Tale of Sinuhe: And Other Ancient Egyptian Poems,
1940-1640 B. C. Trade Paper. Oxford University Press, Inc.
New York, NY. 1999. 332p. Oxford World's Classics Ser.
ISBN:0-19-283966-7, ISBN13: 978-0-19-283966-4.
Dewey:893/.11. LCCN:98-032140.
                                    Audience: u,f.

Parkinson, R. B.   PJ1943.V6 1991
Voices from Ancient Egypt: An Anthology of Middle Kingdom
Writings. Trade Paper. University of Oklahoma Press. Norman,

OK. 1991. 160p. Oklahoma Series in Classical Culture Ser., Vol. 9 ISBN:0-8061-2362-1, ISBN13: 978-0-8061-2362-2. Dewey:893/.1. LCCN:91-007250.

Audience: **u,f.**

Simpson, William Kelly   **PJ1943**
   (Editor)
The Literatutre of Ancient Egypt: An Anthology of Stories, Instructions, and Poetry. Yale University Press. 2003.

Audience: **l,u,f.**

Middle Eastern Languages and Literatures > Hamitic Languages and Literatures > Other Hamitic Languages And Literatures (Coptic, Berber)

Budge, E. A. Wallis   **PJ1949.B83 2002**
Egyptian Tales and Legends: Pagan, Christian, and Muslim. Trade Paper. Dover Publications, Inc. Mineola, NY. 2002. 448p. ISBN:0-486-42235-6, ISBN13: 978-0-486-42235-0. Dewey:893/.13008. LCCN:2002-019207.

Audience: **u,f.**

Middle Eastern Languages and Literatures > Semitic Languages and Literatures > Hebrew > Language

Alcalay, Reuben   **PJ4833 .A4**
The Complete Hebrew-English/English-Hebrew Dictionary. Trade Cloth. French & European Publications, Inc. New York, NY. 1996. 2000p. ISBN:0-7859-9625-7, ISBN13: 978-0-7859-9625-5. Dewey:492.432.

Audience: **l,u,f.**

Alter, Robert   **PJ5017 .A42**
Hebrew and Modernity. Trade Cloth. Indiana University Press. Bloomington, IN. 1994. 208p. ISBN:0-253-30473-3, ISBN13: 978-0-253-30473-5. Dewey:892.4/09. LCCN:93-025423.

Audience: **l,u,f.**

Baron, Salo W.   **DS112.B31523.B37**
High Middle Ages: Hebrew Language and Letters. Trade Cloth. Columbia University Press. New York, NY. 1958. 321p. ISBN:0-231-08844-2, ISBN13: 978-0-231-08844-2. Dewey:909/.04924. LCCN:52-000404.

Audience: **l,u,f.**

Ben-Yehuda, Eliezer   **PJ4831**
   (Editor)
Dictionary and Thesaurus of the Hebrew Language, Set. Trade Cloth. A. S. Barnes & Company, Inc. Stamford, CT. ISBN:0-498-07038-7, ISBN13: 978-0-498-07038-9. Dewey:492.4321.

Audience: **l,u,f.**

Birnbaum, Philip   **PJ4567**
Fluent Hebrew. Trade Cloth. Hebrew Publishing Company. Spencertown, NY. 1966. 491p. ISBN:0-88482-681-3, ISBN13: 978-0-88482-681-1. Dewey:492/.4.

Audience: **g,l,u,f.**

Blau, Joshua   **PJ4551 .B54 1981**
The Renaissance of Modern Hebrew and Modern Standard Arabic: Parallels and Differences in the Revival of Two Semitic Languages. Trade Paper. University of California Press. Berkeley, CA. 1982. Publications in Near Eastern Studies, Vol. 18 ISBN:0-520-09548-0, ISBN13: 978-0-520-09548-9. Dewey:492/.7. LCCN:81-016129.

Audience: **l,u,f.**

Bolozky, Shmuel   **PJ4645.B56 1996**
501 Hebrew Verbs. Trade Paper. Barron's Educational Series, Inc. Hauppauge, NY. 1996. 900p. 501 Verbs Ser. ISBN:0-8120-9468-9, ISBN13: 978-0-8120-9468-8. Dewey:492.4/824/21. LCCN:95-083209.

Audience: **g,l,u,f.**

Brettler, Marc Zvi   **PJ4567.3.B74 2002**
Biblical Hebrew for Students of Modern Israeli Hebrew. Cloth over Boards. Yale University Press. Cumberland, RI. 2001. 368p. Language Ser. ISBN:0-300-08440-4, ISBN13: 978-0-300-08440-5. Dewey:492.4/82421. LCCN:00-050323.

Audience: **u,f.**

Brown, F., et al.   **PJ4833**
The Brown-Driver-Briggs Hebrew and English Lexicon: Coded to Strong's Numbering System. S. Driver & C. Briggs (Authors). Trade Cloth. Hendrickson Publishers, Inc. Peabody, MA. 1996. 1216p. ISBN:1-56563-206-0, ISBN13: 978-1-56563-206-6. Dewey:492.4/321.

Audience: **u,f.**

Chomsky, William &   **PJ4556.K493C46 2001**
   Kimhi, David
David Kimhi's Hebrew Grammar: Mikhlol: Systematically Presented and Critically Annotated. Trade Paper. Bloch Publishing Company. New York, NY. 2001. xxxiv, 427p. ISBN:0-8197-0719-8, ISBN13: 978-0-8197-0719-2. Dewey:492.4/82. LCCN:2001-043565.

Audience: **l,u,f.**

Coffin, Edna A.   **PJ4567.5.C57 1992**
Encounters in Modern Hebrew, Level 1. Trade Cloth. University of Michigan Press. Chicago, IL. 1992. 280p. ISBN:0-472-10124-2, ISBN13: 978-0-472-10124-5. Dewey:492.4. LCCN:90-072019.

Audience: **l,u,f.**

Coffin, Edna A. &   **PJ4567.3.C63 2005**
   Bolozky, Shmuel
A Reference Grammar of Modern Hebrew. Cloth Text. Cambridge University Press. New York, NY. 2005. 462p. Reference Grammars Ser. ISBN:0-521-82033-2, ISBN13: 978-0-521-82033-2. Dewey:492.4/82421. LCCN:2004-051945.

Audience: **u,f.**

De Lange, Nicholas R.   **PJ5016 .H43 2001**
   M. (Editor)
Hebrew Scholarship and the Medieval World. Trade Cloth. Cambridge University Press. New York, NY. 2001. 261p. ISBN:0-521-78116-7, ISBN13: 978-0-521-78116-9. Dewey:492.4/09/02. LCCN:00-031266.

Audience: **u,f.**

Doniach, N. & Kahane,   **PJ4833.O9 1995**
   A.
The Oxford English-Hebrew Dictionary of Current Usage. Cloth Text. Oxford University Press, Inc. New York, NY. 1996. 1118p.

ISBN:0-19-864322-5, ISBN13: 978-0-19-864322-7.
Dewey:492.4/3/21. LCCN:95-021451.
Audience: **g,l,u,f.** *Choice, 1997.*

Even-Shoshan,   **PJ4830**
  Abraham (Editor)
The Complete Hebrew Dictionary in Three Volumes. Cloth Text.
Kiryat Sefer, Ltd. Reseda, CA. 1664p. ISBN:0-318-56919-1,
ISBN13: 978-0-318-56919-2. Dewey:492.4321.
Audience: **l,u,f.**

Glinert, Lewis   **PN6414.G58 1992**
The Joys of Hebrew. Cloth Text. Oxford University Press, Inc.
New York, NY. 1992. 304p. ISBN:0-19-507424-6, ISBN13:
978-0-19-507424-6. Dewey:398.9924. LCCN:92-028624.
Audience: **g,l,u,f.**

Glinert, Lewis   **PJ4567.3.G58 2004**
Modern Hebrew: An Essential Grammar. Ed. 3. Perfect, Paper
over Boards. Routledge. New York, NY. 2005. 304p. Essential
Grammars Ser. ISBN:0-415-70081-7, ISBN13:
978-0-415-70081-8. Dewey:492.4/8421. LCCN:2004-000795.
Audience: **l,u,f.**

Greenberg, Moshe   **PJ4567 .G855**
Introduction to Hebrew. Cloth Text. Prentice Hall PTR. Upper
Saddle River, NJ. 1964. ISBN:0-13-484469-6, ISBN13:
978-0-13-484469-5. Dewey:221.44.
Audience: **l,u,f.**

Halkin, A. S.   **PJ4645**
201 Hebrew Verbs. Trade Paper. Barron's Educational Series,
Inc. Hauppauge, NY. 1977. 448p. ISBN:0-8120-0331-4,
ISBN13: 978-0-8120-0331-4. Dewey:492.45.
Audience: **g,l,u,f.**

Harper, William Rainey   **PJ4567.H33**
Elements of Hebrew by an Inductive Method. Trade Cloth.
Classic Books. Murrieta, CA. 1921. 218p. ISBN:0-7426-4135-X,
ISBN13: 978-0-7426-4135-8. Dewey:492.45.
Audience: **l,u,f.**

Hoffman, Joel   **PJ4545.H58 2004**
In the Beginning: A Short History of the Hebrew Language.
Trade Cloth. New York University Press. New York, NY. 2004.
280p. ISBN:0-8147-3654-8, ISBN13: 978-0-8147-3654-8.
Dewey:492.4/09. LCCN:2004-040255.
Audience: **g,l,u,f.**

Kittel, Bonnie Pedrotti,   **PJ4567.3.K5 2004**
  et al.
Biblical Hebrew. Ed. 2. Victoria Hoffer & Rebecca Abts Wright
(Authors). Cloth over Boards. Yale University Press.
Cumberland, RI. 2004. 528p. Yale Language Ser.
ISBN:0-300-09862-6, ISBN13: 978-0-300-09862-4.
Dewey:492.4/82421. LCCN:2004-040723.
Audience: **u,f.**

Levenston, Edward A.   **PJ4833 .L55**
  & Sivan, Reuban (Editors)
The Megiddo Modern Dictionary: English-Hebrew,
Hebrew-English. Trade Cloth. Hippocrene Books, Inc. New
York, NY. 1983. ISBN:0-318-56935-3, ISBN13:
978-0-318-56935-2. Dewey:492.4321.
Audience: **g,l,u,f.**

Mintz, Alan (Editor)   **PJ4531.U6H4 1993**
Hebrew in America: Perspectives and Prospects. Trade Cloth.
Wayne State University Press. Detroit, MI. 1992. 338p.

American Jewish Civilization Ser. ISBN:0-8143-2351-0,
ISBN13: 978-0-8143-2351-9. Dewey:492.40973.
LCCN:92-013602.
Audience: **l,u,f.**

Orr-Stav, Jonathan &   **PJ4589.L68 2006**
  Lotan, Jon
Learn to Write the Hebrew Script: Aleph Through the Looking
Glass. Trade Paper, Perfect. Yale University Press. Cumberland,
RI. 2005. 176p. Yale Language Ser. ISBN:0-300-11334-X,
ISBN13: 978-0-300-11334-1. Dewey:492.4/82421.
LCCN:2005-042603.
Audience: **g,l,u,f.**

Raizen, Esther   **PJ4567.3.R35 2000**
Modern Hebrew for Beginners: A Multimedia Program for
Students at the Beginning and Intermediate Levels. Yaron
Shemer (Contribution by). Trade Paper. University of Texas
Press. Austin, TX. 2000. 224p. ISBN:0-292-77104-5, ISBN13:
978-0-292-77104-8. Dewey:492.4/82421. LCCN:99-058419.
Audience: **l,u,f.**

Ringvald, Vardit, et al.   **PJ4569**
Brandeis Modern Hebrew. Bonit Porath & Yaron Peleg
(Authors). Trade Cloth. University Press of New England.
Lebanon, NH. 608p. ISBN:1-58465-355-8, ISBN13:
978-1-58465-355-4. Dewey:492.4/82421.
Audience: **l,u,f.**

Saenz-Badillos, Angel   **PJ4545 .S2313 1996**
A History of the Hebrew Language. John Elwolds (Translator),
Shelomo Morag (Foreword by). Trade Cloth. Cambridge
University Press. New York, NY. 1993. 383p.
ISBN:0-521-43157-3, ISBN13: 978-0-521-43157-6.
Dewey:492.4/09. LCCN:93-020367.
Audience: **l,u,f.** *Choice, 1994.*

Yardeni, Ada   **PJ4589.Y3613 2002**
The Book of Hebrew Script: History, Palaeography, Script
Styles, Calligraphy and Design. Trade Cloth. Oak Knoll Press.
New Castle, DE. 2002. 365p. ISBN:1-58456-087-8, ISBN13:
978-1-58456-087-6. Dewey:492/.4/11. LCCN:2002-029266.
Audience: **u,f.**

Middle Eastern Languages and Literatures > Semitic Languages and Literatures > Hebrew > Literature

Ackerman, Susan   **PJ3771.G6A25 2005**
[e] When Heroes Love: The Ambiguity of Eros in the Stories of
Gilgamesh and David. E-Book. Columbia University Press. New
York, NY. 2005. 336p. Religion and Gender Ser.
ISBN:0-231-50725-9, ISBN13: 978-0-231-50725-7.
Dewey:809/.93353.
Audience: **u,f.**

Agnon, Shmuel Yosef   **PJ5050.J6**
The Bridal Canopy. Trade Cloth. Knopf Publishing Group. New
York, NY. 1967. ISBN:0-8052-3020-3, ISBN13:
978-0-8052-3020-8. Dewey:892.43. LCCN:67-014955.
Audience: **g,l,u,f.**

Agnon, Shmuel Yosef   **PJ5050.J6**
A Guest for the Night. Naftali C. Brandwein & Allen
Mandelbaum (Editors), Misha Louvish (Translator). Trade Cloth.
Knopf Publishing Group. New York, NY. 1968.

ISBN:0-8052-3091-2, ISBN13: 978-0-8052-3091-8.
Dewey:892.43. LCCN:68-013723.

Audience: **g,l,u,f.**

Agnon, Shmuel Yosef   PJ5053.A4S52413 1985
A Simple Story. Hillel Halkin (Translator, Afterword by). Trade
Cloth. Knopf Publishing Group. New York, NY. 1987. 256p.
ISBN:0-8052-3999-5, ISBN13: 978-0-8052-3999-7.
Dewey:892.4/35. LCCN:85-002481.

Audience: **g,l,u,f.**

Agnon, Shmuel Yosef &   PJ5053.A4T413 2000
  Harshav, Barbara
Only Yesterday. Cloth Text. Princeton University Press.
Princeton, NJ. 2000. 688p. ISBN:0-691-00972-4, ISBN13:
978-0-691-00972-8. Dewey:892.4/35. LCCN:00-021147.

Audience: **g,l,u,f.**

Agnon, Shmuel Yosef   PJ5053.A4
In the Heart of the Seas: A Story of a Journey to the Land of
Israel. I. M. Lask (Translator), T. Herzl Rome (Illustrator). Trade
Cloth. Knopf Publishing Group. New York, NY. 1966.
ISBN:0-8052-3110-2, ISBN13: 978-0-8052-3110-6.
Dewey:892.4/35. LCCN:66-030349.

Audience: **g,l,u,f.**

Alcalay, Ammiel   PJ5059.E1K48 1996
  (Editor, Introduction by)
Keys to the Garden: New Israeli Writing. Trade Paper. City
Lights Books. San Francisco, CA. 1996. 400p.
ISBN:0-87286-308-5, ISBN13: 978-0-87286-308-8.
Dewey:892.4/08. LCCN:95-024516.

Audience: **g,l,u,f.**

Amichai, Yehuda   PJ5054.A65
Open Closed Open: Poems. Trade Paper. Harcourt Trade
Publishers. New York, NY. 2006. 204p. ISBN:0-15-603050-0,
ISBN13: 978-0-15-603050-2. Dewey:892.4/16.

Audience: **g,l,u,f.**

Amichai, Yehuda   PJ5054.A65
Poems of Jerusalem and Love Poems. Trade Paper. Sheep
Meadow Press, The. Riverdale-on-Hudson, NY. 1992. 277p.
ISBN:1-878818-19-8, ISBN13: 978-1-878818-19-5.
Dewey:892.4/16. LCCN:92-031558.

Audience: **g,l,u,f.**

Amichai, Yehuda   PJ5054.A65S413 1997
Great Tranquillity: Questions and Answers. Glenda Abramson &
Tudor Parfitt (Translators). Trade Paper. Sheep Meadow Press,
The. Riverdale-on-Hudson, NY. 1997. 86p.
ISBN:1-878818-68-6, ISBN13: 978-1-878818-68-3.
Dewey:892.4/16. LCCN:97-032012.

Audience: **g,l,u,f.**

Amichai, Yehuda   PJ5054.A65A2 1996
The Selected Poetry of Yehuda Amichai. Chana Bloch &
Stephen Mitchell (Translators). Trade Cloth. University of
California Press. Berkeley, CA. 1996. 212p. Literature of the
Middle East Ser., Vol. 6 ISBN:0-520-20538-3, ISBN13:
978-0-520-20538-3. Dewey:892.4/16. LCCN:96-018580.

Audience: **g,l,u,f.**

Amichai, Yehuda &   PJ5054.A65
  Harshav, Benjamin
Yehuda Amichai: A Life of Poetry, 1948-1994. Trade Paper.
HarperCollins Publishers. New York, NY. 1995. 504p.

ISBN:0-06-092666-X, ISBN13: 978-0-06-092666-3.
Dewey:892.41. LCCN:94-007683.

Audience: **g,l,u,f.**

Appelfeld, Aharon   PJ5054.O9
The Healer. Trade Paper. Grove/Atlantic, Inc. New York, NY.
1994. 224p. ISBN:0-8021-3357-6, ISBN13: 978-0-8021-3357-1.
Dewey:892.4/36. LCCN:89-025847.

Audience: **g,l,u,f.**

Appelfeld, Aharon   PJ5054.O9
The Immortal Bartfuss. Trade Paper. Grove/Atlantic, Inc. New
York, NY. 1994. 138p. ISBN:0-8021-3358-4, ISBN13:
978-0-8021-3358-8. Dewey:892.4/36. LCCN:87-023111.

Audience: **g,l,u,f.**

Appelfeld, Aharon   PJ5054.A755K3613
Katerina: A Novel. Trade Paper. Knopf Publishing Group. New
York, NY. 2006. 224p. ISBN:0-8052-1198-5, ISBN13:
978-0-8052-1198-6. Dewey:892.4/36. LCCN:2005-049965.

Audience: **g,l,u,f.**

Appelfeld, Aharon   PJ5054.O9
To the Land of the Cattails. Trade Paper. Grove/Atlantic, Inc.
New York, NY. 1994. 148p. ISBN:0-8021-3359-2, ISBN13:
978-0-8021-3359-5. Dewey:892.4/36.

Audience: **g,l,u,f.**

Appelfeld, Aharon   PJ5054.A755U94 1994
Unto the Soul. Random House, Inc. 1993. ISBN:0-679-40611-5,
ISBN13: 978-0-679-40611-2.

Audience: **g,l,u,f.**

Appelfeld, Aharon   PJ5054
The Age of Wonders. Dalya Bilu (Translator). Trade Paper.
David R. Godine Publisher. Boston, MA. 2002. 288p.
ISBN:0-87923-798-8, ISBN13: 978-0-87923-798-1.
Dewey:892.4/36. LCCN:81-047318.

Audience: **g,l,u,f.**

Appelfeld, Aharon   PJ5054.O9
Badenheim 1939. Dalya Bilu (Translator). Trade Paper. David
R. Godine Publisher. Boston, MA. 1980. 160p.
ISBN:0-87923-799-6, ISBN13: 978-0-87923-799-8.
Dewey:892.436. LCCN:80-066192.

Audience: **g,l,u,f.**

Appelfeld, Aharon   PJ5054.O9
For Every Sin. Jeffrey M. Green (Translator). Trade Paper.
Grove/Atlantic, Inc. New York, NY. 1996. 176p.
ISBN:0-8021-3446-7, ISBN13: 978-0-8021-3446-2.
Dewey:892.4/36.

Audience: **g,l,u,f.** *Choice, 1989.*

Appelfeld, Aharon   PJ5054.A755Z47313
The Story of a Life: A Memoir. Aloma Halter (Translator).
Trade Cloth. Knopf Publishing Group. New York, NY. 2004.
208p. ISBN:0-8052-4178-7, ISBN13: 978-0-8052-4178-5.
Dewey:892.4/36 B. LCCN:2004-045306.

Audience: **g,l,u,f.**

Baron, Devorah   PJ5053.B34 A27 2001
The First Day and Other Stories. Trade Paper. University of
California Press. Berkeley, CA. 2001. 264p.
ISBN:0-520-08538-8, ISBN13: 978-0-520-08538-1.
Dewey:892.4/35. LCCN:00-055162.

Audience: **g,l,u,f.**

Bialik, C. N.   PJ5053.B5A6 2004
Selected Poems of C. N. Bialik. Trade Cloth. Overlook Press,
The. New York, NY. 2004. 180p. Jewish Classics Ser.
ISBN:1-58567-343-9, ISBN13: 978-1-58567-343-8.
Dewey:892.4/15. LCCN:2005-298265.
                                        Audience: **g,l,u,f.**

Bialik, Hayyim Nahman   PJ5053.B5 A694
Knight of Onions and Knight of Garlic. Trade Cloth. Hebrew
Publishing Company. Spencertown, NY. 1934. 55p.
ISBN:0-88482-734-8, ISBN13: 978-0-88482-734-4.
Dewey:892.41.
                                        Audience: **g,l,u,f.**

Bialik, Hayyim Nahman   PJ5053.B5
Random Harvest and Other Novellas. David Patterson & Ezra
Spicehandler (Translator, Introduction by). Trade Paper. Toby
Press LLC, The. New Milford, CT. 2005. 160p. Modern Hebrew
Classics Ser. ISBN:1-59264-094-X, ISBN13:
978-1-59264-094-2. Dewey:892.4/35.
                                        Audience: **g,l,u,f.**

Brenner, Rachel   PJ5029.B74 2003
  Feldhay
Inextricably Bonded: Israeli, Arab, and Jewish Writers
Re-Visioning Culture. Trade Cloth. University of Wisconsin
Press. Chicago, IL. 2004. 272p. Studies on Israel
ISBN:0-299-18960-0, ISBN13: 978-0-299-18960-0.
Dewey:892.4/3609358. LCCN:2003-007695.
                                        Audience: **u,f.**

Burnshaw, Stanley   PJ5059.E3M57 2003
  (Editor)
The Modern Hebrew Poem Itself. Ed. 2. Trade Paper. Wayne
State University Press. Detroit, MI. 2003. 232p.
ISBN:0-8143-2485-1, ISBN13: 978-0-8143-2485-1.
Dewey:892.4/1608. LCCN:2001-046706.
                                        Audience: **l,u,f.**

Carmi, T. (Editor,   PJ5040
  Translator)
The Penguin Book of Hebrew Verse. UK-B Format Paperback.
Penguin Group (USA) Inc. New York, NY. 2006. 608p.
ISBN:0-14-042467-9, ISBN13: 978-0-14-042467-6.
Dewey:892.41008.
                                        Audience: **g,l,u,f.**

Castel-Bloom, Orly, et   PJ5054.O9
  al.
Dolly City. Dalya Bilu & Marion Baraitser (Authors). Trade
Cloth. UNESCO Publishing. Paris, 1997. 182p.
ISBN:92-3-103362-X, ISBN13: 978-92-3-103362-9.
Dewey:892.436.
                                        Audience: **g,l,u,f.**

Feldman, Yael S.   PJ5029.F35 1999
No Room of Their Own: Gender and Nation in Israeli Women's
Fiction. Trade Cloth. Columbia University Press. New York, NY.
1999. 248p. Gender and Culture Ser. ISBN:0-231-11146-0,
ISBN13: 978-0-231-11146-1. Dewey:892.4/3099287.
LCCN:99-031641.
                                        Audience: **u,f.**

Goldberg, Leah   PJ5053.G6 A713 1992
On the Blossoming. Miriam B. Sivan (Translator, Afterword by).
Cloth Text. Garland Publishing, Inc. New York, NY. 1992. 84p.
World Literature in Translation Ser., Vol. 22

ISBN:0-8240-0034-X, ISBN13: 978-0-8240-0034-9.
Dewey:892.415. LCCN:92-010598.
                                        Audience: **g,l,u,f.**

Goldberg, Lea   PJ5053.G6
Selected Poetry and Drama. Rachel Tzvia Back & T. Carmi
(Translators). Trade Paper, Perfect. Toby Press LLC, The. New
Milford, CT. 2005. 318p. Modern Hebrew Classics Ser.
ISBN:1-59264-111-3, ISBN13: 978-1-59264-111-6.
Dewey:892.415.
                                        Audience: **g,l,u,f.**

Gouri, Haim   PJ5054.G66I813 1999
The Chocolate Deal. Seymour Simckes (Translator), Geoffrey
Hartman (Foreword by). Trade Paper. Wayne State University
Press. Detroit, MI. 1999. 144p. ISBN:0-8143-2800-8, ISBN13:
978-0-8143-2800-2. Dewey:892.4/36. LCCN:99-013470.
                                        Audience: **g,l,u,f.**

Grossman, David   PJ5054.G728H513 1990
The Smile of the Lamb. Trade Cloth. Farrar, Straus & Giroux.
New York, NY. 1991. 325p. ISBN:0-374-26639-5, ISBN13:
978-0-374-26639-4. Dewey:892.4/36. LCCN:90-003873.
                                        Audience: **g,l,u,f.**

Grossman, David   PJ5054.G728 S54
Words into Flesh. Trade Cloth. Farrar, Straus & Giroux. New
York, NY. 1957. ISBN:0-374-29284-1, ISBN13:
978-0-374-29284-3. Dewey:892.436.
                                        Audience: **g,l,u,f.**

Grossman, David   PJ5054.G728S5413
Be My Knife: A Novel. Vered Almog & Maya Gurantz
(Translators). Cloth over Boards. Farrar, Straus & Giroux. New
York, NY. 2002. 324p. ISBN:0-374-29977-3, ISBN13:
978-0-374-29977-4. Dewey:892.4/36. LCCN:2001-033645.
                                        Audience: **g,l,u,f.**

Grossman, David   PJ5054.G728M5713
Someone to Run With: A Novel. Vered Almog & Maya Gurantz
(Translators). Cloth over Boards. Farrar, Straus & Giroux. New
York, NY. 2004. 352p. ISBN:0-374-26657-3, ISBN13:
978-0-374-26657-8. Dewey:892.4/36. LCCN:2002-029778.
                                        Audience: **g,l,u,f.**

Grossman, David   PJ5054.G728A233 2005
Her Body Knows: Two Novellas. Jessica Cohen (Translator).
Cloth over Boards. Farrar, Straus & Giroux. New York, NY.
2005. 272p. ISBN:0-374-17557-8, ISBN13: 978-0-374-17557-3.
Dewey:892.4/36. LCCN:2004-056267.
                                        Audience: **g,l,u,f.**

Grossman, David   N45
See Under. Betsy Rosenberg (Translator). Trade Paper. Picador.
New York, NY. 2002. 464p. ISBN:0-312-42069-2, ISBN13:
978-0-312-42069-7. Dewey:700.
                                        Audience: **g,l,u,f.**

Grossman, David   PJ5054.G728Y47 1997
The Zigzag Kid. Betsy Rosenberg (Translator). Trade Cloth.
Farrar, Straus & Giroux. New York, NY. 1997. 384p.
ISBN:0-374-29692-8, ISBN13: 978-0-374-29692-6.
Dewey:892.4/36. LCCN:96-049824.
                                        Audience: **g,l,u,f.**

Hareven, Shulamith   PJ5054.H292I713 1993
City of Many Days: A Novel. Hillel Halkin (Translator). Trade
Paper. Mercury House. San Francisco, CA. 1993. 200p.

ISBN:1-56279-050-1, ISBN13: 978-1-56279-050-9.
Dewey:892.4/36. LCCN:93-012726.

Audience: **g,l,u,f.**

Hazaz, Haim   **PJ5053.A4**
Gates of Bronze. S. Gershon Levi (Translator), Robert Alter
(Introduction by). Trade Cloth. Jewish Publication Society.
Dulles, VA. 1975. ISBN:0-8276-0059-3, ISBN13:
978-0-8276-0059-1. Dewey:892.435. LCCN:74-015463.

Audience: **g,l,u,f.**

Hendel, Yehudit   **PJ5054.H454A24 2002**
Small Change. Dalia Bilu, Barbara Harshaw & Marsha
Pomerantz (Translators). Trade Cloth. University Press of New
England. Lebanon, NH. 2005. 160p. Tauber Institute for the
Study of European Jewry Ser. ISBN:1-58465-279-9, ISBN13:
978-1-58465-279-3. Dewey:892.4/36. LCCN:2002-013291.

Audience: **g,l,u,f.**

Hoffmann, Yoel   **PJ5054.H6319L4813**
The Heart Is Katmandu: Novel. Peter Cole (Translator). Trade
Cloth. New Directions Publishing Corporation. New York, NY.
2001. 144p. ISBN:0-8112-1465-6, ISBN13: 978-0-8112-1465-0.
Dewey:892.4/36. LCCN:00-069567.

Audience: **g,l,u,f.**

Hoffmann, Yoel   **PJ5054.H6319S5815**
The Shunra and the Schmetterling. Peter Cole (Translator).
Trade Paper. New Directions Publishing Corporation. New York,
NY. 2004. 128p. ISBN:0-8112-1567-9, ISBN13:
978-0-8112-1567-1. Dewey:892.4/36. LCCN:2004-000950.

Audience: **g,l,u,f.**

Hoffmann, Yoel   **PJ5054.H6319K3813**
Katschen and The Book of Joseph. David Kriss, Alan Treister &
Eddy Levenston (Translators). Trade Cloth. New Directions
Publishing Corporation. New York, NY. 1998. 160p.
ISBN:0-8112-1373-0, ISBN13: 978-0-8112-1373-8.
Dewey:892.4/36. LCCN:97-050300.

Audience: **g,l,u,f.**

Hoffmann, Yoel   **PJ5054.H6319B4713**
Bernhardt. Alan Triester (Translator). Trade Cloth. New
Directions Publishing Corporation. New York, NY. 1998. 192p.
ISBN:0-8112-1389-7, ISBN13: 978-0-8112-1389-9.
Dewey:892.4/36. LCCN:98-025231.

Audience: **g,l,u,f.**

Joseph, Herbert S.   **PJ5043 .M6 1983**
  (Editor)
Modern Israeli Drama: An Anthology. Trade Cloth. Fairleigh
Dickinson University Press. Cranbury, NJ. 1983. 272p.
ISBN:0-8386-3104-5, ISBN13: 978-0-8386-3104-1.
Dewey:892.4/26.08. LCCN:81-065461.

Audience: **l,u,f.**

Ka-Tzetnik   **PZ3.K1613**
Phoenix Over the Galilee. Trade Paper. Penguin Group (USA)
Inc. New York, NY. 1977. ISBN:0-515-04192-0, ISBN13:
978-0-515-04192-7. Dewey:892.4/3/6.

Audience: **g,l,u,f.**

Ka-Tzetnik   **PZ3.K1613**
Star Eternal. Trade Cloth. HarperCollins Publishers. New York,
NY. 1971. ISBN:0-87795-009-1, ISBN13: 978-0-87795-009-7.
Dewey:892.4/3/6. LCCN:75-141639.

Audience: **g,l,u,f.**

Ka-Tzetnik   **PJ5054.O9**
House of Dolls. Moshe M. Kahn (Translator). Trade Paper.
Academy Chicago Publishers, Ltd. Chicago, IL. 1982. 222p.
ISBN:0-583-12248-5, ISBN13: 978-0-583-12248-1.
Dewey:892.4/3/6.

Audience: **g,l,u,f.**

Kaniuk, Yoram   **PJ5054.K326**
Rockinghorse. Richard Flantz (Translator). Trade Cloth.
HarperCollins Publishers. New York, NY. 1977.
ISBN:0-06-012245-5, ISBN13: 978-0-06-012245-4.
Dewey:892.4/3/6. LCCN:76-005546.

Audience: **g,l,u,f.**

Kaniuk, Yoram   **PJ5054.K326Y4413**
The Last Jew: A Novel. Barbara Harshav (Translator). Trade
Cloth. Grove/Atlantic, Inc. New York, NY. 2006. 544p.
ISBN:0-8021-1811-9, ISBN13: 978-0-8021-1811-0.
Dewey:892.4/36. LCCN:2005-051396.

Audience: **g,l,u,f.**

Kaniuk, Yoram   **PJ5054.O9**
The Story of Great Aunt Shlomzion. Zeva Shapiro (Translator).
Trade Cloth. HarperCollins Publishers. New York, NY. 1979.
ISBN:0-06-012259-5, ISBN13: 978-0-06-012259-1.
Dewey:892.4/3/6. LCCN:78-002066.

Audience: **g,l,u,f.**

Kaniuk, Yoram   **PJ5054.K326A6713**
Adam Resurrected. Seymour Simckes (Translator). Trade Paper.
Grove/Atlantic, Inc. New York, NY. 2000. 384p.
ISBN:0-8021-3689-3, ISBN13: 978-0-8021-3689-3.
Dewey:892.4/36. LCCN:99-056655.

Audience: **g,l,u,f.**

Kaniuk, Yoram   **PJ5054.K326B5813**
His Daughter. Seymour Simckes (Translator). Trade Cloth.
George Braziller Inc. New York, NY. 1989. 293p.
ISBN:0-8076-1215-4, ISBN13: 978-0-8076-1215-6.
Dewey:892.4/36. LCCN:88-007496.

Audience: **g,l,u,f.** *Choice, 1989.*

Kashua, Sayed   **PJ5055.38.A84A8713**
Dancing Arabs. Miriam Shlesinger (Translator). Trade Paper.
Grove/Atlantic, Inc. New York, NY. 2004. 240p.
ISBN:0-8021-4126-9, ISBN13: 978-0-8021-4126-2.
Dewey:892.4/37. LCCN:2003-067765.

Audience: **g,l,u,f.**

Kenaz, Yehoshua   **PJ5054.K36H513 2003**
Infiltration: A Novel. Dalya Bilu (Translator). Trade Paper.
Steerforth Press. Hanover, NH. 2003. 608p.
ISBN:1-58195-205-8, ISBN13: 978-1-58195-205-6.
Dewey:892.4/36. LCCN:2003-009891.

Audience: **g,l,u,f.**

Kenaz, Yehoshua   **PJ5054.K36M313 2001**
Returning Lost Loves: A Novel. Dalya Bilu (Translator). Trade
Paper. Steerforth Press. Hanover, NH. 2001. 250p.
ISBN:1-58642-013-5, ISBN13: 978-1-58642-013-0.
Dewey:892.4/36. LCCN:00-012132.

Audience: **g,l,u,f.**

Kovner, Abba   **PJ5054.A65**
Sloan Kettering: Poems. Trade Paper. Knopf Publishing Group.
New York, NY. 2004. 160p. ISBN:0-8052-1145-4, ISBN13:
978-0-8052-1145-0. Dewey:892.4/16.

Audience: **g,l,u,f.**

Kovner, Abba   PJ5054.K6M9 1986
My Little Sister and Selected Poems. Shirley Kaufman
(Translator, Preface by). Trade Cloth. Oberlin College Press.
Oberlin, OH. 2003. 159p. Field Translation Ser., No. 11
ISBN:0-932440-20-7, ISBN13: 978-0-932440-20-4.
Dewey:892.4/16. LCCN:85-073146.
                          Audience: **g,l,u,f.** *Choice, 1986.*

Levin, Hanoch   PJ5054.L38A24 2003
The Labor of Life: Selected Plays. Barbara Harshav (Translator).
Trade Cloth. Stanford University Press. Palo Alto, CA. 2003.
352p. ISBN:0-8047-4858-6, ISBN13: 978-0-8047-4858-2.
Dewey:892.4/26. LCCN:2003-013749.
                                    Audience: **g,l,u,f.**

Megged, Aharon   PJ5054.M352
Foiglman. Trade Cloth. Toby Press LLC, The. New Milford, CT.
2003. 277p. ISBN:1-59264-032-X, ISBN13: 978-1-59264-032-4.
Dewey:892.4/36. LCCN:2004-556483.
                                    Audience: **g,l,u,f.**

Megged, Aharon   PJ5054.M352
Mandrakes from the Holy Land. Toby Press LLC. 2005.
ISBN:1-59264-057-5, ISBN13: 978-1-59264-057-7.
                                    Audience: **g,l,u,f.**

Megged, Aharon   PJ5054.M352
The Living on the Dead. Misha Louvish (Translator). Trade
Paper, Perfect. Toby Press LLC, The. New Milford, CT. 2005.
283p. ISBN:1-59264-133-4, ISBN13: 978-1-59264-133-8.
Dewey:892.4/3/6.
                                    Audience: **g,l,u,f.**

Michael, Sami   PJ5054.M44H3813 2003
A Trumpet in the Wadi: A Novel. Trade Cloth. Simon &
Schuster. New York, NY. 2003. 256p. ISBN:0-7432-4496-6,
ISBN13: 978-0-7432-4496-1. Dewey:892.4/36.
LCCN:2003-042716.
                                    Audience: **g,l,u,f.**

Michael, Sami   PJ5054.M44H3713 1988
Refuge. Edward Grossman (Translator). Trade Cloth. Jewish
Publication Society. Dulles, VA. 1988. 376p.
ISBN:0-8276-0308-8, ISBN13: 978-0-8276-0308-0.
Dewey:892.4/36. LCCN:87-031086.
                                    Audience: **g,l,u,f.**

Mintz, Alan (Editor)   PJ5029.B66 1997
The Boom in Contemporary Israeli Fiction. Trade Cloth.
University Press of New England. Lebanon, NH. 1997. 202p.
The Tauber Institute Ser., No. 24 ISBN:0-87451-820-2, ISBN13:
978-0-87451-820-7. Dewey:892.4/360995694. LCCN:97-003013.
                          Audience: **l,u,f.** *Choice, 1998.*

Mintz, Alan   PJ5020.R39 2002
Reading Hebrew Literature: Critical Discussions of Six Modern
Texts. Trade Cloth. University Press of New England. Lebanon,
NH. 2002. 224p. Tauber Institute for the Study of European
Jewry Ser. ISBN:1-58465-195-4, ISBN13: 978-1-58465-195-6.
Dewey:892.4/09006. LCCN:2002-010155.
                          Audience: **l,u,f.** *Choice, 2003.*

Mintz, Alan L.   PJ5029.M46 2001
Translating Israel: Contemporary Hebrew Literature and Its
Reception in America. Trade Cloth. Syracuse University Press.
Syracuse, NY. 2001. vii, 272p. Judaic Traditions in Literature,
Music and Art Ser. ISBN:0-8156-2900-1, ISBN13:
978-0-8156-2900-9. Dewey:892.4/3609. LCCN:00-049263.
                          Audience: **u,f.** *Choice, 2002.*

Mintz, Ruth F.   PJ5059.E3
Modern Hebrew Poetry: A Billingual Anthology. Ed. 3. Trade
Paper. University of California Press. Berkeley, CA. 1966. 425p.
ISBN:0-520-04781-8, ISBN13: 978-0-520-04781-5.
Dewey:892.4108.
                                    Audience: **u,f.**

Oz, Amos   PJ5054.O9
Don't Call It Night. UK-B Format Paperback. Knopf Publishing
Group. New York, NY. 2004. 200p. ISBN:0-09-949601-1,
ISBN13: 978-0-09-949601-4. Dewey:892.4/36.
                                    Audience: **g,l,u,f.**

Oz, Amos   PJ5054.O9
The Hill of Evil Counsel. Trade Paper. Harcourt Trade
Publishers. New York, NY. 1991. 210p. ISBN:0-15-640275-0,
ISBN13: 978-0-15-640275-0. Dewey:892.4/3/6.
                                    Audience: **g,l,u,f.**

Oz, Amos   PJ5054.O9M513 1972
My Michael. Trade Cloth. Alfred A. Knopf Inc. New York, NY.
1972. vi, 287p. ISBN:0-394-47146-6, ISBN13:
978-0-394-47146-4. Dewey:892.4/36. LCCN:70-171158.
                                    Audience: **g,l,u,f.**

Oz, Amos   PZ7.O984SO 2004
Soumchi. Trade Paper. Toby Press LLC, The. New Milford, CT.
2003. 53p. ISBN:1-59264-038-9, ISBN13: 978-1-59264-038-6.
Dewey:892.4/36.
                                    Audience: **g,l,u,f.**

Oz, Amos   PJ5054.O9L2913 1991
To Know a Woman. Cloth over Boards. Harcourt Trade
Publishers. New York, NY. 1991. 262p. ISBN:0-15-190499-5,
ISBN13: 978-0-15-190499-0. Dewey:892.436.
LCCN:90-005196.
                                    Audience: **g,l,u,f.**

Oz, Amos   PJ5054.O9
Touch the Water, Touch the Wind. Trade Paper. Harcourt Trade
Publishers. New York, NY. 1991. 192p. ISBN:0-15-690772-0,
ISBN13: 978-0-15-690772-9. Dewey:892.4/36.
LCCN:74-012178.
                                    Audience: **g,l,u,f.**

Oz, Amos   PJ5054.O9Z47313 2004
A Tale of Love and Darkness. Nicholas De Lange (Translator).
Cloth over Boards. Harcourt Trade Publishers. New York, NY.
2004. 544p. ISBN:0-15-100878-7, ISBN13: 978-0-15-100878-0.
Dewey:892.4/36 B. LCCN:2004-007302.
                                    Audience: **g,l,u,f.**

Oz, Amos   PJ5054.O9K8413 1988
Black Box. Nicholas R. M. De Lange (Translator). Trade Cloth.
Harcourt Trade Publishers. New York, NY. 1988. 320p.
ISBN:0-15-112888-X, ISBN13: 978-0-15-112888-4.
Dewey:892.4/36. LCCN:87-033525.
                                    Audience: **g,l,u,f.**

Oz, Amos   PJ5054.O9
Elsewhere Perhaps. Nicholas R. M. De Lange (Translator).
Trade Paper. Harcourt Trade Publishers. New York, NY. 1985.
324p. A Helen and Kurt Wolff Bk. ISBN:0-15-628475-8,
ISBN13: 978-0-15-628475-2. Dewey:892.4/3/6.
LCCN:73-008628.
                                    Audience: **g,l,u,f.**

Oz, Amos   PJ5054.O9
Unto Death: Crusade and Late Love. Nicholas R. M. De Lange (Translator). Trade Paper. Harcourt Trade Publishers. New York, NY. 1978. 176p. Harvest Book Ser. ISBN:0-15-693170-2, ISBN13: 978-0-15-693170-0. Dewey:[Fic]. LCCN:77-015963.
Audience: **g,l,u,f.**

Oz, Amos   PJ5054.O9 A8713 1981
Where the Jackals Howl and Other Stories. Nicholas R. M. De Lange & Philip Simpson (Translators). Trade Cloth. Harcourt Trade Publishers. New York, NY. 1981. 228p. A Helen and Kurt Wolff Bk. ISBN:0-15-196038-0, ISBN13: 978-0-15-196038-5. Dewey:892.4/36. LCCN:80-008754.
Audience: **g,l,u,f.**

Oz, Amos   PJ5054.O9M413 1985
A Perfect Peace. Hillel Halkin (Translator). Trade Cloth. Harcourt Trade Publishers. New York, NY. 1985. 400p. A Helen and Kurt Wolff Bk. ISBN:0-15-171696-X, ISBN13: 978-0-15-171696-8. Dewey:892.4/36. LCCN:84-025171.
Audience: **g,l,u,f.**

Pagis, Dan   PJ5054.P32A25 1996
The Selected Poetry of Dan Pagis. Stephen Mitchell (Translator), Robert Alter (Introduction by). Trade Paper. University of California Press. Berkeley, CA. 1996. 160p. Literature of the Middle East Ser., Vol. 7 ISBN:0-520-20539-1, ISBN13: 978-0-520-20539-0. Dewey:892/.416. LCCN:96-014395.
Audience: **g,l,u,f.**

Rabinyan, Dorit   PJ5054.R257S5613 199
Persian Brides: A Novel. Ed. 1. Yael Lotan (Translator). George Braziller. 1998. ISBN:0-8076-1430-0, ISBN13: 978-0-8076-1430-3.
Audience: **g,l,u,f.**

Rabinyan, Dorit   PJ5054.R257H3813
A Strand of a Thousand Pears: A Novel. Yael Lotan (Translator). Random House. 2001. ISBN:0-375-50811-2, ISBN13: 978-0-375-50811-0.
Audience: **g,l,u,f.**

Ramras-Rauch, Gila &   PJ5059.E8F33 1985
  Michman-Melkman, Joseph (Editors)
Facing the Holocaust: Selected Israeli Fiction. Gershon Shaked (Afterword by). Trade Cloth. Jewish Publication Society. Dulles, VA. 1986. 292p. ISBN:0-8276-0253-7, ISBN13: 978-0-8276-0253-3. Dewey:892.4/301/0895694. LCCN:85-012570.
Audience: **g,l,u,f.** *Choice, 1986.*

Ravikovitch, Dahlia   PJ5054.R265A22 1989
The Window: New and Selected Poems. Chana Bloch & Ariel Bloch (Translators), Robert Alter (Foreword by). Library Binding. Sheep Meadow Press, The. Riverdale-on-Hudson, NY. 1989. 133p. ISBN:0-935296-81-6, ISBN13: 978-0-935296-81-5. Dewey:892.4/16. LCCN:88-034896.
Audience: **g,l,u,f.** *Choice, 1989.*

Sasson, Jack M.   PJ310 .S78 1984
  (Editor)
Studies in Literature from the Ancient Near East: Dedicated to Samuel Noah Kramer. Trade Cloth. American Oriental Society. New Haven, CT. 1984. 369p. American Oriental Ser., Vol. 65 ISBN:0-940490-65-X, ISBN13: 978-0-940490-65-9. Dewey:809/.89394. LCCN:86-136854.
Audience: **u,f.**

Shabtai, Yaakov   PJ5054.S2643Z3313
Past Continuous. Dalya Bilu (Translator). Trade Cloth. Jewish Publication Society. Dulles, VA. 1985. 389p. ISBN:0-8276-0239-1, ISBN13: 978-0-8276-0239-7. Dewey:892.4/36. LCCN:84-020097.
Audience: **g,l,u,f.**

Shabtai, Yaakov   PJ5054.S2643S613
Past Perfect. Dalya Bilu (Translator). Trade Cloth. Penguin Group (USA) Inc. New York, NY. 1987. 291p. ISBN:0-670-81308-7, ISBN13: 978-0-670-81308-7. Dewey:892.4/36. LCCN:86-040493.
Audience: **g,l,u,f.** *Choice, 1988.*

Shabtai, Yaakov   PJ5054.S2643U53 2004
Uncle Peretz Takes Off. Dalya Bilu (Translator). Trade Cloth. Overlook Press, The. New York, NY. 2004. 240p. ISBN:1-58567-340-4, ISBN13: 978-1-58567-340-7. Dewey:892.4/36. LCCN:2004-058316.
Audience: **g,l,u,f.**

Shaham, Nathan   PJ5054.S3
The Rosendorf Quartet: A Novel. Trade Paper. Grove/Atlantic, Inc. New York, NY. 1993. 368p. ISBN:0-8021-3316-9, ISBN13: 978-0-8021-3316-8. Dewey:892.4/36. LCCN:91-006482.
Audience: **g,l,u,f.**

Shaked, Gershon   PJ5029
Modern Hebrew Fiction. Emily Miller Budick (Editor), Yael Lotan (Translator). Trade Cloth. Indiana University Press. Bloomington, IN. 2000. 336p. Jewish Literature and Culture Ser. ISBN:0-253-33711-9, ISBN13: 978-0-253-33711-5. Dewey:892.4/3609. LCCN:99-054356.
Audience: **l,u,f.** *Choice, 2001.*

Shalev, Meir   PJ5054.O9
The Blue Mountain. Hillel Halkin (Translator). Trade Paper. Canongate Books. Edinburgh, 2002. 376p. ISBN:1-84195-115-3, ISBN13: 978-1-84195-115-7. Dewey:892.4/36.
Audience: **g,l,u,f.**

Shalev, Meir   PJ5054.S384K413 1999
The Loves of Judith. Barbara Harshav (Translator). Trade Cloth. HarperCollins Publishers. New York, NY. 1999. 320p. ISBN:0-88001-635-3, ISBN13: 978-0-88001-635-3. Dewey:892.4/36. LCCN:98-022747.
Audience: **g,l,u,f.**

Shamir, Moshe   PZ4.S5274 KI
King of Flesh and Blood. David Patterson (Translator). Trade Paper. Hebrew Publishing Company. Spencertown, NY. ISBN:0-85222-220-3, ISBN13: 978-0-85222-220-1. Dewey:892.436.
Audience: **g,l,u,f.**

Shammas, Anton   PJ5054.S414A8913
Arabesques. Vivian Eden (Translator). Trade Cloth. HarperCollins Publishers. New York, NY. 1988. 256p. ISBN:0-06-015744-5, ISBN13: 978-0-06-015744-9. Dewey:892.4/36. LCCN:87-045665.
Audience: **g,l,u,f.** *Choice, 1988.*

Someck, Ronny   PJ5054.S65A23 2002
The Fire Stays in Red: Poems. Moshe Dor & Barbara Goldberg (Translators). Trade Cloth. University of Wisconsin Press. Chicago, IL. 2002. 144p. ISBN:0-299-17900-1, ISBN13: 978-0-299-17900-7. Dewey:892.4/16. LCCN:2002-020689.
Audience: **g,l,u,f.**

Spicehandler, Ezra &   **PJ5059.E1.N4**
  Arnson, Curtis (Editors)
New Writing in Israel. Trade Cloth. Knopf Publishing Group.
New York, NY. 1976. 224p. ISBN:0-8052-3625-2, ISBN13:
978-0-8052-3625-5. Dewey:892.4/08/006. LCCN:75-036497.
            Audience: **g,l,u,f.** *B*

Stern, David & Mirsky,   **BM512.R28 1990**
  Mark J. (Editors)
Rabbinic Fantasies: Imaginative Narratives from Classical
Hebrew Literature. Mimi Gross & Inger J. Grytting
(Illustrators). Cloth Text. Jewish Publication Society. Dulles, VA.
1990. 376p. ISBN:0-8276-0363-0, ISBN13: 978-0-8276-0363-9.
Dewey:892.4/08. LCCN:90-032680.
            Audience: **g,l,u,f.**

Taub, Michael (Editor)   **PJ5043.I87 1996**
Israeli Holocaust Drama. Trade Cloth. Syracuse University
Press. Syracuse, NY. 1996. 456p. ISBN:0-8156-2673-8, ISBN13:
978-0-8156-2673-2. Dewey:892.4/26080358. LCCN:95-010506.
          Audience: **l,u,f.** *Choice, 1997.*

Wallach, Yona   **PJ5054.W26L47 2006**
Let the Words: Selected Poems. Linda Stern Zisquit (Translator).
Trade Paper. Sheep Meadow Press, The. Riverdale-on-Hudson,
NY. 2006. 178p. ISBN:1-931357-34-X, ISBN13:
978-1-931357-34-0. Dewey:892.4/16. LCCN:2005-036254.
            Audience: **g,l,u,f.**

Yehoshua, A. B.   **PJ5054. Y42 1998**
The Continuing Silence of a Poet: The Collected Stories of A.
B. Yehoshua. Paper Text. Syracuse University Press. Syracuse,
NY. 1998. 328p. Library of Modern Jewish Literature
ISBN:0-8156-0559-5, ISBN13: 978-0-8156-0559-1.
Dewey:892.436. LCCN:98-036433.
            Audience: **g,l,u,f.**

Yehoshua, A. B.   **PJ5054.Y42 B513 1977**
Early in the Summer of Nineteen Seventy. Miriam Arad
(Translator). Trade Cloth. Doubleday Publishing. New York, NY.
1977. 165p. ISBN:0-385-02590-4, ISBN13: 978-0-385-02590-4.
Dewey:892.4/3/6. LCCN:76-016262.
            Audience: **g,l,u,f.**

Yehoshua, A. B.   **PN49.Y4413 2000**
The Terrible Power of a Minor Guilt: Literary Essays. Ora
Cummings (Translator). Trade Cloth. Syracuse University Press.
Syracuse, NY. 2000. xxii, 145p. ISBN:0-8156-0656-7, ISBN13:
978-0-8156-0656-7. Dewey:809/.93353. LCCN:00-030086.
          Audience: **g,l,u,f.** *Choice, 2001.*

Yehoshua, A. B.   **PJ5054.Y42M5513 1989**
Five Seasons. Hillel Halkin (Translator). Trade Cloth.
Doubleday Publishing. New York, NY. 1988. 368p.
ISBN:0-385-23130-X, ISBN13: 978-0-385-23130-5.
Dewey:892.436. LCCN:88-010900.
            Audience: **g,l,u,f.**

Yehoshua, A. B.   **PJ5054.O9**
A Late Divorce. Hillel Halkin (Translator). Trade Cloth.
Doubleday Publishing. New York, NY. 1984. 360p.
ISBN:0-385-15574-3, ISBN13: 978-0-385-15574-8.
Dewey:892.4/36. LCCN:82-045830.
            Audience: **g,l,u,f.**

Yehoshua, A. B.   **PJ5054.Y42K3513 2003**
The Liberated Bride. Hillel Halkin (Translator). Cloth over
Boards. Harcourt Trade Publishers. New York, NY. 2003. 576p.

ISBN:0-15-100653-9, ISBN13: 978-0-15-100653-3.
Dewey:892.4/36. LCCN:2003-005360.
            Audience: **g,l,u,f.**

Yehoshua, A. B.   **PJ5054.Y42S4913 2006**
A Woman in Jerusalem. Hillel Halkin (Translator). Cloth over
Boards. Harcourt Trade Publishers. New York, NY. 2006. 256p.
ISBN:0-15-101226-1, ISBN13: 978-0-15-101226-8.
Dewey:892.4/36. LCCN:2005-033435.
            Audience: **g,l,u,f.**

Yehoshua, A. B.   **PJ5054.O9**
The Lover. Philip Simpson (Translator). Trade Cloth. Doubleday
Publishing. New York, NY. 1978. 352p. ISBN:0-385-12134-2,
ISBN13: 978-0-385-12134-7. Dewey:892.4/36.
LCCN:76-051996.
            Audience: **g,l,u,f.**

Yudkin, Leon I. (Editor)   **PJ5012.H65.H43 1993**
Hebrew Literature in the Wake of the Holocaust. Trade Cloth.
Fairleigh Dickinson University Press. Cranbury, NJ. 1993. 131p.
ISBN:0-8386-3499-0, ISBN13: 978-0-8386-3499-8.
Dewey:892.4/09358. LCCN:92-054455.
          Audience: **g,l,u,f.** *Choice, 1994.*

Yudkin, Leon I. (Editor)   **PJ5029 .I87 1993**
Israeli Writers Consider the "Outsider". Trade Cloth. Fairleigh
Dickinson University Press. Cranbury, NJ. 1993. 143p.
ISBN:0-8386-3498-2, ISBN13: 978-0-8386-3498-1.
Dewey:892.4/3609. LCCN:92-054458.
            Audience: **u,f.**

Middle Eastern Languages and Literatures > Semitic Languages and Literatures > Aramaic

Johns, Alger F.   **PJ5213**
A Short Grammar of Biblical Aramaic. Paper Text. Andrews
University Press. Berrien Springs, MI. 1982. 120p. Monograph
Ser. ISBN:0-943872-74-X, ISBN13: 978-0-943872-74-2.
Dewey:492/.29. LCCN:93-072717.
            Audience: **u,f.**

Moosa, Matti   **DS59.S94I3413 2000**
The History of Syriac Literature and Sciences. Trade Cloth.
Passeggiata Press. Pueblo, CO. 2000. xviii, 252p.
ISBN:1-57889-103-5, ISBN13: 978-1-57889-103-0.
Dewey:956.7. LCCN:00-048730.
            Audience: **u,f.**

Robinson, T. H. &   **PJ5423.5 .R6 1981**
  Brockington, L. H. (Editors)
Paradigms and Exercises in Syriac Grammar. Ed. 4. Trade
Paper. Oxford University Press, Inc. New York, NY. 1982. 176p.
ISBN:0-19-815458-5, ISBN13: 978-0-19-815458-7.
Dewey:492/.3. LCCN:81-018723.
            Audience: **u,f.**

Thackston, Wheeler M. Jr.   **PJ5423.T53 1999**
Introduction to Syriac: An Elementary Grammar with Readings
from Syriac Literature. Trade Paper. IBEX Publishers, Inc.
Bethesda, MD. 2000. 228p. ISBN:0-936347-98-8, ISBN13:
978-0-936347-98-1. Dewey:492/.382421. LCCN:99-039576.
            Audience: **u,f.**

Wright, William   **PJ5494**
  (Abridged by)
A Short History of Syriac Literature. Perfect. Gorgias Press,
LLC. Piscataway, NJ. 2001. 308p. ISBN:0-9713097-5-2,
ISBN13: 978-0-9713097-5-3. Dewey:896.

                                    Audience: **u,f.**

Middle Eastern Languages and Literatures > Semitic Languages and Literatures > Arabic > Language

Abboud, Peret   **PJ6307**
Modern Standard Arabic: Intermediate Level. Univ. of Michigan
Dept. of Near Eastern Studies. 1971. ISBN:0-916798-09-7,
ISBN13: 978-0-916798-09-3.

                                    Audience: **l,u,f.**

Abboud, Peter   **PJ6779**
Essential Arabic Grammar: Colloquial Cairo Dialect. Paper Text.
Dover Publications, Inc. Mineola, NY. 1994. 96p.
ISBN:0-486-27873-5, ISBN13: 978-0-486-27873-5.
Dewey:492.7.

                                    Audience: **l,u,f.**

Abboud, Peter F. &   **PJ6111**
  McCarus, Ernest N.
Elementary Modern Standard Arabic. Ed. 2. Cambridge
University Press. 1983.

                                    Audience: **l,u,f.**

Al-Khalesi, Yasin M.   **PJ6823.K43 2001**
Modern Iraqi Arabic: A Textbook. Trade Paper. Georgetown
University Press. Washington, DC. 2001. 272p.
ISBN:0-87840-788-X, ISBN13: 978-0-87840-788-0.
Dewey:492.7/709567. LCCN:2001-023251.

                                    Audience: **l,u,f.**

Bateson, Mary   **PJ6095.B3 2003**
  Catherine
Arabic Language Handbook. Trade Paper. Georgetown
University Press. Washington, DC. 2003. 144p. Georgetown
Classics in Arabic Language and Linguistics Ser.
ISBN:0-87840-386-8, ISBN13: 978-0-87840-386-8.
Dewey:492.7/82421. LCCN:2002-033904.

                                    Audience: **u,f.**

Beeston, A. F. L.   **PJ6073 .B4 2006**
The Arabic Language Today. Book, Other. Georgetown
University Press. Washington, DC. 2006. 144p. Georgetown
Classics in Arabic Language and Linguistics Ser.
ISBN:1-58901-084-1, ISBN13: 978-1-58901-084-0.
Dewey:492.7. LCCN:2005-054443.

                                    Audience: **u,f.**

Beeston, A. F. L.   **PJ6307**
Written Arabic: An Approach to the Basic Structures. Trade
Paper. Cambridge University Press. New York, NY. 1968. 124p.
ISBN:0-521-09559-X, ISBN13: 978-0-521-09559-4.
Dewey:492.7.

                                    Audience: **u,f.**

Blau, Joshua   **PJ4551 .B54 1981**
The Renaissance of Modern Hebrew and Modern Standard
Arabic: Parallels and Differences in the Revival of Two Semitic
Languages. Trade Paper. University of California Press.
Berkeley, CA. 1982. Publications in Near Eastern Studies, Vol.

18 ISBN:0-520-09548-0, ISBN13: 978-0-520-09548-9.
Dewey:492/.7. LCCN:81-016129.

                                    Audience: **l,u,f.**

Brustad, Kristen   **PJ6307.B78 2004**
al-Kitaab fii Ta'allum al-Arabiyya; with DVDs: A Textbook for
Beginning Arabic. Ed. 2. Georgetown University Press. 2004.
ISBN:1-58901-104-X, ISBN13: 978-1-58901-104-5.

                                    Audience: **l,u,f.**

Brustad, Kristen, et al.   **PJ6123.B78 1995**
Alif Baa: Introduction to Arabic Letters and Sounds. Mahmoud
Al-Batal & Abbas Al-Tonsi (Authors). Trade Paper. Georgetown
University Press. Washington, DC. 1995. 224p.
ISBN:0-87840-292-6, ISBN13: 978-0-87840-292-2.
Dewey:492.781/3. LCCN:95-006981.

                                    Audience: **l,u,f.**

Cowan, David   **PJ6307**
An Introduction to Modern Literary Arabic. Cloth Text.
Cambridge University Press. New York, NY. 1958.
ISBN:0-521-04734-X, ISBN13: 978-0-521-04734-0.
Dewey:492.75.

                                    Audience: **l,u,f.**

Cowell, Mark W.   **PJ6813.C65 2005**
A Reference Grammar of Syrian Arabic. Book, Other.
Georgetown University Press. Washington, DC. 2004.
Georgetown Classics in Arabic Language and Linguistics Ser.
ISBN:1-58901-003-5, ISBN13: 978-1-58901-003-1.
Dewey:492.7/09536144.

                                    Audience: **u,f.**

Doniach, N. S. (Editor)   **PJ6640 .O93**
The Oxford English-Arabic Dictionary of Current Usage. Trade
Cloth. Oxford University Press, Inc. New York, NY. 1972. 1,
408p. ISBN:0-19-864312-8, ISBN13: 978-0-19-864312-8.
Dewey:492.7/3/21. LCCN:73-151265.

                                    Audience: **g,l,u,f.**

Erwin, Wallace M.   **PJ6823.E685 2004**
A Basic Course in Iraqi Arabic. Compact Disc, Trade Paper.
Georgetown University Press. Washington, DC. 2004. 424p.
Georgetown Classics in Arabic Language and Linguistics Ser.
ISBN:1-58901-011-6, ISBN13: 978-1-58901-011-6.
Dewey:492.7/709567. LCCN:2003-049539.

                                    Audience: **l,u,f.**

Erwin, Wallace M.   **PJ6823.E7 2004**
A Short Reference Grammar of Iraqi Arabic. Trade Paper.
Georgetown University Press. Washington, DC. 2004. 416p.
Georgetown Classics in Arabic Language and Linguistics Ser.
ISBN:1-58901-010-8, ISBN13: 978-1-58901-010-9.
Dewey:492.7/7/09567. LCCN:2003-049538.

                                    Audience: **u,f.**

Fischer, Wolfdietrich   **PJ6303.F3513 2002**
A Grammar of Classical Arabic. Ed. 3. Jonathan Rodgers
(Translator). Cloth over Boards. Yale University Press.
Cumberland, RI. 2001. 352p. Yale Language Ser.
ISBN:0-300-08437-4, ISBN13: 978-0-300-08437-5.
Dewey:492.7/5. LCCN:00-048714.

                                    Audience: **u,f.**

Harrell, Richard S.   **PJ6763.H315 2004**
A Short Reference Grammar of Moroccan Arabic. Compact
Disc, Trade Paper. Georgetown University Press. Washington,

DC. 2004. 288p. Georgetown Classics in Arabic Language and Linguistics Ser. ISBN:1-58901-009-4, ISBN13: 978-1-58901-009-3. Dewey:492.7/7/0964. LCCN:2003-049544.

Audience: **u,f.**

Harrell, Richard S., et al.   **PJ6770.23**
A Basic Course in Moroccan Arabic. Mohammed Abu-Talib & William S. Carroll (Authors). Book, Other. Georgetown University Press. Washington, DC. 2003. Georgetown Classics in Arabic Language and Linguistics Ser. ISBN:0-87840-388-4, ISBN13: 978-0-87840-388-2. Dewey:492.7/0964.

Audience: **u,f.**

Haywood, J. A. & Nahmad, H. M.   **PJ6307**
A New Arabic Grammar of the Written Language. Trade Cloth. Harvard University Press. Cambridge, MA. 1962. 696p. ISBN:0-674-60851-8, ISBN13: 978-0-674-60851-1. Dewey:492.78242.

Audience: **l,u,f.**

Jones, Alan   **PJ6106**
Arabic Through the Qur'an. Cloth over Boards. Islamic Texts Society. Cambridge, 2005. 352p. ISBN:0-946621-67-5, ISBN13: 978-0-946621-67-5. Dewey:492.7/5.

Audience: **u,f.**

Kendall, Elisabeth   **PJ6680.K42 2005**
The Top 1,000 Words for Understanding Media Arabic. Trade Paper, Perfect. Georgetown University Press. Washington, DC. 2005. 90p. ISBN:1-58901-068-X, ISBN13: 978-1-58901-068-0. Dewey:492.7/2. LCCN:2005-040059.

Audience: **l,u,f.**

McCarus, Ernest N. (Editor), et al.   **PJ6311 .M532**
Formal Arabic. Adil I. Yacoub & Frederic J. Cadora (Editors). Trade Cloth. University of Michigan, Department of Near Eastern Studies. Ann Arbor, MI. 1963. Contemporary Arabic Readers Ser., Vol. III ISBN:0-916798-13-5, ISBN13: 978-0-916798-13-0. Dewey:492.78642.

Audience: **l,u,f.**

McLoughlin, Leslie   **PJ6307**
Colloquial Arabic (Levantine). Trade Paper. Routledge. New York, NY. 1982. 160p. Colloquial Ser. ISBN:0-415-05107-X, ISBN13: 978-0-415-05107-1. Dewey:892.7709569.

Audience: **g,l,u,f.**

Mitchell, T. F.   **PJ6779**
An Introduction to Egyptian Colloquial Arabic. Trade Paper. Oxford University Press, Inc. New York, NY. 1978. 298p. ISBN:0-19-815148-9, ISBN13: 978-0-19-815148-7. Dewey:492/.77.

Audience: **g,l,u,f.**

Mitchell, T. F.   **ND1457.A7**
Writing Arabic: A Practical Introduction to Ruq'ah Script. Paper Text. Oxford University Press, Inc. New York, NY. 1979. 170p. ISBN:0-19-815150-0, ISBN13: 978-0-19-815150-0. Dewey:745.6/199/27. LCCN:78-040804.

Audience: **l,u,f.**

Mitchell, T. F.   **PJ6121.M58 1990**
Pronouncing Arabic. Oxford University Press. 1990. ISBN:0-19-815151-9, ISBN13: 978-0-19-815151-7.

Audience: **l,u,f.**

Nydell, Margaret K.   **PJ6307**
Introduction to Colloquial Arabic. Paper Text. Diplomatic Language Services, Inc. Arlington, VA. 1994. 328p. ISBN:0-9628410-8-0, ISBN13: 978-0-9628410-8-8. Dewey:492.782421.

Audience: **g,l,u,f.**

Rice, Frank A. & Said, Majed F.   **PJ6813R554 2005**
Eastern Arabic: With MP3 Files; An Introduction to Palestinian Arabic. Margaret Nydell (Foreword by). Trade Paper, Compact Disc. Georgetown University Press. Washington, DC. 2005. 432p. Georgetown Classics in Arabic Language and Linguistics Ser. ISBN:1-58901-052-3, ISBN13: 978-1-58901-052-9. Dewey:492.7/7/095691. LCCN:2004-061777.

Audience: **l,u,f.**

Rouchdy, Aleya (Editor)   **PJ6068.U5A89 1992**
The Arabic Language in America. Trade Cloth. Wayne State University Press. Detroit, MI. 1992. 350p. ISBN:0-8143-2283-2, ISBN13: 978-0-8143-2283-3. Dewey:492/.7/0973. LCCN:91-030156.

Audience: **u,f.**

Ryding, Karin C.   **PJ6303.R93 2005**
A Reference Grammar of Modern Standard Arabic. Cloth Text. Cambridge University Press. New York, NY. 2005. 734p. Reference Grammars Ser. ISBN:0-521-77151-X, ISBN13: 978-0-521-77151-1. Dewey:492.7/82421. LCCN:2004-051854.

Audience: **u,f.**

Ryding, Karin C. & Mehall, David   **PJ6111.R933 2005**
Formal Spoken Arabic Basic Course. Ed. 2. Trade Paper, Mixed Media. Georgetown University Press. Washington, DC. 2005. 365p. Georgetown Classics in Arabic Language and Linguistics Ser. ISBN:1-58901-060-4, ISBN13: 978-1-58901-060-4. Dewey:492.7/83421. LCCN:2005-040093.

Audience: **l,u,f.**

Saheb-Ettaba, Mouncef, et al.   **PJ6307.S27**
Arabic Made Easy. Caroline Squire & Random House Staff (Authors). Trade Cloth. David McKay Company, Inc. New York, NY. 1986. x, 246 p. ;p. ISBN:0-679-50905-4, ISBN13: 978-0-679-50905-9. Dewey:492.7/8242. LCCN:57-011081.

Audience: **g,l,u,f.**

Scheindlin, Raymond P.   **PJ6145.S3**
201 Arabic Verbs. Trade Paper. Barron's Educational Series, Inc. Hauppauge, NY. 1978. 224p. 201 Verbs Ser. ISBN:0-8120-0547-3, ISBN13: 978-0-8120-0547-9. Dewey:492/.7/82421. LCCN:77-013695.

Audience: **l,u,f.**

Schulz, Eckehard   **PJ6307.S385 2004**
A Student Grammar of Modern Standard Arabic. Cloth Text. Cambridge University Press. New York, NY. 2005. 264p. ISBN:0-521-83377-9, ISBN13: 978-0-521-83377-6. Dewey:492.7/82421. LCCN:2004-051859.

Audience: **u,f.**

Steingass, F.   **PJ6640 .S7**
English-Arabic Dictionary. Trade Cloth. French & European Publications, Inc. New York, NY. 1990. 466p. ISBN:0-8288-0437-0, ISBN13: 978-0-8288-0437-0. Dewey:492.7/3/2.

Audience: **l,u,f.**

Suleiman, Yasir   DS63.6.S94 2003
The Arabic Language and National Identity: A Study in
Ideology. Trade Paper. Georgetown University Press.
Washington, DC. 2003. 288p. ISBN:0-87840-395-7, ISBN13:
978-0-87840-395-0. Dewey:320.54/089/927.
LCCN:2002-151195.
Audience: **u,f.** *Choice, 2003.*

Thackston, Wheeler M.   PJ6307.T45 1994
An Introduction to Koranic and Classical Arabic: An Elementary
Grammar of the Language. Paper Text. IBEX Publishers, Inc.
Bethesda, MD. 1994. 328p. ISBN:0-936347-40-6, ISBN13:
978-0-936347-40-0. Dewey:492/.782421. LCCN:94-001289.
Audience: **l,u,f.**

Wehr, Hans   PJ6640
A Dictionary of Modern Written Arabic. Ed. 4. J. Milton Cowan
(Editor). Trade Paper. Spoken Language Services, Inc. Ithaca,
NY. 1993. 1301p. ISBN:0-87950-003-4, ISBN13:
978-0-87950-003-0. Dewey:492.7321.
Audience: **g,l,u,f.**

Wright, William   PJ6305
A Grammar of the Arabic Language. Ed. 3. Cambridge
University Press. 1967. ISBN:0-521-09455-0, ISBN13:
978-0-521-09455-9.
Audience: **l,u,f.**

Middle Eastern Languages and Literatures > Semitic Languages and Literatures > Arabic > Literature

                                   PJ7692.E3 B7 1982
Bread, Hashish and Moon: Four Modern Arab Poets. Trade
Cloth. Unicorn Press, Inc. Bryan, TX. 1982. 72p. Keepsake Ser.,
Vol. 9 ISBN:0-87775-134-X, ISBN13: 978-0-87775-134-2.
Dewey:892/.716/08.
Audience: **g,l,u,f.**

Abdullah, Yahya Taher   PJ7805.Y3 A25
The Mountain of Green Tea. Denys Johnson-Davies (Translator).
Trade Paper. Lynne Rienner Publishers, Inc. Boulder, CO. 1983.
130p. ISBN:0-89410-352-0, ISBN13: 978-0-89410-352-0.
Dewey:892/.736. LCCN:82-074250.
Audience: **g,l,u,f.**

Abouzeid, Leila   PJ7808.Z22
  (Author, Translator)
The Director: And Other Stories from Morocco. Elizabeth
Warnock Fernea (Introduction by). Trade Paper, Perfect.
University of Texas Press. Austin, TX. 2006. 130p. Modern
Middle East Literatures in Translation Ser. ISBN:0-292-71265-0,
ISBN13: 978-0-292-71265-2. Dewey:892.737.
LCCN:2005-931342.
Audience: **g,l,u,f.**

Abouzeid, Leila   PJ7808.Z22A3 1998
  (Author, Translator)
Return to Childhood: The Memoir of a Modern Moroccan
Woman. Elizabeth Fernea (Foreword by), Heather Logan Taylor
(As told to). Trade Paper. University of Texas Press. Austin, TX.
1998. 104p. Modern Middle Eastern Literature in Translation
Ser. ISBN:0-292-70490-9, ISBN13: 978-0-292-70490-9.
Dewey:892.7/36 B. LCCN:98-075404.
Audience: **g,l,u,f.**

Abouzeid, Leila   PJ7806.O99Y43 1989
Year of the Elephant: A Moroccan Woman's Journey Toward
Independence. Barbara M. Parmenter (Translator), Elizabeth
Warnock Fernea (Introduction by). Trade Paper. University of
Texas Press. Austin, TX. 1989. 129p. Modern Middle Eastern
Literature in Translation Ser. ISBN:0-292-79603-X, ISBN13:
978-0-292-79603-4. Dewey:[Fic]. LCCN:89-062509.
Audience: **g,l,u,f.**

Adonis, A.   PJ7862.A519
If Only the Sea Could Sleep: Love Poems. Kamal Boullata
(Translator), Mirene Ghossien (Translator, Introduction by).
Trade Cloth. Penguin Group (USA) Inc. New York, NY. 2003.
150p. ISBN:1-931243-29-8, ISBN13: 978-1-931243-29-2.
Dewey:892/.716.
Audience: **g,l,u,f.**

Adonis, A.   PJ7862.A519A24 2000
The Pages of Day and Night. Samuel Hazo (Translator). Trade
Paper. Northwestern University Press. Evanston, IL. 2000. 108p.
ISBN:0-8101-6081-1, ISBN13: 978-0-8101-6081-1.
Dewey:892.7/16. LCCN:00-056638.
Audience: **g,l,u,f.**

Adonis, et al.   PJ7820.A7
Victims of a Map: A Bilingual Anthology of Arabic Poetry.
Mahmud Darwish & Samih al-Qasim (Authors). Trade Paper.
Saqi Books. London, 2006. 168p. ISBN:0-86356-524-7,
ISBN13: 978-0-86356-524-3. Dewey:892.71608.
Audience: **u,f.**

Adonis   PJ7862.A519W313 2004
Time Between Ashes and Roses. Shawkat M. Toorawa
(Translator, Afterword by). Trade Paper. Syracuse University
Press. Syracuse, NY. 2004. 224p. Middle East Literature in
Translation Ser. ISBN:0-8156-0828-4, ISBN13:
978-0-8156-0828-8. Dewey:892.7/16. LCCN:2004-021127.
Audience: **g,l,u,f.**

Al Munif, Abd   PJ7850.U514N513 1988
  Al-Rahman
Endings. Trade Cloth. Quartet Books, Ltd. London, 1993. 152p.
ISBN:0-7043-2651-5, ISBN13: 978-0-7043-2651-4.
Dewey:892/.736. LCCN:88-117338.
Audience: **g,l,u,f.**

Al-Amir, Daisy   PJ7814.M577
The Waiting List: An Iraqi Woman's Tales of Alienation.
Barbara M. Parmenter (Translator), Mona N. Mikhail
(Introduction by). Trade Paper. Center for Middle Eastern
Studies. Minneapolis, MN. 1994. 95p. Modern Middle Eastern
Literature in Translation Ser. ISBN:0-292-79067-8, ISBN13:
978-0-292-79067-4. Dewey:892.
Audience: **g,l,u,f.**

Al-Ashour, Radwa   PJ7814.S514 G4813 2003
Granada: A Novel. William Granara (Translator). Syracuse
University Press. 2003. Middle Eastern Literature in Translation
Series ISBN:0-8156-0765-2, ISBN13: 978-0-8156-0765-6.
Audience: **g,l,u,f.**

Al-Bisatie, Mohamed   PJ7816.I76 H68
Houses behind the Trees. Denys Johnson-Davies (Translator).
American University in Cairo Press. 1996.
Audience: **g,l,u,f.**

Al-Bisatie, Mohamed   PJ7816.I76 A24 1998
A Last Glass of Tea. Denys Johnson-Davies (Translator). Lynne
Rienner Publishers, Inc. 1998.
                                   Audience: **g,l,u,f.**

Al-Daif, Rashid   PJ7846.A46
Dear Mr. Kawabata. Paul Starkey (Translator), Margaret Drabble
(Foreword by). Trade Paper. Quartet Books, Ltd. London, 2000.
176p. ISBN:0-7043-8113-3, ISBN13: 978-0-7043-8113-1.
Dewey:892.7/36.
                                   Audience: **g,l,u,f.**

Al-Ghitani, Gamal   PJ7846.A46
Zayni Barakat. Farouk Abdel Wahab (Translator). Trade Paper.
American University in Cairo Press. New York, NY. 2004. 254p.
ISBN:977-424-872-4, ISBN13: 978-977-424-872-6.
Dewey:892.736.
                                   Audience: **g,l,u,f.**

Al-Hakim, Tawfiq   PJ7828.K52 A24
Plays, Prefaces and Postscripts of Tawfiq Al-Hakim. 2 vols.
Three Continents. 1981. ISBN:0-89410-134-X, ISBN13:
978-0-89410-134-2.
                                   Audience: **g,l,u,f.**

Al-Hakim, Tawfiq   PJ7828.K52S5513 1992
The Prison of Life: An Autobiography. Pierre A. Cachia
(Translator). Trade Cloth. American University in Cairo Press.
New York, NY. 1993. 160p. ISBN:977-424-279-3, ISBN13:
978-977-424-279-3. Dewey:892/.725. LCCN:93-203348.
                                   Audience: **g,l,u,f.**

Al-Hakim, Tawfiq &   PJ7828.K52Y33 1989
  Eban, A. S.
Maze of Justice: Diary of a Country Prosecutor. P. G. Newby
(Introduction by). Trade Cloth. University of Texas Press.
Austin, TX. 1989. 160p. ISBN:0-292-75112-5, ISBN13:
978-0-292-75112-5. Dewey:892/.735. LCCN:88-051739.
                         Audience: **g,l,u,f.** *Choice, 1990.*

Al-Hakim, Tawfiq   PJ7826.I2
The Return of the Spirit. William M. Hutchins (Translator).
Trade Cloth. Lynne Rienner Publishers, Inc. Boulder, CO. 1990.
288p. ISBN:0-89410-425-X, ISBN13: 978-0-89410-425-1.
Dewey:892/.735.
                                   Audience: **g,l,u,f.**

Al-Hakim, Tawfiq   PJ7828.K52A24 1998
In the Tavern of Life and Other Stories. William M. Hutchins
(Editor, Translator). Library Binding. Lynne Rienner Publishers,
Inc. Boulder, CO. 1998. 232p. ISBN:0-89410-648-1, ISBN13:
978-0-89410-648-4. Dewey:892/.735. LCCN:95-019994.
                         Audience: **g,l,u,f.** *Choice, 1998.*

Al-Jahiz, Amir ibn   PJ7575
  Bahir
The Book of Misers: al-Bukhala. R. B. Searjeant (Translator).
Ithaca Press. 2000.
                                   Audience: **g,l,u,f.**

Al-Kharrat, Edwar   PJ7842.H327Y3313
Girls of Alexandria. Trade Cloth. Quartet Books, Ltd. London,
1993. 256p. ISBN:0-7043-7006-9, ISBN13: 978-0-7043-7006-7.
Dewey:893.1. LCCN:93-247790.
                                   Audience: **g,l,u,f.**

Al-Kharrat, Edwar   PJ7842.H327
Rama and the Dragon. Trade Cloth. American University in
Cairo Press. New York, NY. 2002. 340p. ISBN:977-424-676-4,
ISBN13: 978-977-424-676-0. Dewey:896.
                                   Audience: **g,l,u,f.**

Al-Kharrat, Edwar   PJ7846.A46
City of Saffron. Frances Liardet (Translator). Trade Cloth.
Quartet Books, Ltd. London, 1990. 192p. ISBN:0-7043-2693-0,
ISBN13: 978-0-7043-2693-4. Dewey:892.736.
                                   Audience: **g,l,u,f.**

Al-Maghut, Muhammad   PJ7846.A375
Joy Is Not My Profession. Michael Harris (Editor), John Asfour
& Alison Burch (Translator, Introduction by). Trade Paper.
Vehicule Press. Montreal, PQ. 1994. 64p. Signal Editions Ser.
ISBN:1-55065-050-5, ISBN13: 978-1-55065-050-1.
Dewey:892/.716.
                                   Audience: **g,l,u,f.**

Al-Maghut, Muhammad   PJ7820.A7
The Fan of Swords. May Jayyusi & Naomi S. Nye (Translators),
Sakna J. Jayyusi (Introduction by). Trade Cloth. Lynne Rienner
Publishers, Inc. Boulder, CO. 1991. 62p. ISBN:0-89410-685-6,
ISBN13: 978-0-89410-685-9. Dewey:892/.716.
                                   Audience: **g,l,u,f.**

Al-Munif, Abd   PJ7850.U514
  al-Rahman
Cities of Salt. Peter Theroux (Translator). Knopf Publishing
Group. 1989.
                                   Audience: **g,l,u,f.**

Al-Munif, Abd   PJ7850.U514 T3613
  al-Rahman
Variations on Night and Day. Peter Theroux (Translator). Alfred
A. Knopf, Inc. 1994. ISBN:0-679-75551-9, ISBN13:
978-0-679-75551-7.
                                   Audience: **g,l,u,f.**

Al-Munif, Abd   PJ7850.U514
  al-Rahman
Story of a City: A Childhood in Amman. Samira Kawar
(Translator). Quartet Books, Ltd. 1996. ISBN:0-7043-8023-4,
ISBN13: 978-0-7043-8023-3.
                                   Audience: **g,l,u,f.**

Al-Ramly, Lenin   PJ7860.R36
In Plain Arabic: A Play in Two Acts. Esmat Allouba
(Translator). American University in Cairo Press. 1994.
ISBN:977-424-342-0, ISBN13: 978-977-424-342-4.
                                   Audience: **g,l,u,f.**

Al-Saadawi, Nawal   PJ7862.A3
Love in the Kingdom of Oil. Basil Hatim (Translator); Malcolm
Williams (Translator). Saqi Books. 2001. ISBN:0-86356-337-6,
ISBN13: 978-0-86356-337-9.
                                   Audience: **g,l,u,f.**

Al-Saadawi, Nawal   PJ7862.A3 M813 1988
Memoirs of a Woman Doctor. Catherine Cobham (Translator).
Saqi Books. 1988. ISBN:0-86356-184-5, ISBN13:
978-0-86356-184-9.
                                   Audience: **g,l,u,f.**

Al-Saadawi, Nawal   PJ7862.A3 Z47313 1994
Memoirs from the Women's Prison. Marilyn Booth (Translator).
University of California Press. 1994. ISBN:0-520-08887-5,
ISBN13: 978-0-520-08887-0.

Audience: **g,l,u,f.**

Al-Saadawi, Nawal   PJ7862.A3 A3 1999
A Daughter of Isis: the Autobiography of Nawal el Saadawi.
Sherif Hetata (Translator). Zed Books, Ltd. 1999.
ISBN:1-85649-679-1, ISBN13: 978-1-85649-679-7.

Audience: **g,l,u,f.**

Al-Saadawi, Nawal   PJ7862.A3 M313 1985
God Dies by the Nile. Sherif Hetata (Translator). Zed Books,
Ltd. 1985. ISBN:0-86232-295-2, ISBN13: 978-0-86232-295-3.

Audience: **g,l,u,f.**

Al-Saadawi, Nawal   PJ7862.A3 W6 1983
Woman at Point Zero. Sherif Hetata (Translator). Zed Books,
Ltd. 1958.

Audience: **g,l,u,f.**

Al-Sharqawi, Abdel   PJ7862.H27
  Rahman
Egyptian Earth. Ed. 2. D. Stewart (Translator). Trade Paper. I.
B. Tauris & Company, Ltd. London, 1990. 264p.
ISBN:0-86356-261-2, ISBN13: 978-0-86356-261-7.
Dewey:892.736.

Audience: **g,l,u,f.**

Al-Shaykh, Hanan   PJ846.A46
Only in London. Trade Paper. Vintage Anchor Publishing. New
York, NY. 2002. 288p. ISBN:0-385-72121-8, ISBN13:
978-0-385-72121-9. Dewey:892.7/36.

Audience: **g,l,u,f.**

Al-Shaykh, Hanan   PJ7846.A46
Beirut Blues. Catherine Cobhaim (Translator). Trade Paper.
Doubleday Publishing. New York, NY. 1996. 384p.
ISBN:0-385-47382-6, ISBN13: 978-0-385-47382-8.
Dewey:892/.736.

Audience: **l,u,f.**

Al-Shaykh, Hanan   PJ7862.H356.A7613
I Sweep the Sun off Rooftops: Stories. Catherine Cobham
(Translator). Trade Paper. Doubleday Publishing. New York, NY.
1998. 288p. ISBN:0-385-49127-1, ISBN13: 978-0-385-49127-3.
Dewey:892.7/36. LCCN:98-015876.

Audience: **g,l,u,f.**

Al-Shaykh, Hanan   PJ7846.A46
Women of Sand and Myrrh. Catherine Cobham (Translator).
Trade Cloth. Quartet Books, Ltd. London, 1990. 224p.
ISBN:0-7043-2736-8, ISBN13: 978-0-7043-2736-8.
Dewey:892/.736.

Audience: **g,l,u,f.**

Al-Shaykh, Hanan   PJ7862.H356H5513
The Story of Zahra: A Novel. Peter Ford (Translator). Trade
Paper. Doubleday Publishing. New York, NY. 1996. 224p.
ISBN:0-385-47206-4, ISBN13: 978-0-385-47206-7.
Dewey:892/.736. LCCN:93-003678.

Audience: **g,l,u,f.**

Al-Zayyat, Latifah   PJ7876.A99
The Open Door. Marilyn Booth (Translator). American
University in Cairo Press. 2002. ISBN:977-424-698-5, ISBN13:
978-977-424-698-2.

Audience: **g,l,u,f.**

Al-Zayyat, Latifah   PJ7876.A985
The Owner of the House. Sophie Bennett (Translator). Quartet
Books. 1998.

Audience: **g,l,u,f.**

Alem, Raja   PJ7814.L53F3813 2002
Fatma: A Novel of Arabia. Tom McDonough (Contribution by).
Trade Cloth. Syracuse University Press. Syracuse, NY. 2002.
164p. Middle East Literature in Translation Ser.
ISBN:0-8156-0738-5, ISBN13: 978-0-8156-0738-0.
Dewey:892/.736. LCCN:2002-004525.

Audience: **g,l,u,f.** *Choice, 2003.*

Allen, Roger   PJ7510 .A44 1998
The Arabic Literary Heritage: The Development of its Genres
and Criticism. Trade Cloth. Cambridge University Press. New
York, NY. 1998. 475p. ISBN:0-521-48066-3, ISBN13:
978-0-521-48066-6. Dewey:892.709. LCCN:97-027113.

Audience: **g,u,f.**

Allen, Roger   PJ7510 .A43 2000
An Introduction to Arabic Literature. Cloth Text. Cambridge
University Press. New York, NY. 2000. 286p.
ISBN:0-521-77230-3, ISBN13: 978-0-521-77230-3.
Dewey:892.709. LCCN:99-053418.

Audience: **g,l,u,f.** *Choice, 2001.*

Allen, Roger (Editor)   PJ7558.A73 2006
Arabic Literature in the Post-Classical Period. Richards, Donald
(Editor). Cambridge University Press. 2006. Cambridge History
of Arabic Literature ISBN:0-521-77160-9, ISBN13:
978-0-521-77160-3.

Audience: **u,f.**

Arberry, Arthur John   PJ7692.E3
Arabic Poetry: A Primer for Students. Trade Cloth. Cambridge
University Press. Cambridge, 1965. 184p. ISBN:0-521-04037-X,
ISBN13: 978-0-521-04037-2. Dewey:892.71008.

Audience: **u,f.**

Arberry, Arthur John   PJ8453 .A7 1975
  (Compiled by)
A Maltese Anthology. Trade Cloth. Greenwood Publishing
Group, Inc. Portsmouth, NH. 1975. 280p. ISBN:0-8371-8112-7,
ISBN13: 978-0-8371-8112-7. Dewey:892/.7/08.
LCCN:75-008831.

Audience: **u,f.**

Arberry, Arthur John   PJ7655.A7 1967
Modern Arabic Poetry. Trade Cloth. Cambridge University
Press. New York, NY. 1967. 156p. Cambridge Oriental Ser., No.
1 ISBN:0-521-07050-3, ISBN13: 978-0-521-07050-8.
Dewey:892.7/1/008. LCCN:67-105223.

Audience: **u,f.**

Ashtiany, Julia (Editor)   PJ7530 .A18 1990
'Abbasid Belles Lettres. Trade Cloth. Cambridge University
Press. New York, NY. 1990. 533p. Cambridge History of Arabic
Literature Ser. ISBN:0-521-24016-6, ISBN13:
978-0-521-24016-1. Dewey:892/.7/090034. LCCN:89-042575.

Audience: **u,f.** *Choice, 1990.*

Aswany, Ala Al   PJ7814.S926
Yacoubian Building. Humphrey Davies (Translator). Trade
Cloth. American University in Cairo Press. New York, NY.
2005. 272p. ISBN:977-424-862-7, ISBN13: 978-977-424-862-7.
Dewey:892.76.

Audience: **g,l,u,f.**

Awwad, Tawfiq Y.   **PJ7814.W9T313 1995**
Death in Beirut. Leslie McLoughlin (Translator). Trade Paper.
Lynne Rienner Publishers, Inc. Boulder, CO. 1984. 190p.
ISBN:0-914478-87-7, ISBN13: 978-0-914478-87-4.
Dewey:892/.735. LCCN:95-009596.

Audience: **g,l,u,f.**

Badawi, M. M. (Editor)   **PJ7661 .B28**
An Anthology of Modern Arabic Verse. Trade Paper. Oxford
University Press, Inc. New York, NY. 1971. 296p.
ISBN:0-19-920032-7, ISBN13: 978-0-19-920032-0.
Dewey:892.7/1/5. LCCN:73-871528.

Audience: **u,f.**

Badawi, M. M. (Editor)   **PJ7538 .M58 1992**
Modern Arabic Literature. Cloth Text. Cambridge University
Press. New York, NY. 1993. 592p. History of Arabic Literature
Ser. ISBN:0-521-33197-8, ISBN13: 978-0-521-33197-5.
Dewey:892.709005. LCCN:91-041007.

Audience: **l,u,f.**   *Choice, 1993.*

Badawi, M. M.   **PJ7538.B265 1993**
A Short History of Modern Arabic Literature. Trade Cloth.
Oxford University Press, Inc. New York, NY. 1993. 326p.
ISBN:0-19-826542-5, ISBN13: 978-0-19-826542-9.
Dewey:892.709005. LCCN:92-023257.

Audience: **u,f.**   *Choice, 1993.*

Badr, Liyana   **PJ7816.A335**
A Balcony over the Fakihani. P. Clark & Christopher Tingley
(Translators). Trade Cloth. Interlink Publishing Group, Inc.
Northampton, MA. 1993. 128p. Emerging Voices Ser.
ISBN:1-56656-104-3, ISBN13: 978-1-56656-104-4.
Dewey:892/.736. LCCN:92-023387.

Audience: **g,l,u,f.**

Bailey, Clinton   **PJ8214.5.E5B35 1990**
Bedouin Poetry from Sinai and the Negev: Mirror of a Culture.
Oxford University Press. 1991. ISBN:0-19-826547-6, ISBN13:
978-0-19-826547-4.

Audience: **g,l,u,f.**

Bakr, Salwa   **PJ7816.A466A24 1993**
The Wiles of Men and Other Stories. Denys Johnson-Davies
(Translator), Barbara Harlow (Introduction by). Trade Paper.
University of Texas Press. Austin, TX. 1993. 200p.
ISBN:0-292-70800-9, ISBN13: 978-0-292-70800-6.
Dewey:892/.736. LCCN:93-004648.

Audience: **g,l,u,f.**

Baraadah, Muohammad   **PJ7816.A6538D3913**
Fugitive Light: A Novel. Issa J. Boullata (Translator, Foreword
by). Trade Cloth. Syracuse University Press. Syracuse, NY.
2002. xi, 171p. Middle East Literature in Translation Ser.
ISBN:0-8156-0749-0, ISBN13: 978-0-8156-0749-6.
Dewey:892.7/36. LCCN:2002-008074.

Audience: **g,l,u,f.**

Barakat, Halim I.   **PJ7816.A67S513 1990**
Six Days. Bassam Frangieh & Scott McGehee (Translators).
Trade Cloth. Lynne Rienner Publishers, Inc. Boulder, CO. 1990.
121p. ISBN:0-89410-661-9, ISBN13: 978-0-89410-661-3.
Dewey:892/.736. LCCN:90-011283.

Audience: **g,l,u,f.**

Barakat, Halim I.   **PJ7816.A67**
Days of Dust. Ed. 2. Trevor Le Gassick (Translator), Kamal
Boullata (Illustrator), Edward W. Said (Introduction by), Jacques
Berque (Preface by). Trade Paper. Lynne Rienner Publishers,

Inc. Boulder, CO. 1983. 179p. ISBN:0-89410-360-1, ISBN13:
978-0-89410-360-5. Dewey:892.736. LCCN:82-074265.

Audience: **g,l,u,f.**

Barakat, Hoda   **PJ7816.A672H3513**
The Stone of Laughter: A Novel. Sophie Bennett (Translator).
Trade Cloth. Interlink Publishing Group, Inc. Northampton, MA.
1995. 240p. Emerging Voices Ser. ISBN:1-56656-197-3,
ISBN13: 978-1-56656-197-6. Dewey:892/.736.
LCCN:95-014090.

Audience: **g,l,u,f.**   *Choice, 1996.*

Barakat, Hoda   **PJ7816.A672A6413**
Disciples of Passion. Marilyn Booth (Translator). Saddle
Stitched, Cloth over Boards, Dust Jacket. Syracuse University
Press. Syracuse, NY. 2005. 136p. Middle East Literature in
Translation Ser. ISBN:0-8156-0833-0, ISBN13:
978-0-8156-0833-2. Dewey:892.7/36. LCCN:2005-018501.

Audience: **g,l,u,f.**

Bayati, Abd al-Wahhab   **PJ7816.A92**
The Singer and the Moon. Abdullah al-Udhari (Trans.). Ithaca
Press. 1976.

Audience: **g,l,u,f.**

Bayati, Abd al-Wahhab   **PJ7816.A92A23 1991**
Love, Death, and Exile. Bassem K. Frangieh (Trans).
Georgetown University Press. 1990. ISBN:0-87840-217-9,
ISBN13: 978-0-87840-217-5.

Audience: **g,l,u,f.**

Beeston, A. F. L.   **PJ7510 .A8 1983**
(Editor), et al.
Arabic Literature to the End of the Umayyad Period. T. M.
Johnstone, R. B. Serjeant & G. R. Smith (Editors). Trade Cloth.
Cambridge University Press. New York, NY. 1983. 576p.
Cambridge History of Arabic Literature Ser.
ISBN:0-521-24015-8, ISBN13: 978-0-521-24015-4.
Dewey:892/.7/09. LCCN:82-023528.

Audience: **u,f.** *B*

Booth, Marilyn   **PJ8216.S76 1993**
(Translator, Introduction by)
Stories by Egyptian Women: My Grandmother's Cactus. Trade
Paper. University of Texas Press. Austin, TX. 1993. 175p.
ISBN:0-292-70803-3, ISBN13: 978-0-292-70803-7.
Dewey:892/.7301089287. LCCN:92-043065.

Audience: **g,l,u,f.**

Boullata, Issa J. &   **PJ7510.T74 1997**
DeYoung, Terri (Editors)
Tradition and Modernity in Arabic Literature. Cloth Text.
University of Arkansas Press. Fayetteville, AR. 1997. xvii, 285p.
ISBN:1-55728-447-4, ISBN13: 978-1-55728-447-1.
Dewey:892/.709. LCCN:97-006667.

Audience: **u,f.**   *Choice, 1998.*

Boullata, Kamal   **PJ7661 .W66**
(Editor, Translator)
Women of the Fertile Crescent: Modern Poetry by Arab Women.
Trade Cloth. Lynne Rienner Publishers, Inc. Boulder, CO. 1992.
ISBN:0-914478-41-9, ISBN13: 978-0-914478-41-6.
Dewey:892/.7/1608. LCCN:77-003834.

Audience: **g,l,u,f.**

Budge, E. A. Wallis   PJ1949.B83 2002
Egyptian Tales and Legends: Pagan, Christian, and Muslim.
Trade Paper. Dover Publications, Inc. Mineola, NY. 2002. 448p.
ISBN:0-486-42235-6, ISBN13: 978-0-486-42235-0.
Dewey:893/.13008. LCCN:2002-019207.
Audience: **u,f.**

Choukri, Mohamed   PJ7818.H6
Streetwise. Ed Emery (Translator). Cloth over Boards. I. B.
Tauris & Company, Ltd. London, 1996. 164p.
ISBN:0-86356-093-8, ISBN13: 978-0-86356-093-4.
Dewey:892.7/36. LCCN:95-126836.
Audience: **g,l,u,f.**

Cooke, Miriam   PN3448.W3C66 1996
Women and the War Story. Trade Paper. University of California
Press. Berkeley, CA. 1997. 378p. ISBN:0-520-20613-4, ISBN13:
978-0-520-20613-7. Dewey:892/.73609358. LCCN:96-011601.
Audience: **u,f.** *Choice, 1997.*

Darwish, Mahmoud   PJ7820.A7A2 2000
The Adam of Two Edens: Poems. Munir Akash (Editor,
Introduction by), Daniel Moore (Editor), Husain Haddawi, Sinan
Antoon, Sargon Boulos, Ferial Ghazoul, Clarissa Burt, Noel
Abdulahad, Mona Asali van Engen & Tahia Khaled Abdulnasser
(Translators). Trade Paper. Syracuse University Press. Syracuse,
NY. 2001. 203p. ISBN:0-8156-0710-5, ISBN13:
978-0-8156-0710-6. Dewey:892.7/16. LCCN:00-067132.
Audience: **g,l,u,f.**

Darwish, Mahmoud   DS87.53.D36513 1995
Memory for Forgetfulness: August, Beirut, 1982. Ibrahim
Muhawi (Translator). Trade Paper. University of California
Press. Berkeley, CA. 1995. 212p. Literature of the Middle East
Ser. ISBN:0-520-08768-2, ISBN13: 978-0-520-08768-2.
Dewey:956.9204/4. LCCN:94-026351.
Audience: **g,l,u,f.**

Darwish, Mahmud   PJ7820.A7 A22 2003
Unfortunately, It Was Paradise: Selected Poems. Munair Akash
& Carolyn Forche (Editor, Translators), Sinan Antoon & Amira
El-Zein (Translators). Trade Paper. University of California
Press. Berkeley, CA. 2003. 208p. ISBN:0-520-23754-4, ISBN13:
978-0-520-23754-4. Dewey:892/.716. LCCN:2002-068454.
Audience: **g,l,u,f.**

Darwish, Mahmud &   PJ7820.A7
  Johnson-Davies, Denys
Music of Human Flesh. Trade Cloth. Heinemann. Portsmouth,
NH. xix, 71p. ISBN:0-435-99407-7, ISBN13:
978-0-435-99407-5. Dewey:892/.716.
Audience: **g,l,u,f.**

Elmessiri, Abdelwahab   PJ8190.P3
  M. (Editor, Translator)
The Palestinian Wedding: A Bilingual Anthology of
Contemporary Palestinian Resistance Poetry. Kamal Boullata
(Illustrator). Trade Cloth. Lynne Rienner Publishers, Inc.
Boulder, CO. 1982. 249p. ISBN:0-89410-095-5, ISBN13:
978-0-89410-095-6. Dewey:892/.716/08095694.
Audience: **g,l,u,f.**

Frangieh, Bassam K.   PJ6119.F69 2004
Anthology of Arabic Literature, Culture, and Thought from
Pre-Islamic Times to the Present. Trade Cloth. Yale University
Press. Cumberland, RI. 2004. 544p. Yale Language Ser.
ISBN:0-300-10493-6, ISBN13: 978-0-300-10493-6.
Dewey:492.7/86421. LCCN:2004-040855.
Audience: **u,f.**

Ghanem, Fathy   PJ7826.H276R313 1994
The Man Who Lost His Shadow. Trade Cloth. American
University in Cairo Press. New York, NY. 1995. 352p.
ISBN:977-424-347-1, ISBN13: 978-977-424-347-9.
Dewey:892.73/6. LCCN:95-119161.
Audience: **g,l,u,f.**

Habiby, Emile   PJ7828.B53W313 2001
The Secret Life of Saeed: The Pessoptimist. Salma K. Jayyusi &
T. LeGassick (Translators). Trade Cloth. Interlink Publishing
Group, Inc. Northampton, MA. 2004. 192p. Emerging Voices
Ser. ISBN:1-56656-415-8, ISBN13: 978-1-56656-415-1.
Dewey:892/.736. LCCN:2001-039601.
Audience: **g,l,u,f.**

Handal, Nathalie   PJ7694.E3P64 2000
  (Editor)
The Poetry of Arab Women: A Contemporary Anthology. Trade
Cloth. Interlink Publishing Group, Inc. Northampton, MA. 2004.
384p. ISBN:1-56656-374-7, ISBN13: 978-1-56656-374-1.
Dewey:892.7/160809287. LCCN:00-058054.
Audience: **g,l,u,f.**

Haqqi, Yahya   PJ7828.Q7 Q513 2004
The Lamp of Umm Hashim and Other Stories. American
University in Cairo Press. 2004. Modern Arabic Writing Series
ISBN:977-424-788-4, ISBN13: 978-977-424-788-0.
Audience: **g,l,u,f.**

Haqqi, Yahya   PJ7828.Q7
Good Morning! and Other Stories. Miriam Cooke (Translator),
Max Winkler (Illustrator). Trade Cloth. Lynne Rienner
Publishers, Inc. Boulder, CO. 1987. 117p. ISBN:0-89410-334-2,
ISBN13: 978-0-89410-334-6. Dewey:892.736.
LCCN:82-050879.
Audience: **g,l,u,f.**

Himmich, Bensalem   PJ7577
Polymath. Roger Allen (Translator). Trade Cloth. American
University in Cairo Press. New York, NY. 2004. 256p.
ISBN:977-424-821-X, ISBN13: 978-977-424-821-4.
Dewey:892.7/37. LCCN:2004-556654.
Audience: **g,l,u,f.**

Himmich, Bensalem   PR9275.A583
The Theocrat. Roger Allen (Translator). Saddle Stitched, Cloth
over Boards, Dust Jacket. American University in Cairo Press.
New York, NY. 2005. 206p. ISBN:977-424-897-X, ISBN13:
978-977-424-897-9. Dewey:813.
Audience: **g,l,u,f.**

Hovannisian, Richard   PJ7737 .T48 1997
  C. & Sabagh, Georges (Editors)
The Thousand and One Nights in Arabic Literature and Society.
Trade Cloth. Cambridge University Press. New York, NY. 1997.
129p. Levi Della Vida Symposia Ser., No. 12
ISBN:0-521-57397-1, ISBN13: 978-0-521-57397-9.
Dewey:398.22. LCCN:96-005952.
Audience: **u,f.**

Husayn, Taha   PJ7864.A35D39 1997
The Days. Ed. 2. Trade Cloth. American University in Cairo
Press. New York, NY. 2001. 412p. ISBN:977-424-435-4,
ISBN13: 978-977-424-435-3. Dewey:892.78509.
LCCN:98-147757.
Audience: **g,l,u,f.**

Husayn, Taha   PJ7864.A35M813 1993
The Sufferers. Mona El-Zayyat (Translator). Trade Cloth.
American University in Cairo Press. New York, NY. 1993. 144p.
ISBN:977-424-299-8, ISBN13: 978-977-424-299-1.
Dewey:892/.735. LCCN:93-207270.
                              Audience: **g,l,u,f.**

Hussein, M. Kamel   BT453
City of Wrong: A Friday in Jerusalem. Trade Cloth. Oneworld
Publications. Oxford, 1995. 250p. Christianity Ser.
ISBN:1-85168-072-1, ISBN13: 978-1-85168-072-6.
Dewey:232.963.
                              Audience: **g,l,u,f.**

Ibrahim, Sonallah   PJ7838.B7173D43 2001
Zaat. Trade Cloth. American University in Cairo Press. New
York, NY. 2001. 344p. Modern Arabic Writing Ser.
ISBN:977-424-647-0, ISBN13: 978-977-424-647-0.
Dewey:892.7/36. LCCN:2001-304508.
                              Audience: **g,l,u,f.**

Ibrahim, Sun'Allah   PJ7838.B7173L313
The Committee. Mary St. Germain & Charlene Constable
(Translators). Trade Cloth. Syracuse University Press. Syracuse,
NY. 2001. 172p. Middle East Literature in Translation Ser.
ISBN:0-8156-0726-1, ISBN13: 978-0-8156-0726-7.
Dewey:892.7/36. LCCN:2001-049680.
                              Audience: **g,l,u,f.**

Idilbi, Ulfat   PJ7838.D68
My Grandfather's Tale. Trade Paper. Interlink Publishing Group,
Inc. Northampton, MA. 1999. 256p. ISBN:0-7043-8100-1,
ISBN13: 978-0-7043-8100-1. Dewey:892.736.
                              Audience: **g,l,u,f.**

Idilbi, Ulfat   PJ7838.D48D5613 1997
Sabriya: Damascus Bitter Sweet. Peter Clark (Translator). Trade
Cloth. Interlink Publishing Group, Inc. Northampton, MA. 1997.
248p. Emerging Voices Ser. ISBN:1-56656-219-8, ISBN13:
978-1-56656-219-5. Dewey:892/.736. LCCN:96-046045.
             Audience: **g,l,u,f.** *Choice, 1997.*

Idris, Yusuf   PJ7838.D7 Q313 1999
City of Love and Ashes. Trade Cloth. American University in
Cairo Press. New York, NY. 1999. 175p. Modern Arabic Writing
Ser. ISBN:977-424-501-6, ISBN13: 978-977-424-501-5.
Dewey:892.7/36. LCCN:2002-360479.
                              Audience: **g,l,u,f.**

Idris, Yusuf   PJ7838.D7 A22
In the Eye of the Beholder: Tales of Egyptian Life from the
Writings of Yusuf Idris. Trade Paper. Bibliotheca Islamica, Inc.
Minneapolis, MN. 1978. Studies in Middle Eastern Literatures,
No. 10 ISBN:0-88297-038-0, ISBN13: 978-0-88297-038-7.
Dewey:892/.736. LCCN:78-050505.
                              Audience: **g,l,u,f.**

Idris, Yusuf   PJ7838.D7 A236 1990
Rings of Burnished Brass and Other Stories. Catherine Cobham
(Translator). Trade Paper. American University in Cairo Press.
New York, NY. 1992. 156p. ISBN:977-424-248-3, ISBN13:
978-977-424-248-9. Dewey:892.7/36. LCCN:91-960386.
                              Audience: **g,l,u,f.**

Idris, Yusuf   PJ7838.D7A7913 1989
The Cheapest Nights. Wadida Wassef (Translator). Trade Cloth.
Lynne Rienner Publishers, Inc. Boulder, CO. 1991.

ISBN:0-89410-665-1, ISBN13: 978-0-89410-665-1.
Dewey:892/.736. LCCN:78-072967.
                              Audience: **g,l,u,f.**

Irwin, Robert   PJ7694.E1N54 2000
Night and Horses and the Desert: An Anthology of Classical
Arabic Literature. Trade Cloth. Overlook Press, The. New York,
NY. 2000. 462p. ISBN:1-58567-064-2, ISBN13:
978-1-58567-064-2. Dewey:892.708. LCCN:00-042738.
                              Audience: **g,l,u,f.**

Jabra, Jabra Ibrahim &   PJ7840.A322Z468513
  Boullata, Issa J.
Princesses' Street: Baghdad Memories. Trade Cloth. University
of Arkansas Press. Fayetteville, AR. 2005. x, 185p.
ISBN:1-55728-801-1, ISBN13: 978-1-55728-801-1.
Dewey:892.7/8609 B. LCCN:2005-021969.
                              Audience: **g,l,u,f.**

Jabra, Jabra I.   PR9570.I723J34 1990
Hunters in a Narrow Street. Roger Allen (Introduction by).
Trade Paper. Lynne Rienner Publishers, Inc. Boulder, CO. 1990.
227p. ISBN:0-89410-585-X, ISBN13: 978-0-89410-585-2.
Dewey:823. LCCN:86-051010.
                              Audience: **g,l,u,f.**

Jabra, Jabra I.   PJ7840.A322Z46813
The First Well: A Bethlehem Boyhood. Issa J. Boullata
(Translator). Trade Cloth. University of Arkansas Press.
Fayetteville, AR. 2003. 192p. ISBN:1-55728-349-4, ISBN13:
978-1-55728-349-8. Dewey:892/.7809 B. LCCN:95-018662.
             Audience: **g,l,u,f.** *Choice, 1996.*

Janabi, Hatif   PJ7840.A49A24 1996
Questions and Their Retinue. Khaled Mattawa (Translator).
Trade Cloth. University of Arkansas Press. Fayetteville, AR.
2003. xxi, 64p. ISBN:1-55728-431-8, ISBN13:
978-1-55728-431-0. Dewey:892/.716. LCCN:96-012896.
                              Audience: **g,l,u,f.**

Jayyusi, Salma K.   PJ7694.E3M64 1987
  (Editor)
Modern Arabic Poetry: An Anthology. Cloth Text. Columbia
University Press. New York, NY. 1987. 496p.
ISBN:0-231-05272-3, ISBN13: 978-0-231-05272-6.
Dewey:892/.716/08. LCCN:87-000678.
             Audience: **l,u,f.** *Choice, 1988.*

Johnson-Davies, Denys   PJ7694.E8 A73 1983
  (Translator)
Arabic Short Stories. Book, Other. Quartet Books, Ltd. London,
1987. 208p. ISBN:0-7043-2367-2, ISBN13: 978-0-7043-2367-4.
Dewey:892/.7301/08. LCCN:84-670043.
                              Audience: **g,l,u,f.**

Johnson-Davies, Denys   PJ7695.E5
  (Editor, Translator)
Egyptian One-Act Plays. Trade Paper. Lynne Rienner Publishers,
Inc. Boulder, CO. 1981. 118p. Arab Writers Ser.
ISBN:0-89410-347-4, ISBN13: 978-0-89410-347-6.
Dewey:892/.72041/08962.
                              Audience: **g,l,u,f.**

Johnson-Davies, Denys   PJ7694.E8
  (Editor, Translator)
Modern Arabic Short Stories. Ed. 2. Trade Cloth. Lynne Rienner
Publishers, Inc. Boulder, CO. 1989. ISBN:0-914478-99-0,
ISBN13: 978-0-914478-99-7. Dewey:892/.7/301.
                              Audience: **g,l,u,f.**

Kabbani, Nizar　　　　　　　**PJ7820.A7**
Republic of Love: Selected Poems. Nayef Al-Kalali (Translator).
Trade Cloth. Kegan Paul International, Ltd. London, 2003.
240p. ISBN:0-7103-0680-6, ISBN13: 978-0-7103-0680-7.
Dewey:892.716.

Audience: **g,l,u,f.**

Kabbani, Nizar　　　　　　**PJ7858.A2A24 1998**
Arabian Love Poems. Bassam K. Frangieh & Clementina R.
Brown (Translators). Trade Paper. Lynne Rienner Publishers,
Inc. Boulder, CO. 1998. 223p. Three Continents Press Ser.
ISBN:0-89410-881-6, ISBN13: 978-0-89410-881-5.
Dewey:892.71/6. LCCN:98-042796.

Audience: **g,l,u,f.**

Kanafani, Ghassan　　　　　**PJ7842.A5A24 2000**
Palestine's Children: Returning to Haifa and Other Stories.
Barbara Harlow & Karen E. Riley (Translators). Library
Binding. Lynne Rienner Publishers, Inc. Boulder, CO. 2000. vi,
199p. ISBN:0-89410-865-4, ISBN13: 978-0-89410-865-5.
Dewey:892.7/36. LCCN:00-024783.

Audience: **g,l,u,f.**

Kanafani, Ghassan　　　　　**PJ7842.A5R513 1998**
Men in the Sun and Other Palestinian Stories. Hilary Kilpatrick
(Translator). Trade Paper. Lynne Rienner Publishers, Inc.
Boulder, CO. 1998. 117p. ISBN:0-89410-857-3, ISBN13:
978-0-89410-857-0. Dewey:892.7/36. LCCN:98-046345.

Audience: **g,l,u,f.**

Khalifeh, Sahar　　　　　　**PJ7842.H2938**
The Inheritance. Aida Bamia (Translator). Trade Cloth.
American University in Cairo Press. New York, NY. 2005. 256p.
ISBN:977-424-939-9, ISBN13: 978-977-424-939-6. Dewey:892.

Audience: **g,l,u,f.**

Khouri, Mounah A. &　　　　　**PJ7695.E3.K48**
　Algar, Hamid (Editor, Translators)
An Anthology of Modern Arabic Poetry. Trade Cloth. University
of California Press. Berkeley, CA. 1974. xii, 252p.
ISBN:0-520-02234-3, ISBN13: 978-0-520-02234-8.
Dewey:892/.7/1608. LCCN:77-189220.

Audience: **u,f.** *B*

Khoury, Elias　　　　　　**PJ7842.H823B3313**
Gate of the Sun: Bab al-Shams. Humphrey Davies (Translator).
Trade Cloth. Archipelago Books. Brooklyn, NY. 2006. 475p.
ISBN:0-9763950-2-9, ISBN13: 978-0-9763950-2-7.
Dewey:892.7/36. LCCN:2005-021036.

Audience: **g,l,u,f.**

Khoury, Elias　　　　　　**PJ7842.H823R5413**
The Journey of Little Gandhi. Paula Haydar (Translator). Book,
Other. University of Minnesota Press. Minneapolis, MN. 1994.
xx, 194p. ISBN:0-8166-1995-6, ISBN13: 978-0-8166-1995-5.
Dewey:892/.736. LCCN:93-004743.
Audience: **g,l,u,f.** *Choice, 1994.*

Khoury, Elias　　　　　　**PJ7842.H823M3513**
The Kingdom of Strangers. Paula Haydar (Translator). Trade
Cloth. University of Arkansas Press. Fayetteville, AR. 2003. viii,
103p. ISBN:1-55728-433-4, ISBN13: 978-1-55728-433-4.
Dewey:892/.736. LCCN:95-043341.

Audience: **g,l,u,f.**

Khoury, Elias　　　　　　**PJ7842.H823J3413**
Little Mountain. Maia Tabet (Translator), Edward W. Said
(Foreword by). Book, Other. University of Minnesota Press.
Minneapolis, MN. 1989. 124p. Emergent Literatures Ser.

ISBN:0-8166-1770-8, ISBN13: 978-0-8166-1770-8.
Dewey:892/.736. LCCN:89-031940.
Audience: **g,l,u,f.** *Choice, 1989.*

Kilpatrick, Hilary　　　　　**PJ8212.K54**
The Modern Egyptian Novel. Cloth Text. Evergreen Book
Distributors. Los Angeles, CA. 1974. [9], 254 p. ;p.
ISBN:0-903729-04-0, ISBN13: 978-0-903729-04-8.
Dewey:892/.7/3609. LCCN:75-317686.

Audience: **u,f.**

Lustick, Ian S. (Editor)　　　　**DS119.7.R383 1994**
Religion, Culture, and Psychology in Arab-Israeli Relations.
Library Binding. Garland Publishing, Inc. New York, NY. 1994.
416p. Arab-Israeli Relations Ser., Vol. 5 ISBN:0-8153-1585-6,
ISBN13: 978-0-8153-1585-8. Dewey:303.48/25605694.
LCCN:93-048221.

Audience: **u,f.**

Lyall, Charles J.　　　　　**PJ7694.E3 L9 1981**
Translations of Ancient Arabian Poetry. Trade Cloth. Hyperion
Press, Inc. Westport, CT. 1987. 200p. ISBN:0-8305-0042-1,
ISBN13: 978-0-8305-0042-0. Dewey:892/.711/08.
LCCN:79-002872.

Audience: **u,f.**

Mahdi, Mushin &
　Haddawy, Husain
Arabian Nights: The Thousand and One Nights. Trade Cloth.
Alfred A. Knopf Inc. New York, NY. 1992. 464p.
ISBN:0-679-41338-3, ISBN13: 978-0-679-41338-7.
LCCN:91-058701.

Audience: **g,l,u,f.**

Mahfouz, Naguib　　　　　**PJ7846.A46**
Adrift on the Nile. Trade Cloth. Doubleday Publishing. New
York, NY. 1993. 176p. ISBN:0-385-40336-4, ISBN13:
978-0-385-40336-8. Dewey:892/.736.

Audience: **g,l,u,f.**

Mahfouz, Naguib　　　　　**PJ7846.A46A2 2000**
The Beggar, the Thief and the Dogs, Autumn Quail. UK-Trade
Paper. Random House Children's Books. New York, NY. 2000.
480p. The Autumn Quail Ser. ISBN:0-385-49835-7, ISBN13:
978-0-385-49835-7. Dewey:892.7/36. LCCN:00-040145.

Audience: **g,l,u,f.**

Mahfouz, Naguib　　　　　**PJ7846.A46**
Midaq Alley. Trade Cloth. Peter Smith Publisher, Inc. Magnolia,
MA. 2002. ISBN:0-8446-7225-4, ISBN13: 978-0-8446-7225-0.
Dewey:892/.736.

Audience: **g,l,u,f.**

Mahfouz, Naguib　　　　　**PJ7846.A46**
Mirrors. Trade Cloth. American University in Cairo Press. New
York, NY. 2001. 183p. ISBN:977-424-533-4, ISBN13:
978-977-424-533-6. Dewey:892.735.

Audience: **g,l,u,f.**

Mahfouz, Naguib　　　　　**PJ7846.A46Q313 1992**
Palace of Desire. Trade Paper. Random House Children's
Books. New York, NY. 1991. 432p. Cairo Trilogy, Vol. II
ISBN:0-385-26468-2, ISBN13: 978-0-385-26468-6.
Dewey:892/.736. LCCN:91-025147.

Audience: **g,l,u,f.**

Mahfouz, Naguib   PJ7846.A46
Palace Walk. Trade Cloth. Peter Smith Publisher, Inc. Magnolia,
MA. 2002. ISBN:0-8446-7226-2, ISBN13: 978-0-8446-7226-7.
Dewey:892/.736.

Audience: **g,l,u,f.**

Mahfouz, Naguib   PJ7846.A46 G613
God's World: An Anthology of Short Stories. Akef Abadir &
Roger Allen (Translators). Trade Paper. Bibliotheca Islamica,
Inc. Minneapolis, MN. 1973. Studies in Middle Eastern
Literatures, No. 2 ISBN:0-88297-044-5, ISBN13:
978-0-88297-044-8. Dewey:892.736. LCCN:73-079201.

Audience: **g,l,u,f.**

Mahfouz, Naguib   PJ7846.A46
Sugar Street. William M. Hutchins (Translator). Trade Paper.
Random House Children's Books. New York, NY. 1992. 320p.
Cairo Trilogy, Vol. 3 ISBN:0-385-26470-4, ISBN13:
978-0-385-26470-9. Dewey:892/.736. LCCN:92-025362.

Audience: **g,l,u,f.**

Mahfouz, Naguib   PJ7846.A46
Miramar. John Rodenbeck (Editor), Fatma M. Mahmoud
(Translator), Maged El Kommos (Revised by). Trade Paper.
Doubleday Publishing. New York, NY. 1992. 192p.
ISBN:0-385-26478-X, ISBN13: 978-0-385-26478-5.
Dewey:892/.736. LCCN:92-025382.

Audience: **g,l,u,f.**

Mahfouz, Naguib   PJ7846.A46
Children of the Alley: A Novel. Peter Theroux (Translator).
UK-Trade Paper. Doubleday Publishing. New York, NY. 1996.
464p. ISBN:0-385-26473-9, ISBN13: 978-0-385-26473-0.
Dewey:892/.736.

Audience: **g,l,u,f.**

Makar, Ragai N. &   Z3014.L56.M35 1998
  Bloyer, Christen T.
Modern Arabic Literature: A Bibliography. Trade Cloth.
Scarecrow Press, Inc. Lanham, MD. 1998. 270p. Scarecrow
Area Bibliographies Ser., No. 17 ISBN:0-8108-3539-8, ISBN13:
978-0-8108-3539-9. Dewey:016.8/927/09006. LCCN:98-022136.
Audience: **l,u,f.** *Choice, 1999.*

Malti-Douglas, Fedwa   PJ7519.W66 M34
Woman's Body, Woman's Word: Gender and Discourse in
Arabo-Islamic Writing. Princeton University Press. 1991.
ISBN:0-691-06856-9, ISBN13: 978-0-691-06856-5.

Audience: **l,u,f.**

Matar, Muhammad A.   PJ7846.A8756R75 1997
Quartet of Joy. Ferial J. Ghazoul & John Verlenden (Translator,
Preface by). Trade Cloth. University of Arkansas Press.
Fayetteville, AR. 2003. 152p. ISBN:1-55728-487-3, ISBN13:
978-1-55728-487-7. Dewey:892/.716. LCCN:97-026841.

Audience: **g,l,u,f.**

Menocal, Maria Rosa   PJ8417.A5 L58 2000
  (Editor), et al.
The Literature of Al-Andalus. Michael Sells & Raymond P.
Scheindlin (Editors). Trade Cloth. Cambridge University Press.
New York, NY. 2000. 518p. Cambridge History of Arabic
Literature Ser. ISBN:0-521-47159-1, ISBN13:
978-0-521-47159-6. Dewey:892.7/309946. LCCN:00-022599.

Audience: **u,f.**

Meyer, Stefan G.   PJ7577.M49 2001
The Experimental Arabic Novel: Postcolonial Literary
Modernism in the Levant. Cloth Text. State University of New

York Press. Albany, NY. 2000. xviii, 323p. SUNY Series in
Middle Eastern Studies ISBN:0-7914-4733-2, ISBN13:
978-0-7914-4733-8. Dewey:892.7/3609. LCCN:00-041338.

Audience: **u,f.** *Choice, 2001.*

Mikhail, Mona H.   PJ7538.M554 2003
Seen and Heard: A Century of Arab Women in Literature and
Culture. Trade Cloth. Interlink Publishing Group, Inc.
Northampton, MA. 2004. 184p. Bestselling History and Politics
Ser. ISBN:1-56656-463-8, ISBN13: 978-1-56656-463-2.
Dewey:892.7/09352042/0904. LCCN:2003-014171.

Audience: **l,u,f.** *Choice, 2004.*

Milson, Menahem   PJ7846.A46Z7125 1998
Najib Mahfuz: The Novelist-Philosopher of Cairo. Trade Cloth.
Palgrave Macmillan. New York, NY. 1999. 320p.
ISBN:0-312-21518-5, ISBN13: 978-0-312-21518-7.
Dewey:892/.736. LCCN:98-014267.

Audience: **u,f.** *Choice, 1999.*

Mina, Hanna   PJ7846.I48M8613 1997
Sun on a Cloudy Day. Bassam Frangieh & Clementina Brown
(Translators). Trade Paper. Passeggiata Press. Pueblo, CO. 1997.
192p. ISBN:1-57889-044-6, ISBN13: 978-1-57889-044-6.
Dewey:892/.736. LCCN:97-005634.

Audience: **g,l,u,f.**

Mina, Hanna   PJ7846.A46
Fragments of Memory: A Story of a Syrian Family. Olive
Kenny & Lorne Kenny (Translators), Khaldoun Shamaa
(Introduction by). Trade Cloth. Interlink Publishing Group, Inc.
Northampton, MA. 2004. 192p. Emerging Voices Ser.
ISBN:1-56656-547-2, ISBN13: 978-1-56656-547-9.
Dewey:892/.736 B.

Audience: **g,l,u,f.**

Mosteghanemi, Ahlam   PJ7846.O88F39 2004
Chaos of the Senses. Trade Cloth. American University in Cairo
Press. New York, NY. 2004. 240p. Modern Arabic Writing Ser.
ISBN:977-424-670-5, ISBN13: 978-977-424-670-8. Dewey:892.
LCCN:2004-556560.

Audience: **g,l,u,f.**

Moussa, Sabri   PJ7850.U845
Seeds of Corruption. Mona N. Mikhail (Translator). Trade
Paper. Interlink Publishing Group, Inc. Northampton, MA. 2002.
192p. Emerging Voices Ser. ISBN:1-56656-457-3, ISBN13:
978-1-56656-457-1. Dewey:892.736.

Audience: **g,l,u,f.**

Munif, Abd al-Rahman   PJ7850.U514 U3513 1993
The Trench. Peter Theroux (Translator). Knopf Publishing
Group. 1993. ISBN:0-679-74533-5, ISBN13:
978-0-679-74533-4.

Audience: **g,l,u,f.**

Nasrallah, Emily   PJ7852.A69I6513 1997
Flight Against Time. Issa Boullata (Translator). Trade Paper.
University of Texas Press. Austin, TX. 1998. 194p. Modern
Middle Eastern Literature in Translation Ser.
ISBN:0-292-75564-3, ISBN13: 978-0-292-75564-2.
Dewey:892.7/36. LCCN:97-077534.

Audience: **g,l,u,f.**

Nicholson, Reynold A.   PJ7510
A Literary History of the Arabs. Ed. 2. Trade Cloth. Cambridge
University Press. New York, NY. 1930. 538p.

ISBN:0-521-05823-6, ISBN13: 978-0-521-05823-0.
Dewey:892/.709.

Audience: **u,f.** *B*

Nicholson, Reynold A. **PJ418**
Translations of Eastern Poetry and Prose. Paper Text. Classic
Books. Murrieta, CA. 2001. 200p. ISBN:0-7426-9134-9,
ISBN13: 978-0-7426-9134-6. Dewey:892/.7/08.

Audience: **l,u,f.**

Norris, H. T. **PJ7702.A36**
The Adventures of Antar: An Early Arab Epic Approaches to
Arabic. Trade Cloth. Aris & Phillips. Oxford, 1980. 264p.
ISBN:0-85668-161-X, ISBN13: 978-0-85668-161-5.
Dewey:892/.73. LCCN:81-105959.

Audience: **u,f.**

Pinault, David **PJ7737.P56 1992**
Story-Telling Techniques in the Arabian Nights. Trade Cloth.
Brill Academic Publishers, Inc. Boston, MA. 1992. 292p.
Journal of Arabic Literature Supplements Ser., No. 15
ISBN:90-04-09530-6, ISBN13: 978-90-04-09530-4.
Dewey:398.22. LCCN:91-028023.

Audience: **u,f.** *Choice, 1992.*

Quayd, Muhammad Y. **PJ7858.U3H3713 1998**
War in the Land of Egypt. Olive E. Kenny, Lorne Kenny &
Christopher Tingley (Translators). Trade Cloth. Interlink
Publishing Group, Inc. Northampton, MA. 1998. 192p.
Emerging Voices Ser. ISBN:1-56656-227-9, ISBN13:
978-1-56656-227-0. Dewey:892/.736. LCCN:97-021922.

Audience: **g,l,u,f.** *Choice, 1998.*

Rifaat, Alifa **PJ7860.I3/**
Distant View of a Minaret and Other Stories. Trade Paper.
Heinemann. Portsmouth, NH. 1987. 126p. African Writers Ser.
ISBN:0-435-90912-6, ISBN13: 978-0-435-90912-3.
Dewey:892/.736.

Audience: **g,l,u,f.**

Rosenthal, Franz **PN6222.A6R6**
Humor in Early Islam. Paper Text. Textbook Publishers.
Temecula, CA. 2003. x, 154p. ISBN:0-7581-1665-9, ISBN13:
978-0-7581-1665-9. Dewey:892/.7/7008.

Audience: **u,f.**

Salem, Ibtihal **PJ7862**
Children of the Waters. Marilyn Booth (Translator). Trade Paper.
University of Texas Press. Austin, TX. 2003. 132p. Modern
Middle East Literatures in Translation Ser. ISBN:0-292-77773-6,
ISBN13: 978-0-292-77773-6. Dewey:892.7/37.
LCCN:2002-111854.

Audience: **g,l,u,f.**

Salih, Tayeb & **PJ7862.A564B313 1996**
Johnson-Davies, Denys
Bandarshah. Trade Cloth. Kegan Paul International, Ltd.
London, 1996. 120p. UNESCO Collection of Representative
Works ISBN:0-7103-0537-0, ISBN13: 978-0-7103-0537-4.
Dewey:892/.736. LCCN:95-043489.

Audience: **g,l,u,f.**

Salih, Tayeb **PJ7846.A46**
Season of Migration to the North. Denys Johnson-Davies
(Translator). Trade Cloth. Lynne Rienner Publishers, Inc.
Boulder, CO. 1996. 168p. ISBN:0-89410-199-4, ISBN13:
978 0 89410 199 1. Dewey:892/.736. LCCN:90-110140.

Audience: **g,l,u,f.** *Choice, 1990.*

Salih, Tayeb **PJ7862.A564.U7213**
The Wedding of Zein and Other Stories. Denys Johnson-Davies
(Translator), Ibrahim Salahi (Illustrator). Trade Paper. Lynne
Rienner Publishers, Inc. Boulder, CO. 1985. 120p.
ISBN:0-89410-201-X, ISBN13: 978-0-89410-201-1.
Dewey:892/.736. LCCN:90-110915.

Audience: **g,l,u,f.**

Samman, Ghada **PJ7862.A584Q2613**
The Square Moon: Supernatural Tales. Issa J. Boullata
(Translator). Trade Cloth. University of Arkansas Press.
Fayetteville, AR. 2003. 208p. ISBN:1-55728-534-9, ISBN13:
978-1-55728-534-8. Dewey:892.7/36. LCCN:98-030084.

Audience: **g,l,u,f.** *Choice, 1999.*

Samman, Ghada **PJ7862.A584B3913**
Beirut '75. Nancy N. Roberts (Translator). Cloth Text.
University of Arkansas Press. Fayetteville, AR. 1995. 160p.
ISBN:1-55728-383-4, ISBN13: 978-1-55728-383-2.
Dewey:892/.736. LCCN:95-013545.

Audience: **g,l,u,f.**

Samman, Ghada **PJ7862.A584K313 1997**
Beirut Nightmares. Nancy N. Roberts (Translator). Trade Paper.
Quartet Books, Ltd. London, 1998. 268p. ISBN:0-7043-8065-X,
ISBN13: 978-0-7043-8065-3. Dewey:892.7/36.
LCCN:98-159982.

Audience: **g,l,u,f.**

Samman, Ghada **PJ7862.A584L3313**
Night of the First Billion. Nancy N. Roberts (Translator). Trade
Cloth. Syracuse University Press. Syracuse, NY. 2004. 448p.
Middle East Literature in Translation Ser. ISBN:0-8156-0829-2,
ISBN13: 978-0-8156-0829-5. Dewey:892.7/36.
LCCN:2004-020952.

Audience: **g,l,u,f.**

Sayyab, Badr Shakir **PJ7862.A93**
Selected Poems. Nadia Bishai (Trans., Intro.). Third World
Centre for Research and Publishing. 1986.

Audience: **g,l,u,f.**

Schimmel, Annemarie **PJ827**
As Through a Veil: Mystical Poetry in Islam. Paper Text.
Columbia University Press. New York, NY. 1987. 359p.
ISBN:0-231-05247-2, ISBN13: 978-0-231-05247-4.
Dewey:809.1/938297. LCCN:81-012302.

Audience: **u,f.**

Sells, Michael **PJ7694.E3**
(Translator, Introduction by)
Desert Tracings: Six Classic Arabian Odes by 'Alqama,
Shanfara, Labid, 'Antara, Al-A'sha, and Dhu Al-Rumma. Trade
Paper. Wesleyan University Press. Middletown, CT. 1989. 87p.
Wesleyan Poetry in Translation Ser. ISBN:0-8195-1158-7,
ISBN13: 978-0-8195-1158-4. Dewey:892/.1043/08.
LCCN:88-028084.

Audience: **g,l,u,f.** *Choice, 1990.*

Sharouni, Yusuf **PJ7862.H273 A24 1991**
Blood Feud and Other Stories. Denys Johnson-Davies
(Translator). Trade Paper. American University in Cairo Press.
New York, NY. 1992. 137p. ISBN:977-424-268-8, ISBN13:
978-977-424-268-7. Dewey:892/.736. LCCN:92-161496.

Audience: **g,l,u,f.**

Starkey, Paul & **PJ7510.E53 1998**
Mcisami, Julic S. (Editors)
Encyclopedia of Arabic Literature. Paper over Boards.

Routledge. New York, NY. 1998. 896p. ISBN:0-415-06808-8, ISBN13: 978-0-415-06808-6. Dewey:892/.70903 B. LCCN:96-047907.

Audience: **l,u,f.** *Choice, 1998.*

Straley, Dona S.   **Z3014.L56S77 2004**
The Undergraduate's Companion to Arab Writers and Their Web Sites. Trade Paper. Libraries Unlimited, Inc. Westport, CT. 2004. 204p. Undergraduate Companion Ser. ISBN:1-59158-118-4, ISBN13: 978-1-59158-118-5. Dewey:892.7/02854678. LCCN:2004-046582.

Audience: **g,l,u,f.** *Choice, 2005.*

Taher, Bahaa   **PJ7864.A357K4613**
Aunt Safiyya and the Monastery: A Novel. Barbara Romaine (Translator). Trade Paper. University of California Press. Berkeley, CA. 1996. 144p. Literature of the Middle East Ser. ISBN:0-520-20075-6, ISBN13: 978-0-520-20075-3. Dewey:892/.736. LCCN:95-038100.

Audience: **g,l,u,f.** *Choice, 1996.*

Tamir, Zakariya   **PJ7864.A384A25 1985**
Tigers on the Tenth Day and Other Stories. Denys Johnson-Davies (Translator). Book, Other. Quartet Books, Ltd. London, 1993. 128p. ISBN:0-7043-2465-2, ISBN13: 978-0-7043-2465-7. Dewey:892/.736. LCCN:85-118254.

Audience: **g,l,u,f.** *Choice, 1986.*

Tawfiq, Sahar   **PJ7864.A478A6 1995**
Points of the Compass: Stories by Sahar Tawfiq. Marilyn Booth (Translator, Introduction by, Selected by). Trade Cloth. University of Arkansas Press. Fayetteville, AR. 2003. 96p. ISBN:1-55728-385-0, ISBN13: 978-1-55728-385-6. Dewey:892/.736. LCCN:95-017242.

Audience: **g,l,u,f.** *Choice, 1996.*

Telmissany, May   **PJ7846.A46**
Dunyazad. Trade Cloth. Saqi Books. London, 2000. 120p. ISBN:0-86356-552-2, ISBN13: 978-0-86356-552-6. Dewey:892.7/3/6.

Audience: **g,l,u,f.**

Wattar, Tahir   **PJ7870.A8.Z313 2000**
The Earthquake. Trade Cloth. Saqi Books. London, 2000. 184p. ISBN:0-86356-944-7, ISBN13: 978-0-86356-944-9. Dewey:892.7/36.

Audience: **g,l,u,f.** *Choice, 2001.*

Yakhlif, Yahya   **PJ7874.A36.B813 1998**
A Lake Beyond the Wind. M. Jayyusi & C. Tingley (Translators). Trade Cloth. Interlink Publishing Group, Inc. Northampton, MA. 1998. 160p. Emerging Voices Ser. ISBN:1-56656-301-1, ISBN13: 978-1-56656-301-7. Dewey:892.7/36. LCCN:98-041185.

Audience: **g,l,u,f.** *Choice, 1999.*

Yared, NazikSaba   **PJ7874.A77T3713 1997**
Improvisations on a Missing String. Stuart A. Hancox (Translator). Trade Cloth. University of Arkansas Press. Fayetteville, AR. 2003. 112p. ISBN:1-55728-495-4, ISBN13: 978-1-55728-495-2. Dewey:892.7/36. LCCN:97-036782.

Audience: **g,l,u,f.** *Choice, 1998.*

Young, M. J. L.   **DS36.85 .R45 1990**
  (Editor), et al.
Religion, Learning and Science in the 'Abbasid Period. J. D. Latham & R. B. Serjeant (Editors). Trade Cloth. Cambridge University Press. New York, NY. 1991. 611p. History of Arabic

Literature Ser. ISBN:0-521-32763-6, ISBN13: 978-0-521-32763-3. Dewey:909/.097671. LCCN:90-001549.

Audience: **u,f.** *Choice, 1992.*

Youssef, Saadi   **PJ7874.U84A245 2002**
Without an Alphabet, Without a Face: Selected Poems. Khaled Mattawa (Translator). Trade Paper. Graywolf Press. St. Paul, MN. 2002. 216p. ISBN:1-55597-371-X, ISBN13: 978-1-55597-371-1. Dewey:892.7/16. LCCN:2002-102976.

Audience: **g,l,u,f.**

Middle Eastern Languages and Literatures > Semitic Languages and Literatures > Other Semitic Languages and Literatures (Babylonian, Assyrian)

Ackerman, Susan   **PJ3771.G6A25 2005**
🄴 When Heroes Love: The Ambiguity of Eros in the Stories of Gilgamesh and David. E-Book. Columbia University Press. New York, NY. 2005. 336p. Religion and Gender Ser. ISBN:0-231-50725-9, ISBN13: 978-0-231-50725-7. Dewey:809/.93353.

Audience: **u,f.**

Black, Jeremy (Editor),   **PJ3953**
  et al.
The Literature of Ancient Sumer. Graham Cunningham, Eleanor Robson & Gabor Zolyomi (Editors). Trade Cloth. Oxford University Press, Inc. New York, NY. 2005. 320p. ISBN:0-19-926311-6, ISBN13: 978-0-19-926311-0. Dewey:899/.9508. LCCN:2005-295986.

Audience: **u,f.** *Choice, 2005.*

Budge, E. A. Wallis   **PJ3771.G5**
The Babylonian Story of the Deluge and the Epic of Gilgamesh with an Account of the Royal Libraries of Nineveh. Trade Paper. Kessinger Publishing, LLC. Whitefish, MT. 1995. 57p. ISBN:1-56459-572-2, ISBN13: 978-1-56459-572-0. Dewey:935.03.

Audience: **u,f.**

Driver, Godfrey   **PJ3019 .D7 1976**
Semitic Writing: From Pictograph to Alphabet. Ed. 3. Trade Cloth. Oxford University Press, Inc. New York, NY. 1976. 362p. Schweich Lectures on Biblical Archaeology ISBN:0-19-725917-0, ISBN13: 978-0-19-725917-7. Dewey:492. LCCN:77-355545.

Audience: **u,f.**

Fitzmyer, Joseph A.   **BS2395.F573**
The Semitic Background of the New Testament. Paper Text. William B. Eerdmans Publishing Company. Grand Rapids, MI. 1997. 524p. Biblical Resource Ser. ISBN:0-8028-4845-1, ISBN13: 978-0-8028-4845-1. Dewey:225.6. LCCN:97-010581.

Audience: **u,f.**

Foster, Benjamin R.   **PJ3951.B44 2005**
Before the Muses: An Anthology of Akkadian Literature. Ed. 3. Trade Cloth. University Press of Maryland. Bethesda, MD. 2005. xx, 1044p. ISBN:1-883053-76-5, ISBN13: 978-1-883053-76-5. Dewey:892/.1. LCCN:2004-065045.

Audience: **u,f.**

George, Andrew   **PJ4061**
The Epic of Gilgamesh. Library Binding. Sagebrush Education
Resources. Caledonia, MN. 2003. ISBN:0-613-64275-9,
ISBN13: 978-0-613-64275-0. Dewey:899.9/51.

                                        Audience: **g,l,u,f.**

Heidel, Alexander   **PJ3771.G6 H4**
Gilgamesh Epic and Old Testament Parallels. Ed. 2. Trade
Paper. University of Chicago Press. Chicago, IL. 1963. 280p.
ISBN:0-226-32398-6, ISBN13: 978-0-226-32398-5.
Dewey:892.191. LCCN:49-005734.

                                        Audience: **u,f.** *B*

Hetzron, Robert   **PJ3021.S46 1998**
The Semitic Languages. Paper over Boards. Routledge. New
York, NY. 1997. 592p. Routledge Language Family Descriptions
Ser. ISBN:0-415-05767-1, ISBN13: 978-0-415-05767-7.
Dewey:492. LCCN:96-045373.

                                        Audience: **l,u,f.**

Mitchell, Stephen   **PJ3771.G5**
Gilgamesh: A New English Version. Trade Paper. Simon &
Schuster. New York, NY. 2006. 304p. ISBN:0-7432-6169-0,
ISBN13: 978-0-7432-6169-2. Dewey:892/.1.

                                        Audience: **g,l,u,f.**

Sasson, Jack M.   **PJ310 .S78 1984**
(Editor)
Studies in Literature from the Ancient Near East: Dedicated to
Samuel Noah Kramer. Trade Cloth. American Oriental Society.
New Haven, CT. 1984. 369p. American Oriental Ser., Vol. 65
ISBN:0-940490-65-X, ISBN13: 978-0-940490-65-9.
Dewey:809/.89394. LCCN:86-136854.

                                        Audience: **u,f.**

Middle Eastern Languages and Literatures > Armenian Language and Literature

Bardakjian, Kevork B.   **PK8505.B37 2000**
Reference Guide to Modern Armenian Literature, 1500-1920:
With an Introductory History. Trade Cloth. Wayne State
University Press. Detroit, MI. 2000. 714p. ISBN:0-8143-2747-8,
ISBN13: 978-0-8143-2747-0. Dewey:891/.99209.
LCCN:98-043139.

                                        Audience: **u,f.** *Choice, 2001.*

Surmelian, Leon   **PK8547.S27**
(Translator)
Daredevils of Sassoun: The Armenian National Epic. A.
Swallow. 1964.

                                        Audience: **g,l,u,f.**

Surmelian, Leon   **GR271.A75**
Apples of Immortality: Folktales of Armenia. Stewart Irwin
(Illustrator). Library Binding. Greenwood Publishing Group, Inc.
Portsmouth, NH. 1985. 319p. Unesco Collection of
Representative Works ISBN:0-313-23417-5, ISBN13:
978-0-313-23417-0. Dewey:398.21094792. LCCN:82-024260.

                                        Audience: **g,l,u,f.**

Middle Eastern Languages and Literatures > Caucasian Languages and Literatures > Georgian (Grusinian)

Rustaveli, Shota   **PK9169.R8**
The Man in the Panther's Skin: A Romantic Epic. Wardrop,
Marjory Scott (Translator). Literatura de Khelovneba. 1966.

                                        Audience: **u,f.**

Middle Eastern Languages and Literatures > Turkic Languages and Literatures > Turkish (Osmanic): Ottoman and Modern > Language

Alderson, Anthony D. &   **PL191.H6 1984**
Iz, Fahir
The Oxford Turkish-English Dictionary. Ed. 3. Trade Cloth.
Oxford University Press, Inc. New York, NY. 1985. 544p.
ISBN:0-19-864124-9, ISBN13: 978-0-19-864124-7.
Dewey:494/.35321. LCCN:85-170756.

                                        Audience: **l,u,f.**

Erdener, Yldray   **PL179.E73 2004**
101 Turkish Idiomatic Expressions. Trade Cloth. Dunwoody
Press. Hyattsville, MD. 2004. iv, 202p. ISBN:1-931546-02-9,
ISBN13: 978-1-931546-02-7. Dewey:494. LCCN:2004-107776.

                                        Audience: **l,u,f.**

Halman, Talat S.   **PL161 .H3**
201 Turkish Verbs: Fully Conjugated in All the Tenses. Trade
Paper. Barron's Educational Series, Inc. Hauppauge, NY. 1981.
224p. 201 Verbs Ser. ISBN:0-8120-2034-0, ISBN13:
978-0-8120-2034-2. Dewey:494/.3582421. LCCN:80-027006.

                                        Audience: **g,l,u,f.**

Iz, Fahir (Editor), et al.   **PL191.I94 1992**
The Oxford Turkish Dictionary: Turkish-English,
English-Turkish. H. C. Hony & Anthony D. Alderson (Editors).
Trade Cloth. Oxford University Press, Inc. New York, NY. 1993.
1186p. ISBN:0-19-864190-7, ISBN13: 978-0-19-864190-2.
Dewey:494/.35321. LCCN:93-226416.

                                        Audience: **l,u,f.** *Choice, 1993.*

Jaeckel, Ralph &   **PL161.J34 2005**
Erciyes, Gulna Doganata
A Dictionary of Turkish Verbs: In Context and by Theme.
Mehmet Süreyya Er (Contribution by). Trade Paper. Georgetown
University Press. Washington, DC. 2006. 768p.
ISBN:1-58901-057-4, ISBN13: 978-1-58901-057-4.
Dewey:494/.35321. LCCN:2004-061778.

                                        Audience: **u,f.**

Lewis, Geoffrey   **PL123.L4 2000**
Turkish Grammar. Ed. 2. Paper Text. Oxford University Press,
Inc. New York, NY. 2001. 328p. ISBN:0-19-870036-9, ISBN13:
978-0-19-870036-4. Dewey:494/.355. LCCN:00-063688.

                                        Audience: **l,u,f.**

Mardin, Yusuf   **PL127 .M37**
Turkish Phrase Book. Paper Text. Transatlantic Arts, Inc.
Albuquerque, NM. 1970. x, 156p. ISBN:0-7100-6777-1,
ISBN13: 978-0-7100-6777-7. Dewey:494/.35/8242.
LCCN:70-505742.

                                        Audience: **g,l,u,f.**

Redhouse, Sir James PL191
Turkish-English, English-Turkish Dictionary: New Red House. Ed. 12. U.Bhadur Alkim (Editor). Trade Cloth. i. b. d., Ltd. Kinderhook, NY. 1991. 1292p. ISBN:975-413-022-1, ISBN13: 978-975-413-022-5. Dewey:494.3532.

Audience: **l,u,f.**

Wittek, Paul PL125
Turkish Reader. Paper Text. Textbook Publishers. Temecula, CA. 2003. 134p. ISBN:0-7581-9394-7, ISBN13: 978-0-7581-9394-0. Dewey:494.3586.

Audience: **u,f.**

Middle Eastern Languages and Literatures > Turkic Languages and Literatures > Turkish (Osmanic): Ottoman and Modern > Literature

Andrews, Walter G. PL217 .A5
An Introduction to Ottoman Poetry. Trade Cloth. Bibliotheca Islamica, Inc. Minneapolis, MN. 1976. Studies in Middle Eastern Literatures, No. 7 ISBN:0-88297-012-7, ISBN13: 978-0-88297-012-7. Dewey:894.35/1/09. LCCN:74-027615.

Audience: **u,f.**

Andrews, Walter G. PL235.O87 1997
(Editor, Translator), et al.
Ottoman Lyric Poetry: An Anthology. Najaat Black & Mehmet Kalpakli (Editor, Translators). Trade Cloth. University of Texas Press. Austin, TX. 1997. 328p. ISBN:0-292-70471-2, ISBN13: 978-0-292-70471-8. Dewey:894/.35108. LCCN:96-024262.

Audience: **u,f.**

Evin, Ahmet O. PL223 .E95 1983
Origins and Development of the Turkish Novel. Trade Paper. Bibliotheca Islamica, Inc. Minneapolis, MN. 1983. Studies in Middle Eastern Literatures, No. 11 ISBN:0-88297-040-2, ISBN13: 978-0-88297-040-0. Dewey:894/.353/009. LCCN:84-253082.

Audience: **l,u,f.**

Faik, Sait PL248.S288 A2
A Dot on the Map: Selected Stories and Poems. Ilhan Basgoz & Talat S. Halman (Editors). Trade Cloth. Indiana University, Turkish Studies. Bloomington, IN. 1983. 307p. Turkish Studies, Vol. 4 ISBN:0-685-29322-X, ISBN13: 978-0-685-29322-5. Dewey:894/.3533.

Audience: **g,l,u,f.**

Faik, Sait PL248.S288A2 2004
Sleeping in the Forest: Stories and Poems. Jayne L. Warner & Talat S. Halman (Editors). Trade Paper, Perfect. Syracuse University Press. Syracuse, NY. 2004. 199p. Middle East Literature in Translation Ser. ISBN:0-8156-0804-7, ISBN13: 978-0-8156-0804-2. Dewey:894.3533. LCCN:2004-022125.

Audience: **g,l,u,f.**

Furuzan PL248.F9
A Summer Full of Love. Damian Croft (Translator). Trade Paper. Milet Publishing. Chicago, IL. 2004. 176p. ISBN:1-84059-301-6, ISBN13: 978-1-84059-301-3. Dewey:894.3512.

Audience: **g,l,u,f.**

Halman, Talat S. PL271.E5 M6 1976
Modern Turkish Drama: An Anthology. Trade Cloth. Bibliotheca Islamica, Inc. Minneapolis, MN. 1976. Studies in Middle Eastern Literatures, No. 5 ISBN:0-88297-007-0, ISBN13: 978-0-88297-007-3. Dewey:894/.3/52308. LCCN:73-079204.

Audience: **l,u,f.**

Halman, Talat S., et al. PN2 .R44
Turkey: From Empire to Nation. Kathleen Burrill, Anne Paolucci, Metin And, Bedia Turgay-Ahmad, Suheyla Artemel, Ilhan Basgoz, John R. Walsh & Richard Clark (Authors). Trade Paper. Griffon House Publications. Smyrna, DE. 1973. 144p. Review of National Literatures Ser., Vol. 4, No. 1 ISBN:0-918680-62-X, ISBN13: 978-0-918680-62-4. Dewey:894/.35/09. LCCN:77-126039.

Audience: **u,f.**

Halman, Talat S. PL271.E3
(Editor, Introduction by)
Contemporary Turkish Literature: Fiction and Poetry. Trade Cloth. Fairleigh Dickinson University Press. Cranbury, NJ. 1982. 550p. ISBN:0-8386-1360-8, ISBN13: 978-0-8386-1360-3. Dewey:894/.3513/08. LCCN:77-074391.

Audience: **g,l,u,f.** 𝓑

Hikmet, Nazim PL248.H45A235 2002
Beyond the Walls: Selected Poems. Trade Paper. Anvil Press Poetry, Ltd. London, 2001. 256p. ISBN:0-85646-329-9, ISBN13: 978-0-85646-329-7. Dewey:894/.3513. LCCN:2002-318432.

Audience: **g,l,u,f.**

Hikmet, Nazim PL248.H45
A Sad State of Freedom. Trade Cloth. Greville Press, The. Warwick, 1990. 23p. ISBN:0-906887-40-2, ISBN13: 978-0-906887-40-0. Dewey:894.3513.

Audience: **g,l,u,f.**

Hikmet, Nazim PL248.H45
The Epic of Sheik Bedreddin and Other Poems. Randy Blasing & Mutlu Konuk (Translators). Trade Paper. Persea Books, Inc. New York, NY. 1978. ISBN:0-89255-024-4, ISBN13: 978-0-89255-024-1. Dewey:894/.3/513. LCCN:77-076663.

Audience: **g,l,u,f.**

Hikmet, Nazim PL248.H45A6 2002
Poems of Nazim Hikmet. Ed. 2. Randy Blasing & Mutlu Konuk (Translators). Trade Paper. Persea Books, Inc. New York, NY. 2002. 288p. ISBN:0-89255-274-3, ISBN13: 978-0-89255-274-0. Dewey:894/.3513. LCCN:2001-059118.

Audience: **g,l,u,f.**

Hikmet, Nazim PL248.H45R813 1985
Rubaiyat. Randy Blasing & Mutlu Konuk (Translators). Trade Paper. Copper Beech Press. Providence, RI. 1985. 50p. ISBN:0-914278-48-7, ISBN13: 978-0-914278-48-1. Dewey:894/.3513. LCCN:85-015151.

Audience: **g,l,u,f.**

Hikmet, Nazim PL248.H45 M413 1982
Human Landscapes. Randy Blasing & Mutlu Konuk (Translators), Denise Levertov (Introduction by). Trade Paper. Persea Books, Inc. New York, NY. 1993. 325p. Poetry in Translation Ser. ISBN:0-89255-068-6, ISBN13: 978-0-89255-068-5. Dewey:894/.3513.

Audience: **g,l,u,f.**

Iz, Fahir PL271.E8 A67 1978
An Anthology of Modern Turkish Short Stories. Trade Cloth. Bibliotheca Islamica, Inc. Minneapolis, MN. 1978. Studies in

Middle Eastern Literatures, No. 9 ISBN:0-88297-021-6, ISBN13: 978-0-88297-021-9. Dewey:894/.35/301. LCCN:77-089828.

Audience: **g,l,u,f.**

Karasu, Bilge   **PL248.K33G6313 2003**
Garden of the Departed Cats. Trade Paper. New Directions Publishing Corporation. New York, NY. 2004. 240p. ISBN:0-8112-1551-2, ISBN13: 978-0-8112-1551-0. Dewey:894/.3533. LCCN:2003-013221.

Audience: **g,l,u,f.**

Karasu, Bilge   **PL248.K33T713 2002**
Death in Troy. Aron Aji (Translator). Trade Paper. City Lights Books. San Francisco, CA. 2002. 116p. ISBN:0-87286-401-4, ISBN13: 978-0-87286-401-6. Dewey:894/.3533. LCCN:2002-024170.

Audience: **g,l,u,f.**

Karasu, Bilge   **PL248.K33G4313 1994**
Night: A Novel. Guneli Gun (Translator). Trade Cloth. Louisiana State University Press. Baton Rouge, LA. 1994. 152p. ISBN:0-8071-1849-4, ISBN13: 978-0-8071-1849-8. Dewey:894/.3533. LCCN:93-037912.

Audience: **g,l,u,f.** *Choice, 1994.*

Kemal, Yashar   **PL248.P34**
Anatolian Tales. Trade Paper. Writers & Readers Publishing, Inc. New York, NY. 148p. ISBN:0-906495-99-7, ISBN13: 978-0-906495-99-5. Dewey:894/.3533.

Audience: **g,l,u,f.**

Kemal, Yashar   **PL248.Y275D4613 1985**
The Sea-Crossed Fisherman. Trade Cloth. George Braziller Inc. New York, NY. 1985. 286p. ISBN:0-8076-1122-0, ISBN13: 978-0-8076-1122-7. Dewey:894/.3533. LCCN:84-029338.

Audience: **g,l,u,f.**

Kemal, Yashar   **PL248.P34**
They Burn the Thistles: Memed My Hawk, Part II. Trade Paper. Writers & Readers Publishing, Inc. New York, NY. 412p. ISBN:0-906495-47-4, ISBN13: 978-0-906495-47-6. Dewey:894/.3533.

Audience: **g,l,u,f.**

Kemal, Yashar (Author, Introduction by)   **PL248.Y275I513 2005**
Memed, My Hawk. Edouard Roditi (Translator). Trade Paper, Perfect. New York Review of Books, Incorporated, The. New York, NY. 2005. 392p. New York Review Books Classics ISBN:1-59017-139-X, ISBN13: 978-1-59017-139-4. Dewey:894/.3533. LCCN:2005-003745.

Audience: **g,l,u,f.**

Nava'i, Alisher   **PK6451.A5723**
The Language of the Birds. Trade Paper. AuthorHouse. Bloomington, IN. 2006. 156p. ISBN:1-4259-1248-6, ISBN13: 978-1-4259-1248-2. Dewey:891.5511.

Audience: **g,l,u,f.**

Nesin, Aziz   **PN6231.N27 N47 1988**
Tales of Nasrettin Hoca. Trade Paper. Tuttle Publishing. Boston, MA. 2005. 112p. ISBN:975-95481-0-0, ISBN13: 978-975-95481-0-0. Dewey:398. LCCN:89-968656.

Audience: **g,l,u,f.**

Nesin, Aziz   **PL248.N49**
Hayri the Barber Surname. Joseph S. Jacobson (Translator). Trade Paper. Southmoor Studios. Holladay, UT. 2001. ISBN:0-9673703-9-6, ISBN13: 978-0-9673703-9-2.

Audience: **g,l,u,f.**

Nesin, Aziz   **PL248.N43**
Istanbul Boy: The Autobiography of Aziz Nesin. Joseph S. Jacobson (Translator). Trade Paper. Southmoor Studios. Holladay, UT. 2000. 189p. ISBN:0-9673703-5-3, ISBN13: 978-0-9673703-5-4. Dewey:894/.3/58307.

Audience: **g,l,u,f.**

Nesin, Aziz   **PL248.N49**
Memoirs of an Exile. Joseph S. Jacobson (Editor). Trade Paper. Southmoor Studios. Holladay, UT. 2001. 157p. ISBN:0-9673703-8-8, ISBN13: 978-0-9673703-8-5.

Audience: **g,l,u,f.**

Oren, Aras   **PL248.P34**
Please, No Police: A Novella. Teoman Sipahigil (Translator). Trade Paper. Center for Middle Eastern Studies. Minneapolis, MN. 1992. 174p. Modern Middle Eastern Literature in Translation Ser. ISBN:0-292-76038-8, ISBN13: 978-0-292-76038-7. Dewey:894/.3533. LCCN:92-075236.

Audience: **g,l,u,f.**

Pamuk, Orhan   **PL248.P34**
Snow. Trade Cloth. Knopf Publishing Group. New York, NY. 2005. Reading Group Guides ISBN:1-4000-8933-6, ISBN13: 978-1-4000-8933-8. Dewey:894.3533.

Audience: **g,l,u,f.**

Pamuk, Orhan   **PL248.P34B4613 2001**
My Name Is Red. Erdag Goknar (Translator). Trade Cloth. Alfred A. Knopf Inc. New York, NY. 2001. 448p. ISBN:0-375-40695-6, ISBN13: 978-0-375-40695-9. Dewey:894/.3533. LCCN:2001-029866.

Audience: **g,l,u,f.**

Pamuk, Orhan   **PL248.P34K3713 1994**
The Black Book. Guneli Gun (Translator). Trade Cloth. Farrar, Straus & Giroux. New York, NY. 1994. 356p. ISBN:0-374-11394-7, ISBN13: 978-0-374-11394-0. Dewey:894/.353. LCCN:94-004791.

Audience: **g,l,u,f.**

Pamuk, Orhan   **PL248.P34Y4613 1997**
The New Life. Guneli Gun (Translator). Trade Cloth. Farrar, Straus & Giroux. New York, NY. 1997. 296p. ISBN:0-374-22129-4, ISBN13: 978-0-374-22129-4. Dewey:894.3/5/3/3. LCCN:96-045722.

Audience: **g,l,u,f.**

Pamuk, Orhan   **PL248.P34W4713 1991**
The White Castle. Victoria Holbrook (Translator). Trade Cloth. George Braziller Inc. New York, NY. 1991. 162p. ISBN:0-8076-1264-2, ISBN13: 978-0-8076-1264-4. Dewey:894.3533. LCCN:91-000202.

Audience: **g,l,u,f.** *Choice, 1991.*

Seyh Galip   **PL248.S387A28 2005**
Beauty and Love/Seyh Galip; Translated from the Ottoman Turkish with an Introduction and Key by Victoria Rowe Holbrook. Victoria Rowe Holbrook (Translator). Trade Paper. Modern Language Association of America. New York, NY. 2005. 160p. MLA Texts and Translations Ser., 17

ISBN:0-87352-934-0, ISBN13: 978-0-87352-934-1.
Dewey:894/.3512. LCCN:2005-050132.

Audience: **g,l,u,f.**

Sumer, Faruk (Editor), **PL248.K54**
  et al.
Book of Dede Korkut: A Turkish Epic. Ahmet E. Uysal &
Warren S. Walker (Editors). Trade Paper. University of Texas
Press. Austin, TX. 1971. 240p. ISBN:0-292-70787-8, ISBN13:
978-0-292-70787-0. Dewey:398.22.

Audience: **u,f.**

Tanpinar, Ahmet Hamdi **PL248.T234S19513**
The Time Regulation Institute. Ender Gurol (Translator), Berna
Moran (Supplement by). Trade Cloth. Turko-Tatar Press, LLC.
Madison, WI. 2002. 335p. ISBN:1-892381-02-8, ISBN13:
978-1-892381-02-6. Dewey:894/.3533. LCCN:2001-087469.

Audience: **g,l,u,f.**

Veli, Orhan **PL248.K23A27 1989**
I, Orhan Veli. Murat Nemet-Nejat (Translator). Trade Cloth.
Hanging Loose Press. Brooklyn, NY. 1989.
ISBN:0-914610-65-1, ISBN13: 978-0-914610-65-6.
Dewey:894/.3513. LCCN:88-024751.

Audience: **g,l,u,f.**

Walker, Barbara K. **PL246.W35 1990**
The Art of the Turkish Tale. Trade Paper. Texas Tech University
Press. Lubbock, TX. 1993. ISBN:0-89672-316-X, ISBN13:
978-0-89672-316-0. Dewey:398.2/09561. LCCN:90-039477.

Audience: **g,l,u,f.**

Middle Eastern Languages and Literatures > Iranian languages and literatures > Other Iranian languages (Kurdish, Pushtu, etc.)

PK6908.65.E64
Anthology of Contemporary Kurdish Poetry. London: Kurdistan
Solidarity Committee and Yashar Ismail. 1994.
ISBN:0-9524991-0-X, ISBN13: 978-0-9524991-0-7.

Audience: **g,l,u,f.**

Abdulla, Jamal & **PK6905**
  McCarus, Ernest N. (Editors)
Kurdish Short Stories. Trade Cloth. University of Michigan,
Department of Near Eastern Studies. Ann Arbor, MI. 1967. ix,
115p. Kurdish Readers Ser., Vol. 3 ISBN:0-916798-63-1,
ISBN13: 978-0-916798-63-5. Dewey:491.59.

Audience: **l,u,f.**

Ahmadzadeh, Hashem **PK6423.A36 2003**
Nation and Novel: A Study of Persian and Kurdish Narrative
Discourse. Trade Cloth. Uppsala Universitet/Acta Universitatis
Uppsaliensis. Uppsala, 2003. 330p. Studia Iranica Upsaliensia,
No. 6 ISBN:91-554-5514-X, ISBN13: 978-91-554-5514-9.
Dewey:891/.553009. LCCN:2003-504675.

Audience: **u,f.**

Awde, Nicholas **PK6906**
Kurdish-English/English-Kurdish Dictionary and Phrases. Trade
Paper. Hippocrene Books, Inc. New York, NY. 2004. 226p.
ISBN:0-7818-1071-X, ISBN13: 978-0-7818-1071-5.
Dewey:491.597321.

Audience: **l,u,f.**

Blau, Joyce **PK6905**
Kurdish Kurmanji Modern Texts: Introduction, Selection and
Glossary. Wiesbaden: Harrassowitz. 1968.

Audience: **u,f.**

Chyet, Michael L. **PK6906.C44 2003**
Kurdish-English Dictionary. Cloth over Boards. Yale University
Press. Cumberland, RI. 2003. 896p. Yale Language Ser.
ISBN:0-300-09152-4, ISBN13: 978-0-300-09152-6.
Dewey:491/.597321. LCCN:2002-193384.

Audience: **l,u,f.**

Hassanpour, Amir **PK6901 .H37 1992**
Nationalism and Language in Kurdistan, 1918-1985: The
Language Factor in National Development. Trade Cloth. Edwin
Mellen Press, The. Lewiston, NY. 1992. 450p.
ISBN:0-7734-9816-8, ISBN13: 978-0-7734-9816-7.
Dewey:491/.59. LCCN:92-005916.

Audience: **u,f.**

Lennox, Gina & **DS59.K86**
  Mitterand, Danielle
Fire, Snow & Honey: Voices from Kurdistan: Essays, Life
Stories, Poems, Short Fiction and Fables. Halstead. 2001.
ISBN:1-875684-70-0, ISBN13: 978-1-875684-70-0.

Audience: **g,l,u,f.**

MacKenzie, D. N. **PK6909**
Kurdish Dialect Studies 1-2. Oxford University Press. 1961.

Audience: **u,f.**

Meho, Lokman I. & **Z3014**
  Maglaughlin, Kelly L. (Compiled by)
Kurdish Culture and Society: An Annotated Bibliography. Cloth
Text. Greenwood Publishing Group, Inc. Portsmouth, NH. 2001.
384p. Bibliographies and Indexes in Ethnic Studies, No. 9
ISBN:0-313-31543-4, ISBN13: 978-0-313-31543-5.
Dewey:016.305891/597. LCCN:00-063654.

Audience: **l,u,f.** *Choice, 2001.*

Mofty, Soraya (Author, **PK6905**
  Read by)
Easy Way to Kurdish. Cyrus Salam (Read by). Audio Cassette,
Trade Paper. Jeffrey Norton Publishers, Inc. Madison, CT. 1997.
60p. ISBN:0-88432-940-2, ISBN13: 978-0-88432-940-4.
Dewey:491.597.

Audience: **g,l,u,f.**

Mokri, M. **PK6903**
Kurdish-Arabic Dictionary: Al-Hadiyati 'l-Hamidiyah. Trade
Cloth. International Book Centre, Inc. Troy, MI. 1975.
ISBN:0-86685-126-7, ISBN13: 978-0-86685-126-8.
Dewey:491.59.

Audience: **u,f.**

Pikkert, P. (Peter) **PK6903**
A Basic Course in Modern Kurmanji. Genk, Belgium: Alev
Books. 1991.

Audience: **u,f.**

Rizgar, Baran **PK6906**
Kurdish-English, English-Kurdish (Kurmanci) Dictionary. M.F.
Onen. 1993.

Audience: **u,f.**

Rizgar, Baran PK6906
Kurdish-English English-Kurdish Dictionary. Nevin Yavuz (Illustrator). Trade Paper. DIANE Publishing Company. Collingdale, PA. 2005. 400p. ISBN:0-7567-8793-9, ISBN13: 978-0-7567-8793-6. Dewey:491.59.

Audience: **u,f.**

Shakely, Ferhad PK6908.9.K53
Kurdish Nationalism in Mam u Zin of Ahmad-i Khani. Bruxelles: Kurdish Institute of Brussels. 1992.

Audience: **u,f.**

Middle Eastern Languages and Literatures > Iranian languages and literatures > Persian (Farsi) > Language

Amuzegar, Hooshang & PK6235.5.A48 2001
  Amuzegar, Farideh
How to Speak, Read and Write Persian (farsi). Trade Paper, Audio Cassette. IBEX Publishers, Inc. Bethesda, MD. 2003. 285p. ISBN:0-936347-05-8, ISBN13: 978-0-936347-05-9. Dewey:491/.5582421. LCCN:2001-024457.

Audience: **l,u,f.**

Aryanpur-Kashani, PK6379
  Abbas & Aryanpur-Kashani, Manoochehr
The Combined New Persian-English and English-Persian Dictionary. Trade Cloth. Mazda Publishers, Inc. Costa Mesa, CA. 1986. 688p. ISBN:0-939214-29-6, ISBN13: 978-0-939214-29-7. Dewey:491/.55321. LCCN:85-061402.

Audience: **u,f.** *Choice, 1987.*

Elwell-Sutton, L. P. PK6235
Elementary Persian Grammar. Trade Paper. Cambridge University Press. New York, NY. 1963. 234p. ISBN:0-521-09206-X, ISBN13: 978-0-521-09206-7. Dewey:491.5582421.

Audience: **l,u,f.**

Haim, Soleyman PK6381.E5
English-Persian / Persian-English Dictionary Smaller. Cloth Text. IBEX Publishers, Inc. Bethesda, MD. 2004. 1027p. ISBN:964-5545-39-0, ISBN13: 978-964-5545-39-8. Dewey:491.55321.

Audience: **l,u,f.**

Lambton, Ann K. S. PK6379
Persian Vocabulary. Trade Paper. Cambridge University Press. New York, NY. 1953. 406p. ISBN:0-521-09154-3, ISBN13: 978-0-521-09154-1. Dewey:491.55.

Audience: **l,u,f.**

Lambton, Ann PK6235 .L35
  Katharine Swynford. [from old catalog]
Persian Grammar. Paper Text. Textbook Publishers. Temecula, CA. 2003. 275p. ISBN:0-7581-1286-6, ISBN13: 978-0-7581-1286-6. Dewey:491.555.

Audience: **l,u,f.**

Marashi, Mehdi PK6228
Persian Handwriting: Manual for Persian (Farsi) Handwriting. Trade Paper, CD-ROM. IBEX Publishers, Inc. Bethesda, MD. 2003. 240p. ISBN:1-58814-000-8, ISBN13: 978-1-58814-000-5. Dewey:491.5511. LCCN:98-084882.

Audience: **l,u,f.**

Rafiee, Abdi PK6239.5.E5R34 2001
Colloquial Persian: The Complete Course for Beginners. Ed. 2. Trade Paper. Routledge. New York, NY. 2001. 304p. Colloquial Ser. ISBN:0-415-15749-8, ISBN13: 978-0-415-15749-0. Dewey:491.5582421. LCCN:00-062752.

Audience: **l,u,f.**

Steingass, F. PK6379 .S7
Comprehensive Persian-English Dictionary: Including the Arabic Words and Phrases to Be Met with in Persian Literature. Trade Cloth. Munshiram Manoharial Publishers Private, Ltd. New Delhi, 1996. 1548p. ISBN:81-215-0711-1, ISBN13: 978-81-215-0711-0. Dewey:491.5532.

Audience: **l,u,f.**

Stilo, Donald, et al. PK6235
Modern Persian: Spoken and Written. Talattof, Kamran; Clinto, Jerome (Authors). Yale University Press. 2005. ISBN:0-300-10051-5, ISBN13: 978-0-300-10051-8.

Audience: **l,u,f.**

Windfuhr, Gernot L. PK6235
Modern Persian: Intermeditate Level. International Book Center. 1981.

Audience: **u,f.**

Windfuhr, Gernot L. & PK6235 .W5
  Tehranisa
Modern Persian: Elementary Level. Trade Paper. International Book Centre, Inc. Troy, MI. 1981. 377p. ISBN:0-86685-443-6, ISBN13: 978-0-86685-443-6. Dewey:491/.5582421.

Audience: **l,u,f.**

Middle Eastern Languages and Literatures > Iranian languages and literatures > Persian (Farsi) > Literature

Ahmadzadeh, Hashem PK6423.A36 2003
Nation and Novel: A Study of Persian and Kurdish Narrative Discourse. Trade Cloth. Uppsala Universitet/Acta Universitatis Uppsaliensis. Uppsala, 2003. 330p. Studia Iranica Upsaliensia, No. 6 ISBN:91-554-5514-X, ISBN13: 978-91-554-5514-9. Dewey:891/.553009. LCCN:2003-504675.

Audience: **u,f.**

Al Ahmad, Jalal PK6561.A38.M813
The School Principal: A Novel. Trade Cloth. Bibliotheca Islamica, Inc. Minneapolis, MN. 1974. 144p. ISBN:0-88297-008-9, ISBN13: 978-0-88297-008-0. Dewey:891/.55/33. LCCN:75-300709.

Audience: **g,l,u,f.**

Alavi, Bozorg PK6561.A4C513 1989
Her Eyes. Ehsan Yarshater (Editor), John O'Kane (Translator). Trade Cloth. University Press of America, Inc. Lanham, MD. 1989. 222p. Modern Persian Literature Ser., No. 9 ISBN:0-8191-7344-4, ISBN13: 978-0-8191-7344-7. Dewey:891/.5533. LCCN:89-005569.

Audience: **g,l,u,f.** *Choice, 1990.*

Alavi, Bozorg, et al. PK6449.E7 S86 1992
Stories from Iran, 1921-1991: A Chicago Anthology. M. A. Jamalzadeh, Sadeq Chubak, Simin Danishvar & Moni Ravanipur (Authors), Heshmat Moayyad (Editor), John Perry, Judith

Audience: g=general, l=lower division undergraduate, u=upper division undergraduate, f=faculty.

669

Wilkes, Paul Sprachman & Paul Losensky (Translators). Trade Cloth. Mage Publishers, Inc. Washington, DC. 1992. 576p. ISBN:0-934211-28-0, ISBN13: 978-0-934211-28-4. Dewey:891/.553010803. LCCN:91-029041.
Audience: **l,u,f.** *Choice, 1992.*

Arberry, Arthur John   **PK6406.A71994**
Classical Persian Literature. Trade Paper. Taylor & Francis Group. Abingdon, 1995. 464p. ISBN:0-7007-0276-8, ISBN13: 978-0-7007-0276-3. Dewey:891/.5509001. LCCN:94-134343.
Audience: **u,f.**

Arberry, Arthur John   **PK6449.E5 A7**
  (Editor)
Immortal Rose: An Anthology of Persian Lyrics. Library Binding. Gordon Press Publishers. New York, NY. 1976. ISBN:0-8490-2039-5, ISBN13: 978-0-8490-2039-1. Dewey:891.551082.
Audience: **l,u,f.**

Attar, Farid Al-Din   **PK6451.F4M2813 1984**
The Conference of Birds. Afkham Darbandi & Dick Davis (Translator, Introduction by). Trade Paper. Penguin Group (USA) Inc. New York, NY. 1984. 240p. Classics Ser. ISBN:0-14-044434-3, ISBN13: 978-0-14-044434-6. Dewey:891/.5511. LCCN:84-211777.
Audience: **l,u,f.**

Behrangi, Samad   **PZ7.B489LI 1987**
The Little Black Fish and Other Modern Persian Stories. Ed. 2. Mary Hegland & Eric Hooglund (Translators). Trade Paper. Lynne Rienner Publishers, Inc. Boulder, CO. 1987. 106p. ISBN:0-89410-621-X, ISBN13: 978-0-89410-621-7. Dewey:[Fic]. LCCN:87-026680.
Audience: **g,l,u,f.**

Beyaz'i, Bahram, et al.   **PK6449.E6B39 1987**
Modern Persian Drama: An Anthology. Abbas Na'lbandian & Gowhar E. Morad (Authors), Ehsan Yarshater (Editor), Gisele Kapuscinski (Translator). Trade Paper. University Press of America, Inc. Lanham, MD. 1987. 248p. Modern Persian Literature Ser., No. 8 ISBN:0-8191-6579-4, ISBN13: 978-0-8191-6579-4. Dewey:891/.5523/08. LCCN:87-018899.
Audience: **u,f.**

Browne, E. G.   **PK6097**
A Literary History of Persia, Set. Paper over Boards. Taylor & Francis Group. Abingdon, 1999. 2268p. ISBN:0-7007-0406-X, ISBN13: 978-0-7007-0406-4. Dewey:955.
Audience: **u,f.**

Chubak, Sadeq   **PK6561.C45**
Tangsir: A Persian Novel. Perfect. Ketab Corporation. Los Angeles, CA. 1990. 360p. Collection of Works by Sadeq Chubak ISBN:1-883819-64-4, ISBN13: 978-1-883819-64-4. Dewey:891.5533.
Audience: **g,l,u,f.**

Chubak, Sadeq   **PK6561.C45 A2 1981**
Sadeq Chubak: An Anthology. F. R. Bagley (Editor). Cloth Text. Bibliotheca Persica Press. New York, NY. 1982. vii, 286p. Modern Persian Literature Ser., Vol. 3 ISBN:0-88206-048-1, ISBN13: 978-0-88206-048-4. Dewey:891/.5533. LCCN:81-017970.
Audience: **g,l,u,f.**

Chubak, Sadeq   **PK6561.C45S313 1989**
The Patient Stone. Mohammad R. Ghanoonparvar (Translator, Introduction by). Trade Cloth. Mazda Publishers, Inc. Costa

Mesa, CA. 1989. 290p. Persian Literature in Translation, No. 1 ISBN:0-939214-62-8, ISBN13: 978-0-939214-62-4. Dewey:891/.5533. LCCN:89-013102.
Audience: **g,l,u,f.**

Curtis, Vesta Sarkhosh   **BL2270.C87 1993**
Persian Myths. Trade Paper. University of Texas Press. Austin, TX. 1993. 80p. Legendary Past Ser. ISBN:0-292-71158-1, ISBN13: 978-0-292-71158-7. Dewey:398.20935. LCCN:93-060589.
Audience: **l,u,f.**

Daneshvar, Simin   **PK6561.H43**
Savushun: A Novel about Modern Iran. M. R. Ghanoonparvar (Translator). Trade Paper. Mage Publishers, Inc. Washington, DC. 1991. 320p. ISBN:0-934211-31-0, ISBN13: 978-0-934211-31-4. Dewey:891/.5533. LCCN:90-005608.
Audience: **g,l,u,f.**

Daneshvar, Simin   **DK6561.D263 S88 1994**
Sutra and Other Stories. Hassan Javadi & Amin Neshati (Translators). Trade Cloth. Mage Publishers, Inc. Washington, DC. 1994. 192p. ISBN:0-934211-42-6, ISBN13: 978-0-934211-42-0. Dewey:891/.5533. LCCN:94-017049.
Audience: **g,l,u,f.**

Daneshvar, Simin   **PK6561.D263 A25 1989**
Daneshvar's Playhouse: A Collection of Stories. Maryam Mafi (Translator, Afterword by). Trade Cloth. Mage Publishers, Inc. Washington, DC. 1989. 184p. ISBN:0-934211-19-1, ISBN13: 978-0-934211-19-2. Dewey:891/.5533. LCCN:89-002527.
Audience: **g,l,u,f.** *Choice, 1990.*

Daneshvar, Simin   **PK6561.D263S213 1992**
A Persian Requiem. Roxane Zand (Translator). Trade Cloth. George Braziller Inc. New York, NY. 1992. 288p. ISBN:0-8076-1273-1, ISBN13: 978-0-8076-1273-6. Dewey:891/.5533. LCCN:91-040933.
Audience: **g,l,u,f.** *Choice, 1992.*

Davis, Dick   **PK6416.D385 2002**
Panthea's Children: Hellenistic Novels and Medieval Persian Romances. Trade Cloth. Bibliotheca Persica Press. New York, NY. 2002. 113p. Biennial Ehsan Yarshater Lecture Ser., Vol. 3 ISBN:0-933273-65-7, ISBN13: 978-0-933273-65-8. Dewey:891/.55309001. LCCN:2002-014961.
Audience: **l,u,f.**

Farrokhzad, Forough   **PK6561.F264.A24 1982**
Bride of Acacias: Selected Poems of Forugh Farrokhzad. Jascha Kessler & Amin Banani (Translators). Cloth Text. Bibliotheca Persica Press. New York, NY. 1981. 158p. Modern Persian Literature Ser., Vol. 5 ISBN:0-88206-050-3, ISBN13: 978-0-88206-050-7. Dewey:891/.5513. LCCN:82-001156.
Audience: **g,l,u,f.**

Farrokhzad, Forugh   **PK6561.F264**
Another Birth. Susan Sallee (Translator), Hasan Javadi (Introduction by). Trade Paper. Lynne Rienner Publishers, Inc. Boulder, CO. 1981. 144p. ISBN:0-89410-361-X, ISBN13: 978-0-89410-361-2. Dewey:891/.5513.
Audience: **g,l,u,f.**

Ferdowsi   **PK6456.A12R82 1996**
The Tragedy of Sohrab and Rostam: From the Persian National Epic, the Shahname of Abu'l-Qasem Ferdowsi. Jerome W. Clinton (Translator). Trade Paper. University of Washington Press. Seattle, WA. 1996. 224p. Publications on the Near East,

Vol. 3 ISBN:0-295-97567-9, ISBN13: 978-0-295-97567-2. Dewey:891/.5511. LCCN:96-019208.

Audience: **g,l,u,f.**

Firdawsi　　　　　**PK6456.A13D3813 2006**
Shahnameh: The Persian Book of Kings. Dick Davis (Translator). Viking. 2006. ISBN:0-670-03485-1, ISBN13: 978-0-670-03485-7.

Audience: **g,l,u,f.**

Firdawsi　　　　　**PK6456.A1**
The Epic of the Kings: Shah-nama, the National Epic of Persia. Levy, Reuben (Translator). University of Chicago Press. 1967.

Audience: **l,u,f.**

Fitzgerald, Edward　　　　　**PK6513.A1 1997**
Rubaiyat of Omar Khayyam: A Critical Edition. Christopher Decker (Editor). Cloth Text. University Press of Virginia. Charlottesville, VA. 1997. 352p. Victorian Literature and Culture Ser. ISBN:0-8139-1689-5, ISBN13: 978-0-8139-1689-7. Dewey:891/.5511. LCCN:96-024529.

Audience: **g,l,u,f.** *Choice, 1997.*

Ganjavi, Nizami　　　　　**PK6501.Z928 2000**
Poetry of Nizami Ganjavi: Knowledge, Love and Rhetoric. Kamran Talattof & Jerome W. Clinton (Editors). Cloth over Boards. Palgrave Macmillan. New York, NY. 2001. 224p. ISBN:0-312-22810-4, ISBN13: 978-0-312-22810-1. Dewey:891/.5511. LCCN:99-056710.

Audience: **l,u,f.**

Ghanoonparvar,　　　　　**PK6424.C58G48 1993**
Mohammad R.
In a Persian Mirror: Images of the West and Westerners in Iranian Fiction. Trade Cloth. University of Texas Press. Austin, TX. 1993. 191p. ISBN:0-292-72760-7, ISBN13: 978-0-292-72760-1. Dewey:891/.5509321821. LCCN:92-039689.

Audience: **u,f.**

Hafiz, Shamsedin　　　　　**PK6465.Z32C5 1997**
The Divan-I-Hafiz. H. Wilberforce Clarke (Translator), Michael C. Hillmann (Introduction by). Trade Cloth. IBEX Publishers, Inc. Bethesda, MD. 1997. 1011p. Classics of Persian Literature Ser., Vol. 3 ISBN:0-936347-80-5, ISBN13: 978-0-936347-80-6. Dewey:891/.5511. LCCN:96-036660.

Audience: **l,u,f.**

Hafiz　　　　　**PK6465.Z31A7 1993**
Fifty Poems of Hafiz. Arthur John Arberry (Translator). Trade Paper. Taylor & Francis Group. Abingdon, 1995. 220p. ISBN:0-7007-0275-X, ISBN13: 978-0-7007-0275-6. Dewey:891/.5511. LCCN:98-171420.

Audience: **l,u,f.**

Hedayat, Sadeq　　　　　**HD6508 .C657**
Sadeq Hedayat: An Anthology. Franklin J. Havelick (Editor), Theodore Kheel (Introduction by). Cloth Text. Bibliotheca Persica Press. New York, NY. 1979. xiv, 223p. Modern Persian Literature Ser., Vol. 2 ISBN:0-89158-386-6, ISBN13: 978-0-89158-386-8. Dewey:331.89/0973. LCCN:79-004234.

Audience: **l,u,f.**

Hidayat, Sadiq　　　　　**PK6561.H43**
The Blind Owl. Trade Paper. Canongate Books. Edinburgh, 2001. 128p. ISBN:1-84195-194-3, ISBN13: 978-1-84195-194-2. Dewey:891.5533.

Audience: **g,l,u,f.**

Hillman, Michael　　　　　**PK6237.P47 1995**
Persian Fiction Reader. Trade Cloth. Dunwoody Press. Hyattsville, MD. 1996. ISBN:1-881265-36-6, ISBN13: 978-1-881265-36-8. Dewey:491.5586421. LCCN:95-083678.

Audience: **g,l,u,f.**

Hillmann, Michael C.　　　　　**PK6561.F264Z69 1987**
A Lonely Woman: Forugh Farrokhzad and Her Poetry. Trade Cloth. Lynne Rienner Publishers, Inc. Boulder, CO. 1987. 181p. ISBN:0-89410-543-4, ISBN13: 978-0-89410-543-2. Dewey:891/.5513 B. LCCN:86-051008.

Audience: **u,f.** *Choice, 1988.*

I'tisami, Parvin　　　　　**PK6561.I82**
A Nightingale's Lament: Selections from the Poems and Fables of Parvin Etesami (1907-41). Heshmat Moayyad & Margaret A. Madelung (Translators). Trade Paper. Mazda Publishers, Inc. Costa Mesa, CA. 1985. 289p. Iran-e Literary Collection ISBN:0-939214-20-2, ISBN13: 978-0-939214-20-4. Dewey:891.5513. LCCN:84-060071.

Audience: **g,l,u,f.**

Jamalzada, Mohammad A.　　　　　**PK6561.J3**
Once upon a Time. Heshmat Moayyad & Paul Sprachman (Translators). Cloth Text. Bibliotheca Persica Press. New York, NY. 1985. x, 112p. Modern Persian Literature Ser., Vol. 6 ISBN:0-933273-00-2, ISBN13: 978-0-933273-00-9. Dewey:891/.5533.

Audience: **g,l,u,f.**

Kamshad, Hassan　　　　　**PK6423.K3 1996**
Modern Persian Prose Literature. Trade Paper. IBEX Publishers, Inc. Bethesda, MD. 1996. 226p. ISBN:0-936347-72-4, ISBN13: 978-0-936347-72-1. Dewey:891/.553009. LCCN:96-001869.

Audience: **u,f.**

Karimi-Hakkak, Ahmad　　　　　**PK6449.E5 A5**
(Editor, Translator)
An Anthology of Modern Persian Poetry. Cloth Text. Bibliotheca Persica Press. New York, NY. 1978. xiv, 203p. Modern Persian Literature Ser., Vol. 1 ISBN:0-89158-181-2, ISBN13: 978-0-89158-181-9. Dewey:891/.55/1308. LCCN:78-058473.

Audience: **l,u,f.**

Khayyam, Omar　　　　　**MLCS 95/08649 PK6516**
Omar Khayyam's the Rubaiyat: A Literal Translation. Parvine Mahmoud (Translator). Trade Cloth. Carlton Press, Corporation. Bethel, CT. 1996. 64p. ISBN:0-8062-5274-X, ISBN13: 978-0-8062-5274-2. Dewey:891.5511. LCCN:96-230397.

Audience: **l,u,f.**

Khorrami, Mohammad　　　　　**PK6449.E7F43 2000**
Mehdi & Vatanabadi, Shouleh (Editors)
A Feast in the Mirror: Stories by Contemporary Iranian Women. Trade Cloth. Lynne Rienner Publishers, Inc. Boulder, CO. 2000. vii, 235p. ISBN:0-89410-864-6, ISBN13: 978-0-89410-864-8. Dewey:891/.55301089287. LCCN:00-032855.

Audience: **g,l,u,f.** *Choice, 2001.*

Khusraw, Nasir-I　　　　　**DS46.N313**
Nasir-i Khusraw's Book of Travels. Wheeler M. Thackston (Editor). Paper Text. Mazda Publishers, Inc. Costa Mesa, CA. 2001. 312p. Bibliotheca Iranica Ser., Vol. 6:Intellectual Traditions ISBN:1-56859-137-3, ISBN13: 978-1-56859-137-7. Dewey:915.604/54. LCCN:2001-051214.

Audience: **l,u,f.**

Kianush, Mahmud   PK6449.E5M63 1996
  (Author, Translator)
Modern Persian Poetry. Trade Paper. IBEX Publishers, Inc.
Bethesda, MD. 1996. 216p. ISBN:1-873468-35-0, ISBN13:
978-1-873468-35-7. Dewey:891/.551308. LCCN:96-217312.
                                            Audience: l,u,f.

Levy, Reuben   PK6097
An Introduction to Persian Literature. Cloth Text. Columbia
University Press. New York, NY. 1969. 194p.
ISBN:0-231-03177-7, ISBN13: 978-0-231-03177-6.
Dewey:891.5509. LCCN:68-008876.
                                            Audience: l,u,f.

Lorimer, D. L. R.   PZ8.1.P46 2005
  (Editor)
Persian Tales: Fifty-Eight Traditional and Folk Tales from Iran.
Emily Overend Lorimer (Translator). Trade Paper. IBEX
Publishers, Inc. Bethesda, MD. 2006. 360p. Classics of Persian
Literature Ser., vol. 6 ISBN:0-936347-91-0, ISBN13:
978-0-936347-91-2. Dewey:398.20955. LCCN:98-042590.
                                            Audience: l,u,f.

Milani, Farzaneh   PK6413.5.W65M5 1992
Veils and Words: The Emerging Voices of Iranian Women
Writers. Cloth Text. Syracuse University Press. Syracuse, NY.
1992. 320p. Contemporary Issues in the Middle East Ser.
ISBN:0-8156-2557-X, ISBN13: 978-0-8156-2557-5.
Dewey:891/.55099287. LCCN:91-028640.
                                  Audience: l,u,f. Choice, 1993.

Modarres-Sadeqi, Jafar   PK6561.M73.G3713
The Marsh (Gavkhuni). Afkham Darbandi (Translator), Dick
Davis (Preface by). Trade Paper. Mazda Publishers, Inc. Costa
Mesa, CA. 1996. 110p. Bibliotheca Iranica Ser., No. 3:Persian
Fiction in Translation ISBN:1-56859-044-X, ISBN13:
978-1-56859-044-8. Dewey:891/.5533. LCCN:96-044379.
                                            Audience: g,l,u,f.

Mozaffari, Nahid   PK6449.E1S77 2005
Strange Times, My Dear: The PEN Anthology of Contemporary
Iranian Literature. Ahmad Karimi Hakkak (Editor). Trade Cloth.
Arcade Publishing, Inc. New York, NY. 2005. 494p.
ISBN:1-55970-765-8, ISBN13: 978-1-55970-765-7.
Dewey:891/.5508003. LCCN:2004-023527.
                                            Audience: g,l,u,f.

Nizami, N.   PK6501.L33 G4
Story of Layla and Majnun. R. Gelpke (Translator). Trade Paper.
Kazi Publications, Inc. Chicago, IL. 1996. 192p.
ISBN:0-614-21656-7, ISBN13: 978-0-614-21656-1.
Dewey:891/.55/31.
                                            Audience: l,u,f.

Parsipur, Shahrnush   PK6561.H43
Women Without Men: A Novel of Modern Iran. Kamran Talattof
& Jocelyn Sharlet (Translators), Persis Karim (Afterword by).
Trade Paper. Feminist Press at The City University of New
York. New York, NY. 2004. 192p. ISBN:1-55861-452-4,
ISBN13: 978-1-55861-452-9. Dewey:891.5533.
                                            Audience: g,l,u,f.

Pezeshkzad, Iraj   PK6561.P54 D313 1996
My Uncle Napoleon. Dick Davis (Translator). Trade Cloth.
Mage Publishers, Inc. Washington, DC. 1996. 512p.
ISBN:0-934211-48-5, ISBN13: 978-0-934211-48-2.
Dewey:891/.5533. LCCN:96-006255.
                                  Audience: g,l,u,f. Choice, 1997.

Rahimieh, Nasrin   DS266.R277 2001
Missing Persians: Discovering Voices in Iranian Cultural
History. Trade Cloth. Syracuse University Press. Syracuse, NY.
2001. 208p. Gender, Culture, and Politics in the Middle East
Ser. ISBN:0-8156-2753-X, ISBN13: 978-0-8156-2753-1.
Dewey:955. LCCN:2001-020955.
                                  Audience: u,f. Choice, 2002.

Robinson, B. W.   PK6457
The Persian Book of Kings: An Epitome of the Shahnama of
Firdawsi. Paper over Boards. Taylor & Francis Group.
Abingdon, 184p. ISBN:0-7007-1618-1, ISBN13:
978-0-7007-1618-0. Dewey:891.5/1104.
                                            Audience: u,f.

Rumi, Jalaluddin   PJ709
Mathnawi of Jalalu'ddin Rumi: English Translation. Ed. 2.
Reynold A. Nicholson (Editor). Trade Cloth. Gibb Memorial
Trust, The. Cambridge, 2001. ISBN:0-906094-27-5, ISBN13:
978-0-906094-27-3. Dewey:891.5.
                                            Audience: u,f.

Rumi, Jalalu'L-Dein &   PK6480.E5N5 2001
  Nicholson, Reynold A.
Selected Poems of Rumi. Trade Paper. Dover Publications, Inc.
Mineola, NY. 2001. 144p. Thrift Editions Ser.
ISBN:0-486-41583-X, ISBN13: 978-0-486-41583-3.
Dewey:891/.5511. LCCN:00-052302.
                                            Audience: g,l,u,f.

Rumi   PK6480.E5
Mystical Poems of Rumi: Second Selection, Poems 201-400,
Vol. 34. Ehsan Yarshater (Editor), Arthur John Arberry
(Translator). Cloth Text. Bibliotheca Persica Press. New York,
NY. 1979. xiv, 187p. Persian Heritage Ser., Vol. 23
ISBN:0-89158-477-3, ISBN13: 978-0-89158-477-3.
Dewey:891/.5511. LCCN:79-005101.
                                            Audience: g,l,u,f.

Rypka, J.   PK6097 .R913
History of Iranian Literature. Karl Jahn (Editor), P. Van
Popta-Hope (Translator). Trade Cloth. Springer. New York, NY.
1968. 955p. ISBN:90-277-0143-1, ISBN13: 978-90-277-0143-5.
Dewey:891.5.
                                            Audience: u,f.

Sa'di   PK6495.N24
The Gulistan; or Rose-Garden or Shekh Muslihu'd-Din Sadi of
Shiraz: Trubner's Oriental Series. Ed. 2. Edward B. Eastwick
(Editor). Paper over Boards. Routledge. New York, NY. 2001.
352p. ISBN:0-415-24535-4, ISBN13: 978-0-415-24535-7.
Dewey:891.5531.
                                            Audience: l,u,f.

Sa'idi, Ghulam Husayn   PK6561.S27 A23
Dandil: Stories from Iranian Life. Robert Campbell (Translator).
Trade Cloth. Random House, Inc. New York, NY. 1981. 223p.
ISBN:0-394-50511-5, ISBN13: 978-0-394-50511-4.
Dewey:891/.5533. LCCN:80-006042.
                                            Audience: g,l,u,f.

Sa'idi, Ghulam Husayn   PK6561.S27 T313 1984
Fear and Trembling. Minoo Southgate (Translator). Trade Cloth.
Lynne Rienner Publishers, Inc. Boulder, CO. 1993. xxxi, 121p.
ISBN:0-89410-287-7, ISBN13: 978-0-89410-287-5.
Dewey:891/.5533. LCCN:81-051641.
                                            Audience: g,l,u,f.

Schimmel, Annemarie   PK6416.S3513 1992
A Two-Colored Brocade: The Imagery of Persian Poetry. Trade
Cloth. University of North Carolina Press. Chapel Hill, NC.
1992. 558p. ISBN:0-8078-2050-4, ISBN13: 978-0-8078-2050-6.
Dewey:891/.551009. LCCN:92-002642.
                              Audience: **l,u,f.** *Choice, 1993.*

Sharma, Sunil   PK6451.A59
Amir Khusraw: The Poets of Sultans and Sufis. Saddle Stitched,
Cloth over Boards. Oneworld Publications. Oxford, 2005. 140p.
ISBN:1-85168-362-3, ISBN13: 978-1-85168-362-8.
Dewey:891.5511.
                              Audience: **l,u,f.** *Choice, 2006.*

Southgate, Minoo   PK6449.E7M6 1980
  (Editor, Translator)
Modern Persian Short Stories. Trade Cloth. Lynne Rienner
Publishers, Inc. Boulder, CO. 1980. 228p. ISBN:0-89410-032-7,
ISBN13: 978-0-89410-032-1. Dewey:891/.55301/08.
LCCN:79-089930.
                              Audience: **g,l,u,f.**

Talattof, Kamran   PK6415.5.T35 1999
Politics of Writing in Iran: A History of Modern Persian
Literature. Trade Cloth. Syracuse University Press. Syracuse,
NY. 1999. xi, 250p. ISBN:0-8156-2818-8, ISBN13:
978-0-8156-2818-7. Dewey:891/.5509358. LCCN:99-037867.
                              Audience: **u,f.** *Choice, 2000.*

Taraghi, Goli   PK6561.T37
A Mansion in the Sky: And Other Short Stories. Faridoun
Farrokh (Translator). Trade Paper. University of Texas Press.

Austin, TX. 2003. 160p. CMES Modern Middle East Literature
in Translation Ser. ISBN:0-292-70226-4, ISBN13:
978-0-292-70226-4. Dewey:891.5/533.
                              Audience: **g,l,u,f.**

Thackston, Wheeler M.   PK6416.T45 1994
  Jr.
A Millennium of Classical Persian Poetry: A Guide to the
Reading and Understanding of Persian Poetry from the Tenth to
the Twentieth Century. Paper Text. IBEX Publishers, Inc.
Bethesda, MD. 1994. 216p. ISBN:0-936347-50-3, ISBN13:
978-0-936347-50-9. Dewey:891/.551009. LCCN:94-006485.
                              Audience: **u,f.**

Vatanabadi, Shouleh &   PK6449.E7A56 2003
  Khorrami, Mohammad Mehdi (Editors)
Another Sea, Another Shore: Persian Stories of Migration. Trade
Cloth. Interlink Publishing Group, Inc. Northampton, MA. 2004.
256p. Emerging Voices Ser. ISBN:1-56656-511-1, ISBN13:
978-1-56656-511-0. Dewey:891/.5530108355.
LCCN:2003-013525.
                              Audience: **g,l,u,f.**

Yarshater, Ehsan   PK6097.P47 1988
Persian Literature. Cloth Text. State University of New York
Press. Albany, NY. 1988. xi, 562p. ISBN:0-88706-263-6,
ISBN13: 978-0-88706-263-6. Dewey:891/.55/09.
LCCN:87-016613.
                              Audience: **l,u,f.** *Choice, 1989.*

NATIVE AMERICAN STUDIES

Native American studies builds on the usual classic works from anthropology and history to expand the study of the indigenous peoples of North America to include contemporary issues and topics of relevance and importance to understanding the current status of these peoples. Special topics, reflecting common curriculum offerings in Native American/American Indian studies programs, include health and medicine (traditional and western), language revitalization, environmental issues, legal and political issues, women and gender, and literature and film.

Some of these categories are new areas for Indian studies, and the literature on them is growing daily. Future RCL updates will need to pay close attention to this literature, and add new titles as they become core to the field. The RCL sections for more traditional disciplines should be perused for titles pertaining to Native American/American Indian studies.

Since so much of the literature on Indians has been filtered through various non-Indian academic intermediaries and disciplines, several broad, comprehensive Web pages on the contemporary Indian world are included to provide direct student access to Native voices and concerns, offering an alternative perspective to the core literature.

— Lisa Mitten

E98.P76

☐ American Indian and Alaska Native (AIAN) Data and Links (U.S. Census Bureau).
http://factfinder.census.gov/home/aian/index.html

Audience: **g,l,u,f.**

E77.6

☐ Index of Native American Resources on the Internet (WWW Virtual Library American Indians).
http://www.hanksville.org/NAresources/

Audience: **g,l,u,f.**

E98.S7

☐ Indianz.com.
http://www.indianz.com/

Audience: **g,l,u,f.**

GN380

☐ NativeWeb.
http://www.nativeweb.org/

Audience: **g,l,u,f.**

E93

☐ U. S. Bureau of Indian Affairs.
http://www.doi.gov/bureau-indian-affairs.html

Audience: **g,l,u,f.**

Cabalero, Cesar   **Z1251**
The border finder: a border studies bibliography. El Paso: University of Texas at El Paso. 1987.

Audience: **l,u,f.**

Mitten, Lisa   **E98.S7**
☐ Native American Sites.
http://www.nativeculturelinks.com/indians.html

Audience: **g,l,u,f.**

Smithsonian Institution   **E77**
  Staff
Handbook of North American Indians: Southeast, Vol. 14. Perfect. United States Government Printing Office. Washington, DC. 2004. 1042p. ISBN:0-16-072300-0, ISBN13: 978-0-16-072300-1. Dewey:970/.004/97.

Audience: **g,l,u,f.**

Stoddard, Ellwyn R.   **Z1251.S8 B67 1983**
  (Editor), et al.
Borderlands Sourcebook: A Guide to the Literature on Northern Mexico and the American Southwest. Richard L. Nostrand & Jonathan P. West (Editors). Trade Cloth. University of Oklahoma Press. Norman, OK. 1983. 462p. ISBN:0-8061-1718-4, ISBN13: 978-0-8061-1718-8. Dewey:016.979. LCCN:82-040331.

Audience: **l,u,f.**

Sturtevant, William C.   **E77**
  & Damas, David
Handbook of North American Indians: Arctic. Trade Cloth, Box or Slipcased. United States Government Printing Office. Washington, DC. 1985. 845p. ISBN:0-16-004580-0, ISBN13: 978-0-16-004580-6. Dewey:970/.004/97. LCCN:77-017162.

Audience: **g,l,u,f.**

Sturtevant, William C.   **E77 .H25**
  & D'Azevedo, Warren L. (Editors)
Handbook of North American Indians: Great Basin, Vol. 11. Trade Cloth, Box or Slipcased. United States Government Printing Office. Washington, DC. 1986. 868p.

ISBN:0-16-004581-9, ISBN13: 978-0-16-004581-3. Dewey:970/.004/97. LCCN:77-017162.

Audience: **g,l,u,f.**

Sturtevant, William C.   **E77 .H25**
  & Heizer, Robert
Handbook of North American Indians, California, Vol. 8. Trade Cloth, Box or Slipcased. United States Government Printing Office. Washington, DC. 1978. 816p. ISBN:0-16-004574-6, ISBN13: 978-0-16-004574-5. Dewey:970/.004/97. LCCN:77-017162.

Audience: **g,l,u,f.**

Sturtevant, William C.   **E77**
  & Helm, June
Handbook of North American Indians: Subarctic, Vol. 6. Trade Cloth, Box or Slipcased. United States Government Printing Office. Washington, DC. 1981. 853p. ISBN:0-16-004578-9, ISBN13: 978-0-16-004578-3. Dewey:970/.004/97. LCCN:77-017162.

Audience: **g,l,u,f.**

Sturtevant, William C.   **E77 .H25**
  & Ortiz, Alfonso
Handbook of North American Indians: Southwest. Trade Cloth, Box or Slipcased. United States Government Printing Office. Washington, DC. 1983. 884p. ISBN:0-16-004579-7, ISBN13: 978-0-16-004579-0. Dewey:970/.004/97. LCCN:77-017162.

Audience: **g,l,u,f.**

Sturtevant, William C.   **E77**
  & Suttles, Wayne
Handbook of North American Indians: Northwest Coast. Trade Cloth, Box or Slipcased. United States Government Printing Office. Washington, DC. 1990. 793p. ISBN:0-16-020390-2, ISBN13: 978-0-16-020390-9. Dewey:970/.004/97.

Audience: **g,l,u,f.**

Sturtevant, William C.   **E77**
  & Trigger, Bruce G.
Handbook of North American Indians: Northeast, Vol. 15. Trade Cloth, Box or Slipcased. United States Government Printing Office. Washington, DC. 1978. 924p. ISBN:0-16-004575-4, ISBN13: 978-0-16-004575-2. Dewey:970/.004/97. LCCN:77-017162.

Audience: **g,l,u,f.**

Sturtevant, William C.,   **E77 .H25**
  et al.
Handbook of North American Indians: Plateau. Deward E. Walker Jr. & Smithsonian Institution Staff (Authors). Trade Cloth. United States Government Printing Office. Washington, DC. 1998. 807p. ISBN:0-16-049514-8, ISBN13: 978-0-16-049514-4. Dewey:970/.004/97. LCCN:77-017162.

Audience: **g,l,u,f.**

Sturtevant, William C.,   **E78.G73**
  et al.
Handbook of North American Indians: Plains, Set. Deward E. Walker Jr. & Smithsonian Institution Staff (Authors), Raymond J. DeMallie (Editor). Box or Slipcased, Trade Cloth. United States Government Printing Office. Washington, DC. 2001. 1392p. ISBN:0-16-050400-7, ISBN13: 978-0-16-050400-6. Dewey:978.00497. LCCN:77-017162.

Audience: **g,l,u,f.** *Choice, 2002.*

Surtevant, William C.   **E77**
(Editor)
Handbook of North American Indians. Washington: Smithsonian
Institution Press. 1978.
Audience: **g,l,u,f.**

Swagerty, W. R.   **Z1209.2.N67S361984**
(Editor)
Scholars and the Indian Experience: Critical Reviews of Recent
Writings in the Social Sciences. Trade Cloth. Indiana University
Press. Bloomington, IN. 1984. 280p. ISBN:0-253-35095-6,
ISBN13: 978-0-253-35095-4. Dewey:016.970004/97.
LCCN:83-049510.
Audience: **u,f.**

Tiller, Veronica E.   **E93.T55 2005**
(Editor)
Tiller's Guide to Indian Country: Economic Profiles of
American Indian Reservations. Ed. 2. Trade Cloth. Bow Arrow
Publishing Company. Albuquerque, NM. 2000. 1138p.
ISBN:1-885931-04-2, ISBN13: 978-1-885931-04-7.
Dewey:970.004/97. LCCN:2005-012917.
Audience: **g,l,u,f.** *Choice, 2006.*

West, W. Richard Jr.   **E56.A56 1994**
(Foreword by)
All Roads Are Good: Native Voices on Life and Culture. Clara
S. Kidwell (Preface by). Trade Cloth. Smithsonian Institution
Press. Washington, DC. 1994. 224p. ISBN:1-56098-451-1,
ISBN13: 978-1-56098-451-1. Dewey:970.004/97/0074753.
LCCN:94-008236.
Audience: **l,u,f.** *Choice, 1995.*

Art

Bates, Craig D. & Lee,   **E78.C15B28 1990**
Martha J.
Tradition and Innovation: A Basket History of the Indians of the
Yosemite- Mono Lake Area. Trade Cloth. Yosemite Association.
El Portal, CA. 1994. 225p. ISBN:0-939666-54-5, ISBN13:
978-0-939666-54-6. Dewey:746.41/2/08997079447.
LCCN:90-012420.
Audience: **g,l,u.** *Choice, 1992.*

Berlo, Janet Catherine   **E98.A7B47 1998**
& Phillips, Ruth
Native North American Art. Trade Paper. Oxford University
Press, Inc. New York, NY. 1998. 302p. Oxford History of Art
Ser. ISBN:0-19-284218-8, ISBN13: 978-0-19-284218-3.
Dewey:704.03/97. LCCN:99-177938.
Audience: **g,l,u,f.**

Blumer, Thomas John   **E99.C24B58 2004**
Catawba Indian Pottery: The Survival of a Folk Tradition. Trade
Cloth. University of Alabama Press. Tuscaloosa, AL. 2004.
240p. Contemporary American Indian Studies
ISBN:0-8173-1383-4, ISBN13: 978-0-8173-1383-8.
Dewey:738/.089/9752. LCCN:2003-012348.
Audience: **g,l,u,f.** *Choice, 2004.*

Bolz, Peter & Sanner,   **E98.A7B66 1999**
Hans-Ulrich
Native American Art: The Collections of the Ethnological
Museum Berlin. Trade Paper. University of Washington Press.
Seattle, WA. 2000. 240p. ISBN:0-295-97954-2, ISBN13:
978-0-295-97954-0. Dewey:745/.089/97. LCCN:99-069424.
Audience: **u,f.**

Brody, J. J.   **E99.P9B732 1991**
Anasazi and Pueblo Painting. Trade Cloth. University of New
Mexico Press. Albuquerque, NM. 1991. 272p.
ISBN:0-8263-1236-5, ISBN13: 978-0-8263-1236-5.
Dewey:750/.89/974. LCCN:90-023678.
Audience: **u,f.** *Choice, 1991.*

Brody, J. J.   **E99.M76B766 2004**
Mimbres Painted Pottery. Trade Paper. School of American
Research Press. Santa Fe, NM. 2005. 264p.
ISBN:1-930618-27-1, ISBN13: 978-1-930618-27-5.
Dewey:738.3/089/97079. LCCN:2004-009108.
Audience: **g,l,u,f.** *B* *Choice, 2005.*

Brody, J. J.   **E99.P9B744 1997**
Pueblo Indian Painting: Tradition and Modernism in New
Mexico, 1900-1930. Trade Cloth. School of American Research
Press. Santa Fe, NM. 1997. 238p. ISBN:0-933452-45-4,
ISBN13: 978-0-933452-45-9. Dewey:759.189/089/974.
LCCN:96-050100.
Audience: **u,f.** *Choice, 1997.*

Cole, Douglas   **E78.N78C63 1995**
Captured Heritage: The Scramble for the Northwest Coast
Artifacts. Trade Paper. University of Oklahoma Press. Norman,
OK. 1995. 392p. ISBN:0-8061-2777-5, ISBN13:
978-0-8061-2777-4. Dewey:704/.03972. LCCN:95-035735.
Audience: **u,f.** *Choice, 1985.*

Dobkins, Rebecca J., et al.   **E99.M18D393 1997**
Memory and Imagination: The Legacy of Maidu Indian Artist
Frank Day. Frank R. LaPena & Carey T. Caldwell (Authors).
Trade Paper. University of Washington Press. Seattle, WA. 1997.
120p. ISBN:0-295-97612-8, ISBN13: 978-0-295-97612-9.
Dewey:759.13 B. LCCN:96-049341.
Audience: **g,l,u,f.** *Choice, 1997.*

Feest, Christian F.   **E98.A7F44 1992**
Native Arts of North America. Ed. 2. Trade Paper. Thames &
Hudson. New York, NY. 1992. 216p. World of Art Ser.
ISBN:0-500-20262-1, ISBN13: 978-0-500-20262-3.
Dewey:704.0397. LCCN:92-082579.
Audience: **g,l,u,f.**

Hill, Sarah H.   **E99.C5H68 1997**
Weaving New Worlds: Southeastern Cherokee Women and Their
Basketry. Trade Cloth. University of North Carolina Press.
Chapel Hill, NC. 1997. 440p. ISBN:0-8078-2345-7, ISBN13:
978-0-8078-2345-3. Dewey:746.41/2/0899755.
LCCN:96-047882.
Audience: **g,l,u,f.** *Choice, 1997.*

Hill, Tom & Hill,   **E98.A7C74 1994**
Richard W. Sr. (Editors)
Creation's Journey: Native American Identity and Belief. Trade
Cloth. Smithsonian Institution Press. Washington, DC. 1994.
256p. ISBN:1-56098-453-8, ISBN13: 978-1-56098-453-5.
Dewey:745/.089/97073. LCCN:94-004757.
Audience: **l,u,f.** *Choice, 1995.*

Johnson, Tim (Editor)   **E77.5.S65 1998**
Spirit Capture: Photographs from the National Museum of the
American Indian. Trade Paper. Smithsonian Institution Press.
Washington, DC. 1998. 224p. ISBN:1-56098-765-0, ISBN13:
978-1-56098-765-9. Dewey:779.997000497. LCCN:98-004173.
Audience: **g,l,u,f.** *Choice, 1999.*

Lester, Patrick D.   **ND203.L47 1995**
  (Editor)
The Biographical Directory of Native American Painters. Trade
Cloth. University of Oklahoma Press. Norman, OK. 1995. 720p.
ISBN:0-8061-9936-9, ISBN13: 978-0-8061-9936-8.
Dewey:759.1308997. LCCN:95-069012.
           Audience: **g,l,u,f.** *Choice, 1996.*

Lowe, Truman (Editor)   **N6537.M656**
Native Modernism: The Art of George Morrison and Allan
Houser. Trade Paper, Saddle Stitched. University of Washington
Press. Seattle, WA. 2005. 128p. ISBN:0-295-98467-8, ISBN13:
978-0-295-98467-4. Dewey:704.03/970747/074753.
LCCN:2004-007584.
           Audience: **g,l,u,f.** *Choice, 2005.*

Matuz, Roger (Editor)   **E98.A7S8 1998**
St. James Guide to Native North American Artists. Richard W.
Hill Sr. (Foreword by). Trade Cloth. Thomson Gale. Farmington
Hills, MI. 1997. 691p. ISBN:1-55862-221-7, ISBN13:
978-1-55862-221-0. Dewey:704.03/97. LCCN:97-018453.
           Audience: **g,l,u,f.**

M'Closkey, Kathy   **E99.N3M315 2002**
Swept under the Rug: A Hidden History of Navajo Weaving.
University of Arizona, Southwest Center Staff (Contribution by).
Trade Cloth. University of New Mexico Press. Albuquerque,
NM. 2002. 320p. ISBN:0-8263-2831-8, ISBN13:
978-0-8263-2831-1. Dewey:381/.45746/089972.
LCCN:2002-009369.
           Audience: **u,f.** *Choice, 2003.*

Menair, Peter, et al.   **E78.N78M32 1998**
Down from the Shimmering Sky: Masks of the Northwest
Coast. Robert Joseph & Bruce Grenville (Authors). Paper Text.
University of Washington Press. Seattle, WA. 1998. 192p.
ISBN:0-295-97709-4, ISBN13: 978-0-295-97709-6.
Dewey:731/.75/089970795. LCCN:98-015997.
           Audience: **g,l,u,f.** *Choice, 1999.*

Norton, Derek &   **E99.E7N68 2005**
  Reading, Nigel
Cape Dorset Sculpture. Trade Cloth. University of Washington
Press. Seattle, WA. 2005. 144p. ISBN:0-295-98478-3, ISBN13:
978-0-295-98478-0. Dewey:730/.89/9712071952.
LCCN:2004-023553.
           Audience: **g,l,u,f.** *Choice, 2005.*

Paterek, Josephine   **E98.C8**
Encyclopedia of American Indian Costume. Trade Paper. W. W.
Norton & Company, Inc. New York, NY. 1996. 536p.
ISBN:0-393-31382-4, ISBN13: 978-0-393-31382-6.
Dewey:391/.008997.
           Audience: **g,l,u,f.** *Choice, 1994.*

Peterson, Susan   **E98.P8P37 1997**
Pottery by American Indian Women: The Legacy of
Generations. Trade Cloth. Abbeville Press, Inc. New York, NY.
1997. 224p. ISBN:0-7892-0353-7, ISBN13: 978-0-7892-0353-3.
Dewey:738/.082. LCCN:97-012628.
           Audience: **g,l,u,f.**

Power, Susan C.   **E99.W84P69 2004**
Early Art of the Southeastern Indians: Feathered Serpents and
Winged Beings. Trade Cloth. University of Georgia Press.
Athens, GA. 2004. 288p. ISBN:0-8203-2501-5, ISBN13:
978-0-8203-2501-9. Dewey:704.03/97075. LCCN:2003-011154.
           Audience: **g,l,u,f.** *Choice, 2004.*

Reid, Bill   **E99.H2R455 2000**
Solitary Raven: The Selected Writings of Bill Reid. Robert
Bringhurst (Editor). Trade Cloth. University of Washington
Press. Seattle, WA. 2000. 250p. ISBN:0-295-98080-X, ISBN13:
978-0-295-98080-5. Dewey:704.03/972. LCCN:00-048397.
           Audience: **g,l,u,f.** *Choice, 2001.*

Rushing, W. Jackson   **NX512.3.A35**
  (Editor)
Native American Art in the Twentieth Century: Makers,
Meanings and Histories. Trade Paper. Routledge. New York, NY.
1999. 252p. ISBN:0-415-13748-9, ISBN13: 978-0-415-13748-5.
Dewey:700.8/9. LCCN:98-048803.
           Audience: **u,f.** *Choice, 2000.*

Rushing, W. Jackson III   **NB237.H62R87 2004**
Allan Houser: An American Master - Chiricahua Apache
1914-1994. Trade Cloth. Harry N. Abrams, Inc. New York, NY.
2004. 256p. ISBN:0-8109-4326-3, ISBN13: 978-0-8109-4326-1.
Dewey:730/.92. LCCN:2003-021491.
           Audience: **g,l,u,f.** *Choice, 2005.*

Rushing, W. Jackson   **N6538.A4A34 2001**
  (Editor)
After the Storm: The Eiteljorg Fellowship for Native American
Fine Art, 2001. Eiteljorg Museum of American Indians and
Western Art Staff (Contribution by). Trade Paper. University of
Washington Press. Seattle, WA. 2002. xvii, 93p. Eiteljorg
Fellowship Ser. ISBN:0-295-98174-1, ISBN13:
978-0-295-98174-1. Dewey:704.03/97/007477252.
LCCN:2001-041480.
           Audience: **g,l,u.** *Choice, 2002.*

Ryan, Allan J.   **E78.C2R93 1999**
The Trickster Shift: Humour and Irony in Contemporary Native
Art. Trade Cloth. University of Washington Press. Seattle, WA.
1999. 320p. ISBN:0-295-97816-3, ISBN13: 978-0-295-97816-1.
Dewey:704.03/97071. LCCN:99-017663.
           Audience: **l,u,f.** *Choice, 2000.*

Shadbolt, Doris   **E99.H2R457 1999**
Bill Reid. Trade Cloth. University of Washington Press. Seattle,
WA. 1998. 200p. ISBN:0-295-97750-7, ISBN13:
978-0-295-97750-8. Dewey:730/.92. LCCN:98-025897.
           Audience: **g,l,u,f.** *Choice, 1999, 1987.*

Simpson, Georgiana   **E99.N3S56 2003**
  Kennedy
Navajo Ceremonial Baskets: Sacred Symbols, Sacred Space.
Trade Paper. Book Publishing Company, The. Summertown, TN.
2004. 160p. ISBN:1-57067-118-4, ISBN13: 978-1-57067-118-0.
Dewey:746.41/20899726. LCCN:2003-025512.
           Audience: **g,l,u,f.** *Choice, 2004.*

Torrence, Gaylord &   **E98.L4T67 1994**
  Danoff, I. Michael
The American Indian Parfleche: A Tradition of Abstract
Painting. Trade Paper. University of Washington Press. Seattle,
WA. 1994. 272p. ISBN:0-295-97333-1, ISBN13:
978-0-295-97333-3. Dewey:745.53/1/097. LCCN:93-039709.
           Audience: **g,l,u,f.** *Choice, 1994.*

Wardwell, Allen   **E78.N78W283 1996**
Tangible Visions: Northwest Coast Indian Shamanism and Its
Art. Trade Cloth. Monacelli Press, Inc. New York, NY. 1996.
352p. ISBN:1-885254-16-4, ISBN13: 978-1-885254-16-0.
Dewey:704/.03972. LCCN:95-024157.
           Audience: **g,l,u,f.**

Audience: g=general, l=lower division undergraduate, u=upper division undergraduate, f=faculty.

679

Werness, Hope B.   E98.A7W49 2000
Continuum Encyclopedia of Native Art. Trade Cloth. Continuum
International Publishing Group, Ltd. London, 2000. 420p.
ISBN:0-8264-1156-8, ISBN13: 978-0-8264-1156-3.
Dewey:704.03. LCCN:00-021842.

Audience: **g,l,u,f.** *Choice, 2001.*

Education

Adams, David W.   E97.5.A35 1995
Education for Extinction: American Indians and the Boarding
School Experience, 1875-1928. Trade Cloth. University Press of
Kansas. Lawrence, KS. 1997. 408p. ISBN:0-7006-0735-8,
ISBN13: 978-0-7006-0735-8. Dewey:371.97/97.
LCCN:95-007638.

Audience: **l,u.** *Choice, 1996.*

Bensen, Robert (Editor)   E98.C89C55 2001
Children of the Dragonfly: Native American Voices on Child
Custody and Education. Carter Revard (Foreword by). Trade
Cloth. University of Arizona Press. Tucson, AZ. 2001. 280p.
ISBN:0-8165-2012-7, ISBN13: 978-0-8165-2012-1.
Dewey:305.897. LCCN:00-011169.

Audience: **l,u.**

Bloom, John   E98.G2B56 2000
To Show What an Indian Can Do: Sports at Native American
Boarding Schools. Trade Paper. University of Minnesota Press.
Minneapolis, MN. 2005. 176p. Sport and Culture Ser., Vol. 2
ISBN:0-8166-3652-4, ISBN13: 978-0-8166-3652-5.
Dewey:796/.089/97. LCCN:00-008865.

Audience: **u.**

Cajete, Gregory   E96.C35 1994
Look to the Mountain: An Ecology of Indigenous Education.
Trade Paper. Kivaki Press, Inc. Skyland, NC. 1993. 248p.
ISBN:1-882308-65-4, ISBN13: 978-1-882308-65-1.
Dewey:370.897073. LCCN:94-175203.

Audience: **l,u,f.**

Chalcraft, Edwin L. &   E97.65.N4C43 2004
  Collins, Cary C.
ⓔ Assimilation's Agent: My Life As a Superintendent in the
Indian Boarding School System. E-Book. University of
Nebraska Press. Lincoln, NE. 2004. lxvi, 360p.
ISBN:0-8032-0435-3, ISBN13: 978-0-8032-0435-5.
Dewey:371.2/011/092 B. LCCN:2004-000623.

Audience: **g,l,u.** *Choice, 2005.*

Mihesuah, Devon A. &   E97.I464 2004
  Wilson, Angela Cavender
Indigenizing the Academy: Native Scholars and Scholarship on
Natives. Trade Paper. University of Nebraska Press. Lincoln,
NE. 2005. 240p. Contemporary Indigenous Issues Ser.
ISBN:0-8032-8292-3, ISBN13: 978-0-8032-8292-6.
Dewey:378.1/982997. LCCN:2003-020064.

Audience: **u,f.** *Choice, 2005.*

Milloy, John   E96.5
A National Crime: The Canadian Government and the
Residential School System, 1879-1986. Trade Paper. University
of Manitoba Press. Winnipeg, MB. 1999. 424p. Manitoba
Studies in Native History Ser. ISBN:0-88755-646-9, ISBN13:
978-0-88755-646-3. Dewey:371.829/97071.

Audience: **u,f.**

Pratt, Richard Henry   E97.6.C2P89 2004
Battlefield and Classroom: Four Decades with the American
Indian, 1867-1904. Robert Marshall Utley (Editor). Trade Paper.
University of Oklahoma Press. Norman, OK. 2004. 416p.
ISBN:0-8061-3603-0, ISBN13: 978-0-8061-3603-5.
Dewey:973.8 B. LCCN:2004-041232.

Audience: **g,l,u.**

Reyhner, Jon Allan &   E97.R49 2004
  Eder, Jeanne Oyawin
American Indian Education: A History. Trade Cloth. University
of Oklahoma Press. Norman, OK. 2004. 368p.
ISBN:0-8061-3593-X, ISBN13: 978-0-8061-3593-9.
Dewey:371.829/97. LCCN:2003-063420.

Audience: **g,l,u,f.** *Choice, 2005.*

Senese, Guy B.   E97
Self-Determination and the Social Education of Native
Americans. Trade Cloth. Greenwood Publishing Group, Inc.
Portsmouth, NH. 1991. 248p. ISBN:0-275-93776-3, ISBN13:
978-0-275-93776-8. Dewey:370/.8997. LCCN:90-020011.

Audience: **u,f.** *Choice, 1992.*

Environmental Issues

Ali, Saleem H.   E98.L3A35 2003
Mining, the Environment, and Indigenous Development
Conflicts. Trade Cloth. University of Arizona Press. Tucson, AZ.
2003. xxii, 254p. ISBN:0-8165-2312-6, ISBN13:
978-0-8165-2312-2. Dewey:333.2. LCCN:2003-008311.

Audience: **l,u.**

Awiakta, Marilou   E99.C5 A95 1993
Selu: Seeking the Corn-Mother's Widsom. Mary Adair
(Illustrator), Wilma P. Mankiller (Foreword by). Trade Cloth.
Fulcrum Publishing. Golden, CO. 1993. 352p.
ISBN:1-55591-144-7, ISBN13: 978-1-55591-144-7.
Dewey:299/.785. LCCN:93-026645.

Audience: **g,l.**

Bol, Marsha C. &   E98.P5S73 1998
  Carnegie Museum of Natural History Staff (Editors)
The Stars Above, the Earth Below: American Indians and
Nature. Trade Paper. Roberts Rinehart Publishers. Boulder, CO.
1998. 272p. ISBN:1-57098-198-1, ISBN13: 978-1-57098-198-2.
Dewey:304.2/089/97. LCCN:98-005747.

Audience: **g,l.**

Burnham, Philip   E98.L3B87 2000
Indian Country, God's Country: Native Americans and the
National Parks. Trade Cloth. Island Press. Washington, DC.
2000. 384p. ISBN:1-55963-667-X, ISBN13: 978-1-55963-667-4.
Dewey:333.78/3/089973. LCCN:99-050934.

Audience: **g,l,u,f.** *Choice, 2000.*

Cajete, Gregory   E96.C35 1994
Look to the Mountain: An Ecology of Indigenous Education.
Trade Paper. Kivaki Press, Inc. Skyland, NC. 1993. 248p.
ISBN:1-882308-65-4, ISBN13: 978-1-882308-65-1.
Dewey:370.897073. LCCN:94-175203.

Audience: **l,u,f.**

Cajete, Gregory   E59.S35C35 2000
Native Science: Natural Laws of Interdependence. Trade Cloth.
Clear Light Publishers. Santa Fe, NM. 1999. 328p.
ISBN:1-57416-035-4, ISBN13: 978-1-57416-035-2.
Dewey:508.997. LCCN:99-054279.

Audience: **l,u.**

Eichstaedt, Peter H.   **E99.N3E29 1994**
If You Poison Us: Uranium and Native Americans. Murrae
Haynes (Photographer). Trade Cloth. Red Crane Books, Inc.
Santa Fe, NM. 1994. 272p. ISBN:1-878610-40-6, ISBN13:
978-1-878610-40-9. Dewey:363.11/962234932/089.
LCCN:94-007306.
            Audience: **g,l.** *Choice, 1995.*

Gedicks, Al   **GN449.3.G43 2001**
Resource Rebels: Native Challenges to Mining and Oil
Corporations. Trade Cloth. South End Press. Cambridge, MA.
2001. 250p. Native American Studies ISBN:0-89608-641-0,
ISBN13: 978-0-89608-641-8. Dewey:333.8/517.
LCCN:2001-042687.
            Audience: **g,l,u,f.** *Choice, 2002.*

Grinde, Donald &   **E98.L3G74 1995**
   Johansen, Bruce
Ecocide of Native America: Environmental Destruction of
Indian Lands and Peoples. Trade Cloth. Clear Light Publishers.
Santa Fe, NM. 1994. 320p. ISBN:0-940666-52-9, ISBN13:
978-0-940666-52-8. Dewey:333.7/097. LCCN:94-017271.
            Audience: **g,l,u.** *Choice, 1995.*

Hurt, R. Douglas   **E98.A3**
Indian Agriculture in America: Prehistory to the Present. Trade
Paper. University Press of Kansas. Lawrence, KS. 1996. xiv,
290p. ISBN:0-7006-0802-8, ISBN13: 978-0-7006-0802-7.
Dewey:338.1/08997073. LCCN:87-014764.
            Audience: **g,l,u.** *Choice, 1988.*

Krech, Shepard   **E98.P5K74**
Ecological Indian: Myth and History. Library Binding.
Sagebrush Education Resources. Caledonia, MN. 2003.
ISBN:0-613-91414-7, ISBN13: 978-0-613-91414-7.
Dewey:333.7/089/97.
            Audience: **g,l,u,f.**

LaDuke, Winona   **E98.L3L34 1999**
All Our Relations: Native Struggles for Land and Life. Trade
Cloth. South End Press. Cambridge, MA. 1999. 256p. Native
American Studies ISBN:0-89608-600-3, ISBN13:
978-0-89608-600-5. Dewey:333.2. LCCN:99-016813.
            Audience: **g,l.** *Choice, 2000.*

LaDuke, Winona   **E98.R3L33 2005**
Recovering the Sacred: The Power of Naming and Claiming.
Trade Cloth. South End Press. Cambridge, MA. 2005. 0p.
ISBN:0-89608-713-1, ISBN13: 978-0-89608-713-2.
Dewey:299.7. LCCN:2005-012700.
            Audience: **g,l.**

Lambert Colomeda,   **RA448.5.I5L36 1998**
   Lorelei A.
Keepers of the Central Fire: Issues in Ecology for Indigenous
Peoples. Paper Text. Jones & Bartlett Publishers, Inc. Sudbury,
MA. 1998. 256p. ISBN:0-7637-0923-9, ISBN13:
978-0-7637-0923-5. Dewey:613/.089/97. LCCN:97-051179.
            Audience: **l.** *Choice, 1999.*

McCool, Daniel   **KF8210.N37.M38 2002**
Native Waters: Contemporary Indian Water Settlements and the
Second Treaty Era. Trade Cloth. University of Arizona Press.
Tucson, AZ. 2002. 260p. ISBN:0-8165-2227-8, ISBN13:
978-0-8165-2227-9. Dewey:346.7304/32. LCCN:2002-001766.
            Audience: **u,f.**

Shurts, John   **KF8210.N37S55 2000**
Indian Reserved Water Rights: The Winters Doctrine in Its
Social and Legal Context, 1880s-1930s. Trade Cloth. University
of Oklahoma Press. Norman, OK. 2000. 352p. Legal History of
North America Ser., Vol. 8 ISBN:0-8061-3210-8, ISBN13:
978-0-8061-3210-5. Dewey:346.7304/32. LCCN:99-043558.
            Audience: **u,f.** *Choice, 2001.*

Sutton, Imre & Clow,   **E98.T77T78 2001**
   Richmond L. (Editors)
Trusteeship in Change: Toward Tribal Autonomy in Resource
Management. Trade Cloth. University Press of Colorado.
Boulder, CO. 2001. 354p. ISBN:0-87081-622-5, ISBN13:
978-0-87081-622-2. Dewey:333.7/0973. LCCN:2001-002412.
            Audience: **u,f.** *Choice, 2002.*

Weaver, Jace (Editor)   **E98.S67D44 1996**
Defending Mother Earth: Native American Perspectives on
Environmental Justice. Russell Means (Foreword by). Trade
Paper. Orbis Books. Maryknoll, NY. 1996. 220p. Ecology and
Justice Ser. ISBN:1-57075-096-3, ISBN13: 978-1-57075-096-0.
Dewey:305.897/073. LCCN:96-021203.
            Audience: **l,u,f.**

History

Columbia Guides to American History and Culture. New York,
NY.: Columbia University Press. 2001.
            Audience: **g,l,u,f.**

Adams, David W.   **E97.5.A35 1995**
Education for Extinction: American Indians and the Boarding
School Experience, 1875-1928. Trade Cloth. University Press of
Kansas. Lawrence, KS. 1997. 408p. ISBN:0-7006-0735-8,
ISBN13: 978-0-7006-0735-8. Dewey:371.97/97.
LCCN:95-007638.
            Audience: **l,u.** *Choice, 1996.*

Armstrong, William H.   **E99.S3**
Warrior in Two Camps: Ely S. Parker, Union General and
Seneca Chief. Paper Text. Syracuse University Press. Syracuse,
NY. 1990. 256p. Iroquois and Their Neighbors Ser.
ISBN:0-8156-2495-6, ISBN13: 978-0-8156-2495-0. Dewey:921.
            Audience: **g,l,u,f.**

Banner, Stuart   **E98.L3B36 2005**
How the Indians Lost Their Land: Law and Power on the
Frontier. Trade Cloth. Harvard University Press. Cambridge,
MA. 2005. 352p. ISBN:0-674-01871-0, ISBN13:
978-0-674-01871-6. Dewey:333.2. LCCN:2005-043617.
            Audience: **g,l,u,f.** *Choice, 2006.*

Berkhofer, Robert F. Jr.   **E98**
Salvation and the Savage: An Analysis of Protestant Missions
and American Indian Response, 1787-1862. Trade Cloth.
Greenwood Publishing Group, Inc. Portsmouth, NH. 1977. 186p.
ISBN:0-8371-9745-7, ISBN13: 978-0-8371-9745-6.
LCCN:77-022857.
            Audience: **u,f.**

Berkhofer, Robert F. Jr.   **E98.P99 B47 1979**
The White Man's Indian: Images of the American Indian from
Columbus to the Present. Trade Paper. Knopf Publishing Group.
New York, NY. 1979. 304p. ISBN:0-394-72794-0, ISBN13:

Audience: g=general, l=lower division undergraduate, u=upper division undergraduate, f=faculty.

681

978-0-394-72794-3. Dewey:301.15/43/9700497. LCCN:78-011047.

Audience: **g,l,u.**

Brown, Dee E81.B75 2001
Bury My Heart at Wounded Knee: An Indian History of the American West. Ed. 30. Cloth over Boards. Henry Holt & Company. New York, NY. 2001. 512p. ISBN:0-8050-6634-9, ISBN13: 978-0-8050-6634-0. Dewey:970.5. LCCN:00-040958.

Audience: **g,u,f.**

Drinnon, Richard E98.P99D74 1997
Facing West: The Metaphysics of Indian-Hating and Empire-Building. Trade Paper. University of Oklahoma Press. Norman, OK. 1997. 608p. ISBN:0-8061-2928-X, ISBN13: 978-0-8061-2928-0. Dewey:305.8/00973. LCCN:96-038834.

Audience: **g,l,u,f.**

Fenton, William N. E99.I7F453 1998
The Great Law and the Longhouse: A Political History of the Iroquois Confederacy. Trade Cloth. University of Oklahoma Press. Norman, OK. 1998. 808p. Civilization of the American Indian Ser., No. 223 ISBN:0-8061-3003-2, ISBN13: 978-0-8061-3003-3. Dewey:973/.049755. LCCN:97-019842.

Audience: **l,u,f.** *Choice, 1998.*

Friesen, Gerald F1062.F74
The Canadian Prairies: A History. Trade Paper. University of Toronto Press. Toronto, ON. 1987. 820p. ISBN:0-8020-6648-8, ISBN13: 978-0-8020-6648-0. Dewey:971.2.

Audience: **g,l,u,f.** *B*

Hale, Horatio E99.I7
The Iroquois Book of Rites. Trade Paper. Kessinger Publishing, LLC. Whitefish, MT. 2004. ISBN:1-4191-6770-7, ISBN13: 978-1-4191-6770-6. Dewey:974.7004976.

Audience: **g,l,u,f.**

Hoxie, Frederick E. E76.2.E53 1996
(Editor)
Encyclopedia of North American Indians: Native American History, Culture, and Life from Paleo-Indians to the Present. Trade Cloth. Houghton Mifflin Company Trade & Reference Division. Boston, MA. 1996. 768p. ISBN:0-395-66921-9, ISBN13: 978-0-395-66921-1. Dewey:970/.00497. LCCN:96-021411.

Audience: **g,l,u.** *Choice, 1997.*

Johansen, Bruce E. E98
(Editor)
The Encyclopedia of Native American Economic History. Cloth Text. Greenwood Publishing Group, Inc. Portsmouth, NH. 1999. 320p. ISBN:0-313-30623-0, ISBN13: 978-0-313-30623-5. Dewey:330.973/008997. LCCN:98-025733.

Audience: **g,l,u,f.** *Choice, 1999.*

Josephy, Alvin M. Jr. E77.J787 2001
500 Nations: An Illustrated History of North American Indians. Trade Cloth. Random House Value Publishing. New York, NY. 2002. 480p. ISBN:0-517-16394-2, ISBN13: 978-0-517-16394-8. Dewey:970.004/97. LCCN:2001-023623.

Audience: **g,l,u.**

Josephy, Alvin M. Jr. E89.J78 1993
The Patriot Chiefs: A Chronicle of American Indian Resistance. Trade Paper. Penguin Group (USA) Inc. New York, NY. 1993. 384p. ISBN:0-14-023463-2, ISBN13: 978-0-14-023463-3. Dewey:970.004/97 B. LCCN:94-116933.

Audience: **g,l,u.**

Martin, Calvin (Editor) E76.8.A47 1986
The American Indian and the Problem of History. Trade Paper. Oxford University Press, Inc. New York, NY. 1987. 246p. ISBN:0-19-503856-8, ISBN13: 978-0-19-503856-9. Dewey:970.004/97. LCCN:86-008425.

Audience: **u,f.** *Choice, 1987.*

Miller, Christopher L. E78.C64M55 2003
Prophetic Worlds: Indians and Whites on the Columbia Plateau. Chris Friday (Foreword by). Trade Paper. University of Washington Press. Seattle, WA. 2003. 192p. ISBN:0-295-98302-7, ISBN13: 978-0-295-98302-8. Dewey:979.7/02. LCCN:2003-040226.

Audience: **u,f.**

Miller, Jay (Compiled Z1206.M55 1995
by), et al.
Writings in Indian History, 1985-1990. Colin G. Calloway & Richard A. Sattler (Compiled by). Trade Cloth. University of Oklahoma Press. Norman, OK. 1999. 216p. D'Arcy McNickle Center Bibliographies in American Indian History Ser., Vol. 2 ISBN:0-8061-2759-7, ISBN13: 978-0-8061-2759-0. Dewey:016.973/0497. LCCN:95-008776.

Audience: **l,u,f.** *Choice, 1996.*

Morrison, R. Bruce & E78.C2
Wilson, Rod
Native Peoples: The Canadian Experience. Ed. 3. Trade Paper. Oxford University Press, Inc. New York, NY. 2004. 504p. ISBN:0-19-541819-0, ISBN13: 978-0-19-541819-4. Dewey:971.004/97. LCCN:2004-299695.

Audience: **g,l,u.**

Muise, D. A. (Editor) Z1382.R4 1982
A Reader's Guide to Canadian History: Beginnings to Confederation. Paper Text. University of Toronto Press. Toronto, ON. 1982. 256p. ISBN:0-8020-6442-6, ISBN13: 978-0-8020-6442-4. Dewey:016.971. LCCN:82-219054.

Audience: **g,l,u,f.**

Nabokov, Peter E98.G2
Indian Running: Native American History and Tradition. Ed. 2. Trade Paper. Gibbs Smith, Publisher. Layton, UT. 1987. 208p. ISBN:0-941270-41-6, ISBN13: 978-0-941270-41-0. Dewey:70.6. LCCN:87-071658.

Audience: **u,f.**

Ostler, Jeffrey E99.D1O85 2004
The Plains Sioux and U. S. Colonialism from Lewis and Clark to Wounded Knee. Frederick Hoxie & Neal Salisbury (Contribution by). Cloth Text. Cambridge University Press. New York, NY. 2004. 406p. Studies in North American Indian History Ser. ISBN:0-521-79346-7, ISBN13: 978-0-521-79346-9. Dewey:978.004/975243. LCCN:2003-070009.

Audience: **u,f.** *Choice, 2005.*

Patterson, E. Palmer E78.C2
The Canadian Indian: A History Since 1500. Collier-Macmillan Canada, Ltd., Don Mills, Ont.. 1971.

Audience: **g,l,u,f.**

Patterson, E. Palmer; E78.C2
Patterson, Nancy-Lou
The Changing People: A History of the Canadian Indians. Collier-Macmillan Canada Toronto. 1971.

Audience: **g,l,u.**

Pratt, Richard Henry   E97.6.C2P89 2004
Battlefield and Classroom: Four Decades with the American
Indian, 1867-1904. Robert Marshall Utley (Editor). Trade Paper.
University of Oklahoma Press. Norman, OK. 2004. 416p.
ISBN:0-8061-3603-0, ISBN13: 978-0-8061-3603-5.
Dewey:973.8 B. LCCN:2004-041232.

Audience: **g,l,u.**

Prucha, Francis P.   JX235.9
American Indian Treaties: The History of a Political Anomaly.
Trade Paper. University of California Press. Berkeley, CA. 1997.
578p. ISBN:0-520-20895-1, ISBN13: 978-0-520-20895-7.
Dewey:341/.026673. LCCN:93-036297.

Audience: **g,l,u,f.** *Choice, 1995.*

Prucha, Francis P.   G1201.E1P7 1990
Atlas of American Indian Affairs. Cloth Text. University of
Nebraska Press. Lincoln, NE. 1990. 191p. ISBN:0-8032-3689-1,
ISBN13: 978-0-8032-3689-9. Dewey:912.7. LCCN:90-675000.

Audience: **g,l,u,f.** *Choice, 1991.*

Prucha, Francis P.   Z1209.2.U5
A Bibliographical Guide to the History of Indian-White
Relations in the United States. Library Binding. University of
Chicago Press. Chicago, IL. 1977. x, 454p.
ISBN:0-226-68476-8, ISBN13: 978-0-226-68476-5.
Dewey:016.3058/97/073. LCCN:76-016045.

Audience: **l,u,f.**

Prucha, Francis P.   E93.P9654 1995
The Great Father: The United States Government and the
American Indians, Set. Trade Cloth. University of Nebraska
Press. Lincoln, NE. 1995. 1302p. ISBN:0-8032-8734-8, ISBN13:
978-0-8032-8734-1. Dewey:323.1/197/073. LCCN:83-016837.

Audience: **u,f.**

Prucha, Francis P.   Z1209.2.U5.P67 SUPPL
Indian-White Relations in the United States: A Bibliography of
Works Published 1975-1980. Trade Cloth. University of
Nebraska Press. Lincoln, NE. 1982. 179p. ISBN:0-8032-3665-4,
ISBN13: 978-0-8032-3665-3. Dewey:016.3231/197073.
LCCN:81-014722.

Audience: **u,f.**

Prucha, Francis P.   E93 .P9665 1985
The Indians in American Society: From the Revolutionary War
to the Present. Trade Cloth. University of California Press.
Berkeley, CA. 1985. 127p. Quantum Bks., No. 29
ISBN:0-520-05503-9, ISBN13: 978-0-520-05503-2.
Dewey:973/.0497. LCCN:85-001023.

Audience: **g,l,u.** *Choice, 1986.*

Salisbury, Neal   E77.C74 2004
Companion to American Indian History. Philip J. Deloria
(Editor). Trade Paper. Blackwell Publishing, Inc. Malden, MA.
2004. 528p. ISBN:1-4051-2131-9, ISBN13: 978-1-4051-2131-6.
Dewey:970/.00497.

Audience: **l,u,f.**

Shattuck, George C.   KF8228.O45A3 1991
The Oneida Land Claims: A Legal History. Jack Campisi
(Foreword by), Laurence M. Hauptman (Introduction by). Paper
Text. Syracuse University Press. Syracuse, NY. 1991. 288p.
Iroquois and Their Neighbors Ser. ISBN:0-8156-2525-1,
ISBN13: 978-0-8156-2525-4. Dewey:346.7304/32/089975.
LCCN:90-022625.

Audience: **u,f.** *Choice, 1992.*

Smith, Jane F. &   E93.N24
  Kvasnicka, Robert M. (Editors)
Indian-White Relations: A Persistent Paradox. Trade Paper.
Howard University Press. Washington, DC. 2003. 278p.
ISBN:0-88258-094-9, ISBN13: 978-0-88258-094-4.
Dewey:323.1/19/7073. LCCN:75-022316.

Audience: **u,f.**

Spicer, Edward Holland   E78.S7 S6
Cycles of Conquest: The Impact of Spain, Mexico, and the
United States on the Indians of the Southwest 1533. Paper Text.
Textbook Publishers. Temecula, CA. 2003. xii, 609p.
ISBN:0-7581-2831-2, ISBN13: 978-0-7581-2831-7.
Dewey:970.49.

Audience: **l,u,f.**

Sturtevant, William C.   E77 .H25
  & Washburn, Wilcomb E. (Editors)
History of Indian-White Relations. Trade Cloth. Smithsonian
Institution Press. Washington, DC. 1989. 852p. The Handbook
of North American Indians Ser., Vol. 4 ISBN:0-87474-184-X,
ISBN13: 978-0-87474-184-1. Dewey:970/.004/97.
LCCN:77-017162.

Audience: **g,l,u,f.**

Surtees, Robert J.   Z1209.2.C2S91982E92
Canadian Indian Policy: A Critical Bibliography. Trade Paper.
Indiana University Press. Bloomington, IN. 1982. 120p.
Newberry Library D'Arcy McNickle Center for the History of
the American Indian Bibliographical Ser. ISBN:0-253-31300-7,
ISBN13: 978-0-253-31300-3. Dewey:016.3231/197/071.
LCCN:81-048088.

Audience: **g,l,u,f.**

Surtees, Robert J.   E78.C2
The Original People. Holt, Rinehart and Winston of Canada,
Toronto. 1971. ISBN:0-03-925122-5, ISBN13:
978-0-03-925122-2.

Audience: **g,l.**

Swanton, John R.   E85
The Indian Tribes of North America. Trade Paper. Smithsonian
Institution Press. Washington, DC. 1985. 726p. Classics of
Smithsonian Anthropology Ser. ISBN:0-87474-179-3, ISBN13:
978-0-87474-179-7. Dewey:970.004/97. LCCN:52-061970.

Audience: **g,l,u,f.**

Thomas, David Hurst,   E77
  et al.
The Native Americans: An Illustrated History. Jay Miller,
Richard White, Peter Nabokov & Philip J. DeLoria (Authors),
Betty Ballantine & Ian Ballantine (Editors), Alvin M. Josephy
Jr. (Introduction by). Trade Cloth. World Publications, Inc.
North Dighton, MA. 2003. 480p. ISBN:1-57215-303-2, ISBN13:
978-1-57215-303-5. Dewey:970.0049.

Audience: **g,l,u.**

Trigger, Bruce G. &   E85
  Washburn, Wilcomb E. (Editors)
The Cambridge History of the Native Peoples of the Americas,
Set. Trade Cloth. Cambridge University Press. New York, NY.
2000. 4154p. Cambridge History of the Native Peoples of the
Americas Ser. ISBN:0-521-79054-9, ISBN13:
978-0-521-79054-3. Dewey:970.00497.

Audience: **g,l,u,f.**

Utley, Robert Marshall   F596 .U84
Indian, Soldier and Settler: Experiences in the Struggle for the American West. Trade Paper. University of Washington Press. Seattle, WA. 1977. 86p. ISBN:0-295-96055-8, ISBN13: 978-0-295-96055-5. Dewey:978/.02. LCCN:77-018408.
Audience: **g,l.**

Valk, Barbara G.   Z1251.M44V35 1988
   (Editor)
BorderLine: A Bibliography of the United States-Mexico Borderlands. Trade Cloth. University of California, Latin American Center. Los Angeles, CA. 1988. 736p. ISBN:0-87903-112-3, ISBN13: 978-0-87903-112-1. Dewey:016.972/1. LCCN:88-004565.
Audience: **u,f.**

Vecsey, Christopher &   KFN5940.A75I76 1988
   Starna, William A. (Editors)
Iroquois Land Claims. Cloth Text. Syracuse University Press. Syracuse, NY. 1988. 240p. Iroquois and Their Neighbors Ser. ISBN:0-8156-2434-4, ISBN13: 978-0-8156-2434-9. Dewey:346.74704/32. LCCN:87-033621.
Audience: **u,f.** *Choice, 1988.*

Wallace, Anthony F.   E99.S3
The Death and Rebirth of the Seneca. Trade Paper. Knopf Publishing Group. New York, NY. 1972. 416p. ISBN:0-394-71699-X, ISBN13: 978-0-394-71699-2. Dewey:970.3.
Audience: **g,l,u,f.**

White, Richard   E99.A35 W48 1991
The Middle Ground: Indians, Empires, and Republics in the Great Lakes Region, 1650-1815. Frederick E. Hoxie & Neal Salisbury (Contribution by). Cloth Text. Cambridge University Press. New York, NY. 1991. 560p. Studies in North American Indian History ISBN:0-521-37104-X, ISBN13: 978-0-521-37104-9. Dewey:305.8/97/077. LCCN:92-005045.
Audience: **l,u,f.** *Choice, 1992.*

Wilson, Edmund   E99.I7
Apologies to the Iroquois: The Iroquois and Their Neighbors. William N. Fenton (Introduction by). Trade Paper. Syracuse University Press. Syracuse, NY. 1992. 356p. Iroquois and Their Neighbors Ser. ISBN:0-8156-2564-2, ISBN13: 978-0-8156-2564-3. Dewey:305.897/5.
Audience: **g,l,u,f.**

History > Contact and Exploration

Anawalt, Patricia R.   F1219.3.C75
Indian Clothing Before Cortes: Mesoamerican Costumes from the Codices. Jean C. Sells (Illustrator), H. B. Nicholson (Introduction by). Trade Paper. University of Oklahoma Press. Norman, OK. 1990. 252p. Civilization of the American Indian Ser., Vol. 156 ISBN:0-8061-2288-9, ISBN13: 978-0-8061-2288-5. Dewey:391/.00972. LCCN:80-005942.
Audience: **u,f.**

Anderson, Virginia   SF51.A655 2004
   DeJohn
Creatures of Empire: How Domestic Animals Transformed Early America. Trade Cloth. Oxford University Press, Inc. New York, NY. 2004. 336p. ISBN:0-19-515860-1, ISBN13: 978-0-19-515860-1. Dewey:636/.0973. LCCN:2004-043401.
Audience: **g,l,u.**

Arnold, Jeanne E.   E99.C815O75 2001
The Origins of a Pacific Coast Chiefdom: The Chumash of the Channel Islands. Trade Cloth. University of Utah Press. Salt Lake City, UT. 2001. 336p. ISBN:0-87480-674-7, ISBN13: 978-0-87480-674-8. Dewey:979.4/91. LCCN:00-012452.
Audience: **u,f.**

Bailey, Alfred   F1021.B25 1969
   Goldsworthy
The Conflict of European and Eastern Algonkian Cultures 1504-1700: A Study in Canadian Civilization. Trade Cloth. University of Toronto Press. Toronto, ON. 1969. xxiii, 218p. ISBN:0-8020-1506-9, ISBN13: 978-0-8020-1506-8. Dewey:917.1/03/1. LCCN:78-434310.
Audience: **f.** ℬ

Denevan, William M.   E59.P75N37 1992
   (Editor)
The Native Population of the Americas in 1492. Ed. 2. W. George Lovell (Foreword by). Trade Paper. University of Wisconsin Press. Chicago, IL. 1992. 398p. ISBN:0-299-13434-2, ISBN13: 978-0-299-13434-1. Dewey:304.60973. LCCN:91-040042.
Audience: **u,f.**

Hoig, Stanley   F396
Tribal Wars of the Southern Plains. Trade Cloth. University of Oklahoma Press. Norman, OK. 1993. 252p. ISBN:0-8061-2463-6, ISBN13: 978-0-8061-2463-6. Dewey:976. LCCN:92-054154.
Audience: **g,l,u,f.** *Choice, 1993.*

Innis, Harold Adams   F1060.I58 1999
The Fur Trade in Canada. A. J. Ray (Introduction by). Trade Paper. University of Toronto Press. Toronto, ON. 1999. 496p. ISBN:0-8020-8196-7, ISBN13: 978-0-8020-8196-4. Dewey:380.1/456753/0971. LCCN:99-203946.
Audience: **u,f.**

Jennings, Francis   F7J46 1976
The Invasion of America: Indians, Colonialism, and the Cant of Conquest. Trade Paper. W. W. Norton & Company, Inc. New York, NY. 1976. 384p. Norton Library, Vol. N830 ISBN:0-393-00830-4, ISBN13: 978-0-393-00830-2. Dewey:974/.02. LCCN:76-025451.
Audience: **u,f.** ℬ

Jennings, Francis &   E93
   Fenton, William N. (Editors)
The History and Culture of Iroquois Diplomacy: An Interdisciplinary Guide to the Treaties of the Six Nations and Their League. Paper Text. Syracuse University Press. Syracuse, NY. 1995. 296p. Iroquois and Their Neighbors Ser. ISBN:0-8156-2650-9, ISBN13: 978-0-8156-2650-3. Dewey:973/.0497.
Audience: **l,u,f.**

John, Elizabeth A.   E78.S7J64 1996
Storms Brewed in Other Men's Worlds: The Confrontation of Indians, Spanish, and French in the Southwest, 1540-1795. Ed. 2. Trade Paper. University of Oklahoma Press. Norman, OK. 1996. 836p. ISBN:0-8061-2869-0, ISBN13: 978-0-8061-2869-6. Dewey:979/.01. LCCN:96-016504.
Audience: **u,f.**

Josephy, Alvin M. Jr.   E58.A526 1992
America in 1492: The World of the Indian Peoples Before the
Arrival of Columbus. Trade Cloth. Alfred A. Knopf Inc. New
York, NY. 1992. 477p. ISBN:0-394-56438-3, ISBN13:
978-0-394-56438-8. Dewey:970.01/1. LCCN:90-026222.
Audience: **u,f.**

Josephy, Alvin M. Jr.   E103
America in 1492: The World of the Indian Peoples Before the
Arrival of Columbus. UK-Trade Paper. Knopf Publishing Group.
New York, NY. 1993. 496p. ISBN:0-679-74337-5, ISBN13:
978-0-679-74337-8. Dewey:970.01/1. LCCN:92-056363.
Audience: **g,l,u.**

Leacock, Stephen   N5345.L55
The Dawn of Canadian History: A Chronicle of Aboriginal
Canada and the Coming of the White Man. Trade Cloth.
IndyPublish.com. Cambridge, MA. 2002. 120p.
ISBN:1-58827-291-5, ISBN13: 978-1-58827-291-1.
Dewey:709.56.
Audience: **g,l,u,f.**

Ramen, Fred   E35.R36 2005
A Historical Atlas of North America Before Columbus. Library
Binding. Rosen Publishing Group, Incorporated, The. New York,
NY. 2005. 64p. The United States, Historical Atlases of the
Growth of a New Nation Ser. ISBN:1-4042-0203-X, ISBN13:
978-1-4042-0203-0. Dewey:911/.7. LCCN:2004-041877.
Audience: **g,l,u,f.**

Ray, Arthur J.   E78.C2R35 1998
Indians in the Fur Trade: Their Roles as Trappers, Hunters and
Middlemen in the Lands Southwest. Trade Cloth. University of
Toronto Press. Toronto, ON. 1998. 566p. ISBN:0-8020-4133-7,
ISBN13: 978-0-8020-4133-3. LCCN:98-162603.
Audience: **l,u,f.**

History > Colonial Period

Abler, Thomas S.   E99.S3B533 1989
  (Editor, Introduction by, Notes by)
Chainbreaker: The Revolutionary War Memoirs of Governor
Blacksnake As Told to Benjamin Williams. Benjamin Williams
(As told to). Cloth Text. University of Nebraska Press. Lincoln,
NE. 1989. xviii, 306p. American Indian Lives Ser.
ISBN:0-8032-1446-4, ISBN13: 978-0-8032-1446-0.
Dewey:974.7/00497 B. LCCN:88-028085.
Audience: **g,l,u,f.** *Choice, 1990.*

Axtell, James   E45
Beyond 1492: Encounters in Colonial North America. Trade
Cloth. Oxford University Press, Inc. New York, NY. 1992. 400p.
ISBN:0-19-506838-6, ISBN13: 978-0-19-506838-2.
Dewey:970.02. LCCN:91-045411.
Audience: **g,l,u,f.**

Bourne, Russell   E83.67.B74 1990
The Red King's Rebellion: Racial Politics in New England,
1675-1677. Trade Cloth. Simon & Schuster. New York, NY.
1990. 288p. ISBN:0-689-12000-1, ISBN13: 978-0-689-12000-8.
Dewey:973.2/4. LCCN:89-017581.
Audience: **g,l,u,f.** *Choice, 1990.*

Calloway, Colin G.   E92.C18 1986
Crown and Calumet: British-Indian Relations, 1783-1815. Trade
Cloth. University of Oklahoma Press. Norman, OK. 1987. 360p.

ISBN:0-8061-2033-9, ISBN13: 978-0-8061-2033-1.
Dewey:323.1/197/071. LCCN:86-016151.
Audience: **u,f.** *Choice, 1987.*

Cave, Alfred A.   E83.63.C37 1996
The Pequot War. Trade Paper. University of Massachusetts
Press. Amherst, MA. 1996. 232p. Native Americans of the
Northeast Ser., :Culture, History, and the Contemporary
ISBN:1-55849-030-2, ISBN13: 978-1-55849-030-7.
Dewey:973.2/2. LCCN:95-047282.
Audience: **g,l,u,f.** *Choice, 1996.*

Dowd, Gregory Evans   E83.76.D69 2002
War under Heaven: Pontiac, the Indian Nations, and the British
Empire. Trade Cloth. Johns Hopkins University Press.
Baltimore, MD. 2002. 384p. ISBN:0-8018-7079-8, ISBN13:
978-0-8018-7079-8. Dewey:973.2/7. LCCN:2002-000596.
Audience: **u,f.** *Choice, 2003.*

Graymont, Barbara   E99.I7
The Iroquois in the American Revolution. Trade Paper. Syracuse
University Press. Syracuse, NY. 1972. 359p. New York State
Bks. ISBN:0-8156-0116-6, ISBN13: 978-0-8156-0116-6.
Dewey:973.3/43. LCCN:73-170096.
Audience: **g,l,u,f.**

Havard, Gilles   E92.H39 2001
The Great Peace of Montreal of 1701: French-Native Diplomacy
in the Seventeenth Century. Phyllis Aronoff & Howard Scott
(Translators). Trade Cloth. McGill-Queen's University Press.
Montreal, PQ. 2001. xi, 308p. ISBN:0-7735-2209-3, ISBN13:
978-0-7735-2209-1. Dewey:971.01/8. LCCN:2002-489834.
Audience: **u,f.** *Choice, 2002.*

Hoig, Stanley   F396
Tribal Wars of the Southern Plains. Trade Cloth. University of
Oklahoma Press. Norman, OK. 1993. 252p.
ISBN:0-8061-2463-6, ISBN13: 978-0-8061-2463-6. Dewey:976.
LCCN:92-054154.
Audience: **g,l,u,f.** *Choice, 1993.*

Jennings, Francis &   E93
  Fenton, William N. (Editors)
The History and Culture of Iroquois Diplomacy: An
Interdisciplinary Guide to the Treaties of the Six Nations and
Their League. Paper Text. Syracuse University Press. Syracuse,
NY. 1995. 296p. Iroquois and Their Neighbors Ser.
ISBN:0-8156-2650-9, ISBN13: 978-0-8156-2650-3.
Dewey:973/.0497.
Audience: **l,u,f.**

John, Elizabeth A.   E78.S7J64 1996
Storms Brewed in Other Men's Worlds: The Confrontation of
Indians, Spanish, and French in the Southwest, 1540-1795. Ed.
2. Trade Paper. University of Oklahoma Press. Norman, OK.
1996. 836p. ISBN:0-8061-2869-0, ISBN13: 978-0-8061-2869-6.
Dewey:979/.01. LCCN:96-016504.
Audience: **u,f.**

Kupperman, Karen   E59.F53K86 2000
  Ordahl
Indians and English: Facing Off in Early America. Book, Other.
Cornell University Press. Ithaca, NY. 2000. 320p.
ISBN:0-8014-3178-6, ISBN13: 978-0-8014-3178-4.
Dewey:973.2. LCCN:99-052767.
Audience: **g,l,u,f.** *Choice, 2000.*

Lepore, Jill   **E83.67.L46 1998**
The Name of War: King Philip's War and the Origins of American Identity. Trade Cloth. Random House, Inc. New York, NY. 1998. 337p. ISBN:0-679-44686-9, ISBN13: 978-0-679-44686-6. Dewey:973.2/4. LCCN:97-002820.

Audience: **g,l,u,f.**

Merritt, Jane T.   **E78.P4M47 2003**
At the Crossroads: Indians and Empires on a Mid-Atlantic Frontier, 1700-1763. Trade Cloth. University of North Carolina Press. Chapel Hill, NC. 2003. 304p. Published for the Omohundro Institute of Early American History and Culture, Williamsburg, Virginia ISBN:0-8078-2789-4, ISBN13: 978-0-8078-2789-5. Dewey:305.897/0748/09032. LCCN:2002-013318.

Audience: **u,f.** *Choice, 2003.*

Stevens, Laura M.   **E98.M6S75 2004**
The Poor Indians: British Missionaries, Native Americans, and Colonial Sensibility. Book, Other. University of Pennsylvania Press. Philadelphia, PA. 2004. 272p. Early American Studies ISBN:0-8122-3812-5, ISBN13: 978-0-8122-3812-9. Dewey:266/.02341/008997. LCCN:2004-042027.

Audience: **u,f.** *Choice, 2005.*

Taylor, Alan   **E99.I7T299 2006**
The Divided Ground: Indians, Settlers, and the Northern Borderland of the American Revolution. Trade Cloth. Alfred A. Knopf Inc. New York, NY. 2006. 560p. ISBN:0-679-45471-3, ISBN13: 978-0-679-45471-7. Dewey:974.7004/9755. LCCN:2005-043582.

Audience: **g,l,u,f.** *Choice, 2006.*

Vaughan, Alden T.   **F7.V3 1995**
New England Frontier: Puritans and Indians, 1620-1675. Ed. 3. Trade Paper. University of Oklahoma Press. Norman, OK. 1995. 492p. ISBN:0-8061-2718-X, ISBN13: 978-0-8061-2718-7. Dewey:974/.02. LCCN:94-035277.

Audience: **u,f.** *B*

History > Early American

Berkhofer, Robert F. Jr.   **E98**
Salvation and the Savage: An Analysis of Protestant Missions and American Indian Response, 1787-1862. Trade Cloth. Greenwood Publishing Group, Inc. Portsmouth, NH. 1977. 186p. ISBN:0-8371-9745-7, ISBN13: 978-0-8371-9745-6. LCCN:77-022857.

Audience: **u,f.**

Calloway, Colin G.   **E78.W5C43 2003**
One Vast Winter Count: The Native American West Before Lewis and Clark. Trade Cloth. University of Nebraska Press. Lincoln, NE. 2003. 640p. History of the American West Ser. ISBN:0-8032-1530-4, ISBN13: 978-0-8032-1530-6. Dewey:978/.01. LCCN:2003-044757.

Audience: **g,l,u.** *Choice, 2004.*

Hoig, Stanley   **F396**
Tribal Wars of the Southern Plains. Trade Cloth. University of Oklahoma Press. Norman, OK. 1993. 252p. ISBN:0-8061-2463-6, ISBN13: 978-0-8061-2463-6. Dewey:976. LCCN:92-054154.

Audience: **g,l,u,f.** *Choice, 1993.*

Horsman, Reginald   **E93**
Expansion and American Indian Policy, 1783-1812. Trade Paper. University of Oklahoma Press. Norman, OK. 1992. 220p. ISBN:0-8061-2422-9, ISBN13: 978-0-8061-2422-3. Dewey:323.1197. LCCN:91-050858.

Audience: **u,f.**

Jennings, Francis   **F7J46 1976**
The Invasion of America: Indians, Colonialism, and the Cant of Conquest. Trade Paper. W. W. Norton & Company, Inc. New York, NY. 1976. 384p. Norton Library, Vol. N830 ISBN:0-393-00830-4, ISBN13: 978-0-393-00830-2. Dewey:974/.02. LCCN:76-025451.

Audience: **u,f.** *B*

Prucha, Francis P.   **F353**
Broadax and Bayonet: The Role of the United States Army in the Development of the Northwest, 1815-1860. Edward M. Coffman (Introduction by). Trade Cloth. University of Nebraska Press. Lincoln, NE. 1995. 277p. ISBN:0-8032-5151-3, ISBN13: 978-0-8032-5151-9. Dewey:977.02. LCCN:94-044363.

Audience: **u,f.**

Richter, Daniel K.   **E98.F39R53 2003**
Facing East from Indian Country: A Native History of Early America. Trade Paper. Harvard University Press. Cambridge, MA. 2003. 336p. ISBN:0-674-01117-1, ISBN13: 978-0-674-01117-5. Dewey:970/.00497.

Audience: **g,l,u,f.** *Choice, 2002.*

Ronda, James P.   **F592.7.R66 2002**
Lewis and Clark among the Indians. Ed. 2. Trade Cloth. University of Nebraska Press. Lincoln, NE. 2005. 333p. ISBN:0-8032-8990-1, ISBN13: 978-0-8032-8990-1. Dewey:917.804/2. LCCN:2002-017965.

Audience: **g,l,u,f.**

Satz, Ronald N.   **E93.S27 2002**
American Indian Policy in the Jacksonian Era. Trade Paper. University of Oklahoma Press. Norman, OK. 2002. 208p. ISBN:0-8061-3432-1, ISBN13: 978-0-8061-3432-1. Dewey:323.1/197073/09034. LCCN:2001-055696.

Audience: **u,f.**

Sheehan, Bernard W.   **E93**
Seeds of Extinction: Jeffersonian Philanthropy and the American Indian. Trade Paper. W. W. Norton & Company, Inc. New York, NY. 1974. 320p. Norton Library ISBN:0-393-00716-2, ISBN13: 978-0-393-00716-9. Dewey:970.5.

Audience: **u,f.**

Weber, David J.   **F786**
The Mexican Frontier, 1821-1846: The American Southwest under Mexico. Trade Paper. University of New Mexico Press. Albuquerque, NM. 1982. 440p. Histories of the American Frontier Ser. ISBN:0-8263-0603-9, ISBN13: 978-0-8263-0603-6. Dewey:979/.02. LCCN:82-008200.

Audience: **f.** *B*

White, Richard   **E99.A35 W48 1991**
The Middle Ground: Indians, Empires, and Republics in the Great Lakes Region, 1650-1815. Frederick E. Hoxie & Neal Salisbury (Contribution by). Cloth Text. Cambridge University Press. New York, NY. 1991. 560p. Studies in North American Indian History ISBN:0-521-37104-X, ISBN13: 978-0-521-37104-9. Dewey:305.8/97/077. LCCN:92-005045.

Audience: **l,u,f.** *Choice, 1992.*

Formats: Web: ☐   Ebook: 🄴   CD/DVD-ROM: 🐟   BCL3: *B*

History > Removal Period

Green, Michael D.   **E93**
The Politics of Indian Removal: Creek Government and Society
in Crisis. Paper Text. University of Nebraska Press. Lincoln,
NE. 1982. 237p. ISBN:0-8032-7015-1, ISBN13:
978-0-8032-7015-2. Dewey:973/.0497. LCCN:81-014670.
                                           Audience: **u,f.**

Hassrick, Royal B.   **E78.G73**
Sioux: Life and Customs of a Warrior Society. Dorothy B.
Maxwell & Cile M. Back (Contribution by). Trade Paper.
University of Oklahoma Press. Norman, OK. 1988. 394p.
Civilization of the American Indian Ser., No. 72
ISBN:0-8061-2140-8, ISBN13: 978-0-8061-2140-6.
Dewey:978/.00497. LCCN:64-011331.
                                           Audience: **g,l,u.**

Hauptman, Laurence M.   **E540.I3H38 1995**
Between Two Fires: American Indians in the Civil War. Trade
Cloth. Simon & Schuster. New York, NY. 1995. 304p.
ISBN:0-02-914180-X, ISBN13: 978-0-02-914180-9.
Dewey:973.7/3. LCCN:94-042217.
                          Audience: **g,l,u.** *Choice, 1996.*

Hauptman, Laurence M.   **E99.I7.H335 1993**
The Iroquois in the Civil War: From Battlefield to Reservation.
Trade Cloth. Syracuse University Press. Syracuse, NY. 1992.
240p. Iroquois and Their Neighbors Ser. ISBN:0-8156-0272-3,
ISBN13: 978-0-8156-0272-9. Dewey:973/.04975.
LCCN:92-003741.
                            Audience: **u,f.** *Choice, 1993.*

Hoig, Stanley   **F396**
Tribal Wars of the Southern Plains. Trade Cloth. University of
Oklahoma Press. Norman, OK. 1993. 252p.
ISBN:0-8061-2463-6, ISBN13: 978-0-8061-2463-6. Dewey:976.
LCCN:92-054154.
                          Audience: **g,l,u,f.** *Choice, 1993.*

Josephy, Alvin M. Jr.   **E470.9.J66 1993**
Civil War in the American West. Trade Paper. Knopf Publishing
Group. New York, NY. 1993. 288p. Vintage Civil War Library
ISBN:0-679-74003-1, ISBN13: 978-0-679-74003-2.
Dewey:973.7/3. LCCN:92-050622.
                                           Audience: **u,f.**

La Vere, David   **E78.S65**
Contrary Neighbors: Southern Plains and Removed Indians in
Indian Territory. Trade Paper. University of Oklahoma Press.
Norman, OK. 2001. 304p. Civilization of the American Indian
Ser., Vol. 237 ISBN:0-8061-3299-X, ISBN13:
978-0-8061-3299-0. Dewey:975/.00497.
                            Audience: **u,f.** *Choice, 2001.*

Lancaster, Jane F.   **E99.S28L35 1994**
Removal Aftershock: The Seminoles' Struggles to Survive in the
West, 1836-1866. Trade Cloth. University of Tennessee Press.
Knoxville, TN. 1994. 248p. ISBN:0-87049-845-2, ISBN13:
978-0-87049-845-9. Dewey:973/.04973. LCCN:94-000129.
                            Audience: **u,f.** *Choice, 1995.*

McLoughlin, William G.   **93-18532 [E]**
After the Trail of Tears: The Cherokees' Struggle for
Sovereignty, 1839-1880. Trade Paper. University of North
Carolina Press. Chapel Hill, NC. 1994. 456p.
ISBN:0-8078-4433-0, ISBN13: 978-0-8078-4433-5.
Dewey:973/.04975. LCCN:93-018532.
                                           Audience: **u,f.**

Phillips, George   **E78.C15P445 2004**
  Harwood
Bringing Them under Subjection: California's Tejon Indian
Reservation and Beyond, 1852-1864. Trade Cloth. University of
Nebraska Press. Lincoln, NE. 2004. 384p. ISBN:0-8032-3736-7,
ISBN13: 978-0-8032-3736-0. Dewey:979.4004/97.
LCCN:2003-059620.
                          Audience: **u,f.** *Choice, 2005.*

Satz, Ronald N.   **E93.S27 2002**
American Indian Policy in the Jacksonian Era. Trade Paper.
University of Oklahoma Press. Norman, OK. 2002. 208p.
ISBN:0-8061-3432-1, ISBN13: 978-0-8061-3432-1.
Dewey:323.1/197073/09034. LCCN:2001-055696.
                                           Audience: **u,f.**

Utley, Robert Marshall   **E81**
Frontiersmen in Blue: The United States Army and the Indian,
1848-1865. Trade Cloth. University of Nebraska Press. Lincoln,
NE. 1981. 416p. ISBN:0-8032-9550-2, ISBN13:
978-0-8032-9550-6. Dewey:973.6. LCCN:80-027796.
                                           Audience: **l,u,f.**

Utley, Robert Marshall   **E81.U747 1984**
The Indian Frontier of the American West, 1846-1890. Trade
Cloth. University of New Mexico Press. Albuquerque, NM.
1984. 347p. Histories of the American Frontier Ser.
ISBN:0-8263-0715-9, ISBN13: 978-0-8263-0715-6.
Dewey:978/.02. LCCN:83-012516.
                                           Audience: **u,f.**

Utley, Robert Marshall   **E99.D1U9**
Last Days of the Sioux Nation. Trade Cloth. Yale University
Press. Cumberland, RI. 1963. Western Americana Ser., No. 3
ISBN:0-300-01003-6, ISBN13: 978-0-300-01003-9.
Dewey:973/.00497.
                                           Audience: **u,f.**

Weeks, Philip   **E93.W39 2000**
Farewell, My Nation: The American Indian and the United
States in the Nineteenth Century. Ed. 2. Trade Cloth. Harlan
Davidson Inc. Wheeling, IL. 2000. xvi, 266p. The American
History Ser. ISBN:0-88295-956-5, ISBN13: 978-0-88295-956-6.
Dewey:973/.0497. LCCN:00-059635.
                                           Audience: **u,f.**

West, Elliott   **F596**
The Contested Plains: Indians, Goldseekers and the Rush to
Colorado. Trade Paper. University Press of Kansas. Lawrence,
KS. 2000. xxiv, 442p. ISBN:0-7006-1029-4, ISBN13:
978-0-7006-1029-7. Dewey:978.
                          Audience: **l,u,f.** *Choice, 1998.*

History > Manifest Destiny

Clark, Blue   **KF26.5**
Lone Wolf vs. Hitchcock: Treaty Rights and Indian Law at the
End of the Nineteenth Century. Trade Paper. University of
Nebraska Press. Lincoln, NE. 1999. 198p. Law in the American
West Ser. ISBN:0-8032-6401-1, ISBN13: 978-0-8032-6401-4.
Dewey:346.7304/32/08997. LCCN:94-007735.
                            Audience: **u,f.** *Choice, 1995.*

Fritz, Henry E. E93
The Movement for Indian Assimilation, 1860 to 1890. Trade Cloth. Greenwood Publishing Group, Inc. Portsmouth, NH. 1981. 244p. ISBN:0-313-22012-3, ISBN13: 978-0-313-22012-8. LCCN:81-006650.
Audience: **u,f.**

Harring, Sidney L. KF8205 .H37 1994
Crow Dog's Case: American Indian Sovereignty, Tribal Law, and United States Law in the Nineteenth Century. Frederick Hoxie & Neal Salisbury (Contribution by). Trade Paper. Cambridge University Press. New York, NY. 1994. 317p. Cambridge Studies in North American Indian History ISBN:0-521-46715-2, ISBN13: 978-0-521-46715-5. Dewey:347.30613.
Audience: **u,f.** *Choice, 1994.*

Hoig, Stanley F396
Tribal Wars of the Southern Plains. Trade Cloth. University of Oklahoma Press. Norman, OK. 1993. 252p. ISBN:0-8061-2463-6, ISBN13: 978-0-8061-2463-6. Dewey:976. LCCN:92-054154.
Audience: **g,l,u,f.** *Choice, 1993.*

Hoxie, Frederick E. E98.C89H68 2001
A Final Promise: The Campaign to Assimilate the Indians, 1880-1920. Paper Text. University of Nebraska Press. Lincoln, NE. 2001. 350p. ISBN:0-8032-7327-4, ISBN13: 978-0-8032-7327-6. Dewey:323.1/197073/09034. LCCN:2001-045002.
Audience: **g,l,u,f.**

Knight, Rolf E78.B9 K58 1996
Indians at Work: An Informal History of Native Labour in British Columbia 1858-1930. Ed. 2. Trade Paper. New Star Books, Ltd. Vancouver, BC. 1996. 398p. ISBN:0-921586-50-7, ISBN13: 978-0-921586-50-0. Dewey:331.6/9970711.
Audience: **u,f.**

McLoughlin, William G. 93-18532 [E]
After the Trail of Tears: The Cherokees' Struggle for Sovereignty, 1839-1880. Trade Paper. University of North Carolina Press. Chapel Hill, NC. 1994. 456p. ISBN:0-8078-4433-0, ISBN13: 978-0-8078-4433-5. Dewey:973/.04975. LCCN:93-018532.
Audience: **u,f.**

Mooney, James E98.R3M6 1991
The Ghost-Dance Religion and the Sioux Outbreak of 1890. Raymond J. DeMallie (Introduction by). Trade Cloth. University of Nebraska Press. Lincoln, NE. 1991. 531p. ISBN:0-8032-8177-3, ISBN13: 978-0-8032-8177-6. Dewey:299/.77. LCCN:91-024546.
Audience: **u,f.**

Prucha, Francis P. E93.P964
American Indian Policy in Crisis: Christian Reformers and the Indian, 1865-1900. Trade Cloth. University of Oklahoma Press. Norman, OK. 1976. 468p. ISBN:0-8061-1279-4, ISBN13: 978-0-8061-1279-4. Dewey:323.1/19/7073. LCCN:75-004957.
Audience: **u,f.**

Rankin, Charles E. (Editor) E83.876.L44 1996
Legacy: New Perspectives on the Battle of the Little Bighorn. Trade Paper. Montana Historical Society Press. Helena, MT. 1996. 334p. ISBN:0-917298-42-X, ISBN13: 978-0-917298-42-4. Dewey:973.8/2. LCCN:96-024512.
Audience: **g,l,u,f.**

Utley, Robert Marshall E83.866.U87 1985
Frontier Regulars: The United States Army and the Indian, 1866-1891. Trade Paper. University of Nebraska Press. Lincoln, NE. 1984. 494p. ISBN:0-8032-9551-0, ISBN13: 978-0-8032-9551-3. Dewey:973.8. LCCN:84-007484.
Audience: **u,f.** *B*

Utley, Robert Marshall E99.D1S625 1994
The Lance and the Shield: The Life and Times of Sitting Bull. UK-Trade Paper. Ballantine Books. New York, NY. 1994. 432p. ISBN:0-345-38938-7, ISBN13: 978-0-345-38938-1. Dewey:978/.004975/0092 B. LCCN:93-091086.
Audience: **g,l,u.** *Choice, 1993.*

Welch, James & Stekler, Paul E83.876 .W38 1994
Killing Custer: The Battle of the Little Big Horn and the Fate of the Plains Indians. Trade Paper. Penguin Group (USA) Inc. New York, NY. 1995. 320p. ISBN:0-14-025176-6, ISBN13: 978-0-14-025176-0. Dewey:973.8/2.
Audience: **g,l,u.**

Wickett, Murray R. F705.A1W53 2000
Contested Territory: Whites, Native Americans and African Americans in Oklahoma. Trade Cloth. Louisiana State University Press. Baton Rouge, LA. 2000. xvii, 240p. ISBN:0-8071-2584-9, ISBN13: 978-0-8071-2584-7. Dewey:976.6004/96073. LCCN:00-032122.
Audience: **u,f.** *Choice, 2001.*

Wooster, Robert E83.866.W66 1995
The Military and United States Indian Policy, 1865-1903. Trade Cloth. University of Nebraska Press. Lincoln, NE. 1995. 268p. ISBN:0-8032-9767-X, ISBN13: 978-0-8032-9767-8. Dewey:973.8. LCCN:94-043018.
Audience: **u,f.**

History > 20th Century

Abler, Tom (Editor) Z1209.2.C2 A24
Canadian Indian Bibliography Nineteen Sixty to Nineteen Seventy. Trade Cloth. University of Toronto Press. Toronto, ON. 1974. ISBN:0-8020-2092-5, ISBN13: 978-0-8020-2092-5. Dewey:971/.004/97. LCCN:73-085083.
Audience: **l,u,f.**

Banks, Dennis & Erdoes, Richard E99.C6
Ojibwa Warrior: Dennis Banks and the Rise of the American Indian Movement. Trade Paper. University of Oklahoma Press. Norman, OK. 2005. 352p. ISBN:0-8061-3691-X, ISBN13: 978-0-8061-3691-2. Dewey:977.004/97333.
Audience: **g,l,u.** *Choice, 2005.*

Brand, Johanna E99.M6A693 1993
The Life and Death of Anna Mae Aquash. Ed. 2. Trade Paper. Formac Distributing Ltd. Halifax, NS. 1978. 172p. ISBN:1-55028-422-3, ISBN13: 978-1-55028-422-5. Dewey:970/.004/97. LCCN:93-246366.
Audience: **g,l,u.**

Comeau, Pauline & Santin, Aldo E93.C715 1995
The First Canadians: A Profile of Canada's Native People Today. Ed. 2. Trade Paper. James Lorimer & Company Ltd.,

Publishers. Toronto, ON. 220p. ISBN:1-55028-478-9, ISBN13: 978-1-55028-478-2. Dewey:323.1/197071. LCCN:95-231601.

Audience: **g,l,u,f.**

Deloria, Vine Jr.   E93.A44 1985
  (Editor)
American Indian Policy in the Twentieth Century. Trade Cloth. University of Oklahoma Press. Norman, OK. 1985. 272p. ISBN:0-8061-1897-0, ISBN13: 978-0-8061-1897-0. Dewey:323.1/197/073. LCCN:85-001057.

Audience: **u,f.**

Eagle, Adam Fortunate   E78.C15E16 2002
  & Findley, Tim
Heart of the Rock: The Indian Invasion of Alcatraz. Trade Cloth. University of Oklahoma Press. Norman, OK. 2002. 232p. ISBN:0-8061-3396-1, ISBN13: 978-0-8061-3396-6. Dewey:979.4/61. LCCN:2001-048071.

Audience: **g,l,u,f.** *Choice, 2002.*

Grossman, Mark &   KF8203.36.G76 1996
  ABC-CLIO Inc. Staff, Inc
The Native American Rights Movement. Library Binding. ABC-CLIO, Inc. Santa Barbara, CA. 1996. 498p. Clio Companions Ser. ISBN:0-87436-822-7, ISBN13: 978-0-87436-822-2. Dewey:342.73/0872. LCCN:96-036782.

Audience: **g,l,u.** *Choice, 1997.*

Hauptman, Laurence M.   E99.I7.H33
The Iroquois and the New Deal. Trade Cloth. Syracuse University Press. Syracuse, NY. 1988. 276p. Iroquois and Their Neighbors Ser. ISBN:0-8156-2247-3, ISBN13: 978-0-8156-2247-5. Dewey:323.1/197. LCCN:81-021198.

Audience: **u,f.**

Hauptman, Laurence M.   E99.I7H34 1986
The Iroquois Struggle for Survival: World War II to Red Power. Paper Text. Syracuse University Press. Syracuse, NY. 1986. 384p. Iroquois and Their Neighbors Ser. ISBN:0-8156-2350-X, ISBN13: 978-0-8156-2350-2. Dewey:973/.0497. LCCN:85-022306.

Audience: **u,f.** *Choice, 1986.*

Hoxie, Frederick E.   E98.C89H68 2001
A Final Promise: The Campaign to Assimilate the Indians, 1880-1920. Paper Text. University of Nebraska Press. Lincoln, NE. 2001. 350p. ISBN:0-8032-7327-4, ISBN13: 978-0-8032-7327-6. Dewey:323.1/197073/09034. LCCN:2001-045002.

Audience: **g,l,u,f.**

Johnson, Troy   E78.C15J6115 1997
We Hold the Rock: The Indian Occupation of Alcatraz Island, 1969-1971. Trade Paper. Golden Gate National Parks Conservancy. San Francisco, CA. 1997. 64p. ISBN:1-883869-28-5, ISBN13: 978-1-883869-28-1. Dewey:979.4/61. LCCN:96-078731.

Audience: **u,f.**

Johnson, Troy R.   E78.C15A49 1994
  (Editor)
Alcatraz: Indian Land Forever. Trade Cloth. University of California, American Indian Studies Center. Los Angeles, CA. 1994. 144p. Native American Politics Ser., 4 ISBN:0-935626-41-7, ISBN13: 978-0-935626-41-4. Dewey:979.4/61. LCCN:94-077967.

Audience: **g,l,u,f.**

Johnson, Troy R.   E78.C15J612 1996
The Occupation of Alcatraz Island: Indian Self-Determination and the Rise of Indian Activism. Trade Paper. University of Illinois Press. Champaign, IL. 1996. 304p. ISBN:0-252-06585-9, ISBN13: 978-0-252-06585-9. Dewey:979.4/61. LCCN:96-004452.

Audience: **u,f.** *Choice, 1997.*

Johnson, Troy R.   E78.C15 Y68 1995
  (Editor)
You Are on Indian Land: Alcatraz Island, 1969-1971. Trade Cloth. University of California, American Indian Studies Center. Los Angeles, CA. 1995. 160p. Native American Politics Ser., 5 ISBN:0-935626-42-5, ISBN13: 978-0-935626-42-1. Dewey:979.4/61. LCCN:94-079442.

Audience: **g,l,u,f.**

Johnson, Troy R.   E78.C15J612 1996
The Occupation of Alcatraz Island: Indian Self-Determination and the Rise of Indian Activism. Donald Lee Fixico (Foreword by). Trade Cloth. University of Illinois Press. Champaign, IL. 1996. 304p. ISBN:0-252-02254-8, ISBN13: 978-0-252-02254-8. Dewey:979.4/61. LCCN:96-004452.

Audience: **u,f.** *Choice, 1997.*

Knight, Rolf   E78.B9 K58 1996
Indians at Work: An Informal History of Native Labour in British Columbia 1858-1930. Ed. 2. Trade Paper. New Star Books, Ltd. Vancouver, BC. 1996. 398p. ISBN:0-921586-50-7, ISBN13: 978-0-921586-50-0. Dewey:331.6/9970711.

Audience: **u,f.**

Matthiessen, Peter   E93.M46 1992
In the Spirit of Crazy Horse. Martin Garbus (Afterword by). Trade Paper. Penguin Group (USA) Inc. New York, NY. 1992. 688p. ISBN:0-14-014456-0, ISBN13: 978-0-14-014456-7. Dewey:305.897073. LCCN:92-127239.

Audience: **g,l,u,f.**

McCool, Daniel   KF8210.N37.M38 2002
Native Waters: Contemporary Indian Water Settlements and the Second Treaty Era. Trade Cloth. University of Arizona Press. Tucson, AZ. 2002. 260p. ISBN:0-8165-2227-8, ISBN13: 978-0-8165-2227-9. Dewey:346.7304/32. LCCN:2002-001766.

Audience: **u,f.**

Nesper, Larry   E99.C6N47 2002
The Walleye War: The Struggle for Ojibwe Spearfishing and Treaty Rights. Trade Cloth. University of Nebraska Press. Lincoln, NE. 2005. 245p. ISBN:0-8032-8380-6, ISBN13: 978-0-8032-8380-0. Dewey:639.2/1/089973. LCCN:2001-053181.

Audience: **g,l,u,f.** *Choice, 2003.*

Philp, Kenneth R.   E93
  (Editor)
Indian Self-Rule: First-Hand Accounts of Indian-White Relations from Roosevelt to Reagan. Trade Cloth. Howe Brothers. Salt Lake City, UT. 1986. 350p. Current Issues in the American West Ser., Vol. IV ISBN:0-935704-28-0, ISBN13: 978-0-935704-28-0. Dewey:323.1/197073/0904. LCCN:85-021863.

Audience: **g,l,u,f.** *Choice, 1987.*

Philp, Kenneth R.   E93.P55 1999
Termination Revisited: American Indians on the Trail to Self-Determination, 1933-1953. Cloth Text. University of Nebraska Press. Lincoln, NE. 1999. 265p. ISBN:0-8032-3723-5,

ISBN13: 978-0-8032-3723-0. Dewey:323.1/197073/09041.
LCCN:98-039667.

Audience: **u,f.** *Choice, 1999.*

Sayer, John W.   **KF224.B27S39 1997**
Ghost Dancing the Law: The Wounded Knee Trials. Trade
Cloth. Harvard University Press. Cambridge, MA. 1997. 320p.
ISBN:0-674-35433-8, ISBN13: 978-0-674-35433-3.
Dewey:973.8/6. LCCN:97-001227.

Audience: **u,f.**

Smith, Paul Chaat &   **E93.S655 1996**
  Warrior, Robert Allen
Like a Hurricane: The Indian Movement from Alcatraz to
Wounded Knee. Trade Cloth. New Press, The. New York, NY.
1996. 360p. ISBN:1-56584-316-9, ISBN13: 978-1-56584-316-5.
Dewey:979.4/61. LCCN:95-048025.

Audience: **g,l,u,f.** *Choice, 1997.*

Wallis, Michael &   **E99**
  Mankiller, Wilma
Mankiller: A Chief and Her People. Trade Paper. St. Martin's
Press. Gordonville, VA. 2000. 384p. ISBN:0-312-20662-3,
ISBN13: 978-0-312-20662-8. Dewey:973/.04975/0092 B.

Audience: **l,u,f.**

Weaver, Sally M.   **E92.W4**
Making Canadian Indian Policy: The Hidden Agenda,
1968-1970. Paper Text. University of Toronto Press. Toronto,
ON. 1980. 352p. Studies in the Structure of Power
ISBN:0-8020-6403-5, ISBN13: 978-0-8020-6403-5.
Dewey:323.1/197/071.

Audience: **u,f.**

Wilkinson, Charles   **E98.T77W546 2005**
Blood Struggle: The Rise of Modern Indian Nations. Trade
Cloth. W. W. Norton & Company, Inc. New York, NY. 2005.
384p. ISBN:0-393-05149-8, ISBN13: 978-0-393-05149-0.
Dewey:323.1197/073/09045. LCCN:2004-025221.

Audience: **g,l,u,f.**

Languages and Linguistics

Basso, Keith H.   **E99.A6B2295**
Portraits of the Whiteman: Linguistic Play and Cultural Symbols
among the Western Apache. Trade Paper. Cambridge University
Press. New York, NY. 1979. 144p. ISBN:0-521-29593-9,
ISBN13: 978-0-521-29593-2. Dewey:301.2/1. LCCN:78-031535.
Audience: **u,f.** *B*

Buechel, Eugene   **PM1024.Z9L333 2002**
Lakota Dictionary: Lakota-English/English-Lakota, New
Comprehensive Edition. University of Nebraska Press. 2005.
ISBN:0-8032-6199-3, ISBN13: 978-0-8032-6199-0.

Audience: **g,u,f.**

Fernald, Theodore B.   **PM641.A93 2000**
The Athabaskan Languages: Perspectives on a Native American
Language Family. Oxford University Press, Inc. 2000.
ISBN:0-19-511947-9, ISBN13: 978-0-19-511947-3.

Audience: **g,u,f.**

Greenberg, Joseph H.   **P376.G7 1987**
Language in the Americas. Stanford University Press. 1987.
ISBN:0-8047-1315-4, ISBN13: 978-0-8047-1315-3.

Audience: **u,f.**

Hale, Horatio   **E99.I7**
The Iroquois Book of Rites. Trade Paper. Kessinger Publishing,
LLC. Whitefish, MT. 2004. ISBN:1-4191-6770-7, ISBN13:
978-1-4191-6770-6. Dewey:974.7004976.

Audience: **g,l,u,f.**

Hinton, Leanne   **P4.5**
The Green Book of Language Revitalization in Practice: Toward
a Sustainable World. Elsevier Science & Technology Books.
2001. ISBN:0-12-349354-4, ISBN13: 978-0-12-349354-5.

Audience: **g.**

Hinton, Leanne   **PM102.S78 1998**
Studies in American Indian Languages: Description and Theory.
University of California Press. 1998. University of California
Publications in Linguistics ISBN:0-520-09789-0, ISBN13:
978-0-520-09789-6.

Audience: **u,f.**

Holton, Jim   **PM847.H65 2004**
Chinook Jargon: The Hidden Language of the Pacific Northwest.
Adisoft, Inc. 2004. ISBN:0-9674897-0-9, ISBN13:
978-0-9674897-0-4.

Audience: **g,u,f.**

Mithun, Marianne   **PM108 .L35 1999**
The Languages of Native North America. Anderson, S. R..
Cambridge University Press. 1999. Cambridge Language
Surveys Ser. ISBN:0-521-23228-7, ISBN13: 978-0-521-23228-9.
Audience: **u,f.**

Neundorf, Alyse   **PM2008.N48 2005**
Navajo/English Bilingual Dictionary. University of New Mexico
Press. 2005. ISBN:0-8263-3825-9, ISBN13: 978-0-8263-3825-9.
Audience: **g,u,f.**

Riggs, Stephen Return   **PM1021.R48 2004**
Dakota Grammar: With Texts and Ethnography. Minnesota
Historical Society Press. 2004. ISBN:0-87351-472-6, ISBN13:
978-0-87351-472-9.

Audience: **g,u,f.**

Scancarelli, Janine   **PM441.N37 2005**
  (Editor)
Native Languages of the Southeastern United States. University
of Nebraska Press. 2005. Studies in the Anthropology of North
American Indians Series ISBN:0-8032-4235-2, ISBN13:
978-0-8032-4235-7.

Audience: **l,u.**

William C Sturtevant   **E77**
  (Editor)
Handbook of North American Indians, Vol. 17: Languages.
United States Government Printing Office. 1997. Handbook of
North American Indians ISBN:0-16-048774-9, ISBN13:
978-0-16-048774-3.

Audience: **g,u,f.**

Languages and Linguistics > Language Preservation and Revitalization

Hinton, Leanne   **PM501.C2.H56 1996**
Flutes of Fire: Essays on California Indian Languages. Heyday
Books. 1994. ISBN:0-930588-62-2, ISBN13:
978-0-930588-62-5.

Audience: **g.**

Hinton, Leanne   **PB35.H56 2002**
How to Keep Your Language Alive: A Commonsense Approach
to One-on-One Language Learning. Heyday Books. 2002.
ISBN:1-890771-42-2, ISBN13: 978-1-890771-42-3.

Audience: **g.**

Hinton, Leanne   **P40.5.L356G74 2001**
Green Book of Language Revitalization in. Masoro, Edward J..
Elsevier Science & Technology Books. 2001.
ISBN:0-12-349353-6, ISBN13: 978-0-12-349353-8.

Audience: **g.**

Reyhner, Jon Allan   **PM205.S73 2003**
Nurturing Native Languages. Northern Arizona University's
Center for Excellence. 2003. ISBN:0-9670554-3-1, ISBN13:
978-0-9670554-3-5.

Audience: **g,l.**

Politics and Government

Akwesasne Notes   **E99.I7B23 2004**
(Editor)
Basic Call to Consciouness. Trade Paper, Perfect. Book
Publishing Company, The. Summertown, TN. 2005. 160p.
ISBN:1-57067-159-1, ISBN13: 978-1-57067-159-3.
Dewey:323.1/19755. LCCN:2004-005301.

Audience: **g,l,u,f.**

Banner, Stuart   **E98.L3B36 2005**
How the Indians Lost Their Land: Law and Power on the
Frontier. Trade Cloth. Harvard University Press. Cambridge,
MA. 2005. 352p. ISBN:0-674-01871-0, ISBN13:
978-0-674-01871-6. Dewey:333.2. LCCN:2005-043617.

Audience: **g,l,u,f.** *Choice, 2006.*

Brown, Brian E.   **KF8210**
Religion, Law and the Land: Native Americans and the Judicial
Interpretation of Sacred Land. Trade Cloth. Greenwood
Publishing Group, Inc. Portsmouth, NH. 1999. 208p.
Contributions in Legal Studies Ser., No. 94
ISBN:0-313-30972-8, ISBN13: 978-0-313-30972-4.
Dewey:346.7304/32/08997. LCCN:99-033830.

Audience: **u,f.**

Burnham, Philip   **E98.L3B87 2000**
Indian Country, God's Country: Native Americans and the
National Parks. Trade Cloth. Island Press. Washington, DC.
2000. 384p. ISBN:1-55963-667-X, ISBN13: 978-1-55963-667-4.
Dewey:333.78/3/089973. LCCN:99-050934.

Audience: **g,l,u,f.** *Choice, 2000.*

Calloway, Colin G.   **E92.C18 1986**
Crown and Calumet: British-Indian Relations, 1783-1815. Trade
Cloth. University of Oklahoma Press. Norman, OK. 1987. 360p.
ISBN:0-8061-2033-9, ISBN13: 978-0-8061-2033-1.
Dewey:323.1/197/071. LCCN:86-016151.

Audience: **u,f.** *Choice, 1987.*

Canby, William C.   **KF8205.Z9C36 2004**
American Indian Law in a Nutshell. Ed. 4. Trade Paper.
Foundation Press. New York, NY. 2004. 496p. Nutshell Ser.
ISBN:0-314-14640-7, ISBN13: 978-0-314-14640-3.
Dewey:342.73/0872. LCCN:2004-271008.

Audience: **g,l,u.**

Cohen, Felix S., et al.   **KF8205.C6 2005**
Felix S. Cohen's Federal Indian Law. Ed. 4. Nell Jessup Newton
& Bob Anderson (Authors). Trade Cloth. LexisNexis Matthew

Bender. Newark, NJ. 2005. xxxviii, 647p. ISBN:0-327-16444-1,
ISBN13: 978-0-327-16444-9. Dewey:342.7308/72.
LCCN:2005-021550.

Audience: **u,f.**

Comeau, Pauline &   **E93.C715 1995**
Santin, Aldo
The First Canadians: A Profile of Canada's Native People
Today. Ed. 2. Trade Paper. James Lorimer & Company Ltd.,
Publishers. Toronto, ON. 220p. ISBN:1-55028-478-9, ISBN13:
978-1-55028-478-2. Dewey:323.1/197071. LCCN:95-231601.

Audience: **g,l,u,f.**

Deloria, Vine Jr.   **E93.A44 1985**
(Editor)
American Indian Policy in the Twentieth Century. Trade Cloth.
University of Oklahoma Press. Norman, OK. 1985. 272p.
ISBN:0-8061-1897-0, ISBN13: 978-0-8061-1897-0.
Dewey:323.1/197/073. LCCN:85-001057.

Audience: **u,f.**

Deloria, Vine Jr. &   **KF8224.C6 D44 1983**
Lytle, Clifford M.
American Indians, American Justice. Trade Paper. University of
Texas Press. Austin, TX. 1983. 262p. ISBN:0-292-73834-X,
ISBN13: 978-0-292-73834-8. Dewey:347.307109.
LCCN:83-006975.

Audience: **u,f.**

Fenton, William N.   **E99.I7F453 1998**
The Great Law and the Longhouse: A Political History of the
Iroquois Confederacy. Trade Cloth. University of Oklahoma
Press. Norman, OK. 1998. 808p. Civilization of the American
Indian Ser., No. 223 ISBN:0-8061-3003-2, ISBN13:
978-0-8061-3003-3. Dewey:973/.049755. LCCN:97-019842.

Audience: **l,u,f.** *Choice, 1998.*

Green, Michael D.   **E93**
The Politics of Indian Removal: Creek Government and Society
in Crisis. Paper Text. University of Nebraska Press. Lincoln,
NE. 1982. 237p. ISBN:0-8032-7015-1, ISBN13:
978-0-8032-7015-2. Dewey:973/.0497. LCCN:81-014670.

Audience: **u,f.**

Johansen, Bruce E.   **KF8204**
(Editor)
The Encyclopedia of Native American Legal Tradition. Charles
R. Cloud (Foreword by). Cloth Text. Greenwood Publishing
Group, Inc. Portsmouth, NH. 1998. 424p. ISBN:0-313-30167-0,
ISBN13: 978-0-313-30167-4. Dewey:346.7301/3.
LCCN:97-021994.

Audience: **g,u,f.** *Choice, 1998.*

Jones, B. J.   **KF8210.C45J66 1995**
The Indian Child Welfare Act Handbook: A Legal Guide to the
Custody and Adoption of Native American Children. Trade
Paper. American Bar Association. Chicago, IL. 1995. 240p.
ISBN:1-57073-136-5, ISBN13: 978-1-57073-136-5.
Dewey:346.7301/78/08997. LCCN:94-074277.

Audience: **u,f.**

Llewellyn, Karl N. &   **KF8228.C53L59 2002**
Hoebel, E. Adamson
Cheyenne Way: Conflict and Case Law in Primitive
Jurisprudence. Trade Cloth. William S. Hein & Company, Inc.
Buffalo, NY. 2002. ix, 360p. ISBN:1-57588-717-7, ISBN13:
978-1-57588-717-3. Dewey:340.5/2. LCCN:2002-073666.

Audience: **l,u,f.**

Lyons, Oren, et al.   **E151**
Exiled in the Land of the Free: Democracy, Indian Nations and the U. S. Constitution. John Mohawk & Vine Deloria Jr. (Authors), Daniel K. Inouye & Peter Matthiessen (Contribution by). Trade Paper. Clear Light Publishers. Santa Fe, NM. 1997. 428p. ISBN:0-940666-50-2, ISBN13: 978-0-940666-50-4. Dewey:973/.00497. LCCN:91-072479.
Audience: **u,f.** *Choice, 1993.*

McNickle, D'Arcy   **E85**
Native American Tribalism: Indian Survivals and Renewals. Ed. 3. Peter J. Iverson (Editor). Trade Paper. Oxford University Press, Inc. New York, NY. 1993. 208p. ISBN:0-19-508422-5, ISBN13: 978-0-19-508422-1. Dewey:970.00497.
Audience: **u,f.**

Morrison, R. Bruce &   **E78.C2**
  Wilson, Rod
Native Peoples: The Canadian Experience. Ed. 3. Trade Paper. Oxford University Press, Inc. New York, NY. 2004. 504p. ISBN:0-19-541819-0, ISBN13: 978-0-19-541819-4. Dewey:971.004/97. LCCN:2004-299695.
Audience: **g,l,u.**

Philp, Kenneth R.   **E93**
  (Editor)
Indian Self-Rule: First-Hand Accounts of Indian-White Relations from Roosevelt to Reagan. Trade Cloth. Howe Brothers. Salt Lake City, UT. 1986. 350p. Current Issues in the American West Ser., Vol. IV ISBN:0-935704-28-0, ISBN13: 978-0-935704-28-0. Dewey:323.1/197073/0904. LCCN:85-021863.
Audience: **g,l,u,f.** *Choice, 1987.*

Pommersheim, Frank   **E93**
Braid of Feathers: American Indian Law and Contemporary Tribal Life. Trade Paper. University of California Press. Berkeley, CA. 1997. 278p. ISBN:0-520-20894-3, ISBN13: 978-0-520-20894-0. Dewey:973/.0497. LCCN:94-004846.
Audience: **u,f.** *Choice, 1995.*

Prucha, Francis P.   **E93.P964**
American Indian Policy in Crisis: Christian Reformers and the Indian, 1865-1900. Trade Cloth. University of Oklahoma Press. Norman, OK. 1976. 468p. ISBN:0-8061-1279-4, ISBN13: 978-0-8061-1279-4. Dewey:323.1/19/7073. LCCN:75-004957.
Audience: **u,f.**

Prucha, Francis P.   **G1201.E1P7 1990**
Atlas of American Indian Affairs. Cloth Text. University of Nebraska Press. Lincoln, NE. 1990. 191p. ISBN:0-8032-3689-1, ISBN13: 978-0-8032-3689-9. Dewey:912.7. LCCN:90-675000.
Audience: **g,l,u,f.** *Choice, 1991.*

Prucha, Francis P.   **Z1209.2.U5**
A Bibliographical Guide to the History of Indian-White Relations in the United States. Library Binding. University of Chicago Press. Chicago, IL. 1977. x, 454p. ISBN:0-226-68476-8, ISBN13: 978-0-226-68476-5. Dewey:016.3058/97/073. LCCN:76-016045.
Audience: **l,u,f.**

Prucha, Francis P.   **Z1209.2.U5.P67 SUPPL**
Indian-White Relations in the United States: A Bibliography of Works Published 1975-1980. Trade Cloth. University of Nebraska Press. Lincoln, NE. 1982. 179p. ISBN:0-8032-3665-4, ISBN13: 978-0-8032-3665-3. Dewey:016.3231/197073. LCCN:81-014722.
Audience: **u,f.**

Prucha, Francis P.   **E93 .P9665 1985**
The Indians in American Society: From the Revolutionary War to the Present. Trade Cloth. University of California Press. Berkeley, CA. 1985. 127p. Quantum Bks., No. 29 ISBN:0-520-05503-9, ISBN13: 978-0-520-05503-2. Dewey:973/.0497. LCCN:85-001023.
Audience: **g,l,u.** *Choice, 1986.*

Prucha, Francis Paul   **KF8205.D63 2000**
  (Editor)
Documents of United States Indian Policy. Ed. 3. Cloth Text. University of Nebraska Press. Lincoln, NE. 2000. 396p. ISBN:0-8032-3728-6, ISBN13: 978-0-8032-3728-5. Dewey:346.7301/3. LCCN:99-089969.
Audience: **u,f.**

Robertson, G. Lindsay   **KF228.U5R63 2005**
Conquest by Law. Trade Cloth. Oxford University Press, Inc. New York, NY. 2005. 272p. ISBN:0-19-514869-X, ISBN13: 978-0-19-514869-5. Dewey:346.7304/32/08997. LCCN:2004-022795.
Audience: **u,f.** *Choice, 2006.*

Rusco, Elmer R.   **KF8205.R87 2000**
A Fateful Time: Background and Legislation of the Indian Reorganization Act. Cloth Text. University of Nevada Press. Reno, NV. 2000. xv, 363p. Wilbur S. Shepperson Series in History and Humanities ISBN:0-87417-345-0, ISBN13: 978-0-87417-345-1. Dewey:323.1/197073/09. LCCN:00-008554.
Audience: **u,f.** *Choice, 2001.*

Satz, Ronald N.   **E93.S27 2002**
American Indian Policy in the Jacksonian Era. Trade Paper. University of Oklahoma Press. Norman, OK. 2002. 208p. ISBN:0-8061-3432-1, ISBN13: 978-0-8061-3432-1. Dewey:323.1/197073/09034. LCCN:2001-055696.
Audience: **u,f.**

Senese, Guy B.   **E97**
Self-Determination and the Social Education of Native Americans. Trade Cloth. Greenwood Publishing Group, Inc. Portsmouth, NH. 1991. 248p. ISBN:0-275-93776-3, ISBN13: 978-0-275-93776-8. Dewey:370/.8997. LCCN:90-020011.
Audience: **u,f.** *Choice, 1992.*

Smith, Jane F. &   **E93.N24**
  Kvasnicka, Robert M. (Editors)
Indian-White Relations: A Persistent Paradox. Trade Paper. Howard University Press. Washington, DC. 2003. 278p. ISBN:0-88258-094-9, ISBN13: 978-0-88258-094-4. Dewey:323.1/19/7073. LCCN:75-022316.
Audience: **u,f.**

Sokolow, Gary A.   **KF8203.6.S66 2000**
🄴 Native Americans and the Law: A Dictionary. E-Book. ABC-CLIO, Inc. Santa Barbara, CA. 2001. Contemporary Legal Issues Ser. ISBN:1-57607-370-X, ISBN13: 978-1-57607-370-4. Dewey:342.73/0872/03.
Audience: **g,l,u,f.** *Choice, 2001.*

Stubben, Jerry D. &   **E98.T77S78 2005**
  Sokolow, Gary A.
Native Americans and Political Participation. Raymond A. Smith (Editor). Library Binding. ABC-CLIO, Inc. Santa Barbara, CA. 2005. 310p. Political Participation in America Ser. ISBN:1-57607-262-2, ISBN13: 978-1-57607-262-2. Dewey:323/.04208997073. LCCN:2005-025405.
Audience: **u,f.**

Surtees, Robert J.   Z1209.2.C2S91982E92
Canadian Indian Policy: A Critical Bibliography. Trade Paper.
Indiana University Press. Bloomington, IN. 1982. 120p.
Newberry Library D'Arcy McNickle Center for the History of
the American Indian Bibliographical Ser. ISBN:0-253-31300-7,
ISBN13: 978-0-253-31300-3. Dewey:016.3231/197/071.
LCCN:81-048088.

Audience: **g,l,u,f.**

Sutton, Imre & Clow,   E98.T77T78 2001
  Richmond L. (Editors)
Trusteeship in Change: Toward Tribal Autonomy in Resource
Management. Trade Cloth. University Press of Colorado.
Boulder, CO. 2001. 354p. ISBN:0-87081-622-5, ISBN13:
978-0-87081-622-2. Dewey:333.7/0973. LCCN:2001-002412.
Audience: **u,f.** *Choice, 2002.*

U. S. Laws and Statutes   KF8203
  Staff, Statutes
Indian Affairs. Laws and Treaties, Vol. 5. Charles J. Kappler
(Editor). Trade Paper. Books on Demand. Ann Arbor, MI. 891p.
ISBN:0-598-51695-6, ISBN13: 978-0-598-51695-4.
Dewey:342/.73/0872. LCCN:31-003067.

Audience: **g,l,u,f.**

Valk, Barbara G.   Z1251.M44V35 1988
  (Editor)
BorderLine: A Bibliography of the United States-Mexico
Borderlands. Trade Cloth. University of California, Latin
American Center. Los Angeles, CA. 1988. 736p.
ISBN:0-87903-112-3, ISBN13: 978-0-87903-112-1.
Dewey:016.972/1. LCCN:88-004565.

Audience: **u,f.**

Wallis, Michael &   E99
  Mankiller, Wilma
Mankiller: A Chief and Her People. Trade Paper. St. Martin's
Press. Gordonville, VA. 2000. 384p. ISBN:0-312-20662-3,
ISBN13: 978-0-312-20662-8. Dewey:973/.04975/0092 B.
Audience: **l,u,f.**

Washburn, Wilcomb E.   KF8205.W38 1995
Red Man's Land/White Man's Law: The Past and Present Status
of the American Indian. Ed. 2. Trade Paper. University of
Oklahoma Press. Norman, OK. 1995. 320p.
ISBN:0-8061-2740-6, ISBN13: 978-0-8061-2740-8.
Dewey:346.7301/3. LCCN:94-038444.

Audience: **g,u,f.**

Weaver, Sally M.   E92.W4
Making Canadian Indian Policy: The Hidden Agenda,
1968-1970. Paper Text. University of Toronto Press. Toronto,
ON. 1980. 352p. Studies in the Structure of Power
ISBN:0-8020-6403-5, ISBN13: 978-0-8020-6403-5.
Dewey:323.1/197/071.

Audience: **u,f.**

Wilkins, David E.   E98.T77W545 2002
American Indian Politics and the American Political System.
Book, Other. Rowman & Littlefield Publishers, Inc. Lanham,
MD. 2001. 384p. Prismatic Politics Ser., :Race and Ethnicity in
National and Global Politics ISBN:0-8476-9306-6, ISBN13:
978-0-8476-9306-1. Dewey:323.1197/073. LCCN:2001-019738.
Audience: **u,f.** *Choice, 2002.*

Wilkinson, Charles   E98.T77W546 2005
Blood Struggle: The Rise of Modern Indian Nations. Trade
Cloth. W. W. Norton & Company, Inc. New York, NY. 2005.

384p. ISBN:0-393-05149-8, ISBN13: 978-0-393-05149-0.
Dewey:323.1197/073/09045. LCCN:2004-025221.
Audience: **g,l,u,f.**

Wilkinson, Charles F.   KF8205
American Indians, Time, and the Law: Native Societies in a
Modern Constitutional Democracy. Trade Paper. Yale University
Press. Cumberland, RI. 1988. 227p. ISBN:0-300-04136-5,
ISBN13: 978-0-300-04136-1. Dewey:347.302/872.
LCCN:86-009164.

Audience: **u,f.**

Williams, Robert A. Jr.   E93.W755 1997
Linking Arms Together: American Indian Treaty Visions of Law
and Peace, 1600-1800. Trade Cloth. Oxford University Press,
Inc. New York, NY. 1997. 202p. ISBN:0-19-506591-3, ISBN13:
978-0-19-506591-6. Dewey:342.7/3/0872. LCCN:96-023095.
Audience: **u,f.** *Choice, 1997.*

Wooster, Robert   E83.866.W66 1995
The Military and United States Indian Policy, 1865-1903. Trade
Cloth. University of Nebraska Press. Lincoln, NE. 1995. 268p.
ISBN:0-8032-9767-X, ISBN13: 978-0-8032-9767-8.
Dewey:973.8. LCCN:94-043018.

Audience: **u,f.**

Wunder, John R.   KF8205
Retained by the People: A History of American Indians and the
Bill of Rights. New York: Oxford University Press. 1994.
ISBN:0-19-505563-2, ISBN13: 978-0-19-505563-4.

Audience: **l,u,f.**

Politics and Government > Activism

Alan, John (Editor)   E184.A1
Black Brown and Red: The Movement for Freedom among
Black, Chicano, Latino, and Indian. Trade Paper. News &
Letters Committees. Chicago, IL. 1975. 78p.
ISBN:0-914441-09-4, ISBN13: 978-0-914441-09-0.
Dewey:305.800973.

Audience: **l,u.**

Banks, Dennis &   E99.C6
  Erdoes, Richard
Ojibwa Warrior: Dennis Banks and the Rise of the American
Indian Movement. Trade Paper. University of Oklahoma Press.
Norman, OK. 2005. 352p. ISBN:0-8061-3691-X, ISBN13:
978-0-8061-3691-2. Dewey:977.004/97333.
Audience: **g,l,u.** *Choice, 2005.*

Brand, Johanna   E99.M6A693 1993
The Life and Death of Anna Mae Aquash. Ed. 2. Trade Paper.
Formac Distributing Ltd. Halifax, NS. 1978. 172p.
ISBN:1-55028-422-3, ISBN13: 978-1-55028-422-5.
Dewey:970/.004/97. LCCN:93-246366.

Audience: **g,l,u.**

Deloria, Vine Jr.   E93.D35 1985
Behind the Trail of Broken Treaties: An Indian Declaration of
Independence. Trade Paper. University of Texas Press. Austin,
TX. 1985. 310p. ISBN:0-292-70754-1, ISBN13:
978-0-292-70754-2. Dewey:973/.0947. LCCN:84-051686.
Audience: **l,u,f.**

Deloria, Vine Jr.   E93.D36 1988
Custer Died for Your Sins: An Indian Manifesto. Trade Paper.
University of Oklahoma Press. Norman, OK. 1988. 292p.

ISBN:0-8061-2129-7, ISBN13: 978-0-8061-2129-1.
Dewey:973/.0497. LCCN:87-040561.

Audience: **g,l,u,f.** *B*

Eagle, Adam Fortunate   **E78.C15E16 2002**
  & Findley, Tim
Heart of the Rock: The Indian Invasion of Alcatraz. Trade
Cloth. University of Oklahoma Press. Norman, OK. 2002. 232p.
ISBN:0-8061-3396-1, ISBN13: 978-0-8061-3396-6.
Dewey:979.4/61. LCCN:2001-048071.

Audience: **g,l,u,f.** *Choice, 2002.*

Fine-Dare, Kathleen S.   **KF8210.A57F56 2002**
Grave Injustice: The American Indian Repatriation Movement
and NAGPRA. Trade Paper. University of Nebraska Press.
Lincoln, NE. 2002. 250p. Fourth World Rising Ser.
ISBN:0-8032-6908-0, ISBN13: 978-0-8032-6908-8.
Dewey:323.1/197073/09. LCCN:2002-020016.

Audience: **g,u,f.** *Choice, 2003.*

Grossman, Mark &   **KF8203.36.G76 1996**
  ABC-CLIO Inc. Staff, Inc
The Native American Rights Movement. Library Binding.
ABC-CLIO, Inc. Santa Barbara, CA. 1996. 498p. Clio
Companions Ser. ISBN:0-87436-822-7, ISBN13:
978-0-87436-822-2. Dewey:342.73/0872. LCCN:96-036782.

Audience: **g,l,u.** *Choice, 1997.*

Johnson, Troy   **E78.C15J6115 1997**
We Hold the Rock: The Indian Occupation of Alcatraz Island,
1969-1971. Trade Paper. Golden Gate National Parks
Conservancy. San Francisco, CA. 1997. 64p.
ISBN:1-883869-28-5, ISBN13: 978-1-883869-28-1.
Dewey:979.4/61. LCCN:96-078731.

Audience: **u,f.**

Johnson, Troy R.   **E78.C15A49 1994**
  (Editor)
Alcatraz: Indian Land Forever. Trade Cloth. University of
California, American Indian Studies Center. Los Angeles, CA.
1994. 144p. Native American Politics Ser., 4
ISBN:0-935626-41-7, ISBN13: 978-0-935626-41-4.
Dewey:979.4/61. LCCN:94-077967.

Audience: **g,l,u,f.**

Johnson, Troy R.   **E78.C15J612 1996**
The Occupation of Alcatraz Island: Indian Self-Determination
and the Rise of Indian Activism. Trade Paper. University of
Illinois Press. Champaign, IL. 1996. 304p. ISBN:0-252-06585-9,
ISBN13: 978-0-252-06585-9. Dewey:979.4/61.
LCCN:96-004452.

Audience: **u,f.** *Choice, 1997.*

Johnson, Troy R.   **E78.C15 Y68 1995**
  (Editor)
You Are on Indian Land: Alcatraz Island, 1969-1971. Trade
Cloth. University of California, American Indian Studies Center.
Los Angeles, CA. 1995. 160p. Native American Politics Ser., 5
ISBN:0-935626-42-5, ISBN13: 978-0-935626-42-1.
Dewey:979.4/61. LCCN:94-079442.

Audience: **g,l,u,f.**

Johnson, Troy R.   **E78.C15J612 1996**
The Occupation of Alcatraz Island: Indian Self-Determination
and the Rise of Indian Activism. Donald Lee Fixico (Foreword
by). Trade Cloth. University of Illinois Press. Champaign, IL.
1996. 304p. ISBN:0-252-02254-8, ISBN13: 978-0-252-02254-8.
Dewey:979.4/61. LCCN:96-004452.

Audience: **u,f.** *Choice, 1997.*

Johnson, Troy R., et al.   **E78.C15A2 1997**
American Indian Activism: Alcatraz to the Longest Walk. Joane
Nagel & Duane Champagn (Authors). Trade Paper. University
of Illinois Press. Champaign, IL. 1997. 304p.
ISBN:0-252-06653-7, ISBN13: 978-0-252-06653-5.
Dewey:979.4/61. LCCN:97-001877.

Audience: **u,f.**

Lyman, Stanley David,   **E99.O3L96 1991**
  et al.
e Wounded Knee 1973: A Personal Account. Floyd A. O'Neil,
June K. Lyman, Susan McKay & Alvin M. Josephy (Authors).
E-Book. NetLibrary, Inc. Boulder, CO. 1991.
ISBN:0-585-31587-6, ISBN13: 978-0-585-31587-4.
Dewey:978.3/66.

Audience: **u,f.**

Matthiessen, Peter   **E93.M46 1992**
In the Spirit of Crazy Horse. Martin Garbus (Afterword by).
Trade Paper. Penguin Group (USA) Inc. New York, NY. 1992.
688p. ISBN:0-14-014456-0, ISBN13: 978-0-14-014456-7.
Dewey:305.897073. LCCN:92-127239.

Audience: **g,l,u,f.**

Means, Russell & Wolf,   **E99.O3M386 1995**
  Marvin J.
Where White Men Fear to Tread: The Autobiography of Russell
Means. Trade Cloth. St. Martin's Press. Gordonville, VA. 1995.
608p. ISBN:0-312-13621-8, ISBN13: 978-0-312-13621-5.
Dewey:305.897/073/092 B. LCCN:95-023289.

Audience: **g,l,u,f.**

Nagel, Joane   **E98.E85**
American Indian Ethnic Renewal: Red Power and the
Resurgence of Identity and Culture. Trade Paper. Oxford
University Press, Inc. New York, NY. 1997. 320p.
ISBN:0-19-512063-9, ISBN13: 978-0-19-512063-9.
Dewey:305.8/97.

Audience: **g,l,u,f.** *Choice, 1996.*

Nesper, Larry   **E99.C6N47 2002**
The Walleye War: The Struggle for Ojibwe Spearfishing and
Treaty Rights. Trade Cloth. University of Nebraska Press.
Lincoln, NE. 2005. 245p. ISBN:0-8032-8380-6, ISBN13:
978-0-8032-8380-0. Dewey:639.2/1/089973.
LCCN:2001-053181.

Audience: **g,l,u,f.** *Choice, 2003.*

Nielsen, Nancy J.   **E89.N53 1997**
Reformers and Activists. Trade Cloth. Facts On File, Inc. New
York, NY. 1997. 128p. American Indian Lives Ser.
ISBN:0-8160-3440-0, ISBN13: 978-0-8160-3440-6. Dewey:[B].
LCCN:96-041254.

Audience: **g,l,u,f.**

Peltier, Leonard F.   **E99.O3**
Prison Writings: My Life Is My Sun Dance. Harvey Arden
(Editor), Ramsey Clark (Preface by), Chief Arvol Looking
Horse (Introduction by). Trade Paper. St. Martin's Press.
Gordonville, VA. 2000. 243p. ISBN:0-312-26380-5, ISBN13:
978-0-312-26380-5. Dewey:978.1/0049752/0092 B.

Audience: **g,l,u,f.**

Sayer, John W.   **KF224.B27S39 1997**
Ghost Dancing the Law: The Wounded Knee Trials. Trade
Cloth. Harvard University Press. Cambridge, MA. 1997. 320p.
ISBN:0-674-35433-8, ISBN13: 978-0-674-35433-3.
Dewey:973.8/6. LCCN:97-001227.

Audience: **u,f.**

Sherry, John W.   E99.N3S47 2002
Land, Wind, and Hard Words: A Story of Navajo Activism.
Trade Cloth. University of New Mexico Press. Albuquerque,
NM. 2002. 246p. ISBN:0-8263-2281-6, ISBN13:
978-0-8263-2281-4. Dewey:333.73/16/089972.
LCCN:2001-008065.

Audience: **u,f.**

Smith, Paul Chaat &   E93.S655 1996
  Warrior, Robert Allen
Like a Hurricane: The Indian Movement from Alcatraz to
Wounded Knee. Trade Cloth. New Press, The. New York, NY.
1996. 360p. ISBN:1-56584-316-9, ISBN13: 978-1-56584-316-5.
Dewey:979.4/61. LCCN:95-048025.

Audience: **g,l,u,f.** *Choice, 1997.*

Stern, Kenneth S.   KF224.B36S74 1994
Loud Hawk: The United States vs. the American Indian
Movement. Trade Cloth. University of Oklahoma Press.
Norman, OK. 1994. 384p. ISBN:0-8061-2587-X, ISBN13:
978-0-8061-2587-9. Dewey:345.7307. LCCN:93-006175.

Audience: **g,l,u,f.**

Sullivan, Robert   E99.M19S85 2000
A Whale Hunt: Two Years on the Olympic Peninsula with the
Makah and Their Canoe. Trade Cloth. Simon & Schuster. New
York, NY. 2000. ISBN:0-684-08643-3, ISBN13:
978-0-684-08643-9. Dewey:639.2/8/089979079799.
LCCN:00-030108.

Audience: **g,l,u.** *Choice, 2001.*

Politics and Government > The Federal Relationship. Sovereignty and Treaty Rights

Cadwalader, Sandra L.   E93.A34 1984
  & Deloria, Vine Jr. (Editors)
The Aggressions of Civilization: Federal Indian Policy Since the
1880s. Trade Cloth. Temple University Press. Philadelphia, PA.
1984. 272p. ISBN:0-87722-349-1, ISBN13: 978-0-87722-349-8.
Dewey:323.1/197. LCCN:84-000094.

Audience: **u,f.**

Castile   E93.C35 1998
To Show Heart: Native American Self-Determination and
Federal Indian Policy, 1960-1975. Trade Cloth. University of
Arizona Press. Tucson, AZ. 1998. 216p. ISBN:0-8165-1837-8,
ISBN13: 978-0-8165-1837-1. Dewey:323.1/197073/09046.
LCCN:97-033775.

Audience: **u,f.**

Castile, George P.   E93.C35 1998
To Show Heart: Native American Self-Determination and
Federal Indian Policy, 1960-1975. Trade Paper. University of
Arizona, Graduate Library School. Tucson, AZ. 1999. 227p.
ISBN:0-8165-1838-6, ISBN13: 978-0-8165-1838-8.
Dewey:323.1/197073/09046. LCCN:97-033775.

Audience: **u,f.**

Castile, George P. &   E93
  Bee, Robert L. (Editors)
State and Reservation: New Perspectives on Federal Indian
Policy. Trade Cloth. University of Arizona Press. Tucson, AZ.

1992. 259p. ISBN:0-8165-1319-8, ISBN13: 978-0-8165-1319-2.
Dewey:323.1/197073. LCCN:92-008229.

Audience: **u,f.** *Choice, 1993.*

Clark, Blue   KF26.5
Lone Wolf vs. Hitchcock: Treaty Rights and Indian Law at the
End of the Nineteenth Century. Trade Paper. University of
Nebraska Press. Lincoln, NE. 1999. 198p. Law in the American
West Ser. ISBN:0-8032-6401-1, ISBN13: 978-0-8032-6401-4.
Dewey:346.7304/32/08997. LCCN:94-007735.

Audience: **u,f.** *Choice, 1995.*

Cohen, Felix S.   KF8205 .A33
Felix S. Cohen's Handbook of Federal Indian Law. Trade Cloth.
University of New Mexico Press. Albuquerque, NM. 1971.
ISBN:0-8263-0205-X, ISBN13: 978-0-8263-0205-2.
Dewey:342/.73/087. LCCN:79-153935.

Audience: **u,f.**

Deloria, Vine   KF8225.I53 2002
e The Indian Reorganization Act: Congresses and Bills.
E-Book. University of Oklahoma Press. Norman, OK.
ISBN:0-8061-7979-1, ISBN13: 978-0-8061-7979-7.
Dewey:342.73/0872.

Audience: **u,f.**

Deloria, Vine Jr.   E93
  (Editor)
American Indian Policy in the Twentieth Century. Trade Paper.
University of Oklahoma Press. Norman, OK. 1992. 272p.
ISBN:0-8061-2424-5, ISBN13: 978-0-8061-2424-7.
Dewey:323.1/197/073. LCCN:85-001057.

Audience: **g,l,u,f.**

Deloria, Vine Jr.   E93.D35 1985
Behind the Trail of Broken Treaties: An Indian Declaration of
Independence. Trade Paper. University of Texas Press. Austin,
TX. 1985. 310p. ISBN:0-292-70754-1, ISBN13:
978-0-292-70754-2. Dewey:973/.0947. LCCN:84-051686.

Audience: **l,u,f.**

Deloria, Vine Jr. &   KF82021999
  DeMallie, Raymond J.
Documents of American Indian Diplomacy: Treaties,
Agreements, and Conventions, 1775-1979. Trade Cloth.
University of Oklahoma Press. Norman, OK. 1999. 1536p.
Legal History of North America Ser., Vol. 4
ISBN:0-8061-3118-7, ISBN13: 978-0-8061-3118-4.
Dewey:342.73/0872. LCCN:98-045365.

Audience: **g,u,f.** *Choice, 2000.*

Deloria, Vine Jr. &   E98.T77D44 1998
  Lytle, Clifford M.
The Nations Within: The Past and Future of American Indian
Sovereignty. Trade Paper. University of Texas Press. Austin, TX.
1998. 304p. ISBN:0-292-71598-6, ISBN13: 978-0-292-71598-1.
Dewey:323.1/197. LCCN:97-033718.

Audience: **u,f.** **B**

Deloria, Vine Jr. &   KF8210.C5D45 1999
  Wilkins, David E.
Tribes, Treaties, and Constitutional Tribulations. Trade Paper.
University of Texas Press. Austin, TX. 2000. 221p.
ISBN:0-292-71608-7, ISBN13: 978-0-292-71608-7.
Dewey:342.73/0872. LCCN:99-026402.

Audience: **u,f.** *Choice, 2000.*

Deloria, Vine &   KF8210.C5D45 1999
  Wilkins, David E.
Tribes, Treaties and Constitutional Tribulations. Trade Cloth.
University of Texas Press. Austin, TX. 1999. xi, 209p.
ISBN:0-292-71607-9, ISBN13: 978-0-292-71607-0.
Dewey:342.73/0872. LCCN:99-026402.
Audience: u,f.   Choice, 2000.

Harring, Sidney L.   KF8205 .H37 1994
Crow Dog's Case: American Indian Sovereignty, Tribal Law,
and United States Law in the Nineteenth Century. Frederick
Hoxie & Neal Salisbury (Contribution by). Trade Paper.
Cambridge University Press. New York, NY. 1994. 317p.
Cambridge Studies in North American Indian History
ISBN:0-521-46715-2, ISBN13: 978-0-521-46715-5.
Dewey:347.30613.
Audience: u,f.   Choice, 1994.

Jennings, Francis &   E93
  Fenton, William N. (Editors)
The History and Culture of Iroquois Diplomacy: An
Interdisciplinary Guide to the Treaties of the Six Nations and
Their League. Paper Text. Syracuse University Press. Syracuse,
NY. 1995. 296p. Iroquois and Their Neighbors Ser.
ISBN:0-8156-2650-9, ISBN13: 978-0-8156-2650-3.
Dewey:973/.0497.
Audience: l,u,f.

Kappler, Charles J.   KF8203 1972
  (Editor)
Indian Affairs: Laws and Treaties, Set. Library Binding. A M S
Press, Inc. New York, NY. 1971. ISBN:0-404-06710-7, ISBN13:
978-0-404-06710-6. Dewey:342/.73/087. LCCN:78-128994.
Audience: l,u,f.

Kappler, Charles J.   KF8203
  (Editor)
☐ Indian Affairs: Laws and Treaties.
http://digital.library.okstate.edu/kappler/index.htm
Audience: g,l,u,f.

Long, Carolyn N.   KF228.O74L66 2000
Religious Freedom and Indian Rights: The Case of Oregon vs.
Smith. Trade Cloth. University Press of Kansas. Lawrence, KS.
2000. xii, 324p. Landmark Law Cases and American Society
Ser. ISBN:0-7006-1063-4, ISBN13: 978-0-7006-1063-1.
Dewey:342.73/0852. LCCN:00-043652.
Audience: g,u,f.   Choice, 2001.

Mason, W. Dale   E78.N65
Indian Gaming: Tribal Sovereignty and American Politics. Trade
Paper. University of Oklahoma Press. Norman, OK. 2000. 320p.
ISBN:0-8061-3260-4, ISBN13: 978-0-8061-3260-0.
Dewey:795/.089/97.
Audience: g,u,f.

McCool, Daniel   KF8210.N37.M38 2002
Native Waters: Contemporary Indian Water Settlements and the
Second Treaty Era. Trade Cloth. University of Arizona Press.
Tucson, AZ. 2002. 260p. ISBN:0-8165-2227-8, ISBN13:
978-0-8165-2227-9. Dewey:346.7304/32. LCCN:2002-001766.
Audience: u,f.

Nesper, Larry   E99.C6N47 2002
The Walleye War: The Struggle for Ojibwe Spearfishing and
Treaty Rights. Trade Cloth. University of Nebraska Press.
Lincoln, NE. 2005. 245p. ISBN:0-8032-8380-6, ISBN13:

978-0-8032-8380-0. Dewey:639.2/1/089973.
LCCN:2001-053181.
Audience: g,l,u,f.   Choice, 2003.

Otis, Delos S.   KF5660.O85
The Dawes Act and the Allotment of Indian Lands. Francis P.
Prucha (Introduction by). Trade Paper. Books on Demand. Ann
Arbor, MI. 226p. Civilization of the American Indian Ser., No.
123 ISBN:0-8357-8088-0, ISBN13: 978-0-8357-8088-9.
Dewey:333.1/1/09701. LCCN:72-003597.
Audience: l,u,f.

Pevar, Stephen L.   KF8210.C5
The Rights of Indians and Tribes: The Authoritative ACLU
Guide to Indian and Tribal Rights, Third Edition. Ed. 3. Trade
Paper. New York University Press. New York, NY. 2004. 448p.
ISBN:0-8147-6718-4, ISBN13: 978-0-8147-6718-4.
Dewey:342.73087.
Audience: g,l,u,f.

Philp, Kenneth R.   E93.P55 1999
Termination Revisited: American Indians on the Trail to
Self-Determination, 1933-1953. Cloth Text. University of
Nebraska Press. Lincoln, NE. 1999. 265p. ISBN:0-8032-3723-5,
ISBN13: 978-0-8032-3723-0. Dewey:323.1/197073/09041.
LCCN:98-039667.
Audience: u,f.   Choice, 1999.

Porter, Robert O.   KF8205.P64 2005
Sovereignty, Colonialism, and the Future of Indigenous Nations.
Trade Cloth. Carolina Academic Press. Durham, NC. 2004.
806p. ISBN:0-89089-333-0, ISBN13: 978-0-89089-333-3.
Dewey:342.730872. LCCN:2004-112858.
Audience: u,f.

Price, Monroe E. &   KF8204.5.L38 1983
  Clinton, Robert
Law and the American Indian: Readings, Notes and Cases. Ed.
2. Trade Cloth. LEXIS Publishing. Charlottesville, VA. 1983.
885p. Contemporary Legal Education Ser. ISBN:0-87215-554-4,
ISBN13: 978-0-87215-554-1. Dewey:342.73/0872 347.3028.
Audience: u,f.

Prucha, Francis P.   JX235.9
American Indian Treaties: The History of a Political Anomaly.
Trade Paper. University of California Press. Berkeley, CA. 1997.
578p. ISBN:0-520-20895-1, ISBN13: 978-0-520-20895-7.
Dewey:341/.026673. LCCN:93-036297.
Audience: g,l,u,f.   Choice, 1995.

Prucha, Francis P.   E93.P9654 1995
The Great Father: The United States Government and the
American Indians, Set. Trade Cloth. University of Nebraska
Press. Lincoln, NE. 1995. 1302p. ISBN:0-8032-8734-8, ISBN13:
978-0-8032-8734-1. Dewey:323.1/197/073. LCCN:83-016837.
Audience: u,f.

Sharma, Parnesh   KEB529.5.H8S45 1998
Aboriginal Fishing Rights: Laws, Courts, Politics. Trade Paper.
Fernwood Publishing Company, Ltd. Peterborough, ON. 1998.
104p. ISBN:1-895686-98-9, ISBN13: 978-1-895686-98-2.
Dewey:346.71104/6956. LCCN:98-214786.
Audience: u,f.

Shattuck, George C.   KF8228.O45A3 1991
The Oneida Land Claims: A Legal History. Jack Campisi
(Foreword by), Laurence M. Hauptman (Introduction by). Paper
Text. Syracuse University Press. Syracuse, NY. 1991. 288p.
Iroquois and Their Neighbors Ser. ISBN:0-8156-2525-1,

ISBN13: 978-0-8156-2525-4. Dewey:346.7304/32/089975.
LCCN:90-022625.

Audience: **u,f.** *Choice, 1992.*

Shurts, John   **KF8210.N37S55 2000**
Indian Reserved Water Rights: The Winters Doctrine in Its
Social and Legal Context, 1880s-1930s. Trade Cloth. University
of Oklahoma Press. Norman, OK. 2000. 352p. Legal History of
North America Ser., Vol. 8 ISBN:0-8061-3210-8, ISBN13:
978-0-8061-3210-5. Dewey:346.7304/32. LCCN:99-043558.

Audience: **u,f.** *Choice, 2001.*

Vecsey, Christopher &   **KFN5940.A75I76 1988**
Starna, William A. (Editors)
Iroquois Land Claims. Cloth Text. Syracuse University Press.
Syracuse, NY. 1988. 240p. Iroquois and Their Neighbors Ser.
ISBN:0-8156-2434-4, ISBN13: 978-0-8156-2434-9.
Dewey:346.74704/32. LCCN:87-033621.

Audience: **u,f.** *Choice, 1988.*

Wilkins, David E.   **KF8205.W527 1997**
American Indian Sovereignty and the U. S. Supreme Court: The
Masking of Justice. Trade Paper. University of Texas Press.
Austin, TX. 1997. 421p. ISBN:0-292-79109-7, ISBN13:
978-0-292-79109-1. Dewey:342.73/0872. LCCN:97-001988.

Audience: **u,f.** *Choice, 1998.*

Wilkins, David &   **KF8205**
Lomawaima, Tsianina
Uneven Ground: American Indian Sovereignty and Federal Law.
Trade Paper. University of Oklahoma Press. Norman, OK. 2002.
336p. ISBN:0-8061-3395-3, ISBN13: 978-0-8061-3395-9.
Dewey:323.1197073.

Audience: **u,f.**

Literature, Music, Dance, and Film

Adamson, Joni   **PS153.I52A33 2001**
American Indian Literature, Environmental Justice, and
Ecocriticism: The Middle Place. Trade Cloth. University of
Arizona Press. Tucson, AZ. 2000. 213p. ISBN:0-8165-1791-6,
ISBN13: 978-0-8165-1791-6. Dewey:810.9/355.
LCCN:00-010360.

Audience: **g,l,u,f.** *Choice, 2001.*

Berkhofer, Robert F. Jr.   **E98.P99 B47 1979**
The White Man's Indian: Images of the American Indian from
Columbus to the Present. Trade Paper. Knopf Publishing Group.
New York, NY. 1979. 304p. ISBN:0-394-72794-0, ISBN13:
978-0-394-72794-3. Dewey:301.15/43/9700497.
LCCN:78-011047.

Audience: **g,l,u.**

Literature, Music, Dance, and Film > Literature

Alexie, Sherman   **PS3568.O243**
The Lone Ranger and Tonto Fistfight in Heaven. Library
Binding. Sagebrush Education Resources. Caledonia, MN. 1994.
ISBN:0-7857-6949-8, ISBN13: 978-0-7857-6949-1.
Dewey:813.5/4.

Audience: **g,l.**

Allen, Paula Gunn   **PS508.I5 S62**
(Editor)
Song of the Turtle: American Indian Literature, 1974-1994.
Trade Cloth. Ballantine Books. New York, NY. 1996.
ISBN:0-614-96849-6, ISBN13: 978-0-614-96849-1.
Dewey:813/.54080897.

Audience: **l,u,f.**

Birchfield, D. L.   **PS3602.I725F54 2004**
Field of Honor: A Novel. Trade Cloth. University of Oklahoma
Press. Norman, OK. 2004. 224p. American Indian Literature and
Critical Studies, Vol. 48 ISBN:0-8061-3608-1, ISBN13:
978-0-8061-3608-0. Dewey:813/.6. LCCN:2003-063448.

Audience: **g,l,u,f.**

Bruchac, Joseph   **PS591.I55.S66 1983**
(Introduction by)
Songs from This Earth on Turtle's Back: An Anthology of
Poetry by American Indian Writers. Trade Paper. Greenfield
Review Literary Center, Inc. Greenfield Center, NY. 1983. 300p.
ISBN:0-912678-58-5, ISBN13: 978-0-912678-58-0.
Dewey:811/.54/080897. LCCN:82-082420.

Audience: **l,u,f.** *B*

Cheyfitz, Eric   **PS153.I52C573 2006**
The Columbia Guide to American Indian Literatures of the
United States since 1945. Trade Cloth. Columbia University
Press. New York, NY. 2006. 448p. Columbia Guides to
Literature since 1945 Ser. ISBN:0-231-11764-7, ISBN13:
978-0-231-11764-7. Dewey:810.897/009045.
LCCN:2005-045451.

Audience: **l,u,f.**

D'Aponte, Mimi G.   **PS628.I53S48 1999**
(Editor)
Seventh Generation: An Anthology of Native American Plays.
Trade Paper. Theatre Communications Group, Inc. New York,
NY. 1998. 300p. ISBN:1-55936-147-6, ISBN13:
978-1-55936-147-7. Dewey:812/.54080897. LCCN:98-004449.

Audience: **l,u,f.**

Darby, Jaye T. &   **PS628.I53**
Fitzgerald, Stephanie (Editors)
Keepers of the Morning Star: An Anthology of Native Women's
Theater. Trade Cloth. University of California, American Indian
Studies Center. Los Angeles, CA. 2004. 386p. Native American
Theater Ser. ISBN:0-935626-56-5, ISBN13: 978-0-935626-56-8.
Dewey:812/.54080897. LCCN:2003-100128.

Audience: **l,u,f.** *Choice, 2004.*

Day, A. Grove   **PM198**
The Sky Clears: Poetry of the American Indians. Trade Cloth.
Greenwood Publishing Group, Inc. Portsmouth, NH. 1983. 218p.
ISBN:0-313-23883-9, ISBN13: 978-0-313-23883-3. Dewey:897.
LCCN:83-001576.

Audience: **l,u,f.** *B*

Erdrich, Louise   **PS3555.R42T73 1989**
Tracks. Trade Paper. HarperCollins Publishers. New York, NY.
1989. 256p. ISBN:0-06-097245-9, ISBN13: 978-0-06-097245-5.
Dewey:813/.54. LCCN:89-045123.

Audience: **g,l,u,f.** *Choice, 1988.*

Geiogamah, Hanay &   **PS628.I53**
Darby, Jaye T. (Editors)
Stories of Our Way: An Anthology of American Indian Plays.
Trade Paper. University of California, American Indian Studies
Center. Los Angeles, CA. 1999. 503p. Native American Theater

Ser., No. 1 ISBN:0-935626-50-6, ISBN13: 978-0-935626-50-6.
Dewey:812/.5080897.

Audience: **l,u,f.** *Choice, 1999.*

Geiogamah, Hanay   PS3545.I5365
  (Editor)
New Native American Drama: Three Plays. Jeffrey Huntsman
(Introduction by). Trade Paper. University of Oklahoma Press.
Norman, OK. 1980. 158p. ISBN:0-8061-1697-8, ISBN13:
978-0-8061-1697-6. Dewey:812/.54. LCCN:79-004733.

Audience: **l,u,f.** *B*

Glancy, Diane   PS3557.L294A84 2002
American Gypsy: Six Native American Plays. Trade Cloth.
University of Oklahoma Press. Norman, OK. 2002. 224p.
American Indian Literature and Critical Studies, Vol. 45
ISBN:0-8061-3456-9, ISBN13: 978-0-8061-3456-7.
Dewey:812/.54. LCCN:2002-018870.

Audience: **l,u,f.**

Glancy, Diane H.   PS3557.L294P87 1996
Pushing the Bear: A Novel of the Trail of Tears. Trade Cloth.
Harcourt Trade Publishers. New York, NY. 1996. 320p.
ISBN:0-15-100225-8, ISBN13: 978-0-15-100225-2.
Dewey:813/.54. LCCN:95-051020.

Audience: **g,l,u.**

Hobson, Geary (Editor)   PS508.I5 R4 1981
The Remembered Earth: An Anthology of Contemporary Native
American Literature. Trade Paper. University of New Mexico
Press. Albuquerque, NM. 1981. 429p. ISBN:0-8263-0568-7,
ISBN13: 978-0-8263-0568-8. Dewey:810/.8/0897.
LCCN:80-054561.

Audience: **l,u,f.**

Hogan, Linda   PS3568.O243
Mean Spirit. Trade Paper. Ballantine Books. New York, NY.
1991. 384p. ISBN:0-8041-0863-3, ISBN13: 978-0-8041-0863-8.
Dewey:813/.54.

Audience: **g,l,u,f.**

Hollander, John   PS607.A56 1993
  (Editor)
American Poetry: Melville to Stickney, American Indian Poetry,
Folk Songs and Spirituals. Trade Cloth. Library of America,
The. New York, NY. 1993. 1050p. Library of America, Vol. 67
ISBN:0-940450-78-X, ISBN13: 978-0-940450-78-3.
Dewey:811/.308. LCCN:93-010702.

Audience: **g,l,u,f.**

Kilcup, Karen   PS508.I5N374 2000
Native American Women's Writing: An Anthology c. 1800-1924.
Trade Cloth. Blackwell Publishing, Inc. Malden, MA. 2000.
464p. Anthologies Ser. ISBN:0-631-20517-9, ISBN13:
978-0-631-20517-3. Dewey:810.8/09287/08997.
LCCN:99-086315.

Audience: **l,u,f.**

King, Thomas (Editor)   PR9197.33.I53
All My Relations: An Anthology of Contemporary Canadian
Native Fiction. University of Oklahoma Press. 1992. American
Indian Literature and Critical Studies Ser., Vol. 4
ISBN:0-8061-2429-6, ISBN13: 978-0-8061-2429-2.

Audience: **g,l,u,f.**

Least Heat-Moon,   F687.C35
  William
PrairyErth: A Deep Map. Trade Paper. Houghton Mifflin
Company Trade & Reference Division. Boston, MA. 1999.

640p. ISBN:0-395-92569-X, ISBN13: 978-0-395-92569-0.
Dewey:917.81/59.

Audience: **g,l,u,f.**

McAdams, Janet   PS3563.C263I85 2000
The Island of Lost Luggage. Trade Cloth. University of Arizona
Press. Tucson, AZ. 2000. 74p. First Book Awards Ser.
ISBN:0-8165-2056-9, ISBN13: 978-0-8165-2056-5.
Dewey:813/.6. LCCN:99-050807.

Audience: **g,l,u,f.**

Momaday, N. Scott   PS3563.O47H6 1996
House Made of Dawn. Trade Cloth. University of Arizona Press.
Tucson, AZ. 1996. 212p. The Momaday Collection
ISBN:0-8165-1705-3, ISBN13: 978-0-8165-1705-3.
Dewey:813/.54. LCCN:96-031832.

Audience: **g,l,u,f.**

Momaday, N. Scott   E99.K5M64 1996
The Way to Rainy Mountain. Al Momaday (Illustrator). Trade
Cloth. University of Arizona Press. Tucson, AZ. 1996. 88p.
ISBN:0-8165-1701-0, ISBN13: 978-0-8165-1701-5.
Dewey:398.2/089/974. LCCN:96-028570.

Audience: **g,l,u,f.**

Moore, Marijo   GV953.5
Red Woman with Backward Eyes and Other Stories. Trade
Paper. Renegade Planets Publishing. Candler, NC. 2001. 96p.
ISBN:0-9654921-7-6, ISBN13: 978-0-9654921-7-1.
Dewey:796.332.

Audience: **g,l,u,f.**

Northrup, Jim   E99.C6N67 1997
The Rez Road Follies: Canoes, Casinos, Computers, and Birch
Bark Baskets. Trade Cloth. Kodansha America, Inc. New York,
NY. 1997. 208p. ISBN:1-56836-205-6, ISBN13:
978-1-56836-205-2. Dewey:818/.5409 B. LCCN:97-036078.

Audience: **g,l,u,f.**

Ortiz, Simon J.   PS3565.R77
After and Before the Lightning. Trade Cloth. University of
Arizona Press. Tucson, AZ. 1994. 127p. Sun Tracks, :An
American Indian Literary Ser. ISBN:0-8165-1448-8, ISBN13:
978-0-8165-1448-9. Dewey:813/.54. LCCN:94-005761.

Audience: **g,l,u,f.**

Ortiz, Simon J.   PS508.I5.E23 1983
Earth Power Coming: Short Fiction in Native American
Literature. Trade Paper. Dine College Press. Tsaile, AZ. 1983.
299p. ISBN:0-912586-50-8, ISBN13: 978-0-912586-50-2.
Dewey:813/.01/08897. LCCN:83-060959.

Audience: **g,l,u,f.** *B*

Parins, James W.   E99.C5R547 1991
John Rollin Ridge: His Life and Works. Trade Cloth. University
of Nebraska Press. Lincoln, NE. 2003. 260p. American Indian
Lives Ser. ISBN:0-8032-3683-2, ISBN13: 978-0-8032-3683-7.
Dewey:973/.0497502 B. LCCN:90-040464.

Audience: **u,f.** *Choice, 1991.*

Regier, Willis Goth   PS508.I5M37 2005
  (Introduction by)
Masterpieces of American Indian Literature. Trade Paper.
University of Nebraska Press. Lincoln, NE. 2005. 639p.
ISBN:0-8032-8997-9, ISBN13: 978-0-8032-8997-0.
Dewey:810.8/0897. LCCN:2004-025287.

Audience: **l,u.**

Revard, Carter   **PS501.S85 VOL.47**
Winning the Dust Bowl. Trade Cloth. University of Arizona
Press. Tucson, AZ. 2001. xvi, 212p. Sun Tracks, Vol. 47:An
American Indian Literary Ser. ISBN:0-8165-2071-2, ISBN13:
978-0-8165-2071-8. Dewey:810.8 811/.54. LCCN:00-010293.
                                        Audience: **g,l,u,f.**

Revard, Carter C.   **PS3568.E784**
An Eagle Nation. Trade Cloth. University of Arizona Press.
Tucson, AZ. 1993. 123p. Sun Tracks, Vol. 24:An American
Indian Literary Ser. ISBN:0-8165-1403-8, ISBN13:
978-0-8165-1403-8. Dewey:810.8. LCCN:93-012720.
                                        Audience: **g,l,u,f.**

Ridge, John Rollins   **PZ3.R4359 LI**
Joaquin Murieta: The Life and Adventures of Joaquin Murieta,
the Celebrated California Bandit. Paul Reilly (Editor), Yellow
Bird (As told by). Perfect. Poitin. Grass Valley, CA. 2003. 152p.
ISBN:1-59108-000-2, ISBN13: 978-1-59108-000-8.
Dewey:813.3.
                                        Audience: **g,l,u,f.**

Roemer, Kenneth M. &   **PS153.I52C36 2005**
  Porter, Joy (Editors)
The Cambridge Companion to Native American Literature.
Trade Paper, Perfect. Cambridge University Press. New York,
NY. 2005. 365p. Cambridge Companions to Literature Ser.
ISBN:0-521-52979-4, ISBN13: 978-0-521-52979-2.
Dewey:810.9/897. LCCN:2005-044298.
                              Audience: **l,u,f.** *Choice, 2006.*

Silko, Leslie Marmon   **PS3569.I44C4 1986**
Ceremony. Trade Paper. Penguin Group (USA) Inc. New York,
NY. 1986. 272p. Contemporay American Fiction Ser.
ISBN:0-14-008683-8, ISBN13: 978-0-14-008683-6.
Dewey:813'.54. LCCN:85-019216.
                              Audience: **g,l,u,f.** *B*

Silko, Leslie Marmon   **PS3569.I44**
Gardens in the Dunes. Trade Paper. Simon & Schuster. New
York, NY. 2000. 480p. ISBN:0-684-86332-4, ISBN13:
978-0-684-86332-0. Dewey:813/.54.
                                        Audience: **g,l,u,f.**

Silko, Leslie Marmon   **PS3568.O243**
Storyteller. Trade Paper. Arcade Publishing, Inc. New York, NY.
1989. 278p. ISBN:1-55970-005-X, ISBN13: 978-1-55970-005-4.
Dewey:813/.54.
                                        Audience: **g,l,u,f.**

Swann, Brian (Editor)   **E98.F6V665 2004**
Voices from Four Directions: Contemporary Translations of the
Native Literatures of North America. Trade Paper. University of
Nebraska Press. Lincoln, NE. 2005. 608p. ISBN:0-8032-9310-0,
ISBN13: 978-0-8032-9310-6. Dewey:398.2/089/97.
LCCN:2003-019698.
                              Audience: **g,l,u,f.** *Choice, 2004.*

Warrior, Robert   **PS153.I52.W37 2005**
The People and the Word: Reading Native Nonfiction. Trade
Paper, Perfect. University of Minnesota Press. Minneapolis, MN.
2005. 280p. Indigenous Americas Ser. ISBN:0-8166-4617-1,
ISBN13: 978-0-8166-4617-3. Dewey:818/.08.
LCCN:2005-013448.
                              Audience: **l,u,f.** *Choice, 2006.*

Witalec, Janet ;   **PS508.I5N38 1994**
  Chapman, Jeffery ; Giroux, Christopher
Native North American Literature : Biographical and Critical
Information on Native Writers and Orators from the United
States and Canada from Historical Times to the Present. Gale
Research. 1994. ISBN:0-8103-9898-2, ISBN13:
978-0-8103-9898-6.
                                        Audience: **g,l,u.**

Womack, Craig S.   **PS501.S85 VOL.48**
Drowning in Fire. Trade Cloth. University of Arizona Press.
Tucson, AZ. 2001. 280p. Sun Tracks, Vol. 48:An American
Indian Literary Ser. ISBN:0-8165-2167-0, ISBN13:
978-0-8165-2167-8. Dewey:810.8 s 813/.6. LCCN:2001-001221.
                                        Audience: **l,u,f.**

Yellow Robe, William S.   **PS3575.E46W48 2000**
Where the Pavement Ends: Five Native American Plays. Trade
Cloth. University of Oklahoma Press. Norman, OK. 2000. 192p.
American Indian Literature and Critical Studies Ser., Vol. 37
ISBN:0-8061-3265-5, ISBN13: 978-0-8061-3265-5.
Dewey:812/.6. LCCN:00-023468.
                                        Audience: **l,u,f.**

Literature, Music, Dance, and Film > Music

Diamond, Beverley, et al.   **ML3557.D5 1994**
Visions of Sound: Musical Instruments of First Nations
Communities in Northeastern America. M. Sam Cronk &
Franziska Von Rosen (Authors). Trade Paper. University of
Chicago Press. Chicago, IL. 1995. 240p. Chicago Studies in
Ethnomusicology ISBN:0-226-14476-3, ISBN13:
978-0-226-14476-4. Dewey:784.1974/08997. LCCN:94-010337.
                                        Audience: **g,l,u,f.**

Vander, Judith   **ML3557.V34 1997**
Shoshone Ghost Dance Religion: Poetry Songs and Great Basin
Context. Trade Cloth. University of Illinois Press. Champaign,
IL. 1997. 688p. Music in American Life Ser.
ISBN:0-252-02214-9, ISBN13: 978-0-252-02214-2.
Dewey:782.42162/974. LCCN:95-041755.
                                        Audience: **u,f.**

Wright-McLeod, Brian   **ML156.4.I5W75 2005**
The Encyclopedia of Native Music: More Than a Century of
Recordings from Wax Cylinder to the Internet. Perfect, Paper
over Boards, Dust Jacket. University of Arizona Press. Tucson,
AZ. 2005. 450p. ISBN:0-8165-2447-5, ISBN13:
978-0-8165-2447-1. Dewey:016.78162/97/00266.
LCCN:2004-023862.
                              Audience: **l,u,f.** *Choice, 2005.*

Literature, Music, Dance, and Film > Dance

Heth, Charlotte (Editor)   **E59.D35**
Native American Dance: Ceremonies and Social Traditions.
Trade Paper. Fulcrum Publishing. Golden, CO. 1993. 208p.
ISBN:1-56373-021-9, ISBN13: 978-1-56373-021-4.
Dewey:394.3/0897. LCCN:92-034969.
                              Audience: **u,f.** *Choice, 1993.*

Laubin, Reginald &   **GV1796.M35**
  Laubin, Gladys
Indian Dances of North America: Their Importance to Indian Life. Louis R. Bruce (Foreword by). Trade Paper. University of Oklahoma Press. Norman, OK. 1989. 576p. Civilization of the American Indian Ser., No.141 ISBN:0-8061-2172-6, ISBN13: 978-0-8061-2172-7. Dewey:793.3/19789. LCCN:76-040962.
    Audience: **g,l,u,f.**

Literature, Music, Dance, and Film > Film

Aleiss, Angela   **PN1995**
Making the White Man's Indian: Native Americans and Hollywood Movies. Trade Cloth. Greenwood Publishing Group, Inc. Portsmouth, NH. 2005. 232p. ISBN:0-275-98396-X, ISBN13: 978-0-275-98396-3. Dewey:791.43/652997. LCCN:2004-028188.
    Audience: **g,l,u.** *Choice, 2005.*

Aleiss, Angela   **PN1995**
Making the White Man's Indian: Native Americans and Hollywood Movies. Praeger. 2005. ISBN:0-275-98396-X, ISBN13: 978-0-275-98396-3.
    Audience: **g,l,u,f.**

Bataille, Gretchen M. &   **PN1995.9.I48**
  Silet, Charles L. (Editors)
The Pretend Indians: Images of Native Americans in the Movies. Trade Paper. Books on Demand. Ann Arbor, MI. 232p. ISBN:0-608-18795-X, ISBN13: 978-0-608-18795-2. LCCN:79-027432.
    Audience: **g,l,u,f.**

Buscombe, Edward   **PN1995.9.I48**
'Injuns!': Native Americans in the Movies. Trade Paper. Reaktion Books, Ltd. London, 2006. 272p. Reaktion Books - Locations Ser. ISBN:1-86189-279-9, ISBN13: 978-1-86189-279-9. Dewey:791.43652997.
    Audience: **g,l,u,f.**

Hilger, Michael   **PN1995.9.I48**
From Savage to Nobleman: Images of Native Americans in Film. Trade Paper. Scarecrow Press, Inc. Lanham, MD. 2002. 295p. ISBN:0-8108-4456-7, ISBN13: 978-0-8108-4456-8. Dewey:791.43/6520397. LCCN:94-042057.
    Audience: **g,l,u,f.**

Kilpatrick, Jacquelyn   **PN1995.9.I48K56 1999**
Celluloid Indians: Native Americans and Film. Paper Text. University of Nebraska Press. Lincoln, NE. 1999. 261p. ISBN:0-8032-7790-3, ISBN13: 978-0-8032-7790-8. Dewey:791.43/6520397. LCCN:99-017814.
    Audience: **g,l,u,f.** *Choice, 2000.*

Prats, A. J.   **PS374.W4P73 2002**
Invisible Natives: Myth and Identity in the American Western. Book, Other. Cornell University Press. Ithaca, NY. 2002. 344p. ISBN:0-8014-3961-2, ISBN13: 978-0-8014-3961-2. Dewey:791.43/6278. LCCN:2001-006863.
    Audience: **u,f.** *Choice, 2003.*

Rollins, Peter C. &   **PN1995.9**
  O'Connor, John E. (Editors)
Hollywood's Indian: The Portrayal of the Native American in Film. Trade Cloth. University Press of Kentucky. Lexington,

KY. 2003. 264p. ISBN:0-8131-9077-0, ISBN13: 978-0-8131-9077-8. Dewey:791.43/652997. LCCN:2004-266659.
    Audience: **g,l,u,f.**

Singer, Beverly R.   **PN1995.9.I48S56 2001**
Wiping the War Paint off the Lens: Native American Film and Video, Vol. 10. Book, Other. University of Minnesota Press. Minneapolis, MN. 2001. 136p. Visible Evidence Ser., Vol. 10 ISBN:0-8166-3160-3, ISBN13: 978-0-8166-3160-5. Dewey:791.43/6520397. LCCN:2001-001939.
    Audience: **g,l,u,f.**

Religion and Philosophy

Akwesasne Notes   **E99.I7B23 2004**
  (Editor)
Basic Call to Consciouness. Trade Paper, Perfect. Book Publishing Company, The. Summertown, TN. 2005. 160p. ISBN:1-57067-159-1, ISBN13: 978-1-57067-159-3. Dewey:323.1/19755. LCCN:2004-005301.
    Audience: **g,l,u,f.**

Albanese, Catherine L.   **BL2525**
Nature Religion in America: From the Algonkian Indians to the New Age. Martin E. Marty (Foreword by). Trade Paper. University of Chicago Press. Chicago, IL. 1991. 284p. Chicago History of American Religion Ser. ISBN:0-226-01146-1, ISBN13: 978-0-226-01146-2. Dewey:291.2/12/0973. LCCN:89-039561.
    Audience: **u,f.** *Choice, 1991.*

Beck, Peggy V.; Walters,   **E59.R38**
  Anna L. ; Fransisco, Nia
The Sacred: Ways of Knowledge, Sources of Life. Dine College Press. 1989. ISBN:0-912586-24-9, ISBN13: 978-0-912586-24-3.
    Audience: **g,l,u.**

Berkhofer, Robert F. Jr.   **E98**
Salvation and the Savage: An Analysis of Protestant Missions and American Indian Response, 1787-1862. Trade Cloth. Greenwood Publishing Group, Inc. Portsmouth, NH. 1977. 186p. ISBN:0-8371-9745-7, ISBN13: 978-0-8371-9745-6. LCCN:77-022857.
    Audience: **u,f.**

Brown, Brian E.   **KF8210**
Religion, Law and the Land: Native Americans and the Judicial Interpretation of Sacred Land. Trade Cloth. Greenwood Publishing Group, Inc. Portsmouth, NH. 1999. 208p. Contributions in Legal Studies Ser., No. 94 ISBN:0-313-30972-8, ISBN13: 978-0-313-30972-4. Dewey:346.7304/32/08997. LCCN:99-033830.
    Audience: **u,f.**

Collins, John J.   **E98.R3C69 1990**
Native American Religions: A Geographical Survey. Trade Cloth. Edwin Mellen Press, The. Lewiston, NY. 1991. 393p. Native American Studies, Vol. 1 ISBN:0-88946-483-9, ISBN13: 978-0-88946-483-4. Dewey:299/.7. LCCN:90-033942.
    Audience: **l,u,f.**

Deloria, Vine Jr.   **E93.D36 1988**
Custer Died for Your Sins: An Indian Manifesto. Trade Paper. University of Oklahoma Press. Norman, OK. 1988. 292p. ISBN:0-8061-2129-7, ISBN13: 978-0-8061-2129-1. Dewey:973/.0497. LCCN:87-040561.
    Audience: **g,l,u,f.** *B*

Deloria, Vine Jr   **BL262**
Evolution, Creationism, and Other Modern Myths: A Critical
Inquiry. Trade Paper. Fulcrum Publishing. Golden, CO. 2004.
320p. ISBN:1-55591-458-6, ISBN13: 978-1-55591-458-5.
Dewey:291.1/75.
Audience: **u,f.**

Deloria, Vine Jr.   **BL2776.D44 2003**
God Is Red: A Native View of Religion. Ed. 30. Trade Paper.
Fulcrum Publishing. Golden, CO. 2003. 352p.
ISBN:1-55591-498-5, ISBN13: 978-1-55591-498-1.
LCCN:2003-006477.
Audience: **g,l,u,f.**

Deloria, Vine Jr.   **E98.P5D45 1999**
Spirit and Reason: The Vine Deloria, Jr. Reader. Barbara
Deloria, Kristen Foehner & Sam Scinta (Editors). Trade Cloth.
Fulcrum Publishing. Golden, CO. 1999. 400p.
ISBN:1-55591-430-6, ISBN13: 978-1-55591-430-1.
Dewey:970/.00497. LCCN:99-030110.
Audience: **u,f.**

Gulliford, Andrew   **E159.5**
Sacred Objects and Sacred Places: Preserving Tribal Traditions.
Trade Cloth. University Press of Colorado. Boulder, CO. 2000.
307p. ISBN:0-87081-579-2, ISBN13: 978-0-87081-579-9.
Dewey:973/.1.
Audience: **g,l,u,f.** *Choice, 2001.*

Hale, Horatio   **E99.I7**
The Iroquois Book of Rites. Trade Paper. Kessinger Publishing,
LLC. Whitefish, MT. 2004. ISBN:1-4191-6770-7, ISBN13:
978-1-4191-6770-6. Dewey:974.7004976.
Audience: **g,l,u,f.**

Long, Carolyn N.   **KF228.O74L66 2000**
Religious Freedom and Indian Rights: The Case of Oregon vs.
Smith. Trade Cloth. University Press of Kansas. Lawrence, KS.
2000. xii, 324p. Landmark Law Cases and American Society
Ser. ISBN:0-7006-1063-4, ISBN13: 978-0-7006-1063-1.
Dewey:342.73/0852. LCCN:00-043652.
Audience: **g,u,f.** *Choice, 2001.*

Martin, Joel W.   **E98.R3M333 2001**
The Land Looks After Us: A History of Native American
Religion. Trade Paper. Oxford University Press, Inc. New York,
NY. 2001. 172p. ISBN:0-19-514586-0, ISBN13:
978-0-19-514586-1. Dewey:299/.7/09. LCCN:00-066583.
Audience: **u,f.**

Miller, Christopher L.   **E78.C64M55 2003**
Prophetic Worlds: Indians and Whites on the Columbia Plateau.
Chris Friday (Foreword by). Trade Paper. University of
Washington Press. Seattle, WA. 2003. 192p.
ISBN:0-295-98302-7, ISBN13: 978-0-295-98302-8.
Dewey:979.7/02. LCCN:2003-040226.
Audience: **u,f.**

Mooney, James   **E98.R3M6 1991**
The Ghost-Dance Religion and the Sioux Outbreak of 1890.
Raymond J. DeMallie (Introduction by). Trade Cloth. University
of Nebraska Press. Lincoln, NE. 1991. 531p.
ISBN:0-8032-8177-3, ISBN13: 978-0-8032-8177-6.
Dewey:299/.77. LCCN:91-024546.
Audience: **u,f.**

Niehardt, John G. &   **E99.03B48 2000**
Elk, Nicholas Black
Black Elk Speaks: Being the Life Story of a Holy Man of the
Oglala Sioux. Ed. 21. Standing Bear (Illustrator), Vine Deloria
Jr. (Introduction by). Trade Cloth. University of Nebraska Press.
Lincoln, NE. 2000. 300p. ISBN:0-8032-1309-3, ISBN13:
978-0-8032-1309-8. Dewey:978.004/9752 B. LCCN:00-036382.
Audience: **g,l,u,f.**

Prucha, Francis P.   **E93.P964**
American Indian Policy in Crisis: Christian Reformers and the
Indian, 1865-1900. Trade Cloth. University of Oklahoma Press.
Norman, OK. 1976. 468p. ISBN:0-8061-1279-4, ISBN13:
978-0-8061-1279-4. Dewey:323.1/19/7073. LCCN:75-004957.
Audience: **u,f.**

Sullivan, Lawrence   **E98.R3N39 2000**
(Editor)
Native Religions and Cultures of North America: Anthropology
of the Sacred. Trade Cloth. Continuum International Publishing
Group, Ltd. London, 2000. 249p. Anthropology of the Sacred
Ser. ISBN:0-8264-1084-7, ISBN13: 978-0-8264-1084-9.
Dewey:299/.7. LCCN:99-049012.
Audience: **u,f.** *Choice, 2001.*

Underhill, Ruth M.   **E98.R3**
Red Man's Religion: Beliefs and Practices of the Indians North
of Mexico. Trade Paper. University of Chicago Press. Chicago,
IL. 1972. 312p. ISBN:0-226-84167-7, ISBN13:
978-0-226-84167-0. Dewey:299.7. LCCN:65-024985.
Audience: **g,l,u,f.**

Versluis, Arthur   **E98.R3**
Native American Tradition. Trade Cloth. Element Books, Inc.
Boston, MA. 1994. 96p. ISBN:1-85230-572-X, ISBN13:
978-1-85230-572-7. Dewey:299.7.
Audience: **g,l,u,f.**

Wardwell, Allen   **E78.N78W283 1996**
Tangible Visions: Northwest Coast Indian Shamanism and Its
Art. Trade Cloth. Monacelli Press, Inc. New York, NY. 1996.
352p. ISBN:1-885254-16-4, ISBN13: 978-1-885254-16-0.
Dewey:704/.03972. LCCN:95-024157.
Audience: **g,l,u,f.**

Health and Medicine

     RA408.I49
☐ Native Health Databases.
http://hsc.unm.edu/library/nhd/
Audience: **g,l,u,f.**

Alvord, Lori Arviso &   **RD27.35.A45 A3**
Van Pelt, Elizabeth Cohen
The Scalpel and the Silver Bear: The First Navajo Woman
Surgeon Combines Western Medicine and Traditional Healing.
Trade Paper. Bantam Books. New York, NY. 2000. 224p.
ISBN:0-553-37800-7, ISBN13: 978-0-553-37800-9.
Dewey:617/.092/273.
Audience: **g,u,f.**

Dixon, Mim &   **RA448.5.IP766 2001**
Roubideaux, Yvette (Editors)
Promises to Keep: Public Health Policy for American Indians
and Alaska Natives in the 21st Century. Trade Cloth. American

Public Health Association Publications. Washington, DC. 2001. xxi, 311p. ISBN:0-87553-024-9, ISBN13: 978-0-87553-024-6. Dewey:362.1/089/97073. LCCN:2001-093396.

Audience: **u,f.**

Lux, Maureen   **RA412.5.C3**
Medicine That Walks: Medicine, Disease and Canadian Plains Aboriginal People, 1880-1945. Cloth over Boards. University of Toronto Press. Toronto, ON. 2001. 288p. ISBN:0-8020-4728-9, ISBN13: 978-0-8020-4728-1. Dewey:362.1/089/970712.

Audience: **g,u,f.** *Choice, 2002.*

National Library of
Medicine
☐ American Indian Health : An Informational Portal for and about the Health of Native Peoples of the United States.
http://americanindianhealth.nlm.nih.gov/

Audience: **g,l,u,f.**

Rhoades, Everett R.   **RA448.5.I5**
American Indian Health: Innovations in Health Care, Promotion, and Policy. Trade Paper. Johns Hopkins University Press. Baltimore, MD. 2002. 488p. ISBN:0-8018-6904-8, ISBN13: 978-0-8018-6904-4. Dewey:362.1/089/97073.

Audience: **u,f.** *Choice, 2001.*

Trafzer, Clifford E.   **E98.M4M43 2001**
Medicine Ways: Disease, Health, and Survival among Native Americans. Diane Weiner (Editor). Trade Paper. AltaMira Press. Walnut Creek, CA. 2001. 324p. Contemporary Native American Communities Ser., Vol. 5 ISBN:0-7425-0255-4, ISBN13: 978-0-7425-0255-0. LCCN:00-055867.

Audience: **u,f.**

U.S. Commission on   **KF8210**
Civil Rights
☐ Broken Promises: Evaluating the Native American Health Care System.
http://www.usccr.gov/pubs/nahealth/nabroken.pdf

Audience: **g,u,f.**

U.S. Department of   **RA448.5.I5**
Health and Human Services
☐ Indian Health Service.
http://www.ihs.gov/

Audience: **g,l,u,f.**

Vernon, Irene S.   **RA448.5.I5V47 2001**
Killing Us Quietly: Native Americans and HIV/AIDS. Trade Cloth. University of Nebraska Press. Lincoln, NE. 2001. 176p. ISBN:0-8032-4668-4, ISBN13: 978-0-8032-4668-3. Dewey:362.1/969792/0097073. LCCN:2001-027440.

Audience: **u,f.** *Choice, 2002.*

Vogel, Virgil J.   **E59.M4**
American Indian Medicine. Ed. 2. Trade Paper. University of Oklahoma Press. Norman, OK. 1990. 622p. Civilization of the American Indian Ser., Vol. 95 ISBN:0-8061-2293-5, ISBN13: 978-0-8061-2293-9. Dewey:615.882097. LCCN:69-010626.

Audience: **g,u,f.**

Anthropology and Archeology

Ames, Kenneth M. &   **E78.N78**
Maschner, Herbert D.
Peoples of the Northwest Coast: Their Archaeology and Prehistory. Trade Cloth. Thames & Hudson. New York, NY. 1999. 272p. ISBN:0-500-05091-0, ISBN13: 978-0-500-05091-0. Dewey:979/.00497. LCCN:98-060253.

Audience: **u,f.**

Biolsi, Thomas &   **E76.6.I53 1997**
Zimmerman, Larry J. (Editors)
Indians and Anthropologists: Vine Deloria, Jr., and the Critique of Anthropology. Trade Cloth. University of Arizona Press. Tucson, AZ. 1997. 240p. ISBN:0-8165-1606-5, ISBN13: 978-0-8165-1606-3. Dewey:301/.01. LCCN:96-045804.

Audience: **u,f.** *Choice, 1997.*

Bourque, Bruce J.   **E78**
Twelve Thousand Years: American Indians in Maine. Steven L. Cox & Ruth H. Whitehead (Contribution by). Trade Cloth. University of Nebraska Press. Lincoln, NE. 2005. 369p. ISBN:0-8032-6231-0, ISBN13: 978-0-8032-6231-7. Dewey:974.1. LCCN:00-064779.

Audience: **u,f.** *Choice, 2002.*

Bragdon, Kathleen J.   **E78.E2B72 2005**
The Columbia Guide to American Indians of the Northeast. Trade Paper. Columbia University Press. New York, NY. 2005. 352p. ISBN:0-231-11453-2, ISBN13: 978-0-231-11453-0. Dewey:974.00497.

Audience: **g,l,u,f.**

Briggs, Jean L.   **HQ734**
Never in Anger: Portrait of an Eskimo Family. Trade Paper. Harvard University Press. Cambridge, MA. 1970. 416p. ISBN:0-674-60828-3, ISBN13: 978-0-674-60828-3. Dewey:301.42/7. LCCN:75-105368.

Audience: **g,l,u,f.**

Cole, Douglas   **E78.N78C63 1995**
Captured Heritage: The Scramble for the Northwest Coast Artifacts. Trade Paper. University of Oklahoma Press. Norman, OK. 1995. 392p. ISBN:0-8061-2777-5, ISBN13: 978-0-8061-2777-4. Dewey:704/.03972. LCCN:95-035735.

Audience: **u,f.** *Choice, 1985.*

Driver, Harold E.   **E77**
Indians of North America. Ed. 2. Trade Paper. University of Chicago Press. Chicago, IL. 1969. 650p. ISBN:0-226-16467-5, ISBN13: 978-0-226-16467-0. Dewey:970.1. LCCN:79-076207.

Audience: **g,l,u,f.**

Drucker, Philip   **E78.A3D78 1991**
The Native Brotherhoods: Modern Intertribal Organizations on the Northwest Coast. Paper Text. Native American Book Publishers. Hamburg, MI. 1992. 200p. Bureau of American Ethnology Ser. ISBN:1-878592-27-0, ISBN13: 978-1-878592-27-9. Dewey:303.48/2711. LCCN:91-017406.

Audience: **u,f.**

Fitzhugh, William W. &   **GN635.S5C752 1988**
  Chaussonnet, Valerie (Editors)
Anthropology of the North Pacific Rim. Trade Cloth.
Smithsonian Institution Press. Washington, DC. 1994. 368p.
ISBN:1-56098-202-0, ISBN13: 978-1-56098-202-9.
Dewey:306.091823. LCCN:92-038689.

                                             Audience: **u,f.**

Gordon, Bryan   **E78.N79**
People of Sunlight and Starlight: Barrenland Archaeology in the
Northwest Territories. Trade Paper. Canadian Museum of
Civilization/Musee Canadien des Civilisations. Gatineau, PQ.
1996. 300p. Mercury Ser., ASC No. 154 ISBN:0-660-15963-5,
ISBN13: 978-0-660-15963-8. Dewey:930.1097192.

                                 Audience: **u,f.** *Choice, 1997.*

Griffin-Pierce, Trudy   **E78.S7G76 2000**
Native Peoples of the Southwest. Trade Cloth. University of
New Mexico Press. Albuquerque, NM. 2000. xv, 439p.
ISBN:0-8263-1907-6, ISBN13: 978-0-8263-1907-4.
Dewey:979.004/97. LCCN:00-008872.

                                           Audience: **g,l,u,f.**

Hale, Horatio   **E99.I7**
The Iroquois Book of Rites. Trade Paper. Kessinger Publishing,
LLC. Whitefish, MT. 2004. ISBN:1-4191-6770-7, ISBN13:
978-1-4191-6770-6. Dewey:974.7004976.

                                           Audience: **g,l,u,f.**

Hassrick, Royal B.   **E78.G73**
Sioux: Life and Customs of a Warrior Society. Dorothy B.
Maxwell & Cile M. Back (Contribution by). Trade Paper.
University of Oklahoma Press. Norman, OK. 1988. 394p.
Civilization of the American Indian Ser., No. 72
ISBN:0-8061-2140-8, ISBN13: 978-0-8061-2140-6.
Dewey:978/.00497. LCCN:64-011331.

                                           Audience: **g,l,u.**

Hyde, George E.   **E78.W5 H97**
Indians of the High Plains: From the Prehistoric Period to the
Coming of Europeans. Paper Text. Textbook Publishers.
Temecula, CA. 2003. 231p. ISBN:0-7581-1735-3, ISBN13:
978-0-7581-1735-9. Dewey:970.1.

                                           Audience: **g,l,u,f.**

Jenness, Diamond   **E78.C2**
The Indians of Canada. Ed. 7. Trade Paper. University of
Toronto Press. Toronto, ON. 1977. 750p. ISBN:0-8020-6326-8,
ISBN13: 978-0-8020-6326-7. Dewey:971/.004/97.

                                           Audience: **g,l,u,f.**

Johansen, Bruce E.   **KF8204**
  (Editor)
The Encyclopedia of Native American Legal Tradition. Charles
R. Cloud (Foreword by). Cloth Text. Greenwood Publishing
Group, Inc. Portsmouth, NH. 1998. 424p. ISBN:0-313-30167-0,
ISBN13: 978-0-313-30167-4. Dewey:346.7301/3.
LCCN:97-021994.

                                 Audience: **g,u,f.** *Choice, 1998.*

Josephy, Alvin M. Jr.   **E103**
America in 1492: The World of the Indian Peoples Before the
Arrival of Columbus. UK-Trade Paper. Knopf Publishing Group.
New York, NY. 1993. 496p. ISBN:0-679-74337-5, ISBN13:
978-0-679-74337-8. Dewey:970.01/1. LCCN:92-056363.

                                           Audience: **g,l,u.**

Kluckhohn, Clyde &   **E99.N3 K54 1974**
  Leighton, Dorothea C.
The Navaho. Lucy Kluckhohn (Foreword by). Trade Paper.
Harvard University Press. Cambridge, MA. 1973. 374p. Harvard
Paperbacks Ser. ISBN:0-674-60603-5, ISBN13:
978-0-674-60603-6. Dewey:979.1/3/00497. LCCN:62-006779.

                                           Audience: **g,l,u,f.**

Kroeber, A. L.   **E78.C15**
Handbook of the Indians of California. Trade Cloth. Scholarly
Press, Inc. Saint Clair Shores, MI. 1972. 1024p.
ISBN:0-403-00369-5, ISBN13: 978-0-403-00369-3.
Dewey:979.4/00497. LCCN:75-108501.

                                             Audience: **u,f.**

Landes, Ruth   **E51 .C7**
Ojibwa Woman. Trade Cloth. A M S Press, Inc. New York, NY.
Columbia University, Contributions to Anthropology Ser., Vol.
31 ISBN:0-404-50581-3, ISBN13: 978-0-404-50581-3.
Dewey:301.41/2. LCCN:70-082362.

                                           Audience: **g,l,u,f.**

Llewellyn, Karl N. &   **KF8228.C53L59 2002**
  Hoebel, E. Adamson
Cheyenne Way: Conflict and Case Law in Primitive
Jurisprudence. Trade Cloth. William S. Hein & Company, Inc.
Buffalo, NY. 2002. ix, 360p. ISBN:1-57588-717-7, ISBN13:
978-1-57588-717-3. Dewey:340.5/2. LCCN:2002-073666.

                                           Audience: **l,u,f.**

McEwan, Bonnie G.   **E78.S65I52 2000**
  (Editor)
Indians of the Greater Southeast: Historic Archaeology and
Ethnohistory. Trade Cloth. University Press of Florida.
Gainesville, FL. 2000. xvi, 336p. ISBN:0-8130-1778-5, ISBN13:
978-0-8130-1778-5. Dewey:975/.00497. LCCN:99-049534.

                                 Audience: **g,l,u,f.** *Choice, 2001.*

Mooney, James   **E98.R3M6 1991**
The Ghost-Dance Religion and the Sioux Outbreak of 1890.
Raymond J. DeMallie (Introduction by). Trade Cloth. University
of Nebraska Press. Lincoln, NE. 1991. 531p.
ISBN:0-8032-8177-3, ISBN13: 978-0-8032-8177-6.
Dewey:299/.77. LCCN:91-024546.

                                             Audience: **u,f.**

Morgan, Lewis H.   **E99.I7**
The League of the Iroquois. Paper Text. Classic Textbooks.
Murrieta, CA. 1922. 465p. ISBN:1-4047-5160-2, ISBN13:
978-1-4047-5160-6. Dewey:970.3.

                                           Audience: **l,u,f.**

Morrison, R. Bruce &   **E78.C2**
  Wilson, Rod
Native Peoples: The Canadian Experience. Ed. 3. Trade Paper.
Oxford University Press, Inc. New York, NY. 2004. 504p.
ISBN:0-19-541819-0, ISBN13: 978-0-19-541819-4.
Dewey:971.004/97. LCCN:2004-299695.

                                           Audience: **g,l,u.**

Murdock, George P. &   **Z1209.2.N67 M87**
  O'Leary, Timothy J.
Ethnographic Bibliography of North America. Ed. 4. Trade
Cloth. Human Relations Area Files Press, Inc. New Haven, CT.
1975. Bibliographies Ser. ISBN:0-318-53458-4, ISBN13:
978-0-318-53458-9. Dewey:016.97/0004/97. LCCN:75-017091.

                                           Audience: **l,u,f.**

Opler, Morris E.   E99.A6 C46 1983
Apache Odyssey: A Journey Between Two Worlds. Louise S. Spindler & George D. Spindler (Editors). Paper Text. Irvington Publishers. New York, NY. 1983. 320p. Case Studies in Cultural Anthropology ISBN:0-8290-1267-2, ISBN13: 978-0-8290-1267-5. Dewey:970.004/97. LCCN:82-023355.
Audience: **g,l,u,f.**

Parker, Arthur C.   E99.I7
Parker on the Iroquois: Iroquois Uses of Maize and Other Food Plants. William N. Fenton (Editor). Trade Paper. Syracuse University Press. Syracuse, NY. 1981. 478p. ISBN:0-8156-0115-8, ISBN13: 978-0-8156-0115-9. Dewey:970.3. LCCN:68-031036.
Audience: **l,u,f.**

Perttula, Timothy K.   E99.C13 P47
The Caddo Nation: Archaeological and Ethnohistoric Perspectives. Ed. 2. Thomas R. Hester (Foreword by). Trade Paper. University of Texas Press. Austin, TX. 1997. 352p. Texas Archaeology and Ethnohistory Ser. ISBN:0-292-76574-6, ISBN13: 978-0-292-76574-0. Dewey:976/.01.
Audience: **u,f.**

Quimby, George Irving   E78.G7 Q5
Indian Life in the Upper Great Lakes, 11,000 B C to a D 1800. Paper Text. Textbook Publishers. Temecula, CA. 2003. 182p. ISBN:0-7581-2910-6, ISBN13: 978-0-7581-2910-9. Dewey:970.477.
Audience: **g,l,u,f.**

Radin, Paul   E99.W7B56 1999
Crashing Thunder: The Autobiography of an American Indian. Trade Paper. University of Michigan Press. Chicago, IL. 1999. 256p. Ann Arbor Paperbacks Ser. ISBN:0-472-08632-4, ISBN13: 978-0-472-08632-0. Dewey:978.2/0049752 B. LCCN:99-023924.
Audience: **g,l,u,f.**

Rohner, Ronald P. &   E99.K9
  Bettauer, Evelyn C.
The Kwakiutl: Indians of British Columbia. Paper Text. Waveland Press, Inc. Prospect Heights, IL. 1986. 111p. ISBN:0-88133-225-9, ISBN13: 978-0-88133-225-4. Dewey:970.3.
Audience: **g,l,u,f.**

Speck, Frank G.   Q11.C95 NO. 23
Iroquois. Ed. 2. Robert T. Hatt (Foreword by). Trade Paper. Cranbrook Institute of Science. Bloomfield Hills, MI. 1955. 95p. Bulletin Ser., No. 23 ISBN:0-87737-007-9, ISBN13: 978-0-87737-007-9. Dewey:970.3. LCCN:46-002147.
Audience: **g,l,u,f.**

Sullivan, Lawrence   E98.R3N39 2000
  (Editor)
Native Religions and Cultures of North America: Anthropology of the Sacred. Trade Cloth. Continuum International Publishing Group, Ltd. London, 2000. 249p. Anthropology of the Sacred Ser. ISBN:0-8264-1084-7, ISBN13: 978-0-8264-1084-9. Dewey:299/.7. LCCN:99-049012.
Audience: **u,f.** *Choice, 2001.*

Swanton, John R.   E85
The Indian Tribes of North America. Trade Paper. Smithsonian Institution Press. Washington, DC. 1985. 726p. Classics of Smithsonian Anthropology Ser. ISBN:0-87474-179-3, ISBN13: 978-0-87474-179-7. Dewey:970.004/97. LCCN:52-061970.
Audience: **g,l,u,f.**

Tedlock, Barbara   E99.Z9T425 2001
The Beautiful and the Dangerous: Encounters with the Zuni Indians. Trade Cloth. University of New Mexico Press. Albuquerque, NM. 2001. 336p. ISBN:0-8263-2342-1, ISBN13: 978-0-8263-2342-2. Dewey:978.9004/979. LCCN:00-042316.
Audience: **g,l,u,f.**

Thompson, Laura   E0099.H7
The Hopi Way: By Laura Thompson and Alice Joseph. Trade Paper. Books on Demand. Ann Arbor, MI. 155p. Indian Education Research Ser., Vol. 1 ISBN:0-598-98966-8, ISBN13: 978-0-598-98966-6. LCCN:45-001110.
Audience: **g,l,u,f.**

Underhill, Ruth M.   E99.P9U314 1991
Life in the Pueblos. Willard W. Beatty (Editor). Trade Paper. Gibbs Smith, Publisher. Layton, UT. 1991. 168p. ISBN:0-941270-68-8, ISBN13: 978-0-941270-68-7. Dewey:979/.00497. LCCN:90-085644.
Audience: **g,l,u,f.** *Choice, 1992.*

Wallace, Anthony F.   E99.S3
The Death and Rebirth of the Seneca. Trade Paper. Knopf Publishing Group. New York, NY. 1972. 416p. ISBN:0-394-71699-X, ISBN13: 978-0-394-71699-2. Dewey:970.3.
Audience: **g,l,u,f.**

Weslager, Clinton A.   E99.D2 W39
The Delaware Indians: A History. Paper Text. Rutgers University Press. Piscataway, NJ. 1990. 570p. ISBN:0-8135-1494-0, ISBN13: 978-0-8135-1494-9. Dewey:970.3.
Audience: **g,l,u,f.**

Wilson, Edmund   E99.I7
Apologies to the Iroquois: The Iroquois and Their Neighbors. William N. Fenton (Introduction by). Trade Paper. Syracuse University Press. Syracuse, NY. 1992. 356p. Iroquois and Their Neighbors Ser. ISBN:0-8156-2564-2, ISBN13: 978-0-8156-2564-3. Dewey:305.897/5.
Audience: **g,l,u,f.**

Witherspoon, Gary   E99
Navajo Kinship and Marriage. Trade Paper. University of Chicago Press. Chicago, IL. 1996. 145p. Native American Studies in Anthropology ISBN:0-226-90418-0, ISBN13: 978-0-226-90418-4. Dewey:301.42/1/0979.
Audience: **u,f.** *B*

Anthropology and Archeology > Repatriation

Fine-Dare, Kathleen S.   KF8210.A57F56 2002
Grave Injustice: The American Indian Repatriation Movement and NAGPRA. Trade Paper. University of Nebraska Press. Lincoln, NE. 2002. 250p. Fourth World Rising Ser. ISBN:0-8032-6908-0, ISBN13: 978-0-8032-6908-8. Dewey:323.1/197073/09. LCCN:2002-020016.
Audience: **g,u,f.** *Choice, 2003.*

Women and Gender

Awiakta, Marilou   E99.C5 A95 1993
Selu: Seeking the Corn-Mother's Widsom. Mary Adair (Illustrator), Wilma P. Mankiller (Foreword by). Trade Cloth.

Fulcrum Publishing. Golden, CO. 1993. 352p.
ISBN:1-55591-144-7, ISBN13: 978-1-55591-144-7.
Dewey:299/.785. LCCN:93-026645.

Audience: **g,l.**

Bataille, Gretchen M. &   **E98.W8B38 2001**
  Lisa, Laurie (Editors)
Native American Women: A Biographical Dictionary. Ed. 2.
Paper over Boards. Routledge. New York, NY. 2001. 384p.
Biographical Dictionaries of Minority Women Ser.
ISBN:0-415-93020-0, ISBN13: 978-0-415-93020-8.
Dewey:920.72/08997. LCCN:2001-019749.

Audience: **l,u,f.** *Choice, 2001, 1993.*

Bataille, Gretchen M. &   **PS366.A35**
  Sands, Kathleen M.
American Indian Women: Telling Their Lives. Trade Paper.
University of Nebraska Press. Lincoln, NE. 1984. 209p.
ISBN:0-8032-6082-2, ISBN13: 978-0-8032-6082-5.
Dewey:818/.08. LCCN:83-010234.

Audience: **u,f.** *B*

Harjo, Joy (Editor)   **PS508.I5R38 1997**
Reinventing the Enemy's Language: Contemporary Native
Women's Writings of North America. W. W. Norton & Co..
1997. ISBN:0-393-04029-1, ISBN13: 978-0-393-04029-6.

Audience: **g,l,u.**

Hill, Sarah H.   **E99.C5H68 1997**
Weaving New Worlds: Southeastern Cherokee Women and Their
Basketry. Trade Cloth. University of North Carolina Press.

Chapel Hill, NC. 1997. 440p. ISBN:0-8078-2345-7, ISBN13:
978-0-8078-2345-3. Dewey:746.41/2/0899755.
LCCN:96-047882.

Audience: **g,l,u,f.** *Choice, 1997.*

Landes, Ruth   **E51 .C7**
Ojibwa Woman. Trade Cloth. A M S Press, Inc. New York, NY.
Columbia University, Contributions to Anthropology Ser., Vol.
31 ISBN:0-404-50581-3, ISBN13: 978-0-404-50581-3.
Dewey:301.41/2. LCCN:70-082362.

Audience: **g,l,u,f.**

Minesuah, Devon   **E98.W8M54 2003**
  Abbott
Indigenous American Women: Decolonization, Empowerment,
Activism. Cloth Text. University of Nebraska Press. Lincoln,
NE. 2003. 288p. Contemporary Indigenous Issues Ser.
ISBN:0-8032-3227-6, ISBN13: 978-0-8032-3227-3.
Dewey:305.48/897073. LCCN:2002-028767.

Audience: **u,f.**

Roscoe, Will (Editor)   **E98.S48R67 1998**
Changing Ones: Third and Fourth Genders in Native North
America. Trade Cloth. Palgrave Macmillan. New York, NY.
1998. 334p. ISBN:0-312-17539-6, ISBN13: 978-0-312-17539-9.
Dewey:305.308997. LCCN:97-041762.

Audience: **g,l,u,f.** *Choice, 1998.*

Audience: g=general, l=lower division undergraduate, u=upper division undergraduate, f=faculty.

705

URBAN STUDIES

Urban Studies is new to Resources for College Libraries. The Urban Studies section identifies approximately 400 titles that form a core collection appropriate for a four-year college. Materials are primarily intended to meet the needs of students and faculty. The collection of titles is intended to reflect the multi-disciplinary nature of Urban Studies as well as the breadth of topics and approaches that characterize the field. Titles have been selected from a variety of areas that address urban concerns including sociology, history, anthropology, geography, political and policy science, economics, and planning.

The Urban Studies section is limited to English-language titles. It includes major works from the history of urban studies although the emphasis is on recent works. Out-of-print sources, dated sources, and textbooks have not been included except in the case of highly influential works. Web sites have been selected based on their currency, reputation of the agencies that created them, and intended audience.

— Scott Johnston

Reference Works

Z7165.U5

☐ The Index to Current Urban Documents (ICUD).
http://www.urbdocs.com/
Greenwood Publishing Group, Inc.

Audience: **l,u,f.**

☐ Infoshare Online.
http://www.infoshare.org/
Community Studies of New York, Inc.

Audience: **l,u,f.**

☐ Urban Studies & Planning: A SAGE Full-Text Collection.
http://www.sagefulltext.com/
SAGE.

Audience: **l,u,f.**

Caves, Roger W.   **HT108.5**
(Editor)
Encyclopedia of the City. Paper over Boards. Routledge. New York, NY. 2005. XXX, 578p. ISBN:0-415-25225-3, ISBN13: 978-0-415-25225-6. Dewey:307.76/03. LCCN:2004-051142.
Audience: **l,u,f.** *Choice, 2006.*

Marley, David F.   **E18**
Historic Cities of the Americas: An Illustrated Encyclopedia. Library Binding. ABC-CLIO, Inc. Santa Barbara, CA. 2005. 500p. ISBN:1-57607-027-1, ISBN13: 978-1-57607-027-7. Dewey:307.76/097. LCCN:2005-019012.
Audience: **l,u,f.** *Choice, 2006.*

Ness, Immanuel   **HT108.5.N47 1999**
Encyclopedia of World Cities, Set. Library Binding, Trade Cloth. M. E. Sharpe Inc. Armonk, NY. 1998. 768p. ISBN:0-7656-8017-3, ISBN13: 978-0-7656-8017-4. Dewey:307.76/03. LCCN:98-029844.
Audience: **l,u,f.** *Choice, 1999.*

Rusk, David   **HT123.R84 2003**
Cities Without Suburbs: A Census 2000 Edition. Ed. 3. Trade Cloth. Woodrow Wilson Center Press. Washington, DC. 2003. 150p. ISBN:1-930365-13-6, ISBN13: 978-1-930365-13-1. Dewey:307.76/0973. LCCN:2003-006734.
Audience: **l,u,f.**

Shumsky, Neil Larry   **HT123.E5 1998**
ⓔ Encyclopedia of Urban America: The Cities and Suburbs. E-Book. ABC-CLIO, Inc. Santa Barbara, CA. 2002. ISBN:1-57607-500-1, ISBN13: 978-1-57607-500-5. Dewey:307.76/0973/03.
Audience: **l,u,f.**

Van Vliet, Willem   **HD7287.E53 1998**
(Editor)
The Encyclopedia of Housing. Trade Cloth. SAGE Publications, Inc. Thousand Oaks, CA. 1998. 736p. ISBN:0-7619-1332-7, ISBN13: 978-0-7619-1332-0. Dewey:363.5/03. LCCN:98-008949.
Audience: **l,u,f.** *Choice, 1998.*

Vogel, Ronald K.   **HT110**
(Editor)
Handbook of Research on Urban Politics and Policy in the United States, Vol. 28, no. 13. Cloth Text. Greenwood Publishing Group, Inc. Portsmouth, NH. 1997. 464p.

ISBN:0-313-29166-7, ISBN13: 978-0-313-29166-1. Dewey:307.76/0973. LCCN:96-005786.
Audience: **l,u,f.** *Choice, 1997.*

Urban Theory

Benjamin, Walter   **PT2603.E455P33513**
The Arcades Project. Howard Eiland & Kevin McLaughlin (Translators). Trade Cloth. Harvard University Press. Cambridge, MA. 1999. 1088p. ISBN:0-674-04326-X, ISBN13: 978-0-674-04326-8. Dewey:944/.361081. LCCN:99-027615.
Audience: **u,f.** *Choice, 2000.*

Berman, Marshall   **CB425.B458**
All That Is Solid Melts into Air: The Experience of Modernity. Trade Paper. Analytical Psychology Club of San Francisco, Inc. San Francisco, CA. 2000. 416p. ISBN:1-85984-311-5, ISBN13: 978-1-85984-311-6. Dewey:909.82.
Audience: **u,f.** ℬ

Bridge, Gary & Watson,   **HT111.B53 2002**
Sophie (Editors)
The Blackwell City Reader. Trade Cloth. Blackwell Publishing, Inc. Malden, MA. 2002. 600p. Blackwell Readers in Geography Ser. ISBN:0-631-22513-7, ISBN13: 978-0-631-22513-3. Dewey:307.76. LCCN:2002-022630.
Audience: **l,u,f.**

Buck-Morss, Susan   **PT2603.E455**
The Dialectics of Seeing: Walter Benjamin and the Arcades Project. Trade Paper. MIT Press. Cambridge, MA. 1991. 505p. Studies in Contemporary German Social Thought Ser. ISBN:0-262-52164-4, ISBN13: 978-0-262-52164-2. Dewey:193.
Audience: **u,f.** *Choice, 1990.*

Dear, Michael   **HT384.U52L674 2000**
The Postmodern Urban Condition. Trade Paper. Blackwell Publishing, Inc. Malden, MA. 2000. 352p. ISBN:0-631-20988-3, ISBN13: 978-0-631-20988-1. Dewey:307.76/09794/94. LCCN:99-043567.
Audience: **l,u,f.** *Choice, 2000.*

Dear, Michael J.   **HT384.U52L673 2001**
(Editor)
From Chicago to L. A.: Making Sense of Urban Theory. Paper Text. SAGE Publications, Inc. Thousand Oaks, CA. 2001. 456p. ISBN:0-7619-2095-1, ISBN13: 978-0-7619-2095-3. Dewey:307.76/0973. LCCN:2001-000421.
Audience: **l,u,f.** *Choice, 2002.*

Gottdiener, M.   **GN406.G67 1995**
Postmodern Semiotics: Material Culture and the Forms of Postmodern Life. Trade Cloth. Blackwell Publishing, Inc. Malden, MA. 1995. 240p. ISBN:0-631-19215-8, ISBN13: 978-0-631-19215-2. Dewey:306. LCCN:94-014114.
Audience: **u,f.**

Gregory, Derek, et al.   **G70.D379 2006**
David Harvey: A Critical Reader. Noel Castree & Gareth Schott (Authors). Trade Cloth. Blackwell Publishing, Inc. Malden, MA. 2006. 336p. Antipode Book Ser. ISBN:0-631-23509-4, ISBN13: 978-0-631-23509-5. Dewey:910/.01. LCCN:2005-013795.
Audience: **u,f.**

Audience: g=general, l=lower division undergraduate, u=upper division undergraduate, f=faculty.

709

Hanssen, Beatrice   B3209.B58
Walter Benjamin and the Arcades Project. Trade Cloth.
Continuum International Publishing Group, Ltd. London, 2004.
256p. Walter Benjamin Studies ISBN:0-8264-6386-X, ISBN13:
978-0-8264-6386-9. Dewey:193.

Audience: **u,f.**

Lefebvre, Henri   HT151.L375 2003
The Urban Revolution. Trade Cloth. University of Minnesota
Press. Minneapolis, MN. 2003. 176p. ISBN:0-8166-4159-5,
ISBN13: 978-0-8166-4159-8. Dewey:307.76.
LCCN:2002-015036.

Audience: **l,u,f.**

Lefebvre, Henri & Le   HT153.L345 1996
  Bas, Elizabeth
Writings on Cities. Eleonore Kofman (Editor). Trade Paper.
Blackwell Publishing, Inc. Malden, MA. 1995. 264p.
ISBN:0-631-19188-7, ISBN13: 978-0-631-19188-9.
Dewey:307.76. LCCN:95-012470.

Audience: **l,u,f.**

Lefebvre, Henri   BD621
The Production of Space. Donald Nicholson-Smith (Translator).
Trade Paper. Blackwell Publishing, Inc. Malden, MA. 1991.
464p. ISBN:0-631-18177-6, ISBN13: 978-0-631-18177-4.
Dewey:114. LCCN:90-021058.

Audience: **u,f.** *Choice, 1992.*

Low, Setha M.   HT119.T44 1999
Theorizing the City: The New Urban Anthropology Reader.
Trade Paper. Rutgers University Press. Piscataway, NJ. 2004.
432p. ISBN:0-8135-2720-1, ISBN13: 978-0-8135-2720-8.
Dewey:307.76. LCCN:99-017712.

Audience: **l,u,f.**

Short, John Rennie   HT151.S414 2006
Urban Theory: A Critical Assessment. Cloth over Boards.
Palgrave Macmillan. New York, NY. 2006. 272p.
ISBN:1-4039-0658-0, ISBN13: 978-1-4039-0658-8.
Dewey:307.76. LCCN:2006-043255.

Audience: **l,u,f.**

Tonkiss, Fran   HT110
Space, City and Social Theory. Trade Paper. Polity Press.
Cambridge, 2006. 176p. ISBN:0-7456-2826-5, ISBN13:
978-0-7456-2826-4. Dewey:307.76.

Audience: **l,u,f.**

Urban History

Abbott, Carl   F595.A24 1993
The Metropolitan Frontier: Cities in the Modern American West.
Trade Cloth. University of Arizona Press. Tucson, AZ. 1993.
244p. Modern American West Ser. ISBN:0-8165-1129-2,
ISBN13: 978-0-8165-1129-7. Dewey:978.033.
LCCN:93-011035.

Audience: **u,f.** *Choice, 1994.*

Anderson, Kay J.   FC3847.9.C5
Vancouver's Chinatown: Racial Discourse in Canada,
1875-1980. Trade Paper. McGill-Queen's University Press.
Montreal, PQ. 1995. 336p. ISBN:0-7735-1329-9, ISBN13:
978-0-7735-1329-7. Dewey:305.8951071133.

Audience: **u,f.** *Choice, 1992.*

Artibise, A. F.   HN110.W5
Winnipeg: A Social History of Urban Growth, 1874-1914. Trade
Cloth. McGill-Queen's University Press. Montreal, PQ. 1975.
400p. ISBN:0-7735-0202-5, ISBN13: 978-0-7735-0202-4.
Dewey:309.1/7127/402. LCCN:75-325419.

Audience: **u,f.** *B*

Banti, Luisa   DG223.B313
The Etruscan Cities and Their Culture. Erika Bizzari
(Translator). Trade Cloth. University of California Press.
Berkeley, CA. 1974. ISBN:0-520-01910-5, ISBN13:
978-0-520-01910-2. Dewey:913.37/5.

Audience: **u,f.**

Bayor, Ronald H.   F294.A89N424
Race and the Shaping of Twentieth-Century Atlanta. Trade
Paper. University of North Carolina Press. Chapel Hill, NC.
2000. 350p. Fred W. Morrison Series in Southern Studies
ISBN:0-8078-4898-0, ISBN13: 978-0-8078-4898-2.
Dewey:305.8/009758/231. LCCN:95-039552.

Audience: **f.** *Choice, 1996.*

Beauregard, Robert A.   HT123.B33 2002
Voices of Decline: The Postwar Fate of U. S. Cities. Ed. 2.
Paper over Boards. Routledge. New York, NY. 2002. 320p.
ISBN:0-415-93237-8, ISBN13: 978-0-415-93237-0.
Dewey:307.76/0973. LCCN:2002-069661.

Audience: **u,f.**

Boatwright, Mary   DG295.B62 2000
  Taliaferro
Hadrian and the Cities of the Roman Empire. Trade Cloth.
Princeton University Press. Princeton, NJ. 2000. 262p.
ISBN:0-691-04889-4, ISBN13: 978-0-691-04889-5.
Dewey:937.07/092 B. LCCN:99-041096.

Audience: **u,f.** *Choice, 2000.*

Bodnar, John E.   E184.A1B59 1985
The Transplanted: A History of Immigrants in Urban America.
Cloth Text. Indiana University Press. Bloomington, IN. 1985.
320p. Interdisciplinary Studies in History ISBN:0-253-31347-3,
ISBN13: 978-0-253-31347-8. Dewey:305.8/00973.
LCCN:84-048041.

Audience: **l,u,f.** *B* *Choice, 1985.*

Boyd, Herb   F128.68.H3H33 2003
The Harlem Reader: A Celebration of New York's Most Famous
Neighborhood, from the Renaissance Years to the 21st Century.
Trade Paper. Crown Publishing Group. New York, NY. 2003.
336p. ISBN:1-4000-4681-5, ISBN13: 978-1-4000-4681-2.
Dewey:974.7/1. LCCN:2002-151280.

Audience: **u,f.**

Briggs, Asa   HT133
Victorian Cities. Andrew Lees & Lynn H. Lees (Introduction
by). Trade Paper. University of California Press. Berkeley, CA.
1993. 411p. Classics in Urban History Ser., Vol. 2
ISBN:0-520-07922-1, ISBN13: 978-0-520-07922-9.
Dewey:307.7/6/0942/09034. LCCN:92-030443.

Audience: **g,l,u,f.**

Brodsky, Alyn   E748.L23B76 2003
The Great Mayor: Fiorello La Guardia and the Making of the
City of New York. Cloth over Boards. St. Martin's Press.
Gordonville, VA. 2003. 544p. ISBN:0-312-28737-2, ISBN13:
978-0-312-28737-5. Dewey:974.7/1042/092.
LCCN:2003-041007.

Audience: **u,f.**

Burns, Thomas S. &   HT114.U725 2001
Eadie, John W.
Urban Centers and Rural Contexts in Late Antiquity. Trade
Paper. Michigan State University Press. East Lansing, MI. 2001.
xxvii, 379p. ISBN:0-87013-585-6, ISBN13: 978-0-87013-585-9.
Dewey:307.76/0937. LCCN:00-013228.

Audience: **u,f.**

Burrows, Edwin G. &   F128.3.W35 1998
Wallace, Mike
Gotham: A History of New York City to 1898. Trade Cloth.
Oxford University Press, Inc. New York, NY. 1998. 1,408p. The
History of NYC Ser. ISBN:0-19-511634-8, ISBN13:
978-0-19-511634-2. Dewey:974.7/1. LCCN:97-039308.
Audience: **u,f.** *Choice, 1999.*

Cannato, Vincent J.   F128.54.L55
The Ungovernable City: John Lindsay and His Struggle to Save
New York. Trade Paper. Basic Books. New York, NY. 2002.
720p. ISBN:0-465-00844-5, ISBN13: 978-0-465-00844-5.
Dewey:974.7104309.

Audience: **u,f.**

Caro, Robert A.   NA9085.M68
The Power Broker: Robert Moses and the Fall of New York.
Trade Cloth. Alfred A. Knopf Inc. New York, NY. 1974. 1336p.
ISBN:0-394-48076-7, ISBN13: 978-0-394-48076-3.
Dewey:974.7/04/0924 B. LCCN:73-020751.
Audience: **l,u,f.** *B*

Carrillo, Francisco   HT255.K66 2005
Javier (Editor)
Knowledge Cities: Approaches, Experiences, and Perspectives.
Audio, Other. Elsevier Science & Technology Books. Saint
Louis, MO. 2005. 312p. ISBN:0-7506-7941-7, ISBN13:
978-0-7506-7941-1. Dewey:307.76/01/1. LCCN:2005-022281.
Audience: **l,u,f.**

Cassis, Youssef &   HG3881
Bussiere, Eric
London and Paris As International Finance Centres, 1890-2000.
Trade Cloth. Oxford University Press, Inc. New York, NY. 2005.
382p. ISBN:0-19-926949-1, ISBN13: 978-0-19-926949-5.
Dewey:332.1/5/094210904. LCCN:2004-024144.

Audience: **u,f.**

Celik, Zeynep (Editor),   NA9053.S7S82 1994
et al.
Streets: Critical Perspectives on Public Space. Diane Favro &
Richard Ingersoll (Editors), Spiro Kostof (Introduction by).
Trade Paper. University of California Press. Berkeley, CA. 1996.
302p. ISBN:0-520-20528-6, ISBN13: 978-0-520-20528-4.
Dewey:711/.4.
Audience: **l,u,f.** *Choice, 1995.*

Cerchiai, Luca, et al.   DG55.M3C4713 2004
The Greek Cities of Magna Graecia and Sicily. Lorena Jannelli
& Fausto Longo (Authors). Trade Cloth. Oxford University
Press, Inc. New York, NY. 2004. 288p. Antiquities Ser.
ISBN:0-89236-751-2, ISBN13: 978-0-89236-751-1.
Dewey:937/.701. LCCN:2003-023715.

Audience: **u,f.**

Clark, Dennis   F158.9.I6 C55 1981
The Irish in Philadelphia: Ten Generations of Urban Experience.
Trade Paper. Temple University Press. Philadelphia, PA. 1982.
264p. ISBN:0-87722-227-4, ISBN13: 978-0-87722-227-9.
Dewey:974.8/110049162. LCCN:81-018343.
Audience: **u,f.** *B*

Cohen, Lizabeth   HC110.C6C537 2004
A Consumers' Republic: The Politics of Mass Consumption in
Postwar America. Trade Paper. Knopf Publishing Group. New
York, NY. 2003. 576p. ISBN:0-375-70737-9, ISBN13:
978-0-375-70737-7. Dewey:339.4/7/0973. LCCN:2002-141599.
Audience: **l,u,f.**

Connolly, James J.   F73.5.C745 1998
The Triumph of Ethnic Progressivism: Urban Political Culture in
Boston, 1900-1925. Trade Cloth. Harvard University Press.
Cambridge, MA. 1998. 272p. ISBN:0-674-90950-X, ISBN13:
978-0-674-90950-2. Dewey:974.4/61. LCCN:97-038662.
Audience: **u,f.** *Choice, 1999.*

Cronon, William   F548.4 .C85
Nature's Metropolis: Chicago and the Great West. Trade Paper.
W. W. Norton & Company, Inc. New York, NY. 1992. 592p.
ISBN:0-393-30873-1, ISBN13: 978-0-393-30873-0.
Dewey:977.3/11/03.
Audience: **g,l,u,f.** *Choice, 1991.*

Demand, Nancy H.   DF261.T3
Thebes in the Fifth Century. Trade Cloth. Routledge. New York,
NY. 1983. 208p. States and Cities of Ancient Greece Ser.
ISBN:0-7100-9288-1, ISBN13: 978-0-7100-9288-5.
Dewey:938/.4. LCCN:82-016702.

Audience: **u,f.**

Denton, Sally & Morris,   F849.L35D46 2001
Roger
The Money and the Power: The Making of Las Vegas and Its
Hold on America, 1947-2000. Trade Cloth. Alfred A. Knopf Inc.
New York, NY. 2001. 496p. ISBN:0-375-40130-X, ISBN13:
978-0-375-40130-5. Dewey:979.3/135. LCCN:00-062011.
Audience: **l,u,f.** *Choice, 2001.*

Deutsch, Sarah Jane   HQ1439.B7
Women and the City: Gender, Space, and Power in Boston,
1870-1940. Trade Paper. Oxford University Press, Inc. New
York, NY. 2002. 400p. ISBN:0-19-515864-4, ISBN13:
978-0-19-515864-9. Dewey:305.4/09744/61.
Audience: **l,u,f.** *Choice, 2000.*

Drake, St. Clair &   F548.9.N4 D73 1993
Cayton, Horace R.
Black Metropolis: A Study of Negro Life in a Northern City.
William Julius Wilson (Foreword by), Richard Wright
(Introduction by). Trade Paper. University of Chicago Press.
Chicago, IL. 1993. 910p. ISBN:0-226-16234-6, ISBN13:
978-0-226-16234-8. Dewey:305.896/073077311.
LCCN:93-012615.
Audience: **l,u,f.** *B*

Dyos, H. J. & Wolff,   DA533
Michael (Editors)
The Victorian City: Images and Realities, Vol. 2. Trade Cloth.
Routledge. New York, NY. 1973. 1001p. ISBN:0-7100-7383-6,
ISBN13: 978-0-7100-7383-9. Dewey:941/.081.
LCCN:73-076088.
Audience: **l,u,f.** *B*

Esslinger, Dean R.   F534.S7.E77
Immigrants and the City: Ethnicity and Mobility in a 19th
Century Midwestern City. Trade Cloth. Associated Faculty
Press, Inc. New York, NY. 1975. xii, 156p.
ISBN:0-8046-9108-8, ISBN13: 978-0-8046-9108-6.
Dewey:301.32/9/77289. LCCN:75-015947.
Audience: **u,f.** *B*

Fogelson, Robert M.   HT123.F64 2001
Downtown: Its Rise and Fall, 1880-1950. Cloth over Boards.
Yale University Press. Cumberland, RI. 2001. 492p.
ISBN:0-300-09062-5, ISBN13: 978-0-300-09062-8.
Dewey:307.3/3316/0973. LCCN:2001-001628.
Audience: u,f. Choice, 2002.

Fogelson, Robert M.   F869.L857 F64 1993
The Fragmented Metropolis: Los Angeles, 1850-1930. Trade
Paper. University of California Press. Berkeley, CA. 1993. 396p.
Classics in Urban History Ser., Vol. 3 ISBN:0-520-08230-3,
ISBN13: 978-0-520-08230-4. Dewey:979.494.
LCCN:92-029078.
Audience: u,f.

Fong, Timothy P.   F869.M7F68 1994
The First Suburban Chinatown: The Remaking of Monterey
Park, California. Trade Cloth. Temple University Press.
Philadelphia, PA. 1994. 240p. Asian American History and
Culture Ser. ISBN:1-56639-123-7, ISBN13: 978-1-56639-123-8.
Dewey:979.4/93. LCCN:93-020562.
Audience: l,u,f.

Formisano, Ronald P.   F73
Boston, Seventeen Hundred to Nineteen Eighty: The Evolution
of Urban Politics. Constance K. Burns (Editor). Trade Cloth.
Greenwood Publishing Group, Inc. Portsmouth, NH. 1984. 296p.
Contributions in American History Ser., No. 106
ISBN:0-313-23336-5, ISBN13: 978-0-313-23336-4.
Dewey:320.9744/61. LCCN:83-018415.
Audience: u,f.

Fradkin, Philip L.   F869.S357 F735
The Great Earthquake and Firestorms of 1906: How San
Francisco Nearly Destroyed Itself. Trade Paper. University of
California Press. Berkeley, CA. 2006. 435p.
ISBN:0-520-24820-1, ISBN13: 978-0-520-24820-5.
Dewey:979.4/6103. LCCN:2004-018506.
Audience: l,u,f. Choice, 2006.

Frugoni, Chiara   N5975.F7813 1991
A Distant City: Images of Urban Experience in the Medieval
World. William McCuaig (Translator). Trade Cloth. Princeton
University Press. Princeton, NJ. 1991. 250p.
ISBN:0-691-04083-4, ISBN13: 978-0-691-04083-7.
Dewey:709/.02. LCCN:90-008876.
Audience: u,f. Choice, 1991.

Frykenberg, Robert E.   DS486.D3D44 1986
(Editor)
Delhi Through the Ages: Essays in Urban History, Culture and
Society. Cloth Text. Oxford University Press, Inc. New York,
NY. 1988. 564p. ISBN:0-19-561728-2, ISBN13:
978-0-19-561728-3. Dewey:954/.56. LCCN:86-900004.
Audience: l,u,f. Choice, 1989.

Garcia, Matthew   F869.L89A253 2002
A World of Its Own: Race, Labor, and Citrus in the Making of
Greater Los Angeles, 1900-1970. Trade Cloth. University of
North Carolina Press. Chapel Hill, NC. 2002. 352p. Studies in
Rural Culture ISBN:0-8078-2658-8, ISBN13:
978-0-8078-2658-4. Dewey:305.8/009794/94.
LCCN:2001-035879.
Audience: u,f. Choice, 2002.

Garrioch, David   DC729 .G33 2002
The Making of Revolutionary Paris. Trade Cloth. University of
California Press. Berkeley, CA. 2002. 412p.

ISBN:0-520-23253-4, ISBN13: 978-0-520-23253-2.
Dewey:944/.36. LCCN:2001-008255.
Audience: l,u,f. Choice, 2003.

Goldberger, Paul   NA6233.N5
Up from Zero: Politics, Architecture, and the Rebuilding of New
York. Trade Paper. Random House Adult Trade Publishing
Group. New York, NY. 2005. 320p. ISBN:0-8129-6795-X,
ISBN13: 978-0-8129-6795-1. Dewey:725/.23/097471.
Audience: g,l,u,f.

Goldberger, Paul   NA6233.N5W6745 2004
Up from Zero: Politics, Architecture, and the Rebuilding of New
York. Trade Cloth. Random House Adult Trade Publishing
Group. New York, NY. 2004. 288p. ISBN:1-4000-6017-6,
ISBN13: 978-1-4000-6017-7. Dewey:725/.23/097471.
LCCN:2004-046769.
Audience: g,l,u,f.

Gottdiener, Mark   NA712.G68 2001
The Theming of America: American Dreams, Media Fantasies,
and Themed Environments. Ed. 2. Trade Paper. Westview Press.
Boulder, CO. 2001. 216p. ISBN:0-8133-9765-0, ISBN13:
978-0-8133-9765-8. Dewey:720/.47. LCCN:2001-026562.
Audience: u,f.

Grossman, James R.   F548.9.N4
Land of Hope: Chicago, Black Southerners, and the Great
Migration. Trade Paper. University of Chicago Press. Chicago,
IL. 1991. 398p. ISBN:0-226-30995-9, ISBN13:
978-0-226-30995-8. Dewey:977.3/1100496073.
LCCN:88-039125.
Audience: u,f. Choice, 1990.

Hall, Peter   HT166.H349 2002
Cities of Tomorrow: An Intellectual History of Urban Planning
and Design in the Twentieth Century. Ed. 3. Trade Paper.
Blackwell Publishing, Inc. Malden, MA. 2002. 576p.
ISBN:0-631-23252-4, ISBN13: 978-0-631-23252-0.
Dewey:307.1/2/0904. LCCN:2001-052758.
Audience: u,f. Choice, 1989.

Hammack, David C.   F128.47.H2 1982
Power and Society: Greater New York at the Turn of the
Century. Trade Cloth. Russell Sage Foundation. New York, NY.
1982. 450p. ISBN:0-87154-348-6, ISBN13: 978-0-87154-348-6.
Dewey:974.7/1041. LCCN:81-066977.
Audience: u,f. B

Handlin, Oscar   F73.9.A1H3 1991
Boston's Immigrants, 1790-1880: A Study in Acculturation.
Trade Paper. Harvard University Press. Cambridge, MA. 1991.
400p. Belknap Press Ser. ISBN:0-674-07986-8, ISBN13:
978-0-674-07986-1. Dewey:305.8/00974461. LCCN:91-012808.
Audience: l,u,f. B

Hannigan, John A.   HT123.H337 1998
Fantasy City: Pleasure and Profit in the Postmodern Metropolis.
Paper over Boards. Routledge. New York, NY. 1998. 256p.
ISBN:0-415-15097-3, ISBN13: 978-0-415-15097-2.
Dewey:307.76/0973. LCCN:98-023774.
Audience: u,f. Choice, 1999.

Harris, Leslie M.   F128.9.N4H37 2002
In the Shadow of Slavery: African Americans in New York City,
1626-1863. Trade Cloth. University of Chicago Press. Chicago,
IL. 2003. 387p. Historical Studies of Urban America

ISBN:0-226-31774-9, ISBN13: 978-0-226-31774-8.
Dewey:305.896/07307471/09. LCCN:2002-027144.

Audience: **u,f.** *Choice, 2003.*

Harris, Richard   **HT169.C32**
Unplanned Suburbs: Toronto's American Tragedy, 1900 - 1950.
Trade Paper. Johns Hopkins University Press. Baltimore, MD.
1999. 376p. Creating the North American Landscape Ser.
ISBN:0-8018-6282-5, ISBN13: 978-0-8018-6282-3.
Dewey:307.7/6/09713541.

Audience: **u,f.**

Harvey, David   **DC733**
Paris, Capital of Modernity. UK-B Format Paperback.
Routledge. New York, NY. 2005. 384p. ISBN:0-415-95220-4,
ISBN13: 978-0-415-95220-0. Dewey:944/.36107.

Audience: **u,f.**

Hayden, Dolores   **HT168.L6**
The Power of Place: Urban Landscapes As Public History. Trade
Paper. MIT Press. Cambridge, MA. 1997. 320p.
ISBN:0-262-58152-3, ISBN13: 978-0-262-58152-3.
Dewey:307.7/6/0979494. LCCN:94-023424.

Audience: **l,u,f.**

Hohenberg, Paul M. &   **HT131.H58 1995**
Lees, Lynn H.
The Making of Urban Europe, 1000-1994. Ed. 2. Trade Paper.
Harvard University Press. Cambridge, MA. 1995. 448p.
ISBN:0-674-54362-9, ISBN13: 978-0-674-54362-1.
Dewey:307.7/6/094. LCCN:95-009303.

Audience: **u,f.**

Holmes, Urban T. Jr. &   **GT120 .H64 1980**
Neckam, Alexander
Daily Living in the Twelfth Century: Based on the Observations
of Alexander Neckam in London and Paris. Trade Cloth.
Greenwood Publishing Group, Inc. Portsmouth, NH. 1980. 337p.
ISBN:0-313-22796-9, ISBN13: 978-0-313-22796-7.
Dewey:940.1/82. LCCN:80-019991.

Audience: **l,u.**

Hood, Clifton   **TF847.N5H66 2004**
722 Miles: The Building of the Subways and How They
Transformed New York. Trade Paper. Johns Hopkins University
Press. Baltimore, MD. 2004. 336p. ISBN:0-8018-8054-8,
ISBN13: 978-0-8018-8054-4. Dewey:388.4/28/097471.
LCCN:2004-051569.

Audience: **l,u,f.**

Horne, Gerald   **F869.L89N4 1995**
Fire This Time: The Watts Uprising and the 1960's. Trade
Cloth. University Press of Virginia. Charlottesville, VA. 1995.
448p. Carter G. Woodson Institute Series in Black Studies
ISBN:0-8139-1626-7, ISBN13: 978-0-8139-1626-2.
Dewey:979.4/94053. LCCN:95-001630.

Audience: **l,u,f.** *Choice, 1996.*

Isenberg, Alison   **HT123.I74 2004**
Downtown America: A History of the Place and the People Who
Made It. Trade Paper. University of Chicago Press. Chicago, IL.
2005. 464p. Historical Studies of Urban America
ISBN:0-226-38508-6, ISBN13: 978-0-226-38508-2.
Dewey:307.76/0973. LCCN:2003-024058.

Audience: **l,u,f.** *Choice, 2004.*

Jackson, Joy J.   **F379.N557**
New Orleans in the Gilded Age: Politics and Urban Progress,
1880-1896. Ed. 2. Trade Cloth. University of Louisiana at

Lafayette, Center for Louisiana Studies. Lafayette, LA. 1998.
326p. ISBN:1-887366-16-4, ISBN13: 978-1-887366-16-8.
Dewey:309.1/763/355. LCCN:96-084965.

Audience: **u,f.** *B*

Jackson, Kenneth T.   **F128.3.E75 1995**
(Editor)
Encyclopedia of New York City. Cloth over Boards. Yale
University Press. Cumberland, RI. 1995. 1392p.
ISBN:0-300-05536-6, ISBN13: 978-0-300-05536-8.
Dewey:974.7/1/003. LCCN:95-002811.

Audience: **g,l,u,f.** *Choice, 1996.*

Kenoyer, Jonathan M.   **DS425.K43 1998**
Ancient Cities of the Indus Valley Civilization. Paper Text.
Oxford University Press, Inc. New York, NY. 1998. 264p.
ISBN:0-19-577940-1, ISBN13: 978-0-19-577940-0. Dewey:934.
LCCN:98-930419.

Audience: **l,u,f.**

Kenyon, Amy Maria   **HT352.U62D485 2004**
Dreaming Suburbia: Detroit and the Production of Postwar
Space and Culture. Trade Paper. Wayne State University Press.
Detroit, MI. 2004. 224p. African American Life Ser.
ISBN:0-8143-3228-5, ISBN13: 978-0-8143-3228-3.
Dewey:307.76/0973. LCCN:2004-015479.

Audience: **u,f.**

Klein, Menachem   **DS109.95.K55 2001**
Jerusalem: The Future of a Contested City. Trade Cloth. New
York University Press. New York, NY. 2001. 272p.
ISBN:0-8147-4754-X, ISBN13: 978-0-8147-4754-4.
Dewey:956.94/42054. LCCN:2002-416456.

Audience: **l,u,f.** *Choice, 2001.*

Kling, Rob (Editor), et al.   **HN79.C22 O726**
Postsuburban California: The Transformation of Orange County
since World War II. Mark Poster & Spencer C. Olin (Editors).
Trade Paper. University of California Press. Berkeley, CA. 1995.
328p. ISBN:0-520-20160-4, ISBN13: 978-0-520-20160-6.
Dewey:306/.09794/96.

Audience: **l,u,f.**

Kornwolf, James D.   **NA703.K67 2002**
Architecture and Town Planning in Colonial North America.
Georgiana Wallis Kornwolf (Assisted by). Trade Cloth. Johns
Hopkins University Press. Baltimore, MD. 2002. 536p. Creating
the North American Landscape Ser. ISBN:0-8018-5986-7,
ISBN13: 978-0-8018-5986-1. Dewey:711/.4/09730903.
LCCN:00-011535.

Audience: **l,u,f.** *Choice, 2003.*

Kostof, Spiro   **HT111**
City Assembled: The Elements of Urban Form Through History.
Richard Tobias (Illustrator). Trade Paper. Little Brown &
Company. New York, NY. 1999. 320p. ISBN:0-8212-2599-5,
ISBN13: 978-0-8212-2599-8. Dewey:307.7609.

Audience: **l,u,f.**

Kotkin, Joel   **HT111.K65 2005**
The City: A Global History. Trade Cloth. Random House, Inc.
New York, NY. 2005. 256p. Modern Library Chronicles
ISBN:0-679-60336-0, ISBN13: 978-0-679-60336-8.
Dewey:307.76/09. LCCN:2004-058167.

Audience: **g,l,u,f.** *Choice, 2006.*

Land, Myrick & Land,   **F849**
Barbara
A Short History of Las Vegas. Ed. 2. Trade Paper. University of

Nevada Press. Reno, NV. 2004. 288p. ISBN:0-87417-564-X, ISBN13: 978-0-87417-564-6. Dewey:979.3/135. LCCN:2004-268966.

Audience: **l,u,f.**

Lankevich, George   **F128**
New York City: A Short History. Ed. 2. Trade Cloth. New York University Press. New York, NY. 2002. 288p. ISBN:0-8147-5185-7, ISBN13: 978-0-8147-5185-5. Dewey:974.71. LCCN:98-011251.

Audience: **u,f.**

Lewis, Robert   **HC118.M6L49 2000**
Manufacturing Montreal: The Making of an Industrial Landscape, 1850 to 1930. Trade Cloth. Johns Hopkins University Press. Baltimore, MD. 2000. 360p. Creating the North American Landscape Ser. ISBN:0-8018-6349-X, ISBN13: 978-0-8018-6349-3. Dewey:338.4/767/0971428. LCCN:99-050708.

Audience: **u,f.**   *Choice, 2001.*

Lorant, Stefan, et al.   **F159.P657L67 1999**
Pittsburgh, the Story of an American City: The Millennium Edition. Ed. 5. Bruce D. Campbell, Henry Steele Commager, J. Cutler Andrews, John M. Blum, Gerald W. Johnson, Oscar Handlin, Sylvester K. Stevens, Henry David & David Lawrence (Authors). Trade Cloth. Derrydale Press, The. Lanham, MD. 1999. 776p. ISBN:0-9674103-0-4, ISBN13: 978-0-9674103-0-2. Dewey:974.8/86. LCCN:99-066641.

Audience: **u,f.**

Ma, John   **DS155**
Antiochos III and the Cities of Western Asia Minor: With New Preface and Addenda. Trade Paper. Oxford University Press, Inc. New York, NY. 2002. 425p. ISBN:0-19-925051-0, ISBN13: 978-0-19-925051-6. Dewey:939.2. LCCN:99-023236.

Audience: **u,f.**

Mahler, Jonathan   **E743.5**
Ladies and Gentlemen, the Bronx Is Burning: 1977, Baseball, Politics, and the Battle for the Soul of a City. Trade Paper. Picador. New York, NY. 2006. 376p. ISBN:0-312-42430-2, ISBN13: 978-0-312-42430-5. Dewey:974.7/043.

Audience: **l,u,f.**   *Choice, 2006.*

Mann, Barbara E.   **HT147.I7M36 2005**
A Place in History: Modernism, Tel Aviv, and the Creation of Jewish Urban Space. Trade Cloth. Stanford University Press. Palo Alto, CA. 2006. 336p. Stanford Studies in Jewish History and Culture ISBN:0-8047-5018-1, ISBN13: 978-0-8047-5018-9. Dewey:307.76/095694/8. LCCN:2005-022960.

Audience: **l,u,f.**

McDonald, Robert A.   **F1089.5.V22M43 1996**
Making Vancouver, 1863-1913. Trade Cloth. University of Washington Press. Seattle, WA. 1996. 336p. ISBN:0-7748-0555-2, ISBN13: 978-0-7748-0555-1. Dewey:971.1/33. LCCN:96-162574.

Audience: **l,u,f.**   *Choice, 1996.*

McKay, Claude   **F0128**
Harlem: Negro Metropolis. Trade Paper. Books on Demand. Ann Arbor, MI. 277p. ISBN:0-598-56484-5, ISBN13: 978-0-598-56484-9. Dewey:917.471. LCCN:40-032205.

Audience: **l,u,f.** ℬ

Meyer, David R.   **HC105.M576 2003**
The Roots of American Industrialization. Trade Cloth. Johns Hopkins University Press. Baltimore, MD. 2003. 352p. Creating

the North American Landscape Ser. ISBN:0-8018-7141-7, ISBN13: 978-0-8018-7141-2. Dewey:338.0973/09/034. LCCN:2002-005436.

Audience: **l,u,f.**   *Choice, 2004.*

Mollenkopf, John H.   **F128.55.M65 1994**
A Phoenix in the Ashes: The Rise and Fall of the Koch Coalition in New York City Politics. Trade Paper. Princeton University Press. Princeton, NJ. 1994. 320p. ISBN:0-691-03673-X, ISBN13: 978-0-691-03673-1. Dewey:320.9747/1. LCCN:94-233758.

Audience: **l,u,f.**

Muller, Thomas   **JV6471.M85**
Immigrants and the American City. Trade Paper. New York University Press. New York, NY. 1994. 600p. ISBN:0-8147-5506-2, ISBN13: 978-0-8147-5506-8. Dewey:304.873.

Audience: **l,u,f.**   *Choice, 1993.*

Mumford, Lewis   **HT111**
The City in History: Its Origins, Its Transformations and Its Prospects. Trade Paper. Harcourt Trade Publishers. New York, NY. 1968. 784p. ISBN:0-15-618035-9, ISBN13: 978-0-15-618035-1. Dewey:307.7. LCCN:61-007689.

Audience: **l,u,f.** ℬ

Mumford, Lewis   **HT151**
The Culture of Cities. Trade Cloth. Greenwood Publishing Group, Inc. Portsmouth, NH. 1981. 586p. ISBN:0-313-22746-2, ISBN13: 978-0-313-22746-2. Dewey:307.76. LCCN:80-023130.

Audience: **l,u,f.** ℬ

Nash, Gary B.   **F158.9.N4**
Forging Freedom: The Formation of Philadelphia's Black Community, 1720-1840. Trade Paper. Harvard University Press. Cambridge, MA. 1991. 372p. ISBN:0-674-30933-2, ISBN13: 978-0-674-30933-3. Dewey:974.8/1100496073. LCCN:87-023696.

Audience: **u,f.**   *Choice, 1988.*

O'Connor, Thomas H.   **F73.3.O26 2001**
The Hub: Boston Past and Present. Trade Cloth. Northeastern University Press. Boston, MA. 2005. 310p. ISBN:1-55553-474-0, ISBN13: 978-1-55553-474-5. Dewey:974.4/61. LCCN:00-068974.

Audience: **l,u,f.**   *Choice, 2001.*

Osofsky, Gilbert   **F128.68.H3O86 1996**
Harlem - The Making of a Ghetto: Negro New York, 1890-1930. Ed. 2. Trade Paper. Ivan R. Dee Publisher. Blue Ridge Summit, PA. 1996. 295p. ISBN:1-56663-104-1, ISBN13: 978-1-56663-104-4. Dewey:305.896/07307471. LCCN:95-026633.

Audience: **l,u,f.**

Page, Max   **HT168.N5**
The Creative Destruction of Manhattan, 1900-1940. Trade Paper. University of Chicago Press. Chicago, IL. 2001. 317p. Historical Studies of Urban America ISBN:0-226-64469-3, ISBN13: 978-0-226-64469-1. Dewey:307.1/216/0974710904.

Audience: **l,u,f.**   *Choice, 2000.*

Platt, Harold L.   **HT243.U62C486 2004**
Shock Cities: The Environmental Transformation and Reform of Manchester and Chicago. Trade Cloth. University of Chicago Press. Chicago, IL. 2005. 592p. ISBN:0-226-67076-7, ISBN13:

978-0-226-67076-8. Dewey:307.76/09773/11.
LCCN:2004-012103.

Audience: **l,u,f.** *Choice, 2006.*

Rosenzweig, Roy &   **F128.65.C3R67**
Blackmar, Elizabeth
The Park and the People: A History of Central Park. Trade
Cloth. Cornell University Press. Ithaca, NY. 1998. 640p.
ISBN:0-8014-9751-5, ISBN13: 978-0-8014-9751-3.
Dewey:974.71. LCCN:92-007062.

Audience: **g,l,u,f.** *Choice, 1993.*

Rybczynski, Witold   **NA9105**
City Life: Urban Expectations in a New World. Cloth Text.
DIANE Publishing Company. Collingdale, PA. 1998. 256p.
ISBN:0-7881-5517-2, ISBN13: 978-0-7881-5517-8.
Dewey:711/.4/0973.

Audience: **l,u,f.**

Rybczynski, Witold   **SB470.O5R93 1999**
A Clearing in the Distance: Frederick Law Olmsted and
America in the 19th Century. Trade Cloth. Simon & Schuster.
New York, NY. 1999. 480p. ISBN:0-684-82463-9, ISBN13:
978-0-684-82463-5. Dewey:712/.092 B. LCCN:99-018094.

Audience: **g,l,u,f.**

Schaffer, Kristen   **NA737**
Daniel H. Burnham: Visionary Architect and Planner. Scott J.
Tilden (Editor), Paul Rocheleau (Photographer). Trade Cloth.
Rizzoli International Publications, Inc. New York, NY. 2003.
224p. ISBN:0-8478-2533-7, ISBN13: 978-0-8478-2533-2.
Dewey:720.9/2. LCCN:2002-115814.

Audience: **l,u,f.** *Choice, 2004.*

Scullard, Howard H.   **DG55.E87S35 1998**
Etruscan Cities and Rome. Trade Paper. Johns Hopkins
University Press. Baltimore, MD. 1998. 384p.
ISBN:0-8018-6072-5, ISBN13: 978-0-8018-6072-0.
Dewey:937/.5. LCCN:98-008777.

Audience: **u,f.**

Seligman, Amanda I.   **F548.9.A1S45 2005**
Block by Block: Neighborhoods and Public Policy on Chicago's
West Side. Trade Cloth. University of Chicago Press. Chicago,
IL. 2005. 320p. Historical Studies of Urban America
ISBN:0-226-74663-1, ISBN13: 978-0-226-74663-0.
Dewey:977.3/11043. LCCN:2004-016543.

Audience: **l,u,f.** *Choice, 2006.*

Sheppard, Francis   **DA677.S54**
London: A History. Trade Cloth. DIANE Publishing Company.
Collingdale, PA. 2002. 442p. ISBN:0-7567-5459-3, ISBN13:
978-0-7567-5459-4. Dewey:942.1.

Audience: **l,u,f.** *Choice, 1999.*

Shorto, Russell   **F128.4.S56 2004**
The Island at the Center of the World: The Epic Story of Dutch
Manhattan and the Forgotten Colony That Shaped America.
Trade Cloth. Thorndike Press. Waterville, ME. 2004. 622p.
ISBN:0-7862-6835-2, ISBN13: 978-0-7862-6835-1.
Dewey:974.7/102. LCCN:2004-053746.

Audience: **u,f.**

Smith, Michael   **DF920.S65 2004**
Llewellyn
Athens: A Cultural and Literary History. Trade Paper. Interlink
Publishing Group, Inc. Northampton, MA. 2004. 256-264p.

Cities of the Imagination Ser. ISBN:1-56656-540-5, ISBN13:
978-1-56656-540-0. Dewey:949.5/12. LCCN:2004-003243.

Audience: **g,l,u,f.**

Sonnichsen, Charles L.   **E99.H68**
Tucson: The Life and Times of an American City. Donald H.
Bufkin (Illustrator). Trade Paper. University of Oklahoma Press.
Norman, OK. 1987. 383p. ISBN:0-8061-2042-8, ISBN13:
978-0-8061-2042-3. Dewey:979.1/77. LCCN:82-040329.

Audience: **u,f.** *B*

Sorkin, Michael &   **NA9127.N5**
Zukin, Sharon (Editors)
After the World Trade Center: Rethinking New York City. UK-B
Format Paperback. Routledge. New York, NY. 2005. 240p.
ISBN:0-415-94605-0, ISBN13: 978-0-415-94605-6.
Dewey:711/.4/097471.

Audience: **l,u,f.**

Tager, Jack   **HV6483.B6T34 2001**
Boston Riots: Three Centuries of Social Violence. Trade Cloth.
Northeastern University Press. Boston, MA. 2000. xi, 289p.
ISBN:1-55553-461-9, ISBN13: 978-1-55553-461-5.
Dewey:303.6/23/0974461. LCCN:00-041816.

Audience: **u,f.** *Choice, 2001.*

Talen, Emily   **HT165.52**
New Urbanism and American Planning: The Conflict of
Cultures. UK-B Format Paperback. Routledge. New York, NY.
2005. 328p. Planning History and the Environment Ser.
ISBN:0-415-70133-3, ISBN13: 978-0-415-70133-4.
Dewey:307.1/216/0973. LCCN:2005-009165.

Audience: **l,u,f.**

Tarr, Joel A.   **TD180.T37 1996**
The Search for the Ultimate Sink: Urban Pollution in Historical
Perspective. Trade Paper. University of Akron Press, The.
Akron, OH. 1996. 419p. Technology and the Environment Ser.
ISBN:1-884836-06-2, ISBN13: 978-1-884836-06-0.
Dewey:363.73/09173/2. LCCN:96-038383.

Audience: **l,u,f.** *Choice, 1997.*

Taylor, Quintard   **F899.S49N475 1994**
The Forging of a Black Community: Seattle's Central District,
from 1870 Through the Civil Rights Era. Norm Rice (Foreword
by). Trade Paper. University of Washington Press. Seattle, WA.
1994. 376p. The Emil and Kathleen Sick Lecture-Book Series in
Western History and Biography ISBN:0-295-97345-5, ISBN13:
978-0-295-97345-6. Dewey:979.7/77200496073.
LCCN:93-049522.

Audience: **l,u,f.**

Teaford, Jon C.   **HT175.T43 1990**
The Rough Road to Renaissance: Urban Revitalization in
America, 1940-1985. Trade Paper. Johns Hopkins University
Press. Baltimore, MD. 1990. 408p. Creating the North American
Landscape Ser. ISBN:0-8018-4134-8, ISBN13:
978-0-8018-4134-7. Dewey:307.3/416. LCCN:89-049001.

Audience: **u,f.** *Choice, 1991.*

Ward, Stephen V.   **HT325.W37 1998**
Selling Places: The Marketing and Promotion of Towns and
Cities, 1850-2000. UK-B Format Paperback. Routledge. New
York, NY. 1998. 288p. Studies in History, Planning, and the
Environment ISBN:0-419-24240-6, ISBN13: 978-0-419-24240-6.
Dewey:307.76. LCCN:98-004002.

Audience: **l,u,f.**

Weber, Adna F.   HB2161 .W37
Growth of Cities in the Nineteenth Century. Library Binding.
Greenwood Publishing Group, Inc. Portsmouth, NH. 1969.
ISBN:0-8371-4466-3, ISBN13: 978-0-8371-4466-5.
Dewey:301.3/6.

Audience: **l,u,f.**

Weiner, Edward   HE308
Urban Transportation Planning in the United States: An
Historical Overview. Trade Cloth. Greenwood Publishing Group,
Inc. Portsmouth, NH. 1999. 272p. ISBN:0-275-96329-2,
ISBN13: 978-0-275-96329-3. Dewey:388.4/0973.
LCCN:98-038286.

Audience: **l,u,f.** *Choice, 1999, 1987.*

Welter, Volker M. &   HT169.G7
  Whyte, Iain Boyd
Biopolis: Patrick Geddes and the City of Life. Trade Paper. MIT
Press. Cambridge, MA. 2003. 379p. ISBN:0-262-73164-9,
ISBN13: 978-0-262-73164-5. Dewey:711/.4/092 B.

Audience: **l,u,f.** *Choice, 2003, 2002.*

Whitfield, Peter   G1030.W5 2005
Cities of the World: A History in Maps. Trade Cloth. University
of California Press. Berkeley, CA. 2005. 208p.
ISBN:0-520-24725-6, ISBN13: 978-0-520-24725-3.
Dewey:911.1732. LCCN:2005-045003.

Audience: **l,u,f.** *Choice, 2006.*

Wiese, Andrew   E185.86.W436 2005
Places of Their Own: African American Suburbanization in the
Twentieth Century. Trade Paper. University of Chicago Press.
Chicago, IL. 2005. 422p. Historical Studies of Urban America
ISBN:0-226-89625-0, ISBN13: 978-0-226-89625-0.
Dewey:307.74/089/96073.

Audience: **l,u,f.** *Choice, 2004.*

Urban Sociology

Adams, Carolyn   HN80.P5 P477
Philadelphia: Neighborhoods, Division, and Conflict in a
Postindustrial City. Paper Text. DIANE Publishing Company.
Collingdale, PA. 1999. 210p. ISBN:0-7881-6747-2, ISBN13:
978-0-7881-6747-8. Dewey:307.1/416/0974811.

Audience: **l,u,f.**

Amster, Randall   HV4506.T8A67 2004
Street People and the Contested Realms of Public Space.
Library Binding. LFB Scholarly Publishing LLC. New York,
NY. 2004. 246p. Criminal Justice, :Recent Scholarship
ISBN:1-59332-066-3, ISBN13: 978-1-59332-066-9.
Dewey:307.3/3. LCCN:2004-015556.

Audience: **u,f.**

Atkinson, R.   HT175
Gentrification in a Global Context: The New Urban Colonialism.
Gary Bridge (Editor). Paper over Boards. Routledge. New York,
NY. 2005. 320p. Housing and Society Ser. ISBN:0-415-32950-7,
ISBN13: 978-0-415-32950-7. Dewey:305.5.
LCCN:2004-012325.

Audience: **u,f.**

Baily, Samuel L.   JV8131.B34 2004
Immigrants in the Lands of Promise: Italians in Buenos Aires
and New York City, 18701914. Trade Paper. Cornell University
Press. Ithaca, NY. 2004. 336p. ISBN:0-8014-8882-6, ISBN13:
978-0-8014-8882-5. Dewey:305.8/5108212/09034.

Audience: **u,f.**

Berg-Schlosser, Dirk &   HV4028.P88 2002
  Kersting, Norbert (Editors)
Poverty and Democracy: Self-Help and Political Participation in
Third World Cities. Trade Paper. Zed Books, Ltd. London, 2003.
204p. ISBN:1-84277-205-8, ISBN13: 978-1-84277-205-8.
Dewey:321.8. LCCN:2002-027026.

Audience: **l,u,f.** *Choice, 2004.*

Blakely, Edward J. &   HT169.59.U6B53 1997
  Snyder, Mary G.
Fortress America: Gated Communities in the United States.
Trade Cloth. Brookings Institution Press. Washington, DC. 1997.
208p. ISBN:0-8157-1002-X, ISBN13: 978-0-8157-1002-8.
Dewey:307.76. LCCN:97-021231.

Audience: **l,u,f.** *Choice, 1998.*

Body-Gendrot, Sophie   HT321.B65 1999
The Social Control of Cities? Trade Paper. Blackwell
Publishing, Inc. Malden, MA. 2000. 328p. Studies in Urban and
Social Change ISBN:0-631-20521-7, ISBN13:
978-0-631-20521-0. Dewey:307.7/6. LCCN:99-043568.

Audience: **u,f.** *Choice, 2000.*

Bonine, Michael E.   HT384.M628P66 1997
  (Editor)
Population, Poverty, and Politics in Middle East Cities. Trade
Cloth. University Press of Florida. Gainesville, FL. 1997. 384p.
ISBN:0-8130-1474-3, ISBN13: 978-0-8130-1474-6.
Dewey:307.76/0956. LCCN:96-021377.

Audience: **u,f.**

Brenner, Neil & Keil,   HT151
  Roger (Editors)
Global Cities Reader. Trade Paper. Routledge. New York, NY.
2006. XVIII, 438p. Routledge Urban Readers Ser.
ISBN:0-415-32345-2, ISBN13: 978-0-415-32345-1.
Dewey:307.76. LCCN:2005-009601.

Audience: **l,u,f.**

Browning, Rufus P.   E185.615
Racial Politics in American Cities. Ed. 2. Paper Text.
Addison-Wesley Longman, Inc. Boston, MA. 1997. 336p.
ISBN:0-8013-1691-X, ISBN13: 978-0-8013-1691-3.
Dewey:324/.089/9607301732.

Audience: **l,u,f.**

Browning, Rufus P., et al.   E185.615.R214 2002
Racial Politics in American Cities. Ed. 3. Dale Rogers Marshall
& David H. Tabb (Authors). Trade Paper. Longman Publishing.
Boston, MA. 2002. 416p. ISBN:0-321-10035-2, ISBN13:
978-0-321-10035-1. Dewey:324/.089/9607301732.
LCCN:2002-010341.

Audience: **l,u,f.**

Burgess, Ernest W. &   HT108.B8
  Bogue, Donald J. (Editors)
Contributions to Urban Sociology. Library Binding. University
of Chicago Press. Chicago, IL. 1964. ISBN:0-226-08055-2,
ISBN13: 978-0-226-08055-0. Dewey:301.36082.
LCCN:63-021309.

Audience: **l,u,f.** *B*

Burgess, Ernest W. &   HT151
  Bogue, Donald J. (Editors)
Urban Sociology. Paper Text. University of Chicago Press.
Chicago, IL. 1967. ISBN:0-226-08056-0, ISBN13:
978-0-226-08056-7. Dewey:301.3/64/08.

Audience: **l,u,f.**

Burgess, Ernest W. &   HT0108.B8
  Bogue, Donald J. (Editors)
Urban Sociology. Trade Paper. Books on Demand. Ann Arbor,
MI. 335p. Phoenix Bks. ISBN:0-608-20618-0, ISBN13:
978-0-608-20618-9. Dewey:301.3/64/08. LCCN:67-005821.
                                          Audience: l,u,f.

Castells, Manuel   HT151.C377 2001
The Castells Reader on Cities and Social Theory. Ida Susser
(Editor). Trade Paper. Blackwell Publishing, Inc. Malden, MA.
2001. 448p. ISBN:0-631-21933-1, ISBN13: 978-0-631-21933-0.
Dewey:307.76. LCCN:00-069790.
                                          Audience: l,u,f.

Center on Urban   HT108
  Poverty and Social Change, Case Western Reserve
  University
☐ Center on Urban Poverty and Social Change, Case Western
Reserve University.
http://povertycenter.case.edu/
                                          Audience: u,f.

Chauncey, George   HQ76.2.U52
Gay New York: Gender, Urban Culture, and the Making of the
Gay Male World 1890-1940. Trade Paper. Basic Books. New
York, NY. 1995. 496p. ISBN:0-465-02621-4, ISBN13:
978-0-465-02621-0. Dewey:305.9/06642/0973.
                       Audience: g,l,u,f.   Choice, 1994.

Clay, Grady   HT123
Close-Up: How to Read the American City. Trade Paper.
University of Chicago Press. Chicago, IL. 1980. 192p. Phoenix
Book, P863 Ser. ISBN:0-226-10945-3, ISBN13:
978-0-226-10945-9. Dewey:301.36/3/0973. LCCN:79-026307.
                                          Audience: l,u,f.

Cornelius, Wayne A.   JS2137.A2 C67
Politics and the Migrant Poor in Mexico City. Trade Cloth.
Stanford University Press. Palo Alto, CA. 1975. xiv, 319p.
ISBN:0-8047-0880-0, ISBN13: 978-0-8047-0880-7.
Dewey:301.5/92/091724. LCCN:75-000179.
                                          Audience: u,f.

Cressey, Paul G.   GV1624.5.C5 C7 1969
The Taxi-Dance Hall: A Sociological Study in Commercialized
Recreation and City Life. E. W. Burgess (Introduction by), J. F.
Finford (Foreword by). Trade Cloth. Patterson Smith Publishing
Corporation. Montclair, NJ. 1969. Criminology, Law
Enforcement, and Social Problems Ser., No. 76
ISBN:0-87585-076-6, ISBN13: 978-0-87585-076-4.
Dewey:301.5/7. LCCN:69-016236.
                                          Audience: l,u,f.

Davila, Arlene M.   HT178.N5 D38 2004
Barrio Dreams: Puerto Ricans, Latinos, and the Neoliberal City.
Trade Cloth. University of California Press. Berkeley, CA. 2004.
256p. ISBN:0-520-24092-8, ISBN13: 978-0-520-24092-6.
Dewey:307.1/416/097471. LCCN:2003-064572.
                       Audience: u,f.   Choice, 2005.

Davis, Mike   HN80.L7 D38 1992
City of Quartz: Excavating the Future in Los Angeles. Trade
Paper. Knopf Publishing Group. New York, NY. 1992. 480p.
ISBN:0-679-73806-1, ISBN13: 978-0-679-73806-0.
Dewey:306/.09794/94. LCCN:91-050492.
                                          Audience: u,f.

Davis, Mike   E184.S75D36 2000
Magical Urbanism: Latinos Reinvent the U. S. Big City. Trade
Cloth. Analytical Psychology Club of San Francisco, Inc. San
Francisco, CA. 2000. 192p. Haymarket Ser.
ISBN:1-85984-771-4, ISBN13: 978-1-85984-771-8.
Dewey:305.868/073. LCCN:00-698296.
                       Audience: u,f.   Choice, 2001.

Davis, Mike   HT119
Planet of Slums. Trade Cloth. Verso Books. London, 2006.
256p. ISBN:1-84467-022-8, ISBN13: 978-1-84467-022-2.
Dewey:307.76. LCCN:2006-275053.
                                          Audience: l,u,f.

Eade, John & Mele,   HT119.U53 2002
  Christopher (Editors)
Understanding the City: Contemporary and Future Perspectives.
Trade Cloth. Blackwell Publishing, Inc. Malden, MA. 2002.
448p. Studies in Urban and Social Change ISBN:0-631-22406-8,
ISBN13: 978-0-631-22406-8. Dewey:307.76.
LCCN:2002-066641.
                                          Audience: l,u,f.

Ember, Melvin &   HT108.5.E53 2002
  Ember, Carol R. (Editors)
Encyclopedia of Urban Cultures: Cities and Cultures Around the
World. Library Binding. Scholastic Library Publishing. Danbury,
CT. 2002. 2112p. ISBN:0-7172-5698-7, ISBN13:
978-0-7172-5698-3. Dewey:307.76/03. LCCN:2002-070034.
                       Audience: l,u,f.   Choice, 2003.

Fischer, Claude S.   HT111.F56
To Dwell among Friends: Personal Networks in Town and City.
Trade Paper. University of Chicago Press. Chicago, IL. 1982.
459p. ISBN:0-226-25138-1, ISBN13: 978-0-226-25138-7.
Dewey:307. LCCN:81-011505.
                                          Audience: l,u,f.

Gans, Herbert J.   HN80.W497 G36 1982
The Levittowners: Ways of Life and Politics in a New Suburban
Community. Trade Paper. Columbia University Press. New York,
NY. 1982. 474p. ISBN:0-231-05571-4, ISBN13:
978-0-231-05571-0. Dewey:307.7/6/0973. LCCN:82-004375.
                                          Audience: l,u,f.

Gans, Herbert J.   HN80.B7G2 1982
The Urban Villagers. Ed. 2. Trade Cloth. Simon & Schuster.
New York, NY. 1982. 456p. ISBN:0-02-911250-8, ISBN13:
978-0-02-911250-2. Dewey:305.8/51/073. LCCN:82-008577.
                                          Audience: l,u,f.

Garreau, Joel   HT334.U5G37 1991
The Edge City: Life on the New Frontier. Trade Cloth.
Doubleday Publishing. New York, NY. 1991. 560p.
ISBN:0-385-26249-3, ISBN13: 978-0-385-26249-1.
Dewey:307.76/0973. LCCN:91-010548.
                       Audience: l,u,f.   Choice, 1992.

Gottdiener, Mark &   HT109
  Budd, Leslie
Key Concepts in Urban Studies. Cloth Text. SAGE Publications,
Inc. Thousand Oaks, CA. 2005. 200p. SAGE Key Concepts Ser.
ISBN:0-7619-4097-9, ISBN13: 978-0-7619-4097-5.
Dewey:307.7/6. LCCN:2005-276639.
                       Audience: l,u,f.   Choice, 2005.

Gottdiener, Mark &   HT0175.
  Pickvance, Chris G. (Editors)
Urban Life in Transition. Trade Paper. Books on Demand. Ann

Arbor, MI. 1991. 253p. Urban Affairs Annual Reviews Ser., Vol. 39 ISBN:0-608-04310-9, ISBN13: 978-0-608-04310-4. Dewey:307.760973. LCCN:91-025273.

Audience: l,u,f.

Graham, Stephen &   **HT153.G72 2001**
Marvin, Simon
Splintering Urbanism: Networked Infrastructures, Technological Mobilities and the Urban Condition. Trade Paper. Routledge. New York, NY. 2004. 512p. ISBN:0-415-18965-9, ISBN13: 978-0-415-18965-1. Dewey:307.76. LCCN:00-045793.

Audience: u,f.

Gugler, Josef   **HT149.5.U7337 1996**
🄴 The Urban Transformation of the Developing World. E-Book. NetLibrary, Inc. Boulder, CO. 1996. ISBN:0-585-21823-4, ISBN13: 978-0-585-21823-6. Dewey:307.7/6/091724.

Audience: u,f. *Choice, 1997.*

Hayden, Dolores   **HD7293.H39 2002**
Redesigning the American Dream: Gender Housing and Family Life. Trade Paper. W. W. Norton & Company, Inc. New York, NY. 2002. 288p. ISBN:0-393-73094-8, ISBN13: 978-0-393-73094-4. Dewey:363.5/0973. LCCN:2002-066504.

Audience: l,u,f.

Jackson, Kenneth T.   **HT384.U5**
Crabgrass Frontier: The Suburbanization of the United States. Trade Paper. Oxford University Press, Inc. New York, NY. 1987. 406p. ISBN:0-19-504983-7, ISBN13: 978-0-19-504983-1. Dewey:307.7/4/0973.

Audience: l,u,f. 𝓑 *Choice, 1986.*

Jacobs, Jane   **HT123**
The Death and Life of Great American Cities. Paper Text. Textbook Publishers. Temecula, CA. 2003. 458p. ISBN:0-7581-5101-2, ISBN13: 978-0-7581-5101-8. Dewey:307.76/0973.

Audience: l,u,f. 𝓑

Jones-Correa, Michael   **F130.S75J66 1998**
Between Two Nations: The Political Predicament of Latinos in New York City. Book, Other. Cornell University Press. Ithaca, NY. 1998. 272p. ISBN:0-8014-8364-6, ISBN13: 978-0-8014-8364-6. Dewey:305.868/07471. LCCN:97-049415.

Audience: u,f. *Choice, 1999.*

Kennedy, Liam   **HT221**
Race and Urban Space in American Culture. Cloth Text. Fitzroy Dearborn Publishers, Inc. Chicago, IL. 2000. 300p. America in the 20th/21st Century Ser., Vol. 9 ISBN:1-57958-280-X, ISBN13: 978-1-57958-280-7. Dewey:810.932.

Audience: l,u,f. *Choice, 2001.*

Kleniewski, Nancy   **HT108.C523 2004**
(Editor)
Cities and Society. Trade Paper. Blackwell Publishing, Inc. Malden, MA. 2004. 352p. Blackwell Readers in Sociology Ser. ISBN:1-4051-0232-2, ISBN13: 978-1-4051-0232-2. Dewey:307.76. LCCN:2004-050167.

Audience: l,u,f.

Langdon, Philip   **HT352.U6L36 1994**
A Better Place to Live: Reshaping the American Suburb. Cloth Text. University of Massachusetts Press. Amherst, MA. 1994. 288p. ISBN:0-87023-914-7, ISBN13: 978-0-87023-914-4. Dewey:307.1/214/0973. LCCN:93-042348.

Audience: l,u,f. *Choice, 1995.*

Livezey, Lowell W.   **BL2527.C48P83 2000**
(Editor)
Public Religion and Urban Transformation. Trade Cloth. New York University Press. New York, NY. 2000. 364p. Religion, Race, and Ethnicity Ser. ISBN:0-8147-5157-1, ISBN13: 978-0-8147-5157-2. Dewey:200/.9773/11. LCCN:99-050622.

Audience: l,u,f.

Lloyd, Richard D.   **HQ2044.U6L56 2005**
Neo-Bohemia: Art and Commerce in the Post Industrial City. Saddle Stitched, Cloth over Boards. Routledge. New York, NY. 2005. 295p. ISBN:0-415-95181-X, ISBN13: 978-0-415-95181-4. Dewey:306.1. LCCN:2005-008803.

Audience: l,u,f.

Lofland, Lyn H.   **HT151.L6 1998**
The Public Realm: Exploring the City's Quintessential Social Territory. Trade Cloth. Aldine Transaction. Somerset, NJ. 1998. 305p. Communication and Social Order Ser. ISBN:0-202-30607-0, ISBN13: 978-0-202-30607-0. Dewey:307.76. LCCN:97-042290.

Audience: u,f. *Choice, 1998.*

Low, Setha M.   **HT169.59.U6L69 2003**
Behind the Gates: Security and the New American Dream. Paper over Boards. Routledge. New York, NY. 2003. 288p. ISBN:0-415-94438-4, ISBN13: 978-0-415-94438-0. Dewey:307/.0973. LCCN:2002-036620.

Audience: l,u,f. *Choice, 2004.*

Mattingly, Paul H.   **HT352.U62N55 2001**
Suburban Landscapes: Culture and Politics in a New York Metropolitan Community. Center for American Places Staff (Contribution by). Trade Cloth. Johns Hopkins University Press. Baltimore, MD. 2001. 352p. Creating the North American Landscape Ser. ISBN:0-8018-6680-4, ISBN13: 978-0-8018-6680-7. Dewey:307.76/09749/21. LCCN:2001-000676.

Audience: l,u,f.

Merrifield, Andrew   **HT119.M377 2002**
Metromarxism: A Marxist Tale of the City. Paper over Boards. Routledge. New York, NY. 2002. 224p. ISBN:0-415-93348-X, ISBN13: 978-0-415-93348-3. Dewey:307.76. LCCN:2002-024668.

Audience: u,f.

Morton, Margaret   **HV4506.N6M67 1995**
The Tunnel: The Underground Homeless of New York City. Cloth over Boards. Yale University Press. Cumberland, RI. 1995. 160p. The Architecture of Despair Ser. ISBN:0-300-06538-8, ISBN13: 978-0-300-06538-1. Dewey:305.5/68/097471. LCCN:95-004894.

Audience: l,u,f.

Orsi, Robert A. (Editor)   **BL2525.G63 1999**
Gods of the City: Religion and the American Urban Landscape. Cloth Text. Indiana University Press. Bloomington, IN. 1999. 581p. Religion in North America Ser. ISBN:0-253-33499-3, ISBN13: 978-0-253-33499-2. Dewey:200/.973/091732. LCCN:98-048338.

Audience: l,u,f.

Park, Robert Ezra &   **HT123**
Burgess, Ernest W.
The City. Morris Janowitz (Introduction by). Trade Paper. University of Chicago Press. Chicago, IL. 1984. 250p. The Heritage of Sociology Ser., :Midway Reprint

ISBN:0-226-64611-4, ISBN13: 978-0-226-64611-4.
Dewey:307.7/6/0973. LCCN:66-023694.

Audience: **l,u,f.** B

Peterson, Paul E.   **HT123.N45 1985**
(Editor)
The New Urban Reality. Trade Cloth. Brookings Institution
Press. Washington, DC. 1985. 301p. ISBN:0-8157-7018-9,
ISBN13: 978-0-8157-7018-3. Dewey:307.7/6/0973.
LCCN:84-045848.

Audience: **l,u,f.** *Choice, 1985.*

Rae, Douglas W.   **F104.N657R34 2003**
City: Urbanism and Its End. Cloth over Boards. Yale University
Press. Cumberland, RI. 2003. 544p. Yale ISPS Ser.
ISBN:0-300-09577-5, ISBN13: 978-0-300-09577-7.
Dewey:974.6/8043. LCCN:2003-009974.

Audience: **u,f.**

Rodriguez, Joseph A.   **HN80**
City Against Suburb: The Culture Wars in an American
Metropolis. Trade Cloth. Greenwood Publishing Group, Inc.
Portsmouth, NH. 1999. 160p. ISBN:0-275-96406-X, ISBN13:
978-0-275-96406-1. Dewey:306/.09794/6. LCCN:99-021192.

Audience: **l,u,f.**

Sassen, Saskia   **HT321.S28 2006**
Cities in a World Economy. Ed. 3. Paper Text. Pine Forge Press.
Newbury Park, CA. 2006. 288p. Sociology for a New Century
Ser. ISBN:1-4129-3680-2, ISBN13: 978-1-4129-3680-4.
Dewey:330.9173/2. LCCN:2005-034084.

Audience: **l,u,f.**

Sassen, Saskia   **HG184.N5S27 2001**
The Global City: New York, London, Tokyo. Ed. 2. Trade Paper.
Princeton University Press. Princeton, NJ. 2001. 474p.
ISBN:0-691-07063-6, ISBN13: 978-0-691-07063-6.
Dewey:332/.042. LCCN:2001-021130.

Audience: **l,u,f.** *Choice, 1992.*

Saunders, Peter   **HT111.S26 1995**
[e] Social Theory and the Urban Question. Ed. 2. E-Book.
Taylor & Francis Group. Philadelphia, PA. ISBN:0-203-39316-3,
ISBN13: 978-0-203-39316-1. Dewey:307.7/6.

Audience: **l,u,f.**

Self, Robert O.   **F869.O2S455 2005**
American Babylon: Race and the Struggle for Postwar Oakland.
Trade Paper. Princeton University Press. Princeton, NJ. 2005.
408p. Politics and Society in Twentieth Century America Ser.
ISBN:0-691-12486-8, ISBN13: 978-0-691-12486-5.
Dewey:979.4/6600496073.

Audience: **l,u,f.** *Choice, 2004.*

Sennett, Richard   **HT151.S43**
(Compiled by)
Classic Essays on the Culture of Cities. Trade Cloth.
McGraw-Hill Primis Custom Publishing. Hightstown, NJ. 1969.
233p. ISBN:0-390-79668-9, ISBN13: 978-0-390-79668-4.
Dewey:301.3/64. LCCN:71-077533.

Audience: **l,u,f.**

Simmel, Georg   **HM51.S537**
Georg Simmel on Individuality and Social Forms. Donald N.
Levine (Editor). Trade Paper. University of Chicago Press.
Chicago, IL. 1972. 412p. The Heritage of Sociology Ser.,
:Midway Reprint ISBN:0-226-75776-5, ISBN13:
978-0-226-75776-6. Dewey:301. LCCN:78-157146.

Audience: **l,u,f.**

Smith, Michael P. &   **HT110.C65 VOL.7**
Bender, Thomas
City and Nation: Rethinking Place and Identity. Trade Paper.
Transaction Publishers. Somerset, NJ. 2001. 244p. Comparative
Urban and Community Research Ser., Vol. 7
ISBN:0-7658-0871-4, ISBN13: 978-0-7658-0871-4.
Dewey:307.76. LCCN:00-054507.

Audience: **l,u,f.**

Sorkin, Michael   **HT123.V37 1992**
(Editor)
Variations on a Theme Park: The New American City and the
End of Public Space. Trade Paper. Farrar, Straus & Giroux. New
York, NY. 1992. 252p. ISBN:0-374-52314-2, ISBN13:
978-0-374-52314-5. Dewey:307.76/0973. LCCN:91-022976.

Audience: **l,u,f.**

Southall, Aidan   **HT111**
The City in Time and Space. Trade Paper. Cambridge University
Press. New York, NY. 1999. 483p. ISBN:0-521-78432-8,
ISBN13: 978-0-521-78432-0. Dewey:307.76/09.

Audience: **l,u,f.** *Choice, 1999.*

Strauss, Anselm   **HT123 .S786**
Images of the American City. Trade Cloth. Transaction
Publishers. Somerset, NJ. 1976. 306p. ISBN:0-87855-144-1,
ISBN13: 978-0-87855-144-6. Dewey:301.360973.
LCCN:75-043358.

Audience: **l,u,f.** B

Tajbakhsh, Kian   **99-056668**
The Promise of the City: Space, Identity and Politics in
Contemporary Social Thought. Trade Paper. University of
California Press. Berkeley, CA. 2000. 246p.
ISBN:0-520-22278-4, ISBN13: 978-0-520-22278-6.
Dewey:307.76. LCCN:99-056668.

Audience: **l,u,f.** *Choice, 2001.*

Theodorson, George A.   **HT151**
(Editor)
Urban Patterns: Studies in Human Ecology. Trade Cloth.
Pennsylvania State University Press. University Park, PA. 1982.
475p. ISBN:0-271-00297-2, ISBN13: 978-0-271-00297-2.
Dewey:307.7/6. LCCN:81-083145.

Audience: **l,u,f.**

Tönnies, Ferdinand   **HM706.T61613 2001**
Tönnies: Community and Civil Society. Jose Harris (Editor,
Translator), Margaret Hollis (Translator), Raymond Geuss &
Quentin Skinner (Contribution by). Trade Paper. Cambridge
University Press. New York, NY. 2001. 318p. Texts in the
History of Political Thought ISBN:0-521-56782-3, ISBN13:
978-0-521-56782-4. Dewey:305. LCCN:00-046753.

Audience: **l,u,f.**

Vergara, Camilo J.   **HN57.V47 1995**
(Author, Photographer)
The New American Ghetto. Trade Cloth. Rutgers University
Press. Piscataway, NJ. 1995. 200p. ISBN:0-8135-2209-9,
ISBN13: 978-0-8135-2209-8. Dewey:307.3/366/0973.
LCCN:94-045707.

Audience: **l,u,f.** *Choice, 1996.*

Waldinger, Roger   **F128.9.N3**
Still the Promised City?: African-Americans and New
Immigrants in Postindustrial New York. Trade Paper. Harvard
University Press. Cambridge, MA. 1999. 384p.

ISBN:0-674-00072-2, ISBN13: 978-0-674-00072-8.
Dewey:330.9/747/1/00896073.

Audience: **l,u,f.** *Choice, 1997.*

Weber, Max M.   **HT151.W413**
The City. Ed. 2. Don Martindale & Gertrud Neuwirth (Editors).
Trade Paper. Simon & Schuster. New York, NY. 1966. 265p.
ISBN:0-02-934210-4, ISBN13: 978-0-02-934210-7.
Dewey:307.76 21. LCCN:58-006492.

Audience: **l,u,f.** *B*

Welch, Susan, et al.   **F574.D49 A27 2001**
Race and Place: Race Relations in an American City. Timothy
Bledsoe, Michael W. Combs & Lee Sigelman (Authors), Dennis
Chong & James H. Kuklinski (Contribution by). Trade Paper.
Cambridge University Press. New York, NY. 2001. 224p.
Studies in Political Psychology and Public Opinion
ISBN:0-521-79655-5, ISBN13: 978-0-521-79655-2.
Dewey:305.8/009774/34. LCCN:2001-025035.

Audience: **u,f.**

Whyte, William F.   **HV6446.W49 1993**
Street Corner Society: The Social Structure of an Italian Slum.
Ed. 4. Trade Paper. University of Chicago Press. Chicago, IL.
1993. 418p. ISBN:0-226-89545-9, ISBN13: 978-0-226-89545-1.
Dewey:302.340974461. LCCN:92-042262.

Audience: **l,u,f.**

Wilson, William Julius   **HV4045.W55 1987**
The Truly Disadvantaged: The Inner City, the Underclass, and
Public Policy. Trade Cloth. University of Chicago Press.
Chicago, IL. 1993. xii, 252p. ISBN:0-226-90130-0, ISBN13:
978-0-226-90130-5. Dewey:362.5/0973. LCCN:87-010822.

Audience: **l,u,f.** *Choice, 1988.*

Wilson, William Julius   **HV4045.W553 1996**
When Work Disappears: The World of the New Urban Poor.
Trade Cloth. Alfred A. Knopf Inc. New York, NY. 1996. 352p.
ISBN:0-394-57935-6, ISBN13: 978-0-394-57935-1.
Dewey:362.5/0973/091732. LCCN:96-011803.

Audience: **l,u,f.** *Choice, 1997.*

Wirth, Louis   **HM51**
Louis Wirth on Cities and Social Life. Albert J. Reiss Jr.
(Editor). Paper Text. University of Chicago Press. Chicago, IL.
1996. 380p. The Heritage of Sociology Ser., :Midway Reprint
ISBN:0-226-90242-0, ISBN13: 978-0-226-90242-5.
Dewey:301.081. LCCN:64-024970.

Audience: **l,u,f.**

Zukin, Sharon   **HT109.Z85 1995**
The Cultures of Cities. Trade Paper. Blackwell Publishing, Inc.
Malden, MA. 1995. 336p. ISBN:1-55786-437-3, ISBN13:
978-1-55786-437-6. Dewey:307.7/64. LCCN:95-007534.

Audience: **l,u,f.** *Choice, 1996.*

Zukin, Sharon   **HN59.2.Z85 1993**
Landscapes of Power: From Detroit to Disney World. Trade
Paper. University of California Press. Berkeley, CA. 1993. 338p.
ISBN:0-520-08288-5, ISBN13: 978-0-520-08288-5.
Dewey:307.1/2/0973.

Audience: **l,u,f.** *Choice, 1992.*

Zukin, Sharon   **HC110.C6**
Point of Purchase: How Shopping Changed American Culture.
UK-B Format Paperback. Routledge. New York, NY. 2005.
336p. ISBN:0-415-95043-0, ISBN13: 978-0-415-95043-5.
Dewey:306.3/0973.

Audience: **l,u,f.** *Choice, 2004.*

Urban Geography

Badcock, Blair   **HT371**
Making Sense of Cities. Trade Paper. Oxford University Press,
Inc. New York, NY. 2002. 352p. A Hodder Arnold Publication
ISBN:0-340-74224-0, ISBN13: 978-0-340-74224-2.
Dewey:307.76. LCCN:2003-268506.

Audience: **u,f.**

Berry, Brian J.L. &   **GF503.U73 2005**
Wheeler, James (Editors)
Urban Geography in America, 1950-2000: Paradigms and
Personalities. Paper over Boards. Routledge. New York, NY.
2005. 408p. ISBN:0-415-95190-9, ISBN13: 978-0-415-95190-6.
Dewey:307.76/0973. LCCN:2004-029780.

Audience: **l,u,f.**

Brenner, Neil & Keil,   **HT151**
Roger (Editors)
Global Cities Reader. Trade Paper. Routledge. New York, NY.
2006. XVIII, 438p. Routledge Urban Readers Ser.
ISBN:0-415-32345-2, ISBN13: 978-0-415-32345-1.
Dewey:307.76. LCCN:2005-009601.

Audience: **l,u,f.**

Buisseret, David   **G140.E58 1998**
(Editor)
Envisioning the City: Six Studies in Urban Cartography. Trade
Cloth. University of Chicago Press. Chicago, IL. 1998. 196p.
Kenneth Nebenzahl, Jr., Lectures in the History of Cartography
ISBN:0-226-07993-7, ISBN13: 978-0-226-07993-6.
Dewey:912/.19732. LCCN:97-037158.

Audience: **l,u,f.** *Choice, 1998.*

Conzen, M. R. G. &   **HT371**
Conzen, Michael P.
Thinking about Urban Form: Papers on Urban Morphology,
1932-1998. Trade Cloth. Peter Lang Publishing, Inc. New York,
NY. 2005. 310p. ISBN:3-03-910276-1, ISBN13:
978-3-03-910276-1. Dewey:307.76. LCCN:2004-061562.

Audience: **u,f.**

de Souza Briggs, Xavier   **HD7288.76.U5G46 2005**
(Editor)
The Geography of Opportunity: Race and Housing Choice in
Metropolitan America. William Julius Wilson (Foreword by).
Trade Paper, Perfect. Brookings Institution Press. Washington,
DC. 2005. 353p. ISBN:0-8157-0873-4, ISBN13:
978-0-8157-0873-5. Dewey:363.59900973. LCCN:2005-009628.

Audience: **u,f.** *Choice, 2006.*

French, R. A.   **HT145.S58F74 1995**
Plans, Pragmatism and People: The Failure of Soviet City
Planning. Trade Paper. University of Pittsburgh Press.
Pittsburgh, PA. 1996. 233p. Pitt Series in Russian and East
European ISBN:0-8229-6106-7, ISBN13: 978-0-8229-6106-2.
Dewey:307.76/0947. LCCN:95-012855.

Audience: **u,f.** *Choice, 1996.*

Graham, Stephen &   **HT153.G72 2001**
Marvin, Simon
Splintering Urbanism: Networked Infrastructures, Technological
Mobilities and the Urban Condition. Trade Paper. Routledge.
New York, NY. 2004. 512p. ISBN:0-415-18965-9, ISBN13:
978-0-415-18965-1. Dewey:307.76. LCCN:00-045793.

Audience: **u,f.**

Hall, Tim GF125.H35 2006
Urban Geography. Ed. 3. Trade Paper. Routledge. New York, NY. 2006. XIV, 202p. Routledge Contemporary Human Geography Ser. ISBN:0-415-34446-8, ISBN13: 978-0-415-34446-3. Dewey:910/.9173/2. LCCN:2005-020301.

Audience: **l,u,f**.

Harvey, David LC2808.S7B22 2002
Spaces of Capital: Towards a Critical Geography. Paper over Boards. Routledge. New York, NY. 2002. 400p. Studies in Higher Education, Dissertation ISBN:0-415-93248-3, ISBN13: 978-0-415-93248-6. Dewey:378.1/981/0968. LCCN:2001-048408.

Audience: **u,f**.

Harvey, David HB501.H3598 2006
Spaces of Global Capitalism: A Theory of Uneven Geographical Development. Trade Cloth. Verso Books. London, 2006. 140p. ISBN:1-84467-065-1, ISBN13: 978-1-84467-065-9. Dewey:330.12/2. LCCN:2006-002202.

Audience: **u,f**.

Kenny, Judith T. & GF125
Fyfe, Nicholas (Editors)
The Urban Geography Reader. Perfect, Paper over Boards. Routledge. New York, NY. 2005. XIV, 410p. Routledge Urban Readers Ser. ISBN:0-415-30701-5, ISBN13: 978-0-415-30701-7. Dewey:307.76. LCCN:2004-018547.

Audience: **l,u,f**.

Low, Setha M. & GF50.A55 2003
Lawrence-Zuaniga, Denise (Editors)
The Anthology of Space and Place: Locating Culture. Trade Cloth. Blackwell Publishing, Inc. Malden, MA. 2003. 432p. Blackwell Readers in Anthropology Ser., Vol. 4 ISBN:0-631-22877-2, ISBN13: 978-0-631-22877-6. Dewey:304.2. LCCN:2002-071219.

Audience: **l,u,f**.

Maantay, Juliana & HT153.M314 2006
Ziegler, John
GIS for the Urban Environment. John Pickles (Foreword by). Trade Paper. ESRI, Inc. Redlands, CA. 2006. 600p. ISBN:1-58948-082-1, ISBN13: 978-1-58948-082-7. Dewey:307.760285. LCCN:2006-013778.

Audience: **u,f**.

Marcuse, Peter & van HT119.G65 2000
Kempen, Ronald (Editors)
Globalizing Cities: A New Spatial Order? Trade Paper. Blackwell Publishing, Inc. Malden, MA. 2000. 336p. Studies in Urban and Social Change ISBN:0-631-21290-6, ISBN13: 978-0-631-21290-4. Dewey:307.76. LCCN:99-043570.

Audience: **l,u,f**.

Otterstrom, Samuel HT123.G43 2004
A Geographical History of United States City-Systems: From Frontier to the Urban Transformation. Trade Cloth. Edwin Mellen Press, The. Lewiston, NY. 2004. 265p. Mellen Studies in Geography Ser., Vol. 10 ISBN:0-7734-6521-9, ISBN13: 978-0-7734-6521-3. Dewey:307.76. LCCN:2004-040188.

Audience: **u,f**.

Pamuk, Ayse HT166.P333 2006
Mapping Global Cities: GIS Methods in Urban Analysis. Trade Paper. ESRI, Inc. Redlands, CA. 2006. 350p. ISBN:1-58948-143-7, ISBN13: 978-1-58948-143-5. Dewey:307.1/2160285. LCCN:2006-010177.

Audience: **u,f**.

Ravetz, Joe, et al. HT241
Environment and the City. Joe Howe, Clive George & Peter Roberts (Authors). Cloth Text. Routledge. New York, NY. 2007. 248p. Routledge Introductions to Environment Ser. ISBN:0-415-30246-3, ISBN13: 978-0-415-30246-3. Dewey:307.1/416.

Audience: **l,u,f**.

Sassen, Saskia HG184.N5S27 2001
The Global City: New York, London, Tokyo. Ed. 2. Trade Paper. Princeton University Press. Princeton, NJ. 2001. 474p. ISBN:0-691-07063-6, ISBN13: 978-0-691-07063-6. Dewey:332/.042. LCCN:2001-021130.

Audience: **l,u,f**. *Choice, 1992.*

Short, John Rennie HT151.S477 1996
The Urban Order: An Introduction to Urban Geography. Trade Cloth. Blackwell Publishing, Inc. Malden, MA. 1996. 512p. ISBN:1-55786-360-1, ISBN13: 978-1-55786-360-7. Dewey:307.7/6. LCCN:95-000307.

Audience: **l,u,f**.

Smith, Neil & Williams, HT170.G46 1986
Peter (Editors)
Gentrification of the City. Cloth Text. Routledge. New York, NY. 1986. 256p. ISBN:0-04-301201-9, ISBN13: 978-0-04-301201-7. Dewey:307.2. LCCN:85-022889.

Audience: **l,u,f**. *Choice, 1986.*

Soja, Edward W. JC319.S57
The Political Organization of Space. Paper Text. Association of American Geographers. Washington, DC. 1971. CCG Resource Papers, No. 8 ISBN:0-89291-055-0, ISBN13: 978-0-89291-055-7. Dewey:320.9. LCCN:70-135471.

Audience: **l,u,f**.

Soja, Edward W. HT119.S65 2000
Postmetropolis: Studies of Cities and Regions. Trade Paper. Blackwell Publishing, Inc. Malden, MA. 2002. 464p. ISBN:1-57718-001-1, ISBN13: 978-1-57718-001-2. Dewey:307. LCCN:99-047607.

Audience: **l,u,f**.

Soja, Edward W. G70.S62 1989
Postmodern Geographies: The Reassertion of Space in Critical Social Theory. Trade Paper. Analytical Psychology Club of San Francisco, Inc. San Francisco, CA. 1989. 300p. ISBN:0-86091-936-6, ISBN13: 978-0-86091-936-0. Dewey:910/.01. LCCN:88-020578.

Audience: **l,u,f**. *Choice, 1989.*

Steinberg, Steven J. & H62.S7542 2006
Steinberg, Sheila L.
Geographic Information Systems for the Social Sciences: Investigating Space and Place. Cloth Text. SAGE Publications, Inc. Thousand Oaks, CA. 2005. 272p. ISBN:0-7619-2872-3, ISBN13: 978-0-7619-2872-0. Dewey:300/.285. LCCN:2005-007114.

Audience: **l,u,f**.

Tuan, Yi-Fu (Editor) G71.5
Space and Place. Trade Paper. University of Minnesota Press. Minneapolis, MN. 2001. 248p. ISBN:0-8166-3877-2, ISBN13: 978-0-8166-3877-2. Dewey:153.7/52.

Audience: **l,u,f**.

Whitehill, Walter Muir F73.3.W57 2000
(Author, Illustrator)
Boston: A Topographical History. Ed. 3. Trade Cloth. Harvard

Audience: g=general, l=lower division undergraduate, u=upper division undergraduate, f=faculty.

721

University Press. Cambridge, MA. 2000. 432p. Belknap Press Ser. ISBN:0-674-00267-9, ISBN13: 978-0-674-00267-8. Dewey:974.461. LCCN:99-086597.

Audience: **u,f.** *B*

Wilson, David   **HT164**
Cities and Race: America's New Black Ghetto. Paper over Boards. Routledge. New York, NY. 2006. 192p. Questioning Cities Ser. ISBN:0-415-35805-1, ISBN13: 978-0-415-35805-7. Dewey:307.3/3660973. LCCN:2006-009658.

Audience: **u,f.**

Urban Anthropology

Gmelch, George &   **GN395.U725 2002**
  Zenner, Walter P. (Editors)
Urban Life: Readings in the Anthropology of the City. Ed. 4. Paper Text. Waveland Press, Inc. Prospect Heights, IL. 2001. 394p. ISBN:1-57766-194-X, ISBN13: 978-1-57766-194-8. Dewey:307.76. LCCN:2002-277258.

Audience: **l,u,f.**

Leeds, Anthony   **GN395.L44 1994**
Cities, Classes, and the Social Order. Roger Sanjek (Editor). Book, Other. Cornell University Press. Ithaca, NY. 1994. 272p. The Anthropology of Contemporary Issues Ser. ISBN:0-8014-2957-9, ISBN13: 978-0-8014-2957-6. Dewey:307.76. LCCN:93-038934.

Audience: **l,u,f.**

Urban Politics and Public Policy

Abu-Lughod, Janet L.   **HT123.A613 1999**
New York, Chicago, Los Angeles: America's Global Cities. Trade Paper. University of Minnesota Press. Minneapolis, MN. 2001. x, 580p. ISBN:0-8166-3336-3, ISBN13: 978-0-8166-3336-4. Dewey:307.76/0973. LCCN:99-020783.

Audience: **l,u,f.**

Altshuler, Alan A. &   **HN90.C6A668 2003**
  Luberoff, David E.
Mega-Projects: The Changing Politics of Urban Public Investment. Trade Paper. Brookings Institution Press. Washington, DC. 2002. 368p. ISBN:0-8157-0129-2, ISBN13: 978-0-8157-0129-3. Dewey:307.1/416/0973. LCCN:2002-152773.

Audience: **u,f.** *Choice, 2004.*

Banfield, Edward C. &   **JS331 .B28**
  Wilson, James Q.
City Politics. Trade Cloth. Harvard University Press. Cambridge, MA. 1963. 374p. Joint Center for Urban Studies ISBN:0-674-13250-5, ISBN13: 978-0-674-13250-4. Dewey:352.073. LCCN:63-019134.

Audience: **u,f.** *B*

Beito, David T. (Editor),   **JS78.V6 2002**
  et al.
The Voluntary City: Choice, Community, and Civil Society. Deborah Gordon & Alexander Tabarrok (Editors). Trade Cloth. University of Michigan Press. Chicago, IL. 2002. 480p. Economics, Cognition and Society Ser. ISBN:0-472-11240-6, ISBN13: 978-0-472-11240-1. Dewey:307.76. LCCN:2001-006444.

Audience: **u,f.** *Choice, 2003.*

Benjamin, Gerald &   **JS1230**
  Nathan, Richard P.
Regionalism and Realism: A Study of Government in the New York Metropolitan Area. Trade Cloth. Brookings Institution Press. Washington, DC. 2001. 304p. ISBN:0-8157-0088-1, ISBN13: 978-0-8157-0088-3. Dewey:320.8097471.

Audience: **u,f.** *Choice, 2002.*

Capello, Roberta &   **HT321**
  Nijkamp, Peter (Editors)
Urban Dynamics and Growth: Advances in Urban Economics. Trade Cloth. Elsevier Science & Technology Books. Saint Louis, MO. 2005. 900p. Contributions to Economic Analysis Ser. ISBN:0-444-51481-3, ISBN13: 978-0-444-51481-3. Dewey:330.9/1732.

Audience: **u,f.**

Clarke, Susan   **HN49.C6C573 1998**
Work of Cities. Book, Other. University of Minnesota Press. Minneapolis, MN. 1998. 240p. ISBN:0-8166-2892-0, ISBN13: 978-0-8166-2892-6. Dewey:307.1/416/0973. LCCN:98-010858.

Audience: **l,u,f.** *Choice, 1999.*

Cochrane, Allan   **HT133**
Understanding Urban Policy: A Critical Introduction. Trade Paper. Blackwell Publishing, Inc. Malden, MA. 2006. 256p. ISBN:0-631-21121-7, ISBN13: 978-0-631-21121-1. Dewey:307.76. LCCN:2006-018674.

Audience: **l,u,f.**

Colton, Kent W.   **HD7287.3**
Housing in the Twenty-First Century: Achieving Common Ground. Trade Cloth. Harvard University Press. Cambridge, MA. 2003. 528p. Wertheim Publications in Industrial Relations Ser. ISBN:0-674-01093-0, ISBN13: 978-0-674-01093-2. Dewey:363.5/0973.

Audience: **l,u.**

Dahl, Robert   **JS1195.2**
Who Governs?: Democracy and Power in an American City. Ed. 2. Douglas W. Rae (Foreword by). Trade Paper. Yale University Press. Cumberland, RI. 2005. 384p. ISBN:0-300-10392-1, ISBN13: 978-0-300-10392-2. Dewey:320.9746809046.

Audience: **l,u,f.**

Dilworth, Richardson   **HT334.U5D55 2004**
The Urban Origins of Suburban Autonomy. Trade Cloth. Harvard University Press. Cambridge, MA. 2005. 280p. ISBN:0-674-01531-2, ISBN13: 978-0-674-01531-9. Dewey:307.76/4/0973. LCCN:2004-054250.

Audience: **u,f.** *Choice, 2005.*

Dreier, Peter, et al.   **HV4045.D74 2004**
Place Matters: Metropolitics for the Twenty-First Century. Ed. 2. John H. Mollenkopf & Todd Swanstrom (Authors). Trade Paper. University Press of Kansas. Lawrence, KS. 2005. 328p. Studies in Government and Public Policy ISBN:0 7006 1364 1, ISBN13: 978-0-7006-1364-9. Dewey:307.76/0973. LCCN:2004-013599.

Audience: **l,u,f.** *Choice, 2002.*

Elkind, Sarah S.   **HD4464.B67E45 1998**
Bay Cities and Water Politics: The Battle for Resources in Boston and Oakland. Trade Cloth. University Press of Kansas. Lawrence, KS. 1998. viii, 246p. Development of Western Resources Ser. ISBN:0-7006-0907-5, ISBN13: 978-0-7006-0907-9. Dewey:363.6/1/0974461. LCCN:96-012351.

Audience: **l,u,f.** *Choice, 1999.*

Euchner, Charles C. &   **HT123.E83 2003**
  McGovern, Stephen J.
Urban Policy Reconsidered: Dialogues on the Problems and
Prospects of American Cities. Paper over Boards. Routledge.
New York, NY. 2003. 336p. ISBN:0-415-94470-8, ISBN13:
978-0-415-94470-0. Dewey:307.76/0973. LCCN:2002-045467.

                    Audience: **l,u,f.**

Fainstein, Susan S.   **HT178.G72L56365 2001**
The City Builders: Property Development in New York and
London, 1980-2000. Ed. 2. Trade Cloth. University Press of
Kansas. Lawrence, KS. 2004. 326p. Studies in Government and
Public Policy ISBN:0-7006-1132-0, ISBN13:
978-0-7006-1132-4. Dewey:307.76/09421. LCCN:2001-026015.

          Audience: **l,u,f.** *Choice, 2002.*

Fisher, Robert & Kling,   **JA71**
  Joe (Editors)
Mobilizing the Community: Local Politics in the Era of the
Global City, Vol. 41. Trade Paper. SAGE Publications, Inc.
Thousand Oaks, CA. 1993. 338p. Urban Affairs Annual Review
Ser., Vol. 41 ISBN:0-8039-4248-6, ISBN13: 978-0-8039-4248-6.
Dewey:320.

                    Audience: **l,u,f.**

Friedmann, John   **HT384.C6F75 2005**
China's Urban Transition. Trade Cloth. University of Minnesota
Press. Minneapolis, MN. 2005. 196p. ISBN:0-8166-4614-7,
ISBN13: 978-0-8166-4614-2. Dewey:307.76/0951.
LCCN:2004-022458.

           Audience: **u,f.** *Choice, 2006.*

Frug, Gerald E.   **HT167.F78 1999**
ⓔ City Making: Building Communities Without Building Walls.
E-Book. Princeton University Press. Princeton, NJ.
ISBN:1-4008-1168-6, ISBN13: 978-1-4008-1168-7.
Dewey:307.1/216/0973.

          Audience: **l,u,f.** *Choice, 2000.*

Gottdiener, M.   **HT334.U5G66 1994**
The Social Production of Urban Space. Ed. 2. Trade Paper.
University of Texas Press. Austin, TX. 1994. 340p.
ISBN:0-292-72772-0, ISBN13: 978-0-292-72772-4.
Dewey:307.7/6/0973. LCCN:93-039444.

          Audience: **u,f.** *Choice, 1986.*

Gottdiener, Mark   **JS323.G58 1987**
The Decline of Urban Politics: Political Theory and the Crisis of
the Local State. Trade Paper. SAGE Publications, Inc. Thousand
Oaks, CA. 1987. 300p. Library of Social Research, Vol. 162
ISBN:0-8039-2714-2, ISBN13: 978-0-8039-2714-8.
Dewey:320.8/0973. LCCN:86-014020.

                    Audience: **u,f.**

Graham, Stephen   **HT119.C573 2004**
  (Editor)
Cities, War, and Terrorism: Towards an Urban Geopolitics.
Trade Paper. Blackwell Publishing, Inc. Malden, MA. 2004.
416p. Studies in Urban and Social Change ISBN:1-4051-1575-0,
ISBN13: 978-1-4051-1575-9. Dewey:307.76.
LCCN:2004-004244.

          Audience: **l,u,f.** *Choice, 2005.*

Greene, Richard P. &   **GF125.G74 2005**
  Pick, James B.
Exploring the Urban Community: A GIS Approach. Trade Paper.
Prentice Hall PTR. Upper Saddle River, NJ. 2005. 512p.
Prentice Hall Series in Geographic Information Science

ISBN:0-13-017576-5, ISBN13: 978-0-13-017576-2.
Dewey:307.76. LCCN:2005-004926.

                    Audience: **l,u,f.**

Healey, Patsy (Editor),   **HT107.M35 1995**
  et al.
Managing Cities: The New Urban Context. Stuart Cameron,
Simin Davoudi, Stephen Graham & Ali Madani-Pour (Editors).
Trade Cloth. John Wiley & Sons, Inc. Hoboken, NJ. 1995. 332p.
ISBN:0-471-94922-1, ISBN13: 978-0-471-94922-0.
Dewey:307.76. LCCN:94-040240.

          Audience: **l,u,f.** *Choice, 1995.*

Indergaard, Michael   **HD9696.8.U63N745**
Silicon Alley: The Rise and Fall of a New Media District. Paper
over Boards. Routledge. New York, NY. 2004. 256p. Cultural
Spaces Ser. ISBN:0-415-93570-9, ISBN13: 978-0-415-93570-8.
Dewey:338.4/7004678/09747. LCCN:2003-013134.

                    Audience: **l,u,f.**

Isin, Engin F.   **JS67.D45 2000**
Democracy, Citizenship and the Global City: Rights, Democracy
and Place. Paper over Boards. Routledge. New York, NY. 2000.
336p. Innis Centenary Ser. ISBN:0-415-21667-2, ISBN13:
978-0-415-21667-8. Dewey:321.8. LCCN:00-025432.

          Audience: **l,u,f.** *Choice, 2001.*

Judd, Dennis R. &   **JS331.J78 2005**
  Swanstrom, Todd
City Politics: The Political Economy of Urban America. Ed. 5.
Trade Paper. Longman Publishing. Boston, MA. 2005. 464p.
ISBN:0-321-32816-7, ISBN13: 978-0-321-32816-8.
Dewey:320.8/5/0973. LCCN:2005-000456.

                    Audience: **l,u,f.**

Katznelson, Ira   **HT123**
City Trenches: Urban Politics and the Patterning of Class in the
United States. Trade Paper. University of Chicago Press.
Chicago, IL. 1982. 286p. ISBN:0-226-42673-4, ISBN13:
978-0-226-42673-0. Dewey:307.7/6/0973. LCCN:82-008392.

                    Audience: **u,f.**

Kazepov, Yuri (Editor)   **HT131.C56 2004**
Cities of Europe: Changing Contexts, Local Arrangements and
the Challenge to Urban Cohesion. Trade Cloth. Blackwell
Publishing, Inc. Malden, MA. 2005. 368p. Studies in Urban and
Social Change ISBN:1-4051-2133-5, ISBN13:
978-1-4051-2133-0. Dewey:307.76094. LCCN:2004-008399.
          Audience: **l,u,f.** *Choice, 2005.*

Kohn, Margaret   **HT123.K64 2004**
Brave New Neighborhoods: The Privatization of Public Space.
Paper over Boards. Routledge. New York, NY. 2004. 240p.
ISBN:0-415-94462-7, ISBN13: 978-0-415-94462-5.
Dewey:323.44/3/0973. LCCN:2003-022339.

          Audience: **l,u,f.** *Choice, 2004.*

Kweit, Robert W. &   **HT123.K9 1999**
  Kweit, Mary G.
People and Politics in Urban America. Ed. 2. Trade Paper.
Garland Publishing, Inc. New York, NY. 1998. 470p. Garland
Reference Library of Social Science, Vol. 1147
ISBN:0-8153-2606-8, ISBN13: 978-0-8153-2606-9.
Dewey:320.8/5/0973. LCCN:98-006537.

                    Audience: **l,u,f.**

Audience: g=general, l=lower division undergraduate, u=upper division undergraduate, f=faculty.

723

Ladd, Helen F. &　　　　　　**HJ9145.L32 1989**
Yinger, John M.
America's Ailing Cities: Fiscal Health and the Design of Urban
Policy. Trade Cloth. Johns Hopkins University Press. Baltimore,
MD. 1989. 368p. ISBN:0-8018-3767-7, ISBN13:
978-0-8018-3767-8. Dewey:336/.014/73. LCCN:88-013653.
Audience: **l,u,f.** *Choice, 1989.*

Levine, Myron A. &　　　　　　　　**JS323**
Ross, Bernard H.
Urban Politics: Power in Metropolitan America. Ed. 7. Paper
Text. Thomson Wadsworth. Belmont, CA. 2005. 592p.
ISBN:0-534-60487-0, ISBN13: 978-0-534-60487-5.
Dewey:320.850973. LCCN:2005-925536.
Audience: **l,u,f.**

Lewis, Paul G.　　　　　　　　**HT167.L48 1996**
Shaping Suburbia: How Political Institutions Organize Urban
Development. Trade Paper. University of Pittsburgh Press.
Pittsburgh, PA. 1996. 208p. Pitt Series in Policy and
Institutional ISBN:0-8229-5595-4, ISBN13: 978-0-8229-5595-5.
Dewey:307.76/0973. LCCN:95-052088.
Audience: **l,u,f.** *Choice, 1997.*

Ley, David　　　　　　　　**HT178.C2L49 1996**
The New Middle Class and the Remaking of the Central City.
Trade Cloth. Oxford University Press, Inc. New York, NY. 1997.
400p. Oxford Geographical and Environmental Studies
ISBN:0-19-823292-6, ISBN13: 978-0-19-823292-6.
Dewey:305.5/5/0971. LCCN:96-011424.
Audience: **l,u,f.** *Choice, 1998.*

Logan, John R. &　　　　　　　　**HT151**
Molotch, Harvey L. (Editors)
Urban Fortunes: The Political Economy of Place. Trade Paper.
University of California Press. Berkeley, CA. 1988. 383p.
ISBN:0-520-06341-4, ISBN13: 978-0-520-06341-9.
Dewey:307.7/6.
Audience: **u,f.** *Choice, 1987.*

Low, Setha & Smith,　　　　　**HT153.P654 2005**
Neil (Editors)
The Politics of Public Space. Perfect, Paper over Boards.
Routledge. New York, NY. 2005. 200p. ISBN:0-415-95138-0,
ISBN13: 978-0-415-95138-8. Dewey:304.2/3.
LCCN:2005-008804.
Audience: **l,u,f.**

Lowi, Theodore J.　　　　　　　　**JS1234.A1**
At the Pleasure of the Mayor. Trade Cloth. Simon & Schuster.
New York, NY. 1964. ISBN:0-02-919420-2, ISBN13:
978-0-02-919420-1. Dewey:352.07471. LCCN:64-011216.
Audience: **l,u,f.**

Lyons, W. E., et al.　　　　　　　**JS323.L97 1992**
The Politics of Dissatisfaction: Citizens, Services and Urban
Institutions. David Lowery & Ruth Hoogland DeHoog
(Authors), Kenneth S. Meier (Foreword by). Cloth Text. M. E.
Sharpe Inc. Armonk, NY. 1992. 248p. Bureaucracies, Public
Administration, and Public Policy Ser. ISBN:0-87332-898-1,
ISBN13: 978-0-87332-898-2. Dewey:321.80973.
LCCN:91-035287.
Audience: **l,u,f.** *Choice, 1993.*

Mills, Edwin S.　　　　　　　　**HT0321.M5**
Studies in the Structure of the Urban Economy. Trade Paper.
Books on Demand. Ann Arbor, MI. 166p. ISBN:0-598-12040-8,
ISBN13: 978-0-598-12040-3. Dewey:330.9/173/2.
LCCN:71-179873.
Audience: **u,f.**

Mollenkopf, John Hull　　　　　　　　**JS422**
The Contested City. Trade Paper. Princeton University Press.
Princeton, NJ. 1983. 344p. ISBN:0-691-02220-8, ISBN13:
978-0-691-02220-8. Dewey:352/.008/0973. LCCN:83-042568.
Audience: **l,u,f.**

National Research　　　　　　**JS422.N39 1999**
Council Staff
Governance and Opportunity in Metropolitan America:
Governmental Arrangements and Individual Life Chances in
Urban America. Alan Altshuler (Editor). Trade Cloth. National
Academies Press. Washington, DC. 1999. ix, 347p.
ISBN:0-309-06553-4, ISBN13: 978-0-309-06553-5.
Dewey:352.14/0973. LCCN:99-006607.
Audience: **l,u,f.** *Choice, 2000.*

Nivola, Pietro S.　　　　　　**HT384.U5N58 1999**
Laws of the Landscape: How Policies Shape Cities in Europe
and America. Trade Paper. Brookings Institution Press.
Washington, DC. 1999. 126p. Brookings Metropolitan Ser.
ISBN:0-8157-6081-7, ISBN13: 978-0-8157-6081-8.
Dewey:307.76/0973. LCCN:98-058140.
Audience: **l,u,f.**

Noyelle, Thierry J. &　　　　　**HT334.U5 N65 1984**
Stanback, Thomas M. Jr.
The Economic Transformation of American Cities. Trade Cloth.
Rowman & Littlefield Publishers, Inc. Lanham, MD. 1984.
298p. Conservation of Human Resources Ser., Vol. 19
ISBN:0-86598-144-2, ISBN13: 978-0-86598-144-7.
Dewey:330.973. LCCN:83-021292.
Audience: **l,u,f.**

O'Connor, Alice　　　　　　**HT123 .U7454**
(Editor), et al.
Urban Inequality: Evidence from Four Cities. Chris Tilly &
Lawrence Bobo (Editors). Trade Paper. Russell Sage
Foundation. New York, NY. 2003. 564p. ISBN:0-87154-651-5,
ISBN13: 978-0-87154-651-7. Dewey:307.760973.
Audience: **l,u,f.**

Orfield, Myron W.　　　　　**HT334.U5O72 2002**
Metropolitics: A Regional Agenda for Community and Stability.
Trade Cloth. Brookings Institution Press. Washington, DC. 1998.
245p. ISBN:0-8157-6640-8, ISBN13: 978-0-8157-6640-7.
Dewey:307.76/4/0973. LCCN:2001-007582.
Audience: **l,u,f.** *Choice, 1997.*

Pagano, Michael A. &　　　　　**HT175.P32 1995**
Bowman, Ann O.
Cityscapes and Capital: The Politics of Urban Development.
Trade Cloth. Johns Hopkins University Press. Baltimore, MD.
1995. 208p. ISBN:0-8018-5034-7, ISBN13: 978-0-8018-5034-9.
Dewey:307.3/416. LCCN:94-040582.
Audience: **l,u,f.** *Choice, 1996.*

Pagano, Michael A. &　　　　　**HJ9145.P34 1985**
Moore, Richard
Cities and Fiscal Choices: A New Model of Urban Public
Investment. Trade Cloth. Duke University Press. Durham, NC.
1985. xii, 166p. Duke Press Policy Studies

Formats: Web: ☐　Ebook: 🄴　CD/DVD-ROM: 🛞　BCL3: 𝐵

ISBN:0-8223-0653-0, ISBN13: 978-0-8223-0653-5. Dewey:336.02/73. LCCN:85-016211.

Audience: **l,u,f.**   *Choice, 1986.*

Pelissero, John P.   JS331.C54 2003
   (Editor)
Cities, Politics, and Policy: A Comparative Analysis. Trade Paper. CQ Press. Washington, DC. 2002. 350p. ISBN:1-56802-686-2, ISBN13: 978-1-56802-686-2. Dewey:320.8/5/0973. LCCN:2002-015014.

Audience: **l,u,f.**   *Choice, 2003.*

Pinder, David   HT113.P56 2005
Visions of the City: Utopianism, Power, and Politics in Twentieth-Century Urbanism. Trade Cloth. Routledge. New York, NY. 2006. 352p. ISBN:0-415-95310-3, ISBN13: 978-0-415-95310-8. Dewey:307.1/216/0904. LCCN:2005-016223.

Audience: **l,u,f.**

Pritchett, Wendell E.   F129.B7P75 2003
Brownsville, Brooklyn: Blacks, Jews, and the Changing Face of the Ghetto. Trade Paper. University of Chicago Press. Chicago, IL. 2003. 340p. Historical Studies of Urban America Ser. ISBN:0-226-68447-4, ISBN13: 978-0-226-68447-5. Dewey:573.8/719.

Audience: **l,u,f.**   *Choice, 2003, 2002.*

Rabinowitz, Alan   HT1230.R22 2004
Urban Economics and Land Use in America: The Transformation of Cities in the Twentieth Century. Trade Cloth. M. E. Sharpe Inc. Armonk, NY. 2004. 272p. ISBN:0-7656-1410-3, ISBN13: 978-0-7656-1410-0. Dewey:307.76/0973. LCCN:2003-061448.

Audience: **l,u,f.**   *Choice, 2004.*

Ranney, David   HC108.C4R35 2003
Global Decisions, Local Collisions: Urban Life in the New World Order. Trade Cloth. Temple University Press. Philadelphia, PA. 2002. 296p. ISBN:1-59213-001-1, ISBN13: 978-1-59213-001-6. Dewey:330.9773/11. LCCN:2002-070252.

Audience: **u,f.**

Rusk, David   HT123.R843 1999
Inside Game-Outside Game: Winning Strategies for Saving Urban America. Trade Cloth. Brookings Institution Press. Washington, DC. 2001. 384p. A Century Foundation Bk. ISBN:0-8157-7650-0, ISBN13: 978-0-8157-7650-5. Dewey:307.76/0973. LCCN:98-025430.

Audience: **l,u,f.**

Sassen, Saskia (Editor)   HT321.G55 2002
Global Networks Linked Cities. UK-B Format Paperback. Routledge. New York, NY. 2002. 376p. ISBN:0-415-93163-0, ISBN13: 978-0-415-93163-2. Dewey:303.48/34. LCCN:2001-041831.

Audience: **l,u,f.**

Savitch, H. V. &   HT321.S29 2004
   Kantor, Paul
Cities in the International Marketplace: The Political Economy of Urban Development in North America and Western Europe. Trade Paper. Princeton University Press. Princeton, NJ. 2004. 480p. ISBN:0-691-12014-5, ISBN13: 978-0-691-12014-0. Dewey:307.76.

Audience: **l,u,f.**   *Choice, 2003.*

Sayre, Wallace S.   JS1228 .S37
Governing New York City: Politics in the Metropolis. Paper Text. Textbook Publishers. Temecula, CA. 2003. 815p. ISBN:0-7581-4319-2, ISBN13: 978-0-7581-4319-8. Dewey:352.07471.

Audience: **l,u,f.**

Scott, Allen J. (Editor)   HT330.G554
Global City-Regions: Trends, Theory, Policy. Trade Paper. Oxford University Press, Inc. New York, NY. 2002. 486p. ISBN:0-19-925230-0, ISBN13: 978-0-19-925230-5. Dewey:307.76.

Audience: **l,u,f.**

Sharp, Elaine B.   JS331.S46 2005
Morality Politics in American Cities. Yvette Alex-Assensoh, Susan Clarke & Richard DeLeon (As told tos). Perfect, Paper over Boards. University Press of Kansas. Lawrence, KS. 2005. 243p. Studies in Government and Public Policy ISBN:0-7006-1373-0, ISBN13: 978-0-7006-1373-1. Dewey:320.6/0973. LCCN:2004-025499.

Audience: **l,u,f.**   *Choice, 2005.*

Shefter, Martin   HJ9289.N4 S54 1992
Political Crisis - Fiscal Crisis: The Collapse and Revival of New York City. Trade Paper. Edinburgh University Press. Edinburgh, 1992. 270p. ISBN:0-231-07943-5, ISBN13: 978-0-231-07943-3. Dewey:336.747/1. LCCN:91-038495.

Audience: **l,u,f.**   *Choice, 1985.*

Sidney, Mara S.   HD7288.76.U5S53 2003
Unfair Housing: How National Policy Shapes Community Action. Trade Cloth. University Press of Kansas. Lawrence, KS. 2003. xiv, 186p. Studies in Government and Public Policy ISBN:0-7006-1275-0, ISBN13: 978-0-7006-1275-8. Dewey:363.5/5/0973. LCCN:2003-008802.

Audience: **l,u,f.**   *Choice, 2004.*

Stone, Clarence N. &   JS341.P65 1987
   Sanders, Heywood T. (Editors)
The Politics of Urban Development. Trade Cloth. University Press of Kansas. Lawrence, KS. 1987. viii, 312p. Studies in Government and Public Policy ISBN:0-7006-0332-8, ISBN13: 978-0-7006-0332-9. Dewey:320.973. LCCN:87-013311.

Audience: **l,u,f.**   *Choice, 1988.*

Sugrue, Thomas J.   F574.D49N4835 2005
The Origins of the Urban Crisis: Race and Inequality in Postwar Detroit. Ed. 2. I. R. A. Katznelson, Martin Shefter & Theda Skocpol (Editors). Trade Paper, Perfect. Princeton University Press. Princeton, NJ. 2005. 416p. Princeton Studies in American Politics ISBN:0-691-12186-9, ISBN13: 978-0-691-12186-4. Dewey:305.8/00977434. LCCN:2005-047695.

Audience: **l,u,f.**   *Choice, 1997.*

Tangires, Helen   HF5472.U6T36 2002
Public Markets and Civic Culture in Nineteenth-Century America. Trade Cloth. Johns Hopkins University Press. Baltimore, MD. 2003. 296p. Creating the North American Landscape Ser. ISBN:0-8018-7133-6, ISBN13: 978-0-8018-7133-7. Dewey:381/.1/097309034. LCCN:2002-005381.

Audience: **l,u,f.**   *Choice, 2004.*

United Nations: Human   HT151
   Settlements Programme
The State of the World's Cities 2004/2005: Globalization and Urban Culture. Trade Paper. United Nations Publications. New

York, NY. 2005. 216p. ISBN:92-1-131705-3, ISBN13: 978-92-1-131705-3. Dewey:307.76.

Audience: **l,u,f.**

Van Den Berg, Leo, et al.   **HT131**
European Cities in the Knowledge Economy: The Cases of Amsterdam, Dortmund, Eindhoven, Helsinki, Manchester, Munich, Munster, Rotterdam and Zaragoza. Peter M. J. Pol, Willem van Winden & Paulus Woets (Authors). Trade Cloth. Ashgate Publishing, Ltd. Aldershot, 2005. 380p. EURICUR Series (European Institute for Comparative Urban Research) Ser. ISBN:0-7546-4521-5, ISBN13: 978-0-7546-4521-4. Dewey:307.76094. LCCN:2005-924973.

Audience: **l,u,f.**

Wilson, John Q.   **TK5101**
City Politics and Public Policy. Ed. 99. Paper Text. John Wiley & Sons, Inc. Hoboken, NJ. 1968. 300p. ISBN:0-471-94959-0, ISBN13: 978-0-471-94959-6. Dewey:621.38. LCCN:67-030636.

Audience: **l,u,f.**

World Bank Institute   **HT151.C5686 2006**
Staff
Cities in a Globalizing World. Frannie Léautier & Xingzhu Liu (Editors). Trade Paper. World Bank Publications. Washington, DC. 2005. 144p. WBI Learning Resources Ser. ISBN:0-8213-6553-3, ISBN13: 978-0-8213-6553-3. Dewey:307.76. LCCN:2005-057897.

Audience: **l,u,f.**

Urban Architecture

Ladd, Brian   **HT169.G32B4127 1997**
The Ghosts of Berlin: Confronting German History in the Urban Landscape. Trade Cloth. University of Chicago Press. Chicago, IL. 1997. 282p. ISBN:0-226-46761-9, ISBN13: 978-0-226-46761-0. Dewey:307.121. LCCN:96-028562.

Audience: **g,l,u,f.**

Urban Architecture > Urban development and redevelopment

Bunnell, Gene   **NA9108**
Making Places Special: Stories of Real Places Made Better by Planning. Trade Cloth, CD-ROM. American Planning Association. Chicago, IL. 2003. 588p. ISBN:1-884829-58-9, ISBN13: 978-1-884829-58-1. Dewey:307.12160973. LCCN:2001-131721.

Audience: **l,u,f.**

Duany, Andres, et al.   **HT123**
Suburban Nation: The Rise of Sprawl and the Decline of the American Dream. Elizabeth Plater-Zyberk & Jeff Speck (Authors). Trade Paper. Farrar, Straus & Giroux. New York, NY. 2001. 320p. ISBN:0-86547-606-3, ISBN13: 978-0-86547-606-6. Dewey:307.76/0973.

Audience: **l,u,f.** *Choice, 2000.*

Hall, Peter   **HT166.H349 2002**
Cities of Tomorrow: An Intellectual History of Urban Planning and Design in the Twentieth Century. Ed. 3. Trade Paper. Blackwell Publishing, Inc. Malden, MA. 2002. 576p.

ISBN:0-631-23252-4, ISBN13: 978-0-631-23252-0. Dewey:307.1/2/0904. LCCN:2001-052758.

Audience: **u,f.** *Choice, 1989.*

Hayden, Dolores   **HT123**
Building Suburbia: Green Fields and Urban Growth, 1820-2000. Trade Paper. Knopf Publishing Group. New York, NY. 2004. 336p. ISBN:0-375-72721-3, ISBN13: 978-0-375-72721-4. Dewey:307.76/0973.

Audience: **u,f.** *Choice, 2004.*

Holleran, Michael   **F73.37**
Boston's "Changeful Times": Origins of Preservation and Planning in America. Trade Paper. Johns Hopkins University Press. Baltimore, MD. 2001. 352p. Creating the North American Landscape Ser. ISBN:0-8018-6644-8, ISBN13: 978-0-8018-6644-9. Dewey:974.4/61.

Audience: **g,l,u,f.** *Choice, 1999.*

Kayden, Jerold S., et al.   **HT151.K345 2000**
Privately Owned Public Space: The New York City Experience. Municipal Art Society of New York Staff & New York City Department of City Planning (Authors). Trade Cloth. John Wiley & Sons, Inc. Hoboken, NJ. 2000. 360p. ISBN:0-471-36257-3, ISBN13: 978-0-471-36257-9. Dewey:333.33/7/097471. LCCN:00-035193.

Audience: **l,u,f.**

Lynch, Kevin   **NA9108**
The Image of the City. Trade Paper. MIT Press. Cambridge, MA. 1960. 202p. ISBN:0-262-62001-4, ISBN13: 978-0-262-62001-7. Dewey:711.40973.

Audience: **l,u,f.** *B*

Reichl, Alexander J.   **HT168.N5R45 1999**
Reconstructing Times Square: Politics and Culture in Urban Development. Trade Paper. University Press of Kansas. Lawrence, KS. 1999. xii, 240p. Studies in Government and Public Policy ISBN:0-7006-0950-4, ISBN13: 978-0-7006-0950-5. Dewey:307.1/216/097471. LCCN:98-055259.

Audience: **l,u,f.** *Choice, 1999.*

Robbins, Edward &   **HT166.S399 2003**
El-Khoury, Rodolphe (Editors)
Shaping the City: Studies in History, Theory and Urban Design. Paper over Boards. Routledge. New York, NY. 2004. 280p. ISBN:0-415-26188-0, ISBN13: 978-0-415-26188-3. Dewey:307.1/216. LCCN:2002-156108.

Audience: **l,u,f.**

Sorkin, Michael   **HT123.V37 1992**
(Editor)
Variations on a Theme Park: The New American City and the End of Public Space. Trade Paper. Farrar, Straus & Giroux. New York, NY. 1992. 252p. ISBN:0-374-52314-2, ISBN13: 978-0-374-52314-5. Dewey:307.76/0973. LCCN:91-022976.

Audience: **l,u,f.**

Vale, Lawrence J.   **NA4195.V35 1992**
Architecture, Power, and National Identity. Cloth over Boards. Yale University Press. Cumberland, RI. 1992. 350p. ISBN:0-300-04958-7, ISBN13: 978-0-300-04958-9. Dewey:725/.11. LCCN:91-024557.

Audience: **l,u,f.** *Choice, 1992.*

Wagner, Fritz W.   **HT175.U743 1995**
(Editor), et al.
Urban Revitalization: Policies and Programs. Timothy E. Joder

& Anthony J. Mumphrey Jr. (Editors). Trade Paper. SAGE
Publications, Inc. Thousand Oaks, CA. 1995. 248p.
ISBN:0-8039-5870-6, ISBN13: 978-0-8039-5870-8.
Dewey:307.3/4/16/0973. LCCN:94-042555.

Audience: **l,u,f.** *Choice, 1995.*

Weinberg, Adam S., et al.   **HN49.C6W437 2000**
Urban Recycling and the Search for Sustainable Community
Development. David N. Pellow & Allan Schnaiberg (Authors).
Trade Cloth. Princeton University Press. Princeton, NJ. 2000.
236p. ISBN:0-691-05014-7, ISBN13: 978-0-691-05014-0.
Dewey:307.1/4. LCCN:00-021055.

Audience: **l,u,f.** *Choice, 2001.*

Zielenbach, John W.   **HT177.C5Z54 2000**
The Art of Revitalization: Improving Conditions in Distressed
Inner City Neighborhoods. Paper over Boards. Garland
Publishing, Inc. New York, NY. 2000. xi, 308p. Contemporary
Urban Affairs Ser., Vol. 12 ISBN:0-8153-3597-0, ISBN13:
978-0-8153-3597-9. Dewey:307.3/416/0977311.
LCCN:99-043812.

Audience: **l,u,f.** *Choice, 2001.*

Urban Architecture > Urban planning and land use

Bednar, Michael J   **NA9127.W2B43 2006**
L'Enfant's Legacy: Public Open Spaces in Washington, D.C.
Trade Cloth. Johns Hopkins University Press. Baltimore, MD.
2006. 304p. Creating the North American Landscape Ser.
ISBN:0-8018-8318-0, ISBN13: 978-0-8018-8318-7.
Dewey:712/.5/09753. LCCN:2005-016599.

Audience: **u,f.** *Choice, 2006.*

Bruegmann, Robert   **HT371.B74 2005**
Sprawl: A Compact History. Trade Cloth. University of Chicago
Press. Chicago, IL. 2005. 306p. ISBN:0-226-07690-3, ISBN13:
978-0-226-07690-4. Dewey:307.76. LCCN:2005-007591.

Audience: **g,l,u,f.**

Buchwald, Emilie   **NA9053.H76T69 2003**
(Editor)
Toward the Livable City. Trade Paper. Milkweed Editions.
Minneapolis, MN. 2003. 312p. ISBN:1-57131-271-4, ISBN13:
978-1-57131-271-6. Dewey:307.3/416. LCCN:2003-010374.

Audience: **l,u,f.** *Choice, 2004.*

Campbell, Scott &   **HT165.5.R43 2003**
Fainstein, Susan S. (Editors)
Readings in Planning Theory. Ed. 2. Trade Paper. Blackwell
Publishing, Inc. Malden, MA. 2003. 488p. ISBN:0-631-22347-9,
ISBN13: 978-0-631-22347-4. Dewey:307.1/216/0973.
LCCN:2002-066635.

Audience: **l,u,f.**

Couch, Chris, et al.   **HT384**
Urban Sprawl: European patterns and Policy. Lila Leontidou &
Jens Dangschat (Authors), Gerhard Petschel-held (Editor). Trade
Paper. Blackwell Publishing, Inc. Malden, MA. 2007. 272p.
ISBN:1-4051-3917-X, ISBN13: 978-1-4051-3917-5.
Dewey:307.76094.

Audience: **u,f.**

Coupland, A. (Editor)   **HT169.G7**
Reclaiming the City. UK-B Format Paperback. Routledge. New
York, NY. 1996. 308p. ISBN:0-419-21360-0, ISBN13:
978-0-419-21360-4. Dewey:711.4/0941. LCCN:96-070576.

Audience: **u,f.**

Cullingworth, J. Barry   **HD205.C85 1993**
The Political Culture of Planning: American Land Use Planning
in Comparative Perspective. Paper over Boards. Routledge. New
York, NY. 1993. 368p. ISBN:0-415-08812-7, ISBN13:
978-0-415-08812-1. Dewey:711.0973. LCCN:92-018452.

Audience: **l,u,f.**

Ellin, Nan (Editor)   **NA2542.4.A735 1997**
Architecture of Fear. Trade Paper. Princeton Architectural Press.
New York, NY. 1997. 320p. ISBN:1-56898-082-5, ISBN13:
978-1-56898-082-9. Dewey:720/.1/104. LCCN:96-037635.

Audience: **u,f.**

Ford, Larry   **HT167.F675 2003**
America's New Downtowns: Revitalization or Reinvention?
Trade Cloth. Johns Hopkins University Press. Baltimore, MD.
2003. 360p. Creating the North American Landscape Ser.
ISBN:0-8018-7163-8, ISBN13: 978-0-8018-7163-4.
Dewey:307.3/416/0973. LCCN:2002-007933.

Audience: **u,f.** *Choice, 2004.*

Freestone, Robert   **HT166.U7425 2000**
(Editor)
Urban Planning in a Changing World: The Twentieth Century
Experience. Ed. 2. Paper over Boards. Routledge. New York,
NY. 2000. 304p. Studies in History, Planning, and the
Environment ISBN:0-419-24650-9, ISBN13: 978-0-419-24650-3.
Dewey:307.1/216/0904. LCCN:99-087685.

Audience: **l,u,f.**

Frumkin, Howard, et al.   **HT371.F78 2004**
Urban Sprawl and Public Health: Designing, Planning, and
Building for Healthy Communities. Lawrence D. Frank &
Richard Jackson (Authors). Trade Cloth. Island Press.
Washington, DC. 2004. 288p. ISBN:1-55963-912-1, ISBN13:
978-1-55963-912-5. Dewey:307.76. LCCN:2004-002136.

Audience: **l,u,f.** *Choice, 2005.*

Gandy, Matthew   **HT243.U62N74 2002**
Concrete and Clay: Reworking Nature in New York City. Trade
Cloth. MIT Press. Cambridge, MA. 2002. 358p. Urban and
Industrial Environments Ser. ISBN:0-262-07224-6, ISBN13:
978-0-262-07224-3. Dewey:304.2/09747/1. LCCN:2001-054604.

Audience: **l,u,f.** *Choice, 2002.*

Garcia-Mira, Ricardo   **HT151**
(Editor), et al.
Housing, Space and Quality of Life. Jose Romay, J. Eulogio
Real & David L. Uzzell (Editors). Trade Cloth. Ashgate
Publishing, Ltd. Aldershot, 2005. 186p. Ethnoscapes Ser.
ISBN:0-7546-4255-0, ISBN13: 978-0-7546-4255-8.
Dewey:363.5. LCCN:2004-027709.

Audience: **l,u,f.**

Garvin, Alexander   **NA9105.G37 2002**
The American City: What Works, What Doesn't. Ed. 2. Trade
Cloth. McGraw-Hill Professional Publishing. New York, NY.
2002. 560p. ISBN:0-07-137367-5, ISBN13: 978-0-07-137367-8.
Dewey:711/.4/0973. LCCN:2002-026345.

Audience: **l,u,f.** *Choice, 2003.*

Germic, Stephen A.   **E169.1.G458 2001**
American Green: Class, Crisis and the Deployment of Nature in
Central Park, Yosemite and Yellowstone. Trade Cloth. Lexington
Books. Lanham, MD. 2001. 160p. ISBN:0-7391-0228-1,
ISBN13: 978-0-7391-0228-2. Dewey:333.78/3/097309034.
LCCN:00-052030.

Audience: **u,f.** *Choice, 2002.*

Gillespie, Angus K.   NA6233.N5W674 1999
Twin Towers: The Life of New York City's World Trade Center.
Trade Cloth. Rutgers University Press. Piscataway, NJ. 1999.
288p. ISBN:0-8135-2742-2, ISBN13: 978-0-8135-2742-0.
Dewey:725/.23/097471. LCCN:99-015068.
Audience: **g,l,u,f.** *Choice, 2000.*

Grogan, Paul &   HT175.G76 2001
   Proscio, Tony
Comeback Cities: A Blueprint for Urban Neighborhood Revival.
Trade Paper. Westview Press. Boulder, CO. 2001. 320p.
ISBN:0-8133-3952-9, ISBN13: 978-0-8133-3952-8.
Dewey:307.3/416/0973. LCCN:2001-055946.
Audience: **l,u,f.**

Hall, Kenneth B. &   HT167.H29 2001
   Porterfield, Gerald A.
Community by Design: New Urbanism for Suburbs and Small
Communities. Cloth Text. McGraw-Hill Professional Publishing.
New York, NY. 2001. 296p. ISBN:0-07-134523-X, ISBN13:
978-0-07-134523-1. Dewey:307.1/216/0973. LCCN:00-050049.
Audience: **g,l,u,f.**

Hall, Peter   HT166.G7H34 2002
Urban and Regional Planning. Ed. 4. Trade Paper. Routledge.
New York, NY. 2002. 248p. ISBN:0-415-21777-6, ISBN13:
978-0-415-21777-4. Dewey:309.2/62/0941. LCCN:2002-069951.
Audience: **l,u,f.**

Hise, Greg   HT394.L67H57 1997
Magnetic Los Angeles: Planning the Twentieth-Century
Metropolis. Trade Cloth. Johns Hopkins University Press.
Baltimore, MD. 1997. 320p. Creating the North American
Landscape Ser. ISBN:0-8018-5543-8, ISBN13:
978-0-8018-5543-6. Dewey:307.121. LCCN:96-050423.
Audience: **l,u,f.** *Choice, 1998.*

Judd, Dennis R. &   HT123.A6663 2006
   Kantor, Paul
American Urban Politics: The Reader. Ed. 4. Trade Paper,
Perfect. Longman Publishing Group. White Plains, NY. 2005.
417p. ISBN:0-321-12970-9, ISBN13: 978-0-321-12970-3.
Dewey:320.850973. LCCN:2005-017551.
Audience: **l,u,f.**

Kostof, Spiro   NA9090
The City Shaped: Urban Patterns and Meanings Through
History. Trade Paper. Little Brown & Company. New York, NY.
1993. 352p. ISBN:0-8212-2016-0, ISBN13: 978-0-8212-2016-0.
Dewey:711.4/09.
Audience: **l,u,f.**

Leach, Neil (Editor)   HT151
The Hieroglyphics of Space: Understanding the City. Paper over
Boards. Routledge. New York, NY. 2001. 320p.
ISBN:0-415-19891-7, ISBN13: 978-0-415-19891-2.
Dewey:307.7/6.
Audience: **u,f.**

Lejeune, Jean-Francois   NA702.C7813 2005
Cruelty and Utopia. Centre international pour la ville,
l'architecture et le paysage Staff (Contribution by). Trade Paper.
Princeton Architectural Press. New York, NY. 2005. 263p.
ISBN:1-56898-489-8, ISBN13: 978-1-56898-489-6.
Dewey:720/.98/091732. LCCN:2004-015433.
Audience: **u,f.** *Choice, 2005.*

Levy, John M.   HT167.L38 2006
Contemporary Urban Planning. Ed. 7. Trade Paper, Perfect.
Prentice Hall PTR. Upper Saddle River, NJ. 2005. 370p.
ISBN:0-13-193068-0, ISBN13: 978-0-13-193068-1.
Dewey:307.1/216/0973. LCCN:2005-018793.
Audience: **g,l,u,f.**

Low, Nicholas &   HE305.M35 2002
   Gleeson, Brendan (Editors)
Making Urban Transport Sustainable. Cloth over Boards.
Palgrave Macmillan. New York, NY. 2003. 304p. Global Issues
Ser. ISBN:0-333-98198-7, ISBN13: 978-0-333-98198-6.
Dewey:388.4/042. LCCN:2002-028747.
Audience: **l,u,f.** *Choice, 2003.*

MacLaran, Andrew   HT166
   (Author, Editor)
Making Space: Property Development and Urban Planning.
Trade Paper. Oxford University Press, Inc. New York, NY. 2003.
272p. An Arnold Publication ISBN:0-340-80827-6, ISBN13:
978-0-340-80827-6. Dewey:307.1/216. LCCN:2004-559506.
Audience: **l,u,f.**

Marcus, Clare Cooper   NA9070.P45
   & Francis, Carolyn (Editors)
People Places: Design Guidelines for Urban Open Space. Ed. 2.
Trade Paper. John Wiley & Sons, Inc. Hoboken, NJ. 1997. 367p.
ISBN:0-471-28833-0, ISBN13: 978-0-471-28833-6.
Dewey:711.409730904. LCCN:97-001233.
Audience: **l,u,f.**

Marcuse, Peter & van   HT119.G65 2000
   Kempen, Ronald (Editors)
Globalizing Cities: A New Spatial Order? Trade Paper.
Blackwell Publishing, Inc. Malden, MA. 2000. 336p. Studies in
Urban and Social Change ISBN:0-631-21290-6, ISBN13:
978-0-631-21290-4. Dewey:307.76. LCCN:99-043570.
Audience: **l,u,f.**

Marshall, Alex   HT166.M259 2000
How Cities Work: Suburbs, Sprawl, and the Roads Not Taken.
Trade Cloth. University of Texas Press. Austin, TX. 2001. 288p.
Constructs Ser. ISBN:0-292-75239-3, ISBN13:
978-0-292-75239-9. Dewey:307.76. LCCN:00-026691.
Audience: **l,u,f.** *Choice, 2001.*

Melosi, Martin V.   TD223.M45 2000
Sanitary City: Urban Infrastructure in America from Colonial
Times to the Present. Trade Cloth. Johns Hopkins University
Press. Baltimore, MD. 2000. 600p. Creating the North American
Landscape Ser. ISBN:0-8018-6152-7, ISBN13:
978-0-8018-6152-9. Dewey:363.6/1/0973. LCCN:99-029417.
Audience: **l,u,f.** *Choice, 2000.*

Murtagh, William J.   E159.M875 2005
Keeping Time: The History and Theory of Preservation in
America. Ed. 3. Trade Paper. John Wiley & Sons, Inc. Hoboken,
NJ. 2005. 272p. ISBN:0-471-47377-4, ISBN13:
978-0-471-47377-0. Dewey:363.6/9/0973. LCCN:2004-061237.
Audience: **g,l,u,f.**

Neill, William J. V.   HT166.N4218 2004
Urban Planning and Cultural Identity. Paper over Boards.
Routledge. New York, NY. 2003. 272p. The RTPI Library, Vol.
6 ISBN:0-415-19747-3, ISBN13: 978-0-415-19747-2.
Dewey:307.1/216. LCCN:2003-008576.
Audience: **u,f.**

Newman, Peter &   HT166.N48 2004
  Thornley, Andrew
Planning World Cities: Globalization, Urban Governance and
Policy Dilemmas. Cloth over Boards. Palgrave Macmillan. New
York, NY. 2004. 256p. Planning, Environment, Cities Ser.
ISBN:0-333-74869-7, ISBN13: 978-0-333-74869-5.
Dewey:307.1/216. LCCN:2004-052105.

Audience: **l,u,f.** *Choice, 2005.*

Nobel, Philip   NA6233.N5W67488 2005
Sixteen Acres: Architecture and the Outrageous Struggle for the
Future of Ground Zero. Metropolitan Books, Henry Holt and
Co.. 2005. ISBN:0-8050-7494-5, ISBN13: 978-0-8050-7494-9.

Audience: **g,l,u,f.**

Paloscia, Raffaele   HT151.C6344 2004
Contested Metropolis: Six Cities at the Beginning of the 21st
Century. Inura (Editor). Trade Paper. Birkhauser Verlag AG.
CH-4010 Basel, 2004. 304p. ISBN:3-7643-0086-8, ISBN13:
978-3-7643-0086-9. Dewey:307.76. LCCN:2004-301366.

Audience: **l,u,f.**

Peterson, Jon A.   HT167.P47 2003
The Birth of City Planning in the United States: 1840-1917.
Trade Cloth. Johns Hopkins University Press. Baltimore, MD.
2003. 464p. Creating the North American Landscape Ser.
ISBN:0-8018-7210-3, ISBN13: 978-0-8018-7210-5.
Dewey:307.76/0973. LCCN:2002-009870.

Audience: **l,u,f.** *Choice, 2004.*

Rybczynski, Witold   NA9105
City Life: Urban Expectations in a New World. Cloth Text.
DIANE Publishing Company. Collingdale, PA. 1998. 256p.
ISBN:0-7881-5517-2, ISBN13: 978-0-7881-5517-8.
Dewey:711/.4/0973.

Audience: **l,u,f.**

Serageldin, Ismail   CC135.H467 2001
  (Editor), et al.
Historic Cities and Sacred Sites: Cultural Roots for Urban
Futures. Joan Martin-Brown & Ephim Shluger (Editors). Trade
Paper. World Bank Publications. Washington, DC. 2001. 44p.
Bks. ISBN:0-8213-4904-X, ISBN13: 978-0-8213-4904-5.
Dewey:363.6/9. LCCN:00-069698.

Audience: **u,f.** *Choice, 2001.*

Smith, Neil   HT170.S55 1996
The New Urban Frontier: Gentrification and the Revanchist
City. Trade Paper. Routledge. New York, NY. 1996. 288p.
ISBN:0-415-13255-X, ISBN13: 978-0-415-13255-8.
Dewey:305/.091732. LCCN:95-046015.

Audience: **l,u,f.**

Sorensen, Andre   HT166
  (Editor), et al.
Towards Sustainable Cities: East Asian, North American and
European Perspectives on Managing Urban Regions. Peter
Marcotullio & Jill Grant (Editors). Trade Cloth. Ashgate
Publishing, Ltd. Aldershot, 2004. 324p. Urban Planning and
Environment Ser. ISBN:0-7546-3766-2, ISBN13:
978-0-7546-3766-0. Dewey:307.76. LCCN:2003-060707.

Audience: **l,u,f.**

Spirou, Costas &   GV415.S65 2003
  Bennett, Larry
It's Hardly Sportin': Stadiums, Neighborhoods, and the New
Chicago. Trade Paper. Northern Illinois University Press.

DeKalb, IL. 2003. 224p. ISBN:0-87580-305-9, ISBN13:
978-0-87580-305-0. Dewey:725/.827. LCCN:2002-141421.

Audience: **l,u,f.** *Choice, 2003.*

Stein, Jay M. (Editor)   HT167.C565 2004
Classic Readings in Urban Planning. Ed. 2. Paper Text.
American Planning Association. Chicago, IL. 2004. 432p.
ISBN:1-884829-90-2, ISBN13: 978-1-884829-90-1.
Dewey:307.1/216/0973. LCCN:2003-115360.

Audience: **l,u,f.**

Thall, Bob   F548.37.T48 1999
The New American Village. Trade Paper. Johns Hopkins
University Press. Baltimore, MD. 2000. 112p. Creating the
North American Landscape Ser. ISBN:0-8018-6158-6, ISBN13:
978-0-8018-6158-1. Dewey:977.3/11. LCCN:98-049379.

Audience: **l,u,f.**

Vale, Lawrence J. &   HT170.R46 2005
  Campanella, Thomas J.
The Resilient City: How Modern Cities Recover from Disaster.
Trade Cloth. Oxford University Press, Inc. New York, NY. 2005.
390p. ISBN:0-19-517584-0, ISBN13: 978-0-19-517584-4.
Dewey:307.3/416/09. LCCN:2004-049246.

Audience: **l,u,f.** *Choice, 2005.*

Vuchic, Vukan R.   HE308.V83 1999
Transportation for Livable Cities. Cloth Text. Center for Urban
Policy Research. New Brunswick, NJ. 1999. 377p.
ISBN:0-88285-161-6, ISBN13: 978-0-88285-161-7.
Dewey:388.4. LCCN:98-019218.

Audience: **l,u,f.** *Choice, 2000.*

Whyte, William H. Jr.   HT123.E9 1993
  (Editor)
Exploding Metropolis. Trade Paper. University of California
Press. Berkeley, CA. 1993. 212p. Classics in Urban History Ser.
ISBN:0-520-08090-4, ISBN13: 978-0-520-08090-4.
Dewey:307.760973. LCCN:92-028611.

Audience: **l,u,f.**

Willis, Carol   NA6232.W55 1995
Form Follows Finance: Skyscrapers and Skylines in New York
and Chicago. Trade Paper. Princeton Architectural Press. New
York, NY. 1995. 224p. ISBN:1-56898-044-2, ISBN13:
978-1-56898-044-7. Dewey:725/.23/097471. LCCN:95-024297.

Audience: **l,u,f.**

Wilson, William H.   HT167
The City Beautiful Movement. Trade Paper. Johns Hopkins
University Press. Baltimore, MD. 1963. 384p. Creating the
North American Landscape Ser. ISBN:0-8018-4978-0, ISBN13:
978-0-8018-4978-7. Dewey:307.1/2/0973. LCCN:88-028244.

Audience: **l,u,f.** *Choice, 1990.*

Urban Technology > Information Cities

Castells, Manuel   HC79.I55C373 2000
Rise of the Network Society. Ed. 2. Trade Paper. Blackwell
Publishing, Inc. Malden, MA. 2000. 624p. Information Age Ser.,
Vol. 1 ISBN:0-631-22140-9, ISBN13: 978-0-631-22140-1.
Dewey:3303.48/33. LCCN:00-037832.

Audience: **u,f.**

Graham, Stephen   T14.5.C93 2004
  (Editor)
The Cybercities Reader. Trade Paper. Routledge. New York, NY.

Audience: g=general, l=lower division undergraduate, u=upper division undergraduate, f=faculty.

729

2003. 464p. Urban Reader Ser. ISBN:0-415-27956-9, ISBN13: 978-0-415-27956-7. Dewey:303.48/3. LCCN:2003-010584.

Audience: **l,u,f.**

Mitchell, William J.   **HM851**
City of Bits: Space, Place, and the Infobahn. Library Binding. Sagebrush Education Resources. Caledonia, MN. 1996. ISBN:0-613-91148-2, ISBN13: 978-0-613-91148-1. Dewey:303.4/833.

Audience: **l,u,f.**   *Choice, 1996.*

Representation of Cities in Film and Literature

Beuka, Robert   **PS374.S82B48 2004**
SuburbiaNation: Reading Suburban Landscape in Twentieth-Century American Fiction and Film. Trade Paper. Palgrave Macmillan. New York, NY. 2004. 304p. ISBN:1-4039-6340-1, ISBN13: 978-1-4039-6340-6. Dewey:813/.509321733. LCCN:2003-054914.

Audience: **l,u,f.**   *Choice, 2004.*

Brooker, Peter   **PN56.C55B76 2001**
Modernity and Metropolis: Writing, Film and Urban Formations. Cloth over Boards. Palgrave Macmillan. New York, NY. 2002. 242p. ISBN:0-333-80168-7, ISBN13: 978-0-333-80168-0. Dewey:809/.93321732. LCCN:2001-036493.

Audience: **u,f.**   *Choice, 2002.*

Ulin, David L.   **PS572.L6W74 2002**
Writing Los Angeles: A Literary Anthology. Trade Cloth. Library of America, The. New York, NY. 2002. 880p. ISBN:1-931082-27-8, ISBN13: 978-1-931082-27-3. Dewey:810.8/0979494. LCCN:2002-069352.

Audience: **g,l,u,f.**

Representation of Cities in Film and Literature > Film

Barber, Stephen   **PN1995.9.C513**
Projected Cities: Cinema and Urban Space. Trade Paper. Reaktion Books, Ltd. London, 2004. 224p. Locations Ser. ISBN:1-86189-127-X, ISBN13: 978-1-86189-127-3. Dewey:791.43/621732. LCCN:2003-467559.

Audience: **u,f.**

Clarke, David B.   **PN1995.9.C513.C46**
The Cinematic City. Paper over Boards. Routledge. New York, NY. 1997. 264p. ISBN:0-415-12745-9, ISBN13: 978-0-415-12745-5. Dewey:791.43/621732. LCCN:96-031750.

Audience: **l,u,f.**   *Choice, 1998.*

Fitzmaurice, Tony   **PN1995.9.C513**
Screening the City. Trade Cloth. Verso Books. London, 2003. 288p. ISBN:1-85984-690-4, ISBN13: 978-1-85984-690-2. Dewey:791.4/3621732.

Audience: **l,u,f.**   *Choice, 2003.*

Fitzmaurice, Tony &   **PN1995.9.C513C45**
Shiel, Mark (Editors)
Cinema and the City: Film and Urban Societies in a Global Context. Trade Cloth. Blackwell Publishing, Inc. Malden, MA.

2001. 320p. Studies in Urban and Social Change ISBN:0-631-22243-X, ISBN13: 978-0-631-22243-9. Dewey:791.43/621732. LCCN:00-010767.

Audience: **u,f.**

Krause, Linda & Petro,   **NX650.C66G58 2003**
Patrice (Editors)
Global Cities: Cinema, Architecture and Urbanism in a Digital Age. Trade Cloth. Rutgers University Press. Piscataway, NJ. 2003. 208p. New Directions in International Studies ISBN:0-8135-3275-2, ISBN13: 978-0-8135-3275-2. Dewey:307.76/4/090511. LCCN:2002-152301.

Audience: **u,f.**

Rich, Nathaniel   **PN1995.9.F54R48 2005**
San Francisco Noir. Trade Paper. Little Bookroom. New York, NY. 2005. 168p. ISBN:1-892145-30-8, ISBN13: 978-1-892145-30-7. Dewey:791.43/6556. LCCN:2004-026260.

Audience: **l,u,f.**

Sanders, James   **PN1995.9.N49**
Celluloid Skyline: New York and the Movies. Trade Paper. Alfred A. Knopf Inc. New York, NY. 2003. 512p. ISBN:0-375-71027-2, ISBN13: 978-0-375-71027-8. Dewey:791.43/627471.

Audience: **l,u,f.**   *Choice, 2002.*

Silver, Alain & Ursini,   **PN1995.9.F54S57 2005**
James
L. A. Noir: The City as Character. Trade Paper. Santa Monica Press. Santa Monica, CA. 2005. 176p. ISBN:1-59580-006-9, ISBN13: 978-1-59580-006-0. Dewey:791.43/6279494. LCCN:2005-009681.

Audience: **l,u,f.**

Representation of Cities in Film and Literature > Literature

Alter, Robert   **PN3352.C5A48 2005**
Imagined Cities: Urban Experience and the Language of the Novel. Cloth over Boards. Yale University Press. Cumberland, RI. 2005. 208p. ISBN:0-300-10802-8, ISBN13: 978-0-300-10802-6. Dewey:809.3/9321732. LCCN:2004-026801.

Audience: **l,f.**   *Choice, 2005.*

Brewster, Dorothy P.   **PR6045.O72 Z563 1979**
Virginia Woolf's London. Trade Cloth. Greenwood Publishing Group, Inc. Portsmouth, NH. 1979. 120p. ISBN:0-313-20788-7, ISBN13: 978-0-313-20788-4. Dewey:823/.9/12. LCCN:78-026590.

Audience: **g,l,u,f.**

Calvino, Italo   **PQ4809.A45**
Invisible Cities. UK-B Format Paperback. Knopf Publishing Group. New York, NY. 2002. 165p. ISBN:0-09-942983-7, ISBN13: 978-0-09-942983-8. Dewey:853.9/14.

Audience: **g,l,u,f.**

Campbell, James   **PS226.B6C36 1999**
This Is the Beat Generation: New York, San Francisco, Paris. Trade Cloth. Martin Secker & Warburg, Ltd. London, 1999. xi, 320p. ISBN:0-436-20498-3, ISBN13: 978-0-436-20498-2. Dewey:810.9/0054. LCCN:00-302930.

Audience: **g,l,u,f.**

Jurca, Catherine   **PS374.S82J87 2001**
White Diaspora: The Suburb and the Twentieth-Century
American Novel. Trade Cloth. Princeton University Press.
Princeton, NJ. 2001. 246p. ISBN:0-691-05734-6, ISBN13:
978-0-691-05734-7. Dewey:813/.509321733. LCCN:00-058881.
Audience: **u,f.** *Choice, 2002.*

Nead, Lynda   **DA683.N425 2005**
Victorian Babylon: People, Streets and Images in
Nineteenth-Century London. Trade Paper. Yale University Press.
Cumberland, RI. 2005. 264p. ISBN:0-300-10770-6, ISBN13:
978-0-300-10770-8. Dewey:942.1/2.
Audience: **u,f.** *Choice, 2001.*

Rotella, Carlo   **PS228.C54 R68 1998**
October Cities: The Redevelopment of Urban Literature. Trade
Paper. University of California Press. Berkeley, CA. 1998. 370p.
ISBN:0-520-21144-8, ISBN13: 978-0-520-21144-5.
Dewey:810.9/321732. LCCN:97-027980.
Audience: **l,u,f.** *Choice, 1998.*

Schwarz, Daniel R.   **PS3535.U52Z75 2003**
Broadway Boogie Woogie: Damon Runyon and the Making of
New York City Culture. Cloth over Boards. Palgrave Macmillan.
New York, NY. 2003. 352p. ISBN:0-312-23948-3, ISBN13:
978-0-312-23948-0. Dewey:813/.52. LCCN:2002-074885.
Audience: **l,u,f.** *Choice, 2003.*

Squier, Susan M.   **PR6045.O72Z8785 1985**
Virginia Woolf and London: The Sexual Politics of the City.
Trade Cloth. University of North Carolina Press. Chapel Hill,
NC. 1985. 232p. ISBN:0-8078-1637-X, ISBN13:
978-0-8078-1637-0. Dewey:823/.912. LCCN:84-017376.
Audience: **l,u,f.** *B Choice, 1985.*

Wirth-Nesher, Hana   **PS374.C5W57 1996**
City Codes: Reading the Modern Urban Novel. Trade Cloth.
Cambridge University Press. New York, NY. 1996. 256p.
ISBN:0-521-47314-4, ISBN13: 978-0-521-47314-9.
Dewey:809.9/3/321732. LCCN:94-048821.
Audience: **l,u,f.** *Choice, 1996.*

VICTORIAN STUDIES

Victorian Studies emerged as a field in the late 1950s, at a time when literary scholars were turning to the preparation of editions of key Victorian writers and historians were beginning a systematic exploration of the origins and impact of industrialization on British society.

Drawing on pioneering essays on the period by writers like G. M. Young and Humphrey House, the founding of the eponymous journal in 1957 reflected a conviction that only an approach informed by both literary and historical study could adequately take the measure of the world's first fully "modern" society.

This group of core titles focuses, therefore, on works of a distinctly interdisciplinary cast at the expense of some titles with which all serious students of the period should be familiar (standard editions of canonical authors, authoritative social histories, and the like) but that sit squarely within one discipline and are therefore covered under the appropriate RCL sections. Despite its name, Victorian Studies (and this bibliography) looks beyond the Queen's reign to encompass all of the "long nineteenth century," from the 1780s to the end of World War I, in Britain and its empire, but does not include scholarship on America during the same period. The field's early classics are here, as well as the enormously influential studies of women's history that began to appear in the 1970s. These remain accessible and thought-provoking and are included here in the most useful editions available, while the bulk of the list is devoted to a generous sampling of the extraordinary flowering of interdisciplinary work that has appeared over the last twenty years, with an emphasis upon those titles that would work best in the undergraduate classroom. The list also features a sprinkling of primary sources — memoirs, diaries, journalism — that are essential windows into Victorian culture but that, due to their non-canonical nature, do not appear elsewhere in RCL.

— Patrick Leary

AP4

☐ Times Digital Archive, 1785-1985.
http://www.galegroup.com/Times/
Thomson Gale.

Audience: **g,l,u,f.**

Adams, James E., et al.   **DA550.E527 2003**
Encyclopedia of the Victorian Era. Tom Pendergast & Sara
Pendergast (Authors). Trade Cloth. Scholastic Library
Publishing. Danbury, CT. 2003. 1632p. ISBN:0-7172-5860-2,
ISBN13: 978-0-7172-5860-4. Dewey:941.081/03.
LCCN:2003-057101.

Audience: **g,l.** *Choice, 2004.*

Altick, Richard D.   **DA533**
Victorian People and Ideas. Trade Paper. W. W. Norton &
Company, Inc. New York, NY. 1974. 338p.
ISBN:0-393-09376-X, ISBN13: 978-0-393-09376-6.
Dewey:942.081.

Audience: **g,l,u.**

Boase, Frederic   **DA28.1**
Modern English Biography: Containing Many Thousand Concise
Memoirs of Persons Who Have Died since 1850, with an Index
of the Most Interesting Matter. Trade Cloth. Continuum
International Publishing Group, Ltd. London, 2000. 3972p.
ISBN:1-85506-863-X, ISBN13: 978-1-85506-863-6.
Dewey:942/.0099.

Audience: **u,f.**

Briggs, Asa   **DA530.B68**
The Age of Improvement. Paper Text. Textbook Publishers.
Temecula, CA. 2003. xii, 547p. ISBN:0-7581-9471-4, ISBN13:
978-0-7581-9471-8. Dewey:941.07.

Audience: **g,l,u,f.** *B*

Briggs, Asa   **DA560**
Victorian People: A Reassessment of Persons and Themes,
1851-67. Ruari McLean (Illustrator). Trade Paper. University of
Chicago Press. Chicago, IL. 1975. 324p. Chicago Collectors
Editions Ser. ISBN:0-226-07488-9, ISBN13: 978-0-226-07488-7.
Dewey:942.081. LCCN:55-005118.

Audience: **g,l,u,f.** *B*

Clark, G. Kitson   **DA533**
The Making of Victorian England. Trade Paper. Simon &
Schuster. New York, NY. 1972. ISBN:0-689-70049-0, ISBN13:
978-0-689-70049-1. Dewey:942. LCCN:62-051827.

Audience: **g,u,f.** *B*

Dodds, John W.   **DA533.D6**
The Age of Paradox: A Biography of England 1841. Paper Text.
Textbook Publishers. Temecula, CA. 2003. xvii, 509p.
ISBN:0-7581-4836-4, ISBN13: 978-0-7581-4836-0.
Dewey:914.2/03/81.

Audience: **g,l,u,f.**

Gardiner, John   **DA554**
The Victorians: An Age in Retrospect. Trade Cloth. Continuum
International Publishing Group, Ltd. London, 2003. 304p.
ISBN:1-85285-385-9, ISBN13: 978-1-85285-385-3.
Dewey:941/.081/0922.

Audience: **g,l,u,f.**

Hoppen, K. Theodore   **DA560.H58 1998**
The Mid-Victorian Generation 1846-1886. Cloth Text. Oxford
University Press, Inc. New York, NY. 1998. 808p. New Oxford

History of England Ser. ISBN:0-19-822834-1, ISBN13:
978-0-19-822834-9. Dewey:941.081. LCCN:97-018126.

Audience: **g,l,u,f.** *Choice, 1998.*

Houghton, Walter E.   **AI3.W45 1999**
  (Editor)
Wellesley Index to Victorian Periodicals 1824-1900. Compact
Disc. Routledge. New York, NY. 1999. ISBN:0-415-19345-1,
ISBN13: 978-0-415-19345-0. Dewey:052.

Audience: **g,l,u,f.** *Choice, 1999.*

Leary, Patrick   **D1**
☐ Victoria Research Web.
http://victorianresearch.org/

Audience: **g,l,u,f.**

Marsden, Gordon   **HN385.V55 1998**
Victorian Values: Personalties and Perspectives in
Nineteenth-Century Society. Ed. 2. Trade Paper. Longman
Publishing. Boston, MA. 1998. 304p. ISBN:0-582-29289-1,
ISBN13: 978-0-582-29289-5. Dewey:941/.08/0922.
LCCN:98-004601.

Audience: **g,l,u,f.**

Matthew, H. C. G. &   **DA28.D56**
  Harrison, Brian (Editors)
Oxford Dictionary of National Biography. Trade Cloth. Oxford
University Press, Inc. New York, NY. 2004. 61792p.
ISBN:0-19-861411-X, ISBN13: 978-0-19-861411-1.
Dewey:920.041 B. LCCN:2004-005444.

Audience: **g,l,u,f.** *Choice, 2005.*

Mitchell, Sally   **DA550**
Victorian Britain: An Encyclopedia. Trade Cloth. Thomson Gale.
Farmington Hills, MI. 1990. xvi, 986p. ISBN:1-55862-105-9,
ISBN13: 978-1-55862-105-3. Dewey:941.081.

Audience: **g,l,u,f.** *Choice, 1989.*

North, John   **Z6956.E5**
☐ The Waterloo Directory of English Newspapers and
Periodicals, 1800-1900.
http://www.victorianperiodicals.com
Ed. Series 2. North Waterloo Academic Press.

Audience: **g,l,u,f.**

Perkin, Harold   **HN385.P46 1990**
Origins of Modern English Society. Trade Paper. Routledge.
New York, NY. 1985. 480p. Studies in Social History
ISBN:0-415-05922-4, ISBN13: 978-0-415-05922-0.
Dewey:306/.0942. LCCN:90-049632.

Audience: **g,l,u,f.**

Robbins, Keith   **DA533**
Nineteenth-Century Britain: Integration and Diversity. Trade
Paper. Oxford University Press, Inc. New York, NY. 1995. 212p.
Ford Lectures ISBN:0-19-820585-6, ISBN13:
978-0-19-820585-2. Dewey:941.081. LCCN:87-023951.

Audience: **u,f.**

Southall, Humphrey
☐ A Vision of Britain through Time.
http://www.visionofbritain.org.uk/index.jsp
Great Britain Historical GIS Project.

Audience: **g,l,u,f.**

Strachey, Lytton   **DA562.S87 2003**
Eminent Victorians. John Sutherland (Editor). Trade Paper.
Oxford University Press, Inc. New York, NY. 2003. 324p.

Oxford World's Classics Ser. ISBN:0-19-280158-9, ISBN13: 978-0-19-280158-6. Dewey:941.081092/2 B.
Audience: **g,l,u,f.** *B*

Sullivan, Alvin (Editor)   **PN5124**
British Literary Magazines: The Romantic Age, 1789-1836. Cloth Text. Greenwood Publishing Group, Inc. Portsmouth, NH. 1983. 491p. Historical Guides to the World's Periodicals and Newspapers ISBN:0-313-22872-8, ISBN13: 978-0-313-22872-8. Dewey:820/.8. LCCN:82-021136.
Audience: **g,l,u,f.**

Sullivan, Alvin (Editor)   **PN5124**
British Literary Magazines: The Victorian and Edwardian Age, 1837-1913. Cloth Text. Greenwood Publishing Group, Inc. Portsmouth, NH. 1984. 560p. Historical Guides to the World's Periodicals and Newspapers ISBN:0-313-24335-2, ISBN13: 978-0-313-24335-6. Dewey:805. LCCN:82-021136.
Audience: **g,l,u,f.**

Sutherland, John   **PR871**
The Stanford Companion to Victorian Fiction. Trade Paper. Stanford University Press. Palo Alto, CA. 1989. 700p. ISBN:0-8047-1842-3, ISBN13: 978-0-8047-1842-4. Dewey:823/.809/03. LCCN:88-061462.
Audience: **g,l,u,f.** *Choice, 1989.*

Taylor, Miles & Wolff,   **DA550**
Michael (Editors)
The Victorians since 1901: Histories, Representations and Revisions. Cloth over Boards. Manchester University Press. Manchester, 2004. 320p. ISBN:0-7190-6724-3, ISBN13: 978-0-7190-6724-2. Dewey:941.081. LCCN:2004-303594.
Audience: **g,u,f.**

Thompson, F. M.   **DA550.T53 1988**
The Rise of Respectable Society: A Social History of Victorian Britain, 1830-1900. Trade Cloth. Harvard University Press. Cambridge, MA. 1988. 382p. ISBN:0-674-77285-7, ISBN13: 978-0-674-77285-4. Dewey:941.081. LCCN:88-014802.
Audience: **g,l,u,f.** *Choice, 1989.*

Thompson, F. M. L.   **HN385 .C14 1990**
(Editor)
The Cambridge Social History of Britain, 1750-1950: Social Agencies and Institutions, Vol. 3. Trade Cloth. Cambridge University Press. New York, NY. 1990. 496p. ISBN:0-521-25790-5, ISBN13: 978-0-521-25790-9. Dewey:941/.07. LCCN:89-009840.
Audience: **g,l,u,f.** *Choice, 1991.*

Thompson, F. M. L.   **HN385 .C14 1990**
(Editor)
The Cambridge Social History of Britain, 1750-1950: People and Their Environment. Trade Paper. Cambridge University Press. New York, NY. 1992. 392p. ISBN:0-521-43815-2, ISBN13: 978-0-521-43815-5. Dewey:941/.07. LCCN:89-009840.
Audience: **g,l,u,f.**

Thompson, F. M. L.   **HN385 .C14 1990**
(Editor)
The Cambridge Social History of Britain, 1750-1950: Regions and Communities. Alan Armstrong, C. Baber, P. L. Garside & D. W. Howell (Contribution by). Trade Paper. Cambridge University Press. New York, NY. 1992. 608p. ISBN:0-521-43816-0, ISBN13: 978-0-521-43816-2. Dewey:941/.07. LCCN:89-009840.
Audience: **g,l,u,f.**

Tucker, Herbert F.   **PR461.C597 1999**
(Editor)
A Companion to Victorian Literature and Culture. Book, Other. Blackwell Publishing, Inc. Malden, MA. 1999. 512p. Companions to Literature and Culture Ser., Vol. 2 ISBN:0-631-20463-6, ISBN13: 978-0-631-20463-3. Dewey:820.9/008. LCCN:98-019517.
Audience: **g,l,u,f.** *Choice, 1999.*

Williams, Raymond   **DA533.W6 1983**
Culture and Society, 1780-1950. Ed. 2. Trade Cloth. Columbia University Press. New York, NY. 1983. 363p. A Morningside Bk. ISBN:0-231-02287-5, ISBN13: 978-0-231-02287-3. Dewey:306/.4/0941. LCCN:85-005195.
Audience: **g,u,f.** *B*

Young, George M.   **DA550 .Y6 1977**
Portrait of an Age: Victorian England. George K. Clark (Annotations by). Trade Cloth. Oxford University Press, Inc. New York, NY. 1977. 423p. ISBN:0-19-212961-9, ISBN13: 978-0-19-212961-1. Dewey:941.081. LCCN:78-306764.
Audience: **g,l,u,f.**

Historiography

                    Z2016
☐ Royal Historical Society Bibliography.
http://www.rhs.ac.uk/bibl/
Royal Historical Society, Institute of Historical Research, University of London.
Audience: **g,l,u,f.**

Cannadine, David   **HN400.S6**
The Rise and Fall of Class in Britain. Trade Paper. Columbia University Press. New York, NY. 2000. 320p. Leonard Hastings Schoff Lectures ISBN:0-231-09667-4, ISBN13: 978-0-231-09667-6. Dewey:305.5/0941.
Audience: **g,l,u,f.** *Choice, 1999.*

Culler, A. Dwight   **DA3.A1C85 1985**
The Victorian Mirror of History. Trade Cloth. Yale University Press. Cumberland, RI. 1986. 336p. ISBN:0-300-03452-0, ISBN13: 978-0-300-03452-3. Dewey:941/.0072. LCCN:85-011985.
Audience: **l,u,f.**

Taylor, Miles & Wolff,   **DA550**
Michael (Editors)
The Victorians since 1901: Histories, Representations and Revisions. Cloth over Boards. Manchester University Press. Manchester, 2004. 320p. ISBN:0-7190-6724-3, ISBN13: 978-0-7190-6724-2. Dewey:941.081. LCCN:2004-303594.
Audience: **g,u,f.**

Architecture

Atterbury, Paul &   **NA997.P9A4 1994**
Wainwright, Clive (Editors)
Pugin: A Gothic Passion. Trade Paper. Yale University Press. Cumberland, RI. 1995. 328p. ISBN:0-300-06014-9, ISBN13: 978-0-300-06014-0. Dewey:720/.92. LCCN:94-015209.
Audience: **g,l,u,f.** *Choice, 1995.*

Garrigan, Kristine O.   NA2599.8.R8
Ruskin on Architecture: His Thought and Influence. Trade Cloth.
University of Wisconsin Press. Chicago, IL. 1973. 238p.
ISBN:0-299-06460-3, ISBN13: 978-0-299-06460-0.
Dewey:720/.92/4. LCCN:73-002045.
     Audience: **l,u,f.** *B*

Girouard, Mark   NA7620
The Victorian Country House. Trade Cloth. Yale University
Press. Cumberland, RI. 1979. 448p. ISBN:0-300-02390-1,
ISBN13: 978-0-300-02390-9. Dewey:728.8/3/0942.
LCCN:79-064077.
     Audience: **g,l,u,f.**

Art

Altick, Richard D.   PR408.A68A48 1985
Paintings from Books: Art and Literature in Britain, 1760-1900.
Cloth Text. Ohio State University Press. Columbus, OH. 1986.
527p. ISBN:0-8142-0380-9, ISBN13: 978-0-8142-0380-4.
Dewey:700/.941. LCCN:85-021737.
     Audience: **g,l,u,f.** *Choice, 1986.*

Anderson, Patricia   DA533.A574 1991
The Printed Image and the Transformation of Popular Culture,
1790-1860. Trade Cloth. Oxford University Press, Inc. New
York, NY. 1991. 224p. ISBN:0-19-811236-X, ISBN13:
978-0-19-811236-5. Dewey:306.4. LCCN:91-002828.
     Audience: **g,l,u,f.** *Choice, 1992.*

Casteras, Susan P.   N6767.5.V52C37 1987
Images of Victorian Womanhood in English Art. Trade Cloth.
Fairleigh Dickinson University Press. Cranbury, NJ. 1987. 192p.
ISBN:0-8386-3281-5, ISBN13: 978-0-8386-3281-9.
Dewey:760/.04424/0942. LCCN:85-045933.
     Audience: **u,f.** *Choice, 1988.*

Curtis, L. Perry Jr.   DA925.C85 1997
Apes and Angels: The Irishman in Victorian Caricature. Ed. 2.
Trade Cloth. Smithsonian Institution Press. Washington, DC.
1997. 208p. ISBN:1-56098-647-6, ISBN13: 978-1-56098-647-8.
Dewey:305.8/9162/09034. LCCN:96-016744.
     Audience: **g,l,u,f.**

Dale, Peter A.   PR468.S34D35 1989
In Pursuit of a Scientific Culture: Science, Art, and Society in
the Victorian Age. Paper Text. University of Wisconsin Press.
Chicago, IL. 1989. 348p. Science and Literature Ser.
ISBN:0-299-12264-6, ISBN13: 978-0-299-12264-5.
Dewey:820.9/008. LCCN:89-040251.
     Audience: **g,u,f.** *Choice, 1990.*

Elton, Arthur   N8218
Art and the Industrial Revolution. Francis D. Klingender
(Editor). Trade Paper. Academy Chicago Publishers, Ltd.
Chicago, IL. 1981. 272p. ISBN:0-586-08122-4, ISBN13:
978-0-586-08122-8. Dewey:704.94/9/6.
     Audience: **g,l,u,f.**

Garrigan, Kristine O.   NA2599.8.R8
Ruskin on Architecture: His Thought and Influence. Trade Cloth.
University of Wisconsin Press. Chicago, IL. 1973. 238p.
ISBN:0-299-06460-3, ISBN13: 978-0-299-06460-0.
Dewey:720/.92/4. LCCN:73-002045.
     Audience: **l,u,f.** *B*

Green-Lewis, Jennifer   TR15.G69 1996
Framing the Victorians: Photography and the Culture of
Realism. Trade Cloth. Cornell University Press. Ithaca, NY.
1997. 264p. ISBN:0-8014-3276-6, ISBN13: 978-0-8014-3276-7.
Dewey:770/.9/034. LCCN:96-020784.
     Audience: **u,f.** *Choice, 1997.*

Houfe, Simon   NC1479.L47 H68 1984
John Leech and the Victorian Scene. Trade Cloth. Antique
Collectors' Club. Easthampton, MA. 1984. 264p.
ISBN:0-907462-44-8, ISBN13: 978-0-907462-44-6.
Dewey:741.5/092/4. LCCN:84-107389.
     Audience: **u,f.**

Knoepflmacher, U. C. &   DA553
  Tennyson, G. B. (Editors)
Nature and the Victorian Imagination. Trade Cloth. University of
California Press. Berkeley, CA. 1978. xxiii, 519p.
ISBN:0-520-03229-2, ISBN13: 978-0-520-03229-3.
Dewey:304.2/0941. LCCN:76-007761.
     Audience: **g,l,u,f.**

MacLeod, Dianne   N72.S6 M23 1996
  Sachko
Art and the Victorian Middle Class: Money and the Making of
Cultural Identity. Cloth Text. Cambridge University Press. New
York, NY. 1996. 550p. ISBN:0-521-55090-4, ISBN13:
978-0-521-55090-1. Dewey:700.8/622. LCCN:95-024299.
     Audience: **u,f.** *Choice, 1997.*

Maidment, Brian   NE962.M35
Reading Popular Prints 1790-1870. Ed. 2. Trade Paper.
Manchester University Press. Manchester, 2001. 232p.
ISBN:0-7190-3371-3, ISBN13: 978-0-7190-3371-1.
Dewey:769.9/034.
     Audience: **l,u,f.**

Maxwell, Richard   NC978.V53 2002
  (Editor)
The Victorian Illustrated Book. Trade Cloth. University Press of
Virginia. Charlottesville, VA. 2002. 448p. Victorian Literature
and Culture Ser. ISBN:0-8139-2097-3, ISBN13:
978-0-8139-2097-9. Dewey:741.6/4/094109034.
LCCN:2001-007791.
     Audience: **g,l,u,f.**

McGann, Jerome
▢ The Rossetti Archive.
http://www.rossettiarchive.org/
     Audience: **g,l,u,f.**

Meisel, Martin   NX543.M4 1983
Realizations: Narrative, Pictorial, and Theatrical Arts of the
Nineteenth Century. Trade Cloth. Princeton University Press.
Princeton, NJ. 1984. 471p. ISBN:0-691-06553-5, ISBN13:
978-0-691-06553-3. Dewey:700/.942. LCCN:82-012292.
     Audience: **g,u,f.** *B*

Patten, Robert L.   N6797.C78P3 1992
George Cruikshank's Life, Times and Art: 1835-1878. Trade
Cloth. Rutgers University Press. Piscataway, NJ. 1996. 500p.
ISBN:0-8135-1814-8, ISBN13: 978-0-8135-1814-5.
Dewey:741.6/092. LCCN:91-040344.
     Audience: **g,l,u,f.** *Choice, 1996.*

Patten, Robert L.   N6797.C78.P3 1992
George Cruikshank's Life, Times and Art: 1792-1835. Trade
Cloth. Rutgers University Press. Piscataway, NJ. 1992. 550p.

Audience: g=general, l=lower division undergraduate, u=upper division undergraduate, f=faculty.

737

ISBN:0-8135-1813-X, ISBN13: 978-0-8135-1813-8.
Dewey:741.6/092. LCCN:91-040344.

Audience: **g,l,u,f.** *Choice, 1993.*

Ruskin, John   **PR5252.R64 1997**
The Genius of John Ruskin: Selections from His Writings. John
D. Rosenberg (Editor), Herbert F. Tucker (Foreword by). Trade
Paper. University Press of Virginia. Charlottesville, VA. 1998.
576p. Victorian Literature and Culture Ser. ISBN:0-8139-1789-1,
ISBN13: 978-0-8139-1789-4. Dewey:828/.809.
LCCN:97-031013.

Audience: **g,l,u,f.** *B*

Seiberling, Grace &   **TR57.S45 1986**
  Bloore, Carolyn
Amateurs, Photography, and the Mid-Victorian Imagination.
Trade Cloth. University of Chicago Press. Chicago, IL. 1986.
206p. ISBN:0-226-74498-1, ISBN13: 978-0-226-74498-8.
Dewey:770/.942. LCCN:85-020901.

Audience: **g,l,u,f.** *Choice, 1986.*

Strong, Roy   **N6767**
Painting the Past: The Victorian Painter and British History.
Trade Paper. Random House. London, 2004. 256p.
ISBN:1-84413-083-5, ISBN13: 978-1-84413-083-2.
Dewey:758.9/941.

Audience: **u,f.**

Book History

Jones, Aled   **PN5117.J66 1996**
Powers of the Press: Newspapers, Power and the Public in
Nineteenth-Century England. Trade Cloth. Ashgate Publishing,
Ltd. Aldershot, 1996. 244p. The Nineteenth Century Ser.
ISBN:1-85928-132-X, ISBN13: 978-1-85928-132-1. Dewey:072.
LCCN:95-053260.

Audience: **u,f.** *Choice, 1997.*

Sutherland, John   **PR871**
Victorian Fiction: Writers, Publishers, Readers. Ed. 2. Trade
Paper. Palgrave Macmillan. New York, NY. 2005. 224p.
ISBN:1-4039-3985-3, ISBN13: 978-1-4039-3985-2.
Dewey:823/.809. LCCN:2005-049320.

Audience: **u,f.** *Choice, 1995.*

Vincent, David   **LC156.G72E58 1989**
Literacy and Popular Culture: England, 1750-1914. Peter Burke
& Ruth Finnegan (Contribution by). Trade Paper. Cambridge
University Press. New York, NY. 1993. 374p. Studies in Oral
and Literate Culture, No. 19 ISBN:0-521-45771-8, ISBN13:
978-0-521-45771-2. Dewey:302.2/244/0942/09034.

Audience: **g,l,u,f.** *Choice, 1990.*

Book History > Reading

Altick, Richard D.   **Z1003.5.G7A53 1998**
The English Common Reader: A Social History of the Mass
Reading Public, 1800-1900. Ed. 2. Cloth Text. Ohio State
University Press. Columbus, OH. 1998. 468p.
ISBN:0-8142-0793-6, ISBN13: 978-0-8142-0793-2.
Dewey:028/.9/0941. LCCN:98-019581.

Audience: **g,l,u,f.**

Anderson, Patricia   **DA533.A574 1991**
The Printed Image and the Transformation of Popular Culture,
1790-1860. Trade Cloth. Oxford University Press, Inc. New
York, NY. 1991. 224p. ISBN:0-19-811236-X, ISBN13:
978-0-19-811236-5. Dewey:306.4. LCCN:91-002828.

Audience: **g,l,u,f.** *Choice, 1992.*

Blackleeds, Alistair   **Z791.E5B58 1996**
A New History of the English Public Library: Social and
Intellectual Contexts, 1850-1914. Library Binding. Continuum
International Publishing Group, Ltd. London, 1996. 352p.
ISBN:0-7185-0015-6, ISBN13: 978-0-7185-0015-3.
Dewey:027.4/09. LCCN:95-041411.

Audience: **l,u,f.**

Brantlinger, Patrick   **PR868.P68B73 1998**
The Reading Lesson: The Threat of Mass Literacy in
Nineteenth-Century British Fiction. Trade Cloth. Indiana
University Press. Bloomington, IN. 1998. 320p.
ISBN:0-253-33454-3, ISBN13: 978-0-253-33454-1.
Dewey:823/.809. LCCN:98-019906.

Audience: **u,f.** *Choice, 1999.*

Brown, Lucy M.   **PN5117.B76 1985**
Victorian News and Newspapers. Trade Cloth. Oxford
University Press, Inc. New York, NY. 1985. 300p.
ISBN:0-19-822624-1, ISBN13: 978-0-19-822624-6. Dewey:072.
LCCN:86-142738.

Audience: **u,f.** *Choice, 1986.*

Cruse, Amy   **PR461.C7**
The Victorians and Their Reading. Houghton Mifflin. 1935.

Audience: **g,l,u,f.**

Flint, Kate   **Z1039.W65F57 1993**
The Woman Reader, 1837-1914. Cloth Text. Oxford University
Press, Inc. New York, NY. 1993. 384p. ISBN:0-19-811719-1,
ISBN13: 978-0-19-811719-3. Dewey:028/.9082.
LCCN:93-018195.

Audience: **g,l,u,f.** *Choice, 1994.*

Gill, Stephen   **PR5887.3.G55 1998**
Wordsworth and the Victorians. Cloth Text. Oxford University
Press, Inc. New York, NY. 1998. 366p. ISBN:0-19-811965-8,
ISBN13: 978-0-19-811965-4. Dewey:821.7. LCCN:97-040689.

Audience: **g,l,u,f.** *Choice, 1998.*

Haywood, Ian   **PR468.P57H39 2004**
The Revolution in Popular Literature: Print, Politics and the
People, 1790-1860. Gillian Beer (Contribution by). Trade Cloth.
Cambridge University Press. New York, NY. 2004. 348p.
Cambridge Studies in Nineteenth-Century Literature and Culture
Ser., Vol. 44 ISBN:0-521-83546-1, ISBN13: 978-0-521-83546-6.
Dewey:820.9/358. LCCN:2003-065207.

Audience: **u,f.**

Jordan, John O. &   **Z325 .L58 1995**
  Patten, Robert L. (Editors)
Literature in the Marketplace: Nineteenth-Century British
Publishing and Reading Practices. Colin Beer & Gillian Beer
(Contribution by). Trade Paper. Cambridge University Press.
New York, NY. 2003. 352p. Cambridge Studies in
Nineteenth-Century Literature and Culture Ser.
ISBN:0-521-89393-3, ISBN13: 978-0-521-89393-0.
Dewey:070./49/0941.

Audience: **g,l,u,f.**

Loeb, Lori A.   **HF5813.G7L63 1994**
Consuming Angels: Advertising and Victorian Women. Cloth
Text. Oxford University Press, Inc. New York, NY. 1994. 240p.
ISBN:0-19-508596-5, ISBN13: 978-0-19-508596-9.
Dewey:659.1/042/094109034. LCCN:93-046094.
                                    Audience: **l,u,f.** *Choice, 1995.*

McCalman, Iain   **HN400.R3**
Radical Underworld: Prophets, Revolutionaries and
Pornographers in London, 1795-1840. Paper Text. Oxford
University Press, Inc. New York, NY. 1993. 358p.
ISBN:0-19-812286-1, ISBN13: 978-0-19-812286-9.
Dewey:320.9421. LCCN:87-011770.
                                    Audience: **g,l,u,f.** *Choice, 1988.*

Rose, Jonathan   **Z1039.L3R67 2001**
The Intellectual Life of the British Working Classes. Cloth over
Boards. Yale University Press. Cumberland, RI. 2001. 544p.
ISBN:0-300-08886-8, ISBN13: 978-0-300-08886-1.
Dewey:028/.9/0941. LCCN:00-068562.
                                    Audience: **g,l,u,f.** *Choice, 2002.*

Secord, James A.   **QH363.S4 2000**
Victorian Sensation: The Extraordinary Publication, Reception,
and Secret Authorship of Vestiges of the Natural History of
Creation. Trade Cloth. University of Chicago Press. Chicago, IL.
2001. 624p. ISBN:0-226-74410-8, ISBN13: 978-0-226-74410-0.
Dewey:576.8/0941/09034. LCCN:00-009124.
                                    Audience: **g,l,u,f.** *Choice, 2001.*

Sigel, Lisa Z.   **HQ472.G7S54 2002**
Governing Pleasures: Pornography and Social Change in
England, 1815-1914. Cloth Text. Rutgers University Press.
Piscataway, NJ. 2002. 248p. ISBN:0-8135-3001-6, ISBN13:
978-0-8135-3001-7. Dewey:363.4/7/094209034.
LCCN:2001-019801.
                                    Audience: **g,l,u,f.** *Choice, 2003, 2002.*

St. Clair, William   **Z1003.S77 2004**
The Reading Nation in the Romantic Period. Trade Cloth.
Cambridge University Press. New York, NY. 2004. 796p.
ISBN:0-521-81006-X, ISBN13: 978-0-521-81006-7.
Dewey:028/.9. LCCN:2003-060795.
                                    Audience: **g,l,u,f.** *Choice, 2005.*

Stewart, Garrett   **PR878.A79S74 1996**
Dear Reader: The Conscripted Audience in Nineteenth-Century
British Fiction. Trade Paper. Johns Hopkins University Press.
Baltimore, MD. 1996. 472p. ISBN:0-8018-5283-8, ISBN13:
978-0-8018-5283-1. Dewey:823/.809. LCCN:95-052372.
                                    Audience: **u,f.** *Choice, 1997.*

Terry, R. C.   **PR4168**
Victorian Popular Fiction, 1860-80. Cloth Text. Brill Academic
Publishers, Inc. Boston, MA. 1983. 208p. ISBN:0-391-02963-0,
ISBN13: 978-0-391-02963-7. Dewey:823/.8/09.
                                    Audience: **g,l,u,f.**

Turner, Ernest S.   **PN1009.A1 T8 1974**
Boys Will Be Boys. Trade Cloth. Thomson Gale. Farmington
Hills, MI. 1977. ISBN:0-8103-4091-7, ISBN13:
978-0-8103-4091-6. Dewey:823/.03. LCCN:76-175338.
                                    Audience: **g,l,u.**

Vincent, David   **HD8388**
Bread, Knowledge and Freedom: A Study of Nineteenth-Century
Working Class Autobiography. Trade Paper. Routledge. New

York, NY. 1983. 221p. ISBN:0-416-34670-7, ISBN13:
978-0-416-34670-1. Dewey:305.5/62/0941. LCCN:82-014163.
                                    Audience: **g,l,u,f.**

Book History > Authorship

Annan, Noel   **PR5473.S6A88 1984**
Leslie Stephen: The Godless Victorian. Trade Cloth. Random
House, Inc. New York, NY. 1984. 384p. ISBN:0-394-53061-6,
ISBN13: 978-0-394-53061-1. Dewey:828/.809 B.
LCCN:84-042512.
                                    Audience: **g,l,u,f.** ℬ

Bevington, Merle M.   **PN5130.S3B4**
Saturday Review, 1855-1868: Representative Educated Opinion
in Victorian England. Trade Cloth. A M S Press, Inc. New York,
NY. ISBN:0-404-00795-3, ISBN13: 978-0-404-00795-9.
Dewey:52.0942109. LCCN:41-025970.
                                    Audience: **g,u,f.**

Broomfield, Andrea &   **PR1286.W6P76 1996**
  Mitchell, Sally
Prose by Victorian Women: An Anthology. Cloth Text. Garland
Publishing, Inc. New York, NY. 1995. 752p. Garland Reference
Library of the Humanities, Vol. 1893: ISBN:0 8153 1970 3,
ISBN13: 978-0-8153-1970-2. Dewey:828/.8080809287.
LCCN:95-024400.
                                    Audience: **g,l,u,f.** *Choice, 1996.*

Chittick, Kathryn   **PR4582.C48 1990**
Dickens and the Eighteen Thirties. Trade Cloth. Cambridge
University Press. New York, NY. 1990. 222p.
ISBN:0-521-38174-6, ISBN13: 978-0-521-38174-1.
Dewey:823/.8 B. LCCN:90-001404.
                                    Audience: **u,f.** *Choice, 1991.*

Cross, Nigel   **PR451 .C76 1985**
The Common Writer: Life in Nineteenth-Century Grub Street.
Trade Cloth. Cambridge University Press. New York, NY. 1985.
271p. ISBN:0-521-24564-8, ISBN13: 978-0-521-24564-7.
Dewey:820/.9/008. LCCN:84-029247.
                                    Audience: **g,l,u,f.** *Choice, 1986.*

Curran, Eileen
☐ The Curran Index.
http://victorianresearch.org/curranindex.html
Victoria Research Web.
                                    Audience: **u,f.**

Dooley, Allan C.   **PR468.T48D66 1992**
Author and Printer in Victorian England. Cloth Text. University
Press of Virginia. Charlottesville, VA. 1992. 224p. Victorian
Literature and Culture Ser. ISBN:0-8139-1401-9, ISBN13:
978-0-8139-1401-5. Dewey:820.9008. LCCN:92-010420.
                                    Audience: **l,u,f.** *Choice, 1993.*

Elfenbein, Andrew   **PR468.R65 E44 1995**
Byron and the Victorians. Gillian Beer (Contribution by). Trade
Cloth. Cambridge University Press. New York, NY. 1995. 297p.
Studies in Nineteenth-Century Literature and Culture, No. 4
ISBN:0-521-45452-2, ISBN13: 978-0-521-45452-0.
Dewey:820.9/008. LCCN:94-020629.
                                    Audience: **u,f.** *Choice, 1995.*

Gagnier, Regenia PR5824.G34 1986
Idylls of the Marketplace: Oscar Wilde and the Victorian Public. Stanford University Press. 1986. ISBN:0-8047-1334-0, ISBN13: 978-0-8047-1334-4.

Audience: **u,f.**

Gross, John PR63.G7 1992
The Rise and Fall of the Man of Letters: English Literary Life since 1800. Trade Paper. Ivan R. Dee Publisher. Blue Ridge Summit, PA. 1992. 372p. ISBN:1-56663-000-2, ISBN13: 978-1-56663-000-9. Dewey:820.9. LCCN:92-016011.

Audience: **u,f.**

Keating, Peter PR878.S615
The Haunted Study: A Social History of the English Novel 1875-1914. Secker & Warburg. 1989. ISBN:0-436-23248-0, ISBN13: 978-0-436-23248-0.

Audience: **g,l,u,f.**

Martineau, Harriet PR4984.M5 Z463
Harriet Martineaus's Autobiography, Vol. 1. Trade Paper. Kessinger Publishing, LLC. Whitefish, MT. 2005. ISBN:1-4179-7016-2, ISBN13: 978-1-4179-7016-2. Dewey:823/.8.

Audience: **g,l,u,f.**

Martineau, Harriet PR4984.M5 Z463
Harriet Martineaus's Autobiography, Vol. 2. Trade Paper. Kessinger Publishing, LLC. Whitefish, MT. 2005. ISBN:1-4179-7017-0, ISBN13: 978-1-4179-7017-9. Dewey:823/.8.

Audience: **g,l,u,f.**

Maxwell, Richard NC978.V53 2002
(Editor)
The Victorian Illustrated Book. Trade Cloth. University Press of Virginia. Charlottesville, VA. 2002. 448p. Victorian Literature and Culture Ser. ISBN:0-8139-2097-3, ISBN13: 978-0-8139-2097-9. Dewey:741.6/4/094109034. LCCN:2001-007791.

Audience: **g,l,u,f.**

Mermin, Dorothy PR115
e Godiva's Ride: Women of Letters in England, 1830-1880. E-Book. Indiana University Press. Bloomington, IN. 1993. 204p. ISBN:0-253-20824-6, ISBN13: 978-0-253-20824-8. Dewey:820.9/9287/09034. LCCN:92-045186.

Audience: **g,l,u.** *Choice, 1994.*

Mitchell, Sally PR4461.C3Z78 2004
Frances Power Cobbe: Victorian Feminist, Journalist, Reformer. Trade Cloth. University Press of Virginia. Charlottesville, VA. 2004. 400p. Victorian Literature and Culture Ser. ISBN:0-8139-2271-2, ISBN13: 978-0-8139-2271-3. Dewey:070.92 B. LCCN:2003-022365.

Audience: **u,f.**

Nayder, Lillian PR4586.N39 2001
Unequal Partners: Charles Dickens, Wilkie Collins, and Victorian Authorship. Book, Other. Cornell University Press. Ithaca, NY. 2001. 240p. ISBN:0-8014-3925-6, ISBN13: 978-0-8014-3925-4. Dewey:823/.8. LCCN:2001-003445.

Audience: **u,f.** *Choice, 2002.*

Onslow, Barbara PN5124.W58O59 2000
Women of the Press in Nineteenth-Century Britain. Cloth over Boards. Palgrave Macmillan. New York, NY. 2001. 311p.

ISBN:0-312-23602-6, ISBN13: 978-0-312-23602-1. Dewey:070.9/22. LCCN:00-033333.

Audience: **g,l,u,f.** *Choice, 2001.*

Peterson, Linda H. PR788.W65P47 1999
Traditions of Victorian Women's Autobiography: The Poetics and Politics of Life Writing. Trade Cloth. University Press of Virginia. Charlottesville, VA. 1999. 272p. Victorian Literature and Culture Ser. ISBN:0-8139-1883-9, ISBN13: 978-0-8139-1883-9. Dewey:828/.80809492072. LCCN:99-019832.

Audience: **g,l,u,f.** *Choice, 2000.*

Stephens, John Russell PN2594 .S75 1991
The Profession of the Playwright: British Theatre, 1800-1900. Cloth Text. Cambridge University Press. New York, NY. 1992. 274p. ISBN:0-521-25913-4, ISBN13: 978-0-521-25913-2. Dewey:792/.092/241. LCCN:90-025605.

Audience: **l,u,f.** *Choice, 1992.*

Sutherland, J. A. PR878.P78
Victorian Novelists and Publishers. Trade Paper. University of Chicago Press. Chicago, IL. 1996. 260p. ISBN:0-226-78062-7, ISBN13: 978-0-226-78062-7. Dewey:823.09. LCCN:76-008216.

Audience: **g,l,u,f.**

Sutherland, John PR871
The Stanford Companion to Victorian Fiction. Trade Paper. Stanford University Press. Palo Alto, CA. 1989. 700p. ISBN:0-8047-1842-3, ISBN13: 978-0-8047-1842-4. Dewey:823/.809/03. LCCN:88-061462.

Audience: **g,l,u,f.** *Choice, 1989.*

Weiner, Joel H. (Editor) PN5124
Innovators and Preachers: The Role of the Editor in Victorian England. Trade Cloth. Greenwood Publishing Group, Inc. Portsmouth, NH. 1985. 335p. Contributions to the Study of Mass Media and Communications Ser., No. 5 ISBN:0-313-24164-3, ISBN13: 978-0-313-24164-2. Dewey:070.4/1/0941. LCCN:85-017658.

Audience: **u,f.** *Choice, 1986.*

Worth, George J. PN5130.M33W67 2002
Macmillan's Magazine, 1859-1907: No Flippancy or Abuse Allowed. Trade Cloth. Ashgate Publishing, Ltd. Aldershot, 2003. 204p. The Nineteenth Century Ser. ISBN:0-7546-0986-3, ISBN13: 978-0-7546-0986-5. Dewey:052/.0942/09034. LCCN:2002-018516.

Audience: **l,u,f.**

Book History > Publishing

Brake, Laurel PN4759.B73 1994
Subjugated Knowledges: Journalism, Gender, and Literature in the Nineteenth Century. Trade Cloth. New York University Press. New York, NY. 1994. 320p. ISBN:0-8147-1218-5, ISBN13: 978-0-8147-1218-4. Dewey:820.9/008. LCCN:93-031425.

Audience: **u,f.** *Choice, 1994.*

Brake, Laurel (Editor), PN5124.P4N56 2000
et al.
Nineteenth-Century Media and the Construction of Identities. Bill Bell & David Finkelstein (Editors). Cloth over Boards. Palgrave Macmillan. New York, NY. 2001. 405p.

ISBN:0-312-23215-2, ISBN13: 978-0-312-23215-3.
Dewey:302.2/3/09034. LCCN:00-021404.

Audience: **u,f.** *Choice, 2001.*

Brown, Lucy M.   **PN5117.B76 1985**
Victorian News and Newspapers. Trade Cloth. Oxford
University Press, Inc. New York, NY. 1985. 300p.
ISBN:0-19-822624-1, ISBN13: 978-0-19-822624-6. Dewey:072.
LCCN:86-142738.

Audience: **u,f.** *Choice, 1986.*

Dooley, Allan C.   **PR468.T48D66 1992**
Author and Printer in Victorian England. Cloth Text. University
Press of Virginia. Charlottesville, VA. 1992. 224p. Victorian
Literature and Culture Ser. ISBN:0-8139-1401-9, ISBN13:
978-0-8139-1401-5. Dewey:820.9008. LCCN:92-010420.

Audience: **l,u,f.** *Choice, 1993.*

Eliot, Simon   **Z325.E45 1994**
Some Patterns and Trends in British Publishing, 1800-1919. The
Bibliographical Society. 1994. The Bibliographical Society:
Occasional Papers

Audience: **u,f.**

Erickson, Lee   **PR451.E75 1996**
The Economy of Literary Form: English Literature and the
Industrialization of Publishing, 1800-1850. Trade Cloth. Johns
Hopkins University Press. Baltimore, MD. 1996. 224p.
ISBN:0-8018-5145-9, ISBN13: 978-0-8018-5145-2.
Dewey:820.9/007. LCCN:95-017054.

Audience: **g,l,u,f.** *Choice, 1996.*

Feather, John   **Z325.F414 2005**
History of British Publishing. Ed. 2. Paper over Boards.
Routledge. New York, NY. 2005. CCLXX, 10p.
ISBN:0-415-30225-0, ISBN13: 978-0-415-30225-8.
Dewey:070.5/0941. LCCN:2005-004363.

Audience: **g,l,u,f.**

Finkelstein, David   **Z325.W58F36 2002**
The House of Blackwood: Author-Publisher Relations in the
Victorian Era. Trade Cloth. Pennsylvania State University Press.
University Park, PA. 2002. 208p. Penn State Series in the
History of the Book ISBN:0-271-02179-9, ISBN13:
978-0-271-02179-9. Dewey:070.5/0941. LCCN:2002-000501.

Audience: **g,l,u,f.**

Fyfe, Aileen   **BL245.F94 2004**
Science and Salvation: Evangelical Popular Science Publishing
in Victorian Britain. Trade Cloth. University of Chicago Press.
Chicago, IL. 2004. 432p. ISBN:0-226-27647-3, ISBN13:
978-0-226-27647-2. Dewey:261.5/5/094109034.
LCCN:2003-017513.

Audience: **u,f.** *Choice, 2005.*

Gettmann, R. A.   **Z325.B45 G4**
Victorian Publisher. Trade Cloth. Cambridge University Press.
New York, NY. 1960. ISBN:0-521-05072-3, ISBN13:
978-0-521-05072-2. Dewey:655.4421.

Audience: **g,l,u,f.**

Howsam, Leslie   **BV2370.B8 H69 1991**
Cheap Bibles: Nineteenth-Century Publishing and the British
and Foreign Bible Society. Trade Cloth. Cambridge University
Press. New York, NY. 1991. 263p. Studies in Publishing and
Printing History ISBN:0-521-39339-6, ISBN13:
978-0-521-39339-3. Dewey:070.5/0941/09034.
LCCN:90-021900.

Audience: **u,f.**

Howsam, Leslie   **Z325.K35 H69 1998**
Kegan Paul - a Victorian Imprint: Publishers, Books, and
Cultural History. Printed Dust Jacket. University of Toronto
Press. Toronto, ON. 1996. 218p. ISBN:0-8020-4126-4, ISBN13:
978-0-8020-4126-5. Dewey:070.5/0941/09034.
LCCN:99-475827.

Audience: **u,f.**

Howsam, Leslie   **BV2370.B8 H69 1991**
Cheap Bibles: Nineteenth-Century Publishing and the British
and Foreign Bible Society. Terry Belanger & David McKitterick
(Contribution by). Trade Paper. Cambridge University Press.
New York, NY. 2002. 263p. Cambridge Studies in Publishing
and Printing History Ser. ISBN:0-521-52212-9, ISBN13:
978-0-521-52212-0. Dewey:070.5/0941/09034.

Audience: **g,l,u,f.**

Hughes, Linda K. &   **PR468.P37H84 1991**
  Lund, Michael
The Victorian Serial. Cloth Text. University Press of Virginia.
Charlottesville, VA. 1991. 448p. Victorian Literature and Culture
Ser. ISBN:0-8139-1314-4, ISBN13: 978-0-8139-1314-8.
Dewey:820.9/008. LCCN:90-020878.

Audience: **u,f.** *Choice, 1993.*

Jordan, John O. &   **Z325 .L58 1995**
  Patten, Robert L. (Editors)
Literature in the Marketplace: Nineteenth-Century British
Publishing and Reading Practices. Colin Beer & Gillian Beer
(Contribution by). Trade Paper. Cambridge University Press.
New York, NY. 2003. 352p. Cambridge Studies in
Nineteenth-Century Literature and Culture Ser.
ISBN:0-521-89393-3, ISBN13: 978-0-521-89393-0.
Dewey:070./49/0941.

Audience: **g,l,u,f.**

Keating, Peter   **PR878.S615**
The Haunted Study: A Social History of the English Novel
1875-1914. Secker & Warburg. 1989. ISBN:0-436-23248-0,
ISBN13: 978-0-436-23248-0.

Audience: **g,l,u,f.**

Law, Graham   **PR878.P78L39 2000**
Serializing Fiction in the Victorian Press. Cloth over Boards.
Palgrave Macmillan. New York, NY. 2001. 328p.
ISBN:0-312-23574-7, ISBN13: 978-0-312-23574-1.
Dewey:823.8/09. LCCN:00-031124.

Audience: **u,f.** *Choice, 2001.*

Lohrli, Anne   **PN5130.H6L6**
Household Words: A Weekly Journal 1850-1859, Conducted by
Charles Dickens. Table of Contents, List of Contributors and
Their Contributions Based on the Household Words Office Book
in the Morris L. Parrish Collection of Victorian Novelists,
Princeton Uni. Trade Paper. Books on Demand. Ann Arbor, MI.
550p. ISBN:0-598-10228-0, ISBN13: 978-0-598-10228-7.
Dewey:052;. LCCN:71-185722.

Audience: **g,l,u,f.**

Marchand, Leslie A.   **PN5130.A7**
Athenaeum. Library Binding. Hippocrene Books, Inc. New
York, NY. 1970. ISBN:0-374-95280-9, ISBN13:
978-0-374-95280-8. Dewey:52. LCCN:77-120646.

Audience: **g,l,u,f.**

Patten, Robert L.   **PR4583.P29 1978**
Charles Dickens and His Publishers. Cloth Text. Oxford
University Press, Inc. New York, NY. 1978. 518p.

ISBN:0-19-812076-1, ISBN13: 978-0-19-812076-6.
Dewey:823/.8. LCCN:77-030164.

Audience: **g,l,u,f.** *B*

Rose, Jonathan &   **Z326.B673 1991**
  Anderson, Patricia
British Literary Publishing Houses, 1881-1965. Cloth Text.
Thomson Gale. Farmington Hills, MI. 1991. 420p. Dictionary of
Literary Biography Ser. ISBN:0-8103-4592-7, ISBN13:
978-0-8103-4592-8. Dewey:070.5/0941. LCCN:91-031918.

Audience: **g,l,u,f.** *Choice, 1992.*

Shillingsburg, Peter L.   **PR5633.S5 1992**
Pegasus in Harness: Victorian Publishing and W. M. Thackeray.
Cloth Text. University Press of Virginia. Charlottesville, VA.
1992. 320p. Victorian Literature and Culture Ser.
ISBN:0-8139-1397-7, ISBN13: 978-0-8139-1397-1.
Dewey:823.8. LCCN:92-002805.

Audience: **g,l,u,f.** *Choice, 1993.*

Sigel, Lisa Z.   **HQ472.G7S54 2002**
Governing Pleasures: Pornography and Social Change in
England, 1815-1914. Cloth Text. Rutgers University Press.
Piscataway, NJ. 2002. 248p. ISBN:0-8135-3001-6, ISBN13:
978-0-8135-3001-7. Dewey:363.4/7/094209034.
LCCN:2001-019801.

Audience: **g,l,u,f.** *Choice, 2003, 2002.*

Sullivan, Alvin (Editor)   **PN5124**
British Literary Magazines: The Romantic Age, 1789-1836.
Cloth Text. Greenwood Publishing Group, Inc. Portsmouth, NH.
1983. 491p. Historical Guides to the World's Periodicals and
Newspapers ISBN:0-313-22872-8, ISBN13: 978-0-313-22872-8.
Dewey:820/.8. LCCN:82-021136.

Audience: **g,l,u,f.**

Sullivan, Alvin (Editor)   **PN5124**
British Literary Magazines: The Victorian and Edwardian Age,
1837-1913. Cloth Text. Greenwood Publishing Group, Inc.
Portsmouth, NH. 1984. 560p. Historical Guides to the World's
Periodicals and Newspapers ISBN:0-313-24335-2, ISBN13:
978-0-313-24335-6. Dewey:805. LCCN:82-021136.

Audience: **g,l,u,f.**

Sutherland, J. A.   **PR878.P78**
Victorian Novelists and Publishers. Trade Paper. University of
Chicago Press. Chicago, IL. 1996. 260p. ISBN:0-226-78062-7,
ISBN13: 978-0-226-78062-7. Dewey:823.09. LCCN:76-008216.

Audience: **g,l,u,f.**

Thrall, Miriam M.   **PN5130.F7 T5 1934A**
Rebellious Fraser's: Nol Yorke's Magazine in the Days of
Maginn, Thackeray and Carlyle. Trade Cloth. A M S Press, Inc.
New York, NY. ISBN:0-404-06458-2, ISBN13:
978-0-404-06458-7. Dewey:52. LCCN:35-001070.

Audience: **g,l,u,f.**

Vann, J. Don & Van   **PN5124.P4**
  Ardsel, Rosemary
Victorian Periodicals and Victorian Society. Trade Cloth.
Ashgate Publishing Company. Williston, VT. 1994. xii, 370p.
ISBN:0-85967-944-6, ISBN13: 978-0-85967-944-2.
Dewey:052/.09034.

Audience: **g,l,u,f.** *Choice, 1994.*

Weedon, Alexis   **Z325.W425 2003**
Victorian Publishing: The Economics of Book Production for a
Mass Market 1836-1916. Trade Cloth, Mass Market. Ashgate
Publishing, Ltd. Aldershot, 2003. 228p. The Nineteenth Century

Ser. ISBN:0-7546-3527-9, ISBN13: 978-0-7546-3527-7.
Dewey:070.5/0941. LCCN:2002-038374.

Audience: **l,u,f.**

Wiener, Joel H.   **HJ4708.A7**
War of the Unstamped: A History of the Movement to Repeal
the British Newspaper Tax, 1830-1836. Trade Cloth. Cornell
University Press. Ithaca, NY. 1969. xix, 310p.
ISBN:0-8014-0522-X, ISBN13: 978-0-8014-0522-8.
Dewey:336.2/43. LCCN:70-081598.

Audience: **g,l,u,f.**

Wilson, Charles   **Z325.W23W54 1986**
First with the News: A History of W. H. Smith and Son since
1792-1972. Trade Cloth. Doubleday Publishing. New York, NY.
1986. 512p. ISBN:0-385-23503-8, ISBN13: 978-0-385-23503-7.
Dewey:070.5/0941. LCCN:85-020737.

Audience: **g,l,u,f.** *Choice, 1986.*

Worth, George J.   **PN5130.M33W67 2002**
Macmillan's Magazine, 1859-1907: No Flippancy or Abuse
Allowed. Trade Cloth. Ashgate Publishing, Ltd. Aldershot, 2003.
204p. The Nineteenth Century Ser. ISBN:0-7546-0986-3,
ISBN13: 978-0-7546-0986-5. Dewey:052/.0942/09034.
LCCN:2002-018516.

Audience: **l,u,f.**

Class > General

Cannadine, David   **HN400.S6**
The Rise and Fall of Class in Britain. Trade Paper. Columbia
University Press. New York, NY. 2000. 320p. Leonard Hastings
Schoff Lectures ISBN:0-231-09667-4, ISBN13:
978-0-231-09667-6. Dewey:305.5/0941.

Audience: **g,l,u,f.** *Choice, 1999.*

Joyce, Patrick D.   **DA533.J68 1994**
Democratic Subjects: The Self and the Social in
Nineteenth-Century England. Trade Paper. Cambridge University
Press. New York, NY. 1994. 254p. ISBN:0-521-44802-6,
ISBN13: 978-0-521-44802-4. Dewey:942.081.
LCCN:93-037741.

Audience: **u,f.** *Choice, 1995.*

Joyce, Patrick W.   **HN388.E53**
Visions of the People: Industrial England and the Question of
Class, C. 1848-1914. Trade Paper. Cambridge University Press.
New York, NY. 1993. 463p. ISBN:0-521-44797-6, ISBN13:
978-0-521-44797-3. Dewey:305.509.

Audience: **u,f.** *Choice, 1992.*

Keating, Peter (Editor)   **HV245**
Into Unknown England, 1866-1913: Selections from the Social
Explorers. Trade Cloth. Rowman & Littlefield Publishers, Inc.
Lanham, MD. 1976. 320p. ISBN:0-87471-820-1, ISBN13:
978-0-87471-820-1. Dewey:301.44/1. LCCN:76-000964.

Audience: **g,l,u,f.**

Perkin, Harold   **HN385.P46 1990**
Origins of Modern English Society. Trade Paper. Routledge.
New York, NY. 1985. 480p. Studies in Social History
ISBN:0-415-05922-4, ISBN13: 978-0-415-05922-0.
Dewey:306/.0942. LCCN:90-049632.

Audience: **g,l,u,f.**

Phillipps, K. C.   **PE1085.P45 1984**
Language and Class in Victorian England. David Crystal
(Editor). Trade Cloth. Blackwell Publishing, Inc. Malden, MA.

1984. 224p. The Language Library ISBN:0-631-13689-4, ISBN13: 978-0-631-13689-7. Dewey:428. LCCN:84-016717.
Audience: **g,l,u,f.** *Choice, 1985.*

Thompson, F. M.   **DA550.T53 1988**
The Rise of Respectable Society: A Social History of Victorian Britain, 1830-1900. Trade Cloth. Harvard University Press. Cambridge, MA. 1988. 382p. ISBN:0-674-77285-7, ISBN13: 978-0-674-77285-4. Dewey:941.081. LCCN:88-014802.
Audience: **g,l,u,f.** *Choice, 1989.*

Class > Working Class

Anderson, Patricia   **DA533.A574 1991**
The Printed Image and the Transformation of Popular Culture, 1790-1860. Trade Cloth. Oxford University Press, Inc. New York, NY. 1991. 224p. ISBN:0-19-811236-X, ISBN13: 978-0-19-811236-5. Dewey:306.4. LCCN:91-002828.
Audience: **g,l,u,f.** *Choice, 1992.*

Bailey, Peter   **GV75.B33 1978**
Leisure and Class in Victorian England: Rational Recreation and the Contest for Control, 1830-1885. Trade Cloth. University of Toronto Press. Toronto, ON. 1978. x, 260p. Studies in Social History Ser. ISBN:0-8020-2258-8, ISBN13: 978-0-8020-2258-5. Dewey:790/.0941. LCCN:78-040390.
Audience: **g,l,u,f.** *B*

Clark, Anna   **HD8390**
Struggle for the Breeches: Gender and the Making of the British Working Class. Trade Paper. University of California Press. Berkeley, CA. 1997. 432p. Studies on the History of Society and Culture, Vol. 23 ISBN:0-520-20883-8, ISBN13: 978-0-520-20883-4. Dewey:305.5/62/0941. LCCN:93-050835.
Audience: **u,f.**

Cullwick, Hannah   **TX331.C85A33 1984**
The Diaries of Hannah Cullwick, Victorian Maidservant. Liz Stanley (Editor). Trade Cloth. Rutgers University Press. Piscataway, NJ. 1984. 385p. ISBN:0-8135-1070-8, ISBN13: 978-0-8135-1070-5. Dewey:640/.46/0924 B. LCCN:84-011638.
Audience: **g,u,f.**

Higginbotham, Peter
The Workhouse.
http://www.workhouses.org.uk
Audience: **g,l,u,f.**

Himmelfarb, Gertrude   **HV4086.A3H55 1985**
The Idea of Poverty: England in the Early Industrial Age. Trade Paper. Knopf Publishing Group. New York, NY. 1985. 608p. ISBN:0-394-72607-3, ISBN13: 978-0-394-72607-6. Dewey:305.5/69/0941. LCCN:84-040005.
Audience: **u,f.** *B*

James, Louis   **PR878.L3 J3 1974**
Fiction for the Working Man. Trade Paper. Penguin Group (USA) Inc. New York, NY. 1974. xviii, 261p. ISBN:0-14-060037-X, ISBN13: 978-0-14-060037-7. Dewey:823/.8/09. LCCN:75-323006.
Audience: **g,l,u,f.**

Joyce, Patrick   **HC255**
Work, Society, and Politics: The Culture of the Factory in Later Victorian England. Trade Cloth. Ashgate Publishing, Ltd. Aldershot, 1992. 382p. ISBN:0-7512-0008-5, ISBN13: 978-0-7512-0008-9. Dewey:303.48309427.
Audience: **g,l,u,f.** *B*

Joyce, Patrick D.   **DA533.J68 1994**
Democratic Subjects: The Self and the Social in Nineteenth-Century England. Trade Paper. Cambridge University Press. New York, NY. 1994. 254p. ISBN:0-521-44802-6, ISBN13: 978-0-521-44802-4. Dewey:942.081. LCCN:93-037741.
Audience: **u,f.** *Choice, 1995.*

Mayhew, Henry   **HV4086.L66M38 2005**
The London Underworld in the Victorian Period: Authentic First-Person Accounts by Beggars, Thieves and Prostitutes. Trade Paper, Perfect. Dover Publications, Inc. Mineola, NY. 2005. 416p. ISBN:0-486-44006-0, ISBN13: 978-0-486-44006-4. Dewey:305.5/69/0942109034. LCCN:2005-041274.
Audience: **g,l,u,f.**

Mayhew, Henry   **HV4086.L66**
London Labour and the London Poor, Vol. 2. J. D. Rosenberg (Introduction by). Trade Paper. Dover Publications, Inc. Mineola, NY. 1982. 512p. ISBN:0-486-21935-6, ISBN13: 978-0-486-21935-6. Dewey:305.5/69/09421.
Audience: **g,l,u,f.** *B*

Stedman-Jones, Gareth   **HD8390 .J8 1983**
Languages of Class: Studies in English Working Class History 1832-1982. Cloth Text. Cambridge University Press. New York, NY. 1984. 268p. ISBN:0-521-25648-8, ISBN13: 978-0-521-25648-3. Dewey:305.5/62/0942. LCCN:83-007721.
Audience: **u,f.**

Sweetman, John   **PR5101.M39Z**
Bomber Crew: Taking on the Reich. Trade Paper. Little, Brown Book Group Ltd. London, 2005. 288p. ISBN:0-349-11796-9, ISBN13: 978-0-349-11796-6. Dewey:821/.8.
Audience: **g,l,u,f.**

Vincent, David   **HD8388**
Bread, Knowledge and Freedom: A Study of Nineteenth-Century Working Class Autobiography. Trade Paper. Routledge. New York, NY. 1983. 221p. ISBN:0-416-34670-7, ISBN13: 978-0-416-34670-1. Dewey:305.5/62/0941. LCCN:82-014163.
Audience: **g,l,u,f.**

Class > Middle Class

Davidoff, Leonore &   **HT690.G7D38 2002**
Hall, Catherine
Family Fortunes: Men and Women of the English Middle Class, 1780-1850. Ed. 2. Paper over Boards. Routledge. New York, NY. 2003. 616p. ISBN:0-415-29064-3, ISBN13: 978-0-415-29064-7. Dewey:305.5/5/094209033. LCCN:2002-032612.
Audience: **g,l,u,f.** *Choice, 1988.*

Gordon, Eleanor &   **HQ1600.G53G67 2003**
Nair, Gwyneth
Public Lives: Women, Family, and Society in Victorian Britain. Cloth over Boards. Yale University Press. Cumberland, RI. 2004. 328p. ISBN:0-300-10220-8, ISBN13: 978-0-300-10220-8. Dewey:305.5/5/094144. LCCN:2003-014022.
Audience: **g,l,u,f.** *Choice, 2004.*

Gunn, Simon   **DA110.G86 2000**
Public Culture of Victorian Middle Class: Ritual and Authority in the English Industrial City, 1840-1914. Cloth over Boards. Manchester University Press. Manchester, 2001. 224p.

ISBN:0-7190-5715-9, ISBN13: 978-0-7190-5715-1.
Dewey:306/.0942/09034.

Audience: **u,f.** *Choice, 2001.*

Langland, Elizabeth **HT690.G7L35 1995**
Nobody's Angels: Middle-Class Women and Domestic Ideology in Victorian Culture. Book, Other. Cornell University Press. Ithaca, NY. 1995. 288p. Reading Women Writing Ser. ISBN:0-8014-8220-8, ISBN13: 978-0-8014-8220-5. Dewey:305.5/5/082. LCCN:94-024393.

Audience: **g,l,u,f.**

MacLeod, Dianne **N72.S6 M23 1996**
Sachko
Art and the Victorian Middle Class: Money and the Making of Cultural Identity. Cloth Text. Cambridge University Press. New York, NY. 1996. 550p. ISBN:0-521-55090-4, ISBN13: 978-0-521-55090-1. Dewey:700.8/622. LCCN:95-024299.

Audience: **u,f.** *Choice, 1997.*

Peterson, M. Jeanne **HQ1599.E5P48 1989**
Family, Love and Work in the Lives of Victorian Gentlewomen. Trade Cloth. Indiana University Press. Bloomington, IN. 1989. 256p. ISBN:0-253-34427-1, ISBN13: 978-0-253-34427-4. Dewey:305.4/0942. LCCN:88-045389.

Audience: **g,l,u,f.** *Choice, 1989.*

Reader, W. J. (William **HT687**
Joseph)
Professional Men: The Rise of the Professional Classes in Nineteenth-Century England. New York, Basic Books. 1966.

Audience: **g,l,u,f.**

Wahrman, Dror **HT690.G7 W34 1995**
Imagining the Middle Class: The Political Representation of Class in Britain, C. 1780-1840. Trade Cloth. Cambridge University Press. New York, NY. 1995. 442p. ISBN:0-521-47127-3, ISBN13: 978-0-521-47127-5. Dewey:305.5/5. LCCN:94-030858.

Audience: **u,f.** *Choice, 1996.*

Class > Aristocracy

Cannadine, David **HT653.G7C358 1999**
The Decline and Fall of the British Aristocracy. Trade Cloth. Knopf Publishing Group. New York, NY. 1999. 848p. ISBN:0-375-70368-3, ISBN13: 978-0-375-70368-3. Dewey:305.5/2/0941. LCCN:99-022542.

Audience: **g,l,u,f.** *Choice, 1991.*

Davidoff, Lenore **HQ1596 .D38**
The Best Circles. Trade Cloth. Rowman & Littlefield Publishers, Inc. Lanham, MD. 1973. 127p. ISBN:0-87471-428-1, ISBN13: 978-0-87471-428-9. Dewey:301.41/2/0942. LCCN:73-010386.

Audience: **g,l,u,f.**

Girouard, Mark **NA7620**
The Victorian Country House. Trade Cloth. Yale University Press. Cumberland, RI. 1979. 448p. ISBN:0-300-02390-1, ISBN13: 978-0-300-02390-9. Dewey:728.8/3/0942. LCCN:79-064077.

Audience: **g,l,u,f.**

Mandler, Peter **DA655**
The Fall and Rise of the Stately Home. Yale University Press. 1999. ISBN:0-300-07869-2, ISBN13: 978-0-300-07869-5.

Audience: **u,f.**

Crime and Policing

Altick, Richard D. **HV6535.G6**
Deadly Encounters: Two Victorian Sensations. Book, Other. University of Pennsylvania Press. Philadelphia, PA. 2000. 176p. ISBN:0-8122-1756-X, ISBN13: 978-0-8122-1756-8. Dewey:364.1/523/09421. LCCN:86-001511.

Audience: **g,l,u,f.**

Collins, Philip **PR4592.C7C6 1994**
Dickens and Crime. Ed. 3. Trade Paper. Palgrave Macmillan. New York, NY. 1995. 388p. ISBN:0-312-12327-2, ISBN13: 978-0-312-12327-7. Dewey:823/.8. LCCN:94-025477.

Audience: **u,f.**

Curtis, L. Perry **HV6535.G72L663 2001**
Jack the Ripper and the London Press. Cloth over Boards. Yale University Press. Cumberland, RI. 2001. 368p. ISBN:0-300-08872-8, ISBN13: 978-0-300-08872-4. Dewey:070.4/493641523/092. LCCN:2001-002530.

Audience: **u,f.**

Duckworth, Jeannie **HV9145**
Fagin's Children: Criminal Children in Victorian England. Trade Cloth. Continuum International Publishing Group, Ltd. London, 2003. 256p. ISBN:1-85285-391-3, ISBN13: 978-1-85285-391-4. Dewey:364.36094109034. LCCN:2003-273556.

Audience: **l,u,f.** *Choice, 2004.*

Marsh, Joss **PR468.B55M37 1998**
Word Crimes: Blasphemy, Culture, and Literature in Nineteenth-Century England. Trade Cloth. University of Chicago Press. Chicago, IL. 1998. 362p. ISBN:0-226-50690-8, ISBN13: 978-0-226-50690-6. Dewey:820.9353. LCCN:97-049344.

Audience: **u,f.**

Mayhew, Henry **HV4086.L66**
London Labour and the London Poor, Vol. 2. J. D. Rosenberg (Introduction by). Trade Paper. Dover Publications, Inc. Mineola, NY. 1982. 512p. ISBN:0-486-21935-6, ISBN13: 978-0-486-21935-6. Dewey:305.5/69/09421.

Audience: **g,l,u,f.** *B*

Wiener, Martin J. **HV6535.G42E64 2003**
Men of Blood: Violence, Manliness, and Criminal Justice in Victorian England. Cloth Text. Cambridge University Press. New York, NY. 2004. 312p. ISBN:0-521-83198-9, ISBN13: 978-0-521-83198-7. Dewey:364.15/23/094209034. LCCN:2003-048566.

Audience: **u,f.** *Choice, 2004.*

Wiener, Martin Joel **HV6022.G7 W54 1990**
Reconstructing the Criminal: Culture, Law, and Policy in England, 1830-1914. Trade Cloth. Cambridge University Press. New York, NY. 1990. 391p. ISBN:0-521-35045-X, ISBN13: 978-0-521-35045-7. Dewey:364.9/42/09034. LCCN:90-001593.

Audience: **u,f.** *Choice, 1991.*

Zedner, Lucia **HV9649.E5.Z43 1991**
Women, Crime, and Custody in Victorian England. Trade Cloth. Oxford University Press, Inc. New York, NY. 1992. 372p. ISBN:0-19-820264-4, ISBN13: 978-0-19-820264-6. Dewey:364.3/74/082. LCCN:92-136980.

Audience: **g,l,u,f.** *Choice, 1992.*

Economics

Davis, Lance E. &   **HC259 .D38 1986**
  Huttenback, Robert A.
Mammon and the Pursuit of Empire: The Political Economy of
British Imperialism, 1860-1912. Robert Fogel & Stephan A.
Thernstrom (Contribution by). Cloth Text. Cambridge University
Press. New York, NY. 1987. 414p. Interdisciplinary Perspectives
on Modern History Ser. ISBN:0-521-23611-8, ISBN13:
978-0-521-23611-9. Dewey:330.9171/241. LCCN:86-002649.
             Audience: **u,f.** *Choice, 1987.*

Davis, Tracy C.   **PN2599.5.E25 D38 20**
The Economics of the British Stage, 1800-1914. Trade Cloth.
Cambridge University Press. New York, NY. 2000. 524p.
ISBN:0-521-57115-4, ISBN13: 978-0-521-57115-9.
Dewey:338.4/7792/0941. LCCN:00-020381.
             Audience: **g,l,u,f.** *Choice, 2001.*

Finn, Margot C.   **PR830.E37.F66 2003**
  (Author, Contribution by)
The Character of Credit: Personal Debt in English Culture,
1740-1914. Keith Wrightson & Colin Jones (Contribution by).
Trade Cloth. Cambridge University Press. New York, NY. 2003.
374p. Cambridge Social and Cultural Histories Ser., Vol. 1
ISBN:0-521-82342-0, ISBN13: 978-0-521-82342-5.
Dewey:306.3/0942/09033. LCCN:2002-041697.
             Audience: **u,f.** *Choice, 2004.*

Himmelfarb, Gertrude   **HV4086.A3H55 1985**
The Idea of Poverty: England in the Early Industrial Age. Trade
Paper. Knopf Publishing Group. New York, NY. 1985. 608p.
ISBN:0-394-72607-3, ISBN13: 978-0-394-72607-6.
Dewey:305.5/69/0941. LCCN:84-040005.
             Audience: **u,f.** *B*

Himmelfarb, Gertrude   **HV4086.A3**
Poverty and Compassion: The Moral Imagination of the Late
Victorians. Trade Paper. Knopf Publishing Group. New York,
NY. 1992. 475p. ISBN:0-679-74173-9, ISBN13:
978-0-679-74173-2. Dewey:362.5/0942/09034.
LCCN:92-050066.
             Audience: **g,l,u,f.** *Choice, 1992.*

Richards, Thomas   **HC255.R53 1990**
The Commodity Culture of Victorian England: Advertising and
Spectacle, 1851-1914. Trade Cloth. Stanford University Press.
Palo Alto, CA. 1990. 320p. ISBN:0-8047-1652-8, ISBN13:
978-0-8047-1652-9. Dewey:659.1/0941/09034.
LCCN:89-037035.
             Audience: **u,f.** *Choice, 1990.*

Wiener, Martin Joel   **DA533.W59 2004**
English Culture and the Decline of the Industrial Spirit,
1850-1980. Ed. 2. Cloth Text. Cambridge University Press. New
York, NY. 2004. 236p. ISBN:0-521-84376-6, ISBN13:
978-0-521-84376-8. Dewey:942.08. LCCN:2004-052117.
             Audience: **g,l,u,f.**

Education

Chandos, John   **LC1390.C43 1984**
Boys Together: English Public Schools 1800-1864. Trade Cloth.
Yale University Press. Cumberland, RI. 1984. 400p.
ISBN:0-300-03215-3, ISBN13: 978-0-300-03215-4.
Dewey:373.2/22/0941. LCCN:84-040192.
             Audience: **g,l,u,f.** *B*

Dyhouse, Carol   **LC2046.D94 1995**
No Distinction of Sex?: Women in British Universities,
1870-1939. Paper over Boards. Taylor & Francis Group.
Abingdon, 1995. 288p. Women's History Ser.
ISBN:1-85728-458-5, ISBN13: 978-1-85728-458-4.
Dewey:376/.65/0941. LCCN:95-000875.
             Audience: **u,f.**

Honey, J. R.   **LA631.7.H64 1977**
Tom Brown's Universe: The Development of the English Public
School of the 19th Century. Trade Cloth. Crown Publishing
Group. New York, NY. 1978. ISBN:0-8129-0689-6, ISBN13:
978-0-8129-0689-9. Dewey:370/.942. LCCN:76-056585.
             Audience: **g,u,f.**

Lubenow, W. C.   **LF129.5.C34 L83 1998**
The Cambridge Apostles, 1820-1914: Liberalism, Imagination,
and Friendship in British Intellectual and Professional Life.
Trade Cloth. Cambridge University Press. New York, NY. 1998.
480p. ISBN:0-521-57213-4, ISBN13: 978-0-521-57213-2.
Dewey:378.426/59. LCCN:97-035252.
             Audience: **u,f.**

Newsome, David   **LA632**
Godliness and Good Learning: Four Studies on a Victorian
Ideal. Trade Cloth. Transatlantic Arts, Inc. Albuquerque, NM.
1961. ISBN:0-7195-1015-5, ISBN13: 978-0-7195-1015-1.
Dewey:370/.942.
             Audience: **g,l,u,f.**

Rothblatt, Sheldon   **LF118**
The Revolution of the Dons: Cambridge and Society in
Victorian England. Trade Paper. Cambridge University Press.
New York, NY. 1981. 328p. ISBN:0-521-28370-1, ISBN13:
978-0-521-28370-0. Dewey:378.426/59. LCCN:80-041865.
             Audience: **l,u,f.**

Wiener, Martin Joel   **DA533.W59 2004**
English Culture and the Decline of the Industrial Spirit,
1850-1980. Ed. 2. Cloth Text. Cambridge University Press. New
York, NY. 2004. 236p. ISBN:0-521-84376-6, ISBN13:
978-0-521-84376-8. Dewey:942.08. LCCN:2004-052117.
             Audience: **g,l,u,f.**

Empire

Brantlinger, Patrick   **PR463**
Rule of Darkness: British Literature and Imperialism,
1830-1914. Book, Other. Cornell University Press. Ithaca, NY.
1990. 336p. ISBN:0-8014-9767-1, ISBN13: 978-0-8014-9767-4.
Dewey:820.9/008. LCCN:87-047823.
             Audience: **u,f.** *Choice, 1988.*

Burton, Antoinette   **JV1017.P65 2001**
  (Editor)
Politics and Empire in Victorian Britain: A Reader. Cloth over
Boards. Palgrave Macmillan. New York, NY. 2001. 368p.
ISBN:0-312-22997-6, ISBN13: 978-0-312-22997-9.
Dewey:909/.0971241081. LCCN:2001-019448.
             Audience: **g,l,u,f.**

Cannadine, David   **DA16.C28 2001**
Ornamentalism: How the British Saw Their Empire. Trade
Cloth. Oxford University Press, Inc. New York, NY. 2001. 288p.
ISBN:0-19-514660-3, ISBN13: 978-0-19-514660-8.
Dewey:941.08. LCCN:2001-021407.
             Audience: **g,u,f.**

Curtis, L. Perry Jr.   DA925.C85 1997
Apes and Angels: The Irishman in Victorian Caricature. Ed. 2.
Trade Cloth. Smithsonian Institution Press. Washington, DC.
1997. 208p. ISBN:1-56098-647-6, ISBN13: 978-1-56098-647-8.
Dewey:305.8/9162/09034. LCCN:96-016744.

Audience: **g,l,u,f.**

Davis, Lance E. &   HC259 .D38 1986
Huttenback, Robert A.
Mammon and the Pursuit of Empire: The Political Economy of
British Imperialism, 1860-1912. Robert Fogel & Stephan A.
Thernstrom (Contribution by). Cloth Text. Cambridge University
Press. New York, NY. 1987. 414p. Interdisciplinary Perspectives
on Modern History Ser. ISBN:0-521-23611-8, ISBN13:
978-0-521-23611-9. Dewey:330.9171/241. LCCN:86-002649.

Audience: **u,f.** *Choice, 1987.*

Foster, R. F.   DA925.F63
Paddy and Mr. Punch: Connections in Irish and English History.
Trade Paper. Penguin Group (USA) Inc. New York, NY. 1996.
400p. ISBN:0-14-017170-3, ISBN13: 978-0-14-017170-9.
Dewey:941.

Audience: **g,l,u,f.**

Hall, Catherine   DA16.H18 2002
Civilising Subjects: Metropole and Colony in the English
Imagination 1830-1867. Trade Cloth. University of Chicago
Press. Chicago, IL. 2002. 556p. ISBN:0-226-31334-4, ISBN13:
978-0-226-31334-4. Dewey:941.08. LCCN:2002-283737.

Audience: **u,f.**

Milligan, Barry   PR468.O6M55 1995
Pleasures and Pains: Opium and the Orient in
Nineteenth-Century British Culture. Cloth Text. University Press
of Virginia. Charlottesville, VA. 1995. 192p. Victorian Literature
and Culture Ser. ISBN:0-8139-1571-6, ISBN13:
978-0-8139-1571-5. Dewey:820.9/9208. LCCN:94-024140.

Audience: **l,u,f.** *Choice, 1995.*

Porter, Bernard   HN381
The Absent-Minded Imperialists: Empire, Society and Culture in
Britain. Trade Cloth. Oxford University Press, Inc. New York,
NY. 2005. 504p. ISBN:0-19-820854-5, ISBN13:
978-0-19-820854-9. Dewey:941.081. LCCN:2004-019735.

Audience: **g,l,u,f.**

Porter, Bernard   DA16.P67 1996
The Lion's Share: A Short History of British Imperialism,
1850-1995. Ed. 3. Cloth Text. Longman Publishing Group.
White Plains, NY. 1996. 432p. ISBN:0-582-29294-8, ISBN13:
978-0-582-29294-9. Dewey:325.3/41. LCCN:95-050463.

Audience: **g,l,u,f.**

Porter, Bernard   DA16.P67 2004
The Lion's Share: A Short History of British Imperialism,
1850-2004. Ed. 4. Trade Paper. Longman Publishing Group.
White Plains, NY. 2004. 496p. ISBN:0-582-77252-4, ISBN13:
978-0-582-77252-6. Dewey:909/.0971241. LCCN:2004-040108.

Audience: **g,l,u,f.**

Said, Edward W.   PN761.S28 1994
Culture and Imperialism. Trade Paper. Knopf Publishing Group.
New York, NY. 1994. 416p. ISBN:0-679-75054-1, ISBN13:
978-0-679-75054-3. Dewey:809/.894. LCCN:93-043485.

Audience: **g,l,u,f.** *Choice, 1993.*

Gender

Ardis, Ann   PR878.F45A74 1990
New Women, New Novels: Feminism and Early Modernism.
Cloth Text. Rutgers University Press. Piscataway, NJ. 1990.
225p. ISBN:0-8135-1581-5, ISBN13: 978-0-8135-1581-6.
Dewey:823/.809352042. LCCN:90-035039.

Audience: **u,f.** *Choice, 1991.*

Armstrong, Nancy   PR821
Desire and Domestic Fiction: A Political History of the Novel.
Trade Paper. Oxford University Press, Inc. New York, NY. 1990.
310p. ISBN:0-19-506160-8, ISBN13: 978-0-19-506160-4.
Dewey:823/.009. LCCN:86-016482.

Audience: **u,f.** *Choice, 1987.*

Beeton, Isabella   TX145.B54 2000
Mrs. Beeton's Book of Household Management. Nicola Humble
(Editor). Trade Paper. Oxford University Press, Inc. New York,
NY. 2000. 667p. Oxford World's Classics Ser.
ISBN:0-19-283345-6, ISBN13: 978-0-19-283345-7. Dewey:640.
LCCN:99-054236.

Audience: **g,l.**

Boyd, Kelly   PR878.C513B69 2002
Manliness and the Boys' Story Paper in Britain: A Cultural
History, 1855-1940. Cloth over Boards. Palgrave Macmillan.
New York, NY. 2003. 288p. Studies in Gender History Ser.
ISBN:0-333-64172-8, ISBN13: 978-0-333-64172-9.
Dewey:823/.80992826. LCCN:2002-072302.

Audience: **g,l,u,f.**

Broomfield, Andrea &   PR1286.W6P76 1996
Mitchell, Sally
Prose by Victorian Women: An Anthology. Cloth Text. Garland
Publishing, Inc. New York, NY. 1995. 752p. Garland Reference
Library of the Humanities, Vol. 1893: ISBN:0-8153-1970-3,
ISBN13: 978-0-8153-1970-2. Dewey:828/.8080809287.
LCCN:95-024400.

Audience: **g,l,u,f.** *Choice, 1996.*

Casteras, Susan P.   N6767.5.V52C37 1987
Images of Victorian Womanhood in English Art. Trade Cloth.
Fairleigh Dickinson University Press. Cranbury, NJ. 1987. 192p.
ISBN:0-8386-3281-5, ISBN13: 978-0-8386-3281-9.
Dewey:760/.04424/0942. LCCN:85-045933.

Audience: **u,f.** *Choice, 1988.*

Cherry, Deborah   ND467.C45 1993
Painting Women: Victorian Women Artists. Cloth Text.
Routledge. New York, NY. 1993. 344p. ISBN:0-415-06052-4,
ISBN13: 978-0-415-06052-3. Dewey:759.2. LCCN:92-036713.

Audience: **g,l,u,f.**

Clark, Anna   HD8390
Struggle for the Breeches: Gender and the Making of the British
Working Class. Trade Paper. University of California Press.
Berkeley, CA. 1997. 432p. Studies on the History of Society
and Culture, Vol. 23 ISBN:0-520-20883-8, ISBN13:
978-0-520-20883-4. Dewey:305.5/62/0941. LCCN:93-050835.

Audience: **u,f.**

Clarke, Micael M.   PR5642.W6C58 1995
Thackeray and Women. Library Binding. Northern Illinois
University Press. DeKalb, IL. 1995. 250p. ISBN:0-87580-197-8,
ISBN13: 978-0-87580-197-1. Dewey:823/.8. LCCN:94-036979.

Audience: **u,f.** *Choice, 1996.*

Cullwick, Hannah   **TX331.C85A33 1984**
The Diaries of Hannah Cullwick, Victorian Maidservant. Liz
Stanley (Editor). Trade Cloth. Rutgers University Press.
Piscataway, NJ. 1984. 385p. ISBN:0-8135-1070-8, ISBN13:
978-0-8135-1070-5. Dewey:640/.46/0924 B. LCCN:84-011638.
Audience: **g,u,f.**

Cvetkovich, Ann   **PR878.F45 C85 1992**
Mixed Feelings: Feminism, Mass Culture and Victorian
Sensationalism. Paper Text. Rutgers University Press.
Piscataway, NJ. 1992. x, 227p. ISBN:0-8135-1857-1, ISBN13:
978-0-8135-1857-2. Dewey:823/.809352042. LCCN:92-004457.
Audience: **u,f.**

David, Deirdre   **PR469.F44D38 1987**
Intellectual Women and Victorian Patriarchy: Harriet Martineau,
Elizabeth Barrett Browning, George Eliot. Trade Paper. Cornell
University Press. Ithaca, NY. 1989. 265p. ISBN:0-8014-9414-1,
ISBN13: 978-0-8014-9414-7. Dewey:820.9/9287.
LCCN:86-023989.
Audience: **u,f.** *Choice, 1988.*

Davidoff, Lenore   **HQ1596 .D38**
The Best Circles. Trade Cloth. Rowman & Littlefield Publishers,
Inc. Lanham, MD. 1973. 127p. ISBN:0-87471-428-1, ISBN13:
978-0-87471-428-9. Dewey:301.41/2/0942. LCCN:73-010386.
Audience: **g,l,u,f.**

Davis, Tracy C.   **PN2594.D34 1991**
Actresses As Working Women: Their Social Identity in Victorian
England. Paper over Boards. Routledge. New York, NY. 1991.
228p. Gender and Performance Ser. ISBN:0-415-05652-7,
ISBN13: 978-0-415-05652-6. Dewey:306.4/84/082.
LCCN:90-047664.
Audience: **u,f.** *Choice, 1992.*

Dyhouse, Carol   **HQ798 .D85**
Girls Growing up in Late Victorian and Edwardian England.
Trade Cloth. Routledge. New York, NY. 1981. 224p. Studies in
Social History ISBN:0-7100-0821-X, ISBN13:
978-0-7100-0821-3. Dewey:305.2/3/0941. LCCN:81-008578.
Audience: **l,u,f.**

Dyhouse, Carol   **LC2046.D94 1995**
No Distinction of Sex?: Women in British Universities,
1870-1939. Paper over Boards. Taylor & Francis Group.
Abingdon, 1995. 288p. Women's History Ser.
ISBN:1-85728-458-5, ISBN13: 978-1-85728-458-4.
Dewey:376/.65/0941. LCCN:95-000875.
Audience: **u,f.**

Flanders, Judith   **HQ615.F58 2004**
Inside the Victorian Home: A Portrait of Domestic Life in
Victorian England. Trade Cloth. W. W. Norton & Company, Inc.
New York, NY. 2004. 416p. ISBN:0-393-05209-5, ISBN13:
978-0-393-05209-1. Dewey:306/.0942/09034.
LCCN:2003-027693.
Audience: **g,l,u,f.** *Choice, 2005.*

Frost, Ginger S.   **KD754.F76 1995**
Promises Broken: Courtship, Class, and Gender in Victorian
England. Cloth Text. University Press of Virginia.
Charlottesville, VA. 1995. 304p. Victorian Literature and Culture
Ser. ISBN:0-8139-1610-0, ISBN13: 978-0-8139-1610-1.
Dewey:346.42/022. LCCN:95-007637.
Audience: **g,l,u,f.** *Choice, 1996.*

Gilbert, Sandra M. &   **PR115.G5 2000**
Gubar, Susan
The Madwoman in the Attic: The Woman Writer and the
Nineteenth-Century Literary Imagination. Ed. 2. Trade Paper.
Yale University Press. Cumberland, RI. 2000. 768p.
ISBN:0-300-08458-7, ISBN13: 978-0-300-08458-0.
Dewey:820.9/9287/09034. LCCN:99-086038.
Audience: **g,l,u,f.**

Gilmour, Robin   **PR788.U/**
The Idea of the Gentleman in the Victorian Novel. Trade Paper.
Routledge. New York, NY. 1981. 208p. ISBN:0-04-800005-1,
ISBN13: 978-0-04-800005-7. Dewey:823/.8/093520621.
LCCN:81-010869.
Audience: **l,u,f.** ℬ

Gordon, Eleanor &   **HQ1600.G53G67 2003**
Nair, Gwyneth
Public Lives: Women, Family, and Society in Victorian Britain.
Cloth over Boards. Yale University Press. Cumberland, RI.
2004. 328p. ISBN:0-300-10220-8, ISBN13: 978-0-300-10220-8.
Dewey:305.5/5/094144. LCCN:2003-014022.
Audience: **g,l,u,f.** *Choice, 2004.*

Helsinger, Elizabeth K.,   **HQ1599.E5H44**
et al.
The Woman Question: Society and Literature in Britain and
America, 1837-1883: Social Issues. Robin L. Sheets & William
Veeder (Authors). Trade Paper. University of Chicago Press.
Chicago, IL. 1996. 278p. ISBN:0-226-32667-5, ISBN13:
978-0-226-32667-2. Dewey:305.4/0942. LCCN:88-027796.
Audience: **g,l,u,f.**

Helsinger, Elizabeth K.,   **HQ1599.E5H44 1989**
et al.
The Woman Question: Society and Literature in Britain and
America, 1837-1883: Defining Voices. Robin L. Sheets &
William Veeder (Authors). Trade Paper. University of Chicago
Press. Chicago, IL. 1997. 162p. ISBN:0-226-32666-7, ISBN13:
978-0-226-32666-5. Dewey:305.4/0942. LCCN:88-027796.
Audience: **g,l,u,f.**

Helsinger, Elizabeth K.,   **HQ1599.E5H44**
et al.
The Woman Question: Society and Literature in Britain and
America, 1837-1883: Literary Issues. Robin L. Sheets &
William Veeder (Authors). Trade Paper. University of Chicago
Press. Chicago, IL. 1996. 256p. ISBN:0-226-32668-3, ISBN13:
978-0-226-32668-9. Dewey:305.4/0942. LCCN:88-027796.
Audience: **g,l,u,f.**

Holcombe, Lee   **KD760.H64 1983**
Wives and Property: Reform of the Married Women's Property
Law in Nineteenth-Century England. Cloth Text. University of
Toronto Press. Toronto, ON. 1982. 368p. ISBN:0-8020-6476-0,
ISBN13: 978-0-8020-6476-9. Dewey:344.206/4.
LCCN:83-105215.
Audience: **g,l,u,f.**

Honey, J. R.   **LA631.7.H64 1977**
Tom Brown's Universe: The Development of the English Public
School of the 19th Century. Trade Cloth. Crown Publishing
Group. New York, NY. 1978. ISBN:0-8129-0689-6, ISBN13:
978-0-8129-0689-9. Dewey:370/.942. LCCN:76-056585.
Audience: **g,u,f.**

Langland, Elizabeth   **HT690.G7L35 1995**
Nobody's Angels: Middle-Class Women and Domestic Ideology
in Victorian Culture. Book, Other. Cornell University Press.

Audience: g=general, l=lower division undergraduate, u=upper division undergraduate, f=faculty.

747

Ithaca, NY. 1995. 288p. Reading Women Writing Ser. ISBN:0-8014-8220-8, ISBN13: 978-0-8014-8220-5. Dewey:305.5/5/082. LCCN:94-024393.

Audience: **g,l,u,f.**

Lansbury, Coral   **HV4943.G7E535 1985**
The Old Brown Dog: Women, Workers and Vivisection in Edwardian England. Cloth Text. University of Wisconsin Press. Chicago, IL. 1985. 232p. ISBN:0-299-10250-5, ISBN13: 978-0-299-10250-0. Dewey:942.082/3. LCCN:85-040369.

Audience: **u,f.**   *Choice, 1986.*

Loeb, Lori A.   **HF5813.G7L63 1994**
Consuming Angels: Advertising and Victorian Women. Cloth Text. Oxford University Press, Inc. New York, NY. 1994. 240p. ISBN:0-19-508596-5, ISBN13: 978-0-19-508596-9. Dewey:659.1/042/094109034. LCCN:93-046094.

Audience: **l,u,f.**   *Choice, 1995.*

Martineau, Harriet   **PR4984.M5 Z463**
Harriet Martineaus's Autobiography, Vol. 1. Trade Paper. Kessinger Publishing, LLC. Whitefish, MT. 2005. ISBN:1-4179-7016-2, ISBN13: 978-1-4179-7016-2. Dewey:823/.8.

Audience: **g,l,u,f.**

Martineau, Harriet   **PR4984.M5 Z463**
Harriet Martineaus's Autobiography, Vol. 2. Trade Paper. Kessinger Publishing, LLC. Whitefish, MT. 2005. ISBN:1-4179-7017-0, ISBN13: 978-1-4179-7017-9. Dewey:823/.8.

Audience: **g,l,u,f.**

Mermin, Dorothy   **PR115**
ⓔ Godiva's Ride: Women of Letters in England, 1830-1880. E-Book. Indiana University Press. Bloomington, IN. 1993. 204p. ISBN:0-253-20824-6, ISBN13: 978-0-253-20824-8. Dewey:820.9/9287/09034. LCCN:92-045186.

Audience: **g,l,u.**   *Choice, 1994.*

Mitchell, Sally   **PR4461.C3Z78 2004**
Frances Power Cobbe: Victorian Feminist, Journalist, Reformer. Trade Cloth. University Press of Virginia. Charlottesville, VA. 2004. 400p. Victorian Literature and Culture Ser. ISBN:0-8139-2271-2, ISBN13: 978-0-8139-2271-3. Dewey:070.92 B. LCCN:2003-022365.

Audience: **u,f.**

Morgan, Thais E.   **PR464.V53 1990**
  (Editor)
Victorian Sages and Cultural Discourse: Renegotiating Gender and Power. Cloth Text. Rutgers University Press. Piscataway, NJ. 1990. 320p. ISBN:0-8135-1600-5, ISBN13: 978-0-8135-1600-4. Dewey:820.9/32042/09034. LCCN:90-030977.

Audience: **u,f.**

Nelson, Claudia   **PR830.C513N45 1991**
Boys Will Be Girls: The Feminine Ethic and British Children's Fiction, 1857-1917. Cloth Text. Rutgers University Press. Piscataway, NJ. 1991. 216p. ISBN:0-8135-1681-1, ISBN13: 978-0-8135-1681-3. Dewey:823/.8099287. LCCN:90-020004.

Audience: **u,f.**

Nord, Deborah E.   **PR878.W6N67 1995**
Walking the Victorian Streets: Women, Representation, and the City. Trade Cloth. Cornell University Press. Ithaca, NY. 1995.

xiii, 270p. ISBN:0-8014-2392-9, ISBN13: 978-0-8014-2392-5. Dewey:823/.809352042. LCCN:95-010932.

Audience: **l,u,f.**   *Choice, 1996.*

Onslow, Barbara   **PN5124.W58O59 2000**
Women of the Press in Nineteenth-Century Britain. Cloth over Boards. Palgrave Macmillan. New York, NY. 2001. 311p. ISBN:0-312-23602-6, ISBN13: 978-0-312-23602-1. Dewey:070.9/22. LCCN:00-033333.

Audience: **g,l,u,f.**   *Choice, 2001.*

Peterson, Linda H.   **PR788.W65P47 1999**
Traditions of Victorian Women's Autobiography: The Poetics and Politics of Life Writing. Trade Cloth. University Press of Virginia. Charlottesville, VA. 1999. 272p. Victorian Literature and Culture Ser. ISBN:0-8139-1883-9, ISBN13: 978-0-8139-1883-9. Dewey:828/.80809492072. LCCN:99-019832.

Audience: **g,l,u,f.**   *Choice, 2000.*

Peterson, M. Jeanne   **HQ1599.E5P48 1989**
Family, Love and Work in the Lives of Victorian Gentlewomen. Trade Cloth. Indiana University Press. Bloomington, IN. 1989. 256p. ISBN:0-253-34427-1, ISBN13: 978-0-253-34427-4. Dewey:305.4/0942. LCCN:88-045389.

Audience: **g,l,u,f.**   *Choice, 1989.*

Poovey, Mary   **HQ1075.5.G7P66 1988**
Uneven Developments: The Ideological Work of Gender in Mid-Victorian England. Trade Paper. University of Chicago Press. Chicago, IL. 1988. 289p. Women in Culture and Society Ser. ISBN:0-226-67530-0, ISBN13: 978-0-226-67530-5. Dewey:305.3/0942/09034. LCCN:88-004783.

Audience: **u,f.**   *Choice, 1989.*

Robson, Catherine   **PR468.G5R63 2003**
Men in Wonderland: The Lost Girlhood of the Victorian Gentleman. Trade Paper. Princeton University Press. Princeton, NJ. 2003. 264p. ISBN:0-691-11526-5, ISBN13: 978-0-691-11526-9. Dewey:820.9/352054.

Audience: **u,f.**   *Choice, 2001.*

Ross, Ellen   **HQ759.R66 1993**
Love and Toil: Motherhood in Outcast London, 1870-1918. Trade Cloth. Oxford University Press, Inc. New York, NY. 1993. 326p. ISBN:0-19-503957-2, ISBN13: 978-0-19-503957-3. Dewey:306.874/3/094212. LCCN:92-040849.

Audience: **g,l,u,f.**   *Choice, 1994.*

Russett, Cynthia   **QP81.5**
Sexual Science: The Victorian Construction of Womanhood. Trade Paper. Harvard University Press. Cambridge, MA. 1991. 256p. ISBN:0-674-80291-8, ISBN13: 978-0-674-80291-9. Dewey:305.3/09/034.

Audience: **l,u,f.**   *Choice, 1992, 1989.*

Shanley, Mary Lyndon   **KD758**
Feminism, Marriage and the Law in Victorian England, 1850-1895. Trade Paper. Princeton University Press. Princeton, NJ. 1993. 224p. ISBN:0-691-02487-1, ISBN13: 978-0-691-02487-5. Dewey:346.4201/6. LCCN:89-003758.

Audience: **u,f.**

Showalter, Elaine   **PR115 .S5 1999**
A Literature of Their Own: British Women Novelists from Brontë to Lessing. Trade Paper. Princeton University Press. Princeton, NJ. 1998. 382p. ISBN:0-691-00476-5, ISBN13: 978-0-691-00476-1. Dewey:828/.8/099287. LCCN:98-089253.

Audience: **u,f.**   *Choice, 1999.*

Small, Helen PR878.S44
Love's Madness: Medicine, the Novel, and Female Insanity, 1800-1865. Trade Paper. Oxford University Press, Inc. New York, NY. 1998. 274p. ISBN:0-19-818491-3, ISBN13: 978-0-19-818491-1. Dewey:823/.809353. LCCN:95-033313.
Audience: **u,f.** *Choice, 1996.*

Sussman, Herbert PR468.M38S87 1995
Victorian Masculinities: Manhood and Masculine Poetics in Early Victorian Literature and Art. Trade Cloth. Cambridge University Press. New York, NY. 1995. 239p. Studies in Nineteenth-Century Literature and Culture, Vol. 3 ISBN:0-521-46571-0, ISBN13: 978-0-521-46571-7. Dewey:820.9/353. LCCN:94-010268.
Audience: **l,u,f.** *Choice, 1996.*

Taylor, Barbara HQ1206 .T33X 1983B
Eve and the New Jerusalem: Socialism and Feminism in the Nineteenth Century. Trade Cloth. Random House, Inc. New York, NY. 1994. 400p. ISBN:0-86068-258-7, ISBN13: 978-0-86068-258-5. Dewey:305.4/2/09034. LCCN:84-672248.
Audience: **u,f.**

Thompson, Dorothy DA554.T47 1990
Queen Victoria: The Woman, the Monarchy, and the People. Trade Cloth. Knopf Publishing Group. New York, NY. 1990. 192p. ISBN:0-394-53709-2, ISBN13: 978-0-394-53709-2. Dewey:941.081/092 B. LCCN:90-052563.
Audience: **g,l,u,f.**

Tosh, John HQ1090.7.G7T67 1999
A Man's Place: Masculinity and the Middle-Class Home in Victorian England. Cloth over Boards. Yale University Press. Cumberland, RI. 1999. 272p. ISBN:0-300-07779-3, ISBN13: 978-0-300-07779-7. Dewey:305.31/0942/09034. LCCN:98-031422.
Audience: **g,l,u,f.** *Choice, 1999.*

Vicinus, Martha HQ800.2
Independent Women: Work and Community for Single Women, 1850-1920. Trade Paper. University of Chicago Press. Chicago, IL. 1992. 412p. Women in Culture and Society Ser. ISBN:0-226-85568-6, ISBN13: 978-0-226-85568-4. Dewey:305.4/89/652/0942. LCCN:84-016158.
Audience: **u,f.** ℬ *Choice, 1985.*

Vicinus, Martha (Editor) HQ1597
Suffer and Be Still: Women in the Victorian Age. Trade Paper. Indiana University Press. Bloomington, IN. 1973. 256p. ISBN:0-253-20168-3, ISBN13: 978-0-253-20168-3. Dewey:305.4/2/0941. LCCN:71-184524.
Audience: **g,l,u.** ℬ

**Vicinus, Martha
(Editor)** HQ1593
A Widening Sphere: Changing Roles of Victorian Women. Trade Cloth. Indiana University Press. Bloomington, IN. 1977. 352p. ISBN:0-253-36540-6, ISBN13: 978-0-253-36540-8. Dewey:305.4/2/0941. LCCN:76-026433.
Audience: **g,l,u,f.** ℬ

Walkowitz, Judith R. HQ72.G7W33
City of Dreadful Delight: Narratives of Sexual Danger in Late-Victorian London. Catherine R. Stimpson (Foreword by). Trade Cloth. University of Chicago Press. Chicago, IL. 1998. 368p. Women in Culture and Society Ser. ISBN:0-226-87145-2, ISBN13: 978-0-226-87145-5. Dewey:305.4/2/09421/09034. LCCN:91-048153.
Audience: **g,l,u,f.**

Zedner, Lucia HV9649.E5.Z43 1991
Women, Crime, and Custody in Victorian England. Trade Cloth. Oxford University Press, Inc. New York, NY. 1992. 372p. ISBN:0-19-820264-4, ISBN13: 978-0-19-820264-6. Dewey:364.3/74/082. LCCN:92-136980.
Audience: **g,l,u,f.** *Choice, 1992.*

General History

Burn, W. L. DA550
Age of Equipoise: A Study of the Mid-Victorian Generation. Ashgate Publishing Company. 1994. ISBN:0-7512-0296-7, ISBN13: 978-0-7512-0296-0.
Audience: **g,l,u,f.**

Landow, George
☐ The Victorian Web.
http://www.victorianweb.org/
Audience: **g,l,u,f.**

Leary, Patrick D1
☐ Victoria Research Web.
http://victorianresearch.org/
Audience: **g,l,u,f.**

Newsome, David DA550.N49 1997
The Victorian World Picture: Perceptions and Introspections in an Age of Change. Trade Cloth. Rutgers University Press. Piscataway, NJ. 1997. 310p. ISBN:0-8135-2454-7, ISBN13: 978-0-8135-2454-2. Dewey:941.081/072. LCCN:97-015588.
Audience: **g,l,u,f.** *Choice, 1998.*

Sweet, Matthew DA550.S93 2001
Inventing the Victorians. Cloth over Boards. St. Martin's Press. Gordonville, VA. 2001. 288p. ISBN:0-312-28326-1, ISBN13: 978-0-312-28326-1. Dewey:941.081. LCCN:2002-512155.
Audience: **g,l,u,f.**

Intellectual History

Altick, Richard D. DA533
Victorian People and Ideas. Trade Paper. W. W. Norton & Company, Inc. New York, NY. 1974. 338p. ISBN:0-393-09376-X, ISBN13: 978-0-393-09376-6. Dewey:942.081.
Audience: **g,l,u.**

Annan, Noel PR5473.S6A88 1984
Leslie Stephen: The Godless Victorian. Trade Cloth. Random House, Inc. New York, NY. 1984. 384p. ISBN:0-394-53061-6, ISBN13: 978-0-394-53061-1. Dewey:828/.809 B. LCCN:84-042512.
Audience: **g,l,u,f.** ℬ

Ashton, Rosemary DA125.G4A84 1989
Little Germany: German Refugees in Victorian Britain. Trade Paper. Oxford University Press, Inc. New York, NY. 1989. 320p. ISBN:0-19-282562-3, ISBN13: 978-0-19-282562-9. Dewey:941/.00431. LCCN:88-025394.
Audience: **g,l,u,f.**

Berg, Maxine HC79.T4
The Machinery Question and the Making of Political Economy, 1815-1848. Trade Cloth. Cambridge University Press. New York, NY. 1980. 389p. ISBN:0-521-22782-8, ISBN13: 978-0-521-22782-7. Dewey:338/.06. LCCN:79-051223.
Audience: **u,f.** ℬ

Audience: g=general, l=lower division undergraduate, u=upper division undergraduate, f=faculty.

749

Bevington, Merle M.   **PN5130.S3B4**
Saturday Review, 1855-1868: Representative Educated Opinion in Victorian England. Trade Cloth. A M S Press, Inc. New York, NY. ISBN:0-404-00795-3, ISBN13: 978-0-404-00795-9. Dewey:52.0942109. LCCN:41-025970.

Audience: **g,u,f.**

Buckley, Jerome H.   **PR0731.B8**
The Triumph of Time: A Study of the Victorian Concepts of Time, History, Progress, and Decadence. Trade Paper. Books on Demand. Ann Arbor, MI. 198p. ISBN:0-7837-4452-8, ISBN13: 978-0-7837-4452-0. Dewey:820.9008. LCCN:66-021333.

Audience: **g,l,u,f.**

Chandler, Alice   **PR457 .C35**
A Dream of Order: The Medieval Ideal in Nineteenth-Century English Literature. Trade Cloth. University of Nebraska Press. Lincoln, NE. 1970. xii, 278p. ISBN:0-8032-0704-2, ISBN13: 978-0-8032-0704-2. Dewey:820/.9/007. LCCN:69-010413.

Audience: **u,f.**

Collini, Stefan   **DA550.C62 1993**
Public Moralists: Political Thought and Intellectual Life in Britain, 1850-1930. Paper Text. Oxford University Press, Inc. New York, NY. 1993. 388p. ISBN:0-19-820422-1, ISBN13: 978-0-19-820422-0. Dewey:941.08. LCCN:92-041294.

Audience: **g,l,u,f.** *Choice, 1992.*

Culler, A. Dwight   **DA3.A1C85 1985**
The Victorian Mirror of History. Trade Cloth. Yale University Press. Cumberland, RI. 1986. 336p. ISBN:0-300-03452-0, ISBN13: 978-0-300-03452-3. Dewey:941/.0072. LCCN:85-011985.

Audience: **l,u,f.**

Curtis, L. Perry Jr.   **DA925.C85 1997**
Apes and Angels: The Irishman in Victorian Caricature. Ed. 2. Trade Cloth. Smithsonian Institution Press. Washington, DC. 1997. 208p. ISBN:1-56098-647-6, ISBN13: 978-1-56098-647-8. Dewey:305.8/9162/09034. LCCN:96-016744.

Audience: **g,l,u,f.**

David, Deirdre   **PR469.F44D38 1987**
Intellectual Women and Victorian Patriarchy: Harriet Martineau, Elizabeth Barrett Browning, George Eliot. Trade Paper. Cornell University Press. Ithaca, NY. 1989. 265p. ISBN:0-8014-9414-1, ISBN13: 978-0-8014-9414-7. Dewey:820.9/9287. LCCN:86-023989.

Audience: **u,f.** *Choice, 1988.*

Desmond, Adrian   **QE705.G7 D47 1984**
Archetypes and Ancestors: Palaeontology in Victorian London, 1850-1875. Trade Paper. University of Chicago Press. Chicago, IL. 1986. 288p. ISBN:0-226-14344-9, ISBN13: 978-0-226-14344-6. Dewey:560/.9421. LCCN:83-018104.

Audience: **g,l,u,f.**

Garrigan, Kristine O.   **NA2599.8.R8**
Ruskin on Architecture: His Thought and Influence. Trade Cloth. University of Wisconsin Press. Chicago, IL. 1973. 238p. ISBN:0-299-06460-3, ISBN13: 978-0-299-06460-0. Dewey:720/.92/4. LCCN:73-002045.

Audience: **l,u,f.** *B*

Gilbert, Pamela K.   **G1811**
Mapping the Victorian Social Body. Cloth Text. State University of New York Press. Albany, NY. 2004. 245p. SUNY Series,

Studies in the Long Nineteenth Century ISBN:0-7914-6025-8, ISBN13: 978-0-7914-6025-2. Dewey:614.4/0941/09034. LCCN:2003-055013.

Audience: **u,f.**

Gilmour, Robin   **PR461.G55 1993**
The Victorian Period: The Intellectual and Cultural Context of English Literature 1830-1890. Cloth Text. Addison-Wesley Longman, Ltd. Harlow, 1994. 320p. ISBN:0-582-49346-3, ISBN13: 978-0-582-49346-9. Dewey:820.9008. LCCN:92-044545.

Audience: **g,l,u,f.**

Green-Lewis, Jennifer   **TR15.G69 1996**
Framing the Victorians: Photography and the Culture of Realism. Trade Cloth. Cornell University Press. Ithaca, NY. 1997. 264p. ISBN:0-8014-3276-6, ISBN13: 978-0-8014-3276-7. Dewey:770/.9/034. LCCN:96-020784.

Audience: **u,f.** *Choice, 1997.*

Heyck, T. W.   **DA533.H48 1982**
The Transformation of Intellectual Life in Victorian England. Cloth Text. Palgrave Macmillan. New York, NY. 1982. 262p. ISBN:0-312-81427-5, ISBN13: 978-0-312-81427-4. Dewey:942.081. LCCN:82-000840.

Audience: **g,l,u,f.** *B*

Holloway, John   **PR463 .H6**
Victorian Sage: Studies in Argument. Trade Cloth. Shoe String Press, Inc. North Haven, CT. 1962. ISBN:0-208-00593-5, ISBN13: 978-0-208-00593-9. Dewey:820.4.

Audience: **u,f.** *B*

Houghton, Walter E.   **DA533**
Victorian Frame of Mind, 1830-1870. Trade Paper. Yale University Press. Cumberland, RI. 1963. 484p. ISBN:0-300-00122-3, ISBN13: 978-0-300-00122-8. Dewey:941.90981.

Audience: **g,l,u,f.**

Jann, Rosemary   **DA3.A1J36 1985**
The Art and Science of Victorian History. Cloth Text. Ohio State University Press. Columbus, OH. 1985. 272p. ISBN:0-8142-0390-6, ISBN13: 978-0-8142-0390-3. Dewey:907/.2041. LCCN:85-013651.

Audience: **u,f.** *Choice, 1986.*

Jenkyns, Richard   **DA550 .J46**
The Victorians and Ancient Greece. Trade Cloth. Harvard University Press. Cambridge, MA. 1990. 398p. ISBN:0-674-93686-8, ISBN13: 978-0-674-93686-7. Dewey:941.081. LCCN:79-025487.

Audience: **u,f.**

Landow, George
▢ The Victorian Web.
http://www.victorianweb.org/

Audience: **g,l,u,f.**

Landow, George P.   **NX544.A1**
Victorian Types, Victorian Shadows: Biblical Typology in Victorian Literature, Art and Thought. Trade Cloth. Routledge. New York, NY. 1980. 256p. ISBN:0-7100-0598-9, ISBN13: 978-0-7100-0598-4. Dewey:700/.942. LCCN:80-040970.

Audience: **g,l,u,f.**

Levine, P. J. A.   **D13.5.G7L48 2002**
The Amateur and the Professional: Antiquarians, Historians and Archaeologists in Victorian England 1838-1886. Trade Paper.

Cambridge University Press. New York, NY. 2003. 220p. ISBN:0-521-53050-4, ISBN13: 978-0-521-53050-7. Dewey:907.2094109034.

Audience: **u,f.**

Lubenow, W. C.   LF129.5.C34 L83 1998
The Cambridge Apostles, 1820-1914: Liberalism, Imagination, and Friendship in British Intellectual and Professional Life. Trade Cloth. Cambridge University Press. New York, NY. 1998. 480p. ISBN:0-521-57213-4, ISBN13: 978-0-521-57213-2. Dewey:378.426/59. LCCN:97-035252.

Audience: **u,f.**

Marchand, Leslie A.   PN5130.A7
Athenaeum. Library Binding. Hippocrene Books, Inc. New York, NY. 1970. ISBN:0-374-95280-9, ISBN13: 978-0-374-95280-8. Dewey:52. LCCN:77-120646.

Audience: **g,l,u,f.**

Poovey, Mary   DA533.P66 1995
Making a Social Body: British Cultural Formation, 1830-1864. Trade Cloth. University of Chicago Press. Chicago, IL. 1995. 266p. ISBN:0-226-67523-8, ISBN13: 978-0-226-67523-7. Dewey:941.081. LCCN:95-004153.

Audience: **u,f.** *Choice, 1996.*

Postlethwaite, Diana   PR469.P45 P67
Making It Whole: A Victorian Circle and the Shape of Their World. Trade Paper. Ohio State University Press. Columbus, OH. 1985. 282p. ISBN:0-8142-0401-5, ISBN13: 978-0-8142-0401-6. Dewey:820/.9/008. LCCN:84-020677.

Audience: **l,u,f.**

Rauch, Alan   PR878.K54R38 2001
Useful Knowledge: The Victorians, Morality and the March of Intellect. Trade Paper. Duke University Press. Durham, NC. 2001. 304p. ISBN:0-8223-2668-X, ISBN13: 978-0-8223-2668-7. Dewey:823/.809. LCCN:00-010752.

Audience: **u,f.** *Choice, 2002.*

Secord, James A.   QH363.S4 2000
Victorian Sensation: The Extraordinary Publication, Reception, and Secret Authorship of Vestiges of the Natural History of Creation. Trade Cloth. University of Chicago Press. Chicago, IL. 2001. 624p. ISBN:0-226-74410-8, ISBN13: 978-0-226-74410-0. Dewey:576.8/0941/09034. LCCN:00-009124.

Audience: **g,l,u,f.** *Choice, 2001.*

Stocking, George W.   GN308.3.G7
Victorian Anthropology. Trade Paper. Simon & Schuster. New York, NY. 1991. 448p. ISBN:0-02-931551-4, ISBN13: 978-0-02-931551-4. Dewey:301.0941. LCCN:86-018370.

Audience: **l,u,f.**

Taylor, Miles & Wolff,   DA550
  Michael (Editors)
The Victorians since 1901: Histories, Representations and Revisions. Cloth over Boards. Manchester University Press. Manchester, 2004. 320p. ISBN:0-7190-6724-3, ISBN13: 978-0-7190-6724-2. Dewey:941.081. LCCN:2004-303594.

Audience: **g,u,f.**

Turner, Frank M.   DA533 .T87
The Greek Heritage in Victorian Britain. Trade Paper. Yale University Press. Cumberland, RI. 1984. 466p. ISBN:0-300-03257-9, ISBN13: 978-0-300-03257-4. Dewey:941.08. LCCN:80-024013.

Audience: **u,f.**

Wiener, Martin Joel   DA533.W59 2004
English Culture and the Decline of the Industrial Spirit, 1850-1980. Ed. 2. Cloth Text. Cambridge University Press. New York, NY. 2004. 236p. ISBN:0-521-84376-6, ISBN13: 978-0-521-84376-8. Dewey:942.08. LCCN:2004-052117.

Audience: **g,l,u,f.**

Willey, Basil   B1561 .W5 1980
More 19th-Century Studies: A Group of Honest Doubters. Trade Paper. Cambridge University Press. New York, NY. 1980. 304p. ISBN:0-521-28067-2, ISBN13: 978-0-521-28067-9. Dewey:210. LCCN:80-040635.

Audience: **u,f.**

Willey, Basil   B1561 .W52 1980
Nineteenth-Century Studies, Coleridge to Matthew Arnold. Trade Paper. Cambridge University Press. New York, NY. 1980. 296p. ISBN:0-521-28066-4, ISBN13: 978-0-521-28066-2. Dewey:192. LCCN:80-040634.

Audience: **g,l,u,f.**

Winter, Alison   BF1125.W56 1998
Mesmerized: Powers of Mind in Victorian Britain. Trade Cloth. University of Chicago Press. Chicago, IL. 1998. 480p. ISBN:0-226-90219-6, ISBN13: 978-0-226-90219-7. Dewey:154.7/0941/09034. LCCN:98-021833.

Audience: **g,l,u,f.** *Choice, 1999.*

Young, George M.   DA550 .Y6 1977
Portrait of an Age: Victorian England. George K. Clark (Annotations by). Trade Cloth. Oxford University Press, Inc. New York, NY. 1977. 423p. ISBN:0-19-212961-9, ISBN13: 978-0-19-212961-1. Dewey:941.081. LCCN:78-306764.

Audience: **g,l,u,f.**

Language

Chapman, Raymond   PR878.S64 C43 1994
Forms of Speech in Victorian Fiction: Studies in 18th and 19th Century Literature. Ed. 1. Trade Cloth. Longman Publishing Group. White Plains, NY. 1994. 280p. ISBN:0-582-08746-5, ISBN13: 978-0-582-08746-0. Dewey:823.80926. LCCN:93-005699.

Audience: **g,l,u,f.**

Epstein, James A.   DA530.E67 1994
Radical Expression: Political Language, Ritual, and Symbol in England, 1790-1850. Trade Cloth. Oxford University Press, Inc. New York, NY. 1994. 244p. ISBN:0-19-506550-6, ISBN13: 978-0-19-506550-3. Dewey:303.4840942. LCCN:93-020691.

Audience: **u,f.**

Mugglestone, Lynda   PE1074.7.M84 2002
Talking Proper: The Rise of Accent As Social Symbol. Ed. 2. Trade Cloth. Oxford University Press, Inc. New York, NY. 2003. 368p. ISBN:0-19-925061-8, ISBN13: 978-0-19-925061-5. Dewey:306.44/0941. LCCN:2002-032652.

Audience: **u,f.**

Phillipps, K. C.   PE1085.P45 1984
Language and Class in Victorian England. David Crystal (Editor). Trade Cloth. Blackwell Publishing, Inc. Malden, MA. 1984. 224p. The Language Library ISBN:0-631-13689-4, ISBN13: 978-0-631-13689-7. Dewey:428. LCCN:84-016717.

Audience: **g,l,u,f.** *Choice, 1985.*

Literature

Altick, Richard D.   **PR408.A68A48 1985**
Paintings from Books: Art and Literature in Britain, 1760-1900.
Cloth Text. Ohio State University Press. Columbus, OH. 1986.
527p. ISBN:0-8142-0380-9, ISBN13: 978-0-8142-0380-4.
Dewey:700/.941. LCCN:85-021737.
Audience: **g,l,u,f.** *Choice, 1986.*

Bodenheimer,   **PR878.D65**
  Rosemarie
The Politics of Story in Victorian Social Fiction. Trade Paper.
Cornell University Press. Ithaca, NY. 1991. 264p.
ISBN:0-8014-9920-8, ISBN13: 978-0-8014-9920-3.
Dewey:823.8/09355. LCCN:87-017313.
Audience: **u,f.** *Choice, 1988.*

Brantlinger, Patrick   **PR0469.P6B65**
The Spirit of Reform: British Literature and Politics, 1832-1867.
Trade Paper. Books on Demand. Ann Arbor, MI. 1977. 303p.
ISBN:0-7837-4450-1, ISBN13: 978-0-7837-4450-6.
Dewey:820/.9/3. LCCN:76-030537.
Audience: **u,f.** *B*

Buckley, Jerome H.   **PR0731.B8**
The Triumph of Time: A Study of the Victorian Concepts of
Time, History, Progress, and Decadence. Trade Paper. Books on
Demand. Ann Arbor, MI. 198p. ISBN:0-7837-4452-8, ISBN13:
978-0-7837-4452-0. Dewey:820.9008. LCCN:66-021333.
Audience: **g,l,u,f.**

Buckley, Jerome H.   **PR461**
The Victorian Temper: A Study in Literary Culture. Trade Paper.
Cambridge University Press. New York, NY. 1981. 304p.
ISBN:0-521-28448-1, ISBN13: 978-0-521-28448-6.
Dewey:820.9/008. LCCN:81-006142.
Audience: **u,f.**

Chandler, Alice   **PR457 .C35**
A Dream of Order: The Medieval Ideal in Nineteenth-Century
English Literature. Trade Cloth. University of Nebraska Press.
Lincoln, NE. 1970. xii, 278p. ISBN:0-8032-0704-2, ISBN13:
978-0-8032-0704-2. Dewey:820/.9/007. LCCN:69-010413.
Audience: **u,f.**

Clayton, Jay   **PR451.C58 2003**
Charles Dickens in Cyberspace: The Afterlife of the Nineteenth
Century in Postmodern Culture. Trade Cloth. Oxford University
Press, Inc. New York, NY. 2003. 280p. ISBN:0-19-516051-7,
ISBN13: 978-0-19-516051-2. Dewey:823/.8.
LCCN:2002-011755.
Audience: **u,f.** *Choice, 2004.*

Davis, Philip   **PR85.O96 2002**
The Oxford English Literary History: 1830-1880: the Victorians.
Trade Cloth. Oxford University Press, Inc. New York, NY. 2002.
648p. Oxford English Literary History Ser.
ISBN:0-19-818447 6, ISBN13: 978-0-19-818447-8.
Dewey:820.9. LCCN:2002-025038.
Audience: **u,f.** *Choice, 2003.*

Gilbert, Sandra M. &   **PR115.G5 2000**
  Gubar, Susan
The Madwoman in the Attic: The Woman Writer and the
Nineteenth-Century Literary Imagination. Ed. 2. Trade Paper.
Yale University Press. Cumberland, RI. 2000. 768p.
ISBN:0-300-08458-7, ISBN13: 978-0-300-08458-0.
Dewey:820.9/9287/09034. LCCN:99-086038.
Audience: **g,l,u,f.**

Goodlad, Lauren M. E.   **PR468.P57G66 2003**
Victorian Literature and the Victorian State: Character and
Governance in a Liberal Society. Trade Cloth. Johns Hopkins
University Press. Baltimore, MD. 2004. 320p.
ISBN:0-8018-6963-3, ISBN13: 978-0-8018-6963-1.
Dewey:820.9/358. LCCN:2002-154081.
Audience: **u,f.** *Choice, 2004.*

Henkle, Roger B.   **PR468.C65**
Comedy and Culture: England, 1820-1900. Trade Cloth.
Princeton University Press. Princeton, NJ. 1980. 384p.
ISBN:0-691-06428-8, ISBN13: 978-0-691-06428-4.
Dewey:820/.9/17. LCCN:79-003214.
Audience: **u,f.** *B*

Holloway, John   **PR463 .H6**
Victorian Sage: Studies in Argument. Trade Cloth. Shoe String
Press, Inc. North Haven, CT. 1962. ISBN:0-208-00593-5,
ISBN13: 978-0-208-00593-9. Dewey:820.4.
Audience: **u,f.** *B*

Houghton, Walter E.   **AI3.W45 1999**
  (Editor)
Wellesley Index to Victorian Periodicals 1824-1900. Compact
Disc. Routledge. New York, NY. 1999. ISBN:0-415-19345-1,
ISBN13: 978-0-415-19345-0. Dewey:052.
Audience: **g,l,u,f.** *Choice, 1999.*

Jordan, John O. &   **Z325 .L58 1995**
  Patten, Robert L. (Editors)
Literature in the Marketplace: Nineteenth-Century British
Publishing and Reading Practices. Colin Beer & Gillian Beer
(Contribution by). Trade Paper. Cambridge University Press.
New York, NY. 2003. 352p. Cambridge Studies in
Nineteenth-Century Literature and Culture Ser.
ISBN:0-521-89393-3, ISBN13: 978-0-521-89393-0.
Dewey:070./49/0941.
Audience: **g,l,u,f.**

Landow, George
☐ The Victorian Web.
http://www.victorianweb.org/
Audience: **g,l,u,f.**

Landow, George P.   **NX544.A1**
Victorian Types, Victorian Shadows: Biblical Typology in
Victorian Literature, Art and Thought. Trade Cloth. Routledge.
New York, NY. 1980. 256p. ISBN:0-7100-0598-9, ISBN13:
978-0-7100-0598-4. Dewey:700/.942. LCCN:80-040970.
Audience: **g,l,u,f.**

Marchand, Leslie A.   **PN5130.A7**
Athenaeum. Library Binding. Hippocrene Books, Inc. New
York, NY. 1970. ISBN:0-374-95280-9, ISBN13:
978-0-374-95280-8. Dewey:52. LCCN:77-120646.
Audience: **g,l,u,f.**

Pite, Raloh (Editor), et   **DA30**
  al.
Lives of Victorian Literary Figures V: Mary Elilzabeth Braddon,
Wilkie Collins, William Thackeray by Their Contemporaries.
Ed. 3. Judith Fisher, William Baker & Andrew Maunder
(Editors). Trade Cloth. Pickering & Chatto Publishers, Ltd.
London, 2007. 1200p. ISBN:1-85196-819-9, ISBN13:
978-1-85196-819-0. Dewey:941.
Audience: **l,u,f.**

Pite, Ralph (Editor)   **PR451**
Lives of Victorian Literary Figures II: The Brownings, the
Brontes and the Rossettis by Their Contemporaries, Set. Trade
Cloth. Pickering & Chatto Publishers, Ltd. London, 2004.
1432p. ISBN:1-85196-775-3, ISBN13: 978-1-85196-775-9.
Dewey:820.9/008 B. LCCN:2003-022554.
                 Audience: **l,u,f.**

Pite, Ralph (Editor), et al.   **PR462.L585 2005**
Lives of Victorian Literary Figures III: The Carlyles, John
Ruskin and Elizabeth Gaskell by their Contemporaries. Aileen
Christianson, Simon Grimble & Sheila A. McIntosh (Editors).
Trade Cloth. Pickering & Chatto Publishers, Ltd. London, 2005.
1200p. ISBN:1-85196-780-X, ISBN13: 978-1-85196-780-3.
Dewey:820.9/008 B. LCCN:2004-025260.
                 Audience: **l,u,f.**

Pite, Ralph & Mullan, John (Editors)   **PR462.L58 2003**
Lives of Victorian Literary Figures I: George Eliot, Charles
Dickens and Alfred, Lord Tennyson by Their Contemporaries,
Set. Trade Cloth. Pickering & Chatto Publishers, Ltd. London,
2003. 1584p. Lives of Victorian Literary Figures Ser.
ISBN:1-85196-759-1, ISBN13: 978-1-85196-759-9.
Dewey:820.9/008 B. LCCN:2002-030354.
                 Audience: **u,f.**

Pite, Ralph (Editor), et al.   **PS2110.L584 2005**
Lives of Victorian Literary Figures IV: Henry James, Edith
Wharton and Oscar Wilde by Their Contemporaries. John
Mullan & Janet Beer (Editors). Trade Cloth. Pickering & Chatto
Publishers, Ltd. London, 2005. 1200p. ISBN:1-85196-814-8,
ISBN13: 978-1-85196-814-5. Dewey:820.9008.
                 Audience: **l,u,f.**

Reed, John R.   **PR468.S6.R4**
Victorian Conventions. Trade Cloth. Ohio University Press.
Athens, OH. 1975. 574p. ISBN:0-8214-0147-5, ISBN13:
978-0-8214-0147-7. Dewey:820/.9/008. LCCN:73-092908.
                 Audience: **u,f.** ℬ

Shattock, Joanne (Editor)   **Z2011 .N45 1999 PR83**
The Cambridge Bibliography of English Literature: 1800-1900.
Ed. 3. Cloth Text. Cambridge University Press. New York, NY.
2000. 1536p. Cambridge Bibliography of English Literature Ser.,
Vol. 4 ISBN:0-521-39100-8, ISBN13: 978-0-521-39100-9.
Dewey:016.82. LCCN:99-055526.
         Audience: **l,u,f.** *Choice, 2000.*

Shattock, Joanne & Wolff, Michael (Editors)   **PN5124.P4 V49 1982**
The Victorian Periodical Press: Samplings and Soundings. Trade
Cloth. University of Toronto Press. Toronto, ON. 1982. 420p.
ISBN:0-8020-2463-7, ISBN13: 978-0-8020-2463-3.
Dewey:052/.09/034. LCCN:82-184551.
                 Audience: **l,u,f.** ℬ

Stein, Richard L.   **PR461.S78 1987**
Victoria's Year: English Literature and Culture, 1837-1838.
Trade Cloth. Oxford University Press, Inc. New York, NY. 1988.
326p. ISBN:0-19-504922-5, ISBN13: 978-0-19-504922-0.
Dewey:820/.9/008. LCCN:87-017347.
         Audience: **g,l,u,f.** *Choice, 1988.*

Sullivan, Alvin (Editor)   **PN5124**
British Literary Magazines: The Romantic Age, 1789-1836.
Cloth Text. Greenwood Publishing Group, Inc. Portsmouth, NH.

1983. 491p. Historical Guides to the World's Periodicals and
Newspapers ISBN:0-313-22872-8, ISBN13: 978-0-313-22872-8.
Dewey:820/.8. LCCN:82-021136.
             Audience: **g,l,u,f.**

Sullivan, Alvin (Editor)   **PN5124**
British Literary Magazines: The Victorian and Edwardian Age,
1837-1913. Cloth Text. Greenwood Publishing Group, Inc.
Portsmouth, NH. 1984. 560p. Historical Guides to the World's
Periodicals and Newspapers ISBN:0-313-24335-2, ISBN13:
978-0-313-24335-6. Dewey:805. LCCN:82-021136.
             Audience: **g,l,u,f.**

Sutherland, John   **PR871**
The Stanford Companion to Victorian Fiction. Trade Paper.
Stanford University Press. Palo Alto, CA. 1989. 700p.
ISBN:0-8047-1842-3, ISBN13: 978-0-8047-1842-4.
Dewey:823/.809/03. LCCN:88-061462.
       Audience: **g,l,u,f.** *Choice, 1989.*

Thrall, Miriam M.   **PN5130.F7 T5 1934A**
Rebellious Fraser's: Nol Yorke's Magazine in the Days of
Maginn, Thackeray and Carlyle. Trade Cloth. A M S Press, Inc.
New York, NY. ISBN:0-404-06458-2, ISBN13:
978-0-404-06458-7. Dewey:52. LCCN:35-001070.
             Audience: **g,l,u,f.**

Turner, Frank M.   **DA533 .T87**
The Greek Heritage in Victorian Britain. Trade Paper. Yale
University Press. Cumberland, RI. 1984. 466p.
ISBN:0-300-03257-9, ISBN13: 978-0-300-03257-4.
Dewey:941.08. LCCN:80-024013.
                 Audience: **u,f.**

Vann, J. Don & Van Ardsel, Rosemary   **PN5124.P4**
Victorian Periodicals and Victorian Society. Trade Cloth.
Ashgate Publishing Company. Williston, VT. 1994. xii, 370p.
ISBN:0-85967-944-6, ISBN13: 978-0-85967-944-2.
Dewey:052/.09034.
         Audience: **g,l,u,f.** *Choice, 1994.*

Weiner, Joel H. (Editor)   **PN5124**
Innovators and Preachers: The Role of the Editor in Victorian
England. Trade Cloth. Greenwood Publishing Group, Inc.
Portsmouth, NH. 1985. 335p. Contributions to the Study of
Mass Media and Communications Ser., No. 5
ISBN:0-313-24164-3, ISBN13: 978-0-313-24164-2.
Dewey:070.4/1/0941. LCCN:85-017658.
         Audience: **u,f.** *Choice, 1986.*

Wheeler, Michael   **PR468.D42W4 1990**
Death and the Future Life in Victorian Literature and Theology.
Trade Cloth. Cambridge University Press. New York, NY. 1990.
472p. ISBN:0-521-30617-5, ISBN13: 978-0-521-30617-1.
Dewey:820.9/354/09034. LCCN:89-077366.
         Audience: **g,l,u,f.** *Choice, 1991.*

Willey, Basil   **B1561 .W5 1980**
More 19th-Century Studies: A Group of Honest Doubters. Trade
Paper. Cambridge University Press. New York, NY. 1980. 304p.
ISBN:0-521-28067-2, ISBN13: 978-0-521-28067-9. Dewey:210.
LCCN:80-040635.
                 Audience: **u,f.**

Willey, Basil   **B1561 .W52 1980**
Nineteenth-Century Studies, Coleridge to Matthew Arnold.
Trade Paper. Cambridge University Press. New York, NY. 1980.

296p. ISBN:0-521-28066-4, ISBN13: 978-0-521-28066-2.
Dewey:192. LCCN:80-040634.

Audience: **g,l,u,f.**

Literature > Drama

Altick, Richard D.   **DA688**
The Shows of London. Trade Cloth. Harvard University Press.
Cambridge, MA. 1978. 568p. ISBN:0-674-80731-6, ISBN13:
978-0-674-80731-0. Dewey:790.2/09421. LCCN:77-002755.

Audience: **g,l,u,f.** *B*

Booth, Michael Richard   **PN2594 .B58 1991**
Theatre in the Victorian Age. Trade Paper. Cambridge
University Press. New York, NY. 1991. 238p.
ISBN:0-521-34837-4, ISBN13: 978-0-521-34837-9.
Dewey:792/.0941/09034. LCCN:90-021003.

Audience: **g,l,u,f.** *Choice, 1992.*

Davis, Tracy C.   **PN2599.5.E25 D38 20**
The Economics of the British Stage, 1800-1914. Trade Cloth.
Cambridge University Press. New York, NY. 2000. 524p.
ISBN:0-521-57115-4, ISBN13: 978-0-521-57115-9.
Dewey:338.4/7792/0941. LCCN:00-020381.

Audience: **g,l,u,f.** *Choice, 2001.*

Gagnier, Regenia   **PR5824.G34 1986**
Idylls of the Marketplace: Oscar Wilde and the Victorian Public.
Stanford University Press. 1986. ISBN:0-8047-1334-0, ISBN13:
978-0-8047-1334-4.

Audience: **u,f.**

Hadley, Elaine   **PR728.M4H33 1995**
Melodramatic Tactics: Theatricalized Dissent in the English
Marketplace, 1800-1885. Trade Cloth. Stanford University Press.
Palo Alto, CA. 1995. 318p. ISBN:0-8047-2403-2, ISBN13:
978-0-8047-2403-6. Dewey:822/.0527/0907. LCCN:94-042454.

Audience: **u,f.** *Choice, 1996.*

Slater, Michael   **PR4825.J4**
Douglas Jerrold: A Life (1803-1857). Trade Cloth. Gerald
Duckworth & Company, Ltd. London, 2002. 272p.
ISBN:0-7156-2824-0, ISBN13: 978-0-7156-2824-9.
Dewey:822/.8 B. LCCN:2002-483685.

Audience: **g,l,u,f.** *Choice, 2003.*

Literature > Prose

Broomfield, Andrea &   **PR1286.W6P76 1996**
Mitchell, Sally
Prose by Victorian Women: An Anthology. Cloth Text. Garland
Publishing, Inc. New York, NY. 1995. 752p. Garland Reference
Library of the Humanities, Vol. 1893: ISBN:0-8153-1970-3,
ISBN13: 978-0-8153-1970-2. Dewey:828/.8080809287.
LCCN:95-024400.

Audience: **g,l,u,f.** *Choice, 1996.*

Dickens, Charles &   **PR4572.A83S58 1996**
Slater, Michael
The Amusements of the People and Other Papers: Reports,
Essays and Reviews, 1834-1851. Trade Cloth. Ohio State
University Press. Columbus, OH. 1996. 408p.
ISBN:0-8142-0724-3, ISBN13: 978-0-8142-0724-6.
Dewey:824/.8. LCCN:96-024142.

Audience: **g,u,f.** *Choice, 1997.*

James, Louis   **PR878.L3 J3 1974**
Fiction for the Working Man. Trade Paper. Penguin Group
(USA) Inc. New York, NY. 1974. xviii, 261p.
ISBN:0-14-060037-X, ISBN13: 978-0-14-060037-7.
Dewey:823/.8/09. LCCN:75-323006.

Audience: **g,l,u,f.**

Jann, Rosemary   **DA3.A1J36 1985**
The Art and Science of Victorian History. Cloth Text. Ohio State
University Press. Columbus, OH. 1985. 272p.
ISBN:0-8142-0390-6, ISBN13: 978-0-8142-0390-3.
Dewey:907/.2041. LCCN:85-013651.

Audience: **u,f.** *Choice, 1986.*

Levine, George &   **PR783.L4**
Madden, William
Art of Victorian Prose. Trade Cloth. Oxford University Press,
Inc. New York, NY. 1968. ISBN:0-19-500953-3, ISBN13:
978-0-19-500953-8. Dewey:828/.8/08.

Audience: **u,f.**

Levine, P. J. A.   **D13.5.G7L48 2002**
The Amateur and the Professional: Antiquarians, Historians and
Archaeologists in Victorian England 1838-1886. Trade Paper.
Cambridge University Press. New York, NY. 2003. 220p.
ISBN:0-521-53050-4, ISBN13: 978-0-521-53050-7.
Dewey:907.2094109034.

Audience: **u,f.**

Lohrli, Anne   **PN5130.H6L6**
Household Words: A Weekly Journal 1850-1859, Conducted by
Charles Dickens. Table of Contents, List of Contributors and
Their Contributions Based on the Household Words Office Book
in the Morris L. Parrish Collection of Victorian Novelists,
Princeton Uni. Trade Paper. Books on Demand. Ann Arbor, MI.
550p. ISBN:0-598-10228-0, ISBN13: 978-0-598-10228-7.
Dewey:052;. LCCN:71-185722.

Audience: **g,l,u,f.**

Milligan, Barry   **PR468.O6M55 1995**
Pleasures and Pains: Opium and the Orient in
Nineteenth-Century British Culture. Cloth Text. University Press
of Virginia. Charlottesville, VA. 1995. 192p. Victorian Literature
and Culture Ser. ISBN:0-8139-1571-6, ISBN13:
978-0-8139-1571-5. Dewey:820.9/9208. LCCN:94-024140.

Audience: **l,u,f.** *Choice, 1995.*

Onslow, Barbara   **PN5124.W58O59 2000**
Women of the Press in Nineteenth-Century Britain. Cloth over
Boards. Palgrave Macmillan. New York, NY. 2001. 311p.
ISBN:0-312-23602-6, ISBN13: 978-0-312-23602-1.
Dewey:070.9/22. LCCN:00-033333.

Audience: **g,l,u,f.** *Choice, 2001.*

Peterson, Linda H.   **PR788.W65P47 1999**
Traditions of Victorian Women's Autobiography: The Poetics
and Politics of Life Writing. Trade Cloth. University Press of
Virginia. Charlottesville, VA. 1999. 272p. Victorian Literature
and Culture Ser. ISBN:0-8139-1883-9, ISBN13:
978-0-8139-1883-9. Dewey:828/.80809492072.
LCCN:99-019832.

Audience: **g,l,u,f.** *Choice, 2000.*

Picker, John M.   **PR468.S68P53 2003**
Victorian Soundscapes. Trade Paper. Oxford University Press,
Inc. New York, NY. 2003. 232p. ISBN:0-19-515191-7, ISBN13:
978-0-19-515191-6. Dewey:820.9/356. LCCN:2002-035906.

Audience: **u,f.** *Choice, 2004.*

Ruskin, John   PR5252.R64 1997
The Genius of John Ruskin: Selections from His Writings. John
D. Rosenberg (Editor), Herbert F. Tucker (Foreword by). Trade
Paper. University Press of Virginia. Charlottesville, VA. 1998.
576p. Victorian Literature and Culture Ser. ISBN:0-8139-1789-1,
ISBN13: 978-0-8139-1789-4. Dewey:828/.809.
LCCN:97-031013.
Audience: **g,l,u,f.** *B*

Slater, Michael   PR4825.J4
Douglas Jerrold: A Life (1803-1857). Trade Cloth. Gerald
Duckworth & Company, Ltd. London, 2002. 272p.
ISBN:0-7156-2824-0, ISBN13: 978-0-7156-2824-9.
Dewey:822/.8 B. LCCN:2002-483685.
Audience: **g,l,u,f.** *Choice, 2003.*

Literature > Verse

Armstrong, Isobel   PR595.H5 A76 1993
Victorian Poetry: Poetry, Poetics, Politics. Paper over Boards.
Routledge. New York, NY. 1993. 560p. Critical History of
Victorian Poetry Ser. ISBN:0-415-03016-1, ISBN13:
978-0-415-03016-8. Dewey:821.809. LCCN:92-002451.
Audience: **u,f.**

Bristow, Joseph (Editor)   PR591 .C36 2000
The Cambridge Companion to Victorian Poetry. Cloth Text.
Cambridge University Press. New York, NY. 2000. 353p.
Companions to Literature Ser. ISBN:0-521-64115-2, ISBN13:
978-0-521-64115-9. Dewey:821/.809. LCCN:00-020013.
Audience: **l,u,f.** *Choice, 2001.*

Elfenbein, Andrew   PR468.R65 E44 1995
Byron and the Victorians. Gillian Beer (Contribution by). Trade
Cloth. Cambridge University Press. New York, NY. 1995. 297p.
Studies in Nineteenth-Century Literature and Culture, No. 4
ISBN:0-521-45452-2, ISBN13: 978-0-521-45452-0.
Dewey:820.9/008. LCCN:94-020629.
Audience: **u,f.** *Choice, 1995.*

Gill, Stephen   PR5887.3.G55 1998
Wordsworth and the Victorians. Cloth Text. Oxford University
Press, Inc. New York, NY. 1998. 366p. ISBN:0-19-811965-8,
ISBN13: 978-0-19-811965-4. Dewey:821.7. LCCN:97-040689.
Audience: **g,l,u,f.** *Choice, 1998.*

Johnson, Edward D.   PR593 .J6
Alien Vision of Victorian Poetry: Sources of the Poetic
Imagination in Tennyson, Browning and Arnold. Trade Cloth.
Shoe String Press, Inc. North Haven, CT. 1963.
ISBN:0-208-00090-9, ISBN13: 978-0-208-00090-3.
Dewey:821.809.
Audience: **u,f.**

McGann, Jerome
☐ The Rossetti Archive.
http://www.rossettiarchive.org/
Audience: **g,l,u,f.**

Literature > The Novel

Altick, Richard D.   PR878.R4A48 1991
The Presence of the Present: Topics of the Day in the Victorian
Novel. Cloth Text. Ohio State University Press. Columbus, OH.
1991. 854p. Studies in Victorian Life and Literature

ISBN:0-8142-0518-6, ISBN13: 978-0-8142-0518-1.
Dewey:823/.80912. LCCN:90-034806.
Audience: **l,u,f.** *Choice, 1991.*

Ardis, Ann   PR878.F45A74 1990
New Women, New Novels: Feminism and Early Modernism.
Cloth Text. Rutgers University Press. Piscataway, NJ. 1990.
225p. ISBN:0-8135-1581-5, ISBN13: 978-0-8135-1581-6.
Dewey:823/.809352042. LCCN:90-035039.
Audience: **u,f.** *Choice, 1991.*

Armstrong, Nancy   PR821
Desire and Domestic Fiction: A Political History of the Novel.
Trade Paper. Oxford University Press, Inc. New York, NY. 1990.
310p. ISBN:0-19-506160-8, ISBN13: 978-0-19-506160-4.
Dewey:823/.009. LCCN:86-016482.
Audience: **u,f.** *Choice, 1987.*

Baker, William &   PR871
   Womack, Kenneth (Editors)
A Companion to the Victorian Novel. Cloth Text. Greenwood
Publishing Group, Inc. Portsmouth, NH. 2002. 464p. Literary
Companions Ser. ISBN:0-313-31407-1, ISBN13:
978-0-313-31407-0. Dewey:823/.809. LCCN:2001-042326.
Audience: **l,u.** *Choice, 2002.*

Bodenheimer,   PR878.D65
   Rosemarie
The Politics of Story in Victorian Social Fiction. Trade Paper.
Cornell University Press. Ithaca, NY. 1991. 264p.
ISBN:0-8014-9920-8, ISBN13: 978-0-8014-9920-3.
Dewey:823.8/09355. LCCN:87-017313.
Audience: **u,f.** *Choice, 1988.*

Brantlinger, Patrick   PR868.P68B73 1998
The Reading Lesson: The Threat of Mass Literacy in
Nineteenth-Century British Fiction. Trade Cloth. Indiana
University Press. Bloomington, IN. 1998. 320p.
ISBN:0-253-33454-3, ISBN13: 978-0-253-33454-1.
Dewey:823/.809. LCCN:98-019906.
Audience: **u,f.** *Choice, 1999.*

Chapman, Raymond   PR878.S64 C43 1994
Forms of Speech in Victorian Fiction: Studies in 18th and 19th
Century Literature. Ed. 1. Trade Cloth. Longman Publishing
Group. White Plains, NY. 1994. 280p. ISBN:0-582-08746-5,
ISBN13: 978-0-582-08746-0. Dewey:823.80926.
LCCN:93-005699.
Audience: **g,l,u,f.**

Clarke, Micael M.   PR5642.W6C58 1995
Thackeray and Women. Library Binding. Northern Illinois
University Press. DeKalb, IL. 1995. 250p. ISBN:0-87580-197-8,
ISBN13: 978-0-87580-197-1. Dewey:823/.8. LCCN:94-036979.
Audience: **u,f.** *Choice, 1996.*

Cvetkovich, Ann   PR878.F45 C85 1992
Mixed Feelings: Feminism, Mass Culture and Victorian
Sensationalism. Paper Text. Rutgers University Press.
Piscataway, NJ. 1992. x, 227p. ISBN:0-8135-1857-1, ISBN13:
978-0-8135-1857-2. Dewey:823/.809352042. LCCN:92-004457.
Audience: **u,f.**

David, Deirdre (Editor)   PR871 .C17 2001
The Cambridge Companion to the Victorian Novel. Cloth Text.
Cambridge University Press. New York, NY. 2000. 288p.
Companions to Literature Ser. ISBN:0-521-64150-0, ISBN13:
978-0-521-64150-0. Dewey:823/.809. LCCN:00-028928.
Audience: **g,l,u,f.** *Choice, 2001.*

Dickens, Charles &   **PR4572.A83S58 1996**
Slater, Michael
The Amusements of the People and Other Papers: Reports,
Essays and Reviews, 1834-1851. Trade Cloth. Ohio State
University Press. Columbus, OH. 1996. 408p.
ISBN:0-8142-0724-3, ISBN13: 978-0-8142-0724-6.
Dewey:824/.8. LCCN:96-024142.
                          Audience: **g,u,f.** *Choice, 1997.*

Feltes, N. N.   **PR878.C25.F44 1993**
Literary Capital and the Late Victorian Novel. Trade Cloth.
University of Wisconsin Press. Chicago, IL. 1993. 185p.
ISBN:0-299-13660-4, ISBN13: 978-0-299-13660-4.
Dewey:823.809. LCCN:92-035455.
                          Audience: **u,f.** *Choice, 1993.*

Feltes, N. N.   **BV2370.B8**
Modes of Production of Victorian Novels. Trade Paper.
University of Chicago Press. Chicago, IL. 1989. 140p.
ISBN:0-226-24118-1, ISBN13: 978-0-226-24118-0.
Dewey:070.5/0941/09034. LCCN:86-006927.
                          Audience: **u,f.**

Gallagher, Catherine   **PR878.D65**
The Industrial Reformation of English Fiction: Social Discourse
and Narrative Form, 1832-1867. Paper Text. University of
Chicago Press. Chicago, IL. 1996. xvi, 320p.
ISBN:0-226-27933-2, ISBN13: 978-0-226-27933-6.
Dewey:823/.8/09355. LCCN:84-016272.
                          Audience: **u,f.** *Choice, 1986.*

Gettmann, R. A.   **Z325.B45 G4**
Victorian Publisher. Trade Cloth. Cambridge University Press.
New York, NY. 1960. ISBN:0-521-05072-3, ISBN13:
978-0-521-05072-2. Dewey:655.4421.
                          Audience: **g,l,u,f.**

Gilmour, Robin   **PR788.U/**
The Idea of the Gentleman in the Victorian Novel. Trade Paper.
Routledge. New York, NY. 1981. 208p. ISBN:0-04-800005-1,
ISBN13: 978-0-04-800005-7. Dewey:823/.8/093520621.
LCCN:81-010869.
                          Audience: **l,u,f.** *B*

Harvie, Christopher T.   **PR830.P6H37 1991**
Centre of Things: Political Fiction in Britain from Disraeli to
the Present. Paper over Boards. Routledge. New York, NY.
1992. 256p. ISBN:0-04-445593-3, ISBN13: 978-0-04-445593-6.
Dewey:823.009/358. LCCN:90-046071.
                          Audience: **g,l,u,f.** *Choice, 1993.*

Herbert, Christopher   **GN357.H47 1991**
Culture and Anomie: Ethnographic Imagination in the
Nineteenth Century. Trade Cloth. University of Chicago Press.
Chicago, IL. 1991. 374p. ISBN:0-226-32738-8, ISBN13:
978-0-226-32738-9. Dewey:306. LCCN:91-004366.
                          Audience: **u,f.** *Choice, 1992.*

Hughes, Linda K. &   **PR468.P37H84 1991**
Lund, Michael
The Victorian Serial. Cloth Text. University Press of Virginia.
Charlottesville, VA. 1991. 448p. Victorian Literature and Culture
Ser. ISBN:0-8139-1314-4, ISBN13: 978-0-8139-1314-8.
Dewey:820.9/008. LCCN:90-020878.
                          Audience: **u,f.** *Choice, 1993.*

James, Louis   **PR878.L3 J3 1974**
Fiction for the Working Man. Trade Paper. Penguin Group
(USA) Inc. New York, NY. 1974. xviii, 261p.

ISBN:0-14-060037-X, ISBN13: 978-0-14-060037-7.
Dewey:823/.8/09. LCCN:75-323006.
                          Audience: **g,l,u,f.**

Kane, Penny   **HQ614**
Victorian Families in Fact and Fiction. Trade Paper. Palgrave
Macmillan. New York, NY. 1997. 192p. ISBN:0-312-17221-4,
ISBN13: 978-0-312-17221-3. Dewey:306.8/5/0941.
                          Audience: **g,l,u,f.** *Choice, 1995.*

Langland, Elizabeth   **HT690.G7L35 1995**
Nobody's Angels: Middle-Class Women and Domestic Ideology
in Victorian Culture. Book, Other. Cornell University Press.
Ithaca, NY. 1995. 288p. Reading Women Writing Ser.
ISBN:0-8014-8220-8, ISBN13: 978-0-8014-8220-5.
Dewey:305.5/5/082. LCCN:94-024393.
                          Audience: **g,l,u,f.**

Law, Graham   **PR878.P78L39 2000**
Serializing Fiction in the Victorian Press. Cloth over Boards.
Palgrave Macmillan. New York, NY. 2001. 328p.
ISBN:0-312-23574-7, ISBN13: 978-0-312-23574-1.
Dewey:823.8/09. LCCN:00-031124.
                          Audience: **u,f.** *Choice, 2001.*

Lovell, Terry   **PR861**
Consuming Fiction. Cloth Text. Analytical Psychology Club of
San Francisco, Inc. San Francisco, CA. 1987. 188p. Questions
for Feminism Ser. ISBN:0-86091-173-X, ISBN13:
978-0-86091-173-9. Dewey:823/.009. LCCN:87-203939.
                          Audience: **u,f.** *Choice, 1988.*

Miller, D. A.   **PR861**
The Novel and the Police. Trade Paper. University of California
Press. Berkeley, CA. 1989. xv, 222p. ISBN:0-520-06746-0,
ISBN13: 978-0-520-06746-2. Dewey:823/.8/09355.
LCCN:87-025470.
                          Audience: **l,u,f.** *Choice, 1988.*

Nelson, Claudia   **PR830.C513N45 1991**
Boys Will Be Girls: The Feminine Ethic and British Children's
Fiction, 1857-1917. Cloth Text. Rutgers University Press.
Piscataway, NJ. 1991. 216p. ISBN:0-8135-1681-1, ISBN13:
978-0-8135-1681-3. Dewey:823/.8099287. LCCN:90-020004.
                          Audience: **u,f.**

Nunokawa, Jeff   **PR878.D65N86 2003**
The Afterlife of Property: Domestic Security and the Victorian
Novel. Trade Paper. Princeton University Press. Princeton, NJ.
2003. 160p. ISBN:0-691-11467-6, ISBN13: 978-0-691-11467-5.
Dewey:828.8.
                          Audience: **u,f.** *Choice, 1994.*

Pettit, Clare   **PR788**
Patent Inventions: Intellectual Property and the Victorian Novel.
Trade Cloth. Oxford University Press, Inc. New York, NY. 2004.
356p. ISBN:0-19-925320-X, ISBN13: 978-0-19-925320-3.
Dewey:823/.8093554. LCCN:2004-049211.
                          Audience: **u,f.**

Postlethwaite, Diana   **PR469.P45 P67**
Making It Whole: A Victorian Circle and the Shape of Their
World. Trade Paper. Ohio State University Press. Columbus,
OH. 1985. 282p. ISBN:0-8142-0401-5, ISBN13:
978-0-8142-0401-6. Dewey:820/.9/008. LCCN:84-020677.
                          Audience: **l,u,f.**

Formats: Web: ☐   Ebook: **e**   CD/DVD-ROM: ✵   BCL3: *B*

Said, Edward W.   **PN761.S28 1994**
Culture and Imperialism. Trade Paper. Knopf Publishing Group.
New York, NY. 1994. 416p. ISBN:0-679-75054-1, ISBN13:
978-0-679-75054-3. Dewey:809/.894. LCCN:93-043485.
Audience: **g,l,u,f.** *Choice, 1993.*

Showalter, Elaine   **PR115 .S5 1999**
A Literature of Their Own: British Women Novelists from
Brontë to Lessing. Trade Paper. Princeton University Press.
Princeton, NJ. 1998. 382p. ISBN:0-691-00476-5, ISBN13:
978-0-691-00476-1. Dewey:828/.8/099287. LCCN:98-089253.
Audience: **u,f.** *Choice, 1999.*

Small, Helen   **PR878.S44**
Love's Madness: Medicine, the Novel, and Female Insanity,
1800-1865. Trade Paper. Oxford University Press, Inc. New
York, NY. 1998. 274p. ISBN:0-19-818491-3, ISBN13:
978-0-19-818491-1. Dewey:823/.809353. LCCN:95-033313.
Audience: **u,f.** *Choice, 1996.*

Stewart, Garrett   **PR878.A79S74 1996**
Dear Reader: The Conscripted Audience in Nineteenth-Century
British Fiction. Trade Paper. Johns Hopkins University Press.
Baltimore, MD. 1996. 472p. ISBN:0-8018-5283-8, ISBN13:
978-0-8018-5283-1. Dewey:823/.809. LCCN:95-052372.
Audience: **u,f.** *Choice, 1997.*

Sussman, Herbert L.   **PR468.T4 S8**
Victorians and the Machine: Literary Response to Technology.
Trade Cloth. Harvard University Press. Cambridge, MA. 1968.
ISBN:0-674-93705-8, ISBN13: 978-0-674-93705-5.
Dewey:820.9. LCCN:68-014274.
Audience: **g,l,u.**

Sutherland, J. A.   **PR878.P78**
Victorian Novelists and Publishers. Trade Paper. University of
Chicago Press. Chicago, IL. 1996. 260p. ISBN:0-226-78062-7,
ISBN13: 978-0-226-78062-7. Dewey:823.09. LCCN:76-008216.
Audience: **g,l,u,f.**

Sutherland, John   **PR871**
The Stanford Companion to Victorian Fiction. Trade Paper.
Stanford University Press. Palo Alto, CA. 1989. 700p.
ISBN:0-8047-1842-3, ISBN13: 978-0-8047-1842-4.
Dewey:823/.809/03. LCCN:88-061462.
Audience: **g,l,u,f.** *Choice, 1989.*

Sutherland, John   **PR871**
Victorian Fiction: Writers, Publishers, Readers. Ed. 2. Trade
Paper. Palgrave Macmillan. New York, NY. 2005. 224p.
ISBN:1-4039-3985-3, ISBN13: 978-1-4039-3985-2.
Dewey:823/.809. LCCN:2005-049320.
Audience: **u,f.** *Choice, 1995.*

Terry, R. C.   **PR4168**
Victorian Popular Fiction, 1860-80. Cloth Text. Brill Academic
Publishers, Inc. Boston, MA. 1983. 208p. ISBN:0-391-02963-0,
ISBN13: 978-0-391-02963-7. Dewey:823/.8/09.
Audience: **g,l,u,f.**

Tillotson, Kathleen   **PR871**
Novels of the 1840s. Trade Paper. Oxford University Press, Inc.
New York, NY. 1983. 344p. ISBN:0-19-871109-3, ISBN13:
978-0-19-871109-4. Dewey:823/.8/09.
Audience: **g,l,u,f.**

Turner, Ernest S.   **PN1009.A1 T8 1974**
Boys Will Be Boys. Trade Cloth. Thomson Gale. Farmington
Hills, MI. 1977. ISBN:0-8103-4091-7, ISBN13:
978-0-8103-4091-6. Dewey:823/.03. LCCN:76-175338.
Audience: **g,l,u.**

Music

Ehrlich, Cyril   **ML285**
The Music Profession in Britain since the Eighteenth Century: A
Social History. Trade Paper. Oxford University Press, Inc. New
York, NY. 1989. 280p. ISBN:0-19-822743-4, ISBN13:
978-0-19-822743-4. Dewey:780/.941.
Audience: **u,f.** ℬ *Choice, 1986.*

Samson, Jim (Editor)   **ML196 .C36 2001**
The Cambridge History of Nineteenth-Century Music. Cloth
Text. Cambridge University Press. New York, NY. 2001. 788p.
History of Music Ser. ISBN:0-521-59017-5, ISBN13:
978-0-521-59017-4. Dewey:780.9034. LCCN:00-067469.
Audience: **g,l,u,f.** *Choice, 2002.*

Temperley, Nicholas   **ML285.4.L68 1989**
(Editor)
The Lost Chord: Essays on Victorian Music. Trade Cloth.
Indiana University Press. Bloomington, IN. 1989. 192p.
ISBN:0-253-33518-3, ISBN13: 978-0-253-33518-0.
Dewey:781.741. LCCN:88-045456.
Audience: **g,l,u,f.**

Politics

Blake, Robert   **DA554**
Disraeli. Ed. 2. Trade Paper. Prion. London, 1998. 850p. Lost
Treasures Ser. ISBN:1-85375-275-4, ISBN13:
978-1-85375-275-9. Dewey:941/.081/092.
Audience: **g,l,u,f.**

Brantlinger, Patrick   **PR0469.P6B65**
The Spirit of Reform: British Literature and Politics, 1832-1867.
Trade Paper. Books on Demand. Ann Arbor, MI. 1977. 303p.
ISBN:0-7837-4450-1, ISBN13: 978-0-7837-4450-6.
Dewey:820/.9/3. LCCN:76-030537.
Audience: **u,f.** ℬ

Briggs, Asa   **DA560**
Victorian People: A Reassessment of Persons and Themes,
1851-67. Ruari McLean (Illustrator). Trade Paper. University of
Chicago Press. Chicago, IL. 1975. 324p. Chicago Collectors
Editions Ser. ISBN:0-226-07488-9, ISBN13: 978-0-226-07488-7.
Dewey:942.081. LCCN:55-005118.
Audience: **g,l,u,f.** ℬ

Colley, Linda   **DA470**
Britons: Forging the Nation, 1707-1837. Ed. 2. Trade Paper.
Yale University Press. Cumberland, RI. 2005. 448p.
ISBN:0-300-10759-5, ISBN13: 978-0-300-10759-3.
Dewey:941/.07.
Audience: **g,l,u,f.** *Choice, 1993.*

Collini, Stefan   **DA550.C62 1993**
Public Moralists: Political Thought and Intellectual Life in
Britain, 1850-1930. Paper Text. Oxford University Press, Inc.
New York, NY. 1993. 388p. ISBN:0-19-820422-1, ISBN13:
978-0-19-820422-0. Dewey:941.08. LCCN:92-041294.
Audience: **g,l,u,f.** *Choice, 1992.*

Epstein, James A. DA530.E67 1994
Radical Expression: Political Language, Ritual, and Symbol in England, 1790-1850. Trade Cloth. Oxford University Press, Inc. New York, NY. 1994. 244p. ISBN:0-19-506550-6, ISBN13: 978-0-19-506550-3. Dewey:303.4840942. LCCN:93-020691.
Audience: **u,f.**

Finn, Margot C. HN400.R3 F56 1993
After Chartism: Class and Nation in English Radical Politics 1848-1874. Lyndal Roper (Contribution by). Trade Paper. Cambridge University Press. New York, NY. 2004. 375p. Past and Present Publications ISBN:0-521-52598-5, ISBN13: 978-0-521-52598-5. Dewey:322.2/0942/09034.
Audience: **u,f.**

Goodlad, Lauren M. E. PR468.P57G66 2003
Victorian Literature and the Victorian State: Character and Governance in a Liberal Society. Trade Cloth. Johns Hopkins University Press. Baltimore, MD. 2004. 320p. ISBN:0-8018-6963-3, ISBN13: 978-0-8018-6963-1. Dewey:820.9/358. LCCN:2002-154081.
Audience: **u,f.** *Choice, 2004.*

Hadley, Elaine PR728.M4H33 1995
Melodramatic Tactics: Theatricalized Dissent in the English Marketplace, 1800-1885. Trade Cloth. Stanford University Press. Palo Alto, CA. 1995. 318p. ISBN:0-8047-2403-2, ISBN13: 978-0-8047-2403-6. Dewey:822/.0527/0907. LCCN:94-042454.
Audience: **u,f.** *Choice, 1996.*

Hall, Catherine, et al. JN955 .H25 2000
Defining the Victorian Nation: Class, Race, Gender and the British Reform Act of 1867. Keith McClelland & Jane Rendall (Authors). Cloth Text. Cambridge University Press. New York, NY. 2000. 318p. ISBN:0-521-57218-5, ISBN13: 978-0-521-57218-7. Dewey:323/.0941/09034. LCCN:00-709639.
Audience: **u,f.** *Choice, 2001.*

Harvie, Christopher T. PR830.P6H37 1991
Centre of Things: Political Fiction in Britain from Disraeli to the Present. Paper over Boards. Routledge. New York, NY. 1992. 256p. ISBN:0-04-445593-3, ISBN13: 978-0-04-445593-6. Dewey:823.009/358. LCCN:90-046071.
Audience: **g,l,u,f.** *Choice, 1993.*

Haywood, Ian PR468.P57H39 2004
The Revolution in Popular Literature: Print, Politics and the People, 1790-1860. Gillian Beer (Contribution by). Trade Cloth. Cambridge University Press. New York, NY. 2004. 348p. Cambridge Studies in Nineteenth-Century Literature and Culture Ser., Vol. 44 ISBN:0-521-83546-1, ISBN13: 978-0-521-83546-6. Dewey:820.9/358. LCCN:2003-065207.
Audience: **u,f.**

Himmelfarb, Gertrude HV4086.A3H55 1985
The Idea of Poverty: England in the Early Industrial Age. Trade Paper. Knopf Publishing Group. New York, NY. 1985. 608p. ISBN:0-394-72607-3, ISBN13: 978-0-394-72607-6. Dewey:305.5/69/0941. LCCN:84-040005.
Audience: **u,f.** *B*

Joyce, Patrick D. DA533.J68 1994
Democratic Subjects: The Self and the Social in Nineteenth-Century England. Trade Paper. Cambridge University Press. New York, NY. 1994. 254p. ISBN:0-521-44802-6, ISBN13: 978-0-521-44802-4. Dewey:942.081. LCCN:93-037741.
Audience: **u,f.** *Choice, 1995.*

Matthew, H. C. G. DA563.4
(Henry Colin Gray)
Gladstone 1809-1898. Oxford University Press. 1997. ISBN:0-19-820696-8, ISBN13: 978-0-19-820696-5.
Audience: **g,l,u,f.**

Meisel, Joseph S. DA560.M45 2001
Public Speech and the Culture of Public Life in the Age of Gladstone. Trade Cloth. Columbia University Press. New York, NY. 2001. 336p. ISBN:0-231-12144-X, ISBN13: 978-0-231-12144-6. Dewey:941.081. LCCN:2001-028834.
Audience: **u,f.** *Choice, 2002.*

Stein, Richard L. PR461.S78 1987
Victoria's Year: English Literature and Culture, 1837-1838. Trade Cloth. Oxford University Press, Inc. New York, NY. 1988. 326p. ISBN:0-19-504922-5, ISBN13: 978-0-19-504922-0. Dewey:820/.9/008. LCCN:87-017347.
Audience: **g,l,u,f.** *Choice, 1988.*

Thompson, Dorothy DA554.T47 1990
Queen Victoria: The Woman, the Monarchy, and the People. Trade Cloth. Knopf Publishing Group. New York, NY. 1990. 192p. ISBN:0-394-53709-2, ISBN13: 978-0-394-53709-2. Dewey:941.081/092 B. LCCN:90-052563.
Audience: **g,l,u,f.**

Religion

Altholz, Josef L. BR50.E783A57 1994
Anatomy of a Controversy: The Debate over Essays and Reviews. Trade Cloth. Ashgate Publishing, Ltd. Aldershot, 1994. 208p. The Nineteenth Century Ser. ISBN:1-85928-040-4, ISBN13: 978-1-85928-040-9. Dewey:230/.3/09034. LCCN:94-238071.
Audience: **u,f.**

Annan, Noel PR5473.S6A88 1984
Leslie Stephen: The Godless Victorian. Trade Cloth. Random House, Inc. New York, NY. 1984. 384p. ISBN:0-394-53061-6, ISBN13: 978-0-394-53061-1. Dewey:828/.809 B. LCCN:84-042512.
Audience: **g,l,u,f.** *B*

Chadwick, Owen BR759
Victorian Church, Pt.1. Ed. 3. Trade Paper. SCM-Canterbury Press Ltd. London, 1966. 616p. ISBN:0-334-02409-9, ISBN13: 978-0-334-02409-5. Dewey:274.1/081.
Audience: **u,f.**

Fyfe, Aileen BL245.F94 2004
Science and Salvation: Evangelical Popular Science Publishing in Victorian Britain. Trade Cloth. University of Chicago Press. Chicago, IL. 2004. 432p. ISBN:0-226-27647-3, ISBN13: 978-0-226-27647-2. Dewey:261.5/5/094109034. LCCN:2003-017513.
Audience: **u,f.** *Choice, 2005.*

Gosse, Edmund PR4725.G7Z5 2004
Father and Son. Michael Newton (Editor). Trade Paper. Oxford University Press, Inc. New York, NY. 2004. 288p. Oxford World's Classics Ser. ISBN:0-19-284066-5, ISBN13: 978-0-19-284066-0. Dewey:820/.809 B. LCCN:2004-049285.
Audience: **g,l,u,f.**

Hilton, Boyd HC256.5
The Age of Atonement: The Influence of Evangelicalism on Social and Economic Thought 1785-1865. Paper Text. Oxford

University Press, Inc. New York, NY. 1992. 428p.
ISBN:0-19-820295-4, ISBN13: 978-0-19-820295-0.
Dewey:306/.3/0941.

Audience: **g,l,u,f.**

Howsam, Leslie   **BV2370.B8 H69 1991**
Cheap Bibles: Nineteenth-Century Publishing and the British
and Foreign Bible Society. Terry Belanger & David McKitterick
(Contribution by). Trade Paper. Cambridge University Press.
New York, NY. 2002. 263p. Cambridge Studies in Publishing
and Printing History Ser. ISBN:0-521-52212-9, ISBN13:
978-0-521-52212-0. Dewey:070.5/0941/09034.

Audience: **g,l,u,f.**

Lockwood, David   **BX5199.K49A3 1992**
(Editor)
Kilvert, the Victorian: A New Selection from Kilvert's Diaries.
Trade Cloth. Seren Books. Bridgend, 1992. 288p.
ISBN:1-85411-077-2, ISBN13: 978-1-85411-077-0.
Dewey:283/.092 B. LCCN:94-108691.

Audience: **g,l,u,f.**

Newsome, David   **LA632**
Godliness and Good Learning: Four Studies on a Victorian
Ideal. Trade Cloth. Transatlantic Arts, Inc. Albuquerque, NM.
1961. ISBN:0-7195-1015-5, ISBN13: 978-0-7195-1015-1.
Dewey:370/.942.

Audience: **g,l,u,f.**

Schlossberg, Herbert   **DA550.S3 2000**
The Silent Revolution and the Making of Victorian England.
Trade Paper. Ohio State University Press. Columbus, OH. 2000.
x, 405p. ISBN:0-8142-5046-7, ISBN13: 978-0-8142-5046-4.
Dewey:941.081. LCCN:99-056104.

Audience: **u,f.** *Choice, 2000.*

Snell, K. D. M. & Ell,   **BR759 .S54 2000**
Paul S.
Rival Jerusalems: The Geography of Victorian Religion. Trade
Cloth. Cambridge University Press. New York, NY. 2000. 516p.
ISBN:0-521-77155-2, ISBN13: 978-0-521-77155-9.
Dewey:274.2081. LCCN:99-037794.

Audience: **l,u,f.**

Wheeler, Michael   **PR468.D42W4 1990**
Death and the Future Life in Victorian Literature and Theology.
Trade Cloth. Cambridge University Press. New York, NY. 1990.
472p. ISBN:0-521-30617-5, ISBN13: 978-0-521-30617-1.
Dewey:820.9/354/09034. LCCN:89-077366.

Audience: **g,l,u,f.** *Choice, 1991.*

Rural Life

Howkins, Alun   **HN398.E5H69 1991**
Reshaping Rural England: Social History, 1850-1925. Paper
Text. Routledge. New York, NY. 1991. 272p.
ISBN:0-04-445705-7, ISBN13: 978-0-04-445705-3.
Dewey:307.72/0942. LCCN:90-021857.

Audience: **g,l,u,f.**

Thompson, Flora   **PR6039.H653 L3 1983**
The Illustrated Lark Rise to Candleford: A Trilogy. Julian
Shukburgh (Abridged by). Trade Cloth. Random House Value
Publishing. New York, NY. 1984. ISBN:0-517-55187-X,
ISBN13: 978-0-517-55187-5. Dewey:823/.912.
LCCN:83-007763.

Audience: **g,l,u,f.**

Winter, James   **GF551.W56**
Secure from Rash Assault: Sustaining the Victorian
Environment. Trade Paper. University of California Press.
Berkeley, CA. 2002. 354p. ISBN:0-520-22930-4, ISBN13:
978-0-520-22930-3. Dewey:333.7/13/0941/09034.
LCCN:98-043970.

Audience: **l,u,f.**

Science and Medicine

☐ Science in the Nineteenth Century Periodical: An Electronic
Index.
http://www.sciper.org/
Universities of Leeds and Sheffield.

Audience: **g,l,u,f.**

Beer, Gillian   **PR878.E95 B43 2000**
Darwin's Plots: Evolutionary Narrative in Darwin, George Eliot
and Nineteenth-Century Fiction. Ed. 2. George Levine
(Foreword by). Cloth Text. Cambridge University Press. New
York, NY. 2000. 311p. ISBN:0-521-78008-X, ISBN13:
978-0-521-78008-7. Dewey:823.809356. LCCN:99-051377.

Audience: **u,f.**

Dale, Peter A.   **PR468.S34D35 1989**
In Pursuit of a Scientific Culture: Science, Art, and Society in
the Victorian Age. Paper Text. University of Wisconsin Press.
Chicago, IL. 1989. 348p. Science and Literature Ser.
ISBN:0-299-12264-6, ISBN13: 978-0-299-12264-5.
Dewey:820.9/008. LCCN:89-040251.

Audience: **g,u,f.** *Choice, 1990.*

Desmond, Adrian   **QE705.G7 D47 1984**
Archetypes and Ancestors: Palaeontology in Victorian London,
1850-1875. Trade Paper. University of Chicago Press. Chicago,
IL. 1986. 288p. ISBN:0-226-14344-9, ISBN13:
978-0-226-14344-6. Dewey:560/.9421. LCCN:83-018104.

Audience: **g,l,u,f.**

Diamond, Michael   **DA533.D525 2003**
Victorian Sensation, or, the Spectacular, the Shocking, and the
Scandalous in Nineteenth-Century Britain. Trade Cloth. Anthem
Press. Manchester, NH. 2003. 328p. ISBN:1-84331-076-7,
ISBN13: 978-1-84331-076-1. Dewey:941.081.
LCCN:2003-446248.

Audience: **g,l,u,f.**

Fyfe, Aileen   **BL245.F94 2004**
Science and Salvation: Evangelical Popular Science Publishing
in Victorian Britain. Trade Cloth. University of Chicago Press.
Chicago, IL. 2004. 432p. ISBN:0-226-27647-3, ISBN13:
978-0-226-27647-2. Dewey:261.5/5/094109034.
LCCN:2003-017513.

Audience: **u,f.** *Choice, 2005.*

Gilbert, Pamela K.   **G1811**
Mapping the Victorian Social Body. Cloth Text. State University
of New York Press. Albany, NY. 2004. 245p. SUNY Series,
Studies in the Long Nineteenth Century ISBN:0-7914-6025-8,
ISBN13: 978-0-7914-6025-2. Dewey:614.4/0941/09034.
LCCN:2003-055013.

Audience: **u,f.**

Marcus, Steven   **Z1019**
The Other Victorians: A Study of Sexuality and Pornography in
Mid-Nineteenth Century England. Trade Paper. W. W. Norton &
Company, Inc. New York, NY. 1985. 320p.

ISBN:0-393-30236-9, ISBN13: 978-0-393-30236-3.
Dewey:098.1.

Audience: **g,l,u,f.**

Milligan, Barry   **PR468.O6M55 1995**
Pleasures and Pains: Opium and the Orient in
Nineteenth-Century British Culture. Cloth Text. University Press
of Virginia. Charlottesville, VA. 1995. 192p. Victorian Literature
and Culture Ser. ISBN:0-8139-1571-6, ISBN13:
978-0-8139-1571-5. Dewey:820.9/9208. LCCN:94-024140.

Audience: **l,u,f.** *Choice, 1995.*

Oppenheim, Janet   **LA209.2.H87**
Shattered Nerves: Doctors, Patients and Depression in Victorian
England. Trade Cloth. Replica Books. Bridgewater, NJ. 2000.
396p. ISBN:0-7351-0353-4, ISBN13: 978-0-7351-0353-5.
Dewey:370/.973.

Audience: **l,u,f.**

Ritvo, Harriet   **SF53.R58 1987**
The Animal Estate: The English and Other Creatures in the
Victorian Age. Trade Paper. Harvard University Press.
Cambridge, MA. 1987. 368p. ISBN:0-674-03707-3, ISBN13:
978-0-674-03707-6. Dewey:306.4/0942/09034.

Audience: **g,l,u,f.**

Secord, James A.   **QH363.S4 2000**
Victorian Sensation: The Extraordinary Publication, Reception,
and Secret Authorship of Vestiges of the Natural History of
Creation. Trade Cloth. University of Chicago Press. Chicago, IL.
2001. 624p. ISBN:0-226-74410-8, ISBN13: 978-0-226-74410-0.
Dewey:576.8/0941/09034. LCCN:00-009124.

Audience: **g,l,u,f.** *Choice, 2001.*

Small, Helen   **PR878.S44**
Love's Madness: Medicine, the Novel, and Female Insanity,
1800-1865. Trade Paper. Oxford University Press, Inc. New
York, NY. 1998. 274p. ISBN:0-19-818491-3, ISBN13:
978-0-19-818491-1. Dewey:823/.809353. LCCN:95-033313.

Audience: **u,f.** *Choice, 1996.*

Sexuality

Dowling, Linda   **PR468.H65**
Hellenism and Homosexuality in Victorian Oxford. Book, Other.
Cornell University Press. Ithaca, NY. 1996. 192p.
ISBN:0-8014-8170-8, ISBN13: 978-0-8014-8170-3.
Dewey:480/.71/141.

Audience: **u,f.** *Choice, 1994.*

Gallagher, Catherine &   **HQ23.M29 1987**
Laqueur, Thomas (Editors)
The Making of the Modern Body: Sexuality and Society in the
Nineteenth-Century. Trade Cloth. University of California Press.
Berkeley, CA. 1987. xv, 242p. Representation Bks., No. 1
ISBN:0-520-05960-3, ISBN13: 978-0-520-05960-3.
Dewey:305.3. LCCN:86-019361.

Audience: **u,f.**

Gay, Peter   **BF692**
Education of the Senses: The Bourgeois Experiance - Victoria to
Freud. Trade Paper. W. W. Norton & Company, Inc. New York,
NY. 1999. 544p. Bourgeois Experience, Vol. 1:Victoria to Freud
Ser. ISBN:0-393-31904-0, ISBN13: 978-0-393-31904-0.
Dewey:306.7/094/09034. LCCN:83-008187.

Audience: **g,l,u,f.**

Marcus, Steven   **Z1019**
The Other Victorians: A Study of Sexuality and Pornography in
Mid-Nineteenth Century England. Trade Paper. W. W. Norton &
Company, Inc. New York, NY. 1985. 320p.
ISBN:0-393-30236-9, ISBN13: 978-0-393-30236-3.
Dewey:098.1.

Audience: **g,l,u,f.**

Mason, Michael   **HQ18.G7M28 1995**
The Making of Victorian Sexuality. Trade Paper. Oxford
University Press, Inc. New York, NY. 1995. 348p.
ISBN:0-19-285312-0, ISBN13: 978-0-19-285312-7.
Dewey:306.7/0941. LCCN:94-043259.

Audience: **g,l,u,f.**

McCalman, Iain   **HN400.R3**
Radical Underworld: Prophets, Revolutionaries and
Pornographers in London, 1795-1840. Paper Text. Oxford
University Press, Inc. New York, NY. 1993. 358p.
ISBN:0-19-812286-1, ISBN13: 978-0-19-812286-9.
Dewey:320.9421. LCCN:87-011770.

Audience: **g,l,u,f.** *Choice, 1988.*

Sedgwick, Eve K.   **PR409.M/**
Between Men: English Literature and Male Homosocial Desire.
Carolyn G. Heilbrun & Nancy K. Miller (Editors). Paper Text.
Columbia University Press. New York, NY. 1993. 244p. Gender
and Culture Ser. ISBN:0-231-05861-6, ISBN13:
978-0-231-05861-2. Dewey:820.9/353. LCCN:84-017583.

Audience: **u,f.** *Choice, 1985.*

Sigel, Lisa Z.   **HQ472.G7S54 2002**
Governing Pleasures: Pornography and Social Change in
England, 1815-1914. Cloth Text. Rutgers University Press.
Piscataway, NJ. 2002. 248p. ISBN:0-8135-3001-6, ISBN13:
978-0-8135-3001-7. Dewey:363.4/7/094209034.
LCCN:2001-019801.

Audience: **g,l,u,f.** *Choice, 2003, 2002.*

Sweetman, John   **PR5101.M39Z**
Bomber Crew: Taking on the Reich. Trade Paper. Little, Brown
Book Group Ltd. London, 2005. 288p. ISBN:0-349-11796-9,
ISBN13: 978-0-349-11796-6. Dewey:821/.8.

Audience: **g,l,u,f.**

Social Life and Customs

Altick, Richard D.   **DA688**
The Shows of London. Trade Cloth. Harvard University Press.
Cambridge, MA. 1978. 568p. ISBN:0-674-80731-6, ISBN13:
978-0-674-80731-0. Dewey:790.2/09421. LCCN:77-002755.

Audience: **g,l,u,f.** *B*

Altick, Richard D.   **DA533**
Victorian People and Ideas. Trade Paper. W. W. Norton &
Company, Inc. New York, NY. 1974. 338p.
ISBN:0-393-09376-X, ISBN13: 978-0-393-09376-6.
Dewey:942.081.

Audience: **g,l,u.**

Ashton, Rosemary   **DA125.G4A84 1989**
Little Germany: German Refugees in Victorian Britain. Trade
Paper. Oxford University Press, Inc. New York, NY. 1989. 320p.
ISBN:0-19-282562-3, ISBN13: 978-0-19-282562-9.
Dewey:941/.00431. LCCN:88-025394.

Audience: **g,l,u,f.**

Beeton, Isabella   **TX145.B54 2000**
Mrs. Beeton's Book of Household Management. Nicola Humble
(Editor). Trade Paper. Oxford University Press, Inc. New York,
NY. 2000. 667p. Oxford World's Classics Ser.
ISBN:0-19-283345-6, ISBN13: 978-0-19-283345-7. Dewey:640.
LCCN:99-054236.

Audience: **g,l.**

Briggs, Asa   **DA533**
Victorian Things. Trade Paper. Sutton Publishing, Ltd. Stroud,
2003. 448p. ISBN:0-7509-3339-9, ISBN13: 978-0-7509-3339-1.
Dewey:942.081.

Audience: **g,l,u,f.** *Choice, 1989.*

Davidoff, Lenore   **HQ1596 .D38**
The Best Circles. Trade Cloth. Rowman & Littlefield Publishers,
Inc. Lanham, MD. 1973. 127p. ISBN:0-87471-428-1, ISBN13:
978-0-87471-428-9. Dewey:301.41/2/0942. LCCN:73-010386.

Audience: **g,l,u,f.**

Finn, Margot C.   **PR830.E37.F66 2003**
(Author, Contribution by)
The Character of Credit: Personal Debt in English Culture,
1740-1914. Keith Wrightson & Colin Jones (Contribution by).
Trade Cloth. Cambridge University Press. New York, NY. 2003.
374p. Cambridge Social and Cultural Histories Ser., Vol. 1
ISBN:0-521-82342-0, ISBN13: 978-0-521-82342-5.
Dewey:306.3/0942/09033. LCCN:2002-041697.

Audience: **u,f.** *Choice, 2004.*

Flanders, Judith   **HQ615.F58 2004**
Inside the Victorian Home: A Portrait of Domestic Life in
Victorian England. Trade Cloth. W. W. Norton & Company, Inc.
New York, NY. 2004. 416p. ISBN:0-393-05209-5, ISBN13:
978-0-393-05209-1. Dewey:306/.0942/09034.
LCCN:2003-027693.

Audience: **g,l,u,f.** *Choice, 2005.*

Gallagher, Catherine   **PR878.D65**
The Industrial Reformation of English Fiction: Social Discourse
and Narrative Form, 1832-1867. Paper Text. University of
Chicago Press. Chicago, IL. 1996. xvi, 320p.
ISBN:0-226-27933-2, ISBN13: 978-0-226-27933-6.
Dewey:823/.8/09355. LCCN:84-016272.

Audience: **u,f.** *Choice, 1986.*

Gay, Peter   **BF692**
Education of the Senses: The Bourgeois Experiance - Victoria to
Freud. Trade Paper. W. W. Norton & Company, Inc. New York,
NY. 1999. 544p. Bourgeois Experience, Vol. 1:Victoria to Freud
Ser. ISBN:0-393-31904-0, ISBN13: 978-0-393-31904-0.
Dewey:306.7/094/09034. LCCN:83-008187.

Audience: **g,l,u,f.**

Gilmour, Robin   **PR788.U/**
The Idea of the Gentleman in the Victorian Novel. Trade Paper.
Routledge. New York, NY. 1981. 208p. ISBN:0-04-800005-1,
ISBN13: 978-0-04-800005-7. Dewey:823/.8/093520621.
LCCN:81-010869.

Audience: **l,u,f.** *B*

Harrison, Brian H.   **HV5446.H35**
Drink and the Victorians: The Temperance Question in England,
1815-1872. Trade Cloth. Edinburgh University Press. Edinburgh,
1998. 528p. ISBN:1-85331-046-8, ISBN13: 978-1-85331-046-1.
Dewcy:178.

Audience: **g,l,u,f.**

Helsinger, Elizabeth K.,   **HQ1599.E5H44**
et al.
The Woman Question: Society and Literature in Britain and
America, 1837-1883: Social Issues. Robin L. Sheets & William
Veeder (Authors). Trade Paper. University of Chicago Press.
Chicago, IL. 1996. 278p. ISBN:0-226-32667-5, ISBN13:
978-0-226-32667-2. Dewey:305.4/0942. LCCN:88-027796.

Audience: **g,l,u,f.**

Helsinger, Elizabeth K.,   **HQ1599.E5H44 1989**
et al.
The Woman Question: Society and Literature in Britain and
America, 1837-1883: Defining Voices. Robin L. Sheets &
William Veeder (Authors). Trade Paper. University of Chicago
Press. Chicago, IL. 1997. 162p. ISBN:0-226-32666-7, ISBN13:
978-0-226-32666-5. Dewey:305.4/0942. LCCN:88-027796.

Audience: **g,l,u,f.**

Helsinger, Elizabeth K.,   **HQ1599.E5H44**
et al.
The Woman Question: Society and Literature in Britain and
America, 1837-1883: Literary Issues. Robin L. Sheets &
William Veeder (Authors). Trade Paper. University of Chicago
Press. Chicago, IL. 1996. 256p. ISBN:0-226-32668-3, ISBN13:
978-0-226-32668-9. Dewey:305.4/0942. LCCN:88-027796.

Audience: **g,l,u,f.**

Higginbotham, Peter
⌷ The Workhouse.
http://www.workhouses.org.uk

Audience: **g,l,u,f.**

Keating, Peter (Editor)   **HV245**
Into Unknown England, 1866-1913: Selections from the Social
Explorers. Trade Cloth. Rowman & Littlefield Publishers, Inc.
Lanham, MD. 1976. 320p. ISBN:0-87471-820-1, ISBN13:
978-0-87471-820-1. Dewey:301.44/1. LCCN:76-000964.

Audience: **g,l,u,f.**

Lockwood, David   **BX5199.K49A3 1992**
(Editor)
Kilvert, the Victorian: A New Selection from Kilvert's Diaries.
Trade Cloth. Seren Books. Bridgend, 1992. 288p.
ISBN:1-85411-077-2, ISBN13: 978-1-85411-077-0.
Dewey:283/.092 B. LCCN:94-108691.

Audience: **g,l,u,f.**

Logan, Thad   **PR468.H63 L64 2001**
The Victorian Parlour: A Cultural Study. Gillian Beer
(Contribution by). Trade Cloth. Cambridge University Press.
New York, NY. 2001. 304p. Studies in Nineteenth-Century
Literature and Culture, Vol. 30 ISBN:0-521-63182-3, ISBN13:
978-0-521-63182-2. Dewey:820.9/355. LCCN:00-050237.

Audience: **g,u,f.** *Choice, 2002.*

Mayhew, Henry   **HV4086.L66**
London Labour and the London Poor, Vol. 2. J. D. Rosenberg
(Introduction by). Trade Paper. Dover Publications, Inc.
Mineola, NY. 1982. 512p. ISBN:0-486-21935-6, ISBN13:
978-0-486-21935-6. Dewey:305.5/69/09421.

Audience: **g,l,u,f.** *B*

Mitchell, Sally   **DA533**
Daily Life in Victorian England. Cloth Text. Greenwood
Publishing Group, Inc. Portsmouth, NH. 2002. 336p. Daily Life
Through History Ser. ISBN:0-313-32657-6, ISBN13:
978-0-313-32657-8. Dewey:941.081. LCCN:96-002539.

Audience: **g,l,u.**

Peterson, M. Jeanne   **HQ1599.E5P48 1989**
Family, Love and Work in the Lives of Victorian Gentlewomen.
Trade Cloth. Indiana University Press. Bloomington, IN. 1989.
256p. ISBN:0-253-34427-1, ISBN13: 978-0-253-34427-4.
Dewey:305.4/0942. LCCN:88-045389.
                                   Audience: **g,l,u,f.** *Choice, 1989.*

Picker, John M.   **PR468.S68P53 2003**
Victorian Soundscapes. Trade Paper. Oxford University Press,
Inc. New York, NY. 2003. 232p. ISBN:0-19-515191-7, ISBN13:
978-0-19-515191-6. Dewey:820.9/356. LCCN:2002-035906.
                                   Audience: **u,f.** *Choice, 2004.*

Raverat, Gwen   **NE1217.R3 A2**
Period Piece: The Victorian Childhood of Charles Darwin's
Granddaughter. Trade Cloth. Penguin Group (USA) Inc. New
York, NY. 2003. 272p. ISBN:1-904555-12-8, ISBN13:
978-1-904555-12-4. Dewey:769.92.
                                   Audience: **g,l,u.**

Reed, John R.   **PR468.S6.R4**
Victorian Conventions. Trade Cloth. Ohio University Press.
Athens, OH. 1975. 574p. ISBN:0-8214-0147-5, ISBN13:
978-0-8214-0147-7. Dewey:820/.9/008. LCCN:73-092908.
                                   Audience: **u,f.** *B*

Richards, Thomas   **HC255.R53 1990**
The Commodity Culture of Victorian England: Advertising and
Spectacle, 1851-1914. Trade Cloth. Stanford University Press.
Palo Alto, CA. 1990. 320p. ISBN:0-8047-1652-8, ISBN13:
978-0-8047-1652-9. Dewey:659.1/0941/09034.
LCCN:89-037035.
                                   Audience: **u,f.** *Choice, 1990.*

Stein, Richard L.   **PR461.S78 1987**
Victoria's Year: English Literature and Culture, 1837-1838.
Trade Cloth. Oxford University Press, Inc. New York, NY. 1988.
326p. ISBN:0-19-504922-5, ISBN13: 978-0-19-504922-0.
Dewey:820/.9/008. LCCN:87-017347.
                                   Audience: **g,l,u,f.** *Choice, 1988.*

Thompson, F. M. L.   **HN385 .C14 1990**
   (Editor)
The Cambridge Social History of Britain, 1750-1950: Social
Agencies and Institutions, Vol. 3. Trade Cloth. Cambridge
University Press. New York, NY. 1990. 496p.
ISBN:0-521-25790-5, ISBN13: 978-0-521-25790-9.
Dewey:941/.07. LCCN:89-009840.
                                   Audience: **g,l,u,f.** *Choice, 1991.*

Thompson, F. M. L.   **HN385 .C14 1990**
   (Editor)
The Cambridge Social History of Britain, 1750-1950: People
and Their Environment. Trade Paper. Cambridge University
Press. New York, NY. 1992. 392p. ISBN:0-521-43815-2,
ISBN13: 978-0-521-43815-5. Dewey:941/.07. LCCN:89-009840.
                                   Audience: **g,l,u,f.**

Thompson, F. M. L.   **HN385 .C14 1990**
   (Editor)
The Cambridge Social History of Britain, 1750-1950: Regions
and Communities. Alan Armstrong, C. Baber, P. L. Garside &
D. W. Howell (Contribution by). Trade Paper. Cambridge
University Press. New York, NY. 1992. 608p.
ISBN:0-521-43816-0, ISBN13: 978-0-521-43816-2.
Dewey:941/.07. LCCN:89-009840.
                                   Audience: **g,l,u,f.**

Thompson, Flora   **PR6039.H653 L3 1983**
The Illustrated Lark Rise to Candleford: A Trilogy. Julian
Shukburgh (Abridged by). Trade Cloth. Random House Value
Publishing. New York, NY. 1984. ISBN:0-517-55187-X,
ISBN13: 978-0-517-55187-5. Dewey:823/.912.
LCCN:83-007763.
                                   Audience: **g,l,u,f.**

Technology and Information

Picker, John M.   **PR468.S68P53 2003**
Victorian Soundscapes. Trade Cloth. Oxford University Press,
Inc. New York, NY. 2003. 232p. ISBN:0-19-515190-9, ISBN13:
978-0-19-515190-9. Dewey:820.9/356. LCCN:2002-035906.
                                   Audience: **g,l,u,f.** *Choice, 2004.*

Picker, John M.   **PR468.S68P53 2003**
Victorian Soundscapes. Trade Paper. Oxford University Press,
Inc. New York, NY. 2003. 232p. ISBN:0-19-515191-7, ISBN13:
978-0-19-515191-6. Dewey:820.9/356. LCCN:2002-035906.
                                   Audience: **u,f.** *Choice, 2004.*

Sussman, Herbert L.   **PR468.T4 S8**
Victorians and the Machine: Literary Response to Technology.
Trade Cloth. Harvard University Press. Cambridge, MA. 1968.
ISBN:0-674-93705-8, ISBN13: 978-0-674-93705-5.
Dewey:820.9. LCCN:68-014274.
                                   Audience: **g,l,u.**

Urban World

Altick, Richard D.   **DA688**
The Shows of London. Trade Cloth. Harvard University Press.
Cambridge, MA. 1978. 568p. ISBN:0-674-80731-6, ISBN13:
978-0-674-80731-0. Dewey:790.2/09421. LCCN:77-002755.
                                   Audience: **g,l,u,f.** *B*

Briggs, Asa   **HT133**
Victorian Cities. Andrew Lees & Lynn H. Lees (Introduction
by). Trade Paper. University of California Press. Berkeley, CA.
1993. 411p. Classics in Urban History Ser., Vol. 2
ISBN:0-520-07922-1, ISBN13: 978-0-520-07922-9.
Dewey:307.7/6/0942/09034. LCCN:92-030443.
                                   Audience: **g,l,u,f.**

Davis, Tracy C.   **PN2599.5.E25 D38 20**
The Economics of the British Stage, 1800-1914. Trade Cloth.
Cambridge University Press. New York, NY. 2000. 524p.
ISBN:0-521-57115-4, ISBN13: 978-0-521-57115-9.
Dewey:338.4/7792/0941. LCCN:00-020381.
                                   Audience: **g,l,u,f.** *Choice, 2001.*

Desmond, Adrian   **QE705.G7 D47 1984**
Archetypes and Ancestors: Palaeontology in Victorian London,
1850-1875. Trade Paper. University of Chicago Press. Chicago,
IL. 1986. 288p. ISBN:0-226-14344-9, ISBN13:
978-0-226-14344-6. Dewey:560/.9421. LCCN:83-018104.
                                   Audience: **g,l,u,f.**

Dyos, H. J. & Wolff,   **DA533**
   Michael (Editors)
The Victorian City: Images and Realities, Vol. 2. Trade Cloth.
Routledge. New York, NY. 1973. 1001p. ISBN:0-7100-7383-6,

ISBN13: 978-0-7100-7383-9. Dewey:941/.081.
LCCN:73-076088.

Audience: **l,u,f.** *B*

Goodlad, Lauren M. E.   **PR468.P57G66 2003**
Victorian Literature and the Victorian State: Character and
Governance in a Liberal Society. Trade Cloth. Johns Hopkins
University Press. Baltimore, MD. 2004. 320p.
ISBN:0-8018-6963-3, ISBN13: 978-0-8018-6963-1.
Dewey:820.9/358. LCCN:2002-154081.

Audience: **u,f.** *Choice, 2004.*

Jackson, Lee   **DA533**
▢ Dictionary of Victorian London.
http://www.victorianlondon.org/

Audience: **g,l,u,f.**

Nead, Lynda   **DA683.N425 2005**
Victorian Babylon: People, Streets and Images in
Nineteenth-Century London. Trade Paper. Yale University Press.
Cumberland, RI. 2005. 264p. ISBN:0-300-10770-6, ISBN13:
978-0-300-10770-8. Dewey:942.1/2.

Audience: **u,f.** *Choice, 2001.*

Williams, Raymond   **PR409.C5**
The Country and the City. Trade Paper. Oxford University Press,
Inc. New York, NY. 1975. 344p. ISBN:0-19-519810-7, ISBN13:
978-0-19-519810-2. Dewey:820.9/32. LCCN:72-098128.

Audience: **u,f.** *B*

Culture

Altholz, Josef L.   **BR50.E783A57 1994**
Anatomy of a Controversy: The Debate over Essays and
Reviews. Trade Cloth. Ashgate Publishing, Ltd. Aldershot, 1994.
208p. The Nineteenth Century Ser. ISBN:1-85928-040-4,
ISBN13: 978-1-85928-040-9. Dewey:230/.3/09034.
LCCN:94-238071.

Audience: **u,f.**

Altick, Richard D.   **DA688**
The Shows of London. Trade Cloth. Harvard University Press.
Cambridge, MA. 1978. 568p. ISBN:0-674-80731-6, ISBN13:
978-0-674-80731-0. Dewey:790.2/09421. LCCN:77-002755.

Audience: **g,l,u,f.** *B*

Anderson, Patricia   **DA533.A574 1991**
The Printed Image and the Transformation of Popular Culture,
1790-1860. Trade Cloth. Oxford University Press, Inc. New
York, NY. 1991. 224p. ISBN:0-19-811236-X, ISBN13:
978-0-19-811236-5. Dewey:306.4. LCCN:91-002828.

Audience: **g,l,u,f.** *Choice, 1992.*

Auerbach, Jeffrey   **T690.B1A94 1999**
The Great Exhibition of 1851: A Nation on Display. Cloth over
Boards. Yale University Press. Cumberland, RI. 1999. 288p.
ISBN:0-300-08007-7, ISBN13: 978-0-300-08007-0.
Dewey:907.4/421. LCCN:99-032177.

Audience: **g,l,u,f.**

Bailey, Peter   **DA533 .B33 1998**
Popular Culture and Performance in the Victorian City. Trade
Cloth. Cambridge University Press. New York, NY. 1998. 272p.
ISBN:0-521-57417-X, ISBN13: 978-0-521-57417-4.
Dewey:941.081. LCCN:99-174955.

Audience: **g,l,u,f.** *Choice, 1999.*

Buckley, Jerome H.   **PR0731.B8**
The Triumph of Time: A Study of the Victorian Concepts of
Time, History, Progress, and Decadence. Trade Paper. Books on
Demand. Ann Arbor, MI. 198p. ISBN:0-7837-4452-8, ISBN13:
978-0-7837-4452-0. Dewey:820.9008. LCCN:66-021333.

Audience: **g,l,u,f.**

Chandler, Alice   **PR457 .C35**
A Dream of Order: The Medieval Ideal in Nineteenth-Century
English Literature. Trade Cloth. University of Nebraska Press.
Lincoln, NE. 1970. xii, 278p. ISBN:0-8032-0704-2, ISBN13:
978-0-8032-0704-2. Dewey:820/.9/007. LCCN:69-010413.

Audience: **u,f.**

Colley, Linda   **DA470**
Britons: Forging the Nation, 1707-1837. Ed. 2. Trade Paper.
Yale University Press. Cumberland, RI. 2005. 448p.
ISBN:0-300-10759-5, ISBN13: 978-0-300-10759-3.
Dewey:941/.07.

Audience: **g,l,u,f.** *Choice, 1993.*

Elfenbein, Andrew   **PR468.R65 E44 1995**
Byron and the Victorians. Gillian Beer (Contribution by). Trade
Cloth. Cambridge University Press. New York, NY. 1995. 297p.
Studies in Nineteenth-Century Literature and Culture, No. 4
ISBN:0-521-45452-2, ISBN13: 978-0-521-45452-0.
Dewey:820.9/008. LCCN:94-020629.

Audience: **u,f.** *Choice, 1995.*

Elton, Arthur   **N8218**
Art and the Industrial Revolution. Francis D. Klingender
(Editor). Trade Paper. Academy Chicago Publishers, Ltd.
Chicago, IL. 1981. 272p. ISBN:0-586-08122-4, ISBN13:
978-0-586-08122-8. Dewey:704.94/9/6.

Audience: **g,l,u,f.**

Foster, R. F.   **DA925.F63**
Paddy and Mr. Punch: Connections in Irish and English History.
Trade Paper. Penguin Group (USA) Inc. New York, NY. 1996.
400p. ISBN:0-14-017170-3, ISBN13: 978-0-14-017170-9.
Dewey:941.

Audience: **g,l,u,f.**

Haley, Bruce   **PR469.H42**
The Healthy Body and Victorian Culture. Trade Cloth. Harvard
University Press. Cambridge, MA. 1978. 176p.
ISBN:0-674-38610-8, ISBN13: 978-0-674-38610-5.
Dewey:820/.9/35. LCCN:78-006933.

Audience: **g,u,f.**

Haywood, Ian   **PR468.P57H39 2004**
The Revolution in Popular Literature: Print, Politics and the
People, 1790-1860. Gillian Beer (Contribution by). Trade Cloth.
Cambridge University Press. New York, NY. 2004. 348p.
Cambridge Studies in Nineteenth-Century Literature and Culture
Ser., Vol. 44 ISBN:0-521-83546-1, ISBN13: 978-0-521-83546-6.
Dewey:820.9/358. LCCN:2003-065207.

Audience: **u,f.**

Herbert, Christopher   **GN357.H47 1991**
Culture and Anomie: Ethnographic Imagination in the
Nineteenth Century. Trade Cloth. University of Chicago Press.
Chicago, IL. 1991. 374p. ISBN:0-226-32738-8, ISBN13:
978-0-226-32738-9. Dewey:306. LCCN:91-004366.

Audience: **u,f.** *Choice, 1992.*

Homans, Margaret   **DA533.H74 1998**
Royal Representations: Queen Victoria and British Culture,
1837-1876. Trade Paper. University of Chicago Press. Chicago,

IL. 1999. 322p. Women in Culture and Society Ser.
ISBN:0-226-35114-9, ISBN13: 978-0-226-35114-8.
Dewey:941.081. LCCN:98-019836.

Audience: **g,l,u,f.** *Choice, 1999.*

Jenkyns, Richard　　　　　　　**DA550 .J46**
The Victorians and Ancient Greece. Trade Cloth. Harvard
University Press. Cambridge, MA. 1990. 398p.
ISBN:0-674-93686-8, ISBN13: 978-0-674-93686-7.
Dewey:941.081. LCCN:79-025487.

Audience: **u,f.**

Knoepflmacher, U. C. &　　　　　**DA553**
 Tennyson, G. B. (Editors)
Nature and the Victorian Imagination. Trade Cloth. University of
California Press. Berkeley, CA. 1978. xxiii, 519p.
ISBN:0-520-03229-2, ISBN13: 978-0-520-03229-3.
Dewey:304.2/0941. LCCN:76-007761.

Audience: **g,l,u,f.**

Marsden, Gordon　　　　　　　**HN385.V55 1998**
Victorian Values: Personalties and Perspectives in
Nineteenth-Century Society. Ed. 2. Trade Paper. Longman
Publishing. Boston, MA. 1998. 304p. ISBN:0-582-29289-1,
ISBN13: 978-0-582-29289-5. Dewey:941/.08/0922.
LCCN:98-004601.

Audience: **g,l,u,f.**

Martineau, Harriet　　　　　　**PR4984.M5 Z463**
Harriet Martineaus's Autobiography, Vol. 1. Trade Paper.
Kessinger Publishing, LLC. Whitefish, MT. 2005.
ISBN:1-4179-7016-2, ISBN13: 978-1-4179-7016-2.
Dewey:823/.8.

Audience: **g,l,u,f.**

Martineau, Harriet　　　　　　**PR4984.M5 Z463**
Harriet Martineaus's Autobiography, Vol. 2. Trade Paper.
Kessinger Publishing, LLC. Whitefish, MT. 2005.
ISBN:1-4179-7017-0, ISBN13: 978-1-4179-7017-9.
Dewey:823/.8.

Audience: **g,l,u,f.**

Morgan, Thais E.　　　　　　　**PR464.V53 1990**
 (Editor)
Victorian Sages and Cultural Discourse: Renegotiating Gender
and Power. Cloth Text. Rutgers University Press. Piscataway,
NJ. 1990. 320p. ISBN:0-8135-1600-5, ISBN13:
978-0-8135-1600-4. Dewey:820.9/32042/09034.
LCCN:90-030977.

Audience: **u,f.**

Munich, Adrienne　　　　　　　**DA554.M86 1996**
Queen Victoria's Secrets. Trade Cloth. Columbia University
Press. New York, NY. 1996. 276p. ISBN:0-231-10480-4,
ISBN13: 978-0-231-10480-7. Dewey:941/.081/092.
LCCN:95-043737.

Audience: **g,l,u,f.** *Choice, 1996.*

Newsome, David　　　　　　　**DA550.N49 1997**
The Victorian World Picture: Perceptions and Introspections in
an Age of Change. Trade Cloth. Rutgers University Press.
Piscataway, NJ. 1997. 310p. ISBN:0-8135-2454-7, ISBN13:
978-0-8135-2454-2. Dewey:941.081/072. LCCN:97-015588.

Audience: **g,l,u,f.** *Choice, 1998.*

Picker, John M.　　　　　　　**PR468.S68P53 2003**
Victorian Soundscapes. Trade Paper. Oxford University Press,
Inc. New York, NY. 2003. 232p. ISBN:0-19-515191-7, ISBN13:
978-0-19-515191-6. Dewey:820.9/356. LCCN:2002-035906.

Audience: **u,f.** *Choice, 2004.*

Richards, Thomas　　　　　　**HC255.R53 1990**
The Commodity Culture of Victorian England: Advertising and
Spectacle, 1851-1914. Trade Cloth. Stanford University Press.
Palo Alto, CA. 1990. 320p. ISBN:0-8047-1652-8, ISBN13:
978-0-8047-1652-9. Dewey:659.1/0941/09034.
LCCN:89-037035.

Audience: **u,f.** *Choice, 1990.*

Ritvo, Harriet　　　　　　　**SF53.R58 1987**
The Animal Estate: The English and Other Creatures in the
Victorian Age. Trade Paper. Harvard University Press.
Cambridge, MA. 1987. 368p. ISBN:0-674-03707-3, ISBN13:
978-0-674-03707-6. Dewey:306.4/0942/09034.

Audience: **g,l,u,f.**

Sigel, Lisa Z.　　　　　　　**HQ472.G7S54 2002**
Governing Pleasures: Pornography and Social Change in
England, 1815-1914. Cloth Text. Rutgers University Press.
Piscataway, NJ. 2002. 248p. ISBN:0-8135-3001-6, ISBN13:
978-0-8135-3001-7. Dewey:363.4/7/094209034.
LCCN:2001-019801.

Audience: **g,l,u,f.** *Choice, 2003, 2002.*

Turner, Frank M.　　　　　　**DA533 .T87**
The Greek Heritage in Victorian Britain. Trade Paper. Yale
University Press. Cumberland, RI. 1984. 466p.
ISBN:0-300-03257-9, ISBN13: 978-0-300-03257-4.
Dewey:941.08. LCCN:80-024013.

Audience: **u,f.**

Wheeler, Michael　　　　　　**PR468.D42W4 1990**
Death and the Future Life in Victorian Literature and Theology.
Trade Cloth. Cambridge University Press. New York, NY. 1990.
472p. ISBN:0-521-30617-5, ISBN13: 978-0-521-30617-1.
Dewey:820.9/354/09034. LCCN:89-077366.

Audience: **g,l,u,f.** *Choice, 1991.*

Family

Armstrong, Nancy　　　　　　**PR821**
Desire and Domestic Fiction: A Political History of the Novel.
Trade Paper. Oxford University Press, Inc. New York, NY. 1990.
310p. ISBN:0-19-506160-8, ISBN13: 978-0-19-506160-4.
Dewey:823/.009. LCCN:86-016482.

Audience: **u,f.** *Choice, 1987.*

Banks, J.A.　　　　　　　　**JFD 95-8511**
Prosperity and Parenthood. Trade Cloth. Ashgate Publishing
Company. Williston, VT. 1993. 248p. ISBN:0-7512-0267-3,
ISBN13: 978-0-7512-0267-0. Dewey:363.960941.

Audience: **g,l,u,f.**

Chase, Karen &　　　　　　**PR468.H63C48 2000**
 Levenson, Michael H.
The Spectacle of Intimacy: A Public Life for the Victorian
Family. Trade Cloth. Princeton University Press. Princeton, NJ.
2000. 264p. Literature in History Ser. ISBN:0-691-00668-7,
ISBN13: 978-0-691-00668-0. Dewey:823/.809355.
LCCN:99-058479.

Audience: **u,f.** *Choice, 2000.*

Davidoff, Leonore &   **HT690.G7D38 2002**
Hall, Catherine
Family Fortunes: Men and Women of the English Middle Class,
1780-1850. Ed. 2. Paper over Boards. Routledge. New York,
NY. 2003. 616p. ISBN:0-415-29064-3, ISBN13:
978-0-415-29064-7. Dewey:305.5/5/094209033.
LCCN:2002-032612.

Audience: **g,l,u,f.** *Choice, 1988.*

Dyhouse, Carol   **HQ798 .D85**
Girls Growing up in Late Victorian and Edwardian England.
Trade Cloth. Routledge. New York, NY. 1981. 224p. Studies in
Social History ISBN:0-7100-0821-X, ISBN13:
978-0-7100-0821-3. Dewey:305.2/3/0941. LCCN:81-008578.

Audience: **l,u,f.**

Flanders, Judith   **HQ615.F58 2004**
Inside the Victorian Home: A Portrait of Domestic Life in
Victorian England. Trade Cloth. W. W. Norton & Company, Inc.
New York, NY. 2004. 416p. ISBN:0-393-05209-5, ISBN13:
978-0-393-05209-1. Dewey:306/.0942/09034.
LCCN:2003-027693.

Audience: **g,l,u,f.** *Choice, 2005.*

Frost, Ginger S.   **KD754.F76 1995**
Promises Broken: Courtship, Class, and Gender in Victorian
England. Cloth Text. University Press of Virginia.
Charlottesville, VA. 1995. 304p. Victorian Literature and Culture
Ser. ISBN:0-8139-1610-0, ISBN13: 978-0-8139-1610-1.
Dewey:346.42/022. LCCN:95-007637.

Audience: **g,l,u,f.** *Choice, 1996.*

Gosse, Edmund   **PR4725.G7Z5 2004**
Father and Son. Michael Newton (Editor). Trade Paper. Oxford
University Press, Inc. New York, NY. 2004. 288p. Oxford
World's Classics Ser. ISBN:0-19-284066-5, ISBN13:
978-0-19-284066-0. Dewey:820/.809 B. LCCN:2004-049285.

Audience: **g,l,u,f.**

Hammerton, James   **HQ615.H357 1992**
Cruelty and Companionship: Conflict in Nineteenth Century
Married Life. Paper over Boards. Routledge. New York, NY.
1992. 248p. ISBN:0-415-03622-4, ISBN13: 978-0-415-03622-1.
Dewey:306.810942. LCCN:91-045648.

Audience: **g,l,u,f.** *Choice, 1993.*

Hughes, M. Vivian   **DA688**
A London Child of the 1870s. Trade Cloth. Oxford University
Press, Inc. New York, NY. 1977. 148p. Oxford Paperbacks Ser.,
No. 383 ISBN:0-19-281216-5, ISBN13: 978-0-19-281216-2.
Dewey:942.1/081/0924.

Audience: **g,l,u.**

Jalland, Pat   **HQ1593.J34 1986**
Women, Marriage, and Politics, 1860-1914. Trade Cloth. Oxford
University Press, Inc. New York, NY. 1987. 380p.
ISBN:0-19-822668-3, ISBN13: 978-0-19-822668-0.
Dewey:305.4/0941. LCCN:85-028406.

Audience: **l,u,f.** *Choice, 1987.*

Kane, Penny   **HQ614**
Victorian Families in Fact and Fiction. Trade Paper. Palgrave
Macmillan. New York, NY. 1997. 192p. ISBN:0-312-17221-4,
ISBN13: 978-0-312-17221-3. Dewey:306.8/5/0941.

Audience: **g,l,u,f.** *Choice, 1995.*

Langland, Elizabeth   **HT690.G7L35 1995**
Nobody's Angels: Middle-Class Women and Domestic Ideology
in Victorian Culture. Book, Other. Cornell University Press.

Ithaca, NY. 1995. 288p. Reading Women Writing Ser.
ISBN:0-8014-8220-8, ISBN13: 978-0-8014-8220-5.
Dewey:305.5/5/082. LCCN:94-024393.

Audience: **g,l,u,f.**

Nelson, Claudia   **PR830.C513N45 1991**
Boys Will Be Girls: The Feminine Ethic and British Children's
Fiction, 1857-1917. Cloth Text. Rutgers University Press.
Piscataway, NJ. 1991. 216p. ISBN:0-8135-1681-1, ISBN13:
978-0-8135-1681-3. Dewey:823/.8099287. LCCN:90-020004.

Audience: **u,f.**

Nunokawa, Jeff   **PR878.D65N86 2003**
The Afterlife of Property: Domestic Security and the Victorian
Novel. Trade Paper. Princeton University Press. Princeton, NJ.
2003. 160p. ISBN:0-691-11467-6, ISBN13: 978-0-691-11467-5.
Dewey:828.8.

Audience: **u,f.** *Choice, 1994.*

Peterson, M. Jeanne   **HQ1599.E5P48 1989**
Family, Love and Work in the Lives of Victorian Gentlewomen.
Trade Cloth. Indiana University Press. Bloomington, IN. 1989.
256p. ISBN:0-253-34427-1, ISBN13: 978-0-253-34427-4.
Dewey:305.4/0942. LCCN:88-045389.

Audience: **g,l,u,f.** *Choice, 1989.*

Raverat, Gwen   **NE1217.R3 A2**
Period Piece: The Victorian Childhood of Charles Darwin's
Granddaughter. Trade Cloth. Penguin Group (USA) Inc. New
York, NY. 2003. 272p. ISBN:1-904555-12-8, ISBN13:
978-1-904555-12-4. Dewey:769.92.

Audience: **g,l,u.**

Industry and Transportation

Bizup, Joseph   **DA533.B57 2003**
Manufacturing Culture: Vindications of Early Victorian Industry.
Trade Cloth. University Press of Virginia. Charlottesville, VA.
2003. 256p. Victorian Literature and Culture Ser.
ISBN:0-8139-2246-1, ISBN13: 978-0-8139-2246-1.
Dewey:306.3/4/094109034. LCCN:2003-009463.

Audience: **u,f.**

Clark, Anna   **HD8390**
Struggle for the Breeches: Gender and the Making of the British
Working Class. Trade Paper. University of California Press.
Berkeley, CA. 1997. 432p. Studies on the History of Society
and Culture, Vol. 23 ISBN:0-520-20883-8, ISBN13:
978-0-520-20883-4. Dewey:305.5/62/0941. LCCN:93-050835.

Audience: **u,f.**

Elton, Arthur   **N8218**
Art and the Industrial Revolution. Francis D. Klingender
(Editor). Trade Paper. Academy Chicago Publishers, Ltd.
Chicago, IL. 1981. 272p. ISBN:0-586-08122-4, ISBN13:
978-0-586-08122-8. Dewey:704.94/9/6.

Audience: **g,l,u,f.**

Freeman, Michael J.   **HE1041.F74 1999**
Railways and the Victorian Imagination. Cloth over Boards. Yale
University Press. Cumberland, RI. 1999. 272p.
ISBN:0-300-07970-2, ISBN13: 978-0-300-07970-8.
Dewey:385/.09. LCCN:99-020495.

Audience: **g,l,u,f.** *Choice, 2000.*

Gallagher, Catherine   **PR878.D65**
The Industrial Reformation of English Fiction: Social Discourse
and Narrative Form, 1832-1867. Paper Text. University of

Chicago Press. Chicago, IL. 1996. xvi, 320p.
ISBN:0-226-27933-2, ISBN13: 978-0-226-27933-6.
Dewey:823/.8/09355. LCCN:84-016272.

Audience: **u,f.** *Choice, 1986.*

Himmelfarb, Gertrude   **HV4086.A3H55 1985**
The Idea of Poverty: England in the Early Industrial Age. Trade
Paper. Knopf Publishing Group. New York, NY. 1985. 608p.
ISBN:0-394-72607-3, ISBN13: 978-0-394-72607-6.
Dewey:305.5/69/0941. LCCN:84-040005.

Audience: **u,f.** *B*

Schivelbusch, Wolfgang   **HE1021 .S3413 1986**
The Railway Journey: The Industrialization and Perception of
Time and Space. Trade Cloth. University of California Press.
Berkeley, CA. 1986. ISBN:0-520-05812-7, ISBN13:
978-0-520-05812-5. Dewey:385/.09/034. LCCN:86-011226.

Audience: **g,l,u,f.**

Simmons, Jack   **HE3018.S58 1991**
The Victorian Railway. Trade Cloth. Thames & Hudson. New
York, NY. 1991. 416p. ISBN:0-500-25110-X, ISBN13:
978-0-500-25110-2. Dewey:385/.0941. LCCN:90-070206.

Audience: **g,l,u,f.** *Choice, 1991.*

Wiener, Martin Joel   **DA533.W59 2004**
English Culture and the Decline of the Industrial Spirit,
1850-1980. Ed. 2. Cloth Text. Cambridge University Press. New
York, NY. 2004. 236p. ISBN:0-521-84376-6, ISBN13:
978-0-521-84376-8. Dewey:942.08. LCCN:2004-052117.

Audience: **g,l,u,f.**

Winter, James   **GF551.W56**
Secure from Rash Assault: Sustaining the Victorian
Environment. Trade Paper. University of California Press.
Berkeley, CA. 2002. 354p. ISBN:0-520-22930-4, ISBN13:

978-0-520-22930-3. Dewey:333.7/13/0941/09034.
LCCN:98-043970.

Audience: **l,u,f.**

Reform

Brantlinger, Patrick   **PR0469.P6B65**
The Spirit of Reform: British Literature and Politics, 1832-1867.
Trade Paper. Books on Demand. Ann Arbor, MI. 1977. 303p.
ISBN:0-7837-4450-1, ISBN13: 978-0-7837-4450-6.
Dewey:820/.9/3. LCCN:76-030537.

Audience: **u,f.** *B*

Higginbotham, Peter
☐ The Workhouse.
http://www.workhouses.org.uk

Audience: **g,l,u,f.**

Himmelfarb, Gertrude   **HV4086.A3**
Poverty and Compassion: The Moral Imagination of the Late
Victorians. Trade Paper. Knopf Publishing Group. New York,
NY. 1992. 475p. ISBN:0-679-74173-9, ISBN13:
978-0-679-74173-2. Dewey:362.5/0942/09034.
LCCN:92-050066.

Audience: **g,l,u,f.** *Choice, 1992.*

McCalman, Iain   **HN400.R3**
Radical Underworld: Prophets, Revolutionaries and
Pornographers in London, 1795-1840. Paper Text. Oxford
University Press, Inc. New York, NY. 1993. 358p.
ISBN:0-19-812286-1, ISBN13: 978-0-19-812286-9.
Dewey:320.9421. LCCN:87-011770.

Audience: **g,l,u,f.** *Choice, 1988.*

Author Index

B

G

H

I

K

L

M

N

P

S

W

Title Index

C

D

E

F

G

H

J

L

M

N

O

P

S

W

X

Y

Numeric Titles